MW00386581

ALSO FROM ROLLING STONE PRESS

The Rolling Stone Album Guide

The Rolling Stone Illustrated History of Rock & Roll

The Rolling Stone Book of Women in Rock: Trouble Girls

THE Rolling Stone JAZZ & BLUES ALBUM GUIDE

THE

Rolling Stone

JAZZ & BLUES

ALBUM GUIDE

EDITED BY JOHN SWENSON

RANDOM HOUSE
NEW YORK

 Published in the United States by Random House, Inc., New York, and simultaneously in Canada by Random House of Canada Limited, Toronto.

Small portions of this work were originally published in *The Rolling Stone Jazz Record Guide,* published by Random House, Inc., in 1985, and *The Rolling Stone Album Guide,* published by Random House, Inc., in 1992.

Library of Congress Cataloging-in-Publication Data

The Rolling Stone jazz and blues album guide/Rolling Stone.
p. cm.
Includes index.
ISBN 0-679-76873-4
1. Jazz—Discography. 2. Blues (Music)—Discography. 3. Sound recordings—Reviews. I. Rolling Stone (San Francisco, Calif.)
ML156.4.J3R65 1999 781.65′0266—dc21 98-43120
CIP
MN

A Rolling Stone Press Book

Editor: Holly George-Warren
Senior Editor: Shawn Dahl
Assistant Editor: Ann Abel
Editorial Assistant: Carrie Smith

Random House website address: http://www.atrandom.com
Rolling Stone website address: http://www.rollingstone.com
Printed in the United States of America on acid-free paper
2 4 6 8 9 7 5 3
First Edition

ABOUT THE BOOK

HOLLY GEORGE-WARREN

The ROLLING STONE *Jazz and Blues Album Guide* you hold in your hands is the pleasantly plump child of the 1985 volume *The* ROLLING STONE *Jazz Record Guide,* originally conceived and edited by John Swenson. When John approached Rolling Stone Press in March 1993 about creating an expanded, revised edition of the guide, jazz had already begun reaching a new generation of listeners through its own offspring: Exciting young players like Joshua Redman had released debut albums. The avant-garde loft scene that had taken hold in downtown New York in the '70s had spread its reach to the heartland. New strains of jazz were jelling—the sampling of classic jazz riffs was making its way into hip-hop, spawning the mutant subgenre acid jazz. MOR fans had discovered jazz through the recently developed Quiet Storm radio format. And a few artists who'd spent the '80s playing in or listening to rock & roll bands had just begun forming combos that paid homage to classic swing. In New York, scores of listeners who weren't alive when Charlie Parker and Dizzy Gillespie were birthing bebop in Harlem and on West 52nd Street were flocking to the recently inaugurated Charlie Parker Day in the East Village's Tompkins Square Park. On the West Coast, the lounge scene—which celebrated cool jazz, along with its easy-listening offshoot—was pervasive. Record-breaking numbers were descending on New Orleans every spring to attend the New Orleans Jazz and Heritage Festival.

Concurrently, the popularity of blues was reaching epic proportions, with scores of new artists and blues bands bringing back the roots sounds of the Delta and Chicago. Meanwhile, obscure elder statesmen who'd been toiling in anonymity had been discovered and recorded. Blues labels, festivals and venues were proliferating. Because jazz and blues are so irrevocably interlinked, John felt strongly that this guide should encompass both genres. I agreed—as did Jonathan Karp, our very supportive editor at Random House. And so our task began.

First, we looked to the original *Jazz Record Guide* and the 1992 ROLLING STONE *Album Guide* for our initial list of entries. Then we *really* went to town, adding dozens of new jazz and blues artists who'd emerged over the past decade. In addition, we discovered numerous recordings that had fallen out of print when the books were last published and had since been reissued on CD. (Perhaps because of the improvisational nature of jazz, the genre's releases peculiarly tend to go in and out of print at the drop of a hat—some releases in print at the beginning of this project have since gone out of print, only to be reissued again.)

A note about the discographies: For each artist's discography, we made every attempt to include all albums currently available domestically; we also reviewed important foreign releases that have U.S. distribution. (We excluded limited-edition collectors' sets and mail-order–only releases.) Each album's label and release date (not recording date) are provided in the discography; for reissues, we listed the work's original release date (rather than the date of its recording), followed by its current label and (when possible) reissue date. If a CD reissue compiles two original albums, we listed each release date if the years differ. (We used "N.A."—not available—if labels did not include the reissue date on the CD packaging or provide it to us.) When a high-quality (sometimes five-star-caliber) recording is currently unavailable on CD, the entry will most likely note that within the text (and usually give the original label and date info), so the tenacious among our readers can seek it out at used-record stores and flea markets. (We hope, too, that some industrious labels will get the idea to make such albums available again.) Because some of the best recordings can be difficult to find, we've listed in the appendix Web sites through which the CDs can be ordered. We've also included information about locating the product of some of the smaller labels.

Speaking of labels, the majority were very helpful in our quest to listen to and critique as many jazz and blues albums as humanly possible over the past five years. Surprisingly, we often found that the smaller the label and the more limited its resources, the more helpful the staff was.

In addition to our dedicated squad of reviewers, our team consisted of vigilant researchers who fact-checked each entry. Again, this was no easy task—and the labels' help was often invaluable. It's extremely frustrating that many CD guides—both print and electronic versions—are riddled with errors. Whenever possible, the fact checking was completed with the actual release in hand. Invariably, however, mistakes creep in: Should the astute among you find any inaccuracies in the reviews, please notify us in writing (Editor, Rolling Stone Press, 1290 Sixth Avenue, New York, NY 10104).

When choosing what to include under the categories of jazz and blues, we tried to go outside the "traditional" boundaries to an extent. Therefore, a selection of zydeco, punk-blues, acid jazz, country-blues, gospel, R&B and blues-rock artists are here. Though all the reviewers awarded stars to their entries, John Swenson was the ultimate arbiter—so that the star system would consistently and accurately reflect the releases' merits. Consult the chart on page xvi to see the stars' values.

As for the book's organization, it's very straightforward. Entries are arranged in alphabetical order, by the artist's last name or the first letter of a band's name. Within each entry, the discography is listed in chronological order by release date rather than recording date. Anthologies are grouped in the back of the book. We opted to include only a smattering of anthologies, thereby saving the space for individual entries. (Thus, we've excluded soundtracks.) Making the cut are those anthologies of historical importance, which provide the only means for hearing early 78s and 45s. A few overviews give a great introduction to certain subgenres of blues and jazz; these are also here. In addition, we've included sampler sets for labels that have extensive catalogs, as a way to offer a taste of various artists on those labels. Using this book along with the sampler should help you make good selections when adding to your CD library.

And now for the best part: gratitude. This book would not exist without the unflagging energy, nonstop enthusiasm and superhuman expertise of John Swenson. *The Rolling Stone Jazz and Blues Album Guide* has truly been a labor of love (and what labor!) for this esteemed critic and insightful writer. Thank you, John! In addition to writing more than half of the book's entries, he oversaw the editing of the rest of the reviews. Thanks also to those who spent long hours critiquing and writing reviews: Ann Abel, Robert Baird, Bob Blumenthal, Hank Bordowitz, J.D. Considine, Shawn Dahl, Greg Emmanuel, Paul Evans, Ken Franckling, Steve Futterman, Geoffrey Himes, B.R. Hunter, Scott Jordan, Ashley Kahn, Jordan Kessler, David McGee, Tom Miller, Steve Mirkin, Mitch Myers, Ted Panken, Alan Paul, Joe Van Plummer and Jennifer Zoggott. Rolling Stone Press senior editor Shawn Dahl and assistant editor Ann Abel did the lion's share of work editing and collating all the text changes on this massive tome—kudos to them. Editorial assistant Carrie Smith joined us in time to put in many hours of life-saving work. Our former editorial assistant, Greg Emmanuel, gave his fair share as well. Among our small army of fact checkers, one stands out: Peter Kenis went above and beyond to get the facts straight and stayed at the job longer than anyone else. Other fact checkers who put in their time include Joe Van Plummer, Pete Moe, Gina Zucker, Jenny Wesley, Nana Asfour, Rosanna Shokrian, Travis McGee, Noelle Band, Gretchen Lutz, Jeanne Schiltz, Alysha Yagoda, Kelly Keller, Susan Yusef, Ann Zeidner, Tim Siefert and Tom Gogola.

As always, our agent, Sarah Lazin, made this book happen, and Tana Osa-Yande helped in many ways. At Random House, Jon Karp really believed in the project and didn't give up on us. And Dennis Ambrose and his crew gave the book their all. Wenner Media's Jann S. Wenner, Kent Brownridge, John Lagana, Evelyn Bernal, Fred Woodward and Gail Anderson were also crucial to our efforts.

I hate to turn the many notable record-label staffers who assisted us into a laundry list of thanks, but in the interest of saving space . . . We are grateful to: Steve Karas, formerly at A&M; Russ at Accurate; Marc Lipkin at Alligator; Jennifer at Angel; Annie Johnston and Mark Warren at Arhoolie; Tom Ramsey at Arrival; Susan Swan at Atlantic; Kim Ewing at Atlantic Jazz; Christine Kozler at Avenue Jazz; Lisa Hirsch and the late Marilyn Lipsius at BMG; Jason Leopold at BMG/Milan; Alan Caplin at Biograph; Kat Stratton at Black Top; Herb Hells at Blue Chip Jazz; Chris Dray at Blind Pig; Bubba Sullivan at Blues Corner; Jack Worthiemer at Brownstone; Traci M. Taylor at Burnside Records; Jeremy Much, formerly at Capricorn; Glenn Ito at Challenge; Lisa Hershfield at Chesky; Melissa Green and Don McAvoy at Collectables; Chris, Margaret and Kevin Gorr at Columbia Jazz; David Ginochio and Jennifer Jaime at Concord Jazz; Don Lucoff at D.L. Media; Alan Young and Alicia "the Cup" Robles at DaCapo Press; Tracy Cavenaugh and Susan Swain at da Music; Leona at Decca; Doug Engle at Delmark; Roy and Eric Dilts at Delta; Johnny Parth at Document; Jim Eigo at Dreyfus; Byron Hontas at Drive Archive; Neal at ECM; Viviana Chan at EMI; Michael, Rita and Frank at Earwig; Mike Knuth at Enemy; Andy Schwartz and Olga at Epic; Jerry Gordon and Alan Edwards at Evidence; Terri Hinte at Fantasy; Henry

Passman at Genes Adelphi; Hans at Gramavision; Jennifer Levy, Rachel Spartman and David Wallace at GRP; Pete at Hightone; Jamie at Hindsight; Marshall Lamm at Impulse!/GRP; Bob Cummins at India Navigation; Jeff Cargerman at Inside Sounds; Dick Bossi at Intersound; Philip Barker at Jazz Focus; Anna at Jazz Tree; Keith Abel at Jewel/Ronn/Paula; Rob Baure, Donald Elfman and Heather Hayes at Koch; Tom Cording, Jeff Jones and Joann Sloan at Sony Legacy; Thomasine Anderson and Leslie Myers at Malaco; Rick Hallock at Mapleshade; Curt, Kymm Britton, Danielle Levy and Christine Wolff at MCA; Eric Talbert at Motown; Ray and Barney at Muse; Anne Busfield and Rick Lecercq at MusicMasters; Debbie at Nonesuch; Dave at North Country Distributors; Kyle at Other Music; Harry Weinger at PolyGram; Hugh Agner at Private Music; George Buck at Progressive; Anthony at Qualiton; Howard Silvers at Quicksilver; Ron Carter and Kisha Maldonado at Qwest; Kala Feldman and Mark Feldman at Reservoir Music; Cindy, David Dorn and Tom Muzquiz at Rhino; Carrie Murphy and Steve at Rounder; Darcy Myers at Rykodisc; Cindy Byram at Shanachie; Mark Satlof at Shore Fire Media; Rachel Sears at Smithsonian Folkways; Tony Reif at Songline; Yvette Noel-Shure at Sony; Rob at Sphere; Jordan Trachtenberg at Tomato; David C. Broyles at Triloka; Bruce Duff at Triple X; MargAnn Turnipseed at Turnipseed; Bob Sunenblick at Uptown; Meg, Lynette and Georgetee Cartwright at Vanguard; Samantha Black at Verve; Tamra Wilson at Warner Jazz; Chris Courtney at Windham Hill; and Don Kent at Yazoo. Also thanks to Sam's BBQ in Austin, Texas—where the idea for this book was hatched.

Most of all, our gratitude goes to those adventurous players who created the incredible body of work critiqued herein. There are certainly more lucrative pursuits than jazz and blues (in many cases, at least): The enrichment and enjoyment their music has brought to millions of jazz and blues fans around the world is, of course, incalculable.

INTRODUCTION

J O H N   S W E N S O N

I'm sitting in New Orleans on the east bank of the Mississippi River, listening to local radio station WWOZ track a young rap-and-brass band, Coolbone, playing in a style they call brass-hop. The rap is positive, even joyous, and the groove suits the easy interlace of trombone, tuba, trumpet and saxophone. The track segues perfectly into the traditional New Orleans jazz of Doc Cheatham, who recently left the planet after a lifetime in music that stretched across the 20th Century.

It's August 1997, 80 years after the first jazz recording was made by the Original Dixieland Jazz Band. The oily tropical atmosphere saturates New Orleans like a gorged sponge. People rest quietly on the Mississippi levee, watching the hot air move in visible currents above the river as rusty tankers the length of football fields negotiate the tricky crescent S bend that gives the city its nickname.

The levee slopes down away from the river, some 10 feet below sea level at Jackson Square, where a group of black kids play brass-band music for tips from the ubiquitous tourists. The trombonist is a particularly hot soloist; he could very well show up that night at Donna's, the unassuming bar and grill at the other end of the French Quarter on the corner of Rampart Street and St. Ann's, home turf for the current plethora of New Orleans brass bands.

A century ago another generation of young black musicians playing in these same streets was creating the new American music that would become known as jazz. New Orleans, with its tradition of elaborate funerals accompanied by brass bands playing solemn dirges on the way from the church to the burial site, then ecstatic, celebratory music on the way back, became the cradle of jazz. In the years of the Depression and after World War II the brass bands had all but vanished, only to revive in the hands of a few veterans and a new generation eager to bring its own personality to the music. This oldest of traditions was eventually able to assimilate radical new ideas and continue on with more vigor than ever.

The renewed popularity of brass bands illustrates the recombinant nature of jazz itself. The brass-band tradition was particularly strong in New Orleans, as it was throughout the United States, in the latter half of the 19th Century, when the elements that forged jazz finally coalesced after a long period of interaction. Military bands were a dominant feature in occupied New Orleans during and after the War Between the States. The newly emancipated black Americans were among the few New Orleans residents during Reconstruction who interpreted the walking cadence of the marching drums and the high piercing calls of the brass instruments in the military bands as a symbol of freedom rather than oppression.

By the turn of the century the marching band had assumed a new form in the hands of virtuosic musicians whose style of playing led directly to New Orleans jazz. Though this music was played by whites as well as blacks and Creoles, the collective improvisation that lies at the heart of the traditional New Orleans band is similar to the roles played by the various drums in African music.

The brass band was a central element in the foundation of jazz but by no means the only one. Though the itinerant blues singer bears resemblance to the African griot, blues is not simply transplanted African folk music. Neither is jazz simply an African response to the European classical tradition. Jazz and blues are new forms born out of the boiling landscape of an America writhing in the feverish grip of self-actualization. The forms were the result of historically unprecedented cultural interactions in an equally unprecedented setting, the mixture of old and new that New Orleans represented.

The African-Americans who existed at the center of these new forms were the children of a people wrenched from their own society and brought to a new world in subhuman conditions, deprived of their use of language and custom and the celebration of their religion. They were forbidden from bringing musical instruments, particularly the drums that were such an integral part of their life, to the Americas.

But they brought the spirit and character of the culture—the unstoppable groove itself. It was carried in the minds and hearts of the people of the African diaspora, ingeniously adapted to the materials at hand. Plantation slaves chanted work songs rooted in African folk melodies. Church services found the English hymns transmogrified into the intricate call-and-response of gospel singing, which in turn became a blueprint for blues singing. The tools of bondage were magically transformed into carriers of rhythm—picks and hammers became percussion instruments, mule bones became drums, mule jaws with their rattling teeth became shakers.

The intricate language of African polyrhythms survived through any number of struck or plucked instruments and the body rhythms of dancing. These unique characteristics began to surface in American popular culture during the 19th Century as traditional African elements interacted with aspects of European culture to create new American paradigms.

Minstrel shows, the cakewalk and elaborate tap dances became popular in the first half of the 19th Century, leading up to the fusion of European classical notation and African-American rhythms that constituted ragtime. This tradition of assimilation would become a central element in the astonishing adaptability jazz has shown over the last century. Ragtime was not completely jazz, however—the compositions lacked the collective improvisational element that heralded a new approach to music at the beginning of a new century.

Jazz has been responsible for some of the most popular American music of that new century, as well as much of the most progressive. No musical fashion has escaped its assimilative genius. Still, in an American culture with a short history and a lust for disposability, it's hard not to marvel at this music that can effortlessly incorporate the essence of a century of sound into the latest trend on the charts.

Jazz went on to flourish in the cities along the Mississippi River, continuing all the way north to Chicago, in the wide-open territory of Kansas City and the melting pot of New York, a city even more culturally diverse than New Orleans. Jazz spread throughout America, taking hold in Los Angeles in the mid-1930s as the swing era institutionalized the big band as a quintessential symbol of the country, lasting through World War II and becoming a key element of American cultural influence on the rest of the world.

In New York today the big-band tradition still flourishes in the music of working groups like the Mingus Big Band, the Vanguard Orchestra, the Next Legacy Big Band and large groups led by Toshiko Akiyoshi and Maria Schneider, as well as institutionally funded groups at Carnegie Hall and Lincoln Center. Meanwhile the shape of jazz to come is being explored in the vibrant downtown scene centered around the Knitting Factory.

Jazz has produced at least five generations of genius and is currently populated by scores of virtuosic players who will carry the tradition well into the 21st Century. Wynton Marsalis, the New Orleans trumpet maestro who also leads the Lincoln Center jazz program, can boast of a musical legacy that follows an unbroken chain back to the days of recording's prehistory. In 1997 Marsalis became the first jazz musician to win a Pulitzer Prize, for his epic treatment of the African diaspora, *Blood on the Fields.*

Blues, another product of the African diaspora, predates jazz and is an integral part of the jazz tradition while carving out a separate, though often concurrent, route for itself through this century. "Jazz could not exist without blues, although blues does very well on its own," points out the noted jazz historian, record producer and radio host Phil Schaap.

That statement informs the heart of this project. *The Rolling Stone Jazz and Blues Album Guide* is a consumer guide in the tradition of *The Rolling Stone Album Guide,* but it is also a demonstration of how thoroughly this music has inundated our culture and extended itself into a universal language.

Louis Armstrong, the first great jazz improviser to record, was also a consummate blues player who appears on some of Bessie Smith's greatest recordings. You can hear echoes of Armstrong's phrasing and rhythmic approach all through jazz history and by direct or indirect extension in the music of the Harlem Hamfats, Louis Jordan, T-Bone Walker, Bill Haley, Cream, Johnny Winter, Jimi Hendrix, Stevie Ray Vaughan and the current crop of blues newcomers including Little Jimmy King, Melvin Taylor, Jonny Lang and Monster Mike Welch.

Jazz and blues permeate American music in virtually all its forms, from the classical applications of George Gershwin to the blue yodels of Jimmie Rodgers. Fashion-conscious hip-hop fans might be surprised to discover how much rap has in common with the field hollers of plantation slaves in the antebellum South.

While the branches of jazz are diverse, the roots remain fundamentally anchored by blues. The stream is so pure that such innovations as bop (Charlie Parker's first recording session as a leader included the blues "Now's the Time") and free jazz (Ornette Coleman and John Coltrane shared blues-band backgrounds) are directly connected to blues.

The overwhelming majority of rock's many stylistic variations are blues-based, a fact that remains a great irony of the 1970s punk revolution, which claimed to be overthrowing one set of musical values only to replace them with a virtual mirror image of the same influences once removed.

Without Louis Armstrong and Muddy Waters there could have been no Rolling Stones. There could also have been no Sex Pistols, no Police, no Nirvana, no Jamiroquai, no Fugees.

The pantheon of guitar heroes who surfaced out of British rock in the 1960s and 1970s share common influences. Eric Clapton, Jimmy Page, Jeff Beck, Pete Townshend of the Who and Dave Davies of the Kinks, along with dozens of others, all listened to the same blues records and developed a style within a remarkably narrow range. American teenage audiences who were not aware of John Lee Hooker and Albert King thought these ingenious Britons had invented this fantastic music.

Rock & roll culture was unaware of its debt to jazz largely because of generational differences. Jazz became the mainstream American popular music during the first half of the 20th Century. Teenagers listening to rock & roll in the 1950s saw the music of the previous generation as the enemy without realizing that the musical similarities were greater than the differences. The schoolteacher in the J.D. film *Blackboard Jungle* believed that if the leather-clad rockers in his class got a chance to listen to his bop records they could actually hear how Charlie Parker's blues "Now's the Time" anticipated the rock beat as it later showed up in "The Hucklebuck." But the kids weren't interested in listening to the records; it was more fun simply to break them.

Two generations down the road, those *Blackboard Jungle* kids are pushing retirement and tuning in to Kenny G and Boney James on one of the many "soft jazz" easy-listening radio stations around the country. Their grandchildren have revived the atmospheric West Coast jazz of Chet Baker and elevated it to the neonoir status of "lounge music."

The cultural war between rock & roll and jazz was not a one-way street. Mainstream jazz advocates deeply resented being forced off the charts by newcomers and resisted innovations in jazz as well. When Miles Davis arrived at a new sound combining his jazz background with the new possibilities offered by amplified instruments and unusual instrumentations, the Brahmins howled that he had sold out. Fusion is still scorned by many who never acknowledged its creative triumphs or recognized how its ongoing influence has helped jazz to stay fresh as it moves into the new millennium.

We can't settle those arguments—in fact, such differences of opinion are part of the internal conversation this book provides by including a score of critics whose tastes vary widely. We can offer the reader an honest guide through the extremely tangled undergrowth of regularly available catalogs at the average record store.

When the last edition of this book was released in 1985, CDs barely existed. As we've moved into the CD era, recording catalogs have been turned inside out: Many of the vinyl albums reviewed in the first *Jazz Record Guide* are no longer in print, while other recordings by the same artists then unavailable have since been rereleased. Often the availability of key titles seems almost arbitrary.

Jazz records in particular frequently are issued in limited-edition sets (Mosaic Records, a superb packager, comes to mind) that sell out immediately. We've therefore left out these recordings; serious jazz fans should get on the Mosaic mailing list (35 Melrose Place, Stamford, CT 06902; [203] 327-7111) to obtain these rare gems while they're briefly available. Only rarely have we included hard-to-find import albums. Rather than torture you with reviews of great albums you'll never be able to buy, we instead hope to guide you through the vast number of titles currently available in the stores.

The history of jazz and blues runs like an interstate highway through the 20th Century, stopping at plenty of familiar territory but blazing even more new trails as it goes along. Heading into its second century of existence, this music has grown into an international phenomenon whose practitioners recognize no boundaries, be they creative, commercial, racial, sexual or geographic. Although virtually all of the music's original players and innovators are gone, every style and form has been passed down to a new generation of players blessed with a heart for the past, an ear for the present and an eye toward the future. This vast landscape of unbridled invention has never been better represented historically than it is today. To explore this territory, lingering at moments of wonder and awesome beauty, has been a labor of love. Trace the journey along with us, and you're sure to find music that will nourish your soul.

RATINGS

★★★★★

Classic: Albums in this category are essential listening for anyone interested in the artist under discussion or the style of music that artist's work represents.

★★★★

Excellent: Four-star albums represent peak performances in an artist's career. Generally speaking, albums that are granted four or more stars constitute the best introductions to an artist's work for listeners who are curious.

★★★

Average to Good: Albums in the three-star range will primarily be of interest to established fans of the artist being discussed. This middle range, by its very nature, requires the most discretion on the part of the consumer.

★★

Fair to Poor: Albums in the two-star category either fall below an artist's established standard or are, in and of themselves, failures.

★

Disastrous: Albums in the range of one star or less are wastes of vital resources. Only masochists or completists need apply.

REVIEWERS AND THEIR CORRESPONDING INITIALS

Ann Abel — A.A.
Robert Baird — R.B.
Bob Blumenthal — B.B.
Hank Bordowitz — H.B.
J.D. Considine — J.D.C.
Shawn Dahl — S.D.
Greg Emmanuel — G.E.
Paul Evans — P.E.
Ken Franckling — K.F.
Steve Futterman — S.F.
Holly George-Warren — H.G.-W.
Geoffrey Himes — G.H.
B.R. Hunter — B.R.H.
Scott Jordan — S.J.
Ashley Kahn — A.K.
Jordan Kessler — J.K.
David McGee — D.M.
Tom Miller — T.M.
Steve Mirkin — S.M.
Mitch Myers — M.M.
Ted Panken — T.P.
Alan Paul — A.P.
John Swenson — J.S.
Joe Van Plummer — J.V.P.
Jennifer Zoggott — J.Z.

THE Rolling Stone JAZZ & BLUES ALBUM GUIDE

GREG ABATE

★★★ **Bop City—Live at Birdland (Candid, 1991)**
★★★ **Abate Straight Ahead (Candid, 1993)**
★★★½ **My Buddy (Seaside, 1994)**
★★★½ **Dr. Jekyll and Mr. Hyde (Candid, 1995)**
★★★½ **Live at Chan's (with Dan Moretti) (Brownstone, 1995)**
★★★★ **Bop Lives! (Blue Chip Jazz, 1996)**
★★★ **Broken Dreams (Seaside, 1997)**
★★★½ **Happy Samba (Blue Chip Jazz, 1998)**

After two years as a section player in the Ray Charles Orchestra and the revived Artie Shaw band, saxophonist Greg Abate (b. 1947) boldly stepped into bebop in the late 1980s. It was a natural fit for Abate, who plays all of the reed instruments well but acknowledges the alto as his true musical voice.

His intense playing has matured and his skills as a writer and bebop arranger have grown steadily since *Bop City—Live at Birdland,* his first recording as a leader. While *Bop City* and *Abate Straight Ahead* match him with top-flight New York rhythm sections (and special guest Claudio Roditi on the latter), several of his latest homegrown recordings sustain more interest.

My Buddy was made with several fellow New Englanders as a tribute to Jackie Stevens, a 1960s tenor marvel in Woody Herman's band who hasn't picked up a horn in three decades because of a skein of personal problems. Stevens's musical spirit still glows through the efforts of Abate, who was the driving force on this session, which includes seven of Jack's very fine tunes.

Dr. Jekyll and Mr. Hyde is a live club recording with Richie Cole. Abate wrote more than a dozen tunes with Cole in mind as his front-line foil in what became a spirited cutting and quoting session. The only nonoriginal is their blazing baritone-and-alto rendition of "Tommyhawk," a little-recorded Johnny Mandel bop chart from the early 1950s. *Live at Chan's,* recorded with saxophonist Dan Moretti and Brazilia, moves Abate forcefully into the Latin context he began exploring with Roditi on earlier sessions.

Bop Lives! is Abate's best work to date. He is teamed with an all-star rhythm section of Kenny Barron, Rufus Reid and Ben Riley and trumpeter Roditi, whose presence tempers and focuses the alto player's abundant energy. *Broken Dreams,* another Stevens-inspired session, cofeatures tenor saxophonist Frank Tiberi. There's less Latin fire but more depth to Abate's approach on *Happy Samba,* recorded with pianist Mark Soskin, bassist Harvie Swartz, drummer Ed Uribe and *conguero* Wilson "Chembo" Corniel. — K.F.

JOHN ABERCROMBIE

★★★★½ **Timeless (with Jack DeJohnette and Jan Hammer) (ECM, 1974)**
★★★★ **Gateway (ECM, 1975)**
★★★★ **Sargasso Sea (ECM, 1976)**
★★★★ **Characters (ECM, 1977)**
★★★★ **Gateway 2 (ECM, 1978)**
★★★★ **Night (ECM, 1984)**
★★★★ **Current Events (ECM, 1986)**
★★★ **Getting There (ECM, 1987)**
★★★ **John Abercrombie/Marc Johnson/Peter Erskine (ECM, 1988)**
★★★★ **Animato (ECM, 1989)**
★★★½ **Once Upon a Time (New Albion, 1989)**
★★★★ **Works (ECM, 1991)**

★★★ **While We're Young (ECM, 1992)**
★★★ **November (ECM, 1993)**
★★★ **Speak of the Devil (ECM, 1994)**
★★★★★ **Homecoming (ECM, 1995)**
★★★★ **In the Moment (ECM, 1995)**
★★★½ **Solar (Quicksilver, 1996)**
★★★½ **Tactics (ECM, 1997)**

Guitarist John Abercrombie (b. 1944), from Port Chester, New York, came out of a stint at the Berklee College of Music during the early 1960s with a dazzling technique informed by a self-taught genius for emotional expression. By the end of the 1960s, Abercrombie was pursuing the panstylistic ideas of the era as a founding member of Dreams, then in the 1970s with the bands of Chico Hamilton, Jeremy Steig, Gil Evans, Gato Barbieri, Billy Cobham and Jack DeJohnette.

Abercrombie and DeJohnette were a perfect match, both players of meticulous technical prowess with vivid stylistic imaginations. From the moment of their first collaboration on the brilliant *Timeless,* a trio session featuring some of Jan Hammer's best recorded playing, the bond between Abercrombie and DeJohnette is obvious. The two went on to make the quieter *Gateway* and its follow-up, *Gateway 2,* with bassist Dave Holland. The trio reunited for the stellar *Homecoming* and *In the Moment.* Abercrombie and DeJohnette also teamed up on *Night,* with Hammer and tenor saxophonist Michael Brecker.

Sargasso Sea is an atmospheric electric/acoustic guitar-and-piano duet recording with Ralph Towner. They reprised the effort on the now unavailable *Five Years Later. Characters* is a rare solo outing from Abercrombie that shows him to be one of the brightest instrumental lights of his generation.

Current Events was the first in a series of records with the trio of drummer Peter Erskine and bassist Marc Johnson backing Abercrombie's increasingly adventurous guitar work, which he expanded into synthesizer textures. Saxophonist Michael Brecker makes it a quartet on *Getting There.* Abercrombie's electronic experiments reach new heights in his next trio, with Vince Mendoza on synths and Jon Christensen on drums, featured in the otherworldly *Animato.* Yet another trio, with drummer Adam Nussbaum and keyboardist Dan Wall, appears on *While We're Young, Speak of the Devil* and *Tactics.* Erskine and Johnson return, with saxophonist John Surman, on *November. Solar* finds Abercrombie collaborating with guitarist John Scofield.

— J.S.

MUHAL RICHARD ABRAMS

★★★ **Levels and Degrees of Light (1967; Delmark, 1991)**
★★★★ **Sightsong (Black Saint, 1976)**
★★★★ **1-OQA+19 (Black Saint, 1978)**
★★ **Spihumonesty (Black Saint, 1980)**
★★★★★ **Mama and Daddy (Black Saint, 1980)**
★★★★★ **Blues Forever (Black Saint, 1982)**
★★★★★ **Rejoicing with the Light (Black Saint, 1983)**
★★★ **View from Within (Black Saint, 1985)**
★★★★ **Colors in Thirty-Third (Black Saint, 1987)**
★★★★ **Young at Heart/Wise in Time (Delmark, 1989)**
★★★ **The Hearinga Suite (Black Saint, 1990)**
★★★★½ **Blu Blu Blu (Black Saint, 1991)**
★★★ **Familytalk (Black Saint, 1993)**
★★★★ **Duet (with Amina Claudine Myers) (Black Saint, 1993)**
★★★★½ **One Line, Two Views (New World, 1995)**
★★★ **Think All, Focus One (Black Saint, 1996)**

Richard Abrams (b. 1930) was a mainstay on the Chicago club scene during the 1950s, supporting a wide range of visiting jazz stars on piano. Along with another visionary jazz pianist, Sun Ra, Abrams went on to forge a Chicago jazz revolution in the 1960s, beginning with his 1961 Experimental Band, then with the Association for the Advancement of Creative Musicians (AACM) in 1965. With the AACM, Abrams (who began calling himself Muhal at the decade's end) encouraged a new generation of Chicago-based jazz musicians to explore myriad avant-garde styles that were always firmly rooted in black-music tradition. Abrams's albums all have moments of incandescence but often possess fathomless unexplored musical depths beneath the surface.

Levels and Degrees of Light features AACM mainstays Anthony Braxton and Maurice McIntyre on a set that begins with promise but unravels into an undifferentiated wall of sound. *Young at Heart/Wise in Time* showcases Abrams as a solo artist and a stellar AACM quintet of Abrams, Leo Smith, Henry Threadgill, Lester Lashley and Thurman Barker.

The currently unavailable *Things to Come from Those Now Gone* captures Abrams and the AACM in 1972 running the gamut among chamber ballads, hard bop, electronics, mock opera and high energy. It's fascinating, but there are too many bits and pieces. *Sightsong* is a more successful survey from 1975, with Art Ensemble bassist Malachi Favors along to help Abrams explore the AACM's roots.

Abrams's recording activity picked up noticeably from the end of 1977, which is not to say that his albums are easy to find. The two 1978 sessions on Arista/Novus are out of print, and the Black Saint recordings are Italian imports. By all means look for the Black Saints, for Abrams made his best records for that label. The constant shifting of instrumental situations and emotional attitudes hasn't always worked in Abrams's music; sometimes, as on the synthesizer- and voice-laden *Spihumonesty,* what should be a good band doesn't come up with much. But Abrams the small-group leader has never sounded better than on the numerologically titled *1-OQA + 19,* where Anthony Braxton and Henry Threadgill are the saxophonists and Steve McCall is on drums.

Abrams's finest achievement in any format may be *Mama and Daddy;* this ambitious set of compositions for a 10-piece group, with its masterful blends of brass, strings and percussion, has a balance in its glowing execution evocative of chamber music.

Duet is a surprisingly lyrical and diverse encounter with pianist Amina Claudine Myers, while the currently unavailable *Afrisong* contains the best of Abrams's early solo work recorded for Japanese release in 1975. His crowning achievement, however, is *Blues Forever,* a set of orchestral performances expanding on the ideas heard on *Mama and Daddy. Rejoicing with the Light* uses many of the same voices as *Mama* and *Blues.*

On *View from Within* and *Colors in Thirty-Third* Abrams returns to smaller-band settings. *Colors* features the magnificent rhythm-section accompaniment of bassist Fred Hopkins and drummer Andrew Cyrille, who are back in the driver's seat for the large-band rendition of *The Hearinga Suite.*

Blu Blu Blu brings orchestral music into the 1990s with a vengeance, moving effortlessly inside and beyond the tradition. *One Line, Two Views* is an extraordinary exploration into a conception that melds African, jazz and modern classical elements into a coherent whole, a perfect example of how Abrams manages to create not just the music he plays but the creative environment in which it lives.
— B.B./J.S.

WILLIAM ACKERMAN

★★★ **In Search of the Turtle's Navel (Windham Hill, 1976)**
★★ **It Takes a Year (1977; Windham Hill, 1986)**
★★ **Childhood and Memory (Windham Hill, 1979)**
★★★ **Passage (Windham Hill, 1981)**
★★★ **Past Light (Windham Hill, 1983)**
★★★ **Conferring with the Moon (Windham Hill, 1986)**
★★ **Imaginary Roads (Windham Hill, 1988)**
★★ **The Opening of Doors (Windham Hill, 1992)**

Guitarist William Ackerman (b. 1949) formed the Windham Hill label in the '70s after getting positive response to his solo acoustic-guitar experiments, first heard on *In Search of the Turtle's Navel.* Little did the record industry realize that this was the beginning of a gilt-edged commercial trend, New Age music. Ackerman's meticulously performed chamber-jazz outings have their own pristine virtues, which should not be minimized by association with much of the bland music they inspired. The first recordings are solo efforts, but by *Passage* Ackerman has expanded his format to include several duet pieces. *Past Light* employs even more elaborate settings, among them a collaboration with the Kronos Quartet. *Conferring with the Moon* includes highly effective use of a cello section. — J.S.

FAYE ADAMS

★★★ **Shake a Hand: Golden Classics (Collectables, 1988)**

Among the virtues that led Atlantic Records to sign Joe Morris's Blues Cavalcade in the early 1950s was its lead singer, blues belter Faye Adams (b. Faye Tuell, 1932). When the Cavalcade broke up, Adams signed with the small Herald label and immediately cut three R&B hits: "Shake a Hand," "I'll Be True" and "Hurts Me to My Heart." Adams's readings had both power and subtlety, conveying equal degrees of anger and hurt in a single phrasing. At the same time as she struck a cynic's stance with regard to the ways of the heart, she also revealed a tender, loving soul that imbued her best work with the emotional pull of torch songs. *Shake a Hand: Golden Classics* shows off the range of her interpretive skills to moving effect. The big hits are here, as well as some interesting obscurities on the order of "The Hammer (Keeps a-Knockin)." — D.M.

GEORGE ADAMS

★★★★ **Sound Suggestions (ECM, 1979)**
★★★★ **Hand to Hand (with Dannie Richmond) (Soul Note, 1980)**
★★★★ **Gentlemen's Agreement (with Dannie Richmond) (Soul Note, 1983)**
★★★★★ **Live at the Village Vanguard, Vol. 1 (with Don Pullen) (Soul Note, 1985)**
★★★★½ **Live at the Village Vanguard, Vol. 2 (with Don Pullen) (Soul Note, 1986)**
★★★★ **Original Phalanx (DIW, 1987)**
★★★ **Nightingale (Blue Note, 1989)**
★★★½ **America (Blue Note, 1990)**
★★★½ **Old Feeling (Blue Note, 1991)**
★★★½ **Don't Lose Control (with Don Pullen) (Soul Note, 1991)**

George Rufus Adams (1940–1992) was a tenor saxophonist of extraordinary power, range and vision who excelled at exploring the coloratura possibilities of experimental big-band work and was a tireless innovator in bands with coleader pianist Don Pullen. Adams also played flute and bass clarinet, as well as singing a blues-influenced vocal from time to time.

Adams's honking, earthy tone was the product of an imagination that linked the gutbucket blues of Howlin' Wolf and Lightnin' Hopkins with the big-voiced tenor of Coleman Hawkins and a sense of exploration that was clearly post–John Coltrane. He played with Gil Evans and was featured in the Roy Haynes band before joining forces with Charles Mingus along with Pullen and drummer Dannie Richmond during the mid-1970s, an association that was to shape Adams's music until the end of his life. He was an essential member of Mingus Dynasty. Later in the '70s Adams worked in the McCoy Tyner band and made a major contribution to the Evans album *Priestess.*

The Adams-Pullen band, with Richmond on drums and Cameron Brown on bass, carried the Mingus message forward into new terrain, but as new acoustic music it was overlooked by an American record industry fixated on fusion projects. Several European labels picked up the slack, notably Italy's Soul Note, which documented this unit's extraordinary contribution to jazz history, particularly on the two outstanding live sets from New York's Village Vanguard, recorded in 1983. *Don't Lose Control* is an earlier (1979) live recording by the quartet. *Hand to Hand,* an Adams-Richmond project, was recorded in Italy during a 1980 Mingus Dynasty tour, with that group's Hugh Lawson on piano, Richmond's brother Mike on bass and the Mingus stalwart Jimmy Knepper on trombone. This lineup reconvened in New York in 1983 to make the *Gentlemen's Agreement* album.

Though out of print, *Sound Suggestions* is an important recording, a sextet session powered by the rhythm section of bassist Dave Holland, drummer Jack DeJohnette and pianist Richie Beirach. Several excellent records recorded with Pullen for the import label Timeless—*Melodic Excursions, Earth Beams* and *Life Line*—are also out of print, but the quartet date *City Gates* and the quintet *Paradise Space Shuttle* are still available. *Original Phalanx* documents the group Phalanx that Adams formed with guitarist James Blood Ulmer. Adams continued to perform with the Mingus Dynasty band up until his death. By the time the American record industry caught up with Adams in his final years, this tenor giant had his eye on the past rather than the future. The three Blue Note albums contain curious attempts at pop crossover and outright nostalgia. Best moment: "Take Me Out to the Ball Game" from *America.* — J.S.

JOHNNY ADAMS

★★★★ **From the Heart (Rounder, 1984)**
★★★ **After Dark (Rounder, 1986)**
★★★★ **Room with a View of the Blues (Rounder, 1988)**
★★★★★ **I Won't Cry: From the Vaults of Ric/Ron Records (Rounder, 1991)**
★★★★ **Johnny Adams Sings Doc Pomus: The Real Me (Rounder, 1991)**
★★★★ **Good Morning Heartache (Rounder, 1993)**
★★★★ **The Verdict (Rounder, 1995)**
★★★★½ **One Foot in the Blues (Rounder, 1996)**

Johnny Adams (1932–1998), "the Tan Canary," shares with Aaron Neville the reputation as the greatest of the modern New Orleans singers. He grew up singing gospel in various New Orleans choirs before teaming up with the 18-year-old Mac Rebennack to record an electrifying Number One local hit with the soulful blues ballad "(Oh Why) I Won't Cry" for Ric/Ron Records in 1959. *I Won't Cry: From the Vaults of Ric/Ron Records,* a collection of his recordings for that label reissued as a package for the first time in the '90s, offers a glimpse into the golden age of the New Orleans recording industry. Rebennack's influence as a producer is all over this material, but Adams's amazingly dramatic performances—the striking falsetto on "Oh So Nice," the slow blues buildup of "You Can Make It If You Try," the desperation of "Lonely Drifter"—are the product of a supreme talent.

Adams was badly used by Ric owner Joe Ruffino, who blocked an attempt by Berry Gordy Jr. to sign Adams to Motown, where he may well have become a household name. He recorded sporadically for small labels until the mid-'80s, when he began making a series of excellent records for Rounder. *From the Heart* reunited him with Rebennack, now Dr. John, as a writer, along with songs by Doc Pomus and Sam Cooke. *Walking on a Tightrope,* a brilliant reading of Percy Mayfield material, and *Johnny Adams Sings Doc Pomus: The Real Me* demonstrate what a superb interpreter Adams can be.

Adams's elegant, theatrical voice can ferret emotional nuances from even the most familiar material. On *Good Morning Heartache* the 62-year-old Adams showed another side of his talent by recording an album of jazz standards with a big band of New Orleans musicians playing charts arranged by Wardell Quezergue. Exercising perfect control over his voice as it darts in and out of the band's colorations, he maintains the relaxed poise of a true veteran. *The Verdict,* another jazz session, features small bands composed of New Orleans stars. *One Foot in the Blues,* recorded only months before Adams was diagnosed with incurable prostate cancer, shows that he was still in top form on a jazz/blues set that includes three Percy Mayfield compositions and guest performances from Dr. Lonnie Smith on Hammond B-3 organ, Jimmy Ponder on guitar, Shannon Powell on drums and Donald Harrison Jr. on saxophone. — J.S.

PEPPER ADAMS

★★★ **My One and Only Love (West Wind Jazz, 1957)**
★★★ **Pepper Adams Quintet (VSOP, 1957)**
★★★ **10 to 4 at the 5-Spot (1958; Original Jazz Classics, 1993)**
★★★★ **Plays Charles Mingus (Fresh Sound, 1963)**
★★★ **Encounter! (1968; Original Jazz Classics, 1996)**
★★★ **Twelfth and Pingree (Enja, 1975)**
★★★★★ **Reflectory (Muse, 1978)**
★★★★★ **The Master (Muse, 1980)**
★★★ **Conjuration: Fat Tuesday's Session (Reservoir, 1983)**
★★★★ **California Cookin' (Interplay, 1991)**
★★★ **The Cool Sound of Pepper Adams (Savoy, 1993)**
★★★★★ **Urban Dreams (Quicksilver, N.A.)**

Pepper Adams (1930–1986) fully applied Charlie Parker's swift bop conception to the baritone saxophone. In an era dominated by the cool, even-tempered melodiousness of Gerry Mulligan, Adams was heard as the fiery alternative. Springing out of Detroit in the mid-'50s, Adams quickly established himself on the New York scene through his gutsy work with a quintet he co-led with Donald Byrd (*10 to 4 at the 5-Spot*) and numerous sideman dates for Blue Note and Prestige. He later did impressive work with Charles Mingus (*Blues and Roots*) and the Thad Jones/Mel Lewis band. Adams's early work on the West Coast can be heard on *My One and Only Love* and *Pepper Adams Quintet; The Cool Sound of Pepper Adams* is a typically exuberant early-'60s workout with a fine supporting cast including Elvin and Hank Jones.

By the '70s, Adams had hit his stride in a series of recordings marked by intriguing song selection, arrangements and soloist/ensemble interaction. Three remarkable pianists are crucial to Adams's best work of the period: Roland Hanna (*Reflectory*), Tommy Flanagan (*The Master*) and Jimmy Rowles (*Urban Dreams*). Each session is exquisitely balanced between hard-bop cooking and Adams's muscular introspection on well-chosen ballads. His untimely death caught Adams at the peak of his powers. — S.F.

C.C. ADCOCK

★★★½ **C.C. Adcock (Island, 1994)**

The eponymous debut album from Louisiana swamp-rocker C.C. Adcock (b. 1969) packs the synergy of two disparate attitudes: the crank-it-up brashness befitting a young rock & roller and a heartfelt and mature reverence for the rich musical traditions of his home state. Adcock's swaggering tremolo-drenched guitar playing recalls Jimmie Vaughan's ultracool tone and deadly precision in the early days of the

Fabulous Thunderbirds, especially on the roadhouse rockers "Cindy Lou" and "Good Lovin' Do Right Lil' Lady," while his fondness for vintage bullet microphones gives Adcock's vocals the crackling sheen of a 1950s radio broadcast. His cover choices are impeccable—Bo Diddley's "Beaux's Bounce," Art Neville's "I'm Just a Fool to Care" and Arthur Alexander's "Sally Sue Brown"—and marked with equal inspiration from rockabilly, R&B, zydeco, cajun and swamp pop. Adcock's originals are catchy, too. — S.J.

CANNONBALL ADDERLEY

★★★ **Presenting Cannonball (1955; Savoy, 1995)**
★★★★★ **Somethin' Else (1958; Blue Note, 1992)**
★★★½ **Portrait of Cannonball (1958; Original Jazz Classics, 1989)**
★★★★ **Things Are Getting Better (1958; Original Jazz Classics, 1993)**
★★★★ **Cannonball and Coltrane (1959; EmArcy, 1988)**
★★½ **Cannonball Takes Charge (1959; Landmark, 1987)**
★★★ **In San Francisco (1959; Original Jazz Classics, N.A.)**
★★★★ **Them Dirty Blues (1960; Landmark, 1987)**
★★★½ **What Is This Thing Called Soul (1960; Original Jazz Classics, 1994)**
★★★ **Cannonball and the Poll Winners (1960; Landmark, 1986)**
★★★½ **At the Lighthouse (1960; Landmark, 1986)**
★★★ **Know What I Mean (1961; Original Jazz Classics, 1987)**
★★★★ **African Waltz (1961; Original Jazz Classics, 1993)**
★★★ **Cannonball Adderley Quintet Plus (1961; Original Jazz Classics, 1988)**
★★★½ **Compact Jazz: Cannonball Adderley (1962; EmArcy, N.A.)**
★★★½ **In New York (1962; Original Jazz Classics, 1987)**
★★★½ **Cannonball in Europe! (1962; Landmark, 1987)**
★★★ **Jazz Workshop Revisited (1962; Landmark, 1987)**
★★★ **Cannonball's Bossa Nova (1962; Landmark, 1987)**
★★★½ **Dizzy's Business (1963; Milestone, 1993)**
★★★★ **Nippon Soul (1963; Original Jazz Classics, 1990)**
★★★ **Cannonball in Japan (1966; Capitol, 1990)**
★★★★ **Mercy, Mercy, Mercy (1966; Capitol, 1995)**
★★★ **Country Preacher (1969; Capitol, 1994)**
★★★ **Inside Straight (1973; Original Jazz Classics, 1992)**
★★★★ **The Best of Cannonball Adderley: The Capitol Years (Capitol, 1991)**
★★★½ **Paris, 1960 (Pablo, 1997)**

Cannonball Adderley (1928–1975) took the free-blowing message Charlie Parker gave alto players and used it to simple yet devastating effect in pioneering the soul-jazz movement, an offspring of bop heavily accented by R&B and gospel. His sense of melody and groove-oriented rhythm brought Adderley from recognition as a young lion alongside John Coltrane in Miles Davis's band (the two saxophonists engage in sublime dialog on the epochal Davis recording *Kind of Blue*) to mainstream pop stature with the 1967 hit "Mercy, Mercy, Mercy!" lifted right off the live recording of the same name.

Born in Tampa, Florida, Adderley came to New York with his cornet-playing brother, Nat, in 1955 and made an immediate impression on the club circuit as a Parker disciple with a flair for dramatic, emotional solos. The unknown saxophonist took the stage at the Cafe Bohemia to jam with Oscar Pettiford's group. Shortly afterward, he was in the studio for his first session, *Bohemia After Dark,* a date led by drummer Kenny Clarke but designed to showcase the new jazz star. Two weeks later Adderley recorded his first session as a leader—an era represented on *Presenting Cannonball.*

The first Adderley quintet with Nat on cornet recorded for EmArcy but broke up in 1957. In the two years before he re-formed the group with his brother, Adderley made a series of hot quintet albums with a variety of quality players as well as contributing to Davis's *Milestones* and *Kind of Blue.* Davis appears on the top-flight *Somethin' Else* with Art Blakey on drums, Sam Jones on bass and Hank Jones on piano. Blakey also contributes on the excellent *Things Are Getting Better,* with Wynton Kelly on piano, Milt Jackson on vibes and Percy Heath on bass. *Portrait of Cannonball* features pianist Bill Evans, drummer Philly Joe Jones, bassist Sam Jones and trumpeter Blue Mitchell. All of these albums used players from the Davis band; *Cannonball and Coltrane* is the Davis band without Miles.

The re-formed Adderley-brothers quintet included pianist Bobby Timmons, bassist Sam Jones and drummer Louis Hayes. *Them Dirty Blues* introduces Timmons's soul classic "Dat Dere" and Nat's immortal "Work Song." *Paris, 1960* is a spirited live session with Victor Feldman instead of Timmons and a killer version of Oscar Pettiford's "Bohemia After Dark."

Adderley's popularity led him to record in other settings besides the working group. The magnificent big-band outing *African Waltz* won a pair of Grammy Awards. *Know What I Mean* is a quartet session with Bill Evans on piano, Percy Heath on bass and Connie Kay on drums. *Cannonball and the Poll Winners* was a popular all-star session featuring Wes Montgomery on guitar and the regular quintet's next pianist, Victor Feldman, who appears on *At the Lighthouse*, *What Is This Thing Called Soul* and *Quintet Plus.*

Adderley's impressive run took another leap with the addition of keyboardist Joe Zawinul and reed player Yusef Lateef to the lineup. Zawinul's thirst for the groove and compositional ability ("Mercy, Mercy, Mercy!," "Country Preacher") was a perfect fit in this powerful unit, and Lateef brought tenor saxophone, flute and oboe into the mix. This configuration can be heard on *In New York*, *In Europe*, *Jazz Workshop*, *Dizzy's Business* and *Nippon Soul.* — J.S.

NAT ADDERLEY

★★★½ **That's Nat (Savoy, 1955)**
★★★★ **Branching Out (1958; Original Jazz Classics, 1994)**
★★★½ **Much Brass (1959; Original Jazz Classics, 1995)**
★★★★½ **Work Song (1960; Original Jazz Classics, 1989)**
★★★★ **That's Right! (1960; Original Jazz Classics, 1994)**
★★★★ **In the Bag (1962; Original Jazz Classics, 1991)**
★★ **Don't Look Back (1976; SteepleChase, 1995)**
★★★ **On the Move (1983; Evidence, 1993)**
★★★★ **Blue Autumn (1983; Evidence, 1992)**
★★★★ **Autumn Leaves (1990; Evidence, 1994)**
★★★ **The Old Country (Enja, 1990)**
★★★ **Talkin' About You (Landmark, 1990)**
★★★ **We Remember Cannon (In + Out, 1991)**
★★★ **Workin' (Timeless, 1992)**
★★★ **Mercy, Mercy, Mercy (Evidence, 1997)**

As part of the group led by his brother Cannonball Adderley, cornet and trumpet player Nat Adderley (b. 1931) spearheaded the gospel- and blues-influenced soul-jazz movement of the early '60s. Nat was already working in an engaging Dizzy Gillespie–inspired style on the Savoy sides. *Branching Out* is a red-hot 1958 session with Johnny Griffin on tenor sax. In 1960, using his brother's associates Bobby Timmons on piano, Louis Hayes on drums and Sam Jones on cello, as well as Wes Montgomery on guitar and Percy Heath on bass, Adderley wrote and recorded the soul classic "Work Song," which subsequently became popularized in cover versions.

That's Right!, from later in 1960, pits Nat against "the Big Sax Section"—brother Cannonball, Yusef Lateef, Jimmy Heath, Charlie Rouse and Tate Houston. The Adderley brothers traveled to Cosimo Matassa's studio in New Orleans in 1962 to cut *In the Bag* with a local band led by pianist Ellis Marsalis. The reissue features a fascinating attempt at the New Orleans dance tune "The Popeye," originally released as a single by Spider Johnson and His Popeye Band, with Harold Battiste replacing Marsalis.

The live Keystone Korner recordings *On the Move* and *Blue Autumn* document a solid lineup featuring Sonny Fortune on alto sax, Larry Willis on piano, Walter Booker on bass and Jimmy Cobb on drums. By 1990 Vincent Herring had assumed the alto-sax chair for *The Old Country* and *Talkin' About You,* but the best recording from this era is the live set recorded at Sweet Basil with both Fortune and Herring, *Autumn Leaves.* — J.S.

RON AFFIF

★★★½ **Ron Affif (Pablo, 1993)**
★★★★ **Vierd Blues (Pablo, 1994)**
★★★★ **52nd Street (Pablo, 1996)**
★★★★ **Ringside (Pablo, 1997)**

Guitarist Ron Affif (b. 1965) is a virtuosic improviser in the tradition of Joe Pass and Wes Montgomery, one of the few guitarists of his generation seemingly untouched by the fusion revolution. His note articulation at high speed is remarkable, but the phrases always swing with a bop or blues feel, and he mixes tempos deftly, displaying keen emotional sense on ballads.

Affif was raised in Pittsburgh by a musical family. His father, Charlie Affif, was a friend of Miles Davis, and his uncle Ron Anthony taught him to play and gave him his first guitar. He moved to Los Angeles in 1984 and recorded a now unavailable debut album before moving to New York in 1989.

Affif worked in a variety of contexts in New York, honing his skills until he was ready to make his Pablo debut, a mixture of standards and several originals that marked him as a developing talent.

The guitarist came into his own with the outstanding *Vierd Blues,* a Davis tribute offering some unique interpretations of the Miles trademarks "So What," "Blue in Green," "All Blues," "Four" and "Seven Steps to Heaven" and ending with his own "Homage to Miles." Uncle Ron sits in on a couple of tracks.

52nd Street is the work of a major artist coming into the confidence of his prime. Affif dazzles on such historic tracks as Oscar Pettiford's "Bohemia After Dark," the swing standard "Stompin' at the Savoy," Charlie Parker's "Yardbird Suite" and "Steeplechase" and the Tadd Dameron composition "Tadd's Delight." Affif closes the proceedings with "Eric's Zinc Bar Blues," a tribute to the tiny club where he held forth on Monday nights with a trio fleshed out by bassist Essiet Essiet and drummer Jeff "Tain" Watts. Essiet is also on hand, along with drummer Colin Bailey, for *Ringside,* recorded before a live audience at the Fantasy Studio in Berkeley, California. The flow and energy of Affif's live performance is caught well here, especially on the opening tandem of "If I Were a Bell" and "Don't Make Me Pull That Tongue Out." — J.S.

AIR

★★★★ **Live Air (Black Saint, 1980)**
★★★★ **Air Mail (Black Saint, 1981)**
★★★★ **Air Song (India Navigation, 1982)**
★★★ **New Air: Live at Montreal International Jazz Festival (Black Saint, 1984)**
★★★ **New Air: Air Show No. 1 (Black Saint, 1986)**

Saxophonist Henry Threadgill, bassist Fred Hopkins and drummer Steve McCall formed Air in Chicago in 1971. Until 1976, when they began appearing regularly in New York, Air quietly developed their strengths, recording two stunning albums for the Japanese Whynot label. *Air Song,* the first of these, appeared domestically in 1982. From the time their American recording activity began in earnest in 1978, Air was elevated to the ranks of those permanent bands that had developed something special.

Among Air's virtues are the classic sax, bass, drums lineup, a willingness to explore all manner of material, attention to detail at even the most collectively heated junctures and the earth-moving Hopkins/McCall rhythm section. This trio doesn't make bad records but has tended to be most impressive when avoiding side-long performances. The currently unavailable *Air Time* is probably the best single-album indication of the band's range, which encompasses the heroic ("Keep Right On Playing . . .") and the whimsical ("G.v.E.," on which Threadgill plays his array of hubcaps, the hubkaphone).

Still, if one Air album belongs in every collection, it is *Air Lore,* a 1979 performance of Scott Joplin rags and Jelly Roll Morton tunes that is currently unsurpassed as a statement of historical homage from the perspective of the frontiers and should be a priority reissue project.

One of the best jazz albums of 1982, *80 Degrees Below '82* (also currently unavailable), captures the telepathic agreement of Air's members in full glory. McCall left the trio in early 1983. Threadgill and Hopkins continued to perform with various drummers. The two New Air sets are with drummer Pheeroan AkLaff. — B.B.

AIRTO

★★★ **Seeds on the Ground (One Way, 1971)**
★★★★ **Dafos (with Mickey Hart) (Rykodisc, 1984)**
★★★★ **Three Way Mirror (Reference, 1985)**
★★★★ **The Magicians (Concord Vista, 1986)**
★★★★ **The Sun Is Out (Concord Vista, 1987)**
★★★★ **The Best of Airto (Legacy, 1994)**

Percussionist/singer Airto Moreira (b. 1941) was a child prodigy in his native Brazil before joining the Sambalanco Trio, then leading his own band, Quarteto Novo, with multi-instrumentalist Hermeto Pascoal. He emigrated to the United States, working with Moacir Santos in the late 1960s before becoming a fusion star with the Miles Davis group and the original Return to Forever lineup.

Airto's virtuosic command of Brazilian rhythms, innovative use of aboriginal percussion instruments and awesome technical ability made him one of the most sought-after session percussionists in the early 1970s.

He went on to form a solo band featuring his wife, vocalist Flora Purim. The pair combined for a very original sound based on the rich folk traditions of Brazilian music but constantly evolving into new realms through Airto's flights of percussive fancy and Purim's wordless vocal style.

Airto has been in and out of the recording studio, but much of his work, including several good outings for CTI, has passed out of circulation. Of what is available, *The Magicians,* a large band outing, *Three Way Mirror,* with tenor saxophonist/flautist Joe Farrell, a cohort from the CTI days, and *The Sun Is Out* are particularly good. All three feature Purim.
— J.S.

TOSHIKO AKIYOSHI

★★★★★ **The Toshiko Akiyoshi/Lew Tabackin Big Band (Novus, 1976)**
★★★ **Finesse (1978; Concord Jazz, N.A.)**
★★★½ **Interlude (Concord Jazz, 1987)**
★★★★ **Remembering Bud: Cleopatra's Dream (Evidence, 1992)**
★★★★★ **Carnegie Hall Concert (Columbia, 1992)**
★★★★ **Desert Lady—Fantasy (Columbia, 1994)**
★★★★ **Maybeck Recital Hall Series, Vol. 36 (Concord Jazz, 1995)**

As an Asian woman, Toshiko Akiyoshi (b. 1929) had to overcome the most thoroughgoing of prejudices to become accepted as a jazz performer and bandleader. She had to be that much better than her peers to be treated as more than just a novelty act, and indeed she is now lauded for her accomplished playing and considered one of the best contemporary big-band composers for the richness of her orchestral colors, the originality of her arrangement ideas and the rhythmic sophistication of her bands as a total organism.

Born in Manchuria, China, the classically trained Akiyoshi returned to Japan with her family after World War II. There she played piano in dance halls, and in 1951 began leading her own jazz group in Tokyo, where she was discovered two years later by Oscar Peterson during a Jazz at the Philharmonic tour.

By 1956, when Akiyoshi arrived in the United States to study at the Berklee College of Music, she was generally acknowledged as Japan's leading jazz musician and accorded mainstream status as a Bud Powell disciple. During the 1950s and '60s she made a series of now unavailable small-group and solo albums, married and had a child with saxophonist Charlie Mariano and studied and played with the Charles Mingus Jazz Workshop. Akiyoshi's career revived in the mid-1970s after she married saxophonist/flautist Lew Tabackin and moved to the West Coast, where she became the leader of a critically acclaimed and award-winning rehearsal orchestra of top Los Angeles session musicians with Tabackin as the principal soloist. The Novus edition collects material from four albums recorded during this period—*Long Yellow Road*, *Insights*, *Kogun* and *Road Time.*

Finesse, on the other hand, showcases Akiyoshi's talents in a trio setting, with drummer Jake Hanna, who played in her trio when she was at Berklee, and bassist Monty Budwig. The set mixes standards and originals with a Jelly Roll Morton tune and material that dates back to her days starting out in Japanese dance halls.

None of Akiyoshi's 1980s work with the big band is currently available in the United States, including the exceptional *Tanuki's Night Out*, *Wishing Peace* and the Mingus tribute *Farewell to Mingus.* Thus a key element in the band's history, when Akiyoshi and Tabackin returned to New York and recruited a new group of players, is unrepresented here. *Interlude,* a 1987 trio with bassist Dennis Irwin and drummer Eddie Marshall, includes several originals contrasted against Count Basie, Duke Ellington, standards and a classical piece.

Remembering Bud—Cleopatra's Dream was originally recorded for a Japanese label in 1990 at two separate trio sessions with bassists George Mraz and Ray Drummond and drummers Lewis Nash and Al Harewood. The album is a tribute to one of Akiyoshi's key influences, pianist Bud Powell.

The 1991 *Carnegie Hall Concert,* celebrating the 35th anniversary of Akiyoshi's arrival in the United States, was a triumphant moment for the composer, whose vibrant, Ellington-like orchestrations are handled deftly by a band clearly inspired by the sensitivity of her vision.

Akiyoshi distinguished herself as a soloist on her back-to-the-roots Maybeck Recital Hall concert, part of the essential Concord Jazz solo-piano series recorded at that venue. Her own

"The Village" is followed by Ellington's "Come Sunday" in an obvious homage. After a delightful cover of Dizzy Gillespie's "Con Alma," Akiyoshi goes on to perform a thoughtful series of standards before closing with another Ellington composition, "Sophisticated Lady," her own "Quadrille, Anyone?" and her tribute to the master, Powell's "Tempus Fugit." — J.S.

JOE ALBANY

★★★★ **The Right Combination (1957; Original Jazz Classics, 1990)**
★★★★ **Bird Lives! (Storyville, 1978)**
★★★★ **Portrait of an Artist (Elektra Musician, 1982)**

A great musician whose tragic life kept his recorded output to a minimum, Joe Albany (1924–1988) was one of the top bop pianists of the mid-1940s. He worked with Charlie Parker's band as well as with Lester Young and, later, Charles Mingus. The Atlantic City, New Jersey, native had a deep harmonic intelligence and an expressive style but was severely limited by a heroin addiction. *The Right Combination* is a reissue of a solid session with Warne Marsh on tenor saxophone. It was the only recording Albany was able to make between 1957 and 1971.

Bird Lives! is the most characteristic of Albany's recordings, a Parker tribute that recalls their days together turning the music world upside down. *Portrait of an Artist,* his last record, shows that Albany was still a spectacular player whose conception, even into the '80s, was far from dated. As with so many of his contemporaries, Albany's talents were ignored at home, forcing him to emigrate to Europe for large portions of his life. From this era, look for the out-of-print *Two's Company,* duet recordings with bassist Niels-Henning Ørsted Pedersen; *Proto-Bopper;* and the live *Birdtown Birds.* — J.S.

HOWARD ALDEN

★★ **Swing Street (Concord Jazz, 1988)**
★★★ **The Howard Alden Trio (with Ken Peplowski and Warren Vache) (Concord Jazz, 1989)**
★★★½ **The Alden-Barrett Quintet Salutes Buck Clayton (Concord Jazz, 1989)**
★★★★★ **Snowy Morning Blues (with Monty Alexander) (Concord Jazz, 1990)**
★★★ **13 Strings (with George Van Eps) (Concord Jazz, 1991)**
★★★★ **Misterioso (Concord Jazz, 1991)**
★★★★ **Hand-Crafted Swing (with George Van Eps) (Concord Jazz, 1992)**
★★★ **A Good Likeness (Concord Jazz, 1993)**
★★ **Concord Duo Series, Vol. 3 (with Ken Peplowski) (Concord Jazz, 1993)**
★★★½ **Seven and Seven (with George Van Eps) (Concord Jazz, 1993)**
★★★ **Fujitsu-Concord 25th Jazz Festival—Silver Anniversary Set (Concord Jazz, 1994)**
★★★★ **Your Story: The Music of Bill Evans (with Frank Wess) (Concord Jazz, 1994)**
★★★½ **Encore! (with Ken Peplowski) (Concord Jazz, 1995)**
★★★★ **Concord Jazz Guitar Collective (with Frank Vignola, Jimmy Bruno) (Concord Jazz, 1995)**
★★★★ **Keepin' Time (with George Van Eps) (Concord Jazz, 1996)**
★★★★ **Take Your Pick (Concord Jazz, 1997)**
★★★½ **Full Circle (with Jimmy Bruno) (Concord Jazz, 1998)**

Guitarist and banjo player Howard Alden (b. 1958) grew up in Southern California but shunned contemporary pop, gravitating instead toward the strong rhythms and recognizable melodies of swing jazz and the American songbook. He absorbed a tremendous repertoire of tunes while developing a clean and warm single-note melodic style in the tradition of Barney Kessel and his teacher, Howard Roberts.

A summer stint in Atlantic City with vibraphonist Red Norvo's band in 1979 hooked him on a music career. In 1982, Alden moved permanently to New York, where he found plenty of work on the mainstream scene. Pianist Joe Bushkin guaranteed him two months as a sideman at his Hotel Carlyle gig. That led to a succession of strong musical partnerships—with cornetist Ruby Braff, with clarinetist Kenny Davern and with trombonist Dan Barrett as coleader of a quintet. He also found a seat in Buck Clayton's jazz orchestra.

Since the mid-1980s, Alden has recorded extensively for the Concord Jazz label, including fine work as a sideman with Braff and saxophonist Ken Peplowski and on several Concord all-star sessions. All showcase his sunny tone, modern harmonic sense and elegant, structured solos.

Among his early recordings, the Alden-Barrett salute to Buck Clayton, his *Snowy Morning Blues* collaboration with pianist Monty Alexander and the wide-ranging trio session *Misterioso* are strongest.

Since 1991 Alden has also made four fine recordings with one of his guitar heroes, fellow Californian George Van Eps, a master of chordal playing whose style complements Alden's single-note strengths. Working with Van Eps prompted Alden to get his own seven-string guitar and strengthen his harmonic playing.

With strong aid from Frank Wess on tenor and flute, Alden's trio reveals new facets in the Bill Evans songbook on *Your Story: The Music of Bill Evans.* Supported by a rhythm section on several selections, *Encore!* is the best of his collaborations with Peplowski. Alden's *Concord Jazz Guitar Collective* appearance with Jimmy Bruno and Frank Vignola is a very fine showcase for each of them, one that continues the guitar swing-summit tradition that Concord began in the 1970s with Charlie Byrd, Herb Ellis and Barney Kessel.

Alden leaves his fellow guitarists behind on *Take Your Pick,* a mighty swing session in which he alternates between electric and acoustic seven-string guitars. He also has fresh company from drummer Bill Goodwin, tenor-saxophone/flute player Lew Tabackin and pianist Renee Rosnes. Alden and Bruno blend hot and cool styles as they team up mightily with bassist Michael Moore and drummer Alan Dawson on *Full Circle,* a package that includes a bonus CD of *Jazz/Concord,* the 1972 Joe Pass–Herb Ellis–Ray Brown–Jake Hanna quartet session that was the label's first release. — K.F.

MONTY ALEXANDER

★★★★★ **Montreux Alexander (Verve, 1977)**
★★★ **Facets (1980; Concord Jazz, 1991)**
★★★★ **Ivory & Steel (Concord Picante, 1980)**
★★★ **Trio (Concord Jazz, 1981)**
★★★★ **Triple Treat (Concord Jazz, 1982)**
★★½ **Full Steam Ahead (Concord Jazz, 1985)**
★★★½ **Threesome (Soul Note, 1986)**
★★★ **Jamboree (Concord Picante, 1988)**
★★★ **Triple Treat II (Concord Jazz, 1988)**
★★★ **Triple Treat III (Concord Jazz,1989)**
★★★★★ **The River (Concord Jazz, 1990)**
★★★ **Caribbean Circle (Chesky, 1992)**
★★★ **Steamin' (Concord Jazz, 1995)**
★★★★ **Maybeck Recital Hall Series, Vol. 40 (Concord Jazz, 1995)**
★★★½ **Yard Movement (Island Jamaica Jazz, 1996)**
★★★★ **To the Ends of the Earth (Concord Picante, 1996)**
★★★★ **Echoes of Jilly's (Concord Jazz, 1997)**

Jamaican-born pianist Monty Alexander (b. 1944) has made his Caribbean heritage an integral part of his musical personality, blending its rhythmic flavor and accents into his invigorating sound. Most available recordings find this former Milt Jackson and Ray Brown sideman in the comfortable confines of the jazz trio, an influence absorbed from Nat Cole and Oscar Peterson, in whose hard-swinging jazz lineage Alexander has blossomed since arriving in the United States in 1961.

Twenty years after its recording at Switzerland's world-class Montreux Jazz Festival in 1976, *Montreux Alexander* remains one of Alexander's most essential recordings. It established him as a potent force on his first appearance at a major European jazz festival with bassist John Clayton and drummer Jeff Hamilton. As if burning versions of "Battle Hymn of the Republic" and "Work Song" weren't enough, Alexander even makes Morris Albert's wretched pop song "Feelings" interesting.

Trio and the joyous *Triple Treat* recordings with bassist Ray Brown and guitarist Herb Ellis are top-notch, with violinist Johnny Frigo guesting on the second and third volumes. *Threesome* teams Alexander with bassist Niels-Henning Ørsted Pedersen and drummer/vocalist Grady Tate.

His larger-band recordings, ranging from quintet to sextet, blend jazz with his roots for the *Ivory & Steel* and *Jamboree* sessions featuring steel drummers Othello Molineaux and Boogsie Sharpe. *Ivory & Steel* adds Caribbean spice to several terrific jazz chestnuts, including a wonderful "Impressions"/"So What" medley, while the *Jamboree* repertoire leans more toward the islands. *Caribbean Circle* is a somewhat overdone blend of Caribbean influences and singsong autobiography, rescued by hot playing on several tracks with Frank Foster, Slide Hampton, Anthony Jackson, Jon Faddis and Wynton Marsalis (making a cameo under the alias E. Dankworth).

The River, a trio session with bassist John Clayton and drummer Ed Thigpen, draws on spirituals and traditional hymns for its upbeat inspiration. Alexander's visit to Maybeck Recital Hall, part of Concord's acclaimed solo-piano series, showcases his breadth, depth and vibrant roots. *Yard Movement* returned Alexander to the setting of his 1976 Montreux triumph for a buoyant session with, among others, Jamaican guitarist Ernest Ranglin, a collaborator since the late 1950s. *To the Ends of the Earth* is Alexander's third "Ivory and Steel" collaboration, a jazz-meets-the-steel-pans session enhanced by the forceful presence of alto saxophonist Antonio Hart and trombonist Steve Turre. Recorded with bassist John Patitucci and drummer Troy Davis, *Echoes of Jilly's* is a tribute session featuring swinging instrumental versions of tunes made famous by Frank Sinatra. — K.F.

LOREZ ALEXANDRIA

★★★ **Band Swings Lorez Sings (King, 1957)**
★★★ **Singing Songs Everybody Knows (King, 1960)**
★★★½ **May I Come In (Muse, 1991)**
★★★½ **I'll Never Stop Loving You (Muse, 1993)**
★★★½ **Star Eyes (Muse, 1996)**

Trained as a gospel singer in her native Chicago, Lorez Alexandria (b. 1929) made a series of records for King in the 1950s and early '60s. Her Billie Holiday–influenced sound owed as much to Lester Young's protocool jazz saxophone style as to any other vocalist (check out *Lorez Sings Pres,* an unavailable King release).

Alexandria went on to sing in a more emotive style, reaching back to her gospel roots. Two out-of-print 1970s releases, *Deep Roots* and an album of Johnny Mercer songs, are worth seeking out.

Alexandria began to perform more frequently in her 60s and enjoyed a renaissance in the studio with a trio of albums for Muse produced by saxophonist Houston Person, whose tenor accompanies Alexandria's emotional delivery perfectly. *I'll Never Stop Loving You* includes an epic performance of "For All We Know." — J.S.

CARL ALLEN

★★★ **The Pursuer (Atlantic Jazz, 1994)**
★★★ **Testimonial (Atlantic Jazz, 1995)**

Drummer Carl Allen, born in Milwaukee in 1961, was musical director with Freddie Hubbard's band and also played with Sonny Stitt, James Moody, Jackie McLean and Billy Taylor before joining forces with saxophonist Vincent Herring in 1988 to pursue new projects.

A straight-ahead sextet session, *The Pursuer* features Herring and trumpeter Marcus Printup. *Testimonial* is a gospel-influenced album highlighted by "Tuesday Night Prayer Meeting" and Duke Ellington's "Come Sunday." Herring adds tenor to his usual array of alto and soprano saxes, and the high-energy New Orleans trumpeter Nicholas Payton excels in his role. Special guests include bassist Christian McBride, Cyrus Chestnut on organ and piano and Mark Whitfield on guitar. — J.S.

GERI ALLEN

★★★ **Segments (DIW, 1989)**
★★½ **In the Year of the Dragon (JMT, 1989)**
★★★ **Live at the Village Vanguard (DIW, 1991)**
★★★½ **The Nurturer (Blue Note, 1991)**
★★★ **Maroons (Blue Note, 1992)**
★★★½ **Twenty One (Blue Note, 1994)**
★★★½ **Eyes . . . in the Back of Your Head (Blue Note, 1997)**

A sought-after accompanist on piano, Geri Allen (b. 1957) has worked with Oliver Lake, Betty Carter and Ornette Coleman, among others. Much of her early (pre-1990) solo work has fallen out of print. Look for the solo outing *Homegrown* and *In the Middle,* which features her mentor, Marcus Belgrave, Was (Not Was) stalwart Rayse Biggs and a cast of M-Base colleagues.

Segments and *In the Year of the Dragon* catch Allen in a trio of rotating leadership she shared with Charlie Haden and Paul Motian. At *Segments'* spirited best—a lyrical reading of "I'm All Smiles," a sparkling interpretation of Ornette's "Law Years," and the title track—the disc is full of swing and nuance. Unfortunately, not all of the album produces such sublime moments.

Dragon is more even but has far less fire. Haden's bluesy "See You at Per Tutti's" and Bud Powell's lively "Oblivion" are the highlights. Both of these recordings tend to meander, as does the trio's Vanguard date. Tunes like "Mumbo Jumbo" and "Fiasco" live up to their names, free-form improvisations that don't go anywhere. Reprises of the title track from

Dragon and "A Prayer for Peace" work better, as does the Monk-ish "Vanguard Blues."

The Nurturer features Belgrave and Kenny Garrett. The results are at once sweeter and surprisingly more direct than the previous trio recordings, especially on the two tracks by Lawrence Williams, "No. 3" and "It's Good to Be Home Again."

Maroons kicks off with the first of three takes on "Feed the Fire," worth repeating as it's the best thing on the album, especially the first, all-too-short, Latin-esque dual-drum track. A version of "No More Mr. Nice Guy," a tune she did on *Dragon,* propelled by drummer Tani Tabbal, eventually swings ferociously, as does "Bed-Sty." In general, the tunes featuring Tabbal and Dwayne Dolphin epitomize jazz flexibility. While the expanding and contracting band sizes work nicely, the playing from one track to another is wildly uneven.

Moving back to a trio format, Allen hooked up with producers Teo Macero and Herb Jordan (her only outside producers on any of the reviewed CDs here) and a radically different rhythm section of Ron Carter and Tony Williams for *Twenty One.* Combining percussive impetus with consistency, the trio swings and sways in about equal measures. Even tepid tracks like "In the Morning" retain internal logic, and her swinging "Tea for Two" shows where you can take a hoary standard when you blow the dust off.

After becoming Ornette Coleman's choice for the first pianist to work with him in nearly four decades, Allen came back with *Eyes . . . in the Back of Your Head.* On this album of solos, duets and an occasional trio, experimental from the first note, she explores the piano inside and out, venturing into Henry Cowell territory on "Windows to the Soul." The album brings to mind a paraphrase of John Philpot Curran's adage—eternal vigilance (to the meter and melody) is the cost of freedom (in jazz). Coleman knows this instinctively (might come from all those years of playing R&B), as he illustrates on his duets with Allen, the rambling but bluesy "The Eyes Have It" and the almost liquid-sounding "Vertical Flowing." Percussionist Cyro Baptista also keeps up the groove on "Mother Wit" and the trio with Allen's husband, trumpeter Wallace Roney, on "Dark Eyes." Actually, the vigilance of everyone involved, even Coleman, occasionally slips. Then freedom turns to anarchy. These occasions are rare, and Allen has never sounded more willing to take chances. — H.B.

HARRY ALLEN

★★★	**How Long Has This Been Going On? (Progressive, 1989)**
★★½	**Are You Having Any Fun? A Celebration of the Music of Sammy Fain (Audiophile, 1991)**
★★★	**My Little Brown Book: A Celebration of Billy Strayhorn's Music, Vol. 1 (Progressive, 1994)**
★★★	**The Intimacy of the Blues: A Celebration of Billy Strayhorn's Music, Vol. 2 (Progressive, 1994)**
★★★	**A Night at Birdland, Vol. 1 (Nagel-Heyer, 1994)**
★★★★★	**Jazz Im Amerika Haus, Vol. 1 (Nagel-Heyer, 1994)**
★★	**Blue Skies: Jazz Ballads from the 1930s to Today (John Marks, 1994)**
★★★	**A Night at Birdland, Vol. 2 (Nagel-Heyer, 1995)**
★★★★	**Harry Allen Meets the John Pizzarelli Trio (BMG Japan, 1996)**
★★★	**A Little Touch of Harry (Mastermix, 1997)**
★★★★½	**Tenors Anyone? (BMG Japan, 1997)**
★★★½	**Here's to Zoot (BMG Japan, 1997)**
★★★	**The Music of the Trumpet Kings (with Randy Sandke) (Nagel-Heyer, 1997)**

Stylistically and geographically, tenor saxophonist Harry Allen (b. 1966) grew up in the shadow of fellow Rhode Islander Scott Hamilton, a strong influence despite their 12-year age gap. Producer George Wein summoned Allen, then 16, to the stage to sit in with his Newport Jazz Festival All Stars—including Hamilton—in 1983. Allen hasn't looked back, developing into a confident and mature New York–based swing player.

The two-volume Billy Strayhorn–tribute series, with frequent musical partner Keith Ingham on piano, bassist Dennis Irwin and two Hamilton quintet veterans, guitarist Chris Flory and drummer Chuck Riggs, showcases Allen's facile range. Both volumes rediscover several neglected Strayhorn gems.

A Night at Birdland, Vols. 1 and *2,* recorded at Hamburg's Birdland jazz club in 1993, are swinging collaborations with a quintet cofeaturing trumpeter Randy Sandke and propelled by drummer Oliver Jackson, who was one of Allen's primary mentors. They turned out to be Jackson's final recordings before his passing at age 61.

Jazz Im Amerika Haus, on Hans Nagel-Heyer's independent German label, is one to seek out no matter how difficult. This live Hamburg club session with John Bunch, Dennis Irwin and Duffy Jackson documents Allen's step forward with a frisky style prodded by veteran big-band drummer Jackson. Allen's work on the great Basie-band blowing tune "The King" has a searing energy reminiscent of Paul Gonsalves's historic 1956 "Diminuendo and Crescendo" extended moment at Newport with the Ellington band. *Blue Skies,* recorded with the same personnel as *Amerika Haus,* is flawed by poor recording quality.

Allen's Japanese release with producer/guitarist John Pizzarelli's trio reflects his continuing growth as a hard-swinging tenor soloist emerging from the shadows of Zoot Sims, Stan Getz and Scott Hamilton.

Allen turns standards into more than standard fare, as shown on *A Little Touch of Harry,* which teams him with the all-star rhythm section of Kenny Barron, George Mraz and Al Foster. *Tenors Anyone?* is an excellent rematch with Pizzarelli's trio, with which Allen has a special empathy. (Check out his interpretation of "America, the Beautiful.") *Here's to Zoot* brings Allen together with former Sims collaborators Dave McKenna, Michael Moore and Jake Hanna. *The Music of the Trumpet Kings* pairs Allen and trumpeter Randy Sandke with the RIAS Big Band Berlin, directed by trombonist Jiggs Whigham. — K.F.

LEE ALLEN

★★★★ **Walkin' with Mr. Lee (1958; Collectables, 1990)**

Lee Allen (1927–1994) would be a shoo-in for the Rock and Roll Hall of Fame if sidemen commanded half the adulation of their bandleaders. Saxophonist Allen was one of the core New Orleans rhythm & blues musicians utilized in the Crescent City's fertile recording scene in the '50s. Allen's fingerprints—and impeccably crafted and swaggering solos—are all over the legendary Little Richard songs "Tutti Frutti" and "Lucille," as well as tracks from T-Bone Walker, Big Joe Turner, Charles Brown and countless others. In the twilight of his career 30 years later, his youthful vigor and old-school swing found a new audience on recordings by revivalists the Blasters.

Allen did make a small batch of recordings as a bandleader, scoring a national hit in 1958 with his tenor-saxophone signature piece, "Walkin' with Mr. Lee." The Collectables CD contains that anthem and 13 more instrumental R&B gems, all powered by Allen's joyful phrasing and vibrant tone and a crack New Orleans band. "Chuggin," "Boppin' at the Hop" and "Big Horn Special" are perfectly chosen song titles and show Allen's impressive range. There's more greatness where this set comes from—the omission of the glorious groove "Rockin' at Cosimo's" is a shame—on a handful of out-of-print 45s well worth tracking down. — S.J.

LUTHER ALLISON

★★★ **Love Me Papa (Evidence, 1992)**

★★★ **Serious (Blind Pig, 1994)**

★★★★ **Soul Fixin' Man (Alligator, 1994)**

★★★★ **Blue Streak (Alligator, 1995)**

★★★½ **The Motown Years 1972–1976 (Motown, 1996)**

★★★½ **Reckless (Alligator, 1997)**

Arkansas-born Luther Allison (1939–1997), the 14th of 15 children, moved as a teenager to Chicago, where he absorbed the thriving blues scene, witnessing performances by Muddy Waters and Howlin' Wolf. Though he played in several bands with his siblings in the early- to mid-'50s, Allison's first substantive gig came in 1957 as bassist in a band fronted by Jimmy Dawkins. Allison went on to do session work with Magic Sam and others starting in 1963, but it wasn't until 1967 that he played his first session as a guitarist on a recording by harmonica player Shakey Jake.

Five years later Allison became the first blues player contracted to the Motown imprint Gordy, which released a trio of soul/blues albums by the guitarist. These albums, entitled *Bad News Is Coming* (1972), *Luther's Blues* (1974) and *Night Life* (1976), are compiled on *The Motown Years.* Each album features Allison backed by a progressively larger cast of players, and the later songs get swamped by too many all-star session players (Richard Tee, Dr. John, the Brecker Brothers) and overproduction. Highlights from this collection include an urgent version of Willie Dixon's "Easy Baby," a slow, smooth rendition of Roosevelt Sykes's "Drivin' Wheel" and the funky original "Into My Life," all of which emanate from the 1974 release. When the Gordy albums failed to take off, Allison moved abroad.

In Europe Allison recorded for various labels throughout the late '70s and '80s, becoming a star in his adopted home of Paris and throughout the world—everywhere except America.

Chronicling a December 1977 session originally released on France's Black and Blue label, *Love Me Papa* was reissued in America on CD by Evidence. Consisting primarily of scorching slow blues, the album features Allison on guitar and vocals, as well as harmonica on one track. Backed by a quartet (guitar, bass, organ and drums), Allison's passionate playing burns from the outside in. Highlights include the title song, a rendition of Big Bill Broonzy's "Key to the Highway," and three previously unreleased bonus tracks, including Elmore James's wrenching, bubbling "Standing at the Crossroads."

A more varied effort is *Soul Fixin' Man,* which was cut in Memphis at Ardent Studios and was at that time Allison's first domestically recorded album in almost two decades. Produced by Jim Gaines (Santana, Stevie Ray Vaughan, Albert Collins), the release exudes a funky, contemporary feel without sacrificing the integrity of the music. On selected tracks Allison is joined by Another Blessed Creation Choir; on others his sound is bolstered by the Memphis Horns (Wayne Jackson on trumpet and trombone and Andrew Love on saxophone). Ranging stylistically from Chicago blues ("Soul Fixin' Man") to blues rock ("I Want to Know") to Memphis soul ("She Was Born That Way") to world music ("Freedom"), the album veers wildly but maintains the common thread of Allison's scathing electric guitar and vocal skills.

With most tracks produced by Gaines, *Blue Streak* comprises soul-inflected blues and gutbucket performances. The Memphis Horns make another stellar showing, adding a sultry layer of sound and serving as a change of pace from Allison's guitar histrionics. In fact, the four tracks on which they appear ("What's Going On in My Home?," "Think with Your Heart," "Midnight Creeper" and "You Don't Know") are among the album's best. Allison's fine acoustic-slide work on "Should I Wait" is a refreshing departure for the usually plugged-in guitarist, as is the rapid, organ-drenched shuffle of "I Believe in You," penned by Allison and James Solberg (who produced two other tracks). Both Alligator recordings have served to reinstate Allison's stature in his homeland, as has *Serious,* a diverse collection of aching blues, rock and soul. — B.R.H.

MOSE ALLISON

★★★★★ **Back Country Suite (1957; Original Jazz Classics, 1991)**
★★★★½ **Local Color (1957; Original Jazz Classics, 1990)**
★★★★½ **Greatest Hits (1957; Original Jazz Classics, 1988)**
★★★½ **Creek Bank (Prestige, 1958)**
★★★½ **Autumn Song (1959; Original Jazz Classics, 1996)**
★★★½ **The Best of Mose Allison (1962; Atlantic, 1988)**
★★★ **I Don't Worry About a Thing (1962; Rhino, 1993)**
★★★ **Middle Class White Boy (1982; Discovery, 1994)**
★★★★ **Lessons in Living (1982; Discovery, 1994)**
★★★½ **Ever Since the World Ended (Blue Note, 1987)**
★★★ **My Backyard (Blue Note, 1990)**
★★★★★ **Allison Wonderland: The Mose Allison Anthology (Rhino, 1994)**
★★★ **Earth Wants You (Blue Note, 1994)**
★★★★ **Pure Mose (32 Jazz, 1996)**
★★★½ **Down Home Piano (Original Jazz Classics, 1997)**
★★★½ **Jazz Profile (Blue Note, 1997)**
★★★½ **Gimcracks and Gewgaws (Blue Note, 1997)**

Mose Allison (b. 1927) grew up in the Mississippi Delta town of Tippo, where he schooled himself on the deep blues of Sonny Boy Williamson (Rice Miller) and Lightnin' Hopkins, the popular rhythm & blues of Louis Jordan and the blues poetry of Percy Mayfield. By 1950, he was working in Louisiana's piano-playing, singing-professor tradition, leading a trio out of Lake Charles. The format gave Allison plenty of scope as both lead instrumentalist and vocal improvisor and he has stuck with it over the years with few variations.

Allison honed a soulful keyboard style with one foot in swamp music and the other in the ever-surprising harmonic territory of Bud Powell, but his real strength, as it turned out, was his songwriting.

The self-styled country boy arrived in New York in 1956 just in time to become a patron saint of the Beats. *Back Country Suite,* the musical saga of a country boy's visit to Gotham, sold poorly at first but has since become a Beat-era icon.

Allison's shoot-from-the-hip attitude is best summed up in "Your Mind Is on Vacation," the ultimate scorching of a nightclub heckler. Gnossos Pappadopoulis, hero of Richard

Farina's Beat novel *Been Down So Long It Looks Like Up to Me,* played an Allison record as the selected soundtrack throughout his constant Kerouac hustle. Later, Allison's "Young Man Blues" showed its versatility as a hard-rock remake for the Who.

Allison's playing, stage presence, song selection and instrumentation have been remarkably consistent despite the numerous changes that the music scene around him has undergone over the years. *Local Color*, *Creek Bank*, *Autumn Song* and *Down Home Piano* document Allison's early days recording for Prestige as a bop-era pianist who also sang. By the time of his Atlantic debut, *I Don't Worry About a Thing,* his vocal style is fully developed. The Rhino reissues cover this most popular phase of his career. *Allison Wonderland* is indispensable.

Allison exerted a profound influence on the rock era but his own fortunes waned through the '60s and '70s as he released a series of albums on Atlantic, ending with the acclaimed but unfortunately out-of-print *Your Mind Is on Vacation* in 1976. Allison didn't record for another six years, but 32 Jazz released the live *Pure Mose* to document his late '70s work.

He continued on into the '80s, recording solid records for Elektra Musician (reissued by Discovery): *Middle Class White Boy,* a studio set with a commercial blues/pop slant and a fine band led by Joe Farrell on tenor and flute and Phil Upchurch on guitar; and *Lessons in Living,* a live set from the 1982 Montreux Jazz Festival with a rocking fusion quintet featuring Jack Bruce on bass, Billy Cobham on drums, Eric Gale on guitar and Lou Donaldson on alto sax.

Age has failed to dampen either Allison's wit or skill on his recent Blue Note albums. *Ever Since the World Ended* is a bristling session with Arthur Blythe on alto sax and Kenny Burrell on guitar; *Earth Wants You,* with John Scofield on guitar, Joe Lovano on alto sax and Randy Brecker on trumpet, features an over-65 Allison devilishly dubbing himself a "Certified Senior Citizen." *Jazz Profile* collects tracks from those two and *My Backyard. Gimcracks and Gewgaws* includes a witty rewrite of his famous "Young Man Blues," this time around as "Old Man Blues." —J.S.

ALLMAN BROTHERS BAND

★★★★½ **The Allman Brothers Band (Capricorn, 1969)**
★★★★ **Idlewild South (Capricorn, 1970)**
★★★★★ **Allman Brothers Band at Fillmore East (Capricorn, 1971)**
★★★★★ **Eat a Peach (Capricorn, 1972)**
★★★½ **Brothers and Sisters (Capricorn, 1973)**
★★★ **Win, Lose or Draw (Capricorn, 1975)**
★★★ **Enlightened Rogues (Capricorn, 1979)**
★★★★ **Dreams (Polydor, 1989)**
★★★★ **Live at Ludlow Garage, 1970 (Polydor, 1990)**
★★★½ **Seven Turns (Epic, 1990)**
★★★★ **Shades of Two Worlds (Epic, 1991)**
★★★★ **An Evening with the Allman Brothers Band (Epic, 1992)**
★★★★ **Where It All Begins (Epic, 1994)**
★★★★ **2nd Set (Epic, 1995)**

The Allman Brothers Band became one of the most influential groups in mainstream American music for its ability to appropriate the blues lexicon while striving toward the improvisational goals codified by the experiments of the Miles Davis, John Coltrane, Cannonball Adderley lineup in *Kind of Blue.* The two-guitar front line of Duane Allman (1946–1971) and Dickey Betts (b. 1943) bypassed the stock approaches commonly used by rock guitarists in favor of more hornlike strategies based on modal improvisations and freewheeling harmonic substitutions.

The band's roots are in evidence on the first disc of the career retrospective *Dreams,* where B.B. King is presented as a paradigm and the first steps of a two-guitar vamp over polyrhythms are set out. Gregg Allman (b. 1947) emerged as one of the signature vocalists of his generation on *The Allman Brothers Band,* contributing riveting performances on "Dreams" and "Whipping Post." *Idlewild South* continues the development, adding the gospel element of "Revival" to the mix.

The band arrives at a full realization of its power on the epochal *At Fillmore East.* The rhythm section of Butch Trucks (b. ca. 1945) and Jai Johanny Johanson (b. 1944) set down rippling patterns for an astonishing interplay between Duane Allman, Betts and the virtuosic bassist Berry Oakley (1948–1972), with Gregg Allman's soulful vocals and Hammond B-3 washes providing foundation. The recasting of Blind Willie McTell's "Statesboro Blues" demonstrates the group's brilliant arrangement strengths, while the inventive instrumental flights on Willie Cobb's "You Don't Love Me,"

Betts's "In Memory of Elizabeth Reed" and Gregg Allman's "Whipping Post" reveal an almost spiritual improvisational genius.

Eat a Peach picked up right where *At Fillmore East* left off, with "Mountain Jam," nearly 35 minutes of improvisational bliss. The record also includes the band's crackling arrangement of Sonny Boy Williamson (Rice Miller)'s "One Way Out" and a beautiful Betts melody that would become a staple of live performances, "Blue Sky." The band's live performances during this era blew fresh and unpredictable night after night, as the archival *Live at Ludlow Garage* demonstrates.

Both Duane Allman and Oakley were dead by the time the band's next album, *Brothers and Sisters,* was released, yet the group managed to continue on with studio help from Les Dudek and a new live arrangement strategy built around a second keyboardist, the versatile and virtuosic Chuck Leavell. The records became more condensed and song-oriented, and Gregg's singing took on a tragic, mournful cast that yielded chilling performances of "Wasted Words," from *Brothers,* and Muddy Waters's "Can't Lose What You Never Had," from *Win, Lose or Draw.*

The band eventually split up, but the four surviving original members regrouped for an engaging reunion, *Enlightened Rogues,* that was charged by the enthusiasm of the brotherhood but eventually found lacking in terms of both material and the lineup's ability to do more than reflect past glories on the subsequent (now deleted) *Reach for the Sky* and *Brothers of the Road.*

Allman and Betts led separate bands during the 1980s, Allman continuing in the Brothers tradition and Betts trying out several ideas, including an excellent fusion outing, *Pattern Disruptive.* This band, featuring brilliant young guitarist Warren Haynes and bassist Allen Woody, was so good that in 1989 Allman decided to join forces and take another crack at the Brothers.

Seven Turns proved that the decision was sound, but by *Shades of Two Worlds* the band was rivaling its greatest moments, with Haynes and Woody effectively channeling Duane Allman and Oakley rather than simply aping the style. Gregg Allman was revitalized on the powerful "End of the Line," and the band soared to its improvisational heights once again on "Kind of Bird."

With Haynes and Woody revitalizing the band's sound, Betts playing better than ever and percussionist Marc Quinones from Spyro Gyra added into the mix, the Brothers were playing so well live that they returned to the magic of *Fillmore East* on the excellent *Where It All Begins*, *An Evening with the Allman Brothers Band* and *2nd Set.* — J.S.

LAURINDO ALMEIDA

★★★★ **Brazilliance, Vol. 1 (World Pacific, 1953)**
★★★½ **Brazilliance, Vol. 2 (World Pacific, 1958)**
★★★ **Chamber Jazz (Concord Jazz, 1978)**
★★★ **Artistry in Rhythm (Concord Jazz, 1983)**
★★★ **Otra Vez (Concord Jazz, 1991)**

Brazilian guitarist Laurindo Almeida (1917–1995) was one of the first musicians to employ Brazilian musical conceptions in a jazz context. After a successful career as a classical and pop guitarist in Brazil, Almeida joined the Stan Kenton Orchestra in 1947. His 1953 collaboration with saxophonist Bud Shank, *Brazilliance, Vol. 1,* melded Brazilian popular music with improvisational jazz in a style that was considered revolutionary at the time. Another historic moment came in the (now out-of-print) 1964 set with the Modern Jazz Quartet, *Collaboration.*

Over the last two decades of his life Almeida recorded in a variety of contexts for Concord. *Chamber Jazz* mixes his classical and jazz influences on selections such as "Unaccustomed Bach." *Artistry in Rhythm* is a trio date with percussionist Milt Holland and bassist Bob Magnusson. — J.S.

BARRY ALTSCHUL

★★★★ **For Stu (Soul Note, 1981)**
★★★½ **That's Nice (Soul Note, 1986)**
★★★★ **Virtuosi (Soul Note, 1992)**

Percussionist/drummer Barry Altschul (b. 1943) is a player of awesome technique and versatility who teamed with Dave Holland to form one of the strongest rhythm sections playing experimental jazz during the '70s. They were part of Circle, with Chick Corea and Anthony Braxton, as well as the section on records by Braxton, Sam Rivers and Paul Bley. Perhaps their finest work together, though, was on Holland's wonderful *Conference of the Birds.*

Holland was around once again for Altschul's now deleted 1977 set *You Can't Name Your Own*

Tune, along with Sam Rivers on flute, tenor and soprano saxophone, Muhal Richard Abrams on piano and George Lewis on trombone. Also sadly unavailable is *Another Time, Another Place,* an even more impressive record sparked by the performances of Arthur Blythe on alto sax, Ray Anderson on trombone, Anthony Davis on piano and Abdul Wadud on cello. "Crepuscule: Suite for Monk" is a stunning tribute to that master composer, climaxing with a stirring version of "Epistrophy." Altschul has made several recordings for Soul Note, the best of which, *For Stu* (with Ray Anderson on trombone, Anthony Davis on piano and Rick Rozie on bass), is still available. Another recently reissued gem is the 1967 free-jazz set *Virtuosi,* with pianist Paul Bley and bassist Gary Peacock. — J.S.

HERB ALPERT

★★ **The Lonely Bull (A&M, 1962)**
★★ **Whipped Cream & Other Delights (A&M, 1965)**
★★ **Going Places (A&M, 1965)**
★★★ **Greatest Hits (A&M, 1970)**
★★ **Greatest Hits, Vol. 2 (A&M, 1973)**
★★ **Four Sider (A&M, 1973)**
★★ **Rise (A&M, 1979)**
★★ **Keep Your Eye on Me (A&M, 1987)**
★★ **Classics, Vol. 20 (A&M, 1987)**
★★ **Under a Spanish Moon (A&M, 1988)**
★★ **My Abstract Heart (A&M, 1989)**
★★ **North on South Street (A&M, 1991)**
★★ **Midnight Sun (A&M, 1992)**
★★★ **Second Wind (Almo Sounds, 1996)**
★★ **Passion Dance (Almo Sounds, 1997)**

Herb Alpert (b. 1935) may be the best example of a musician with a limited jazz vocabulary whose genius for pop reduction transcends cliché to become the soundtrack of its time. Despite possessing a thin, unimpressive tone, while leading the pop-jazz group Tijuana Brass he evolved a trumpet style that is instantly recognizable and (not always happily) widely imitated. Alpert's marketing savvy in developing commercial hooks launched a record company (he's the A in A&M) on the strength of the 1962 hit single "The Lonely Bull." Other hits followed—"A Taste of Honey," "Spanish Flea" (*The Dating Game* theme) and "This Guy's in Love with You," on which he also sings.

Alpert switched his attention from the band to the record company during the 1970s, while releasing the occasional recording. In 1979 he enjoyed a postdisco comeback with the Number One hit "Rise," which featured a thicker tone and more elaborate arrangement strategy and owed a massive debt to Chuck Mangione, whose "Feel So Good" was the blueprint for Alpert's new sound. *Second Wind* found Alpert playing with renewed vigor in front of a funk-oriented group designed to appeal to acid-jazz buffs. Alpert's playing is virtually invisible by contrast on the pop salsa set *Passion Dance.* — J.S.

ALBERT AMMONS

★★★★★ **Le Hot Club de France: Master of Boogie (Milan/BMG, 1992)**
★★★★★ **Albert Ammons 1936–39 (Classics, 1993)**

Chicago-born Albert Ammons (1907–1949) was a great solo pianist whose proficiency at playing the eight-to-the-bar rhythm figures he learned from Pinetop Smith and Meade Lux Lewis made him one of the kings of boogie-woogie. He began recording in 1936 while still in Chicago, and in 1938, during the height of the boogie-woogie craze, he went to New York to establish himself at Café Society, where he worked as a team with pianist Pete Johnson. Ammons was one of the best practitioners of the genre.

The Classics set contains 18 solo pieces, including the wild "Boogie Woogie Stomp," and two sessions with his band the Rhythm Kings. *Le Hot Club de France: Master of Boogie* was a session from December 23, 1938, featuring piano exchanges with Pete Johnson and Meade Lux Lewis as well as the legendary Count Basie rhythm section of Jo Jones on drums and Walter Page on bass. Big Bill Broonzy joins in on guitar and vocals. — J.S.

GENE AMMONS

★★★★ **Young Jug (1952; GRP, 1994)**
★★★★ **Red Top (1953; Savoy, 1994)**
★★★★★ **The Happy Blues (1956; Original Jazz Classics, 1991)**
★★★★ **Jammin' with Gene (1956; Original Jazz Classics, 1991)**
★★★★ **Jammin' in Hi-Fi with Gene Ammons (1957; Original Jazz Classics, 1992)**
★★★★ **Funky (1957; Original Jazz Classics, 1987)**
★★★★ **The Big Sound (1958; Original Jazz Classics, 1991)**

★★★★ **Blue Gene (1958; Original Jazz Classics, 1985)**
★★★★ **Boss Tenor (1960; Original Jazz Classics, 1988)**
★★★ **Live! In Chicago (1961; Original Jazz Classics, 1992)**
★★★ **Jug (1961; Original Jazz Classics, 1992)**
★★★★ **Greatest Hits, Vol. 1: The Sixties (1961; Original Jazz Classics, 1988)**
★★★½ **Up Tight! (1961; Prestige, 1995)**
★★★ **Bad! Bossa Nova (1962; Original Jazz Classics, 1989)**
★★★★ **Groove Blues (1968; Original Jazz Classics, 1992)**
★★★★ **Gentle Jug, Vol. 2 (1969; Prestige, 1995)**
★★★★★ **The Gene Ammons Story: The 78 Era (Prestige, 1992)**
★★★★ **The Gene Ammons Story: Organ Combos (Prestige, 1992)**
★★★★ **The Gene Ammons Story: Gentle Jug (Prestige, 1992)**
★★★★ **Soul Summit (Prestige, 1992)**

Tenor saxophonist Gene Ammons (1925–1974) was the son of boogie-woogie piano player Albert Ammons, and the blues tradition that his father represented can be heard throughout Gene's recording career, which spanned from bebop into soul jazz and funk.

A warm, big-toned player, Ammons comes out of the Coleman Hawkins/Herschel Evans tenor tradition, although many critics have pointed out that his phrasing and melodic sense derive from the seemingly antithetical influence of Lester Young.

While he was still a teenager during the early '40s Ammons began playing with a local band led by King Kolax. Between 1944 and 1947 Ammons was part of Billy Eckstine's legendary big band, which included at various points during Ammons's tenure such players as Charlie Parker, Sonny Stitt, Dexter Gordon, Dizzy Gillespie, Fats Navarro, Miles Davis, Lucky Thompson and Art Blakey. Ammons was the featured soloist in Eckstine's band, and his trade-offs with Dexter Gordon were memorable. It was Stitt, however, who would go on to become Ammons's partner after the two left Eckstine. In the meantime Ammons replaced Stan Getz in Woody Herman's big band at the end of the '40s.

Between 1950 and 1952 Ammons and Stitt co-led a fantastic group notable for its tenor battles. This music still sounds fresh and exciting today and can be heard on *The Gene Ammons Story: The 78 Era.* Stitt left in 1952, and Ammons continued the group on his own, scoring a popular hit in 1953 with "Red Top," which you can hear on the Savoy compilation *Red Top.*

Throughout the '50s Ammons led a number of blowing jam sessions with consistently great musicians. Excellent selections from this era can be heard on *The Big Sound* and *Groove Blues,* dates featuring John Coltrane playing alto sax, Pepper Adams (baritone), Paul Quinichette (tenor), Jerome Richardson (flute), George Joyner, a.k.a. Jamil Nasser (bass), Art Taylor (drums) and Mal Waldron (piano). *The Happy Blues* is a '56 set featuring Jackie McLean on alto sax, Art Farmer on trumpet, Duke Jordan on piano, Addison Farmer on bass, Art Taylor on drums and Candido playing congas. *Jammin' with Gene,* another '56 classic, adds Donald Byrd's trumpet and replaces Jordan with Waldron and Addison Farmer with Doug Watkins.

The Gene Ammons Story: Organ Combos, which covers tracks from several albums, has Ammons working with organists Jack McDuff and Johnny "Hammond" Smith. *Jammin' in Hi-Fi with Gene Ammons* features McLean, Waldron, Kenny Burrell on guitar, Idrees Sulieman on trumpet and the hot congas of Ray Barretto. *Funky* includes Burrell, McLean, Waldron and Farmer. *Blue Gene* uses Adams, Sulieman, Waldron and Barretto. *Soul Summit* is a blistering exchange with Stitt, McDuff and Charlie Persip on drums.

In the early '60s Ammons recorded frequently in an impressive variety of musical contexts with generally favorable results. There were a couple of reunions with Stitt, a lot of small organ combos, including *Live! In Chicago,* the quartet ballads on *Gentle Jug* and the quartets, quintets and sextets augmented by conga drums or bongos, *Boss Tenor, Bad! Bossa Nova* (a misnomer) and several others that have never been made available on CD but are worth cranking up the turntable for.

From 1958 until 1960 and then from late 1962 until the end of the decade Ammons was off the scene serving a prison term on a narcotics charge. In the last five years of his life he went back into the studio for a number of sessions and was also caught live on several recordings. Tragically, none of this material is currently available. *The Boss Is Back* is a triumphant return, *Brother Jug* and *The Black*

Cat are fine sessions, *The Chase* is a tenor battle with Dexter Gordon from 1970 and *You Talk That Talk* and *Together Again for the First Time* are Ammons's final pair of collaborations with Stitt. Ammons recorded *Goodbye,* with Nat Adderley on cornet, Kenny Drew on piano, Sam Jones on bass, Louis Hayes on drums, Gary Bartz on alto sax and Barretto on congas, five months before his death. — J.S.

DAVID AMRAM

★★★★ **Havana–New York: The Historic U.S.-Cuban Musical Exchange of 1977 (Flying Fish, 1977)**
★★★½ **Pull My Daisy . . . and Other Jazz Classics (Premier, 1995)**
★★★ **The Manchurian Candidate (Premier, 1997)**
★★★★½ **No More Walls (Flying Fish, 1997)**

Versatile instrumentalist/composer David Amram (b. 1930) is one of the few jazz French horn players. In the '50s he played with Lionel Hampton, Sonny Rollins, Charlie Mingus, Oscar Pettiford and Kenny Dorham. In 1962 he composed the soundtrack to *The Manchurian Candidate.* In 1966 he became the first composer-in-residence at the New York Philharmonic. Amram's best and most ambitious recording, *No More Walls,* mixes classical, jazz and folk elements deftly. *Havana–New York* is a spirited Latin jazz session with Thad Jones, Pepper Adams and Irakere joining in. *David Amram's Latin Jazz Celebration,* a similar session that has come and gone on the Elektra Musician label, is also recommended. *Pull My Daisy* references the Robert Frank Beat film Amram scored in the '50s, with Jack Kerouac providing narration. — J.S.

FRANCK AMSALLEM

★★★★ **Another Time (1992; Challenge/A, 1997)**
★★★½ **Regards (Free Lance, 1994)**
★★★★ **Is That So? (Sunnyside, 1996)**

French pianist Franck Amsallem was born in 1961 in Oran, Algeria, was raised in Nice, France, and moved in 1981 to the United States, where he has become part of the thriving Brooklyn jazz scene. Amsallem's piano style combines the perfect technique engendered by years of classical study with the rhythmic variation and sense of surprise essential to worthwhile jazz playing. His influences range over a wide area that encompasses the pointillist melodic sense of Bill Evans, the harmonic architecture of Thelonious Monk and the dramatic chordal clusters of McCoy Tyner.

Another Time, originally available as *Out a Day,* shows off Amsallem's skills. Bassist Gary Peacock and drummer Bill Stewart provide stalwart accompaniment on this debut that invited comparisons to Keith Jarrett. *Regards* is an impressive quartet session with tenor/soprano saxophonist Tim Ries. Amsallem and Ries had been working together for well over a decade when they recorded *Is That So?* with drummer Leon Parker. This trio seems to be in telepathic communion as it spins through a series of Amsallem and Ries compositions that reveal the harmonic sophistication of their classical training and the subtle dialog of their collective improvisations. — J.S.

CAT ANDERSON

★★★★ **Cat Anderson Plays W.C. Handy (Black and Blue, N.A.)**

William Alonzo "Cat" Anderson (1916–1981) learned to play trumpet at a South Carolina orphanage before hitting the road in a variety of settings. He had achieved moderate success on his own when Duke Ellington hired him in 1944 to feature his octave-leaping range and penchant for searing high notes epitomized by his showcase "El Gato." Anderson left Ellington in 1971 to do studio work and lead his own recording groups, which he did sporadically. The Black and Blue album culls material from two sessions in 1977 and 1978 and shows Anderson in a much more varied role than casual fans of his work with Ellington might recognize. — J.S.

ERNESTINE ANDERSON

★★★½ **Ernestine Anderson (1958; Verve, 1992)**
★★★★ **Hello Like Before (Concord Jazz, 1977)**
★★★★ **Live from Concord to London (Concord Jazz, 1978)**
★★★½ **Sunshine (Concord Jazz, 1980)**
★★★★ **Never Make Your Move Too Soon (Concord Jazz, 1981)**
★★★★ **Big City (Concord Jazz, 1983)**
★★★ **When the Sun Goes Down (Concord Jazz, 1985)**
★★★★ **Be Mine Tonight (Concord Jazz, 1987)**
★★★★ **Boogie Down (Concord Jazz, 1990)**
★★★★ **Great Moments with Ernestine Anderson (Concord Jazz, 1993)**

★★★½ **Now and Then (Warner Bros., 1993)**
★★★★ **Blues Dues & Love News (Warner Bros., 1996)**

Ernestine Anderson (b. 1928) began singing in rhythm & blues bands in the late 1940s, but it wasn't until 1959, after knocking around in both the United States and Europe singing in a variety of contexts, that she came to widespread public attention, winning the *Down Beat* "New Star" award. Anderson went on to win acclaim for her 1960s Mercury recordings but decided to perform in Europe rather than buck the rock trend sweeping the United States.

Bassist Ray Brown convinced Anderson to come out of semiretirement in 1976 with *Hello Like Before,* the first in a series of solid recordings for Concord. Her comeback began at the 1976 Concord Jazz Festival, a performance documented on *Live from Concord to London,* along with tracks recorded at Ronnie Scott's club in London. She shows off her blues chops on the Grammy-nominated *Never Make Your Move Too Soon* and works hand in glove with pianist Hank Jones on the beautiful *Big City.*

Anderson's abilities beyond the blues are also in evidence on *Be Mine Tonight,* where she is matched with Benny Carter's eloquent alto-sax playing and fronts the Clayton-Hamilton Jazz Orchestra on *Boogie Down. Great Moments with Ernestine Anderson* collects highlights from Anderson's Concord recordings.

On Warner Bros. Anderson returned to a rootsier style, brilliantly captured on the Stix Hooper–produced live set *Blues, Dues & Love News,* which ranges from a terrific version of Miles Davis's "All Blues" to a cover of Sting's "Sister Moono." — J.S.

MILDRED ANDERSON

★★★½ **Person to Person (1960; Original Blues Classics, 1993)**
★★★ **No More in Life (1960; Original Blues Classics, 1995)**

Though Mildred Anderson learned to sing in an urban gospel choir connected with Brooklyn's Antioch Baptist Church, her style is unmistakably country, a deliberately hoarse and expressive contralto devoid of the slickness usually associated with female nightclub vocalists. She developed her style in New York clubs during the late '40s and early '50s before joining organist Bill Doggett. In 1953 Anderson scored her biggest hit with Doggett, the anguished ballad "No More in Life."

Anderson went on to work with trumpeter Hot Lips Page before returning to the gospel-related Hammond B-3 organ–group sound for her Prestige recordings (rereleased on Original Blues Classics). Her robust tone is particularly well suited to organ accompaniment. *Person to Person* pits her against organist Shirley Scott in tenor saxophonist Eddie "Lockjaw" Davis's band with a swinging rhythm section of bassist George Duvivier and Arthur Edgehill. *No More in Life* reprises her trademark hit along with blues standards like "Roll 'Em Pete" and two originals in a lineup featuring gospel organist Robert Banks and tenor saxophonist Al Sears. — J.S.

PINK ANDERSON

★★★★ **Gospel, Blues and Street Songs (with Rev. Gary Davis) (Original Blues Classics, 1991)**
★★★★ **Carolina Blues Man, Vol. 1 (Original Blues Classics, 1992)**
★★★★ **The Blues of Pink Anderson: Ballad and Folk Singer, Vol. 3 (Original Blues Classics, 1995)**

Piedmont bluesman Pink Anderson (1900–1974), born and raised in South Carolina, was a primary purveyor of rural blues. Subtle yet highly emotive, Anderson's style was characterized by his ragged guitar playing and matter-of-fact vocal work. He traveled with the Indian Remedy Company's medicine show and others from 1915 to 1945.

Anderson splits *Gospel, Blues and Street Songs* with the Rev. Gary Davis. Anderson's seven tracks recorded in Charlottesville, Virginia, in May 1950 include versions of "The Ship *Titanic,*" "John Henry" and "Wreck of the Old 97."

Carolina Blues Man, Vol. 1, recorded for Prestige's Bluesville label in April 1961 in Anderson's hometown, Spartanburg, features his inimitable treatment of a variety of traditional tunes, including "Big House Blues" and "Mama Where Did You Stay Last Night." Also performed here are compositions by Brownie McGhee ("Meet Me in the Bottom") and Joe Williams ("Baby Please Don't Go"), which Anderson personalizes in his rough-hewn manner.

Ballad and Folk Singer, Vol. 3 also was recorded in Spartanburg in August 1961, and includes nine solo tracks, among them "Boweevil," "I Will Fly Away" and "The Kaiser." Anderson would gain a degree of fame several years after the recording of this album when his name became the well-publicized inspiration behind the first half of Pink Floyd's moniker. — B.R.H.

WESSELL ANDERSON

★★★★ **New Orleans Collective (with Nicholas Payton, Peter Martin, Christopher Thomas and Brian Blade) (1992; Evidence, 1995)**
★★★½ **Warmdaddy in the Garden of Swing (Atlantic, 1994)**
★★★½ **The Ways of Warmdaddy (Atlantic, 1996)**

Wessell "Warmdaddy" Anderson (b. 1966) plays the alto and soprano saxophones with rhythmic ingenuity, lyric imagination and a pure, resonant sound in all the registers. Best known for his association with the Wynton Marsalis Septet from 1988 to 1994 and the Lincoln Center Jazz Orchestra, Anderson has made recordings that explore many permutations of the blues—the blues as such and the blues as a worldview. Firsthand involvement in the structures of classic jazz have imparted to him a bird's-eye view of older styles; he's equally comfortable referencing the melodic nuance of Johnny Hodges (and *his* antecedent, Sidney Bechet), the unpredictable phrasing of Charlie Parker, the straight-to-the-gut attack of Sonny Stitt, the urbane fire of Cannonball Adderley, the harmonic spirituality of John Coltrane. A Brooklyn native who's resided in Louisiana for over a decade, Anderson spices Northern sophistication with Southern soulfulness; he relishes the challenge of trying to say something fresh within the tradition.

New Orleans Collective (Anderson; Nicholas Payton, trumpet; Peter Martin, piano; Christopher Thomas, bass; Brian Blade, drums), an intriguing concept record, is an energetic session with dynamic grooves and spirited solos. Anderson's five compositions include an effective funeral function, a few variations on Crescent City–style blues and an affecting Johnny Hodges homage.

Warmdaddy in the Garden of Swing, Anderson's strong debut as a leader, presents him in a modernist vein. Anderson, Marsalis band mates Eric Reed (piano) and Ben Wolfe (bass), and Louisianan Donald Edwards (drums) nimbly explore a variety of tempos, time signatures, timbres and structures on eight challenging Anderson originals and one by Edwards.

On *The Ways of Warmdaddy* Anderson implacably tackles solo saxophone ("Mood Indigo"), the trio format ("Rockin' in Rhythm" and two originals), attended by bassist Taurus Mateen and Edwards on drums, three quartets with patriarch Ellis Marsalis and a quintet track with trumpeter Antoine Drye. The sparer format yields a concise, mature, personal document, entwining old and new.

Anderson also performs on most of Wynton Marsalis's recordings since 1988. — T.P.

THE ANIMALS

★★★★★ **The Best of the Animals (1966; ABKCO, N.A.)**
★★★ **Best of Eric Burdon and the Animals (Polydor, 1991)**

While the Beatles and their Merseybeat cohorts sparked the British Invasion by wedding American rock & roll to the English sounds of skiffle and vaudeville music, among Brit '60s titans, the Animals were second only to the Rolling Stones in mining the blues. And with Eric Burdon as one of the toughest singers the British Isles ever produced, the band lived up to its name. This was 12-bar fare and raw R&B delivered like a cannon shot: Burdon exploded, but with Alan Price—a big fan of jazz organist Jimmy Smith—handling expert keyboards, the band fired with precision.

The original Animals fell apart in 1966, and a new band, Eric Burdon and the Animals, debuted. Burdon moved to California, embraced psychedelia and ditched R&B. *The Best of the Animals* covers the essentials of the original band, from the blues standard "House of the Rising Sun" to the anthemic "It's My Life." The band's transitional period is anthologized on the Polydor set, which has fewer blues and more of the San Francisco sound. — P.E.

AQUARIUM RESCUE UNIT

★★★★ **Col. Bruce Hampton & the Aquarium Rescue Unit (Capricorn, 1992)**
★★★ **Mirrors of Embarrassment (Capricorn, 1993)**
★★★★ **In a Perfect World (Intersound, 1994)**

This genre-hopping group slips easily from blues into fusion, newgrass and space music with virtuosic conviction. Masterminded by guitarist visionary Bruce Hampton, whose influences range from Son House to Sun Ra, the Aquarium Rescue Unit debuted with a scorching live album highlighted by versions of Booker White's "Fixin' to Die," the gospel traditional "Working on a Building," Les McCann's "Compared to What" and a handful of originals. Guitarist Jimmy Herring hurls chorus after chorus of brilliant guitar improvisations against the post-Pastorius funk of bassist Oteil Burbridge, with drummer Apt. Q258 and percussionist Count M'Butu keeping the energy level in the red zone, and Matt Mundy adding mandolin, doubled by Hampton on his "chazoid," a customized electric mandolin.

Mirrors of Embarrassment is a studio set highlighted by "No Ego's Under Water," "Lost My Mule in Texas," "Shoeless Joe" and "Trondossa." Hampton turned the band leadership over to Herring for *In a Perfect World,* a burnished fusion effort featuring magnificent performances from Herring and Oteil Burbridge, whose brother Kofi plays flute, keyboards and piano on the record. — J.S.

JAMES ARMSTRONG

★★★ **Sleeping with a Stranger (Hightone, 1995)**

James Armstrong (b. 1964) is a popular Los Angeles–based blues guitar player and vocalist whose rock-influenced histrionics are well grounded in blues fundamentals. The product of a musical family on both sides, Armstrong studied under guitarist Irving Ashby, who played with Nat King Cole. Armstrong's song "The Bank of Love" was featured on the soundtrack of *Hear No Evil. Sleeping* is a collaboration with Hightone's producer/songwriter Bruce Bromberg. — J.S.

LIL HARDIN ARMSTRONG

★★★★ **Chicago: The Living Legends (1961; Original Jazz Classics, 1993)**

The first important woman instrumentalist in jazz history, Lil Hardin Armstrong (1902–1971) was hired by King Oliver in 1920 to play piano in his legendary Creole Jazz Orchestra. Louis Armstrong joined the group in 1922 and married Lil two years later. Armstrong always credited her, even after the two divorced, with encouraging him to pursue his own trumpet style. She was a member of Armstrong's two groundbreaking small-group recording bands of the mid- to late 1920s, the Hot Five and the Hot Seven. A classically trained pianist, Hardin Armstrong also wrote such early jazz standards as "Struttin' with Some Barbecue" and "Hotter Than That."

After the divorce Armstrong continued to work as an accompanist to vocalists as well as leading her own studio bands. She also found some success as a writer: "Just for a Thrill" was recorded by Ray Charles, Peggy Lee and Kay Starr.

The 1961 album, originally recorded for Riverside as part of the Chicago Living Legends series, documents the fortuitous accident that occurred when Armstrong's band showed up for its session while the Earl Hines group was finishing one. The two bands combined for a delirious traditional New Orleans jazz romp showing this expressive ensemble style had lost none of its energy. In addition to "Muskrat Ramble," "Royal Garden Blues" and "Basin Street Blues," Armstrong's own "Clip Joint" is included, giving her a chance to show off her enthusiastic vocal style. — J.S.

LOUIS ARMSTRONG

★★★½ **Satchmo at Symphony Hall (1951; MCA, 1977)**
★★★½ **Louis Armstrong Plays W.C. Handy (1954; Columbia, 1986)**
★★★ **Satch Plays Fats (Columbia, 1955)**
★★★ **Ella & Louis (Verve, 1956)**
★★★ **Louis Armstrong Meets Oscar Peterson (Verve, 1957)**
★★★★ **Satchmo Serenades (MCA, 1960)**
★★★½ **Louis Armstrong Sings the Blues (1962; RCA Bluebird, 1993)**
★★★★½ **Louis Armstrong & Duke Ellington: The Complete Louis Armstrong–Duke Ellington Sessions (1963; Roulette Jazz/EMI, 1990)**
★★★ **Hello, Dolly! (MCA, 1964)**
★★★★ **The Best of Louis Armstrong (1965; MCA, 1980)**
★★★★ **What a Wonderful World (1968; MCA, 1988)**
★★★★★ **Louis Armstrong and King Oliver (1974; Milestone, 1992)**
★★ **Mostly Blues (Olympic, 1974)**
★★★ **The Best of Louis Armstrong (1975; Vanguard, 1991)**
★★ **The Essential Louis Armstrong (1976; Vanguard, 1987)**
★★★ **An Evening with Louis Armstrong and His All Stars (GNP Crescendo, 1977)**
★★★ **Louis and the Big Bands, 1928–30 (1987; Disques Swing, 1990)**
★★★★ **Pops (RCA Bluebird, 1987)**

★★★ **Compact Jazz (Verve, 1987)**
★★★★★ **The Hot Fives, Vol. 1 (Columbia, 1988)**
★★★★★ **The Hot Fives & Hot Sevens, Vol. 2 (Columbia, 1988)**
★★★★ **Stardust (Portrait Masters/CBS, 1988)**
★½ **What a Wonderful World (RCA Bluebird, 1988)**
★★★★ **The Best of the Decca Years, Vol. 1: The Singer (Decca, 1989)**
★★★★★ **The Hot Fives & Hot Sevens, Vol. 3 (Columbia, 1989)**
★★★★ **Louis Armstrong & Earl Hines, Vol. 4 (Columbia, 1989)**
★★★½ **Laughin' Louie: Louis Armstrong and His Orchestra (1932–1933) (RCA Bluebird, 1989)**
★★★★ **Pops: The 1940s Small Band Sides (RCA Bluebird, 1989)**
★★★★ **The Best of the Decca Years, Vol. 2: The Composer (Decca, 1990)**
★★★★ **Louis Armstrong of New Orleans (Decca, 1990)**
★★½ **Mack the Knife (Pablo, 1990)**
★★★★ **Louis Armstrong's Greatest Hits (Curb, 1990)**
★★★★★ **Louis Armstrong, Vol. 5: Louis in New York (Columbia, 1990)**
★★★★★ **Louis Armstrong, Vol. 6: St. Louis Blues (Columbia, 1991)**
★★★½ **I Like Jazz: The Essence of Louis Armstrong (Columbia/Legacy, 1991)**
★★★ **Compact Jazz 5: An American Songbook (Verve, 1991)**
★★½ **Jazz Round Midnight (Verve, 1991)**
★★★½ **C'est Si Bon (Tomato, 1991)**
★★★½ **Rhythm Saved the World (Decca, 1991)**
★★★ **Sugar (RCA Bluebird, 1992)**
★★★★★ **Jazz Tribune No. 43: Louis Armstrong at Town Hall: The Complete Town Hall Concert 17 May 1947 (RCA Bluebird, 1992)**
★★★ **The California Concerts (Decca, 1992)**
★★★ **The Essential Louis Armstrong (Verve, 1992)**
★★★★ **Jazz Tribune No. 20: Young Louis Armstrong (1930–1933) (RCA Bluebird, 1993)**
★★★★★ **Louis Armstrong, Vol. 7: You're Driving Me Crazy (Columbia/Legacy, 1993)**
★★★★ **Heart Full of Rhythm (Decca, 1993)**
★★★½ **Louis and His Friends (GNP Crescendo, 1993)**
★★★★ **Highlights from His Decca Years (Decca, 1994)**
★★★★★ **Portrait of the Artist as a Young Man 1923–1934 (Columbia/Legacy, 1994)**
★★½ **Verve Jazz Masters 1 (Verve, 1994)**
★★★½ **Louis Armstrong's All-Time Greatest Hits (MCA, 1994)**
★★½ **Swing That Music (Drive Archive, 1994)**
★★★★ **16 Most Requested Songs (Columbia/Legacy, 1994)**
★★★ **What a Wonderful World: The Elisabethville Concert (Milan, 1994)**
★★★ **The Essential Louis Armstrong (LaserLight, 1995)**
★★★ **Louis Armstrong & His Orchestra Vol. 3: Pocketful of Dreams (Decca, 1995)**
★★★★ **From the Big Band to the All Stars (1946–1956) (RCA, 1995)**
★★★ **Butter and Eggman (Tomato, 1995)**
★★★★ **This Is Jazz 1 (Columbia/Legacy, 1996)**
★★★½ **Struttin' (Drive Archive, 1996)**
★★½ **When the Saints Go Marchin' In (LaserLight, 1996)**
★★½ **Singin' 'n' Playin' (LaserLight, 1996)**
★★★½ **Please Don't Talk About Me When I'm Gone (LaserLight, 1997)**
★★★★½ **High Society: Louis Armstrong and King Oliver with Bessie Smith (Tradition/Rykodisc, 1997)**
★★★ **Now You Has Jazz: Louis Armstrong at MGM (Rhino, 1997)**

The Louis Armstrong legend is as daunting as his catalog is broad and deep. The respected and much honored jazz authority Dan Morgenstern has observed: "The whole vocabulary of mature jazz was based on Armstrong's phrases, Armstrong rhythms, Armstrong transformations." While Elvis Presley and the Beatles continue to inspire new generations of rock artists and exert an impact on popular culture, and Duke Ellington brooks few comparisons as a contemporary composer, no other individual artist or group of the 20th Century approaches the continuing sweep of Armstrong's influence on jazz and popular music. As an innovator and visionary, he is, simply, a one-man Mount Rushmore.

Born in New Orleans and raised in one of the city's poorest sections, Armstrong (1901–1971) had ended his formal schooling in fifth grade and was making money on the streets, playing dice games and singing with a vocal quartet he had formed with three friends. At age 12 he was in reform school, the Colored Waif's Home, serving an indeterminate sentence. Yet this unfortunate turn of events proved fortuitous. In the structured environment of the home he found a direction and purpose, which blossomed when he joined its band, first playing tambourine, then drums, then alto horn, and finally the cornet, his instrument of choice all along.

The jazz Armstrong was hearing in New Orleans in his early teens was a music in transition, played in different styles by different types of bands. Those with older musicians tended to favor a relatively restrained repertoire of popular songs, marches, plantation songs and rags played sturdily and with gusto but lacking rhythmic sophistication; younger players favored a looser rhythmic approach heralding a transition in jazz's basic character, pointing toward the swing era.

After leaving the Waif's Home in 1914 or 1915, Armstrong lived for a while with his father, then returned to his mother's home and was out on his own by his midteens, working odd jobs around New Orleans and eventually entering the nascent Crescent City jazz scene by sitting in with bands playing the local honky-tonks. In 1917 Joe "King" Oliver, who was playing cornet in Kid Ory's band, then regarded as the best around, took Armstrong under his wing and became his sponsor and mentor. Although their playing styles were dissimilar, Oliver's advice helped Armstrong shape his sound, and his support enabled the young apprentice to gain better jobs around town—when he moved to Chicago, Oliver recommended that Armstrong replace him in Ory's band.

Eventually Ory relocated to California; Armstrong chose to stay home in New Orleans and began a three-year-plus tenure playing on riverboats with Fate Marable's band, whose lineup included several musicians who would join Armstrong in the pantheon of jazz pioneers, including bassist Pops Foster, clarinetist Johnny Dodds, drummer Baby Dodds, and guitarist Johnny St. Cyr. In the coming years these players would join other great New Orleans musicians who had preceded them in a northward exodus to Chicago. Armstrong was one of the last to leave, finally lured away in 1922 when King Oliver offered him a spot in the Creole Jazz Band. Over the next decade Armstrong would produce the body of work, both instrumentally and vocally, that not only changed the course of jazz and popular music of the time but continues to cast its shadow over jazz musicians and jazz music today. A number of titles offer overviews of the 1923–33 period, either in whole or in part; all come with the highest recommendation. Those confused about which titles to own are advised to spring for them all, because none are totally inclusive but all are absolutely essential. And lest anyone be misled into thinking that this music is to be enjoyed purely for the technical mastery on display, understand that these recordings remain vital, energetic and emotionally compelling these many decades hence.

In the spring of 1923 the Creole Jazz Band was extended an offer to record for the Gennett Record Company in Richmond, Indiana. That same year the band also waxed sides for the Okeh, Columbia and Paramount labels. The work on Milestone's *Louis Armstrong and King Oliver* ranks with Jelly Roll Morton's Gennett sides, also cut in 1923, as the most important documents in early jazz. Oliver's band at this juncture included Armstrong, Honoré Dutrey on trombone, Johnny Dodds on clarinet, Lil Hardin (later Mrs. Louis Armstrong) on piano, Stump Evans and Charlie Jackson on saxophones, Bill Johnson and Johnny St. Cyr on banjos and Baby Dodds on drums. On this outing their work is ragged and Armstrong's role dicey. He does little more than support Oliver's leads and offer a passing commentary when given an opportunity. In the 40-plus sides he cut with Oliver, Armstrong took only four solos; three of them are here, including "Chimes Blues," with his first recorded solo (a rather conservative, close-to-the-melody effort on behalf of a winning song), Jelly Roll Morton's "Froggie Moore" and one of two takes of "Riverside Blues." Also note three King Oliver's Creole Jazz Band tracks on disc one of the essential four-disc boxed set, *Portrait of the Artist as a Young Man 1923–1934,* including "Chimes Blues," "Snake Rag" (with a raucous double-cornet break between Oliver and Armstrong) and "Tears," an Armstrong-Hardin composition with Armstrong featured on nine extraordinary breaks, each one varying slightly from and building on the one preceding it.

As history records it, Lil Hardin made it her mission to ensure that, once in Chicago, Armstrong found the fame for which he seemed destined as a musician. In 1924, with Oliver's band disintegrating, the Armstrongs were offered a spot in Fletcher Henderson's band in New York. There they met Clarence Williams, a bandleader who used both Armstrongs during the couple's year in New York. These recordings were issued under the group names Clarence Williams's Blue Five and Red Onion Jazz Babies. For years the Blue Five recordings had been virtually impossible to find, but seven are included on disc one of *Portrait of the Artist as a Young Man 1923–1934.* Several Red Onions sides are heard on *Louis Armstrong and King Oliver.* In the Red Onions the key instrumentalist, apart from Armstrong himself, was the inventive Sidney Bechet on soprano saxophone. Bechet's bold style is overpowering and doubtless spurred Armstrong to more inspired performances. The two instrumentalists drive "Cake Walking Babies from Home" with relentless, breakneck propulsion; "Terrible Blues" shows Armstrong's instinctive mastery of theme and variation and stands as one of his most compelling solos on record. Yet another facet of his artistry is revealed on "Texas Moaner Blues," when his support of Alberta Hunter's hard-edged vocals demonstrates the great sensitivity he brought to his work with blues vocalists. The Blue Five recordings contained on *Portrait* feature the perky, husky-voiced vocalist Eva Taylor (Clarence Williams's wife) on three cuts; one of these, the hit "Everybody Loves My Baby," includes an electrifying plunger-muted solo from Armstrong at the end of the song. On another Blue Five cut, "Changeable Daddy of Mine," featuring vocalist Margaret Johnson, Armstrong delivers a breathtaking series of double-time solo passages, the last of which served as the model for one of his most celebrated solo flights, the opening cadenza in the jazz monument "West End Blues," recorded in 1928 and included on *Portrait*'s disc three.

Armstrong's year in New York also found him working numerous sessions; disc one of *Portrait* does a good job of cataloging these by rounding out the record of the artist's myriad activities during this fertile period. Included here are cuts with the fine blues singer Maggie Jones, the Southern Seranders (presumed to be Fletcher Henderson's band recording under a different name) and, most important, Bessie Smith, on the epochal version of "St. Louis Blues" and the moving "Sobbin' Hearted Blues."

By 1925 Armstrong reigned supreme among New Orleans musicians, an artist both envied and emulated by his peers. His year in New York had found him broadening his music and sharpening his instrumental attack—his range seemed limitless, and he had the physical gifts to sustain astonishing solo flights into the trumpet's upper register. This, coupled with his innate discipline and his breadth of influences, made his solos as unpredictable as they were groundbreaking in their sense of structure and exhilarating logic. These virtues alone made Armstrong a formidable figure; but when his energy and indomitable personality were factored into the mix, he stood alone.

In November 1925 Armstrong returned to Chicago and to the Okeh studio, first to do some session work (with, among others, blues singer Bertha "Chippie" Hill, heard on discs one and two of the *Portrait* boxed set, the latter disc containing Armstrong's heartbreaking solo on Hill's "Pleadin' for the Blues" from 1926) and then to cut the sessions that would change the jazz landscape forever. The label heads at Okeh, thinking Armstrong could grab a share of the pop market with his music, went along with his idea to assemble a band of New Orleans players working in Chicago strictly for recording purposes—not unusual now but unheard of in 1925, when bands appearing on records also worked together outside the studio. Thus the birth of the Hot Five.

The original lineup included Edward "Kid" Ory on trombone, Johnny Dodds on clarinet, Johnny St. Cyr on banjo, Lil Armstrong (the native Tennessean was the sole non–New Orleans musician on the date) on piano and Armstrong himself on cornet. Over the next three years this configuration's ranks would shift to include Baby Dodds on drums, Pete Briggs on tuba, Lonnie Johnson on guitar, Fred Robinson on trombone, Jimmy Strong and Jimmy Noone on clarinets, Earl "Fatha" Hines on piano, Mancy Carr on banjo, Zutty Singleton on drums, Dave Wilborn on banjo and guitar, and Don Redman on clarinet and alto saxophone—exceptional musicians all. Over the course of three years and some 60 sides, their music was issued as Louis Armstrong and His Hot Four, Louis Armstrong and His Hot Five, Louis Armstrong and His Hot Seven; other configurations were recorded as the Louis Armstrong Stompers, Louis Armstrong and His Savoy Ballroom Five, and Johnny Dodds's Black Bottom Stompers, but it was the "Hot" sessions that made Armstrong a nationally known figure—beloved and respected by blacks and whites, intellectuals and common folk alike—and changed the course of 20th Century music as well. For one, the Hot Five (et al.), while rooted in New Orleans ensemble-jazz traditions, emphasized solos to a degree then unprecedented in jazz history; and in Armstrong, Johnny Dodds, Kid Ory, Lonnie Johnson, Don Redman and Earl Hines, the group had several of the most distinctive instrumental voices of the time. Being surrounded by artistry of this high caliber brought out the best in Armstrong.

The list of achievements Armstrong wrought with these musicians is staggering, even in abbreviated form: Armstrong introduced scat singing on record (it was a technique common in New Orleans music well before Armstrong's time but seems to have remained strictly a Crescent City phenomenon) and became the absolute master of the form in the Hot Five's first hit, "Heebie Jeebies"; pioneered the stop-time chorus in "Cornet Chop Suey"; built a song on breaks and used his voice as an instrument on "Skid-Dat-De-Dat"; demonstrated a mastery of breath, time and tone on 1927's "Potato Head Blues" that remains a standard for every cornet and trumpet player who followed him and on the aforementioned "West End Blues" (1928), a tune written by King Oliver on which Armstrong and the Hot Five delivered a work of high art. He opened with a stunning cadenza—a masterful display of triplet runs into the stratosphere and the odd quarter note rumbling low, played in a quirky, zigzag rhythm pattern that is uniquely Armstrong's—sang some nonsense syllables in a warm, comforting voice that summoned images of a lazy summer afternoon under a shade tree, then locked into some breathtaking, delicately nuanced solo sparring with Hines, whose sensitive, succinct right-hand runs engaged Armstrong's keening solos in a heartbreaking dialog. The whole affair is suffused with near-palpable melancholy—a perfect marriage of technique and feeling in a mesmerizing 3 minutes, 16 seconds.

While the *Portrait* boxed set offers a highlight reel of Hot Four, Five and Seven recordings, this period is best appreciated in the more inclusive seven-volume Columbia Jazz Masterpieces Louis Armstrong collection, the first three of which contain 48 of the 60 sides cut by the Hot Five and the Hot Seven. Vol. 4, *Louis Armstrong & Earl Hines,* rounds out this period in its singular focus on the work these two pioneering instrumentalists made during their brief time together under the rubricks Hot Five and Savoy Ballroom Five. This latter volume includes some of jazz's enduring classics, such as "Weather Bird," on which Hines and Armstrong egg each other on with chase choruses and other spirited conceits in a rousing summit session, "St. James Infirmary," "Basin Street Blues," "Tight Like This" and "West End Blues."

In 1929 Armstrong returned to New York and began fronting a band led by the pianist Luis Russell. This association brought him together with a number of superb instrumentalists also in Russell's employ, including trombonist Jack Teagarden, who soon began adapting many of Armstrong's techniques to his own instrument, string bassist Pops Foster and the inventive guitarist Eddie Lang. For most of the next two decades Armstrong would stick to a big-band lineup, surrounding himself with top-flight musicians and solidifying his standing as the preeminent figure in jazz. When he went into the studio with Russell's band on March 5, 1929, he was recognized as a revolutionary on his instrument; when he took the lead vocal on "I Can't Give You Anything but Love," he staked his claim as a peerless vocalist as well. In this performance his muted and open trumpet solos bookend a vocal that is the extension of his instrumental approach. He stretches phrases, bends notes, scats a shotgun flurry of lyrics, leans in cozily and caresses all the tenderness out of a lyric line; his interpretation is warm and languid, witty and engaging all at once.

The most expansive survey of Armstrong's work with Russell is in the 11 cuts on *St. Louis Blues* (Vol. 6 of the Columbia Jazz Masterpieces Armstrong collection), which features 3 takes of the formidable title track and a wonderful, campy vocal duet with Hoagy Carmichael on the latter's song "Rockin' Chair," a model for the shtick Armstrong would employ most effectively with Jack Teagarden in the years ahead. Other Russell-band sides are on *Portrait*'s disc three, on *Louis in New York* (Vol. 5 of the Columbia Jazz Masterpieces set) and on Disques Swing's *Louis and the Big Bands 1928–30.*

By this time Armstrong had taken to the musical stage as well, gaining notice from legitimate theater critics for his interpretation of "Ain't Misbehavin'" in the revue *Hot Chocolates,* with songs composed by its star, Fats Waller. Each night when he finished his Broadway performance, Armstrong would go uptown to Connie's Inn nightclub in Harlem and participate in a truncated version of the show for the after-hours crowd. There he was backed by Carroll Dickerson's band, which included Pete Briggs on tuba and his ex–Hot Five mate Earl Hines on piano. Some of the *Hot Chocolates* selections are found on *Louis and the Big Bands, 1928–30* and *Louis in New York,* and three choice numbers are on disc three of *Portrait.* At this point, while he is still performing remarkable feats with the melodic and harmonic structure of songs in his trumpet solos, Armstrong is cutting a rather wide swath as a vocalist as well. Both *Louis in New York* and *St. Louis Blues* keep a sharp focus on the artist's growth as a singer at a time when the refinements in his vocal style were coming as rapidly as his solo trumpet innovations.

In the summer of 1930 Armstrong was holding forth in California, at Frank Sebastian's Cotton Club in Culver City as part of a band led by veteran saxophonist Les Hite. This group's fine musicians included young Lionel Hampton, then a drummer doubling on vibraphones. Recording with Hite between October 1930 and March 1931, Armstrong cut eight sides, all of them interesting. Seven are included on the seventh and final volume of the Columbia Jazz Masterpieces series, *You're Drivin' Me Crazy.* More pop hits of the day were showing up in Armstrong's repertoire now, and a couple of those—"Memories of You" and "You're Lucky to Me"—get near-definitive treatments here. The former is notable for Hampton's breezy vibe soloing—his first on record—and for another stellar vocal performance by Armstrong, again displaying a master stylist's command of tempo, phrasing and nuance in his reading. Among the other cuts here is one of the most revelatory from this period, "Sweethearts on Parade," a vehicle for one of the most adventurous trumpet solos Armstrong had attempted on record to this point.

The remaining 11 cuts on *You're Drivin' Me Crazy* date from Armstrong's brief tenure in 1931 with a Chicago band led by Zilner Randolph. This group's landmark recordings include a loping rendition of "Walkin' My Baby Back Home" and "When It's Sleepy Time Down South," the latter a staple in Armstrong's repertoire until the end of his life, although the clumsily executed original version would seem to mark it for instant obscurity.

On the *Portrait* boxed set, disc four documents both the Les Hite sessions and those with Zilner Randolph's band; as per the latter, disc four includes not only those sides found on *You're Drivin' Me Crazy* but other cuts as well, including the immortal renditions of "Stardust" (plus an alternate take of same) and "Between the Devil and the Deep Blue Sea," on which Armstrong's trumpet and voice are virtually a single instrument, poignant, resonant, deep and heartfelt. Not the least of disc four's virtues is its inclusion of Louis and Lil Armstrong's sole recording with Jimmie Rodgers, the father of modern country music, on his 1930 side "Blue Yodel No. 9," marking the first time a country musician had worked with black artists on record. It was also the last time Louis and Lil played together before their marriage broke up. Given Armstrong's increasing profile as a vocalist at this juncture, this is probably the best place to recommend the Portrait Masters title, *Stardust,* for its focus on Louis the singer. In addition to two takes of "Stardust" and "Between the Devil and the Deep Blue Sea," this recommended collection includes other songs that loom large in the artist's oeuvre, such as "Chinatown, My Chinatown," "Georgia on My Mind," "I Got Rhythm" and "All of Me."

In 1932 Armstrong left Columbia and signed with RCA, where he continued his big-band work, cutting some good sides here and there with fine musicians; more often, though, he found himself saddled with mediocre sidemen and unchallenging material. In addition, when he signed he had recently returned from a withering European tour and was not only physically fatigued but his embouchure was damaged by the punishment he had been inflicting on his lips from the time he picked up the cornet at the Waif's Home, where he was untutored in the proper alignment of the lips on the mouthpiece and the correct use of the muscles around the lips in producing tones.

Two RCA albums, *Laughin' Louie: Louis Armstrong and His Orchestra (1932–1933)* and the double-disc Jazz Tribune volume, *Young Louis Armstrong (1930–1933),* provide careful overviews of his years at that label. Over the course of these recordings we hear Armstrong, who was nearing the peak of his worldwide popularity, adopting a statelier, more conservative approach as an instrumentalist. Rather than improvising upper-register solo flights that left listeners and fellow players gaping open-mouthed at his technical facility, he stayed close to the melody line and favored a more introspective tone, one still rife with the yearning, tenderness and exuberance that marked his most personable work of earlier years.

The first RCA sides, heard on both titles listed above, find Armstrong supported by one of the best bands he would play with during the '30s, with a solid rhythm section anchored by legendary jazz drummer Chick Webb and including Elmer James on bass. Mezz Mezzrow, who played bells on "Hobo You Can't Ride This Train," has remarked upon the sorry condition of Louis's lip during these recordings, but that doesn't stop Pops from getting off a warm, muted solo to enliven a pleasant pop ditty "That's My Home," or a straightforward, jumping solo near the end of the rousing "Hobo." Elsewhere Armstrong's supporting cast includes Teddy Wilson on piano, Bud Johnson on clarinet and tenor sax, Elmer Whitlock and Zilner Randolph on trumpet, Scoville Browne and George Oldham on clarinet and alto saxophones, Bill Oldham on bass and Yank Porter on drums, among others. On some 1933 sessions, drummer Sid Catlett sits in on what was one of his first recording sessions. Though the results are uneven, the better moments are well worth savoring, especially in light of Armstrong's delicate physical condition, which he seems to have ignored near the end of the '33 sessions. He delivers a winning vocal on "Don't Play Me Cheap" and follows it with a herky-jerky solo on which he strains and stretches but finally reaches a last, aching high note.

In 1935 Armstrong signed with Decca Records, where his work with big bands produced a number of high points in his catalog of recordings but also found him falling back on gimmickry, engaging in pointless vocal and instrumental histrionics that show the artist at his most self-involved. *Heart Full of Rhythm,* the double-disc *Highlights from His Decca Years*, *Rhythm Saved the World* and *Pocketful of Dreams* offer ample evidence of the aesthetic peaks and valleys of the 1936–38 years; while the low points are embarrassing coming from a performer of Armstrong's stature, there is also an ample amount of inspired playing, some of it nearly on a par with the Hot Five and Hot Seven performances. Among the 16 tracks on *Louis Armstrong of New Orleans* are 10 cuts recorded between 1936 and 1940 with various big-band configurations. There are three cuts arranged by Luis Russell in 1938 and 1940 sessions, highlighted by a terrific, swinging version of "When the Saints Go Marchin' In," Armstrong's first and still definitive version of this well-worn chestnut. In an interesting reconsideration of an early Jelly Roll Morton hit, "Wolverine Blues," Armstrong engages in a near-song-length trumpet solo in which he first states the melody and then deconstructs it artfully again and again as the song winds down, without ever returning to the original theme—a remarkable performance that surely served notice to the day's young, hotshot trumpeters that Pops could still perform feats his descendants had yet to imagine.

Another 1940 session finds Armstrong and Russell joined by Sidney Bechet on four engaging cuts. Notable here is the swinging interplay between Bechet and Armstrong on "Perdido Street Blues" and Bechet's warm, vibrant solo in support of Armstrong's heartfelt vocal on the melancholy "2:19 Blues." This disc is rounded out by 1950 sessions with Jack Teagarden on trombone, Barney Bigard on clarinet, Earl Hines on piano, Arvell Shaw on bass and Cozy Cole on drums; a 1927 date with Johnny Dodds's Black Bottom Stompers ("Wild Man Blues"); and two 1926 cuts credited to Lil's Hot Shots, whose lineup is actually that of the Hot Five.

In addition to its valuable focus on Armstrong's writing, *The Best of the Decca Years, Vol. 2: The Composer* includes the original and only recording Armstrong made of "Satchel Mouth Swing," a lively 1938 orchestral track that led one wag to refer to the principal artist as Satchmo, a nickname that stuck and became the one by which most of the general public knew Armstrong in later decades as he became one of the most popular entertainers in the world. That and 3 other of the 13 tracks here date from 1936 to 1939, with the Louis Armstrong Orchestra numbering among its outstanding members Luis Russell, Henry "Red" Allen, Sid Catlett and Pops Foster.

On a lesser note but still of interest is the rare Olympic issue, *Mostly Blues,* a return to the traditional New Orleans style of jazz mounted for a radio show produced on December 12, 1938, by disc jockey Martin Block. The all-star lineup Block assembled to accompany Armstrong included Jack Teagarden, Bud Freeman, Al Casey, Fats Waller and two of Waller's stalwart sidemen, guitarist Al Casey and drummer Slick Jones. As promising as this sounds, the date was a disaster; some spirited playing ensued, but Armstrong pretty much clowned his way through the proceedings, and Waller, no stranger to outlandish showmanship, uncharacteristically retreated into a barely audible support role. Teagarden stands out with some inspired soloing, but the session is notable mostly for the first and sole meeting on record of Armstrong and Waller. Two songs from this date, "Jeepers Creepers" and "Tiger Rag," are also contained on Drive Archive's *Swing That Music,* which is otherwise devoted to live tracks from 1947 to 1949.

At the outset of the 1940s Armstrong's career was going into decline, his only a few years after he had broken down some barriers for black artists by being featured in several Hollywood films and making extended trips abroad to entertain U.S. troops. As a musician, though, he was facing other obstacles that were proving even tougher to overcome than show-business bigotry. His lips were deteriorating further, and his style of jazz had fallen out of favor both with the public and with other musicians. The end of World War II also marked the demise of the big-band era, both in jazz and in rhythm & blues, with bandleaders in both genres stripping their ensembles down to quartets, quintets and sextets and stepping up the rhythmic pulse to suit the rapidly evolving pace of postwar society. Bebop, rather than traditional and swing jazz, was the favored mode of communication among young musicians, whose advanced harmonies and odd rhythms (odd, that is, by the standards of traditional and swing jazz) signaled as much a change in style and attitude as did their political militancy, which further alienated them from the old guard. Armstrong cast a critical eye on the upstarts.

By 1947, though, even Armstrong was changing with the times. In February he played a well-received show at Carnegie Hall, half of which featured him fronting Edmond Hall's sextet, half leading a big band in what turned out to be the latter configuration's final appearance. Drive Archive's *Struttin'* documents the sextet's portion of the show and finds Armstrong in fairly good form instrumentally (especially on a lighthearted version of "Lazy River," on which the delicacy of Armstrong's soloing is a joy to hear) and at his most engaging vocally. In May he was booked at New York's Town Hall with a small band comprising some of jazz's finest traditional players, who were the first of many incarnations of the Armstrong All Stars: trombonist and vocalist Jack Teagarden, pianist Dick Cary, bassist Bob Haggart, drummers Sid Catlett and George Wettling, trumpeter Bobby Hackett and clarinetist Peanuts Hucko. Energized and ebullient, Armstrong played and sang with renewed conviction, spurred his sidemen on with comic insults (in the middle of his stirring vocal on "Back O' Town Blues" he shouts, "Shut up, boy," at one of his colleagues, goes back to singing, then sends the song home with a wailing trumpet solo) and was his usual gregarious, engaging self as the show's master of ceremonies.

A month later some of these same musicians, supplemented by baritonist Ernie Caceres and bassist Jack Lesberg, joined Armstrong for another scintillating show at New York's Winter Garden Theater. The proof is in the pudding on two highly recommended live albums, *Louis Armstrong at Town Hall: The Complete Town Hall Concert 17 May 1947* from the RCA Jazz Tribune Series, a release of many virtues, including an easygoing vocal duet between Armstrong and Teagarden on Hoagy Carmichael's "Rockin' Chair" and the concert's finale, "Jack Armstrong Blues," previously unavailable on the import of this title but included here, even though the recording equipment had overheated and was drowning out the performance in static; and the bulk of the cuts on the aforementioned *Swing That Music.*

Still another scintillating document from the late '40s is the RCA Bluebird title *Louis Armstrong Sings the Blues,* a survey of several of Armstrong's finest vocal performances (some live) from 1946 and 1947, save for three cuts from 1933 (including "St. Louis Blues"). In this collection are two numbers featured in the 1947 film *New Orleans,* with featured musical artists on the order of Armstrong, Billie Holiday, Kid Ory, Barney Bigard, Woody Herman's band, Meade Lux Lewis and Zutty Singleton.

Pops, *Pops: The 1940s Small Band Sides* and *Sugar* trace the mid- to late-'40s evolution of Armstrong's small bands. *Pops* includes three 1947 tracks recorded in Los Angeles for the New Orleans film with Armstrong's accompanists including Kid Ory, Barney Bigard and bassist Red Callender, along with other 1946–47 sessions with many of the same musicians Armstrong used at Town Hall and the Winter Garden; *Sugar* combines tracks from the 1947 Los Angeles and New York recordings heard on *Pops* with four tracks from the Town

Hall concert, which has the effect of driving the listener back to *Pops* and the Town Hall concert disc (*Jazz Tribune No. 43*) for more of this excellent playing.

This seeming rebirth remains evident on a November 1947 concert at Boston's Symphony Hall, although, in Armstrong's case, not to the degree heard on the Town Hall and Winter Garden performances. On the CD version of *Satchmo at Symphony Hall* (three tracks have been deleted from the 1977 double-LP release, which combined the original cuts issued on several 45s in 1951), the most scintillating moments come at the outset, with a rousing "Mahogany Hall Stomp" opening the night, followed by a winsome, moody take on "Black and Blue," on which Armstrong gives a wonderful midrange solo, then a deep, heartbreaking vocal. The mood lightens with the buoyant "Royal Garden Blues," with Armstrong's angular solo leading the way. Elsewhere, Barney Bigard offers a lovely, haunting clarinet solo on "Body and Soul"; the entire sextet (Armstrong, Bigard, Teagarden, pianist Dick Cary, drummer Sid Catlett and bassist Arvell Shaw) gets into a Dixieland rave-up on "Muskrat Ramble"; and vocalist Velma Middleton demonstrates why she was so despised by critics with a flat, amateurish reading of "Since I Fell for You" that drags the band down with her.

From the '50s up to his death in 1971, Armstrong toured constantly and profitably with the All Stars, whose lineup remained remarkably stable over the decades. The recorded output from this time, though, is inconsistent, and much of what remains in print is not studio recordings but live albums and compilations of work from various periods of Armstrong's career. Even so, many songs are duplicated from album to album, reflecting the settled nature of Armstrong's post-'40s repertoire. Arguably the best work he did in the mid-'50s, the Decca four-volume *Satchmo: A Musical Autobiography,* is out of print. A brief association with Verve produced some interesting small-band recordings, some featuring Ella Fitzgerald engaging in wonderful duets with Armstrong and others teaming Armstrong with a small combo comprising Oscar Peterson, Herb Ellis, Ray Brown and Louis Bellson. This latter contingent played with admirable taste and *simpatía* and is heard in peak form on the *Compact Jazz 5* album: *An American Songbook* contains seven tracks with the Peterson, Ellis, Brown, Bellson group and four others with an orchestra in a CD-i format that includes artist profiles, photos, interviews, discography and lyrics.

One of the better live efforts is GNP Crescendo's *Louis and His Friends,* recorded in 1951 at the Pasadena Civic Auditorium. For one, this is an endlessly entertaining set replete with assured but heartfelt playing, compelling ambiance and thoughtful interpretations of well-worn material. As always, Pops is the most genial of hosts, but his musical efforts are aided mightily by Jack Teagarden and especially Barney Bigard, and pianist Charlie Lavere (Earl Hines had left the All Stars earlier in the year) gets in some good licks along the way as well. This was one of Armstrong's strongest small-band lineups, but both Teagarden and Bigard would make amicable partings from the All Stars the next year, although Bigard would return and leave again two more times over the next decade and a half.

In this final era of his career, Armstrong never again enjoyed the musical intimacy he had developed over the productive years with Teagarden and Bigard, who on their own instruments were very nearly the equal of Armstrong the trumpeter in his prime; and in Teagarden he had an onstage foil and superb covocalist the likes of which had not graced his bands before the big Texan's arrival and would not after his departure. As a final document of this association, *Louis and His Friends* is a worthy, rewarding effort.

Vol. 1 of MCA's *Best of the Decca Years,* subtitled *The Singer,* belongs in this period as well. Apart from a 1937 track recorded with the Mills Brothers, "In the Shade of the Old Apple Tree," and 1949's "Blueberry Hill"—this cover of Glenn Miller's 1940 hit became Armstrong's first pop hit (it peaked at #24 on the *Billboard* chart), seven years before Fats Domino turned it into his biggest-selling single—the other 11 tracks are from the 1950s and show Pops's consummate skill as an interpreter, whether the material be jazz- or pop-oriented. Of note here: a duet with Louis Jordan, whose Tympany Five anticipated the All Stars of the late '40s and defined the approach of rhythm & blues combos of the '50s, on "You Rascal You," a bit of boisterous fun; a languorous interpretation of "La Vie en Rose" that compares favorably with the immortal Edith Piaf recording of same; and the touching "It's All in the Game," a 1951 track recorded with Gordon Jenkins's orchestra, as on "Blueberry Hill."

A 1954 Columbia release, *Louis Armstrong*

Plays W.C. Handy, features some solid playing by the post-Teagarden All Stars, including Bigard, who had returned in 1953, pianist Billy Kyle, drummer Barrett Deems, bassist Arvell Shaw, vocalist Velma Middleton and, stepping into Teagarden's large shoes and doing a superb job, James "Trummy" Young. Vocalist Middleton, target of critics' barbs since her arrival in Armstrong's big band in 1942, acquits herself well here on several duets, adopting a bland, pop-oriented approach rather than the more adventurous jazz stylings that defeated her on earlier recordings. Inspired playing is the order of the day on Milan's *What a Wonderful World: The Elisabethville Concert,* recorded live in Africa in 1960. Although Armstrong was playing his trumpet less and less in concert as a result of the deteriorating condition of his lips, he still gets off a soaring, upper-register wail on "Tiger Rag," and Trummy Young and Barney Bigard enliven the show with their distinctive sound signatures throughout.

By far the most unexpected event in Armstrong's career was its reinvigoration in 1964 when he recorded the title song from the Broadway play *Hello, Dolly!* for Kapp Records. Released in February, it entered the pop chart at #76 and began a steady climb, finally displacing the Beatles' "Can't Buy Me Love" atop the chart on May 9. A hastily recorded album, *Hello, Dolly!* followed the single's path, reaching Number One in early June. Also released on Kapp, that album is now on MCA and includes splendid versions of "A Kiss to Build a Dream On," "Moon River" and "It's Been a Long, Long Time," introducing a new generation to the wonders of Armstrong the vocal interpreter.

Though in ill health through much of the mid- and late '60s, Armstrong had one more transcendent performance left in him. In 1968 the timeless, bittersweet ballad, "What a Wonderful World," a single he recorded with veteran jazz producer Bob Thiele (who cowrote the song), topped the British singles chart and was followed stateside with a like-titled album featuring Armstrong, his band—trombonist Tyree Glenn, clarinetist Joe Muranyi, pianist Marty Napoleon, bassist Buddy Carter, drummer Danny Barcelona—and a large string section on a variety of pop- and Broadway-oriented tunes, including "Cabaret" (a minor hit single), "Hellzapoppin'" and "Dream a Little Dream of Me." Two albums titled *What a Wonderful World* exist in Armstrong's catalog, but the 1968 release is the one to own. The Bluebird *What a Wonderful World* is a collection of 1970 Thiele-produced sessions, among the last Armstrong recorded, that find the artist awash in some horrifying string and orchestral arrangements.

Sifting through Armstrong's hits collections and other compilations is almost as difficult as sorting out the wheat from the chaff among the live albums. Still, some can be singled out as best buys. At the top of the list among hits collections would be Columbia/Legacy's *16 Most Requested Songs* and *This Is Jazz 1.* Despite the former's pedestrian title, it is a thoughtful, well-annotated collection of Armstrong's better Columbia recordings. Columbia executive George Avakian, who was instrumental in directing Armstrong's career at the label in the 1950s, provides interesting song-by-song anecdotes detailing the stories behind the stories of each recording. This collection includes the original 1956 recording of "Mack the Knife," a Top 20 single for Armstrong that remains one of his signature songs. *This Is Jazz 1* is a sampler of key recordings from the '20s and '30s but hardly a substitute for any of the powerful albums from that period.

Tomato's *Butter and Eggman* covers the years 1929 to 1959 in 17 tracks, some of them familiar fare ("Do You Know What It Means to Miss New Orleans?," "La Vie en Rose," "Old Rockin' Chair"), some interesting left-field selections, such as the duets with Ella Fitzgerald on Gershwin's "Summertime" and with Austrian vocalist Gabriele Clonisch on "Onkel Satchmo's Lullaby." Another Tomato title, *C'est Si Bon,* is an overview of Armstrong the live performer in 16 tracks ranging from 1934's big-band recording of "St. Louis Blues" to several of the Teagarden-Bigard-era All Stars performances and rounded out by several Armstrong evergreens—"Mack the Knife," "Hello, Dolly!," "Blueberry Hill," "A Kiss to Build a Dream On," "That's My Desire"—recorded live in Europe in 1967 with the final edition of the All Stars.

After being hospitalized following a heart attack in the spring of 1971, Armstrong returned to his home in Astoria, New York, to recuperate. On July 6, two days after celebrating his putative birthday with former All Star Tyree Glenn, he died in his sleep. But his voice wasn't stilled. Eighteen years later, his 1967 recording of "What a Wonderful World" became a stateside hit after being a featured number on the soundtrack of the film *Good Morning, Vietnam* (1989). As Dan Morgenstern notes in his essay accompanying *Portrait of the Artist as a Young*

Man, "Louis would have been pleased. He didn't realize he was immortal." — D.M.

DESI ARNAZ

★★★★ **The Best of Desi Arnaz the Mambo King (RCA, 1992)**
★★★ **Desi Arnaz & Chico Marx: Big Bands of Hollywood (LaserLight, 1992)**
★★★★ **Babalu (RCA, 1996)**

Beloved as Lucy Ricardo's ever-beleaguered husband, Ricky, Desi Arnaz (1917–1986) had another life before *I Love Lucy* was even a distant dream, and a productive one it was. To Xavier Cugat goes the distinction of igniting an American craze for Latin-flavored, big-band dance music in the 1940s, but it was his protégé Arnaz who brought that particular strain of exotica to its fullest flower. Whereas Cugat incorporated Latin stylings into a pop approach, Arnaz did the reverse, favoring a harder-edged, percussive Latin sound with echoes of romantic, orchestral American pop. Both Cugat and Arnaz were beholden to the fiery Cuban bandleader Machito, whose raw, blistering sound was too ethnic to be commercially palatable for American tastes of the time but found popular appeal when recast in the big-band format by his acolytes. In turn, Arnaz's success in the late '40s opened the door in the '50s for another tough-minded Cuban bandleader, Perez Prado, from whose band sprang the towering Mongo Santamaria, who has brought Afro-Cuban music to its aesthetic, spiritual and philosophical apex in succeeding decades.

The Best of Desi Arnaz the Mambo King and *Babalu* chart Arnaz's landmark recordings from 1946 to 1949, when his orchestra was lighting mambo fires on both coasts in frequent nightclub appearances. Recorded when rhythm & blues was moving into high gear, country had produced a rawboned offshoot called honky-tonk and several of the century's greatest popular singers were coming of age, Arnaz's music embraced the spirit of adventure redolent in these other styles. Engaging wordplay, string arrangements that are lush and romantic without being gooey, vibrant, pulsating Latin percussion, pronounced brass and reed sections and strong, involved vocal performances (most by Arnaz, some by his personable female vocalist, Jane Harvey) mark these distinctive performances. In any role, Arnaz is a dominant personality, whether directing the band through a challenging instrumental ("Tico Tico," with its breathtaking brass-woodwind-keyboard-strings sparring matches) or stepping out to put across lyrics in English and Spanish. And though his voice wasn't an awe-inspiring instrument, that dark baritone could be warm and friendly on the mambos, seductive and dreamy on the love songs.

Elsewhere, novelties such as 1947's "You Can in Yucatan" allow Arnaz a vocal display of the comedic genius he would bring to his role as Ricky Ricardo in the next decade. Original recordings of songs from the TV show—"The Straw Hat Song," "Guadalajara," "Babalu"—are on both discs, unexpurgated and more overtly Latin in feel than the versions Ricky Ricardo's orchestra performed. His signature song, "Babalu," for example, is heard in all its dramatic glory, with three conga drummers beating out a forceful polyrhythm before Arnaz and orchestra come in, alternately boisterous and tender. Singing in Spanish, Arnaz shows off his belting style to admirable effect, then settles into a soft, crooning passage, before exploding into a shouting call-and-response with his chorus as the congas raise the ante again with their infectious polyrhythmic urgency. From first cut to last, the proceedings are informed by Arnaz's impeccable musicianship, grand sense of style and genial personality.

LaserLight's entry is evenly split between recordings by Arnaz's band and the one led by Chico Marx in the 1940s. Standouts among Arnaz's seven cuts are a lush, irresistible version of Cole Porter's "Begin the Beguine" and the Egan/Whiting chestnut "Till We Meet Again," one of Arnaz's warmest, most sincere readings on record. — D.M.

BILLY BOY ARNOLD

★★★★½ **More Blues on the South Side (1964; Original Blues Classics, N.A.)**
★★★★ **I Wish You Would (Charly, 1980)**
★★★★ **Ten Million Dollars (1984; Evidence, N.A.)**
★★★★ **Back Where I Belong (Alligator, 1993)**
★★★★ **Going to Chicago (Testament, 1995)**
★★★★ **Eldorado Cadillac (Alligator, 1995)**

The great Chicago harmonica player, vocalist and songwriter Billy Boy Arnold (b. 1935) was a protégé of John Lee "Sonny Boy" Williamson before working the streets with Ellas McDaniel during the early 1950s. Arnold applied the nickname Bo Diddley to his sidekick and played harmonica on some of the early Chess sessions.

The inventive Arnold wrote a number of memorable tunes, including "Diddley Daddy," "I Wish You Would," "I'm Gonna Move," "Oh Baby," "Two Drinks of Wine" and "You Don't Love Me No More," among others. His 1950s recordings for Vee-Jay Records (reissued on the Charly collection) became a favorite source for rock bands looking for blues material to cover.

His recordings are consistently great, which makes their scarcity all the more unfortunate. His first album, *More Blues on the South Side,* was recorded by a quintet boasting some of the best Chicago blues players of the early 1960s, including guitarist Mighty Joe Young and pianist Lafayette Leake. Bassist Jerome Arnold, another of the 16 kids in Billy's family, took time off from his work with the Butterfield Blues Band to join in on this session.

Incredibly, Arnold is represented by only one album over a nearly 30-year span, the 1984 French recording *Ten Million Dollars,* later reissued by Evidence. This is another top-flight set, with guitarists Jimmy Johnson and John "Mad Dog" Watkins burning a groove alongside Arnold's soulful harmonica work.

Arnold has made a spectacular comeback in the 1990s on Alligator records. *Back Where I Belong* finds him in ripe form backed by the Los Angeles blues band the Taildraggers.

Nothing could prepare the listener for the awesome glory of *Eldorado Cadillac,* however. At the age of 60, after a life of early accomplishment followed by decades of obscurity, Arnold produced his finest work, a gripping series of performances in a two-guitar octet led by the spectacularly *simpático* performance of guitarist Bob Margolin. Arnold's cool, knowing vocals are the essence of blues sensibility on terrific new songs like "Sunday Morning Blues," "Don't Stay Out All Night," "Mama's Bitter Seed" and "Man of Considerable Taste." Arnold's harmonica work is even more impressive. His full-throated, single-note blasts and bleeding tremolos bring the listener thrillingly back to the earliest days of harmonica virtuosity. — J.S.

HORACEE ARNOLD

★★★★ **Tribe (Columbia, 1973)**

★★★★ **Tales of the Exonerated Flea (Columbia, 1974)**

Drummer Horacee Arnold (b. 1937) apprenticed with Bud Powell, Charles Mingus, Stan Getz and Chick Corea before recording his first LP as a leader, *Tribe.* A beautiful record, *Tribe* offers superb Afro-Latin accompaniment from percussionists David Friedman and Ralph McDonald, reedmen Joe Farrell and Billy Harper, bassist George Mraz and acoustic-guitar virtuoso Ralph Towner. *Tales of the Exonerated Flea* is closer to a pure fusion outing featuring excellent performances from Jan Hammer (synthesizer), John Abercrombie and Towner (guitars), Dom Um Romao (percussion) and Sonny Fortune (soprano sax and flute). Though both recordings are unavailable at this writing, they are worth searching out and may well be included in the ongoing Legacy reissues.
— J.S.

JAMES "KOKOMO" ARNOLD

★★★½ **Complete Recorded Works in Chronological Order, Vol. 1 (1930–1935) (Document, 1991)**

★★★ **Complete Recorded Works in Chronological Order, Vol. 2 (1935–1936) (Document, 1991)**

★★★ **Complete Recorded Works in Chronological Order, Vol. 3 (1936–1937) (Document, 1991)**

★★½ **Complete Recorded Works in Chronological Order, Vol. 4 (1937–1938) (Document, 1991)**

★★★★ **Bottleneck Guitar Trendsetters of the 1930s (Yazoo, 1992)**

Before 2 Live Crew, before Rick James or Prince, there was Kokomo Arnold (1901–1968). In the world of slide-guitar blues, he was as nasty as he wanted to be, infusing such off-color ribaldry as "Busy Bootin'," "Salty Dog" and "Feels So Good" with a furious rhythmic sense and frantic slide play. The least polished and easily most manic of Chicago's first generation of slide guitarists (Tampa Red and Casey Bill Weldon were his peers), Arnold recorded close to a hundred titles between 1930 and '38, as a solo act, in piano accompaniments with the likes of Roosevelt Sykes and Peetie Wheatstraw ("The Devil's Son-in-Law") and in small-band settings. The Yazoo title catches him at his raucous best, though his stylistic limitations become pronounced in the exhaustive Document series. Disgruntled over years of unpaid royalties, Arnold laid down his bottleneck guitar in 1938 for a more lucrative career as a bootlegger, a protogangsta to the end. — A.K.

ART ENSEMBLE OF CHICAGO

★★★ **A Jackson in Your House/Message to Our Folks (1969; Affinity, N.A.)**

★★★½ **Live at Mandel Hall (1972; Delmark, 1991)**

★★★★ **Nice Guys (1979; ECM, 1987)**
★★★★★ **Full Force (1980; ECM, 1988)**
★★★★ **Urban Bushmen (1982; ECM, 1988)**
★★★ **The Complete Live in Japan, 1984 (DIW, 1988)**
★★★ **The Third Decade (ECM, 1985)**
★★★ **Vol. 1: Ancient to the Future (DIW, 1987)**
★★★ **Naked (DIW, 1988)**
★★★★ **The Alternate Express (DIW, 1989)**
★★★ **Live at the Sixth Tokyo Music Joy 90 (DIW, 1990)**
★★★½ **Dreaming of the Masters Suite (DIW, 1990)**
★★★★ **Thelonious Sphere Monk: Dreaming of the Masters, Vol. 2 (DIW, 1992)**
★★★½ **Art Ensemble of Soweto (DIW, 1992)**
★★★½ **Tutankhamun (Black Lion, 1994)**
★★★★ **Coming Home Jamaica (Atlantic, 1998)**

One of the most important developments in 1960s jazz came from the dramatic new concepts of self-expression championed by the Chicago-based Association for the Advancement of Creative Musicians. The AACM was only one of a number of movements toward a new definition of jazz during that eventful decade, but no group came closer to redefining the nature of the music. Its disciples went on to form the Black Artists Group in St. Louis and the loft-jazz movement in New York.

The best known of the AACM groups, the Art Ensemble of Chicago epitomized the AACM search for music beyond category and often played with unconventional instruments drawn from a variety of sources and a performance aesthetic that insisted on unpredictability.

Alto saxophonist Roscoe Mitchell (b. 1940) first organized the group in 1966, with trumpeter Lester Bowie (b. 1941) and bassist Malachi Favors (b. 1937). All of them also played the assortment of little instruments that became the Art Ensemble trademark. At the close of the decade Joseph Jarman (b. 1937) joined and the group switched from Mitchell's leadership to the collective Art Ensemble of Chicago.

A band dedicated to such lofty and unorthodox standards of creativity had difficulty finding outlets for its work and has a current catalog with glaring omissions. None of the original group's recordings are in print. Early masterpieces such as *People in Sorrow* as well as *Art Ensemble of Chicago with Fontella Bass* and *Les Stances à Sophie,* both of which feature outstanding singing from Bass, are not available.

In 1970 drummer Famoudou Don Moye (b. 1946) joined the group. The ensemble released two albums on Atlantic between *Live at Mandel Hall,* its 1972 homecoming concert in Chicago following a European residence, and 1978's *Nice Guys,* the beginning of a fruitful relationship with ECM, a label with the kind of recording standards that suited the subtleties of the group's approach.

Full Force is highlighted by the ear-opening extended composition "Magg Zelma" and an effective Charles Mingus homage, "Charlie M." *Urban Bushmen,* a live recording from 1980, presents the Art Ensemble at its best, developing a vision that ties African talking percussion directly to free jazz.

Five more years elapsed before the disappointing *Third Decade,* which not coincidentally ended the band's relationship with ECM. The year 1985 also marked the start of the band's enduring if not always satisfying relationship with the Japanese label DIW.

The Complete Live in Japan suffers compared with previous live efforts, as does *Live at the Sixth Tokyo Music Joy 90.* The studio effort *Naked* features some good playing, but *Ancient to the Future* goes over the top with embarrassing covers of Jimi Hendrix and Bob Marley. The band must have sensed that it went off the rails, judging from the high quality of the ensuing release, *The Alternate Express,* and its magnificent centerpiece, "Kush."

Art Ensemble of Soweto is an interesting if somewhat pro forma collaboration with the South African vocal group Amabutho. Pianist Cecil Taylor joins for what has to be one of the strangest Thelonious Monk tributes ever ventured, *Dreaming of the Masters, Vol. 2,* with its beautifully wrenching version of "'Round Midnight." The *Dreaming of the Masters Suite* follows the historic tribute mode into John Coltrane territory. The Art Ensemble resurfaced (minus Jarman) in time for the millennium with *Coming Home Jamaica,* a joyous release on Atlantic. Bowie and Mitchell's unique voices blend merrily with the lush Caribbean rhythms of the Favors/Maye rhythm section. — J.S.

DOROTHY ASHBY

★★ **Jazz Harpist (1957; Savoy, 1993)**
★★ **In a Minor Groove (1958; Prestige, 1992)**

It was through sheer virtuosity that Detroit-born Dorothy Ashby (1932–1986) overcame the skepticism engendered by her decision to play harp as a jazz soloist. Though she was schooled in bebop, her influence has ranged into the free-jazz and world-music styles of musicians as diverse as Alice Coltrane and Zusann Kali Fasteau. Frank Wess plays flute on these two albums, which suffer from a lack of intensity and rhythmic coherence in the overall band sound. — J.S.

HAROLD ASHBY

★★★ **The Viking (Gemini, 1989)**
★★★ **What Am I Here For? (Criss Cross, 1990)**
★★★ **I'm Old Fashioned (Stash, 1991)**
★★★ **On the Sunny Side of the Street (Timeless, 1992)**

Harold Ashby (b. 1925) was Duke Ellington's last star tenor saxophonist—a bighearted soloist with a breathy sound redolent of Ben Webster. Ashby's distinctive work is featured on Ellington's *Togo Brava Suite* and *The Afro-Eurasian Eclipse.* Ashby still had it together in the '80s and '90s and found himself in reliable company. *The Viking* employs the sympathetic pianist Norman Simmons; *What Am I Here For?* has the solid modernist backing of Mulgrew Miller, Rufus Reid and Ben Riley, while *I'm Old Fashioned* utilizes the great Modern Jazz Quartet drummer Connie Kay. — S.F.

BRIAN AUGER

★★½ **Definitely What! (1968; One Way, 1994)**
★★★ **Befour (RCA, 1970)**
★★★ **Brian Auger's Oblivion Express (RCA, 1971)**
★★★ **A Better Land (RCA, 1971)**
★★½ **Second Wind (RCA, 1972)**
★★★ **Closer to It (1973; One Way, 1995)**
★★½ **Straight Ahead (1974; One Way, 1995)**
★★½ **Reinforcements (RCA, 1975)**
★★½ **Encore (with Julie Tippitts) (One Way, 1978)**
★★½ **Here and Now (One Way, 1984)**
★★★ **The Best of Brian Auger's Oblivion Express (Chronicles, 1996)**

A British jazz organist whose early live work featured Rod Stewart, Long John Baldry and the cool-voiced Julie Driscoll, Brian Auger (b. 1939) hit his stride with the trailblazing *Befour,* from 1970. While the classical playing on the record was tasty, it was the swinging material that kicked: Influenced by Jimmy Smith and Herbie Hancock, Auger's precocious fusion was tough and smart.

His next three albums were kicky stuff, too. *Oblivion Express* featured "Dragon Song" by Auger's friend John McLaughlin; the band Oblivion Express moved into directions far funkier than Trinity had imagined (its then–lead singer, Alex Ligertwood, would go on to join Santana). *Closer to It,* heavily influenced by Auger's love for Marvin Gaye, was slick and sharp, and as jazz-rock fusion began gathering adherents, Auger shared his rightful place on stages with Return to Forever and the Mahavishnu Orchestra. — P.E.

LYNN AUGUST

★★ **Zydeco Groove (Maison de Soul, 1989)**
★★★ **It's Party Time (Maison de Soul, 1990)**
★★★★ **Creole Cruiser (Black Top, 1992)**
★★★½ **Sauce Piquante (Black Top, 1993)**

Lynn August was born in 1948 in Lafayette, ground zero of the French Louisiana zydeco scene, but zydeco wasn't his first love. Blind from before his first birthday, August was initially drawn to the rhythm & blues of Ray Charles, Fats Domino and Sam Cooke. He became a professional drummer as a teenager and in 1959 joined the band of Esquerita (a.k.a. Eskew Reeder), the makeup-wearing, piano-pounding, squealing New Orleans singer who so greatly influenced Little Richard and eventually convinced August to switch to keyboards and vocals.

When zydeco began its long comeback in the late '70s, August (much like his ex–band mate Buckwheat Zydeco) made the switch from R&B to the indigenous swamp music. He played organ for zydeco accordionist Marcel Dugas from 1977 to 1979 before launching his solo career.

Zydeco Groove is hampered by an underwhelming rhythm section and August's tentative vocals. With *It's Party Time,* however, he realized he didn't have to choose between R&B and zydeco but could combine them in ways that showed off his soulful voice. Although the low-budget approach to recording mars the results, August emerges as an impressive singer equally comfortable with a New Orleans second-line beat or a South Louisiana two-step.

These influences all come together on *Creole Cruiser,* a terrific zydeco album on which the strength of August's vocals and accordion riffs is finally equaled by the rhythm section and the engineering. Backed by Meters bassist George Porter Jr. and zydeco guitarist Selwyn Cooper, August captures the fiery drive of Clifton Chenier on some numbers and the infectious giddiness of Fats Domino on others. He gives two examples of jure—an ancient, prezydeco, a cappella chant—and he sings the traditional "Josephine Is Not My Woman" in Creole French. His tribute-in-song to the car on the album cover, "'58 Pink Cadillac," begins with a French exclamation but then jumps into a Larry Williams–like vocal. When August covers Bobby Bland's "Blind Man," you realize just how good a singer he is.

The same formula is applied to the follow-up, *Sauce Piquante,* with nearly equal success. This album features guitar solos from New Orleans bluesman Snooks Eaglin and August's own rocking squeeze-box solo on Little Richard's "Slippin' and Slidin' (Peepin' and Hidin')." — G.H.

CLAIRE AUSTIN

★★★ **Claire Austin Sings "When Your Lover Has Gone" (Original Jazz Classics, 1991)**

This fascinating record presents the work of Claire Austin (b. 1918), a blues neoclassicist whose unique singing style unites qualities ranging from the subtle emotional shifts of Billie Holiday back through the more formalized power of Bessie Smith. *When Your Lover Has Gone* collects three sessions, including a raucous set of classic blues accompanied by a small group with the great trombonist Kid Ory at the helm, and an atmospheric session of Holiday-like performances backed by an extremely supportive band featuring guitarist Barney Kessel, drummer Shelly Manne and trumpeter Bob Scobey. — J.S.

JESSE "WILD BILL" AUSTIN

★★★½ **Steel Trap (Roesch, 1992)**
★★★★ **Baby's Back (Roesch, 1995)**

Jesse "Wild Bill" Austin (1930–1996) broke in as a blues shouter at age 14 with Wynonie Harris in the 1940s and later worked with Percy Mayfield; his best solo work 50 years later still retains a swing sensibility. After years of obscurity, he was rediscovered and recorded in Connecticut by Joe Roesch, who founded Roesch Records to record Austin.

On both albums, horn sections balance Austin's trademark organ and big, rough vocals. He may not have a beautiful voice, but he sings with feeling and brings a lot of experience and energy to the mix. — J.Z.

TEODROSS AVERY

★★★ **In Other Words (GRP, 1994)**
★★★★ **My Generation (Impulse!, 1996)**

Born in 1973 near California's Bay Area, Teodross Avery carried his tenor sax into Oakland and San Francisco jazz clubs as a teenager and boldly asked to sit in with visiting heavyweights including Art Blakey, Donald Byrd, Elvin Jones and the Marsalis brothers. While Avery was at Boston's Berklee College of Music, people took even more notice of the kid with the swaggering tenor sound (best exemplified by the track "One to Love") and the floating yet biting soprano.

In Other Words was recorded with his regular working quartet in June 1994, weeks after Avery completed his junior year at Berklee. Trumpeter Roy Hargrove provides additional front-line sparkle. It is an auspicious debut for a Joe Henderson student whose composition skills show as much promise as his playing. *My Generation* is more conceptual, teaming Avery on various tracks with guitarists John Scofield, Mark Whitfield and Peter Bernstein. — K.F.

ROY AYERS

★★★★ **Evolution: Anthology (Polydor, 1970)**
★★★ **Mystic Voyage (with Ubiquity) (Polydor, 1975)**
★★★ **Everybody Loves the Sunshine (with Ubiquity) (Polydor, 1976)**
★★★½ **Nasté (BMG, 1995)**
★★★ **The Best of Roy Ayers (Polydor, 1997)**

Roy Ayers, born in Los Angeles in 1940, was a multi-instrumentalist child prodigy who by his early 20s was coleading his own band with Hampton Hawes. Coming to prominence as the vibraphonist on albums by Herbie Mann, Ayers evolved from a strict Afro-Cuban style into a world-music prototype on the 1967 release *Impressions of the Middle East.* During his stay with Mann he recorded a pair of solo albums, which were consolidated into the excellent but now out-of-print *Daddy Bug and Friends.* He worked with Mann through the also unavailable 1971 release *Memphis Two Step.*

Ayers went on to form Ubiquity, a progressive

funk-jazz group that cut a serious groove on such sessions as *Red, Black and Green*, *Mystic Voyage*, *Everybody Loves the Sunshine* and *Tear to a Smile.* As Ayers moved increasingly into keyboard and synth arrangements, his music became more pop-oriented, represented by the 1982 single "Turn Me Loose" from the *Feeling Good* album. The historic 1981 collaboration with Afro-beat master Fela Anikulapo Kuti, *Africa, Center of the World,* is now out of print, as are *Red, Black and Green*, *Tear to a Smile,* and *Feeling Good,* but a survey of his Polydor recordings is available on *Evolution: Anthology.*

Despite his commercial success, Ayers had a hard time consolidating his career. Subsequent titles on Columbia are not in print, and Ayers's 1990s recordings for Ichiban are available only as cassettes.

Ayers came back into the commercial mainstream as a guest on the acid-jazz breakthrough recording *Jazzmatazz* in 1993. *Nasté* gives him a chance to demonstrate the range of his musical interests, concentrating on a computerized rhythmic groove that gives him ample space to solo on both vibes and keyboards, experiment with some Afro-pop grooves, get down with James Moody on soprano sax and vocalize an exchange of pillow talk with the sultry-voiced Wunmi Olaiya. As good as this music is, some will have a point in refusing to acknowledge it as jazz, especially when some of Ayers's best playing is simply unavailable. — J.S.

ALBERT AYLER

★★★ **My Name Is Albert Ayler (1963; Black Lion, 1996)**
★★★½ **Witches and Devils (1964; Freedom, 1990)**
★★★★ **Spiritual Unity (ESP, 1964)**
★★★★ **Spirits Rejoice (ESP, 1965)**
★★★★ **Vibrations (with Don Cherry) (1973; Freedom, 1987)**
★★★ **Live at Lorrach/Paris 1966 (hat Art, 1986)**
★★★★ **Love Cry (Impulse!, 1991)**
★★★½ **Goin' Home (Black Lion, 1995)**

After mastering his skills—a grand tone, a shimmering vibrato—in rhythm & blues settings, Albert Ayler (1936–1970) went on to blaze trails with assertive free jazz, hitting his zenith in the mid-'60s. Influenced as clearly by folk and Mexican melodies as by the blues, this tenor-saxophone wizard began recording with Sunny Murray and working alongside trumpeter Don Cherry and pianist Cecil Taylor while refining his own style. Misunderstood stateside, he spent time in Europe (the credible *My Name Is Albert Ayler* was recorded with Swedish players) before embarking on a series of signature dates on the ESP label. *Spiritual Unity* is the strongest exemplar of the period; with Ayler, Murray on drums and bassist Gary Peacock bonding on a set of unadorned power, it's one of the classics of free jazz. *Witches and Devils* is nearly as fine, as is *Spirits Rejoice* (which highlights Call Cobbs's harpsichord). As Ayler's titles underline, the musician soared on flights into the music—his best early work, in particular, was strongly spiritual (check, also, the stirring gospel fare on *Goin' Home*). *Vibrations* features standout playing from Cherry while Ayler alternates on tenor and alto. By 1966, Ayler was again exploring—this time, on *Live at Lorrach,* he harkens back to the halcyon days of New Orleans, but he fractures the melodies, making of them very much his own fierce poetry. On *Love Cry* he adds vocals to three tracks, and the maneuver is at least intriguing. His later work, featuring rock guitar and a return to his R&B roots, again showed promise, but his peak remains his '60s canon. Sadly, Ayler's body was found in New York Harbor in 1970. — P.E.

AZYMUTH

★★★ **Light as a Feather (Milestone, 1980)**
★★★ **Telecommunication (Milestone, 1981)**
★★★ **Cascades (Milestone, 1982)**
★★★ **Rapid Transit (Milestone, 1983)**
★★★ **Flame (Milestone, 1984)**
★★★ **Spectrum (Milestone, 1985)**
★★ **Tightrope Walker (Milestone, 1986)**
★★★ **Crazy Rhythm (Milestone, 1987)**
★★★ **Carioca (Milestone, 1988)**

Azymuth is a Brazilian group combining samba and bossa nova influences with pop jazz arrangements for an airy sound that has proved to be commercially successful. Keyboardist and producer José Roberto Bertrami (b. 1946), bassist Alex Malheiros (b. 1946) and drummer Ivan Conti (b. 1946) form the basis of the band, which is augmented with additional percussionists and flautist José Carlos Bignora on *Cascades.* The consistency of the band's conception is a plus for those who find this original style engaging, but it draws attention to the fact that Azymuth has no compelling improvisational leader to make it more than a run-of-the-mill jazz combo. — J.S.

CHET BAKER

★★★½ Witch Doctor (1953; Original Jazz Classics, 1991)
★★½ Chet Baker and Strings (1954; Legacy, 1998)
★★½ Grey December (1955; Pacific Jazz, 1992)
★★★ In Paris 1 (1955; Verve, N.A.)
★★★ In Paris 2 (1955; Verve, N.A.)
★★★ In New York (1958; Original Jazz Classics, 1988)
★ It Could Happen to You (1958; Original Jazz Classics, 1987)
★★½ Introduces Johnny Pace (1958; Original Jazz Classics, 1990)
★★★ Chet (1959; Original Jazz Classics, 1987)
★★★ Chet Baker Plays the Best of Lerner & Loewe (1959; Original Jazz Classics, 1984)
★★★ In Milan (1959; Original Jazz Classics, 1989)
★★ With Fifty Italian Strings (1959; Original Jazz Classics, 1991)
★★ Somewhere over the Rainbow (1962; RCA, 1992)
★★★ Baker's Holiday (1965; EmArcy, N.A.)
★★½ She Was Too Good to Me (1974; CBS, N.A.)
★★ Live in Paris/Live in Nice (1975; Esoldun, 1984)
★★★ Live at Nick's (1978; Criss Cross, N.A.)
★★ Live in Chateauvallon—1978 (1978; Esoldun, N.A.)
★★½ No Problem (1979; SteepleChase, N.A.)
★★ Someday My Prince Will Come (1979; SteepleChase, 1994)
★★½ The Touch of Your Lips (1979; SteepleChase, N.A.)
★★★ Daybreak (1979; SteepleChase, 1995)
★★★ Once upon a Summertime (1980; Original Jazz Classics, 1989)
★ Nightbird (West Wind, 1980)
★★★½ Chet Baker and the Boto Brasilian Quartet (1981; Dreyfus, 1991)
★★★ Peace (1982; Enja, 1990)
★★½ Out of Nowhere (1982; Milestone, 1991)
★ Live in Sweden (Dragon, 1983)
★★★ Blues for a Reason (Criss Cross, 1984)
★★½ Strollin' (Enja, 1985)
★★ When Sunny Gets Blue (SteepleChase, 1986)
★★★ Live at Ronnie Scott's (DRG, 1987)
★ Live in Tokyo (1987; Evidence, 1996)
★★½ My Favorite Songs (Enja, 1988)
★★★ Let's Get Lost: The Best of Chet Baker Sings (Pacific Jazz, 1989)
★★★ Compact Jazz (EmArcy, 1989)
★★ Jazz Round Midnight (Verve, 1990)
★★ Two a Day (Dreyfus, 1991)
★★½ Little Girl Blue (Philology, 1992)
★★ A Night at the Shalimar (Philology, 1992)
★★★ Boston, 1954 (Uptown, 1992)
★★★★ Best of Chet Baker Plays (Pacific Jazz, 1992)
★★ In Bologna (Dreyfus, 1992)
★★★★ The Pacific Jazz Years (Pacific Jazz, 1993)
★★★ My Funny Valentine (Philology, 1994)

★★½ **Jazz Masters 32 (Verve, 1994)**
★★½ **Young Chet (Pacific Jazz, 1995)**
Trumpet/flügelhorn player and vocalist Chesney "Chet" Baker (1929–1988) established his reputation as one of the best young trumpeters on the West Coast in the early 1950s through club dates with Charlie Parker and a subsequent residence in Gerry Mulligan's pianoless quartet. Baker's earliest solo work, reissued on the Pacific Jazz label, includes plenty of top-flight alto-sax work from Art Pepper. *Witch Doctor,* which was recorded with the area's highest-rated group, the Lighthouse All-Stars, depicts Baker as one of the more successful Miles Davis imitators of the time. The soft, lyrical trumpet style that served Baker so well on these tracks deteriorates over the years, and though he adapted with some moments of grace, Baker all too often fell back on his early reputation, making picking through his recorded output a tortuous affair.

Beginning the first of numerous European stays in late 1955, Baker became a huge star abroad and recorded on the Continent as much if not more than any other American jazz expatriate, often in less than spectacular form with earnest but pedestrian European accompanists. He became a cult figure, then a star, on the basis of his mystique (heroin chic) and a haunting vocal style, expressing an innocent beauty that eventually clotted into Herb Alpert–style pablum. Baker embodied the myth of the beautiful loser, codified in the lachrymose "Everything Happens to Me" (*In Paris 2*, *Jazz Masters 32*). The vocal whine evident on *Grey December* gravitates from Frank Sinatra to Pat Boone by the time of *It Could Happen to You.* When Baker concentrated on his playing and was physically capable (his wasted lifestyle led to an incident in which his teeth were knocked out, disabling his playing), moments of beauty ensued. Baker's legend bears some similarity to that of Billie Holiday's; the 1965 *Baker's Holiday* offers a convincing tribute to Lady Day.

The mid-1950s Paris sessions, with a small group highlighted by the gifted pianist Richard Twardzik, solidified Baker's European credentials. *In Milan* is an earnest set backed by two capable Italian lineups. Back home, *In New York* teamed Baker with Johnny Griffin on tenor, Al Haig on piano, Paul Chambers on bass and Philly Joe Jones on drums. *Chet* is a fine session with Herbie Mann on tenor sax and flute, Pepper Adams on baritone sax, Bill Evans on piano, Kenny Burrell on guitar and Connie Kay or Philly Joe Jones on drums. Most of the same group came back for the *Lerner & Loewe* session.

Once upon a Summertime is valuable, if only for the rhythm section of bassist Ron Carter, drummer Mel Lewis and pianist Harold Danko. *Daybreak* finds Baker on a drummerless session with bassist Niels-Henning Ørsted Pedersen, who also appears on *Someday My Prince Will Come* and *No Problem.*

Baker's diffident trumpet phrasing is perfectly suited to the gentle rhythms of the Boto Brasilian Quartet, leaving listeners to wonder why he didn't try more of the same. *Peace* benefits from good compositions from vibist/marimba player Dave Friedman, with Buster Williams on bass and Joe Chambers on drums.

Blues for a Reason features saxophonist Warne Marsh. *My Funny Valentine* consists of seven treatments of the tune, popularized for the jazz audience by Miles Davis, with various groups. *Live at Ronnie Scott's* features a vocal by Van Morrison on "Send in the Clowns." *Little Girl Blue* is Baker's final recording session, backed by the Space Jazz Trio. — J.S.

GINGER BAKER

★★★★½ **Going Back Home (Atlantic, 1994)**
★★★★ **Falling off the Roof (Atlantic, 1996)**
Drummer Ginger Baker (b. 1939) grew up in London playing with some of the most influential English blues and jazz bands of the 1960s, including Alexis Korner's Blues Incorporated, the Graham Bond Organisation and Cream. The last band, a trio with guitarist Eric Clapton and bassist Jack Bruce, established Baker among the premier drummers of the rock era. His solo feature in Cream's "Toad" revealed Baker to be an unabashed disciple of Gene Krupa, whose drum solo on the Benny Goodman swing classic "Sing, Sing, Sing" electrified the previous generation of hot-music fans.

Baker went on to explore African drumming, recording crossover work with his own band, Air Force. Through much of the '70s and '80s, Baker recorded sporadically, mostly with African musicians. In 1994 he returned to top form with *Going Back Home,* an excellent postfusion trio album with guitarist Bill Frisell and bassist Charlie Haden, musicians whose musical imaginations provide the perfect landscape for Baker's inspired forays into the sonic netherworld. This group went on to make another terrific record, *Falling off the Roof,* which includes guest appearances from guitarist

Jerry Hahn and virtuosic banjo player Bela Fleck. —J.S.

LAVERN BAKER

★★★★ **LaVern Baker Sings Bessie Smith (1958; Atlantic, 1988)**
★★★★★ **Soul on Fire: The Best of LaVern Baker (Atlantic, 1991)**
★★★ **Live in Hollywood '91 (Rhino, 1991)**
★★★½ **Woke Up This Mornin' (DRG, 1992)**

If anyone came to her profession with an unassailable pedigree, it was LaVern Baker (1929–1997). Born Delores Williams in Chicago, the niece of Memphis Minnie, Baker started her recording career in 1950 with the Eddie Penigar Band. Those sides were unissued, but a year later she appeared on three Okeh singles as Bea Baker, then billed herself as Little Miss Sharecropper and recorded for National, RCA Victor and Columbia. In 1952, using the name LaVern Baker, she joined Todd Rhodes and His Orchestra and recorded for King; she signed to Atlantic the following year. There she delivered a sultry slice of urgent R&B, "Soul on Fire," a cataclysmic performance that found Baker employing a stunning array of vocal tools ranging from a deep, longing blues growl to tearful glottal stops to wanton, upper-register shouts. It was a portent of things to come. In early '55 she had her first hit, "Tweedlee Dee," which had a near-three-month run on the pop chart, peaking at #14; between 1956 and 1963 she placed six more singles in the Top 50, with 1956's "Jim Dandy" rising to the Top 20 and 1958's wrenching "I Cried a Tear" peaking at #6 in its five-month chart run.

As her Aunt Minnie had done more than 20 years earlier, Baker stepped into a man's world, making a lasting impression on fans and on female vocalists who came after her. Hers was a voice that would not be denied, whether she was belting out an up-tempo pop hit or probing the nuances of Doc Pomus's poignant blues ballad "My Happiness Forever," which demands the singer put across equal measures of resilience and vulnerability from one phrase to another. And on the rare occasions when she got hold of a song that took her back to her Baptist church roots, as she did on Leiber-Stoller's "Saved," she could testify with the best, using her big, booming voice to proclaim the Lord's goodness and mercy for all to hear.

The Atlantic years are succinctly documented on *Soul on Fire*. The other essential document from this time is the one that best reveals the depth and breadth of Baker's artistry: *LaVern Baker Sings Bessie Smith* links the former most dramatically to the latter's legacy, not merely by its title but by the intelligence and personality of Baker's interpretations. Here she is by turns bawdy ("Baby Doll"), strong and independent ("I Ain't Gonna Play No Second Fiddle," "Young Woman's Blues"), vulnerable ("Empty Bed Blues," "After You've Gone") and bowed but proud ("Nobody Knows You When You're Down and Out"). Among a stellar supporting cast of players, Buck Clayton on trumpet and Vic Dickenson on trombone stand out with solo turns that buttress Baker's tour de force with eloquent instrumental commentaries. In asserting her heritage, Baker tells anyone who will listen that this music defines her. She sings Bessie Smith in grand style—but the control, phrasing and attitude are all LaVern Baker, whose best-known work barely suggests her great gift as an artist.

When the hits stopped coming in the '60s, Baker continued touring and recording before dropping out of sight by decade's end. When found almost 20 years later, she was happily engaged as the entertainment director of a U.S. military NCO club in the Philippines, where she had been raising a family and performing for GIs. In 1988 she returned to the States to participate in Atlantic's 40th birthday celebration at Madison Square Garden—where she brought the house down. Gradually she made her way back, performing selected concert dates, cutting "Slow Rollin' Mama" for the 1988 *Dick Tracy* soundtrack, then following her friend and former Atlantic artist Ruth Brown in the starring role in Broadway's *Black and Blue.* In early 1991 she was elected to the Rock and Roll Hall of Fame and followed that honor with her return to recording.

Live in Hollywood '91 is the resulting document of her early comeback, a live performance recorded at Hollywood's Cinegrill Club in the Roosevelt Hotel. The years have been kind to her voice; here it sounds even more powerful than it does on some of the Atlantic sides, and age has lent it an earthy huskiness that deepens the feeling she brings to bluesier material like "Tomorrow Night," a song identified with Lonnie Johnson. Biggest surprise: the venerable "Tennessee Waltz" done up in a strutting tempo, with Baker tossing off the verses as if she were engaged in idle chitchat; then she swoops and glides through the chorus, her voice suddenly exposing the hurt and longing she feels below the surface—a remarkable performance.

Six months after her Cinegrill performance, Baker ended her 20-year exile from records by cutting a studio album in New York with a host of top-flight musicians, among them guitarist Cornell Dupree, bassist Chuck Rainey, drummer Bernard Purdie and powerhouse Ronnie Cuber, who manhandles the baritone sax in delivering one sterling solo after another. True to her versatile nature, Baker assays a wide range of material. Blues and R&B dominate the proceedings, with the torch reading of "Body and Soul" standing out, although she one-ups herself on "Trouble in Mind," going low for some deep blues, as Dupree and Cuber support her with well-crafted, emotion-packed solos. Elsewhere, she makes a good, lusty run at the Bee Gees' "To Love Somebody," imbuing the song with a bold eroticism uncommon to most interpretations. She does Otis Redding proud with a fiery take on "Can't Turn You Loose," then closes out the proceedings with another reading of "Tennessee Waltz," again done up-tempo but with her performance even more nuanced than on her live album. There are a few missteps here—the treatments of Eddie Floyd's "Knock on Wood" and William Bell's "You Don't Miss Your Water" are a bit too stolid in their arrangements, and Baker sounds unduly restrained as a result. Hard to quibble with either of the '91 albums, though. LaVern Baker is a gem of the rarest kind. — D.M.

LONG JOHN BALDRY

★★★ **Let the Heartaches Begin/Wait for Me (1968/1969; Beat Goes On, 1995)**
★★★½ **It Still Ain't Easy (Stony Plain, 1991)**
★★★½ **On Stage Tonight—Baldry's Out! (Stony Plain, 1993)**
★★★½ **Right to Sing the Blues (Stony Plain, 1996)**

English-born blues singer and guitarist Long John Baldry (b. 1941) learned the ropes touring with Ramblin' Jack Elliott in the 1950s and became one of the founders of England's 1960s blues scene, working with Alexis Korner's Blues Incorporated (see *R&B from the Marquee*) and the Cyril Davies R&B All Stars before forming his own group. His greatest notoriety came as the leader of Steampacket, which gave Rod Stewart his start. *Let the Heartaches Begin/Wait for Me* is a twofer reissue of late-'60s material made for Pye records.

In the early 1970s Baldry emigrated to Canada, where he made a living doing voice-overs before recording his 1991 comeback album, *It Still Ain't Easy,* with help from guitarist Amos Garrett, saxophonist Lucky Peterson and vocalists Bobby King and Terry Evans. The live *On Stage Tonight—Baldry's Out!* shows that Baldry still has what it takes as a club performer. *Right to Sing the Blues* features a guest shot from Colin James, who wrote the title track, and a bonus interview touching on Baldry's recollections of his early days. — J.S.

MARCIA BALL

★★★½ **Soulful Dress (Rounder, 1983)**
★★★ **Hot Tamale Baby (Rounder, 1986)**
★★★ **Gatorhythms (Rounder, 1989)**
★★★ **Blue House (Rounder, 1994)**
★★★½ **Let Me Play with Your Poodle (Rounder, 1997)**
★★★★★ **Sing It! (Rounder, 1998)**

One of the grande dames of the Austin scene, Marcia Ball (b. 1949) seems at once the most self-conscious of that city's trio of honky-tonk legends (the others being Angela Strehli and Lou Ann Barton) and the most free-swinging. It's an odd combination, to be sure, and it makes for music that seems less than the sum of its parts, albeit frequently engaging. Her Texiana piano style sounds better the farther east her references take her, all the way to New Orleans.

The clarity of Ball's singing and the preciseness of her diction keep the focus on the message rather than the messenger by establishing what feels at times like an emotional distance from her material. But listen closely and you'll find she allows you full access to her world. On *Soulful Dress,* she moves on through 10 songs that describe the emotional roller-coaster she's been riding in trying to come to grips with this thing called love. Selected song titles tell the tale: "Made Your Move Too Soon," "My Mind's Made Up," "Soul on Fire," "Don't Want No Man." Blues ballads and contemporary honky-tonk stylings further recommend an album that is both personally revealing and musically buoyant.

Hot Tamale Baby follows in its predecessor's footsteps, both in theme and style. No questioning the commitment evident in Ball's lyric readings, but there's little to distinguish this effort from *Soulful Dress,* except that the band seems to be pumping away at about twice the volume.

Gatorhythms, on the other hand, finds Ball

exploring the rhythms of her native Louisiana while remaining in a Lone Star state of mind. She's also credited as coproducer and wrote 7 of the 10 songs on the album. In laying her soul ever barer, Ball offers up two powerful ballads, "The Power of Love" and "Find Another Fool," that find the artist admitting vulnerability, even insecurity, in her search for a significant other. Throw in some fine, rocking tracks on the order of "How Can You Carry On" and the zydeco-flavored "Daddy Said," and *Gatorhythms* becomes a document of growth, personal as well as artistic, and something to build on.

Which she does effectively on *Blue House* and *Let Me Play with Your Poodle,* each album offering more ruminative, introspective songs of serious lyric intent than can be found on Ball's early efforts. A beautiful version of Randy Newman's "Louisiana" closes out *Poodle* on a reflective note, suggesting an artist on a journey of intense self-discovery. There's plenty of playfulness on both albums, but it's those quieter moments that linger after the last song has played out. Suddenly she sounds like she's discovered a new world, a transformation that is reflected in the rigor of her instrumental support and the intensity of her personal reminiscences. Ball's facility for working closely within the group is best applied on the astonishingly great *Sing It!,* a collaboration with Tracy Nelson and both singers' prime influence, New Orleans R&B great Irma Thomas. The three trade off lead vocals, back one another up expertly and join together in jubilant gospel fervor on the title track. For someone who's been around awhile, Marcia Ball seems to have begun anew. And what a start it is. — D.M.

BILLY BANG

★★★★ Rainbow Gladiator (1981; Soul Note, 1993)
★★★ Invitation (1982; Soul Note, 1993)
★★★½ The Fire from Within (Soul Note, 1985)
★★★½ Live at Carlos 1 (1987; Soul Note, 1993)
★★★ A Tribute to Stuff Smith (Soul Note, 1993)
★★★★ Commandment (No More, 1997)
★★★½ Bang On! (Justin Time, 1997)

Classically trained violinist Billy Bang (b. 1947) studied with Leroy Jenkins before embarking on his own quest into uncharted musical territory. Bang's early (out-of-print) solo recording, *Distinction Without a Difference* on Hat Hut, is worth seeking out.

After working in several duo settings, most notably with baritone and alto saxophonist Charles Tyler, Bang came into his own leading the quintets that recorded *Rainbow Gladiator* and *Invitation,* which also featured Tyler. Pianist Michele Rosewoman excelled on the heady *Gladiator,* which swings with a mad, dazzlingly surreal intensity.

The Fire from Within uses percussionists Thurman Barker and Charles Bobo Shaw for more North African shadings, a style conducive to Bang's approach and very effective in clubs, as *Live at Carlos 1* demonstrates. The Stuff Smith tribute is an ethereal session recorded with Sun Ra at a point where the pianist's health was failing but his spirit was as impish as ever. *Bang On!* is a quartet date with pianist D.D. Jackson, drummer Ronnie Burrage and bassist Akira Ando. On *Commandment* Bang employs the full scope of his considerable imagination in a solo suite addressed to Alain Kirili's sculptures, ranging from "Swing Low Sweet Chariot" to compositions by Sun Ra and Butch Morris.

Bang is also a sought-after collaborator on special projects such as the String Trio of New York, of which he is a founder, as well as a sideman with Marilyn Crispell, Material and others. — J.S.

PATRICIA BARBER

★★★ Split (Floyd, 1989)
★★★ A Distortion of Love (Antilles, 1992)
★★★★ Cafe Blue (Premonition, 1994)
★★★★ Modern Cool (Premonition, 1998)

Chicago-based Patricia Barber (b. 1955) is a singer/pianist whose eclectic sound is both exotic and understated. Her piano work is artful and excellent on its own terms, but it's Barber's hypnotic vocal distillation of songs that turns repeat listeners into ardent fans. It has been that way since 1984 at Chicago's Gold Star Sardine Bar, and more recently at the Green Mill jazz club. She has been a regular at Europe's North Sea Jazz Festival since 1989. The daughter of a jazz saxophonist, Floyd "Shin" Barber, she majored in classical piano and psychology in college before turning her talents to jazz.

Her self-produced and -released debut recording, *Split,* displays the promise of an evolving personal style. That style boldly reaches its potential on *A Distortion of Love,* with a hired-gun band including bassist Marc Johnson, drummer Adam Nussbaum and guitarist Wolfgang Muthspiel. Original treatments of "Summertime," "You Stepped Out of a Dream" and Smokey Robinson's "My Girl" are exquisite, as are several of her avant-garde instrumentals.

Cafe Blue and *Modern Cool* offer a similar range of eclectic, intellectual material in which Barber is in the hip company of longtime band mates, bassist Michael Arnopol (with her since 1981) and drummer Mark Walker, plus the rangy guitarist John McLean. Trumpeter Dave Douglas joins the crowd for *Modern Cool,* which captures her growth as a writer, one who is concerned with high anxiety heading into the 21st Century. — K.F.

GATO BARBIERI

★★½ **In Search of Mystery (ESP, 1967)**
★★★★ **Chapter One: Latin America (MCA Jazz, 1973)**
★★★★½ **Chapter Three: Viva Emiliano Zapata (1974; GRP, 1992)**
★★★½ **Caliente! (A&M, 1976)**
★★★ **Ruby, Ruby (1978; A&M, 1989)**
★★★ **Tropico (1978; A&M, 1989)**
★★★★ **Gato . . . Para Los Amigos (1983; Signature/CBS Special Products, 1989)**
★★★½ **Qué Pasa (Columbia, 1997)**
★★★ **Fire and Passion (A&M, N.A.)**

Argentinian saxophonist Gato Barbieri (b. 1934) developed a full-throated, passionate tone combining the energy of John Coltrane's saxophone innovations and the romantic melodicism of South American folk music. He began his career playing with Lalo Schifrin in Argentina and Brazil, then moved into the throes of commitment to the free-jazz movement, joining Don Cherry's lineup for *Complete Communion* and swinging for the outside fence on the ESP session. He went on to experiment in a duet setting with Dollar Brand/Abdullah Ibrahim on the out-of-print session *Confluence.*

Barbieri then made a series of albums that explored the roots of his own musical, cultural, and political history, beginning with the out-of-print but worthwhile *The Third World.* Most of this material is unavailable; *Bolivia, El Pampero* and the stirring *Under Fire* are all worth searching out.

Fortunately two of the titles from Barbieri's Latin America cycle are still in print. *Chapter One: Latin America,* a Buenos Aires session featuring top South American musicians, represents the full realization of Barbieri's efforts to carve out his own niche in jazz history.

Chapter Three: Viva Emiliano Zapata is a sequence of songs from Latin America embellished with lush orchestrations from master arranger Chico O'Farrill and Barbieri's vibrato-rich tone.

Barbieri moved to A&M and producer Herb Alpert, who crafted a slick and star-studded studio package for "El Gato" that resulted in the hit *Caliente!* and its transparent remake attempts, *Fire and Passion*, *Ruby, Ruby* and *Tropico.* No matter how much his sound was being manipulated in the studio in search of commercial success, Barbieri remained an electrifying live performer, as *Para Los Amigos* amply demonstrates. Barbieri made a dramatic comeback in *Qué Pasa,* an effective collaboration with keyboardist/programmer Philippe Saisse that placed his expressive sound in a contemporary setting. — J.S.

CHARLIE BARNET

★★★½ **Cherokee (1958; Evidence, 1993)**
★★★½ **More Charlie Barnet (1959; Evidence, 1995)**
★★★★ **Cherokee (RCA Bluebird, 1992)**
★★★★★ **Drop Me Off in Harlem (Decca, 1992)**
★★★ **Giants of the Big Band Era (Magma, 1994)**
★★★ **Swell and Super (Drive Archive, 1996)**
★★★ **Skyliner (Topaz Jazz, 1996)**

Big-band leader/saxophonist Charlie Barnet (1913–1991) led one of the most popular swing bands during the 1930s and '40s by eschewing the precision and slickness of the Benny Goodman and Glenn Miller approach in favor of an emotional style calculated to appeal to the youthful dance audience.

Barnet had a beautiful tone, particularly on his Johnny Hodges–inspired alto-saxophone playing, a terrific ear for good musicians and a dedication to the virtues of putting together integrated bands. The Bluebird *Cherokee* collects recordings on that label from 1939 to 1941. *Drop Me Off in Harlem* covers his 1942–46 bands, lineups that included Roy Eldridge, Buddy DeFranco, Dodo Marmarosa, Al Haig, Barney Kessel and Dizzy Gillespie.

The rest of these sides are less interesting rehashes of career highlights, with the exception of the two Evidence reissues of Barnet's late-1950s recordings. At a time when interest in big-band jazz was waning, Barnet was still sizzling along. *Cherokee* offers some interesting soprano work from Barnet and features a brass section that includes Charlie Shavers and Clark Terry. *More Charlie Barnet* utilizes Phil Woods on alto, Shavers in the brass section and bassists Milt Hinton, George Duvivier and Wendell Marshall. — J.S.

RAY BARRETTO

★★★★ **Carnaval (1962; Fantasy)**
★★★★ **La Cuna (1979; Columbia Jazz, 1995)**
★★★★ **Handprints (Concord Picante, 1991)**
★★★★ **Live in New York (Messidor, 1992)**
★★★★ **Ancestral Messages (Concord Picante, 1993)**
★★★★ **Taboo (Concord Picante, 1994)**
★★★½ **My Summertime (Owl, 1995)**
★★★★ **Contact (Blue Note, 1997)**

Ray Barretto (b. 1929) was already a highly respected jazz-session percussionist when he clicked with the catchy 1963 hit single "El Watusi." The irresistible charanga rhythm and stirring flute melodies made it a masterpiece of pop simplicity, establishing Barretto's working band, which he has led ever since while recording dozens of albums, most now out of print domestically.

Barretto's charanga band made several joyful records during these years, with Ray's fierce conga attack earning him the nickname "Mr. Hard Hands." Barretto has gone on to become one of the kings of salsa, and his orchestra has provided some of the music's liveliest moments, as *Live in New York* so amply demonstrates. *Carnaval* collects much of Barretto's early work. *La Cuna* is a reissue of a lush, Creed Taylor–produced project. Search for the great *Tomorrow: Barretto Live*, *Charanga Moderna* and the incendiary *Acid.*

In the 1990s Barretto enjoyed a renaissance leading the Latin-jazz small group New World Spirit, featuring the fine saxophonist Adam Kolker. — J.S.

KENNY BARRON

★★★½ **Peruvian Blue (1974; 32 Jazz, 1998)**
★★½ **Scratch (1985; Enja, 1992)**
★★½ **New York Attitude (1985; Uptown, 1996)**
★★★ **What If (Enja, 1986)**
★★★ **Live at Fat Tuesday's (Enja, 1988)**
★★★½ **The Only One (Reservoir, 1991)**
★★★★ **Lemuria-Seascape (Candid, 1991)**
★★★★½ **Maybeck Recital Hall Series, Vol. 10 (Concord Jazz, 1991)**
★★★★ **The Moment (Reservoir, 1992)**
★★★★★ **People Time (with Stan Getz) (Verve, 1992)**
★★★★ **Sambao (Verve, 1993)**
★★★½ **Other Places (Verve, 1994)**
★★★★★ **Wanton Spirit (Verve, 1995)**
★★★½ **Swamp Sally (Verve, 1996)**
★★★★ **Things Unseen (Verve, 1997)**
★★½ **Soft Spoken Here (32 Jazz, 1997)**
★★★ **First Half Highlights (32 Jazz, 1997)**
★★★ **Night and the City (with Charlie Haden) (Verve, 1998)**

Pianist Kenny Barron (b. 1943) has been in strong demand as a mainstream and bebop session player throughout the 1970s, '80s and '90s because of his versatility, natural melodicism and clean, precise style. He regards Tommy Flanagan, Bud Powell, Thelonious Monk and Wynton Kelly as key influences.

Barron was a quick learner in his native Philadelphia. He began studying piano at age 12 under the tutelage of Ray Bryant's sister. At 14 he played his first paying gig alongside his big brother, saxophonist Bill Barron, in the Mel Melvin orchestra. After finishing high school in 1961 he moved to New York and worked extensively with Roy Haynes and Dizzy Gillespie. Other musical liaisons soon followed, with Freddie Hubbard, Ron Carter, Stanley Turrentine, Milt Jackson and Stan Getz.

In the early 1980s, Barron founded the quartet Sphere with bassist Buster Williams, drummer Ben Riley and tenor saxophonist Charlie Rouse to play the music of Thelonious Monk as well as their own tunes. They disbanded upon Rouse's death in 1988.

Soft Spoken Here is a two-CD reissue of the Muse recordings *Sunset to Dawn* (1973) and *Golden Lotus* (1982), by 32 Jazz, which intends to make all of Barron's early Muse works available on CD in the near future. *Sunset to Dawn* features Barron on both acoustic and electric piano. *Golden Lotus* is also a fine showcase for saxophonist John Stubblefield. *First Half Highlights* compiles nine diverse tracks by Barron for a variety of labels as a leader or sideman, vintage 1960s–'80s. It includes one tune by Sphere.

Since he started recording as a leader in the 1970s, Barron has built a body of work with consistent excellence. His very best include trio sessions with Riley and bassist Ray Drummond

(*The Only One* and *Lemuria-Seascape*) and with Rufus Reid and Victor Lewis (*The Moment*), the Brazilian-jazz–inspired *Sambao,* his solo showcase in Concord's historically important Maybeck Recital Hall Series; and *Wanton Spirit,* a wide-ranging trio session with Roy Haynes and Charlie Haden.

Swamp Sally is one of the most wide-ranging and eclectic recordings Barron has made, though its inventive multitracked duets with percussionist/guitarist Mino Cinelu may seem a bit extreme for many fans of Barron's mainstream work. *Things Unseen* takes Barron deeper into new stylistic territory. With John Stubblefield, John Scofield, Eddie Henderson and violinist Naoko Terai aboard, the ride is exhilarating. It also shows that while Barron is at the top of his game, he isn't coasting. Recorded at New York's Iridium jazz club with bassist Charlie Haden in 1996, *Night and the City* pairs two of the great instrumentalists in jazz today—and displays Barron's sensitive and imaginative way with ballads.

Also key to any collection is *People Time,* the best example of Barron as partner/accompanist. The two-disc set documents four evenings of performances by Getz and Barron at Copenhagen's Cafe Montmartre in March 1991. It turned out to be Getz's last recording and last public performances, three months before his death from cancer. — K.F.

LOU ANN BARTON

★★★ Old Enough (1982; Antone's, 1992)
★★★★ Read My Lips (Antone's, 1989)

When Asylum Records released her 1982 debut album, *Old Enough,* produced by Jerry Wexler and Glenn Frey, it seemed ordained that Texas native Lou Ann Barton (b. 1954) ultimately would be hailed as one of the greatest blues and country singers of her generation. She had it all—looks, presence, attitude, a whiskey-soaked voice that told searing tales of betrayal, faithlessness and high times. She sang as if Patsy Cline, Carla Thomas and Arlene Smith had all been in her gene pool. Though well reviewed, *Old Enough* failed to catch the public's fancy, and Barton, beset by personal and professional crises, retreated to the Lone Star State and out of the spotlight. A second album, the now out-of-print *Forbidden Tones,* surfaced in 1986 and disappeared almost before anyone knew it existed. Subsequently the news out of Austin was invariably distressing with regard to her sporadic attempts to rekindle a once promising career.

Come 1989, Barton got it together in remarkable form. Recording *Read My Lips* for the Austin-based Antone's label, she delivered a set of scorching performances that remind us not of what she might have been but of what she is—a natural-born singer whose hard-won wisdom sounds earned in spades. Her version of Barbara Lynn's "You'll Lose a Good Thing" is a wonder of self-assurance. Jimmy Reed's "Shake Your Hips" offers her a chance to deliver some low-down blues in her most suggestive voice, while "It's Raining," a signature song for Irma Thomas, becomes a masterpiece of loss and longing when Barton's throaty delivery is augmented by David "Fathead" Newman's mournful sax lines. "Rocket in My Pocket" and "Let's Have a Party" are served up as the forceful rockers they are.

Guitarist Jimmie Vaughan gets the record off to a blazing start with his stinging, Albert King–style lead work on "Sugar Coated Love" and also offers some wry commentaries in support of Barton's playful rendition of Slim Harpo's "Te Ni Nee Ni Nu." — D.M.

GARY BARTZ

★★★ Monsoon (1988; SteepleChase, 1994)
★★★ Shadows (Timeless, 1993)
★★★½ Precious Energy (Mapleshade, 1993)
★★★ Episode One: Children of Harlem (Challenge, 1993)
★★★★½ The Red and Orange Poems (Atlantic, 1995)
★★★★ The Blues Chronicles: Tales of Life (Atlantic, 1996)

Gary Bartz (b. 1940) grew up in Baltimore idolizing Charlie Parker and was already a precociously talented hard-bop alto saxophonist when he came up in the mid-1960s playing with Max Roach, Art Blakey and McCoy Tyner. He became a major star as a featured soloist in the early 1970s Miles Davis group documented on *Live/Evil.* He has played in numerous other contexts over the years, from the blues of Buddy Guy to the experimental music of Cindy Blackman and the classic repertoire of the Mingus Big Band.

Bartz, who also plays soprano saxophone, clarinet and flute, was always a passionate blues player who frequently jumped the rails into free expression and the harmonic experiments of Ornette Coleman and John Coltrane. On his own Bartz also anticipated the jazz/rap synthesis with his spoken-word application of Langston

Hughes poetry to his own music on *I've Known Rivers,* a live recording from the Montreux Jazz Festival that is currently unavailable.

His spoken-word ideas didn't always flower so majestically, however, and at one point in the 1970s Bartz was making disco records with novelty raps like the LP *The Shadow Do* and doing very little playing of merit.

Bartz returned to his musical roots in the 1980s, recording for several labels, reestablishing himself as a major voice on the alto. *Precious Energy* is a good live session from 1987 with a band co-led by vocalist Leon Thomas, who wrote most of the material, and featuring trumpeter Eddie Henderson. Unfortunately, most of his best recordings from this period, on Candid, are currently unavailable, but 1990's outstanding live *There Goes the Neighborhood!* is worth searching out.

Bartz made a spectacular return to major-label status with *The Red and Orange Poems,* a beautiful set with Eddie Henderson on trumpet and flügelhorn, John Clark on French horn, Mulgrew Miller on piano, Dave Holland on bass and Greg Bandy on drums.

Bartz revisited his love for genre mixing on *Blues Chronicles,* adding reggae and rap to the mix but not forgetting about the overall playing performance. The result is a kind of street-life concept album that works extremely well, with great support from vocalist Jon Hendricks and keyboardist Cyrus Chestnut. — J.S.

COUNT BASIE

★★★★½ **One O'Clock Jump (1937; MCA, 1990)**
★★★★ **Brand New Wagon (1947; RCA Bluebird, 1990)**
★★★★ **April in Paris (Verve, 1955)**
★★★★★ **Count Basie Swings, Joe Williams Sings (with Joe Williams) (Verve, 1955)**
★★★½ **The Greatest! (with Joe Williams) (Verve, 1957)**
★★★★★ **Count Basie at Newport (1957; Verve, 1989)**
★★★★½ **Sing Along with Basie (1958; Roulette, 1991)**
★★★★ **One More Time (1959; Roulette, 1991)**
★★★★ **Basie Swings, Bennett Sings (with Tony Bennett) (1959; Roulette, 1990)**
★★★★ **Kansas City Suite: The Music of Benny Carter (1960; Roulette, 1990)**
★★★½ **Count Basie and the Kansas City 7 (1962; Impulse! 1987)**
★★★★ **Count Basie in Sweden (1962; Roulette, 1991)**
★★★½ **Li'l Ol' Groovemaker . . . Basie! (Verve, 1963)**
★★★ **Blues Alley (1968; LaserLight, 1996)**
★★★ **Basic Basie (Verve/MPS, 1970)**
★★★ **High Voltage Basie (Verve/MPS, 1970)**
★★½ **Loose Walk (with Roy Eldridge) (1972; Pablo, 1988)**
★★★★★ **The Best of Count Basie (MCA, 1973)**
★★★ **Basie Jam (1973; Pablo, 1987)**
★★★½ **The Bosses (with Joe Turner) (1974; Original Jazz Classics, 1994)**
★★★ **For the First Time (1974; Pablo, 1987)**
★★★ **The Basie Big Band (Pablo, 1975)**
★★★ **Fun Time (1975; Pablo, 1991)**
★★★★ **Jam Session at Montreux, 1975 (1975; Pablo, 1987)**
★★★ **For the Second Time (1975; Original Jazz Classics, 1990)**
★★★ **Basie Jam 2 (1976; Original Jazz Classics, 1991)**
★★½ **Basie Jam #3 (1976; Original Jazz Classics, 1992)**
★★★ **I Told You So (1976; Original Jazz Classics, 1995)**
★★★ **Basie & Zoot (with Zoot Sims) (Original Jazz Classics, 1976)**
★★★★ **Satch & Josh (with Oscar Peterson) (1976; Pablo, 1988)**
★★★ **Satch & Josh . . . Again (with Oscar Peterson) (1977; Pablo, 1987)**
★★½ **The Timekeepers (with Oscar Peterson) (1978; Original Jazz Classics, 1983)**
★★½ **Yessir, That's My Baby (with Oscar Peterson) (1978; Pablo, 1987)**
★★★½ **Milt Jackson/Count Basie and the Big Band, Vol. 1 (1978; Original Jazz Classics, 1992)**
★★★½ **Milt Jackson/Count Basie and the Big Band, Vol. 2 (1978; Original Jazz Classics, 1992)**
★★★ **Get Together (1979; Pablo, 1987)**
★★★ **On the Road (1979; Original Jazz Classics, 1995)**
★★★★ **The Best of Count Basie (Pablo, 1980)**

★★★½ **Kansas City Shout (1980; Pablo, 1987)**
★★½ **Warm Breeze (Pablo, 1981)**
★★½ **Kansas City 6 (1981; Original Jazz Classics, 1990)**
★★★★ **Farmer's Market Barbecue (1982; Original Jazz Classics, 1992)**
★★★½ **Prime Time (Pablo, 1987)**
★★★ **Live in Japan, '78 (Pablo, 1987)**
★★★ **88 Basie Street (Original Jazz Classics, 1987)**
★★½ **Fancy Pants (Pablo, 1987)**
★★½ **Me and You (Original Jazz Classics, 1987)**
★★★ **Mostly Blues . . . and Some Others (Pablo, 1987)**
★★★★ **The Essential Count Basie, Vol. 1 (1936–1939) (Columbia, 1987)**
★★★★★ **The Essential Count Basie, Vol. 2 (1939–1940) (Columbia, 1987)**
★★★★½ **The Essential Count Basie, Vol. 3 (1940–1941) (Columbia, 1988)**
★★½ **Basie and Friends (Pablo, 1988)**
★★★ **Count Basie Big Band: Montreux '77 (Original Jazz Classics, 1989)**
★★★½ **Count Basie Jam: Montreux '77 (Original Jazz Classics, 1989)**
★★★½ **The Standards (1963–70) (Verve, 1989)**
★★★★★ **The Complete Roulette Live Recordings of Count Basie and His Orchestra (1959–62) (Mosaic, 1991)**

One of the few big-band leaders to remain a vital force in jazz long after the big-band era itself had become a memory, William "Count" Basie (1904–1984) was a pivotal figure in American popular music. Where other bands in the 1930s seemed to place most of their emphasis on melody and ensemble work, Basie's band stressed rhythm and solos. To that extent, the Basie ensemble operated more like a combo than a big band, often relying on riff-based arrangements that simply provided a launching pad for improvisation. Moreover, the kind of material the Basie band specialized in—lean, blues-based songs powered by an aggressive, hard-swinging backbeat—set the stage for jump-blues outfits like those led by Louis Jordan, Big Joe Turner, Eddie "Cleanhead" Vinson, Jack McVea or Bull Moose Jackson. From there it was but a short jump to rock & roll.

To be honest, though, what led Basie to that sound was happenstance as much as anything else. Born in Red Bank, New Jersey, Basie was playing organ in a touring vaudeville show when he found himself stranded in Kansas City. Working his way into that city's jazz scene, he played first with the Blue Devils, a band led by trumpeter Oran "Hot Lips" Page, before joining up with Bennie Moten's Kansas City Orchestra. It was with Moten that Basie made his first recordings, which are collected on Bluebird's *Basie Beginnings;* although the playing tends mostly to the "stomp" style popular in the Midwest at that time, it's clear that there's something more to the band, especially in the way Basie's piano filters Midwestern blues through the wit of Fats Waller. Listen closely, and it's easy to hear the beginnings of the Basie sound in the insistent, bass-driven pulse of "Moten Swing."

Moten died in 1935 (during a tonsillectomy, of all things), and Basie put together a group of his own, drawing on some of his old Moten band mates (alto saxophonist Jack Washington, trombonist Dan Minor and bassist Walter "Big Un" Page) as well as some hot new players (most notably tenor saxophonist Lester Young, trumpeter Buck Clayton and drummer Jo Jones). Instead of using the fancy ensemble writing that was the norm then, the Basie band often worked off of "head arrangements"—loose, casually organized charts with parts worked out cooperatively among the band members—letting the groove do most of the work. And work it did. When critic and talent scout John Hammond heard the band during a radio broadcast in early 1936, he was instantly smitten and rushed to get the Basie band signed. Unfortunately, he only got a quintet performance of "Lady Be Good" on wax for Columbia (it's on *The Essential Count Basie, Vol. 1*) before Basie, short on cash, signed the band with Decca. Financially, it was a bum deal (it took the intervention of the musicians' union for Basie to earn any royalties), but musically it's hard to argue with the results. At this writing, there isn't much in print from those sessions; *One O'Clock Jump* includes the classic riff tune "One O'Clock Jump," which became the band's signature, as well as "Topsy," "Good Morning Blues" (with Jimmy Rushing on vocals) and the fiery "John's Idea," but it lacks the breadth of MCA's *The Best of Count Basie,* a 24-tune compilation comprising such classics as "Cherokee," "Every Tub," "Jumpin' at the Woodside," "You Can Depend on Me" and "Swinging at the Daisy Chain." It's an absolutely essential collection but not currently available on CD.

In 1939 Basie finally got free of his Decca deal and went over to Columbia, where he cut the material assembled on the three volumes of *The Essential Count Basie.* Although the tunes lack the pop appeal of the Decca material, the playing is far more exciting, as the band's soloists—particularly Lester Young—truly come to the fore. All three volumes are good, but *Vol. 2* is especially fine, featuring a classic pair of performances by Count Basie's Kansas City 7 ("Dickie's Dream," featuring trombonist Dicky Wells, and "Lester Leaps In," one of Young's most memorable recordings) as well as the full-band classics "Tickle Toe," "Blow Top" and "Super Chief."

Basie went to RCA in 1947 but with a much different band. Young and Clayton were gone and Washington was dead, and though the rhythm section retained its flavor, the horn arrangements grew brash and brassy, adding tremendous kick to tunes like the Jimmy Rushing blues "Brand New Wagon" or the red-hot "House Rent Boogie." *Brand New Wagon* offers a fair sampling of this period in the band's development but doesn't include any of the band's popular novelty numbers, like its chart-topping cover of Jack McVea's "Open the Door, Richard" or the topical "Did You See Jackie Robinson Hit That Ball?"

Basie folded his band in 1950 and worked strictly with small ensembles for the next two years before assembling a new band to record for Norman Granz's Verve label (of the albums he recorded during this period, only a handful are available at this writing). Again, it's the rhythm section that determines the character of the band, and new drummer Sonny Payne puts real punch into the familiar Basie groove. Payne is admirably explosive on the title track to *April in Paris*—no doubt a factor in making the song Basie's last Top 40 hit—but he shines even brighter on *Count Basie Swings, Joe Williams Sings,* where his forthright backbeat helps this collection of blues pack a wallop that rivals even Joe Turner's finest (the Basie/Williams version of "Every Day I Have the Blues" actually went to #2 on the R&B charts). Unfortunately, the Basie/Williams album *The Greatest!* has nowhere near the sizzle of its predecessor, but *Count Basie at Newport* more than makes up, flanking Williams with such all-star alumni as Lester Young, Roy Eldridge and Jo Jones.

In 1957 Basie moved to Roulette Records, where he and arranger Neal Hefti (who is probably better known for the *Batman* TV theme than for his stunning big-band writing) immediately showed their versatility through the lovely ballad "Li'l Darling" (from *The Atomic Mr. Basie,* which is out of print at this writing). Basie recorded fairly extensively for Roulette, cutting everything from thematically focused albums like *Kansas City Suite* to one-off collaborations with such singers as Tony Bennett (on the wonderful *Basie Swings, Bennett Sings*) and Sarah Vaughan (*Basie, Vaughan,* also out of print at this writing). Perhaps the most unusual of these is *Sing Along with Basie,* in which Basie and Williams are joined by Lambert, Hendricks and Ross for vocalized versions of Basie classics like "Tickle Toe" and "Every Tub." But the best of the Roulette recordings are the live albums culled from performances at Miami's Americana Hotel in 1959, New York's Birdland in 1961 and the Grona Lund amusement park in Stockholm in 1962. Not only does the band swing beautifully, but the solos—particularly those by trumpeter Harry "Sweets" Edison, trombonist Al Grey, and above all saxophonists Frank Wess and Frank Foster—show that there was much more to this band than a great book. Of the original albums, only *Count Basie in Sweden* is currently in print, but even if the others are reissued, *The Complete Roulette Live Recordings* is still preferable, both for its completeness (its eight CDs offer over six and a half hours of music) and its ability to convey a sense of what this band was like in concert.

In many senses, the Roulette years were the Basie band's high-water mark, for the group would never again attain such a consistent level of greatness. That's not to say the Basie band didn't have its moments, but after 1962 they didn't always come when expected. For instance, the Quincy Jones charts on *Li'l Ol' Groovemaker . . . Basie!* are certainly nothing to sneeze at, but frankly the band at that period seems to have more snap when backing Frank Sinatra on albums like *Sinatra-Basie* and *It Might as Well Be Swing.*

Perhaps the most problematic of Basie's recordings, though, are the ones he made for Pablo, the label Verve founder Granz launched in the early '70s. Here the problem is sheer volume; Granz recorded 30-odd albums' worth of Basie material in the 12 years before his death. Naturally, not every note is golden. Granz did have some good ideas, and some of the small-group recordings—particularly the trio album *For the First Time,* the lively *Basie Jam* and *Satch & Josh,* the first of the Oscar Peterson collaborations—are pleasant surprises. His big-band albums, however, are a mixed lot, with the feisty *Prime Time* and the nostalgic *Montreux '77* being the only standouts. — J.D.C.

SIDNEY BECHET

★★★★ **Sidney Bechet: Jazz at Storyville (1971; Black Lion, N.A.)**
★★★★ **The Legendary Sidney Bechet (GNP Crescendo, 1976)**
★★★★★ **Master Musician (1976; RCA, N.A.)**
★★★★★ **Great Original Performances 1924–1938 (ABC, 1989)**
★★★½ **Compact Jazz: Sidney Bechet and Friends (EmArcy, 1989)**
★★★★★ **The Complete Sidney Bechet Vols. 1 and 2 (1932–1941) (RCA, 1992)**
★★★★★ **The Best of Sidney Bechet (Blue Note, 1994)**
★★★★ **An Introduction to Sidney Bechet: His Best Recordings 1923–1941 (Best of Jazz, 1994)**
★★★★★ **Double Dixie (with Muggsy Spanier) (Drive Archive, 1994)**
★★★★★ **Louis Armstrong and Sidney Bechet in New York 1923–1925 (Smithsonian, N.A.)**

Soprano saxophonist/clarinetist Sidney Bechet (1897–1959) was, along with Louis Armstrong, the greatest individual voice in early jazz. Bechet grew up in New Orleans during the second generation following Reconstruction, and though he was born into a relatively prosperous and socially established Creole family, he found the avenues to professional employment closed to him because he was the wrong color.

Music was one of the few outlets open to Bechet, and he became the most audacious soloist and conceptualizer of his era. He refused to accept the traditional role of the clarinet as a support instrument to the trumpet in New Orleans ensemble jazz. Instead he invented a soloing style that made the instrument the lead voice in the ensemble, often wresting the role away from whoever was playing trumpet in the ensemble. This innovation is as important as any single development in jazz history.

A child prodigy on clarinet, he was a New Orleans legend by age 15 and an early jazz missionary by 1916, when he brought his sensational sound to Chicago. A 1919 European sojourn turned Bechet into an international star. He returned to the United States in 1922, by this time just as accomplished on the soprano saxophone as on the clarinet.

Bechet's big-voiced tone and stunningly inventive improvisational skills made him a force to be reckoned with in any context. Even Armstrong was extended to his limits in ensemble work with Bechet, as evidenced on the two tracks from *Great Original Performances 1924–1938.* On the 1924 recording of "Mandy, Make Up Your Mind," Bechet plays with ridiculous dexterity on the unwieldy double-reeded bass sarrusophone, a virtuosic move that prompts Armstrong to counter with a solo of such terse brilliance one can only assume Dippermouth knew he was up against the staunchest competition. For more of the interaction between these two giants, check out the Smithsonian release *Louis Armstrong and Sidney Bechet in New York 1923–1925.*

Bechet's clarinet work is the king influence on swing players such as Benny Goodman. As a saxophonist, Bechet virtually closed the book on the straight horn, which would see no further developments until Steve Lacy bridged New Orleans jazz and Thelonious Monk, thus paving the way for the fantastic constructs of John Coltrane's soprano playing.

Bechet played briefly in Duke Ellington's band in New York during the early 1920s, but by 1925 he was back in Europe, playing in La Revue Nègre with Josephine Baker, then in Russia in 1926. In 1928 he joined Noble Sissle's band in Paris, where his taste for wild nightlife eventually landed him in prison.

Back in New York, Bechet and trumpeter Tommy Ladnier formed the sensational New Orleans Feetwarmers for a residence at the Savoy Ballroom. This band's 1932 recordings kick off *Master Musician* and *The Complete Sidney Bechet,* both of which take Bechet through 1941 and feature such giants as Earl Hines, Red Allen, Willie "the Lion" Smith, Rex Stewart and Kenny Clarke. This set also includes "Sidney Bechet's One Man Band," an audacious bit of invention that finds Bechet overdubbing six separate parts in the studio.

The Blue Note *Best of Sidney Bechet* includes material from the late 1930s to the 1950s with a variety of lineups featuring jazz legends Bunk Johnson, Meade Lux Lewis, Sid Catlett and Frankie Newton.

Bechet's brilliance remained in service to the New Orleans ensemble during the swing era, when his approach went out of style, but the drummerless chamber ensemble, the Bechet-Spanier Big Four, which recorded in 1940, was a key element in spurring the traditional-jazz revival that took place during that decade. Cornetist Muggsy Spanier was the perfect foil for Bechet's scene-stealing proclivities, and the group was rounded out by Tommy Dorsey Band guitarist Carmen Mastren and former Ellington bassist Wellman Braud. This band is well documented on *Double Dixie,* which includes Bechet's wild solo on "China Boy." The CD also includes a fine Spanier-led set from 1957.

Though he was undoubtedly one of the greatest and most colorful figures in jazz history, Bechet was never given his due in the United States and chose to live in France, where he was regarded as a genius, from 1951 until his death, returning infrequently to perform in the United States. During that time he recorded a number of albums, which are for the most part unavailable. *Jazz at Storyville* is an important reunion with master New Orleans trombonist Vic Dickenson recorded live in 1953. *Sidney Bechet and Friends* collects Bechet performances with a variety of European musicians from 1949 to 1956. — J.S.

JEFF BECK

★★★½ **Truth (Epic, 1968)**
★★½ **Beck-Ola (Epic, 1969)**
★★★ **Rough and Ready (Epic, 1971)**
★★ **Jeff Beck Group (Epic, 1972)**
★★ **Beck Bogert Appice (Epic, 1973)**
★★★★ **Blow by Blow (Epic, 1975)**
★★½ **Wired (Epic, 1976)**
★ **Jeff Beck with the Jan Hammer Group Live (Epic, 1977)**
★★½ **There & Back (Epic, 1980)**
★★★½ **Flash (Epic, 1985)**
★★½ **Jeff Beck's Guitar Shop (Epic, 1989)**
★★★★ **Beckology (Epic, 1991)**
★★★ **Crazy Legs (Epic, 1993)**
★½ **Frankie's House (Epic Soundtrax, 1993)**
★★★ **Best of Beck (Epic, 1995)**

Between his thoroughgoing command of the fret board and his daredevil feel for feedback and distortion, Jeff Beck's playing is rarely less than astonishing. But Beck (b. 1944) lacks the vision and determination necessary to convert that instrumental intensity into any viable group chemistry, a weakness that has kept his solo career from amounting to much more than a few dazzling moments scattered through a lot of disappointing music.

Perhaps the closest he's ever come to fronting a band that could balance and enhance his strengths as a soloist was with the group he formed after leaving the Yardbirds. Because both singer Rod Stewart and bassist/guitarist Ron Wood had enough presence and confidence to hold their own ground against Beck, the music they made together was often as cohesive as it was exciting. *Truth,* despite a tendency to confuse showboating with ambition, is an excellent example of the heights Beck and his band mates could achieve; had they continued in this vein, they could in time have eclipsed even the mighty Led Zeppelin. Unfortunately, it was not to be; although *Beck-Ola* features a couple of amusingly energized Elvis covers ("Jailhouse Rock" and "All Shook Up"), the group's attempts to add a heavier edge to its sound only succeed in making the music more lugubrious.

After losing Stewart and Wood to the Faces, Beck opted for a funkier approach with his next group, built around jazz-oriented keyboardist Max Middleton and David Clayton-Thomas imitator Bob Tench. It wasn't an ideal match; *Rough and Ready* stumbles whenever faced with a ballad but otherwise offers a passable gloss on the sort of vaguely improvisatory white soul Traffic made popular. But *Jeff Beck Group* pushes the band's mannerisms to the point of self-parody. Beck then tried the power-trio approach, but the results, as embodied by *Beck Bogert Appice,* aren't much better, offering all the self-indulgence of Cream but none of the focus or pop appeal. (A concert recording from this period, *Beck Bogert Appice Live,* is even more embarrassing but was released only in Japan.)

By rights, Beck's next attempt at reinvention—this time as a fusion-jazz star—ought to have been just as disastrous as the last three, but thanks to producer George Martin, the all-instrumental *Blow by Blow* emerges as one of the most listenable and consistent albums of the guitarist's career. An eloquent player with absolutely nothing to say, Beck isn't much of a jazzman, but Martin works around the guitarist's limitations, elegantly framing the solos with sympathetic rhythm arrangements and lush string orchestrations.

With *Wired,* Beck leaps into the deep end, abandoning all his *Blow by Blow* playmates except Middleton to work with Mahavishnu Orchestra alumni Jan Hammer and Narada

Michael Walden. Beck plays gamely, but it's really Hammer's album, since his synth solos are what ultimately galvanize the group. *Jeff Beck with the Jan Hammer Group Live* would seem a natural outgrowth of this collaboration, but the actual results are a mess, with Beck getting by on feedback and flash while Hammer's group tries to hold the music together. *There & Back* returns Beck to the studio with a more sympathetic set of collaborators (Hammer, drummer Simon Phillips, keyboardist Tony Hymas) but still goes nowhere.

Astonishingly, Beck's next album, *Flash,* is a pop outing with Wet Willie alumnus Jimmy Hall singing on most tracks. Thanks to producers Nile Rodgers and Arthur Baker, it's consistent and accessible but throws sparks only when the guitarist reunites with Rod Stewart for a version of "People Get Ready." Bored, Beck went back to fusion and the empty acrobatics of *Jeff Beck's Guitar Shop,* but that didn't last. His next album, *Crazy Legs,* is a tribute to Gene Vincent and the Bluecaps guitarist Cliff Gallup that finds Beck playing in classic rockabilly style with the Big Town Playboys, while the soundtrack album *Frankie's House* finds him working in enough different styles (R&B, New Age, semimetal) to show off his versatility but without enough focus for the music to make much of an impression.

Although not quite a career summation, the boxed set *Beckology* includes highlights from the above, as well as Beck's first recordings (with the Tridents), a good sampling of his Yardbirds material and a smattering of arcana. It's not perfect, but then, no collection representative of Beck's solo career could be. — J.D.C.

JOE BECK

★★★½ **Beck & Sanborn (with David Sanborn) (CTI, 1975)**
★★★ **Relaxin' (Digital Music Products, 1984)**
★★★ **Friends (Digital Music Products, 1986)**
★★★ **Back to Beck (Digital Music Products, 1988)**
★★★ **The Journey (Digital Music Products, 1991)**
★★★ **Finger Painting (Wavetone, 1995)**

Guitarist Joe Beck (b. 1945) came out of Philadelphia and established himself as a proficient sideman in the 1960s working with Paul Winter, Charles Lloyd, Gary McFarland, Chico Hamilton, Miles Davis and Gil Evans. He went on to become a staff arranger and a key figure in the CTI productions of the 1970s, coleading *Upon This Rock* and *Penny Arcade* with Joe Farrell.

Beck's edgy take on fusion and ability to adapt to different circumstances are marks of a talented musician, but his solo albums lack the vision of a leader with something to say. The collaboration with alto saxophonist Sanborn worked surprisingly well, but as fusion's star waned, so did Beck's. — J.S.

LEON BIX BEIDERBECKE

★★★★ **Vol. 1: Singin' the Blues (Columbia Jazz Masterpieces, 1990)**
★★★★★ **Vol. 2: At the Jazz Band Ball (Columbia Jazz Masterpieces, 1990)**
★★★★★ **And the Chicago Cornets (Milestone, 1992)**
★★★★★ **Bix Beiderbecke (1924–1927) (Classics, 1994)**
★★★★★ **Bix Beiderbecke (1927–1930) (Classics, 1994)**
★★★★ **The Indispensable Bix Beiderbecke (1924–1930) (RCA Bluebird, 1995)**
★★★★ **Singin' the Blues (Drive Entertainment, 1995)**

Among other things, Bix Beiderbecke (1903–1931) is a fount of clichés concerning musicians. He was the original sensitive white student who sought his own voice through the example of black masters, the prototype of serious artist hemmed in by commercial mediocrity, the grand alcoholic wipeout. F. Scott Fitzgerald might have invented the trumpeter's life as a Jazz Age parable. Beiderbecke's music has a moody and fragile existence of its own, one that provided a complement to Louis Armstrong's bravura and first hinted at less blues-centered implications for jazz.

Of the available Beiderbecke albums, *And the Chicago Cornets* and *Bix Beiderbecke (1924–1927)* have the earliest recordings by the rambunctious Wolverines, a Midwest combo in love with the sound of the early white bands from New Orleans. These sets also offer the contrasting example of other young white cornetists, Jimmy McPartland and Muggsy Spanier.

Singin' the Blues and *At the Jazz Band Ball* contain particularly important material covering 1927–28. Here the trumpeter is teamed with his good friend and perfect partner, C-melody saxophonist Frankie Trumbauer, plus assorted other greats. *Bix Beiderbecke* (*1927–1930*) includes the overblown pop music of Paul Whiteman's orchestra (where Beiderbecke finished his career as a featured soloist), which warrants a place of honor for Beiderbecke's impressionistic piano solo, "In a Mist." *Singin' the Blues* and *The Indispensable* are "hits" packages. — B.B./J.S.

RICHIE BEIRACH

★★★ **Antarctica (1985; Evidence, 1994)**
★★★ **Emerald City (1987; Evidence, 1994)**
★★★ **Maybeck Recital Hall Series, Vol. 19 (Concord Jazz, 1992)**
★★★ **Self Portraits (CMP, 1992)**
★★★ **Trust (Evidence, 1996)**

Classically trained keyboardist Richie Beirach (b. 1947) came to prominence as part of Dave Liebman's Lookout Farm group of the mid-'70s and went on to develop some of the most intriguing approaches to electronic jazz composition. He has since recorded frequently in a solo context, bringing his otherworldly visions to the appropriately titled *Antarctica* solo project, an icy landscape if there ever was one. *Emerald City,* an album of duets with guitarist John Abercrombie, continues to explore this eerie sonic terrain. The out-of-print *Elegy for Bill Evans* is worth searching out. — J.S.

CAREY BELL

★★★½ **Last Night (One Way/MCA, 1973)**
★★½ **Harpslinger (1988; JSP, 1995)**
★★★½ **Mellow Down Easy (with Tough Luck) (Blind Pig, 1991)**
★★★ **Harpmaster (JSP, 1993)**
★★★★ **Goin' on Main Street (Evidence, 1994)**
★★★ **Heartaches and Pain (Delmark, 1994)**
★★★ **Carey Bell's Blues Harp (Delmark, 1995)**
★★★½ **Deep Down (Alligator, 1995)**
★★★ **Good Luck Man (Alligator, 1997)**

Blues-harp virtuoso Carey Bell (b. 1936) cut his teeth under the tutelage of Little Walter Jacobs and later played with Muddy Waters, Willie Dixon, John Lee Hooker and Lowell Fulson, among others. The Macon, Mississippi, native's debut as a bandleader can be heard on *Carey Bell's Blues Harp,* originally recorded in 1969. Released in 1995 with several bonus tracks, the album features Jimmy Dawkins on guitar and Pinetop Perkins on piano. Bell smolders through eight originals and catches fire on the covers, including Dixon's "I'm Ready," Junior Wells's "Everything's Up Tight" and Mel London's "I Cry So Much."

In 1973 Bell cut *Last Night,* paying tribute to the author of the title track, Little Walter, and featuring Muddy Waters singing on "Mean Mistreater." Spearheaded by the guitar playing of Eddie Taylor, Bell's band does a fine job on such tracks as "Love Pretty Women" and "She's 19 Years Old."

Heartaches and Pain—recorded in 1977 but not released domestically until years later—was produced by legendary Chess A&R man Ralph Bass and represents Bell's fine blowing and improvisational skills, as well as his somewhat weak singing voice. The refreshing *Mellow Down Easy* finds Bell backed by Maryland blues quartet Tough Luck, a group of hungry young players who give and take in equal proportion. Bell's harp work is stinging, notably on several songs associated with Waters: "Short Dress Woman," originally written for Waters in 1964 by reed player J.T. Brown; "Walkin' Thru the Park," composed by the man himself; the title track by Waters's longtime bassist Willie Dixon; and "Walkin' by Myself," credited to Waters's guitarist Jimmy Rogers.

Goin' on Main Street has been rescued from obscurity by Evidence, which released the album domestically in 1994. Originally on Germany's L+R label, the recording, for the most part, dates to June 1982. Featuring Bell's sons Lurrie and Carey Junior, who play guitar and bass respectively, all of the tracks from this session were written or cowritten by the elder Bell, except "I Am Worried," penned by Lurrie. The reissue includes two bonus tracks (Magic Sam's "I Need You So Bad" and Buddy Guy's "Man and the Blues"), recorded live in 1981, with Lurrie Bell on guitar alongside the legendary Hubert Sumlin.

Lurrie Bell's guitar is also on *Harpmaster,* released by the English JSP label. *Harpslinger* is a quartet session recorded in London with English musicians in 1988. *Deep Down* opens with a breakneck-tempo version of Little Walters's "I Got to Go." Lurrie again joins his father on this effort, as does Alligator Records label mate Lucky Peterson on piano. The combo works through seven of Bell's originals, including the sultry "Let Me Stir in Your Pot" and the metallic, slow-burning lament "Must I

Holler?" Closing the album is "Easy" by Big Walter Horton, another influence on Bell's playing: There's no doubt Horton would appreciate the "full-tilt boogie" treatment Bell and company give his song. — B.R.H.

LURRIE BELL

★★★★★ Mercurial Son (Delmark, 1995)
★★★★ 700 Blues (Delmark, 1997)

Guitarist Lurrie Bell (b. 1958) literally grew up in the Chicago blues scene—his father is the blues-harmonica great Carey Bell, his cousin is Eddy "the Chief" Clearwater and his four brothers all play as well. Their grandfather is the piano-playing Lovie Lee.

After doing some session work, Bell founded the Sons of Blues with harmonica player Billy Branch. He went on to record with Koko Taylor, Son Seals, Big Walter Horton and others before making his 1989 debut, the hard-to-find *Everybody Wants to Win.* With *Mercurial Son,* Bell seemed to appear from out of nowhere with an intense, unique approach to blues guitar playing. His sense of internal rhythms allows for some startling dynamic shifts as he plays, from bursts of combination-punch phrasing to stretches of ringing silence where the blank sonic space screams for resolution.

700 Blues continues Bell's remarkable development on a varied program from B.B. King ("I've Got Papers on You, Baby," "All Over Again"), Jimmy Reed ("Found Love," "You Got Me Dizzy"), Howlin' Wolf ("How Many More Years"), Muddy Waters ("Honey Bee") and Professor Longhair ("She Walks Right In"). Bell's own title track and "I'll Be Your .44" fit naturally alongside these classics. — J.S.

JESSE BELVIN

★★★★ Yesterdays (RCA, 1975)
★★★★★ Jesse Belvin: The Blues Balladeer (Specialty, 1990)
★★★★★ Goodnight My Love (Flair/Virgin, 1991)

Had Jesse Belvin (1932–1960) survived a head-on automobile accident and gone on to produce the ambitious work that seemed the logical progression of his career path, his name might be as well known as that of his contemporary Sam Cooke, who picked up more than a few notions from Belvin's singing style and masterful control of audiences. Belvin the vocalist possessed the sensuous, smoky voice and precise enunciation associated with Nat King Cole and Billy Eckstine, but his musical roots were in gospel. Born in Texarkana, Arkansas, and raised in Los Angeles, he became a member of his church choir at age seven and immediately impressed the congregation.

As his career evolved, Belvin explored not only rhythm & blues but pop and jazz, traditional group harmony and even doo-wop. This he did not only on his own recordings but also as a writer. Prolific and eloquent, Belvin clouded his history by writing many songs and then selling the rights; it's amazing anything survived with his credit on it, but many important sides have; Belvin married a woman who was a writer, too, and understood the value of copyrights. She made sure her husband got his due, both in dollars and cents and in the name below the title.

The other problem in tracking Belvin's career is that he had little regard for contracts and showed up on numerous labels in various guises. His career began in 1951 with the release of some solo sides on the Hollywood-based Recorded label and as part of a vocal group fronting his friend Big Jay McNeeley's orchestra for Imperial Records. Called Three Dots & a Dash, the quartet's personnel included Marvin Phillips, with whom Belvin struck up a productive friendship. Belvin, Phillips and another singer moved to Specialty in 1952. Belvin cut some solo sides and a single with Phillips, credited to Marvin & Jesse, that gained some attention in the R&B market. The duo with Phillips was ended when Belvin was drafted into the Army. While in the service, he wrote "Earth Angel," which was subsequently recorded by the Penguins and became an early crossover smash, selling over a million copies shortly after its release in late 1954. (Following the single's success, a dispute arose over the songwriting credits and was settled with Belvin being awarded a one-third share in the royalties.) Upon completing his tour of duty, Belvin returned to recording in Los Angeles. Over the next few years his studio ramblings produced single releases under his own name as well as the Gassers, the Sheiks, the Californians and Jesse Belvin and the Sharptones; he even sat in with the Shields on that group's 1958 hit "You Cheated." Every so often he would drop in at Specialty, cut a wonderful track or two (most written on the spot) and hit the road. Wherever he went he left behind one enthralling performance after another.

The Specialty disc encompasses 24 Belvin sides, some solo, some recorded with Phillips (including their self-penned 1953 Top 10 R&B hit "Dream Girl"); rounding out the collection are seven tracks Belvin cut in the early '50s for Dolphin, a Los Angeles record store and label whose in-house recordings were given away free to every customer who bought one major-label release. That these freebies surfaced in any form is a fortuitous development in mapping the evolution of Belvin's artistry. Among them is an exquisite solo version of "Dream Girl." In addition to Belvin's Specialty tracks, *The Blues Balladeer* contains a number of previously unissued, undated demos.

In 1956 Belvin moved to Modern, where his near-two-year stay was fruitful on many fronts, not least for producing the most enduring song he recorded under his or any other name: the incandescent ballad "Goodnight My Love," a Top 10 R&B single in '56, the sign-off song on Alan Freed's popular radio show and a model of smooth, heartfelt singing that sounds as fresh 40 years later as it did when new. *Goodnight My Love* brings the Modern years to life again, complete with the original "Goodnight My Love" (which Belvin cowrote and then sold his rights to for $400, according to legend) and a bluesier alternate take, as well as the lively jump R&B and forward-looking doo-wop sides he cut with the Cliques (who bear an uncanny vocal similarity to the Cadets of "Stranded in the Jungle" fame, especially on this set's "I'll Mess You Up") and a topical R&B space-age novelty number, "My Satellite," credited to Jesse Belvin and the Space Riders. Other revelations include an interesting version of the Sam Cooke hit "You Send Me," on which Belvin adopts a yearning but resigned tone, as if acknowledging the inevitable end of a love affair rather than its hopeful beginning; a lush, orchestrated Christmas love song, "I Want You with Me Christmas"; and three previously unreleased R&B torch songs, the sad and lonesome "Beware," "What Can I Do Without You" and "I'll Make a Bet," all featuring Belvin employing his entire vocal range, from a rich bass to a pinched falsetto.

From Modern, Belvin journeyed to RCA, where he had his only major pop hit, "Guess Who," a Top 40 single in 1959, written by his wife, Jo Anne. Comprised of a dozen tracks recorded in the months preceding his death (five being released here for the first time), *Yesterdays* hints at what may have been ahead for Belvin, particularly the new tracks that find him working with accomplished jazz instrumentalists such as Mel Lewis, Red Callender (with whose orchestra Belvin had recorded during his Dolphin tenure), Howard Roberts, Shelly Manne and Barney Kessel. Belvin had some of these players work out on the smoky gospel blues "It Could've Been Worse." Apart from featuring one of Belvin's most measured vocals, this cut breaks all the barriers, incorporating a little of everything—jazz, blues, gospel, pop—without settling squarely in any one camp. To get a sense of the range of moods and attitudes Belvin was exploring at this transitional stage, consider the inclusion in his repertoire of pop standards by Johnny Mercer/Harold Arlen ("Blues in the Night") and Cole Porter ("In the Still of the Night," "It's All Right with Me")—a laconic version of "Summertime" is included on the Flair/Virgin CD—and then consider that one of Belvin's two originals, the hit ballad "Guess Who," begs comparison to the sophisticated offerings Belvin selected as cover versions. Ultimately one thinks of Buddy Holly, Ritchie Valens, Sam Cooke—men who, like Belvin, seemed destined to create truly groundbreaking music, if only they had lived. The evidence here suggests Belvin may well have outdistanced them all. — D.M.

SATHIMA BEA BENJAMIN

★★★½ Love Light (1988; Enja, 1990)
★★★★ Southern Touch (Enja, 1992)
★★★★★ A Morning in Paris (Enja, 1997)

Jazz vocalist/songwriter Sathima Bea Benjamin (b. 1936) began singing as a teenager in her native South Africa, where mixed ancestry meant she was repressively classified as "colored" under that country's old apartheid system. She met her husband, pianist Abdullah Ibrahim, then known as Dollar Brand, at a 1959 local concert where he accompanied her on a Duke Ellington tune. As racial conditions worsened, the couple fled South Africa in 1962, settling in Switzerland, then New York. They returned to South Africa briefly in 1970 and again in 1976 for the births of their two children. Benjamin didn't perform again in South Africa until after the inauguration of Nelson Mandela in 1994.

With a keen sense of rhythm and melody, Benjamin doesn't float above the accompaniment as many vocalists do; rather, her cool and clear phrasing weaves in and out of the instrumentation, completing a fine musical tapestry. Benjamin refuses to perform or record with anything less than an outstanding and empathetic rhythm section. *Love Light,* recorded with pianist Larry Willis, bassist Buster Williams, drummer Billy Higgins and saxophonist Ricky Ford, and *Southern Touch,* with pianist Kenny Barron, Williams and Higgins, are both very strong showcases for Benjamin's work. *Love Light* mixes standards and exquisite originals, while *Southern Touch* is a pure standards album infused with African rhythms and a pointed emphasis on the emotion of the lyrics.

Released 34 years after it was recorded, the excellent and historically significant *A Morning in Paris* documents Benjamin's first recordings, made in 1963 at Duke Ellington's invitation after he heard her sing several nights earlier in Zurich. The tapes, which were never issued, resurfaced in 1994. Stylistically in full bloom, Benjamin was backed by Ibrahim's trio, with Ellington and Billy Strayhorn each accompanying her on two tracks and Svend Asmussen adding exotic guitarlike pizzicato touches on violin. — K.F.

TONY BENNETT

★★★★ **Basie Swings, Bennett Sings (with Count Basie) (Roulette, 1959)**
★★★★ **I Left My Heart in San Francisco (Columbia, 1962)**
★★★★ **I Wanna Be Around (1963; Columbia, 1995)**
★★★★ **Who Can I Turn To (1964; Columbia, 1995)**
★★★ **The Movie Song Album (Columbia, 1966)**
★★★★ **Snowfall: The Tony Bennett Christmas Album (Columbia, 1968)**
★★★ **Something (1970; Columbia, 1995)**
★★★★ **Tony Bennett's All-Time Greatest Hits (Columbia, 1972)**
★★★★ **The Tony Bennett/Bill Evans Album (1975; Fantasy, 1990)**
★★★ **The Rodgers and Hart Songbook (1976; DRG, 1987)**
★★★★ **Together Again: Tony Bennett & Bill Evans (1977; DRG, 1986)**
★★★ **The Special Magic of Tony Bennett (1979; DRG, 1988)**
★★★★ **16 Most Requested Songs (Columbia, 1986)**
★★★★ **The Art of Excellence (Columbia, 1986)**
★★★★ **Bennett/Berlin (Columbia, 1987)**
★★★★★ **Tony Bennett Jazz (Columbia, 1987)**
★★★★ **Astoria: Portrait of an Artist (Columbia, 1990)**
★★★★★ **Forty Years: The Artistry of Tony Bennett (Columbia/Legacy, 1991)**
★★★★★ **Perfectly Frank (Columbia, 1992)**
★★★★ **Steppin' Out (Columbia, 1993)**
★★★★ **The Essence of Tony Bennett (Columbia/Legacy, 1993)**
★★★½ **MTV Unplugged (Columbia, 1994)**
★★★★ **Here's to the Ladies (Columbia, 1995)**
★★★★ **Tony Bennett on Holiday (Columbia, 1997)**

That Tony Bennett is as popular, if not more so, in the mid-'90s as he has been at any other time in his 40-plus years in show business is more than testimony to the power of persistence or to the MTV generation appreciating his individual sense of style as a mark of unassailable cool. When he sings, Bennett, by the very personal nature of his lyric readings, creates new worlds and reveals the heart's deepest desires. Making listeners conscious of their lives to the point where they examine their own values is something that important artists do as a matter of course. In a world increasingly confused about matters of personal responsibility and personal relationships, and struggling with issues relating to intimacy and romance, here is a man who stands for something, whose texts reveal an egalitarian worldview informed by a moral code of selflessness, compassion, respect and sensitivity. Apart from these philosophical, abstract virtues, there is something more concrete about Tony Bennett's music that has resulted in this artist standing the test of time: He has never lost sight of the wisdom proffered by two early mentors, Frank Sinatra and Count Basie—to wit, insist on singing the best songs (Sinatra) and "economy of line, keep it simple, keep it swingin' " (Basie).

Exhibit A in defense of the above observations is the four-disc boxed set *Forty Years: The Artistry of Tony Bennett,* released in 1991. Its 87 songs, beginning with Bennett's first single, 1950's overblown "Boulevard of Broken Dreams," to 1989's "When Do the Bells Ring for Me," show songwriter credits from the pantheon: notably Jule Styne, Richard Rodgers, Johnny Mercer, Cole Porter, Kurt Weill, Harold Arlen, Ira Gershwin, Cy Coleman/Carolyn Leigh, Carl Sigman, Gordon Jenkins, Jerome Kern, Oscar Hammerstein, Johnny Mandel,

Betty Comden/Adolph Green, Jimmy Van Heusen and Hank Williams (whose "Cold, Cold Heart" Bennett and producer Mitch Miller transformed with strings and a pop arrangement into a single that had a six-week run atop the pop chart in 1951, the first country-to-pop mutation embraced by the masses). He worked well with a number of producers ("some terrible, some terribly artistic," he writes in his liner notes) whose styles varied, including Mitch Miller, Ernie Altschuler, Helen Keane, Teo Macero and his own son, Danny Bennett, and found a comfort zone where he could deliver honest performances. And it never hurts to have the kind of backing Bennett was blessed with during these years, particularly that of his longtime (since 1956) piano accompanist and musical director, Ralph Sharon, the Count Basie Orchestra, Bill Evans, Jo Jones, Jimmy Rowles, Joe La Barbera, Zoot Sims—a mile-long list of the finest musicians of the day. And this litany hasn't yet accounted for the superb arrangers on these sessions, such as Robert Farnon, Torrie Zito, George Siravo, Marion Evans and others.

Obviously the boxed set documents the breadth and depth of Bennett's art in all its remarkable variety. His first producer, Mitch Miller, knew nothing of subtlety, favoring instead a big, bright sound, full of rising strings, orchestral crescendos, and big-voiced backup singing. Still, Bennett had a productive run with Miller, as disc one of this set shows. Elsewhere, though, the textures become richer as new producers and arrangers pass through, and Bennett becomes a singer, as opposed to the belter he often had to be under Miller's aegis. In this light, disc four is a revelation, as it showcases Bennett in more austere settings, digging deep into his lyrics and delivering again and again with deeply felt but introspective probings of the human condition, particularly with regard to feelings of love and the passing of time. The apex of this 22-song disc—and the entire boxed set, some might argue—is 3 songs cut in 1975 with the evocative pianist Bill Evans providing the sole instrumental support. On his solo forays Evans steps out, but gingerly, with atmospheric, discursive variations on the theme, then backs off when Bennett returns, supporting the vocalist's moody deliberations with solemn right-hand fills.

The boxed set becomes the jumping-off point for all of Bennett's work in the years leading up to his 1990s "rediscovery." For one, the artist himself is now engaged in a reconsideration and repackaging of his catalog, with titles reissued as the Tony Bennett Master Series. These are perfect products of their times: 1963's *I Wanna Be Around* (comprising the entire original *I Wanna Be Around* album and seven tracks from another '63 long-player, *This Is All I Ask*) captures the mood of American pop in its final, florid orchestral stage before the British Invasion and rock & roll in general took control of the radio and of the American cultural mainstream; 1964's *Who Can I Turn To,* released at the height of Beatlemania, reads like a troubled internal monolog conducted in the aftermath of a love affair gone south, with the material reflecting the appropriate contrasting moods, from desolation ("Who Can I Turn To [When Nobody Needs Me]") to tearful reflection ("There's a Lull in My Life") to the determination to move on ("The Best Thing to Be Is a Person," a blues ballad that closes the album as an optimistic philosophical bookend to the opening title track); on 1970's *Something* Bennett finds his emotional touchstones in contemporary material such as the George Harrison–penned title track; Lennon/McCartney's "The Long and Winding Road"; a swinging version of Fred Neil's "Everybody's Talkin'"; and a deliberate, almost conversational reading of the Bacharach/David gem "Make It Easy on Yourself," to which Bennett imparts a mature acceptance of the inevitable while also suggesting the bombastic emotion found in the Walker Brothers' 1965 hit version and the poignancy of Dionne Warwick's 1970 hit.

Astoria, an autobiographical song cycle, is a special entry in the Bennett catalog, with the songs carefully chosen to reflect the ideas and moods of the singer's formative years in New York, where he was born Anthony Dominick Benedetto in 1926 to immigrant Italian parents. That Bennett is at his most reflective on this album is indicative of the degree to which this material reaches into his marrow as he takes stock of a world long passed but lovingly recalled.

Astoria provides perspective on a life, *Tony Bennett Jazz* on a career. As the boxed set indicates, Bennett has blurred the lines between jazz and pop singing by working effectively in both styles. On *Jazz* he assays an assortment of sides cut between 1954 and 1967, adding grist to the argument that he ranks with the best jazz singers of any generation; along the same lines, his two after-hours summits with Bill Evans,

The Tony Bennett/Bill Evans Album and *Together Again,* are treasures barely hinted at even by the exceptional cuts on the boxed set. Other recommended forays into more pronounced jazz encounters include *The Rodgers and Hart Songbook,* on which Bennett is accompanied by the Ruby Braff–George Barnes Quartet, and the scintillating *Basie Swings, Bennett Sings* with Count Basie and His Orchestra.

Bennett/Berlin teams the master interpreter with a set of Irving Berlin tunes less obvious than one might imagine, despite the inclusion of "White Christmas." Focusing on several melancholy entries in the Berlin canon, Bennett in effect delivers a concept album quite moving in its depictions of shattered love. The 1986 album *The Art of Excellence* finds a low-key, dispassionate Bennett ruminating over aspects of love in a performance enlivened by a humorous, topical call-and-response duet with Ray Charles on "Everybody Has the Blues."

Snowfall: The Tony Bennett Christmas Album is an engaging affair, much of it recorded in London in 1968 with an orchestra and a choir conducted and arranged by the respected Robert Farnon. Situating the artist in a variety of settings—with a small combo, backed by an orchestra and with full choir and orchestra—it allows him to display his big, stentorian singing style as well as the more subtle, sensitive approach he employs on his best pop albums. The title song is a first-rate evocation of the Yule ambiance, with Bennett's gentle voice rising over a swirling wash of woodwinds and strings, establishing a comfortable mise-en-scène for the forthcoming traditional carols and holiday fare. A Christmas medley comprising of "We Wish You a Merry Christmas," "Silent Night," "O Come, All Ye Faithful," "Jingle Bells" and "Where Is Love" is a marvel of contrasting moods—reverent and celebratory—and impassioned ensemble singing, with Bennett sometimes harmonizing with the choir, at other times soaring magnificent and proud above their smooth crooning, thus imparting to the proceedings an unusual degree of emotional edge.

Given that he had 33 Top 40 singles between 1951 and 1965, with all but 3 rising into the Top 30, the purely commercial aspect of Bennett's art demands some sort of representation. And so it is that three greatest hits–type compilations exist. *Tony Bennett's All-Time Greatest Hits* and *16 Most Requested Songs* assemble the most successful singles in their respective packages, while *The Essence of Tony Bennett* aspires to an elevated plateau. On the latter, timeless moments such as "Because of You," "Solitaire" and "I Left My Heart in San Francisco" are present and accounted for, but so are less obvious but equally scintillating entries. From the adventurous (and now out-of-print) 1957 album *The Beat of My Heart* comes "Wave"—slow, churning, with sad, angular tenor-sax lines and portentous swells of strings suggesting doom, as Bennett checks in with a morose vocal—intriguing in all its details. Ditto for "Yesterday I Heard the Rain" with its hint of Latin influence.

From the first quiet notes and heartfelt lyrics of "Time After Time," the opening track on *Perfectly Frank,* it's apparent something special is going on. And something is: This is Tony Bennett paying homage to Frank Sinatra, the man who, in a *Life* magazine article in the '60s, called Bennett his favorite singer and has since extolled his virtues many times over. With the singer sensitively backed by the Ralph Sharon Trio, these intimate readings are direct and passionate, the ambiance is strictly late-night, small-club, and the theme is romance. Warming up to the challenge of the album's concept, Bennett tackles trademarked Sinatra fare such as "Nancy" and "One for My Baby" as well as less prominent selections in the Chairman of the Board's repertoire, gives it all a respectful, swinging spin and for a moment owns each of the 24 tracks. No mere masterful tribute, *Perfectly Frank* is a vivid demonstration of a peerless interpreter at the top of his game. His first studio effort after the *Forty Years* boxed set returned him to the public eye in a major way, *Perfectly Frank* was the launching of an artistic renaissance that has continued unabated through the mid-'90s.

Fred Astaire, best known through his film roles as the epitome of upper-crust elegance and a dancer nonpareil, had a unique way with a song that marked him as a formidable stylist, very nearly the equal of the giants of his generation. His range would not wow anyone, and his singing voice was soothing but not especially rich in colors. Yet he understood and knew how to sell the sophisticated lyrics he sang, be they celebrations of high life (Irving Berlin's "Steppin' Out with My Baby") or high romance (George and Ira Gershwin's "He Loves and She Loves"). In the wake of his tribute to the singer's singer, Bennett tipped his hat to the stylist's stylist in a collection of Astaire chestnuts, *Steppin' Out.* American popular song gets no better than this, with 18 tracks written by Irving Berlin, the Gershwins, Arthur Schwartz/Howard Dietz, Cole Porter and A.J. Lerner. Again backed by the Ralph Sharon Trio, Bennett finds new points of personal reference in the Astaire canon as he explores the worldly-wise texts of Cole Porter's "I Concentrate on You" and the Gershwins' "Nice Work If You Can Get It," the latter being an especially nice bit of work as the mood (and tempos) change from the jaunty, cocky opening bars into a solemnly described account of love's end.

Continuing to pay tribute to those who influenced him, Bennett surfaced again in 1995 with *Here's to the Ladies,* 18 songs otherwise associated with some of the top female vocalists of the past half century—the likes of Billie Holiday, Peggy Lee, Rosemary Clooney, Sarah Vaughan, Margaret Whiting, Ella Fitzgerald, Dinah Washington and others—expertly executed by the Ralph Sharon Trio supplemented by a big band and an orchestra. This, then, is hardly the low-key affair à la the Sinatra and Astaire tributes, but rather one given to big emotions expressed with bravado and a heart attuned to unexpected twists and turns. The unstudied enthusiasm he brings to some well-worn material, such as "People," "Sentimental Journey," "God Bless the Child" and "Somewhere Over the Rainbow" bespeaks an artist working at the peak of his capacity.

With Sharon on piano and backed by an unobtrusive orchestra, Bennett focused his attention solely on Billie Holiday in the 1997 release *Tony Bennett on Holiday.* While hardly sharing Lady Day's sense of the tragic, Bennett finds common ground by way of introspection and meditation, delivering wistful reflections on love's odd, unexpected turns. Ambiance counts for much here, and Bennett, who coproduced with his son Danny, keeps things resolutely quiet, his vocals floating free with feathery tenderness across the medium-cool soundscape. An electronic duet between Bennett and Billie Holiday on "God Bless the Child" (the only track produced by Phil Ramone, the architect of Frank Sinatra's *Duets* albums) sounds as pasted-together as it really is.

MTV Unplugged documents Bennett's transformation into alternative-rock icon with his appearance on the in-concert show that gives this album its name. Here Bennett and the Sharon Trio work out on a compelling set of classics, including "Old Devil Moon," "Fly Me to the Moon (in Other Words)" and "Body and Soul," as well as the signature songs (which also qualify as classics) "Rags to Riches" and "I Left My Heart in San Francisco." Elvis Costello and k.d. lang make guest appearances, the latter harmonizing nicely with Bennett on a medium-cool version of "Moonglow" and taking her own well-considered solo turns; the less said about Costello's affected performance the better.
— D.M.

TAB BENOIT

★★★ Nice and Warm (Justice, 1992)
★★★½ What I Live For (Justice, 1994)
★★★★ Standing on the Bank (Justice, 1995)
★★★★ Live: Swampland Jam (Justice, 1997)

Tab Benoit, born in Louisiana in 1967, is a passionate guitarist, soulful singer and talented songwriter. His somewhat distorted electric-guitar tone, though, can result in an unpleasantly smeared attack. He's at his best on numbers other than slow blues, which just aren't his strength. Benoit's acoustic work on Lightnin' Hopkins's "Shining Moon" (*Nice and Warm*) and his own "Somehow" (*What I Live For*) is outstanding, as are the songs where he shows his Southern roots and New Orleans flavor. Each album employs a slightly different configuration of musicians. Paul English's keyboards highlight *Nice and Warm* and *Standing on the Bank;* Kenny Aronoff's drumming on *What I Live For* is masterful. Benoit shows his maturation as a player and arranger with *Standing on the Bank,* which is studded with catchy hooks, and the exciting *Live: Swampland Jam,* where he stakes his claim as a major blues force. — J.Z.

GEORGE BENSON

★★★★ The New Boss Guitar of George Benson with the Brother Jack McDuff Quartet (1964; Prestige, 1990)
★★★★ Beyond the Blue Horizon (1970; Columbia, 1987)
★★★ Body Talk (1974; Columbia, 1989)
★★★ Bad Benson (1974; Columbia, 1988)
★★★★ Benson and Farrell (1976; Columbia, 1988)
★★★★ Good King Bad (1976; Columbia, 1989)

★★★½ **Breezin' (Warner Bros., 1976)**
★★★½ **George Benson in Concert: Carnegie Hall (1977; Columbia, 1988)**
★★★ **In Flight (1977; Warner Bros., 1996)**
★★★ **Weekend in L.A. (Warner Bros., 1978)**
★★ **Livin' Inside Your Love (Warner Bros., 1979)**
★★ **Give Me the Night (Warner Bros., 1980)**
★★★½ **The George Benson Collection (1981; Warner Bros., 1988)**
★★ **In Your Eyes (Warner Bros., 1983)**
★★ **20/20 (Warner Bros., 1985)**
★★ **While the City Sleeps (Warner Bros., 1986)**
★★★½ **White Rabbit (1987; Legacy, 1995)**
★★ **Twice the Love (Warner Bros., 1988)**
★★★ **Tenderly (Warner Bros., 1989)**
★★ **Big Boss Band Featuring the Count Basie Orchestra (Warner Bros., 1990)**
★★★ **I Like Jazz: The Essence of George Benson (Legacy, 1993)**
★★★ **The George Benson Cookbook (Legacy, 1994)**
★★★½ **It's Uptown with the George Benson Quartet (Legacy, 1994)**

George Benson (b. 1943) came out of Pittsburgh to play with organist Jack McDuff's band in the early 1960s. McDuff was featured on his Prestige debut, but by 1965 Benson was leading his own band featuring organist Lonnie Liston Smith and Ronnie Cuber on baritone sax. Benson's octave-jumping solo style, influenced by Wes Montgomery and Charlie Christian, made him one of the most promising players of his generation.

After Montgomery's death in 1968, producer Creed Taylor fashioned a series of pop-jazz albums around Benson's playing, cushioning his sound with layers of strings and selecting pop hits for Benson to cover in instrumental versions. This was a cruel musical joke for a player of such caliber that Miles Davis tapped him for *Miles in the Sky,* but the principals laughed all the way to the bank.

Throughout this period, Benson never let his playing flag (these albums have been reissued on Columbia), even in the blandest of settings, and when he hooked up with a spirited collaborator such as saxophonist/flautist Joe Farrell (on *Benson and Farrell*), Benson's musicality was freed to soar. *Beyond the Blue Horizon,* a stripped-down session backed by bassist Ron Carter and drummer Jack DeJohnette, gives Benson's playing plenty of room.

Breezin' placed Benson back in a small-group mode, and the result was the first platinum-selling album in jazz history. With *In Flight* Benson was reintroduced as a vocalist (he'd begun as a singer in the 1950s) as well, another shrewd commercial move that muzzled his strongest creative instincts. His cover of "Nature Boy" proves that his ability to follow in the footsteps of Christian and Montgomery doesn't translate to Nat King Cole. *Weekend in L.A.* is an enjoyable live set that gives his sweet playing its due.

For the most part, Benson's subsequent recordings treat jazz as an unwelcome spice on his musical table. Even *Tenderly,* an overt attempt to reestablish his jazz credentials by bringing in heavy hitters McCoy Tyner and Ron Carter for an album of standards, is choked by overproduction. The most disappointing outing is a tepid collaboration with the Frank Foster–led Basie band, *Big Boss Band.* Benson's live work continues to impress, but his records, unfortunately, mask his brilliance. — J.S.

BUSTER BENTON

★★★★½ **Blues at the Top (Evidence, 1993)**
★★★½ **Spider in My Stew (Ronn, 1994)**
★★★½ **That's the Reason (Ronn, 1995)**

Vocalist/guitarist Buster Benton (1932–1996) made the migration from the Deep South to the urban North that characterized an entire generation of blues players, moving from his birthplace of Texarkana, Arkansas, to Chicago. An original writer with an expressive, Bobby Bland–influenced vocal style and a strong, rhythm-centered guitar style, Benton is equally capable of building a groove to a powerful peak and caressing a slow blues with intense feeling. In the 1970s he recorded a minor hit for the Jewel label, "Spider in My Stew," which is included on the compilation of the same name. *Blues at the Top,* a compilation from two 1980s sessions featuring contributions from the outstanding harpist Billy Branch, guitarist Carlton Weathersby, pianist Lafayette Leake and drummer Odie Payne, is a prime example of the vitality of the Chicago blues scene over the decades. — J.S.

BUNNY BERIGAN

★★★½ **Portrait of Bunny Berigan (ASV, 1992)**

★★★★★ **The Pied Piper (1934–40) (RCA Bluebird, 1995)**
★★★ **On Your Toes (Drive Archive, 1996)**

One of the greatest of the big band trumpeters, Rowland Bernart "Bunny" Berigan (1908–1942) grew up in a musical family, playing violin and trumpet in his grandfather's orchestra. Berigan replaced Bix Beiderbecke in the Paul Whiteman orchestra at the beginning of the 1930s and went on to join the Dorsey Brothers band (material featured on *Portrait of Bunny Berigan*), then Benny Goodman's orchestra, where he was featured on the hits "King Porter Stomp" and "Sometimes I'm Happy," then Tommy Dorsey's band, where he crafted memorable solos on "Marie" and "Song of India."

In 1937 Berigan left Dorsey to organize his own band, scoring a huge hit with "I Can't Get Started." He rejoined Dorsey briefly in 1940 before trying his hand as a leader again, but failing health exacerbated by acute alcoholism led to his untimely death from pneumonia. *The Pied Piper,* the best of Berigan's Bluebird recordings leading his own group and as a sideman, is an essential jazz album that demonstrates why Berigan's name is listed with the top trumpeters of his generation. — J.S.

TIM BERNE

★★★ **The Ancestors (Soul Note, 1983)**
★★★ **Mutant Variations (Soul Note, 1984)**
★★★★ **Diminutive Mysteries (JMT, 1993)**
★★★ **Nice View (with Caos Totale) (JMT, 1994)**

Alto saxophonist Tim Berne (b. 1954) is a sonic experimenter whose dedicated risk taking has produced some very interesting results. Unusual charts and instrumental lineups characterize all of his recordings, but Berne always chooses a great drummer to keep things focused. Paul Motian's Zen-like drums and percussion highlight *The Ancestors* and *Mutant Variations;* the eclectic Joey Baron takes over on *Diminutive Mysteries.* A tribute to Berne's teacher and main influence, Julius Hemphill, *Mysteries* collects seven Hemphill compositions (and one Berne piece), wonderfully played by a group fronted by Berne on alto and baritone saxophone and David Sanborn on alto and soprano sax. — J.S.

GENE BERTONCINI

★★★★★ **Art of the Duo (with Michael Moore) (Stash, 1987)**
★★★★ **Two in Time (with Michael Moore) (Chiaroscuro, 1995)**
★★★★ **Someone to Light Up My Life (Chiaroscuro, 1997)**

Guitarist Gene Bertoncini (b. 1937) is perhaps best known for his refined session work on albums by Paul Desmond, Hubert Laws, Paul Winter and Wayne Shorter. His work with bassist Michael Moore is jazz's premier chamber jazz. By interpreting classical pieces along with jazz, popular standards and bossa nova, Bertoncini and Moore produce an unpretentious synthesis that exposes the organic connections between these worlds of music. Both are virtuosos (Bertoncini often plays the classical guitar) whose gifts lie in their exquisite musicianship and restrained lyricism. The duo's first (out-of-print) collaborations, *Bridges* and *Close Ties,* should be searched for, but *Art of the Duo* is a fine compilation that draws on *Ties* and the excellent *O Grande Amor* and *Strollin'* (both unavailable). *Two in Time* finds them exploring standards with patented taste and precision. *Someone to Light Up My Life* is a superb collection of Bertoncini's interpretations of compositions by Antonio Carlos Jobim. — S.F.

BIG JOE AND THE DYNAFLOWS

★★★ **Good Rockin' Daddy (Powerhouse, 1991)**
★★★ **Cool Dynaflow (Tramp, 1991)**
★★★ **Layin' in the Alley (Black Top, 1994)**
★★ **Mojo (with Jeff Sarli) (Wildchild, 1994)**
★★★★ **I'm Still Swingin' (Severn, 1998)**

Washington, D.C., native Joe Maher (b. 1953) adopted the musical moniker "Big Joe" not only to name-check his hero Big Joe Turner but also to reference his own imposing size behind the drums. Maher's style has gradually evolved into jump blues; as a drummer, he could have supplied the crisp swing that made the blues of Turner, Louis Jordan and Wynonie Harris "jump"; as a singer, Maher has the big, booming baritone of his role models. After displaying his talents in two notable D.C. blues bands, the Uptown Rhythm Kings and Tom Principato and Powerhouse, Big Joe launched his own ensemble.

Good Rockin' Daddy, Maher's debut as a leader, features contributions from Principato, keyboardist Deanna Bogart and several former Uptown Rhythm Kings (including future Iguana Derek Huston). Maher dominates the proceedings, though, with his warm, expansive vocals and relaxed groove. In contrast to so many jump-blues revival bands who tend to rush the tempos and mug shamelessly on the punch lines, Maher knows the counterintuitive secret: The more you relax, the more exciting the jump blues are. He applied that same approach to *Cool Dynaflow,* which showcases 10 original numbers, most of which hold their own next to the debut's cover tunes.

Layin' in the Alley documents Maher's appealingly understated jump-blues approach, particularly on his "Big Legs," which turns a potential insult into a compliment, and his nice-and-easy version of Turner's "Oke-She-Moke-She-Pop." Maher's longtime bassist Jeff Sarli, who has also worked with guitarists Bill Kirchen and John Mooney, conceived and produced *Mojo,* which emphasizes the sophisticated cocktail blues associated with Percy Mayfield and Charles Brown. Two Mayfield compositions are featured, as are selections from Duke Ellington and Charlie Rich, but Maher's voice isn't well suited to the husky intimacy of the arrangements. Maher raids the New Orleans R&B treasure chest of Dave Bartholomew's book for *I'm Still Swingin',* covering "Playgirl," Bad Luck Blues," "Gumbo Blues" and "One Night of Sin."
— G.H.

BIG SANDY AND HIS FLY-RITE BOYS

★★★½ Fly Right with . . . (Dionysus, 1989)
★★★ Jumping from 6 to 6 (Hightone, 1994)
★★★ Swingin' West (Hightone, 1995)

Big Sandy (b. Robert Williams, 1965) and His Fly-Rite Boys play up-tempo country, blues, swing and rockabilly with a dash of early rock & roll thrown in for good measure. Extremely competent but not bracingly original, the group has a honky-tonk sound that owes a debt to the melancholia of Hank Williams, the hiccupping swagger of Elvis Presley and the jump and jive of Cab Calloway.

The group's debut, *Fly Right with . . .* is credited to Big Sandy and the Fly-Rite Trio. It showcases the band's swinging sound and contains liner notes that could have appeared in the '50s, diffidently describing the songs as a "delightful mix" and the album as "a solid sender." Included here are jumping originals like "Don't Desert Me," "Hot Water" and the twangy "Missouri Gal."

Jumping from 6 to 6 contains 16 tracks, including covers of Williams's "Weary Blues from Waitin'" and Jimmy Reed's "When I Found You" and such originals as the amusing "Different Girl," on which the protagonist tells his ex that he's had a different lover every night since she left him. Also included here is "Who, Tell Me Who?," which sounds like Elvis in Hawaii, with the slippery steel-guitar work of Lee Jeffriess, who also authored a drunken instrumental called "Barnyard Beatnik," one of the album's best songs.

Like its predecessor, *Swingin' West* was produced by ex-Blaster Dave Alvin, and it picks up where *Jumping from 6 to 6* left off. The album certainly doesn't lack swing, and its songs are tightly arranged and performed, with a dash of humor. The self-effacing "Music to Her Ears" proclaims that the singer "can't carry a tune in a bucket" but his baby likes it anyway. Jeffriess contributes a snappy, jazzy instrumental, "Murphy's Law," with a deceptive complexity that distinguishes it from the rest of the album. *Swingin' West* closes with "The New Ball," a celebration of music, moonshine, pickup trucks and women. Big Sandy and His Fly-Rite Boys mine familiar territory both musically and lyrically, but their earnest approach and commitment to the music rescues them from the jaws of mediocrity. — B.R.H.

"BIG TIME" SARAH

★★★½ Lay It on 'Em Girls (Delmark, 1993)
★★★★ Blues in the Year One-D-One (Delmark, 1996)

"Big Time" Sarah Streeter (b. 1953) has the kind of powerful, vibrato voice that could lead a band in the days before amplification. Working as a bartender and bouncer at B.L.U.E.S. on Chicago's North Side in the 1970s, Streeter would sing with the band, usually fronted by Sunnyland Slim, during jam sessions. By the end of the decade, she was touring under her own name. In 1989 she formed BTS Express and recorded a pair of albums that offer an accurate account of her galvanic stage presence.

Lay It on 'Em Girls is packed with Willie Dixon tunes highlighted by the title track and the adapted "Hoochie Coochie Woman," but the big moment on the set is Sarah's rip-roaring version of George Gershwin's "Summertime." The triumphant *Blues in the Year One-D-One* showcases Sarah's strengths on material ranging from hard blues ("You Don't Love Me Baby," "Ain't Nobody's Business," "Little Red Rooster," "Down Home Blues") to R&B ("Hound Dog," "Cadillac Assembly Line," "Woke Up This Morning") to funk (the title track and "Chicken Heads") and gospel ("Steal Away"). The recording features an outstanding performance from guitarist Emery Williams, who died before it was released. — J.S.

ACKER BILK

- ★ **Best of Acker Bilk, Vol. 1 (GNP Crescendo, 1978)**
- ★ **Best of Acker Bilk, Vol. 2 (GNP Crescendo, 1984)**
- ★ **The Magic Clarinet of Acker Bilk (K-Tel International, 1986)**
- ★★ **Acker Bilk Plays Lennon & McCartney (GNP Crescendo, 1987)**
- ½ **The Best of Acker Bilk: His Clarinet & Strings (GNP Crescendo, 1989)**

A leader of the trad-jazz movement in England in the late '50s while fronting his Paramount Jazz Band, clarinetist Acker Bilk (b. 1929) achieved stateside renown for a hot minute in 1962 with a lilting, languorous, haunting instrumental, "Stranger on the Shore," a Number One pop single. In the following two years he was little more than a blip on the radar screen and dropped out of sight when the young British Invasion–era rockers undermined trad (which was little more than New Orleans jazz with lame rhythms) in England and pushed Bilk's generation off the U.S. charts. Bilk has never been long off record, but any semblance of jazz in his work has disappeared. His in-print recordings are elevator music—sweet, melodic, innocuous, utterly unchallenging and lacking anything in the way of personality. Worse still, his lovely original recording of "Stranger on the Shore" is absent from the above-listed albums (check out any number of oldies anthologies; it invariably shows up). Instead, the *Best of* titles offer inferior rerecordings of "Stranger" featuring Bilk's clarinet meandering through soppy string arrangements or, in the case of the track on the 1989 album, becoming a secondary voice to the strings and to annoying guitar filigrees that effectively destroy the song's delicate mood, which was precisely what made it so compelling an instrumental in the first place. Elsewhere Bilk tackles such uninspiring fare as "Feelings," "We've Only Just Begun," and "Eres Tu." At least on the *Lennon & McCartney* album his song selection is surprising, as he assays some of each writer's solo work ("Imagine" and "Woman" from Lennon; "Mull of Kintyre" and "Pipes of Peace" from McCartney) as well as their putative collaborations ("World Without Love," "Here, There & Everywhere"). These too turn into MOR fodder. Not much to hang your hat on here. — D.M.

ELVIN BISHOP

- ★★★ **The Best of Elvin Bishop: Crabshaw Rising (1972; Epic, 1987)**
- ★★★ **Juke Joint Jump (1975; One Way, 1996)**
- ★★★ **Live! Raisin' Hell (One Way, 1977)**
- ★★★½ **Big Fun (Alligator, 1988)**
- ★★★★½ **Don't Let the Bossman Get You Down! (Alligator, 1990)**
- ★★★½ **Sure Feels Good: The Best of Elvin Bishop (Polydor, 1992)**
- ★★★★ **Tulsa Shuffle: The Best of Elvin Bishop (Legacy, 1994)**
- ★★★★ **Ace in the Hole (Alligator, 1995)**
- ★★★★ **The Skin I'm In (Alligator, 1998)**

Tulsa, Oklahoma, native Elvin Bishop (b. 1942) studied at the University of Chicago but got his real education playing guitar on the city's South Side as part of the Paul Butterfield Blues Band, teaming with Mike Bloomfield in one of the most spectacular two-guitar lineups in blues history (see the Butterfield band's *East-West*), then held the guitar chair when Butterfield added horns for the group's *The Resurrection of Pigboy Crabshaw.*

Bishop's first solo efforts are summarized on Epic's *The Best of Elvin Bishop* but are put in a larger and far more satisfying context on *Tulsa Shuffle.* In the 1970s Bishop developed a new identity at Capricorn Records as a down-home Southern blues rocker. His distinctive sound added flair to what was often a monochromatic approach to recording at Capricorn, where formless boogie and blatant Allman Brothers imitations were the rule of the day. *Juke Joint Jump* pretty well sums up Bishop's Southern strategy, and *Live! Raisin' Hell* demonstrates what a fine showman Bishop can be. In an odd twist, Bishop's Capricorn career took a lurching move into pop with the addition of sweet vocalist Mickey Thomas and the resultant hit "Fooled Around and Fell in Love." Thomas eventually moved on to join Jefferson Starship.

Bishop returned to the blues in the 1980s, making a strong comeback album on Alligator, *Big Fun.* Back in comfortable territory, he proceeded to record the masterful *Don't Let the Bossman Put You Down,* a rocking tour de force of blues and R&B that balances updated interpretations of classic songs with originals, all delivered by Bishop with unflagging enthusiasm and wit. His droll, conversational singing carries the narrative while his solos, mixtures of fat slide figures and razor-edged single-line bursts, strike a variety of tones against imaginative arrangements and great execution from his band. Bishop continued his strong run with Alligator on the sizzling *Ace in the Hole,* featuring a brilliant guest spot from Charlie Musselwhite on harmonica, and *The Skin I'm In,* with Musselwhite and Norton Buffalo sitting in on harmonica and Joe Louis Walker on guitar. — J.S.

NEAL BLACK

★★★★ Neal Black and the Healers (1992; Deluge, 1994)
★★★★ Black Power (Dixiefrog, 1994)

Neal Black (b. 1959) is a Texas blues guitarist who can sling it with the best of them but has an unusually broad harmonic palette acquired from his jazz training. There is no better two-guitar lineup than Black and Gib Wharton, who plays steel guitar on both of these albums, in a sublime interplay more reminiscent of the Texas tenor battles than any guitar analogy. Black's Mississippi growl is used in service of a songwriting skill that may well be his greatest talent. The debut includes some of the best blues writing in recent years—the chilling "I Don't Get the Blues," the blistering "Hell on the Highway" and a mournful "Somebody Call Mama." *Black Power,* which features cameos from John Sebastian, Johnnie Johnson, Jimmy Vivino and Michael Merritt, includes another handful of originals highlighted by "Misery," "Sometimes You Get Lucky" and "Hard Way." — J.S.

CINDY BLACKMAN

★★½ Arcane (Muse, 1988)
★★★ Trio Plus Two (Free-Lance, 1992)
★★★★ Code Red (Muse, 1993)
★★★ Telepathy (Muse, 1994)
★★★★ The Oracle (Muse, 1996)

Cindy Blackman (b. 1959) is a virtuosic drummer with four-limbed independence who navigates a broad spectrum of rhythmic approaches. A keen student of drum styles, Blackman incorporates Max Roach's crystal-clear rhythmic patterns, Art Blakey's innovative polyrhythmic structures and Tony Williams's integrated, orchestral approach to the tones of the trap kit. A sharp intelligence and keen aural reflexes mark all of Blackman's work; she inhabits a sound world of her own devising.

Blackman's tentative debut, *Arcane,* is a quintet alternating top-shelf saxophonists Kenny Garrett and Joe Henderson next to trumpeter Wallace Roney, pianist Larry Willis and bassist Buster Williams.

Her range and individuality emerge on two very different 1990 recordings. *Trio Plus Two* is more free-form, exploring rock, jazz and Latin territory with energy-guitar sound shaper David Fiuczynski, fluid bassist Santi Debriano, articulate saxophonist Greg Osby and Latin percussion master Jerry Gonzalez. *Code Red,* a rhythmic tour de force dedicated to Art Blakey, elicits some of the most powerful performances on record up to that time from trumpeter Wallace Roney and alto saxophonist Steve Coleman. Veteran pianist Kenny Barron enacts a dance of perpetual counterstatement with Blackman's surging rhythms, and Lonnie Plaxico holds it all together. Where *Trio Plus Two* explores the implications of Tony Williams's Lifetime innovations within the Blackman prism, *Code Red* recodes Williams the Milesian and '80s group leader to remarkable effect. This one is delightful over repeated listenings.

Telepathy documents a working ensemble, with more textural drumming from Blackman than on the earlier sessions. She pushes and prods Jacky Terrasson on piano and Antoine Roney on tenor and soprano saxophone through post-Bird Miles ("Well, You Needn't," recorded in 1959) and "Tune Up" (1953). This is interesting material that would have benefited from more assertive improvisations by her talented but inexperienced cohorts.

Oracle assembles an all-star unit of improvisers at the peak of their powers (Gary Bartz, alto and soprano saxophone; Kenny Barron, piano; Ron Carter, bass) interpreting five Blackman originals, Quincy Jones's ballad "Who Needs Forever?" Sam Rivers's modern standard "Beatrice" and the Billie Holiday vehicle "Crazy He Calls Me" with collective focus, fire, imagination and flair. The ensemble sound bears Blackman's indelible stamp; she's refined her conception to assert idiomatic individuality in a multiplicity of contexts. — T.P.

ED BLACKWELL

★★★★ What It Is (Enja, 1993)
★★★★★ What It Be Like? (Enja, 1994)

New Orleans percussionist Ed Blackwell (1929–1992) developed a unique style based on the traditions of his city's blues and second-line drumming and adapted to contemporary jazz rhythms. Part of New Orleans's post–World War II nascent bop scene, Blackwell worked with tenor saxophonist Harold Battiste, clarinetist Alvin Batiste and pianist Ellis Marsalis before becoming a key New Orleans R&B drummer in the 1950s, appearing on numerous sessions backing Huey "Piano" Smith, Earl King, Ray Charles and others.

Blackwell came to prominence in the jazz world as a member of Ornette Coleman's historic early-1960s group, appearing on the classic albums *This Is Our Music* and *Free Jazz,* among others. He went on to record with Coleman associates Charlie Haden and Don Cherry as well as John Coltrane, Eric Dolphy and Anthony Braxton.

Despite scant documentation, Blackwell is regarded by those he played with as one of the finest drummers of his generation and a pioneer in applying African drumming techniques to jazz performance. Both *What It Is* and *What It Be Like?* demonstrate Blackwell's fascination with an African-jazz musical concept. *What It Is* features Carlos Ward on alto saxophone, Graham Haynes on cornet and Mark Helias on bass. *What It Be Like?* adds Cherry's trumpet for a sublime send-off to a truly original musical force. Two Blackwell/Cherry collaborations, the two-part recording *Mu* and *El Corazón,* are well worth searching out. — J.S.

SCRAPPER BLACKWELL

★★★★½ The Virtuoso Guitar of Scrapper Blackwell (Yazoo, 1991)

Francis "Scrapper" Blackwell (1903–1962) successfully combined the powerful, rhythmic strumming of country blues with the sophisticated, melodic phrasing of urban blues. While his bass-string thumping stemmed from his roots in rural North Carolina, his treble-string runs reflected the urbanity of Indianapolis, where he spent most of his adult life. There, in the mid-1920s, he began a longtime collaboration with piano-playing vocalist Leroy Carr. Between 1928 and 1935 the duo cut more than a hundred singles for Vocalion, including the wildly popular "How Long How Long Blues." Carr and Blackwell complemented each other well; Carr's rumbling piano work filled out the low end, allowing Blackwell to construct complex solos in the upper register.

Blackwell also recorded with Bertha "Chippie" Hill, Georgia Tom Dorsey, Black Bottom McPhail and Tommy Bradley. In addition, he waxed numerous solo recordings, including "Kokomo Blues," which served as the basis for Robert Johnson's "Sweet Home Chicago."

A good cross section of Blackwell's material from this period is included on the Yazoo collection, though the bulk of his recordings with Carr, including "How Long" and *How Long Blues* can be found under Carr's name. Following Carr's death in 1935, Blackwell stopped recording for more than 20 years, until he was rediscovered during the late '50s. In 1960 he cut an excellent album for Prestige/Bluesville, but it's currently out of print. In 1962, just as a blues revival kicked into high gear, Blackwell was gunned down by an unknown assailant, his comeback nipped in the bud. — J.K.

BLIND BLAKE

★★★★★ Ragtime Guitar's Foremost Fingerpicker (Yazoo, 1990)
★★★★ Complete Recorded Works, Vol. 1 (1926–1927) (Document, 1991)
★★★★ Complete Recorded Works, Vol. 2 (1927–1928) (Document, 1991)
★★★★ Complete Recorded Works, Vol. 3 (1928–1929) (Document, 1991)
★★★★ Complete Recorded Works, Vol. 4 (1929–1932) (Document, 1991)
★★★★ The Best of Blind Blake (Collectables, 1995)

One of the most talented bluesmen of his generation, Arthur "Blind" Blake (ca. 1890–ca. 1933) is also one of the most enigmatic; historians speculate he may have been born Arthur Phelps in Jacksonville, Florida. What is certain, though, is Blake's remarkable range and expressiveness as a singer and guitarist. Rather than adhering to one style of music, he was adept at 8-, 12-, and 16-bar blues as well as rag, stomp and breakdown instrumentals. Blake also incorporated pop ditties and multistructured songs into his repertoire. Between 1926 and 1932 Blake recorded more than 100 tracks in various capacities, from solo artist to accompanying guitarist with Ma Rainey, Irene Scruggs and Papa Charlie Jackson, among others. Blake made no more recordings after 1932, which lends credence to conjecture that he died sometime shortly thereafter.

Blake's legacy remains preserved today by six sets of recordings. They vary in sound quality, but all present a solid picture of his versatility and skill as a player. The Yazoo set offers the best sound, while the Document series sacrifices sonic quality (at times the music is barely discernible over the cracks and pops) in favor of comprehensiveness, featuring 100 tracks in chronological order. *The Best of Blind Blake* is a poorly annotated but useful overview of his career.

Ragtime Guitar's Foremost Fingerpicker contains 23 tracks of various styles, including "Skeedle Loo Doo Blues," the original recording of the rag standard later recorded by Big Bill Broonzy, among others. Also present is the 12-bar "C.C. Pill Blues," where Blake provides muted accompaniment to Johnny Dodds's clarinet and Jimmy Bertrand's slide whistle. The set's other highlights include the complex blues picking of "Come On Boys Let's Do That Messin' Around," "Police Dog Blues" and "Diddie Wah Diddie."

Complete Recorded Works, Vol. 1 includes among its 26 tracks "Dying Blues," on which Blake's guitar accompanies a vocal performance by Leola Wilson, and "Buck-Town Blues," which finds Blake backed by a kazoo band. *Vol. 2* features 25 tracks, including the solo "You Gonna Quit Me Blues" and, with Blake on guitar and Elzadie Robinson on vocals, "Pay Day Daddy Blues" and "Elzadie's Policy Blues." All tracks on the first two volumes were cut in Chicago; *Vol. 3* includes recordings made in Chicago and Richmond, Indiana. Among them are "Sweet Papa Low Down," on which Blake's guitar is accompanied by Bertrand's xylophone, and "Hookworm Blues," one of several tracks on which Blake is backed by an unknown pianist. *Vol. 4* chronicles the last 24 tracks Blake recorded, the majority of which were cut in Grafton, Wisconsin. Highlights include "Fancy Tricks," with Blake's guitar backing vocalist Laura Rucker, and "Diddie Wah Diddie No. 2," which is musically identical to the original but lyrically quite different; in this "sequel" Blake learns the meaning of the song's mysterious title. — B.R.H.

EUBIE BLAKE

★★★ **Memories of You (Biograph, 1990)**
★★★★ **Tricky Fingers (Quicksilver, 1994)**
★★★★★ **Eighty-Six Years of Eubie Blake (Legacy, 1998)**

Over the course of his 85 years in show business, pianist James Herbert "Eubie" Blake (1883–1983) saw it all—the rise of ragtime, the beginnings of jazz, the vaudeville circuit, Broadway and beyond. He lived to be obsolete more than once and made dramatic comebacks on at least two occasions.

A better-than-average ragtime pianist during that music's heyday, Blake wrote several classic ragtime compositions and covered standards like Scott Joplin's "Maple Leaf Rag" before making it big in the 1910s as a nightclub performer and as a vaudeville act with Noble Sissle. In the 1920s he and Sissle cowrote a number of hit shows and popular songs, including "Memories of You" and "I'm Just Wild About Harry."

Considering the enormous range of his career, Blake recorded infrequently. *Memories of You* offers some piano rolls he recorded before World War I. The best representation of his work is the comprehensive *Eighty-Six Years of Eubie Blake.* — J.S.

ART BLAKEY

★★★★★ **A Night at Birdland, Vol. 1 (1954; Blue Note, 1987)**
★★★★★ **A Night at Birdland, Vol. 2 (1954; Blue Note, 1987)**
★★★★★ **At the Café Bohemia, Vol. 1 (1955; Blue Note, 1985)**
★★★★★ **At the Café Bohemia, Vol. 2 (1955; Blue Note, 1987)**
★★★★ **Midnight Session (1957; Savoy, 1991)**
★★★★★ **The Jazz Messengers with Thelonious Monk (1958; Atlantic Jazz, N.A.)**
★★★★★ **Moanin' (1958; Blue Note, 1987)**
★★★★★ **At the Jazz Corner of the World (1959; Blue Note, 1994)**
★★★★½ **The Big Beat (1960; Blue Note, N.A.)**
★★★★½ **Like Someone in Love (Blue Note, 1960)**
★★★★ **Meet You at the Jazz Corner of the World (Blue Note, 1960)**
★★★★★ **A Night in Tunisia (1960; Blue Note, 1989)**
★★★★★ **Art Blakey and the Jazz Messengers (1961; Impulse! 1987)**
★★★★ **Mosaic (1961; Blue Note, 1987)**
★★★★ **Buhaina's Delight (1962; Blue Note, 1992)**
★★★★ **Three Blind Mice, Vol. 1 (1962; Blue Note, 1990)**
★★★★ **Three Blind Mice, Vol. 2 (1962; Blue Note, 1990)**
★★★★ **Caravan (1962; Original Jazz Classics, 1987)**

★★★★ A Jazz Message (1963; Impulse! 1986)
★★★★ Ugetsu (1963; Original Jazz Classics, 1989)
★★★★★ Free for All (1964; Blue Note, 1988)
★★★★ Kyoto (1964; Original Jazz Classics, 1990)
★★★½ Buttercorn Lady (Limelight, 1964)
★★★½ Child's Dance (1973; Prestige, 1994)
★★★ In My Prime, Vol. 1 (Timeless, 1978)
★★★★ In This Korner (1978; Concord Jazz, 1992)
★★★ A Night in Tunisia (Philips, 1979)
★★★★ Album of the Year (Timeless, 1981)
★★★½ Straight Ahead (1981; Concord Jazz, 1990)
★★★½ Keystone 3 (Concord Jazz, 1982)
★★★★ New York Scene (Concord Jazz, 1984)
★★★ Blue Night (Timeless, 1985)
★★★★ Live at Kimball's (Concord Jazz, 1985)
★★★★ Live at Ronnie Scott's, London (DRG, 1985)
★★★½ Live in Stockholm 1960 (DIW, 1987)
★★★★★ Magical Trio 1 (with Ray Brown and James Williams) (EmArcy, 1987)
★★★ Not Yet (Soul Note, 1988)
★★★★★ The Best of Art Blakey and the Jazz Messengers (Blue Note, 1989)
★★★ Feel the Wind (Timeless, 1989)
★★★ Chippin' In (Timeless, 1990)
★★★ I Get a Kick Out of You (Soul Note, 1990)
★★★★ Art Collection: The Best of Art Blakey and the Jazz Messengers (Concord Jazz, 1992)
★★★★★ The History of Art Blakey and the Jazz Messengers (Blue Note, 1992)
★★★★ Dr. Jeckyle: Live at Sweet Basil (Evidence, 1992)
★★★★ Hard Champion (Evidence, 1992)
★★★ New Year's Eve at Sweet Basil (Evidence, 1992)
★★★½ In Sweden (Evidence, 1993)
★★★★★ Hard Bop/Paris Concert (Collectables, 1995)
★★★★ Mission Eternal (Prestige, 1995)
★★★★½ The Art of Jazz: Live in Leverkusen (In + Out, 1996)
★★★½ Moanin' (LaserLight, 1997)

The magnitude of the impact drummer/bandleader Abdullah Ibn Buhaina Art Blakey (1919–1990) had on the history of jazz is hard to calculate because he chose to apply his influence in a different direction from that of most of the music's other outstanding figures. Though Blakey was one of the greatest teachers and influences in jazz, his focus was on the playing itself, particularly the live performances of his band, the Jazz Messengers, and his genius was as an accompanist—coaxing, goading and firing up his pupils to achieve artistic greatness. No single jazz figure has had a more profound personal impact on a greater number of musicians. As a bandleader Blakey rivals Fletcher Henderson, Duke Ellington, Count Basie and Miles Davis in terms of nurturing virtuosic jazz stars.

Blakey's first edition of the Messengers defined the hard-bop style that would rule for nearly two decades, and even when fusion eclipsed it, Blakey stuck with the style and passed it on to each new member of the group. Blakey is thus single-handedly responsible for the bop revival of the 1980s and '90s as well, having nurtured in his band the key figures in that resurgence.

Blakey was also one of the greatest drummers ever, an indefatigable maelstrom of thundering polyrhythms whose power would levitate the Messengers nightly. Blakey's explosive backbeat was the engine of these relentless units, and when he slammed his foot on the gas, the band rocked with sleek, swinging drive. He could unleash sustained press rolls with astonishing speed, punctuated by the thunder of his bass-drum bombs and the lightning of his crashing hi-hat cymbals. More than anything, though, Blakey's conception was firmly grounded in the blues and gospel elements at the root of black American music and the layered, interwoven rhythms of African drumming.

The Pittsburgh-born Blakey began his career as a pianist, switching to drums as a sub for an ailing band mate. He played with Fletcher Henderson, Mary Lou Williams and, from 1944 to '47, with Billy Eckstine, performing alongside Charlie Parker, Dizzy Gillespie, Fats Navarro, Gene Ammons and Sarah Vaughan.

After working as a leader as well as in groups led by Lucky Millinder, Buddy DeFranco and the groundbreaking Thelonious Monk, Blakey put together a quintet co-led by pianist Horace Silver and featuring trumpeter Clifford Brown, alto saxophonist Lou Donaldson and bassist

Curley Russell. This group recorded the sensational *A Night at Birdland* sets in February 1954. Later that year Silver was the leader on the first official Jazz Messengers session, with Kenny Dorham on trumpet, Hank Mobley on tenor and Doug Watkins on bass. Under Blakey's leadership the same band recorded the historic 1955 sessions *At the Café Bohemia,* which ushered in the hard-bop era.

Through the rest of the decade Blakey's bands were awesome units that presaged the roots-oriented soul-jazz movement of the early 1960s. One of the key figures in that style, pianist Bobby Timmons, contributed the new standard "Moanin'" to the Blakey book. On that same session prolific tenor saxophonist Benny Golson penned "Are You Real," "Along Came Betty," "The Drum Thunder Suite" and the classic "Blues March." The brilliant trumpeter Lee Morgan and bassist Jymie Merritt completed the lineup on the Blue Note album *Moanin'*.

That same working unit is on the live half of the twofer *Hard Bop/Paris Concert; Hard Bop* consists of 1956 studio sessions featuring Bill Hardman on trumpet and Jackie McLean on alto; that lineup is also on *Midnight Session,* from March 1957. *At the Jazz Corner of the World* is the Morgan/Timmons/Merritt group with Hank Mobley on tenor. The *Jazz Messengers with Thelonious Monk* is a classic 1957 date with Hardman and tenor saxophonist Johnny Griffin covering Monk's "Evidence," "In Walked Bud," "Blue Monk," "I Mean You" and "Rhythm-a-Ning."

Tenor saxophonist Wayne Shorter joined Morgan to make a perfectly balanced front line on the 1960 recordings *The Big Beat*, *Like Someone in Love*, *Meet You at the Jazz Corner of the World*, *Live in Stockholm 1960* and the epochal *A Night in Tunisia.* This group also appears on the out-of-print classic *The Freedom Rider.* On *Art Blakey and the Jazz Messengers* the lineup was expanded into the perfect sextet with the addition of the brilliantly matched Curtis Fuller on trombone. The seemingly limitless talent of the young Freddie Hubbard took over the trumpet spot in the group, and Cedar Walton replaced Timmons. This edition of the Messengers added the beautiful ballad approach epitomized by "Invitation" alongside the funky romps of the group's trademark style. Fuller's sprightly composition "A La Mode" virtually defines the Messengers' sound.

Blakey and the Messengers enjoyed a period of stability and international commercial success as a working group during the early 1960s, a time when jazz was losing most of the ground it once held at the center of America's popular music. This group recorded *Three Blind Mice*, *Mosaic* and *Buhaina's Delight,* then with Reggie Workman replacing Merritt in 1962, *Caravan*, *Ugetsu*, *Free for All* and *Kyoto.* Shorter, Fuller, Hubbard and Walton all contributed enduring compositions to the Messengers' repertoire during this period.

Morgan rejoined the group in place of Hubbard for the out-of-print 1964 session *Indestructible!* In 1963 Blakey also recorded a side project without the Messengers, *A Jazz Message,* a quartet date with McCoy Tyner on piano, Sonny Stitt on alto and tenor saxophone and Art Davis on bass.

Blakey's fortunes declined with those of acoustic jazz as the 1960s progressed and the constantly shifting nature of the Messengers' personnel reflected his difficulty getting the band domestic record deals. A stint with Limelight resulted in the mellower face of the Messengers on *Buttercorn Lady,* with Chuck Mangione on trumpet and featuring the recording debut of pianist Keith Jarrett. *Moanin'* documents the 1968 edition of the Messengers, with Hardman back on trumpet, Billy Harper's fiery tenor-saxophone work, Julian Priester on trombone, Ronnie Mathews on piano and Lawrence Evans on bass.

Child's Dance and *Mission Eternal* collect tracks from early-1970s versions of the Messengers, bands including Walton, trumpeter Woody Shaw, pianist John Hicks, bassist Stanley Clarke and trombonist Steve Turre. These groups, which also featured Latin percussion and guitar, showed the band trying to expand its sound.

On *In This Korner,* a 1978 release recorded live at the Keystone Korner, the Messengers return to the sextet format with Bobby Watson's alto, Dave Schnitter's tenor and Valery Ponomarev's trumpet on the front line, and James Williams on piano and Dennis Irwin on bass. The same lineup recorded the muscular *Night in Tunisia* and a marathon 18-minute version of the title track.

Watson and Williams stuck around for the 1981 edition of the Messengers, with Wynton Marsalis on trumpet, Bill Pierce on tenor and Charles Fambrough on bass. That group recorded *Album of the Year*, *In Sweden* and *Straight Ahead.*

On *Keystone 3,* a live set from 1982, Donald Brown replaces Williams on piano and Marsalis is joined by brother Branford on alto in place of Watson.

The last classic lineup of Jazz Messengers made its way through the mid-1980s with Terence Blanchard on trumpet, Donald Harrison on alto saxophone, Jean Toussaint on tenor saxophone, Mulgrew Miller on piano and Lonnie Plaxico on bass. Blanchard, Harrison and Miller all contributed good compositions to *New York Scene.* The same group recorded *Live at Ronnie Scott's* and *Live at Kimball's* in 1985. *New Year's Eve at Sweet Basil* and *Dr. Jeckyle: Live at Sweet Basil* were also recorded live at the end of that year with trombonist Tim Williams added to the lineup.

Hard Champion combines tracks from another 1985 live date by the Harrison/Blanchard band with the brief Blakey-penned title theme, recorded in 1987 with Philip Harper on trumpet, Kenny Garrett on alto, Javon Jackson on tenor, Benny Green on piano and Peter Washington on bass.

The Art of Jazz: Live in Leverkusen is a wonderful lifetime-tribute concert recorded two days before Blakey's 70th birthday with a collection of jazz stars who started out with the Messengers over the years, including Golson, Shorter, McLean, Fuller, Hubbard and Blanchard. The big-band blowout was a fitting cap to Blakey's brilliant career. — J.S.

TERENCE BLANCHARD

★★★ Terence Blanchard (Columbia, 1991)
★★★½ Simply Stated (Columbia, 1992)
★★★★ The Malcolm X Jazz Suite (Columbia, 1993)
★★★½ The Billie Holiday Songbook (Columbia, 1994)
★★★★ The Heart Speaks (Columbia, 1996)

Trumpeter Terence Blanchard (b. 1962) followed Wynton Marsalis from New Orleans to New York and a stint with Art Blakey's Jazz Messengers, where he combined with alto saxophonist Donald Harrison to form the last great front line Blakey assembled before his death. Harrison and Blanchard went on to work as a duo before embarking on solo careers.

On his debut as a bandleader, Blanchard took a more soulful approach than Marsalis. Produced by Wynton's brother Delfeayo, the recording features Branford Marsalis and Sam Newsome on tenor saxophone, Bruce Barth on piano, Rodney Whitaker on bass and Jeff Watts and Troy Davis on drums. That same lineup minus the Marsalis brothers plus Billy Kilson on drums and Antonio Hart on alto saxophone appears on *Simply Stated,* an engaging mix of Blanchard originals such as "Little Miss Olivia Ray" and the title track, covers of the classics "Dear Old Stockholm" and "When It's Sleepytime Down South" and a medley that begins with Blanchard's "Glass J" and ends with Ornette Coleman's "Lonely Woman." *The Malcolm X Jazz Suite* is Blanchard's most profound work, an exercise in spiritual questing that recalls the contemplative tone of Miles Davis's *Kind of Blue.* Newsome, Barth and Davis are joined this time by bassist Tarus Mateen.

The Billie Holiday Songbook documents a 1993 concert with Blanchard's regular quartet joined by vocalist Jeanie Bryson performing songs associated with Billie Holiday. The creatively restless Blanchard moved on again, making an ambitious album of Brazilian music, *The Heart Speaks,* with vocalist Ivan Lins adding an ethereal touch to the proceedings.
— J.S.

BOBBY "BLUE" BLAND

★★★★★ The Best of Bobby Bland (1972; MCA, 1974)
★★★★★ Two Steps from the Blues (1973; MCA, 1989)
★★★ Dreamer (MCA, 1974)
★★★ Ain't Nothing You Can Do (MCA, 1974)
★★★ Here's the Man (MCA, 1974)
★★★★ B.B. King & Bobby Bland: Together for the First Time Live (MCA, 1974)
★★★★ The Soul of the Man (MCA, 1974)
★★★★ The Best of Bobby Bland, Vol. 2 (MCA, 1974)
★★★ Call on Me (MCA, 1974)
★★★ Introspective of the Early Years (MCA, 1974)
★★ B.B. King & Bobby Bland: Together Again . . . Live (1976; MCA, 1990)
★★★ Reflections in Blue (MCA, 1977)
★★★ I Feel Good, I Feel Fine (MCA, 1979)
★★★ Members Only (Malaco, 1985)
★★★ After All (Malaco, 1986)
★★★ Blues You Can Use (Malaco, 1987)

★★★ **First Class Blues (Malaco, 1987)**
★★★★ **Midnight Run (Malaco, 1989)**
★★★ **Portrait of the Blues (Malaco, 1991)**
★★★★★ **I Pity the Fool: The Duke Recordings, Vol. 1 (MCA, 1992)**
★★★ **Years of Tears (Malaco, 1993)**
★★★★★ **Turn On Your Love Light: The Duke Recordings, Vol. 2 (MCA, 1994)**

Less celebrated than his contemporary B.B. King (for whom he served briefly as valet and chauffeur) and lacking King's major-label support, Bobby "Blue" Bland (b. 1930) has a lot more than staying power going for him. Although nearly 50 years have passed since his early, scuffling days working joints on Memphis's Beale Street with King, Roscoe Gordon and Johnny Ace, he has quietly become one of the best-selling and most frequently charting R&B artists of all time, well ahead of some of his celebrated peers. That he rarely visits the charts anymore in these his later years is irrelevant, because from time to time in his current stint with the Mississippi-based Malaco label he has delivered albums that approach the quality of the formidable work he did during his reputation-establishing 20-year affiliation with Duke Records.

Born near Memphis, the young Robert Calvin Bland received his first lessons in direct, heartfelt singing while a member of various church groups in town; in the late '40s he took to Beale Street and began honing a singular vocal approach out of the gospel, blues and early R&B that had become his artistic touchstones. Bland didn't, and doesn't, have a big, powerful voice. Rather, his was the quiet storm of postwar blues—forceful and determined in a macho kind of way on the up-tempo numbers but with an underlying tenderness that could put the hurt in a ballad to a degree approached in his peer group only by B.B. King. Along the way he developed the earmarks of a master stylist as well in his subtle use of nuance to suggest deeper feelings roiling below the surface of his dignified demeanor. Although his artistic growth was far from complete when he cut his first sides at Sam Phillips's Memphis Recording Service in 1951, he sounds every bit the assured vocalist, recording in his hometown backed by musician friends from Roscoe Gordon's band. In 1954 he was signed to the Houston-based Duke label, teamed with players unfamiliar to him (Johnny Board and His Orchestra), and lost nary a step—in fact, Board brought a big, ambitious sound to Bland's sessions by way of a prominent horn section and an organist and vibraphonist whose embellishments added a jazz feel to the arrangements, prompting even richer-textured performances from Bland. Such was the genesis of a signature style that embraced not only florid, emotionally charged blues (and borderline pop) ballads but also hard-driving blues and jump-blues orchestrations, extending a tradition pioneered in the '30s by Big Joe Turner and the boogie-woogie cats from Kansas City.

In 1955 he began recording in Houston with a small orchestra led by trumpeter/arranger Joe Scott, who in the years ahead would assume a critical role in the sound and sensibility peculiar to Bland's music. The early years produced some powerful music—in 1956 a wrenching torch number, "You or None," rendered with Percy Mayfield–inspired cool sensuality, and an explosive performance on "Time Out" (from '55) in which he charges into his high register and wails like a Sonny Boy Williamson harmonica solo—but his breakthrough would not come until 1957, with a shuffling bit of R&B clairvoyance in "Farther Up the Road," notable for the spitfire dialog between Bland lusting for revenge and guitarist Pat Hare firing off portentous-sounding four-bar riffs around him before launching into an angry, serpentine solo attack. Upon its release that August the song bolted up the charts and stayed at Number One for two weeks. At the same time that "Farther Up the Road" was introducing him to a larger audience, it was also establishing a unique storytelling style, not exclusive to Bland but employed most effectively by him on many of his most memorable sides. Bland begins his tale in progress and proceeds to hurtle toward a dénouement while filling in minute—but not all—details of the story's first act, in effect shifting the timeline to create drama around key sentiments such as "Farther on up the road/Someone's gonna hurt you/Like you hurt me." From this point forward, Bland's Duke recordings were notable for the diversity of their arrangements and his inventive vocal stylings. Whether he was shouting over a pulsating, horn-driven, Ray Charles–style arrangement ("Close to You," from 1960) or crooning sensitively on a moody, lilting ballad ("Two Steps from the Blues," 1960), he was believable and affecting.

An exemplary reissue program has restored order to Bland's Duke recordings, thanks primarily to the two essential well-annotated two-disc collections, *I Pity the Fool: The Duke Recordings, Vol. 1* and *Turn On Your Love Light: The Duke Recordings, Vol. 2.* The ultimate aim of this program is to bring the entirety of Bland's 20-year Duke recording history to the market in chronological order, including alternate takes, rarities and previously unissued sides. Of the sets here, *I Pity the Fool* focuses on the years 1952–1960, *Turn On Your Love Light* the years 1960–1964, with the former having more informative liner information with regard to chart histories, career outline, biographical details and so forth.

Lower-budget Duke retrospectives include the single CDs *The Best of Bobby Bland* (includes "Farther Up the Road" and two other certified Bland classics in "I Pity the Fool"—his second Number One R&B single, from 1960—and "Turn On Your Love Light"); *The Best of Bobby Bland, Vol. 2; The Soul of the Man,* a nice sampling of gospel-oriented, minor-key blues; and *Introspective of the Early Years,* featuring Bland in a raw mode, backed by a small combo and centered on rather downbeat fare.

Among the non–greatest-hits albums, the one absolute must-have is *Two Steps from the Blues,* one of the most powerful R&B albums ever recorded. From the rawboned confessional blues of the opening title song to the final, touching "I've Been Wrong So Long," this concept album, devoted to intimate reflections on love and longing, is so personal and atmospheric it comes off as R&B's answer to Sinatra's brilliant forays into thematic unity, *Only the Lonely* and *In the Wee Small Hours.* Check out the aching plea "Lead Me On" for a heartbreaking sample of this artist's deeply felt balladeering style—this one's strictly Mount Olympus in grandeur.

Aging as gracefully as his friend B.B. King, Bland, after some fallow years on ABC in the mid- to late '70s (the highs and lows of which are encapsulated on the two live albums noted above, now on MCA), found a home on Malaco and has stayed the course with gospel-soul stylings and exemplary song selection in a traditional R&B vein. A good starting point for this era is *First Class Blues,* something of a greatest-hits package comprising several tracks from Bland's first two Malaco albums, *After All* and *Members Only,* as well as fresh interpretations of "Two Steps from the Blues" and another Bland evergreen from the Duke years, "St. James Infirmary." On a fervent interpretation of "In the Ghetto," Bland, all soul on ice, gives a slow, deliberate reading that has the effect of making vivid the overwhelming desperation of inner-city life. The inspired *Midnight Run* and *Portrait of the Blues* and especially 1993's *Years of Tears* show the mature vocalist in splendid form, working his turf, moving hearts, and sounding as involved in his material as he was at the outset of his career. — D.M.

CARLA BLEY

★★★★★ **Escalator over the Hill (JCOA, 1972)**
★★★½ **Tropic Appetites (Watt, 1973)**
★★★½ **13 & 3/4 (with Michael Mantler) (Watt, 1975)**
★★★½ **Dinner Music (Watt, 1977)**
★★★½ **European Tour, 1977 (Watt, 1978)**
★★★★ **Musique Mecanique (Watt, 1979)**
★★★★★ **Social Studies (ECM, 1980)**
★★★★ **Live! (ECM, 1982)**
★★★½ **Heavy Heart (Watt, 1984)**
★★★½ **Night-Glo (Watt, 1985)**
★★★½ **Sextet (Watt, 1987)**
★★★½ **Duets (1988)**
★★★½ **Fleur Carnivore (Watt, 1989)**
★★★★ **Orchestra Jazz Siciliana Plays the Music of Carla Bley (xtraWATT, 1990)**
★★★★ **The Very Big Carla Bley Band (Watt, 1991)**
★★★½ **Go Together (Watt, 1993)**
★★★½ **Big Band Theory (Watt, 1993)**
★★★½ **Songs with Legs (with Andy Sheppard, Steve Swallow) (ECM, 1995)**
★★★★ **The Carla Bley Big Band Goes to Church (Watt, 1996)**

A wry, subversive talent, Carla Bley (b. 1938) masterminded one of the most outlandish musical events of the '70s: *Escalator over the Hill,* a work that took several years to record and clocked in at a playing time of more than three conventional albums. Pianist/organist Bley, after all, flashes intimidating, high-art credentials—cofounder of the Jazz Composers Orchestra Association (JCOA), she'd played with Pharoah Sanders, written music for vibraphonist Gary Burton and built up a reputation as one of the more interesting post–Ornette Coleman players even before she released *Escalator.* Uniting such diverse figures as Gato Barbieri and Linda Ronstadt, Warhol star Viva and John McLaughlin, Jack Bruce, Charlie Haden and Don Cherry, the epic is jazz fusion that sounds nothing like either the African and blues-derived menace of Miles Davis's *Bitches Brew* nor the dilutions of such popularizers as Chuck Mangione or Jean-Luc Ponty. Instead, with its libretto by poet Paul Haines, its virtuosic playing and cryptic humor, *Escalator* is postmodern opera—difficult, intense, often abstract. And gorgeous.

Nothing Bley has done since that breakthrough has flourished such Olympian power, but every record she's made is provocative. Whether working out dense, majestic brass arrangements with her big band or recording austerely lovely duets with bassist Steve Swallow, she combines a jazz player's sense of freedom with the complex intelligence of a modern classical composer. *Sextet* features some of her nicer melodies; *Musique Mecanique,* with its standout 12-minute "Jesus Maria and Other Spanish Strains," combines the graceful ambiance of chamber music with the heat of jazz (bassist Charlie Haden, a regular contributor, turns in outstanding work, as does guitarist Eugene Chadbourne). *Tropic Appetites* highlights the exceptional vocals of Julie Tippetts (formerly Julie Driscoll, whose early fame came with Brian Auger in the '60s); with husband Michael Mantler, *13 & 3/4* is brilliant large-ensemble music, its intricacy and sweep emblematic of much of the music Bley and Mantler offer on their record label, Watt. Bley at her most approachable can be found on 1991 versions of her "greatest hits," performed by the Orchestra Jazz Siciliana; *Social Studies* (1980) comes closest to *Escalator* in artistic derring-do. With 18 musicians going strong, *The Very Big Carla Bley Band* is also impressive; note the 15-minute highlight, "The United States." *The Carla Bley Big Band Goes to Church* is another outstanding large-group outing, recorded live at the Umbria Jazz Festival in Italy. — P.E.

PAUL BLEY

★★★★ **Introducing Paul Bley (1953; Original Jazz Classics, 1985)**
★★★★ **Solemn Meditation (1958; GNP Crescendo, N.A.)**
★★★½ **Paul Bley with Gary Peacock (1963; ECM, N.A.)**
★★★½ **Footloose (1963; Savoy, 1995)**
★★★½ **Paul Bley Quintet (1964; ESP, N.A.)**
★★★½ **Closer (1966; ESP, N.A.)**
★★★★ **Open, to Love (1973; ECM, N.A.)**
★★★ **Alone, Again (1975; I.A.I., 1994)**
★★★★ **Axis (1977; I.A.I., 1993)**
★★★ **Tango Palace (Soul Note, 1983)**
★★★½ **Fragments (ECM, 1986)**
★★★½ **Notes (Soul Note, 1987)**
★★★½ **The Paul Bley Quartet (ECM, 1988)**
★★★½ **Bebopbebopbebopbebop (SteepleChase, 1989)**
★★★★ **Memoirs (Soul Note, 1989)**
★★★ **12 (+6) in a Row (Hat Hut, 1991)**
★★★★ **Japan Suite (I.A.I., 1992)**
★★★½ **Double Time (Justin Time, 1994)**
★★★½ **In the Evenings Out There (ECM, 1994)**
★★★½ **Synth Thesis (Postcards, 1994)**
★★★½ **Outside In (Justin Time, 1995)**
★★★★ **Sweet Time (Justin Time, 1995)**
★★★½ **Paul Bley/NHØP (SteepleChase, 1995)**
★★★½ **Time Will Tell (ECM, 1995)**
★★★½ **Modern Chant (MusicMasters, 1996)**
★★★½ **Solo Piano (SteepleChase, N.A.)**

Canadian pianist Paul Bley (b. 1932) is a prolific and exacting player whose vast and underappreciated catalog swings wildly in and out of print. His style is sparse yet constantly brimming with ideas; he simply never overplays his hand, choosing to enunciate his melodies in the most unsparing manner while setting them in rich harmonic contexts. Sometimes his playing has the stark clarity of an idea whose time has come; elsewhere it is full of implication and poetic allusion. He is a master of understatement who gives the impression of always being in complete control of even the most abstract material.

Bley's 1953 debut couldn't have been couched in a more impressive setting than this trio with Charles Mingus on bass and Art Blakey on drums. By the end of the decade he was challenging the hegemony of bop in the musings of *Solemn Meditation* and in a quartet featuring alto saxophonist Ornette Coleman (see the currently unavailable *Live at Hillcrest*).

In the early 1960s on the ESP dates and later with ECM, Bley became one of the most convincing exponents of free jazz. He worked in several fine trios during the 1960s. *Closer* features bassist Steve Swallow and drummer Barry Altschul performing several compositions by Bley's wife, Carla. Though the marriage didn't last, over the years Paul Bley continued to be one of his ex-wife's greatest interpreters. *Paul Bley with Gary Peacock* is a trio session with Peacock on bass and either Paul Motian or Billy Elgart on drums. *Footloose* uses Swallow and drummer Pete LaRoca.

Bley experimented with the tonal possibilities offered by synthesizers in the 1970s, but his most fruitful work was at the solo piano. The sleek beauty of *Open, to Love* was a triumph of the kind of music ECM was championing, and *Axis* was a thoroughly enjoyable recording. During that decade, he also formed his own production company, Improvising Artists, Inc., and put out records by Sam Rivers and Sun Ra, as well as his own.

In the 1980s Bley worked in group contexts in between recording such solo outings as *Tango Palace* and *Solo Piano. Fragments* and *The Paul Bley Quartet* introduce Bley's collaboration with John Surman on soprano and baritone saxophones and bass clarinet, Bill Frisell on guitar and Motian on drums. Surman reappears on the 1993 set *In the Evenings Out There,* a quartet with Peacock on bass and Tony Oxley on drums.

Bassist Niels-Henning Ørsted Pedersen proved to be a capable partner for Bley on *Paul Bley/NHØP. Bebopbebopbebopbebop* is another trio session with Bob Cranshaw on bass and Keith Copeland on drums. On *12 (+6) in a Row* Bley experiments with 12-tone in an unusual trio setting with Hans Koch on a variety of reed instruments and Franz Koglmann on flügelhorn. *Memoirs* is a superb trio session with bassist Charlie Haden and drummer Motian playing a mixture of original compositions alongside those of Thelonious Monk and Ornette Coleman. Another atmospheric trio date, *Time Will Tell,* employs bassist Barre Phillips and saxophonist Evan Parker.

Bley has recorded a series of albums in recent years for the Canadian-based Justin Time records. Look for solo efforts *Solo, Changing Hands* and *Sweet Time* and a pair of stunning duets, *Double Time,* with soprano saxophonist and clarinetist Jane Bunnett, and *Outside In,* with guitarist Sonny Greenwich. *Hands On,* another expansive solo set from 1993, balances around the 12-minute-plus "Three Fifth." On *Synth Thesis* Bley juggles solo piano and synthesizer textures. *Modern Chant* is Bley's fascinating interpretation of Gregorian chant in a trio with David Eyges on electric cello and Bruce Ditmas on drums. — J.S.

RORY BLOCK

★★★ **High Heeled Blues (1981; Rounder, 1989)**
★★★ **Rhinestones and Steel Strings (1983; Rounder, 1990)**
★★½ **Blue Horizon (1983; Rounder, 1989)**
★★★ **I've Got a Rock in My Sock (1986; Rounder, 1989)**
★★★½ **House of Hearts (Rounder, 1987)**
★★★½ **Best Blues and Originals (Rounder, 1987)**
★★★½ **Mama's Blues (Rounder, 1991)**
★★★ **Ain't I a Woman (Rounder, 1992)**
★★★ **Angel of Mercy (Rounder, 1994)**
★★★★ **When a Woman Gets the Blues (Rounder, 1995)**
★★★ **Tornado (Rounder, 1996)**
★★★★ **Confessions of a Blues Singer (Rounder, 1998)**

Country-blues interpreter, guitarist and songwriter Rory Block, born a cobbler's daughter in 1949, grew up in New York City's Greenwich Village. As a musician she has proven to be both talented and prolific, releasing a number of fine albums that combine her own compositions with traditional fare by the likes of Robert Johnson, Skip James and Charley Patton. Her auspicious Rounder debut, *High Heeled Blues,* was coproduced by Block and John Sebastian. Highlights include her renditions of Johnson's "Walkin' Blues" and "Travelin' Blues," as well as James's "Devil Got My Man" and the original "Since You've Been Gone."

Rhinestones and Steel Strings features Willie Brown's "Future Blues" and the Rev. Gary Davis's "Sit Down on the Banks." Block's own strong originals include "Lovin' Fool" and "God's Gift to Women," with the Persuasions supplying background vocals. *Blue Horizon* also has some solid tracks, such as Davis's "Feel Just Like Goin' On" and her own "Catastrophe Rag." *I've Got a Rock in My Sock* contains another good crop of originals, such as "Gypsie Boy," upon which Stevie Wonder plays harmonica, and the title track, with David Bromberg on fiddle. Taj Mahal also makes a guest appearance, playing harmonica on two tracks (Patton's "Moon's Goin' Down" and Willie Brown's "M & O Blues"). Consisting mostly of originals, the melancholy *House of Hearts* is dedicated to Block's son, Thiele, who died in a car crash at age 20. Block's voice is anguished and wrenchingly beautiful on the title track, a requiem for her son. Also outstanding is "Bonnie Boy," with David Grisman on mandolin.

Best Blues and Originals compiles tracks

from Block's work up to that point, excluding *House of Hearts. Mama's Blues* features Robert Johnson's "Terraplane Blues" and Tommy Johnson's "Big Road Blues." Several Block originals stand out, though: "Got to Shine" and the title track, on which Jorma Kaukonen plays electric guitar. *Ain't I a Woman* features special guest guitarist Mark Knopfler on Block's "Faithless World." Other originals include the longing "Sisters" and the pensive "Never Called Your Name," upon which John Sebastian's harmonica leads the way.

On *Angel of Mercy* Block writes about the road ("I'll Be Gone"), a homeless mother ("Somebody's Baby"), greed ("It Ain't Right") and the perils of the music business ("Big Bad Agent Man"). Though the songs are intriguing, the album's slick production makes it less effective than her other, more rough-hewn releases. *When a Woman Gets the Blues* is a terrific return to Block's rootsy ethos. With the exception of one track, the album contains exclusively classic blues covers: Son House's "Preaching Blues," Kid Bailey's "Rowdy Blues," Skip James's "Cypress Grove" and "Be Ready When He Comes" and Blind Willie McTell's "T'Ain't Long for Day."

Tornado again finds Block mining emotionally charged issues for inspiration. Dedicated to Nicole Brown Simpson, "Gone Woman Blues" uses mournful slide-guitar work and an arsenal of sighs and moans to create a ghostly effect. As on almost all her albums, guest musicians appear on *Tornado,* including Mary Chapin Carpenter, David Lindley, Jerry Marotta and Paul Shaffer. Block is in top form on *Confessions of a Blues Singer,* covering Robert Johnson, Charley Patton, Bukka White, Furry Lewis and Blind Willie McTell, along with songs telling her own sagas. — B.R.H.

BLOOD, SWEAT AND TEARS

★★★★ **Child Is Father to the Man (1968; Columbia, 1994)**
★★★★ **Blood, Sweat and Tears (1969; Columbia, 1992)**
★ **Blood, Sweat and Tears 3 (1970; Columbia, 1986)**
★★ **Greatest Hits (Columbia, 1972)**
★ **New Blood (Columbia, 1972)**
★ **No Sweat (Columbia, 1973)**
★★★ **Live & Improvised (Legacy, 1991)**
★★★½ **What Goes Up! The Best of Blood, Sweat and Tears (Legacy, 1995)**

Blood, Sweat and Tears started out in 1967 as a fusion of jazz, blues and folk elements spearheaded by vocalist/arranger Al Kooper and guitarist Steve Katz from the groundbreaking 1960s group the Blues Project. Its stellar cast of young jazz-session players included drummer Bobby Colomby, saxophonist Fred Lipsius and trumpeters Randy Brecker and Lew Soloff.

Child Is Father to the Man is an ingenious blend of elements that merits praise if only for introducing the Beatles generation to the music of Charlie Parker. It is a canny melding of pop song structures with jazz arrangements that proved to be very influential.

By the time of *Blood, Sweat and Tears* the formula had evolved into a pop juggernaut behind the histrionic vocals of David Clayton-Thomas. The result was a string of hit singles—"Spinning Wheel," "And When I Die" et cetera—spun through a gorgeous concept album. But the spontaneity had been hammered out of the music, and the group went on to more commercial success offset by increasingly self-parodistic music. — J.S.

MIKE BLOOMFIELD

★★★ **Super Session (with Al Kooper, Stephen Stills) (Columbia, 1968)**
★★★ **It's Not Killing Me (Columbia, 1969)**
★★★ **The Live Adventures of Mike Bloomfield and Al Kooper (Columbia, 1969)**
★★½ **Try It Before You Buy It (Columbia, 1973)**
★★★ **Triumvirate (Columbia, 1973)**
★★★ **Mill Valley Session (Polydor, 1976)**
★★★ **Analine (Takoma, 1977)**
★★★ **If You Love These Blues, Play 'Em as You Please (Guitar Player, 1977)**
★★★ **Mike Bloomfield (Takoma, 1978)**
★★½ **Between a Hard Place and the Ground (Takoma, 1980)**
★★½ **Living in the Fast Lane (Waterhouse, 1981)**
★★★½ **Cruisin' for a Bruisin' (Takoma, 1981)**
★★★½ **Bloomfield (Columbia, 1983)**
★★★½ **Blues, Gospel and Ragtime Guitar Instrumentals (Shanachie, 1993)**
★★★½ **"Don't Say That I Ain't Your Man!" Essential Blues, 1964–1969 (Legacy, 1994)**

His attack stinging, his tone bell-like, Mike Bloomfield (1944–1981) was a guitarist's guitarist. After an acoustic apprenticeship in Chicago clubs alongside vocalist Nick Gravenites and Charlie Musselwhite on harmonica, Bloomfield gained fame with the Paul Butterfield Blues Band and their hard Chicago blues—urban, fast and very electric. With a style based on the lean power of B.B. King, he was capable of very fluid runs and fills, and his solos were breathtakingly precise. The Electric Flag (again with Gravenites) provided his best backdrop; their innovative mix of blues rock and horn-driven jazz provoked some of his tastiest playing and, with *A Long Time Comin'* (#31 pop), a measure of chart success, but he left the group a year after joining. Subsequently, he never found exactly the right vehicle for his talents. His playing with Al Kooper was graceful and exciting, but Kooper couldn't really keep pace with him, and *Triumvirate,* a collaboration with John Hammond and Dr. John, was all-pro blues—but the one-shot band played things safe. Solo, he turned out solid records—the best being *It's Not Killing Me* and *Cruisin' for a Bruisin',* but they lacked the fire he'd found when teamed with musicians of equal stature. *If You Love These Blues,* an instructional guide to blues guitar, earned him a Grammy in 1977 and yet served, too, to remind listeners that here was an awesome player in search of a band.

The 1983 Bloomfield compilation, released two years after he was found dead in a car in San Francisco, victim of a drug overdose, provides the best overall intro; it collects his finest work with Butterfield, the Electric Flag and Kooper, as well as some previously unreleased gems. Focusing specifically on the blues, the Legacy and Shanachie collections are also recommended. — P.E.

THE BLUES BROTHERS

★★★½ Briefcase Full of Blues (Atlantic, 1978)
★ Made in America (Atlantic, 1980)
★★★ The Blues Brothers (Original Soundtrack) (Atlantic, 1980)
★★★ The Best of the Blues Brothers (Atlantic, 1981)

Credit or blame for the Blues Brothers belongs to Delbert McClinton, whose late-night blues jams at New York's Lone Star Cafe in the mid-'70s convinced a pair of music-loving comedians that they could become a whiteface Sam and Dave. John Belushi and Dan Aykroyd were right—their commercial status as *Saturday Night Live* stars gave them the clout to indulge their wildest fantasies, and their true love of the music gave them the sense to get the kind of instrumental backing that record producers don't usually give TV stars. Just as he realized how good it felt to sing in front of McClinton's band, Belushi knew how much fun it would be to have the Stax band, led by Steve Cropper and Donald "Duck" Dunn, backing him up.

Belushi's vocal liabilities didn't prevent the band from playing its mightiest on the live *Briefcase Full of Blues,* which became a Number One album on the strength of an awesome groove and the fact that it was one of the key party albums of its era. The music so thoroughly re-creates the excitement of the Stax revues that a good vocalist would push it toward a five-star rating. The band's strengths could not sustain Belushi as a front man beyond the initial enthusiasm of his conception—all the intensity and back flips in the world can't make up for a lack of musical vision. In the end Belushi's performance was essentially that of the drunk guy jumping onstage at the frat party. It's worth noting that the House of Blues in New Orleans, part of the restaurant chain that grew out of the Jake and Elwood experience, has featured a Monday-night jam in which local college kids are encouraged to do just that. — J.S.

BLUES QUEEN SYLVIA

★★★½ Midnight Baby (Evidence, 1994)

"Blues Queen" Sylvia Lee Burton Embry (1941–1991) sang in a powerful, high-pitched voice and easily adapted traditional blues tropes to her own confessional style. Born in Arkansas, she moved to Chicago, where she became a fixture on the local blues scene, playing and singing with her husband, John Embry, and eventually joining the Jimmy Dawkins band. Dawkins returns the favor as the guitarist on *Midnight Baby,* recorded in 1983. The powerful voice that made Sylvia a mainstay of the Antioch Baptist Church gospel choir is in good form here on 11 originals, and Dawkins provides gritty support. — J.S.

BLUESIANA TRIANGLE

★★★★ Bluesiana Triangle (Windham Hill, 1990)
★★★½ Bluesiana II (Windham Hill, 1991)

Producer Joe Ferry put together like-minded musicians for this project, teaming legendary jazz drummer Buhaina Art Blakey with New Orleans pianist/vocalist Mac "Dr. John" Rebennack, David "Fathead" Newman on saxophones and flute, Essiet Okon Essiet on bass and Joe Bonadio on percussion. From the Newman instrumental "Heads Up" to Dr. John arrangements of New Orleans chestnuts "Life's a One Way Ticket," "Shoo Fly Don't Bother

Me" and a down-home "When the Saints Go Marchin' In," the band cuts a terrific groove. The session turned out to be one of Blakey's last hurrahs, capped off by Buhaina singing a hoarse, tearful "For All We Know."

Bluesiana II is a tribute to the late Blakey with Will Calhoun joining the lineup on drums, trombonist Ray Anderson and a second bassist, Jay Leonhart. Rebennack brought six compositions to this set, including "For Art's Sake," written with Anderson. Calhoun's "Tribute to Art" closes out the proceedings. — J.S.

HAMIET BLUIETT

★★★½ **Dangerously Suite (1981; Soul Note, 1993)**
★★★½ **Ebu (Soul Note, 1984)**
★★★½ **Live at Carlos I (1986; Just a Memory, 1997)**
★★★★ **Clarinet Family (Black Saint, 1987)**
★★★★ **Resolution (Black Saint, 1991)**
★★★★ **Nali Kola (Soul Note, 1993)**
★★★½ **Sankofa/Rear Garde (Soul Note, 1993)**
★★★★½ **Young Warrior, Old Warrior (Mapleshade, 1995)**
★★★★ **Bluiett's Barbecue Band (Mapleshade, 1996)**
★★★★ **Live at the Village Vanguard: Ballads and Blues (Soul Note, 1997)**
★★★★★ **Live at the Knitting Factory (Knitting Factory Records, 1998)**

Hamiet Bluiett (b. 1940) is a master of two underutilized instruments: baritone saxophone and alto clarinet. His depth-plumbing baritone work earned him a chair in the Charles Mingus band, and he is a distinctive voice in the influential World Saxophone Quartet. Bluiett is also a sought-after accompanist on many challenging recording projects.

On his own, Bluiett has worked with great sidemen as he's evolved a sound based on eclecticism and exploration of the avenues between jazz and African music. *Ebu* is a solid session with pianist John Hicks, bassist Fred Hopkins and drummer Marvin "Smitty" Smith. *Clarinet Family* is a bold exploration of the colorations produced by various clarinet players accompanied by the rhythm section of Hopkins and drummer Ronnie Burrage. The great bassist Hopkins also appears on the excellent *Resolution,* with pianist Don Pullen and percussionist Famoudou Don Moye. Bluiett's experiments with African influences started on a small scale with the 1981 session *Dangerously Suite,* which features drummer Chief Bey, and by the time of the remarkably powerful 1987 recording *Nali Kola,* he was leading a band with a dense African percussion section and poet Quincy Troupe adding declamations.

In the early 1990s Bluiett collaborated with guitarist Ted Dunbar in a quartet with bassist Clint Houston and drummer Ben Riley. The 1994 live recording *Live at the Village Vanguard: Ballads and Blues* rates the edge over the studio session *Sankofa/Rear Garde. Young Warrior, Old Warrior* is a stirring sextet date that pits Bluiett's baritone against Mark Shim's tenor saxophone and Jack Walrath's trumpet, backed by the superb rhythm section of pianist Larry Willis, bassist Keter Betts and drummer Jimmy Cobb. *Bluiett's Barbecue Band* is an engaging crossover outing that reaches back into gospel roots and R&B influences for a lively, danceable mix.

In the late 1990s Bluiett found himself performing frequently in a variety of small and large group contexts at New York's downtown mecca for avant-garde jazz, the Knitting Factory. *Live at the Knitting Factory,* recorded at the 1997 New York Jazz Festival, documents Bluiett's mind-blowing Bluiett Baritone Saxophone Group, which gathers four baritone players—Bluiett, James Carter, Patience Higgins and Alex Harding—with Ronnie Burrage kicking it all along on drums. This group rivals the interplay Bluiett enjoys with the World Saxophone Quartet. — J.S.

ARTHUR BLYTHE

★★★★ **The Grip (India Navigation, 1977)**
★★★★½ **Bush Baby (Adelphi, 1977)**
★★★½ **Metamorphosis (India Navigation, 1977)**
★★★½ **Lenox Avenue Breakdown (Columbia, 1979)**
★★★ **In the Tradition (Columbia, 1979)**
★★★★★ **Illusions (Columbia, 1980)**
★★★★★ **Blythe Spirit (Columbia, 1981)**
★★★★ **Elaborations (Columbia, 1982)**
★★★★ **Light Blue: Arthur Blythe Plays Thelonious Monk (Columbia, 1983)**
★ **Put Sunshine in It (Columbia, 1985)**
★★ **Da-Da (Columbia, 1986)**
★★★★½ **Basic Blythe (Columbia, 1988)**
★★★ **Hipmotism (Enja, 1991)**

★★★ **Retroflection: Live at the Vanguard (Enja, 1994)**
★★★ **Calling Card (Enja, 1996)**
In the late '60s and early '70s, a vital and innovative jazz scene sprang up in Los Angeles, with older players such as John Carter and Horace Tapscott schooling younger players like David Murray, James Newton and saxophonist Arthur Blythe. Unlike musicians in New York, where the battle lines between boppers and avant-gardists were stubbornly defended, the Angelinos were determined to erase boundaries. Why not play with the harmonic freedom of Ornette Coleman *and* the creamy tone of Johnny Hodges?

Arthur Blythe (b. 1940) could do both, and when he moved to New York in 1974, he turned heads with solos that began with bluesy riffs and developed into long, elegant lines that snaked inside and out of conventional harmony but always maintained a fat, oleogenous tone.

Blythe recorded with Tapscott in L.A. and played with Chico Hamilton and Gil Evans in Manhattan. His first albums as a leader, *The Grip* and *Metamorphosis,* are both taken from the same concert at a New York club and introduce an unusual band that included Bob Stewart on tuba (harkening back to New Orleans), Abdul Wadud on cello (alluding to European chamber music) and Muhamad Abdullah on congas (representing African roots). The music is imperfectly recorded and relentlessly "outside" but often quite compelling.

Bush Baby, a trio album by Stewart, Abdullah and "Black Arthur Blythe," is a more lucid statement of this early period. In this stripped-down setting, the lyricism of Blythe's writing and soloing comes through much more forcefully.

Raves in the press led to a contract with Columbia. The major-label debut, *Lenox Avenue Breakdown,* featured such notable musicians as Newton, James Blood Ulmer, Cecil McBee and Jack DeJohnette, and expansive, intoxicating music, if not the dark shadows and angularity of the early work. *In the Tradition* found Blythe proving his "inside" credentials playing tunes by Ellington, Coltrane and Waller with the Air rhythm section (bassist Fred Hopkins and drummer Steve McCall) and pianist Stanley Cowell.

If those sessions were more admirable than thrilling, they did set up the triumph of *Illusions.* On this album, Blythe used both his traditional quartet (Hopkins, McCall and pianist John Hicks) and his chamber ensemble (Stewart, Ulmer, Wadud and drummer Bobby Battle), incorporating all his vocabularies—bop, free jazz, swing, blues, gospel and R&B—into six original tunes that roiled with tension, which he then released in cathartic solos. The subsequent *Blythe Spirit,* which added Gershwin, Garner and gospel tunes to the originals, employed the same approach with most of the same musicians (Kelvyn Bell replaced Ulmer) and similarly exhilarating results.

Elaborations, featuring the quintet of Blythe, Stewart, Wadud, Battle and Bell, was almost as good if not quite as intense. On *Light Blue* the same pianoless band tackled six Monk compositions (including the rarely heard "We See" and "Coming on the Hudson"), with revealing results. After so much good music, Blythe made the dreaded commercial move with the synth-soaked *Put Sunshine in It,* a bad album by any standard. Not much better was *Da-Da,* which included two more fusion exercises, a tuba-guitar ensemble tune and three piano-combo numbers.

Blythe closed out his Columbia tenure with the controversial *Basic Blythe,* which found the saxophonist backed by a piano trio and string section. Many heard another commercial sellout, but Bob Friedman's ambitious string charts bring out both the lush sensuality and harsh blues in Blythe's playing and create romanticism in the best sense.

Blythe became the great avant-garde hope when he signed with Columbia, and his failure to grab the brass ring left many of his former supporters feeling betrayed. The saxophonist settled into a comfortable career as a coleader in such cooperative groups as the Leaders, Roots and the World Saxophone Quartet. He returned to the studio as a leader with *Hipmotism,* a respectable but unambitious project that reunites him with Bell, Stewart and World Sax partner Hamiet Bluiett.

Retroflection and *Calling Card* are both taken from the same June 1993 live performances at New York's Village Vanguard. They feature a terrific rhythm section (Hicks, McBee and Battle) and confident, sumptuous playing by the leader, but no challenges are pursued and no new territory is opened. — G.H.

CLAUDE BOLLING

★★★★ **Suite for Flute and Jazz Piano Trio (Milan, 1975)**

★★ **Concerto for Classic Guitar and Jazz Piano Trio (Milan, 1975)**
★★★ **Suite for Violin and Jazz Piano Trio (Milan, 1977)**
★★★ **Picnic Suite (CBS, 1980)**
★★★ **Jazz à la Française (CBS, 1984)**
★★★ **Jazz Brunch (CBS, 1988)**
★★ **Bolling Plays Ellington: Black, Brown, and Beige (Milan, 1990)**
★★ **Cross Over U.S.A. (Milan, 1993)**
★★★ **The Victory Concert (Milan, 1994)**
★ **Enchanting Versailles (Milan, 1995)**
★★★ **Vintage Bolling (Milan, 1995)**
★★★ **A Drum Is a Woman (Milan, 1996)**
★ **Cinema Dreams (Milan, 1996)**

For decades, the fusion of classical music and jazz into the very ephemeral compositions of the Third Stream often meant a dense and deeply theoretically based music. In the mid-1970s French composer and bandleader Claude Bolling (b. 1930) turned this equation inside out. Rather than running toward the more esoteric strains of jazz and classical, Bolling took the lighter side of the two musics, invited French virtuoso flautist Jean-Pierre Rampal along and created *Suite for Flute and Jazz Piano Trio.* Clean and nearly Baroque, it opened doors for similar sounds (such as that of Free Fall) over the next decade or so before burning itself out. The Rampal record may well have been the best, with tunes in 5/4 time to emulate Bach and Brubeck simultaneously. While the recording is somewhat stilted, Bolling and his trio manage to coax an enormous amount of swing out of the classical musician.

Bolling capitalized on the success of this double-platinum album with other classical virtuosi. The brass version, *Toot Suite* (with Maurice Andre) has fallen out of print, but the *Picnic Suite,* with Rampal's flute and Alexandre Lagoya on guitar, remains in the Sony Music catalog, and the *Concerto for Classic Guitar and Jazz Piano Trio* and *Suite for Violin and Jazz Piano Trio* have recently been reissued. Part of the problem with these recordings is that Bolling's compositions use very similar melodic and compositional elements to create a jazz ambiance. Although they sound fresh on the first album, they start to get tired in the later versions.

Nor does Alexandre Lagoya's guitar work exude the sensual charm of Rampal's flute, even when they're working together. Rampal still swings, as does Bolling's trio. On this work and the guitar concerto, the classical technique keeps Lagoya's solo passages sounding stiff. Ironically, some of his comping on the *Picnic Suite* actually swings.

So does Pinchas Zukerman's violin. His playing seems to have energized Bolling on *Suite for Violin and Jazz Piano Trio,* but the idea no longer sounds fresh. The compositions also lean more heavily on the classical chops of Zukerman than the jazz affectations of Bolling. Nothing can make the violinist sound like an improviser.

The concept gets another workout on the thematic *Cross Over U.S.A.,* three different groups playing songs with U.S. cities and states in the titles. While Bolling gets in a few good ragtime licks, the overall effect is tired. *Vintage Bolling* is a collection of these small-band outings.

Bolling displays some of these characteristics playing with just a trio on *Jazz à la Française.* Familiar phrases from the classical recordings crop up in the compositions, which can either be perceived of trademark licks or as signifying a paucity of ideas. His playing and writing show off his encyclopedic knowledge of the jazz piano, from Albert Ammons to Bill Evans, but they feel excessively academic. Despite the romantic nature of most of the pieces and the excellent technique, even despite the innate swing, the work lacks warmth.

In addition to these smaller bands Bolling leads one of the more creative contemporary big bands, a 20-piece group that assayed some of Bolling's favorite music, Duke Ellington's large-band works. Their version of "Black, Brown, and Beige," while faithful to the spirit of the original, lacks its spark and subtlety. The big band's version of "A Drum Is a Woman" swings a lot harder, mostly thanks to the vocals and the live context. Jeffrey Smith, singing all the male roles in Duke's cantata, is especially powerful, bringing great vitality to such underappreciated Ellington tunes as "You Better Know It." In the French version of the album, the great Manu Dibango performs these parts.

When it's not assaying Ellington, the big band proves a mighty swinging organization for *The Victory Concert.* Its tribute to the end of the World War II years (1944–45) captures the exuberance of the swing era and tinges it with nostalgia, like the cover of "Begin the Beguine" right from the Artie Shaw charts. The finale, "Flyin' Home," captures the sheer excitement of this flag-waver.

Bolling's charts veer into banality on *Cinema*

Dreams, comprising jazz arrangements of movie themes. Some of the song choices are too obvious, like the torchy "As Time Goes By," the "Pink Panther" theme, the tired arrangement of "Everybody Wants to Be a Cat" and the cheesy vocal arrangement of "Old Devil Moon." There are a couple of pleasant surprises—the totally uncharacteristic readings of "La Strada" and "A Pair of Twins" (from *The Young Girls of Rochefort*) shine like baubles in this sea of dross.

Bolling returned to the classical half of the equation for *Enchanting Versailles,* an album of his composed works. These retro, romantic chamber works (two trios, a duet and a sonata for solo guitar) are inoffensive but soporific. — H.B.

GRAHAM BOND

★★★ **Solid Bond (Warner Bros., 1970)**
★★ **Holy Magick (Vertigo, U.K., 1971)**
★★ **We Put the Magick on You (Mercury, 1974)**
★★ **This Is Graham Bond (Philips, U.K., 1978)**
★★★ **Live at Klook's Kleek (Decal/Charly, 1990)**

A gruff and burly presence on the English pop scene in the early '60s, Graham Bond (1937–1974) was instrumental in spurring British interest in R&B. Beginning as a jazz saxophonist with a special devotion to Charles Mingus, he switched to organ and vocals when joining with drummer Ginger Baker, double-bassist Jack Bruce and guitarist John McLaughlin (all three graduates of Alexis Korner's Blues Incorporated) as the Graham Bond Organisation. *Solid Bond* (now out of print) features Bond on alto and piano as well as organ, playing in 1963 at the ultrahip nightclub Klook's Kleek. The extended jazz cuts (Sonny Rollins's "Doxy," Bond and McLaughlin's "The Grass Is Greener") are only capable, but the R&B stuff kicks—as their later careers obviously proved, Bond's musicians were first-rate, and their promise is readily apparent even at this early date.

Live at Klook's Kleek, a 1965 club date, is even stronger. The album's production values are primitive, but the crude sound and smoke-and-ale ambiance only add atmosphere to a session of fierce blues and jazz-tinged soul. Baker, in particular, comes across as a monster, and Bond's deep voice thunders. Always a catalyst and cult figure, never a star, Bond suffered through heroin addiction in the '60s and then, in 1971, formed Holy Magick with his wife, singer Diane Stewart. Divorce soon followed, and Bond's preoccupation with the occult reached the point of obsession (he began believing he was the son of black magician Aleister Crowley). He died mysteriously, under the wheels of a (parked) subway train. — P.E.

JUKE BOY BONNER

★★★★ **Life Gave Me a Dirty Deal (Arhoolie, 1993)**

Weldon "Juke Boy" Bonner (1932–1978) grew up in rural Texas during the Depression and migrated to Houston, where he discovered and emulated Lightnin' Hopkins, developing an open-ended boogie guitar style to accompany his story-songs about personal experiences and his philosophical observations about life. Working as a one-man human jukebox in neighborhood taverns, he also played rack harmonica in response to his vocal lines.

During his convalesence from a stomach operation in 1963, Bonner wrote poetry and became a regular contributor to the Houston newspaper *Forward Times.* When he became healthy enough to perform again, he began setting these poems to music. The material on *Life Gave Me a Dirty Deal,* recorded between 1967 and '69, offers an extraordinarily personal account of a nearly destitute black musician in Houston. The stark detail of songs like "Going Back to the Country," "Stay Off Lyons Avenue" and "Over Ten Years Ago" offers an amazingly vivid glimpse into the bleak life and indomitable spirit of one of the most creative itinerant blues musicians in history. — J.S.

ROY BOOK BINDER

★★★½ **Bookeroo! (Rounder, 1988)**
★★★½ **Roy Book Binder and the Hillbilly Blues Cats (Rounder, 1992)**
★★★½ **Live Book . . . Don't Start Me Talkin' . . . (Rounder, 1994)**

Roy Book Binder (b. 1943) is a singer, guitarist and storyteller whose infatuation with prewar country blues led him to travel and study with the Rev. Gary Davis in the '60s and with Pink Anderson in the early '70s. Book Binder subsequently recorded several albums that chronicle his fine playing and arranging and contain tunes by some of the greatest country/blues songsters. Dobro master Jerry Douglas produced and played on *Bookeroo!,* which features such noted bluegrass players as guitarist Russ Barenberg and bassist Edgar Meyer, underscoring the fact that country, blues, folk and bluegrass are very closely related forms. Included here are songs like the overtly phallic "Cigarette Blues," which was recorded in 1936 by Bo Carter, a man Book Binder describes in the liner notes as "master of the single entendre." There's also a jaunty version of Ray Charles's and Percy Mayfield's "Tell Me How Do You Feel" and a matter-of-fact reading of Merle Haggard's "Nobody Knows I'm Hurtin'."

On *The Hillbilly Blues Cats* Book Binder fronts a tasteful duo of harmonica honker Rock Bottom and bassist Billy Ochoa, who roll through a mixture of original and cover songs, as well as interpretations of five public-domain numbers. Included here is a Dave Van Ronk–inspired version of "One Meat Ball," a tune Josh White brought to the masses in 1945. The trio also does a graceful version of Blind Willie McTell's most famous song, "Statesboro Blues," and a rendition of Happy Traum's "Mississippi John"—a tribute to the immortal Mississippi John Hurt—on which Book Binder's guitar line echoes the lick from Hurt's "My Creole Belle." Recorded in Athens, Ohio, in 1993, *Live Book* captures Book Binder's raw musical skills and storytelling abilities. His monolog preceding a version of "Candy Man" is a revealing and humorous account of his first meeting with the Rev. Davis. Throughout this solo acoustic effort, Book Binder displays an intrinsic skill on such songs as Davis's "Hesitation Blues," which segues neatly into "That Old-Time Religion" because, according to Book Binder, that's how he learned it.

— B.R.H.

JAMES BOOKER

★★★★ **Junco Partner (1976; Hannibal, 1993)**
★★★★ **New Orleans Piano Wizard: Live! (1981; Rounder, 1983)**
★★★★ **Classified (Rounder, 1983)**
★★★★★ **Spiders on the Keys (Rounder, 1993)**
★★★★★ **Resurrection of the Bayou Maharajah (Rounder, 1993)**
★★★½ **The Lost Paramount Tapes (DJM, 1995)**
★★★★ **Gonzo: More Than All the 45s (Night Train, 1996)**

A classically trained pianist, the late James Booker (1939–1983) is as revered in New Orleans as fellow native sons Louis Armstrong and Professor Longhair. Booker moved away from classical and into gospel and blues by the time he was 12, when he landed his own radio show; at 14 he made his first record, "Doing the Hambone," for Imperial. Producer Dave Bartholomew subsequently employed Booker as a session player, sometimes using his keyboard wizardry to support Fats Domino's studio vocals. After graduating high school, Booker went on the road with Joe Tex, whose label, Ace, hired the pianist to do sessions. As Booker's reputation grew, so did the touring offers, and Booker was eager to please. At one point he went out impersonating Huey "Piano" Smith, who hated to travel but had contractual commitments for shows beyond New Orleans.

Finally, in 1960, Booker hit with "Gonzo" (the title became an all-too-appropriate nickname for Booker himself), but rather than pursue a solo career he continued over the next 15 years to tour as a sideman with the day's most important R&B names. *Gonzo* collects Booker's early singles, recorded for various labels between 1954 and 1962. "Doing the Hambone" is the earliest example of Booker's precocious piano style, but "Gonzo," "Beale Street Popeye" and "The Duck" showcase an original at work. In 1977 a promoter convinced Booker to perform a series of solo concerts in Europe. An instant success, Booker went on to cut one studio and three live albums for European labels.

A heroin addict for many years, Booker was given to strange behavior that fueled his legend. One night he is reputed to have pulled a gun onstage and threatened to shoot himself if customers didn't start filling up the tip jar. In the last year of his life, claiming to be bored with the piano, he took a job typing and filing at New Orleans City Hall. On the day sessions were to begin for his *Classified* album, he refused to play the rehearsed material and instead tore into some jazz and classical material that went nowhere; on the second day, he deposited himself in a corner of the studio and would not move. Finally his producer and sax player lifted him bodily onto his piano stool and ordered him to play. Two days later, he did.

A pair of Booker albums were released in the United States before his death from intestinal bleeding and heart and lung failure. *Junco Partner,* Booker's first full-length studio LP, was recorded in 1975 and displays the full range of his talent, from New Orleans standards like the title track and "Make a Better World" to "Sunny Side of the Street," a Chopin waltz, his own

"Blues Minuet" and Liberace's theme song, "I'll Be Seeing You." *New Orleans Piano Wizard: Live!* was recorded in Zurich and originally released in Germany. Mischievous in performance, Booker offers "Something Stupid"—a choice indicative of Booker's unabashed love for a wide range of music, especially pop and rock—as a march, but injects a quote from "Tea for Two" at the end before closing it out with a bombastic cadenza. In that sense, Booker was always good for a laugh, but he could also get deep into material that touched his emotions on a more fundamental level. His teary-eyed vocal on Percy Mayfield's "Please Send Me Someone to Love" has the feel of something being pulled from a part of his soul that outsiders were rarely allowed to see.

Despite the tumultuous circumstances surrounding its recording, *Classified* is a wry, intelligent work. Having assimilated the styles of the long line of influential New Orleans pianists, Booker shows off the full panoply of technique at his command. "Professor Longhair Medley," comprising "Bald Head" and "Tipitina," is jaunty, bluesy, evocative, searching; the medley is a form Booker used often to explore a range of common emotional and tonal colors within a single, extended piece rather than playing each song separately. After assaying Roger Miller's "King of the Road," Booker reaches into the Sinatra canon again for a poignant instrumental version of "Angel Eyes" that is a smooth melding of blues and classical influences.

Ten years after Booker's death, Rounder released two must-have titles, *Spiders on the Keys* and *Resurrection of the Bayou Maharajah,* culled from more than 60 hours of tapes recorded at New Orleans's Maple Leaf Bar between 1977 and 1982. Having separated the wheat from the chaff, producers Scott Billington and John Parsons have delivered, in Billington's words, "what you might have heard if you got lucky and caught one of Booker's best Maple Leaf sets, for his inconsistency in those years could weed out all but the most patient fans." *Spiders* is an all-instrumental collection best exemplified in its variety by, say, the way an exhilarating, syncopated version of "Eleanor Rigby" gives way to an impressionistic bebop interpretation of "Malagueña." Or the contrast between a Baroque rendition of "A Taste of Honey" and a lilting, lyrical (and for Booker, minimalist) exploration of "Over the Rainbow." Despite all his right-hand flourishes (and one recalls with some amusement how he would cite Liberace as an influence), Booker always kept the melody in sight; indeed, he favored songs with strong, memorable melodies. Much of the emotional pull of his work comes less from the technical mastery he displayed than from the great heart evident in his restless search to find even more beauty deep below the surface of songs already beloved for that quality.

The companion set, *Resurrection,* highlights vocal performances over instrumental ones and shows Booker at his most engaging, moaning the blues, mimicking other instruments, yodeling, shouting out some rock & roll, chastising the audience and turning lyrics inside out like a jazz singer who subverts the harmonic and melodic line to unearth nuances of new meaning in well-worn material. One of Booker's finest recorded vocal performances is here in "Papa Was a Rascal" (there's a lesser take of it on the *Spiders* album). At song's end he tempers the New Orleans rock & roll mode he's in by reverting to a slow blues while lamenting, "My papa was a rascal/Why can't I be one too?" before picking up the pace again. It's a startling, revelatory moment, made more so by the fury with which his right hand attacks the keys, glissandos cascading one over the other until slowly winding down to silence.

One of Booker's most powerful recorded moments is his bleak interpretation of "St. James Infirmary," which starts in the grave and stays there. Casting himself as the jilted lover who sees no future in the wake of his woman's leaving, Booker mourns in a high and trembling voice, "She's gone/Let's just say they gonna bless her/Wherever she may be," then takes it home with a series of minor-chord glissandos.

The liner booklet for *Spiders* cites Booker's explanation to a newspaper reporter as to why he went to work for City Hall (the liner notes for both Maple Leaf Bar albums include a number of amazing and hilarious anecdotes of Booker's oddities as witnessed over the years by his friends and associates). Said Booker: "You don't want to stay with piano all the time. Too much piano ain't good for you. Too much water ain't good for you, either. It makes you drown." Fans will agree, though, that with Booker and these four fine albums, there was never too much piano. — D.M.

BOOKER T. AND THE MG'S

★★★½ **Green Onions (1962; Atlantic, 1991)**

★★★ **Soul Dressing (1965; Atlantic, 1991)**

★★★ **And Now! Booker T. and the MG's (1966; Rhino/Atlantic, 1992)**
★★★½ **Back to Back (Stax, 1967)**
★★★★ **The Best of Booker T. and the MG's (Atlantic, 1968)**
★★★ **Doin' Our Thing (1968; Rhino/Atlantic, 1992)**
★★★½ **Hip Hug-Her (1968; Rhino/Atlantic, 1992)**
★★★ **Soul Limbo (Stax, 1968)**
★★★ **Uptight (Stax, 1968)**
★★★ **The Booker T. Set (Stax, 1969)**
★★★ **McLemore Avenue (Stax, 1970)**
★★★ **Melting Pot (Stax, 1971)**
★★★★ **Booker T. and the MG's Greatest Hits (Atlantic, 1974)**
★★★ **Memphis Sound (Warner Bros., 1975)**
★★★ **Union Extended (Warner Bros., 1976)**
★★★½ **Time Is Tight (Warner Bros., 1976)**
★★★ **Universal Language (Asylum, 1977)**
★★½ **Try and Love Again (A&M, 1978)**
★★★½ **That's the Way It Should Be (Columbia, 1994)**

Adding sinew and polish to the Memphis Sound, Booker T. and the MG's ("MG" = Memphis Group) honed their skills by backing Otis Redding and a host of Stax all-stars and recording as part of the Mar-Keys. The soul of efficiency, the quartet boasted virtuosic players adamant in their insistence that less is more. One of the inventors of funk guitar, Steve Cropper flourished rhythm work that formed a deft series of trebly, swift riffs; his telegraphic leads never overstated. Donald "Duck" Dunn rarely relied on the blues tropes of most R&B players—his bass, instead, provided essential punctuation. Al Jackson's spare drumming was soul music's counterpart to that of Rolling Stone Charlie Watts. Only Booker T. Jones, a teenage wunderkind when he started at Stax, was a more expansive talent—and the eloquence of his organ lent the band's records an insinuating grace.

The band's '60s instrumentals are its masterworks. "Green Onions" (#3 pop), "Time Is Tight" (#6 pop), "Hip Hug-Her," "Groovin'" and "Soul Limbo" are singles that can't be improved upon. While something of a curio, *McLemore Avenue,* featuring covers of all the songs on the Beatles' *Abbey Road,* remains interesting. With standout covers of "It Was Just My Imagination" and "I Can't Stand the Rain," the 1994 reunion set rekindles the old spark. All of the Stax records have worthwhile cuts; and each of the best-of compilations is timeless, elegant funk. — P.E.

LESTER BOWIE
★★ **Numbers 1 & 2 (Nessa, 1968)**
★★★★ **Fast Last! (Muse, 1974)**
★★★½ **Rope-a-Dope (Muse, 1976)**
★★★★½ **The 5th Power (Black Saint, 1978)**
★★★½ **From the Roots to the Source (Soul Note, 1980)**
★★★ **All the Magic/The One and Only (ECM, 1983)**
★★★★ **The Great Pretender (ECM, 1988)**
★★★ **Works (ECM, 1989)**
★★★½ **My Way (DIW, 1990)**
★★ **Duet (with Phillip Wilson) (I.A.I., 1993)**
★★★ **Not Two Live (Gowi, 1995)**

LESTER BOWIE'S BRASS FANTASY
★★★★½ **I Only Have Eyes for You (ECM, 1985)**
★★★★ **Avant Pop (ECM, 1986)**
★★★½ **Twilight Dreams (Venture/Virgin, 1988)**
★★★½ **Serious Fun (DIW, 1989)**
★★★½ **The Fire This Time (In + Out, 1995)**

LESTER BOWIE'S NEW YORK ORGAN ENSEMBLE
★★★ **The Organizer (DIW, 1991)**
★★★★ **Funky T, Cool T (DIW, 1991)**

In pop music it's not unusual to find singers and musicians with limited technical skills who succeed by the sheer force of their personality and innovations, but it's always been rare in jazz. Such a rarity, however, is Lester Bowie (b. 1941), a mediocre technical trumpeter but a performer so charismatic and a conceptualist so fiercely original that he overshadows dozens of trumpeters who can play rings around him.

Best known as a member of the Art Ensemble of Chicago, Bowie has carved out a solo career where his personality and obsessions emerge forcefully. Bowie's stage presence—he wears a long, white doctor's smock and pointy goatee and dances between trumpet parts—underscores his belief that African-American music is about more than just the music: It should include elements of ritual, theater and showmanship. Even on his recordings, where the visual element is missing, the emphasis on ritual comes through, for the focus is not on tricky chord changes and show-off solos but on moody atmospherics, exploratory quests, mournful dirges, determined processionals and joyful shouts.

The Art Ensemble's motto is "Great black music, ancient to the future," and Bowie selects from that spectrum the forms most reflective of ritual–Third World ceremonial music, gospel hymns, gutbucket blues, New Orleans brass parades and rhythm & blues dances.

Bowie was born in Frederick, Maryland, but grew up in St. Louis. As the photographs on the cover of *All the Magic/The One and Only* testify, his father, uncles and grandfather all played in pre–World War II brass bands. The younger Bowie played in school, Air Force and local hard-bop bands before hitting the road with such R&B stars as Albert King, Aretha Franklin, the Temptations and Fontella Bass (whom he married). He even traveled with an old-fashioned tent show, Leon Claxton's Harlem Revue.

In 1966, Bowie landed in Chicago, where he met pianist/composer Muhal Richard Abrams and his Association for the Advancement of Creative Musicians. Inspired by the group's willingness to try unusual approaches to jazz, the young trumpeter began rehearsing with other AACM members and in 1969 in Paris formed the Art Ensemble of Chicago with the bassist Malachi Favors and saxophonists Joseph Jarman and Roscoe Mitchell. (Percussionist Don Moye joined in 1970.)

Bowie's first album as a leader is 1968's *Numbers 1 & 2,* which is actually a prototype for the Art Ensemble, as it includes four of the eventual five members. The free-form explorations seem tentative, as if the musicians are seeking a sound they haven't found yet.

Fast Last! is far more focused. The 1974 session includes Bowie's old St. Louis compadres—alto saxophonist Julius Hemphill, his kid brother Joseph Bowie on trombone and drummer Phillip Wilson—plus two mainstreamers, pianist John Hicks and bassist Cecil McBee. The humor is already evident in a long drumroll piece called "F Troop Rides Again" and an affectionately irreverent reading of "Hello, Dolly!" Bowie's instinct for the perfect flamboyant gesture also makes itself felt on two wonderful Hemphill compositions.

Almost as good is *Rope-a-Dope,* which features a title song as unorthodox as the Muhammad Ali boxing strategy it's named after. Favors, Moye and Joe Bowie also help the leader turn the brass-band tradition inside out on their version of "St. Louis Blues."

The 5th Power assembles a great band (Favors, Wilson, Arthur Blythe and Amina Myers) behind Bowie and finds them in an expansive, exclamatory mood. The highlight is the 18-minute version of the old hymn "God Has Smiled on Me," which begins with Myers's vocal and follows with Bowie and Blythe testifying on their horns. Bowie experiments further with vocals on *From the Roots to the Source;* gospel-soul singers Fontella Bass and David Peaston prove they can wail as wildly as any avant-garde horn player.

From there the next logical step was R&B. *The Great Pretender* took its title from a 16-minute version of the Platters' 1956 hit single, which featured Bowie's trumpet braying and twisting notes like an R&B singer improvising an endless, maddened coda. The album also features three of Bowie's most lyrical free-jazz pieces.

I Only Have Eyes for You was also named after an old R&B hit, the Flamingos' 1959 doo-wop arrangement of the standard, but it's most noteworthy for introducing Lester Bowie's Brass Fantasy, a nonet of four trumpets, two trombones, tuba, French horn and drums. Based on the format of New Orleans brass parade bands, the Brass Fantasy sounded like the Dirty Dozen Brass Band but took considerably more liberties with the form. "Coming Back, Jamaica," for example, was "When the Saints Go Marching In" set to a reggae beat, while "When the Spirit Returns" was a hymn done as a slow-motion burlesque vamp.

In 1983 Bowie released a double album with two titles and two very different sets of music. The first disc, *All the Magic,* is a quintet date with two R&B tunes, a loosey-goosey tribute to Louis Armstrong, Albert Ayler's "Ghosts" and three rather abstract Bowie originals. The second disc, *The One and Only,* consists of a dozen short, unaccompanied, mostly unrewarding pieces, including "Miles Davis Meets Donald Duck," which sums up the simultaneous seriousness and irreverence of Bowie's aesthetic—not to mention his often quacking tone. *Works* anthologizes of tracks from Bowie's previous ECM albums, but the selections don't make a lot of sense as either a best-of or an introduction.

Avant Pop, *Twilight Dreams*, *Serious Fun* and *The Fire This Time* were all vehicles for Bowie's brass bands, which had developed a choirlike sense of harmony and rapport. There were plenty of R&B songs, such as "Blueberry Hill" and "Thriller," several jazz-funk originals and even a Willie Nelson tune. Trombonist Steve Turre stepped forward as a dominant figure, composing the majestic "Emperor" as well as tributes to Machito and Duke Ellington and playing solos that were as moving as they were unorthodox. *The Fire This Time,* recorded at a Swiss nightclub in 1992 the day after the L.A. Rodney King riots, reprised many of the studio numbers in even more boisterous versions.

In addition to Brass Fantasy and the Art Ensemble, Bowie also played with a superb sextet called the Leaders. In 1991 he unveiled yet another outfit, Lester Bowie's New York Organ Ensemble, devoted to his quirky take on the jazz-soul organ trios led by the likes of Jimmy Smith, "Groove" Holmes and Jack McDuff. In the organ role, he cast his old friend Myers and surrounded her with Turre, Wilson, Moye and a then unknown Detroit saxophonist named James Carter. The group sounds tentative and underrehearsed on *The Organizer* but clicks into focus on *Funky T, Cool T,* which finds Carter blowing strong and Bowie blowing strange over the organ/drum groove. — G.H.

EDDIE BOYD

★★★★ Eddie Boyd and His Blues Band (1967; Deram, 1994)

★★★★ Five Long Years (Evidence, 1994)

One thing about any record label—there's room for only so many stars. On the all-too-crowded roster of Chicago's Chess Records it was inevitable that certain deserving artists would be overlooked in favor of their better-known blues colleagues. Pianist/singer Eddie Boyd, born in 1914 in Mississippi, was one of those unfortunate few, and after scoring a number of blues hits in the early '50s, he eventually followed the Memphis Slim route: touring Europe and then relocating there.

Buoyed by self-consciously jazzy vocals and economic piano playing, Boyd's style seems to have taken the urbane influence of Leroy Carr and Memphis Slim and added in a liberal dose of Billy Eckstine. His classics (and Top 10 R&B hits)—"Third Degree" and the languid "24 Hours" (with rim shots striking off the clock beats)—confirm Boyd's lyrical prowess and are well worth checking out on Chess's *The Blues* series (Vols. 4 and 5, respectively). "Hard Headed Woman," "It's Miserable to Be Alone" and his signature, "Five Long Years," are available on the Paula collection *Chicago Piano 1951–58 from Cobra and Job.*

British blues producer Mike Vernon put Boyd together with some of the biggest names on England's blues scene for *Eddie Boyd and His Blues Band.* The all-star cast includes Peter Green on guitar, John Mayall on harp, John McVie on bass and Aynsley Dunbar on drums. *Five Long Years* is a strong, postexile session featuring Boyd on piano and organ, Buddy Guy on guitar, a Chicago rhythm section and guest vocals by Big Mama Thornton. Recorded in the United Kingdom in 1965, it features many tunes written by Boyd but not previously recorded.
— A.K.

JOANNE BRACKEEN

★★★★ Fi-Fi Goes to Heaven (Concord Jazz, 1986)

★★★★ Maybeck Recital Hall Series, Vol. 1 (Concord Jazz, 1989)

★★★★ Where Legends Dwell (Ken, 1991)

★★★★½ Breath of Brazil (Concord Picante, 1991)

★★★★ Take a Chance (Concord Picante, 1994)

★★★★ Power Talk (Turnipseed, 1994)

★★★★½ Turnaround (Evidence, 1995)

Pianist Joanne Grogan (b. 1938) made a name for herself among musicians in the late 1950s on West Coast performances with musicians such as Dexter Gordon, Harold Land and Charles Lloyd. After marrying saxophonist/trumpeter Charles Brackeen, she started a second phase of her career in New York, garnering a tremendous response to her work with Woody Shaw, Dave Liebman, Art Blakey's Jazz Messengers, Joe Henderson and Stan Getz, among others.

By the late 1970s Brackeen was a budding star, mesmerizing audiences with her incredible stylistic range and technique, often in duo and trio performances at Manhattan piano bars such as Bradley's and Top of the Gate. Brackeen can shift from powerful rhythmic crescendos reminiscent of McCoy Tyner to lucid, bare-bones Chick Corea–style melodies during a performance that is seldom less than romantic.

Unfortunately, much of Brackeen's early work is unavailable. Look for the out-of-print *Ancient Dynasty*, *Special Identity* and *Snooze.* Of the material available, *Fi-Fi Goes to Heaven* demonstrates her compositional strength, *Maybeck Recital Hall Series* documents a stunning solo recital and *Where Legends Dwell* is a beautiful trio date with stalwart accompanists Eddie Gomez on bass and Jack DeJohnette on drums.

Recorded at New York's Sweet Basil in 1992

with Cecil McBee on bass, Marvin "Smitty" Smith on drums and Donald Harrison on alto saxophone, *Turnaround* is a superb quartet performance. The Ornette Coleman–written title track showcases Brackeen at her best.

On *Breath of Brazil* Brackeen expands her scope into works by Antonio Carlos Jobim, Gilberto Gil and Egberto Gismonte, as well as making her own comment on the Brazilian tradition with three originals including the title track. Brackeen was certainly familiar with Brazilian music through her work with Getz, but her thorough assimilation of the style, with Eddie Gomez on bass, Duduka Da Fonseca on drums and Waltino Anastácio on percussion, remains a remarkable achievement. *Take a Chance,* titled after one of Brackeen's best compositions, reassembles the same group. *Power Talk* is a tour-de-force live performance recorded in New Orleans in 1994 with bassist Ira Coleman and drummer Tony Reedus.
— J.S.

CARMEN BRADFORD

★★★½ **With Respect (Evidence, 1995)**

Vocalist Carmen Bradford (b. 1960) is the daughter of singer Melba Joyce and trumpet player Bobby Bradford, who replaced Don Cherry in the Ornette Coleman Quartet. Bradford's influences tend toward classic blues and R&B, although she also emulates the more formal style of Ella Fitzgerald. Her affinity for the blues made her a natural to front the Count Basie band for nine years, but on her own she handles a more pop-oriented program deftly. *With Respect* benefits from the presence of pianist Cedar Walton, a superb accompanist who nurtures Bradford along beautifully, especially on the duet "Maybe Now." — J.S.

RUBY BRAFF

★★★½ **Hustlin' and Bustlin' (Black Lion, 1988)**
★★★ **Me, Myself and I (Concord Jazz, 1989)**
★★★ **Bravura Eloquence (Concord Jazz, 1990)**
★★★ **Hear Me Talkin' (Black Lion, 1991)**
★★★½ **Ruby Braff and His New England Songhounds, Vol. 1 (Concord Jazz, 1991)**
★★★½ **Ruby Braff and His New England Songhounds, Vol. 2 (Concord Jazz, 1992)**
★★★ **Very Sinatra (Red Baron, 1993)**
★★★ **Live at the Regattabar (Arbors, 1994)**
★★★ **Cornet Chop Suey (Concord Jazz, 1994)**
★★½ **Controlled Nonchalance at the Regattabar, Vol. 1 (Arbors, 1994)**
★★½ **Controlled Nonchalance at the Regattabar, Vol. 2 (Arbors, 1996)**

Ruby Braff (b. 1927) is an excellent traditional trumpet/cornet player who was overlooked when he arrived on the scene in the '50s, playing with traditional players like Vic Dickenson, Pee Wee Russell, Bud Freeman and Urbie Green, because his style was considered out of date. Despite such obvious influences as Louis Armstrong and Bobby Hackett, Braff's approach has always remained personal and full of conviction.

Hustlin' and Bustlin' is a blazing set with Dickenson's trombone in full voice. *Hear Me Talkin'* is another hot outing with a crack British trad group. *Very Sinatra* features excellent accompaniment from keyboardist Dick Hyman. The Concord releases document a return to top form in a trio format and the outstanding sextet dates with the New England Songhounds—pianist Dave McKenna, tenor saxophonist Scott Hamilton, bassist Frank Tate, guitarist Howard Alden and drummer Alan Dawson. — J.S.

BILLY BRANCH

★★★½ **Live '82 (1982; Evidence, 1994)**
★★★★ **Where's My Money? (1984; Evidence, 1995)**

Vocalist/harmonica player Billy Branch (b. 1951) grew up in Los Angeles and moved to Chicago at age 17, just in time to take part in the blues explosion that was taking over the city. The young harmonicist sat in all over town, learning techniques from Junior Wells, James Cotton, Big Walter Horton and Carey Bell.

Branch went on to play in bands led by Jimmy Walker and Willie Dixon before cofounding the S.O.B.s (Sons of Blues) band, sharing the front-man position with guitarist/vocalist Lurrie Bell (Carey's son). *Live '82* is an uneven live set recorded during a European tour, highlighted by some terrific harmonica work from Branch.

Where's My Money?, a studio effort, is much more polished, with Jimmy Walker guesting on piano and vocals. Branch shows himself to be a more-than-capable vocalist on the title track and takes on Little Walter's harp legacy with the fiery instrumental "Son of Juke." The band, in excellent form throughout, does a bang-up job converting James Brown's "Sex Machine" into a funk medley of Brown themes. — J.S.

BRAND NEW HEAVIES

★★ **The Brand New Heavies (Delicious Vinyl/Capitol, 1991)**
★★★★ **Heavy Rhyme Experience, Vol. 1 (Delicious Vinyl/Capitol, 1992)**
★★½ **Brother/Sister (Delicious Vinyl/Capitol, 1994)**
★★ **Excursions: Remixes & Rare Grooves (Delicious Vinyl/Capitol, 1995)**
★½ **Original Flava (Acid Jazz/Hollywood, 1995)**

Playing funky jazz-influenced house music, guitarist Simon Bartholomew, bassist Andrew Levy and drummer/keyboardist Jan Kincaid pioneered the British acid-jazz scene with their group Brand New Heavies, which also helped to popularize the soulful blend of R&B, jazz, funk and hip-hop in the United States. Brand New Heavies' stateside self-titled debut opens with a virtual statement of purpose called "BNH," an instrumental track with a slow retro-'70s funk groove complemented by a complex, horn-accented rhythm pattern. On other cuts, featured vocalist N'Dea Davenport matches the Heavies' soulful playing with her own fervent style.

Heavy Rhyme Experience, Vol. 1 marks a vast improvement in the group's sound. Not unlike Guru's *Jazzmatazz, Heavy Rhyme* pairs the Brand New Heavies with some of rap's biggest stars, and the ferment they create is almost unmatched in similar pairings. In what feels like a live jam session rather than a studio affair, the guest rappers bring out the funkiest side of the Heavies and vice versa. Black Sheep, Pharcyde, Gang Starr and Grand Puba are among the coconspirators who give each track a unique flavor whether it be reggae, complex rhyming or even a hard-core gangsta style, while the Heavies improvise their own dirty funk.

On *Brother/Sister,* the Heavies return to the sonic realm of their debut, this time with Davenport a full-fledged band member. The improvisational fun of *Heavy Rhyme* does turn up on the opener, "Have a Good Time," with clearly funkier rhythms than on the first record.

Excursions: Remixes & Rare Grooves combines remixes and unreleased material; however, the remixes fail to improve the tracks, and some just simply fall flat. More of a dance/R&B affair and overall a limp recording, *Excursions* is for the clubhound and collector only, delivering its best track in "Country Funkin'." Reissued stateside by Hollywood Records, *Original Flava* collects older material originally available only in the United Kingdom. Many of the tracks feature Kincaid on vocals, illustrating that his move to the drum kit was a wise one. — G.E.

ANTHONY BRAXTON

★★★★★ **Three Compositions of New Jazz (1968; Delmark, 1989)**
★★★★ **For Alto (1969; Delmark, 1990)**
★★★½ **In the Tradition, Vol. 1 (Inner City, 1974)**
★★★½ **In the Tradition, Vol. 2 (Inner City, 1976)**
★★★★ **Creative Orchestra Music 1976 (1976; RCA Bluebird, 1987)**
★★★★ **Anthony Braxton Live (1976; RCA Bluebird, 1988)**
★★★½ **One in Two—Two in One (with Max Roach) (Hat Hut, 1979)**
★★★★ **Alto Saxophone Improvisations (Arista, 1979)**
★★★½ **Open Aspects '82 (hat Art, 1982)**
★★★½ **Six Compositions: Quartet (Antilles, 1982)**
★★★★ **Composition 113 (PolyGram Imports, 1984)**
★★★★ **Seven Standards 1985, Vol. I (Magenta/Windham Hill, 1985)**
★★★★ **Seven Standards 1985, Vol. II (Magenta/Windham Hill, 1986)**
★★★★★ **Six Monk's Compositions (1987; Black Saint, 1988)**
★★★ **Duets Vancouver 1989 (Music and Arts Programs of America, 1990)**
★★★★★ **Dortmund (Quartet—1976) (Hat Hut, 1991)**
★★★ **Eugene (1989) (Black Saint, 1991)**
★★★★ **Eight Compositions: Hamburg 1991 (Music and Arts Programs of America, 1992)**
★★★ **8 Duets (Music and Arts Programs of America, 1992)**
★★★ **Willisau (Quartet) (Hat Hut, 1992)**
★★★★ **Open Aspects 1982 (Duo) (Hat Hut, 1993)**
★★★★ **Wesleyan (12 Alto Solos) (Hat Hut, 1993)**
★★★★ **4 (Ensemble) Compositions—1992 (Black Saint, 1993)**
★★★★ **Twelve Compositions (Music and Arts Programs of America, 1994)**

★★★★ **Together Alone (with Joseph Jarman) (Delmark, 1994)**
★★★★ **Creative Orchestra Music 1976 (Koln 1978) (Hat Hut, 1995)**
★★★★ **Charlie Parker Project 1993 (Hat Hut, 1995)**
★★★★ **Solo Piano (Standards) 1995 (No More Records, 1995)**
★★★★ **Yoshi's 1994 (Music and Arts Programs of America, 1996)**
★★★★ **Composition No. 173 (Black Saint, 1996)**
★★★★ **Braxton at the Leipzig Gewandhaus (Music and Arts Programs of America, 1996)**
★★★★ **Piano Quartet (Music and Arts Programs of America, 1996)**

While Anthony Braxton's expert readings of Clifford Brown and Paul Robeson pieces on *Seven Standards 1985, Vol. I* and of John Coltrane, Thelonious Monk and Charlie Parker works on *Vol. II* demonstrate unequivocably his mastery of jazz that's recognizable to the conventional listener, this saxophonist is best considered as a titan of the avant-garde. Unabashedly intellectual, Braxton (b. 1945) has committed his daunting musical theories to print—the combined eight volumes of *Tri-Axium Writing* and *Composition Notes*—and the sounds those texts explicate have generally been just as challenging as his prose. The blues basis of much of his music can lure the novice; the man's virtuosity on woodwinds from clarinet to all sorts of saxes is undeniable; Braxton's industry is intimidating. And his fusion of post–Ornette Coleman jazz and contemporary classical music (finding a rough match in the sensibility of Cecil Taylor) is the very definition of "demanding."

The double album *For Alto* (1969) is early Braxton, unaccompanied, intense and, for all but the most fearless free-jazz follower, well-nigh inscrutable. By the time of *The Complete Braxton* (a 1971 Arista recording, now out of print), the composer, in league with Chick Corea, Barry Altschul and Dave Holland, had incorporated the influence of such modern European giants as Stockhausen, Schoenberg and Varèse—and was beginning to work in the orchestral idiom. *Creative Orchestra Music 1976* is the triumph of that style; it's sweeping, colorful and overwhelmingly ambitious. The unavailable *New York (Fall 1974)* may be the most accessible Braxton—a saxophone quartet blowing brave new sound. *Dortmund (Quartet—1976)* is also approachable: With bassist Dave Holland, trombonist George Lewis and drummer Barry Altschul, Braxton turns in a fragmented circus march and plays with a kind of exultation that puts muscle behind his theory. Both *Six Compositions: Quartet* and *Open Aspects '82* offer pieces that can be enjoyed by nonmusicologists; *Six Monk's Compositions* comes closest to planet Earth jazz.

For the tougher stuff, listeners are directed to two masterworks. *Twelve Compositions* is live thunder: Countermelodies abound, the players work at intentional cross purposes and pianist Marilyn Crispell matches Braxton at conveying a musical complexity that reflects a fierce, very private intelligence. *Charlie Parker Project 1993* is awesome in its ambition: Rather than attempting anything close to Bird's trademark sound, Braxton attempts instead a reading of Bird's high-flying, boundary-breaking motivation; he doesn't play Parker so much as become Parker's struggle. And he leaves you breathless. — P.E.

JOSHUA BREAKSTONE

★★★½ **Evening Star (Contemporary, 1989)**
★★★ **Self-Portrait in Swing (Contemporary, 1990)**
★★★ **9 by 3 (Contemporary, 1991)**
★★★½ **Walk, Don't Run (Evidence, 1993)**
★★★★ **Remembering Grant Green (Evidence, 1996)**
★★★ **Let's Call This Monk! (Double-Time, 1997)**

Guitarist Joshua Breakstone (b. 1955) has a rich, hornlike tone and plays in a rhythmic style influenced by Lee Morgan's and Clifford Brown's trumpet playing and Charlie Parker's approach to alto saxophone.

The New Jersey native played in rock bands while studying jazz technique with Sal Salvador, then attended Berklee College of Music in Boston. Breakstone worked as a sideman in the early 1980s around New York clubs, playing with Warne Marsh, Emily Remler, Dave Schnitter, Aaron Bell and Vic Juris.

Breakstone's first album, 1983's *Wonderful!,* with pianist Barry Harris, was issued on the Canadian Sonora label; his second *4/4=1* (1984), with Kenny Barron on piano, was released on Mobile Fidelity. Both are currently hard to find. *Evening Star* was the second release in a four-record stay with Contemporary (the first, *Echoes,* is no longer in print).

Breakstone's quintet on *Evening Star* includes legendary pianist Tommy Flanagan and trombonist Jimmy Knepper and is rounded out by bassist Dave Shapiro and drummer Keith Copeland.

Breakstone's regular rhythm section of bassist Dennis Irwin and drummer Kenny Washington returned for *Self-Portrait in Swing,* which also reunited Breakstone with Barron, and *9 by 3.* Barron, Irwin and Washington all shine on a tribute to the Ventures, *Walk, Don't Run.* Breakstone pays homage to the great jazz guitarist Grant Green on the splendid *Remembering Grant Green,* with organist Jack McDuff guesting. — J.S.

LENNY BREAU

★★★★★ Five O'Clock Bells/Mo' Breau (Genes, 1987)
★★★★ Last Sessions (Genes, 1988)

Guitarist Lenny Breau (1941–1984) possessed a delicate, exquisitely beautiful tone, which he seemed to caress from the strings, combined with a technical dexterity that often had him sounding as if he were playing more than one guitar at a time. A jazz player by avocation, he languished on the Nashville session scene before making these recordings toward the end of a tragic life plagued by drug addiction. His poetic lyricism is best heard on the magnificent *Five O'Clock Bells,* part of the Genes twofer with *Mo' Breau.*

Breau adapted the fingerpicking style he learned from Chet Atkins records as a youth to jazz improvisation, using all of his fingers simultaneously, like a keyboardist. His customized guitar, fitted with a classical neck, allowed him to chord at higher octaves than with a regular guitar, an ability used to great advantage on "Visions." His masterful use of harmonic overtones is best heard on "Five O'Clock Bells."

Last Sessions is another worthwhile demonstration of his prowess. A cassette-only trio session, *Lenny Breau Trio,* is also available. — J.S.

MICHAEL BRECKER

★★★★★ Michael Brecker (Impulse!, 1987)
★★★½ Don't Try This at Home (Impulse!, 1988)
★★★½ Now You See It . . . (Now You Don't) (Impulse!, 1990)
★★★★★ Tales from the Hudson (Impulse!, 1996)
★★★★ Two Blocks from the Edge (Impulse!, 1998)

Tenor saxophonist Michael Brecker (b. 1949) has carved out a remarkable career as both an innovator and popularizer of jazz during a period when the most successful of his peers have resolutely gazed at the past. By the time he recorded as a leader, Brecker had established himself in a wide variety of contexts, from the protofusion band Dreams to the soul jazz of the Horace Silver group to the funk of the Brecker Brothers (the group he formed with his brother Randy on trumpet) to large-band work with Gil Evans and Frank Zappa. Brecker also worked with the group Steps Ahead and appeared on countless sessions.

Michael Brecker is an auspicious debut, an all-star quintet session with guitarist Pat Metheny, keyboardist Kenny Kirkland, bassist Charlie Haden and drummer Jack DeJohnette. Brecker really lights a fire under this lineup with a challenging, hard-blowing performance. He features his electronic saxophone more prominently on *Don't Try This at Home* and *Now You See It . . . (Now You Don't).* Brecker pays homage to the immortal John Coltrane on *Tales from the Hudson,* which includes a guest appearance from McCoy Tyner on two tracks, including the outstanding "Song for Bilbao." — J.S.

BRECKER BROTHERS

★★★ The Brecker Brothers (One Way, 1975)
★★ Back to Back (One Way, 1976)
★★★½ Don't Stop the Music (One Way, 1977)
★★★★ Heavy Metal Be-Bop (One Way, 1978)
★★ Detente (One Way, 1980)
★★ Straphangin' (One Way, 1981)
★★★★ The Brecker Brothers Collection, Vol. 1 (Novus/RCA, 1990)
★★★ The Brecker Brothers Collection, Vol. 2 (Novus/RCA, 1991)
★★★★ Return of the Brecker Brothers (GRP, 1992)
★★★ Out of the Loop (GRP, 1994)

The Breckers were the most ubiquitous New York session players during the heyday of the 1970s fusion era. Randy (b. 1945) was Miles Davis's peer on electronic trumpet; Michael (b. 1949) was recognized as being among the best of countless young tenor saxophonists. In addition to their lengthy list of credentials with some of the top bands of the time, the two played together in the watershed fusion group Dreams.

The two formed the Brecker Brothers band with other New York sessioneers and proceeded to track a first album calculated to appeal to the dance-music audience. They gave themselves a commercial leg up when "Sneakin' Up Behind You" became a minor hit. The formula took over as the group went on, turning the playing into processed funk. The band remained vital in live performance, however, as *Heavy Metal Be-Bop* indicates, and there are enough high points to make *The Brecker Brothers Collection, Vols. 1 and 2* interesting.

The Brothers continued to explore the boundaries between acoustic and electric jazz, and by the time of *Return of the Brecker Brothers,* it's clear that they had found the key to balancing the forms without going too far in either direction. Randy's trumpet effects and Michael's lyricon work fit subtly into the overall conception. Both musicians continue to flourish as acoustic and electric performers (Randy has been sitting in with the Mingus Big Band), proving that fusion does not have to be a dead end for all players. — J.S.

TERESA BREWER

★ Live at Carnegie Hall and Montreux, Switzerland (Sony, 1978)
★ I Dig Big Band Singers (Doctor Jazz, 1983)
★ The Best of Teresa Brewer (MCA, 1983)
★★ What a Wonderful World (Signature, 1989)
★ 16 Most Requested Songs (Legacy, 1991)
★★ Memories of Louis (Red Baron, 1991)
★★ Softly I Swing (Red Baron, 1992)
★ American Music Box, Vol. 2: The Songs of Harry Warren (Red Baron, 1993)
★ Music! Music! Music! The Best of Teresa Brewer (Varese Sarabande/MCA, 1995)

Teresa Brewer (b. 1931) is a pop singer who began to dabble as a jazz vocalist after meeting her husband, producer Bob Thiele. Thiele's encouragement and connections put Brewer in some enviable settings where her flimsy understanding of the jazz form and self-consciously cute voice betrayed her. *The Best of Theresa Brewer* reissues her 1950s pop hits for Coral. They, along with *Live at Carnegie Hall and Montreux, Switzerland* and *I Dig Big Band Singers,* are frighteningly bad. She comes closest to pulling it off on the pop-jazz set *What a Wonderful World,* with violinist Stéphane Grappelli and trumpeter Ruby Braff providing magnificent support, and on *Memories of Louis,* with Braff, Bucky Pizzarelli on guitar and Grady Tate on drums. *Softly I Swing* is worth it for the moment on "It's the Talk of the Town" when Brewer lays out and tenor saxophonist David Murray channels Ben Webster while Tate, bassist Ron Carter and pianist Kenny Barron caress the solo home. — J.S.

DEE DEE BRIDGEWATER

★★★½ Live in Montreux (Verve, 1992)
★★★ Keeping Tradition (Verve, 1993)
★★★★ Love and Peace: A Tribute to Horace Silver (Verve, 1995)

Vocalist Denise "Dee Dee" Bridgewater (b. 1950), whose married name came from trumpeter Cecil Bridgewater, first came to prominence in the mid-1970s as the featured singer in the Thad Jones/Mel Lewis orchestra, then crossed over to pop stardom as part of the cast of *The Wiz,* for which she won a Tony Award.

In addition to her interpretive abilities, Bridgewater is a master of the art of the wordless vocal. After working in the pop mode, she returned to an active jazz career in Europe in 1986 and has released a series of recordings for Verve in the 1990s.

The *Live in Montreux* set documents her immense popularity at European jazz festivals and her debt to Sarah Vaughan. *Keeping Tradition* and *Love and Peace: A Tribute to Horace Silver* are studio sessions recorded in Paris with European bands. The latter features guest performances from Horace Silver on piano and Jimmy Smith on organ for a program of Silver tunes including "Song for My Father," "The Jody Grind" and "Nica's Dream." — J.S.

NICK BRIGNOLA

★★★ Raincheck (Reservoir, 1988)
★★★★ On a Different Level (Reservoir, 1990)
★★★½ What It Takes (Reservoir, 1991)
★★★ It's Time (Reservoir, 1992)

★★★ **Live at Sweet Basil—First Set (Reservoir, 1993)**
★★★★ **Like Old Times (with Claudio Roditi) (Reservoir, 1994)**
★★★½ **The Flight of the Eagle (Reservoir, 1996)**
★★★ **Poinciana (Reservoir, 1998)**

Nick Brignola (b. 1936) plays virtually all of the woodwind instruments very well, but the baritone saxophone is his best-known musical voice. He has a husky and authoritative sound on his preferred horn, sometimes biting in its intensity yet producing cogent, melodic solos. Brignola prefers quality to sheer quantity of notes.

With the passing of Gerry Mulligan in 1996, Brignola ascended to first among equals in the cadre of active mainstream/bop baritone players. Ironically, he took up the big horn at age 19 only because his alto was being fixed and the musical repairman had only a bari to lend him. He took to it at once.

While studying at Berklee College of Music, he worked with Boston modernists Charlie Mariano and Herb Pomeroy, then went on tour with trumpeter Ted Curson's band and the Woody Herman Orchestra. In addition to making his own recordings, he has worked with guitarist Sal Salvador, alto player Phil Woods's Little Big Band and the Mingus Superband.

All of Brignola's available discs feature him in small-band formats with pianist Kenny Barron leading most of the all-star rhythm sections. Bassists George Mraz and Dave Holland, drummers Jack DeJohnette, Billy Hart and Dick Berk, and trumpeters Randy Brecker and Brazilian Claudio Roditi fit into the equation at various times.

On a Different Level is an all-baritone session with Barron, Holland and DeJohnette exploring a diverse array of tunes. *What It Takes,* with Brecker aboard as guest horn man, shows Brignola's range on soprano, alto, baritone and clarinet.

It's Time is a radical "trio" session, with Brignola playing 10 different horns. Through overdubbing, he creates his own voicelike woodwind ensemble with up to 13 horn tracks, depending on the supporting mood he is trying to create. Extended solos and a strong groove on *Live at Sweet Basil—First Set* make for compelling listening. Trumpeter Claudio Roditi helps stoke the fire on *Like Old Times.*

Brignola is also very strong on *The Flight of the Eagle,* with four originals—including a Mulligan tribute tune, "Gerrylike"—and excellent updates of Billy Taylor's "Diz" and three standards. The quartet session *Poinciana* offers Brignola's take on his favorite new and old standards. In some cases the material is tired, and the soloing lacks the fire of Brignola's finest works. — K.F.

BOB BROOKMEYER

★★★½ **The Dual Role of Bob Brookmeyer (1955; Original Jazz Classics, 1990)**
★★★½ **Back Again (Gazell, 1978)**
★★★ **Oslo (Concord Jazz, 1987)**

Though he began his musical career in the 1950s as a pianist, Bob Brookmeyer (b. 1929) eventually became known for his sleek, mellifluous valve-trombone playing with Gerry Mulligan in the later part of the decade. *The Dual Role of Bob Brookmeyer* references both of his instrumental strengths and features guitarist Jimmy Raney and drummer Mel Lewis.

Brookmeyer went on to join Lewis as a charter member and arranger of the Thad Jones/Mel Lewis orchestra. Brookmeyer, Lewis and Jones team up with pianist Jimmy Rowles and bassist George Mraz for a spirited reunion on *Back Again.* Also look for the out-of-print *Bob Brookmeyer and Friends* and *With Mel Lewis and the Jazz Orchestra.* — J.S.

LONNIE BROOKS

★★★½ **Sweet Home Chicago (1976; Evidence, 1992)**
★★★½ **Bayou Lightning (Alligator, 1979)**
★★★ **Turn On the Night (Alligator, 1981)**
★★★ **Hot Shot (Alligator, 1983)**
★★★½ **Wound Up Tight (Alligator, 1986)**
★★★★ **Live from Chicago: Bayou Lighting Strikes (Alligator, 1988)**
★★★ **Satisfaction Guaranteed (Alligator, 1991)**
★★★ **Let's Talk It Over (Delmark, 1993)**
★★★ **Roadhouse Rules (Alligator, 1996)**
★★★½ **Deluxe Edition (Alligator, 1997)**

Born Lee Baker Jr. in Dubuisson, Louisiana, in 1933, master blues guitarist Lonnie Brooks didn't begin playing until he was in his 20s. He made his first recordings under the pseudonym Guitar Jr. for a small Louisiana label in the late 1950s. Though he moved to Chicago in 1959 and recorded under the name Lonnie Brooks for Mercury, Chess and Capitol (notably, the now deleted 1969 LP *Broke and Hungry*), among other labels, he didn't become well known in the States for several decades.

In the early 1970s Brooks found an

appreciative audience in Europe; *Sweet Home Chicago,* recorded in France in 1975, features Brooks's fiery guitar work accompanied by a stellar band, including guitarist Hubert Sumlin, pianist Willie Mabon and drummer Fred Below. Brooks covers familiar territory here, from a loose-limbed version of the title track to a duel between Brooks and Sumlin on Brooks's "Two Guitar Shuffle." Versions of "Crosscut Saw" and Lowell Fulson's "Reconsider Baby" show up here. Also cut in the '70s, *Let's Talk It Over* includes eight tracks, six of which were written by Brooks.

Bayou Lightning marks the beginning of Brooks's relatively long relationship with the U.S. independent label Alligator. Upon its release in 1979, Brooks was hailed as the great "new" guitar hope (of course, he'd already been gigging steadily for 20 years). The album lives up to the hype. Simmering slow blues like "In the Dark" cohabitate with funky numbers like "Voodoo Daddy," which discusses a young man's fear that his fiancée's father might put a spell on him. Other supernaturally tinged songs include a version of Willie Dixon's "I Ain't Superstitious." *Turn On the Night* features a large ensemble of players, including a full horn section. Its songs are mostly penned by Brooks, including "Inflation," "Mother Nature" and "Don't Go to Sleep on Me," a plea for love after a hard week of work.

Hot Shot is a high-energy album that finds the guitarist back with a small combo consisting of keyboards, bass and drums; tenor saxophonist Abb Locke appears on two tracks. Several originals are featured (credited to "Baker"), including "Mr. Hot Shot" and the long-unavailable "Family Rules," as well as Otis Blackwell's "Back Trail" and J.B. Lenoir's "One More Shot." Another small-combo album, *Wound Up Tight* features the smoking guitar work of Johnny Winter on two songs, including the title track and the rollicking "Got Lucky Last Night."

Live from Chicago, recorded at the B.L.U.E.S., Etcetera club over three days in November 1987, has a presence lacking in Johnson's studio work. Highlights include "Eyeballin'," "One More Shot" and a hyperfast version of Freddie King's "Hideaway," during which Brooks can be heard to say, "Get me another drink, I need it bad." *Live from Chicago* paints a titillating, accurate picture of what it's like to be in a dark, smoky Chicago club with guitar-fueled blues hitting from every angle. On *Satisfaction Guaranteed* Brooks welcomes into the fray his son Ronnie Baker Brooks, playing lead guitar on two tracks (he also played rhythm on *Live from Chicago*). Ronnie does a vocal turn on "Like Father, Like Son," which he also wrote; Koko Taylor makes a special vocal appearance on "If the Price Is Right," a tune written by father and son.

Roadhouse Rules finds Brooks performing six originals, including the muscular, midtempo "Backbone Man," the plaintive "I Need a Friend" and the rollicking "Treat Me Like Your Dog." Accompanied by Sugar Blue on one track ("Roll of the Tumbling Dice") and the Memphis Horns on another ("Too Little, Too Late"), Brooks sings and wields his axe on *Roadhouse Rules* with the characteristic dexterity that has come to define this cagey blues veteran.
— B.R.H.

BIG BILL BROONZY

★★★★ Feelin' Low Down (GNP Crescendo, 1973)
★★★★ Big Bill Broonzy and Washboard Sam (1986; Chess, 1991)
★★★★ Big Bill Broonzy Sings Folk Songs (Smithsonian Folkways, 1989)
★★★★★ Good Time Tonight (Columbia, 1990)
★★★★★ The Young Big Bill Broonzy 1928–1935 (Yazoo, 1991)
★★★★★ Do That Guitar Rag 1928–35 (Yazoo, 1991)
★★★★★ The 1955 London Sessions (Collectables, 1994)
★★★½ Baby, Please Don't Go (Drive Archive, 1994)
★★★★★ The Complete Bluebird Recordings (1934–1935) (RCA Bluebird, 1995)
★★★★ Black, Brown & White (Evidence, 1995)
★★★½ Treat Me Right (Tradition, 1996)

An important transitional link between acoustic country blues and electrified urban blues, Big Bill Broonzy (1893–1958), born in Mississippi and raised in Arkansas, helped shape the force that became Chicago blues. After completing a tour of duty in the Army, Broonzy moved to the Windy City in 1920. A fiddle player at that time, he switched to guitar and began playing the instrument as if born to it; he was often seen in the company of local stars such as Blind Lemon Jefferson and Sleepy John Estes. Even among this crowd, his style was distinctive. His basic, fundamental guitar accompaniment was highlighted by stark, single-string solos and forceful chording; his smooth but plaintive singing voice, which could move easily from a world-weary moan to a mellow, sanguine tone, was suited to deliver self-penned songs focused on the travails of big-city life, social inequities and hard times with women. More than any guitarist of his time, he made effective use of silence as a dramatic component of his music, sometimes employing only a few strong, angular retorts to punctuate key lyric sections. And he was prolific: At his death in 1958, more than 300 songs had been copyrighted with his name as composer.

Although Broonzy recorded for several small labels—including Paramount and Melotone—in the late '20s, it was his affiliation with Bluebird in 1934 and 1935 that established him in the front ranks of contemporary blues artists. White audiences picked up on his work following his appearance on the "From Spirituals to Swing" show at New York's Carnegie Hall in 1938, when he scorched the place with "Done Got Wise" and "Louise, Louise," backed by a band that included Albert Ammons, Walter Page and Jo Jones. Broonzy, a last-minute replacement on the bill for Robert Johnson, who had been found poisoned in Mississippi, made the most of his moment, and his career hit high gear afterward. The essential Bluebird recordings are collected on *The Complete Bluebird Recordings (1934–1935).*

Broonzy's early years are well documented on the Yazoo and Columbia collections. The Yazoo discs focus primarily on solo acoustic or duet recordings from 1928 to 1935, whereas Columbia's *Good Time Tonight* offers both acoustic and combo recordings spanning the years 1930 to 1940. A notably delicious treat recommending *Do That Guitar Rag 1928–35* is the inclusion of four bawdy numbers featuring scintillating musical dialogs between Broonzy on guitar and Georgia Tom Dorsey on piano (obviously before he saw the light and began writing the songs that defined modern gospel music), supporting Jane Lucas's sassy vocalizing. Those who doubt that the line between country music and country blues is exceedingly thin need only listen to Broonzy's "I Can't Be Satisfied," a 1930 recording (available on both *The Young Bill Broonzy* and *Good Time Tonight*) that is the model for Ernest Tubb's 1942 hit "You Nearly Lose Your Mind." Take it a step further and check out his recordings made in 1953 with bassist Ernest "Big" Crawford, Washboard Sam, guitarist Lee Cooper and pianist Memphis Slim. As heard on Chess's *Big Bill Broonzy and Washboard Sam,* these sound like nothing so much as gutbucket rockabilly, pure and simple.

An engaging live performance is captured on *Black, Brown & White,* with seven tracks recorded in concert in Antwerp, Belgium, in 1952 and six others recorded in 1955 at a friend's house in Brussels. Playing acoustic or with pianist Blind John Davis, Broonzy samples virtually every type of song in his repertoire. Topical songs are represented by the brutal title track, with its light, lilting rhythm quite at odds with the lyrics' frontal assaults on racism and a flat-out demand to put an end to Jim Crow; elsewhere, Broonzy eases comfortably into the pop strains of "Who's Sorry Now," energizing it with a ragtime rhythm; "Big Bill Blues" shows the artist in a deep-blues, self-referential, self-pitying mode; and his interpretation of W.C. Handy's "Careless Love" is played like a Delta blues and phrased like a country song.

That Broonzy never left his social conscience behind is indicated on the opening track of the first-rate *1955 London Sessions,* "When Do I Get to Be Called a Man," an explicit litany of the sacrifices a man had made for his country and what his country had withheld in return—dignity, for one; respect, for another. Apart from the solo acoustic sides, Broonzy is teamed here with a septet on some bluesy, boozy performances with a decidedly New Orleans feel about them, notably "Southbound Train," with trumpeter Leslie Hutchinson blowing piercing, muted fills. Other treats here include a remarkable, florid solo instrumental version of "St. Louis Blues" and a take on "Glory of Love" on which Broonzy showcases a personable style with a pop song and a deft touch in supporting himself on guitar. Finally, a superb collection is rounded out by the harrowing "Joe Turner Blues," a traditional song adapted by Broonzy and introduced with his oral reminiscence of Southern folkways—how people tell time by poking a stick in the ground—and human compassion as related in the story of a white man picking up a stranded black man on the highway and giving him a home on his farm. When the set winds down with a medley of Leroy Carr's "In the Evening" and Broonzy's classic "Going Down This Road Feeling Bad," all the human emotions have been in play in what was a memorable two days in the Pye Studios in London in 1955. *Baby, Please Don't Go* suffers only from a lack of adequate liner information, but what's there indicates these 10 tracks were recorded between 1952 and 1956. Among the key tracks: "Ridin' On Down (Mule

Ridin')," a rare Broonzy talking blues, made more potent by being rooted in personal experience; a driving instrumental version of "St. Louis Blues"; a dramatic interpretation of "Backwater Blues (I Got Up One Mornin' Blues)" that is not only one of the most haunting tracks Broonzy ever recorded but ranks with Bessie Smith's version in terms of the profound sense of loss the singer communicates. A bouncing, lighthearted take on Merle Travis's "Sixteen Tons" closes out the CD, Broonzy coming on rather jocular, as if owing his soul to the company store weren't no big deal to a man who knew something about hard times.

Feelin' Low Down is a set of acoustic sides, raw and potent, but it lacks dates and session information. Apart from that oversight, its 14 cuts feature vintage Broonzy in many moods on songs ranging from his own moving originals (including "Big Bill Blues" and "Lonesome Road Blues") to stirring covers, such as the heavyweight treatment he gives the traditional folk number "John Henry." Before he died of throat cancer in 1958, Broonzy had helped ignite a folk and blues revival in this country that brought attention to many of his contemporaries who might otherwise have died in obscurity. Today he is far less known among the general public than, say, Robert Johnson, but his most penetrating and personal songs remind us of the important issues of his time that remain relevant to our own. Similarly, but with far better annotation, the Smithsonian Folkways entry, *Big Bill Broonzy Sings Folk Songs,* collects some recordings Broonzy made for the Folkways label near the end of his life as well as several live tracks, some featuring Pete Seeger on harmony vocals and banjo, all of which underscore the remarkable breadth and depth of Broonzy's repertoire, whether it be an intimate, revealing original song or a tender reading of a pop chestnut such as "Glory of Love," the album's closer. — D.M.

CHARLES BROWN

★★★½ **Boss of the Blues (1964; Mainstream/Legacy, 1993)**
★★★★ **One More for the Road (1986; Alligator, 1989)**
★★★★ **All My Life (Bullseye Blues, 1990)**
★★★★★ **Driftin' Blues: The Best of Charles Brown (Collectables, 1992)**
★★★★ **Someone to Love (Bullseye Blues, 1992)**
★★★★ **Blues and Other Love Songs (Muse, 1992)**
★★★★ **Just a Lucky So and So (Bullseye Blues, 1994)**
★★★★ **Blues n' Brown (Jewel, 1995)**

Late night, lights down low, bottle of wine, someone to dream with and Charles Brown, blues elegance personified—now there's a scenario suitable for any true romantic. Blues and R&B have had any number of outstanding boudoir balladeers, but Charles Brown (1922–1999) always brought a special warmth and engaging personality to his efforts and thus carved out for himself an exalted place among his peers and, for a few years in the late '40s and early '50s, the general public as well.

Born in Texas City, Texas, Brown showed an early aptitude for science as well as music. He was a star pupil through high school, matriculated at Prairie View A&M College and earned a B.S. in chemistry, math and education. After graduation, though, his burgeoning interest in music led him to Los Angeles (where another Texan, T-Bone Walker, had been ruling the R&B roost since the early '40s) and an association with Eddie Williams and Johnny Moore in a group they called the Three Blazers. Of their three wonderful voices, none stood out more than Brown's in its laconic grace and soothing timbre (comparable to Nat King Cole's "smoky gray" quality), attributes made more effective by the singer's unerring sense of propriety with regard to a lyrical phrase—gingerly kneading key words or stretching them over a few beats to draw out an underlying feeling—and frugal use of ornamentation (deep bass dips or a conversational or recitative style) for greatest emotional impact.

The Three Blazers hit it big out of the box in 1946 with "Drifting Blues," a song Brown had written in high school; they remained in the upper reaches of the R&B chart for over three years. Brown went solo in '48, though, and on his own, he wrote and recorded numerous upper-level R&B–chart singles—six in 1949 alone—including two Number Ones (1949's "Trouble Blues" and 1951's "Black Night"). Meanwhile, a Christmas song he wrote and recorded with the Three Blazers in 1947, the melancholy "Merry Christmas, Baby," was becoming a seasonal classic, charting every year in the first three years after its release. While "Drifting Blues" is regarded as his signature song, "Merry Christmas, Baby" has lived on in numerous cover versions, by far the most powerful being Elvis Presley's tour de force of blues vocalizing on his *Elvis Sings the Wonderful World of Christmas* LP. *Driftin'*

Blues: The Best of Charles Brown is the must-have CD charting these fruitful years.

Brown's chart run ended in 1952, although he continued recording for Aladdin into the late '50s. After dropping out of the recording scene, Brown continued an active touring schedule. He was playing at a San Francisco club in 1963 when the president of Mainstream Records stumbled upon him and signed him. Although he was backed by a string section and Don Sebesky's opulent, Nelson Riddle–style arrangements in an effort to move him into the pop field, Brown's Mainstream work went virtually unnoticed. Of late, some of the sessions have resurfaced on the Mainstream/Legacy CD, *Boss of the Blues,* and they are wonderful. "I Won't Cry Anymore" is a heartbreaking ballad of lost love that Brown brings home with a probing, stoic vocal; on an interpretation of Johnny Ace's "Pledging My Love," Brown's direct, determined vow plays beautifully off the soaring strings to create a longing ambiance with a fatalistic undertow; by contrast, Brown, with the impressionistic noodlings of pianist Roger Kellaway acting as a distinguished counterpoint, delivers Lonnie Johnson's 1948 hit "Tomorrow Night" in a silky, suggestive tone, all hope and longing. This is Quiet Storm about 20 years before Smokey Robinson pioneered the style.

Boss of the Blues combines all the tracks from Brown's first Mainstream album with several bonus tracks from other sessions in a fine 16-track set. Once in a blue moon Brown's other Mainstream album, *Driftin' Blues,* will show up in cutout bins, and it's a bargain at any price. In addition to the title track, the LP features moving, low-key interpretations of "Our Day Will Come," "Days of Wine and Roses," "More" and—get this—"Go Away Little Girl" (yes, the Number One single from 1962 as recorded by the oleaginous Steve Lawrence).

So low-profile he seemed to have dropped off the earth during the 1970s and 1980s, Brown in fact stayed on the road and every so often found a small label here or there that was happy to have him for a moment. *Blues n' Brown,* released in 1995, is a 10-song collection of low-down blues—most of them cowritten by Brown—recorded at the Modern/Kent studios in Los Angeles in 1971, with producer Maxwell Davis, who had been behind the board for most of Brown's sterling Aladdin work, back in the fold. With Johnny Moore joining him on guitar, Brown dips freely into his signature sound for some soul-searching ruminations on faithless love but also does a convincing, rousing turn in a Memphis-soul style on "I Don't Know." Brown's voice is a bit ragged here, but its shopworn quality is more endearing than distracting, particularly on heartfelt love songs on the order of the album's opening gem, "For You."

One More for the Road is Alligator's 1989 reissue of a 1986 album originally released on the Blue Side label. Here Brown explored a typical potpourri of songs, not the least being a couple of his own (the album's slow-grooving opener, "I Cried Last Night," is especially strong) as well as songs otherwise associated with Frank Sinatra, Charlie Rich and Nat King Cole. Whatever the source material, it all came out blues, and Brown proved here that his instinct for a lyric's hidden meaning remained undiminished.

Praise the Lord for Bullseye Blues, which has done a great service if only for giving Jimmy McCracklin and Charles Brown a place to record. It has done that, to the benefit of both artists. Brown's first Bullseye effort, *All My Life,* is another smooth, assured outing showing off the artist's interpretive powers. Throughout these sessions his vocals, more resonant, more nuanced, more ambivalent than on any of his other recordings, reflect a stronger sense of love as an impermanent state.

Possibly as a response to the harder edge of *All My Life, Someone to Love* is soft, mellow, back-to-the-boudoir fare, beginning with the Brown–Bonnie Raitt duet on the title track, which finds the two singers engaged in the vocal equivalent of long, meaningful looks into each other's eyes, and discreet, under-the-table hand-holding. Love in all its forms is the theme, from the hopeful posturing on "Tell Me You'll Wait for Me," to the yearning plea of hopeless infatuation, "Don't Drive Me Away" (underscored by Danny Caron's brief, sizzling guitar solo), to the resigned, down-child moan of rejection Brown adopts on "I Want to Go Home." The centerpiece of all this is a refreshing, jazzy, minor-key reconsideration of Brenda Holloway's pop-soul classic "Every Little Bit Hurts," with Brown working some interpretive magic on the lyrics—drawing out the phrases in a weary voice that suggests a man at the end of his emotional rope—while supplying Monk-like suggestive chording over which Bonnie Raitt's slide-guitar lines evoke the singer's cry of the heart.

The same year he recorded *Someone to Love,* Brown slipped into a San Francisco studio for three days and came back with *Blues and Other Love Songs,* produced by the formidable tenor saxophonist Houston Person, who lent his distinctive touch to five of the songs, including a barn-burning workout on his version of "One Mint Julep." Backed on half of the 10 songs by a trio of bass, drums and guitar, Brown takes an approach here that is more brooding than usual; it's also more penetrating in its self-recrimination. On record Brown has rarely been more potent than he is here on two numbers featuring his dark, woebegone vocal accompanied solely by his spare, haunting piano fills, "Who's Beating My Time" and "I've Got a Right to Cry." Elsewhere Brown turns in a scintillating take on Thelonious Monk's "'Round Midnight," a taut, angular display of jazz interpretation that is as gripping in its shifting emotional content as it is in its deft execution.

Brown's last Bullseye release, *Just a Lucky So and So,* is a more ornate affair in that Brown is backed not only by a small combo but also by the Crescent City Horns (the album was recorded in New Orleans) and the New Orleans Strings. The pleasing result is a combination of the best of the Mainstream style with the small-combo midnight blues of *Someone to Love.* The prevailing mood—despite songs on the order of "Gloomy Sunday" and "I Won't Cry Anymore"—is upbeat and swinging, à la the title track, which is cut from the cloth of '30s and '40s big-band swing. Of note: Brown reprises his 1951 chart topper, "Black Night," with the strings and the combo alternately roaring and whispering in bracing support of his changing moods. In the 50 years spanning his recording career, Charles Brown saw most of his peers disappear from the scene altogether, forced out by failing health, changing trends, general ennui or combinations thereof. He, however, always strived to be in a growth phase, as a singer exploring a wide range of emotional textures reflecting his own broad range of life experiences, and as a pianist stripping away the frills in his style to the choicest phrases needed to move the song forward. Brown continued to deliver great work up until his death. — D.M.

CLARENCE "GATEMOUTH" BROWN

★★★★ **Gate's on the Heat (1973; Verve, 1993)**
★★★★ **Alright Again (Rounder, 1981)**
★★★½ **One More Mile (Rounder, 1983)**
★★★★ **The Original Peacock Recordings (Rounder, 1983)**
★★★★ **Pressure Cooker (Alligator, 1986)**
★★★½ **Real Life (Rounder, 1987)**
★★★★ **Texas Swing (Rounder, 1987)**
★★★★ **Standing My Ground (Alligator, 1989)**
★★★★ **No Looking Back (Alligator, 1992)**
★★★★ **Just Got Lucky (Evidence, 1993)**
★★★★ **The Man (Verve, 1994)**
★★★★½ **Long Way Home (Verve, 1996)**
★★★★½ **Gate Swings (Verve, 1997)**

Born in Vinton, Louisiana, in 1924, Clarence "Gatemouth" Brown grew up in Texas. He learned music early, eventually playing a variety of instruments—guitar, fiddle, mandolin, drums, bass and harmonica. After first recording in 1947 for Aladdin, Brown cut more than 50 sides for Peacock between 1947 and 1960, showcasing his mixture of country, soul, blues, jazz and Cajun music. His popularity waned in the '60s, as rock & roll rose in popularity.

Brown reappeared in 1973 with a performance at the Montreux Jazz Festival and the album *Gate's on the Heat.* Among its several stellar tracks are an ultrafunky version of Percy Mayfield's "River's Invitation" and two cuts featuring the Memphis Horns and the London Strings Orchestra. Other highlights include versions of W.C. Handy's "St. Louis Blues" and a swirling "Funky Mama," as well as the originals "Please Mr. Nixon" and "Louisiana Breakdown," an instrumental recorded live at Montreux.

Of Brown's five '80s albums on Rounder, *Alright Again* garnered a Grammy. Featuring 10 contemporary blues, including a reworking of Lou Donaldson's "Alligator Boogaloo," it is one of Brown's best releases, with fine horn charts and Brown's fevered guitar and fiddle work. *Texas Swing* collects tracks from *Alright Again* and *One More Mile. The Original Peacock Recordings* highlights Brown's early recordings, which influenced such Texan guitarists as Albert Collins and Johnny Copeland. Rife with high-powered guitar and smoldering, jazzy horn arrangements, the album includes "Pale Dry Boogie," "Dirty Work at the Crossroads," "Rock My Blues Away" and incendiary instrumentals like "Okie Dokie Stomp" and "Boogie Uproar."

The swinging *Pressure Cooker* compiles tracks culled from five jazzy albums Brown recorded in 1973 for the French label Disques Black and Blue. Notable are "She Winked

Her Eye," "My Time Is Expensive" and "Just Lippin'," which features Al Grey on trombone. Various cuts also include Texas tenor-sax man Arnett Cobb, Kansas City pianist Jay McShann and pioneering jazz organist Milt Buckner. Though there are no repeated tracks, the first 11 songs on *Just Got Lucky* were also culled from the same sessions that yielded *Pressure Cooker.* The album's three additional tracks were recorded in Nice, France, in 1977. Though it features primarily the same backing musicians, *Just Got Lucky* has a decidedly more bluesy feel than *Pressure Cooker* and is just as compelling. Highlights include the Brown originals "Long Way Home," "It's Mean" and the laid-back "Here I Am."

Recorded in New Orleans and environs, *Standing My Ground* clearly absorbed some of that city's indigenous musical artistry. Playing piano and drums on one track each, Brown is joined by a host of Louisiana players, including Terrance Simien on accordion. Notable are the Brown originals "Louisiana Zydeco" and "Born in Louisiana" (with the autobiographical lines "I was born in Louisiana/And raised on the Texas side"). There is also an authoritative reading of "Got My Mojo Working."

No Looking Back again boasts some fine, punchy horn arrangements and Gatemouth's diffuse mixture of swing, bop, blues and the like. It contains three John D. Loudermilk compositions, the funky "Dope," the humorous "Alligator Eating Dog" and the ballad "I Will Be Your Friend," which includes Brown's vocal duet with folkie Michelle Shocked. Other highlights are an interpretation of Duke Ellington's "C-Jam Blues" and five excellent Brown originals. *The Man,* again features diverse, compelling material, such as Bill Doggett's horn-spiked shuffle "Honky Tonk," Louis Jordan's "Early in the Morning" and Hank Williams's "Jambalaya," on which Cajun accordion master Jo-El Sonnier sings and plays. Sonnier's accordion can also be heard on Link Davis's "Big Mammou" and one other track. Also worth mentioning are Delbert McClinton's "Solid Gold Plated Fool" and Brown's own "There You Are."

Long Way Home finds Brown entertaining an array of A-list players, including Eric Clapton, Leon Russell and Ry Cooder. On the Clapton/Russell classic "Blues Power," Brown and Russell trade vocal verses while Clapton characteristically embroiders the track with his fiery, bent-string work. Also noteworthy are Brown's renditions of the Bobby Charles ballad "Here I Go Again," with Brown, Maria Muldaur and Charles himself sharing the vocal chores, and the incisive "Mean and Evil," a Russell composition. Another highlight is the Brown-penned "Dockside Boogie," an off-kilter instrumental romp with Cooder's mandolin providing a rhythmic framework for Amos Garrett's seamless guitar solo; Bob Dylan's "Don't Think Twice"; J.J. Cale's "Don't Cry Sister" (featuring Sonny Landreth on National steel guitar); and a foreboding, snail's tempo version of "Tobacco Road," on which Loudermilk—the song's author—handles the vocal.

Gate Swings is a supercharged, horn-embellished work that recalls big-band blues recordings of the late '40s and includes impeccably punchy versions of tunes like Fleecie Moore's "Caldonia," Percy Mayfield's "River's Invitation" and Count Basie's "One O'Clock Jump." The only thing that's more impressive than the album's tasteful, razor-sharp playing is the joy that drips from every riff.
— B.R.H.

CLIFFORD BROWN

★★★★ **Memorial Album (1953; Blue Note, 1985)**
★★★★★ **The Best of Clifford Brown/Max Roach in Concert (1954; GNP, 1989)**
★★★★ **Clifford Brown and Max Roach (1954; Verve, 1990)**
★★★ **Best Coast Jazz (1954; Verve, 1997)**
★★★★★ **Brown and Roach Inc. (1954; Verve, 1997)**
★★★★ **Study in Brown (1955; Verve, 1990)**
★★★ **Clifford Brown with Strings (1955; Verve, 1997)**
★★★★★ **More Study in Brown (1955; Verve, 1997)**
★★★★★ **At Basin Street (1956; Verve, 1997)**
★★★½ **Memorial (1956; Original Jazz Classics, 1987)**
★★★★★ **The Beginning and the End (1973; Columbia, 1994)**
★★★★ **The Immortal Clifford Brown (Blue Note, 1988)**
★★★★ **Big Band in Paris (Original Jazz Classics, 1989)**
★★★★★ **Quartet in Paris (Original Jazz Classics, 1989)**

★★★★ **Sextet in Paris (Original Jazz Classics, 1989)**
★★★★★ **Brownie: The Complete EmArcy Recordings of Clifford Brown (EmArcy, 1989)**
★★★★ **Compact Jazz (Verve, 1990)**
★★★★ **Jazz 'Round Midnight (Verve, 1993)**
★★★★★ **The Complete Blue Note and Pacific Jazz Recordings of Clifford Brown (Blue Note, 1995)**
★★★★ **Jazz Masters 44 (Verve, 1995)**
★★★½ **Alone Together: The Best of the Mercury Years (Verve, 1995)**
★★★★ **Jam Session (Verve, 1997)**
★★★½ **Jams 2 (Verve, 1997)**

Clifford Brown (1930–1956) was generally considered one of the greatest trumpeters in jazz history, and a threat to reigning trumpet stars Dizzy Gillespie and Miles Davis, when he was killed in an automobile accident along with the pianist in his band, Richie Powell, and Powell's wife after a June 26, 1956, performance in Philadelphia. A throng of posthumous albums added additional weight to his reputation, and his legend has survived to this day despite only a few years of recordings.

Brown's main influences were Fats Navarro and Gillespie, but his overall conception was fresh and evolving. As it stands, his influence can be heard in the music of many of the important trumpeters who've followed him.

Born in Wilmington, Delaware, Brown began playing trumpet in 1945 and excelled in school, winning a scholarship to Maryland State University. In a terrible foreshadowing of his fate, Brown was seriously injured in a June 1950 automobile accident that sidelined him until 1951. He made his recording debut with an R&B band, Chris Powell and the Five Blue Flames, in 1952. Two tracks recorded with that group are included on *The Beginning and the End.* The remainder of the release documents Brown's final recording, made the day before he died.

Brown played with Tadd Dameron in 1953 before joining Lionel Hampton's group. He recorded tracks from the Blue Note *Memorial Album* during that year, as well as the . . . *In Paris* sessions for Prestige. *Quartet* showcases Brown with French musicians, *Sextet* with alto saxophonist Gigi Gryce in the mix, and *Big Band* with Gryce, Art Farmer and Quincy Jones involved. The Original Jazz Classics *Memorial* is a posthumous assemblage of two 1953 sessions, one with Tadd Dameron, the other featuring Brown and Art Farmer on trumpets fronting the Swedish All Stars.

The Complete Blue Note and Pacific Jazz Recordings of Clifford Brown collects some of Brown's 1953 studio work and some important 1954 West Coast recordings that feature beautiful interplay with tenor saxophonist Zoot Sims.

In the less than two years before his death, Brown recorded prolifically for EmArcy with the groundbreaking group he co-led with drummer Max Roach. Bud Powell's brother Richie on piano and Harold Land or Sonny Rollins on tenor saxophone rounded out this group. This material, as well as several side projects Brown was involved in, is collected on the meticulously gathered 10-CD set *Brownie,* which includes 10 performances never before released. All the Verve recordings are included in this package.

The Brown/Roach band is one of the key groups in jazz history, notable for the spectacular solo playing and ensemble work of the individuals and Brown's compositional genius. One can only imagine what the writer of "Daahoud" might have come up with as he matured. — J.S.

JAMES BROWN

★★★ **Please Please Please (King, 1959)**
★★½ **Try Me (King, 1959)**
★★★★ **Think (King, 1960)**
★★½ **The Amazing James Brown (King, 1961)**
★★★★ **James Brown Presents His Band (King, 1961)**
★★★½ **Excitement Mr. Dynamite (King, 1962)**
★★½ **James Brown and His Famous Flames Tour the U.S.A. (King, 1962)**
★★★★★ **Live at the Apollo (King, 1963)**
★★★ **Prisoner of Love (King, 1963)**
★★★★ **Pure Dynamite! (King, 1964)**
★★½ **Showtime (Smash, 1964)**
★★½ **Grits and Soul (Smash, 1964)**
★★★★ **Papa's Got a Brand New Bag (King, 1965)**
★★½ **James Brown Plays James Brown Today and Yesterday (Smash, 1966)**
★★★★ **I Got You (I Feel Good) (King, 1966)**
★★★ **Mighty Instrumentals (King, 1966)**

★★★ James Brown Plays New Breed (The Boo-Ga-Loo) (Smash, 1966)
★★★½ It's a Man's, Man's, Man's World (King, 1966)
★★ Christmas Songs (King, 1966)
★★★ Handful of Soul (Smash, 1966)
★★ The James Brown Show (Smash, 1967)
★★★★ James Brown Sings Raw Soul (King, 1967)
★★★ James Brown Plays the Real Thing (Smash, 1967)
★★★ Live at the Garden (King, 1967)
★★★ Cold Sweat (King, 1967)
★★½ James Brown Presents His Show of Tomorrow (King, 1968)
★★★★ I Can't Stand Myself (When You Touch Me) (King, 1968)
★★★★ I Got the Feelin' (King, 1968)
★★★ James Brown Plays Nothing but Soul (King, 1968)
★★★★★ Live at the Apollo, Vol. 2 (King, 1968)
★★★★★ Say It Live and Loud: Live in Dallas 1968 (1968; Polydor, 1998)
★★★½ Thinking About Little Willie John and a Few Nice Things (King, 1968)
★★ A Soulful Christmas (King, 1968)
★★★★ Say It Loud, I'm Black and I'm Proud (King, 1969)
★★ Gettin' Down to It (King, 1969)
★★★ It's a Mother (King, 1969)
★★★★ Ain't It Funky (King, 1970)
★★★½ Soul on Top (King, 1970)
★★★★½ It's a New Day So Let a Man Come In (King, 1970)
★★★★½ Sex Machine (King, 1970)
★★½ Hey, America (King, 1970)
★★★½ Super Bad (King, 1971)
★★ Sho Is Funky Down Here (King, 1971)
★★★★ Hot Pants (Polydor, 1971)
★★★★ Revolution of the Mind: Live at the Apollo, Vol. 3 (Polydor, 1971)
★★★★½ There It Is (Polydor, 1972)
★★★★★ Soul Classics (1972; Polydor, 1997)
★★★½ Get on the Good Foot (Polydor, 1972)
★★ Black Caesar (Polydor, 1973)
★★ Slaughter's Big Rip-off (Polydor, 1973)
★★★★ The Payback (Polydor, 1974)
★★★★ Hell (Polydor, 1974)
★★★½ Reality (Polydor, 1975)
★★★★★ Soul Classics, Vol. 2 (1975; Polydor, 1997)
★★★ Sex Machine Today (Polydor, 1975)
★★ Everybody's Doin' the Hustle and Dead on the Double Bump (Polydor, 1975)
★★★ Hot (Polydor, 1976)
★★★½ Get Up Offa That Thing (Polydor, 1976)
★★★ Body Heat (Polydor, 1976)
★★½ Mutha's Nature (Polydor, 1977)
★★★★★ Solid Gold (Polydor UK, 1977)
★★½ Jam 1980's (Polydor, 1978)
★★★ Take a Look at Those Cakes (Polydor, 1979)
★★ The Original Disco Man (Polydor, 1979)
★★½ People (Polydor, 1980)
★★★ Hot on the One (Polydor, 1980)
★★★★ Soul Syndrome (1980; Rhino, 1991)
★★ Nonstop! (Polydor, 1981)
★★½ The Greatest Hits Live in Concert (1981; Sugar Hill, 1991)
★★★½ Bring It On! (Churchill/Augusta Sound, 1983)
★★★½ Gravity (Scotti Bros., 1986)
★★★★½ James Brown's Funky People (Polydor, 1986)
★★★★½ In the Jungle Groove (Polydor, 1986)
★★★½ I'm Real (Scotti Bros., 1988)
★★★★ James Brown's Funky People, Part 2 (Polydor, 1988)
★★★★ Motherlode (Polydor, 1988)
★★★ Soul Session Live (Scotti Bros., 1989)
★★★★½ Roots of a Revolution (Polydor, 1989)
★★★★ Messing with the Blues (Polydor, 1990)
★★★★★ Star Time (Polydor, 1991)
★★★ Love Over-Due (Scotti Bros., 1991)
★★★★★ 20 All-Time Greatest Hits! (Polydor, 1991)
★★★ The Greatest Hits of the Fourth Decade (Scotti Bros., 1992)
★★★★½ Love, Power, Peace: Live at the Olympia, Paris 1971 (Polydor, 1992)
★★★ Universal James (Scotti Bros., 1993)
★★★★★ Soul Pride: The Instrumentals (1960–1969) (Polydor, 1993)
★★★★ Live at the Apollo 1995 (Scotti Bros., 1995)

★★★★★ **Foundations of Funk: A Brand New Bag, 1964–1969 (Polydor, 1996)**
★★★★★ **J B 40 (Polydor, 1997)**
★★★★★ **Funk Power: A Brand New Thang (Polydor, 1997)**
★★★★★ **Make It Funky: The Big Payback (Polydor, 1997)**

James Brown (b. 1933) was astonishingly productive during the first four decades of his recording career, churning out more than 90 albums (give or take a few anthologies) as a singer, bandleader or instrumentalist; many are great, and nearly all are worth hearing. And even though none of the 44 singles he put into the Top 40 pop chart ever made it to Number One—indeed, only two cracked the Top 5—in retrospect, that seems to reflect worse on the pop audience than it does on his music.

Brown has long boasted that his best ideas were years ahead of their time, and recent history has borne him out. Hip-hop borrowed freely from his back catalog, as rappers like Rob Base, Kool Moe Dee, Eric B. and Rakim and Hammer all powered singles with beats Brown produced as many as 20 years earlier. They weren't the only ones; by the early '90s the churning-fatback pattern immortalized in Brown's "Funky Drummer (Part One)" (1969) was a staple among club-savvy alternative-rock acts. Even Michael Jackson's celebrated moonwalk was little more than an update of a Brown move called the camel walk.

Dealing with a body of work so wide-ranging and important is not easy, particularly for those starting from scratch. Certainly, there are greatest-hits albums available, of which *20 All-Time Greatest Hits!* is the best buy. Fortunately, due to the multiplicity of reissues, fans can now listen to Brown's history by specific periods. Those interested in some of the lesser hits, particularly from his funk-fueled late-'60s and early-'70s work, may want to augment *20 All-Time Greatest Hits!* with *J B 40*, *Funk Power* or the spectacular *Foundations of Funk: A Brand New Bag, 1964–1969.* And those who think of Brown only as a singer need to hear *Soul Pride,* a collection of instrumental tracks that not only show how Brown's interests extended from R&B into jazz but that also document his surprising strengths as a keyboardist.

The single best introduction to Brown's work is *Star Time,* a wonderfully annotated, admirably representative four-CD boxed set that follows Brown's career from "Please Please Please," his 1956 debut, to "Unity," a 1984 collaboration with hip-hop godfather Afrika Bambaataa. In addition to including all the intervening hits, it restores some singles to their full-length versions, offers a fair amount of non-LP material and includes several illuminating rarities, among them the previously unreleased original version of "Papa's Got a Brand New Bag." Five stars barely describe its greatness.

Apart from such compilations, however, much of Brown's original catalog remains out of print at this writing. That's not to say these titles are unavailable; some can be found as Japanese or German imports, and others may still appear (although often at a premium) on the used-album market.

Brown's early recordings—though far from being his best work—have been the most consistently obtainable until now. Perhaps the best overview of this period can be heard on Solid Smoke's now deleted albums, *The Federal Years, Part 1* and *Part 2,* which include all of Brown's hits from 1956 to '60, plus a representative slice of his other work from that time. Greater depth can be had from the 42-song *Roots of a Revolution* (focusing on 1956–1962, with two songs each from '63 and '64), but this set purposely excludes Brown's best-known titles under the assumption that serious fans would already have them.

Then there are the original albums themselves. Of these, *Think* is by far the best, in part because it has the highest hit quotient ("Think," "I'll Go Crazy" and "Good Good Lovin' "), but mostly because it offers Brown's most distinctive work to that point, particularly in its chugging title tune. *Please Please Please,* despite including Brown's first single, the raw, gospel-inflected "Please Please Please," and his first R&B chart topper, the more traditional R&B tune "Try Me," is mostly given over to derivative material like "Chonnie-on-Chon" and "Let's Make It." *Try Me,* which was first reissued in 1964 as *The Unbeatable James Brown,* repeats "Try Me" but otherwise leans more toward the blues, thanks to songs like "I Want You So Bad (You Made Me Love You)" and "Messing with the Blues," while *The Amazing James Brown* shows off the increasing proficiency of his band through gritty titles like "Dancin' Little Thing" and "Come over Here." With *James Brown Presents His Band,* Brown moves into the instrumental realm and delivers his epochal remake of Jimmy Forrest's "Night Train," but *Excitement Mr. Dynamite* (which has also been available as *Shout and Shimmy*) returns Brown and company to the hard-hitting vocal approach of *Think,* even to the point of repeating "Good Good Lovin'."

At that point, though, Brown was still better known for his live show than for his recordings, a fact that explains the somewhat misleading title to the studio album *James Brown and His Famous Flames Tour the U.S.A.* Incredibly, King Records president Syd Nathan felt there was no market for a real James Brown live album, so the singer went ahead and recorded *Live at the Apollo* on his own; it turned out to be the album that finally put him on the map. And no wonder. An astonishing document, it doesn't just present the hits but it shows off the incredible precision of Brown's band as well as the uncanny bond he had with his audience. *Pure Dynamite!,* an even more energetic set recorded before a raucously appreciative crowd at Baltimore's Royal Theater, followed a year later, and Brown would release 11 more live albums after that, including 3 more recorded at the Apollo: *Live at the Apollo, Vol. 2,* with its itchy, intense rendition of "There Was a Time"; *Revolution of the Mind: Live at the Apollo, Vol. 3;* and the Papa's-still-got-it *Live at the Apollo 1995.* Also worth seeking out is *Love, Power, Peace: Live at the Olympia, Paris 1971,* in which Brown's band shows off its discipline and complete mastery of the groove. Because Brown toured with a large revue, *The James Brown Show* puts its emphasis on the other players in the show, including his band; likewise, *James Brown Presents His Show of Tomorrow* features only two tracks by Brown, with the rest given over to members of the revue. Brown also put out a couple of "faked" live albums—studio recordings with audience noise dubbed in later. Perhaps the most notorious of these was *Showtime* (fortunately, its best tunes appear without embellishment on *Messing with the Blues*), but *Super Bad* repeats the ruse, as does the first half of the double album *Sex Machine,* although the loping, hypnotic groove generated by his band on "Give It Up or Turnit Loose" makes such fakery almost forgivable. This material was rereleased without the fake applause on *Funk Power.*

Brown later admitted that his model for *Live at the Apollo* was Ray Charles's concert recording *In Person.* That wasn't his only nod to Brother Ray; *Prisoner of Love,* with its string sweetening and choral cushioning, is self-consciously in the vein of Charles's ABC recordings—although Brown remains far too raw a singer to seem much at home in these MOR arrangements. No matter; the direction Brown takes with *Papa's Got a Brand New Bag* would soon leave Charles in the dust, at least from an R&B perspective. This, in effect, is the birth of funk, as Brown's songs grow lean and repetitious, with fewer and fewer chord changes and a greater emphasis on rhythmic tension. Granted, nothing else on the album takes that idea quite as far as its two-part title tune, but that was more than enough. The revolution truly had begun.

Actually, Brown suggests in his autobiography that the revolution had actually begun with *Out of Sight,* an album he recorded for Smash shortly before *Brand New Bag,* but a legal battle between Brown, King Records and Smash resulted in a court order withdrawing the album shortly after its release (the single "Out of Sight" can be found on *Star Time*). Lost when *Out of Sight* was removed from the picture was a track entitled "I Got You (I Feel Good)," but Brown, typically, turned the situation to his advantage and recut the song with a harder groove; both versions of the song can be found on *Star Time,* but the funkier and more familiar of the two is the centerpiece of *I Got You* (*I Feel Good*). *Out of Sight* was reissued on CD in 1995. Brown didn't cut down on his balladry during this period, however. *It's a Man's, Man's, Man's World* certainly has its share of funk, including "Ain't That a Groove," but there's room enough for the slow ones, including the male-chauvinist title track and a tearfully intense number called "The Bells." Likewise, *James Brown Sings Raw Soul* alternates rhythmically intense tunes like "Money Won't Change You" and "Let Yourself Go" with soppy ballads. Even the unstoppable groove of "Cold Sweat"—which with its driving, monolithic bass pulse and exquisite Maceo Parker sax break was a milestone almost as important as "Papa's Got a Brand New Bag"—is flanked on *Cold Sweat* with MOR numbers like "Mona Lisa" and "Nature Boy" as well as a smattering of rock & roll oldies.

Of course, some of that was simply a reflection of Brown's determined eclecticism. Like Ray Charles, Brown refused to see himself as a one-dimensional musician and regularly fleshed out his albums with material that ranged far afield from the sound of his singles. Sometimes he did whole albums of such songs, like *Thinking About Little Willie John and a Few*

Nice Things, a tribute to the seminal R&B stylist that boasts a touching cover of Little Willie John's "Talk to Me," but is padded with instrumentals. He also flirted with jazz, trying his hand at lounge singing with the Dee Felice Trio on *Gettin' Down to It* and recording *Soul on Top* with the Louis Bellson big band.

But Brown's most consistent sideline was playing organ, piano and even drums. Although Brown is by no means a master technician, his solos are remarkably fluid and at their best compare well against the work of jazz-funk players like Les McCann and Ramsey Lewis. In all, Brown released 11 instrumental albums between 1961 and '71; some, like *James Brown Plays New Breed*, *James Brown Plays the Real Thing* and *James Brown Plays James Brown Today and Yesterday* feature his funky, Jimmy McGriff–style organ solos; others, like *Mighty Instrumentals*, *James Brown Plays and Directs the Popcorn* and *Ain't It Funky,* put the emphasis on his band. Most have been unfairly written off as inconsequential, but as the anthology *Soul Pride* reminds us, the music is often quite good, particularly on rhythm-centered tunes like "Soul Pride," from *The Popcorn.* Nor should we forget the albums he produced for his backing band, the J.B.'s, and their various spin-offs, a sampling of which is spread between *James Brown's Funky People* and *James Brown's Funky People, Part 2.* (The former also includes Lyn Collins's "Think [About It]," which was the basis for rapper Rob Base's "It Takes Two" rhythm bed, while the latter has Bobby Byrd's original "I Know You Got Soul," which Eric B. and Rakim later reconfigured.)

With *Say It Loud, I'm Black and I'm Proud* Brown states what had long been implicit in his music; the black-power sentiment of the title tune generated a certain amount of controversy at the time, but the album isn't all politics, as the loping "Licking Stick" makes clear. Brown's band was getting funkier with each passing month; even his outtakes are astonishing, as evidenced by the selection on *Motherlode. It's a New Day So Let a Man Come In* is especially strong, thanks to "Give It Up or Turnit Loose," a mesmerizing (and heavily sampled) workout with interlocking guitar and bass patterns, as well as such lesser greats as "It's a New Day" and "Let a Man Come In and Do the Popcorn." But many of Brown's hottest singles from this period—"Funky Drummer," for instance—didn't make it to album until Brown began to be anthologized in the '80s and '90s. Some of these tracks turn up in remixes on *In the Jungle Groove,* a DJ-oriented release that augments "Funky Drummer" with a three-minute "Bonus Beat Reprise." Still, *Star Time* offers the choicest selection as well as the most complete versions of these tracks, an important consideration when dealing with singles like "Mother Popcorn," which fades out during Maceo Parker's tenor solo on *The CD of JB* but appears in its full glory (all 6:18 minutes' worth) on *Star Time.*

Hot Pants includes a salacious version of the title track. *There It Is* is even better, with both "I'm a Greedy Man" and the marvelously kinetic "Talkin' Loud and Sayin' Nothing," plus the dark message number "King Heroin." After the double album *Get on the Good Foot,* Brown released several unlistenable soundtracks; but *The Payback* merits a hearing; from there, he went straight to *Hell,* a somewhat mixed double album. By this point, Brown was losing his edge, and as he tried to adjust to the disco era, his albums grew increasingly spotty. Some, like the remake-oriented *Sex Machine Today* or the uncharacteristic *Everybody's Doin' the Hustle and Dead on the Double Bump,* are conceptual failures, while others—*Body Heat*, *Mutha's Nature*, *Jam 1980's* or *People*—are simply uninspired. Still, he has his moments: *Hot,* which Brown claimed was copied by David Bowie on "Fame"; *Get Up Offa That Thing,* with its breathlessly insistent title tune; "For Goodness Sakes, Look at Those Cakes," his amusingly lusty tribute to feminine assets on *Take a Look at Those Cakes.* With *The Original Disco Man,* he even comes to terms with disco itself (check the backing vocals on "It's Too Funky in Here"), and he proves on *Soul Syndrome* that he could imitate the Miami sound as well as anyone.

By the early '80s, Brown was in limbo, with no label and a waning audience. He recorded a live album at Studio 54; entitled *The Greatest Hits Live in Concert* (originally *Live in New York*), it isn't even as good as the live Japan date *Hot on the One,* recorded a year earlier. He tried going independent, releasing the pleasantly retro *Bring It On!* through the tiny Augusta Sound label; it's a good album but heard by almost no one. He even went Hollywood for a time, appearing in and contributing to the soundtracks of *The Blues Brothers* and *Dr. Detroit;* the latter has the more interesting musical performance. But it wasn't until he cut "Living in America" for the soundtrack to *Rocky IV* that Brown was

able to reestablish himself. Ironically, part of the reason "Living in America" works is that it plays off the clichéd James Brown–isms that had come back into vogue; in a sense, Brown was just imitating himself, as he is through the rest of *Gravity. I'm Real* takes the opposite approach, with Brown complaining about rappers ripping him off (musically, that is), over rhythm tracks largely built around—ahem—sampled James Brown records. *Soul Session Live* is the soundtrack from a Cinemax special that offers more stars (Aretha Franklin, Joe Cocker, Wilson Pickett) than memorable music, but *Universal James,* recorded after Brown's release from prison on traffic and assault charges, is a return to form that boasts a sharp new band and a classic sense of material.
— J.D.C.

NAPPY BROWN

★★★½ **Don't Be Angry (Savoy, 1984)**
★★★ **Tore Up (1984; Alligator, 1990)**
★★★½ **Something Gonna Jump Out the Bushes! (Black Top, 1988)**

Hailing from Charlotte, North Carolina, Napoleon "Nappy" Brown Culp (b. 1929) made his mark as an urban blues singer with a series of fierce singles for Savoy in the mid-'50s, most of them written by the prolific Rose Marie McCoy. Typical of the fate befalling most black artists in the '50s, two of Brown's best efforts, "Don't Be Angry" and "Pitter Patter," received more exposure when covered by white artists (the Crew Cuts with "Don't Be Angry" and Patti Page with "Piddily Patter Patter"), although Brown's version of "Don't Be Angry" did rise to #25 on the pop chart before the Crew Cuts chop-blocked him. That Brown had something going for him as a vocalist is amply demonstrated on the Savoy collection, *Don't Be Angry.* On tracks cut between 1954 and 1956, Brown shows off his ingratiating vocal style on a host of first-rate tracks. His varying backing support is exemplary throughout: boogie-woogie master Sam Price on piano; Panama Francis and Milt Hinton comprise the formidable rhythm section; the redoubtable Mickey Baker does the job on guitar; and the saxophone lineup includes both Big Al Sears and Budd Johnson.

Brown remained active on the club circuit as a working blues act and wound up on record again in the '80s, courtesy of Alligator and Black Top. Both albums have their merits, but Black Top's *Something Gonna Jump Out the Bushes!* is the more impressive of the two. Here Brown is in both great, gruff voice—a tinge of B.B. King's sweetness here, Howlin' Wolf's crustiness there—and good humor. As he has throughout his recording career, Brown attracts good musicians, notably here Anson Funderburgh, whose serpentine, razor-sharp guitar lines are one of this album's constant pleasures. — D.M.

RAY BROWN

★★★ **The Big Three (with Milt Jackson and Joe Pass) (1975; Original Jazz Classics, 1994)**
★★★★ **Something for Lester (1977; Original Jazz Classics, 1989)**
★★★½ **Montreux '77 (with Milt Jackson) (1977; Original Jazz Classics, 1989)**
★★★★★ **As Good as It Gets (with Jimmy Rowles) (Concord Jazz, 1978)**
★★★ **Live at the Concord Jazz Festival, 1979 (Concord Jazz, 1979)**
★★★★★ **Tasty! (with Jimmy Rowles) (Concord Jazz, 1980)**
★★★ **A Ray Brown 3 (Concord Jazz, 1982)**
★★★ **Soular Energy (Concord Jazz, 1985)**
★★★ **Don't Forget the Blues (Concord Jazz, 1986)**
★★★★ **Magical Trio 1 (with Art Blakey and James Williams) (EmArcy, 1987)**
★★★ **Summer Wind (Concord Jazz, 1990)**
★★ **Brown's Bag (Concord Jazz, 1991)**
★★★★ **Moore Makes 4 (Concord Jazz, 1991)**
★★★★ **Ray Brown's New Two Bass Hits (with Pierre Boussaguet) (Capri, 1992)**
★★★ **3 Dimensional (Concord Jazz, 1992)**
★★★★ **Bassface (Telarc, 1993)**
★★★★ **Don't Get Sassy (Telarc, 1994)**
★★★★ **Black Orpheus (Evidence, 1994)**
★★★★★ **Seven Steps to Heaven (Telarc, 1995)**
★★★★ **Some of My Best Friends Are . . . the Piano Players (Telarc, 1995)**
★★★★ **Some of My Best Friends Are . . . the Sax Players (Telarc, 1996)**

No other bassist in the world sounds like Ray Brown. With his cavernous sound, woody tone and superbly musical approach to his instrument, Brown (b. 1926) is one of the most respected jazzmen to emerge from the postwar generation. A constantly in-demand sideman since the late '40s, Brown can be heard on thousands of recordings with practically every major mainstream jazz artist. His '50s stint with Oscar Peterson's trio and extensive session work with Verve highlight his superb gifts, and his marvelous playing also can be heard on Concord Jazz recordings throughout the last three decades.

Some of Brown's most inspirational performances can be heard on *Tasty!* and *As Good as It Gets,* duet recordings with pianist Jimmy Rowles. These two men get inside each other's skin, and their interaction is both exciting and deeply moving. Brown also cut a wonderful duet session, the out-of-print *This One's for Blanton,* with Duke Ellington in 1972.

Brown's own small-group work on Concord has always featured fine players and graceful arrangements, but the quality of his recent work on Telarc is particularly high. Both *Some of My Best Friends Are . . . the Piano Players* and *Some of My Best Friends Are . . . the Sax Players* are delightful, while *Seven Steps to Heaven,* with Brown's regular pianist Benny Green, is typical of the jubilantly swinging recordings Brown is producing as his first half century in jazz comes to a close. — S.F.

ROY BROWN

★★★★ **Good Rocking Tonight (Quicksilver, 1982)**
★★★★★ **Good Rocking Tonight: The Best of Roy Brown (Rhino, 1994)**
★★★★ **The Complete Imperial Recordings (Capitol, 1995)**

Vocalist Roy Brown (1920–1981) melded the cry of the blues to the fervor of gospel, then tossed in a dash of Bing Crosby–style crooning. His signature style—shouting, wailing, relentlessly rhythmic—bridged the hard-charging R&B of the late '40s and early '50s and early country- and blues-influenced rock & roll.

Recording in New Orleans in the late '40s, Brown played a key role in the development of Crescent City rock & roll; he went on to influence the blues scene in the early '50s, informing the work of B.B. King and Bobby "Blue" Bland. A flamboyant showman, Brown taught his contemporaries a thing or two about stirring up an audience.

Brown is represented domestically by three fine albums, two focusing on the critical studio sides of the early years, and one showcasing the artist in a live setting nearly three decades after "Good Rocking Tonight" put him on the American music map. Rhino's *Good Rocking Tonight: The Best of Roy Brown* collects the essential DeLuxe singles, from the enduring title track to 1951's rousing "Big Town," and adds four noncharting tracks released on the King label, as well as his last big R&B hit, 1957's "Let the Four Winds Blow." This is prime Roy Brown, delivering bighearted boisterous workouts like "Mighty Mighty Man" as well as heart-wrenching blues ballads such as " 'Long About Midnight," on which the subtlety and nuance of his vocal attack is little short of breathtaking.

"Let the Four Winds Blow," the template for an even bigger hit by Brown's Imperial label mate Fats Domino, is by far the best known of the 20 sides Brown recorded under the aegis of the masterful producer, writer, bandleader and trumpeter Dave Bartholomew. Only 14 of these were issued, but all 20 can be found on *The Complete Imperial Recordings.* Many of the tracks here are quintessential New Orleans rock & roll, in the style Bartholomew had perfected with Domino. While chart success greeted only "Let the Four Winds Blow," this collection shows that Brown's music was still as lively and vital as ever, even if public attention had drifted.

Finally, *Good Rocking Tonight,* a live performance from the early '70s, provides further evidence of Brown's undiminished talent. All Brown's children are in the grooves here: The soulful cries that punctuate the opener, "Travelin' Blues," lead us to Bobby Bland; "Love for Sale," a tender, mournful blues, features the clear, precise, pained diction that also marks B.B. King's vocal style; the macho swagger of "Good Rocking Tonight"—indeed, the falsetto cries throughout the album—reveal a deep root of Presley's style.

Brown died of a heart attack shortly after raising the roof at the 13th New Orleans Jazz and Heritage Festival. The work he left behind constitutes a remarkable legacy. — D.M.

RUTH BROWN

★★★ **Gospel Time (1963; Lection/Mercury, 1989)**
★★½ **Fine Brown Frame (1968; Capitol, 1993)**
★★★ **Have a Good Time (Fantasy, 1988)**

★★★★ **Blues on Broadway (Fantasy, 1989)**
★★★★★ **Miss Rhythm: Greatest Hits and More (Atlantic, 1989)**
★★★½ **Fine and Mellow (Fantasy, 1991)**
★★★★ **The Songs of My Life (Fantasy, 1993)**
★★★★★ **Rockin' in Rhythm: The Best of Ruth Brown (Rhino, 1996)**
★★★★ **R+B=Ruth Brown (Bullseye Blues, 1997)**

To say that Ruth Brown put Atlantic Records on the map is an understatement. Her first hit, 1949's "So Long," was only the second for the nascent label; over the next decade Brown, with a style rooted in gospel and legitimate swing, racked up 23 more R&B hits, leading one wag to dub Atlantic "the house that Ruth built." In all, she recorded more than 80 songs between 1949 and 1961, leaving the label that year as its best-selling artist.

Born Ruth Weston in 1928 in Portsmouth, Virginia, Brown worked in the fields by day and by night sang at church. She began her professional career in 1947 as a vocalist with Lucky Millinder's Big Band, and a year later she went solo when Atlantic cofounders Ahmet Ertegun and Herb Abramson offered her a contract following a roof-raising performance at the Crystal Cavern in Washington, D.C. In those days and on her Atlantic recordings her vocal timbre was light and airy, but the blues inflections and impeccable sense of phrasing are already evident. Age and experience deepened her voice, bringing out the lusty belter in her. This evolution is dramatically illustrated on the 40-track, two-CD Atlantic retrospective, *Miss Rhythm,* which includes not only her best-known songs (such as "[Mama] He Treats Your Daughter Mean," "5-10-15 Hours," "Wild, Wild Young Men," "Lucky Lips," "This Little Girl's Gone Rockin' "), but lesser-known—though no less inspired—singles (notably "Have a Good Time," the gospel-influenced "I Can See Everybody's Baby" and "As Long as I'm Moving") and three previously unreleased tracks, including a swinging performance on "It's All for You."

The essential single-disc overview, *Rockin' in Rhythm: The Best of Ruth Brown,* contains two studio tracks not on *Miss Rhythm* ("Mend Your Ways," a 1953 B side notable mainly for being Atlantic's first stab at overdubbed vocals; and a stomping, swinging Top 10 R&B hit from 1956, "Sweet Baby of Mine," one of Brown's sassiest vocals on record) as well as two rare live cuts of "(Mama) He Treats Your Daughter Mean" and "Oh What a Dream," both from a 1959 performance in Atlanta.

Brown went on to cut two albums for Philips; one of these, *Gospel Time,* was recorded in Nashville with producer Shelby Singleton and some of Music City's top session players. Brown sounds transported, declaiming and testifying as if she were literally back in the church. An apt illustration of the point where gospel intersects R&B, *Gospel Time* finds Brown putting new spins on such well-worn items as "Just a Closer Walk with Thee" and "Peace in the Valley."

Eventually Brown fell on hard times and dropped out of the business. Spurred by Miles Davis's support, she resumed her career, ultimately to greater achievement than she had known in the '50s. She is no longer simply a recording artist but an actress as well, with a Tony Award to her credit, presented in 1989 for her performance in the Broadway musical *Black and Blue.* This new phase of Brown's career has been buttressed by the renewal of her recording career as well. A live album, *Have a Good Time,* features several imposing performances, including irrepressible updates of three Atlantic gems, "5-10-15 Hours," "Have a Good Time" and "(Mama) He Treats Your Daughter Mean." The stunning *Blues on Broadway* features Brown delivering a version of "Good Morning Heartache" that compares favorably to Billie Holiday's. A 1997 release, *R+B=Ruth Brown,* finds her blending some sturdy R&B and pop gems (e.g., "Break It to Me Gently," "Love Letters," "I'm Gonna Move to the Outskirts of Town") with some tough but relatively obscure items on the order of Willia Mabon's "I Don't Know" and Doc Pomus's "Destination Heartache" in what becomes a seamless and idiosyncratic statement of purpose. Minus her mesmerizing personal testimonies, this studio effort captures much of the high drama and lascivious good humor that inform Brown's club performances these days.

Fine and Mellow showcases the blues singer in Brown: In Holiday's swinging title track, she adopts an insouciant tone, spits out the lyrics detailing her woes with a two-timing man, then turns tender and earthy when the narrative comes around to warm nights in the sack. By contrast, she comes on haggard and world-weary on the evocative Doc Pomus blues "A World I Never Made." The actress in Brown tells all we need to know about the struggling, marginally talented artist of Pomus's song, bereft and broke in an unforgiving urban nightmare, who finally, reluctantly, sees the light. Probing each lyric phrase for meaning, Brown manages to recast the number in the darkest, most hopeless terms, never easing up on her character.

The Songs of My Life is a semiautobiographical journey through good times and bad by a woman who has seen her fair share of both. Brown may sing more consistently deeper on *Fine and Mellow,* but the raw nerves she displays on the song selection here bespeak a work that cuts deep into her own experiences both in philosophical, ruminative overviews (à la "The Songs of My Life" and Arthur Prysock's "I Wonder Where Our Love Has Gone") and in homages to other artists whose counsel inspired and guided her along the way. Holiday, whose path Brown crossed as a young lady then beginning her career, is honored in an in-your-face version of "God Bless the Child." Brown also revitalizes Lena Horne's signature song, "Stormy Weather," with a deliberate, woebegone reading that is the vocal equivalent of the clouds opening up and "raining all the time." With a fine band lending low-profile, note-perfect support, and harmonica virtuoso William Galison sculpting feathery, tear-stained lines above Brown's lamentations, the song pays tribute to Horne's breathtaking original even as Brown nearly makes it her own. Blessed by Rodney Jones's sensitive production and arrangements, Brown describes a life lived full measure every time she sings. She closes *Songs* with the pop classic "I'll Be Seeing You," all deep longing and poetic yearning. Accompanied only by Mike Renzi on piano, Brown displays the tender heart and the resilient spirit buoying her throughout the bumpy ride that has been her life and career. An amazing woman, vibrant and vital, is fully revealed on disc. — D.M.

TOM BROWNE

★★ **Mo' Jamaica Funk (Hip Bop, 1994)**
★★ **Another Shade of Browne (Hip Bop, 1996)**

Trumpeter Tom Browne (b. 1954) learned from masters like Jimmy Nottingham and Roy Eldridge while a student of New York's High School of Music and Art yet has had little difficulty tailoring his sound to the demands of the dance floor. After building his reputation as a sideman with Sonny Fortune and Lonnie Liston Smith he made his pop-jazz debut covering hits, then scored his own huge hit, "Funkin' for Jamaica," from the out-of-print *Love Approach.* After a lengthy retirement Browne resurfaced with an unabashed attempt at a sequel, *Mo' Jamaica Funk.* — J.S.

DAVE BRUBECK

★★★★ **Jazz at the College of the Pacific (1953; Fantasy, 1987)**
★★★★ **Stardust (1953; Fantasy, 1990)**
★★★½ **Jazz Goes to College (1954; Columbia, 1989)**
★★★ **The Last Set at Newport (1958; Atlantic, 1973)**
★★★½ **Gone with the Wind (1959; Columbia, 1987)**
★★★★½ **Time Out (Columbia, 1960)**
★★★½ **A la Mode (1960; Fantasy, 1985)**
★★★½ **Brubeck/Mulligan/Cincinnati (1971; MCA, 1990)**
★★★ **Two Generations of Brubeck (Atlantic, 1973)**
★★★½ **We're All Together for the First Time (Atlantic, 1973)**
★★★ **Brubeck and Desmond—1975: The Duets (Horizon, 1975)**
★★★ **All the Things We Are (Atlantic, 1976)**
★★★ **25th Anniversary Reunion (A&M, 1977)**
★★½ **Concord on a Summer Night (Concord Jazz, 1982)**
★★★½ **Dave Brubeck/Paul Desmond (1982; Fantasy, 1990)**
★★★★ **Twenty-Four Classic Original Recordings (1982; Fantasy, 1990)**
★★★ **Reflections (Concord Jazz, 1986)**
★★★★ **The Dave Brubeck Quartet Featuring Paul Desmond in Concert (Fantasy, 1986)**
★★★½ **Music from "West Side Story" (Columbia, 1986)**
★★★ **Blue Rondo (Concord Jazz, 1987)**
★★★ **Moscow Night (Concord Jazz, 1988)**
★★★★ **The Great Concerts (Columbia, 1988)**
★★★½ **Jazz Impressions of New York (Columbia, 1990)**
★★★ **Quiet as the Moon (MusicMasters, 1991)**
★★★ **Time Signature (Columbia, 1991)**
★★★½ **Late Night Brubeck, Live from the Blue Note (Telarc, 1994)**
★★★ **Just You, Just Me (Telarc, 1994)**

★★★ **Nightshift, Live at the Blue Note (Telarc, 1995)**
★★★½ **Young Lions & Old Tigers (with Joshua Redman, Christian McBride, Joe Lovano, Michael Brecker, George Shearing and Gerry Mulligan) (Telarc, 1995)**
★★★ **In Their Own Sweet Way (Telarc, 1997)**

Critics may bitch about Dave Brubeck's (b. 1920) braininess—having studied with Darius Milhaud, the pianist was as influenced by classical music as he was by jazz tradition, and it's apparent that he thinks when he swings. But he was smart enough to collaborate in his essential outfit, the Dave Brubeck Quartet, with a highly intuitive alto saxophonist, Paul Desmond, whose introspective style lent airy grace to Brubeck's often high technique. And the Quartet were pioneers.

At the vanguard of the West Coast school (whose members favored a cool style, in contrast to bebop's frenzy), Brubeck's quartet was among the first to experiment with novel time signatures. Desmond's "Take Five," off *Time Out,* was played in 5/4 time, a rhythm today's braver jazzers take for granted; Brubeck's "Blue Rondo à la Turk" was played in 9/8—yet while Max Roach and Benny Carter, among others, had tried out unorthodox rhythms, the Brubeck Quartet was popular enough that its movement beyond traditional 4/4 gained broad impact.

The Quartet's college concerts, beginning in the 1950s, were tremendously influential for turning suburbanites into knowledgeable insiders; for many, Brubeck was the first experience of any jazz beyond Dixieland (*Jazz Goes to College,* with its phenomenal Desmond solo "Balcony Rock," epitomizes the appeal). *Time Signature,* four CDs, best introduces the man and his casual magic: Clean, supple melody meets strong, easy swing. Fantasy has reissued good volumes of early Dave: *Stardust*, *Twenty-Four Classic Original Recordings* and especially *Jazz at the College of the Pacific* and anything featuring Paul Desmond hold up well. Columbia's reissues, *Music from "West Side Story"* and *The Great Concerts* present the Quartet at its finest; along with *Jazz Impressions of New York,* they show off, too, Brubeck's tuneful gifts. *All the Things We Are* finds Brubeck contending with radical composer Anthony Braxton; *We're All Together for the First Time* and *Brubeck/Mulligan/Cincinnati* pair the pianist with saxist Gerry Mulligan; the later Brubeck, primarily on Concord, continues in the very tasteful style of his early work. — P.E.

JACK BRUCE

★★★★ **Songs for a Tailor (1969; Polydor, 1989)**
★★★★ **Things We Like (1970; Polydor, 1989)**
★★★½ **Harmony Row (1971; Harmony, 1989)**
★★★ **Out of the Storm (1974; Polydor)**
★★★ **How's Tricks (1977; Polydor, 1989)**
★★★ **Will Power (Polydor, 1989)**
★★★ **A Question of Time (Epic, 1989)**

Classically trained bassist, cellist and vocalist Jack Bruce (b. 1943) studied at the Royal Scottish Academy of Music before playing jazz and blues with Alexis Korner's Blues Incorporated and the Graham Bond Organisation, where he met drummer Ginger Baker. Bruce went on to join John Mayall's Bluesbreakers, with guitarist Eric Clapton. Bruce, Clapton and Baker later formed the improvisation-oriented rock band Cream. Bruce's innovative bass playing in this group did much to influence fusion; after Cream he worked with Michael Mantler and Carla Bley in the JCOA Orchestra to make *Escalator over the Hill.*

Songs for a Tailor and *Things We Like* showcase Bruce at his best. The former includes two compositions Bruce couldn't adapt to Cream's needs, "Weird of Hermiston" and "The Clearout." The latter is an outstanding fusion session with guitarist John McLaughlin, reeds player Dick Heckstall-Smith and drummer Jon Hiseman. The rest of Bruce's solo output is erratic, but his playing is always worth a listen. Drummer Simon Phillips is an adept partner on *How's Tricks. A Question of Time* features another song originally written for Cream, "Hey Now Princess." — J.S.

BILL BRUFORD

★★★½ **Feels Good to Me (Editions EG, 1977)**
★★★ **One of a Kind (Editions EG, 1979)**
★★ **The Bruford Tapes (Editions EG, 1979)**
★★ **Gradually Going Tornado (Editions EG, 1980)**
★★★ **Master Strokes, 1978–1985 (Editions EG, 1986)**
★★★½ **Earthworks (Editions EG, 1987)**

★★★ **Dig (Editions EG, 1989)**
★★★ **All Heaven Broke Loose (Editions EG, 1991)**
★★ **Earthworks Live Stomping Ground (Venture/Caroline, 1994)**

Drummer Bill Bruford (b. 1949) once said that the reason he joined the rock band Yes was that he thought he was joining a jazz band. Since then, he's straddled the worlds of progressive rock (Genesis, King Crimson, UK) and progressive British fusion (National Health). Throughout, Bruford has brought his own ideas and talents to the fusion arena.

Feels Good to Me races full-bore into fusion, with former National Health band mate Dave Stewart, guitarist Allan Holdsworth and bassist Jeff Berlin making up the core of the band. Not content merely to set the beat, Bruford contributes some biting vibes and marimba work as well. One of the recording's nicer surprises is Annette Peacock's vocals, especially on "Back to the Beginning." While some of the compositions meander a bit, the extremely strong performances more than take up the slack.

Although the core band on *One of a Kind* is the same, the material and energy aren't as potent, and Peacock is absent. On the plus side, Bruford spins out compositions like "Fainting in Coils," a remarkably labyrinthine bit of music. With the rest of the material less dense, Holdsworth stretches out.

The live *Bruford Tapes* basically rehashes the same material, with John Clark filling Holdsworth's spot quite nicely. This quartet also plays on *Gradually Going Tornado* (informed by Bruford's Genesis residency rather than his jazz inclinations), which features the lovely "Palewell Park" and fusion number "Joe Frazier." Nicely summarizing the Bruford band, *Master Strokes, 1978–1985* includes a Bruford collaboration with Patrick Moraz.

After a few intense years with the revamped King Crimson, Bruford returned to jazz, forming the Earthworks band with some of England's best young players, including Loose Tubes keyboardist and trumpeter Django Bates, bassist Mick Hutton and saxophonist Iain Bellamy, with old mate Dave Stewart producing and occasionally adding keyboards. Creating some of the best experimental fusion of the 1980s, Bruford began using samples such as a slamming door and timpani on a MIDI drum set, with the meters varying from densely complex to moderate fours and the playing following suit.

Dig solidifies the direction of the debut. The rhythm track of "Dancing on Frith Street" would border on Third Stream if it wasn't so outright funky and concerned with pop forms (like reggae). Tim Harries's fretless electric bass fits in well with this spirit of innovation, but the compositions are not as strong, nor the playing as puissant, as on the debut.

All Heaven Broke Loose builds on the strength of both albums, with the loose-limbed experimentation and pop cops added to Bruford's muscular and intelligent work on his MIDI drums. *Earthworks Live Stomping Ground* had a similar genesis to *The Bruford Tapes* in that they were both originally set for radio broadcast. The sonics 20 years down the road are far better, but the band seems to meander a bit live, lacking the intensity of the studio recordings. — H.B.

RUSTY BRYANT

★★★★ **Rusty Bryant Returns (1969; Original Jazz Classics, 1995)**
★★★½ **Legends of Acid Jazz (Prestige, 1996)**

Tenor/alto saxophonist Royal "Rusty" Bryant (b. 1929) developed a honking, Gene Ammons–influenced tenor style that worked to great effect on several 1950s hits, particularly "Night Train," and led a soul-jazz/R&B group featuring vocalist Nancy Wilson. Bryant recorded eight albums for Prestige, most of them enjoyably soulful outings. The terrific *Rusty Bryant Returns* and *Legends of Acid Jazz* are the only ones left in print. — J.S.

B SHARP JAZZ QUARTET

★★★ **B Sharp Jazz Quartet (MAMA, 1994)**
★★★★ **Mirage (MAMA, 1995)**
★★★★ **Searching for the One (MAMA, 1996)**
★★★½ **Tha Go 'Round (MAMA, 1997)**

The B Sharp Jazz Quartet was formed in 1990 in Crenshaw, an artsy, predominantly African-American neighborhood in Los Angeles, by a team of players committed to using the postbop tradition, hard-swinging blues and today's funk rhythms to present spirited original and classic material. The band began with drummer Herb Graham Jr., saxophonist Randall Willis, pianist Eliot Douglass and bassist Reggie Carson.

The quartet's eponymous debut is marked by highly charged playing and a distinctive group sound, with Graham (coleader with Willis) writing five of the nine wide-ranging originals that lead into a warm, challenging rendition of John Coltrane's "Naima." By the time *Mirage* was recorded, Rodney Lee had moved into the keyboard slot (adding B-3 organ to the mix as well as piano). Ex–Basie-band singer Carmen Bradford's scatting, chanting presence adds to the cohesive spirit of B Sharp's second disc.

B Sharp's third recording brought another personnel change as bassist Osama Afifi joined Graham, Willis and Lee. *Searching for the One* further strengthened the group's collective voice, with even more urban music influences surfacing in their bold sound and all-original material. *Tha Go 'Round* extends the band's acoustic commitment and development.

— K.F.

ROY BUCHANAN

★★½ **Roy Buchanan (Polydor, 1972)**
★★½ **Second Album (1973; Polydor, 1988)**
★★★½ **That's What I Am Here For (Polydor, 1974)**
★★★½ **In the Beginning (1974; Polydor, 1988)**
★★½ **Live Stock (1975; Polydor, 1988)**
★★★ **A Street Called Straight (Atlantic, 1976)**
★★★ **Loading Zone (Atlantic, 1977)**
★★½ **You're Not Alone (Atlantic, 1978)**
★★½ **My Babe (Waterhouse, 1980)**
★★★½ **When a Guitar Plays the Blues (Alligator, 1985)**
★★½ **Dancing on the Edge (Alligator, 1986)**
★★★ **Hot Wires (Alligator, 1988)**
★★★★ **Sweet Dreams: The Anthology (Polydor, 1992)**
★★★½ **Guitar on Fire: The Atlantic Sessions (Rhino, 1993)**

Chiefly a blues player, his style based on the stinging clarity of Albert and B.B. King, Telecaster master Roy Buchanan (1923–1988) was also capable of almost demonic virtuosity—jazz flourishes and lightning runs—and of combining both passion and precision. His passion, however, was an introspective one—he was neither an innovator nor a crowd pleaser. Instead, his playing was always highly personal, concentrated and intense.

Beginning by backing up rockabilly greats Dale Hawkins and Ronnie Hawkins, Buchanan then did sessions before going solo. He retained a sideman's sensibility—playing, not vision, remained his forte. His first release blueprinted a pattern from which he would seldom depart—blues, countryish rockers and the occasional spiritual (his father was a preacher). Nearly all of the lengthy instrumental passages are exciting, but until the arrival of blue-eyed soulster Bill Sheffield, on *In the Beginning,* he worked with mediocre singers, and he never found a good drummer until he recorded for Atlantic. Buchanan himself attempted vocals only rarely on record, and with embarrassing results: His monotonous blues delivery proved how demanding that superficially simple style can be; when he tried for a ballad, he often sang off-key. On "The Messiah Will Come Again," from *Roy Buchanan,* he settled for talking—to only marginally better effect.

That's What I Am Here For, with its Hendrix tribute ("Hey Joe") and its varied song selection, holds up well, as does *In the Beginning* (its full horn section lends interest). Arif Mardin's classy production helps elevate *A Street Called Straight,* and *Loading Zone,* produced by Stanley Clarke, is probably Buchanan's most ambitious work—he ranges from a jazzlike density to a swooning grace (although unimaginative strings and harp glissandos clutter the mix). Much more straightforward, the Alligator albums are Buchanan returning to his metier—the blues. The *Sweet Dreams* collection is the place to start; *Guitar on Fire* also blazes.

— P.E.

BUCKWHEAT ZYDECO

★★★ **One for the Road (1979; Paula/Flyright, N.A.)**
★★★ **100% Fortified Zydeco (Black Top, 1983)**
★★ **Turning Point (Rounder, 1984)**
★★½ **Waitin' for My Ya-Ya (Rounder, 1985)**
★★★ **Zydeco Party (Rounder, 1987)**
★★★★ **On a Night Like This (Island, 1987)**
★★★½ **Taking It Home (Island, 1988)**
★★★★ **Where There's Smoke, There's Fire (Island, 1990)**
★★★½ **On Track (Charisma, 1992)**
★★★ **Choo Choo Boogaloo (Warner Bros., 1994)**
★★★★ **Trouble (Atlantic, 1997)**

One of several pretenders to Clifton Chenier's throne, Stanley "Buckwheat" Dural Jr. (b. 1947) is a journeyman blues player and competent zydeco accordionist whose recordings, though seldom exceptional, are rarely less than entertaining. He actually began his professional career as an R&B organist and is a fair soloist in the Jimmy McGriff mold, as "Jasperoux" (from *100% Fortified Zydeco*) attests. As a zydeco accordionist, though, he's an oddity. Though he clearly knows the repertoire (no surprise, considering the time he spent as part of Chenier's Red Hot Louisiana Band), Buckwheat's approach to the traditional material is considerably less convincing than his Creole-style takes on pop tunes, as he shows with his version of Mungo Jerry's "In the Summertime" (*100% Fortified Zydeco*). Unfortunately, it was a while before this truth dawned on any of his producers. Hence, *Turning Point* meanders from bayou funk (the title tune) to halfhearted rock ("Tutti Frutti"), while *Waitin' for My Ya-Ya* alternates between the classic New Orleans rhythms of "My Feet Can't Fail Me Now" or "Tee Nah Nah" and such oddities as a reggae-style version of Lee Dorsey's "Ya Ya." (*Zydeco Party* combines the best moments of *Turning Point* and *Waitin' for My Ya-Ya* with a fiery performance of "Hot Tamale Baby.")

On a Night Like This, however, solves most of Buckwheat's problems. Not only does producer Ted Fox wisely emphasize the resilient groove of Buckwheat's rhythm section, which creates a pulse that puts plenty of punch into "Ma 'Tit Fille," but he also matches Buckwheat with a handful of stunningly appropriate covers, including the Blasters' "Marie Marie," Booker T.'s "Time Is Tight" and the Dylan title tune. Both *Taking It Home* and *Where There's Smoke, There's Fire* continue in that vein, although the mostly traditional *Taking It Home* offers but a single cover, a version of Derek and the Dominos' "Why Does Love Got to Be So Sad." *Where's There Smoke,* on the other hand, not only pairs Buckwheat with Los Lobos's David Hidalgo, it even brings in Dwight Yoakam for an inspired "Hey, Good Lookin'." But *On Track* is neither as ambitious nor as successful, despite a sterling rendition of "The Midnight Special." *Choo Choo Boogaloo* is an engaging children's record. *Trouble* puts it all together with a tremendous set of zydeco originals. — J.D.C.

ALEX BUGNON

★★★ **Love Season (RCA, 1989)**
★★★ **Head over Heels (RCA, 1990)**
★★★ **107° in the Shade (RCA, 1991)**
★★★ **This Time Around (RCA, 1993)**
★★★½ **Tales from the Bright Side (RCA, 1995)**

Jazz/R&B keyboardist Alex Bugnon (b. 1959) grew up absorbing a wide range of jazz influences at the legendary festival in his hometown of Montreux, Switzerland. He took up the keyboards under the direction of Herbie Hancock, then went to the Berklee College of Music in Boston. Bugnon grounded his conception by working with a gospel group and playing in the R&B bands of Najee, James Ingram, Patti Austin, Freddie Jackson and Keith Sweat. His combination of jazz harmonies with funk rhythms pulled *Love Season* to #2 on the R&B charts. *Tales from the Bright Side* is more eclectic, featuring a tribute to his mentor, "Mr. Hancock," some acoustic performances and the stately "Waltz in G Minor." — J.S.

JANE BUNNETT

★★★½ **Spirits of Havana (Denon, 1992)**
★★★★ **The Water Is Wide (Evidence, 1994)**
★★★★ **Jane Bunnett and the Cuban Piano Masters (World Pacific, 1996)**
★★★★½ **Chamalongo (Blue Note, 1998)**

Jane Bunnett (b. 1955) is a fully realized stylist on both flute and soprano saxophone, working the edges between hard bop and free jazz while transcending any particular influences. Trained on classical piano in her native Toronto, Bunnett was inspired by Charles Mingus to become a jazz musician. Her flute playing combines the abstract blues of Eric Dolphy with the precocious freedom of Rahsaan Roland Kirk.

Bunnett studied soprano with contemporary master Steve Lacy, who imparted some of his unique understanding of how to play the demanding compositions of Thelonious Monk. These lessons were well learned, as the lucid treatments of Monk's "Pannonica" and "Brake's Sake" demonstrate on *The Water Is Wide.* The album also features "Serenade to a Cuckoo," a beautiful tribute to Kirk, and several of Bunnett's own works, including the uplifting "Elements of Freedom." In addition to solid contributions from her husband, trumpeter Larry Cramer, the band includes longtime collaborator Don Pullen on piano, Billy Hart on drums, Kieran Overs on bass and vocalists Sheila Jordan and Jeanne Lee on the moving version of the traditional title cut. Throughout the 1990s, Bunnett made multiple trips to Cuba to work with and record some of the island's most notable players. *Spirits of Havana* teams her with singer Merceditas Valdes and pianists Hilario Duran, Frank Emilio Flynn and Gonzalo

Rubalcaba. *Jane Bunnett and the Cuban Piano Masters* features Bunnett in a variety of settings with Flynn and José Maria Vitier. These first Cuban albums were steeped in Afro-Cuban jazz; *Chamolongo* includes many of the same players but focuses on the rhythms of traditional Cuban folkloric music and the chants of Santeria, an Afro-Cuban tradition. Bunnett weaves her flute and soprano saxophone through the rich rhythms and melodic tapestry built by her Cuban collaborators rather than superimposing her own sensibility on the music. — J.S./K.F.

ERIC BURDON

★★★ **The Greatest Hits of Eric Burdon and the Animals (MGM, 1969)**
★★½ **Eric Burdon Declares War (1970; Rhino, 1992)**
★★★ **Wicked Man (GNP, 1988)**

After singing top-notch R&B with the original Animals, the brilliant, brawling Eric Burdon (b. 1941) moved to California, where he reconstructed himself as an ultrahippie. His new band, Eric Burdon and the Animals, were nothing like the original crew—they made novelty singles, albums awash in psychedelic clichés and strange, overheated epics. Their out-of-print albums are hard to find, but *The Greatest Hits of Eric Burdon and the Animals* covers the essentials. It's a strange collection but in some ways compelling—Burdon is so fervent a vocalist that he makes even a slight single like "Sky Pilot," with its phase-shifter effects and clunky antiwar message, sound almost significant, and when he goes for broke on an operatic treatment of the Bee Gees' "To Love Somebody" or Ike and Tina Turner's "River Deep, Mountain High," he achieves the thrilling, almost surreal melodrama of a mad, latter-day Gene Pitney.

Then, reclaiming his passion for black music, Burdon began working with a California funk outfit in 1970. "Spill the Wine" was the first, and very infectious single, released by Eric Burdon and War, and found on *Eric Burdon Declares War.* A follow-up double album, *Black Man's Burdon* (out of print), however, was embarrassingly inflated, and the exhausted singer left War to its own devices. War flourished; Burdon floundered. Recording with one of his idols, blues legend Jimmy Witherspoon, he turned in a credible performance on *Guilty!* (now out of print), but the '70s as a whole were a wasteland for the singer.

The Eric Burdon Band was basically a washout. Burdon reunited with the original Animals and flourished briefly in the early '80s, then put out the solo album *Wicked Man* (1988). Recorded with a cast of nobodies, the record features solid, undistinguished playing—but Burdon's voice sounds, as always, remarkable. A certain pathos attends his remake of the Animals' classic "House of the Rising Sun"—that of a brilliant talent, lost and nearly forgotten, except by the diehard fans who continue to attend his sporadic live performances. — P.E.

SOLOMON BURKE

★★★★ **The Best of Solomon Burke (1965; Atlantic, 1989)**
★★★½ **Soul Alive (Rounder, 1984)**
★★★ **A Change Is Gonna Come (Rounder, 1986)**
★★★½ **Home Land (Bizarre/Straight, 1991)**
★★★★ **Home in Your Heart: The Best of Solomon Burke (Rhino, 1992)**
★★★ **Let Your Love Flow (Shanachie, 1993)**
★★★½ **Soul of the Blues (Black Top, 1993)**
★★★½ **Live at the House of Blues (Black Top, 1994)**
★★★ **Into My Life You Came (Savoy, N.A.)**
★★★ **Lord, We Need a Miracle (Savoy, N.A.)**

Born in 1936 to a church family in Philadelphia, pioneering soul artist Solomon Burke was occupying the pulpit and singing solo in the choir by the age of 9, hosting a gospel radio show by age 12, and making secular and gospel records by age 19. By the time he got his big break with Atlantic in 1960, at age 24, he was in full command of a vocal style that could convincingly sell virtually any type of song, be it gospel, country, R&B, or the nascent gospel/R&B mutation termed soul. The lessons he had learned preaching the gospel—specifically, how to modulate his voice for maximum emotional impact—were put to good use when he got hold of an evocative song lyric, as evidenced by a string of Atlantic hits (both R&B and pop) between 1961 and 1967. His first was "Just Out of Reach (of My Two Open Arms)," a country song to which Burke gave an R&B spin on the strength of his smooth, crooning style. His Atlantic tenure shows him to be a one-of-a-kind singer: He could affect a big, gravelly baritone that came on like a Rev. James Cleveland firestorm or, as the occasion demanded, a suave, cool, gentleman's croon à la Brook Benton, and he could do it all in convincing fashion. His most enduring hit, 1965's "Got to Get You Off My Mind," couples a bouncy Memphis-style soul groove to the sort of measured pop-soul crooning that had been effectively employed by Sam Cooke on his trailblazing singles of the late '50s and early '60s. While *The Best of Solomon Burke* is an excellent overview of the artist's most important recordings, the more inclusive title is the two-CD anthology *Home in Your Heart,* containing all of the hits and some relatively obscure pleasures among its 39 cuts from 1962 to 1968. Check out Burke at his deceptively weary best on his self-penned "Dance Dance Dance."

Always staying close to his gospel roots, Burke has continued recording and performing. *Into My Life You Came* and *Lord, We Need a Miracle* are by turns fire and brimstone and soothing and meditative, with the message coming through loud and clear regardless of the approach. Burke's two Rounder releases bring him back to the secular world. *Soul Alive* is a live album that catches him in one of his feistier moods, ranging across a broad spectrum of material that includes several of his Atlantic sides and stirring interpretations of songs identified with other legends, such as Little Richard's "Send Me Some Lovin' " (the studio version is on *Home in Your Heart*), "He'll Have to Go" (Jim Reeves), "I Almost Lost My Mind" (Ivory Joe Hunter) and "I Can't Stop Loving You" (Ray Charles). *A Change Is Gonna Come,* a studio album, is a spotty attempt at updating Burke's sound. When it works, it's startling—his take on the title track is given added resonance by the sadness, almost resignation, in his delivery; there's a world of pain in that voice. *Home Land* shows Burke in fine form, singing with conviction on the hard-hitting "Baby Please Don't Cry" and a powerful version of Otis Redding's "Try a Little Tenderness." *Let Your Love Flow* fills in one of the gaps in Burke's recording history by reissuing 10 of the artist's late-'70s recordings. Produced by Swamp Dogg, the tracks—all but one written by the estimable Jerry Williams Jr.—run the gamut from boisterous funk-soul replete with burbling electric piano ("Boo Hoo Hoo [Cra-Cra-Craya]") to tender R&B ballads ("Sidewalks, Fences and Walls") to richly ornamented TSOP-style disco ("Please Don't You Say Goodbye to Me"). Gliding effortlessly through the various stylistic approaches the material demands, Burke is rather breathtaking in his command of shading and timbre, using these tools to personalize the readings in a heartfelt way. Best example: the Otis Redding–influenced ballad "The More," which finds Burke turning a placid folk melody into the stuff of revelation with a gritty, pleading vocal.

Burke's most recent efforts are solid outings, one in the studio, one live, the latter being compelling enough to have been awarded a 1995 Handy Award as Soul/Blues Album of the Year. In both instances New Orleans is the mise en scène, and the Crescent City's horn sections and second-line rhythms are a nice fit with Burke's varied approach. On *Soul of the Blues,* he reworks some blues evergreens into an R&B mode without losing the je ne sais quoi that made the songs memorable in the first place. Willie Dixon's "My Babe" sets the tone for the album, with Burke adopting a wry, wary persona. Mark "Kaz" Kazanoff's robust harmonica soloing pays homage to Little Walter's original version, while drummer Herman V. Ernest III lays down a solid, second-line beat. A roaring, big-band take on Roy Brown's "Good Rockin' Tonight" follows, before Burke mellows out again on a straightforward, testifying blues reading of Guitar Slim's "Sufferin' Mind." So it goes—a refreshing blend of big-voiced shouting and silky, seductive crooning, with the New Orleans musicians supplying the precise amounts of gris-gris and restraint to make the most of the moment. *Live at the House of Blues* documents a quintessential Burke concert, which incorporates a good amount of preacherly testifying, engaging flirtations with female audience members and all the vocal tools Burke needs to shout it out or sing it sweet and low (a medley of "If You Need Me"/"Tonight's the Night"/"I Almost Lost My Mind" blends both approaches to shattering effect). A solid, winning effort all around—not the least of its virtues being the tireless backing of the Souls Alive Orchestra—the House of Blues show proves Burke the performer to be every bit as potent as he was during his glory years on Atlantic. — D.M.

EDDIE BURNS

★★★★ Detroit (Evidence, 1993)

Eddie Burns (b. 1928) grew up in the country-blues heartland of Mississippi, where he was raised by his grandparents because his father was a traveling musician. Taught by his father on harmonica and guitar, Burns moved during World War II to Clarksdale, Mississippi, where he played with Sonny Boy Williamson (Rice Miller) and Pinetop Perkins. After the war Burns moved to Detroit, where he recorded a few singles and played with John Lee Hooker into the '50s. He built a strong local following in various Detroit clubs and recorded for a number of minor labels. Burns worked days to support his family and played music on the side, doing club dates and the occasional European tour. *Detroit,* the only Burns material currently available, was recorded in 1993 with his working quartet. Burns is in good voice on a mix of originals ("When I Get Drunk" could become a classic) and covers, including an excellent version of Hooker's "Boom Boom." His clean, single-note guitar playing and precision harp work are impressive. — J.S.

R.L. BURNSIDE

★★★★ **Sound Machine Groove (1981; HMG/High Tone, 1997)**
★★★ **Bad Luck City (Fat Possum, 1991)**
★★★★ **Too Bad Jim (Fat Possum, 1994)**
★★★★ **A Asspocket of Whiskey (with the Jon Spencer Blues Explosion) (Matador, 1996)**
★★★★ **Mr. Wizard (Fat Possum/Epitaph, 1997)**

Mississippi blues guitarist R.L. Burnside (b. 1926) learned to play music from his neighbor, as often happens in the rural South. What distinguishes Burnside's case, however, is that his teacher was none other than Mississippi Fred McDowell. Burnside has gone on to become one of the most accomplished performers of the traditional country blues emanating from Mississippi's northern hills, a style that relies on the relationship between terse rhythmic ideas and speech patterns. The songs evolve slowly, twisting and elongating with slashing rhythms and gutbucket lyrics. Unlike standard 8- or 12-bar blues, Burnside's songs have their changes dictated by his internal sense of time. Cueing each section only when he sees fit gives Burnside's performances a linear quality and makes them more identifiable by their rhythmic nuances than by their melodies or harmonies.

Indigenous to Mississippi's Desoto, Panola, Tate and Marshall counties, Burnside's music doesn't easily translate into the electrified realm due to its textural subtlety and droning, one-chord riffing. Masterfully, however, Burnside makes the transition, and his second Fat Possum release bears testament to that fact. Produced by Robert Palmer and recorded primarily at Junior Kimbrough's juke joint in Chulahoma, Mississippi, Burnside is joined by a battery of local players such as drummer Calvin Jackson and guitarist Kenny Brown. Their sympathetic yet impassioned playing inhabit such traditional fare as "Shake 'em on Down," "Old Black Mattie" and "Going Down South." Other songs that Burnside and company make their own include two by Lightnin' Hopkins, "Death Bell Blues" and "Short Haired Woman."

Burnside's debut, *Sound Machine Groove,* and his first Fat Possum release, *Bad Luck City* (now out of print), both feature the Sound Machine, his family band, which included sons Joseph, Daniel and Dwayne Burnside. *Sound Machine Groove* was a lost classic of juke joint blues until High Tone reissued it with three additional tracks. *Bad Luck City* showcases the contemporary side of Burnside, who performs a number of classic blues such as John Lee Hooker's "Boogie Chillun'," Howlin' Wolf's "Killing Floor" and Bo Diddley's "You Don't Love Me." These standards appear alongside originals like "Burnside's Blues" and the title track. *Bad Luck City* has a flair, but it surely doesn't have the mystique and voodoo that characterize *Too Bad Jim,* underscoring Burnside's "progression" from contemporary blues to the more provincial—albeit more interesting—music for which he will be remembered.

A Asspocket of Whiskey was recorded in February 1996, in Holly Springs, Mississippi. The release finds Burnside plying his trade with the Jon Spencer Blues Explosion, a young, bassless New York City rock trio. If seemingly unorthodox, the combination of master and protégé is bracing, as guitarists Spencer and Judah Bauer and drummer Russell Simins lay down some sinister grooves behind Burnside's slashing guitar and smoky vocals. Standout tracks include the manic "Snake Drive" and a slow, agonizing version of "Walking Blues."

An assemblage of tracks recorded at various locations between September 1994 and November 1996, *Mr. Wizard* again features Spencer and company on two tracks. The album's finest moments, though, are those in which Burnside is joined with guitarist Kenny Brown and his grandson, drummer Cedric Burnside. One such tune is a shuffling, electrified instrumental in honor of his mentor, titled "Tribute to Fred," which was recorded at an interesting locale: Jimmy's Auto Care in Oxford, Mississippi. — B.R.H.

KENNY BURRELL

★★★★ **All Night Long (with Donald Byrd) (1956; Original Jazz Classics, 1990)**
★★★★ **All Day Long (with Donald Byrd) (1957; Original Jazz Classics, 1990)**
★★★ **Kenny Burrell (1957; Original Jazz Classics, 1992)**
★★★★ **Kenny Burrell and John Coltrane (1958; Original Jazz Classics, 1987)**
★★★ **Blue Lights, Vol. 1 (1958; Blue Note, 1989)**
★★★★ **On View at the Five Spot Cafe (1959; Blue Note, 1987)**
★★★ **Midnight Blue (1963; Blue Note)**
★★★★ **Crash! (1963; Prestige, 1994)**
★★★★ **Ellington Is Forever, Vol. 1 (1975; Fantasy, 1993)**
★★★★ **Ellington Is Forever, Vol. 2 (1975; Fantasy, 1994)**
★★★½ **Tin Tin Deo (Concord Jazz, 1977)**
★★★ **When Lights Are Low (Concord Jazz, 1979)**
★★★ **Live at the Village Vanguard (Muse, 1980)**
★★★ **Listen to the Dawn (Muse, 1980)**
★★★★ **Bluesin' Around (Columbia, 1983)**
★★★½ **Two Guitars (with Jimmy Raney) (1986; Original Jazz Classics, 1992)**
★★★ **Guiding Spirit (Contemporary, 1990)**
★★★½ **Sunup to Sundown (Contemporary, 1991)**
★★½ **Moon and Sand (Concord Jazz, 1992)**
★★★★ **Midnight at the Village Vanguard (1993; Evidence, 1995)**
★★★½ **Then Along Came Kenny (1994; Evidence, 1996)**

Guitarist Kenny Burrell (b. 1931) hails from Detroit, where he built a solid reputation backing Candy Johnson, Count Belcher, Tommy Barnett and Dizzy Gillespie as well as leading his own groups. A facile, bluesy guitarist with an elegant rhythmic sense, Burrell owes obvious debts to Django Reinhardt and Charlie Christian, but his soulful, easy-swinging playing style has carved its own mark, moving deftly from postbop to R&B. After moving to New York in the late 1950s, Burrell led a number of hot improvisational "blowing" sessions with a variety of groups from quintets to larger units.

All Night Long and *All Day Long* typify the spirit of these blowing sessions, with Donald Byrd's trumpet sharing the lead and bassist Doug Watkins and drummer Arthur Taylor anchoring the rhythm section. Saxophonists Hank Mobley and Jerome Richardson join the front line on *Night,* with pianist Mal Waldron filling out the section. Tommy Flanagan takes over keyboards on *Day,* while Frank Foster adds his tenor saxophone to the lineup. *Two Guitars* features the personnel from *Night* with Jackie McLean as the reedman and second guitarist Jimmy Raney sitting in.

Kenny Burrell uses the all-Detroit rhythm section of Flanagan on piano, Watkins on bass and Elvin Jones on drums, with Cecil Payne playing baritone saxophone. Flanagan is back on the quintet session *Kenny Burrell and John Coltrane,* along with Paul Chambers on bass and Jimmy Cobb on drums, for a fascinating contrast of Coltrane's intensity against the diffidence of Burrell's approach.

At the end of the 1950s and into the 1960s Burrell recorded for several labels in a variety of contexts, most of which attempted to mine the popular soul-jazz style. *On View at the Five Spot Cafe* and *Blue Lights, Vol. 1* benefited from the presence of drummer Art Blakey, who kicked Burrell's playing along nicely.

Crash! teams Burrell with jazz/blues organist Jack McDuff. *Moonglow* and *Out of This World,* both now out of print, feature legendary tenor saxophonist Coleman Hawkins. *Bluesin' Around* collects several unreleased sessions for Columbia, two of which include tenor star Illinois Jacquet. *Midnight Blue* puts Burrell in the *sympatico* context of Stanley Turrentine's soulful tenor.

Burrell's most uncharacteristic album during this era is the beautiful *Guitar Forms,* built around exquisite Gil Evans charts rather than the usual head arrangements. Like so much essential jazz, this Verve recording is, inexcusably, out of print.

Burrell worked with smaller groups during the '70s, relying on Jerome Richardson's sax and flute work as the other solo voice for most of the now deleted Fantasy sets (look for *Both Feet on the Ground*, *Up the Street* and *Sky Street*). His best work during this period is the two-volume Duke Ellington tribute, *Ellington Is Forever, Vols. 1* and *2,* which used Ellington sidemen along with musicians like Jimmy Smith and Nat Adderley paying homage to the great composer's influence.

Burrell went on to work with different trios to achieve some warm, open-ended results, which can be found on the Concord Jazz and Muse sets. *Tin Tin Deo,* with bassist Reggie Johnson and drummer Carl Burnett, is an especially good session.

Guiding Spirit, a live Village Vanguard quartet date, features vibraphonist Jay Hoggard. *Sunup to Sundown* recalls those early blowing sessions with a burning lineup of pianist Cedar Walton, bassist Rufus Reid, drummer Lewis Nash and percussionist Ray Mantilla. Burrell shows that he's only getting better with age on the magnificent live set *Midnight at the Village Vanguard. Then Along Came Kenny* is more live material from the Vanguard. — J.S.

GARY BURTON

★★★½ 3 in Jazz (1963; RCA, 1995)
★★★★ A Genuine Tong Funeral (1968; One Way, 1997)
★★★★★ Crystal Silence (with Chick Corea) (1973; ECM, 1987)
★★★★ The New Quartet (ECM, 1973)
★★★★ Ring (ECM, 1974)
★★★½ Hotel Hello (with Steve Swallow) (ECM, 1975)
★★★★ Dreams So Real (ECM, 1976)
★★★★ Passengers (ECM, 1977)
★★★ Real Life Hits (ECM, 1985)
★★★ Whiz Kids (ECM, 1986)
★★★ Tennessee Firebird (Bear Family, 1989)
★★★ Green Apple (Moon, 1989)
★★★½ Reunion (ECM, 1990)
★★★½ Right Time—Right Place (with Paul Bley) (GNP Crescendo, 1991)
★★★★ Works (ECM, 1994)
★★★ It's Another Day (GRP, 1994)
★★★ Gary Burton and the Berklee Allstars (JVC, 1995)
★★★ Face to Face (GRP, 1995)
★★★ Collection (GRP, 1996)
★★★ Departure (Concord Jazz, 1997)

Vibraphonist Gary Burton (b. 1943) is one of the most influential players of his generation, a four-mallet soloist of amazing dexterity and expression. After attending the Berklee College of Music he quickly established himself in the jazz world as a virtuoso performer and composer with George Shearing and Stan Getz and, by 1967, as a bandleader with guitarist Larry Coryell, bassist Steve Swallow and drummer Bob Moses.

Burton's protofusion group recorded 13 albums for RCA, most of which are now unavailable, as is much of the fine work he did for Atlantic. Try to find the overview *Artist's Choice.* Fortunately, Carla Bley's opera, *A Genuine Tong Funeral,* a 1968 RCA recording with Coryell, Swallow and special guests Steve Lacy on soprano sax, Gato Barbieri on tenor, Mike Mantler on trumpet, Jimmy Knepper on trombone, Howard Johnson on tuba and Bley on keyboards, has recently been reissued.

Burton's lyricism and chamber-music sensibility were tailor-made for the style that producer Manfred Eicher developed at ECM in the 1970s, and Burton became a frequent contributor on Eicher's recordings and other musicians' dates.

Burton's ECM debut, *Crystal Silence,* a series of magnificent duets with pianist Chick Corea, picks up where his best work on Atlantic left off and is arguably a recording high point for both musicians, whose deft touch and lyricism complement each other perfectly. *The New Quartet* introduces guitarist Michael Goodrick, bassist Abraham Laboriel and drummer Harry Blazer on a number of compositions by Corea, Swallow, Carla Bley and longtime Burton songwriter Michael Gibbs.

Burton's most prolific year was 1974. In May he reunited with Swallow from his old quartet for a duet album, *Hotel Hello,* then collaborated with Gibbs on the now out-of-print *In the Public Interest,* a project of Gibbs compositions scored for a large (22 musicians) ensemble. Then, in a four-day period that July, Burton recorded two albums for Eicher; the first was *Ring,* with a group consisting of Goodrick, new guitarist Pat Metheny, percussionist Bob Moses and two bassists, Swallow and Eicher's star instrumentalist, Eberhard Weber. After recording that set he returned to the studio with guitarist Ralph Towner to make a duet record, *Matchbook,* mostly of Towner's compositions (including the Winter Consort standard "Icarus"). The album closes with a stately reading of the Charles Mingus elegy for Lester Young, "Goodbye Pork Pie Hat." This gem is also currently out of print.

Dreams So Real uses the Moses/Swallow rhythm section and guitarists Goodrick and Metheny on a selection of Carla Bley material. *Passengers* combines drummer Dan Gottlieb with bassists Weber and Swallow and guitarist Metheny, with the latter contributing three songs and Swallow and Weber one each. The high point is Corea's "Sea Journey," illustrating Burton's special affinity for Corea's light-spirited melodicism. *Times Square* (currently unavailable) benefits from some strong songwriting by Swallow. *In Concert* (unavailable) reunites Burton with Corea in a sublime exchange. *Real Life Hits* introduces pianist Makoto Ozone. *Works* is a solid overview of Burton's ECM years.

In 1971, Burton began teaching at the Berklee College of Music, where in the 1980s he brought promising students into the recording process on *Whiz Kids* and *Gary Burton and the Berklee Allstars. Reunion* is a quintet date with Metheny, pianist Mitch Forman, bassist Will Lee and drummer Peter Erskine. *Right Time—Right Place* is a series of duets and solos recorded in Copenhagen with pianist Paul Bley. — J.S.

HENRY BUTLER

★★ **Fivin' Around (Impulse!, 1986)**
★★★★ **The Village (Impulse!, 1988)**
★★★★ **Orleans Inspiration (Windham Hill, 1990)**
★★★★ **Blues and More, Vol. 1 (Windham Hill, 1992)**
★★★ **For All Seasons (Atlantic Jazz, 1996)**
★★★★½ **Blues After Sunset (Black Top, 1998)**

Henry Butler (b. ca. 1946) is a blind pianist from New Orleans who made his debut in 1986 at age 39 with *Fivin' Around,* a flute-heavy postbop excursion, largely faceless save for a version of "Giant Steps" with strings and a reading of the spiritual "I Want Jesus to Walk with Me" sung in his rich bass voice. *The Village* highlights his extraordinary improvisations on piano, as well as those of multiwind player John Purcell. It also showcases wonderfully melodic and inventive compositions like "Joanna." He even takes a side trip into samba with "Expressions of Quietude" and rag (complete with a tuba) on a version of "The Entertainer."

After a two-year hiatus, Butler took an entirely new approach with *Orleans Inspiration,* recorded live at Tipitina's with Meter Leo Nocentelli. A paean to Butler's roots, the album's original compositions blend seamlessly with a couple of Professor Longhair songs, variations on a theme by Stephen Foster and even a tune from *West Side Story.* Most important, it gives Butler license to cut loose, exploring the upper reaches of his voice and treading the fine line between soul, rock and jazz.

Blues and More, Vol. 1 is a solo piano exploration of the blues at the heart of all Butler's music, a deeply felt performance from an inspired player. Butler's astonishing panstylistic mastery of the entire history of New Orleans piano, bridging stride, swing, bop, traditional jazz, gospel, soul, blues, funk and second-line continues to evolve on *Blues After Sunset,* recorded for the New Orleans–based Black Top Records. — H.B.

WILD CHILD BUTLER

★★★ **Lickin' Gravy (Rooster Blues, 1986)**
★★★★ **These Mean Old Blues (Bullseye Blues, 1991)**
★★★ **Stranger (Bullseye Blues, 1994)**

The legend goes that George "Wild Child" Butler (b. 1936) was so tough he got his nickname from his mother, and the down-home blues he turns out on guitar and harmonica back the story up. An itinerant musician, he started working the juke-joint circuit in his home state of Alabama in the late 1950s, followed by residencies in Houston, New Orleans and Chicago through the 1960s and '70s, recording occasionally for Shaw, Jewel and Mercury Records.

Butler moved to Canada in the 1980s and finally made it back into the studio in the 1990s, recording in London for Bullseye. An impressive comeback, *These Mean Old Blues* is powered by Butler's thick-noted guitar playing, soul-dripping harp licks and impassioned singing. His raspy, Howlin' Wolf–style vocal on "Crack House Woman" is the real sound of the blues. — J.S.

THE PAUL BUTTERFIELD BLUES BAND

★★★★ **The Paul Butterfield Blues Band (Elektra, 1965)**
★★★★★ **East-West (Elektra, 1966)**
★★★★ **The Resurrection of Pigboy Crabshaw (1968; Elektra, 1989)**
★★★ **In My Own Dream (Elektra, 1968)**
★★★ **The Butterfield Blues Band Live (Elektra, 1971)**
★★★★ **Golden Butter: The Best of the Paul Butterfield Blues Band (Elektra, 1972)**
★★★ **Strawberry Jam (Winner, 1995)**
★★★½ **The Original Lost Elektra Sessions (Rhino, 1995)**

PAUL BUTTERFIELD

★★★ **It All Comes Back (1973; Rhino, 1987)**
★★★ **Better Days (1973; Rhino, 1987)**

★★ **Put It in Your Ear (1976; Rhino, 1987)**
★★ **North South (1981; Rhino, 1987)**
★★½ **The Legendary Paul Butterfield Rides Again (Amherst, 1986)**

Never megasellers, Butterfield & Co. still were highly influential in offering '60s rock & roll kids a first, authentic taste of the Chicago blues of the band's hometown. With nimble harp and workmanlike vocals, Paul Butterfield (1942–1987) served as emissary of the magic of Otis Rush, Little Walter and Buddy Guy, mainstreaming their sound for mid-America without condescension or the archivist's overreverence. But his ensemble's strength was guitarists—the group helped mold Mike Bloomfield and Elvin Bishop into premier players. Zest and modesty marked Butterfield's approach—he was a faithful aspirant to the singing of his black mentors, not an original stylist—and while his mission may have seemed more instructive than creative, he played like no pedant. With sharp solos by Bishop and Bloomfield, *East-West* shows precocious skill and confidence. Even with Bloomfield departed, *The Resurrection of Pigboy Crabshaw* shows Butterfield dealing from his strengths. On the nine minutes of "Driftin' and Driftin'," a horn section featuring David Sanborn cooks tastily; "Born Under a Bad Sign" rocks; and on "Pity the Fool" Butterfield sounds freer than he ever would again. The record's R&B pep shows a progress away from the careful attack of the first two albums—and a casual verve the singer would never recover. *Strawberry Jam* highlights the band at its improvisatory best; *The Original Lost Elektra Sessions* unearths previously unreleased takes from the outfit's peak period.

It All Comes Back and *Better Days* are post–Blues Band projects—able but unremarkable. Only by the time of *Put It in Your Ear* and *North South,* however, did Butterfield appear to be running out of steam. The first is a misguided crossover bid overloaded with strings and stellar guests (Levon Helm, Eric Gale, Bernard Purdie); the second should've worked—a partnership with Al Green's producer, Willie Mitchell. Instead, it sinks in a soup of strained funk. — P.E.

JAKI BYARD

★★★★ **Out Front! (1964; Original Jazz Classics, 1994)**
★★★ **With Strings! (Prestige, 1968)**
★★★★ **There'll Be Some Changes Made (Muse, 1973)**
★★★★ **To Them—To Us (Soul Note, 1982)**
★★★ **Foolin' Myself (Soul Note, 1989)**
★★★ **Empirical (Muse, 1990)**
★★ **Phantasies II (with the Apollo Stompers) (Soul Note, 1991)**
★★★★ **Maybeck Recital Hall Series, Vol. 17 (Concord Jazz, 1992)**
★★★★ **Live! (Prestige, 1992)**

In his best playing, pianist Jaki Byard (1922–1999) created a seamless continuum of jazz, freely mixing stride, gospel, bop, modal and any number of other disparate genres, bridging musical styles with unself-conscious elegance. Like his former employer Charles Mingus, Byard was blessed with a sly sense of humor; his recordings are equally inventive and gleeful. This playful and slightly irreverent quality is best found on his solo albums: *There'll Be Some Changes Made*, *To Them—To Us* and *Maybeck Recital Hall Series, Vol. 17.* Wildly imaginative and stunningly performed, they feature a diverse set of show tunes, jazz standards, gospel songs and even transformed pop numbers.

Byard's small-group sessions on Original Jazz Classics all have their moments; out-of-print standouts are *Freedom Together,* with the marvelous rhythm section of bassist Richard Davis and drummer Alan Dawson, and *Experience,* with that other great musical eccentric Rahsaan Roland Kirk. Byard, along with Davis and Dawson, also can be heard to great effect on recordings by saxophonists Booker Ervin and Eric Kloss. — S.F.

DON BYAS

★★★ **A Night in Tunisia (Black Lion, 1963)**
★★★ **Walkin' (Black Lion, 1963)**
★★★★★ **Savoy Jam Party: The Savoy Sessions (Savoy, 1995)**
★★★★ **Don Byas: 1944–1945 (Classics, 1996)**
★★★★ **Tenor Giant (Drive Archive, 1996)**

The ferocious tenor work of Don Byas (1912–1972) is one of the key links between the swing and bop eras. His advanced harmonic knowledge and awesome command of his instrument make for some of the most stimulating listening from that transitional period. After an impressive stint with Count Basie as Lester Young's replacement, Byas hit 52nd Street just when the bop movement was taking off. He was in the "first" bop band with Dizzy Gillespie and Oscar Pettiford and participated in some important recording sessions of the time. The essential *Savoy Jam*

Party documents Byas's exuberant work and features able support from bassist Slam Stewart and such early bop legends as trumpeter "Little" Benny Harris and pianist Clyde Hart. *Don Byas: 1944–1945* and *Tenor Giant* also showcase his classic early blowing.

Byas spent the last 20 years of his life in Europe—fine Byas playing from this period can be heard on the Black Lion recordings. The excellent but sadly out-of-print *Tribute to Cannonball* was a summing-up recording for the great tenorist and includes grand playing by two bop giants: pianist Bud Powell and drummer Kenny Clarke. — S.F.

CHARLIE BYRD

★★★ **Jazz Recital (1957; Savoy, 1993)**
★★★ **Midnight Guitar (Savoy, 1957)**
★★★ **Guitar Artistry of Charlie Byrd (Riverside, 1960)**
★★★ **At the Village Vanguard (1961; Original Jazz Classics, 1991)**
★★★★ **Bossa Nova Pelos Pássaros (1963; Original Jazz Classics, 1992)**
★★★ **Byrd at the Gate (1963; Original Jazz Classics, 1987)**
★★★ **Brazilian Byrd (1965; Legacy, 1994)**
★★½ **Bluebyrd (1979; Concord Jazz, 1991)**
★★½ **Sugarloaf Suite (Concord Picante, 1980)**
★★½ **Isn't It Romantic (Concord Jazz, 1984)**
★★★ **Byrd and Brass (Concord Jazz, 1986)**
★★★½ **It's a Wonderful World (Concord Jazz, 1989)**
★★★ **Charlie Byrd (LaserLight, 1990)**
★★★ **The Bossa Nova Years (Concord Picante, 1991)**
★★½ **Charlie Byrd and the Washington Guitar Quintet (Concord Concerto, 1992)**
★★★ **Moments Like This (Concord Jazz, 1994)**
★★★ **Aquarelle (with the Washington Guitar Quintet) (Concord Jazz, 1994)**
★★½ **Du Hot Club de Concord (Concord Jazz, 1995)**
★★★ **Classical Byrd (Milestone, 1997)**
★★★★ **Latin Byrd (Milestone, N.A.)**

Guitarist Charlie Byrd, born in Virginia in 1925, is known mostly for his pioneering influence on and promotion of Brazilian jazz, despite his classical training. Impressed by the indigenous music of Brazil while on a Latin American concert tour in the early '60s, Byrd helped popularize bossa nova in the United States via recordings with Stan Getz as well as on his own. An accomplished classical guitarist whose purity of technique is widely acclaimed, Byrd studied under Segovia, owes a stylistic debt to Charlie Christian and played in Woody Herman's orchestra before adopting Brazilian music. Despite his varied background, the Brazilian trademark has stuck with him.

Byrd's early records are straightforward acoustic sessions. *Bossa Nova Pelos Pássaros* features the hit "Meditation." *Latin Byrd* is a compilation covering such standard bossa nova titles as "One-Note Samba," "Desafinado" and "Carnaval."

Byrd at the Gate is a mainstream-jazz session with trumpeter Clark Terry guesting. Much of the Concord material features Byrd in trio settings, often with the gas on very low flame. *Byrd and Brass,* with the Annapolis Brass Quintet, is an interesting matchup. *It's a Wonderful World* benefits from Scott Hamilton's generous tenor-saxophone work. — J.S.

DONALD BYRD

★★★ **First Flight (1955; Delmark, 1990)**
★★★★ **Byrd's Word (1955; Savoy, 1991)**
★★★½ **Byrd in Hand (1959; Blue Note, 1995)**
★★★★ **Free Form (1961; Blue Note, 1986)**
★★★ **Groovin' for Nat (1962; Black Lion, 1990)**
★★★ **A New Perspective (1963; Blue Note, 1988)**
★★★ **Electric Byrd (1970; Blue Note, 1996)**
★★★★ **Fancy Free (1971; Blue Note, 1993)**
★★★ **Blackbyrd (1973; Blue Note, 1992)**
★★★½ **Motor City Scene (1986; Bethlehem, 1994)**
★★★½ **Fuego (Blue Note, 1987)**
★★½ **Harlem Blues (Landmark, 1988)**
★★½ **Getting Down to Business (Landmark, 1990)**
★★½ **A City Called Heaven (Landmark, 1991)**
★★★½ **The Best of Donald Byrd (Blue Note, 1992)**
★★½ **Love Byrd: Donald Byrd and 125th Street, N.Y.C. (Discovery, 1994)**
★★★½ **Kofi (Blue Note, 1995)**

Trumpet/flügelhorn player Donald Byrd (b. 1932) was among the group of promising young jazz musicians who came from Detroit to New York City in the mid-1950s. His hot, full-toned trumpet playing with George Wallington and then Art Blakey's Jazz Messengers in '55 and '56 made him a sought-after session player and leader. He recorded with alto saxophonist Gigi Gryce in the Jazz Lab Quintet and with flügelhornist Art Farmer and saxophonist Pepper Adams (on *Motor City Scene*).

First Flight features Yusef Lateef on tenor saxophone and Barry Harris on piano. *Byrd's Word* is a sharp date with Frank Foster on tenor, Hank Jones on piano, Paul Chambers on bass and Kenny Clarke on drums. Saxophonists Charlie Rouse and Adams join the front line on *Byrd in Hand.* Jackie McLean sits in on *Fuego,* and *Free Form* features Wayne Shorter on tenor and Herbie Hancock on piano.

The advent of fusion in the late 1960s led to across-the-board experimentation with electronics, and Byrd joined in with *Fancy Free.* He went on to become one of the more successful crossover jazz artists in the '70s, playing the hard funk epitomized on his later Blue Note records. These records featured the Blackbyrds group, which later recorded on its own, netting the huge hit "Walking in Rhythm." Though the grooves were solid, Byrd's playing became trite and cliché-ridden.

Byrd's attempt to regain the form of his youth on the well-appointed Landmark sessions placed him in the right context for jazz, but when he reached for the old verve, it simply wasn't there.
— J.S.

DONNA BYRNE

★★★ **Sweet and Lovely (Ol' Socks, 1990)**
★★★★ **Let's Face the Music and Dance (Stash, 1994)**
★★½ **It Was Me (Daring Records, 1996)**
★★★½ **Walking on Air (with Herb Pomeroy) (Arbors, 1997)**
★★★★ **Byrnin' (Ol' Socks, 1998)**

Boston-based Donna Byrne (b. 1950) is a selfless singer, preferring subtlety to brassiness, and delivering heartfelt songs with clear, rhythmic phrasing and a cool demeanor. She gives her talented band mates—usually including pianist Dave McKenna, guitarist Gray Sargent and trumpeter Herb Pomeroy—ample space to solo and mingle musically. As a result, she has won a legion of followers and the respect of the finest instrumentalists in and around New England.

Byrne's debut session, *Sweet and Lovely,* captures the essence of her charming, knowing and unfettered style, all of which make for a singer of substance. *Let's Face the Music and Dance* adds reedman Dick Johnson on an exploration of solid, beautiful tunes.

Pomeroy, Sargent, Ken Peplowski (on tenor sax and clarinet) and pianist Bill Cunliffe are aboard for *It Was Me.* Their instrumental work is strong, and Byrne's voice is in good form on this material—a strong departure for Byrne from the obvious standards. In a couple of cases, it's a difficult stretch.

Walking on Air, a session partnered with Pomeroy, is outstanding for the collective personality and maturity this band (with McKenna, Sargent, bassist Marshall Wood and drummer Jim Gwin) has developed above and beyond its members' stunning individual talents. *Byrnin'* is a no-frills, no-horns session with a piano trio that showcases the singer's versatility and broad taste in popular music. Newcomer Tim Ray adds tremendous depth and creativity at the piano. — K.F.

GEORGE CABLES

★★★ **Cables' Vision (1979; Original Jazz Classics, 1992)**
★★★ **Phantom of the City (Contemporary, 1985)**
★★★½ **By George: The Music of George Gershwin (Contemporary, 1987)**
★★★½ **Night and Day (DIW, 1991)**
★★★½ **Maybeck Recital Hall Series, Vol. 35 (Concord Jazz, 1994)**

A well-respected and sought-after accompanist, pianist George Cables (b. 1944) joined Billy Cobham and Steve Grossman in the Jazz Samaritans when he was 18, showing the influences of both Herbie Hancock and Thelonious Monk. He's worked with some of jazz's best sax players, including Sonny Rollins, Dexter Gordon, Frank Morgan and Joe Henderson.

Cables' Vision captures his influences. His duet with Bobby Hutcherson on Hutcherson's "The Stroll" captures the song's tricky Monk-ish rhythms and changes. However, "Morning Song" sounds like a musical outtake from a Steely Dan album.

Phantom of the City is a trio session with bassist John Heard and drummer Tony Williams. *By George: The Music of George Gershwin* takes on Gershwin with a trio and solo performances. In this homage and expansion, Cables takes harmonic and melodic liberties, like the Monk quotes in the solo on "I Got Rhythm" and the chord expansion in "Bess, You Is My Woman Now." His solo version of "Someone to Watch Over Me" is a study in lyricism and dynamism for the piano.

He reprises the latter two tunes during his turn playing the Maybeck Recital Hall Series. "Bess, You Is My Woman Now" sounds similar, hardly missing the bass and drums. He gets even more adventurous in this context, going as far as playing stride. He also does a beautiful rendition of one of his best compositions, "Helen's Song."
— H.B./J.S.

CACHAO

★★★½ **Master Sessions, Vol. 1 (Crescent Moon/Epic, 1994)**
★★★★ **Master Sessions, Vol. 2 (Crescent Moon/Epic, 1995)**

Israel Lopez (b. 1918), better known as Cachao, is one of the acknowledged masters of Afro-Cuban jazz, equally adept as composer, instrumentalist (bass) and arranger. Combine Duke Ellington's elegance and breadth with Charles Mingus's prowess, and you have some idea of the reverence and esteem with which Cachao is held among Latin musicians. Like Astor Piazzolla in tango and Caetano Veloso in Brazilian pop, Cachao has both refined and expanded the language of his genre.

With almost none of his Latin albums in print and those that are available not widely distributed (Salsoul's *Dos,* released in 1994, is the most readily available but is not recommended, due in part to its stingy running time), American listeners are left with the two *Master Sessions* albums. Not that this is any sort of consolation prize; either album would be a worthy addition to a collection. The brainchild of actor/producer Andy Garcia and executive producer Emilio Estefan Jr., the albums are an obvious labor of love, bringing Cachao into the studio with a mixed group of Latin, American and European musicians, including reed player Paquito D'Rivera, guitarist Nelson Gonzalez, flautist Nestor Torres and trombonist Jimmy Bosch.

The results are consistently exciting and eminently listenable. Either album is worth having, but if you must choose, *Master Sessions, Vol. 2* has a slight advantage, both for its three jams (especially the sly "Spoon Lips," where Cachao steadily increases the tempo) and for its "Africa Suite," which finds an exuberant compromise between African rhythms and Western melody and manages to turn the section "Over the Rainbow" into a samba, without lapsing into camp as it might in the hands of a lesser musician. — S.M.

CAB CALLOWAY

★★★★½ **Cab Calloway and the Missourians 1929–1930 (JSP, N.A.)**
★★★ **Cab Calloway 1930–1942 (Best of Jazz, N.A.)**
★★★★ **Cab Calloway 1930–1931 (Classics, N.A.)**
★★★★ **Cab Calloway 1931–1932 (Classics, N.A.)**
★★★★ **Cab Calloway 1932 (Classics, N.A.)**
★★★½ **Cab Calloway 1932–1934 (Classics, N.A.)**
★★★★ **Cab Calloway 1934–1937 (Classics, N.A.)**
★★★★ **Cab Calloway 1937–1938 (Classics, N.A.)**
★★★½ **Cab Calloway 1938–1939 (Classics, N.A.)**
★★★★ **Cab Calloway 1939–1940 (Classics, N.A.)**
★★★★ **Cab Calloway 1940 (Classics, N.A.)**
★★★ **Cab Calloway 1940–1941 (Classics, N.A.)**
★★★ **Cab Calloway 1941–1942 (Classics, N.A.)**
★★½ **Cab Calloway '44 (Magnetic, N.A.)**
★★★ **The Best of the Big Bands (Sony, 1990)**
★★★ **Cab Calloway Featuring Chu Berry (Sony, 1993)**
★★★ **Are You Hep to the Jive? (Sony, 1994)**
★★★ **Cab Calloway and Company (Bluebird, 1994)**
★★★ **Cruisin' with Cab (Topaz Jazz, 1995)**
★★★ **Get with Cab (West Wind, N.A.)**

Bandleader/singer Cab Calloway (1907–1994) is well known as a jazz novelty figure from cartoon soundtracks, as a composer of marijuana tributes and as the goggle-eyed, high-stepping Hi-De-Ho man. Although these caricatures helped build a popular legend for Calloway, they obscured the fact that he was a terrific bandleader whose organizations always played the hottest material and featured some of the brightest instrumental lights of the era, including saxophonists Chu Berry and Hilton Jefferson, trumpeters Dizzy Gillespie and Jonah Jones and drummer Cozy Cole.

Calloway led another band, called the Alabamians, before taking over the Missourians. The Missourians played in a wild, frenetic style that pounded rather than swung the beat. Though much of the *Cab Calloway and the Missourians* disc is instrumental, it includes 10 electrifying performances from Calloway, including a tour de force rendition of the staple song of the era, "St. Louis Blues."

The first of the Classics compilations overlaps with the *Missourians* disc. Calloway's band matched the intensity of any other 1930s working jazz band, led by his inspired persona singing "Minnie the Moocher," "St. James Infirmary," "St. Louis Blues" and the rest. Though "Minnie the Moocher" was one of Calloway's signatures, the other tracks were identified with Louis Armstrong, and Calloway took Armstrong on directly. He did it again on *Cab Calloway 1931–1932,* with smoking versions of "Kickin' the Gong Around" and "You Rascal You" and a band featuring Doc Cheatham on trumpet.

Calloway classics "Reefer Man" and "The Man from Harlem" can be found on *Cab Calloway 1932*; *Cab Calloway 1932–1934* includes "Harlem Camp Meeting," another version of "Minnie the Moocher" and "Doin' the New Lowdown" with the Don Redman Orchestra. Tenor-sax man Ben Webster and bassist Milt Hinton are showcased on *Cab Calloway 1934–1937;* and tenor saxophonist Chu Berry and guitarist Danny Barker join in on *Cab Calloway 1937–1938.*

Not only did Calloway lead one of the swing era's hottest bands, he looked forward to the next thing when he hired trumpeters Dizzy Gillespie and Mario Bauza, who appear on the material dating from 1939 to 1941; Jonah Jones is on trumpet for the last set.

The World War II years broke up Calloway's last great band, as Gillespie went off to seed the next generation of great jazz musicians. Calloway continued on with panache and elegance, even after he had passed the point where most performers would have devolved into self-parody. As late as the 1980s and the

Blues Brothers film, the Hi-De-Ho man could still single-handedly work his magic — J.S.

MICHEL CAMILO

★★½ **Why Not? (1986; Evidence, 1992)**
★★★ **Suntan (1987; Evidence, 1992)**
★★★ **Michel Camilo (Portrait, 1988)**
★★★★ **On Fire (Epic, 1989)**
★★★½ **On the Other Hand (Epic, 1990)**
★★★★ **Rendezvous (Columbia, 1993)**
★★★★★ **One More Once (Columbia, 1994)**
★★★★ **Thru My Eyes (Tropijazz, 1997)**

Pianist Michel Camilo (b. 1952) was schooled in the classical-music tradition in his native Santo Domingo, where at age 16 he became the youngest member of the Dominican Republic's national symphony orchestra. He was a percussionist then, and percussive elements fuel his jazz—a warm, joyous sound filled with Latin fire.

In 1979 Camilo moved to New York, where he worked with the group French Toast in the studio and with Cuban reedmen Paquito D'Rivera and Tito Puente. Soon afterward, his composition "Why Not?" won a Grammy for the Manhattan Transfer.

Camilo's earliest recordings, made for Japan's King label in 1986 and 1987 and reissued for U.S. release by Evidence in 1992, showcase his formidable talent and a musical concept that has grown stronger with age and experience. Electric bassist Anthony Jackson and drummer Dave Weckl are aboard in both the debut septet session *Why Not?* and his *Suntan.* They are also key players on many of his subsequent recordings.

His most formidable showcase, *One More Once* features a Latin/bop jazz-orchestra setting and arrangements for Camilo's finest compositions, including "Why Not?" and "Caribe." The small-group session *Thru My Eyes* puts Camilo's personal twists on beloved jazz standards from Sonny Rollins, Horace Silver, Dizzy Gillespie, Herbie Hancock, Chick Corea and others. — K.F.

EDDIE C. CAMPBELL

★★★½ **Let's Pick It (Evidence, 1993)**
★★★½ **That's When I Know (Blind Pig, 1994)**
★★★½ **King of the Jungle (Rooster Blues, 1996)**

Guitarist/vocalist Eddie Campbell (b. 1939) moved at about age 10 to Chicago, where he became a protégé of Magic Sam. After playing with Jimmy Reed, Koko Taylor and Willie Dixon during the 1970s, Campbell emigrated to Europe. *Let's Pick It* was recorded in 1984 in the Netherlands with the Dutch blues band Tip On In. The group backs Campbell well on a dozen tracks, including two Magic Sam covers, "All My Whole Life" and "Love Me with a Feeling." Campbell's icy-clean tone and penchant for intense note clusters reflect the inspiration of Magic Sam, but songs like "Cold and Hungry," "Messin' with My Pride" and the nifty instrumental "Double Dutch" demonstrate he has his own style as well. "Sister Taught Me Guitar" from *That's When I Know* shows Campbell to be an original writer with a gift for storytelling. *King of the Jungle* covers well-known material such as "Poison Ivy," "The Red Rooster" and "Cheaper to Keep Her" and features the novelty tune "Santa's Messin' with the Kid." — J.S.

JOHN CAMPBELL

★★★½ **A Man and His Blues (1988; Crosscut, 1994)**
★★★★ **One Believer (Elektra, 1991)**
★★★ **Howlin' Mercy (Elektra, 1993)**

John Campbell (1952–1993), like Robert Johnson 30 years before him, sang and played as if he had hellhounds on his trail. Born in Shreveport, Louisiana, Campbell grew up in Texas and began playing blues after a drag-racing accident claimed his right eye, developing an aggressive and rhythmic fingerpicking style modeled after Lightnin' Hopkins. Campbell subsequently moved to New York City, where a chance meeting with contemporary blues guitarist Ronnie Earl initiated his first recording.

An impressive debut, *A Man and His Blues* features a well-chosen mix of solo acoustic numbers and group efforts bolstered by Earl and ex–Muddy Waters harpist Jerry Portnoy. Campbell's voice has a lived-in quality rare for a bluesman in his 30s, and his deep, intricate six-string work on "Deep River Rag" reveals an innate understanding of the use of space for maximum emotional effect.

Campbell underwent a major stylistic change on his first major-label release, *One Believer,* reemerging as a mysterious figure obsessed with the spirit world. His voice became a rabid snarl, and he pumped up the volume and unleashed some hell-bent slide-guitar playing. The songs are spine-chilling: "Devil in My Closet," "Angel of Sorrow," "Tiny Coffin" and "World of

Trouble" illustrate Campbell's ability to tap into the unknown with scary authenticity.

Howlin' Mercy attempts to lead that journey further, with mixed results. Full-throttle covers of Memphis Minnie's/Led Zeppelin's "When the Levee Breaks" and the traditional "Saddle Up My Pony" are supercharged slide workouts, but on tracks like "Ain't Afraid of Midnight" Campbell's over-the-top vocal delivery borders on self-parody. Campbell's unexpected death from a heart attack at age 41 fostered speculation over the influence of his supernatural beliefs but, more important, robbed contemporary blues of an original voice. — S.J.

CANNED HEAT

★★★★ **Canned Heat (Liberty, 1967)**
★★★★ **Boogie with Canned Heat (Liberty, 1968)**
★★★ **Living the Blues (Liberty, 1969)**
★★ **Hallelujah (Liberty, 1969)**
★ **Vintage Heat (Janus, 1970)**
★★★½ **Live in Europe (Liberty, 1970)**
★★★½ **Future Blues (Liberty, 1970)**
★★★★ **Hooker 'n' Heat (1971; EMI, 1991)**
★★½ **Live at the Topanga Corral (Wand, 1971)**
★★ **Historical Figures and Ancient Heads (United Artists, 1972)**
★★ **New Age (United Artists, 1973)**
★★ **One More River to Cross (Atlantic, 1974)**
★★★ **Infinite Boogie: John Lee Hooker and Canned Heat (Rhino, 1986)**
★★★ **John Lee Hooker and Canned Heat Recorded Live at the Fox Venice Theatre (Rhino, 1986)**
★★★½ **The Best of Canned Heat (EMI, 1987)**
★★ **Reheated (Dali, 1990)**
★★★ **Uncanned! The Best of Canned Heat (EMI, 1994)**

No '60s band was more cognizant of blues roots than Canned Heat. An accomplished folklorist, guitarist Al Wilson scoured the Deep South for survivors from the country-blues era, becoming a master of the music's distinctive styles, and lead singer Bob Hite was an avid blues collector who knew all the material by heart. Providing the vision for Canned Heat, Wilson and Hite forged a modern style out of the same elements used by Muddy Waters's classic 1950s band.

Following in Waters's footsteps, the group opens its 1967 debut with a burning cover of "Rollin' and Tumblin'." Great versions of "Bullfrog Blues," "Dust My Broom" and "Help Me" showcase lead guitarist Henry Vestine and the airtight rhythm section of bassist Larry Taylor and drummer Frank Cook. Adolpho de la Parra replaced Cook on the magnificent *Boogie with Canned Heat,* highlighted by an anthemic cover of "On the Road Again."

By this time, Canned Heat had become something of a pop phenomenon and began to suffer from the musical excesses of the era. *Living the Blues* is split between the tight arrangements the band had perfected on its first two albums, including the hit single and Woodstock theme song "Going Up the Country," and the kind of overplayed jam that was becoming the cliché of the moment, including a ridiculously bloated 40-minute-long "Refried Boogie."

The band never regained the terseness of its original conception, although it remained a powerful live act, proven by the excellent *Live in Europe* and particularly *Hooker 'n' Heat,* where the band's mistakes of excess become virtues in the company of John Lee Hooker, who clearly enjoyed the collaboration.

Future Blues features an aggressive reading of Wilbert Harrison's "Let's Work Together." The rest of the group's career is a slow spiral into obscurity, an eerie parallel to the fate of the original country-blues music the late Hite and Wilson both loved. — J.S.

GUS CANNON

★★★★★ **Complete Recorded Works, Vol. 1 (1927–28) (Document, N.A.)**

This record documents the earliest recordings of Gus "Banjo Joe" Cannon and his Jug Stompers, who codified a jug-band tradition whose influence still reverberates today throughout contemporary music, from blues to folk to hip-hop. Cannon played banjo like a woodchopper, hitting the strings with a fierce rhythmic intensity that matched the ribald enthusiasm of his singing, whistling, jug blowing and kazoo playing. He exuded an energy and love of playing on these sides that is incredibly infectious. His 1927 duets (as Banjo Joe) with guitarist Blind Blake include such classics as "Poor Boy, Long Ways from Home," the great story-song "Madison Street Rag" and the hilarious "My Money Never Runs Out," material ripe for sampling. The Stompers were a trio with Cannon, the brilliant harmonica player

Noah Lewis and guitarist Ashley Thompson.
— J.S.

CAPTAIN BEEFHEART

★★★ **The Legendary A&M Sessions (1965; A&M, 1984)**
★★★ **Mirror Man (1965; One Way, 1990)**
★★★★ **Safe as Milk (1967; Buddah, 1970)**
★★½ **Strictly Personal (1968; Blue Thumb, 1985)**
★★★½ **Trout Mask Replica (1969; Reprise, 1970)**
★★★★ **Lick My Decals Off, Baby (1970; Bizarre, 1991)**
★★★½ **The Spotlight Kid/Clear Spot (1972; Reprise, 1990)**
★★½ **Unconditionally Guaranteed (1974; Blue Plate/Caroline, 1990)**
★★ **Bluejeans and Moonbeams (1974; Blue Plate/Caroline, 1990)**
★★★★ **Shiny Beast (Bat Chain Puller) (1978; Bizarre, 1991)**
★★★★½ **Doc at the Radar Station (Virgin, 1980)**
★★★★ **Ice Cream for Crow (1982; Blue Plate/Caroline, 1990)**

Even though he turned his back on music to pursue painting more than a decade ago, Captain Beefheart (b. Don Van Vliet, 1941) still casts a long shadow across popular music's avant-garde. Although his albums have never sold well, their influence has been enormous, and his work has been a touchstone for bands ranging from Devo to Pere Ubu to the Clash. Yet Beefheart's music is often misunderstood even by his fans, who seem dazzled by its virtuosic weirdness without understanding any of its underlying structure or stylistic discipline.

Beefheart's musical roots are in blues and R&B, and fairly conventional fare at that (though it wasn't seen that way at the time). He made his first recordings for A&M and enjoyed some popular success through a raucous remake of the Bo Diddley hit "Diddie Wah Diddie." A&M didn't see much commercial potential in his subsequent work, however, and quickly dropped him; "Diddie Wah Diddie" and five other tunes were later released with the oddly self-congratulatory title *The Legendary A&M Sessions.*

Reorganizing his Magic Band, Beefheart added 19-year-old Ry Cooder to the lineup and cut *Safe as Milk,* an astonishing combination of soulful conventionality and audacious invention. Cooder's guitar playing is especially engaging, blessed with a fluidity that grounds the music in the blues even while pulling it away from the predictability of most white blues bands' efforts. But the most startling thing about this album is its range, which stretches from the doo-wop–derived harmonies of "I'm Glad" to the throbbing, trancelike "Abba Zaba," to the snarling roar of "Electricity." With *Strictly Personal,* Beefheart—this time without Cooder—tried to expand on *Milk*'s approach, but the album was remixed and cuted-up while he was on tour in Europe, enraging Beefheart (and justly so). As such, only the live *Mirror Man* presents his post-Cooder band in its unvarnished prime; though the playing is first-rate, the performances ramble interminably.

Refusing to relinquish artistic control ever again, Beefheart brought in old friend Frank Zappa (the two had met while in their teens) to produce the sorely overrated *Trout Mask Replica.* Musically, much of what Beefheart does here is stunning, merging the melodic plasticity of early Delta blues with the disjointed interplay of free-form improvisation. But Zappa's production undoes much of that, both by working to reveal the inherent artifice of the recording process (for instance, the mistakes-and-all intro to "Pena," in which Beefheart is heard coaching one of his cohorts through a piece of poetry) and mixing Beefheart's voice so high that it almost obscures the magic his band is working (as on "Dachau Blues"). Thus, despite occasionally amazing moments, like "Sugar n' Spikes" and "Dali's Car," the album's superficial weirdness overwhelms the band's brilliantly warped take on the blues.

Beefheart restores the music's balance on the self-produced *Lick My Decals Off, Baby,* where the music is often just as challenging as on *Trout Mask Replica* but far easier to follow. Here every move the band makes stands out, whether it be the vocal wit of "Smithsonian Institute Blues," the gnarled instrumental interplay of "Peon" or the free-blowing dissonance of "Flash Gordon's Ape." With *The Spotlight Kid,* though, the chemistry between his rhythm section and guitarists remains as volatile as ever, but the melodic structure verges almost on hard-rock normalcy, particularly on "I'm Gonna Booglarize You Baby" and "Alice in Blunderland." *Clear Spot* continues Beefheart's move toward the mainstream but doesn't quite coalesce, despite engaging moments like the New Orleans–style "Nowadays a Woman's Gotta Hit a Man." Still, even that seems brilliant compared with *Unconditionally Guaranteed* and *Bluejeans and Moonbeams,* where his increasingly watered-down sound robs his music of its essential energy.

Fortunately, Beefheart is back on course with *Shiny Beast (Bat Chain Puller)*. Thanks to the jazz-schooled assurance of his sidemen, the album includes some of Beefheart's most eloquent instrumental work ("Ice Rose") while still finding room for such pop-friendly titles as "Harry Irene." *Doc at the Radar Station* isn't quite as easygoing, what with the anxious stop-start pulse of "Dirty Blue Gene" and the ominously grinding "Making Love to a Vampire with a Monkey on My Knee," though the music remains disarmingly approachable, even hooky at times ("Hot Head"). Beefheart's last album, *Ice Cream for Crow,* brings him full circle, as his final Magic Band returns to the blues-based sound of *Safe as Milk.* There's still quite a lot of jazz in the mix (check the confident swing of the instrumental "Semi-Multicoloured Caucasian"), and the gritty slide-guitar riffs roiling beneath the title tune rank among his most memorable.
— J.D.C.

CHUCK CARBO

★★★ **Drawers Trouble (Rounder, 1993)**
★★★ **The Barber's Blues (Rounder, 1995)**

Vocalist Hayward "Chuck" Carbo (b. 1926) provides a good example of the seemingly ubiquitous nature of music in New Orleans. The singing barber actually has a long musical history dating back to his work in the 1950s with the vocal group the Spiders. *The Barber's Blues* is an all–New Orleans session ranging from R&B to jazz—on "The Very Thought of You," Carbo's voice is answered by a flügelhorn solo. The album features three Dr. John/Doc Pomus compositions including the atmospheric "Black Widow" and Carbo's own Carnival tribute "Hey, Mardi Gras! (Here I Am)." The accompaniment includes local keyboard prodigy Davell Crawford and former Ray Charles band guitarist Eugene Ross. — J.S.

CHUBBY CARRIER AND THE BAYOU SWAMP BAND

★★★ **Boogie Woogie Zydeco (Flying Fish, 1991)**
★★★½ **Dance All Night (Blind Pig, 1993)**
★★★½ **Who Stole the Hot Sauce? (Blind Pig, 1996)**

Accordion player Roy "Chubby" Carrier (b. 1967) formed his own zydeco band in 1989 after a stint playing with Terrance Simien and the Mallet Playboys. His debut, *Go Zydeco Go,* is currently unavailable. His next release, *Boogie Woogie Zydeco,* delivers on the promise of its title, serving up 15 mostly up-tempo tracks of accordion- and washboard-driven fun. Carrier originals like "Young Creole Man" and "Allons Dancez" defy the listener to sit still, while a version of Boozoo Chavis's "Dog Hill" threatens to bring down the roof. "Be Fair to the People" and "Sherrie" are slower numbers that highlight Carrier's soulful vocals.

Dance All Night finds Carrier performing zydeco readings of songs by Bob Wills and Tommy Duncan ("Stay a Little Longer"), Clifton Chenier ("Tule Ton Son Ton") and Bobby Bland ("Turn On Your Love Light") and is guaranteed to thrill anyone with a pulse. *Who Stole the Hot Sauce?* follows suit, with the churning, the funky and the burning. Offering testimony to Carrier's wide-ranging musical taste, covers of War's funky "Cisco Kid" and Pete Townshend's mellifluous "Squeeze Box" are interspersed with more traditional zydeco fare like the title track, the Carrier-penned "Luziana Feeling" and Clifton Chenier's "Zydeco Sont Pas Sale." — B.R.H.

BARBARA CARROLL

★★★½ **Live at the Hotel Carlyle (DRG, 1991)**
★★★ **This Heart of Mine (DRG, 1994)**
★★★ **Everything I Love (DRG, 1996)**
★★★½ **The Music of Jerome Kern (After 9, 1996)**

The legendary performances of pianist Barbara Carroll (b. 1925) at New York's Hotel Carlyle earned her a cult status akin to that of the better-known Bobby Short, but her approach is more attuned to playing than entertaining, as documented on her 1991 live album. The Worcester, Massachusetts, native was a pioneer on 52nd Street, becoming one of the first women instrumentalists to break into the bop scene. Her touch and emotional depth sprang from a musical affinity with Bud Powell, and she remains a great interpreter of standards, as the Jerome Kern tribute amply demonstrates.
— J.S.

BENNY CARTER

★★★★ **Jazz Giant (1958; Original Jazz Classics, 1987)**
★★★ **Swingin' the '20s (1958; Original Jazz Classics, 1988)**

★★★★★ **Further Definitions (1961; Impulse!, 1986)**
★★★½ **BBB & Co. (with Ben Webster and Barney Bigard) (1962; Original Jazz Classics, 1992)**
★★★★ **The King (1976; Pablo, 1996)**
★★★★ **Carter, Gillespie, Inc. (with Dizzy Gillespie) (1976; Original Jazz Classics, 1992)**
★★★½ **Wonderland (1977; Pablo, 1987)**
★★★★ **Montreux '77 (1978; Original Jazz Classics, 1989)**
★★★ **'Live and Well in Japan! (1978; Original Jazz Classics, 1992)**
★★★★ **1928–1952 (Bluebird, 1979)**
★★★ **Summer Serenade (Storyville, 1980)**
★★★½ **A Gentleman and His Music (Concord, 1985)**
★★★½ **All Stars (with Nat Adderley and Red Norvo) (Gazell, 1985)**
★★★★ **Benny Carter Meets Oscar Peterson (Pablo, 1987)**
★★★★ **Central City Sketches (MusicMasters, 1987)**
★★★★ **In the Mood for Swing (MusicMasters, 1988)**
★★★ **My Kind of Trouble (Pablo, 1989)**
★★★ **Over the Rainbow (MusicMasters, 1989)**
★★★½ **My Man Benny, My Man Phil (with Phil Woods) (MusicMasters, 1990)**
★★★½ **Cookin' at Carlos I (MusicMasters, 1990)**
★★★★ **1929–1933 (Classics, 1991)**
★★★★ **1933–1936 (Classics, 1991)**
★★★★ **1936 (Classics, 1991)**
★★★★ **1937–1939 (Classics, 1991)**
★★★★ **1940–1941 (Classics, 1991)**
★★★½ **All of Me (RCA Bluebird, 1991)**
★★★★ **All That Jazz—Live at Princeton (MusicMasters, 1991)**
★★★ **Harlem Renaissance (MusicMasters, 1992)**
★★★★ **Legends (MusicMasters, 1993)**
★★★★ **An Introduction to Benny Carter: His Best Recordings: 1929–1940 (Best of Jazz, 1993)**
★★★★ **Elegy in Blue (MusicMasters, 1994)**
★★★★ **The Best of Benny Carter (MusicMasters, 1995)**
★★★★ **The Best of Benny Carter (Pablo, N.A.)**

Composer, arranger, bandleader, alto saxophonist and trumpeter Benny Carter (b. 1907) is a figure of such brilliance in jazz history that his reputation has been somewhat obscured by the number of different directions he's followed, which explains why he's less known to the general public than to his legions of musician admirers. Throughout his career, Carter has gone an unorthodox route that has often seen him using his musical abilities in the service of others rather than enhancing his own name.

The mostly self-taught, New York–born musician was influenced in his youth by trumpeter Bubber Miley and played with Fletcher Henderson, Chick Webb, the Chocolate Dandies and McKinney's Cotton Pickers. Though Carter is known as one of the finest alto saxophonists in jazz history, his trumpet playing is also influential; he's recorded on clarinet and trombone, and he's played piano as well.

Carter's 1933 group featured pianist Teddy Wilson, tenor saxophonist Chu Berry, trombonist Wilbur DeParis and drummer Sid Catlett. He spent time in Europe during the rest of the 1930s, frequently doing arrangements for England's BBC radio. His recorded work from this period can be heard on *1936* and *1937–1939.*

During the 1940s Carter was back in the United States leading bands that included Dizzy Gillespie, Miles Davis, Buddy Rich, Max Roach, J.J. Johnson and Joe Albany. From the mid-1940s until the end of the 1950s, Carter was a much-in-demand Hollywood arranger and composer of film and television soundtracks. He recorded with small bands occasionally during this time, to best effect on the Original Jazz Classics reissues of his Contemporary sides. *Jazz Giant* was recorded in 1957 and '58 with a group including Ben Webster on tenor sax and Barney Kessel on guitar. *Swingin' the '20s,* a 1958 session, is a quartet with the great pianist Earl Hines, bassist Leroy Vinnegar and drummer Shelly Manne.

Carter's most important album may well be the classic 1961 set *Further Definitions,* sublime music from a lineup including Coleman Hawkins (a crony dating back to the Chocolate Dandies days) and Charlie Rouse on tenor saxophones, Phil Woods and Carter on altos, Jo Jones on drums, Jimmy Garrison on bass, Dick Katz on piano and John Collins on guitar.

Carter's playing remained fresh into the 1970s and '80s on a number of fine albums for Pablo including *The King,* a sextet session with vibist Milt Jackson, guitarist Joe Pass and pianist

Tommy Flanagan; the collaborations with Dizzy Gillespie and Oscar Peterson; and the red-hot live 1977 session from Montreux.

Incredibly, Carter seemed to pick up steam in his 80s with a remarkable series of recordings for MusicMasters: *Central City Sketches,* a tribute organized around the American Jazz Orchestra; *In the Mood for Swing,* a sextet date with Gillespie, pianist Roland Hanna, bassist George Mraz and drummer Louie Bellson; and *Over the Rainbow,* a saxophone cornucopia with Herb Geller joining Carter on alto, Jimmy Heath and Frank Wess on tenors and Joe Temperley on baritone.

All That Jazz is a sizzling concert recorded at Princeton University, where Carter had first performed 62 years earlier with Fletcher Henderson. *Legends* pairs him with another swinging octagenarian, trumpeter Doc Cheatham, and *Elegy in Blue* is a moving tribute to departed colleagues. — J.S.

BETTY CARTER

★★★★ **'Round Midnight (1963; Atlantic, 1992)**
★★★★★ **Finally (1969; Blue Note, 1991)**
★★★★ **At the Village Vanguard (1971; Verve, 1993)**
★★★★★ **The Betty Carter Album (1976; Verve, 1992)**
★★★★★ **The Audience with Betty Carter (1980; Verve, 1988)**
★★★★ **Look What I Got (Verve, 1988)**
★★★★ **Whatever Happened to Love? (Verve, 1989)**
★★★★ **Compact Jazz (Verve, 1990)**
★★★★ **Droppin' Things (Verve, 1990)**
★★★★ **It's Not About the Melody (Verve, 1992)**
★★★★ **I Can't Help It (GRP, 1992)**
★★★★ **Inside Betty Carter (Capitol, 1993)**
★★★★ **Feed the Fire (Verve, 1994)**
★★★★ **Meet Betty Carter and Ray Bryant/Little Susie (Collectables, 1995)**
★★★ **I'm Yours, You're Mine (Verve, 1996)**
★★★★½ **Meet Betty Carter and Ray Bryant (Legacy, 1996)**

Jazz history is filled with great vocalists, none more inventive than the astonishingly fresh Betty Carter (1930–1998). Refusing to work out of stock modes or be typecast as a band-fronting canary, Carter developed an improviser's approach to her material, disassembling each line of a song and reconstructing it in a new form with the cunning, grace and soul of a virtuoso.

Carter was born Lillie Mae Jones in Flint, Michigan, and became part of the flourishing Detroit jazz scene of the 1940s and '50s. She joined up with Charlie Parker's band and then with Lionel Hampton's while still in her teens, earning the nickname "Betty Bebop" for her superb scat-singing ability, and recorded a version of "The Hucklebuck" with Hampton's group. She later appeared on the King Pleasure recording of "Red Top."

Her first session as a leader, *Meet Betty Carter,* with Ray Bryant on piano, is available in two versions. Carter fans will want the Legacy version, with its attractive booklet and material not on the original release. The Collectables set is a twofer combining the album with Bryant's own recording, *Little Susie.*

I Can't Help It is a 1958 date with pianist Wynton Kelly originally recorded for the Texas-based Peacock label and reissued with additional material. The title track and "What a Little Moonlight Can Do" document Carter's growth into a major artist. (See also *Ray Charles and Betty Carter,* reviewed under the Ray Charles entry.)

Unsatisfied with the way the record industry was dealing with her, Carter severed her ties to it in early 1971 and proceeded to release albums on her own Bet-Car label. Several of those titles have been reissued on Verve. The great live set *At the Village Vanguard* was originally called *Betty Carter* and includes her legendary performance of "Body and Soul." *The Betty Carter Album* showcases her ability as a writer, with songs like "I Can't Help It" and "Happy."

The Audience with Betty Carter, a two-disc set recorded live in San Francisco in 1979, is the best representation of Carter's flair for suspending time in live performance, engaging the audience in her creative process. Her spellbinding presence and the musical sleight of voice she performs with brilliant accompaniment from pianist John Hicks, bassist Curtis Lundy and drummer Kenny Washington give this recording a reputation as one of the greatest jazz-vocal albums ever made. On another live recording, *Whatever Happened to Love?,* Carter's band is augmented by strings on four tracks.

Carter became a full-fledged star in the 1980s and recorded consistently for Verve until her death. The useful compendium *Compact Jazz* covers the period between 1976 and 1987. On *Look What I Got* she appears with two trios, one led by pianist Benny Green, the other by Stephen Scott, and both follow her inventions with precision feel.

Droppin' Things documents two 1990 shows at New York City's Bottom Line. Carter sings in several contexts here, performing a medley of "Stardust" and "Memories of You" in a duet with pianist Geri Allen and backed by her trio—Marc Cary on piano, Tarus Mateen on bass and Gregory Hutchinson on drums—the rest of the way. On three Carter originals—"Droppin' Things," "Open the Door '90" and the inspired "Dull Day (In Chicago)"—and one other song, trumpeter Freddie Hubbard and tenor-sax man Craig Handy join the lineup.

Pianists John Hicks, Mulgrew Miller and Cyrus Chestnut each accompany Carter on *It's Not About the Melody. Feed the Fire* recorded Carter at a 1993 concert at London's Royal Festival Hall with Allen on piano, Dave Holland on bass and Jack DeJohnette on drums. A group led by pianist Xavier Davis highlights "East of the Sun," "Lonely House" and the title track of *I'm Yours, You're Mine.* — J.S.

BO CARTER

★★★★ **Banana in Your Fruit Basket (Yazoo, 1991)**
★★★★★ **Twist It Babe 1931–1940 (Yazoo, 1992)**

Vocalist/multi-instrumentalist Armenter "Bo Carter" Chatmon (1893–1964) was one of the most important country-blues players both on his own and as a member of the Mississippi Sheiks. His father, Henderson, a freed slave, was an accomplished fiddler who taught his children to play various instruments. His brother Sam was also a member of the Mississippi Sheiks, recording on his own and playing in a family dance band made up of as many as seven of the brothers. The Chatmon brothers were also half brothers to the great Delta-blues guitarist Charley Patton.

Bo Carter sang, wrote and played banjo, bass, violin, guitar and clarinet in an eclectic style influenced by everything from 19th Century traditional material to blues, ragtime, minstrel tunes, hokum, bawdy blues and topical folk songs. He played with the family band before the loss of his eyesight forced him to develop his own solo recording style.

His virtuosic guitar, accompanied by his sophisticated harmonic sense and brilliant arrangement strategies, allowed Carter to invent new forms as he went along, to fashion his own style. He has influenced the string-band and jug tradition as well as the work of such country-blues performers as Tommy Johnson and John Hurt.

The essential *Twist It Babe* collects his versions of Mississippi Delta blues. *Banana in Your Fruit Basket* features songs with witty double-entendre lyrics. — J.S.

JAMES CARTER

★★★★½ **J.C. on the Set (DIW/Columbia, 1994)**
★★★ **Jurassic Classics (DIW/Columbia, 1995)**
★★★★★ **The Real Quietstorm (Atlantic Jazz, 1995)**
★★★½ **Conversin' with the Elders (Atlantic Jazz, 1996)**
★★★★ **In Carterian Fashion (Atlantic Jazz, 1998)**

While the public fawns over some of his talented contemporaries, saxophonist James Carter (b. 1969) does more without fuss to tear down the stylistic partitions within jazz. Carter's music—raw and polished, romantic and spiritual, hot and cool—and his boundless imagination blend swing jazz, bebop, the often raucous R&B shouts of the Texas tenors, the freedom espoused by avant-garde players and the deep spirituality that inspired John Coltrane. He credits Don Byas as a primary influence. Carter played with the defunct Detroit-based avant-garde ensemble Griot Galaxy, then worked in trumpeter Wynton Marsalis's band, which led to opportunities with the Lincoln Center Jazz Orchestra, the Mingus Big Band, trumpeter Lester Bowie's New York Organ Ensemble and the Julius Hemphill sextet.

Carter's first three recordings featured a stable, bold quartet, rounded out by fellow Detroiters Craig Taborn on piano, Jaribu Shahid on bass and Tani Tabbal on drums. His debut recording, *J.C. on the Set,* showcases his swaggering individuality on his originals, Sun Ra and Byas tunes and baritone-sax reconstructions of "Caravan" and "Sophisticated Lady." *Jurassic Classics* roars through seven standards. Warmth, a touch of romanticism and a unified approach strengthen his performance on *The Real Quietstorm.*

Conversin' with the Elders is less a showcase of his bold individualism and more an opportunity for Carter to honor, and mingle

ideas with, players who have been a strong influence on him, including trumpeters Bowie and Harry "Sweets" Edison and saxophonists Larry Smith, Buddy Tate and Hamiet Bluiett. *In Carterian Fashion,* a session built around three different B-3 organ–based ensembles with Henry Butler, Cyrus Chestnut and Taborn, reinforces Carter's deep roots, stylistic versatility and bold forward-looking spirit.
— K.F.

JOHN CARTER

★★★ **Flight for Four (Flying Dutchman, 1969)**
★★★ **West Coast Hot (1969; Novus, 1991)**
★★★ **Self-Determination Music (Flying Dutchman, 1971)**
★★★½ **Night Fire (Black Saint, 1981)**
★★★★½ **Dauwhe (Black Saint, 1982)**
★★★½ **Suite of Early American Folk Pieces for Solo Clarinet (Moers, 1985)**
★★★★★ **Castles of Ghana (1986; Gramavision, 1994)**
★★★★½ **Dance of the Love Ghosts (1987; Gramavision, 1994)**
★★★★ **Southern Bells (with the Clarinet Summit) (Black Saint, 1987)**
★★★★★ **Fields (1988; Gramavision, 1994)**
★★★★ **Comin' On (Hat Hut, 1989)**
★★★★★ **Shadows on a Wall (1989; Gramavision, 1994)**

John Carter (1929–1991) died relatively unknown except to critics and fellow musicians, who hailed him as one of the most important jazz composers and bandleaders of the '80s. It was in that decade that he recorded the five suites (each a full album) of his masterwork, "Roots and Folklore: Episodes in the Development of an American Folk Music." This expansive evocation of African-American history recalled the extended forms and descriptive writing of Duke Ellington and Charles Mingus but used the enlarged musical vocabulary of Ornette Coleman and Cecil Taylor.

Carter was born about six months before Coleman, both natives of Fort Worth, Texas. They played alto sax together in high school with such friends as drummer Charles Moffett and tenor saxophonist Dewey Redman. Carter, though, pursued a career as a public-school music teacher and wound up in Los Angeles in the early 1960s. On weekends he performed on the city's struggling avant-garde jazz scene and formed an enduring partnership with trumpeter Bobby Bradford, who briefly replaced Don Cherry in Coleman's band without any loss of fire or invention.

The early, Coleman-esque collaborations between Carter and Bradford can be heard on *Flight for Four*, *West Coast Hot* and *Self-Determination Music*; *Comin' On* is a later collaboration, from a 1988 live show.

In 1974 Carter switched from alto sax to clarinet exclusively and finally escaped Coleman's shadow to find his own, powerful voice. Drawing on the classical tradition as well as the inside and outside jazz traditions, Carter achieved a keening, yearning quality on his instrument, whether he was working in the glowing, warm tones of the lower register or the piercing squeaks of the upper range.

In the 1980s he convened the Clarinet Summit, an unaccompanied clarinet quartet including New Orleans legend Alvin Batiste, former Ellington sideman Jimmy Hamilton and West Coast prodigy David Murray, and they reinvigorated the instrument's flagging reputation with *Southern Bells.* Carter also recorded a solo clarinet album, *Variations.*

Carter launched his ambitious historical series in 1982 with *Dauwhe.* Named after a goddess of African mythology, the album conjures up an imagined, precolonial Africa with some of Carter's loveliest writing, full of eerie, dreamlike harmonies played by Carter, Bradford, flautist James Newton, tubaist Red Callender and oboist/soprano saxophonist Charles Owens.

The second installment, *Castles of Ghana,* evokes the social disintegration caused by the European invasion and intertribal warfare. Darker still, *Dance of the Love Ghosts* examines the Middle Passage of the slave trade through an octet of two clarinets (Carter and Marty Ehrlich), two brass instruments (Bradford and Count Basie trombonist Benny Powell), two string players (violinist Terry Jenoure and bassist Richard Davis) and two percussionists (Mothers of Invention keyboardist Don Preston and Cecil Taylor drummer Andrew Cyrille). Carter expertly uses these four pairs of instruments to clash and resolve.

With Fred Hopkins of Air replacing Davis, the same octet completed the series, growing tighter and stronger all the time. *Fields,* which deals with the experiences of the transplanted Africans in the American South, is the most personal of the five suites, for Carter draws on the experiences of his Texas relatives and the surviving music of that era to inform his ingenious structure of notated and improvised sections.

Climaxing with *Shadows on a Wall,* a study of the migration of African-Americans from the rural South to the urban North, the suite sounds positively Ellingtonian as Carter touches on hot jazz, swing, bop and gospel and gathers everything he has learned into a stunning whole. — G.H.

RON CARTER

★★★★ **Where? (with Eric Dolphy and Mal Waldron) (1961; Original Jazz Classics, 1990)**
★★★★ **Blues Farm (CTI, 1973)**
★★★ **Spanish Blue (1975; CTI, 1987)**
★★★ **Yellow and Green (CTI, 1976)**
★★½ **Pastels (1976; Original Jazz Classics, 1991)**
★★★½ **Third Plane (with Herbie Hancock and Tony Williams) (1977; Original Jazz Classics, 1992)**
★★★½ **Peg Leg (1978; Original Jazz Classics, 1991)**
★★★ **Patrao (1980; Original Jazz Classics, 1993)**
★★★★ **Etudes (1983; Discovery, 1994)**
★★★★ **Live at Village West (with Jim Hall) (Concord Jazz, 1984)**
★★★★ **Telephone (with Jim Hall) (Concord Jazz, 1985)**
★★★★ **Uptown Conversation (Rhino, 1989)**
★★★½ **Standard Bearers (Ron Carter and friends) (Original Jazz Classics, 1989)**
★★★½ **Panamanhattan (1991; Evidence, 1994)**
★★★ **Ron Carter Meets Bach (Blue Note, 1992)**
★★★ **Friends (Blue Note, 1993)**
★★★ **Jazz, My Romance (Blue Note, 1994)**
★★★½ **Mr. Bow-Tie (Blue Note, 1996)**

Ron Carter (b. 1937) is one of the finest bassists to emerge in the postbop era, a model of consistency and taste who can accompany virtually anyone with lyrical, melodically inventive rhythms. Though best known for his work with the legendary Miles Davis quintet that also included Wayne Shorter, Herbie Hancock and Tony Williams, he has been a ubiquitous session figure, appearing on hundreds of records.

Carter's solo albums are examples of how vital small-ensemble jazz can sound without pandering to commercial tastes, just concentrating on superb playing, arrangement and song selection. *Where?* features Eric Dolphy on alto saxophone, bass clarinet and flute, Mal Waldron on piano, George Duvivier on bass (Carter also plays cello on the date) and Charles Persip on drums. *Uptown Conversation* features some of Carter's best electric-bass work and accompaniment from pianist Herbie Hancock and drummer Billy Cobham.

The strength of Carter's musical convictions really comes across on *Blues Farm* and his other CTI recordings, which successfully avoid the overbearing arrangements that have marked many of the label's trademark releases.

Carter went on to make a series of modestly excellent records in the 1970s and '80s. He reunites with Hancock and Williams on the spirited *Third Plane. Live at Village West* and *Telephone* feature magnificent duets with guitarist Jim Hall. Carter formed a quartet with Williams on drums, Art Farmer on flügelhorn and Bill Evans on saxophone for the beautiful *Etudes.*

An adventurous duet with accordionist Richard Galliano, recorded live to two-track in a Paris record store, resulted in the romantic *Panamanhattan.* In the '90s Carter went on to make another series of fine albums on the Blue Note label, highlighted by *Mr. Bow-Tie,* which features an inspired performance from pianist Gonzalo Rubalcaba. — J.S.

VALERIE CARTER

★★★ **Just a Stone's Throw Away (Columbia, 1977)**
★★½ **The Way It Is (Countdown/Unity, 1996)**

Someone should've told Valerie Carter (b. ca. 1958) that women blues singers aren't supposed to be polite. When Carter, whose voice has backed hits by Linda Ronstadt, Jackson Browne, Cher and others, takes the spotlight as a solo artist, she sounds tentative—as if she's still afraid to command too much attention. Carter's music isn't bad—just boring.

After several years as a West Coast folkie, Carter recorded two solo albums for Columbia in the '70s (*Wild Child* is now out of print). *Just a Stone's Throw Away* showcases Carter the chanteuse with an impressive range. She sings with gusto, especially on the sexy "Ooh Child" and "A Stone's Throw Away."

Her return to solo work nearly 20 years later lacks confidence. *The Way It Is* does offer a well-chosen selection of songs and some stellar guest vocalists. Four tracks cowritten by Carter sound slight compared to the seven she covers, including Van Morrison's "Into the Mystic" (with Lyle Lovett's heartfelt vocals making it a real standout), Earth, Wind and Fire's "That's the Way of the World" and Tom Waits's "Whistle Down the Wind." Other contributors—James Taylor, Ronstadt and Browne among them—add the passion and emotion that Carter's voice is lacking here. — A.A.

MARC CARY

★★★½ **Cary On (Enja, 1995)**
★★★★ **Listen (Arabesque, 1996)**
★★★½ **The Antidote (Arabesque, 1998)**

Pianist Marc Cary was born in 1967 in New York but raised near Washington, D.C., where he studied at the Oxendine Music Academy and the Duke Ellington School of the Arts as well as with pianist John Malachi. He moved smoothly into the New York jazz scene in 1989 by touring for two years with singer Betty Carter and working in the final incarnation of drummer Arthur Taylor's postbop band, Taylor's Wailers. Cary also became a forceful member of young trumpeter Roy Hargrove's quintet, both as pianist and songwriter, and worked with saxophonist Abraham Burton (another Wailers alumnus) before making his first recording as a leader. In 1995 he joined singer Abbey Lincoln's touring band.

Hargrove and tenor saxophonist Ron Blake are key figures on the solid *Cary On,* which consists primarily of very personal compositions filled with beauty and nuance. Blake, along with trumpeter Terell Stafford and flautist Yarborough Charles Laws, swings on the septet session *Listen.* The band's strengths lie in its ensemble playing and musical range. With *The Antidote,* Cary continues to move further into his own conceptual territory rather than dazzling with his excellent playing. With the addition of percussionist Daniel Moreno, his band adds to his bold, diverse and often daring material. — K.F.

TOMMY CASTRO

★★★ **Exception to the Rule (Blind Pig, 1996)**
★★★ **Can't Keep a Good Man Down (Blind Pig, 1997)**

Tommy Castro (b. 1955) is the exception to the rule that nothing but swing and jump blues is coming out of the West Coast blues scene. This is ferocious blues rock, intense and propulsive, if less than deep and packing few surprises. It's loud, hard and mostly fast. Still, if it's a bar-band sound, it's a first-rate one. Castro has a great voice, a fiery guitar style and tremendous energy. The band is tight and strong, and Keith Crossan's tenor-saxophone work fits perfectly. A great live performer, Castro is a bit less interesting on record, though these albums will certainly get a party going in a hurry. — J.Z.

CATFISH KEITH

★★★½ **Pepper in My Shoe! (Fish Tail, 1991)**
★★★★ **Jitterbug Swing (Fish Tail, 1992)**
★★★★ **Cherry Ball (Fish Tail, 1993)**
★★★★ **Fresh Catfish (Fish Tail, 1995)**

Catfish Keith (b. 1962) interprets and delivers acoustic blues with ease and energy. He wears old-time styles like a comfortable suit, never self-conscious or theatrical. These four albums were recorded directly to two-track, lending real intimacy to the sound—you can hear Keith's feet stomping in accompaniment to his masterful bottleneck steel. When he puts down the steel for a small-bodied ragtime guitar, his picking ranks with the very best, as on a guitar arrangement of Fats Waller's "12th Street Rag" from *Jitterbug Swing.*

The albums combine his own arrangements of traditional Delta pieces with originals; a wide range of artists are covered, including Bo Carter, Johnny Shines, Blind Willie Johnson, Mississippi John Hurt, Oscar "Buddy" Woods, John Lee Hooker and Bukka White. From *Jitterbug Swing* on, Keith provides highly entertaining and informative liner notes with a sentence or two about each tune and credits to the artists who influenced his originals (he is clearly honoring his forebears, not just showing off what he knows). Keith also has a sweet tooth for island sounds; a couple of Joseph Spence and Hawaiian tunes turn up.

A first-rate entertainer, not a stodgy re-creator, Keith sings with a voice that is adequate, gritty and growling, though a bit more mellow and easy by *Fresh Catfish,* and his Skip James falsetto is marvelous. — J.Z.

PHILIP CATHERINE

★★★ **I Remember You (Criss Cross, 1991)**

★★★★ Spanish Nights (Enja, 1992)
★★★★ The Art of the Duo (Enja, 1993)

An accomplished instrumentalist in a number of different contexts, guitarist Philip Catherine (b. 1942) has worked with bop saxophonist Dexter Gordon as well as with fusion bands such as Passport. He was also prominent in French violinist Jean-Luc Ponty's early-'70s European band and played with the Dutch-based fusion group Focus. Though Catherine is an accomplished electric-fusion player, none of his work in this style is currently in print.

Spanish Nights is a lush session with bassist Niels-Henning Ørsted Pedersen and the Royal Copenhagen Chamber Orchestra, recorded live in 1989. *I Remember You* features a trio with Tom Harrell. Pedersen, who has a special affinity for Catherine's ethereal touch, collaborates again with the guitarist on *The Art of the Duo.*

Out-of-print titles to look for are *The Viking,* another fine Pedersen date, and *Twin House,* an acoustic duet with Larry Coryell. — J.S.

CEPHAS AND WIGGINS

★★★★½ Dog Days of August (Flying Fish, 1984)
★★★★ Guitar Man (Flying Fish, 1989)
★★★★ Flip, Flop and Fly (Flying Fish, 1992)
★★★★ Sweet Bitter Blues (Evidence, 1994)
★★★★★ Cool Down (Alligator, 1996)

Guitarist John Cephas (b. 1930) is the foremost practitioner of the southeastern Piedmont blues guitar style, as well as a walking blues encyclopedia who will reference Blind Lemon Jefferson and Skip James as if he knew them personally. In tandem with the sympathetic harmonica playing of the much younger Phil Wiggins (b. 1954), Cephas works his magic like an updated Brownie McGhee, tossing off reworked old songs or newly written material, singing with a deep, gospel-influenced voice and punctuating it all with his intricately picked guitar structures.

The two had been working together for nearly a decade (see the early-1980s compilation *Sweet Bitter Blues*) when they recorded the landmark *Dog Days of August.* The album brought the work of the late, brilliant country-blues master Skip James ("Cherryball," "Hard Time Killing Floor Blues"), as well as such traditional American myths as "John Henry" and "Stagerlee" back into performance circulation alongside original material, as if the ensuing half century hadn't passed.

Guitar Man includes tributes to Blind Boy Fuller ("Weeping Willow"), Blind Blake ("Police Dog Blues") and Furry Lewis ("Brownsville"), with the Wiggins-penned title track, a live favorite at the group's concerts. *Flip, Flop and Fly* expands the group's repertoire into rhythm & blues and its instrumentation to include piano, clarinet and bass, but the highlights are the original songs "The Backbiter" and "Evil Twin Blues."

Cool Down shows Cephas and Wiggins adapting country blues to the 21st Century. Their version of James's "Special Rider" will make the hairs on the back of your neck stand on end. Cephas sings it in James's high, ghostly voice, and Djimo Kouyate plays an intricate response line on the kora. The effect must be heard to be believed. Elsewhere on this classic record Cephas and Wiggins roll across the breadth of their abilities, with pianist Darryl Davis starring in accompaniment on Blind Boy Fuller's "Screaming and Crying." Wiggins's decrial of urban violence on "Cool Down" shows that the blues can still speak as effectively to the street as it did at the beginning of the century. — J.S.

JOE CHAMBERS

★★★ Phantom of the City (Candid, 1993)

Drummer/keyboardist Joe Chambers (b. 1942) moved to New York and became one of Blue Note's top session drummers in the mid-1960s. A mainstay of Bobby Hutcherson's late-'60s band, Chambers also recorded with Eric Dolphy, Freddie Hubbard, Lou Donaldson, Andrew Hill and Joe Henderson. He later joined the Max Roach percussion ensemble M'Boom. *Phantom of the City,* recorded live at New York's Birdland in 1991, places Chambers drumming in a quintet with Philip Harper on trumpet, Bob Berg on tenor saxophone, George Cables on piano and Santi Debriano on bass. The out-of-print Muse set *Double Exposure,* a series of duets with organist Larry Young, is worth searching out. — J.S.

PAUL CHAMBERS

★★★★½ Whims of Chambers (1956; Blue Note, 1996)
★★★★ Paul Chambers Quintet (1957; Blue Note, 1996)

Bassist Paul Chambers (1935–1969) was best known for his work with the classic Miles Davis groups of the late 1950s and early 1960s. Schooled in the then-thriving Detroit jazz scene,

Chambers was an expressive and rock-solid addition to any rhythm section. He made a handful of albums as a leader, but his root skills were as an accompanist. Even on albums under his own name, it's the sidemen who bring the marquee potential.

Whims of Chambers is a sextet session with the star-studded lineup of tenor saxophonist John Coltrane, trumpeter Donald Byrd, pianist Horace Silver, guitarist Kenny Burrell and drummer Philly Joe Jones. Byrd also plays on *Paul Chambers Quintet,* along with tenor saxophonist Clifford Jordan, pianist Tommy Flanagan and drummer Elvin Jones. — J.S.

THOMAS CHAPIN

★★★½ **Third Force (1991; Knitting Factory Works, 1994)**
★★★½ **Anima (Knitting Factory, 1992)**
★★★★½ **Insomnia (Knitting Factory Works, 1993)**
★★★½ **I've Got Your Number (Arabesque, 1994)**
★★★★ **You Don't Know Me (Arabesque, 1995)**
★★★★ **Menagerie Dreams (Knitting Factory, 1996)**
★★★★ **Haywire (Knitting Factory, 1996)**
★★★★★ **Sky Piece (Knitting Factory, 1998)**

Multi-instrumentalist Thomas Chapin (1957–1998) was one of the leading lights of the downtown New York jazz scene in the late 1980s and '90s, a superb technician on a variety of saxophones and flutes with a thirst for new experience that led him to explore the history and future of jazz simultaneously. A protégé of saxophonist Jackie McLean at the Hartt College of Music, Chapin studied with pianist Kenny Barron at Rutgers University, led the Lionel Hampton orchestra for six years during the 1980s and was a featured sideman in Chico Hamilton's group before forming his own trio with bassist Mario Pavone and drummer Steve Johns (later replaced by Michael Sarin), performing at the downtown Manhattan new-jazz mecca, the Knitting Factory.

Chapin, the third artist signed by Knitting Factory Works, recorded a series of augmented trio and quartet dates combining the improvisational responsibility of small-group settings with the architectural detail of large-band arrangements. *Third Force* unleashes his otherworldly take on swing in the free surroundings of trio work. *Insomnia* is a terrific live recording from the Knitting Factory in which the trio is augmented by a five-piece horn section, showcasing Chapin's arrangement ability. *I've Got Your Number* is a traditional set featuring pianist Ronnie Matthews. *You Don't Know Me* explores African rhythmic contexts, including a beautiful collaboration with trumpeter Tom Harrell on "Kaokoland." *Menagerie Dreams* runs the gamut from post–Charlie Parker through a decidedly unusual take on Thelonious Monk and a dramatic recasting of Ellingtonia. The witty *Haywire* adds a string section to the trio format for the epic vision of "The Devil's Hopyard." *Sky Piece* is a recording of indescribable beauty, made while Chapin was battling the leukemia that eventually caused his death. The sparse world-music settings feature Chapin's eerily expressive flute playing in sonorous, spiritually driven trio arrangements. — J.S.

BOBBY CHARLES

★★★★★ **Bobby Charles (1972; Stony Plain, 1994)**
★★★½ **Wish You Were Here Right Now (Stony Plain, 1995)**

Bobby Charles (b. 1938) is one of America's mysterious talents, a brilliant songwriter and soulfully idiosyncratic singer who has shied away from live performing throughout his career. A Louisiana native raised on the sounds of New Orleans rhythm & blues and Cajun melodies, Charles first made a splash when Bill Haley and the Comets scored a hit with his now-famous composition "See You Later, Alligator." Charles went on to write songs for Fats Domino—including "Walkin' to New Orleans" and "Before I Grow Too Old"—that affirmed him as a powerful creative force.

Charles did record a masterpiece of his own, and it is one of the greatest "lost" albums rescued by a CD reissue. *Bobby Charles,* recorded in Woodstock, New York, with members of the Band and a supporting roster of stellar guest musicians including Dr. John, Amos Garrett and David Sanborn, sounds like a Louisiana companion to the legendary collaboration between the Band and Bob Dylan on *The Basement Tapes:* Charles's molasses-slow vocals and backwoods phrasing suggest a born-on-the-bayou Dylan. On songs like "I Must Be in a Good Place Now," "He's Got All the Whiskey" and "Save Me Jesus," the rural South comes alive in Charles's swampy tales of fishing, liquor and redemption, anchored by Levon Helm's earthy drumming and Garth Hudson's accordion and organ flourishes.

The reclusive Charles resurfaced strongly two decades later with *Wish You Were Here Right Now,* which features cameos from friends such as Neil Young and Willie Nelson. His gift for memorable tales remains undiminished; "Not Ready Yet" is a defiant bachelor's anthem, while "Promises, Promises (The Truth Will Set You Free)" slings a workingman's arrow at politicians. Charles's voice still oozes rural charm, and slide-guitar wizard Sonny Landreth shines on the Charles classic "The Jealous Kind" and the Carnival chronicle "The Mardi Gras Song." — S.J.

RAY CHARLES

★★★★ **Ray Charles (a.k.a. Hallelujah, I Love Her So) (Atlantic, 1957)**
★★★½ **The Great Ray Charles (1957; Rhino, 1993)**
★★★ **Soul Brothers/Soul Meeting (with Milt Jackson) (1957/1961; Rhino, 1989)**
★★★ **Yes Indeed! (Atlantic, 1958)**
★★★★ **What'd I Say (Atlantic, 1959)**
★★★★½ **The Genius of Ray Charles (1959; Rhino, N.A.)**
★★½ **The Genius Hits the Road (ABC-Paramount, 1960)**
★★★ **Dedicated to You (ABC-Paramount, 1961)**
★★★ **The Genius After Hours (1961; Rhino, 1993)**
★★★★½ **Genius + Soul = Jazz (1961; Rhino, 1988)**
★★★★ **Ray Charles and Betty Carter (1961; Dunhill Compact Classics, 1988)**
★★★★ **The Genius Sings the Blues (Atlantic, 1961)**
★★★★ **Do the Twist! (a.k.a. The Greatest!) (Atlantic, 1961)**
★★★★★ **Modern Sounds in Country and Western Music, (1962; Rhino, 1988)**
★★★★★ **Greatest Hits (ABC-Paramount, 1962)**
★★★★★ **Modern Sounds in Country and Western Music, Vol. 2 (ABC-Paramount, 1962)**
★★★★ **Ingredients in a Recipe for Soul (1963; Dunhill Compact Classics, 1990)**
★★★½ **Sweet & Sour Tears (ABC-Paramount, 1964)**
★½ **Have a Smile with Me (ABC-Paramount, 1964)**
★★★★ **Live in Concert (ABC-Paramount, 1965)**
★★★ **Country and Western Meets Rhythm and Blues (a.k.a. Together Again) (ABC-Paramount, 1965)**
★★★½ **Crying Time (ABC-Paramount, 1966)**
★★★ **Ray's Moods (ABC-Paramount, 1966)**
★★ **Listen (ABC, 1967)**
★★★ **A Portrait of Ray (ABC, 1968)**
★★½ **I'm All Yours, Baby (ABC, 1969)**
★★★★ **Doing His Thing (ABC, 1969)**
★★★ **My Kind of Jazz (Tangerine, 1970)**
★★½ **Love Country Style (ABC, 1970)**
★★★½ **The Best of Ray Charles (1970; Rhino, N.A.)**
★★★ **Volcanic Action of My Soul (ABC-Paramount, 1971)**
★★★★★ **A 25th Anniversary in Show Business Salute (ABC, 1971)**
★★★★ **A Message from the People (ABC, 1972)**
★★½ **Through the Eyes of Love (ABC-Paramount, 1972)**
★★★ **Jazz Number II (Tangerine, 1973)**
★★½ **Come Live with Me (Crossover, 1974)**
★★★★ **Renaissance (Crossover, 1975)**
★★ **My Kind of Jazz, Part 3 (Crossover, 1975)**
★★★★★ **Porgy and Bess (with Cleo Laine) (1976; RCA, 1989)**
★★★ **True to Life (Crossover/Atlantic, 1977)**
★★½ **Love & Peace (Crossover/Atlantic, 1978)**
★★★ **Ain't It So (Crossover/Atlantic, 1979)**
★★★ **Brother Ray Is at It Again (Crossover/Atlantic, 1980)**
★★★ **Wish You Were Here Tonight (Columbia, 1983)**
★★ **Do I Ever Cross Your Mind (Columbia, 1984)**
★★½ **Friendship (Columbia, 1984)**
★★ **The Spirit of Christmas (Columbia, 1985)**
★★ **From the Pages of My Mind (Columbia, 1986)**
★★★★ **Live (Rhino, 1987)**

★★★★ **His Greatest Hits, Vol. 1 (Rhino, 1988)**
★★★★ **His Greatest Hits, Vol. 2 (Rhino, 1988)**
★★½ **Just Between Us (Columbia, 1988)**
★★ **Seven Spanish Angels and Other Hits (Columbia, 1989)**
★★★★★ **Anthology (Rhino, 1989)**
★½ **Would You Believe? (Warner Bros., 1990)**
★★★★★ **Ray Charles 1954–1966 (Time-Life Music, 1991)**
★★★★★ **The Birth of Soul: The Complete Atlantic Rhythm & Blues Recordings, 1952–1959 (Rhino, 1991)**
★★★ **My World (Warner Bros., 1993)**
★★ **Ain't That Fine (Drive Archive, 1994)**
★★★★½ **The Best of Ray Charles: The Atlantic Years (Rhino, 1994)**
★★★★½ **Blues + Jazz (Rhino, 1994)**
★★½ **The Early Years (Tomato, 1994)**
★★★★ **Classics (Rhino, 1995)**
★★★½ **Berlin, 1962 (Pablo, 1996)**
★★★★ **Strong Love Affair (Qwest, 1996)**
★★★★★ **Genius & Soul: The 50th Anniversary Collection (1947–93) (Rhino, 1997)**
★★★★★ **The Complete Country & Western Recordings 1959–1986 (Rhino, 1998)**

One of popular music's most protean talents, Ray Charles (b. 1930) has tried almost every imaginable style in his 50-odd years as a recording artist, building a body of work that includes not only classic R&B and rock numbers but also forays into country, jazz and even middle-of-the-road pop. His heartfelt eclecticism has resulted in some astonishing music, but it has also led to enough misguided and mediocre work to make even the most sympathetic listener wish that the singer's judgment were as sterling as his talent.

Charles made his first recordings in 1947–48 and began releasing singles on the Downbeat label (it eventually became Swingtime) in '49. These sides have been assembled in low-cost packages of varying content and quality; to that extent, *The Early Years* and *Ain't That Fine* are typical, offering minimal fidelity and little or no recording information; habitués of bargain bins and used-record stores will surely find others. Musically, the value of these collections is marginal, as Charles's earliest singles owe much to the sound of Charles Brown or Nat King Cole. But the singer's maturity is immediately apparent, even if his future greatness is not.

As such, the Ray Charles story begins, for all intents and purposes, in 1952, when his contract with Swingtime was purchased by Atlantic Records. Atlantic was where Charles's sound finally came into focus, and where he recorded his first—and in many ways most influential—R&B hits, although it took a few years for him to build up to that point. Those interested in a chronological view of his progress should proceed directly to the triple-disc boxed set *The Birth of Soul,* which finds the young singer/pianist starting with more-or-less conventional blues (e.g., "The Sun's Gonna Shine Again") and jump tunes ("Mess Around" or "Jumpin' in the Morning") before hitting on the formula that would beget "I Got a Woman," "Hallelujah I Love Her So" and other breakthrough singles. What makes these singles so affecting is the way they fuse jump-blues rhythm work to a gospel-inflected vocal, an approach that electrified pop fans (but scandalized churchgoers, who felt its marriage of secular and spiritual was nothing short of sacrilege). "I Got a Woman," "Mess Around" and "Hallelujah I Love Her So" are all on *Ray Charles,* although lesser tunes like "Funny (But I Still Love You)" and "Losing Hand" are just as interesting, if only for Mickey Baker's growling guitar work. *Yes Indeed!* adds Charles's first Top 40 hit, "Swanee River Rock (Talkin' 'Bout That River)," as well as the similarly soulful "Leave My Woman Alone" and "Lonely Avenue," while *What'd I Say* delivers the singer's first Top 10 pop hit, the supercharged call-and-response number "What'd I Say," as well as the churchy "Tell All the World About You" and a surprisingly swinging version of the Scottish folk song "My Bonnie." "I Believe to My Soul" and "Hard Times" are the highlights of *The Genius Sings the Blues,* but the album flanks those performances with lesser numbers from Charles's earliest sessions for the label. (*The Birth of Soul* includes everything on these four albums, which have been deleted but are widely available on import.) *Live* augments the 1958 recording *Ray Charles at Newport* with six selections recorded a year later (and originally released on *Ray Charles in Person*) and is a stunning testament to the power of Charles's live band, particularly Margie Hendrix of the Raeletts.

Even though his commercial success was

strictly with R&B tunes, Atlantic considered Charles as much a jazz musician as a pop star. He had been playing jazz since he was a kid, often with Quincy Jones, who arranged parts of *The Genius of Ray Charles*. No surprise, then, that his Atlantic discography contains almost as much instrumental work as vocal. Unfortunately, his Atlantic jazz sessions have been packaged and repackaged with other albums over the years so that it takes some work to sort it all out. However, the CDs listed from Rhino are the most available. *The Great Ray Charles* is a soulful, small-band session featuring his horn players, particularly alto saxophonist David "Fathead" Newman. Two tunes from *The Genius After Hours* have been added to the Ray Charles and Milt Jackson double CD *Soul Brothers/Soul Meeting,* although the individual albums *Soul Brothers* ('57) and *Soul Meeting* ('61) are also in print.

Perhaps the most important of his albums for Atlantic is *The Genius of Ray Charles*—not because it's full of hits (it isn't) or contains his best work for the label (it doesn't), but because it introduces the musical approach he would follow for much of the '70s. Although *The Genius of Ray Charles* puts him in front of a big band, the sound he pursues is nothing like that of the swing-era bands or even the jazzy, large-ensemble sound singers like Frank Sinatra or Dean Martin went for; instead, what Charles comes up with is a curious hybrid between the brassy R&B of his pop-oriented recordings and the showy schmaltz favored by the era's middle-of-the-road acts. Hence, Charles bounces from the powerhouse blues of "Let the Good Times Roll" or "Two Years of Torture" to overblown and gimmicky renditions of fare like "Alexander's Ragtime Band," although at times—"Come Rain or Come Shine" comes to mind—he's able to incorporate elements of both. (Be aware, however, that the album is abysmally recorded, with frequent overmodulation muddying its brasher moments.)

Whether it's worth sifting through these titles is, of course, another issue entirely. Charles isn't a bad jazz pianist, but neither is he an especially inspiring one, being generally more adept at rhythm work and accompaniment than strict improvisation. Then again, these aren't terribly demanding jazz dates, either, tending more toward the sort of soul-jazz groovesmanship of Ramsey Lewis or Ahmad Jamal, with only the Milt Jackson collaborations managing to push the playing beyond the pedestrian. Some of that can be chalked up to the fact that *Soul Brothers* and *Soul Meeting* find Charles playing with a better class of musician (Oscar Pettiford, Connie Kay, Kenny Burrell, Art Taylor), but it helps that both feature Charles on alto saxophone, an instrument that brings out much of the same soulful passion that informs his singing. Those wanting a convenient overview should look for *Blues + Jazz,* a double-disc set that, tellingly, is evenly split between vocal-based blues tracks and jazz instrumentals.

Charles jumped to ABC Records in 1960, negotiating a deal that gave him, among other things, full ownership of the masters themselves. Ironically, Charles's control of these recordings is part of the reason most of his albums from this era have been out of print for years—despite the fact that this period produced his biggest hits, including such singles as "Hit the Road Jack" and "Unchain My Heart." Granted, most (but not all) of Charles's Top 40 hits from this period have been collected on the two Rhino CDs, *His Greatest Hits, Vol. 1* and *His Greatest Hits, Vol. 2,* but considering that this was when Charles first began to think in terms of albums instead of singles and planned his recordings with that in mind, serious listeners have little choice but to seek out the used-record market.

Still, it helps to shop carefully, for in the early '60s Charles had an unfortunate fondness for conceptually organized albums, an approach that often led to trouble. His first album for ABC, for instance, was a collection of place-name songs called *The Genius Hits the Road,* which on the one hand boasts "Georgia on My Mind," perhaps his greatest ballad performance ever, and on the other drags in such dreck as "Moon Over Miami" and an appallingly gimmicky "Deep in the Heart of Texas." *Dedicated to You* focuses on songs featuring women's names in their titles; *Sweet & Sour Tears* offers songs about crying; *Have a Smile with Me* goes for allegedly funny songs like "Two Ton Tessie" and "The Man with the Weird Beard"; and so on. Most seem a trifle forced, but when Charles gets ahold of a theme that grabs him musically—say, the various shades of blue on *Crying Time,* particularly "Let's Go Get Stoned"—the results are amazing.

Nowhere is that more the case than on *Modern Sounds in Country and Western Music,* an album of country songs performed Ray Charles–style. This wasn't unknown territory for the singer, as he'd grown up listening to country music and even played piano in a hillbilly band, but what makes the album work is his ability to transform these songs. Consider, for instance, the way he turns Floyd Tillman's twangy "It Makes No Difference Now" into a jaunty, horn-driven blues or adds a jazzy edge to Hank Williams's "Hey, Good Lookin'." But it was his sturdily straightforward reading of the Don Gibson hit "I Can't Stop Loving You" that struck the strongest chord with the pop audience. Even more stunning is his soulful take on "You Are My Sunshine," from *Modern Sounds in Country and Western Music, Vol. 2,* which treats it as a groove tune, with solid rhythm work and scintillating interplay with the Raeletts. But then, Charles's second *Modern Sounds* album is generally superior to the first, both because its balladry is smoother (as with his version of Williams's "Your Cheatin' Heart"), and because the blues tunes rock harder (check his smoldering rendition of Gibson's "Don't Tell Me Your Troubles"). Both albums can be found on *The Complete Country & Western Recordings 1959–1986,* along with *Country and Western Meets Rhythm and Blues,* his third country-style album, which includes his funky approach to Buck Owens's "I've Got a Tiger by the Tail" and Bill Monroe's "Blue Moon of Kentucky," as well as various country tracks from the mid-80s.

As he did at Atlantic, Charles continued to make jazz albums. *Genius + Soul = Jazz* is by far the best of the lot, since its big-band-and-organ arrangements retain much of the sound of his pop albums, but the low-key and swinging *Ray Charles and Betty Carter* also shines, particularly when the two genially spar through "Baby, It's Cold Outside." There are also a few jazzy moments on *Live in Concert,* much as there were on his Newport album for Atlantic. But his self-indulgent '70s jazz albums are easily ignored, apart from the funkier moments of *My Kind of Jazz* (in particular, "Booty Butt").

By the mid-'60s, much of Charles's output was solidly middle-of-the-road, with a heavy emphasis on string-laden ballads. That's not to say he'd abandoned the soul side of his sound, just that it grew ever more compartmentalized, as with *A Portrait of Ray,* which is split into separate slow and up-tempo sides. Still, Charles doesn't get significantly funky again until *Doing His Thing,* an album that's long on groove but short on songs (although the interplay between Charles and Jimmy Lewis on "If It Wasn't for Bad Luck" is delightful).

A Message from the People pushes even further toward a progressive-soul sound, thanks to its playful treatment of the New Seekers' "Look What They've Done to My Song, Ma" and John Denver's "Take Me Home, Country Roads." But the album's real strength is its approach to social issues, and it's hard not to be moved by his performance of "America the Beautiful" or "Abraham, Martin, and John" (in fact, Charles seems on the verge of tears when singing about Robert Kennedy). It's a tough album to top, though *Renaissance,* with its gospelized renditions of both Stevie Wonder's "Livin' for the City" and Randy Newman's "Sail Away," certainly comes close.

By the mid-'70s, Charles was better known for what he'd done than what he was doing. That didn't stop him from making good records, of course—the *Porgy and Bess* he recorded with Cleo Laine is easily one of the best pop performances those songs have seen, at times surpassing even the legendary Louis Armstrong–Ella Fitzgerald version—but the good ones were becoming increasingly rare. He returned to Atlantic in 1977 and released four albums, none of which particularly demand hearing, though they have their moments: his "Oh, What a Beautiful Morning" from *True to Life,* for instance; the quasi-disco "You 20th Century Fox" from *Love & Peace,* a genuine hoot; the way he rephrases the Dobie Gray hit "Drift Away" on *Ain't It So.*

There was worse to come, however. Charles jumped to Columbia in 1983, where he proceeded to turn himself into a country singer. It wasn't a complete transformation, of course; *Just Between Us* is mostly blues and features a rollicking "Save the Bones for Henry Jones," recorded with Lou Rawls and Milt Jackson, while *The Spirit of Christmas* reverts to the MOR plus R&B formula that served him so well in the '60s. When Charles did sing country for Columbia, though, he sang it straight, without any of the R&B overtones that marked his first C&W experiments. And frankly, the music gains nothing from his fidelity. If anything, the reverse is true, as most of these albums are indistinguishable from the Music Row hack work Charles's producer, Billy Sherrill, churned out for his other clients. Granted, the singer does occasionally rise above the production-line predictability of his material, as when he breathes life into "3/4

Time" on *Wish You Were Here Tonight* or joins Merle Haggard in savoring the loneliness of a "Little Hotel Room" on *Friendship.* Still, saying that these albums aren't entirely bad hardly counts as a recommendation. *Would You Believe,* Charles's first Warner Bros. release, isn't much cause for hope, since it sounds less like a finished album than a collection of demos, but considering that the singer followed it with a Pepsi commercial that was more popular than any of his recent recordings, it seems far too early to count him out for good.

Given the breadth of Charles's output, it might seem that the best introduction would be a well-balanced best-of album. For years, dedicated fans spent fortunes on import copies of *A 25th Anniversary in Show Business Salute,* a long out-of-print 35-song compilation that drew upon both his Atlantic and ABC recordings. Fortunately, *Genius & Soul: The 50th Anniversary Collection* makes that unnecessary. Drawing from the full range of his career, beginning with the Downbeat singles and going all the way up to his recent work for Warner Bros., its five CDs offer a faultless overview of his vocal work (though the set ignores the instrumental side of his career). The Time-Life Rhythm & Blues series' more modest *Ray Charles 1954–1966* is a cheaper option, since its 22 songs draw on both the Atlantic and ABC catalogs (no Columbia country or Qwest material, though); too bad it's a subscription-only item. Of the Atlantic collections, while *The Greatest Ray Charles* delivers the basic hits, *The Best of Ray Charles* has none, tending to showcase his jazz side. An excellent collection, *Anthology* includes the ABC hits and others from the '60s and '70s. — J.D.C.

BOOZOO CHAVIS

★★★★ **Louisiana Zydeco Music (Maison de Soul, 1986)**

★★★½ **Boozoo Zydeco (Maison de Soul, 1987)**

★★★½ **Zydeco Homebrew (1989; Maison de Soul, 1992)**

★★★★ **Zydeco Live! Direct from Richard's Club, Lawtell, Louisiana (with Nathan and the Zydeco Cha-Chas) (Rounder, 1989)**

★★★★ **Zydeco Trail Ride (Maison de Soul, 1990)**

★★★ **The Lake Charles Atomic Bomb (Original Goldband Recordings) (Rounder, 1990)**

★★★½ **Boozoo, Chavis (Elektra Nonesuch, 1991)**

★★★½ **Boozoo, That's Who! (Rounder, 1993)**

★★★★½ **Live! At the Habibi Temple, Lake Charles, Louisiana (Rounder, 1994)**

★★★½ **Hey Do Right! (Antone's, 1997)**

When modern zydeco emerged from the mists of swamp blues and Cajun and Creole "zodico" music after World War II, two smash singles made the new sound the favorite dance music in the African-American communities of French Louisiana. In 1955 Clifton Chenier had a hit with "Ay-Te Te Fee" for Specialty and began the career that made him the "King of Zydeco." But a year earlier Wilson "Boozoo" Chavis (b. 1930) had enjoyed an even bigger hit with "Paper in My Shoe" on the Goldband/Folk-Star label. His career almost ended right there.

Chenier and Chavis represented two very different styles of zydeco. Chenier played a piano accordion and wrote melodic songs in the style of such blues heroes as T-Bone Walker and Joe Liggins. Chavis, by contrast, played the old-fashioned, Cajun button accordion and adapted local folk materials into hypnotic chants that emphasized a stomping beat. It was analogous to the difference between Sam Cooke and James Brown. Today, half a century later, the Louisiana zydeco scene is still split into two camps—Chenier's musical heirs and Chavis's. In the '90s the Chavis camp was in ascendancy as such blatant imitators as Beau Jocque, Keith Frank, Zydeco Force and Chris Ardoin ruled the Gulf Coast.

Chavis was born in Lake Charles, Louisiana, not far from his current home in Dog Hill. His father was a tenant farmer who played accordion on weekends, and the younger Chavis soon mastered the squeeze box, too. As a youngster he played house parties with Creole fiddler Morris Chenier, Clifton's uncle. Chavis's reputation spread, and producer Eddie Shuler invited him to make a single. "Paper in My Shoe," based on a story that Boozoo had no socks and wore shoes with holes in them to school, is widely hailed as the first modern zydeco record, and it sold more than 100,000 copies.

Chavis and Shuler feuded over money from that day onward, but Chavis recorded enough singles between 1954 and 1960 to make the 14-song compilation *The Lake Charles Atomic Bomb,* released in 1990. The fidelity of the recordings is ragged, the intonation is hit-or-miss and the songwriting is primitive, but the stomping, two-step beat and singsong choruses are so mesmerizing that one can understand why Chavis was a star of the local dance halls.

Chavis finally got so fed up with not being paid that he quit the music business for 24 years. Except for the occasional local gig, he hung up his accordion and devoted himself to raising and training racehorses, a successful business he continues to this day. It was only when the Cajun and zydeco revival gathered steam in the mid-'80s and Chavis started hearing his imitators on the radio and at festivals that the godfather of zydeco decided to jump back into the ring.

Chavis hit the dance-hall circuit again in 1984 and two years later released his first recordings in 26 years and his first-ever album, *Louisiana Zydeco Music.* Accompanied by his sons, nephews and neighbors, Chavis recut his signature tune and unveiled such compositions as "Dog Hill" (about his hometown) and "Leona Had a Party" (about his wife). The music was still simple and riveting, but the singer/accordionist had more control of it than he'd had in the Goldband/Folk-Star days.

The formula didn't change much as Chavis continued to boil down older songs into his own simplified stomp sound. *Zydeco Trail Ride* contains his deliciously naughty sing-along "I Want to Play with Your Poodle" and his infectious zydeco arrangement of the Bob and Earl hit "Harlem Shuffle." *Zydeco Live! Direct from Richard's Club, Lawtell, Louisiana* captures Chavis in his natural element—a Louisiana dance hall full of partyers—on half an album (Nathan and the Zydeco Cha-Chas have the other half), including a raucous version of his risqué put-down song "Deacon Jones."

An even better performance document is *Live! At the Habibi Temple, Lake Charles, Louisiana,* which presents most of Chavis's best-known songs in pumped-up, speeded-up arrangements. This album is the best introduction to Chavis's work.

By 1991, Chavis's fans had grown in number to include several well-known rock musicians. NRBQ keyboardist Terry Adams agreed to produce Boozoo Chavis for Elektra Nonesuch's "American Explorer" series, which was designed to introduce obscure but gifted regional musicians to the rest of the country. Picking songs from every phase of Chavis's career, Adams didn't mess with the arrangements but achieved an optimal balance of dance-hall energy and state-of-the-art fidelity. Unfortunately, Adams also allowed some of the numbers to degenerate into loose jamming.

More controlled is *Boozoo, That's Who!,* which Adams also produced. *Hey Do Right!,* produced by Adams as well, features Chavis's best crop of new songs in some time. But it was his revival of an old song, the witty, catchy, insult-filled two-step "You're Gonna Look Like a Monkey" that became the album's hit. And on "Message from the Master" Chavis declares that all the young musicians "want to put me in the pasture/but I want them to know one thing/I'm still the master." Indeed he is. — G.H.

DOC CHEATHAM

★★★½ **Highlights in Jazz Presents Echoes of Harlem (with George Kelly) (Stash, 1986)**
★★★★ **The Eighty-Seven Years of Doc Cheatham (Columbia, 1993)**
★★★★ **Swinging Down in New Orleans (Jazzology, 1994)**
★★★ **Butch and Doc (Daring, 1994)**
★★★★ **Doc Cheatham and Nicholas Payton (Verve, 1997)**

It's hard to fathom that in 1993 when Adolphus "Doc" Cheatham (1905–1997) made his major-label debut as a bandleader, cutting probably his finest album, it had been some 70 years since his recording debut with Ma Rainey. At the time of his death Cheatham was the only still-active trumpet player on the scene before Louis Armstrong—who remains the primary influence on Cheatham's remarkably clear-toned, ever-soulful blowing.

An alumnus of the bands of Cab Calloway, Billie Holiday and Benny Goodman, Cheatham was a late bloomer, who didn't blossom as a soloist until after he turned 70. Twenty years later he was still going strong (in fact, he had played a gig only days before his death). *The Eighty-Seven Years of Doc Cheatham* features Cheatham performing more or less the standard set he delivered every Sunday afternoon at New York's Sweet Basil. *Butch and Doc* features Cheatham in duets with pianist Butch Thompson. The results are typically charming but ultimately a tad boring. Cheatham's last recording, *Doc Cheatham and Nicholas Payton,* paired him with one of the brightest young trumpeters on the New Orleans scene. The two performed together in one of the highlights of the 1997 Jazz and Heritage Festival. — A.P.

C.J. CHENIER AND THE RED HOT LOUISIANA BAND

★★★ **My Baby Don't Wear No Shoes (1988; Arhoolie, 1992)**
★★★½ **I Ain't No Playboy (Slash, 1992)**
★★★½ **Too Much Fun (Alligator, 1995)**
★★★½ **The Big Squeeze (Alligator, 1996)**

Clayton Joseph ("C.J.") Chenier (b. 1957), the son of zydeco king Clifton Chenier, joined his father's Red Hot Louisiana Band as saxophonist when he was 20. When Clifton died in 1987, C.J. took over leadership, playing accordion and alto sax and singing. His first recorded effort as bandleader, *My Baby Don't Wear No Shoes,* keeps alive his father's sound: Clifton wrote three of the album's songs, including the sensual "Blue Flame Blues" and swirling "Banana Man," on which C.J.'s impassioned vocal and accordion work evoke his father's spirit. A C.J. original, the busy "I'm All Shook Up" is another highlight.

I Ain't No Playboy mines similar territory; it swings and bites, veering from romantic to frenetic. Along with songs by Clifton and C.J. is a version of Z.Z. Top's "Sharp Dressed Man," where the spacious, accordion-driven sound works surprisingly well. *Too Much Fun* opens with the raucous "Man Smart, Woman Smarter," and quickly evolves into the funky, serrated "Bad Luck" and the swampy "Louisiana Down Home Blues," complete with French lyrics. The album hangs together more as a whole than its predecessors do. The addition of the Memphis Horns on four tracks also gives the music a more sophisticated, svelte sound.

The Big Squeeze is another fine effort by Chenier, who rips through 14 tunes, including a version of his father's slow blues "The Moon Is Rising" and a strangely jaunty rendition of the Arthur Alexander classic "Every Day I Have to Cry Some." Of the originals on the disc, the laid-back, flute-laden instrumental "Mon Cher 'Tite Bebe" stands out. C.J. will forever remain in the shadow of his groundbreaking father, but as a bandleader and player he's made remarkable steps toward establishing a formidable legacy of his own. — B.R.H.

CLIFTON CHENIER

★★★½ **Bayou Blues (Specialty, 1970)**
★★ **Out West (1972; Arhoolie, 1991)**
★★★★★ **Bogalusa Boogie (1975; Arhoolie, 1990)**
★★★½ **The King of Zydeco Live at Montreux (1975; Arhoolie, 1990)**
★★ **Boogie in Black & White (Jin, 1976)**
★★★★ **Boogie 'n' Zydeco (Maison de Soul, 1977)**
★★½ **New Orleans (GNP Crescendo, 1978)**
★★★ **King of Zydeco (Home Cooking, 1980)**
★★★★ **I'm Here! (Alligator, 1982)**
★★★ **Country Boy Now Grammy Award Winner 1984! (Maison de Soul, 1984)**
★★★★½ **60 Minutes with the King of Zydeco (Arhoolie, 1986)**
★★★½ **Live at St. Mark's (Arhoolie, 1989)**
★★★★★ **Louisiana Blues & Zydeco (Arhoolie, 1990)**
★★★★★ **Bon Ton Roulet & More (Arhoolie, 1990)**
★★★★ **King of the Bayous (Arhoolie, 1992)**
★★★★★ **Clifton Chenier Sings the Blues (Arhoolie, 1992)**
★★★ **Live! at the Long Beach and San Francisco Blues Festivals (Arhoolie, 1993)**
★★★★½ **Zodico Blues & Boogie (Specialty, 1993)**
★★★★★ **Zydeco Dynamite: The Clifton Chenier Anthology (Rhino, 1993)**
★★★½ **Bayou Soul (Maison de Soul, N.A.)**

Muddy Creole French lyrics, stuttering accordion runs jumping from R&B boogies to slow waltzes, with swampy blues guitar and moody saxophone fills, plus a scratchy push-pull rhythm propagated by bottle openers scraped against a corrugated metal bib called a rub board—these are the elements that define the irresistible, sweat-inducing dance music of West Louisiana's Creole population. In the land of the bayous, accordionist and singer Clifton Chenier (1925–1987) was modern zydeco's creator and first major star—successfully arranging the marriage of Cajun French tunes with the blues and R&B he heard on the radio and jukeboxes of his native Opelousas and then taking the new sound to the world. With his brother Cleveland playing rub board at his side, a groove R&B band behind him and an Imperial-margarine crown perched on his head, Chenier reigned supreme until his death. *Vive le roi!*

Chenier's body of work is a vast one replete with oft-repeated material, scattered among various independent labels with varying production standards. The best and only full-career overview is the excellent double-disc *Zydeco Dynamite*—covering selections of his entire oeuvre from 1955 to '84, from boogies and hard-driving rockers to waltzes and slow blues. Chenier's label-specific discs stretch from his earliest extant recordings for L.A.'s Specialty label in 1955, through his long-standing association in the '60s and '70s with Arhoolie, to his latter-day efforts for regional Louisiana companies and his Grammy-winning swan song on Chicago's Alligator.

With an urgency and surprisingly sharp production for the day, *Zodico Blues & Boogie* packs together Chenier's entire mid-'50s output for Specialty (including all of the tracks on *Bayou Blues*). The 20-track collection features all his hit singles ("I'm on My Way [Back Home to My Best Friend])," "Eh, Petite Fille"—also called "Ay-Te Te Fee"), adding unissued tracks, second takes and outtakes and showing off a very young Phillip Walker on guitar and a blues-based band hip to the various '50s R&B sounds and rhythms.

For 20 years beginning in 1964 with most of the tracks on the excellent down-and-rootsy *Louisiana Blues & Zydeco* (an absolute must for swamp-blues fans), Arhoolie recorded and released Chenier's music on a nonexclusive basis. His best-of anthologies from the label's archives—especially *Bon Ton Roulet & More* and *60 Minutes with the King of Zydeco*—collect the high points of his mid-'60s to early-'70s session work and are surefire party starters.

In an unfortunate effort to extend the amount of music on CD reissues, Arhoolie has randomly cut up and repackaged a few of its Chenier titles, juxtaposing material from various incongruous sessions. Two thirds of the tracks on *Clifton Chenier Sings the Blues,* for instance, a fine collection of '60s soul-influenced zydeco with a sprinkling of swamp pop, date from 1969, while the rest are from a funk-fueled New Orleans session in 1977 (which include a young Stanley Dural—a.k.a. Buckwheat Zydeco—on keyboards). *Bogalusa Boogie* is a happy exception, presenting the complete 1975 session that resulted in Chenier's best album of the '70s, fired by arguably his strongest band ever: John Hart (tenor), Paul Senegal (guitar), Joe Brouchet (bass), Robert St. Julian (drums) and, of course, Cleveland Chenier (rub board). More pastiche than successful fusion, *Out West* dates from 1972 and remains an unconvincing attempt at updating Chenier's sound by recording him with Elvin Bishop's distorted rock-blues guitar.

Chenier's live recordings all catch the free-spirited, entertainer side of Chenier's personality and the far-reaching appeal of his music. Intense and intimate, *St. Mark's* is a great snapshot of a nonstop dance party from a small hall in California in 1971, with a rough-and-bluesy edge showing on tracks like "Bad Luck and Trouble" and wonderful crowd interaction. *The King of Zydeco Live at Montreux* captures him having fun speaking French with a Swiss audience in Montreux in 1975, while *Live! at the Long Beach and San Francisco Blues Festivals* presents Chenier in less urgent, more polished performances at two West Coast blues festivals in 1982 and '83.

An excellent example of how a roots-based artist can benefit from modern-day production values, *I'm Here!* is a blistering late-career set with fresh songs ("I'm the Zydeco Man," "The New Zydeco" and a cover of Glenn Miller's "In the Mood"), a hard-hitting backup band and full horn section (son C.J. on alto sax) and inspired performances that did not betray Chenier's worsening health at the time. — A.K.

DON CHERRY
★★★★ Symphony for Improvisers (1966; Blue Note, 1994)
★★½ Dona Nostra (ECM, 1994)
WITH ED BLACKWELL
★★★★½ El Corazón (ECM, 1982)
WITH OLD AND NEW DREAMS
★★★★ Old and New Dreams (Black Saint, 1977)
★★★★★ Old and New Dreams (ECM, 1979)
★★★½ Playing (ECM, 1988)
★★★ A Tribute to Blackwell (Black Saint, 1990)
WITH CODONA (Collin Walcott and Nana Vasconcelos)
★★★½ Codona (ECM, 1979)
★★★ Codona 2 (ECM, 1981)
★★★★ Codona 3 (ECM, 1983)

Even after his death, Don Cherry (1936–1995) continues to defy labels. Performing and/or recording with a range of musicians stretching from Ornette Coleman and John Coltrane to Lou Reed and Brazilian percussionists, he was a multi-instrumentalist (but primarily pocket trumpeter), world-music visionary (but mainly jazz improviser) and Oklahoma-born global voyager (but listed in the New York City phone book). A child of the first wave of the free-jazz avant-garde (as one fifth of Ornette Coleman's revolutionary 1959 ensemble), Cherry had a democratic approach that found common ground in the notion that music is forever re-creating itself, disassociating itself from what has just been played, wherein any and all sounds, rhythms, textures and traditions could (and did) find their way into his music.

Currently retail shelves do unfair service to Cherry's varied recorded legacy. His earliest works with Coleman on Atlantic are readily available (especially the well-annotated Rhino reissues). His supporting role with other saxophonists such as Albert Ayler, Archie Shepp and Sonny Rollins can still be found, with Cherry matching his well-hewn and fluidly spoken approach to the avant-garde flag bearers of the day.

Of Cherry's own groundbreaking mid-'60s Blue Note recordings as leader—*Symphony for Improvisers*, *Complete Communion* and *Where Is Brooklyn?*—only *Symphony* remains in print. It features stellar experimental support from Argentinian saxophonist Gato Barbieri, German vibist Karl Berger, drummer Ed Blackwell and Pharoah Sanders on tenor sax and piccolo. (The Mosaic boxed set of the three albums is also, sadly, out of print.)

By the late '60s, Cherry's interests and travels had exploded globally, and over the next decade he recorded a few titles in a variety of flavors and production standards for a variety of labels. None of these—including *Relativity Suite*, *Hear and Now* and *Don Cherry*—are currently in print.

In 1979 Cherry established a fruitful association with ECM, bringing a number of jazz and world-music projects to the European-based label. Common to these latter titles was Cherry's role as co-realizer (rather than leader) and a strong presence of folk music from around the globe. Seeking a minimalist departure from his earlier work, Cherry in his own playing—on trumpet, melodica and even doussn'gouni—developed a haunting, reverb-heavy feel.

Old and New Dreams was the name of a critically successful but regrettably short-lived late-'70s reunion of Coleman's groundbreaking collective (less Ornette)—with Cherry, Dewey Redman, Ed Blackwell and Charlie Haden. The group yielded four albums that harkened back to their earlier sense of collective, intimate improvisation but with an added political and world-music slant. The eponymous set on Black Saint from 1977 bristles with new ideas and a reinvigorated sense of the group as a leaderless democracy—Redman's "Dewey's Tune," Haden's "Chairman Mao" and Cherry's joyous "Next to the Quiet Stream" are all standout performances proving the quartet's unspoken communication—while Redman's title track points to the exotic heights reached on the next release.

Laced with Third World rhythms and melodies, the 1979 *Old and New Dreams* release on ECM is fueled by stellar compositions contributed by each member, plus two venerable Coleman chestnuts (the brilliantly evocative "Lonely Woman" and bebop-with-a-twist "Open or Close") with a particularly left political/ecological slant: Blackwell's "Togo" and Cherry's "Guinea" play off traditional folk melodies, while Haden's atmospheric bass-and-whale conversation, "Song for the Whales" (with a haunting burst of melody toward the end), exhibits the artistic depth and subtlety that Paul Winter's similar experiments only hint at. Cherry's playing is sharp throughout, particularly on "Lonely Woman" and with the Indian sonorities he intertwines with Redman's musette on the latter's "Orbit of La-Ba."

The other two Old and New Dreams albums reveal the group at their live best. *Playing* is a 1980 Austrian concert, with Cherry showing off punchy and pristine chops on a few Coleman tunes (the hurtling "Happy House" and the disjointed "Broken Shadows" particularly), Haden's catchy title track and Cherry's own "Mopti," which with its folkish melody paints a delicate African tableau. *A Tribute to Blackwell* is taken from the 1987 Atlanta festival celebrating the New Orleans–born drummer Ed Blackwell, again featuring mostly Coleman material, with solid, live versions of such Old and New Dreams tracks as Blackwell's "Togo" and "Dewey's Tune."

Contemporaneously, Cherry created the jazz/world-beat triumvirate Codona with Brazilian percussionist Nana Vasconcelos and multi-instrumentalist Collin Walcott from the group Oregon. Their three titles all feature well-focused moments of cross-cultural conversation, mixing and matching a battery of traditional and modern instruments (sitar, berimbau, hand drums, dulcimer, trumpet, tabla, etc.) on tunes ranging from childlike sing-along chants to complex and eerie Eastern and Indian melodies. Though inspiration is found on all three volumes, *Codona 2* is a trifle indulgent in its vocal tapestries, but the last album refines the formula almost to perfection, sparked by rhythmic gems ("Hey Da Ba Doom"), a crystalline sitar prayer ("Lullaby") and a railroad blues on berimbau with Cherry singing of his Oklahoma roots ("Clicky Clacky").

El Corazón comes off more like an informal

set of inspired medleys caught on tape than a structured session, finding Cherry jumping midtune from pocket trumpet to piano and melodica, back in the "in" pocket with Ed Blackwell, whose dance-worthy New Orleans roots are also manifest. The two create a sparse world where melodies float in and out like chance visitors: Monk's "Bemsha Swing" is an old friend dropping by, while "Roland Alphonso" suitably echoes the reggae sax pioneer and the title track conjures a weird Western soundtrack. *Dona Nostra,* a loose, schematic session recorded in 1993 with a Norwegian jazz outfit led by sax man Lennart Åberg never catches fire, remaining a passive canvas of impressions and smoke. "Fort Cherry" and Coleman's "Race Face" are contrastingly interesting but cannot save this all-too-ECM monochromatic palette. — A.K.

CHERRY POPPIN' DADDIES

★★ **Ferociously Stoned (Space Age Bachelor Pad Records, 1994)**
★★ **Rapid City Muscle Car (Space Age Bachelor Pad Records, 1994)**
★★ **Kids on the Street (Space Age Bachelor Pad Records, 1996)**
★★ **Zoot Suit Riot (Universal, 1997)**

This clever outfit from Eugene, Oregon, built a local reputation as a so-called ska group before breaking out nationally as the so-called swing band behind the hit album *Zoot Suit Riot;* in fact, the group plays neither style. The Daddies are a lounge act with arrangements inspired by Louis Jordan's popular jump-blues style, but without the performing excitement of Jordan's band. The Daddies' rhythms are mechanical and metronomic, like the soundtrack for an exercise video, rather than subtle and swinging. Originally recording for a label named after lounge guru Esquivel's description of his own music, the Daddies write sharply sarcastic tunes that are tightly rehearsed and performed with the precision of a Broadway musical cast. Singer Steve Perry utilizes a stagy, camp persona that is all surfaces; he's the perfect frontman for a video-generation band that has about as much to do with swing music as does Chuck Berry.
— J.S.

CYRUS CHESTNUT

★★★ **Nut (1992; Evidence, 1996)**
★★½ **Another Direction (1993; Evidence, 1996)**
★★★★ **Revelation (Atlantic, 1994)**
★★★ **The Dark Before the Dawn (Atlantic, 1995)**
★★★★ **Earth Stories (Atlantic, 1996)**
★★★★ **Blessed Quietness (Atlantic, 1996)**

Pianist Cyrus Chestnut (b. 1963) is a thoroughly schooled musician with a formidable two-handed technique whose approach blends aspects of, among others, Art Tatum, Bud Powell, Ahmad Jamal, Wynton Kelly and McCoy Tyner. He revels in articulating imaginative twists on the often formulaic genres of classic jazz. Chestnut's thoughtfully constructed, fluid compositions don't so much recode the tradition as address it head-on, avoiding clichés if not always cuteness. A swinging communicator, he has the gift of creating melodic hooks out of complex ideas without condescension.

Another Direction, produced for the Japanese market (with presumably little autonomy in tune selection), is three originals and five standards exquisitely executed in a mechanical manner by the trio of Chestnut, bassist Christian McBride and drummer Carl Allen.

Chestnut's four domestic releases (on Atlantic) are personal statements with a strong narrative quality. *Revelation* presents nine bright Chestnut originals and two covers, cutting through chiaroscuroed nostalgia to address gospel, blues, KC-4/4 swing, bebop, modality and European romantic classicism with fresh perspectives, accompanied empathetically by bassist Chris Thomas and drummer Clarence Penn.

On *The Dark Before the Dawn* Chestnut seems mired in a profusion of references. The homages have a derivative, calculated quality—clever variations on particular stylistic antecedents approached from a certain distance. His brilliant technique seems to overshadow fresh ideas. Chestnut incorporates some of the more hackneyed aspects of Ahmad Jamal's orchestrational approach to the piano trio, sabotaging masterfully executed passages with reflexive in-jokes, like the Basie cliché tag that concludes the Bud Powell–inspired "Call Me Later." It's beautifully performed, however, by the Swiss-watch–tight trio (Steve Kirby on bass and Penn on drums).

Earth Stories is a strong, well-conceived recording with more dynamic variation than its predecessors. Chestnut offers two solo tracks (the Jelly Roll Morton–inspired "Nutman's Invention #1" and the Tatum-esque "Gomez"), a three-horn orchestration ("Cooldaddy's

Perspective"), the standard "East of the Sun and West of the Moon" (which opens with a clever quote from Barry Harris's "Nascimento") and six originals for the trio (Kirby and drummer Alvester Garnett) ranging from ebullient to meditative.

Chestnut spent more years apprenticing than many of his contemporaries, including two years with Betty Carter. His forceful, contextual comping and bold solos give him great cachet as a sideman, where he reaches for areas that his CDs don't always explore. Some recordings to check out: Harrison-Blanchard's *Black Pearl* (Columbia, 1988); Donald Harrison's *Indian Blues* (Candid, 1992); Betty Carter's *It's Not About the Melody* (Verve, 1992); Steve Wilson's *Step Lively* (Criss Cross, 1993); the Joris Teepe/Don Braden Quintet's *Pay as You Earn* (Mons, 1993); Vincent Herring's *Don't Let It Go* (MusicMasters, 1995); Roy Hargrove's *With the Tenors of Our Time* (Verve, 1994); Christian McBride's *Gettin' to It* (Verve, 1995); and Kathleen Battle's *So Many Stars* (Sony Classical, 1995). — T.P.

CHICAGO

★★★★ **Chicago Transit Authority (Columbia, 1969)**
★★★½ **Chicago II (Columbia, 1970)**
★★★ **Chicago III (Columbia, 1971)**
★ **Chicago at Carnegie Hall (Columbia, 1971)**
★★★ **Chicago V (Columbia, 1972)**
★★ **Chicago VI (Columbia, 1973)**
★★ **Chicago VII (Columbia, 1974)**
★ **Chicago VIII (Columbia, 1975)**
★★ **Chicago's Greatest Hits (Columbia, 1975)**
★ **Chicago X (Columbia, 1976)**
★ **Chicago XI (Columbia, 1977)**
★★½ **Hot Streets (Columbia, 1978)**
★ **Chicago 13 (Columbia, 1979)**
★ **Chicago XIV (Columbia, 1980)**
★ **Chicago's Greatest Hits, Vol. II (Columbia, 1981)**
★ **Chicago 16 (Warner Bros./Full Moon, 1982)**
★★ **If You Leave Me Now (Columbia, 1983)**
★ **Chicago 17 (Warner Bros./Full Moon, 1984)**
★ **Chicago 18 (Warner Bros., 1986)**
★ **Chicago 19 (Reprise, 1988)**
★ **Chicago's Greatest Hits 1982–89 (Reprise, 1989)**
★★★ **Group Portrait (Columbia/Legacy, 1991)**

Chicago began its career as talented, enthusiastic musicians with jazz aspirations, a solid blues base, an ambitious composer/keyboardist in Robert Lamm and a capable group of soloists whose ensemble work overshadowed their individual virtuosity, a fact that the band's clever arrangements didn't make too obvious.

The first album is a gem of its kind, an exciting set that showcased the post-Hendrix lead-guitar work of Terry Kath, who carried the group instrumentally with hard-riffing support from the brass section and the strong rhythm section powered by drummer Danny Seraphine. Kath kept the intensity high on the follow-up, which featured more adventurous charts in service of lengthy suites that began to subject the band to charges of pretentiousness, a tendency that continued on *Chicago III,* where some good material and proficient playing couldn't overcome the feeling of stagnation setting in.

Live at Carnegie Hall is a terrible album that exposed the band's instrumental limitations to disastrous effect, a humiliation the players never overcame. Though Lamm tried to stop the band's creative implosion with one of his most innovative songs, "A Hit by Varese," (*Chicago V*), the presence of "Saturday in the Park" was the real augur of the band's future direction.

Chicago devolved into a lounge act, the very type of band the group had begun its life parodying. After Kath—the closest thing to a virtuoso in the group—died in a gun accident, the band replaced him with Donnie Dacus, but it still lacked a strong lead instrumental voice. Though the muse didn't completely desert the group, as the occasional well-crafted hit single proved, any attempt to maintain musical credibility outside of the pop world did. — J.S.

CHARLIE CHRISTIAN

★★★★ **The Genius of the Electric Guitar (Columbia, 1987)**
★★★★★ **The Immortal Charlie Christian (LaserLight, 1993)**

To Eddie Durham, who played in bands headed by Benny Moten, Jimmie Lunceford and Count Basie, goes the distinction of being the first practitioner of the amplified electric guitar.
To Charlie Christian (1919–1942) goes the distinction of being the visionary who most fully explored the electric's sonic palette. Recording

with Benny Goodman's band between 1939 and 1942 (he died of tuberculosis at 23), Christian redefined his instrument's role in the band context and in the process rendered obsolete the acoustic guitar in the jazz ensemble.

Inspired and influenced by the lyricism of tenor saxophonist Lester Young, Christian, who played tenor sax also, adopted a similar style in constructing a singular approach to technique, melody and harmony, which brought the guitar out of its traditional role as supporting player and into the spotlight. To Christian, the guitar was a solo instrument, pure and simple. Sustained legato phrases; improvisations based on the passing chords played between a song's root harmonies; and a tonal style that rendered the guitar's sound comparable to that of a reed instrument were Christian-pioneered innovations that propelled jazz into the modern age.

What remains domestically of Christian's recordings are Columbia's 16-song CD of tracks cut with the Goodman band, LaserLight's 10-cut live set, plus 5 live cuts on Vanguard's two-CD set *From Spirituals to Swing.*

The Immortal Charlie Christian, recorded at Henry Minton's Harlem nightclub in May 1941, finds Christian teaming with some of the best musicians of his time, including Dizzy Gillespie, Thelonious Monk, Kenny Clarke, trumpeters Joe Guy and Hot Lips Page, tenor saxophonist Don Byas, pianist Kenny Kersey and bassist Nick Finton, whose solid, inventive support is one of the evening's treats. Then playing with Benny Goodman, Christian would often retreat to Minton's after hours to jam with other musicians. By the personnel present at this session, it's obvious Minton's club drew at least the upper crust of the jazz world, and there's little here that will disappoint fans of any of the above-named artists. Christian, as was his wont, stays unobtrusively in the background, then creeps in with a sly, witty solo and gracefully fades out as another player steps forward. In no way does he dominate the session—with Gillespie and Monk around, that would have been a difficult task for anyone—but his soloing is economical and swinging throughout. He and Gillespie engage in a humorous dialog on "Swing to Bop," with Christian picking tentative, teasing notes that are echoed by Gillespie, as if neither one knows whose turn it is. "Guy's Got to Go" offers a splendid showcase of Christian's inventive approach, as he kicks off the song with an extended solo incorporating a series of Lonnie Johnson–style single-note runs, then broadens the palette with double-note chords and distorted vamping over a steady rhythmic pulse laid down by Clarke and Finton, before giving way to an exultant chorus and solos by trumpeters Guy and Page and sax man Byas. The finest bit of ensemble work comes at the session's close, on the Oscar Hammerstein/Jerome Kern pop classic "All the Things You Are." Gillespie keys the mood with an airy, delicate, searching solo, Monk checks in with a moody, angular retort cutting against the rhythmic grain, Christian glides in for eight bars of trebly yearning, concise and to the point, before bowing gracefully to another Gillespie solo, this one a flurry of ascending notes building to a linear, major-mode restatement of the wistful opening theme.

The Genius of the Electric Guitar does its job well—"Rose Room" and "Waiting for Benny" (the latter cut during a rehearsal when the musicians were indeed anticipating an appearance by their tardy leader) provide exciting indications of where Christian was taking his instrument—and the live cuts recorded in 1939 are stirring in their way.

Fans are urged to be on the lookout for Columbia's 1972 double-LP release, *Solo Flight: The Genius of Charlie Christian,* currently out of print. Of its 28 cuts, 3 are credited to the Charlie Christian Quintet, recorded privately in Minneapolis in 1939. Here Christian is allowed ample opportunity to develop his solo ideas, and the results are striking. On "I Got Rhythm" he turns the melody inside out, then backtracks, alternating between the staccato style that was common among guitarists before his arrival on the scene and the legato style that became his signature. "Stardust" shows Christian at his most lyrical, stretching out long, yearning lines with the gentlest of touches. "Tea for Two" finds the quintet back in the up-tempo mode of "I Got Rhythm," with Christian fashioning an elegant, angular retort to Jerry Jerome's Young-style tenor-sax voicings. That so little of Christian's artistry is available in the first place elevates *The Genius of the Electric Guitar* to the indispensable plateau; however, *Solo Flight* best demonstrates the wide scope of that genius.

— D.M.

JUNE CHRISTY

★★★ Something Cool (1955; Capitol, 1991)

★★★★ Duet (1955; Blue Note, N.A.)

★★★ **Misty Miss Christy (1956; Capitol, 1992)**
★★★½ **Gone for the Day (1957; Blue Note, 1998)**
★★★ **Song Is June (1958; Blue Note, 1997)**
★★★ **"Impromptu" (1977; Discovery/Sire/WEA Antone's, 1993)**
★★★ **June Christy with the Kentones Uncollected (Hindsight, 1986)**
★★★ **June Christy, Vol. 2 (1987; Hindsight, 1994)**
★★★½ **Day Dream (Blue Note, 1995)**
★★★ **Through the Years (Hindsight, 1995)**
★★★½ **Best of June Christy (Blue Note, 1996)**

What cool-jazz vocalist June Christy (1925–1990) lacked in technique she made up for in mood, providing thousands of 1950s, mid-America art-school couples with makeout music. After getting her start singing with the Stan Kenton Orchestra (replacing Anita O'Day), Christy recorded numerous torchy solo albums for Capitol, personifying that label's cool-jazz sound. She's at her best putting her sultry spin on standards, particularly when backed by Kenton alone on the piano, as on the lovely *Day Dream* (originally recorded in the '50s and reissued on CD with four unreleased tracks) and the wonderful *Duet.* Some of Christy's most successful recordings, including her solo debut *Something Cool,* where she's backed by an orchestra conducted by her major '50s collaborator Pete Rugolo, have been reissued on CD (and include the original period cover illustrations of the pony-tailed blonde). Christy's *Gone for the Day,* a collection of songs about being outdoors during the various seasons of the year—kitschy, but fun. *June Christy with the Kentones* documents 1946 live radio performances. Latter-day June, with a slightly huskier voice, can be heard backed by the Lou Levy Sextet on *"Impromptu."* —H.G.-W.

ERIC CLAPTON

★★★½ **Eric Clapton (Polydor, 1970)**
★★★ **Eric Clapton's Rainbow Concert (Polydor, 1973)**
★★★★★ **461 Ocean Boulevard (Polydor, 1974)**
★★★ **There's One in Every Crowd (Polydor, 1974)**
★★½ **E.C. Was Here (Polydor, 1975)**
★★★ **No Reason to Cry (Polydor, 1976)**
★★★★★ **Slowhand (Polydor, 1977)**
★★★½ **Backless (Polydor, 1978)**
★★★½ **Just One Night (Polydor, 1980)**
★★★ **Another Ticket (Polydor, 1981)**
★★★★ **Timepieces (The Best of Eric Clapton) (Polydor, 1982)**
★★★½ **Timepieces, Vol. 2: Live in the Seventies (Polydor, 1982)**
★★★★ **Money and Cigarettes (Warner Bros., 1983)**
★★★½ **Behind the Sun (Warner Bros., 1985)**
★★★ **August (Warner Bros., 1986)**
★★★★★ **Crossroads (Polydor, 1988)**
★★★★ **Journeyman (Reprise, 1989)**
★★★ **24 Nights (Reprise, 1991)**
★★★½ **Rush (Reprise, 1992)**
★★★ **Unplugged (Reprise, 1992)**
★★★★★ **From the Cradle (Reprise, 1994)**
★★★★★ **The Cream of Clapton (Polydor, 1995)**
★★★ **Pilgrim (Reprise, 1998)**

Eric Clapton (b. 1945) was the most influential player of the 1960s British blues movement, a consolidation of American blues styles from the Mississippi Delta to Memphis, Texas and Chicago. Clapton demonstrated an almost classical stylistic formality, a genius for glib improvisation and a complete mastery of the array of volume and distortion effects allowed by the latest technological advances.

Clapton's understanding of guitaristic dynamics is clear from his early work with the experimental rock band the Yardbirds; his instinct for blues is obvious from his work with John Mayall, particularly on the album *Bluesbreakers,* a virtual primer for British blues players.

By the time Clapton founded Cream in 1967, the phrase "Clapton Is God" was scrawled on London walls, reflecting his Zeus-like facility of hurling lightning bolts of crackling electric blues from the strings of his guitar. Clapton's tone with Cream was monumental, screechingly loud and played with awesome velocity. His handling of effects, particularly the wah-wah pedal, broke entirely new ground. It's all there on the 1995 *The Cream of Clapton* compilation.

That version of Clapton did not survive the 1960s. Clapton emerged as a solo artist in 1970 with a far more understated approach to guitar playing and the goal of featuring his vocals more prominently. Though Clapton earned his reputation with his guitar, he owes his solo career to his voice. As a solo artist his singing has carried his most popular work, from the frenetic gospel groove of "After Midnight" to the pointed melancholy of "Old Love." In fact, his least interesting solo recordings tend to be those that most emphasize his solos—an irony, perhaps, but also a testament to the fact that Clapton today is more than just another guitar hero.

Compared with his work with Cream, the playing on *Eric Clapton* is lighter-toned and rhythmically streamlined. The album was recorded with musicians he'd met while a part of Delaney and Bonnie and Friends (he was a featured player on the duo's 1970 release, *On Tour*) and boasts similar blues-and-gospel overtones. Although his lithe, understated vocals make the most of "Blues Power" and a cover of J.J. Cale's "After Midnight," Clapton seems somewhat overwhelmed by the size of the band; perhaps that's why he grabbed the rhythm section—Bobby Whitlock, Carl Radle and Jim Gordon—and ran off to form Derek and the Dominos. But that band fell apart in 1971, and Clapton, beset by depression and a heroin problem, wasn't heard from until 1973, when Pete Townshend organized the star-studded (but generally forgettable) *Eric Clapton's Rainbow Concert.*

Joining forces with producer Tom Dowd, Clapton went to Florida to record *461 Ocean Boulevard,* the album that first showed his pop-star potential. Although the material isn't obviously commercial, being given mainly to blues (Robert Johnson's "Steady Rollin' Man"), oldies (Johnny Otis's "Willie and the Hand Jive") and reggae ("I Shot the Sheriff," by Bob Marley), Clapton's affectless delivery is almost irresistible, cutting to the heart of the blues while avoiding the sort of guttural mannerisms most pop listeners found off-putting. The album was a massive success, but its standard wasn't easy to maintain. *There's One in Every Crowd,* for instance, virtually duplicates its predecessor's approach, but with considerably less success, and the difference is mostly a matter of writing. After all, no amount of reggae groove is going to make Clapton's "Don't Blame Me" as memorable a song as "I Shot the Sheriff."

After a passable live album, *E.C. Was Here,* Clapton returned to the studio in search of a new direction. *No Reason to Cry* wasn't quite it; despite a duet with Bob Dylan ("Sign Language") and a backing band that includes Ron Wood, Robbie Robertson and Georgie Fame, the only track that really works is the amiable, calypso-tinged "Hello, Old Friend." So Clapton ditched the all-star approach and took a low-key tack to his next recording, *Slowhand.* Bingo—the best album of his career. Working with his own band and once again relying more on the songs than the groove, Clapton seems utterly at home, from the wistful balladry of "Wonderful Tonight" to the stoned shuffle of "Cocaine" (yet another Cale composition). And though there's plenty of blowing room on the album—check the slide work on his version of Arthur Crudup's "Mean Old Frisco"—the fact that the writing is so strong always leaves him with a solid foundation from which to build.

Backless tries hard to re-create that balance but falls short in spite of a few lovely songs ("Tell Me That You Love Me" in particular) and some inspired rhythm work (especially on the Marcy Levy feature, "Roll It"). As had by then become customary, it was time for another live album, but *Just One Night* improves on the usual, thanks to a crack new band that keeps Clapton on his toes through the extended versions of "Double Trouble" and "Cocaine." Unfortunately, that dynamic didn't quite translate to the studio, and apart from the quietly dramatic title tune, *Another Ticket* is a disappointment.

Clapton changed labels soon after, a switch that prompted a predictable round of best-ofs. Apart from a non-LP version of "Knockin' on Heaven's Door," *Timepieces* boasts few surprises; *Timepieces, Vol. 2: Live in the Seventies* is easily ignored.

Meanwhile, Clapton's new deal was already producing impressive changes. Although *Money and Cigarettes* was something of a letdown commercially, it's anything but a disappointment musically, thanks to a comfortable collection of songs and a backing band that includes slide virtuoso Ry Cooder and Stax session man Duck Dunn. Charmingly unassuming, it's classic Clapton. *Behind the Sun,* on the other hand, is perhaps the guitarist's most daring effort, a (mostly) Phil Collins–produced project that finds him gamely trying everything from guitar synthesizer (on "Never Make You Cry") to what can only be described as 12-bar art rock (on "Same Old Blues"). Unfortunately, not everyone appreciated such risk taking, and Warner Bros. honchos Ted Templeman and Lenny Waronker later added three tracks—including "Forever

Man"—to increase the album's commercial appeal. Perhaps that's why *August,* also partially produced by Collins, backs off a bit from its predecessor's innovations and does nothing more radical than adding a layer of synths to its version of Robert Cray's "Bad Influence." (It does, however, include "Tearing Us Apart," a stunning duet with Tina Turner that ranks among Clapton's finest vocal performances.)

Any such failings, however, were completely forgotten with *Crossroads,* a career-spanning, 73-song retrospective that includes all of Clapton's most memorable recordings, from his days with the Yardbirds to the *August* sessions. It's an absolutely stunning collection—so monumental, in fact, that Clapton himself probably felt at a loss to follow it. Tellingly, *Journeyman* seems by the very nature of its title to shrug off any implications of greatness and as such turns out to be a remarkably relaxed and satisfying album. But Clapton's work with composer/arranger Michael Kamen on the now out-of-print *Homeboy* soundtrack in 1989, coming on the heels of similarly symphonic contributions to the *Lethal Weapon II* score, opens yet another direction for the guitarist, one that he pursues on his own with his score to *Rush.* Where he'll take it is hard to say, but judging from the multiensemble live album, *24 Nights*—in which the guitarist performs with a quartet, a nonet, a blues band and a Kamen-conducted orchestra—Clapton isn't ruling out any possibilities.

Unplugged is a banal acoustic set from the MTV show of the same name that became a huge hit on the strength of its tepid updating of "Layla" as an easy-listening hit. As if in penance, Clapton went on to pay homage to the blues giants who taught him how to play on *From the Cradle.* — J.D.C./J.S.

SONNY CLARK

★★★★ **Sonny's Crib (Blue Note, 1957)**
★★★★ **Sonny Clark Trio (Blue Note, 1957)**
★★★★★ **Cool Struttin' (Blue Note, 1958)**
★★★★ **High Fidelity (Time, 1960)**
★★★★ **Leapin' and Lopin' (Blue Note, 1961)**
★★★ **Oakland, 1955 (Uptown, 1995)**

Pianist Sonny Clark (1932–1963) was one of the most popular sidemen of the '50s and early '60s, performing with, among others, Buddy DeFranco, Serge Chaloff, Curtis Fuller, Johnny Griffin and notably Dexter Gordon, who considered Clark his favorite accompanist.

Clark's own *Cool Struttin'* and *Leapin' and Lopin'* stand out among the innumerable blowing sessions of the time due to Clark's relaxed, Bud Powell–influenced playing, worthy compositions and solid contributions from Jackie McLean on alto saxophone and Art Farmer on flügelhorn on *Cool Struttin'* and tenor-sax man Charlie Rouse and drummer Billy Higgins on *Leapin' and Lopin'.* Two trio sessions, *High Fidelity,* with Max Roach on drums and George Duvivier on bass, and *Sonny Clark Trio,* with Paul Chambers on bass and Philly Joe Jones on drums, are also fine examples of Clark's art. *Sonny's Crib* features John Coltrane on tenor saxophone. — S.F.

W.C. CLARK

★★★½ **Heart of Gold (Black Top, 1994)**
★★★½ **Texas Soul (Black Top, 1996)**

The godfather of the Austin, Texas, blues scene, W.C. Clark (b. ca. 1940) learned to sing by listening to gospel music and learned to play guitar from a wide range of blues players working out of East Austin. By the late 1950s he was leading a popular local group at the Victory Grill, a long-standing gig that deeply influenced Jimmie Vaughan. After playing bass on tour with Joe Tex, Clark returned to Austin to form the group Southern Feeling with Angela Strehli and Denny Freeman. He went on to play bass in Stevie Ray Vaughan's Triple Threat Revue, which featured vocalist Lou Ann Barton.

Heart of Gold covers all the bases in Clark's musical history, from the Isaac Hayes–David Porter soul classic "Where There's Smoke There's Fire" to the rhythm & blues of Latimore's "Let's Straighten It Out" and Clark's own brand of blues, epitomized by "Cold Shot," originally written for Stevie Ray Vaughan, "Heart of Gold" and the set-closing "The Blues Is at Hand." The album uses Clark's group augmented by Austin's top session players and cameo performances by Stevie Ray Vaughan's rhythm section of bassist Tommy Shannon and drummer Chris Layton. Shannon and Layton return for the solid *Texas Soul,* which features more of Clark's originals and a beautiful version of Willie Nelson's "Funny How Time Slips Away." — J.S.

KENNY "KLOOK" CLARKE

★★★ **Telefunken Blues (1955; Savoy, 1992)**
★★★½ **Bohemia After Dark (1955; Savoy, 1993)**

★★★½ Kenny Clarke Meets the Detroit Jazz Men (1956; Savoy, 1994)
★★★★ Pieces of Time (Soul Note, 1984)
★★★½ In Paris, Vol. 1 (DRG, 1986)
★★★ The Paris Bebop Sessions (Vogue Disques, N.A.)
WITH THE CLARKE-BOLAND BIG BAND
★★★ Handle with Care (Atlantic, 1962)
★★★ Open Door (1967; Muse, 1975)
★★★½ Fire, Heat, Soul and Guts (1967; Prestige, 1969)
★★½ Let's Face the Music (1968; Prestige, 1970)
★★½ Latin Kaleidoscope (1968; Prestige, 1970)
★★★ Famous Orchestra (Supraphon, 1969)
★★★ At Her Majesty's Pleasure (Black Lion, 1970)
★★★½ En Concert: Avec Europe 1 (RTE-2, 1995)

Drummer Kenneth Spearman "Kenny (Klook)" Clarke (1914–1985) was a rhythmic innovator in jazz progressionalism. An experienced musician with knowledge of the piano, Clarke, who worked before World War II with the Edgar Hayes Big Band, Sidney Bechet and Louis Armstrong, was grounded in the idiomatic drum styles of the 1930s. He was the first to codify the implications of the odd accents and disjunctive meters conjured by tappers, lindy-hoppers and jitterbuggers booted by the black big bands of the 1930s. Around 1940, in after-hours sessions at Minton's Playhouse in Harlem, he, Thelonious Monk and Dizzy Gillespie worked out the next phase of rhythm and harmony in jazz.

Clarke was already keeping time on the snare and accenting with the bass drum on the 1941 tape recordings of Charlie Christian playing after hours at Minton's (which can be heard on *Live Sessions at Minton's Playhouse* on Jazz Anthology). He explores Afro-Cuban rhythms with Cuban hand-drummer Chano Pozo on the 1947 recordings of Dizzy Gillespie's big band (available on Gillespie's 1995 RCA Victor boxed set). On late-'40s recordings with Tadd Dameron, Fats Navarro and Howard McGhee (on Navarro and Dameron's 1995 Blue Note boxed set) he's the penultimate swinging small-group drummer; his subtle propulsion is the heart of Miles Davis's *Birth of the Cool.*

In February 1948 he and Gillespie went to Paris, where he eventually settled, and remained there for several months, performing with a variety of bands. Two of the three dates that comprise *The Paris Bebop Sessions* are from this period. The first (March 1948) is a sextet featuring personnel from the Gillespie band (Benny Bailey on trumpet, Cecil Payne on baritone sax, John Brown on alto sax, Al McKibbon on bass) performing tight arrangements on two Charlie Parker originals and a pair of Kenny Clarke compositions. The second (May 1948) is a Clarke-led date with trumpeter Howard McGhee; McGhee's sidemen Jimmy and Percy Heath on alto sax and bass; Jesse Powell on tenor sax; John Lewis on piano; and John Collins on guitar. It's strong blowing; Clarke unifies everything.

Residing in America until 1956, he was a founding member and drummer of the Modern Jazz Quartet. He inspired and played on many recording sessions, including those of Charlie Parker (1951's *Swedish Schnapps* on Verve), Miles Davis (1954's *With the Modern Jazz Giants* and *Walkin'* on Prestige), Jay Jay Johnson (*The Eminent Jay Jay Johnson, Vols. 1* and *2* on Blue Note) and Thelonious Monk (1955's *Monk Plays Ellington* on Riverside).

From 1954 to 1956 Clarke was house drummer at Savoy Records (Hank Jones was house pianist), where he served as nominal leader on several dates. Sideman appearances of note: 1955's *Presenting Cannonball Adderley;* Nat Adderley's *That's Nat;* and Hank Jones's *Trio*, *Quartet/Quintet* and *Bluebird.* And in 1956: Milt Jackson's *Second Nature* and *From Opus de Jazz to Jazz Skyline;* Joe Wilder's *Wilder 'n' Wilder;* and Frank Wess's *North, East, South . . . and Wess!*

Telefunken Blues juxtaposes a Clarke-led November 1954 neobop ensemble (fronted by youngsters Frank Morgan on alto saxophone, Walter Benton on tenor saxophone and Modern Jazz Quartet partner and Gillespie associate Milt Jackson on vibraphone, with Los Angeles–based pianist Gerald Wiggins and bassist Percy Heath performing nobly on blues and rhythm changes) with a smoldering, textured, Ernie Wilkins–led 1955 sextet (featuring Basie's front-liner Frank Wess on tenor sax, Henry Coker on trombone and Charlie Fowlkes on baritone sax, backed by Milt Jackson's strong comping piano).

Bohemia After Dark from June 1955 is best known as Cannonball Adderley's striking recording debut, with Nat Adderley on cornet, Donald Byrd on trumpet and Jerome Richardson on tenor sax and flute. Throughout the recording (and any recording he appeared on), Clarke subsumes his mastery of every aspect of drum technique to the needs of the ensemble; with the superlative rhythm section of Horace Silver and Paul Chambers, he swings the band unerringly through a range of tempos and textures.

Kenny Clarke Meets the Detroit Jazz Men is an intelligently presented, varied program featuring four young Detroit musicians (Pepper Adams on baritone sax, Kenny Burrell on guitar, Tommy Flanagan on piano and Paul Chambers on bass) who had recently settled in New York.

Clarke returned to Europe in 1956; he lived there until his death in 1985. *In Paris, Vol. 1* culls sessions for Swing Records from 1957, with a French band, and 1960, with American-expatriate tenor saxophonists Lucky Thompson and Don Byas, both in top form. The well-arranged recordings with the French ensemble showcase aspects of Clarke's style. In 1957 he spurred one of Miles Davis's most ebullient recordings, the soundtrack to Louis Malle's debut film, *L'Ascenseur pour l'Échafaud (Elevator to the Gallows).* Between 1957 and 1963 Clarke worked frequently in trios with seminal bop pianist Bud Powell.

In 1961 Clarke joined Belgian pianist, composer and arranger Francy Boland as coleader of a multinational big band comprising American-expatriate all-stars and strong European musicians. The likes of Johnny Griffin, Tony Coe, Derek Humble, Sahib Shihab, Billy Mitchell, Benny Bailey, Idrees Sulieman, Art Farmer, Kenny Wheeler, Dusko Goykovich and Ake Persson enhance Boland's blend of Ellington-like concentration on environments for the soloist and a Basie-Kenton–like power-band aesthetic. Perhaps the most interesting of their recordings listed here are *Fire, Heat, Soul and Guts,* featuring a reunion of two-tenor pair Johnny Griffin and Eddie "Lockjaw" Davis, and *At Her Majesty's Pleasure,* a jazz suite by Boland.

In the '70s Clarke established a drum school in Paris and continued to work as a sideman. He appears on a powerful 1970 Lockjaw Davis–Johnny Griffin reunion date, *Tough Tenors. Invitation,* from 1974 on Spotlite, is a superb trio side with seminal bop pianist Al Haig.

Compellingly capping Clarke's recorded legacy is *Pieces of Time,* a singular encounter between the patriarch of contemporary trap-kit drumming and Andrew Cyrille, Milford Graves and Famoudou Don Moye on a huge array of percussion, exploring a range of idioms, textures and colors. Two compositions by Cyrille, one by Moye, one by Graves, one by Clarke and concluding solo statements by each are included. — T.P.

STANLEY CLARKE

★★★★ **Children of Forever (One Way, 1973)**
★★★★ **Stanley Clarke (1974; Epic, 1980)**
★★½ **Journey to Love (1975; Epic, 1980)**
★½ **School Days (1976; Epic, 1980)**
★★★ **I Wanna Play for You (Epic, 1979)**
★ **Rocks, Pebbles and Sand (Epic, 1980)**
★★½ **The Clarke/Duke Project (with George Duke) (Epic, 1981)**
★ **Let Me Know You (Epic, 1982)**
★★½ **The Clarke/Duke Project, Vol. 2 (with George Duke) (Epic, 1983)**
★★½ **Time Exposure (Epic, 1984)**
★★½ **Find Out! (Epic, 1985)**
★★ **Hideaway (Portrait, 1986)**
★★★ **If This Bass Could Only Talk (Portrait, 1988)**
★★★½ **Live 1976–1977 (Epic, 1991)**
★★★ **East River Drive (Epic, 1993)**
★★★ **Live at the Greek (Slamm Dunk, 1994)**
★★★ **At the Movies (Epic Soundtrax, 1995)**

Among the most gifted bassists of his generation, Stanley Clarke (b. 1951) is as adept on double bass as on electric, something that marks him as a more versatile (if not quite as influential) player than Jaco Pastorius, his closest rival. Like Pastorius, who made several noteworthy recordings with Joni Mitchell, Clarke has also made inroads into rock & roll, playing with both Jeff Beck and Keith Richards's New Barbarians. But where Pastorius merely flirted from afar, Clarke actively courted the pop market, and that made for a very different sort of recording career. His early albums, in fact, painted him as a serious jazzbo—both *Stanley Clarke* and *Journey to Love* include compositions for double bass and string section (*Journey*'s offering is even pretentiously titled "Concerto for Jazz/Rock Orchestra")—but what sets *Stanley Clarke* above the rest is the quality of its lineup, which includes Jan Hammer, Bill Connors and Tony Williams. With *School Days,* Clarke moves closer to rock, but his belief in bass as a lead instrument keeps him from having much success with the style; as *Rocks, Pebbles and Sand* makes plain, Clarke is a mediocre rocker and an abysmal singer. Fortunately, he's a terrific collaborator; his work with George Duke is funkier by far. *The Clarke/Duke Project,* for instance, may not have much in the way of hits, but it does have the right attitude (loose, loopy and on the one) and a killer version of "Louie Louie." Even without Duke, Clarke had his moments; for instance, *Find Out!* is daring enough to try "Born in the U.S.A." as rap (and it works, too).

Still, Clarke's most satisfying recordings are those that forget commercial considerations and simply let him blow. *If This Bass Could Only Talk* is full of such star turns, from the stirring rendition of "Goodbye Pork Pie Hat" to the Gregory Hines collaboration on the title tune. And though *Live 1976–1977* reprises much of the material found on *Stanley Clarke*, *Journey to Love* and *School Days,* the playing is superior to most of the studio recordings. — J.D.C.

WILLIAM CLARKE

★★★½ **Blowin' Like Hell (Alligator, 1990)**
★★★★ **Serious Intentions (Alligator, 1992)**
★★★½ **Groove Time (Alligator, 1994)**
★★★½ **The Hard Way (Alligator, 1996)**

Los Angeles–based William Clarke (1951–1996) was a keen student of Little Walter and the Chicago blues scene who fronted a hard-edged band with his blistering harmonica playing and gruff vocals. Clarke spared no energy in live performance, and his tenacity shows through on his records, highly enjoyable sets that helped propel the 1990s blues revival. Clarke was a gifted songwriter, whose best songs are found on *Serious Intentions* ("Pawnshop Bound," "Chasin' the Gator"), which also features a burning version of Nat Adderley's "Work Song." Clarke died of a heart attack. — J.S.

BUCK CLAYTON

★★★★ **The Classic Swing of Buck Clayton (1946; Original Jazz Classics, 1990)**
★★★★ **Buck and Buddy (with Buddy Tate) (1960; Original Jazz Classics, 1992)**
★★★★ **Goin' to Kansas City (with Tommy Gwaltney's Kansas City Nine, Charlie Byrd and Dicky Wells) (1960; Original Jazz Classics, 1990)**
★★★½ **Buck and Buddy Blow the Blues (with Buddy Tate) (1961; Original Jazz Classics, 1995)**
★★★½ **Buck Clayton Meets Joe Turner (Black Lion, 1965)**
★★★★ **A Buck Clayton Jam Session (1974; Chiaroscuro, 1989)**
★★★★ **A Buck Clayton Jam Session: 1975 (1975; Chiaroscuro, 1995)**
★★★ **The Essential Buck Clayton (Vanguard, 1977)**

Trumpeter Wilbur "Buck" Clayton (1911–1991) was part of the legendary Count Basie lineup from 1936 until he joined the Army in 1943. Clayton was a strong, melodically inventive soloist who epitomized the stylistic strengths of the swing era. During the postwar remainder of the 1940s Clayton contributed to a large number of jam sessions led by himself and others, a tradition he continued for decades. The Chiaroscuro albums, recorded in the mid-1970s with longtime cohorts such as Doc Cheatham and Joe Newman on trumpet; Urbie Green and Vic Dickenson on trombone; Earle Warren and Lee Konitz on alto saxophone; Budd Johnson, Buddy Tate and Zoot Sims on tenor; Joe Temperley on baritone; Earl Hines and Tommy Flanagan on piano; Milt Hinton on bass; and Gus Johnson and Mel Lewis on drums, show how hot these sessions could get.

The Classic Swing of Buck Clayton was recorded shortly after Clayton got out of the military and consists of sessions with Buck Clayton's Big Eight, a cross-generational band with Trummy Young and Dicky Wells playing trombone and the young Billy Taylor playing some great piano; Buck Clayton's Big Four, with guitarist Tiny Grimes; and Trummy Young's Big Seven featuring Buck Clayton, led by the trombonist and featuring Cozy Cole on drums.

The sessions with tenor saxophonist Tate are warm reunions of two stalwart Basie-ites. *Goin' to Kansas City* is a hot tribute to the wide-open town where Clayton first hooked up with Basie and another compatriot from that band, Dicky Wells, who also plays in this nonet assembled by traditional jazz scholar and multi-instrumentalist Tommy Gwaltney.

Clayton was a great accompanist to singers—he played on many of the classic Billie Holiday sides and had a long-term musical relationship with Jimmy Rushing—so it's no surprise that his style fit hand-in-glove with Joe Turner's on the Black Lion release, *Buck Clayton Meets Joe Turner.* — J.S.

JAY CLAYTON

★★★ **Beautiful Love (Sunnyside, 1995)**

Vocalist Jay Clayton (b. 1941) is known for the abstraction of her technique, using wordless vocals to evoke program music of great melodic and rhythmic sophistication. She has appeared in a number of currently out-of-print avant-garde projects, most notably the Vocal Summit group with Urszula Dudziak, Norma Winstone and Michele Hendricks, and has recorded with sound-as-sound practitioners Steve Reich and John Cage. *Beautiful Love* is an album of duets with pianist Fred Hersch. Look for the cutout *All-Out* on Anima Records, a session with soprano saxophonist Jane Ira Bloom and bassist Harvie Swartz. — J.S.

EDDY CLEARWATER

★★★★ **Blues Hang Out (1989; Evidence, 1992)**
★★★½ **A Real Good Time (Rooster Blues, 1990)**
★★★½ **Help Yourself (Blind Pig, 1992)**
★★★½ **The Chief (Rooster Blues, 1994)**
★★★★ **Black Night (Storyville, 1995)**
★★★½ **Boogie My Blues Away (Delmark, 1995)**
★★★★ **Mean Case of the Blues (Bullseye Blues, 1997)**

Eddy Harrington, born in 1935 in Macon, Mississippi, would later become known as Eddy "the Chief" Clearwater, thanks to Chicago drummer "Jump" Jackson, who bestowed the nickname on the young southpaw guitarist (he often wore an Indian headdress). Clearwater is a play on Muddy Waters's name. Though early in his career Clearwater was pigeonholed as a Chuck Berry imitator, he later became recognized as a peer of such Chicago West Side sound pioneers as Otis Rush and Buddy Guy. Clearwater's innovative and soulful guitar style mixes blues, C&W and '50s rock & roll.

Blues Hang Out, initially issued in France, features a smoldering version of T-Bone Walker's "Stormy Monday Blues," with Big Time Sarah on vocals. Also included is a jumping cover of Leiber and Stoller's "Hound Dog" and the raucous, Berry-esque original "Lay My Guitar Down." *Help Yourself,* with a title track by Jimmy Reed, contains a streamlined, reverb-soaked version of Otis Rush's classic "All Your Love" as well as a number of terrific originals, such as "Chicago Weather Woman" and the smooth "Crossover."

Boogie My Blues Away, comprising tracks recorded in 1977 and previously unavailable domestically, consists of eight original tunes produced by Ralph Bass, who helped launch the careers of James Brown and Little Esther, among others. Notable are the rockin' title track, the solemn "Came Up the Hard Way" and "Mayor Daley's Blues," with lyrics complaining that Chicago's then-mayor and President Carter don't have the time "to come out here and listen to these blues we're puttin' out."

Black Night is a live recording from 1976 with Jimmy Dawkins on guitar, Sylvester Boines on bass and Fred Below on drums covering blues classics such as "Hoochie Coochie Man," "Rock Me Baby," "Every Day I Have the Blues," "The Things I Used to Do" and "You Don't Have to Go." *A Real Good Time* is a live album compiled from two Indiana shows. *The Chief* is a solid studio effort with contributions from Lurie Bell on guitar, Carey Bell on harmonica and Lafayette Leake on piano. Clearwater is in good form on *Mean Case of the Blues,* leading a horn-augmented band with excellent support from Billy Branch on harmonica. — B.R.H.

CLARENCE CLEMONS

★★★ **Peacemaker (Zoo, 1995)**

Saxophonist Clarence Clemons (b. 1942) was one of the most successful practitioners of the vibrato-rich King Curtis tenor style as a member of Bruce Springsteen's E Street Band. Clemons demonstrates a wider range of musical interests on his own with *Peacemaker,* playing in a style closer to John Coltrane on a series of world-music–inspired compositions. — J.S.

REV. JAMES CLEVELAND

★★★ **This Sunday in Person: James Cleveland with the Angelic Gospel Choir (Savoy, 1961)**
★★★ **Rev. James Cleveland with the Angelic Choir, Vol. 2 (Savoy, 1962)**
★★★★★ **Peace Be Still: Rev. James Cleveland with the Angelic Choir, Vol. 3 (Savoy, 1963)**
★★★ **Songs of Dedication (Savoy, 1968)**
★★★★ **I Stood on the Banks of Jordan: Rev. James Cleveland with the Angelic Choir, Vol. 4 (Savoy, 1970)**
★★★ **In the Ghetto: Rev. James Cleveland and the Southern California Community Choir (Savoy, 1973)**
★★★ **Give It to Me: Rev. James Cleveland and the Southern California Community Choir (Savoy, 1973)**

★★★ **Tomorrow (with the Charles Fold Singers) (Savoy, 1978)**
★★★★ **Lord Let Me Be an Instrument: James Cleveland with the Charles Fold Singers, Vol. 4 (Savoy, 1979)**
★★★★★ **James Cleveland Sings with the World's Greatest Choirs (Savoy, 1980)**
★★★★ **This Too Will Pass: James Cleveland, Charles Fold and the Charles Fold Singers (Savoy, 1983)**
★★★ **Jesus Is the Best Thing That Ever Happened to Me (with the Charles Fold Singers) (Savoy, 1990)**
★★★★★ **Touch Me (with the Charles Fold Singers) (Savoy, 1990)**
★★★★ **Give Me My Flowers: James Cleveland with the Angelic Choir, Vol. 5 (Savoy, N.A.)**
★★★★ **James Cleveland and the Angelic Choir, Vol. 8—Part 2: Recorded Live (Savoy, N.A.)**
★★★★ **Merry Christmas from James Cleveland and the Angelic Choir (Savoy, N.A.)**
★★★★★ **James Cleveland with the Gospel Chimes (Savoy, N.A.)**
★★★½ **Jesus Is the Best Thing (Savoy, N.A.)**

While the above listings indicate but a portion of the prolific Rev. James Cleveland's (b. 1932) extensive Savoy catalog, these selections limn the most important era of his long career. Inspired and influenced by the singing of Mahalia Jackson, the forthright poetry of Thomas A. Dorsey's songs and the inventive, genre-jumping piano stylings of Roberta Martin, Cleveland, a third-generation modern gospel singer, absorbed the music that preceded him, took what he liked and set out re-creating it to address the changing times.

While he worked with a number of groups in the '50s, Cleveland's stature within the gospel community grew mightily on the strength of his powerhouse singing, blues-tinged arrangements and eloquent songwriting. His most important early association was with the Gospel Chimes, who already boasted three of the top young singers of the day in Jessy Dixon, Lee Charles and Claude Timmons. Dixon was a formidable figure, well versed in pop and R&B mannerisms, with a physical presence to match Cleveland's. Listening to their aggressive give-and-take on *James Cleveland and the Gospel Chimes,* one hears gospel melding into soul and the roots of a new male-duo style that would reach its apex with the emergence of Sam and Dave in Memphis a decade later. (At the same time, his full-bore gospel shouting on "Walking with the King" prefigures the Wilson Pickett style.)

In 1960 Cleveland joined the Voices of Tabernacle, a progressive Detroit choir with which he ushered in the modern gospel sound on a recording of the Soul Stirrers' "The Love of God" that became a gospel best-seller. Signed to Savoy, Cleveland had moderate success with the Gospel Chimes and the Gospel All Stars but finally hit his stride when teamed with the Angelic Choir. To this association he brought his young organist from the Cleveland Singers, one Billy Preston, whose soulful accompaniment moved Cleveland to his most possessed performances. *Vol. 3* of the Angelic Choir recordings proved to be a breakthrough record. Propelled by the stunning title song, "Peace Be Still," the album catapulted Cleveland into the gospel pantheon, where he achieved a measure of wealth and fame virtually without parallel in the black gospel world.

Visions of Sam Cooke dancing in his head, Cleveland entertained the thought of transforming himself into a pop singer; when that hot minute had passed, he was back in the church, at home with the music that spoke to him on the most fundamental level. It has been his practice to record before live church audiences, and though some of these efforts leave much to be desired in sound quality, they also add compelling context to the performances. *James Cleveland Sings with the World's Greatest Choirs* is an apt summation of the master's breadth. It includes a selection with the Voices of Tabernacle, one each with 15 others, including the Southern California Community Choir, the Angelic Choir and the Voices of Christ—in essence an overview of the modern choir movement.

The releases with the Charles Fold Singers are recommended without qualification. All live recordings, these performances have moments of tenderness (on "Lord Let Me Be an Instrument" Cleveland gives a controlled, deeply felt reading that would be the envy of Jerry "the Iceman" Butler), but the dominant mode is fire. Cleveland is relentless in pushing the emotional envelope, and the choir gives it right back. The unidentified female soloist on *Touch Me* deserves her own solo recording: She closes out the service with a scalding treatment of "If You Have the Faith" with a force rivaled only by Aretha Franklin. This is not an exaggeration—she must be heard to be believed. — D.M.

ROSEMARY CLOONEY

★★★★★ **Love (1963; Reprise Archives, 1994)**
★★★ **Everything's Coming Up Rosie (Concord Jazz, 1977)**
★★★ **Rosie Sings Bing (Concord Jazz, 1978)**
★★★ **Here's to My Lady (Concord Jazz, 1979)**
★★★★ **Rosemary Clooney Sings the Lyrics of Ira Gershwin (Concord Jazz, 1980)**
★★★ **With Love (Concord Jazz, 1981)**
★★★★ **Rosemary Clooney Sings the Music of Cole Porter (Concord Jazz, 1982)**
★★★ **My Buddy (Concord Jazz, 1983)**
★★★ **Rosemary Clooney Sings the Music of Harold Arlen (Concord Jazz, 1983)**
★★★★ **Rosemary Clooney Sings the Music of Irving Berlin (Concord Jazz, 1984)**
★★★★ **Rosemary Clooney Sings Ballads (Concord Jazz, 1985)**
★★★ **Rosemary Clooney Sings the Music of Jimmy Van Heusen (Concord Jazz, 1986)**
★★★★ **Rosemary Clooney Sings the Lyrics of Johnny Mercer (Concord Jazz, 1987)**
★★★ **Show Tunes (Concord Jazz, 1989)**
★★★★ **16 Most Requested Songs (Legacy, 1989)**
★★★½ **For the Duration (Concord Jazz, 1991)**
★★★ **Girl Singer (Concord Jazz, 1992)**
★★★½ **Do You Miss New York? (Concord Jazz, 1993)**
★★★ **Still on the Road (Concord Jazz, 1994)**
★★★★★ **Demi-Centennial (Concord Jazz, 1995)**
★★★★★ **Dedicated to Nelson (Concord Jazz, 1996)**

Rosemary Clooney's personal history of triumph, near-tragic decline and glorious comeback is every bit as stirring as the music she's made throughout her career. Signed to Columbia, Clooney (b. 1928) became one of America's most popular singers in the 1950s, a superb stylist in an era rife with same, an interpreter of such immediate intimacy and alluring grace that she belongs in a pantheon whose ranks include only a handful of artists on the order of Frank Sinatra, Ella Fitzgerald, Dinah Washington, Tony Bennett, Nat King Cole, Sarah Vaughan—the list isn't long. Even so, her Columbia years were marked by a certain schizophrenia in that producer Mitch Miller's insistence on Clooney cutting songs with novelty appeal tended to obscure her tremendous vocal gift. Fluff such as "Come On-a My House" (a Number One single in 1951), "Botch-a-Me" and "Mambo Italiano" went far toward defining her public image, despite her success with deeper, more sophisticated material on the order of "You'll Never Know," a Top 20 single in 1953, and the wistful "Hey There," a Number One in 1954. Yet Miller's formula worked on a pure commercial level—worked to the tune of 24 Top 40 singles between 1951 and 1954. With this part of her career coinciding with the last great era of the classic American pop song before rock & roll pushed it off the charts and, in large part, off the airwaves, Clooney's husky, shaded, seductive voice remains one of the most resonant echoes of a time when lyricists reached for the poetry in life and found graceful, sensitive singers to herald their coming.

The essential pop-song overview is *16 Most Requested Songs,* complete with "Come On-a My House," "Hey There," "Tenderly," "Half as Much," "You'll Never Know," "Too Young," "I Could Have Danced All Night"—performed with such insight and beauty as to rewrite these well-worn (even then) tunes into personal statements. Moving to RCA in the late '50s, Clooney found success elusive but was given an opportunity, in 1961, to fashion an album on her own terms. She selected the material and then was teamed with her dream arranger, Nelson Riddle. Twelve songs and a performance for the ages later, she was told RCA had canceled the album's release.

Cut to 1963—Sinatra signs her to his Reprise label, buys the master tapes of the album that was to have been titled *Love,* and releases it. *Thud.* Cut to 1994—and it surfaces again, from the Reprise Archives vault. What were they thinking at RCA? *Love* is an American pop classic on every level. Riddle, justifiably lauded for his lush, intriguing arrangements for Sinatra, met a kindred spirit in Clooney, whose smart phrasing and impeccable timing (riding exuberantly along with the melody line on a giddy song, lingering behind the beat to heighten the subtext of a poignant verse) underscored the lyrics' most revelatory insights and were in turn burnished to a heartbreaking glow by Riddle's subtle counterthemes. The song selection indicates an intent on Clooney's part to explore the nature of love from the interior—the delicate, almost whispered remembrances of yesterday's passion; the throaty, sensual melismas; the deliberate, plainsong accounts of the heart's unfathomable movements; all suggest a singer with an emotionally charged involvement in the material, as if these were diary entries. Few albums in the pop canon compare to *Love* in terms of the sheer artistry exhibited throughout and the sense of an artist's most intimate feelings being laid bare on the disc.

As her popularity ebbed, Clooney came undone, turning to pills and alcohol to ease the fall. A 1968 singing engagement in Reno, Nevada, ended prematurely after she launched into an onstage tirade directed at the audience. A medical team took her in restraints to a Los Angeles hospital, where she was remanded to a psychiatric ward for four weeks. Upon her release, she laid the foundation for a comeback with the aid of her friend Bing Crosby, who added her as an opening act on every concert he played during the last year and a half of his life (he died in 1977).

That year also marked her return to recording with a set of standards, *Everything's Coming Up Rosie,* for the Concord Jazz label, an association that has endured for nearly 20 years and produced a number of remarkable recordings. This period has seen her concentrate on the jazz and pop songs that are her natural métier and in the process has reestablished her as one of the peerless vocalists of the past half century. Working from a breadth and depth of experience unusual even by show-business standards, Clooney rummages through her songs' rich texts more fearlessly than she did in her younger days. You don't have to know much of her background to appreciate the sense of renewal she brings to "Ding Dong! The Witch Is Dead," of all things, on *Rosemary Clooney Sings the Music of Harold Arlen.* By the same token, the dark clouds hanging over her clipped, terse reading of the opening lines of the Johnny Mercer/Victor Schertzinger standard "I Remember You" (on *Rosemary Clooney Sings the Lyrics of Johnny Mercer*) bespeaks a moving sense of time lost.

Describing the highlights of Clooney's Concord Jazz catalog is a book unto itself. Certainly the *Rosemary Clooney Sings* albums are required listening. This is not to dismiss the others, though. The poignant *For the Duration* includes readings of "I'll Be Seeing You" and Cole Porter's "You'd Be So Nice to Come Home To" that stand up to any other singer's. On *Here's to My Lady,* she pays stirring tribute to Billie Holiday, not by emulating Lady Day but by interpreting her repertoire in the Clooney style, which, as it turns out, has a familiar longing quality about it.

Recent years have seen theme albums of a different sort, these being more introspective journeys into the Clooney saga, all sensitively produced for small combos (and an occasional orchestra) by John Oddo. *Girl Singer* celebrates the world of Clooney's earlier career; her confident sashay through "It Don't Mean a Thing (If It Ain't Got That Swing)"/"I'm Checking Out" recalls the triumph of her 1956 album with Duke Ellington, the now-out-of-print classic *Blue Rose. Do You Miss New York?* is a well-considered collection of songs with Big Apple connections (Broadway, the Cotton Club, etc.).

Two of Clooney's strongest efforts are 1995's *Demi-Centennial* and 1996's *Dedicated to Nelson.* The former celebrates the singer's 50 years in show business in a song cycle that charts not merely the course of a career but a full life, beginning with the lilting Irish melody of "Danny Boy" that harkens back to the Clooney family's origins, followed by "The Coffee Song," sung with Cathi Campo, daughter of Rosemary's sister Betty. In 1945, billing themselves as the Clooney Sisters, 17-year-old Rosemary and 13-year-old Betty performed regularly on Cincinnati's WLW radio station, with "The Coffee Song" one of the constants on their bill of fare. Thus a reminiscence in song, gaily done, that honors both the beginning of an important career and the memory of a departed sister, whose perky voice her daughter has inherited. Other friends are summoned with equal vividness: "I Left My Heart in San Francisco" is a tender gesture toward former Columbia label mate Tony Bennett, with whom Clooney used to joust for chart prominence in the early '50s; "White Christmas" pays touching tribute to Bing Crosby, with whom she costarred in *Holiday Inn,* the film from which springs this

Irving Berlin Christmas classic; in a gently rendered "Falling in Love Again" Clooney adopts an aloof, quizzical tone, at once distant and wanting, in evoking the otherworldly spirit of Marlene Dietrich. Most touching, Nelson Riddle is remembered in the elegant wash of strings supporting Clooney's heartfelt delivery of "How Will I Remember You," the Carl Sigman song that was the emotional flashpoint of the *Love* album.

Which turns out to be the appropriate bridge to a full-blown tribute to Riddle, *Dedicated to Nelson,* that brings dignity to this benighted conceit. In 1956 and 1957 Riddle was the musical director for Clooney's popular TV show, for which he wrote hundreds of scores. For this album Clooney reviewed the show's audio tapes and selected 16 songs she felt best exemplified the pinnacle of their work together. Lacking any written scores, however, Clooney's producer/musical director John Oddo (with Eddie Karam and David Berger) had to transcribe the arrangements directly from the TV programs; because some were written only as short, transitional pieces, he then had to flesh these out into full-length numbers. Oddo did a superb job in finding Riddle's voice in the new passages, if only by adhering to the master's preference of disdaining harmonic and melodic verbosity in favor of concise, emotionally gripping notes, phrases and themes. Clooney responds with some of her most engaging and engaged singing on record. The marvelous, weary vibrato in her voice on "Limehouse Blues" resonates with barely concealed despair; at the other end of the spectrum, her jaunty but sedate rendering of "We're in the Money" delivers bravado without boorishness; in the closing bars of "Do You Know What It Means to Miss New Orleans?" she executes an octave leap without undermining the narrative's moody ambiance—a nice bit of vocal tightrope-walking at a delicate moment. The album closes on a note of unwavering commitment, with Clooney digging deep on the Harold Arlen/Johnny Mercer evergreen "Come Rain or Come Shine." Her gritty declamation of the lyric "I'm with you/Come rain or come shine" speaks volumes about the heart informing Rosemary Clooney's work. — D.M.

ARNETT COBB

★★★★ **Blow, Arnett, Blow (with Eddie "Lockjaw" Davis) (1959; Original Jazz Classics, 1994)**

★★★½ **Party Time (1959; Original Jazz Classics, 1995)**

★★★ **Smooth Sailing (1959; Original Jazz Classics, 1995)**

★★★ **Blue and Sentimental (with the Red Garland Trio) (1960; Original Jazz Classics, 1993)**

★★★½ **Show Time (with Dizzy Gillespie and Jewel Brown) (Fantasy, 1988)**

★★★ **Live in Paris (Esoldan, 1989)**

★★★ **Tenor Tribute I (Soul Note, 1993)**

★★★ **Tenor Tribute II (Soul Note, 1993)**

★★★ **Arnett Blows for 1300 (Delmark, 1994)**

★★★ **Arnett Cobb and the Muse All Stars: Live at Sandy's (Muse, 1996)**

Arnett Cobb (1918–1989), the "Wild Man of the Tenor Sax," was born in Houston, Texas, and came up during the 1930s. He closed out the decade as the featured saxophonist in Milton Larkins's band before replacing Illinois Jacquet in Lionel Hampton's organization in 1942.

Cobb's five years with Hampton earned him his nickname, and he has recorded sporadically between illnesses and accidents since he left Hampton in '47. Most of this material is out of print, but the 1959 tenor matchup with Eddie "Lockjaw" Davis, *Blow, Arnett, Blow,* provides all the testimony to Cobb's playing ability you need. Cobb and Davis muscle their way through this record with George Duvivier on bass and Arthur Edgehill on drums pushing the tenor battle to its limits.

Party Time features Ray Bryant on piano and Art Taylor on drums. *Smooth Sailing* showcases Cobb's warm ballad style, as does part of *Blue and Sentimental,* which combines the unavailable *Sizzlin'* and *Ballads by Cobb.* — J.S.

WILLIE COBBS

★★★½ **Down to Earth (Rooster Blues, 1994)**

Country-blues harpist/vocalist Willie Cobbs (b. 1932) spent an itinerant career singing gospel, then playing juke joints in his native Arkansas, knocking around Maxwell Street with Little Walter during the post–World War II Chicago blues scene, then relocating to Memphis, where he put out his claim to fame, the snappy put-down "You Don't Love Me." Junior Wells, the Allman Brothers and John Hammond were among the many of Cobbs's admirers who saw fit to cover the song, but for most of his career Cobbs himself was relegated to recording a string of obscure singles. *Down to Earth* presents him in solid form backed by a driving Memphis rhythm section. His new version of "You Don't Love Me," with additional lyrics, is worth the wait. — J.S.

BILLY COBHAM

★★★★ **Spectrum (1973; Rhino, 1992)**
★★★★½ **The Best of Billy Cobham (Rhino, 1987)**
★★★ **Billy's Best Hits (GRP, 1988)**
★★★★ **The Traveler (Evidence, 1994)**

After serving a decade-long apprenticeship backing R&B bands and playing with Horace Silver, Dreams and Miles Davis, drummer Billy Cobham (b. 1944) enjoyed the powerful early-'70s propulsion of the Mahavishnu Orchestra. That enabled him to leave the band with superstar credentials, which were immediately justified by his first solo album, *Spectrum,* a high-water mark in the history of jazz-rock fusion.

Spectrum eschewed Mahavishnu's cerebrations for a gut punch, and Cobham pushed the late rock guitarist Tommy Bolin to his finest moments as a soloist, producing a hit single, "Stratus," in the process.

Cobham then formed a band around soloists John Abercrombie on guitar, Randy Brecker on trumpet and Michael Brecker on saxophone. For three albums, *Crosswinds*, *Total Eclipse* and *Shabazz,* they played strong material with sublime fervor. Although these titles are no longer in print, highlights appear on Rhino's *The Best of Billy Cobham.*

With expectations higher for Cobham's next band, Spectrum, with its stellar lineup of bassist Doug Rauch, keyboardist George Duke and guitarist John Scofield, its attempt to incorporate '70s funk led to unfortunate results. The band's collective energy didn't sustain the chops of the individual musicians, and Cobham's soloing, while still impressive, couldn't be as inventive as it once was.

Cobham retrenched for *Magic* (now out of print), a shrewd move that speaks well of his judgment as a bandleader, and came up with an understated yet commercial session featuring instrumental support from keyboardist Joachim Kuhn, guitarist Pete Maunu, bassist Randy Jackson, percussionists Pete and Sheila Escovedo and clarinetist Alvin Batiste.

Cobham went on to form the Glass Menagerie band, an outstanding postfusion unit comprising guitarist Dean Brown, bassist Tim Landers and keyboardist Gil Goldstein. That group's 1982 Montreux Festival recording, *Smokin',* is now out of print.

Though still in demand as a session player, Cobham's fortunes waned as mainstream jazz took a neoconservative turn against fusion. *Billy's Best Hits* is nothing special. Like so many talented musicians in jazz history, Cobham couldn't find a U.S. record deal and had to leave the country to make his music. *The Traveler,* an imaginative tour de force of Cobham's strengths as a composer and bandleader, demonstrates that his talent never waned along with his music-industry cachet.

In the late 1990s Cobham resurfaced as the leader of the Jazz Is Dead project, a group featuring Aquarium Rescue Unit guitarist Jimmy Herring and dedicated to performing unusual arrangements of Grateful Dead compositions. — J.S.

AL COHN

★★★★ **The Progressive Al Cohn (1953; Savoy, 1995)**
★★★★ **Broadway (1954; Original Jazz Classics, 1993)**
★★★★★ **Body and Soul (with Zoot Sims) (1973; Muse, 1988)**
★★★★ **Motoring Along (with Zoot Sims) (Gazelle, 1974)**
★★★★★ **Play It Now (Xanadu, 1975)**
★★★ **Be Loose (Biograph, 1976)**
★★★★★ **America (Xanadu, 1977)**
★★★★★ **Heavy Love (with Jimmy Rowles) (Xanadu, 1978)**
★★★★ **No Problem (Xanadu, 1980)**
★★★★ **Nonpareil (1981; Concord Jazz, 1992)**
★★★★ **Overtones (Concord Jazz, 1982)**
★★★★ **Standards of Excellence (Concord Jazz, 1984)**
★★★★ **Either Way (Evidence, 1992)**

Al Cohn (1925–1988) was one of the finest tenor-saxophone players to come under the spell of Lester Young in the late '40s. Cohn went on to find his own voice, richly toned and relentlessly swinging, establishing himself as a first-rate mainstream saxophonist. Cohn's early individuality can be found on *The Progressive Al Cohn*, *Be Loose* and *Broadway.* In the late '50s Cohn hooked up with fellow tenorist and ex–Woody Herman big-band mate Zoot Sims, a union that continued sporadically until Cohn's death. Cohn wrote and arranged intricate charts featuring their faultless unison playing,

interspersed with focused solo spots. The masterpiece of the Sims/Cohn partnership may well be 1973's *Body and Soul,* where they are backed by a superlative rhythm section: drummer Mel Lewis, bassist George Duvivier and pianist Jaki Byard. Cohn continued to lead sessions during this peak period, and some of the supreme moments of his career are contained on *Play It Now* and *America. Heavy Love,* a duet with pianist Jimmy Rowles, is a marvel of empathy. And as the Concord Jazz recordings *Nonpareil*, *Overtones* and *Standards of Excellence* prove, Cohn was still playing marvelously in the last decade of his life.
— S.F.

FREDDY COLE

★★★ I'm Not My Brother, I'm Me (Sunnyside, 1991)
★★★ Live at Birdland West (LaserLight, 1992)
★★★ Always (Fantasy, 1995)
★★★ A Circle of Love (Fantasy, 1996)
★★★½ To the Ends of the Earth (Fantasy, 1997)

Freddy Cole (b. 1931), the younger brother of Nat King Cole, has an instantly recognizable voice full of charm and emotional heft. His best record, *To the Ends of the Earth,* is a collection of standards with great support from Cyrus Chestnut on piano, Joe Locke on vibes, George Mraz on bass and Steve Berrios on drums.
— J.S.

HOLLY COLE

★★ Blame It on My Youth (Manhattan, 1992)
★ Don't Smoke in Bed (Manhattan, 1993)
★★★ Temptation (Metro Blue, 1995)
★★★½ It Happened One Night (Metro Blue, 1996)
★★★ Dark Dear Heart (Blue Note, 1997)

Singer Holly Cole (b. 1963), a jazz-scene darling in her native Canada, has a vocal style that actually fits more into the adult-pop category despite the jazz backing provided by her band mates. For 10 years, pianist Aaron Davis and bassist David Piltch have provided a substantial cushion for her captivating voice and dark humor.

On *Blame It on My Youth,* the jazz-inspired chanteuse twists standards into something so offbeat it makes humorless purists cringe; "On the Street Where You Live" sounds as if it's sung by the obsessive woman stalking Jerry Lewis in *The King of Comedy.* And even a Joe Henderson cameo can't rescue *Don't Smoke in Bed* from banal mediocrity.

Consisting entirely of Tom Waits songs, *Temptation* is fulfilling, however, because of its cohesiveness and musicality—and strong aid from Davis, Piltch and harmonica ace Howard Levy. Recorded live in Montreal, *It Happened One Night* reprises some of the more interesting material from Cole's three prior sessions and sounds more heartfelt. The enhanced CD also includes four interactive CD-ROM sessions, including two music videos. *Dark Dear Heart* offers a broader range of material, to which her enhanced band gives an alternative-rock feel, and invites comparisons to the work of fellow Canadian Sarah McLachlan. — K.F.

NAT KING COLE

★★★★ Nat King Cole Sings for Two in Love (1953; Capitol, 1987)
★★★ Unforgettable (1953; Capitol, 1990)
★★★★ The Christmas Song (1954; Capitol, 1990)
★★★★ The Piano Style of Nat King Cole (1955; Capitol Jazz, 1993)
★★★★ Just One of Those Things (and More) (1957; Capitol, 1991)
★★★★ After Midnight (1957; Capitol, 1978)
★★★★ Love Is the Thing (1957; Capitol, 1987)
★★★★ The Very Thought of You (1958; Capitol, 1987)
★★★★ To Whom It May Concern (Capitol, 1959)
★★★½ Wild Is Love (1960; Capitol, 1993)
★★★★ Ramblin' Rose (1962; Capitol, 1991)
★★★ Nat "King" Cole Sings/George Shearing Plays (1962; Capitol, 1991)
★★★ Love Is Here to Stay (Capitol, 1974)
★★★★★ Hit That Jive, Jack (Decca, 1990)
★★★★ Cole, Christmas & Kids (Capitol, 1990)
★★★★ Capitol Collectors Series (Capitol, 1990)
★★★★★ Jumpin' at Capitol: The Best of the Nat King Cole Trio (Rhino, 1990)
★★★★★ The Nat King Cole Story (Capitol, 1991)

★★★★ Big Band Cole (Capitol Jazz, 1991)
★★★★★ Nat King Cole: The Trio Recordings (LaserLight, 1991)
★★★★★ The Unforgettable Nat King Cole (Capitol, 1992)
★★★★ Jazz Encounters (Capitol Jazz, 1992)
★★★★★ Nat "King" Cole (Capitol, 1992)
★★★★★ The Complete Capitol Recordings of the Nat King Cole Trio (Capitol, 1993)
★★★★ Lush Life: Nat King Cole with the Pete Rugolo Orchestra (Capitol Jazz, 1993)
★★★★★ The Billy May Sessions (Capitol Jazz, 1993)
★★★★★ The Greatest Hits (Capitol, 1994)
★★★★★ Great Gentlemen of Song: Spotlight on Nat King Cole (Capitol, 1995)
★★★★★ The King Cole Trio: The MacGregor Years, 1941–1945 (Music and Arts Programs of America, 1995)
★★★★★ The Best of the Nat King Cole Trio: The Instrumental Classics (Capitol Jazz, 1995)
★★★★★ The Best of the Nat King Cole Trio: The Vocal Classics (1942–46) (Capitol Jazz, 1995)

Before the term *superstar* was coined, there was Nat King Cole (1919–1965), whose broad-based appeal transcended all boundaries of race, age, gender and musical preference to a degree rivaled only by the internationally beloved Louis Armstrong. The record shows 86 singles and 17 albums in the Top 40 between 1943 and 1964, encompassing a repertoire of ballads, jazz instrumentals, Spanish folk songs, gospel songs, Christmas carols, pop standards and what might now be termed pop rock. That's but part of the story.

Born Nathaniel Adams Coles in Montgomery, Alabama, the young Nat grew up in the gospel world, playing piano and organ as a child in a Chicago church presided over by the Rev. Edward James Coles—his father—after the family moved there in 1923. In his formative years he could be found outside the Grand Terrace Cafe, absorbing every note of the jazz performances going on inside, particularly those of his idol, the formidable jazz pianist Earl "Fatha" Hines. In the mid-'30s, after disbanding his own group, Cole joined his older brother Eddie's band, Eddie Cole's Solid Swingers, and appeared on that group's early recordings before marrying and striking out on his own again.

He wound up in California, knocking around from club to club, his career in low gear, until he got what he thought would be his big break. In 1937 he formed a trio with an inventive guitarist named Oscar Moore and bassist Wesley Prince (later replaced by Johnny Miller) and was booked into Los Angeles's Swanee Inn for a four-week run. Six months later the trio was still packing the Swanee and Nat had been dubbed "King Cole" by the club owner.

Signed to Decca in 1940, the King Cole Trio cut 16 sides, all unsuccessful commercially but important signposts to Cole's future. As collected on *Hit That Jive, Jack,* these recordings showcase both the trio's engaging instrumental approach as well as the range of material Cole the vocalist could negotiate. The swinging dialogs between the musicians set up solo passages that are models of tasty economy, with the bass settling in steady at the bottom, as Moore constructs deft, lofting lines built on octave chords and legato single-string runs modeled after Charlie Christian's, while Cole comps gently behind him, then steps forward for a solo turn that invariably surprises in its combination of chordal leaps, arpeggio runs and impressionistic right-hand fills.

As a vocalist, Cole had already perfected the smooth delivery that served him so effectively when he moved toward pop-oriented jazz in later years. Rather than breathtaking range, he developed an impeccable sense of phrasing; like all masterful vocalists, a bent note here or a subtle change in timbre there communicated worlds in the way of deep feeling and point of view. Warm, sensitive, convivial, his voice remains one of the most wondrous instruments in all of American music. In *Hit That Jive, Jack,* he's heard romping through the title song, a stylistic precursor to his definitive 1946 recording of Bobby Troup's "(Get Your Kicks on) Route 66"; on "That Ain't Right" he delivers a straight-ahead blues performance; "Sweet Lorraine," Cole's first recorded vocal performance, and "This Will Make You Laugh" are aching, lovely ballads given delicate treatments that underscore their tender sentiments.

In late 1942 the trio cut a hit single, "All for You," which was released on three different labels (Excelsior, Atlas and Premiere) and led to their signing a year later with the nascent

Capitol label, where Cole remained up to his death. The trio continued recording into the early '50s but was pretty much history by 1955. What they left behind in the way of recordings sound not the least bit aged, testimony to the musicians' remarkable versatility and not least of all to Cole's own skill as an arranger. Some purists regard these as Cole's finest work, a view that insults the great arrangers he worked with in the '50s and '60s and also seems to blissfully disregard the pop directions suggested by much of the repertoire. Still, this trio was so potent that the hardliners' myopia is somewhat understandable.

To hear the combo in its purest jazz mode, check out *The Best of the Nat King Cole Trio: The Instrumental Classics,* on which the foundation is being laid for Cole's pop heroics of the '50s and '60s, and study *The Best of the Nat King Cole Trio: The Vocal Classics (1942–46),* on which Cole is nothing less than superb in his delivery of classic fare such as "I'm Thru with Love," "Sweet Lorraine," "Straighten Up and Fly Right," the above-mentioned definitive "(Get Your Kicks on) Route 66" and a most telling signpost, 1946's sweet and lovely "(I Love You) For Sentimental Reasons," Cole's first Number One single.

Many of the 16 tracks on Rhino's *Jumpin' at Capitol* can be found on the 22-track *The Vocal Classics,* but the former is recommended for two performances: a stirring instrumental take on Cole Porter's "What Is This Thing Called Love," featuring a scintillating, angular guitar solo from Oscar Moore—popping notes, bending strings, darting in with two- and three-note chords—wrapped around Cole's propulsive piano commentary; and a romping R&B shouter, "For You My Love," a stylistic departure for the trio, which is joined here by saxophonist Charlie Barnet (who gets off a wonderful, honking solo midway), trumpeter Ernie Royal and vocalist Nellie Lutcher, whose harder style is a pleasing foil to Cole's velvety crooning.

The trio also appeared frequently on radio, and completists are advised to check cutout and import bins for some of these recordings, specifically: *The Complete Early Transcriptions of the King Cole Trio 1938–1941,* a four-disc set on Vintage Jazz Classics, which documents the group's first five years; *Straighten Up and Fly Right,* also on Vintage Jazz Classics, comprising radio broadcasts from 1942 to '48, with Frank Sinatra as guest vocalist; and *The King Cole Trio 1938–39,* on Savoy, a collection of radio transcriptions, some of which had appeared only on 78s before this now also out-of-print release.

Most impressive, LaserLight's five-disc box, *Nat King Cole: The Trio Recordings,* shows the remarkable evolution of the trio and of Cole as he honed a signature vocal style in the early- to mid-'40s. Despite its skimpy liner notes, this set becomes essential on the strength of its material alone: These recordings date from 1941 to 1945, when the trio recorded voluminously for C.P. MacGregor Transcription, a West Coast outfit that provided program material for radio broadcast. In addition to studio recordings, the trio is heard on a number of tracks from V-Disc sessions, some obscure live recordings from 1955–67 and a few sides featuring vocalist Anita O'Day.

An unassuming but not unattractive package, *Nat King Cole: The Trio Recordings* is one of the Cole catalog's diamonds in the rough. The MacGregor years are rounded out in the four-disc collection from Music and Arts Programs of America, *The King Cole Trio: The MacGregor Years, 1941–1945.* Naturally there is some duplication of material between this and the LaserLight package, but the Music and Arts set contains a greater selection of the trio's work backing not only Anita O'Day but also Anita Boyer, the Barrie Sisters and perky Ida James, and in doing so offers additional opportunity to marvel at the subtle power of Cole's work as an accompanist.

A 1992 release, *Jazz Encounters,* further emphasizes Cole's versatility in its 21 numbers recorded between 1945 and 1950 in a series of all-star sessions. The trio is heard accompanying Woody Herman (in a strictly vocalist role) on a personable version of "My Baby Just Cares for Me" and a strictly-for-laughs take of "Mule Train," complete with Gene Orloff sawing away on fiddle. Stan Kenton Orchestra arranger Pete Rugolo, who would go on to play a critical role in Cole's development as a pop vocalist in the '50s, makes his first appearance with the artist on a 1947 cut, "Leap Here" (included in two versions, one a previously unissued alternate take). This features Cole accompanying the winners of *Metronome* magazine's annual jazz poll, among them Dizzy Gillespie and Buddy Rich, in a session that brought a touch of bebop to a swing outing. Those who remember Jo Stafford for her rich, atmospheric pop ballads will hear something new in her three cuts here, among her first Capitol sides. "Baby, Won't You

Please Come Home" shows her swinging gracefully through an arrangement featuring an evocative solo from trumpeter Ray Lynn; it's followed by "Cindy," in a country-swing treatment marked by a sprightly instrumental dialog between Cole and Lynn. One of the rare treats here is the session pairing the King Cole Trio on three cuts with the man who signed them to Capitol, Johnny Mercer, otherwise regarded as one of America's great pop songwriters. The wry, cool duets between Cole and Mercer on "Save the Bones for Henry Jones" and "My Baby Likes to Be-Bop" show two first-rate stylists at their most ingratiating.

Although they would continue recording sporadically into the early '50s, the trio—now with Irving Ashby on guitar and Joe Comfort on bass—began a graceful exit from Cole's history in 1949 when Pete Rugolo came on board as musical director, an association that endured for three years and is showcased on *Lush Life: Nat King Cole with the Pete Rugolo Orchestra.* Although he had recorded a few sides with orchestral arrangements earlier in the decade (notably in 1946 with "The Christmas Song," the Mel Torme–penned Yule standard that Cole retired on the strength of a rich, heartfelt vocal resonating with benevolent spirit and comforting nostalgia for the Yuletide season's symbolic rituals—a Currier & Ives scene set to music that rose to #3 on the pop chart; and 1948's "Nature Boy," a Number One single featuring Cole solo backed by Frank DeVol's Orchestra, a most dramatic harbinger of things to come), Cole always returned to the piano, guitar and bass lineup as his meat and potatoes.

When Stan Kenton took a year off in 1948, freeing Rugolo, Cole and Capitol seized the opportunity to journey down what all the evidence indicated would be a fruitful path. As heard on *Lush Life,* Rugolo and Cole managed this without undermining the integrity of the trio recordings; that is, many of the orchestral arrangements evoked the mood and temperament of the trio's work by mingling Cole's piano solos and Ashby's robust guitar fills with strings, horns, understated percussion and pop-style background voices. Elsewhere, Rugolo's deployment of Latin percussion, blaring horn lines and string arpeggios clearly mark these deftly executed, artistically sound sessions as an aural line in the sand over which the trio would rarely step in the years ahead.

In 1958 Cole returned to the big-band format long enough to deliver a classic album, *Welcome to the Club,* recorded with the Count Basie Orchestra (sans Basie—Gerald Wiggins replaced him on piano). This is heard in its entirety on *Big Band Cole,* along with five tracks recorded between 1950 and 1961 with the Stan Kenton Orchestra (Pete Rugolo, arranger), including "Orange Colored Sky," a #5 single from 1950, and the Shorty Rogers–arranged Latin-flavored burner "Jam-bo," with clanging percussion, vibrant polyrhythms courtesy Jack Costanza on bongos, and tart, angular piano retorts interjected by Cole himself, all of it redolent of the Big Hunk of America/Little Bit of Cuba mainstream stylings pioneered in the 1940s by Desi Arnaz, Xavier Cugat and Perez Prado.

Pete Rugolo looms even larger in the Cole saga than the *Lush Life* sessions might indicate. In 1950 Cole cut his third Number One single, the haunting "Mona Lisa," backed by Lex Baxter's orchestra. The arrangement, however, had been ghostwritten for Baxter by a then-unknown named Nelson Riddle. Rugolo imparted this information to Cole, who then brought Riddle on as his musical director—for some 10 years and approximately 250 songs. With Cole, Riddle built lasting monuments in the '50s and '60s, as he did with Frank Sinatra, Peggy Lee and Rosemary Clooney. Along the way, Cole also worked with two other arranger giants, Billy May and Gordon Jenkins, both of whose individual styles were as distinctive as Riddle's. In broad generalizations, Riddle, though identified with a lush, string-laden sound, was the most parsimonious of the three, preferring succinctly stated themes and counterthemes, sustained legato washes of strings, sotto voce keyboards and delicate, poignant woodwind passages. Jenkins was given more to opulence and soaring emotions ostentatiously displayed by the orchestra as a single entity rather than having instruments contributing parts to create the whole; even so, he was capable of great subtlety within this style: Listen to the delicate moods he sustains on *The Very Thought of You* and *Love Is The Thing,* creating an almost unbearable tension by supporting Cole's probing, introspective readings with muted orchestrations that achieve grandiosity through sparseness. May, by contrast, was the most overtly swinging and macho, if you will, of the three; as a link both to Cole's jazz-trio origins and to big-band R&B stylings, he eased Cole's seamless passage into the rock & roll era. Where Riddle and Jenkins wrung every ounce of feeling out of the strings, May, a former trumpet player, came on with horns—alto, tenor and baritone saxophones, trumpets, muted cornets, tubas, trombones—to provide emotional ballast even to tender love songs.

With these arrangers, Cole developed the art of the concept album, a song collection consciously built on a single theme and requiring a specific mood be maintained from first cut to last. Although Sinatra and Riddle are credited with producing the first such effort, 1953's *Songs for Young Lovers,* Cole and Riddle's *Nat King Cole Sings for Two in Love* actually preceded the Sinatra LP (the CD release of the album contains an extra song not included on the original release, "You Stepped Out of a Dream," conducted by, yes, Pete Rugolo).

Two other Riddle/Cole collaborations remain in print: the moving *To Whom It May Concern,* a collection of ballads exploring the vagaries of love; and *Wild Is Love,* manifesting an intriguing idea in which writers Dotty Wayne and Ray Rasch composed 14 songs (only a dozen could be contained on the original 1960 LP; the additional two have been added to the CD) centered on the emotional experience of a single love affair, each one carrying the narrative line forward even as the individual compositions stand as complete works unto themselves. Cole delivered the above-mentioned pair of albums, which probe the idea of love as a philosophical conceit, conducting an internal dialog examining the purpose of it all. Typically, the Billy May sessions are bright and buoyant affairs, showing off Cole in gregarious voice, his whimsical readings harkening back to the endearing novelty tunes the King Cole Trio cut in its heyday. Typical of May's approach is *Just One of Those Things (and More)* (the parenthetical title reference alludes to the presence of three bonus tracks from Cole's big-band album *Let's Face the Music and Dance*), an upbeat exercise released after the somber, reflective, Riddle-conducted *Love Is the Thing.* Available as a single CD, all of its tunes are contained as well on the double-disc overview, *The Billy May Sessions,* which traces the Cole-May relationship from its hit beginnings with 1952's "Walkin' My Baby Back Home" (#8 on the pop chart) to the sessions that produced their final, first-rate collaboration, 1961's *Let's Face the Music and Dance.* Among the standard Cole fare, however, are a couple of oddities from 1957: "With You on My Mind," cowritten by Cole with his wife's sister, Charlotte Hawkins, is energized by a distinctly doo-wop–flavored arrangement; and "Send for Me," wherein Cole affects a swaggering vocal in an arrangement that blends Plas Johnson's honking R&B sax solos with guitarist John Collins's rock & roll–style octave chord fills.

Although he was solidly established in the pop market by the early '50s, Cole occasionally gravitated back to his roots as an instrumentalist. Between 1952 and 1956 he cut three albums on which he was the featured pianist. One, 1952's easygoing *Penthouse Serenade,* is now out of print. *The Piano Style of Nat King Cole* from 1955 teams him with a studio orchestra conducted by Nelson Riddle on a set of standards that are almost evenly divided between tender, romantic tunes awash with strings (the beautiful "Imagination" being a standout) and swinging, upbeat numbers with Cole's graceful keyboard runs supported by brass and woodwinds. *The Piano Style of Nat King Cole* finds the titular artist and the orchestra engaging in some interesting byplay and getting down with some challenging improvisational passages that invigorate the proceedings in unexpected ways. The third piano album, 1957's *After Midnight,* finds Cole backed by the trio of guitarist John Collins, bassist Charlie Harris and drummer Lee Young (brother of tenor-sax giant Lester Young), with four outstanding guest soloists enlivening the proceedings: Harry "Sweets" Edison on trumpet, Willie Smith on alto sax, Juan Tizol on valve trombone and Stuff Smith on violin. The mellow, casual feel of the sessions and the frequent sparks of instrumental brilliance recall the King Cole Trio's finest hours, a point hammered home by Cole's relaxed, jaunty reading of "Sweet Lorraine"—that trio chestnut—which sets up a warm, muted solo from Edison, followed by a lilting, robust single-string commentary by Collins, which bows gracefully to Cole's own feathery, arpeggio-rich variation on the theme. Smith shines on four numbers, notably "Sometimes I'm Happy," where his angular solos are all Appalachia by way of 52nd Street—a stirring fusion of folk and country styles played both as a harmonizing voice and protesting counterpoint to Cole's lead vocals.

Cole's 1961 summit meeting with George Shearing, *Nat "King" Cole Sings/George Shearing Plays,* might have been better conceived as a piano duet. While the Shearing

Quintet's cool style is in the pocket with Cole's instincts as a romantic balladeer, the affair as a whole stays pretty much in low gear, despite a beautiful opening take on "September Song."

Those interested less in charting the course of Cole's artistic development and more in getting all the big hits in one place can choose from a variety of desirable titles. *Capitol Collectors Series* is designed to document the chart successes and does so admirably in 20 cuts. The two-disc *Nat King Cole Story,* originally released as a multiple-album package in the early '60s, offers a wide-ranging survey of Cole's recordings in different veins dating from his early efforts on the label. Several of the defining hits are here—"Mona Lisa," "Nature Boy," "The Christmas Song," "Unforgettable," "Walkin' My Baby Back Home"—in addition to some interesting, lesser-known sides, such as the Brook Benton–penned "Looking Back" and the gospel-styled "Oh, Mary, Don't You Weep" (arranged by Gordon Jenkins). *The Unforgettable Nat King Cole* and *The Greatest Hits* have pluses and minuses: *Unforgettable* has "That Sunday, That Summer," but *Hits* has "Answer Me, My Love"; *Unforgettable* has "Autumn Leaves," but *Hits* has "Walkin' My Baby Back Home"; *Unforgettable* has the original recording of the title song; *Hits* has the original "Unforgettable" *and* the putative "duet" with Natalie Cole.

The indispensable *Great Gentlemen of Song: Spotlight on Nat King Cole* is not the greatest-hits package its title might imply; rather, it includes five songs from the Basie Orchestra sessions (three are included on the *Big Band Cole* album); three songs from the overlooked 1961 album of love songs, *Touch of Your Lips;* selections from one of Cole's final masterpieces, *Where Did Everyone Go?;* and an obscure Cole/Riddle gem, "Should I?," making its first appearance on record in 40 years. Not to overlook the breadth of the man's artistry, Cole's out-of-print excursions into Spanish-language songs, *Cole Espanol* and *More Cole Espanol,* have their pop virtues and some challenging moments when Cole, singing in Spanish or Portuguese, is backed by a marimba band on songs indigenous to Latin America.

Few performers are as identified with Christmas music as is Nat King Cole, thanks to his monumental performance of "The Christmas Song," and it's fitting that both of his Yule albums, *The Christmas Song* and *Cole, Christmas & Kids,* rank with the finest seasonal fare ever recorded. While the former's title song gives it a higher profile, the latter (which reprises "The Christmas Song") has some terrific moments that capture the Yuletide spirit of reflection and hope for renewal with the coming new year. Of note are two arrangements by Pete Rugolo, "Frosty the Snowman" and "The Little Christmas Tree," which invest these tried-and-true standards with a bit of jazz swing.

Ultimately, the big enchiladas of the Cole catalog are the four-disc boxed set, *Nat "King" Cole,* featuring 100 songs, some previously unreleased as of 1992, and a 60-page booklet with extensive liner notes, discography, sessionography and rare photos of Cole at work and at play; and *The Complete Capitol Recordings of the Nat King Cole Trio*, which, for those with deep pockets—to the tune of $300-plus—is the winning ticket. On 18 CDs, this set charts 349 songs recorded between 1942 and 1961, many of which had been out of print for years or never released at all before this 1991 issue. In addition, the entire *After Midnight* sessions are here, as well as 56 rare Cole Trio radio transcriptions. An accompanying 64-page booklet includes all the pertinent session information and even goes the extra mile with a cross-indexed song list. For completists and historians, this exhaustive overview is a godsend; for those who would prefer not to break the bank, a representative collection of Cole's remarkable and enduring art can be assembled from the single- and double-disc titles listed above without omitting any critical performances. — D.M.

RICHIE COLE

★★★	**New York Afternoon (Muse, 1977)**
★★★★	**Alto Madness (Muse, 1978)**
★★★	**Hollywood Madness (1979; Muse, 1994)**
★★★★½	**Side by Side (with Phil Woods) (1980; Muse, 1991)**
★★★	**Pure Imagination (Concord, 1987)**
★★★	**Popbop (Milestone, 1987)**
★★★	**Signature (Milestone, 1988)**
★★★★	**Bossa International (Milestone, 1990)**
★★★	**Yakety Madness! (with Boots Randolph) (LaserLight, 1992)**
★★★	**Profile (Heads Up, 1993)**
★★★★	**Kush: The Music of Dizzy Gillespie (Heads Up, 1995)**

★★★ **West Side Story (MusicMasters, 1996)**

Saxophonist Richie Cole (b. 1948) studied under Phil Woods and emerged as one of the most popular young alto players in the bop tradition initiated by Charlie Parker. The Trenton, New Jersey, native also plays tenor and baritone, but his alto style is his trademark.

Cole recorded a series of hot, eccentric sessions for Muse in the 1970s and early '80s. His early Muse sides, *New York Afternoon* and *Alto Madness,* feature vocalist Eddie Jefferson. On *Hollywood Madness* Cole used vocals by the Manhattan Transfer and Tom Waits as well as Jefferson.

Cole went on to make a series of saxophone-battle albums, the best of which, *Side by Side,* pairs him with Woods and features Eddie "Lockjaw" Davis on tenor, John Hicks on piano, Walter Booker on bass and Jimmy Cobb on drums. *Yakety Madness!* is an oddball country-fusion set with saxophonist Boots Randolph. Other "battles," with Eric Kloss and Art Pepper, are now out of print.

Pure Imagination is a quintet session spotlighting Cole's playing backed by his working group—guitarist Vic Juris, bassist Ed Howard, drummer Victor Jones and percussionist Ray Mantilla. A series of recordings for Milestone followed, the best of which, *Bossa International,* pairs Cole with Hank Crawford on alto and features some magnificent playing from guitarist Emily Remler.

Kush: The Music of Dizzy Gillespie features Cole on tenor matched with Paquito D'Rivera on alto and clarinet and a big brass section featuring four trumpets, French horn, trombone, bass trombone and tuba. The session flies through such Gillespie standards as "Be-Bop," "Birk's Works," "Salt Peanuts" and "Con Alma." — J.S.

DEBORAH COLEMAN

★★★½ **Takin' a Stand (New Moon Blues, 1994)**
★★★★ **I Can't Lose (Blind Pig, 1997)**

Deborah Coleman (b. 1956) grew up playing a mixture of Jimi Hendrix–influenced rock and R&B in her native Virginia. After retiring from music to raise a family, Coleman returned to action in 1985, collaborating in the all-female rock band Moxxie, then in the R&B group Misbehavin' and finally as a solo artist playing blues.

Coleman's developing skills as a guitarist and her talents as a vocalist and songwriter enabled her to become a fixture on the mid-Atlantic blues scene. Her debut album, *Takin' a Stand,* on the Chapel Hill, North Carolina–based New Moon Blues label, showcases her bar-band eclecticism. *I Can't Lose,* her first straightforward-blues effort, proves that Coleman has complete control over the form and the scope for enough improvement to make her one of the genre's stars somewhere down the road. — J.S.

GEORGE COLEMAN

★★★½ **Playing Changes (Jazz House, 1979)**
★★★★ **Manhattan Panorama (1983; Evidence, 1992)**
★★★★ **At Yoshi's (1987; Evidence, 1992)**
★★★½ **My Horns of Plenty (Verve, 1992)**

George Coleman (b. 1935) is one of the most overlooked tenor-saxophone giants in jazz history. He's in tough company, of course, but for such a prodigious talent he is woefully underrecorded.

Coleman's moment in the spotlight came when he was a member of the Miles Davis Quintet, recording with that group in 1963 and 1964 on *Seven Steps to Heaven, Four and More, My Funny Valentine, In Europe* and *In Antibes.*

A soulful, aggressive yet beautifully swinging improviser, Coleman has also played with Max Roach, Elvin Jones (as part of a fantastic front line with Frank Foster, as on *Coalition*), Herbie Hancock, Horace Silver, Lee Morgan, Jimmy Smith and others.

Playing Changes documents a live set from 1979 at Ronnie Scott's in London. The Evidence reissues, *Manhattan Panorama* and *At Yoshi's,* are two magnificent sides, part live, part studio, originally recorded in the 1980s. Aside from one alto-saxophone piece, "Harlem Nocturne," on *Manhattan Panorama,* this is Coleman playing tenor sax at his best. Both albums feature superb accompaniment from pianist Harold Mabern, who went to the same Memphis high school as Coleman. Mabern also plays on *My Horns of Plenty.* — J.S.

ORNETTE COLEMAN

★★★★ **Something Else!!! (1958; Original Jazz Classics, 1988)**
★★★★★ **The Shape of Jazz to Come (Atlantic, 1959)**

★★★★ Tomorrow Is the Question (1959; Original Jazz Classics, 1988)
★★★★★ This Is Our Music (Atlantic, 1961)
★★★★★ Free Jazz (Atlantic, 1961)
★★★★ Ornette! (Atlantic, 1962)
★★★★½ At the "Golden Circle" Stockholm, Vol. 1 (1965; Blue Note, 1987)
★★★★½ At the "Golden Circle" Stockholm, Vol. 2 (1965; Blue Note, 1987)
★★★★ Ornette on Tenor (1966; Atlantic, 1962)
★★★★ New York Is Now! (1968; Blue Note, 1990)
★★★★ The Art of the Improvisers (1970; Atlantic Jazz, 1988)
★★★★ Twins (1971; Atlantic, 1981)
★★★★★ Dancing in Your Head (1977; A&M, 1988)
★★★★ Virgin Beauty (with Prime Time) (Portrait, 1988)
★★★★★ Beauty Is a Rare Thing: The Complete Atlantic Recordings (Rhino, 1993)
★★★★ Tone Dialing (with Prime Time) (Harmolodic/Verve, 1995)

Alto saxophonist Ornette Coleman (b. 1930) discovered a personal style of astonishing expressiveness—paying no heed to rules, the genius founded an entire school of jazz, and as a kind of avant-garde trickster god of modern jazz he continues to delight, befuddle and challenge.

Coleman in the late '50s, abetted by his powerhouse quartet (Charlie Haden on bass, Don Cherry on trumpet, Billy Higgins on drums), soared out of a firm grounding in the blues to revolutionize jazz through "harmolodics"—his own term for a radical style of playing that disregarded the chord changes of any given piece of music and abandoned the soloist to pure melodic improvisation. *Free Jazz* was the triumph of the maneuver: With a double quartet starring Cherry, Eric Dolphy and Freddie Hubbard, the album was one long (37-minute) explosion of contending, conjoining solos. *Beauty Is a Rare Thing,* a remarkable six-disc package, collects the whole of Coleman's Atlantic-period trailblazing: From *The Shape of Jazz to Come* and *Free Jazz* to *Ornette!* and *Ornette on Tenor,* this remains astonishing music—sheer improvisational daring.

The early Coleman recordings, *Something Else!!!* and *Tomorrow Is the Question,* spurred on by the saxophonist's long-standing stint at New York's Five Spot, are straighter fare—but not by much. At the time, Coleman confounded purists by often playing a plastic alto; his daring counterpart, Don Cherry, used a pocket trumpet—and the duo, with the expert backing of Haden and Higgins, came on like mad, brilliant kids. The post–*Free Jazz* work of the middle '60s (the two Golden Circle sets, primarily) refined the gains Coleman had made with his forays into unchained melody—check the unavailable *Great London Concert* (with Coleman blazing not only on alto but also on violin), the two volumes of *At the "Golden Circle" Stockholm* (live fireworks), *Love Call* (with John Coltrane's great rhythm section, drummer Elvin Jones and bassist Jimmy Garrison) and *New York Is Now!* (a companion piece to *Love Call*); an excellent early-'70s curio, out of print at this point, was *Skies of America* (1972), a vast, 21-part symphonic piece that introduced harmolodics in an orchestral setting. *Dancing in Your Head* (1977) brought another breakthrough, as Coleman turned himself loose on a very funky version of rock-jazz fusion; he continued to experiment throughout the '80s with an electric ensemble (paired guitars, basses, drum kits), Prime Time. *Opening the Caravan of Dreams* is the out-of-print masterwork, but the tough tracks on *Virgin Beauty* and *Tone Dialing* also bristle with energy. — P.E.

STEVE COLEMAN

WITH THE FIVE ELEMENTS
★★★★ The Tao of Mad Phat (Novus, 1993)
★★★★½ Def Trance Beat (Modalities of Rhythm) (Novus, 1995)
★★★½ Curves of Life (RCA Victor, 1996)
WITH THE METRICS
★★★ The Way of the Cipher (RCA Victor, 1995)
★★★½ A Tale of 3 Cities (Novus, 1995)
WITH THE MYSTIC RHYTHM SOCIETY
★★½ Myths, Modes and Means (RCA Victor, 1997)
★★★★ The Sign and the Seal (RCA Victor, 1997)

Architect of the Brooklyn-spawned M-Base Collective formula of shifting, funk-fueled rhythms laced with angular, avant-garde soloing, alto saxist Steve Coleman (b. 1956) dances the line between the Poles of Parker (Charlie and Maceo, that is). For the most part, he convincingly maintains this delicate balance, though his repetitive and looplike lengthier jams occasionally veer toward a weary fusion trance.

Born in Chicago and schooled in such

diverse, New York–based outfits as the Thad Jones/Mel Lewis orchestra and the Cecil Taylor Unit, Coleman formed M-Base Collective in 1981. The group has since yielded a bumper crop of modern-day talent, such as singer Cassandra Wilson, trumpeter Graham Haynes, trombonist Robin Eubanks, keyboardist Geri Allen, drummer Marvin "Smitty" Smith and members of Coleman's working units, the Five Elements, the Metrics and the world-music–focused ensemble Mystic Rhythm Society.

For his first bandleading effort (for the German-based JMT label), Coleman recruited a strong rhythmic underpinning in pianist Andy Milne, guitarist David Gilmore, bass man Reggie Washington and drummer "Smitty" Smith (later replaced by Gene Lake, son of saxophonist Oliver), known collectively as the Five Elements, which has become Coleman's most recorded group. As a side project, Coleman collaborated with bassist Dave Holland on 1985's *Sine Die* for Sting's Pangaea label (currently unavailable domestically). In 1990 Coleman began a lengthy association with various BMG-group jazz labels.

Coleman's first two Five Elements albums for Novus (currently out of print), *Black Science* and *Drop Kick,* lay an urgent, hard-hitting framework for the more polished productions to come. The latter features compelling nuggets like the mood piece "The Journeyman" (with vocals by Cassandra Wilson) and the kickoff tune "Ramses" (with clarinet support from Don Byron).

The French division of BMG remains Coleman's strongest champion, arranging and recording him in 1995 at Paris's Hot Brass Club and releasing a boxed set that gives equal time to all three of Coleman's performance groups. (Stateside the discs were released separately.)

Curves of Life (featuring the Five Elements) is the most satisfying disc of the three, with such tunes as "Country Bama" bristling with David Murray's guest tenor, moving from a leisurely stated, choppy melodic line replete with a popping electric-bass line to a coda of New Orleans–ish cacophony. "The Gypsy" is too short, only suggesting the emotional depth of Coleman's horn play in a spare, open setting, and Thelonious Monk's " 'Round Midnight" is deconstructed in a jaunty, almost offhand way, pulling the song piecemeal through a stop-start, snare-driven blender. "I'm Burnin' Up" features a rap trio, trading lyrics and licks with Coleman, copying his choppy phrasing and throwing it back in style.

On *Myths, Modes and Means,* Coleman debuted his world-beat–conscious Mystic Rhythm Society, augmenting his jazz unit with various percussionists, an Indian vocalist, a New York rapper and a koto player. But his attempts at cross-cultural mixology prove more pasted pastiche than successful integration, though the improvisatory gifts of new sidemen trumpeter Ralph Alessi and keyboardist Vijay Iyer are clearly revealed. Exceptions are the brief and bouncy "Numerology" and the successful alto-sax/Indian-song dialog of "Transits."

On the hip-hop tip with the third disc, *The Way of the Cipher* introduced the Metrics, Coleman's jazz crew accompanied by an able and gear-shifting rap trio: Kokayi, Sub Zero and Black Indian. Nine tracks are featured, exploring the common ground between free-form, improvised funk (drummer Lake repeatedly proves his endless store of chops, as on "Fast Lane") and the power of well-thought-out, almost overly academic lyrics. Well performed and appropriately loose-limbed, the experiment never gels sufficiently to achieve the convincing and in-your-face level of other similar voices-and-live-band approaches to the genre (Brand New Heavies, Branford Marsalis's Buckshot LeFonque). The other (more convincing) Metrics release, a six-track studio EP titled *A Tale of 3 Cities,* retains the Five Elements' snaky rhythms while adding minimal studio wizardry and bringing the rappers to the fore. Check out the irresistible drive on "Get Open" and "Left to Right."

Back on the jazz track, the Five Elements' *Def Trance Beat* begins to break out of Coleman's narrow mold with strong compositional play and arrangements that feed material like "Dogon" and the excellent album opener, "Flint." Guest percussionists and Ravi Coltrane's tenor tastefully fill in blank spaces on the funk canvas, adding needed sonic variety. Compellingly, the album points to a future direction that could expand and spur on Coleman's creative progress.

Further supported by BMG France, Coleman realized a seven-year dream in 1996 by journeying with the Mystic Rhythm Society to Havana, recording with the percussion and vocal folklore group AfroCuba de Matanzas. *The Sign and the Seal* was the mixed result, replete with extensive explanations of cultural commonality, though the juxtaposition of jibaro chants and Brooklyn rap tends to emphasize distance and difference. Again, pensive and emotive pieces prove the prize: The softly spoken "Saudade" is underwhelming in its poetry. As Coleman continues to draw on a kaleidoscopic array of influences, intermittently the musical blender threatens to burst. — A.K.

ALBERT COLLINS

★★★★ **Truckin' with Albert Collins (1969; MCA, 1992)**
★★★★ **Ice Pickin' (Alligator, 1978)**
★★★½ **Frostbite (1980; Alligator, 1990)**
★★★★★ **Frozen Alive (1981; Alligator, 1990)**
★★★★ **Don't Lose Your Cool (Alligator, 1983)**
★★★★ **Live in Japan (Alligator, 1984)**
★★★★★ **Showdown! (with Johnny Copeland and Robert Cray) (Alligator, 1985)**
★★★★ **Cold Snap (Alligator, 1986)**
★★★★ **The Complete Imperial Recordings (EMI, 1991)**
★★★★ **Collins Mix (The Best of Albert Collins) (Pointblank, 1993)**
★★ **Live (with Barrelhouse) (Munich, 1995)**
★★★★ **Live 92–93 (Pointblank, 1995)**
★★★½ **The Iceman Cometh (Collectables, 1996)**

Albert Collins (1932–1993) is nothing short of an American legend, a man literally born in a log cabin who went on to become one of the most distinctive voices in the great tradition of Texas blues guitarists. An inspiration to a generation of blues and rock players who came after him (Jimi Hendrix consistently cited him as a huge influence), he implemented stage innovations that have since become commonplace.

Collins, "the Master of the Telecaster," like a number of other blues greats, played his instrument in an unorthodox style, giving him an instantly recognizable sound. He achieved a high-pitched, biting tone through his use of a capo on the seventh and eighth frets of his guitar neck. His style also included a particularly effective use of dynamics, especially in live settings, where he could quiet a raucous blues audience to a whisper by playing softer and softer passages that the audience would strain to hear before blasting back with a screaming run of razor-sharp notes. He was also famous for using long guitar cords that allowed him to wander through the audience. His storytelling abilities were unparalleled, and he had a knack for working contemporary themes into his songwriting.

Collins picked up his earliest blues influences from his cousin, another Leona, Texas, native and one of the codifiers of Texas blues, Lightnin' Hopkins, who taught him to play in D-minor and E-minor tunings. This helped Collins exploit his treble-heavy tone and low-volume dynamics.

Collins moved to Houston in 1939. By 1948, the teenage Collins was leading his first band, the Rhythm Rockers, on the Houston bar scene. Among his band members were alto saxophonist/arranger Henry Hayes, Illinois Jacquet's father, and pianist Johnny Watson, who went on to fame as Johnny "Guitar" Watson. Collins played the Gulf Coast circuit, working with Louis Armstrong and members of Fats Domino's band in New Orleans.

With Bill Doggett, Duane Eddy, Link Wray and fellow Houstonian Clarence "Gatemouth" Brown all releasing instrumental hits in the 1950s, Collins decided to coin his own sound, recording a Fenton Robinson tune, "The Freeze," in 1958. His alternately biting, high-pitched tone and its drop-off to a barely audible counterpart depicts the song's title.

In 1959 Collins cut "De Frost," but it was the next single, "Frosty," that would sell more than a million copies in 1962, establishing his reputation. Collins followed with a long series of theme instrumentals through the early 1960s; of these, "Frostbite," "Sno-Cone" and "Don't Lose Your Cool" would become staples of his live act. *Truckin' with Albert Collins* summarizes this era.

Collins moved to Kansas City in the mid-1960s, where he came under the influence of guitarist Grant Green and organists Jimmy Smith and Jimmy McGriff. He began to add even more soul and improvisational punch to his live performances as the leader of a band that included Buddy Miles.

Bob Hite of Canned Heat caught Collins at a 1968 Houston club date and helped him sign to Imperial Records. Music from the Imperial albums *Love Can Be Found Anywhere* (*Even in a Guitar*), *Trash Talkin'* and *The Compleat Albert Collins* is collected in the excellent double-CD reissue *The Complete Imperial Recordings,* which features Collins in supercharged R&B and zydeco settings as well as playing straight blues.

Although Collins made the transformation from a 1950s-style single instrumentalist to a front man with a penchant for crowd-pleasing dramatics and storytelling, his career waned in the 1970s without a hit single, and the record industry lost interest. *The Iceman Cometh* is a live recording with a pickup band from the early '70s.

Alligator Records, the Chicago-based independent blues label, revived Collins's career with the brilliant comeback album *Ice Pickin'*, featuring his crack Chicago band, the Icepickers, including tenor saxophonist A.C. Reed, guitarist Larry Burton and drummer Casey Jones. After a slightly less forceful follow-up, *Frostbite,* Collins finally documented the electricity of his live performances with the incredible *Frozen Alive.*

The suave *Don't Lose Your Cool,* with one of Collins's patented story-songs, "But I Was Cool!," was followed by another hot performance recording, *Live in Japan.* The Grammy-winning monster jam session *Showdown!* pits Collins against his protégés from the 1950s, Johnny Copeland, and the 1970s, Robert Cray. One of the best blues albums of the 1980s, *Showdown!* is available as a Mobile Fidelity gold disc, as is *Cold Snap,* which features the Uptown Horns and Collins's pal from the '70s, organist Jimmy McGriff.

Collins Mix compiles newly recorded tracks from his Alligator recordings and one new cut. *Live* is a European live set from 1978 marred by a local band that can't keep up with Collins. *Live 92–93,* with the Icebreakers backing him on some of the last performances of his life, captures Collins giving it everything he had until the bitter end. — J.S.

CAL COLLINS

★★★½ Ohio Style (Concord Jazz, 1991)

Guitarist Cal Collins (b. 1933) grew up in Indiana playing bluegrass and country music. By age 13, he had developed an interest in jazz guitar and became an excellent Django Reinhardt–style swing player. During a stay with the Benny Goodman Orchestra he came to the attention of mainstream-jazz fans and has subsequently led his own groups based in Cincinnati. He has recorded a number of albums for Concord, but only *Ohio Style,* with Jerry Van Blair on flügelhorn, Lou Lausche on bass and Tony Sweet on drums, remains in print. Look for the solo *Cross Country* and the live *Interplay* with Herb Ellis. — J.S.

ALICE COLTRANE

★★★½ Ptah, the El Daoud (1970; Impulse!, 1996)
★★★★ Journey in Satchidananda (1971; Impulse!, 1997)

Alice McLeod (b. 1937) grew up in Detroit as a Bud Powell–influenced pianist and played with the Terry Gibbs quartet in the early 1960s before joining John Coltrane's group in 1966. She played in his last groups and appeared on the records *Live at the Village Vanguard Again!, Live in Japan,* and *Expression.* She married Coltrane in 1965 and after his death in 1967 continued to lead her own band with several of the same musicians.

Her currently available albums reflect her deep interest in Indian music and spirituality, which she shared with her husband. In that sense her recordings carry some of the ambiance of John Coltrane's devotional music. *Ptah, the El Daoud* features Joe Henderson on tenor saxophone and Pharoah Sanders on tenor sax and alto flute, with a rhythm section of Ron Carter on bass and Ben Riley on drums. Sanders, another member of the final Coltrane band, really does seem to channel that group's spirit on these recordings.

Sanders plays magnificently on the darkly meditative *Journey in Satchidananda,* which should not be overlooked simply because of its dedication to the much maligned swami. The mix of Sanders's Eastern modalities on soprano saxophone with the spooky atmosphere evoked by the droning combination of oud, tamboura, Alice's hypnotic keyboard and harp work and Cecil McBee's bass patterns does transport the listener to another realm. Drummer Rashied Ali, another of John Coltrane's final musical companions, makes an important contribution. The album closes with a terrific live performance, "Isis and Osiris," from the Vanguard, with Charlie Haden replacing McBee on bass. — J.S.

JOHN COLTRANE

★★★★ Blue Train (1957; Prestige, 1996)
★★★½ Interplay for 2 Trumpets and 2 Tenors (1957; Original Jazz Classics, 1992)
★★★½ Wheelin' & Dealin' (1957; Original Jazz Classics, 1991)
★★★½ Coltrane (1957; Original Jazz Classics, 1987)
★★★½ Traneing In (1957; Original Jazz Classics, 1985)
★★★★ Soultrane (1958; Original Jazz Classics, 1987)
★★★½ Cattin' with Coltrane and Quinichette (1959; Original Jazz Classics, 1990)
★★★★★ Giant Steps (Atlantic, 1960)

★★★½ **Lush Life (1960; Original Jazz Classics, 1987)**
★★★★★ **Coltrane Jazz (Atlantic, 1961)**
★★★★★ **My Favorite Things (Atlantic, 1961)**
★★★½ **Africa/Brass (1961; Impulse!, 1988)**
★★★½ **Settin' the Pace (1961; Original Jazz Classics, 1987)**
★★★★ **Olé Coltrane (1962; Atlantic, 1989)**
★★★★ **Coltrane Plays the Blues (Atlantic, 1962)**
★★★★★ **Live at the Village Vanguard (1962; Impulse!, 1990)**
★★★★ **Coltrane (1962; Impulse!, 1987)**
★★★★ **Standard Coltrane (1962; Original Jazz Classics, 1990)**
★★★½ **Ballads (1963; Impulse!, 1995)**
★★★★½ **John Coltrane and Johnny Hartman (1963; Impulse!, 1995)**
★★★½ **Stardust (1963; Original Jazz Classics, N.A.)**
★★★½ **Dakar (1963; Original Jazz Classics, 1989)**
★★★★ **Coltrane's Sound (1964; Atlantic, 1990)**
★★★★ **Crescent (1964; Impulse!, 1987)**
★★★½ **The Believer (1964; Original Jazz Classics, 1996)**
★★★½ **Black Pearls (1964; Original Jazz Classics, 1989)**
★★★★★ **A Love Supreme (1965; Impulse!, 1986)**
★★★½ **The John Coltrane Quartet Plays (Impulse!, 1965)**
★★★★★ **Ascension (Impulse!, 1965)**
★★★½ **Bahia (1965; Original Jazz Classics, 1989)**
★★★★ **The Last Trane (1965; Original Jazz Classics, 1989)**
★★★★ **The Avant-Garde (with Don Cherry) (Atlantic, 1966)**
★★★★½ **Meditations (1966; Impulse!, 1990)**
★★★★ **Expression (1967; Impulse!, 1993)**
★★★★ **Live at the Village Vanguard Again! (Impulse!, 1967)**
★★★½ **Om (1967; Impulse!, 1995)**
★★★½ **Transition (1970; Impulse!, 1993)**
★★★½ **Live in Seattle (1971; Impulse!, 1994)**
★★★½ **Sun Ship (1971; Impulse!, 1995)**
★★★★★ **The Best of John Coltrane, His Greatest Years (1972; Impulse!, 1982)**
★★★★★ **The Best of John Coltrane, His Greatest Years, Vol. 2 (1972; Impulse!, 1982)**
★★★★★ **The Art of John Coltrane (The Atlantic Years) (1973; Atlantic, 1991)**
★★★½ **Live in Japan (1973; Impulse!, 1991)**
★★★ **Countdown (1974; Atlantic, 1985)**
★★★½ **Africa/Brass, Vol. 2 (1974; Impulse!, 1988)**
★★★★ **Interstellar Space (1974; Impulse!, 1991)**
★★★★ **The Gentle Side of John Coltrane (1975; Impulse!, 1991)**
★★★★½ **First Meditations (1977; Impulse!, 1992)**
★★★★ **Afro Blue Impressions (1977; Pablo, 1993)**
★★★½ **The Paris Concert (1979; Original Jazz Classics, 1987)**
★★★½ **The European Tour (1980; Pablo, 1988)**
★★★½ **Bye Bye Blackbird (1981; Original Jazz Classics, 1992)**
★★★½ **The Best of John Coltrane (1983; Pablo, 1991)**
★★★★ **From the Original Master Tapes (MCA, 1985)**
★★★★ **John Coltrane and the Jazz Giants (Prestige, 1986)**
★★★★ **A Blowing Session (with Johnny Griffin and Hank Mobley) (Blue Note, 1988)**
★★★½ **The Prestige Recordings (Prestige, 1991)**
★★★★★ **The Art of John Coltrane (Blue Note, 1992)**
★★★★ **The Major Works of John Coltrane (Impulse!, 1992)**
★★★★★ **A John Coltrane Retrospective: The Impulse Years (Impulse!, 1992)**
★★★½ **Dear Old Stockholm, (Impulse!, 1993)**
★★★½ **Newport '63 (Impulse!, 1993)**
★★★★ **The Last Giant: The John Coltrane Anthology (Rhino, 1993)**
★★★★ **The Bethlehem Years (Bethlehem, 1994)**
★★★★★ **The Heavyweight Champion: The Complete Atlantic Recordings (Rhino, 1995)**
★★★★½ **Stellar Regions (Impulse!, 1995)**

If Duke Ellington stands as a kind of jazz Tolstoy—expansive, the polyglot master of any number of musical tongues, a spiritual man wise also to the ways of the world, a commander who nonetheless charmed crowds—John Coltrane (1926–1967) was Dostoyevsky: enigmatic, introspective, a genuine mystic, a gentle sufferer whose 41 years were marked by intense private agony, a trailblazer heedless of an audience. *A Love Supreme* (recorded in 1964) is Coltrane at his peak: The tenor saxophonist, the most influential since the early '50s, whose technical prowess freed him to play as many as a thousand notes a minute, turns in dazzling, ferocious variations on a simple four-note theme. Backed by the best of his regular quartets (pianist McCoy Tyner, drummer Elvin Jones and bassist Jimmy Garrison) with help from Archie Shepp on tenor, Coltrane is working the modal style he encountered first as a sideman for Miles Davis; it's the innovator experimenting with polytonality—playing in two keys simultaneously. He's also returning in spirit to one of his original sources: the transcendent yet visceral passion of African-American spiritual music. He recorded *Ascension* with a powerhouse of horn players (Shepp, Pharoah Sanders, John Tchicai, Marion Brown, Freddie Hubbard, Dewey Johnson); the entire record is one long cut of post–Ornette Coleman free jazz—the soloists periodically erupt from a blizzard of sheer rhythm, then return to passages of free ensemble blowing (two versions, each clocking in at around 40 minutes, are available on *The Major Works*). Incredibly demanding, these albums are musical abstract expressionism—they offer very little to hold on to except absolute soul power—and they make real the prayer Coltrane wrote for the liner notes of *A Love Supreme.* "ELATION-ELEGANCE-EXALTATION/All From God."

Achieving these fearsome heights, of course, took time, pain and work. And the early career of John Coltrane was notable for its quality of blazing: an addict and compulsive overeater, addicted to, among other things, the Life Savers that rotted his teeth, causing him extreme irritation whenever he played, this was a musician whose aesthetic discipline was equally obsessive—Trane simply couldn't stop practicing (sometimes 12 hours daily), refining his aggressive tenor and sweeter alto-sax work on jazz standards and in company first with Dizzy Gillespie and then with Miles Davis. Starting as a hard-bop player after the school of Charlie Parker, he perfected in the late '50s (*Giant Steps*, *Coltrane*, *Blue Train*, *Lush Life*) a jagged, lightning-fast delivery that came to be termed "sheets of sound." *Giant Steps,* with its gorgeous ballad playing on "Naima" (named for his first wife), was the saxophonist's breakthrough and the most accessible of his classics; while Sonny Rollins continued for a while as a rival instrumentalist, Coltrane emerged as a powerfully individual creator. With its beautiful extended soprano playing on the title cut, *My Favorite Things* brought him a mass audience as well as critical acclaim—it was a following that he would occasionally revisit (*The Gentle Side of John Coltrane*) but soon outdistance with the two volumes of *Africa/Brass*—forays into more challenging meters and chord structures that often were more suggested than stated outright.

Next came Trane's modal work. With alto titan Eric Dolphy beside him on such albums as *Olé Coltrane*, *Live at the Village Vanguard* and the currently unavailable *Impressions,* he explored the possibilities of anchoring his solos on a given single scale rather than on chord changes; this is trance music, and the trance state it induces is of a whirling, dizzying variety. Heading toward his mid-'60s summit, Coltrane had evolved into what poet LeRoi Jones termed "a scope of feeling." If Louis Armstrong's keynote was very human joy, Ellington's a bittersweet nostalgia and Parker's a rush of exhilaration, Coltrane had become a player whose every musical gesture was one of the soul in turmoil—the archetypal seeker, he kept pushing harder, diving deeper. He was helped immeasurably in his quest by his classic quartet—Elvin Jones and Jimmy Garrison, at last a rhythm section both subtle and fierce enough to challenge him, and McCoy Tyner, a pianist capable of scattering notes with a speed and dexterity that nearly matched Trane's own. *Om,* with its sharp sax trade-offs with Pharoah Sanders, and *Meditations* and *First Meditations* (alternate sessions of basically the same pieces), with their spare and lovely titles ("The Father and the Son and the Holy Ghost," "Love," "Consequences," "Serenity," "Compassion") were the major works Coltrane made after *A Love Supreme* and *Ascension.* On these, the rhythms of percussionist Rashied Ali are looser, more expansive than Jones's, allowing Trane to soar into the ether (but a little of the gripping tension is lost). *Interstellar Space* was his last long flash of genius—a rhythmic evocation of the dance of planets.

The Impulse! *Retrospective* boxed set and

Rhino's *The Heavyweight Champion* are both terrific—the former highlighting Coltrane's later, fevered experimentation, the latter capturing (complete with outtakes) the somewhat sweeter Atlantic period. By now, most of Coltrane can be found either in its original version or in reissues. Among the standouts: *Blue Train* (a sextet set presaging brilliance to come); *Coltrane Jazz* (gorgeous in the vein of *Giant Steps*); *Coltrane Plays the Blues* (six takes on the blues); *Crescent* (profoundly sad beauty); *The John Coltrane Quartet Plays* (Coltrane explodes a version of "Chim Chim Cheree"—from *Mary Poppins*!); *Live at the Village Vanguard Again!* (great piano from Trane's second wife, Alice); *Expression* (Trane on flute).

Along with Miles Davis and Charles Mingus, Coltrane was the major figure in modern jazz. From him came technique in superabundance, passionate innovation, titanic ambition—and a kind of sacred savagery. — P.E.

EDDIE CONDON

★★ In Japan (Chiaroscuro, 1977)
★★★ Dixieland Jam (Columbia, 1989)
★★½ The Dr. Jazz Series, Vol. 1 (Storyville, 1993)
★★★ Eddie Condon and His Dixieland All Stars (Decca, 1994)
★★★ Eddie Condon 1938–40 (Classics, 1994)
★★★½ Town Hall Concerts, Vol. 1 (Jazzology, 1995)
★★★½ Town Hall Concerts, Vol. 2 (Jazzology, 1995)
★★★½ Town Hall Concerts, Vol. 3 (Jazzology, 1995)
★★★½ Town Hall Concerts, Vol. 4 (Jazzology, 1995)
★★★½ Town Hall Concerts, Vol. 5 (Jazzology, 1995)
★★★ Windy City Jazz (Pearl, 1995)
★★★ Chicago Style: Original Mono Recordings (Living Era, 1996)

Albert Edwin "Eddie" Condon (1905–1973), rhythm guitarist, banjo player and raconteur, did much to popularize traditional New Orleans jazz in Chicago during the '20s as part of the McKenzie-Condon Chicagoans, then in New York as part of Red McKenzie's Mound City Blue Blowers. He championed the pell-mell rhythmic approach to Dixieland that became known as Chicago-style.

Condon arranged countless jam sessions, wrote extensively about jazz (he's as well known for his outrageous quotes as for his playing) and ran the important New York jazz club that bore his name. The *Town Hall Concerts* series documents the kind of spirited, free-form sessions he would organize and features some of his most musical cronies, including Pee Wee Russell on clarinet, Hot Lips Page on trumpet and vocals and Bobby Hackett on cornet.

Trombonist Jack Teagarden, another regular, appears on *Chicago Style.* Another compatriot, tenor saxophonist Bud Freeman, shines on *Eddie Condon and His Dixieland All Stars.* It's worth searching for the out-of-print Condon/Freeman collaboration *The Commodore Years. Dixieland Jam* catches a free-spirited session by the house band at Condon's. — J.S.

HARRY CONNICK JR.

★★★½ Harry Connick, Jr. (Columbia, 1987)
★★★ 20 (Columbia, 1988)
★★★★ When Harry Met Sally (Columbia, 1989)
★★ We Are in Love (Columbia, 1990)
★★½ Lofty's Roach Souffle (Columbia, 1990)
★★ Blue Light, Red Light (Columbia, 1991)
★★ 11 (Columbia, 1992)
★★★½ 25 (Columbia, 1992)
★★ She (Columbia, 1994)
½ Star Turtle (Columbia, 1996)

The Marsalis clan might have paved the way for jazz's youth movement, but it was Harry Connick Jr. (b. 1967) who most blatantly capitalized on it. *Harry Connick, Jr.,* recorded when the pianist was just 19, shows tremendous promise; despite obvious debts to Thelonious Monk and James Booker, Connick clearly had a voice of his own (although, as *Lofty's Roach Souffle* would later suggest, he hasn't a clue how to develop it). With *20,* Connick adds a Sinatra-style croon to his repertoire, but it's *When Harry Met Sally* that makes the most of it, fleshing out his café-society piano-and-vocals act with lush, Gershwinesque orchestration. Both *We Are in Love* and *Blue Light, Red Light* try the same trick but with Connick writing the tunes; Cole Porter he ain't. Perhaps that's why he went back to his roots with his next two releases—literally in the case of *11,* which takes its title from his age at the time of the recording and confirms that he was a child prodigy but doesn't make us care. By contrast, *25* is a thoughtful (and quite enjoyable) update on *20* and does quite a lot to restore his credibility as an improviser. Still, with *She* and *Star Turtle,* the point becomes moot as Connick abandons jazz altogether for New Orleans–style funk sessions that are to the Meters as catsup is to Tabasco. *Star Turtle* compounds the insult by adding in a narrative provided by a, er, talking turtle. Stay far away. — J.D.C.

CHRIS CONNOR

★★★½ **Chris Connor Sings the George Gershwin Almanac of Song (1957; Atlantic, 1989)**
★★★ **Jazz Date with Chris Connor (1958; Rhino, 1994)**
★★★ **Sweet and Swinging (Audiophile, 1978)**
★★★½ **Lover Come Back to Me (1981; Evidence, 1995)**
★★★½ **Classic (Contemporary, 1986)**
★★★½ **Chris (1986; Bethlehem, 1994)**
★★★ **New Again (Contemporary, 1988)**
★★★ **As Time Goes By (Enja, 1992)**

Chris Connor (b. 1927) grew up in Kansas City, Missouri, dreaming of singing in the Stan Kenton Orchestra. In 1949 she moved to New York and was hired by the Claude Thornhill orchestra, then by Jerry Wald, before following in the footsteps of her two key influences, June Christy and Anita O'Day, by joining the Kenton band in 1952.

Though she stayed with Kenton for less than a year, Connor made a lasting impact in the band, stamping the ballad "All About Ronnie" as her own. In 1953 she embarked on a solo career, making a series of albums for Bethlehem and Atlantic. *Chris* collects under her own name Connor's first recordings, including a Sy Oliver–arranged remake of "All About Ronnie." The excellent double disc *Chris Connor Sings the George Gershwin Almanac of Song* exhibits her fronting a variety of support groups. Also look for the out-of-print 1960 Atlantic recording *Double Exposure,* with Maynard Ferguson.

Connor recorded sporadically during the '60s and '70s. Her renaissance arrived with the highly acclaimed comeback album *Classic,* featuring Paquito D'Rivera on saxophone. Her voice has lost none of its range, yet age has added to its expressiveness.

Lover Come Back to Me, an intimate performance recorded at the New York club Sweet Basil in 1981, demonstrates Connor's ability to hold an audience spellbound. — J.S.

BILL CONNORS

★★★ **Theme to the Guardian (1975; ECM, 1994)**
★★★★ **Step It (1985; Evidence, 1994)**
★★★ **Double Up (1986; Evidence, 1994)**
★★★★ **Assembler (1987; Evidence, 1994)**

The searing, pinpoint guitar playing of Bill Connors (b. 1950) in the original, tightly arranged, electric version of *Return to Forever* helped define the jazz-rock fusion guitar style in the 1970s. Fans of his intense delivery will be surprised at the subdued, classically influenced acoustic records he went on to make at ECM, although only *Theme to the Guardian* remains in print.

Connors returned to the electric-trio format in the 1980s for a series of outstanding recordings later reissued by Evidence. *Step It,* with bassist Tom Kennedy and drummer Dave Weckl, was coproduced by Steve Khan, who also sits in on guitar. When Weckl left to join Chick Corea's Elektric Band, Connors replaced him with drummer Kim Plainfield. This unit really hit its stride on *Assembler,* with Kennedy's six-string bass working the counterpoint to Connor's legato note bursts, which are phrased so closely that they sound like unbroken lines or searing blurts of sound. — J.S.

RY COODER

★★½ **Ry Cooder (1970; Warner Archives, N.A.)**
★★★ **Into the Purple Valley (Reprise, 1972)**
★★★½ **Boomer's Story (Reprise, 1972)**
★★★ **Paradise and Lunch (Reprise, 1974)**
★★★★ **Chicken Skin Music (Reprise, 1976)**
★★½ **Jazz (Warner Bros., 1978)**
★★½ **Bop Till You Drop (Warner Bros., 1979)**
★★ **Borderline (Warner Bros., 1980)**
★★ **The Slide Area (Warner Bros., 1982)**
★★★ **Paris, Texas (Warner Bros., 1984)**
★★ **Crossroads (Warner Bros., 1986)**
★★½ **Get Rhythm (Warner Bros., 1987)**
★★★ **A Meeting by the River (with Vishwa Mohan Bhatt) (Water Lily Acoustics, 1993)**
★★★ **Music by Ry Cooder (Warner Archives, 1995)**

To say that Ry Cooder (b. 1947) is an extremely gifted musician is not only an understatement, but misleading as well. Certainly, Cooder has achieved an extraordinary level of technical proficiency in his playing, but what truly makes his music exceptional is the degree of stylistic expertise he has attained. Simply put, Ry Cooder can play damn near anything, from slide guitar to mandolin to banjo, saz or tiple, or any style, be it gospel, folk, blues, calypso, Tex-Mex or Hawaiian slack-key guitar. But if Cooder's ability is unquestionable, his taste is not. Despite his credentials, which include studio work with Taj Mahal, the Rolling Stones, Captain Beefheart and Eric Clapton, Cooder's own work ranges in quality from the intriguingly experimental to the utterly embarrassing.

Why this is the case isn't entirely clear, but it must have to do with the guitarist's willingness to try anything. That seems to be the undoing of his debut, *Ry Cooder.* Although the album has its moments, including Randy Newman's acrid "Old Kentucky Home" and a delightfully unadorned mandolin version of Sleepy John Estes's "Goin' to Brownsville," it also ends up lumbered with the overwrought arrangements of "One Meatball" and Lead Belly's "Pig Meat." Fortunately, Cooder scales back for *Into the Purple Valley,* and the music improves immensely. Cooder still can't help tinkering with the arrangements, but this time around, the unexpected touches—for instance, the celesta in "Denomination Blues"—work in his favor. But the best moments, like the traditional "Billy the Kid" or his slide-guitar rendition of Woody Guthrie's "Vigilante Man," are generally straightforward, presenting each song with minimal ornamentation.

Both *Boomer's Story* and *Paradise and Lunch* proceed in a similar vein, with minor variations and occasional cameos. Cooder brings in Sleepy John Estes for a version of "President Kennedy" on *Boomer's Story,* although that album's highlight is probably Cooder's slide-guitar treatment of "Dark End of the Street." For *Paradise and Lunch,* Earl "Fatha" Hines is on hand to add stride-piano flourishes to "Diddie Wah Diddie." But *Chicken Skin Music* takes this guest-star strategy to new levels by bringing in two exceptional and distinctive players: Tex-Mex accordion legend Flaco Jimenez and Hawaiian slack-key guitar whiz Gabby Pahinui. It's marvelous enough when the music is geared to their specialties, but when Cooder changes the context—by using Jimenez for a rendition of Ben E. King's "Stand by Me," say—the results are stunning. Sadly, *Jazz* doesn't quite meet *Chicken Skin Music*'s standard. Even though it includes tunes by Jelly Roll Morton and Bix Beiderbecke, *Jazz* isn't a jazz album. Nor does Cooder intend it to be, since he's far more interested in showing parallels between Morton's *habaniera* and the Bahamanian guitar style of Joseph Spence. And it makes for a fascinating lesson, if a tad too pedantic to be truly entertaining.

With *Bop Till You Drop,* Cooder makes a serious wrong turn, applying his rootsy eclecticism to material culled from rock and R&B. It's not a particularly novel approach for him—*Purple Valley,* for instance, included a version of the Drifters' "Money Honey"—but it brings out the worst in his music. *Bop,* at least, is able to balance its excesses with refreshingly rootsy instrumentals like "I Think It's Going to Work Out Fine"; *Borderline,* on the other hand, goes completely off the deep end. "Down in the Boondocks," "634-5789" and "Crazy 'Bout an Automobile (Every Woman I Know)" are songs that barely needed to be remade, much less reinvented as false nostalgia. Cooder downplays that tendency on *The Slide Area,* offering a blues-shuffle treatment of "Blue Suede Shoes" but otherwise sticking with more modern material like the Little Feat–ish "I'm Drinking Again" or "UFO Has Landed in the Ghetto." But *Get Rhythm* finds him fiddling with the oldies again, slogging through an overblown boogie makeover of "All Shook Up" and a version of Johnny Cash's "Get Rhythm" done as imitation doo-wop.

Uneven as those albums are, Cooder was still making great music during this period—he just happened to be doing it for movie studios instead of record companies. Cooder was no stranger to soundtrack work, having contributed to both *Performance* and *Candy* before cutting his first solo album, but it wasn't until he provided some Southwestern atmosphere in 1980 for Walter Hill's *The Long Riders* (now out of print) that his soundtrack career truly got into gear. Ironically, Cooder actually wound up making better rock records for movies than he did for himself; if you can find the out-of-print 1981 soundtrack *The Border,* compare it with *The Slide Area* or *Get Rhythm,* and it's obvious that the focused demands of film scoring bring out the best in his playing. *Paris, Texas* is eloquently atmospheric, conveying a palpable sense of the town's barren landscape. *Crossroads* is too heavy on overstuffed blues, but the out-of-print 1989 soundtrack *Johnny Handsome* gets everything right, from the ominous quiet of the "Main Theme" to the

jaunty good mood of "Clip Joint Rhumba."
— J.D.C.

COOLBONE

★★★★½ **Brass-Hop (Hollywood, 1997)**

The New Orleans brass-band tradition so radically updated by the ReBirth Brass Band, Dirty Dozen Brass Band and the scores of new mobile aggregations that have followed takes on further transformation in the hands of this octet led by trombonist Steve "Coolbone" Johnson. With lead rapper and trumpeter Eric "Cash Us" Clay in the pocket, Coolbone deftly and effectively combines the brass-band bump with hip-hop flava.

Clay, from Louisville, Kentucky, studied trumpet at the University of New Orleans. He joined the band as an instrumentalist but soon started to lay his witty raps into the mix, excelling on a rap dedicated to his cousin Muhammad Ali, "Float Like a Butterfly," and on the Guru-mixed single "Nothin' but Strife."

Andre Carter, formerly with the Treme Brass Band, also doubles on trumpet and vocals, taking the lead on the Bill Withers groove "Use Me."

The nucleus of the group is the Johnson brothers: Steve, who centers the sound with his phat trombone playing, and little brother Ronell "Roo" Johnson, whose tuba playing creates an unusually dense bottom. Both brothers grew up in the middle of the brass-band culture and played in numerous local groups, including the Young Olympia Brass Band and its offshoot, the Soul Rebels. Their experience and collective vision provide a refreshing glimpse into the future of one of the oldest American musical traditions. — J.S.

JOHNNY COPELAND

★★★★★ **Texas Twister (Rounder, 1983)**
★★★★★ **Showdown! (with Albert Collins and Robert Cray) (Alligator, 1985)**
★★★★★ **When the Rain Starts Fallin' (Rounder, 1988)**
★★★★ **Ain't Nothing but a Party (Rounder, 1988)**
★★★ **Boom Boom (Rounder, 1990)**
★★★ **The Copeland Collection, Vol. 1 (Collectables, 1991)**
★★★ **The Copeland Collection, Vol. 2 (Collectables, 1992)**
★★★½ **The Three Sides of Johnny Clyde Copeland (Collectables, 1993)**
★★★ **Flyin' High (Verve, 1993)**
★★★ **Catch Up with the Blues (Verve, 1994)**
★★★ **Jungle Swing (Verve, 1996)**

Johnny Clyde Copeland (1937–1997) was a popular Houston-based guitarist and vocalist during the 1950s and '60s, charting regional blues and rock & roll hits during that period. *The Copeland Collection, Vol. 1* consists of material from this era. A former boxer, Copeland has a powerful voice and a thick, sustained guitar tone with a dynamic rhythmic feel derived from his years as a rhythm guitarist with Albert Collins.

Though he continued to play Texas clubs throughout the soul era, (see *Collection, Vol. 2*), Copeland fell through the cracks during the 1970s, eventually resurfacing in New York. He was a key figure in the blues revival of the 1980s after releasing the five-star 1981 record *Copeland Special,* which presented him as a tough Texas front man with a crack rhythm section and a horn lineup that included jazz saxophonists Arthur Blythe, Byard Lancaster and George Adams.

Copeland Special, the equally great *Make My Home Where I Hang My Hat,* the original *Texas Twister* and the epochal *Bringin' It All Back Home,* recorded in Africa with indigenous musicians, are only available on cassette, but the material is packaged together on two CDs, *Texas Twister* and *When the Rain Starts Fallin'.*

The Grammy-nominated *Ain't Nothing but a Party* documents the intensity of Copeland's live performances during the 1980s, but *Boom Boom* marks a downturn in Copeland's studio work that continued onto the star-studded (Dr. John, etc.) but clinical-sounding *Flyin' High.*

Meanwhile, in 1988 and 1989, Copeland was the subject of a live documentary recorded in Texas, *The Three Sides of Johnny Clyde Copeland.* The CD of the same name collects live material recorded for the video.

Catch Up with the Blues marks a comeback that also saw Copeland playing on two tracks of Randy Weston's *Volcano Blues. Jungle Swing,* recorded while Copeland was battling heart disease, revisits some of the material from *Bringin' It All Back Home*—unsuccessfully.

Copeland also appears with Collins and Robert Cray on the classic Alligator release *Showdown!* — J.S.

SHEMEKIA COPELAND

★★★★ **Turn the Heat Up (Alligator, 1998)**

The daughter of the late blues singer Johnny Copeland knows the blues inside-out despite her tender age; Shemekia Copeland (b. 1979) watched her father go through a painful and debilitating heart condition and attended him in concert during his last years, spelling him during shows when he had to take a break and subbing for him when he couldn't make it at all. Those who've seen her grow into this role marvel at the strides she's made in such a short time. She is infused with the spirit of her father's art and gifted with a magnificent voice to deliver it.

On her stunning debut, *Turn the Heat Up,* she is backed by former members of her father's band, some of whom are now regulars in New York's best studio band, run by guitarist Jimmy Vivino and featured as the Max Weinberg Seven on *Late Night With Conan O'Brien.* Bassist Michael Merritt and drummer Jimmy Wormworth would make any singer sound good, and they offer Copeland a rhythmic trampoline from which to work. A clear heir to the female blues vocal throne once dominated by Bessie Smith and now occupied by Etta James and Koko Taylor, Copeland is a blues voice for the next millennium. — J.S.

CHICK COREA

★★★★½ **Now He Sings, Now He Sobs (1968; Blue Note, 1988)**
★★★★½ **The Song of Singing (1970; Blue Note, 1985)**
★★★½ **Circling in Blue (Blue Note, 1970)**
★★★ **A.R.C. (1971; ECM, 1988)**
★★★★ **Circle Paris Concert (ECM, 1971)**
★★★★★ **Piano Improvisations, Vol. 1 (1971; ECM, 1987)**
★★★★★ **Piano Improvisations, Vol. 2 (1972; ECM, 1987)**
★★★★★ **Crystal Silence (with Gary Burton) (1973; ECM, 1987)**
★★★★ **Inner Space (1974; Atlantic, 1988)**
★★★★½ **Chick Corea (Blue Note, 1975)**
★★½ **My Spanish Heart (Polydor, 1976)**
★★ **Musicmagic (Columbia, 1977)**
★★ **Mad Hatter (Verve, 1978)**
★★★½ **Circulus (Blue Note, 1978)**
★★ **Secret Agent (Polydor, 1978)**
★★★ **Friends (1978; Polydor, 1991)**
★★★½ **Delphi 1 (Polydor, 1979)**
★★ **Tap Step (Stretch, 1980)**
★★★½ **Chick Corea and Gary Burton: In Concert, Zurich, October 28, 1979 (1980; ECM, 1987)**
★★★½ **Three Quartets (Stretch, 1981)**
★★★★★ **Trio Music (ECM, 1982)**
★★★ **Touchstone (Stretch, 1982)**
★★★½ **Again and Again (Elektra Musician, 1983)**
★★★ **Children's Songs (ECM, 1984)**
★★★½ **Chick Corea and Steve Kujala: Voyage (ECM, 1985)**
★★★★★ **Works (ECM, 1985)**
★★★★½ **Trio Music, Live in Europe (ECM, 1986)**
★★★½ **Early Days (Denon, 1986)**
★★★½ **Early Circle (Blue Note, 1992)**
★★★½ **Play (with Bobby McFerrin), (Blue Note, 1992)**
★★★ **Expressions (GRP, 1994)**
★★★½ **Live in Montreux (Stretch, 1994)**
★★★½ **Time Warp (Stretch, 1995)**
★★★½ **Music Forever and Beyond (GRP, 1996)**
★★★½ **Remembering Bud Powell (Stretch, 1997)**
★★★★ **Chick Corea & Origin, Live at the Blue Note (Stretch, 1998)**

WITH RETURN TO FOREVER

★★★★½ **Return to Forever (1972; ECM, 1988)**
★★★★ **Light as a Feather (Polydor, 1972)**
★★★★★ **Hymn of the Seventh Galaxy (1972; Polydor, 1991)**
★★★ **Where Have I Known You Before (Polydor, 1974)**
★★ **No Mystery (Polydor, 1975)**
★★★½ **The Leprechaun (Polydor, 1976)**
★★★ **Romantic Warrior (1976; Columbia, 1990)**
★★★★ **The Best of Return to Forever (Columbia, 1980)**

WITH THE AKOUSTIC BAND

★★★ **The Chick Corea Akoustic Band (GRP, 1989)**
★★★ **Akoustic Band: Alive (GRP, 1991)**

WITH THE ELEKTRIC BAND

★★★ **Chick Corea Elektric Band (GRP, 1986)**
★★ **Light Years (GRP, 1987)**
★★★ **Eye of the Beholder (GRP, 1988)**
★★★ **Inside Out (GRP, 1990)**
★★½ **Alive (GRP, 1991)**
★★½ **Beneath the Mask (GRP, 1991)**
★★½ **Paint the World (as Elektra Band II) (GRP, 1993)**

A keyboard prodigy—he has been playing since the age of four—Chick Corea (b. 1941) remains a pianist of singular freshness and precision, but he's best known as one of the first popularizers of jazz-rock fusion. Corea started with Mongo

Santamaria, Stan Getz and Herbie Mann, playing Latin-inflected jazz before recording a breakthrough 1968 set: *Now He Sings, Now He Sobs.* With Miroslav Vitous on bass and Roy Haynes on drums, *Now He Sings* is dazzling. In '68 as well, Corea began a three-year stint with Miles Davis, exploring in detail the possibilities of the Fender Rhodes electric piano. He then took up with bassist Dave Holland and Barry Altschul for music of a more cerebral turn (*The Song of Singing*), before adding avant-garde saxophonist Anthony Braxton to the lineup (as Circle, the group released trailblazing work in the late '60s, such as *Circle Paris Concert* and *Circulus*).

At the start of the '70s, Corea recorded two volumes of solo *Piano Improvisations:* Lovely albums, they stand as his classics—few players have ever achieved anything close to his tone, which manages to be lush as well as clean, sweet and very romantic. These first-take albums remain unparalleled examples of Corea's genius for melody. They were followed by the equally gorgeous duet album with vibraphonist Gary Burton, *Crystal Silence.*

With Return to Forever, Corea, fresh from his tenure with Miles, unleashed pyrotechnics on electric keyboards (Rhodes, Mini-Moog, etc.). With its primary personnel consisting of drummer Lenny White, bassist Stanley Clarke and guitarist Bill Connors (later Al DiMeola), the group was a monster; with Corea's composing now in full bloom, they offered Latin rhythms played with rock intensity. *Hymn of the Seventh Galaxy* is fusion as it was intended to be, polytechnical but exuberant—and while their breezier work (usually with Brazilian vocalist Flora Purim) hasn't the sizzle of the scorching stuff, *Return to Forever* and *Light as a Feather* were pathfinding examples of the new hybrid.

In the late '70s and early '80s, Corea's group sets alternated between expert fluff (*Friends*) and cornball excitement (*My Spanish Heart*); his solo-piano *Delphi 1,* while featuring a nice side of tributes to Art Tatum, hadn't quite the freshness of the *Piano Improvisations.* He came back strong, however, with *Trio Music* and its in-concert counterpart, *Trio Music, Live in Europe;* reunited with Vitous and Haynes, he again swung with a powerful grace, and he solidified his relationship with ECM Records, the label that released his best '80s music (check, especially, the pristine *Works*).

More recently, the keyboardist, recording with zest, has come up with two expert outfits, the Elektric Band and the Akoustic Band, which reveal both his strengths and his weaknesses. The Elektric stuff is corny compared to RTF at its toughest; the Akoustic is far more copacetic. *Play,* a set with Bobby McFerrin, including a reworking of Corea's classic "Spain," is sweet and clean; Corea's albums on his own label, Stretch, have as always featured terrific playing—even if the material is sometimes lackluster.

In 1996 Corea toured with Roy Haynes, Kenny Garrett, Christian McBride, Joshua Redman and Wallace Roney to celebrate the music of pianist Bud Powell, and followed with a recording putting their fresh stamp on his works. In early 1998, he went back on the road with Origin, a new band of daring younger acoustic players, to push his own improvisational urge. It included bassist Avishai Cohen, drummer Adam Cruz, trombonist Steve David and saxophonists Steve Wilson and Bob Sheppard. The sextet's first major gig was a weeklong run at the Blue Note in New York, which was documented on *Chick Corea & Origin.* Their creative chemistry yielded a musical intensity comparable to the leader's work with Getz, Davis and Return to Forever.

Corea's energy, his compositional flair and especially his astonishing range—perhaps no other player has matched his equal brilliance on both acoustic and electric keyboards—qualify him as a contemporary master. — P.E./K.F.

LARRY CORYELL

★★★½	**Lady Coryell (Vanguard, 1969)**
★★★★½	**Spaces (1970; Vanguard, 1989)**
★★★★	**Larry Coryell and the Eleventh House at Montreux (Vanguard, 1974)**
★★★★	**The Essential Larry Coryell (1975; Vanguard, 1988)**
★★★½	**Standing Ovation (Mood, 1978)**
★★★½	**Comin' Home (Muse, 1986)**
★★★	**Equipoise (Muse, 1986)**
★★★★	**Toku Do (Muse, 1987)**
★★★	**Shining Hour (Muse, 1989)**
★★★½	**The Dragon Gate (Shanachie, 1989)**
★★★½	**American Odyssey (DRG, 1990)**
★★★★	**Twelve Frets to One Octave (Shanachie, 1991)**
★★★★	**Bolero (Evidence, 1993)**
★★★	**Fallen Angel (CTI, 1993)**
★★★	**I'll Be Over You (CTI, 1995)**
★★★★	**Spaces Revisited (Shanachie, 1997)**

Among the most gifted soloists to emerge since the 1960s, guitarist Larry Coryell (b. 1943) brilliantly improvises and adeptly synthesizes styles, from classical to jazz, blues, country and rock. One of the brightest lights of the fusion era, Coryell's reputation was systematically trashed by those who treated fusion as a form of musical Stalinism to be expunged from history. These New Age moldy figs succeeded in burying a lot of great music, and Coryell's history is a prime example of the wrongs resulting from their efforts.

The Galveston, Texas, native studied at the University of Washington in Seattle before moving to New York in 1965, where he was understudy to Gabor Szabo in Chico Hamilton's band. Coryell made his recording debut on the fine Hamilton album *The Dealer.* In '66 Coryell cofounded the experimental prefusion group Free Spirits with Jim Pepper and Bob Moses, then joined the Gary Burton Quartet for the recordings *Duster*, *Lofty Fake Anagram* and *Gary Burton in Concert.* Coryell also toured with Herbie Mann and recorded on the hit album *Memphis Underground* before forming his own group in 1969 with saxophonist Steve Marcus and keyboardist Mike Mandel.

Lady Coryell is a tour de force debut showcasing the guitarist's range and technique, covering ground from Chet Atkins to Jimi Hendrix and beyond in a swirling exploration of the noise-guitar style being mined by others from Hendrix to Sonny Sharrock. The record is marred by Coryell's unfortunate attempts at singing, and it seems odd that this one is still in print while the superior efforts from the same era, *Coryell*, *Larry Coryell at the Village Gate* and the superb *Real Great Escape,* are unavailable.

Spaces, a sublime fusion all-star collaboration with guitarist John McLaughlin, keyboardist Chick Corea, bassist Miroslav Vitous and drummer Billy Cobham, features Coryell's most tasteful and subdued playing since his days with Chico Hamilton and Gary Burton.

From there Coryell turned to the full-blast electric fusion group Eleventh House. Though this was Coryell's grasp at the brass ring, only a live recording from the Montreux Jazz Festival remains available from this period.

Coryell disbanded the group in the mid-1970s and concentrated on playing acoustic guitar, displaying his prowess on such beautiful but currently unavailable sessions as *The Restful Mind,* with Oregon and its *sympatico* guitarist Ralph Towner; *Tributaries,* with guitarists Joe Beck and John Scofield; and *Twin House,* with guitarist Philip Catherine. *Standing Ovation,* with Indian violinist L. Subramaniam, documents Coryell's fascination with Indian classical music.

Fortunately, the magical *Bolero* is still available; this collection of acoustic solos and duets with guitarist Brian Keane includes a majestic performance of Ravel's signature composition as well as the prelude from "Le Tombeau de Couperin." Coryell's audacious mastery of the flamenco idiom adds another facet to his dazzling virtuosity. The solo acoustic *Twelve Frets to One Octave* displays Coryell's acoustic dexterity in the full flower of its imagination.

The Muse sets, *Comin' Home*, *Equipoise*, *Toku Do* and *Shining Hour,* represent a return to the traditional-jazz small-group format for Coryell. The best of these straight-ahead sessions, *Toku Do,* features Stanley Cowell on piano, Buster Williams on bass and Beaver Harris on drums weaving their spells on standards such as "'Round Midnight," "Sophisticated Lady" and "My Funny Valentine."

To this day, Coryell remains a crucially undervalued resource as his recent work for CTI and Shanachie demonstrates. The currently unavailable 1992 release *Live from Bahia,* a powerful recording of Brazilian music, is worth searching out. *Spaces Revisited* is a terrific reunion with Cobham. — J.S.

TOM COSTER

★★★½ **Did Jah Miss Me?!? (Head First/JVC, 1993)**
★★½ **From Me to You (JVC, 1993)**
★★★ **Gotcha!! (Head First/JVC, 1993)**
★★★★ **Let's Set the Record Straight (JVC, 1993)**
★★★ **The Forbidden Zone (JVC, 1994)**
★★★ **From the Street (JVC, 1996)**

During his long-running '70s collaboration with Santana, keyboardist Tom Coster (b. 1941) established himself as one of the most imaginative fusion conceptualists, a master of a variety of keyboards. As a solo artist Coster went through a period of reliance on synthesizers and a search for a commercial formula, which led to overconceptualized, brackish music. On the best of his work, particularly *Did Jah Miss Me?!?* and *Let's Set the Record Straight,* with its excellent contribution from tenor saxophonist Bob Berg, Coster lets his natural inclinations toward a swinging Latin-jazz groove flow like sweet spring water, recalling the exhilaratingly lucid simplicity he employed with Santana. — J.S.

ELIZABETH COTTEN

★★★★ **Freight Train and Other North Carolina Folk Songs and Tunes (1958; Smithsonian Folkways, 1989)**

Chapel Hill, North Carolina, native Elizabeth Cotten (1892–1987) learned to play guitar and banjo at an early age, performing with her brothers until she was about 12, when she followed in her mother's footsteps and became a housekeeper. She subsequently gave up music for over 25 years except for occasional performances in church, and it was not until late 1957 that her homespun music was properly recorded and documented by Mike Seeger for Folkways Records. A formidable guitarist and banjo player, Cotten played several styles of music, displaying an amazing facility and diversity. Her voice had a fragile, slightly ragged tone, but her playing was always sweet and true.

Freight Train contains songs recorded in 1957–58 during Seeger's half dozen visits to Cotten's home in Washington, D.C. The album's title track is Cotten's one original, a blues song in which she displays the single-string, country-ragtime picking for which she is best remembered. Also included are a number of traditional North Carolina folk, blues and gospel songs performed on both banjo and guitar. Cotten's adaptation of "Going Down the Road Feeling Bad" is particularly chilling, as her high, lonesome voice echoes the song's doleful sentiments. Also notable are the country blues "Ain't Got No Honey Baby Now" and "Here Old Rattler Here"/"Sent for My Fiddle Sent for My Son"/"George Buck," a medley of lightning-tempo dance songs that Cotten performs on five-string banjo. Another blues number, "Oh Babe It Ain't No Lie," displays Cotten's unforgettably plaintive, desperate vocal tone.

Cotten retired from housekeeping in 1970 and toured regularly in the late '70s, eventually relocating to Syracuse, New York, where she died in 1987. The Smithsonian has two other Folkways recordings available on cassette by mail order (*Shake Sugaree* and *When I'm Gone*). The album for which she won a Grammy in 1984, *Elizabeth Cotten Live!* (Arhoolie, 1983), is now out of print. A fine player, singer and interpreter, she had an unmistakable influence on pickers like Jerry Garcia, who often performed songs closely associated with Cotten, such as "Oh Babe It Ain't No Lie" and "Going Down the Road Feeling Bad." — B.R.H.

JAMES COTTON

★★★★ **Cut You Loose! (1968; Vanguard, 1988)**
★★★★½ **High Compression (Alligator, 1984)**
★★★★ **Live from Chicago—Mr. Superharp Himself! (Alligator, 1986)**
★★★★½ **Live at Antone's Nightclub (Antone's, 1988)**
★★★★ **Take Me Back (Blind Pig, 1989)**
★★★★ **Harp Attack! (Alligator, 1990)**
★★★★ **Mighty Long Time (Antone's, 1991)**
★★★★ **Three Harp Boogie (Tomato, 1993)**
★★★★ **Living the Blues (Verve, 1994)**
★★★★½ **The Best of the Verve Years (Verve, 1995)**
★★★★½ **Deep in the Blues (Verve, 1996)**

After Little Walter, James Cotton (b. 1935) checks in as the boss of Chicago blues harmonica players. Raised in the depths of the Depression in Tunica, Mississippi, Cotton started playing harmonica after hearing Sonny Boy Williamson (Rice Miller) on the radio. He later ran away from home to join up with Williamson, who took Cotton as a protégé and gave him exposure on the King Biscuit Time radio show.

From there Cotton gigged with various Memphis-area bands, including that of Howlin' Wolf, and recorded for Sun in 1953 and '54, joining up with Muddy Waters the same year. He recorded and toured with Waters for well over a decade before forming his own group in 1966.

Though he was unquestionably one of the greatest classic-blues harp players, Cotton was more interested in promoting himself as a singer and stage personality, using gimmicks like multiple back flips during solos to whip up an audience. The lack of focus on his musical direction led to some disastrous moments in the studio. Fortunately, the least flattering recordings have slipped into oblivion, leaving in print a smaller but select catalog that shows Cotton in top form.

The Best of the Verve Years shrewdly collects material recorded for that label, using the entire *James Cotton Blues Band* session from 1967, a statement of purpose from a player out to prove he had a good musical reason for leaving Muddy's band. *Three Harp Boogie* also draws tracks from *Blues Band* along with an acoustic session with Paul Butterfield and Billy Boy Arnold on harp and Elvin Bishop on guitar.

Cut You Loose!, recorded in San Francisco in 1968 with a West Coast horn section and a guest shot from Guitar Junior, features a great reading of the Percy Mayfield classic "River's Invitation." Blues stars who've lost their way trying to negotiate the pop maze have a habit of revisiting first-outing triumphs in new recordings for Alligator Records, the Chicago-based label started by blues lover Bruce Iglauer. Cotton rebounded from some uneven years with the stunning *High Compression,* which features killer support from guitarist Magic Slim and pianist Pinetop Perkins.

Take Me Back assembles a crack band from two generations of blues stalwarts, with Sam Lawhorn and John Primer on guitars, Pinetop Perkins on piano, Sam Lay on drums and Bob Anderson on bass. *Live at Antone's Nightclub* shows Cotton putting it all on the line for another blues-loving label, this one named after the Austin nightclub. The supporting cast here includes Perkins again along with former Cotton sidemen Matt Murphy and Luther Tucker on guitars, and Muddy Waters's rhythm section of Calvin Jones on bass and Willie Smith on drums. This session worked so well that Antone's tried it again on *Mighty Long Time* with a new cast, including guitarists Hubert Sumlin and Jimmie Vaughan, that ends up sounding almost as good.

Harp Attack! is a shrewd bit of Alligator packaging in the summit-meeting style used on the guitar-based hit *Showdown!* Here Cotton is joined on harp by Junior Wells, Carey Bell and Billy Branch. The only drawback is that with all those harp players around, Cotton decided to showcase his vocals. As a singer, Cotton is still a great harp player. He returned to Verve in the 1990s and enjoyed a serious revival of his fortunes with the driving *Living the Blues,* featuring contributions from Dr. John, Joe Louis Walker and Lucky Peterson, and the Grammy-winning *Deep in the Blues,* with another great performance by Walker. — J.S.

CURTIS COUNCE

★★★ **Landslide (1956; Original Jazz Classics, 1991)**

★★★ **Sonority (1956; Contemporary, 1989)**

★★★★ **You Get More Bounce with Curtis Counce (1957; Original Jazz Classics, 1988)**

★★★ **Carl's Blues (1960; Original Jazz Classics, 1990)**

Curtis Counce (1926–1963) was one of the most sought-after hard-bop bassists on the West Coast jazz scene of the post–World War II era, a master accompanist in the Jimmy Blanton tradition who could ride a walking bass pattern through the hottest hard-bop grooves.

The Kansas City native settled in Los Angeles in the 1940s and went on to play with a wide range of artists including Edgar Hayes, Billy Eckstine, Bud Powell, Buddy DeFranco, Teddy Charles, Wardell Gray, Hampton Hawes, Herb Geller and Clifford Brown.

Counce went on to lead his own quintet during the 1950s, the period represented by these albums. His band included the stalwarts Harold Land on tenor saxophone and Frank Butler on drums, with either Elmo Hope or Carl Perkins on piano. These Contemporary/Original Jazz Classics reissues are all good examples of the emotional blowing sessions that existed alongside the "cool" sound often associated with the California players of the period. — J.S.

COUSIN JOE

★★★ **Bad Luck Blues (Evidence, 1994)**

New Orleans piano—now there's a crowded barrelhouse. From the early jazz of Jelly Roll Morton and Tuts Washington to the syncopated R&B of Professor Longhair and Allen Toussaint, to the boogie-woogie of Fats Domino and Dr. John, the keyboard masters of the Crescent City abound. Along with Champion Jack Dupree, that other court jester of the 88s, "Cousin Joe" Pleasant (1907–1989) was one of the first straight-ahead blues masters exported from New Orleans, delivering a repertoire of blues songs and boogies rife with a warm, gritty voice, an infectious humor and a good-time spirit.

Cousin Joe hit New York in 1942, becoming somewhat of a token Southern-blues piano player awash in a sea of bebop and small-band jazz, but he hit it big with the wry "Lightnin' Struck the Poorhouse." His subsequent recordings for DeLuxe, Imperial, Savoy, King and other labels of the day further revealed his bent for low-down laughs and ironic social commentary: "Box Car Shorty," "Chicken a la Blues," "Too Tight to Walk Loose" and

"Beggin' Woman Blues" (with the immortal line "She's got a handful of gimme and a mouthful of much obliged"). *Bad Luck Blues,* the only title available at this writing, was recorded in 1971 and is a reworking of old numbers with noted guitarists Clarence "Gatemouth" Brown and Jimmy Dawkins. — A.K.

STANLEY COWELL

★★★ We Three (DIW, 1987)
★★★★ Sienna (SteepleChase, 1989)
★★★½ Back to the Beautiful (Concord Jazz, 1989)
★★★½ Departure (SteepleChase, 1990)
★★★★ Maybeck Recital Hall Series, Vol. 5 (Concord Jazz, 1990)
★★★ Close to You Alone (DIW, 1991)
★★★½ Bright Passion (SteepleChase, 1993)
★★★½ Solo Piano (SteepleChase, 1994)
★★★ Live (SteepleChase, 1995)
★★★★ Brilliant Circles (Black Lion, 1995)
★★★½ Mandara Blossoms (SteepleChase, 1996)
★★★★½ Regeneration (Strata-East, N.A.)
★★★★½ Musa-Ancestral Streams (Strata-East, N.A.)

Stanley Cowell (b. 1941) is an imposing composer and pianist who recorded in the late '60s and early '70s with Marion Brown, Max Roach and Charles Tolliver before experimenting with his own albums, some of which have been released on the label he set up with Tolliver, Strata-East. This is some of his best work, particularly *Regeneration* and the solo *Musa-Ancestral Streams*. Other out-of-print titles on Galaxy and ECM are also worth getting. *Brilliant Circles* is an excellent 1969 sextet date with Woody Shaw on trumpet, Tyrone Washington on reeds and flute, Bobby Hutcherson on vibes, Reggie Workman on bass and Joe Chambers on drums.

Cowell, an accomplished sideman and member of the Heath Brothers band, has played in a wide range of settings, from the splendid *Maybeck Recital Hall Series* solo outing to the Bud Powell–styled trio session *Close to You Alone,* with bassist Cecil McBee and drummer Ronnie Burrage, to a series of trio, quintet and sextet recordings for SteepleChase.

Sienna, a trio recording with Ron McLure on bass and Keith Copeland on drums, includes a remarkable cover of Thelonious Monk's "Evidence." — J.S.

DAVELL CRAWFORD

★★★½ Let Them Talk (Rounder, 1995)

New Orleans keyboardist Davell Crawford (b. 1975) shows off his prodigious talents on an impressive debut album that suffers only from the eagerness of a young virtuoso whose dazzling skills sometimes flood the borders into overplaying. There's no question about his understanding of the New Orleans tradition, however. The grandson of '50s R&B star Sugar Boy Crawford and great-nephew of Lionel Hampton has been one of the brightest younger lights of the Crescent City music scene for years, directing two of New Orleans's best choirs and performing numerous jazz and R&B gigs.

Crawford attempts to show the full range of his talents on *Let Them Talk,* fronting a hard-driving R&B band featuring saxophonists Alvin "Red" Tyler and Fred Kemp, tabbing the 75 voices of the John F. Kennedy Senior High School Choir for the rousing gospel effort "Can't Nobody Do Me Like Jesus" and demonstrating (on three solo tracks) that the chain of New Orleans pianists leading back through the century to Jelly Roll Morton remains unbroken. — J.S.

HANK CRAWFORD

★★★ After Hours (1967; Atlantic, 1992)
★★★½ Indigo Blue (1983; Milestone, 1991)
★★★½ Midnight Ramble (1983; Milestone, 1991)
★★★★½ Soul Survivors (Milestone, 1986)
★★½ Mr. Chips (Milestone, 1987)
★★★ Steppin' Up (Milestone, 1987)
★★★½ Night Beat (Milestone, 1989)
★★★ On the Blue Side (Milestone, 1989)
★★★½ Groove Master (Milestone, 1990)
★★★ Portrait (Milestone, 1991)
★★★½ South-Central (Milestone, 1993)
★★★½ Heart and Soul: The Hank Crawford Anthology (Rhino, 1994)
★★★★ Tight (Milestone, 1996)
★★★★ After Dark (Milestone, 1998)

Hank Crawford (b. 1934) started out working with a number of blues bands before joining the Ray Charles band, where he played baritone and alto saxophone (his main instrument) and served as musical director and arranger. Working off his blues and R&B foundation, he made a series of albums under his own name in the '50s and '60s for Atlantic. In the '70s Crawford made several more albums for CTI, which are currently unavailable.

The Milestone albums, recorded in the '80s and '90s, represent a return to Crawford's blues roots for an incendiary soul-jazz groove. *Indigo Blue*, *Midnight Ramble*, *Night Beat*, *Groove Master*, *Heart and Soul* and *South-Central* all feature Dr. John on piano. Check out the cassette-only *Down on the Deuce* (Milestone, 1984), with Cedar Walton on piano.

Sessions with organist Jimmy McGriff—*Soul Survivors*, *Steppin' Up* and *On the Blue Side*—breathe new life into the irresistible groove of the classic organ combo. *Soul Survivors,* with Mel Lewis and Bernard Purdie on drums and one of the best performances guitarist George Benson ever cut in the studio, is a must-have.

Tight is an excellent career overview showcasing Crawford's great ballad style on several tracks and a blues groove on others, kicked by a group that includes a number of Crawford's longtime friends—Melvin Sparks on guitar, Howard Johnson on baritone saxophone, David Newman on tenor saxophone and flute and Idris Muhammad on drums. Crawford digs even deeper into his Memphis roots on the blues-drenched *After Dark,* which features another gritty performance from Sparks and heavy fatback drumming from Bernard Purdie.
— J.S.

ROBERT CRAY

★★★ Too Many Cooks (1980; Tomato, 1989)
★★★★ Bad Influence (High Tone, 1983)
★★★ False Accusations (High Tone, 1985)
★★★★★ Showdown! (with Albert Collins and Johnny Copeland) (Alligator, 1985)
★★★ Strong Persuader (Mercury, 1986)
★★★ Don't Be Afraid of the Dark (Mercury, 1988)
★★★★ Midnight Stroll (Mercury, 1990)
★★★★½ I Was Warned (Mercury, 1992)
★★★½ Shame + A Sin (Mercury, 1994)
★★★½ Some Rainy Morning (Mercury, 1995)

Born in Georgia in 1953 and raised in Tacoma, Washington, Robert Cray had about-perfect timing when Tomato issued his first recordings in 1980. Stevie Ray Vaughan was a little over two years away from re-proving the commercial viability of blues as played by someone other than Eric Clapton, but Cray's early work served notice that some new voices had something to say. Steeped in the entire history of electric blues, Cray absorbed the best it had to offer—notably Muddy Waters and Albert Collins—and melded his distinctive robust sound to Memphis soul à la Stax/Volt, complete with horns. Moreover, he, like Vaughan, has a powerful presence as both a singer and a writer. His original songs as well as those he covers disdain the stereotypical bluesman's pose of being forever put-upon by conniving women. While the vagaries of love remain a lyrical focus, Cray, ever the sensitive modern man, looks inward for solutions and is quick to admit his own failings in personal relationships. He's not the only contemporary blues artist to do this, but few of his peers state their cases more eloquently.

As a solo recording artist and as the leader of the Robert Cray Band, Cray has been unusually consistent. While his unqualified masterpiece is yet to come, his catalog shows solid, sometimes spectacular moments from an artist producing an impressive body of work as time goes on. The Tomato albums are small-combo affairs featuring a saxophonist and trumpeter augmenting the Cray quintet of piano, bass, drums, guitar and harmonica, and their feel is strictly South Side Chicago (Robert Cray does Pepper's Lounge) in the wee small hours. That lean, mean sound reached its apex on the High Tone entries, particularly 1983's *Bad Influence,* a searing, intense bible of the blues that features some of Cray's most impassioned vocals and startling guitar work. Coming as it did in the same year as Vaughan's debut album, *Bad Influence* was a welcome antidote to the synth-pop and fashion bands then taking over the pop market.

The fashion bands came and went, but the blues and Cray pushed on. A move to Mercury in 1986 found him broadening out his sound and going foursquare into Memphis soul, complete with the addition of the esteemed Memphis Horns. *Midnight Stroll* and *I Was Warned* are the standouts here. Of the two, the latter is most recommended, as its sustained cloudy-day ambiance lends emotional pull to Cray's introspective lyrics and stinging, supple lead lines.

Of note to blues-guitar enthusiasts is the Alligator *Showdown!* summit meeting teaming Cray with Albert Collins ("the Master of the Telecaster") and Johnny Copeland ("the Texas Twister"), two now deceased blues masters who had an incalculable impact on Cray's style. On one cut, "T-Bone Shuffle," each virtuoso takes a vocal and guitar solo, and when they've finished their thundering they've reclaimed the past and put the present in new perspective. Cray fans can't afford to be without this recording.

Cray pays homage to another of his touchstones when he sits in with B.B. King on the latter's 1993 all-star blowout, *Blues Summit.* On this must-have, Cray is featured delivering a warm, down-home vocal and trebly, serpentine guitar solo on the boisterous album-opening shuffle, "Playin' with My Friends." This sets the tone for an inspired series of duets between King and the likes of John Lee Hooker, Irma Thomas, Buddy Guy, Ruth Brown, Lowell Fulson and others. In short, wherever and whenever Robert Cray shows up, good things happen. — D.M.

PEE WEE CRAYTON

★★★ **Things I Used to Do (Vanguard, 1971)**

★★★★★ **Pee Wee's Blues: The Complete Aladdin and Imperial Recordings (Capitol, 1996)**

In the late '40s, Texas-born Connie Curtis "Pee Wee" Crayton (1914–1985) took a $125 investment in a first-generation Epiphone amplified guitar and—along with friend and mentor T-Bone Walker—pioneered the guitar's role as *the* lead instrument of electric blues and R&B. With a series of chart-topping instrumentals on the Modern label ("Blues After Hours," "Texas Hop"), Crayton forged an approach that added a more gritty and urgent edge to Walker's big-band blues. In turn, Crayton influenced an entire generation of electric stringpickers, from B.B. King and Lowell Fulson to Clarence "Gatemouth" Brown and Chuck Berry (whose instrumental "Deep Feeling" owes a truckload to Crayton's classic "Blues After Hours").

Sadly, the Modern titles have yet to be collected on one package—"Blues After Hours" can, however, be found on Rhino's *Blues Masters, Vol. 1: Urban Blues,* and "Texas Hop" appears on Rhino's *Blues Masters, Vol. 3: Texas Blues.* Crayton's subsequent recordings from 1951 to 1955 for the Imperial and Aladdin labels —featuring bouncy and bountiful production polish from New Orleans bandmaster Dave Bartholomew—can be found on the excellently annotated Capitol collection. The 20-track package covers the full breadth of Crayton's blues palette: proto–rock & roll guitar workouts ("Do Unto Others"), lilting blues ("Win-O") and strollin' Louisiana R&B ("Runnin' Wild").

The late '50s saw Crayton signed to Vee-Jay, yielding the R&B hit "Peace of Mind"—yet to be rereleased on CD. In 1971 he recorded the rather loose small-band effort on Vanguard, reprising several past hits of his own and of others. — A.K.

CREATIVE CONSTRUCTION COMPANY

★★★ **Creative Construction Company (Muse, 1970)**

★★★ **Creative Construction Company, Vol. 2 (Muse, 1970)**

Born out of the creative foment of the Association for the Advancement of Creative Musicians, the Creative Construction Company was a short-lived sextet of Chicago musicians—violinist Leroy Jenkins (b. 1932), saxophonist Anthony Braxton (b. 1945), trumpeter Leo Smith (b. 1941), pianist Muhal Richard Abrams (b. 1930), drummer Steve McCall (b. 1933) and bassist Richard Davis (b. 1930). Only Davis was not a direct participant in the experiments of the AACM, but his improvisational abilities made him a welcome addition to this lineup.

Both of these albums were recorded at the same concert, a 1970 performance at Peace Church in New York's Greenwich Village. Each comprises a single composition by Jenkins, probed, tested and reveled in according to the new music visions and improvisational demands that characterize virtually all of the AACM's work. "Muhal," the Abrams tribute that makes up the first volume, provides a useful glimpse of the conceptual heights these dedicated musicians scaled in their quest for new jazz horizons. — J.S.

ARTHUR "BIG BOY" CRUDUP

★★★★ **Mean Ole Frisco (1957; Collectables, 1990)**

★★★ **Look on Yonder's Wall (Delmark, 1968)**

★★★ **Crudup's Mood (Delmark, 1970)**

★★★ **That's All Right Mama (RCA Bluebird, 1992)**

Forest, Mississippi–born Arthur "Big Boy" Crudup (1905–1974) spent his early life working a variety of manual-labor jobs before deciding at age 32 to take up the guitar and play the country blues that had become his passion. Even at his best Crudup the player can sound amateurish—he was given to striking the wrong notes, playing in the wrong key—but Crudup the vocalist had a brooding authority that could not be denied. Signed to Bluebird in 1941, he cut more than 80 songs over the next 15 years and was a consistent presence on the R&B chart, despite never being more than a regional success. It was Crudup's fate to enter into legend at the dawn of the rock & roll era, in 1954, when Elvis Presley cut his song "That's All Right" as his first single for Sun Records. After moving to RCA in 1956, Presley dipped into the Crudup catalog for two more songs, "So Glad You're Mine" and "My Baby Left Me."

All four of Crudup's in-print albums are commendable efforts. The absolute must-have is Collectables' *Mean Ole Frisco,* a reissue of an album Crudup cut for the Fire label in 1957. The 12 tracks are remakes of songs Crudup wrote (excluding the title song) and recorded for Bluebird, including "That's All Right," "So Glad You're Mine" and "Rock Me Baby." While hardly peak Crudup, the two Delmark albums have the loose, easy ambiance of an artist completely at home with his material and himself. *Look on Yonder's Wall* finds Crudup reprising "That's All Right" in fine, understated fashion. For a sampling of Crudup's Bluebird recordings, look for the deleted 1971 LP from RCA *Father of Rock 'n' Roll.* — D.M.

THE CRUSADERS

★★★ **Pass the Plate (1971; Mojazz, 1994)**
★★ **Hollywood (1972; Mojazz, 1994)**
★★ **At Their Best (1973; Motown, 1992)**
★★★★ **Scratch (1974; GRP, 1997)**
★★★★ **Southern Comfort (1974; GRP, 1997)**
★★★★ **Chain Reaction (1975; GRP, 1997)**
★★★½ **Those Southern Knights (1976; GRP, 1988)**
★★★ **The Best of the Crusaders (MCA, 1976)**
★★★ **Street Life (MCA, 1979)**
★★★ **Healing the Wounds (1991; GRP, 1997)**
★★★★ **The Golden Years (GRP, 1992)**
★★★★ **Way Back Home (Blue Thumb/MCA, 1996)**

The Crusaders—drummer Stix Hooper (b. 1938), keyboardist Joe Sample (b. 1939), saxophonist/bassist Wilton Felder (b. 1940) and trombonist Wayne Henderson (b. 1939)—grew up listening to and playing jazz and R&B in their native Texas before moving in the late '50s to California, where they dubbed themselves the Jazz Crusaders and made a number of excellent records. The currently out-of-print Blue Note album *Young Rabbits* collects some of their best moments from the '60s.

In the early '70s the group dropped *Jazz* from its name, hired guitarist Larry Carlton and proceeded to record a series of highly successful pop-jazz albums, even scoring a sizable hit single with the instrumental "Put It Where You Want It" from *The Crusaders I.* That LP and *The 2nd Crusade* (both out of print) as well as *Scratch*, *Chain Reaction* and *Southern Comfort* represent the group at its creative best—they played commercial, accessible music without compromising their musical identity. *Way Back Home* is an excellent career overview.

Following the departure of Henderson in 1975, the band's sound became more formulaic and less convincing, and by the 1980s the Crusaders had devolved into making producer-oriented pop records. "Street Life," an urban-radio hit, was the group's final high point. Sample and Felder continued to use the name into the early '90s, recording with a variety of sidemen, but the Crusaders no longer lived up to the name. — J.S.

CURLEW

★★★½ **Live in Berlin (Cuneiform, 1992)**
★★★★ **Bee (Cuneiform, 1992)**
★★★★ **A Beautiful Western Saddle (Cuneiform, 1993)**
★★★★★ **Paradise (Cuneiform, 1996)**
★★★★★ **Fabulous Drop (Cuneiform, 1998)**

There's no telling what you might hear on a Curlew album, from Albert Ayler–inspired saxophone improvisations to reggae grooves, outer space R&B, Zappa-esque guitar solos, soothing world-music sonorities or full-bore heavy-metal vamps. Most likely the music will include unusual intonation, cross melodies, rhythms that slice against one another like a Vegomatic and the constant sound of surprise. Much of the downtown New York new-jazz scene of the 1990s owes a debt to this band's experiments.

Curlew began in 1979 when mystic saxophonist/composer George Cartwright decided to expand into a band format the work he was doing with the like-minded experimental reed player Michael Lytle. Cartwright called on guitarist Davey Williams, whose blues background with Johnny Shines gave him a sharp rhythmic sense to complement with his penchant for exploring weird tones, cellist Tom Cora, drummer Pippin Barnett and keyboardist Wayne Horvitz. *Live in Berlin* shows the Cartwright/Williams collaboration moving into uncharted territory. The same group, without Horvitz but with Ann Rupel on bass, recorded *Bee,* with its memorable opening track, "The March (or Ornette Went to Miles' House and They Didn't Get Along)." Amy Denio joins in on vocals for *A Beautiful Western Saddle.* Samm Bennett takes over the drums and guitarist Chris Cochrane signs on for the nearly commercial *Paradise;* drummer Kenny Wolleson replaces Bennett on *Fabulous Drop. Paradise* and *Fabulous Drop* are astonishingly great recordings with Cartwright, Williams and Cochrane taking jaw-dropping turns on a set of compositions that put the listener through numerous contortions to keep up. — J.S.

TED CURSON

★★★★ **Plenty of Horn (1962; Boplicity, 1994)**
★★★½ **Ted Curson Plays Fire Down Below (1962; Original Jazz Classics, 1990)**
★★★★½ **Tears for Dolphy (1964; Black Lion, 1994)**
★★★½ **'Round About Midnight (with Dizzy Reece) (Trend/Discovery, 1989)**
★★★★ **Traveling On (Evidence, 1997)**

Roughly hewn and gingerly phrased aptly describe the horn work of Ted Curson (b. 1935), a premier postbop trumpeter who draws on a rich vocabulary of blues and Afro-Cuban, as well as cool and free jazz. Sideman for a wide range of leaders, Curson is also notable for a number of important recordings as a bandleader.

Graduating from the same Philadelphia high school as John Coltrane, Curson was urged to move to New York by Miles Davis, who had heard him perform. He finally made the jump in 1955, landing first with a Latin band, then with Mal Waldron; in 1959 he had, according to Curson, "one concert, one record date and a whole year of rehearsing" with Cecil Taylor. The next year found Curson in the ranks of Mingus's Jazz Workshop, journeying to Europe as the fifth member of the legendary team of Mingus, Richmond, Ervin and Dolphy. Atlantic's *Mingus at Antibes* (available on Rhino) best captures Curson's free awakenings.

On Curson's first excursions as leader (particularly on *Plenty of Horn*), he retained his "cool" influence not only as a composer (tunes like "Flatted Fifth" and "Nosruc" are exceptional) but also as a varied stylist who introduced the four-valve piccolo trumpet to the jazz idiom. In 1962 he assembled a solid rhythm section of pianist Gildo Mahones, bassist George Tucker and drummer Roy Haynes for the mellow, ballad-laden *Plays Fire Down Below.*

Curson relocated to Europe from the mid-'60s through most of the '70s, recording some of his most significant work. In 1965 he joined forces with tenor saxophonist Bill Barron on the excellent *Quicksand* (for Atlantic, currently out of print). He later put two titles to wax: His cool side shines on the currently unavailable *Flip Top,* recorded with the Zagreb Radio Orchestra; his strongest and best-conceived album, *Tears for Dolphy,* reveals Curson back home in the hurtling rhythms typical of Mingus.

Recorded between 1978 and '80 but released almost a decade later, *'Round About Midnight* is a hard-driving but unevenly produced dual-trumpet session. The set finds Curson in fine company, matching licks with Jamaican trumpeter Dizzy Reece and receiving strong rhythmic support from drummer Roy Haynes and bassist Ray Drummond, among others, who add both polish and fire to such standards as "Walkin'," "Pent Up House" and the title track (a showcase for Drummond's expressive soloing ability), as well as Curson's own free-form "Snake Johnson" and tender, lighthearted ballad "Marjo."

The recent *Traveling On* is easily Curson's best in years: well produced, well programmed, a solid reconfirmation of his blues and Latin postbop roots. Revived originals like the soulful "Lin's Garden," the somber "Tears for Dolphy" and the minor-key "Flatted Fifth" excel with hard-hitting rhythm backup (Ray Drummond again on bass, Misako Kano on piano, Sylvia Cuenca on drums and a host of Latin percussionists). The nine-track outing further benefits from the sensitive sax work of Mark Gross—musical director of the Duke Ellington Group—and draws on Curson's Dizzy-like vocal talents ("Flip Flop and Fly," "Watermelon Man" and "The Saints Go Marching In"). — A.K.

ANDREW CYRILLE

★★★★ **Metamusician's Stomp (Soul Note, 1978)**
★★★★ **Nuba (with Jeanne Lee and Jimmy Lyons) (Black Saint, 1979)**
★★★½ **Special People (Soul Note, 1981)**
★★★ **The Navigator (Soul Note, 1983)**
★★★★½ **Pieces of Time (Soul Note, 1984)**

★★★★ **Something in Return (with Jimmy Lyons) (Black Saint, 1988)**
★★★ **Burnt Offering (with Jimmy Lyons) (Black Saint, 1991)**
★★★½ **Galaxies (with Vladimir Tarasov) (Music and Arts Programs of America, 1991)**
★★★★½ **X Man (Soul Note, 1994)**

"The new, free, creative black drumming definitely has a beginning, and that was it!" proudly declared drummer/percussionist Andrew Cyrille (b. 1939) on a live 1974 now out-of-print recording. Like Art Blakey before him, Cyrille has preached such a message through his experimental approach to solo and collective improvisation, drawing from his many years accompanying Cecil Taylor's free excursions as well as the timeless African tradition of drummer-as-leader. Cyrille prefers the label "metamusician," underscoring his spearheading role as primary collaborator, when not actually leading.

Cyrille's jazz path has run high and low, in and out. Through the '60s he played with Illinois Jacquet, Coleman Hawkins, Mary Lou Williams and Nigerian master drummer Olatunji and is best known for his 11-year association with Taylor. He struck out on his own in the '70s, initially performing with other drummers—Rashied Ali, Milford Graves, Famoudou Don Moye of the Art Ensemble. He founded his own educational foundation and label, the Institute of Percussive Studies. IPS released a number of fine jazz explorations, notably 1975's revolutionary and improvised collage *Celebration* by the collective Maono ("may-o-no," "feelings" in Swahili), which included Cyrille, vocalist Jeanne Lee, tenor man David S. Ware, trumpeter Ted Daniel and others.

By 1978, Maono had been distilled to its strongest elements, a quartet of Daniel, Ware and bassist Nick DiGeronimo, with Cyrille as leader and primary composer. *Metamusician's Stomp* swings through a wide arc of experimental and accessible styles and reveals Cyrille's considerable compositional vision, particularly on the title track and the bebop-bordering-on-anarchy of "5-4-3-2."

The last 15 years have seen Cyrille recording almost exclusively for the Italian Black Saint/Soul Note labels. *Special People* features the same lineup as *Metamusician's Stomp* but lacks its fire and focus, though offering a satisfying mix of originals and covers (Ornette Coleman's "A Girl Named Rainbow," John Stubblefield's "Baby Man"). *The Navigator* adds pianist Sonelius Smith, drops Ware and takes a straight-ahead turn—with Cyrille withdrawing to a more collaborative position. *Pieces of Time* is a drummers-only quartet in an orgy of jazz and African rhythms, featuring the collective efforts of Cyrille, Graves, Moye and bebop legend Kenny Clarke (liner notes by Max Roach, fittingly).

The evocative, mood-setting *Nuba* finds Cyrille in a trio with vocalist Jeanne Lee and Cecil Taylor Unit alumnus Jimmy Lyons on alto sax. Lee and Lyons sound alternately like cooing lovers and dueling altos, while Cyrille's percussion paints atmospheric backdrops. The spontaneously charged give-and-take of Cyrille's rhythmic propulsion and Lyons's long-breathed riffing is the focus of two posthumously released in-concert duets, *Something in Return* (1981) and *Burnt Offering* (1982). (Lyons died in 1986.) The former features more compositionally based improvisation, kicking off with a brilliant outtake on "Take the A Train," while Lyons's "Fragments I" tosses and retosses melodic references in a compelling sound salad. The title track on the latter, more jam-focused release is a mammoth, 23-minutes-plus instrumental dialog that builds up steam as each player ups the artistic ante, reaching a satisfying conclusion. *Galaxies* is a live and charged percussion discussion, catching Cyrille in a 1990 concert with Russian drummer Vladimir Tarasov, as the two find common ground (and fun on Coltrane's "One Up, One Down") using rhythm, instrumental textures (great cymbal work) and space.

Back in straight time, Cyrille collected a fleet guitar, flute, bass and drums quartet for 1994's *X Man;* "Knowing How to Listen" could be its subtitle, as the group displays the interplay of a unit with decades of experience together (in actuality, the grouping derived from the guitarless trio performing at an Ed Blackwell benefit a year previously). The interlocking of Alix Pascal's nylon-stringed picking, James Newton's pensive flute work, Cyrille's whispered cymbal-and-snare play and Anthony Cox's sensitive underpinning make for a disc that balances mellow and mature, sparse and sublime. — A.K.

TONY DAGRADI

★★★ **Lunar Eclipse (Gramavision, 1982)**
★★★ **Dreams of Love (Rounder, 1988)**
★★★★ **Live at the Columns (Turnipseed, 1994)**

Reed player Tony Dagradi (b. 1953) got his start playing in R&B horn sections with Marvin Gaye, Ike and Tina Turner and Archie Bell and the Drells before moving to New Orleans to pursue his own musical course in the late '70s. His Astral Project group, heard on *Lunar Eclipse,* features Dagradi's tuneful compositions and intelligent yet accessible playing on tenor and alto sax and clarinet. *Dreams of Love* also features his soprano-saxophone work backed by Steve Masakowski on guitar and David Torkanowski on piano. Dagradi has also played with Professor Longhair and the Carla Bley band. *Live at the Columns,* recorded with Dagradi's working trio of James Singleton on bass and John Vidacovich on percussion, captures the improvisational magic of this lineup's regular performances at the Garden District Hotel and adds another chapter to the great New Orleans live-music tradition. — J.S.

TADD DAMERON

★★★½ **Fontainebleau (1956; Original Jazz Classics, 1987)**
★★★ **Mating Call (with John Coltrane) (1957; Original Jazz Classics, 1992)**
★★★ **The Magic Touch (1962; Original Jazz Classics, 1990)**

Better known as a songwriter ("Good Bait," "Our Delight," "The Squirrel" and "On a Misty Night") and arranger (for Count Basie, Dizzy Gillespie and Sarah Vaughan, among others), Tadd Dameron (1917–1965) released only four albums under his name, the three listed above and the out-of-print and very rare *Tribute to Clifford Brown* (1955). His St. Louis–based small bands of the '40s and early '50s included such greats as Miles Davis (whose *Birth of the Cool* sessions were influenced by Dameron's ideas), Fats Navarro, Milt Jackson and Kai Winding.

Above all, Dameron the musician was a proponent of beauty. His piano playing and arrangements on the two large-band albums, *Fontainebleau* and *The Magic Touch,* share a light, elegant quality. The horns—trumpet, trombone, and baritone, tenor and alto saxes—appear to float above the rhythm section but still give the soloists (especially Kenny Dorham on trumpet) room to move. *Fontainebleau*'s title suite has a limpid grace, while the skittish "Delirium" and sultry "Bula-Beige" allow tenor saxophonist Joe Alexander room to stretch out.

In a small-group setting, *Mating Call* showcases Dameron's sprightly side. The insistent title song and charging blues "Super Jet" bristle with an unbridled energy. Even "On a Misty Night," which is performed on *The Magic Touch* with a lulling romanticism, swings with a muscular vitality. While the rhythm section (bassist John Simmons and drummer Philly Joe Jones) is superlative, the lion's share of credit goes to John Coltrane, whose passionate playing, clearly influenced by Sonny Rollins and Sonny Stitt, soars above Dameron's melodies. — S.M.

HAROLD DANKO

★★½ **Mirth Song (with Rufus Reid) (1982; Sunnyside, 1991)**
★★ **Shorter by Two (with Kirk Lightsey) (1983; Sunnyside, 1989)**

★★ Ink and Water (1985; Sunnyside, 1996)
★★★ Alone but Not Forgotten (Sunnyside, 1989)
★★★ Next Age (SteepleChase, 1994)
★★★½ After the Rain (SteepleChase, 1995)
★★★★ New Autumn (SteepleChase, 1996)
★★★★ The Feeling of Jazz (SteepleChase, 1996)
★★★ Tidal Breeze (SteepleChase, 1997)

Pianist and composer Harold Danko (b. 1947), an evocative modernist at the keyboard, has performed or recorded through the years with Chet Baker, Gerry Mulligan, the Thad Jones/Mel Lewis orchestra, Lee Konitz, Clark Terry and Woody Herman. He performs most frequently with his own quartet featuring tenor saxophonist Rich Perry, bassist Scott Colley and drummer Jeff Hirshfield. He's also a busy jazz educator on the faculty of the Manhattan School of Music and the New School, both in New York.

Danko's two earliest Sunnyside sessions are flawed by the format, not the musicality of the pairings or the material. While well intended, the Wayne Shorter tribute, *Shorter by Two,* is ill-served by a two-piano treatment. *Ink and Water* is a series of solo-piano improvisations inspired by the concept of *sumie* painting—Japanese ink-and-water pictures resulting from the spontaneous release of what the artist sees with his "inner eye."

Alone but Not Forgotten is a romantic trio-plus-strings session. *Next Age* and the much stronger *New Autumn* feature Danko's working quartet on a wide stylistic range of original compositions. Danko's solo recording *After the Rain* explores the rich harmonies and melodic flow of 14 John Coltrane compositions, while *The Feeling of Jazz* tackles the music Coltrane and Duke Ellington explored in their historic 1962 studio summit. *Tidal Breeze* showcases eight of Danko's challenging original compositions, performed by his regular quartet of Perry, Colley and Hirshfield — K.F.

KENNY DAVERN

★★★½ Soprano Summit in Concert (with Bob Wilber) (Concord, 1976)
★★★½ Soprano Summit Live at Concord '77 (with Bob Wilber) (1977; Concord Jazz, 1991)
★★★½ One Hour Tonight (MusicMasters, 1988)
★★★★ I'll See You in My Dreams (MusicMasters, 1989)
★★★½ Stretchin' Out (Jazzology, 1989)
★★★½ My Inspiration (MusicMasters, 1992)
★★★★ East Side, West Side (Arbors, 1994)
★★★ Never in a Million Years (with Dick Wellstood) (Challenge, 1995)

When you listen to Kenny Davern (b. 1935) snake his way through a blues tune or blow a cool, slinky toe-tapping number like "Comes Love" (from *One Hour Tonight*), it's hard to understand why the clarinet fell so far out of favor in the jazz world. In Davern's hands, at least, it is a keenly expressive, highly emotive, distinctly laid-back instrument. All of Davern's sessions, including *My Inspiration,* which features a full string section (usually to good effect), have the spontaneous kick of live gigs. *One Hour Tonight* and *I'll See You in My Dreams,* recorded at the same 1988 session, feature guitarist Howard Alden in a virtually coheadlining role, with the pair displaying telepathically sympathetic playing throughout. The Wilber sessions document concerts, with both leaders splitting their time between clarinet and soprano sax. Generally, each Davern album paints a vivid picture of an unheralded virtuoso. — A.P.

DEBBIE DAVIES

★★★★ Picture This (Blind Pig, 1993)
★★★★ Loose Tonight (Blind Pig, 1994)
★★★★ I Got That Feeling (Blind Pig, 1997)

Guitarist/vocalist Debbie Davies (b. 1952) learned her craft backing Albert Collins for three years and has proved a more-than-capable leader since going out on her own. Her nimble, carefully structured lead-guitar style reflects the architectural values that grow out of a superb rhythm-guitar orientation. Her vocals are strong and expressive, but her prime asset is great songwriting, which contemporizes the battle of the sexes that lies at the heart of blues lyrics without resorting to clichés.

The title track of *Picture This* is a gem of a song that remains one of the highlights of her sets. *Loose Tonight,* with bassist Danny Klein joining the band, contains several excellent originals: "Give It Up," "This Man Is Killin' Me" and "A Mother's Blues," a complex lament that could well become a classic.

"How many more cuts can a country endure?" Davies demands on the terrific "Howlin' at the

Moon," the contemporary blues that leads off *I Got That Feeling* with the force of a slap in the face from the working women of America. The title track is a cover of a Collins song done as a guitar-and-vocal duet with another former Collins guitarist, Coco Montoya. Tab Benoit also duets with Davies on the blues ballad "Let the Heartaches Begin." — J.S.

ANTHONY DAVIS

★★★★ **Song for the Old World (India Navigation, 1978)**
★★★★ **Of Blues and Dreams (Sackville, 1978)**
★★★★★ **Hidden Voices (1980; India Navigation, 1997)**
★★★★★ **Episteme (1981; Gramavision, 1995)**
★★★★★ **I've Known Rivers (1982; Gramavision, 1994)**
★★★★ **Variations in Dreamtime (India Navigation, 1982)**
★★★★★ **Hemispheres (1983; Gramavision, 1994)**
★★★★ **Middle Passage (Gramavision, 1984)**
★★★★ **Ghost Factory (1988; Gramavision, 1994)**
★★★★★ **Trio² (1989; Gramavision, 1994)**
★★★★ **Lady of the Mirrors (N.A.; India Navigation, 1991)**
★★★★ **X: The Life and Times of Malcolm X (Gramavision, 1992)**

Pianist Anthony Davis (b. 1951) came to be regarded as a major new voice on his instrument during the late 1970s, after his work with such important new musicians as Leo Smith, Oliver Lake, Leroy Jenkins and Barry Altschul. As the new decade began, he also rose to the forefront of those young black musicians placing increasing emphasis on compositional (as opposed to improvisational) elements in their music.

A sense of Davis's pianistic roots in Duke Ellington, Thelonious Monk and Cecil Taylor, as well as his ingenuity in the jazz-combo format, can be gleaned from his earlier band albums. *Song for the Old World,* with vibist Jay Hoggard, bassist Mark Helias and drummer Ed Blackwell, is a strong debut, introducing a craggy postmodernism that suggests Andrew Hill's Blue Note work (Hill is the subject of one piece). *Hidden Voices,* with stunning writing and a consistently high level of solos, features the quintet Davis co-led with flautist James Newton; trombonist George Lewis appears as "special guest." After the solo title performance, *Of Blues and Dreams* presents yet another quartet, this one setting the leader's piano against the stark sonorities of Leroy Jenkins on violin and Abdul Wadud on cello.

By 1980, Davis was stressing predetermined compositional devices that channel the performer's creative impulses, trying to move from predominantly improvised music to a greater compositional/improvisational balance. *Lady of the Mirrors,* an album of piano solos, is thus an extremely contained recital, with the strongly melodic written themes encouraging nuances as much as outright variations. *Episteme* features an octet that develops sonorities heard earlier on *Hidden Voices* and *Of Blues and Dreams* within a context that also suggests turn-of-the-century impressionism and contemporary minimalism.

Davis remained prolific through 1983, as duet albums with Hoggard and Newton, previously available only in Europe, appeared in America; newer work was released by American labels. *I've Known Rivers* is a chamber-jazz trio with compositions by all three (Davis, Newton, Wadud) participants. *Variations in Dreamtime* is a larger-ensemble album, less compelling than *Episteme. Hemispheres* is a solo outing conceptualized in collaboration with choreographer Molissa Fenley and featuring beautiful playing.

Middle Passage is another compelling solo outing. *Ghost Factory* is a gamelan-influenced recording with the Kansas City Symphony Orchestra. *Trio²* (as in the mathematical function) reunites the *I've Known Rivers* group for another contemplative chamber-jazz session. *X: The Life and Times of Malcolm X* is an ambitious three-act, two-CD opera about the black religious leader, with strong performances from Marty Erlich, J.D. Parran and John Purcell on flutes and reeds, Herb Robertson on trumpet, Arthur Baron on trombone and Abdul Wadud on cello. — B.B./J.S.

BLIND JOHN DAVIS

★★★½ **Blind John Davis (Evidence, 1994)**

Pianist Blind John Davis (1913–1985) was a skilled boogie and blues player who was also able to arrange and had an encyclopedic knowledge of popular material, which made him a valued session leader from the 1930s on. Between 1937 and 1942 he played on more than 100 recordings by a variety of blues artists including Sonny Boy (John Lee) Williamson, Big Bill Broonzy, Tampa Red, Memphis Minnie, Sunnyland Slim, Lonnie Johnson and Washboard Sam.

Although he recorded six sides for Vocalion in 1938 with guitarist George Barnes, some trio dates in the early 1950s and several hours for the Library of Congress, there is little trace of Davis on record: A 1950s Vogue album, two 1970s German albums and a session for Oldie Blues are currently unavailable. *Blind John Davis,* recorded in Chicago in 1983, shows him still in full command of a rolling barrelhouse style, playing with the stately grace of a master. — J.S.

EDDIE "LOCKJAW" DAVIS

★★★★½ **The Eddie "Lockjaw" Davis Cookbook, Vol. 1 (1958; Original Jazz Classics, 1991)**
★★★★ **Smokin' (1958; Original Jazz Classics, 1992)**
★★★½ **Jaws (1958; Original Jazz Classics, 1993)**
★★★½ **The Eddie "Lockjaw" Davis Cookbook, Vol. 2 (1958; Original Jazz Classics, 1991)**
★★★½ **The Eddie "Lockjaw" Davis Cookbook, Vol. 3 (1958; Original Jazz Classics, 1992)**
★★★½ **Jaws in Orbit (1959; Original Jazz Classics, 1992)**
★★★★ **Trane Whistle (1960; Original Jazz Classics, 1990)**
★★★½ **Afro-Jaws (1961; Original Jazz Classics, 1989)**
★★★ **Straight Ahead (1976; Original Jazz Classics, 1991)**
★★★★ **Montreux '77 (1977; Original Jazz Classics, 1989)**
★★★½ **The Best of Eddie "Lockjaw" Davis (1980; Pablo, 1991)**
★★★★ **Gentle Jaws (Prestige, 1995)**
★★★★ **Streetlights (Prestige, 1995)**

Tenor saxophonist Eddie "Lockjaw" Davis (1922–1986) was a strong link to the Coleman Hawkins–Ben Webster tenor sound, particularly on ballads, and a thrilling player on blues and up-tempo numbers. Davis's big-voiced sound served him well in the large bands he grew up playing with in New York, beginning with Cootie Williams's in 1942, followed by stints with Lucky Millinder, Andy Kirk and Louis Armstrong. Between dates as a leader, Davis had a starring role in several Count Basie lineups during the 1950s and '60s and again in the '70s.

Davis's biggest success came fronting an incendiary blues-based group with organist Shirley Scott, bassist George Duvivier, drummer Arthur Edgehill and flautist/saxophonist Jerome Richardson. This group debuted on *The Eddie "Lockjaw" Davis Cookbook* and went on to make *Smokin',* the other two *Cookbook* dates, *Jaws* (without Richardson), *Jaws in Orbit* (with trombonist Steve Pulliam) and part of the beautiful ballad collection *Gentle Jaws,* which also includes a session Davis recorded with pianist Red Garland's trio, with Sam Jones on bass and Arthur Taylor on drums.

Trane Whistle places Davis in front of a terrific big band with arrangements by Oliver Nelson and Ernie Wilkins, a setting made for Davis's larger-than-life sound. *Afro-Jaws* is a quartet session augmented with percussion from Ray Barretto and a Clark Terry–led trumpet section on two tracks.

After the memorable early-1960s "tough tenors" quintet with Johnny Griffin, Davis returned to the tenor-organ formula on *Streetlights* backed by guitarist Paul Weeden's trio, which included organist Don Patterson, Duvivier and drummer Billy James.

Davis was still going strong in the '70s on a series of Pablo releases. *Straight Ahead* was recorded with the Tommy Flanagan trio; *Montreux '77* captures a live quartet set with Oscar Peterson on piano, Ray Brown on bass and Jimmie Smith on drums. — J.S.

GUY DAVIS

★★★ **Dreams About Life (Smithsonian Folkways, 1978)**
★★★½ **Stomp Down Rider (Red House, 1995)**

Actor/singer Guy Davis (b. 1952), the son of actors Ossie Davis and Ruby Dee, grew up in the affluent suburbs of Westchester County, New York, fascinated by the tales of black folk history in the South. Davis has pursued a career combining his acting and musical skills.

Though he recorded his first album in the 1970s, it wasn't until the 1990s that his career began to take off. In 1991 he performed on Broadway in *Mulebone,* then in 1993 played the lead role in the off-Broadway production of *Robert Johnson: Trick the Devil.* Davis then developed the one-man show *In Bed with the Blues: The Adventures of Fishy Waters. Stomp Down Rider* mixes Davis's engaging originals

with covers of Mississippi blues classics.
— J.S.

LARRY DAVIS

★★★½ **Blues Knights (with Byther Smith) (1986; Evidence, 1994)**
★★★ **I Ain't Begging Nobody (1987; Evidence, 1993)**
★★★★ **Sooner or Later (Bullseye Blues, 1992)**

The late Larry "Totsy" Davis (1936–1994) seems destined to be known as the composer of "Texas Flood," the song that launched Stevie Ray Vaughan's career. There's nothing inherently wrong with this—the song is, after all, a modern blues classic—but Davis's own recordings deserve considerably more attention than they've ever received. A gifted songwriter, he was also an effective and lyrical though not flashy lead guitarist, with a distinctly distorted tone, and one of blues' most emotive singers, capable of delivering a big soul ballad as well as anyone. *Sooner or Later* is his best, most consistent effort, but all of his soul-blues albums are quite good: "Giving Up on Love," from *I Ain't Begging Nobody,* is as fine a blues vocal performance as you'll hear anywhere. *Blues Knights* is top-notch but is a split album with Byther Smith, another criminally underknown bluesman, and thus contains only four Davis tracks. Davis's fine debut album, *Funny Stuff,* has yet to make it to CD. — A.P.

REV. GARY DAVIS

★★★★★ **Pure Religion and Bad Company (1957; Smithsonian Folkways, 1991)**
★★★★½ **Harlem Street Singer (1960; Original Blues Classics, 1992)**
★★★½ **Say No to the Devil (1961; Original Blues Classics, 1990)**
★★★★ **At Newport (Vanguard, 1967)**
★★★★ **O'Glory: The Apostolic Studio Sessions (1973; Genes, 1996)**
★★★ **Good Morning Blues (with Lead Belly and Dan Smith) (Biograph, 1990)**
★★★★ **Complete Recorded Works 1935–1949 (Document, 1991)**
★★★½ **From Blues to Gospel (Biograph, 1992)**
★★★★★ **Blues & Ragtime (Shanachie, 1993)**
★★★★★ **The Complete Early Recordings of Rev. Gary Davis (Yazoo, 1994)**

Born in Laurens County, South Carolina, Gary Davis (1896–1972) was equal parts musician and preacher. Blinded as a young boy by a physician's blunder, Davis became an accomplished musician by his early teens, playing banjo, harmonica and guitar. In the late '20s he moved to Durham, North Carolina, where he met and influenced Blind Boy Fuller, who recorded several songs he'd been taught by Davis. Davis claimed to have been ordained as a minister as early as 1933. His predilection for performing religious songs was strong—his first recording sessions in 1935 were marked by his refusal, after cutting two blues numbers, to perform any more of "the devil's music" for the rest of the session.

Regardless of the type of music Davis played, his great skill as a guitarist was comparable to that of Blind Lemon Jefferson, Blind Blake and Blind Willie Johnson. A "guitarist's guitarist" of the highest order, he influenced numerous contemporary players, including Ry Cooder, Stefan Grossman, Jerry Garcia and Jorma Kaukonen. Into his truly unique sound Davis incorporated many styles, from jazz and gospel to blues, ragtime and minstrel-show songs, resulting in impassioned, technically dazzling recordings. He had a rare ability to embellish guitar phrases with speedy, multinote clusters, and he frequently used melodic guitar lines to finish a vocal phrase, particularly in a song's refrain. Davis's scratchy vocals varied according to the type of material he performed: When doing blues, he spoke-sang the lyrics over interesting guitar arrangements; on religious numbers he fervently shouted the lyrics; on medicine-show songs he sang more melodically but never with the verve that characterized his gospel singing.

Davis's earliest recordings can be found on both *Complete Recorded Works 1935–1949* and *The Complete Early Recordings of Rev. Gary Davis.* Though the two albums have similar track listings, the Yazoo title has comprehensive liner notes and slightly better sound quality. The Document set presents the recordings in chronological order, capturing Davis's first two secular numbers ("I'm Throwin' Up My Hands" and "Cross and Evil Woman Blues") and his subsequent religious recordings. Some of Davis's most riveting material can be found on these albums, including "You Can Go Home," "I Am the True Vine" and "I Am the Light." Also among the many notable tracks are "Civil War March," recorded in New York City circa 1945, the tragic "Lord I Wish I Could See," cut on July 26, 1935, and "I Saw the Light," the only Davis recording to feature a voice other than his own. In this case, Bull City Red, a.k.a. George Washington, handled the vocal chores, while Davis provided brilliant backing on his National steel guitar. (He used the National for the 1935 sessions and a Gibson acoustic for the 1949 recordings.) Both sets include "I Can't Bear My Burden by Myself" and "Meet Me at the Station," from 1949.

There are also quite a few Davis recordings from the '50s and '60s, when the aging musician was rediscovered during the folk revival. On *Pure Religion and Bad Company,* every song was written, adapted or arranged by Davis. Recorded in June 1957 in New York City and originally issued only in the United Kingdom, it was Davis's third album. He infused every track with a resounding emotional wallop; highlights include the wordless Carolina blues "Mountain Jack," the dark, foreboding "Moon Goes Down" and the ragtime-inflected instrumental "Hesitation Blues," a perfect illustration of Davis's fluid fingerpicking style. Religious tracks include "Right Now," "Runnin' to the Judgment," "Time Is Drawing Near" and "Crucifixion."

At Newport, recorded at the folk festival in July 1965, documents Davis's throaty growl and virtuosity on 6- and 12-string guitar; his vocal performances are rawer and his guitar skills even more compelling than on earlier recordings. Davis runs through signature instrumentals like "Buck Dance" and "Twelve Sticks" and tackles the vocally wrenching "Samson and Delilah (If I Had My Way)" and "I Won't Be Back No More." Also riveting are Davis's remarkable versions of "Death Don't Have No Mercy" and "You Got to Move." Ironically, even on compositions that mine the depths of despair, Davis's unshakable faith in music and God shines through, offsetting each song's dark cloud with a silver lining.

Davis's two Bluesville albums still in print (on Original Blues Classics), *Harlem Street Singer* and *Say No to the Devil,* were recorded in New Jersey in 1960 and 1961 respectively, and both have a heavily spiritual feel, as virtually every song is religious in nature. *Say No to the Devil* features Davis's simmering, muted harmonica work on several songs, lending an aura of swampy mystery to tracks like "Hold On to God's Unchanging Hand" and "No One Can Do Me Like Jesus." In general, *Say No* has a more pessimistic, sedated sound than *Harlem Street Singer,* which benefits from stronger material such as the joyous "I Belong to the Band," the anthemic "I Am the Light of This World" and one of Davis's signature songs, "Twelve Gates to the City."

Good Morning Blues compiles recordings by Davis, Lead Belly and Dan Smith. Davis's five songs, cut on March 17, 1971 (less than a year before his death), include interesting versions of two Davis classics—a 12-string instrumental "Candy Man" and a rendition of "Hesitation Blues" with vocals. Other tracks cut by Davis at the same session can be heard on *From Blues to Gospel.* Here Davis played the 12-string exclusively, running through both secular and religious material, including the dirgelike "Eagle Rocking Blues," on which Davis, jilted by a lover, evokes a decidedly nonspiritual sentiment: "I'm gonna get drunk/Tell everything I know." Also found on this set are old favorites like "Cocaine Blues" and "Down by the River," which is the same song as "I Won't Be Back No More" but more introspective and subdued than the bursting-at-the-seams version found on *At Newport.*

A majority of Davis's nonsecular material shows up on *Blues & Ragtime.* The album showcases his ragtime guitar style, which is very regimented and uncompromising but never short of brilliant. The tracks were recorded at various locations between 1962 and 1966 and include extended treatments of "Hesitation Blues," "She's Funny That Way" and "Whistlin' Blues." The only religious track on the album is the gorgeous "Children of Zion." Another standout is the instrumental "Twelve Sticks," on which an audience can be heard to collectively gasp at the speed and clarity of some of Davis's guitar runs.
— B.R.H.

MILES DAVIS

★★★ **Bopping the Blues (1946; Black Lion, 1987)**
★★★★ **Dig (1951; Original Jazz Classics, 1991)**
★★★½ **Miles Davis and Horns (1953; Original Jazz Classics, 1989)**
★★★ **At Last! (with the Lighthouse All-Stars) (1953; Original Jazz Classics, 1985)**
★★★★ **Blue Haze (1954; Original Jazz Classics, 1988)**
★★★★ **Bags' Groove (1954; Original Jazz Classics, 1987)**

★★★★ Walkin' (1954; Original Jazz Classics, 1987)
★★★½ Musings of Miles (1955; Original Jazz Classics, 1988)
★★★★ The New Miles Davis Quintet (1955; Original Jazz Classics, 1982)
★★★★ Green Haze (1955; Prestige, 1976)
★★★½ Blue Moods (1955; Original Jazz Classics, 1990)
★★★★★ 'Round About Midnight (1955; Columbia, 1987)
★★★★★ Cookin' with the Miles Davis Quintet (1956; Original Jazz Classics, 1987)
★★★★★ Relaxin' with the Miles Davis Quintet (1956; Original Jazz Classics, 1987)
★★★★★ Workin' with the Miles Davis Quintet (1956; Original Jazz Classics, 1987)
★★★★½ Steamin' with the Miles Davis Quintet (1956; Original Jazz Classics, 1989)
★★★★★ Workin' and Steamin' (1956; Prestige, 1974)
★★★★★ Miles Davis (1956; Prestige, 1972)
★★★★ Miles Davis, Vol. 1 (1956; Blue Note, 1988)
★★★★½ Miles Davis, Vol. 2 (1956; Blue Note, 1990)
★★★★½ Miles Ahead (1957; Columbia, 1997)
★★★ Miles and Monk at Newport (1958; Columbia, 1994)
★★★★★ Porgy and Bess (1958; Columbia, 1987)
★★★★ '58 Sessions (1958; Columbia/Legacy, 1991)
★★★★ L'Ascenseur pour L'Echafaud (1958; Verve, 1989)
★★★★ Milestones (1958; Columbia, 1987)
★★★★★ Kind of Blue (1959; Columbia, 1987)
★★★½ Live in Stockholm (with Sonny Stitt) (1960; Secret, 1989)
★★★★★ Sketches of Spain (1960; Columbia, 1987)
★★★★ Someday My Prince Will Come (1961; Columbia, 1990)
★★★★ Friday Night at the Blackhawk (1961; Columbia, 1988)
★★★★ Saturday Night at the Blackhawk (1961; Columbia, 1988)
★★★★½ At Carnegie Hall (Columbia, 1961)
★★★★ Live Miles: More Music from the Legendary Carnegie Hall Concert (1961; Columbia, 1987)
★★½ Quiet Nights (1963; Columbia, 1997)
★★★★ Seven Steps to Heaven (1963; Columbia/Legacy, 1992)
★★★★ Miles Davis in Europe (Columbia, 1963)
★★★½ My Funny Valentine (Columbia, 1964)
★★★★ "Four" & More (Columbia, 1964)
★★★★ Miles in Tokyo (CBS Japan, 1964)
★★★★ Miles in Berlin (CBS Germany, 1964)
★★★★ Heard 'Round the World (1964; Columbia, 1983)
★★★★½ E.S.P. (1965; Columbia/Legacy, 1991)
★★★★★ The Complete Live at the Plugged Nickel (1965; Columbia, 1995)
★★★★ Highlights from the Plugged Nickel (1965; Columbia, 1995)
★★★½ Cookin' at the Plugged Nickel (1965; Columbia, 1987)
★★★★ Miles Smiles (1966; Columbia/Legacy, 1992)
★★★½ Sorcerer (1967; Columbia, 1993)
★★★★★ Nefertiti (1967; Columbia, 1990)
★★★½ Miles in the Sky (1968; Columbia, 1993)
★★★★½ Filles de Kilimanjaro (1968; Columbia, 1990)
★★★★★ In a Silent Way (1969; Columbia, 1987)
★★★★½ Greatest Hits (Columbia, 1969)
★★★★★ Bitches Brew (1969; Columbia, 1987)
★★★★★ A Tribute to Jack Johnson (1970; Columbia, 1992)
★★★★½ Live-Evil (1971; Columbia, 1997)
★★★½ On the Corner (1972; Columbia, 1993)
★★★★ Tallest Trees (Prestige, 1972)
★★★½ In Concert: Live at Philharmonic Hall (1972; Columbia/Legacy, 1997)
★★★★ Basic Miles: Classic Performances (Columbia, 1973)
★★★★½ Facets (Columbia, 1973)
★★★★ Get Up with It (Columbia, 1974)
★★★ Big Fun (Columbia, 1974)
★★★½ Water Babies (Columbia, 1976)
★★★★½ Agharta (1976; Columbia, 1991)
★★★★★ Pangaea (1976; Columbia, 1990)

★★★★ **Circle in the Round (1979; Columbia/Legacy, 1991)**
★★★★ **Directions (Columbia, 1981)**
★★★½ **The Man with the Horn (Columbia, 1981)**
★★★★ **We Want Miles (Columbia, 1982)**
★★★½ **Star People (Columbia, 1983)**
★★★★ **Decoy (Columbia, 1984)**
★★★★½ **Aura (1984; Columbia, 1989)**
★★★ **You're Under Arrest (Columbia, 1985)**
★★★★½ **Miles Davis and the Jazz Giants (Prestige, 1986)**
★★★★ **Tutu (Warner Bros., 1986)**
★★★★½ **Siesta (Warner Bros., 1987)**
★★★★½ **Collectors' Items (Prestige, 1987)**
★★★★★ **Miles Davis Chronicle: The Complete Prestige Recordings (Prestige, 1987)**
★★★★ **Ballads (Columbia, 1988)**
★★★★½ **The Columbia Years 1955–85 (Columbia, 1988)**
★★★½ **First Miles (Savoy, 1989)**
★★★★★ **Birth of the Cool (Capitol, 1989)**
★★★½ **Miles Davis and the Modern Jazz Giants (Original Jazz Classics, 1989)**
★★★ **Amandla (Warner Bros., 1989)**
★★★★ **Compact Jazz (Verve, 1989)**
★★★ **The Essence of Miles Davis (Columbia/Legacy, 1991)**
★★½ **Dingo (with Michel Legrand) (Warner Bros., 1991)**
★★★ **Doo Bop (Warner Bros., 1992)**
★★★★ **Live in Japan 1981 (Sony Japan, 1992)**
★★★★★ **Live at Montreux (Warner Bros., 1993)**
★★★★½ **The Blue Note and Capitol Recordings (Blue Note, 1993)**
★★★★ **1969 Miles: Festiva de Juan Pins (Sony Japan, 1993)**
★★★★ **Ballads and Blues (Blue Note, 1996)**
★★★★ **Bluing: Miles Davis Plays the Blues (Prestige, 1996)**
★★★★★ **Miles Davis and Gil Evans: The Complete Columbia Studio Recordings (Columbia, 1996)**
★★★★ **Live Around the World (Warner Bros. 1996)**
★★★ **At Fillmore: Live at Fillmore East (Columbia, 1997)**
★★★ **Black Beauty: Miles Davis Live at Fillmore West (Columbia, 1997)**
★★★½ **Dark Magus (Columbia, 1997)**
★★★★★ **The Miles Davis Quintet, 1965–68: The Complete Columbia Studio Recordings (Columbia/Legacy, 1998)**

Inarguably one of the most important jazz musicians who ever lived, Miles Davis (1926–1991) started out at the top and managed to stay there for the rest of his 46-year career. As a soloist, his ideas were startlingly original and his tone utterly unmistakable; as a leader, he often recognized talent well before anyone else, and he knew how to get the most out of almost any sideman.

But it was as a stylist that Davis had his greatest impact. Most jazzmen are lucky if they can be linked to even a single formal breakthrough; Davis can be credited with several. After the teenage trumpeter graduated from Charlie Parker's groundbreaking quintet, he turned bebop's frenetic virtuosity on its head with a series of small-group recordings introducing what came to be known as "cool" jazz. A few years later, he and his quintet had swapped cool's languid lyricism for a tougher, more intense sound and were acknowledged leaders in the hard-bop movement. Next came his embrace of modality, which shifted his improvisational emphasis from chord changes and harmonic structure to a scale-based approach that gave soloists a whole new musical vocabulary. Then, after being among the first to incorporate electric instruments in a jazz rhythm section, he abandoned the music's traditional dependence on swing and began working with rock- and funk-based rhythms, in the process setting the groundwork for such fusion bands as Weather Report, Return to Forever and the Mahavishnu Orchestra.

Davis, like most jazzmen, began his career as a sideman and had played in Billy Eckstine's big band and Charlie Parker's quintet before making his recording debut in 1945 with saxophonist Herbie Fields, a session that would have been quickly forgotten had Davis not become so famous later. Those tunes are included on *First Miles,* along with the first recordings actually issued under Davis's own name. Cut with Parker and a rhythm section featuring John Lewis and Max Roach, it follows the basic form of straight bebop, but the young trumpeter's voice can already be heard in its adventurous writing and measured phrasing. It's far preferable to *Bopping the Blues,* a sideman date finding Davis blowing blues obbligati behind singers Earl Coleman and Ann Baker.

Still, the sessions that made Davis's

reputation as a leader are the ones collected under the title *Birth of the Cool.* Using either an octet or nonet, Davis and arranger Gil Evans generate a sound that conveys the coloristic range of a big band while maintaining a chamber-music sense of dynamics; moreover, because the playing manages to employ all the harmonic sophistication of bebop while trading its instrumental flash for more leisurely, contemplative soloing, it produced jazz that was far closer to the depth and consideration of art music than anything that had gone before. And though these recordings hardly stand as a commercial breakthrough, their influence is incalculable, as groups ranging from the Modern Jazz Quartet to the Gerry Mulligan/Chet Baker quartet to the Stan Kenton Orchestra all learned from them.

Ironically, the Davis nonet existed only for the *Cool* project, which, like most of his early-'50s output, was the product of one-off recording sessions. The same is true of the boppish Blue Note dates compiled as *Miles Davis, Vol. 1* and *Vol. 2* and the deliciously unconventional *Blue Haze,* recorded with Charles Mingus for Debut. Even Davis's work for Prestige, the label for which he most frequently recorded during this period, was varied and episodic. Admittedly, that had its advantages, as a session with Thelonious Monk (included, variously, on *Bags' Groove, Tallest Trees* and *Miles Davis and the Jazz Giants*) makes plain. *Chronicle* traces Davis's days with Prestige admirably, including all his sessions as a leader as well as four tunes recorded under Lee Konitz's name, and is a boon to anyone who wants a comprehensive overview of the period without having to endure the inevitable redundancies caused by 30 years of repackaging.

Those interested only in the highlights, however, should skip ahead to 1955, when Davis introduces saxophonist John Coltrane into his hard-bop quintet. Although Coltrane's contributions are relatively low-key on *The New Miles Davis Quintet*, his aggressive, questing solos offer a dynamic contrast to the acerbic economy of Davis's playing. Add in the wry elegance of the rhythm section (Red Garland, Paul Chambers and the incomparable Philly Joe Jones), and these albums—*Cookin' with the Miles Davis Quintet, Relaxin' . . . , Workin' . . .* and *Steamin' . . .* (which also are collected on the twofers *Miles Davis* and *Workin' and Steamin'*)—constitute the best of his work for that label.

This version of the quintet followed Davis when he moved to Columbia Records and can be heard on the lovely *'Round About Midnight.* But the album that truly introduces Davis's Columbia period is *Miles Ahead,* which features a large ensemble under the direction of Davis's old *Birth of the Cool* collaborator, Gil Evans. Theirs is an uncommonly sympathetic pairing, for Evans's coloristic approach to arranging brings out the best in Davis's dark, warm tone (particularly when the trumpeter switched to flügelhorn), while Evans's inventive voicings seem to inspire Davis to ever more brilliant improvisations. Together they produced material for a half dozen albums, and apart from the halfhearted bossa nova of *Quiet Nights,* it's uniformly excellent. *Porgy and Bess,* a setting of selections from the Gershwin opera, was particularly popular in its time, but their masterwork is undoubtedly *Sketches of Spain,* a recording of unparalleled grace and lyricism. (A concert rendition of its "Concierto de Aranjuez" appears on *Live Miles.*) *The Complete Columbia Studio Recordings* augments the original albums with exquisite outtakes, plus enough rehearsal material to appreciate just how exacting Evans could be.

Davis continued his small-group work, of course, adding alto saxophonist Cannonball Adderley on *Milestones* and the Miles side of *Miles and Monk at Newport* and replacing Garland and Jones with, respectively, pianist Bill Evans and drummer James Cobb for *'58 Sessions.* (Davis also appears as a sideman on Adderley's *Somethin' Else* at this time.) Good as these albums are, they're minor work compared to *Kind of Blue.* This is where Davis introduces the concept of modal improvisation, in which the soloist works from a predetermined set of scales instead of extrapolating a line off a song's chord changes; but it isn't the theoretical breakthrough that makes this worth hearing—it's the charged spontaneity of the performances that makes the album so continually rewarding. Even after a thousand replays, this music remains startlingly vital.

John Coltrane would spend the rest of his life refining the concepts introduced on that album, but he'd do it without Davis's help; the swinging and incisive *Someday My Prince Will Come* is his last album with the trumpeter, as Hank Mobley is added on tenor at that point (and is the only saxophonist on the two *In Person* albums). In addition to George Coleman, yet another new tenor man, *Seven Steps to Heaven* introduces what is widely considered to be Davis's greatest rhythm section ever: pianist

Herbie Hancock, bassist Ron Carter and drummer Tony Williams. Although much younger than Davis's previous cohorts (Hancock was 23, Carter 25 and Williams just 17), this trio plays with astonishing energy and insight, and the sheer physicality of their live work—as heard on *Miles in Europe*, *My Funny Valentine* and *"Four" & More*—is breathtaking.

Coleman's input is somewhat more irregular, although his best work (as on much of *"Four" & More,* his last album with the group) recalls the fire of Coltrane. Saxophonist Sam Rivers adds an interesting twist to *Live in Tokyo,* but it's not until Art Blakey alumnus Wayne Shorter joins, on *Live in Berlin,* that Davis finds a saxophonist whose harmonic imagination matches his own. (Both the Tokyo and Berlin dates have been collected on *Heard 'Round the World.*) *Live at the Plugged Nickel* shows how Shorter fits into the format established with Coleman, though *The Complete Live at the Plugged Nickel*—which spreads two full nights of music over eight CDs—offers an excellent picture of how he and the others were more than happy to push those boundaries. From there, the music grows ever more daring, from the angularity of *E.S.P.* through the moody eloquence of *Nefertiti,* until it seems to tug at the very seams of mainstream jazz.

For Davis, however, those albums marked the end of an era, for with *Miles in the Sky* and *Filles de Kilimanjaro,* he begins to move away from swing-based rhythms and toward the electric, backbeat-driven sound of rock and funk. He wasn't entirely a pioneer in this regard, as Williams had already been toying with rock rhythms in his own group, Lifetime. Nor was this as radical a departure as it seemed at the time. Perhaps the greatest revelation to be found in *The Miles Davis Quintet, 1965–68: The Complete Studio Recordings* is how naturally some of the rock-inflected ideas of *Miles in the Sky* and *Filles de Kilimanjaro* emerged from the ostinato-based compositions found on *E.S.P.* and *Nefertiti.* In that respect, the biggest initial change was instrumentation.

But as Davis expanded on those rock influences, diving deeper into the rhythms while maintaining the same sort of harmonic complexity he'd long been using, he began to shape an entirely new sound. *In a Silent Way* is a step beyond the quintet approach of *Filles de Kilimanjaro,* relying on more amplification, a larger ensemble (including guitarist John McLaughlin, on loan from Williams's Lifetime, and keyboardists Joe Zawinul and Chick Corea) and a rambling, riff-based approach to composition. It was quite a departure; only the album's relative quiet kept jazz purists from considering it complete apostasy on Davis's part.

There was no ignoring the implications of *Bitches Brew,* however. Where *In a Silent Way* merely flirts with funk, *Bitches Brew* openly courts its rhythmic insistence; naturally, the jazz community was in an uproar over the album. Yet this is by no means a pop record, for Davis's compositions remained harmonically challenging, while his ensemble (which augmented the electric guitar, keyboards and Fender bass with soprano sax and bass clarinet) seems to have been assembled mostly for its coloristic range. A better view of what Davis's working band sounded like at that time can be found on the more conventional *1969 Miles: Festiva de Juan Pins.* Even so, the die was cast, and Davis's subsequent albums draw more and more obviously from rock reference points, from the bluesy guitar of *Jack Johnson* to the spacey, Sly Stone–style funk of *On the Corner.*

It wasn't just the sound of the music that had changed. Davis had also taken a cue from rock's approach to record making, and began to assemble his albums from cleverly spliced snippets instead of whole performances; the results could be jarringly kaleidoscopic, but nonetheless these releases included their share of gems, like the Keith Jarrett electric-piano solo in "Funky Tonk" (from *Live-Evil*) or Pete Cosey's searing guitar solo in "Maiysha" (from *Get Up with It*). Any doubts about Davis's vision as a leader were quickly quelled by *Agharta* and *Pangaea,* two live albums culled from a single day's performance in Osaka, Japan. Alternately audacious, poetic, hypnotic and abrasive, these albums (particularly *Pangaea*) captured the risk-taking genius of Davis's band in riveting detail and have worn better over time than any of his '70s albums.

They were also his last recordings of the decade, thanks to an auto accident that sent him on a downward spiral of ill health and chemical dependence. Not that his absence kept Columbia from releasing new albums, as the vault-scrounging *Circle in the Round* and *Directions* make plain. Nor was his return to action, in the form of *The Man with the Horn,* much cause for hope, inasmuch as it relies overmuch on hackneyed attempts at commerciality like the title tune. Still, Davis soon found his footing;

the live *We Want Miles* is a considerable improvement, and thanks to his unfailing taste in bright young sidemen, Davis's output through *You're Under Arrest* is solid and consistent. Still, only *Aura*—an adventurous big-band suite conceived by Danish jazzman Palle Mikkelborg—offers anything in the way of revelation.

Davis left Columbia for Warner Bros. in 1985; Columbia's response (or was it revenge?) was to issue *The Columbia Years,* a 30-year retrospective that culls most of the obvious highlights but shortchanges both Davis's electric period and his Evans albums. *Tutu,* his first Warner album, is a one-on-one pairing with producer/multi-instrumentalist Marcus Miller (who played bass in Davis's comeback band); it's good, but not as impressive as their second outing, a soundtrack album called *Siesta* that marvelously updates the Iberian groove of *Sketches of Spain.* Davis's other Warner soundtrack, *Dingo,* released shortly after his death, is also intriguing—in part because it includes his first attempts in 23 years at traditional, bop-derived jazz, but mostly because the film's plot features Davis as a jazz legend who inspires a young trumpeter, whose part, musically, was played by Chuck Findley (there's as much Findley on the album as there is Davis). Davis didn't entirely swear off contemporary music, as the rap-oriented *Doo-Bop* found him trying to show he was hep to hip-hop, but its lack of first-class rappers greatly weakens the album. *Live at Montreux,* however, finds him playing the old Gil Evans charts with Quincy Jones conducting; although hardly an improvement on the originals, it was obviously a heartfelt performance and an appropriate coda to his career. — J.D.C.

RICHARD DAVIS

★★★ Now's the Time (1973; Muse, 1989)
★★★ Persia My Dear (with Roland Hanna and Frederick Waits) (DIW, 1987)
★★★ One for Frederick (Hep, 1989)
★★★ Live at Sweet Basil (Evidence, 1994)

Richard Davis (b. 1930) is one of the most important of the bassists who helped extend the instrument's role during the early '60s. His Blue Note work with Andrew Hill, Bobby Hutcherson and Joe Henderson is simply breathtaking. Breaking up time, making use of double stops and daring runs, all the while retaining an authentic grainy tone, Davis simultaneously calls attention to himself and remains eminently supportive. In addition to his jazz work, he distinguished himself with a magnificent performance on Van Morrison's epochal *Astral Weeks* album.

Davis's own *Now's the Time* is a marathon blowing session with Clifford Jordan and Marvin "Hannibal" Peterson; *Live at Sweet Basil* features Ricky Ford and Cecil Bridgewater for additional intense playing. *Persia My Dear,* a trio session co-led by pianist Roland Hanna and drummer Frederick Waits, captures Davis in typically fine form. — S.F.

JIMMY DAWKINS

★★★★½ Fast Fingers (Delmark, 1969)
★★★★ All for Business (1971; Delmark, 1990)
★★★½ Hot Wire 81 (1981; Evidence, 1994)
★★★ Kant Sheck Dees Bluze (Earwig, 1991)
★★★½ Tribute to Orange (Evidence, 1993)
★★½ Blues and Pain (Wild Dog Blues, 1994)
★★½ B Phur Real (Wild Dog Blues, 1995)
★★★½ Blues from Iceland (Evidence, 1995)

Guitarist Jimmy Dawkins, born in 1936 in Tchula, Mississippi, was inspired at an early age by Guitar Slim and Smiley Lewis. Moving to Chicago in 1955, he forged alliances with the likes of Otis Rush and Magic Sam, helping to create the influential West Side sound.

Dawkins began recording as a solo artist in 1969, cutting the seminal *Fast Fingers* for Delmark. In 1971 that record was awarded the Grand Prix du Disque de Jazz by the Hot Club of France, and Dawkins was on his way to becoming an international blues sensation. *All for Business* features Rush on guitar and the vocals of Andrew "Big Voice" Odom, who had previously sung on several Earl Hooker recordings. Highlights include the saxophone-spiked (courtesy of reedman Jim Conley) "Moon Man" and a steaming, instrumental version of "Sweet Home Chicago."

Hot Wire 81 features Dawkins leading a quartet consisting of second guitar, bass and drums. Rereleased by Evidence after being previously available only on France's Isabel label, the album benefits from its spontaneity: Recorded in Paris in 1981 with no rehearsal, such songs as the up-tempo "Peeper's Music" and "My Way" illustrate Dawkins's string-bending best. The linear "Roc-Kin-Sole" strongly recalls John Lee Hooker, while the low-down, slow blues "Welfare Line" relates an eight-minute tale of poverty. *Kant Sheck Dees Bluze* features Dawkins flanked by such great musicians as pianist "Professor" Eddie Lusk, bassist Johnny B. Gayden and vocalist Nora Jean Wallace, who sings on two tracks, the soulful, melodic "A Love Like That" and the slow scorcher "My Man Loves Me."

Another fine Evidence reissue, *Tribute to Orange* combines tracks from two Dawkins recording sessions in France—one in 1971 and the other three years later. The album's first eight cuts feature Dawkins in cahoots with Clarence "Gatemouth" Brown and New Orleans pianist Cousin Joe. A highlight is "You've Got to Keep On Trying," which originally appeared on Dawkins's debut. The album's last five tracks reprise the Dawkins half of an LP he shared with Big Voice Odom, featuring the guitarist backed by Otis Rush, organist Jerome Van Jones, bassist James Green and drummer Robert Plunkett. Notable are "It Serves You Right to Suffer" (an adaptation of Percy Mayfield's "Memory Pain") and the album's only cover song, an instrumental take on Bobby Gentry's "Ode to Billy Joe."

The two Wild Dog Blues albums find Dawkins up to his same tricks, singing the blues and playing his heart out. *B Phur Real* features a horn section, adding pizzazz to the arrangements. While the playing is right on, the songs are unspectacular. *Blues from Iceland* documents three nights of Dawkins performances in 1991 at the Púlsinn Music Club in Reykjavík. Backed by a cast of Icelandic musicians, including Gudmundur Pétursson and "Blue Ice" Bragason on guitars, Dawkins runs through songs like Willie Cobbs's "You Don't Love Me," J.B. Hutto's "Too Much Alcohol," Sonny Boy Williamson (Rice Miller)'s "Help Me" and Willie Nelson's "Nightlife." — B.R.H.

BLOSSOM DEARIE

★★★½ **Give Him the Ooh La La (1957; Verve, 1998)**
★★★½ **Once upon a Summertime (1958; Verve, 1992)**
★★★½ **May I Come In? (1964; Capitol, 1984)**
★★★ **Blossom Dearie Sings (Daffodil, 1974)**
★★★ **Blossom Dearie (Daffodil, 1975)**
★★★ **My New Celebrity Is You (Daffodil, 1976)**
★★★½ **Winchester in Apple Blossom Time (Daffodil, 1977)**
★★★ **Needlepoint Magic (Daffodil, 1979)**
★★★ **Et Tu Bruce (Daffodil, 1984)**
★★★ **Songs of Chelsea (Daffodil, 1988)**
★★★★ **Blossom Dearie (Verve, 1989)**
★★★ **Tweedledum and Tweedledee (Daffodil, 1991)**
★★★★ **Verve Jazz Masters 51 (Verve, 1996)**

Singer Blossom Dearie (b. 1926) began performing in New York in the 1940s with Woody Herman and Alvino Rey before moving to Paris in 1952, where she and Annie Ross formed a vocal group called the Blue Stars, which evolved into the Swingle Singers. She returned to the United States later in the '50s as the leader of nightclub trios, now featuring her rhythmically inventive piano playing and light, witty vocals. The eponymous Verve set, placing Dearie in the sympathetic hands of bassist Ray Brown and drummer Jo Jones, documents this part of her career well. *Once upon a Summertime,* recorded in 1958, includes guitarist Mundell Lowe and quirky covers of "Tea for Two" and "If I Were a Bell."

Despite building a pop cult following in the 1960s behind such novelty tunes as "Peel Me a Grape," "I'm Hip," "Sweet Georgie Fame" and "Hey John" (written for John Lennon), Dearie found herself without a recording contract in the 1970s and began issuing recordings on her own Daffodil label. Highlights of this work include *Blossom Dearie*; *Winchester in Apple Blossom Time,* a collection of great ballad readings; the live *Needlepoint Magic* and *Et Tu Bruce;* and *Tweedledum and Tweedledee,* with musical director Mike Renzi. — J.S.

JOEY DEFRANCESCO

★★ **All of Me (Columbia, 1989)**
★★★½ **Where Were You (Columbia, 1990)**
★★ **Part III (Columbia, 1991)**
★★ **Reboppin' (Columbia, 1992)**
★★★ **Live at the Five Spot (Columbia, 1993)**
★★ **All About My Girl (Muse, 1994)**
★★★ **The Street of Dreams (Big Mo, 1995)**
★★ **It's About Time (with Jack McDuff) (Concord Jazz, 1996)**

A picture in the insert of *It's About Time* speaks volumes. Jack McDuff sits at an organ, on his lap a chubby 10-year-old with a pageboy haircut. In the intervening years, that boy, Joey DeFrancesco (b. 1971), has carved his own niche as a jazz organ player while remaining McDuff's acolyte. He placed third in the first Thelonious Monk Competition, toured Europe with Miles Davis and played keyboards on "Cobra," from Davis's *Amandla,* all before he turned 20.

Though DeFrancesco's debut album, *All of Me,* suffers from callow choices of material ("Close to You") and overblown arrangements, his next, the all-star extravaganza *Where Were You,* is a vast improvement. Recorded at the renowned Van Gelder studios, the session features guest appearances by Milt Hinton, Kirk Whalum, John Scofield and Illinois Jacquet. Presented as a young artist among his new peers, DeFrancesco holds his own, but the big-band-and-organ tracks do get bogged down at points. DeFrancesco is at his best on the bouncy "Red Top."

Part III features almost exclusively DeFrancesco's touring band, which suits him well. He works in a trio with drummer Byron Landham and guitarist Paul Bollenback, and as part of a quintet, adding trumpeter Jim Henry and tenor saxophonist Glenn Guidone. Though producing the record himself may have been ill-advised, it does allow DeFrancesco the leeway to work out on both piano and trumpet.

Reboppin' ranges from an introspective reading of John Coltrane's "Naima" to a swinging version of "Someday My Prince Will Come," offering Bollenback many moments in which to shine, both compositionally and with a new sense of confidence in his playing. The set also features the appropriately titled "Family Jam," on which DeFrancesco's father and brother join the act. *Live at the Five Spot* showcases DeFrancesco with his on-again off-again saxophone player Robert Landham. Grover Washington Jr., several players from *Where Were You* and DeFrancesco's regular band join in on the set of standards. DeFrancesco's musical maturation is evident in the scope of the tunes he chooses to cover, from Sonny Stitt's ethereal "The Eternal One" and Coltrane's sophisticated "Impressions" to the perennials "All of Me" and "Moonlight in Vermont." Washington has them rocking in the aisles through "Work Song," while Jacquet turns in a velvety "Embraceable You."

DeFrancesco's collaboration with Houston Person, *All About My Girl,* is not as successful. There is a pretty version of "When Sonny Gets Blue," but the only thing that generates the kind of soul both players are capable of is the saxless take of Charlie Parker's "Donna Lee." *Street of Dreams* finds the trio (with an occasional large horn section) concentrating again on covers, with the exception of one Bollenback composition. More important, it expands DeFrancesco's horizons in several ways. In addition to playing piano, organ and trumpet, he also exhibits a penchant for Frank Sinatra–influenced singing. Horace Ott's big-band charts shine, and DeFrancesco displays far more spirit than he did with Person.

On *It's About Time,* old master McDuff and his upstart protégé face off in an hourlong cutathon. When the two organists trade licks on "Pork Chops and Pasta," it's tough to pinpoint who's who. — H.B.

ALEX DE GRASSI

★★★ **Turning: Turning Back (Windham Hill, 1978)**
★★★ **Slow Circle (Windham Hill, 1979)**
★★★ **Clockwork (Windham Hill, 1981)**
★★★ **Southern Exposure (Windham Hill, 1983)**
★★★ **Deep at Night (Windham Hill, 1991)**
★★★★ **Windham Hill Retrospective (Windham Hill, 1992)**
★★★ **The World's Getting Loud (Windham Hill, 1993)**

Alex de Grassi (b. 1952) is a talented guitarist who combines jazz theory and composition with folk and classical playing techniques for a smooth, fluid sound characteristic of the Windham Hill style of chamber jazz, meticulously performed and recorded. His approach anticipated much of the New Age music style, but his playing never glosses into the emotional vapidity that has been the downfall of New Age in its guise as musical Prozac. — J.S.

JACK DEJOHNETTE

★★½ **The DeJohnette Complex (1968; Original Jazz Classics, 1991)**
★★★½ **Ruta and Daitya (with Keith Jarrett) (1973; ECM, 1993)**
★★★★½ **Timeless (with John Abercrombie and Jan Hammer) (ECM, 1974)**
★★★ **Sorcery (1974; Original Jazz Classics, 1994)**
★★★★ **New Directions (1978; ECM, 1992)**

★★★★ **Special Edition (ECM, 1979)**
★★★★ **New Directions in Europe (1980; ECM, 1988)**
★★★★★ **Album Album (ECM, 1984)**
★★★ **The Jack DeJohnette Piano Album (Landmark, 1985)**
★★★ **Parallel Realities (MCA, 1990)**
★★★★ **Music for the Fifth World (Blue Note, 1992)**
★★★½ **Extra Special Edition (Blue Note, 1995)**
★★★★ **Dancing with Nature Spirits (ECM, 1996)**
★★★★ **Oneness (ECM, 1998)**

Drummer/percussionist Jack DeJohnette (b. 1942) first came to widespread public attention as part of Charles Lloyd's late-1960s quartet and then worked with Miles Davis's groundbreaking early-'70s band. His eclectic style was perfectly suited to the myriad turns that characterized fusion, and his earliest solo albums show off his forceful, R&B–influenced side. Guitarist John Abercrombie's big-voiced, propulsive playing provides an exciting counterpoint to DeJohnette's fast-handed attack.

The ECM albums show DeJohnette moving away from the power style and overkill of virtually all late-'70s fusion drumming; instead, he explored increasingly subtle textures, while never quite neglecting his hypnotic propulsion reminiscent of Tony Williams in one of the classic Miles Davis Quintet lineups. Abercrombie appears on the now out-of-print *Untitled* and *New Rags* and the brilliant *New Directions* and *New Directions in Europe* (with trumpeter Lester Bowie and bassist Eddie Gomez).

In the early '80s DeJohnette formed the spectacular acoustic band Special Edition. The sublime quartet session *Special Edition* pits David Murray's tenor saxophone and bass clarinet against Arthur Blythe's alto, with DeJohnette and bassist Peter Warren offering inspired accompaniment. The out-of-print *Tin Can Alley* and *Inflation Blues* don't match *Special Edition*'s intensity, but *Album Album,* with its front line of Murray, John Purcell and Howard Johnson, surpasses it. *The Jack DeJohnette Piano Album* showcases DeJohnette on his second instrument.

DeJohnette continued to experiment with musical textures into the 1990s, with the excellent but unavailable *Earth Walk*; *Parallel Realities,* which includes Herbie Hancock and Pat Metheny; *Music for the Fifth World,* with guitarists John Scofield and Vernon Reid; *Extra Special Edition,* featuring vocalist Bobby McFerrin; *Dancing with Nature Spirits,* with Steve Gorn on flute, soprano saxophone and clarinet and Michael Cain on keyboards; and *Oneness,* with Cain, Jerome Harris on guitar and Don Alias on percussion. — J.S.

PETER DELANO

★★★ **Peter Delano (Verve, 1993)**
★★★★ **Bite of the Apple (Verve, 1994)**

The rapid emergence of pianist Peter Delano (b. 1976) on the major-league jazz scene in his native New York can be attributed as much to fascination with his youth as to his obvious sheer talent and solid musical contributions. A strong improviser and composer, he writes material that is wide-ranging in style and approach, yet he almost disappeared after these two recordings.

His eponymous debut, made when he was 16, teams Delano with trumpeter Tim Hagans, saxophonists Gary Bartz and Michael Brecker and an equally strong rhythm section. All but three tunes are Delano originals. His solo version of Benny Golson's "I Remember Clifford" and a duet with Brecker on "Reminiscence" show the depth of his Keith Jarrett–like improvisational skills.

Bite of the Apple focuses on Delano's imprint as writer and player. The session employs five combinations of established players—including Bartz, Hagans, tenor saxophonists Chris Potter and Craig Handy, vibist Joe Locke and bassist Gary Peacock—to cover a range of original material arranged by Delano with Bob Belden. The constant shift in personnel is not a distraction on this recording; rather, it provides some stylistic variation for the listener. — K.F.

THE PAUL DELAY BAND

★★★½ **Take It from the Turnaround . . . (Evidence, 1996)**
★★★★ **Ocean of Tears (Evidence, 1996)**
★★★★ **Nice & Strong (Evidence, 1998)**

Harmonica master Paul deLay (b. 1952) has been a fixture on the Portland, Oregon, blues scene since the early 1970s. His strikingly original chromatic harmonica work is his calling card, but a near-fatal cocaine habit and a prison sentence for dealing gave deLay compelling subject matter for some exceptional songwriting.

The Paul deLay Band recorded several independent albums of cover material during the

1980s. *Take It from the Turnaround . . .* is a compilation from two albums recorded between the time deLay was busted and his incarceration. *Ocean of Tears,* recorded after his release, is a classic blues album informed by the sense of being overcome by doom yet redeemed by the life-affirming message in the music. The band continues in this vein on *Nice & Strong,* with deLay's harmonica playing as exciting as ever and the stalwart group accompanying him with fervor. — J.S.

EUMIR DEODATO

★★ **Prelude (1972; Sony, 1997)**
★★ **Live at the Felt Forum (1973; Sony, 1989)**

Composer, arranger and keyboardist Eumir de Almeida Deodato (b. 1942) was one of Brazil's top arrangers in the late 1960s before moving to the United States to write arrangements for Frank Sinatra, Aretha Franklin, Bette Midler, Roberta Flack, Björk and others, as well as doing soundtrack work. His thick, busy disco-jazz arrangements made him a natural for dance-oriented music, and he scored a huge success with his 1973 arrangement of "2001 (Also Sprach Zarathustra)," which earned him two Grammys and the somewhat dubious distinction of being named a top jazz artist by *Billboard* and *Playboy.* His dated, over-the-top style has gone the way of coke spoons. — J.S.

DEREK AND THE DOMINOS

★★★★★ **Layla and Other Assorted Love Songs (RSO, 1970)**
★★★½ **In Concert (RSO, 1973)**
★★★½ **The Layla Sessions/20th Anniversary Edition (Polydor, 1990)**
★★★★ **Live at the Fillmore (Polydor, 1994)**

An astonishing evocation of unrequited love, "Layla" is almost as celebrated for its real-life circumstances as for its emotionally involving sound. Written for the most part by Eric Clapton (b. 1945) and inspired by the classical Persian love poem "The Story of Layla and Majnun," the song sprang from a love triangle between Clapton, his best friend (George Harrison) and the best friend's wife (Pattie Boyd). Heavy stuff, to be sure; indeed, Clapton later admitted that "being Derek was a cover for the fact that I was trying to steal someone else's wife." Of course, everyone knew Derek was Eric, just as they knew that the Dominos were the rhythm section Clapton had picked up through his association with Delaney and Bonnie. But it was just as obvious that the pain and longing expressed in the single was real, and that genuine show of emotion puts an edge on Clapton's vocals and fire in his guitar playing, helping his churning rhythm work throw sparks against the tart counterpoint of Duane Allman's slide. But it's Jim Gordon's stately, pastoral piano figure that has the final word, adding an air of hope and transcendence that seems almost to answer the pleas of the opening verses. Rarely do love songs provide such a sense of redemption.

That isn't the only place such anguish comes across on *Layla and Other Assorted Love Songs*—"Have You Ever Loved a Woman" and "Why Does Love Got to Be So Sad" spring to mind—but the album isn't just an exploration of love denied. Instead, *Layla* is ultimately about the transformation of the blues. "Bell Bottom Blues," for instance, distills the pop-blues approach of Blind Faith and Cream; "Tell the Truth" brings to fruition the white-soul groove Clapton mastered with Delaney and Bonnie, while the exquisitely arranged "Little Wing" pulls a pathos from the song that even Hendrix missed.

As with any masterpiece, it wasn't easy achieving such clarity of vision, and anyone wishing to hear just how much mediocre music had to be thrown away in making the album need only listen through the almost two and a quarter hours of outtakes and jam sessions included in *The Layla Sessions.* Although this 20th-anniversary–issue boxed set will doubtless be of interest to guitar fiends (thanks to more than an hour's worth of Clapton/Allman jams) and Clapton collectors, the sheer volume of material seems almost to lessen the original album's achievement. *In Concert* at least has the advantage of a slightly different set list, including Blind Faith's "Presence of the Lord" and three songs from Clapton's first solo album, but you're better off with *Live at the Fillmore,* which augments the *In Concert* lineup with five additional performances from the same shows, including "Little Wing" and an illuminating take on "Crossroads." — J.D.C.

PAUL DESMOND

★★★★ **East of the Sun (1959; Discovery, N.A.)**
★★★½ **Two of a Mind (1962; Victor Jazz, 1996)**
★★★½ **Take Ten (1963; RCA Bluebird, 1993)**

★★★★ **Paul Desmond & the Modern Jazz Quartet (1972; Red Baron, 1993)**
★★★ **Skylark (1974; CTI, 1988)**
★★★ **Pure Desmond (1975; CTI, 1987)**
★★★★ **Like Someone in Love (1975; Telarc, 1992)**
★★★ **Late Lament (RCA Bluebird, 1987)**
★★★★ **Easy Living (RCA Bluebird, 1990)**
★★★ **The Best of Paul Desmond (Legacy, 1990)**
★★½ **Paul Desmond Quintet and Voices (Original Jazz Classics, 1992)**
★★★★ **Polka Dots and Moonbeams (RCA Bluebird, 1992)**

Alto saxophonist Paul Desmond (1924–1977) was a mainstay of the West Coast "cool" jazz style epitomized by his collaboration with Dave Brubeck in Brubeck's groundbreaking quartet. Desmond's trademark, slyly melodic approach explores the high harmonics of the alto, a virtual definition of the cool-jazz sound. Most of Desmond's contributions to jazz came via the Brubeck quartet, but his own recordings add color and substance to the scope of his work.

East of the Sun is a sublime collaboration with the like-minded guitarist Jim Hall and the rhythm section from the Modern Jazz Quartet, bassist Percy Heath and drummer Connie Kay. *Two of a Mind* pairs Desmond with saxophonist Gerry Mulligan on sessions with drummer Connie Kay or Mel Lewis. *Take Ten* features him with Hall and Kay again. *Easy Living* collects tracks recorded between 1963 and '65 with Hall, Kay and various bassists; *Polka Dots and Moonbeams* covers most of the same material.

Desmond fits the MJQ's chamber-jazz approach hand in glove on *Paul Desmond & the Modern Jazz Quartet.* He began working with producer Creed Taylor in the 1960s; those records are no longer in print, but Desmond's later work with Taylor at CTI remains available. *Skylark* features guitarist Gabor Szabo, bassist Ron Carter and drummer Jack DeJohnette. Guitarist Ed Bickert joins Carter and Kay behind Desmond on *Pure Desmond.*

Desmond's epitaph is a marvelous live recording from Toronto's Bourbon Street jazz club, reissued as *Like Someone in Love,* a quartet session with Bickert, bassist Don Thompson and drummer Jerry Fuller. — J.S.

DETROIT JUNIOR

★★★★ **Turn Up the Heat (Blue Suit, 1996)**

Pianist Detroit Junior (b. Emery Williams Jr., 1932) worked behind John Lee Hooker, Amos Milburn, Roscoe Gordon and Eddie Boyd but is probably best known for his work with Howlin' Wolf and with Wolf's band after the singer's death in 1971. Williams got his name when, unbeknownst to him, Beat Baby Records pressed his first single ("Money Tree," 1960) and affixed the new name to the label. It was chosen because he was from Detroit (although he'd moved to Chicago in 1956) and he was a "junior." It was a surprise when he heard it on a jukebox, and he said, "You've got somebody else's name on my tune!"

Turn Up the Heat finds him stepping out front, backed by a superb combo including guitarist Maurice John Vaughn, trombonist B.J. Emery and bassist Freddie Dixon (Willie's son). The entire band and, indeed, the entire sound of the album falls in line behind Junior's gravelly voice and boogie-woogie piano; it sounds like a mid-1960s urban-blues classic, without the self-consciousness or glaring anachronisms of re-creators. He serves up pure, low-down and rootsy blues, without a hint of rock or funk. Ten of the 12 songs are first-rate originals; covers of "Killing Floor" and "Bad Bad Whiskey" are given respectful treatment, with Junior accompanying himself on piano. — J.Z.

AL DI MEOLA

★★★ **Land of the Midnight Sun (Columbia, 1976)**
★★★ **Elegant Gypsy (Columbia, 1977)**
★★★½ **Casino (1978; Columbia/Legacy, 1992)**
★★★★ **Friday Night in San Francisco (1980; Columbia/Legacy, 1993)**
★★★★ **Splendido Hotel (1980; Columbia/Legacy, 1990)**
★★★★ **Electric Rendezvous (1982; Columbia/Legacy, 1986)**
★★★ **Tour de Force (Columbia, 1982)**
★★★★ **Scenario (Columbia, 1983)**
★★★ **Soaring Through a Dream (1985; EMI Manhattan, 1993)**
★★★★ **Kiss My Axe (Mesa Bluemoon, 1991)**
★★★★ **World Sinfonia (Mesa Bluemoon, 1991)**
★★★ **The Best of Al Di Meola (Blue Note, 1992)**
★★★ **Heart of the Immigrants (Mesa Bluemoon, 1993)**

★★★★ **The Essence of Al Di Meola (Columbia/Legacy, 1994)**
★★★ **Orange and Blue (Mesa Bluemoon, 1994)**
★★★★ **Acoustic Anthology (One Way, 1995)**
★★★★ **Electric Anthology (One Way, 1995)**

After serving a celebrated apprenticeship with Chick Corea and Stanley Clarke in Return to Forever, Al Di Meola (b. 1954) went on to immediate solo success. *Land of the Midnight Sun*, *Elegant Gypsy* and *Casino* showcase Di Meola's unique acoustic- and electric-guitar-playing skills, as well as his commercial use of jazz, Latin and fusion ideas. Di Meola won a series of awards, including *Guitar Player* magazine's "Best Jazz Guitar" prize 12 times, including 5 consecutive years (1977–81).

Di Meola's ties to Corea led to fine moments, like their interpretation of "Señor Mouse" on *Casino* and a reunion of the two players on *Splendido Hotel. Electric Rendezvous* features bassist Anthony Jackson, drummer Steve Gadd and keyboardist Jan Hammer in one of his better post-Mahavishnu sessions. Hammer also excels on *Scenario,* which includes drummers Phil Collins and Bill Bruford and bassist/stick player Tony Levin. *Acoustic Anthology*, *Electric Anthology* and *The Essence of Al Di Meola* are good representations of the Columbia material.

Though Di Meola generated some of the more interesting synth-guitar ideas of the fusion era, his acoustic playing remains a strong aspect of his style, and it served as a bit of a refuge from the '80s antifusion sensibility that developed as the form was abused. The live acoustic *Friday Night in San Francisco,* featuring John McLaughlin and Paco De Lucia, is a magnificent recording, but the subsequent live electric *Tour de Force* pales by comparison.

Kiss My Axe showcases Di Meola's best electric work of the 1990s, although his new textures with synthesizers and other instruments make *Heart of the Immigrants* and *Orange and Blue* valuable. His finest moment, however, comes on the sublime acoustic recording *World Sinfonia,* which includes three tangos dedicated to Astor Piazzolla. — J.S.

MANU DIBANGO

★★★ **Gone Clear (Mango/Antilles, 1980)**
★★★ **Ambassador (Mango/Antilles, 1981)**
★★★ **Afrijazzy (Enemy, 1987)**
★★★ **Wakafrika (Giant, 1994)**

Manu Dibango, born in 1933 in Douala, Cameroon, is a soprano saxophonist who produced an international hit in 1973 with the catchy instrumental "Soul Makossa." Despite the fact that he failed to reproduce the hit formula on subsequent releases, Dibango built a career as "the Soul Makossa Man," becoming a staple of the West African recording industry centered in Abidjan, directing the Ivoirian television orchestra and touring the world. These recordings show him in consistently appealing form, mining a pleasant synthesis of African rhythms, jazz fusion and reggae instrumental stylings. — J.S.

VIC DICKENSON

★★ **Trombone Cholly (Sonet, 1976)**
★★★★ **The Essential Vic Dickenson (1977; Vanguard, 1995)**
★★★★ **Gentleman of the Trombone (Storyville, 1992)**
★★★★ **Vic Dickenson Plays Bessie Smith: "Trombone Cholly" (Gazell, 1976)**

A distinctive and original trombonist whose career started in the 1930s, Ohio-born Vic Dickenson (1906–1984) worked with the Bennie Moten, Benny Carter and Count Basie bands. After World War II he concentrated on playing in small Dixieland combos, which is what you'll find on *Trombone Cholly,* but Dickenson could also play excellent small-band swing as on *Gentleman of the Trombone,* supported by Buddy Tate on tenor saxophone and George Duvivier on bass. — J.S.

WALT DICKERSON

★★★★ **This Is Walt Dickerson! (1961; Original Jazz Classics, 1993)**
★★★★ **A Sense of Direction (1961; Original Jazz Classics, 1992)**
★★★★ **Relativity (1962; Original Jazz Classics, 1993)**
★★★½ **Serendipity (1976; SteepleChase, 1994)**
★★★★ **Shades of Love (1977; SteepleChase, 1997)**
★★★★ **Visions (with Sun Ra) (1978; SteepleChase, 1995)**
★★★★ **Tenderness (with Richard Davis) (N.A.; SteepleChase, 1995)**

Though he is among the most daringly creative of the post–Milt Jackson vibraphonists, Walt Dickerson (b. 1931) remains largely ignored by jazz historians, who have been far kinder to easier-to-digest players. Dickerson brings an uncompromisingly percussive and searching approach to vibes.

His longtime collaborator, drummer Andrew Cyrille (on the Original Jazz Classics reissues and other, out-of-print work), matches Dickerson's energetic thirst and manic precision. He's also recorded a treasure trove of SteepleChase material, including the beautiful solo-vibes outing *Shades of Love* and a magnificent series of duets with Sun Ra on piano (*Visions*) and bassist Richard Davis (*Tenderness*). Other duet sessions, with guitarist Pierre Dørge (*Landscape with Open Door*) and Davis (*Divine Gemini*) are no longer available. *To My Queen,* another out-of-print recording with pianist Andrew Hill, is also worth seeking out. — J.S.

BO DIDDLEY

★★★ **Bo Diddley (1958; Chess, 1986)**
★★★★ **Bo Diddley/Go Bo Diddley (1958/1959; Chess, 1987)**
★★★ **In the Spotlight (1960; Chess, 1987)**
★★★★ **Bo Diddley Is a Gunslinger (1963; Chess, 1989)**
★★ **Two Great Guitars: Bo Diddley & Chuck Berry (1964; Chess, 1986)**
★★ **The London Bo Diddley Sessions (1973; Chess, 1989)**
★ **Bo Diddley Live (1975; Triple X, 1994)**
★★½ **The Mighty Bo Diddley (1985; Triple X, 1994)**
★★★★ **The Super Super Blues Band: Bo Diddley, Muddy Waters & Howlin' Wolf (Chess, 1986)**
★★★★ **Superblues: Bo Diddley, Muddy Waters and Little Walter (Chess, 1986)**
★★★★ **His Greatest Sides (Chess, 1986)**
★★★★★ **The Chess Box (Chess, 1990)**
★★ **This Should Not Be (Triple X, 1992)**
★★½ **Promises (Triple X, 1994)**
★★ **A Man Amongst Men (Code Blue/Atlantic, 1996)**
★★★★ **His Best (Chess, 1997)**

In the beginning, Bo Diddley (b. 1928) took a simple shave-and-a-haircut-six-bits rhythm and covered it with layer upon layer of rhythmic variation, courtesy of Jerome Green's maracas and his own heavily tremoloed guitar on which he played two different rhythms simultaneously. Having created form, he added complexity in myriad harmonic and textural conceits. Then he brought his world to life in song by blending gospel and blues, then spicing these bedrock ingredients with quotes from black street-corner culture ("Say Man" being an early example of Diddley's use of "the dozens," ritualized insults, boasts and dares). Bringing it all home in a deep, confident baritone vocal strut, the fellow born Ellas McDaniel in McComb, Mississippi, became the absolute ruler of his dominion, an artist whose sound remains a touchstone for rock & roll guitarists *and* percussionists, and whose standing as "500 percent more man," as he asserted in one of his memorable lyric flights, remains unassailed four decades after "Say Man" became his sole Top 40 hit.

The logical place to begin assessing Bo Diddley's work is *The Chess Box,* two discs containing 45 tracks recorded between 1955 and 1968, including all the best-known songs—"Who Do You Love," "I'm a Man"/"Bo Diddley," "Mona," "Say Man" and an extended version of "Signifying Blues"—as well as a host of alternate takes, B sides and previously unreleased tracks. In the accompanying booklet, critic Robert Palmer offers a rigorous, authoritative dissection of Diddley's music that demands the artist's oeuvre be reconsidered in serious musicological terms.

The Chess Box may be the alpha and omega of Diddley's catalog, but anyone inspired by Palmer's essay to look for further justification of Diddley's genius will find ample rewards in other available Chess titles. *Bo Diddley Is a Gunslinger* comes highly recommended for its first-rate performances, notable among them being "Ride On Josephine," which finds Diddley doing Berry (Chuck, that is) and opening with a riff copped by Lonnie Mack for his own take on Berry's "Memphis." Diddley's streamroller version of "Sixteen Tons," coupling the famous beat to an angry, menacing vocal, is a classic. Also on the A list is *The Super Super Blues Band,* teaming Diddley with Muddy Waters and Howlin' Wolf on a fabulous set of raw, electric blues, with all three participants toasting one another at every turn. For sheer drive, few albums approach the jiving, juking, incendiary summit meeting heard on *Superblues.* Diddley, Waters and Little Walter Jacobs play like men on a mission, talking trash and spurring one another to more resonant performances. The version of Diddley's "Who Do You Love" included here is the model for the raging, near-meltdown performance of the tune that Diddley delivered on the *La Bamba* soundtrack. Jacobs blows low and mean behind Diddley and Waters on "I'm a Man," as the two guitarists spar instrumentally and verbally.

Another supersession captured on tape, *Two Great Guitars,* teams Diddley and Chuck Berry on four extended instrumental tracks that are pretty much in the sound-and-fury-signifying-nothing category. Diddley's first two album releases, *Bo Diddley* and *Go Bo Diddley,* are now available in a twofer CD and represent in 24 tracks prime early Diddley; this is a good alternative to the more expensive boxed set for anyone on a limited budget or with only a casual interest in Diddley's work, as it contains a number of the best-known sides ("Bo Diddley," "I'm a Man," "Who Do You Love," "Say Man") as well as scintillating items such as "Diddie Wah Diddie" and "Before You Accuse Me."

The London Bo Diddley Sessions, recorded in 1973 (six of its nine tracks in London, with bassist Roy Wood of the Move being the most prominent guest artist), finds Diddley addressing Memphis soul, reggae and Sly Stone pop funk without much success, although "Get Out of My Life" is a nice dip into classic soul music's mellow side.

In recent years Diddley has found a home on Triple X Records, with fair to middlin' results. At the desultory end of the scale, *Bo Diddley Live,* originally released in 1975, is five tracks of pointless jamming over steadily percolating P-Funk–influenced rhythms. At no point in this mess does Diddley distinguish himself on guitar, and one can only imagine how dreary a night it must have been for the audience as the noodling went on ad nauseum, rarely broken up by flashes of the headliner's lyrical wit or hilarious self-aggrandizing. Five songs comprise this album, the shortest running slightly under 10 minutes, the longest a shade over 12 minutes.

Cut to 10 years later, and Diddley releases *The Mighty Bo Diddley,* a stronger effort in that it features some good new original songs and a few instrumental sparks from Diddley himself. Lascivious as ever, Diddley busts a move on the now aging Mona's sister, in "Mona, Where's Your Sister," and gets in the face of an imagined competitor in "I Don't Know Where I've Been," an up-tempo 12-bar blues effort that would have been right at home in Muddy Waters's repertoire. Before taking off on a stinging solo turn, Diddley warns, "I'm gonna make my guitar fit yo' head like a baseball cap!" One of the real treats on any Diddley album comes here, near the end, in a slow, deep, eight-bar blues, "Evil Woman," featuring a shouting, exasperated lead vocal—all B.B. King in style—and a series of concise, crying guitar solos, tart and angular with nary a superfluous note, that demonstrate the depth of feeling sometimes lost in the customary flash. Caveat emptor—at this point Diddley began displaying a social conscience in his lyrics, and these efforts, while well-meaning, are uniformly embarrassing. "Ain't It Good to Be Free" would like to have been Diddley's take on Merle Haggard's "The Fightin' Side of Me," but it has nothing of the latter's wit or sense of purpose; "Gotta Be a Change" and "I Don't Want Your Welfare" might have been compelling in third-person anecdotal form rather than first-person invective.

On *This Should Not Be* Diddley catalogs the social ills he sees around him—singling out hunger and homelessness—and extends the message of "this should not be" to every nation in the world. The sentiment is laudable, but the guitarist is buried beneath the electronic grooves almost to the point of being inaudible. And what is a Bo Diddley album without Bo Diddley's guitar?

The title of his 1994 album, *Promises,* keyed to the song of the same name about a woman's duplicity, is more directly related to the overall theme of the promise life holds for those who keep their heads on straight and stay straight at the same time. The title cut kicks off the set in sizzling fashion, with Tuck Tucker's soaring lap-steel lines adding some country funk to the foot-stomping Diddley beat. Diddley the writer delivers one of his strongest melodies ever, and Diddley the singer accommodates it with a powerful, rocking vocal as the band wails behind him.

While retooling his signature rhythm for the electronic age in the braggadocio "I'm Gonna Get Your Girlfriend," Diddley addresses the younger generation in blunt terms on two songs inveighing against the lure of the street ("Kids Don't Do It" and "Hear What I'm Sayin'"), then closes out the album with a troubling, nightmare scenario suggested by the national colloquies on date rape, "She Wasn't Raped." — D.M.

DIRTY DOZEN BRASS BAND

★★★★ Live: Mardi Gras in Montreux (Rounder, 1986)
★★★★ Voodoo (CBS, 1989)
★★★½ The New Orleans Album (Columbia, 1990)

★★★★ **Open Up: Whatcha Gonna Do for the Rest of Your Life? (Columbia, 1992)**
★★★★½ **Jelly (Columbia, 1993)**
★★★★ **This Is Jazz 30 (Columbia/Legacy, 1997)**

The Dirty Dozen Brass Band, a New Orleans Mardi Gras tradition, has featured such brass-band believers as drummers Benny Jones and Lionel Batiste and several other members of the Batiste family. Every year the band members would march through Treme and other black districts, dressed in drag and accompanied by the Baby Dolls, a group of courtesans. These wild frolics developed into the original Dirty Dozen Brass Band, a freewheeling combination of traditional New Orleans marching-band styles and quotes from and tributes to bop-era musicians like Thelonious Monk and Dexter Gordon, as well as bits of popular culture appropriated from television and the street.

Live: Mardi Gras in Montreux accurately captures the mayhem of the Dozen's live performance, right down to the band's zany cop of the theme song from *The Flintstones. Voodoo* expands the party to include Dr. John, Branford Marsalis and Dizzy Gillespie; New Orleans R&B greats Eddie Bo and Dave Bartholomew are featured on *The New Orleans Album,* which goes over the top by bringing Elvis Costello along for the ride. On *Open Up: Whatcha Gonna Do for the Rest of Your Life?* the band shows itself to be an evolving musical force, without the distraction of musical guest stars, as trumpeter Gregory Davis, trombonist Charles Joseph and baritonist Roger Lewis emerge as gifted writers as well as improvisers. In a brilliant conceptual stroke, the band returned to the primary source of the New Orleans jazz tradition, Jelly Roll Morton, for the material on *Jelly,* and emerged with its finest recording. *This Is Jazz 30* is an excellent compilation culled from the Columbia recordings. — J.S.

DIVA

★★★ **Something's Coming (Perfect Sound, 1995)**
★★★½ **Leave It to DIVA (DIV Ltd., 1997)**

The 15 women of DIVA, also known as "No Man's Band," are breaking through instrumental jazz's glass ceiling with their solid musicianship and collective sound. Drummer Sherrie Maricle leads the big band, which was formed in 1993 by producer Stanley Kay, a veteran manager and onetime backup drummer for Buddy Rich. *Something's Coming* and *Leave It to DIVA* contain a fine mix of big-band standards and originals written for the group, whose primary soloists include trumpeter Ingrid Jensen, tenor saxophonist Virginia Mayhew and alto players Carol Chaikin and Laura Dreyer. — K.F.

DIXIE DREGS

★★★ **What If (Capricorn, 1978)**
★★★ **Night of the Living Dregs (Capricorn, 1979)**
★★★ **Bring 'Em Back Alive (Capricorn, 1992)**
★★★ **Full Circle (Capricorn, 1994)**
★★★ **King Biscuit Flower Hour Presents Dixie Dregs (King Biscuit Flower Hour/BMG, 1997)**

Formed by guitarist Steve Morse (b. 1954) and bassist Andy West (b. 1954) as a rock band called the Dixie Grits, what eventually became the Dixie Dregs materialized after both musicians attended the University of Miami music school. Using school mates Rod Morgenstein (b. 1957) on drums and Allen Sloan on violin along with ex-Grits keyboardist Steve Davidowski, the Dregs made several albums that were heavily influenced by the Mahavishnu Orchestra and Jeff Beck. The part-live *Night of the Living Dregs* is a good representation of the band's proclivities during the 1970s; *King Biscuit Flower Hour Presents Dixie Dregs* is more of the same.

T. Lavitz replaced Davidowski on keyboards for their now unavailable Arista albums, including the 1982 release *Industry Standard,* on which virtuoso violinist Mark O'Connor (b. 1962) had replaced Sloan.

The group's style centered around Morse's guitar playing, arrangements and production strategies. Morse split to pursue a solo career in the mid-'80s, then brought the band out of mothballs in the 1990s only to discover that this variation on fusion had gone the way of the dinosaurs. — J.S.

BILL DIXON

★★★★ **Bill Dixon in Italy, Vol. 1 (Soul Note, 1980)**
★★★★ **Bill Dixon in Italy, Vol. 2 (Soul Note, 1981)**
★★★★ **November 1981 (Soul Note, 1982)**
★★½ **Thoughts (Soul Note, 1987)**
★★★½ **Son of Sisyphus (Soul Note, 1990)**
★★★ **Vade Mecum (Soul Note, 1994)**

Trumpet/flügelhorn player Bill Dixon (b. 1925), a distinguished educator, composer and visual artist, has been an influential behind-the-scenes shaper of contemporary music. The Massachusetts native emerged in the late 1950s as part of Cecil Taylor's groundbreaking unit and went on to play with Archie Shepp and Don Cherry in developing the emerging New York loft-jazz scene. In the late '60s he moved to New England, developing one of the most successful black-music programs in history at Bennington College.

Dixon's brooding, introspective playing offers a stark contrast to the prolix tendencies of many of his contemporaries and brings gravity to his own recordings. Both volumes of *Bill Dixon in Italy* use an unusual three-trumpet format; *November 1981* features a two-bass quartet. *Son of Sisyphus,* with its low-pitched, tuba-powered quartet, also features Dixon on piano and—from the world-weary title to his paintings on the cover—pretty well sums up his artistic vision. Look for the out-of-print *Intents and Purposes.*
— J.S.

FLOYD DIXON

★★★★★ **Marshall Texas Is My Home (Specialty, 1991)**
★★★½ **Wake Up and Live! (Alligator, 1996)**

Vocalist and pianist Floyd Dixon (b. 1929) became an innovator in the Charles Brown–influenced West Coast blues sound that evolved in the late '40s. Dixon's sometimes introspective fare includes elements of jump blues and boogie but is also informed by jazz and pop sensibilities.

The excellent *Marshall Texas Is My Home* chronicles the career of the man who wrote and performed the original version of "Hey, Bartender." Its 22 tracks, recorded between 1953 and 1957, include the particularly engaging half dozen songs cut on October 6, 1953, by Dixon and a menacing, swinging combo: tenor-sax men Joe Howard and Carlos Bermudez, guitarist Charles Norris, bassist William K. Hadnott and drummer Rudolph Pitts. Dixon's tense piano figures stab at sax-supplied grooves on the two instrumentals "Carlos" and "Instrumental Shuffle." Other standouts include a previously unreleased ballad, "Time Brings About a Change," the admonishment to busybodies, "Nose Trouble," and the heavenly "Reap What You Sow," featuring Dixon's honeyed vocals.

The 16 tracks on the recent *Wake Up and Live!* include updated versions of classic numbers like "Hey, Bartender," "Don't Send Me No Flowers in the Graveyard" and "Rockin' at Home," as well as newer songs such as "Got the Blues So Bad," "Skeet's California Sunshine," "A Dream" and "Mean and Jealous Man." The album has a decidedly '50s vibe—even the new songs with references to Brooke Shields and Oprah Winfrey sound as if they could have been written in Dixon's prime. — B.R.H.

WILLIE DIXON

★★★★ **Willie's Blues (1959; Original Blues Classics, 1990)**
★★★★ **I Am the Blues (Columbia/Legacy, 1970)**
★★ **Hidden Charms (Bug/Capitol, 1988)**
★★★★★ **The Chess Box (Chess, 1988)**
★★★ **The Big Three Trio (Columbia, 1990)**
★★★★★ **The Original Wang Dang Doodle (MCA, 1995)**

Without ever establishing a style of his own as distinctive as that of the artists with whom he worked, Willie Dixon (1915–1992) became one of the architects of urban blues on the strength of his skills as a songwriter, bandleader, musician, arranger, producer and diplomat. In these roles Dixon reigned supreme at Chess Records in the 1950s and early 1960s, when he worked in one capacity or another with every significant artist on the label blessed with an abundance of same. Even a cursory listing of his many songwriting credits indicates the breathtaking scope of his contributions to American music and to the language of the blues: "My Babe," "You Shook Me," "Back Door Man," "Little Red Rooster," "Spoonful," "Wang Dang Doodle," "I Can't Quit You Baby," "Hoochie Coochie Man," "You Can't Judge a Book by Its Cover," "Seventh Son," "I Just Want to Make Love to You." Muddy Waters, Howlin' Wolf, Little Walter, Bo Diddley, Lowell Fulson and Jimmy Witherspoon are only the most prominent of the musicians in Dixon's debt. They and others are heard on the two-disc boxed set from Chess, which is as essential a blues overview as any on the market. It's impossible to listen to the 36 tracks here and then understate Dixon's stature.

Oddly, Dixon's solo work was the least of his accomplishments. As a musician and producer, he was beyond reproach. Vocally he was genial, even moving on occasion, but he never sounded as completely immersed in and defined by his material as did, for example, Muddy Waters and Howlin' Wolf. The zone these and other artists inhabited, in which passion, pain and technique came together in one explosive package, is one Dixon visited in other capacities but not on his own releases.

That said, it should be added that Dixon's recordings have some stirring, if not transcendent, moments. The earliest of these, Columbia's *Big Three Trio,* finds Dixon near the outset of his career, joined by Leonard Caston and Ollie Crawford in a trio purveying blues-tinged popular music in the style of the Mills Brothers. Among the interesting tracks here is the Dixon/Caston–penned "If the Sea Was Whiskey," the first verse of which has shown up in countless songs, most notably "Rollin' and Tumblin'."

Original Blues Classics has reissued Dixon's first album as a bandleader, *Willie's Blues,* recorded in 1959 and featuring the redoubtable Memphis Slim on piano. Imbued with a dark, after-hours ambiance, the album is by far Dixon's strongest solo recording. Here the solid rhythm section, formed by Dixon on standup bass and Gus Johnson on drums, constructs a strong foundation for some exciting solo excursions courtesy Slim, guitarist Wally Richardson and tenor-sax man Al Ashby. Dixon's stuttering vocal on "Nervous" is one of his most effective on record, and one of the better tracks is the loping "Youth to You," a thinly disguised reworking of "I Just Want to Make Love to You."

I Am the Blues features Dixon's own interpretations of nine of his best-known songs and for this reason alone becomes a good companion volume to the Chess box and the other extensive MCA overview, *The Original Wang Dang Doodle,* featuring tracks cut between 1954 and 1990. His final studio album, *Hidden Charms,* is a pleasant if unspectacular outing. "The blues is about life," he once said. "If it ain't about life, it ain't the blues." When death brought an end to his remarkable career in 1992, Willie Dixon had walked it like he talked it, staying true to his own maxim right up to the end of his days. — D.M.

JOHNNY DODDS

★★★★★ The Chronological Johnny Dodds 1926–40 (Classics, 1991)

Johnny Dodds (1892–1940) pioneered the early role of the clarinet in small jazz groups. Born in New Orleans, Dodds was in Kid Ory's legendary New Orleans band by 1911. He played with King Oliver's Chicago groups in the 1920s, including the historic 1923 dates that featured Oliver and Louis Armstrong on cornets, trombonist Honore Dutrey, Dodds's brother Baby on drums, Lil Hardin on piano and Bill Johnson on banjo, but he reached his pinnacle as part of Armstrong's Hot Five and Hot Seven recording dates. A four-CD set, *The Chronological Johnny Dodds 1926–40* features tracks recorded with the New Orleans Wanderers and Bootblacks (the Hot Five lineup with George Mitchell subbing for Armstrong on cornet). — J.S.

ERIC DOLPHY

★★★★ Outward Bound (1960; Original Jazz Classics, 1987)
★★★★ Out There (1960; Original Jazz Classics, 1982)
★★★★ Far Cry (1961; Original Jazz Classics, 1989)
★★★★ At the Five Spot, Vol. 1 (1961; Prestige, 1991)
★★★★ At the Five Spot, Vol. 2 (1961; Prestige, 1991)
★★★★ Great Concert (with Booker Little) (Prestige, 1961)
★★★½ Here and There (1961; Prestige, 1991)
★★★½ Eric Dolphy in Europe, Vol. 1 (1961; Original Jazz Classics, 1989)
★★★½ Eric Dolphy in Europe, Vol. 2 (1961; Original Jazz Classics, 1989)
★★★½ Eric Dolphy in Europe, Vol. 3 (1961; Original Jazz Classics, 1989)
★★★★ Memorial Album: Eric Dolphy and Booker Little Recorded Live at the Five Spot (1961; Original Jazz Classics, 1989)
★★★ The Berlin Concerts (1961; Enja, 1989)
★★½ Iron Man (1963; Restless, 1992)
★★½ Conversations (1964; Metrotone, 1992)
★★★½ Last Date (1964; Fontana, 1986)
★★★★★ Out to Lunch (1964; Blue Note, 1987)
★★½ Vintage Dolphy (GM, 1986)
★★★★ The Essential Eric Dolphy (Prestige, 1986)
★★★★ Other Aspects (Blue Note, 1987)
★★½ Candid Dolphy (Candid, 1990)
★★★ Stockholm Sessions (Enja, 1990)

★★★★½ The Complete Prestige Recordings (Prestige, 1995)

Though he died at age 36, jazz impressionist Eric Dolphy (1928–1964) left behind recordings of a deep and haunting loveliness. An intellectual, introspective musician, Dolphy played solos—on alto saxophone, flute and, in particular, bass clarinet—that were careful, intricate work, his sensibility recalling high European romanticism (such as Debussy and modern classical composers) nearly as easily as very cerebral bebop. However, unlike some of the practitioners of the sweeter West Coast sound or followers of Gunther Schuller's Third Stream movement (with its attempt to explore the possibilities of classical music), Dolphy always conveyed a signature passion, sometimes disturbing, ever intense.

Starting out as a Charlie Parker–style player with Chico Hamilton and then working with Charles Mingus, Dolphy debuted as a leader on *Outward Bound*; the title track was solidly grounded in the blues, but a version of "Glad to Be Unhappy" suggested Dolphy's capacity for a subtler lyricism, and on "Green Dolphin Street" his bass-clarinet work broke exciting new ground. With his sidemen including Freddie Hubbard on trumpet and Jackie Byard on piano, Dolphy drew comparison to Ornette Coleman—but while the young player's style was indeed marked by a "free" approach that superficially resembled Coleman's, it was more inward-turning. *Out There,* with phenomenal cello work by Ron Carter, emphasized Dolphy's finesse; the album's last cut, "Feathers," exemplifies his profound delicacy. This disc also reveals a strong Mingus influence.

He collaborated next with Booker Little, a trumpet prodigy whose best work came close to paralleling Dolphy's in its lucid drive (Little died three years before Dolphy, at age 23). *Far Cry, Memorial Album* and *At the Five Spot, Vols. 1* and *2* feature the fruit of the alliance; *Far Cry*'s "Mrs. Parker of K.C. (Bird's Mother)" and "Ode to Charlie Parker" are reflective gems. With *Out to Lunch,* Dolphy swung harder and more freely; on such standouts as the title track and the Thelonious Monk tribute, "Hat and Beard," he tests to the utmost the awesome talents of Freddie Hubbard, Bobby Hutcherson on vibes, bassist Richard Davis and a very young Tony Williams on drums. *Out to Lunch* remains one of the watershed albums of the period: Here rhythm is emancipated from time signature, solos catch fire off of sketchy melodies rather than the 12-bar structure of the blues or the chord changes of standards. Cecil Taylor, Ornette Coleman, John Coltrane—*Out to Lunch* incorporates elements of each of their innovations while still serving as Dolphy's own triumph.

Feeling unappreciated in this country, Dolphy left for Europe shortly after *Out to Lunch.* A few years before, with a somewhat naive Danish rhythm section, he'd played the series of Copenhagen concerts that ended up as the three volumes of *Eric Dolphy in Europe*—and had found a very receptive audience. Dying in Berlin of diabetes-related heart problems, Dolphy was cut down before he'd had a chance to fully develop his remarkable gifts.

His character one of rare sweetness (he was known to practice along with chirping birds on his windowsill—a Franciscan move), Dolphy worked ferociously and recorded prodigiously (nearly 20 sides in 1960 alone). His discography, then, can be confusing, a jumble of original releases and reissues. Among the standouts are *Other Aspects* (on "Jim Crow" Dolphy dazzles on three horns), *The Essential Eric Dolphy* (a good intro for newcomers), *Last Date* (especially "Epistrophy") and *The Complete Prestige Recordings* (a very craftily assembled boxed set). The undiluted power of the man's art can be found on an unaccompanied bass-clarinet version of Billie Holiday's "God Bless the Child," from *Eric Dolphy in Europe, Vol. 1.* Staggering. — P.E.

LOU DONALDSON

★★★ Alligator Bogaloo (1967; Blue Note, 1987)
★★★ Lush Life (Blue Note, 1967)
★★★ Hot Dog (1969; Blue Note, 1994)
★★★ Everything I Play Is Funky (1970; Blue Note, 1995)
★★★ Pretty Things (1970; Blue Note, 1993)
★★½ Forgotten Man (Timeless, 1981)
★★★ Sweet Poppa Lou (Muse, 1981)
★★★ Blues Walk (Blue Note, 1987)
★★★½ Play the Right Thing (Milestone, 1991)
★★★½ Birdseed (Milestone, 1992)
★★★½ The Best of Lou Donaldson, Vol. 1 1957–1967 (Blue Note, 1993)
★★★½ Caracas (Milestone, 1994)
★★★½ Sentimental Journey (Columbia, 1995)
★★★½ Blue Breakbeats (Blue Note, 1998)

Alto saxophonist Lou Donaldson (b. 1926) shares with virtually all of his instrumental contemporaries a debt to Charlie Parker, but his sweet, self-assured style provides him with a strong signature. He worked with hard-bop musicians including Milt Jackson, Thelonious Monk, Parker, Sonny Stitt, Art Blakey and Horace Silver before leading his own groups, which were almost always soulful, swinging blues-based outfits, although sometimes the fare got a bit stale.

Donaldson's small-group blowing sessions for Blue Note pretty well defined, without inventing, that genre. The out-of-print *Quartet/Quintet/Sextet* finds him grooving with like-minded company such as trumpeters Kenny Dorham and Blue Mitchell, pianists Silver and Elmo Hope, bassist Percy Heath and drummers Blakey and Art Taylor. *Blues Walk* features basic soul-jazz formulas driven by Ray Barretto's congas; *Alligator Bogaloo* offers a take on New Orleans R&B with Melvin Lastie Sr. playing cornet and Lonnie Liston Smith on organ. The quintet dates *Hot Dog* and *Pretty Things* and the sextet date *Everything I Play Is Funky* are heavy on the groove, while *Lush Life* showcases Donaldson's expressive ballad playing in the company of trumpeter Freddie Hubbard, reed players Wayne Shorter and Pepper Adams, pianist McCoy Tyner, bassist Ron Carter and drummer Al Harewood.

Donaldson got lost in the shuffle during the 1980s as his soul-jazz conception was overshadowed by other styles. While *Forgotten Man* sounds fairly tepid, *Sweet Poppa Lou* is a highlight of this era, with Herman Foster on piano along with Idris Muhammad on drums and Calvin Hill on bass.

Producer Bob Porter encouraged Donaldson to return to his traditional strength on the wonderful series of 1990s comeback albums, *Play the Right Thing*, *Birdseed* and *Caracas.* Donaldson reprises some of his old favorites and revisits Parker with Dr. Lonnie Smith burning it up on the organ. Smith also excels on *Sentimental Journey,* as does guitarist Peter Bernstein. Blue Note decided to mine Donaldson's soul-jazz history for the 1990s acid-jazz set with *Blue Breakbeats,* which collects such grooves as "Turtle Walk" and "Brother Soul." — J.S.

DOROTHY DONEGAN

★★★ **The Dorothy Donegan Trio Live at the 1990 Floating Jazz Festival (Chiaroscuro, 1991)**
★★★ **The Incredible Dorothy Donegan Trio (Chiaroscuro, 1992)**
★★★ **The Dorothy Donegan Trio (Chiaroscuro, 1993)**

Whatever musical talent Chicago-born singer/pianist Dorothy Donegan (b. 1924) brought to the table, it was overshadowed by her vaudevillian career as a nightclub entertainer. Donegan mixed humor and outlandish visual displays with crowd-pleasing technical turns from boogie-woogie to classical-music themes overplayed as jazz numbers.

The pyrotechnics mask an interesting style, however, as these three sessions prove. Each features Donegan's trio with a guest trumpeter added—Dizzy Gillespie on *The Incredible Dorothy Donegan Trio* and *Live at the 1990 Floating Jazz Festival,* Clark Terry on *The Dorothy Donegan Trio.* — J.S.

DR. JOHN

★★★★½ **Gumbo (1972; Alligator, 1986)**
★★★½ **In the Right Place (1973; Atco, 1990)**
★★½ **Hollywood Be Thy Name (United Artists, 1975)**
★★★★ **Dr. John Plays Mac Rebennack (1981; Clean Cuts, 1988)**
★★★★ **The Brightest Smile in Town (1983; Clean Cuts, N.A.)**
★★★★ **The Ultimate Dr. John (Warner Bros., 1987)**
★★½ **In a Sentimental Mood (Warner Bros., 1990)**
★★★★★ **Goin' Back to New Orleans (Warner Bros., 1992)**
★★★★½ **Mos' Scocious: Anthology (Rhino, 1993)**
★★★★ **Television (GRP, 1995)**
★★★½ **The Very Best of Dr. John (Rhino, 1995)**
★★★½ **Right Place, Wrong Time and Other Hits (Rhino Flashback, 1997)**
★★★★ **Trippin' Live (Surefire, 1997)**

Mac Rebennack (b. 1940) began his musical career as a guitarist and pianist on the New Orleans R&B scene of the '50s and eventually followed Earl Palmer, Harold Battiste and other N.O. session players to the Los Angeles studio scene in the mid-'60s. And in a very real way, the musical persona Rebennack assumed for his solo career—that of Dr. John Creaux, the Night Tripper—was a product of the collision between Louisiana Creole funk and West Coast hippie mysticism.

That fusion didn't always take, of course, as heard on several out-of-print albums marked by hallucinatory grooves and hippie foolishness. In truth, Dr. John didn't really hit his stride until he returned to roots with *Gumbo,* which offers funky updates of classic New Orleans R&B numbers like "Iko Iko," "Junko Partner," Professor Longhair's classic "Tipitina" and a medley of Huey Smith hits. From there it's an easy jump to the second-line funk of *In the Right Place,* which was recorded with the Meters and produced by Allen Toussaint; it contains Dr. John's only Top 10 single, "Right Place Wrong Time." *The Ultimate Dr. John* compiles highlights from *Gris Gris*, *Gumbo, Remedies* and *Desitively Bonnaroo,* but not necessarily the tunes every fan would have chosen. Apparently tiring of the voodoo shtick, Dr. John tries a bit of straight-up rock & roll revivalism with *Hollywood Be Thy Name,* a mostly live album that offers mildly spiced renditions of oldies like "The Way You Do the Things You Do" and "Yesterday" along with a few Dr. John originals; it's second-rate rock despite the first-rate band.

Yet just when it seemed Dr. John had exhausted all his options, he brought his skills back into focus with *Dr. John Plays Mac Rebennack,* a solo-piano session that brings him back home to the New Orleans piano stylings he cut his teeth on; essential listening, if only for "Memories of Professor Longhair." *The Brightest Smile in Town* not only maintains its predecessor's momentum but actually broadens the music's scope with a few standards like "Come Rain or Come Shine." But *In a Sentimental Mood,* though it boasts a coy "Makin' Whoopee" recorded with Rickie Lee Jones, wastes too much energy on large-scale arrangements that overwhelm both the singer and the songs.

The Grammy-winning *Goin' Back to New Orleans* is Dr. John's ingeniously eccentric history of New Orleans music from Gottschalk to the Mardi Gras Indians, second-line parades and burning Louisiana rhythm & blues. *Television* is a hard-edged funk session. The double-disc *Mos' Scocious* is the definitive Dr. John anthology. *Trippin' Live* is an incendiary set from Ronnie Scott's club in London.

— J.D.C.

PIERRE DØRGE

★★★★ **Different Places, Different Bananas (Olufsen, 1989)**
★★★★ **Brikama (SteepleChase, 1992)**
★★★★½ **Karawane (Olufsen, 1993)**
★★★★ **Polar Jungle Orchestra (Ulo, 1994)**

Danish guitarist, bandleader and composer Pierre Dørge (b. 1946) possesses one of the most inventive musical imaginations in the world jazz community. The conservatory-trained Dørge strips down musical language, then restructures it in a fabulous manner. He brings together an intensive personal study of African artistic structures, Arabic trance music, Balinese gamelan theory and various ethnic musics from around the world—from Siberia to Greenland—and uses his passion for jazz to bring it all into focus. In the late 1960s, Dørge's guitar work was already remarkable during his stay with the John Tchicai group, and it continues to be an interesting featured voice in various editions of his New Jungle Orchestra, a large group, featuring Irene Becker on keyboards, which has taken several forms since its inception in the early 1980s.

On the astonishing *Karawane* Dørge envisions a merger of Ellington's Harlem Jungle Orchestra with the loping, hypnotic rhythms of Nigerian juju music. *Different Places, Different Bananas* is the orchestra's deadpan reading of a world where the logical direction of history evolved from Fats Waller to Sun Ra, while guitar solos Frank Zappa wouldn't have hesitated to sample ring through the arrangements. *Polar Jungle Orchestra* expands Dørge's vision to include a musical marriage of Tibetan and Greenland Inuit music with jazz in an otherworldly, chant-oriented recording sparsely orchestrated with bass clarinet, French horn and two guitars.

Dørge made history when the Danish government named his group the official state orchestra of Denmark, the first time the honor had been bestowed on a nonclassical artist. He has also participated as the Danish representative of the coveted JazzPar award.

— J.S.

KENNY DORHAM

★★★★ **Kenny Dorham Quintet (1953; Original Jazz Classics, 1993)**
★★★ **'Round About Midnight at the Cafe Bohemia (1956; Blue Note, 1995)**
★★★ **2 Horns, 2 Rhythm (1957; Original Jazz Classics, 1990)**
★★★★ **Jazz Contrasts (1957; Original Jazz Classics, 1992)**
★★★★ **Quiet Kenny (1959; Original Jazz Classics, 1987)**

★★★ **Blue Spring (1959; Original Jazz Classics, 1990)**
★★★ **Jazz Contemporary (Bainbridge, 1960)**
★★★ **The Kenny Dorham Memorial Album (1960; Xanadu, 1976)**
★★★★★ **Whistle Stop (1961; Blue Note, 1994)**
★★★ **Osmosis (Black Lion, 1961)**
★★★ **Showboat (Bainbridge, 1961)**
★★★★ **Una Mas (Blue Note, 1963)**
★★★ **Scandia Skies (1963; SteepleChase, 1995)**
★★★ **Short Story (1963; SteepleChase, 1993)**
★★★★ **Trumpeta Toccata (Blue Note, 1964)**
★★★ **Matador/Inta Somethin' (Blue Note, 1991)**
★★★★ **The Best of the Blue Note Years (Blue Note, 1996)**

Through the exquisitely controlled eloquence of his playing, trumpeter Kenny Dorham (1924–1972) helped transform the fierce language of hard bop into a more free-flowing, lyrical expression. Having worked with Charlie Parker, Thelonious Monk and Bud Powell by the late 1940s, Dorham was acknowledged as a talented and valued sideman. His big break came when he replaced Clifford Brown in Art Blakey's band. Dorham again replaced Brown in Max Roach's band after Brown was killed in an automobile accident.

Dorham emerged from Roach's band a distinct horn voice, having perfected a confident, rounder tone that lent a measured, warm edge to his playing. His peak work came in the late 1950s and early '60s. *Jazz Contrasts* employs saxophonist Sonny Rollins, drummer Roach and harpist Betty Glamman. *Quiet Kenny,* a low-key collection of ballads and blues, captures Dorham at his most poised and emotive. A definitive hard-bop outfit, drummer Philly Joe Jones, bassist Paul Chambers, pianist Kenny Drew and saxophonist Hank Mobley kick 1961's *Whistle Stop* into overdrive.

Dorham proves himself a compelling soloist in his supporting work on Blue Note for frequent partner, saxophonist Joe Henderson; Dorham's most enduring composition, "Blue Bossa," gets its debut on Henderson's 1963 recording *Page One.* Dorham never abandoned the lyrical bop style he developed, and his later work remained solid and affecting. His later Blue Note recordings find Dorham stretching out over modernist forms supported by vanguard players. — S.F.

THE DORSEY BROTHERS

★★½ **Live in the Meadowbrook October 28, 1955 (Jazz Hour, N.A.)**
★★★★ **Best of the Big Bands (Columbia/Legacy, 1992)**

The Dorsey Brothers, clarinetist/alto saxophonist Jimmy (1904–1957) and trombonist/trumpeter Tommy (1905–1956), were notorious battlers who had a hard time staying in a band with each other but enjoyed tremendous success together and separately through the swing era, eventually becoming the subject of the Hollywood biopic *The Fabulous Dorseys.*

Best of the Big Bands collects the 1932–34 Columbia sessions of the band that included Tommy Dorsey and Glenn Miller on trombones, Jimmy Dorsey on clarinet and alto sax, Bunny Berigan on trumpet, Joe Venuti on violin and Mildred Bailey on vocals. This group was a hot outfit in the tradition of the big swing bands of the era. *Live in the Meadowbrook,* recorded shortly before the brothers died, reflects wanly on what this band was about in its heyday. — J.S.

TOM DORSEY

★★★ **Come On Mama Do That Dance (Yazoo, 1992)**
★★★½ **Georgia Tom: Complete Recorded Works, Vol. 1 (1928–1930) (Document, 1992)**
★★★★ **Georgia Tom: Complete Recorded Works, Vol. 2 (1930–1934) (Document, 1992)**
★★★★ **Precious Lord (Legacy, 1994)**

Of the many stories that tell of the blues/gospel, profane/sacred diametric in the legacy of black music—Little Richard, Aretha Franklin, Al Green—none is as emblematic or poignant as the story of pianist/composer Georgia Tom, a.k.a. Thomas A. Dorsey (1899–1993). By applying the blues and ragtime sensibilities popular in the '20s to a sacred context, Dorsey helped to create the more rhythmic and compelling modern-day gospel-music tradition. He was also one of the first black composers who successfully pursued a career through the publishing, rather than the recording, end of the music business.

Born near Atlanta and moving north in the late '10s, Dorsey became one of the leading pianists and songwriters in the urban-based hokum-blues idiom—combining blues, rags and more sophisticated, upbeat styles into a short but influential six-year legacy of recordings well chronicled on the Document sets. His groundbreaking work with Tampa Red, Bertha "Chippie" Hill and Frankie Jaxon and as a recording artist in his own right yielded such ribald classics as "Eagle Ridin' Papa," "The Duck's Yas Yas Yas" and the notoriously huge 1920s hit "It's Tight Like That." *Come On Mama Do That Dance* illustrates the wide variety of contexts in which Dorsey performed, including a taste of the gospel conversion that was to come in 1932's "If You See My Saviour" and "How About You."

Dorsey's 1932 one-way crossover to gospel music exclusively—which was to unleash a creative font of gospel standards ("Precious Lord" and "Peace in the Valley," among many others)—was sealed by the devastating loss of his wife and baby during childbirth. By melding blues and ragtime chord changes to an intimate, first-person view of salvation in his lyrics—and establishing and maintaining a publishing company that tracked his songs—Dorsey created music that touched millions; one of every four modern gospel standards was written by Dorsey, according to some sources. *Precious Lord* is an excellent survey of that effect, with the cream of the Dorsey songbook interpreted by a wide gamut of gospel legends: singers (Marion Williams, Sallie Martin, R.H. Harris), harmony quartets (Dixie Hummingbirds) and choirs (the Alex Bradford Choir). The documentary *Say Amen, Somebody* is an especially personal portrait of the aging composer, who was captured playing, preaching and listening to an old Georgia Tom recording.

— A.K.

TOMMY DORSEY

★★★ **All Time Hit Parade Rehearsals (1944; Hep, N.A.)**
★★★ **Live in Hi-Fi at Casino Garden (1946; Jazz Hour, 1992)**
★★½ **Sentimental (1973; MCA, 1982)**
★★★ **The Best of Tommy Dorsey (1975; RCA, 1992)**
★★★★ **Tommy Dorsey/Frank Sinatra: All Time Greatest Hits, Vol. 1 (RCA Bluebird, 1988)**
★★★★ **Tommy Dorsey/Frank Sinatra: All Time Greatest Hits, Vol. 2 (RCA Bluebird, 1988)**
★★★★ **Tommy Dorsey/Frank Sinatra: All Time Greatest Hits, Vol. 3 (RCA Bluebird, 1989)**
★★★½ **Oh! Look at Me Now and Other Hits (RCA, 1990)**
★★★★ **Yes, Indeed! (RCA Bluebird, 1990)**
★★★★ **Tommy Dorsey/Frank Sinatra: All Time Greatest Hits, Vol. 4 (RCA Bluebird, 1990)**
★★★★ **The 17 Number Ones (RCA, 1990)**
★★ **The Best of Tommy Dorsey and His Orchestra (Curb, 1991)**
★★★ **The Great Tommy Dorsey (Pearl, 1991)**
★★½ **Jazz Collector Edition, Vol. 1 (LaserLight, 1991)**
★★★ **Jazz Collector Edition, Vol. 2 (LaserLight, 1991)**
★ **Tommy Dorsey and David Rose (LaserLight, 1992)**
★★★★ **Stardust (RCA Bluebird, 1992)**
★★★ **Stop, Look & Listen (Living Era, 1993)**
★★★ **The Post-War Era (RCA Bluebird, 1993)**
★★★ **Tommy Dorsey and His Greatest Band (Jasmine, 1994)**
★★★½ **Having a Wonderful Time (RCA Bluebird, 1994)**
★★★★ **I'll Be Seeing You (RCA, 1994)**
★★★★★ **The Song Is You (with Frank Sinatra) (RCA Bluebird, 1994)**
★★★ **Giants of the Big Band Era (Magma, 1994)**
★★★½ **Tommy Dorsey's Greatest Hits (RCA Victor, 1996)**
★★★★ **Love Songs (with Frank Sinatra) (RCA Victor, 1997)**
★★★★ **Well Git It! (Jass, N.A.)**
★★★ **1942 War Bond Broadcasts (Jazz Hour, N.A.)**
★★ **The One and Only Tommy Dorsey (RCA Camden Classics, N.A.)**

Trombonist Tommy Dorsey (1905–1956) was one of the most popular swing-band leaders. His career began in the early 1920s, playing with his brother, saxophonist/clarinetist Jimmy Dorsey, in local Pennsylvania bands. The brothers went on to join the Gene Goldkette Orchestra, then the Paul Whiteman Orchestra, before emerging as successful session players on radio broadcasts at the end of the decade. Tommy was also an in-demand trumpet player on sessions, but it was on the trombone that he achieved his trademark sound, with his technical facility and deep, buttery tone.

In 1934 the brothers formed the Dorsey Brothers Orchestra, featuring Glenn Miller's arrangements; in less than a year, because of musical differences, Tommy went off on his own. While Jimmy continued to lead the band, Tommy took over what had been singer Joe Haymes's orchestra. From its first recordings in 1935 the Tommy Dorsey Orchestra crafted tight, well-disciplined pop songs that were mostly novelty tunes or maudlin vehicles for romantic leads to sing in films. "I'm Getting Sentimental Over You" became Dorsey's theme song and earned him the nickname "the Sentimental Gentleman of Swing."

Despite Dorsey's frankly commercial sensibility, his trombone playing is rich and beautiful, his phrasing and musical imagination excellent. Vocalist Edythe Wright provides some of the best settings for the group during the mid-to-late '30s, although her male counterpart, Jack Leonard, sounds dated now. "Marie" and the instrumental "Song of India" joined the lengthy list of Dorsey-band hit singles. But Dorsey really cut loose with his small group, the Clambake Seven, whose lineup at times included Pee Wee Erwin on trumpet, Bud Freeman on tenor sax, Johnny Mince on clarinet, Howard Smith on piano, Carmen Mastren on guitar, Gene Traxler on bass and Dave Tough on drums; unfortunately, this material is generally overlooked on reissues in favor of shoddy repackagings of the same big hits over and over, often with little attention paid to sound quality. *Having a Wonderful Time* includes the small-band recordings.

Of the in-print overviews, *Yes, Indeed!* does the best job of showcasing the band's musical rather than commercial strengths. Dorsey's most famous hit, the memorable instrumental "Boogie Woogie," an arrangement of the Pinetop Smith classic, came in 1938. The best way to hear Dorsey's other hits is the carefully remastered *17 Number Ones.*

Dorsey hit a creative peak in the 1940s leading a band featuring the young singer Frank Sinatra, whose voice was part extension, part foil to Dorsey's trombone phrasing. Sinatra's distinctive style was formed in this association. At its finest, the Dorsey band featured the young Sinatra on vocals, the powerhouse drumming of Buddy Rich and the well-crafted arrangements of Sy Oliver and Alex Stordahl. The *All Time Greatest Hits* volumes include all of Dorsey's commercially released recordings from 1940 to '42. Sinatra's voice on these tracks is at its purest, reaching for notes, dropping in stunning technical displays, free from the stylistic clichés that would eventually plague (and enrich) him. *Stardust* covers the same ground, as does *Oh! Look at Me Now and Other Hits.* The outstanding boxed set *The Song Is You* covers the Sinatra years in exhaustive detail, including live performances and previously unreleased studio tracks. *I'll Be Seeing You* is a sampler from the box.

The post-Sinatra Dorsey band was capable of generating tremendous excitement live, as the mad, burning grooves of *Well Git It!* demonstrate. *The Post-War Era* covers the Dorsey band's studio efforts in the mid-1940s. Shlock never totally deserted Dorsey's commercial side, however, as the abysmal *Tommy Dorsey and David Rose* (including a version of "My Dog Has Fleas") proves.
— J.S.

DAVE DOUGLAS

★★★★ **Parallel Worlds (Soul Note, 1993)**
★★★★ **In Our Lifetime (New World, 1995)**
★★★★ **Constellations (with the Tiny Bell Trio) (Hat Hut, 1995)**
★★★★ **Five (Soul Note, 1996)**

Trumpeter Dave Douglas (b. 1963) is an original thinker who has successfully translated his influences into bold new concepts incorporating elements of world music and the avant-garde. *Parallel Worlds* contrasts the strings of Mark Feldman's violin, Erik Friedlander's cello and Mark Dresser's string bass with Douglas's trumpet and Michael Sarin's drums on a mixture of original material and works by Duke Ellington, Anton Webern and Igor Stravinsky.

The Tiny Bell Trio consists of the highly unusual lineup of trumpet, guitar (Brad Schoeppack) and drums (Jim Black). Douglas puts himself on the spot in this context on *Constellations* and delivers virtuosic results. *Five* uses another inventive string section to invoke the Third Stream's synthesis of classical and jazz forms using the same lineup as *Parallel Worlds* except for Drew Gress replacing Dressler on bass.

Douglas pays tribute to trumpeter Booker Little on *In Our Lifetime* with stellar accompaniment from Chris Speed on tenor saxophone and clarinet, Josh Roseman on trombone, Marty Erlich on bass clarinet, Uri Caine on piano, James Genus on bass and Joey Baron on drums. — J.S.

K.C. DOUGLAS

★★★½ **K.C.'s Blues (1961; Original Blues Classics, 1990)**
★★★★ **Big Road Blues (1961; Original Blues Classics, 1994)**

A gentler, more hushed member of the Lightnin' Hopkins school of fingerpicked blues, Oakland-based K.C. Douglas (1913–1975) was liberated from obscurity during the early '60s by Arhoolie Records founder Chris Strachwitz. Born in Mississippi, Douglas developed a strong country style, training at the hands of Delta blues legend Tommy Johnson.

Douglas recorded more R&B-ish material, including 1954's "Mercury Boogie," for San Francisco's Rhythm label in the '50s. These recordings are currently unavailable on CD. Both *K.C.'s Blues* and *Big Road Blues* are derived from one 1961 session for Bluesville, capturing Douglas in a solo, folk-purist context. The latter features a couple of Tommy Johnson classics and other blues standards. — A.K.

KENNY DREW

★★★ **Kenny Drew Trio (1956; Original Jazz Classics, 1992)**
★★★ **This Is New (1956; Original Jazz Classics, 1990)**
★★★★ **Trio/Quartet/Quintet (1957; Original Jazz Classics, 1988)**
★★★ **Pal Joey (1957; Original Jazz Classics, 1992)**
★★★ **Kenny Drew Plays the Music of Harry Warren and Harold Arlen (1957; Milestone, 1995)**
★★★★ **Duo (SteepleChase, 1973)**
★★★★ **Duo 2 (1974; SteepleChase, 1996)**
★★★★ **Duo Live in Concert (1974; SteepleChase, 1994)**
★★★ **If You Could See Me Now (SteepleChase, 1974)**
★★★ **Morning (1975; SteepleChase, 1995)**
★★★ **In Concert (SteepleChase, 1977)**
★★★ **Ruby My Dear (SteepleChase, 1977)**
★★★★ **Lite Flite (1977; SteepleChase, 1992)**
★★★ **Home Is Where the Soul Is (Xanadu, 1980)**
★★★ **For Sure! (Xanadu, 1981)**
★★★ **It Might as Well Be Spring (Soul Note, 1982)**
★★★ **Your Soft Eyes (Soul Note, 1982)**
★★★ **And Far Away (Soul Note, 1983)**
★★★★ **Undercurrent (Blue Note, 1987)**
★★★ **Everything I Love (SteepleChase, 1991)**
★★★ **Dark Beauty (SteepleChase, 1994)**
★★★ **Solo-Duo (Storyville, 1996)**

An expatriate living in Denmark, pianist Kenny Drew (1928–1993) had roots back to the early bop era. After working with a host of jazz legends including Lester Young and Charlie Parker, Drew established himself as a valuable session player and occasional leader during the 1950s. The Original Jazz Classics recordings (originally released on Riverside) capture the youthful enthusiasm of a funky bopper with nice assists from Paul Chambers and Philly Joe Jones on *Kenny Drew Trio* and Donald Byrd and Wilbur Ware on *This Is New. Undercurrent* is a solid hard-bop session with Freddie Hubbard.

Drew moved to Europe in 1961 and by the '70s was recording regularly for SteepleChase and later Soul Note. The accomplished results feature excellent playing from such sidemen as the great Danish bassist Niels-Henning Ørsted Pedersen and Belgian guitar virtuoso Philip Catherine. — S.F.

PAQUITO D'RIVERA

★★★ **A Taste of Paquito (1985; Legacy, 1994)**
★★★ **Manhattan Burn (Columbia, 1987)**
★★★ **Celebration (Columbia, 1988)**
★★★½ **Tico! Tico! (Chesky, 1989)**
★★★½ **Havana Cafe (Chesky, 1991)**
★★★★ **Reunion (Messidor, 1991)**
★★★★ **La Habana–Rio Connexion (Messidor, 1991)**
★★★★★ **Paquito D'Rivera Presents Forty Years of Cuban Jam Session (Messidor, 1993)**
★★★★ **A Night in Englewood (with the United Nation Orchestra) (Messidor, 1994)**
★★★★ **Portraits of Cuba (Chesky, 1996)**

Multi-instrumentalist Paquito D'Rivera, born in Cuba in 1948, was a key member of the historic Orquestra Cubana de Musica Moderna but came to prominence during the thaw in relations between the United States and Cuba in the late '70s, when he was part of the popular Cuban group Irakere. Irakere can be heard on the *Havana Jam* anthologies that document the historic 1979 Havana concerts where the best of Cuba's musicians played with U.S. jazz and pop groups. D'Rivera also made two domestically released albums with Irakere before defecting from Cuba in 1980 to begin his solo recording career. His virtuosic alto-saxophone playing burns throughout his Columbia efforts, including the now out-of-print *Paquito Blowin'*, *Live at Keystone Korner*, *Mariel* and *Why Not!*

The Chesky recordings place D'Rivera in a comfortable setting that melds South American rhythms with hard-bop soloing. On *Tico! Tico!* he showcases some fine clarinet playing, on *Havana Cafe* his soprano-sax work.

D'Rivera is completely in his element on the outstanding Messidor recordings, which fully integrate South American and Afro-Cuban styles into his postbop conception. *Reunion* brings him back together with trumpeter Arturo Sandoval, his band mate in both the Orquestra and Irakere. *Paquito D'Rivera Presents Forty Years of Cuban Jam Session* is an astonishing project, a collection of 23 of the world's finest Cuban players in a variety of settings, which offers an overview of the music's history.

An additional important musical contribution of D'Rivera's is his work with the United Nation Orchestra, which he has directed since previous leader Dizzy Gillespie's death in 1993. *A Night in Englewood* is a United Nation Orchestra recording under D'Rivera's direction dedicated to Gillespie's memory. *Portraits of Cuba* is an engaging tribute to D'Rivera's homeland.

— J.S.

GEORGE DUKE

★ **Don't Let Go (1978; Epic, 1991)**
★★★ **Reach for It (1978; Epic/Legacy, 1991)**
★★★½ **A Brazilian Love Affair (1979; Epic/Legacy, 1990)**
★★½ **Master of the Game (Epic, 1979)**
★★½ **The Clarke/Duke Project (with Stanley Clarke) (Epic, 1981)**
★★★ **Dream On (1982; Epic, 1991)**
★★½ **The Clarke/Duke Project, Vol. 2 (with Stanley Clarke) (Epic, 1983)**
★★ **Guardian of the Light (Epic, 1983)**
★★★ **Rendezvous (Epic, 1991)**
★★ **Snapshot (Warner Bros., 1992)**
★★★ **Illusions (Warner Bros., 1995)**
★★★ **The Best of George Duke (Epic, 1996)**
★★★½ **Muir Woods Suite (Warner Bros., 1996)**
★★★½ **Is Love Enough? (Warner Bros., 1997)**

Classically trained keyboardist George Duke (b. 1946) began his career leading various groups on the West Coast club circuit. After a brief stint with Don Ellis, he joined Frank Zappa's band, where he started playing synthesizer, the instrument he's become known for. During and immediately following his stay in Zappa's band, Duke recorded his first solo outings, the now unavailable *George Duke*, *The Aura Will Prevail* and *I Love the Blues—She Heard My Cry.* Between Zappa projects, Duke joined the Cannonball Adderley band, which brought his playing into more of a soul-jazz style.

Duke switched to a contemporary R&B style upon joining forces with Billy Cobham in 1975, playing some heavy James Brown– and Sly Stone–influenced funk. The combination of players should have been fruitful, but it wasn't, as the now unavailable *Live on Tour in Europe* painfully demonstrates.

Duke extended the funk strategy with better results on the Epic albums. He finally achieved his goal—a hit single—with "Reach for It," a chanting, danceable blues-funk pattern strongly reminiscent of Sly Stone's "Stand," then broke from the formula to make *A Brazilian Love Affair,* an album that recalls his greatest talents.

Duke enjoyed success in the 1980s as a producer, in a series of collaborations with bassist Stanley Clarke (including the fine *Clarke/Duke Project, Vols. 1* and *2*) and on the solo albums *Dream On* and *Rendezvous. Muir Woods Suite,* an interesting classical-jazz mix, was recorded with Clarke at the Montreux Jazz Festival; on *Is Love Enough?* Duke effectively veers back into pop/funk territory, deftly mixing his synthesizer colorations with the slow-burning groove of the excellent title cut, several effective vocal arrangements, the TV theme from *The Malcolm and Eddie Show* and one jazz instrumental, "Back in the Day."

— J.S.

CHAMPION JACK DUPREE

★★★½ **Back Home in New Orleans (Bullseye Blues, 1990)**
★★★★½ **Forever and Ever (Bullseye Blues, 1991)**
★★★★½ **One Last Time (Bullseye Blues, 1993)**

★★★★ **New Orleans Barrelhouse Boogie (Columbia/Legacy, 1993)**

New Orleans native William "Champion" Jack Dupree (1910–1992) perfected a barrelhouse, boogie-woogie piano style that would influence such famed Crescent City players as Professor Longhair, Fats Domino and Allen Toussaint, among others.

Back Home in New Orleans, filled with Dupree's songs about drinking, eating, traveling and chasing women, finds the garrulous pianist accompanied by a terrific New Orleans band, including legendary tenor saxophonist Alvin "Red" Tyler. With a laid-back feel, sinewy grooves and loose-yet-tight playing, the band provides a solid underpinning for songs like the cautionary "When I'm Drinkin'," the lamenting "Broken Hearted" and "Calcutta," which Dupree cowrote with Roosevelt Sykes. Another highlight is the improvisational talking blues "Freedom."

Companion pieces *Forever and Ever* and *One Last Time* (Dupree's last recording before his death) underscore the fact that the pianist was in full command of his musical faculties until the end. *Forever and Ever* features such great songs as an implosive version of Eddie Boyd's "Third Degree" and Dupree's own "Dupree Special," which he taught to Professor Longhair. Stellar tracks on *One Last Time* include "Early in the Morning" and Sykes's "She's Jail Bait," as well as Dupree's "Big Leg Emma." Both albums include fine work by Dupree's band, particularly guitarist Kenn Lending and bassist Walter Payton Jr.

New Orleans Barrelhouse Boogie is a fabulous retrospective of Dupree's early-'40s output for the Okeh label. Including 11 previously unissued tracks, the album's 25 cuts were recorded between June 1940 and November 1941. Though Dupree's later recordings were more stylistically diverse, this anthology brings into clear perspective his influential style, as well as his formidable skills as a player and performer. — B.R.H.

JOHNNY DYER

★★★½ **Jukin' (Blind Pig, 1983)**
★★★½ **Listen Up! (with Rick Holmstrom) (Black Top, 1994)**
★★★½ **Shake It! (with Rick Holmstrom) (Black Top, 1995)**

Following in the footsteps of Muddy Waters, Johnny Dyer (b. 1938) learned to play the blues while living on the Stovall plantation in Rolling Fork, Mississippi. He developed a harmonica style patterned after Little Walter Jacobs and in 1958 moved to Los Angeles, where he began playing duets with George "Harmonica" Smith and founded his own band, Johnny Dyer and the Blue Notes.

Dyer stopped performing in the early 1960s but came out of retirement in the '80s to record *Jukin',* composed of a song originally released on the Murray Brothers label and four additional tracks, one of which features Smith. Dyer went on to record with guitarist Rick Holmstrom from Rod Piazza and the Mighty Flyers, a fortuitous collaboration that produced the exciting jam sessions *Listen Up!* and *Shake It!*
— J.S.

DOMINIQUE EADE

★★★½ **The Ruby and the Pearl (Accurate, 1991)**
★★★ **My Resistance Is Low (Accurate, 1995)**
★★★ **When the Wind Was Cool (RCA Victor, 1997)**

Vocalist Dominique Eade (b. 1958) approaches jazz more as an instrumentalist than as an out-front singer, which gives her luminescent voice a distinctive style. Whether singing or scatting, her music thrives on risky interaction with other players as she bends, shapes and places notes. Eade developed her art within the fertile Boston jazz scene as both student (at the Berklee College of Music and the New England Conservatory's Third Stream department) and teacher.

In her very strong debut, *The Ruby and the Pearl,* with pianist Stanley Cowell, bassist John Lockwood, drummer Alan Dawson and saxophonist Allan Chase, Eade adds her own poignant words to Billy Strayhorn's musical epitaph "Blood Count." *My Resistance Is Low,* with pianist Bruce Barth, bassist George Mraz and drummer Lewis Nash, is more daring and difficult to absorb but well worth the effort. *When the Wind Was Cool* consists of cool explorations of classic songs associated with 1950s Stan Kenton band singers June Christy and Chris Connor. — K.F.

SNOOKS EAGLIN

★★★ **Blues from New Orleans, Vol. 1 (Storyville, 1958)**
★★★ **Country Boy Down in New Orleans (1958; Arhoolie, 1991)**
★★★ **New Orleans Street Singer (1958; Storyville, 1994)**
★★★ **Possum up a Simmon Tree (Arhoolie, 1971)**
★★★½ **Baby, You Can Get Your Gun! (Black Top, 1987)**
★★★★ **Out of Nowhere (Black Top, 1989)**
★★★ **Teasin' You (Black Top, 1992)**
★★★ **Soul's Edge (Black Top, 1995)**
★★★½ **The Complete Recordings (Capitol, 1995)**

A very appealing New Orleans blues and rock & roll guitarist, Eaglin (b. 1936) finds his strength in his sense of humor—and his total saturation in the roots music that formed him (as a former member of Allen Toussaint's first band, his Crescent City credibility is unassailable). His '50s recordings were faithful country blues; later he went electric and rocked harder. With Fats Domino's rhythm section along for the ride, *Baby, You Can Get Your Gun!* is tough and rollicking; *Out of Nowhere,* featuring Smiley Lewis's "Playgirl," is even zestier. A very nimble player, his style informed both by jump-jazz swing and deep blues grit, Snooks also sings up a storm. *Teasin' You* rekindles the fire of Lloyd Price's "Baby, Please Come Home"; *Soul's Edge* gives up a righteous version of Hank Ballard's "Thrill on the Hill" and features excellent spiritual fare—yet another example of Eaglin's encyclopedic range. — P.E.

JON EARDLEY

★★★ **Hollywood to New York (Original Jazz Classics, 1990)**

Trumpeter Jon Eardley (b. 1928) grew up steeped in the classic swing tradition passed on from his father, Bill Eardley, who played cornet in bands led by Paul Whiteman and Isham Jones. Jon, who was featured in the Gerry

Mulligan band before making his recording debut as a leader, demonstrates a disciplined tone and strong melodic sense.

Hollywood to New York collects two EPs, the first recorded in Los Angeles on Christmas Day, 1954, with a sympathetic trio featuring outstanding bass work from Red Mitchell and strong writing from Eardley. The second session, a March 1955 date with the Phil Woods rhythm section and saxophonist J.R. Monterose, features two Tadd Dameron numbers, including "Sid's Delight," a tribute to Eardley's strongest influence, Fats Navarro. — J.S.

CHARLES EARLAND

★★★★ **Black Talk! (1970; Original Jazz Classics, 1995)**
★★★★ **Leaving This Planet (1974; Prestige, 1993)**
★★★½ **Front Burner (Milestone, 1988)**
★★★½ **Third Degree Burn (Milestone, 1989)**

Keyboardist Charles Earland (b. 1941) grew up in South Philadelphia and started out playing alto, tenor and baritone saxophone, influenced by local jazz heroes the Heath Brothers. By the time he was 17, Earland was the featured tenor saxophonist in organist Jimmy McGriff's group. He switched to organ in the early 1960s and led his own R&B and soul-jazz combos through the decade. In 1968–69 he was the organist in Lou Donaldson's band.

Earland's solo breakthrough came on *Black Talk!,* recorded with the Donaldson rhythm section of Melvin Sparks on guitar and Idris Muhammad on drums and augmented by trumpeter Virgil Jones, tenor saxophonist Houston Person and congero Buddy Caldwell. This was one of the hottest albums of the '70s, with the lengthy jam on "More Today Than Yesterday" and the tidy signature track "The Mighty Burner" generating massive airplay.

Earland's Hammond B-3 style, with its insistent, ahead-of-the-beat bass lines and percussive effects, as well as his subsequent interest in synthesizer textures made him an early giant of the fusion era. His stature is illustrated on the exciting and influential *Leaving This Planet,* an extended set of 10 lengthy pieces with solid grooves laid down by Earland on organ, synths, clavinet, electric piano and soprano sax; Dr. Patrick Gleeson on synths; terrific contributions from Freddie Hubbard and Eddie Henderson on trumpets; Joe Henderson on tenor; Dave Hubbard on alto flute and soprano and tenor sax; Mark Elf and Eddie Arkin on guitars; and Harvey Mason on drums.

After gravitating into more overtly R&B and pop styles in the 1970s and '80s, Earland returned to the organ-combo format at the end of the '80s. On *Front Burner* Earland reunites with Virgil Jones in his classic format, with Bill Easley on tenor, Bobby Broom on guitar, Rudy Williams on drums and Frank Colon on conga. The result is still a high-quality groove, lacking only the sense of discovery found in the earlier material. *Third Degree Burn* is another fine session with Broom and Williams returning behind an all-star front line of Lew Soloff on trumpet, Grover Washington Jr. on soprano sax and David Newman on tenor.

Earland has made many other records that have yet to be rereleased on CD, but with the recent resurgence of interest in soul jazz and dance-oriented grooves it seems only a matter of time before he enjoys an overdue revival. — J.S.

HARRY "SWEETS" EDISON

★★★★ **Pres and Sweets (with Lester Young) (1955; Verve, 1991)**
★★★★ **Jawbreakers (1962; Original Jazz Classics, 1991)**
★★★½ **Oscar Peterson and Harry "Sweets" Edison (1975; Original Jazz Classics, 1992)**
★★★½ **Edison's Lights (1976; Original Jazz Classics, 1994)**
★★★ **Simply Sweets (1978; Original Jazz Classics, 1987)**
★★★ **For My Pals (Pablo, 1988)**
★★★½ **Oscar Peterson + Harry Edison + Eddie "Cleanhead" Vinson (Pablo, 1988)**
★★★ **"Sweets" for the Sweet (Collectables, 1996)**
★★★½ **The Best of Harry Edison (Pablo, N.A.)**

From 1938 to 1950 trumpeter Harry "Sweets" Edison (b. 1915) was a mainstay in Count Basie's greatest bands. Lester Young gave him the nickname "Sweets" as a reference to his airy, melodious style. Edison's relaxed approach to the blues proved a perfect match for another Basie-ite, tenor saxophonist Eddie "Lockjaw" Davis. The two first teamed up on *Jawbreakers,* a date so memorable that they would reprise it more than a decade later on a series of Pablo recordings, including *Edison's Lights* (which also includes Basie) and *Simply Sweets* (both now reissued on Original Jazz Classics). Edison's durability showed him leading a session well into his 70s on the enjoyable *For My Pals.* — J.S.

HONEYBOY EDWARDS

★★★★ **Crawling Kingsnake (Testament, 1977)**
★★★★ **Old Friends (with Floyd Jones, Kansas City Red, Sunnyland Slim and Big Walter Horton) (1981; Earwig, 1993)**
★★★★ **White Windows (1989; Evidence, 1993)**
★★★★ **Delta Bluesman (Earwig, 1992)**

Honeyboy Edwards, born David Edwards in 1915 in Shaw, Mississippi, was a contemporary of Son House and a student of Big Joe Williams. He played with the shadowy Robert Johnson during the summer of 1937 and spent a short time with Muddy Waters in 1939.

An important link to the Delta blues, Edwards's first recordings, by Alan Lomax in 1942 for the Library of Congress, are reproduced almost in their entirety on the compilation *Delta Bluesman.* Then 27, Edwards exhibited an ability to play several styles of music, including ragtime, traditional work songs and biting Delta blues. Combining 27 recordings from 4 sessions, *Delta Bluesman* begins with Lomax's July 1942 introduction of Edwards as "one of the best guitar players in the country," whereupon the artist launches into Arthur Phelps's "Roamin' and Ramblin' Blues." A standout Edwards original is "The Army Blues," on which he blows an insistent rack harmonica, reinforcing his dexterous acoustic-slide work and matter-of-fact vocals.

Rounding out *Delta Bluesman* are sides cut in 1979 and 1991. The solitary 1979 track, a version of Big Joe Williams's "Bad Whiskey and Cocaine," includes backing by Kansas City Red on drums and Floyd Jones on second acoustic guitar. The latter tracks feature a band consisting of Carey Bell (harmonica), Sunnyland Slim (piano), Aron Burton (bass) and Robert Plunkett (drums). *Crawling Kingsnake* includes versions of "Just Like Jesse James" and "Sweet Home Chicago" and a revealing interview with Pete Welding about Robert Johnson and Tommy Johnson.

White Windows, a reissue of a 1989 release on the Blue Suit label, consists of a solo Edwards playing acoustic and electric guitars and occasionally harmonica. The album contains three originals, among them "Drop Down Mama," a song he recorded for Leonard Chess in 1953. The song was never released as a single, claims Edwards, because Muddy Waters—who was also recording for Chess at the time—claimed its slide work was too similar to his own and put pressure on the label owner to squelch the song. Nevertheless, here Edwards covers Waters's "Don't Say I Don't Love You," as well as compositions by Roosevelt Sykes, Walter Davis and Robert Jr. Lockwood. The album's best song, however, is a rollicking version of Bukka White's "Shake 'Em on Down," which displays Edwards's instrumental dexterity and woozy vocals.

While not a proper Edwards solo release, *Old Friends* is a worthy collective effort that unites Edwards with Floyd Jones (on bass), Kansas City Red, Sunnyland Slim and harmonica ace Big Walter Horton. Cut in 1979 and 1980, these sessions (some of Horton's and Jones's final recordings) marked the first time Edwards had recorded with a band since the infamous "Drop Down Mama" sessions in the early '50s. With six additional tracks, the album contains compositions from each player, including four by Edwards, whose distinctive keening voice and dizzying guitar are unmistakable against the sultry backing groove provided by his accomplished colleagues. — B.R.H.

ROY ELDRIDGE

★★★★★ **Roy and Diz (1954; Verve, 1994)**
★★★ **Jazz Maturity (1954; Original Jazz Classics, 1994)**
★★★½ **Mexican Bandit Meets Pittsburgh Pirate (with Paul Gonsalves) (1973; Original Jazz Classics, 1992)**
★★★½ **Oscar Peterson and Roy Eldridge (1975; Original Jazz Classics, 1994)**
★★★ **Happy Time (1975; Original Jazz Classics, 1991)**
★★★★ **The Trumpet Kings at Montreux '75 (1975; Original Jazz Classics, 1990)**
★★★ **What It's All About (1976; Original Jazz Classics, 1995)**
★★★★ **Montreux '77 (1977; Original Jazz Classics, 1989)**
★★★★★ **The Nifty Cat (New World, 1986)**
★★★★★ **Little Jazz (Columbia, 1989)**
★★★★★ **Uptown (Columbia, 1990)**
★★★★★ **After You've Gone (Decca, 1991)**
★★★★★ **Little Jazz: Best of the Verve Years (Verve, 1994)**

★★★★ **The Big Sound of Little Jazz (Topaz Jazz, 1995)**
★★★★ **In Paris (Vogue Disques, 1995)**

Considering that Roy Eldridge (1911–1989) was indisputably the best and most influential trumpet player of the swing era's glory days, the sparse documentation of his career is a source of great frustration for his fans. The Pittsburgh-born Eldridge came to New York in 1930, where he played with several groups at Small's Paradise in Harlem before joining Teddy Hill's band, followed by stints with Connie's Hot Chocolates and McKinney's Cotton Pickers. The Columbia recording *Little Jazz* (titled after his nickname) samples Eldridge's work in various contexts from 1935 to '40. His work with outfits led by Hill, Fletcher Henderson and Teddy Wilson are highlights, showcasing his high-register pyrotechnics, relentless swing and melodic invention. *The Big Sound of Little Jazz* covers much of the same era.

Uptown collects a series of terrific performances by Eldridge as part of the Gene Krupa orchestra. The bulk of the material is from 1941 to '42 and features some of the finest moments in vocalist Anita O'Day's career as well. Check out the drums-trumpet breaks in "That Drummer's Band." Four tracks from 1949 flesh out the set. *After You've Gone* collects Eldridge's excellent recordings for Decca leading his own orchestra from 1943 to '46, with three tracks from 1936 included. By the end of the 1940s, touring big bands, except for the most successful groups, had lost their popularity, and Eldridge adjusted by leading smaller combos. The fine small-group session *In Paris,* from 1950, features saxophonist Zoot Sims.

Eldridge recorded prolifically for Verve during the 1950s, though you wouldn't know it by what's currently available. The Verve *Little Jazz* provides a useful sample of this era. *Roy and Diz* documents the profound impact Eldridge had on the next great trumpet star in jazz history, his protégé Dizzy Gillespie.

During the '60s Eldridge got plenty of work as a sideman and toured the world with the Jazz at the Philharmonic orchestra, but he virtually disappeared as a leader on record. He remained capable of greatness when given the chance, though, as demonstrated on the fine 1970 recording *The Nifty Cat,* a sextet session featuring Benny Morton on trombone and Oliver Jackson on drums.

Eldridge enjoyed a renaissance in the 1970s, playing with such veteran stars as pianist Oscar Peterson, vibraphonist Milt Jackson, bassist Ray Brown and drummer Louie Bellson. The Trumpet Kings, a trio comprising Eldridge, Gillespie and Clark Terry, come off well on the live *Trumpet Kings at Montreux '75,* and Eldridge sounds particularly good on *Montreux '77* in a quartet setting with Peterson, bassist Niels-Henning Ørsted Pedersen and drummer Bobby Durham. — J.S.

ELECTRIC FLAG

★★★★★ **Long Time Comin' (Columbia, 1968)**
★★ **The Electric Flag (Columbia, 1969)**
★★★ **The Best of the Electric Flag (Columbia, 1970)**
★★½ **The Band Kept Playing (Atlantic, 1974)**
★★★ **Old Glory: The Best of Electric Flag (Legacy, 1995)**

A San Francisco supergroup boasting former Butterfield Blues Band guitarist Mike Bloomfield as its ace, the Electric Flag also featured such dynamite players as Mitch Ryder, Steve Miller, keyboardist Barry Goldberg, bassist Harvey Brooks (ex-Dylan, Doors), saxophonist Herbie Rich and drummer Buddy Miles (Nick Gravenites, the quintet's other mainstay, was an earnest singer but a better writer). At the Monterey Pop Festival they introduced the jazz-rock sound that made their first album a minor classic. The group's blues were mainly Bloomfield's show—and a great one. But it was with mid-tempo numbers that the band sounded most distinctive; experimenting with an aggressive horn section, the Flag succeeded, where Blood, Sweat and Tears and Chicago failed, at creating a new kind of swing that lost no rock power. Yet the Flag's stellar technique never overwhelmed its passion.

Without Bloomfield, the band's second record, *The Electric Flag,* was weak, and hence, both *Best of* compilations suffer. Reuniting with Dr. John's Bonaroo Brass and the Muscle Shoals Horns in 1974 seemed promising, but the original drive was lacking. — P.E.

MARK ELF

★★½ **Mark Elf Trio (Alerce, 1995)**
★★★★ **The Eternal Triangle (Jen Bay, 1996)**
★★★½ **A Minor Scramble (Jen Bay, 1997)**
★★★ **Trickynometry (Jen Bay, 1998)**

The talent of guitarist Mark Elf (b. 1949), a player blessed with a strong, joyful sense of swing, has propelled him into opportunities playing with Dizzy Gillespie, Jon Hendricks and Jimmy Heath. In the late 1970s and early '80s, he worked the soul-jazz circuit with saxophonist Lou Donaldson and organists Charles Earland and Jack McDuff. Heavily inspired by guitarists Tal Farlow and Jimmy Raney as well as numerous horn players, Elf's biting, single-note hard-bop style is marked by fluid melodic lines. His recordings have been impressive not only for his playing, but also for his musical concepts and choice of material.

Mark Elf Trio, recorded in Chile with a South American rhythm section, spotlights Elf's talent as a soloist. On his tour de force, *The Eternal Triangle,* recorded in 1988 but not released until 1996, Elf matches talents with Heath, pianist Hank Jones, drummer Ben Riley and bassist Ray Drummond. *A Minor Scramble,* cut in two phases, teams Elf with a mix of younger talents: Half of the tracks feature bassist Peter Washington and drummer Louis Nash; the remainder showcase pianist Benny Green, trumpeter Nicholas Payton, saxophonist Eric Alexander, bassists Dennis Irwin and Neal Miner and drummer Gregory Hutchinson in varying combinations. *Trickynometry* is similar in approach and tone, leaning more toward originals. — K.F.

KURT ELLING

★★★ **Close Your Eyes (Blue Note, 1995)**
★★★★ **The Messenger (Blue Note, 1997)**

Singer Kurt Elling, born in Chicago in 1967, has an innovative vocalese style that gives a Generation X twist to his world-roaming improvisations. The leaps of logic involved in some of his vocal feats veer into wild realms of musical intuition. In his debut, *Close Your Eyes,* Elling, philosopher, human beatbox and bop lifer all in one, presents a serious talent searching for direction.

The Messenger follows with a powerfully focused vision epitomized by a truly original version of "Nature Boy," done up-tempo with an exultant scat solo; the ambitious three-part suite of "The Beauty of All Things," "The Dance" and "Prayer for Mr. Davis"; a breathtaking vocalese breakdown of a Dexter Gordon solo, "Tanya Jean"; and a duet with Cassandra Wilson on the Zombies' hit "Time of the Season."
— J.S.

DUKE ELLINGTON

★★★★ **Hi-Fi Ellington Uptown (Columbia, 1953)**
★★★★ **The 1953 Pasedena Concert (1953; GNP Crescendo, 1988)**
★★★★ **The 1954 Los Angeles Concert (1954; GNP Crescendo, 1988)**
★★★★ **The 1952 Seattle Concert (1954; RCA Bluebird, 1995)**
★★★★★ **Duke Ellington and His Orchestra at Newport (1956; Columbia, 1987)**
★★★★ **Ellington Indigos (1957; Columbia, 1989)**
★★★★★ **Black, Brown and Beige (1958; RCA Bluebird, 1988)**
★★★★★ **Ellington Jazz Party (1959; Columbia, 1987)**
★★★★★ **Side by Side (with Johnny Hodges) (Verve, 1959)**
★★★★ **Blues in Orbit (1960; Columbia Jazz Masterworks, 1988)**
★★★½ **First Time! The Count Meets the Duke (with Count Basie) (Columbia, 1961)**
★★★★★ **Duke Ellington and John Coltrane (1962; Impulse!, 1988)**
★★★★★ **Duke Ellington Meets Coleman Hawkins (1962; Impulse!, 1986)**
★★★★ **Duke Ellington and His Orchestra Featuring Paul Gonsalves (1962; Original Jazz Classics, 1991)**
★★★★★ **The Great Paris Concert (Atlantic, 1963)**
★★★★★ **Back to Back: Duke Ellington and Johnny Hodges Play the Blues (Verve, 1963)**
★★★★ **Francis A. Sinatra and Edward K. Ellington (1967; Reprise, 1998)**
★★★½ **70th Birthday Concert (Blue Note, 1969)**
★★★½ **Latin American Suite (1970; Original Jazz Classics, 1990)**
★★★★ **Orchestral Works (1970; MCA, 1989)**
★★★½ **Togo Brava Suite (Blue Note, 1971)**
★★★★★ **The Afro-Eurasian Eclipse (1971; Original Jazz Classics, 1991)**
★★★½ **Up in Duke's Workshop (1972; Pablo, 1991)**
★★★★ **The Ellington Suites (1972; Original Jazz Classics, N.A.)**
★★★★ **It Don't Mean a Thing . . . (with Teresa Brewer) (1973; Columbia, 1981)**

★★★½ Yale Concert (1973; Original Jazz Classics, 1991)
★★★★½ Duke's Big 4 (1974; Pablo, 1988)
★★★½ The Pianist (1974; Original Jazz Classics, 1992)
★★★★★ Second Sacred Concert (1974; Prestige, 1990)
★★★★½ This One's for Blanton (with Ray Brown) (1975; Original Jazz Classics, 1994)
★★★★ The Ellington Suites (1976; Original Jazz Classics, 1990)
★★★½ The Intimate Ellington (1977; Original Jazz Classics, 1992)
★★★★★ The Duke Ellington Carnegie Hall Concerts: January 1943 (1977; Prestige, N.A.)
★★★★★ The Duke Ellington Carnegie Hall Concerts: December 1944 (1977; Prestige, N.A.)
★★★★★ The Duke Ellington Carnegie Hall Concerts: January 1946 (1977; Prestige, N.A.)
★★★★½ The Duke Ellington Carnegie Hall Concerts: December 1947 (1977; Prestige, N.A.)
★★★★½ The Best of Duke Ellington (1980; Pablo, 1991)
★★★★ The All-Star Road Band (1983; CBS Special Products, 1989)
★★★★ The All-Star Road Band, Vol. 2 (1983; CBS Special Products, 1989)
★★★★½ Piano Duets: Great Times! (with Billy Strayhorn) (1984; Original Jazz Classics, N.A.)
★★★★ New Mood Indigo (1985; CBS Special Products, 1989)
★★★★ Harlem (Pablo, 1985)
★★★★ Duke Ellington/Happy Reunion (Sony Music Special Products, 1985)
★★★★ The Intimacy of the Blues (1986; Original Jazz Classics, 1991)
★★★½ Money Jungle (Blue Note, 1986)
★★★★★ Duke Ellington: The Blanton-Webster Band (RCA Bluebird, 1986)
★★★★ And His Mother Called Him Bill (RCA Bluebird, 1987)
★★★★ Compact Jazz: Duke Ellington and Friends (Verve, 1987)
★★★½ In the Uncommon Market (Pablo, 1987)
★★★★ Back Room Romp (Portrait, 1988)
★★★★½ The Far East Suite: Special Mix (1988; RCA Bluebird, 1995)
★★★★★ The Great Ellington Units (RCA Bluebird, 1988)
★★★½ The Feeling of Jazz (Black Lion, 1988)
★★★★ The Piano Album (Capitol, 1989)
★★★★ The Best of Duke Ellington (Signature, 1989)
★★★★★ Braggin' in Brass: The Immortal 1938 Year (Portrait, 1989)
★★★★ Duke Ellington Live! (EmArcy, 1989)
★★★★★ Four Symphonic Works (MusicMasters, 1989)
★★★½ Live at the 1956 Stratford Festival (Music and Arts Programs of America, 1989)
★★★★ Solos, Duets and Trios (RCA Bluebird, 1990)
★★★★ Three Suites (Columbia, 1990)
★★★★ The Brunswick Era, Vol. 1: (1926–1929) (MCA, 1990)
★★★★½ The Brunswick Era, Vol. 2: The Jungle Band (MCA, 1990)
★★★★ Jungle Nights in Harlem (RCA Bluebird, 1991)
★★★★★ The Okeh Ellington (Columbia, 1991)
★★★★★ The Essence of Duke Ellington (Columbia/Legacy, 1991)
★★★★★ The Duke's Men: Small Groups, Vol. 1 (Columbia/Legacy, 1991)
★★★★ Reminiscing in Tempo (Columbia/Legacy, 1991)
★★★½ Hot Summer Dance (Red Baron/Sony, 1991)
★★★★ Jubilee Stomp (RCA Bluebird, 1992)
★★★½ Jungle Style (1927–1938) (Black and Blue, 1992)
★★★★★ Masterpieces (1938–1940) (Black and Blue, 1992)
★★★½ The Young Duke (Pearl, 1992)
★★★★★ The Best of Duke Ellington: Original Capitol Recordings (Curb/CEMA, 1992)
★★★★ The "Collection" 46–47 Recordings (Hindsight, 1992)
★★★½ Happy Birthday Duke! (LaserLight, 1992)
★★★★ Things Ain't What They Used to Be (LaserLight, 1993)
★★★★ Duke's Men, Vol. 2 (Columbia Jazz Masterworks, 1993)

★★★½ **The Great London Concerts (MusicMasters, 1993)**
★★★★ **Compact Jazz: Ella Fitzgerald and Duke Ellington (Verve, 1993)**
★★★★ **The Indispensable Duke Ellington and the Small Groups, Vols. 9 and 10 (RCA Bluebird, 1994)**
★★★★ **The Great Chicago Concerts (MusicMasters, 1994)**
★★★★★ **16 Most Requested Songs (Columbia/Legacy, 1994)**
★★★★★ **Early Ellington: The Complete Decca Recordings (Decca, 1994)**
★★★★ **Giants of the Big Band Era (Magma, 1994)**
★★★★★ **Duke Ellington and His Orchestra Live at Newport 1958 (Legacy, 1994)**
★★★½ **Sir Duke (Drive Archive, 1994)**
★★★★ **Swing, Vol. 2 (ABC Music, 1994)**
★★★★ **Verve Jazz Masters 4 (Verve, 1994)**
★★★★ **Beyond Category: The Musical Genius of Duke Ellington, (RCA, 1994)**
★★★★ **Duke Ellington, Vol. 2: Swing 1930–1938 (ABC Music, 1994)**
★★★½ **Duke Ellington and His Great Vocalists (Columbia/Legacy, 1995)**
★★★★ **Best of the Big Bands (Columbia/Legacy, 1995)**
★★★★½ **Live at the Whitney (Impulse!, 1995)**
★★★★ **The Indispensable Duke Ellington, Vols. 5 and 6 (RCA Bluebird, 1995)**
★★★★ **The Indispensable Duke Ellington, Vols. 11 and 12 (RCA Bluebird, 1995)**
★★★★ **New York Concert: In Performance at Columbia University (MusicMasters, 1995)**
★★★★ **In a Mellotone (RCA, 1995)**
★★★★★ **The Best of Duke Ellington (Blue Note, 1995)**
★★★½ **The Duke Plays Ellington, Vol. 1 (Topaz Jazz, 1995)**
★★★★ **This Is Jazz 7 (Columbia/Legacy, 1996)**
★★★★ **Greatest Hits (RCA Victor, 1996)**
★★★★ **Ellington at Basin Street East (Music and Arts Programs of America, 1996)**
★★★½ **Through the Roof (Drive Archive, 1996)**
★★★★ **The Popular Duke Ellington (RCA Victor, 1997)**

SERIES
★★★★ **1924–1927 (Classics, 1991)**
★★★★ **1927–1928 (Classics, 1991)**
★★★★ **1928 (Classics, 1991)**
★★★★ **1928–1929 (Classics, 1991)**
★★★★ **1929 (Classics, 1991)**
★★★★ **1929–1930 (Classics, 1991)**
★★★★ **1930 (Classics, 1991)**
★★★★★ **1937 (Classics, 1993)**
★★★★★ **1938–1939 (Classics, 1994)**
★★★★★ **1939 (Classics, 1994)**
★★★★★ **1939, Vol. 2 (Classics, 1994)**
★★★★★ **1939–1940 (Classics, 1994)**
★★★★★ **1940, Vol. 2 (Classics, 1995)**

THE PRIVATE COLLECTION
★★★★ **Vol. 1 (Studio Sessions, Chicago, 1956) (Saja, 1989)**
★★★★ **Vol. 2 (Dance Concerts, California, 1958) (Saja, 1989)**
★★★★ **Vol. 3 (Studio Sessions, New York, 1962) (Saja, 1989)**
★★★★ **Vol. 4 (Studio Sessions, New York, 1963) (Saja, 1989)**
★★★★★ **Vol. 5 (The Suites) (Saja, 1989)**
★★★★ **Vol. 6 (Dance Dates, California, 1958) (Saja, 1989)**
★★★★ **Vol. 7 (Studio Sessions, 1957 and 1962) (Saja, 1989)**
★★★★ **Vol. 8 (Studio Sessions, 1957, 1965, 1966, 1967) (Saja, 1989)**
★★★★ **Vol. 9 (Studio Sessions, New York, 1968) (Saja, 1989)**
★★★★ **Vol. 10 (New York and Chicago, 1965, 1966, 1971) (Saja, 1989)**

Arguably America's greatest composer, Duke Ellington (1899–1974) made the most melodic, ambitious and sophisticated jazz imaginable. He both epitomized and transcended the form; the blue notes and swing rhythm of jazz, its blues structures and nightclub ethos—they're found in abundance in the whole of Duke, but prolific as Picasso (Ellington penned over 2,000 pieces) and just as unlimited in stylistic range, he inhabits the high, free air of genius and can't be confined (classical listeners detect echoes of Bach, Delius, Stravinsky, Ravel). Although, oddly enough, his interest in music didn't intensify to passion until after his high school years, Edward Kennedy Ellington was stellar equally in the late '20s (his Cotton Club days), the early '40s and the mid-'50s (his '60s work isn't far off the mark). Indeed, Duke is ultimately not merely a musician but the bearer of a certain complex spirit—polished but full of gentle pathos, elegant, romantic, witty. And, as is true of only a few titans (Mozart, again Picasso), the man was remarkably consistent in his greatness—so much so that the star ratings above are "accurate" only in a relative way. Virtually everything Ellington recorded is of great value; his output was voluminous (even the above listing is selective, concentrating on the more available offerings).

Influenced by Willie "the Lion" Smith and James P. Johnson, Ellington was a terrific, percussive pianist (check the rare 1972 solo recital *Live at the Whitney,* also *The Piano Album* and *The Pianist*), but his primary instrument was the large ensemble, the orchestra or big band (astonishingly, he kept his band generally intact for 50 years). At any given time, that band featured up to eight dynamite soloists—among the stars count saxophonists Johnny Hodges (king of smooth), Ben Webster (a magnificent growler) and speed demon Paul Gonsalves; trumpeters Cootie Williams and Ray Nance; trombonist Joe Nanton; clarinetist Barney Bigard; bassist Jimmy Blanton (more or less the inventor of modern jazz bass). The Ellington sound combined staggering musical intelligence with intuitive character study: Duke wrote not for generic players but for his specific, longtime stars. Each was given great encouragement and one primary dictate: Ellington's famous motto, It don't mean a thing if it ain't got that swing.

Getting a grip on Ellington takes work, not because his music was ever inaccessible, but because there's simply so much of it. A felicitous start might be with the songs: At indelible verse-chorus-verse Ellington rivals the Gershwins, Jerome Kern, Cole Porter. *16 Most Requested Songs* collects the pips, from "Mood Indigo," "Don't Get Around Much Anymore" and "Do Nothing Till You Hear from Me" to "Satin Doll" and "Take the A Train" (along with "East St. Louis Toodle-o," Duke's signature tune, and a hot example of his longtime collaboration with arranger/composer Billy Strayhorn). Then there's any number of best-of packages, all decent: combining *The Best of Duke Ellington* on Signature, with Columbia/Legacy's *The Essence of Duke Ellington* nets a brisk intro—"Sophisticated Lady," "Solitude," "Dimuendo and Crescendo in Blue (The Wailing Interval)" span music from the '30s to the '50s, and as short pieces they flourish the composer's melodic gifts and remarkable concision. Try also *This Is Jazz 7,* RCA's *Greatest Hits,* Blue Note's *Best of* and Verve's *Jazz Masters 4.*

For the early work—so beat-happy, it earned the name "jungle music"—note *The Okeh Ellington* and its 50 cuts of embryonic (1927–30) greatness, as well as the Decca three-disc *Early Ellington. The Indispensable Duke* series offers the '40s Ellington at his finest; the band is fearless. Verve's *Duke Ellington and Friends* is nice, too—this is Duke a little later on, with Ella Fitzgerald, Billy Strayhorn on piano, tenor saxophonist Ben Webster and drummer Louis Bellson turning in late-'50s–early-'60s versions of the Ellington classics. Both volumes of *The All-Star Road Band* series are copacetic: With the Ellington heavyweights blowing in a dance setting, "Perdido," "Take the A Train" and other hits come across with an assured, easy grace. Romantics might find a good entry into the elegiac Ellington with *Ellington Indigos:* 1957 vignettes of great tenderness and charm—"Autumn Leaves," "Willow Weep for Me" and the album's other cuts often bring Duke's piano uncharacteristically to the fore, and Johnny Hodges plays like a dream. *It Don't Mean a Thing* is a fine Ellington for song lovers—a collaboration with ace vocalist Teresa Brewer, it captures an essential mood of the master for listeners scared off by long solos. Braver sorts then should dive into *Ellington at Newport.* His best-selling album, it captures a groundbreaking live performance in which tenor saxophonist Paul Gonsalves blazes through 27 choruses of "Dimuendo and Crescendo in Blue"—breathtaking, and for more along the same lines, pick up *Featuring Paul Gonsalves.*

Grounded in the blues, Ellington forayed into all but the most passing or outre forms of jazz; he was at home, as well, in the European classical tradition, and as his career progressed, he concentrated more heavily on longer pieces in which the form extended far beyond jazz structure. At the opposite end of the introductory work are the Ellington monuments. Duke's own favorites were his *Sacred Concerts* of the late '60s. Some jazz listeners who place a premium on improvisation don't dig them, but the combination of some of Ellington's strongest sidemen, gospel choirs and solo vocalists remains inspiring. Portrait's *Braggin' in Brass: The Immortal 1938 Year* includes among its 32 gems a strong "Black and Tan Fantasy"—first recorded in 1927, the piece was an early example of Ellington's trailblazing incorporation of the jazz player's improvisational skills within a completely structured piece. Ellingtonians—

and few jazz masters have been better served by champions and scholars—often argue that his orchestra reached its peak in the '40s when such long-form landmarks as "Liberian Suite" and "Ko-Ko" were unveiled—and, along with *The Blanton-Webster Band,* Prestige's four volumes of the ensemble's four *Carnegie Hall Concerts* make the claim hard to refute. The 1943 set is the most impressive, debuting "Black, Brown and Beige," the first of Duke's massive, extended pieces. *Four Symphonic Works* includes a version of that milestone, as well as "Harlem," "New World a-Comin'" and "Three Black Kings," works that may not rank among Duke's greatest but that help point out his mastery of the orchestral idiom (note, too, the fine *Orchestral Works* on MCA Classics). Another impressive collection of the Ellington orchestra at its height is Bluebird's *Black, Brown and Beige,* with its 58 selections from the 1944–1946 period.

Jazz Party and *Blues in Orbit* are effervescent, and *First Time!,* a Basie collaboration, brings Duke, still cooking, into the '60s (*The Great Paris Concert* is the decade's live band at its finest; see also *The Far East Suite*). His pairings both with John Coltrane and Coleman Hawkins are sharp representative work of that decade; by the '70s, with notable exceptions (*The Afro-Eurasian Eclipse*), even this indefatigable master was ever so slightly slowing down. *Duke's Big 4* presents the lion in winter—recorded with only three other remarkable players (Joe Pass on guitar, Ray Brown on bass, Louis Bellson on drums), it highlights Ellington's often overlooked playing. The amazing thing about Ellington is that all of his creative periods bore remarkable fruit, and virtually any of his recordings bears the stamp of genius. Die-hards will want to explore two remarkable series, the Classics year-by-year collection of pre-'40s wonders and Saja's *The Private Collection* of later work (1956–1971). — P.E.

DON ELLIS

★★★½ **New Ideas (1961; Original Jazz Classics, 1990)**
★★★★ **How Time Passes (Candid, 1988)**
★★★½ **Out of Nowhere (Candid, 1988)**
★★★★★ **Electric Bath (GNP Crescendo, 1994)**

Trumpeter/bandleader Don Ellis (1934–1978) was influenced by his classical training and residencies in a series of big bands during the 1950s, including work with Charlie Barnet, Lionel Hampton and Maynard Ferguson. In the 1960s, at the beginning of his prolific recording career, he was constantly trying out different ideas, working with unusual time signatures, rock and avant-garde ideas and interesting applications of world-music concepts (see "Turkish Bath" from *Electric Bath*). This experimentation led to some uneven work and spotty availability, but what does remain in print includes some of his best work.

His early-'60s small-group efforts were hailed at the time as major statements in the Third Stream movement, which utilized complex time signatures and orchestral textures that had previously been considered antithetical to the concept of swing. In his notes to *How Time Passes,* a quartet date with pianist/alto saxophonist Jaki Byard, bassist Ron Carter and drummer Charlie Persip, Gunther Schuller states that Ellis was paralleling the ideas of German composer Karlheinz Stockhausen. *New Ideas,* which adds vibraphonist Al Francis to the same lineup, was partially inspired, according to Ellis himself, by John Cage. *Out of Nowhere* is a fascinating reading of standards by a drummerless trio with pianist Paul Bley and bassist Steve Swallow.

Though Ellis worked mostly in big-band settings where his arrangement skills really took over, only *Electric Bath* remains in print as an example of this era of his work. Fortunately, it is a fitting testament to his status as a groundbreaking conceptualist who was eager to utilize the newest ideas in dynamics, material and electronic effects. *Electric Bath* was an extremely influential album in the late 1960s, and it endures as an example of the free-spirited attitude of the times. Look for the out-of-print *Autumn* for more along these lines. — J.S.

HERB ELLIS

★★★½ **Nothing but the Blues (1958; Verve, 1994)**
★★★½ **Together! (1963; Koch, 1995)**
★★★ **Jazz/Concord (with Joe Pass, Ray Brown and Jake Hanna) (1973; Concord Jazz, 1992)**
★★★ **Seven, Come Eleven (with Joe Pass, Ray Brown and Jake Hanna) (1973; Concord Jazz, 1992)**
★★★ **Soft Shoe (with Ray Brown) (1974; Concord Jazz, 1988)**
★★★ **After You've Gone (with Ray Brown) (1975; Concord Jazz, 1988)**
★★★★ **Hot Tracks (with the Ray Brown Sextet) (1976; Concord Jazz, 1988)**

★★★ **Poor Butterfly (with Barney Kessel) (1977; Concord Jazz, 1995)**
★★ **Windflower (with Remo Palmier) (1978; Concord Jazz, 1996)**
★★★ **Doggin' Around (with Red Mitchell) (Concord Jazz, 1989)**
★★★½ **Roll Call (Justice, 1991)**
★★★½ **Texas Swings (Justice, 1994)**
★★★½ **Down-home (Justice, 1996)**

Guitarist Herb Ellis (b. 1921) grew up in Texas and became a leading exponent of the Charlie Christian style of electric guitar. His slick, single-note lines carried Christian's tradition into the 1950s and beyond. Ellis may have made his most significant contribution as a member of pianist Oscar Peterson's drummerless trio, which also included bassist Ray Brown, and Ellis's association with Brown continued for decades afterward.

Ellis went on to lead his own groups, producing some high-quality performances. *Nothing but the Blues* presents Ellis fronting a group with bassist Brown, all-star trumpeter Roy Eldridge and tenor saxophonist Stan Getz. *Together!,* the reissue of a hot 1963 session featuring violinist Stuff Smith, is another good example of this period. Ellis took time off for session work before recording a series of albums for Concord, the best of which are his reunions with Brown and the sessions with like-minded guitarist Joe Pass.

In the 1990s Ellis returned to his Texas roots on Justice with great success, first on the wide-ranging *Roll Call,* then on the Bob Wills tribute *Texas Swings. Down-home* is a spirited session with the Justice all-stars—pianist Stefan Karlsson, trumpeter Rebecca Coupe Franks, drummer Sebastian Whittaker and bassist David Craig. — J.S.

TINSLEY ELLIS

★★★ **Cool on It (with the Heartfixers) (1986; Alligator, 1991)**
★★★½ **Georgia Blue (Alligator, 1988)**
★★★★ **Fanning the Flames (Alligator, 1989)**
★★★★ **Trouble Time (Alligator, 1992)**
★★★★★ **Storm Warning (Alligator, 1994)**
★★★½ **Fire It Up (Alligator, 1997)**

Tinsley Ellis (b. 1957), one of the best blues guitarists to emerge from the post–Allman Brothers style of Southern blues-rock eclecticism, is a keen student of Freddie King, Buddy Guy, Magic Sam, the Rolling Stones and the Allmans. He also incorporates the Texas blues of T-Bone Walker and Albert Collins into his style, and tends to play with a more powerful attack, making every note say something even in the fastest of runs.

Ellis built his reputation in the early 1980s as the leader of the popular Georgia blues-rock band the Heartfixers, which also included singer/mouth harpist Chicago Bob Nelson, before going out on his own. The great *Live at the Moonshadow* is, unfortunately, out of print, but *Cool on It* is a good representation of the Heartfixers' approach, which was based more on a stripped-down hard-blues sound than on expository soloing.

Over the years, Ellis developed a harmonic approach that suggested jazz-guitar influences as well and became known for a high-intensity slide-guitar style that made him a sought-after commodity on the blues club scene, where he logs more than 200 dates a year leading his own band.

Georgia Blue is an impressive solo debut with horns framing Tinsley's guitar arrangements. *Fanning the Flames* turns up the heat on a set that gives a good account of what Ellis's live performances sound like. Guitarist Peter Buck of R.E.M. makes a guest appearance on "Sign of the Blues" on *Trouble Time.*

Storm Warning is simply one of the best blues albums of the 1990s, one unbelievably biting solo after another as Ellis is freed to soar as the lead voice by the presence of second guitarist Oliver Wood and a cameo from a future guitar star, Derek Trucks. Other contributors to this awesome set include keyboardist Chuck Leavell and percussionist Count M'Butu from the Aquarium Rescue Unit. On *Fire It Up* Ellis returns to a single-guitar format. The highlight of the album is an outstanding cover of Fleetwood Mac's "One Sunny Day." — J.S.

PETER ERSKINE

★★★★ **Peter Erskine (1982; Original Jazz Classics, 1991)**
★★★½ **Transition (Denon, 1987)**
★★★★ **Motion Poet (Denon, 1988)**
★★★★ **Aurora (Denon, 1989)**
★★★★ **Sweet Soul (RCA/Novus, 1991)**
★★★½ **You Never Know (ECM, 1993)**
★★★★ **Time Being (ECM, 1994)**
★★★★ **History of the Drum (Interworld, 1995)**
★★★½ **As It Is (ECM, 1996)**

Peter Erskine (b. 1954) made an immediate impact as a big-band drummer in the early 1970s with the Stan Kenton Orchestra and went on to play in the Maynard Ferguson band before joining Weather Report at the height of its popularity in the late 1970s. A much-in-demand session drummer since leaving Weather Report in 1982, Erskine also boasts a formidable record as a leader. His self-titled debut album demonstrates his taste and versatility; the outstanding session band includes tenor saxophonist Michael Brecker, trumpeter/flügelhornist Randy Brecker, vibist Mike Mainieri, pianist Kenny Kirkland and bassist Eddie Gomez.

Transition offers an imaginative series of program pieces and a glimpse at the John Abercrombie trio (guitarist Abercrombie, drummer Erskine, bassist Marc Johnson) on "My Foolish Heart." *Motion Poet* also features Abercrombie and Johnson, along with several horn sections incorporating multiple French horns and trumpets.

Aurora, an outstanding trio recording with tenor saxophonist/bass clarinetist Marty Krystall and bassist Buell Neidlinger, is augmented by Don Preston on synthesizer. *Sweet Soul* finds Erskine leading another excellent lineup with trumpeter Randy Brecker, tenor/soprano saxophonist Joe Lovano, tenor saxophonist Bob Mintzer, guitarist John Scofield, pianist/organist Kenny Werner and bassist Johnson.

The African diaspora inspired Erskine to write the spellbinding program piece *History of the Drum* for the Kokuma African-Caribbean Dance Theater, and it was expanded into this full-length album. The delicacy and precision of Erskine's technique is much in evidence on *You Never Know*, *Time Being* and *As It Is,* the trio albums with pianist John Taylor and bassist Palle Danielsson. — J.S.

BOOKER ERVIN

★★★★ **Exultation! (1963; Original Jazz Classics, 1994)**
★★★★ **The Blues Book (1964; Original Jazz Classics, 1993)**
★★★★ **The Song Book (1964; Original Jazz Classics, 1993)**
★★★★★ **The Freedom Book (1964; Original Jazz Classics, 1995)**
★★★★★ **The Space Book (1964; Original Jazz Classics, 1996)**
★★★★ **Groovin' High (1964; Original Jazz Classics, 1996)**
★★★★ **Setting the Pace (1965; Prestige, 1993)**
★★★★ **The Trance (Original Jazz Classics, 1965)**
★★★★ **Heavy! (Original Jazz Classics, 1966)**

Tenor saxophonist Booker Ervin (1930–1970) was never a formalist innovator, but his earthy, blues-drenched sound and nonstop energy made him popular with some of the most advanced bandleaders of the 1960s, including Charles Mingus and Andrew Hill.

Everything that Ervin did has healthy doses of his supercharged horn, but the recordings in his *Book* series remain the classics. On *The Freedom Book* and *The Space Book* Ervin collaborates with one of the great rhythm sections in jazz history. Pianist Jaki Byard, bassist Richard Davis and drummer Alan Dawson attack standards and blues with an intensity and cohesiveness remarkable for a group that existed only in the studio. — S.F.

SLEEPY JOHN ESTES

★★★★½ **Broke and Hungry (1964; Delmark, 1995)**
★★★★ **Complete Recorded Works, Vol. 1 (1929–1937) (Document, 1990)**
★★★★ **Complete Recorded Works, Vol. 2 (1937–1941) (Document, 1990)**
★★★★ **The Legend of Sleepy John Estes (Delmark, 1990)**
★★★★ **Electric Sleep (Delmark, 1991)**
★★★★★ **I Ain't Gonna Be Worried No More (1929–1941) (Yazoo, 1992)**

Sleepy John Estes (né John Adams Estes, 1904–1977) began to play music in his native Tennessee in his preteens and around 1920 teamed up with mandolin player Yank Rachell, beginning a relationship that would last a lifetime. Estes's powerful voice and Rachell's soaring playing were the focal points of their acoustic country blues, and they cut tracks in Memphis in 1929 and 1930. Working with various personnel in Chicago and New York over the next decade, Estes recorded and plied his trade until he was "rediscovered" in the '60s.

Offering the best sound quality of any Estes release, *Broke and Hungry* finds the emotive singer backed by Rachell, harmonica and jug ace Hammie Nixon (with whom he'd recorded as early as 1935) and guitarist Mike Bloomfield (who later formed Electric Flag and the Butterfield Blues Band). Recorded in 1964, the album has a down-home feel, with songs reflecting the plight of an itinerant bluesman; Estes's vocal expressiveness contains a stamp of authenticity that can only be gained by experience. Highlights include his "Black

Mattie," Arthur "Big Boy" Crudup's "So Glad I'm Livin'" and several songs from the public domain, including the title track, "3:00 Morning Blues" and "The Girl I Love."

Compiled by Austrian Johnny Parth for his Document label are two volumes of Estes's early works. Assembled in chronological order, the first set's 24 tracks span recordings made from 1929 to 1937 and include such keening Estes classics as "Street Car Blues," "Poor John Blues" and "Down South Blues," perhaps the best song on either volume. Four cuts feature Rachell on vocals. *Vol. 2* comprises 26 tracks recorded from 1937 to 1941 and including such highlights as "Airplane Blues," "Liquor Store Blues" and "Mailman Blues." *Electric Sleep* is a 1968 recording with Sunnyland Slim on piano, Jimmy Dawkins on guitar, Odie Payne Jr. on drums, Earl Hooker on bass and Carey Bell on harp.

Yazoo's *I Ain't Gonna Be Worried No More* is the best Estes anthology currently available. While far from representing his complete body of work, the album collects 23 masterpieces, including "Milk Cow Blues," which features the steady playing of Rachell and pianist Jab Jones. "Someday Baby Blues" was later performed by Big Joe Williams and Muddy Waters, among others, and was the basis for Big Maceo's "Worried Life Blues." "Floating Bridge," which recounts Estes's near drowning in the '30s, is a fine example of his compelling autobiographical writing style. — B.R.H.

KEVIN EUBANKS

★★★★ **Guitarist (Discovery, 1983)**
★★½ **The Searcher (GRP, 1989)**
★★★ **Promise of Tomorrow (GRP, 1990)**
★★★½ **Turning Point (Blue Note, 1992)**
★★★½ **Spirit Talk (Blue Note, 1993)**
★★★½ **Spiritalk 2: Revelations (Blue Note, 1995)**
★★★½ **Live at Bradley's (Blue Note, 1996)**
★★★ **The Best of Kevin Eubanks (GRP, 1996)**

Guitarist Kevin Eubanks (b. 1957) has fought throughout his career to keep his talent and imagination free from the market demands for video soundtracks and smooth jazz. He's seen small victories along the way, but it's been a losing battle, and he finally surrendered outright by accepting the musical-director position at *The Tonight Show.*

Eubanks attempted to embrace fusion's stylistic diversity on a now deleted debut, *Face to Face,* that showcased him on solo-acoustic pieces, "The Novice Bounce" and the Miles Davis/Bill Evans classic "Blue in Green"; standards ("Yesterdays"); and foot-to-the-floor band arrangements like "Inner-Vision." Eubanks backed away from fusion on the Blue Note releases and proved himself a technically capable if somewhat unimaginative straight-ahead jazz player. *Spirit Talk* features solid contributions from brother Robin Eubanks on trombone, Kent Jordan on flute, Dave Holland on bass and Marvin "Smitty" Smith on drums. *Live at Bradley's* is an engaging session from the defunct New York club. — J.S.

JAMES REESE EUROPE

★★★★ **James Reese Europe with His 369th U.S. Infantry "Hell Fighters" Band (Memphis Archives, 1996)**

James Reese Europe (1880–1919), a classically trained pianist, bandleader, composer and arranger who also played mandolin and violin, helped found the Clef Club, a powerful organization of New York's top black musicians. In 1912 he led a Clef Club sold-out revue at Carnegie Hall.

Europe began collaborating with pianist Eubie Blake and vocalist Noble Sissle in 1916, but the trio was separated that same year when Europe and Sissle enlisted in the 15th New York Infantry, six months before the United States's official entry into World War I. Europe put together his military brass band, which was nicknamed "the Hell Fighters" for fighting heroically in the trenches, and the group won praise as "the best military band in Europe."

Two weeks after returning home in 1919, the Hell Fighters entered the studio to fulfill a contract with the Pathé Freres Phonograph Company, for whom all 24 cuts on *James Reese Europe with His 369th U.S. Infantry "Hell Fighters" Band* were recorded. The songs are largely played in a military-band format, with much pomp and patriotic fervor and yet with an inventive playfulness, sophistication and laid-back swing.

Several Europe originals, as well as W.C. Handy's "St. Louis Blues," a Stephen Foster medley, "Plantation Echoes," Rachmaninoff (Op. 3, No. 2) via George L. Cobb's "Russian Rag" and Bob Carleton's traditional jazz standard "Ja Da," are heard in this eclectic set. Nine tracks, including "On Patrol in No Man's Land" and "My Choc'late Soldier Sammy Boy," feature Sissle's brilliant vocals.

Two days after these sessions were completed, Europe was mortally stabbed in the neck with a penknife by a crazed drummer backstage during a concert at Boston's Mechanics Hall. — J.V.P.

BILL EVANS

★★★★ **New Jazz Conceptions (1956; Original Jazz Classics, 1988)**
★★★★★ **Everybody Digs Bill Evans (1958; Original Jazz Classics, 1997)**
★★★★★ **Portrait in Jazz (1960; Original Jazz Classics, 1987)**
★★★★★ **Explorations (1961; Original Jazz Classics, N.A.)**
★★★★★ **Sunday at the Village Vanguard (1961; Original Jazz Classics, N.A.)**
★★★★★ **Waltz for Debby (1961; Original Jazz Classics, 1994)**
★★★★ **Bill Evans at the Village Vanguard (1961; Riverside, N.A.)**
★★★★½ **How My Heart Sings! (1962; Original Jazz Classics, N.A.)**
★★★★½ **Moonbeams (1962; Original Jazz Classics, 1990)**
★★★★ **Undercurrent (with Jim Hall) (1962; Blue Note, 1988)**
★★½ **Interplay (1962; Original Jazz Classics, 1987)**
★★★½ **Loose Blues (1962; Milestone, 1992)**
★★★ **On Green Dolphin Street (1962; Milestone, 1995)**
★★★½ **Bill Evans at Shelly's Manne-Hole (1963; Original Jazz Classics, 1987)**
★★★★ **The Solo Sessions, Vol. 1 (1963; Milestone, 1989)**
★★★★ **The Solo Sessions, Vol. 2 (1963; Milestone, 1992)**
★★★ **Conversations with Myself (1964; Verve, 1997)**
★★★★ **Trio, '64 (1964; Verve, 1997)**
★★★★ **Stan Getz & Bill Evans (1964; Verve, 1987)**
★★★½ **Trio, '65 (1965; Verve, 1993)**
★★★½ **Paris 1965 (Royal Jazz, 1965)**
★★★ **Bill Evans Trio with Symphony Orchestra (Verve, 1965)**
★★★½ **Bill Evans Trio at Town Hall (1966; Verve, 1987)**
★★★★ **Intermodulation (with Jim Hall) (Verve, 1966)**
★★★½ **Alone (1968; Verve, 1988)**
★★★★ **At the Montreux Jazz Festival (1968; Verve, 1986)**
★★★½ **What's New (Verve, 1969)**
★★★½ **Jazzhouse (1969; Milestone, 1988)**
★★★½ **You're Gonna Hear from Me (Milestone, 1969)**
★★★★ **Montreux II (1970; CTI, 1989)**
★★½ **The Bill Evans Album (1971; Columbia, 1996)**
★★★★★ **The Tokyo Concert (1973; Original Jazz Classics, 1990)**
★★★★★ **Blue in Green (1974; Milestone, 1991)**
★★★★ **But Beautiful (with Stan Getz) (1974; Milestone, 1996)**
★★★ **Live in Europe, Vol. 1 (EPM, 1974)**
★★★ **Live in Europe, Vol. 2 (EPM, 1974)**
★★★★ **Re: Person I Knew (1974; Original Jazz Classics, 1992)**
★★★★ **Since We Met (1974; Original Jazz Classics, 1991)**
★★★½ **Intuition (with Eddie Gomez) (1974; Original Jazz Classics, N.A.)**
★★★ **Symbiosis (1974; Verve, 1995)**
★★★½ **Eloquence (1975; Original Jazz Classics, 1994)**
★★★★ **Montreux III (with Eddie Gomez) (1975; Original Jazz Classics, 1991)**
★★★★ **The Tony Bennett/Bill Evans Album (1975; Original Jazz Classics, 1990)**
★★★★ **Alone (Again) (1976; Original Jazz Classics, 1988)**
★★★ **Quintessence (1976; Original Jazz Classics, 1992)**
★★★★ **Crosscurrents (1977; Original Jazz Classics, 1992)**
★★★½ **I Will Say Goodbye (1977; Original Jazz Classics, N.A.)**
★★★½ **New Conversations (Warner Archives, 1978)**
★★★ **Affinity (Warner Bros., 1979)**
★★★½ **Consecration I (1980; Timeless, 1990)**
★★★½ **Consecration II (1980; Timeless, 1990)**
★★★★ **You Must Believe in Spring (Warner Bros., 1981)**
★★½ **Moods Unlimited (with Hank Jones and Red Mitchell) (1982; Evidence, 1993)**
★★★★★ **The Complete Riverside Recordings (Riverside, 1985)**
★★★★ **Compact Jazz (Verve, 1987)**
★★★★½ **The Complete Fantasy Recordings (Fantasy, 1989)**
★★★★ **Empathy/A Simple Matter of Conviction (Verve, 1990)**
★★★½ **Jazz 'Round Midnight (Verve, 1993)**

★★★½ **Verve Jazz Masters 5 (Verve, 1994)**
★★★★ **The Best of Bill Evans on Verve (Verve, 1995)**
★★★★ **The Best of Bill Evans Live (Verve, 1996)**
★★★★★ **Turn Out the Stars (Warner Bros., 1996)**
★★★★½ **Highlights from Turn Out the Stars (Warner Bros., 1996)**
★★★★½ **Bill Evans: Secret Sessions (Milestone, 1996)**
★★★½ **Letter to Evan (Dreyfus, 1996)**
★★★½ **Turn Out the Stars (Dreyfus, 1996)**
★★★★★ **The Complete Bill Evans (Verve, 1997)**

Bill Evans (1929–1980), one of the most virtuosic and emotionally expressive pianists in jazz history, was playing professionally by age 16. Attending Southeastern Louisiana College just outside New Orleans and far from the burgeoning jazz scene on the East Coast, he absorbed some of Bud Powell's influence without ever completely embracing bebop. A cool, intellectual player, Evans united bop's sophisticated chording with a unique, hornlike phrasing style. He would often shape a song's melody with a series of single notes that were smaller parts of a much larger whole, while repeating brief phrases in pursuit of what he called "the science of building a line." Extending bop's idea of freeing the left hand from the traditional rhythmic responsibility, he would sustain chords to create a harmonic bottom to support or offset his melodic explorations. Evans excelled at playing softer, more melancholy ballads and was always most at home in a trio with bass and drums.

While Evans recorded as a leader in 1956, he first came into the spotlight as part of the Miles Davis band that recorded 1959's immortal *Kind of Blue.* Although he was part of that group for only eight months, the experience gave him a great deal of confidence and he quickly blossomed into a world-class player. Evans recorded prolifically until his death, and the overall quality of his output tends to be excellent.

New Jazz Conceptions quietly introduces Evans to the jazz world. Accompanied by bassist Teddy Kotick and drummer Paul Motian, Evans is obviously influenced by Bud Powell but has already begun developing his own unique style. With a gentle touch and seemingly inscrutable wisdom, Evans swings well and tackles a nice mix of standards, originals and Tadd Dameron's bop gem "Our Delight." The follow-up, *Everybody Digs Bill Evans,* is far more impressive. Along with bassist Sam Jones and drummer Philly Joe Jones (no relation), Evans attacks the piano with boppish urgency and startling phrasing. The solo renditions of "Peace Piece" and "Lucky to Be Me" showcase Evans's tender side, while the exuberant interpretations of Gigi Gryce's "Minority" and Sonny Rollins's "Oleo" are absolutely bracing.

The invigorating *Portrait in Jazz* introduces the first classic Bill Evans Trio. Evans, bassist Scott LaFaro and drummer Paul Motian display a tremendous amount of empathy and anticipation for one another's playing. With an expressive sound almost as distinctive as Evans's, LaFaro influenced numerous musicians as well as helping to define the sound of piano trios in the '60s. The trio's interpretations of "Autumn Leaves" and "When I Fall in Love" are certainly definitive. *Explorations* cannot be held in any less esteem. Evans, LaFaro and Motian are telepathic on tunes like "Haunted Heart," "Nardis" and "How Deep Is the Ocean." Evans's interplay with LaFaro creates "simultaneous improvisation," and the trio seemed unable to record anything that wasn't an instant classic.

Sunday at the Village Vanguard, *Waltz for Debby* and *Bill Evans at the Village Vanguard* were all recorded in one outstanding night at the famous Manhattan jazz club and reveal the legendary trio at its collective peak. *Bill Evans at the Village Vanguard* is docked a notch due to the fact that it is merely a composite rerelease of the famous live session. More vibrant than the earlier studio work, the Village Vanguard date was this particular trio's swan song. Ten days after recording at the Vanguard, LaFaro died in an auto accident at the age of 25. His contrapuntal playing and walking bass lines were never more prominent than here, and these recordings endure as a testament to the void he left behind.

Evans and Motian returned to the studio in 1962 with Chuck Israels on bass and produced the excellent *How My Heart Sings!* and *Moonbeams. How My Heart Sings!* emphasizes more upbeat numbers, while *Moonbeams* showcases ballads. Israels replaces LaFaro ably, and the new trio produces top-quality stuff, but momentum and chemistry suffer, and the abrupt change in personnel signals a transition period for Evans.

Undercurrent features Evans and guitarist Jim Hall, whose light touch and impeccable sense of time make him an ideal foil for Evans, and the recording is an unqualified success. The two perform some elegant ballads and overt swing numbers amid a variety of standards. Evans returns to this successful duo on *Intermodulation,* but *Interplay* does not fare as well. Showcasing a quintet that includes trumpeter Freddie Hubbard and Hall, this loose date offers decent jazz but sounds little like a real Bill Evans album.

Loose Blues is a definite improvement, reminiscent of Evans's work on Davis's *Kind of Blue.* Assisted by tenor saxophonist Zoot Sims and a sparkling Hall, this interesting session features Evans's own compositions from start to finish. Evans returns to the style and format that suited him best on *At Shelly's Manne-Hole,* his last album for Riverside, featuring a trio of Israels and Larry Bunker. While the rhythm section pales in comparison with the old LaFaro-Motian team, Evans's playing is no less impeccable.

The two volumes of *The Solo Sessions* were recorded on the same day, and both are marvelous examples of Evans alone in the studio. Evans would go on to record other solo albums in his time but nothing much better than these two.

The Complete Riverside Recordings includes a tremendous amount of Bill Evans at his best. This extraordinary, comprehensive collection supplants all the earlier Riverside, Original Jazz Classics and Milestone releases. In the course of a very prolific period, Evans recorded the unconventional *Conversations with Myself,* on which he overdubs three-way piano discussions. Innovative and mildly controversial, the experiment was deemed a success and was revisited on the out-of-print *Further Conversations with Myself* and the even smoother *New Conversations.*

On *Trio '64,* virtuoso bassist Gary Peacock and Motian join Evans and evoke the classic LaFaro trio. Well-arranged and quite energetic, *Trio '65* isn't on the same level as Evans's best trio dates, but it's always a pleasure to hear Evans perform Thelonious Monk's "'Round Midnight." Israels and drummer Arnold Wise hold up their end quite well, as Evans shines on inspired versions of classics like "I Should Care" and "Spring Is Here."

Shifting ever so slightly in both tone and focus, the two trio albums *Empathy/A Simple Matter of Conviction* (now available on one CD) feature the irrepressible Shelly Manne on drums. Monty Budwig plays bass on *Empathy,* but the introduction of bassist Eddie Gomez on *A Simple Matter of Conviction* stains the trio's high-quality performance. Evans returns to the healing solitude of the recording studio on *Alone.* While a little bit dry, the recording proves nobody plays solo piano like Bill Evans. Evans does this again to even greater effect in 1975 with *Alone (Again). At the Montreux Jazz Festival* is an energetic live recording that features bassist Gomez along with the idiosyncratic Jack DeJohnette on drums. A quality session, it's the only recorded collaboration between Evans and DeJohnette.

Compact Jazz, Jazz 'Round Midnight, Jazz Masters 5, The Best of Bill Evans on Verve and *The Best of Bill Evans Live* compile previously released material. All are very good, and some include tunes that are currently unavailable on single discs. *The Complete Bill Evans,* a particularly fantastic boxed set, contains Evans's entire Verve catalog, making the smaller collections almost moot.

Jazzhouse and *You're Gonna Hear from Me* are both culled from a live concert at the Jazzhus Montmartre in Denmark. The concert is notable for the debut of Bill Evans's second important trio of Gomez and new drummer Marty Morell. *Montreux II* finds this trio coming together; Morell is more than snappy, and Gomez attacks the bass while both remain thoroughly attentive to Evans. Evans's own playing, of course, remains as brilliant as ever.

The Tokyo Concert and *Blue in Green* show the trio of Evans, Gomez and Morell at the top of their game. Evans's harmonically sophisticated playing overflows with expressive nuance and intricate technique. *But Beautiful* adds the great, romantic tenor of Stan Getz to the already in-sync trio with marvelous results. Getz and Evans communicate well and push each other to great musical heights.

Since We Met and *Re: Person I Knew* are both excellent trio sessions recorded in two nights at the Village Vanguard. As usual, the Vanguard brings out the best in Evans, and his latest sidemen are passionately responsive. Unfortunately, Morell would leave the group soon after these albums were recorded. *Intuition* features duets between Evans and Gomez, a lovely concept that needed a little more time to come to complete fruition. *Eloquence,* a half-solo, half–Evans/Gomez-duet recording, finds Evans playing some electric piano that adds very little to the proceedings. On *Montreux III* Gomez and Evans hit their stride as a musical couple: Exquisite, intuitive and instructive, Gomez adheres to Evans, and both players are in exceptional form.

The Tony Bennett/Bill Evans Album finds the two jazz giants in great confluence; Bennett is in fine voice, and Evans sounds suitably inspired. *Quintessence* brings veteran jazzmen Harold Land and Kenny Burrell into the picture along with bassist Ray Brown and drummer Philly Joe Jones. While not a classic, this worthwhile session still shows Evans to be a formidable bandleader.

The superior Lennie Tristano homage *Crosscurrents* features saxophonists Lee Konitz and Warne Marsh. Both *I Will Say Goodbye* and *You Must Believe in Spring* spotlight yet another fine version of the Bill Evans Trio, this time with drummer Eliot Zigmond adding to standout cuts like "Dolphin Dance" and "Theme from *M*A*S*H.*" *The Complete Fantasy Recordings* comprehensively documents latter-era Evans. *Affinity* is a well-played curiosity piece with harpist Toots Thielemans and young bass virtuoso Marc Johnson.

An out-of-print album, *The Paris Concert,* presents the third (and final) significant Bill Evans Trio: Evans along with Marc Johnson and Joe LaBarbera. Evans compared this group's intimate camaraderie to that of his famous trio with LaFaro and Motian. The intuitive and powerful rhythm section served Evans until his death. *Consecration I* and *Consecration II* feature this group live at the Keystone Korner in San Francisco. The fluid playing continues, with Evans in particularly great form. The Dreyfus recordings, *Turn Out the Stars* and *Letter to Evan,* were recorded live during a week in London at Ronnie Scott's jazz club. These performances were made just a month before Evans's death, and the trio's sensitive playing is quite notable.

The Warner recording of *Highlights from Turn Out the Stars* is an excellent sampler from the phenomenal six-CD set *Turn Out the Stars.* Recorded over four nights in 1980, this is a perfect farewell for the legendary pianist as LaBarbera and Johnson accompany Evans on his final visit to the place where it all began.

Secret Sessions is an eight-CD set documenting an overview of Evans's work at the Village Vanguard from 1966 through 1975. This beautiful package contains all previously unreleased material, making it another essential collection for the Bill Evans fanatic. — M.M.

BILL EVANS

★★★ **The Alternative Man (1985; Blue Note, 1996)**
★★★ **Push (Lipstick, 1994)**
★★★ **Live in Europe (Lipstick, 1995)**
★★★ **Escape (Escapade, 1996)**

Tenor/soprano saxophonist Bill Evans (b. 1958) came to prominence as part of Miles Davis's *Man with the Horn* band in the early 1980s, and carried that group's postfusion funk into *The Alternative Man,* which includes the Davis tribute "Miles Away." After making several now unavailable albums, Evans reinvented himself in the 1990s as an acid-jazz bandleader. Both in the studio and on *Push* and *Live in Europe,* Evans and his band successfully blend hip-hop rhythms and rap with his instrumental vision. On *Escape* Evans combines the two approaches with help from trumpeter Wallace Roney, guitarist Lee Ritenour and MC 900 Ft Jesus. — J.S.

GIL EVANS

★★★★ **Gil Evans & Ten (1957; Original Jazz Classics, 1989)**
★★★★★ **Out of the Cool (1962; Impulse!, 1986)**
★★★★ **The Individualism of Gil Evans (1965; Verve, 1988)**
★★★ **Blues in Orbit (1972; Enja, 1990)**
★★★ **Tokyo Concert (West Wind Jazz, 1976)**
★★★★ **Priestess (1977; Antilles, 1991)**
★★★ **Little Wing (1978; West Wind Jazz, 1989)**
★★★ **Anti-Heroes (with Lee Konitz) (1980; Verve, 1992)**
★★★★ **Paris Blues (with Steve Lacy) (1987; Blue Note, 1994)**
★★★★ **Live at Sweet Basil (Evidence, 1992)**
★★★★ **Live at Sweet Basil, Vol. 2 (Evidence, 1992)**
★★★★ **In Memoriam: Bud and Bird (with the Monday Night Orchestra) (Evidence, 1992)**
★★★★ **Farewell (Evidence, 1992)**
★★★★ **Live at the Public Theater, Vol. 1 (Evidence, 1994)**
★★★★ **Live at the Public Theater, Vol. 2 (Evidence, 1994)**
★★★★★ **Miles Davis and Gil Evans: The Complete Columbia Studio Recordings (Columbia, 1996)**

Keyboardist Gil Evans (1912–1988), one of the most creative conceptualists, arrangers and bandleaders in postbop jazz, had already carved out a reputation through his work with Claude Thornhill and Miles Davis before recording under his own name. During the late 1940s, when the bop scene was in full swing on New York's 52nd Street, Evans's apartment was an open-door hangout for bop's elite. It was there that Evans and Miles Davis devised plans to design music for a larger-scale group with a more challenging chromatic range, an idea that resulted in Davis's influential *Birth of the Cool* nonet sessions.

Evans's genius emerges clearly on the monumental archive project *The Complete Columbia Studio Recordings,* a behind-the-scenes look at his working relationship with Davis during the period between 1957 and 1968, when Evans arranged and Davis starred on the large-band recordings *Miles Ahead*, *Porgy and Bess*, *Sketches of Spain* and *Quiet Nights.* The team's work rivals the orchestrations of Duke Ellington and Charles Mingus with the subtlety, range and bluesy audacity Evans summons up in his colorations and his sense of where the hearts of his soloists' passions lie.

Throughout his recordings, Evans explores uncharted territory in the company of some of the most gifted musicians around, all of whom play as if their lives depended on it. Despite the high level of risk-taking this music demanded, there are few failed moments amid the torrent of disciplined self-discovery.

For his first recording as a leader, *Gil Evans & Ten,* Evans turned to another forward thinker, soprano saxophonist and Thelonious Monk scholar Steve Lacy, and to dependable alto saxophonist Lee Konitz, to front a group anchored by the magnificent bassist Paul Chambers. *Out of the Cool,* a flat-out jazz masterpiece, exemplifies the amazing creative strides made in the tumultuous creative ferment of the 1960s. The orchestra, powered by bassist Ron Carter and drummers Elvin Jones and Charlie Persip, swings as a well-oiled unit yet is notable for the individualism of its parts, like the soulful articulations of Jimmy Knepper's trombone or the weird sonorities of Johnny Coles's trumpet.

Coles and Lacy reappear on *Individualism* as part of several sprawling ensembles that show Evans moving in more open-ended directions with a band concept pointed beyond studio work. *Blues in Orbit* introduces Howard Johnson's great baritone saxophone and tuba playing, colors that Evans would use greedily in future lineups.

By the 1970s, Evans's concerts were epochal events, and some wisely considered the music important enough to document on the spot before it disappeared. These live performances are just about all that remain of Evans's legacy from that period until the end of his life.

Evans was in the first stages of organizing a joint project with guitarist Jimi Hendrix and had come up with tentative arrangements for some Hendrix material when the project was terminated by Hendrix's death. *Tokyo Concert* offers a glimpse at what could have been another historic combination, but guitarist Ryo Kawasaki is a poor substitute for Hendrix, and on *Little Wing* Evans interprets Hendrix without a guitar in the group—not such a bad idea when his main soloist is the remarkable tenor saxophonist George Adams.

On *Priestess* Evans has all his guns blazing—Adams, Johnson, Knepper, trumpeter Lew Soloff, alto saxophonists David Sanborn (in the finest recorded moments of his somewhat overrated career) and Arthur Blythe and keyboardist Pete Levin. Levin and Evans combined on some dazzling double-keyboard effects for the rest of the band's run.

The *Live at the Public Theater* recordings document a stellar lineup with Jon Faddis and Hannibal Marvin Peterson joining trumpeter Soloff, saxophonists Blythe and Hamiet Bluiett, trombonist George Lewis, keyboardists Levin and Masabumi Kikuchi and drummer Billy Cobham. *Vol. 1* features an excellent "Up from the Skies"; *Vol. 2* an inspired pairing of "Stone Free" and "Orange Was the Color of Her Dress."

Evans closed out his life leading the Monday Night Orchestra at New York's Sweet Basil jazz club. This shifting lineup is represented on the two *Sweet Basil* recordings, *Bud and Bird* and *Farewell,* all of which demonstrate this band's brilliant unpredictability. Each has its moments: "Voodoo Chile" and the Charlie Parker tribute "Blues in C" on *Live at Sweet Basil;* the subtle reggaefication of "Friday the 13th" and Johnson's meaty baritone lines on "Prelude to Stone Free" on *Live at Sweet Basil, Vol. 2;* the title track and "Groove from the Louvre" on *Bud and Bird;* and Hiram Bullock's take-on-Jimi guitar work on *Farewell*'s "Little Wing."

Aside from his big-band work, Evans recorded several excellent duet albums: *Paris Blues* with Lacy, and *Heroes* and *Anti-Heroes* with Konitz. *Heroes* is no longer available, joining such out-of-print gems as *Into the Hot*, *Big Stuff*, *There Comes a Time*, *Pacific Standard Time* and *Svengali.* — J.S.

THE FABULOUS THUNDERBIRDS

★★★½ **The Fabulous Thunderbirds (Takoma, 1979)**
★★★ **What's the Word (Chrysalis, 1980)**
★★★½ **Butt Rockin' (Chrysalis, 1981)**
★★★ **T-Bird Rhythm (Chrysalis, 1982)**
★★★★ **Tuff Enuff (Epic, 1986)**
★★★ **Hot Number (Epic, 1987)**
★★★ **Powerful Stuff (Epic, 1989)**
★★★ **Walk That Walk, Talk That Talk (Epic, 1991)**
★★★★ **The Essential Fabulous Thunderbirds Collection (Chrysalis, 1991)**
★★★★ **Hot Stuff: The Greatest Hits (Epic, 1992)**
★★★★ **Roll of the Dice (Private Music, 1995)**
★★★ **High Water (High Street, 1997)**

Solid, sometimes spectacular, always rousing, the Fabulous Thunderbirds have aged gracefully and with remarkable consistency. Over the course of a recording history spanning more than a decade and half, only stalwart vocalist and harmonica master Kim Wilson remains from the original lineup. While the loss of so exemplary a player as founding guitarist Jimmie Vaughan, who departed in 1990, is not easily overcome, Wilson has stepped up and delivered credible work, growing impressively as a vocalist and writer along the way, and always finding *simpatico* instrumental support. The Fabulous Thunderbirds are not the powerhouse band they were in the mid-'80s—may not even be a band in the true sense but more a conceit for Wilson's forays into hard-edged Texas blues rock—but T-Birds fans need not sit around pining for the old days yet.

The T-Birds surfaced in 1979 on an eponymous album for Takoma, then moved to Chrysalis and cut three blues-rock smokers that inspired a loyal following without ever making much impact on the charts. Switching labels in 1986 changed all that, as *Tuff Enuff* became a bona fide hit album, propelled by the title-track single featuring Wilson's strutting vocal married to a churning, grungy rhythm and a slightly menacing, minor-key–style ambiance. Although the band called Austin home and carried the flag of Austin music to the rest of the world, the musicians drew inspiration from sources both in and outside the Lone Star State. Jimmie Vaughan might quote T-Bone Walker one minute and in the next travel to Mississippi for a B.B. King– or Muddy Waters–inspired commentary. Lead singer Wilson would rumble and roar through the songs, then go to the harmonica and rip a solo straight out of Little Walter.

A typical T-Birds long-player mixes blues chestnuts with original songs written primarily by Wilson. Chrysalis has assembled a good cross section of highlights on *The Essential Fabulous Thunderbirds Collection,* but digging deeper into the catalog and checking out the pleasures of *The Fabulous Thunderbirds* or *Butt Rockin'* is recommended. Nick Lowe came aboard as producer for *T-Bird Rhythm* and polished the sound without undercutting the force of the band's take-no-prisoners attack. Produced by Dave Edmunds, *Tuff Enuff* is a hard-polished, mature work notable for the darker-edged material from Wilson's pen, ever optimistic and always suggesting that Wilson swagger but displaying a streak of pessimism—or perhaps realism—over the inevitable course of love and life.

With Vaughan's departure, the challenge ahead remained as it always was: to find interesting avenues of expression within the stylistic parameters of the blues. Post-Vaughan, *Walk That Walk, Talk That Talk* found the reconstituted T-Birds (with former Roomful of Blues guitarist Duke Robillard in Vaughan's place) treading water, despite a couple of interesting moments. The Epic era is effectively summarized in *Hot Stuff: The Greatest Hits,* which has the added pleasure of two new tracks, "Got Love If You Want It" and a firestorm of a take on Willie Dixon's "You Can't Judge a Book by Its Cover," featuring Wilson in a punishing vocal assault backed by a relentless and unforgiving rhythm section.

Then Wilson retreated, cutting two fine solo albums in '93 and '94 (*Tigerman* and *That's Life,* respectively) before assembling a new T-Birds lineup. Teamed with producer Danny Kortchmar, who has done commendable work as a session guitarist but is not generally known for his facility as a blues player, Wilson and the T-Birds (whose lineup includes drummer Fran Christina, who joined the band in 1980 and remained for the entire Vaughan-era ride) roared again on *Roll of the Dice.* Throughout, Wilson properly carries the show with his writing, singing and inspired harmonica work; he is blessed with solid rhythm support (with Kortchmar on guitar) and gets inspired performances from guitarists Kid Ramos and David Grissom. The title track is in the "Tuff Enuff" mold, an obvious appeal to radio, but Wilson's sapient vocal, touting risk taking and self-reliance as the only sensible approaches to life, is as chilling as it is authoritative. The surprising cover of Them's hit "Here Comes the Night" soars over an arrangement offering the Spectoresque grandeur of Bruce Springsteen's "Backstreets," with Wilson wailing in protest over his girl falling for another man; it's as close as anyone has come to reducing a well-regarded Van Morrison performance to a footnote. Amazing as this cut is, Wilson nearly tops himself on "I Don't Wanna Be the One," a blues lament he cowrote with Jerry Williams. On an album replete with passionate playing and open-veined singing, these are Homeric moments. There's still life in the old boys yet. — D.M.

JON FADDIS

★★★ **Legacy (Concord Jazz, 1986)**
★★★ **Into the Faddisphere (Epic, 1989)**
★★★ **Hornucopia (Epic, 1991)**
★★★★ **Jon & Billy (with Billy Harper) (Evidence, 1993)**

Trumpeter Jon Faddis (b. 1953) is a Dizzy Gillespie protégé whose facility with the highest end of the trumpet register is unparalleled among other members of his generation. Called on to participate in myriad Gillespie tributes, Faddis invariably blows everyone else off the stage. He was playing with Gillespie at age 21, worked as a featured soloist with Lionel Hampton and the Thad Jones/Mel Lewis orchestra and currently plays with the Carnegie Hall Jazz Band, which regularly cuts the Wynton Marsalis–led Lincoln Center Jazz Orchestra in head-to-head competition.

For all his accomplishments as a sideman, Faddis has a surprisingly thin catalog as a leader. *Hornucopia* features him hopping genres, fronting the complex orchestration of "Highfive," growling the blues in accompaniment to vocalist Vivian Cherry on "Reckless Blues," topping a funk fusion vamp on "Ahbeedunseedja," handling the emotional gospel of "I Surrender All," heading into Miles Davis territory on "Dewey's Dance" and trading licks with Diz on "Rapartee." For all the dazzle, there's a lack of focus, which similarly clouds *Into the Faddisphere.* No such problems mar the highly emotive *Jon & Billy,* with the great tenor saxophonist Billy Harper. Look for the out-of-print *Youngblood* on Pablo. — J.S.

JOHN FAHEY

★★★½ **Death Chants, Breakdowns and Military Waltzes (Takoma, 1962)**
★★★½ **Dance of Death and Other Plantation Favorites (Takoma, 1964)**
★★★½ **John Fahey Guitar (Takoma, 1967)**
★★★½ **Blind Joe Death (Vanguard, 1967)**
★★★ **The Yellow Princess (Vanguard, 1969)**
★★★½ **Fare Forward Voyagers (1973; Shanachie, 1992)**
★★★½ **The Transfiguration of Blind Joe Death (Takoma, 1973)**
★★★½ **The Essential John Fahey (Vanguard, 1974)**
★★★½ **John Fahey/Leo Kottke/Peter Lang (Takoma, 1974)**
★★★★ **The Best of John Fahey (1959–1977) (Takoma, 1977)**
★★★½ **Live in Tasmania (Takoma, 1981)**
★★★½ **Let Go (Varrick, 1985)**
★★★½ **Rain Forests, Oceans and Other Themes (Varrick, 1985)**

★★★½ **I Remember Blind Joe Death (Varrick, 1987)**
★★★½ **God, Time and Causality (Shanachie, 1990)**
★★★½ **Old Fashioned Love (Shanachie, 1990)**
★★★½ **Old Girlfriends and Other Horrible Memories (Varrick, 1992)**
★★★½ **The Return of the Repressed: The John Fahey Anthology (Rhino, 1994)**

Recording for more than three decades, Maryland acoustic guitarist John Fahey (b. 1939) has alternated between country blues and Celtic folk; he also pens classically derived melodies. An archivist who wrote his Ph.D. thesis about bluesman Charley Patton and helped bring Skip James and Bukka White to wide notice, Fahey brings a scholar's care to his music—but he's no pedant. Generally unaccompanied, with no overdubs, his albums are complex tapestries of sound; his virtuosity is less a matter of speed or novel rhythm than of tone—Fahey's guitar resounds like no other. A very consistent artist—the assured delivery of "Old Southern Medley" from 1973's *The Transfiguration of Blind Joe Death* isn't dissimilar to his rousing take on Eric Clapton's "Layla" (*Let Go*)—he's kept his standards very high throughout the years. Gorgeous mood music, trance-inducing and rapturous, Fahey's albums deserve a larger audience. The Rhino collection is a good place to start, but any of the individual CDs is deserving — P.E.

TAL FARLOW

★★★★ **The Return of Tal Farlow: 1969 (1969; Original Jazz Classics, 1989)**
★★★ **Sign of the Times (Concord Jazz, 1992)**
★★★ **Chromatic Palette (Concord Jazz, 1994)**
★★★ **Cookin' on All Burners (Concord Jazz, 1996)**

Guitarist Tal Farlow (1921–1998) forged a reputation in the late 1940s as a Charlie Christian–style guitarist with lightning speed and bop harmonic sense. He played with Red Norvo and in Artie Shaw's small groups until the late '50s, when he went into semiretirement. *The Return of Tal Farlow* is just that, a celebrated quartet set that sees Farlow recapture his legendary status. His subsequent albums provide solid representations of his chops, but so many other guitarists have come along since he started that his pioneering status as a virtuoso is undervalued. — J.S.

ART FARMER

★★★★ **The Art Farmer Septet (1954; Original Jazz Classics, N.A.)**
★★★★ **Early Art (1955; Original Jazz Classics, N.A.)**
★★★★ **When Farmer Met Gryce (with Gigi Gryce) (1955; Original Jazz Classics, N.A.)**
★★★½ **The Art Farmer Quintet Featuring Gigi Gryce (1955; Original Jazz Classics, 1987)**
★★★½ **2 Trumpets (with Donald Byrd) (1956; Original Jazz Classics, N.A.)**
★★★★ **Farmer's Market (1957; Original Jazz Classics, 1989)**
★★★★ **Modern Art (1958; Blue Note, 1991)**
★★★★ **Portrait of Art Farmer (1958; Original Jazz Classics, 1988)**
★★★½ **Meet the Jazztet (1960; Chess, 1990)**
★★★ **Live at the Half Note (1964; Rhino, 1995)**
★★★ **Gentle Eyes (1972; Mainstream, 1993)**
★★★ **On the Road (1976; Original Jazz Classics, 1990)**
★★★ **A Work of Art (Concord Jazz, 1982)**
★★★ **Warm Valley (1983; Concord Jazz, 1992)**
★★★ **Maiden Voyage (Denon, 1983)**
★★★½ **Back to the City (1986; Original Jazz Classics, 1995)**
★★★★★ **Something to Live For: The Music of Billy Strayhorn (Contemporary, 1987)**
★★★★ **Blame It on My Youth (Contemporary, 1988)**
★★★★ **Ph.D. (Contemporary, 1989)**
★★★½ **Central Avenue Reunion (Contemporary, 1990)**
★★★★ **The Best of Art Farmer (Columbia/Legacy, 1990)**
★★★ **Ambrosia (Denon, 1993)**
★★★★ **Live at Sweet Basil (with Clifford Jordan) (Evidence, 1994)**

Lyricism is Art Farmer's (b. 1928) raison d'être. Although he can swing with the best of them, this trumpeter/flügelhornist's real contribution is to the art of the ballad. His gorgeous tone, impeccable taste and incredible control make him one of the great storytellers in jazz history.

Trumpeters in the 1950s had two stylistic role models: Miles Davis and his introspective musings and Clifford Brown, with his fiery flash. The material on Farmer's mid-'50s releases, *2 Trumpets*, *The Art Farmer Septet*, *Early Art*, *When Farmer Met Gryce*, *The Art Farmer Quintet Featuring Gigi Gryce* and *Farmer's Market,* finds Farmer working on a synthesis that eventually leans toward Davis. He used Davis's example to develop his own form of finely honed lyricism and laconic swing, working out a personal means of expression that is always involving and never overly derivative. *Portrait of Art Farmer* finds him in a favorite surrounding, his horn-plus-rhythm section, which gave him plenty of space while avoiding the familiar two-horned-unit sound of the time.

In 1960, after working for Horace Silver and Gerry Mulligan and becoming one of the New York scene's most adaptable sidemen, Farmer organized the Jazztet with the talented saxophonist/composer Benny Golson, with whom he'd already worked on *Modern Art.* The lineup on *Meet the Jazztet*—Curtis Fuller on trombone, McCoy Tyner on piano, Art's brother Addison Farmer on bass and Lex Humphries on drums—was short-lived, but both Golson and Fuller would reunite with Farmer on the excellent live recordings from New York's Sweet Basil nightclub in February 1986, *Back to the City* and *Real Time.* The latter features a magnificent version of the ballad "Autumn Leaves."

Farmer's post-Jazztet band featured a more unique roster; the brilliant and wholly sympathetic guitarist Jim Hall replaced both the pianist and the second horn. The tonal color is as arresting as the setting; Farmer was now using the darker-toned flügelhorn exclusively. The Atlantic recordings of this swinging chamber-jazz group, which also includes Steve Swallow on bass, are represented by *Live at the Half Note;* look for the impressive but out-of-print *To Sweden with Love* and *Sing Me Softly of the Blues* for more.

Before leaving for an extended stay in Europe, Farmer formed another important group, a more typical bop quintet with piano and two horns. What made it exceptional was the still-undervalued saxist Jimmy Heath. *The Best of Art Farmer* includes material from *The Time and the Place,* a 1967 live recording that testifies to this band's range; they could ease heartbreak from "The Shadow of Your Smile," then rage into a heated workout on "Blue Bossa."

Age only intensified Farmer's genius for expressive ballads. During the late 1980s he made several great recordings with tenor saxophonist Clifford Jordan—*Something to Live For*, *Blame It on My Youth* and *Ph.D. Something to Live For,* a collection of Billy Strayhorn compositions, is a masterpiece. Farmer teamed up with tenor saxophonist Frank Morgan on *Central Avenue Reunion.* — S.F.

JOE FARRELL

★★★★ Sonic Text (1979; Original Jazz Classics, 1993)
★★★½ Skate Board Park (1979; Xanadu, 1995)
★★★★ Darn That Dream (1982; Drive Archive, 1994)

Tenor and soprano saxophonist/flautist Joe Farrell (1937–1986) was a mainstay at CTI and a frequent sideman on engaging 1960s and '70s sessions with Chick Corea, Elvin Jones and a variety of other artists.

Unfortunately, little of Farrell's excellent reed and flute work remains in print. His strong out-of-print debut features Corea on keyboards, John McLaughlin on guitar, Dave Holland on bass and Jack DeJohnette on drums. Freddie Hubbard adds fine trumpet and flügelhorn to Farrell's playing on the engaging quintet session *Sonic Text. Darn That Dream* features alto saxophonist Art Pepper on three tracks. The out-of-print *Moon Germs*, *Upon This Rock* and *Benson and Farrell* offer more examples of this overlooked player's work. — J.S.

ZUSAAN KALI FASTEAU

★★★½ Bliss (Flying Note, 1986)
★★★½ Beyond Words (Flying Note, 1987)
★★★½ Affinity (Flying Note, 1988)
★★★★★ Worlds Beyond Words (Flying Note, 1989)
★★★★ Prophecy (Flying Note, 1993)

Multi-instrumentalist Zusaan Kali Fasteau (b. 1956) is a truly syncretic musician with strong technical training in jazz improvisation and classical theory. Her thirst for genre-transcending interactions with world music has been nurtured by forays into Africa, Asia and India to study and perform indigenous musics. As a result, Fasteau's work lies beyond simple classification, though her post-Coltrane improvisational style and her choice of such accompanists as drummers Rashied Ali and Andrew Cyrille and saxophonists Dewey

Redman, Oliver Lake and Archie Shepp place it closest to jazz. More than one critic has suggested that she is the logical successor to Coltrane's quest for a universal music.

The mostly solo *Bliss* and *Affinity* find Fasteau working her way through the recording process and moving in fascinating directions on a variety of woodwinds, soprano saxophone, ney (a microtonal Indian reed instrument) and an exotic vocal style. On *Beyond Words,* with Ali and bassist Bob Cunningham, Fasteau's lithe soprano-saxophone work and four-octave vocal range dominate the proceedings.

Worlds Beyond Words, her best work, features Ali, Cunningham, Elizabeth Panzer on harp, James C. Jamison II on guitar, David Cornick on percussion and Paul Leake on tabla. Fasteau is astonishing on soprano sax, piano, ney, shakuhachi and kaval flutes, mizmar, sanza, voice and berimbau. Her interactions with Ali on "From Above" and "Beyond Words" are stellar, but she reaches the high point on the otherworldly "Priestess," a solo tour de force on four mizmars.

A particularly demanding album, *Prophecy* ventures even further into the thick forests of world music while incorporating synthesizer textures. Oscar Brown III plays bass, as does William Parker, who doubles on balafon. Three percussionists and a violinist also accompany Fasteau, who adds cello, sheng, moursin, synthesizer, drums, tympani and gong to her instrumental repertoire. — J.S.

WILTON FELDER

★★★ **Nocturnal Moods (Par, 1991)**

As a member of the Crusaders, saxophonist/bassist Wilton Felder (b. 1940) developed the distinctive R&B–influenced instrumental groove that made the band famous. Much of his solo work, like the Crusaders' later albums, generally suffers from lack of both musical conviction and strong direction as Felder searches for a commercial sound that can satisfy his musical ambitions, but *Nocturnal Moods* presents Felder in good form, reunited with Crusaders band mate Wayne Henderson, who produced this outing. — J.S.

MAYNARD FERGUSON

★★★ **Live in Stereo at Peacock Lane, Hollywood (Jazz Hour, 1957)**
★★★★ **Two's Company (Roulette, 1961)**
★★★ **Live from San Francisco (Avenue Jazz, 1983)**
★★ **Storm (Avenue Jazz, 1983)**
★★★ **I Like Jazz: The Essence of Maynard Ferguson (Columbia/Legacy, 1993)**
★★★ **Live from London (Avenue Jazz, 1994)**
★★★½ **These Cats Can Swing! (with Big Bop Nouveau) (Concord Jazz, 1995)**
★★★★ **One More Trip to Birdland (with Big Bop Nouveau) (Concord Jazz, 1996)**
★★★ **Verve Jazz Masters 52 (Verve, 1996)**

Trumpeter Maynard Ferguson (b. 1928) moved to the United States at the end of the 1940s after building a solid reputation as a bandleader in Canada. During the early 1950s he was a featured soloist known for his high-register pyrotechnics in the Stan Kenton big band. In 1956 Ferguson led the Birdland Dream Band, an outfit whose deleted Bluebird recordings represent his best work. He has led various bands off and on ever since, always featuring his technically proficient work in front of a skilled band employing a variety of arrangements. *Two's Company* boasts a stellar lineup including tenor and soprano saxophonist/flautist Joe Farrell, pianist Jaki Byard, drummer Rufus Reid and vocalist Chris Connor.

After entering a period of semiretirement in the '70s, Maynard began a strong comeback in the '80s, leading bands of young players. His Big Bop Nouveau Band is an in-demand '90s touring outfit. *These Cats Can Swing!* features an imaginative arrangement of "Caravan" that employs an impressive brass chart highlighted by Ferguson trading Spanish-nuanced lines with saxophonists Chip McNeill and Matt Wallace. The band's vocal efforts leave something to be desired, however.

Ferguson and Big Bop Nouveau revisit his greatest moments on *One More Trip to Birdland,* playing stirring versions of "Manteca," "Milestones" and "It Don't Mean a Thing If It Ain't Got That Swing" and updating the concept with a version of Joe Zawinul's "Birdland." — J.S.

GARRISON FEWELL

★★★★★ **A Blue Deeper Than the Blue (Accurate, 1993)**
★★★★ **Are You Afraid of the Dark? (Accurate, 1995)**
★★★½ **Reflection of a Clear Moon (with Laszlo Gardony) (Accurate, 1997)**

Garrison Fewell (b. 1953) labored in near anonymity for almost 20 years as a Berklee College of Music guitar teacher until the release of his 1993 debut, *A Blue Deeper Than the Blue,* which showcases his virtuosity and cerebral swing.

Are You Afraid of the Dark? shows Fewell extending far beyond the mainstream, with Middle Eastern musical tones and colors showering his "Journey to the East Suite," as well as a stunning tribute medley to Ravel and Jimi Hendrix.

The guitarist teamed with pianist Laszlo Gardony, who has become a musical soul mate, on *Dark* and *Reflection of a Clear Moon* (the latter a 1995 Hungarian National Radio live-concert broadcast made in Gardony's native Budapest). Their exotic interplay and improvisation on six extended originals make *Moon* a noteworthy addition to the challenging art of the jazz duo. — K.F.

ELLA FITZGERALD

★★★★★ **Ella Fitzgerald Sings the Cole Porter Songbook, Vol. 1 (Verve, 1956)**
★★★★★ **Ella Fitzgerald Sings the Cole Porter Songbook, Vol. 2 (Verve, 1956)**
★★★★ **Ella and Louis (Verve, 1956)**
★★★★★ **Ella Fitzgerald Sings the Rodgers and Hart Songbook, Vol. 1 (Verve, 1957)**
★★★★★ **Daydream: The Duke Ellington Songbook (1957; Verve, 1988)**
★★★½ **Jazz at the Philharmonic: Ella Fitzgerald (1957; Verve, 1985)**
★★★★ **Ella Fitzgerald at the Opera House (1957; Verve 1986)**
★★★★½ **Ella and Louis Again (Verve, 1957)**
★★★★★ **Porgy and Bess (Verve, 1958)**
★★★★★ **The Best of Ella Fitzgerald (1958; MCA, 1973)**
★★★★★ **The Best of Ella Fitzgerald, Vol. 2 (1958; MCA, 1977)**
★★★½ **Ella in Rome: The Birthday Concert (1958; Verve, 1988)**
★★★★½ **The Irving Berlin Songbook, Vol. 1 (1958; Verve, 1986)**
★★★★½ **The Irving Berlin Songbook, Vol. 2 (1958; Verve, 1986)**
★★★★★ **Ella Fitzgerald Sings the George and Ira Gershwin Songbook (1959; Verve, 1978)**
★★★★½ **Mack the Knife: The Complete Ella in Berlin (1960; Verve, 1985)**
★★★★ **Ella Swings Brightly with Nelson (with Nelson Riddle) (Verve, 1961)**
★★★½ **Ella Returns to Berlin (1961; Verve, 1991)**
★★★★½ **Ella Fitzgerald Sings the Harold Arlen Songbook, Vol. 1 (1961; Verve, 1988)**
★★★★½ **Ella Fitzgerald Sings the Harold Arlen Songbook, Vol. 2 (1961; Verve, 1988)**
★★★½ **Ella Swings Gently with Nelson (with Nelson Riddle) (Verve, 1962)**
★★★★ **Ella and Basie (Verve, 1963)**
★★★★½ **Ella Fitzgerald Sings the Jerome Kern Songbook (1964; Verve, 1985)**
★★★★ **Ella Fitzgerald Sings the Johnny Mercer Songbook (Verve, 1964)**
★★★★ **Ella at Duke's Place (Verve, 1965)**
★★★½ **Brighten the Corner (1967; Capitol, 1991)**
★★★★½ **Ella Fitzgerald and Louis Armstrong (1972; Verve, 1984)**
★★★½ **Ella in London (1974; Pablo, 1987)**
★★★ **Take Love Easy (with Joe Pass) (1974; Pablo, 1987)**
★★★½ **Montreux '75 (1975; Pablo, 1987)**
★★★★ **Ella and Oscar (with Oscar Peterson) (1975; Pablo, 1987)**
★★★½ **Fitzgerald and Pass . . . Again (1976; Pablo, 1988)**
★★★½ **Ella Fitzgerald with the Tommy Flanagan Trio, Montreux '77 (1977; Pablo, 1989)**
★★★½ **Lady Time (1978; Pablo, 1988)**
★★★½ **Dream Dancing (with Cole Porter) (1978; Pablo, 1987)**
★★★½ **A Classy Pair: Ella Fitzgerald Sings, Count Basie Plays (1979; Pablo, 1982)**
★★★½ **Fine and Mellow (1979; Pablo, 1987)**
★★★★ **A Perfect Match: Ella & Basie (with Count Basie) (1980; Pablo, 1987)**
★★★★ **Digital III at Montreux (with Joe Pass and Count Basie) (Pablo, 1980)**
★★★★ **Ella Abraça Jobim: Ella Fitzgerald Sings the Antonio Carlos Jobim Songbook (1981; Pablo, 1991)**
★★★ **The Best Is Yet to Come (Pablo Today, 1982)**

★★★½ **Speak Love (with Joe Pass) (1983; Pablo, 1987)**
★★★½ **Ella à Nice (1983; Pablo Live, 1990)**
★★★½ **Nice Work If You Can Get It (with Andre Prévin) (1983; Pablo, 1987)**
★★★½ **Easy Living (with Joe Pass) (Pablo, 1986)**
★★★★½ **The Best of Ella Fitzgerald (Pablo, 1988)**
★★★½ **Ella: Things Ain't What They Used to Be (and You Better Believe It) (Reprise, 1989)**
★★★½ **Jazz 'Round Midnight (Verve, 1990)**
★★★½ **All That Jazz (Pablo, 1990)**
★★★★★ **The Intimate Ella (Verve, 1990)**
★★★★★ **The Essential Ella Fitzgerald: The Great Songs (Verve, 1992)**
★★★★★ **The Complete Ella Fitzgerald Songbooks (Verve, 1993)**
★★★★★ **The First Lady of Song (Verve, 1993)**
★★★★ **Compact Jazz: Ella Fitzgerald and Duke Ellington (Verve, 1993)**
★★★★ **Best of Ella Fitzgerald: Her Original Capitol Recordings (Curb, 1993)**
★★★★★ **The 75th Birthday Celebration: The Original Decca Recordings (Decca, 1993)**
★★★★★ **Best of the Songbooks (Verve, 1993)**
★★★★★ **Pure Ella (Decca, 1994)**
★★★★ **The War Years (1941–1947) (Decca, 1994)**
★★★★ **The Concert Years (Pablo, 1994)**
★★★★½ **The Best of the Songbooks: The Ballads (Verve, 1994)**
★★★★ **Jazz 'Round Midnight Again (Verve, 1995)**
★★★★★ **Ella: The Legendary Decca Recordings (Decca, 1995)**
★★★★★ **The Early Years, Part 1 and Part 2 (Decca, 1995)**
★★★★★ **Daydream: Best of the Duke Ellington Songbook (Verve, 1995)**
★★★★★ **The Jazz Sides: Verve Jazz Masters 46 (Verve, 1995)**
★★★★½ **Oh, Lady Be Good! Best of the Gershwin Songbook (Verve, 1996)**
★★★★½ **Love Songs: Best of the Verve Song Books (Verve, 1996)**

The antithesis of flash, "First Lady of Song" Ella Fitzgerald (1918–1996) is the steadiest of the great jazz singers. Other titans of the form lent their readings of American standards a very personal stamp; ultimately, whatever the repertoire, Sinatra sang Sinatra, Billie Holiday sang Billie Holiday. Not Ella Fitzgerald. With a modesty rare in a talent so huge, she let nothing get in the way of the music—her voice unsurpassably clear, she remained resolutely faithful to the song itself. Perhaps the premier scat singer, Fitzgerald obviously could breathtakingly improvise (the given talent of any jazz great), but her essential genius lay in capturing the mood of any of the awesome number of classic songs that she delivered.

Born and orphaned just after World War I, Fitzgerald hooked up in the 1930s with Chick Webb, big-band leader and volcanic drummer. The husband-and-wife team scored a gigantic hit in 1938 with "A-Tisket, A-Tasket," making Fitzgerald an instant star—and, unusual for the time, the band became a crossover success, appealing not only to the black audience they'd gained at New York's Savoy Ballroom but to whites as well. After Webb's death, the strong-willed if affable Fitzgerald held the band together for a couple of years before going solo—and then working with almost all of the greatest of her peers.

On Decca, up until the mid-'50s, Fitzgerald could be considered at least as much a pop singer as a jazz one; she never let go of her capacity to swing, but the range of her material and her warm way with it transcended the confines of "hipness." *Ella: The Legendary Decca Recordings* (four CDs) gives us the material of that period in detailed form; highlights are available on *The Early Years, Part 1 and Part 2* and *The 75th Birthday Celebration,* both capable.

In 1955, Fitzgerald moved over to Verve, the label founded by her manager, Norman Granz, the "Jazz at the Philharmonic" impresario. There she sharpened her jazz edge while simultaneously embarking on a series of definitive recordings of Broadway classics that earned her lasting critical and popular success. These songbooks are not only the essence of Fitzgerald but the most thorough and uncompromising catalog of the standards of American popular song. Cole Porter, Rodgers and Hart, Duke Ellington, Jerome Kern, the Gershwins and Harold Arlen all get treated with a respect that raises even their slighter songs to a level of irresistible enjoyment; the orchestras, whether led by Buddy Bregman or Nelson Riddle, really cook—and Fitzgerald's exuberance is a thing of wonder. All of the sets are worth checking out—as is a later follow-up, the Jobim "songbook," *Ella Abraça Jobim*—but, for sheer, stunning grace, the Cole Porter, Rodgers and Hart, Gershwin and Ellington records have the edge. *The Complete Ella Fitzgerald Songbooks* takes up 16 discs (all of them terrific); however, any number of reissues highlight selections available by composer.

Fitzgerald performed with vigor throughout the '60s but sat out a while in the early '70s due to eye surgery. When she returned she did so with full force. Whether singing with Count Basie or longtime cohort Oscar Peterson on piano, with ultrasmooth guitarist Joe Pass, with a full orchestra or the excellent Tommy Flanagan Trio, she maintained her poise and elegance—her classicism made human, however, through her zest, charm and exemplary ease.

A strong intro to the later Fitzgerald is provided by the Pablo *Best of Fitzgerald*. A representative sample of her '70s period, it features orchestral settings and small-combo work, as well as examples of her collaborations with Joe Pass (Pass fans should also check out *Speak Love*, *Fitzgerald and Pass . . . Again* and *Digital III at Montreux*). *Nice Work If You Can Get It* is an assured Gershwin outing with André Previn that shows Fitzgerald still delivering strongly. With Benny Carter on alto sax and Clark Terry on trumpet, *All That Jazz* is the roar and purr of a lion in winter—her voice has obviously aged, but her skill and zest are unassailable.

Other recommendations: for Fitzgerald backed by solo piano, *Pure Ella* and *The Intimate Ella*. The Louis Armstrong pairings (including *Porgy and Bess*) unite two national treasures. And *The First Lady of Song* features three CDs of her best Verve offerings. — P.E.

FLAMIN' AMY AND SWEET POTATA

★★★ **Soul Kiss (Blue Frog, 1995)**

Vocalist Amy Coleman (b. 1960) is a popular presence on the Northeast club circuit, backed here by the solid all-woman trio Sweet Potata, who deliver a tough-edged, no-apologies version of the blues from a female perspective. Guitarist Eve Moon, whose solo work is now out of print, carries the soloing burden well, and bassist Joyous Perrin and drummer Kathleen Breitenfeld hold up their end of the bargain. The band's strength is its songwriting, from the title track, cowritten by Moon and Steve Jordan, to "Love Me Tonight," written by Coleman and "Wild" Bill Durkin, Perrin's "Real Bad Lie" and the terrific Moon/Coleman collaborations "Blood from a Stone" and "Turning to Stone." Flamin' Amy and Sweet Potata split up in early 1997, with Coleman forming the Flamin' Amy Coleman Band. — J.S.

TOMMY FLANAGAN

★★★★ **The Cats (1957; Original Jazz Classics, 1983)**
★★★★ **The Tommy Flanagan Trio (1960; Original Jazz Classics, 1985)**
★★★ **The Tokyo Recital (1975; Original Jazz Classics, 1992)**
★★★ **Montreux '77 (1977; Original Jazz Classics, 1989)**
★★★★ **The Best of Tommy Flanagan (1977; Pablo, 1991)**
★★★ **Something Borrowed, Something Blue (1978; Original Jazz Classics, 1990)**
★★★★ **Our Delights (1979; Original Jazz Classics, 1992)**
★★★★ **Ballads and Blues (1979; Enja, 1993)**
★★★★ **Confirmation (1979; Enja, 1991)**
★★★★ **Super Session (1980; Enja, 1993)**
★★★★ **The Magnificent (Progressive, 1981)**
★★★★★ **Thelonica (Enja, 1987)**
★★★★½ **Jazz Poet (Timeless, 1990)**
★★★★★ **Beyond the Bluebird (Timeless, 1991)**
★★★★ **Eclypso (Enja, 1993)**
★★★★ **Flanagan's Shenanigans (Storyville, 1994)**
★★★★ **Lady Be Good . . . For Ella (Verve, 1994)**
★★★½ **Sea Change (Evidence, 1997)**
★★★½ **Sunset and the Mockingbird (Blue Note, 1998)**

Pianist Tommy Flanagan (b. 1930) is one of the greatest accompanists in jazz history, a master with perfect touch, empathy for his surroundings and an unerring sense of when to step out to the front of an arrangement and when to move subtly through its shadows. A product of the rich Detroit jazz tradition, Flanagan played with Billy Mitchell, Milt Jackson and Kenny Burrell before moving in 1956 to New York, where he eventually became famous as an accompanist with Tony Bennett and for his magnificent work with Ella Fitzgerald. A superb band pianist as well, Flanagan has played with

Miles Davis, Sonny Rollins (*Saxophone Colossus*) and John Coltrane (*Giant Steps*) and led various trios.

Flanagan's work as a leader is consistently superb right from the beginning; *The Cats* is a fine session with Coltrane and Burrell. *The Tommy Flanagan Trio* introduces his standard trio format, with a bassist (Tommy Potter) and drummer (Roy Haynes). Bassist Keter Betts and drummer Bobby Durham appear on *Montreux '77* and *The Tokyo Recital;* Jimmie Smith replaces Durham on *Something Borrowed, Something Blue. Our Delights* is a marvelous series of duets with fellow Detroit pianist Hank Jones, and it's worth looking for the cassette-only sequel, *More Delights.*

Flanagan teams up with the perfectly matched bassist George Mraz and drummer Elvin Jones on *Eclypso* and *Confirmation.* Red Mitchell replaces Mraz on *Super Session,* but Mraz returns, this time with drummer Al Foster, on *The Magnificent,* then with Kenny Washington for *Jazz Poet* and finally with Burrell and drummer Lewis Nash for the Detroit tribute record *Beyond the Bluebird. Ballads and Blues* finds Flanagan dueting with Mraz.

One of Flanagan's greatest recordings is the sublime *Thelonica,* a tribute to Thelonious Monk and the jazz patron Baroness Pannonica de Koenigswarter. This trio date features Mraz and drummer Art Taylor. Flanagan, a winner of the Danish Jazzpar award, collaborates with Scandinavian musicians, including the great tenor saxophonist Jesper Thilo, on *Flanagan's Shenanigans.*

Flanagan reprises the songs that most remind him of his tenure with Ella Fitzgerald on *Lady Be Good,* where he is backed by Nash and bassist Peter Washington. — J.S.

BELA FLECK

★★★★ **Crossing the Tracks (Rounder, 1979)**
★★★ **Natural Bridge (Rounder, 1982)**
★★★★ **Double Time (Rounder, 1983)**
★★★ **Deviation (Rounder, 1984)**
★★★★ **In Roads (Rounder, 1986)**
★★★★ **Daybreak (Rounder, 1987)**
★★★★ **Places (Rounder, 1987)**
★★★½ **Drive (Rounder, 1988)**
★★★★ **Bela Fleck and the Flecktones (Warner Bros., 1990)**
★★★★ **Flight of the Cosmic Hippo (Warner Bros., 1991)**
★★★½ **UFO Tofu (Warner Bros., 1992)**
★★★★ **Three Flew over the Cuckoo's Nest (Warner Bros., 1993)**
★★★★½ **Tales from the Acoustic Planet (Warner Bros., 1995)**
★★★★★ **Live Art (Warner Bros., 1996)**
★★★★ **Tabula Rasa (with V.M. Bhatt and Jie-Bing Chen) (Water Lily Acoustics, 1996)**

Bela Fleck (b. 1958) is a banjo virtuoso, and that in itself is a fairly singular achievement. But what truly makes his music exceptional is the way he has applied his astonishing ability to such unlikely ends. Sure, he plays bluegrass and is a wizard at fleet-fingered Scruggs-style picking. But he's equally at home in bebop, fusion or any of the hybrid folk styles that have grown up around the new acoustic movement.

As such, though many of his albums start off with what might be considered a traditional bluegrass sound, where they end up is often impossible to predict. *Crossing the Tracks,* for instance, seems relatively straightforward when Fleck is left to the likes of "Dear Old Dixie" or "Texas Barbecue" but heads into uncharted territory when he and his playmates rip through the jazzy changes of Chick Corea's "Spain." It's an astonishing bit of playing but it hardly prevents Fleck from ending the album with a wonderful old-timey tune called "Ain't Gonna Work Tomorrow." And though the music isn't quite as audacious on *Natural Bridge,* the musicians on hand—an all-star lineup including David Grisman, Mark O'Connor and Ricky Scaggs—keep the music from ever getting dull. (Selections from these albums, as well as from a trio album with Tony Trischka and Bill Keith called *Fiddle Tunes for Banjo,* can be found on the CD compilation *Daybreak.*)

Double Time finds Fleck moving into the new acoustic camp with a set of ingenious, genre-hopping duets. Some, like "Sweet Rolls," with fellow picker John Hartford, are fairly traditional, while others—for instance, the electronically embellished "Light Speed"—are anything but. Still, the most interesting tracks are those like "Ladies and Gentlemen" (with cellist Darol Anger) that draw from traditional styles but take a wholly unique approach. In fact, Fleck's playing is so exciting in such circumstances that it's almost a disappointment to hear him revert to the relatively traditional sound of *Deviation*—almost, but not quite. *Deviation* may be more like a bluegrass album than *Double Time* is, but because Fleck cut the album with his then–band mates in the New

Grass Revival, there's plenty of experimentation in the playing. But *In Roads* more than makes up, for though it maintains a strong sense of roots, it pushes Fleck in a variety of new directions, from the quiet Celtic melancholy of "Ireland" to the jazzy interplay of the vibes-driven "Perplexed." (Highlights from these three albums can be found on the CD compilation *Places.*)

Fleck's last album for Rounder, *Drive,* is also something of a farewell to bluegrass. Masterfully played and featuring such stalwart soloists as Mark O'Connor, Jerry Douglas and Tony Rice, it neatly sums up Fleck's past but offers not a clue about his future. No wonder. *Bela Fleck and the Flecktones* is built around one of the oddest ensembles in improvised music, a quartet that includes Howard Levy on harmonica and keyboards, Victor Lemonte Wooten on electric bass and Roy "Future Man" Wooten on Synth-axe/Drumitar, an electronic gizmo that's part guitar, part synth and part drum machine. Given the unorthodox nature of the instrumentation, it follows that the music would be similarly singular—and it is. Fleck may touch on many of the same sources from which he's always drawn, but the music invariably pushes in an unexpected direction. "Half Moon Bay," for instance, starts out as a lovely neofolk waltz but somehow sidesteps into a bit of bebop; "Sinister Minister" flirts with funk even as Fleck fingerpicks Scruggs-style arpeggios; and "Reflections of Lucy" is a jazzy reverie that somehow backs into "Lucy in the Sky with Diamonds."

Flight of the Cosmic Hippo and *UFO Tofu* continue in that vein; *Hippo* is typically eclectic, successfully essaying from "Michelle" to "The Star-Spangled Banner," but *Tofu* seems overarranged at times, with the title tune verging on the ain't-we-hot? bombast of progressive rock. Levy left the group at this point, and *Three Flew over the Cuckoo's Nest* consequently takes a different tack. Not only is Fleck using synth triggers to alter the tone of his banjo, but his playing with the Wootens sounds at times like fairly tasteful fusion (particularly "Vix 9" and "Bumpershoot"), though the band gets quite funky during Victor Wooten's rap-inflected "The Message." Bruce Hornsby and Branford Marsalis sit in on some tracks.

Tales from the Acoustic Planet finds a solo Fleck (though the Wootens show up on more than half the tunes) reconciling his new acoustic roots with some of his later experiments. Chick Corea, Paul McCandless, Jerry Douglas, Edgar Meyer, Sam Bush and Branford Marsalis are among the guests—and that breadth of talent says something about how far afield the music wanders. Good as it is, though, the double CD *Live Art* is even better, drawing from a similar range of talent (plus Levy and Hornsby) and pulling more from all the players, especially Corea and Bush. *Tabula Rasa* bridges even more styles, as Fleck joins vina virtuoso V.M. Bhatt and er-hu player Jie-Bing Chen for a set of performances that somehow link Indian, Chinese and Appalachian folk traditions. Could it be that Fleck is only just getting warmed up? — J.D.C.

RICKY FORD

★★★★★ Loxodonta Africana (1977; New World, 1997)
★★★ Saxotic Stomp (Muse, 1988)
★★★½ Manhattan Blues (Candid, 1990)
★★★½ Hard Groovin' (Muse, 1991)
★★★★ Ebony Rhapsody (Candid, 1991)
★★★ Hot Brass (Candid, 1992)
★★★ Tenor Madness Too! (Muse, 1995)

Tenor saxophonist Ricky Ford (b. 1954) grew up in Boston and attended the New England Conservatory of Music before making his professional mark with Jaki Byard, the Duke Ellington Orchestra, Charles Mingus and Abdullah Ibrahim, among others. His full, intense playing on both traditional and avant-garde material is his own conception, although it owes a stylistic debt to Dexter Gordon and Sonny Rollins. He also possesses the leadership qualities of a gifted composer.

Ford's debut, *Loxodonta Africana,* is powered by the great rhythm section of bassist Richard Davis and drummer Dannie Richmond. The unavailable *Manhattan Plaza* is a magnificent showcase for Byard, and the also-deleted *Flying Colors* finds Byard exploring Thelonious Monk and Duke Ellington material. *Saxotic Stomp,* with James Spaulding on alto saxophone and flute and Charles Davis on baritone, *Hard Groovin',* with trumpeter Roy Hargrove, and *Tenor Madness Too!* are less interesting than the out-of-print *Shorter Ideas*, *Tenor of the Times* and *Interpretations.*

Manhattan Blues and *Ebony Rhapsody* are sublime quartet sessions with Byard, bassist Milt Hinton and drummer Ben Riley. Also look for the out-of-print *African-American Blues* on Candid. — J.S.

JIMMY FORREST

★★★★ **Forrest Fire (1960; Original Jazz Classics, 1993)**
★★★ **Sit Down and Relax with Jimmy Forrest (1961; Original Jazz Classics, 1996)**
★★★ **Most Much! (1961; Original Jazz Classics, 1989)**
★★★ **Out of the Forrest (1961; Original Jazz Classics, 1994)**
★★★★ **Heart of the Forrest (1978; Muse, 1996)**
★★★★ **Soul Street (Original Jazz Classics, 1998)**

Tenor saxophonist Jimmy Forrest (1920–1980) is best known for recording the often covered R&B hit "Night Train," but this hard-blowing, soulful instrumentalist was a veteran of several of the best big bands and numerous hard-bop sessions. Forrest accomplished the rare feat of playing in both the Duke Ellington and Count Basie bands, but he was at his best in smaller combos, where he could really cut loose. *Forrest Fire* is a torrid session with Larry Young on Hammond B-3 organ, Thornel Schwartz on guitar and Jimmie Smith on drums. *Heart of the Forrest,* a 1978 live recording, features organist Shirley Scott. *Out of the Forrest* adds Joe Zawinul on piano. *Soul Street,* recorded between 1958 and 1962, includes quintet and sextet lineups and tracks with Oliver Nelson. — J.S.

JOEL FORRESTER

★★★½ **No . . . Really! (Koch, 1997)**

Finally, the more hidden of the two creative helmsmen behind New York's favorite little big band of the '80s—the Microscopic Septet—resurfaces with an album of his own. Pianist/composer Joel Forrester (b. 1946) remains true to his original, ebullient vision—his playing still prankish and playful, his compositions lurching with loungelike Latin leanings, giddy with a barrelful of Monk-ishness. It's a vision that also zestfully balances sincerity and caprice—bebop-style tracks like "Dodo," "Your Political Movie" and the semimocking "Don't Ask Me Now" poke and prod expectations with little melodic twists, surprising turns of phrase, double intros and false endings.

Featuring a streamlined unit called People Like Us—including fellow former Micros Dave Hofstra on bass and Dave Sewelson guesting intermittently on baritone sax, plus legendary "out" drummer Denis Charles and new recruit Claire Daly also on baritone—*No . . . Really!* is the first of at least four promised (and promising) Forrester titles on the Koch jazz label. — A.K.

SONNY FORTUNE

★★★★ **Four in One (Blue Note, 1994)**
★★★★ **A Better Understanding (Blue Note, 1995)**
★★★½ **From Now On (Blue Note, 1996)**

Tenor and alto saxophonist/flautist Sonny Fortune (b. 1939) hit the New York jazz scene in the late 1960s as a sideman with Elvin Jones, then Mongo Santamaria. In the early 1970s Fortune was part of the powerful McCoy Tyner unit that recorded *Sahara,* and later in the decade he joined the Miles Davis group for *Agharta* and *Pangaea.* He also played on the hit album *The Other Side of Abbey Road* with George Benson.

Fortune has made a number of albums as a leader, most of which are out of print. Look for *Awakening,* an A&M cutout, and *Monk's Mood.* His career has been revived on Blue Note in the 1990s: *Four in One,* an album of Thelonious Monk compositions, features pianist Kirk Lightsey, bassists Buster Williams and Santi Debriano and drummers Billy Hart and Ronnie Burrage. *A Better Understanding,* another fine set with Hart, includes a great performance from pianist Kenny Barron. — J.S.

FRANK FOSTER

★★½ **The House That Love Built (1982; SteepleChase, 1995)**
★★★★ **Two for the Blues (with Frank Wess) (1984; Original Jazz Classics, 1993)**
★★★½ **Frankly Speaking (with Frank Wess) (Concord Jazz, 1985)**
★★½ **The Frank Foster Non-Electric Company (EPM, 1989)**
★★★★ **Shiny Stockings (Denon, 1993)**
★★★★ **Leo Rising (Arabesque, 1997)**

Tenor saxophonist Frank Benjamin Foster (b. 1928) replaced Eddie "Lockjaw" Davis in Count Basie's band in 1953 and immediately became one of the band's driving instrumental forces. Over the next decade in the group, Foster wrote more than 100 charts for Basie and teamed up with saxophonist/flautist Frank Wess as the double-barreled "Two Franks," whose nickname inspired the Neal Hefti classic of the same name. After Basie's death in 1984, Foster took over the direction of the band in 1986, effectively sacrificing his own career as a leader.

On *Two for the Blues* and *Frankly Speaking,* Foster and Wess front a quintet that also includes pianist Kenny Barron, bassist Rufus Reid and drummer Marvin "Smitty" Smith. Foster's presence alone makes *The Frank Foster Non-Electric Company* and *The House That Love Built* notable. *Shiny Stockings* documents the big band Foster led in the 1970s before taking over the Basie organization. *Leo Rising* is a strong small-group date recorded after Foster stopped leading the Basie band. Look for the out-of-print *No Count,* a 1957 small-band session with Foster and Wess minus the Count but still swinging mightily. Fellow Basie-ite Henry Coker joins in on trombone. — J.S.

ARETHA FRANKLIN

★★★½ **Unforgettable (1964; Columbia/Legacy, 1995)**
★★★★★ **I Never Loved a Man (the Way I Love You) (1967; Rhino, 1995)**
★★★ **Aretha Arrives (1967; Rhino, 1993)**
★★★★★ **Lady Soul (1968; Rhino, 1995)**
★★★½ **Aretha Now (1968; Rhino, 1993)**
★★★ **Aretha in Paris (1968; Rhino, 1994)**
★★★½ **Soul '69 (1969; Rhino, 1993)**
★★★★ **Aretha's Gold (Atlantic, 1969)**
★★★½ **This Girl's in Love with You (1970; Rhino, 1993)**
★★★½ **Spirit in the Dark (1970; Rhino, 1993)**
★★★½ **Greatest Hits (Atlantic, 1971)**
★★★ **Live at Fillmore West (1971; Rhino, 1993)**
★★★½ **Young, Gifted and Black (1972; Rhino, 1993)**
★★★★★ **Amazing Grace (1972; Rhino, 1993)**
★★★ **The Great Aretha Franklin: The First 12 Sides (1972; Columbia, 1988)**
★★★½ **All-Time Greatest Hits (Columbia, 1972)**
★★½ **Hey Now Hey (The Other Side of the Sky) (1973; Rhino, 1994)**
★★★ **The Best of Aretha Franklin (1973; Rhino, 1985)**
★★★ **Let Me in Your Life (1974; Rhino, 1994)**
★★★ **With Everything I Feel in Me (Atlantic, 1974)**
★ **You (Atlantic, 1975)**
★★ **Sparkle (1976; Rhino, 1992)**
★★★ **Ten Years of Gold (Atlantic, 1976)**
★★ **Sweet Passion (Atlantic, 1977)**
★★ **Almighty Fire (Atlantic, 1978)**
★★ **La Diva (Atlantic, 1979)**
★★ **Aretha (Arista, 1980)**
★★★ **Love All the Hurt Away (Arista, 1981)**
★★★ **Jump to It (Arista, 1982)**
★★½ **Sweet Bitter Love (Columbia, 1982)**
★★★½ **Get It Right (Arista, 1983)**
★★★½ **Aretha's Jazz (Atlantic, 1984)**
★★★½ **Who's Zoomin' Who (Arista, 1985)**
★★★ **Aretha Sings the Blues (Columbia, 1985)**
★★★★★ **30 Greatest Hits (Rhino, 1986)**
★★½ **Aretha (Arista, 1986)**
★★★ **After Hours (Columbia, 1987)**
★★★★ **One Lord, One Faith, One Baptism (Arista, 1987)**
★★★ **Through the Storm (Arista, 1989)**
★★★ **What You Get Is What You Sweat (Arista, 1991)**
★★★★★ **Queen of Soul: The Atlantic Recordings (Rhino, 1992)**
★★★½ **Jazz to Soul (Columbia/Legacy, 1992)**
★★★★★ **The Very Best of Aretha Franklin, Vol. 1 (Rhino, 1994)**
★★★★★ **The Very Best of Aretha Franklin, Vol. 2 (Rhino, 1994)**

"Lady Soul" could have triumphed at virtually any form of popular music: Her supple mezzosoprano has astonishing range, and both her passion and technique are remarkable. Daughter of Detroit's Rev. C.L. Franklin, a preacher whose many albums of sermons earned him the name "the Million-Dollar Voice," Aretha Franklin (b. 1942) was inspired to pursue a singing career by hearing Clara Ward; throughout her life, she'd deem gospel greats Ward and Mahalia Jackson her mentors (and her own move from sacred to secular music was patterned after another friend's, Sam Cooke's). She could swing, too, as hard as any jazz diva, and her feel for the blues was equally sure. But it's as the R&B queen, the doyenne of that '60s soul music that combined all of the above elements, that she gained fame.

At Columbia, beginning in 1961, Franklin initially was forced into the mold of a pop singer, covering easy fare like "Over the Rainbow." Her work for that label—now on *The First 12 Sides,* four reissues and *Jazz to Soul*—merely anticipates her coming glory; glossy arrangements can't bury her brilliant piano playing and innate vocal power. Great work, especially a tribute to Dinah Washington, still surfaced.

It was by joining in 1966 with Atlantic Records vice president Jerry Wexler and the famed Muscle Shoals studio players that Franklin found her true voice; backed by a surging rhythm section and punching horns, she turned loose her gospel piano and sang with such graceful abandon that she became recognized as one of the handful of inventors of hard-core soul. Motown achieved symphonic sweep and sweet melodicism; in contrast, Franklin's music—assisted in production by Wexler, Tom Dowd and Arif Mardin—would be consistently tougher, rawer and arguably, much deeper.

I Never Loved a Man (the Way I Love You) is a staggering introduction to the new Franklin. Her "Respect" knocked cold even the Otis Redding original; and with the title track, "Do Right Woman—Do Right Man," "Dr. Feelgood" and "Save Me," this was music of absolute, fluid assurance. The record may stand as the greatest soul album of all time.

"Baby I Love You" enlivens the capable *Aretha Arrives,* but *Lady Soul* is another masterpiece, producing the hits "(You Make Me Feel Like) A Natural Woman," "(Sweet Sweet Baby) Since You've Been Gone" and, most significantly, "Chain of Fools." With Franklin singing with swagger, and background vocals (featuring her sister, Carolyn) recalling the Staple Singers, the song encapsulates her soul style—as catchy as any early rock & roll number, it resounds with wiser force.

Aretha Now showed that the singer could transform pop into soul; infusing Burt Bacharach's "I Say a Little Prayer" with swing, she adds edge to the delicate melody. And *Soul '69* proves her to be a jazz singer of rare intelligence and dimension. With great takes on Sam Cooke's "Bring It on Home to Me" and Big Maybelle Smith's "Ramblin'" and a tight brass section led by King Curtis, *Soul '69*'s highlights can be found on *Aretha's Jazz.* That compilation also presents the better work from Franklin's later orchestral jazz set with Quincy Jones, *Hey Now Hey (The Other Side of the Sky).*

The early '70s marked the end of Franklin's titanic period. *Greatest Hits* offers "Spanish Harlem" and a gospel "Bridge over Troubled Water." *Young, Gifted and Black* presents the spare, urgent "Rock Steady" and the lovely "Day Dreamin'." *Live at Fillmore West* finds her collaborating with Ray Charles. All these records are confident; none, however, matches the majesty of her two-album gospel magnum opus, *Amazing Grace.* Backed by James Cleveland and the Southern California Community Choir, *Grace* is Franklin transcendent, returning to the source of her own—and soul music's—earliest inspiration.

In 1981 Franklin came back from a series of bland, sometimes discofied albums in which she often sounds bored or exhausted, with *Love All the Hurt Away*—a funky pop near-triumph. While not of the caliber of the Atlantic sides, it shows off her newly energized singing—and paves the way for her commercial reemergence with *Who's Zoomin' Who.* In many ways a rock record (despite a cameo by Dizzy Gillespie), *Zoomin'* may be lyrically slight, but it kicks—check the duet with the Eurythmics, Carlos Santana's guitar solo and sax work by Clarence Clemons. With help from the Mighty Clouds of Joy, Jesse Jackson and Mavis Staples, *One Lord, One Faith, One Baptism* reasserts Franklin's gospel prowess—it's her best record in more than a decade.

Franklin remains the spirit of soul—a singer of genius. Nearly all of her 1967–72 releases are essential R&B; the excellent *Queen of Soul,* a four-CD boxed set, presents Franklin at her finest. — P.E.

MICHAEL FRANKS

★★½ **The Art of Tea (Reprise, 1976)**
★★½ **Sleeping Gypsy (Warner Bros., 1977)**
★★ **Burchfield Nines (Warner Bros., 1978)**
★★ **Tiger in the Rain (Warner Bros., 1979)**
★★ **One Bad Habit (Warner Bros., 1980)**
★★½ **Skin Dive (Warner Bros., 1985)**
★★ **The Camera Never Lies (Warner Bros., 1987)**
★★ **Previously Unavailable (DRG, 1989)**
★★ **Blue Pacific (Reprise, 1990)**
★★ **Dragonfly Summer (Reprise, 1993)**
★★ **Abandoned Garden (Warner Bros., 1995)**

Parlaying extremely user-friendly jazz lite, Michael Franks (b. 1944) has evolved a formula—ultraclean production, soft vocals either winsome or coyly seductive, tasty sax fills and hummable tunes heavy on wordplay. His songs covered by the Carpenters and Melissa

Manchester, his own albums turned out by session vets and fusion stalwarts, Franks consistently offers a kind of "call of the mild"—his music is tasteful, charming and the antithesis of risk.

Franks featured the Crusaders on *The Art of Tea* and its cutesy, minor hit "Popsicle Toes," played with Brazilian musicians on *Sleeping Gypsy* and with Brenda Russell and Ron Carter on *Skin Dive*—but his casts of players don't alter his sound. Again and again, he hits the same note—a note of a pastel, designer shade.
— P.E.

NNENNA FREELON

★★★½ **Nnenna Freelon (Columbia, 1992)**
★★★ **Heritage (Columbia, 1993)**
★★★ **Listen (Columbia, 1994)**
★★★★ **Shaking Free (Concord Jazz, 1996)**
★★★ **Maiden Voyage (Concord Jazz, 1998)**

North Carolina–based Nnenna Freelon (b. 1956) is an engaging singer, blessed with a warm and pure tone and a strong sense of musicality, but within the ranks of jazz singers, she is more a storyteller than a vocal gymnast. Freelon's Grammy-nominated eponymous debut—made with an all-star jazz big band plus strings—shows her to be a fine interpreter of standards and creator of new songs. On *Heritage* she reinterprets neglected standards with support of a premier rhythm section—pianist Kenny Barron, bassist Christian McBride and drummer Lewis Nash—plus two horns.

The more artful *Listen* brings out her talents as a lyricist and songwriter. It adds her words to Wayne Shorter's "Footprints" (reworked as "Song of Silent Footprints") and the McCoy Tyner ballad "Aisha." Freelon cuts loose on the aptly titled *Shaking Free,* the first recording made with her regular working band—pianist Bill Anschell, bassist John Brown and drummer Woody Williams with supplemental support from percussionist Alex Acuña, guitarist Scott Sawyer and saxophonist Ricky Woodard. *Maiden Voyage* is Freelon's most eclectic work to date, presenting a range of women's songs about life, love and understanding. Participating musicians include Herbie Hancock, Joe Beck, Bob Mintzer, Dave Valentin, Danny Gottlieb and Sammy Figueroa. — K.F.

CHICO FREEMAN

★★★★ **Beyond the Rain (1978; Original Jazz Classics, 1991)**
★★★★★ **Spirit Sensitive (1978; India Navigation, 1988)**
★★★ **No Time Left (1979; Black Saint, 1993)**
★★★★ **Destiny's Dance (1982; Original Jazz Classics, 1994)**
★★★½ **Live at Ronnie Scott's (1986; DRG, 1994)**
★★★★ **Freeman & Freeman (India Navigation, 1989)**
★★★★ **Chico (India Navigation, 1991)**
★★★★ **Up and Down (Black Saint, 1992)**
★★½ **Threshold (In + Out, 1993)**
★★★★ **Still Sensitive (India Navigation, 1995)**
★★★★ **Focus (Contemporary, 1995)**
★★★★★ **The Emissary (Clarity, 1996)**

Multi-instrumentalist Chico Freeman (b. 1949) is perhaps the most flexible of the generation of tenor-saxophone stars who emerged in the 1970s, a searching player who has surrounded himself with great musicians throughout his career. Freeman's sensibility was formed in part by his father, the outstanding Chicago tenor saxophonist Von Freeman, as well as his close contact with the local blues scene and his association with the experimental musicians of Chicago's Association for the Advancement of Creative Musicians. In addition to his jazz work, Freeman has played with the Temptations; the Four Tops; Earth, Wind and Fire; Tito Puente and Celia Cruz. As a result he is equally at home on traditional and free-jazz sessions and always willing to bridge the gap into other musical disciplines.

Unfortunately one of Freeman's greatest albums, *Kings of Mali,* is currently unavailable. The record has an Afrocentric theme and benefits from outstanding performances by vibraphonist Jay Hoggard and pianist Anthony Davis as well as Freeman's work on soprano sax and flutes. Another currently unavailable recording, *Peaceful Heart, Gentle Spirit,* showcases Freeman's considerable abilities as a writer as well as his stunning clarinet and bass-clarinet playing.

Fortunately, the exquisite ballad album, *Spirit Sensitive,* on which Freeman handles gentler material with the touch of a legendary master, remains in print. The lineup of Freeman on tenor and soprano, bassist Cecil McBee, pianist John Hicks and drummers Billy Hart and Famoudou Don Moye was so successful that the session was reprised, with Winard Harper instead of Hart, on *Still Sensitive.*

Other Freeman albums, including a number

of now deleted sessions, have their ups and downs. *Destiny's Dance* is a sextet outing featuring Wynton Marsalis and Bobby Hutcherson at the top of their games. The live *Freeman & Freeman,* recorded at New York's Public Theater in 1981, with Chico and Von fronting a crack lineup of McBee, drummer Jack DeJohnette and pianist Kenny Barron (and Muhal Richard Abrams guesting on piano for one track), is a thoroughly satisfying family reunion, far better than the out-of-print Columbia release *Fathers and Sons.*

Freeman's early-1990s band, Brainstorm, attempted to merge pop and jazz ideas with an unstated but obvious eye toward mainstream commercial success. The result is the maddening pastiche of *Threshold,* which buries some great instrumental moments and a superb assist from vocalist Urszula Dudziak (see the inventive "Duet") with pro forma electronics, funk bass supplied by New Kids on the Block bassist Dave Dyson and stupid rapping sequences squeezed on like so much catsup.

Focus matches Freeman's tenor against Arthur Blythe's careening alto saxophone in a spirited quintet format with pianist George Cables, bassist Santi Debriano and drummer Yoron Israel. *The Emissary* may be Freeman's greatest achievement, the closest he's come to utilizing all the disparate elements of his musical education in service of a coherent vision. Working with the Josh Jones Latin Jazz Ensemble, Freeman varies from the tribute to Idris Muhammad, "The Spirit Catcher," to the exotic arrangement of the title track to the flamenco-inspired "Murcia" to a reggae take on the Delfonics hit "La La Means I Love You" to the Afro-Cuban rundown of "The Streets Got Me Weeping" to a world-music approach to the Earth, Wind and Fire composition "I'll Write a Song for You" to wonderful African drumming sequences from Babou Sagna to a showstopping version of the immortal Miles Davis/Victor Feldman theme "Seven Steps to Heaven."
— J.S.

DAVID FRIESEN

★★★½ Returning (Burnside, 1993)
★★★½ Remembering the Moment (Soul Note, 1994)
★★★★ Concord Duo Series, Vol. 8 (with Denny Zeitlin) (Concord Jazz, 1995)

David Friesen (b. 1942) is a virtuosic bassist and a subtly accomplished composer. *Returning* is a series of beautifully understated duets with bassist/pianist Glen Moore. Livelier fare, *Remembering the Moment* features tenor saxophonist Jim Pepper, trombonist Julian Priester, pianist Mal Waldron and drummer Eddie Moore. Friesen has also recorded duet LPs with guitarist John Stowell and pianist Denny Zeitlin. — J.S.

BILL FRISELL

★★★★ In Line (ECM, 1983)
★★★ Rambler (ECM, 1985)
★★★½ Smash & Scatteration (with Vernon Reid) (Rykodisc, 1986)
★★★★ Lookout for Hope (ECM, 1988)
★★★½ Works (1988; ECM, 1994)
★★★½ Before We Were Born (Elektra Musician, 1989)
★★★ Is That You? (Elektra Musician, 1990)
★★★★ Where in the World? (Elektra, 1991)
★★★ Have a Little Faith (Nonesuch, 1993)
★★★ This Land (Nonesuch, 1994)
★★★ Go West: Music for the Films of Buster Keaton (Nonesuch, 1995)
★★★ Live (Gramavision, 1995)
★★★ The High Sign/One Week: Music for the Films of Buster Keaton (Nonesuch, 1995)
★★★ Quartet (Nonesuch, 1996)
★★★½ Nashville (Nonesuch, 1997)

Being a capable technician and resourceful improviser isn't enough for jazz guitarists these days; in addition to providing the right notes, they must also have a handle on all the right sounds. But that's one of the things Bill Frisell (b. 1951) does best, shaping his tone with such skill that it almost seems three-dimensional. That's one of the reasons he's such a sought-after sideman, and it's no accident that half of the selections on *Works* are taken from other leaders' recordings (interested listeners should definitely seek out any of the recordings by Bass Desires, the Marc Johnson–led quartet that uses Frisell in tandem with guitarist John Scofield). Still, Frisell's output as a leader is nothing to sniff at. *In Line,* a lusciously reflective collection of solos and duets (the latter with bassist Arild Andersen), offers perhaps the clearest view of his playing, followed by *Smash & Scatteration,* a wittily coloristic collaboration with Living Colour guitarist Vernon Reid. On the other end of the spectrum is *Rambler,* which finds Frisell flanked by trumpeter Kenny Wheeler, tubaist Bob Stewart, drummer Paul Motian and bassist

Jerome Harris; impressive as the interplay often is, it can be hard to get past the occasionally odd ensemble textures.

Frisell records most frequently with quartets, though. His own Bill Frisell Band—cellist Hank Roberts, bassist Kermit Driscoll and drummer Joey Baron—is featured on *Lookout for Hope*, *Where in the World?* and parts of *Before We Were Born,* with *Lookout* being the most approachable and *Where?* the most daring. *Is That You?,* recorded with pianist Wayne Horvitz, is also intriguing, though its atmospheric improvisation is not as dynamic or consistent as the albums with Frisell's own band. On *Nashville* Frisell goes for a bluegrass feel and uses dobro great Jerry Douglas, along with banjo and mandolin. — J.D.C.

BLIND BOY FULLER

★★★★★ **Truckin' My Blues Away (Yazoo, 1990)**
★★★★★ **East Coast Piedmont Style (Columbia/Legacy, 1991)**
★★★★ **Complete Recorded Works, Vol. 1 (1935–1936) (Document, 1992)**
★★★½ **Complete Recorded Works, Vol. 2 (1936–1937) (Document, 1992)**
★★★½ **Complete Recorded Works, Vol. 3 (1937) (Document, 1992)**
★★★★ **Complete Recorded Works, Vol. 4 (1937–1938) (Document, 1992)**
★★★★ **Complete Recorded Works, Vol. 5 (1938–1940) (Document, 1992)**
★★★★½ **Complete Recorded Works, Vol. 6 (1940) (Document, 1992)**
★★★★★ **Get Your Yas Yas Out (Indigo, 1996)**

Born Fulton Allen in North Carolina, Blind Boy Fuller (1908–1941) became one of the most influential East Coast bluesmen, as well as one of the most commercially successful blues players, of the 1930s. His style was imitated by such players as Brownie McGhee, whose early records bore the moniker "Blind Boy No. 2." An unparalleled entertainer and singer, Fuller had a penchant for taking material from different sources (such as guitar riffs from peers like Blind Blake and Blind Lemon Jefferson) and making it his own. Between 1935 and 1940 Fuller recorded 135 tracks, many of which were credited to James Baxter Long, who discovered Fuller and marketed his records (along with those of other local bluesmen) in a Durham, North Carolina, department store.

Though all of Fuller's recorded output is available on the Document volumes, the cream of the crop is on *East Coast Piedmont Style* and *Truckin' My Blues Away.* The former, a collection of songs recorded between 1935 and 1939, features, for the most part, Fuller solo with his guitar. Exceptions are two tracks ("Rag, Mama, Rag" and "Baby You Gotta Change Your Mind") with fret man Rev. Gary Davis, who has been credited with helping Fuller mold his style; six tracks with George Washington ("Bull City Red") on washboard; and one, "I'm a Stranger Here," with Sonny Terry on harmonica.

Truckin' My Blues Away covers the same period as *East Coast* and features two of the same tracks ("Untrue Blues" and "Walkin' My Troubles Away"). Highlights of *Truckin'* include Fuller's "Meat Shakin' Woman" and "You Can Never Tell," on which he purloins licks from Blind Lemon Jefferson's "Bad Luck Blues" and Blind Blake's "Early Morning Blues," respectively. The album concludes with one of Fuller's very popular double-entendre songs, "Sweet Honey Hole." With its terrific music and R. Crumb cover art, *Truckin' My Blues Away* is an enticing package. *Get Your Yas Yas Out,* a collection of songs recorded from 1935 to 1940, duplicates some of the *East Coast* material but features more collaborations with Sonny Terry on harmonica.

As with all Document titles, *Complete Recorded Works* presents Fuller's work in chronological order, from his debut session on July 23, 1935 (although the cover mistakenly says September 23, 1935), to his last on June 19, 1940. His final sessions are particularly interesting because they include Fuller's first forays into religious themes. Included on the sixth disc is a version of Rev. Gary Davis's "Twelve Gates to the City" as well as such spirituals as "Must Have Been My Jesus," "Jesus Is a Holy Man" and "Precious Lord." Fuller apparently made a religious conversion in the last year of his life, reportedly believing that his health problems were God's punishment for his singing the blues. Nevertheless, his last session ends with the decidedly secular "Night Rambling Woman." — B.R.H.

CURTIS FULLER

★★½ **New Trombone (1957; Original Jazz Classics, 1993)**
★★★★ **Blues-ette (1959; Savoy, 1991)**
★★★½ **The Curtis Fuller Jazztet (1959; Savoy, N.A.)**
★★★½ **Images of Curtis Fuller (1960; Savoy, N.A.)**
★★★½ **Imagination (1960; Savoy, 1995)**

★★★ **Blues-ette II (Savoy, 1993)**
★★★ **Jazz . . . It's Magic! (Savoy, 1996)**
Trombonist Curtis Fuller (b. 1934) grew up in Detroit, where he played with Kenny Burrell and Yusef Lateef in the mid-1950s before moving in 1957 to New York, where he quickly became a sought-after sideman. He played with Miles Davis and Lester Young, worked and recorded with Gil Evans and the Benny Golson/Art Farmer Jazztet and recorded with John Coltrane, Bud Powell, Paul Quinichette, Blue Mitchell and others.

New Trombone is nothing special. *Blues-ette,* with Golson on tenor, is another story, a perfectly balanced lineup with pianist Tommy Flanagan, bassist Jimmy Garrison and drummer Al Harewood.

Golson and trumpeter Thad Jones fill out the front line on *Imagination,* with Garrison and pianist McCoy Tyner from Coltrane's band. *The Curtis Fuller Jazztet* features Golson, trumpeter Lee Morgan, pianist Wynton Kelly, bassist Paul Chambers and drummer Charlie Persip. *Images of Curtis Fuller* employs trumpeters Morgan and Wilbur Harden, tenor saxophonist/flautist Lateef and Tyner and Garrison in the rhythm section. — J.S.

JESSE FULLER (THE LONE CAT)
★★★★★ **Jazz, Folk Songs, Spirituals, & Blues (1958; Original Blues Classics, 1993)**
★★★★½ **The Lone Cat (1961; Original Blues Classics, 1990)**
★★★★★ **San Francisco Bay Blues (1963; Original Blues Classics, 1991)**
★★★★★ **Jesse Fuller's Favorites (1964; Original Blues Classics, 1990)**
★★★★ **'Frisco Bound (Arhoolie, 1991)**
★★★★★ **Brother Lowdown (Fantasy, 1992)**
Jonesboro, Georgia–born Jesse Fuller (1896–1976) didn't become a professional musician until he reached his mid-50s, when he quickly garnered an international following with his one-man traveling show and infectious songwriting. In performance, Fuller sang and accompanied himself on a battery of instruments played simultaneously: 12-string guitar, harmonica, kazoo, cymbals and a huge 6-string bass called a fotdella (his own invention) that he played with his foot. A one-man musical wrecking crew, the gruff-voiced Fuller played a mixture of folk, blues, pop, ragtime and religious music.

Jazz, Folk Songs, Spirituals, & Blues contains both original and traditional fare, including work songs ("Linin' Track," "Take This Hammer"), a prison song ("99 Years"), blues ("Hesitation Blues," Fuller's own "Memphis Boogie"), a folk ballad ("Stagolee") and jazzy instrumentals ("Fingerbuster" and the Original Dixieland Jazz Band's "Tiger Rag"). Be the song an original or an interpretation, it receives Fuller's unmistakable stamp, with high-quality playing and remarkable singing.

The Lone Cat is also chockful of great songs of all kinds and showcases Fuller's versatility and originality; even a novelty song like "The Monkey and the Engineer" is indelibly delightful as performed by Fuller. Selections range from a waltz ("Down Home Waltz") to a pop hit from the '20s ("Runnin' Wild"), but Fuller saves the best for the last track, "Buck and Wing," where he tap dances while picking out the song on guitar.

Fuller's second commercial recording session is documented on *'Frisco Bound* (his first resulted in the rare 10-inch *Working on the Railroad*). He uses a knife for a slide on his 12-string to play the spirituals "Amazing Grace," "Hark from the Tomb" and "As Long as I Can Feel the Spirit." Other notable tracks include a rag called "Finger Twister" and a version of "Motherless Children." The CD reissue of *'Frisco Bound* includes six songs recorded at an Ithaca, New York, performance in November 1962 and four previously unreleased cuts. Among the live selections is a classic version of "San Francisco Bay Blues," Fuller's signature song.

The last 12 of 26 tracks on *Brother Lowdown* are the same songs and performances as on *Jesse Fuller's Favorites* and include covers of Blind Boy Fuller ("Red River Blues"), Leroy Carr ("How Long Blues"), Hudson Whittaker ("Stranger Blues") and Big Bill Broonzy ("Key to the Highway"). The performances are upbeat, again highlighting Fuller's interpretive dexterity and skillful arrangements. His rendition of "Midnight Special" is as understated and compelling as any recorded. *Brother Lowdown*'s first 14 tracks include an up-tempo "San Francisco Bay Blues" and renditions of W.C. Handy's "Beale Street Blues" and Ivory Joe Hunter's "Let Me Hold You in My Arms Tonight." Other highlights include "Crazy Waltz" (which appears on *San Francisco Bay Blues* as "Crazy About a Woman") and "Animal Farm," an amalgamation of children's stories.

San Francisco Bay Blues is another winner. In addition to the title track, the set includes "Morning Blues" and "Whoa Mule," an amusing tale about a crazy mule who "kicked a fella in the bottom of the neck." The churning "Midnight Cold" is a classic Fuller tale of a lopsided relationship. — B.R.H.

LOWELL FULSON

★★★ **River Blues (1949; Arhoolie, 1991)**
★★★★½ **Hung Down Head (1970; Chess, 1991)**
★★★½ **It's a Good Day (Rounder, 1988)**
★★★½ **Hold On (Bullseye Blues, 1992)**
★★★ **One More Blues (Evidence, 1993)**
★★★ **San Francisco Blues (Black Lion, 1993)**
★★★★ **Tramp/Soul (Flair/Virgin, 1993)**
★★★ **Everyday I Have the Blues (Night Train, 1994)**
★★★½ **Sinner's Prayer (Night Train, 1995)**
★★★ **Them Update Blues (Bullseye Blues, 1995)**
★★½ **My Baby (Jewel, 1996)**

Were it just for his seminal and enduring recordings of "Reconsider Baby" and the protofunk classic "Tramp," guitarist, singer and songwriter Lowell Fulson (b. 1921) would be assured status in the American music pantheon. Since his arrival in 1946, Fulson's fruitful career has long influenced the influencers—B.B. King is the most obvious inheritor of his vocal and guitar approach (adopting Fulson's "Three O'Clock in the Morning" and "Every Day I Have the Blues" to his early canon), while Elvis Presley, Ray Charles, Eric Clapton, Otis Redding and even the Artist Formerly Known as Prince have chosen to rerecord his material. Straight out of the swing-driven Texas-blues mold shared by T-Bone Walker and Charles Brown, with a heady dose of Billy Eckstine cool, Fulson proved a blues stalwart who kept coming back—recording for a large number of labels over the years (Swingtime, Aladdin, Checker and Kent being the most notable) and bouncing back onto the R&B charts again and again over the first three decades of his career. It's a career that continues strongly through today, as Fulson maintains a blues patriarchal role onstage and in the studio.

From the outset, Fulson established an urbane big-band blues sound with warm vocals and tasteful picking from his hollow-body guitar. His earliest recordings were released between 1946 and 1952 on the L.A.-based Swingtime R&B label, where he recorded a number of trend-setting big-band blues—"Three O'Clock in the Morning," "Every Day I Have the Blues," "Blue Shadows," "Guitar Shuffle"—often with studio help from his brother Martin on second guitar (pianists Lloyd Glenn and Jay McShann and saxophonist Stanley Turrentine would also pass through early incarnations of his band). Capricorn's *Swingtime Records Story* boxed set offers a number of hits from this era, while Arhoolie's to-be-reissued-on-CD *River Blues* title collects 14 more Swingtime tracks, without overlap. Further studies of this period are available on the Night Train and Black Lion albums.

In 1968 Fulson established a long association with Jewel/Paula Records head and longtime fan Stan Lewis, who produced his best-seller "Reconsider Baby" (mysteriously available only on various anthologies and boxed sets) and other notable sides for Chess Records. Collected by Fulson himself in 1970, the career-high release *Hung Down Head* (now, sadly, out of print) features the best from the period 1954–61, including "Tollin' Bells," "It's All Your Fault Baby," "Low Society" and "I Want to Know."

Lewis later oversaw Fulson's expansion in the '60s to a more funk orientation, as his songwriting began to break out of the strict blues format; *Tramp/Soul* is a two-for-one, must-have reissue featuring the best tracks of Fulson's late-'60s period, with "Year of '29," "Black Nights," "Little Angel" and the well-known title track. *My Baby* is also from this period but warrants a pass, with such dated and ill-advised experiments as distorted rock guitar and a cover of "Why Don't We Do It in the Road."

Jumping 17 years to a domestic release of a 1984 French session with sympathetic support from Phillip Walker and his band (an appropriately chosen second-generation ensemble from Los Angeles), *One More Blues* is back in the blues bag and firing on all cylinders, with a front line of guitar, tenor, piano and organ. Fulson provided funky, hard-driving new material like "Hot Mama" and "I Can't Stand It," a convincing reprisal of "Guitar Shuffle" and covers of Jimmy Witherspoon's "Jump Children" and Mercy Walton's "One Room Country Shack." Most significant is Fulson's successful songwriting collaboration with bassist Dennis Walker, yielding the plaintive, road-weary "Ten More Shows" and "One More Blues," and the after-show romantic refusal "Thanks for the Offer."

Since the late '80s, Fulson has operated mostly in the Rounder Records orbit, with success on a first-time pairing with old Swingtime label mate Jimmy McCracklin and a crack L.A. rhythm-and-horns ensemble on *Hold On.* It's his strongest of recent years, covering a wide stylistic range consistently—from shuffles ("Quicker the Better"), slow, heartfelt blues ("It's No Need") and two great contributions from McCracklin's creative and wry worldview: "Real Name Is Danger Zone" and "Love Is the Bottom Line."

Assisted by a veteran New Orleans horn section and Boston-based keyboardist Ron Levy, *It's a Good Day* flows with a comfortable groove, rerecording a number of hard-hitting originals from his '84 French Phillip Walker session—like "Ten More Shows." But at times it seems the years are catching up with his smooth vocal delivery as a rougher edge begins to show, with his trademark melisma a little tired. But his guitar work is unabated—"Blues and My Guitar" and "One More Blues" attest to the smoldering fire that his guitar can still engender. *Them Update Blues* is a rawer and more urgent session—relying on an open-spaced set with tasteful horn support from Memphis horn masters Wayne Jackson (trumpet, trombone) and Andrew Love (tenor). — A.K.

ANSON FUNDERBURGH AND THE ROCKETS FEATURING SAM MYERS

★★★ **Rack 'Em Up (Black Top, 1989)**
★★★ **Tell Me What I Want to Hear (Black Top, 1991)**
★★★★ **Thru the Years (Black Top, 1992)**
★★★★½ **Live at the Grand Emporium (Black Top, 1994)**
★★★★½ **That's What They Want (Black Top, 1997)**

Guitarist Anson Funderburgh (b. 1955) and his band, the Rockets, were a good-timey fixture on the southern roadhouse circuit until they teamed up with singer/harmonica player Sam Myers (b. 1936), a dynamic frontman who turned this outfit into a killer live unit. *Thru the Years* covers the band's work from 1981 to 1991, showing its development with Myers. *Live at the Grand Emporium* is a sizzling no-holds-barred set recorded at Kansas City's most important club. *That's What They Want,* the band's studio masterpiece, is highlighted by Funderburgh's Albert Collins tribute, "Mudslide," Myers's cover of Muddy Waters's "The Meanest Woman" and rousing versions of Eddie Bo's New Orleans classic "Oh-Oh" and Willie Dixon's "I Don't Play." — J.S.

KENNY G

★ **Kenny G (Arista, 1982)**
★ **G-Force (Arista, 1983)**
★ **Gravity (Arista, 1985)**
★★ **Duotones (Arista, 1986)**
★ **Silhouette (Arista, 1988)**
★ **Live (Arista, 1989)**
★★ **Breathless (Arista, 1992)**
★ **The Moment (Arista, 1996)**

As a jazz player, Kenny G (b. 1956) is at once the biggest-selling saxophonist in history and the justifiable target of scorn from anyone paying more than casual attention to the music. As a pop figure he's a genre-bending giant whose appropriation of jazz elements into an easy-listening mix opened up a whole new audience through the institutionalization of lite-jazz radio programming, the new form of Muzak.

Seattle native Kenneth Gorelick is often mistakenly called a fusion musician because he appeared on one album by Jeff Lorber Fusion, but the key to his success was the realization that fusion was a musician's medium. This student accountant's most telling influence was as a touring member of Barry White's Love Unlimited Orchestra, where he learned the commercial value of stage presence and watered-down funk vamps set to romantic themes.

Thus did Kenny G become the preeminent jazz star of the video age with a kinetic, aisle-dancing delivery and glittering smile that whited out the blandness of his thin, watery soprano-sax sound. His astonishing lack of musical expressiveness amid the showy posturing is the stuff of genius—he may well become the Lawrence Welk of the 21st Century. After the ballad "Songbird" from *Duotones* became a #4 pop hit, Kenny G was sought after as a guest star with pop divas Aretha Franklin, Natalie Cole and Whitney Houston. *Breathless,* at 8 million sales and counting, is a juggernaut for international jazz marketers in the 1990s.

— J.S.

JAN GARBAREK

★★★★ **Afric Pepperbird (1971; ECM, 1994)**
★★★ **Sart (1971; ECM, 1994)**
★★★ **Triptykon (1973; ECM, 1994)**
★★★★ **Witchi-Tai-To (with Bobo Stenson) (1974; ECM, 1994)**
★★★★½ **Belonging (with Keith Jarrett) (1974; ECM, 1994)**
★★★ **Luminessence (with Keith Jarrett) (1975; ECM, 1989)**
★★★ **Arbour Zena (with Keith Jarrett) (1975; ECM, 1989)**
★★★ **Dansere (with Bobo Stenson) (1976; ECM, 1994)**
★★★ **Dis (1977; ECM, 1994)**
★★★★ **My Song (with Keith Jarrett) (1977; ECM, 1987)**
★★★ **Photo with Blue Sky (1979; ECM, 1994)**
★★★ **Paths, Prints (1982; ECM, 1994)**
★★★ **Wayfarer (1983; ECM, 1994)**
★★★ **It's OK to Listen to the Gray Voice (1984; ECM, 1994)**
★★ **All Those Born with Wings (1986; ECM, 1994)**
★★★ **Legend of the Seven Dreams (1988; ECM, 1994)**
★★★★ **I Took Up the Runes (1990; ECM, 1994)**
★★★ **Ragas and Sagas (1992; ECM, 1994)**

★★★ **Twelve Moons (1993; ECM, 1994)**
★★★ **Madar (ECM, 1994)**
★★★★ **Officium (ECM, 1994)**
★★★ **Visible World (ECM, 1995)**

Jan Garbarek (b. 1947) is a Norwegian saxophonist/flautist who studied the Lydian Chromatic Concept of Tonal Organization with theorist/bandleader George Russell, under whose auspices the challenging *Esoteric Circle* was made (the album is available through import by DA Music).

Garbarek was among the first musicians approached by producer Manfred Eicher when he was conceptualizing what would become ECM, and Garbarek's debut, the wild and woolly *Afric Pepperbird,* is one of the sheer triumphs of the early ECM catalog, featuring some excellent Terje Rypdal guitar work and the precision rhythm section of bassist Arild Anderson and drummer Jon Christensen. *Sart* uses the same group, adding pianist Bobo Stenson, who is also present on the lyrical *Witchi-Tai-To* and the elegant *Dansere.*

Garbarek worked steadily for ECM over the years, recording much of his greatest work, including the dazzling *Belonging,* as a sideman with pianist Keith Jarrett. Two other collaborations with Jarrett, the quartet date *My Song* and *Luminessence,* which features Jarrett's scoring for the Sundfunk Symphony Orchestra, are available under Jarrett's name.

Dis pairs Garbarek with guitarist Ralph Towner. *Photo with Blue Sky* employs the dry pointillism of Bill Connors. *Wayfarer* and *Paths, Prints* benefit from the dazzling textures of guitarist Bill Frisell and bassist Eberhard Weber.

All Those Born with Wings, Garbarek's solo outing, lacks the sense of focus that characterizes most of his work. *Legend of the Seven Dreams* is a trio session with keyboardist Rainer Bruninghaus and percussionist Nana Vasconcelos.

The fascinating *I Took Up the Runes* finds Garbarek exploring his Scandinavian roots. More recently he has delved deeply into world-music projects, working with musicians from Pakistan on *Ragas and Sagas* and Anouar Brahem and Shaukat Hussain on *Madar.*

Garbarek also paralleled ECM's interest in the 1990s with developing a classical-music profile. *Officium* is a medieval music collaboration with the vocal group the Hilliard Ensemble recorded live in a monastery in the Austrian Alps. Garbarek's ability to find the heart of this music and bring his own vision to it is a startling revelation. — J.S.

LASZLO GARDONY

★★★½ **Changing Standards (Sunnyside, 1993)**
★★★★ **Breakout (Avenue Jazz, 1994)**
★★★½ **Reflection of a Clear Moon (with Garrison Fewell) (Accurate, 1997)**

Laszlo Gardony (b. 1956) began improvising on the piano in his native Hungary at age five, two years before he began lessons on the instrument in which he has developed a distinctive, forceful voice. After touring Europe as a successful session player, he grew tired of the limitations of the Hungarian jazz scene.

Gardony moved to the United States in 1983 and studied further at the Berklee College of Music in Boston. He joined the Berklee faculty in 1987, the year he won first prize at the Jacksonville Jazz Festival's Great American Jazz Piano Competition. *Changing Standards* is an aptly named solo-piano session in which Gardony reworks an array of jazz and popular chestnuts, giving each a brilliant, spontaneous new feel dominated by a propulsive rhythm, thick chords and dark tonal clusters.

His aggressive quintet session *Breakout* is a buoyant fusion of mostly original material and unusual instrumentation—Gardony's piano, the highly inventive Mick Goodrick on guitar, Stomu Takeishi on electric bass, George Jinda on African percussion and Satoshi Takeishi on taiko drums and other exotic percussion.

The pianist teamed up with guitarist Garrison Fewell, a frequent collaborator, on *Reflection of a Clear Moon.* The Hungarian National Radio live-concert broadcast was made in Budapest in 1995. Their combined musical chemistry and improvisation on six extended originals make this a noteworthy addition to the challenging art of the jazz duo. — K.F.

HANK GARLAND

★★★★ **Jazz Winds from a New Direction (1960; Collectors Series, 1995)**

Jazz Winds from a New Direction not only represents the first session of guitarist Hank Garland (b. 1930) as a jazz leader after a career of Nashville country session work, it also introduces the prodigious talent of vibraphonist Gary Burton, then only 17. With Dave Brubeck's drummer Joe Morello and bassist Joe Benjamin along for the ride, Burton and Garland engage in an ecstatic dialog throughout the record. The exchange between Garland and Burton shines in particular on "All the Things You Are" and the 7:50-minutes-long blues "Riot-Chorus," inspired by the 1960 riots that closed down that year's Newport Jazz Festival. — J.S.

RED GARLAND

- ★★★½ **A Garland of Red (1956; Original Jazz Classics, 1991)**
- ★★★½ **Groovy (1957; Original Jazz Classics, 1987)**
- ★★★★ **All Mornin' Long (1957; Original Jazz Classics, 1987)**
- ★★★½ **Red Garland's Piano (1957; Original Jazz Classics, 1987)**
- ★★★★ **Soul Junction (1957; Original Jazz Classics, 1990)**
- ★★★½ **Dig It! (1958; Original Jazz Classics, 1989)**
- ★★★★ **High Pressure (1958; Original Jazz Classics, 1989)**
- ★★★½ **Rojo (1958; Original Jazz Classics, 1993)**
- ★★★★ **Manteca (1958; Original Jazz Classics, 1990)**
- ★★★½ **All Kinds of Weather (1959; Original Jazz Classics, 1991)**
- ★★★½ **Red in Blues-Ville (1959; Original Jazz Classics, 1993)**
- ★★★ **At the Prelude, Vol. 1 (1959; Prestige, 1993)**
- ★★★ **Moodsville, Vol. 1 (with Eddie "Lockjaw" Davis) (1960; Original Jazz Classics, 1989)**
- ★★★ **Bright and Breezy (1961; Original Jazz Classics, 1995)**
- ★★★½ **Solar (1962; Original Jazz Classics, 1992)**
- ★★★ **When There Are Grey Skies (1962; Original Jazz Classics, 1991)**
- ★★★½ **Crossings (1977; Original Jazz Classics, 1990)**
- ★★★ **Red Alert (1977; Original Jazz Classics, 1991)**
- ★★★ **Rediscovered Masters, Vol. 1 (Original Jazz Classics, 1992)**
- ★★★ **Rediscovered Masters, Vol. 2 (Original Jazz Classics, 1992)**

(William) Red Garland (1923–1984) was a lyrical and passionate pianist with a unique harmonic sense who excelled as an accompanist and improviser. He came to prominence as part of Miles Davis's late-'50s quintet.

A Garland of Red, a reissue of his first album for Prestige, uses bassist Paul Chambers and drummer Art Taylor from the Davis band in a sublime interplay. The same trio appears on *Groovy*, *Red Garland's Piano*, *Manteca* and *All Kinds of Weather.* Garland's compositional strength and harmonic flow enabled him to excel in this kind of trio format, in which he worked extensively. Garland also worked with John Coltrane in the Davis band and went on to tap Coltrane for some of his greatest recordings as a leader—*All Mornin' Long*, *Soul Junction*, *High Pressure* and *Dig It!*

Garland continued to record in a trio format, sometimes bringing in another voice for the front line. *Moodsville, Vol. 1* utilizes the tenor giant Eddie "Lockjaw" Davis on several tracks. *Crossings* is a better-than-average session featuring bassist Ron Carter and drummer Philly Joe Jones. — J.S.

ERROLL GARNER

- ★★ **1944, Vol. 2 (1944; Classics, 1995)**
- ★★★½ **Separate Keyboards (with Billy Taylor) (1945; Savoy, N.A.)**
- ★★★ **Serenade to Laura (1945; Savoy, 1994)**
- ★★★★ **The Original Misty (1954; EmArcy, 1988)**
- ★★★★½ **Concert by the Sea (1970; Columbia, 1987)**
- ★★★★ **Compact Jazz (Verve, 1987)**
- ★★ **Long Ago and Far Away (Columbia, 1987)**
- ★★★ **Mambo Moves Garner (EmArcy, 1988)**
- ★★★★ **Easy to Love, Collection 1 (EmArcy, 1988)**
- ★★★★ **Dancing on the Ceiling, Collection 2 (EmArcy, 1989)**
- ★★★★ **Too Marvelous for Words, Collection 3 (EmArcy, 1990)**
- ★★★ **Jazz 'Round Midnight (Verve, 1990)**
- ★★★½ **Body and Soul (Legacy, 1991)**
- ★★★ **Penthouse Serenade (Savoy, 1993)**
- ★★★ **Yesterdays (Savoy, 1994)**
- ★★★★ **Solos (Legacy, 1994)**
- ★★★★ **That's My Kick/Gemini (Telarc, 1994)**
- ★★★★ **The Essence of Erroll Garner (Legacy, 1994)**
- ★★ **Verve Jazz Masters 7 (Verve, 1994)**
- ★★★ **Magician/Gershwin and Kern (Telarc, 1995)**

★★★ **Moon Glow (Tradition/Rykodisc, 1996)**

★★★ **Now Playing—A Night at the Movies/Up in Erroll's Room—The Brass Bed (Telarc, 1996)**

In the 1940s pianist Erroll Garner (1921–1977) moved from his Pittsburgh home to New York, where he was featured in bassist Slam Stewart's band before embarking on his own recording career. The poorly recorded *1944* is for die-hards only; early Garner comes across much better on the Savoy sides, which have been issued and reissued in a dizzying number of configurations. A self-taught musician, Garner had a unique style firmly rooted in the strong harmonic foundation of another Pittsburgh jazz hero, Earl Hines, but capable of the raucous wit and overt showmanship of Fats Waller.

Garner alternates a pulsing change between softly stated figures and pounding arpeggios so forceful that the piano often sounds distorted in recordings. His right-hand flourishes are extremely decorative as he rolls through each chord, while his left turns steady, stabbing punctuation. His composition "Misty" is one of the most famous jazz pieces ever written and has become a hit single for a number of other musicians.

Garner recorded prolifically during the 1950s and '60s, and this material comprises the bulk of his currently available albums, most of which are compilations. *That's My Kick* and *Gemini,* a twofer, combines two hot dates, one from '67 and one from '72. The classic is *Concert by the Sea,* a September 1955 West Coast live date with regular accompanists Denzil Best on drums and Eddie Calhoun on bass. The sparse settings of Garner's trio set his virtuosic playing off forcefully on trademark pieces such as "I'll Remember April," "Autumn Leaves" and "They Can't Take That Away from Me."

The Essence of Erroll Garner, *Compact Jazz* and the EmArcy *Collections* do the most justice to Garner's reputation. *Verve Jazz Masters 7* is a halfhearted slap at the same material, and it ends up full of holes. — J.S.

CARLOS GARNETT

★★★ **Black Love (Muse, 1974)**

★★★ **Resurgence (Muse, 1996)**

Panamanian saxophonist Carlos Garnett (b. 1938) played in a variety of late-1960s and early-'70s jazz and fusion groups with Freddie Hubbard, Art Blakey, Miles Davis, Pharoah Sanders, Robin Kenyatta and Norman Connors. His debut, *Black Love,* comes closest in spirit to the music he made with Connors.

Garnett's approach to fusion did not go in the predictable direction. Instead he explored the overlapping elements in a variety of different North and Central American musics. The results are often engaging and even emotionally challenging, with Garnett's tough, direct playing as the focal point. *Black Love* shows him working with some of the ideas from his stint with Connors and contains an outstanding vocal performance from Dee Dee Bridgewater.

Unfortunately, there's a giant hole in Garnett's catalog between his debut and the 1996 title *Resurgence.* Garnett's robust tenor-sax playing over a rich bed of drums and percussion is still the main event, but these two records alone offer a very incomplete picture of his work. The currently unavailable *Journey to Enlightenment* and particularly the Sun Ra–influenced *Cosmos Nucleus* must be heard if one is to truly appreciate Garnett's vision. — J.S.

KENNY GARRETT

★★ **Presence of Love (Atlantic Jazz, 1989)**

★★★ **African Exchange Student (Atlantic Jazz, 1990)**

★★★★ **Black Hope (Warner Bros., 1992)**

★★★★★ **Trilogy (Warner Bros., 1995)**

★★★★ **Pursuance: The Music of John Coltrane (with Pat Metheny) (Warner Bros., 1996)**

★★★★ **Songbook (Warner Bros., 1997)**

★★★★ **General Music Project II (Evidence, 1998)**

Alto saxophonist Kenny Garrett (b. 1960) spent five years as a member of Miles Davis's final band, where he honed his skills as a soloist. As a result, his playing often is marked by freewheeling, risk-taking intensity.

Garrett grew up in a musical household in Detroit, where his father was a tenor player. His strong jazz foundation was reinforced during a three-year stint in the Duke Ellington Orchestra, starting in 1978. Moving to New York in 1982, he worked in the Mel Lewis Jazz Orchestra, with Art Blakey, Freddie Hubbard and the Blue Note developmental band OTB before Davis hired him in 1986.

Presence of Love, recorded with Davis band mates, has romance as its muse but is weak despite the trumpeter's cameos on two tracks. Garrett comes into his own as a writer and soloist on *African Exchange Student,* with strong aid from sidemen including Mulgrew Miller, Ron Carter and Elvin Jones. *Black Hope* showcases Garrett on alto and soprano in formats ranging from solo showcase to sextet. Tenor master Joe Henderson is a serious foil on two Garrett originals and a spitfire quasi salute to Davis on "Bye Bye Blackbird."

Trilogy consists mostly of standards given fresh twists and very strong soloing in what is Garrett's most formidable showcase to date as he explores the depths of his melodicism. *Pursuance: The Music of John Coltrane* is a strong quartet session in which guitarist Pat Metheny complements and at times stretches the alto saxophonist's melodic intensity. The fiery quartet session *Songbook,* consisting entirely of original compositions, showcases Garrett's standing as the most intense alto-sax soloist on the scene today *General Music Project II* is a 1994 date in which Garrett is joined by Charnett Moffett on bass, Charles Moffett on drums and Cyrus Chestnut on keyboards. — K.F.

DANNY GATTON

★★★ Redneck Jazz (NRG, 1978)
★★★ Unfinished Business (1978; NRG, 1991)
★★★ 88 Elmira Street (Elektra, 1991)
★★★★ New York Stories (Blue Note, 1992)
★★★½ Cruisin' Deuces (Elektra, 1993)
★★★★ Relentless (Big Mo, 1994)
★★★½ Redneck Jazz Explosion (NRG, 1995)

Danny Gatton (1945–1994) had speed, chops and wild eclecticism to burn. An avid user of effects before they were widely accepted, he could make his guitar sound like a B-3 organ or ring like a bell.

Redneck Jazz aptly demonstrates his genre-bending approach, from a funk cover of "Ode to Billy Joe" to a swinging version of "Rock Candy." The latter finds Gatton doing his best to approximate an organ duet with veteran pedal-steel virtuoso Buddy Emmons. Gatton and Emmons took such a shine to each other that they played a number of dates in 1978 as the Redneck Jazz Explosion. The album by that name (released after Gatton's death in 1994) captures the venerable Nashville cat and the upstart fret man sounding like they're having the time of their lives at a New Year's Eve show on Gatton's home turf in D.C.

Unfinished Business shows Gatton at war with his unresolved inclinations, alternating jazz standards like his Les Paul–verized version of "Cherokee" with electrified bluegrass like "Nit Pickin'." "Sleepwalk" and "Sky King" provide media for his muscular guitaristics, but technique overcomes emotion too often for greatness on this set.

88 Elmira Street introduces elements of surf music and R&B to Gatton's already complicated musical gestalt, sounding like the Bar Kays go to the beach, especially on the cover of "Quiet Village."

Despite the recording debut of Joshua Redman and the presence of Roy Hargrove, *New York Stories* is Gatton's record, from the Chuck Berry–meets–Horace Silver opening of "Dolly's Ditty" to the "Blue Monk" cop of "Mike the Cat." Other than *Redneck Jazz Explosion,* it is the most focused record he has made, with the focus decidedly on jazz.

Although couched in similar terms to *88 Elmira Street*, *Cruisin' Deuces* alternates rockabilly pop like "Sun Medley" with a very dark "Harlem Nocturne" and a version of "Sky King" superior to the one on *Unfinished Business.*

Relentless, Gatton's collaboration with organist (and former Miles Davis sideman) Joey DeFrancesco may be some of the rockingest music either ever played. It also represents one of the rare instances where all of Gatton's firepower is concentrated and homogenized enough to transcend its myriad influences. Both players seem to be operating under Willie Dixon's assertion that jazz is just the blues played real fast. — H.B.

BRUCE GERTZ

★★★ Blueprint (1992; Evidence, 1997)
★★★★½ Third Eye (Ram, 1994)
★★★★ Discovery Zone (Ram, 1996)

Bruce Gertz (b. 1952), a longtime Berklee College of Music faculty member, is an exceptional player of both the acoustic and electric bass. Based in Boston, he is a versatile and rock-solid player who has worked regularly with guitarists John Abercrombie, Bill Frisell, Mick Goodrick and Mike Stern and with saxophonists George Garzone, Jerry Bergonzi and the late Jimmy Mosher. He was a member of Bergonzi's first formidable quartet, Con Brio, starting in 1979. He has toured with Maynard Ferguson, Gary Burton and Dave Brubeck.

Gertz moved into the spotlight by assembling his own special-occasion band of longtime collaborators—Abercrombie, Bergonzi, pianist Joey Calderazzo and drummer Adam

Nussbaum—to put an ensemble stamp on his own tunes.

Blueprint is a very good introduction to his energetic and solid contemporary compositions, a session in which Gertz emerges as a forceful player who gives his colleagues wide latitude. With two additional years of growth and fresh material, *Third Eye,* the live concert recording with the same personnel, is even better.

Discovery Zone puts this harmonically inventive ensemble's imprint on a fine range of standards and original material. — K.F.

STAN GETZ

★★★★ **At Storyville, Vols. 1 and 2 (1953; Blue Note, 1990)**
★★★ **At the Shrine (Verve, 1954)**
★★★ **Hamp and Getz (Verve, 1955)**
★★★★ **Diz and Getz (Verve, 1955)**
★★★ **Stan Getz and J.J. Johnson at the Opera House (1957; Verve, 1987)**
★★★ **Getz Meets Mulligan in Hi-Fi (1957; Verve, 1991)**
★★★ **Stan Getz and the Oscar Peterson Trio (Verve, 1958)**
★★★★ **Focus (1961; Verve, 1984)**
★★★ **Big Band Bossa Nova (Verve, 1962)**
★★★★ **Jazz Samba (Verve, 1963)**
★★★½ **Jazz Samba Encore! (with Luiz Bonfa) (Verve, 1963)**
★★★★ **Getz/Gilberto (with João Gilberto) (Verve, 1963)**
★★★ **Stan Getz with Cal Tjader (Original Jazz Classics, 1963)**
★★★★ **Getz Au Go Go featuring Astrud Gilberto (Verve, 1964)**
★★★★ **Getz/Gilberto #2 (with João Gilberto) (Recorded Live at Carnegie Hall) (1964; Verve, 1993)**
★★★★ **Stan Getz & Bill Evans (1964; Verve, 1987)**
★★★½ **Stan Getz with Guest Artist Laurindo Almeida (1966; Verve, 1984)**
★★★★½ **Sweet Rain (Verve, 1967)**
★★★ **Dynasty (1971; Verve, 1989)**
★★★ **The Best of Two Worlds Featuring Joao Gilberto (Columbia, 1976)**
★★★ **Live at Montmartre, Vol. 1 (SteepleChase, 1977)**
★★★★ **Stan Getz Presents Jimmie Rowles: The Peacocks (1977; Columbia/Legacy, 1994)**
★★★ **Sextet Utopia (West Wind Jazz, 1978)**
★★★ **Autumn Leaves (Koch, 1980)**
★★★ **The Dolphin (Concord Jazz, 1981)**
★★★ **Spring Is Here (1981; Concord Jazz, 1992)**
★★★½ **Pure Getz (Concord Jazz, 1982)**
★★★ **Line for Lyons (Gazell, 1983)**
★★★ **Live at Montmartre, Vol. 2 (SteepleChase, 1986)**
★★★★½ **Compact Jazz (Verve, 1987)**
★★★½ **Serenity (1987; EmArcy, 1991)**
★★★½ **The Lyrical Stan Getz (Columbia, 1988)**
★★★½ **Anniversary! (EmArcy, 1989)**
★★★ **The Brothers (Original Jazz Classics, 1989)**
★★★★★ **The Bossa Nova Years (The Girl from Ipanema) (Verve, 1989)**
★★★★ **For Musicians Only (with Dizzy Gillespie and Sonny Stitt) (Verve, 1989)**
★★★★ **Billy Highstreet Samba (EmArcy, 1990)**
★★ **Apasionado (A&M, 1990)**
★★★ **Early Stan (Original Jazz Classics, 1991)**
★★★ **Prezervation (Original Jazz Classics, 1991)**
★★★ **Stan Getz Quartets (Original Jazz Classics, 1991)**
★★★★ **The Roost Quartets (Roulette, 1991)**
★★★★ **The Best of the Roost Years (Roulette, 1991)**
★★★★ **Stan Getz (LaserLight, 1991)**
★★★★ **The Artistry of Stan Getz, Vol. 1 (Verve, 1991)**
★★★ **Stan Getz with Strings (Verve, 1992)**
★★★★ **People Time (with Kenny Barron) (Verve, 1992)**
★★★½ **The Essential Stan Getz: The Getz Songbook (Verve, 1992)**
★★★★ **The Artistry of Stan Getz, Vol. 2 (Verve, 1993)**
★★★★ **Jazz 'Round Midnight (Verve, 1993)**
★★★½ **I Like Jazz: The Essence of Stan Getz (Legacy, 1993)**
★★★★ **The New Collection (Columbia/Legacy, 1993)**
★★★★ **Nobody Else but Me (Verve, 1994)**
★★★½ **Jazz Masters 8 (Verve, 1994)**
★★★★ **Jazz Masters 25 (with Dizzy Gillespie) (Verve, 1994)**

★★★ **Cool Velvet: Stan Getz and Strings/Voices (Verve, 1995)**
★★★½ **Blue Skies (Concord Jazz, 1995)**
★★★½ **Stan Getz Quartet Live in Paris (Dreyfus, 1996)**
★★★★ **The Song Is You (LaserLight, 1996)**
★★★ **Stan Getz with European Friends (LaserLight, 1996)**
★★★ **East of the Sun: The West Coast Sessions (Verve, 1996)**
★★★★★ **A Life in Jazz: A Musical Biography (Verve, 1996)**
★★★½ **Stan Getz Plays (Verve, N.A.)**

Beginning his career as a talented and imaginative disciple of Lester Young's approach to the tenor saxophone, Stan Getz (1927–1991) developed into one of the most lyrical, romantic stylists of his era.

His first major recognition came as part of the Woody Herman band in the late '40s, when he and Zoot Sims, Al Cohn and Serge Chaloff were nicknamed the "Four Brothers." Getz, the most popular of the four, soon went out on his own. His cool, relaxed yet rhythmically interesting style is influenced heavily by Young and Charlie Parker, and even though he is known for his understated, breathy tone, Getz could blow surprisingly hot when the mood struck him, and his accessible style is echoed in a lot of West Coast session reed players.

The Brothers reunites Getz with Sims and Cohn and, like *Early Stan*, *Prezervation* and *Stan Getz Quartets,* features Getz in small-combo bop sessions from the late 1940s and early '50s. The Roost material (on *The Best of the Roost Years*), with sidemen including Horace Silver or Al Haig on piano and Roy Haynes on drums, collects the cream of his early-1950s work.

Getz continued successfully in a postbop vein, often teaming up with costars such as Dizzy Gillespie, Oscar Peterson and Gerry Mulligan (on Verve), as one of the most visible tenor saxophonists of the 1950s. The collaborations with Gillespie—the 1953 session *Diz and Getz,* the 1956 meeting with Sonny Stitt, *For Musicians Only,* and the *Jazz Masters 25* compilation—are particularly good. Getz emigrated to Copenhagen in 1958, building a loyal following in Europe before returning to the United States in 1961. *Stan Getz with European Friends* was recorded during his residence in Copenhagen.

Getz proceeded to change his musical contexts to fit the concept of his playing. *Focus,* a brilliant collaboration with arranger Eddie Sauter, showcased Getz in a new setting. He plays soaring, hypnotically rhythmic lines against the lush, exotic string and woodwind arrangements. The Creed Taylor–produced project prefigured much of the work Taylor would go on to oversee in the years to come.

With guitarist Charlie Byrd, Getz recorded an album of Brazilian tunes, *Jazz Samba,* that started a bossa nova jazz craze when Antonio Carlos Jobim's "Desafinado" became a hit single. He produced the best samba records in the company of Jobim and guitarist Joao Gilberto, scoring a hit with "The Girl from Ipanema" from *Getz/Gilberto,* for which he won four Grammy Awards. His samba work is collected briefly in *Jazz 'Round Midnight,* in a definitive greatest-hits format on *Compact Jazz* and in superb detail on *The Bossa Nova Years.*

Rather than stay exclusively with the hit formula, Getz kept moving, trying different things in between the record-industry demands for more bossa nova sessions. He recorded a stunning set with pianist Bill Evans accompanied by drummer Elvin Jones and bassists Ron Carter and Richard Davis. Getz put together a touring band with vibraphonist Gary Burton, bassist Steve Swallow and drummer Roy Haynes, a trio that went directly from playing with Getz to forming one of the first fusion groups, the Gary Burton Quartet, with guitarist Larry Coryell. The Getz/Burton combination can be heard on the studio recording *Nobody Else but Me.*

The strikingly beautiful *Sweet Rain,* recorded with the then–relatively unknown pianist Chick Corea, is a highlight of this period. *The Song Is You* is a 1969 quartet recording with Stanley Cowell on piano, Miroslav Vitous on bass and Jack DeJohnette on drums. Getz recorded the excellent *Stan Getz Presents Jimmie Rowles: The Peacocks* in New York during 1975.

Getz also returned to Europe for a period during the 1970s, recording with European musicians on *Dynasty* and *Live at Montmartre, Vol. 1.* In the 1980s he recorded a series of fine records for Concord, highlighted by the exquisite *Pure Getz. Stan Getz Quartet Live in Paris* is a posthumously released session from 1982 with Jim McNeely on piano, Marc Johnson on bass and Victor Lewis on drums. The LaserLight *Stan Getz* is an album of standards recorded with European orchestras, including the excellent Danish Radio Big Band.

Toward the end of his life Getz was still able

to play with sublimely cool passion on *Anniversary!* and *Serenity,* with Kenny Barron on piano, Rufus Reid on bass and Victor Lewis on drums. Though Getz plays for all he's worth on *Apasionado,* the Herb Alpert production does him no favors. Getz finished up his recording life with appropriate dignity on the moving *People Time,* a two-disc collection of duets with Barron.

Of the several compilations on the market, *A Life in Jazz* provides the best overview of Getz's work. — J.S.

DIZZY GILLESPIE

★★★★ **Bird and Diz (with Charlie Parker) (1950; Verve, 1986)**
★★★★ **Roy and Diz (with Roy Eldridge) (1954; Verve, 1994)**
★★★ **Diz and Getz (with Stan Getz) (1955; Verve, N.A.)**
★★★★ **At Newport (1957; Verve, 1992)**
★★★½ **Duets (with Sonny Rollins and Sonny Stitt) (1958; Verve, 1988)**
★★★ **Sonny Side Up (with Sonny Rollins and Sonny Stitt) (1958; Verve, 1986)**
★★★½ **Gillesiana/Carnegie Hall Concert (1961; Verve, 1993)**
★★★ **And Double 6 of Paris (1963; Verve, N.A.)**
★★★ **Jambo Caribe (1964; Verve, 1998)**
★★★½ **Swing Low, Sweet Cadillac (Impulse!, 1967)**
★★½ **The Trumpet Kings Meet Joe Turner (1975; Pablo, 1990)**
★★½ **Dizzy's Big 4 (1975; Pablo, 1990)**
★★ **The Trumpet Kings at Montreux (1975; Pablo, 1990)**
★★★½ **Dizzy Gillespie Y Machito: Afro-Cuban Jazz Moods (1976; Pablo, 1990)**
★★★ **Dizzy Gillespie Jam (1977; Pablo, 1989)**
★★½ **The Trumpet Summit Meets the Oscar Peterson Big Four (1980; Pablo, 1990)**
★★★½ **The Best of Dizzy Gillespie (1980; Pablo, 1987)**
★★ **The Alternate Blues (Pablo, 1982)**
★★★ **To a Finland Station (with Arture Sandoval) (1983; Original Jazz Classics, 1992)**
★★★½ **Dee Gee Days (1951–52) (Savoy, 1985)**
★★★★★ **Groovin' High (1945–46) (Musicraft, 1986)**
★★★★★ **One Bass Hit (1945–46) (Musicraft, 1986)**
★★★★★ **Dizziest (1946–49) (RCA, 1987)**
★★★★½ **Compact Jazz (1954–64) (Mercury, 1987)**
★★★ **Oscar Peterson and Dizzy Gillespie (Pablo, 1987)**
★★★★ **For Musicians Only (with Stan Getz and Sonny Stitt) (Verve, 1989)**
★★★★ **Max and Dizzy: Paris 1989 (with Max Roach) (A&M, 1989)**
★★★ **To Bird with Love: The Diamond Jubilee Recordings Live at the Blue Note (Telarc, 1992)**
★★★ **To Diz with Love: The Diamond Jubilee Recordings Live at the Blue Note (Telarc, 1992)**
★★★½ **Dizzy's Diamonds: The Best of the Verve Years (Verve, 1992)**
★★★½ **Groovin' High (Drive Archive, 1994)**
★★★½ **Verve Jazz Masters 10 (Verve, 1994)**
★★★★ **Verve Jazz Masters 25 (with Stan Getz) (Verve, 1994)**
★★★ **Jazz Collector Edition: Dizzy Gillespie, Sarah Vaughan, and Charlie Parker (LaserLight, 1994)**
★★★★★ **The Complete RCA Victor Recordings (1937–1949) (RCA, 1995)**
★★★★ **The Cool World/Dizzy Goes Hollywood (Verve, 1996)**
★★★½ **Dizzier and Dizzier (RCA Victor, 1996)**
★★★½ **Greatest Hits (RCA Victor, 1996)**
★★½ **Bird Songs: The Final Recordings (Telarc, 1997)**
★★★ **Talkin' Verve (Verve, 1997)**
★★★½ **Ultimate Dizzy Gillespie (Verve, 1998)**

Mention John Birks "Dizzy" Gillespie (1917–1993), and the association that immediately comes to mind is Charlie "Yardbird" Parker—as in Bird and Diz, bebop's most famous and photogenic pairing. They first worked together as members of the Earl Hines Orchestra in 1943, and from there went to Billy Eckstine's legendary (and short-lived) protobop big band. Like Parker, Gillespie had already been building a reputation for musical audacity, and the adventurous harmonies he essayed on "Pickin' Up the Cabbage"—which he wrote for and recorded with Cab Calloway's band—show that he was moving beyond the boundaries of swing as early as 1940.

But it wasn't until Parker and Gillespie joined the coterie of like-minded nonconformists on the 52nd Street jazz scene that the two truly came into their own. Gillespie was the first to land a recording contract, and in 1945 he and a small group featuring Parker cut some sides for Guild, including "Groovin' High," "Shaw Nuff," "Hot House" and "Salt Peanuts." These sessions, included on *Groovin' High,* typify the inspired abandon of the bebop style, and Gillespie seemed uniquely suited to its demands. It wasn't just his technique that did it, although his range, dexterity and precision never ceased to amaze; it was also the strength of his ideas, the way his quicksilver phrases and daredevil flourishes suggested a world of rhythmic and harmonic possibility.

Gillespie also had bandleader ambitions, and as bebop's star began to rise, he assembled an orchestra of his own to try and pick up where Eckstine's big band left off. Its legacy was enormous—this, for example, was where Milt Jackson, John Lewis, Percy Heath and Kenny Clarke coalesced into what would become the Modern Jazz Quartet—but despite the artistic achievement of its recordings (collected on *One Bass Hit*), the Gillespie band was unable to make a go of it commercially. Fortunately, Gillespie was not one to give up, and by 1947 he had assembled yet another big band, which found him working to incorporate Afro-Cuban rhythms into the bop vocabulary. Again, Gillespie's band hardly racked up major-league sales, but its music was first-rate, particularly on such classic sides as "Manteca," "Cubana Be" and "Cubana Bop" (all of which can be found on *Dizziest*). *The Complete RCA Victor Recordings* (*1937–1949*) is the definitive recording from these years and belongs in any serious jazz fan's collection.

By 1950, though, Gillespie had been shown the door by RCA. Finding himself without a deal, he took matters into his own hands and formed a label of his own, Dee Gee, whose output is collected on *Dee Gee Days.* Gillespie's recordings during this phase of his career were nowhere near as audacious as his earlier efforts; indeed, his increasing reliance on vocals (mostly by Joe Carroll, although Freddy Strong, Melvin Moore and Diz himself contributed at times) suggests a growing awareness of audience expectations. Even so, Gillespie generally maintained his artistic standards, whether with the vigorous bop workout on "Tin Tin Deo" or the playful Louis Armstrong impression of "Confession (Pop's)."

Eventually, Gillespie signed with Norman Granz's Verve label, where he experimented with everything from Latin jazz to straight blowing sessions. *At Newport,* a 1957 big-band gig at the Newport Jazz Festival, is a notable live recording from this period. Most of the Verve material runs to straight-ahead blowing sessions, such as the Sonny Rollins/Sonny Stitt albums *Duets* and *Sonny Side Up,* and while little of the music is as revelatory as the trumpeter's early work, he's a nimble enough improviser to keep things interesting throughout. Still, the quintessential Gillespie album from this period has to be *Swing Low, Sweet Cadillac,* a concert recording with a blend of wit, groove and virtuosity that is typical of his live act.

After a few deservedly forgotten attempts at jazz pop in the early '70s, Gillespie rejoined Granz, who by then had founded Pablo. Sadly, the majority of what he recorded for the label is disappointingly slapdash, tending toward extremely casual jam-session sides. *Afro-Cuban Jazz Moods* is a notable exception, however, with Gillespie and percussionist Machito offering a credible re-creation of the great 1947 big-band sessions. *To Bird with Love* and *To Diz with Love* document Gillespie's final performance, at New York's Blue Note nightclub. — J.D.C.

LARRY GOLDINGS

★★★★ The Intimacy of the Blues (Verve, 1991)
★★★½ Caminhos Cruzados (Novus/RCA, 1994)
★★★ Light Blue (Minor Music, 1995)
★★★★★ Whatever It Takes (Warner Bros., 1995)
★★★ Big Stuff (Warner Bros., 1996)
★★★½ Awareness (Warner Bros., 1997)

Larry Goldings (b. 1968), son of a Boston criminal lawyer, studied classical piano as a youngster and was first introduced to jazz at a summer music camp. Through their recordings, he fell under the spell of Oscar Peterson, Dave McKenna and Keith Jarrett before moving to New York to further his musical studies and work his way into the jazz scene.

As he toured successively with Jon Hendricks, saxophonist Christopher Hollyday and guitarist Jim Hall, he also became deeply interested in the Hammond B-3 organ, the instrument of choice for his recordings as a leader. His B-3 work soon earned him a spot in the J.B. Horns touring band led by R&B saxophonist Maceo Parker.

Goldings attacks the organ differently from most R&B-based and soul-jazz players. In his hands it swings with a blues feeling and surgical precision. Each organ recording also showcases Goldings's exemplary partners, guitarist Peter Bernstein and drummer Bill Stewart. Each session is strengthened by their collective spirit.

Tenor saxophonist David "Fathead" Newman joins on two tracks of *The Intimacy of the Blues,* while *Light Blue* is strictly a trio outing. Tenor player Joshua Redman guests on the Latin-tinged *Caminhos Cruzados,* which is also aided by Brazilian percussionist Guilherme Franco. Redman, Parker, David Sanborn, trombonist Fred Wesley (another J.B. Horns alumnus) and bassist Richard Patterson guest on the high-energy, funk-filled *Whatever It Takes.*

Big Stuff is a transitional recording for Goldings, who still has Bernstein and Stewart aboard but less available due to their other commitments. As a result, his lineup also includes guitarist Kurt Rosenwinkle, tenor saxophonist John McKenna, drummer Idris Muhammad and, again, percussionist Franco. Because *Big Stuff* covers more stylistic bases, it lacks some of the B-3 punch its predecessors had. Goldings is moving toward a true band sound rather than a showcase for one instrument.

Awareness is Goldings's reminder that he was a pianist first and that the instrument remains an integral part of his musical psyche. He gets extraordinary support from bassist Larry Grenadier and drummer Paul Motian on this fine, subtler trio session. — K.F.

BENNY GOLSON

★★★½ **Benny Golson's New York Scene (1957; Original Jazz Classics, N.A.)**
★★★★ **The Other Side of Benny Golson (1958; Original Jazz Classics, 1990)**
★★★★ **Gone with Golson (1959; Original Jazz Classics, 1995)**
★★★★ **Groovin' with Golson (1959; Original Jazz Classics, 1992)**
★★★★ **Gettin' with It (1960; Original Jazz Classics, 1995)**
★★★½ **California Message (1981; Timeless, 1990)**
★★★★ **This Is for You, John (Timeless, 1984)**
★★★½ **Time Speaks (Timeless, 1985)**
★★★½ **Stardust (Denon, 1988)**
★★★½ **Benny Golson Quartet Live (Dreyfus, 1991)**
★★★★ **I Remember Miles (1993; Evidence, 1996)**
★★★★ **Domingo (Dreyfus, 1994)**
★★★ **Benny Golson Quartet (LaserLight, 1996)**
★★★★ **Remembering Clifford (Milestone, 1997)**
★★★ **The Modern Touch (N.A.; Original Jazz Classics, N.A.)**

Saxophonist, arranger, composer and bandleader Benny Golson (b. 1929) has been a master of styles over a career that has taken him through swing, blues and bop to the realms of expressionistic acoustic jazz. He's composed and arranged such standards as "Killer Joe," "I Remember Clifford," "Whisper Not" and "Stablemates." He's also put together a number of memorable groups, including the Jazztet, which he co-led with trumpeter Art Farmer. He was a key member of one of Art Blakey's greatest Jazz Messengers lineups and assembled a Blakey tribute band.

The Philadelphia native was trained in both blues playing, with Bull Moose Jackson, and jazz, with Tadd Dameron, Lionel Hampton and Dizzy Gillespie. He came into his own as a member of the Jazz Messengers, contributing four numbers to the band's classic *Moanin',* including "Along Came Betty" and "Blues March."

His first album, *Benny Golson's New York Scene,* is a collection of elegant performances by quintets and nonets featuring Farmer, pianist Wynton Kelly and bassist Paul Chambers. Blakey joins his former band mate for the incendiary *Groovin' with Golson,* which also includes the wonderful trombone playing of Curtis Fuller, who would go on to become a member of the Jazztet. Fuller also contributes mightily to *The Other Side of Benny Golson, Gone with Golson* and *Gettin' with It.*

Golson's arrangement skills led to the greener pastures of studio work during the height of the fusion era, but he returned in the 1980s to lead several groups. *California Message* reunited him with Fuller. *This Is for You, John* paid tribute to Golson's close friend John Coltrane, with an outstanding lineup of Pharoah Sanders battling Golson on tenor, Cedar Walton on piano, Ron

Carter on bass and Jack DeJohnette on drums. *Time Speaks* puts trumpeters Freddie Hubbard and Woody Shaw on the front line. Hubbard is even better on *Stardust,* which also features beautiful piano work from Mulgrew Miller, who returns on LaserLight's *Benny Golson Quartet.* Golson made a pair of fine albums for the French Dreyfus label: the live quartet date from a 1989 performance in Italy and the 1991 set *Domingo,* another reunion with Fuller.

Golson's abilities as an arranger are never more in evidence than on the magnificent *I Remember Miles,* a tribute in which Golson manages to climb inside the spirit of the classic Davis groups of the 1950s. With stalwart sidekicks Fuller and Miller joined by bassist Ray Drummond, drummer Tony Reedus and trumpeter Eddie Henderson taking Miles head on, this sextet captures the spirit of what many fans consider Davis's finest moments. *Remembering Clifford* extends the tribute series with a sextet session dedicated to the memory of trumpeter Clifford Brown. "Brown Immortal," Golson's "Five Spot After Dark" and "Tito Puente," which adds percussionists Puente and Carlos "Patato" Valdes, are the highlights.
— J.S.

PAUL GONSALVES

★★★★ **Gettin' Together (1961; Original Jazz Classics, 1987)**
★★★ **Just A-Sittin' and A-Rockin' (1970; Black Lion, 1991)**
★★★½ **Paul Gonsalves Meets Earl Hines (1972; Black Lion, 1993)**
★★★½ **Mexican Bandit Meets Pittsburgh Pirate (1973; Original Jazz Classics, 1992)**

Tenor saxophonist Paul Gonsalves (1920–1974) played in Boston-area bands until he enlisted in military service during World War II. Upon his discharge he worked with the Count Basie and Dizzy Gillespie bands before joining the Duke Ellington Orchestra in 1950. An aggressive player firmly rooted in the basics of the Coleman Hawkins tradition but looking toward bop and modal approaches to soloing, Gonsalves was one of the main soloists in the Ellington band through the 1950s, delivering a legendary solo during "Diminuendo and Crescendo in Blue" at the 1956 Newport Jazz Festival.

On his own, the underrecorded Gonsalves showed that he had more to offer than a big-band chair could allow. He solos fiercely on *Gettin' Together,* nearly blowing cornetist Nat Adderley off the date, then pulls out his big-toned Hawkins chops for a beautiful ballad reading with pianist Wynton Kelly, bassist Sam Jones and drummer Jimmy Cobb gently accompanying him.

Just A-Sittin' and A-Rockin' brings Gonsalves together with fellow Ellingtonians Ray Nance on trumpet and violin and Norris Turney on alto saxophone and clarinet. Gonsalves and pianist Earl Hines interact superbly on their Black Lion recording. Trumpeter Roy Eldridge plays the Pittsburgh Pirate to Gonsalves's Mexican Bandit on another exquisite session. The CD reissue includes a bit of Ellingtonia, "Satin Doll," that didn't make it to the original release. — J.S.

JERRY GONZALEZ

★★★★ **Ya Yo Me Curé (1981; Sunnyside, 1995)**
★★★★ **Rumba Para Monk (Sunnyside, 1989)**
★★★½ **Earthdance (Sunnyside, 1991)**
★★★½ **Moliendo Café: To Wisdom the Prize (Sunnyside, 1992)**
★★★½ **Crossroads (Milestone, 1994)**
★★★★ **Pensativo (Milestone, 1995)**
★★★★½ **Fire Dance (Milestone, 1996)**

Percussionist and trumpeter Jerry Gonzalez (b. 1949) and bassist Andy Gonzalez have played in a variety of salsa, jazz and rock bands since the late 1960s, when they emerged from the tough South Bronx neighborhood nicknamed Fort Apache by local police.

In the early 1970s the brothers played in pianist Eddie Palmieri's band, bringing a jazz mix to Palmieri's salsa sound. From there the brothers joined percussionist Manny Oquendo to form Libre, then in the early 1980s put together their own Fort Apache Band. Fort Apache has ranged in size from small groups to a 15-piece orchestra and included such esteemed players as percussionists Gene Golden, Nicky Marrero, Steve Berrios and Flaco Hernandez, trombonist Steve Turre, the late pianist Jorge Dalto and saxophonists Mario Rivera and Wilfredo Velez.

Ya Yo Me Curé is a large-ensemble version of the band that mixes the traditional, rhythmic compositions of vocalist and percussionist Frankie Rodríguez with exotic renditions of the jazz classics "Caravan," "Nefertiti" and "Evidence" with "The Lucy Theme" thrown in for good luck.

By the end of the 1980s, the band was honed down to a quintet; the lineup of *Rumba Para Monk* includes the Gonzalez brothers, Berrios, pianist Larry Willis and tenor saxophonist

Carter Jefferson. This historic exploration of Monk themes meets halfway between jazz and salsa, creating memorable versions of such Monk compositions as "Monk's Mood," "Nutty," "Misterioso" and "Jackie-ing."

Joe Ford joined the band on alto and soprano saxophones for *Earthdance* and *Moliendo Café,* a mixture of originals and standards. *Earthdance* features more Monk ("Let's Call This") as well as compositions by another band favorite, Wayne Shorter ("Fe Fi Fo Fum"), and Ron Carter ("81") plus several originals, including Ford's title track.

Jefferson died in 1993 and was replaced by John Stubblefield on tenor for *Crossroads,* an album of mostly originals that reflects the band's deeper exploration of its Afro-Caribbean roots. By the time of *Pensativo,* Stubblefield had become a prime voice in the group, contributing the strong original "Midnight Train." Ford was right there with him, writing "Give It Some Thought" and "Heidi Ho," and the band added to its body of Monk compositions with a cover of "Ruby, My Dear."

Fire Dance, recorded at Blues Alley in Washington, D.C., over a three-day engagement in 1996, really captures the spirit of the Fort Apache Band. The group's interaction with the enthusiastic live audience lifts it to another level here, and the front line of Stubblefield, Ford and Gonzalez produces one of the most distinctive sounds to come from this generation of bands.

— J.S.

BENNY GOODMAN

★★★★★ **The Carnegie Hall Jazz Concert (1938) (1950; Columbia, 1987)**
★★★½ **B.G. in Hi Fi (1954; Capitol, 1989)**
★★½ **Benny Rides Again (1959; MCA, 1988)**
★★★ **Swing, Swing, Swing (1963; RCA, 1987)**
★★★½ **Together Again (1963; RCA, 1987)**
★★½ **The King Swings (1974; Star Line, 1993)**
★★★ **Pure Gold (RCA Bluebird, 1975)**
★★½ **Live at Carnegie Hall 1978: 40th Anniversary Concert (Verve, 1978)**
★★★ **The Great Benny Goodman (Columbia, 1981)**
★★★ **Sing, Sing, Sing (RCA Bluebird, 1986)**
★★★½ **Benny Goodman's 1934 Bill Dodge All-Star Recordings (Circle, 1987)**
★★★ **Compact Jazz (Verve, 1987)**
★★★ **The Benny Goodman Sextet (Columbia, 1987)**
★★★★ **Roll 'Em (Columbia, 1987)**
★★★½ **Slipped Disc 1945–46 (Columbia, 1988)**
★★★½ **Clarinet a la King (Columbia, 1988)**
★★★ **All the Cats Join In (Columbia, 1988)**
★★★ **Benny Goodman (RCA Special Products, 1988)**
★★★½ **Airplay (Signature, 1989)**
★★★★½ **The Benny Goodman Sextet Featuring Charlie Christian: 1939–41 (Columbia, 1989)**
★★★ **The Early Years (Biograph, 1989)**
★★★★ **The Yale University Music Library Archives, Vol. 1 (MusicMasters, 1989)**
★★★½ **The Yale University Music Library Archives, Vol. 2: Live at Basin Street (MusicMasters, 1989)**
★★★ **The Yale University Music Library Archives, Vol. 3: Big Band in Europe (MusicMasters, 1989)**
★★★ **The Small Groups: 1941–1945 (Columbia, 1989)**
★★★★ **Avalon: The Small Bands, Vol. 2 (RCA Bluebird, 1990)**
★★ **Best of the Big Bands (Columbia, 1990)**
★★ **Greatest Hits (Curb, 1990)**
★★ **The Yale University Music Library Archives, Vol. 4: Big Band Recordings (MusicMasters, 1990)**
★★★ **The Yale University Music Library Archives, Vol. 5 (MusicMasters, 1990)**
★★★ **The Yale University Music Library Archives, Vol. 6: Live at Rainbow Grill (MusicMasters, 1991)**
★★★ **I Like Jazz: The Essence of Benny Goodman (Legacy, 1991)**
★★★ **Jazz Collector Edition—Benny Goodman Orchestra (LaserLight, 1991)**
★★★★★ **The Birth of Swing (RCA Bluebird, 1991)**
★★★★ **B.G. & Big Tea in NYC (Decca, 1992)**
★★★ **The Yale University Music Library Archives, Vol. 7: Florida Sessions (MusicMasters, 1992)**
★★★★ **Benny Goodman and His Orchestra, 1935 (Classics, 1992)**

★★★ **Best of the Big Bands Featuring Helen Forrest (Legacy, 1992)**
★★★★ **Jazz Collector Edition—Let's Dance (LaserLight, 1992)**
★★★ **Stompin' at the Savoy (RCA Bluebird, 1992)**
★★★★ **On the Air (1937–1938) (Legacy, 1993)**
★★★ **16 Most Requested Songs (Legacy, 1993)**
★★★ **Benny Goodman and His Orchestra, 1928–1931 (Classics, 1993)**
★★★ **Benny Goodman and His Orchestra, 1931–1933 (Classics, 1993)**
★★½ **Best of the Big Bands Featuring Peggy Lee (Legacy, 1993)**
★★★½ **Swing, Swing, Swing (MusicMasters, 1993)**
★★★★ **The Harry James Years, Vol. 1 (RCA Bluebird, 1993)**
★★★ **The Yale University Music Library Archives, Vol. 8 (MusicMasters, 1993)**
★★★★ **Benny Goodman and His Orchestra, 1934–1935 (Classics, 1994)**
★★★ **Swing Sessions 1945–46 (Hindsight, 1994)**
★★★★ **The Indispensable Benny Goodman, Vols. 3 and 4 (RCA Bluebird, 1994)**
★★★ **The Yale University Music Library Archives, Vol. 9: Live at Basin Street, 1954 (MusicMasters, 1994)**
★★½ **Verve Jazz Masters 33 (Verve, 1994)**
★★★½ **Stompin' (Drive Archive, 1995)**
★★★★ **The Indispensable Benny Goodman, Vols. 5 and 6 (RCA Bluebird, 1995)**
★★★★ **The Indispensable Benny Goodman (RCA Bluebird, 1995)**
★★★★ **Benny Goodman and His Orchestra, 1935–1936 (Classics, 1995)**
★★★★ **Benny Goodman and His Orchestra, 1936 (Classics, 1995)**
★★★ **Best of the Big Bands: Benny Goodman and His Great Vocalists (Legacy, 1995)**
★★ **The Benny Goodman Story (Capitol, 1995)**
★★★★ **The Complete Small Combinations (1935–1937) (RCA, 1995)**
★★★★ **The Harry James Years, Part 2 (RCA Bluebird, 1995)**
★★★ **The Yale University Music Library Archives, Vol. 10 (MusicMasters, 1995)**
★★ **Undercurrent Blues (Capitol, 1995)**
★★★½ **The King of Swing (MusicMasters, 1996)**
★★★ **Great Vocalists of Our Time (RCA, 1996)**
★★★ **Greatest Hits (RCA Victor, 1996)**
★★★ **This Is Jazz 4 (Legacy, 1996)**
★★★★★ **The Complete RCA Victor Small Group Recordings (RCA, 1997)**
★★★½ **Way Down Yonder 1943–1944 (Stash, N.A.)**

Clarinetist and bandleader Benny Goodman (1909–1986) is the justifiably named "King of Swing" for kicking off the swing era with a 1935 national tour heading a big band that was wildly accepted by dance audiences. His technical proficiency as an organizer and leader, his brilliance as an individual soloist and his insistence on the concept that jazz was best approached as an integrated form all contributed to his stature as a jazz visionary and true American hero. At a time when blacks were not permitted to participate with whites in professional sports, Goodman was championing black stars in his band in an unambiguous stance against segregation.

Goodman grew up in Chicago, where he started playing professionally by age 12, performing in a variety of bands. He joined the Ben Pollack band in Los Angeles, where he cut his first sides as a leader; these can be heard on Classics' *Benny Goodman and His Orchestra, 1928–1931*. Goodman moved to New York to work as a session musician, playing saxophone as well as clarinet in a variety of contexts (see *B.G. & Big Tea in NYC* and *Benny Goodman and His Orchestra, 1931–1933*).

The first real Benny Goodman band was formed in 1934 to perform on the weekly radio program "Let's Dance." Featuring one of the hottest trumpet players in jazz, Bunny Berigan, and, by early 1935, the outstanding Gene Krupa on drums, the band played burning dance music supplied by its contract arranger, Fletcher Henderson, whose own bands provided the blueprint for swing. *Benny Goodman's 1934 Bill Dodge All-Star Recordings*, *Jazz Collector*

Edition—Let's Dance, The Early Years and *Benny Goodman and His Orchestra 1934–1935* cover this period.

Accounts of the 1935 tour indicate that the band wasn't going over well at most stops and was discouraged to the point of breaking up—until reaching the West Coast, where a well-received Oakland date was followed by the historic August 21 show at the Palomar Ballroom in Los Angeles. The story goes that after a lackluster first set of "safe" tunes at the Palomar, Krupa (or perhaps it was Berigan) said to Goodman, "If we're gonna go down, let's go down swingin'." The next set was packed with Henderson arrangements, and when Berigan took his solo on "King Porter Stomp," the ecstatic response ushered in the swing era. This material is on *The Birth of Swing*, *The Indispensable Benny Goodman* and *Benny Goodman and His Orchestra 1935–1936* and *1936*.

At the same time that Goodman was honing his big-band style he was also working with Krupa and pianist Teddy Wilson in the superb trio format that allowed these master musicians to interact in complete communion. By August of 1936 vibraphonist Lionel Hampton was added to the lineup to make it a quartet. These trio and quartet recordings are collected in their entirety on *The Complete RCA Victor Small Group Recordings.*

The Goodman big band went on to a residency at the Congress Hotel in Chicago, while swing became a national craze. Goodman continued to record in both big-band lineups, using primarily Henderson's arrangements, and with the smaller group in the studio for RCA Victor into 1939, material collected on the *Complete RCA Victor Small Group Recordings* and *The Harry James Years* sets.

Meanwhile, Columbia had the rights to live recordings of the Goodman band from the same period. *Airplay* and *On the Air* are superb collections of air checks recorded between 1936 and 1938 that document the band in all of its glory.

The Carnegie Hall Jazz Concert, possibly the most famous live show in jazz history, is the triumphant 1938 performance that caught Goodman at the height of his popularity and included the crowd-pleasing histrionics of Krupa's massively influential drum solo on "Sing Sing Sing."

In 1939 Goodman signed to Columbia for studio recordings as well. He continued to lead the big band until 1944, when he disbanded the group, but a wartime recording ban limited the amount these groups set down in the studio. Columbia did record some sides in the early 1930s, before Goodman signed with RCA Victor, and continued to record him after the recording ban was lifted in 1944.

Roll 'Em covers air shots and some of the 1939 studio sides for Columbia. *Clarinet à la King,* named after the Eddie Sauter arrangement of a popular Goodman tune, tracks the band from '39 to '41 with such soloists as guitarist Charlie Christian and trumpeter Cootie Williams. *All the Cats Join In* covers the war years. *The Small Groups: 1941–1945* covers trios to sextet recordings made immediately before and after the wartime ban. *Slipped Disc 1945–46* covers more sextet dates with Wilson, Red Norvo and Slam Stewart.

The most amazing Columbia studio recordings are those on *The Benny Goodman Sextet Featuring Charlie Christian,* some of which feature Henderson at the piano. These tracks go far beyond the harmonic climate of swing and suggest the eventual direction in which postwar jazz would move: bop. Christian's guitar playing on these sides is a revelation.

Goodman's post-1940s efforts, despite his continued ability to play excellent clarinet, suffer from the nostalgic hero worship still associated with his glory days, a fall-off in the dance-oriented rhythms that added so much to the band's live presentation and the inevitable problems associated with playing a greatest-hits set over and over, night after night.

Though most of the records don't bear comparison with his greater works, *B.G. in Hi-Fi* is a particularly good set that stands out for the committed performance of the assembled band, particularly Ruby Braff and Charlie Shavers on trumpets, George Duvivier on bass and Bobby Donaldson and Jo Jones on drums. *Together Again* is a 1963 reunion of the classic quartet of Goodman, Wilson, Hampton and Krupa.

The Benny Goodman Story, the companion LP to the 1955 film in which Steve Allen played Goodman, is a textbook example of how self-mythologizing can embarrass an artist. The *Live at Carnegie Hall 1978* set is a recording of the 40th-anniversary performance of the historic '38 Carnegie Hall show and is not to be confused with the original, as nostalgic remakes shoulder aside a Beatles tune.

Some of the best later Goodman albums are the *Yale University Music Library Archives* sets culled from his private collection. *Vol. 1,* which collects material from 1955 to shortly before his death in 1986, is the most rewarding.

The numerous Benny Goodman best-of collections tend to duplicate one another with the obvious tracks and are generally worth less than the classic '30s sides on the aforementioned albums. — J.S.

DEXTER GORDON

★★★ **The Resurgence of Dexter Gordon (Jazzland, 1960)**
★★★★ **Doin' Allright (Blue Note, 1961)**
★★★★★ **Dexter Calling (Blue Note, 1961)**
★★★★½ **A Swingin' Affair (Blue Note, 1962)**
★★★★½ **Go! (Blue Note, 1962)**
★★ **Cry Me a River (SteepleChase, 1962)**
★★★★★ **Our Man in Paris (Blue Note, 1963)**
★★★★ **One Flight Up (Blue Note, 1964)**
★★★ **Billie's Bounce (SteepleChase, 1964)**
★★★ **After Midnight (SteepleChase, 1965)**
★★★½ **Gettin' Around (Blue Note, 1965)**
★★★★ **Body and Soul (1967; Black Lion, 1988)**
★★★½ **Both Sides of Midnight (1967; Black Lion, 1988)**
★★½ **Take the A Train (1967; Black Lion, 1996)**
★★★½ **The Tower of Power! (1969; Original Jazz Classics, 1993)**
★★★ **Dexter Gordon (1969; Original Jazz Classics, 1994)**
★★★ **At Montreux (with Junior Mance) (1970; Prestige, 1987)**
★★★½ **The Jumpin' Blues (Original Jazz Classics, 1970)**
★★★★ **The Panther! (1970; Original Jazz Classics, 1992)**
★★★ **Generation (1972; Original Jazz Classics, 1994)**
★★★½ **The Apartment (SteepleChase, 1974)**
★★★★½ **Stable Mable (SteepleChase, 1975)**
★★★ **Swiss Nights, Vol. 1 (SteepleChase, 1975)**
★★★ **Swiss Nights, Vol. 2 (SteepleChase, 1975)**
★★★ **Swiss Nights, Vol. 3 (SteepleChase, 1975)**
★★★★ **Biting the Apple (SteepleChase, 1976)**
★★★½ **Homecoming: Live at the Village Vanguard (1976; Legacy, 1990)**
★★★★ **Lullaby for a Monster (SteepleChase, 1976)**
★★★ **True Blue (1977; Xanadu, 1994)**
★★★ **Midnight Dream (West Wind Jazz, 1977)**
★★★★ **Gotham City (Columbia, 1980)**
★★★ **American Classic (1982; Discovery, 1993)**
★★★★ **The Other Side of 'Round Midnight (Blue Note, 1985)**
★★★½ **The Best of the Blue Note Years (Blue Note, 1988)**
★★★½ **Ballads (Blue Note, 1991)**
★★★★ **Dexter Rides Again (Savoy, 1992)**
★★★ **Daddy Plays the Horn (Bethlehem, 1994)**
★★★½ **Dexter Gordon Featuring Joe Newman (Monad, 1995)**
★★★★ **The Complete Blue Note Sixties Sessions (Blue Note, 1996)**
★★★½ **Blue Dex: Dexter Gordon Plays the Blues (Prestige, 1996)**
★★★ **Backstairs (E.J.'s, N.A.)**
★★★★½ **The Complete Dial Sessions (Stash, N.A.)**

Dexter Gordon (1923–1990) is generally accepted as one of the more accomplished tenor saxophonists in jazz history. He left his Los Angeles home to join Lionel Hampton's band at the tender age of 17, hooking up with Illinois Jacquet for the first of his many "tenor battles."

Gordon joined up with Billy Eckstine's big band in 1944 for a short but significant period. Here, alongside soon-to-be innovators like Dizzy Gillespie and Charlie Parker, Gordon established himself as the first bebop tenor player. Combining the influence of Lester Young's tenor playing with the harmonic advancements of Charlie Parker, Gordon made a huge impact on future saxophone stars like John Coltrane and Sonny Rollins.

After leaving Eckstine's band Gordon bounced between both coasts, hanging with the beboppers on 52nd Street in New York and doing tenor battles with Wardell Gray in Los Angeles.

Gordon's early sides on Savoy and Dial clarify exactly what all the critical fuss was about. On *Dexter Rides Again* Gordon shoots straight from the hip along with young lions like Tadd Dameron, Art Blakey, Bud Powell and Max Roach. *The Complete Dial Sessions* captures Gordon embroiled in a classic West Coast date with both Wardell Gray and tenor player Teddy Edwards.

Due to personal and legal problems related to drugs, Gordon barely recorded at all in the 1950s, and *The Resurgence of Dexter Gordon* was just that. Produced by Cannonball Adderley, this recording marked the first of Gordon's two great comebacks. With a cast of near-anonymous sidemen, Gordon showed that a decade of relative inactivity had not diminished his playing powers in the least.

Between 1961 and 1965, Gordon recorded a handful of excellent albums for Blue Note. *Doin' Allright* is a swinging, bluesy affair featuring Freddie Hubbard on trumpet and Horace Parlan on piano. Gordon sounds robust and in control, already emerging as an elder statesman of jazz.

Dexter Calling is a hot quartet date that unites Gordon with an old Los Angeles comrade, pianist Kenny Drew. Gordon's tenor sound is monstrous, and with no other horn player in sight, he takes the lead beautifully. With great playing, the advanced compositions of "Drew" and three Gordon originals from the jazz musical *The Connection,* this is essential Dex. *A Swingin' Affair* and *Go!* are more of the same. Once again, the quartet format highlights Gordon's saxophone strength. While the players involved are occasionally overwhelmed by Dexter, these two discs are more than worthwhile.

It was around this time that Dexter moved to Europe and made Copenhagen his home base. While his first album for SteepleChase, *Cry Me a River,* is a disappointment, and his European group is ineffective, *Our Man in Paris* is by all contrasts a knockout and another essential album. With a trio featuring Pierre Michelot on bass and Kenny Clarke on drums, Gordon tears things up and wears his bebop crown proudly (check out his killer version of "A Night in Tunisia"). *One Flight Up* is more quality Dex and features an all-star quintet with Gordon, Kenny Drew, trumpeter Donald Byrd, drummer Art Taylor and the wonderful European bassist Niels-Henning Ørsted Pedersen.

Gordon's SteepleChase output improved somewhat with *Billie's Bounce.* Surrounding himself with accomplished players like pianist Tete Montoliu and the reliable Pedersen, Gordon was becoming more comfortable in his adopted homeland. *Body and Soul* and *Both Sides of Midnight* were recorded in the same day, and both albums have held up well over the years. They document a late-1960s Gordon playing at full strength along with Drew, Pedersen and Albert "Tootie" Heath on drums.

The Tower of Power! and *Dexter Gordon* (originally released as *More Power!*) hark back to the tenor battles of old with James Moody occupying the second-tenor chair on a few of the tunes. While *The Tower of Power!* is the better of the two, the solid playing of pianist Barry Harris, drummer Tootie Heath and bassist Buster Williams energizes both of these blowing sessions. Recorded while visiting the United States to play the Newport Jazz Festival, *The Panther!* features an evocative version of "Body and Soul" and shows a mature Dexter in the company of pianist Tommy Flanagan, bassist Larry Ridley and the excellent Alan Dawson on drums.

Generation is another solid Prestige date (rereleased on Original Jazz Classics) that reunites Dexter with trumpeter Freddie Hubbard. While *The Apartment* is less than fantastic for mid-1970s Dexter, *Stable Mable* is a near classic. With great contributions from Horace Parlan and Niels-Henning Ørsted Pedersen, the group runs through standards written by Duke Ellington, Miles Davis and, of course, Charlie Parker. The *Swiss Nights* recordings continue in a similar vein, and although the series is stretched thin over three volumes, they are still worth the purchase.

Biting the Apple signals Gordon's lauded return to America, this time for keeps. More than three full decades into his career, he stands tall with Barry Harris, bassist Sam Jones and drummer Al Foster. *Homecoming: Live at the Village Vanguard* respectfully documents Dexter Gordon's second triumphant comeback.

Lullaby for a Monster is a decent trio session and one of Gordon's final SteepleChase recordings. *Gotham City* is a sturdy blues album that unites Dexter with drummer Art Blakey, bassist Percy Heath and pianist Cedar Walton and includes guest appearances by George Benson and Woody Shaw.

The Other Side of 'Round Midnight is music from the film *'Round Midnight,* which cast Gordon as an erratic American jazzman living in Europe. The music is surprisingly top-notch and features a virtual Who's Who in the world of jazz.

The Best of the Blue Note Years and *Ballads* are both quality compilations mining Gordon's excellent Blue Note albums, but they don't add anything new to his recorded legacy. *Blue Dex* is another compilation documenting Gordon's blues roots but again contains no new material. *Dexter Gordon Featuring Joe Newman* is an energetic live gig recorded in Chicago in 1976. Joe Newman is an able contributor on trumpet, and the rhythm section of pianist Jodie Christian, drummer Wilbur Campbell and bassist Eddie DeHase is right on time.

True Blue is little more than a decent jam session that features Gordon in yet another celebrated tenor battle, this time with veteran saxophonist Al Cohn. — M.M.

EARL GRANT

★★½ **The End (MCA Special Products, 1983)**
★★ **Winter Wonderland (MCA Special Products, N.A.)**

Although known primarily as a pianist and organist, classically trained Earl Grant (1931–1970) hit the Top 10 in 1963 for the first and only time in his career with "The End," a single lacking even a hint of keyboards in its instrumental lineup. It did have a moving vocal performance by Grant to recommend it, so much so as to make his low profile as a singer all the more puzzling. While "The End" is done in the smooth crooning style of Nat King Cole, another song, "A Closer Walk," shows him equally at home in a gospel mode. In addition to including these tracks, *The End* is rounded out with several lush instrumentals, as well as some blues-tinged piano solos. Grant's Christmas offering, *Winter Wonderland,* offers no surprises in its seasonal fare but remains a pleasant outing nonetheless, thanks to the artist's engaging sincerity. — D.M.

STÉPHANE GRAPPELLI

★★★ **Violins No End (1957; Original Jazz Classics, N.A.)**
★★★ **Afternoon in Paris (Verve, 1971)**
★★★ **Shades of Django (Verve, 1975)**
★★★ **Best of Stéphane Grappelli (Vanguard, 1975)**
★★★ **Satin Doll (1975; Vanguard, 1987)**
★★★ **Tivoli Gardens, Copenhagen, Denmark (with Joe Pass and Niels-Henning Ørsted Pedersen) (1979; Original Jazz Classics, 1990)**
★★★ **Skol (with Oscar Peterson) (1979; Original Jazz Classics, 1990)**
★★★ **Stéphane Grappelli and David Grisman Live (Warner Bros., 1981)**
★★★ **At the Winery (Concord Jazz, 1981)**
★★★ **Vintage 1981 (Concord Jazz, 1981)**
★★★ **Stephanova (with Marc Fosset) (Concord Jazz, 1983)**
★★ **Just One of Those Things (Angel, 1984)**
★★★★ **Bringing It Together (with Toots Thielemans) (Cymekob, 1984)**
★★★ **Together at Last (with Vassar Clements) (Flying Fish, 1987)**
★★ **Play Berlin, Kern, Porter, Rodgers & Hart (with Yehudi Menuhin) (EMI U.K., 1988)**
★★ **Play "Jealousy" and Other Great Standards (with Yehudi Menuhin) (EMI U.K., 1988)**
★★★ **Olympia '88 (Atlantic, 1988)**
★★★ **Jazz 'Round Midnight (Verve, 1989)**
★★ **My Other Love Is Solo Piano (CBS, 1990)**
★★★★ **One on One (with McCoy Tyner) (Milestone, 1990)**
★★★★ **Live in Tokyo (Denon, 1991)**
★★★ **85 and Still Swinging: Live at Carnegie Hall (with the Rosenberg Trio) (Angel, 1993)**
★★★ **Live 1992 (Verve, 1993)**
★★★ **First Class (with the Bolling Big Band) (Milan, 1993)**
★★★ **So Easy to Remember (Omega, 1993)**
★ **Stéphane Grappelli and Michel Legrand (Verve, 1993)**
★★★ **Verve Jazz Masters 11 (Verve, 1994)**
★★★ **Live at the Blue Note (Telarc, 1996)**
★★★★ **Flamingo (Dreyfus, 1996)**
★★★ **Parisian Thoroughfare (LaserLight, 1997)**
★★★ **Reunion (with Mortin Taylor) (Honest, 1997)**
★★★ **Stéphane Grappelli Plays Jerome Kern (GRP, N.A.)**
★★ **Anything Goes: The Music of Cole Porter (with Yo-Yo Ma) (CBS, N.A.)**
★★★ **Compact Jazz: Stéphane Grappelli (with Jean-Luc Ponty) (Verve, N.A.)**

French violinist Stéphane Grappelli (1908–1997) performed up until his death, and while he may have lost some of his fire as he neared age 90, he never lost his flair. One of the most elegant and eloquent improvisers in jazz for very nearly as long as jazz has existed, his bow spun lyrical curlicues on themes ranging from Gershwin to Sonny Rollins to Fats Waller to Stevie Wonder—and this in the course of just one concert.

Grappelli played professionally since his teens, on both piano and violin. He earned his stripes on the latter, in the legendary Quintette du Hot Club de France, alongside Django Reinhardt. From the late '30s he worked extensively with George Shearing, and in the '40s he reteamed with Reinhardt. While he led sessions from the '30s through the '60s, Grappelli's available recorded output is somewhat spotty. His repertoire, mostly hoary standards, veritably tumbles off Grappelli's fingers, yet he has such tremendous affection for the songs that they rarely sound stale, which is amazing considering "Lady Be Good" was his theme song for nigh on 50 years, and he probably played "Blue Skies" and "Nice Work If You Can Get It" for nearly as long. Indeed, some of Grappelli's standards appear in better than half a dozen versions. For this reason, most of Grappelli's live recordings are virtually interchangeable, with much of the same material and often the same players. The *Live in Tokyo* set, however, swings the hardest and sounds the best, with the Blue Note set running a close second on the strength of Bucky Pizzarelli's seven-string guitar work—a fine foil for Grappelli.

Jazz 'Round Midnight gives a chronological glimpse of Grappelli's career, covering recordings from the 1930s through the 1970s, including some great tunes with Reinhardt. The *Verve Jazz Masters 11* set is even better, both sonically and because of the detailed annotation. The enhanced sound, however, stems from the fact that the tracks come from far more recent Verve recordings, especially the very good album with Diz Disley, *Shades of Django.* A couple of tracks from that session overlap both CDs, but the original is worth seeking out as it contains most of Grappelli's favorite tunes in generally excellent performances.

Satin Doll, which merges the Vanguard *Best of Stéphane Grappelli* with an album no longer available as a single release, refreshingly features Grappelli's quintet (organ, piano, guitar, bass and drums) as much as Grappelli himself. Tunes like "Ain't Misbehavin'," powered by Kenny Clarke on percussion, show just how fiercely and elegantly Grappelli's band could swing, though on certain tunes, like "Body and Soul" and "My Funny Valentine," Eddy Louis's organ becomes overbearing.

Parisian Thoroughfare uses tracks from Grappelli's days with Disley, as well as others ranging from 1961 through 1975. It features such diverse players as Clarke, Slam Stewart and Johnny Guarnieri. Unfortunately, like the *Jazz 'Round Midnight* set, the sound is uneven.

While a big band might swamp and sunder a lesser soloist, *First Class,* with the Bolling Big Band, affords a musical experience roughly equivalent to sitting in a well-worn leather easy chair. This has all the charm of a 1940s big-band session, a feel Claude Bolling clearly wanted to capture in his arrangements, yet it also maintains up-to-the-minute, discreet audio clarity. The music swings with grace and fire.

Grappelli does not fare as well in his recording with Michel Legrand and orchestra. The arrangements go way over the treacle line—this is beautiful music in the worst sense of the phrase, Grappelli's violin constantly buried under the overbearing orchestrations. Grappelli's elder-statesman status had other detrimental effects: *My Other Love Is Solo Piano* features Grappelli at the keyboard, where he displays the feeling of a violin virtuoso expressed with the technique of Chico Marx.

Grappelli has recorded with a wide variety of players in some interesting contexts. Pairing Grappelli with country-violin virtuoso Vassar Clements borders on genius, though the recording *Together at Last* only half lives up to the potential. In terms of what they play, some of the choices are inspired: "Alabamy Bound" captures the country ambiance while tapping Grappelli's Berlin roots. On the other hand, "I Can See Clearly Now" is lost on most of the band, especially the rhythm section.

Working with harmonica virtuoso Toots Thielemans might seem odd for Grappelli, but *Bringing It Together* is one of his finest albums. Even Thielemans's whistling on "You'd Be So Nice to Come Home To" complements Grappelli's playing. Listening to the pair swap fours on "Bye Bye Blackbird" opens the window on what jazz is all about.

Yo-Yo Ma valiantly tries to keep up with Grappelli's band's improvisational approach on *Anything Goes,* but he drags things down with his lovely yet ultimately uninspired playing. Similarly, when Grappelli collaborates with

Yehudi Menuhin, the classical violinist has clearly walked into the wrong arena. Some songs, like the tango title track of *Play "Jealousy"* work better, just by their semiclassical nature, than the *Play Berlin, Kern, Porter, Rogers & Hart* recording. Menuhin plays some colorful ornamentations, but they hardly sound like jazz.

Since his days with Reinhardt, Grappelli has demonstrated an affinity for string-on-string work with guitarists. *Stephanova* pairs him with longtime collaborator Marc Fosset on guitar for an uncluttered duet set. Fosset has rarely swung harder, propelling some terrific performances out of Grappelli. Grappelli's outings with Fosset's predecessor, Martin Taylor, tend to lilt more than swing; Taylor's virtuosity, however, seems to push Grappelli. Even more satisfying, the repertoire on *Reunion* leans on Taylor originals and, with a few exceptions, covers that appear less frequently in Grappelli's oeuvre, with "I Thought About You" and "Drop Me Off in Harlem" sounding especially wonderful. This recording also deserves mention for its unparalleled warmth.

Grappelli improvises beautifully on his *Tivoli Gardens* live recording with Niels-Henning Ørsted Pedersen and Pablo Records mainstay guitarist Joe Pass. After ripping through the first four tunes, however, they seem to lose steam, catching fire again only at the end, on a version of "I Get a Kick Out of You."

One On One brings out the best in both Grappelli and McCoy Tyner. As he would with Michel Petrucciani some years later, Grappelli controls most of the repertoire and seems to enjoy the challenge of keeping up with Tyner's gospel-inflected postbop style. Neither musician really compromises, yet they find a highly complementary middle ground and both sound like they're having an enormous amount of fun doing it.

Grappelli and Jean-Luc Ponty play together only twice on their *Compact Jazz* compilation. Their versions of Sonny Rollins's "Pent-Up House" and Ponty's blues "Summit Soul" find the veteran's taste pitted against the younger player's fire to excellent musical advantage. It also features a couple of dynamic tracks of Grappelli with Larry Coryell and Philip Catherine, one of the best guitar matchups ever. Both Ponty and Grappelli get their own tracks, and sometimes the differences are jarring.

Some of the best available studio recordings of Grappelli come from his days with Concord in the 1980s. While perhaps not as energetic as some of the earlier recordings, they sound great and generally swing. *Vintage 1981* offers many of the usual suspects ("Paper Moon," "Honeysuckle Rose") in a two-guitar-and-bass setup that mimics the Quintette du Hot Club de France instrumentation, albeit without the virtuosity or intensity.

An 85th-birthday celebration, *So Easy to Remember* finds Grappelli joined by Pizzarelli, Kenny Burrell, drummer Grady Tate and bassist Ron Carter, who create a genuinely relaxed session, rife with standards like "God Bless the Child" and "You Brought a New Kind of Love to Me."

On 1996's *Flamingo,* with Michel Petrucciani, Roy Haynes and George Mraz, Grappelli covers artistic territory similar to his earlier work with Tyner. He plays his favorites, like "Sweet Georgia Brown" and "I Got Rhythm," but in a decidedly postbop context. The result is refreshing, but everyone's playing sounds somewhat reserved. Generally, the spate of Grappelli recordings made in the years before his death not only allowed him to accept the jazz world's accolades but found him in fine enough fettle to fully participate in each outing. — H.B.

BENNY GREEN

★★	**Prelude (Criss Cross, 1988)**
★★	**In This Direction (Criss Cross, 1989)**
★★★	**Lineage (Blue Note, 1990)**
★★★★★	**Greens (Blue Note, 1991)**
★★★★	**Testifyin'! Live at the Village Vanguard (Blue Note, 1992)**
★★★½	**That's Right! (Blue Note, 1993)**
★★★★	**The Place to Be (Blue Note, 1994)**
★★★★½	**Kaleidoscope (Blue Note, 1997)**
★★★★	**Oscar and Benny (with Oscar Peterson) (Telarc, 1998)**

Steeped in the many facets of the jazz-piano tradition, Benny Green (b. 1963) grew up in the San Francisco Bay Area and worked there professionally as a teenager with trumpeter Eddie Henderson and bassist Chuck Israels. When he arrived in 1982 from Berkeley, California, he quickly emerged as one of the most impressive young modernists on the New York jazz scene. Beginning in 1983, he spent four years in singer Betty Carter's band, then two more with the Jazz Messengers before working with trumpeter Freddie Hubbard (recording with each of those leaders) and forming his own trio. Since 1990 he has been busy as both a sideman and a leader. In the former role, he worked extensively in bassist

Ray Brown's trio. As an emerging young leader, Green won a significant endorsement in 1993 when Oscar Peterson awarded him "protégé" recognition.

While his earliest recordings for the Dutch label Criss Cross are worthy debuts in quintet and trio formats, Green's first Blue Note recording, *Lineage,* shows his rapid maturation as an interpreter and player with an explosive style. Things gelled even more on his next three trio sessions, *Testifyin'!* (recorded live at the Village Vanguard), *That's Right!,* with bassist Christian McBride and drummer Carl Allen, and *The Place to Be,* which showcases his formidable range and sensitivity in solo, duo and trio formats. On three tunes the trio is augmented by a six-man horn section. Green is less the hotshot pianist and more the composer, bandleader and conceptualist on *Kaleidoscope,* an all-star showcase for original material with supporting roles for saxophonists Antonio Hart and Stanley Turrentine and guitarist Russell Malone.

Oscar and Benny is of historical significance within the piano legacy tradition as much as it is of high musical quality. There is a seamless blending of styles and inspirations by a grand master and his talented disciple, backed by Ray Brown and Gregory Hutchinson. It shows Green has grown far beyond protégé. — K.F.

GRANT GREEN

★★★	**Reaching Out (1961; Black Lion, 1989)**
★★★½	**Green Street (1961; Blue Note, 1995)**
★★★★	**Grantstand (1961; Blue Note, 1987)**
★★★★	**Born to Be Blue (1962; Blue Note, 1989)**
★★★★½	**Idle Moments (1963; Blue Note, 1987)**
★★★★	**Feelin' the Spirit (1963; Blue Note, 1987)**
★★★★	**Matador (1965; Blue Note, 1990)**
★★★★	**Carryin' On (1969; Blue Note, 1995)**
★★★	**Green Is Beautiful (1970; Blue Note, 1994)**
★★★★	**Alive! (1970; Blue Note, 1993)**
★★★★	**Live at the Lighthouse (1972; Blue Note, 1998)**
★★★★	**Solid (1979; Blue Note, 1995)**
★★★★	**The Best of Grant Green, Vol. 1 (Blue Note, 1993)**
★★★★	**His Majesty King Funk/Up (with Donald Byrd) (Verve, 1995)**
★★★½	**The Best of Grant Green, Vol. 2 (Blue Note, 1996)**
★★★★	**A Tribute to Grant Green (Evidence, 1998)**

One of the most influential players of his generation, St. Louis guitarist Grant Green (1931–1979) was a contemporary of Wes Montgomery's who went in the opposite direction, into single-line improvisations and driving, blues-based soul-jazz turns. Green could play ballads with Charlie Christian–like delicacy as well, but it was his amazingly tactile rhythmic style that was so arresting. He could do more with a single note or phrase than a much more technically dazzling player could with an entire score. Green's solos would hammer home an idea until the flurry of staccato notes built up a secondary, internal rhythm, like a drum accenting itself. Set against the right rhythm section, this effect was often astonishing and never failed to lift an audience to its feet, not to mention getting his bassist and drummer worked up.

In the 1950s Green woodshedded in local St. Louis jazz and R&B groups, then played on Jimmy Forrest's *All the Gin Is Gone* before coming in the early '60s to New York, where he worked in several organ combos before his clean, driving rhythmic style made him a prized sideman on many of the soulful records produced at the time on the Blue Note label (by Hank Mobley, Herbie Hancock and Lee Morgan, among others).

Green went on to great success as a leader, making a series of hard-grooving records himself. *Reaching Out* is the reissue under Green's name of a session led by drummer Dave Bailey for Jazztime records. *Grantstand* shows Green in full flight leading a spirited quartet with tenor saxophonist and flautist Yusef Lateef, organist Jack McDuff and drummer Al Harewood.

Born to Be Blue showcases Green's abilities on ballad tempos, where he unveils the melodic side of his playing in a quintet setting flanked by tenor saxophonist Ike Quebec and pianist Sonny Clark. *Idle Moments* is a stone classic, with tenor player Joe Henderson, vibist Bobby Hutcherson, pianist Duke Pearson, bassist Bob Cranshaw and returning drummer Harewood. Hutcherson and Henderson color Green's style exquisitely, and the alternate version of "Django" on the reissue, sacrificed at first for length considerations, is a treat.

Green draws on the deep soul of his gospel roots for the intense *Feelin' the Spirit,* with

Herbie Hancock getting down on piano and bassist Butch Warren and drummer Billy Higgins holding nothing back. Green is feeling his oats on *Matador* in the company of bassist Bob Cranshaw and John Coltrane band mates McCoy Tyner on piano and Elvin Jones on drums, even doing his own version of "My Favorite Things."

His Majesty King Funk/Up is a reissue of two LPs recorded in the mid-'60s just as Green was centering himself in the funk-jazz mode that made its dramatic return in the 1990s as acid jazz. These roots-drenched sessions feature topical themes and foot-to-the-floor rhythm sections. Organist Larry Young and percussionist Candido star on the first session, which produced "The Selma March" and "The Cantaloupe Woman." Trumpeter Donald Byrd coleads the second, heading an all-star cast including Hancock, Candido, Jimmy Heath, saxophonist Stanley Turrentine and drummer Grady Tate.

Solid augments the *Matador* lineup with alto saxophonists Henderson and James Spaulding. *Carryin' On* is another out-and-out funk session covering tracks by the Meters and James Brown with a rhythm section powered by Jimmy Lewis's electric bass and Idris Muhammad's drums. *Green Is Beautiful* uses a similar sound on a mixed bag of material from Brown's "Ain't It Funky Now" to pop tracks "A Day in the Life" and "I'll Never Fall in Love Again."

Green was best heard in live performance, and *Alive!* shows why. This session, a sextet with Muhammad burning on the drums, Claude Bartee riffing on tenor saxophone, William Bivens on vibes, Ronnie Foster on organ and Joseph Armstrong on conga all playing in service to the groove, allows Green to work his magic on funk vamps like "Let the Music Take Your Mind" and "Sookie, Sookie." More of the same can be heard on *Live at the Lighthouse. A Tribute to Grant Green* is a monster session in Green's memory. Organist Larry Goldings and drummer Idris Muhammad anchor the trio for guitarists Greg Green, Dave Stryker, Peter Bernstein, Ed Cherry, Russell Malone and Mark Whitfield. — J.S.

AL GREY

★★★★ **Things Are Getting Better All the Time (with J.J. Johnson) (1984; Original Jazz Classics, 1992)**
★★★½ **Al Grey and Jesper Thilo Quintet (Storyville, 1986)**
★★★ **The New Al Grey Quintet (Chiaroscuro, 1988)**
★★★ **Live at the Floating Jazz Festival (Chiaroscuro, 1991)**
★★★½ **Centerpiece: Live at the Blue Note (Telarc, 1995)**

Big-band veteran trombonist Al Grey (b. 1925) has worked with Benny Carter, Dizzy Gillespie, Lionel Hampton, Jimmie Lunceford and Count Basie's late-1950s bands, which featured him prominently. He's recorded well but infrequently as a leader, bringing his enthusiasm, sense of humor and traditional plunger-mute technique to each setting.

The New Al Grey Quintet finds him surrounded by youngsters, including his son, trombonist Mike Grey, on an engaging session. The date with Danish saxophonist Jesper Thilo fronting a Scandinavian quintet has a classic quality to it—Thilo's Ben Webster–influenced tenor playing joins Grey's in a reprise of swing-era joys. *Live at the Floating Jazz Festival* is an entertaining session recorded on the S.S. *Norway* with a bonus track of interview material.

Centerpiece finds Grey at age 69 still banging it out in a lively set from the Blue Note with another old-timer, trumpeter Harry "Sweets" Edison, tenor saxophonist/flautist Jerome Richardson, pianist Junior Mance, bassist Ben Brown and frequent Grey sideman drummer Bobby Durham. — J.S.

BIG MIKE GRIFFIN

★★★½ **Back on the Streets Again (Waldoxy, 1992)**
★★★½ **Gimme What I Got Comin' (Waldoxy, 1993)**
★★★★ **Sittin' Here with Nothing (Waldoxy, 1995)**

Oklahoma native Mike Griffin (b. 1957) moved to Nashville in the mid-1980s, and by the end of the decade, the 350-pound, 6-foot-10½-inch guitarist/vocalist established himself as one of that music town's hottest blues guitarists. Griffin has a powerful voice, string-bending capabilities reminiscent of Albert King and a crowd-pleasing slide-guitar technique.

He is backed on the first two albums by his working group, the Unknown Blues Band. On *Back on the Streets Again* the group is augmented by the Muscle Shoals Horns and a guest shot from vocalist Dorothy Moore. *Gimme What I Got Comin'* features a terrific cover of Big Joe Turner's "T.V. Mama."

Sittin' Here with Nothing was recorded at the Muscle Shoals studios with session masters David Hood on bass and Clayton Ivey on keyboards. The studio works its magic on Griffin's guitar sound, from the ripping slide of the title track to the jazz-influenced runs on "He Can't Do It." Hood frames Griffin's work masterfully, and the interchange between Griffin's guitar and Ivey's sinister Hammond B-3 sounds like a cross between a Blue Note organ trio blowing session and a Stax-Volt B side.
— J.S.

JOHNNY GRIFFIN

★★★★ **Johnny Griffin Sextet (1958; Original Jazz Classics, 1994)**
★★★★★ **Way Out! (1958; Original Jazz Classics, 1995)**
★★★★½ **The Little Giant (1959; Original Jazz Classics, 1995)**
★★★ **The Big Soul Band (1960; Original Jazz Classics, 1990)**
★★★★ **White Gardenia (1961; Original Jazz Classics, 1995)**
★★★★ **Tough Tenor Favorites (1962; Original Jazz Classics, 1995)**
★★★½ **The Man I Love (Black Lion, 1988)**
★★★★ **A Blowing Session (with John Coltrane and Hank Mobley) (Blue Note, 1988)**
★★★½ **The Cat (Antilles, 1991)**
★★★ **Chicago, New York, Paris (Verve, 1995)**
★★★★★ **Return of the Griffin (Original Jazz Classics, 1996)**

A classic hard-bop musician, Johnny Griffin (b. 1928) was featured on late-'50s recordings by Art Blakey's Jazz Messengers and Thelonious Monk and considered the fastest tenor player around (this during the rise of John Coltrane). *Johnny Griffin Sextet*, *Way Out!* and *The Little Giant,* some of his best sessions from this period, reveal Griffin and his wrenching tone in all their explosive glory. Part of *A Blowing Session* is a bit long on sound and fury, as Griffin and Coltrane race while Mobley tries to keep up. *The Big Soul Band* attempts commercialism, with Griffin backed by big band and strings. A Billie Holiday tribute, *White Gardenia,* shows off Griffin's strengths as a ballad player.

For three years, beginning in 1960, Griffin led a quintet with fellow tenor Eddie "Lockjaw" Davis, and the pair turned out consistently gritty battles. All of their recordings are exciting but plagued by watery piano solos from the likes of Junior Mance. *Tough Tenor Favorites* is all that's available on CD now, but the live releases from this group are worth watching out for.

Like his friend Dexter Gordon, Griffin spent more than a decade in Europe before beginning to divide his time between continents. *The Man I Love* is a live effort from his European period. Unlike Gordon, however, Griffin has not seen his fire tempered by age. Rather, Griffin has learned to effectively use his past frenzy as part of an expanded arsenal that has made him more commanding in other areas, such as ballad playing.

Return of the Griffin, the first of his back-in-the-U.S.A. sessions, captures his then-current range with an excellent quartet. The unavailable 1978 recording *Bush Dance* is also recommended. Griffin has continued to be a vibrant performer well into the 1990s; his albums demonstrate the consistent quality of his playing. — B.B.

GROOVE COLLECTIVE

★★★½ **Groove Collective (Giant Step/Reprise, 1994)**
★½ **We the People (Giant Step/Impulse!, 1996)**

New York's Groove Collective emerged from the downtown scene known as Giant Step, a nomadic acid-jazz dance party. The collective began loosely in 1990—in a manner that reflects the band's hybrid sound—with all types of players adding a myriad of musical elements. Founding members flautist Richard Worth, DJ Smash and rapper/MC Nappy G quickly attracted a bassist, keyboardist and drummer; as the size of the band increased, so did its following. A pivotal addition was vibes man Bill Ware, whose background in more traditional jazz led him to add similar players to the mix. Groove Collective, like the city that conceived it, is a true melting pot of styles.

Recorded in one night with Steely Dan producer Gary Katz, the group's debut captures the band's live sound, successfully translating its loose improvisational style to record. With 10 musicians and as many tracks, the songs range from the largely R&B stylings of "Watchugot" to the smooth funk and jazz of "Ms. Grier." In between are any number of other musical styles including Latin, Afro-Cuban beat and rap; however diverse the mix, the album holds together through the quality of the playing and strong jazz riffing epitomized by the track "Rahsaanasong." All the while, Ware's vibes anchor the musical squalls.

We the People lacks the forceful edge of the first recording. Gone is the playful nature of Groove Collective's live performance, and in its place is a much more slickly produced, almost primarily R&B record. The strength of the band's jazz and Latin-tinged playing is almost completely buried by the slow sheen of tracks like "Fly" and "Lift Off," which sound more appropriate for an elevator than for the dance floor. — G.E.

STEFAN GROSSMAN

★★★★ **Guitar Landscapes (Shanachie, 1990)**

★★★½ **Yazoo Basin Boogie (Shanachie, 1991)**

★★★★ **Black Melodies on a Clear Afternoon (Shanachie, 1991)**

★★★★ **Love, Devils and the Blues (Shanachie, 1992)**

★★★½ **Shining Shadows (Shanachie, 1992)**

WITH JOHN RENBOURN

★★★½ **The Three Kingdoms (Shanachie, 1987)**

★★★★ **Snap a Little Owl (Shanachie, 1988)**

★★★½ **Live (Shanachie, 1990)**

A guitar disciple of the late Rev. Gary Davis, Stefan Grossman (b. 1945) has gone on to become one of the world's foremost players and proselytizers of traditional roots music. Grossman got his start in the mid-'60s, releasing his first two solo endeavors, *Aunt Molly's Murray Farm* and *The Gramercy Park Sheik,* in England. Showcasing his burgeoning guitar and arranging skills, these albums were springboards for Grossman, who subsequently made several records for Transatlantic, the first of which was entitled *Yazoo Basin Boogie.* However, the album bearing that name today is a compilation of traditional country blues, rags and originals culled from his Transatlantic stint. Except for one song ("Mississippi Blues #2," which features an overdubbed guitar solo), the album comprises solo guitar tracks, including the ebullient "Buck Dance," inspired by the Gary Davis, Mance Lipscomb and Mississippi John Hurt versions. Also included is Grossman's first original guitar instrumental, the country-blues–inflected "Roberta," which he penned in 1964.

On Grossman's releases with Pentangle alumnus and fellow picker John Renbourn, the playing is uniformly amazing, spotlighting their similar musical sensibilities and marked stylistic differences. While Grossman's playing is rhythmically based, Renbourn's is grounded in melody, making the pair a formidable tandem. *The Three Kingdoms* is its most understated and contemplative album, featuring duets on six tracks, including a somber reading of Thelonious Monk's "'Round Midnight." Another highlight is the labyrinthine, harmonics-laden "Rites of Passage," one of three tracks cowritten by the duo. A compilation of tracks recorded by Renbourn and Grossman for the Kicking Mule label (which Grossman cofounded in the early '70s), *Snap a Little Owl* has an up-tempo sheen that spotlights the duo's eclecticism and improvisational virtuosity. Both musicians perform on 8 of the 13 instrumentals, including the precious "Idaho Potato" and the darkly evocative "The Drifter." *Live,* featuring both duet and solo performances, includes blues, Irish fare and Charles Mingus's "The Shoes of the Fisherman's Wife Are Some Jive Ass Slippers."

Guitar Landscapes contains Grossman's signature tune, the tense, jazzy, country-blues instrumental "Tightrope." Several songs feature Grossman solo, but others (including a beautiful three-part medley called "Under the Volcano") were cowritten with Renbourn, who shows up on this and one other track playing six-string guitar. *Shining Shadows* comprises solely tracks written or arranged by Grossman, while *Love, Devils and the Blues* is also a solo album of blues influenced by Jesse Fuller, Professor Longhair and Blind Lemon Jefferson. *Black Melodies on a Clear Afternoon,* another compilation, reprises tracks recorded from 1972 to '75 for Grossman's Kicking Mule solo albums, featuring songs taken from or inspired by black music in the early 1900s. Here Grossman is occasionally joined by the Blind Blake–esque guitarist Ton Van Bergeyk, who adds punch to Jelly Roll Morton's "King Porter Stomp" and Cow Cow Davenport's "Atlanta Rag." Also included on this 34-track album are versions of well-known compositions like "Bill Bailey," "C.C. Rider" and "Spoonful." — B.R.H.

STEVE GROSSMAN

★★★½ **Some Shapes to Come (1974; One Way, 1994)**

★★★ **Standards (DIW, 1985)**

★★★★ **Way Out East, Vol. 1 (1985; Red, 1993)**

★★★½ **Love Is the Thing (1986; Red, 1995)**
★★★★ **Way Out East, Vol. 2 (1988; Red, 1993)**
★★★ **Katonah (DIW, 1989)**
★★★ **My Second Prime (Red, 1991)**
★★★★ **Do It (Dreyfus, 1991)**
★★★★½ **In New York (Dreyfus, 1993)**
★★★★ **Time to Smile (Dreyfus, 1994)**
★★★★ **Bouncing with Mr. A.T. (Dreyfus, 1996)**

Brooklyn native Steve Grossman (b. 1951) is a self-taught tenor/soprano saxophonist with a high-energy tenor style influenced by John Coltrane and Sonny Rollins. He was a sensation in Miles Davis's 1969–70 group, playing relentlessly on the hard-edged *A Tribute to Jack Johnson, At the Fillmore* and *Live-Evil.* He later worked with Elvin Jones and Lonnie Liston Smith before forming an experimental cooperative with Gene Perla and Don Alias in the mid-'70s.

Grossman's frenetic, spiritually driven style is well represented on his records. The solid *Some Shapes to Come* includes fine keyboard work from ex–Mahavishnu Orchestra member Jan Hammer (see also the out-of-print *Terra Firma*). *Way Out East, Vols. 1* and *2,* explosive trio sessions, feature bassist Juni Booth and drummer Joe Chambers. *Love Is the Thing* is a good quartet date with pianist Cedar Walton, bassist David Williams and drummer Billy Higgins.

Grossman's recent work for Dreyfus is exemplary, particularly on the magnificent *In New York,* which pits him against pianist McCoy Tyner, bassist Avery Sharpe and drummer Art Taylor — J.S.

GIGI GRYCE

★★★★ **When Farmer Met Gryce (with Art Farmer) (1955; Original Jazz Classics, N.A.)**
★★★★ **Gigi Gryce and the Jazz Lab Quintet (1957; Original Jazz Classics, 1991)**
★★★ **The Hap'nin's (1960; Original Jazz Classics, 1995)**
★★★ **Saying Somethin'! (1960; Original Jazz Classics, 1994)**
★★★★ **The Rat Race Blues (1960; Original Jazz Classics, 1991)**
★★★★ **Nica's Tempo (Savoy, 1991)**

Alto saxophonist/flautist Gigi Gryce (né Basheer Quism, 1927–1983) was an exceptionally gifted player who managed to evolve a blues-based personal style during the Charlie Parker era without being swamped by Parker's conception. Classically trained at the Boston Conservatory and in France under a Fulbright scholarship, he was in high demand as a composer and arranger.

In the early 1950s Gryce was based in New York, playing with Max Roach and Howard McGhee before joining the Lionel Hampton orchestra. By the decade's end, he was performing with the Jazz Lab Quintet, which he put together with trumpeter Donald Byrd. *Gigi Gryce and the Jazz Lab Quintet* features Byrd and drummer Art Taylor.

The Hap'nin's and *Saying Somethin'!* are quintet dates with drummer Granville "Mickey" Roker. *The Rat Race Blues* shows Gryce at his best, on a quintet date with outstanding performances from trumpeter Richard Williams and Roker once again at the drum kit. A star-studded session, *Nica's Tempo* features large-band arrangements and four tunes by a quartet of Thelonious Monk on piano, Gryce on alto, Percy Heath on bass and Art Blakey on drums. Trumpeter Art Farmer, baritone saxophonist Cecil Payne, pianist Horace Silver, bassist Oscar Pettiford and drummers Kenny Clarke and Blakey participate in the large-band session. — J.S.

VINCE GUARALDI

★★★ **Vince Guaraldi Trio (1956; Original Jazz Classics, 1987)**
★★★ **A Flower Is a Lovesome Thing (1957; Original Jazz Classics, N.A.)**
★★★ **Jazz Impressions (1962; Original Jazz Classics, N.A.)**
★★★★ **Jazz Impressions of "Black Orpheus" (1965; Original Jazz Classics, 1990)**
★★★★ **The Latin Side of Vince Guaraldi (1965; Original Jazz Classics, 1996)**
★★★½ **"In Person" (1965; Original Jazz Classics, 1997)**
★★★★ **A Charlie Brown Christmas (1965; Fantasy, 1988)**
★★★ **A Boy Named Charlie Brown (1969; Fantasy, 1989)**
★★★★ **Greatest Hits (1980; Fantasy, 1989)**

Along with Bill Evans and Ramsey Lewis, the late Vince Guaraldi (1928–1976) helped define a school of jazz piano that emphasized melodic improvisation and a heightened concern for the lyric line. He was less an innovator than an explorer rooting around in pop songs for some new way to express a human emotion. His records are distinguished not only by impeccable choices of material—including his own impressionistic compositions—but also by easy conversation among the various instruments (he most often worked with a trio). Although not highly regarded by jazz critics, Guaraldi suffered no such indignities among his peers. His lyricism and graceful, swinging style—honed during his years with the Woody Herman and Cal Tjader groups—were well suited to exotica, and throughout his career he was associated with and championed gifted and important artists such as Mongo Santamaria and Bola Sete. He appears with Tjader on one key cut of Santamaria's *Afro Roots* album and recorded two acclaimed albums with Sete.

Two events brought Guaraldi's music out of the jazz world into the popular marketplace. One was the Top-40 charting of his self-penned single "Cast Your Fate to the Wind," an instrumental suffused with haunting melancholy that became a hit in 1963 (and was also a regional hit in an orchestral cover version by the Sounds Orchestra); the other was his scoring for several Charlie Brown TV specials. These latter provided the sympathetic underpinning to the *Peanuts* characters' endless quest for truth and meaning in everyday life and played easy on the ears but were challenging in their ever-changing emotional colors. None was more perfectly conceived than the score for *A Charlie Brown Christmas,* a collection of sweet (but not cloying) melodies, seductive rhythms and reflective moods that captured the spirit of the holiday season about as well as any artist ever has on record (Dickens might say Guaraldi knew how to keep Christmas well, if any man alive possessed the knowledge).

At the time of his death in 1976, Guaraldi was far better known to the general public for his Charlie Brown scores than for any of the estimable work he had done in the '50s and early '60s. It's out there for the sampling, and what a window it provides into an unusual artist's world. The stirring *Jazz Impressions of "Black Orpheus"* features four tracks from the score of the film *Black Orpheus* that bring Guaraldi back to his twin interests of American jazz and Latin music and the African influence shared by both. This album also marks the first appearance on record of "Cast Your Fate to the Wind" and includes as well a heartbreaking rendition of Henry Mancini/Johnny Mercer's "Moon River." *The Latin Side of Vince Guaraldi* melds the artist's taste for unusual textures with his impeccable ear for ingratiating—and ofttimes haunting—melodies. Lush, penetrating treatments of Henry Mancini's "Mr. Lucky" theme and "What Kind of Fool Am I?" open the album. Beautiful songs both, each one is made more compelling by the addition of subtle conga and timbale interplay with the basic Guaraldi quartet. A gentle, swaying bossa nova treatment of "Corcovado" is given added plushness by an understated string quartet playing straight, classical-style counterpoint to Guaraldi's nimble right-hand excursions into hidden corners of the unforgettable melody line. The bright, bossa nova bounce of "Star Song" and the sumptuous but introspective "Whirlpool," both Guaraldi originals rife with soaring emotions, sound like the blueprints for the original Charlie Brown score Guaraldi composed the same year this album was originally released.

For sheer lyricism, Guaraldi is at his peak on *A Flower Is a Lovesome Thing.* In addition to Billy Strayhorn's beautiful title song, Guaraldi also assays a Gershwin tune ("Looking for a Boy"), Bobby Troup's "Lonely Girl," Romberg Hammerstein's "Softly, As in a Morning Sunrise" and "Willow Weep for Me," in addition to offering a fine tune of his own, "Like a Mighty Rose." The out-of-print *Live at El Matador,* one of two albums he made with Bola Sete, is essential listening for anyone interested not only in the legendary Brazilian guitarist but also in the inspired interplay of ideas from disparate cultures. The reissued *"In Person"* restores to print a scintillating live performance, heavy on Brazilian rhythms, recorded in Sausalito, California, in 1962, with Guaraldi's trio supplemented by guitarist Eddie Duran and percussionist Benny Velarde. These tight, lyrical instrumental ruminations and reconsiderations showcase Guaraldi's deft assimilation of folk and pop song styles indigenous to the Americas, North and South; moreover, the inspired instrumental interplay on numbers such as Oscar Castro-Neves's "Chora Tua Tristeza" and Antonio Carlos Jobim's "Outra Vez" anticipates the inventive, heartfelt dialogs he would soon strike up with Bola Sete.

Greatest Hits guides the listener around Guaraldi's palette, which includes standards, movie themes, a couple of the *Black Orpheus* tracks, "Cast Your Fate to the Wind" and Charlie Brown music. — D.M.

GUITAR SHORTY

★★★★ Topsy Turvy (Black Top, 1993)
★★★★ Get Wise to Yourself (Black Top, 1995)

The well-traveled but underrecorded David "Guitar Shorty" Kearney (b. 1939) was a fixture on the legendary New Orleans blues and R&B scene at the Dew Drop Inn. Known for his wild stage antics and fierce playing, the Houston-born, Florida-raised guitarist mastered the T-Bone Walker shuffle and Albert King string bending. He got his nickname as a 14-year-old whiz kid fronting house bands in Florida blues clubs, then played second guitar in the Otis Rush band and worked with R&B acts like Ray Charles and Sam Cooke during the 1950s.

In the '60s he moved to Seattle, where he married Jimi Hendrix's stepsister and subsequently discovered that Hendrix considered him an important influence. During the 1970s and '80s Guitar Shorty lived in Los Angeles and recorded for minor labels. The Black Top releases find him still in top form. *Get Wise to Yourself* mixes fine originals such as the title track and "I'm the Clean Up Man" with a tribute to Albert King on "Born Under a Bad Sign" and a great version of the Willie Mitchell classic "I Don't Know Why." — J.S.

GUITAR SLIM

★★★★ The Things That I Used to Do (1970; Specialty, 1988)
★★★★ The Atco Sessions (Atlantic, 1987)
★★★★★ Sufferin' Mind (Specialty, 1991)

Only 32 when he died, Guitar Slim (né Eddie Jones, 1926–1959) had all the tools: His songwriting was literate, insightful and brutally honest, sparing no one, least of all himself; his singing was a marvel of expressiveness, his rough voice capable of unusual emotional impact whether he was exploring a down-and-dirty blues or working out in an up-tempo groove; his guitar playing was fired by emotion and infallible instincts. On the indisputably great "The Things I Used to Do," from 1953, his piano player was the young Ray Charles; their teaming resulted in a masterpiece of self-recrimination and hinted at Charles's groundbreaking work ahead. "The Things I Used to Do" spent 14 weeks in the Number One spot on the R&B chart and remains one of the genre's keystones.

Specialty's *Sufferin' Mind* collects the tracks from 1970's *The Things I Used to Do,* adds 13 more and becomes in 26 tracks (cut between 1953 and 1955) an important map in tracing the blues roots of R&B and the R&B roots of rock & roll. In Slim's Specialty work one hears tradition honored and new standards set, especially in the hyperkinetic vocal delivery that would later characterize rock & roll artists such as Little Richard (who owes Slim no small debt) and Jerry Lee Lewis. "The Things I Used to Do," "Story of My Life" and "Sufferin' Mind" paint a picture of a tortured soul doomed to live his life alone.

In 1956 Slim moved to Atlantic subsidiary Atco and recorded extensively in New Orleans and New York until 1958, but the label released only four singles prior to his death. Those, plus the remaining unissued sides, comprise the stunning *Atco Sessions.* Slim's pain is palpable in the gruff shouts and stinging guitar lines on "I Won't Mind at All," and he croons plaintively in "If I Had My Life to Live Over." A remarkable document this, in all respects. — D.M.

BUDDY GUY

★★★½ I Left My Blues in San Francisco (1967; Chess, 1987)
★★ This Is Buddy Guy! (Vanguard, 1968)
★★★★ A Man and the Blues (1969; Vanguard, 1987)
★★★½ I Was Walking Through the Woods (1970; Chess, 1989)
★★★ Buddy and the Juniors (MCA, 1970)
★★★ Hold That Plane (Vanguard, 1972)
★★★ Breaking Out (1980; JSP, 1991)
★★★½ Stone Crazy! (Alligator, 1981)
★★★ DJ Play My Blues (1981; JSP, 1995)
★★★ Buddy Guy (Chess, 1983)
★★★½ Damn Right, I've Got the Blues (Silvertone, 1991)
★★★ The Complete Chess Studio Recordings (Chess, 1992)
★★★★ My Time After a While (Vanguard, 1992)
★★★★★ The Very Best of Buddy Guy (Rhino, 1992)
★★★ Feels Like Rain (Silvertone, 1993)
★★★½ Southern Blues 1957–63 (Paula, 1994)
★★★ Slippin' In (Silvertone, 1994)
★★★½ Live at the Checkerboard Lounge, Chicago, 1979 (JSP, 1995)
★★★ Live: The Real Deal (Silvertone, 1996)
★★★★ Buddy's Blues (Chess, 1997)

WITH JUNIOR WELLS

★★★½ Buddy Guy & Junior Wells Play the Blues (1972; Rhino, 1992)
★★ Live in Montreux (1977; Evidence, 1992)
★★★★ Drinkin' TNT 'n' Smokin' Dynamite (1981; Blind Pig, 1988)
★★★ Alone and Acoustic (1981;

Alligator, 1991)
★★★ **The Original Blues Brothers (Magnum, 1991)**

Buddy Guy's manic, over-the-top guitar playing and singing were prime influences on a host of rock players, notably Jimi Hendrix and Eric Clapton, who experienced his whirlwind energy live in concert. In the studio, however, Chess Records never really allowed Guy (b. George Guy in 1936, in Lettsworth, Louisiana) to be his own, untethered self or to develop as a studio artist, releasing a series of singles and using him as a session musician to back greats like Muddy Waters and Sonny Boy Williamson (Rice Miller). Guy likes to tell the story that Leonard Chess approached him after hearing Hendrix and bent down, put his posterior in the air and said, "Go ahead and kick me. You been trying to sell me this shit for 12 years." By then, Guy had decided to move on to Vanguard Records.

I Left My Blues in San Francisco and *I Was Walking Through the Woods* exemplify Guy's frustrations with Chess: Both albums, while slightly inconsistent, are treasure troves of great tracks cut as early as 1960 but not released as albums until 1967 and 1970, respectively. *Walking* is particularly strong, with Guy performing songs like "First Time I Met the Blues" and "My Time After a While" with an urgent, tightly coiled tension. Both albums are included on *The Complete Chess Studio Recordings,* which is a little too complete for its own good, including out-of-key songs, untuned guitars, dance-pop triflings and other tracks that never should have seen the light of day. *Buddy's Blues* also collects the Chess recordings. Guy's earliest sides—including a two-cut demo he recorded for Chess before leaving his Louisiana home—are collected on *Southern Blues 1957–63,* which illustrates how early his trademark guitar and vocal mannerisms were developed.

Guy finally recorded a proper album with *A Man and the Blues.* Backed by rock-ribbed Chicago vets, including Waters's master pianist Otis Spann, Guy probes the outer reaches of control without going over the edge into histrionics. He takes slow blues like "Sweet Little Angel" and "One Room Country Shack" at a tense simmer, rocks up "Mary Had a Little Lamb" and lets loose on "Just Playing My Axe"—a masterpiece of controlled frenzy. Recorded the same year, the live *This Is Buddy Guy!* is extremely uneven. Better is *Hold That Plane,* an oft-overlooked album featuring an interesting band, including pianist Junior Mance (with whom he also cut *Buddy and the Juniors*). Selections from these three albums, as well as tracks from Guy's backing work with Junior Wells, comprise *My Time After a While.* Rhino's appropriately named *The Very Best of Buddy Guy* collects tracks from every period of Guy's career into an extremely satisfying overview.

Guy was woefully underrecorded throughout the '70s and '80s. *Stone Crazy!* is the sole representative of his work during this era, and though somewhat self-indulgent, it's an adrenaline-fueled, rough-edged gem. As evidenced by the abundance of Guy compilations in recent years, he has experienced a major renaissance this decade. The turning point was *Damn Right, I've Got the Blues,* a fine album on which Guy manages to not be overwhelmed by such guest stars as Jeff Beck, Eric Clapton and Mark Knopfler or the occasionally overbearing arrangement. The more relaxed follow-up, *Feels Like Rain,* is equally good for the most part, except for the ill-considered pairings with Travis Tritt and Paul Rodgers. *Slippin' In* finds Guy settling into a solid groove, with some sparkling interplay between Guy and ex–Chuck Berry keyboardist Johnnie Johnson. *Live: The Real Deal* is a strong, high-energy live set marred by Guy's sometimes annoying guitar tone.

Guy and longtime partner Junior Wells cut several albums as co–front men. *Drinkin' TNT 'n' Smokin' Dynamite* is the best, capturing an excellent 1974 performance, with a band including pianist Pinetop Perkins and Rolling Stones bassist Bill Wyman. *Buddy Guy & Junior Wells Play the Blues,* a recently rediscovered 1970 album coproduced by and featuring Clapton, is somewhat uneven, with the rhythm section occasionally sounding anesthetized, but its best material is very good, indeed. Wells shines on *Live in Montreux,* but Guy's playing is somewhat sloppy throughout. *Alone and Acoustic* is ultimately boring—a tad too low-key—but fans will certainly find it interesting to hear Guy playing unplugged. — A.P.

CHARLIE HADEN

★★★★★ **Liberation Music Orchestra (1970; Impulse!, 1996)**
★★★★ **As Long as There's Music (Artists House, 1976)**
★★★★★ **Closeness (A&M, 1976)**
★★★★ **The Golden Number (A&M, 1977)**
★★ **Magico (ECM, 1979)**
★★★ **Folk Songs (ECM, 1980)**
★★★★ **The Ballad of the Fallen (ECM, 1982)**
★★★½ **Rejoicing (with Billy Higgins and Pat Metheny) (1984; ECM, 1994)**
★★★★½ **Quartet West (Verve, 1987)**
★★★ **Etudes (Soul Note, 1987)**
★★ **Silence (Soul Note, 1988)**
★★★ **In Angel City (Verve, 1988)**
★★★★ **Montreal Tapes (Verve, 1989)**
★★★ **First Song (Soul Note, 1990)**
★★★ **Dream Keeper (Blue Note, 1990)**
★★★ **Haunted Heart (Verve, 1992)**
★★★ **Always Say Goodbye (Verve, 1993)**
★★★★ **Steal Away (Verve, 1994)**
★★★ **Now Is the Hour (Verve, 1995)**
★★★½ **Night and the City (Verve, 1996)**
★★★★ **Beyond the Missouri Sky (Short Stories) (Verve, 1997)**

Charlie Haden (b. 1937) established a role for the bass in nonchordal improvised music through his startling plucking and strumming technique and his work with Ornette Coleman. He spent most of his career through the early 1980s playing with Coleman and Keith Jarrett, but he also released excellent recordings of his own. His masterpiece, *Liberation Music Orchestra,* is a musical and political statement touching on the Spanish Civil War, Vietnam and the Chicago Democratic convention, with a railing orchestra containing Carla Bley (who arranged), Don Cherry, Gato Barbieri and others. *Closeness,* by contrast, joins the bassist with Jarrett, Coleman, Alice Coltrane and Paul Motian in four stunning duets.

Haden has continued to contrast his remarkable instrumental duets with small-group recordings, including Old and New Dreams (the cooperative quartet of Ornette Coleman alumni) and larger group sessions. *The Golden Number* uses the duet format, this time with Archie Shepp, Hampton Hawes, Cherry and Coleman (on trumpet). Haden's duets with the late pianist Hampton Hawes on *As Long as There's Music* place the bassist in a more traditional musical setting than usual and afford an uncommonly sensitive glimpse of the sadly underrated Hawes.

Haden also recorded (and toured Europe) occasionally with Magico, a trio completed by Norwegian saxophonist Jan Garbarek and Brazilian guitarist/pianist Egberto Gismonti. Unfortunately, *Magico* featured some of the most static and uninvolving music in the ECM catalog, a far cry from any of these musicians' best work. *Folk Songs,* the group's second album, is a better record than *Magico* because the tracks are shorter.

Haden assembled a new edition of the Liberation Music Orchestra, featuring original mainstays Cherry, Bley, tenor saxophonist Dewey Redman, drummer Paul Motian and newcomers such as guitarist Mick Goodrick, to record the emotionally charged *Ballad of the Fallen.*

Haden's next project, *Quartet West,* became his working band, with tenor saxophonist Ernie Watts, New Zealand pianist Alan Broadbent and drummer Billy Higgins. The concept behind this band was to explore 1940s and '50s Los Angeles jazz, particularly in relation to Haden's passion for film noir. Higgins was replaced by drummer Larance Marable for the quartet's recordings *In Angel City*, *Haunted Heart* and *Always Say Goodbye*.

Meanwhile Haden worked with a trio featuring Motian and pianist Geri Allen on *Etudes* and another trio with Motian and pianist Paul Bley on *Montreal Tapes*. The reconvened Liberation Music Orchestra recording *Dream Keeper* was a less successful idea, falling short of the grandeur present in the previous LMO projects.

Haden returned to duet projects with great success, particularly on *Steal Away,* a gospel-influenced exercise with pianist Hank Jones, and *Beyond the Missouri Sky (Short Stories),* with guitarist Pat Metheny. Look for another great duet set, the out-of-print *Time Remembers One Time Once.* Haden's duets with pianist Denny Zeitlin provide one of the finest forums for his resonant, highly emotional conception. The intelligent program also underscores Zeitlin's fondness for the late Bill Evans. — B.B./J.S.

JERRY HAHN

★★★ **Time Changes (Enja, 1995)**

Adept guitarist Jerry Hahn (b. 1940) was one of the brighter lights in fusion's early years. The Midwest native, a graduate of Wichita State University, played with John Handy in the mid-1960s, then joined the Gary Burton Quintet later in the decade before forming his own group, Jerry Hahn Brotherhood. Also a member of Ginger Baker's current band, Hahn has made solo recordings in a variety of contexts over the years, but *Time Changes,* his first outing in two decades, is the only one currently in print. *Moses,* an out-of-print set on Fantasy, is worth looking for. — J.S.

JIM HALL

★★★★ **Where Would I Be? (1971; Original Jazz Classics, 1991)**
★★★ **Alone Together (with Ron Carter) (1972; Original Jazz Classics, 1991)**
★★★★ **Concierto (1975; Columbia, 1997)**
★★★ **Concierto de Aranjuez (1981; Evidence, 1992)**
★★★★ **Circles (Concord Jazz, 1981)**
★★★ **Jim Hall's Three (Concord Jazz, 1986)**
★★★ **These Rooms (Denon, 1988)**
★★★★ **All Across the City (Concord Jazz, 1989)**
★★★★ **Live at Town Hall, Vol. 1 (MusicMasters, 1990)**
★★★★ **Live at Town Hall, Vol. 2 (MusicMasters, 1990)**
★★★ **Subsequently (MusicMasters, 1991)**
★★★½ **Something Special (MusicMasters, 1993)**
★★★★ **Dialogues (Telarc, 1995)**
★★★★ **Textures (Telarc, 1996)**
★★★★ **Panorama: Live at the Village Vanguard (Telarc, 1997)**

Lyrical invention, subtle swing and an uncompromising dedication to jazz mark the understated guitar of Jim Hall (b. 1930), one of the instrument's greatest stylists. The above albums are consistent and never less than engaging.

Where Would I Be? is a quartet date with drummer Airto Moreira; Hall blows with calm assurance on a program heavily weighted with compositions by the guitarist and his wife. *Alone Together* is a live duo set with bassist Ron Carter. Both musicians are masters, but the consistently low-key mood detracts from the polished playing.

Concierto has the distinction of being one of the most substantial records ever cut according to the CTI formula. A stellar band (Carter, Chet Baker, Paul Desmond, Roland Hanna and Steve Gadd) blows politely with Hall on a few tracks, then expands beneficially on arranger Don Sebesky's reworking of "Concierto de Aranjuez."

Concierto de Aranjuez places Hall with the David Matthews orchestra. *Circles*, *Jim Hall's Three* and *These Rooms* are all trio dates, with the latter augmented by Tom Harrell's trumpet on three tracks.

Hall stepped out on the adventurous quartet date *All Across the City,* with Gil Goldstein pushing him along on keyboards. That lineup, with bassist Steve LaSpina and drummer Terry Clarke, also appears on *Live at Town Hall, Vols. 1* and *2,* along with guest guitarists Peter Bernstein, John Scofield, Mick Goodrick and John Abercrombie.

Hall's adventurous side appears once again on *Dialogues,* which pits him against such advanced thinkers as Harrell, Goldstein, tenor saxophonist Joe Lovano and guitarists Bill Frisell and Mike Stern. He returns to his fascination with the Third Stream marriage of jazz and classical music on the beautiful, stately *Textures.* Always at home in a jazz context, Hall treats his fans to a delightful live session from the jazz mecca on *Panorama: Live at the Village Vanguard.* —B.B./J.S.

CHICO HAMILTON

★★★★ **Gongs East (Discovery, 1990)**
★★★★ **The Dealer (Impulse!, 1990)**
★★★★ **Man from Two Worlds (GRP, 1993)**

Drummer Forestorn "Chico" Hamilton (b. 1921) played with Lionel Hampton, Lester Young, Gerry Mulligan's pianoless quartet and Count Basie, while also serving as accompanist to Lena Horne and dubbing film soundtracks like *The Road to Bali.* In 1955 Hamilton began leading his own band, which appeared in films in 1957 (*The Sweet Smell of Success*) and 1959 (*Jazz on a Summer's Day*). The latter group featured the young Eric Dolphy on alto saxophone, flute and bass clarinet. Dolphy also appears on *Gongs East.*

One of the most distinctive drummers of his era, Hamilton thrived on rhythmic versatility and magnificent touch rather than the power approach that was far more popular at the time. Hamilton introduced exciting young players in his bands during the 1960s. *Man from Two Worlds* features one of his most popular lineups, with Charles Lloyd on tenor and alto saxophone and flute and Gabor Szabo on guitar. Hamilton went on to introduce guitarist Larry Coryell to the jazz world on *The Dealer,* which features the Coryell showstopper "Larry of Arabia." — J.S.

SCOTT HAMILTON

★★½ **Bob Wilber and the Scott Hamilton Quintet (1977; Chiaroscuro, 1993)**
★★★ **Scott Hamilton Is a Good Wind Who Is Blowing Us No Ill (1977; Concord Jazz, 1992)**
★★★ **Scott Hamilton, 2 (1978; Concord Jazz, 1994)**
★★★½ **No Bass Hit (1979; Concord Jazz, 1991)**
★★★★ **Tenorshoes (1980; Concord Jazz, 1990)**
★★★ **Tour de Force (with Al Cohn and Buddy Tate) (1982; Concord Jazz, 1990)**
★★ **Close Up (1982; Concord Jazz, 1991)**
★★★ **In Concert (1984; Concord Jazz, 1991)**
★★★ **The Second Set (Concord Jazz, 1985)**
★★★½ **A Sailboat in the Moonlight (Concord Jazz, 1986)**
★★★★ **Soft Lights and Sweet Music (with Gerry Mulligan) (Concord Jazz, 1986)**
★★★★ **Major League (Concord Jazz, 1986)**
★★½ **Uptown (with Maxine Sullivan) (Concord Jazz, 1987)**
★★★ **The Right Time (Concord Jazz, 1987)**
★★★ **A Sound Investment (with Flip Phillips) (Concord Jazz, 1987)**
★★★ **A First (with Ruby Braff) (Concord Jazz, 1988)**
★★★ **It's a Wonderful World (with Charlie Byrd) (Concord Jazz, 1989)**
★★★★★ **Scott Hamilton Plays Ballads (Concord Jazz, 1989)**
★★★ **Radio City (Concord Jazz, 1990)**
★★★★ **At Last (with Gene Harris) (Concord Jazz, 1990)**
★★★ **Race Point (Concord Jazz, 1992)**
★★★★½ **Groovin' High (with Ken Peplowski and Spike Robinson) (Concord Jazz, 1992)**
★★★ **Concord All Stars on Cape Cod (Concord Jazz, 1992)**
★★★★★ **Scott Hamilton with Strings (Concord Jazz, 1993)**
★★★★ **East of the Sun (Concord Jazz, 1993)**
★★★★★ **Organic Duke (Concord Jazz, 1994)**
★★★½ **Live at Brecon Jazz Festival (Concord Jazz, 1995)**
★★★ **My Romance (Concord Jazz, 1996)**
★★★★ **After Hours (Concord Jazz, 1997)**
★★★½ **The Red Door (Concord Jazz, 1998)**

Tenor saxophonist Scott Hamilton (b. 1954) arrived on the New York scene in 1976 from his native Providence, Rhode Island, like a breath of fresh air. With a sound echoing the era of Coleman Hawkins, Ben Webster, Don Byas and Lester Young, the mature-sounding Hamilton wasn't intentionally thumbing his nose at the modernists. He just preferred the swing style and the great songs of the '20s, '30s and '40s. With the encouragement of Roy Eldridge and early partnerships with cornetist Warren Vaché, Hamilton helped spark a much needed swing-jazz revival a full decade before the music world took notice of Wynton Marsalis, yet his contributions in that regard have often been overlooked.

While stretching the seams of swing at every opportunity, Hamilton has also had a lifelong affinity for the blues that electrifies his playing. His slightly shifting style has always been filled with assurance and a conversational melodicism. Since signing with Concord Jazz in 1977, Hamilton has recorded a steady stream of sessions, virtually all of which remain in print. *Scott Hamilton Is a Good Wind Who Is Blowing Us No Ill, Scott Hamilton, 2* and *Tenorshoes* showcase his early poise and maturity, as do pairings with guests Flip Phillips, Maxine Sullivan, Gerry Mulligan, Charlie Byrd and Ruby Braff.

Since 1989, Hamilton has developed into an even more compelling player, often seeking out new contexts for his rich sound. The best include *Scott Hamilton Plays Ballads,* with longtime associates John Bunch, Phil Flanigan, Chris Flory and Chuck Riggs; *Scott Hamilton with Strings,* arranged and conducted by Alan Broadbent; and *Organic Duke,* a quartet session with Mike LeDonne on organ, Dennis Irwin on bass and Riggs on drums. *After Hours* reveals a new, darker edge to Hamilton's melodic tenor. The romance-tinged mix of blues and ballads finds him in the splendid company of pianist Tommy Flanagan, bassist Bob Cranshaw and drummer Lewis Nash. Hamilton more than meets the challenges of a duo project on *The Red Door,* a Zoot Sims tribute with guitarist Bucky Pizzarelli, veteran of a similar 1975 recording with Sims.

Hamilton has also been a mainstay on a large outpouring of Concord Jazz All Star recordings made in California, Japan and on Cape Cod, as well as several Newport Jazz Festival All Stars sessions. — K.F.

JAN HAMMER

★★★ **The Early Years (1974–1977) (Nemporer, 1986)**
★★ **Escape from Television (MCA, 1988)**
★★ **Beyond the Mind's Eye (Miramar, 1992)**
★★★ **Drive (Miramar, 1995)**
★★★★½ **Timeless (with John Abercrombie and Jan Hammer) (ECM, 1994)**

Czech keyboardist Jan Hammer (b. 1948) was classically trained at the Prague Conservatory and went on to pursue jazz studies at the Berklee College of Music. He began his jazz career accompanying Sarah Vaughan but soon moved into the headier realms of fusion as a charter member of the Mahavishnu Orchestra in the early 1970s.

Hammer went on to make the spectacular *Timeless* in 1974 with guitarist John Abercrombie and drummer Jack DeJohnette. On his own, Hammer made a series of heavily conceptualized synthesizer albums for Nemporer, which are anthologized on *The Early Years (1974–1977).*

In the '80s Hammer did soundtrack music for the television series *Miami Vice,* collected on *Escape from Television; Beyond the Mind's Eye* features solo keyboards with vocal backing, and *Drive* joins Hammer with guitarist Jeff Beck and Michael Brecker on trumpet and flügelhorn. — J.S.

JOHN HAMMOND

★★ **John Hammond (1963; Vanguard, 1992)**
★★ **Big City Blues (1964; Vanguard, 1995)**
★★★ **So Many Roads (1965; Vanguard, 1993)**
★★ **Country Blues (1965; Vanguard, 1995)**
★★★½ **I Can Tell (1968; Atlantic, 1992)**
★★½ **John Hammond: Solo (1976; Vanguard, 1992)**
★★½ **Frogs for Snakes (Rounder, 1982)**
★★★ **John Hammond Live (Rounder, 1988)**
★★½ **Nobody but You (Rounder, 1988)**
★★★½ **Got Love If You Want It (Pointblank, 1992)**
★★★½ **Trouble No More (Pointblank, 1994)**
★★★½ **Found True Love (Virgin, 1996)**

Touring relentlessly for more than 30 years, vocalist/guitarist John Hammond (b. 1942) has become an almost archetypal journeyman blues hero—and, as is true of the greats he zealously emulates, he only gets better with age.

Son of recording-industry legend John Hammond Sr., the younger Hammond specializes in very faithful covers of country blues. A powerful, distinctive voice, fine guitar work (with an emphasis on bottleneck) and tasteful song selection characterize his albums. So consistent is his approach that the energetic take on, say, Muddy Water's "Sail On," off *Nobody but You,* or any of the unaccompanied acoustic gems from his '90s releases hardly differ in spirit from his early-'60s renderings of Robert Johnson and Blind Willie McTell. *I Can Tell* (with Robbie Robertson and Bill Wyman) is the best and most electric of his earlier albums still available (look for the out-of-print *Southern Fried,* featuring Duane Allman); *John Hammond Live* kicks, too.

Hammond has continued to attract impressive

guests (John Lee Hooker on *Got Love If You Want It;* Charles Brown on *Trouble No More*), but it's the man's own zest, goodheartedness and understated skill that make his work a dependable delight. —P.E.

LIONEL HAMPTON

★★★½ **Just Jazz (Decca, 1958)**
★★★★ **You Better Know It!!! (1965; Impulse!, 1994)**
★★★ **Where Would I Be? (1971; Original Jazz Classics, 1991)**
★★★ **Lionel Hampton with Dexter Gordon (Who's Who in Jazz, 1977)**
★★★ **Lionel Hampton and Friends: Telarchive (Telarc, 1977)**
★★★★★ **The Complete Lionel Hampton, Vols. 1 & 2 (1985; RCA, 1994)**
★★ **Sentimental Journey (Atlantic, 1986)**
★★★★ **Compact Jazz (Verve, 1987)**
★★★½ **Live at the Metropole Cafe (1960–1961) (Hindsight, 1989)**
★★★ **Mostly Blues (MusicMasters, 1989)**
★★★★★ **Lionel Hampton's Jumpin' Jive (1937–39), Vol. 2 (RCA Bluebird, 1990)**
★★★★ **Flying Home 1942–45 (Decca, 1990)**
★★ **Mostly Ballads (MusicMasters, 1990)**
★★★ **Lionel Hampton and the Golden Men of Jazz—Live at the Blue Note (Telarc, 1991)**
★★ **Just Jazz—Live at the Blue Note (Telarc, 1992)**
★★★★★ **Tempo and Swing (RCA Bluebird, 1992)**
★★★½ **Lionel Hampton and Friends: Rare Recordings, Vol. 1 (Telarc, 1992)**
★★★½ **Vintage Hampton (Telarc, 1993)**
★★★★ **Midnight Sun (Decca, 1993)**
★★★★ **Lionel Hampton and the Just Jazz All Stars (GNP Crescendo, 1993)**
★★★½ **Flying Home (Drive Archive, 1993)**
★★★½ **Reunion at Newport 1967 (RCA Bluebird, 1993)**
★★★★ **Verve Jazz Masters 26 (Verve, 1994)**
★★★ **Good Vibes (Jazz World, 1994)**
★★★ **In Paris (Vogue Disques, 1995)**
★★★ **For the Love of Music (MoJazz, 1995)**
★★★ **Slide Hamp Slide (Drive Archive, 1995)**
★★★★ **Greatest Hits (RCA Victor, 1996)**
★★★★★ **Hamp: The Legendary Decca Recordings (Decca, 1996)**
★★★ **Hamp's Boogie (LaserLight, 1996)**

Vibraphonist, drummer, pianist, vocalist and bandleader Lionel Hampton (b. 1908) has the distinction of fronting the longest-running big band of the 20th Century by virtue of having survived the other leaders whose bands continued on after their deaths. Though he may not have been the very first jazz vibraphonist, he turned the instrument into a virtuosic jazz voice whose influence can be heard in every vibraphonist who came after him.

Hampton was also a consummate entertainer, a singer of limited range who used his interpretive, rhythmic and improvisational skills to tremendously crowd-pleasing effect, making his band a popular attraction and ensuring a string of hits. For an indication of his vocal genius, just listen to the way he sings the pop throwaway "The Object of My Affection" on *The Complete Lionel Hampton, Vols. 1 and 2.*

As a bandleader, Hampton's entertainer instincts caused many critics to undervalue his work, but he was a rhythmic visionary, a strict adherent to the backbeat who loved the propulsive power of twin basses in his band lineup and the fastest, wildest solos. As such, Hampton was a precursor of the post–World War II R&B boom, which in turn set the stage for rock & roll.

Hampton always surrounded himself with terrific players but usually preferred to lead them by the sheer force of his own example rather than by carefully rehearsed arrangements. As a result, some of his studio recordings have an offhand approach that tolerates abrupt tempo shifts and messy ensemble work. The musicians make up for technical glitches by playing with abandon—a swing style that has found a new generation of fans in the late 1990s.

In recent years Hampton's rhythms have tended toward slower, more luxuriant tempos, but his own playing, amazingly, has never lost its emotion even as he devolved into a reflection of his own style. When forced to surrender control of the proceedings to producers looking for jump starts, however, Hampton sometimes found his interests poorly served.

Born in Louisville, Kentucky, Hampton was raised in Birmingham, Wisconsin, and Chicago, then moved to Los Angeles in 1927. He switched from drums to vibes with the Les Hite Orchestra fronted by Louis Armstrong, and made his first recording on that instrument in 1930. He recorded with Benny Goodman in

1936 as part of the legendary quartet with Teddy Wilson and Gene Krupa. By the time he formed his own outfit in 1940, Hampton had already been leading pickup recording dates featuring some of the biggest names in jazz recruited from some of the top bands in the business.

The Complete Lionel Hampton, Lionel Hampton's Jumpin' Jive and *Tempo and Swing* document late-1930s Bluebird sessions with the likes of trumpeters Cootie Williams, Ziggy Elman, Jonah Jones, Harry James, Dizzy Gillespie and Red Allen (and Rex Stewart on cornet); alto saxophonists Johnny Hodges and Benny Carter; tenor saxophonists Coleman Hawkins, Herschel Evans, Chu Berry, Ben Webster and Budd Johnson; bassists John Kirby and Milt Hinton; and drummers Gene Krupa, Cozy Cole, Sonny Greer, Jo Jones, Sid Catlett and Zutty Singleton.

In 1942 Hampton released the epochal hit "Flying Home," with a honking tenor solo played by Illinois Jacquet that changed the course of history by creating the paradigm for the saxophone style of R&B and early rock. The Decca discs document this era of Hampton's work. *Midnight Sun* shows that Hampton was incorporating ideas associated with the bop revolution into his band's book. Hampton appears on only one cut of 1958's *Just Jazz,* playing brilliantly on the ballad "Stardust" as part of a 1947 live recording of four lengthy jams. The rest of Hampton's performance on that 1947 night is included on the incendiary *Lionel Hampton and the Just Jazz All Stars,* which concludes with a wild 11:40-minute version of "Flying Home."

In Paris is a 1953 live jam session, mixing relaxed trios with Billy Mackell on guitar and Monk Montgomery on electric bass and a full rhythm section augmented by a four-piece horn section. *Verve Jazz Masters 26* collects 1953 and '54 small-group recordings with then–whiz-kid pianist Oscar Peterson. More Hampton/Peterson collaborations from '54 and '55 are included on the collection of small-band Hampton recordings on *Compact Jazz.*

You Better Know It!!! is a fine small-group session with the star-studded cast of trumpeter Clark Terry, tenor saxophonist Ben Webster, pianist Hank Jones, bassist Milt Hinton and drummer Osie Johnson. Hampton's big band could still kick it, as *Reunion at Newport 1967* proves.

Mostly Blues, recorded in 1988, edges its follow-up, *Mostly Ballads,* simply because Hampton has such a great feel for the blues. On the *Lionel Hampton and the Golden Men of Jazz* sessions Hampton sounds nostalgic. *For the Love of Music* is a sad stab at smooth jazz. RCA's *Greatest Hits* includes vintage 1939–40 material and several useful recordings from 1956. *Slide Hamp Slide* collects finger-burning 1944 sides and hot 1960s recordings with three lukewarm 1977 tracks. *Lionel Hampton and Friends* and *Vintage Hampton* are recordings from the 1960s and '70s with various all-star lineups. — J.S.

HERBIE HANCOCK

★★★★½ **Takin' Off (1962; Blue Note, 1996)**
★★★ **Inventions and Dimensions (1963; Blue Note, 1988)**
★★★★ **Empyrean Isles (1964; Blue Note, 1990)**
★★★★½ **Maiden Voyage (1965; Blue Note, 1990)**
★★★½ **Speak Like a Child (1968; Blue Note, 1987)**
★★★½ **Headhunters (1972; Columbia, 1997)**
★★★★★ **Sextant (1973; Columbia, 1998)**
★★★ **Thrust (1974; Columbia, 1998)**
★★★★ **Dedication (1974; Columbia, 1997)**
★★★★ **Man-Child (1975; Columbia, 1988)**
★★½ **Death Wish (1975; One Way, 1996)**
★★★ **Secrets (1976; Columbia, 1988)**
★★★★ **V.S.O.P. Quintet (1977; Legacy, 1997)**
★★★★ **The Herbie Hancock Trio (1977; Legacy, 1997)**
★★★½ **Tempest in the Colosseum (1977; Legacy, 1997)**
★★½ **Feets Don't Fail Me Now (1979; Columbia, 1991)**
★★★★ **The Best of Herbie Hancock (1979; Columbia, 1986)**
★★★ **The Piano (1980; Legacy, 1997)**
★★★½ **Greatest Hits (1980; Columbia, 1990)**
★★½ **Monster (1980; Tristar, 1994)**
★★★½ **The Quartet (1981; Columbia, 1991)**
★★ **Lite Me Up (1982; Tristar, 1994)**
★★★★ **Future Shock (Columbia, 1983)**
★★★★½ **Sound-System (Columbia, 1984)**
★★★★ **Perfect Machine (Columbia, 1988)**
★★★★★ **The Best of Herbie Hancock (Blue Note, 1988)**
★★★½ **A Jazz Collection (Columbia, 1991)**
★★★★ **Cantaloupe Island (Blue Note, 1994)**
★★★★½ **Mwandishi: The Complete Warner**

Bros. Recordings (Warner Bros., 1994)

★★ Jammin' with Herbie (Prime Cuts, 1995)
★★★ Dis Is da Drum (Mercury, 1995)
★★★½ New Standard (Verve, 1996)
★★★★ In Concert (with Chick Corea) (Legacy, 1997)
★★★★½ 1 + 1 (with Wayne Shorter) (Verve, 1997)
★★★★ Jazz Profile (Blue Note, 1997)
★★★★½ The Complete '60s Sessions (Blue Note, 1998)
★★★ Gershwin's World (Verve, 1998)
★★★ Return of the Headhunters! (Verve, 1998)
★★★★ This Is Jazz 35 (Legacy, 1998)

Jazz critics tend to see Herbie Hancock (b. 1940) as having a split personality. Put him on piano with an acoustic rhythm section, and he's a jazz classicist, blessed with the same genius that fired the legendary Miles Davis Quintet of the mid-'60s. Surround him with electronic instruments, on the other hand, and he immediately becomes Mr. Sellout, a gadget-obsessed pop wannabe who'll willingly prostitute his talent for a few minutes on the charts.

Needless to say, the truth is somewhat less extreme. For one thing, although Hancock's acoustic work can, indeed, be brilliant, it's also true that his traditional playing has a tendency to rely more on competence than inspiration. Likewise, though some of his electronic albums can push their dance-driven rhythms past the point of monotony, others find him at his most resourceful and creative, and easily rank with the best of his work.

But the bottom line is simply that Hancock has always had an equal fondness for both funk and straight jazz. That much is evident in the sound of *Takin' Off,* his first solo outing. Recorded before he joined the Davis quintet, most of the album is given over to standard-issue hard bop. "Watermelon Man," however, finds Hancock and his session mates playing the sort of funky jazz for which Horace Silver was known (though even Silver rarely got this soulful); it wasn't pop, exactly, but it showed potential.

"Blind Man, Blind Man," from the unavailable *My Point of View,* is in some ways an extension of the "Watermelon Man" groove, and benefits from the inclusion of guitarist Grant Green in the ensemble. But Hancock, no doubt influenced by his association with Davis (whose quintet he joined in 1963), grew more interested in toying with form than playing to a mass audience, and his subsequent sessions for Blue Note are far less pop-friendly. Ironically, one of those recordings, "Cantaloupe Island," became an acid-jazz touchstone in the 1990s in a sampled version by Us3.

That doesn't mean they aren't tuneful: The dreamy "Maiden Voyage," for instance, quickly became something of a jazz standard. But *Inventions and Dimensions* (which was briefly available under the title *Succotash*) proffers loosely structured experiments with Latin rhythms; *Empyrean Isles* and *Maiden Voyage* are Davis-influenced small-group sessions with Freddie Hubbard on trumpet; while *Speak Like a Child* uses a slightly larger ensemble to extend the coloristic possibilities of his music. Blue Note's *The Best of Herbie Hancock* highlights the best of his Blue Note recordings.

Hancock went electric after leaving Blue Note, and his sound changed radically, recalling the rock-influenced sound of Davis's *Bitches Brew* but augmenting it with instrumental arrangements. It wasn't exactly jazz rock and neither was it traditional jazz, yet it captured the strengths of both. The unavailable *Mwandishi* is dark and dreamy, all rolling rhythms and swirling electronics, while the sonic tapestry of the out-of-print *Crossings* conveys an almost otherworldly sense of atmosphere, particularly on the haunting, synth-colored "Quasar." But *Sextant* is the standout, thanks to its richly detailed sound and intricate interplay. *Mwandishi*, *Crossings* and the out-of-print *Fat Albert Rotunda* are collected on *Mwandishi: The Complete Warner Bros. Recordings.*

Those albums may have introduced changes in Hancock's sound, but it was the stripped-down sound of *Headhunters*—or, more accurately, the pop credibility he earned through the success of "Chameleon"—that changed the course of his career. *Headhunters* isn't an R&B album per se, but clearly the die was cast, as each subsequent album got funkier and funkier. *Thrust* plays down the more abstract elements that rounded out *Headhunters,* emphasizing the music's pulse, while *Man-Child* introduced R&B session men to the mix, adding depth to the groove without compromising the improvised content. (These are the albums emphasized in Columbia's *The Best of Herbie Hancock.*)

Yet despite his pop success (*Headhunters*, *Thrust* and *Man-Child* all cracked the Top 40), Hancock wasn't about to divorce himself from jazz. *Secrets* sought to strike a balance between the two, but it was with *V.S.O.P. Quintet,* that Hancock truly tried to turn back the clock. Recorded with his old Davis band mates—Wayne Shorter, Ron Carter and Tony Williams, plus Hubbard on trumpet—it featured much the same sound as the Davis Quintet's classic recordings, though little of their fire or daring. Still, the album went over well enough with jazz traditionalists that Hancock began to live a musical double life, recording acoustic albums (*The Quartet*, *The Herbie Hancock Trio* and *In Concert*) and electric albums simultaneously.

Unfortunately, that separation led Hancock to believe that his nonacoustic albums ought to be more like real R&B sessions. Big mistake: *Monster* and *Lite Me Up* are hopelessly hokey. Mercifully, hip-hop and high technology eventually saved the day. With *Future Shock,* Hancock uses drum machines, digital synths and DJ Grandmixer D.ST. to conjure the sound of the urban jungle, an approach that turned "Rockit" into a club-level hit. *Sound-System* adds a world-beat flavor to the mix, thanks to Hancock's use of Gambian griot Foday Musa Suso, while *Perfect Machine* relies on P-Funk bassist Bootsy Collins and Ohio Player Leroy "Sugarfoot" Bonner for its edge.

Hancock once again failed in a head-on move for the mainstream with the condescending *Dis Is da Drum* and the pop star–pandering *New Standard.* On the latter, he began an association with Verve that led to the adventurous *1 + 1,* a series of duets with Wayne Shorter that the label buried, and *Gershwin's World,* an uncomfortable hitchhike on the composer's centennial bandwagon.

In addition to his solo career, Hancock has also been doing soundtrack work since 1966, when he scored Michelangelo Antonioni's *Blow Up.* His contributions can be heard in films ranging from *Death Wish* to the elegiac *'Round Midnight,* a score that's just as jazz-soaked and moody as the film itself. — J.D.C.

W.C. HANDY

★★★ **W.C. Handy's Memphis Blues Band (Memphis Archives, 1994)**

Regarded as "the Father of the Blues," cornetist, bandleader, composer and arranger William Christopher Handy (1873–1958) was instrumental in documenting the form. In the 1930s he became the first to notate the idiom, thereby bringing it to mass audiences.

As a teenager in Alabama, Handy obtained a rotary-valve cornet from a traveling circus and learned in secret, studying such forms as the polka, the schottische, the mazurka and the york. He headed for Chicago in 1893 and eventually made his way to Henderson, Kentucky, where he joined forces with Mahara's Colored Minstrels and toured the United States and Cuba. Hired by E.H. "Boss" Crump, the Memphis political giant, to play at his campaign rallies in 1909, Handy penned "Mister Crump." The song was later renamed "The Memphis Blues" and became phenomenally popular in 1912. After being swindled out of the rights to "The Memphis Blues," Handy established his own publishing company in Memphis with bank cashier and songwriting partner Harry H. Pace. The duo wrote a barrage of hits, eclipsing the success of "The Memphis Blues" with "St. Louis Blues" and "Yellow Dog Blues," which can be heard on *W.C. Handy's Memphis Blues Band.* As an active member of ASCAP (American Society of Composers, Authors and Publishers) Handy went on to control a successful publishing business and become a great champion of composers' rights.

Despite Handy's prolific output as a composer and countless recordings of his music by such artists as Louis Armstrong, Duke Ellington, Machito, Django Reinhardt and Sun Ra, he left little recorded legacy of his own. For the numbers on *W.C. Handy's Memphis Blues Band,* cut over several sessions for Columbia Records in New York between 1917 and 1923, Handy assembled a 13-piece band including four veterans from his original Memphis band: cellist Henry Graves, tubaist/bassist Archie Walls, clarinetist Nelson Kincaid and xylophonist/drummer Jasper Taylor. Taylor's work is simply outstanding on such numbers as "Fuzzy Wuzzy Rag," "That Jazz Dance" and the stellar "Moonlight Blues." — J.V.P.

ROLAND HANNA

★★★★ **Perugia (Freedom Records, 1974)**
★★★★ **Persia My Dear (DIW, 1987)**
★★★★ **Duke Ellington Piano Solos (MusicMasters, 1991)**
★★★ **Round Midnight (Town Crier, 1993)**
★★★ **Plays Gershwin (LaserLight, 1993)**
★★★★ **Maybeck Recital Hall Series, Vol. 32 (Concord Jazz, 1994)**

Pianist Roland Hanna (b. 1932) possesses a highly romantic style that colors his florid excursions. Because of his prodigious, orchestral approach, Hanna prefers to record solo, and *Perugia*, *Duke Ellington Piano Solos* and *Maybeck Recital Hall Series* are recommended. *Persia My Dear,* a trio date with bassist Richard Davis and drummer Frederick Waits, includes some of Hanna's finest small-group work. — S.F.

KIP HANRAHAN

★★★★½ Desire Develops an Edge (American Clave, 1983)
★★★½ Days and Nights of Blue Luck Inverted (American Clave, 1987)
★★★ Tenderness (American Clave, 1990)
★★★ Exotica (American Clave, 1994)
★★★ All Roads Are Not Enough (American Clave, 1995)
★★★ A Thousand Nights a Night (American Clave, 1997)

Kip Hanrahan (b. 1954) describes himself not as a bandleader or producer but as the musical equivalent of a film director, and odd as that job description might seem, it fits. Like a director, Hanrahan expresses himself not through personal action but by choosing those who will carry each part; also, like a director, Hanrahan uses these other people to bring a distinctly personal vision into being. Music isn't film, however, nor is improvising jazz the same thing as acting from a script, which perhaps explains why Hanrahan's albums seem so tempestuous. *Desire Develops an Edge* is a real stunner, an album that bridges jazz, rock and Caribbean music without seeming to strain; it also boasts one of the best vocal performances Jack Bruce has ever given. *Days and Nights of Blue Luck Inverted* is well-enough cast (particularly on the jazz end) that the performance easily overcomes any weaknesses in the script. — J.D.C.

ROY HARGROVE

★★★ Diamond in the Rough (Novus, 1990)
★★★ Public Eye (Novus, 1991)
★★★ The Vibe (Novus, 1992)
★★★ The Tokyo Sessions (Novus, 1992)
★★★★ Beauty and the Beast (Novus, 1993)
★★★ Of Kindred Souls (Novus, 1993)
★★★★ Live in Concert (Novus, 1993)
★★★ Approaching Standards (Novus, 1994)
★★★ Tenors of Our Time (Verve, 1994)
★★★★ Family (Verve, 1995)
★★★★★ Parker's Mood (Verve, 1995)
★★★★ Habana (Verve, 1997)

One of the young lions of the 1990s, trumpeter Roy Hargrove (b. 1969) has had the dubious pleasure of growing up musically as a high-profile leader. After several years of lighting up the New York jazz scene sitting in with nearly everyone, the 20-year-old Hargrove made his debut as a leader in 1990 with *Diamond in the Rough.*

Separate bands of older and younger players back Hargrove: Charles Fambrough, John Hicks and Al Foster are all of the previous generation, while Antonio Hart, Ralph Peterson Jr., Geoff Keezer and others represent the new breed of jazz traditionalists. *Diamond* offers outstanding playing and clean technique and tone; the compositions by Hargrove and Keezer stand up surprisingly well in the company of Thelonious Monk, Benny Golson and Rodgers and Hammerstein.

Public Eye takes this approach even further, mixing such well-known tunes as "September in the Rain," "What's New" and a storming, high-speed "Crazeology" with high-powered originals like the title track and "Lada." With the sole exception of Billy Higgins, the players on this recording hadn't reached their 30th birthdays, but the byplay of Hargrove and Hart provides the kind of exchange usually associated with seasoned veterans. Not long after, Hargrove and Hart took that interplay to Tokyo, recording with some Japanese contemporaries. *The Tokyo Sessions* takes a clean, crisp approach to a set of standards that run from a Chet Baker–inspired "But Not for Me" to a no-frills "Work Song."

Following that recording, George Wein put together a pride of the young lions headed by Hargrove for the Newport Jazz Festival. You can hear the results on *Jazz Futures,* a swinging octet show with Hart, Marlon Jordan, Tim Warfield, Benny Green, Christian McBride, Mark Whitfield and Carl Allen. A field day for lovers of standards, the recording features these young players laying into the songs of their ancestors—"Stardust," "Blue Moon," "Bewitched, Bothered and Bewildered" and "You Don't Know What Love Is"—with extraordinary verve. Hargrove, Hart and Jordan turn parts of Hargrove's showcase, "Public Eye," into a storm of free improvisation.

With all this work together, Hargrove's dialog with Hart grew even stronger by the time they tracked *The Vibe.* Here the youthful core quintet plays with the more seasoned Frank Lacy, Jack McDuff, David "Fathead" Newman and Branford Marsalis, who don't swing as hard as their counterparts.

Hart's absence (he moved on to a solo career) doesn't much affect the live *Of Kindred Souls.* The band swings fiercely, except on bassist

Rodney Whitaker's languid ballads "Mothered" and "For Rockelle." Hargrove or group members wrote all but two of the tunes, which tend toward tonal introspection, but "Gentle Wind," "The Left Side" and "Homelife Revisited" pack in the postbop fury.

Hargrove moved to Verve in 1994, where the label tried to package the 25-year-old horn player as a veteran (not unreasonable for an artist with half a dozen of his own albums and a vast amount of guest appearances). *Tenors of Our Time* pairs him with veteran saxophonists Joe Henderson, Stanley Turrentine and Johnny Griffin and fellow young stars Joshua Redman and Branford Marsalis. Pianist Cyrus Chestnut stands out, though the soulful "Greens at the Chicken Shack," with Johnny Griffin, and "Soppin' the Biscuit," with Turrentine, also shine.

Family similarly uses several stars with little focus; Wynton Marsalis, David "Fathead" Newman, Christian McBride, Walter Booker, John Hicks and Lewis Nash sit in with parts of Hargrove's working quintet. The album's saving graces are the fiercely bopping "Firm Roots" and the almost eerily introspective Booker/Hargrove duet on "Ethiopia." It's also amusing to guess who's playing what on the Marsalis/Hargrove feature, Fats Navarro's "Nostalgia."

With a drumless trio consisting of Hargrove, McBride and pianist Stephen Scott, the Bird tribute *Parker's Mood* is about as focused a recording as you can get, showing how a decade of seasoning has matured and centered these musicians. A brilliant choice of material, studiously avoiding the obvious, doesn't hurt their cause. All three players handle Parker's rocky terrain with fleet agility, Hargrove assaying Bird's lines on his horn as if they were made for trumpet. The antithesis of nearly everything that precedes it, this collection of jazz masterpieces by a jazz master represents the apex of Hargrove's output.

Habana takes Hargrove 180 degrees from anything he has done previously. The album matches an all-star Afro-Cuban rhythm section, featuring Chucho Valdes on piano, against an impressive horn section of Frank Lacy, Gary Bartz and David Sanchez. Most notably, though, Russell Malone's electric guitar occupies almost as much space as Hargrove's horn. — H.B.

JAMES HARMAN

★★★ **Thank You Baby (Enigma, 1983)**
★★★ **Those Dangerous Gentlemens (Rhino, 1987)**
★★★ **Extra Napkins (Riviera, 1988)**
★★★½ **Strictly Live . . . in '85! (Riviera, 1990)**
★★★★ **Do Not Disturb (Black Top, 1991)**
★★★★ **Two Sides to Every Story (Black Top, 1993)**
★★★★½ **Takin' Chances (Cannonball, 1998)**

James Harman (b. 1946) grew up in Alabama singing gospel and listening to the blues, but he didn't begin playing seriously until moving to Los Angeles in 1972, when he organized a house band to run jam sessions at the Ash Grove. There he learned what it takes to front a blues band while playing behind such veterans as T-Bone Walker, Big Joe Turner and Eddie "Cleanhead" Vinson.

Harman began featuring his own vocals and harp work on record in the 1980s, first with the EP *This Band Won't Behave,* on his own Icepick label, then with his solid, roots-oriented Enigma debut, *Thank You Baby,* the more radio-friendly *Those Dangerous Gentlemens* and the roadhouse-style *Extra Napkins. Strictly Live . . . in '85!* shows that Harman still delivers something special live that the studio sides can't quite capture.

Once he signed with the New Orleans–based Black Top label, however, Harman found his band sound in the studio with the smoking *Do Not Disturb.* Highlights include the title track, "Motel King" and "Icepick's Confessions." *Two Sides to Every Story* is another high-energy outing. Harman switched labels again for *Takin' Chances,* a stunning set with contributions from guitarists Bob Margolin, Junior Watson and Kid Ramos. — J.S.

BILLY HARPER

★★★★ **Jon & Billy (1974; Evidence, 1993)**
★★★★½ **Black Saint (Black Saint, 1975)**
★★★★ **Billy Harper in Europe (Soul Note, 1979)**
★★★ **Destiny Is Yours (SteepleChase, 1994)**
★★★★★ **Somalia (Evidence, 1995)**

Tenor saxophonist Billy Harper (b. 1943) began singing gospel in his native Texas when he was very young and was playing the saxophone by the time he was 14. He performed with marching bands and local jazz and R&B groups before enrolling in the jazz program at North Texas State University.

Harper's Coltrane-esque intensity was immediately noticed when he arrived on the

New York jazz scene in the mid-1960s, and he found work with Gil Evans, Art Blakey, Lee Morgan, Donald Byrd, Max Roach, Elvin Jones and the Thad Jones/Mel Lewis orchestra. Though jobs as a sideman were plentiful, Harper found little work for his own acoustic quintet and eventually concentrated on performing and recording outside the United States despite maintaining a residence in New York.

Jon & Billy, a top-flight set recorded with trumpeter Jon Faddis, includes keyboardist Roland Hanna, bassist George Mraz, drummer Motohiko Hino and kalimbaist Cecil Bridgewater. The historic *Black Saint* was the first release on the label of the same name, with pianist Joe Bonner, trumpeter Virgil Jones, bassist David Friesen and drummer Malcolm Pinson.

Another quintet session, *Billy Harper in Europe* features trumpeter Everett Hollins, pianist Fred Hersch, bassist Louis Spears and drummer Horacee Arnold. *Destiny Is Yours* is one of several hard-to-find and uneven recordings Harper made for the Danish SteepleChase label.

Somalia, a lengthy masterwork that heralded Harper's triumphant return to widespread U.S. attention, plumbs the depth of spirituality in Harper's playing alongside trumpeter Eddie Henderson, pianist Francesca Tanksley, bassist Louie "Mbiki" Spears and drummers Horacee Arnold and Newman Taylor Baker. — J.S.

SLIM HARPO

★★★★ **The Best of Slim Harpo: Scratch My Back (Rhino, 1989)**
★★★★ **Hip Shakin': The Excello Collection (Excello, 1994)**
★★★★ **The Scratch (Excello, 1996)**

The ambitious Slim Harpo (né James Isaac Moore, 1924–1970) made sure all his eggs weren't solely in music's basket. In his late teens, the Lobdell, Louisiana, native worked as a longshoreman in New Orleans, then migrated to Baton Rouge, where he worked as a contractor and, in his later years, ran his own trucking company. At the same time, he pursued his music career; for the better part of his professional life he was affiliated with guitarist Lightnin' Slim, with whom he performed club and concert dates; Slim also sat in on some of Harpo's recording sessions, notably those that produced the 1961 Top 40 hit "Rainin' in My Heart" and the enduring double-entendre classic "Scratch My Back," a Number One R&B single and Top 20 pop single in 1966.

That so many rock artists have covered Harpo's songs (the Rolling Stones, the Kinks, Van Morrison and Them, Dave Edmunds [in Love Sculpture], the Jeff Beck–era Yardbirds, Alex Chilton and the Moody Blues, who took their name from a Harpo track) is unsurprising in light of the evidence: The man had a homegrown, stone-natural feel for the big beat in his blues. That combination conspired to lift him out of obscurity with the aforementioned hit singles. One of life's little pleasures is to get caught up in the smoky ambiance of Harpo's recordings without realizing you're falling victim to an infectious vocal style. With only the slightest twist, his laconic delivery can mutate from playful but devilish one moment ("Baby, Scratch My Back," "I'm a King Bee") to pleading and pain-wracked the next ("Rainin' in My Heart"). One of the most subversive singers ever, Slim Harpo was an original. — D.M.

TOM HARRELL

★★★★ **Moon Alley (Criss Cross, 1986)**
★★★★★ **Stories (Contemporary, 1988)**
★★★★½ **Sail Away (Contemporary, 1989)**
★★★ **Form (Contemporary, 1990)**
★★★½ **Visions (Contemporary, 1991)**
★★★ **Passages (Chesky, 1992)**
★★★★½ **Upswing (Chesky, 1993)**
★★★ **Cape Verde (Mons, 1993)**
★★★★★ **Labyrinth (RCA Victor, 1996)**
★★★★ **The Art of Rhythm (RCA Victor, 1998)**

Without any fuss and fanfare, Tom Harrell (b. 1946), a prolific writer and gifted player, built a reputation among jazz cognoscenti as one of the finest and most melodic trumpet players in modern jazz. That recognition began during his 1973–77 tenure in Horace Silver's band, grew in Mel Lewis's Village Vanguard big band and Charlie Haden's Liberation Music Orchestra and blossomed with the Phil Woods Quintet from 1983 to '89. The encouragement and creative warmth of Woods's band gave Harrell the confidence and perseverence to become a leader in his own right. That tenure also afforded the public the opportunity to better understand the music of Harrell, who has schizophrenia.

Each available recording teams Harrell with some of the best players in jazz, colleagues who are drawn to a writer of postbop standards-in-the-making. His indelible melodies, filled with beauty and depth, are so strong that as a composer he looms as the Horace Silver of the baby boom generation. *Moon Alley* matches him with alto saxophonist Kenny Garrett, pianist

Kenny Barron, bassist Ray Drummond and drummer Ralph Peterson on a session spotlighting some of the leader's fine originals.

Though there are fiery moments, a pensive mood touched with melancholy dominates his best writing on *Stories,* with tenor saxophonist Bob Berg and guitarist John Scofield aboard. Much the same feeling permeates *Sail Away,* with a band that includes Joe Lovano, Dave Liebman, John Abercrombie and James Williams. *Form* teams Harrell with Lovano, pianist Danilo Perez, Haden and drummer Paul Motian. *Visions* is an all-star sampler, consisting of material not included in the three prior recordings.

On *Passages,* Harrell explores his interest in Latin rhythms and the thick horn lines associated with a big band. This sextet session again features Lovano and Perez. *Cape Verde* is one of several recordings Harrell made in a quintet co-led with Swiss saxophonist George Robert, a frequent European collaborator.

Upswing, with Woods and Lovano aboard as special guests, recaptures the fiery energy that marked Harrell's work in Silver's quintet. Harrell takes that momentum one step higher on *Labyrinth,* an extraordinary session showcasing his writing for a larger ensemble. His band here, with Lovano, Don Braden, Kenny Werner, Steve Turre and Billy Hart among the key collaborators, stretches from 5 to 10 members. *The Art of Rhythm* combines his distinctive, gorgeous melodies with a variety of Brazilian, flamenco, swing and Afro-Caribbean rhythms. His band mates include saxophonists Dewey Redman, David Sanchez and Greg Tardy, guitarists Mike Stern and Romero Lubambo and pianist Danilo Perez.

Harrell's emergence as an important jazz composer is also celebrated on a fine trio recording by Finnish drummer Klaus Suonsaari and two other Scandinavian jazz players, bassist Niels-Henning Ørsted Pedersen and pianist Niels Lan Doky. While his horn is not present on the Jazz Alliance session *Suonsaari, Pedersen, Lan Doky Play the Music of Tom Harrell,* Harrell rearranged each tune for the trio. Nine of his finest compositions are included. — K.F.

BARRY HARRIS

★★★ **At the Jazz Workshop (1960; Original Jazz Classics, 1985)**

★★★ **Preminado (1961; Original Jazz Classics, 1990)**

★★★ **Luminescence! (1967; Original Jazz Classics, 1997)**

★★★★ **Maybeck Recital Hall Series, Vol. 12 (Concord Jazz, 1991)**

★★★★ **Confirmation (with Kenny Barron) (Candid, 1992)**

Pianist Barry Harris (b. 1929) is a proselytizer for bebop in its classic state. Although he qualifies as a second-generation bopper (his early recordings date from the mid-'50s), Harris carries on the unadulterated traditions of Charlie Parker and Bud Powell with his elegant and unmannered playing. Replacing Powell's freneticism with easeful lyricism, Harris speaks the music of the late '40s through his own voice. The swinging trio recordings, *At the Jazz Workshop* and *Preminado,* are standouts among Harris's earlier work. Several LP-only Xanadu recordings are excellent examples of Harris's consummate artistry in a straightforward bebop mode.

Confirmation matches Harris with another brilliant pianist, Kenny Barron, for a spirited tête-à-tête. *Maybeck Recital Hall Series* demonstrates Harris's magic as a solo performer. — S.F.

BEAVER HARRIS

★★★★ **In:Sanity (1976; Black Saint, 1996)**

★★★★ **Beautiful Africa (1979; Soul Note, 1994)**

Drummer Beaver Harris (1936–1991) distinguished himself as a sideman with Albert Ayler, Thelonious Monk, Archie Shepp, Sonny Rollins, Dexter Gordon, Gato Barbieri and Roswell Rudd. Harris could play at the highest energy levels, excelling in his support of power saxophonists reaching for the outer limits, but his polyrhythmic sense and overall balance remained astonishingly acute even in the wildest settings.

As one of the leaders of the 360 Degree Music Experience, Harris recorded a number of thoughtful and technically demanding projects that searched for common ground in the rhythms of world music. His work was never courted by the major labels and is unfortunately mostly unavailable. *In:Sanity* is a "live" studio session from 1976 with a large band including steel drums, sitar, Latin percussion and a reed section headlined by Hamiet Bluiett on baritone saxophone, clarinet and flute and Azar Lawrence on tenor. *Beautiful Africa,* featuring Ken McIntyre on bassoon and alto saxophone, is a fascinating piece of program music tracing

Harris's account of the history of jazz from an Afrocentric perspective.

Search out Harris's masterpiece, the out-of-print *From Ragtime to No Time,* one of the most important explorations of the history of jazz rhythms ever recorded. — J.S.

COREY HARRIS

★★★★ **Between Midnight and Day (Alligator, 1995)**
★★★★★ **Fish Ain't Bitin' (Alligator, 1997)**

Guitarist Corey Harris, born in Colorado in 1969, combines a studied interest in the Delta blues masters with a clear understanding of the possibilities offered by world music, experience gleaned from a stay in Cameroon and honed playing the streets of his adopted home, New Orleans. His slide technique is among the most impressive of the young blues musicians recording today.

Harris shows himself to be a virtuosic blues stylist on *Between Midnight and Day,* a debut that balances eclectic originals ("Roots Woman") with classics such as Charley Patton's "Pony Blues." Harris expands his vision on *Fish Ain't Bitin'* to the point where he no longer interprets the Delta blues tradition but lives inside it. His own compositions mesh effortlessly with relaxed versions of classic blues by Blind Lemon Jefferson, Son House, Memphis Minnie and Blind Willie Johnson. His awesome reading of the traditional "Frankie and Johnnie" works as a virtual rite of passage into the realms of blues legend. The addition of trombone and tuba as rhythmic/melodic elements on Harris originals like "High Fever Blues" and the title track is part of New Orleans's exciting contemporary movement fusing the unfettered rhythms of Delta blues with the New Orleans brass-band tradition. —J.S.

EDDIE HARRIS

★★★★½ **The Electrifying Eddie Harris/Plug Me In (1967/1968; Rhino, 1993)**
★★★★ **Swiss Movement (with Les McCann) (1969; Rhino, 1993)**
★★★½ **Live in Berlin (Timeless, 1989)**
★★★★ **The Best of Eddie Harris (Rhino, 1989)**
★★★★ **Artists Choice: The Eddie Harris Anthology (Rhino, 1993)**
★★★ **The In Sound/Mean Greens (Rhino, 1993)**
★★★½ **There Was a Time: Echo of Harlem (Enja, 1993)**
★★★ **Funk Project: Listen Here! (Enja, 1993)**
★★★ **Dancing by a Rainbow (Enja, 1996)**

Though multi-instrumentalist Eddie Harris (1936–1996) first became known to the public through a 1960 ballad hit, a cover of the theme music for the film *Exodus,* his best work was recorded for Atlantic later in his career.

Harris became one of the first jazz musicians to successfully adapt electronic effects to his tenor saxophone with *The Electrifying Eddie Harris,* which featured the space-funk classic "Listen Here" and is now available as a Rhino twofer with another fine set, *Plug Me In.* Harris also collaborated with keyboardist Les McCann on the funk-jazz classic *Swiss Movement* and recorded many more albums for Atlantic, most of which are uneven and out of print. The anthologies collect his bright moments from this era.

Harris's early success proved a curse when he bounced around from one gimmick to the next looking to regain his commercial status and ended up making music that was beneath him. *Live in Berlin* demonstrates that he never lost his ability, just his context, and Harris was set for a modest but decidedly musical comeback in the '90s beginning with the terrific *There Was a Time,* featuring pianist Kenny Barron, bassist Cecil McBee and drummer Ben Riley. — J.S.

WYNONIE HARRIS

★★★★★ **Bloodshot Eyes: The Best of Wynonie Harris (Rhino, 1994)**
★★★★★ **Wynonie Harris 1944–1945 (Classics, 1996)**
★★★★ **Everybody Boogie! (Delmark, 1996)**

Wynonie Harris (1915–1969) was a powerful blues singer whose inventive phrasing and facility with the open-ended lyrics of blues improvisation made him a hot commodity in the 1940s fronting bands led by Johnny Otis, Illinois Jacquet and Lionel Hampton. The versatile Harris could shout the blues like Jimmy Rushing or syncopate it like Louis Jordan. The same qualities led him to a successful solo career in the decade immediately following World War II, beginning with the hit record "Who Threw the Whiskey in the Well?" Harris became a popular solo artist, singing songs loaded with double entendre about whiskey, money and sex.

Unfortunately, Harris is only sporadically represented on CD, but these releases afford a good overview. The Classics set covers his recordings with Lucky Millinder, Otis, Jacquet and others and features the early hits, including "Who Threw the Whiskey in the Well?" *Everybody Boogie!* documents his early days as a blues singer on Apollo Records (1945) backed by jazz players such as Jacquet, Bill Doggett, Charles Mingus and Oscar Pettiford. The title track, "Somebody Changed the Lock on My Door" and "Wynonie's Blues" are standouts.

Bloodshot Eyes covers the period between 1947 and 1955, when Harris recorded his most famous material for King, including "Good Rockin' Tonight," "Bloodshot Eyes" and "All She Wants to Do Is Rock," employing a band that included trumpeters Hot Lips Page and Cat Anderson and providing a discernible bridge between jazz and rock & roll via the blues. Other Harris sides can be heard on import compilations from Ace, Charly and Route 66.
— J.S.

DONALD HARRISON

★★★★½ Nouveau Swing (Impulse!, 1997)

Alto saxophonist Donald Harrison (b. 1960) is the son of Donald Harrison Sr., a major player in the New Orleans Mardi Gras Indian nation. One of the many young New Orleanians who were tutored by New Orleans maestro Ellis Marsalis, the talented junior Harrison continued his studies at the Berklee College of Music and began an impressive recording career as part of Art Blakey and the Jazz Messengers, alongside trumpeter Terence Blanchard, who went on to co-lead a group with Harrison.

Harrison has recorded prolifically as a sideman, but only one of his albums as a leader, *Nouveau Swing,* is currently available. The release gives a good account of Harrison's strengths as an improviser and a groove merchant as he engagingly mixes a variety of Gulf Coast rhythmic patterns, staying closest to home on the hopping second-line march of "Duck's Groove." His *Indian Blues* (Candid, 1992), a five-star classic with his father calling down the Mardi Gras spirits on a set that includes "Cherokee," "Uptown Ruler," "Big Chief" and "Indian Red," needs to be back in print. — J.S.

ANTONIO HART

★★½ For the First Time (Novus, 1991)
★★★ Don't You Know I Care (Novus, 1992)
★★★★ For Cannon and Woody (Novus, 1993)
★★★ It's All Good (Novus, 1995)
★★★★ Here I Stand (Impulse!, 1997)

Compatriate and school chum of Roy Hargrove, Antonio Hart (b. 1969) is one of the young lions of 1990s jazz. His work as the reed voice of Hargrove's early bands and on these records shows this generation's decidedly retro postbop leanings.

For Cannon and Woody, a tribute to Cannonball Adderley and Woody Shaw, is his best solo recording and makes his roots abundantly clear. The playing, especially on the Adderley compositions, tends to lean more heavily on the blues than on his other outings. Hart performs Shaw's "Organ Grinder" with a stellar nonet featuring the likes of Mulgrew Miller, Ray Drummond, Victor Lewis, Craig Handy, Steve Turre and Robin Eubanks. With backup like that, it's little surprise that Hart shines so well.

Here I Stand is Hart's impressive debut for Impulse! fronting a quartet augmented by various guest stars including Robin Eubanks on trombone and Shirley Scott on keyboards.
— H.B.

JOHNNY HARTMAN

★★★ All of Me (1957; Bethlehem, 1993)
★★★★ I Just Dropped by to Say Hello (1963; Impulse!, 1995)
★★★★½ John Coltrane and Johnny Hartman (1963; Impulse!, 1995)
★★★★ The Voice That Is (1964; Impulse!, 1995)
★★★½ Unforgettable (1966; Impulse!, 1995)
★★★ Songs from the Heart (1987; Bethlehem, 1994)
★★★ This One's for Tedi (Audiophile, 1989)
★★★ For Trane (Blue Note, 1995)

Singer Johnny Hartman (1923–1983) had one of the most distinctive voices in jazz, a lush sound perfectly suited to ballads and slow standards. Hartman was able to strike a romantic tone without ever sounding corny and was particularly well cared for at Impulse!.

I Just Dropped by to Say Hello features an all-star cast including tenor-saxophonist Illinois Jacquet, pianist Hank Jones, guitarists Jim Hall and Kenny Burrell, bassist Milt Hinton and drummer Elvin Jones. Hank Jones also appears on *The Voice That Is* and *All of Me*; *Unforgettable* features saxophonist Teddy

Edwards, guitarist Herb Ellis, bassist Ray Brown and drummer Shelly Manne. *For Trane* was recorded live in Tokyo with trumpeter Terumasa Hino guesting. — J.S.

HAMPTON HAWES

★★★ **Piano: East/West (1953; Original Jazz Classics, 1991)**
★★★½ **The Trio, Vol. 1 (1955; Original Jazz Classics, 1987)**
★★★½ **The Trio, Vol. 2 (1956; Original Jazz Classics, 1987)**
★★★½ **Everybody Likes Hampton Hawes/The Trio, Vol. 3 (1956; Original Jazz Classics, 1990)**
★★★★ **All Night Session, Vol. 1 (1956; Original Jazz Classics, 1991)**
★★★½ **All Night Session, Vol. 2 (1957; Original Jazz Classics, 1991)**
★★★½ **All Night Session, Vol. 3 (1958; Original Jazz Classics, 1991)**
★★★★ **For Real! (1958; Original Jazz Classics, 1992)**
★★★ **Four! (1958; Original Jazz Classics, 1988)**
★★★ **The Green Leaves of Summer (1964; Original Jazz Classics, 1990)**
★★★ **Here and Now (1965; Original Jazz Classics, 1991)**
★★★ **The Seance (1966; Original Jazz Classics, 1990)**
★★★ **Blues for Bud (1969; Black Lion, 1990)**
★★★ **Something Special (1976; Contemporary, 1995)**
★★★ **Hampton Hawes at the Piano (1976; Original Jazz Classics, 1996)**
★★★ **I'm All Smiles (Original Jazz Classics, 1994)**

Pianist Hampton Hawes (1928–1977) began his career in the late 1940s gigging around his native Los Angeles with Big Jay McNeely. Hawes's bop-era keyboard style was influenced tremendously by Charlie Parker, with whom Hawes played in Howard McGhee's early-'50s band. Hawes worked with Wardell Gray and Dexter Gordon before being drafted, and when he returned to the scene in 1955 he began recording in earnest.

The *Trio* sets, with bassist Red Mitchell and drummer Chuck Thompson, date from 1955 and 1956 and lead off with the jamming standard "I Got Rhythm" on *Vol. 1.* The *All Night Session* sides, recorded in '56, also include Mitchell, along with drummer Bruz Freeman and guitarist Jim Hall. *Vols. 1* and *2* feature inspired takes of several Dizzy Gillespie tunes ("Groovin' High," "Two Bass Hit," "Blue 'n' Boogie," "Woody 'n' You").

For Real! is a hot '58 session with bassist Scott LaFaro, drummer Frank Butler and tenor saxophonist Harold Land. *The Green Leaves of Summer*, *Here and Now* and *The Seance* are all trio albums from the mid-'60s. Hawes began playing electric as well as acoustic piano during the '70s with very good results, as the unavailable *Playin' in the Yard* indicates. On his last recording, *Hampton Hawes at the Piano,* Hawes returned to the acoustic-trio format he had become known for in the '50s, accompanied by bassist Ray Brown and drummer Shelly Manne.

Hawes was a gifted player who never got the credit he deserved; his soulful blues base kept his music emotionally grounded without being cliché-ridden. His moving autobiography, *Raise Up off Me,* is well worth reading. — J.S.

COLEMAN HAWKINS

★★★ **The Hawk Returns (1954; Savoy, 1993)**
★★★ **Cool Groove (1955; Drive Archive, 1996)**
★★★ **The Hawk in Paris (1956; Bluebird, 1993)**
★★★½ **At the Opera House (1957; Verve, 1994)**
★★★ **The Genius of Coleman Hawkins (1957; Verve, 1986)**
★★★★ **The Hawk Flies High (1957; Original Jazz Classics, 1984)**
★★★★ **Soul (1958; Original Jazz Classics, 1989)**
★★★½ **Coleman Hawkins Meets the Big Sax Section (1958; Savoy, 1994)**
★★★½ **Coleman Hawkins Encounters Ben Webster (1959; Verve, 1988)**
★★★ **The High and Mighty Hawk (1959; London, 1988)**
★★★½ **Hawk Eyes (1959; Original Jazz Classics, 1988)**
★★★ **Bean Stalkin' (1960; Pablo, 1988)**
★★★★ **At Ease with Coleman Hawkins (1960; Original Jazz Classics, 1985)**
★★★½ **Coleman Hawkins All Stars Featuring Joe Thomas and Vic Dickenson (1960; Original Jazz Classics, 1996)**
★★★½ **Coleman Hawkins with the Red Garland Trio (1960; Original Jazz Classics, 1990)**

★★★½ **The Hawk Relaxes (1961; Original Jazz Classics, 1992)**
★★★★ **Night Hawk (with Eddie "Lockjaw" Davis) (1961; Original Jazz Classics, 1990)**
★★★½ **Jam Session in Swingville (with Pee Wee Russell) (1961; Prestige, 1992)**
★★★ **Coleman Hawkins and Confreres (1961; Verve, 1988)**
★★★ **Hawkins! Eldridge! Hodges! Alive! (with Roy Eldridge) (1962; Verve, 1992)**
★★★ **Coleman Hawkins in Concert with Roy Eldridge (1962; BandStand, 1992)**
★★★★★ **Duke Ellington Meets Coleman Hawkins (1962; Impulse!, 1986)**
★★★ **Hawk Talk (1963; Tradition/Rykodisc, 1996)**
★★★ **Wrapped Tight (1965; Impulse!, 1991)**
★★★½ **Sirius (1966; Original Jazz Classics, 1995)**
★★★★½ **Body and Soul (RCA Victor, 1986)**
★★★★ **The Complete Coleman Hawkins (Mercury, 1987)**
★★★ **In a Mellow Tone (Original Jazz Classics, 1988)**
★★★ **The Big Three (with Ben Webster and Lester Young) (Signature, 1989)**
★★★★ **Hollywood Stampede (Capitol, 1989)**
★★★ **Desafinado (Impulse!, 1990)**
★★★ **Masters of Jazz, Vol. 12 (Storyville, 1990)**
★★★★½ **The Indispensable Coleman Hawkins: "Body and Soul" (1927–1956) (RCA Bluebird, 1992)**
★★★★½ **April in Paris (RCA Bluebird, 1992)**
★★★½ **The Hawk in Europe (ASV, 1992)**
★★★★ **Rainbow Mist (Delmark, 1992)**
★★★½ **Bean and the Boys (Prestige, 1993)**
★★★ **Body and Soul Revisited (Decca, 1993)**
★★★½ **Coleman Hawkins in the '50s (GRP, 1993)**
★★★ **Live at the London House, Chicago (Jasmine, 1993)**
★★★ **Song of the Hawk (Pearl, 1994)**
★★★ **Somebody Loves Me (Four Star, 1994)**
★★★½ **Verve Jazz Masters 34 (Verve, 1994)**
★★★ **In Paris (with Johnny Hodges) (Vogue Disques, 1995)**
★★★ **Body and Soul (Topaz Jazz, 1995)**
★★★★ **Coleman Hawkins: A Retrospective (1929–1963) (RCA Bluebird, 1995)**
★★★ **Supreme (Enja, 1995)**
★★★ **Today and Now (Impulse!, 1996)**
★★★ **Passin' It Around (Jazz Hour, 1996)**
★★★ **Solitude (Dove Audio, 1996)**
★★★½ **Greatest Hits (RCA Victor, 1996)**

A contemporary of Louis Armstrong, tenor saxophonist Coleman Hawkins (1904–1969) was strongly influenced by Armstrong's sharp, swingingly rhythmic style during his early days with the Fletcher Henderson band (1924), when Armstrong was also with that outfit. But Hawkins soon developed his own hard-hitting, full-throated style and is widely considered the first tenor soloist of note. He certainly had a lot to do with the tenor sax becoming as popular a jazz instrument as the trumpet. In fact, Hawkins influenced virtually every tenor player after him and carved out a style that would dominate jazz for a decade, until Lester Young popularized a cooler, more relaxed approach.

Hawkins was quickly acknowledged as the world's greatest tenor player during his stint with Henderson, which lasted until 1934 and is best documented on the RCA compilations. After a five-year stay in Europe (see *The Hawk in Europe* and *Song of the Hawk*), he returned to the United States in 1939 and recorded his most famous track, "Body and Soul," introducing an approach for reworking standard ballads that would become the favorite format for the tenor-saxophone showcase. *April in Paris* and the RCA Victor *Body and Soul* offer the best of this work.

A consummate musician with a mind open to experimentation, Hawkins embraced the small-combo bebop era of the '40s when many of his big-band contemporaries disdained it. In almost every context, Hawkins managed to turn convention into a statement of his playing's warm, rich personality. His influence continued on into the jump-blues and R&B eras as well as through Sonny Rollins.

Hawkins's '40s work shows him moving easily between swing and bop formats. *The Complete Coleman Hawkins* collects all of his 1944 recordings for Keynote, including alternate takes, with swing all-stars including saxophonist Don Byas, trumpeters Roy Eldridge and Buck Clayton, trombonist Jack Teagarden, pianists

Teddy Wilson and Earl Hines, bassist Billy Taylor and drummer Cozy Cole.

That same year Hawkins made a series of recordings for Apollo, collected as *Rainbow Mist.* Here he sits in with the Georgie Auld Orchestra, cuts small-group sides as a coleader with saxophonist Ben Webster, who had replaced Hawkins in the Fletcher Henderson band, and leads his own band with bop pioneers Dizzy Gillespie on trumpet and Max Roach on drums.

In 1945 Hawkins returned to California for the first time since the 1920s and recorded *Hollywood Stampede* with his working band—trumpeter Howard McGhee, pianist Sir Charles Thompson, bassist Oscar Pettiford and drummer Denzil Best. *Bean and the Boys,* another bop-era compilation, runs into the late '50s and features Thelonious Monk, Roach, Milt Hinton and Pepper Adams.

The mid-1950s recording *Coleman Hawkins Meets the Big Sax Section* features Count Basie saxophonists Frank Foster and Frank Wess along with Basie-ites Marshall Royal on alto sax and Freddie Green on guitar. Several live recordings from the mid-'50s are currently available: *The Hawk in Paris,* which includes songs lauding the City of Lights but was actually recorded at New York's Webster Hall; *At the Opera House,* a hot session with Eldridge, Lester Young, Stan Getz, J.J. Johnson, John Lewis, Oscar Peterson, Percy Heath and Connie Kay; and *Coleman Hawkins in the '50s,* material from seven Decca sessions recorded between 1951 and 1958 featuring Hawkins in contexts from small groups to an orchestra.

The one overriding characteristic of Hawkins's playing, whether on blues, ballads, swing or bop, is an emotional depth and richness, which when translated through the church would eventually become known as soul. Hawkins's playing was the embodiment of soul, and the contexts that gave him the best outlet for that emotion created some of the high points of his later career.

While Verve and Impulse! were searching for the right context for Hawkins (leading to more fruitful sessions with Webster on *Coleman Hawkins Encounters Ben Webster* and *Coleman Hawkins and Confreres* as well as the *Verve Jazz Masters 34* compilation), Riverside and Prestige were putting him in the nascent soul-jazz context, where Hawkins lived up to his several nicknames with a vengeance. Many of these sides, reissued under the Original Jazz Classics imprint, make up some of Hawkins's best work.

The Hawk Flies High is a well-paced session with trombonist J.J. Johnson and trumpeter Idrees Sulieman matching the relaxed intensity of Hawkins's playing while Jo Jones caresses the beat with brush strokes, Oscar Pettiford executes perfectly counterweighted bass runs and guitarist Barry Galbraith phrases chords like a piano accompanist.

Soul features Hawkins alone on the front line, accompanied by guitarist Kenny Burrell, pianist Ray Bryant, bassist Wendell Marshall and drummer Osie Johnson. Bryant and Johnson return for *Hawk Eyes.* Of the 1960 recordings, *At Ease with Coleman Hawkins* is a relaxed quartet date with pianist Tommy Flanagan augmenting the Marshall/Johnson rhythm section; *Coleman Hawkins All Stars Featuring Joe Thomas and Vic Dickenson* adds Thomas and Dickenson to the same lineup; and the Red Garland Trio set is a more spirited piano-quartet session. *The Hawk Relaxes* features the unusual (for Hawkins) rhythm section of bassist Ron Carter and drummer Andrew Cyrille. *Night Hawk* is a blazing tenor battle between Hawkins and another of his disciples, Eddie "Lockjaw" Davis. *In a Mellow Tone* culls ballads from the Original Jazz Classics recordings.

Hawkins also made several impressive recordings for Pablo in the '60s. *Bean Stalkin'* puts Hawkins in the company of Eldridge, Byas, Jones and Benny Carter, among others. There is hardly a more moving record than *Sirius,* a disc made a few years before Hawkins's death. Even when ill health had enfeebled him, he still managed to express powerful emotion through his saxophone. — J.S.

ERSKINE HAWKINS

★★★★ **Tuxedo Junction (RCA Bluebird, 1992)**

★★★ **1941–1945 (Classics, 1996)**

Trumpeter/bandleader Erskine Hawkins (1914–1993) led a band in his hometown of Birmingham, Alabama, before moving in 1934 to New York, where he became a popular favorite based on his ability to hit high notes à la Louis Armstrong and his band's sense of swing for hot dancing. By the end of the '30s, the Hawkins band was regularly featured at the Savoy Ballroom and had recorded a series of hits for Bluebird, the biggest of which was "Tuxedo Junction." *1941–1945* is highlighted by another of his more popular tunes, "Holiday for Swing." — J.S.

SCREAMIN' JAY HAWKINS

★★★ **Voodoo Jive: The Best of Screamin' Jay Hawkins (Rhino, 1990)**
★★★ **Cow Fingers and Mosquito Pie (Epic/Legacy, 1991)**
★★½ **Live and Crazy (Evidence, 1992)**
★★★ **I Put a Spell on You (Collectables, 1993)**
★★½ **Stone Crazy (Bizarre/Rhino, 1993)**

Although he had only one major hit, the man born Jalacy Hawkins in Cleveland in 1929 and immortalized in the music world as Screamin' Jay Hawkins made his mark by way of a wild-man persona. Carried onstage in a flaming coffin, he would emerge decked out in a suit of the unlikeliest color and pattern, a silk cape flowing down his back, a human skull in one hand. And then he would sing, or rather perform, delivering his repertoire with a full array of shrieks, manic laughter, mock-frightened stutters and general verbal chaos.

Before he began his musical career (playing piano and singing) with the Tiny Grimes Band in 1952, his chief accomplishments had been winning the Golden Gloves championship in 1943 and the Alaska middleweight championship in 1949. After leaving Grimes, he put in a stint with the Leroy Kirkland Band and, in 1954, went on the road with Fats Domino. Opting for a solo career, he got himself on the map in 1956 with "I Put a Spell on You," which still retains its manic luster. The cuts on *Voodoo Jive: The Best of Screamin' Jay Hawkins*, *I Put a Spell on You* and *Cow Fingers and Mosquito Pie* show him to be a marginal R&B singer who was at his best when he didn't really have to sing: "I Put a Spell on You," recorded when Hawkins and his band were drunk, is mostly ominous growls and ghostly laughs. *Voodoo Jive* also includes two of Hawkins's rare recordings done pre-"Spell"—"(She Put the) Wamee (On Me)" and "This Is All"—that find him playing it straight. He might have made a name for himself as an R&B vocalist had he kept to this early path; after "Spell" he seemed in relentless pursuit of the bizarre, which resulted in one other minor hit, Leiber and Stoller's "Alligator Wine," a 1958 single that is fairly unremarkable by the songwriters' standards. Among *Cow Fingers'* oddities are a swinging pop version of Cole Porter's "I Love Paris" that degenerates into some insensitive parodies of other countries' languages and "There's Something Wrong with You," which may be much funnier than Hawkins intended. *I Put a Spell on You* might be considered a companion volume to *Cow Fingers,* with its standards (more Porter; a Latin-tinged "Temptation," with Hawkins doing his best Billy Eckstine impersonation; and a comical reading of "You Made Me Love You" that sounds inspired by Spike Jones), traditional material (a schizoid "Ol' Man River" and a dignified, introspective take on "Swing Low, Sweet Chariot") and curious fare such as "Take Me Back to My Boots and Saddle."

Thanks to well-reviewed appearances in the films *American Hot Wax* (1978) and *Mystery Train* (1989), Hawkins's career has been revived periodically through the years. Age has deepened his voice, and on *Live and Crazy,* recorded in 1988 at the Hotel Meridien Paris Etoile, he sounds remarkably like Big Joe Turner on the swinging cuts ("The Whammy," "Yellow Coat"), as he does on some of the tracks on *Stone Crazy.* In the end, though, Screamin' Jay is unmistakably himself—a colorful, lovable personality and a singer of modest virtues burdened with an unfortunate predilection for undercutting his best vocals with silly sound effects and sophomoric humor. — D.M.

TED HAWKINS

★★★★ **Watch Your Step (1982; Rounder, 1994)**
★★★★ **Happy Hour (1986; Rounder, 1994)**
★★★★★ **The Next Hundred Years (DGC, 1994)**
★★★★½ **Songs from Venice Beach (Evidence, 1995)**

To Ted Hawkins (1936–1995), music was a vehicle for truth, beauty, reflection and redemption. Though he died in the midst of receiving long-overdue public attention, the former street musician's stirring recordings are a vivid reminder of his immense talent. Listening to Hawkins's craft—a blur of folk, R&B, country and soul—one is struck immediately by its simplistic veneer. But like a mirror reflecting its own image, it reveals layers of complexity with repeated listenings. Hawkins's passion reverberates, magnifying the implicit meaning of his lyrics, which betray a lifetime of yearning, ambition, triumph and tragedy. His words are invitations to the intimate recesses of the soul, and his guileless, sand-tattooed vocal delivery makes every image resonate. With this conviction and sensitivity to emotional detail, Hawkins's work is timeless. Its revelatory nature is sometimes bittersweet but always compelling.

Hawkins's professional career began in 1966

with a single issued on Money Records. He went on to record more than a dozen songs for producer Bruce Bromberg (future founder of Hightone Records) in 1971, but these wouldn't be released until years later. In the interim Hawkins established a reputation as a street performer on the boardwalk of Venice Beach, California. When Rounder Records put out Hawkins's early-'70s recordings as *Watch Your Step* in 1982, it only hinted at the infectious edge his songs would later attain. The album contains all originals, including two versions of the title track—one a solo acoustic performance, the other horn-injected and electrified. The soulful "Bring It Home Daddy" sounds as if it could have been recorded by Sam Cooke; the mournfully beautiful ballad "I Gave Up All I Had" features Hawkins's wife, Elizabeth, on vocals.

Again produced by Bromberg (with Dennis Walker), *Happy Hour* finds Hawkins's performances as grainy and impassioned as ever. He's joined by a quartet dubbed "the Angry Old Men" on three songs and the electric blues guitar of Night Train Clemons on two others. Highlights include two terrific covers, the elegiac Steve Gillette/Dave MacKechnie–penned title track and Curtis Mayfield's "Gypsy Woman," on which Hawkins's elastic falsetto provides a striking contrast to his standard guttural evocations. Also notable are "The Constitution," Hawkins's ode to freedom, and "California Song," a quintessentially American tale of a couple's desire to fulfill their own manifest destiny. On the latter, Hawkins is again joined by his wife, whose ragged-but-perfect vocals help establish the song's sad and hopeful tone.

Hawkins's crowning achievement is *The Next Hundred Years,* which introduced the artist to the masses. Concurrently mysterious and confessional, the album is a masterful journey from the heart of Mississippi to the California sea and back again. Every song, from the longing "Green Eyed Girl" to the plain-spoken "Good and the Bad" and "Ladder of Success," is testament to the power of Hawkins's voice and the universal sentiments of his work. Hawkins's only album with high production values and diverse instrumentation (courtesy of a host of renowned session players), *The Next Hundred Years* features lap steel, cello and Hawaiian guitar, all residing neatly in the mix, their timbre providing sharp relief to Hawkins's sandpapery growl. His graceful and convincing interpretations of songs by Jesse Winchester ("Biloxi"); Russ Hull, Mary Shurtz and Michael Pierce ("There Stands the Glass"); and John Fogerty ("Long as I Can See the Light") are peerless.

The posthumously released *Songs from Venice Beach,* culled from some 1985 sessions, was previously available in two volumes in Europe, where it helped establish Hawkins's reputation much earlier than in the States. Uncharacteristically, this release comprises primarily covers and features Hawkins in a solo setting, playing guitar and singing. The one original, "Ladder of Success," stands resoundingly on its own among such classics as "Having a Party," "Somebody Have Mercy," "Just My Imagination," "Too Busy Thinking About My Baby" and "Gypsy Woman."

Tragically, Hawkins was entering the twilight of his life when he was "discovered" by America. Just as *The Next Hundred Years* was achieving critical and commercial success, Hawkins died of a stroke at age 58 (on January 1, 1995). It was a cruel but somehow fitting end for an artist who had endured such sorrow and joy during his life. In the final analysis, Hawkins's own "Big Things" serves as a proper eulogy to a singer whose songs will live on forever: "I've got big things to do/Too soon my life will be through." Too soon, indeed.

— B.R.H.

ROY HAYNES

★★★★½ **We Three (1958; Original Jazz Classics, 1985)**
★★★★½ **Out of the Afternoon (1962; Impulse!, 1996)**
★★★★ **Cracklin' (1963; Original Jazz Classics, 1994)**
★★★★ **True or False (1986; Evidence, 1992)**
★★★★ **When It's Haynes It Roars! (Dreyfus, 1993)**
★★★★ **Homecoming (Evidence, 1994)**
★★★★½ **Te Vou! (Dreyfus, 1994)**
★★★★ **My Shining Hour (Storyville, 1995)**
★★★★ **Just Us (Original Jazz Classics, 1996)**

Roxbury, Massachusetts, native Roy Haynes (b. 1925) is a superb technician and one of the most musically accomplished postwar drummers. Though his style was originally inspired by Jo Jones's playing with Count Basie, Haynes made a name for himself during the bop revolution via its headquarters on 52nd Street in New York.

The list of musicians Haynes played with is a bop-era Who's Who: Charlie Parker, John Lewis, Lester Young, Sonny Rollins, Thelonious Monk, Kai Winding, Phineas Newborn, Miles Davis, Lennie Tristano, George Shearing, Lee Konitz and Sarah Vaughan, to name just a few; he's also played with Ella Fitzgerald, Louis Armstrong and Billie Holiday.

Haynes went on to sub for Elvin Jones in John Coltrane's classic quartet, was part of the historic prefusion Gary Burton Quartet with Larry Coryell and collaborated on Chick Corea's great *Now He Sings, Now He Sobs.* Haynes also led his own group, the Hip Ensemble.

Partly because of his value as a supporting player, Haynes has been a sought-after session star and is thus underrecorded as a leader. As with so many of his contemporaries, Haynes's work is not easy to come by, but the late-1950s/early-1960s New Jazz releases (reissued on Original Jazz Classics) *Cracklin',* with Booker Ervin, and the trio set *We Three,* with pianist Phineas Newborn Jr. and bassist Paul Chambers, as well as *Out of the Afternoon,* with Rahsaan Roland Kirk and Tommy Flanagan, are highly recommended.

Almost 25 years elapsed before the release of *True or False,* a live 1986 recording from Paris with Haynes's group at the time, bassist Ed Howard, tenor saxophonist Ralph Moore and pianist David Kikoski. Haynes remains a vital force on the scene in the 1990s and is well represented by the live 1992 recording at Scullers' Jazz Club, *Homecoming,* and the terrific *Te Vou!* with Kikoski, bassist Christian McBride, guitarist Pat Metheny and alto saxophonist Donald Harrison. In 1994 Haynes was awarded the coveted Danish Jazzpar prize.
— J.S.

KEVIN HAYS

★★★ Seventh Sense (Blue Note, 1994)
★★★½ Go Round (Blue Note, 1995)

New York pianist/composer Kevin Hays (b. 1968) took advantage of his hometown's rich jazz heritage and learned by watching and playing with some of the best in the business. He became a regular at Bradley's and the Knickerbocker (the Greenwich Village piano bars that have served a steady diet of some of the greatest pianists in jazz history) and frequently sat in at trumpeter Ted Curson's after-hours jam sessions at the Blue Note.

Hays worked as a sideman with Nick Brignola, Joshua Redman, Benny Golson, Eddie Henderson, Donald Harrison, Roy Haynes, Joe Henderson and Bob Belden before making his own records as a leader. His acoustic debut, *Seventh Sense,* was well received, but Hays expanded his band's lineup and went in a more adventurous direction on *Go Round,* a rich sonic landscape strongly influenced by Miles Davis's fusion experiments. Hays has gone on to work with Sonny Rollins. — J.S.

JEFF HEALEY BAND

★★★ See the Light (Arista, 1988)
★★★½ Hell to Pay (Arista, 1990)
★★½ Feel This (Arista, 1992)
★★½ Cover to Cover (Arista, 1995)

A gifted, idiosyncratic player, Jeff Healey (b. 1966) not only taught himself blues guitar but developed a lap-based technique giving him astonishing control over his phrasing and vibrato. Not that such virtuosity always translates into memorable music; *See the Light,* for instance, is technically dazzling but too often descends into bar-band theatrics. *Hell to Pay* is more consistent, though the celebrity cameos—like George Harrison's appearance on an overwrought "While My Guitar Gently Weeps"—detract from straight-up rockers like "Something to Hold On To." Ironically, some of Healey's best playing can be found on the soundtrack of an otherwise forgettable Patrick Swayze film called *Road House,* though it's questionable whether hearing Healey's take on "Hoochie Coochie Man" is worth suffering through the tunes Swayze himself sings.
— J.D.C.

THE HEATH BROTHERS

★★★ Passing Thru . . . (Columbia, 1978)
★★★ In Motion (Columbia, 1979)
★★★ Live at the Public Theater (Columbia, 1980)
★★★ Expressions of Life (Columbia, 1981)
★★★★ Brotherly Love (1982; Antilles, 1991)
★★★½ Brothers and Others (1984; Antilles, 1991)
★★★½ As We Were Saying . . . (Concord Jazz, 1997)

This very talented family band—featuring saxophonist and composer Jimmy (b. 1926), bassist Percy (b. 1923) and at times drummer Albert (b. 1935)—has simply never been able to rise to its potential. The ingredients are certainly in place: Jimmy is one of modern jazz's best writers, Percy is a legendary bassist, Stanley Cowell, another good composer, has filled the piano chair from the outset and the other sidemen (guitarist Tony Purrone, drummers Keith Copeland and, after Albert's departure, Akira Tana) have never been less than first-rate. But the Heath Brothers play it safe. They don't take full advantage of Cowell's presence and continually opt for Jimmy's most commercial material. On a few tracks from *Live at the Public Theater* and *Expressions of Life* the group has even allowed Jimmy's son Mtume to insert some truly forgettable funk. Yet these last albums contain moments of comfortable blowing, and Jimmy manages to slip little twists into even his most innocuous pieces. *Passing Thru . . .* was the best of a consistently okay lot until the band's recording career was substantially upgraded in 1982 with *Brotherly Love,* which eschews gimmicks and allows the quintet to open up for its strongest recital yet. *Brothers and Others* continues that healthy trend. *As We Were Saying . . .* reunites the original lineup of the three brothers and Cowell with strong support from Mark Elf on guitar, Slide Hampton on trombone and Jon Faddis on trumpet and flügelhorn. — B.B.

JIMMY HEATH

★★★★½ **Really Big! (1960; Original Jazz Classics, 1992)**
★★★½ **The Thumper (1960; Original Jazz Classics, 1994)**
★★★★ **The Quota (1961; Original Jazz Classics, 1995)**
★★★½ **On the Trail (1964; Original Jazz Classics, 1995)**
★★★★ **Love and Understanding (1973; Xanadu, 1995)**
★★★½ **The Time and the Place (Landmark, 1994)**
★★★½ **You or Me (SteepleChase, 1995)**

Part of the Philadelphia-based Heath family, saxophonist/flautist Jimmy Heath (b. 1926) started playing in the late 1940s with Howard McGhee, then with Dizzy Gillespie, Kenny Dorham, Miles Davis and Gil Evans. Originally an alto player, he was so much under the sway of Charlie Parker's innovations that he was nicknamed "Little Bird" until he switched to tenor. Also known and in demand as a gifted arranger and writer ("C.T.A." and "Gingerbread Boy"), Heath has recorded intermittently while working for Chet Baker, Art Blakey, Davis and Nat Adderley, among others.

From 1959 into the 1960s, Heath made a number of excellent records for Riverside, which have been reissued on the Original Jazz Classics label. *Really Big!* is a large-band set with his brother Percy Heath (the subject of Jimmy's "Big P") on bass and Cannonball and Nat Adderley in the group. He was in top form during the 1970s, both on his own projects (including such gems as the out-of-print *Jimmy* and the vinyl-only *Picture of Heath*) and as the main writer and soloist of the Heath Brothers (with bassist Percy and drummer Albert). The remarkably consistent Heath continues to record high-quality records powered by his distinctive tenor sound. — J.S.

MICHAEL HEDGES

★★½ **Breakfast in the Field (Windham Hill, 1981)**
★★½ **Aerial Boundaries (Windham Hill, 1984)**
★★ **Watching My Life Go By (Windham Hill, 1985)**
★★★ **Live on the Double Planet (Windham Hill, 1987)**
★★★★ **Taproot (Windham Hill, 1990)**
★★★ **The Road to Return (Windham Hill, 1994)**
★★★½ **Oracle (Windham Hill, 1996)**

Perhaps no contemporary guitarist pushed genre boundaries as much as Michael Hedges (1954–1997). Once described as the guy who thinks the guitar is a percussion instrument, Hedges explored the full range of his instrument's possibilities. A master of obscure and oblique tunings, he also possessed astonishing acoustic technique. Tragically, Hedges was killed in a car accident not far from his home in Mendocino County, California, in December 1997.

On his debut, *Breakfast in the Field,* Hedges mostly offers the kind of blandishments the Windham Hill label and producer William Ackerman made famous, despite his genuinely strange trio featuring George Winston (piano) and Michael Manring (fretless bass). Notable exceptions include "The Funky Avocado," which somehow lives up to its name, and "Lenono," a tribute to the martyred Beatle. On that tune, the trio actually gels. *Aerial Boundaries* finds Hedges opening up his artistic vision of the guitar a bit more and exposing some of his roots, but the material sounds tenuous. Its

"Spare Change" explores some electronic treatments of acoustic guitar, and his unique take on Neil Young's "After the Gold Rush" features Manring taking the melody on bass.

Hedges made a semipop move with the vocal album *Watching My Life Go By,* singing his own songs and covering Dylan's "All Along the Watchtower." Hedges has a pleasant-enough voice, but it really doesn't add to his main asset, his startling guitar technique.

Live, standing alone onstage with his acoustic guitars in a variety of bizarre tunings, Hedges always displayed a keen sense of humor. This comes through on *Live on the Double Planet,* which showcases his musical mischief on pop tunes like the Beatles' "Come Together."

Taproot proffers lovely melodies, moody guitar and brilliant playing, not only on his main axe but on piano, whistle and various synthesizers. With all the electronics and studio wizardry, the album still manages to sound as organic as the theme. Mike Moore adds a variety of winds, which work particularly well on the Traffic-esque "Scenes." David Crosby and Graham Nash add sweet harmony backing vocals to his musical setting of e.e. cummings's poem "i carry your heart." This approach carries over to his next album of vocals, *The Road to Return.* More fully realized than *Watching My Life Go By,* it lacks the verve of *Taproot.*
— H.B.

JESSIE MAE HEMPHILL

★★★★ **She-Wolf (1981; Hightone, 1997)**
★★★★ **Feelin' Good (Hightone, 1997)**

Como, Mississippi–native Jessie Mae Hemphill (b. 1934) was a wonder to see live. Keeping the beat with a foot tambourine, she played a mean electric guitar and sang her own personal blues with an eerie mournfulness in her melismatic vocals. Unfortunately, Hemphill had to stop performing in 1993 when she suffered a stroke.

On *She-Wolf,* recorded in 1979–80, she used a second guitarist (the album's producer, musicologist David Evans), drums and a diddley bow—described in the liner notes by Evans as "an instrument of African origin consisting of a horizontal strand of broom wire strung on the side of a house, with two bottles serving as bridges, played by striking the string with a finger while sliding a bottle along its length." The diddley bow's haunting sound completely puts across the melancholy in such numbers as "Take Me Home with You, Baby." Keeping blues traditions alive, Hemphill's evocative material includes her own songs and those taught to her by her musical relatives: Aunt Rosa Lee Hemphill ("Bullyin' Well" and "Honey Bee") and her grandfather ("Crawdad Hole"). Her own "Married Man Blues" captures the feisty spirit of Memphis Minnie. Hemphill gives each song's origins in the notes to *She-Wolf* (the title track was inspired by Howlin' Wolf).

Feelin' Good, also recorded with Evans, won the 1991 W.C. Handy Award for best traditional female blues album. It documents more of Hemphill's Delta-blues-meets-fife-and-drum-band style. — H.G.-W.

JULIUS HEMPHILL

★★★★ **Reflections (1975; Freedom, 1995)**
★★★★ **Raw Materials and Residuals (1977; Black Saint, 1993)**
★★★ **Flat-Out Jump Suite (1980; Black Saint, 1994)**
★★★★ **Julius Hemphill Big Band (Elektra Musician, 1988)**
★★★★ **Fat Man and the Hard Blues (Black Saint, 1991)**
★★★½ **Live from the New Music Cafe (Music and Arts Programs of America, 1992)**
★★★½ **Five Chord Stud (Black Saint, 1994)**

Julius Hemphill (1940–1995) was an important saxophonist from the Midwestern collective movement. Born in Fort Worth, Texas, he was a founding member of St. Louis's Black Artists Group and made some fine independent recordings in the early '70s.

Reflections, a reissue of *'Coon Bid'Ness* (originally released on Hemphill's Mbari label), comprises the lengthy "Hard Blues," recorded in 1972 with Hemphill's St. Louis–based band, and four tracks recorded in 1975 in New York, where Hemphill had become an integral part of the loft-jazz scene. *Dogon A.D.,* a prophetic conjunction of new music and funk also from 1972 with the St. Louis band, including trumpeter Baikida E.J. Carroll, cellist Abdul Wadud and drummer Philip Wilson, is currently unavailable. Hemphill subsequently became the primary compositional force behind the exceptional World Saxophone Quartet.

Even when his improvisation fell short, Hemphill remained a challenging writer and conceptualizer. *Raw Materials and Residuals* features his alto sax (his primary horn) in an excellent trio completed by Wadud and percussionist Don Moye. On *Flat-Out Jump*

Suite Hemphill plays tenor and flute, in front of another fine band with trumpeter Olu Dara, Wadud and drummer Warren Smith. The program is extremely well plotted, but Hemphill's playing isn't particularly inspired. The currently unavailable *Roi Boye and the Gotham Minstrels,* a solo piece with prerecorded tape accompaniment, is simply too much of a good idea that would have functioned better contrasted with some of Hemphill's other pieces.

Julius Hemphill Big Band offers a thorough example of the range of his musical imagination, from the abstractions of "Drunk on God" to the gutbucket blues of "C/Saw" and the vividly programmatic "Bordertown," with its echoes of Charles Mingus and Miles Davis. This awesome lineup consists of Hemphill on alto and soprano saxophones, K. Curtis Lyle's spoken-word vocals, Marty Ehrlich on alto and soprano saxophones and flute, John Purcell and John Stubblefield on soprano and tenor saxophones and flute, J.D. Parran on baritone saxophone and flute, David Hines and Rasul Siddik on trumpet, Vincent Chancey and John Clark on French horn, Frank Lacy on trombone, David Taylor on bass trombone, Jack Wilkins and Bill Frisell on electric guitars, Jerome Harris on bass, Ronnie Burrage on drums and Gordon Gottlieb on percussion.

Hemphill left the World Saxophone Quartet in 1990 and put together the saxophone sextet of Marty Ehrlich, Andrew White, James Carter, Sam Furnace and Carl Grubbs, who burn their way through the excellent *Fat Man and the Hard Blues.* Illness forced Hemphill to quit playing in 1993, but the saxophone sextet of Tim Berne, Ehrlich, Furnace, Carter, White and Fred Ho performs his compositions on *Five Chord Stud.* — B.B./J.S.

EDDIE HENDERSON

★★★½ **Phantoms (SteepleChase, 1994)**
★★★★ **Inspiration (Milestone, 1995)**

Trumpeter/flügelhornist Eddie Henderson (b. 1940) first gained fame as one of the main soloists in Herbie Hancock's early-'70s fusion band, a direct parallel to the innovative electric band Miles Davis put together after dissolving the classic '60s quintet of which Hancock was a member. Henderson went on to make two fusion albums for Capricorn before shifting to Blue Note in the mid-'70s to produce a funkier jazz along the lines of the Donald Byrd recordings of the era. Both the Capricorn and the Blue Note recordings are now out of print.

Like many jazz musicians before him, Henderson became an artistic expatriate, recording for the Danish SteepleChase label. *Inspiration* documents his triumphant return to domestic recording with a powerful quintet featuring vibraphonist Joe Locke, pianist Kevin Hays, bassist Ed Howard and drummer Lewis Nash. — J.S.

FLETCHER HENDERSON

★★★★ **Fletcher Henderson & the Dixie Stompers (1925–1928) (Disques Swing, 1991)**
★★★½ **Under the Harlem Moon (ASV, 1992)**
★★★★★ **The Fletcher Henderson Story: A Study in Frustration (Columbia/Legacy, 1994)**
★★★★ **Tidal Wave (Decca, 1994)**
★★★★ **The Indispensable Fletcher Henderson (RCA Bluebird, 1995)**
★★★★ **The Crown King of Swing (Savoy, 1995)**
★★★ **Live at the Grand Terrace Chicago 1938 (Jazz Unlimited, 1996)**

Innovative bandleader and pianist Fletcher Henderson (1897–1952) was an accomplished science student with a degree from Atlanta University when he arrived in New York in 1920 to pursue a career in chemistry. Discrimination prevented Henderson from finding work in the sciences, so he turned to music—playing with W.C. Handy; as the studio pianist at Black Swan Records; and as the leader of the group backing up singer Ethel Waters.

Henderson began leading his own band in 1923 and became a Broadway sensation the following year, beginning a long run as the featured attraction at Roseland. A true precursor to the swing era, his was the first popular jazz big band, featuring the greatest names in the business: Coleman Hawkins, Louis Armstrong, Benny Carter, Tommy Ladnier, Rex Stewart and Don Redman, who provided many of the groundbreaking arrangements. Later, brother Horace Henderson also contributed arrangements, but Fletcher's arrangements as used by Benny Goodman's orchestra are the underpinnings of the swing-band sound.

The Fletcher Henderson Story, a three-disc set of material recorded for Columbia from 1923 to 1938, best covers this heyday of Henderson's band. *Fletcher Henderson & the Dixie Stompers* collects a series of recordings from 1925 to 1928 made by the Henderson band under a thin pseudonym that did little to disguise the unmistakable presence of stars like Hawkins, Ladnier and Stewart.

The Crown King of Swing, a series of 1931 recordings for the Crown label, was recorded during the band's residence at the famed Harlem nightspot Connie's Inn. Once again, Hawkins blows the roof off on "Tiger Rag," and Stewart plays an exquisite trumpet part on a gorgeous version of Hoagy Carmichael's "Stardust."

Under the Harlem Moon includes material recorded by a band featuring Hawkins and Stewart in the mid-1930s. *Tidal Wave* and *The Indispensable Fletcher Henderson* collect material recorded by the Henderson band for Bluebird between 1927 and 1936; *Indispensable* covers almost all of the releases during this period, including some less-than-wonderful novelty pieces. The band includes such greats as Hawkins, Stewart, Buster Bailey, Benny Morton, Edgar Sampson and John Kirby playing classic arrangements of such warhorses as "I'm Crazy 'Bout My Baby (and My Baby's Crazy 'Bout Me)," "Sugar Foot Stomp," "You Rascal You," "Limehouse Blues," "Tidal Wave" and "Memphis Blues."

Live at the Grand Terrace Chicago 1938 documents a later version of the band far less powerful than it was in its heyday. Too bad some of the earlier lineups weren't preserved like this. In fact, considering Henderson's importance in jazz history, he was woefully underrecorded, and what has been kept poorly represents the band's reputation in live performance and the staggering collective reputation of its personnel. The subtitle of *The Fletcher Henderson Story: A Study in Frustration*—the best Henderson collection—sums up the problem. — J.S.

JOE HENDERSON

★★★★ **In 'n Out (1964; Blue Note, 1994)**
★★★★ **Inner Urge (1964; Blue Note, 1989)**
★★★★ **Mode for Joe (1966; Blue Note, N.A.)**
★★★½ **The Kicker (1967; Original Jazz Classics, 1990)**
★★★½ **Tetragon (1968; Original Jazz Classics, 1995)**
★★★ **Multiple (1973; Original Jazz Classics, 1993)**
★★★ **The Elements (with Alice Coltrane) (1973; Original Jazz Classics, 1996)**
★★★ **Canyon Lady (1973; Original Jazz Classics, 1997)**
★★★ **Relaxin' at Camarillo (1980; Original Jazz Classics, 1993)**
★★★ **Mirror, Mirror (1980; Verve, 1993)**
★★★ **The State of the Tenor (1985; Blue Note, 1994)**
★★★ **Page One (Blue Note, 1988)**
★★★★ **The Best of the Blue Note Years (Blue Note, 1991)**
★★★ **Lush Life: The Music of Billy Strayhorn (Verve, 1992)**
★★★ **So Near, So Far (Musings for Miles) (Verve, 1993)**
★★★ **Four! (with the Wynton Kelly Trio) (Verve, 1994)**
★★★ **The Milestone Years (Milestone, 1994)**
★★★ **Double Rainbow: The Music of Antonio Carlos Jobim (Verve, 1995)**
★★★ **Big Band (Verve, 1996)**
★★★ **Straight, No Chaser (Verve, 1996)**
★★★½ **Ballads and Blues (Blue Note, 1997)**
★★★ **Porgy and Bess (Verve, 1997)**

Joe Henderson (b. 1937) represents the first generation of jazzmen influenced more by John Coltrane and Sonny Rollins than by Charlie Parker. As a young tenorist in the post–*Kind of Blue/Giant Steps* era, Henderson was fully comfortable with modal forms and emulated the big "sheets of sound" blowing style that Coltrane had popularized.

In 'n Out, *Inner Urge* and *Mode for Joe* are long-winded and often lacking in focus but still impressive, if mainly because of the extraordinary company Henderson was keeping—Richard Davis, McCoy Tyner and Elvin Jones were frequent rhythm mates, and Kenny Dorham often filled in as the extra horn. The open-ended themes of the late '60s and '70s encouraged Henderson to squander his energies in excessive and ill-suited projects. The best albums of this period are the most traditional, *Tetragon* and *The Kicker,* with Henderson backed by a tight rhythm section working out on sharp, concisely organized material. Both are collected in *The Milestone Years,* along with other sides as a leader and some important sessions as a sideman.

Henderson showed signs of rebirth in the '80s, continuing in a more orderly vein and surrounding himself with seasoned players—Chick Corea, Ron Carter and Billy Higgins on *Mirror, Mirror;* Richard Davis and Tony

Williams on parts of *Relaxin' at Camarillo.* He continued to pursue a more conservative role in the '90s, returning to familiar themes with programs of music by Billy Strayhorn, Miles Davis, Antonio Carlos Jobim and Thelonious Monk, and a showcase of his New York–based big band. — S.F.

WAYNE HENDERSON

★★★½ **Back to the Groove (Par, 1992)**
★★★½ **Sketches of Life (Par, 1993)**

Trombonist Wayne Henderson (b. 1939) recorded close to 40 albums with the Crusaders before leaving that band in 1977 to produce records and develop his solo recording career. His biggest production credit has been the introduction of saxophonist Ronnie Laws, but Henderson's own disco-influenced outings of the time were quickly forgotten. His 1990s reunion with Crusaders tenor saxophonist Wilton Felder in the Next Crusade band, documented on *Back to the Groove,* was a welcome return to the blues-based strengths of the band's Texas roots. *Sketches of Life* is another album with Next Crusade. — J.S.

JON HENDRICKS

★★★½ **Cloudburst (Enja, 1972)**
★★★ **Love (Muse, 1982)**
★★★★ **Boppin' at the Blue Note (Telarc, 1995)**

Vocalese virtuoso Jon Hendricks (b. 1921) made his reputation with the vocal group Lambert, Hendricks and Ross and that group's magnificent vocal reconstruction of Count Basie standards, *Sing a Song of Basie.* On his own, Hendricks varies his programs away from sheer vocalese, doing some scat singing and band work. The out-of-print *Evolution of the Blues* offers his marvelous account of jazz history. The extraordinary live album *Boppin' at the Blue Note* features all-star backing from trumpeter Wynton Marsalis, trombonist Al Grey, tenor saxophonist Benny Golson and altoist Red Holloway. Marsalis even contributes some of his own scat singing to this joyous event. — J.S.

JIMI HENDRIX

★★★★★ **Are You Experienced? (1967; MCA, 1993)**
★★★★★ **Axis: Bold as Love (1968; MCA, 1993)**
★★★★★ **Electric Ladyland (1968; MCA, 1993)**
★★★★★ **Smash Hits (Reprise, 1969)**
★★★★ **Band of Gypsys (1970; Capitol, 1995)**
★★★★ **Otis Redding/Jimi Hendrix Experience: Historic Performances Recorded at the Monterey International Pop Festival (Reprise, 1970)**
★★★★ **The Cry of Love (Reprise, 1971)**
★★★½ **Rainbow Bridge (Reprise, 1971)**
★★★½ **Hendrix in the West (Reprise, 1972)**
★★★ **War Heroes (Reprise, 1972)**
★★★ **Soundtrack from the Film, Jimi Hendrix (Reprise, 1973)**
★★★ **Crash Landing (Reprise, 1975)**
★★★ **Midnight Lightnin' (Reprise, 1976)**
★★★★ **The Essential Jimi Hendrix, Vol. 1 (Reprise, 1978)**
★★★★ **The Essential Jimi Hendrix, Vol. 2 (Reprise, 1979)**
★★★½ **Nine to the Universe (Reprise, 1980)**
★★★½ **The Jimi Hendrix Concerts (Warner Bros., 1982)**
★★★½ **Band of Gypsys 2 (Capitol, 1986)**
★★★½ **Jimi Plays Monterey (Reprise, 1986)**
★★★½ **Johnny B. Goode (Capitol, 1986)**
★★★★ **Live at Winterland (Rykodisc, 1987)**
★★★★ **Radio One (Rykodisc, 1988)**
★★★½ **Lifelines: The Jimi Hendrix Story (Reprise, 1990)**
★★★★ **Stages 1967–1970 (Reprise, 1991)**
★★★★ **Blues (MCA, 1994)**
★★★½ **Voodoo Soup (MCA, 1995)**

As did Django Reinhardt with the jazz acoustic, Charlie Christian with the jazz electric and Elmore James with bottleneck, Jimi Hendrix (1942–1970) virtually redefined his instrument—the rock electric guitar. Feedback, distortion, wah-wah, tremolo, sustain—the sonic vocabulary of the amplified six-string was never the same after this left-handed wizard expanded it. Even fed without effects, however, directly into his amp, Hendrix's Stratocaster signature—blues-based yet surging into jazz improvisation—was unmistakable: On his softest passages, a superabundance of almost fearsome energy shines through.

More than a monstrous player, though, Hendrix was a psychic force. No one since Elvis Presley had so effectively fused the black and white strains of American music—from his own heritage Hendrix drew upon the earthiness of those blues greats who initially inspired him (Muddy Waters, Elmore James, B.B. King) as well as the experimentalism of jazz and its tendency toward the ethereal; he grooved also on the majestic sweep of classical music—and, in his maturity, he found a wordsmith mentor in Bob Dylan (whose surrealist poetry suggested a parallel to the mind-expanding music that Hendrix, an inventor of psychedelia, perfected). Hendrix's singing, underrated but highly suggestive—and in its emotive depth an apt partner to his playing—hinted, like all fine bluesmen's, at worlds of experience. And underlying the wordplay and the wall of sound was a universal message—of spirit/flesh union, of sensuality and transcendence, of music as emancipation from genre, color lines and the limits, even, of life itself. Jazz rock would have been unthinkable without Hendrix. Contemporary titans—Miles Davis, Gil Evans, Frank Zappa, Pete Townshend—accorded him the deepest respect, and the shadow he cast continues today to lengthen.

The Seattle-born ex-paratrooper began by backing up B.B. King, Little Richard and the Isley Brothers. He hit his stride in England; with bassist Noel Redding (a former lead guitarist whose playing felicitously betrayed its grounding in melody) and jazz-styled drummer Mitch Mitchell, the interracial Jimi Hendrix Experience was launched. After a trailblazing single, a cover of the traditional "Hey Joe," *Are You Experienced?* was the Summer of Love debut, and it comes on like unearthly madness: The psychedelic anthem "Purple Haze," "I Don't Live Today," "Manic Depression" and "Fire" wedded feedback and arrogant dexterity to lyrics sprung from primal wondering, lust and fear.

Axis: Bold as Love plunges deeper. Ballads ("Little Wing") meet twisted blues—the songs blur together, metaphorically implying Hendrix's creative impatience and forecasting his later ventures into jazz expansiveness. With Steve Winwood, Buddy Miles and Jack Casady guest-starring, *Electric Ladyland* is a double-album manifesto—Hendrix flashing unbridled ambition. The chord progressions of "Burning of the Midnight Lamp"—with Jimi on harpsichord and, on guitar, achieving the wonder of a wah-wah pedal employed elegantly—echo Bach; "Crosstown Traffic" catches the Experience thunderously rocking; "All Along the Watchtower" became Hendrix's classic Dylan cover; and with "Voodoo Child (Slight Return)," the songwriter exhumed gris-gris lore to fashion himself as a figure of mock-cosmic luminosity. As if exhausted, then, at having moved heaven and earth, the Experience imploded.

Mitchell held on long enough to join Hendrix and new bassist Billy Cox (an ex-Army buddy of Hendrix's) for an appearance at Newport, but the legendary Woodstock gig (including the fiery "Star Spangled Banner") was performed by an ad hoc ensemble, the Electric Sky Church, and by the time of the live *Band of Gypsys,* the drummer's post had been taken by the bombastic Buddy Miles. For once fronting an all-black band, Hendrix tackled funk. "Machine Gun" and "Message of Love" were Gypsy's fierce highlights, yet while the power trio achieved incendiary force, it lacked melody—and aesthetic richness suffered as a result.

Hendrix died in 1970, choking on vomit following barbiturate and alcohol intoxication, during a period of seeming creative transition. He'd been moving away from rock, returning to blues, delving deeper into funk and studying jazz fusion (he'd planned to record with both Miles Davis and jazz arranger Gil Evans). *The Cry of Love,* however, shows the star, playing with Mitchell and Cox, at his most assured: "Ezy Rider" and "Angel" are the tough and tender faces of the genius at his most winning.

Then a flood of posthumous albums began. Of the live work, *Radio One*, *Live at Winterland,* the Hendrix side of the Otis Redding/Jimi Hendrix Monterey set and the four-CD *Stages 1967–1970,* a concert retrospective, are the most exciting. *Crash Landing* and *Midnight Lightnin'* represent a faintly bizarre bid by Hendrix curator Alan Douglas to boost the legacy—with studio players, he overdubbed tracks atop unreleased late-period originals to come up with "Jimi Does Fusion." The ethics of this strategy remain debatable, but Hendrix sounds great (the Douglas-produced *Nine to the Universe,* a record of the guitarist jamming with jazz organist Larry Young on two tracks, is rawer but sharper). Most of the reissues, rarities and novelty packagings of the canon—their number now tops 200—are fodder for devotees: *Smash Hits* is the tightest best-of; *The Essential Jimi Hendrix, Vols. 1* and *2* are shoddily compiled; *Blues* handily recycles the rootsy highlights; the four-CD *Lifelines* is crammed with standards and alternate takes, but the inclusion of Hendrix interviews is problematic—while interesting, they impede the music's flow. — P.E.

DEBORAH HENSON-CONANT

★★★½ **Round the Corner (1987; Laika/DNA, 1994)**
★★ **On the Rise (GRP, 1989)**
★★★ **Caught in the Act (GRP, 1990)**
★★★½ **Talking Hands (GRP, 1991)**
★★★★ **Budapest (1993; DNA, 1995)**
★★½ **Naked Music (Laika/DNA, 1994)**
★★★½ **Just for You (Laika/DNA, 1995)**
★★ **Alter Ego (Golden Cage, 1996)**

Deborah Henson-Conant (b. 1953) has done more than any other player in the past 25 years to bring the harp out of the symphony setting and into the jazz realm. In 1982 the California native was living in Boston and playing background music at a local restaurant when she grew tired of that lonely pursuit and asked the jazz trio in the lounge next door if she could sit in and improvise. The harp world hasn't been the same since, as Henson-Conant opened up the instrument as a jazz vehicle much in the way harpist Andreas Vollenweider attracted legions of New Age followers.

Henson-Conant expanded the harp's vocabulary, playing it with a devilish, no-holds-barred attack. She adds percussive touches and supplements her bluesy playing at times with a fine, dreamy voice. She performs in a variety of settings including solo, trio and occasionally as a featured artist with top orchestras including the Boston Pops and Pittsburgh Symphony Pops. *Round the Corner,* her earliest available recording, was reissued on CD in 1994 and will hold the most interest for jazz fans because of its jazz-standards repertoire.

When she affiliated herself with GRP, Henson-Conant's recordings took on a decidedly contemporary/pop flavor. Special EFX coleaders Chieli Minucci (guitar) and George Jinda (percussion) became frequent recording partners, adding lush and exotic shadings, percussion and rhythms to her extensive original material.

Budapest, recorded with Minucci, Jinda, bassist Victor Bailey and saxophonist Mark Johnson, boasts a solid concept and cohesive playing. *Naked Music* features Henson-Conant alone on harp and vocals. A live trio set in Germany in 1994, *Just for You,* is unmatched in its intensity and its range of original material, with "Baroque Flamenco" and "Danger Zone" as highlights. *Alter Ego* includes less jazz and more vocals as Henson-Conant presents original tunes and new twists on traditional material.

— K.F.

WOODY HERMAN

★★★ **Wildroot (1958; Tradition/Rykodisc, 1996)**
★★★ **The Herd Rides Again (1958; Evidence, 1992)**
★★★ **Herman's Heat and Puente's Beat (1958; Evidence, 1992)**
★★★ **The Raven Speaks (1972; Original Jazz Classics, 1991)**
★★½ **Thundering Herd (1974; Original Jazz Classics, 1995)**
★★★ **Woody Herman Presents, Vol. 1: A Concord Jam (1980; Concord Jazz, 1990)**
★★★ **Woody Herman Presents, Vol. 2: Four Others (1981; Concord Jazz, 1993)**
★★★ **Feelin' So Blue (1981; Original Jazz Classics, 1997)**
★★½ **World Class (Concord Jazz, 1982)**
★★½ **Live at the Concord Jazz Festival (Concord Jazz, 1982)**
★★★ **Woody Herman Presents, Vol. 3: A Great American Evening (1983; Concord Jazz, 1996)**
★★½ **50th Anniversary Tour (Concord Jazz, 1986)**
★★½ **Woody's Gold Star (Concord Jazz, 1987)**
★★★ **The Best of the Decca Years (MCA, 1988)**
★★★★ **The Thundering Herds 1945–1947 (Columbia, 1988)**
★★★½ **The Third Herd: Early Autumn (Discovery, 1988)**
★★★ **The Best of Woody Herman and His Orchestra (Curb, 1990)**
★★★ **The Best of the Big Bands (Columbia, 1990)**
★★★★ **Blues on Parade (GRP, 1991)**
★★ **Northwest Passage, Vol. 2 (Jass, 1991)**
★★★½ **Early Autumn (RCA Bluebird, 1992)**
★★★ **The Early Woody Herman (Pearl, 1992)**
★★★½ **Live at Peacock Lane Hollywood, January 13, 1958 (Jazz Hour, 1992)**
★★★ **Keeper of the Flame: Complete Capitol Recordings of the Four Brothers (Capitol, 1992)**
★★ **Crown Royal (LaserLight, 1992)**
★★ **Jazz Collector Edition (LaserLight, 1992)**

★★★½ **Woody Herman and Friends/Monterey Jazz Festival (Concord Jazz, 1992)**
★★★½ **Live in Stereo at Marion, June 8, 1957 (Jazz Hour, 1992)**
★★½ **The Best of Woody Herman and His Big Band: The Concord Years (Concord Jazz, 1993)**
★★★ **Blue Flame (LaserLight, 1993)**
★★★ **Caldonia (Four Star, 1994)**
★★★½ **The Essence of Woody Herman (Columbia/Legacy, 1994)**
★★½ **Blowin' Up a Storm (Drive Archive, 1994)**
★★ **Giants of the Big Band Era (Magma, 1994)**
★★★ **Jazz Classics (Aurophon, 1995)**
★★½ **The Fourth Herd/The New World of Woody Herman (Mobile Fidelity, 1995)**
★★½ **At the Woodchopper's Ball (Living Era, 1995)**
★★★ **Verve Jazz Masters 54 (Verve, 1996)**
★★★ **1963 Summer Tour (Jazz Hour, N.A.)**
★★ **Giant Steps (N.A.; Original Jazz Classics, N.A.)**

Clarinetist and big-band leader Woody Herman (1913–1987) recorded scores of albums, which haven't been maintained with any sense of historical urgency or concern for the best material. The in-print recordings primarily consist of frequent repackagings of the best-known "hits" recorded in 1945 and 1946 by the Thundering Herd band. This material runs to Herman's arrangements of pop tunes from the hot "Caldonia" to the saccharine "I've Got the World on a String," often sung by Herman himself.

Herman honed his abilities as an interpreter of pop material in Tom Gerun's and Isham Jones's West Coast bands of the 1930s. By 1936, he had assembled his first group, the Band That Plays the Blues, debuting opposite Count Basie at the Roseland Ballroom. *Blues on Parade* documents the recordings this band made for Decca between 1937 and 1942. This is some of the hottest playing Herman ever presided over, including a rocking version of King Oliver's "Doctor Jazz," the spirited title track and 1939's million-seller "Woodchopper's Ball."

Herman assembled the first of the series of Herds in the early 1940s, updating his sound to stay in touch with the kind of voicings Ellington and Basie were using by including new arrangers like Neal Hefti. The classic Thundering Herd, which included at various times such stalwarts as trumpeter Shorty Rogers, trombonist Bill Harris, tenor saxophonists Flip Phillips, Stan Getz and Zoot Sims, baritone saxophonist Serge Chaloff, pianist Jimmy Rowles, vibist Red Norvo and drummers Dave Tough and Buddy Rich, inspired Igor Stravinsky to write his *Ebony* Concerto and is best represented on *The Thundering Herds 1945–1947.*

That collection ends with the first appearance of the famed "Four Brothers"—saxophonists Getz, Sims, Chaloff and Herbie Steward (later replaced by Al Cohn)—who epitomized the cool fire of the legendary Second Herd, of which very little evidence remains in print. *Keeper of the Flame* covers some of these sessions from 1948 and 1949 and includes saxophonist Gene Ammons. Discovery's *Early Autumn,* from the early 1950s, continues several aspects of the Four Brothers band and features the updated Four Others. Herman's Herds continued a punishing touring and recording schedule through the '50s and are caught in particularly good form on the live recordings *Live at Peacock Lane Hollywood* and *Live in Stereo at Marion.*

Though most of the Herds continued to play the same collection of songs over and over with different instrumentation, there were some good moments. *The Herd Rides Again* is a solid late-'50s recapitulation of the first Herd; its companion piece, *Herman's Heat and Puente's Beat,* culls a select group of players from the big band and places them alongside Tito Puente on timbales and Ray Barretto on congas for a spirited Latin-jazz session.

The Bluebird *Early Autumn* is a live 1976 recording from Carnegie Hall featuring Getz, Sims and Joe Lovano on saxophones. *Woody Herman and Friends/Monterey Jazz Festival* is another highlight, a 1979 set with Getz, Dizzy Gillespie, Woody Shaw and Slide Hampton joining in.

Toward the end of his life Herman made a series of recordings for Concord Jazz that featured some engaging moments. *Woody Herman Presents, Vol. 1: A Concord Jam* includes fine performances from Scott Hamilton on tenor and Dave McKenna on piano. *Woody Herman Presents, Vol. 2: Four Others* brings back Herd veterans Cohn, Phillips and Sal Nistico. —J.S.

FRED HERSCH

★★★ **Sarabande (Sunnyside, 1987)**
★★★½ **Heartsongs (Sunnyside, 1990)**
★★★ **Evanessence (1990; Evidence, 1998)**
★★½ **Forward Motion (Chesky, 1991)**
★★★½ **Red Square Blue (Angel/EMI, 1993)**
★★★★★ **Dancing in the Dark (Chesky, 1993)**
★★★★ **Last Night When We Were Young: The Ballad Album (Classical Action, 1994)**
★★★★½ **Maybeck Recital Hall Series, Vol. 31 (Concord Jazz, 1994)**
★★★½ **The Fred Hersch Trio Plays . . . (Chesky, 1994)**
★★★ **I Never Told You: Fred Hersch Plays Johnny Mandel (Varese Sarabande, 1995)**
★★★★ **Slow Hot Wind (with Janis Siegel) (Varese Sarabande, 1995)**
★★★★★ **Point in Time (Enja, 1995)**
★★★½ **Beautiful Love (with Jay Claton) (Sunnyside, 1995)**
★★★★ **Passion Flower (Nonesuch, 1996)**
★★★ **Thirteen Ways (GM, 1997)**
★★★½ **Thelonious: Fred Hersch Plays Monk (Nonesuch, 1998)**

A stalwart sideman and accompanist for many years, pianist Fred Hersch (b. 1953) emerged in the early 1990s as one of the finest modernists in jazz, extending the harmonic beauty and counterpoint associated with the late Bill Evans.

Arriving in 1977 on the New York jazz scene from his native Cincinnati, he built his credentials in the bands of Stan Getz, Charlie Haden, Toots Thielemans, James Moody, Joe Henderson and Art Farmer. Hersch has made more than 80 recordings in various capacities: sideman, leader, producer, soloist, conceptualist. He accelerated his creative output in 1994 after disclosing that he was HIV-positive, explaining: "One can't be honest as a musician and dishonest as a person."

Hersch's first two trio albums for Sunnyside are strong showcases from which he developed a vibrant recording career as a leader. While bassist Charlie Haden ups *Sarabande*'s star power, *Heartsongs,* with bassist Michael Formanek and drummer Jeff Hirschfield, is the stronger session.

Red Square Blue, a beautiful jazz-meets-the-classics project, features Thielemans, James Newton and Phil Woods playing impressions of works by the greatest Russian composers. *Dancing in the Dark,* a standards session with longtime band mates bassist Drew Gress and drummer Tom Rainey, stands as one of his finest recordings. His first solo album, *Vol. 31* in Concord's acclaimed Maybeck Recital Hall series, is another prime showcase.

The Fred Hersch Trio Plays . . . honors the music of 10 of his favorite jazz composers, ranging from Duke Ellington to Ornette Coleman, while *I Never Told You* is a solo-piano tribute to Johnny Mandel. Hersch's strength as an empathetic partner/accompanist powers *Slow Hot Wind,* a duo recording with the Manhattan Transfer's Janis Siegel.

Point in Time, featuring trio, quartet and quintet performances with saxophonist Rich Perry and trumpeter Dave Douglas, is extraordinary. Hersch pays homage to composer/lyricist Billy Strayhorn with solo, trio, piano-duet and trio-plus-strings tracks on *Passion Flower. Thirteen Ways,* with Michael Moore on clarinets and alto sax and Gerry Hemingway on drums, is one of Hersch's most wide-ranging adventures, blending avant-garde improvisations and playful new twists on standards. Originally released in Japan, *Evanessence* is Hersch's heartfelt tribute to Evans. It was recorded in a trio with Formanek and Hirschfield, with Toots Thielemans and Gary Burton as special guests on several tracks.

Hersch was the driving force behind the all-star recording *Last Night When We Were Young.* More than a dozen top jazz players donated their time to participate in the project, an AIDS-benefit recording. Hersch plays on most tracks. Hersch goes solo on *Thelonious: Fred Hersch Plays Monk* for an exquisite personal journey through 13 of Monk's challenging originals.
— K.F.

AL HIBBLER

★★★★ **For Sentimental Reasons (Open Sky, 1984)**
★★★★ **After the Lights Go Down Low (Atlantic, 1989)**

In 1955 Al Hibbler (b. 1915) cut the original version of "Unchained Melody" (later a hit for the Righteous Brothers) and staked a claim on it that he has never relinquished. He had two Top 25 singles and three in the Top 10, but after '56 chart success eluded him. Hibbler's gruff style cut with sly humor sometimes brings to mind Louis Armstrong, and he also shares baritone Billy Eckstine's sense of grandeur when delivering a tender lyric. At his rollicking best, Hibbler was completely unpredictable—swooping, growling, moving freely up and down his vocal range, uncovering multiple personalities in the most straightforward material. An ardent Spike Jones fan, Hibbler couldn't resist working up his own variation on musical mayhem when tackling melody, harmony, rhyme and reason, especially when he got hold of something on the order of "Gee Baby, Ain't I Good to You" or the pair of Fats Waller songs he weaves into a gut-busting medley on *For Sentimental Reasons.*

Hibbler was anything but a novelty vocalist, though; every flourish had a purpose. Often he simply played it straight. At those moments he was the crooner's crooner, an elegant stylist who could caress and coax a lyric with deeply felt understanding. He honed his chops as the singer in Duke Ellington's band in the 1940s before embarking on a solo career in 1950. In the ensuing decade, he recorded for RCA, Columbia, Atlantic and Decca, the latter being the home port of his mid-'50s hits (Atlantic bought the masters of "After the Lights Go Down Low," a Top 10 hit for Hibbler in 1956, included on the like-titled 1989 album). Hibbler's career as a recording artist hit the skids briefly in 1963 after he was arrested while participating in a civil rights march in Birmingham, Alabama, where he led protesters in singing "You'll Never Walk Alone." Frank Sinatra brought him back into the fold by tendering him the first contract on the newly formed Reprise label. No hits materialized, but Sinatra's gesture allowed Hibbler to reestablish himself on the club circuit.

After the Lights Go Down Low is vintage early Hibbler, fronting four different orchestras in sessions recorded in 1950 and 1951. Material runs the gamut from soft ballads ("Dedicated to You") to slow, grinding love songs (the title track, "Autumn Winds") and some rugged blues ("Blues Came Falling Down"). *For Sentimental Reasons* is latter-day Hibbler, circa 1982, when his voice was still mellifluous but far more low-down than it was in his younger days. Hibbler works it like the seasoned pro he is, investing the lyrics with humor, heartache and a certain elevated perspective born of advancing years. He's accompanied by the aptly named Hank Jones All-Stars—Jones on piano, Buddy Tate on tenor sax and clarinet, Milt Hinton on bass and Oliver Jackson on drums. Their versatility is well suited to Hibbler's individual style. Unfortunately, "Unchained Melody" is nowhere to be found on either of these albums, which are all that remain in print of Hibbler's recordings. Both are splendid outings, however, one capturing a great singer in his restless youth, honing his style; the other revelatory of the subtle adjustments he made with age. — D.M.

BARBECUE BOB HICKS

★★★★ **Complete Recorded Works, Vol. 1 (1927–1928) (Document, 1991)**
★★★★ **Complete Recorded Works, Vol. 2 (1928–1929) (Document, 1991)**
★★★★½ **Complete Recorded Works, Vol. 3 (1929–1930) (Document, 1991)**
★★★★★ **Chocolate to the Bone (Yazoo, 1992)**

Guitarist Robert "Barbecue Bob" Hicks (1902–1931) became one of the most popular Atlanta-based bluesmen of the '20s. Recording his propulsive 12-string slide work and clever lyrics for Columbia beginning in 1927, he became one of the most successful blues artists on that label until his death four years later. Hicks's percussive guitar attack and intriguing arrangements, documented by several excellent recordings, made him unique among his Geogian musical peers.

Complete Recorded Works, Vols. 1–3 cover Hicks's complete recording career in chronological order, from March 1927 until December 1930. Of the 65 tracks, the vast majority feature Hicks performing solo on 12-string guitar and singing. The other tracks include occasional appearances by his brother Charley Lincoln on guitar (*Vols. 1* and *3*) and Nellie Florence on vocals (*Vol. 2*). On two tracks Hicks is joined by a duo consisting of guitarist Curly Weaver and harmonica player Buddy Moss (*Vol. 3*), collectively calling themselves the Georgia Cotton Pickers.

Chocolate to the Bone collects Hicks's best sides. Included here are classic tracks like "Motherless Chile Blues" and "Mississippi Heavy Water Blues," as well as the previously unissued "Twistin' Your Stuff" and "She Shook Her Gin." The Georgia Cotton Pickers join Hicks on the Georgia standard "She's Coming Back Some Cold Rainy Day" and the Blind Blake hit "Diddle-Da-Diddle." — B.R.H.

BILLY HIGGINS

★★★½ **Rejoicing (with Charlie Haden and Pat Metheny) (1984; ECM, 1994)**

★★★★ **Mr. Billy Higgins (1985; Evidence, 1993)**
★★★★ **Billy Higgins Quintet (1993; Evidence, 1997)**
One of the most important drummers in the hard-bop–to–free-jazz era and beyond, Billy Higgins (b. 1936) has played on scores of important recordings by other artists, most notably Ornette Coleman, but has few titles as a leader available domestically. Higgins's association with Coleman stretches back to 1959—and he was part of the historic 1961 *Free Jazz* session—and continues into the 1990s.

Higgins was a mainstay on 1960s Blue Note sessions, recording with Lee Morgan, Jackie McLean, Hank Mobley, Dexter Gordon, Herbie Hancock, John Coltrane, Bobby Hutcherson, tenor saxophonist Harold Land and pianist Cedar Walton, among others. He remains a much-in-demand sideman, recording with such varied artists as Abbey Lincoln, Pat Martino, Steve Turre and Bheki Mseleku, and he and Walton continue to work together in the excellent group Eastern Rebellion.

Mr. Billy Higgins is a sharp quartet session with bassist Tony Dumas, who worked with Higgins as the rhythm section on an Art Pepper date, pianist William Henderson and multi-instrumentalist Gary Bias, who lays out extensively on this recording, which features three of his compositions. *Billy Higgins Quintet* matches Higgins with bassist David Williams and several longtime session associates—Walton, Land and trumpeter Oscar Brashear. Higgins also has several recordings on the Italian Red label—*Once More*, *3/4 for Peace* and *Soweto*. — J.S.

CHUCK HIGGINS

★★★½ **Pachuko Hop (Specialty, 1992)**
Tenor saxophonist Chuck Higgins (b. 1924) moved from his hometown of Gary, Indiana, to Los Angeles as a child and grew up witnessing the swing era translate itself into West Coast R&B during the 1940s. Like so many saxophonists of his generation, Higgins was inspired by the galvanic Illinois Jacquet solo on the 1942 Lionel Hampton hit "Flying Home."

Higgins formed a small band with arrangements patterned after the Louis Jordan sound and scored a regional hit in 1952 with "Pachuko Hop." The piano player in this band would go on to fame as Johnny "Guitar" Watson. The 1954 and '56 recordings on *Pachuko Hop* show the Higgins band in raw, rocking form, with Higgins blowing furiously on "One Chord Instrumental" and "Rock." — J.S.

ANDREW HILL

★★★★ **Smokestack (1963; Blue Note, 1995)**
★★★★ **Judgment! (1964; Blue Note, 1994)**
★★★★★ **Point of Departure (1964; Blue Note, 1988)**
★★★★ **From California with Love (Artists House, 1979)**
★★★★½ **Faces of Hope (Soul Note, 1980)**
★★★★ **Strange Serenade (Soul Note, 1980)**
★★★★ **Shades (Soul Note, 1987)**
★★★ **Verona Rag (Soul Note, 1987)**
Pianist Andrew Hill (b. 1937), a consummate modern jazz artist who played an important part in the postbop movement of the late '50s and early '60s, has been sadly neglected in the United States. A music-theory scholar and an extraordinarily disciplined analyst, he possesses an encyclopedic, detailed knowledge of jazz idioms inside and out. His tonalities and rhythmic ideas, reminiscent at times of Cecil Taylor, are inventive yet remain grounded in tradition.

Hill can move through many styles from radically different epochs of jazz history in a single piece and make it work. Monk-ish spiked-chord voicings and phrasing across the time and dynamic planes characterize the playing field, but even Hill's most cerebral explorations retain the vibrancy of his solid feel for tempo and counterpoint. In some ways his earlier style anticipates the work of Anthony Braxton; a powerful intellect shapes angular forms, and an inquisitive spirit propels them into forward motion. His quietly insistent music has a certain quality of abstraction that makes for challenging and invigorating listening.

Hill grew up in Chicago, playing at the age of 16 with Charlie Parker and studying composition with Paul Hindemith. Following early-'60s work with Rahsaan Roland Kirk in L.A., he moved to New York. The classic Blue Note albums, recorded by Rudy Van Gelder, contain brilliant and uncompromising ensemble work with some of the best in the business, especially Eric Dolphy, Joe Henderson, Kenny Dorham and Tony Williams on *Point of Departure.*

For much of the past two decades, Hill has chosen not to perform due to insufficient recognition and support, settling in California and doing valuable work in music education and music therapy. Although he has had too few opportunities to record in America, Hill has long had a large and enthusiastic following in Europe, and the later Soul Note recordings were produced in Italy. *Shades* has Clifford Jordan's sax and a swinging rhythm section of Rufus Reid and Ben Riley. Of the three solo CDs, *Faces of Hope* is more sensitive, bold and assured than *From California with Love* or *Verona Rag;* "Bayside 1" and "Bayside 2" display astonishing pedal control, articulation and use of space. — T.M.

MICHAEL HILL

★★★½ **Bloodlines (Alligator, 1994)**
★★★½ **Have Mercy (Alligator, 1996)**
★★★½ **New York State of Blues (Alligator, 1998)**

Michael Hill, born in 1952 and raised in New York's South Bronx, both preserves and updates the blues by flavoring it with a variety of African and African-American music. His strong social conscience is evident throughout his work. For Hill, the blues is not a museum piece but a response to contemporary problems. As illustrated on *Bloodlines*, *Have Mercy* and *New York State of Blues,* he writes intelligent, strong and diverse songs (sometimes in collaboration with his bassist brother, Kevin, and drummer Tony Lewis) and delivers them with a searing guitar sound and an emotional vocal style a touch less gritty than his message. — J.Z.

Z.Z. HILL

★★★½ **Down Home (Malaco, 1981)**
★★★½ **The Rhythm and the Blues (Malaco, 1982)**
★★★½ **Greatest Hits (Malaco, 1990)**

In the 1970s and '80s Texas-born R&B vocalist Z.Z. Hill (1935–1984) turned out singles stamped with a suave and subtle delivery. "I Found Love," "You Don't Love Me"—his music insinuated, rather than shouted; his lean style was more swinging than rocking. *Down Home*'s "Cheating in the Next Room" enjoyed an astonishingly successful run on the R&B charts in 1982, but his crossover appeal—despite the accessibility of first-rate material like "Please Don't Make Me (Do Something Bad to You)"—remained limited. The greatest-hits collection is strong; even where the arrangements are less than inventive, Hill's singing smoothly triumphs. — P.E.

EARL "FATHA" HINES

★★★ **A Monday Date (1961; Original Jazz Classics, 1994)**
★★★ **Blues in Thirds (1965; Black Lion, 1989)**
★★★½ **Paul Gonsalves Meets Earl Hines (1972; Black Lion, 1993)**
★★★ **Masters of Jazz, Vol. 2 (1974; Storyville, 1990)**
★★★ **Earl Hines in New Orleans (1977; Chiaroscuro, 1996)**
★★★★½ **Earl Hines Plays Duke Ellington (New World, 1988)**
★★★½ **Live at the Village Vanguard (Columbia, 1988)**
★★★ **Way Down Yonder in New Orleans (Biograph, 1989)**
★★★ **Live at the New School (Chiaroscuro, 1989)**
★★★★ **Tour De Force (Black Lion, 1990)**
★★★ **Jazz Collector Edition: Earl Hines and His Orchestra (LaserLight, 1991)**
★★★½ **Jazz Collector Edition: Piano Solos (LaserLight, 1992)**
★★★★ **Tour De Force Encore (Black Lion, 1992)**
★★★ **Live at the Crescendo (GNP Crescendo, 1992)**
★★★ **Reunion in Brussels (Red Baron, 1992)**
★★★ **Here Comes Earl "Fatha" Hines: Spontaneous Explorations (Red Baron, 1993)**
★★★ **Earl Hines Septet (LaserLight, 1993)**
★★★ **Hines Shines (LaserLight, 1993)**
★★★ **Honor Thy Fatha (Drive Archive, 1994)**
★★★ **Fatha (Pearl, 1994)**
★★★★ **The Indispensable Earl Hines, Vol. 5 & 6 (1944–1966) (RCA Bluebird, 1994)**
★★★½ **Earl Hines and the Duke's Men (Delmark, 1994)**
★★★★ **Another Monday Date (Prestige, 1995)**
★★★★ **Grand Reunion (Verve, 1995)**
★★★ **Savoy Blues (Four Star, 1995)**
★★★ **Swingin' Away (Black Lion, 1995)**
★★★ **One for My Baby: The Music of Harold Arlen (Black Lion, 1995)**
★★★ **Piano Man! (Living Era, 1995)**
★★★½ **Fatha's Blues (Tradition/Rykodisc, 1996)**

★★★½ **Earl Hines Plays Cole Porter (New World, 1996)**
★★★½ **At Home (Delmark, 1997)**
★★★ **Hines Shines (Bescol, 1997)**
Pianist Earl Hines (1905–1983), along with Jelly Roll Morton, codified the standard vocabulary of jazz piano. He'd already studied classical piano and excelled in stride, ragtime and early jazz techniques when he joined forces in 1927–1928 with Louis Armstrong to make the single most historic series of jazz recordings ever. These tracks defined the nature of a new kind of jazz showcasing virtuoso soloists as opposed to the collective approach of traditional New Orleans playing up until that time. The like-minded Armstrong and Hines—Hines later said he tried to play the piano as if it were a cornet—were the voices that emerged from these records, and the rest of the jazz world took decades to fully assimilate their direction.

Hines could have gone on to acclaim as a solo pianist but chose to concentrate on leading a band instead. From late 1928 to the post–World War II era, the Hines big band broadcast from the Grand Terrace in Chicago. The band bridged the era from swing to bebop, featuring swing saxophonists Jimmy Mundy and Budd Johnson in the early days, then protoboppers Charlie Parker and Dizzy Gillespie at the end of its run. After disbanding his group in 1948 Hines rejoined Armstrong until 1951, then went back out on his own, recording in both solo and small-group contexts for the rest of his life.

Since Hines virtually invented jazz piano playing, he influenced everyone who came after him in one way or another, although Art Tatum (and by extension Oscar Peterson) and Cecil Taylor are generally considered direct disciples. Nevertheless, his catalog is in utter disarray. Much of the newly available material has been released as bootlegs.

Little of Hines from the 1950s remains in print, with the notable exception of *Another Monday Date,* which collects two mid-'50s recordings, one of Fats Waller songs recorded with a quartet, the other a Hines solo recording. Much of the current catalog consists instead of recordings made by Hines after a critically acclaimed New York engagement in 1964 that prompted a revival of interest in his music. Fortunately he remained a great entertainer and a vibrant player until the very end of his career, whether leading small combos, often in recapitulations of the glory years, or on his ever-inventive solo outings.

The group recordings are a mixed bag, although Hines himself is always worth a listen. One highlight is *Earl Hines and the Duke's Men,* with Johnny Hodges, Jimmy Hamilton, Ray Nance, Flip Phillips, Sonny Greer, Rex Stewart, Harry Carney, Oscar Pettiford and Cat Anderson; *Live at the Village Vanguard,* with Budd Johnson, Eddie Locke and Gene Ramey, is another gem. The two-disc *Grand Reunion,* recorded at the Vanguard in 1965, features the Hines trio with bassist George Tucker and drummer Oliver Jackson Jr., augmented by Coleman Hawkins and Roy Eldridge.

Of the solo records, the two *Tour De Force* sessions; *One for My Baby,* a collection of Harold Arlen tunes; and the magnificent *Earl Hines Plays Duke Ellington* are particularly recommended. One of the greatest indications of Hines's remarkable talent is that the Ellington sessions, recorded in the 1970s, match the brilliance of his early work recorded nearly 50 years before. *At Home,* an engaging 1969 recording, was made on Hines's favorite piano, a 1904 Steinway, in his Oakland, California, home. *Piano Solos,* recorded in 1974 at an informal gathering at the home of concert pianist Saralee Halprin, also shows Hines in top form on a collection of 20th Century standards stretching back to 1919's "Alice Blue Gown."
— J.S.

EDDIE HINTON

★★★½ **Cry and Moan (Bullseye Blues, 1991)**
★★★½ **Very Blue Highway (Bullseye Blues, 1993)**
Sometimes called "the white Otis Redding," singer, songwriter and guitarist Eddie Hinton (1944–1995) gained his reputation in the mid- to late '60s on the Southern soul scene, where he recorded prolifically as a session man with the Muscle Shoals rhythm section and wrote songs that would be covered by the likes of Aretha Franklin, the Box Tops and Percy Sledge, among others. At one point Hinton lived with Duane Allman, but he later refused invitations to join the nascent Allman Brothers Band as its lead singer. Hinton would record *Very Extremely Dangerous* in 1978 for Capricorn and a European release called *Letters from Mississippi* in '85, but both are unavailable domestically. *Cry and Moan* features 12 Hinton originals, which showcase his gruff, passionate vocals and guitar playing, including a swampy, organ- and percussion-dominated tune called "The Well of

Love" and the Sam Cooke–esque "Make It Easy on Me" and "Good Times."

Very Blue Highway is another fine collection of R&B, blues, soul and rock tunes, including the surging "Poor Ol' Me," on which the Memphis Horns (Andrew Love on tenor sax and Wayne Jackson on trombone and trumpet) add punchy, syncopated filigrees to the mix. Other standouts include the low-down title track, the ebullient "Let It Roll" and the Joe South–penned "Standin' In," on which Hinton's voice wavers near the emotional threshold as it imparts the song's lonely message, bringing us that much closer—as does all passionately rendered singing—to the deep recesses of the artist's soul. — B.R.H.

MILT HINTON

★★ **The Modern Art of Jazz (1956; Biograph, 1991)**
★★★★★ **Old Man Time (Chiaroscuro, 1990)**
★★★ **The Trio: 1994 (Chiaroscuro, 1994)**
★★★★ **Laughing at Life (Columbia, 1995)**

Milt Hinton, the dean of active bass players, qualifies as a national treasure. Born in 1910, he grew up in Chicago, where his mother was Nat Cole's piano teacher. He switched from violin to bass while in high school and was active on the jazz scene from the early 1930s. He spent 16 years, from 1936 to 1951, in Cab Calloway's high-profile swing orchestra.

When Calloway stopped touring, Hinton settled down and became one of the busiest studio players in New York, recording in both popular and jazz contexts. As such, he became one of the most heavily recorded jazz musicians of all time, making more than 1,200 sessions ranging from Louis Armstrong's All Stars to Charles Mingus, from Billie Holiday to Leontyne Price to Aretha Franklin, from Paul Anka to Paul McCartney. For most of his career he has also carried a camera with him. Two books of his vital and insightful documentary photographs are in print.

Possessing an uncanny sense of time, Hinton plays in a swinging, timeless style filled with humor and joy. One of the earliest bass soloists, Hinton has influenced players on the instrument in every decade since the 1930s and is held in high esteem as a soloist and role model. He advanced the slapping style of early New Orleans bass players by developing his own double- and triple-slap techniques.

The Modern Art of Jazz is a compilation of Dawn Records material recorded in 1956 by shifting combos led by Hinton, pianist Hank Jones and bassist Oscar Pettiford. It documents a busy time in Hinton's career but doesn't showcase him.

The *Old Man Time* double-disc project teams Hinton in seven 1989–90 recording sessions with Doc Cheatham, Dizzy Gillespie, Clark Terry, Flip Phillips, Buddy Tate, Derek Smith, Bobby Rosengarden, Danny Barker, Lionel Hampton, Cab Calloway and Joe Williams. The 19 musical tracks are supplemented by two lengthy and fascinating "Jazzspeak" career reflections.

Hinton is senior partner on *The Trio: 1994,* a fine small-band session with pianist Derek Smith and drummer Bobby Rosengarden. *Laughing at Life* celebrates Hinton's playing style and endearing vocals with help from trumpeter Jon Faddis and tenor saxophonist Harold Ashby. On the finale, "The Judge and the Jury," Hinton lovingly trades solos with fellow bassists Lynn Seaton, Brian Torff, Santi Debriano and Rufus Reid. — K.F.

FRED HO

★★★ **Tomorrow Is Now! (1985; Soul Note, 1993)**
★★★ **Monkey: Part One (Koch, 1996)**
★★★ **Monkey: Part Two (Koch, 1997)**

AS FRED HOUN AND THE AFRO-ASIAN MUSIC ENSEMBLE

★★★ **We Refuse to Be Used and Abused (Soul Note, 1988)**
★★★ **The Underground Railroad to My Heart (Soul Note, 1994)**
★★★ **Yes Means Yes, No Means No (Koch, 1998)**

Composer/baritone saxophonist Fred Ho (b. 1957), a.k.a. Fred Houn, has made a series of adventurous recordings, both on his own and as leader of the Afro-Asian Music Ensemble. *Monkey: Part One* is an intriguing if somewhat baffling piece of music excerpted from what he describes as "my Afro-Asian multimedia musical, *Journey Beyond the West: The New Adventures of Monkey.*" Ho leads the work, which is based on a tale of a trickster from 16th-Century Chinese folklore, on baritone saxophone and flute. Also featured are an unusual combination of Western and Eastern instrumentation and Cindy Zuoxin Wang's Mandarin Chinese vocals floating eerily over the mix. *Part Two* concludes that musical experiment. The group recordings consist of baritone, tenor, alto and soprano saxes, with piano, bass and drums, and are also an unusual jazz-meets-world-music study of Chinese folk themes. "Yes Means Yes, No Means No, Whatever She Wears, Wherever She Goes" is an antirape suite that makes up the bulk of the album titled after it.

Ho's earlier albums mix originals with revolutionary political themes and exotic arrangements of traditional material. *The Underground Railroad to My Heart* includes fascinating versions of "Caravan" and "Auld Lang Syne." *Tomorrow Is Now!* is highlighted by the title suite. *We Refuse to Be Used and Abused* is an overt call for a revolution of the oppressed. — J.S.

THE HOAX

★★★½ **Sound Like This (Code Blue/Atlantic, 1995)**

The Hoax—lead guitarist Jon Amor, bassist Robin Davey, vocalist Hugh Coltman, second guitarist Jess Davey and drummer Dave Rauburn—provides everything one might wish for in a blues-rock band: hook-filled original songs written with a good command of blues vocabulary, hot harp work, strong guitars and solid vocals. The youthful band's tremendous reception in its native England has created interest in a third generation of British blues players. A good introduction to an ensemble of considerable talent, *Sound Like This* captures much of the energy of the band's exciting live shows. — J.Z.

LEONARD HOCHMAN

★★★½ **Until Tomorrow (Brownstone, 1995)**
★★★★ **Manhattan Morning (Jazzheads, 1996)**

Saxophonist Leonard Hochman (b. 1933) worked steadily in New York and on the road in the 1950s with Phil Woods, Charlie Barnet, Kai Winding, Kenny Clarke and Al Haig, yet he recorded only sparingly as a sideman. This swinging reed player packed away his horns in the early 1960s to support his family and start a successful music-instrument rental business near Boston.

Hochman's Rip Van Winkle–like re-emergence in 1989 led to *Until Tomorrow,* his first recording as a leader. It's a fine showcase for Hochman's confident, masterful sound on tenor and bass clarinet, and it reflects his blues roots and a lyricism reminiscent of Dexter Gordon and Gene Ammons. The album was also one of drummer Alan Dawson's last recordings. Hochman teamed up with pianist Kenny Barron, bassist Harvie Swartz, drummer Victor Lewis and vibist Joe Locke on *Manhattan Morning,* a showcase for his deep swing sound on a variety of standards, underrecorded tunes and originals. — K.F.

ART HODES

★★★ **Up in Volly's Room (1972; Delmark, 1993)**
★★★★ **Apex Blues (Jazzology, 1982)**
★★★ **Live! from Toronto's Café des Copains (Music and Arts Programs of America, 1989)**
★★★ **Midnight Blue (Jazzology, 1990)**
★★★★ **Pagin' Mr. Jelly (Candid, 1990)**
★★★★ **The Jazz Record Story (Jazzology, 1991)**
★★★½ **Hodes' Art (Delmark, 1994)**
★★★ **Americana (Music and Arts Programs of America, 1994)**
★★★ **Keepin' Out of Mischief Now (Candid, 1995)**
★★★½ **Hot 'n' Cool Blues (Parkwood, 1996)**

Chicago-based pianist Art Hodes (1904–1993) played in the '20s and '30s with groups led by Wingy Manone, Frank Teschemacher, Bud Freeman and others. In the '40s he became a promoter of traditional jazz via radio shows; his own label, Jazz Record; and his own magazine, *The Jazz Record.* Hodes's unabashed enthusiasm for hot jazz as he played it led bop enthusiasts to attack him as a reactionary.

Hodes was not just a moldy fig but a disciple of the austere, communicative playing logic of Jelly Roll Morton and James P. Johnson. His simple, direct manner is profoundly moving on the solo tribute to Morton, *Pagin' Mr. Jelly.* The excellent *Apex Blues,* produced in 1944 for radio release by Milt Gabler, showcases legendary clarinetist Mezz Mezzrow and drummer Danny Alvin. Hodes makes the case for his music most convincingly on the Jazzology compilation *The Jazz Record Story,* which collects a series of trio, quintet and sextet performances by Hodes originally issued on 78s in the '40s.

Up in Volly's Room is a trio outing featuring clarinetist Volly Defaut. Raymonde Burke's clarinet and Pops Foster's bass work small pleasures on "Struttin' with Some Barbecue" from *Hodes' Art.* Saxophonist Jim Galloway and clarinetist Kenny Davern grace *Americana.*

Live! from Toronto's Café des Copains pairs Hodes and Galloway in a duet session. *Hot 'n' Cool Blues,* an appropriately titled series of 1988 duets with trumpeter Marcus Belgrave, covers such familiar material as "Blue Monk," "Watermelon Man," "Creole Love Call" and "C.C. Rider" and shows that Hodes played with intense feeling until the end of his life.

Hodes can also be heard on the Rhino collection *Chicago Jazz Summit.* He made many other recordings that are now unavailable: Look for the wonderful collaboration with bassist Milt Hinton, *Just the Two of Us,* and the limited-edition Mosaic release *The Complete Blue Note Art Hodes Sessions.* — J.S.

JOHNNY HODGES

★★★ **Hawkins! Eldridge! Hodges! Alive! (with Roy Eldridge and Coleman Hawkins) (1962; Verve, 1992)**
★★★★ **Everybody Knows Johnny Hodges (Impulse!, 1992)**
★★★ **Caravan (Prestige, 1992)**
★★★ **Johnny Hodges at Sportpalast, Berlin (Pablo, 1993)**
★★★★ **Verve Jazz Masters 35 (Verve, 1994)**
★★★★★ **Hodge Podge (Legacy, 1995)**
★★★★★ **Passion Flower (RCA Bluebird, 1995)**
★★★ **In Paris (with Coleman Hawkins) (Vogue Disques, 1995)**
★★★★ **Triple Play (RCA Victor, 1996)**
★★★★ **Used to Be Duke (Verve, N.A.)**

Johnny Hodges (1907–1970) was the first distinctive alto-saxophone soloist in jazz history and the primary influence on his instrument until the arrival of Charlie Parker. Equally important, Hodges was the definitive Duke Ellington sideman and, with the exception of four years in the early '50s when he led his own, mid-sized band, was featured in the Ellington Orchestra from 1928 until his death.

Always a masterful ballad and blues player, Hodges was also a convincing "hot" soloist who doubled on soprano saxophone at the start of his career. Most of his work, then and afterward, was done within the Ellington band, but Duke had a habit in the pre–World War II years of showcasing his featured players in small-group sessions under their own names while providing much of the material and the piano accompaniment.

Hodge Podge, from 1938–39, and *Passion Flower,* from 1940–46, are stellar examples of small-band Ellingtonia, with the latter album (collecting the early-'40s RCA sessions under Hodges's own name) especially valuable. *Caravan,* an album's worth of 1947 Hodges sessions plus some 1950–51 small bands with Hodges's replacement, Willie Smith, shows that the format did not prove as successful in later years.

The Hodges approach turned predictable and often listless after the passage of time, as the rehash of Ellington material from the 1961 Berlin concert demonstrates. There were moments, however, such as *Used to Be Duke,* a '54 small-group recording featuring trumpeter Shorty Baker, trombonist Lawrence Brown, tenor saxophonist/clarinetist Jimmy Hamilton and John Coltrane in a supporting ensemble role, and such other orchestral efforts as the late-'50s *Big Sound* (now unavailable) and the mid-'60s *Everybody Knows Johnny Hodges.*

To really hear Hodges, of course, consult virtually any important Ellington album. He is also well served in the 1944 trio recordings contained on *Shelly Manne and His Friends* (not the 1956 session of the same name). — B.B./J.S.

SILAS HOGAN

★★★½ **Trouble: The Best of the Excello Masters (Excello, 1995)**

Silas Hogan (1911–1994) is an unjustly overlooked contributor to the Louisiana swamp-blues canon. A deceptively laconic singer who warbled like a sober Jimmy Reed, Hogan also turned in reliable guitar work that shows traces of his electric label mate Slim Harpo and the acoustic influence of Blind Lemon Jefferson. Hogan was a fixture of the still-vibrant Baton Rouge blues scene for four decades and a mainstay of the Southern festival circuit up until his death at age 82.

Trouble: The Best of the Excello Masters collects Hogan's best work from the early '60s. All the mainstays of the Excello sound are here: a loping rhythm section of muddy drums and understated bass, meat-and-potatoes rural harmonica playing and guitar lines wrapped in a thin current of fuzz tones. What distinguishes Hogan is his clever songwriting; he can describe unflinchingly the squalor of rats and roaches in his kitchen in "Trouble at Home Blues" or address the universal need for love in "Everybody Needs Somebody." A deep sense of foreboding pervades Hogan's peak moments: The apocalyptic metaphor that hovers through "Dark Clouds Rollin'" and an unsettling knock on the door in "Early One Morning" are chilling. — S.J.

JAY HOGGARD

★★★★ **Solo Vibraphone (1978; India Navigation, 1992)**
★★★★ **Under the Double Moon (with Anthony Davis) (PA/USA, 1980)**
★★★ **Rain Forest (1981; Original Jazz Classics, 1994)**

The most impressive vibes player of his era, Jay Hoggard (b. 1954) belongs to a new generation of musicians who see no irreconcilable differences between totally uncompromising and blatantly commercial styles. As a result, Hoggard tends to record music that is merely pleasant, as on his currently unavailable GRP recordings and the better but still spotty *Rain Forest.*

Hoggard makes his strongest impression in intimate duo and solo performance settings. He and pianist Anthony Davis share a true affinity and interpret each other's music sensitively on *Under the Double Moon.* The best introduction to Hoggard's talents, however, remains his first recording, *Solo Vibraphone,* a 1978 concert taped at New York's Public Theater. Here, church touches, Latin and African influences, social consciousness and romantic tenderness all come together in a stunning solo program where "May Those Who Love Apartheid Burn in Hell," a memorial to Stephen Biko, coexists with music from *The Wiz.*

Oddly, none of Hoggard's later work is currently in print. The worthwhile *Mystic Winds, Tropical Breezes,* featuring Davis and other fine players, proves that Hoggard has the presence to lead a small, uncompromising combo. A series of recordings for Muse, including *Overview*, *The Little Tiger*, *In the Spirit*, *Love Is the Answer* and *A Night in Greenwich Village* is out of print due to the recent sale and projected reorganization of that catalog. — B.B./J.S.

DAVE HOLE

★★★ **Short Fuse Blues (Alligator, 1992)**
★★★ **Working Overtime (Alligator, 1993)**
★★★½ **Steel on Steel (Alligator, 1995)**
★★★½ **Ticket to Chicago (Alligator, 1997)**

Australian slide virtuoso Dave Hole (b. 1948) has his perseverance and an accident, along with considerable talent, to thank for his success. As a child in Perth, Australia, Hole taught himself guitar by listening to Jimi Hendrix, Eric Clapton, Blind Willie Johnson and Elmore James. When he broke his little finger playing football, he could play only by putting the slide on his index finger and hanging his hand over the top of the guitar neck. By the time his finger healed, he'd grown used to the style and liked its effects. Now his inventive overhand slide work is something of a trademark and one of the reasons that his live performances are popular. Hole toured Western Australia in the '70s and '80s, and in 1990 he financed and recorded his debut, *Short Fuse Blues.* He sent a copy to *Guitar Player* magazine, which wrote a rave review and feature story and passed the CD along to Alligator's Bruce Iglauer. When Iglauer released the album, he made Hole the label's first overseas signing.

Hole's is an admirable debut, especially from a player who grew up in an isolated city where he had trouble finding blues albums, let alone performers or teachers. On the 14 originals and covers, Hole offers powerful solos, smoldering tone and impressive leaps. While the album works well, the closer, a cover of Hendrix's "Purple Haze," makes it clear that Hole hasn't quite found his own sound yet. He's slowly remedying that, and each album reveals a more distinctive voice. On *Working Overtime* and *Steel on Steel,* Hole's playing has gotten more pained and more playful, and he's replaced most of the covers with originals. And the remaining covers, including Muddy Waters's "I Can't Be Satisfied" on *Overtime,* are interpretations, not mere copies. *Ticket to Chicago* is literally that—Hole flew to Chicago and recorded with some of the city's players. Keyboardist Tony Z., bassist Johnny B. Gayden and drummer Ray "Killer" Allison (and horn and harmonica players on a few tracks) contribute to a full, expressive album. — A.A.

BILLIE HOLIDAY

★★★★ **Lady Sings the Blues (1956; Verve, 1990)**
★★★ **Songs for Distingué Lovers (1957; Verve, 1984)**
★★★★ **Lady in Satin (1958; Columbia, 1986)**
★★★★ **The Last Recordings (1959; Verve, 1988)**
★★★★ **The Original Recordings (Columbia, 1973)**
★★★★ **The Silver Collection (Verve, 1984)**
★★★★ **From the Original Decca Masters (MCA Jazz, 1986)**

★★★★ **The Billie Holiday Songbook (Verve, 1986)**
★★★★ **Compact Jazz (Verve, 1987)**
★★★★ **The Quintessential Billie Holiday, Vol. 1 (1933–1935) (Columbia, 1987)**
★★★★ **The Quintessential Billie Holiday, Vol. 2 (1936) (Columbia, 1987)**
★★★★★ **The Quintessential Billie Holiday, Vol. 3 (1936–1937) (Columbia, 1988)**
★★★★★ **The Quintessential Billie Holiday, Vol. 4 (1937) (Columbia, 1988)**
★★★★ **Lady's Decca Days, Vol. 1 (MCA Jazz, 1988)**
★★★★ **Lady's Decca Days, Vol. 2 (MCA Jazz, 1988)**
★★★★★ **The Quintessential Billie Holiday, Vol. 5 (1937–1938) (Columbia, 1989)**
★★★½ **Compact Jazz: Live! (Verve, 1990)**
★★★★½ **The Quintessential Billie Holiday, Vol. 6 (1938) (Columbia, 1990)**
★★★★½ **The Quintessential Billie Holiday, Vol. 7 (1938–1939) (Columbia, 1990)**
★★★★½ **The Quintessential Billie Holiday, Vol. 8 (1939–1940) (Columbia, 1991)**
★★★★½ **The Quintessential Billie Holiday, Vol. 9 (1940–1942) (Columbia, 1991)**
★★★½ **I Like Jazz: The Essence of Billie Holiday (Columbia/Legacy, 1991)**
★★★★★ **The Complete Decca Recordings (Decca, 1991)**
★★★ **The Legacy (1933–1958) (Columbia/Legacy, 1991)**
★★★★ **Lady in Autumn: The Best of the Verve Years (Verve, 1991)**
★★★½ **Billie's Best (Verve, 1992)**
★★★★★ **The Complete Billie Holiday on Verve (1945–1959) (Verve, 1993)**
★★★½ **Solitude: The Billie Holiday Story, Vol. 2 (Verve, 1993)**
★★★★ **16 Most Requested Songs (Columbia/Legacy, 1993)**
★★★½ **Recital by Billie Holiday: The Billie Holiday Story, Vol. 3 (Verve, 1994)**
★★★ **First Issue: The Great American Songbook (Verve, 1994)**
★★★★ **Verve Jazz Masters 12 (Verve, 1994)**
★★★½ **Jazz at the Philharmonic (Verve, 1994)**
★★★ **Jazz 'Round Midnight (Verve, 1994)**
★★★½ **Lady Sings the Blues: The Billie Holiday Story, Vol. 4 (Verve, 1995)**
★★★½ **Music for Torching: The Billie Holiday Story, Vol. 5 (Verve, 1995)**
★★★½ **At Carnegie Hall: The Billie Holiday Story, Vol. 6 (Verve, 1995)**
★★★½ **All or Nothing at All: The Billie Holiday Story, Vol. 7 (Verve, 1995)**
★★★★ **Verve Jazz Masters 47: Billie Holliday Sings Standards (Verve, 1995)**
★★★½ **Billie Holiday's Greatest Hits (Decca, 1995)**
★★★½ **Love Songs (Columbia/Legacy, 1996)**
★★★ **This Is Jazz 15 (Columbia/Legacy, 1996)**
★★★ **Priceless Jazz Collection (GRP, 1997)**
★★★★ **The Complete Commodore Recordings (Commodore, 1997)**

Epitomizing as dramatically as does Charlie Parker the saga of jazz genius as tragic soul, the story of Billie Holiday (1915–1959)—especially her ghostwritten autobiography, *Lady Sings the Blues*—reads like a Dostoyevsky novel: Raped at age 11 by a neighbor (some accounts say cousin), she was sent to a home for wayward girls; in her teens she spent several months jailed for prostitution. Inspired by hearing Louis Armstrong's "West End Blues," she began singing in New York's rough-and-tumble speakeasies of the early '30s; championed by Columbia A&R giant John Hammond, she was famous by middecade, Lester Young dubbing her "Lady Day." Her 1939 recording of the riveting "Strange Fruit," a harrowing account of a Deep South lynching, made Holiday famous—typically, the notes her signature song sounded were those of grief, admonition and terror. Heroin and a luckless love life began wearing her down in the '40s; with career success had come song pluggers and aesthetic compromise—all of Tin Pan Alley's hack writers dogged Holiday to sing their tunes. Her personality a tense mix of rebel and victim, Holiday's life was wholly struggle: Self-destructive, incandescent, she died at 44. And she left music that, at its finest, works like a depth charge—few singers of any genre approach her intensity; few, either, possess the skill that, for however brief a time, she once commanded.

Remarkably, Holiday's voice wasn't the natural force that some stars (Sarah Vaughan, Ella Fitzgerald) have been given. She didn't scat; she was never flashy. Instead, her greatness lay in how she deployed her voice. By 1937, she was in full control of her style, hitting notes against the beat the way jazz horn players do (an early influence was Armstrong's trumpet), she shaped rhythmic lines ingeniously—and interpreted lyrics with intuitive savvy. Humor, sass, toughness and yearning informed her staggering emotive repertoire; Holiday was expert at laying bare the essence of a great lyric or, alternately, at tossing off a mediocre one with such happy virtuosity that the words were elevated into pure swinging sound.

Two massive, worthwhile compilations cover Holiday. Columbia's *Quintessential Billie Holiday* series chronicles her 1933–1942 heyday; her sessions are grounded on the elegant piano work of Teddy Wilson, and her range of sidemen extends to such legends as clarinetist Artie Shaw and saxophonist Lester Young; she cut a few sides, too, with the orchestras of both Benny Goodman and Count Basie (sadly, just a very few radio broadcasts remain of her Basie recordings). *Vol. 1* kicks things off strongly ("What a Little Moonlight Can Do" especially shines); *Vol. 2* showcases Shaw, Johnny Hodges and Holiday in a small-combo setting. *Vols. 3, 4* and particularly *5* are the crème de la crème; at the peak of her powers and teaming up with Young and trumpeter Buck Clayton, Holiday soars. *The Legacy* boxed set is necessarily patchy in trying to condense the strengths of all nine of the *Quintessential* series; it does, however, include such standouts as "I Must Have That Man," "Having Myself a Time," "God Bless the Child," "Summertime" and "Long Gone Blues." Holiday's later work continues to divide listeners—some fans of her blues-based numbers scorn her experiments with string arrangements, others consider her interpretive approach occasionally melodramatic or strained, and devotees of Holiday's early, clearer tone find disturbing the roughness that comes into her voice in the mid-1940s. Listen to *The Complete Billie Holiday on Verve (1945–1959),* a 10-CD collection (each volume was also released singly, though the set contains otherwise unavailable rehearsal material), and discover remarkable music that, for all its hit-and-miss technique (sometimes poorly chosen material or overwhelming instrumentation), is an astonishing spiritual autobiography—at times, Holiday's singing is the very voice of pain, loss and hard experience. *Billie's Best* commendably encapsulates the Verve *Complete.* Her sidemen (Ben Webster on tenor, Benny Carter on alto, Charlie Shavers on trumpet) are often stellar; the live sets—including *Jazz at the Philharmonic* and *At Carnegie Hall*—are candid and sharp. *Lady in Autumn* also reviews the Verve years, and it's a bittersweet triumph; in fact, it's often against the lush backdrop of a full orchestra that she achieves her most eerie effect—her singing is acid splashed against velvet. Those who appreciate the fearsome, agonized Holiday might also check out *Lady in Satin* and *The Last Recordings:* Ray Ellis's somewhat soupy arrangements serve (who knows how intentionally?) to set off Lady Day's singing in ways that can provoke feelings of real terror. Striking the balance between Holiday's early finesse and her final raw, cathartic agony is *The Complete Commodore Recordings,* two CDs of gems and alternate takes that cover the period (1939) of her greatest confidence. *The Complete Decca Recordings,* two CDs, is a wonderful starting place for novices: It's Holiday, 1944–1950, on a relatively even keel, at her most accessible—great standards delivered in a very personal manner. Its 50 selections include her first outings with strings, and while the tight arrangements allow scant room for the sidemen to stretch out, Holiday's voice is at its strongest.

Of Holiday's additional live work, fine examples can be found on Verve's *Billie Holiday Live.* Of the perplexing plethora of samplers and best-of sets, *Verve Jazz Masters 12,* reflecting Holiday at her least anguished, and Legacy's *16 Most Requested Songs* are recommended.

— P.E.

JOE HOLIDAY

★★★½ Mambo Jazz (Original Jazz Classics, 1991)

Sicilian-born, Newark, New Jersey–bred tenor saxophonist Joseph A. Befumo, a.k.a. Joe Holiday (b. 1925), displays a smooth capacity to swing on the up-tempo numbers and a supple, breathy tone on ballads. *Mambo Jazz* features Billy Taylor on piano and organ.

— J.S.

DAVE HOLLAND

★★★★★ Conference of the Birds (1972; ECM, 1988)

★★★★ Dave Holland/Sam Rivers (1976; I.A.I., 1992)

★★★★ **Dave Holland/Sam Rivers, Vol. 2 (1977; I.A.I., 1992)**
★★★½ **Emerald Tears (1979; ECM, 1996)**
★★★★ **Life Cycle (1982; ECM, 1988)**
★★★★½ **Jumpin' In (1984; ECM, 1988)**
★★★½ **Seeds of Time (ECM, 1987)**
★★★★ **The Razor's Edge (ECM, 1988)**
★★★½ **Triplicate (ECM, 1988)**
★★★★ **Extensions (ECM, 1990)**
★★★★½ **Dream of the Elders (ECM, 1995)**

British bassist and cellist Dave Holland (b. 1946) was a key member of Miles Davis's 1968 protofusion band and went on to become one of his generation's most important new-music bassists. He was a key figure in ECM's early development, excelling on the spectacular interchange with saxophonists Sam Rivers and Anthony Braxton and drummer Barry Altschul, *Conference of the Birds.*

Holland recorded mostly as a sideman through the 1970s, continuing a fruitful association with Rivers and Braxton. *Emerald Tears* is a solo-bass album; *Life Cycle* is an exquisite solo-cello recital. Holland returned to leading a crack quintet on *Jumpin' In,* which features Steve Coleman on alto saxophone and flute, Kenny Wheeler on trumpet and flügelhorn, Julian Priester on trombone and Steve Ellington on drums. Marvin "Smitty" Smith came in for Ellington as of *Seeds of Time;* Robin Eubanks subs for Priester on *The Razor's Edge.* Holland cut back to a quartet with Coleman, Eubanks and Smith for *Extensions,* and a trio with Coleman and drummer Jack DeJohnette for *Triplicate.*

Holland is superb on the quartet session *Dream of the Elders,* conversing glibly with Steve Nelson on vibraphone, Eric Person on alto and soprano saxophone and Gene Jackson on drums. Vocalist Cassandra Wilson contributes a fine reading of Holland's arrangement on "Equality," a Maya Angelou poem. — J.S.

RON HOLLOWAY

★★★½ **Slanted (Milestone, 1994)**
★★★★ **Scorcher (Milestone, 1996)**

Washington, D.C. tenor saxophonist Ron Holloway (b. 1953) built an impressive reputation as a sideman in a variety of musical settings before making his debut as a leader. A strong disciple of Sonny Rollins and John Coltrane, Holloway played with Gil Scott-Heron and avant-rocker Root Boy Slim and was a featured soloist in Dizzy Gillespie's final group from 1989 to 1993.

Slanted showcases Holloway's full, open tone and proves him a capable bandleader with a group of D.C.-area musicians who support him enthusiastically. He demonstrates his chops by undertaking the difficult task of putting his own stamp on one of the most covered tunes in jazz history, "Caravan," and the standard "Autumn Leaves." Holloway also wrote the title track as a tribute to Thelonious Monk.

Scorcher shows Holloway developing as a leader on an aptly titled set that features a crack band augmented with Joey DeFrancesco on Hammond B-3 organ and featuring Gil Scott-Heron on two tracks. This album offers something to both hard-bop fans and acid-jazz heads. — J.S.

THE HOLLYWOOD FLAMES

★★★★½ **The Hollywood Flames (Specialty, 1992)**

Bobby Byrd, Curley Dinkens, Willie Ray Rockwell and David Ford—the four singers who would become the first batch of Hollywood Flames—met in the Watts section of Los Angeles in 1949. Using variations on the Flames name until 1952, the quartet would later splinter, becoming a vehicle for a revolving cast of characters that would establish the ensemble as one of the most important Los Angeles vocal R&B groups of the '50s. Onetime Hollywood Flame Bobby Day would later go on to solo success with "Rockin' Robin."

The Hollywood Flames documents recordings made by the group from early 1952 to June 1959, featuring tracks released on Specialty, Fidelity and Ebb Records (with the exception of three previously unissued cuts). Included are such gems as "W-I-N-E," "Buzz, Buzz, Buzz," "I'll Be Seeing You" and "Let's Talk It Over." With the group performing songs both a cappella and backed by musicians, *The Hollywood Flames* is an exceptional snapshot of one of the West Coast's most respected doo-wop and R&B vocal groups. — B.R.H.

THE HOLMES BROTHERS

★★★★ **In the Spirit (Rounder, 1990)**
★★★★ **Where It's At (Rounder, 1991)**
★★★★ **Jubilation (Realworld, 1992)**
★★★★ **Soul Street (Rounder, 1993)**
★★★★ **Promised Land (Rounder, 1997)**

When Wendell and Sherman Holmes (b. 1943 and 1939) made their recording debut in 1990, they had been playing without fanfare in the New York City area for 20 years. That music this powerful could escape attention for so long is one of life's mysteries. The brothers' original material and cover choices betray deep gospel roots, from which they find affinity with a broad range of styles in the same emotionally charged mode, from Stax-Volt's Memphis-bred soul to gospel-pop-soul fusions à la Sam Cooke to electrified urban blues to traditional country.

The other factor in the mix is the brothers' longtime partner, drummer and vocalist Popsy Dixon. His is the otherworldly falsetto that plays so well off his mates' aggressive stylings, adding tenderness and delicacy to the more boisterous outings and a smooth edge to the spirited ensemble singing. His lead vocal on *In the Spirit*'s "The Final Round" finds him declaiming like Otis Redding and soaring like Curtis Mayfield, all in the same song. His prowess is vividly displayed on *Jubilation,* a collection of spiritually oriented classics upon which the band is joined by some of world music's finest vocalists and musicians. "Amazing Grace," however well-worn, is reborn in the brothers' startling version. "Gonna do a little song here that hits you where you live," one of the brothers announces at the outset. Beneath Sherman's gravel-voiced, pain-wracked testifying, an organ chord rumbles; over it, Gib Wharton sneaks in on pedal steel, his aching lines swirling ominously around the vocals. After Wharton steps to the fore with a wailing solo so stark and haunting it would make angels weep, Dixon enters, his falsetto piercing the heavens in heartfelt surrender. Urged on by the brothers to "Sing it, Popsy! Bring it on down!," Dixon reveals unimagined nuances in a text too often taken for granted.

Jubilation lives up to its title at every turn. If it isn't Dixon supplying the stirring emotion, one or both of the brothers bring it home. "I Want Jesus to Walk with Me" is dirgelike and chilling, much in the mold of the Chosen Gospel Singers' "Prayer for the Doomed." Wendell Holmes, every bit as persuasive with a guitar in his hands as he is as a singer, adds counterpoint voice in the form of spitfire blasts of notes, suggesting the torment of a troubled, searching soul crying out for relief. Elsewhere, matters lighten up. Another evergreen, "Will the Circle Be Unbroken," is transformed into a jaunty East Africa–by-way-of-Appalachia hoedown, thanks to a trio of guitarists from Remmy Ongala's Orchestre Super Matimila.

Another solid effort, *Soul Street* features the brothers' signature array of soul, country, R&B and gospel numbers, including three new original songs by Wendell and/or Sherman. Jimmy Reed's catalog provides two of the peak moments, first in a churning, urgent take on "How Can I Love You," with Wendell crafting slinky, longing guitar lines in support of Sherman's pleading vocal. On the other Reed number, the rocker "Down in Virginia," Wendell and Sherman swing loose and carefree on an ebullient vocal duet spiced by Wendell's roughneck blues soloing, working his way up and down the neck, jettisoning notes in true rave-up style—Wendell Holmes by way of Albert Collins by way of Jimmy Reed. A tasty, gospel-tinged version of Dallas Frazier's "There Goes My Everything," notable both for the vocal approach and for the way guest Alison Krauss's moaning fiddle solos heighten Wharton's weeping protests on pedal steel. Throw in "To Make a Long Story Short," a beautiful ballad of lost love cocomposed by Dan Penn, and the meditative gospel closer, "Walk in the Light," and you're left with your soul in flight yet again, and the certainty that the Holmes Brothers can do no wrong.

Following a four-year absence, the brothers returned in 1997 with *Promised Land,* a journey into deep-gospel and classic R&B stylings, melding forceful originals such as Wendell Holmes's growling "Easy Access" with inspired cover choices along the lines of Tom Waits's "Train Song," delivered as apocalyptic reverie by Popsy Dixon. Strong, soul-shaking stuff, in true Holmes Brothers style. — D.M.

RICHARD "GROOVE" HOLMES

★★★★ **Groovin' with Jug (1961; Pacific Jazz, 1989)**
★★★½ **Soul Message (1965; Original Jazz Classics, 1988)**
★★★ **Misty (1966; Original Jazz Classics, 1992)**
★★★ **Blues All Day Long (Muse, 1989)**
★★★ **Hot Tat (Muse, 1991)**
★★★ **Blue Groove (Prestige, 1994)**
★★★ **Legends of Acid Jazz (Prestige, 1997)**

Organist Richard "Groove" Holmes (1931–1991) turned out the bluesiest Hammond B-3 organ-trio sound this side of Jimmy Smith. He moved from lush lounge laments to high-intensity soul-jazz settings as if they were all of a piece. He also recorded a hit version of Erroll Garner's "Misty," originally on *Soul Message,* then as the title cut of a subsequent release.

Holmes was at his best in the company of hardworking tenor saxophonist Gene Ammons, as in *Groovin' with Jug*. Trumpeter Blue Mitchell and guitarist Pat Martino make guest appearances on *Blue Groove*; *Blues All Day Long* features tenor saxophonist Houston Person. — J.S.

RICK HOLMSTROM

★★★½ Lookout! (Black Top, 1996)

Lookout, an excellent instrumental blues record, features an all-star cast of young West Coast blues players led by Rick Holmstrom (b. 1965), the guitar wizard currently with the Mighty Flyers. The rest of that band and its leader, harmonica virtuoso Rod Piazza, are all on board, as is Holmstrom's former teammate, harpist Johnny Dyer. Check out Holmstrom's two albums as a coleader with Dyer, *Listen Up!* and *Shake It!*. — J.S.

EARL HOOKER

★★★★ Two Bugs & a Roach (Arhoolie, 1990)
★★★★★ Blue Guitar (Paula, 1991)
★★★★ Play Your Guitar Mr. Hooker (Black Top, 1993)

Earl Hooker (1930–1970) was the undisputed king of the smooth, single-string slide-guitar style. With uncanny accuracy Hooker (cousin to John Lee) could make a guitar whine, whinny and wail across a full range of emotions and colors. Distilling a kit bag of influences and effects (including Western swing, jazz, hands-on tutelage by Robert Nighthawk and later experimentation with the wah-wah pedal), Hooker invented a sound that, by the '60s, put him in demand as a session player and recording artist and labeled him *the* blues guitarist's guitarist in Chicago.

Since Hooker recorded for so many different, independent labels—from his first single for King in the early '50s ("Race Track Blues"/"Blue Guitar Blues")—it's almost impossible to gather the many gems he fashioned as leader or sideman. He had a penchant for using his smooth, sophisticated guitar work to recraft popular R&B numbers ("The Hucklebuck," "Tanya," "Something You Got") and to fashion his own stinging instrumentals ("Off the Hook"). His signature sound is unmistakable behind Muddy Waters ("You Shook Me"), Junior Wells ("Messin' with the Kid") and other Chicago stalwarts. A boxed-set overview of the Hook's accomplishments is long overdue.

That said, *Blue Guitar* comes closest to such a dream collection, including excellent efforts as leader ("Universal Rock," "Blues in D Natural," "Off the Hook" and the title track) and as sideman with various vocalists: honky-tonker Lillian Offitt ("Lotta Lovin'") and singer/sax man A.C. Reed ("This Little Voice"). The mature Hooker guitar genius bristles on each and every track, showing off his treble-heavy trademark sound while at his strongest.

The other available albums offer Hooker's output both before and just after his prime, when he began to succumb to tuberculosis (hence the *Two Bugs* in the Arhoolie title, which documents a 1968 session and a few tracks from his early years in Memphis). *Play Your Guitar Mr. Hooker* collects his sessions from 1964 to 1968, with a variety of vocalists, including Hooker and A.C. Reed again. — A.K.

JOHN LEE HOOKER

★★★★ House of the Blues (1959; Chess, 1987)
★★★½ That's My Story: John Lee Hooker Sings the Blues (1960; Riverside, 1991)
★★★★½ The Country Blues of John Lee Hooker (1960; Original Blues Classics, 1991)
★★★★★ John Lee Hooker Plays & Sings the Blues (1961; Chess, 1989)
★★★★ Boogie Chillun' (1962; Fantasy, 1972)
★★★★ Burning Hell (1964; Original Blues Classics, 1992)
★★★ Urban Blues (1967; MCA, 1993)
★★★★ The Real Folk Blues (1968; Chess, 1987)
★★★★★ Goin' Down Highway 51 (Specialty, 1971)
★★★★ Mad Man Blues (Chess, 1971)
★★★½ Endless Boogie (MCA, 1971)
★★★ Hooker 'n' Heat: Canned Heat and John Lee Hooker (1971; EMI, 1991)
★★★ Never Get Out of These Blues Alive (MCA, 1972)
★★★★ Black Snake (Fantasy, 1977)
★★★ The Cream (Tomato, 1978)
★★★★ That's Where It's At! (1979; Stax, 1990)
★★★★ Sad and Lonesome (Muse, 1979)
★★★★ Lonesome Road (MCA, 1983)
★★★ Infinite Boogie: John Lee Hooker and Canned Heat (Rhino, 1986)
★★★ John Lee Hooker and Canned Heat

Recorded Live at the Fox Venice Theatre (Rhino, 1986)
★★★★★ **The Best of John Lee Hooker (GNP Crescendo, 1987)**
★★★★ **Gotham Golden Classics (Collectables, 1989)**
★★★★ **The Healer (Chameleon, 1989)**
★★★★ **Alone (Tomato, 1989)**
★★★★ **Detroit Blues 1950–1951: John Lee Hooker/Eddie Burns (Collectables, 1991)**
★★★ **More Real Folk Blues: The Missing Album (Chess, 1991)**
★★★★ **Mr. Lucky (Charisma/Pointblank, 1991)**
★★★★ **The Best of John Lee Hooker 1965 to 1974 (MCA, 1991)**
★★★★★ **The Ultimate Collection: 1948–1990 (Rhino, 1991)**
★★★★ **Boom Boom (Pointblank, 1992)**
★★★★ **Graveyard Blues (Specialty, 1992)**
★★★½ **Get Back Home (Evidence, 1992)**
★★★★ **Everybody's Blues (Specialty, 1993)**
★★★★★ **The Legendary Modern Recordings, 1948–1954 (Flair/Virgin, 1993)**
★★★★★ **The Early Years (Tomato, 1994)**
★★★½ **King of the Boogie (Drive Archive, 1994)**
★★★★★ **Alternative Boogie: Early Studio Recordings, 1948–1952 (Capitol Blues Collection, 1995)**
★★★★ **Chill Out (Pointblank, 1995)**
★★★★ **The Very Best of John Lee Hooker (Rhino, 1995)**
★★★½ **His Best Chess Sides (Chess, 1997)**
★★★★ **Don't Look Back (Pointblank, 1997)**

John Lee Hooker was born near Clarksdale, Mississippi, in 1917, but his blues were born farther south, thanks to his stepfather, Will Moore, who was raised in Louisiana and played a style of blues built on a one-chord droning tone, relentless vamping, and stinging, lower-string punctuations. Blind Lemon Jefferson, Blind Blake and Charley Patton often visited Moore at his house, but their effect on Hooker was virtually nil—Moore's music possessed him and is the most direct influence on a style that became one of the touchstones of blues-based rock & roll. In fact, Hooker is now at that point in life when all his "children" are paying homage to their inspiration. In his excellent latter-day releases, *The Healer*, *Mr. Lucky*, *Boom Boom* and *Chill Out,* Hooker is joined by Bonnie Raitt, Albert Collins, Robert Cray, Keith Richards, Carlos Santana, Los Lobos, George Thorogood, Booker T. Jones, Johnnie Johnson, John Hammond, Charlie Musselwhite, a new incarnation of Canned Heat, Ry Cooder, Johnny Winter and others in what amounts to Hooker's whistlestop tour through 25-plus years of rock music bearing his signature in the voices of other players. In his recent resurgence, he has been well served by producer Roy Rogers, who hasn't let the marquee names overwhelm the proceedings. Indeed, *Chill Out*'s best moments feature not the all-stars but Hooker alone with his guitar, carving out some savage blues all on his own.

Hooker's signature sound, though, isn't easily copied, since its only pattern is no pattern at all. Vamping and droning are its constants, but Hooker regularly breaks down the 12-bar structure in order to extend his story to a conclusion only he envisions; moreover, his fingering and chording follow no discernible logic, and time is without question a moving thing almost from bar to bar. Then Hooker brings everything home with his brooding, low-down vocals, which hint at some impending danger even in the brightest moments.

After working odd jobs and playing music as a sideline in Memphis and Cincinnati in the late '30s and early '40s, Hooker moved to Detroit. There he made some recordings for Bernard Besman, a local distributor who had his own small label, Sensation, but who leased the first masters to the folks at Modern and proceeded to work extensively in the studio with the artist over the next five years. From that first session, "Boogie Chillun'" broke out in 1948 and reportedly sold over a million copies; its success loosed on the world an insistent, brooding, pulsating rhythm—built on a simple ostinato figure played slightly behind the beat—that both heralded the coming of a distinctive new artist and brought traditional blues into step with the accelerating pace of America's postwar society. Thereafter Hooker's masters were leased to a variety of labels and issued with the artist identified by a variety of names: Delta John, Texas Slim, the Booker Man, even John Lee Booker. Regardless of the name on the labels, most of the songs (and certainly the most effective) featured only Hooker accompanied by his electric guitar and his own foot stomping, in large part because his unusual approach to a song's structure and rhythm made it difficult for other musicians to stay in step with him.

Apart from the late '80s and '90s albums,

Hooker's most noted band sessions are those he cut in 1970 with blues revivalists Canned Heat, now reissued in a two-CD set by EMI, *Hooker 'n' Heat,* and on Rhino's *Infinite Boogie* (same albums, different titles). Rhino's catalog features as well a live album, *John Lee Hooker and Canned Heat,* featuring Hooker, Canned Heat and, on backup vocals, the Chambers Brothers. In its original incarnation with 300-pound lead singer Bob Hite and ace guitarist/vocalist Al Wilson (both are now deceased), Canned Heat was the foremost exponent of Hooker-style boogie in a blues-rock setting.

Nothing, however, supplants Hooker solo or with minimal backing. His finest records through the years have benefited from a stark approach that elevates the mood of his most personal stories. Rhino's *The Ultimate Collection: 1948–1990* supports this theory even as it shows Hooker sometimes effective in a broader setting. Guitarist Eddie Kirkland, who provided exemplary support on several Hooker sessions, is heard here in good form on "Think Twice Before You Go," and again on a 1968 track, "Back Biters and Syndicators," which also features Louis Myers on harmonica, Eddie Taylor on bass and Al Duncan on drums. Similarly, "You Know I Know," a track from Hooker's marvelous *The Real Folk Blues,* finds him backed by one of his early accompanists, guitarist Eddie Burns, as well as Lafayette Leake on piano, Willie Dixon on bass and the incomparable Fred Below on drums.

You don't have to be a purist to appreciate the power of Hooker's earliest sides cut in Detroit. These represent the darkest, rawest tales in the artist's literature as well as his most acerbic slants on life as black Americans knew it in the immediate postwar years. Some of these have the feel of having been carefully prepared and worked out; others are ragged and improvisational. All are powerful statements. Numerous first-rate overviews of this period are now in print, and it's difficult to recommend one over the other. However, as a complete package, the Capitol Blues Collection's three-disc survey of the Besman-produced sessions, *Alternative Boogie: Early Studio Recordings, 1948–1952,* is hard to beat. In addition to 56 recordings, including some alternate and previously unreleased takes, the set comes with an informed liner essay by Pete Welding and a short piece by Bernard Besman himself, who lays out his argument that Hooker's music is so distinctive it cannot be called blues at all but rather should be designated "early Americana." Less ambitious but no less essential is the 24-track single-CD survey *The Legendary Modern Recordings, 1948–1954.* Other key titles that round out Hooker's early years on various labels include *Detroit Blues 1950–1951,* with solo recordings by Hooker and by Eddie Burns (Hooker's tracks are also available separately in Collectables' *Gotham Golden Classics*); two fine Specialty titles, *Graveyard Blues* (from 1948–50, its 20 cuts produced by Besman and released on his Sensation label) and *Everybody's Blues* (a handful of solo Hooker tracks from 1950–51 and others from 1954 recorded for Specialty). Deeper into the '50s, another exemplary package comes by way of the 31-track, double-disc Tomato set, *The Early Years,* also graced by a Pete Welding essay and covering Hooker's band recordings for the Vee-Jay label from 1955 to 1964. On this set the stellar Vee-Jay artist Jimmy Reed is heard blowing a mean harmonica and playing guitar on a few cuts; Hooker is backed by horns on a 1961 session; and the Vandellas sing backup vocals on two cuts from 1963. An overview that takes Hooker from his solo days into his first band sides is available by way of GNP Crescendo's well-considered *The Best of John Lee Hooker.*

The development of Hooker's style within a band context is demonstrated on the sides dating from the late '50s forward. Not that the style developed all that much—Hooker is resolutely Hooker to this day; what's interesting is how other musicians respond to the challenge posed by his unorthodox sense of song structure. Some of the strongest work from this period was done for the Riverside label, starting in 1959 with the potent, stark solo renderings on *The Country Blues of John Lee Hooker,* wherein the Hooker boogie is displaced by a blues style redolent of the Delta. From those same sessions comes *Burning Hell,* issued first in England (and even there not until 1964) and unavailable stateside until its release on CD in 1992. In 1960 producer Orrin Keepnews cut Hooker with bassist Sam Jones and drummer Louis Hayes, rhythm masters recruited from Cannonball Adderley's band, for *That's My Story: John Lee Hooker Sings the Blues.* Of interest here is Hooker's "I Need Some Money," which showed up in slightly different form as "Money (That's What I Want)," a Top 30 pop single that year for Barrett Strong. Also new to the catalog as of 1991, although it was recorded in 1966 as the follow-up to the outstanding *Real Folk Blues* album for Chess, is *More Real Folk Blues.* Equally as engaging as its predecessor, *More Real Folk Blues* finds Hooker plugged in and working with a band on some of the most overt efforts he made at chart success. This is a mixed bag, but Hooker does an interesting take on "Mustang Sally & GTO," basing his version on the original "Mustang Sally" cut by Mack Rice in 1965, over a year before Wilson Pickett hit pay dirt with it. One of Hooker's final '60s recording sessions took place in Paris in late November 1969; some of these sides were issued on a Black and Blue import; these plus six other previously unreleased songs comprise Evidence's *Get Back Home.* Among the interesting oddities here: John Lee having a boisterous go at "Hi Heel Sneakers" and a reconsideration of Jimmie Rodgers's "T.B. Blues" in which Hooker's vocal takes on a penetrating Bukka White–style vibrato. Sessions from 1967 and 1969 comprise *Urban Blues,* which finds Hooker dipping ever so slightly into social commentary on the dark, turgid "Motor City Is Burning" (from 1967) and, less successfully, on "I Gotta Go to Vietnam" (a previously unreleased track from 1969); the latter, which borrows generously from "Rollin' and Tumblin'," percolates along steadily but delivers more in its powerhouse riffing (with Earl Hooker's snarling wah-wahed guitar lines most prominent) than in its ho-hum narrative.

Payback time begins in the '70s with the Canned Heat sessions and continues with the above-mentioned guest artists populating his latest recordings. Additionally, *Never Get Out of These Blues Alive* teams Hooker with a band whose numbers are bolstered on several cuts by Elvin Bishop on slide guitar, Mark Naftalin on piano and, on the title track, Naftalin, Bishop and Van Morrison, the latter sharing lead vocals with Hooker. 1971's *Endless Boogie* brings Steve Miller on board to add some pungent electric-guitar lines to the proceedings, although it is harmonica wizard Dave Berger who steals the show with his Little Walter–style wails and moans. *The Cream* is four sides of live, prime Hooker, recorded in 1977 with a band featuring Charlie Musselwhite on harmonica. *(. . . Alone)* is now available only on cassette from Specialty and contains sides cut between 1948 and 1951 with Bernard Besman in Detroit; *Alone* is a two-disc live album on Tomato featuring Hooker solo at New York City's Hunter College (unfortunately, there is no indication on the album or in the liner copy of when this recording was made). As for single-CD overviews, both Chess and Rhino have top-notch samplers of Hooker's work, with Chess's covering the years 1965 to 1974, while Rhino's *The Very Best of John Lee Hooker* ranges from the original Modern recording of "Boogie Chillun'" through representative tracks from the '50s and '60s cut for Modern, Vee-Jay, Riverside, Impulse!, Chess and Bluesway, plus a side from the 1971 *Hooker 'n' Heat* album and an interesting take on Robert Johnson's "Terraplane Blues" recorded for Roy Rogers's 1987 release, *Sidewinder.* It can be argued that Hooker has rarely varied his tried-and-true formula; but nearly 50 years after that formula was first heard on record, the man's "early Americana" sounds as vital and stirring as ever. — D.M.

WILLIAM HOOKER

★★ Shamballa (Knitting Factory Works, 1994)
★★½ Radiation (Homestead, 1994)
★★★ Armageddon (Homestead, 1995)
★★★½ The Gift of Tongues (Knitting Factory Works, 1996)

Passionate to a fault and filled with a thunderous, intense physicality, drummer William Hooker (b. ca. 1960) is exemplary in his ability to bridge genres, having worked with musicians from New York's downtown improvisational-jazz scene, DJs, rockers, and electronic-music artists, even when it leads him into uncharted territory. Though sometimes undisciplined, his searching music frequently makes for compelling listening.

Shamballa finds Hooker attempting to rationalize Elliott Sharp's thin, spidery skronk with Thurston Moore's more muscular rock. There are moments when he succeeds, but all too often the album veers into indulgent wank.

Radiation and *Armageddon* are more successful meldings of genres: The former at times is a modernization of the viscous guitar and horn funk of Miles Davis's *On the Corner,* while the latter, as one might expect from its title, is a more viscerally rhythmic exercise.

The Gift of Tongues is Hooker's strongest album, due to the strength of his collaborators, Sonic Youth's Lee Ranaldo and harpist Zeena Parkins. The three play forcefully, with Ranaldo's guitar and Parkins's amplified harp providing the alpha and omega to Hooker's elemental drumming. — S.M.

ZAKIYA HOOKER

★★½ Flavors of the Blues (Pointblank, 1996)

Songstress Zakiya Hooker (b. Vera Lee Hooker, ca. 1955) has the blues in her blood. The daughter of John Lee Hooker has lived the blues as well: a short marriage, single motherhood, one son killed in an auto accident and another in jail. After taking the name Zakiya (Swahili for "intelligence" and Hebrew for "pure, exonerated"), Hooker met producer Ollan Christopher in 1987, beginning a musical and romantic partnership (the two are now married). Her first public appearance came in a 1991 duet with her father.

Flavors of the Blues is certainly a passable album but not a very daring one. Hooker's voice veers between burnished and twangy. The album is bookended by fine performances, beginning with a jazz-tinged cover of Robert Johnson's "Stones in My Passway" and ending with the solid "Bit by Love (Hard Times)," which features her father. The energy lags on the other eight tracks (including four Hooker cowrote), however; her torch songs don't smolder as much as they flicker. — A.A.

ELMO HOPE

★★★★ Meditations (1955; Original Jazz Classics, 1991)
★★★★ Hope Meets Foster (1955; Original Jazz Classics, 1991)
★★★ Trio and Quintet (1957; Blue Note, 1991)
★★★★★ Elmo Hope Trio (1959; Original Jazz Classics, 1990)
★★★★ Hope-Full (1961; Original Jazz Classics, 1995)
★★★★ Homecoming (1961; Original Jazz Classics, 1993)
★★★★★ The Final Sessions (1966; Evidence, 1996)
★★★★ The All-Star Sessions (Milestone, 1989)

Pianist Elmo Hope (1923–1967) was overshadowed by his main influences, Bud Powell and Thelonious Monk, but he remained a bright, individual player with a strong compositional sense whose recorded output withstands the test of time. *Meditations* finds Hope in his best context, leading a trio, in this case with Monk sidemen John Ore on bass and Willie Jones on drums. Art Taylor replaces Jones on *Hope Meets Foster,* with Frank Foster on tenor saxophone and Freeman Lee on trumpet.

The All-Star Sessions, from 1956 and 1961, puts Hope in the company of John Coltrane, Donald Byrd, Jimmy Heath and Philly Joe Jones. With *Elmo Hope Trio,* a superb date with Jimmy Bond on bass and Frank Butler on drums, Hope pays his ultimate tribute to Monk and Powell. His selection of notes is impeccable throughout, and his touch is so sure that a listener feels familiar with him immediately.

The Final Sessions serves as a fitting epitaph for an underrated musician whose beautiful legacy has been obscured by the passage of time. Evidence lovingly restored these sessions, originally released in two volumes, in their entirety, including full takes of previously edited performances (check out "Punch That" and several alternate takes). Ore is the bassist throughout, with Clifford Jarvis or Philly Joe Jones on drums. — J.S.

LIGHTNIN' HOPKINS

★★★★★ Lightnin' Hopkins (1959; Smithsonian Folkways, 1990)
★★★★★ Last Night Blues (with Sonny Terry) (1960; Original Blues Classics, 1992)
★★★★ Autobiography in Blues (Tradition, 1960)
★★★★ The Best of Lightnin' Hopkins (Prestige, 1960)
★★★★ Blues in My Bottle (1961; Original Blues Classics, 1990)
★★★★ How Many More Years I Got (1962; Fantasy, 1989)
★★★★ Smokes Like Lightning (1962; Original Blues Classics, 1992)
★★★ Goin' Away (1963; Original Blues Classics, 1990)
★★★★ Soul Blues (1964; Original Blues Classics, 1991)
★★★★ Double Blues (1964; Fantasy, 1989)
★★★½ The Hopkins Brothers: Lightnin', Joel & John Henry (1964; Arhoolie, 1991)
★★★ Hootin' the Blues (1964; Original Blues Classics, 1995)
★★★ Free Form Patterns (1968; Collectables, 1993)
★★★★ Los Angeles Blues (1969; Rhino, 1995)
★★★ It's a Sin to Be Rich (Verve, 1972)
★★★ The Legacy of the Blues, Vol. 12: Lightnin' Hopkins (GNP Crescendo, 1976)

★★★★ **Mojo Hand/Golden Classics (Collectables, 1987)**
★★★ **An Anthology of the Blues, Part 1: Drinkin' in the Blues (Collectables, 1988)**
★★★ **An Anthology of the Blues, Part 2: Prison Blues (Collectables, 1988)**
★★★ **An Anthology of the Blues, Part 3: Mama and Papa Hopkins (Collectables, 1988)**
★★★ **An Anthology of the Blues, Part 4: Nothing but the Blues (Collectables, 1988)**
★★★★ **The Herald Recordings—1954 (Collectables, 1988)**
★★★★★ **Texas Blues (Arhoolie, 1989)**
★★★ **The Lost Texas Tapes, Vol. 1 (Collectables, 1989)**
★★★ **The Lost Texas Tapes, Vol. 2 (Collectables, 1989)**
★★★ **The Lost Texas Tapes, Vol. 3 (Collectables, 1989)**
★★★★ **The Lost Texas Tapes, Vol. 4 (Collectables, 1989)**
★★★ **The Lost Texas Tapes, Vol. 5 (Collectables, 1989)**
★★★★★ **The Gold Star Sessions, Vol. 1 (Arhoolie, 1990)**
★★★★★ **The Gold Star Sessions, Vol. 2 (Arhoolie, 1990)**
★★★★★ **The Complete Aladdin Recordings (EMI America, 1991)**
★★★★★ **The Complete Prestige/Bluesville Recordings (Prestige, 1991)**
★★★ **Lightnin' Strikes Back (Collectables, 1991)**
★★★ **Lightnin' Hopkins Strikes Again (Collectables, 1991)**
★★★ **Lonesome Life (Collectables, 1992)**
★★★★ **The Herald Recordings—1954, Vol. 2 (Collectables, 1992)**
★★★★★ **Mojo Hand: The Lightnin' Hopkins Anthology (Rhino, 1993)**
★★★½ **Lightnin'! (Arhoolie, 1993)**
★★★★ **The Swarthmore Concert (Original Blues Classics, 1993)**
★★★ **Cadillac Man (Drive Archive, 1994)**
★★★★ **Po' Lightnin' (Arhoolie, 1995)**

Sam "Lightnin'" Hopkins (1912–1982) left behind a voluminous collection of country and urban blues as personal and topical as that of any artist of his time. He recorded solo acoustic; he recorded with small backing groups of anywhere from one to four players, some playing acoustic instruments, some playing electric. He talked some of his blues, he sang most of them. In narrative and ambiance, his acoustic sides reflect the country life and attitudes he stayed close to from the cradle to the grave; his band sides burn with the fierce energy of rock & roll, as if the artist were acknowledging the quickening pace of society around him. From his songs you sense the man: witty, acerbic, truculent, deep-feeling, confident, loyal, generous, somewhat sentimental, sensitive, engaged in the world and sexually unforgiving. In his art he remained true to what he knew, and for ill or good there is abundant testimony by which to judge the giant called Lightnin'.

Born in the Texas farming community of Centerville, north of Houston, Hopkins grew up in a large family, one of five boys and one girl. His musician father, Abe, was killed (according to Lightnin', no stranger to mythmaking) in a dispute over a card game when Sam was three, but he had long since passed his love of music on to his children; Sam and his older brothers Joel and John Henry all had special gifts as musicians, but Sam was the one who emerged from the pack with the most unique voice. A cigar box and chicken wire served as his first guitar, when he was eight years old; he was still new at the instrument when he met Blind Lemon Jefferson at a Baptist church meeting and picked up some tricks of the trade from the Texas blues master. His youth was spent not in school but on the streets and in clubs or at social events—anyplace he could pick up some cash for playing music. At one point in his wandering young years he again crossed paths with Blind Lemon Jefferson and served as his guide for a short time.

Apart from Jefferson, his most important musical association in his formative years was with his cousin, blues vocalist Alger Alexander, who recorded in the 1920s as "Texas" Alexander. His improvisational, rhythmically irregular songs necessitated that any guitarist supporting him be quick enough to execute the proper changes without advance notice. Lonnie Johnson had worked with Alexander, and young Sam Hopkins no doubt raised his own game quickly in accompanying his cousin. In 1946 Sam was discovered by a talent scout for the Aladdin label and sent to Los Angeles to record with pianist Wilson "Thunder" Smith. "Thunder and Lightnin'" made a single, "Katie Mae Blues," that did well in the Houston area, and Hopkins returned to the Aladdin studio, where he would cut 41 more sides between 1946 and 1948; these are now collected on the double-CD set *The Complete Aladdin Recordings,* one of the critical early documents in Hopkins's recording history.

As good as those Aladdin sides are—and some, such as the rocking "Play with Your Poodle," a song written and originally recorded by Tampa Red, are not only extremely powerful but even forward-looking—vintage Hopkins can be found on other labels during these early years as well. After returning from California to Houston, he was signed to the local Gold Star label. A single issued in 1947, "Short Haired Woman" backed with "Big Mama Jump," sold a respectable 40,000 copies; a follow-up single, "Baby Please Don't Go," doubled that number, and Hopkins was off on a recording career that found him leaving many children with many labels. If he is not the most frequently recorded blues artist in history, as some scholars have suggested, he is most certainly near the top of the list, as his ever-growing CD catalog attests.

Women figure prominently in Hopkins's songs, although they are generally regarded with derision. But Hopkins was also something of a social commentator in that his songs observed the events unfolding in the world around him. "Tim Moore's Farm" describes in explicit detail the hard life of a black field hand; the song became a local hit and led Moore to show up at one of Hopkins's shows and demand he cease singing the number whenever he was in the area. "Bud Russell Blues" is a scalding account of the chief transfer agent (who is also immortalized in Lead Belly's "Midnight Special") for the Texas State Prison System whose job it was to transfer convicts to a central location from which they would be assigned to work camps; having spent some time working on the Houston Prison Farm's road gang, Hopkins knew whereof he sang. In later songs he limned the hazards of the approaching jet age in "DC-7," and in "Happy John Glenn Blues" he celebrated the personal triumph of the Clean Marine's triple orbit of the earth. With his gift for meter and rhyme, Hopkins was known also to make up songs on the spot from ideas supplied by his audience.

Arhoolie's *Gold Star Sessions* document the beginnings of his career (1947–1950), when he was recording an unusually broad variety of material. For example, in the midst of the fairly traditional folk blues on *Vol. 1,* Hopkins launches into "Zolo Go," accompanying himself on organ. The title is a phonetic misspelling of *zydeco,* and this is one of the early recorded examples of that genre, cut several years before Clifton Chenier first appeared on record.

From the 1950s, Hopkins is represented by a set of recordings made for the Herald label, now issued on Collectables as *The Herald Recordings—1954* and *The Herald Recordings —1954, Vol. 2,* and by Smithsonian Folkways' *Lightnin' Hopkins,* recorded in 1959 when he was rediscovered in Houston by blues scholar and producer Samuel Charters. Setting up a tape recorder in Hopkins's drab living quarters, Charters held the microphone in his hand while the artist produced one remarkable performance after another.

One of Hopkins's most productive periods occurred between 1960 and 1964 when he recorded for the Prestige label. Obviously the seven-disc boxed set, *The Complete Prestige/Bluesville Recordings,* is a must-have title, since it is true to its mission (it even includes a remarkable live performance recorded in 1963 at Swarthmore College, also now available as a single CD, and a revealing 1964 interview with Hopkins conducted by Charters). These seven discs bring together everything that Hopkins was as an artist—as a man, for that matter—in performances recorded solo and with small groups (for the most part dubbed in after Hopkins had recorded his parts; still, the sensitive backing support—and it was a tough job, given Hopkins's irregular sense of rhythm—is neither an encumbrance nor lacking for inspiration), and have the added benefit of an informative reminiscence by Charters of Hopkins's career and his own search for the artist in the late '50s. As for individual Prestige titles (most rereleased on Original Blues Classics), *Smokes Like Lightning* is highly recommended, both for the quality of the songs—"Prison Farm Blues" is one of the bleakest portraits any bluesman ever painted about the bleakest of places they could and often did land—and for folklorist/producer Mack McCormick's liner notes. McCormick, who was also Hopkins's agent and manager, had a volatile relationship with his charge, and his feelings boiled over during these sessions, resulting in what Charters terms (in his booklet accompanying *The Complete Prestige/Bluesville Recordings*), "the most hostile set of notes anyone has ever written as a back liner for an album."

Tastes vary, but *Last Night Blues,* with Sonny Terry sitting in on harmonica and singing one song (with Leonard Gaskin on bass and Belton Evans on drums), sounds like quintessential Lightnin'. His vocals are crisp and clear, full of feeling, and he's right there on guitar, strong and cutting and propulsive, as Terry's harmonica snakes its way through the melody line, energizing Hopkins's every lick. *Hootin' the Blues* is a live album from 1962, recorded at the Second Fret in Philadelphia and featuring an etiology of the blues ("Blues Is a Feeling") and an original instrumental dialog imagining a musical interchange between Lightnin' and Ray Charles ("Me and Ray Charles").

Post-Prestige, Hopkins continued label jumping, producing several interesting recordings over the next few years, particularly for Arhoolie, whose founder, blues authority Chris Strachwitz, is an unabashed Hopkins fan. In addition to returning the Gold Star recordings to print, Strachwitz did blues fans the great favor of recording Lightnin' with his brothers John Henry and Joel, at John Henry's home in Waxahachie, Texas, in 1964. This was something of a family reunion, since John Henry had not been in touch with his siblings or mother in years when they located him and showed up at his house that February. Lightnin' had long acknowledged John Henry as the best entertainer and singer in the family, and while his music here lacks Lightnin's depth of feeling, he still demonstrates an engaging way with a song, a quick wit and a strong, personable voice. Joel is less convincing, but then, this is mostly a showcase for Lightnin' and John Henry. As heard on *The Hopkins Brothers,* this was a reunion full of laughter, love and some melancholy over time passed—Lightnin's disc-opening "See About My Brother John Henry" is about as sad as blues gets.

Other Arhoolie titles may not have the emotional pull of the Hopkins brothers set but are worthy examples of the variety of blues Lightnin' was proffering in his later years. Particularly recommended is *Po' Lightnin',* a collection culled mostly from previously issued recordings dating from 1961, '62, '67 and '69, as it features some electrified Lightnin' as well as the artist accompanying himself on organ on two scintillating tracks and on piano on three tracks. *Lightnin'* collects several 1969 tracks that were released on the Poppy and Tomato labels, as well as previously issued Arhoolie sides from 1967, one featuring the artist backed by a small band.

In 1968 Hopkins recorded *California Mudslide* (*and Earthquake*) for the Vault label, which has now been reissued by Rhino as *Los Angeles Blues.* This spare, elegant recording finds Hopkins in a mellow mood, topical as ever with the title song and "California Mudslide" and reworking his first Aladdin single, "Katie Mae" into the delicately tempered "Rosie Mae"; getting introspective on "Change My Way of Living" and "No Education," the latter owing its existence to Bukka White's "Parchman Farm Blues"; working out a nice organ boogie on "Los Angeles Boogie"; and reprising (on organ) one of the few gospel songs he recorded, "Jesus, Would You Come By Here," which is heard in its 1952 RPM incarnation, "Needed Time," on Rhino's essential two-CD overview *Mojo Hand: The Lightnin' Hopkins Anthology* and on the aforementioned *Po' Lightnin'* as "Jesus Will You Come By Here."

One of the most interesting entries in the catalog is Tradition's *Autobiography in Blues.* Consciously designed to show the different aspects of the artist's approach to songs, its tracks include traditional fare such as "Trouble in Mind Time," which Hopkins personalized to express his own point of view; self-penned songs that became staples of his repertoire ("Short Haired Woman . . . Time," "75 Highway . . . Time"); and a group of songs lacking defined structure or lyrics that Hopkins would create anew with each performance ("Get Off My Toe . . . Time").

Collectables' four-volume *Anthology of the Blues* series is culled from the Everest label's vaults and takes Hopkins from the late '50s into the early '60s. Another Collectables title, *Mojo Hand,* features some of Hopkins's most searing guitar work, close-miked and violent in its intensity, produced by Bobby Robinson, whose Fire and Fury labels were home to some of the greatest blues and R&B artists of the '50s.

From later years comes the *Legacy of the Blues* entry, which in 1976 reunited Hopkins with Samuel Charters for what proved to be one of the artist's final recording sessions. An intriguing five-volume series titled *The Lost Texas Tapes* may be (there's no annotation) recordings Hopkins made in Houston in the '70s for the Home Cooking label (Collectables has two other Home Cooking releases in its Hopkins catalog, both interesting, in *Lonesome Life* and *Lightnin' Hopkins Strikes Again*). *Vols. 1* through *3* are Hopkins solo; *4* and *5* bring on guest artists. *Vol. 4* is a live recording, a true down-home effort done in a club or restaurant;

patrons are heard conversing in the background, and on one track a cash register rings as Hopkins plays. He's accompanied by Curley Lee, who blows mean and low harmonica fills throughout and engages Hopkins in some humorous but cutting between-songs banter.

Finally, for those who really want some sense of the path of Hopkins's career, run, don't walk, to the above-mentioned Rhino set, *Mojo Hand: The Lightnin' Hopkins Anthology.* This well-annotated double-CD set contains 41 cuts, ranging from the original "Katie Mae Blues" cut for Aladdin with Thunder Smith in 1946 to a 1974 track previously released on a Swedish blues album. In all, around 20 labels are represented here, including relative rarities issued on World Pacific, Ivory, Specialty, Decca and Jewel. Among other things, this set shows that no matter the passing of time and trends, Hopkins remained true to his style and never ran out of things to say or to say in a compelling way. — D.M.

SHIRLEY HORN

★★★ **Loads of Love/Horn with Horns (1963; Verve, 1990)**
★★★★ **Travelin' Light (1965; Impulse!, 1994)**
★★★½ **I Thought About You: Live at Vine Street (1977; Verve, 1992)**
★★★½ **Close Enough for Love (Verve, 1989)**
★★★★½ **You Won't Forget Me (Verve, 1991)**
★★★½ **Here's to Life: Shirley Horn with Strings (Verve, 1992)**
★★★½ **Light Out of Darkness: A Tribute to Ray Charles (Verve, 1993)**
★★★ **I Love You, Paris (Verve, 1994)**
★★★½ **The Main Ingredient (Verve, 1996)**

Vocalist/pianist Shirley Horn (b. 1934) was a popular Washington, D.C.–area performer in the 1950s. Her spare technique on ballads, where she seemed much more interested in the intervals between notes and phrases than in chord progressions themselves, won praise from the like-minded Miles Davis, who encouraged her to record.

Horn's earliest recordings, from 1963, feature her just as a vocalist and are collected on *Loads of Love/Horn with Horns. Travelin' Light* is an excellent session with alto saxophonist/flautist Frank Wess, guitarist Kenny Burrell and trumpeter Joe Newman.

Horn resurfaced on record in the late 1970s with a series of beautifully understated but hard-to-come-by import recordings—look for *A Lazy Afternoon*, *All Night Long* and *Violets for Your Furs.* She enjoyed a full-scale U. S. comeback with a series of Verve albums beginning with the live *I Thought About You. You Won't Forget Me* is a beautifully atmospheric record featuring guest spots from longtime admirer Miles Davis and young lion Wynton Marsalis on trumpets. Marsalis also appears on *Here's to Life,* where the string-heavy production detracts from the stark drama of Horn's vocals.

The Main Ingredient is an interesting live remote recording made in Horn's home with a variety of lineups from the trio with bassist Charles Ables and drummer Steve Williams on "The Look of Love" and "Looking at You!" to trios augmented by Roy Hargrove on flügelhorn, Buck Hill and Joe Henderson on tenor saxophone (together and separately), Ables on guitar and Steve Novosel on bass. — J.S.

LENA HORNE

★★★½ **Watch What Happens! (1969; DCC, 1990)**
★★★ **Lena Goes Latin and Sings Your Requests (DRG, 1987)**
★★★ **Stormy Lady (LaserLight, 1989)**
★★★ **Stormy Weather: The Legendary Lena (1941–1958) (RCA Bluebird, 1990)**
★★★ **The Best of Lena Horne: All Original Recordings (Curb, 1993)**
★★★ **Love Is the Thing (RCA, 1994)**
★★★ **We'll Be Together Again (Blue Note, 1994)**
★★★½ **The Lady and Her Music: Live on Broadway (Qwest, 1995)**
★★★★ **An Evening with Lena Horne: Live at the Supper Club (Blue Note, 1995)**
★★★ **Lena Soul (EMI America, 1996)**
★★★ **Lena in Hollywood (EMI America, 1996)**

Vocalist Lena Horne (b. 1917) began her career in the 1930s as a dancer and singer at the Cotton Club before breaking in as a singer with Noble Sissle. She then recorded with Sidney Bechet and Charlie Barnet before becoming a movie star in *Cabin in the Sky* and *Stormy Weather.* She went on to outstanding success in supper clubs and larger venues and on Broadway, starring in *Jamaica* in the late '50s.

Horne's wit, savvy and theatrical ability allow her to excel in the tony environs of high society, but she always has the feel of a jazz singer; in a musical rather than theatrical context, as in *Watch What Happens!* with guitarist Gabor Szabo, another side of her great talent emerges. Capable of great things well into her 70s, Horne is showcased spectacularly on the Quincy Jones–produced *The Lady and Her Music: Live on Broadway* and the Grammy-winning *An Evening with Lena Horne: Live at the Supper Club,* both of which feature an all-star backing band. — J.S.

WALTER "SHAKY" HORTON

★★★★ **The Soul of Blues Harmonica (1964; Chess, 1987)**
★★★½ **Johnny Shines with Big Walter Horton (1969; Testament, 1995)**
★★★★ **Big Walter Horton with Carey Bell (1972; Alligator, 1989)**
★★★ **Fine Cuts (1978; Blind Pig, 1990)**
★★★ **Can't Keep Lovin' You (Blind Pig, 1984)**

Harmonica ace Walter Horton (1917–1981), professionally known as "Shaky" or "Big Walter," was born in Horn Lake, Mississippi. Raised in Memphis, he moved to Chicago in the early '50s and worked as a sideman for a number of Chess artists, including Muddy Waters, Willie Dixon and Otis Rush. He also cut sides under his own name on various small Chicago labels but did not release his first proper LP, *The Soul of Blues Harmonica,* until 1964. The album comprises originals like "Hard Hearted Woman" and "Friday Night Stomp" and his Chi-Town colleagues' songs, like Waters's "It's Alright," Dixon's "Good Moanin' Blues" and Big Joe Turner's "Wee Baby Blues." Buddy Guy plays guitar throughout, and Dixon handles vocal duties on two tracks.

Big Walter Horton with Carey Bell features Horton backed by a band including Eddie Taylor on guitar. A young Carey Bell plays second harmonica and occasionally bass on this session, which finds the two masterful players dueling on eight Horton originals, including the rough-hewn instrumentals "Lovin' My Baby" and "Have Mercy." *Fine Cuts,* recorded in 1977, collects some of Horton's last recordings. Backed by a band including guitarist and sometime piano player John Nicholas, Horton runs through a battery of standards like "We Gonna Move to Kansas City," "Worried Life Blues" and Duke Ellington's "Don't Get Around Much Anymore." *Can't Keep Lovin' You* is a posthumous compilation of recordings by Horton, an artist who'll be remembered as one of the greatest blues harp players. — B.R.H.

HOT TUNA

★★½ **Hot Tuna (1970; RCA, N.A.)**
★★★★ **First Pull Up—Then Pull Down (1971; RCA, N.A.)**
★★★½ **Burgers (1972; RCA, N.A.)**
★★★½ **The Phosphorescent Rat (1973; RCA, 1989)**
★★★ **America's Choice (1975; RCA, 1990)**
★★★ **Yellow Fever (1975; RCA, 1990)**
★★★½ **Hoppkorv (1976; RCA, 1996)**
★★★ **Double Dose (1977; Edsel, 1995)**
★★★ **Splashdown (Relix, 1984)**
★★★ **Historic Hot Tuna (Relix, 1985)**
★★★ **Pair a Dice Found (Epic, 1990)**
★★★½ **Live at Sweetwater (Relix, 1992)**
★★★ **Live at Sweetwater Two (Relix, 1993)**
★★★★ **Classic Acoustic Hot Tuna (Relix, 1996)**
★★★★ **Classic Electric Hot Tuna (Relix, 1996)**
★★★ **Splashdown Two (Relix, 1997)**

Originally begun as a side project, Hot Tuna was formed by Jefferson Airplane's instrumental powerhouse, guitarist Jorma Kaukonen (b. 1940) and bassist Jack Casady (b. 1944). The two went for laid-back authenticity with the blues, unlike the Airplane's other spinoff, the glossy Jefferson Starship. Kaukonen and Casady deserve credit for exposing the work of the Rev. Gary Davis to a larger public, for proselytizing for country blues as a whole and for generating an in-concert atmosphere of funky geniality and casual virtuosity. The live *First Pull Up—Then Pull Down* shows what Hot Tuna is capable of at its best on "John's Other," "Candy Man," "Keep Your Lamps Trimmed and Burning" and "Come Back Baby."

But the band suffered, after a while, from too coy a modesty in its approach. With the Airplane, Casady and Kaukonen were dangerous, risky players; as Hot Tuna, they grinned and boogied, but seldom blazed. Kaukonen's vocals were rarely more than a diffident mumble, and the structure of blues itself, rather than rewarding Casady's capacity for experimentation, seemed too often to lock him into clichés. After an acoustic self-titled debut, they added ex–Airplane violinist, Papa John Creach (1917–1994), and cranked up the amps. Both maneuvers helped greatly to create a more varied sound; Kaukonen began writing more (if somewhat shapeless) songs, and *The Phosphorescent Rat* and *Hoppkorv* were solid. Their blues, however, seldom had the soul or bite of the original versions. The live work, more recent and more fluid, tends to offer more excitement than the studio sets. — P.E.

SON HOUSE

★★★★★ **Father of the Delta Blues: The Complete 1965 Sessions (1965; Columbia/Legacy, 1992)**
★★★★★ **Son House (Arhoolie, 1973)**
★★★★ **The Real Delta Blues (Blue Goose, 1979)**
★★★★★ **Delta Blues: The Original Library of Congress Sessions from Field Recordings 1941–1942 (Biograph, 1991)**
★★★★★ **Delta Blues and Spirituals (Capitol Blues Collection, 1995)**
★★★★★ **Son House and Blind Lemon Jefferson (Biograph, N.A.)**

Son House's blues universe is like no other Delta artist's, and to some his music is without parallel in its spiritual force. Born in Riverton, Mississippi, and raised in Tallulah, Louisiana, the forever-restless Eddie "Son" House (1902–1988) returned to his native state periodically in his teens in what now seems a search for peace of mind that would consume him throughout his life. A devout churchgoer from childhood, by age 15 he was a dedicated Baptist preacher who loved and sang gospel music but scorned the blues for its evocations of immorality and slovenly behavior.

In his mid-20s, though, House heard the music with new ears, perhaps because he was on his way to living out the very tales he so despised as he rambled aimlessly from town to town throughout the South, preaching, riding the rails, working a variety of manual-labor jobs, designing his next getaway. From a wandering Mississippi guitarist named Willie Wilson he learned the fundamentals of the bottleneck style that would lend his music its eerie, edgy quality. In another bluesman, Rubin Lacey (or Lacy), he heard the guitar being used almost as a second, inner voice, its hard-flailed chords crying out heartache as Lacey sang dark tales relating the ongoing battles in his soul between the sacred and the profane. In Lyon, he stumbled on James McCoy, whose songs "My Black Mama" and "Preachin' the Blues" House mastered, then rewrote into what are now regarded Delta-blues classics (the former in turn served as the foundation for Robert Johnson's "Walkin' Blues"). With these songs as a springboard, House soon found himself with a fast-flourishing occupation playing Delta juke joints.

In 1928, at the moment his career was gaining some momentum, House shot a man to death after the fellow had opened fire in a juke joint where House was performing. Sent to the notorious Parchman Prison Farm, he was pardoned after serving a year; from that experience came another House monument, "Mississippi County Farm Blues," whose tune was adapted from the great Blind Lemon Jefferson's "See That My Grave Is Kept Clean." Ordered by a judge to leave Clarksdale, House made his way north to Lula, where he met and befriended Charley Patton, then the reigning giant of Delta blues. The two performed together locally, and when Patton was preparing for a recording session for the Paramount label in Grafton, Wisconsin, he recommended the company record House as well as Willie Brown, an extraordinary guitarist who was then Patton's musical partner, and a piano-playing teenage girl, Louise Johnson, to whom Patton had taken a fancy. These sessions produced a number of remarkable recordings, but for House the most important upshot was the beginning of a deep friendship and musical pairing with Willie Brown that endured for 20 years. In the early '30s, one of House's and Brown's acolytes was young Robert Johnson, who would sit in with them on harmonica, all the while studying the guitarists' styles as his own began taking shape.

More important to House's high standing in the blues pantheon was a 1941 trip through the Delta by a team of field recordists (Alan Lomax among them) working on a documentary project cosponsored by Fisk University and the Library of Congress. These recordings, capturing House at his artistic peak, were followed by another session with the same team a year later (House then moved to Rochester, New York, where he stayed into the '70s). Son House gets no better than on Biograph's *Delta Blues* set.

While he had his share of songs about faithless lovers and general feelings of doom and degradation, House, more so even than Robert Johnson, found his soul in a constant tug-of-war between God and the Devil (a reason, perhaps, for his frequent returns to the pulpit), and this battle gave House's music a moral depth rarely encountered in any music, let alone Delta blues. "Preachin' Blues" may be the most explicit delineation of this war, but spiritual conflict shadows him in almost every circumstance. As powerful as the lyrics are in detail and imagery, it is House's deep, gravelly voice, haunted and haunting, that brings the message home with steely authority. Behind all this are some rather simple guitar stylings, by Delta standards—no showy polyrhythms, no startling key changes, no sweeping single- or double-string solo runs; rather, House wielded his slide as if it were on the left hand of God: It slashed, it wailed, it howled, it moaned, it wept. In the end, these rather fundamental parts created a mesmerizing whole.

When Willie Brown died in the mid-'50s, House lost interest in music completely. After moving to Rochester, he pretty much retired from music, preferring various day jobs (railroad porter, cook, etc.) to playing without Brown. The blues scholars who tracked him down in 1964 were shocked to learn he didn't even own a guitar anymore. Coaxed out of retirement, House began playing to enthusiastic audiences all over the country and in 1965 was signed to Columbia Records. The resulting sessions, first issued on vinyl as *Father of Folk Blues,* are now collected on the two-CD set *Father of the Delta Blues: The Complete 1965 Sessions.* Here he reprises many of the songs that established his legend—"Death Letter," "Preachin' Blues," "Pony Blues," "Louise McGhee"—along with more recent fare, including the touching, loving elegy "President Kennedy." House is a bit rusty in spots—a blown lyric here, a fumbled guitar lick there—but the imperfections are endearing glitches in otherwise remarkable performances. House enthusiasts will also want to track down the long-out-of-print classic *The Real Delta Blues,* as it is the earliest document of the artist's comeback years. The tracks here come from some private recordings made in 1964 at the time of House's rediscovery and include outstanding versions of "Pony Blues" and "Mississippi County Farm Blues" (the latter performance so resounding it suggests the memory of his Parchman confinement remained fresh in House's mind).

The House legacy is rounded out beautifully by Capitol's *Delta Blues and Spirituals,* which wraps four blues songs and four spirituals around a pair of insightful House monologs explaining in folk poetry—which was general conversation for Son House—the link between the two musical styles. "You can sing the blues in church if you use the words right—the verses and the words, *the meanings of it*—you can sing it in church," House tells an appreciative audience before launching into a growling, protesting version of "Between Midnight and Day," with Canned Heat's Al Wilson (one of those instrumental in House's rediscovery and latter-day prominence) moaning the blues behind him on harmonica. Recorded in a London club in 1970, this set shows House's spirit undiminished and the battles far from over. Check out the powerful take on "I Want to Go Home on the Morning Train," where House gets so deep into his spiritual quest that the title sentiment becomes a desperate plea rendered with thundering moral authority.

Although House struggled on performing as his health permitted, by the mid-'70s he had played his last show. He moved in with relatives in Detroit, was later taken to a rest home and died there on October 19, 1988, leaving behind a body of work rarely equaled, never surpassed. His guitar is in the Delta Blues Museum in Clarksdale; his voice is in the wind. — D.M.

HOWLIN' WOLF

★★★★★ **Howlin' Wolf (1962; Chess, 1987)**
★★★★★ **Moanin' in the Moonlight (1964; Chess, 1986)**
★★★★ **Poor Boy (Chess, 1965)**
★★★★★ **The Real Folk Blues (1966; Chess, 1988)**
★★★★★ **Evil (Chess, 1967)**
★★★★ **Live and Cookin' (at Alice's Revisited) (1967; Chess, 1992)**
★★★★★ **More Real Folk Blues (1967; Chess, 1988)**
★★★★ **The London Sessions (1971; Chess, 1989)**
★★★★ **The Back Door Wolf (Chess, 1973)**
★★★★ **Change My Way (1977; Chess, 1990)**
★★★★★ **His Greatest Sides, Vol. 1 (Chess, 1986)**
★★★★★ **Howlin' Wolf/Moanin' in the Moonlight (Chess, 1987)**
★★★★ **Cadillac Daddy: Memphis Recordings, 1952 (Rounder, 1987)**
★★★★ **Howling Wolf Rides Again (Flair, 1991)**
★★★★★ **The Chess Box (Chess, 1991)**
★★★★ **Ain't Gonna Be Your Dog: Chess Collectables, Vol. 2 (Chess, 1994)**
★★★★ **Chicago Blue (Tomato, 1995)**

★★★★ **The Legendary Masters Series (Aim, 1995)**
★★★★ **Bluesmaster (MCA, 1996)**
★★★★ **Howlin' Wolf: His Best (Chess, 1997)**

Along with his lifetime rival, Muddy Waters, Howlin' Wolf (1910–1976) was the archetypal Chicago bluesman—raw, electric, deep and continually astonishing. Born Chester Burnett, the singer-guitarist was raised in Mississippi, absorbing the country-blues tradition of Robert Johnson and Charley Patton. Learning the harmonica style of his teacher, Sonny Boy Williamson (Rice Miller), he formed his first band in 1948 in Memphis with James Cotton and Junior Parker; he'd later play with Ike Turner, Willie Dixon and other genre greats. While seldom recording as a guitarist, he gripped listeners with his voice in the early '50s; moving to Chicago, he recorded a series of seminal electrified singles whose appeal was their sheer visceral power. A performer known for keening like his namesake and cavorting onstage on all fours, as well as for his intimidating physical presence, the gigantic Wolf was indeed a force of nature.

The Chess Box is, by far, the best collection. Not only is it comprehensive—extending from 1951 to 1973, its three CDs feature 71 songs—but its roster of rarities and of all Wolf's hits (most of them written by Willie Dixon) makes it indispensable. "Smokestack Lightnin'," "I Ain't Superstitious," "Killing Floor" and "Back Door Man" are preternaturally moving music, by turns sly and terrifying, spooky, profane and wise. *The London Sessions* is a good late collaboration with Eric Clapton, Steve Winwood, Charlie Watts and Bill Wyman; *Cadillac Daddy* collects hard-to-find gems from Wolf's earliest recording career. All the Chess records are worth seeking out.

Among individual albums, *Howlin' Wolf* and *Moanin' in the Moonlight* (available as a twofer) are the great, early standouts: Songs like "How Many More Years" and "Wang Dang Doodle" would form the basis of the Chicago-blues repertoire. Fortunate in working with two stellar guitarists, Willie Johnson and Hubert Sumlin, and guest stars ranging from James Cotton to Ike Turner (on piano), Wolf was consistent in his greatness. Note, particularly, *The Real Folk Blues* (selected singles from 1956 to 1965, all heavily electric), *Ain't Gonna Be Your Dog* (rare takes), *Howlin' Wolf Rides Again* (Wolf in Memphis in the early '50s) and *Evil* (perhaps his toughest set). — P.E.

FREDDIE HUBBARD

★★★½ **Minor Mishap (1961; Black Lion, 1961)**
★★★★½ **Ready for Freddie (1961; Blue Note, 1995)**
★★★★½ **The Artistry of Freddie Hubbard (1962; GRP, 1996)**
★★★★½ **Hub-Tones (1962; Blue Note, 1985)**
★★★★ **Breaking Point (1964; Blue Note, 1991)**
★★★★★ **The Night of the Cookers (1965; Blue Note, 1994)**
★★★★ **Backlash (1967; Rhino, 1986)**
★★★★ **Red Clay (1970; CTI, 1987)**
★★★ **First Light (1972; CTI, 1987)**
★★½ **Sky Dive (1972; CTI, 1988)**
★★★½ **Freddie Hubbard in Concert (with Stanley Turrentine) (1974; CTI, 1987)**
★★★ **Outpost (1981; Enja, 1987)**
★★½ **Born to Be Blue (1982; Original Jazz Classics, 1992)**
★★½ **Face to Face (with Oscar Peterson) (1982; Original Jazz Classics, 1987)**
★★★ **The Best of Freddie Hubbard (Pablo, 1982)**
★★★★½ **The Best of Freddie Hubbard: The Blue Note Years (Blue Note, 1989)**
★★★ **The Best of Freddie Hubbard (Legacy, 1990)**
★★★★ **Bolivia (MusicMasters, 1991)**
★★★★ **Blues for Miles (1992; Evidence, 1996)**
★★★½ **Live at Fat Tuesday's (MusicMasters, 1992)**
★★★ **Live at Concerts by the Sea (LaserLight, 1994)**
★★★ **Back to Birdland (Drive Archive, 1994)**
★★★½ **Keystone Bop: Sunday Night (Prestige, 1994)**
★★★★ **MMTC (Monk, Miles, Trane and Cannon) (MusicMasters, 1995)**
★★★★ **The Freddie Hubbard and Woody Shaw Sessions (Blue Note, 1995)**
★★★ **Keystone Bop, Vol. 2: Friday/Saturday (Prestige, 1996)**

Trumpet/flügelhornist Frederick Dewayne "Freddie" Hubbard (b. 1938) came out of Indianapolis in the late 1950s to almost instant stardom as part of the new thing in jazz: hard bop and beyond into modal playing, freedom of expression, soul jazz and, within a few years, the first inklings of fusion. By the mid-'60s, Hubbard had played with Sonny Rollins, Eric Dolphy, Ornette Coleman and Oliver Nelson and spent several years in a featured role with Art Blakey's Jazz Messengers. He appeared on some of the decade's watershed albums—Coleman's *Free Jazz,* Dolphy's *Out to Lunch,* Rollins's *East Broadway Rundown,* Nelson's *Blues and the Abstract Truth,* Blakey's *Mosaic, Free for All, Ugestsu* and *Kyoto,* John Coltrane's *Ascension* and Herbie Hancock's *Maiden Voyage.*

Capable of making vital contributions to the different styles of the above albums, Hubbard obviously lies beyond simple characterization, but his distinguishing style did set him apart from the era's other young lion of the trumpet, Lee Morgan. Hubbard replaced the hard-blowing Morgan in Blakey's band, inviting comparisons that revealed Hubbard as possessing a more melismatic sound that made him Clifford Brown's spiritual heir. Hubbard's lines had punch, but he remained interested in maintaining rhythmic flow.

Hubbard had begun recording as a leader even before joining Blakey, and his outstanding early output is still well represented. *Ready for Freddie* and *Hub-Tones* are spirited hard-bop sessions with Hubbard in audaciously great form; *Breaking Point* veers more toward the experimental music he was making with Dolphy and Coleman. Blue Note's *The Best of Freddie Hubbard* includes tracks from his first four albums on that label; *The Artistry of Freddie Hubbard* reissues Impulse! recordings featuring Sun Ra Arkestra tenor saxophonist John Gilmore. *Minor Mishap* is inferior to the rest of the material from this period.

No single album captures the mystique of the hard-bop era better than *The Night of the Cookers,* an incendiary septet performance before a beautifully responsive audience at Brooklyn's Club La Marchal. Hubbard and Morgan engage in a trumpet battle for the ages, with James Spaulding, a Hubbard mainstay at Blue Note, refereeing on alto sax and flute. The rhythm section—pianist Harold Mabern, bassist Larry Ridley, drummer Pete la Roca and conga player Big Black—pretty well tears the joint down.

By the late 1960s, Hubbard was recording for Atlantic, a label that had made the transition from jazz and rhythm & blues to the extremely popular soul music and blues-rock. His rhythm sections started emphasizing the backbeat as Hubbard pursued his own take on soul, most successfully on *Backlash,* the only in-print album from that period. Hubbard's classic "Little Sunflower" debuts here.

The mass success Hubbard sought at Atlantic eluded him there; he found it instead at CTI in the early 1970s, beginning with the masterful *Red Clay* and the Grammy-winning *First Light.* But success leads to formulization and, all too often, vapidity, a problem with too many of CTI's overproduced '70s releases, like *Sky Dive.*

The demands of a more pop-oriented audience led Hubbard away from his artistic strengths into indifference and inappropriate settings through a series of generally uneventful and mostly unavailable recordings for several labels. The exception was his participation in the inspired VSOP project, which gathered some of the best-known contemporary players—Hubbard, keyboardist Hancock, saxophonist Wayne Shorter, drummer Tony Williams and bassist Ron Carter—not to create a fusion supergroup but to play acoustic jazz.

A return to Blue Note in the mid-1980s saw Hubbard in vintage form on *Double Take* and *The Eternal Triangle* (both available on *The Freddie Hubbard and Woody Shaw Session*), spectacular trumpet collaborations with Woody Shaw made even better by the presence of alto saxophonist/flautist Kenny Garrett and pianist Mulgrew Miller. Hubbard's musical restlessness and eclecticism has subsequently led him through a diverse run of projects with more hits than misses. The *Blues for Miles* tribute demonstrates the breadth of Hubbard's technique, from the open-throated shouts of New Orleans jazz to the muted introspection of Davis's ballad style, and the MusicMasters recordings *Bolivia* and *MMTC (Monk, Miles, Trane and Cannon)* are unqualified successes.

Hubbard remains a top draw in concert, especially on the European festival circuit, and never lets too many years go by without a live document of his playing. But as good as some of them are, none can improve on *The Night of the Cookers.* — J.S.

JOE "GUITAR" HUGHES

★★★★ **If You Want to See the Blues (Black Top, 1989)**

★★★★ **Texas Guitar Slinger (Bullseye Blues, 1996)**

Joe "Guitar" Hughes (b. 1938) grew up in Houston, where he learned to play guitar from Johnny "Guitar" Watson and Clarence "Gatemouth" Brown. In 1954 Hughes formed the Dukes of Rhythm with another local guitarist, Johnny Copeland. Later in the '50s he set up the house band at Shady's Playhouse, backing up the various blues stars who would come through town. In 1958 he played on the

Albert Collins session that produced "The Freeze" and recorded his own first singles as well. Though he made records for local mogul Huey Meaux, none of Hughes's singles became hits. In 1963 he joined Grady Gaines's Upsetters, then played with Bobby "Blue" Bland in 1965 and was featured on Bland's recordings for Duke until 1967. He finished off the '60s working with the Dallas-based Al "T.N.T." Braggs before returning to Houston, where he played local clubs through the '70s. During the '80s Hughes eventually found work in Europe, largely on the strength of collectors who prized his obscure recordings from the '50s and '60s.

If You Want to See the Blues reveals a consummate blues professional who, even in his 50s, plays with youthful fire and passion. The album consists of two sessions, one with a tight New Orleans quintet, the other with a Houston band including a seven-piece horn section. Hughes uses his smooth, near vibratoless vocals expertly on a wide range of material, including several well-written originals. He dances along the strings of his Gibson hollow-body guitar with a light, clear tone reminiscent of B.B. King.

Texas Guitar Slinger sounds like the work of a different man: Hughes goes for the gruffer vocal approach and stinging, sustained guitar tone of his Houston roots. The record is dedicated to Copeland, and it sounds as if some of the raw power of Copeland's approach to Texas blues rubbed off on Hughes — J.S.

BOBBI HUMPHREY

★★★ **City Beat (Malaco, 1989)**
★★★ **The Best of Bobbi Humphrey (Blue Note, 1992)**

Texan flautist Bobbi Humphrey (b. 1950) played with Herbie Mann and Hubert Laws before hitting it big with a series of Blue Note R&B/disco–jazz albums (now out of print but anthologized on *The Best of Bobbi Humphrey*). Her aggressive soloing in dance-music settings yielded crossover success on the pop charts, a recording contract with Epic and sessions with Sly Stone and Stevie Wonder. Humphrey began singing as well and descended into a smooth-jazz groove that led to radio airplay but encouraged lame (now unavailable) recordings. — J.S.

PERCY HUMPHREY

★★★★ **Percy Humphrey's Crescent City Joymakers (1961; Original Jazz Classics, 1994)**

Trumpeter Percy Humphrey (1905–1995) directly linked the prejazz New Orleans music tradition to the 1990s—he was the grandson of Jim Humphrey, a 19th Century New Orleans cornet teacher whose pupils filled the ranks of that city's jazz bands. On *Percy Humphrey's Crescent City Joymakers,* the band, a re-creation of the early jazz groups that played on the backs of wagons, offers a spirited run-through of a traditional session, featuring such chestnuts as "Milenberg Joys," "Weary Blues," "Bucket's Got a Hole in It" and "All the Gals Like the Way I Ride." Humphrey continued playing regularly for decades at Preservation Hall with his clarinetist brother Willie and never lost the good-time fire that charges this music with mythic power. — J.S.

ALBERTA HUNTER

★★★½ **Alberta Hunter with Lovie Austin's Blues Serenaders (1961; Original Blues Classics, 1988)**
★★★½ **Songs We Taught Your Mother (with Lucille Hegamin and Victoria Spivey) (1961; Original Blues Classics, N.A.)**
★★★★ **Amtrak Blues (Columbia, 1980)**
★★★½ **The Glory of . . . Alberta Hunter (Columbia, 1985)**
★★★½ **The Legendary Alberta Hunter: The London Sessions 1934 (Swing/DRG, 1991)**

Alberta Hunter (1895–1984) enjoyed thriving runs as a vocalist at the opposite ends of her professional life. Born in Memphis, she ran away to Chicago in 1911 and, within a few years, became one of the most popular early blues singers, recording with Ray's Dreamland Orchestra in 1921, then with Fletcher Henderson's band. She went on to star opposite Paul Robeson in the London stage production of *Showboat* and became a popular theatrical attraction, achieving dazzling success on the London stage and worldwide fame before retiring from show business in 1956 to become a nurse.

Alberta Hunter with Lovie Austin's Blues Serenaders reunites Hunter with pianist Austin, her onetime Chicago accompanist, for a one-shot recording. In 1977 Hunter returned to active performing, singing regularly at the Cookery in New York. She remained a thoroughly entertaining performer and a consummate blues singer to the end of her life, as the excellent *Amtrak Blues* attests. — J.S.

CHARLIE HUNTER

★★★½ **Charlie Hunter Trio (Mammoth, 1993)**

★★★ **Bing Bing Bing! (Blue Note, 1995)**

★★★ **T.J. Kirk (as T.J. Kirk) (Warner Bros., 1995)**

★★★ **Ready . . . Set . . . Shango! (Blue Note, 1996)**

★★★½ **Return of the Candyman (Blue Note, 1998)**

Charlie Hunter (b. 1968) plays such a mean and distinctive guitar, it's easy to overlook the amount of technique that goes into it. On his custom eight-string instrument, he keeps bass and rhythm patterns going even through his solo spots. In addition to his own recordings, Hunter played in the influential rap group Disposable Heroes of Hiphoprisy with Michael Franti.

The trio—with drummer Jay Lane and tenor saxophonist David Ellis—debuts with an eponymous album produced by Les Claypool of the funk-metal band Primus. "20, 30, 40, 50, 60 Dead" fuses bop and funk in a contemporary homage to Barney Kessel; "Dance of the Jazz Fascists," apart from being one of jazz's greatest titles since Mingus stopped naming tunes, swings mightily, with Ellis doing his best Sonny Rollins over an extended vamp climaxed with Latin percussion; Hunter's ambitious solo arrangement of Mingus's "Fables of Faubus" sounds like three guitarists are playing.

On *Bing Bing Bing!* Hunter makes the upper end of his guitar sound like an organ. His "Greasy Granny" is clearly inspired by Horace Silver, while "Bullethead" sounds like Prime Time, with Hunter referencing both James Blood Ulmer and Jamaaladeen Tacuma. On *T.J. Kirk,* which he describes as "Plays the Music of Thelonious Monk, James Brown and Rahsaan Roland Kirk," Hunter presents a quartet doing just that—sometimes all at once, blending "I Got to Move" with "In Walked Bud" and "Cold Sweat" with "Rip Rig and Panic." The group brings a rock edge to these composers, as in the grunge version of "Epistrophy." *Ready . . . Set . . . Shango!* lacks the manic energy of Hunter's earlier recordings but does show a compositional craftiness and melodic maturity the others wanted. *Return of the Candyman* is an easy-grooving quartet featuring Stefon Harris on vibraphone. — H.B.

IVORY JOE HUNTER

★★★★ **7:TH Street Boogie (Route 66, 1977)**

★★★★ **Jumping at the Dew Drop (Route 66, 1980)**

★★★★ **I'm Coming Down with the Blues (1989; Collectables, 1993)**

★★★★ **Since I Met You Baby: The Best of Ivory Joe Hunter (Razor & Tie, 1994)**

A blues singer who moved easily in country and pop circles, Ivory Joe Hunter (1914–1974) was one of the most distinctive stylists of the '40s and '50s, with 20 charting singles between 1945 and 1960; his soothing sound goes down as well today as it did in his own time. Born to a guitar-playing preacher father and gospel-singing mother in Kirbyville, Texas, Hunter had 13 siblings, all of whom were musically inclined: His four sisters sang locally, and each of his nine brothers was an accomplished pianist or drummer. Unsurprisingly, Hunter's entrance into the music world was through spirituals, which he sang in church choirs and as a member of several gospel quartets during his high school years in Port Arthur, Texas. But in his home state Hunter was surrounded by masters of the barrelhouse-piano style, and his own playing began reflecting this influence, as well as that of stride and sophisticated jazz keyboardists such as Duke Ellington and Fats Waller.

In 1933 the 19-year-old Hunter, singing "Stagolee," was recorded by Alan Lomax for the Library of Congress (Hunter is identified as Ivory Joe White on the disc). During the Depression years, Hunter fashioned a steady living playing pop and jazz in white clubs, where the pay was considerably higher than that being offered in black venues. As his stature grew on the circuit, Hunter began drawing top-flight musicians to his band, among them Illinois Jacquet and Arnett Cobb. With the onset of World War II, Hunter migrated to California, where he decided to form his own record label. At his first session in 1945 he was accompanied by pianist Charles Brown, guitarist Johnny Moore and bassist Eddie Williams, who became the Three Blazers and had a chart-topping single that year in Brown's self-penned "Drifting Blues." Despite good sales, Hunter's single, a version of Leroy Carr's "Blues at Sunrise" backed with "You Taught Me Love," was the only release on the short-lived Ivory label (then licensed to Exclusive).

Hunter next surfaced as the founder and sole artist on the Pacific label, where he cut several fine efforts with some of the Bay Area's top musicians, including guitarist Pee Wee Crayton.

In 1948 he had a Number One R&B hit with "Pretty Mama Blues." After folding Pacific, Hunter migrated to the King label in 1947 and became the MGM label's first R&B act in 1950, an honor he returned by writing and recording a Number One single right off the bat in "I Almost Lost My Mind," a lazy, yearning, after-hours blues notable for Hunter's silky vocal and Taft Jordan's haunting, upper-register muted trumpet lines wafting eerily through the stratosphere. That single, which was also a success in a 1950 cover version by Floyd Tillman (and would have a four-week run atop the pop chart in 1956 in a lugubrious interpretation by Pat Boone), kicked off a chart run of some nine years for Hunter, a period when he was a regular presence on the R&B chart and a frequent visitor to the pop side as well.

By the time he got to King, the Hunter style was pretty well set. While the up-tempo, barrelhouse songs remained vital in his repertoire, he was at his most dazzling in a quieter, ballad mode, where his soothing voice, crisp diction and measured phrasing were well suited to dreamy love songs and the gentle angst of bluesy weepers on the order of "I Almost Lost My Mind." His recording bands were no different in quality from his earlier groups, featuring such commanding musicians as tenor-sax man Budd Johnson, guitarists Mickey Baker and Al Caiola, drummer Joe Marshall and orchestral leader Ray Ellis, who shaped many of the tasteful, understated string arrangements on Hunter's memorable late-'50s recordings.

In 1954 Hunter signed with Atlantic, but his early up-tempo sides met with lukewarm response. Going to his strength, Hunter, though a prolific writer, opted to cover "A Tear Fell," which rose to #15 on the R&B chart in 1956 and set the stage for the latter-year success of a beautiful new Hunter love ballad, the lilting "Since I Met You Baby," which topped the R&B chart and peaked at #12 on the pop side. Before his Atlantic tenure ended in 1958, he had one more crossover hit in "Empty Arms," a country-flavored lament of lost love rendered in Hunter's deepest, most despairing tone.

The peak years of Hunter's career are well documented on *Since I Met You Baby: The Best of Ivory Joe Hunter,* which begins with 1949's "Since I Met You Baby," touches on other MGM entries and devotes most of its running time to the Atlantic sides, hits and otherwise (these being remarkable in some cases, such as "Love Is a Hurting Game"), through 1958.

Completists, though, are urged to search high and low for two import titles on the Route 66 label, *7:TH Street Boogie* and *Jumping at the Dew Drop.* The former contains the essential early years of Hunter's career, including 1945's "Blues at Sunrise" with the Three Blazers and the sides cut for Pacific and King through 1950. *Jumping at the Dew Drop* picks up where *7:TH Street Boogie* leaves off, encompassing tracks Hunter cut between 1947 and 1952 for Pacific (or Four Star, which bought Hunter's 32 Pacific masters, reissued some titles and issued others for the first time), King and MGM.

Post-Atlantic, Hunter had short, unsuccessful stints on Dot and Epic (with a pure pop effort, *The Return of Ivory Joe Hunter,* in 1971). In 1968 he returned to his native Texas and cut the sides that comprise *I'm Coming Down with the Blues.* Most of the tracks are Hunter originals written for this album, in addition to revamped versions of "I Almost Lost My Mind" and "Empty Arms." Hunter's in good form here, his voice strong and assured and his performances always engaging. Ever versatile, he offers a new country song, "The Cold Gray Light of Dawn," as well as a classically constructed pop number, "The Masquerade Is Over," though in-the-pocket '50s-style R&B is the rule. For a truly inspired Hunter performance, check out his live track on *The Johnny Otis Show Live at Monterey!* (Epic/Legacy), wherein he delivers a heartbreaking version of "Since I Met You Baby." At the time of his death from lung cancer in 1974 Hunter claimed to have written more than 2,000 songs. Those that remain in print reveal the beautiful soul of an elegant, distinguished artist, a class act in every respect. — D.M.

LONG JOHN HUNTER

★★★½ Ride with Me (1992; Alligator, 1998)

★★★★½ Border Town Legend (Alligator, 1996)

★★★★ Swinging from the Rafters (Alligator, 1997)

Guitarist/vocalist Long John Hunter (b. 1931) takes his place alongside such Texas blues legends as Albert Collins, Clarence "Gatemouth" Brown and Johnny Copeland with the firebrand album *Border Town Legend,* incredibly only the second full-length recording of his career. Decades of playing 12-hour gigs at bucket-of-blood bars along the Texas/Mexico border gave him plenty of opportunity to develop a crowd-pleasing style forged out of ringing guitar histrionics and gruff, arresting vocals. *Ride with Me* brought Hunter into the Texas-blues mainstream, but *Border Town Legend* marks him as a true original.

Swinging from the Rafters is designed to showcase Hunter's guitar playing, but even more impressive is the fact that on his third album Hunter is still relying on original material written by himself and producers Tary Owens and John Foose. — J.S.

ROBERT HURST III

★★★½ Robert Hurst Presents: Robert Hurst (DIW/Columbia, 1993)
★★★ One for Namesake (DIW/Columbia, 1994)

Bassist with Wynton Marsalis, Tony Williams and Branford Marsalis in the 1980s and early '90s, young veteran of numerous sessions and presently in *The Tonight Show* band, Robert Hurst (born in Detroit in 1964) is known for his strong sense of time, resonant sound and keen harmonic ear. Until the appearance of his two DIW/Columbia recordings, few knew of his gifts as a composer and group shaper.

Robert Hurst Presents: Robert Hurst assembles the Branford Marsalis Quartet (Marsalis on tenor, alto and soprano sax and clarinet, Kenny Kirkland on piano, Jeff Watts on drums) augmented by luminous trumpeter Marcus Belgrave, Hurst's musical mentor and first employer (Belgrave hired him for gigs at age 14). Strong ensemble writing, shifting tempos and rhythmic patterns, waltzes, ballads, variations on the blues and a chops-demonstration solo on Thelonious Monk's "Evidence" mark this intriguing debut. *One for Namesake* is an ambitious exploration of the trio format, with Kenny Kirkland and Detroit drum master Elvin Jones performing 10 Hurst originals and Dave Brubeck's "In Your Own Sweet Way." A muddy sound obscures the interplay between Hurst and Jones, who never quite seem to link up. An inconsistent session that contains inspired moments and tentative plateaus, it is nonetheless very much worth hearing.

Hurst also appears as a sideman on recordings including *The Ellis Marsalis Trio* (Blue Note, 1991), Geri Allen's *The Nurturer* (Blue Note, 1991), Tony Williams's *Native Heart* (Blue Note, 1990) and Kenny Kirkland's *Kenny Kirkland* (GRP, 1991), as well as several Branford Marsalis releases: *Renaissance* (1987), *Crazy People Music* (1990), *The Beautyful Ones Are Not Yet Born* (1991), *I Heard You Twice the First Time* (1992) and *Bloomington* (1993), all on Columbia. — T.P.

MISSISSIPPI JOHN HURT

★★★★½ The Immortal Mississippi John Hurt (Vanguard, 1967)
★★★★ The Best of Mississippi John Hurt (1970; Vanguard, 1987)
★★★★ Last Sessions (Vanguard, 1972)
★★★½ Today! (Vanguard, 1987)
★★★★★ 1928 Sessions (Yazoo, 1990)
★★★★★ Avalon Blues 1963 (Rounder, 1991)

Unlike many rural bluesmen of the early 1900s, John Hurt (1893–1966) didn't play music that focused on life's harshness. Instead, his songs were understated and intricate, discussing hardships with a wit and subtlety ahead of its time. While in his early teens, Hurt performed at local dances and parties, but most of his life he worked as a farmer. Okeh Records persuaded him to cut 13 tracks in Memphis and New York in 1928, but he quickly returned to Avalon, Mississippi, his beloved home. Hurt would be "rediscovered" by blues scholars in the '60s, leading to acclaimed recordings and performances, prospects he had rejected 50 years earlier.

Hurt's bucolic lifestyle was reflected in his music, a restrained array of traditional folk, religious and work songs that could be loosely termed country blues. His style, which relied on strict, fluid fingerpicking patterns, rhythmic smoothness and sweet, unforced vocals, was truly unique. Whereas most bluesmen used their voices as a primary rhythmic tool, Hurt was one of the first Delta musicians to use guitar for that purpose. Defining a song's accents with deft, inflexible picking patterns, Hurt's guitar playing became solid accompaniment rather than ornamentation.

This refined technique can be heard on the wonderful *Avalon Blues 1963,* one of Hurt's first recording efforts after his "rediscovery." In his 70s, Hurt runs through signature originals like "Avalon Blues," "Richland Woman Blues," "Spanish Fandango" and "My Creole Belle" with spry picking. Produced by Patrick Sky for Vanguard Records, both *Today!* and *The Immortal Mississippi John Hurt* feature fine performances of a variety of traditional and original material. The former, featuring "Pay Day" and "Spike Driver's Blues," unfortunately suffers from inferior sound quality. The latter is much more satisfying sonically, as Sky plays second guitar on two tracks.

The Best of Mississippi John Hurt documents the majesty of a latter-day Hurt performance. Recorded in 1965, at Oberlin College, the album's 21 tracks and nearly 70 minutes of music are compelling testimony to Hurt's humility, grace and popularity. A particularly poignant moment occurs when a woman in the audience calls for "Candy Man," one of Hurt's finest compositions. Softly repeating the title, Hurt launches into a playfully inspired version. At concert's end, he humbly asks the throng to sing along on "You Are My Sunshine," concurrently displaying his modesty and charisma. *Last Sessions* was recorded on two separate occasions in 1966, just months before his death of a heart attack that November. Again produced by Sky, who doubles on guitar on two tracks, the release features many songs never before recorded by Hurt, including versions of Bukka White's "Poor Boy, Long Ways from Home," Lead Belly's "Irene" and Hurt's own "Trouble, I've Had It All My Days."

An authentic, monumental work, *1928 Sessions,* comprising 13 originals, is a rare recorded testament to what has been called black household music, the rural, secular fare played strictly for the musician's entertainment rather than for financial gain or social acceptance (unlike much other blues-based music of its time). Hurt's finest, unadulterated output is represented here, including "Stack o' Lee Blues," "Big Leg Blues" and "Praying on the Old Camp Ground." *1928 Sessions* is truly an intimate, brilliant-sounding album that no serious fan of great songs, innovative guitar playing or rural blues should be without.
—B.R.H.

BOBBY HUTCHERSON

★★★★½ **Dialogue (1965; Blue Note, 1995)**
★★★★★ **Components (1965; Blue Note, 1994)**
★★★★½ **Happenings (1966; Blue Note, 1998)**
★★★★ **Oblique (1967; Blue Note, 1995)**
★★★★½ **San Francisco (1971; Blue Note, 1994)**
★★★★ **Solo/Quartet (1982; Original Jazz Classics, 1990)**
★★★ **Master of the Art (with Woody Shaw) (Elektra Musician, 1982)**
★★★½ **Night Music (with Woody Shaw) (Elektra Musician, 1983)**
★★★ **Good Bait (Landmark, 1985)**
★★★★ **Color Schemes (Landmark, 1986)**
★★★★½ **In the Vanguard (Landmark, 1987)**
★★★★ **Cruisin' the Bird (Landmark, 1988)**
★★★½ **Ambos Mundos (Both Worlds) (Landmark, 1989)**
★★★½ **Landmarks (A Compilation: 1984–86) (Landmark, 1991)**
★★★★½ **Mirage (Landmark, 1991)**
★★★★★ **Farewell Keystone (Evidence, 1992)**
★★★½ **Acoustic Masters II (Atlantic Jazz, 1994)**

Bobby Hutcherson (b. 1941) revolutionized the vibraphone as a jazz instrument, building on Milt Jackson's advances to make the instrument an angular, harmonically astute alternative (or adjunct) to the piano in the challenging postbop arrangements of the 1960s and beyond. In the early '60s, after moving to New York, the California native became a sought-after sideman who provided an unforgettable counterpoint to Eric Dolphy's saxophone, flute and bass clarinet on the landmark *Out to Lunch* in 1964.

In addition to being a ubiquitous sideman on Blue Note sessions, Hutcherson had a conceptual resourcefulness and compositional genius that made him a natural leader. He recorded a series of classic albums beginning with the experimental 1965 session *Dialogue,* with tenor saxophonist Sam Rivers and pianist Andrew Hill. *Components* is a tour de force recording with some of the brightest young stars of the era, including pianist Herbie Hancock, trumpeter Freddie Hubbard, bassist Ron Carter, drummer Joe Chambers and flautist/alto saxophonist James Spaulding. Hancock also figures prominently on *Happenings* and *Oblique.*

Back on the West Coast in the late '60s, Hutcherson co-led a superb quintet with tenor saxophonist Harold Land. This little-regarded unit, one of the undiscovered treasures in jazz history, is unfortunately represented only by *San Francisco,* a fusion-straddling outing energized by Joe Sample's electric piano. This collaboration made several other fine albums—look for *Total Eclipse*, *Medina*, *Blow Up* and the terrific *Head On.*

In the '70s, Blue Note placed Hutcherson in some less-than-flattering settings, the results of which have disappeared over the years. He returned to his more experimental side with a new label, Contemporary, for the stunning *Solo/Quartet;* half of the recording consists of overdubbed vibe and marimba parts with various other percussion instruments, while the rest features the McCoy Tyner trio.

Good Bait invites comparisons between Branford Marsalis and Land. Hutcherson wrests control for himself on the surefooted *Color Schemes,* with pianist Mulgrew Miller, bassist John Heard, drummer Billy Higgins and percussionist Airto supporting him. Hutcherson waxes virtuosic on the quartet recording *In the Vanguard:* This venerable club inspires a musical genius to reach beyond the perceived limits of the time.

Landmarks is an otherwise decent compilation marred by material from *Good Bait.* Hutcherson returns to sharing the front line with a saxophone on *Cruisin' the Bird,* this time with Ralph Moore on tenor and soprano. *Ambos Mundos* explores his fascination with Latin jazz, offering spectacular marimba work on a version of "Besame Mucho." *Mirage,* another quartet session of near-miraculous beauty, centers on a dialog between Hutcherson's vibes and marimba and Tommy Flanagan's piano. Another joint-leaders outing, *Acoustic Masters II* features drummer Lenny White, reeds player/flautist Craig Handy, trumpeter/flügelhornist Jerry Gonzalez, pianist Mulgrew Miller and bassist Ron Carter. *Farewell Keystone* is a stirring reunion with Land in a lineup with Oscar Brashear on trumpet and flügelhorn, Billy Higgins on drums, Buster Williams on bass and Cedar Walton on piano. — J.S.

J.B. HUTTO

★★★★ Masters of the Modern Blues (1967; Testament, 1995)
★★★ Hawk Squat! (1968; Delmark, 1994)
★★★★ Slidewinder (1973; Delmark, 1990)
★★★★½ Slideslinger (1982; Evidence, 1992)
★★★½ Slippin' and Slidin' (Varrick/Rounder, 1983)

"The Hawk" is what Chicagoans have dubbed the icy, ferocious wind that sweeps off Lake Michigan and chills the city to the bone. Slide master Joseph Benjamin "J.B." Hutto (1926–1983) called his band the Hawks, an apt description of the effect made by his blistering, vocallike slide style and rough-hewn singing—"an icepick to the forehead" is how *Living Blues* once put it à la Frank Zappa. An unabashed acolyte from the Elmore James school of slide, Hutto carried on that intense tradition with a ferocity and singlemindedness shared only with the likes of Hound Dog Taylor. A series of well-recorded, widely distributed albums in the '60s established Hutto as the genre's premier slide man.

His first full album project is *Masters of the Modern Blues,* which bridles with all the energy and set-list variety of hardworking South Side blues outfits: Guitarist Johnny Young and harmonicist Big Walter Horton help "Pet Cream Man," "Blues Stay Away from Me" and the Latin-tinged "My Kind of Woman" shine. Culled from a series of late-'60s sessions, *Hawk Squat!*—though helped along by Sunnyland Slim on organ and Maurice McIntyre on sax—is an uneven effort, suffering from inadequate rhythm backup and apparently falling victim to one-take-itis.

Hutto's *Slidewinder* is easily one of the decade's most convincingly solid and complete slide albums, boasting his last great Chicago-based band (Lee Jackson on guitar and the irrepressible Bombay Carter on drums) as well as his songwriting. "Blues Do Me a Favor" and "Precious Stone" reveal a knack for blues metaphor and intimacy unforeseen on his previous albums. After Hound Dog Taylor passed away in the late '70s, Hutto inherited his bassless backup band, the Houserockers (Brewer Phillips and Ted Harvey), for one (unfortunately out-of-print) title on Boston's Baron label.

Hutto found his way to Boston in the early '80s, hooking up with a younger, more rock-infused band, the New Hawks. *Slideslinger* brilliantly captures his road-tested quartet, with Steve Coveney's rhythm-guitar work providing appropriately distorted counterpoint to Hutto's blistering leads. Hard-driving numbers like "I Feel Good" and "Combination Boogie" show off his hard-driving side, while he ably handles heartrending ballads like "Lone Wolf." Though the blues world lost Hutto to cancer in 1983, he recorded a handful of projects in his last year: In March he tastefully expanded the New Hawks lineup with a Roomful of Blues reeds-and-rhythm unit; *Slippin' and Slidin'* is the result. As well, a compelling version of "Summertime" saw light on Baron, giving the Gershwin chestnut its most raucous reading since Janis Joplin. In the years since Hutto's passing, his nephew Little Ed continues to carry the electric-slide torch. — A.K.

ABDULLAH IBRAHIM
(DOLLAR BRAND)

★★★½ **Duke Ellington Presents the Dollar Brand Trio (1964; Reprise, 1997)**
★★★★½ **African Piano (1969; ECM, 1989)**
★★★ **The Banyana: Children of Africa (1976; Enja, 1990)**
★★★½ **Echoes from Africa (1979; Enja, 1990)**
★★ **Africa: Tears and Laughter (1979; Enja, 1996)**
★★★½ **Live at Montreux (1980; Enja, 1990)**
★★★½ **Zimbabwe (1983; Enja, 1990)**
★★★ **South Africa (1983; Enja, 1993)**
★★★★ **Water from an Ancient Well (1985; Tiptoe, 1992)**
★★★ **African Dawn (Enja, 1987)**
★★★ **Mindif (Enja, 1988)**
★★★★½ **African River (Enja, 1989)**
★★★ **Mantra Mode (Tiptoe, 1991)**
★★★ **Desert Flowers (Enja, 1992)**
★★★½ **Good News from Africa (Enja, 1994)**
★★★ **African Marketplace (Discovery, 1994)**
★★★ **Yarona (Tiptoe, 1995)**
★★★ **Knysna Blue (Tiptoe, 1995)**

A South African expatriate, pianist Abdullah Ibrahim (born Adolph Johannes Brand in 1934, a.k.a. Dollar Brand), has had a subtle but profound influence on modern music. His knowledge of and sympathy for African music makes him a firsthand practitioner of the styles and feelings many other musicians have adopted from afar, while his wide-ranging control of rhythmic dynamics and melodic improvisation mark him as a musical modernist.

In 1960–61 he led his own group, the Jazz Epistles, including Hugh Masekela on trumpet, which in 1960 was the first black group in South Africa to record a jazz LP. In the mid-1960s Ibrahim began recording internationally as Dollar Brand at the encouragement of Duke Ellington, who sponsored his first visits to the United States and produced his impressive debut, *Duke Ellington Presents the Dollar Brand Trio.* In the United States Ibrahim became involved in the free-jazz movement, meeting Don Cherry, whose interest in world music paralleled his own, and playing with John Coltrane and Elvin Jones. He adopted the name Abdullah Ibrahim after converting to Islam in 1968. Unfortunately, many of his extensive 1960s and early-'70s recordings, which include a number of very good solo-piano outings, are currently unavailable. An exception is the best of these, *African Piano,* one of his most important works.

Available Ibrahim recordings primarily consist of small-group settings. A trio date, *The Banyana* features bassist Cecil McBee and drummer Roy Brooks. *Echoes from Africa* is a moving collection of duets with fellow expatriate Johnny Mbizo Dyani on bass and African bells. Both musicians vocalize with spine-tingling results. This collaboration can also be heard on *Good News from Africa.*

On the live set from Montreux, Ibrahim begins a magnificent collaboration with alto saxophonist/flautist Carlos Ward, whose playing sensibilities mesh perfectly with his. The leader also plays soprano saxophone on this date for a pointedly Arabic musical reference. Ward lights up the fine *Zimbabwe,* but the partnership reaches its zenith on *Water from an Ancient Well,* which also includes trombonist Dick Griffin, tenor saxophonist Ricky Ford, baritone saxophonist Charles Davis, bassist David Williams and drummer Ben Riley. Ward appears on *African Marketplace* as well.

African Dawn is a solo-piano recording from 1982, while *Mindif* is a sextet with a front line composed of trombonist Benny Powell, Ricky Ford on tenor and soprano saxophone and Craig Handy on tenor and flute. Generally considered Ibrahim's best larger-group album, *African River* is a sublime effort highlighted by the performances of John Stubblefield on flute and tenor saxophone, Horace Alexander Young on soprano, alto and piccolo and the great Howard Johnson on baritone sax and tuba. The lineup also features trombonist Robin Eubanks, bassist Buster Williams and drummer Brian Adams. *Mantra Mode* was recorded in Cape Town with local musicians; the solo outing *Desert Flowers* features Ibrahim's synthesizer experiments; *Yarona* is a live trio date recorded at New York's Sweet Basil; and *Knysna Blue* is another solo outing. — J.S.

THE INK SPOTS

★★★★★ **The Best of the Ink Spots (MCA, 1980)**
★ **Just Like Old Times (Open Sky, 1982)**
★★★★ **Greatest Hits: 1939–1946 The Original Decca Recordings (MCA, 1989)**
★½ **Java Jive (LaserLight, 1992)**
★½ **Truck Stop Country (Jewel, 1996)**

Founded in 1934, the Ink Spots pioneered a pop-oriented group-harmony approach that translated into consistent chart success from 1939 through 1951 and became the key link between the vocal trios featured in the swing big bands and doo-wop's golden era in the '50s. The group's trademark was the contrasting voices of lead tenor Bill Kenny and bass singers Orville Jones and Herb Kenny (the latter joining in 1944 after Jones's death). Tenor Bill Kenny, he of the impeccable control and diction in his highest register, was the singer's singer, a master of technique with a peerless sense of drama.

The Best of the Ink Spots is the most complete overview of the trio remaining in print. With 24 essential tracks, it has 9 more songs than the otherwise excellent *Greatest Hits* album. "We'll Meet Again," "Until the Real Thing Comes Along," "I Cover the Waterfront" and "It Is No Secret" are among the songs unavailable on *Greatest Hits* that rank as definitive performances. Both sets, though, include the original versions of songs that were '50s and '60s hits for the Platters—"My Prayer," "To Each His Own," "If I Didn't Care" and "I'll Never Smile Again"—and one that has become a staple of the risible Manhattan Transfer's repertoire, "Java Jive."

Just Like Old Times features a latter-day configuration of the Ink Spots formed by original member Ivory "Deek" Watson. The harmonies are smooth, the material only passable and lead singer Gene Miller's Kenny-style vocal posturing misses the mark. Accept no substitutes. Similarly, *Java Jive* presents some vintage Ink Spots songs sung by a group whose members are unidentified in the liner copy (neither are the recording dates), but whose lead singer has some Kenny affectations absent the heart-tugging delicacy of the real thing. *Truck Stop Country* is what its title suggests, an attempt at a mainstream country album (even down to a sad reworking of the original Ink Spots' "If I Didn't Care"). Devoid of personnel information, this effort finds the group hewing to safe, MOR arrangements and tight, bland harmonies. — D.M.

ITSLYF

★★★★★ **Hep Caolin (PAO, 1995)**

Itslyf, a visionary transglobal octet from Austria, India and the United States, melds ethno-jazz-world music with interactive computer music. *Hep Caolin*'s 13 tracks conjure detailed imaginative programs, with multi-instrumentalist Paul Zauner leading the ensemble and Franz Hackl writing much of the material and playing trumpet and flügelhorn. Other members include guitarist David Gilmore, saxophonist Gottfried Stoger, bassist Fima Ephron, drummer Thomas Lang and tabla player Pawan Kumar. They met at the Jak Jazz Festival in Jakarta, Indonesia, and formed a partnership.

Zauner studied piano in his hometown of Passau on the Austro-German border and moved at age 20 to Vienna, where he played piano in blues bands and took up the trombone. He became a founder of Blue Brass Connection in 1985, recording "Cool Affairs" with that group; he also appears on David Murray's *Last of the Hipmen.* In 1993 he played on *Beginnings,* by jazz/world-music ensemble Abstract Truth.

Hackl, a composer, educator and performer on trumpet and flügelhorn, studied at the Vienna Conservatory and the Manhattan School of Music. He has orchestrated soundtrack material and served as musical consultant for a number of film scores while exploring the boundaries between classical, pop and jazz. Hackl has recorded in a wide variety of settings, with Dave Taylor, John Clark, Thomas Larcher and many others. He designs and crafts his own brass instruments and develops interactive computer-music installations.

Brooklyn-based Gilmore has recorded with the Black Rock Coalition, Steve Coleman and the Five Elements, Muhal Richard Abrams, Cassandra Wilson, Greg Osby and the M-Base Collective, among others. His performance credits include appearances with Geri Allen, Kevin Eubanks, Don Byron, Larry Coryell, Von Freeman, Branford Marsalis and David Murray. Stoger has worked with Joe Zawinul, Lee Konitz, Kenny Werner and others. The versatile Ephron also plays with Lost Tribe and the Screaming Headless Torsos. A premier Austrian session drummer, Lang has recorded in many styles, including a stint with the pop group Falco. Kumar, one of the most respected tabla players in the world, currently teaches in Jakarta and works extensively with Jalu Pratidina.

Hep Caolin is highlighted by the burning funk progressions of the ambitious centerpiece "TKAG," the elegiac "Go South," Hackl's jubilant, antiphonous "KSKG" and a terrific Hackl arrangement of Ron Carter's "Eighty One." Kumar on tabla and Pratidina on kendang bring the listener through the dusty overlands of five riveting interludes that act as sonic passageways between the album's episodic sections. — J.S.

JACKIE AND ROY

★★★ **Spring Can Really Hang You Up the Most (1955; Black Lion, 1988)**
★★★ **We've Got It: Music of Cy Coleman (Discovery, 1986)**
★★★ **One More Rose: A Tribute to Alan Lerner (Audiophile, 1989)**
★★ **An Alec Wilder Collection (Audiophile, 1990)**
★★★ **Forever (MusicMasters, 1995)**
★★★ **East of Suez (Concord Jazz, 1996)**

Vocalists Jackie Cain (b. 1928) and Roy Kral (b. 1921) were part of the post–World War II Chicago jazz scene, singing with Charlie Ventura, then on their own since 1949. Kral also plays piano and has arranged much of their material to be lounge-friendly: Jackie and Roy have been a staple of the Las Vegas nightclub circuit. Their trademark sound consists of unison vocal lines informed by bop-era harmonics. A dependable ballad singer, Cain also possesses the requisite range and emotional commitment to the material.

Spring Can Really Hang You Up the Most features guitarist Barney Kessel, bassist Red Mitchell and drummer Shelly Manne. The collections of selected writers' material are generally well done—an album of Stephen Sondheim compositions is currently unavailable. The duo successfully revisits its heyday on *Forever,* fronting a large band in a John Simon production aimed at the pop market, where this duo really belonged all along. — J.S.

D.D. JACKSON

★★★½ **Peace-Song (Justin Time, 1995)**
★★★★ **Rhythm-Dance (Justin Time, 1996)**

Canadian-born, conservatory-trained pianist/composer D.D. Jackson (b. 1967) is surely one of New York's most promising young stars. Spirited and spiritual, his rhythmically inventive compositions and energetic technique incorporate wide-ranging influences (from classical romanticism to bebop, Latin and R&B) and reveal a zealous devotion to his chosen holy trinity of jazz inventors. Particularly from Don Pullen (with whom he studied until Pullen's passing in 1995), Jackson inherited a dramatic flair for full-keyboard sweeps and staccato bursts of song, while adding an aggressive, percussive attack and a folklike melodic sense he gleaned from Thelonious Monk and South Africa's Abdullah Ibrahim. That he has so skillfully balanced a sense of jazz daring and experimentation with a rootsy, compositional skill is a compliment to his growing talent.

Recruiting an experienced and equally versatile rhythm section from his native Ottawa (bassist John Geggie and drummer Jean Martin), Jackson cut his first two albums in a trio setting with the erstwhile addition of saxophonist David Murray (whom he met while both were on tour with bandleader Kip Hanrahan). *Peace-Song* is a solid and surprisingly unified freshman effort given the vast stylistic bases he chooses to cover, from the introspective, Chick Corea sound of "Wisps of Thought" to the gospel flavor of the title track to the comical ending of "For Monk-Sake." The follow-up, *Rhythm-Dance,* takes a more energetic and rhythmically expansive approach, adding loose-limbed, Third World beats on the title track and "No Boundaries" and allowing himself sentimental room on catchy, pop-melodic exercises like "Nuevo Canción" and "Guitar Song." — A.K.

DUFFY JACKSON

★★★★ **Swing! Swing! Swing! (Milestone, 1995)**

Florida-based drummer Duffy Jackson (b. 1953) learned to play from his father, Chubby Jackson, bassist with the Woody Herman band. Duffy quickly garnered a reputation as a child prodigy, studying with Gene Krupa and Louie Bellson. At age 14 he broke in playing a guest spot with the Buddy Rich band and at 18 began touring with Lena Horne. Jackson's versatile technique and powerful swing are well presented on *Swing! Swing! Swing!* in a mixture of small-group and big-band settings featuring strong compositions from Jackson and Todd DelGuidice. — J.S.

JAVON JACKSON

★★★ **Me & Mr. Jones (Criss Cross, 1992)**
★★★★ **When the Time Is Right (Blue Note, 1994)**
★★★ **For One Who Knows (Blue Note, 1995)**
★★★ **A Look Within (Blue Note, 1996)**
★★★½ **Good People (Blue Note, 1997)**
★★★★ **Burnin' (with Billy Pierce) (Criss Cross, 1997)**

Tenor saxophonist Javon Jackson (b. 1965) was fortunate to have spent nearly three years in the final edition of drummer Art Blakey's Jazz Messengers, where he rapidly developed his own musical personality. The former Berklee College of Music student, raised in Denver, also put in serious time in the bands of Betty Carter, Elvin Jones and Freddie Hubbard before starting to record on his own in 1992.

While Wayne Shorter and Sonny Rollins are among his influences, Jackson has a sure, blues-steeped sound of his own and keeps stretching his stylistic comfort range.

Jackson is backed by pianist James Williams, bassist Christian McBride and drummer Elvin Jones on *Me & Mr. Jones,* a solid introduction to his playing and his musical preferences. Betty Carter produced Jackson's 1994 release, *When the Time Is Right,* a quartet session with appearances by singer Dianne Reeves and alto player Kenny Garrett.

Jackson's most progressive recordings to date, *For One Who Knows* and *A Look Within,* reflect his growth as a soloist and interpreter with a stretch in material and instrumentation. The title track of *For One Who Knows* is a searing loft-jazz original that reveals a deeply emotional facet. The eclecticism is carried a step further on *A Look Within,* featuring cameos by singer Cassandra Wilson and organ player Dr. Lonnie Smith.

Jackson continued to break away from the straight-ahead jazz mold on *Good People,* bringing organ whiz John Medeski and ex–Living Colour guitarist Vernon Reid along to help explore a variety of stylistic influences. While not released until 1997, the 1991 recording *Burnin',* a collaboration with his Berklee College of Music mentor, Billy Pierce, is a very strong example of Jackson's abilities. He rises to every challenge Pierce throws his way. — K.F.

MAHALIA JACKSON

★★★ **Bless This House (Columbia, 1963)**
★★½ **Mahalia Jackson: Greatest Hits (Columbia, 1963)**
★★★½ **Mahalia Jackson Sings the Best-Loved Hymns of Dr. Martin Luther King, Jr. (Columbia, 1968)**
★★ **Christmas with Mahalia (Columbia, 1968)**
★★ **Mahalia Jackson Sings America's Favorite Hymns (Columbia, 1971)**
★★ **The Great Mahalia Jackson (Columbia, 1972)**
★★★★ **How I Got Over (Columbia, 1976)**
★★★★★ **I Sing Because I'm Happy (1976; Smithsonian Folkways, 1992)**
★★★★★ **Gospels, Spirituals & Hymns (Columbia/Legacy, 1991)**
★★★★★ **Mahalia Jackson, Vol. 2 (Columbia/Legacy, 1992)**
★★★★ **Silent Night: Gospel Christmas with Mahalia Jackson (LaserLight, 1992)**
★★★★★ **Go Tell It on the Mountain (Arrival, 1993)**
★★★★ **Live at Newport 1958 (Columbia/Legacy, 1994)**
★★★★ **The Essence of Mahalia Jackson (Columbia/Legacy, 1994)**
★★★ **Mahalia Sings Songs of Christmas (Columbia/Legacy, 1995)**
★★★★★ **The Best of Mahalia Jackson (Columbia/Legacy, 1995)**

Atop the gospel mountain, Mahalia Jackson's stature is such that her neighboring titans (Thomas A. Dorsey excepted) are diminished by comparison. Inspired by Bessie Smith's haunted, brooding testifying, Jackson (1911–1972) developed a muscular style that coupled the blues sensibility of a woman forever 'buked and scorned with a deeply held conviction of salvation by grace of a higher power she knew in her own fashion. Indeed, being stubborn, contentious and not altogether a model of propriety herself, the God-fearing Jackson had good cause for coming on as an emotional firestorm, since such an approach reflected the inner turmoil rocking her as she sought to stay the sacred course in an increasingly profane world. When she sang, it all came together: Hers was the blues singer's voice inveighing against profligacy; the folksinger's voice broadcasting the unceasing trials of the disenfranchised; the gospel singer's voice heralding the unconditional love, mercy and forgiveness God promised in the Good Book. Though some important trailblazers preceded her—notably Sister Rosetta Tharpe—it was Jackson who most profoundly melded the complex emotional hues of deep blues to gospel music. Not content to stop there, she then relayed the good news as she had shaped it to the ears and hearts of a secular, multiracial audience, reaching numbers unprecedented in her day, or ours.

Born in New Orleans, Jackson grew up singing in church; although she was surrounded and fascinated by jazz and blues (Bessie Smith and Ma Rainey on the phonograph; Louis Armstrong and King Oliver sitting in at neighborhood lawn parties), she found in gospel's texts the peace that surpasses all understanding, a source of strength she leaned on and learned from in enduring the suffocating, unrelenting racism directed at Southern blacks. (Her eye fixed on the goal beyond, she disdained the blues, she once said, "because when you finished, you still had the blues.") Working numerous odd jobs to help support her family, she finally migrated north to Chicago in 1927, anticipating better opportunities in a more tolerant climate. While working as a maid, she joined the choir at the Greater Salem Baptist Church, quickly was elevated to a soloist's spot, and then moved over to join a quartet, the Johnson Singers. As her reputation spread through the Windy City's church community, she was introduced to Thomas A. Dorsey (who was then engaged in nothing less than building the foundation of modern gospel with his original hymns) and joined him in a duo playing at church meetings.

In 1937, the same year she began working with Dorsey, she recorded a few sides for Decca that gained little notice; nine years and many appearances with Dorsey later, she was signed to the Apollo label and recorded Herbert Brewster's "I Will Move On Up a Little Higher." It sold half a million copies, and the snowball effect took hold: She appeared on Studs Terkel's Chicago radio show, was booked to sing in New York City churches, performed before a gathering of music experts from the nation's finest schools and, in 1952, made a tour of Europe in the wake of her Apollo recording "I Can Put My Trust in Jesus," being honored as a masterpiece by the French government. From her first notes on record, she projected an image of a woman of moral force and unwavering faith.

After being out of print for many years, 10 of the original Apollo recordings surfaced in 1993 on the unassuming *Go Tell It on the Mountain*. These are works of inestimable beauty and power, recorded when Jackson's voice was a big, booming instrument, to be sure, but also a supple one, well able to scale the high end of her register in piercing fashion. Although neither "I Will Move On Up" nor "I Can Put My Trust in Jesus" is included, there's plenty here of a revealing nature. The stately, commanding reading of "Go Tell It on the Mountain" brings new meaning to this evergreen's jubilant message. On "Beautiful Tomorrow" she is joined by a small instrumental combo and a male quartet (the liner copy contains no personnel info or recording dates, an unfortunate lapse) for some exhilarating call-and-response vocal face-offs. With an organ rumbling low behind her, Jackson makes moving personal testimony of "I Gave Up Everything to Follow Him," in an interpretation that best demonstrates exactly what she took from Bessie Smith in the way of a moaning, blues-drenched cry of the soul; this is followed immediately by a take on "Just as I Am" in which she employs nearly every weapon in her arsenal: swoops, shouts, foreboding guttural moans, diction precise and clipped as appropriate, or swaggering, loose and bluesy, rife with bent notes and phrases stretched tantalizingly into illuminating subtextual messages.

In 1954 she made the jump to the big time, signing with Columbia Records and hosting her own radio show. From 1954 up to her death, she was the most popular gospel artist in the world. But as her fame and influence spread, so were efforts made to smooth out her rough edges, to rein in the full-frontal emotional assault of her singing style. Sensing an opportunity to tap into a broader audience than had theretofore been thought possible for a gospel artist, Columbia saddled Jackson with syrupy string arrangements and sometimes a full orchestra (the most egregious example being the mercifully out-of-print *Power and the Glory,* with arrangements by Percy Faith, the very model of the corporate studio hack). And yet Jackson surmounted almost every obstacle placed in her path; each of her albums has its profound, moving moments, even if few are totally successful or fully representative of the breadth and depth of her artistry. On the low end of the spectrum, *The Great Mahalia Jackson* stands as a worst-case example of Columbia's mishandling of a great artist. Songs such as "Danny Boy," "Sunrise, Sunset" and "What the World Needs Now Is Love" have their virtues—and their messages—but the only way they would make sense in Jackson's repertoire would be in radically reconsidered treatments, which these are not. *Bless This House* is closer to the mark. Here Jackson is backed by a basic rhythm section and the always sensitive accompaniment of her longtime pianist, Mildred Falls; she brings the house down with fiery testifying on "God Knows the Reason Why," "Trouble of the World" and Dorsey's towering "Precious Lord." Only a preposterous male quartet—a pop conceit that sounds like it was cooked up by Columbia's then–A&R director Mitch Miller—undercuts a number of otherwise stellar performances.

A woman of deep conviction, Jackson threw herself into a number of social causes and was a bulwark of support to her friend Dr. Martin Luther King Jr. during the civil rights movement of the '50s and '60s. The commitment she felt to the cause is evident in the thunder she delivers on *Mahalia Jackson Sings the Best-Loved Hymns of Dr. Martin Luther King, Jr.* Rumbling up from the deepest part of her being, her voice resonates with unassailable authority as she limns 100-plus years of shameful American history in what ultimately is a vision of triumph, fully realized by an artist bringing to bear on the issues of her time the entire weight of her considerable vocal prowess and indefatigable sense of purpose. "We Shall Overcome," sung like a victory march, and a stately, prayerful reconsideration of "Precious Lord" are but two examples among many of Jackson's powerful and unexpected interpretations forcing the listener to hear familiar songs with new ears.

Recent reissues and boxed sets have eliminated much of the ephemera from Jackson's catalog, leaving a tight focus on her pure gospel work during the Columbia years. These collections, however, are weighted toward material from the late '50s through the '60s; *How I Got Over,* a 1976 release, fills something of a gap in being culled from 1954 radio performances, supplemented by songs from a 1963 television appearance, the earliest of the lot showcasing Jackson in the ebullient form she displayed on her Apollo recordings. The first boxed set, the two-disc *Gospels, Spirituals & Hymns,* tracks Jackson in 36 songs from the mid-'50s into the late '60s, in a variety of settings, from orchestral ("If I Can Help Somebody") to small combo (including the Falls/Jones Ensemble, with Mildred Falls on piano and Ralph Jones on organ, and Milt Hinton playing bass on the 1956 recording of "Trouble of the World") to solo piano (Mildred Falls, exquisite as always); some songs demand she do nothing more than sing ("Dear Lord, Forgive"); others call upon her tremendous facility as an improviser and underscore the unusual communication she and Falls shared. The repertoire on this and the *Vol. 2* box, balanced between bedrock Negro spirituals ("Roll, Jordan, Roll") and standard hymns (with six Dorsey compositions), effectively showcases her graceful integration of fundamental texts with her progressive sense of phrasing and rhythmic interplay between voice and instruments. Both boxes are blessed by Dr. Horace Clarence Boyer's detailed annotation, which analyzes the musical complexity of Jackson's approach while reminding the listener that the message carried in that great voice is really the point.

The Essence of Mahalia Jackson and *The Best of Mahalia Jackson* are single-CD (and lower-priced) alternatives to the boxed sets; the 12 songs on the former and the 16 songs on the latter can be found on the boxes; *Best of* also includes an interesting experiment recorded in 1958 with Jackson fronting Duke Ellington and His Orchestra on "Part IV (23rd Psalm)." This is the rebuttal to anyone arguing that Jackson was little more than a belter. Here she sings/speaks the text of the 23rd Psalm with breathtaking sensitivity to the poetry's pacing and nuances, as behind her the Ellington Orchestra establishes a respectful ambiance, be it delicate, melodic Gershwin-style passages or searching, atonal interludes. For this alone, *Best of* is a must-have, even if one opts for both boxes.

A number of live performances are included on the boxed sets, some from Jackson's epochal 1958 appearance at the Newport Jazz Festival, where she was backed by the Mildred Falls Trio, except on "Keep Your Hand on the Plow," where

Ellington and His Orchestra join her. The performance in its entirety is captured on *Live at Newport 1958,* recorded on a day when everything was working right. In addition to the Ellington track, two towering performances recommend this disc: The first number, "An Evening Prayer," sets the mood by way of Jackson's stately, deliberate, penitent reading, which lends it the aura of a statement of moral purpose; a couple of cuts later she storms her way through the self-penned "I'm on My Way," a sprightly, syncopated dialog with Falls that positively rocks the joint even as it makes an explicit spiritual vow.

While a case can be made that all we need to know about Mahalia Jackson we can learn from her music, her spoken words, as heard on the Smithsonian Folkways release *I Sing Because I'm Happy,* are equally gripping. Here Jackson sings only four songs—"He's Got the Whole World in His Hand," "Joshua Fit the Battle of Jericho," "I Sing Because My Soul Is Happy" and "The Lord's Prayer"—which are interspersed between interviews conducted in 1952 by independent filmmaker Jules Schwerin. These were to form the basis of a film rooted in the black experience, centering on Jackson's life and work. Abandoned in 1957 for lack of funds, the film, *Got to Tell It,* was finally produced in 1975 with CBS-TV's sponsorship; in 1992 Schwerin used his interviews with Jackson again as the foundation for his biography, *Got to Tell It: Mahalia Jackson, Queen of Gospel,* for which this cassette release is a companion. Anyone who would pretend to understand this great American artist—musically, spiritually, emotionally—must spend some time with her painful, sometimes horrifying but often loving reminiscences about growing up black and poor in the South. It's impossible, for instance, to listen to her cool recollection of the sanctioned random violence visited on blacks by whites during Mardi Gras and ever again view that event the same way. On the other hand, her forceful, clearheaded view of gospel music—"these songs are the staff of life"—will energize your spirit, driving you back to the recordings for even more sustenance courtesy of Mahalia's incandescent soul. This is an essential historical musical document, nearly the equal of the harrowing *Blues in the Mississippi Night* (Rykodisc), Alan Lomax's 1946 interviews with Sonny Boy (John Lee) Williamson, Big Bill Broonzy and Memphis Slim in which the three stellar bluesmen talk in graphic detail about the horrors of their lives and those of other blacks in Mississippi, well before the civil rights movement further inflamed racial tensions in the Magnolia State. — D.M.

MICHAEL GREGORY JACKSON

★★★★ **Karmonic Suite (I.A.I., 1993)**

Guitarist Michael Gregory Jackson (b. 1953) was a mainstay of the New York loft-jazz scene of the 1970s and '80s, playing extensively with artists like Oliver Lake, David Murray and Leo Smith, all of whom appear on the out-of-print *Clarity.* Jackson played on a number of his own, now unavailable records as well, but his masterpiece is *Karmonic Suite,* a series of high-level duets with Lake. Jackson plays guitar, flute, marimba, gongs and percussion and adds spoken-word vocals, while Lake contributes alto and soprano saxophone and flute. — J.S.

MILT JACKSON

★★★★ **In the Beginning (1948; Original Jazz Classics, 1991)**
★★★★ **Milt Jackson (1952; Blue Note, N.A.)**
★★★ **Milt Jackson Quartet (1955; Original Jazz Classics, N.A.)**
★★★½ **Jackson's Ville (1956; Savoy, 1993)**
★★★★ **The Jazz Skyline (1956; Savoy, 1993)**
★★★★ **Plenty, Plenty Soul (1957; Atlantic, 1989)**
★★★★ **Bags' Opus (1959; Blue Note, 1991)**
★★★ **Big Bags (1962; Original Jazz Classics, 1989)**
★★★½ **Bags Meets Wes! (1962; Original Jazz Classics, 1987)**
★★★½ **Invitation (1963; Original Jazz Classics, 1987)**
★★★★ **Live at the Village Gate (1963; Original Jazz Classics, 1988)**
★★★ **Olinga (1974; CTI, 1988)**
★★★ **Sunflower (1974; CTI, 1987)**
★★★½ **Mostly Duke (1975; Original Jazz Classics, 1991)**
★★★★ **The Big 3 (with Joe Pass and Ray Brown) (1975; Original Jazz Classics, 1994)**
★★★½ **Milt Jackson Big 4 at the Montreux Jazz Festival 1975 (1975; Original Jazz Classics, 1996)**
★★ **Feelings (1976; Original Jazz Classics, 1990)**
★★★ **Fuji Mama (West Wind Jazz, 1976)**

★★★½ **Montreux '77 (with Ray Brown) (1977; Original Jazz Classics, 1989)**
★★★½ **Soul Fusion (1977; Original Jazz Classics, 1992)**
★★½ **Sings and Plays "Soul Believer" (1978; Original Jazz Classics, 1992)**
★★★½ **Milt Jackson/Count Basie and the Big Band, Vol. 1 (1978; Original Jazz Classics, 1992)**
★★★½ **Milt Jackson/Count Basie and the Big Band, Vol. 2 (1978; Original Jazz Classics, 1992)**
★★★½ **The Ellington Album: "All Too Soon" (1980; Original Jazz Classics, 1990)**
★★★ **Bags' Bag (1980; Original Jazz Classics, 1988)**
★★★½ **The Best of Milt Jackson (1980; Pablo, 1987)**
★★★ **Big Mouth (1981; Original Jazz Classics, 1995)**
★★★½ **Night Mist (1981; Original Jazz Classics, 1995)**
★★★½ **A London Bridge (1982; Pablo, 1988)**
★★★★ **Memories of Thelonious Sphere Monk (1982; Original Jazz Classics, 1995)**
★★★½ **Ain't but a Few of Us Left (1982; Original Jazz Classics, 1993)**
★★★½ **Jackson, Johnson, Brown & Company (1983; Original Jazz Classics, 1996)**
★★★★ **Soul Route (1984; Pablo, 1987)**
★★★★ **It Don't Mean a Thing If You Can't Tap Your Foot to It (1984; Original Jazz Classics, 1991)**
★★★½ **Brother Jim (Pablo, 1985)**
★★★½ **Bebop (Rhino, 1988)**
★★★ **Soul Brothers/Soul Meeting (with Ray Charles) (Rhino, 1989)**
★★★ **That's the Way It Is (Impulse!, 1989)**
★★★½ **For Someone I Love (Original Jazz Classics, 1989)**
★★★ **The Harem (MusicMasters, 1991)**
★★★ **Statements (GRP, 1993)**
★★★½ **Meet Milt Jackson (Savoy, 1993)**
★★★ **Roll 'Em Bags (Savoy, 1993)**
★★★ **Opus De Jazz (Savoy, 1993)**
★★★ **Howard McGhee and Milt Jackson (Savoy, 1993)**
★★★ **Reverence and Compassion (Qwest, 1993)**
★★★ **The Prophet Speaks (Qwest, 1994)**
★★★ **Burnin' in the Woodhouse (Qwest, 1995)**
★★★½ **Sa Va Bella (Qwest, 1997)**

Vibraphonist Milt Jackson (b. 1923) grew up in Detroit, influenced by the gospel music he heard at his mother's church. Self-taught on the guitar from age 7, Jackson took formal piano training at 11, and by the time he was in high school, he was singing in the glee club and church choir and playing xylophone, violin and drums as well. Jackson switched to vibraphone after witnessing a performance by Lionel Hampton.

In 1945 Jackson joined Dizzy Gillespie's band, where he became one of bebop's leading lights, alongside band mate Charlie Parker on saxophone. Through the remainder of the '40s and the early '50s, Jackson played with Howard McGhee, Tadd Dameron, Thelonious Monk, Woody Herman and Coleman Hawkins, before rejoining the Gillespie outfit.

In 1952 Jackson, pianist John Lewis, bassist Percy Heath and drummer Kenny Clarke left Gillespie's band and formed the Modern Jazz Quartet. Jackson's thorough musicality and strength as an ensemble player helped the MJQ establish a new kind of jazz closely associated with classical chamber music. At the same time, he retained his roots in gospel and blues, sides of his playing personality that have been more fully explored on his solo work.

In the Beginning is a set co-led by Jackson and saxophonist Sonny Stitt with MJQ partners Lewis and Clarke also contributing, as well as trombonist J.J. Johnson and percussionist Chano Pozo, among others. The Blue Note *Milt Jackson* includes recordings made under Thelonious Monk's leadership and sides with Lewis, Clarke and Lou Donaldson. *Milt Jackson Quartet* is the MJQ with Horace Silver instead of Lewis on piano in a looser session.

The Savoy sessions include some terrific material: *Jackson's Ville* and *The Jazz Skyline* both feature great work from tenor saxophonist Lucky Thompson, pianist Hank Jones, drummer Clarke and bassist Wendell Marshall; on *Meet Milt Jackson* Thompson shares the front line with Julius Watkins on French horn while Clarke and bassist Walter Bishop man the rhythm section; on *Opus De Jazz* Frank Wess sits in on tenor saxophone and flute.

Thompson returns on half of *Plenty, Plenty Soul* as part of a quintet with trumpeter Joe Newman, bassist Oscar Pettiford and drummer Connie Kay. The rest of the session is an all-star aggregation with Newman, Cannonball

Adderley on alto sax, Frank Foster on tenor, Sahib Shihab on baritone, Jimmy Cleveland on trombone, Horace Silver on piano, Percy Heath on bass and Art Blakey on drums. *Bags' Opus,* with trumpeter Art Farmer, tenor saxophonist Benny Golson, pianist Tommy Flanagan, bassist Paul Chambers and drummer Connie Kay, really swings.

With the MJQ making it big in the 1960s, Jackson used his solo dates as get-togethers with his favorite players to lay out on the side. *Big Bags* is a big-band date featuring Nat Adderley on cornet and trumpet, Clark Terry on trumpet, James Moody on tenor sax, Hank Jones on piano, Ron Carter on bass and Philly Joe Jones on drums. On *Bags Meets Wes!* Jackson and guitarist Wes Montgomery are backed by pianist Wynton Kelly, bassist Sam Jones and Philly Joe Jones. *Invitation* is a sextet with Jimmy Heath on tenor and Kenny Dorham on trumpet; *Live at the Village Gate* pares it down to a quintet, with Heath taking a bigger share of the soloing.

In the '70s Jackson's proclivity for the impromptu jam was the perfect attitude for the roll-the-tape philosophy Norman Granz had at Pablo. Like most of Pablo's session stars, Jackson recorded voraciously for that label, both as a leader and sideman, and he was never at a loss for something to say in this context. The only down moments come with the strings-attached *Feelings* and *Sings and Plays "Soul Believer,"* in which Milt proves that as a vocalist, he's still a great vibraphone player. Highlights of the Pablo era include his meeting with Count Basie, the Thelonious Monk and Duke Ellington tributes, the collaboration with Joe Pass and Ray Brown on *The Big 3* and the smoking *It Don't Mean a Thing If You Can't Tap Your Foot to It,* with Brown, pianist Cedar Walton and drummer Mickey Roker.

Jackson offers consistently enjoyable listening well into the 1990s, with a string of releases on Quincy Jones's Qwest label. The best of these, *Sa Va Bella,* is a tribute to Jackson's favorite female singers, with guest vocalist Etta Jones.
— J.S.

RONALD SHANNON JACKSON

★★★★ Mandance (Antilles, 1982)
★★★ Barbeque Dog (Antilles, 1983)
★★★ Taboo (Venture, 1990)
★★★★½ Red Warrior (Axiom, 1990)
★★★½ Shannon's House (Koch, 1997)

Ronald Shannon Jackson (b. 1940) was the drummer in Prime Time, Ornette Coleman's first electric "harmolodic" ensemble, and has spent most of his solo career spinning variations on the funk-oriented free jazz he played with Coleman. That's not to say Jackson's work merely clones Coleman's, for Jackson's albums with his Decoding Society (a group that for many years included Living Colour guitarist Vernon Reid) are as a rule more rigorously arranged, with a greater emphasis on composition than on collective improvisation. Jackson's writing particularly stands out on *Mandance,* which makes excellent use of instrumental textures. Apparently, though, the balance between cogent song structures and open improvisation is not an easy one to maintain, as *Taboo* seems stifled by its overinvolved arrangements. On the other hand, the guitar-crazed *Red Warrior* offers an inspired blend of organization and anarchy and is easily the most visceral of these albums. — J.D.C.

WILLIS JACKSON

★★★ Call of the Gators (1950; Delmark, 1992)
★★★ Please Mr. Jackson (1959; Original Jazz Classics, 1988)
★★★ Bar Wars, Willis Jackson with Pat Martino (1978; Muse, 1990)
★★★ Gentle Gator (Prestige, 1995)
★★★ Willis Jackson with Pat Martino (Prestige, 1995)
★★★ Single Action (1995; Muse, 1995)

Willis "Gator Tail" Jackson (b. 1932) grew up in Miami, where his reputation as a hard-blowing tenor saxophone player led to a tour with the Cootie Williams band. Jackson starred in that outfit, where he earned his nickname, then fronted his own groups and made his recording debut with *Call of the Gators.*

His organ combos have consistently been among the most listenable groups in the genre, and Jackson has, as a result, become an extremely durable recording artist, making some soulful records in the late 1950s and '60s for Prestige and featuring Jack McDuff's swinging organ accompaniment on *Please Mr. Jackson.* By 1974, Jackson started recording a series of sessions with organists Carl Wilson, Charles Earland and Mickey Tucker and some fine guitar playing from Pat Martino. These albums hold few surprises—Jackson alternates between cooking, up-tempo tracks, where he plays with a rhythmic dexterity inspired by Lester Young and Charlie Parker, and emotional ballads delivered with a deep, expressive Coleman Hawkins sound. All that's currently available of this output are *Bar Wars, Willis Jackson with Pat Martino* and *Single Action.* — J.S.

CHRISTIAN JACOB

★★★ **Maynard Ferguson Presents Christian Jacob (Concord Jazz, 1997)**

Conservatory-trained pianist Christian Jacob (b. 1958) left the limited jazz opportunities in his native France in 1983 to study at Boston's Berklee College of Music. He graduated two years later, immediately joined its jazz faculty and was soon touring occasionally with vibes player Gary Burton. In 1990 Jacob signed on as musical director with trumpeter Maynard Ferguson's Big Bop Nouveau band. *Maynard Ferguson Presents Christian Jacob,* an impressive debut with bassist John Patitucci and drummer Peter Erskine, finds this lyrical player exploring standards and offering poignant and classical-tinged originals. — K.F.

ILLINOIS JACQUET

★★★★½ **Illinois Jacquet (1963; Columbia/Legacy, 1995)**
★★★★ **Bottoms Up (1968; Original Jazz Classics, 1989)**
★★★★ **The King! (1968; Original Jazz Classics, 1995)**
★★★★ **The Soul Explosion (1969; Original Jazz Classics, 1991)**
★★★★ **The Blues: That's Me! (1970; Original Jazz Classics, 1991)**
★★★★½ **Jacquet's Got It! (Atlantic, 1988)**
★★★½ **Loot to Boot (LaserLight, 1991)**
★★★½ **The Comeback (Black Lion, 1991)**
★★★★½ **Flying Home (RCA Bluebird, 1992)**

Jean Battiste "Illinois" Jacquet was born in Broussard, Louisiana, in 1922 and moved with his family to Houston, where he grew up steeped in the blues and playing soprano and alto sax. After playing in Texas bands led by Milton Larkins, Jacquet moved in 1941 to Los Angeles. There he caught on as a tenor player in Lionel Hampton's band and was immortalized for his heart-stopping high-register solo on "Flying Home"—regarded as the watershed moment when jazz anticipated the postwar R&B and prerock bands that would feature honking saxophones played at high volume with screeching high notes. The high-register distortion technique was later adopted by a number of the early-'60s free-jazz experimenters.

Not simply a showboat, Jacquet is a consummate player, capable of terrific emotional deliveries on ballads and always deeply at home in the blues. He played with Cab Calloway and Count Basie and was a featured member of the Jazz at the Philharmonic orchestra in the 1940s as well as leading his own combos.

Flying Home collects small-group sessions from 1947–50 with a live version of "Flying Home" recorded with Hampton at the 1967 Newport Jazz Festival. *Illinois Jacquet,* a small-band swing session from 1962, features Jacquet on tenor and alto, along with trumpeter Roy Eldridge, trombonist Matthew Gee, baritonists Leo Parker and Cecil Payne, pianist Sir Charles Thompson, guitarist Kenny Burrell, drummer Jo Jones and bassist George Duvivier. The CD reissue includes five previously unreleased tracks.

By the end of the '60s, Jacquet had quite naturally become aligned with the roots-oriented soul-jazz movement, and the Original Jazz Classics releases show him in relaxed and commanding form on a series of sessions that range from swing to blues. *Bottoms Up* is a terrific quartet session with pianist Barry Harris, bassist Ben Tucker and drummer Alan Dawson. *The King!* features Joe Newman on trumpet, Milt Buckner on keyboards, Billy Butler on guitar, Al Lucas on bass and tuba, Jo Jones on drums and Montego Joe on percussion. Here a Basie/Ellington session is augmented by Billy Taylor's easy-swinging blues "I Wish I Knew How It Would Feel to Be Free."

The Blues: That's Me! features the great Wynton Kelly on piano, Tiny Grimes on guitar, Buster Williams on bass and Oliver Jackson on drums. In addition to his tenor work, Jacquet plays an eerie bassoon part on "'Round Midnight." *The Soul Explosion* is a larger-band session, with Jacquet joined on the front line by Frank Foster on tenor and Cecil Payne on baritone and a trumpet section led by Newman. This unit blasts through the title track and plays a riveting version of "St. Louis Blues."

Loot to Boot collects '70s material from the Lester archives and features organists Jimmy McGriff and Wild Bill Davis. *Jacquet's Got It!* is the recorded testimony of Jacquet's big band, a unit he continues to front with varying personnel late into the 1990s. With arrangements by Wild Bill Davis, Eddie Barefield and Phil Wilson, Jacquet digs into the tradition of the Hampton, Calloway and Basie bands and adds a healthy helping of his own work. His working unit is augmented for the recording by trumpeter Jon Faddis, alto saxophonist Marshall Royal, bassist Milt Hinton and drummer Duffy Jackson. The CD includes a bonus version of "Flying Home."

Jacquet has always been a big-band player at heart, and after serving as an artist-in-residence at Harvard in the mid-1980s he was able to organize a big band around his students and other young jazz talent. This continuing project has led to a series of successful American and European tours. — J.S.

AHMAD JAMAL

★★★★ **Poinciana (1955; Portrait, 1989)**
★★★★ **At the Pershing: But Not for Me (1958; Chess, 1988)**
★★★★ **Ahmad's Blues (1958; GRP, 1994)**
★★★½ **Poinciana (1963; Chess, 1992)**
★★★ **The Awakening (1970; GRP, 1997)**
★★★ **Freeflight (1971; Impulse!, 1993)**
★★★ **Night Song (1980; MoJazz, 1994)**
★★★ **Digital Works (Rhino, 1985)**
★★★½ **Live at Montreal Jazz Festival 1985 (Rhino, 1986)**
★★★ **Rossiter Road (Rhino, 1986)**
★★★½ **Crystal (Rhino, 1987)**
★★★ **Pittsburgh (Rhino, 1989)**
★★★½ **Live in Paris '92 (Verve, 1993)**
★★★★ **Chicago Revisited: Live at Joe Segal's Jazz Showcase (Telarc, 1993)**
★★★ **I Remember Duke, Hoagy & Strayhorn (Telarc, 1994)**
★★★½ **The Essence, Part 1 (Verve, 1996)**

Born in Pittsburgh in 1930, Ahmad Jamal was a child prodigy, performing in concert by the age of 11. An early follower of Art Tatum, he nevertheless developed a style antithetical to Tatum's, playing with a variety of jazz and pop groups before forming his famed trio with bassist Israel Crosby and drummer Vernell Fournier in the 1950s. This group enjoyed unusual success with pristine chamber-music pieces like "Poinciana," built around Jamal's sparse, restrained phrasing, which left huge structural gaps in the arrangement that could be artfully filled by his rhythm section or left blank for rhythmic emphasis and a kind of relaxed tension. This approach, wildly successful on *At the Pershing* and the live *Ahmad's Blues* and well demonstrated on the Portrait *Poinciana,* was a tremendous influence on Miles Davis, who incorporated it into his own playing, drawing attention to Jamal at every opportunity.

By the beginning of the 1970s, Jamal was working with another classic trio, bassist Jamil Nasser and drummer Frank Gant, which can be heard on *The Awakening* and *Freeflight,* recorded at Montreux with Jamal playing electric piano. Through the rest of the decade Jamal dabbled in electronics and other attempts at modernizing his sound. None of this material remains in print, but recordings of some similar directions he pursued in the '80s while under contract with Atlantic are still available. Using a trio-and-percussion format with shifting personnel during the '80s, Jamal recorded the overproduced *Digital Works,* the undernourished *Rossiter Road* and *Pittsburgh* and an exquisite orchestral set, *Crystal.* Sandwiched in between these was the stirring live performance from Montreal.

Jamal's magic seems to work best in live performance, and he returned with more such triumphs in the early 1990s: *Live in Paris '92* and *Chicago Revisited,* the latter reminiscent of *At the Pershing,* with bassist John Heard and drummer Yoron Israel. Jamal and Nasser are reunited on *The Essence, Part 1,* with drummer Idris Muhammad, percussionist Manolo Badrena and tenor saxophonist George Coleman. — J.S.

BOB JAMES

★ **Explosions (ESP, 1965)**
★★ **One (1974; Warner Bros., 1995)**
★★ **Two (1975; Warner Bros., 1995)**
★★ **Three (1976; Warner Bros., 1995)**
★ **Four (1977; Warner Bros., 1995)**
★ **Heads (1977; Warner Bros., 1995)**
★ **Touchdown (Warner Bros., 1978)**
★ **Lucky Seven (1979; Warner Bros., 1995)**
★★ **One on One (with Earl Klugh) (1979; Warner Bros., 1993)**
★ **"H" (1980; Warner Bros., 1995)**
★ **Sign of the Times (Warner Bros., 1981)**
★ **All Around the Town (Warner Bros., 1981)**
★ **Hands Down (1982; Warner Bros., 1995)**
★★ **Two of a Kind (Capitol, 1982)**
★ **Foxie (1983; Warner Bros., 1995)**
★ **The Genie (1983; Warner Bros., 1995)**
★★ **12 (1984; Warner Bros., 1995)**
★★ **Rameau (Warner Bros., 1984)**

★ **The Swan (1985; Warner Bros., 1995)**
★★ **Double Vision (with David Sanborn) (Warner Bros., 1986)**
★ **Obsession (Warner Bros., 1986)**
★ **Ivory Coast (Warner Bros., 1988)**
★★½ **Grand Piano Canyon (Warner Bros., 1990)**
★★ **Cool (Warner Bros., 1992)**
★ **Restless (Warner Bros., 1994)**
★ **Straight Up (Warner Bros., 1996)**

Quincy Jones discovered keyboardist Bob James (b. 1939) at the 1962 Notre Dame Jazz Festival at a time when James was a strident practitioner of avant-garde posturing. James began his recording career in 1963 with the now deleted *Bold Conceptions* and followed it with *Explosions,* a self-consciously avant-garde trio effort for ESP that features cheesy sound effects mixed with the playing. Over the course of James's career, the sound effects—if not always the music—improved.

Under Jones's influence, James moved in a more mainstream direction, working as a sideman before resurfacing in the 1970s as a designer of Muzak jazz, helping define CTI's easy-listening style and later bringing the same ideas to Columbia, then to his own Tappan Zee label. James's work helped kill the best instincts of fusion music and anticipate the vapidity of the New Age and smooth-jazz formats. He's a skilled technician and sonic craftsman, so his works are filled with glossy streams of ear candy. James had such success in selling his efforts that Warner Bros. eagerly reissued virtually every flyspeck of his work, although it's hard to imagine why anyone would want more than one of his wallpaperlike CDs in a collection.

As a leader James is almost invisible, with results that are remarkably similar to albums he produces for others. Where the usual complaint is that James's style mutes the personality of the musician he's doctoring up, in his own case there's so little playing personality to begin with that the muting process is nowhere near as traumatic. Therefore, his early 1970s work sounds more like a vehicle for saxophonist Grover Washington Jr.; his collaboration with guitarist Earl Klugh, *One on One,* led to a Grammy; a reprise on *Two of a Kind,* then a similar project with David Sanborn, *Double Vision,* took another Grammy.

James's pretensions also led him to dabble in classical music. Perhaps his most outlandish outing is *Rameau*'s "switched-on" versions of pieces written by the Baroque composer Jean-Philippe Rameau. James attempted to make up for some of his offenses against jazz with the *Grand Piano Canyon* album, but he had already reached his ultimate moment in history as the composer of the theme from the TV series *Taxi.*
— J.S.

BONEY JAMES

★★ **Trust (Warner Bros., 1994)**
★★ **Backbone (Warner Bros., 1994)**
★★★ **Seduction (Warner Bros., 1995)**
★★½ **Sweet Thing (Warner Bros., 1997)**

Boney James (b. 1961) is the most successful of the post–Kenny G pop-jazz instrumentalists, dominating the new adult contemporary radio with a blandly pleasant, undemandingly smooth-jazz style loosely inspired by the once fashionable Quiet Storm format. This Massachusetts-born saxophonist has been working out of Los Angeles as an R&B and fusion session player in the Grover Washington Jr./David Sanborn style since the mid-1970s. His sound evolved into the smooth-jazz bag just in time to capitalize on the form's heyday in the mid-1990s.

James's second album, *Backbone,* topped the new adult contemporary charts, and its follow-up, *Seduction,* defined the genre, spending four months atop both the NAC and smooth-jazz charts. James, an unlikely sexual icon, attempted to extend his base on *Swing Thing* into pop vocals (along with Al Jarreau on the title track) and acid jazz. — J.S.

ELMORE JAMES

★★★★ **Elmore James/John Brim: Whose Muddy Shoes (1969; MCA, 1991)**
★★★★ **Street Talkin' (with Eddie Taylor) (1975; Muse, 1988)**
★★★★★ **Red Hot Blues (Quicksilver, 1982)**
★★★★ **Let's Cut It: The Very Best of Elmore James (Flair/Virgin, 1987)**
★★★★ **The Complete Fire and Fury Sessions, Part 1 (Collectables, 1989)**
★★★★ **The Complete Fire and Fury Sessions, Part 2 (Collectables, 1989)**
★★★★ **The Complete Fire and Fury Sessions, Part 3 (Collectables, 1989)**
★★★★ **The Complete Fire and Fury Sessions, Part 4 (Collectables, 1989)**
★★★★ **Dust My Broom (Tomato, 1991)**
★★★★★ **The Complete Elmore James Story (Capricorn, 1992)**

★★★★★ **The Classic Early Recordings 1951–1956 (Flair/Virgin, 1993)**
★★★★★ **The Sky Is Crying: The History of Elmore James (Rhino, 1993)**
★★★★ **Golden Classics: Guitars in Orbit (Collectables, N.A.)**

Few sounds in any musical genre are more immediately identifiable or more influential than Elmore James's wailing slide guitar. His is a voice that shadows the playing of virtually every important British blues guitarist from the 1960s onward and informs the styles of great American blues guitarists such as Duane Allman, Stevie Ray Vaughan and Michael Bloomfield, to name but three prominent acolytes.

Born of sharecropper parents in Richland, Mississippi, and reared on Delta blues, James (1918–1963) was playing guitar at age 12; in his teens he began traveling around the region in the company of Sonny Boy Williamson (Rice Miller) and Robert Johnson. James's first hit, recorded surreptitiously in 1951 for the Trumpet label (frightened of studio technology, James was coaxed into rehearsing with Williamson; as they played, Trumpet founder Lillian McMurray rolled tape), was a version of Johnson's "Dust My Broom." By 1939 James was playing dances with a lineup that included another guitarist, a trumpet player, a drummer and a saxophonist in one of the earliest attempts by any of the Delta-blues players to bring horns into a band lineup. Following a tour of duty in the Navy (1943–1947), James returned to Mississippi and again hooked up with Williamson for dances and occasional appearances on Miller's King Biscuit Flour–sponsored radio show in Helena, Arkansas. By this time James was playing electric guitar, employing a little voltage to enhance what he did best—that is, using the slide guitar as a cry of the soul. A prolific songwriter as well, his lyrics were incisive, eloquent blues poetry about bad love affairs, tempestuous personal relationships and intimations of mortality, with vivid descriptions of torment, desire and mean mistreaters.

After moving to Chicago in 1952, James and his band the Broomdusters—a group whose power and instrumental brilliance were matched only by the musical giants then populating Muddy Waters's band in the same city—were signed to the Meteor label and proceeded to record for a variety of other small labels in subsequent years as they traveled back and forth from Mississippi to Chicago until James's death from a heart attack in 1963. Much of James and company's ferocious music is now available domestically in both single-tape or -CD configurations and boxed sets.

Among the single-CD issues of James's work, *Whose Muddy Shoes* is recommended for the tracks recorded at Chess in 1953 and 1960. Among these is another version of "Dust My Broom" and an homage to one of James's principal influences, T-Bone Walker, by way of a scorching interpretation of "Stormy Monday." Six tracks are devoted to the underrated Chicago bluesman John Brim, whose band included Robert Jr. Lockwood, Willie Dixon and, on a couple of cuts, Little Walter Jacobs. *Red Hot Blues* and *Golden Classics: Guitars in Orbit* are strong compendiums of James's best-known recordings, while Muse's *Street Talkin'* divides 14 tracks between James and Eddie Taylor, the latter being accompanied here by his longtime partner Jimmy Reed as well as Hubert Sumlin. *Let's Cut It* is in the vein of a greatest-hits album, although it does contain an alternate take of "Hawaiian Boogie" among its predictable fare. *Dust My Broom* is a survey of latter-day James featuring 15 key tracks recorded between 1959 and 1963.

The most succinct overview of James's art through the years is provided by *The Sky Is Crying: The History of Elmore James.* "Dust My Broom" is here, as well as sides James recorded between 1951 and 1960 for Chess, Flair, Atlantic, Kent, Chief, Sphere Sound, Fire and Flashback. Apart from the sheer emotional impact of the songs themselves, this set's great virtue is in showcasing both the breadth and depth of James's music. "Something Inside Me," from 1960, is a beautiful slow blues; in "Sunny Land," from 1954, he one-ups Muddy Waters with a tricky stop-time arrangement and abandons the slide in favor of dark, robust single- and double-string solo lines; on the propulsive instrumental "Hawaiian Boogie," James interjects some searing slide solos along the way as the band rocks relentlessly ahead with J.T. Brown's soaring tenor sax leading the way; "Sho' Nuff I Do" finds James right at home on a standard eight-bar blues (and backed by Ike Turner's Kings of Rhythm horn section); and in a glorious pairing, James's guitar comes wailing in behind Big Joe Turner on the one-off Atlantic session that produced Turner's gutbucket blues howler "T.V. Mama"—the Delta meets Kansas City; "Madison Blues" finds James in a talking-blues mode on a track once again distinguished by J.T. Brown's stuttering tenor-sax solo and James's deep, descending slide retorts. Critical perspective is provided in the liner notes by Robert Palmer.

More exhilarating in quantity and quality are the two boxed sets; taken together, these form virtually all of James's recording history for the various labels whose studios he graced. The three-CD boxed set, *The Classic Early Recordings 1951–1956,* includes the original "Dust My Broom" as well as the blistering early sides he cut in 1952 with a band whose piano player was the formidable Ike Turner, he of the ferocious right hand that seems to bring out the best in James, particularly on the explosive "Please Find My Baby." (Turner shows up as lead guitarist on a 1954 cut, the instrumental "Canton Mississippi Breakdown.") In addition to cuts by James and the Broomdusters, the set also contains several sides crediting James and his band as accompanying the Bep Brown Orchestra and Little Johnny Jones & the Chicago Hound Dogs. The three discs comprise a journey of remarkable artistic growth within the limited framework of the blues.

Between 1960 and 1962 James recorded prolifically for the New York City–based Fire, Fury and Enjoy labels headed by Bobby Robinson. Collectables has assembled the Fire and Enjoy sides in four volumes, each sold separately and absent any biographical or session information—instead, the music carries the day. On the other hand, the thoroughly annotated two-CD boxed set, *The Complete Elmore James Story,* features 50 tracks from the various Robinson labels in what stands as the artist's last will and testament. Though in failing health during these years, James cut some monuments—"Look on Yonder Wall"; an urgent, pleading "One Way Out" (later a staple of the Allman Brothers' repertoire); "Shake Your Moneymaker"; and the blistering "Sky Is Crying" (without question a Mount Rushmore performance)—all of which are here. But as often happens with great artists (particularly those who wrestle with evolving a signature sound as musical trends change around them), some of the gems are to be found in lesser-known tracks that reveal something of the shape of the future. Recording in New York, Chicago and New Orleans, James and Robinson sometimes buttressed the band with R&B-style horn support (check out "Person to Person"), and in some instances James tossed the slide away and got down to playing tough, straight-ahead lead-guitar solos, rooted in urban blues but redolent of the Delta, thus prefiguring by about a decade the ringing, determined cry of Southern-rock guitarists. — D.M.

ETTA JAMES

★★★★ **At Last! (1961; Chess, 1987)**
★★★★ **The Second Time Around (1961; Chess, 1989)**
★★★ **Etta James Rocks the House (1963; Chess, 1986)**
★★★★ **Tell Mama (1968; Chess, 1988)**
★★ **Come a Little Closer (1974; Chess, 1986)**
★★★ **Deep in the Night (1978; Bullseye Blues, 1996)**
★★★★ **R&B Dynamite (1986; Flair/Virgin, 1991)**
★★★ **Her Greatest Sides, Vol. 1 (Chess, 1986)**
★★★ **Blues in the Night: The Early Show (with Eddie "Cleanhead" Vinson) (Fantasy, 1986)**
★★★★ **Blues in the Night: The Late Show (with Eddie "Cleanhead" Vinson) (Fantasy, 1986)**
★★★★ **The Sweetest Peaches (Chess, 1988)**
★★★★★ **The Sweetest Peaches: The Chess Years, Vol. 1 (1960–1966) (Chess, 1988)**
★★★★★ **The Sweetest Peaches: The Chess Years, Vol. 2 (1967–1975) (Chess, 1988)**
★★★ **Seven Year Itch (Island, 1988)**
★★★ **Stickin' to My Guns (Island, 1990)**
★★★ **The Gospel Soul of Etta James (AJK, 1990)**
★★★ **The Right Time (Elektra, 1992)**
★★★½ **How Strong Is a Woman: The Island Sessions (4th and Broadway, 1993)**
★★★★★ **The Essential Etta James (Chess, 1993)**
★★★★★ **Mystery Lady: Songs of Billie Holiday (Private Music, 1994)**
★★★★★ **Live from San Francisco (On the Spot/Private Music, 1994)**
★★★★½ **Time After Time (Private Music, 1995)**
★★★★ **These Foolish Things: The Classic Balladry of Etta James (Chess, 1995)**
★★★★ **Her Best (Chess, 1997)**
★★★ **Love's Been Rough on Me (Private Music, 1997)**

Born in Los Angeles in 1938 to parents of Italian and African-American descent, Etta James (née Jamesetta Hawkins) came by her blues naturally and remains, three decades after her first hit, a formidable vocal presence. She began singing professionally at age 15 in a vocal trio with two female friends; together they had written an answer song to Hank Ballard's early R&B sagas "Work with Me Annie" and "Annie Had a Baby." After Johnny Otis heard the girls, who called themselves the Creolettes, sing "Roll with Me Henry" during one of his dates in San Francisco, he took Etta to Los Angeles and had her record the song. Under the name the Peaches and released on the Modern label as "The Wallflower" (radio stations objected to the original title), the single rose to #2 on the R&B chart and was also successful in a sanitized pop version by Georgia Gibbs retitled again as "Dance with Me Henry." A follow-up single, "Good Rockin' Daddy," reached the Top 20 of the R&B charts but faded quickly. So did James's career at Modern, despite her having cut several other first-rate sides as the '50s progressed. James's Modern recordings are now available on the reissue *R&B Dynamite.*

In 1959 James relocated to Chicago and signed with the Chess label, where one of the A&R directors was Harvey Fuqua, founder of the Moonglows and a solo recording artist who had a history with James, having cut a duet with her on Modern ("I Hope You're Satisfied"). At Chess James produced the performances on which her legend rests. Her work there was exceedingly beautiful—impassioned, intelligent, deeply felt—but also personal and painful in its telling. She cried out in song, telling tales of faithless love and ceaseless heartbreak (stories she described in explicit detail in her highly praised autobiography, *Rage to Survive,* published in 1994); even her upbeat numbers seemed tinged by sadness, mirroring the emotional roller coaster that was her interior life.

Several Chess compilations offer powerful evidence that James lived the blues. Completists are advised to check out the superbly annotated (by David Ritz, who cowrote James's autobiography) two-CD, 44-song set issued in 1993, *The Essential Etta James,* for the broadest overview of the enduring work she did for the Argo, Chess and Cadet labels from 1960 through 1975. Here James is heard successfully adapting her style to the changing trends in black music, working with some of the best producers and arrangers of her time as well as first-rate songwriters (the subtlety and personality she brings to her performances of several Randy Newman songs cut in the early '70s indicate she might well be that fabled songwriter's preeminent interpreter); whatever the style, whomever the composer, the hurt is always near the surface.

During her Chess tenure she also turned to recording pop standards in her singular, bluesy style; *These Foolish Things: The Classic Balladry of Etta James* (again with liner notes by David Ritz) charts this compelling strain of her artistry. The dozen cuts on *Vol. 1* of *The Sweetest Peaches* sets rank among the best R&B singles of the '60s. A sampling of the titles maps out James's barren emotional landscape during this period: "All I Could Do Was Cry," "Fool That I Am," "I Wish Someone Would Care," "Pushover." Her self-penned "Stop the Wedding" was a Top 40 pop hit in 1962, enabling James to dive headfirst into the good life. She wound up a drug addict, and her music assumed a harsh, bitter edge (it's a long road that leads from "All I Could Do Was Cry" to a tough cover version of Jimmy Reed's unapologetic "Baby What You Want Me to Do") as her life fell into disarray.

Though 1963 found her delivering a rousing live album, *Etta James Rocks the House,* recorded at a small Nashville night spot with a band whose members are unidentified, James was then in an emotional free fall. Eventually she headed back to California, went into rehab and came out clean. Seeking to reinvigorate her music, she journeyed south, to Sheffield, Alabama, and the Muscle Shoals Sound Studios. Soul music was the order of the day, and some of the best was coming out of that northern Alabama facility where Aretha Franklin, Percy Sledge, Wilson Pickett and a host of other top artists had cut some of their most important sides. *Tell Mama* and four tracks on *Vol. 2* of *The Sweetest Peaches* reveal the wisdom of this move: *Tell Mama* is one of the decade's exceptional albums; it yielded two Top 30 hits in the title song and the Otis Redding–penned "Security" and includes several potent performances.

In the early '70s James was teamed with rock-oriented producer Gabriel Mekler, whose credits included Janis Joplin, Three Dog Night and Steppenwolf. *Come a Little Closer* (along with cuts on *The Sweetest Peaches: Vol. 2* and on *The Essential Etta James*) was the upshot, but only the above-mentioned Randy Newman–penned songs stand out. James's earthy, mature vocals were as potent as ever, but Mekler's glossy arrangements weren't a good fit with the singer's intense approach. Following another near-disastrous bout with drugs and another round of rehab, James left Chess. But like LaVern Baker and Ruth Brown, great ladies of '50s R&B who later hit tough times artistically and personally before rebounding on the strength of their voices and sheer determination, James was not about to be undone by shifting trends. In 1978 she signed to Warner Bros. and delivered the Jerry Wexler–produced *Deep in the Night* (now available on Bullseye Blues), which pointed her in the right direction again professionally.

James came all the way back with her live album, *Blues in the Night,* recorded in Los Angeles in 1986 with a band that included alto saxophonist Eddie "Cleanhead" Vinson. Here her version of "At Last" is as moody and affecting as the original, and on "Misty" she demonstrates that her exemplary touch on pop standards has not been diminished by time or personal misfortune. A companion volume, *The Late Show,* is even better, with a rollicking version of "Baby What You Want Me to Do" and fervent renditions of her former Modern label mate B.B. King's "Sweet Little Angel" and of "I'd Rather Go Blind" that are further enlivened by blues solos from guitarist Shuggie Otis.

Of her two Island albums, *Stickin' to My Guns* best shows her adapting a hard R&B approach to a contemporary funk-rock sound. Produced by Barry Beckett, one of the stalwarts of the famed Muscle Shoals rhythm section who played on James's sessions there, the album includes songs that run the gamut from rock to country soul. James sounds at home throughout, albeit harder than on any of her recent albums—but then, it's been that kind of life. *How Strong Is a Woman,* on the 4th and Broadway label, is an 11-track anthology culled from the two Island releases.

As it turned out, the Island years were but a prelude to greater glories for Etta James. In 1993 she was inducted into the Rock and Roll Hall of Fame; a year later, after signing with Private Music, she delivered the best album of her long career in the Grammy-winning *Mystery Lady: Songs of Billie Holiday.* For James, this was both an homage to an artist whose personal traumas mirrored those James had battled and overcome throughout her life and an artistic challenge of the highest order. Though her style isn't as winsome and delicate as Holiday's, the sultry, longing quality with which James invests a lyric adds rich subtext to some of Holiday's signature songs. "Lover Man," "The Man I Love," "Body and Soul," "I'll Be Seeing You"—these chestnuts are reinvigorated by way of thoughtful, reflective interpretations. The assembled musicians, directed by pianist/arranger Cedar Walton, display impressive sensitivity to the vocalist's mood—on "Lover Man," so poignantly rendered by James, the sole support is in the form of Josh Sklair's minimalist chording and a feathery trumpet line floating through the song's midsection. This cut exemplifies the near-perfect marriage of song selection, performance and arrangement that is *Mystery Lady.*

So how do you follow a masterpiece? With *Time After Time,* a smart move that finds James going back to one of her strengths, pop standards done in a blues/jazz vein, again with Cedar Walton arranging and playing piano and largely the same musician lineup as accompanied her on *Mystery Lady.* Here James is given room to stretch out vocally; where *Mystery Lady* is remarkable for its sustained, hypnotic, low-key ambiance, *Time After Time* finds the vocalist breaking free on occasion and showing off her belter's side to spectacular effect—the explosion of emotion at the close of "Don't Go to Strangers" is one of James's most forceful statements on record, and she follows that with a swaggering, sassy romp through "Teach Me Tonight." Elsewhere, she goes deep and soulfully into a song—the deliberate, wan reading of "My Funny Valentine" being a case in point—and summons a wealth of contradictory emotions in evoking love's complex and constantly shifting moods, again plumbing her own experience to impart some hard-earned wisdom to her listeners.

The same strategy, in effect, was applied to 1997's *Love's Been Rough on Me.* Described by James in her liner notes as "a country record" (it was recorded in Nashville, with, for the most part, Nashville-based musicians, and produced by now–Nashville-based Barry Beckett), this one's the bluesiest country record anyone's likely to cut in Music City these days—Wynonna would recognize it as a country record, because its R&B flavor hits close to what she's moving closer to in her solo career, and the Mavericks would appreciate the extra-country influences James brings to bear on the songs (particularly the Gretchen Peters–penned title track), but the list then grows short.

Although it was recorded in 1981, *Live from*

San Francisco wasn't released until 1994. It fills in the "lost years" of the '80s, when she was virtually off record and back where she spent part of her childhood ("It brought out the wild child in me," she says of the town in David Ritz's liner notes here) and where she could always find a loyal audience, no matter the arc of her career at the moment. Recorded at the Boarding House, one of James's regular haunts, the occasion finds the artist in a blues frame of mind, singing from the gut and basically adopting a scorched-earth policy to every song on the set list. This is one powerful outing, one of the greatest blues performances ever captured in a live setting. Who would've guessed that "Take It to the Limit," that dreaded song by the dreaded Eagles, could be reconsidered as a blues stomp incorporating a gospel call-and-response section at its close? In a roaring version of "Baby What You Want Me to Do" James uses the instrumental break to do her vocal imitation of Jimmy Reed's harmonica solo. Throw in a tender moment on her interpretation of Kiki Dee's "Sugar on the Floor," and you get a well-rounded set of emotional peaks and valleys, superbly rendered by an artist who may have been forgotten by the industry but still had, as time proved, plenty left to say. — D.M.

SKIP JAMES

★★★★★ **Skip James Today! (1966; Vanguard, 1991)**
★★★★★ **Devil Got My Woman (1968; Vanguard, 1991)**
★★★★★ **Greatest of the Delta Blues Singers (Biograph, 1992)**
★★★★★ **She Lyin' (Adelphi, 1993)**
★★★★★ **Complete Early Recordings—1930 (Yazoo, 1994)**
★★★★★ **Skip's Piano Blues (Adelphi, 1996)**

Born in Bentonia, Mississippi, and raised on a plantation, Nehemiah "Skip" James (1902–1969) stands as the most influential practitioner of the haunting Bentonia-style Delta-blues form. Distinguished by minor keys, odd tunings and lyrics reflecting a fixation on death and bedevilment, Bentonia blues is not for the faint of heart. But James's music is at times so buoyant and percussive that the listener could be forgiven for dancing at the apocalypse described in the songs' lyrics and brought home forcefully by the artist's plaintive, high-pitched moaning.

A compelling writer, James buttressed his verbal skill with breathtaking mastery of both the guitar and the piano. His intricate fingerpicking style influenced folk, bluegrass and country-blues artists alike, his contemporary disciples including virtuosos such as John Fahey and Leo Kottke. In his own time—his first recordings were done for the Paramount label in 1931 (18 of the 26 he claims to have recorded are chronicled on the mislabeled Yazoo set, *Complete Early Recordings—1930*)—James left his mark on Robert Johnson by way of such songs as the frightening "22-20 Blues," which Johnson transformed into an equally disturbing "32-20 Blues"; James's monumental "Devil Got My Woman" shows up in the melody and guitar accompaniment of Johnson's "Hellhound on My Trail," and one verse is incorporated into Johnson's "Come On in My Kitchen." He also was one of the few Delta-blues artists to use the keyboard as effectively and unpredictably as he did the guitar in embroidering or commenting on his narratives. On "Mistreating Child Blues" (from *Devil Got My Woman*), he employs percussive right-hand chording, walking bass lines and staccato bursts of single-note runs both to underscore his gloomy mood and to shift the ambiance to an almost jocular tone, as if the artist were mocking his plight at the same time that he bemoans it. By all accounts, James was a man who harbored and was fearless in expressing deep resentments toward a society that placed limits on how much he could achieve as a black man in the South. Seen in this light, his musical arrangements, pitting instrument against voice in revealing counterpoint, tell a shameful tale.

The Yazoo album shows James at his best, accompanying himself on piano and guitar. A writer conscious of the effect certain musical constructions had on his audience's emotions, James set down in blunt, lyrical detail his generally pessimistic view of the world and drove his points home with dazzling musicianship designed to "deaden the mind," as he said, of anyone paying attention to him. Those who did heard him sing in "Hard Luck Child" of a childhood made lonely by his father's abandonment; when his 16-year-old bride deserted him for another man, his woe produced a masterpiece, "Devil Got My Woman." On those rare occasions when happiness visited, it confounded him, as he sang on "I'm So Glad" (later covered by Cream): "I'm so glad/I don't know what to do." Although the Paramount label was short-lived and James's recordings ill distributed, his work got around enough to make an impact on his contemporaries. Many in the Delta region had an opportunity to see him perform in person, as he traveled widely in his younger days, working variously in day jobs as a bootlegger, a manual laborer and a music teacher (for a time he ran his own music school in Jackson, Mississippi, but his temperament was unsuited for the politesse demanded of someone trying to build a business—a harsh taskmaster, he had a dispiriting habit of referring to his students as "dummies"), while spending his nights playing juke joints, white parties and, for a time, piano for a dollar an hour at a Memphis whorehouse.

As abruptly as James had come on the blues scene, so did he disappear. Less than a year after his Paramount sessions, James's father, preaching the gospel, returned and persuaded his son to enter a Baptist seminary he ran in Plano, Texas. Tired of "the music racket," James joined up with his father on the Southern revival circuit before forming a touring gospel group, the Dallas Texas Jubilee Singers. For over 20 years he left the blues behind, never recording, never playing for public consumption the music that was becoming the stuff of legend among blues aficionados. Eventually he left the gospel trail, and in 1964 he was located, ill with cancer, in a Philadelphia hospital. John Fahey was among those who tracked him down, along with Henry Vestine, who would later join Canned Heat. With their support, James played the 1964 Newport Folk Festival, thus beginning the second and final phase of his career as a blues artist. The Biograph, Adelphi and Vanguard albums are the remaining documents attesting to the depth and emotional pull of James's artistry in his latter years.

Devil Got My Woman is a must-have on the strength of the title track alone but is also recommended, along with Biograph's *Greatest of the Delta Blues Singers,* for its inclusion of "Sickbed Blues," an account of James's battle with cancer. Both the Biograph entry and *Skip James Today!* include another new James song reflecting on his illness, "Washington D.C. Hospital Center Blues."

She Lyin' is a stirring collection of 1964 recordings (some of them live) that are at their most haunting on the title song and on a reprise of "Devil Got My Woman," and at their most lacerating on "Hard Time Killin' Floor Blues." *Skip's Piano Blues,* recorded either in 1964 or '65 (the liner notes list both years), rounds out the picture of the artist in its total focus on James at the piano. In a dozen cuts James demonstrates an idiosyncratic sensibility that blends dollops of ragtime, stride and boogie-woogie while transposing his striking guitar stylings to the keyboard—Bentonia blues played on the 88s. The tracks range from quintessential James blues numbers (the eerie "All Night Long," a matter-of-fact "22-20 Blues," "Vicksburg Blues") to a gentle, reflective gospel tune, "Walking the Sea," all performances revealing the troubled soul reflected in James's eyes in his dour cover photo. Bill Holland's liner notes do a superb job of breaking down the intricacies of James's approach without being so highfalutin as to be recondite to the musically untutored listener.

When it came to communicating deep, inner torment, Skip James bowed to no one save Robert Johnson. Well ahead of his 1964 rediscovery, and certainly by the time the onslaught of cancer overtook him five years later, he had secured a lofty perch in blues history. In the end, he achieved much of what he felt society had denied him in his younger years. That he had so little time to enjoy his ascent makes his life read like nothing so much as a Skip James song. — D.M.

JOSEPH JARMAN

★★★★ Song for (1966; Delmark, 1991)
★★★★ Egwu-Anwu (with Famoudou Don Moye) (1978; India Navigation, 1997)
★★★★ Black Paladins (Black Saint, 1980)
★★★ Earth Passage—Density (with Famoudou Don Moye) (Black Saint, 1981)
★★★★ The Magic Triangle (with Don Pullen and Famoudou Don Moye) (Black Saint, 1993)
★★★★ Together Alone (with Anthony Braxton) (Delmark, 1994)
★★★★ As If It Were the Seasons (Delmark, 1996)

Multi-instrumentalist Joseph Jarman (b. 1937) was a prime mover of the Association for the Advancement of Creative Musicians (AACM), the influential 1960s Chicago-based musical collective, and a member of the AACM's best-known group, the Art Ensemble of Chicago.

The Delmark sessions were early paradigms of the AACM style and as such were extremely influential albums. Jarman's alto-saxophone playing is the main feature, although he does take time throughout these works to exhort listeners with various chants and incantations.

Compared with some of the other free-jazz records of the mid-'60s, *Song for* sounds relatively accessible, with solid performances from Bill Brimfield on trumpet, Fred Anderson on tenor, Christopher Gaddy on piano and marimbas, Charles Clark on bass and Thurman Barker and Steve McCall on drums. *As If It Were the Seasons* brings Anderson, Clark and Barker back as part of a bigger band including tenor saxophonist John Stubblefield, trumpeter John Jackson, trombonist Lester Lashley, flautist Joel Brandon, pianist/oboist Muhal Richard Abrams and vocalist Sherri Scott.

Egwu-Anwu and *Earth Passage—Density* are probing collaborations with percussionist Famoudou Don Moye. Johnny Dyani sings and plays bass and piano on *Black Paladins. The Magic Triangle* is a fine set, with Moye and pianist Don Pullen. Jarman and fellow avant-garde reed player Anthony Braxton trade ideas on *Together Alone.* — J.S.

AL JARREAU

★★★	**We Got By (Reprise, 1975)**
★★	**Glow (Reprise, 1976)**
★½	**Look to the Rainbow: Live in Europe (Warner Bros., 1977)**
★½	**All Fly Home (Warner Bros., 1978)**
★★★	**This Time (Warner Bros., 1980)**
★★★½	**Breakin' Away (Warner Bros., 1981)**
★★★	**Jarreau (Warner Bros., 1983)**
★★	**High Crime (Warner Bros., 1984)**
★★½	**In London (Warner Bros., 1985)**
★★★	**L Is for Lover (Warner Bros., 1986)**
★★★	**Heart's Horizon (Reprise, 1988)**
★★★	**Heaven and Earth (Reprise, 1992)**
★★★	**Tenderness (Reprise, 1994)**
★★★½	**The Best of Al Jarreau (Warner Bros., 1996)**

Al Jarreau (b. 1940) isn't a jazz singer, just a jazzy one, a soul stylist whose taste in vocal ornamentation runs not to the usual range of gospel-derived melisma but to a sort of scat-style improvisation. It's an odd sound, and definitely something of an acquired taste, particularly since Jarreau's choice in scat syllables runs mostly to "oing," "enngh" and "baoww," as if he'd modeled his sound on the twanging of rubber bands. That's not a problem on *We Got By,* on which the songs (written by Jarreau) provide enough of a framework to keep his vocalisms in check. But the cover-packed *Glow* is another matter, for Jarreau's renditions of "Fire and Rain" and "Your Song" shed no light on the songs themselves, instead emphasizing the peculiarity of his sound. Still, it's nowhere near the annoyance *Look to the Rainbow* is, as Jarreau's mannerisms run amok through these live versions of Paul Desmond's "Take Five" and his own "We Got By." By *All Fly Home,* Jarreau's aesthetic is so muddled that "She's Leaving Home" is played as soul while "(Sittin' on) The Dock of the Bay" is treated with the antiseptic respect of art rock.

Fortunately, producer Jay Graydon comes aboard for *This Time* and straightens things out. Rather than jettison Jarreau's jazziness, Graydon focuses the singer's approach so the album ends up stressing tuneful material like Chick Corea's "Spain (I Can Recall)" and Jarreau's own "Never Givin' Up." But it's *Breakin' Away* that pays the biggest dividends, for this album finds Jarreau strutting his stuff through a demanding (but listenable) version of Dave Brubeck's "Blue Rondo a la Turk" but making the most of his pop smarts on "We're in This Love Together." All told, it's probably the singer's most balanced album, though both *Jarreau* and *High Crime* have their points, particularly when the singer stresses his pop side.

Although the live *In London* makes up a bit for the indulgences of *Look to the Rainbow,* it adds little to the singer's catalog. *L Is for Lover* is another story, though, for this Nile Rodgers–produced album rounds out its funky foundation with melodies intricate enough to give Jarreau something to chew on, an approach that's more inventive and just as listenable as the kind of conventional funk dispensed by *Heart's Horizon.* — J.D.C.

KEITH JARRETT

★★★½	**Somewhere Before (1969; Atlantic, 1988)**
★★★★	**Facing You (1971; ECM, 1994)**
★★★★	**Fort Yawuh (1973; Impulse!, 1990)**
★★★	**In the Light (1973; ECM, 1994)**
★★★½	**Ruta and Daitya (with Jack DeJohnette) (1973; ECM, 1993)**
★★★★	**Solo Concerts (1973; ECM, 1994)**
★★★★	**Death and the Flower (1974; Impulse!, 1994)**
★★★★½	**Belonging (with Jan Garbarek) (1974; ECM, 1994)**
★★★	**Luminessence (with Jan Garbarek) (1975; ECM, 1989)**
★★★	**Arbour Zena (with Jan Garbarek) (1975; ECM, 1989)**

★★★★ **The Köln Concert (1975; ECM, 1987)**
★★★★ **The Survivors' Suite (1976; ECM, 1987)**
★★★ **Sun Bear Concerts (1976; ECM, 1994)**
★★★ **Staircase (1977; ECM, 1987)**
★★★★ **Silence (1977; Impulse!, 1992)**
★★★★ **My Song (with Jan Garbarek) (1977; ECM, 1987)**
★★★ **Nude Ants (1979; ECM, 1987)**
★★½ **Eyes of the Heart (1979; ECM, 1994)**
★★½ **Invocations/The Moth and the Flame (1980; ECM, 1994)**
★★★ **Sacred Hymns of G.I. Gurdjieff (1980; ECM, 1994)**
★★★ **Dark Intervals (1980; ECM, 1994)**
★★★ **Concerts (1982; ECM, 1994)**
★★★½ **Spheres (1986; ECM, 1994)**
★★★★ **Standards, Vol. 1 (ECM, 1987)**
★★★★ **Standards, Vol. 2 (ECM, 1987)**
★★★ **Standards Live (ECM, 1987)**
★★★ **Changes (ECM, 1987)**
★★★ **Spirits, Vols. 1 & 2 (ECM, 1987)**
★★★½ **Book of Ways (1987; ECM, 1996)**
★★★★ **Still Live (ECM, 1988)**
★★★½ **Works (1988; ECM, 1994)**
★★★★ **Changeless (ECM, 1989)**
★★★★ **Personal Mountains (1989; ECM, 1996)**
★★½ **Paris Concert (ECM, 1990)**
★★★ **Tribute (ECM, 1991)**
★★★★ **The Cure (ECM, 1992)**
★★★★ **Vienna Concert (ECM, 1992)**
★★★★ **Bye Bye Blackbird (ECM, 1993)**
★★★½ **At the Deer Head Inn (ECM, 1994)**
★★★★ **Foundations: The Keith Jarrett Anthology (Rhino, 1994)**
★★★½ **Standards in Norway (ECM, 1995)**
★★★★½ **At the Blue Note: The Complete Recordings (ECM, 1995)**
★★★★ **At the Blue Note Saturday June 4th, 1994—1st Set (ECM, 1995)**
★★★★ **Mysteries: The Impulse Years 1975–1976 (Impulse!, 1996)**
★★★½ **La Scala (ECM, 1997)**
★★★★ **The Impulse Years: 1973–1974 (Impulse!, 1997)**

The work of prolific and ambitious Keith Jarrett (b. 1945) has made him the most celebrated pianist of his generation. Jarrett was already a genre-crossing prodigy upon his late-1960s recording debut as part of the Charles Lloyd quartet, which also included the equally talented drummer Jack DeJohnette. Jarrett and DeJohnette thus began a creative relationship that, pushing 30 years, continues to cover new ground.

Jarrett was quickly offered his own contract as a leader and went into the studio with bassist Charlie Haden and drummer Paul Motian to make *Somewhere Before;* the title's reference to déjà vu indicates Jarrett's interest in joining musical and parapsychological elements, territory to which he would consistently, though not always effectively, return. More from this era is available on *Foundations.* The addition of tenor saxophonist Dewey Redman led to the great group sessions on *Fort Yawuh*, *The Survivors' Suite* and the out-of-print *Expectations,* among others.

Meanwhile, Jarrett was establishing himself as a top gun on the solo-piano circuit, releasing a precocious number of compelling solo performances, including *Facing You*, *Solo Concerts*, *The Köln Concert,* the inventive clavichord recording *Book of Ways* and the extraordinary organ recording on *Spheres.* Jarrett's abilities to shape and extend his pieces into seemingly endless variations led him deeper and deeper, past Fats Waller and Art Tatum, through Cecil Taylor, into improvisations that eventually enveloped him in the mind-numbing alternate universe of the six-CD *Sun Bear Concerts.*

Jarrett became the marquee performer on producer Manfred Eicher's ECM label, which in addition to giving him carte blanche on his most extravagant solo fantasies allowed him free reign to record in a series of small-group contexts, including duets with guitarist Ralph Towner and the superb *Ruta and Daitya,* with DeJohnette. The emotional range of his earlier work was hardened and fired by a new association with Norwegian saxophonist Jan Garbarek on *Belonging*, *Luminessence*, *Arbour Zena* and *My Song.* The sympathetic rhythm section of bassist Palle Danielsson and drummer Jon Christensen completes the lineup on *Personal Mountains,* recorded live in Tokyo in 1979. *Nude Ants* is a less successful New York recording by the same quartet the following month.

Jarrett reunited with DeJohnette in 1983 as part of an eager, magnificent trio with another ECM artist, bassist Gary Peacock, to make a series of outstanding sonic explorations—including the *Standards* sequence, *Changes,* the experimental *Changeless*, *Still Live*, *Tribute* and

The Cure. The trio continued triumphantly into the 1990s, even as Jarrett was making solo albums of material by his favorite classical composers. *Bye Bye Blackbird* is a stunning tribute to Miles Davis, who employed the young Jarrett in one of his most challenging fusion lineups. After Motian sat in for DeJohnette at the *Deer Head* recording, the trio reconvened for the stunning *At the Blue Note Saturday June 4th, 1994,* leaving the listener to wonder where they could possibly go from there. *Works* attempts the impossible task of reducing Jarrett's output to a single disc of music.

Jarrett is one of the central figures in ECM's continuing strategy of refusing to recognize any boundaries between traditional jazz and classical music, a landscape where J.S. Bach, Thelonious Monk and Jarrett are all searching for a common musical truth. Jarrett's recordings of *The Well-Tempered Clavier*, *French Suites* and *The Goldberg Variations* may not offer the ultimate proof of the strategy's success, but on *Vienna Concert* Jarrett's solos take on a decidedly Bach-inspired soul. Maybe it's a long way from the church to the conservatory, but Keith Jarrett certainly found that passage.
—J.S.

JAZZ JAMAICA

★★★★ Skaravan (Hannibal, 1996)

Modern jazz shares common ground with many other musical styles—particularly those powered by the same reed, horn and rhythm instrumentation. That Jamaican ska has been flowing in the wake of the melodies and tight horn arrangements of New York's bop and postbop jazz scene is well known—one need only hear Don Drummond's groundbreaking work with the early-'60s Skatalites to hear that connection. Jazz Jamaica is a modern-day, London-based septet that has reforged and expanded that link, covering tastefully chosen jazz tunes and their own compositions with a lineup that is a Who's Who of ska/reggae veterans and pedigreed Jamaican musicians.

Led by bassist Gary Crosby (nephew of ska guitarist Ernest Ranglin and a former member of England's Jazz Warriors), Jazz Jamaica features among its floating membership strong Kingston credentials: trombonist Rico Rodriguez (Bob Marley, the Specials), saxophonist Michael Rose (Dennis Brown, Paul Simon) and trumpeter Eddie "Tan-Tan" Thornton (Aswad). *Skaravan* sparkles with promise, a strong rookie outing that boosts the musical cross-pollination with high-powered originals ("Bridge View," "Ramblin'"), ska traditionals ("Peanut Vendor," Drummond's "Don Cosmic") and ska remakes (Charlie Parker's "Barbados" and Duke Ellington's "Caravan"). At this writing, a package featuring ska covers of Blue Note classics is on deck for release by Jazz Jamaica. — A.K.

JAZZ PASSENGERS

★★★ Broken Night/Red Light (Crépescule, 1987)
★★★★ Deranged & Decomposed (Crépescule, 1988)
★★★ Implement Yourself (New World, 1990)
★★★½ Live at the Knitting Factory (Knitting Factory Works, 1991)
★★★★ Plain Old Joe (Knitting Factory Works, 1993)
★★★★ In Love (High Street, 1994)
★★★★½ Individually Twisted (32 Jazz, 1996)

Consistently inventive and compellingly postmodernist, the Jazz Passengers blend hard-bop, free, Latin and cabaret influences with an infection of Lower East Side experimentalism and an affection for borscht-belt humor. The Passengers were cofounded by the nucleus of alto saxophonist Roy Nathanson and trombonist Curtis Fowlkes, who met in the Big Apple Circus band and later worked in the second Lounge Lizards lineup. With an evocative, floating membership of stellar soloists (guitarist Marc Ribot and vibist Bill Ware), solid rhythm section (bassist Brad Jones and drummer E.J. Rodriguez) and eclectic vocalists (Elvis Costello, Jeff Buckley, Deborah Harry and Fowlkes himself), the band has garnered a fan base that includes jazz, avant-garde and alternative-rock aficionados.

A decade of label hopping has not helped the band's cause but has yielded a number of finely crafted, worthwhile titles. *Broken Night/Red Light* and *Deranged & Decomposed,* both released on a Belgian label, capture the anarchic yet convincing interlocking of the unusual combination of vibes, sax, guitar, trombone and violin. The latter is an especially dizzying mosaic of original tunes, weird covers and improvised invocations of New York's downtown scene: "Tikkun" shows off the emotional depth of Nathanson's songwriting and his own klezmer-leaning sax work, while a blue-light reworking of the disco ballad "Salty Tears" features Fowlkes's disarmingly gentle vocals. *Implement Yourself* is more compositionally conscious, with contributions by most of the group: Nathanson's gear-shifting "Augie the Rat" and Jones's rocking "Cha-Ha" act as serious counterpoint to the mockingly suave album closer, Cole Porter's "Easy to Love."

Live at the Knitting Factory, documenting three early-'91 club dates (minus Ribot), presents a strong band overview with a number of "hits" from the Passenger songbook, a pair of covers and material from the group's theatrical production "Jazz Passengers in Egypt," performed by an expanded lineup with tuba, sampler and second drummer. *Plain Old Joe* presents the group back in the studio, fully focused, balancing polished performance pieces like "Robbie" and "Blues for Helen" with hard-rocking out-stepping numbers ("Inzane") and spoken-word vocal excursions ("Honer B. Half-steppin'," the Nathanson/Fowlkes duet "If I Were a Bell" and the Brad Jones–penned title track).

In Love, shining with neocabaret creations by the music-and-lyrics team of Nathanson and actor/producer David Cale, successfully works as a song-oriented album with the Passengers playing host to various and varied vocal guests, including Jeff Buckley, Debbie Harry, Little Jimmy Scott, Mavis Staples, Jenni Muldaur and Freedy Johnston, among others. Standouts include "Imitation of a Kiss" (sung by Scott), "Jolly Street" (Buckley), "Dog in Sand" (Harry) and the seductive, sirenlike invitation of "Swim to Me" (John Kelly).

Individually Twisted, which finds the Passengers fronted by the ballad-friendly voice of Debbie Harry, is the group's strongest release to date, with reprised material ("Imitation of a Kiss" and a parodic, doo-woppish take on the Blondie hit "The Tide Is High") plus writing and vocal contributions from Elvis Costello: the sultry "Aubergine" and his love-and-betrayal duet with Harry on "Doncha Go Away Mad" (based on a melody by Illinois Jacquet called "Black Velvet," with lyrics added for the version popularized by Stan Kenton). "Angel Eyes" and "Li'l Darlin'" both emphasize just how far Harry's lyric handling and vocal dexterity have progressed, while the former unveils the tender violin playing of new member Rob Thomas. An overdue revival of Cannonball Adderley's "Jive Samba" reveals the finely honed postbop instrumental interplay of the Passengers.

— J.S.

THE JAZZHOLE

★★★ **The Jazzhole (Blue Moon, 1994)**
★★★ **And the Feeling Goes 'Round (Blue Moon, 1995)**

A revolving door of vocalists, rappers and instrumentalists adds intriguing elements to the Jazzhole's mélange of jazz gesture and hip-hop style. At its core is an interesting combination of digital whiz Marlon Saunders's programmed hip-hop grooves and John Pondel's clever guitar and bass work (and multi-instrumentalist Kevin DiSimone on *The Jazzhole*). This music's existence offers further proof of jazz's endless adaptability to pop-culture taste and production fads. On its own, it's a dead end, although the principals would most likely feel better if it was called a cul-de-sac. Don't forget to bongo.

— J.S.

JAZZMATAZZ

★★★★ **Jazzmatazz, Vol. 1 (Chrysalis/EMI, 1993)**
★★½ **Jazzmatazz, Vol. 2: The New Reality (hosted by Guru) (Chrysalis/EMI, 1995)**

Jazzmatazz is a successful experiment by Gang Starr rapper Guru (b. Keith Elam, 1966), blending jazz and hip-hop by enlisting the performing and producing talents of a number of star performers. The hypnotic and infectious *Jazzmatazz, Vol. 1* features Guru's brand of mellow-voiced rapping, which blends nicely over soft jazz rhythms. Acting as MC, he introduces his concept and players, then segues into "Loungin'," a track that sets the record's vibe as trumpeter Donald Byrd backs Guru's deep-furrowed funk. Other contributors to *Vol. 1* include saxophonist Courtney Pine, virtuoso vibist Roy Ayers and singer N'dea Davenport (Brand New Heavies), and these collaborators sound comfortable in an experimental role. Guru wisely doesn't try to bring all the collaborators into the studio at once but lets each track evolve around an individual contributor.

In 1995 Guru reincarnated Jazzmatazz with *Vol. 2: The New Reality,* which features about three times as many guest artists. Unfortunately, this is the album's undoing—the kind of focus that exists on the first record gets lost in the crowd here. Gone is the singular player tinkering with Guru in the studio, and in its place are slick acid-jazz outfits like the Solsonics and Jamiroquai recording tracks that are all too similar to the average '90s funk/dance band.

Overall, it's still worth a listen, especially the kinetic fun of "Watch What You Say" with Chaka Khan and Branford Marsalis and the funky "For You" with vocals and bass by Me'Shell Ndegéocello. — G.E.

BLIND LEMON JEFFERSON

★★★★★ **Blind Lemon Jefferson (1974; Milestone, 1992)**
★★★★★ **King of the Country Blues (Yazoo, 1988)**
★★★ **Penitentiary Blues (Collectables, 1989)**
★★★★ **Moanin' All Over (Tradition, 1996)**
★★★★★ **Son House and Blind Lemon Jefferson (Biograph, N.A.)**

Among the influential guitarists of the 1920s, only Lonnie Johnson claims a stature comparable to that of Blind Lemon Jefferson (ca. 1897–1929 or 1930), the first in a long line of great blues guitarists hailing from Texas. An original voice, Jefferson produces unpredictable riffs and irregular rhythms that seem to have sprung organically from his own genius, free from any easily pinpointed influence. At once amazed and baffled by Jefferson's recondite style, his peers began working variations on it, but ultimately no one sounded like the master himself in full flower. As a writer, Jefferson was given to the dark, brooding tales common among country-blues artists, but he was also a wise and often witty observer of his own life and the follies he saw all around him. "See That My Grave Is Kept Clean" and "Easy Rider Blues" are Jefferson originals that have become blues classics. Jefferson recorded steadily from 1926 until his death.

The Yazoo and Milestone albums are highly recommended, as both offer a broad overview of the artist's best work with little duplication of tracks and fine annotation. By comparison, the nine-track *Penitentiary Blues* duplicates a few of the songs on the Milestone set, and its generic annotation fails to provide any information about the album itself. Aficionados, however, will find the two versions of "Black Snake Moan" interesting, as well as the starkly rendered title song. The import bins offer the best option for completists in the form of Document's four-volume *Complete Recorded Works* set. — D.M.

EDDIE JEFFERSON

★★★★ **Letter from Home (1962; Original Jazz Classics, 1988)**
★★★★ **The Jazz Singer (1964/1965; Evidence, 1993)**
★★★★ **Body and Soul (1968; Original Jazz Classics, 1989)**
★★★★ **Come Along with Me (1969; Original Jazz Classics, 1991)**
★★★★ **Things Are Getting Better (1974; Muse, 1996)**
★★★★ **Godfather of Vocalese (1976; Muse, 1990)**

Edgar "Eddie" Jefferson (1918–1979) pioneered the technique of writing lyrics to famous instrumental jazz solos in the '30s, an approach later popularized by King Pleasure and Lambert, Hendricks and Ross. He first made records in the 1950s, on his own and as part of saxophonist James Moody's group. The earliest material here, *The Jazz Singer,* was recorded between 1959 and 1961, while the rest dates from the 1960s and early '70s.

Jefferson's approach often adds surprising illumination to the original performances on which his songs are based. His adaptation of the James Moody solo "Moody's Mood for Love," derived in turn by Moody from the standard "I'm in the Mood for Love," became a cult item in its King Pleasure version.

The Prestige and Riverside reissues (on Original Jazz Classics) show Jefferson's classic touch primarily on bop standards. *Letter from Home* has an impressive backing cast including Clark Terry and Ernie Royal on trumpets, Moody and Johnny Griffin on saxophones, Wynton Kelly and Joe Zawinul on keyboards and Sam Jones on bass. Moody also contributes to *Body and Soul,* while trumpeter Bill Hardman and saxophonist Charles McPherson are on *Come Along with Me.*

Jefferson continued to cover bop tunes and standards in the 1970s for Muse but also updated his adaptations to contemporary material. On the reissue of *Things Are Getting Better,* Jefferson handles Miles Davis's "Bitches Brew" and Sly Stone's "Thank You (Falettinme Be Mice Elf Agin)." *Still on the Planet* from 1976 was reissued as *Godfather of Vocalese.* While on tour in 1979, Jefferson was murdered outside a Detroit nightclub. — J.S.

JOHNNY JENKINS

★★★★★ **Ton Ton Macoute (1972; Capricorn, 1997)**
★★★½ **Blessed Blues (Capricorn, 1996)**

With tasty blues slide guitar (courtesy of Duane Allman), a funk rhythm section (drummer Butch

Trucks and bassist Berry Oakley), sharp, whiplike percussion (Eddie Hinton and Jai Johanny Johanson) and his own deep Southern, half-spoken vocals, Johnny Jenkins (b. 1939) created a thick, swampish masterpiece with his legendary (and frustratingly obscure) album *Ton Ton Macoute.* Long out of print (and recently liberally sampled by Beck), the collector's item was a weird but irresistible amalgam of blues and country songs (material ranged from Dr. John's "I Walk on Gilded Splinters" and Bob Dylan's "Down Along the Cove" to John Loudermilk's "Bad News" and Chris Kenner's "Sick and Tired"), Southern soul grooves and New Orleans voodoo music, all anchored by funky rock rhythms. It also proved to be the Macon, Georgia, guitarist's one and only recording in 25 years and the pinnacle of a short-lived Southern zeitgeist: what Atlantic producer Jerry Wexler dubbed "swamp rock" to describe the early-'70s blues-based, soul-influenced but basically rock sound that Eric Clapton, the Allman Brothers, Doug Sahm and Dr. John were all playing and sharing.

The recent reissue of this classic album gives overdue credit to the upside-down–guitar-playing, left-handed bandleader who founded the legendary '60s R&B group the Pinetoppers, out of which came Otis Redding and whose performances inspired another southpaw string master: Jimi Hendrix (they jammed together once in 1969). An unfortunate fear of flying sidelined Jenkins's career after his singular flash of brilliance, relegating him to home life and intermittent appearances on the Southern soul circuit.

With the help of longtime friend and Capricorn head Phil Walden, *Blessed Blues* marks Jenkins's welcome reintroduction in 1996, with a set of blues originals and standards (Sonny Boy Williamson [Rice Miller]'s "Don't Start Me to Talkin'," Muddy Waters's "Can't Lose What You Ain't Never Had," a Latin reworking of Blind Willie McTell's "Statesboro Blues") and support from a proud Alabama assemblage of studio R&B veterans, notably pianist Chuck Leavell, saxophonist/organist Randall Bramblett, bassist David Hood and drummer Bill Stewart. More straight-ahead than his past, genre-mixing tour de force, it shows off his still-strong heartfelt vocal prowess and features his string-bending talents on the Mickey Baker–ish "Miss Thing" and on his longtime anthem, "The Pinetopper Theme." —A.K.

LEROY JENKINS

★★★★ Mixed Quintet (Black Saint, 1979)
★★★★ Urban Blues (Black Saint, 1984)
★★★★ The Legend of Ai Glatson (Black Saint, 1991)
★★★½ Themes & Improvisations (1992; CRI, 1995)
★★★★★ Lifelong Ambitions (Black Saint, 1993)
★★★½ Leroy Jenkins Live! (Black Saint, 1993)

Violinist Leroy Jenkins (b. 1932) was part of the Midwest avant-garde collective of the 1960s, and then a major player in New York's 1970s loft-jazz scene, which has transmuted in part into the postmodern eclecticism of the Knitting Factory program. Also a member of the highly regarded Revolutionary Ensemble, Jenkins is a conceptual innovator and completely nontraditional player, and has consequently been ignored by the mainstream record industry. On *Mixed Quintet* he plays violin and viola in a group with Marty Ehrlich on bass clarinet, James Newton on flute, John Clark on French horn and J.D. Parran on clarinet. *Urban Blues* provides yet another example of the deep interrelation between the blues and avant-garde. Its uncompromising rhythmic flow and sonic edginess is common to both forms, and Jenkins is clearly right at home leading the group Sting through this program of avant-garde spirituals. *The Legend of Ai Glatson* is a trio session with pianist Anthony Davis and percussionist Andrew Cyrille. *Themes & Improvisations* features a violin section, viola, cello, trombone, bassoon, trumpet, French horn, flute, clarinet, bass and piano over the course of four lengthy pieces. *Lifelong Ambitions* is a stirring live duet performance with pianist Muhal Richard Abrams recorded in 1977 at New York's Washington Square Church. *Leroy Jenkins Live!* uses a conventional rhythm section and synthesizer textures. — J.S.

INGRID JENSEN

★★★★ Vernal Fields (Enja, 1995)
★★★★ Here on Earth (Enja, 1997)

The auspicious debut by Canadian trumpeter and flügelhornist Ingrid Jensen (b. 1966) followed her studies at the Berklee College of Music and three years of teaching and performing on the wide-open European jazz scene, where she was encouraged by Art Farmer. She returned to New York in 1994, where her fresh, confident sound earned her substantial work with the all-woman big band DIVA, the Maria Schneider Jazz Orchestra and the bands of Guillermo Klein and Magali Souriau.

Vernal Fields teams her with saxophonists Steve Wilson and George Garzone, pianist Bruce Barth, bassist Larry Grenadier and drummer Lenny White. Her soaring flights of power and musical grace are showcased within a collective spirit that also illuminates the talents of her sister, Christine Jensen, a composer who provided three of the nine tunes. While *Vernal Fields* seemed like a tough act for a rookie to follow, *Here on Earth* is even stronger in focus and performance, aided by the company of pianist George Colligan, saxophonist Gary Bartz and singer Jill Seifers. Ingrid Jensen stands out as one of the finest young trumpeters to surface in the 1990s. — K.F.

ANTONIO CARLOS JOBIM

★★★★ **Francis Albert Sinatra and Antonio Carlos Jobim (1967; Reprise, 1998)**
★★★½ **Wave (1968; A&M, 1989)**
★★★ **Stone Flower (1971; Legacy, 1990)**
★★★ **Elis and Tom (with Elis Regina) (1974; Verve, 1990)**
★★★½ **Urubu (1976; Warner Archives, 1996)**
★★★ **The Wonderful World of Antonio Carlos Jobim (1978; Discovery, 1986)**
★★★½ **Terra Brasilis (1980; Warner Archives, 1996)**
★★★ **E Convidados (Verve, 1986)**
★★★ **Passarim (Verve, 1987)**
★★★ **Echoes of Rio (RCA, 1989)**
★★★ **Verve Jazz Masters 13 (Verve, 1994)**
★★★★ **The Man from Ipanema (Verve, 1995)**
★★★ **The Girl from Ipanema: The Antonio Carlos Jobim Songbook (Verve, 1996)**
★★★ **Antonio Carlos Jobim and Friends (Verve, 1996)**
★★★½ **Composer (Warner Archives, 1996)**
★★★ **The Composer Plays (Verve, 1997)**
★★★ **The Art of Antonio Carlos Jobim (Verve, N.A.)**
★★★ **Compact Jazz (Verve, N.A.)**

Composer, guitarist and vocalist Antonio Carlos Jobim (1927–1994) was a unique stylist who drew from the lyricism of the Brazilian folk tradition to develop a signature sound that captured the imagination of the music world in the 1960s. A gifted improviser and superb melodist, Jobim delivered his music in a half whisper that gave a sense of restraint and sophistication to passionate sensations, a stylistic approach that appealed to the urbane sensibilities of jet-setters who embraced the bossa nova craze.

Jobim wrote the book on bossa nova, creating durable standards such as "One-Note Samba," "The Girl from Ipanema," "Wave," "Corcovado," "Desafinado" and "Jazz Samba," several of which were popularized by saxophonist Stan Getz and the team of vocalist Astrud and guitarist João Gilberto. A boxed set, *The Man from Ipanema* collects all the hits as well as showcasing Jobim's further guitaristic and atmospheric talents.

Jobim's limitations as a performer mar much of the Verve material recorded under his own name, but the later work rereleased by Warner Archives presents him in lush orchestral settings arranged by Claus Ogerman and Nelson Riddle. — J.S.

LITTLE WILLIE JOHN

★★★★ **Sure Things (King, 1987)**
★★★★ **Mister Little Willie John (King, 1988)**
★★★★★ **Fever: The Best of Little Willie John (Rhino, 1993)**
★★★★ **All 15 Chart Hits (King, 1995)**

One of the eeriest, most tortured but oddly buoyant voices in the history of rhythm & blues belonged to Little Willie John (né William Edgar John, 1937–1968), who lived fast, died young (at 30, officially of a heart attack, while imprisoned on a manslaughter charge) and left an extraordinary legacy that won him entry into the Rock and Roll Hall of Fame in 1996. Born in Arkansas, raised in Detroit, he began singing as a child with his family's gospel group, the United Four. From there he went on his own to compete in amateur shows, and at 14 he toured with Paul "Hucklebuck" Williams's orchestra for a year, then was given the boot when Williams got fed up with the youngster's unruly behavior. John was then signed to King Records.

Hits came immediately for the nearly 18-year-old John, beginning with "All Around the World" (#5 R&B), a blues ballad on which his urgent, pleading tenor style is fully formed. The near-palpable pain in his voice sounded earned, not learned, as if he was conscious of something terrible gaining on him, as if he was always, as he declared in one of his most moving performances, "suffering with the blues." Style and feeling came together in resonant fashion on his fourth King single, the troubled, deliberate "Fever," a Number One R&B single and a Top 30 entry on the pop side in 1956. For two years Little Willie John's work was as distinctive as any produced at the time in the popular genres.

True to the personality of a man who had his share of personal problems outside the studio, much of John's material seems double-edged. The beautiful "Talk to Me, Talk to Me," a Top 20 pop single and Top 5 R&B single from 1958, evolves from a gentle nudge to a desperate plea; the propulsive, dreamy "Sleep" juxtaposes a bright melody and bouncing rhythm against lyrics suggesting that only in dreams can comfort be found; "It Only Hurts a Little While" means to say that it hurts forever.

Fever: The Best of Little Willie John consists of 20 strong tracks and informative annotation that not only recounts career particulars but also clarifies the details of the sad final days, including an account of the after-hours party at which John plunged a knife into the chest of a much larger man who had slugged him, and the reigning theories regarding John's mysterious death. Included are the essential John tracks, from "Fever," "Sleep" and "Talk to Me, Talk to Me" to the tortured "Big Blue Diamonds" and a blues-rock rave-up with Hank Ballard, "I Like to See My Baby." Despite the visage of the smiling, handsome young man pictured on the CD's cover, gazing bright-eyed beyond the camera's lens to a future that seemed promising beyond all measure, this was an artist with hellhounds on his trail from the cradle to the grave. — D.M.

MABLE JOHN

★★★★ **Stay Out of the Kitchen (Stax/Fantasy, 1993)**

Though a relative unknown, Mable John (b. 1930) possessed one of the great soulful voices of the 1960s. The sister of the great Little Willie John recorded a few sides for Berry Gordy's Tamla label, before finding her rightful place at Stax, backed by its legendary house band from 1966 to 1968. The superb *Stay Out of the Kitchen* collects John's handful of Stax singles as well as never-before-released tracks. Produced by Isaac Hayes and David Porter, the album brilliantly showcases John's sultry, simmering vocals on a range of material, from bluesy shuffles to tearful ballads to up-tempo shake-a-tail-feather numbers. John cowrote some of her most memorable songs, including the sassy "Able Mable" (it's sort of the "sister" song to "Fever," and was cowritten with her brother—who made that song a hit). — H.G.-W.

BLIND WILLIE JOHNSON

★★★★★ **Praise God I'm Satisfied (Yazoo, 1976)**

★★★★★ **Sweeter as the Years Go By (Yazoo, 1990)**

★★★★★ **The Complete Recordings of Blind Willie Johnson (Legacy, 1993)**

Born with the century, Texan Blind Willie Johnson (1900–1950) made blues with a heightened, urgent purpose. Let others worry about shaking their moneymakers or dusting their brooms: Johnson's goal was beyond all that—nothing less than God was the object of his desire. Learning his craft on a cigar-box guitar, he became a country-blues evangelist and a "race records" giant, spreading the gospel by means of bottleneck guitar and a singing style of absolute directness. In 1950, after his house burned down, Johnson caught pneumonia. A hospital turned him away (because of his blindness!), and he died, ending a long, remarkable career.

Disregard the primitive lo-fi sound with its occasional pops and hisses, and concentrate instead on genius in the raw. Thirty selections strong, *The Complete Recordings of Blind Willie Johnson* is an authentic masterpiece; among its highlights are "Jesus Make Up My Dying Bed" and "You're Gonna Need Somebody on Your Bond"—but every cut is worthy.

Masterpieces, too, are the Yazoo collections. Both feature material recorded between 1927 and 1930 and boast exemplary notes. *Praise God I'm Satisfied* focuses on Johnson's slide guitar; *Sweeter as the Years Go By* features his fingerpicking style. His playing would influence musicians for years to come, but it's his singing that's truly riveting. "John the Revelator," "If I Had My Way I'd Tear the Building Down" and "Can't Nobody Hide from God" reveal the agony and joy of a soul given over to struggle with things divine. — P.E.

J.J. JOHNSON

★★★★ **Sonny Stitt/Bud Powell/J.J. Johnson (1949; Original Jazz Classics, 1992)**

★★★★★ **Four Trombones: The Debut Recordings (1953; Prestige, 1990)**

★★★★½ **J.J., Inc. (Columbia, 1960)**

★★★★ **The Great Kai and J.J. (1961; Impulse!, 1988)**

★★★½ **Proof Positive (Impulse!, 1964)**
★★★ **Yokohama Concert (with Nat Adderley) (1977; Pablo, 1997)**
★★★½ **Concepts in Blue (1981; Original Jazz Classics, 1992)**
★★★★ **Things Are Getting Better All the Time (with Al Grey) (1984; Original Jazz Classics, 1992)**
★★★★½ **The Trombone Master (Columbia, 1989)**
★★★★★ **The Eminent Jay Jay Johnson, Vol. 1 (Blue Note, 1989)**
★★★★★ **The Eminent Jay Jay Johnson, Vol. 2 (Blue Note, 1989)**
★★★ **Standards: Live at the Village Vanguard (Antilles, 1991)**
★★★½ **Quintergy: Live at the Village Vanguard (Antilles, 1991)**
★★★★ **Trombone by Three (with Kai Winding and Bennie Green) (Original Jazz Classics, 1992)**
★★★★ **Vivian (Concord Jazz, 1992)**
★★★★ **Jazz Quintets (Savoy, 1993)**
★★★ **Let's Hang Out (Verve, 1993)**
★★ **Tangence (Verve, 1995)**
★★★½ **The Brass Orchestra (Verve, 1997)**
★★★★ **Jay and Kai (Savoy, N.A.)**

J.J. Johnson (b. 1924), one of the masters of modern jazz trombone, gave the instrument a new role with his soft, supple lines and fleet, bop-inspired articulation. After working in the big bands of Benny Carter and Count Basie during the first half of the 1940s, the Indianapolis native began playing bop in 1946 with Dizzy Gillespie's band and leading his own small groups. The Savoy *Jazz Quintets* includes the historic recordings "Coppin' the Bop" and "Jay Jay."

Trombone by Three includes four tracks from a 1949 Johnson session with Sonny Rollins on tenor saxophone, Kenny Dorham on trumpet, John Lewis on piano, Leonard Gaskin on bass and Max Roach on drums.

The sessions collected on *The Eminent Jay Jay Johnson, Vols. 1* and *2* represent a bop milestone featuring heavyweight lineups with Clifford Brown on trumpet, Hank Mobley on tenor saxophone, Jimmy Heath on tenor and baritone saxophones, Kenny Clarke on drums, Wynton Kelly, John Lewis and Horace Silver on piano and Paul Chambers, Percy Heath and Charles Mingus on bass.

Johnson, a great composer and arranger as well, experimented with multitrombone recordings at different times over the years beginning with the remarkable *Four Trombones,* a 1953 session with Kai Winding, Bennie Green and Willie Dennis backed by a rhythm section of Mingus on bass, Arthur Taylor on drums and Lewis on piano. This groundbreaking recording was made for Debut, the progressive-jazz label owned by Mingus and Roach.

Johnson went on to fame as part of a marvelous trombone team with Winding in 1954, recording for Savoy, then at greater length for Columbia, and years later reuniting for an Impulse! session. Though the Savoy and Impulse! recordings are available, the Columbia releases are all out of print at this writing.

Working with small groups, Johnson also made a series of outstanding recordings for Columbia in the 1950s and '60s that were influential not only in jazz circles but in pop arrangements as well. *J.J., Inc.,* a sextet recording from 1961 with Clifford Jordan on tenor sax and Freddie Hubbard on trumpet joining Johnson on the front line, was an obvious major influence arrangement-wise on the jazz-rock band Chicago. *The Trombone Master* collects material from four Columbia sessions, but the rest of this great output is currently unavailable. Mosaic collected all the Columbias in a limited-edition boxed set that is virtually impossible to find.

Proof Positive is a good mid-1960s recording with John Coltrane band members McCoy Tyner on piano and Elvin Jones on drums augmented by Toots Thielemans in a relatively rare performance on guitar.

Johnson went into semiretirement from jazz during the 1970s to write and arrange for film and television. *Yokohama Concert* is a live recording from 1977 with a group featuring Nat Adderley. *Concepts in Blue* features Clark Terry on trumpet and flügelhorn and Ernie Watts on tenor and alto saxophones. *Things Are Getting Better All the Time* is another trombone summit, this time with fellow Basie-ite Al Grey.

Johnson jumped into the 1990s with *Standards* and *Quintergy,* live recordings from the Village Vanguard with Ralph Moore on saxophones, Stanley Cowell on piano, Rufus Reid on bass and Victor Lewis on drums. Johnson-band stalwart Moore also appears on the larger-group side *Let's Hang Out.*

Johnson's best 1990s work is the exquisite collection of ballads, *Vivian,* recorded in his classic quintet format with Johnson's tone enveloping the session. *Tangence* is a disappointing outing with the Robert Farnon orchestra. *The Brass Orchestra* showcases

Johnson's abilities with large-band orchestration much more effectively, although it's a shame that the terrific 1960s set *Say When: J.J. Johnson and His Big Bands* is not available.
— J.S.

JAMES P. JOHNSON

★★★★ Carolina Shout (Biograph, 1988)
★★★★ Snowy Morning Blues (Decca, 1991)
★★★★ 1921–1928 (Classics, 1992)
★★★★ 1928–1938 (Classics, 1992)
★★★★ 1938–1942 (Classics, 1993)
★★★★ 1943–1944 (Classics, 1995)
★★★★ 1944 (Classics, 1995)
★★★★½ 1944, Vol. 2 (Classics, 1995)

Born in New Brunswick, New Jersey, James P. Johnson (1894–1955) became known as the "Father of Stride Piano." A pivotal player in the evolution of jazz, he influenced such giants as Fats Waller, Duke Ellington and Thelonious Monk. Primarily influenced by classical composers like Rachmaninoff and Liszt, Johnson was very interested in traditional composition, and he did it well, writing a piano concerto ("Jasmine"), a long choral work (*Yamacraw*) and an opera with a libretto by poet Langston Hughes (*De Organizer*). He also composed the impressionistic, four-part *Symphony Harlem* in 1932. In short, Johnson was a prolific cultural figure in the first half of 20th Century America.

Carolina Shout is a digital recording of Johnson's piano rolls played on a 1910 Steinway. Comprising entirely rolls made from May 1917 to June 1925, the album includes such original "ticklers" as "Steeplechase Rag," "Harlem Strut" and the mesmerizing "Eccentricity," which Johnson referred to as a "syncopated waltz." W.C. Handy's "Ole Miss Blues" is also notable. *Snowy Morning Blues* covers a wider span of Johnson's career, 1930 to 1944; of its four earliest recordings, culled from a January 1930 session for Brunswick, the most interesting is "What Is This Thing Called Love?" a Cole Porter composition that Johnson brilliantly personalizes. The rest of *Snowy Morning Blues* comprises tracks cut at various 1944 sessions not long after Johnson had a stroke; there's a drummer to help him keep time, but his playing doesn't sound like it's suffered appreciably. Included are several Waller compositions: "Honeysuckle Rose," "Squeeze Me" and "Ain't Misbehavin'." Other highlights are the ebullient "I'm Gonna Sit Right Down and Write Myself a Letter" and breakneck-tempo versions of "Carolina Shout" and "Keep Off the Grass."

The Classics series is a complete, six-disc compilation of Johnson's works. Mostly solo-piano performances, *1921–1928* also includes appearances by Cootie Williams on trumpet and Waller on piano, among others, while *1928–1938* features two tracks with trumpeter King Oliver and five with Pee Wee Russell on clarinet. Of particular note are four tracks on *1944, Vol. 2,* which feature Johnson with Max Kaminsky and His Jazz Band, an outfit whose central player is guitarist Eddie Condon. These tracks, particularly "Eccentric (the Eccentric Rag)," show the ensemble's swinging cohesion and its ability to handle an unconventionally structured song, even at a speedy tempo.
— B.R.H.

JIMMY JOHNSON

★★★★ Johnson's Whacks (1979; Delmark, 1991)
★★★ North/South (Delmark, 1983)
★★★★ Bar Room Preacher (Alligator, 1985)
★★★½ I'm a Jockey (Verve, 1995)

Born Jimmy Thompson in Missouri in 1928, the brother of soul singer Syl Johnson, Jimmy Johnson is a major-league Chicago artist who has never really made it out of the minors, despite pioneering a blues/R&B fusion that propelled Robert Cray to fame and became a de rigueur sound of the '80s. Johnson's lack of acclaim is probably due largely to a relatively late start (he didn't record his first album as a leader until the late '70s, after years of playing in cover bands, then backing the likes of Jimmy Dawkins and Otis Rush) and a reluctance to tour nationally (no doubt exacerbated by a tragic 1988 car crash that killed his longtime bassist Larry Exum and one other band member). He is, however, a fluid West Side guitarist, a unique, high-pitched singer and a humorous, wide-ranging writer whose songs are more in the tradition of pop or country than blues. His tunes display a coherent worldview that is cynical without being bitter and incorporate hearty doses of rock, R&B, country and even reggae and disco. His forays into the latter, in fact, mar *North/South,* an otherwise excellent album.

Johnson's other three recordings are all top-notch. *Bar Room Preacher* gets the nod over *Johnson's Whacks* due mostly to superior production and a fuller guitar sound. *I'm a Jockey,* Johnson's return to recording after a nine-year layoff, finds him in fine fettle, backed by a swinging jazz horn section and displaying all facets of his broad style, though it leans a little too heavily on soul standards rather than Johnson's own compositions. — A.P.

JOHNNIE JOHNSON

★★★½ **Blue Hand Johnnie (1988; Evidence, 1993)**
★★★ **Johnnie B. Bad (Elektra Nonesuch, 1991)**
★★★½ **That'll Work (with the Kentucky Headhunters) (Elektra Nonesuch, 1993)**
★★★ **Rockin' Eighty-Eights (with Clayton Love and Jimmy Vaughn) (Modern Blues Recordings, 1995)**
★★★★ **Johnnie Be Back (MusicMasters, 1995)**

As Chuck Berry's original pianist, Johnnie Johnson (b. 1924) was a pivotal—though underappreciated—player in the early architecture of rock & roll. Adding his barrelhouse licks to such classics as "Maybelline," "Oh, Carol" and "School Days," among others, Johnson created a sound that would later be emulated by many. Influenced by such greats as Meade "Lux" Lewis and Earl "Fatha" Hines, Johnson subsequently showcased his pile-driving, two-fisted style on several rollicking solo endeavors, welcoming a number of hotshot sidemen to bolster his attack.

Johnnie B. Bad, released as part of Elektra Nonesuch's "American Explorer" series, features Keith Richards, Eric Clapton and several members of NRBQ. The album's best song is an ode to spirits called "Tanguray," in which a woozy shuffle and festive backing vocals evoke the intimacy of a barroom sing-along. Though its performances are uniformly excellent, the album as a whole suffers from inconsistent material.

Blue Hand Johnnie, originally released on the Pulsar label in 1988, lacks the big-name support of Johnson's other offerings but has a down-home feel that suits his stabbing keyboard work to a tee. Several tracks feature the unspectacular vocals of Barbara Carr and/or Stacy Johnson, yet the album is redeemed by a laid-back instrumental version of "C.C. Rider" and another supple, rolling instrumental called "O.J. Blues." Also present is Johnson's own "Son's Dream," recorded live at the Missouri River Blues Festival in 1990. *That'll Work* is a 12-track collaboration between Johnson and country-rock and blues twangers the Kentucky Headhunters. Standouts include the surging, saxophone-bolstered "Sunday Blues" and the swinging "Feel," which proclaims, "It don't matter how much you've got/It's what you do with it when the band gets hot"). *Rockin' Eighty-Eights* showcases the talents of Johnson and two other St. Louis–area pianists—Clayton Love and Jimmy Vaughn—who played with such figures as Ike Turner, Little Milton and Albert King. Recorded in 1990, the album includes four tracks by each pianist; a highlight is Johnson's silken, slow rendition of Isaac Hayes's "Bluebird" with Vernon Guy on vocals.

On *Johnnie Be Back* Johnson welcomes a veritable army of prominent artists, including Buddy Guy, Al Kooper, John Sebastian, James Wormworth, Jimmy Vivino (who produced the effort), Max Weinberg, Steve Jordan and Phoebe Snow. The combination of fine material and blistering playing makes this Johnson's finest offering, as he and the band rip through versions of Billy Boy Arnold's "Rockinitis," Leiber and Stoller's "Kansas City" and Little Johnnie Taylor's "If You Love Me Like You Say." Also differentiating it from other Johnson albums is the fine vocal work: Johnson, Snow and (particularly) Vivino add a solid punch to the well-arranged songs, which benefit from tasty, no-nonsense blues playing and stripped-down instrumentation. — B.R.H.

LARRY JOHNSON

★★★★ **Fast and Funky (1971; Baltimore Blues Society, 1997)**
★★★★ **Midnight Hour Blues (1972; Biograph, 1995)**

A student of Rev. Gary Davis, Larry Johnson, born in Georgia in 1938, is the contemporary standard bearer of Piedmont-style country blues. His speedy, clean picking and deep, rich vocals are extremely skillful and altogether genuine. On *Midnight Hour Blues* there isn't a weak cut among the 11, but "Mama-Less Rag" and "Saturday Evening Blues" are particularly wonderful. John Hammond adds attractive embellishments on National steel and harp but is not absolutely necessary here. The Baltimore Blues Society rerelease of Johnson's other '70s classic, *Fast and Funky,* features more of the same extraordinary picking and singing.
— J.Z.

LONNIE JOHNSON

★★★ **Blues by Lonnie Johnson (1960; Original Blues Classics, N.A.)**

★★★★ **Blues and Ballads (with Elmer Snowden) (1960; Original Blues Classics, 1990)**
★★★★ **Idle Hours (with Victoria Spivey) (1961; Original Blues Classics, 1987)**
★★★★ **Losing Game (1961; Original Blues Classics, 1991)**
★★★★ **Another Night to Cry (1963; Original Blues Classics, 1992)**
★★★★ **The Complete Folkways Recordings (1982; Smithsonian Folkways, 1993)**
★★★★★ **Steppin' on the Blues (Columbia, 1990)**
★★★★★ **He's a Jelly Roll Baker (RCA Bluebird, 1992)**
★★★★ **Blues, Ballads and Jumpin' Jazz, Vol. 2 (with Elmer Snowden) (Original Blues Classics, 1993)**

Raised in a musical family of 13 kids in New Orleans, Alonzo "Lonnie" Johnson (1889–1970) was playing guitar and violin in a band with his father and a brother by his late teens, as well as performing solo and accompanying jazz trumpeter Punch Miller at various venues of ill repute in the Crescent City's red-light district. Johnson took off for England in 1917 as part of a musical touring revue hired to entertain American soldiers abroad. Tragedy struck at home when the Spanish-flu epidemic claimed most of his family, including his father, whose passing spelled the end of the Johnson family band. On his return to the States, Johnson journeyed to St. Louis, where he was gainfully employed as a musician with various riverboat bands. By the time he made his first recordings in 1925 (as a member of Charlie Creath's Jazz-O-Maniacs, a St. Louis–based group), he had already gained a measure of local fame by winning first prize in an eight-week blues-singing contest at St. Louis's Booker T. Washington Theatre. From the mid- to late '20s he enhanced his reputation with professional work on recording sessions with Louis Armstrong's Hot Five (1925) and the Duke Ellington Orchestra (1927) and on the strength of some envelope-pushing instrumental duets (two of which are available on *Steppin' on the Blues*) with guitar virtuoso Eddie Lang (who was billed as Blind Willie Dunn). The style Johnson developed—fluid, lyrical single-string runs, unusual chordings, double-note harmonic passages—brought the guitar into the forefront as a solo instrument. His infallible technique, graceful lyricism and harmonic sophistication resonate in the work of some of history's most celebrated jazz and blues guitarists, with Django Reinhardt, Charlie Christian, Robert Johnson, Robert Jr. Lockwood, Albert King and B.B. King being only the most obvious heirs to the Johnson tradition.

Johnson's wanderings took him on the road with Bessie Smith in 1929; the following year to New York City, where he hosted a radio show; to Cleveland for five years beginning in 1932; and finally, in 1937, to Chicago. In 1939 he was signed to Bluebird, and over the next five years he cut 34 sides that established him as one of the era's best-selling blues artists. Twenty of the Bluebird tracks can be heard on *He's a Jelly Roll Baker,* a collection carefully assembled and well annotated by music writer Billy Altman. Although this represents Johnson's first full-blown efforts as a solo recording artist, his style was fully formed and from here on would vary hardly a whit as he moved from label to label in the ensuing years. Despite minimal accompaniment (sometimes only one other musician, at most two, among them Lil Armstrong on piano on seven tracks), Johnson eschews flash and quantity for substance and quality in his guitar support: Bursts of staccato single-string voicings or an elongated, wailing series of notes serve as a sort of Greek chorus to the tales of woe he spins about faithless lovers and dark moods, his instrumental asides so subtle that the guitar's crying voice and Johnson's own weary timbre become almost as one. None of which really prepares the listener for his surges of sustained instrumental brilliance—such as the angry solo fusillade that propels the determined narrative of "Get Yourself Together" and the alternating angular and linear solos that heighten the wild emotions of Johnson's pop-influenced "That's Love."

Still, *He's a Jelly Roll Baker* is most valuable for what it reveals of Johnson's songwriting skill, by far the most overlooked aspect of the man's art and understandably so, given the long shadow he casts as a guitarist. But the prolific Johnson left behind hundreds of original tunes that testify to his urban sophistication as well as his innate feel for country lore. There seemed to be no forum alien to him: He could write and play country blues with breathtaking command, step into a small combo or big band and deliver a well-observed slice of city life in a jazz setting or caress a pop confection—either an original or a cover—with appealing and convincing conviction. (Check out his wonderful take on Irving Berlin's "How Deep Is the Ocean" on *The*

Complete Folkways Recordings and his urbane, vibrato-filled crooning on his own "In Love Again" from *He's a Jelly Roll Baker.*)

Johnson's pre-Bluebird years are documented in part on Columbia's stellar *Steppin' on the Blues,* which captures the artist in some of his peak performances from 1925 through 1932. Two of the above-mentioned Johnson/Lang duets are here ("Have to Change Keys [to Play These Blues]" and "Guitar Blues"), as well as two tracks featuring country-blues artist Texas Alexander and two teaming Johnson in a duet with the formidable Victoria Spivey, joined by Clarence Williams on piano. Apart from these treasures, the album is pure, undiluted Lonnie Johnson blues, with the man accompanying himself on guitar and sometimes with a piano player sitting in.

Post-Bluebird, Johnson had a productive stint with King Records, which produced the 1948 R&B hit "Tomorrow Night." Then, with America and its popular music picking up steam in the post–World War II years, Johnson dropped out of sight. When rediscovered by blues scholar Chris Albertson in the late '50s, he was employed as a janitor at the Ben Franklin Hotel in Philadelphia. Albertson got Johnson back on record with 1960's *Blues by Lonnie Johnson,* an honest effort by an artist undiminished by time or changing musical trends. His reputation restored, Johnson spent the decade recording, playing to enthusiastic audiences at home and, especially, overseas and in the late '60s operating and performing at his own Home of the Blues Club in Toronto, where he had moved in 1965.

The final phase of Johnson's recording career is well documented in all its variety. It's hard to single out any one disc over another, so rich are the treasures contained in each title. *Idle Hours* teams Johnson with Victoria Spivey again, more than three decades after they had made their first duet recordings. Here, in their advanced years, they exhibit the chemistry that sparked their earlier work. Spivey's spunk is the perfect complement to Johnson's burnished, mellow vocals, and some of Johnson's acoustic-guitar solos rank among the tastiest he ever laid down in the studio. Though both were seasoned warriors by the time of this 1961 session, Spivey and Johnson prove that age is no barrier to passion as they spar and flirt their way through two Spivey-composed tunes, "Idle Hours" and "Long Time Blues."

In a brilliant move, Albertson took Johnson into the studio in 1960 with Elmer Snowden, a guitarist of considerable repute whose first group, formed in 1921, included Duke Ellington on piano. Over the next two decades the personnel in Snowden's various groups comprised a virtual Jazz Hall of Fame, their numbers including Count Basie, Fats Waller, Chick Webb, Jimmy Lunceford and others. A sought-after session player, Snowden recorded with many of the great blues and jazz artists of his time, not the least of them being Bessie Smith. Backed with admirable sensitivity by former Ellington bassist Wendell Marshall, Johnson and Snowden delivered showcase performances. While his guitar work is stately, fiery or melancholy as the material demands (always with that edge of personality that made his style so distinctive), Johnson's singing is the big news on *Blues and Ballads.* Whether it's on his own "Haunted House," the album's atmospheric opener, or Bessie Smith's deep-blues lament "Back Water Blues," Johnson works the lyrics like a master stylist, shading his phrasings to add complexity to the emotional content, bending notes to heighten the suggestion of unresolved inner turmoil or swaggering along ahead of the beat, cocky and free of conflict. Compare the hilarious, suggestive reading he gives of his own "Jelly Roll Baker" here, in 1960, to the original, classic track recorded in 1942 and featured on the Bluebird collection.

The companion collection, *Blues, Ballads and Jumpin' Jazz,* features guitar duets on 6 of its 10 tracks, with Snowden dominating the proceedings and Johnson settling into the role of a complementary, often secondary voice. This was the first time since his late-'20s duets with Eddie Lang that Johnson had found himself teamed with a guitarist of comparable harmonic and melodic sense and the technical skill to execute some equally adroit moves on the fret board. The result was a convivial jam session, marked by occasions of instrumental grandeur (Snowden's fancy, staccato picking on the album opener, "Lester Leaps In," a staple of tenor-sax legend Lester Young's repertoire), great good humor (Snowden's sprightly soloing and Johnson's rich comping on the infectious "On the Sunny Side of the Street") and deep feeling (Johnson's powerful vocal on "New Orleans Blues"). It's indicative of this album's many riches that the between-songs patter between Johnson and Snowden is worth the price of admission, regardless of the music it supports.

The Prestige years (rereleased on Original Blues Classics) are rounded out by *Another*

Night to Cry. Accompanying himself on guitar, with no other musicians aboard, Johnson works his way through 11 original ballads and blues, including a beautiful instrumental, "Blues After Hours," a scintillating blend of single-string and angular solo runs, double-note phrases and evocative augmented chords holding the piece together. Although the sessions were four years apart, *Another Night to Cry* seems something of a companion piece to *The Complete Folkways Recordings.* On the latter, Johnson is again featured solo, and its 24 tracks form an overview of the artist's tastes, ranging from low-down, country-style blues (the wrenching "Tears Don't Fall No More") to classic American pop ballads ("What a Difference a Day Makes") to prototypical urban blues of the most tortured and psychologically revealing sort (as in his reprise of "Falling Rain Blues," his first Okeh recording). What Johnson left behind—his guitar work, his singing, his spoken comments captured on tape—bespeaks a man of great heart and rare sensitivity. Any one of his recordings proves the point. — D.M.

LUTHER "GUITAR JUNIOR" JOHNSON

★★★★ **Luther's Blues (1976; Evidence, 1992)**
★★★ **I Want to Groove with You (Bullseye Blues, 1990)**
★★★ **It's Good to Me (Bullseye Blues, 1992)**
★★★ **Country Sugar Papa (Bullseye Blues, 1994)**
★★★½ **Slammin' on the West Side (Telarc, 1996)**

Luther "Guitar Junior" Johnson, born in Mississippi in 1939, moved to Chicago in the mid-'50s and played in bands fronted by Big Mama Thornton and Muddy Waters. Since the '80s, he has led his own band. His first recording as bandleader was actually made in 1976, when he enlisted Waters's then-band–guitarist Bob Margolin, harmonica player Jerry Portnoy, pianist Pinetop Perkins, bassist Calvin Jones and drummer Willie Smith—to back him. Originally released on a French label, the work was issued domestically in 1992. *Luther's Blues* displays Johnson's authoritative skills as a guitarist and as a leader when the combo runs through Jimmy Smith's swinging instrumental "Back at the Chicken Shack" and Robert Johnson's rollicking "Sweet Home Chicago." Also notable are versions of Junior Parker's "Mother-in-Law," Little Walter's "Better Watch Yourself" and Guitar Junior's own "Come Baby."

I Want to Groove with You features seven Johnson originals, as well as covers like Eddie Taylor's "Young Boy Blues" and Waters's "Red Beans." Johnson's sidemen, the Magic Rockers—"Sax" Gordon Beadle on tenor and baritone sax, Joe Krown on keys, Buster Paterson on bass and "Spider" Webb and Glenn Rogers splitting duties on the drums—provide fine backing, but they're not as dynamic as the combo that worked on *Luther's Blues.* Still, Johnson's guitar work and vocals are raw and solid. Beadle and Krown also adorn *It's Good to Me,* another smoldering effort by Johnson and company. The outfit tears the stuffing out of Howlin' Wolf's "I'm Leaving You" and finesses its way through Sonny Boy Williamson's (Rice Miller) "In My Younger Days." The cooking instrumental title track is a Johnson original, as are "Raise Your Window" and "Come On Back to Me."

Country Sugar Papa offers up more of the same competent blues, played by some of the foremost contemporary purveyors of the form. Highlights are seven Johnson originals, as well as Magic Sam's "You Belong to Me." *Slammin' on the West Side* is something of a departure for Johnson, who introduces elements of funk, jump blues and country blues. The disc finds the guitarist backed by an outstanding New Orleans rhythm section—namely, founding Meters bassist George Porter Jr. and Dr. John's sometime drummer Herman Ernest. The unit sounds loose yet tight on the Johnson original "Every Woman Needs to be Loved" and yields some classic N'Awlins funk on the Johnson-penned "It's Good to Me." Other highlights include Junior Parker's "Stranded" and "She's Lookin' Good," a hit for Wilson Pickett in 1967. — B.R.H.

LUTHER "HOUSEROCKER" JOHNSON

★★½ **Houserockin' Daddy (Wild Dog Blues/Ichiban, 1991)**

Luther "Houserocker" Johnson, born in 1939 in Atlanta, is one of three prominent bluesmen named Luther Johnson and a skilled acoustic bottleneck-slide guitarist. His debut, *Takin' a Bite Outta the Blues,* is available only on cassette. His second album, *Houserockin' Daddy,* includes Jimmy Reed's "I'm Mr. Luck," "You Know I Love You, Baby" and "Don't Say That No More." Also on this decent release are faithful interpretations of Howlin' Wolf's

"Rockin' Daddy" and Otis Hicks and J.D. Miller's "Bad Luck Blues." The one original is a slow blues, "A Fool's Advice." The Houserocker is joined on this date by a combo called the Shadows, whose competent playing provides a solid backdrop for his fine guitar work and gritty vocals. — B.R.H.

LUTHER "SNAKE" JOHNSON

★★★½ Lonesome in My Bedroom (Evidence, 1992)

★★★½ On the Road Again (Evidence, 1994)

Not to be confused with either Luther "Guitar Junior" or "Houserocker" Johnson, guitarist Luther "Snake" Johnson (1934–1976) was born in Georgia and moved to Chicago in the early '60s, where he played with Elmore James, Otis Spann and Muddy Waters, among others. The two available titles spotlight his Waters-influenced guitar sound and assertive vocal style, which are certainly proficient, if not wholly original. Recorded in 1975 just three months before his death, *Lonesome in My Bedroom* finds Johnson backed by an outstanding band, including guitarists Hubert Sumlin and Lonnie Brooks, who rip through tunes like the impassioned, minor-key title track and the rollicking "She's My Babe." Also of note is Johnson's spare, electrified solo rendition of "Please Don't Take My Baby Nowhere," a tense, linear original reminiscent of John Lee Hooker.

The stark *On the Road Again* finds Johnson performing solo-electric versions of songs by Eddie Jones ("Things I Used to Do"), B.B. King ("Rock Me Baby") and Jimmy Reed ("You've Got Me Runnin'") as well as four by Willie Dixon, including the sinister "Back Door Man" and the keening "Little Red Rooster," on which Johnny Shines lends some razor-edge slide-guitar salvos. — B.R.H.

ROBERT JOHNSON

★★★★★ King of the Delta Blues Singers (Columbia, 1961)

★★★★★ King of the Delta Blues Singers, Vol. 2 (Columbia, 1970)

★★★★★ The Complete Recordings (Columbia, 1990)

The man who casts a giant shadow over blues history finally got his just due in the 1990s when the two-CD boxed set, *The Complete Recordings,* was certified platinum and rested comfortably on the album chart. If ever American music produced a voice that death could not still, it is Robert Johnson's, who left behind only 41 recordings (12 of them alternate takes), all cut over the course of four days in 1936 and 1937.

Born out of wedlock on May 8, 1911, in Hazlehurst, Mississippi, Johnson (d. 1938) learned the blues by studying and incorporating stylistic elements of the great Delta bluesmen all around his part of the state: Charley Patton, the acknowledged father of the Delta blues and a riveting, relentlessly rhythmic guitarist whose exploration of the instrument's tonal possibilities opened new avenues of expression; Son House, possibly the most gifted of Delta guitarists, whose bottleneck technique enabled him to shape the instrument's sound into another voice, as Johnson would later do to stunning effect; Willie Brown, House's friend and also a superior guitarist, from whom Johnson doubtless learned as well (indeed, Johnson refers to him as "my friend-boy Willie Brown" in "Cross Road Blues"); Lonnie Johnson, whose single-string style Johnson quotes from liberally on "Malted Milk" and "Drunken Hearted Man." The list of influences is lengthy and exhaustive, given the variety of styles Johnson ate up. His singular genius was to take this multitude of approaches, assimilate them and create something so unique in voice that it seemed to have no antecedents at all.

Which is not to suggest that only Johnson's guitar work is remarkable. Breathtaking it is, but it's the instrument's piercing wail in service to the artist's anguished, sometimes tortured tales that elevates the complete package to a rarified plateau. Rarely has an artist opened a vein and bled so profusely, admitting to visions of the hounds of hell giving chase ("Hellhounds on My Trail"), of the torments of the flesh ("Terraplane Blues," "Phonograph Blues"), of the loneliness and pain of the drifter's life. Moreover, Johnson's women herein are real flesh and bone, not metaphors or symbols. Names are named—Beatrice, Willie Mae, Bernice, Thelma, Ida Belle—and promises are made, although Johnson's tone of voice suggests even he disbelieves the truth of what he vows to deliver. His lyrics are rife with a desperation and awareness of the moment capable of transporting the listener into the dark heart of Johnson's inner turmoil, where the hurt and isolation become palpable. The songs have been widely covered and credibly so by Muddy Waters, Elmore James, Big Joe Williams,

Johnny Shines, Cream, the Rolling Stones and others. While splendid in their own right, these cover versions pale when measured against the degree of tension and heightened sense of drama with which Johnson imbues his own readings.

The boxed set includes a handsome book with priceless photographs and a complete sessionography and discography. Keith Richards and Eric Clapton submit short appreciations of Johnson's influence on their own music, and music historian Stephen C. LaVere details specifics of Johnson's recording sessions in convincing fashion. The curious, though, are advised to turn to more compelling (and trustworthy) portraits and appraisals of Johnson's life: See Peter Guralnick's *Searching for Robert Johnson,* Robert Palmer's *Deep Blues* or Samuel Charters's *Robert Johnson.* On the other hand, the cassette versions of the original *King of the Delta Blues Singers* releases contain no liner information whatsoever, for those who wish to be freed of context and history. Scavengers should be on the lookout for the vinyl version of *Vol. 2,* as it contains a sensible essay on Johnson by blues authority Pete Welding.

Finally, consider this: In one momentous session Johnson cut "Cross Road Blues," "Walkin' Blues," "Last Fair Deal Gone Down," "Preachin' Blues" and "If I Had Possession Over Judgment Day." Has any other single recording date ever produced such a quantity of music so beautiful, so tortured, so insular and obsessive in its concerns with sin and certain damnation and so historically resonant? No. Johnson is out there all alone, vividly explicating a world where all options have been closed out, where the last fair deal has gone down irrevocably. Recorded over a half century ago, this music haunts like great poetry and is equally ageless. — D.M.

TOMMY JOHNSON

★★★★½ **Complete Recorded Works in Chronological Order (1928–1929) (Document, 1988)**

★★★★★ **Canned Heat Blues: Masters of the Delta Blues (with Furry Lewis and Ishman Bracey) (RCA Bluebird, 1992)**

Overshadowed by better-known Delta bluesmen like Charley Patton and Robert Johnson (no relation), Tommy Johnson (1896–1956) wrote and recorded a handful of creative and intensely original tunes later revived by such blues-based rockers as Bonnie Raitt and Canned Heat (the latter actually drew its name from Johnson's song of alcohol addiction). All surviving the test of time, his "Big Road Blues," "Cool Drink of Water Blues" and "Maggie Campbell Blues" are emotionally evocative with Johnson's trademark falsetto and at times jaunty with a ragtime feel, belying a more urban influence (he grew up near Jackson, Mississippi).

The Bluebird anthology collects his 1928 Victor recordings (including the aforementioned songs), but Johnson proved a free agent, recording for more than one label, and his 1929 Paramount recordings—including tracks with a pared-down New Orleans jazz band and the sublime "Boogaloosa Woman"—are collected on the Document title as well. If neither anthology proves available, a number of Johnson gems can be found on such Yazoo anthologies as *Legends of the Country Blues* ("Canned Heat") and *Jackson Blues 1928–1938* ("Bye Bye Blues"). — A.K.

PHILLIP JOHNSTON

★★★★½ **Take the Z Train (with the Microscopic Septet) (1983; Koch, 1997)**

★★★★ **Big Trouble (with Big Trouble) (Black Saint, 1993)**

★★★★ **The Unknown (with Big Trouble) (Avant, 1994)**

★★★½ **Flood at the Ant Farm (with Big Trouble) (Black Saint, 1996)**

★★★★½ **Normalology (Eighth Day Music, 1997)**

★★★★ **The Needless Kiss (with Transparent Quartet) (Koch Jazz, 1998)**

As time-defying as his genre juggling can be, saxophonist and composer Phillip Johnston (b. 1955) could rightly be classified as the H.G. Wells of the jazz world. His chosen instrument is most often a tightly knit reed-based outfit, first with the "surrealistic swing" of the Microscopic Septet (co-led by the equally inspired pianist Joel Forrester) and later with his own ensembles, Big Trouble and the drumless Transparent Quartet. His vocabulary is one of surprise and seduction: Jump blues lead into waltzes; Dixieland marches become free-edged blowing; and strangely familiar—yet more often just strange—melodies captivate, recede and reappear.

Throughout the '80s, Johnston's Micros neatly distilled big-band charts, playful humor and reverence for a wide range of musical saints (Bechet to Beefheart) into a seven-man unit that could swing through a dizzying array of arrangements and rhythm shifts with jaw-dropping accuracy. They boasted a sax-only front line (soprano through baritone) with an erstwhile tuba-blowing bass man, and their album titles likewise defined a peculiar jazz view: *Take the Z Train*, *Let's Flip!*, *Off Beat Glory* and *Beauty Based on Science (The Visit)* (only the first has made it to CD; the rest are overdue for reissue).

In the '90s Johnston widened his sonic palette to include electric guitar, brass, synthesizer and a more focused compositional approach—as well as throwing in the artfully chosen cover. With tongue still planted firmly in cheek, Johnston dubbed his main performance unit Big Trouble, recruiting versatile keyboardist/composer Joe Ruddick and reed man/composer Robert DeBellis, keeping Micros bassist David Hofstra and adding stellar players such as trombonist Steve Swell and percussionist Kevin Norton. Big Trouble's self-titled debut pays tribute to heroes Steve Lacy ("Hemline"), Herbie Nichols ("Step Tempest," "12 Bars") and cartoon-music maestro Raymond Scott ("Powerhouse"), while including originals like "Natural Confusion"/"Waltz of the Untouched," a visually evocative, jaunty Johnston journey suggesting pictures and places.

On *Flood at the Ant Farm,* Johnston unties the jazz mooring and steers directly into Third Stream/classical currents. Lacy's "Hemline" makes a second, transformed appearance, and in the generous sampling of new material—highlighted by such compelling Ruddick contributions as "Heaven, Hell or Hoboken" and "Advertisement for a Dream"—the humor seems elevated from feet to head, rife with inside musical jokes, self-referential asides and rhythmic nudges. *Normalology* finds Johnston back in a nameless reeds-and-rhythm format with added electric guitar, dusting off 13 unrecorded chestnuts from the old Micros songbook, including "Lobster Leaps In," "Almost Right," "Life's Other Mystery" and "Got Lucky." *The Needless Kiss,* another Lacy-inspired title, is a quartet recording with Ruddick, Hofstra and vibraphonist Mark Josefsberg.

Given the theatrical and visual quality of his music, it is no surprise that Hollywood has begun to call upon Johnston's talents. He has scored American and European features (Paul Mazursky's *Faithful,* Philip Haas's *The Music of Chance* and Doris Dörrie's *Paradiso, Money*). *The Unknown* (on John Zorn's Avant label) features music composed and recorded for the rediscovered Tod Browning film from the silent era, starring Lon Chaney and 18-year-old Joan Crawford. Though silent-film music could be cliché-ridden and limited to context (and still can be in pretentious revivals), this album stands on its own, tastefully finding the balance between the creepy and the jazzy, the swinging and the silver-screen sentimental. — A.K.

ELVIN JONES

★★★★ **Elvin! (1962; Original Jazz Classics, 1995)**
★★★★ **Illumination! (with Jimmy Garrison) (1963; Impulse!, 1998)**
★★★★ **Dear John C. (1965; Impulse!, 1993)**
★★★ **Heavy Sounds (1968; Impulse!, 1989)**
★★★½ **At This Point in Time (1973; Blue Note, 1998)**
★★★★ **On the Mountain (1975; One Way, 1994)**
★★★★ **Very Rare (1979; Evidence, 1993)**
★★★★ **Love and Peace (Evidence, 1982)**
★★★ **Elvin Jones in Europe (Enja, 1992)**
★★★ **Youngblood (Enja, 1992)**
★★★ **Going Home (Enja, 1993)**
★★★ **Live at the Village Vanguard, Vol. 1 (Landmark, 1993)**
★★★ **When I Was at Aso-Mountain (Enja, 1993)**
★★★ **It Don't Mean a Thing (Enja, 1994)**
★★★ **Live at the Village Vanguard (Enja, 1995)**

One of the most powerfully rhythmic drummers alive, Elvin Jones (b. 1927) is a jazz virtuoso who has influenced the full range of modern percussionists. Jones played with Miles Davis and Sonny Rollins, but his work in the 1960s with John Coltrane earned him a secure place in music history, and his solo career, while not always consistent, features some fine moments. Unfortunately, a shockingly large number of these are out of print, leading to an unrepresentative catalog.

Elvin!, recorded in 1961–62, is a spirited family affair with brothers Thad on cornet and Hank on piano joined by Frank Wess on flute, Frank Foster on tenor sax and Art Davis on bass. Foster and Wess, the fabulous "two Franks" since their stays with Count Basie, made up a great front line for Jones, but this is the only taste of that pairing available in print. Foster and George Coleman later teamed up with Jones in another fine combination, but none of their excellent work is currently available. Look for the wonderful *Coalition* on vinyl.

Hank returns on *Dear John C.,* splitting piano duties with Roland Hanna in a quartet rounded out by alto saxophonist Charlie Mariano and bassist Richard Davis. Foster is on *Heavy Sounds* without Wess, and he turns in fine moments, but the record is marred by some jarring stabs at commercialism lowlighted by Jones on guitar.

On the Mountain, a 1975 fusion session with Jan Hammer on keyboards and Gene Perla on bass, really hits the mark, superbly utilizing the fierce energy and surging cross rhythms of Jones's style in support of one of Hammer's better performances.

The Evidence reissue of *Very Rare* is particularly noteworthy for the bonus track of Jones's reunion with one of his finest recorded moments, Coltrane's "A Love Supreme." *Love and Peace* is the real thing, a joyful reunion with fellow Coltrane quartet mainstay pianist McCoy Tyner, adding Richard Davis on bass and Pharoah Sanders on tenor. Unfortunately the lineup has one player too many when guitarist Jean-Paul Bourelly gets in the way.

Jones hasn't always made the best choices in selecting band members, particularly in recent years as he's tried to work newer players into his Jazz Machine concept. The propulsion is always there, but the destination is often vague. Meanwhile, many fine sides on Blue Note and Impulse! are MIA. — J.S.

ETTA JONES

★★★★	**Don't Go to Strangers (1960; Original Jazz Classics, 1991)**
★★★½	**Something Nice (1961; Original Jazz Classics, 1994)**
★★★	**So Warm (1961; Original Jazz Classics, 1996)**
★★★	**Love Shout (1963; Original Jazz Classics, 1997)**
★★★★	**My Mother's Eyes (1977; 32 Jazz, 1997)**
★★★★	**The Melody Lingers On (High Note, 1997)**
★★★½	**My Buddy: Songs of Buddy Johnson (High Note, 1998)**
★★★★½	**Doin' What She Does Best (32 Jazz, 1998)**

The emotionally intense and versatile singer Etta Jones (b. 1928) has been working for 50 years with sporadic success but a survivor's will. Her early records reflect a catalog of influences, but her trump card was the effective Billie Holiday–influenced angst in her delivery. The title song of *Don't Go to Strangers* was her definitive recording for many years. Subsequent albums unsuccessfully attempted to position her in the pop market, and she disappeared until making a strong comeback on the Muse label (now reissued on 32 Jazz) in the 1970s with a more distinctive approach to interpretation and the ever-soulful support from her husband Houston Person on saxophone. *My Mother's Eyes* is an important 32 Jazz reissue; *Doin' What She Does Best* collects her best material from the Muse releases. *The Melody Lingers On* is an excellent quartet session featuring Person and a fine performance from violinist Tom Aaff. Jones continued her resurgence in the late 1990s as a featured performer at various New York nightclubs. — J.S.

HANK JONES

★★★	**Quartet/Quintet (Savoy, 1955)**
★★★★	**The Jazz Trio (Savoy, 1955)**
★★★	**Rockin' in Rhythm (Concord Jazz, 1977)**
★★½	**Just for Fun (1977; Original Jazz Classics, 1990)**
★★★★★	**Tiptoe Tapdance (1978; Original Jazz Classics, 1992)**
★★½	**Moods Unlimited (with Bill Evans and Red Mitchell) (1982; Evidence, 1993)**
★★★★	**Lazy Afternoon (Concord Jazz, 1989)**
★★★★★	**The Oracle (EmArcy, 1989)**
★★★½	**Hank Jones Trio with Mads Vinding and Al Foster (Storyville, 1991)**
★★★★½	**Maybeck Recital Hall Series, Vol. 16 (Concord Jazz, 1992)**
★★★½	**Flowers for Lady Day (with the Great Jazz Trio) (1992; Evidence, 1996)**
★★★★	**Handful of Keys (Verve, 1992)**
★★★★★	**Upon Reflection: The Music of Thad Jones (Verve, 1993)**
★★★★	**Sarala (with Cheick-Tidiane Seck) (Verve, 1995)**
★★★½	**Hank Jones with the Meridian String Quartet (LaserLight, 1997)**

The venerable and versatile pianist Hank Jones (b. 1918) has made scores of recordings as a sideman with some of the biggest names in jazz history and has been acknowledged as one of the greatest accompanying pianists for vocalists ever since taking over that role with Ella Fitzgerald from the late 1940s through 1953. Jones has also recorded a number of albums as a leader, only a few of which are currently available—fortunately, his best work is in print.

Born in Mississippi, Jones was raised in Detroit along with younger brothers Thad and Elvin, who also went on to jazz stardom. He moved to New York in 1944, at a crucial time in jazz history—when the swing era was still driving American popular music but bop was consuming the imaginations of the brightest young players working in jazz. Jones was comfortable in both realms, making him a sought-after player who could back up the hard swing of Hot Lips Page and work hand in glove with Charlie Parker.

Jones's earliest work as a leader is on Savoy, where he was part of the house band along with drummer Kenny Clarke. Clarke is on *Quartet/ Quintet,* which shows Jones working in his preferred format of piano, drums and bass (Eddie Jones), with trumpeters Donald Byrd and Matty Dice sitting in. In fact, Jones's own lead voicings sound better on *The Jazz Trio,* with Clarke and bassist Wendell Marshall and featuring a beautiful version of "My Funny Valentine." Jones also recorded a fine solo outing for Savoy that is currently unavailable.

Through the 1960s into the mid-'70s, Jones worked as a house musician at CBS Records while freelancing as a sideman. One of his most important side gigs during this period was as the pianist for the big band his brother Thad co-led with Mel Lewis. The couple of albums he recorded as a leader during this period are no longer in print.

The Jones catalog resurfaces with the 1977 trio outing *Rockin' in Rhythm,* which features Ray Brown on bass and Jimmie Smith on drums. Unfortunately the outstanding 1976 *Solo Piano* on the All Art label is currently unavailable. *Just for Fun* also has Brown on bass with drummer Shelly Manne and guitarist Howard Roberts. *Tiptoe Tapdance,* a solo album made up mostly of spirituals, shows Jones at his most contemplative. Jones also made his Broadway debut in the late 1970s, playing piano in *Ain't Misbehavin',* a musical based on the songs of Fats Waller.

In the 1980s *Moods Unlimited* unsuccessfully teamed him up with Bill Evans, a soloing star in Miles Davis's band, on soprano and tenor saxophone and Red Mitchell on bass. Jones and Mitchell were far better by themselves on the out-of-print *Duo,* from 1987. *Lazy Afternoon* is an inspired session with bassist Dave Holland, drummer Keith Copeland and Ken Peplowski on alto saxophone and clarinet.

Jones seemed to pick up steam in his 70s, beginning with the exquisite 1989 session with Holland on bass and Billy Higgins on drums, *The Oracle.* The deft handling of standards and Monk on the solo *Maybeck Recital Hall Series* is Jones at his best; similarly, *Handful of Keys* is an inspired retrospective covering one of Jones's deepest influences, Fats Waller. *Hank Jones Trio with Mads Vinding and Al Foster* is part of the high-quality Jazzpar series, which fosters interactions between American and Danish musicians. Bassist Vinding interacts superbly with Jones and drummer Foster.

Upon Reflection, recorded with brother Elvin on drums and George Mraz on bass, is a sublime tribute to the brilliance of Thad Jones as a writer and arranger. *Sarala* is a fascinating project and a complete departure for Jones, who collaborates with Malian Cheick-Tidiane Seck and the Mandinkas in a stunning whirlwind of piano, organ, percussion, vocals, stringed instruments and flutes. It's jazz as world music without exoticism, as Jones's lucid, conversational tones find natural grooves inside the undulating polyrhythms woven by the African musicians.

Jones also leads the Great Jazz Trio, in which he recruits various rhythm sections for a series of up-and-down outings. The best of these recordings is the Billie Holiday tribute, *Flowers for Lady Day,* with Mraz on bass and Roy Haynes on drums.

Jones can also be heard on albums by Ella Fitzgerald, Big Maybelle, Coleman Hawkins, Carrie Smith, Ernestine Anderson, Nancy Wilson, Curtis Lundy, Milt Jackson, Miles Davis, Billie Holiday, Lester Young, Abbey Lincoln, Gerry Mulligan, Betty Carter, Shirley Horn, Louie Bellson, Zoot Sims, Jesse Davis, Kenny Clarke, Mark Elf, Hank Mobley, Grover Washington Jr., Lionel Hampton, Stan Getz, J.J. Johnson, Buck Clayton, Johnny Hartman, Ben Webster, Chet Baker, Rahsaan Roland Kirk, Benny Goodman and Emily Remler, among others. — J.S.

JO JONES

★★★★ **The Essential Jo Jones (1977; Vanguard, 1995)**

★★★★ **The Main Man (1977; Original Jazz Classics, 1995)**

Jonathan "Jo" Jones (1911–1985) anchored the Count Basie band during some of its most influential years, from 1936 to 1948, playing a light, rhythmically loose but sturdy beat characterized by his unique cymbal and brush work. Considered one of the greatest drummers in jazz history, Jones went on to back the biggest stars in the field, from Ella Fitzgerald to fellow Basie-ite Lester Young, Illinois Jacquet and the Jazz at the Philharmonic jam sessions.

Jones was so in demand as an accompanist that he had little time or inclination to work as a leader, but when he did, the results were excellent. He was the heartbeat of the Basie band and arguably the most influential drummer in the history of jazz. *The Essential Jo Jones* collects tracks from his two Vanguard albums, playing with a number of players from his Basie days including the Count himself. *The Main Man* is more of the same, with guest appearances by Freddie Green, Harry Edison, Eddie "Lockjaw" Davis and Vic Dickenson. — J.S.

LEROY JONES

★★★★ Mo' Cream from the Crop (NOPTEE/Columbia, 1995)

Prodigiously talented New Orleans trumpeter Leroy Jones (b. 1958) came out of a Crescent City musical family and by age 13 was a member of Danny Barker's Fairview Baptist Church Christian Marching Band. His precocious talents soon made him lead trumpet in that group and led him to such honors as playing "Little Louis Armstrong" at Super Bowl VI. Jones went on to form the Hurricane Brass Band and the more contemporary quintet New Orleans' Finest while studying early New Orleans music as a member of the Louisiana Repertory Jazz Ensemble. Jones has also toured with Eddie "Cleanhead" Vinson and was a featured soloist in Harry Connick Jr.'s big band.

Mo' Cream from the Crop showcases the breadth of Jones's experience as well as his formidable chops. Whether he's playing Duke Ellington's "Mood Indigo," a classic New Orleans set piece or an original, his sound is steeped in the trumpet tradition first established (at least on record) by Armstrong. Trombonist Lucien Barbarin, the grand-nephew of New Orleans drummer Paul Barbarin, serves as an inspired accompanist. — J.S.

PAUL "WINE" JONES

★★½ Mule (Fat Possum, 1995)

With a style honed in Mississippi roadhouses, Paul "Wine" Jones (b. 1946) sounds as if he grew up in a vacuum—his writing, singing and playing owe almost nothing to modernity. *Mule* could just as easily have been recorded in 1955 as 1995.

Most impressive is Jones's guitar playing, characterized by a stringy, tart moaning sound and his ability to slide from quick Chicago-style runs to thick modal chords. On *Mule* his songwriting is less distinctive, with "Diggin' Momma's Taters," a rewrite of Magic Sam's "Digging My Potatoes"; the syncopated rhythms of "My Baby Got Drunk," owing Howlin' Wolf; "Mad Dog on My Trail," an electrified Robert Johnson; and the staggered riffs of "Coal Black Mare," recalling John Lee Hooker. Backed by a superb band (especially redoubtable drummer Sam Carr), Jones is at his best as a live performer. While there is no denying his talents on *Mule,* the album makes clear Jones has yet to develop a voice of his own. — S.M.

PHILLY JOE JONES

★★★ Blues for Dracula (1958; Original Jazz Classics, 1991)
★★★★ Showcase (1960; Original Jazz Classics, 1990)
★★★★ Drums Around the World: Big Band Sounds (1961; Original Jazz Classics, 1991)
★★★ Mo' Joe (1968; Black Lion, 1991)

Philly Joe Jones (1923–1985) was the quintessential hard-bop drummer. His principal fame grew out of his membership in the classic Miles Davis groups of 1955–58, and he was also a constantly in-demand session player who can be found on scores of important recordings from the '50s and '60s.

Jones was a brilliant drummer and a highly skilled musician whose talents as a composer, arranger and occasional pianist are best revealed on *Showcase. Drums Around the World* features an expanded band including Cannonball Adderley, Benny Golson and Curtis Fuller; *Blues for Dracula* is a sassy small-group date that highlights Jones's celebrated Bela Lugosi imitation; and *Mo' Joe* finds Jones leading a British group with Kenny Wheeler and Harold McNair. In the early '80s, Jones organized Dameronia, a nonet dedicated to preserving the music of bop-era arranger/composer Tadd Dameron. Let's hope Dameronia's near-perfect tribute, *Look Stop and Listen,* with guest Johnny Griffin, will reemerge soon. — S.F.

QUINCY JONES

★★★½ **Quintessence (1961; Impulse!, 1986)**
★★★½ **Body Heat (A&M, 1974)**
★★ **The Dude (A&M, 1981)**
★★★½ **Compact Jazz (Verve, 1987)**
★★★★ **Back on the Block (Qwest, 1990)**
★★★½ **This Is How I Feel About Jazz (Impulse!, 1992)**
★★★★ **Miles and Quincy Live at Montreux (Qwest, 1993)**
★★★ **Q's Jook Joint (Qwest, 1995)**
★★★½ **Q Live in Paris Circa 1960 (Qwest, 1996)**

Composer, arranger and trumpeter Quincy Jones (b. 1933) grew up in Seattle, befriended Ray Charles, played trumpet in Lionel Hampton's early '50s group (alongside such greats as Clifford Brown and Art Farmer), but soon grew more interested in writing and arranging. He worked in A&R at Mercury for seven years, producing Sarah Vaughan and Dinah Washington as well as pop acts like Lesley Gore. His arrangements at Mercury, for his own big bands and for Dizzy Gillespie and Count Basie, concentrated on updating big-band swing rather than exploring dissonant tonalities and the experimental ideas that fascinated many of his contemporaries in the '50s and '60s. *Quintessence* and *Compact Jazz* collect his jazz sessions from this era.

Jones demonstrated a gift for courting mass acceptance while maintaining a high level of musicality in his approach. This led to more prestigious, if musically uneventful, freelance work with the likes of Sammy Davis Jr., Frank Sinatra and Andy Williams. It also led to such film scores as *The Pawnbroker*, *Mirage*, *Cactus Flower*, *The Getaway*, *In the Heat of the Night*, *The New Centurions* and the Oscar-nominated *In Cold Blood,* as well as various television themes (*Sanford and Son*, *Ironside*, *Roots*).

Jones's '70s and '80s work was as glib and successful as his film/TV approach. He moved effortlessly from MOR orchestrations to disco/funk in 1974 with the hit album *Body Heat,* featuring the Brothers Johnson as the rhythm section. Jones went on to produce the Brothers Johnson's own highly commercial records, as well as subsequent chart-toppers by Roberta Flack, Donna Summer and Michael Jackson (including *Thriller*). He also produced the star-studded U.S.A.-for-Africa project, "We Are the World." Unfortunately, two of his best A&M albums, *Smackwater Jack* and *Walking in Space,* are unavailable. One of Jones's lesser-known projects deserves special mention. *Black Requiem,* a 1971 orchestral piece put together with Ray Charles, traces the history of the African-American experience in the United States in a large-scale performance including Charles, an 80-voice choir and the Houston Symphony Orchestra.

Jones went on to start his own label, Qwest, producing albums for Lena Horne (*The Lady and Her Music*) and Sinatra (*L.A. Is My Lady*). His solo projects became more adventurous in the 1990s, incorporating rapper Big Daddy Kane and hip-hop beats into the production of *Back on the Block* and ranging across the breadth of R&B's stylistic range on *Q's Jook Joint.* Jones also assembled a final tribute to the career of Miles Davis on *Miles and Quincy Live at Montreux,* a touching send-off to the already-enfeebled Davis. — J.S.

THAD JONES

★★★★ **The Magnificent Thad Jones (1956; Blue Note, 1987)**
★★★★ **After Hours (with Kenny Burrell and Frank Wess) (1957; Original Jazz Classics, 1992)**
★★★★★ **The Fabulous Thad Jones (1958; Original Jazz Classics, 1991)**
★★★★ **Mean What You Say (with the Pepper Adams Quintet) (1966; Original Jazz Classics, 1991)**
★★★½ **Live at Montmartre, Copenhagen (Storyville, 1978)**
★★★ **Three and One (SteepleChase, 1984)**
★★★ **Greetings and Salutations (with Mel Lewis and Jon Faddis) (Passport, 1995)**

Trumpet/flügelhornist Thad Jones (1923–1986) was part of the Charles Mingus–led musicians' collective that produced the Debut series of recordings, a member of one of the most popular versions of the Count Basie Orchestra and co-leader of the durable Thad Jones/Mel Lewis orchestra, which established at New York's Village Vanguard a long-running Monday night residency that is still going as the Vanguard Jazz Orchestra.

The Fabulous Thad Jones introduces Jones as a leader on a Debut title with him leading one group featuring Mingus and drummer Max Roach, and another with Mingus, pianist Hank Jones, drummer Kenny Clarke and Frank Wess on tenor saxophone and flute. *The Magnificent*

Thad Jones collects small-group recordings, a duet with guitarist Kenny Burrell and a version of "April in Paris," a Number One hit in 1955 for the Basie Orchestra. *After Hours* is a 1957 recording with Wess, Burrell, pianist Mal Waldron, bassist Paul Chambers and drummer Art Taylor. *Mean What You Say* is a 1966 release with baritone saxophonist Pepper Adams's group, which included Mel Lewis on drums. Jones plays flügelhorn on this session, which also features pianist Duke Pearson and bassist Ron Carter.

Jones spent the last years of his life in Europe, where he recorded *Greetings and Salutations* with the Swedish Radio Jazz Group, *Live at Montmartre, Copenhagen* with the Danish Radio Big Band and the quartet session *Three and One.* — J.S.

JANIS JOPLIN

★★★★ **I Got Dem Ol' Kozmic Blues Again Mama! (Columbia, 1969)**
★★★★ **Pearl (1971; Columbia, 1995)**
★★★ **Joplin in Concert (Columbia, 1972)**
★★★ **Janis Joplin's Greatest Hits (1973; Columbia, 1995)**
★★★★ **Janis (1974; Columbia/Legacy, 1993)**
★★ **Farewell Song (Columbia, 1982)**
★★★ **Pearl/Cheap Thrills (Columbia, 1986)**
★★★★★ **18 Essential Songs (Columbia/Legacy, 1995)**
★★★½ **Live at Winterland (with Big Brother and the Holding Company) (Columbia/Legacy, 1998)**

Her voice made Janis Joplin (1943–1970) the greatest white female blues singer; her legendary hard living (she died at age 27 of a heroin overdose) confirmed her status as a mythic figure: part old-school blues desperado, part self-incendiary rocker.

Her voice, however, was a natural wonder: raw, amazingly powerful and capable of conveying astonishing hurt. She exploded first at the 1967 Monterey Pop Festival—jettisoning conventional notions of both sex appeal and orthodox popular singing, the Texas vagabond shrieked and wailed over fevered but formless blues riffing by Big Brother and the Holding Company, whom she'd soon outgrow.

With its horns and tight soulsters, *I Got Dem Ol' Kozmic Blues Again Mama!* provides an intriguing context: Her unleashed delivery shocks even more effectively when backed by crack players (from Big Brother she'd brought along only guitarist Sam Andrew). Adding quivering heart to the sturdy pop skeleton of the Bee Gees' "To Love Somebody" and thunder to Jerry Ragovoy's "Try," she was now balancing a Big Mama Thornton fervor with an Aretha Franklin sense of timing.

Released posthumously, *Pearl,* the album that bears her nickname, finds her moving easily into that other highly emotional roots genre, country music—her take on Kris Kristofferson's "Me and Bobby McGee" remains definitive—but she still musters true blues anguish on Ragovoy's "Cry, Baby." The 1968 album Joplin recorded with Big Brother, *Cheap Thrills,* was reissued with her most successful solo album, *Pearl,* on one CD in 1986. Both *Janis* and *18 Essential Songs* provide excellent overviews. Joplin survives not only as a singer but as a sympathetic, if harrowing, archetype. Too rushed to develop the casual confidence of Billie Holiday or Bessie Smith, she remains a signature singer of the hell-bent blues. — P.E.

CLIFFORD JORDAN

★★★★ **Blowing in from Chicago (1957; Blue Note, 1994)**
★★★★ **Bearcat (1962; Original Jazz Classics, 1990)**
★★★ **Highest Mountain (1975; Muse, 1994)**
★★★★★ **Down Through the Years (Milestone, 1992)**
★★★★ **Live at Ethel's (Mapleshape, 1993)**
★★★½ **Masters from Different Worlds (with Ran Blake) (Mapleshade, 1994)**
★★★★ **Clifford Jordan and the Magic Triangle: On Stage, Vol. 1 (SteepleChase, 1995)**
★★★★ **Clifford Jordan and the Magic Triangle: On Stage, Vol. 2 (SteepleChase, 1995)**
★★★★ **Spellbound (N.A.; Original Jazz Classics, 1992)**

Tenor and alto saxophonist and flautist Clifford Jordan (1931–1993) grew up in Chicago playing with schoolmates Johnny Griffin, Richard Davis and John Gilmore before gigging locally with bands led by Max Roach and Sonny Stitt. Jordan arrived in New York in the mid-'50s as part of Horace Silver's band and became part of that city's thriving jazz scene. *Blowing in from Chicago,* with Gilmore, Silver and drummer Art Blakey, dates from this period.

In the '60s Jordan played as a sideman with J.J. Johnson, Roach and Charles Mingus, among others. He also led some fine dates, which are only sporadically available. *Bearcat* and *Spellbound* document the beginnings of a long association with pianist Cedar Walton, who was a most sympathetic partner for Jordan. Unfortunately, *Starting Time,* with Kenny Dorham on trumpet, is currently out of print.

Though Jordan recorded prolifically, his catalog is in shambles. All that remains from the beginning of the 1970s to the '90s is a single title from his extensive Muse output, *Highest Mountain,* and the import-only two-volume *On Stage,* with Walton, bassist Sam Jones and drummer Billy Higgins.

In his last years Jordan led an outstanding big band, which played weekly engagements in New York when not on the road at festivals. Fortunately, this fruitful coda to a rich musical life was recorded and remains available on *Down Through the Years.* — J.S.

DUKE JORDAN

★★★ **Do It Yourself Jazz, Vols. 1 & 2 (Savoy, 1993)**

★★★ **Trio & Quintet (Savoy, 1993)**

Pianist Duke Jordan (b. 1922) is probably best known for his subtle and supportive work with Charlie Parker in the mid-'40s. Jordan relocated to Denmark in the '70s after making some fine recordings, including the currently out-of-print *Jor-du* (whose title track is his most enduring composition); *Do It Yourself Jazz*; *Trio & Quintet,* featuring drummer Art Blakey; and the unavailable all-star *Flight to Jordan,* with its admired title track. — S.F.

LOUIS JORDAN

★★★★ **One Guy Named Louis: The Complete Aladdin Sessions (1954; Capitol Jazz, 1992)**

★★★★★ **The Best of Louis Jordan (1975; MCA, 1989)**

★★ **I Believe in Music (1980; Evidence, 1992)**

★★★½ **No Moe! Louis Jordan's Greatest Hits (Verve, 1992)**

★★★★★ **Five Guys Named Moe: The Decca Recordings (MCA, 1992)**

★★★★★ **Just Say Moe! Mo' of the Best of Louis Jordan (Rhino, 1992)**

★★★★ **Rock 'n Roll Call: Louis Jordan and His Tympany Five (RCA Bluebird, 1993)**

Born in Brinkley, Arkansas, jump-blues pioneer Louis Jordan (1908–1975) got his start in show business playing with minstrel groups and wound up playing alto saxophone in 1936 in Chick Webb's band, whose vocalist, Ella Fitzgerald, took over the band when Webb died in 1939. Jordan went out on his own, founding the group that evolved into the beloved Tympany Five (although its membership regularly swelled to a few pieces beyond the basic quintet)—its belovedness being indicated by the public's insatiable hunger for Jordan's good-time, big-beat waxings for Decca between 1942 and 1951, when more than 50 of his singles became Top 10 R&B hits, with 18 going to Number One. He was also one of the few black artists of that period to make a significant dent in the pop market: In the five years between 1944 and 1949 he had 19 Top 30 pop hits, 9 of these rising into the Top 10; 1944's "G.I. Jive" topped the pop chart for two weeks in May, and its flip side, "Is You Is or Is You Ain't (Ma' Baby)," topped out at #2 for three weeks in July. Among other black musical artists, only Nat King Cole, then with his trio, rivaled Jordan's popularity as a crossover artist. You snuggled to Cole; you kicked out the jams to Jordan. Between the two of them, they covered all the bases: Cole's music was dignified, refined and tenderhearted, even when it swung, and Cole could croon a love ballad with any of the gifted interpreters of his generation; Jordan, whose music was every bit as sophisticated as Cole's, simply let the good times roll, limning in his witty lyrics the comedic situations common to the human experience, engaging in punning wordplay that bounced hipsters' jargon off the King's English, and keeping the rhythm high-spirited, hot and pulsating, buttressing it all with call-and-response parts, hand clapping and sundry verbal exhortations of pure pleasure. In his arrangements were elements of blues, jazz, gospel, classic pop, even Latin harmonic ideas. By the early '50s, when his Olympian chart run ended, his music had at once laid the foundation for R&B and defined the spirit of early rock & roll.

The first and exceedingly brilliant period of Jordan's career is surveyed on two MCA albums, *The Best of Louis Jordan* and *Five Guys Named Moe: The Decca Recordings.* In addition to the classic Jordan entries ("G.I. Jive," "Is You

Is or Is You Ain't [Ma' Baby]"), many of the lower-profile tunes here are scintillating. For an idea of Jordan's stylistic versatility, check out the nodding vocal and the sassy spoken dialog on "What's the Use of Getting Sober (When You Gonna Get Drunk Again)" and the smooth blues crooning on "Don't Let the Sun Catch You Crying" (not the Gerry and the Pacemakers song). A later track, "I Want You to Be My Baby," written by Jon Hendricks, requires more complex, jazz-rooted phrasing, and Jordan pulls it off with considerable aplomb and winning humor. At the same time, he could get deep inside himself for a straight blues rendering of Jimmie Cox's chestnut "Nobody Knows You When You're Down and Out."

Jordan left Decca in 1954 for a year's stay at Aladdin but produced no hits, despite the consistent high quality of the 21 sides he recorded between January and April. The proof's in the pudding of *One Guy Named Louis: The Complete Aladdin Sessions.* Jordan's quirky individuality is in abundant evidence here: Although today's audience might suggest he needs some consciousness-raising, his feisty upbraiding of his unidentified female partner in "Gal, You Need a Whippin'" is played strictly for laughs, with the woman giving as good as she gets. "It's Hard to Be Good Without You" showcases the sensitive, silky-smooth crooner that Jordan could be when the occasion demanded, as it does here when the band gives him quiet, lilting background support in establishing a warm pop-blues ambiance. The album's rollicking opener, "Whiskey Do Your Stuff," is notable both for Jordan's mock-pleading vocal and for its composer being Shifte Henri, who is perhaps best known for being referenced in Leiber and Stoller's "Jailhouse Rock" ("Shifte Henri said, 'For Heaven's sake . . .' "). "Dreamy" is hardly a term used much in discussing Jordan's work, but it's the appropriate adjective to describe one of his most affecting performances, on the lovely song of devotion "Till We Two Are One." All in all, *One Guy Named Louis* shows the master's touch undiminished at the dawn of the rock & roll era even as it was falling out of commercial favor with the advent of harder-edged musical approaches by artists both black and white.

Jordan's odyssey next took him to RCA in 1955 and '56, where he recorded for the label's subsidiary X and Vik labels, now represented by 12 tracks on *Rock 'n Roll Call.* "Bananas," from 1955, is an interesting foray into Latin rhythmic flourishes within the pop format, albeit a bit softer in execution than the same style as pioneered by Desi Arnaz in the mid-'40s. Effective as he was, though, even the master showman Arnaz couldn't match Jordan for sheer ability to sell a song; if nothing else, these midperiod Jordan sides demonstrate his growing artistry as a vocalist whose appeal rested more on the degree to which he brought a character to life in song—in a sense, assuming the lead role of an actor in a play—and less on technical vocal brilliance. Attitude and energy were the tickets, and Jordan had both in ample quantities. Yet, as he demonstrated on "Till We Two Are One," he could employ his rather limited but personable vocal instrument to potent effect on softer, introspective material, as he does here on the melancholy "Where Can I Go."

Over the next few years, Jordan jumped from label to label—Mercury, Tangerine (he was signed by Ray Charles), Warwick, Blues Spectrum, Pzazz—without success. *I Believe in Music* documents the artist's last recordings, made in the early '70s with a small combo comprising the stellar tenor-sax man Irv Cox, pianist Duke Burrell, bassist John Duke and drummer Archie Taylor. Interestingly, four undated tracks find him teaming with brothers Louis and Dave Meyers (guitar and bass, respectively) and the legendary Chicago blues drummer Fred Below. In the early '50s this trio billed itself as the Aces, and at one time it employed Junior Wells as its harmonica player, before Wells left to join Muddy Waters's band and the Aces went on the road backing Little Walter Jacobs. With the Aces, Jordan takes off on a wondrous, soaring alto-sax solo to juice up the two-part instrumental "Groovin' in Paris"; on "Something for Fred" the quartet gets into a jump-blues rave-up, all instrumental, and closes out with a surging, minor-key blues, "Something for Louis," which allows Jordan room for a rough-hewn, moody sax solo, offering it up as a testifying lead voice, before Louis Meyers works the length of the neck and back on a pointed, protesting guitar solo. With the quintet on the first 11 tracks, Jordan sounds somewhat weary, and his humor is a bit strained. Updated versions of "Caldonia," "Saturday Night Fish Fry," "Is You Is or Is You Ain't (Ma' Baby)" and "I'm Gonna Move to the Outskirts of Town" are pleasant, inconsequential, workmanlike efforts on an album marred only by Jordan's valiant but failed attempt to make a personal statement of Mac Davis's "I Believe in Music," a song so vapid it begs to be consigned to history's dustbin. It shows up again, in a live version from late '73, on Rhino's otherwise excellent overview *Just Say Moe!,* a 20-track highlight reel beginning with a circa-1943 V-Disc issue of "Five Guys Named Moe," with stops along the way at Decca, Aladdin, X, Mercury (five cuts), the European Black Lion label ("A Man Ain't a Man," recorded in 1962 with British jazz star Chris Barber and his band), Tangerine, Pzazz and, yes, that Mac Davis cover, which is notable only for being one of the last recordings made of Jordan before his death from a heart attack. In recent years a hit Broadway revue of his songs, *Five Guys Named Moe,* and his induction into the Rock and Roll Hall of Fame brought Jordan's music the acclaim it warranted for breaking new ground in American popular music. — D.M.

VIC JURIS

★★★ **For the Music (Jazzpoint, 1991)**
★★★ **Night Tripper (SteepleChase, 1994)**
★★★ **Pastels (SteepleChase, 1996)**

New Jersey guitarist Vic Juris (b. 1953) played on records by Barry Miles and Eric Kloss before making his 1978 debut album, the out-of-print *Roadsong.* His loping, bluesy style is sometimes similar to that of his infuences, Wes Montgomery and Larry Coryell, but his playing has its own character. The only in-print albums available are the quartet sessions *Night Tripper* and *Pastels* and the Jazzpoint release *For the Music,* but Juris made a number of engaging sides for Muse—check out *Bleecker Street, Horizon Drive* and the aforementioned debut. — J.S.

CANDYE KANE

★★★ **Home Cookin' (Antone's, 1994)**
★★½ **Knockout (Discovery/Antone's, 1995)**
★★★½ **Diva La Grande (Discovery/Antone's, 1997)**

Equal parts Etta James, Patsy Cline and performance artist Annie Sprinkle, Candye Kane (b. 1965) is a unique blues stylist. As a musician, feminist, sexual libertine, actress and devoted wife and mother, this big mama wears her colorful past proudly. From stripper and welfare mom in East L.A., Kane has evolved into an uninhibited performer whose style blends Southern California, southern Texas and Southern Comfort.

The voluptuous Ms. Kane's appeal lies not so much in her voice or her musical craft (those are more than passable but not strong enough to set her above the numerous blues divas headlining Texas honky-tonks) but in her ballsy, in-your-face persona. Here's a woman unafraid to sing about sexism, homophobia and censorship, and her campy delivery saves her from sounding remotely didactic. Therefore, Kane is at her best when at her bawdiest. *Home Cookin',* produced by her husband, Tom Yearsley, and his Paladins band mate Dave Gonzales, hints at the raucous fun to come. Manifestoes like "Catch an Honest Man" and "Seven Men a Week" stand out amid more timid fare, like the cloying Andrews Sisters–inspired "Babylon Boogie." *Knockout* takes a bit of a step backward, into sweeter territory. Her covers of Bob Dylan's "Watching the River Flow" and Rickie Lee Jones's "Easy Money" are nice enough but rather tame. The rambunctious *Diva La Grande* features more originals and the welcome return of her chutzpah, in the form of raunchy ditties such as "Gifted in the Ways of Love," "All You Can Eat (and You Can Eat It All Night Long)" and "I'm in Love with a Girl." — A.A.

KEB' MO'

★★★½ **Keb' Mo' (Okeh/Epic, 1994)**
★★½ **Just Like You (Okeh/Epic, 1996)**

With equal nods to Taj Mahal and Robert Johnson, Keb' Mo' (b. Kevin Moore, 1951) is one of a new breed of artists whose work is inspired by that of legendary bluesmen. His debut includes two Robert Johnson songs ("Kindhearted Woman Blues" and "Come On in My Kitchen") as well as an original ("Angelina") that sounds as if it could have been recorded by the Rising Sons, Mahal's mid-'60s group. Five tracks feature nothing more than Keb' Mo' 's straightforward vocals and acoustic guitar; the rest of the album introduces his slick, tasteful band, comprised of James "Hutch" Hutchinson (Bonnie Raitt's regular bassist), keyboardist Tommy Eyre and drummer Laval Belle. *Keb' Mo'* won a W.C. Handy Blues Award for country/acoustic blues album.

Just Like You finds Keb' Mo' making a self-conscious attempt at appealing to the same audience that catapulted Raitt to stardom. Accordingly, the album's songs, while well played, lack the emotional punch and urgency that characterized his debut. Raitt and Jackson Browne make vocal appearances on the title track, which—like a number of other nonsolo tunes on the album ("Dangerous Mood," "I'm on Your Side," "The Action")—seem watered-down and tame. A Keb' Mo' original spiritual, "Hand It Over," however, and his "Momma, Where's My Daddy" have an authenticity that shows Keb' Mo' may be capable of carrying

Johnson's shadowy Delta vision into the new millennium instead of taking the high road to pop stardom. — B.R.H.

GEOFF KEEZER

★★★ **Waiting in the Wings (Sunnyside, 1989)**
★★½ **Curveball (Sunnyside, 1990)**
★★★½ **Here and Now (Blue Note, 1991)**
★★★★ **World Music (DIW/Columbia, 1992)**

Pianist Geoff Keezer (b. 1970) made his recording debut and signed on with drummer Art Blakey's last edition of the Jazz Messengers a few months shy of his 18th birthday. The son of piano teachers from Eau Claire, Wisconsin, Keezer fell under the strong guidance of producer/pianist James Williams and has worked regularly as a sideman to Art Farmer whenever the horn master visits the United States.

Keezer has emerged as a contemplative player and writer of great skill who enhances every musical setting in which he works. The piano-and-vibes up-front pairing on Keezer's early Sunnyside recordings make the second work, *Curveball,* overly familiar. Vibist Steve Nelson is less obtrusive on *Here and Now,* which is a stronger work throughout.

World Music, a trio collaboration with bassist James Genus and drummer Tony Reedus (with percussionist Rudy Bird sitting in on two tracks), swings as hard as its predecessors and is stronger for the musical risks taken. — K.F.

ED KELLY

★★★★ **Ed Kelly and Pharoah Sanders (1979; Evidence, 1993)**

Pianist Ed Kelly, born in Texas in 1935, was strongly rooted in gospel before moving to Oakland, California, where he has been a mainstay of the local jazz scene for more than 30 years. He has recorded infrequently but shines on this date, originally released in 1979 as *Ed Kelly and Friend.* Kelly knew Pharoah Sanders from the early 1960s when they played together in Oakland. Sanders is presented in the quiet, lush surroundings of ballads like "Rainbow Song" and Sam Cooke's "You Send Me" as well as on the more up-tempo "Newborn." The album includes the first recording of Sanders's well-known song "You've Got to Have Freedom." In addition, the reissue includes material recorded in 1992 by Kelly's quintet as well as three solo pieces, including a nice cover of Thelonious Monk's "Well, You Needn't." — J.S.

WYNTON KELLY

★★★★ **Piano (1958; Original Jazz Classics, 1989)**
★★★★ **Kelly Blue (1959; Original Jazz Classics, 1989)**
★★★ **It's All Right (Verve, 1964)**
★★★ **Full View (1967; Original Jazz Classics, 1996)**
★★★ **Last Trio Session (Delmark, 1988)**
★★½ **Piano Interpretations (Blue Note, 1991)**
★★½ **Takin' Charge (Le Jazz, 1996)**
★★½ **Live (Collectables, 1997)**

Pianist Wynton Kelly (1931–1971) was well known as a sparkling accompanist, appearing on some of the finest albums by Miles Davis and Cannonball Adderley, as well as working with Dizzy Gillespie, Dinah Washington and Lester Young. Kelly never really got his due as a leader, however. *Piano Interpretations,* Kelly's debut as a leader, is a trio session from 1951 with Oscar Pettiford playing bass on some tracks and Lee Abrams on drums.

Piano and *Kelly Blue,* both cut for Riverside, display him at his swinging best—subtly bluesy and ever inventive. Kelly is reunited on *Kelly Blue* with bassist Paul Chambers and drummer Jimmy Cobb, the rhythm section he played with in the Davis group that recorded *Kind of Blue.*

Kelly also recorded several excellent albums for Vee-Jay Records that go in and out of print. *Last Trio Session* (recorded in 1969) is another reunion with Cobb and Chambers and features lots of great playing. Few rhythm sections in the history of modern jazz top this trio. Unfortunately, some of that playing is wasted on lame pop tunes or inappropriate rock covers, including, unbelievably, "Light My Fire" and "Yesterday." — A.P.

RODNEY KENDRICK

★★★★ **The Secrets of Rodney Kendrick (Verve, 1993)**
★★★★½ **Dance World Dance (Verve, 1994)**
★★★★½ **Last Chance for Common Sense (Verve, 1996)**

Best known as the piano player for jazz vocalist Abbey Lincoln during her early-'90s tours, Rodney Kendrick (b. 1960) has since established himself as a distinctive voice in contemporary jazz. Son of pianist Jimmy Kay Kendrick, who backed Sonny Stitt, Illinois Jacquet and others, the younger Kendrick inherited a formidable talent for the ivories and proved himself as a sideman with Clark Terry, J.J. Johnson, Wynton Marsalis and George Benson, to name a few. It's his restless solo albums, though, that make him one of the most exciting young jazz players on the scene today. His love for all kinds of music and a healthy respect for tradition give his work its basis, but an adventurous spirit and copious talents place Kendrick a cut above the pack of prodigious young players now pushing jazz into the 21st Century.

Kendrick's first effort, *The Secrets of Rodney Kendrick,* shows an atypical maturity apparent not only in his playing skills but through his composing and arranging. Stylistically, the album is informed by bop and hard bop, but its rhythmic emphasis aligns it with Latin jazz as much as with Charlie Parker. Joining Kendrick on the album are such luminaries as trumpeter Roy Hargrove, cornet player Graham Haynes and alto saxophonist Kenny Garrett, among others. Standout tracks include a spare rendition of Randy Weston's "Berkshire Blues," on which Kendrick is joined by bassist Tarus Mateen and drummer Turu Alexander; another Weston cover, "Ganawa in Paris," explodes into a rhythmic platform for three percussionists. Kendrick's compositions "Slide the World into Place," "Sharon" and "Slick Exit" all have an immediacy that must be heard, while the ensemble's Monk-ish treatment of Miles Davis's "Dig" is lent a solid authenticity by Garrett's fine alto work.

On *Dance World Dance,* Kendrick's compositional skills step dramatically to the fore, with 8 originals out of 10 tracks. Again accompanied by a list of distinguished players, including Haynes, bassist Michael Bowie, and alto-sax player Arthur Blythe, Kendrick displays impeccable taste and ability. A highlight is "Santeria," whose intriguing theme could be the soundtrack to an espionage thriller. Yoron Israel's metronomic drumming keeps Kendrick's playing grounded on this track, but just barely. The wonderful "Son Is" finds Blythe and Haynes doubling up to play the tune's serpentine theme, with Kendrick providing a silken piano solo that yields to incendiary cornet and alto-saxophone solos respectively. Weston's "The Last Day" is also included on *Dance World Dance,* giving Kendrick a chance to stretch out as he attacks the song in a solo setting. *Last Chance for Common Sense* is subdivided by several brief yet seductive rhythmic workups ("Rodney's Rhythms" Parts 1–7). Featuring "Led Astray," a composition by Kendrick's wife, Rhonda Ross (daughter of Diana), *Last Chance* includes an exceptional stable of players, namely, Dewey Redman on tenor sax and Tim "Bone" Williams on trombone. — B.R.H.

WILLIE KENT

★★★½ Ain't It Nice (Delmark, 1991)
★★★★ Too Hurt to Cry (Delmark, 1994)
★★★★ Long Way to Ol' Miss (Delmark, 1996)

Willie Kent (b. 1936) is a Chicago bandleader who writes contemporary blues material and sings in an urgent, vibrato-drenched style. He grew up in Mississippi listening to the blues on radio, in juke joints and on his front porch. He moved to Chicago at age 14 and by the end of the 1950s was playing bass regularly on that city's blues circuit. Playing with Little Walter in the 1960s, Kent became much in demand as a sideman. From the 1970s on, he played with many bands and sporadically as a leader but recorded infrequently.

Kent's rolling bass lines are well complemented by Tim Taylor's aggressive drumming on *Ain't It Nice* and *Too Hurt to Cry;* Baldhead Pete is the more in-the-pocket drummer on *Long Way to Ol' Miss.* Kenny Barker completes the rhythm section with percussive piano playing and chordal organ washes.

Ain't It Nice features solid performances from Luther "Slim" Adams and Jacob Dawson on guitars and "Mad Dog" Lester Davenport on harmonica. *Too Hurt to Cry* uses the same rhythm section, with Willie Davis joining Dawson on guitar and Johnny B. Moore guesting on "Blues Train" and "911." The album also uses Billy Branch on harmonica for six cuts and a brass section led by Malachi Thompson on trumpet and featuring Sonny Seals on tenor saxophone and Steve Berry on trombone. On *Long Way to Ol' Miss,* Davis is the carry-over guitarist, with Vernon "Chico" Banks also playing guitar except on two tracks where James Wheeler guests. — J.S.

STAN KENTON

★★½ New Concepts of Artistry in Rhythm (1952; Blue Note, 1990)
★★ Kenton in Hi-Fi (1956; Blue Note, 1992)
★★★ Cuban Fire! (1957; Blue Note, 1991)

★★★ The Ballad Style of Stan Kenton (1958; Blue Note, 1997)
★ West Side Story (1961; Blue Note, 1994)
★★★ Kenton Live from the Las Vegas Tropicana (1961; Blue Note, 1996)
★★★½ Retrospective (Blue Note, 1992)
★★★ Kenton '51 (Storyville, 1993)
★★★½ The Best of Stan Kenton (Blue Note, 1995)
★★★ City of Glass (Blue Note, 1995)
★★ Adventures in Time (Blue Note, 1997)
★★★ Innovations Orchestra (Blue Note, 1997)
★★★ Jazz Profile (Blue Note, 1997)

Keyboardist/bandleader Stan Kenton (1912–1979) led a controversial West Coast big band known less for swing than for its eclecticism and flair for the dramatic. Kenton attempted to apply 20th Century classical-music theory to jazz arrangements, using adventurous harmonics, massed strings and bombastic brass sections keyed by the roar of five trombones. He was a tireless promoter of jazz and a visionary who attracted excellent players eager to face the challenge of playing his difficult arrangements.

The band's theme, "Artistry in Rhythm," is also the title of the 1943 album that brought it widespread attention. Much of Kenton's '50s output featured overstuffed bands playing overblown arrangements of compositions with such pretentious titles as "Concerto to End All Concertos."

When not too ponderous or commercial, Kenton's music can prove surprisingly listenable. The four-disc *Retrospective* and the Blue Note *Best of Stan Kenton* present him well and include the performances of such past and future stars as vocalists Anita O'Day and June Christy; saxophonists Stan Getz, Richie Kamuca, Lee Konitz, Zoot Sims, Art Pepper, Bud Shank and Vido Musso; trumpeter Maynard Ferguson, whose high notes were a showpiece of the band's dynamics; trombonist Kai Winding; guitarist Sal Salvador; and drummers Shelly Manne and Mel Lewis.

The live *Kenton '51* and *Kenton Live from the Las Vegas Tropicana* document good moments for the band. Kenton's most glaring problem, the inability of his bands to develop an exciting rhythmic pulse, is overcome by the addition of an Afro-Cuban percussion section on the lively *Cuban Fire!* — J.S.

JACK KEROUAC

★★★★ The Jack Kerouac Collection (Rhino, 1989)

Taking their cue from Charlie Parker's hard bop, Jack Kerouac (1922–1969) and the rest of the late-'50s loose confederacy of rebel mystics and road scholars who called themselves the Beats attempted a kind of jazz-in-prose; they wanted language—word music—that would flow out, inspired and unedited, and capture the exhilaration of a Parker improvisation. Kerouac's *On the Road* (1957) was the novel that delivered the Beat message with the truest of pop power—its irresistible prose celebrated appetite (food, sex, drink, drugs) while insisting, too, that the spirit must be fed. A beautiful three-disc set, gloriously annotated and filled with tributes, *The Jack Kerouac Collection* presents the writer reading verse that lauds trains, the moon, Mexico and Charlie Parker, delivering thoughts on the Beat Generation and scatting riffs from *On the Road.* The affable Steve Allen comps piano as Jack moans and declaims; elsewhere, Al Cohn and Zoot Sims accompany him as he turns out American haiku and short "blues" poetry. Producers Bob Thiele and Bill Randle leave the tape going during the sessions—and some of Kerouac's offhand comments are nearly as appealing as his poems. What emerges is the soul of the man, expansive, errant and desperately alive. — P.E.

DAVE KEYES

★★★ Rockin' Rhythm and Blues (Keyesland, 1994)

Keyboard ace Dave Keyes (b. 1956) is best known for his work behind Sleepy LaBeef and Bo Diddley and in the band of *Smokey Joe's Cafe,* the Broadway revue of Leiber and Stoller songs. Keyes is a strong songwriter and a competent vocalist. *Rockin' Rhythm and Blues* is an entertaining effort that mixes slow blues, R&B rockers and the New Orleans–style pieces that are his forte. The arrangements are tight and energetic, and the sidemen are first-rate, particularly guitarists Marc Shulman and Jeff Pevar and drummer Frank Pagano. Of the eight originals on the album, the R&B stroll "Signed with Heartache" and the New Orleans tribute "Fess and the Dr." are standouts. — J.Z.

STEVE KHAN

★★★ Let's Call This (Mesa Bluemoon, 1991)
★★★ Headline (Mesa Bluemoon, 1992)

★★★ **Crossings (Verve, 1994)**
★★★ **The Collection (Legacy, 1994)**
Guitarist Steve Khan (b. 1947) was exposed to the music business while growing up in Los Angeles as the son of lyricist Sammy Cahn. By the 1970s, he was a sought-after player on pop, R&B and jazz dates, playing on hundreds of sessions including recordings by James Brown, Steely Dan, Billy Joel, the Brecker Brothers and Billy Cobham. He formed his own group, Eyewitness, in the early 1980s but never got anywhere with it. His early material is collected on the Legacy reissue. A player of great taste and range, Khan nevertheless suffers from the classic session player's lament, a lack of presence as a leader. The Mesa Bluemoon releases both feature fine support from bassist Ron Carter. *Crossings* benefits from the presence of saxophonist Michael Brecker. —J.S.

FRANKLIN KIERMYER

★★★★½ **Solomon's Daughter (Evidence, 1994)**
★★★½ **Kairos (Evidence, 1996)**
Drummer Franklin Kiermyer (b. 1956) starts out on fast-forward with this astonishing high-energy quartet, working off the model of John Coltrane's spiritually driven music in the final phase of his '66 quintet. Kiermyer calls this "American ecstatic music," as apt a description of this beyond-free transcendentalism as any. Filling the role of Coltrane on *Solomon's Daughter* is Pharoah Sanders in one of the finest moments of a career spent searching for the interstices of spiritual awakening and musical freedom. — J.S.

JUNIOR KIMBROUGH

★★★★ **All Night Long (Fat Possum, 1992)**
★★★ **Sad Days, Lonely Nights (Fat Possum, 1994)**
★★★★ **Do the Rump! (HMG/Hightone, 1997)**
Junior Kimbrough (1930–1998) hypnotized his listeners with relentless, one-chord workouts. Applying the jackhammer force of a heavy-metal group, he locked into grooves befitting a funk band, but his music was nothing if not the blues. Born in Hudsonville, Mississippi, Kimbrough operated one of the area's most popular house parties since the 1980s. Despite his local renown, he recorded infrequently before he met journalist and author Robert Palmer in the late '80s. *Do the Rump!* collects some of his rare '80s recordings with the Soul Blues Boys. After including him in the film *Deep Blues* and its soundtrack, Palmer produced two albums for Kimbrough, both of which were cut live at his juke joint. *All Night Long* features wonderfully spare arrangements that somehow manage to carry Kimbrough's enormously heavy music. Less powerful is his follow-up, *Sad Days, Lonely Nights,* which mostly just reiterates the raucous sound unleashed on *All Night Long.* — J.K.

KING CURTIS

★★★ **The New Scene of King Curtis (1960; Original Jazz Classics, 1992)**
★★★ **King Soul (Prestige, 1960)**
★★ **Soul Meeting (Prestige, 1960)**
★★★ **Trouble in Mind (1961; Original Blues Classics, 1992)**
★★★★ **Live at the Fillmore West (Atco, 1971)**
★★★ **Jazz Groove (Prestige, 1973)**
★★★★ **King Curtis & Champion Jack Dupree: Blues at Montreux (Atlantic, 1973)**
★★★★ **Soul Twist & Other Golden Classics (Collectables, 1989)**
★★ **Enjoy . . . The Best of King Curtis (Collectables, 1990)**
★★★★ **Instant Soul: The Legendary King Curtis (Razor & Tie, 1994)**
★★★½ **Night Train (Prestige, 1995)**
Born Curtis Ousley in Fort Worth, Texas, in 1934, King Curtis was steeped in gospel music from an early age, thanks to his father, who played guitar in a sanctified church band. He was all of 10 years old when he heard Louis Jordan playing saxophone on the radio and found his life's path suddenly made clear. Breaking in on alto sax, he later moved to the tenor, put a band together and began working local clubs. Inspired and influenced by a host of tenor-sax giants—including Lester Young, Illinois Jacquet, Arnett Cobb, Dexter Gordon, Gene Ammons, Stan Getz and Coleman Hawkins—Curtis developed an individual and versatile style that found him equally at home in high-minded jazz bands that placed a premium on improvisation and in house-rockin' R&B outfits whose sole purpose was to get the audience on its feet and keep it there. His was a macho sound with heart, deep and probing like Young in the lower register, crystalline and crying like Getz in its upper register.

Jazz, gospel, blues, R&B—Curtis had the

whole package together by the mid-'50s when he emigrated to New York and began doing session work for Atlantic Records. All he accomplished over the next few years was to help define the spirit of early rock & roll and R&B with his now widely emulated honking, stuttering tenor solos; later he made an effortless transition into soul. "Yakety Yak," the Coasters' 1958 chart-topping single, introduced the Curtis sound to the masses. His session credits included dates with, in addition to the Coasters, many of the top R&B and soul artists of his day, among them Aretha Franklin, whose band he led on some of the most important soul recordings in history. He also wrote "Reminiscing" for Buddy Holly and played on the track.

At the same time he was becoming one of the most in-demand session men around, Curtis was pursuing a solo career but with little commercial success. Staying close to his R&B and gospel roots, he cut several pleasing albums, none of them monuments but each graced by often-inspired performances from top-flight musicians. *The New Scene of King Curtis*, *King Soul* and *Soul Meeting* (the latter two were combined as the 1973 reissue *Jazz Groove*) find him leading a deft combo comprising Wynton Kelly, Paul Chambers, Nat Adderley and Oliver Jackson. These fairly tame sides have their moments—the tender ballad "Willow Weep for Me" and the gospel-rooted "Little Brother Soul" on *The New Scene* are standouts—but taken as a whole are ingratiating rather than gripping in execution. *Soul Twist & Other Golden Classics* is a fine sampling of Curtis's lesser-known but no less exemplary work as a session player and as the leader of his own group, the Noble Knights, who recorded for the Enjoy label. That group's lone hit is here (#1 R&B, #17 pop), 1962's bona fide dance-hall burner "Soul Twist," one of the great rock & roll instrumentals, powered by an insinuating groove, memorable melody, inspired ensemble work (Curtis's guitarist at this time was Billy Butler, who had made an indelible mark himself in 1956 with his soloing on Bill Doggett's big hit "Honky Tonk") and a full-frontal assault of a sax solo by Curtis that gives new definition to *stuttering.* "Soul Twist" was forever immortalized by being named in Sam Cooke's lyrics to "Having a Party."

Live at the Fillmore West is Curtis the bandleader at his absolute best on a night when his extraordinary players included Bernard Purdie, Jerry Jemmott and Cornell Dupree. The powerful communication between these musicians produces a set that is a model of intelligent choices made without sacrificing spontaneity and fire. The same could be said for the live album, *Blues at Montreux,* which teams Curtis with the great New Orleans piano player Champion Jack Dupree on six original songs, five cowritten by the two principals. Another side of Curtis gets ample exposure on *Trouble in Mind,* a reissue of an album originally recorded for the Tru-Sound label in 1961. Instead of tenor, Curtis played alto sax on most of the cuts; more significant, he made an impressive debut as a vocalist and showed an agile, personable touch on material ranging from the low-down "Trouble in Mind" to the spirited "But That's Alright." There's a bit of Ray Charles in his voice (emphasized by the background vocals of three former Raelettes) but some of Freddie King's nasality as well. He even gets down as a guitarist on "Ain't Nobody's Business." On the strength of *Trouble in Mind* it's possible to see the full dimension of Curtis's talent, although nothing supplants the roar of that mighty tenor sax.

Prestige has done collectors a favor by packing two of Curtis's other Tru-Sound albums, *Old Gold* and *It's Party Time with King Curtis,* into the single-disc *Night Train* set. These are all-instrumental affairs with a theme. The former is a clutch of reconsidered evergreens ranging from a languid reading of "Fever" to a bouncing "The Hucklebuck." *It's Party Time* takes Curtis back to his dance-hall roots, backed by the likes of tenor saxophonist Sam "The Man" Taylor, organist Ernie Hayes, pianist Paul Griffin, guitarist Billy Butler, bassist Jimmy Lewis and drummer Ray Lucas. Butler, alternately twangy and robust, offers a lesson in concise soloing on the woozy "Easy-Like," a dreamy setup for "Hot Saxes," the battle of the honking saxophones that follows hard on its heels. For slow grindin' or hot steppin', *It's Party Time* is hard to top.

A more recent overview of Curtis's solo work is contained on *Instant Soul.* "Soul Twist" is here in all its glory, but the disc focuses more on the artist's latter-day work, through the '60s up to 1970. So many choice moments—few get any better than 1964's wistful "Soul Serenade," whose many engaging moments include Cornell Dupree's haunting ascending-chord ostinatos kicking off the song in languid fashion and then settling in as a perky counterpoint to Curtis's searching, soaring lead solo. Most of the album, though, consists of cover versions of recognizable hits by other artists; Curtis's genius was to render his as an entirely credible alternative voice in interpreting popular material. There's evidence aplenty to back up that assertion, particularly in the cuts recorded in Memphis and Muscle Shoals with stalwarts such as Duane Allman on guitar (a searing take on "The Weight") and the strictly powerhouse rhythm section of drummer Roger Hawkins and bassist David Hood pushing matters ahead. On the import side, Bear Family offers *Blow Man, Blow!,* a three-CD box of material Curtis cut for Capitol during his 1962–1965 tenure, including 16 previously unreleased tracks. The Capitol years are otherwise unrepresented on domestic releases. — D.M.

ALBERT KING

★★★★★ **Born Under a Bad Sign (Atlantic, 1967; NA)**
★★★★ **King of the Blues Guitar (1968; Atlantic, 1977)**
★★★ **Live Wire Blues Power (1968; Stax, 1979)**
★★★ **Door to Door (with Otis Rush) (1969; Chess, 1991)**
★★★ **Jammed Together: Albert King, Steve Cropper, Pop Staples (1969; Stax, 1988)**
★★★★ **Years Gone By (1969; Stax, 1982)**
★★★★ **Lovejoy (1970; Stax, 1990)**
★★★ **I'll Play the Blues for You (1972; Stax, 1987)**
★★★ **I Wanna Get Funky (1973; Stax, 1987)**
★★★★ **Albert Live (Utopia, 1977)**
★★★ **The Blues Don't Change (1977; Stax, 1992)**
★★★ **New Orleans Heat (Tomato, 1979)**
★★★ **Montreux Festival (Stax, 1979)**
★★★ **Chronicle: Albert King/Little Milton (Stax, 1979)**
★★½ **Blues for Elvis (Stax, 1981)**
★★★½ **Crosscut Saw: Albert King in San Francisco (1983; Stax, 1992)**
★★★★½ **I'm in a Phone Booth, Baby (1984; Stax, 1991)**
★★ **The Lost Session (Stax, 1986)**
★★★ **The Best of Albert King (Stax, 1986)**
★★★ **Blues at Sunrise (Stax, 1988)**
★★★★★ **Let's Have a Natural Ball (Modern Blues, 1989)**
★★½ **Truckload of Lovin' (Tomato, 1989)**
★★½ **I'll Play the Blues for You (Tomato, 1989)**
★★★½ **Live (Tomato, 1989)**
★★½ **King Albert (Tomato, 1989)**
★★ **Albert (Tomato, 1989)**
★★★ **Wednesday Night in San Francisco (Live at the Fillmore) (Stax, 1990)**
★★★ **Thursday Night in San Francisco (Live at the Fillmore) (Stax, 1990)**
★★★★★ **The Ultimate Collection (Rhino, 1993)**
★★★ **Blues at Sunset (Live at Wattstax and Montreux) (Stax, 1993)**
★★★★ **Funky London (Stax, 1994)**
★★½ **The Tomato Years (Tomato, 1994)**

Born in Indianola, Mississippi, Albert King (1923–1992) (no relation to B.B., though he chose the surname after hearing B.B.'s early-'50s hit "Three O'Clock Blues") shaped a singular style of blues guitar that echoed Elmore James and Robert Nighthawk in its ferocious, razor-edged assault but was also distinguished by steely single-string lead lines, muscular phrasing and a tender heart à la Lonnie Johnson and T-Bone Walker. Tuning to an open E-minor chord, King, a lefty, played the guitar as strung for a right-handed player but upside down, executing the most amazing string bending known to humankind by pulling down across the fret board until he reached *le note juste.* But rather than rely on flash, King was about solidity—basic, straight-ahead, indefatigable drive minus filigree or ostentatious displays of technique. If this sounds like a description of, say, Stevie Ray Vaughan as well, then you must be acquainted with the King family tree.

Though he first recorded in the early '50s for the Parrot label, King remained fairly obscure even in blues circles until signing with the St. Louis–based Bobbin label in 1959. There he turned out some raucous sides that found him blazing away on guitar in front of a jump band outfitted with a saxophone section and a piano player, thus laying the foundation for his startling breakthrough the next decade. A 1961 single, "Don't Throw Your Love on Me So Strong," became a national R&B hit but of the one-shot variety. Frustrated by his holding pattern on Bobbin (and on the King label, to which Bobbin had leased some of Albert's sides, now available, along with some tracks cut for Parrot, on the Chess 1969 reissue *Door to Door*), King moved to the East St. Louis–based Coun-Tree label. Working with a quintet (complete with organ), King cut four sides, released as two singles, that garnered some solid airplay in the Midwest and created a demand for King on the concert circuit. Two years later he jumped at an offer from Memphis's Stax label and made an immediate and lasting impact on blues history. For the next two decades plus, while under contract to Stax and Tomato, he delivered a remarkable number of high-quality albums that adhered to no formula save that of remaining adventurous within the context of an identifiable sound signature.

Backed by Booker T. and the MG's and the redoubtable Memphis Horns, King came out of the gate strong and stayed that way. His 1967 album, *Born Under a Bad Sign,* is a blues monument, but on other long-players he gave free reign to his eclectic musical interests and recast the unlikeliest material into ringing personal statements. "Crosscut Saw" and the title song are legendary tracks from *Born Under a Bad Sign*—performances blending infallible musicianship and deeply felt emotion to such a degree that an entire new generation of blues guitarists was inspired by his example. Moreover, he was unafraid to be tender and vulnerable, something of a prototypical Sensitive Man of his day. While his stellar guitar work and blues growl get most of the attention, his warm-hearted voice could be soulful and penetrating on romantic ballads. A somewhat flaccid tribute to Elvis Presley, *Blues for Elvis,* is a case in point: King is defeated by "Jailhouse Rock" and "Heartbreak Hotel," but he elevates "Love Me Tender" by recasting it as a gospel-soul number.

Blues remained the bedrock of King's repertoire, though; nothing could supplant his downright dangerous take on Howlin' Wolf's "Killing Floor" (on *Years Gone By*) or T-Bone Walker's "Call It Stormy Monday" (on *Thursday Night in San Francisco,* the second volume of a sensational two-volume live collection, the first volume being, naturally enough, *Wednesday Night in San Francisco*). No single Stax album is definitive King in the way the out-of-print *Born Under a Bad Sign* is definitive King, but each one has its virtues.

The Lost Session stands as an interesting but failed experiment teaming King with John Mayall in a halfhearted move toward jazz. The rocking *Lovejoy* finds King journeying to Muscle Shoals for five tracks of greasy North Alabama soul. Both of the above-mentioned live albums cut in San Francisco are recommended as chronicles of the man's sheer force in a concert setting; a 1983 San Francisco recording (the City by the Bay was a frequent destination for King from the '60s on) originally issued as *San Francisco '83* has been repackaged with two previously unissued tracks as *Crosscut Saw: Albert King in San Francisco.* Here King, in a comfortable setting fronting a quartet, puts his personal spin on Muddy Waters's "Honey Bee" and delivers an earnest but playful reading of B.B. King's "Ask Me No Questions," highlighted by his own tart, robust single-string solos. The sly humor that marked some of King's best work is in abundant evidence here too, notably on a semitalking blues, "They Made the Queen Welcome," a humorous recounting of the queen of England's visit to California during a season of steady rain—King making the point in his matter-of-fact way that even royalty can get the blues. On a more somber note, "Floodin' in California" finds King worrying over the hardships the rain was working on the California populace, an unsettling bit of reportage underscored by Tony Llorens's furious piano soloing—something like a torrential downpour of notes cascading from the keyboard—and King's own stinging guitar lines swirling around the track. Other than the line "I'm wonderin'/Will a matchbox hold my clothes," King's "Match Box Blues" bears no resemblance either to Blind Lemon Jefferson's or Carl Perkins's "Matchbox" songs; rather, King's seven-minutes-plus tale is a cautionary one, mostly spoken, about the dangers lurking in the roadhouse, where jealousy and murder can put a damper on one's good time. Previously unissued tracks include another version of "Crosscut Saw," recast in a funkier, more upbeat groove than the original, and a King original, "Why You So Mean to Me," a Chicago-style jump blues notable for a guitar solo in which King bends notes into the stratosphere, fires off series of staccato blasts and for good measure tosses in some lyrical single- and double-note runs.

Blues at Sunset is a worthy companion to the San Francisco live albums in that its performances, recorded at the Wattstax and Montreux festivals in 1972 and 1973, respectively, rank with some of King's finest on record, particularly the smoking Wattstax side; the Montreux side is poorly recorded, but King's solos cut through the muddy mix enough to make this recognizable as a night when the artist was feeling the spirit.

The *Funky London* compilation is a collection

of nine tracks, six previously unissued, recorded at the Stax studio between 1970 and 1974. True to the title, the feel here is one of sustained grooving, whether it be on the mellow fatback of "Sweet Fingers," the driving "Finger on the Trigger" or the scorching, urgent soloing over a pulsating rhythm section in "Funky London," which boasts the added surprise of a tasty flute solo rising wispily out of the funk-and-blues stew. Throw in a quintessential blues ballad, "Lonesome," with King delivering one of his most heartfelt vocals on record, and the result is a crown jewel of the artist's Stax tenure.

On *I'm in a Phone Booth, Baby,* the past and the present meet in a smoldering rendition of Robert Cray's "Phone Booth," notable both for King's swaggering vocal and Steve Douglas's crying sax solos. Elsewhere, King tears into the Elmore James standards "Dust My Broom" and "The Sky Is Cryin'," offering in the latter some exquisite, lyrical solo fills as a complement to his weary vocal. King, who produced this album, sounds fresh and vital here—witness the number of times he breaks into laughter and easy banter with the band—and the material is among the strongest on any of his Stax albums. Not the least of *Phone Booth*'s virtues are Douglas's exceptional horn charts, which allow the players ample room for their own soul testifying without undermining the songs' blues foundation.

Post-Stax, King found new life on the Tomato label, where he periodically hit the right groove but also made some terrible mistakes. How to explain, for example, bringing in producer/arranger Bert de Coteaux, who had done some arranging early in his career for B.B. King but was then best known for his work with disco artists? Which leads directly to atrocities such as "Guitar Man," the opening cut on *Albert,* with its thumping bass line and pop background vocals. *Albert* improves when King blazes through a couple of Willie Dixon numbers, "I'm Ready" and the reliable "My Babe," although the setting—a blaring horn section and those female popsters backing him up—is a bit too Baroque. Another Coteaux production, *Truckload of Lovin',* finds room for King's guitar in its mix of strings, cooing chorines and burbling synths, but barely. And Albert sounds very bored.

New Orleans Heat takes King to the Crescent City and to producer Allen Toussaint for a flawed but often gripping melding of jazz and blues, one of the more interesting side trips on King's blues highway. By far his best work on Tomato comes on two live albums, *Live,* recorded in Montreux, and *I'll Play the Blues for You,* an October 1977 recording featuring King on four numbers and John Lee Hooker on five. Both of these outings showcase King with a small combo and horns and in fine voice throughout. Despite its brevity, King's set on *I'll Play the Blues for You* is one of his strongest on record, beginning with a scorching rendition of "Born Under a Bad Sign," then mellowing out for a fine, understated vocal caress of "The Very Thought of You"; this sets the stage for the fireworks that explode on "I Worked Hard," wherein King declares himself in need of some TLC after a long, hard day of manual labor, and emphasizes the point with some astounding soloing: quick bursts of brief, electric phrases on the low end of the neck give way to a wailing lament played in the upper register, all of it forming an intricate latticework of sharp-edged retorts as the horns quote Ray Charles's "Night and Day" riff behind him. Exiting on a philosophical note, King offers his most sensitive counsel to the lovelorn on "I'll Play the Blues for You" (mistakenly titled "When You Down" on the CD case). When he's not busy seducing with words, King lets loose with a furious solo, working the length of the neck, now playing against the beat, now pushing it ahead, now turning it inside out as he holds forth with a rumbling, angular discourse on the top strings only—a stunning display of instrumental virtuosity. Apart from these live efforts, King's tenure on Tomato is given apt summation on *The Tomato Years* in 14 tracks from the artist's various long-players, including live cuts from Montreux (but none from *I'll Play the Blues for You*).

Two other compilations also provide overviews of more critical eras in King's history. *Let's Have a Natural Ball* on Modern Blues contains material from the Bobbin and King years, a must-have title for any serious blues enthusiast. Speaking of must-haves, the Rhino two-disc *Ultimate Collection* is a comprehensive overview of the entirety of King's career, beginning with a Parrot side from 1954, "Be on Your Merry Way," and including four Coun-Tree recordings. A healthy dose of Stax work is here, and rightly so, as well as a smattering of Tomato entries. King died of a heart attack in 1992 in Memphis, where he had taken up residence after several years in Illinois. "Would you believe I invented Blues Power?" he used to ask his audiences before dazzling them with an inspired solo full of scintillating, startling twists and turns, as if answering his own question—something he continues to do on the recordings he left behind, rendering the question moot, as it was when first posed. — D.M.

B.B. KING

★★★★★ **Live at the Regal (1965; MCA, 1997)**
★★★★ **Blues Is King (1967; MCA, 1990)**
★★★★ **Lucille (1968; MCA, 1992)**
★★★★ **The Electric B.B. King: His Best (1968; MCA, 1988)**
★★★★ **Live & Well (1969; MCA, N.A.)**
★★★★ **Completely Well (1969; MCA, N.A.)**
★★★★ **The Incredible Soul of B.B. King (1970; Kent, 1987)**
★★★★ **Indianola Mississippi Seeds (1970; MCA, 1989)**
★★★ **Live in Cook County Jail (1971; MCA, N.A.)**
★★★ **B.B. King in London (1971; MCA, 1994)**
★★★½ **Guess Who (1972; MCA, 1991)**
★★★★ **Back in the Alley: The Classic Blues of B.B. King (1973; MCA, N.A.)**
★★★★ **The Best of B.B. King (1973; MCA, 1987)**
★★★★ **To Know You Is to Love You (1973; MCA, 1991)**
★★★ **Friends (ABC, 1974)**
★★★★ **B.B. King & Bobby Bland: Together for the First Time Live (MCA, 1974)**
★★★★ **Lucille Talks Back (1975; MCA, 1990)**
★★½ **B.B. King & Bobby Bland: Together Again . . . Live (1976; MCA, 1990)**
★★★★ **King Size (ABC, 1977)**
★★★ **Midnight Believer (with the Crusaders) (1978; MCA, 1989)**
★★★ **Take It Home (MCA, 1979)**
★★★★ **Live "Now Appearing" at Ole Miss (MCA, 1980)**
★★★★ **Great Moments with B.B. King (MCA, 1981)**
★★★★★ **There Must Be a Better World Somewhere (MCA, 1981)**
★★★★ **Love Me Tender (MCA, 1982)**
★★★★ **Blues 'n' Jazz (MCA, 1983)**
★★★ **Six Silver Strings (MCA, 1985)**
★★★★★ **The Best of B.B. King, Vol. 1 (1986; Flair/Virgin, 1991)**
★★★★★ **Do the Boogie! B.B. King's Early 50s Classics (Flair/Virgin, 1988)**
★★★ **King of the Blues 1989 (MCA, 1989)**
★★★★ **Live at San Quentin (MCA, 1990)**
★★★★ **There Is Always One More Time (MCA, 1991)**
★★★½ **Spotlight on Lucille (Flair/Virgin, 1991)**
★★★½ **Live at the Apollo (GRP, 1991)**
★★★★★ **Singin' the Blues/The Blues (Flair/Virgin, 1991)**
★★★★★ **The Fabulous B.B. King (Flair/Virgin, 1991)**
★★★★★ **Heart and Soul: A Collection of Blues Ballads (Pointblank/Virgin, 1992)**
★★★★★ **My Sweet Little Angel (Flair/Virgin, 1992)**
★★★★★ **King of the Blues (MCA, 1992)**
★★ **Heart to Heart: Diane Schuur & B.B. King (GRP, 1994)**
★★★★½ **Blues Summit (MCA, 1993)**
★★★★★ **How Blue Can You Get? Classic Live Performances 1964 to 1994 (MCA, 1996)**
★★★★ **Deuces Wild (MCA, 1997)**
★★★★ **Blues on the Bayou (MCA, 1998)**
★★★★★ **Greatest Hits (MCA, 1998)**
★★★★ **The Unexpected . . . Instrumental B.B. King . . . Just Sweet Guitar (N.A.; Kent, N.A.)**

Eventually the superlatives overwhelm. B.B. King (b. 1925) is a great blues singer; a list of the most influential guitarists in history would include his name near the top; whether he's fronting a small combo or a full-blown orchestra, his instincts rarely lead him astray and his leadership is compelling; as a songwriter he has penned several blues classics, including "Paying the Cost to Be the Boss," "Why I Sing the Blues," "Sweet Sixteen" and "Sweet Little Angel."

In arriving at an individual voice, King stayed true to the blues while incorporating into his music elements of other musical styles he enjoyed. Born Riley B. King in Itta Bena, Mississippi, he sang in gospel quartets and on street corners in his youth; in the '40s he often worked with a group of musicians that included singer Bobby Bland and pianist Johnny Ace, all holding forth at a café in West Memphis, Arkansas. At that time King's guitar technique was primordial, being derivative of both Blind Lemon Jefferson and T-Bone Walker. Attempts to master the single-string solo flights developed by Walker, Lonnie Johnson, Eddie Lang and Charlie Christian led him to Robert Jr. Lockwood, who was playing a less ornate style of Delta blues on the electric guitar without diminishing the form's powerful emotional pull. In a fortuitous bit of timing, King, while studying with Lockwood, landed a job as a disc jockey on Memphis's WDIA, which in the late '40s became the first U.S. radio station to feature an all-black format. At WDIA King gained a reputation for playing the hippest records in town; as an added "bonus" for listeners, he put to good use the lessons he had learned from Lockwood and others by accompanying the records he played on the air.

WDIA was King's springboard to a recording career, thanks to the station bosses, who went to bat for their popular DJ in encouraging the powers that be at Nashville's Bullet Records to record King. Two singles were released in 1949, the first being an homage to his wife, "Miss Martha King." In 1950 he was signed to the nascent RPM label, a West Coast operation headed by Jules Bihari, one of the founders of Modern Records, and home to many of the day's R&B greats. For the next year King recorded his RPM sides at Sam Phillips's new Memphis Recording Service studio; his commercial breakthrough came in 1952, when a cover version of Lowell Fulson's 1948 hit "3 O'Clock Blues" hit Number One on the R&B chart.

For the next six years King carved out a place for himself on the blues circuit by touring constantly—as he continues to do—and cutting some potent tracks for RPM, which later became Kent (and sometimes marketed albums on the budget Crown label). Each step of the way King was refining his art: With his supple young voice he could effect the deep, husky timbre that made "3 O'Clock Blues" so poignant or a bright, almost reedy tenor sound that was especially effective on love ballads such as 1952's "You Know I Love You" and lighthearted, upbeat jump-blues tunes on the order of 1954's "You Upset Me Baby." At the same time, his guitar playing became more individual, as the obvious influences on his style were reshaped into a unique, memorable sound that was more than the sum of its parts. It had technical facility to recommend it—crisp, clean, trilling notes, economical phrasing, masterful use of harmonics and dynamics to create fascinating textures—but also that indefinable something that speaks to the great feeling guiding the player's fingers across the fret board. He called his guitar Lucille; and when Lucille talked, she added depth to the joys and fears, dreams and nightmares revealed in King's songs.

In 1961 King signed with ABC-Paramount Records, at the urging of Fats Domino, then moved to ABC's Bluesway label in 1968, back to ABC in 1970 when Bluesway was discontinued, and on to MCA after it absorbed ABC in 1979. There he resides today. Remarkably, his lengthy recording career has produced only a handful of mediocre albums, each of which was followed by an outstanding one, lest anyone think he was slipping. He has gone from playing roadhouses to colleges to arenas to Vegas, always staying with the blues, winning new converts along the way and becoming an international ambassador for the music, beloved here and abroad much in the way Louis Armstrong was in his day. Working with arranger Johnny Pate at ABC, King fashioned the sound he adheres to today: orchestral, with a prominent brass section, a powerhouse rhythm section, strings used sparingly for maximum emotional impact, and King's guitar and voice hot and out front, where each belongs. Over the years a few variations have been worked on this setup, but only a few: His 1978 album with the Crusaders, *Midnight Believer,* is all soft edges and mellow moods, a bit more in the jazz mold than blues, and lacking the grit of the straight-ahead blues efforts; four years later he went foursquare into boudoir soul with the gentle stylings collected on *Love Me Tender,* a well-sustained effort at romantic balladeering on which a tougher mind-set would have been inappropriate.

Thanks to an ambitious reissue campaign by the Flair/Virgin label, much of King's early recorded work for Modern/RPM/Kent has been returned to print, along with a good number of previously unissued sides. Amazingly, only a handful of tracks are duplicated from disc to disc, rendering each title essential in tracing the evolution of one of America's most prolific and influential musical artists. Start with *Singin' the Blues/The Blues,* a twofer combining King's first two Crown album releases. Much of King's mid- to late-'50s sessions were in Los Angeles, under the aegis of veteran arranger and orchestra leader Maxwell Davis, who understood the complexities of King's style and surrounded him with L.A.'s top session players to execute some ambitious big-band arrangements in service to the blues. Plas Johnson and Bumps Meyers were among the horn players who put the juice to the jump numbers, while stride-piano great Willard McDaniels offered another eloquent solo voice as bassist Ralph Hamilton and drummers Jesse Sailes and Jessie Price kept the bottom steady. These players fit King like a glove, inspiring some of his most thoughtful guitar excursions and pushing him in new directions at the same time. *Singin' the Blues* opens with a blazing T-Bone Walker–style assault—all distortion and hard-picked single-string runs—ahead of King's plaintive vocal on "Please Love Me." "3 O'Clock Blues" is here, as well as the earliest versions of two other King classics in his own rich, double-entendre ballad "Sweet Little Angel" (a #6 R&B hit a year later in a different version) and Memphis Slim's "Every Day I Have the Blues," with which King scored a Top 10 R&B hit in 1955 and subsequently made his own with a driving arrangement and direct, personal lyric reading. *The Blues* didn't produce any comparable monuments, but it did showcase King and his stellar studio band in peak form on up-tempo rousers ("Ruby Lee"), slow blues grinders ("Past Day") and breakneck boogie-woogie straight from the Kansas City school ("Boogie Woogie Woman," fueled by Willie McDaniels's boisterous solos).

Elsewhere, *The Best of B.B. King, Vol. 1* and *The Fabulous B.B. King* come closest to being greatest-hits packages from the early era. Both contain "3 O'Clock Blues," "Please Love Me," "You Upset Me Baby," "Every Day I Have the Blues" and the first "Sweet Little Angel"; the latter, though, is the only currently available King CD to include "On My Word of Honor," one of King's earliest Crown hits. Rounding out the picture from the King/Modern/Kent era, three other Flair/Virgin releases highlight specific aspects of King's artistry. *My Sweet Little Angel* features 21 songs, many recorded by Maxwell Davis (or label head Joe Bihari) with King and his touring band in Chicago, Houston, Little Rock and Memphis. The feel, then, is rawer than it is on the L.A. studio sides Davis supervised, and gives us an idea of what it must have been like to experience King in a small-club setting at this seminal stage of his career. From these recordings came the hit versions of "Sweet Little Angel" and "Crying Won't Help You" (Top 15 R&B, 1956), both included here, and a searing bit of R&B balladry, "Please Accept My Love," a #9 R&B hit from 1958 featuring King doing his best Jesse Belvin–style pleading on the lyrics. In addition to a number of nonhit singles from the Crown/Kent years, *My Sweet Little Angel* offers some surprises in the form of alternate takes and rare tracks, such as King's foray into big-band swing on "Shake Yours"; a speed-picked instrumental, "String Bean," a jam session outtake on which King shows a deft touch with Les Paul–style runs; and "Recession Blues," a humorous self-pitying blues notable for being cut at King's only session for Chess Records in what proved to be an aborted attempt to jump labels in 1958.

Though its title might indicate its content to be familiar material, *Do the Boogie! B.B. King's Early 50s Classics* includes a number of sides that have been out of print or available only on bootlegs. For example, the version of "Every Day I Have the Blues" included here is an alternate take of the R&B hit heard on other King albums in the Flair/Virgin catalog. Other treats include the Louis Jordan–style weeper "I Gotta Find My Baby," featuring a tasty vibraphone solo (uncredited), and "Woke Up This Morning (My Baby's Gone)," with an uncredited conga player adding a zesty Latin flavor to the R&B ambiance. Among this album's many selling points is its now classic cover photo of King onstage, decked out in white coat, white shirt, tie, two-tone shoes and Bermuda shorts.

King's tender side is the focus of *Heart and Soul: A Collection of Blues Ballads*. Again, the chart hits are supplemented by previously unissued alternate takes, B sides and otherwise obscure singles. King fans will be fascinated by the artist's efforts at melding blues, R&B and pop stylings on several tracks. "You Can't Fool My Heart" finds him supported by the smooth-crooning Kings Men and an insinuating shuffle beat as he delivers an urgent warning in warm, silky tones; similarly, on "Please Accept My Love" King produces a crooning, heartfelt lover's pledge of everlasting commitment as the Vocal Chords buttress him with steady, harmonized "oohs" and the backing band adds ballast in the form of a steady-rolling groove. In yet another departure, the Duke Ellington evergreen "Don't Get Around Much Anymore" won't make anyone forget versions cut by great pop artists such as Rosemary Clooney and Tony Bennett, but King, backed by the Tommy Dorsey Orchestra, gives it a casual but confident treatment, seeming nonchalant even as he imbues the lyrics with precisely enough tension to deliver their inherent melancholy. If nothing else, *Heart and Soul* shows that later efforts, such as the aforementioned *Midnight Believer* and *Love Me Tender* albums, are consistent with and rooted in a long-standing, broad stylistic definition of the blues universe.

No less essential to the complete picture of the artist as a young man is the reissue of a number of early instrumentals in two packages, *The Unexpected . . . Instrumental B.B. King . . . Just Sweet Guitar* on the revived Kent label and *Spotlight on Lucille,* on Flair. The former's eight tracks and the latter's even dozen comprise a capsule lesson in the development of King's guitar technique. On these tracks King quotes all his influences but also stakes out new territory peculiar to his own consolidation of the styles he cut his teeth on. Again, some of the more lyrical, languorous passages prefigure the assimilation of pop sensibilities heard on *Heart and Soul* and periodically throughout King's career. The Flair CD should be stocked in fine music stores everywhere; finding the Kent release will take some legwork, since it was issued in the early '90s by a Nashville-based company that is now out of business.

King's ABC and Bluesway years (released on MCA) show his sound being refined in some cases for obvious runs at the Top 100 chart and in others staying close to the harder-edged material of his early years. Examples of the latter occur most often on his live albums, all of which have some tough moments despite some inconsistency. At the top of the must-have list is the extraordinary 1964 set from Chicago's Regal, *Live at the Regal,* on which King's superior musicianship is on vivid display as is his exemplary rapport with his audience. Stirring performances of "Every Day I Have the Blues," "Sweet Little Angel" and "Woke Up This Morning" key the show, but the highlight is the hilarious "Help the Poor," which, far from being a socially conscious screed, is B.B.'s own hapless plea for help in rehabilitating his battered soul in the aftermath of a love war. *Together for the First Time . . . Live,* teaming King with fellow trailblazer Bobby "Blue" Bland, is a spectacular outing itself, as these two towering figures in American music burn their way through a repertoire that includes "3 O'Clock Blues," "Driftin' Blues," "Goin' Down Slow" and a medley composed in part of "Rock Me Baby," "Driving Wheel" and "Chains of Love." The second King/Bland summit pales in comparison, even though the two titular artists manage a few sparks along the way.

Those less inclined to wade through all the live albums have a splendid alternative in *How Blue Can You Get?* Opening with four powerhouse cuts from *Live at the Regal* (the first, a searing version of "Every Day I Have the Blues," sets an imposing standard that King keeps topping as the disc plays on), the double CD makes stops in Cook, Mississippi; Tokyo; Germany; and England; Gladys Knight engages King in a moving duet of Percy Mayfield's "Please Send Me Someone to Love" and Bobby Bland helps King get the joint rocking on "Let the Good Times Roll." It's peak B.B. throughout, all wheat, no chaff, and one of the few live albums from any performer that can be considered essential to a complete understanding of his or her artistry.

By 1970 King was a well-established, reliable figure on the concert circuit, and the blues revival of the '60s had brought him a large, multiracial audience. The big crossover breakthrough he seemed poised for as the decade began occurred with *Completely Well,* produced by Bill Szymczyk, who was later behind the board for most of the Eagles' albums. *Completely Well* has its share of bedrock blues, but it is at this point that King's guitar becomes a secondary player—not unheard, but diminished in the overall mix—to the big, booming orchestral arrangements, some by Bert de Coteaux, the man who later tried to put the disco beat to Albert King's blues. The players are changing too, with young rockers stepping in for guest turns backing King: Leon Russell, Carole King, Joe Walsh and Russ Kunkel all show up on early-'70s albums; on *B.B. King in London* the backing band includes Gary Wright, Klaus Voorman, Jim Keltner, Ringo Starr, Dr. John and Jim Gordon. Being well known doesn't necessarily translate to being a sympathetic and idiomatically convincing blues player; yet many of these albums are solid, mainly on the strength of King's fervent, impassioned performances. *Completely Well* yielded the song with which King may well be best identified by the general public in the brooding "Thrill Is Gone," wherein the emotional devastation apparent in King's voice is underscored by a spooky bass triplet ostinato and an unsettling, quiet wash of strings. King's pointed guitar solos—hard-edged and direct, with nary a hint of benevolence—cry out in anguish as the music builds to an angry crescendo; the ensuing slow fade suggests a spiritual exhaustion of profound depth. This is a complete performance, near-perfect in every aspect, and it stands the test of time. Peaking at #15 on the pop chart, it remains King's biggest pop hit, and a worthy one at that.

Come 1981 King's music took another turn, this one being of a philosophical rather than a stylistic nature. With the masterpiece *There Must Be a Better World Somewhere,* the artist set out on the path he continues to follow today, exploring not only the roots of his music but also chronicling his own worldview in far more personal terms than he had to this point. As the starting point for this autobiographical inspection, *There Must Be a Better World Somewhere* offers in its title song, written by Doc Pomus and Dr. John, King's first recorded testimony of a socially conscious nature. It's presented here in metaphorical terms, but it's hardly a stretch to hear the subtext as a commentary on various social ills; ever-present, here and on other songs, is a sense of tomorrow bringing compassion and selflessness to its time. Challenged by these rich texts, King responded with his best-realized vocal performances ever, subtle and tender on the contemplative passages, warm and hearty on the up-tempo numbers.

Shortly after *There Must Be a Better World Somewhere,* King assembled another group of fine players with ties to his past—baritone saxophonist Fred Ford is one of Memphis's legendary horn virtuosos, and pianist Lloyd Glenn began his career about the same time King was cutting his first records—and delivered *Blues 'n' Jazz,* a bit of musical archeology that harkened to the RPM/Kent days in its big-band approach. After ushering in the '90s with another scorching live album, *Live at San Quentin,* King dug down deep for *There Is Always One More Time,* another optimistic message arising out of despairing circumstances. True to the romantic in him, Doc Pomus, whose songs, whether blues or rock & roll, were nothing if not bighearted and generous in their feelings toward others, wrote the title song, one of his most hopeful but poignant tracts, as he lay dying of cancer. King, a longtime friend of Pomus's, gives it a performance for the ages, honoring its composer with the forcefulness of his heartfelt reading. The mood thus set, King explores the rest of the material like a master vocal stylist, finding hidden realms of emotion in unlikely places.

The Phil Ramone–produced *Heart to Heart,* teaming King with jazz vocalist Diane Schuur, is an odd affair that never quite takes off. Schuur's reedy voice doesn't harmonize well with King's, and her performances tend to be overwrought, studied and fighting the brass-heavy arrangements all the way. The song selection is good—Don Gibson's "I Can't Stop Loving You," Aretha Franklin's "Spirit in the Dark," "Try a Little Tenderness," "It Had to Be You," Irving Berlin's "I'm Putting All My Eggs in One Basket"—but the execution leaves something to be desired, at least when Schuur comes in. It sounds like King was doing someone a favor here, but the gesture wasn't returned in kind. *Blues Summit* is a series of scintillating duets with titans on the order of Buddy Guy, Irma Thomas, Lowell Fulson, Koko Taylor, Ruth Brown, Robert Cray, Etta James, John Lee Hooker and others. Picking out highlights is almost impossible—each cut has something to recommend it. Vocally and instrumentally, King is at the top of his game here, energized by his partners, playing and singing with a fervor conspicuous by its absence on *Heart to Heart.* The sassy, innuendo-rich sparring between he and Katie Webster on a boiling rework of Ivory Joe Hunter's "Since I Met You Baby" is everything the sessions with Diane Schuur were not in terms of emotional spark between two artists and the sense that each was nudging the other to get down and get it. Similarly, the vocal set-to between King and Koko Taylor on a steadily percolating version of Chris Kenner's "Something You Got" is gritty and engaging, with Lee Allen supporting the singers' spirited dialog with some honking sax solos and the trio of Maxine Waters, Julia Tillman Waters and Maxayne Lewis raising a ruckus with their gospel-style background choruses. On a mellow note, King takes to the pulpit for some spoken testifying about life its own self on a feisty duet with Etta James—who gives as good as she gets—Big Jay McNeely's hit "There's Something on Your Mind." A summit in the truest sense of the word occurs on the dark, haunting treatment given the Willie Dixon/J.B. Lenoir classic "You Shook Me," which teams King with John Lee Hooker. Though working in disparate styles, the two bluesmen find much common ground here in sharing their respective harsh accounts of being in love's death grip, spicing these frank admissions with pungent guitar breaks in their identifiable instrumental voices.

King delivered another summit session in 1997 with *Deuces Wild,* working out on some tried-and-true material with a roster of veteran and young artists. For the most part the set works, and King's performances, both as guitarist and vocalist, are among his most impassioned in recent years. Tracy Chapman holds her own and more on a wrenching retake of "The Thrill Is Gone"; Eric Clapton and King get down for some steady grooving on "Rock Me Baby"; Marty Stuart turns in a gritty take on "Confessin' the Blues"; D'Angelo reaches down for a tough, blistering performance of "Ain't Nobody Home"; and Joe Cocker stands toe-to-toe with King for a blistering duet on "Dangerous Mood." Mick Hucknall is out of his league on Percy Mayfield's beautiful "Please Send Me Someone to Love," but King saves the day with a warm, tender vocal; on "Cryin' Won't Help You Babe," lightweights David Gilmour and Paul Carrack produce performances so bland as to be laughable; and congenial as it is, "Keep It Coming," a new song cowritten by King and Heavy D, never catches fire, despite some trenchant soloing on B.B.'s part. All in all, though, *Deuces Wild* shows King in fine fettle.

Ultimately, the four-disc boxed set *King of the Blues* provides the sweeping, exhaustive survey of a remarkable blues odyssey. Its 77 tracks begin with the previously unavailable (on any domestic release) Bullet single "Miss Martha King," which began King's career in 1949, and trace the course of King's high points with RPM, Kent, ABC/Bluesway and MCA, concluding with a 1992 version of "Since I Met You Baby" cut for Gary Moore's *After Hours* album. With only eight tracks from the RPM/Kent years, this set hardly makes the Flair/Virgin titles superfluous, any more than its 30 tracks previously unreleased on CD render other individual titles insignificant. This is a smart box in that it hits the high points—"The Thrill Is Gone," "Paying the Cost to Be the Boss," "3 O'Clock Blues," "Every Day I Have the Blues," "Sweet Little Angel," "There Must Be a Better World Somewhere," et al.—but also offers seven previously unreleased tracks and a dozen others that are considerably off the beaten path, such as the 1964 treatment of the Bill Doggett/Louis Jordan gem "Never Trust a Woman," which makes its first appearance here as an album track. In toto, this amounts to nearly five hours of music, all of it fascinating as a short course in the evolution of a great American artist. Better yet, as *Blues Summit* and *Blues on the Bayou* indicate, there's more where this came from.

— D.M.

EARL KING

★★★½ **Glazed (Black Top, 1990)**
★★★★ **Sexual Telepathy (Black Top, 1990)**
★★★★ **Hard River to Cross (Black Top, 1993)**
★★★★ **New Orleans Street Talkin' (Black Top, 1997)**

Guitarist Earl King (b. 1934) is one of the more eccentric blues artists to emerge from the hotbed of eccentricity that is New Orleans. A prolific writer, best known for his catchy and oft covered "Trick Bag," and a wild, electrifying guitarist with an idiosyncratic approach to tunings that has driven sidemen to distraction, King is a true original whose early work is unfortunately unavailable.

The good news is that the New Orleans–based Black Top label has given King a new opportunity to record beginning with *Glazed,* a set backed by Roomful of Blues and featuring a handful of King specialties, including "There's Been Some Lonely, Lonely Nights" and "Mardi Gras in New Orleans." King is in top form on *Sexual Telepathy,* with running partner George Porter Jr. on bass and the like-minded Snooks Eaglin on guitar. *Hard River to Cross,* another session featuring Eaglin and Porter, offers more of the same. *New Orleans Street Talkin'* collects tracks from the first three Black Top releases.

— J.S.

FREDDIE KING

★★★ **Freddie King Sings (1961; Modern Blues, 1989)**
★★★½ **Getting Ready (1972; DCC, 1989)**
★★★½ **The Texas Cannonball (1934–1976) (1972; DCC, 1990)**
★★★ **Live at the Texas Opry House (1976; Collectables, 1992)**
★★★½ **The Best of Freddie King (1977; DCC, 1990)**
★★★★ **Just Pickin' (Modern Blues, 1989)**
★★★★★ **Hide Away: The Best of Freddie King (Rhino, 1993)**
★★★ **King of the Blues (Shelter/EMI, 1995)**
★★★ **Live at the Electric Ballroom, 1974 (Black Top, 1996)**

Mixing country and urban blues with a genuine feeling for traditional country music, Texas-born Freddie King (1934–1976) was one of the touchstones of modern blues, particularly as practiced by a generation of English blues guitarists led by Eric Clapton and Jeff Beck. King's reference points as an instrumentalist were pioneering electric-blues guitarists Muddy Waters, B.B. King and T-Bone Walker. His style was forceful and aggressive, blues picked hard on heavy-gauge strings, but he also possessed a keen sense of phrasing and an unerring feel for using space to heighten the effect of his solos.

Although he had recorded for some small, Chicago-based labels in the early and mid-'50s, his career was jump-started upon his 1960 signing to Cincinnati's King-Federal company. A year later he hit the Top 30 with "Hideaway," a rocking instrumental built on a Hound Dog Taylor boogie and incorporating quotes from Jimmy McCracklin's "The Walk" and Henry Mancini's "The Peter Gunn Theme." The song, now an oft recorded blues standard, set the stage for a host of memorable instrumentals that showcased King's restless drive to find new modes of expression within the blues framework.

His strength as an instrumentalist was so overpowering as to diminish his genuinely affecting vocal style, which was easy and friendly but also moving in its upper register, where King reached for some Skip James–style effects. *Freddie King Sings* makes a convincing case for the instrumentalist as vocalist, wherein King's voice is heard at its most effective in powering things along on up-tempo numbers; he was less compelling on slower tunes but could still get it together in a mighty way from time to time—his emotional reading of "Have You Ever Loved a Woman," for example, is a marvel of quiet agony. The King-Federal years are well documented on *Just Pickin',* which contains the tracks from the artist's two all-instrumental albums for the label, including the original "Hideaway" and another stellar performance in "San-Ho-Zay."

After leaving King-Federal in the early '60s, King continued touring but was without a record deal and struggling, until his rediscovery by British blues artists later in the decade. Back in the limelight, he signed with Atlantic subsidiary Cotillion in 1968; two King Curtis–produced albums (*Freddie King Is a Blues Master* and *My Feeling for the Blues,* both from 1969, both now out of print) were commercial and aesthetic failures—King's guitar took a distant backseat to the work of some of the peerless backing musicians, such as David "Fathead" Newman, Cornell Dupree and Jerry Jemmott—but succeeded in setting the stage for the final, fruitful period of King's recording career. Leon Russell and Denny Cordell signed King to their fledgling Blue Thumb subsidiary, Shelter, and breathed new life into his music by letting King do it his way. Commercial success eluded King during his Shelter tenure as well, but as an artist he had found his way, and Russell provided a setting that backed King's steely soloing with rocking funk-flavored and gospel-rooted support. *Getting Ready* and *The Texas Cannonball* bring two of his three Shelter long-players back into the catalog, but the smart buy is the 1995 double-CD set *King of the Blues,* whose 41 tracks include both of the aforementioned Shelter albums as well as the still-out-of-print *Woman Across the River,* his third and final Shelter LP (a misguided effort in which King's guitar goes low-profile in the mix), and six previously unreleased tracks from the Shelter years (notable among these being a wrenching take on Steve Winwood's blues weeper "It Hurts Me Too," with King shining both on his terse guitar solos and especially on the wailing lead vocal). In 1974 King left the troubled Shelter label and signed, at Eric Clapton's suggestion, with RSO, where he recorded two albums that remain, mercifully, out of print. On these, *Burglar* and *Larger Than Life,* someone decided that King needed the benefit of ornate production, and the result is as woeful as could be imagined.

A solid overview of King's work through the years, *Hide Away: The Best of Freddie King* includes his smoking debut recordings for the El-Be label in 1957 (two strong vocal efforts, "Country Boy" and "That's What You Think," the former appearing domestically for the first time), the key King-Federal sides, a couple of Shelter tracks and, for good measure, a King Curtis–produced Cotillion track. Two mid-'70s live albums, Collectables' 1992 reissue of Home Cooking's *Live at the Texas Opry House* (documenting a 1976 show in Houston) and Black Top's *Live at the Electric Ballroom, 1974* (recorded in Atlanta), are the best antidotes to King's lackluster studio work from these years. King is at his electric best on both occasions, singing with gritty authority and playing with fire and feeling; further recommending the Rounder release is the only recording that has surfaced of King playing acoustic (his version of "Dust My Broom" being a moment to cherish). The live albums do an important job of rounding out the picture of the latter-day Freddie King, a superb artist who was floundering on record but who could still step onstage and deliver the goods with the best of his generation. — D.M.

LITTLE JIMMY KING

★★★★ **Little Jimmy King & the Memphis Soul Survivors (Bullseye Blues, 1991)**

★★★★½ **Something Inside of Me (Bullseye Blues, 1994)**

★★★★ **Soldier for the Blues (Bullseye Blues, 1997)**

Little Jimmy King (b. 1968) is the late Albert King's protégé but is also mightily influenced by Jimi Hendrix. The result is a hard-biting left-handed blues style characterized by searing string-bending technique learned from Albert and embellished with flamboyant runs and distortion effects inspired by Hendrix. "King's Crosstown Shuffle," from *Little Jimmy King & the Memphis Soul Survivors,* delivers the goods with panache; King drags his quartet through this session with his impressive performance. On *Something Inside of Me* King is teamed with a rhythm section that knows exactly where he's going—bassist Tommy Shannon and drummer Chris Layton were Stevie Ray Vaughan's band mates, and here King shows himself as a player of Vaughan's caliber without sounding as if he's copying him. *Soldier for the Blues* moves more in a classic R&B direction under the influence of legendary Hi Records producer Willie Mitchell. — J.S.

MORGANA KING

★★★ **For You, For Me, Forever More (1956; Mercury, 1992)**

★★★ **Simply Eloquent (1965; Muse, 1987)**

★★★ **Everything Must Change (1979; Muse, 1987)**

★★ **Looking Through the Eyes of Love (1982; Muse, 1995)**

★★ **Another Time, Another Space (Muse, 1988)**

★ **This Is Always (Muse, 1994)**

Vocalist Morgana King (b. 1930) began her career at New York nightclubs as a highly touted jazz singer with a finely tuned sense of swing and strong command of her material. Her strengths are apparent on *For You, For Me, Forever More,* with pianist Hank Jones. King moved into pop territory with a hit version of "A Taste of Honey," then realized her ambitions as an actress in the *Godfather* films. Unfortunately, her pop and screen success poisoned her jazz singing as her delivery sank to Vegas-showroom levels. — J.S.

TEDDI KING

★★★ **Lovers and Losers (with the Loonis McGlohon Trio) (1978; Audiophile, 1991)**

Vocalist Teddi King (1929–1977) made a number of fine recordings backed by such respected accompanists as pianists George Shearing, Marian McPartland and Dave McKenna, but *Lovers and Losers* is her only title in print. — J.S.

RAHSAAN ROLAND KIRK

★★★½ **Introducing Roland Kirk (1960; Chess, 1990)**

★★★½ **Kirk's Works (1961; Original Jazz Classics, 1990)**

★★★★ **We Free Kings (1961; Mercury, 1986)**

★★★ **Domino (1962; Mercury, 1986)**

★★★★ **The Inflated Tear (1968; Rhino, 1998)**

★★★ **Volunteered Slavery (1969; Rhino, 1993)**

★★★ **Blacknuss (1972; Rhino, 1993)**

★★★★ **Bright Moments (1973; Rhino, 1993)**

★★★★ **The Case of the 3-Sided Dream in Audio Color (1975; Atlantic, 1987)**

★★★★★ **"Rahsaan": The Complete Mercury Recordings of Roland Kirk (Mercury, 1990)**

★★★★ **Rip, Rig and Panic/Now Please Don't You Cry, Beautiful Edith (Verve, 1990)**

★★★★ **Does Your House Have Lions: The Rahsaan Roland Kirk Anthology (Rhino, 1993)**

★★★½ **Verve Jazz Masters 27 (Verve, 1994)**

★★★★ **Simmer, Reduce, Garnish & Serve: The Warner Bros. Recordings (Warner Bros., 1995)**

★★★★ **Talkin' Verve: Roots of Acid Jazz (Verve, 1996)**

★★★★ **(I, Eye, Aye) Live at Montreux (Rhino, 1996)**

★★★★ **Dog Years in the Fourth Ring (32 Jazz, 1997)**

★★★★★ **Aces Back to Back (32 Jazz, 1998)**

★★★½ **A Standing Eight (32 Jazz, 1998)**

Of the many great portraits of multi-instrumentalist Rahsaan Roland Kirk (1936–1977), a series stands out: the big, blind woodwind master splendiferous in the raffish top hat and tails of those New Orleans players whose sad, ecstatic funeral marches hark back to the earliest days of jazz. Kirk, never ranking as a titan of the music, embodied the tradition—so overbrimming was his musical energy that the image of the man blowing three instruments simultaneously has come to encapsulate his combination of happy virtuosity and furious zeal.

But Kirk was hardly a reverent archivist. Whether experimenting with a post–Ornette Coleman free style, turning in a graceful arrangement of a Villa-Lobos piece or swinging hard with the Quincy Jones Orchestra on a version of "Peter Gunn," Kirk made accessible, engaging music; he crammed his sound full of surreal humor, unafraid to be perceived as pop, and played with a visceral power. While his standard instrument was tenor sax, some fans preferred his breathy flute work—and his arsenal included English horn, trumpet, clarinet, manzello and stritch. *"Rahsaan,"* Mercury's excellent 10-CD compilation, is Kirk in his 1961–65 prime; his quartet work, particularly when the lineup includes pianist Wynton Kelly and drummer Elvin Jones, is tough, smart and engaging. While Kirk's hard-bop background ensures that his music never lacks drive, he is a great, raunchy player on (relatively) straightforward blues, and his ballad work cuts deep. The nifty curio piece, *The Case of the 3-Sided Dream in Audio Color*—along with its diversity of cover material ("The Entertainer," "High Heel Sneakers," "Bye Bye Blackbird")—highlights Kirk's humor ("Echoes of Primitive Ohio and Chili Dogs") and incorporates strange interludes of spoken dreams and sound effects.

Among the other stellar individual albums, *Kirk's Works* features great flute interplay with organist Jack McDuff; *We Free Kings* wonderfully captures Kirk's three-horns-at-once pyrotechnics. *(I, Eye, Aye)* is a rowdy 1972 live set at Montreux; both *Volunteered Slavery* and *Blacknuss* are Black Power celebrations, the former assertive (a John Coltrane medley is a standout), the latter (a collection of pop covers) joyous. *Bright Moments* covers the waterfront—nose flute, New Orleans fare and Kirk's signature piece, the title tune.

Along with the big boxed set, there are other good compilations: *Does Your House Have Lions* offers two CDs that range from Kirk's tributes to John Coltrane and Miles Davis to a stunning fusion of "Sentimental Journey" and "Going Home." *Simmer, Reduce, Garnish & Serve* collects highlights from his last three albums (especially nice is Kirk's nod to a major influence, tenor saxophonist Johnny Griffin). *Rip, Rig and Panic/Now Please Don't You Cry, Beautiful Edith* is actually two of Kirk's mid-'60s albums reissued, but it may as well be a compilation—the man shows off a witty mastery of nearly every conceivable jazz style. *Talkin' Verve* is an approachable overview and a good starting point for beginners.

Joel Dorn, Kirk's producer during some of his most fruitful recordings at Atlantic, has assembled a series of outstanding Kirk sessions on his own 32 Jazz label. *Dog Years in the Fourth Ring* collects some amazing live material with the long out-of-print classic *Natural Black Inventions: Root Strata*. *Aces Back to Back* anthologizes *Left & Right*, *Rahsaan Rahsaan*, *Prepare Thyself to Deal with a Miracle* and *Other Folks' Music*. *A Standing Eight* collects his last three releases. — P.E.

EDDIE KIRKLAND

★★★★½ It's the Blues Man! (1962; Original Blues Classics, 1993)
★★★½ All Around the World (Deluge, 1992)
★★★½ Some Like It Raw (Deluge, 1993)
★★★★ Have Mercy (Evidence, 1993)
★★★½ Where You Get Your Sugar? (Deluge, 1995)

Eddie "Blues Man" Kirkland was born in Jamaica in 1928 and raised in Alabama. He moved to Detroit in 1943 and five years later lent his guitar, and occasionally his vocals, to a number of recordings by John Lee Hooker. Kirkland went on to record his debut single in 1952 and a decade later teamed up with legendary tenor-saxophone honker King Curtis and his band to record the seminal—though often overlooked—*It's the Blues Man!* Buoyed by the second tenor sax of Oliver Nelson and propulsive guitar work by Billy Butler, Kirkland's guitar, harmonica and voice leap to the fore on 14 originals, including the swinging, earnest "I'm Goin' to Keep Loving You" and the sensual "Baby You Know It's True." Curtis and company keep their accompaniment loose and smooth throughout, while Kirkland's grainy vocals and shuffling guitar filigrees answer the band's bedrock grooves with a prickly, immediate counterpoint.

Have Mercy includes another fine batch of originals, such as the plaintive, harmonica-drenched "Young Man Young Woman Blues," the crisply funky "Tomorrow May Bring a Better Day" and the reggae-tinged "Golden Sun." Making a prominent appearance on *Have Mercy* are the Ikettes, whose gospel-edged, three-part vocals lend the album a measured, soulful feel. *All Around the World* comprises 11 originals on which Kirkland is backed by nearly 20 different musicians. His most prominent sideman is none other than Hooker himself, who adds his distinctive guitar and voice to two tracks, "There's Gonna Be Some Blues" and "Big City Behind the Sun."

Some Like It Raw was recorded live over three days at a Vancouver club called the Yale Hotel. Backed by a unit known as the Energy Band—guitarist Billy Boardman, bassist Timo Shanko and drummer Ray Anthony—Kirkland whips through searing originals like "Don't Fool with That Bag" and "Lonely Street" and well-known covers such as "Every Day I Have the Blues" and "Got My Mojo Working." Kirkland sounds as good as ever on *Where You Get Your Sugar?,* which features nine originals and a gritty interpretation of "C.C. Rider." The album underscores Kirkland's uncompromising sound, which is as raw as it was in the early '60s—relying primarily on his barbed voice and guitar. Notable tunes include the relentlessly soulful "Our Love, So Beautiful," the jagged "Lover Bone" and the stinging, organ-saturated "Pity on Me." — B.R.H.

KENNY KIRKLAND

★★★★ **Kenny Kirkland (GRP, 1991)**
★★★ **Jazz from Keystone: Thunder & Rainbows (Sunnyside, 1993)**

An experienced pianist with an expansive harmonic palette and a deep understanding of rhythm, Kenny Kirkland (1955–1998) became well known to the jazz public for his work in the Wynton Marsalis Quintet of the early '80s and the Branford Marsalis Quartet of the late '80s into the '90s, and his tenure in *The Tonight Show* band with Branford.

On his eponymous debut, Kirkland unveils his capacious scope with a balanced program. He inhabits with ease the world of clavé on distinctive performances of Bud Powell's "Celia," Thelonious Monk's "Criss Cross," Wayne Shorter's "Ana Maria" and the original "Blasphemy" (with the incomparable rhythm section of Andy Gonzalez on bass, Steve Berrios on trap drums and Jerry Gonzalez and Don Alias on congas and percussion) and the floating mutable rhythmic concept of Miles Davis's 1963–74 rhythm sections. Kirkland's compositions synthesize and unify the language of Herbie Hancock, Wayne Shorter and Keith Jarrett. Branford Marsalis (particularly effective on soprano sax), Charnett Moffett or Bob Hurst on bass and Jeff Watts on drums play with wit and élan.

Jazz from Keystone is a three-way affair among Kirkland, bassist Charles Fambrough and Watts that explores a range of rhythms, tempos and textures. There are originals by Watts and Fambrough, interpretations of Keith Jarrett's "Rainbow" and Wayne Shorter's "Black Nile" and a way up-tempo version of "You and the Night and Music." — T.P.

JOHN KLEMMER

★★★ **Touch (MCA, 1975)**
★★★ **Cry (1978; MCA, 1989)**
★★★ **Arabesque (MCA, 1978)**
★★★ **Brazilia (MCA, 1979)**
★★★½ **Mosaic: The Best of John Klemmer (GRP, 1996)**

Saxophonist/flautist John Klemmer, born in Chicago in 1946, studied under Stan Kenton and was featured soloist in Don Ellis's band before forming his own combo in the '70s. On his first albums, Klemmer was obviously influenced by John Coltrane and made several attempts to incorporate social-protest themes into the program of his music, all to little avail. Klemmer later went heavily into the use of an Echoplex and other electronic effects on his saxophone, making his sound too gimmicky to hold up over repeated listenings. — J.S.

ERIC KLOSS

★★★★★ **Eric Kloss and the Rhythm Section (Prestige, 1993)**

When Eric Kloss (b. 1949) first hit the scene in the mid-'60s, his youth and blindness were talked about as much as his prowess on the alto saxophone. Teamed with some of the great rhythm sections of the day and often collaborating with guitarist Pat Martino, Kloss plays with assurance and adventurousness (his output bearing a noticeable similarity to the later work of Arthur Blythe).

Kloss recorded several albums for Prestige in the late '60s and early '70s, but very little remains in print. The unavailable *Grits and Gravy* and *In the Land of Giants* feature pianist Jaki Byard, drummer Alan Dawson and bassist Richard Davis—a spectacular studio-only rhythm team—with tenor giant Booker Ervin thrown in on *Giants* to stir things up even more. Kloss branches out further on the also out-of-print *Consciousness!* and *To Hear Is to See!* (now packaged together as *Eric Kloss and the Rhythm Section*) by employing the backbone of Miles Davis's vanguard band: bassist Dave Holland, drummer Jack DeJohnette and pianist Chick Corea. — S.F.

LEE KONITZ

★★★ **Konitz (1954; Black Lion, N.A.)**
★★★½ **Jazz at Storyville (1956; Black Lion, N.A.)**
★★★★★ **Live at the Half Note (1959; Verve, 1994)**
★★★★★ **The Lee Konitz Duets (1967; Original Jazz Classics, N.A.)**
★★★★ **Altissimo (1973; West Wind Jazz, 1992)**
★★★★ **I Concentrate on You (with Red Mitchell) (1974; SteepleChase, 1995)**
★★★★ **Jazz a Juan (1974; SteepleChase, 1996)**
★★★½ **Figure and Spirit (1976; Progressive, N.A.)**
★★★★ **Windows (1977; SteepleChase, 1995)**
★★★★ **Yes, Yes, Nonet (1979; SteepleChase N.A.)**
★★★½ **Dovetail (Sunnyside, 1983)**
★★★ **Live at Laren (Soul Note, 1984)**
★★★ **Ideal Scene (Soul Note, 1986)**
★★★★ **Round and Round (1988; MusicMasters, 1995)**
★★★ **The New York Album (Soul Note, 1988)**
★★★★ **Zounds (Soul Note, 1991)**
★★★★ **Subconscious-Lee (Original Jazz Classics, 1992)**
★★★½ **Lunasea (Soul Note, 1992)**
★★★★ **Jazz Nocturne (1992; Evidence, 1994)**
★★★★★ **Rhapsody (1993; Evidence, 1995)**
★★★★ **Leewise (1993; Storyville, 1995)**
★★★½ **Paul Motian/Lee Konitz on Broadway, Vol. 3 (Jazz Music Today, 1993)**
★★★★ **Rhapsody II (1994; Evidence, 1996)**
★★★½ **In Paris (Vogue Disques, 1995)**
★★★½ **Lullaby of Birdland (Candid, 1995)**
★★★★ **Brazilian Rhapsody (MusicMasters, 1996)**
★★★½ **Chicago and All That Jazz (LaserLight, 1996)**

Lee Konitz (b. 1927) has been among the purest jazz improvisers for more than a half century. He emerged in the late '40s as a member of Claude Thornhill's band, where his alto-sax solos demonstrated how the instrument could be played in a modern style without mimicking Charlie Parker. Soon he was studying and working with Lennie Tristano (some of their important collaborations are on *Subconscious-Lee*), while becoming a featured soloist in Miles Davis's *Birth of the Cool* band and a leader in his own right.

The now deleted *Ezz-thetic,* with Davis as a sideman on four tracks, captures Konitz's early style. *In Paris* is made up of sessions from 1953 and '54 with Bob Brookmeyer, Red Mitchell and French musicians recording, among other things, multiple takes of "I'll Remember April," "All the Things You Are" and "These Foolish Things." The Black Lion discs are mid-1950s sessions from the quartet featured at the Boston club Storyville and recorded by George Wein.

Live at the Half Note is his outstanding 1959 recording with frequent collaborators Warne Marsh on tenor sax, Bill Evans on piano, Jimmy Garrison on bass and Paul Motian on drums.

Konitz went into a period of semiretirement in the early 1960s before returning in 1965. He went on to make one of his greatest albums, 1967's *Duets,* encounters with a diverse group of musicians including Jim Hall, Ray Nance, Joe Henderson and Karl Berger.

Like many jazz musicians, Konitz was forced to go to Europe for much of his career to be appreciated. His unique sound was extremely influential there, and he was able to find many opportunities to record for a variety of European labels; the results include *I Concentrate on You,* a beautiful collection of duets with bassist Red Mitchell, and *Jazz a Juan,* a superb quartet effort with pianist Martial Solal, bassist Niels-Henning Ørsted Pedersen and drummer Daniel Humair. On *Figure and Spirit* Konitz returns to the Tristano style with saxophonist Ted Brown, pianist Albert Dailey, bassist Rufus Reid and drummer Joe Chambers.

In 1975 Konitz formed a nine-piece band for occasional club work in New York, and after a disappointing debut album on Roulette, the group found its audience, once again, in Europe, where it turned out two well-written and well-played efforts, *Yes, Yes, Nonet* and *Live at Laren,* featuring trombone great Jimmy Knepper, John Eckert on trumpets and flügelhorn, Sam Burtis on tuba, Ronnie Cuber on baritone saxophone and clarinet, Harold Danko on piano and Billy Hart on drums.

Windows is a solid session of duets with pianist Hal Galper. On *Dovetail* Konitz plays alto, tenor and soprano saxophones in a trio with Danko and bassist Jay Leonhart. Danko is also on *Ideal Scene,* along with bassist Rufus Reid and drummer Al Harewood. *Round and Round* is an excellent quartet recording with pianist Fred Hersch, bassist Mike Richmond and drummer Adam Nussbaum, featuring top-notch versions of "Someday My Prince Will Come" and "Giant Steps."

During the 1990s Konitz finally gained American appreciation and has handled his elder-statesman status with typical voracity. Among his most challenging works, *Zounds* finds Konitz doubling on alto and soprano in a nontraditional soundscape with Kenny Werner on piano and synthesizer, Ron McClure on bass and Bill Stewart on drums. *Lullaby of Birdland* is a more straightforward set recorded live in 1991 with pianist Barry Harris, bassist Calvin Hill and drummer Leroy Williams.

On *Lunasea* Konitz showcases his pianist, Peggy Stern, performing several of her compositions with guitarist Vic Juris, bassist Harvie Swartz and drummer Jeff Williams. *Jazz Nocturne* is a beautiful session of standards recorded with pianist Kenny Barron, bassist James Genus and drummer Kenny Washington.

Rhapsody is a masterpiece, the best Konitz album since *The Lee Konitz Duets* and one built around similar principles. A series of duets, trios and quartets, some with vocals, the album ranges through a fantastic sequence of moods and features exquisite interaction among Konitz on alto, soprano and tenor and pianist Stern; vocalists Helen Merrill, Jay Clayton and Judy Niemack; guitarist Bill Frisell; baritone saxophonist Gerry Mulligan; clarinetist Jimmy Giuffre; bassists Gary Peacock and Ben Allison; drummers Paul Motian and Jeff Williams; Clark Terry on flügelhorn and Joe Lovano on a variety of reeds. *Rhapsody II* continues the idea with lineups including Terry and harmonica virtuoso Toots Thielemans.

Konitz's beautiful tone and rhythmic sophistication as an improviser are a perfect match with the softly undulating rhythms of Brazilian music. *Brazilian Rhapsody* is a magnificent set with Stern, vocalist Adela Dalto, acoustic guitarist Romero Lubambo, bassist Dave Finck, drummer Duduka Dafonseca and percussionist Waltinho Anastacio. — B.B./J.S.

ALEXIS KORNER

★★★ **R&B from the Marquee (1962; Mobile Fidelity Ultradisc, 1996)**

Even though Alexis Korner (1928–1984) had played jazz for more than a decade, he braved the opposition of Britain's trad-jazz followers by setting up the Ealing Rhythm & Blues Club in London in 1962. *R&B from the Marquee* documents this era. To various degrees, virtually all of England's later blues enthusiasts, from the Rolling Stones and the Animals to Manfred Mann and Cream, owe Korner a debt. Korner's Blues Incorporated—whose alumni include Charlie Watts, reedman Dick Heckstall-Smith (later with John Mayall) and Jack Bruce, among others—released several albums, which are now out of print. — P.E.

DIANA KRALL

★★★ **Stepping Out (Justin Time, 1993)**
★★★½ **Only Trust Your Heart (GRP, 1995)**
★★★★ **All for You (Impulse!, 1996)**
★★★★ **Love Scenes (Impulse!, 1997)**

Stylistically, Canadian singer and pianist Diana Krall (b. 1964) owes debts to pianists Ahmad Jamal and Gene Harris and singer/pianist Nat King Cole. Bassist Ray Brown heard her playing piano in a restaurant in her hometown near Vancouver, British Columbia, and quickly became a mentor, encouraging her to move to Los Angeles to study with Jimmy Rowles and Alan Broadbent. Rowles urged Krall to develop her singing as well. She moved to New York in 1990. Her soulful voice complements her confident and vibrant piano skills so much that they become an artful package.

Krall's debut recording, *Stepping Out,* is a forceful trio session with John Clayton on bass and Jeff Hamilton on drums. Mentor Ray Brown (splitting bass duties with Christian McBride) stops by on "Only Trust Your Heart," which offers more ensemble and stylistic variety. Tenor saxophonist Stanley Turrentine is special guest.

The Grammy-nominated *All for You* is a Nat Cole tribute recording that Krall made after a 1995 Canadian summer jazz-festival tour with guitarist Russell Malone and bassist Paul Keller. With a few twists of meaning, it's another fine example of the way in which the talented singer and pianist lets her music breathe and encourages musical conversation within her bands. Malone and McBride return with Krall on *Love Scenes,* which is a bit more laid-back than its predecessors but is strengthened by her continuing maturing and the trio's cohesiveness. Krall's teasing update of "Peel Me a Grape" is a highlight. — K.F.

CORNELIUS CLAUDIO KREUSCH

★★★ **The Vision (Enja, 1994)**
★★★★ **Black Mud Sound (Enja, 1995)**
★★★½ **Scoop (ACT, 1998)**

Pianist Cornelius Claudio Kreusch, born in Germany in 1968, was first exposed to jazz at age 10 when he heard one of his mother's music students playing boogie-woogie. He began studying seriously as a young teenager with Munich-based expatriate Mal Waldron and made his first European solo concert tour at 16. He has also studied with Russian pianist Leonid Chizhik and Americans Joanne Brackeen and Jaki Byard.

Based in New York since 1995, Kreusch was a finalist that year in the Great American Jazz Piano Competition at the Jacksonville Jazz Festival in Florida. Kreusch's energetic music combines modern modal concepts with a funky, rhythmic groove.

The Vision is a trio session with drummer Marvin "Smitty" Smith and bassist Nate McBride. They are accompanied on three tracks by Thomas Grimes, whose rap-style poetry Kreusch melds into his musical vision. The more powerful *Black Mud Sound,* a quartet session with Smith, bassist Anthony Cox and saxophonist Kenny Garrett, is rich in energy and soaring improvisation. The term and band name Black Mud Sound refers to Kreusch's artistic vision that music is "of all colors and becomes one with all people." — K.F.

GENE KRUPA

★★★½ **Krupa and Rich (with Buddy Rich) (1955; Verve, 1994)**
★★★★★ **Drummer Man (Verve, 1986)**
★★★★★ **Compact Jazz (with Teddy Wilson and Lionel Hampton) (Verve, 1987)**
★★★½ **Drum Boogie (Columbia/Legacy, 1993)**
★★★ **Let Me Off Uptown (Drive Archive, 1996)**

Of all of jazz's swing-era drummer/leaders—Chick Webb, Buddy Rich—none proved as flamboyant, spotlight-grabbing or matinee-star good-looking as Gene Krupa (1909–1973). Featured skin man with Benny Goodman and later leader of his own aggregation, Krupa brought the drum seat front and center, making how one performed as important as how one functioned as a timekeeper. His best-known work with his own orchestra was neither deep nor subtle and did not rewrite jazz history. But Krupa's band laid down the blueprint for and popularized the freewheeling, flag-waving rhythms that would hurtle America into the R&B and rock & roll era 10 years later. At its height in the early '40s, with featured support from Roy Eldridge on trumpet and Anita O'Day on vocals, they simply created some of the most spirited and rocking music to come out of the swing era.

Born in Chicago, Krupa began his career as a Dixieland drummer with the Austin High Gang, which also included young Benny Goodman. Sticking with Goodman on his ascent to stardom, it was not long before the spotlight began to capture the dark-haired, energetic presence behind the cymbals, particularly during his feature solo on the swing anthem "Sing, Sing, Sing." A proven crowd pleaser in a band that could feature only one star, Krupa drafted his own group and set off under his own name in 1938.

Recording first for Brunswick and Okeh, then from 1939 on with Columbia, Krupa's band began to find its own energetic stride with both originals and hit-parade covers. Featuring 16 of the band's best numbers from 1940 and '41, *Drum Boogie* kicks with standout selections like the title track, "Who?" and "Blue Rhythm Fantasy" (all showcasing Krupa's drum work), vocals like "Yes! My Darling Daughter" and "There'll Be Some Changes Made" (ditto for singer Irene Daye) and arrangement-driven swingers like "Tuxedo Junction" and "St. Louis Blues."

As telling as this collection is, it mysteriously does not include, and thus cannot begin to compare with, the high-water mark achieved by Krupa's band in mid-1941 when Eldridge and O'Day took over trumpet and vocal duties, respectively. The best of these tracks—"Green Eyes," "After You've Gone," "Ball of Fire," "Rockin' Chair" and the O'Day/Eldridge repartee hit "Let Me Off Uptown" (with her immortal exhortation "Well, blow, Roy, blow!")—have not been reissued under Krupa's name as such. For these classics, one should track down two Roy Eldridge best-ofs on the Columbia/Legacy label—*Little Jazz* or *Uptown* (featuring Anita O'Day), the latter cobilled with the Gene Krupa Orchestra.

A highly questionable drug bust interrupted Krupa's career and sidelined his orchestra in 1943, and upon his release, he fell back to a supporting role in the bands of Benny Goodman and Tommy Dorsey. By the late '40s, the swing era had begun to wane and a new small-group sound called bebop was stealing the jazz spotlight, but Krupa was still able to re-form his big band in '44 and return to the stage. *Let Me Off Uptown* catches live, 12-track radio broadcasts of Krupa's big band in 1949, featuring Eldridge along with singer Delores Hawkins and a much younger and modern ensemble. The classics—"After You've Gone" especially—still jump, and trombonist Frank Rosolino adds his vocal talents on a wry "Pennies from Heaven" and the frenetic scat piece "Lemon Drop." The maestro himself shows off his rhythm chops on "Gene's Boogie"; the aptly named "Gee Bop" bristles with beboppish harmonies; and added percussion support flavors the Latin set closer "Samaba."

By 1951 Krupa had folded his big band, touring out the decade with various small groups and other orchestras. Derived from the "drum battle" feature of the mid-'50s Jazz at the Philharmonic shows, *Krupa and Rich* is a hard-driving, star-crammed session from 1955. Krupa and Buddy Rich actually perform together on only one track (the 13-plus minutes of "Bernie's Tune"), joined by Eldridge and Dizzy Gillespie (trumpets), Illinois Jacquet and Flip Phillips (saxophones), Oscar Peterson (piano), Herb Ellis (guitar) and Ray Brown (bass). With most rough and rambunctious edges unfortunately trimmed by producer Quincy Jones, *Drummer Man* is a reunion set from 1956 with Eldridge and O'Day celebrating their past glory with a 12-song set including all the hits ("Let Me Off Uptown," "Rockin' Chair," etc.) and a couple of Krupa showcases ("Drum Boogie," "Wire Brush Stomp"). — A.K.

SMOKIN' JOE KUBEK

★★★★ **Steppin' Out Texas Style (Bullseye Blues, 1991)**
★★★★½ **Chain Smokin' Texas Style (Bullseye Blues, 1992)**
★★★★ **Texas Cadillac (Bullseye Blues, 1994)**
★★★½ **Cryin' for the Moon (Bullseye Blues, 1995)**
★★★½ **Got My Mind Back (Bullseye Blues, 1996)**

Smokin' Joe Kubek (b. 1956) grew up in the Dallas suburb of Oak Cliff, Texas, along with Jimmy and Stevie Ray Vaughan, all players schooled firmly in the Texas blues tradition of T-Bone Walker and Freddie King. Kubek was in King's firebrand group when the master died of a sudden heart attack in 1976.

In 1988 Kubek teamed up with vocalist/guitarist Bnois King, whose Junior Parker–style vocal delivery and Grant Green–influenced Gibson hollow-body jazz guitar style meshed dramatically with Kubek's biting Fender Stratocaster single-note sound and searing slide technique. The group soon became one of the hottest acts on the Texas roadhouse circuit, which led to the raw, roadworthy debut. Producer Ron Levy added his Hammond B-3 organ sound and a saxophone to *Chain Smokin' Texas Style,* then stripped the band down to its touring lineup for the terse *Texas Cadillac. Cryin' for the Moon* and *Got My Mind Back* show the band continuing to develop its style with original material while staying close to the grit of its basic sound. — J.S.

STEVE KUHN

★★ **Looking Back (Concord Jazz, 1990)**
★★½ **Maybeck Recital Hall Series, Vol. 13 (Concord Jazz, 1991)**
★★★ **Years Later (Concord Jazz, 1992)**
★★★ **Seasons of Romance (Postcards, 1995)**
★★½ **Remembering Tomorrow (ECM, 1995)**

Steve Kuhn (b. 1938), a pianist with perfect pitch and a wide knowledge of jazz repertoire, has a well-trained ear for tunes, quoting them liberally at times. Influenced by Horace Silver, his sound falls within the lyrical Bill Evans vein but expressively remains close to the surface. He plays in a fluid improvisational style, emphasizing melodic right-hand runs that occasionally veer into dissonance or bebop lines, with only lightly voiced comping in the left hand. Kuhn's solos often begin with a single line or simple idea, which is then developed in greater harmonic complexity and rhythmic or dynamic drive.

After studying classical piano in Boston, Kuhn joined the first John Coltrane quartet (before McCoy Tyner). He was a notable performer with the Stan Getz quartet during the bossa nova craze from 1961 to 1963. He also worked with Kenny Dorham and did a mid-'60s stint with Art Farmer and Steve Swallow.

Kuhn has concentrated on trio work for much of his career, achieving a modest degree of renown in the late '80s with Ron Carter. He made a generally well-regarded series of albums for ECM in the '70s, and two early-'80s LPs highlighted original compositions with open improvisation by a quartet that included Sheila Jordan singing Kuhn's original lyrics. His repertoire since has comprised largely standards, and much of his later recorded output is hard to obtain. The playing on the above recordings, too tasteful and laid-back to be truly exciting or engaging, tends toward pedestrian but otherwise nondescript background music.

On *Looking Back* Kuhn finds a pleasantly bland groove with drummer Lewis Nash and bassist David Finck. "Emmanuel," an obscurity by Michel Colombier, makes a sweetly plaintive encore. *Years Later* offers the same trio's latter-day interpretations of Kuhn's favorite tunes from his youth. *Maybeck Recital Hall Series, Vol. 13,* the pianist's first solo album since 1976, captures a meandering Berkeley recital. Highlights are a sparsely expressive modal passage improvised on Miles Davis's "Solar" and a musing, introspective "Meaning of the Blues." — T.M.

FELA ANIKULAPO KUTI

- ★★★ **Live with Ginger Baker (1971; Celluloid, 1985)**
- ★★★½ **Music of Fela (1972; Makossa International, 1975)**
- ★★★ **Music of Fela, Vol. 2 (1974; Makossa International, 1975)**
- ★★★ **Upside Down (1976; Celluloid, 1990)**
- ★★★ **Unnecessary Begging (1976; Makossa International, 1972)**
- ★★★★ **Zombie (1976; Mercury, 1977)**
- ★★★½ **No Agreement (1977; Celluloid, 1985)**
- ★★★ **Shuffering and Shmiling (1978; Celluloid, 1985)**
- ★★★ **Music of Many Colours (with Roy Ayers) (1980; Celluloid, 1986)**
- ★★★★ **Black President (1981; Capitol, 1984)**
- ★★★★ **Original Sufferhead (1981; Capitol, 1984)**
- ★★★★★ **Original Sufferhead (1981; Shanachie, 1991)**
- ★★★½ **Live in Amsterdam (Capitol, 1984)**
- ★★★½ **Army Arrangement (Celluloid, 1985)**
- ★★★★ **Army Arrangement: Original Version (Celluloid, 1985)**
- ★★★★ **Teacher Don't Teach Me Nonsense (Mercury, 1986)**
- ★★★ **Beasts of No Nation (Shanachie, 1989)**
- ★★★★ **O.D.O.O. (Shanachie, 1990)**
- ★★★★ **Black Man's Cry: Classic Fela (Shanachie, 1992)**

A lot of musicians fancy themselves threats to the establishment, but few can claim to be the genuine annoyance Fela Anikulapo Kuti (1938–1997) was to various Nigerian regimes during the last three decades of his life. (He died from heart failure, although he had suffered from AIDS.) In 1977, for instance, his personal compound outside Lagos was attacked and razed by troops acting on orders of the nation's military government; in 1984 he was imprisoned (by a subsequent military government) on spurious currency charges and languished in jail for two years until yet another government freed him. And the source of his troubles, almost without exception, was his music—specifically, his bitingly political lyrics, raucous tenor-sax solos and the insistently hypnotic beat that carried those words to his audience over more than 50 albums.

For listeners outside Nigeria, Fela's political harangues aren't always easy to follow, particularly since he sang in a combination of English and patois. But his sound—a blend of high life, jazz and American soul that he dubbed "Afro-beat"—needs no translation.

With so much to choose from (even given the limited U.S. release of his albums), it's hard to know where to start. Few of Fela's albums offer more than two songs—which is not as miserly as it seems, considering that the average Fela tune clocks in at 15 minutes or longer—meaning that most of his albums emphasize a single groove. His output is surprisingly consistent, meaning that almost any Fela title will be worth hearing. *Zombie* is a particularly fine example of his '70s band, boasting sharp horn work (including his own raspy sax solos) and a loping, muscular pulse; the feisty *Original Sufferhead* and *Black President* (which features the catchy "I.T.T.") are also recommended. Of his more recent material, both versions of *Army Arrangement* are good, but the original version has a little more edge than Bill Laswell's beefed-up remix. And though *Beasts of No Nation* is a bit spotty, the brutally relentless *O.D.O.O.* is one of his strongest albums to date.

Still, the best buys at this point tend to be CD compilations like Shanachie's reissue of *Original Sufferhead,* which includes "Original Sufferhead" itself as well as all of the Capitol album *Black President,* thereby delivering a sizable serving of prime Afro-beat. *Black Man's Cry* includes "Zombie." Also worth seeking are any of the four-volume Fela series on the French Baya label, which packages much of his '70s output in double-length CDs. — J.D.C.

L.A. 4

★★ **Scores! (1975; Concord Jazz, 1988)**
★★ **Concierto de Aranjuez (Concord Jazz, 1976)**
★★ **Watch What Happens (1978; Concord Jazz, 1990)**
★★½ **Just Friends (1978; Concord Jazz, 1990)**
★★★ **Live at Montreux (1979; Concord Jazz, 1996)**
★★ **Zaca (1980; Concord Jazz, 1993)**
★★ **Montage (1981; Concord Jazz, 1994)**
★★ **Executive Suite (Concord Jazz, 1983)**

This quartet of capable musicians—saxophonist Bud Shank, guitarist Laurindo Almeida, bassist Ray Brown and drummer Jeff Hamilton—play an easy-listening 1970s amalgam of classical-influenced and Latin-American jazz. Despite some fine playing, especially from Shank, the whole is decidedly less than the sum of the parts here. If this is to your taste, however, there are a number of titles from this group, the best being *Live at Montreux.* — J.S.

KATIA LABEQUE

★★★★ **Little Girl Blue (Dreyfus, 1996)**

The innovative *Little Girl Blue* pairs French classical-piano virtuoso Katia Labeque (b. ca. 1952) with a series of master jazz pianists in a unique approach to the familiar duet format. Labeque plays a series of famous jazz solos transcribed by musicologist Brian Priestly and accompanied by jazz pianists who improvise around her performances. Chick Corea joins her on Bill Evans's "We Will Meet Again." Herbie Hancock accompanies her (and his own 1964 solo as part of the Miles Davis group) on "My Funny Valentine." Other duets match Labeque with Joe Zawinul, Gonzalo Rubalcaba, Michel Camilo and Joey DeFrancesco. — J.S.

STEVE LACY

★★★★★ **Soprano Sax (1958; Original Jazz Classics, 1991)**
★★★★★ **Reflections: Steve Lacy Plays Thelonious Monk (1959; Original Jazz Classics, 1990)**
★★★★★ **The Straight Horn of Steve Lacy (1960; Candid, 1991)**
★★★★★ **Evidence (1961; Original Jazz Classics, 1990)**
★★★★★ **School Days (Hat Hut, 1975)**
★★★ **Trickles (Black Saint, 1976)**
★★★ **High, Low and Order (1977; hat Art, 1990)**
★★★★ **Sidelines (I.A.I., 1977)**
★★ **Troubles (Black Saint, 1979)**
★★★★★ **The Way (Hat Hut, 1979)**
★★★★ **Songs (1981; hat Art, 1987)**
★★★ **The Flame (Soul Note, 1982)**
★★★★ **Only Monk (Soul Note, 1986)**
★★★½ **The Condor (Soul Note, 1986)**
★★★★ **Morning Joy (Live at Sunset Paris) (1986; hat Art, 1990)**
★★★★ **Collaboration (with Gil Evans and Helen Merrill) (EmArcy, 1988)**
★★★½ **The Window (Soul Note, 1988)**
★★★★ **More Monk (Soul Note, 1989)**
★★★ **Flim-Flam (hat Art, 1991)**
★★★ **Itinerary (hat Art, 1991)**
★★★ **Remains (Hat Hut, 1992)**
★★★★ **Vespers (Soul Note, 1993)**
★★★★ **Revenue (Soul Note, 1994)**
★★★½ **Actuality (Cavity Search, 1996)**

Steve Lacy, born Steven Lackritz in 1934, was the first important soprano saxophonist since

Sidney Bechet. In the 1950s, when no other modern player was using the horn, Lacy devoted himself to it exclusively and made his mark with direct, melodically coherent playing while in the bands of Cecil Taylor, Gil Evans and Thelonious Monk.

Soprano Sax was Lacy's first album as a leader. *The Straight Horn of Steve Lacy* finds his soprano interacting with the baritone saxophone of Charles Davis in front of a rhythm section of fellow Monk-ites, bassist John Ore and drummer Roy Haynes, playing Monk, Cecil Taylor and Charlie Parker compositions.

As the 1960s began, Lacy organized a quartet with trombonist Roswell Rudd (heard on *School Days*) that devoted itself exclusively to Monk's compositions. *Reflections,* which predates the quartet, is an excellent all-Monk recital that includes Mal Waldron on piano and Elvin Jones on drums. *Evidence,* with Don Cherry as the second horn and music by Monk as well as Duke Ellington and Billy Strayhorn, is another excellent album from this period.

Since 1970 Lacy has lived in Europe, where most of his available albums were recorded, often with his quintet (Steve Potts, alto and soprano sax; Irène Aebi, violin, cello and voice; Kent Carter, bass and cello; Oliver Johnson, drums). The band's music, a mix of free playing, Monk-ish angularity and repetition akin to "process" composers Philip Glass and Steve Reich, is best represented on *The Way,* a complete performance of Lacy's "Tao" song cycle, and the out-of-print *Prospectus,* with Lacy expanding to a septet that includes trombonist George Lewis.

Other examples of Lacy's highly consistent playing can be found in his solo albums *Only Monk, More Monk* and the out-of-print *Clinkers.* Another currently unavailable title worth looking for is *Capers,* a hard-blowing trio performance made in New York with former Cecil Taylor compatriot Dennis Charles on drums and the late Ronnie Boykins (Sun Ra's bassist). Also look for *Ballets,* which allows listeners to experience Lacy both solo and with his group.

Lacy is a loyal collaborator, and some of his best-recorded work has been done with old friends. The out-of-print *Regeneration,* where he and Rudd return to the music of Monk and Herbie Nichols in a quintet setting, stands out, as do the knotty duets with Mal Waldron on the currently unavailable *Snake Out.* In 1995, having been awarded a MacArthur grant, Lacy wrote a book, *Findings,* about the technique of playing soprano saxophone. — B.B.

BIRELI LAGRENE

★★★★ **15 (1982; Antilles/Verve, 1991)**
★★★ **Acoustic Moments (Blue Note, 1991)**
★★★ **Standards (Blue Note, 1993)**
★★★ **My Favorite Django (Dreyfus, 1995)**

Bireli Lagrene (b. 1966) was just 13 when he recorded *Routes to Django* (currently out of print), which documented his miraculous command of legendary Gypsy guitarist Django Reinhardt's romantically expressive and technically awesome acoustic-guitar style. In the late '80s Lagrene signed to Blue Note and began making fusionesque recordings featuring his electric-guitar playing, but something was lost in the translation. Concentrate on Lagrene when he himself is concentrating on playing jazz and Reinhardt standards with an acoustic instrument—his still-exceptional gifts reveal themselves. — S.F.

CLEO LAINE

★★ **I Am a Song (1973; RCA, 1994)**
★★★½ **Live at Carnegie Hall (RCA, 1974)**
★★ **A Beautiful Thing (1974; RCA, 1994)**
★★ **Born on a Friday (RCA, 1976)**
★★½ **Cleo at Carnegie Hall: The 10th Anniversary Concert (RCA, 1983)**
★★ **That Old Feeling (CBS, 1985)**
★★½ **Cleo Sings Sondheim (RCA, 1988)**
★★★½ **Cleo's Choice (GNP Crescendo, 1988)**
★★ **Woman to Woman (RCA, 1990)**
★★★½ **Jazz (RCA, 1991)**
★★½ **Blue and Sentimental (RCA, 1992)**
★★★½ **Solitude (RCA, 1995)**

Cleo Laine, born Clementina Dinah Campbell in 1927, established herself as one of England's most technically proficient singers when she began fronting the John Dankworth Big Band in 1952. She married Dankworth in 1958 and shortly afterward began a parallel career in the theater, recording a series of now unavailable records with literary themes like *Shakespeare and All That Jazz* and *What the Dickens!*

The well-received *Live at Carnegie Hall* gives an accurate picture of Laine's range as she emotes her way through a variety of musical settings and theatrical stances that bridge the enormous gap between the Bessie Smith scorcher "Gimme a Pigfoot" and Stephen Sondheim's Broadway tearjerker "Send in the Clowns."

Laine lands somewhere between pop and jazz throughout these recordings. *Cleo at Carnegie Hall* won a Grammy in 1986. *Woman to Woman* features songs by female composers. *Cleo's Choice* and *Jazz* are both albums of jazz standards. *Blue and Sentimental* features a duet with Joe Williams and guest appearances from Gerry Mulligan and George Shearing. On *Solitude* Laine is backed by the Duke Ellington Orchestra under Mercer Ellington's direction. — J.S.

OLIVER LAKE

★★★★★ **Heavy Spirits (1975; Black Lion, 1997)**
★★★★★ **Holding Together (1976; Black Saint, 1991)**
★★★★ **The Prophet (Black Saint, 1980)**
★★★★ **Clevont Fitzhubert (A Good Friend of Mine) (Black Saint, 1981)**
★★★★ **Expandable Language (Black Saint, 1985)**
★★★★ **Gallery (Gramavision, 1986)**
★★★★ **Compilation (Gramavision, 1990)**
★★★★★ **Again and Again (Gramavision, 1991)**
★★★★★ **Boston Duets (Music and Arts Programs of America, 1992)**
★★★★ **Edge-ing (Black Saint, 1994)**
★★★★ **Dedicated to Dolphy (Black Saint, 1996)**
★★★★ **The Matador 1st and 1st (Passin' Thru, 1997)**

Multi-instrumentalist Oliver Lake (b. 1942), best known for his distinctive voice on the alto saxophone, is a key figure in contemporary jazz. The St. Louis native cofounded the influential Black Artists Group (BAG) with Julius Hemphill, then became a mainstay of the New York loft-jazz scene in the 1970s before cofounding one of the most important jazz groups of the 1980s, the World Saxophone Quartet.

Heavy Spirits shows Lake's versatility in a variety of settings, including a solo performance, accompanied by a string section and cofronting a quintet with trumpeter Olu Dara. *Holding Together* is a superb session with the brilliant bassist Fred Hopkins, drummer Paul Maddox and guitarist Michael Gregory Jackson powering Lake's compositions.

A powerful quintet recording with Baikida Carroll on trumpet and flügelhorn, Donald Smith on piano, Jerry Harris on bass and Pheeroan ak Laff on drums, *The Prophet* is dedicated to the spirit of Eric Dolphy, with three Dolphy compositions, including two from the epochal *Out to Lunch!,* "Hat and Beard" and "Something Sweet, Something Tender." *Dedicated to Dolphy* explores the relationship further. The same group recorded *Clevont Fitzhubert,* with Lake showcasing himself on soprano saxophone.

Lake assembles the terrific rhythm section of Hopkins and ak Laff, with pianist Geri Allen, for *Expandable Language* and *Gallery.* Guitarist Kevin Eubanks turns in a fine performance on the former; Rasul Siddik adds trumpet to the latter.

Compilation is a good collection of material from *Gallery, Jump Up, Impala* and *Otherside* (the latter three are out of print).

Lake's ability to work both inside and outside of conventional structures keeps his work from ever getting into a rut. The exquisitely beautiful *Again and Again* is a relatively conventional quartet outing with ak Laff at his subtle best and two masters of touch, bassist Reggie Workman and pianist John Hicks.

Boston Duets, recorded live with pianist Donal Leonellis Fox, features Lake on saxophones and flute and delivering some masterful spoken-word incantations on "Seque Blues." The two musicians, who deliberately kept rehearsal for the event sparse in order to maximize the improvisational qualities of these compositions, play in sublime contrasts and communions, shifting abruptly from free passages to elegantly phrased themes, blues cries and contemplative modes. It all ends with an exploration of Thelonious Monk's "Rhythm-a-Ning." The concert's overall effect is stunning, clearly the work of improvisational and compositional masters.

The Matador is a spoken-word and saxophone-solo project offering a vivid description of a character on one of the most hectic crossroads on Manhattan's Lower East Side. — J.S.

LAMBERT, HENDRICKS AND ROSS

★★★★ **Sing a Song of Basie (1958; Impulse!, 1992)**
★★★ **Everybody's Boppin' (Legacy, 1989)**
★★★ **Twisted: The Best of Lambert, Hendricks and Ross (Rhino, 1992)**

★★★★ **The Hottest New Group in Jazz (Columbia/Legacy, 1996)**

Taking a cue from the popularity of vocalese as originated by Eddie Jefferson and King Pleasure, Dave Lambert (1917–1966), Jon Hendricks (b. 1921) and Annie Ross (b. 1930) joined together for the recording project *Sing a Song of Basie,* with Hendricks putting words to Count Basie instrumental tracks. Masterful production from Creed Taylor allowed the group to overdub lines and build up intricate sections and even mimic the tenor-sax exchanges of Frank Foster and Frank Wess. The project was so successful that the group went on to perform live and make a number of other records in the same style before breaking up in 1962. Ross scored a huge hit with her vocalese version of Wardell Gray's "Twisted," which is included along with some of the Basie tracks on the Rhino repackaging of the same name.

The Hottest New Group in Jazz, a title taken from a rave review in *Down Beat* magazine, collects the three records Lambert, Hendricks and Ross made for Columbia between 1959 and 1961, augmented by four previously unissued 1962 tracks. *Hottest* features a great version of the Bobby Timmons classic "Moanin'," Hendricks's "Gimme That Wine" and a "Summertime" based on the Miles Davis/Gil Evans version. Also included are the trio's Ellington tribute and *High Flying,* after the Randy Weston composition "Hi-Fly." — J.S.

HAROLD LAND

★★★★ **Harold in the Land of Jazz (1958; Original Jazz Classics, 1988)**
★★★★ **The Fox (1959; Original Jazz Classics, 1988)**
★★★★ **Eastward Ho! Harold Land in New York (1960; Original Jazz Classics, 1990)**
★★★★ **Xocia's Dance (Sue-Sha's Dance) (Muse, 1981)**
★★★ **A Lazy Afternoon (Postcard, 1995)**

Tenor saxophonist Harold Land was born in Texas in 1928 and raised in California, but he shares many of the characteristics of the hard-edged, blues-based Texas tenor players. He came to prominence as a member of the Max Roach/Clifford Brown band in the mid-1950s, then moved back to Los Angeles, where he established a strong local reputation and made a series of hard-bop recordings, eventually coleading a strong group with vibraphonist Bobby Hutcherson. *Eastward Ho!* features Kenny Dorham on trumpet. *The Fox* mixes Land originals with four compositions by pianist Elmo Hope. *Xocia's Dance* is a reunion date with Hutcherson. Land mellowed on the ballads-and-strings recording *A Lazy Afternoon.* — J.S.

ART LANDE

★★★ **Red Lanta (ECM, 1973)**
★★★ **Rubisa Patrol (ECM, 1976)**
★★ **We Begin (ECM, 1987)**

Pianist Art Lande (b. 1947) grew up in the United States but was discovered in Europe during the mid-'70s by ECM founder Manfred Eicher, who teamed him with saxophonist/flautist Jan Garbarek on *Red Lanta.* Lande's impressionistic piano playing was a natural match with Garbarek's ethereal style. Lande followed with *Rubisa Patrol,* a quartet effort featuring trumpeter Mark Isham and Bill Douglas on bass and bamboo flute. This band's atmospherics anticipate world music's multiculturalism. Lande and Isham on synth trumpet delve into the even more abstract realms of New Age music on *We Begin.* Lande fans should look for the out-of-print solo-piano album *The Eccentricities of Earl Dant.* — J.S.

SONNY LANDRETH

★★½ **Blues Attack (1981; AVI, 1996)**
★★ **Down in Louisiana (1985; Epic, 1993)**
★★★½ **Outward Bound (Zoo/BMG, 1992)**
★★★★ **South of I-10 (Zoo/BMG, 1995)**

Pity the guitarist who has to fill Ry Cooder's shoes—unless he's Lafayette, Louisiana's Sonny Landreth (b. 1951). When John Hiatt needed a guitar foil to replace Cooder after their collaboration on Hiatt's 1987 breakthrough *Bring the Family,* Landreth stepped in and helped make Hiatt's 1988 *Slow Turning* a masterpiece. A lengthy tenure as the six-stringer in zydeco king Clifton Chenier's band nurtured Landreth's gift for succinct accompaniment and improvisation, but Landreth's trump card is his unique fretting, an original blending of bottleneck Delta blues and Chet Atkins–like picking that gives his slide playing a wide-open, soaring quality. Before his association with Hiatt opened the door for his major-label debut, *Outward Bound,* Landreth had already recorded the two independent efforts *Blues Attack* and *Down in Louisiana,* both later rereleased. This pair of early releases offers only limited glimpses into Landreth's potential: *Blues Attack* is a homey acoustic collection of classic material like Big Bill Broonzy's "Key to the Highway," though the title track is a powerhouse staple of Landreth's live shows. Tentative vocals are the weakness here, the same problem that holds back *Down in Louisiana*'s full-band approach (harmonica player Mel Melton's journeyman singing on various tracks doesn't help either, though the record is notable for the first appearance of Landreth's "Congo Square," later covered by the Neville Brothers). *Outward Bound* introduced Landreth to the world and showed his previously hidden gift for studio wizardry. Songs like "Soldier of Fortune" and "Sacred Ground" present Landreth's glorious slide playing glimmering in a swirl of effects, adding resonance to his blossoming songwriting skills. John Hiatt guests on "New Landlord" and "Common-Law Love"—two torqued-up barnburners—and Landreth's vocals show a new confidence and maturity.

All Landreth's gifts come together on *South of I-10,* a thematic exploration of southern Louisiana featuring special guests Mark Knopfler, Allen Toussaint and ex-Subdude Tommy Malone. The album boasts something for everyone: Landreth reclaims "Congo Square" with a definitive spooky version, sears the instrumental slide showcase "Native Stepson" and goes *mano a mano* with Toussaint on the slide-and-piano "Mojo Boogie." "Cajun Waltz" is a tender and affecting love song, and the autobiographical title track fondly recalls his days with Chenier, noting, "South of I-10/We really had it made." It's enchanting music like Landreth's that draws almost half a million fans to the New Orleans Jazz and Heritage Festival each year. — S.J.

JONNY LANG

★★★½ **Lie to Me (A&M, 1997)**
★★★★ **Wander This World (A&M, 1998)**

Jonny Lang's music belies his age. His voice may have changed only recently, but this kid (b. 1981) sings the blues like a grown-up, with a gritty, weathered voice and fierce guitar work to match. Though some of Lang's popularity may have initially stemmed from his videogenic looks—then-flowing blond locks and pouty lips—he's proved himself an impressive and serious musician. If nothing else, his obvious respect for the blues and R&B traditions makes him worth a listen.

Lie to Me affirms Lang's conviction that it doesn't take a lifetime of pain to make a guitar weep. Songwriting may be another story, however. Thankfully, Lang cowrote only 2 of his debut's 12 tracks. He's far more impressive covering Sonny Boy (John Lee) Williamson's "Good Morning Little School Girl" or Ike Turner's "Matchbox" or blazing through tunes by his keyboard player Bruce McCabe than he is leading his band through his own less-than-memorable love songs. The songwriting shows improvement and more maturity on Lang's very strong follow-up, *Wander This World,* which again showcases his soulful vocals and fiery guitar work. — A.A.

PRINCE LASHA

★★★★ **Firebirds (with Sonny Simmons) (1967; Original Jazz Classics, 1995)**

Multi-instrumentalist Prince Lasha, born William Lawsha in 1929, came out of the same high school class in Fort Worth, Texas, that produced Ornette Coleman and King Curtis—and it shows. Steeped in the emotional directness of blues playing, he shoots for the kind of spiritual zeal in his alto-saxophone and flute playing that characterized the finest moments of the experimental new music that thrived in the '60s and '70s before neotraditionalism steamrollered that movement during the Reagan era.

Lasha settled in the San Francisco Bay Area during the '60s and became an important part of the regional jazz scene there, playing frequently with another free-thinking multi-instrumentalist, Sonny Simmons. Simmons and Lasha shoot for the stars on the spectacular alto dialog *Firebirds.* The pair also appear on *Illumination!* (Elvin Jones and Jimmy Garrison Sextet) and the magnificent *Journey to Zoar.* Also look for the out-of-print gem *Firebirds Live at Berkeley Jazz Festival.* — J.S.

YUSEF LATEEF

★★★½ **Jazz Moods (1957; Verve, N.A.)**
★★★★ **Prayer to the East (1957; Savoy, N.A.)**
★★★ **Before Dawn (1958; Verve, N.A.)**
★★★½ **Other Sounds (1959; Original Jazz Classics, 1992)**
★★★½ **Cry!/Tender (1960; Original Jazz Classics, 1991)**
★★★★ **The Three Faces of Yusef Lateef (1960; Original Jazz Classics, 1992)**
★★★★½ **The Centaur and the Phoenix (1960; Original Jazz Classics, 1992)**
★★★★ **Eastern Sounds (1961; Original Jazz Classics, 1991)**
★★★★ **Live at Pep's (1964; Impulse!, 1993)**

★★★½ **The Blue Yusef Lateef (1968; Atlantic, 1992)**
★★★★ **Into Something (1969; Original Jazz Classics, 1992)**
★★★½ **The Gentle Giant (1972; Atlantic, 1987)**
★★★½ **The World at Peace (YAL, N.A.)**
★★★★★ **Every Village Has a Song: The Yusef Lateef Anthology (Rhino, N.A.)**
★★★★½ **The Man with the Big Front Yard (32 Jazz, 1998)**

Yusef Lateef (b. 1920), a multi-instrumentalist master of a large variety of reeds and flutes, grew up influenced by the swing tradition, the huge, warm tone of Coleman Hawkins on tenor saxophone and the hard blues of the jump band tenor honkers. He is a virtuoso on flutes from all over the world and the greatest oboe player in jazz history, with a restless musical spirit that always seeks new sounds to explore. Years before the terms fusion or world music were coined, Lateef was obsessed with combining folk music from other cultures with jazz.

Lateef was an integral part of the Detroit jazz scene of the 1950s, making his debut as a leader there. *Before Dawn* and *Jazz Moods* document Lateef as a well-developed tenor saxophone stylist leading a Detroit band consisting of trombonist Curtis Fuller, pianist Hugh Lawson, bassist Ernie Farrow and drummer Louis Hayes. On *Cry!/Tender* Lateef plays tenor, flute and oboe in two quintet settings, one with trumpeter Lonnie Hillyer, the other with flügelhornist Wilbur Harden. *Other Sounds* shows Lateef moving into experiments with Middle Eastern music on his own "Minor Mood" and "Mahaba" while still playing with Harden, Lawson, Farrow and drummer Oliver Jackson. These same players take the concept even further on *Prayer to the East,* with its atmospheric title track moving perfectly into "Night in Tunisia."

In 1959 Lateef moved to New York, where he began playing with some of the best local players and became a sought-after sideman and leader. Charles Mingus called on him for his versatility, Randy Weston for his knowledge of African music and Cannonball Adderley for the soulful fire of his playing. *The Three Faces of Yusef Lateef,* his first New York session as a leader, plays on his triple-threat improvisational skills on tenor, flute and oboe on a mixed program of jazz standards and experiments like "Lateef Minor 7th." *The Centaur and the Phoenix* is a fascinating session with Lateef playing the bassoonlike argol along with tenor, flute and oboe, fronting a horn section made up of Fuller, Clark Terry and Richard Williams on trumpets, Tate Houston on baritone sax and Josea Taylor on bassoon, and a rhythm section commandeered by Joe Zawinul on piano.

Lateef reaches into more delicate territory on the fully realized *Eastern Sounds,* a quartet date with Barry Harris on piano in which the individual songs work together effectively to form a kind of suite. He adds some gorgeous bamboo flute work to his list of accomplishments. *Into Something* heads aggressively back into mainstream bop territory with a quartet including Harris and drummer Elvin Jones, but Lateef's four originals make it anything but a stylistically conservative recording. *Live at Pep's,* a hot Philadelphia quintet date from 1964, documents Lateef's great live sound (including his mastery of the oboe-derived shenai) as well as his popularity with contemporary black audiences of the time.

Lateef's Atlantic albums were vertiginous rides, offering in equal measure breakthroughs and experimental failures. *The Blue Yusef Lateef* and *The Gentle Giant* each have their moments, but the compilations of Lateef's work that include a broader sampling of his Atlantic recordings are preferable. *The Man with the Big Front Yard* is the best overview of his Atlantic sides. *Every Village Has a Song: The Yusef Lateef Anthology* is even better because it covers his whole career. *The World at Peace* is a soothing world-music ensemble recording released on Lateef's own YAL label. — J.S.

AZAR LAWRENCE

★★★ **Bridge into the New Age (1977; Prestige, 1994)**
★★★ **Summer Solstice (1978; Prestige, 1995)**

A dead-earnest Coltrane disciple, tenor and soprano saxophonist Azar Lawrence (b. 1953) grew up in Los Angeles playing the violin, then alto saxophone before reaching a career high point as sideman with both the Elvin Jones and the McCoy Tyner bands during 1973. Solo albums show him in a similar light, carrying the influence of Coltrane into the more populist realms of '70s funk and proto–trance jazz. — J.S.

RONNIE LAWS

★★★ **Pressure Sensitive (1975; Blue Note, 1995)**
★★ **Fever (1976; Blue Note, 1993)**
★★ **Pressure (1979; Rhino, 1993)**

★★ **Mirror Town (Columbia, 1986)**
★★ **All Day Rhythm (Columbia, 1987)**
★★★ **Deep Soul (Par, 1992)**
★★★ **The Best of Ronnie Laws (Blue Note, 1992)**
★★★ **Brotherhood (Intuition, 1995)**
★★½ **Natural Laws (Capitol, 1995)**
★★½ **Tribute to the Legendary Eddie Harris (Blue Note, 1997)**

Ronnie Laws (b. 1950) came out of the Houston blues/jazz scene emulating soul-jazz saxophonists like David "Fathead" Newman while being influenced by other locals—from his flautist brother Hubert to the Jazz Crusaders. Ronnie is equally at home playing blues, R&B, jazz and rock styles; he's performed as a sideman with Hugh Masekela and Earth, Wind and Fire. His solo recordings never overcame the fusion/disco formula that dominated jazz albums produced by major labels in the 1970s and 1980s, but his emotional, groove-oriented playing animates at least part of each album and works to good effect on *Pressure Sensitive, The Best of Ronnie Laws, Deep Soul* and *Brotherhood.* — J.S.

LAZY LESTER

★★★★ **Harp and Soul (Alligator, 1988)**
★★★★★ **I Hear You Knockin'! The Excello Singles (Excello, 1994)**

Leslie "Lazy Lester" Johnson (b. 1933) developed a Jimmy Reed–inspired harmonica style that became one of the staples of the southern-Louisiana sound coined by producer Jay Miller in Crowley, Louisiana, during the 1950s and '60s. From 1957 to 1966 Johnson was a mainstay in Miller's studio, playing harmonica, guitar, washboard and percussion on a variety of sessions. Johnson's "cardboard box" percussion technique can be heard on a number of sides, including some of Slim Harpo's hits, and he played harmonica on Lightnin' Slim's records as well as in his touring band.

As Lazy Lester, Johnson recorded a series of regional hits, including "I'm a Lover, Not a Fighter," "I Hear You Knockin' " and "Sugar Coated Love," that were later covered by younger fans in rock and blues bands such as the Kinks, Dave Edmunds and the Fabulous Thunderbirds. This material is collected on the Excello compilation.

Johnson moved to Pontiac, Michigan, in the mid-1970s and began to tour again in the 1980s after the Thunderbirds focused attention on him by covering his songs and featuring him at the New Orleans Jazz and Heritage Festival. In 1987 he made a comeback album, the currently out-of-print *Lazy Lester Rides Again,* backed by the English band Blues 'n Trouble.

Johnson is in top form once more on *Harp and Soul,* backed by an all-star support cast including guitarist Kenny Neal and Muscle Shoals alumnus Pete Carr. — J.S.

LEAD BELLY

★★★★★ **Lead Belly's Last Sessions (1953; Smithsonian Folkways, 1994)**
★★★ **Leadbelly Sings Folk Songs (1968; Smithsonian Folkways, 1989)**
★★★ **Leadbelly (Capitol, 1969)**
★★★★ **Alabama Bound (RCA, 1989)**
★★★ **Bourgeois Blues: Golden Classics (Collectables, 1989)**
★★★★ **Defense Blues: Golden Classics, Part Two (Collectables, 1990)**
★★★★ **King of the Twelve-String Guitar (Columbia/Legacy, 1991)**
★★★★★ **Lead Belly, Vol. 1: Midnight Special (Rounder, 1991)**
★★★★★ **Lead Belly, Vol. 2: Gwine Dig a Hole to Put the Devil In (Rounder, 1991)**
★★★★★ **Lead Belly, Vol. 3: Let It Shine on Me (Rounder, 1991)**
★★★★★ **Lead Belly, Vol. 4: The Titanic (Rounder, 1994)**
★★★★★ **Lead Belly, Vol. 5: Nobody Knows the Trouble I've Seen (Rounder, 1994)**
★★★★★ **Lead Belly, Vol. 6: Go Down Old Hannah (Rounder, 1994)**
★★★★ **Storyteller Blues (Drive Archive, 1994)**
★★★★ **Lead Belly Memorial Album, Vols. 1 and 2: The Stinson Collector's Series (Collectables, 1995)**
★★★★ **Lead Belly Memorial Album, Vols. 3 and 4: The Stinson Collector's Series (Collectables, 1995)**
★★★ **Lead Belly Party Songs & Sings and Plays: The Stinson Collector's Series (Collectables, 1995)**
★★★★★ **Where Did You Sleep Last Night: Lead Belly Legacy, Vol. 1 (Smithsonian Folkways, 1996)**
★★★★★ **Bourgeois Blues: Lead Belly Legacy, Vol. 2 (Smithsonian Folkways, 1997)**

Perhaps no sentiment better describes the hardscrabble life of Louisiana-born Huddie

Ledbetter (ca. 1885–1949), popularly known as Lead Belly (at the family's request, the nickname is now spelled as two words), than the title of the fifth of Rounder's six volumes of his music, *Nobody Knows the Trouble I've Seen.* Born in a small town near the Arkansas, Louisiana and Texas borders, Lead Belly grew up working the fields (and attending school—a luxury made possible by his father having risen above the rank of sharecropper to become a landowner himself) and, as he matured, making the most of his free Saturday nights by hanging out at the local square dances, called sukey jumps. Inspired by the music he heard at these functions, he took up guitar, harmonica and accordion; at the same time, he began writing songs and recasting in his own style old folk songs, field hollers, dance numbers and gospel shouts meant to entertain the weekend revelers. Blessed with a steel-trap memory, he amassed a repertoire numbering hundreds of songs new and old, many of these topical numbers reflecting turn-of-the-century rural folkways—a rich and priceless diary of an otherwise poorly documented culture.

By his early teens Lead Belly was on the road, wandering around the South and playing his music wherever he could find an audience. Sometime between 1912 and 1915 he befriended Texas blues giant Blind Lemon Jefferson, and the two traveled and played together "for years," by Lead Belly's own account. Unfortunately, Lead Belly's hair-trigger temper surfaced easily in the heated environment of the sukey jumps, and jail became something of a second home for him in his late teens, when a series of minor infractions landed him on the wrong side of the law. He killed a man in a dispute over a woman and in 1918 was sentenced to 30 years at the Shaw Prison Farm in Texas. He was paroled in 1925 after playing for Governor Pat Neff during one of the latter's tours of the prison camp. Back he went to rambling, scuffling and supporting himself through his music. In 1930 he was convicted of assault with intent to murder and was incarcerated at the Louisiana State Penitentiary in Angola, with no parole date in sight.

In 1933 folklorists John Lomax and his son Alan were touring the South, recording blues, work, religious and folk songs for the Library of Congress, an assignment that often took them into prisons, where the black inmates proved to be a rich source of the roots material they were seeking. At Angola they found Lead Belly, a mother lode they had not anticipated discovering. By this time Lead Belly had learned maybe thousands of songs; given the hard times he knew, his material, original and otherwise, was exceptional in many ways but especially for the great humanity and worldly, wry sense of humor informing his tales. The Lomaxes recorded him, helped secure a pardon for him in 1935, then brought him to New York, where he worked for a while as John Lomax's chauffeur. A year later Lead Belly married his longtime female companion, Martha Promise, and settled in New York City. An instant hit in the clubs and throughout the Northeast, he was embraced by the important folk artists of the time, notably Pete Seeger and Woody Guthrie, which earned him the enmity of conservative critics, who castigated him as "the darling of the old Left." In 1940 he took an apartment in lower Manhattan and joined the Headline Singers, whose members included Woody Guthrie, Sonny Terry and Brownie McGhee. At that time he began recording his songs for various labels and even made one short film, *Three Songs by Leadbelly,* in 1945. For the Library of Congress he recorded 135 songs, dating back to the prison sessions; other than that, his most productive association was with Moses Asch's labels beginning in 1941, for which he reprised, in slightly different form, many of the songs he had recorded for the Lomaxes but also brought in a trove of new numbers. He toured constantly following the end of World War II and was performing in Europe in late '49 when the ravages of Lou Gehrig's disease forced him to return to New York, where he died on December 6.

The wealth of recordings Lead Belly left behind offers abundant opportunities to examine the full breadth and depth of the man's music. At the top of the list are the 1994 four-disc boxed set *Lead Belly's Last Sessions* and Rounder's six-volume collection of Lomax-recorded work. The former, originally issued as a pair of two-record sets in 1953, presents a breathtaking overview of both the artist and his art. Recorded over the course of three nights in 1949 in the apartment of his friend Frederic Ramsey Jr., a noted folk-music enthusiast/scholar, *Lead Belly's Last Sessions* is presented with virtually no editing and all the songs sequenced on disc in the order of their performance, with between-songs patter included. This is Lead Belly at work, to be sure, but also relaxed and voluble—

the man was a born storyteller. Over the course of 96 songs, he relates the folklore behind nearly every song's origin or offers some telling anecdote from his own life that relates to the music about to be played. At times he is accompanied by his wife, Martha, but the largest part of this set is the pure, unadulterated, solo folk artist in full flower. Encouraged to go where the muse took him, Lead Belly essays everything from work songs to folk songs to sacred songs to bawdy songs to topical material with sociological bite to the baldly commercial fare that is equal parts folk- and pop-influenced. Treasures abound: Listen to the strong, heartfelt singing, the vitality evident in his conversation, the ringing, percussive 12-string guitar work and try to imagine Lead Belly as a man nearing the end of his life; it doesn't seem possible.

Of the Rounder sets, *Midnight Special* documents Lead Belly's earliest Library of Congress sessions, including those recorded while he was still in prison. Like *Last Sessions,* this presents the entire scope of Lead Belly's repertoire: The blues and work ballads of *Vols. 1* and *2* lead to *Vol. 3*'s (*Let It Shine on Me*) spiritually oriented material and protest songs. *The Titanic* centers largely on topical numbers, such as the title track, and musings about specific people and places ("Blind Lemon Blues," "Mister Tom Hughes' Town," "Henry Ford Blues"), as does *Nobody Knows the Trouble I've Seen,* which includes "Rock Island Line" and the two-part chronicle of a headline-making event, "The Hindenburg Disaster." The set closes on an introspective note with *Go Down Old Hannah,* a collection of spiritual songs ("Amazing Grace," "Old Time Religion") and folk monuments such as "John Henry." Curiously, the final three Rounder volumes lack specific information about the song selections and in fact reprint the same liner notes from disc to disc—a common practice among budget labels but unusual for a company as dedicated to roots history as Rounder.

Between the Library of Congress recordings and the *Last Sessions* set come the years when Lead Belly recorded for Moses Asch, who issued the songs on his Asch, Disc, Solo, Signature and Folkways labels. *Where Did You Sleep Last Night* and *Bourgeois Blues* are the first two releases of a planned three-CD reissue of Lead Belly/Asch sessions previously issued on four Folkways LPs. These two single-disc versions contain most of the tracks from three of the original four vinyl releases of *Lead Belly Legacy* (*Vol. 2* also contains tracks from the Folkways LP *Midnight Special,* including the title song). Recorded between 1941 and 1946, the selections range from a 1943 recording of "Irene" with Sonny Terry sitting in on harmonica; autobiographical songs such as "Cotton Fields," "Bring a Little Water Sylvie" and "4, 5 and 9" (the last an account of Lead Belly's mistreatment at the hands of bigoted Hollywood executives, with accompaniment provided by Terry, Brownie McGhee on guitar, Pops Foster on bass and the great stride pianist Willie "the Lion" Smith); sukey-jump tunes; children's play songs; spirituals (a powerful "Let It Shine on Me," "Meeting at the Building"); and blues. On most of the tracks Lead Belly is heard with only his 12-string (one of the fascinating exceptions to this rule is his button-accordion work behind his vocal on "Sukey Jump [Win' Jammer]"), but on a few tracks, as noted above, some interesting musicians join the sessions. In addition, both releases include a detailed booklet complete with abbreviated biography (and in the case of *Vol. 2,* an appreciation penned by Woody Guthrie); notes on songs, personnel and recording dates; a bibliography; and an archivist's explanations of the technology employed during the original recordings and in the latter-day audio-restoration process.

In the mid-'40s Asch was partners with Herbert Harris of the Stinson Recording Company. When they split up, Harris was given some of the Lead Belly masters, which have surfaced on the Stinson label in four volumes titled *Memorial.* These feature the artist, his bold voice and his 12-string guitar in a variety of contexts encompassing virtually every type of song Lead Belly played. *Vol. 1* is a program of work songs, blues and spirituals; *Vol. 2,* more of the same, with Lead Belly playing piano-concertina as well as 12-string; *Vol. 3* is a collection of previously unreleased masters and once-rare tracks; *Vol. 4* finds Lead Belly telling his life story in song, traveling from the cotton fields to prison to the urban jungle (some of this material is duplicated on Collectables' *Bourgeois Blues*).

Alabama Bound chronicles the artist's commercially unproductive stint with the Victor and Bluebird labels, which nonetheless produced some interesting fare, even if it didn't catapult Lead Belly to the popular acclaim he sought. Of note here are eight tracks recorded in 1940 with the Golden Gate Jubilee Quartet, who would become one of that decade's most influential gospel groups. As always, the quality and variety of material, along with Lead Belly's own performances, are spellbinding. The excellent *King of the Twelve-String Guitar* restores to print Lead Belly's first commercial sessions, recorded in 1935. *Leadbelly Party Songs & Sings and Plays* and *Leadbelly Sings Folk Songs* both find the artist whooping it up with other artists, including Woody Guthrie, Cisco Houston, Sonny Terry and, on *Sings and Plays,* Josh White. The 16-track *Storyteller Blues* and *Defense Blues* both include material available on better-annotated sets but are solid if perfunctory overviews of specific aspects of the artist's sensibility, particularly with regard to highly personal songs and other, more socially conscious fare such as that found on *Defense Blues.* In whatever form it shows up, the music made by this complex, proud artist is rarely less than compelling, almost always instructive in its observations of the human condition and cautionary in suggesting America be diligent in applying its Constitution's promise to the disenfranchised among its populace. — D.M.

BRYAN LEE

★★★½ **Live at the Old Absinthe House Bar . . . Friday Night (Justin Time, 1997)**
★★★½ **Live at the Old Absinthe House Bar . . . Saturday Night (Justin Time, 1998)**

New Orleans blues guitarist Bryan Lee (b. 1945) has been a fixture on the Bourbon Street scene for many years, burning it up night after night with his Jump Street Five and often jamming with visiting blues and rock stars. The Old Absinthe House bar, the New Orleans landmark where Lee's was the house band, was razed under cover of night and replaced by a frozen daiquiri bar in 1997. Fortunately, Lee had documented his performances at the Old Absinthe House, including a jam session with Louisiana guitarist Kenny Wayne Shepherd, before its demise. Lee and the Jump Street Five have moved their act down Bourbon Street to the Opera House, but their magic nights at the Old Absinthe House can be relived on these energetic recordings. — J.S.

PEGGY LEE

★★★ **Miss Peggy Lee (Columbia, 1957)**
★★★★½ **Beauty and the Beat! Peggy Lee with George Shearing (1959; Capitol Jazz, 1992)**
★★★ **Basin Street East Proudly Presents Peggy Lee (1961; Blue Note, 1995)**
★★½ **Let's Love (Atlantic, 1974)**
★★★½ **Mirrors (A&M, 1975)**
★★★ **Close Enough for Love (DRG, 1979)**
★★★ **The Best of Peggy Lee (MCA, 1980)**
★★★★ **Capitol Collectors Series: The Early Years (Capitol, 1990)**
★★★ **The Peggy Lee Songbook: There'll Be Another Spring (MusicMasters, 1990)**
★★★ **All-Time Greatest Hits (Curb, 1990)**
★★★★★ **Love Held Lightly: Rare Songs by Harold Arlen (Angel, 1993)**
★★★★ **Black Coffee and Other Delights: The Decca Anthology (Decca, 1994)**
★★★★★ **Spotlight on Peggy Lee (Capitol, 1995)**

As well as being one of the major popular singers of her generation, Peggy Lee, born Norma Delores Egstrom in Jamestown, North Dakota, in 1920, is also a songwriter of note whose work includes both pop songs and film scores; she was a persuasive enough actress to have been nominated for an Academy Award for Best Supporting Actress in 1955's *Pete Kelly's Blues,* starring and directed by Jack Webb (who played a jazz musician—clearly Lee added some much-needed authenticity to the music scenes). When rock & roll pushed classic American pop off the charts in the '50s, her career remained strong, as if she fit right in with the new sensibility. In short, her professional achievements are remarkable by any standard, and perhaps more so in light of her tortured personal history of four failed marriages, a childhood marred by the early death of her mother and her father's subsequent remarriage to a woman who physically and verbally abused her, and numerous debilitating health problems over the years.

That Lee has enjoyed the public's enduring affection is unsurprising. Her voice is a comforting but beguiling purr, delicate and suggestive all at once, most commanding of attention when she cuddles up to a lyric or affects an easy, sensuous swagger that lends a touch of blue to her phrasing. Passionate and sensual, Lee projects high romance, stylish living and the allure of sustained desire. When in 1941 Benny Goodman saw her in Chicago and signed her to sing in his band, she had been knocking around the hinterlands and in small-time California clubs for some seven years; but in that time she had perfected a vocal approach that would become her trademark: throaty, intimate phrasing that imparted the barely contained heat of sexual longing.

A 1943 release, "Why Don't You Do Right?," brought Lee her first national attention, but it was 1945's "Waitin' for the Train to Come In," a pop hit that peaked at #4 and was on the chart for 14 weeks, that begat an astounding run of hit singles, over two decades' worth (35 reaching the Top 30 in the bountiful period between 1945 and 1954), culminating in 1969's detached, chilling reading of Leiber and Stoller's melancholy "Is That All There Is?," a Top 20 pop single. Of all her many scintillating performances, though, the one with which she is most readily identified is her 1958 Top 10 interpretation of "Fever," done in a smoldering, yearning style. The song had been a hit in 1956 in a considerably more upbeat version by Little Willie John, but Lee added some new lyrics of her own and emoted in a sultry, come-on voice that was direct and to the point in its expressed desire for physical intimacy right now.

The first of Lee's two productive tenures at Capitol Records is given a wide overview on the Capitol Collectors Series entry *The Early Years,* which covers the period from 1945 to 1950; a newer Capitol release, *Spotlight on Peggy Lee,* focuses on her second stay at Capitol (1958–1969). The latter's 18 tracks include "Fever," here in a stereo mix from the original three-track recording, previously released only on an EP, now long out of print; and a powerful, heartbreaking reading of the Jule Styne/Sammy Cahn pop classic "It's Been a Long, Long Time." These two eras bookend a two-year stint (1952–1954) at Decca, chronicled in depth on *Black Coffee and Other Delights: The Decca Anthology.* During this period she remained a perennial Top 30 presence and recorded some first-rate sides with Gordon Jenkins's orchestra, including 1952's #3 single "Lover."

Although most of Lee's Capitol albums are out of print, supplanted by the two collections noted above, the Capitol Jazz imprint has recently brought two landmark efforts back into the catalog. Of these the most impressive is *Beauty and the Beat!,* the 1959 live album Lee cut with the exemplary George Shearing Quintet, whose guitar-piano-vibes lineup, buttressed by an unobtrusive rhythm section, was as impressive on hard-swinging numbers as it was on mellow fare that demanded a feather-light approach (Shearing's guitarist, by the way, was Toots Thielemans); taking a page out of the Cal Tjader and Vince Guaraldi textbooks, Shearing incorporated into his repertoire some rhythmic experiments, particularly those of an Afro-Cuban nature. On this album he brings on conga master Armando Peraza to add some propulsion to his own lively "Mambo in Miami" instrumental interlude and to the feisty ensemble work on Duke Ellington's "Satin Doll"; he also provides some dash to a Latinized version of Cole Porter's "Always True to You in My Fashion," as he engages Shearing in some friendly instrumental sparring while Lee's airy vocal soars over it all like a cornet lead line. Elsewhere, Lee guides the audience through a range of emotional experiences, from the giddy "Do I Love You?" and the witty put-downs of "Get Out of Town" (both Cole Porter numbers) to tender evocations of a woman coming to grips with lost love on "All Too Soon," a beautiful Carl Sigman/Duke Ellington meditation, to her self-penned "There'll Be Another Spring," a statement of hope and resurrection sung with a broken heart. It's not enough to say that Lee's voice gets under the skin; more important, she puts on a virtuoso display of her blues singer's gift for turning a phrase in such a way that new worlds are revealed. The CD reissue also contains a bonus in two additional studio tracks cut shortly after the live date, Rodgers and Hart's "Nobody's Heart (Belongs to Me)," performed with the Shearing trio; and a Hammerstein/Kern gem, "Don't Ever Leave Me," with Lee accompanied only by Shearing on what stands as one of her most intimate, vulnerable performances on record.

By comparison, *Basin Street East Proudly Presents Peggy Lee* cannot match the mastery on display in *Beauty and the Beat!* Part live and part studio recordings, *Basin Street East* finds Lee backed by a 12-piece band and more inclined toward up-tempo material (although the powerful version of "Fever" here is reason enough to own this recording). Her singing is fine throughout—indeed, apart from "Fever," the touching rendition of Cahn/Van Heusen's "The Second Time Around" is one of her most affecting vocals from this time—but on the whole the date lacks the intimacy of her summit with Shearing. This may be unfair to some musicians who exhibit commendable sensitivity to Lee's style, and to the versatility Lee demonstrates on material ranging from pop to jazz to R&B (a couple of lukewarm Ray Charles covers), but the whole is a bit less than the sum of its parts.

In the '70s Lee recorded for several labels, producing some interesting moments without cracking the charts. A 1974 Atlantic album, *Let's Love,* teamed her with Paul McCartney, who wrote and produced the title track. Strangest of the lot is *Mirrors,* an album that was unusual in its time and remains so today. A grandiose Leiber and Stoller production with a full orchestra and an offbeat repertoire of quasi-art songs written especially for Lee, *Mirrors* finds the singer much in her "Is That All There Is?" mold—detached, a bit cynical, weary of the game, struggling to trust her increasingly rare sunny moods (an attitude best expressed in "Feeling Too Good Today Blues"). In the final song, "Longings for a Simpler Time," Lee's icy summary of the album's theme is delivered in a voice haunted by her history. (*Mirrors* would seem to be the prototype for Lee's ill-fated autobiographical Broadway musical from 1983, *Peg,* which opened to devastating reviews and promptly closed. Its most memorable number: a childhood reminiscence titled "One Beating a Day [Maybe More].")

In recent years her physical woes have mounted. In addition to battling diabetes, she is plagued by a respiratory ailment so severe that she requires an oxygen tent wherever she travels; she also has a heart ailment and has been confined to a wheelchair since a mid-'80s onstage fall at Caesars Palace in Las Vegas. Yet the voice and the intellect have not been stilled. This is evident most abundantly on a 1988 recording released on Angel in 1993, *Love Held Lightly: Rare Songs by Harold Arlen.* Perhaps the most blues-influenced of all the giants of American popular-song composers, Arlen found his most formidable interpreter in Lee, who instinctively understood where the blues met pop in Arlen's compositions; moreover, she knew how to render the elegant phrases penned by his all-star lyricists (Ted Koehler, E.Y. Harburg and Johnny Mercer being foremost among equals) into deeply felt murmurings of the heart. All but five of the 14 songs on *Love Held Lightly* are heard here for the first time; and while Lee is backed at times by a nonet, the musicians slip in unobtrusively behind her feathery, searching vocals and give the affair the feel of an intimate, small-club recital that winds up changing a listener's perspective on life and love. This powerful material, some of it penned for unproduced stage and film musicals, becomes, in Lee's hands, a whole, a personal statement culled from disparate sources and turned into a singular monument to great artistry.

The year 1990 saw the release of *The Peggy Lee Songbook: There'll Be Another Spring,* a reconsideration of some of the artist's personal favorites among the hundreds of classic American pop songs she has performed and recorded. Despite her infirmities, Lee's voice retains a seductive charm and her spirit remains strong. Adversity, she has said, "was, and remains, a central theme in my life." Few have made so much of it in song or taught us so much about staying strong in the process. — D.M.

MICHEL LEGRAND

★★★½ I Love Paris (1954; Columbia/Legacy, 1994)
★★★★ Legrand Jazz (1960; Verve, N.A.)
★★★ Michel Legrand at Shelly's Manne-Hole (1968; Verve, 1989)
★★★ Le Jazz Grand (1978; DCC, 1990)
★★★ After the Rain (1982; Original Jazz Classics, 1994)
★★★ Michel Plays Legrand (LaserLight, 1993)
★★★ The Warm Shade of Memory (Evidence, 1995)
★★★ Paris Was Made for Lovers (Laserlight, 1997)

Pianist/composer Michel Legrand was born in Paris, in 1932 and studied classical orchestration, which influenced his work as a film-score composer/arranger as well as his excursions into jazz. *I Love Paris* is an album of songs about Paris, with Miles Davis guesting on trumpet. His most important release, *Legrand Jazz,* features arrangements of jazz classics, including "Jitterbug Waltz," "Night in Tunisia," "Stompin' at the Savoy" and "'Round Midnight," with a stellar cast including Davis, Art Farmer, Donald Byrd and Ernie Royal on trumpets, John Coltrane, Ben Webster and Phil Woods on saxophones and Bill Evans and Hank Jones on piano. — J.S.

J.B. LENOIR

★★★★ His J.O.B. Recordings 1951–54 (1989; Relic, 1994)
★★★★ Vietnam Blues: The Complete L&R Recordings (Evidence, 1995)

J.B. Lenoir (1929–1967) was an extremely talented singer, guitarist and songwriter whose career was hampered by the fact that he wrote songs of overt political protest during the repressive era of the 1950s and early 1960s. *His J.O.B. Recordings 1951–1954* displays Lenoir in his earliest sessions, backed by pianist Sunnyland Slim and guitarist Johnny Shines. *Vietnam Blues: The Complete L&R Recordings* features Fred Below on drums and Willie Dixon on bass. — J.S.

RON LEVY

★★★ **Ron Levy's Wild Kingdom (Black Top, 1987)**
★★★ **Safari to New Orleans (Black Top, 1988)**
★★★½ **B-3 Blues and Grooves (Bullseye Blues, 1993)**
★★★★ **Zim Zam Zoom: Acid Blues on B-3 (Bullseye Blues, 1996)**

The musical career of blues keyboardist Ron Levy, born Reuvin Zev ben Yehoshua Ha Levi in 1951, has spanned nearly three decades and a wide array of genres, from traditional New Orleans–style tunes to the self-proclaimed first-ever acid blues. At 17, he left his native Boston and for eight years backed blues Kings—first Albert, then B.B. From 1976 to 1984 Levy worked with both his own band and Luther "Guitar Junior" Johnson. Then he spent three years with Roomful of Blues and started appearing as a New Orleans session player.

In 1987 Levy released his debut album with his band Wild Kingdom, featuring Roomful alumni (including Greg Piccolo and Ronnie Earl) and members of the Fabulous Thunderbirds (such as Jimmie Vaughan and Kim Wilson). *Ron Levy's Wild Kingdom* and its follow-up, *Safari to New Orleans,* offer fine up-tempo blues tunes and an impressive array of musicians, but Levy's songs aren't particularly memorable.

By the time of his third album in 1993, Levy had also cofounded and was serving as musical director of Rounder subsidiary Bullseye Blues and was producing albums, writing songs and playing sessions for a variety of artists. For his own *B-3 Blues and Grooves,* Levy's style changed considerably, turning from roadhouse blues with vocals to an entirely instrumental set. His capable approach to the B-3 organ delivers some deliciously funky grooves. With *Zim Zam Zoom,* his new sound evolved a step further, becoming looser and incorporating the freer rhythms and dissonant chords of acid jazz to create what he calls acid blues. Whatever they're called, Levy's organ soul-jazz jams are thoroughly groovy. — A.A.

GEORGE LEWIS

★★★★ **George Lewis with Kid Shots (1944; American Music, N.A.)**
★★★★ **George Lewis at Herbert Otto's Party (1949; American Music, 1994)**
★★★★ **The Beverly Caverns Sessions, Vol. 1 (1953; Good Time Jazz, N.A.)**
★★★ **The Beverly Caverns Sessions, Vol. 2 (1953; Good Time Jazz, N.A.)**
★★★ **George Lewis with Guest Artist Red Allen (1955; American Music, 1994)**
★★★★ **Jazz in the Classic New Orleans Tradition (1956; Original Jazz Classics, 1991)**
★★★ **Jazz at Vespers (1957; Original Jazz Classics, N.A.)**
★★★★ **George Lewis of New Orleans (1958; Original Jazz Classics, 1994)**
★★★★ **George Lewis and His New Orleans Stompers (Blue Note, 1998)**

New Orleans clarinet player George Lewis (1900–1968) was an important figure in the resurgence of interest in traditional jazz that took place during the 1950s. This material is best represented on *The Beverly Caverns Sessions Vols. 1* and *2* and *Jazz in the Classic New Orleans Tradition.* He had been a vibrant performer in the genre since the 1920s with such venerable outfits as the Eureka Brass Band but didn't record as a leader until 1943, when he made the Blue Note recordings included on *George Lewis and His New Orleans Stompers. George Lewis of New Orleans* comprises material recorded in 1946 with the Original Zenith Brass Band and the Eclipse Alley Five. — J.S.

GEORGE LEWIS

★★★ **The Imaginary Suite (with Douglas Ewart) (Black Saint, 1973)**
★★★★★ **Homage to Charles Parker (Black Saint, 1979)**
★★★★ **Changing with the Times (New World, 1993)**
★★★★ **Monads (Black Saint, N.A.)**
★★★★★ **The George Lewis Solo Trombone Record (Sackville, N.A.)**

Trombonist/composer George Lewis (b. 1952) is representative of a generation of black musicians prepared and determined to draw upon the most challenging aspects of all musical forms, including electronics and the European tradition. Lewis's own background includes early membership in Chicago's Association for the Advancement of Creative Musicians (AACM), a degree in philosophy from Yale, touring with diverse leaders (Count Basie, Carla Bley, Anthony Braxton, Gil Evans) and direction of the New York experimental composers' forum the Kitchen.

Excluding *The George Lewis Solo Trombone* (one of the finest solo efforts on any wind instrument), most of Lewis's music employs synthesizers, plus a kind of writing—extremely slow-moving textures and situations—in which the soloist is subordinated to the ensemble development. This does not necessarily sound like jazz as even avant-garde fans know it, but it results in stimulating and surprisingly warm contemporary music nonetheless.

Monads is perhaps the best introduction to Lewis's music, with two sextet pieces, a duet by composer/reedman Douglas Ewart (the pair also have an entire album of duets) and one piece where Lewis is bracketed by two pianos.

Ewart is also featured prominently on *Changing with the Times,* a series of pieces set to poetry and monologs relating to the African-American experience.

The out-of-print *Chicago Slow Dance,* by a quartet including Richard Teitelbaum on synthesizer, finds Lewis expanding his techniques to an album-length piece—a convincing effort but one bettered by the excellent *Homage to Charles Parker.* On this work, another quartet (with Ewart, Teitelbaum and Anthony Davis) explores the blues and a more harmonically static form in music that points the way to the future. — B.B./J.S.

MEADE "LUX" LEWIS

★★★ **The Blues Piano Artistry of Meade Lux Lewis (1961; Original Jazz Classics, 1990)**
★★★★ **1939–54 (Story of Blues, 1991)**
★★★★ **Barrelhouse Piano (Jasmine, 1992)**
★★★★ **1927–39 (Classics, 1993)**
★★★★ **1939–41 (Classics, 1994)**
★★★★ **1941–44 (Classics, N.A.)**
★★★★ **Mary Lou Williams and Meade Lux Lewis (Collectables, 1995)**
★★★★ **Tidal Boogie (Tradition, 1996)**

Meade "Lux" Lewis (1905–1964) was one of the best-known practitioners of barrelhouse piano, which he learned in his native Chicago under the influence of Jimmy Yancey. He hit his high point in 1929 with the hard-driving "Honky-Tonk Train Blues," which became his trademark and made him one of the first kings of boogie-woogie, a craze that hung on powerfully. The consistency of Lewis's approach is still apparent on *The Blues Piano Artistry of Meade Lux Lewis,* one of his last recordings. — J.S.

MEL LEWIS

★★★½ **Mel Lewis Sextet (1957; VSOP, 1997)**
★★★½ **Live at the Village Vanguard (1980; DCC, 1991)**
★★★½ **Mel Lewis Jazz Orchestra (1980; Columbia, 1991)**
★★★★ **20 Years at the Village Vanguard (Atlantic, 1986)**
★★★★ **Definitive Thad Jones, Vol. 1 (MusicMasters, 1988)**
★★★ **Definitive Thad Jones, Vol. 2 (MusicMasters, 1988)**
★★★★ **The Lost Art (MusicMasters, 1989)**
★★★½ **To You: A Tribute to Mel Lewis (MusicMasters, 1991)**

Drummer Mel Lewis (1929–1990) developed his remarkable technique for piloting a big band with Gerry Mulligan and Dizzy Gillespie before forming in 1965 with trumpeter Thad Jones a big band that went on to enduring popularity and critical acclaim.

The Jones/Lewis band, though woefully underrecorded, became a fixture at New York's Village Vanguard on Monday nights, where it still flourishes in loving memory of its two departed bandleaders (Jones left the group in 1979 for Europe and died there in '86). The Vanguard live sets and *To You,* a posthumous tribute to Lewis, are noteworthy, as is *Vol. 1* of the Thad Jones tributes.

Lewis's subtle, commanding sense of swing never deserted him, as *The Lost Art,* a magnificent septet date that was one of his final recordings, reveals. On that session Lewis expertly demonstrates the lost art of brush playing, offering a soulful alternative to the monochromatic din of amplified, computerized percussion. — J.S.

RAMSEY LEWIS

★★★½ **The In Crowd (1965; Chess, 1990)**
★★★½ **Maiden Voyage (and More) (1968; GRP, 1994)**
★★★ **Blues for the Night Owl (1972; Columbia, 1981)**
★★★½ **The Best of Ramsey Lewis (1973; Columbia, 1981)**

★★★ **Golden Hits (1973; Columbia, 1989)**
★★★ **Sun Goddess (1974; Columbia, 1987)**
★★★ **Tequila Mockingbird (1977; Columbia, 1987)**
★★★ **Les Fleurs (Columbia, 1979)**
★★★ **Three-Piece Suite (Columbia, 1981)**
★★★½ **Reunion (Columbia, 1982)**
★★★ **Live at the Savoy (Columbia, 1982)**
★★★ **The Two of Us (with Nancy Wilson) (Columbia, 1984)**
★★★ **Keys to the City (Columbia, 1987)**
★★★ **A Classic Encounter (Columbia, 1988)**
★★★ **The Greatest Hits of Ramsey Lewis (Chess, 1989)**
★★★ **We Meet Again (with Billy Taylor) (Columbia, 1989)**
★★★ **Urban Renewal (Columbia, 1989)**
★★★ **The Electric Collection (Columbia, 1991)**
★★★ **Ivory Pyramid (GRP, 1992)**
★★★ **Sky Islands (GRP, 1993)**
★★★ **Between the Keys (GRP, 1996)**
★★★½ **Consider the Source (Chess, 1996)**
★★★ **This Is Jazz 27 (Columbia/Legacy, 1997)**

Chicago's classically trained keyboardist Ramsey Lewis (b. 1935) hit it big in the early '60s with highly commercial jazz covers of pop tunes (Dobie Gray's "The In Crowd," the McCoys' "Hang On Sloopy")—a formula he would continue into the next decade (Stevie Wonder's "Living for the City") and beyond. Starting off as pianist in a standard jazz trio (among its members, Earth, Wind and Fire main man Maurice White), Lewis demonstrated ultracompetent technique and radio savvy, scoring hits with a pop audience few trad players managed to connect with; Chess's *The Greatest Hits of Ramsey Lewis* collects his early acoustic period (1962–1967), and it's nice, if unsurprising, music (check out, as well, *Consider the Source*). Collaborating with Earth, Wind and Fire on *Sun Goddess,* Lewis tackles fusion, making a sort of gentleman's agreement with stylish funk. *Tequila Mockingbird* finds the player deeper into fuzak—the record sold well, his electronic-keyboard work always melodic though never inventive. Lewis continued along these lines for a very long time, only to emerge in 1989 with *We Meet Again,* his strongest album since *Reunion* (with his original rhythm section). A fine, acoustic collaboration with Billy Taylor, *We Meet Again* is a sharp, no-frills set of jazz standards. In the '90s he's recycled some of his hits on *Ivory Pyramid* and *Sky Islands* alongside new material—working always with crack musicians, his albums offer safe, consistent enjoyment. — P.E.

DAVE LIEBMAN

★★★ **Energy of the Chance (Heads Up, 1988)**
★★★ **Setting the Standard (Red, 1992)**
★★★ **Miles Away (Owl/Blue Note, 1994)**
★★★★ **Songs for My Daughter (Soul Note, 1995)**
★★★ **Homage to John Coltrane (Owl/Blue Note, 1996)**
★★★★ **Voyage (Evidence, 1996)**
★★★½ **Return of the Tenor: Standards (Double-Time, 1996)**
★★★½ **New Vista (Arkadia, 1997)**
★★★ **Dave Liebman Plays Cole Porter (Red, N.A.)**

Saxophonist and flautist Dave Liebman (b. 1946) worked in the horn section of the jazz-rock band Ten Wheel Drive before building his reputation as a jazz sideman with Elvin Jones, John McLaughlin and the early-'70s Miles Davis fusion bands.

Liebman's first outing as a leader, *Open Sky,* with bassist Frank Tusa, drummer Bob Moses, pianist Richard Beirach and Liebman on soprano sax, marked him as a force to be reckoned with among the legions of John Coltrane disciples. This record is no longer available, as is the case with the magnificent *Lookout Farm* and the excellent recordings *Pendulum* and *Drum Ode.*

What is available gives an incomplete picture of Liebman's talents. *Energy of the Chance* is just okay. *Homage to John Coltrane* and *Miles Away* are flawed tributes. *Dave Liebman Plays Cole Porter* and *Setting the Standard* are unadventurous looks at a shared tradition that show Liebman's abilities with the canon of standards but say little about his original talents.

On the highly personal *Songs for My Daughter* we finally hear Liebman's genius in the currently available catalog. Liebman is a player with something to say, and it's compelling to hear him unleash honest emotions without regard to the consequences.

Voyage finds Liebman's '90s band—Phil Markowitz on piano and keyboards, Vic Juris on guitars, Tony Marino on basses, Jamey Haddad on drums and Café on percussion—at the top of its form on a mixed program. There are originals by Markowitz and Liebman, as well as Coltrane's "The Drum Thing" and the Herbie Hancock classic "Maiden Voyage." — J.S.

JIMMY LIGGINS

★★★★½ Jimmy Liggins & His Drops of Joy (Specialty, 1990)

★★★½ Rough Weather Blues, Vol. 2 (Specialty, 1992)

With characteristic honking sax solos and boogie bass lines, jump blues constituted the urban, riff-driven transitional stage between jazz and R&B, linking the big-band blues of Count Basie and the pumping rock & roll of Little Richard. In a short 10-year span, ushered in by the likes of Illinois Jacquet and Louis Jordan during World War II, the blues jumped, jived and claimed the commercial charts. Six of those years—1947 to '53—belonged to the brothers Liggins.

Guitarist Jimmy Liggins (1922–1983) was the younger and more blues-focused of the two. His rhythm-and-booze anthem "Drunk" remains a staple of the genre, and his gutsy and inventive arrangements launched a number of his other tunes ("Teardrop Blues," "Careful Love") onto the *Billboard* charts. These songs, along with other examples of his more raucous side ("Saturday Night Boogie-Woogie Man," "Shuffle Shuck") are packed into Specialty's excellent *Jimmy Liggins & His Drops of Joy.*

Rough Weather Blues, Vol. 2 is a noteworthy companion for any student of the jump blues, offering a window on the jazz-R&B bridge that Liggins's band so faithfully explored. Included are test versions of hit tunes, blues that give ample space to Jimmy's distorted guitar playing ("Low Down Blues," "Pleading My Cause"), unnamed instrumentals and a rather back-alley version of the bebop classic "Now's the Time." Beyond his Specialty output, Jimmy is represented by four tracks for Aladdin that have yet to surface. — A.K.

JOE LIGGINS

★★★★★ Joe Liggins & the Honeydrippers (Specialty, 1990)

★★★½ Dripper's Boogie, Vol. 2 (Specialty, 1992)

More jazz-oriented and more the tunesmith than his younger brother, Jimmy, Joe Liggins (1915–1987) rode the R&B charts with a number of jaunty dance songs, ballads and other self-penned jump numbers that still stand as timeless classics of the era.

A veteran of Los Angeles–based jazz bands led by such luminaries as Illinois Jacquet, Joe joined his brother at Specialty in 1950, bringing along a songbook bulging with titles that had already hit for the black-owned independent Exclusive. Unable to make the transition from 78s to 45s, the smaller label had folded, and Specialty signed Joe to rerecord his biggest numbers, "The Honeydripper" and "I've Got a Right to Cry," as well as newer chart-topping jump anthems like "Pink Champagne" (1950's Number One R&B record of the year), "Little Joe's Boogie," "Frankie Lee" and a jazzy cover of the novelty tune "Rag Mop." All these and more—including the way suave sax/guitar workout "Tanya"—are featured on Specialty's *Joe Liggins & the Honeydrippers,* volume, an absolute must for all who are looking to get—or already are—hep to the jive.

For the completist, *Dripper's Boogie, Vol. 2* resurrects 20 more tracks from the archives, including two versions of the instrumental "Little Joe's Boogie." — A.K.

KIRK LIGHTSEY

★★★★ Shorter by Two (Sunnyside, 1983)

★★★½ Lightsey 1 (1983; Sunnyside, 1994)

★★★½ Lightsey Live (Sunnyside, 1986)

★★★★ Everything Is Changed (Sunnyside, 1987)

★★★★ From Kirk to Nat (Criss Cross, 1991)

★★★★★ Goodbye Mr. Evans (Evidence, 1996)

Pianist Kirk Lightsey (b. 1937), well inspired by the blues-rich jazz heritage of his hometown, Detroit, brings the soul and wit of hard bop to a style that never overplays its hand. Lightsey's architectural sense of line and color allows him to reinvent classic compositions from the 1950s and 1960s by Wayne Shorter on *Shorter by Two,* a series of piano solos and duets with Harold Danko.

Lightsey's ideas as a bandleader are as imaginative as his arrangements. *Everything Is Changed* uses the dappling shades of Jerry Gonzalez on trumpet and flügelhorn, Jerry Routch on French horn and Famoudou Don Moye and Chico Freeman on percussion.

From Kirk to Nat, inspired by the classic Nat King Cole Trio, may be the ultimate test of the originality of Lightsey's musical conception. Cole's style, so lucid and filled with simple melodic truths, defies interpretation without cliché. Yet Lightsey manages to shine his own light through this material, taking a cue from his old band mate Chet Baker in his approach to singing "Close Enough for Love," one of two vocals on the album.

Goodbye Mr. Evans is a major statement by the brilliant trio of Lightsey, bassist Tibor Elekes and Moye again on drums. Lightsey is freed from traffic here and weaves a spell augmented by the hypnotic pace of Elekes's bass playing and the multimetrical through-the-pulse time of Moye's drumming. Lightsey's own "Habiba" stands out in a program that includes brilliant takes on Thelonious Monk, Dave Brubeck and Chopin and a medley of "Freedom Jazz Dance," "Pinocchio," "Temptation" and "Giant Steps." — J.S.

LIL' ED AND THE BLUES IMPERIALS

★★★½ **Roughhousin' (Alligator, 1986)**
★★★★½ **Chicken, Gravy & Biscuits (Alligator, 1989)**
★★★ **What You See Is What You Get (Alligator, 1992)**

Slide guitarist Lil' Ed Williams (b. 1955) and his Blues Imperials' first Chicago gig earned them all of six dollars. It would be a while after that night at Big Duke's Blue Flame in 1975 before they found success. For the next decade, they kept their day jobs washing cars and driving school buses while playing clubs on Chicago's West Side. Things looked up when they caught the attention of Alligator Records' Bruce Iglauer, who invited them to play on a sampler album featuring Chicago's young blues talent.

The house-rockin' party band—Williams, bass man James "Pookie" Young (Williams's half brother), second guitarist Dave Weld and drummer Louis Henderson—went into the studio and surprised everyone. After laying down their track for the album, the band kept right on playing their steaming blues. Iglauer offered them a recording contract on the spot, and three hours later they'd recorded 30 songs, with no overdubs or second takes. Ten of those became *Roughhousin',* a lively album that captures the energetic, raw spirit of the evening.

Soon the band was winning rave reviews and playing in festivals and on stages throughout North America, Europe and Japan. By 1989, Weld and Henderson had left the band, and Mike Garrett and Kelly Littleton had taken their respective places. The new lineup released *Chicken, Gravy & Biscuits,* an even more zealous and tighter set (probably benefiting from more recording time and some second takes). Along with the outstanding originals, this collection of rollicking blues includes a cover of "20% Alcohol," by Williams's uncle and first guitar teacher, bluesman J.B. Hutto.

Unfortunately, *What You See Is What You Get* doesn't have much of the earlier albums' spunk. Although the addition of sax man Eddie McKinley injects some energy, Williams and the boys sound tired, playing slow blues that don't grind so much as they plod. — A.A.

ABBEY LINCOLN

★★★ **Affair . . . A Story of a Girl in Love (1956; Blue Note, 1993)**
★★★½ **That's Him! (1957; Original Jazz Classics, 1988)**
★★★ **It's Magic (1958; Original Jazz Classics, 1991)**
★★★★ **Abbey Is Blue (1959; Original Jazz Classics, 1987)**
★★★★ **Straight Ahead (Candid, 1961)**
★★½ **People in Me (1973; Verve, 1993)**
★★½ **Talking to the Sun (1983; Enja, 1993)**
★★★ **Abbey Sings Billie Live! (Enja, 1987)**
★★★ **The World Is Falling Down (Verve, 1990)**
★★★★ **You Gotta Pay the Band (with Stan Getz) (Verve, 1991)**
★★★ **Abbey Sings Billie, Vol. 2 (Enja, 1992)**
★★★ **Devil's Got Your Tongue (Verve, 1993)**
★★★ **When There Is Love (Verve, 1994)**
★★★ **A Turtle's Dream (Verve, 1995)**
★★★ **Who Used to Dance (Verve, 1997)**

Abbey Lincoln (b. 1930) began her career as a cabaret performer and actress but adapted well to a jazz role under the tutelage of drummer Max Roach, who featured her prominently on the historic *Freedom Now Suite,* one of the clarion-call works of the new jazz movement of the 1960s. (Lincoln and Roach were married at the time, as well.)

That's Him! is an impressive session featuring Sonny Rollins and Kenny Dorham with beautiful piano accompaniment from Wynton Kelly and a rhythm section completed by Roach and bassist Paul Chambers. Though several of the same players return for *It's Magic,* the session lacks the focus of *That's Him!* Lincoln went on to the creative triumph of *Abbey Is*

Blue, however, which anticipated her contribution to *Freedom Now. Straight Ahead* uses the same front line as *Freedom Now*—Booker Little on trumpet, Julian Priester on trombone, Coleman Hawkins and Walter Benton on tenor sax—augmented by Eric Dolphy on alto, bass clarinet and flute. Archie Shepp provides fine tenor-saxophone accompaniment to Lincoln on one of several Billie Holiday tributes, *Painted Lady.*

Lincoln's career went into eclipse in the 1970s, with only *People in Me,* a record of mostly her own compositions, surviving. After returning to her inspiration, Billie Holiday, on the Enja sets, Lincoln enjoyed a renaissance at Verve in the 1990s. The best example of her work from this period is *You Gotta Pay the Band.* — J.S.

HIP LINKCHAIN

★★★★ **Airbusters (1987; Evidence, 1993)**

Willie Richard (1936–1989) grew up in Mississippi, taking the nickname Hip Linkchain and learning the country-blues canon from his father and older brother. He moved to Chicago in the early 1950s and played electric blues. As a result, Linkchain's gruff, untutored style combines the accompaniment virtuosity of country blues with the rough-edged groove of the rootsiest urban blues, one step removed from the circuit of roadhouses and juke joints. He made several small-label recordings over the years before breaking through in Europe during the 1980s.

Airbusters showcases Linkchain's driving guitar work, relaxed vocals and talent for original composition with 10 originals, including "House Cat Blues," "Keep On Searching," "Take Out Your False Teeth" and "Fugitive." — J.S.

MANCE LIPSCOMB

★★★★ **Texas Songster (Arhoolie, 1989)**
★★★ **Texas Songster, Vol. 2 (Arhoolie, 1994)**
★★★ **Texas Blues Guitar (Arhoolie, 1994)**

Mance Lipscomb (1895–1976) not only chronicled the myth of the blues but lived it—he took time for his music only after 12-hour days of sharecropper's field work. Yet in the near–half century before he first entered a studio, he'd amassed a vast canon of ballads and jubilees, traditional country blues and vintage period pieces: "Sugar Babe," "Ella Speed," "Angel Child" and "I'm Looking for My Jesus" showcase the subtlety of his conversational singing style and slide-guitar work. Almost always, Lipscomb recorded with no accompaniment other than his guitar—and the music he made, whether witty, racy, haunting or rocking, retains the power of utter directness. With its 22 selections combining his out-of-print debut album and a portion of another unavailable recording, *Texas Songster* provides the best introduction to this classic bluesman. — P.E.

LITTLE BUSTER AND THE SOUL BROTHERS

★★★½ **Right on Time! (Bullseye Blues, 1995)**

Like the Holmes Brothers and Mighty Sam McClain, Little Buster, born Edward Forehand in 1942, successfully brought deep, bluesy soul into the 1990s. Buster moved at age 16 from North Carolina to Long Island, where he and his Soul Brothers played local clubs for 30 years before landing a contract with Bullseye Blues. On their debut, *Right on Time,* Buster and his group effectively recall the music of Otis Redding ("First You Cry") and Al Green ("What Do I Have to Do"), as well as the late-1960s work of B.B. King ("My Darling"). Yet Buster does more than revisit the sounds of the past: His impassioned vocals and his band's tight playing make his music sound fresh, even to jaded ears. — J.K.

LITTLE CHARLIE AND THE NIGHTCATS

★★ **All the Way Crazy (Alligator, 1987)**
★★ **Disturbing the Peace (Alligator, 1988)**
★★½ **The Big Break! (Alligator, 1989)**
★★★ **Captured Live (Alligator, 1991)**
★★★ **Night Vision (Alligator, 1993)**
★★½ **Straight Up! (Alligator, 1995)**
★★★ **Deluxe Edition (Alligator, 1997)**
★★★ **Shadow of the Blues (Alligator, 1998)**

West Coast blues guitarist Little Charlie Baty (b. 1953) and his group of Nightcats began to coalesce in 1976 when Baty first teamed with harmonica player, vocalist and primary songwriter Rick Estrin (b. 1950). The duo soon added two more players to the fray—drummer Dobie Strange and bassist Jay Peterson—and released their first album a little more than a decade later. By that time, the group had established itself as a solid live draw in California, where they were famous for their sweat-soaked, infinitely danceable gigs. Baty, Estrin and Strange have stayed together throughout, and although Peterson departed after the third album (he was replaced by Brad Lee Sexton), the combo has maintained a consistent sound throughout its career. The band's music consists of straight blues, swing instrumentals, '40s and '50s R&B tunes and even a bit of rockabilly—anything to keep the faithful grooving.

While showcasing the band's fine playing, *All the Way Crazy* also illustrates that the group's original songs lack a certain punch. Musically similar, *Disturbing the Peace* is, again, filled with excellent performances and forgettable songs. *Captured Live* more accurately portrays Little Charlie's appeal. Recorded at two California clubs, the album puts into perspective the combo's effect on a smoky roomful of ecstatic fans. Highlights include an Estrin original, "Rain," and a gutbucket reading of "Crawling Kingsnake." *Night Vision,* produced by guitarist Joe Louis Walker, features a horn section for the first time. With stronger material than on previous efforts, the album's highlights include "My Next Ex-Wife," "Sure Seems Strange" and the humorous "Can't Keep It Up." *Straight Up!* features more of the same formula that has kept Little Charlie in business for two decades. The band's forte is clearly playing in a live setting, where its tight ensemble work and fine instrumental skills can take on a life of their own. — B.R.H.

LITTLE MILTON

★★★½ **If Walls Could Talk (1969; Chess, 1988)**
★★★★ **Grits Ain't Groceries (1969; Stax, 1989)**
★★★ **Waiting for Little Milton (1973; Stax, N.A.)**
★★★ **What It Is (1973; Stax, 1989)**
★★★★ **Greatest Hits (1973; Malaco, 1995)**
★★★ **Blues 'n Soul (1974; Stax, 1989)**
★★½ **Tin Pan Alley (1975; Stax, 1989)**
★★★ **Friend of Mine (1977; Collectables, 1993)**
★★★ **Walkin' the Back Streets (1981; Stax, 1989)**
★★★½ **The Blues Is Alright! (1982; Evidence, 1993)**
★★★½ **Movin' to the Country (Malaco, 1987)**
★★★½ **Back to Back (Malaco, 1988)**
★★★ **Too Much Pain (Malaco, 1990)**
★★★★½ **Sun Masters (Rounder, 1990)**
★★★ **Strugglin' Lady (Malaco, 1992)**
★★★ **Me For You, You For Me (Collectables, 1993)**
★★★★★ **Welcome to the Club: The Essential Chess Recordings (MCA, 1994)**
★★★★ **Bobbin' Blues Masters, Vol. 1 (Collectables, 1994)**
★★★½ **Bobbin' Blues Masters, Vol. 2 (Collectables, 1994)**
★★★½ **I'm a Gambler (Malaco, 1994)**
★★★ **Live at Westville Prison (Delmark, 1995)**
★★★ **Little Milton's Greatest Hits (Malaco, 1995)**
★★★½ **Cheatin' Habit (Malaco, 1996)**
★★★ **Count the Days (601, 1997)**
★★★★★ **Greatest Hits (Chess, 1997)**
★★★ **For Real (Malaco, 1998)**
★★★ **Reality (Malaco, 1998)**

Guitarist, vocalist and songwriter Milton Campbell (b. 1934) has spent his life at the forefront of the development of R&B from the blues. As a teen in Mississippi, he performed with Delta blues greats Sonny Boy Williamson (Rice Miller) and Willie Love; he signed to Sun Records in 1953 and began recording with Ike Turner; in 1959, he started his own R&B label (Bobbin') and two years later joined Chess subsidiary Checker. There, beginning in 1961, he scored a string of R&B hits, including "So Mean to Me," "Feel So Bad" and two that crossed over to the pop charts, "We're Gonna Make It" and "Who's Cheating Who?" His gospel-inflected, soulful vocals found another perfect home at Stax, where he began recording in 1971, showing the smoother side of his soulful sound. He's continued making music ever since; for the past 15 years he's been consistently releasing gutsy blues-drenched albums on the Delta independent Malaco.

You can't go wrong with most of Little Milton's extensive catalog. Each phase of his career is represented on CD. Highlights include the Turner-backed recordings for Sun on *Sun Masters,* where Milton is at his most unrestrained. His Bobbin' releases are collected in two volumes on Collectables. Arguably, his finest work was for Checker; part of the Chess 50th Anniversary Series, 1997's *Greatest Hits* consists of 16 crucial tracks, including all the Checker hits. *Welcome to the Club: The Essential Chess Recordings* is more extensive, with two CDs worth of great cuts. (The Malaco hits package compiles 14 of Milton's favorite latter-day tracks.) Milton's Stax sides find the singer in fine form, though the label was beginning to founder and the albums tend to be a little overproduced, giving Milton a slicker vocal sound. Check out *Grits Ain't Groceries* to compare the soulman's style for Stax against the Chicago blues version he cut for Checker in 1968 (then backed by Donny Hathaway on keyboards). He made a foray into the funkier '70s soul sound on *Friend of Mine,* recorded for the small Florida label, T.K., that was the home of K.C. and the Sunshine Band. Keyboardist Lucky Peterson leads Milton's band on the 1983 live prison date. Little Milton's numerous Malaco recordings are also consistently good. Standouts include *Cheatin' Habit* and *I'm a Gambler.* All document a veteran who's never lost the ability to soulfully render a song and get heartbreak out of a guitar. — H.G.-W.

LITTLE WALTER

★★★★★ **The Best of Little Walter (1958; Chess, 1986)**
★★★★★ **Hate to See You Go (1969; Chess, 1990)**
★★★★ **Boss Blues Harmonica (1973; Chess, 1984)**
★★★★ **Little Walter and Otis Rush: Live in Chicago (Quicksilver, 1982)**
★★★★ **The Blues World of Little Walter (Delmark, 1983)**
★★★★ **Superblues: Bo Diddley, Muddy Waters and Little Walter (Chess, 1986)**
★★★★ **The Best of Little Walter, Vol. 2 (Chess, 1989)**
★★★★★ **The Essential Little Walter (Chess, 1993)**
★ **Blues Masters (with Otis Rush) (Tomato, 1994)**
★★★★★ **Blues with a Feeling: Collectables, Vol. 3 (Chess, 1995)**
★★★★ **His Best (Chess, 1997)**

The title of the late Little Walter's Chess release *Boss Blues Harmonica* could hardly be more appropriate. He is acknowledged by blues scholars as the greatest of all blues harmonica players, and his lofty standing rests on the twin poles of skill and invention.

Born near Marksville, Louisiana, Little Walter Jacobs (1930–1968) began playing professionally at age 12 in clubs and on the streets of New Orleans and Monroe. Two years later he migrated north to join the growing blues community in Helena, Arkansas. At that time his playing was redolent with the influences of the two Sonny Boy Williamsons—John Lee Williamson and Rice Miller—but he was also studying the jump blues of Count Basie and Louis Jordan and emulating Jordan's saxophone lines on the harmonica. In Helena he was befriended by Miller and for a while had his own radio show on KFFA, where Miller was holding forth on King Biscuit Time. A restless sort, Jacobs traveled around the South for a couple of years before heading to Chicago in 1947 in the company of Delta bluesman Honeyboy Edwards. Compared with other harmonica players of the day, Jacobs was way ahead of the game, incorporating into his vocabulary various jazz and jump-blues quotations and demonstrating a breathtaking command of intricate melodic patterns.

Almost immediately upon his arrival in the Windy City, Jacobs was working sessions, first with Othum Brown for the Ora Nelle label, then with guitarist Jimmy Rogers for Regal. Through Rogers Jacobs met Muddy Waters, who was becoming Chicago blues' king of the hill. In 1950 he got the call to join Waters's first electric bands for Chess sessions; for five years the volatile harp man's soloing was like a searing second voice to Waters's own in a group that redefined the urban-blues sound for the modern age and laid the last stones to the foundation on which rock & roll was built.

After pestering the Chess brothers to let him record solo, Jacobs got his chance at the end of a Waters session in 1952, when he and the band recorded a stomping instrumental, "Your Cat Will Play," that they had been using as a theme song at the beginning and end of live dates. Retitled "Juke" and issued on Chess's Checker subsidiary, the single was atop the R&B chart by September of 1952, and it stayed there for eight weeks. The sound of Jacobs's amplified harmonica was a thing of wonder, underscoring his absolute mastery of inflection and tone and legitimizing the instrument as a lead voice. Having the biggest hit ever recorded at that time by any of the Delta or Chicago bluesmen, Jacobs left Waters's band midtour to go on his own, backed by a band called the Aces (later renamed the Jukes and boasting a formidable drummer in Fred Below, who would later join Waters), whose harmonica player, Junior Wells, then replaced Jacobs in Waters's band. After a string of nine R&B Top 10 hits, "Juke" was followed by another Number One single, the steady-grooving Willie Dixon–penned "My Babe," which introduced Jacobs's amiable, rough-hewn vocal style, still one of the most underrated aspects of his artistry. Between 1952 and 1958 Jacobs recorded 14 Top 10 R&B hits, a number matched only by Muddy Waters during the same period.

There's no shortage of Little Walter overviews available now; some are more comprehensive than others, naturally, but all afford a good bang for the buck. At the top of the recommended list are two double-CD collections, *The Essential Little Walter* and *Blues with a Feeling: Collectables, Vol. 3.* With surprisingly little duplication of tracks, these packages embrace Jacobs's vital '50s recordings and various band configurations (an ill-tempered man, Jacobs was notoriously difficult to work with, hence a bit of a revolving door when it came to sidemen) and a sampling of his less successful '60s recordings (he had only three Chess sessions between 1960 and 1966), when he was joined by Otis Spann, Luther Tucker and Buddy Guy, among other notables. As a generalization, *The Essential Little Walter*'s 46 tracks represent many of his official Checker singles, along with a smattering of previously unreleased or domestically unissued recordings; *Blues with a Feeling* reverses that formula on its 40 tracks, among these being an alternate take of "Juke" and a growling, brooding alternate version of 1959's "Blue and Lonesome," with Tucker's trembling, spare guitar lines lending a dangerous ambiance in support of Jacobs's desperate vocal and tortured chromatic harp runs.

Those in search of some mostly unadulterated Jacobs vocalizing are directed to *The Best of Little Walter, Vol. 2,* which is top-heavy with some of his most forceful singing, including "Key to the Highway" and the troubling "Boom Boom (Out Go the Lights)." *Hate to See You Go* is a single-CD overview encompassing the years 1952–1960 with instrumental lineups ranging from the early Muddy Waters–Jimmy Rogers configuration to the latter-era groups that featured Robert Jr. Lockwood and, for a moment, Buddy Guy on guitars. Bo Diddley makes an appearance here on his own "Roller Coaster."

Delmark's *The Blues World of Little Walter* fills a gap in that it contains Jacobs's earliest Chicago recordings, made for the Parkway label in January of 1950 and later released on Regal. Its eight tracks feature Jacobs on guitar and harmonica, Muddy Waters and Baby Face Leroy Foster, another Delta bluesman who was part of Waters's first steady band. This group was originally billed as the Baby Face Trio but was identified as the Little Walter Trio on the Regal label. Tracks include two pounding versions of "Rollin' and Tumblin'."

One of Jacobs's final recording efforts for Chess was a mid-'60s summit with Waters and Bo Diddley on the *Superblues* album, a work that has not fared well with blues purists but has some undeniable inspiration working for it. The three principals play like men with hellhounds on their trail, talking trash and spurring one another to deeper performances. The version of Diddley's "Who Do You Love" here is the model for the raging, near-meltdown performance of the tune that Diddley delivers on the soundtrack for *La Bamba.* Jacobs blows low and mean behind Diddley and Waters on the exciting take of "I'm a Man," as the two guitarists spar instrumentally and verbally.

Tomato's *Blues Masters* is a poorly recorded live set, with each artist featured on four cuts recorded in England in the early '60s. Jacobs sounds at the end of his rope here, his voice ragged and flat, his harmonica solos rudimentary and uninvolved, his unidentified band slogging away behind him unsympathetically (particularly the ham-handed drummer). Jacobs sounds awful here, well past his prime; for a better sampling of Little Walter live, check out the rare Quicksilver title *Little Walter and Otis Rush: Live in Chicago.* Even here, though, the ravages of time are evident, despite the persuasive performances. A sad truth, that, since he was a young man of 37 when he died in a violent street fight. The candle he burned at both ends did not last the night, but it gave off a beautiful light.

— D.M.

BOOKER LITTLE

★★★★½ Plus Four (1958; Blue Note, 1991)
★★★★★ Out Front (Candid, 1961)
★★★★ Booker Little and Friend (Bethlehem, 1995)

Before his untimely death at 23 from uremia, Booker Little (1938–1961) was already recognized among his peers as a brilliant trumpeter and a daring and innovative composer/arranger. Chiefly remembered today from his recordings with Max Roach and Eric Dolphy, Little has been too long overlooked and his work too little appreciated despite its belated influence. On his last two albums, particularly *Out Front,* Little began to expand the tonal and metric boundaries of jazz. Unlike Ornette Coleman's groundbreaking work of the same time, Little's employed written arrangements and ensemble playing as well as solo improvisation, predating many of the later structural concerns formulated by progressive jazz artists.

Early examples of Little's precocious trumpet playing can be found on Vee-Jay's *Fantastic Frank Strozier,* an invigorating hard-bop session that featured the saxophonist leader with the Miles Davis rhythm section of the time, and the exceptional, out-of-print *Booker Little,* which teams him with another innovator who passed too quickly, bassist Scott LaFaro. Little's first album, *Plus Four,* is also extremely worthwhile.

A deep melancholy pervades *Out Front,* with its moody off-kilter horn charts and Little's deeply expressive playing. The involvement of Roach and Dolphy (who responds with some of his most heartfelt improvisations) is invaluable throughout the recording. *Out Front* remains an extremely moving masterwork that makes Little's demise all the more regrettable.

Booker Little and Friend (also known, at times, by the more poetic title *Victory and Sorrow*) isn't quite the event that *Out Front* is, but Little continues his formal interests and plays beautifully on it. Little's superb work with Roach (including *We Insist! Freedom Now Suite* and *Percussion Bitter Sweet*) and Dolphy (particularly the live recordings from the Five Spot club) is essential listening. — S.F.

JOHNNY LITTLEJOHN

★★★★½ **Chicago Blues Stars (1968; Arhoolie, 1991)**

John Littlejohn Funchness (1931–1994) learned to play blues growing up in the country near Jackson, Mississippi, and became one of the mainstays of the urban-blues scene around Chicago during the 1950s. His debut shows him to be a master of the form, adapting traditional tunes to his own devices and covering Willie Dixon, J.B. Lenoir and Elmore James, whose slide-guitar influence is one of Littlejohn's several signature stylistic elements. Littlejohn is also an impressive single-note player, strong on the melody and making every note count. His vibrato-free vocal delivery may be the most impressive aspect of his style, however—deep, clear and articulate, with the kind of theatrical control shared only with the very greatest of his peers. The backing band, two tenor saxophonists, rhythm, bass and drums, chops at the groove with just enough roughness about the edges to suit the sound. — J.S.

CHARLES LLOYD

★★★★½ **Forest Flower/Soundtrack (1967/1969; Rhino, 1994)**
★★★½ **A Night in Copenhagen (1983; Blue Note, 1985)**
★★½ **Fish Out of Water (ECM, 1989)**
★★½ **Notes from Big Sur (ECM, 1991)**
★★½ **The Call (ECM, 1993)**
★★½ **All My Relations (ECM, 1995)**

In 1967 Charles Lloyd (b. 1938) was widely heralded as the jazz musician most likely to bridge the gap to younger, rock-oriented audiences. His beautiful, evocative tenor-saxophone playing and fiery flute work had distinguished him in a number of sideman situations, most notably in Chico Hamilton's group. Lloyd's own quartet was magnificent, featuring two of the most expansive, imaginative young players on the scene, drummer Jack DeJohnette and pianist Keith Jarrett, along with the mature, sure-handed accompaniment of bassist Cecil McBee. During the mid-'60s this group left European audiences gasping in its wake and performed several memorable West Coast concerts. Its brightest moment came at the 1966 Monterey Jazz Festival, the set recorded in *Forest Flower* (combined with the live LP *Soundtrack*).

Lloyd's popularity led to a number of other records in the late '60s and early '70s, all of which are presently unavailable. Despite its dated title, *Love-In,* another live set, is particularly worthwhile but hard to find. Lloyd went into semiretirement during the '70s to devote his life to spiritual pursuits but returned to the stage in the early '80s. Of the several live sets recorded during this period, *A Night in Copenhagen,* with a guest appearance from vocalist Bobby McFerrin, remains in print.

Lloyd returned to the studio at the end of the decade to record the first of a series of albums for the ECM label, supported by some of Europe's finest accompanists. His playing is still engaging, but its post–John Coltrane stylings no longer seem quite as riveting. — J.S.

JOE LOCKE

★★★ **Moment to Moment: The Music of Henry Mancini (Milestone, 1995)**

★★★ **Sound Tracks (Milestone, 1997)**
★★★½ **Slander (and Other Love Songs) (Milestone, 1998)**

Vibraphonist Joe Locke (b. 1959) began playing as a teenager in Rochester, New York, taking private lessons from students at the Eastman School of Music. Locke was an accompanist on 1970s dates with Pepper Adams and Billy Hart as well as a sideman in organ-based groups led by Groove Holmes and Jack McDuff.

In the 1980s Locke distinguished himself as a member of the Mingus Big Band and with Kenny Barron, Freddy Cole, Jerry Gonzalez and others. He also began a recording career that led to six difficult-to-find albums on the SteepleChase label and two even more obscure recordings.

Moment to Moment is an acoustic quartet date with pianist Billy Childs, bassist Eddie Gomez and drummer Gene Jackson playing a series of Henry Mancini compositions. Locke's ability to see through cliché to the heart of a piece is evident on his probing arrangement of "Moon River." *Sound Tracks* continues the movie-music angle with such varied material as "The English Patient," the theme from *M*A*S*H*, "The Sounds of Silence" (*The Graduate*), "The Shadow of Your Smile" (*The Sandpiper*) and "Tara's Theme" from *Gone with the Wind. Slander (and Other Love Songs)* is a solid quintet recording mixing Locke originals with fine covers of Stevie Wonder ("Tuesday Heartbreak") and Joni Mitchell ("Blue").
— J.S.

ROBERT JR. LOCKWOOD

★★★ **Steady Rollin' Man (Delmark, 1973)**
★★★ **Hangin' On (with Johnny Shines) (Rounder, 1980)**
★★★ **Mr. Blues Is Back to Stay (with Johnny Shines) (Rounder, 1981)**
★★★★½ **Johnny Shines and Robert Lockwood (Paula, 1991)**
★★★½ **Contrasts (Trix, 1993)**
★★★½ **Plays Robert & Robert (Evidence, 1993)**

Though he is commonly identified as Robert Johnson's stepson and pupil, Robert Jr. Lockwood (b. 1915), whose earliest musical training was on the pump organ, learned from Johnson and moved on to develop his own style and voice. Inspired by the single-string technique of Lonnie Johnson and the innovations of electric-guitar pioneer Charlie Christian, Lockwood enlarged the blues he learned from Robert Johnson as a teenager in Helena, Arkansas. As his career progressed through associations with Johnson, Sonny Boy Williamson (Rice Miller) and other blues masters of his time, Lockwood's restless intellect led him to explore jazz stylings (songs such as "Sheik of Araby" and "Stardust" became staples in his repertoire) while absorbing the rhythmic and harmonic innovations being pioneered by Count Basie and Christian.

In the early '40s Lockwood moved to Chicago for a brief period and cut some powerful sides for Bluebird, including "Take a Little Walk with Me," perhaps the closest he has ever come to having a signature song. Returning to Helena after the Bluebird sessions, Lockwood became a regular on blues powerhouse KFFA's King Biscuit Time and, later, on the Mother's Best Flour show, on which he fronted a small combo complete with a small brass section. As his popularity rose, he took to the road, dropping anchor in St. Louis for a moment and finally returning to the Memphis area, where he played mentor to Muddy Waters and B.B. King, among others. The early '50s found him back in Chicago and recording again, although his solo efforts failed to gain much recognition; to greater profit he found himself in demand as a session player and had steady work backing many of the Chess label's stellar artists at the dawn of the rock & roll era. Still, on his own he had brought an urban, jazzy sophistication to the raw Delta style and thus charted new paths for the generations of blues artists following him.

Steady Rollin' Man, recorded in 1973 with a trio, has the moody, haunting feel of the Delta embedded in its stinging urban blues. Of particular note is Lockwood's version of Robert Johnson's "Rambling on My Mind." It honors the original's sense of the moment, while striking a more languid pace that allows Lockwood time to develop some interesting single-string commentaries in the style of one of his chief influences, Lonnie Johnson. *Hangin' On* and *Mr. Blues Is Back to Stay* team Lockwood with fellow Delta bluesman and former Johnson sideman Johnny Shines for two memorable albums that show both musicians taking the blues in all sorts of surprising directions.

Plays Robert & Robert, recorded in 1982 in Paris, features Lockwood accompanying himself on 12-string guitar on a repertoire almost evenly split between songs composed by Johnson and Lockwood, with a rousing version of Ma Rainey's "C.C. Rider" being the lone title not by

Robert or Robert. Here Lockwood's mastery of the 12-string Delta style is on vivid display—check out the propulsive instrumental "Lockwood's Boogie" for a breathtaking example of same—as are the connections between his singular, ornate voicings and the rhythmically complex Johnson style. Read what you will into it, but Lockwood's own songs are performed with more verve and commitment than are the Johnson numbers, and the versions of the Bluebird classics, "Take a Walk with Me" and "Little Boy Blue," are as strong and impassioned as the original (and still out-of-print) recordings.

"Little Boy Blue" gets another stirring treatment as the opening cut on the Trix LP, *Contrasts,* with Lockwood's rich harmonic runs and robust, popping single-string flights bringing new urgency to this sturdy tune. As always, Lockwood's guitar work is scintillating—and it's buttressed on several cuts here by some stellar supporting work from bassist Gene Schwartz, drummer George Cook and tenor saxophonist Maurice Reedus, whose smoky, languid solo on "Come Day, Go Day" is one of the album's sensuous treats—but as anyone who has seen Lockwood live in his later years will attest, the man's singing has become wondrous and moving in its alternately weary and feisty way. No great technical instrument, Lockwood's voice has a certain *gravitas* in its pinched, resigned tone, but on sprightly fare, such as the buoyant version of "Mr. Down Child" included here, he adopts a winning, friendly tone to get the job done. Regardless of the approach, he sings with authority and personality, and to a far greater degree than he did in his youth. — D.M.

JOE LOCO

★★★★ **Loco Motion (Fantasy, 1994)**

Pianist José "Joe Loco" Estevez (1921–1988) arranged and played with Afro-Cuban and Puerto Rican bands led by Machito, Tito Puente, Xavier Cugat and Noro Morales before popularizing the mambo with his own group in the 1950s. *Loco Motion* is taken from two sessions, one of *pachangas* played by a group including Mongo Santamaria on congas, Willie Bobo on timbales and a violin section, the other a small group playing Loco's catchy arrangements of pop standards. — J.S.

JEFF LORBER

★★½ **Worth Waiting For (Verve, 1993)**

★★½ **West Side Stories (Verve, 1994)**

★★½ **State of Grace (Verve, 1996)**

Multi-instrumentalist/producer Jeff Lorber (b. 1952) is one of the key figures in the jazz world of the 1980s and 1990s for his commercial instincts rather than his playing ability. In fact, the Berklee College of Music graduate is a prime example of the pitfalls of conservatory training as a route into jazz. On his now unavailable 1980s fusion albums for Arista, Lorber showcases his dazzling technical mastery of the keyboard and an eclectic bag of influences but rarely sounds emotionally convincing.

Lorber's danceable blend of funk, Latin and jazz elements proved to be an unerring commercial formula for some of his own work and dozens of other production products but ends up sounding empty. The Verve sides collect top-flight support from various session players and showcase Lorber on piano, synthesizer, organ, guitar, bass and percussion, all busily leading the listener on the road to nowhere. Lorber is one of the people who gave fusion a bad name. — J.S.

LOUISIANA RED

★★½ **Midnight Rambler (Tomato, 1989)**

★★ **The Lowdown Back Porch Blues (Collectables, 1991)**

★★★½ **The Best of Louisiana Red (Evidence, 1995)**

Louisiana Red, born Iverson Minter in 1936, is a postwar bluesman who first drew national attention in the early '60s with recordings on Roulette and Atco. Some of his output on various imprints over the years survives on three albums that put into perspective the career of this adept guitarist and songwriter whose influences include Muddy Waters, Elmore James and John Lee Hooker.

Midnight Rambler, recorded over a period of months in 1975, is divided into two sessions: summer and, more captivating, winter. It features acoustic slide guitar and guttural, howling vocals on harrowing tracks like "Sweetblood Call" ("I have a hard time missin' you baby/With my pistol in your mouth") and "Death of Ealase." Also included here are Slim Harpo's "King Bee" and the original "Too Poor to Die," one of the best songs he has ever written.

The Best of Louisiana Red, comprising tracks recorded between 1965 and 1973 by Atlantic Records cofounder Herb Abramson, showcases Louisiana Red's artistry more effectively than any available recording. Performing a mixture

of covers and originals with a varying ensemble, he shines. His guitar and voice sound warm and natural as he runs through standards by Waters, Willie Dixon and Arthur "Big Boy" Crudup, as well as his poetic, starkly original "Red's Dream," "Red's New Dream" and the disturbing, autobiographical "Story of Louisiana Red."
— B.R.H.

THE LOUNGE LIZARDS
★★★ The Lounge Lizards (Editions EG/Caroline, 1981)
★½ Live 79/81 (Roir, 1985)
★★★½ Live in Tokyo—Big Heart (Antilles/Island, 1986)
★★★★ No Pain for Cakes (Antilles/Island, 1987)
★★★ Voice of Chunk (Lagarto, 1989)
★★½ Live in Berlin 1991, Vol. I (Intuition, 1993)
★★½ Live in Berlin 1991, Vol. II (Intuition, 1995)
JOHN LURIE SOLO
★★ Stranger Than Paradise & the Resurrection of Albert Ayler (Crammed Discs, 1985)
★★ Down by Law & Variety (Intuition, 1987)
THE JOHN LURIE NATIONAL ORCHESTRA
★★ Men with Sticks (Lagarto/Crammed Discs, 1993)

The Lounge Lizards is an intriguing combo that glides above free verse, bop, big band, blues, funk, rock and swings in a cacophonous blend of them all. The downtown New York–based Lizards are led principally by saxophonist John Lurie (b. 1950), an accomplished player, composer, bandleader, actor and film scorer.

The band's debut features Lurie's brother Evan, whose organ bursts are echoed by drummer Anton Fier's syncopated rhythms. But just as suddenly as the noise begins, it recedes, making way for a sexy solo from Lurie. The three dominate the affair; guitarist Arto Lindsay, an interesting player in his own right, is highly underused. Consisting chiefly of Lurie compositions, the set also includes two excellent reworkings of Thelonious Monk classics.

The redundant *Live 79/81,* recorded primarily with the same band, suffers from poor recording quality. The dynamic *Live in Tokyo—Big Heart* features an expanded Lounge Lizards, benefiting greatly from the additions of trombonist Curtis Fowlkes (the Jazz Passengers) and sax player Roy Nathanson. Guitarist Marc Ribot shows off his chops on the surflike "Punch and Judy Tango," a track that also showcases a solo by its author, Evan Lurie.

Expanding their ranks yet again on *No Pain for Cakes,* the Lizards are joined by percussionist E.J. Rodriguez. The understated "Bob and Nico" would be appropriate for the closing credits of a noir thriller—not unlike Lurie's haunting solo soundtrack work. With the same lineup, *Voice of Chunk* features heavy blues guitar by Ribot on the title track.

The pair of *Live in Berlin 1991* albums feature an entirely new lineup, with only John Lurie remaining. This new troupe, featuring free-formist Billy Martin (later of Medeski, Martin and Wood), adapts the Lizards' boisterous and energetic approach. — G.E.

JOE LOVANO
★★★½ Landmarks (Blue Note, 1991)
★★★½ Sounds of Joy (Enja, 1992)
★★★½ From the Soul (Blue Note, 1992)
★★★★ Universal Language (Blue Note, 1993)
★★★★ Tenor Legacy (Blue Note, 1994)
★★★★★ Rush Hour (Blue Note, 1995)
★★★½ Worlds (Evidence, 1995)
★★★★½ Quartets: Live at the Village Vanguard (Blue Note, 1996)
★★★★★ Celebrating Sinatra (Blue Note, 1997)
★★★★½ Flying Colors (with Gonzalo Rubalcaba) (Blue Note, 1997)
★★★★½ Trio Fascination Edition One (Blue Note, 1998)

Saxophonist/clarinetist Joe Lovano (b. 1952) is a central figure in the 1990s jazz renaissance, a player steeped in tradition who is nevertheless well beyond the stylistic captivity of an interpreter, an experimenter conversant in the developments of free and modal jazz but, most important, a man who understands that music is about emotional communication and that technique and style can only exist in service to that communication. Like Coleman Hawkins, Ben Webster and Lester Young, to whom he's been compared, Lovano is an end in himself, a living definition of jazz. It's easy to understand why he's accomplished the unusual feat of generating both critical and popular approval, winning "Jazz Artist of the Year" in *Down Beat*'s 1996 critics poll and "Jazz Musician of the Year" in its readers poll of the same year.

Lovano grew up in Cleveland under the

influence of his father, saxophonist Tony "Big T" Lovano. The younger Lovano studied at Berklee College of Music, then honed his soul-jazz chops in organist Lonnie Smith's band. He went on to play with another groove-oriented organist, "Brother" Jack McDuff, before joining the Woody Herman big band in the late '70s. He spent the '80s as a mainstay in the Mel Lewis orchestra and as a crucial partner to drummer Paul Motian. He was also a key member of guitarist John Scofield's band and a sought-after sideman on the New York scene, working with Carla Bley, Elvin Jones, Charlie Haden and Lee Konitz.

Worlds, a live recording from the French Amiens festival in 1989, shows Lovano at his experimental best as a bandleader. Lovano plays tenor and soprano saxophones and alto clarinet, and key collaborators Motian and guitarist Bill Frisell are joined by the distinctive soprano singing of Lovano's wife, Judi Silvano, with bassist Henri Texier, trumpeter Tim Hagans and trombonist Gary Valente. On *Sounds of Joy,* a trio date with bassist Anthony Cox and drummer Ed Blackwell, Lovano expands his tonal range by playing alto saxophone in emulation of Ornette Coleman.

Landmarks and *From the Soul* established Lovano's credentials as a mainstream postbop musician who could play ballads with the grace and subtlety of the masters. On *From the Soul* he even covers the Hawkins watermark "Body and Soul." *Universal Language* is an eclectic sextet featuring Hagans, Silvano, pianist Kenny Werner, bassist Scott Lee and drummer Jack DeJohnette; its mixture of voice, brass and woodwinds in the arrangements shows Lovano headed off into more complex soundscapes. On *Tenor Legacy,* a solid outing with a great rhythm section—pianist Mulgrew Miller, bassist Christian McBride, bassist Lewis Nash and percussionist Don Alias—Lovano's sound takes on new dimensions with the addition of yet another second-generation tenor star, Joshua Redman. The extraordinary *Rush Hour,* Lovano's historic collaboration with composer Gunther Schuller, was a logical step from *Universal Language* and was nominated for a "Best Large Ensemble" Grammy.

Quartets: Live at the Village Vanguard documents two of Lovano's engagements at the legendary jazz club, where he is one of the most popular bandleaders, leading his lineup through a weeklong stand there at least once a year since 1992. The first lineup on this recording includes trumpeter Tom Harrell, bassist Anthony Cox and drummer Billy Hart playing a program of mostly originals. The second brings back Miller, McBride and Nash to play compositions by John Coltrane, Thelonious Monk and Miles Davis.

Celebrating Sinatra is actually a kind of sequel to *Rush Hour,* an astonishing creative rereading of some highlights from the Sinatra songbook. Manny Albam's orchestrations are ingenious explorations of the melodic and harmonic possibilities of this material, and the use of Silvano's voice as a color in the arrangements is brilliant. On certain lines she'll float in like a piccolo, vocalizing an instrumental line, then she'll sing a few lines like a distant accompanist, lay out for a chorus and return scatting. Lovano himself plays in soft, breathing voices, little phrases reminiscent of some of Young's subtle parts. This is one of the essential recordings of its time. Lovano continued on his red-hot roll with the stirring duet recording with pianist Gonzalo Rubalcaba, *Flying Colors,* and the all-star trio set with bassist Dave Holland and drummer Elvin Jones, *Trio Fascination Edition One.* — J.S.

FRANK LOWE

★★★ **Frank Lowe and His Friends (1973; ESP, N.A.)**
★★★★ **The Flam (1976; Black Saint, 1993)**
★★★★ **Exotic Heartbreak (1982; Soul Note, 1994)**
★★★★ **Live from Soundscape (DIW, 1994)**

Tenor saxophonist Frank Lowe (b. 1943) grew up in Memphis listening to blues and R&B and became interested in jazz through the influence of the free-jazz movement while living in San Francisco. He played with Sun Ra in the late '60s, then in Alice Coltrane's band in the early '70s. Lowe's powerful, free-blowing style used every nuance of the saxophone and experienced gut-wrenching searches throughout his career. He played with Don Cherry, Lester Bowie, Rashied Ali, Carla Bley and Milford Graves.

Frank Lowe and His Friends, with Joseph Jarman on alto and soprano, represents Lowe in his most intense free-jazz period on a set that still sounds way out there. *The Flam* is a much more tightly focused set with Leo Smith on trumpet, Joseph Bowie on trombone, Alex Blake on bass and Charles Bobo Shaw on drums. *Exotic Heartbreak* and *Live from Soundscape* both feature Amina Claudine Myers on piano and Butch Morris on cornet. — J.S.

JON LUCIEN

★★ **Listen Love (Mercury, 1991)**
★★ **Mother Nature's Son (Mercury, 1993)**

Multi-instrumentalist and singer Jon Lucien (b. 1942) was raised by his musician father on the island of St. Thomas. His engaging calypso-jazz style and phrasing inspired by Miles Davis enabled Lucien to transform his baritone into a facile pop instrument. By the time of *Listen Love* and *Mother Nature's Son,* his approach had devolved into mindless easy-listening music. Search out *Song for My Lady* to find out what Lucien is really about. — J.S.

BOBBY LYLE

★★★ **Night Breeze (1985; Evidence, 1992)**
★ **Ivory Dreams (Atlantic, 1989)**
★ **The Journey (Atlantic, 1990)**
★ **Pianomagic (Atlantic, 1991)**
★ **Secret Island (Atlantic Jazz, 1992)**
★ **Rhythm Stories (Atlantic Jazz, 1994)**

Keyboardist Bobby Lyle (b. ca. 1945) plays jazz/funk with lots of conviction but little subtlety. He has straddled genres and instrumentation from George Benson to Sly Stone and from organ to synthesizer. The Atlantic recordings are essentially worthless, the twisted product of record-industry vampires who feed off musicians dying for a shot at the big time. *Night Breeze* shows Lyle in his element, grooving along with fusion-driven bass support from Stanley Clarke. Lyle clearly relishes playing the Chick Corea ("Spain") and John Coltrane ("Naima") compositions in the set. — J.S.

GLORIA LYNNE

★★★★ **Miss Gloria Lynne . . . (1958; Evidence, 1992)**
★★★ **A Time for Love (Muse, 1990)**
★★★ **No Detour Ahead (Muse, 1993)**
★★½ **Golden Classics (Collectables, N.A.)**

Born in New York in 1931 and raised on gospel music as a young member of the Mother A.M.E. Zion Church, Gloria Lynne may well have been ill-served by her mid-'60s success as a pop artist. At heart a jazz singer in the Sarah Vaughan mold (although she cites Ella Fitzgerald and Mahalia Jackson as her primary influences), Lynne had a Top 30 pop hit in 1964 with the melancholy "I Wish You Love" and, through 1965, added several lower-charting singles to her résumé. Pop's up-tempo grooves weren't the free-swinging ones that suited her sense of time, however, and its ballads tended to restrict her interpretive skill, which needed room to breathe. The somewhat hyperbolic liner notes to *A Time for Love* credit her with inspiring romantic female pop-jazz balladeers from Roberta Flack to Anita Baker. But Lynne's own moment in the spotlight was too brief for the public to have much sense of her achievements or a memory of her influence on succeeding generations of vocalists.

The best support for the argument that she was much more than her hit single suggested actually came several years ahead of its success, when she began recording for Everest Records. In 1992 Evidence rereleased her first album, *Miss Gloria Lynne . . .* , cut in 1958 with a solid cast of musicians (including Kenny Burrell on guitar and Milt Hinton on bass) providing the sensitive, impeccable support she deserved. At this time there was no pretense of pop ambition—the album is a display of jazz-influenced balladeering and swinging of the first order, with Lynne pushing the musicians and they her in a dazzling display of musical chops being exercised to their limit. Consider the lively workout on "Perdido," wherein Lynne dashes off the lyrics in great good humor, then goes into a scatting mode as Jo Jones steps up on the brushes and Eddie Costa answers eloquently in kind on the vibes. By contrast, the enduring standard "I Don't Know Why" offers Lynne a chance to show off the probing, heartfelt way she has with a ballad, delicately bending notes and tossing off deep blues asides, then leaving room for Sam Taylor to come in with a tenor-sax solo that adds the proper searching mood to underscore the singer's perplexed, love-besotted state of mind. Some of the tracks here appear on *Golden Classics,* which also contains "I Wish You Love" and three other charted singles.

After a long hiatus, Lynne returned at the outset of the '90s with the graceful *A Time for Love,* another ballad-heavy effort on which she is supported by superb players, among them guitarist David Spinozza, drummer Alan Schwartzberg, percussionist Sammy Figueroa, Pat Rebillot on electric piano and Sonny Fortune and Frank Vacari on saxophones. Testimony to her egalitarian point of view, developed through experience in the peaks and valleys of a life in showbiz, is on display in two songs partly credited to her as a writer—a touching paean to the sweet memory of a lost love, "Lend Me Yesterday," rendered without bitterness; and an easy swinging come-on to romance, "Come Get Your Share."

Lynne's 1993 effort, *No Detour Ahead,* finds her teamed with writer, producer and arranger Nat Adderley Jr., duly celebrated for his exceptional work with Luther Vandross over the years. Adderley clearly understands Lynne and provides her with a variety of settings that allow her room to move. The opener, a solid, funky, steady-grooving take on Lionel Richie's "Hello," threatens to sink Lynne in a sea of swirling instruments each intent on making its mark on the track at her expense. But her resourceful approach, alternately declamatory and wistful, carries the day with an elegant interpretation of lyrics rife with ambiguity. At the other end of the scale, Adderley checks in on piano with a series of angular, melodic retorts (à la Ramsey Lewis or Vince Guaraldi) to Lynne's yearnings on the song "Free." In this slight but effective confection, the repetition of the title sentiment, sung in a distant, hopeful tone, takes on an even more resonant and moving quality as Lynne and Adderley's dialog roots below the lyrics' surface for the darker emotions suggested in their text. A worthy, interesting effort by an underrated vocalist yet to be given her just due. — D.M.

JIMMY LYONS

★★★ Wee Sneezawee (Black Saint, 1984)
★★★★ Give It Up (Black Saint, 1985)

Alto/baritone saxophonist/flautist Jimmy Lyons (1932–1986) spent most of his career collaborating with pianist Cecil Taylor, playing on the landmark recordings *Unit Structures, Conquistador* and *Spring of Two Blue Jays,* among others.

The breakneck speed of his vamps and light-as-a-feather tone that characterize his work with Taylor are carried over into his solo efforts. The spirited dogfight with trumpeter Enrico Rava on *Give It Up,* with bassoonist Karen Borca tracing the outlines of the exchange, is as heady a mix as many of Ornette Coleman's similar exercises. Borca's ghostly genius is also much in evidence on *Wee Sneezawee.*

As have many challenging jazz albums, all too much of Lyons's work disappeared as he played it. He was not well documented in his lifetime, and what was recorded has, for the most part, lapsed into unavailability. Try to find his magnificent duets with fellow Taylor band mate Andrew Cyrille on drums, on *Something in Return* and *Burnt Offering.* — J.S.

JOHNNY LYTLE

★★★ Happy Ground (Muse, 1991)
★★★ Moonchild (Muse, 1992)
★★★ Possum Grease (Muse, 1995)

The solid, blues-oriented instrumental grooves of vibraphonist Johnny Lytle (b. 1932) made him part of the soul/jazz movement of the '60s via a hit single and album, *The Village Caller,* which remains in print (Riverside) only in vinyl. Lytle's later sets for Muse present him in solid form and good company. — J.S.

WILLIE MABON

★★★ Chicago Blues Session! (1979; Evidence, 1995)

Pianist/songwriter Willie Mabon's (1925–1985) suave, jazz-honed approach to Chicago blues hid razor-sharp lyrics and street attitude in such songs as "The Seventh Son," "I'm Mad" and "Poison Ivy." Schooled in Chicago's late-'40s/early-'50s jazz circles—Benny Carter, Gene Ammons and Tom Archia (with whom he later recorded)—Mabon took a Cripple Clarence Lofton number, retooled it as "I Don't Know" and established a semipermanent home for himself among the blues heavyweights at Chess Records. His best work from that era can still be found scattered among various Chess anthologies like *The Blues* (*Vols. 4* and *5*).

In the early '60s Mabon recorded for a number of smaller Chicago R&B labels, striking paydirt with tunes like "Just Got Some" and "I'm the Fixer." Languishing in America, he toured Europe and moved there by the decade's end, recording a number of albums. He often returned to his native Chicago and in 1979 cut the sessions that resulted in *Chicago Blues Session!,* a performance of his songbook that is ably aided by guitarists Hubert Sumlin and Eddie Taylor but ultimately less than compelling. One tantalizing version of his signature tune can be found on the anthology *Atlantic Blues: Piano* (Rhino, 1991) with Mick Jagger on harmonica. — A.K.

MAGIC DICK AND JAY GEILS

★★★½ Bluestime (Rounder, 1994)
★★★★ Little Car Blues (Rounder, 1996)

Magic Dick (b. Dick Salwitz in 1945) and Jay Geils (b. Jerome Geils in 1946) were cofounders of the J. Geils Band, one of the most popular American groups of the 1970s and '80s. Formed out of the duo's love of classic blues from the post–World War II era, the band evolved to develop a more soul-influenced format before reaching its commercial peak as a synth-driven pop group in the '80s.

Bluestime finds Magic Dick and Geils returning to their roots, playing small-group urban blues from the 1940s and '50s framed by Geils's carefully measured guitar structures and highlighted by Dick's high-intensity Little Walter groove and surprisingly deft vocals. The band has blossomed in live performance since its debut and sports a formidable sound on *Little Car Blues*. — J.S.

MAGIC SAM

★★★★½ West Side Soul (1968; Delmark, 1990)
★★★★★ Black Magic (1969; Delmark, 1994)
★★★½ Live (1981; Delmark, 1990)
★★★½ 1957–1966: West Side Guitar (Paula, 1991)
★★★ Give Me Time (Delmark, 1991)
★★★½ Magic Touch (Black Top, 1993)
★★★★½ The Late Great Magic Sam (Evidence, 1995)

Like a Roman candle, Samuel "Magic Sam" Maghett (1937–1969) burned brightly for a tantalizingly brief period. When he died suddenly of a heart attack at age 32, Maghett took with him a guitar and vocal style that had come to epitomize Chicago's gritty West Side sound. Magic Sam's legacy has grown since his untimely death, as elements of his style can clearly be heard in such modern-day bluesmen as Jimmy Dawkins, Lonnie Brooks and Luther "Guitar Jr." Johnson, to name but a few.

Though Magic Sam released only two proper

LPs, the seminal *West Side Soul* and *Black Magic,* his importance has proven conversely proportional to his recorded output. Maghett first recorded for the Cobra label in 1957 and 1958, cutting sides like the slow blues "All Your Love," the rapid-fire, minor-picking "Love Me with a Feeling" and the robust "Easy Baby," a signature tune found on several of his recordings. These tracks are included on *1957–1966: West Side Guitar,* Paula's compendium of 21 songs featuring Maghett backed by the likes of Willie Dixon, Otis Spann, Mighty Joe Young and Shakey Jake, among others. Well played and historically intriguing, *1957–1966* is an overview of Magic Sam's pre-Delmark career, also documenting sides he cut for Chief in 1960 and for Crash in 1966. Though illuminating Magic Sam's formidable talents, the retrospective doesn't hold together as a fully realized album.

On the other hand, *West Side Soul* finds Magic Sam near his pinnacle. Recorded in July and October 1967, the release features Maghett leading a band including Mighty Joe Young on second guitar and Stockholm Slim on piano. This ensemble digs deeply into Maghett originals like "All of Your Love" and the instrumental "Lookin' Good," as well as versions of Robert Johnson's classic "Sweet Home Chicago" and Junior Parker's "I Feel So Good (I Wanna Boogie)." An enduring piece of work from an artist who had Mississippi in his heart but Chicago in his head, *West Side Soul* was 1968's only blues record to earn a five-star review in *Down Beat.*

Black Magic takes *West Side Soul* a notch further. Recorded in October and November 1968 and released one year later, this classic LP finds Magic Sam accompanied by an ensemble consisting of Eddie Shaw on tenor sax, Young on guitar, Lafayette Leake on piano, Mack Thompson on bass and Odie Payne Jr. playing drums. Featuring "Easy Baby," the foreboding, saxophone-soaked "It's All Your Fault," the svelte instrumental "San-Ho-Zay" and an impassioned version of Bo Diddley's "You Don't Love Me, Baby," *Black Magic* sadly proved to be Magic Sam's epitaph. On the verge of a major commercial breakthrough, Maghett died just one month after the album's release.

Since Maghett's death, a number of his recordings have been issued. *Live* chronicles performances in 1963, 1964 and 1969, including his explosive appearance at the Ann Arbor Blues Festival in August 1969. On this date Maghett leads a group consisting of bassist Bruce Barlow and Butterfield Blues Band drummer Sam Lay—making for the most compelling cuts on the album, though the 1964 tracks, featuring Eddie Shaw and A.C. Reed on dueling tenor saxophones, come close. *Live* puts into perspective Magic Sam's musical development and ability to direct ensembles of supremely talented musicians.

Magic Touch captures a December 1966 gig at Sylvio's in Chicago. Sam is accompanied by a hot ensemble—harpist Shakey Jake and the rhythm section from his not-yet-recorded *Black Magic*—though the recording has shaky sound quality. Intriguingly, this recording features only one song ("All Your Love") included on *West Side Soul,* which was recorded the next year.

Give Me Time depicts Maghett as solo artist, having been recorded on a portable tape machine at home in January 1968. Spotlighting his sensational vocal and guitar skills, unadorned by an electric band, the album places Magic Sam on a par with both Sam Cooke and Muddy Waters. Though the sound isn't of pristine studio quality, it has a presence that can only be attained by an off-the-cuff session. With the sounds of his kids in the background, Maghett runs through blues classics including Dixon's "I Can't Quit You Baby," Little Walter Jacobs's "You're So Fine" and B.B. King's "Sweet Little Angel." On "Come into My Arms," Magic Sam's guitar playing is accompanied by the vocal work of Eddie Boyd.

The most fully realized of the Maghett posthumous releases is Evidence's *The Late Great Magic Sam.* Comprising studio tracks recorded in 1963 and 1964 and two live tracks from London's Royal Albert Hall in 1969, the album includes material never before released domestically. Backed by the thick, syrupy organ textures of Johnny "Big Moose" Walker and the rock-solid bass-and-drums combination of Mack Thompson and Bob Richey, respectively, Magic Sam delivers definitive versions of originals like "All Your Love" and "Baby You Torture My Soul." Another instrumental original, "Trying to Make It," sounds like the missing link between Booker T. and the MG's and the Meters; also notable are versions of Robert Higgenbotham's "High-Heel Sneakers" and James A. Lane's "Back Door Friend," which were recorded under the supervision of Willie Dixon. *The Late Great Magic Sam* stands as compelling testimony to the taste and skill of an artist who was struck down before his time, leaving only speculation as to the heights he could have achieved. — B.R.H.

MAGIC SLIM AND THE TEARDROPS

★★★ **Highway Is My Home (1978; Evidence, 1992)**
★★★½ **Raw Magic (Alligator, 1982)**
★★★½ **Grand Slam: Essential Boogie (Rooster Blues, 1982)**
★★★ **Gravel Road (Blind Pig, 1990)**
★★★ **Born Under a Bad Sign (Storyville, 1994)**
★★★½ **Scufflin' (Blind Pig, 1996)**

Magic Slim, born Morris Holt in 1937 in Mississippi, is a Chicago club fixture, but his music reeks of Mississippi juke joints. Magic Slim and his Teardrops play big, meaty, straight-down-the-middle-of-the-dirt-road electric blues, a funky, grinding mix of Albert King, Hound Dog Taylor and Magic Sam—definitely not music for the crossover-minded. The not-so-slim Slim (he stands 6 feet 4 inches and tips the scale somewhere near 270 pounds) is certainly not a master of subtlety, nor is he a flashy guitarist. He does, however, possess one of the most powerful finger vibratos around and is not shy about shaking the hell out of his Fender Jazzmaster. He sings in a similarly straightforward gruff voice. The beauty of Slim's music is its straight-ahead kick and the *simpatico* playing of the Teardrops. On the earlier albums, Slim and his second guitarist play interlocking counterpoint that creates one big, mean guitar sound, best exemplified on *Raw Magic* and *Grand Slam: Essential Boogie.* On later albums, with the more fluid John Primer playing second guitar, the sound is somewhat more linear, heard to excellent effect on *The Blues of the Magic Man* (on the U.K. label Wolf, which has released several other Magic Slim recordings). As Slim is a master of consistency, each of his albums achieves a sort of raw, rough-hewn grace, making any of them a good place to start. — A.P.

TAJ MAHAL

★★★½ **The Natch'l Blues (Columbia, 1969)**
★★★★ **Giant Step/De Old Folks at Home (1969; Columbia, 1989)**
★★★½ **The Best of Taj Mahal, Vol. 1 (1972; Columbia, 1981)**
★★★ **Mo' Roots (Columbia, 1974)**
★½ **Taj (Gramavision, 1986)**
★★★ **Shake Sugaree (Music for Little People, 1988)**
★★★½ **Mule Bone (Gramavision, 1991)**
★★★ **Like Never Before (Private Music, 1991)**
★★★★½ **Taj's Blues (Columbia/Legacy, 1992)**
★★★★½ **Rising Sons Featuring Taj Mahal and Ry Cooder (Columbia/Legacy, 1992)**
★★★½ **Dancing the Blues (Private Music, 1993)**
★★ **World Music (Columbia/Legacy, 1993)**
★★★ **Live at Ronnie Scott's, London (DRG, 1996)**
★★★ **Phantom Blues (Private Music, 1996)**
★★★★ **Señor Blues (Private Music, 1997)**

Singer and multi-instrumentalist Taj Mahal (b. Henry Saint Claire Fredricks in 1942) grew up in Springfield, Massachusetts. His voracious appetite for mixing styles has yielded varying degrees of musical success, but his ambitious and prolific output speaks for itself. Originally a rural-blues revivalist in the early '60s, Mahal was influenced by the Rev. Gary Davis, Robert Johnson and Sonny Terry. Over three decades, Mahal has carved a unique niche for himself among contemporary blues performers, and his influence has had an effect not only on that genre, but on folk and world music as well.

In 1964, joined by then-fledgling guitarist Ry Cooder, Mahal formed an electric band, the Rising Sons. Finally issued in 1992, *Rising Sons* documents the band's mostly unreleased material, including ground-shaking, amphetamine-tempo versions of Blind Willie McTell's "Statesboro Blues" and the previously released "Candy Man" by Gary Davis. Other gems include Bob Dylan's "Walkin' Down the Line" and Willie Dixon's ".44 Blues." Of the original tunes, the most interesting are those written by guitarist Jesse Lee Kincaid, particularly the resoundingly Beatle-esque "The Girl with Green Eyes" and the strikingly surreal, quavering "Sunny's Dream." After the Rising Sons split up in 1966, Mahal pursued the solo career that has lasted into the '90s.

Mahal's eponymously titled 1967 solo debut is out of print. His next efforts, *The Natch'l Blues* and *Giant Step/De Old Folks at Home* (a double LP on one CD), represent the balance of his '60s solo output. The former is a shuffling, electrified blues album complete with spare, harmonica-spiked arrangements and passionate singing. Included here are such originals as "Good Morning, Miss Brown," "Done Changed My Way of Living" and "I Ain't Gonna Let Nobody Steal My Jellyroll." Mahal demonstrates his genius for rearranging traditional material on "Corinna." Guesting on this album is pianist Al Kooper.

Giant Step comprises nine songs, two thirds of which are covers, including Goffin/King's "Take a Giant Step," Lead Belly's "Keep Your Hands Off Her" and Robbie Robertson/Garth Hudson's "Bacon Fat." Mahal, who sings and plays banjo, harmonica and National steel guitar, leads a versatile, sympathetic band with Davis on guitar. The solo *De Old Folks at Home* features Mahal's gruff and breathless a cappella reading of Lead Belly's "Linin' Track," his ragtime rendition of "Stagger Lee" and the definitive version of "Fishin' Blues," which was written by Henry Thomas but is now more frequently associated with Mahal.

The tracks on *The Best of Taj Mahal, Vol. 1* primarily highlight his blues material, including a harmonica-drenched version of Sleepy John Estes's "Leaving Trunk." Also present is a live recording of Mahal's horn-driven instrumental "Ain't Gwine Whistle Dixie (Any Mo')." Rounding out the album is one of Mahal's first excursions into reggae, his version of the Slickers' "Johnny Too Bad."

Mahal's next effort, *Mo' Roots,* is essentially a reggae record featuring such heavyweight guests as Wailer Aston "Familyman" Barrett playing piano on a version of Bob Marley's "Slave Driver." Also covered is Jamaican songwriter Bob Andy's "Desperate Lover." The only misplaced exceptions to the reggae theme are the hard, funky soul of "Big Mama," the Louisiana lilt of "Cajun Waltz" and the flowery, faux-Latino "Why Did You Have to Desert Me?," which could have found acceptance several years later when disco was in full swing. Though the album has a respectfully genuine feel, it sorely lacks the deeply spiritual aspect of the best roots-reggae music.

The Caribbean theme continues on *Taj,* an ill-advised departure from Mahal's roots-flavored formula. This contrived salute to the islands is filled with flaccid electronic instrumentation and calypsoesque tunes that make Mahal sound more like Jimmy Buffett. Even the Robert Mapplethorpe cover photos, the presence of such guests as Babatunde Olatunji and a Mighty Sparrow composition ("Everybody Is Somebody") cannot rescue this effort.

Mahal's next two releases are different still. *Shake Sugaree* is a children's album; *Live at Ronnie Scott's, London,* recorded at the legendary club in September 1988, includes a wide sampling of Mahal's palette, from the soca of "Local Local Girl" and "Everybody Is Somebody" to the 12-bar "Big Blues" and the country blues of "Staggerlee." *Mule Bone* is the soundtrack for the play of the same name written by Zora Neale Hurston and Langston Hughes. Mahal composed every song except one, while Hughes contributed most of the lyrics. With a tasteful, crisp production, *Mule Bone* consists primarily of blues-based songs; highlights include the Meters-esque "Graveyard Mule (Hambone Rhyme)," the lazy blues of "Me and the Mule" and the herky-jerky "Song for a Banjo Dance."

Taj's Blues compiles Mahal's hard-core blues output, spotlighting songs from his first solo album including a midtempo "Statesboro Blues" and Sleepy John Estes's "Everybody's Got to Change Sometime." Both songs feature prime axe work by Ry Cooder and Jesse Ed Davis. Also notable are Mahal's reading of Mississippi John Hurt's "Frankie & Albert," with the Pointer Sisters on backing vocals, and a solo version of Elmore James's "Dust My Broom."

Dancing the Blues benefits from its choice of material; though there are two originals, Mahal sounds most at home covering songs by Fats Domino ("Going to the River," "I'm Ready"), Jerry Leiber and Artie Butler ("Down Home Girl") and Percy Mayfield ("Stranger in My Own Home Town"). Backed by players known primarily in the rock & roll arena (pianists Ian McLagan and Bill Payne and drummer Richie Hayward), Mahal turns in credible performances of classic songs. *World Music* reprises much of Mahal's reggae, calypso and nonblues output. *Phantom Blues* features Eric Clapton's guitar on two tracks and the vocals of Bonnie Raitt, "Sir" Harry Bowens, "Sweet Pea" Atkinson and Terry Forsythe on several others. Mahal and company run through a battery of covers, including Doc Pomus's "Lonely Avenue" and Jessie Hill's "Ooh Poo Pah Doo." All in all a passable blues album, *Phantom Blues* nonetheless sounds sanitized-for-AOR-radio when compared with Mahal's earlier blues efforts.

Señor Blues is a resounding return to form for Mahal. His choice of material seems to more naturally suit his skills as a player and vocalist; the Horace Silver–penned title track is smoky and insistent—not quite boiling, but simmering and shimmering behind Mick Weaver's Hammond B-3 work and the urgent insertions of the Texacalli Horns. Other highlights include a swinging version of Hank Williams's "Mind Your Own Business" and an ultrafunky reading of the Steve Cropper/Otis Redding gem "Mr. Pitiful." — B.R.H.

KEVIN MAHOGANY

★★★ **Double Rainbow (Enja, 1993)**
★★★½ **Songs and Moments (Enja, 1994)**
★★★★ **You Got What It Takes (Enja, 1995)**
★★★ **Kevin Mahogany (Warner Bros., 1996)**
★★★★ **Another Time, Another Place (Warner Bros., 1997)**

Vocalist Kevin Mahogany (b. 1958) blends jazz, pop and R&B styles effortlessly into an accessible mix that is both commercial and musical. The Kansas City native received his greatest recognition as an actor portraying a singer patterned after Big Joe Turner in Robert Altman's film *Kansas City,* but he was ready for the exposure, having already recorded several impressive albums for Enja. *Songs and Moments* benefits from the sympathetic accompaniment of pianist John Hicks, drummer Marvin "Smitty" Smith and bassist Ray Drummond.

You Got What It Takes features Mahogany's best singing, including a duet with Jeanie Bryson, "Baby You Got What It Takes," and a scat-happy interpretation of "Route 66." His eponymous major-label debut showcases a mature vocal style accompanied sympathetically by pianist James Weidman, organist Larry Goldings and pop/jazz saxophonist Kirk Whalum. Mahogany underscores his film persona with a performance of "Yesterday I Had the Blues." *Another Time, Another Place* is a tour de force of stylistic range, from the adventurous vocalizations of "Big Rub" to the old-style ballad cream of "Nature Boy" to a pop duet with the vocally challenged singing cowboy hat Randy Travis, a dramatic gesture pulled off with generosity and guts. — J.S.

MIKE MAINIERI

★★★ **Wanderlust (NYC, 1992)**
★★★ **Man Behind Bars (NYC, 1995)**
★★★★ **An American Diary (NYC, 1996)**
★★ **White Elephant 1 (NYC, 1996)**
★ **White Elephant 2 (NYC, 1996)**
★★★★ **An American Diary: The Dreaming (NYC, 1997)**

WITH STEPS AHEAD

★★★ **Magnetic (Elektra, 1986)**
★★ **NYC (Intuition, 1989)**
★★ **Yin-Yang (NYC, 1992)**
★★★★ **Live in Tokyo, 1986 (NYC, 1994)**
★★★ **Vibe (NYC, 1995)**

Far more influential than his recorded output suggests, producer, composer, record-company owner and vibraphonist Mike Mainieri (b. 1938) has worked with artists ranging from Paul Whiteman (as a 14-year-old prodigy) to Charlie Hunter. As a leader, he seems of two minds, showing fusion can sound as creative and exciting as acoustic jazz, and demonstrating his chops and roots as a mainstream player. But whatever he's playing, he rarely loses sight of the music's history or his vision of its future.

A great many of his early recordings remain out of print, though Mainieri has started releasing them on his own label, NYC, as he acquires his masters. The first *White Elephant* sessions, recorded between 1969 and 1972, showcase his fusion big-band project. Steve Gadd, Ronny Cuber, the Brecker Brothers, Tony Levin, Warren Bernhardt, Joe Beck, David Spinozza, John Faddis, Lou Soloff and dozens more play jazzy, funky free-form rock, much heavier on the fills and improvisation than Blood, Sweat and Tears, though less vocally intense. The second *White Elephant* set strays dangerously close to MOR rock, except for a funky version of "Auld Lang Syne." *Wanderlust* features fusion mainstays Steve Kuhn, Peter Erskine and Don Grolnick along with Jeremy Steig, Levin, the Breckers and Kaz Watanabe.

Several of these players appear on Steps Ahead albums as well. *Magnetic* sets the pattern of using the best and freshest fusioners, introducing Dianne Reeves's shining vocals on the title track and presenting Kenny Kirkland in fusion mode. The mainstays of the session are veterans Erskine and Victor Bailey, who help him create a Weather Report–like sound, mixing catchy themes and rhythms with some inspired improvising; unfortunately, the vibes often get lost in the mix. The album includes a fusion version of "In a Sentimental Mood." *Live in Tokyo, 1986* takes that song and much of the other *Magnetic* material on the road with Michael Brecker, Mike Stern, Daryl Jones and Steve Smith for a smoking set: These versions of the tunes have many of *Magnetic*'s strengths with few of its flaws. Brecker rarely sounds better, and Mainieri shows he can play vibes with the best keyboard players. This band plays in the studio on *NYC,* with Bendik replacing Brecker. Bendik is the only holdover from this band to play on *Yin-Yang,* along with fusion upstarts Rachel Z., Steve Smith and Jeff Andrews, but the album is none the stronger for it.

On the completely solo-in-the-studio *Man Behind Bars,* the stripped-down, vibes-in-front approach and well-used hand percussion serve Mainieri well; this recording has an exotic, almost primitive sound on material ranging from Wayne Shorter's "E.S.P." and John Coltrane's "Equinox" to Mainieri's own hip-hoppy tribute to Jeremy Steig, "Satyr Dance." Mainieri's reading of "All the Things You Are" presages *An American Diary* in style and content, if not in verve.

With players like Bailey and Z., *Vibe* feels like a reunion but doesn't reach its potential, although Mainieri exhibits fine piano chops on the reprise of "Miles Away" and the band's reading of "Green Dolphin Street" is somewhat unique. On *An American Diary,* Mainieri, Joe Lovano, Eddie Gomez and Peter Erskine play their impressions of John Cage, Charles Ives and Roger Sessions as well as actual compositions by Samuel Barber, Leonard Bernstein, Aaron Copland and Frank Zappa. The band dabbles in folk forms, spirituals and other music.

On *An American Diary: The Dreaming* Marc Johnson takes over the bass duties and George Garzone ably fills Joe Lovano's spot. One of the finer moments of this looser recording is a trio version of the lovely ballad "An American Tale." Other highlights include Arto Tuncboyan's small but magical percussive touches on a number of the compositions, excelling on his duet with Mainieri, "Dear, My Friend"; David Tronzo's surprisingly violinlike slide guitar; Noa's dreamlike vocals; and the harp of Mainieri's wife, Dee Carstensen, on the ethereal "Los Dos Lorettas." — H.B.

DAVID MALONE

★★★★ I Got the Dog in Me (Fat Possum, 1995)

Mississippi hill-country guitarist David Malone (b. 1965) has the kind of raw, eclectic style that develops out of the Deep South juke joints where anything goes. The son of another blues original, Junior Kimbrough, Malone started performing at his father's club at age six.

Malone's no-nonsense approach to blues feeling was tempered by a long stretch of hard time at Mississippi's Parchman Farm prison, where he played in the prison band and was discovered by *Deep Blues* author Robert Palmer. Malone had developed an intense blues style shot through with R&B and soul vocalizations and the rawest edge of popular music. The title track of *I Got the Dog in Me,* with its blood-curdling howls and stinging, acerbic guitar lines, tells you all you need to know about this uncompromising talent. — J.S.

JUNIOR MANCE

★★★★ At the Village Vanguard (1961; Original Jazz Classics, 1996)
★★★ Softly as in a Morning Sunrise (Enja, 1995)
★★★ Blue Mance (Chiaroscuro, 1995)
★★★½ At Town Hall (Enja, 1996)
★★★ At Town Hall, Vol. 2 (Enja, 1997)

Pianist Julian "Junior" Mance (b. 1928) is a Chicago-based player in the tradition of the barrelhouse blues pianists who have flourished there. He made the transition to bop accompaniment but is best served in the live trio format that lets him roll the keys. By age 19 he had made a name for himself in the Gene Ammons band and went on to play with Lester Young, Dinah Washington, Cannonball Adderley, Dizzy Gillespie and the Eddie "Lockjaw" Davis/Johnny Griffin band. *At the Village Vanguard* shows Mance at his best, leading a trio in live performance. That was still his strength 35 years later, as the *At Town Hall* recordings prove. — J.S.

CHUCK MANGIONE

★★★ Hey Baby! (with Gap Mangione) (1961; Original Jazz Classics, 1991)
★★★ Spring Fever (with Gap Mangione) (1961; Original Jazz Classics, 1992)
★★★ Recuerdo (1962; Original Jazz Classics, 1991)
★★★½ Land of Make Believe (1973; Mercury, 1988)
★★ Chase the Clouds Away (1975; Rebound, 1996)
★★ Feels So Good (1977; A&M, 1983)
★★★ Fun and Games (1980; Rebound, 1994)
★★ Love Notes (1982; Columbia, 1986)

★★ **Journey to a Rainbow (Columbia, 1983)**
★★★½ **The Best of Chuck Mangione (A&M, 1985)**
★★ **Save Tonight for Me (Columbia, 1986)**
★★★½ **Classics, Vol. 6 (A&M, 1987)**
★★ **Eyes of the Veiled Temptress (Columbia, 1988)**
★★★½ **Greatest Hits (A&M, 1996)**

Trumpeter/flügelhornist Chuck Mangione (b. 1940) played in Art Blakey's band from 1965 to '67 after leading his own group, the Jazz Brothers, in the early '60s with his brother Gap Mangione on keyboards. *Hey Baby!* and *Spring Fever,* both featuring tenor saxophonist Sal Nistico, document that period, as does the solid quintet session *Recuerdo,* with flautist/alto saxophonist Joe Romano, pianist Wynton Kelly, bassist Sam Jones and drummer Louis Hayes.

Though his earliest work is well represented, Mangione's best records are no longer in print. The deleted *Friends and Love,* a live recording from 1971, is a fine piece of multistylistic writing and direction in which Mangione combined his own band with the Rochester Philharmonic Orchestra and established his solo career. A few similar projects followed.

Mangione hit a commercial high point during that era in collaboration with vocalist Esther Satterfield on "Land of Make Believe," which has since become a standard. Mangione's solid quartet albums for Mercury feature Gerry Niewood's excellent soprano-saxophone work, fine playing by Mangione and consistently good session backing. Unfortunately the only one of this series remaining in print is *Land of Make Believe.* Mangione's A&M recordings (some of which have been reissued by Rebound) are exceedingly glib; despite his musical taste and sense for commercial hooks ("Feels So Good"), the records remain unrewarding. The Columbia releases are even worse, and the best-of packages all cover the same material. — J.S.

MANHATTAN JAZZ QUINTET

★★★★ **Manteca (1992; Evidence, 1995)**

A cooperative group of musicians best known for their ubiquitous presence as sidemen and session players, the Manhattan Jazz Quintet features trumpeter Lew Soloff, tenor saxophonist George Young, pianist David Matthews and several different drummers and bassists. *Manteca,* recorded live at New York's Sweet Basil, has Eddie Gomez on bass and Peter Erskine on drums. The set offers a spirited rundown of bop-era classics including "Cherokee," "Stella by Starlight" and the Dizzy Gillespie–signature title track, a showcase for each player's dexterous soloing. — J.S.

THE MANHATTAN TRANSFER

★½ **Jukin' (1971; One Way, 1993)**
★★½ **The Manhattan Transfer (Atlantic, 1975)**
★★ **Pastiche (Atlantic, 1978)**
★★½ **Extensions (Rhino, 1979)**
★★★ **Bodies and Souls (Rhino, 1983)**
★★½ **Bop Doo-Wopp (Rhino, 1984)**
★★★½ **Vocalese (Rhino, 1985)**
★★★ **Manhattan Transfer Live (Rhino, 1987)**
★★ **Brasil (Rhino, 1987)**
★★★★ **The Offbeat of Avenues (Sony, 1991)**
★★★½ **Anthology: Down in Birdland (Rhino, 1992)**
★★★ **The Very Best of the Manhattan Transfer (Rhino, 1994)**
★★ **Tubby the Tuba (Summit, 1994)**
★★ **Tonin' (Atlantic, 1995)**
★★★ **Man-Tora! Live in Tokyo (Rhino, 1996)**
★★★½ **Swing (Atlantic, 1997)**

Few pop vocal groups can sing as well as the Manhattan Transfer, particularly when it comes to the sort of close-harmony vocalese popularized by Lambert, Hendricks and Ross. Trouble is, the Transfer—particularly in its early years—often rounds out its bebop numbers with forays into doo-wop, novelty tunes and campy nostalgia, an approach that may be rewarding commercially but doesn't hold up to repeated listenings. From *The Manhattan Transfer* through *The Very Best of the Manhattan Transfer* (out of print), the group's taste for gimmicky, recherché material runs at least as strong as its interest in jazz; only the out-of-print *Mecca for Moderns,* which includes the charming "Boy from New York City" as well as a poignant rendition of "A Nightingale Sang in Berkeley Square," is worth enduring from start to finish (though *The Very Best of,* which also includes "Four Brothers" and the band's zippy take on Weather Report's "Birdland," is also a reasonable buy). Both *Bodies and Souls* and *Bop Doo-Wopp* up the jazz quotient while maintaining a strong interest in pop marginalia. But *Vocalese,* which includes cameos by Jon Hendricks, Bobby McFerrin and the Four

Freshmen, finds the group utterly in its element and trying hard to meet the impossibly high standards set by Lambert, Hendricks and Ross. And though the wonderfully sung *Brasil,* which features English-language versions of songs by Djavan, Gilberto Gil, Ivan Lins and Milton Nascimento, is undercut by its annoyingly inane lyrics, *The Offbeat of Avenues* balances imaginative numbers like the bebop/hip-hop fusion of "What Goes Around Comes Around" with jazz workouts like Jon Hendricks's setting of Miles Davis's "Blues for Pablo."

Man-Tora! Live in Tokyo is an impressive performance of some of the group's best-known material. *Tubby the Tuba* is a children's album. *Tonin'* pays tribute to such influences as the Four Seasons and the Young Rascals. *Swing* successfully updates such big-band staples as "King Porter Stomp," "Down South Camp Meetin'" and "Choo Choo Ch' Boogie." *The Very Best of the Manhattan Transfer* is a greatest-hits collection. *Anthology* is a two-CD overview of the band's career musical highlights. — J.D.C.

HERBIE MANN

★★★ **Herbie Mann Plays (1954; Bethlehem, 1992)**

★★★ **Flute Soufflé (with Bobby Jaspar) (1957; Original Jazz Classics, 1992)**

★★★ **Just Wailin' (1958; Original Jazz Classics, 1996)**

★★★★ **At the Village Gate (Atlantic, 1961)**

★★★★ **Memphis Underground (1969; Atlantic, 1987)**

★★★ **The Best of Herbie Mann (1970; Atlantic, 1987)**

★★★★ **Push Push (1971; Atlantic, 1989)**

★★★½ **Caminho de Casa (Chesky, 1990)**

★★★ **Yardbird Suite (Savoy, 1993)**

★★★★ **The Evolution of Mann: The Herbie Mann Anthology (Rhino, 1994)**

★★★ **Verve Jazz Masters 56 (Verve, 1996)**

Throughout his career, innovative flautist and shrewd bandleader Herbie Mann (b. 1930) has consistently been able to anticipate as well as cash in on musical fashions. His playing, though highly refined and adaptable to a wide range of circumstances, is almost always subjugated to the context of its settings, which are carefully conceptualized around various world musics, ethnic themes or crack studio bands.

Mann, a Brooklyn native, began his recording career in 1954 with *Herbie Mann Plays.* By the end of the decade he had established himself internationally and was working in Hollywood, where he also scored soundtracks for television. His studies of world music and his childhood exposure to salsa led Mann to organize a series of Afro-Cuban groups that continued on to large-scale success.

These Afro-Cuban bands, epitomized by the classic *At the Village Gate,* featured such great percussionists as Carlos "Patato" Valdes, Ray Barretto, Babatunde Olatunji, Ray Mantilla, Willie Bobo and Armando Peraza. Mann's records from this period are consistently interesting. He also made a series of important proto–world-music records, most notably *Impressions of the Middle East.* Unfortunately, little from Mann's classic period remains in print. Look for such gems as *The Common Ground, Flautista, Brazil Blues* and *Standing Ovation at Newport.* Otherwise, highlights can be heard on *The Best of Herbie Mann* and the two-CD retrospective *The Evolution of Mann.*

Mann's panstylistic bent was the perfect attitude for the '60s' burgeoning fusion movement, and such future fusion stars as pianist Chick Corea, vibraphonist Roy Ayers, bassist Miroslav Vitous and guitarists Larry Coryell and Sonny Sharrock played with him. His understanding of and affinities with rhythm & blues led to the watershed *Memphis Underground.* This commercial and artistic success starred Mann with Coryell, Ayers and Sharrock backed by a Memphis rhythm section whose steamy groove provided a link between jazz, R&B and rock. The title track was also a hit single. Mann followed the album with similar attempts, most of which failed to capture its magic. The only one to approach it, *Push Push,* featured young session guitarist Duane Allman. The CD reissue includes a version of "Funky Nassau" not on the original.

Mann's popularity went into eclipse by the end of the 1970s and through the '80s, but he returned to form in the '90s with a series of albums that recapitulated some of his earlier triumphs. *Caminho de Casa* is the only available indication of Mann's recent significant exchanges with Brazilian musicians. Several other new titles are already out of print, including *Deep Pockets,* which places Mann back in the soul/R&B groove with such players as tenor saxophonist David "Fathead" Newman and keyboardist Les McCann, and *Peace Pieces,* a beautiful collection of Bill Evans covers with

Randy Brecker assisting on flügelhorn. The Evans project proves that even as he approaches 70, Mann hasn't lost his characteristic ability to reinvent himself. — J.S.

WOODY MANN

★★★★ **Stories (Greenhays, 1994)**
★★★★½ **Stairwell Serenade (Acoustic Music, 1995)**
★★★½ **Heading Uptown (Shanachie, 1997)**

Acoustic guitarist Woody Mann (b. 1952) is well schooled in several forms of music: He studied classical at Juilliard and NYU, jazz with Lennie Tristano and blues in the living room of Rev. Gary Davis. He creates his own style from these varied influences, preserving the integrity of each element while dovetailing them into one another.

Mann's playing is astonishingly clean without being sterile; he avoids the pitfall of playing like a scholar and infuses every riff and note with feeling. His vocal on *Stories* is adequate, folksingerish rather than bluesy. A new arrangement of Blind Boy Fuller's "Sweet Soul Music" features jazzy passing-tone riffs spliced in between the blues licks, and the lovely instrumental original "Lisboa" flows seamlessly from jazz to blues to chamber-music filigrees. *Stairwell Serenade* collects original instrumental compositions and offers a feast of tasteful colors, flavors and homages to inspirations as diverse as Joseph Spence, Eddie Lang, Tristano and Davis. "Country Fair" demonstrates Mann's mastery of Davis's idiom. — J.Z.

SHELLY MANNE

★★★ **Shelly Manne & His Friends (1944; Signature, 1993)**
★★★½ **Deep People (1952; Savoy, 1993)**
★★★★ **"The Three" and "The Two" (1954; Original Jazz Classics, 1992)**
★★★ **Shelly Manne & His Men, Vol. 1: The West Coast Sound (1955; Original Jazz Classics, N.A.)**
★★ **My Fair Lady (1956; Original Jazz Classics, 1988)**
★★★ **Shelly Manne & His Friends, Vol. 1 (1956; Original Jazz Classics, 1992)**
★★★ **More Swinging Sounds (1956; Original Jazz Classics, 1992)**
★★★ **Shelly Manne & His Men: Swinging Sounds, Vol. 4 (1956; Original Jazz Classics, 1996)**
★★★ **Bells Are Ringing (1958; Original Jazz Classics, 1996)**
★★★★★ **Shelly Manne & His Men at the Black Hawk, Vol. 1 (1959; Original Jazz Classics, 1991)**
★★★ **Shelly Manne & His Men at the Black Hawk, Vol. 2 (1959; Original Jazz Classics, 1991)**
★★★ **Shelly Manne & His Men at the Black Hawk, Vol. 3 (1959; Original Jazz Classics, 1991)**
★★★★ **Shelly Manne & His Men at the Black Hawk, Vol. 4 (1959; Original Jazz Classics, 1991)**
★★★ **Shelly Manne & His Men at the Black Hawk, Vol. 5 (1959; Original Jazz Classics, 1991)**
★★★★ **At the Manne-Hole, Vol. 1 (1961; Original Jazz Classics, 1992)**
★★★ **At the Manne-Hole, Vol. 2 (1961; Original Jazz Classics, 1992)**
★★★★ **2-3-4 (1962; Impulse!, 1994)**
★★★ **Alive in London (1970; Original Jazz Classics, 1993)**
★★ **Interpretations of Bach and Mozart (Trend, 1980)**

Said to have played on well more than a thousand jazz albums, drummer Shelly Manne (1920–1984) had one of the most prolific recording careers of all jazz musicians. While this statistic may have worked against him on some sessions, he was a fresh, swinging and dedicated artist, schooled in the big-band tradition but far more at home in bop-style small combos, where he could fully express his interest in accents and more subtle playing. Manne was a principal force in the various Stan Kenton bands of the 1940s, an organization largely identified with the West Coast sound of the 1950s, but he also recorded on adventurous small-group sets with Ornette Coleman (*Tomorrow Is the Question!*) and Sonny Rollins (*Way Out West*).

His earliest available material is on Signature's *Shelly Manne & His Friends,* a reissue of sessions led by clarinetist Barney Bigard, alto saxophonist Johnny Hodges and pianist Eddie Heywood, with Don Byas on tenor and Ray Nance on violin. Manne's advanced (for that time) drumming personality, especially his superior brushwork, makes the reissue under his name logical. *Deep People* sees Manne powering a larger band with Art Pepper on alto and Jimmy Giuffre and Bob Cooper on tenor.

After a film appearance in 1955's *The Man with the Golden Arm,* Manne fronted his own groups and wasted little time cashing in on his commercial reputation. His capability for producing fast-selling fodder was epitomized by

My Fair Lady, where pianist André Previn and bassist Leroy Vinnegar join him in Muzak-like runthroughs of "Get Me to the Church on Time," "With a Little Bit of Luck" and so on.

Despite such commercial forays, Manne led a terrific small combo notable for its front line of tenor saxophonist Richie Kamuca and trumpeter Joe Gordon. This band is heard to beautiful effect on the live *Shelly Manne & His Men at the Black Hawk* recordings, which document three nights of performances at that San Francisco club. Bassist Monty Budwig and pianist Victor Feldman mesh neatly into Manne's bopish conception, especially on the exceptional first volume, which features a wonderful Kamuca solo on "Summertime." All the CD reissues include bonus tracks. Kamuca also plays on the *At the Manne-Hole* recordings, which are just a cut below. *2-3-4* finds Manne in a quartet setting with tenor giant Coleman Hawkins, pianist Hank Jones and bassist George Duvivier. — J.S.

MARACA Y OTRA VISIÓN

★★★½ Havana Calling (Qbadisc, 1996)

Cuban flautist Orlando "Maraca" Valle (b. 1966) leads Otra Visión, one of the most popular young jazz groups in Havana. Their debut, *Havana Calling,* fuses contemporary and traditional folkloric elements.

In 1987 Maraca first began playing in a band with vocalist Bobby Carcassés, followed by stints with pianist Emiliano Salvador's group Nueva Visión and then with Irakare. He's also recorded with Roy Hargrove and Steve Coleman. Otra Visión includes his flautist wife, Céline Valle, trumpeter Alexander Brown, alto saxophonist Irving Acao, pianist Yan Carlos Artime, bassist Oscar Rodríguez, percussionist Robert Vizcaíno and drummer Juan Carlos. The album also features a number of Cuban jazz luminaries.

Havana Calling's eight tracks offer an eclectic menu—Cedar Walton's "Bolivia" revisited as a Cuban *comparsa* (carnival parade song); "Monte Adentro," a smooth *guajira;* "La Vela," a sultry bolero with Spanish vocals from Maraca's brother Yumurí; and "Nueva Era," an astounding percussion showcase. — A.A.

BOB MARGOLIN

★★½ Down in the Alley (Alligator, 1993)
★★★ My Blues and My Guitar (Alligator, 1995)
★★★ Up & In (Alligator, 1997)

A modern blues guitarist with one foot planted firmly in the '50s sound, Bob Margolin (b. 1949) is a veteran of Muddy Waters's '70s band, having performed on nine of his albums. His solo efforts, credited to "Steady Rollin'" Bob Margolin, pay homage to Waters, his musical mentor. Available on cassette only, *Chicago Blues* includes performances by Jimmy Rogers, Kim Wilson and Pinetop Perkins, among others. *Down in the Alley* features Waters's "Look What You Done" (with a guest spot by guitarist Ronnie Earl), as well as a number of Margolin originals. Among these, standouts include "Now Who's the Fool" and "Boston Driving Blues," showcasing Margolin's slashing guitar work and his band's pounding rhythm section.

My Blues and My Guitar contains a variety of original and cover material, including Leiber and Stoller's "Drip Drop," Willie Dixon's "The Same Thing," Snooky Pryor's "Peace of Mind" (on which Pryor sings and plays harmonica) and the humorous original "Maybe the Hippies Were Right." Margolin's considerable talents are well framed on the excellent *Up & In,* which features several numbers from previous albums with fresh arrangements. "The Window," originally on *Chicago Blues,* gets an extra kick in this version. Two more updates from the same album, "She and the Devil" and "Not What You Said Last Night," appear here in versions with pianist Pinetop Perkins. Margolin was the guitarist on Muddy Waters's version of "Why Are People Like That?" He revisits the tune here with an expanded version that adds new lyrics to Bobby Charles's original. — B.R.H.

MARK THE HARPER

★★★½ Man on a Mission (Turquoise City, 1996)

Popular New York City blues bandleader Mark Weitzman (b. 1960) works to his strengths on this solid debut, which showcases his fine harmonica work and considerable songwriting skills. Harper also handles lead vocals in front of an all-star New York lineup featuring the brilliant guitarist Arthur Neilson of the Guitar Guys from Hell, saxophonist Crispin Cioe, trumpeter Larry Etkin of the Uptown Horns and vocalists Jerry "Slapmeat Johnson" Dugger and Pat Cisarano. — J.S.

BRANFORD MARSALIS

★★★ Scenes in the City (Columbia, 1984)
★★★ Royal Garden Blues (Columbia, 1986)

★★★½ **Renaissance (Columbia, 1987)**
★★★ **Random Abstract (Columbia, 1988)**
★★★½ **Trio Jeepy (Columbia, 1989)**
★★★★ **Crazy People Music (Columbia, 1990)**
★★★ **The Beautyful Ones Are Not Yet Born (Columbia, 1991)**
★★★★ **I Heard You Twice the First Time (Columbia, 1992)**
★★★ **Bloomington (Columbia, 1993)**
★★★½ **Buckshot LeFonque (Columbia, 1994)**
★★★ **Loved Ones (with Ellis Marsalis) (Columbia, 1996)**

After nearly three years as host of *The Tonight Show*'s house band, Branford Marsalis (b. 1960) was one the most visible jazz musicians in the world. The eldest son of pianist Ellis Marsalis, Branford Marsalis served a brief apprenticeship (on baritone) with Art Blakey in 1980 and another (on alto) in 1981, then worked with his brother Wynton Marsalis's quintet from 1981 through 1985.

A commanding tenor and soprano saxophonist, Marsalis has a technique that enables him to tear through the most complex rhythmic patterns and harmonic sequences with disarming fluency. He's assimilated the stylistic essence of tenor players ranging among Lester Young's across-the-beat riffs, Ben Webster's breathy timbral romances, Sonny Rollins's wit and invention in developing a theme, John Coltrane's complex rhythmical scales, Wayne Shorter's singular harmonic universe and Dewey Redman's harmolodic blues shouts. He's absorbed Charlie Parker's rhythmic disjunctiveness and has no trouble shedding chords à la Ornette Coleman and hurtling headlong into hyperspace improvisations based on the barest framework ("structured burnout," he terms it).

Marsalis's gift of playing effectively in any idiom tends to obscure the fact that, unlike most of his sources, he's often not a particularly gifted melodic improviser. His ability to reference his sources at a moment's notice without plagiarizing their content leads to facile, by-the-numbers improvising (albeit at the highest technical level). Hip, witty and highly literate, Marsalis relies on devices like programmatic titles, in-jokes, encoded inference, genre juxtaposition and extramusical dramatic content to elucidate the narrative. Though music is his idiom, it doesn't seem sufficient to encompass all he wants to say. Yet, when Marsalis is on, particularly when he has a foil, it's hard to think of any of his contemporaries who do it better.

Marsalis's recordings are uneven; all contain at least one or two remarkable performances, and at least two are fully realized works. His humorous debut, *Scenes in the City,* and its updated version of the Mingus title composition prefigure his careerlong use of a parallel narrative line; he selects a program displaying an array of styles and techniques. Marsalis begins to clarify his vision as a group leader on *Royal Garden Blues;* however, six of the seven tunes, ranging from the title track (performed with a modernist sensibility) to the post–Shorter/Hancock/James Black compositions of the Marsalis brothers and pianist Kenny Kirkland, are played by different rhythm sections, so the session lacks focus.

On *Renaissance,* drummer Tony Williams joins Marsalis, Kirkland and bassist Bob Hurst on six tracks (Marsalis, Herbie Hancock and Buster Williams perform as a trio on Jimmy Rowles's "The Peacocks"), performing two Williams originals, a Marsalis original, four standards and a roaring "Just One of Those Things." Marsalis's clear soprano-saxophone technique is particularly impressive. *Random Abstract,* with Kirkland on piano, Delbert Felix on bass and Lewis Nash on drums, employs the same effective mix of standards and originals; there's a remarkable extended Keith Jarrett/Jan Garbarek–style improvisation on Ornette Coleman's "Lonely Woman."

Trio Jeepy, a two-album trio set with 78-year-old bassist Milt Hinton, elaborates an encyclopedic grasp of saxophone styles on seven standards and three originals. *Crazy People Music* features Marsalis's working quartet of Kirkland, Hurst and drummer Jeff Watts. With pianist Kirkland providing form as foil and master comper, Marsalis lets his imagination soar on a beautifully balanced, interactive set. *The Beautyful Ones Are Not Yet Born* is a step back, with a rote quality, although the title composition and "Cain and Abel," a lengthy chase between Branford and Wynton Marsalis, are exceptional performances.

I Heard You Twice the First Time is a successful programmatic release dealing with different aspects of the blues, vernacular to art. B.B. King, John Lee Hooker and the cast of *The Piano Lesson* explore work song, Delta folk, Chicago electric, urban contemporary and contemporary blues extensions. *Bloomington* articulates Marsalis's trio concept of improvising tabula rasa throughout a set, with only the barest structural parameters. The trio of Marsalis, Hurst and Watts plays with virtuosity, energy and ingenuity; without any unifying orchestrational devices, the performance becomes an exercise in extended jazz techniques. This set is considered a landmark recording of contemporary jazz by a number of the stronger young jazz musicians. *Buckshot LeFonque,* Marsalis's second programmatic release of the '90s, sets jazz improvisers like Marsalis and Roy Hargrove against the context of current black poetry, from Maya Angelou to rap, set to contemporary rhythms. — T.P.

DELFEAYO MARSALIS

★★★ **Pontius Pilate's Decision (Novus, 1992)**

★★★ **Musashi (Evidence, 1997)**

Arguably one of the most important jazz producers of the 1980s and '90s (for the records he did with his older brothers), Delfeayo Marsalis (b. 1965) made his solo debut as a trombone player with *Pontius Pilate's Decision,* an ambitious, star-studded recording. One track features all four of the musical Marsalis brothers, including younger brother Jason on drums. The harmonically demanding record frequently swings but just as frequently falls victim to its own excesses. *Musashi* was recorded in Tokyo with a Japanese rhythm section augmented by Mark Gross on alto and soprano saxophones and featuring guest shots from Branford and Ellis Marsalis. — H.B.

ELLIS MARSALIS

★★★ **A Night at Snug Harbor (1989; Evidence, 1995)**

★★★ **Piano in E: Solo Piano (Rounder, 1991)**

★★½ **From Bad to Badder (with the American Jazz Quintet) (Black Saint, 1991)**

★★★½ **The Ellis Marsalis Trio (Blue Note, 1991)**

★★★½ **Heart of Gold (Columbia, 1992)**

★★★½ **Whistle Stop (Columbia, 1994)**

★★½ **Joe Cool's Blues (with Wynton Marsalis) (Columbia, 1995)**

★★★ **Loved Ones (with Branford Marsalis) (Columbia, 1996)**

Jazz-dynasty father Ellis Marsalis (b. 1934) is an accomplished, imaginative pianist who possesses a broad rhythmic vocabulary and distinctively blends New Orleans vernacular piano styles with a post–Bud Powell harmonic sensibility that reaches to Herbie Hancock and beyond. He limns a song with the piano in the manner of Nat King Cole's piano trio, performs it with Oscar Peterson–style precision, works it with the orchestrational attitude of Ahmad Jamal and swings it in the relaxed post-Powell manner of '50s stylists Red Garland and Wynton Kelly. A tenor saxophonist who switched to piano in his teens, a student of jump-band rhythm & blues styles and Charlie Parker, Marsalis since the '50s and '60s has been a paragon of modernist sensibility and tradition-bound New Orleans, as well as an important jazz educator.

Marsalis and like-minded clarinetist Alvin Batiste, drummer Edward Blackwell, tenor saxophonist Nat Perrilliat and drummer/composer James Black pioneered contemporary jazz in the Crescent City. (They would later become the American Jazz Quintet.) Marsalis, Blackwell and Batiste recorded a handful of now out-of-print albums in the late '50s and early '60s, notably their debut, *AFO Quintet,* which holds particular interest as a showcase for Batiste's bright tone and clever compositions and Blackwell's clearly articulated, smoothly modulated rhythmic patterns. Also unavailable is *Monkey Puzzle,* a major statement that presents compositions by Black that are unique for their constantly shifting rhythmic signatures and distinctive phrasing, with strong improvisations by Perrilliat on one of his rare recordings.

In 1982 Black and Marsalis appeared with the next generation (Wynton and Branford Marsalis) on the deleted *Fathers and Sons,* featuring intense performances of four Ellis Marsalis compositions. The gravitas of the New Orleans modernists comes clearly into focus on the retrospective *Whistle Stop,* 12 superb compositions primarily by Black and Batiste, performed by Branford Marsalis on tenor and soprano sax with bassist Bob Hurst and drummer Jeff Watts.

Loved Ones features four Ellis Marsalis solos and 10 duos with Branford; the one original and 13 standards dedicated to various real and imaginary women are performed with elegance and nuance. On *Joe Cool's Blues* Marsalis delivers four rather perfunctory, gentle trio versions (and one band/vocal arrangement) of Vince Guaraldi compositions, juxtaposed with eight originals performed by the Wynton Marsalis Septet.

From Bad to Badder, a live American Jazz Quintet recording, reunites Marsalis with his '50s partners; despite bright moments, it's a disorganized session that ends just as the players begin to cohere. The Snug Harbor session features Marsalis with strong local saxophonists Rick Margitza and Tony Dagradi performing original material, and a strong guest turn by New Orleans native Donald Harrison on "I Can't Get Started." The CD also features the somewhat awkward recording debut of 15-year-old Nicholas Payton, backed by Art Blakey on a Harrison variant of the "52nd Street Theme." Marsalis provides strong soloing and comping throughout. Also from the mid-'80s is *Piano in E,* a beautifully paced solo concert performance before a New Orleans audience.

The strong trio recordings of the early '90s take Marsalis out of a local context and place his considerable skills as interpreter and improviser in perspective. On *The Ellis Marsalis Trio,* young veterans Bob Hurst and Jeff Watts are adept accompanists on an intriguing program of waltzes, ballads and swingers, six standards and five Marsalis or James Black originals. Most of *Heart of Gold* features Marsalis in a highly interactive trio with bassist Ray Brown and drummer Billy Higgins. Their no-holds-barred treatments of "Surrey with the Fringe on Top," "Love for Sale" and "Sweet Georgia Brown" reach the highest level of trio improvising. The youngest Marsalis, then-14-year-old drummer Jason, has a few opportunities to display his fast hands and accurate touch, particularly on "Dr. Jazz," but the level of interaction inevitably drops off. — T.P.

WYNTON MARSALIS

★★½ **Wynton Marsalis (Columbia, 1982)**
★★ **Think of One (Columbia, 1983)**
★★½ **Hot House Flowers (Columbia, 1984)**
★★★½ **Black Codes (from the Underground) (Columbia, 1985)**
★★★ **J Mood (Columbia, 1986)**
★★★ **Live at Blues Alley (Columbia, 1986)**
★★★ **Marsalis Standard Time, Vol. 1 (Columbia, 1987)**
★★★½ **The Majesty of the Blues (Columbia, 1989)**
★★★★ **Standard Time, Vol. 3: The Resolution of Romance (Columbia, 1990)**
★★★★ **Tune In Tomorrow (Columbia, 1990)**
★★★½ **Standard Time, Vol. 2: Intimacy Calling (Columbia, 1991)**
★★★ **Thick in the South: Soul Gestures in Southern Blue, Vol. 1 (Columbia, 1991)**
★★★ **Uptown Ruler: Soul Gestures in Southern Blue, Vol. 2 (Columbia, 1991)**
★★★ **Levee Low Moan: Soul Gestures in Southern Blue, Vol. 3 (Columbia, 1991)**
★★★★ **Blue Interlude (Columbia, 1992)**
★★★★★ **Citi Movement (Columbia, 1993)**
★★★½ **In This House, on This Morning (Columbia, 1994)**
★★½ **Joe Cool's Blues (with Ellis Marsalis) (Columbia, 1995)**
★★★½ **Blood on the Fields (Columbia, 1997)**
★★★½ **Jump Start and Jazz (Sony Classical, 1997)**

As the leading light of the neotraditionalist movement in jazz, trumpeter Wynton Marsalis (b. 1961) has inspired countless young musicians, encouraged those critics who feared that fusion would be the death of jazz and brought new glamour to the music he champions. And though it would be hard to imagine a more appropriate hero for the movement—Marsalis, after all, is attractive, intelligent, articulate and accomplished—it would be just as hard to find an artist who better typifies what's wrong with neotraditional jazz.

That's not to say that Marsalis hasn't made good albums; indeed, he has. Marsalis, even when he finds his own voice and forges his own sound, turns out to have little to say that the past masters he reveres didn't say better.

Perhaps that's why his classical recordings have been his most consistently satisfying. His orchestral debut, a pairing of Haydn and Hummel concertos, offers ample proof of his flawless technique and warm tone; unlike Al Hirt or Doc Severinsen, Marsalis sounds completely at home with the classical repertoire. Half a dozen symphonic recordings followed, highlights of which were released on the now unavailable *Portrait of Wynton Marsalis* (1988). Also worth seeking out is the now out-of-print *Carnaval,* a 1987 collection of turn-of-the-century cornet favorites recorded with the Eastman Wind Ensemble. As a technical showcase, it's hard to beat, for he whips through such crowd pleasers as "The Flight of the Bumblebee" and "Moto Perpetuo," as well as giving a flawless reading of Jean-Baptiste Arban's notoriously demanding "Variations sur 'Le Carnaval de Venise.' " But *Carnaval* is also interesting because it finds Marsalis harkening back to an earlier age in American music—something his jazz recordings have done from the start.

Marsalis's first Columbia session was with a rhythm section led by Herbie Hancock, portions of which appear on *Wynton Marsalis* (the rest can be found on Hancock's album *Quartet*). Along with bassist Ron Carter and drummer Tony Williams, Hancock played in the classic mid-'60s quintet of Miles Davis, and this session found Marsalis working much the same territory Davis pioneered. Except that where Davis's playing was sparse, lyrical and harmonically incisive, Marsalis was brash but mechanical, offering solos that were more technically challenging than Davis's but considerably less eloquent. That pattern holds throughout the trumpeter's early albums. With his own quintet, both on *Wynton Marsalis* and *Think of One,* his playing is ambitious but unconvincing; for the most part, it's older brother Branford on tenor and pianist Kenny Kirkland who come off as the group's great soloists. But they take a backseat on *Hot House Flowers,* an album of high-class mood music that finds Wynton once again chasing ghosts—in this case, Clifford Brown, whose *With Strings* this lushly orchestrated album emulates.

Black Codes (from the Underground) finally pulls the Marsalis quintet into focus, filling the music with fire. Unfortunately, that fire didn't burn long, as Branford and Kenny Kirkland left soon after to tour with Sting. As a result, *J Mood* was recorded with a quartet featuring pianist Marcus Roberts, a group Marsalis would maintain through *Live at Blues Alley.* But as much as this coolly cerebral lineup suits the trumpeter's conservatism, the performances are mannered and unconvincing. With *The Majesty of the Blues,* however, Marsalis finally latches on to a sense of tradition that is both more forgiving of cliché and less prone to icy intellectuality. Now working with a sextet, Marsalis emphasizes the collective groove of old-fashioned New Orleans jazz. It isn't vintage jazz, exactly—though his use of banjo and clarinet makes for some very explicit echoes—so much as an attempt to tap what Marsalis sees as an ongoing tradition in African-American music: namely, the blues. It doesn't always work—"Premature Autopsies (Sermon)," for all its good intentions, seems hokey and unauthentic—but it obviously reinvigorates the trumpeter.

Standard Time, Vol. 3 follows through with a meditation on melody that is midwifed by father Ellis Marsalis (filling in on piano for Roberts); the performances may not be earthshaking, but they are wonderfully nuanced. But it's the semi-Ellingtonian sweep of *Tune In Tomorrow* that really shows Marsalis's ambition. Even if some of it sounds like film scoring (which, in fact, it is), his writing has the kind of heart many of his earlier albums lack, making it remarkably easy to love.

It's when Marsalis tries to apply that approach to a less idiomatic style that he runs into trouble. As cultural theory, his three-volume *Soul Gestures in Southern Blue* series is admirably ambitious, but as music, it works only occasionally. Despite a markedly more soulful groove (particularly on *Uptown Ruler* and *Levee Low Moan*), Marsalis and company have trouble pulling these performances out of the theoretical realm, suggesting that his latest notion of "tradition" is as contrived as the one that fed his earlier albums.

Blue Interlude is an impressive series of set pieces, performed brilliantly by Marsalis's working septet, with Wessell Anderson on alto saxophone, Todd Williams on sax and clarinet, Wycliff Gordon on trombone, Marcus Roberts on piano, Reginald Veal on bass and Herlin Riley on drums. *In This House, on This Morning* is a fascinating but long-winded tribute to the gospel experience.

Citi Movement, a score to accompany the ballet *Griot New York,* shows Marsalis making a quantum leap as a composer capable of scoring and arranging extended programmatic works that sizzle on their own but add up to an even greater whole when listened to together. This is the next step Marsalis needed to take to expand his Ellington-influenced vision into large-group music for a new millennium.

Marsalis took on his greatest role as the head of the Lincoln Center Jazz Program, writing for the Lincoln Center Jazz Orchestra and directing a series of educational programs. On one hand Marsalis is perhaps the best educator jazz has ever known. His ability to work with children's themes is amply evident on *Joe Cool's Blues,* a lightweight but pleasant diversion into the soundtrack music from the *Peanuts* cartoons.

On the big stage Marsalis needed to add middlebrow entertainment and gravitas to the mix in order to satisfy the stuffed-shirt crowd. He undertook his most massive project, the jazz oratorio *Blood on the Fields,* covering the dead-serious subject of slavery with such bombastic pomp and circumstance that he was awarded a Pulitzer Prize for his effort, the kind of honor that Ellington himself was never afforded. Unfortunately, *Blood*'s ambitions far outstrip the ultimately bloated and disappointing recorded performance of a work that is far more impressive on paper, and may yet be due for its definitive performance. *Jump Start and Jazz,* a classical release, is curiously static but is illuminated by a guest shot from the venerable Harry "Sweets" Edison on trumpet. — J.D.C.

PAT MARTINO

★★★★★ **El Hombre (1967; Original Jazz Classics, 1990)**
★★ **Strings! (1968; Original Jazz Classics, 1991)**
★★★ **East! (1968; Original Jazz Classics, 1990)**
★★★½ **Baiyina (The Clear Evidence) (1968; Original Jazz Classics, 1989)**
★★★ **Desperado (1970; Original Jazz Classics, 1991)**
★★★★ **Live! (Muse, 1973)**
★★★½ **Consciousness (Muse, 1975)**
★★★ **Footprints (1975; 32 Jazz, 1997)**
★★★ **Exit (Muse, 1977)**
★ **The Return (Muse, 1987)**
★★★★ **Interchange (Muse, 1994)**
★★★ **The Maker (Evidence, 1995)**
★★★½ **Nightwings (Muse, 1996)**
★★½ **Cream (32 Jazz, 1997)**
★★★ **All Sides Now (Blue Note, 1997)**
★★★½ **Head and Heart (32 Jazz, 1998)**
★★★½ **We'll Be Together Again (32 Jazz, 1998)**
★★★★ **Stone Blue (Blue Note, 1998)**

Ever since he burst on the scene in the 1960s as "the Kid," Pat Martino (b. 1944) has been regarded as a member of the modern jazz guitar pantheon, a godlike hero for emerging players. As he moved beyond work as a sideman for several top jazz organists, the Philadelphia native brought a new approach to postbop guitar with his sustained, often dark, melodic lines played at lightning speed. Eastern influences crept into his music and remained there through his 1970s fusion phase.

Martino's stunning debut, *El Hombre,* is an organ-drenched session that introduced him to jazz audiences and hinted at his shift from a straight-ahead melodic style to a distinctive linear approach. *Strings!* includes some stunning Martino solos but suffers from flawed ensemble playing. *East!* incorporates Indian influences on the title track of this intense bop session. *Baiyina (The Clear Evidence)* expands Martino's moody, eastward orientation. *Desperado* is a 12-string showcase for the near-bionic intensity of his solos.

Live! is the strongest of Martino's available 1970s recordings, fusing his bop lines with an electric rhythm section. Its diverse material ranges from a stunning cover of the pop hit "Sunny" to Martino's own "The Great Stream," one of the few first-phase tunes he brought into the 1990s. *Consciousness* is also strong, with tremendous versions of "Impressions," "Along Came Betty" and "Both Sides Now." *Head and Heart* is a two-CD compilation of *Live!* and *Consciousness.* A mellower Martino sound comes to the fore on *Footprints,* a stylistic tribute to Wes Montgomery. Several key recordings from this phase have recently been reissued by 32 Jazz, including *We'll Be Together Again,* a soft duet session with pianist Gil Goldstein. Martino fans can only hope the same resuscitation awaits his fusion-tinged Warner Bros. albums *Joyous Lake* and *Starbright.*

In 1980 Martino underwent emergency neurosurgery to repair a congenital brain aneurysm that had caused several years of misdiagnosed seizures and depression. The surgery saved his life but temporarily stole his memory, triggering a 15-year near absence from recording and performing, while he slowly relearned the guitar and his musical style by studying his own vintage recordings. He made several low-key Jersey Shore appearances under his given name, Pat Azzara, to test his skills, which led to a trio gig at New York's Bottom Line and a follow-up live recording at Fat Tuesday's. That premature session, *The Return,* will interest only completists. The 32 Jazz compilation *Cream* includes some of the best tracks from six of Martino's Muse albums between 1972 and 1987.

The bop-oriented *Interchange* signaled that Martino was back to his musical self, supported by a strong new rhythm section. Peppered with the unconventional harmonic and tonal concepts that he first used three decades earlier, *The Maker* has a darker sound. *Nightwings,* a powerful, upbeat session, is augmented by the tenor-sax interplay of Bob Kenmotsu. *All Sides Now* is notable for Martino's company as much as the range of his playing. His versatility and love of his instrument is showcased in pairings with jazz guitarists Charlie Hunter, Tuck Andress, Kevin Eubanks, Les Paul, Mike Stern and Michael Hedges, rocker Joe Satriani and singer Cassandra Wilson, with whom Martino duets on "Both Sides Now." Twenty-two years later, *Stone Blue* brought Martino together with *Joyous Lake* band mates Kenwood Dennard and Delmar Brown plus young tenor ace Eric Alexander and bassist James Genus for a strong session with the cohesive band sound for which Martino seems to have been searching since emerging from the darkness. There's even an updated version of his classic "Joyous Lake" composition. — K.F.

HUGH MASEKELA

★★½ **Reconstruction (1970; Mojazz, 1994)**
★★★½ **Hugh Masekela & the Union of South Africa (1971; Mojazz, 1994)**
★★★★ **Uptownship (Novus, 1989)**
★★ **Beatin' Aroun de Bush (Novus, 1992)**
★★★★½ **Hope (Triloka, 1994)**
★★★★ **The Lasting Impressions of Ooga-Booga (Verve, 1996)**

One of South Africa's most significant musical exports, jazz trumpeter and pop singer Hugh Masekela (b. 1939) is an ebullient, playful showman, an early multiculti craftsman and a hit maker both with his 1968 instrumental "Grazing in the Grass" and as a featured member of Paul Simon's *Graceland* entourage. Masekela boasts a bright, strident trumpet sound and staccato phrasing, tending toward the R&B, song-oriented edge of the jazz spectrum. Divinely touched at an early age in the form of a trumpet sent to him by Louis Armstrong, Masekela arrived in New York in 1960 on a scholarship to the Manhattan School of Music. In his native South Africa he had already led a jazz band as an integral member of the Jazz Epistles, an all-star unit featuring pianist Dollar Brand, trombonist Jonas Gwangwa and legendary alto-sax man Kippie Moeketsi. (An eponymous Epistles album has been issued on the Gallo import label.)

Masekela's earliest recording available domestically is *The Lasting Impressions of Ooga-Booga* (actually a joining of two MGM albums, 1965's *The Americanization of Ooga-Booga* and 1968's *The Lasting Impression of Hugh Masekela.* Culled from an excellent 1965 engagement at New York's Village Gate with an American rhythm section (notably Larry Willis on piano), the 13 mostly original tracks herein define a career path, remolding traditional Zulu folk melodies in a small-band jazz context, with political and cultural consciousness-raising commentary throughout.

In 1968 Masekela burst to the top of the charts with the irresistibly charged instrumental "Grazing in the Grass" on the Uni label. A successful fusion of late-'60s soul and his distinctive machine-gun melodic approach, the track is to be found on various reissue collections, most notably Rhino's *Rock Instrumental Classics, Vol. 4.* Three years later Motown was inspired to create the Chisa imprint for Masekela's subsequent albums, *Reconstruction* and *Hugh Masekela & the Union of South Africa.* The former is more of a pop experiment, emphasizing his raspy vocals on some ill-conceived covers ("You Keep Me Hangin' On," "I Will") with a few redeeming, African-rooted songs ("Make Me a Potion," "Woza"). Uniting with homebrothers Gwangwa and saxophonist/composer Caiphus Semenya, Masekela created a true early-'70s timepiece with the latter album, in both musical and social posture, while achieving a convincing mix of funk, Zulu and jazz sonorities. Gwangwa's "Shebeen" and Semenya's "Caution!" are well crafted and strongly played.

With his star on the rise again in the late '80s as a result of the Simon association, Masekela netted a deal with BMG's Novus label. *Uptownship* is easily his strongest latter-career studio effort, with flügelhorn added to his battery and various *Graceland* alumni in attendance (significantly bassist Baghiti Khumalo, keyboardist Tony Cedras and guitarist John Slelowane). The title track is a superb Masekela original, and the '50s Afro-pop hits he resurrects—particularly "Egoli" and "Emavungweni"—form a satisfying link to his roots-based, early career direction. *Beatin' Aroun de Bush* loses direction in an overpolished and synthesized morass; fortunately, the production whitewash doesn't totally smother compelling tunes like Cedras's "Ngena Ngena" or Masekela's "Sekunjalo."

Hope is an accurate document of Masekela's high-energy and stylistically far-reaching live shows. Recorded at Washington, D.C.'s Blues Alley and featuring a young-and-hungry, mostly

African band, the crowd-pleasing selections review his career (with excellent liner notes on each song), including the timeless "Grazing in the Grass," Fela Kuti's Nigerian high-life anthem "Lady," the tender South African jazz classic "Ntjilo Ntjilo" and a dark, fist-raising version of the protest song "Stimela." — A.K.

MATERIAL

★★★★ **Seven Souls (Triloka, 1990)**
★★★★ **The Third Power (Axiom, 1991)**
★★★★½ **Hallucination Engine (Axiom, 1994)**

In its original incarnation, Material was a floating rhythm section built around bassist Bill Laswell, keyboardist Michael Beinhorn and drummer Fred Maher, New York–based musicians whose music freely crossed the boundaries of jazz, rock and the avant-garde. Their earliest efforts, compiled on the out-of-print *Temporary Music,* flirted with the relationship between stasis (as represented by Laswell's repetitious, funk-influenced bass lines) and change (as manifested in most of the other instruments, particularly Beinhorn's keyboards and tapes); the album's mixture of rhythm and noise is sometimes bracing but too often self-indulgent. Sometime after these sessions, the group tried to apply its rhythmic strengths to more commercial ends and cut a fiercely catchy dance single, "Busting Out," with vocalist Nona Hendryx. That experience isn't much reflected in *Memory Serves* (also out of print), which extends the experimentalist approach of *Temporary Music* through looser song structures and more inventive guest soloists (including guitarists Sonny Sharrock and Fred Frith, trombonist George Lewis and alto saxophonist Henry Threadgill), but the unavailable *One Down* finds the group—by then minus Maher—returning to a funk-grounded approach. But because Material sees R&B as a means rather than an end, the songs here invariably push the envelope of popular music, with such wonderfully unexpected results as "Take a Chance," an edgily aggressive dance tune again featuring Hendryx, and "Memories," a lovely ballad that contrasts Archie Shepp's tenor-sax howls against Whitney Houston's soulfully assured singing.

It was almost seven years before another album arrived under the Material imprimatur, by which point Beinhorn was also gone. Although funk beats are once again used to tie the music's disparate elements together, the songs on *Seven Souls* play off a sort of pan-Arabic melodic base; guests include singer Fahiem Dandan, violinists Simon Shaheen and Lakshminarayana Shankar and narrator William Burroughs. As for *The Third Power,* it's a Material album in name only, with Laswell handling production chores but no playing duties, and an all-star cast—Bootsy Collins, the Jungle Brothers, Bernie Worrell, Sly Dunbar, Robbie Shakespeare—generating the same reggae-funk style featured on Dunbar and Shakespeare's Laswell-produced solo albums. *Hallucination Engine* features the outstanding 1994 edition of Material, in which Laswell concocts a heady mix of world music and electronica played by a stellar cast of musicians from around the globe. — J.D.C.

KEIKO MATSUI

★★½ **A Drop of Water (White Cat/Unity, 1987)**
★★½ **Under Northern Lights (MCA, 1989)**
★★½ **No Borders (MCA, 1990)**
★★★ **Night Waltz (Sin-Drome, 1991)**
★★★ **Cherry Blossom (White Cat/Unity, 1992)**
★★★½ **Doll (White Cat/Unity, 1994)**
★★★½ **Sapphire (White Cat/Unity, 1995)**
★★★ **Dream Walk (Countdown/Unity, 1996)**

Japanese keyboardist Keiko Matsui (b. 1961) combines classical piano training with a celebration of heritage instrumentation and an ability to groove. Her soundscapes explore electronics and spiritualism without resorting to New Age clichés. Her compositions are peppered with influences from Mozart and Chopin to Chick Corea and Keith Jarrett.

Matsui's evocative instrumentals have made her America's top-selling female contemporary jazz artist and won her the 1997 Essence Award from the American Society of Young Musicians. The former child piano prodigy first applied her formal training in an all-female band, then began a solo career with the help of her husband and producer, Kazu Matsui, who contributes shakuhachi (traditional Japanese bamboo flute) to her recordings.

Matsui chooses studio-crafted precision over improvisation, but it's hard to deny her music's graceful beauty and power, especially in her later work. (Such guests as saxophonist Paul Taylor and songwriter Jeff Day add complexity to her more recent CDs.) Transcending the formulaic, *Cherry Blossom* features solid playing and composing, particularly on the experimental and funky "Walking on the Bridge" and "Crescendo." *Doll* packs more of the same punch, with Kazu Matsui's flute on "Moroccan Ashes" making that track a standout.

Sapphire continues to mix traditional jazz motifs and organic sounds like chimes and woodwinds that evoke running water or wind through trees. Vocals on two songs detract from the melodic immediacy of Matsui's compositions; instrumentals like "Dragon Wings" and the title track communicate more effectively. Similarly, the impressionistic music on *Dream Walk* doesn't need the package's high-tech enhanced CD gimmickry. If bass samples from John Patitucci ("A Cat on the Chimney") and Marcus Miller ("Fire in the Desert" and others) and haunting classical overtones ("Mask") don't impress you, it's doubtful that CD-ROM gadgetry will. — A.A.

TURK MAURO

★★★ **Hittin' the Jug: The Music of Gene Ammons (Milestone, 1995)**
★★★ **The Truth (Milestone, 1997)**

Saxophonist Turk Mauro (b. 1944) was a featured sideman in the Buddy Rich band and a member of the house band at New York's Blue Note and Half Note clubs before moving to Paris in 1987. He returned to the United States in 1994 and settled in south Florida, where he came to the attention of producer Bob Weinstock. *Hittin' the Jug* is a lively soul-jazz tribute to Gene Ammons, featuring the propulsive drumming of Duffy Jackson and solid organ and piano work from Dr. Lonnie Smith. *The Truth* showcases Mauro's compositional chops on another fiery session of blues- and funk-based jazz. "Kitty Kat Blues" and "Boppin' with Bob" offer a glimpse into the Miami-area jazz scene. — J.S.

JOHN MAYALL

★★½ **John Mayall Plays John Mayall (1965; London, 1988)**
★★★★½ **Bluesbreakers—John Mayall with Eric Clapton (1965; Mobile Fidelity, 1994)**
★★★½ **Crusade (1967; London, 1987)**
★★★ **Raw Blues (1967; London, 1987)**
★★★ **The Blues Alone (1967; Polydor, 1988)**
★★★½ **A Hard Road (1967; London, 1987)**
★★★½ **Bare Wires (1968; Polydor, 1988)**
★★★½ **Blues from Laurel Canyon (1969; Polydor, 1989)**
★★★★ **Looking Back (1969; Polydor, 1990)**
★★★ **Thru the Years (1972; London, 1991)**
★★ **New Year, New Band, New Company (1975; One Way, N.A.)**
★★ **Notice to Appear (1976; One Way, N.A.)**
★★ **A Banquet in Blues (1976; One Way, N.A.)**
★★ **Lots of People (1977; One Way, N.A.)**
★★ **A Hard Core Package (1977; One Way, N.A.)**
★★★½ **Primal Solos (1977; London, N.A.)**
★★ **Last of the British Blues (1978; One Way, N.A.)**
★★ **Behind the Iron Curtain (GNP Crescendo, 1986)**
★★ **Chicago Line (Island, 1988)**
★★★★ **Archives to Eighties (Polydor, 1988)**
★★ **A Sense of Place (Island, 1990)**
★★★½ **London Blues, 1964–1969 (Polydor, 1992)**
★★★½ **Room to Move, 1969–1974 (Polydor, 1992)**
★★★½ **Wake Up Call (Silvertone, 1993)**
★★★ **The 1982 Reunion Concert (One Way, 1994)**
★★★ **Cross Country Blues (One Way, 1994)**
★★★ **Spinning Coin (Silvertone, 1995)**
★★★ **Blues for the Lost Days (Silvertone, 1997)**
★★½ **Drivin' On: The ABC Years (MCA, 1998)**

The early-'60s British blues movement—training ground for such guitar gunslingers as Eric Clapton, Mick Taylor, Peter Green and numerous others—had as its first populizer the fine singer and better harmonica player John Mayall (b. 1933). His bands, in fact, served as informal academies in the then-arcane arts of Sonny Boy Williamson (Rice Miller) and J.B. Lenoir—their graduates also include primo bassists Jack Bruce and John McVie and drummers Aynsley Dunbar and Mick Fleetwood; basically, almost every English player in search of a tougher sound than skiffle or folk gravitated toward Mayall's sphere. Constantly shifting his personnel—more than nine groups from 1963 to 1967 alone—Mayall was a guiding light who offered his players generous room to move. Their efforts and continuing influence made abundantly clear the debt rock owes to the blues.

John Mayall Plays John Mayall reveals the musician's skill on harmonica and his very reverent approach to the blues: In the early days, even his originals rarely broke from the classic 12-bar pattern. On *Bluesbreakers—John Mayall with Eric Clapton,* ex-Yardbird Clapton blazes, delivering Chicago blues with precocious command; it stands as one of Mayall's toughest sets. With *Crusade,* the teenage Mick Taylor is highlighted—his fluid leads anticipate the brilliance he'd develop with the Rolling Stones—and Mayall begins experimenting with a horn section. The elegant *Bare Wires,* an early attempt at jazz-rock fusion, remains one of Mayall's more interesting records; its horns, by Dick Heckstall-Smith and Chris Mercer, are especially fine, and Mayall's vocals, never his strong suit, gain in breathy, haunting appeal. Peter Green, who with Mayall vets John McVie and Mick Fleetwood would leave to form Fleetwood Mac, enlivens *A Hard Road;* his playing is spare, fierce and supple. On *Blues from Laurel Canyon,* a conceptual album offering Mayall's musings about L.A., the sound is soft, jazz-inflected and moody.

While many of his records are now mainly of historical interest, they provide fascinating glimpses of talents in embryo, and they certainly testify to Mayall's industry and influence. And, while much of the work released after *Thru the Years* is primarily for Mayall fanatics, he enjoyed a creative resurgence with 1993's *Wake Up Call*, featuring guest turns by Mavis Staples, Mick Taylor and Buddy Guy. *London Blues, 1964–1969*, *Room to Move 1969–1974*, *Looking Back* and *Primal Solos* offer good overviews. *Archives to Eighties* is an intriguing curio: Mayall updates badly mixed tracks featuring Clapton, Taylor and violinist Sugarcane Harris—the new sound is excellent, and the record provides a good intro to the vast Mayall canon. — P.E.

PERCY MAYFIELD

★★★★	**The Best of Percy Mayfield (Specialty, 1976)**
★★★	**Please Send Me Someone to Love (Intermedia, 1982)**
★★★★★	**Poet of the Blues (Specialty, 1989)**
★★★★	**For Collectors Only (Specialty, 1991)**
★★★★★	**Percy Mayfield, Vol. 2: Memory Pain (Specialty, 1992)**

As a songwriter, Percy Mayfield (1920–1984) evinced a command of language and a deep and tragic understanding of love's mercurial, often contradictory emotions; when he sang, his friendly, soulful delivery had all the comfort of a blazing fire on a cold night. Truly earning the honorific "Poet of the Blues," Mayfield was a prolific and potent writer whose original songs on the Specialty label propelled him to R&B chart success in the early- to mid-'50s and have been covered often by some of America's finest singers, notably Ray Charles, for whose Tangerine label Mayfield became an artist and staff writer in the early '60s. Charles's Tangerine period includes several Mayfield compositions, the best known being the rollicking "Hit the Road, Jack."

A good sampling of Mayfield's early work remains in print. Specialty has four albums in its catalog, including the 12-song *Best of Percy Mayfield* set dating from 1970 and the more recent 25-song retrospectives, *Poet of the Blues* and *Percy Mayfield, Vol. 2: Memory Pain,* the latter two lovingly assembled and annotated by Billy Vera. *Poet* renders *The Best of* superfluous, containing as it does everything on the earlier release plus 13 additional tracks, all dating from 1950 to 1954. His lyrics bespeaking a man who was all raw nerves, Mayfield tackled topics that were rarely addressed in popular music in the '50s. Consider the first track on *Poet:* In feel and presentation, "Please Send Me Someone to Love," a Number One single from 1950, sounds like a yearning love song—until Mayfield hammers home the key lyric: "If the world don't put an end to this damnable sin/Hate will put the world in flame." He was singing of racial prejudice, then a topic sensibly ignored by black artists aiming to break into the pop charts. Mayfield's singing equals the task he set for himself as a writer. In laid-back fashion he twists and turns lyrics to achieve an emotional effect that doubles their impact and raises compelling questions as to their true intent.

Opening with an alternate take of "Please Send Me Someone to Love," as if sounding the theme for the 24 tracks to come, *Memory Pain* takes Mayfield from 1950 into 1960, the latter year represented solely by the previously unreleased a cappella demo Mayfield cut on "Hit the Road, Jack." It is on this set that Mayfield sounds most dispossessed, most despairing of anyone finding him worthy of sympathy, much less love.

As a live recording, Intermedia's *Please Send Me Someone to Love* occupies a hallowed place in the Mayfield catalog. Unfortunately, there is no liner information regarding when, where and with whom Mayfield is performing. Given that his voice has dropped some from the Specialty years, this set must date from his later recording years. Regardless, he is in fine shape here, joking with the band and the audience but always taking care to bring the goods home when it's time to sing. Mayfield went on to record for Tangerine, RCA, Brunswick and, for one Johnny "Guitar" Watson–produced single in 1974, Atlantic. Sadly, nothing remains in print from those years. — D.M.

CECIL McBEE

★★★ **Alternate Spaces (1979; India Navigation, 1996)**
★★★ **Flying Out (1983; India Navigation, 1997)**
★★★★ **Unspoken (Palmetto, 1997)**

Cecil McBee (b. 1935) is an exceptionally talented bassist who came to prominence in the 1960s and is still highly sought after. He was a member of the popular Charles Lloyd group of the mid-'60s and became a valued sideman for Blue Note recordings with Jackie McLean, Grachan Moncur III and Wayne Shorter, among others.

McBee began leading his own sessions in the '70s: *Alternate Spaces* and *Flying Out,* which features a provocative front line of violin, cello and cornet, document this period. He went on to play with everyone worth playing with—hear him on Chico Freeman's *Spirit Sensitive,* a quintet date featuring an invigorating duet between McBee and the gifted saxophonist—and the experience manifests itself in his maturing talents as a composer. *Unspoken* gathers some promising young players, including drummer Matt Wilson, who attack McBee's engaging compositions with gusto.
— S.F.

CASH McCALL

★★★★ **No More Doggin' (1985; Evidence, 1995)**

Morris Dollison Jr. (b. 1941) was already an accomplished singer and guitarist, having played with the Gospel Songbirds and recorded R&B singles as Maurice Dollison, when he scored a hit as Cash McCall with 1966's "When You Wake Up." As McCall, he has recorded sporadically ever since.

A gifted songwriter whose material has been covered by a wide range of people, McCall primarily plays his own songs on *No More Doggin'*. The title track, a B.B. King–inspired up-tempo blues by Roscoe Gordon, includes a stinging guitar solo from McCall and is the set's only cover. McCall heads into Howlin' Wolf territory on "Mojo Women"; the sparse "I'll Be There" recalls his gospel roots; and "European Holiday" is an inventive travelog celebrating the joys of being an American bluesman abroad.
— J.S.

LES McCANN

★★★★ **Swiss Movement (with Eddie Harris) (1969; Rhino, 1993)**
★★ **Much Les (1969; Rhino, 1993)**
★★ **Layers (1973; Rhino, 1993)**
★★★★ **Relationships: The Les McCann Anthology (Rhino, 1993)**
★★★ **On the Soul Side (MusicMasters, 1994)**
★★★ **Listen Up! (MusicMasters, 1996)**

Keyboardist/vocalist Les McCann (b. 1935) helped popularize the soul-jazz sound of the early 1960s, playing bluesy vamps in a mostly trio format and singing with a down-home vocal delivery. By the end of the decade, he had honed this formula into a crowd-pleasing style, captured live at the Montreux Jazz Festival with *Swiss Movement,* his career high point, with tenor saxophonist Eddie Harris and including the definitive version of "Compared to What," the Gene McDaniels hit that became McCann's signature.

McCann made several attempts at broadening his commercial base, including adding strings (on *Much Les*) and synthesizers (*Layers*), none of which worked. Only recently has he returned to his tried-and-true soul-jazz style, reprising his bright moments with Harris in *On the Soul Side* and working with keyboardists George Duke and Billy Preston on *Listen Up!* — J.S.

SUSANNAH McCORKLE

★★★½ **No More Blues (Concord Jazz, 1989)**
★★★½ **Sabia (Concord Jazz, 1990)**
★★★★ **I'll Take Romance (Concord Jazz, 1992)**
★★★ **From Bessie to Brazil (Concord Jazz, 1993)**
★★★½ **From Broadway to Bebop (Concord Jazz, 1994)**
★★★ **Easy to Love: The Songs of Cole Porter (Concord Jazz, 1996)**
★★★ **The Songs of Johnny Mercer (Jazz Alliance, 1996)**

Vocalist Susannah McCorkle (b. 1946), a native Californian, got her start in Europe, then emerged in the 1970s in New York to great acclaim as a top-notch interpreter of classics from all corners of the landscape. Her tributes to Harry Warren and E.Y. "Yip" Harburg are out of print, along with the masterful Grammy-nominated *People That You Never Got to Love,* but her album of Johnny Mercer songs remains available.

McCorkle has excelled at Concord, receiving tremendous support from guitarist Emily Remler on *No More Blues* and *Sabia* and from tenor saxophonist/flautist Frank Wess on *I'll Take Romance. From Bessie to Brazil* is more of a pop record, while *From Broadway to Bebop* does just what the title says, ranging across material from *Guys and Dolls* to "Moody's Mood." — J.S.

JIMMY McCRACKLIN

★★★ **High on the Blues (1971; Stax, 1991)**
★★★★ **My Story (Bullseye Blues, 1991)**
★★★★ **A Taste of the Blues: West Coast Blues Summit (Bullseye Blues, 1994)**

A church-bred blues pianist, writer and vocalist who began recording in 1945, St. Louis native Jimmy McCracklin (b. 1921) had a Top 10 hit in 1958 with "The Walk," inspiring the dance craze of the same name. While "The Walk" proved to be his sole foray into the top of the pop chart as a recording artist, he remained a reliable presence on the R&B chart and on the concert circuit; at the same time, his songs began finding their way into other artists' repertoires. His 1967 song "Tramp" was a hit in versions by Lowell Fulson, Otis Redding and Carla Thomas and, more recently, Salt-n-Pepa. He wound up in Memphis in 1971, cutting the propulsive *High on the Blues* with producers Al Jackson, the stalwart drummer of Booker T. and the MG's, and Willie Mitchell, founder of Hi Records and writer/producer for Al Green. Here McCracklin emerges with a strong album that modulates nicely between the strutting and the slow blues of his reputation and straight-ahead Southern soul.

Throughout the '70s, McCracklin migrated from small label to small label, then bowed out of the recording scene in the '80s, although he continued making public appearances. In 1990 he found a new home at Bullseye Blues and has since delivered two strong albums of quintessential McCracklin blues. His first, *My Story,* was recorded in New Orleans, which clearly suits McCracklin. The opening cut, "Tomorrow," uses the mood and feel of a gospel song—right down to Ron Levy's steady, droning organ chords. McCracklin digs deep for his most mournful blues voice and finds himself standing toe-to-toe with Irma Thomas, one of the Crescent City's finest vocalists, who engages him in a spirited dialog, thundering the female retort to the man's hangdog musings. This fiery duet sets the tone for the rest of the album, which ranges from a warm reminiscence in soul of "Mama and Papa" to a gritty B.B. King–style urban-blues plea on the title track to the lowest of low-down blues ("Stuck with Loneliness") to a strutting funk workout ("Just a Matter of Time") that closes the album on a philosophical note.

On *A Taste of the Blues* McCracklin works his own interesting variations on Southern funk, traditional soul and gutbucket blues. He is joined on various cuts by guitarists Lowell Fulson and Smokey Wilson, all-around-threat Johnny Otis on vibes and, on the poignant slow blues "Yesterday Is Gone," the overlooked Barbara Lynn, whose brooding, husky vocals recall Dinah Washington's. As the cut with Lynn and the powerful, mournful title track demonstrate, McCracklin, singing in a smoky baritone, can deliver heartbreak with the best of 'em, his lyric readings pregnant with subtext. Along the way the various instrumentalists add their own two cents' worth to the mix: On "Not the Right Thing" Fulson energizes a grinding track with angular, punchy solo lines; Wilson and fellow guitarist Larry Davis shine on "Outside Help," one keeping a steady-rolling, chicken-scratching riff going throughout, while the other offers counterpoint in the form of steely, protesting lead lines. — D.M.

MISSISSIPPI FRED McDOWELL

★★★★★ **You Gotta Move (1964; Arhoolie, 1994)**
★★★★★ **Good Morning Little Schoolgirl (1964; Arhoolie, 1994)**
★★★★ **My Home Is in the Delta (with Annie Mae McDowell) (1965; Testament, 1995)**
★★★★ **Long Way from Home (1966; Original Blues Classics, 1990)**
★★★★★ **I Do Not Play No Rock 'n' Roll (1969; Capitol, 1995)**

★★★★½ This Ain't No Rock n' Roll (1969; Arhoolie, 1995)
★★★★ Amazing Grace (1969; Testament, 1994)
★★★★ Shake 'Em on Down (Tomato, 1989)
★★★½ When I Lay My Burden Down (with Furry Lewis and Rev. Robert Wilkins) (Biograph, 1994)
★★★★ Live at the Mayfair Hotel (Infinite Zero/American, 1995)
★★★★½ Mississippi Fred McDowell (Rounder, 1995)

"Mississippi" Fred McDowell (ca. 1904–1972) was actually born in Rossville, Tennessee. He learned to play guitar by watching others, like his mentor, Eli Green, but he didn't own a guitar until around 1940. In 1959 McDowell, then a farm laborer and tractor driver, was "discovered" by folklorist Alan Lomax, who immediately recorded his slicing bottleneck guitar and purely emotive voice, dubbing him the last of the great Delta blues masters. Indeed, McDowell's sound was an extension of the great Mississippi blues players, from Robert Johnson to Charley Patton to Son House. McDowell would enjoy his newly found popularity through the blues revival of the '60s, recording several albums and performing internationally. He even lived to see one of his songs, "You Gotta Move," recorded by the Rolling Stones before his death.

Of the available McDowell titles, none is more compelling than the Arhoolie releases *You Gotta Move* and *Good Morning Little Schoolgirl.* Both comprise recordings made by Arhoolie owner Chris Strachwitz, who was introduced to McDowell by Lomax. The former includes tracks recorded at McDowell's house near Como, Mississippi, in 1964. Among the standouts are "Kokomo Blues," "Fred's Worried Life Blues" and the haunting "Write Me a Few Lines," which McDowell learned from Eli Green. Another highlight is a version of "When I Lay My Burden Down," with McDowell's slicing slide work and his wife, Annie Mae, on vocals. The absolute gems are two duets by McDowell and Eli Green, recorded at Green's home near Holly Springs, Mississippi, in early 1965. Both songs ("Brooks Run into the Ocean" and "Bull Dog Blues") were written by Green and have a special luminescence that can only be attained between teacher and pupil.

Good Morning Little Schoolgirl contains 22 tracks (13 previously unreleased), half of which are designated "the blues" (solo McDowell on guitar) and the other half labeled "church songs" (McDowell on vocals and guitar plus vocals by Annie Mae and several members of their congregation). With McDowell's slide prevalent throughout, there isn't a bad song on the album. Blues highlights include "Drop Down Mama," "Fred's Ramblin' Blues" and "I Looked at the Sun"; notable religious tracks are "Get Right Church," "I'm Going over the Hill" and an intriguing ensemble version of "You Gotta Move" that drips with emotion.

Mississippi Fred McDowell was lovingly recorded in 1962 at McDowell's home by Dick Spottswood, a graduate student who trekked from Washington, D.C., for that purpose. Not released until the early '80s in Britain, the album remained unissued domestically until 1995. McDowell was at his best that day, with his exquisite slide work and urgent vocals bringing to life "John Henry," "Kokomo Blues" and "Shake 'Em on Down." Judging from the excellent sound quality, it could have been recorded yesterday. *My Home Is in the Delta* was recorded in 1963 and '64 with Annie Mae and was previously issued on Testament in 1965. The CD includes four previously unreleased tracks, including the mournful "Six White Horses," the insistent "Down on Dankin's Farm" and the sprightly "Big Road Blues."

Long Way from Home, recorded in late 1966 at UCLA, again features McDowell performing solo on his famous slide guitar. Included here are the McDowell original "Gravel Road Blues" and versions of "John Henry," Kokomo Arnold's "Milk Cow Blues" and Amos Easton's "Sail On, Little Girl." *This Ain't No Rock n' Roll* is an interesting departure for McDowell, marking the first time he was recorded playing electric guitar and backed (on eight songs) by a small group (guitarist Mike Russo, bassist John Kahn and drummer Bob Jones). The remainder of the album consists of 10 electrified tracks that McDowell cut at Strachwitz's house in 1968 with drummer John Francis (on 4 songs) and an uncredited harmonica player (probably Steve Talbot) on "Mama Said I'm Crazy." Of these previously unreleased tracks, 6 feature McDowell playing solo electric guitar.

I Do Not Play No Rock 'n' Roll was recorded and released by Capitol in 1969. The 1995 reissue is a double-disc package, comprising the original album as well as songs from the same sessions that appeared on an obscure album released by the Just Sunshine label. The discs have a relaxed feel, as McDowell runs through his signature tunes (Big Joe Williams's "Baby Please Don't Go," "Good Morning Little Schoolgirl," "Jesus Is on the Mainline") as well as previously unreleased versions of several songs and alternate versions of others. Playing electric guitar, McDowell is backed by bass and drums, giving the songs the blunt, accessible feel that helped endear him to the masses.

Amazing Grace's subtitle, "Mississippi Delta Spirituals by the Hunter's Chapel Singers of Como, Mississippi," tells the story. Originally recorded in 1966, the album consists of emotionally charged spirituals sung by McDowell, his wife and three members of their church (Fannie Davis, Grace Bowden and James Collins). Included here are fantastic versions of "Going over the Hill," with vocals by Annie Mae, and "Back Back Train," featuring Mississippi Fred's somnambulant lead vocal. Throughout, McDowell's slide guitar serves as a keening cocoon for the vocal ensemble's over-the-top incantations.

Shake 'Em on Down is a different kind of album altogether. Recorded live at the famed Gaslight club in New York City in 1971, the performance was one of McDowell's last. Bassist Tom Pomposello adds texture to McDowell's electric-guitar playing. Highlights include the title track (written by McDowell and Alan Lomax), upon which Pomposello plays second guitar, "Mercy," "White Lightnin'" and a smoky version of "Baby Please Don't Go." *Live at the Mayfair Hotel* documents a 1969 London show and includes solo-electric versions of Mance Lipscomb's "Evil Hearted Woman" and Willie Dixon's "My Babe" alongside originals like "61 Highway" and "Red Cross Store Blues." — B.R.H.

JACK McDUFF

- ★★★½ **Tough 'Duff (with Jimmy Forrest) (1960; Original Jazz Classics, 1995)**
- ★★★★★ **The Honeydripper (1961; Original Jazz Classics, 1995)**
- ★★★½ **Screamin' (1962; Original Jazz Classics, 1996)**
- ★★★★ **Brother Jack Meets the Boss (with Gene Ammons) (1962; Original Jazz Classics, 1995)**
- ★★★ **Live! (1963; Prestige, 1995)**
- ★★★ **The Reentry (Muse, 1989)**
- ★★★½ **Color Me Blue (Concord Jazz, 1992)**
- ★★★½ **Write On, Capt'n (Concord Jazz, 1993)**
- ★★★ **The Heatin' System (Concord Jazz, 1995)**
- ★★★ **It's About Time (Concord Jazz, 1996)**

Organist "Brother" Jack McDuff (b. 1926) was one of several distinctive organ-combo leaders to emerge in the 1960s in the wake of Jimmy Smith's success. The Hammond B-3 combo, with its huge sound, its connection to the church and its gospel roots, was especially popular in the black clubs of the time and became a strong influence on many of the late-'60s rock bands, who took advantage of the B-3's intense coloration and ability to stand up to amplified guitars.

McDuff was one of the masters of the form, playing in a concise, gospel- and blues-inspired style most often accompanied by saxophone, guitar and drums, while the organ's pedals took care of the bass lines. *Tough 'Duff* and *The Honeydripper* feature the well-matched Jimmy Forrest on tenor saxophone; the latter uses guitarist Grant Green, another developing soul-jazz giant. *Brother Jack Meets the Boss* features the great tenor saxophonist Gene Ammons. *Screamin'* features guitarist Kenny Burrell, while *Live!* documents George Benson's several years in the McDuff band.

The organ combo fell out of popularity in the '70s, and although he kept recording with hit-and-miss results as he looked for a niche, none of McDuff's recordings from that time remain in print. *The Reentry* is a solid late-1980s set with tenor saxophonist Houston Person, trumpeter Cecil Bridgewater and drummer Grady Tate. McDuff revived his career in the '90s, reuniting with Benson on *Color Me Blue,* working with a larger band on *Write On, Capt'n,* featuring his young touring band on *The Heatin' System* and hooking up with Joey DeFrancesco for a cross-generational organ battle on *It's About Time.*

Much of McDuff's classic 1960s Prestige output is currently unavailable but well worth searching out. Titles to look for include *Live at the Jazz Workshop, Hot Barbecue, Steppin' Out* and especially *Rock Candy.* — J.S.

BOBBY McFERRIN

- ★★½ **Bobby McFerrin (Elektra Musician, 1982)**
- ★★½ **The Voice (Elektra Musician, 1984)**
- ★★★ **Spontaneous Inventions (Blue Note, 1986)**
- ★★ **Simple Pleasures (EMI Manhattan, 1988)**

★★★ **Medicine Music (EMI USA, 1990)**
★★★ **Hush (with Yo-Yo Ma) (Sony Masterworks, 1992)**
★★★ **Play (with Chick Corea) (Blue Note, 1992)**
★★½ **Paper Music (Sony, 1995)**
★★½ **Bang! Zoom (Blue Note, 1996)**

When Bobby McFerrin (b. 1950) turns loose his one-man a cappella band in company with a truly massive talent, the result can be delightful—check him on *Play* with Chick Corea exuberantly duetting his way through "'Round Midnight" and "Autumn Leaves." *Spontaneous Inventions,* with Wayne Shorter, also is fun; and his takes on Bach and Rachmaninoff with stellar cellist Yo-Yo Ma (*Hush*) are fresh as well. But a little of McFerrin goes a mighty long way. Arresting when he began in the mid-'80s—he'd croon, scat and grunt, thumping percussively on his chest, stomach and whatnot—he made a case, with his strange talent, for the human body itself as an instrument. Yet while he's far too middlebrow-tasteful ever to come off as a novelty act, he's held back exactly by such tastefulness. His own tunes are sprightly enough, but his Lennon/McCartney covers (on *Spontaneous Inventions* and *Simple Pleasures*) are merely funky Muzak; in fact, he rarely interprets a tune—he just reformats it. *Simple Pleasures* includes the perky "Don't Worry, Be Happy"—a song with the zing of a well-crafted advertising jingle; *Medicine Music* features McFerrin's best originals ("Soma So De La De Sase" and a version of the 23rd Psalm), but Bobby's weakness is that—like so many other instrumental virtuosos—he produces great sounds but doesn't have much to say. — P.E.

BROWNIE McGHEE AND SONNY TERRY

★★★ **California Blues (1957; Fantasy, 1990)**
★★½ **The 1958 London Sessions (1958; Collectables, 1994)**
★★★½ **Brownie McGhee and Sonny Terry Sing (1958; Smithsonian Folkways, 1990)**
★★★ **Midnight Special (1960; Fantasy, 1989)**
★★★★ **Just a Closer Walk with Thee (1960; Original Blues Classics, 1991)**
★★½ **At Sugar Hill (1963; Original Blues Classics, 1991)**
★★½ **At the 2nd Fret (1963; Original Blues Classics, 1993)**
★★½ **Blues Masters Series, Vol. 5 (1972; Storyville, 1991)**
★★★ **Sonny and Brownie (1973; Mobile Fidelity, 1995)**
★★½ **Hometown Blues (1974; Mainstream, 1990)**
★★★ **Back to New Orleans (Fantasy, 1989)**
★★½ **Blowin' the Fuse (Collectables, 1990)**
★★★½ **The Folkways Years, 1945–1959 (Smithsonian Folkways, 1991)**
★★½ **Po' Boys (Drive Archive, 1994)**
★★★★½ **Climbin' Up (Savoy, 1995)**
★★★½ **Rediscovered Blues (with Lightnin' Hopkins and Big Joe Williams) (Capitol, 1995)**
★★★ **The Bluesville Years: Mr. Brownie & Mr. Sonny (Prestige, 1996)**

BROWNIE McGHEE

★★★½ **Brownie's Blues (1962; Original Blues Classics, 1990)**
★★★★½ **The Complete Brownie McGhee (Columbia/Legacy, 1994)**

SONNY TERRY

★★★½ **Sonny's Story (1960; Original Blues Classics, 1990)**
★★½ **Chain Gang Blues (1976; Collectables, 1990)**
★★★★★ **Whoopin' (Alligator, 1984)**
★★★★ **Woody Guthrie Sings Folk Songs (with Lead Belly, Cisco Houston and Bess Hawes) (Smithsonian Folkways, 1989)**
★★★★ **Sonny Is King (Original Blues Classics, 1990)**
★★★★ **Lead Belly Sings Folk Songs (with Woody Guthrie and Cisco Houston) (Smithsonian Folkways, 1991)**
★★★½ **The Folkways Years, 1944–1963 (Smithsonian Folkways, 1991)**
★★★★ **Whoopin' the Blues: The Capitol Recordings 1947–1950 (Capitol, 1995)**

During their long careers together and apart, guitarist Brownie McGhee (1915–1996) and harpist Sonny Terry (1911–1986) played everything from electrified urban blues to Lead Belly folk tunes, from Broadway musicals to Delta blues, but the core of their sound and enduring legacy is the Piedmont blues. McGhee was a master of the intricate, ragtime-influenced patterns that defined the style, and when he sang his warm baritone had the flexibility to handle the hillbilly, Tin Pan Alley, gospel and jazz flavors that were all part of the hybrid Piedmont sound. Terry's trademark, octave-jumping, "whooping" style on the harmonica enabled him to emphasize the melodic embellishments of the Piedmont style and to play trumpetlike counterpoint to his rough, growling voice.

Separate accidents at ages 11 and 16 robbed Terry of his sight, and he was forced to abandon farming for music. After playing a few years in medicine shows and on the street corners of North Carolina, he met singer/guitarist Blind Boy Fuller in Wadesboro in 1934. They became a team based in Durham, North Carolina, and traveled periodically to New York to record.

Walter Brown McGhee was born in Knoxville, Tennessee, and by his early 20s he had overcome a childhood case of polio to hitchhike all over the Southeast, playing music for blacks and whites. In 1939 McGhee met Fuller and Terry. McGhee absorbed Fuller's repertoire and style so well that after the old man died in 1941, the protégé was billed on his early recordings as Blind Boy Fuller #2. McGhee's 1940–41 recordings under his own name and under the names of Blind Boy Fuller #2 and Brother George and His Sanctified Singers were reissued in 1994 as the two-disc, 47-song package *The Complete Brownie McGhee.* It remains one of the finest Piedmont-blues collections ever released.

Producer John Hammond Sr. discovered Terry playing on the streets of Durham and invited him to participate in 1938's groundbreaking From Spirituals to Swing concert at Carnegie Hall. The show not only introduced an urban, educated audience to regional African-American music but also introduced Terry to the possibilities of playing for such an audience. He went back to North Carolina for a few years and replaced Fuller with McGhee as a duo partner, but by 1942, he had convinced his new cohort to make the move to New York. There they found a flourishing scene that mixed rural, working-class performers and urban, leftist intellectuals—a scene that included Woody Guthrie, Pete Seeger, Blind Gary Davis, Cisco Houston, Lead Belly and Josh White.

During the '40s and '50s Terry's and McGhee's recordings fell into two categories. For their new bohemian audience, they stuck to acoustic, country blues with an emphasis on sing-along melodies and evocative narratives. For the working-class black audience they found in their new home, they imitated the popular sounds of the day, often using drums and electric guitars to reinforce the dance rhythms.

Terry was at his most folk-flavored on two Folkways albums, *Woody Guthrie Sings Folk Songs* and *Lead Belly Sings Folk Songs.* Producer Moses Asch's partiality to rural simplicity is also reflected on Terry's *The Folkways Years, 1944–1963* and McGhee's *The Folkways Years, 1945–1959.* The songwriting is, of course, at a higher level on the Guthrie and Lead Belly collections, but there are more actual blues amid the ballads and folk sing-alongs on the Terry and McGhee sets. The duo's more urban, commercial efforts are captured on two collections that contradict their reputation as quaint rustics. *Whoopin' the Blues: The Capitol Recordings 1947–1950* showcases Terry with two different bands, one featuring legendary jazz drummer Baby Dodds and Brownie's brother Sticks McGhee on guitar, the other featuring Brownie himself on guitar, Melvin Merritt on piano or drums and "Big Chief" Ellis on piano. The arrangements were neither as full-bodied as contemporary hits by Louis Jordan and Joe Liggins nor as sparse as Blind Boy Fuller's older hits. Because they fell somewhere in between, the spirited, double-entendre vocals and raucous dance rhythms were unlike anything else at the time.

In 1949 Sticks McGhee scored a major R&B hit for Atlantic with "Drinkin' Wine Spo-Dee-O-Dee," and his brother Brownie was determined to follow suit. Brownie never got as big a hit, but between 1952 and '55 he cut a distinctive series of 78s that updated the Piedmont blues with electric guitar (played by the legendary Mickey Baker on four cuts) and drums in much the same way that Muddy Waters was simultaneously updating the Delta blues. Those sides are collected on *Climbin' Up,* which is dominated by McGhee's vocals and compositions even though it's cocredited to Terry.

While Terry and McGhee were striking out in their attempts at R&B hits, they were having success in a very different realm. Terry had landed a part in the 1947 Broadway production of *Finian's Rainbow.* McGhee was then cast in the 1955 Broadway production of Tennessee Williams's *Cat on a Hot Tin Roof* and in Langston Hughes's *Simply Heaven* in 1957. These parts made them famous as country-blues traditionalists, and when the country-blues craze spread through college campuses and urban folk societies in the late '50s and early '60s, the duo was recorded by nearly every folk and blues enthusiast with a portable tape recorder.

In 1957 folk collectors Barbara Dane and Max Weiss convinced Terry and McGhee to go into Oakland's Jenny Lind Hall to record 38 songs from their acoustic-duo repertoire. The dozen gospel numbers were issued as *Just a Closer Walk with Thee,* the duo's only all-spiritual package and one of their finest albums. As always, McGhee is the smooth voice and Terry the rough one. The other 26 songs were divided into two albums, *Sonny Terry and Brownie McGhee* and *Blues and Shouts,* which were later combined into *California Blues.* The repertoire is dominated by folk songs such as "John Henry" and "Motherless Child" and is less forceful than the similar *Brownie McGhee and Sonny Terry Sing* on Folkways, where the presence of drummer Gene Moore gives the session a rhythmic verve. Fantasy recorded a similar collection of folk material in 1959 and released it as *Down Home Blues.* The following year jazz drummer Roy Haynes joined the duo on a blues-dominated set, *Blues in My Soul,* but Haynes was buried in the mix until he was barely audible. These two albums were later combined as *Back to New Orleans.*

At the end of 1959 the pair recorded *Blues Is a Story,* a strong set of classic tunes such as "Baby Please Don't Go," "Key to the Highway" and "Twelve Gates to the City," dominated by McGhee. The following summer, producer Ed Michel was so impressed by a four-way house-party concert by Terry, McGhee, Lightnin' Hopkins and Big Joe Williams that he took them into the studio the next day. The resulting album, *Down South Summit Meeting,* is dominated by Hopkins but features some delightfully informal banter and lick swapping among the four friends. *Blues Is a Story, Down South Summit Meeting* and Williams's *Hand Me Down My Old Walking Stick* were later reissued as the two-disc set *Rediscovered Blues.*

On *Brownie's Blues* second guitarist Bennie Foster and a hard-blowing Terry reinforce the driving beat behind McGhee's vocals. The rocking *Sonny Is King* finds Terry backed by Hopkins, a bassist and a drummer and features frankly sexual songs. In the same vein is *Sonny's Story,* which reunites Terry with Sticks McGhee, drummer Belton Evans and second harmonica player J.C. Burris.

After 1960 the duo began to repeat themselves, delivering the same Piedmont menu of blues, rags, folk songs and hymns that were expected of them but without the same spark. *At the 2nd Fret* exemplifies their standard live show. *Mr. Brownie and Mr. Sonny* is an anthology of their earlier Bluesville recordings. The Storyville albums are European sessions, and the Archive and Collectable anthologies are poorly annotated packages of more folk material.

A notable later album is 1973's *Sonny and Brownie,* which put Terry and McGhee into the studio with the likes of Arlo Guthrie, John Mayall, Michael Franks and Earth, Wind and Fire's Al McKay to sing songs by Franks, Sam Cooke and others. Some of the collaborations are uneasy, but the versions of Curtis Mayfield's "People Get Ready" and Randy Newman's "Sail Away" are priceless.

The Johnny Winter–produced *Whoopin' the Blues* is an extraordinary recording that places Terry in one of the most vital contexts of his career. Winter is at his best here, fired by the born-again role of Delta blues guitarist he cast for himself on the series he recorded with Muddy Waters. Though in his 70s, Terry sounds like a brash youngster here, with Winter inspiring him along with bassist Willie Dixon and Terry's protégé Styve Homnick on drums.
— G.H.

HOWARD McGHEE

★★★½ Maggie's Back in Town (1961; Original Jazz Classics, 1992)
★★★½ Howard McGhee and Milt Jackson (Savoy, 1993)
★★★★ Maggie (Savoy, 1995)

Trumpeter Howard McGhee (1918–1987) straddled the swing and bop eras with a style influenced by Roy Eldridge and Fats Navarro. In the early 1940s he worked with Lionel Hampton, then Andy Kirk, where he had his own feature, "McGhee Special." He went on to play with Charlie Barnet, Count Basie, Coleman Hawkins and Jazz at the Philharmonic in the '40s. *Maggie* and *Howard McGhee and Milt Jackson* show him at peak form leading his own bop combos in the 1950s before his career was derailed by chronic drug addiction. McGhee returned to form in 1961 to make the fine *Maggie's Back in Town.* — J.S.

JIMMY McGRIFF

★★★★ Tribute to Count Basie (1966; LaserLight, 1996)

★★★★ **Countdown (1983; Milestone, 1991)**
★★★★ **The Starting Five (Milestone, 1986)**
★★★★ **Blue to the 'Bone (Milestone, 1988)**
★★★★ **Jimmy McGriff at the Apollo (Collectables, 1989)**
★★★½ **A Toast to Jimmy McGriff's Golden Classics (Collectables, 1989)**
★★★★ **Blues for Mr. Jimmy (Collectables, 1990)**
★★★ **In a Blue Mood (Headfirst, 1991)**
★★★ **McGriff's Blues (K-Tel, 1994)**
★★★½ **Right Turn on Blue (Telarc, 1994)**
★★★½ **Blues Groove (Telarc, 1996)**
★★★★ **Jimmy McGriff at the Organ (Collectables, 1996)**
★★ **Topkapi (Collectables, 1996)**
★★★★ **One of Mine (Collectables, 1996)**
★★★½ **I've Got a Woman (Collectables, 1996)**
★★★★ **Funkiest Little Band in the Land (LaserLight, 1996)**
★★★★ **The Dream Team (Milestone, 1997)**

Jimmy McGriff (b. 1936) grew up in the jazz- and blues-rich Philadelphia area, where the Hammond B-3 organ combo became a trademark of the city's sound by the time McGriff became a club-scene regular. McGriff studied organ at Combe College in Philadelphia and Juilliard in New York, going on to play in duets with organist Richard "Groove" Holmes and in a handful of other settings, choosing a more blues-based, rhythmic approach to the instrument than many of his flashier counterparts.

McGriff scored a national hit in 1962 with his first recording, a cover of the Ray Charles staple "I've Got a Woman." The Collectables series showcases a youthful-sounding McGriff from 1963 to the middle of that decade burning in small-combo settings, in a quartet of organ, guitar (Larry Frazier), drums (Willie St. Jenkins) and tenor saxophone (Rudolph Johnson). *Topkapi* suffers from an obtrusive string arrangement, as does the compilation *A Toast to Jimmy McGriff's Golden Classics.* McGriff gets to stretch his blues and swing his chops on the big-band *Tribute to Count Basie. Funkiest Little Band in the Land* is a compilation of tracks recorded between 1968 and 1974.

McGriff had the benefit of the sympathetic producer Bob Porter during the '80s at Milestone. *Countdown* revisits Basie again for two classic Frank Foster arrangements, "Down for the Count" and "Shiny Stockings." *The Starting Five* is a jazz-funk outing consisting of drummer Bernard Purdie, guitarists Mel Brown and Wayne Boyd and tenor and alto saxophonist David "Fathead" Newman. *Blue to the 'Bone* includes trombonist Al Grey, saxophonist Bill Easley, guitarist Melvin Sparks and drummer Purdie. In the 1990s McGriff made the blues-steeped *In a Blue Mood,* featuring covers of Booker T.'s "Hip Hug-Her" and Booker T.'s and William Bull's "Born Under a Bad Sign" (neither of which is on the compilation *McGriff's Blues,* which also includes material from *You Ought to Think About Me*). The collaboration between McGriff and great alto saxophonist Hank Crawford was a fortuitous pairing—they rip it up on *Right Turn on Blue* and *Blues Groove. The Dream Team* revisits *The Starting Five* concept with Red Holloway on saxophones replacing Wayne Boyd's second guitar and Porter rooting them all on from the producer's chair. The extended vamps really turn up the heat, climaxing with "Things Ain't What They Used to Be," an ironic title given the vitality of this music. It's also worth finding the currently unavailable collaborations with Holmes, *Giants of the Organ in Concert* and *Black and Blues.* — J.S.

DAVE McKENNA

★★★ **Solo Piano (1973; Chiaroscuro, 1994)**
★★★★ **The Dave McKenna Quartet (with Zoot Sims) (1974; Chiaroscuro, 1991)**
★★★½ **No Bass Hit (1979; Concord Jazz, 1991)**
★★★★★ **Giant Strides (1979; Concord Jazz, 1994)**
★★★★★ **Left Handed Complement (1980; Concord Jazz, 1992)**
★★★ **A Celebration of Hoagy Carmichael (1983; Concord Jazz, 1994)**
★★★½ **Dancing in the Dark and Other Music of Arthur Schwartz (Concord Jazz, 1986)**
★★★★ **Major League (Concord Jazz, 1986)**
★★★ **My Friend the Piano (Concord Jazz, 1987)**
★★★ **No More Ouzo for Puzo (Concord Jazz, 1989)**
★★★★ **Maybeck Recital Hall Series, Vol. 2**

(Concord Jazz, 1990)
★★★★ **Shadows 'n' Dreams (Concord Jazz, 1991)**
★★★★★ **Concord Duo Series, Vol. 2. (with Gray Sargent) (Concord Jazz, 1993)**
★★★ **A Handful of Stars (Concord Jazz, 1993)**
★★★ **Easy Street (Concord Jazz, 1995)**
★★★ **Sunbeam and Thundercloud (with Joe Temperley) (Concord Jazz, 1996)**
★★★ **You Must Believe in Swing (with Buddy DeFranco) (Concord Jazz, 1997)**

For decades, other first-tier jazz pianists have been in awe of Dave McKenna (b. 1930), who blends a superb sense of rhythmic swing and an encyclopedic command of American-songbook tunes from the 1920s to the present. He draws mightily from the stride-piano era of "walking" bass lines, strumming chords and tempos bop pianists relegated to their bassists and drummers. He developed his strong left-hand style out of necessity: He was self-taught and needed a rhythm section for his inventive melodic and harmonic ideas.

In 1947 McKenna moved to Boston and joined Boots Mussulli's band. A stint with Charlie Ventura led to his joining Woody Herman's orchestra for a year and a half in the early 1950s. After a tour of duty with the Army in Korea, he worked with Buddy Rich, Gene Krupa, Stan Getz, Zoot Sims, Bobby Hackett and Eddie Condon. He has recorded in many group settings, including a classic series of four live recordings that Hackett and Vic Dickenson made for Chiaroscuro during a 10-night gig at New York's Roosevelt Grill, and numerous Concord Jazz all-star sessions in the United States and Japan.

His own 1974 Chiaroscuro *Quartet* session features Sims in a delightful series of standards, including a duet version of "I Cover the Waterfront." Two of his finest small-group sessions are *No Bass Hit* and *Major League,* both with tenor saxophonist Scott Hamilton and drummer Jake Hanna. McKenna's forte has been the solo sessions that spotlight his grand style and penchant for spinning out thematic medleys based on song titles or other common denominators. The very best showcases of his formidable style are *Giant Strides, Left Handed Complement* and the more recent *Shadows 'n' Dreams.*

His musical partnership with Boston-based guitarist Gray Sargent comes to the fore on *Concord Duo Series, Vol. 2.* McKenna and baritone saxophonist Joe Temperley bring great feeling and musical colorings to their enjoyable *Sunbeam and Thundercloud* summit. Temperley shifts to soprano sax and bass clarinet for two tunes. McKenna's equally fine pairing with Buddy DeFranco was a natural leap from the clarinetist's 1950s duo recordings with powerhouse pianists Art Tatum and Oscar Peterson. — K.F.

JOHN McLAUGHLIN

★★★★ **Extrapolation (1969; Verve, 1991)**
★★★★ **Devotion (1970; Metrotone, 1992)**
★★★★ **My Goal's Beyond (1970; Rykodisc, 1987)**
★★★½ **Where Fortune Smiles (1971; One Way, 1994)**
★★★★ **Electric Guitarist (1978; Columbia/Legacy, 1990)**
★★ **Electric Dreams (1979; Columbia/Legacy, 1992)**
★★★ **The Best of John McLaughlin (Columbia, 1980)**
★★★ **Adventures in Radioland (1987; Verve, 1993)**
★★★½ **Live at the Royal Festival Hall (Verve, 1990)**
★★★½ **Que Alegria (Verve, 1992)**
★★★ **Compact Jazz (Verve, 1993)**
★★★★ **After the Rain (Verve, 1995)**
★★★ **The Promise (Verve, 1996)**
★★★★ **The Heart of Things (Verve, 1997)**

WITH THE MAHAVISHNU ORCHESTRA

★★★★★ **The Inner Mounting Flame (1971; Columbia, 1988)**
★★★★★ **Birds of Fire (1973; Columbia, 1986)**
★★★ **Between Nothingness and Eternity (1973; Columbia, 1987)**
★★ **Apocalypse (1974; Columbia, 1990)**
★★ **Visions of the Emerald Beyond (1975; Columbia, 1991)**
★★ **Inner Worlds (1976; Columbia/Legacy, 1994)**

English guitarist John McLaughlin (b. 1942) helped define the fusion style in its 1970s heyday and is one of the most influential musicians of his generation. With minimal classical training on the piano, he began at age 11 playing blues guitar by listening to records and was soon attracted to the complexities of jazz playing.

McLaughlin demonstrates awesome technical and compositional virtuosity as an acoustic and electric guitarist on his early records. His first recording, *Extrapolation,* with baritone and soprano saxophonist John Surman, bassist Brian Odgers and drummer Tony Oxley, is considered a watershed album in European jazz. Surman also appears on *Where Fortune Smiles* along with vibraphonist Karl Berger, bassist Dave Holland and drummer Stu Martin.

McLaughlin went on to showcase his virtuosic electric-guitar work as part of the Tony Williams Lifetime (see *Emergency*) and with Miles Davis circa *In a Silent Way, Bitches Brew* and *Jack Johnson. Devotion* is a quartet featuring drummer Buddy Miles and another Lifetime member, organist Larry Young.

The brilliant *My Goal's Beyond* is the first full-scale exploration of McLaughlin's attempt to marry his interest in the interrelatedness of music and spirituality of the master musicians of India with the dazzling technique he developed as a European virtuoso. In addition to some of McLaughlin's most sublime acoustic solo performances, that album features bassist Charlie Haden, saxophonist Dave Liebman, percussionist Airto Moreira, two Indian musicians and two future members of McLaughlin's Mahavishnu Orchestra, drummer Billy Cobham and violinist Jerry Goodman.

The Mahavishnu Orchestra, which also included bassist Rick Laird and keyboardist Jan Hammer, established a high-water mark for fusion with its first two albums, *The Inner Mounting Flame* and *Birds of Fire.* The band's swooping, vertiginous attack layers lines of molten melodic intensity drawn one moment from a Charlie Parker solo, the next from an Indian raga, in blazing call-and-response fashion among electric guitar, violin and synthesizer, phrased so closely together at points as to sound tonally indistinguishable. It's astonishing music, but the band lost direction after its initial burst of creativity and became one of fusion's reigning clichés. After the live *Between Nothingness and Eternity,* subsequent Mahavishnu sets sound like parodies of the band's original intent. McLaughlin's collaboration with Narada Michael Walden, *Inner Worlds,* is unrefreshing. Even the presence of L. Shankar, McLaughlin's partner in the sublime Shakti recordings, cannot save *Electric Dreams.*

McLaughlin went on to record with fellow Sri Chinmoy disciple Carlos Santana on the now deleted *Love, Devotion, Surrender* before reaching another creative high point with Shakti.

On a roll, he next recorded several fine albums in both electric and acoustic contexts, all of which are currently out of print. Look for *Mahavishnu* and the acoustic *Belo Horizonte* and *Friday Night in San Francisco.* In the 1990s McLaughlin made a series of recordings beginning with *Live at the Royal Festival Hall,* a trio session with bassist Kai Eckhardt and percussionist Trilok Gurtu, and *Que Alegria,* the same trio augmented by another bassist, Dominique De Piazza. *After the Rain* is a superb trio set with drummer Elvin Jones and organist Joey DeFrancesco. *The Promise* attempts to move in a pop direction with such guest stars as Sting and guitarists Jeff Beck and Al DiMeola. Fans of McLaughlin's extrovert side will thrill to the no-holds-barred onslaught of *The Heart of Things* with its celebratory album-opener "Acid Jazz." — J.S.

JACKIE McLEAN

★★★½ **Lights Out! (1956; Original Jazz Classics, 1990)**
★★★½ **4, 5 and 6 (1956; Original Jazz Classics, N.A.)**
★★★ **Jackie's Pal (with Bill Hardman) (1956; Original Jazz Classics, N.A.)**
★★★½ **A Long Drink of the Blues (1957; Original Jazz Classics, 1987)**
★★★½ **Alto Madness (with John Jenkins) (1957; Original Jazz Classics, N.A.)**
★★★ **Jackie McLean & Co. (1957; Original Jazz Classics, N.A.)**
★★★½ **Makin' the Changes (1957; Original Jazz Classics, 1985)**
★★★ **McLean's Scene (1957; Original Jazz Classics, N.A.)**
★★★½ **Strange Blues (1957; Original Jazz Classics, N.A.)**
★★★★ **New Soil (1959; Blue Note, 1989)**
★★★★ **Jackie's Bag (1960; Blue Note, N.A.)**
★★★★★ **Let Freedom Ring (1962; Blue Note, N.A.)**
★★★½ **Right Now (1965; Blue Note, 1991)**
★★★½ **Demon's Dance (1967; Blue Note, N.A.)**
★★★ **New and Old Gospel (1967; Blue Note, N.A.)**
★★★½ **Live at the Montmartre (1972; SteepleChase, 1995)**
★★★ **The Source (1973; SteepleChase, N.A.)**
★★★ **The Meeting (1973; SteepleChase,**

1995)

★★★ **New York Calling (1974; SteepleChase, N.A.)**

★★★½ **Dynasty (Triloka, 1990)**

★★★ **Rites of Passage (Triloka, 1991)**

★★★ **Rhythm of the Earth (Antilles, 1992)**

★★★½ **Hat Trick (Blue Note, 1996)**

One of the more distinctive alto saxophonists to emerge from the hard-bop crowd of the late '50s, Jackie McLean (b. 1932) has a sound notable for its sharp, acid tone and overwhelming intensity. The New York native grew up in the same Harlem neighborhood as saxophone giants Sonny Rollins and Bud Powell and drummer Art Taylor. McLean worked in Rollins's band in 1948 and 1949 and spent the next decade playing with Miles Davis, Charles Mingus and Art Blakey's Jazz Messengers. While each of these bandleaders had a profound influence on McLean's musicianship, his close affiliation with Charlie Parker dominated the early part of his career. McLean spent a good deal of time with Parker and even shared a saxophone with him at the end of Parker's life. Unfortunately, McLean also emulated Parker's legendary appetite for drugs, which caused him numerous personal problems and prevented him from legally performing in Manhattan nightclubs during the 1960s.

Lights Out!, *4, 5 and 6* and *Jackie's Pal* were all recorded in 1956 and display a rapidly maturing McLean mastering the hard-bop idiom. Along with musicians like drummer Art Taylor, trumpeter Donald Byrd and pianist Mal Waldron, McLean plays extremely well, but the shadows of Parker and the other bop innovators loom heavily over these sessions. *Alto Madness* finds McLean and John Jenkins in a raw and obvious tribute to Parker, who had died just two years earlier. While McLean's idiosyncratic alto sound was firmly in place, he was by his own admission still lacking in original ideas. *Makin' the Changes* also finds McLean still playing standards and other tunes from Parker's repertoire.

New Soil shows McLean in transition from hard bop to the challenging excursions he called "the New Thing." Harmonically adventurous while still steeped in the blues, McLean, Donald Byrd and pianist Walter Davis Jr. lead a tough, disciplined quintet through some serious postbop changes. *Jackie's Bag* continues his pursuit of a unique sound while playing with capable, if only moderately innovative players. On tunes like "Quadrangle," McLean straddles old and new musical constructs with a bracing, bittersweet tone.

On *Let Freedom Ring,* McLean attains the compositional maturity, and along with stalwart Davis, bassist Herbie Lewis and drummer Billy Higgins, he reveals an affinity with Ornette Coleman and settles comfortably into his postbop phase. McLean's alto playing is more urgent than ever on three lengthy originals and one Bud Powell composition. While *Right Now* and *Demon's Dance* are not necessarily the best of Jackie's latter Blue Note albums, both maintain the neofree aesthetic he established on *Let Freedom Ring.* Out-of-print classics like *A Fickle Sonance*, *One Step Beyond*, *It's Time* and *Destination Out* are also well worth purchasing. *New and Old Gospel* is noteworthy for the unlikely summit of McLean and Coleman on trumpet.

In the early 1970s McLean recorded some decent albums for SteepleChase—*Live at the Montmartre* is clearly the best of these. With pianist Kenny Drew, bassist Bo Stief and drummer Alex Riel, McLean romps through a lively version of "Parker's Mood" and proves he hadn't lost his hard-bop dexterity. *The Source* and *The Meeting* are less eventful blowing sessions featuring McLean with another of his idols, Dexter Gordon. *New York Calling* introduces Jackie's son, Rene McLean, on tenor and soprano saxophones. Jackie and Rene reunite on the robust *Dynasty.* While Rene claims the lion's share of the writing and adds flute to his own arsenal, Jackie still presides over the session. *Rhythm of the Earth* shows the two McLeans as a viable recording unit with trumpeter Roy Hargrove. — M.M.

BIG JAY McNEELY

★★★ **Swingin' (1964; Collectables, 1990)**

★★★ **Live at Birdland—1957 (Collectables, 1992)**

Redoubtable tenor-sax man Big Jay McNeely (b. 1927) had a reputation as a nonpareil live showman in the late 1950s and early '60s. The cover photo on *Swingin'*, a collection of singles cut for the Swingin' label during the period, tells it all: McNeely spread-eagle, flat on his back onstage, blowing for all he's worth, as teens bop in the aisles. Of the 16 cuts here, 5 are previously unissued; the one that really counts is an uncut version of "There Is Something on Your Mind," a 1959 Number One R&B hit featuring the band's vocalist, Little Sonny Warner, in a wrenching performance that is all dread anticipation, wonderfully played. *Swingin'* shows McNeely and his band doing as the title indicates and mellowing out to good effect as well. It's nothing revolutionary but was guaranteed good rocking in its time.

For a taste of what a McNeely club date was like, check out *Live at Birdland—1957,* captured on a two-track Ampex at Seattle's Birdland, one of the main stops on the chitlin' circuit. The lively set includes sizzling renditions of "Flying Home" and Ray Charles's "I Got a Woman" (with Warner in good form vocally); a frenetic "Deacon's Hop" (a Number One R&B single for McNeely in 1949); an irresistible take of Bill Doggett's "Honky Tonk" with tenor saxophonist Clifford Scott excelling in a featured role; and a thoughtful, passionate reading from Warner on the love pledge "My Darling Dear," bringing the show home with a nice, meditative touch. All in all, *Live at Birdland* shows off everything good about McNeely's band, minus the visual aspect. — D.M.

JIM McNEELY

★★★ **The Plot Thickens (Muse, 1979)**
★★★ **Winds of Change (SteepleChase, 1989)**
★★★½ **Maybeck Recital Hall Series, Vol. 20 (Concord Jazz, 1992)**
★★★½ **East Coast Blowout (Lipstick, 1994)**

Pianist Jim McNeely (b. 1949) is a sure-handed, witty melodist with a strong compositional sense, which are the right attributes for an accompanist (with Stan Getz, Phil Woods and others) or a leader. *The Plot Thickens* is a quintet date featuring bassists Mike Richmond and Jon Burr, drummer Billy Hart and guitarist John Scofield, who stands out. An ambitious session recorded in Cologne, Germany, *East Coast Blowout* features Scofield, bassist Marc Johnson, drummer Adam Nussbaum and the WDR Big Band. *Winds of Change* is a trio album with Mike Richmond on bass and Kenny Washington on drums playing McNeely originals and a cover of Thelonious Monk's "Bye-Ya." McNeely's subtle but effective talents as a solo performer come to the fore on *Maybeck Recital Hall Series, Vol. 20.* — J.S.

MARIAN McPARTLAND

★★★ **From This Moment On (Concord Jazz, 1979)**
★★★ **At the Festival (1980; Concord Jazz, 1994)**
★★★½ **Willow Creek and Other Ballads (Concord Jazz, 1985)**
★★★★ **Marian McPartland Plays the Music of Billy Strayhorn (Concord Jazz, 1987)**
★★★★ **Marian McPartland Plays the Benny Carter Songbook (Concord Jazz, 1990)**
★★★★ **Maybeck Recital Hall Series, Vol. 9 (Concord Jazz, 1991)**
★★★ **Concert in Argentina (Jazz Alliance, 1992)**
★★★ **Marian McPartland Plays the Music of Alec Wilder (Jazz Alliance, 1992)**
★★★★½ **Piano Jazz with Eubie Blake (Jazz Alliance, 1993)**
★★★★ **Piano Jazz with Dizzy Gillespie (Jazz Alliance, 1993)**
★★★½ **Piano Jazz with Bill Evans (Jazz Alliance, 1993)**
★★★ **Piano Jazz with Rosemary Clooney (Jazz Alliance, 1993)**
★★★½ **Piano Jazz with Teddy Wilson (Jazz Alliance, 1993)**
★★★ **Piano Jazz with Dave Brubeck (Jazz Alliance, 1993)**
★★★★½ **In My Life (Concord Jazz, 1993)**
★★★½ **Piano Jazz with Milt Hinton (Jazz Alliance, 1994)**
★★★½ **Piano Jazz with Benny Carter (Jazz Alliance, 1994)**
★★★ **Piano Jazz with Mercer Ellington (Jazz Alliance, 1994)**
★★★ **Piano Jazz with Stanley Cowell (Jazz Alliance, 1994)**
★★★ **Piano Jazz with Dick Hyman (Jazz Alliance, 1994)**
★★★ **Piano Jazz with Red Richards (Jazz Alliance, 1994)**
★★★ **Piano Jazz with Bobby Short (Jazz Alliance, 1994)**
★★★ **Piano Jazz with Clark Terry (Jazz Alliance, 1994)**
★★★ **Piano Jazz with Barbara Carroll (Jazz Alliance, 1994)**
★★★ **Piano Jazz with Dick Wellstood (Jazz Alliance, 1994)**
★★★★ **A Sentimental Journey (Jazz Alliance, 1994)**
★★★★ **Marian McPartland Plays the Music of Mary Lou Williams (Concord Jazz, 1994)**
★★★ **Piano Jazz with Henry Mancini (Jazz Alliance, 1995)**
★★★★ **Piano Jazz with Dave McKenna**

(Jazz Alliance, 1995)
★★★½ **Piano Jazz with Amina Claudine Myers (Jazz Alliance, 1995)**
★★★ **Piano Jazz with Kenny Burrell (Jazz Alliance, 1995)**
★★★½ **Piano Jazz with Alice Coltrane (Jazz Alliance, 1995)**
★★★½ **Piano Jazz with Mary Lou Williams (Jazz Alliance, 1995)**
★★★ **Piano Jazz with Jack DeJohnette (Jazz Alliance, 1995)**
★★★ **Piano Jazz with Jess Stacey (Jazz Alliance, 1995)**
★★★ **Ambiance (Jazz Alliance, 1995)**
★★★ **Piano Jazz with Les McCann (Jazz Alliance, 1996)**
★★★ **Piano Jazz with Lionel Hampton (Jazz Alliance, 1996)**
★★★½ **Piano Jazz with Oscar Peterson (Jazz Alliance, 1996)**
★★★½ **Live at Yoshi's Nightspot (Concord Jazz, 1996)**

British-born pianist Marian McPartland (b. 1920) is an extraordinary musician whose wide-reaching talents are obscured by the fact that her great 1950s work is out of print. She moved to the United States after marrying trumpeter Jimmy McPartland and worked in a group with her husband in the 1940s before leading her own trios.

McPartland became an in-demand lounge stylist whose command of standards and expressive ballad style made her a favorite at New York's Hickory House. McPartland went on to be a jazz activist and educator, working with various jazz-appreciation groups and civic organizations to further the music. She formed her own label, Halcyon, in the late 1960s, recording among other things compositions written for her by Alec Wilder.

McPartland's most enduring legacy may well be her remarkable long-running radio program, Piano Jazz, a talk/music show in which she interacts verbally and musically with jazz greats, unearthing unusually fresh perspectives and some astonishing musical moments as well. Her ability to get inside the myriad styles of her subjects shows the depth of McPartland's musicality in a way her own recordings never could. Jazz Alliance has released a number of these shows, and highlights are the historic piece with Eubie Blake, whose anecdotal memory goes back to the beginnings of jazz; the fascinating exchange with Mary Lou Williams; the sympathetic portrait of Dave McKenna; and the sessions with Dizzy Gillespie, Oscar Peterson, Amina Claudine Myers and Alice Coltrane.

The rest of McPartland's output begins in 1974 with the recording of two live sets that would later be released on Jazz Alliance. *Concert in Argentina* documents the South American tour McPartland put together that year with herself and three other pianists, Teddy Wilson, Ellis Larkins and Earl Hines. *A Sentimental Journey* is a wonderful live reunion with Jimmy McPartland featuring saxophonist Buddy Tate and trombonist Vic Dickenson, the only available example of McPartland's traditional jazz playing. McPartland displays her deft handling of standards in the trio format with *From This Moment On. Willow Creek and Other Ballads* is a beautiful set of solo piano. McPartland's architectural sense makes her particularly adept at interpreting an album's worth of other people's material—her summation of Billy Strayhorn's work is superb. Listen to the way she deconstructs "Take the A Train" and makes her own comments on this well-known piece. The Benny Carter tribute was done with the cooperation of the master himself, who adds his alto saxophone to McPartland's trio. The Maybeck live set is McPartland at her solo-piano best, mixing standards with originals and Ornette Coleman's "Turnaround." McPartland is the perfect musician to summarize the career of Mary Lou Williams, another woman whose passion for jazz ran the gamut from swing to free without missing a beat.

In My Life, a trio set augmented by the underrated Chris Potter on alto and tenor saxophones, demonstrates the wide range of McPartland's musical interests, from the simple melody of the Lennon/McCartney ballad "In My Life" and the standards "What's New" and "Moon and Sand" to the spiritual exercises of John Coltrane's "Red Planet" and "Naima," the metablues of Ornette Coleman's "Ramblin'," two of her own compositions, including "For Dizzy," and the traditional jazz of "Singing the Blues," a staple of her years with Jimmy. This album stands out as a document of McPartland's varied and considerable talents, a vision that encompasses most of jazz history. — J.S.

CHARLES McPHERSON

★★★ **Bebop Revisited! (1964; Original Jazz Classics, 1992)**
★★★ **Con Alma! (1965; Original Jazz**

Classics, 1995)
★★★ **Live at the Five Spot (1966; Prestige, 1995)**
★★★★★ **Beautiful (Xanadu, 1975)**
★★★★ **Live in Tokyo (Xanadu, 1977)**
★★★★ **First Flight Out (Arabesque, 1994)**
★★★★ **Come Play with Me (Arabesque, 1995)**
★★★ **From This Moment On! (N.A.; Original Jazz Classics, 1997)**

Since his first recordings in the mid-'60s, Charles McPherson (b. 1939), the man whose former employer Charles Mingus once cited as his favorite alto saxophonist, has been keeping alive the ghost of Charlie Parker. Not that McPherson hasn't incorporated important new aspects into his style over the years, but the blues-filled language and soulful bop energy of Bird will always be McPherson's spiritual cornerstone.

Bebop Revisited! and *Con Alma!* are substantial sets filled with powerful second-generation bop playing from McPherson and first-rate sidemen including pianist Barry Harris (on both recordings) and tenor saxophonist Clifford Jordan (on *Bebop*). *Live in Tokyo* features brisk up-tempo playing from a perfect team of bebop specialists (Harris, bassist Sam Jones and drummer Leroy Williams), but *Beautiful* may be McPherson's midperiod masterpiece—his ballad readings are assured and charged with emotion.

McPherson had a tremendous second wind in the '90s. *Come Play with Me* and *First Flight Out* are exceptional recordings, proving that McPherson is not only at the top of his game but more individual and inventive than ever. — S.F.

CARMEN McRAE

★★★ **Alive! (1965; Legacy, 1994)**
★★★★½ **The Great American Songbook (1972; Atlantic, 1993)**
★★★ **You Can't Hide Love (1976; Blue Note, 1993)**
★★★½ **Live at Ronnie Scott's (1977; DRG, 1994)**
★★★★ **Any Old Time (1986; Denon, 1990)**
★★★½ **Carmen McRae (1987; Bethlehem, 1994)**
★★★ **Fine and Mellow: Live at Birdland West (Concord Jazz, 1988)**
★★★★ **Carmen Sings Monk (Novus, 1990)**
★★★★ **Sarah: Dedicated to You (Novus, 1991)**
★★★★ **Here to Stay (Decca, 1992)**
★★★★ **Carmen McRae Sings Great American Songwriters (Decca, 1993)**
★★★½ **Velvet Soul (LaserLight, 1993)**
★★★★ **I'll Be Seeing You (Decca, 1995)**
★★★★ **The Best of Carmen McRae (Blue Note, 1995)**
★★★★ **For Lady Day, Vol. 1 (Novus, 1995)**
★★★★ **For Lady Day, Vol. 2 (Novus, 1995)**
★★★★ **Carmen McRae Sings "Lover Man" and Other Billie Holiday Classics (Legacy, 1997)**

Vocalist Carmen McRae (1922–1994) started out as a teenager inspired by the passion and soul of Billie Holiday and went on to become one of the great ladies of jazz interpretation, with a distinctive, powerful yet witty style of her own.

A native New Yorker, McRae sang with the Benny Carter, Count Basie and Mercer Ellington bands in the 1940s, appearing with Ellington as Carmen Clarke after marrying drummer Kenny Clarke. Clarke was part of the group of musicians who were developing bop in nightly jam sessions at Minton's, and McRae performed at the club during intermissions and soaked up the harmonic advances her compatriots were developing.

By the time McRae signed with Decca in the mid-1950s, she was a formidable vocal talent who really knew her way around the songbooks of America's standards composers. *Here to Stay, I'll Be Seeing You* and *Carmen McRae Sings Great American Songwriters* are good representations of this era in a variety of contexts.

Most of McRae's 1960s work is out of print, but the spectacular *Great American Songbook,* with stellar accompaniment from guitarist Joe Pass and pianist Jimmy Rowles, is still available. Legacy has reissued her great 1961 session, *Carmen McRae Sings "Lover Man" and Other Billie Holiday Classics,* with two additional tracks.

Of the 1970s McRae still available, *Velvet Soul* features Zoot Sims on tenor and the Ronnie Scott's set shows McRae in audience-pleasing form. Her Blue Note catalog is reduced to *You Can't Hide Love* and the useful *Best of Carmen McRae.*

McRae was still a force to be reckoned with in her 60s, paying tribute to her onetime idol on the *For Lady Day* material recorded live at the Blue Note in 1983, using her Clifford Jordan–led quintet masterfully on *Any Old Time* and adding lyrics to Monk on *Carmen Sings Monk,* with longtime Monk tenor saxophonist Charlie Rouse and Jordan (soprano, tenor) offering support in two different lineups.

McRae was pushing 70 when she recorded *Sarah: Dedicated to You,* a Sarah Vaughan tribute with Shirley Horn accompanying on piano. This superb demonstration of McRae's mature skills turned out to be a fitting swan song for one of the greatest jazz vocalists. — J.S.

JAY McSHANN

★★★½ **Going to Kansas City (1972; New World, 1987)**
★★★★ **Vine Street Boogie (Black Lion, 1974)**
★★★ **After Hours (Storyville, 1977)**
★★★ **Best of Friends (JSP, 1982)**
★★★★ **Paris All-Star Blues: A Tribute (MusicMasters, 1992)**
★★★ **Some Blues (Chiaroscuro, 1992)**
★★★★ **Hootie & Hicks/Missouri Connection (Reservoir, 1992)**
★★★★★ **1941–1943 (Classics, 1996)**
★★★★ **Hootie's Jumpin' Blues (Stony Plain, 1997)**
★★★½ **1944–1946 (Classics, 1998)**
★★★ **Havin' Fun (Sackville, 1998)**
★★★ **My Baby with the Black Dress On (Chiaroscuro, 1998)**

The real and original Hootie, pianist Jay McShann (b. 1916) is one of the key transitional figures in jazz, a swing veteran who was a main element in the "territory" scene centered in Kansas City during the 1930s. One of McShann's claims to fame is that he hired the fledgling Charlie Parker in 1939. McShann's band was the stuff of legend (check out the hot *1941–1943,* which includes his influential hit "Confessin' the Blues"), but he had to dissolve it when he was drafted in 1944, and then drifted into relative obscurity.

McShann enjoyed a renaissance in the 1970s and went on to record more than 20 albums, which make up the bulk of his extant catalog. He has also become a prolific accompanist. *Going to Kansas City* is a set with dueling tenor saxophonists Buddy Tate and Julian Dash. *Vine Street Boogie* is a spectacular solo set from the 1974 Montreux Jazz Festival. In 1989 McShann assembled a takeoff on his classic big band for *Paris All-Star Blues: A Tribute,* using trumpeters Clark Terry and Terence Blanchard, tenor saxophonists Jimmy Heath, James Moody and Hal Singer, alto saxophonists Benny Carter and Phil Woods and drummer Mel Lewis. *Hootie & Hicks* is a piano duet with John Hicks, recorded in 1992. Even pushing 90, McShann can still really bring it on, as *Hootie's Jumpin' Blues* (with a band led by guitarist Duke Robillard), *Havin' Fun* (duets with bassist Major Holley) and the solo-piano recording *My Baby with the Black Dress On* prove. — J.S.

BLIND WILLIE McTELL

★★★★ **Pig 'n Whistle Red (1950; Biograph, 1993)**
★★★★ **Last Session (1966; Original Blues Classics, 1992)**
★★★★★ **The Early Years 1927–1933 (Yazoo, 1989)**
★★★★ **Complete Recorded Works, Vol. 1 (1927–31) (Document, 1990)**
★★★★ **Complete Recorded Works, Vol. 2 (1931–33) (Document, 1990)**
★★★½ **Complete Recorded Works, Vol. 3 (1933–35) (Document, 1990)**
★★★★½ **Blind Willie McTell 1927–1935 (Yazoo, 1991)**
★★★★½ **Atlanta Twelve String (Atlantic, 1992)**
★★★★½ **The Definitive Blind Willie McTell (Columbia/Legacy, 1994)**
★★★½ **Masters of the Country Blues (with Lead Belly) (Biograph, 1996)**

The Japanese have a name, *ningen kokuho,* for officially recognized human treasures, honored for being a living high-water mark of a particular, time-honored art form, usually one that has all but passed. During his lifetime, in recordings that took place almost every five years from his first sessions in 1927, Blind Willie McTell (ca. 1901–1959) proved to be such a stellar repository of the acoustic blues and ragtime tradition. His tunes inspired and provided material for the likes of the Allman Brothers and Taj Mahal, but by the end of his long and prolific career, McTell's own performances were enjoyed almost exclusively by patrons of a small Atlanta barbecue joint.

McTell was born blind around the turn of the century in rural Georgia, to a musical family. Traveling with minstrel shows while still a teenager, he absorbed a wide variety of the day's acoustic music: blues, rags, minstrel songs and early hillbilly music. Originally a 6-string player, he soon developed an affinity for Atlanta's hallmark 12-string guitar. But relegating him to a specific blues school that included guitarists Charley Lincoln and

Barbecue Bob is like defining Duke Ellington only as a swing bandleader—McTell transcended his genre and location, creating highly original songs and stamping his peculiar Georgia drawl and guitar mastery on whatever melody or style he adopted.

The Yazoo collections cover the best of McTell's first recordings from 1927 to '35 for a variety of labels: *The Early Years 1927–1933* is an absolute must-have for any music collector, featuring deep-and-lonesome blues ("Broke Down Engine Blues," the tender mood-painting "Love Changing Blues" and the well-known "Statesboro Blues"), upbeat, suggestive rags ("Warm It Up to Me," "Southern Can Is Mine") and dexterous guitar showcases like "Travelin' Blues." The excellent companion album, *Blind Willie McTell 1927–35,* offers just as wide an emotional range and evidence of McTell's artistry, switching in and out of slide mode on "Atlanta Strut" and teaming up with blues singer Ruth Day on two tracks. For archivists, Columbia's *The Definitive Blind Willie McTell* is a two-disc package covering his entire 41-track catalog for Columbia, Okeh and Vocalion with the most complete and up-to-date liner notes of any collection. That said, it's unfortunate that McTell's Victor sides (which include many of the highlights mentioned above) do not show up here, though the technically inferior, imported Document series corrals McTell's entire 69-track early output.

After the '30s, McTell forwent an itinerant career in favor of performing around Atlanta, and his recordings tended less toward the deeper Delta blues and favored a street singer's choice of fingerpicked hokum and rag numbers. *Masters of the Country Blues* collects 13 songs from his 1940 hotel-room session for the Library of Congress. Later McTell standards such as "Kill It Kid Rag" and "Dying Crapshooters Blues" make their first appearance, while he reserves his deft slide work almost exclusively for spiritual material; "I Got to Cross the River Jordan" and "Amazing Grace" are among the standout offerings from this session.

The 1949 *Atlanta Twelve String* session comes from Atlantic Records' earliest years and marks the first instance of modern audio technology catching up with McTell's career—his booming 12-string guitar finally rings through like a bell, and his matured vocals are clear and strong. Notable are the slowed-down version of his slide piece "Broke Down Engine Blues" and the most compelling recording of his classic "Dying Crapshooter," which is Rabelaisian in its lyrical detail. The music on *Pig 'n Whistle Red* (McTell's epithet derived from a barbecue joint that became his primary performance venue) was produced by the Regal blues label in 1950, with second-guitar support from fellow Atlantan Curley Weaver. Of special interest are an updated, duet version of his 1933 slide showcase "Savannah Mama," the pop song "Honey It Must Be Love" and two very different takes of the '20s Tin Pan Alley tune "Pal of Mine," revealing his strong improvisational abilities.

McTell recorded his swan song in 1956: *Last Session* was first issued on Prestige 10 years later. Loose, conversational and still fleet-fingered, McTell provided a last glimpse of his ragtime accuracy and fun-loving choice of tunes. He ably handles Blind Blake's "That Will Never Happen No More" and an energetic slide approach to Charlie Jackson's "Salty Dog," while revealing a continuing passion for early country songs with a vocal version of "Wabash Cannonball." But his reading of fellow Georgian Tom Dorsey's "Beedle Um Bum" is this set's guitar/vocal tour de force. McTell's penchant for the good life caught up with him, and he died overweight and diabetic. He was ignominiously buried in a mismarked grave. — A.K.

MEDESKI, MARTIN AND WOOD

★★★½ Notes from the Underground (1992; Accurate, 1994)
★★★★½ It's a Jungle in Here (Gramavision, 1993)
★★★ Friday Afternoon in the Universe (Gramavision, 1995)
★★★★ Shack-Man (Gramavision, 1996)
★★★ Bubblehouse (Gramavision, 1997)

There's a telling moment on Medeski, Martin and Wood's second album: An off-beat version of the obscure Thelonious Monk chestnut "Bemsha Swing" rolls along its merry, slippery, syncopated path until midway through trumpeter Steve Bernstein's solo, when it suddenly shifts into a slow-drag "Lively Up Yourself"—convincingly the most natural transition in the world. When they're on, these guys create punchy, sparse, cross-referencing, groove-heavy, keyboard-based jazz—kind of like Booker T. drunk on *Bitches Brew.*

MMW is the well-integrated and seemingly seamless union of keyboardist John Medeski, bassist Chris Wood and drummer/percussionist

Billy Martin, which originated from a jam series at New York's Village Gate in the early 1990s, followed by a stint in John Lurie's latter-day Lounge Lizards. The group has defined its own particular brand of funky improvisation, carving its way out of the ofttimes provincial New York downtown music scene and appealing to fans of alternative rock.

The group's albums thus far form an accurate progress chart of the band's growth, starting with the more piano-focused and self-conscious jazz of their excellent debut. *It's a Jungle in Here* delivers a looser, trio-plus-guests package, showing off Medeski's organ prowess and the big ears and diverse influences of the band (the aforementioned Marley/Monk fusion and John Coltrane's "Syeeda's Song Flute" hold equal sway alongside King Sunny Ade's "Moti Mo" and funk-fueled originals). A more sparse, open feel was developed on the trio-only *Friday Afternoon in the Universe* ("Last Chance to Dance Trance" is an eye-opener to Medeski's compositional magic), and *Shack Man* unleashes the more rocking, rhythmic kaleidoscope their live shows have always promised, with Medeski wailing on a variety of keyboards and Wood stretching out on acoustic and electric bass and acoustic guitar.

Bubblehouse, an interesting five-track EP featuring remixes of various tracks off *Shack-Man,* only underscores the obvious: With the proper studio coaxing MMW's jams are just one step from contemporary dance-floordom. Atmospheric, foot-tapping manipulations by the likes of DJ Olive (on the time-shifting "Bubblehouse" and moody "Spy Kiss") and DJ Logic (the foreboding "Dracula" with John Zorn's alto sax) add an ambient patina to the band's already sparse funk workouts. — A.K.

BRAD MEHLDAU

★★★½ **Introducing Brad Mehldau (Warner Bros., 1995)**
★★★★ **The Art of the Trio, Vol. 1 (Warner Bros., 1997)**
★★★★ **Live at the Village Vanguard: The Art of the Trio, Vol. 2 (Warner Bros., 1998)**
★★★★ **Songs: The Art of the Trio, Vol. 3 (Warner Bros., 1998)**

Classically trained pianist Brad Mehldau (b. 1970) rose to prominence as part of Joshua Redman's backing group. On *Introducing Brad Mehldau* he reunites with Redman sidemen Christian McBride on bass and Brian Blade on drums for rundowns of "Prelude to a Kiss," Cole Porter's "From This Moment On" and two originals, "London Blues" and "Say Goodbye." Mehldau demonstrates his classical leanings on several other tracks. The *Art of the Trio* series places Mehldau with bassist Larry Grenadier and drummer Jorge Rossy, his group before joining Redman's band. This is an even better setting for Mehldau, who mixes his love for striking melodies, harmonic invention and an eclecticism that can take him from Rodgers and Hart to Radiohead in the same session. — J.S.

MEMPHIS MINNIE

★★★★ **Memphis Minnie & Kansas Joe Complete Recorded Works, Vol. 1 (1929–30) (Document, 1991)**
★★★★ **Memphis Minnie & Kansas Joe Complete Recorded Works, Vol. 2 (1930–31) (Document, 1991)**
★★★★ **Memphis Minnie & Kansas Joe Complete Recorded Works, Vol. 3 (1931–32) (Document, 1991)**
★★★★ **Memphis Minnie & Kansas Joe Complete Recorded Works, Vol. 4 (1933–34) (Document, 1991)**
★★★★ **Complete Recorded Works, Vol. 1 (1935) (RST/Document, 1991)**
★★★★ **Complete Recorded Works, Vol. 2 (1935–36) (RST/Document, 1991)**
★★★★ **Complete Recorded Works, Vol. 3 (1937) (RST/Document, 1991)**
★★★★ **Complete Recorded Works, Vol. 4 (1938–39) (RST/Document, 1991)**
★★★★ **Complete Recorded Works, Vol. 5 (1940–41) (RST/Document, 1991)**
★★★★ **Complete Post-War Recordings, Vol. 1 (1944–46) (Wolf/Document, 1991)**
★★★★ **Complete Post-War Recordings, Vol. 2 (1946–47) (Wolf/Document, 1991)**
★★★★ **Complete Post-War Recordings, Vol. 3 (1949–53) (Wolf/Document, 1991)**
★★★★½ **Hoodoo Lady (1933–1937) (Legacy, 1991)**
★★★★ **Early Rhythm & Blues from the Rare Regal Sessions (Biograph, 1994)**

Guitarist/blues singer Lizzie "Memphis Minnie" Douglas (1897–1973) was born in Algiers, Louisiana, the eldest of 13 children. She would go on to become one of the most respected female country-blues singers of all time, influencing such artists as Big Mama Thornton and Mance Lipscomb, among others. In 1929 Douglas and then-husband Kansas Joe McCoy first recorded in Memphis; the following year the duo relocated to Chicago to record their hard-edged blues for Vocalion. Their musical relationship has been meticulously reconstructed on four chronological discs by Austria's Document Records, capturing the couple's complete output—a mixture of solo and duet numbers—from 1929 to 1934. In addition to 15 sides they cut for Decca in late 1934, the discs include such gems as "Crazy Cryin' Blues," "Memphis Minnie-Jitis Blues" and the poignant "Moanin' the Blues," the last track the duo cut together.

Minnie would go on to record prolifically over the next 19 years, cutting sides with such figures as Little Son Joe, Sunnyland Slim and Little Brother Montgomery. One of the earliest blues artists to switch to electric guitar, she was playing electric dates in the early '40s. The RST and Wolf sets were also spearheaded by Document chief Johnny Parth and chronologically cover Minnie's output from 1935 to 1953. With more than 150 tracks on eight discs, the series is the most complete document of her career ever assembled. The Biograph compilation *Early Rhythm & Blues from the Rare Regal Sessions* includes five Memphis Minnie tracks, among them two takes of Big Bill Broonzy's "Night Watchman Blues." It's a fine set that captures the magic of the Regal label, an imprint that lasted less than three years yet caught the sound of the blues just as the form was becoming more urban and electrified.

— B.R.H.

MEMPHIS SLIM

★★★★ **Blue This Evening (1960; Black Lion, 1991)**
★★★★ **Raining the Blues (1960; Fantasy, 1989)**
★★★★ **Steady Rolling Blues (1961, Original Blues Classics, 1988)**
★★★★½ **All Kinds of Blues (1961; Original Blues Classics, 1990)**
★★★½ **Alone with My Friends (1961; Original Blues Classics, 1996)**
★★★½ **In Paris: Baby Please Come Home! (with Willie Dixon) (1962; Original Blues Classics, 1996)**
★★★★ **The Real Folk Blues (1966; Chess, 1988)**
★★★ **Mother Earth (1972; One Way, 1994)**
★★★ **Memphis Heat (with Canned Heat) (1973; Verve, 1994)**
★★★ **In Paris: Sonny Boy Williamson and Memphis Slim (GNP Crescendo, 1973)**
★★★½ **Legacy of the Blues, Vol. 7 (GNP Crescendo, 1990)**
★★★½ **Bawdy Blues (Original Blues Classics, 1991)**
★★★★½ **Lonesome (Drive Archive, 1994)**
★★★½ **Live at Ronnie Scott's (1986; DRG, 1994)**
★★★★ **Chicago Blues Master, Vol. 1 (with Muddy Waters) (Capitol, 1995)**
★★★★½ **The Bluebird Recordings 1940–1941 (RCA, 1997)**

Peter "Memphis Slim" Chatman (1915–1988) was a terrific barrelhouse-influenced pianist, a gifted vocalist and a great songwriter whose flair for theatrics saw him perform successfully in a variety of contexts over his career. He left his native Memphis for Chicago in the late 1930s, where he began making records. *The Bluebird Recordings* document his early-1940s work in Chicago.

The Real Folk Blues collects singles mostly recorded in Chicago in 1950–51 with bass, drums and a pair of saxophones. On his trademark "Mother Earth," the Vagabonds add backing vocals typical of the period.

Raining the Blues (a pair of 1960 albums, *Just Blues* and *No Strain,* originally recorded for Bluesville) finds Slim accompanied by bass, drums and harmonica and includes "Beer Drinking Woman," the original LP title tracks and "Motherless Child." *Bawdy Blues* compiles several artists' work from 1956 to 1961, including four Memphis Slim tracks.

On the 1961 session *Steady Rolling Blues,* Slim accompanies himself on piano and organ and does great versions of Leroy Carr's "Mean Mistreatin' Mama" and James Oden's "Goin' Down Slow." Slim's piano is rocking on another 1961 solo outing, *All Kinds of Blues,* featuring the steamy "Grinder Man Blues" and "Churnin' Man Blues," a moving version of "Mother Earth" and "Frankie and Johnny Boogie."

In 1960 Slim toured Europe for the first time, where he was greeted as a living legend. *Blue This Evening,* recorded in London with guitarist Alexis Korner, is a statement of purpose on Slim's part. By 1962 he had moved his base to Paris, which he called home until his death. He still recorded whenever possible, often while on tour in the United States.

Lonesome is a 1961 set with a small band featuring guitarist Matt Murphy; all but 3 of the 12 tunes are Memphis Slim originals, including "Cold Blooded Woman," "It's Been Too Long" and "I'm Lost Without You."

Mother Earth is a reissue of a 1972 session originally recorded for Buddah Records, and *Legacy of the Blues, Vol. 7* is a solid 1975 recording produced by Clyde Otis. The *Live at Ronnie Scott's* set shows that Slim's talents never failed him. — J.S.

JOHNNY MERCER

★★★★★ **An Evening with Johnny Mercer (DRG, 1977)**
★★★ **Two of a Kind: Johnny Mercer/Billy May & His Orchestra/Bobby Darin (1985; Atlantic, 1990)**
★★★★★ **Capitol Collectors Series (Capitol, 1989)**
★★★★ **Johnny Mercer Sings Johnny Mercer (Everest, N.A.)**

Johnny Mercer (1909–1976) is so towering a figure as a songwriter that his lengthy, productive career as a recording artist is easily overlooked. Born in Savannah, Georgia, Mercer demonstrated a flair for creative wordplay at a young age, writing his first song when he was 15. From the beginning, his lyrics balanced a love of language at its most elegant with the colloquialisms he picked up in his youth from his black Gullah-speaking friends in Georgia.

His first chart hit came in 1938, and he remained a constant in the Top 40 into the early '50s. During that time he was writing some of the greatest popular songs in history, cofounding Capitol Records and signing artists who would make their own lasting contributions to the type of music his work had helped shape: Nat King Cole, Jo Stafford, Peggy Lee and Margaret Whiting, among others. Mercer wrote, by most estimates, more than 1,000 songs, some of which were hits several times over and in different eras ("Goody Goody" was a Number One single for Benny Goodman in 1936 and a Top 20 single in an entirely new version by Frankie Lymon in 1957; "Fools Rush In [Where Angels Fear to Tread]" was a Number One single for Glenn Miller and His Orchestra in 1940, a Top 30 single for Brook Benton in 1960, and a Top 20 single for Ricky Nelson in 1963).

Capitol's *Collectors Series,* with its detailed liner notes, provides a memorable journey for any devotee of the popular song. Oddly, Mercer wrote only eight of the 20 tracks on this set, although all of them were hits. His contributions range from the novelty "Strip Polka" to three gems cowritten with Harold Arlen ("Blues in the Night," which also features Jo Stafford in one of her first recorded vocals, "Ac-Cent-Tchu-Ate the Positive" and the saloon classic "One for My Baby"). Mercer the vocalist, whose engaging vibrato and conversational folksiness more than compensated for his limited range, assays the same wide spectrum of subject matter he favored as a writer. "Zip-a-Dee-Doo-Dah," "Winter Wonderland" and "Sugar Blues" are all delivered with remarkable sensitivity to mood and texture.

Two of a Kind teams Mercer with Bobby Darin during the latter's phase as a pop singer. Throughout his career Darin made a habit of reinventing himself, always with interesting results. Here he and Mercer team up for a classic "swinging" affair keyed by a witty collection of mostly lesser-known Tin Pan Alley chestnuts. The feel is informal and jovial throughout; Billy May's arrangements are witty or sensitive as the material demands but always uncluttered and in service of the singers' individual quirks; and the featured artists display endearing camaraderie and compatible styles, both personal and musical. Mercer cowrote only four of the dozen tracks, with the most familiar being "Bob White."

More difficult to find but no less essential is Everest's *Johnny Mercer Sings Johnny Mercer.* This release contains no liner information or session notes to date the recordings or identify the players, but the richer tone of Mercer's voice would pinpoint it as coming considerably later than the tracks on the Capitol album (1942–49)—at least 1962, since "Days of Wine and Roses" is here, written that year for the like-titled movie. Note the jaunty treatment Mercer gives "Moon River," the haunting theme song (with Henry Mancini music) from *Breakfast at Tiffany's.* Apart from these two gems, Mercer offers his own treatments of "You Must Have Been a Beautiful Baby," "Goody Goody," "That Old Black Magic," "Tangerine," "Come Rain or Come Shine" and "Satin Doll."

DRG's *An Evening with Mercer* is as delightful as it is indispensable. For many years New York City's 92nd Street Y has presented the Lyrics and Lyricists Series, featuring in-person interviews/performances with composers of all stripes. Mercer was the focus on March 14, 1971; Richard Leonard accompanied him on piano, and as vocalists he enlisted the aid of the redoubtable Margaret Whiting and Robert Sands. Although *An Evening with Johnny Mercer* is an edited version of the complete presentation, it feels like an entire evening. Mercer proves himself a master raconteur, reeling off the names of the towering artists he met and worked with over the years as if they were average Joes but never taking himself too seriously. He escorts the audience on a journey through his career from day one, playing snippets of songs along the way and spicing up the narrative with revealing (and otherwise unpublished) stories-behind-the-stories of Hollywood in the '30s and '40s, of his recording career and the characters whose paths his crossed. Nothing quite compares to the finale, when Mercer performs what he calls "my bread-and-butter songs:" "Goody Goody," "Jeepers Creepers," "Satin Doll," "You Must Have Been a Beautiful Baby," "That Old Black Magic," "I Remember You," "Laura," "Dream," "One for My Baby," "Blues in the Night," "I Wanna Be Around," "Charade" and "The Summer Wind"—to name just a few. — D.M.

HELEN MERRILL

★★★★★ **Helen Merrill (with Clifford Brown) (1955; EmArcy, 1992)**
★★★ **Dream of You (with Gil Evans) (1956; EmArcy, 1992)**
★★★★ **The Complete Helen Merrill on Mercury (Verve, 1986)**
★★★★ **Collaboration (with Gil Evans and Steve Lacy) (EmArcy, 1988)**
★★★★ **Just Friends (with Stan Getz) (EmArcy, 1989)**
★★★ **Duets (with Ron Carter) (EmArcy, 1989)**
★★★½ **Clear Out of This World (Antilles, 1992)**
★★★★★ **Brownie: Homage to Clifford Brown (Verve, 1994)**
★★★ **You and the Night and the Music (Verve, 1998)**

The vocal style of Helen Merrill (b. 1930) has been enchanting listeners ever since she made her exquisite debut album in 1954 with arranger Quincy Jones and trumpeter Clifford Brown's sextet. Her cool, smoky vocals have always had a lingering warmth. They have strengthened with age, experience and a steadfast sense of what she wants to sing—and with whom she wants to sing it.

Born in New York to Yugoslavian immigrants, Merrill was attracted to the jazz scene as a teenager and received encouragement from many players, including Miles Davis and Bud Powell. For most of her career she has enjoyed far more popularity in Europe and Japan than on her native soil.

The 62-song, four-disc boxed set, *The Complete Helen Merrill on Mercury,* encompasses everything she recorded for EmArcy between 1954 and 1958, including her session with Brown and her first recording with arranger Gil Evans as well as an unreleased strings date conducted by Hal Mooney. Some of these early Mercury (EmArcy) recordings also remain available as individual CDs. Her *Dream of You* project with Evans was expanded in the CD reissue to include her first recordings in 1954 with the Johnny Richards Orchestra, which were released originally as singles.

Her second session with Evans three decades later, *Collaboration,* features many of the same tunes performed with maturity, new feelings and enhanced sound quality capturing every nuance of her voice.

Merrill maintains her high standards on succeeding sessions with Ron Carter (whose bass illuminates her voice) and Stan Getz. The quintet session *Clear Out of This World* features two of her favorite horn players, trumpeter Tom Harrell and saxophonist Wayne Shorter.

Merrill's 1994 tribute to Brown teams the singer with an ace rhythm section (Kenny Barron on piano, Rufus Reid on bass, Victor Lewis on drums) and four of the finest trumpeters working in the 1990s—Roy Hargrove, Harrell, Wallace Roney and Lew Soloff. She has recorded so infrequently in the 1990s that every Merrill session is awaited with anticipation by her fans. *You and the Night and the Music* has some very strong moments and solid support from Harrell, Charlie Haden and Paul Motian, among others. But it suffers from inconsistent treatment of the material. — K.F.

BIG MACEO MERRIWEATHER

★★★★½ **The King of Chicago Blues Piano (Arhoolie, 1992)**

Major "Big Maceo" Merriweather (1905–1953) taught himself piano, then moved from Georgia (where he grew up) to Detroit in 1924, playing house parties and the like. It was not until 1941—at the urging of his wife—that he traveled to Chicago in search of a recording contract. There he met talent scout Lester Melrose and guitarist Tampa Red, both of whom helped him cut his first tracks at age 36. Five years later, Merriweather had a stroke that virtually ended his piano-playing career, but by then he had already recorded some of the most enduring piano blues of all time, influencing the work of Otis Spann, among others.

Merriweather's piano style relied heavily on his left hand, which accentuated his songs' bass lines. A wonderfully expressive singer with a soft, smoky voice, Merriweather had a healthy respect for blues players who had preceded him; he took Sleepy John Estes's "Someday Baby," for example, and turned it into "Worried Life Blues," a song that has been covered by innumerable blues artists. Though he recorded with other bluesmen—among them Big Bill Broonzy—on various sessions, the only available testament to Merriweather's skills as a bandleader is *The King of Chicago Blues Piano.* Documenting six sessions from 1941 to 1945, the release includes such gems as "Chicago Breakdown" and "Big Road Blues," an interpretation of a song by Tommy Johnson. Other particularly engaging tracks on this 25-cut release are "Worried Life Blues" and "County Jail Blues," a song recently given new life by Eric Clapton. Tampa Red plays guitar on every track (and supplies vocals on the fantastic "Can't You Read"), and Merriweather can often be heard exhorting him, "Now play it, Mr. Tampa." Other musicians on various tracks include bassist Alfred Elkins and drummers Melvin Draper, Tyrell Dixon, Chick Sanders and Clifford "Snag" Jones. — B.R.H.

THE METERS

★★★★	**Good Old Funky Music (Rounder, 1990)**
★★★★	**Look-Ka Py Py (Rounder, 1990)**
★★★½	**Uptown Rulers! The Meters Live on the Queen Mary (Rhino, 1992)**
★★★½	**The Meters Jam (Rounder, 1992)**
★★★★★	**Funkify Your Life: The Meters' Anthology (Rhino, 1995)**
★★★★	**The Best of the Meters (Mardi Gras, 1996)**

Long the premier R&B rhythm section in New Orleans, the Meters—guitarist Leo Nocentelli, keyboardist Art Neville, bassist George Porter Jr., drummer Joseph "Zigaboo" Modeliste and, eventually, percussionist Cyril Neville—worked with producer Allen Toussaint on dozens of sessions, backing Dr. John, LaBelle, Robert Palmer and others. They also made quite a few records in their own right, recording three albums for Josie between 1968 and '71 before signing with Reprise in 1972. *Good Old Funky Music* and *Look-Ka Py Py* draw from this period, in which the Meters went from operating as a funkier version of the MG's to formulating their own synthesis of James Brown funk and New Orleans second-line syncopations. Of the two albums, *Look-Ka Py Py* is the funkier effort, although the "Rock 'n' Roll Medley" on *Good Old Funky Music* has its charms but contains neither "Cissy Strut" or "Sophisticated Cissy," two of the combo's biggest hits.

Unfortunately, the Meters' six albums for Reprise are long out of print. Unlike the all-instrumental albums for Josie, these sessions add vocals in an attempt to enhance the group's pop appeal; while that works well enough on titles like *Rejuvenation* (1974), which includes the classic "Hey Pocky a-Way" and *Fire on the Bayou* (1975), it also led to such embarrassments as the foolishly topical "Disco Is the Thing Today" on *Trick Bag.*

The Meters performed *Uptown Rulers! The Meters Live on the Queen Mary* at a Paul McCartney–hosted 1975 cruise party; judging from the band's set, it's obvious that fun was had by all. *Funkify Your Life* is an essential two-disc anthology that collects all the Meters' best work. *The Best of the Meters* is a condensed version, packaging 12 classic Meters grooves. *The Meters Jam* consists of previously unissued cover tunes. — J.D.C.

PAT METHENY

★★★★½	**Bright Size Life (ECM, 1975)**
★★★½	**Watercolors (1977; ECM, 1994)**
★★★★	**Pat Metheny Group (1978; ECM, 1994)**
★★★★	**New Chautauqua (1979; ECM, 1994)**
★★★½	**American Garage (1979; ECM, 1994)**
★★★★★	**80/81 (1980; ECM, 1994)**
★★★★½	**As Falls Wichita, So Falls Wichita Falls (1981; ECM, 1994)**
★★★★	**Offramp (1982; ECM, 1994)**
★★★½	**Travels (1983; ECM, 1994)**
★★★★½	**First Circle (1984; ECM, 1994)**
★★★½	**Rejoicing (with Charlie Haden and Billy Higgins) (1984; ECM, 1994)**
★★★	**The Falcon and the Snowman (Capitol/EMI America, 1985)**
★★★★★	**Song X (with Ornette Coleman) (Geffen, 1986)**
★★★★	**Still Life (Talking) (Geffen, 1987)**

★★★½ **Letter from Home (Geffen, 1989)**
★★★★★ **Question and Answer (Geffen, 1990)**
★★★★ **Secret Story (Geffen, 1992)**
★★★★ **Road to You—Recorded Live in Europe (Geffen, 1993)**
★★★★ **Zero Tolerance for Silence (Geffen, 1994)**
★★★★ **We Live Here (Geffen, 1995)**
★★★★ **Quartet (Geffen, 1996)**
★★★★ **Imaginary Day (Warner Bros., 1997)**

A singular presence among fusion musicians, Pat Metheny (b. 1954) is one of the very few guitarists of his generation who can be said to have a genuinely individual voice. Avoiding the speed-demon pyrotechnics of most post-McLaughlin jazz guitarists, Metheny delivers solos that are evenly paced and lyrical, while his tone—full-bodied and warm, making exquisite use of chorusing to soften its edges—is unmistakable.

Bright Size Life, recorded when Metheny was 21 and an alumnus of the Gary Burton Quintet, is an astonishingly precocious debut. Featuring bassist Jaco Pastorius and Burton Quintet drummer Bob Moses, its music is airy and conversational, yet with a solidity that speaks of even greater music to come; the trio's version of Ornette Coleman's "Round Trip/Broadway Blues" is particularly stunning. Metheny introduced his own quartet over his next few albums, and these recordings—*Watercolors, Pat Metheny Group* and *American Garage*—expand upon the sound of his debut, most notably through the keyboard colorings of Lyle Mays, who functions less as Metheny's foil than as his copilot. *Pat Metheny Group* is the most satisfying of these, thanks in no small measure to the writing, particularly "Jaco" and the stately, shimmering "San Lorenzo."

New Chautauqua finds the guitarist sparring with himself in a lovely series of multitracked guitar pieces. Still, Metheny seemed to relish the challenge of playing with other musicians in other contexts. Hence, *80/81,* on which the young guitarist goes head-to-head with bassist Charlie Haden, drummer Jack DeJohnette and tenor saxophonists Dewey Redman and Michael Brecker—heavy company, indeed. Metheny more than holds his own, and the level of communication is remarkably high, as exemplified by the first of the "Two Folk Songs."

Teaming up with Mays again for *As Falls Wichita, So Falls Wichita Falls,* Metheny moves into a new arena of expression. Although the selections are seemingly structured as duets, with embellishments by Brazilian percussionist Nana Vasconcelos, Vasconcelos actually plays an integral role in the proceedings, fleshing out the colors of the title tune and even providing the melody (vocally) for "Estupenda Gráca." *Offramp* introduces a new bass player, Steve Rodby, and Vasconcelos pops up again, adding tremendously to the flavor of "Barcarole." Still, the group's growing reliance on percussion isn't quite as noteworthy as Metheny's embrace of the guitar synthesizer and synclavier guitar, devices that increase the timbral range available to him but at some cost, as the guitarist often ends up with the same sounds as a keyboard synth player but none of the technical advantages. Metheny mostly avoids the synth guitar for *Rejoicing,* a trio date with Haden and drummer Billy Higgins, but when he does resort to it, the grandiloquent, trumpetlike tone he gets for "The Calling" suggests he sees the added electronics as a sort of arranging tool.

First Circle, which adds percussionist Pedro Aznar to the lineup, confirms that suspicion, opening with the Carla Bley–ish "Forward March" and proceeding through a series of tightly arranged tunes that seem to point as much to Metheny and Mays's compositional sense as to their improvisational skills. It's an approach not unlike that taken by Weather Report (although its sound is utterly dissimilar), and his score for *The Falcon and the Snowman* has no trouble expanding it to cinematic scale. (There's also a vocal by David Bowie on "This Is Not America.") Metheny gets even more ambitious on *Still Life (Talking),* adding wordless vocals that lend a dreamy, soaring feel to tunes like "Minuano (Six Eight)"; *Letter from Home* relies on more conventional string orchestration for its occasional bits of textural oomph.

Metheny's most exciting recordings remain those in which he surrounds himself with older, more established players—as in *Song X,* a vigorous, challenging collaboration with Ornette Coleman that recalls the bracingly cacophonous recordings Coleman made in the late '60s and early '70s. Or *Question and Answer,* a far more accessible date featuring Metheny in a trio setting, with bassist Dave Holland and drummer Roy Haynes, whose hard-swinging polyrhythms push the guitarist to new heights.

Secret Story explores Asian and Brazilian sonic terrain with Metheny on a variety of instruments including guitar, electric sitar, trumpet and flügelhorn, various synthesizers, keyboards and percussion instruments. He employs a full brass section alongside such guests as harpist Toots Thielemans, pianist Gil Goldstein and bassist Charlie Haden. *The Road to You* is a live sextet outing from 1993 that won the 1994 Grammy for Best Contemporary Jazz Performance. On *Imaginary Day* Metheny continues to find fresh inspiration in world music. — J.D.C.

GLENN MILLER

★★★ **The Original Reunion of the Glenn Miller Band (1962; GNP Crescendo, 1986)**
★★★ **A Memorial (1969; RCA Bluebird, 1991)**
★★★ **Pure Gold (1975; RCA Bluebird, 1988)**
★★★★ **Chattanooga Choo Choo: The #1 Hits (1981; RCA Bluebird, 1991)**
★★ **In the Digital Mood (1983; GRP, 1991)**
★★★ **A Legendary Performer (RCA Bluebird, 1987)**
★★★ **Best of Glenn Miller (RCA Bluebird, 1988)**
★★★ **The Unforgettable Glenn Miller and His Orchestra (RCA Bluebird, 1988)**
★★★★ **The Popular Recordings (1938–42) (RCA Bluebird, 1989)**
★★★ **War Broadcasts (LaserLight, 1991)**
★★★ **Major Glenn Miller and the Army Air Force Band (LaserLight, 1991)**
★★★★ **The Complete Glenn Miller, Vols. 1–13 (RCA Bluebird, 1991)**
★★★ **Best of the Big Bands: Evolution of a Band (Legacy, 1992)**
★★★ **The Carnegie Hall Concert (RCA Bluebird, 1992)**
★★★ **Moonlight Serenade (RCA Bluebird, 1992)**
★★★ **On the Alamo (Drive Archive, 1995)**
★★★½ **The Essential Glenn Miller (RCA Bluebird, 1995)**
★★★ **The Spirit Is Willing 1939–1942 (RCA Bluebird, 1995)**
★★★★ **Greatest Hits (RCA Victor, 1996)**
★★★ **The Lost Recordings (RCA Victor, 1996)**
★★★ **More Greatest Hits (Victor Jazz, 1996)**
★★★ **Live in Europe (LaserLight, 1997)**
★★★ **Tuxedo Junction (LaserLight, 1997)**
★★★ **The Miller Sound Lives Forever (LaserLight, 1997)**

Trombonist/bandleader Glenn Miller (1904–1944) began his career as a jazz player, working sessions and joining the Dorsey Brothers as a soloist and arranger in 1934. By the time he began successfully leading his own bands in 1938, Miller had developed an arrangement strategy based on a smooth, clarinet-rooted reed section that became the trademark sound of a string of hits, including the band's theme, "Moonlight Serenade," as well as "In the Mood," "Little Brown Jug" and "Sunrise Serenade."

Miller's popularity led to a common paradox—though he became one of the most popular figures in jazz history, his musical importance is insignificant to the point where many historians have simply omitted him from the story of jazz. In fact, his creamy band sound and precise, disciplined arrangements were the essence of the "sweet" big-band style that was privately ridiculed by the era's top musicians.

Miller's bands were notable for their lack of great soloists—his concept had little use for them—but he surrounded himself with superb technicians of studio quality. The letter-perfect performances that ensued were appropriate to the kind of pop material Miller chose to cover, songs picked for their commercial potential rather than musical interest. As a result, his recordings are monolithic in their bland competence; never poorly done and never, ever, exciting.

All of this is not to say that Miller was a poor musician; on the contrary, he was a player and arranger of considerable talents. But aside from his signature reed section of three saxophones and clarinet playing in unison, he left his most creative moments behind when he formed his own organization. His commercial efforts did much to popularize jazz to an audience less interested in playing than in song selection.

Miller's hits are the most enduring representation of his work. Jazz or not, they remain icons of the late 1930s and World War II era, when such soothing bromides as "Moonlight Serenade" provided a tonic for troubled times. The hits selections and complete boxes are recommended as a look into American history, if nothing else. All on RCA, *The Complete Glenn Miller* is a 13-disc boxed set; *The Essential Glenn Miller* contains a fairly long booklet and two discs; *The Popular*

Recordings is another multidisc set; and *Chattanooga Choo Choo: The #1 Hits* is a handy single disc.

When the band played "King Porter Stomp," its emotional deficiencies were obvious, but the middlebrow fodder, patriotic tunes, covers of songs from *The Wizard of Oz* and later hits "Indian Summer," "Stardust," "My Melancholy Baby," "Tuxedo Junction" and "Pennsylvania 6-5000" show where the bread was buttered. Other directions, like the "swinging the classics" versions of "Anvil Chorus" and "Song of the Volga Boatmen," provide little interest.

Miller enlisted in 1942 to lead an Army band (until his plane disappeared in 1944 and was never found) that would become one of the Allies' most powerful propaganda weapons. Miller fashioned wartime material such as "The White Cliffs of Dover," "Keep 'Em Flying," "On the Old Assembly Line," "Shh, It's a Military Secret," "When Johnny Comes Marching Home," "Soldier Let Me Read Your Letter" and "That's Sabotage" as well as playing countless benefit shows and live performances. A lot of this material was recorded and has made its way into circulation. Although some might find the broadcast chatter appealing (*War Broadcasts* features Miller—through an interpreter—speaking to Nazi Germany about the virtues of American jazz), none of it breaks out of the musical straitjacket Miller fastened over his outfit. — J.S.

STEVE MILLION

★★★★ **Million to One (Palmetto, 1995)**
★★★★ **Thanks a Million (Palmetto, 1997)**

Keyboardist Steve Million (b. 1954) came to public attention in his hometown of Chicago in 1990 as the leader of Monk's Dream, a unique Thelonious Monk tribute trio comprising Million on piano, Hammond B-3 organist Mike Kocous and drummer Robert Shy. Million's debt to Monk is in evidence on *Million to One,* but the versatile pianist demonstrates a broader range leading an excellent quintet of Randy Brecker on trumpet and flügelhorn, Chris Potter on saxophones, Michael Moore on bass and Ron Vincent on drums. The same lineup appears on the equally fine *Thanks a Million,* nine Million originals and the title track, a Gus Kahn standard. — J.S.

MINGUS BIG BAND

★★★★★ **Mingus Big Band 93: Nostalgia in Times Square (Dreyfus, 1993)**
★★★★½ **Gunslinging Bird (Dreyfus, 1995)**
★★★★★ **Live in Time (Dreyfus, 1996)**
★★★★½ **Que Viva Mingus! (Dreyfus, 1997)**

New York's best working band through the 1990s, the Mingus Big Band has consistently drawn large and varied crowds of music fans to New York's Fez nightclub for its Thursday residency. Like adventurers in a bottomless cave, exploring the vast interstices of Charles Mingus's sprawling musical imagination, the dozens who've contributed to these remarkable recordings have done as much to promote the genius of Mingus's vision as those who played with him when he lived. Unlike most tribute bands, the Mingus Big Band doesn't imply the absence of its guiding light. Instead, Mingus feels vividly present in the Big Band's highly emotive performances.

Mingus's widow, Sue Mingus, has been the offstage hand guiding the direction of the Mingus repertory since his passing. Mingus Dynasty, which began as a small group, evolved over the years into a large-band prototype for the Mingus Big Band. By the time *Mingus Big Band 93: Nostalgia in Times Square* was released, the group had already mastered a healthy portion of the Mingus book and was paced by textured arrangements from Sy Johnson, trumpeter Jack Walrath and baritone saxophonist Ronnie Cuber. Other stalwart brass and reed players in this star-studded cast include trumpeters Randy Brecker and Ryan Kisor, trombonists Art Baron and Frank Lacy, alto saxophonist Steve Slagle and tenor saxophonists John Stubblefield, Chris Potter and Craig Handy. *Gunslinging Bird* features largely the same players on such Mingus gems as "Fables of Faubus" and "Reincarnation of a Lovebird." *Live in Time* is a gorgeous two-CD document of the band's in-person magic. *Que Viva Mingus!* concentrates on the Latin-jazz side of the Mingus book, including versions of "Dizzy Moods," "Ysabel's Table Dance" and "Los Mariachis" from the album Mingus claimed was the best he'd ever made, *Tijuana Moods.* — J.S.

CHARLES MINGUS

★★★★ **The Jazz Experiments of Charles Mingus (1955; Bethlehem, 1984)**
★★★½ **Jazzical Moods (with John LaPorta) (1955; Original Jazz Classics, 1995)**
★★★★ **Mingus at the Bohemia (1955; Original Jazz Classics, 1991)**

★★★ **Intrusions (1955; Drive Archive, 1994)**
★★★★ **The Charles Mingus Quartet Plus Max Roach (1955; Original Jazz Classics, 1990)**
★★★★★ **Pithecanthropus Erectus (1956; Atlantic, 1981)**
★★★½ **Jazz Composers Workshop: Charles Mingus (1956; Savoy, 1992)**
★★★★ **East Coasting (1957; Bethlehem, 1982)**
★★★★½ **The Clown (1957; Atlantic, 1984)**
★★★★½ **Blues and Roots (Atlantic, 1959)**
★★★★★ **Mingus Ah Um (1959; Columbia, 1991)**
★★★½ **Jazz Portraits (Mingus in Wonderland) (1959; Blue Note, 1994)**
★★★★★ **Mingus Dynasty (1959; Columbia/Legacy, 1994)**
★★★★ **Mingus Revisited (EmArcy, 1960)**
★★★★★ **Mysterious Blues (1961; Candid, 1989)**
★★★★½ **Oh Yeah (1961; Atlantic, 1988)**
★★★★★ **New Tijuana Moods (1962; RCA Bluebird, 1986)**
★★★★★ **The Black Saint and the Sinner Lady (1962; Impulse!, 1986)**
★★★★½ **Mingus, Mingus, Mingus, Mingus, Mingus (1963; Impulse!, 1995)**
★★★½ **Mingus Plays Piano (1963; Mobile Fidelity, 1990)**
★★★★★ **The Great Concert of Charles Mingus (1964; Musicdisc, 1995)**
★★★½ **Right Now: Live at the Jazz Workshop (1964; Original Jazz Classics, 1990)**
★★★★★ **Town Hall Concert (1964; Original Jazz Classics, 1991)**
★★★½ **Charles Mingus Plus Max Roach (1965; Original Jazz Classics, 1990)**
★★★★★ **Let My Children Hear Music (1971; Columbia/Legacy, 1992)**
★★★½ **Charles Mingus and Friends in Concert (Columbia, 1972)**
★★★★ **Changes One (1974; Rhino, 1993)**
★★★★ **Changes Two (1974; Rhino, 1993)**
★★★½ **Mingus Moves (1974; Atlantic, 1993)**
★★★★ **At Carnegie Hall (Atlantic, 1976)**
★★★★★ **Mingus at Antibes (1976; Atlantic, 1986)**
★★★½ **Three or Four Shades of Blues (1977; Atlantic, 1989)**
★★★★ **Shoes of the Fisherman's Wife (Columbia, 1988)**
★★★★★ **The Complete Debut Recordings (Debut, 1990)**
★★★★★ **Epitaph (Columbia, 1990)**
★★★★ **Debut Rarities, Vol. 1 (Original Jazz Classics, 1992)**
★★★★ **Debut Rarities, Vol. 2 (Original Jazz Classics, 1992)**
★★★★ **Debut Rarities, Vol. 3 (Original Jazz Classics, 1992)**
★★★★ **Debut Rarities, Vol. 4 (Original Jazz Classics, 1992)**
★★★★½ **Thirteen Pictures: The Charles Mingus Anthology (Rhino, 1993)**
★★★½ **A Modern Jazz Symposium of Music and Poetry with Charles Mingus (Bethlehem, 1994)**
★★★½ **This Is Jazz 6 (Columbia/Legacy, 1996)**

While portly, pipe-smoking Charles Mingus (1922–1979) stands as the best jazz bassist besides Oscar Pettiford, he's remembered more significantly as the idiom's most original composer since Duke Ellington. As the title of his brilliant, if sometimes fanciful, stream-of-consciousness 1970 autobiography, *Beneath the Underdog,* suggests, Mingus saw himself as a resolute outsider, an embattled figure of too vast a dimension to be contained by conventional categories. While his consistent inventiveness in some ways proved him right, the blustery promethean was also a past master of the tradition—the entire history of jazz lay easily under his dexterous fingertips. And while his methods were demanding and his persona blunt, Mingus, again like Ellington, is noteworthy in that so much of his music, for all of its innovative force, offers such sheer accessible joy (beginners might start with the *Thirteen Pictures* compilation). Since his death from Lou Gehrig's disease, Mingus has assumed his rightful place in the jazz pantheon.

Schooled by his stepmother in church music (gospel would remain an abiding influence), Mingus worked for a while with Red Norvo and his cool-jazz outfit before forming the Debut record label in the early '50s. Fantasy's expertly annotated 12-CD set of 169 selections from 1951 to 1958, *The Complete Debut Recordings,* offers stellar examples of nascent greatness, from wondrous standards (Cole Porter's "What Is This Thing Called Love?") to original manifestoes ("Bass-ically Speaking"). Fantasy issued individual CDs culled from the set in the 1992 series *Debut Rarities, Vols. 1–4.*

Mingus truly cut loose, however, with *Mingus Ah Um* and its rollicking highlight, "Better Git It in Your Soul," which soon became his theme song, and with his first true groundbreaker, *Pithecanthropus Erectus.* The latter's title track was an early instance of his compositional approach: a loosely metaphorical "tale" of pride going before a fall, it showed how Mingus often wrote music to illustrate a very specific, often elusive emotional state. And the playing, with its gospel influence, its whoops and hollers, displayed the characteristic Mingus exuberance (check *The Clown* for similar joys). *Blues and Roots* was also a trailblazer—a nine-piece outfit delving deep into states of rich intensity. *Tijuana Moods* (repackaged and better edited as *New Tijuana Moods*), with the castanet-crazed "Ysabel's Table Dance," continued to demonstrate the man's equal cunning and passion; the record, too, with drummer/soul mate Dannie Richmond and saxophonist Shafi Hadi, showed that part of Mingus's greatness lay in his skill in choosing sidemen—Mingus cited *Tijuana* as his own favorite album, but throughout his career, he always chose as high points work from his most recent period. *The Black Saint and the Sinner Lady* and *Mingus Dynasty* solidified his strengths—a fierce swing, a novel voicing of instruments and a "narrative" sense of composition. While a mere bagatelle in the context of his overall achievement, *Mingus Plays Piano* is interesting: Even without his primary instrument, his distinctiveness comes through. For more typical strength, pick up *Mingus at Antibes,* with standout reed work from Eric Dolphy. And end your tour of the bassist's early glory days with *Oh Yeah* (guest star Rahsaan Roland Kirk shines on everything from tenor sax to siren) and *The Great Concert* (a half hour of "Fables of Faubus," an antisegregationist manifesto, will knock you flat).

The end of the '60s was hard on Mingus. He wandered the streets for a period of nearly three years, believing himself to be going mad. Recovering, he went on to produce exceptional, if inconsistent, music in the '70s—*Let My Children Hear Music* (repackaged on *Shoes of the Fisherman's Wife,* with selections from the 1959 standout *Mingus Dynasty*) ranks with his triumphs. *Mingus at Carnegie Hall* showcases a remarkable outfit starring Kirk and trumpeter Jon Faddis on a long workout of "Perdido": *Changes One* and *Changes Two* are also '70s triumphs—their passions ranging from the political ("Remember Rockefeller at Attica") to the romantic ("Duke Ellington's Sound of Love"). The great composer is fondly remembered on the fittingly titled *Epitaph,* the first recordings of Mingus's orchestral works in their entirety (first essayed in 1962), reconstructed by Gunther Schuller. — P.E.

BLUE MITCHELL

★★★★ **Big 6 (1958; Original Jazz Classics, 1991)**
★★★★ **Out of the Blue (1959; Original Jazz Classics, 1991)**
★★★★ **Blue Soul (1959; Original Jazz Classics, 1992)**
★★★★½ **Blues on My Mind (1959; Original Jazz Classics, 1988)**
★★★★ **Blue's Moods (1960; Original Jazz Classics, 1994)**
★★★½ **Smooth as the Wind (1961; Original Jazz Classics, 1996)**
★★★★½ **A Sure Thing (1962; Original Jazz Classics, 1995)**
★★★½ **The Cup Bearers (1963; Original Jazz Classics, 1994)**

Trumpeter Richard "Blue" Mitchell (1930–1979) was one of several discoveries made by fellow Floridian Julian "Cannonball" Adderley. Producer Orrin Keepnews signed Mitchell to Riverside Records in 1958 after seeing him jam with Adderley in a Miami nightclub. Mitchell demonstrated a limpid midregister tone phrased lazily across the beat yet always in rhythmic control and a solid connection to the blues, making him a perfect recruit for the soul-jazz revolution Cannonball was leading. The Original Jazz Classics reissues document part of the brief but immensely satisfying Riverside era.

Mitchell's debut, *Big 6,* places him in fast company—Curtis Fuller on trombone, Johnny Griffin on tenor sax, Wynton Kelly on piano, Wilbur Ware on bass and Philly Joe Jones on drums—and showcases his lyrical ballad style on "There Will Never Be Another You." On the lively *Out of the Blue,* Kelly remains, with Benny Golson replacing Griffin, Art Blakey instead of Philly Joe and either Paul Chambers or Sam Jones on bass. The CD version also includes "Studio B" from the unavailable *New Blue Horns* session with Cedar Walton on piano. The *Blue Soul* sextet is Kelly, Fuller, Philly Joe, Jimmy Heath on tenor and Sam Jones on bass.

Blues on My Mind compiles tracks from all three albums.

Mitchell joined Horace Silver's band in 1958 and stayed with that group during its prime. On *Blue's Moods* Mitchell brought in drummer Roy Brooks, a Silver band mate, to complete a quartet lineup with Kelly and Sam Jones. The moody quintet outing *The Cup Bearers* was recorded with the rest of the Silver quintet—Brooks, bassist Gene Taylor and tenor saxophonist Junior Cook—and Walton instead of Silver.

A Sure Thing is a vibrant large-group recording highlighted by tenor saxophonist Jimmy Heath's arrangements of Wes Montgomery's "West Coast Blues" and Jay McShann's "Hootie Blues." Drummer Albert "Tootie" Heath joins Kelly and Jones. The horns on this session—including Mitchell on trumpet, Heath on tenor, Pepper Adams and Pat Patrick on baritones, Jerome Richardson on alto and flute and Julius Watkins on French horn—achieve some truly beautiful colors.

Mitchell remained an in-demand session player throughout his life, playing with Adderley, Johnny Griffin, Lou Donaldson and John Mayall, among others. — J.S.

RED MITCHELL

★★★★ **Presenting Red Mitchell (1957; Original Jazz Classics, 1992)**
★★½ **Moods Unlimited (with Bill Evans and Hank Jones) (1982; Evidence, 1993)**
★★★★ **Hear Ye! (Atlantic, 1993)**

Red Mitchell (1927–1992) was one of jazz's greatest bassists. A mainstay of the West Coast recording studios during the '50s, Mitchell's inventive work can be sampled on scores of albums, but a superior introduction is his playing on pianist Hampton Hawes's recordings of that era. More of his advanced bass work can be heard on Ornette Coleman's early Contemporary recording *Tomorrow Is the Question!*

Unfortunately, Mitchell rarely stepped out as a leader during this period. *Presenting Red Mitchell* is a late-'50s bop-oriented set featuring the legendary saxophonist James Clay, pianist Lorraine Geller and drummer Billy Higgins. *Hear Ye!* captures the dynamic band that the bassist co-led with the hard-driving tenor saxophonist Harold Land. Mitchell later spent time in Scandinavia during the late '60s and '70s.

As stunning as his earlier work was, Mitchell reached new peaks during the last three decades of his life; check out the 1985 Contemporary sessions Mitchell co-led with pianist Jimmy Rowles, and *Three For All* with pianist Tommy Flanagan and saxophonist Phil Woods—if you can find them.

Mitchell was also a masterful duet player. First-rate examples of *simpatico* one-on-one interaction include encounters with pianists Rowles and Roger Kellaway; guitarists Joe Pass, Jim Hall, Joe Beck and Joe Puma, saxophonist Lee Konitz and trumpeter Clark Terry. — S.F.

ROSCOE MITCHELL

★★★★ **Sound (1966; Delmark, 1996)**
★★★½ **3×4 Eye (1981; Black Saint, 1994)**
★★★★ **Roscoe Mitchell and the Sound and Space Ensembles (Black Saint, 1984)**
★★★ **The Flow of Things (Black Saint, 1986)**
★★★½ **Live at the Knitting Factory (Black Saint, 1990)**
★★★½ **Duets and Solos (Black Saint, 1993)**
★★½ **This Dance Is for Steve McCall (Black Saint, 1993)**
★★★½ **First Meeting (Knitting Factory Works, 1995)**
★★★ **Hey, Donald (Delmark, 1995)**
★★★★ **Sound Songs (Delmark, 1997)**

Roscoe Mitchell (b. 1940) is one of the more influential musician/composers to emerge from the free-jazz wave of the mid-1960s. His group, the Art Ensemble of Chicago, has existed since 1967 and, while enduring several personnel changes and wholesale moves to both Europe and New York, remains one of the finest composites in contemporary jazz.

A multi-instrumentalist of the highest order, Mitchell plays flute and all manner of saxophones as well as percussion and a wealth of "little instruments" that he has collected over the years. Mitchell is also a great organizer and helped found, along with innovators like Richard Abrams and Anthony Braxton, Chicago's Association for the Advancement of Creative Musicians.

An incredibly strong and intellectually rigorous saxophonist, Mitchell has always been a proponent of extended solo improvisation, a discipline that would eventually become an accepted measuring stick for many a free player. His fierce grasp of multiphonics, circular breathing and harmonic overtones anticipated much of the avant-garde's modern experimentation.

Mitchell has recorded somewhat sporadically as a leader, and a number of his albums are long out of print. Prime examples of Mitchell's compositions, like "Nonaah" and "The Maze," are extremely hard to find but well worth seeking out. Luckily, Mitchell's classic first album, *Sound,* is available on CD. With an additional take of "Ornette" and the restoration of the two versions of "Sound" that had been edited and combined on the LP, this is definitive free jazz from 1966. Accompanied by Lester Bowie and Malachi Favors of the Art Ensemble and fellow AACM members Lester Lashley and Maurice McIntyre, Mitchell forges an ambitious vision for solo and group improvisation alike. *3×4 Eye* introduces the Sound Ensemble, a hand-picked group of inspired young musicians who play quite zealously under Mitchell's direction. Hugh Ragin on trumpet and Spencer Barefield on guitar are sensitive sidemen along with percussionist Tani Tabbal and bassist Jaribu Shahid. Mitchell's improvisational orchestrations reveal his formidable abilities as a composer as well as an outstanding instrumental soloist.

Mitchell willfully expands his band's lineup on *Roscoe Mitchell and the Sound and Space Ensembles.* Spanning funk, avant-garde and lyrical interludes and utilizing strange reed instruments, a classical singer and Mitchell's unbridled saxophone virtuosity, this disc is both exhilarating and exhausting. Mitchell's open-ended compositional agenda is a serious challenge to the players involved but certainly not without its rewards.

The Flow of Things finds Mitchell in a quartet setting along with the late Steve McCall on drums, resident Chicagoan Jodie Christian on piano and Malachi Favors on bass. Breaking little new ground, this date showcases Mitchell's volatile sax playing juxtaposed against Christian's more conventional piano style. The disc's three extended versions of the title track invite us to witness the composer's instrumental endurance as well as his personal variations on a single theme.

Live at the Knitting Factory finds the Sound Ensemble becoming even more intuitive as a group. Hugh Ragin shows particular growth as a soloist and is the perfect foil for Mitchell's demanding expressions on soprano and alto. Featuring an ambitious version of "Nonaah" and the energetic "The Reverend Frank Wright," Mitchell's voracious compositions seem to evolve with a life of their own. While the playing is still not quite in the Art Ensemble's league, it is clear that Roscoe Mitchell is a compelling force in any situation.

Duets and Solos is Mitchell sharing the stage with his old AACM mate Muhal Richard Abrams. Featuring a 26-minute piano solo by Abrams and a 15-minute saxophone interlude by Mitchell, this is prime, AACM-inspired musicianship. Cerebral and intense, the disc's finest moments emerge during the lengthy and evocative duets. Still, Abrams's piano work is practically regal and Mitchell always thrives in a solo context.

This Dance Is for Steve McCall introduces yet another one of Mitchell's highbrow ensembles, the Note Factory. Featuring young free-jazzers Matthew Shipp on piano and William Parker on bass along with the old Sound Ensemble rhythm section, this band had yet to fully coalesce by the time this session was recorded.

Hey, Donald is dedicated to the late saxophonist Donald Myrick. Myrick was a member of the AACM and also in the original Earth, Wind and Fire. Accompanied by Favors, Jodie Christian and Albert "Tootie" Heath, Mitchell leads the quartet through a fairly balanced set of free-form and straight-ahead jazz. Christian's piano-playing is best suited to the mainstream cuts like "Walking in the Moonlight," which was written by Mitchell's father. Highlights include four separate duets with bassist Malachi Favors, who has been a consistent ally to Mitchell for more than three decades.

Sound Songs is an imposing double disc that brings the saxophonist full circle. Including live Midwest performances and studio recordings replete with overdubs, this solo tour de force is a culmination of Roscoe Mitchell's forays into unaccompanied performance. Playing a huge variety of instruments including bells, whistles and even a bamboo saxophone, Mitchell comes up with almost two hours of incredibly imaginative blowing all by his lonesome. From the pastoral beauty of "Fallen Heroes" to the naked intensity of "Full Frontal Saxophone," *Sound Songs* captures Roscoe Mitchell at the top of his game. — M.M.

HANK MOBLEY

★★★ **Tenor Conclave (1956; Original Jazz Classics, N.A.)**

★★★ **Messages (1956; Prestige, 1989)**

★★★★ **Hank Mobley and His All Stars (1957; Blue Note, 1996)**

★★★ **Peckin' Time (1958; Blue Note, 1988)**
★★★★ **Soul Station (1960; Blue Note, 1987)**
★★★ **Roll Call (Blue Note, 1961)**
★★★½ **Workout (1961; Blue Note, 1990)**
★★★ **Another Workout (Blue Note, 1962)**
★★★½ **No Room for Squares (1964; Blue Note, 1989)**
★★★½ **A Caddy for Daddy (1965; Blue Note, 1990)**
★★★ **Dippin' (1965; Blue Note, 1988)**
★★★★ **A Slice of the Top (1966; Blue Note, 1995)**
★★★ **Hi Voltage (Blue Note, 1967)**
★★★ **Reach Out! (1968; Blue Note, 1997)**
★★★★ **The Best of Hank Mobley: The Blue Note Years (Blue Note, 1996)**

Hank Mobley (1930–1986), a dependable but not always inspired tenorist, was a perennial sideman of the '50s and '60s. For a musician who flourished during the hard-bop period, Mobley's playing could be flaccid and lazy rather than funky and biting. His greatest asset seems to have been an ability to adapt to different musical settings; he can be heard with such distinctive leaders as Max Roach, Art Blakey and Miles Davis.

His own records are mostly solid but not indispensable blowing sessions with contributions from up-and-comers like Lee Morgan, Donald Byrd, Kenny Dorham and Jackie McLean. *Hank Mobley and His All Stars* features Horace Silver on piano, Blakey on drums, Milt Jackson on vibes and Doug Watkins on bass. *Soul Station,* a quartet date with Blakey, is a standout.

Mobley always held his own in the fast company he kept, but the majority of his work is professional rather than memorable. The major exception is *A Slice of the Top,* a great 1966 date with arrangements by Duke Pearson and support from Lee Morgan, McCoy Tyner and Billy Higgins. By this time, Mobley had been touched, as had most tenorists, by the work of John Coltrane. This modernist bent added verve and aggressiveness to Mobley's chops; he never sounded better.

Look for the currently out-of-print *Third Season.* — S.F.

THE MODERN JAZZ QUARTET

★★★★ **Modern Jazz Quartet (1951; Savoy, 1993)**
★★★★ **MJQ (1954; Original Jazz Classics, N.A.)**
★★★★½ **Django (1955; Original Jazz Classics, 1987)**
★★★½ **Concorde (1955; Original Jazz Classics, 1987)**
★★★★ **Fontessa (1956; Atlantic Jazz, 1987)**
★★★★ **No Sun in Venice (1957; Atlantic Jazz, 1987)**
★★★★ **At Music Inn, Vol. 2 (with Sonny Rollins) (1958; Atlantic Jazz, 1989)**
★★★ **Odds Against Tomorrow (Blue Note, 1959)**
★★★½ **Pyramid (1960; Atlantic Jazz, 1987)**
★★★★ **Lonely Woman (1962; Atlantic Jazz, 1987)**
★★★½ **The Comedy (1962; Atlantic Jazz, 1989)**
★★★½ **Blues at Carnegie Hall (1966; Atlantic Jazz, 1993)**
★★ **Blues on Bach (1973; Atlantic Jazz, 1987)**
★★★★½ **The Complete Last Concert (1974; Atlantic Jazz, 1989)**
★★★½ **Together Again! Live at Montreux Jazz Festival '82 (1982; Pablo, 1987)**
★★★ **"Echoes": Together Again (1984; Pablo, 1987)**
★★★★ **Topsy: This One's for Basie (1985; Pablo, 1987)**
★★★★ **The Artistry of the Modern Jazz Quartet (Prestige, 1986)**
★★½ **Three Windows (Atlantic Jazz, 1987)**
★★★½ **Compact Jazz: The Modern Jazz Quartet Plus (Verve, 1987)**
★★★½ **The Best of the Modern Jazz Quartet (Pablo, 1988)**
★★★½ **A 40th Anniversary Celebration (Atlantic Jazz, 1994)**
★★★★½ **MJQ40: The Boxed Set (Atlantic, 1991)**
★★★★★ **Dedicated to Connie (Atlantic Jazz, 1995)**

The Modern Jazz Quartet was an ensemble that developed thanks to the many ambiguities of jazz in the early '50s. As Dizzy Gillespie's rhythm section in 1951, John Lewis, Milt Jackson, Ray Brown and Kenny Clarke performed as a quartet in order to provide a break for the rest of Dizzy's hard-blowing big band. Featuring the hot, bop-styled soloing of vibraharpist Milt Jackson, the group began to play its own gigs as the Milt Jackson Quartet. Bassist Ray Brown soon left the band and was replaced by the talented Percy Heath.

Pianist and main composer John Lewis developed the crux of the MJQ's sound. In stark contrast with Milt Jackson's outgoing musical style, Lewis's aim was to recontextualize standard improvisations in jazz by instituting formal structures into the music. Using European compositions of the Renaissance and Baroque periods as his models, Lewis created strict arrangements for himself and his three musical partners. Slowly wresting the artistic control away from Jackson, Lewis dictated the tempo, key and meter of their music with the authority of a neoclassical composer.

As the MJQ began to institute the formalization of standard jazz forms, the dichotomy of styles between Jackson and Lewis began to pay some very high dividends. The group now called itself the Modern Jazz Quartet, and Jackson varied the traditional role of jazz vibes by injecting his vibrato-laden bop solos over the top of Lewis's cool, intellectual blueprints. Anchored by the restrained, swinging groove of Kenny Clarke and Percy Heath, the creative tension afforded this group some exciting (and novel) musical moments. Eventually, the MJQ would become one of the more popular groups in contemporary jazz and perform all over the world for sold-out crowds.

The band's first album, *Modern Jazz Quartet,* is essential MJQ. With Lewis's spare piano style as prime counterpoint for Milt Jackson's aggressive vibraharp solos, the rough foreshadowing of what was to be called "chamber jazz" had quietly begun. Kenny Clarke, who would stay with the band for only a short time, is here in all his bebop glory.

MJQ continues on the path the band had tentatively established on the first album and is another illuminating picture of the group's formative years. With Jackson still steeped in the blues and bebop, his dynamic use of quiet space had yet to fully emerge and his careful sculpting of melodic lines was only beginning to take hold.

With *Django* Lewis's stylistic agenda finally blossoms. "Django" would become a signature tune, and along with other classics on this record, like "La Ronde" and "Milano," it would remain in the band's repertoire for decades. Creating a near-perfect symmetry between Lewis and Jackson, the two men take turns improvising quite freely within the composition's formal structure. Kenny Clarke sounds exuberant on his last session with the band, and Percy Heath steps to the front on Dizzy Gillespie's "One Bass Hit." Lewis's piano style is suitably bluesy at times, and the whole session glimmers like gold. *Concorde* brings new drummer Connie Kay into the fold, where he would justly remain until his death in 1994. More understated than his predecessor Clarke, Kay contributed cymbal work that would become essential to the band's sound and lend a brisk, swinging effectiveness to Lewis's compositions. Jackson's playing displays great depth—he would soon become acknowledged as one of jazz's more exciting soloists.

Fontessa is even more formal, as Lewis explores the fugue and other manifestations of European influence on the "Fontessa Suite." There are some lovely ballads by Jackson, a bit of blues and some bebop to round things out.

No Sun in Venice is an interesting score written by Lewis for a Roger Vadim film and features the bold composition "The Golden Striker." *At Music Inn, Vol. 2* is just one of the many high-profile collaborations that the MJQ would engage in over the years. Sonny Rollins appears on only two tunes, the swinging version of Milt Jackson's "Bags' Groove" and an extended interpretation of Dizzy Gillespie's "A Night in Tunisia." The rest of this session is classic Modern Jazz Quartet. A medley of "Stardust," "I Can't Get Started" and "Lover Man" is brilliantly conceived and very well played. John Lewis does some fine comping behind Milt Jackson on Charlie Parker's "Yardbird Suite."

Pyramid shows the Quartet thriving in tuxedos. The blues-ridden title cut was written by Ray Brown and stretches over 10 majestic minutes. Ever the musical architect, Lewis puts the band through its paces on a stunning version of "Django," Jim Hall's "Romaine" and a lovely interpretation of "How High the Moon."

European Concert is a souvenir of the MJQ's first sojourn overseas. Running through all the favorite selections, this collection (sadly available only on cassette) shows the MJQ at its best. Strong, concise solos are juxtaposed against glorious, almost regal arrangements. Compositions by both Lewis and Jackson blend with old standards as well as classics by Ellington and Monk. Connie Kay is inventive on the drums as he and Percy Heath lay down a firm, understated foundation.

Lonely Woman features a memorable version of Ornette Coleman's imposing composition. While some of Lewis's work here was intended for orchestral accompaniment, the group does just fine on its own. *The Comedy* fully extends some of the European classical ideas first explored on *Fontessa.* Using concepts derived from the 16th Century, the Italian comedy receives an interesting jazz interpretation courtesy of Lewis and his crew. Guest starring Diahann Carroll on "La Cantatrice," this album is as ambitious as it is pretentious. Take away the context, however, and all you have left is some swinging, muscular jazz.

Blues at Carnegie Hall is another quality live date that features some very hot soloing by Jackson. The band is in fine shape, and the players listen closely to one another during the ensemble interludes. *The Complete Last Concert* resulted when Jackson decided that 22 years of John Lewis's formal structure was just about enough. Clearly inspired and unaware that they would regroup seven years later, the band gives it everything, with excellent results, traversing blues, bop, ballads and Third Stream music with equal aplomb, while Jackson plays like a demon.

The live reunion performance *Together Again! Live at Montreux Jazz Festival '82* sounds like the MJQ had never been apart. While the band may not have been as vital as it once was, it still knew the tunes and did them better than anybody else. By contrast, the studio reunion *"Echoes": Together Again* was dull. After 30 years, the quartet had finally begun to sound a bit tired.

The problem was solved on *Topsy: This One's for Basie.* Starting things off with the "Reunion Blues," Lewis shows he still has a canny sense of humor, and Jackson's unaccompanied version of "Nature Boy" is superb. With a nod to the Count and another remake of "Milano," this is classic MJQ, again.

Three Windows features the MJQ along with the New York Chamber Symphony. Composed and conducted by Lewis, this date incorporates the music from *No Sun in Venice* into a triple fugue. Naturally, this session doesn't swing all that much and is for die-hard chamber-jazz freaks only.

A 40th Anniversary Celebration hosts a number of all-star guests including Wynton and Branford Marsalis, Freddie Hubbard, Phil Woods and Bobby McFerrin. Unfortunately, the ailing Connie Kay was unable to attend and was replaced by the dependable Mickey Roker.

A beautiful boxed set highlighting the MJQ from all points in the band's career, *MJQ40* includes previously out-of-print sessions and guest appearances by many a jazz great—an ideal retrospective collection.

Dedicated to Connie was released following Connie Kay's death. Recorded in Slovenia in 1959, it may be the MJQ's finest live recording. Perfect in every way, this double disc consists of standards and originals, all performed with luminescent grace. Kay is his usual tasteful self, and Jackson, Heath and Lewis are just impeccable. *Compact Jazz: The Modern Jazz Quartet Plus* combines 1957 live recordings of classic MJQ material with two fine Milt Jackson sessions that include Oscar Peterson on piano. Disjointed sequencing disrupts any real sense of continuity here but does not ruin an otherwise interesting memento. — M.M.

CHARNETT MOFFETT

★★★ Net Man (Blue Note, 1987)
★★★★ The General Music Project (Evidence, 1994)
★★ Planet Home (Evidence, 1995)
★★★½ Still Life (Evidence, 1997)

Jazz fans associate bassist Charnett Moffett with the 1980s crop of "young lions," those 20-something players dedicated to postbop traditionalism. What Charnett Moffett (b. 1957) shared with the leaders of that pack and former bosses Wynton and Branford Marsalis is his status as a second-generation jazzman. His father, drummer Charles Moffett, appears on several of his recordings. Indeed, his name is a conjunction of his father's first name and the first name of the best man at his father's wedding—Ornette Coleman.

As a sideman, Charnett has worked, mostly on double bass, with such formidable leaders as Ornette Coleman, Courtney Pine, Arturo Sandoval and Pharoah Sanders. More possessed than Branford's brand of what-the-hell musical adventurism, many of his recordings suffer from gratuitous eclecticism. Additionally, his solo career finds him more eager to play the electric bass, perhaps as a reaction to his sideman restrictions. On his earlier recordings, he can't seem to decide whether he really wants to play the bass or the guitar.

He certainly treats the electric bass like a lead instrument on *Net Man,* with interesting results. He does a sweet cover of "Mona Lisa" backed by Kenny Kirkland's 10-fingered orchestra. His father and brother join him for "Softly as in a Morning Sunrise," which, along with "Swing Bass," shows off his postbop pedigree. Conversely, "For You" and "Nett Man" offer a peek at his fuzak side.

This side gets full play on *Planet Home.* The generally good playing—especially on Moffett's part—often lacks puissance due to the generally bland material. Moffett does some nice arco work on *Home*'s "Free Your Mind" after making his bass sound like a Spanish guitar. He plays melodic, guitarlike lines on the piccolo electric bass, often double-tracking the full-sized fretless bass to provide the bottom. When he doesn't add the bottom, the music lacks punch. This direction climaxes with his take on the Jimi Hendrix arrangement of the "Star Spangled Banner."

It took his dad to pull Charnett back into the postbop framework with *The General Music Project.* In addition to the elder Moffett, Geri Allen and Kenny Garrett spark this swinging set. Allen adds some lush and luscious piano to Moffett's "Cathedral." The Ornette Coleman–inspired "Happy Dream" gives Garrett a chance to stretch out. In general, the more collaborative effort brings out the best in everyone.

Still Life splits the difference between Moffett's high-energy, low-input solo work and the balladic bop of *The General Music Project.* He eschews most of the weaker elements of his previous solo recordings, working with a strong bottom, often provided by Rachel Z.'s synthesizers, and interesting melodic ideas. He solos exquisitely on both the double bass and electric, giving this set a stylistic range from traditional piano trio ("Full Circle") to the electronic powerhouse cover of Michael Jackson's "Heal the World." A duo of quick tracks, "Universal Beat" and "Scrambled Eggs," offer Coleman-like blasts of concentrated improvisation. On the solo track "Spiritual Bubbles," he goes from arco to high-speed pizzicato. Rachel Z. displays some remarkable piano work. She also spices up what could have been banal backing beds of synth with a few remarkable samples, like the basso vox humana that wafts through "Journey." This is how a sideman cuts loose. — H.B.

THELONIOUS SPHERE MONK

★★★★★ **Thelonious Monk Plays Duke Ellington (1955; Original Jazz Classics, 1987)**
★★★★½ **The Unique (1956; Original Jazz Classics, 1987)**
★★★★★ **Brilliant Corners (1956; Original Jazz Classics, 1987)**
★★★★★ **Monk's Music (1957; Original Jazz Classics, 1993)**
★★★★ **Thelonious Monk with John Coltrane (1957; Original Jazz Classics, N.A.)**
★★★★½ **Mulligan Meets Monk (1957; Original Jazz Classics, N.A.)**
★★★★ **Thelonious Himself (1958; Original Jazz Classics, 1987)**
★★★★★ **Art Blakey's Jazz Messengers with Thelonious Monk (1958; Atlantic, N.A.)**
★★★★ **Thelonious in Action (1958; Original Jazz Classics, 1988)**
★★★★★ **Misterioso (1958; Original Jazz Classics, 1989)**
★★★★★ **Thelonious Monk Orchestra at Town Hall (1959; Original Jazz Classics, N.A.)**
★★★★½ **5 by Monk by 5 (1959; Original Jazz Classics, 1989)**
★★★★ **Alone in San Francisco (1959; Original Jazz Classics, 1987)**
★★★★ **Thelonious Monk Quartet Plus Two at the Blackhawk (1960; Original Jazz Classics, N.A.)**
★★★★ **Monk's Dream (Columbia, 1963)**
★★★★ **Criss-Cross (1963; Columbia/Legacy, 1993)**
★★★★ **Live at Newport 1963 (with Miles Davis Live at Newport 1958) (1963; Columbia/Legacy, 1994)**
★★★★½ **Big Band and Quartet in Concert (1964; Columbia/Legacy, 1994)**
★★★★ **Solo Monk (1965; Columbia/Legacy, 1992)**
★★★★★ **Straight, No Chaser (1967; Columbia/Legacy, 1996)**
★★★★★ **Underground (1968; Columbia, 1988)**
★★ **Monk's Blues (1969; Columbia/Legacy, 1994)**
★★★★ **The Complete London Collection (1971; Black Lion, 1996)**
★★★★ **Thelonious Monk and the Jazz Giants (1987; Milestone, N.A.)**
★★★ **The Giants of Jazz in Berlin '71 (EmArcy, 1988)**
★★★★ **The Composer (Columbia, 1988)**
★★★½ **Standards (Columbia, 1989)**
★★★½ **Straight, No Chaser (soundtrack) (Columbia, 1989)**
★★★★½ **Genius of Modern Music, Vol. 1 (Blue Note, 1989)**
★★★★★ **Genius of Modern Music, Vol. 2 (Blue Note, 1989)**
★★★★★ **The Best of Thelonious Monk (Blue Note, 1991)**
★★ **The Essence of Thelonious Monk (Columbia/Legacy, 1991)**

★★★½ **Live at the Five Spot Discovery! (Blue Note, 1993)**
★★★★★ **The Complete Blue Note Recordings (Blue Note, 1994)**
★★★★ **This Is Jazz 5 (Columbia/Legacy, 1996)**
★★★★ **Thelonious Monk Trio (N.A.; Original Jazz Classics, N.A.)**
★★★★★ **Monk (N.A.; Original Jazz Classics, N.A.)**
★★★★ **Thelonious Monk/Sonny Rollins (N.A.; Original Jazz Classics, N.A.)**
★★★★ **Monk in France (N.A.; Original Jazz Classics, N.A.)**
★★★★ **Monk in Italy (N.A.; Original Jazz Classics, N.A.)**
★★★★★ **Thelonious Monk Memorial Album (Milestone, N.A.)**
★★★★ **San Francisco Holiday (Milestone, N.A.)**
★★★★★ **The Complete Riverside Recordings (Riverside, N.A.)**

In the uppermost circle of jazz genius—where rule-defying originality, technical skill and universal appeal converge—Thelonious Monk's signature beret still hangs. With a glorious, insular logic all his own, Monk (1917–1982) refracted and rebuilt the common language of the idiom, while rooting his music firmly in the jazz tradition (a key to appreciating Monk is through his studied stride style and Art Tatum–like flourishes alongside his time-defying eccentricities). His fractured vocabulary resounds with jagged melodic lines, idiosyncratic voicings and chords, staccato rhythms, endowing even the silence and anticipation between notes with meaning and weight. Monk's compositions and performances—the two are inseparable parts of a singular vision—held stylistic opposites in a creative balance: playful and solemn, abnormal and accessible, simple as a nursery rhyme yet compositionally and rhythmically as complex as the bebop he first performed publicly.

In dark glasses and goatee, dancing a shuffle onstage during sidemen solos, Monk epitomized the eccentric, ofttimes misunderstood jazz genius that became his legend (he remains one of the very few jazz artists to make the cover of *Time*). Critic John S. Wilson once hailed him as becoming "increasingly lucid" in the mid-'50s, but rather what had evolved by then were the ears of jazz musicians and audiences alike, who had learned to look past Monk's peculiar melodies, titles and aloof behavior and understand how he had almost single-handedly reinvented the role of the composer in jazz. More than any modern-age composer, Monk's inventions resonate in the recordings and repertoire of today's jazz world.

As daunting as Monk's voluminous output can be, it is best approached by dividing his career into roughly four stages: as budding new composer on Blue Note, then as the "High Priest of Bebop" on Prestige, followed by his seminal recordings on Riverside and finally his later, veteran years on Columbia. It's difficult to find anything in his catalog that's not up to Monk's standard, though when his music was "arranged" or was caught in lackluster live performance, it may warrant a pass. All the more often Monk's titles are uncannily consistent, and on the occasions his career intersected with the titans of his age—Milt Jackson, Miles Davis, Sonny Rollins, Coleman Hawkins, John Coltrane, even Pee Wee Russell—the heavens opened and jazz history was made. An advisable starter set would include *The Best of Thelonious Monk*, *Brilliant Corners* and *Underground,* for example. If just one album is preferred, Milestone's *Thelonious Monk Memorial Album* gets the pick, as the disc covers a wide range of years, flavors and contexts—solo, sideman, quintet, big band and live—with reverential and revealing liner notes.

Born in North Carolina but transplanted to Manhattan as a child, Monk grew up in the cradle of the New York jazz scene of the '20s and '30s, influenced by successive styles: from stride and boogie through big band and bebop. Precocious and talented, Monk soon took to the scene. A product of the bebop era—and a house pianist at some of the legendary late-night jams in Harlem—Monk was first recorded in 1941 at Minton's Playhouse, where he played in the company of an impressive, all-star lineup including Charlie Christian, Don Byas, Kenny Clarke and others. These recordings have been released on a variety of independent labels, as were studio recordings Monk made between 1941 and '46, as sideman with Cootie Williams, Coleman Hawkins and even Dizzy Gillespie. The majority of these recordings are not that easily found and reveal little of the compositional genius about to burst forth. Two 1944 recordings do stand out from Monk's preleader days: Coleman Hawkins's "Flyin' Hawk," with the budding piano style present in a generous solo, and the Monk evergreen "'Round Midnight" as released in its initial recording by the Cootie Williams big band.

By 1947, the young Blue Note label opted to take a chance with the young composer. Armed with almost a decade's worth of compositions, Monk first entered the studio as a leader in his two favorite studio contexts: with Art Blakey holding down the drum chair in both (a rhythmic association that was oft repeated). Monk's own playing is bright and supple, though on certain titles one can discern the challenge of the complex charts on his sidemen (e.g., "Evonce" and "Thelonious"). *Genius of Modern Music, Vol. 1* covers Monk's 1947 sessions, offering classics like "Ruby, My Dear," "In Walked Bud," covers of "Nice Work If You Can Get It" and "April in Paris" as well as many alternate takes. *Vol. 2* spans Monk's studio return in 1951 and '52—first as support to an incredible Milt Jackson quintet, then as leader of his own bop-based sextet with Kenny Dorham (trumpet), Lou Donaldson (alto), Lucky Thompson (tenor), Nelson Boyd (bass) and Max Roach (drums). Monk's music shines with the more mature and confident backup group ("Four in One," "Skippy," "Let's Cool One," "Straight, No Chaser"); the blues scale-chase of "Criss-Cross" by Monk and Jackson marks this as an absolute classic.

Crowned with the "High Priest" mantle, Monk jumped to the Prestige label in 1952, recording three titles as leader and a number of tracks with label mates Miles Davis and Sonny Rollins. With Blakey and Roach again on skins, *Thelonious Monk Trio* shows off Monk's continuing writing genius ("Blue Monk," "Trinkle Tinkle" and "Bye-Ya," the last shimmering with Blakey's Latin-tinged cymbal play) as well as the sheer physicality of his performance range: from the hard-pounding "Monk's Dream" to his first, hauntingly sweet cover of "Just a Gigolo."

Monk stands as his first true "blowing" session and most compelling Prestige title. Culled from studio dates with either Frank Foster or Rollins on tenor, Julius Watkins on French horn and Ray Copeland on trumpet, it features extended takes on new tunes "Hackensack," "Let's Call This," "Think of One" and the overlooked gem "Locomotive," supplying ample solo room for all involved. *Thelonious Monk/Sonny Rollins* follows suit with generously long takes of Monk's "Friday the 13th" and the standards "The Way You Look Tonight" and "I Want to Be Happy" plus the unveiling of two more Monk chestnuts in trio format: "Work" and "Nutty."

Monk's seven years with Riverside (1955–1962) arguably constitute his most prolific, expansive and focused period—yielding a catalog that proffers the master at the top of his craft, working in a variety of contexts and with a number of all-star sidemen, and never missing the mark. The relationship kicked off with a conscious effort to respin less-than-mainstream Monk in a more traditional mold—what better way to let him prove his mettle than on material by the genre's most respected composer? With sensitive support from Oscar Pettiford and Kenny Clarke, *Thelonious Monk Plays Duke Ellington* remains an absolute must for any jazz-piano fan—jaw-dropping in its consistent inventiveness (Monk had retreated with a stack of sheet music to plan his approach), jaunty rather than overly reverential and again offering a satisfying staging of his individual stride style. Noteworthy moments include Monk's teasing the melody out of slower ballads like "Sophisticated Lady" and "Solitude"; his oh-so-serious intro to "I Got It Bad and That Ain't Good" swinging free into a Pettiford solo; and the manner in which he takes full advantage of the stuttering theme to "It Don't Mean a Thing If It Ain't Got That Swing" in making it his own.

The Unique was step two in Riverside's plan to establish Monk's in-the-pocket credibility, and with Art Blakey rejoining for this looser—both in concept and performance—collection of jazz standards, Monk allows himself a little more fun on his sophomore project recorded in 1956. A stride workout of "Honeysuckle Rose" receives a glib, sardonic edge; a humorously simple unveiling of "Tea for Two" gets progressively complicated and interesting; and the flag-waving album opener, "Liza," is handled with a light, fleet touch.

An absolute jazz classic, *Brilliant Corners,* recorded in '56, offers a full five-course serving of Monk's compositional genius—blues, ballads, a solo standard and experiments (such as his sole celeste performance on record: the deliciously gentle "Pannonica"). *Brilliant Corners* marked his first horn-filled project in almost three years (featuring Sonny Rollins, Clark Terry and altoist Ernie Henry) and the first Riverside title to feature his own, mostly new compositions. The title track literally growls and bellows (very Charles Mingus–like in its employment of brash, animal effects by the horn line), to the playful strut of "Ba-Lue Bolivar Ba-Lues-Are" (the soloist's show-off track on the album) and the Latin-esque blues reworking of "Bemsha Swing," with Max Roach riding along on drums and timpani and Paul Chambers on bass.

Nineteen fifty-seven proved to be a—if not *the*—banner year for Monk. Having finally found and established his own audience, he began the year by taking his first chance with an almost exclusively solo-piano effort on *Thelonious Himself* (the sole trio track, "Monk's Mood," features the first instance of his all-too-brief association with John Coltrane). The album works as an introspective document that windows the internal workings of Monk's deconstructive/reconstructive world—first as implied through pensive covers of tunes like "I Don't Stand a Ghost of a Chance," "All Alone" and his own "Functional," then as made obvious on the CD bonus track of an unedited 22-minute session tape of "'Round Midnight," filled with false starts and studio conversation.

Monk's strongest performance on another's studio date (he also lent support to Sonny Rollins and Clark Terry sessions during the '50s) is the Atlantic title that was recorded in '57 under Art Blakey's name (*Art Blakey's Jazz Messengers with Thelonious Monk*). But it is Monk who easily steals the stage, providing almost all the material and spirited solos. "Evidence," "Rhythm-a-Ning" and a show-stopping "In Walked Bud" make this a must-have title, along with a bristling Messengers lineup of Johnny Griffin on tenor, Bill Hardman on trumpet and Spanky DeBrest on bass.

Monk's Music—recorded and released in mid-'57 with the now legendary red-wagon cover—has been heralded as Monk's most accomplished balance of tradition and forward-looking innovation, replete with new numbers like his soon-to-be stage theme "Epistrophy," "Crepuscule with Nellie" and even a century-old English hymn (the minute-long "Abide with Me.") The band reflected this Janus-like vision, with the twin tenors of Coltrane and Coleman Hawkins, altoist Gigi Gryce, trumpeter Ray Copeland, bassist Wilbur Ware and Blakey again in the drum chair. If there is one album that focuses clearly on Monk's small-group artistry, mixing instrumental colors and soloist strengths, this is it. As focused as it is on one horn player, *Thelonious Monk with John Coltrane* serves as a solid second volume to *Monk's Music*—including alternate versions of "Epistrophy" and "Off Minor" from the same sessions with the same band. Also featured are quartet treatments (with Coltrane, Ware and drummer Shadow Wilson) of "Nutty," "Ruby, My Dear," "Trinkle Tinkle" and a lengthy solo version of "Functional."

With the all-important New York City cabaret card back in his pocket (he had lost it in 1951 due to a bum narcotics charge), Monk was back in the live spotlight in 1957, with a successful summerlong residency at the East Village's Five Spot featuring Coltrane's maturing "sheets of sound" approach. The recently uncovered and released *Live at the Five Spot Discovery!* (recorded by Naima Coltrane on a portable recorder) stands as a highly interesting—though not high-fidelity—historical snapshot of that significant clash of styles, as the two visionaries commingle and collide over high-powered versions of "Trinkle Tinkle," "In Walked Bud" and "I Mean You." As 1957 ran out, Monk ran into another sax collaboration of significance, recording *Mulligan Meets Monk* with Ware again on bass and Shadow Wilson on drums. It was to be a one-time encounter exploring the baritone sonorities on such material as "I Mean You," "Straight, No Chaser," "Rhythm-a-Ning" and an appropriately mood-setting "'Round Midnight." Also added were covers of "Sweet & Lovely" and "Decidedly." (The CD reissue includes rare alternate takes.)

With as exhausting an output as Monk achieved in 1957, it is small wonder that the remainder of his Riverside years produced almost all live recordings. The exceptions were both from 1959: *5 by Monk by 5,* a punchy quintet effort that delivered a strong platter of established and first-time Monk material: "Jackie-ing," "Straight, No Chaser," "Played Twice," "Ask Me Now" and "I Mean You." *5* is also significant for being Monk's first studio collaboration with his most consistent sideman, tenor saxophonist Charlie Rouse, who would work with him for 10 years; they are joined by bassist Sam Jones, drummer Art Taylor and cornetist Thad Jones. Following in '59 is the loose-limbed solo excursion *Thelonious Alone in San Francisco,* a one-take cakewalk relative to the consciously wrought *Thelonious Himself*—with Monk again sharing his ebullient side on perhaps his quirkiest choice of covers: "You Took the Words Right Out of My Heart," "There's Danger in Your Eyes, Cherie," alongside his own, most tender creations—"Pannonica," "Reflections."

Riverside's live offerings are culled from four distinct late-'50s projects. *Thelonious In Action* and *Misterioso* derive from a 1958 Five Spot date with the Johnny Griffin/Ahmed Abdul-Malik/Roy Haynes quartet, providing one of the most accurate, you-are-there recordings in terms of spontaneity, atmosphere and sequencing (the former offers three bonus CD tracks, while the latter captures the inventive personal styles of one of Monk's strongest units). *Thelonious Monk Orchestra at Town Hall* documents Monk's 1959 unrehearsed, big-band baptism, featuring an all-star 10-piece orchestra of saxophonists Phil Woods and Pepper Adams and a full brass complement (trumpeter Donald Byrd, along with French horn, tuba and trombone) all joining Monk regulars Rouse, Taylor and Jones and bringing life to the charts of arranger Hall Overton on "Friday the 13th," "Monk's Mood," "Thelonious" and three others. *Thelonious Monk Quartet Plus Two at the Blackhawk* finds Monk in 1960 with an expanded horn lineup of trumpeter Joe Gordon, tenors Charlie Rouse and Harold Land, bassist John Ore and drummer Billy Higgins (with brilliant two-tenor arrangements on "Four in One.") Finally, 1961 saw Monk in Europe with a quartet of Charlie Rouse, bassist John Ore and Frankie Dunlop (Monk's other strong unit); *Monk in France* and *Monk in Italy* chronicle that tour with no overlap of material between them and highlight Rouse's raspy tenor work.

Of Riverside's compilations, the Orrin Keepnews–produced *Thelonious Monk Memorial Album* is the excellently annotated and well-chosen collection mentioned at the top of this entry. Keepnews was beginning his own career as Monk's producer; his unflagging dedication during and after Monk's lifetime cannot be overstated—and it shows. *Thelonious Monk and the Jazz Giants* picks the best from Monk's encounters with fellow titans Rollins, Coltrane, Griffin, Mulligan, Hawkins and others. Spanning 1958 through '61, *San Francisco Holiday* is easily the strongest overview of live Monk in a single volume, featuring unissued and alternate takes from all of his solo, quartet, sextet and big band concerts recorded by Riverside, including a spirited "Bye-Ya"/"Epistrophy" from an ultrarare Five Spot recording with Art Blakey and Johnny Griffin. The 15-CD boxed set *The Complete Riverside Recordings* is an exhaustive (and expensive) item for jazz completists and archivists with good taste.

In 1961 Monk achieved the highest tier then attainable by a recording jazz artist—a contract with Columbia Records, joining the exalted (and commercially viable) ranks alongside Miles Davis and Dave Brubeck. With his best-known material already written and his legendary status intact, Monk spent seven years largely reexploring his own material and adopted standards—now and again penning a new classic—in a somewhat formulaic approach.

By past pattern more than current design, Monk's Columbia catalog is the least respectful of the artist's original vision—random or thematic repackagings of Monk's Columbia music abound. The CD issues of his original titles for the label were themselves loosely culled from a wide range of recording dates, and often tracks were severely edited to fit into the long-player format. Current Columbia plans are to release Monk's entire output session by session, unedited, unearthing as many unreleased and alternate takes as may be found.

Straight, No Chaser is the first and stellar example of that intention—a thorough investigation of the late-1966 and early-'67 sessions that yielded the original '67 album with Rouse, bassist Larry Gales and drummer Ben Riley. Beyond the restored full-length versions of "Japanese Folk Song," "We See" and the title track, as well as "Locomotive," "Between the Devil and the Deep Blue Sea" and Ellington's "I Didn't Know About You," three more tracks were rescued and added: Monk's "Green Chimneys," another take of "I Didn't Know About You" and the unusual two-minute "This Is My Story, This Is My Song."

With the odd bonus track, Monk's other notable studio titles for Columbia remain available as initially issued. His best-selling label debut, *Monk's Dream,* from early 1963, is a bluesy, blustery collection of originals like "Bye-Ya," "Bolivar Blues," "Five Spot Blues" and the title track, with "Bright Mississippi" the only new unveiling. Compelling solo renderings of "Body and Soul" and a hauntingly delicate take on "Just a Gigolo" round out the mostly quartet date. Recorded in the same period with the same Rouse/Ore/Dunlop lineup, *Criss-Cross* revives a well-chosen selection of long-buried Monk gems like "Hackensack," "Eronel," "Think of One" and the title track—with an unreleased take of "Pannonica" on the CD reissue. 1965's *Solo Monk,* the third of Monk's four career solo albums, posits an elegance on "These Foolish Things" and "Introspection," conjuring the jovial spirit of Fats Waller on warhorses like "I'm Confessin'" and including Monk's own "Ask Me Now" and the new "Monk's Point."

Underground is as well-known for its staged basement-photo cover (which won a 1968 Grammy) and fictional biography of artist-as-freedom-fighter as it is for its excellent performances and sublimely simple melodies. With fresh material ("Raise Four," "Boo Boo's Birthday," "Easy Street," "Green Chimneys" and the catchy, loping "Ugly Beauty") and the quartet of Rouse, Gales and Riley (add Jon Hendricks's vocal on a lyricized version of "In Walked Bud"), the album is Monk's last fully realized studio effort. Unfortunately, his Columbia years end with *Monk's Blues,* an ill-conceived big-band session from 1968 Hollywood wherein such Monk classics as "Let's Cool One" and "Rootie Tootie" were—as they say in the business—*produced.* Lost in dated, over-the-top arrangements that flatten their nuances and rhythmic subtleties, the tunes are overwhelmed by their milieu, becoming cliché-driven, TV in-themes. An interesting solo slant on "'Round Midnight" attempts to save the project, being its only redeeming track.

Two live Monk titles are currently out on Columbia, while two more were released during his tenure at the label. The historic 1963 Newport Festival set (sandwiched in a double CD with a 1958 Miles Davis performance—the original art director did all possible to convince that the two had performed together) is a straight blowing gig devoid of the by-now requisite standards. It is most significant for the surprise appearance of swing clarinetist Pee Wee Russell on "Blue Monk" and "Nutty," again underscoring just how "of the tradition" Monk's music was, even then. The double-disc set *Big Band and Quartet in Concert* was Monk's third project for the label, his second and arguably most successful recording with a large group, providing proof as to how much his music had become part of the common jazz vocabulary. Documenting a 1963 Lincoln Center evening of Monk in different contexts, the large group—including Phil Woods and Eddie Bert from his '59 Town Hall gig, with newcomers like saxophonists Steve Lacy and Gene Allen—is lithe and well oiled, ably handling the most difficult rhythm shifts ("Four in One" and "Evidence" are awesome knuckle-busters), while the quartet pieces ("Misterioso," "Played Twice") and an evocative solo reading of "Darkness on the Delta" shine.

Of the compilations, *This Is Jazz 5* stands out as a solid introduction title to Monk's Columbia material, while *The Composer* and *Standards* are good thematic bookends to Monk's original and interpretive facets. The soundtrack to the excellent 1989 documentary *Straight, No Chaser* opens a collector's trove of reprocessed material from the 1967–68 European and New York live footage contained in the movie, plus the original home recording of "Pannonica" from 1956. *The Essence of Thelonious Monk,* an extremely stingy seven-track best-of, merits a pass.

Monk's last tour of Europe took place in 1971 with an all-star company of Dizzy Gillespie, Sonny Stitt, Al McKibbon and Art Blakey and yielded his swan song (on record at least). *The Giants of Jazz in Berlin '71* finds the touring ensemble delivering a straight-ahead reading of "'Round Midnight" with some fine soloing, but the performance does not match the music's historical significance. However, Monk's London solo and trio session (with old cohorts McKibbon and Blakey)—now fully collected in the Black Lion three-disc boxed set—captures the lion in winter, in a conclusive outpouring of material and mastery. It would seem too easy to find an air of finality hanging over these tracks, but more so than before, Monk's solo work does stand out with profound emotion and a peculiar sobriety: "Little Rootie Tootie" becomes less a romp and more a slowed-down, mock-stride piece; "Jackie-ing" sounds discreetly thoughtful; and whereas Monk's handling of "Nice Work If You Can Get It" had been a quirky bebop-band arrangement in '47 for Blue Note (available on *Genius of Modern Music, Vol. 1*) and a free-flowing stride piece for Columbia in '64 (on *Standards*), Monk performs it in '71 with rich chords and a sense of maturity: His signature rhythmic and discordant surprises are kept to a minimum, raising their value within the piece. It is as if the various aspects of Monk's musical personality—his angularity, his traditional reverence and playful irreverence—find a restful equilibrium, building the piece until the wistful "In Walked Bud" quote at the coda, followed by an eerie ellipsis of three repeated riffs leading nowhere.

Mention should be made of the large number of Monk's live-performance recordings that float in and out of availability. The majority are semiauthorized, if at all, and are dubbed from live '60s concerts outside the United States. For archivists and devotees, a description of these can be found on a well-researched Web site: *www.achilles.net/~howardm/tsmonk.html.*

As Monk's trick bag has provided ample material for countless recording projects—jazz and nonjazz alike—there are a few albums

devoted exclusively to Monk's songbook that beg mention. Soprano saxophonist Steve Lacy, band mate and acolyte, waxed two atmospheric and stellar titles in the late '50s/early '60s (*Reflections* and *Evidence*). In 1984 Lacy joined a jazz, rock and creative-music roster for producer Hal Willner's tribute *That's the Way I Feel Now*—an A&M two-disc set sadly out of print. On it, electric guitars, a cappella voices and layered studio wizardry interpret Monk's music alongside more standard jazz instrumentation—NRBQ, Donald Fagen, Joe Jackson and Was (Not Was) join Lacy, Barry Harris and Carla Bley in a testament to the far-reaching influence of Monk's music. More recently, Jerry Gonzalez recast a number of Monk's tunes in a sharply focused, Latin-jazz mold on *Rhumba Para Monk* (Sunnyside, 1995).
— A.K.

T.S. MONK

★★★½ Take One (Blue Note, 1991)
★★★★ Changing of the Guard (Blue Note, 1993)
★★★★ The Charm (Blue Note, 1995)
★★★★★ Monk on Monk (N2K, 1997)

Thelonious Monk Jr. (b. 1949) studied with Max Roach and played drums in his father's band in his early 20s, organized the modestly successful rhythm-and-rock band T.S. Monk in his 30s, then returned to the music of his father and his peers with a vengeance in his 40s. Monk is right there on *Take One,* a sextet session with a particularly memorable contribution from pianist Ronnie Mathews. His sextet is in peak form on *Changing of the Guard.* Trumpeter/arranger Don Sickler is joined on the front line by alto saxophonist Bobby Porcelli and tenor/soprano saxophonist Willie Williams, with bassist Scott Colley really locking in with Monk and Mathews. The same group recorded the fine album *The Charm.*

Monk on Monk is in a class by itself, a spiritual meeting of the generations, realized with the attention to detail and sense of history appropriate to a moment whose time has come. In celebration of what would have been Monk Sr.'s 80th birthday, Monk Jr. assembled a program of songs his father wrote about the people in his life, including one about himself, "Little Rootie Tootie." Special guests from Dad's era, including trumpeter Clark Terry, saxophonists Jimmy Heath and Wayne Shorter and bassist Ron Carter, sit in with the T.S. Monk Sextet. Monk also asked some of his contemporaries to play, from pianist Herbie Hancock and bassist Dave Holland to trumpeters Arturo Sandoval, Roy Hargrove and Wallace Roney and singers Dianne Reeves and Kevin Mahogany. — J.S.

LITTLE BROTHER MONTGOMERY

★★★★ Tasty Blues (1960; Original Blues Classics, 1992)
★★★ South Side Blues (with Mama Yancey and others) (1961; Original Blues Classics, 1993)
★★★ Chicago: The Living Legends: Piano, Vocal and Band Blues (1961; Original Blues Classics, 1993)
★★★½ At Home (Earwig, 1991)
★★★★ Goodbye Mister Blues (Delmark, 1993)
★★★★★ Complete Recorded Works in Chronological Order (1930–1936) (Document, 1992)

Except for maybe Roosevelt Sykes, Eurreal "Little Brother" Montgomery (1906–1985) stands as the only blues piano player who boasted a career that stretched from his humble barrelhouse beginnings in Louisiana (drawing much inspiration from the ragtime/early jazz that flowered alongside the blues) to finally achieving legendary status in the '60s and '70s. Rich, vibrato vocals and jazz-tinged rolls, flourishes and rock-steady boogies all constitute the Montgomery sound. Though both he and Jelly Roll Morton were students of noted New Orleans bandleader Clarence Desdune, Montgomery opted for a more straight-ahead blues course.

Montgomery's initial recordings—"No Special Rider Blues" and "Vicksburg Blues"—were waxed for Paramount in 1930 and are currently available only on *Complete Recorded Works* on the import Document label. His subsequent recordings for Victor in 1935 and '36—including a reworking of his hit "Vicksburg Blues No. 2"—have been repeatedly reissued and then cut out, but the Document album also includes these tracks, capturing the inventive and stylistically broad Montgomery at his youthful prime. In one mammoth Victor session in 1936, he recorded 23 songs—17 are included on this album. Highlights abound: the Morton-like stomp and stop time of "Crescent City Blues," the rollicking ragtime of "Farish Street Jive" and a slew of deep, down-home blues that define the cutting edge of early blues piano.

Cut to almost 20 years later, and Montgomery had relocated to Chicago, where he continued to perform in both jazz and blues contexts, influencing a generation of piano players. Of the many tracks he recorded over the next two decades (the majority for various independent labels), only a few scattered songs are available on a variety of piano collections, notably *Atlantic Blues: Piano* (Rhino, 1991), featuring 1951's "Talkin' Boogie."

By the early '60s, Montgomery's fame had reached international audiences; as his music matured and became more introspective, Montgomery drew attention from jazz collectors by way of a few albums for the Prestige and Riverside labels. *Tasty Blues* lives up to its title, with the piano master in a trio setting (Lafayette Thomas standing out on guitar), laying down a mellow groove and proffering well-chosen titles (including reworkings of his classic "Vicksburg Blues" and "No Special Rider").

Goodbye Mister Blues features Montgomery's State Street Swingers (including trombonist Preston Jackson and banjoist Ikey Robinson) breathing life into a number of Crescent City standards ("South Rampart St. Parade," "Struttin' with Some Barbecue") and second-line blues. On the other hand, *Chicago,* a 1961 live Montgomery showcase in an earlier Dixieland context, is well recorded and performed yet comes off like a Bourbon Street tourist trap on a slow night. *South Side Blues* is a weak anthology of various second-rate Chicago trad-jazz bands, with Montgomery accompanying old-school blues wailers Mama Yancey and Henry Benson.

At Home peruses the last 15 years of Montgomery's life, with solo and band performances, reprising some of his better-known instrumentals (including his version of "Pinetop's Boogie Woogie") and an appropriate final track for the Louisiana-born legend: "Do You Know What It Means to Miss New Orleans?" — A.K.

WES MONTGOMERY

★★★★ **The Wes Montgomery Trio (1959; Original Jazz Classics, 1987)**
★★★★★ **The Incredible Jazz Guitar of Wes Montgomery (1960; Original Jazz Classics, 1987)**
★★★½ **Movin' Along (1960; Original Jazz Classics, 1988)**
★★★★ **So Much Guitar! (1961; Original Jazz Classics, 1987)**
★★★★ **Full House (1962; Original Jazz Classics, 1987)**
★★★½ **Bags Meets Wes! (with Milt Jackson) (1962; Original Jazz Classics, 1987)**
★★★ **Portrait of Wes (1963; Original Jazz Classics, 1990)**
★★★★ **Boss Guitar (1963; Original Jazz Classics, 1989)**
★★★★ **Fusion! (1963; Original Jazz Classics, 1989)**
★★★ **Guitar on the Go! (1963; Original Jazz Classics, 1991)**
★★★½ **Movin' Wes (1964; Verve, 1986)**
★★★ **Goin' Out of My Head (1965; Verve, 1986)**
★★★ **Smokin' at the Half Note (with Wynton Kelly) (1965; Verve, 1987)**
★★★ **Bumpin' (1965; Verve, N.A.)**
★★★ **Tequila (1965; Verve, N.A.)**
★★★ **California Dreamin' (1966; Verve, 1986)**
★★★ **The Dynamic Duo (with Jimmy Smith) (1966; Verve, N.A.)**
★★★ **A Day in the Life (1967; A&M, 1986)**
★★½ **Down Here on the Ground (1968; A&M, 1987)**
★★½ **Road Song (1968; A&M, 1986)**
★★★★★ **The Silver Collection (Verve, 1984)**
★★★★★ **The Artistry of Wes Montgomery (Riverside, 1986)**
★★★★ **Wes Montgomery Plays the Blues (Verve, 1988)**
★★★★ **The Alternative Wes Montgomery (Milestone, 1989)**
★★★ **Classics, Vol. 22 (A&M, 1991)**
★★★½ **Far Wes (Pacific Jazz, 1990)**
★★★★ **The Complete Riverside Recordings (Riverside, 1993)**
★★★½ **Jazz 'Round Midnight (Verve, 1994)**
★★★★ **Verve Jazz Masters 14 (Verve, 1994)**
★★★★ **Impressions: The Verve Jazz Sides (Verve, 1995)**
★★★★ **Talkin' Verve: Roots of Acid Jazz (Verve, 1996)**

By the early '60s, Wes Montgomery (1923–1968) had become the most successful jazz guitarist since Charlie Christian. Achieving a very distinctive, somewhat muted sound by playing with his thumb, Montgomery was a dazzling technician, capable of very fleet solos wherein entire octaves took the place of single notes. None of the ferocity of later, rock-inflected players (John McLaughlin, Steve Morse) characterized his playing, but his style finds echoes in George Benson and the mellower work of Al DiMeola. "Mellow," in fact, became synonymous with "Montgomery" in the popular mind, due mainly to his best-selling mid-'60s albums. Awash in harps and strings, the later Wes seemed, to his early followers, severely compromised—and his fluid licks (in E-Z form) became the standard repertoire of lounge guitarists.

The prime Montgomery (1959–1963), however, is still great jazz. A strong debut, *The Wes Montgomery Trio* was followed by the significantly more challenging *Incredible Jazz Guitar of Wes Montgomery.* Swinging hard on Sonny Rollins's "Airegin" and elegantly on Dave Brubeck's "In Your Own Sweet Way," the guitarist was pushed past the point of mere dexterity by such smart sidemen as pianist Tommy Flanagan and the deft brother rhythm section of bassist Percy and drummer Albert Heath. "West Coast Blues," strongly influenced by Django Reinhardt, is Montgomery at his finest. *Full House* is a standout 1962 live set boosted by tenor saxophonist Johnny Griffin and players on loan from the contemporary Miles Davis Sextet, pianist Wynton Kelly, bassist Paul Chambers and drummer Jimmy Cobb. Sharp compilations, *The Artistry of Wes Montgomery* and *The Alternative Wes Montgomery* do a good job of capturing the essence of the prepop period. *The Complete Riverside Recordings* boxed set, carefully annotated and replete with the many alternate takes this perfectionist demanded, is also grand.

While some of the Verve sides represent Montgomery's soporific nadir, that label boasts, in *The Silver Collection,* some great small-group sessions featuring organist Jimmy Smith and, with Don Sebesky's arrangement of "Here's That Rainy Day," the kind of intelligent orchestration that the guitarist was rarely fortunate enough to find later. The prophetic *Fusion!* set the pattern for the Wes-and-Strings fare to come. From this point until his death, Montgomery took it easy, turning out album after orchestrated album of unchallenging, classy background music. For its sweet renderings of Beatles tunes and for the presence of such strong sidemen as Herbie Hancock and Ron Carter, *A Day in the Life* is interesting; of the later Wes, *Verve Jazz Masters 14* is the best.
— P.E.

TETE MONTOLIU

★★★★ **Body and Soul (1971; Enja, 1993)**
★★★½ **Songs for Love (1974; Enja, 1992)**
★★★½ **Tete! (1974; SteepleChase, 1995)**
★★★ **The Music I Like to Play, Vol. 1 (Soul Note, 1987)**
★★★ **The Music I Like to Play, Vol. 2 (Soul Note, 1989)**
★★★★ **The Music I Like to Play, Vol. 3 (Soul Note, 1991)**
★★★½ **The Man from Barcelona (Timeless, 1992)**
★★★ **A Spanish Treasure (Concord Jazz, 1992)**
★★★ **The Music I Like to Play, Vol. 4 (Soul Note, 1993)**

Vincente "Tete" Montoliu (1933–1997) was a blind Catalan pianist whose virtuosic playing combined the dazzling technique of Art Tatum with the harmonic sophistication of bop and the warmth and melodicism of Spanish folk song. Classically trained under the influence of his father, who played with the Barcelona symphony, Montoliu was tutored in jazz by family friend Don Byas. In the 1960s Montoliu backed touring American jazz players, including Roland Kirk, Archie Shepp and Don Cherry, before beginning his own recording career as a leader.

Body and Soul is a sublime live trio date with bassist George Mraz and drummer Joe Nay. *Songs for Love* is a dazzling solo performance. *Tete!* is a trio recording with bassist Niels-Henning Ørsted Pedersen and drummer Albert "Tootie" Heath. Montoliu made a number of other solo and trio recordings in the 1970s and early '80s, which are currently unavailable.

The four volumes of *The Music I Like to Play* feature more of Montoliu's mature, expansive solo work; *Vol. 3,* a joint tribute to Thelonious Monk and Bud Powell, is a masterful set of interpretations. Montoliu works with the sympathetic Mraz again on the trio session *The Man from Barcelona,* with drummer Lewis Nash. *A Spanish Treasure* features another trio, this time with bassist Rufus Reid and drummer Akira Tana. — J.S.

COCO MONTOYA

★★★★ **Gotta Mind to Travel (Blind Pig, 1995)**
★★★ **Ya Think I'd Know Better (Blind Pig, 1996)**
★★★★ **Just Let Go (Blind Pig, 1997)**

Guitarist Coco Montoya (b. 1951) broke into the blues world as Albert Collins's drummer, learned guitar from Collins, and spent 10 years honing his art in John Mayall's Bluesbreakers before striking out on his own in the mid-'90s. His style is melodic and piercing, and he is possessed of a truly wonderful voice, with a richness rarely heard in the tenor range outside an opera house.

Gotta Mind to Travel mixes originals and covers, including a rocking update of the title song (written by Collins), and features guest shots from Collins and Mayall. The originals "Too Much Water" and "Love Jail" are standouts, both minor-key blues that show off Montoya's abilities as guitarist and vocalist to great effect. Montoya is less well framed on *Ya Think I'd Know Better,* which includes only one original (the title cut), though two rockers by David McKnight, "Monkey See, Monkey Do" and "Tumbleweed," are particularly enjoyable.

On *Just Let Go* Montoya is in top form, leading his quartet through a program of intelligent originals ("What's Done Is Done," "My Side of the Fence," "Mother and Daughter") and the Collins tribute/cover "Do What You Want to Do." — J.Z.

MOONDOG

★★★★ Moondog (1956; Original Jazz Classics, 1990)
★★★★ More Moondog/The Story of Moondog (1956/1957; Original Jazz Classics, 1991)
★★★★ Sax Pax for a Sax (Atlantic, 1997)

While he is usually filed with the classical composers, Moondog (b. Louis Hardin, 1916), the New York street performer known for his eccentric, Rasputin-like appearance, recorded three albums of ethereally sensual music for Riverside in the late 1950s. While these albums lack the blues-based chord structures and improvisational spirit of jazz (they are closer to art songs), they are connected to jazz by their small-group settings and rhythmic sophistication.

Moondog draws from many sources, such as a Native American drum pattern buttressing a Rachmaninoff-style piano ("Caribea") and Cuban percussion providing counterpoint to a violin duo ("Trees Against the Sky"). Inspired by found sounds, Moondog incorporated the rhythms of a tap dancer, surf crashing on a beach, and street conversation: The album's only constant is the complete absence of 4/4 time, with time signatures ranging from 7/4 to the almost impossible to follow 1/4.

Even further out there, *More Moondog/The Story of Moondog* (two Prestige albums reissued on a single CD) features Moondog's fluidly polyrhythmic percussion played on his unique inventions, the trimba (a triangular drum) and the yukh (a suspended log hit with rubber mallets), among other instruments. Like field recordings from an alternate universe, Moondog music was recorded in his natural habitat, the street. Highlights include the shimmering, Eastern-textured "Conversation and Music at 51st Street and 6th Ave." and "Tugboat Toccata," featuring modal piano and whistles.

Moondog disappeared from the streets of New York in the '60s and from the record shelves after 1971. Many fans assumed he had died. But he resurfaced (in Germany) in late 1997, confounding expectations with *Sax Pax for a Sax.* The warm brass sound and jaunty tunes ("Paris" could easily fit into the soundtrack of *Funny Face*) might sound like Ellington or *Birth of the Cool*–era Miles, but the dizzyingly complex counterpoint of the arrangements is vintage Moondog.

Certainly, Moondog is not for the faint of heart or those who want music with a strong melodic or chordal base. But for listeners willing to take the plunge, these CDs offer an experience not soon forgotten. — S.M.

JOHN MOONEY

★★ Comin' Your Way (1979; Blind Pig, 1990)
★★ Telephone King (1983; Powerhouse, 1985)
★★★½ Sideways in Paradise (with Jimmy Thackery) (1985; Blind Pig, 1993)
★★★½ Late Last Night (Bullseye Blues, 1990)
★★★★ Testimony (Domino, 1992)
★★★★½ Travelin' On (1992; Crosscut/Blue Rockit, 1995)
★★★★ Against the Wall (House of Blues, 1996)
★★★★ Dealing with the Devil (RFR, 1997)

Innovative blues guitarist John Mooney (b. 1955) can legitimately claim spiritual lineage with Delta blues patriarch Son House. As a teenager in Rochester, New York, Mooney met the elder statesman and became House's protégé and friend, absorbing his acoustic fingerpicking and slide-guitar style as well as his window-rattling voice. When he settled in New Orleans in 1976, the musical riches of the Crescent City began seeping into his music.

Comin' Your Way and *Telephone King* feature rolling piano touches and boogie-woogie and ragtime arrangements, but Mooney's forced hipster vocals give both efforts the feel of '40s-era novelty records. *Late Last Night,* the first breakthrough of a previously unimaginable style, has become Mooney's calling card: a wicked fusion of uncompromising Delta blues and New Orleans second-line funk. In this setting Mooney's voice rises to the challenge, taking a savage, feral step into Howlin' Wolf territory.

Testimony brilliantly pulls together all of Mooney's references, from the greasy electric-slide work of "I Plead Guilty" and the stutter-stop syncopation of Professor Longhair's "In the Night" to the House-esque "I Wish I Was in Heaven Sittin' Down." Meters bassist George Porter Jr. and pianist Dr. John help stoke the fires, and Mooney's songwriting skills shine on a reworked version of Robert Johnson's "Lil' Queen o' Spades." *Sideways in Paradise* teams Mooney with fellow guitar guru Jimmy Thackery for a free-spirited acoustic session featuring joyous romps through Bukka White's "Jitterbug Swing" and a handful of sharp originals.

Travelin' On documents a scorching live trio performance. Mooney's self-penned title track next to a frenetic version of James Booker's "Junco Partner"—both clocking in at over seven minutes long—show a man moving forward by drawing power from the past. *Against the Wall* continues that trend, using percussion fills on "Sacred Ground" to augment classic images of the Mississippi River and the levee, and a Bob Dylan–like narrative rarely found in blues on "3 Sides (2 Every Story)." Coming full circle, Mooney's "Late on in the Evening" sounds like a lost Son House track. — S.J.

FRANK MORGAN

★★★½ **Frank Morgan (1955; GNP Crescendo, 1991)**
★★★★ **Easy Living (Original Jazz Classics, 1985)**
★★★ **Lament (Contemporary, 1987)**
★★★½ **Bebop Lives! (Contemporary, 1987)**
★★★ **Yardbird Suite (Contemporary, 1988)**
★★★★ **Major Changes (with McCoy Tyner) (Contemporary, 1988)**
★★★ **Mood Indigo (Antilles, 1989)**
★★★★ **Reflections (Contemporary, 1989)**
★★★ **A Lovesome Thing (Antilles, 1990)**
★★★ **You Must Believe in Spring (Antilles, 1992)**
★★★ **Quiet Fire (with Bud Shank) (Contemporary, 1992)**
★★★ **Listen to the Dawn (Antilles, 1993)**
★★★ **Love, Lost and Found (Telarc, 1995)**

Alto saxophonist Frank Morgan was born in Minneapolis in 1933 to a musical family—his father, Stanley Morgan, played guitar with the Ink Spots—but was raised in Los Angeles, where he became inspired to play saxophone after hearing Charlie Parker. After debuting in the Freddie Martin big band, Morgan became a fixture of the post–World War II bop scene on Central Avenue and went on to record with Wardell Gray, Teddy Charles, Sonny Clark and Milt Jackson.

Morgan's career was on the rise after the release of his very good eponymous debut, but he was soon relegated to the scandal sheets and musical obscurity during a series of jail terms resulting from various drug busts. Morgan remained musically inactive for 30 years before returning with the triumphant (if ironically titled) *Easy Living.* He proceeded to turn out a series of fine albums. *Lament* is a quartet date with pianist Cedar Walton, bassist Buster Williams and drummer Billy Higgins. *Bebop Lives!* adds flügelhornist Johnny Coles to that lineup. *Major Changes* features pianist McCoy Tyner. *Yardbird Suite* pays tribute to bop's alto king, Charlie Parker; the terrific *Reflections* features Joe Henderson on tenor; *Mood Indigo,* Wynton Marsalis on trumpet. Morgan continued to make solid if sometimes unspectacular music into the 1990s, his best effort being *You Must Believe in Spring,* in which he teams up in piano-duet settings with Kenny Barron, Hank Jones, Roland Hanna, Tommy Flanagan and Barry Harris. — J.S.

LEE MORGAN

★★★★ **Introducing Lee Morgan (1956; Savoy, 1991)**
★★★★ **Dizzy Atmosphere (with Wynton Kelly) (1957; Original Jazz Classics, 1991)**
★★★★ **Candy (1958; Blue Note, 1987)**
★★★★ **Take Twelve (1962; Original Jazz Classics, 1989)**
★★★★★ **The Sidewinder (1963; Blue Note, 1989)**
★★★★ **Tom Cat (1964; Blue Note, 1990)**
★★★★½ **Search for the New Land (1964; Blue Note, 1987)**
★★★★½ **The Rumproller (1965; Blue Note, 1989)**
★★★★★ **The Gigolo (1965; Blue Note, 1989)**
★★★★ **Cornbread (1966; Blue Note, 1988)**

★★★★ **Caramba (1968; Blue Note, 1996)**
★★★★★ **The Best of Lee Morgan (Blue Note, 1988)**
★★★★★ **Live at the Lighhouse (Fresh Sound, 1996)**
★★★★★ **Jazz Profile (Blue Note, 1997)**

Trumpeter Lee Morgan (1938–1972) was discovered and hung with the tag "the new Clifford Brown" after Brown's death in 1956; he recorded his first album when he was just 18 years old. That same year he joined Dizzy Gillespie's big band and was featured on Gillespie's most famous tune, "A Night in Tunisia." Morgan rose quickly, leading six Blue Note sessions in two years, and added solos to John Coltrane's *Blue Train,* among other session work. In 1958 he joined Art Blakey's Jazz Messengers, eventually becoming music director, before dropping out in 1961 to kick his heroin addiction. In 1963 he roared back with *The Sidewinder,* whose title track became one of the most covered jazz-funk tunes of all time. Morgan's career ended in 1972, when his common-law wife walked into a gig at Slug's in New York and shot him to death.

Introducing Lee Morgan finds the young trumpeter in a quintet with tenor player Hank Mobley and pianist Hank Jones. His comeback album, *The Sidewinder,* includes a funky title track, which he tried to replicate on the less successful *The Rumproller.*

In the mid- to late '60s Morgan recorded a string of straight-ahead albums that nearly equaled the peerless quality of his first run. These sessions are filled almost exclusively with originals, and instead of packing in notes, Morgan took care to lengthen and shape the lines of his solos. *Tom Cat* finds the trumpeter in a quintet featuring McCoy Tyner and Morgan's sometime employer Art Blakey. Recorded with a sextet, *Search for the New Land* is a moody masterpiece, the title tune being one of Morgan's finest compositions, and the ballad "Melancholee," not far behind. Wayne Shorter adds much to the proceedings.

Cornbread mixes its slightly funky title cut and straight-ahead numbers and sports a muscular quartet featuring Herbie Hancock, alto saxophonist Jackie McLean and tenor saxophonist Hank Mobley. The ballad "Ceora" is perhaps Morgan's most affecting melody. *Caramba* features a quintet of Morgan, tenor saxophonist Bennie Maupin, pianist Cedar Walton, bassist Reggie Workman and drummer Billy Higgins working its way through a program of Morgan compositions, the best of which, "Suicide City," "Cunning Lee" and "Soulita," show just how far Morgan had come as a writer.

Recorded in 1970 at the Lighthouse Cafe in Hermosa Beach, California, *Live at the Lighthouse* is one of the more enlightening jazz resurrections in recent memory. Most of the material (9 of 13 cuts) on this three-CD set was never before released, including a version of "The Sidewinder" and a rendition of Morgan's "Speedball" with Jack DeJohnette on drums. Underrated tenor saxophonist Bernie Maupin is a force throughout.

The Best of Lee Morgan collects nine cuts from the Blue Note albums, including "The Sidewinder," "The Rumproller" and "I Remember Clifford." *Jazz Profile* pares the number of tracks to six, though it has only one in common with *The Best of Lee Morgan.*
— R.B.

JOE MORRIS

★★★★ **Sweatshop (Riti, 1990)**
★★★★ **Flip and Spike (Riti, 1992)**
★★★★ **Illuminate (Leo Lab, 1995)**
★★★★ **Elsewhere (Soul Note, 1996)**
★★★★ **You Be Me (Soul Note, 1997)**
★★★★ **Antennae (Aum Fidelity, 1997)**
★★★★ **Like Rays (Knitting Factory Works, 1998)**

Guitarist Joe Morris (b. ca. 1960) is part of a new wave of avant-garde jazz artists who eschew the easy money available to those willing to go the conservative retro route promoted by the major labels in favor of an exploratory direction that expands the music's scope and aesthetic influence. This pursuit ironically places Morris closer to the spirit of the once-radical originators of past decades than to the contemporary musicians who imitate their styles. Morris has applied his experiments to new approaches to technique, composition and interpretation. He constantly shifts directions as he tries different setups.

Sweatshop is a relatively loud and aggressive set of high-energy funk jazz, with Sebastian Steinberg on electric bass and Jerry Deupree on drums. Steinberg is back on acoustic bass on *Flip and Spike,* as he was for Morris's first two (currently unavailable) recordings. Morris changes his group context on the out-of-print *Symbolic Gesture,* forming a new trio with Nate McBride on acoustic bass and Curt Newton on drums. This group forces Morris to play in different patterns, bypassing traditional structures in favor of bursts of notes connected by an entropic logic, single-line clusters of melodic ideas whose plasticity breathes inside each composition.

Heading off into yet another direction, *Illuminate* is a quartet session with bassist William Parker, alto saxophonist Rob Brown and drummer Jackson Krall. Parker, a sideman in Ornette Coleman's group and an important member of Manhattan's Lower East Side new-music scene, is the perfect partner for Morris in his uncompromising search for new sounds and approaches. The two team up again on *Elsewhere* in another quartet with pianist Matthew Shipp and drummer Whit Dickey. Morris returns to the McBride/Deupree trio on *Antennae. Like Rays* features a very different trio, with pianist Hans Poppel and saxophonist Ken Vandermark. This unit's conceptual improvisations add new wrinkles to the seemingly endless vistas of Morris's imagination. — J.S.

VAN MORRISON

★★★½ **Blowin' Your Mind (1967; Columbia/Legacy, 1995)**
★★★★★ **Astral Weeks (Warner Bros., 1968)**
★★★★★ **Moondance (Warner Bros., 1970)**
★★★½ **His Band and Streetchoir (Warner Bros., 1970)**
★★★½ **Tupelo Honey (1971; Polydor, 1997)**
★★★★ **Saint Dominic's Preview (1972; Polydor, 1997)**
★★★½ **T.B. Sheets (1972; Columbia, 1990)**
★★ **Hard Nose the Highway (1973; Polydor, 1997)**
★★★★ **It's Too Late to Stop Now (1974; Polydor, 1997)**
★★★ **Veedon Fleece (1974; Polydor, 1997)**
★★★ **A Period of Transition (1977; Polydor, 1997)**
★★★½ **Wavelength (1978; Polydor, 1997)**
★★★★ **Into the Music (1979; Warner Bros., 1990)**
★★½ **Common One (1980; Warner Bros., 1991)**
★★½ **Beautiful Vision (Warner Bros., 1982)**
★ **Inarticulate Speech of the Heart (Warner Bros., 1983)**
★★★½ **A Sense of Wonder (Mercury, 1985)**
★★★★ **Live at the Grand Opera House Belfast (Mercury, 1985)**
★★★★ **No Guru, No Method, No Teacher (Mercury, 1986)**
★★★ **Poetic Champions Compose (Mercury, 1989)**
★★★★ **Avalon Sunset (Mercury, 1989)**
★★★½ **Enlightenment (Mercury, 1990)**
★★★★ **The Best of Van Morrison (Polydor, 1990)**
★★★½ **Bang Masters (Epic, 1991)**
★★★½ **Hymns to the Silence (Polydor, 1991)**
★★★½ **The Best of Van Morrison, Vol. 2 (Polydor, 1993)**
★★★½ **Too Long in Exile (Polydor, 1993)**
★★★½ **A Night in San Francisco (Polydor, 1994)**
★★★½ **Days Like This (Polydor, 1995)**
★★★½ **Tell Me Something (Verve, 1996)**
★★★½ **How Long Has This Been Going On? (Verve, 1996)**
★★★ **The Healing Game (Polydor, 1997)**
★★★★ **The Philosopher's Stone (Polydor, 1998)**

Whether singing R&B, Celtic music or gospel, Van Morrison (b. 1945) both defines and transcends the genres he mines. For inspiration, he returns again and again to the blues—and his improvisatory style, of lyrics drawn out or repeated, of words relished as much for their sound as their sense, owes a significant debt to jazz. Fronting the Irish soulsters Them, he debuted with Bert Berns's "Here Comes the Night," Big Joe Williams's "Baby Please Don't Go"—and his own "Gloria," a propulsive 1966 rocker. A year later, he went solo with the summery pop of "Brown Eyed Girl." Though not quite as memorable, "Spanish Rose" and "Send Your Mind" had a catchy perfection most bands never achieve. Having mastered the form, he moved on, releasing *Astral Weeks* and *Moondance,* two masterpieces from whose differing sensibilities all his later work would flow.

Astral Weeks shattered the constraints of radio pop. Recorded in a 48-hour fever, the record's mood is blue, wise and yearning, its music combining jazz rhythms and freer structures, impressionist strings and woodwinds, and Morrison voicing his lyrics like a misty, Celtic soul singer gifted with a virtuosic sense of drama. The words he alternately declaims, pants and slurs are a kind of Beat poetry and sketches for semisurreal short stories; the atmosphere is pervaded also by the influence of Dylan Thomas and Dylan, Bob. Bassist Richard Davis and drummer Connie Kay support this panstylistic mix with superb rhythmic structures.

Moondance is a bolder flip side. Countering *Astral Weeks*'s trance state and its wash of song tumbling into song, *Moondance* is a flourish of individual set pieces—brash soul, jazz excursions, ballads. The best of Morrison's more accessible works, it formed the mold for the horn-driven, bass-heavy R&B that Morrison would later employ to balance the orchestral metafolk music he premiered with *Astral Weeks.* "Into the Mystic," from *Moondance,* merges the two methods—and the complementary sides of Morrison's psyche—more satisfyingly than anything he's done since.

With its snappy single "Domino" and the jaunty "Blue Money," *His Band and Streetchoir* is a minor *Moondance. Tupelo Honey* is as comfortable as Morrison gets; a countryish record, it's sweet without getting cloying. *Saint Dominic's Preview,* with "Listen to the Lion" and "Almost Independence Day," marks a return to a darker intensity; "Jackie Wilson Said (I'm in Heaven When You Smile)" represents the R&B side of the equation. Of Morrison's other '70s albums, *Hard Nose the Highway* is his vaguest and weakest; *T.B. Sheets,* with its standout, harrowing title song, comprises recordings from *Blowin' Your Mind; Veedon Fleece* seems confused; *A Period of Transition* is tentative; and *It's Too Late to Stop Now* (a live set) and *Into the Music* are pretty terrific, the latter broadcasting the overt spirituality that would pervade his work in the '80s. *Common One* captures the turn toward literary pretensions that dogged Morrison for a while; *Inarticulate Speech of the Heart* is a puzzling about-face—mainly, it's an album of weak jazz-rock instrumentals. From *A Sense of Wonder* to *Hymns to the Silence,* much of Morrison's output has been, in spirit if not in letter, gospel music.

In the '90s Morrison turned again toward rootsy American fare. *Too Long in Exile* features an outstanding duet with John Lee Hooker ("Gloria"); the 22-cut live *A Night in San Francisco,* with jazz-rock organist Georgie Fame, boasts tough versions of "Stormy Monday" and "Good Morning Little Schoolgirl" as well as "Jumpin' with Symphony Sid." Also with Fame, *How Long Has This Been Going On?* turns bluesward (check, especially, "Blues in the Night"), and with Ben Sidran helping out, *Tell Me Something* offers tribute to the great jazz lyricist Mose Allison. *The Philosopher's Stone* is a fascinating collection of previously unissued material spanning Morrison's career and featuring his talents on guitar, saxophone and harmonica. — P.E.

JELLY ROLL MORTON

★★★★★ **Jelly Roll Morton, 1923/24 (1974; Milestone, N.A.)**
★★★★★ **The Pearls (RCA Bluebird, 1988)**
★★★★ **Blues and Stomps from Rare Piano Rolls (Biograph, 1989)**
★★★★★ **The Jelly Roll Morton Centennial: His Complete Victor Recordings 1926–1930 (RCA Bluebird, 1990)**
★★★★★ **Jelly Roll Morton, Vol. 1: The Pianist and the Composer (Smithsonian Folkways, 1991)**
★★★★½ **Mr. Jelly Lord (Tomato, 1991)**
★★★★★ **Jelly Roll Morton, Vol. 2: Chicago: The Red Hot Peppers (Smithsonian Folkways, 1991)**
★★★★ **Jelly Roll Morton, Vol. 3: New York, Washington and the Rediscovery (Smithsonian Folkways, 1991)**
★★★★ **Jelly Roll Morton: Original Versions of the Music Inspiring Jelly's Last Jam & Other Morton Classics (RCA Bluebird, 1992)**
★★★★★ **Kansas City Stomp: The Library of Congress Recordings, Vol. 1 (Rounder, 1993)**
★★★★★ **Anamule Dance: The Library of Congress Recordings, Vol. 2 (Rounder, 1993)**
★★★★★ **The Pearls: The Library of Congress Recordings, Vol. 3 (Rounder, 1993)**
★★★★★ **Winin' Boy Blues: The Library of Congress Recordings, Vol. 4 (Rounder, 1993)**
★★★★★ **Birth of the Hot: The Classic Chicago "Red Hot Peppers" Sessions 1926–27 (RCA Bluebird, 1995)**
★★★½ **The Piano Rolls (Nonesuch, 1997)**

Jelly Roll Morton (1890–1941) backed up his claim of having invented jazz with a body of work that reveals him to be an extraordinary, even visionary composer, bandleader, arranger and musician. Once, while in a philosophical mode, he posited that the piano "should always be an imitation of a jazz band," thus distilling in epigrammatic form his genius even as he issued the challenge to which jazz pianists have attempted to respond since Morton made his first recordings in the early '20s.

In scope, Morton's achievements are astounding. His music closed out the ragtime era, ushered in the jazz age and prefigured the swing era, when the principles Morton had established were redefined and expanded. Along with Louis Armstrong's Hot Five, Morton's Red Hot Peppers combo, which recorded between 1926 and 1930, elevated jazz into high art—"America's classical music," as pundits would later term it—on the strength of composition, ensemble playing and inspired soloing of a caliber unparalleled in the popular arena. With the Peppers, Morton pioneered the then-novel idea of storyboarding his sessions from first note to last, by drilling his band mates in advance on the placement of solos and the basic arrangements. Contrary to conventional wisdom, Morton believed careful attention to structure heightened rather than diminished the spontaneity of improvisation. Some 70 years later, the soundness of this fundamental principle is borne out by his music's gripping vitality and still-luminous soul.

Of Creole extraction, Morton was born Ferdinand Joseph Lematt (according to his baptism certificate published in the liner booklet of *The Jelly Roll Morton Centennial* collection, but referred to in other citations as LeMethe, LaMenthe, Lamothe and variations thereof) in New Orleans. By his teens, he was working clubs in Storyville, the city's notorious red-light district, and acquiring a reputation as a peerless piano player as he absorbed ragtime, stomps, blues and the Spanish and French music he heard all over town. He also picked up an attitude along the way—he made sure everyone knew of his achievements and even wrote a song about himself, called "Mr. Jelly Lord," that pretty much said it all—and was styling at every turn, surrounding himself with beautiful women, dazzling the commonfolk with his expensive, tailored suits and sporting a million-dollar smile that revealed a diamond embedded in one tooth. Stricken with wanderlust, he left behind remarkable and influential recordings made in Chicago, New York and Richmond, Indiana, with the finest musicians of the '20s and '30s. These are to jazz what *The Bristol Sessions* are to country music, what Elvis Presley's Sun recordings are to rock & roll: a look at a music's past being transformed into something new and more reflective of a society in transition.

In 1912 Morton left New Orleans for what he thought would be greener pastures on Chicago's South Side. He did manage to get his first song, 1915's "The Jelly Roll Blues," published there, but his career was in a holding pattern otherwise. Restless, he moved on to California, where for the next seven years he made his home in Los Angeles, fronting his own bands and, for a while, performing with the Spikes Brothers, who had a hit with the Morton song "Wolverine Blues." Yet Morton failed to persuade anyone to record him or to publish his growing catalog of original compositions. In 1923 he went back to Chicago, where the Melrose Brothers publishing company gave him his long-sought opportunity. At the suggestion of Walter Melrose, he took up residence at the Starr Piano Company in Richmond, Indiana, and over two days in June 1923 recorded six original compositions that were issued on the Melroses' Gennett label. He returned to Richmond in January 1924 and cut 11 more solo sides, 9 of which were released. Near midyear 1924, he made 13 piano rolls for the Vocalstyle Company in Cincinnati, recutting some of the Gennett numbers, although many of these were recast through subtle changes in melodic and harmonic structure, in true Jelly Roll fashion of never playing the same song the same way twice. Upon being released, the Vocalstyle rolls found a large audience, and the Morton legend had begun to take shape.

The double-LP *Jelly Roll Morton, 1923/24* collects the first recordings Morton ever made, including all of the now-legendary Gennett solo-piano sides. These indispensable documents find Morton putting into practice his theory about approaching the piano as a jazz band unto itself. Bob Greene's detailed liner notes explain the specific and altogether revolutionary techniques being employed by Morton on various cuts, such as his left hand working out trombone and percussion parts while the right hand plays shimmering cornet and clarinet lead lines. In addition to four unaccompanied piano solos recorded in Chicago, sides three and four feature Morton's first small-band recordings, which mark the break with ragtime styles pioneered by Scott Joplin and also show Morton lending musical ideas worked out on the piano to other instrumentalists (for example, the band breaks on 1923's "Big Fat Ham" are the same as those on his 1924 solo-piano recording of the same song, then titled "Big Foot Ham"). A serious musician but one who always remembered to have a good time while he was at it, Morton even employs a kazoo player (W.E. Burton) to good effect on several of the small-combo cuts.

At this early stage of his career, Morton demonstrates a sweeping command of technique and structure, but his boundless genius for buoyant, rich melodies nearly overshadows the other startling musical innovations heard here. "Frog-I-More Rag," "Wolverine Blues," "Jelly Roll Blues," the Joplin-esque "Stratford Hunch"—these are so redolent of a particular time and place in American history it's as if they rose up whole out of the earth and somehow found their way to Morton's keyboard. *1923/24* amply documents all of these wonders, but Biograph's *Blues and Stomps from Rare Piano Rolls* is recommended as well as a lower-priced overview of the critical Gennett and Vocalstyle recordings (two of the Biograph tracks, "Pep" and "The Naked Dance," do not feature Morton on piano but rather are reconstructions of songs he recorded originally on phonograph records that arranger John Farrell has transcribed in Morton's style on piano rolls).

The early period of Morton's work is represented as well on *Jelly Roll Morton, Vol. 1: The Pianist and the Composer,* the first installment of a three-volume Morton retrospective. Its 18 songs span the years 1923 to 1926, encompassing titles originally issued on Gennett, Paramount, Rialto, Autograph, Vocalion and Vocalstyle. Despite the duplication of material on some other Morton entries, this disc's booklet offers a solid musicological analysis, courtesy of classical pianist Kitty Fassett, of the artist's style with reference to song origins, harmony, melody, structure, texture, rhythm and performance. There's no shortage of informative liner notes with Morton's recordings, but Fassett's, though a bit on the academic side, stand out for their insight into the connections between the artist's original music and the early blues, ragtime and march music on which he built his empire.

Milestone's other entry in the Jelly Roll Morton saga is an out-of-print two-album set of recordings made in Richmond by the remarkable New Orleans Rhythm Kings in 1922 and 1923; Morton sits in on eight songs, marking this as the first racially mixed jazz recording session. The greater story here, though, is less Morton's contribution and more the inspired clarinet work throughout by Leon Rappolo, who was on to some groundbreaking lyrical ideas, and the forward-looking contributions of progressive trumpeters Paul Mares and George Brunis.

In 1926, Morton began a fruitful relationship with the Victor label that produced, over the next four years, some of the most important jazz-ensemble recordings in the genre's history. His band during these years was billed as the Red Hot Peppers, and its shifting early membership comprised many of New Orleans's finest musicians. The first group included Kid Ory on trombone, Omer Simeon on clarinet, Johnny St. Cyr on banjo and guitar, John Lindsay on bass, Andrew Hilaire on drums, George Mitchell (the only non–New Orleans player) on cornet; later Peppers configurations would find Morton joined by giants on the order of Barney Bigard (clarinet), the brothers Dodds—clarinetist Johnny and drummer Warren (commonly referred to as "Baby")—guitarist Bud Scott and alto saxophonist Paul "Stump" Evans, among others.

The Peppers' sessions from September 1926 to June 1927 represent the apotheosis of Morton's brilliance. First, he brought together musicians he had admired; although none of them had ever played together in a band before, Morton recognized something in their individual styles that he felt would translate into superior ensemble work. For these players he wrote and arranged a clutch of songs marked by scintillating melodies, ingratiating syncopation and memorable riffing, and then gave the musicians—himself included—room to make forceful solo statements. What resulted was music remarkable not only in sheer technical terms but equally so in its ebullient spirit and sly wit—whether the numbers be driving, joyous interludes such as the two-strain rag "Black Bottom Stomp" (the first number the Peppers ever recorded, and one of their best) or more lighthearted, sentimental fare such as "Someday Sweetheart," the full range of human feeling evident in each theme and variation still exerts a tremendous emotional pull.

A number of releases do a good job of documenting Morton's Peppers and immediate post-Peppers recordings, and all are blessed with well-researched annotation to guide the listener through this exhilarating, history-making era. The most complete set is *The Jelly Roll Morton Centennial: His Complete Victor Recordings,* issued in 1990 to honor the artist's 100th birthday. Its five CDs contain Morton's complete Victor (and thus Red Hot Peppers) sessions as a bandleader from 1927 up to and including some of the rather lugubrious final recordings he made in 1939, two years before his death, with Jelly Roll Morton's New Orleans Jazzmen (with Zutty Singleton on drums and Sidney Bechet on soprano sax). In contrast to the other Peppers recordings here, the *Centennial* collection includes alternate takes.

Bluebird's *The Pearls* (named after one of Morton's most vibrant, complex solo-piano numbers) is an abridged version of *Centennial,* with 23 tracks ranging from Red Hot Peppers sides to a sampling of Morton's trio and orchestra recordings made during the Victor years. The aptly titled *Birth of the Hot* focuses solely on the Peppers' Chicago recordings, the heart of the legacy. Despite its title, *Jelly Roll Morton, Vol. 2: Chicago: The Red Hot Peppers* includes a New York session from 1928, as well as two other 1928 sides composed by Morton ("Ham and Eggs," "Buffalo Blues") on which he is featured as a sideman with Johnny Dunn and His Band.

Mr. Jelly Lord ranges from early Peppers dates to the aforementioned Johnny Dunn session, and boasts its own rarity in "I'm Alone Without You," a bright jazz-pop number on which Morton makes a guest appearance with Wingy Manone and His Orchestra, an outfit featuring Dicky Wells on trombone, Artie Shaw on clarinet, Bud Freeman on tenor sax and Frank Victor on guitar—a slight confection, this, but notable for the brisk, personable solo statements offered by Victor and Morton when their turns come around.

The '30s were a barren time for Morton, as Louis Armstrong spearheaded revolutionary changes in the style of jazz Morton had pioneered. Hit hard by the Depression, Morton, despondent and nearly broke, was reduced to playing piano, tending bar, and sometimes cooking at the Jungle Inn in Washington, D.C. Between 1930 and 1938 he had no new music published and was a forgotten figure in American music. Then in 1938 the Library of Congress's folk archivist, Alan Lomax, stumbled upon him and persuaded him to record his reminiscences about early New Orleans music. What resulted was a dozen 10-inch albums' worth of stories and songs detailing the whole of Morton's life and career, from the earliest street music of his youth to the glory years with the Peppers and into the present day; from Storyville whorehouses to elegantly appointed urban penthouses; from bawdy songs to languorous ballads to rags to blues to stomps to marches—everything that he had learned, built on, reconstructed, redefined or created from his own fertile and restless musical intellect. About the only quibble one could muster with regard to Rounder's four indispensable Library of Congress volumes would be the set's preponderance of music to dialog, because Morton, clearly energized by this opportunity, comes off as the best sort of history teacher—informed, insightful, witty and impassioned about his subject matter.

The Pearls (not to be confused with the like-titled Bluebird CD) is a collection of outstanding piano pieces, including classics on the order of "The Pearls" and "Wolverine Blues," but its focal point is the mesmerizing "Murder Ballad." This seven-part song, each part four-minutes-plus in length, is about as close to straight blues as Morton got on record, being an account of an unfaithful lover, done with a moody, stark accompaniment—all mournful, minor-key musings—sounding for all the world like the greatest blues song Bessie Smith never recorded.

Morton the vocalist is also featured prominently on *Anamule Dance,* mostly on songs he composed, apart from a couple of interesting takes on Ma Rainey's "C.C. Rider." To make a musical point, he offers a snippet of John Philip Sousa's "Stars and Stripes Forever," making clear the connection between the type of stomps Morton made famous and the march tempos that inspired his experiments in this form.

Winin' Boy Blues offers more solo-piano pieces, some of these being slightly altered from the original versions in reflecting his absorption of then-current ideas regarding harmonic and melodic structure. Besides imparting important history, the Lomax recordings remind us that the artist, although justifiably honored as a bandleader, pianist, composer and arranger, was a compelling vocalist as well. Here he comes off as one of the great blues singers of his era, his ragged voice resonating deep feeling and his phrasing displaying the nuance that comes with a profound understanding of subtext as a lyric phrase's most revealing component.

Inspired by the Library of Congress sessions, Morton attempted, without success, to revive his recording career. Modern jazz had passed him by, but this later work, collected on *Jelly Roll Morton, Vol. 3: New York, Washington and the Rediscovery,* has an undeniable vitality that may have sounded out of date in the late '30s but is gripping today. Understandably, a darker hue tinged Morton's work by this time, and the sad course his life had taken, while evident even in some of the sprightly solo-piano passages, is most pronounced in the melancholic ambiance of more ruminative numbers such as "Mamie's Blues," a deep, haunting, Spanish-inflected blues. Included on this set are two recordings from 1938 that were issued on the Jazz Man label, founded by Ahmet and Nesuhi Ertegun, and seven songs produced by Gordon Mercer and Alan Lomax that were issued in 1939 under the title *Jelly Roll Morton's New Orleans Memories.* These latter songs are piano instrumentals and piano-and-vocal numbers performed largely in a New Orleans–blues style that predates the jazz era—yet another window into a bygone age, courtesy of an artist who lived through it and then changed it forever.

In 1940 Morton moved to Los Angeles in hopes of attempting a comeback. Ill health limited his performing to two days a week, though, and he slipped back into obscurity. He died on July 10, 1941, and was buried in an unmarked grave, with a handful of musician friends in attendance. Except to jazz aficionados, he was pretty much a forgotten figure until the 1991 Broadway production of his life story, *Jelly's Last Jam,* rekindled interest in his formidable body of work. Now there is much to celebrate, as the discography here indicates. — D.M.

SAL MOSCA

★★★★ **A Concert (1979; Jazz, 1990)**

Pianist Sal Mosca (b. 1927) studied at the New York College of Music as well as with Lennie Tristano, whose style he closely approximates. He performed on his own and with Lee Konitz during the 1950s before devoting most of his time to teaching. His only available recording, the solo-piano outing *A Concert,* features his own compositions as well as Tristano's "Lennie Bird" and "Dreams" and the Duke Ellington standard "Prelude to a Kiss." — J.S.

PAUL MOTIAN

★★★ **Psalm (1982; ECM, 1994)**
★★★ **The Story of Maryam (Soul Note, 1984)**
★★★½ **Jack of Clubs (Soul Note, 1985)**
★★★★½ **Misterioso (Soul Note, 1987)**
★★★★ **Monk in Motian (Verve, 1988)**
★★★ **Motian on Broadway, Vol. 1 (Verve, 1989)**
★★★½ **Motian on Broadway, Vol. 2 (Verve, 1990)**
★★★★ **One Time Out (Soul Note, 1990)**
★★★★ **Bill Evans: Tribute to the Great Post-Bop Pianist (Verve, 1991)**
★★★★ **Motian in Tokyo (Jazz Music Today, 1992)**
★★★½ **Paul Motian/Lee Konitz on Broadway, Vol. 3 (Jazz Music Today, 1993)**
★★★½ **Paul Motian and the Electric BeBop Band (Polydor, 1993)**
★★★ **It Should Have Happened a Long Time Ago (ECM, 1994)**
★★★½ **Trioism (Jazz Music Today, 1994)**
★★★★ **Reincarnation of a Love Bird (Jazz Music Today, 1994)**
★★★★ **At the Village Vanguard (Jazz Music Today, 1996)**

Percussionist Paul Motian (b. 1931) developed a subtle, polyrhythmic approach during the 1950s and earned his reputation for "touch" as the drummer with the Bill Evans trio from 1959 to 1964. Motian is indeed a master of coaxing unusual tonalities from percussion instruments, as both his out-of-print debut, *Le Voyage,* and its follow-up, *Psalm,* demonstrate.

Psalm also introduced Motian's basic unit, built around tenor saxophonist Joe Lovano and guitarist Bill Frisell. On its own or augmented by other players, this unit produces a chimeric sound poised between the nuances of harmony and rhythm as Evans explored them and the frisson of new electric music. *Psalm* builds the unit to a quintet with the addition of bassist Ed Schuller and tenor and alto saxophonist Billy Drewes. By the time of *Jack of Clubs,* Jim Pepper replaced Drewes, playing tenor and soprano with Lovano. This band went on to make the magnificent Thelonious Monk tribute *Misterioso.*

The Monk concept extended through *Monk in Motian,* a project that brought in tenor saxophonist Dewey Redman and pianist Geri Allen for a fine set including versions of "Epistrophy" and "Straight, No Chaser," but the set lacked a little of the first try's magic. Monk continued to be a wellspring of influence, however, as the trio tackled "Monk's Mood" on *One Time Out.* Redman later guested on the *Trioism* session.

The Bill Evans tribute, another sublime effort, is a quartet with bassist Marc Johnson. The *Motian on Broadway* series replaces Johnson with Charlie Haden on a choice selection of standards that showcase the unit in traditional settings. Lee Konitz joins in playing soprano and alto sax on *Vol. 3. It Should Have Happened a Long Time Ago,* the dramatic *Motian in Tokyo* and *At the Village Vanguard,* a great live set from 1995, are pure trio outings. Motian moved in other directions in the 1990s as well, unveiling the raucous Electric BeBop Band featuring tenorist Joshua Redman, guitarists Brad Schoeppach and Kurt Rosenwinkel and bassist Stomu Takeishi. The concept reached a high point with the amazing music on *Reincarnation of a Love Bird* with Chris Potter on alto and tenor, Chris Cheek on tenor, Rosenwinkel and Wolfgang Muthspiel on guitar, Steve Swallow on bass and Don Alias on percussion. — J.S.

ALPHONSE MOUZON

★★★ **Morning Sun (1981; Tenacious, 1996)**
★★ **By All Means (1981; Tenacious, 1993)**
★★★ **Distant Lover (1982; Tenacious, 1996)**
★★ **Back to Jazz (1985; Tenacious, 1993)**
★★★ **The Sky Is the Limit (1985; Tenacious, 1996)**
★★ **Love Fantasy (1987; Tenacious, 1993)**
★★ **Early Spring (1988; Tenacious, 1993)**
★★½ **As You Wish (1989; Tenacious, 1995)**
★★★ **The Best of Alphonse Mouzon (Black Sun/Celestial Harmonies, 1989)**
★★ **The Survivor (Tenacious, 1992)**
★ **On Top of the World (Tenacious, 1994)**
★★½ **The Night Is Still Young (Tenacious, 1996)**

Drummer/keyboardist Alphonse Mouzon (b. 1948) played in a variety of jazz, R&B and Broadway show bands during the late 1960s before joining the Roy Ayers band, playing on the first Weather Report album and powering McCoy Tyner's band through *Sahara, Song for My Lady, Song of the New World* and *Enlightenment.* He went on to form Eleventh House with guitarist Larry Coryell, a fusion highlight that springboarded his solo career.

When he's on his own, Mouzon's powerful drumming skills never seem to do him justice as he experiments with synthesizers and exotic arrangements. He has recorded prolifically, and his '80s work has recently been reissued. *Morning Sun* features keyboardist Herbie Hancock, guitarist Lee Ritenour, tenor saxophonist Michael Brecker, flautist Hubert Laws and trumpeter Freddie Hubbard. *Distant Lover* uses Hancock, Ritenour, Brecker and Hubbard along with saxophonist Tom Scott and bassist Stanley Clarke. *The Sky Is the Limit* reunites Mouzon with Coryell. *As You Wish* and *The Survivor* are uneven efforts bolstered by the presence of multi-instrumentalist Gary Meek. All too much of this, though, is aural wallpaper. — J.S.

GEORGE MRAZ

★★★★½ **Jazz (Milestone, 1996)**
★★★★ **My Foolish Heart (Milestone, 1996)**
★★★★ **Bottom Lines (Milestone, 1997)**

Widely regarded as one of the greatest contemporary jazz bassists, conservatory-trained Czech George Mraz (b. 1944) emigrated to America in 1968. Since then, his flawless time, probing technique and ability to excel in any context have made him one of the most in-demand accompanists and, ironically, prevented him from actively pursuing a solo career. Pianists in particular have been impressed with Mraz's graceful touch and his ability to listen and assimilate—marks of the greatest accompanists. Tommy Flanagan, Oscar Peterson, Bill Evans and Hank Jones each sought him out, and he has also worked with Joe Henderson, the Thad Jones/Mel Lewis orchestra, Stan Getz, Mick Goodrick, John Abercrombie, Jack DeJohnette and dozens of other jazz stars in a variety of contexts.

Jazz, his first American release, reunites Mraz with longtime collaborators Richie Beirach on piano and Billy Hart on drums (they played with Mraz in the group Quest as well). The same trio recorded *My Foolish Heart,* a nice mix of originals and standards with good performances of Thelonious Monk's "Ask Me Now" and Miles Davis's "Blue in Green." *Bottom Lines* is a cleverly designed set of compositions by bassists, including three Mraz originals and works by Jaco Pastorius, Buster Williams, Marcus Miller, Ron Carter, Charles Mingus and Steve Swallow. — J.S.

BHEKI MSELEKU

★★★ **Timelessness (Verve, 1994)**
★★★★ **Meditations (Verve, 1994)**
★★★★ **Star Seeding (Verve, 1995)**
★★★½ **Beauty of Sunrise (Verve, 1997)**

Spirituality abounds in the music of South African pianist/saxophonist Bheki Mseleku (b. 1955). Like Abdullah Ibrahim, John Coltrane and Pharoah Sanders, he believes that music is a healing force. A native of Durban in South Africa's Natal province, Mseleku springs from a musical family and is self-taught on piano and saxophone (often playing them simultaneously) and guitar. He fled his homeland's racial oppression in the late 1970s, moving to Sweden. In 1985 he relocated to London, where his music captivated jazz fans and players.

Mseleku's original music combines jazz with South African township music, gospel and meditative chants. Stylistically, his piano playing draws strong influences from Chick Corea's finest acoustic work. The import-only *Celebration* was made in London with drummer Marvin "Smitty" Smith and bassist Michael Bowie, who first sat in with Mseleku when they were playing different rooms at Ronnie Scott's jazz club, plus saxophonists Courtney Pine, Jean Toussaint and Steve Williamson. Bowie and Smith are also on *Timelessness,* a wide-ranging showcase with one-track cameos by Joe Henderson, Abbey Lincoln, Pharoah Sanders, Rodney Kendrick and Elvin Jones.

Meditations presents the full force of his spiritual music in two extended original suites (32 and 14 minutes long) recorded live at the 1992 Bath International Jazz Festival. This solo session features Mseleku on piano, tenor and vocals. *Star Seeding* is Mseleku's most cohesive small-group work, on which he plays piano, tenor sax and guitar accompanied by bassist Charlie Haden and drummer Billy Higgins. His poignant and graceful tenor complements his strong keyboard work and invokes the musical spirit of Stan Getz. Mseleku limits himself to piano and vocals on *Beauty of Sunrise,* a strong group session spotlighting his composing more than his playing. — K.F.

IDRIS MUHAMMAD

★★★★★ **Kabsha (1980; Evidence, 1994)**
★★★★ **Legends of Acid Jazz (Prestige, 1996)**

Master drummer Idris Muhammad (b. Leo Morris, 1939) grew up in New Orleans, surrounded by music. His father played banjo; he and his brothers were all drummers. During the 1950s and early '60s the versatile musician played in a variety of contexts in New Orleans and New York, working with Larry Williams, Dee Clark and Lloyd Price. Through the 1960s he played with Jerry Butler, Lou Donaldson and in the band for the Broadway production of *Hair.* Muhammad worked with Roberta Flack before visiting India and Pakistan and then signing up with Kudu Records, recording several out-of-print albums on that label.

The outstanding *Kabsha* is powered by his meticulously expressive drumming, a style in which propulsive qualities and tonality carry equal weight. The powerfully articulate runs on the title track show Muhammad at his best. The group assembled for this date is something special—George Coleman and Pharoah Sanders split the saxophone duties down the middle, with both players appearing on two takes of Coleman's "GCCG Blues." Bassist Ray Drummond hangs in telepathically with Muhammad and contributes "Little Feet," a delightful variation on John Coltrane's "Giant Steps." The CD reissue adds two alternate takes to the original release. *Legends of Acid Jazz* concentrates on Muhammad's soul-jazz work in an effort to introduce him to a new audience of beat-oriented samplers who will no doubt revel in his grooves. — J.S.

MARIA MULDAUR

★★★½ **Maria Muldaur (1973; Reprise, 1993)**
★★★ **Waitress in a Donut Shop (1974; Reprise, 1993)**
★★★½ **Louisiana Love Call (Black Top, 1993)**
★★★½ **Meet Me at Midnite (Black Top, 1994)**
★★★★ **Fanning the Flames (Telarc, 1996)**

Originally hidden in the obscurity of the Jim Kweskin Jug Band, Maria Muldaur (b. 1943) emerged with a remarkable major-label debut, *Maria Muldaur.* The sly swing of "Midnight at the Oasis" provided her a giant hit, but her graceful, blues-inflected singing made every cut delightful. It helped, of course, that among her sidemen were such monster players as Clarence White, Ry Cooder, David Grisman and Dr. John—but it was in her smart song selection, too, that Muldaur revealed her great taste. With numbers by Dolly Parton, Wendy Waldman and Jimmie Rodgers, the record was lovely and polished, an urbane, folksy triumph. The out-of-print *Sweet Harmony* was even craftier, its jazzier grooves displaying real confidence. Jazz legend Benny Carter provides horn arrangements for *Waitress in a Donut Shop,* but the singer sounds a little ill at ease; other now unavailable '70s and early-'80s records are tepid, glossy funk or didactic gospel. Her Black Top albums, however, especially *Louisiana Love*

Call, with Aaron Neville and Dr. John, are solid, blues-based fare.

By the time of *Fanning the Flames,* Muldaur had remade herself as a veteran blues diva whose voice, deepened and broadened with age, carries the worldly-wise character of her singing into classic territory. Muldaur is right at home sharing vocals with such guests as Johnny Adams, Mavis Staples and Bonnie Raitt.

— P.E.

GERRY MULLIGAN

★★★ **Mulligan Plays Mulligan (1951; Original Jazz Classics, 1982)**
★★★ **Gerry Mulligan Quartet (with the Chubby Jackson Big Band) (1953; Original Jazz Classics, 1992)**
★★★★ **California Concerts, Vol. 1 (1954; Pacific Jazz, 1988)**
★★★ **California Concerts, Vol. 2 (1954; Pacific Jazz, 1988)**
★★★ **Reunion (1957; Pacific Jazz, 1988)**
★★★★ **Mulligan Meets Monk (1957; Original Jazz Classics, 1987)**
★★★ **Getz Meets Mulligan in Hi-Fi (1957; Verve, 1991)**
★★★★★ **The Gerry Mulligan Songbook (1958; Pacific Jazz, 1995)**
★★★ **Mulligan (1958; LaserLight, 1996)**
★★★ **Gerry Mulligan Meets Ben Webster (1959; Verve, 1995)**
★★★★★ **What Is There to Say? (1959; Columbia/Legacy, 1994)**
★★ **Night Lights (1965; Mercury, 1998)**
★★ **Idol Gossip (Chiaroscuro, 1976)**
★★★★ **Walk on the Water (DRG, 1980)**
★★★ **Soft Lights and Sweet Music (Concord Jazz, 1986)**
★★★★½ **At Storyville (Pacific Jazz, 1990)**
★★★★ **Gerry Mulligan and the Concert Jazz Band (Verve, 1990)**
★★★★★ **The Best of the Gerry Mulligan Quartet with Chet Baker (Pacific Jazz, 1991)**
★★★★ **Re-Birth of the Cool (GRP, 1992)**
★★★★ **Paraiso (Telarc, 1993)**
★★★½ **Dream a Little Dream (Telarc, 1994)**
★★★★ **Dragonfly (Telarc, 1995)**
★★★★ **In Paris, Vol. 1 (Vogue Disques, 1995)**
★★★★ **In Paris, Vol. 2 (Vogue Disques, 1995)**
★★★★★ **The Complete Pacific Jazz Recordings of the Gerry Mulligan Quartet with Chet Baker (Pacific Jazz, 1996)**
★★★★ **Gerry Mulligan Tentet and Quartet (GNP Crescendo, 1996)**
★★★★ **This Is Jazz 18 (Columbia/Legacy, 1996)**
★★★★★ **Legacy (N2K Encoded Jazz, 1996)**
★★★ **Meets the Saxophonists—Silver Collection (Verve, N.A.)**

Gerry Mulligan (1927–1996) was one of the most important baritone saxophonists in jazz history and a writer, arranger and leader of great impact. Raised in Philadelphia, he came to New York as a talented young arranger adept at taking bop themes and applying them to big-band charts, as he did in 1946 for Gene Krupa's band. In 1948 Mulligan worked in Miles Davis's nonet and a year later was a key figure in Davis's *Birth of the Cool* sessions, contributing three compositions—"Venus De Milo," "Jeru" and "Rocker"—and two arrangements. Yet it was Mulligan's innovative 1952–53 pianoless quartet with trumpeter Chet Baker that made his reputation as one of the founders of the West Coast or cool-jazz style, which contrasted the robust intensity of bop with a more airy, relaxed approach.

The Mulligan/Baker quartet can be heard in almost complete form on *The Complete Pacific Jazz Recordings* box. Mulligan/Baker material also appears on *Gerry Mulligan Tentet and Quartet* and the Original Jazz Classics *Gerry Mulligan Quartet.*

Mulligan Plays Mulligan features earlier work, including several titles for a medium-sized group and a long jam with tenor saxophonist Allen Eager. Baker was replaced by valve trombonist Bob Brookmeyer by the time of the 1954 live recordings *In Paris* and *California Concerts, Vols. 1* and *2.* Brookmeyer also appears on the 1956 sessions *At Storyville* before Baker and Mulligan get together again on the unsatisfying *Reunion.* A more interesting recording, *Mulligan Meets Monk* puts Mulligan in the company of pianist Thelonious Monk in a quartet setting, recording "'Round Midnight," "Rhythm-a-Ning," "Sweet and Lovely," "Decidely," "Straight, No Chaser" and "I Mean You." The reissue includes several alternate takes.

The Gerry Mulligan Songbook revisits the *Birth of the Cool* sessions, reuniting Mulligan with Lee Konitz to record some of the same compositions and charts. *Mulligan* is a series of 1958 quartet, quintet and sextet units featuring drummer Mel Lewis, trumpeters Art Farmer and Ruby Braff, tenor saxophonist Bud Freeman, pianist Billy Taylor, vibist Dave Samuels and bassist George Duvivier. Mulligan's elegant late-'50s quartet work is featured on *What Is There to Say?* (with Farmer) and *Meets Ben Webster.*

Mulligan the orchestra leader returned in the early 1960s with *Gerry Mulligan and the Concert Jazz Band* and the uninteresting *Night Lights. Walk on the Water* is a more tempered set by the revived 1980 band notable for its extensive sampling of Mulligan's writing. *Soft Lights and Sweet Music* is a session with tenor saxophonist Scott Hamilton.

In his 60s, Mulligan enjoyed a revival of his fortunes in the studio, making a series of fine albums in the years before his death. *Re-Birth of the Cool* revisits his early triumphs one last time with a band featuring Wallace Roney on trumpet, Phil Woods on alto saxophone and John Lewis on piano. *Paraiso* is a long-overdue project matching Mulligan's smooth, legato tone to its natural affinities with Brazilian music. Mulligan recorded a quartet date, *Dream a Little Dream,* before ending his career with the lush *Dragonfly,* a session featuring his working quartet augmented by a five-piece brass section and guest soloists including Grover Washington Jr. on soprano and tenor saxophones, John Scofield on guitar, Dave Samuels on vibes and Warren Vaché on cornet.

Two posthumous collections do justice to Mulligan's memory. *This Is Jazz 18* combines material from *What Is There to Say?* with a 1974 reunion concert with Chet Baker, a track recorded live with Dave Brubeck's band and a 1962 recording from the unavailable album *Jeru.* The magnificent *Legacy* covers the length of Mulligan's career in a single disc, sampling his work with Miles Davis, including otherwise unavailable live recordings and ending with two of Mulligan's compositions in special recordings by others that Mulligan coproduced in the last weeks of his life. — J.S.

MARK MURPHY

★★★ **Rah (1961; Original Jazz Classics, 1993)**
★★★ **That's How I Love the Blues! (1962; Original Jazz Classics, 1989)**
★★★ **Mark Murphy Sings (1975; Muse, 1995)**
★★★★ **Stolen Moments (1978; Muse, 1992)**
★★★★ **Bop for Kerouac (with Richie Cole) (Muse, 1981)**
★★★ **Beauty and the Beast (Muse, 1985)**
★★★½ **Kerouac Then and Now (Muse, 1986)**
★★★★ **Night Mood (Milestone, 1987)**
★★★★ **September Ballads (Milestone, 1988)**
★★★★ **What a Way to Go (Muse, 1990)**
★★★★ **I'll Close My Eyes (Muse, 1994)**
★★★★½ **Stolen . . . and Other Moments (32 Jazz, 1997)**
★★★½ **Song for the Geese (RCA Victor, 1997)**

Syracuse, New York, native Mark Murphy (b. 1932) was a classically trained vocalist before turning to jazz. After earning degrees in music and acting at Syracuse University, Murphy moved to New York City, where he would perform Gilbert and Sullivan one night and sing at the Apollo Theatre's amateur night the next. In the late 1950s Murphy began his recording career, making a series of albums for Decca and Capitol that are now out of print, but his early-'60s Riverside recordings are available on Original Jazz Classics. In the mid-'70s, after spending nine years in London, Murphy returned home to record a number of albums for Muse.

Murphy's fans agree that he has one of the most inventive vocal styles in jazz history but differ when it comes to his penchant for mixing music with theatrics, particularly his fondness for doing readings of the Beat poets. *Bop for Kerouac,* with alto saxophonist Richie Cole, is an engaging mixture of bop standards interspersed with Kerouac readings. *Kerouac Then and Now* also includes Lord Buckley material. Murphy's Milestone recordings are magnificent vocal sets: *September Ballads* collects what Murphy calls "contemporary standards" that showcase his rich baritone and shrewd harmonic sense, and *Night Mood* brings Murphy into Brazilian territory backed by Azymuth, alto saxophonist Frank Morgan and trumpeter Claudio Roditi. *Stolen . . . and Other Moments* is an outstanding collection of Murphy's Muse recordings, the best introduction to his work. — J.S.

MATT "GUITAR" MURPHY

★★½ **Way Down South (Antone's, 1990)**
★★½ **The Blues Don't Bother Me (Roesch, 1996)**

By virtue of his taut playing with such heavyweights as Muddy Waters, Bobby Bland, Howlin' Wolf and Memphis Slim, Chicago bluesman Matt "Guitar" Murphy has well earned his reputation as a sideman. Born in Mississippi in 1929, Murphy found fame in the '80s thanks to his work on the *Blues Brothers* movie and soundtrack. *Way Down South* illuminates his skill and versatility as a musician. But despite the album's tight ensemble playing and sometimes burning guitar work by Murphy and his brother Floyd, their songs are primarily instrumental and not particularly memorable. *The Blues Don't Bother Me* is more of the same. — B.R.H.

DAVID MURRAY

★★½ **Last of the Hipman (Red, 1976)**
★★★½ **Live at the Peace Church (Danola, 1976)**
★★★½ **Flowers for Albert (1976; India Navigation, 1997)**
★★★ **Penthouse Jazz (Circle, 1977)**
★★★½ **Solomon's Sons (with James Newton) (Circle, 1977)**
★★★ **Low Class Conspiracy (Adelphi, 1978)**
★★★ **Holy Siege on the Intrigue (Circle, 1978)**
★★★½ **Live at the Lower Manhattan Ocean Club, Vols. 1 & 2 (1978; India Navigation, 1989)**
★★★ **Let the Music Take You (1978; EPM Musique, 1993)**
★★★ **Conceptual Saxophone (Cadillac, 1978)**
★★★ **Organic Saxophone (Palm, 1978)**
★★½ **Sur-Real Saxophone (Horo, 1978)**
★★½ **Interboogieology (Black Saint, 1978)**
★★★★ **The London Concert (Cadillac, 1979)**
★★★ **The People's Choice (Cecma, 1979)**
★★★★ **3D Family (1980; Hat Hut, 1989)**
★★★ **Solo Live, Vol. 1 (Cecma, 1980)**
★★★ **Solo Live, Vol. 2 (Cecma, 1980)**
★★★★★ **Ming (Black Saint, 1980)**
★★★★½ **Sweet Lovely (Black Saint, 1980)**
★★★★★ **Home (Black Saint, 1982)**
★★★★★ **Murray's Steps (Black Saint, 1982)**
★★★★★ **Morning Song (Black Saint, 1984)**
★★★ **Children (Black Saint, 1985)**
★★★★ **Live at Sweet Basil, Vol. 1 (Black Saint, 1985)**
★★★★ **Live at Sweet Basil, Vol. 2 (Black Saint, 1986)**
★★★★½ **I Want to Talk About You (Black Saint, 1986)**
★★★★½ **N.Y.C. 1986 (1986; DIW, 1993)**
★★★★★ **New Life (Black Saint, 1987)**
★★★★★ **Hope Scope (Black Saint, 1987)**
★★★★★ **The Healers (with Randy Weston) (Black Saint, 1987)**
★★★★½ **Lovers (DIW, 1988)**
★★★½ **In Our Style (with Jack DeJohnette) (DIW, 1988)**
★★★★★ **The Hill (Black Saint, 1988)**
★★★★½ **Deep River (DIW, 1989)**
★★★★★ **Ming's Samba (Portrait, 1989)**
★★★★ **Ballads (DIW, 1990)**
★★★★ **Spirituals (DIW, 1990)**
★★★★ **Sketches of Tokyo (with John Hicks) (DIW, 1990)**
★★★½ **Daybreak (with Dave Burrell) (Gazell, 1990)**
★★½ **Golden Sea (with Kahil El'Zabar) (Sound Aspects, 1990)**
★★★½ **Remembrances (DIW, 1991)**
★★★ **Tea for Two (with George Arvanitas) (Fresh Sounds, 1991)**
★★★ **The Offering (with the Bobby Battle Quartet) (Mapleshade, 1991)**
★★★ **Sunrise, Sunset (with the Bob Thiele Collective) (Red Baron, 1991)**
★★★★½ **In Concert (with Dave Burrell) (Victo, 1992)**
★★★★ **Death of a Sideman (DIW, 1992)**
★★★★ **Special Quartet (DIW, 1992)**
★★★★½ **Shakill's Warrior (DIW, 1992)**
★★★★½ **A Sanctuary Within (Black Saint, 1992)**
★★½ **Black & Black (Red Baron, 1992)**
★★½ **MX (Red Baron, 1992)**
★★★★★ **David Murray Big Band Conducted by Lawrence "Butch" Morris (DIW, 1992)**
★★★★ **Real Deal (with Milford Graves) (DIW, 1992)**
★★★★ **Lucky Four (Tutu, 1993)**
★★★★ **Ballads for Bass Clarinet (DIW, 1993)**
★★★★★ **Picasso (DIW, 1993)**
★★★★ **Fast Life (DIW, 1993)**
★★★ **Jazzosaurus Rex (Red Baron, 1993)**
★★★★ **Body & Soul (Black Saint, 1993)**
★★★★★ **Brother to Brother (with Dave Burrell) (Gazell, 1993)**
★★★ **Jazzpar Prize (with Pierre Dørge's New Jungle Orchestra) (Enja, 1993)**

★★★ **Blue Monk (with Aki Takase) (Enja, 1994)**
★★★★ **Saxmen (Red Baron, 1994)**
★★★ **Live '93 Acoustic Octofunk (Sound Hills, 1994)**
★★★ **The Tip (DIW, 1994)**
★★★★ **Tenors (DIW, 1994)**
★★★★½ **Shakill's II (DIW, 1994)**
★★★½ **For Aunt Louise (DIW, 1995)**
★★★½ **Jug-a-Lug (DIW, 1995)**
★★★★★ **South of the Border (DIW, 1995)**
★★★ **Ugly Beauty (with Donal Fox) (Evidence, 1995)**
★★★ **Dark Star: The Music of the Grateful Dead (Astor Place, 1996)**
★★★★½ **The David Murray/James Newton Quintet (DIW, 1996)**

Arguably one of jazz's greatest tenor saxophonists, David Murray (b. 1955) dominated the 1980s as thoroughly as Charlie Parker dominated the '40s. If he has never achieved Parker's notoriety and legend, it's because very few people were paying attention to progressive, acoustic jazz in the '80s, a decade distracted by commercial fusion and hard-bop nostalgia. While nobody was watching, however, Murray developed a personal voice of astonishing power and boldness on the tenor sax and bass clarinet.

Devoted to sax heroes as conservative as Paul Gonsalves and as radical as Albert Ayler, Murray is the greatest synthesizer since Charles Mingus, composing enchanting melodies and swinging them with fluid ease, then taking them into the furthest realms of abstraction and dissonance and bringing them back to the music's roots in blues and gospel. His main mission, though, has been to continue the work left undone by John Coltrane's death and push the possibilities of improvisation to the limit by playing long, complex solos free of pat phrases and favorite licks. Equally important has been his execution: He gets a rich, expansive sound from his horn and can hum on ballads as effectively as he can shout on fast tunes.

Born in Berkeley, Murray came of age in a California scene where the boundaries between the mainstream and the avant-garde were blessedly blurred. At Southern California's Pomona College he played with critic, drummer and teacher Stanley Crouch, cornetist Lawrence "Butch" Morris, clarinetist John Carter and saxophonist Arthur Blythe. By the time he moved to New York in 1975, he could already play with a brashness backed up by chops. He quickly gravitated to the experimental loft scene, presided over by Sam Rivers and Sunny Murray and invigorated by the recent arrival of Air and the Art Ensemble of Chicago.

He began recording soon after arriving in New York, teaming with Morris (*Last of the Hipman*); Crouch and Air bassist Fred Hopkins (*Live at the Peace Church*); Morris, Hopkins, Crouch and Charles Mingus pianist Don Pullen (*Flowers for Albert*); Hopkins, drummer Phillip Wilson and AEC trumpeter Lester Bowie (*Live at the Lower Manhattan Ocean Club, Vols. 1* and *2* and *Low Class Conspiracy*); and Cecil Taylor, drummer Andrew Cyrille and bassist Johnny Dyani (*3D Family*). On these efforts, Murray already has a strong, original voice on his saxophone but little sense of how to shape it. As a result, his best recordings are the trio sessions, where form counts less and inspired blowing more.

Murray's breakthrough came in 1980 when he finally found a way to combine the gospel-rooted melodicism of his youth with the edgy intensity of the lofts. He created an octet around the core of his old pal Morris, Air drummer Steve McCall and saxophonist Henry Threadgill. Morris had already become Murray's indispensable right-hand man, not only as a piercing cornet foil to his fat sax tone but, more important, as an arranger who kept Murray's explosive ideas in a coherent pattern. The octet recorded three albums—*Ming, Home* and *Murray's Steps*—that rank with the decade's very best. All three recycle Murray's compositions from earlier recordings, but now the tunes have an elegance that equals their energy. The sheer poignancy of the ballads for his then-wife, Ming, and his parents' "Home" illustrate how Murray had matured into a vanguard composer with a populist streak.

With different personnel, the octet remained Murray's most effective vehicle, as he proved on such majestic albums as *New Life, Hope Scope* and *Picasso,* but it was just a scaled-down version of the big band of Murray's dreams. Only occasionally was he able to pull together a jazz orchestra, but when he did, it had the octet's sturdy architecture but with a far more expansive palette. *Live at Sweet Basil, Vols. 1* and *2* capture the energy of the big band, but the sound is so bad it spoils the effect. Much better is the studio album *David Murray Big Band Conducted by Lawrence "Butch" Morris,* a sumptuous sonic feast that demonstrates how a community can accommodate independent action and still unite at crucial junctures. Just as inspiring was 1995's big-band project, *South of the Border.*

In the '80s Murray applied his newfound arranging ability to his small combos as well. Two of the best are *Morning Song* and *Ming's Samba,* both of which feature New Orleans drummer Ed Blackwell, an Ornette Coleman alumnus. Murray had often hinted at New Orleans parade rhythms and Coleman's untethered melodies, but Blackwell's presence brings these influences to the fore. *The Hill,* a trio session with the old-guard rhythm section of Richard Davis and Joe Chambers, includes tunes by Duke Ellington and Billy Strayhorn and started talk of Murray as a neotraditionalist. In fact, he was subsuming all of jazz history in his brawny Ben Webster–like tone, joining Jelly Roll Morton's polyphony and Coleman's harmolodics, Ellington's swing and Mingus's postbop modalism.

Murray recorded a series of unaccompanied duo albums with such pianists as John Hicks (*Sketches of Tokyo*), Dave Burrell (*Brother to Brother*), Randy Weston (*The Healers*), George Arvanitas (*Tea for Two*), Aki Takase (*Blue Monk*) and Donal Fox (*Ugly Beauty*). Of these, the most important are *The Healers,* which realizes the hymnlike qualities of Weston's compositions, "The Healers" and "Blue Moses," and *Brother to Brother,* which digs into the very origins of jazz to show how much one can say with a minimum of notes.

Murray's mother had been a church pianist, and as he passed age 30, he began exploring the gospel influences of his childhood. With Burrell and assorted rhythm sections, Murray recorded *Spirituals*, *Remembrances* and *Deep River,* all albums that evoke the African-American church through traditional hymns and/or new compositions in the same vein. He even convinced pianist Pullen to switch to a churchlike organ for two similar albums, *Shakill's Warrior* and *Shakill's II.*

By the start of 1989, Murray was the dominant figure in the vanguard but had still never released an album as a bandleader on a major U.S. label. That finally changed when Portrait, a short-lived Columbia jazz subsidiary, released *Ming's Samba;* Columbia itself signed a licensing agreement (which has since lapsed) to release some, but not all, of Murray's many albums on the Japanese label DIW, and veteran producer Bob Thiele signed Murray to his Columbia-distributed Red Baron label. Murray's recordings for Red Baron are, for the most part, minor additions to his catalog, as he struggles valiantly to maintain his dignity in albums of show tunes, Thiele compositions and dubious movie tie-ins. The one exception is *Special Quartet,* which finds Murray living out his Coltrane fantasies with half of the classic Coltrane Quartet (pianist McCoy Tyner and drummer Elvin Jones), with wonderful results.

In the mid-'90s Murray formed an eight-piece jazz-funk band anchored by Miles Davis's keyboardist Robert Irving III. This group made a surprisingly successful tribute to the Grateful Dead, *Dark Star,* and Murray recorded two other albums of R&B-influenced originals, *The Tip* and *Jug-a-Lug,* with other lineups. If Murray never succumbed to fusion clichés, however, he never rose to the heights of his original octet either. Far more impressive is his reunion with his old California buddy on *The David Murray/James Newton Quintet.* Murray remains most known for his work with the superb World Saxophone Quartet. His best works, though, are his '80s recordings with the octet, big band, quartet and piano duos, and they are well worth whatever effort it takes to track them down. — G.H.

CHARLIE MUSSELWHITE

★★★★★ Stand Back! Here Comes Charlie Musselwhite's Southside Band (Vanguard, 1967)
★★★½ Stone Blues (1968; Vanguard, 1992)
★★★ Tennessee Woman (1969; Vanguard, 1994)
★★★ The Harmonica According to Charlie Musselwhite (1978; Blind Pig, 1994)
★★★★ Memphis Charlie (Arhoolie, 1989)
★★★½ Ace of Harps (Alligator, 1990)
★★★½ Signature (Alligator, 1991)
★★★★★ In My Time (Alligator, 1994)
★★★ Blues Never Die (Vanguard, 1994)
★★★★½ Rough News (EMD/Virgin, 1997)

Charlie Musselwhite, born in Kosciusko, Mississippi, in 1944, moved with his family to Memphis, where he received a firsthand introduction to the blues from the many performers who proliferated around Beale Street in the 1950s. He learned to play guitar from Will Shade of the Memphis Jug Band. Musselwhite moved on his own to Chicago, where he started playing harmonica at local clubs alongside such blues greats as Little Walter Jacobs, Muddy Waters, Willie Dixon and Buddy Guy. Though the blues were played in black clubs, the scene was integrated to the point where young whites like Musselwhite and Paul Butterfield became part of the developing blues identity.

Musselwhite appeared on the historic Vanguard anthology *Chicago: The Blues Today!* before recording his first album as a leader, the classic *Stand Back!,* with veteran Chess Records tub man Fred Below on drums, Harvey Mandel on guitar and Barry Goldberg on keyboards. Musselwhite recorded three more albums for Vanguard (a self-titled recording is out of print) and a couple more on obscure labels before reaching another creative high point with two fine recordings for Arhoolie, *Takin' My Time* and *Goin' Back Down South,* the latter featuring some of his guitar work. Both are now unavailable, but highlights are collected on *Memphis Charlie.* Through the late '70s and '80s Musselwhite's career waned as he made an unspectacular series of albums for various small labels. Of these, *The Harmonica According to Charlie Musselwhite* is the best.

Musselwhite made a strong comeback on Alligator in the 1990s, beginning with the excellent *Ace of Harps. Signature* is a worthy follow-up, but Musselwhite then put together his best album since *Stand Back!,* the ambitious career retrospective *In My Time.* Released on his 50th birthday, the album covers all aspects of Musselwhite's life in music, beginning with a set of country blues done solo, then a Chicago session with the full band, and finally two moving songs with the Five Blind Boys on vocals.

Rough News is an impressive set from Musselwhite's late-'90s touring band, highlighted by the incendiary title track and "Both Sides of the Fence." Guest stars include guitarists Cesar Rosas, Junior Watson, Kid Ramos and Fenton Robinson. — J.S.

MELTON MUSTAFA

★★★★ Boiling Point (Contemporary, 1996)

★★★★ St. Louis Blues (Contemporary, 1997)

Boiling Point, the auspicious debut by big-band leader and trumpeter Melton Mustafa (b. 1947), followed years of gigging in a variety of contexts and pursuing an academic career that has led him to the directorship of the music department of Miami's African Heritage Cultural Arts Center. The Miami native played all kinds of music in street bands as a teenager and began professionally as a section player in R&B bands backing Frank Williams, Sam and Dave, Betty Wright, Latimore and Lloyd Price among others. He did session work and played in the Uptown Funk All Stars with Jaco Pastorius, who later tabbed Mustafa for his post–Weather Report project Word of Mouth.

Mustafa studied jazz theory at the Berklee College of Music and Florida A&M before playing with Ira Sullivan, the Duke Ellington Orchestra and Bobby Watson. His most formative experience, though, came during a stint with the Count Basie Orchestra when trumpeter Thad Jones was its leader. The Basie style is dominant on the groove-oriented *Boiling Point,* although Mustafa also works in Afro-Cuban rhythms and modal improvisation schemes. *St. Louis Blues,* featuring Jesse Jones Jr. on alto and soprano saxophones and flute, includes an extended big-band arrangement of the title track and a number of engaging compositions by Mustafa highlighted by "To You, Miles" and "The Sound of Soul." — J.S.

AMINA CLAUDINE MYERS

★★★★★ The Circle of Time (Black Saint, 1984)

★★★★ Jumping in the Sugar Bowl (Minor Music, 1984)

★★★★ Duet (with Muhal Richard Abrams) (Black Saint, 1993)

Pianist Amina Claudine Myers (b. 1943) is a virtuosic performer whose importance in the jazz world is obscured by her low-profile presence in the CD racks. Myers has not been treated well by the record industry, and the few recordings she has made are difficult to find. Those who know Myers's work with her own group or as the dazzling centerpiece of Charlie Haden's Liberation Music Orchestra realize that she belongs in the pantheon of greats.

The Circle of Time, a trio recording with bassist Don Pate and drummer Thurman Barker, *Jumping in the Sugar Bowl* and *Duet,* with Muhal Richard Abrams, are the only Myers releases currently available, although *Salutes Bessie Smith* (on Leo) is well worth searching out. Myers's soulful combination of blues and gospel sources and a search for freedom outside traditional harmonic frameworks characterize players with connections to the Association for the Advancement of Creative Musicians. *The Circle of Time* stands among the finest AACM-related recordings, as the blues and gospel roots of "Louisville," "Plowed Fields" and "Do You Wanna Be Saved?" evolve into "The Clock" and "The Circle of Time." *Jumping in the Sugar Bowl* is another excellent trio session with bassist Thomas Palmer and percussionist Reggie Nicholson. — J.S.

MILTON NASCIMENTO

★★★★ **Clube de Esquina (1972; Blue Note, 1995)**
★★★★ **Milagre dos Peixes (1973; Capitol/Intuition, 1992)**
★★★★★ **Milton (A&M, 1976)**
★★★★ **Clube da Esquina, Vol. 2 (1978; Blue Note, 1995)**
★★★ **Sentinela (1980; Verve, 1990)**
★★★★ **Ănimă (1982; Verve, 1990)**
★★★½ **Encontros e Despedidas (Verve, 1985)**
★★★★ **Yauarête (1987; Columbia, 1988)**
★★★½ **A Arte de Milton Nascimento (Verve, 1988)**
★★★½ **Miltons (1988; Columbia, 1989)**
★★★★ **Txai (Columbia, 1990)**
★★★½ **Noticias do Brasil (Tropical Music, 1992)**
★★★ **Missa dos Quilombos (Verve, 1992)**
★★★★ **Angelus (Warner Bros., 1994)**
★★★★ **Amigo (Warner Bros., 1996)**
★★★★★ **Nascimento (Warner Bros., 1997)**

One of Brazil's most talented singer/songwriters, Milton Nascimento (b. 1942) is blessed with one of pop music's most perfect voices—rich and soulful in its lower register, angelically pure in falsetto—as well as the sort of melodic instincts that can exploit such a voice to its fullest. Understandably, that combination has made him a superstar in his homeland, where his recordings are treated with the fervor and respect Americans once lavished on Stevie Wonder. Yet even though numerous attempts have been made to translate Nascimento's appeal into American terms, he remains a cult artist at best in this country, a situation that is less an indictment of U.S. pop fans than a reflection of how quintessentially Brazilian Nascimento's music is.

That's not to say he's strictly a samba singer, mind you. Like many Brazilian musicians who came up under the sway of *tropicalismo,* Nascimento was as in awe of the Beatles as any American rock fan; indeed, the first selection on *Milton* is a version of the Lõ Borges tune "Para Lennon e McCartney." But Nascimento's first American album, *Courage* (now out of print), gives his songs the same lush backing that had been lavished on similar efforts by samba stars like Antonio Carlos Jobim. Consequently, the album, though listenable enough, fails to offer any real sense of Nascimento's talents.

It would take seven years before he assembled another album for U.S. consumption, but Nascimento's Brazilian output improved steadily, offering a masterful synthesis of Brazilian pop styles, from the childlike cadences of "Ponta de Areia" (from the unavailable *Minas*) to the hypnotic primitivism of "Promessas do Sol" (from *Geraes*) and the dramatic splendor of "Milagre dos Peixes" (from *Milagre dos Peixes*). In 1975 Nascimento was featured on the Wayne Shorter album *Native Dancer,* and Shorter returned the favor a year later by appearing—along with Herbie Hancock—on *Milton*. A wonderfully alluring album, it neither diluted Nascimento's sound nor made it seem in any way foreign, and the versions of "Raca" and "The Call (A Chamada)" rival the Brazilian originals. But the now deleted *Journey to Dawn,* which backs away from *Milton*'s jazzy insouciance, isn't quite as exciting, and Nascimento's option with A&M was not renewed.

Not that this lack of U.S. success adversely affected his output at home. In fact, *Ănimă* is one of his most assured efforts, showing with "As Várias Pontas de Uma Estrela" that Nascimento could easily hold his own even against such an eminence as Caetano Veloso. Shorter returns for three cameos on the out-of-print live album *A Barco dos Amantes,* while Pat Metheny adds some delightfully coloristic guitar to "Vidro e Corte" on *Encontros e Despedidas* (although that album's highlight is undoubtedly the Winnie Mandela tribute "Lágrima do Sul"). Nascimento's most inspired pairing, though, is with Paul Simon on *Yauarête,* on which Simon adds an exquisite harmony part to "O Vendedor de Sonhos." Overall, *Yauarête* is Nascimento's most balanced American release since *Milton,* although the winningly exotic *Txai* has its moments, particularly the hauntingly emotional "Yanomami e Nós."

The *Clube de Esquina* albums are classic Brazilian material from the 1970s. *Angelus* includes guest appearances by jazz stars Wayne Shorter, Pat Metheny, Jack DeJohnette, Ron Carter and Herbie Hancock. *Amigo* is an ambitious live recording of Nascimento's 1994 Brazilian concert with a full orchestra and children's chior. *Nascimento* is nothing short of a masterpiece, a spiritually evocative statement of purpose from the master vocalist and composer who won the 1998 Grammy for Best World Music Album. — J.D.C.

FATS NAVARRO

★★★★ Fats Navarro Featured with the Tadd Dameron Band (1948; Milestone, 1989)
★★★★ Memorial (Savoy, 1993)
★★★★ Nostalgia: Fats Navarro Memorial No. 2 (Savoy, 1995)
★★★★★ The Complete Blue Note and Capitol Recordings of Fats Navarro and Tadd Dameron (Blue Note, 1995)

Theodore "Fats" Navarro (1923–1950) was a cometlike talent whose immediate impact briefly rivaled that of any of his trumpet-playing peers, including Dizzy Gillespie, before he succumbed to tuberculosis (aggravated by heroin abuse).

Navarro's confident, big-toned style relied less on high-register pyrotechnics than on a stunning ability to improvise at length with precocious originality. His imaginative solos told bold, lengthy stories. Unfortunately, Navarro left behind a legend without much documentation. *Memorial* and *Nostalgia: Fats Navarro Memorial No. 2,* from 1946 and 1947, collect his earliest works, including a memorable session with Bud Powell on piano, Kenny Dorham joining Navarro on trumpet, Sonny Stitt on alto saxophone and Kenny Clarke on drums.

Fats Navarro Featured with the Tadd Dameron Band includes a 1948 radio-broadcast transcript of a band with the excellent rhythm section of Dameron on piano, Curley Russell on bass and Clarke on drums. *The Complete Blue Note and Capitol Recordings* covers Navarro's last sides, from 1947 to 1949, which were with several Dameron-led bands, and a quintet session featuring Powell and Sonny Rollins.
— J.S.

KENNY NEAL

★★★ Big News from Baton Rouge!! (Alligator, 1988)
★★★ Devil Child (Alligator, 1989)
★★★★ Walking on Fire (Alligator, 1991)
★★★ Bayou Blood (Alligator, 1992)
★★★ Hoodoo Moon (Alligator, 1994)
★★★ Deluxe Edition (Alligator, 1997)

One of a handful of young musicians determined to bring majesty back to the blues, Kenny Neal (b. 1957) is a second-generation bluesman; his father, Raful Neal, was a well-known Baton Rouge harp player. Kenny's first instrument was the piano, and he went on to learn bass, harmonica and his primary instrument, the guitar. Neal made his debut album at age 30, releasing *Big News from Baton Rouge!!,* which is punctuated by his forceful guitar and harmonica work. He also coauthored many of the songs ("Baby Bee," "Outside Looking In") with producer Bob Greenlee, whose Kingsnake label originally released the work before Alligator picked it up. *Devil Child,* whose sound and personnel lineup is similar to its predecessor's, also features the King Snake Horns and keyboardist Lucky Peterson; in addition, there's a cameo by Edgar Winter, who plays alto sax on Neal and Greenlee's "I Owe It All to You." Along with Neal's own material, *Devil Child* features his father's remorseful "Change My Way of Livin'."

Walking on Fire was made around the same time as Neal starred in *Mule Bone,* a Broadway play written by Langston Hughes and folklorist Zora Neale Hurston. Neal's acoustic guitar and harmonica are backed by bassist Russell Jackson and drummer Tony Coleman, professionally known as Silent Partners. Additional players include James Brown alumni

Fred Wesley on trombone and Maceo Parker on alto sax. The album includes two Hughes poems set to Neal's music, "Morning After" and "Bad Luck Card"; other standout tracks include "Look but Don't Touch" and "Blues Stew."

Similar efforts, *Bayou Blood* and *Hoodoo Moon,* remain in the spirit of his first two releases—modern, swinging, hard-driving and well-played electric blues. Sticking to his proven formula, Neal utilizes virtually the same musicians who have been at his side since the late '80s. He had a hand in penning almost every song on both albums, and the quality of most of these tracks is high. — B.R.H.

CHICAGO BOB NELSON

★★★ **Back to Bogalusa (King Snake, 1996)**

"Chicago" Bob Nelson (b. 1943) plays harmonica and sings in a style closer to the Louisiana backwoods than to Chicago's South Side, but he's a galvanic performer nonetheless. In the 1980s he fronted the legendary Southeast roots band the Heartfixers along with guitarist Tinsley Ellis. Ellis returns the favor on *Back to Bogalusa,* adding his hard-hitting playing to Nelson's gritty performance. "Came Home This Morning," "Swamp Jump" and the title track are among the highlights of this engaging recording. — J.S.

OLIVER NELSON

★★★ **Meet Oliver Nelson (1959; Original Jazz Classics, 1992)**
★★★ **Taking Care of Business (1960; Original Jazz Classics, 1991)**
★★★★ **Screamin' the Blues (1960; Original Jazz Classics, 1991)**
★★★★ **Soul Battle (1960; Original Jazz Classics, 1992)**
★★★ **Nocturne (1960; Original Jazz Classics, 1992)**
★★★ **Main Stem (with Joe Newman) (1961; Original Jazz Classics, 1992)**
★★★ **Afro/American Sketches (1961; Original Jazz Classics, 1993)**
★★★★★ **The Blues and the Abstract Truth (1961; Impulse!, 1995)**
★★★★ **Straight Ahead (1961; Original Jazz Classics, N.A.)**
★★★★ **Sound Pieces (1966; GRP, 1991)**
★★★ **Verve Jazz Masters 48 (Verve, 1995)**
★★★★ **More Blues and the Abstract Truth (Impulse!, 1997)**

Oliver Nelson (1932–1975) was a forceful, straightforward soloist on a variety of reed instruments; he was also an extremely skilled composer/arranger whose works still sound fresh and relevant decades later.

During the early '60s Nelson made several records, including *Straight Ahead* and *Screamin' the Blues,* in small combos featuring the brilliant Eric Dolphy on flute, alto sax and bass clarinet. Drummer Roy Haynes and bassist George Duvivier provide sympathetic accompaniment as the Nelson/Dolphy collaboration soars majestically through these tracks. It's hard to imagine a pair of soloists better suited to each other, as Dolphy's pulling angularity and Nelson's controlled, logical aggression create a fantastic ebb and flow of colors.

Nelson used the same rhythm section on *Soul Battle,* a cutting session on tenors among Nelson, King Curtis and Jimmy Forrest, as well as on *Nocturne,* one of two sessions with vibraphonist Lem Winchester (the other is *Taking Care of Business*).

Dolphy also appears on the epochal *Blues and the Abstract Truth,* Nelson's most famous work. This all-star session includes Haynes on drums, Paul Chambers on bass, Bill Evans on piano, Freddie Hubbard on trumpet and George Barrow on baritone saxophone.

Nelson's later works gravitated more toward big-band arrangements and featured less and less of his own soloing, which makes them that much less interesting. The reissue of *Sound Pieces* adds several tracks, including two quartet pieces, not on the initial release.

Nelson became a sought-after composer of film scores and television themes (*The Six Million Dollar Man*) toward the end of his life. — J.S.

THE NEVILLE BROTHERS

★★½ **The Neville Brothers (1978; One Way, 1995)**
★★★★ **Fiyo on the Bayou (1981; A&M, 1987)**
★★★ **Live at Tipitina's 1982 (1985; Rhino, 1998)**
★★★★½ **Treacherous: A History of the Neville Brothers (Rhino, 1988)**
★★★★ **Yellow Moon (A&M, 1989)**
★★★★ **Brother's Keeper (A&M, 1990)**
★★★½ **Treacherous Too! (Rhino, 1991)**
★★★ **Family Groove (A&M, 1994)**

★★★★ **Live on Planet Earth (A&M, 1994)**
★★★ **Mitakuye Oyasin Oyasin (A&M, 1996)**
★★★★ **The Very Best of the Neville Brothers (Rhino, 1997)**

In a just world, great bands would make great albums, bad bands would make bad ones, and the pop charts would mark the difference. And in such a world, the Neville Brothers would all but own the hit parade. Unfortunately, life doesn't quite work that way, which may be why the Nevilles—despite having a fearsomely soulful lead singer, flawless harmony vocals and the finest rhythm section in New Orleans—have never achieved a level of success commensurate with their talent. Although the four Neville brothers, Aaron (b. 1941), Art (b. 1937), Charles (b. 1939) and Cyril (b. 1948), had been kicking around the New Orleans music scene since the mid-'50s, when Aaron and Art were members of the Hawketts, the Neville Brothers as such didn't come together as a band until after the quartet had united behind the Wild Tchoupitoulas. What made the Tchoupitoulas album so exciting was the ease with which the group meshed contemporary funk licks with traditional Mardi Gras parade rhythms. But there's almost no sign of that sound on *The Neville Brothers,* on which the group wastes its time on such calculated attempts at R&B currency as "Dancin' Jones" (an insipid paean to the Rolling Stones) and "Vieux Carré Rouge" (a pleasant but pedestrian soul ballad). Only "All Nights, All Right" and a version of John Hiatt's "Washable Ink" save the album from irrelevancy.

Fiyo on the Bayou puts the band back on track. Some of its punch can be attributed to the addition of guitarist Leo Nocentelli (who'd played in the Meters with Art and Cyril) to the rhythm section, but the real secret to this album's success is the shift in focus away from the R&B charts and toward the Crescent City. Apart from "Mona Lisa" and "The Ten Commandments of Love," a pair of oldies included to frame Aaron's otherworldly tenor, the songs are mostly traditional, lending the album a rootsy richness. Yet despite rave reviews, *Fiyo on the Bayou* was barely a blip on the pop charts; likewise, the stunning *Neville-ization,* which documents the group's legendary live act, failed to reach beyond the faithful and has gone out of print. (*Live at Tipitina's 1982* offers additional material from the same concert.)

By this point, the Nevilles' past appeared far more promising than their future—hence the intoxicating nostalgia of *Treacherous,* which mixes early solo singles by Art, Aaron and Cyril with selections from *The Wild Tchoupitoulas, The Neville Brothers* and *Fiyo on the Bayou. Treacherous Too!* continues in that vein, with more solo stuff and excerpts from *Neville-ization.* But just when it seemed the Nevilles would never find a way to reconcile their sound with the modern pop market, the group went into the studio with producer Daniel Lanois, emerging with the triumphant *Yellow Moon,* an album that manages to find room for such contemporary touches as rap ("Sister Rosa," a tribute to civil rights figure Rosa Parks) without compromising or corrupting the Nevilles' identity. Having found their formula, the Nevilles went back for more on *Brother's Keeper,* which may lack the eerie atmospherics of *Yellow Moon* but otherwise maintains its musical balance, thanks to touches like the low-key funk of "Witness" or the thick, dark harmonies of "Brother Blood."

Family Groove attempts to recapture the band's funk roots but panders to questionable commercial instincts with an uninspired cover of Steve Miller's "Fly Like an Eagle." *Live on Planet Earth* effectively captures the drive and range of the band's concerts. Back in the studio, however, the band flounders on *Mitakuye Oyasin Oyasin* (All My Relations), which is notable primarily for a good cover of Bill Withers's "Ain't No Sunshine." *The Very Best of the Neville Brothers* is a fine anthology, a good place to start if you don't have any of their albums. — J.D.C.

JAMES NEWTON

★★★★ **Paseo del Mar (India Navigation, 1978)**
★★★★★ **The Mystery School (India Navigation, 1980)**
★★★★★ **Axum (ECM, 1981)**
★★★★★ **James Newton (Gramavision, 1982)**
★★★★ **Portraits (India Navigation, 1982)**
★★★★ **Luella (Gramavision, 1983)**
★★★★ **The David Murray/James Newton Quintet (DIW, 1996)**

James Newton (b. 1953) is a virtuosic instrumentalist who chose to devote himself to the flute exclusively and thus became the most impressive new voice on the instrument in years.

His talent for blowing, in the more or less standard small-band configuration, is well documented on both *Paseo del Mar,* featuring a strong rhythm section with Abdul Wadud's cello in place of bass, and pianist Anthony Davis's *Hidden Voices* (Davis and Newton also appear on *Crystal Texts,* their duo album for the Moers label).

In addition to his abilities as a soloist of fire and precision in the Eric Dolphy manner, Newton has also participated in efforts to blend notated music with improvisation. *The Mystery School* features his writing for a woodwind quintet completed by clarinet, oboe or English horn, bassoon and tuba. All of the players are skilled Californians like Newton, and the program is one of the most convincing and warm in this genre. (See also another Davis recording, *I've Known Rivers*—chamber jazz at its finest—featuring the trio of Newton, Davis and Wadud.)

Newton's varied recordings continue to place him among the most consistent and fascinating musicians of the era. For a suggestion of Newton's range, the solo recital *Axum,* the more straight-ahead *James Newton* and *Luella* taken together should make the point. His recent releases, 1994's *Suite for Frida Kahlo* and 1997's *Above All Is Above All* are on the tiny Audioquest and Contour labels, respectively, and are difficult to find. — B.B.

HERBIE NICHOLS

★★★★ Love, Gloom, Cash, Love (1957; Bethlehem, 1994)

★★★★★ The Complete Blue Note Recordings (Blue Note, 1997)

Undeservedly caught in the shadows that fall among such '50s titans as Bud Powell, Bobby Timmons and Thelonious Monk, pianist/composer Herbie Nichols (1919–1963) was one of the most original and intensely nonformulaic voices of his day. His oeuvre was not as well covered or prolific as either Timmons's or Monk's (definitely a comment on its singularity and complexity), and his personal story not as tortured as Powell's (Nichols succumbed to leukemia), but the few sessions he recorded as leader show off his genius and secure him a permanent seat in the jazz composers pantheon.

New York–born of Caribbean heritage, Nichols was an introspective and well-read intellectual who gathered influence from both sides of the Atlantic: Scarlatti and Bartók, James P. Johnson and other stride masters all held equal sway in his ears, including the postbop angularities of his contemporaries.

One hundred seventy compositions cram the Nichols songbook, but only 42 were recorded by Nichols, who fortunately worked with the best rhythm men at his side. Bassist Chocolate Williams and drummer Shadow Wilson add rhythmic drive to his few, earliest sides as a leader for Hi-Lo in 1952 ("Who's Blues," "Nichols & Dimes"), which hint at the compositional genius to come and have, thankfully, been preserved on the Savoy anthology *The Modern Jazz Piano Album.*

Nichols's later, best-known compositional forays were recorded mostly for Blue Note in 1955 and '56. Offbeat classics like "House Party Starting," "Terpsichore," "2300 Skiddoo" and the off-the-wall, unpredictable "The Gig" all exhibit the jagged melodic lines, stop-start rhythm shifts, playfulness and humor that are standard Nichols delights. All these titles and others (including his best-known tune, "Lady Sings the Blues") are collected on the three-CD set of master and alternate takes. The 48 tracks, which feature bassists Al McKibbon and Teddy Kotick and drummers Art Blakey and Max Roach, constitute the pinnacle of Nichols's genius. (All is truly better than nothing at all, and though pricey, *The Complete Blue Note Recordings* really is the best—and virtually only—choice on the racks.)

Love, Gloom, Cash, Love reveals Nichols in 1957 equally well accompanied by George Duvivier and Dannie Richmond and includes such stellar compositions as "Portrait of Ucha," the waltzlike title track and well-executed covers (particularly "All the Way" and "Too Close for Comfort") that catch him in a slightly more mainstream but no less individual light.

Though Nichols recorded exclusively in trio format, an expanded lineup was an unfulfilled dream. In 1995 the Buell Neidlinger–produced *Blue Chopsticks* on K2B2 Records satisfied Nichols's hospital-phone request to the bassist/cellist to have his strongest tunes recorded in a horns-and-strings context. The first of two notable tributes, this collection, a four-star session, further reveals Nichols's classical underpinnings, rhythm play and compositional mastery. Pianist Frank Kimbrough leads the Herbie Nichols Project (saxist/clarinetist Ted Nash, trumpeter Ron Horton, bassist Ben Allison and drummer Jeff Ballard) on the other tribute, *Love Is Proximity* (Soul Note, 1997), which is a less academic, more interpretive, freewheeling collection. — A.K.

ROBERT NIGHTHAWK

★★★★ **Masters of Modern Blues (with Houston Stackhouse) (1968; Testament, 1994)**

★★★½ **Live on Maxwell Street (1980; Rounder, 1991)**

If Elmore James lit the flame that fires electric slide guitar to this day, Robert Nighthawk (né Robert Lee McCullum, 1909–1967) took that flame and made it blow cool, giving it depth and subtlety. A master of the single-string slide style, tutoring Earl Hooker and influencing many other slidesters to come, Nighthawk was the stepping stone between the hokum Chicago blues of Tampa Red and the deeper, amplified style of Muddy Waters and his generation.

It's no surprise, then, that he began his career in the '30s as Robert Lee McCoy, a Bluebird label mate of Red's, leading the Nighthawk Trio. (His recordings as leader from this era can be found on the import label Wolf/Document.) But Nighthawk's most compelling work—updated Delta standards like "Maggie Campbell," deep blues like "Black Angel Blues," and the sublime "Crying Won't Help You"—are his Aristocrat, Chess and United recordings of the late '40s and early '50s. The five-star *Bricks in My Pillow* collects the best of his United tracks, and although available only on vinyl or cassette, it remains the only reissue of his material from this period. Many of these songs and more were redone in 1964 for the excellent Testament set, *Masters of Modern Blues,* with able support from guitarist Johnny Young and harmonicist Big John Wrencher. Blues archivist Norman Dayron caught the live 1964 set, with Carey Bell replacing Wrencher and Robert Whitehead on drums. The interview and home recording of "Kansas City" ending *Live on Maxwell Street* is as intimate a snapshot of a bluesman sharing his craft as one can get—easily worth the price of admission. — A.K.

THE NIGHTHAWKS

★★½ **Open All Night (1976/1977; Genes, 1995)**

★★★ **Live (1976/1977; Genes, 1995)**

★★ **Jacks & Kings, Vols. 1 and 2 (1978/1979; Genes, N.A.)**

★★★ **Ten Years Live (1983; Varrick/Rounder, 1991)**

★★½ **Rock 'n' Roll (1983; Varrick/Rounder, 1990)**

★½ **Hard Living (Varrick/Rounder, 1986)**

★★ **Best of the Nighthawks (Genes, 1990)**

★★½ **Trouble (Powerhouse, 1991)**

★★½ **Rock This House (Big Mo, 1993)**

★★★ **Pain & Paradise (Big Mo, 1996)**

★★★ **Times Four (Genes, 1997)**

★★★ **Side Pocket Shot (Genes, 1997)**

Formed in Washington, D.C., in 1972 by vocalist and harp player Mark Wenner and guitarist Jimmy Thackery, the Nighthawks mix Chicago-influenced blues, R&B and rock, and have earned the dubious distinction of "the world's greatest bar band." *Open All Night* features the Nighthawks running through competent versions of standards like "Big Boss Man" and "Shake Your Money Maker," while one track, "Red Hot Mama," was recorded live with Pinetop Perkins on piano. *Jacks & Kings Vols. 1 and 2* compiles two previously released Adelphi LPs onto one disc. Special guests include Perkins, Bob Margolin and Luther "Guitar Junior" Johnson, among others, as the group runs through spirited though forgettable versions of Chuck Berry's "Little Queenie," Elmore James's "The Sky Is Crying" and Percy Mayfield's "Love Me or Leave Me."

Ten Years Live showcases the Nighthawks' original material, including the funky "Metropolitan Avenue," the raucous "Jenny Lou" and the tense, slide-guitar–fueled "Destination," on which Thackery does his best impersonation of Elvis Presley's vocal style. *Rock 'n' Roll* was originally released on Aladdin Records, and it unleashes another diverse mixture of material, from Willie Dixon's "Bring It on Home" to Whitfield and Strong's "Can't Get Next to You" to Jagger and Richards's "Memo from Turner." On *Hard Living* the Nighthawks welcome keyboardist/vocalist Greg Wetzel into the lineup. The release contains only one original, as the group again finds different sources for material, including Jesse Winchester ("High Ball"), Eddie Hinton ("Yeah Man") and the Everly Brothers ("The Price of Love"). But despite its solid material, this record sounds derivative at best and at worst uninspired, as if the smoke in all those bars is finally getting the combo down.

Best of the Nighthawks taps the band's six Adelphi LPs for its songs, while *Trouble* is the group's first album after the departure of Thackery, who is replaced on guitar by Danny Morris. Margolin also adds his guitar talents to the album, which benefits from the lineup switch. *Rock This House* is a live album recorded in Virginia, showcasing the group's forte: its live show. You can almost feel the sweat dripping from the ceiling as the Nighthawks run through a bevy of up-tempo numbers. With yet another guitarist, Pete Kanaras, *Pain & Paradise* shows a freshness in its funkified version of Frank Zappa's "Trouble Comin' Every Day" and Dixon's "Same Thing." Never short on skillful players, the Nighthawks are a primary example of a band whose spirited fare translates much better in a live setting than it does on album. — B.R.H.

RED NORVO

★★ **Live from the Blue Gardens (1942; MusicMasters, 1992)**
★★★½ **Good Vibes (1944; Drive Archive, 1997)**
★★★ **The Red Norvo Trio (1954; Original Jazz Classics, 1991)**
★★★ **The Forward Look (1957; Reference, 1991)**
★★½ **The Red Norvo Trios (Prestige, 1995)**
★★★½ **The Red Norvo Trio with Tal Farlow and Charles Mingus (Savoy, 1995)**

Illinois's Red Norvo (b. 1908) has enjoyed a long career in the mainstream of jazz vibraphone playing. As a house musician at NBC Radio in the early 1930s, Norvo played with many of the great swing bands. Among his credits he claims the first jazz mallet solos on record, dating from 1933. Norvo and his first wife, singer Mildred Bailey, formed a popular duo ("Mr. and Mrs. Swing") in the late '30s. Norvo sticks to xylophone (his first professional instrument) on the World War II–era *Live from the Blue Gardens,* a radio transcription of dance music played by a 19-piece wind orchestra that includes vocalists Helen Ward and Kay Allen. With Lionel Hampton's success as a vibist and the instrument's louder volume, Norvo permanently switched to vibraphone in 1943, the year most of the tracks on *Good Vibes* were recorded. The recordings feature smaller bands (mostly an octet and some extra tracks with a sextet).

In 1949 Norvo moved to California and formed his first trio. From then on he led numerous small groups, characteristically trios with guitar and bass, and intermittently withdrew from the music scene. Norvo's early-'50s trios, first with Charles Mingus and Tal Farlow and later with Red Mitchell and Jimmy Raney, were standouts. His combo act became a Las Vegas lounge staple during the mid- to late '50s.

A measure of commercial success did not prevent the vibist from fashioning some sophisticated music. Norvo plays middle-of-the-road, old-fashioned standards with a lively feel and a style ranging from hot swing to bebop lite. But he is no moldy fig, as his use of altered scales and unusual melodic embellishments demonstrates. His four-mallet vibe style together with guitar and bass create a linear, melodic sound with a thin, shimmering timbre and a rhythmic propulsion midway between stomp and swing. The formula can get pretty hokey but generally comes off well thanks to Norvo's dexterity and some of the great musicians who worked with him.

On the trio recordings, Mitchell's work is consistently excellent, while the combination of Farlow's melodic agility and lightning runs with Mingus's clarity and strength carries the vibist's comping and leads most admirably.

The Forward Look captures a cooking New Year's Eve show by Norvo's quintet (a group he'd formed to play Vegas with Frank Sinatra), recorded impromptu and complete with crowd ambiance on an early three-channel stereo tape recorder. — T.M.

NRBQ

★★★½ **Scraps (1972; Rounder, 1994)**
★★★★ **Uncommon Denominators (1992; Rounder, N.A.)**
★★★½ **All Hopped Up (1977; Rounder, 1994)**
★★★★ **At Yankee Stadium (1978; Mercury, 1988)**
★★★ **Kick Me Hard (1979; Rounder, 1989)**
★★★★ **Tiddlywinks (1980; Rounder, 1989)**
★★★ **Grooves in Orbit (1983; Rhino, 1990)**
★★★ **Tapdancin' Bats (1983; Rhino, 1990)**
★★★ **God Bless Us All (Rounder, 1987)**
★★★ **Diggin' Uncle Q (Rounder, 1989)**
★★★★½ **Peek-a-Boo: The Best of NRBQ 1969–89 (Rhino, 1990)**
★★★½ **Stay with We: The Best of NRBQ (Columbia, 1993)**
★★★★ **Tokyo: Recorded Live at On Air West Tokyo (Rounder, 1997)**
★★★★ **You're Nice People You Are (Rounder, 1997)**

★★★★ **You Gotta Be Loose (Rounder, 1998)**

There are not many musicians with the imagination, courage and chops to even attempt to bring together as many musical styles as has keyboardist/composer Terry Adams with his 30-year-old-and-counting combo NRBQ. Begun as the New Rhythm and Blues Quintet in 1967 (later to become a Quartet), the 'Q has always dug deep into the musical landscape, particularly the rich motherlodes of jazz and blues. Devotees of the avant-jazz of Sun Ra's Arkestra and Thelonious Monk, the band (Joey Spampinato on vocals and bass, Tom Ardolino on drums and, most recently, Johnny Spampinato on vocals and guitar) can careen effortlessly from the complex melodies and rhythms inspired by the latter (Arkestra members sometimes guest-star at 'Q gigs) to the meaty rawness of blues shouters. Somehow, when this deep-seated musical variety was woven into their own repertoire, the result proved seamless and NRBQ remain one of the finest examples of ace ensemble musicianship to this day.

The band's once-extensive catalog unfortunately is only available in bits and pieces on CD. Still, every phase of its career can be heard on what exists. The original group, with guitarist Steve Ferguson and vocalist Frank Gadler, can be heard on the Columbia anthology *Stay with We,* which covers the years 1969 through 1971 and includes a cover of Sun Ra's "Rocket #9" and some cuts from an early collaboration with Carl Perkins. Guitarist/songwriter/vocalist Al Anderson joined in 1971 (with first Ferguson, then Gadler departing), and the band's repertoire became a mixed bag of Anderson and Adams material. Anderson veered more toward country blues and Adams leaned toward avant-garde jazz (though both have written plenty of catchy pop-rock songs); all of the above can be found on the rollicking *Scraps,* eclectic *All Hopped Up* (upon which current drummer Tom Ardolino joined) and superb *At Yankee Stadium,* the best of the group's '70s releases in print. Rhino's excellent, two-CD *Peek-a-Boo* culls all the greatest cuts from the '70s and '80s albums.

Since Anderson left the group in 1994, the band has continued to perform with Joey Spampinato's brother on guitar. Throughout, Adams has pursued other projects, including compiling the Thelonious Monk album *Always Know* in 1979, producing albums for Boozoo Chavis and Johnnie Johnson and touring and recording with Carla Bley.

God Bless Us All, Diggin' Uncle Q, Tokyo and *You Gotta Be Loose* capture NRBQ doing what they do best: rocking the house with their incomparable mix of R&B, blues, jazz, pop, avant-garde and rock & roll. — H.G.-W.

ANITA O'DAY

★★★ **This Is Anita (1956; Verve, N.A.)**
★★ **Pick Yourself Up with Anita O'Day (1956; Verve, 1992)**
★★★ **Anita O'Day Sings the Most (1957; Verve, N.A.)**
★★★ **I Get a Kick Out of You (1975; Evidence, 1993)**
★★½ **Mello'day (1978; GNP Crescendo, 1992)**
★★ **In a Mellow Tone (DRG, 1989)**
★★★ **Anita O'Day Sings the Winners (Verve, 1990)**
★★★½ **Anita O'Day Swings Cole Porter (Verve, 1991)**
★★★½ **Anita O'Day at Vine Street Live (DRG, 1991)**
★★★½ **I Told Ya I Love Ya, Now Get Out (Signature, 1991)**
★★ **Compact Jazz (Verve, 1993)**
★★★ **Rules of the Road (Pablo, 1993)**
★★★ **Verve Jazz Masters 49 (Verve, 1995)**
★★★ **Jazz 'Round Midnight (Verve, 1997)**

Vocalist Anita O'Day (b. 1919) began singing during the swing era, earning great popularity in the early 1940s fronting Gene Krupa's powerful dance band. O'Day's full-bodied, husky voice and blues feeling stood in dramatic contrast to the standard white female vocalist sound of the time. In 1944 and '45 she further enhanced her reputation while fronting the Stan Kenton Orchestra, recording the celebrated "And Her Tears Flowed Like Wine."

I Told Ya I Love Ya, Now Get Out is a collection of some of the earliest recordings O'Day made under her own name in the late '40s. By the 1950s, she was recording for Verve while in the throes of a deep heroin and alcohol addiction, as related in her autobiography, *High Times, Hard Times.* The best examples of this work are *Anita O'Day Sings the Most* and the compilation *Anita O'Day Swings Cole Porter,* a collection of big-band recordings done for the label.

O'Day's comeback years following a self-imposed exile to cure her addiction produced several impressive recordings. The dazzle of her youth was tempered by a survivor's knowledge that added emotional depth to her performances, particularly on *I Get a Kick Out of You, Anita O'Day At Vine Street Live* and *Rules of the Road.* — J.S.

DAVID O'ROURKE

★★★★½ **The Prize (Night Town, 1997)**

Irish guitarist David O'Rourke (b. 1954) is a gifted player and visionary bandleader who performed with various groups in the New York area before releasing his debut as a leader, *The Prize.* The natural flow of his rhythmically supple style shows his dedication to Grant Green, while his harmonic sophistication and compositional strength reflect the influence of Wes Montgomery, Pat Martino and Joe Pass.
— J.S.

ODETTA

★★★★ **Odetta Sings Ballads and Blues (1956; Tradition/Rykodisc, 1996)**
★★★★½ **Odetta and the Blues (1962; Original Blues Classics, 1991)**
★★★½ **At Town Hall (1963; Vanguard, 1992)**
★★★★ **My Eyes Have Seen (Vanguard, 1963)**

★★★★ The Essential Odetta (Vanguard, 1973)

★★★★ The Tin Angel (Original Blues Classics, 1993)

Born in Birmingham, Alabama, in 1930, folk-blues legend Odetta Gordon got her professional start in San Francisco in the early '50s. With her resonant contralto and repertoire of work songs, blues, folk standards, spirituals and love ballads, she soon established a reputation on the club circuit as an electrifying performer.

In 1953–1954 Odetta played at a Bay Area club called the Tin Angel, where she met singer and banjo player Larry Mohr, who soon began backing her. *The Tin Angel,* recorded during that time, features several of the duo's live performances (notably "No More Cane on the Brazos" and Woody Guthrie's "The Car-Car Song") along with studio tracks. Highlights include Lead Belly's "Old Cotton Fields at Home," which spotlights their fantastic vocal harmonies and Mohr's metronomic banjo work, and a parched version of Sam Gary and Josh White's "Timber," one of six previously unissued tracks.

Odetta Sings Ballads and Blues features the solo Odetta's voice and guitar, a combination that sounds as compelling today as it did 40 years ago. Among the highlights are "Alabama Bound," "Jack O' Diamonds" and the transcendent California gold-rush anthem "Santy Anno," which Odetta belts out with an unbridled authority. A suite of "Oh Freedom," "Come and Go with Me" and "I'm on My Way" closes the album, leaving the listener spiritually refueled, yet ready to hear more.

Odetta and the Blues is a woozy, impassioned success, with the playing of Buck Clayton (trumpet), Vic Dickenson (trombone) and Herb Hall (clarinet) giving it a liquid, New Orleans–jazz pulse, while Dick Wellstood's piano playing and arrangements lend a sprightly, woozy snap to the proceedings. Odetta covers Leroy Carr's "How Long Blues," Jimmie Cox's "Nobody Knows You When You're Down and Out" and the work of such classic female blues singers as Ma Rainey ("Yonder Comes the Blues"), Ida Cox ("Hard, Oh Lord") and her biggest influence, Bessie Smith ("Weeping Willow Blues").

Both *At Town Hall* and *My Eyes Have Seen,* with Odetta backed by Bill Lee on bass, emphasize her folk-music repertoire. The former includes spirituals ("Let Me Ride," "He's Got the Whole World in His Hands," "What Month Was Jesus Born In"), work songs ("Take This Hammer," "Timber") and a trilogy of children's songs. *My Eyes Have Seen* features similar material, such as fantastic versions of "Motherless Children," "Ox Driver Song" and "Battle Hymn of the Republic." *The Essential Odetta* collects her career high points, including such traditional fare as "If I Had a Hammer," "Another Man Done Gone," "No More Auction Block for Me" and a version of Jimmy Driftwood's "He Had a Long Chain On."
— B.R.H.

ANDREW "BIG VOICE" ODOM

★★★★½ Feel So Good (1983; Evidence, 1993)

★★★★ Goin' to California (Flying Fish, 1992)

Andrew "Big Voice" or "B.B." Odom (1936–1991) is virtually unrecognized as one of the greatest blues singers of his generation. His uncanny resemblance to B.B. King led him to be nicknamed "B.B. Junior," but Odom was no cheap knockoff; his gospel training and sweet, powerful voice enabled him to transcend the King influence into his own realm of creative soulfulness.

Originally from Denham Springs, Louisiana, Odom sang in Albert King's St. Louis–based band during the 1950s before moving in 1960 to Chicago, where he became a fixture on the local blues scene until his death, playing constantly at clubs and at the Maxwell Street market on Sundays.

Odom recordings, however, are rare. He sang with Earl Hooker's band, then with Jimmy Dawkins, and made several currently unavailable recordings under his own name for minor labels.

Feel So Good, fortunately, is a masterpiece, recorded in 1982 for the French label Isabel. The title track, a spirited, gospel-influenced romp, is one of five Odom songs on the set. (Though it is listed as the opening number in the liner notes, it is actually the last track on this reissue.) The key to understanding Odom's relationship to King is that while he was unafraid to pay tribute to the influence on up-tempo numbers, recording King's "Woke Up This Morning," he had his own strengths as well, excelling on the sultry, tension-filled slow blues of "I Made Up My Mind" and "Reconsider Baby." With Magic Slim and John Primer on guitars and Lucky Peterson on piano and organ, Odom gets superb backing for his impassioned vocals; Slim's solo on "Memo Blues," Odom's elegy to a fallen friend, is a classic in its own right. Little Milton also contributes to the session, sharing the vocals with Odom on "Mother-in-Law Blues." *Goin' to California* was recorded with the Canadian blues band the Gold Tops the year before Odom died. — J.S.

OLD AND NEW DREAMS

★★★★★ Old and New Dreams (Black Saint, 1976)
★★★ Old and New Dreams (1979; ECM, 1994)
★★★★★ Playing (1982; ECM, 1994)
★★★★ A Tribute to Blackwell (Black Saint, 1990)

The excellent cooperative quartet of former Ornette Coleman sidemen Don Cherry (pocket trumpet, piano), Dewey Redman (tenor sax, musette), Charlie Haden (bass) and Ed Blackwell (drums) rates a separate listing of its own. The quartet's repertoire remained strong from its debut on Black Saint to its dissolution in 1990, with a fairly even mix of music contributed by Coleman and originals from within the band.

The ECM *Old and New Dreams* is a bit disappointing, however, with too much stress on ethnic re-creations and whale-song impressions and a version of "Lonely Woman" that suffers by comparison with the original. Things are back on track with *Playing,* a 1980 Austrian concert with the musicians concentrating once again on intense blowing. Redman is particularly impressive here, a forceful presence in a position that could have passed as a mere stand-in slot for Coleman.

Though gravely ill at the time of the 1990 live recording *A Tribute to Blackwell,* the drummer excels and dominates the proceedings here, with a dynamic performance of Coleman's "Happy House," originally recorded by the group on *Playing.* — B.B.

SY OLIVER

★★★★ Oliver's Twist/Easy Walker (1960/1962; Mobile Fidelity, 1995)

Trumpeter and arranger Melvin James "Sy" Oliver (1910–1988) came to prominence as a performer and arranger with the Tommy Dorsey band. Beside the relentless swing his arrangements generate, their clear, intuitive lines have a conversational flow that encourages harmonic ingenuity and allows the players plenty of room to move inside the powerful rhythms. Though Oliver wrote commercial swing arrangements, his conception was so forward-looking that, in the late '90s, the Mingus Big Band still explores the contours of his work at its weekly jazz workshops at the New York nightclub the Fez. — J.S.

OREGON

★★★★ Music of Another Present Era (1973; Vanguard, 1988)
★★★½ Distant Hills (1974; Vanguard, 1991)
★★★★ Winter Light (1974; Vanguard, 1990)
★★★ Friends (1977; Vanguard, 1995)
★★★ Out of the Woods (1978; Discovery, 1992)
★★★ Roots in the Sky (1979; Discovery, 1992)
★★★★ Oregon (1983; ECM, 1994)
★★★½ Crossing (1985; ECM, 1994)
★★½ Ecotopia (1987; ECM, 1994)
★★★ The Essential Oregon (Vanguard, 1991)
★★★½ Beyond Words (Chesky, 1995)
★★★½ Northwest Passage (Intuition, 1997)

The members of Oregon originally began playing together as part of the Paul Winter Consort, but Oregon ended up eclipsing its parent group. Ralph Towner, Paul McCandless, Glen Moore and Collin Walcott all played a wide range of instruments, but the primary sound consists of Towner's guitars, McCandless's reeds, Moore's bass and Walcott's percussion. The band's use of Indian percussion, Eastern modalities and classical compositional formalities makes it an innovator in world music, but the improvisational elements stay close to the conventions of jazz.

The Vanguard albums consist of dreamlike program music, apparently closely aligned to cultural trends of the 1970s but in retrospect far more universal. *Music of Another Present Era* and *Distant Hills* are dramatic introductions to Towner's impressionistic soundscapes. *Winter Light* is highlighted by a transcendent performance of Jim Pepper's Native American jazz hymn "Witchi-Tai-To." *The Essential Oregon* is an unsatisfying overview of the Vanguard years.

The band's sensibility turned out to be prescient. Oregon fit the aesthetic direction of ECM hand in glove, and indeed the individual members went on to be involved in many other

ECM projects. *Oregon* found the band reinventing itself in the sleek world of studio postmodernism; the world had caught up to the band's exacting vision of a music without borders. *Crossing* is slightly less compelling, and whether this was a momentary lapse will never be known because Walcott died in a car crash just before the album's release; Tabla specialist Trilok Gurtu replaced him, but Oregon fell into a lengthy creative slump. McCandless, Towner and Moore rekindled their collective fire on the 1990s recordings *Beyond Words* and *Northwest Passage*. — J.S.

EDWARD "KID" ORY

★★★★ Kid Ory's Creole Jazz Band (1955; Good Time Jazz, 1992)
★★★★★ The Legendary Kid (1956; Good Time Jazz, 1990)
★★★★ This Kid's the Greatest (1962; Good Time Jazz, 1992)
★★★½ Favorites! (Good Time Jazz, 1986)
★★★★★ Kid Ory's Creole Jazz Band 1944/45 (Good Time Jazz, 1991)
★★★★ Kid Ory's Creole Jazz Band 1954 (Good Time Jazz, 1991)

Groundbreaking musical stylist, bandleader and trombonist Edward "Kid" Ory (1886–1973) eventually became a musical historian whose importance remains underrecognized. Ory is almost solely responsible for creating the trombone's crucial role in Dixieland ensemble playing, providing the deep, resonant foundation for the cornet/trumpet and clarinet interlace, gliding behind and through the chunking banjo/drums rhythm section to add that magical, slinky syncopation and codifying the growling drive and ribald humor for which New Orleans jazz came to be known.

Ory's band was, along with Freddie Keppard's group, one of the first of the great Dixieland ensembles in New Orleans right after the turn of the century. With cornetist Joseph "King" Oliver as his featured soloist, Ory's band terrorized local groups who engaged in bandwagon cutting sessions on the streets of New Orleans to promote their gigs. Louis Armstrong recalled having his group embarrassed by Ory, and when Oliver moved to Chicago, Armstrong replaced him in the Creole Band. Ory's groups also included a series of great clarinetists—Johnny Dodds, Sidney Bechet, Jimmie Noone and George Lewis.

Despite Ory's tremendous reputation as a bandleader, the only material available from his heyday as the greatest trombonist of 1920s jazz is as a sideman. But what a sideman! Ory is featured on recordings with Oliver, Jelly Roll Morton's Red Hot Peppers and Louis Armstrong's Hot Five, appearing on his own song "Muskrat Ramble."

Ory retired from performing in the 1930s, only to make a dramatic comeback in the mid-'40s, when he was one of the most influential figures spearheading the then-controversial Dixieland revival. The albums listed above begin in that period, starting with *Kid Ory's Creole Jazz Band 1944/45,* recorded by Nesuhi Ertegun for Crescent. These recordings, featuring Mutt Carey on trumpet, Omer Simeon on clarinet, Buster Wilson on piano, Bud Scott on banjo and vocals, Ed Garland on bass and several different drummers, mark a milestone in jazz history, offering some of the first proof that, rather than a passing fad linked to pop styles, jazz was informed by a classical tradition of its own, worth not just preserving but reviving as well.

Subsequent albums show that on both Dixieland and blues material Ory remained a vital player into his 70s and was certainly one of the more brilliant lights in American music. — J.S.

ANDERS OSBORNE

★★★½ Break the Chain (Rabadash, 1994)
★★★½ Which Way to Here (Okeh, 1995)
★★★★ Live at Tipitina's (Shanachie, 1997)

When he moved to New Orleans from his native Sweden in 1987, Anders Osborne (b. 1966) sounded like Lowell George reincarnated. Osborne possesses the best qualities of the late beloved Little Feat founder and front man: He's a gifted songwriter with an idiosyncratic voice steeped in free-flowing phrasing, and his slide-guitar playing slinks along the musical path blazed on classic George compositions such as "Two Trains." These traits are especially in evidence on Osborne's *Break the Chain,* an independently produced release worth tracking down for hook-filled songs such as "I'm Back In" and "Right on the Money."

Osborne's major-label debut, *Which Way to Here,* finds him moving away from the Little Feat comparisons by using a broader musical canvas. There's still a healthy chunk of funky New Orleans–influenced rhythms on "Pleasin' You" and "Burnin' on the Inside," but Osborne also presents two beautiful acoustic-based tracks, the autobiographical "Limestone Bay" and the tender ballad "Don't Leave Me." "Blame It on a Few" is a frank assessment of the Crescent City's street-singing scene, with a bluesy, boozy arrangement to match. "What's Going On Here (Big Lies)" is the stunner of the album, a powerful slice of blue-eyed soul that's still smoldering as it fades at the six-minute mark. *Live at Tipitina's* documents Osborne's ingenious combination of Delta blues with New Orleans second-line brass band music. — S.J.

JOHNNY OTIS

★★★ The New Johnny Otis Show (Alligator, 1981)
★★★★ The Capitol Years (Capitol, 1989)
★★★★ Spirit of the Black Territory Bands (Arhoolie, 1992)
★★★★★ The Johnny Otis Show Live at Monterey! (Epic/Legacy, 1993)
★★★★★ The Complete Savoy Recordings with Johnny Otis (Savoy, N.A.)

Johnny Otis, born John Veliotes in 1921 of Greek immigrant parents who settled in Vallejo, California, is a true renaissance figure in music history. For one, he had the talent to be a major artist in his own right (his 1958 Top 10 hit "Willie and the Hand Jive" is a classic), and indeed, he recorded prolifically for Savoy and Capitol and was a bona fide star on the R&B circuit. As a songwriter, he has cut a wide swath: He wrote all of Esther Phillips's early hits on Savoy, as well as "Dance with Me, Henry" with Etta James, "Every Beat of My Heart" for Gladys Knight and "So Fine" for the Fiestas. He's also credited with producing Big Mama Thornton's early version of Leiber and Stoller's "Hound Dog."

In the big picture, Otis has been the most selfless of artists, content to boost others' careers without ever seeming to push his own, except behind the scenes. He was one of the first, if not *the* first, to package blues and R&B artists and take them on the road as a traveling all-star show. A smart judge of artistry, Otis, in his revues, typically featured some unknown singer bound for glory. Esther Phillips, Hank Ballard, Jackie Wilson, Little Willie John, Etta James and Big Mama Thornton were only a few of the names with whom Otis was associated (or vice versa) in the '50s.

Otis's early recordings, available on the Capitol and Savoy releases, represent some of the finest examples of early rhythm & blues. A multi-instrumentalist, Otis began his career in 1939 as a drummer with the West Oakland Houserockers; throughout the '40s he toured the country in various big bands before forming the Johnny Otis Orchestra in 1945 and cutting a national hit with "Harlem Nocturne," a beautiful, noirish instrumental modeled on a Duke Ellington arrangement of the original Earle Hagen song. Touring with the likes of the Ink Spots and Louis Jordan, Otis and his band became a big-ticket item; by 1950 he was the best-selling R&B recording artist in the country, even as he followed other big bands in paring down to a smaller configuration—getting leaner as the music itself did so—and moved toward a rawer, bluesier sound. *The Complete Savoy Recordings* documents this fruitful early era of Otis's career and will convince any doubters that he stood toe-to-toe with the era's finest big bands. The leaner, built-for-speed period, which produced the eternally fresh "Willie and the Hand Jive" and other distinguished late-'50s efforts, is the focus of *The Capitol Years.*

Being in or out of the spotlight never seems to bother Otis. When his style of music was pushed off the charts in the '60s, he surfaced now and then with an all-stops-out show that was at once a glorious celebration of hard-driving R&B and of roots rock & roll, with his gifted guitarist son, Shuggie, standing out among the stellar cast of instrumentalists. Offstage, other pursuits occupied Otis's time: He became a community activist, was a preacher for a while, a painter, a sculptor. Still, music remains a focal point, and there are three fine albums in print that show Otis and his troupe in splendid form through the years. In 1970 he appeared at the Monterey Jazz Festival with a lineup that overshadowed even his finest aggregations in the '40s or '50s. Beginning with a rousing version of "Willie and the Hand Jive," *The Johnny Otis Show Live at Monterey!* provides a note-perfect showcase for some of the acknowledged giants of R&B: No sooner have the last notes of "Hand Jive" ended than does Esther Phillips step forward for a tough version of "Cry Me a River." Joe Turner retires the nickname "Boss of the Blues" on two cuts, "I Got a Gal" and "Plastic Man." One of the set's most elegant touches comes courtesy of the gentleman singer Ivory Joe Hunter, who offers a mellow, moving reprise of his hit "Since I Met You Baby," and a couple of cuts later Roy Brown comes blowing in with a torrid "Good Rockin' Tonight." It goes on: Roy Milton rocks the house on two cuts; alto-sax innovator Eddie "Cleanhead" Vinson blows up a storm on his hit, "Kidney Stew"; Pee Wee Crayton launches into a raging take on "The Things I Used to Do." Can't beat this one, no matter how fine an effort is made on *The New Johnny Otis Show,* which is primarily a showcase for Shuggie Otis, minus artists the caliber of those on *Live at Monterey!* There's still plenty of fire and feeling in these grooves, but the performances hardly rank with those of Turner, Hunter, Brown, Milton and others at Monterey.

In 1992 Otis went all the way back to his roots with a loving evocation and invocation of the big-band era in *Spirit of the Black Territory Bands.* The title refers to the hundreds, maybe thousands, of bands that operated a scale or two below the big names like Count Basie and Duke Ellington. Unable to afford national tours, these groups became stars in their geographical region, or territory, and rarely ventured beyond those boundaries. Having honed his chops in a number of territory bands in the '30s and '40s before going solo, Otis here pays tribute to the bracing dance music of the era preceding R&B's big-beat explosion. Lacking much original material, or playing before audiences that wanted to swing to the hot tunes of the day, the territory bands fashioned their repertoires accordingly. Thus, Count Basie's hard-driving "Swinging the Blues" opens the show here, followed by a smooth, loping "Margie," with Otis's hangdog vocal echoing as if it were reflecting off the walls of a huge ballroom. Elsewhere the band assays Duke Ellington ("The Mooche," "Sophisticated Lady" and "Creole Love Call") and Count Basie; gets down with some Kansas City boogie-woogie by way of Jay McShann's "Jumpin' the Blues," notable for Otis's sprightly workout on vibes and Brad "Baba" Pie's punchy guitar solos; and, for good measure, hauls out "Harlem Nocturne" for alto saxophonist Clifford Solomon to strut his stuff on by way of a deliberate, dark solo. This era may have vanished, but the music has lost none of its potency. — D.M.

JACK OWENS

★★★★★ **It Must Have Been the Devil (1971; Testament, 1995)**

★★★★★ **The Last Giants of the Mississippi Blues: Jack Owens & Eugene Powell (Wolf, 1993)**

Some maps don't even bother indicating the location of Bentonia, Mississippi, on the edge of the Delta, off Highway 49, on Route 433, between Jackson and Yazoo City. Devoid of stoplights, this quiet little town of modest houses and aging storefronts is hardly a tourist mecca, but it nonetheless occupies an honored position in blues history—enough so that it draws a fair share of blues enthusiasts every year to a dilapidated wooden house off a rugged dirt road on the outskirts of town. In warm weather the sole resident of this house can be found sitting on his front porch, often clad in a tan jacket that matches the color of his vinyl rocking chair, making him and his chair seem one and the same from a distance. Up close the man is indeed slight, and weathered, but steely-eyed and confident in his manner. If he is comfortable with the strangers who come to pay their respects, he welcomes them onto his porch, answers their questions and finally (after negotiating some remuneration for his time), eases an ancient acoustic guitar onto his lap and sends up a piercing, bone-chilling wail that surely can be heard across the cotton fields and into the town square. The man is Jack Owens (b. 1904), and he is, as the title of one his albums asserts, one of "the Last Giants of Mississippi Blues."

Bentonia's high standing in the blues world rests on its indigenous music. The Bentonia style is defined by its minor modes, myriad complex tunings, intricately picked guitar accompaniments, eerie, moaning vocals and lyrical focus on death, violence, the supernatural and, oh yes, unfaithful women. Skip James is the Bentonia-blues standard bearer, having brought it into the world at large with his 1931 sessions for Paramount; as well, Robert Johnson's "Hellhound on My Trail" and "Come On in My Kitchen" incorporate elements of James's "Devil Got My Woman." But there was a time when only people around Bentonia knew about Skip James; and if they knew about Skip James, they also knew about his running buddy, Jack Owens (who refers to his late friend as "Skippy" and was once married to the sister of James's wife).

One of Bentonia's most colorful characters, Owens, unlike James, never sought greener pastures elsewhere. He stayed put, farming by day, running a juke joint out of his house on weekends. As the proprietor, he not only supplied food, drink and a jukebox but became the evening's live entertainment, often performing for his customers with the sterling, uncanny harmonica support of his longtime friend and comic foil, Benjamin "Bud" Spires, son of noted Chicago bluesman Arthur "Big Boy" Spires. (In between and sometimes during songs, Spires would regale the customers with "toasties," his term for his original jokes and poems, some of which actually have punch lines.) Today the juke joint is long gone, but Owens and Spires are still around; in recent years, as blues scholars have taken note of their presence, the two musicians have on occasion journeyed away from Bentonia to play at blues festivals as far away as Seattle. Most of their shows, however, occur on Owens's front porch.

In 1970 Owens was recorded at his house by researcher David Evans, who had tracked him down in the mid-'60s after James had mentioned him in an interview. Released on vinyl in 1971, those selections (plus five others) are now available on the Testament CD, *It Must Have Been the Devil,* complete with Evans's original liner notes. Anyone familiar with Skip James's work will be struck by both the similarities and the differences in the two artists' styles. While their voices and lyrical themes are identifiably Bentonian, Owens's writing is more open-ended, less given to beginning-middle-end story development than to anecdotal observations about people and places; working in tandem with his moans, cries and swirling guitar lines, his tales gain urgency through atmosphere—Owens doesn't so much tell you what it's like to feel the devil working in your life but sets you down in a world where the air you breathe is charged with near-palpable evil. As much as any bluesman who has ever been recorded, his music recognizes a connection between humans and the sky above, the land below, the invisible, omnipotent God who brings life and death and the dark forces that speak to our basest natures.

Instrumentally, Owens attacks the guitar in a fashion James eschewed, constructing some ambitious, dexterous, sharp-picked fingerings, all hard angles, hammer-ons, stinging single notes and searing double-note bursts of feeling. And yet his playing has bounce and drive—sometimes the tempo shifts from bar to bar, but there is a pronounced rhythmic thrust to every song: The juke joints' patrons, after all, were fond of dancing, and Owens endeavored to keep his customers satisfied.

It Must Have Been the Devil contains a good number of the songs most identified with Owens—the anguished "Cherry Ball"; the field holler–styled "Can't See, Baby"; "Hard Times," a surging workout featuring guitar and harmonica in a fierce duel; the gently rendered, poignant tale of lost love "Jack Ain't Had No Water"; and of course, "It Must Have Been the Devil," his account of evil doings afoot—either inspired by or the model for James's "Devil Got My Woman"—that is the essence of deep blues, Bentonia division.

The 11-track import, *The Last Giants of Mississippi Blues,* features 7 recorded in 1980–81, 4 from 1991 and 10 tracks recorded during the same period by Eugene Powell, a Utica, Mississippi, bluesman born in 1908 whose style is equal parts Texas and the Delta, although not as riveting lyrically as Owens's. Owens is captured completely solo on six tracks; the songs recorded in 1991 team him with Spires. "Cherry Ball" is reprised here, as is "Hard Times" (twice, with and without Spires) and "Devil" (also twice, with and without Spires). Among the interesting fare: "You Leavin'," all irregular rhythm and restless mood, set up by single- and double-string runs and sliding bass notes; "No Lovin'," with its John Lee Hooker–style vamping; and the remarkable guitar-harmonica sparring between Spires and Owens on "Cool Water," in which Spires—who is most adept at reading and responding to Owens's unusual style—weaves chords and single-note exclamations around and through Owens's high, plaintive cries and busy treble-string solo runs. Today Owens and Spires sound pretty much as they do on these 1991 tracks, and they're happy to play for folks who come through Bentonia searching for them. Cash and a couple of bottles of whiskey get the music started; what happens next will change you.

— D.M.

FRANKIE PARIS

★★★½ **Right Around the Corner (Bahoomba, 1997)**

Singer Frankie Paris (b. 1941) has been a fixture on the New York blues scene for the past 20 years as one of the most frequent performers at the late, lamented all-night blues club Dan Lynch's. His tough, serrated-edge vocals are well-documented here, backed by his working quartet supported by the Blues Brothers' Alan "Mr. Fabulous" Rubin on trumpet and "Blue Lou" Marini on tenor saxophone. — J.S.

JON PARIS

★★★½ **Rock the Universe (Fountainbleu, 1995)**

Jon Paris (b. 1948), best known as a talented sideman who has worked with the likes of Johnny Winter and Robert Gordon, fronts his own band when he isn't on the road. His first solo recording, *Rock the Universe* is blues-based rock along the lines of Chuck Berry and early Rolling Stones. His originals fit seamlessly into the genre; a few carefully chosen covers are treated with feeling and respect.

Paris is a first-rate guitarist and a fine vocalist and blows some great harp, too. He shows off solid slide chops on an excellent version of Berry's "Deep Feeling," joined by Berry's pianist, Johnnie Johnson. The album doesn't quite capture the energy of Paris's live shows, which might well be an impossible task, but it does showcase the many talents of a well-rounded performer. — J.Z.

CHARLIE PARKER

★★★★ **Jazz at the Philharmonic 1946 (1946; Verve, 1992)**

★★★½ **Bird on 52nd Street (1948; Original Jazz Classics, 1984)**

★★★★ **Jazz at the Philharmonic 1949 (1949; Verve, 1993)**

★★★★ **Bird and Diz (with Dizzy Gillespie) (1950; Verve, 1986)**

★★★★ **Bird at St. Nick's (1950; Original Jazz Classics, 1983)**

★★★★ **At Storyville (1953; Blue Note, 1988)**

★★★★★ **Jazz at Massey Hall (1953; Original Jazz Classics, 1986)**

★★★★ **Bird at the Hi-Hat (1954; Capitol, 1993)**

★★★½ **Now's the Time (1957; Verve, N.A.)**

★★★★★ **Charlie Parker (1977; Verve, 1998)**

★★★★★ **Bird: The Savoy Recordings (Master Takes, 1944–1948) (Savoy, 1986)**

★★★★ **Compact Jazz (Verve, 1987)**

★★★★★ **Bird: The Complete Charlie Parker on Verve (Verve, 1988)**

★★★½ **BeBop & Bird, Vol. 1 (Hipsville/Rhino, 1988)**

★★★½ **BeBop & Bird, Vol. 2 (Hipsville/Rhino, 1988)**

★★★★ **Bird: The Original Recordings of Charlie Parker (Verve, 1988)**

★★★★★ **The Complete Charlie Parker Savoy Studio Sessions (Savoy, 1988)**

★★★½ **Charlie Parker Jam Session (Verve, 1990)**

★★★½ **The Cole Porter Songbook (Verve, 1991)**

★★★★ **Swedish Schnapps (Verve, 1991)**

★★★★ **Jazz 'Round Midnight (Verve, 1991)**

★★★ **Best of the Bird (Legacy, 1991)**

★★★★ **The Charlie Parker Story (Savoy, 1991)**

★★★★ **The Genius of Charlie Parker (Savoy, 1991)**

★★★ **Charlie Parker Memorial, Vol. 1 (Savoy, 1991)**
★★★ **The Essential Charlie Parker (Legacy, 1992)**
★★★★ **Compact Jazz: Charlie Parker Plays the Blues (Verve, 1992)**
★★★ **Charlie Parker Memorial, Vol. 2 (Savoy, 1993)**
★★★★ **Evening at Home with the Bird (Savoy, 1993)**
★★★★ **Bird Returns (Savoy, 1993)**
★★★★ **The Immortal Charlie Parker (Savoy, 1993)**
★★★ **Cravin' the Bird (Drive Archive, 1994)**
★★★★ **Verve Jazz Masters 15 (Verve, 1994)**
★★★★ **Verve Jazz Masters 28 (Verve, 1994)**
★★★★ **Bird with Strings: The Master Takes (Verve, 1995)**
★★★★ **Bird's Best Bop on Verve (Verve, 1995)**
★★★ **South of the Border (Verve, 1995)**
★★★★ **Confirmation: The Best of Charlie Parker (Verve, 1995)**
★★★ **Newly Discovered Sides (Savoy, 1996)**
★★★★★ **The Legendary Dial Masters (City Hall, 1996)**
★★★ **Bird Is Free (Collectables, 1997)**
★★★ **Bird Symbols (Collectables, 1997)**
★★★ **Happy Bird (Collectables, 1997)**
★★★ **Once There Was Bird (Collectables, 1997)**
★★★★ **Yardbird Suite: The Ultimate Charlie Parker Collection (Rhino, 1997)**

Bebop was the beginning of modern jazz, a turning point that marked its transition from dance pop to art music, and though many musicians contributed to this transformation, none galvanized this new style the way Charlie Parker (1920–1955) did. It wasn't just that he was a brilliant improviser, whose quicksilver solos suggested a world of rhythmic and harmonic possibilities; Parker's status as a jazz legend also owes more than a little to the disparity between his astonishing creativity and his dissolute personal life. Indeed, for some fans the myth matters almost as much as the music, and their hunger for pieces of that myth—especially outtakes, live recordings, even fragments of solos—has filled the Parker discography with albums of dubious origin, fidelity and worth. Complicating matters further is the fact that Parker's studio recordings have been issued and reissued in various permutations over the years, with one major chunk—his recordings for the long-defunct Dial label—frequently out of print. As such, his discography is constantly in flux, as sub–bootleg-quality concert albums drift on and off the market and his studio output goes through periodic repackaging. So rather than take a strict chronological approach, this entry will break down Parker's recorded legacy into four pieces: the Savoy recordings, the Dial recordings, the Verve recordings and a general look at air checks, concert recordings and other arcana.

As with most jazz musicians, Parker made his initial recordings as a sideman, first as a member of the Jay McShann band in 1940 and then, in 1944, as part of a quintet fronted by guitarist and vocalist Tiny Grimes. He also recorded a handful of seminal bebop sides—including performances of "Groovin' High," "Salt Peanuts" and "Hot House"—with Dizzy Gillespie, but these were all issued under Gillespie's name and can be found on *Groovin' High* (Musicraft, 1986). But the first recordings to be credited to Parker himself were a handful of tunes for Savoy by Charlie Parker's Ree Boppers, in 1945. Like most of Parker's output, these tracks—along with others recorded for Savoy in 1947–1948, are available in two packages: *Bird: The Savoy Recordings (Master Takes, 1944–1948)* and *The Complete Charlie Parker Savoy Studio Sessions.* What's the difference? With the former, what you get are the singles originally released by Savoy, including "Now's the Time," "Donna Lee," "Ko-Ko" and "Ah-Leu-Cha." But with *The Complete Charlie Parker Savoy Studio Sessions,* you get all that plus the alternate takes, fragments and false starts; moreover, there is similarly exhaustive coverage offered of Parker's sideman dates with Tiny Grimes and Miles Davis. However they're packaged, though, the Savoy recordings represent some of Parker's most consistent work—rich, bluesy and inventive, it finds him playing from strengths both in terms of his ideas and his technique. Nor are the players in his bands anything to scoff at, particularly trumpeter Miles Davis, whose harmonic agility is impressive even at this early stage.

Four months after his first Savoy session, Parker was in California recording for Ross

Russell's newly formed Dial label. These include some of Parker's most assured performances as well as some of his most troubled. Parker was deeply into drugs and turned up at his second Dial session stoked to the gills; the results, including a wobbly "Lover Man" and a disjointed, almost out-of-time reading of "The Gypsy," are deeply depressing. Tracks recorded at other Dial sessions, like "Ornithology," "Moose the Mooche," "Drifting on a Reed" and—especially—"Relaxin' at Camarillo," are truly wondrous to hear, however. Unfortunately, the complete Dial recordings (which include important 1948 New York sessions) were last in print in the late '70s, when Warner Bros. released them as *Charlie Parker,* a six-LP boxed set in anticipation of a Parker bioflick starring Richard Pryor (the film, *Bird,* was eventually made with Forest Whitaker in the title role). Highlights of the Dial dates (including the tracks mentioned above) can be found on *The Legendary Dial Masters;* an odd assortment of Dial sessions have been mixed in with the live recordings on the two-volume *BeBop & Bird.* But copies of *Charlie Parker* are well worth seeking out until another complete edition is issued.

Overall, though, Parker's largest and most diverse recordings are on Norman Granz's Verve label. These range from the freewheeling *Jazz at the Philharmonic* jams to combo dates, and from "cubop" big-band recordings with Machito and his orchestra to the lushly arranged *Bird with Strings* session. For a brief introduction, it's hard to beat *Bird: The Original Recordings of Charlie Parker,* a single CD that manages to offer samplings of all sides of his Verve output. Other recommended single albums from this period include the flashy but fun *Bird and Diz,* while the three-volume *Verve Years* sets (on LP and cassette only) cover all the highlights in chronological order. Still, serious listeners owe it to themselves to hear *Bird: The Complete Charlie Parker on Verve,* a 10-CD set with surprisingly little flab and a wealth of previously unreleased material; it's especially fascinating to hear failed experiments like the Gil Evans–arranged 1953 session that found Bird accompanied by strings and mixed chorus (including Dave Lambert and Annie Ross).

From there, we move to the dicey realm of concert recordings. Buying a Charlie Parker live album is often like making a deal with the devil—you may hear some incredible playing, but you pay for the privilege in bad sound and dubious credits. *Jazz at Massey Hall* is the only exception, and this quintet recording—featuring Gillespie, Bud Powell, Charles Mingus, Max Roach and Parker, billed for contractual reasons as "Charlie Chan"—is one of the very best; *At Storyville* is also relatively well recorded, though the playing isn't quite as sparkling. But *Bird on 52nd Street* and *Bird at St. Nick's* offer stalwart performances with abysmal sound; there's heavy distortion throughout the "Live at Birdland" portions of *BeBop & Bird.* — J.D.C.

JUNIOR PARKER

★★★★ **The Best of Junior Parker (MCA, 1973)**
★★★½ **Mystery Train (Rounder, 1990)**
★★★★ **Junior's Blues: The Duke Recordings, Vol. 1 (MCA, 1992)**

The circuitous route that brought West Memphis, Arkansas, native Herman "Junior" Parker (1932–1971) to prominence in the R&B field originated in an impulse. During a 1948 concert, Sonny Boy Williamson (Rice Miller) asked his audience if there was a harmonica player in the house. Parker jumped onstage, and a career was under way. He toured the rest of the year with Williamson and in 1949 joined Howlin' Wolf's band (featuring Ike Turner on piano), which he was fronting two years later after Wolf began a short-lived retirement. By 1952 he had his own group, the Blue Flames, and a recording contract with Modern. But it was a move to Memphis's Sun label in 1953 that got things going full throttle, when Parker's self-penned "Feelin' Good," a driving boogie assault in the style of John Lee Hooker, became a substantial R&B hit.

But though Parker could sell a raucous workout, his deep, hoarse, rough-edged voice was an effective instrument when employed in service of a sorrowful blues lyric, as is demonstrated to good effect on the flip side of "Feelin' Good," a jazzy, urban lament titled "Fussin' and Fightin' (Blues)." In fact, Parker's Sun tenure, brief as it was, showed him to have considerable potential as a balladeer that was insufficiently exploited throughout his career. No matter what else he did at Sun, though, Parker's place in history was secured by way of an eerie, recondite slow blues he wrote and recorded in 1953, "Mystery Train." It's not quite a shuffle, not quite a boogie, but a little of both; Parker's vocal is all dark tones and conflicting emotions, as if he were describing an event he fears but has accepted as inevitable; baritone-sax player Kenneth Banks approximates the train's steady drone of a warning whistle; and the lyrics extend the inscrutability of it all by leaving open the question of whether the lover Parker sings of is dead, leaving him or coming back. Two years later Elvis Presley stood in the same studio where Parker had recorded and, with Scotty Moore on guitar and Bill Black on bass, reconsidered "Mystery Train" in terms so emotionally and instrumentally searing that his and his band's performance became something akin to a gold standard by which all other rock & roll recordings would be measured. Rounder's *Mystery Train* encompasses the title song and eight other Parker Sun recordings (four of them making their first appearance on a domestic release), as well as three Sun cuts by James Cotton, including the epochal, defiant 1954 recording of "Cotton Crop Blues," featuring guitarist Pat Hare's blistering solo; and two previously unissued Hare solo recordings ("Bonus Pay" and the prescient "I'm Gonna Murder My Baby," which he did—murder his girlfriend, that is—six years later, for which he was sentenced to 99 years in prison; one of the most gifted of the many exceptional musicians who walked into the Memphis Recording Service studio on Union Avenue, he died behind bars in 1980).

In 1954 Parker jumped to the Duke label, where he had a productive decadelong stay that saw him landing consistently in the upper reaches of the chart as he lit the transitional path from R&B to rock & roll, both in his swaggering, bluesy vocal style and in the work of his newly acquired guitarist, Hare, whose forceful style and use of distortion as a complementary voice marked his forward-looking sound. Parker's Duke years are chronicled on two sets from MCA, *The Best of Junior Parker* and the more ambitious *Junior's Blues: The Duke Recordings, Vol. 1.* Both sets include the artist's three Top 10 R&B hits: "Next Time You See Me" (1957), "Annie Get Your Yo-Yo" (1962) and the towering "Driving Wheel" (1961). Of note as well is Parker's "Stand By Me," which in feel and sentiment would seem to have been the inspiration for the like-titled Ben E. King classic from 1961.

Recording for a variety of small labels (and one major, Capitol) after leaving Duke, Parker managed no further major hits, although his singles from time to time did edge onto the R&B chart. He died following surgery for a brain tumor. Though his post-Duke recordings are now out of print, versions pop up now and then and are worthwhile, if not essential, investments. — D.M.

LEON PARKER

★★★ Above & Below (Epicure/Columbia, 1994)
★★★★ Belief (Columbia, 1996)
★★★ Awakening (Columbia, 1998)

Drummer Leon Parker (b. 1965) gained much attention in the 1990s for tossing aside many elements of the traditional jazz drum kit, paring down his tools to a bass drum, a snare and a lonely flat-top ride cymbal. With those barest of essentials, he offers a full creative rhythmic palette for band mates and listeners.

Parker's debut recording, *Above & Below,* was made with Ugonna Okegwo on bass and percussionist Adam Cruz and pianist Jacky Terrasson (plus David Sanchez, Mark Turner and Joshua Redman sharing saxophone duties). *Belief* employs a larger band, including alto saxophonist Steve Wilson, trumpeter Tom Harrell and trombonist Steve Davis, to showcase Parker's groove and concept as an interactive composer. On *Awakening,* Parker takes a more worldly approach to his music, abandoning his pared-down drum kit for a varied palette that includes percussion instruments from the Caribbean, Africa and South America—congas, a snare, shakers, bowls, marimbas and, on one track, piano—as he explores a variety of sounds and rhythms. — K.F.

MACEO PARKER

★★★★ Roots Revisited (Verve, 1990)
★★★★ Mo' Roots (Verve, 1991)
★★★★½ Life on Planet Groove (Verve, 1992)
★★★½ Southern Exposure (Novus, 1994)
★★★½ Funk Overload (Verve, 1998)

"We play 2 percent jazz, 98 percent . . . *funky stuff,*" declares veteran R&B alto man Maceo Parker (b. 1943) during the live set on *Life on Planet Groove,* revealing the same irresistible, downhome formula that he developed in the groundbreaking funk groups of James Brown, George Clinton and Bootsy Collins. An adept and versatile player favoring the repeated riffs and urgency of the funk edge of the jazz continuum, Parker has finally become a star in his own right, leading one of today's most consistent and dynamic mergings of contemporary funk and instrumental jazz.

Parker first appeared on record at age 21 when his drummer brother Melvin brought him into James Brown's Famous Flames. By the late '60s, as Brown pared down his syncopated R&B big-band style and created the foundation of modern-day funk, Parker had progressed to a more fluid, freer style on alto, lacing his aggressive, upper-register solos into such seminal hits as "Sex Machine."

Through the '70s and '80s, Parker moved in and out of Brown's ever-changing funk groups ("Over the years he has quit and been fired more times than either one of us can count," wrote Brown in '86), worked with such defining second-generation funk ensembles as George Clinton's Parliament-Funkadelic and Bootsy Collins's Rubber Band and led his own band the JB's with fellow Brown luminaries Pee Wee Ellis on tenor and Fred Wesley on trombone. *Funky Good Time* adequately collects Parker's most relevant work as a leader from this period, including the grindworthy singles "Doing It to Death," "Soul Power '74" and "Cross the Track (We Better Go Back)."

When Brown was incarcerated in 1988, Parker established his own group with Ellis and Wesley, signed to Verve and redefined his tight, groove-based approach with a looser, more jazzy feel. *Roots Revisited* and the follow-up, *Mo' Roots,* are contemporary classics—a horns-organ-and-groove rhythm section delivering satisfying mixes of great instrumental workouts and funkified jazz/soul standards. *Life on Planet Groove* captures Parker's band in high, European flight, delivering a sweat-inducing mix of old JB's chestnuts and latter-day funk tunes.

New Orleans provides the framework for *Southern Exposure,* more an exercise in all-funk promise than actual musical fulfillment. On it, Parker meets members of that other seminal funk band, the Meters, and second-lines through a version of "Mercy, Mercy, Mercy" with the Rebirth Brass Band. Ultimately, Parker's current craft is best seen, heard and felt live. *Funk Overload* (with intermittent rap assistance from Maceo's son Corey) holds onto that live spirit and further proves that Parker can still blister and blow. — A.K.

WILLIAM PARKER

★★★ **Zo (with Matthew Shipp) (1993; 2.13.61/Thirsty Ear, 1997)**

★★½ **Flowers Grow in My Room (with the Little Huey Creative Music Orchestra) (Centering, 1994)**

★★★★ **In Order to Survive (Black Saint, 1995)**

★★★★ **Testimony (Zero In, 1996)**

★★★★★ **Compassion Seizes Bed-Stuy (Homestead, 1996)**

Hailed by the *Village Voice* as no less than "the most consistently brilliant free jazz bassist of all time," William Parker (b. 1952) studied with such legendary bass figures as Milt Hinton and Jimmy Garrison. Evolving from a long association through the '80s and '90s with avant-garde architect Cecil Taylor, Parker has become one of the most fierce experimental voices in the current New York jazz scene. He continues to work with Taylor and a series of fellow travelers—saxophonists David Ware and Charles Gayle, violinist Billy Bang and pianist Matthew Shipp—through jazz's free and uncharted waters.

Flowers Grow in My Room marks Parker's earliest (currently available) leadership effort, fronting his big band, the Little Huey Creative Music Orchestra, which features more than 20 players on some tracks. A risky venture that has challenged the best avant-garde bandleaders (Charlie Haden, Gunter Hampel and Sun Ra all come to mind), any large "free" orchestra can ofttime slip, like a behemoth struggling to find its full, unified throttle, spotlighting individual instrumental voices more than a collective, improvised vision. Parker has Little Huey bouncing in and out of this rut, and for the fortunate inclusion of violinist Billy Bang, baritone saxophonist Joe Ruddick, vibraphonist Gregg Bendian and other strong performers, the project offers more promise of cohesion than is actually realized.

As a small-group leader, Parker has recorded a relatively stronger trio of live albums. *Compassion Seizes Bed-Stuy* and the solo-bass project *Testimony* jump in and out of print as these small labels struggle to stay alive. More easily available is *In Order to Survive,* which kicked off the trilogy and was recorded in 1993 at New York's Roulette performance space and Knitting Factory with a tight and empathetic cadre of "out" players sharing Parker's improvised vision: well-known trombonist Grachan Moncur III, alto saxophonist Rob Brown, trumpeter Lewis Barnes, pianist Cooper Moore, drummer Denis Charles and percussionist Jackson Krall. A clear indication of the magic that can spontaneously flow from a well-honed, free-focused ensemble working through prearranged themes and melodic phrases, the recording offers two tracks that stand out: the sparse, impressionistic "Anast in Crisis Mouth Full of Fresh Cut Flowers" and the intense and mammoth improvisation "Testimony of No Future," wherein Parker's bass work grows from an insistent whisper to a bowed growl. Also worth mentioning is Krall's creative percussion palette, adding spice and dimension to the mood piece "The Square Sun."

Compassion Seizes Bed-Stuy is a more expansive and articulate outing, again in a quartet context, with alto saxist Rob Brown, pianist Cooper Moore and drummer Susie Ibarra. "For Robeson" is the disc's most evocative piece—sparse and schematic—while "Unrestricted (For Julius Hemphill)" showcases Moore's pensive keyboard work; the boogie-driven "Goggles" is an entertaining detour and return to the improvisation thoroughfare.
— A.K.

REBECCA PARRIS

★★★½ A Passionate Fling (1984; Shira, 1996)
★★★ Live at Chan's (with Phil Wilson) (1985; Shira, 1998)
★★★★ Love Comes and Goes (Entertainment Exclusives, 1991)
★★★★ Spring (MusicMasters, 1993)
★★★ It's Another Day (with Gary Burton) (GRP, 1994)
★★½ A Beautiful Friendship (Altenburgh, 1995)

In the mid-1980s, after several youthful decades of work in theater as well as rock and pop singing, Rebecca Parris (b. 1951) turned her full attention to jazz, where she found a welcome niche for her big, bold and expressive sound. Parris is not a cabaret singer in the classic sense; her delivery is rooted in soaring emotion. A touch of theatricality enhances her ability to hold the full attention of an audience without it seeming overdone or contrived.

Parris's first three recordings, *A Passionate Fling, Live at Chan's* with Phil Wilson and *Double Rainbow* with Eddie Higgins, were self-released on LP and long out of print; in 1996 she began to reissue them on CD. *A Passionate Fling* and *Live at Chan's* hold up well and include her powerful treatments of a wide array of American songbook and jazz standards.

Love Comes and Goes is a forceful showcase for Parris and the talented songwriter Carroll Coates, who penned the elegant "London by Night" and six other tunes on the session.

Parris landed with MusicMasters for *Spring,* which is her best effort to date. Backed by a Latin-tinged band and the underrated pianist George Mesterhazy, she offers a wide range of material, including the definitive recording of a great new standard, "First Time on a Ferris Wheel."

Gary Burton's crystalline vibes complement her husky alto on *It's Another Day,* a project with more pop-oriented material and an instrumental feel. The strongest jazz vehicles are Parris's scatting interplay with Burton on "Au Privave" and her interpretation of Dori Caymmi's ballad "We Can Try Love Again."

A Beautiful Friendship teams Parris with drummer Kenny Hadley's fine Boston-based big band. Her vocals are in fine form, but the sparks expected from a big-band collaboration are absent. It's as if solos that might have intensified the effort either weren't encouraged or vanished after the fact in an effort to create short, radio-friendly tracks. — K.F.

JOE PASS

★★★½ The Trio (with Oscar Peterson and Niels-Henning Ørsted Pedersen) (1973; Pablo, 1987)
★★★ Two for the Road (with Herb Ellis) (1974; Original Jazz Classics, 1992)
★★★★★ Virtuoso (1974; Pablo, 1987)
★★★ Take Love Easy (with Ella Fitzgerald) (1974; Pablo, 1987)
★★★★ Portraits of Duke Ellington (with Ray Brown and Bobby Durham) (1974; Pablo, 1988)
★★★ Joe Pass at the Montreux Jazz Festival 1975 (1975; Original Jazz Classics, 1997)
★★★★ The Big Three (with Milt Jackson and Ray Brown) (1975; Original Jazz Classics, 1994)
★★★★ Virtuoso #2 (1976; Pablo, 1987)
★★½ Porgy and Bess (with Oscar Peterson) (1976; Original Jazz Classics, 1994)
★★★½ Fitzgerald and Pass . . . Again (with Ella Fitzgerald) (1976; Pablo, 1988)
★★★ Quadrant (1977; Original Jazz Classics, 1990)
★★★★ Virtuoso #3 (1977; Original Jazz Classics, 1992)
★★½ Montreux '77 (1977; Original Jazz Classics, 1989)
★★★ Tudo Bem! (1978; Original Jazz Classics, 1992)

★★★ **Chops (with Niels-Henning Ørsted Pedersen) (1978; Original Jazz Classics, 1993)**
★★★ **Tivoli Gardens, Copenhagen, Denmark (with Stéphane Grappelli and Neils-Henning Ørsted Pedersen) (1979; Original Jazz Classics, 1990)**
★★★★ **I Remember Charlie Parker (1979; Original Jazz Classics, 1990)**
★★★ **Digital III at Montreux (with Count Basie and Ella Fitzgerald) (Pablo, 1980)**
★★★ **Ira, George and Joe (1982; Original Jazz Classics, 1995)**
★★★ **Blues for Two (with Zoot Sims) (1982; Original Jazz Classics, 1991)**
★★★½ **Speak Love (with Ella Fitzgerald) (1983; Pablo, 1987)**
★★★★ **We'll Be Together Again (with J.J. Jackson) (1984; Original Jazz Classics, 1996)**
★★★½ **Easy Living (with Ella Fitzgerald) (Pablo, 1986)**
★★★ **University of Akron Concert (Pablo, 1987)**
★★★ **Whitestone (Pablo, 1988)**
★★★ **The Best of Joe Pass (1987; Pablo, 1991)**
★★★½ **Blues for Fred (Pablo, 1988)**
★★★ **One for My Baby (Pablo, 1989)**
★★★ **Summer Nights (Pablo, 1990)**
★★★ **Appassionato (Pablo, 1991)**
★★★★ **Virtuoso Live! (Pablo, 1992)**
★★★ **Songs for Ellen (Pablo, 1993)**
★★★★ **Virtuoso #4 (Pablo, 1993)**
★★★ **Joe Pass and Co.: Joe Pass Quartet Live at Yoshi's (Pablo, 1993)**
★★★ **My Song (Telarc, 1993)**
★★★ **Finally: Live in Stockholm (Verve, 1993)**
★★★½ **Duets (with John Pisano) (Pablo, 1996)**
★★★ **Nuages: Live at Yoshi's, Vol. 2 (Pablo, 1997)**
★★★★ **Guitar Virtuoso (Pablo, 1997)**
★★★★ **The Best of Joe Pass (Pacific Jazz/Blue Note, 1997)**

Joe Pass (né Joseph Anthony Passalaqua, 1929–1994) is generally considered one of the finest jazz guitarists in history. His clean, melodic tone, understated dynamic sense, eschewal of gimmickry and formidable improvisational abilities were obvious to the jazz critics who voted him the top new star in *Down Beat*'s 1963 poll despite the fact that Pass hadn't recorded as a leader at that point.

Pass was discovered by Richard Bock, owner of Pacific Jazz Records, while the guitarist was a resident at California's Synanon drug rehabilitation center. Bock released Pass's jazz debut on a record called *Sounds of Synanon* in 1962, and Pass then went on to play on a number of Pacific Jazz dates led by Gerald Wilson, Bud Shank, Les McCann and Groove Holmes, among others (some of which appear on the Blue Note *Best of Joe Pass*).

The Complete "Catch Me" Sessions, from '63 and now unavailable, marks Pass's debut as a leader on beautiful quartet recordings featuring Clare Fischer's sturdy and sympathetic piano accompaniment. Another currently unavailable classic, *For Django,* is a moving tribute to the Belgian guitarist who was the greatest influence on Pass.

The bulk of Pass material since the 1970s has been recorded for Pablo (*Guitar Virtuoso* is a four-disc boxed set compiling his recordings from 1973 to 1992), where he also appeared on numerous sessions headed by Oscar Peterson, Duke Ellington, Dizzy Gillespie, Sarah Vaughan and Ella Fitzgerald. He has, in fact, suffered a bit in this context from being overrecorded.

Pass's debt to pianist Art Tatum is well repaid on the *Virtuoso* solo sets, the first of which, recorded in November 1973, remains the most impressive (the 1993 *#4* release contains outtakes from that first session). Other notable solo recordings include *Montreux '77, I Remember Charlie Parker, Songs for Ellen* and *Blues for Fred.*

Pass has also varied his solo outings on Pablo with a number of duet and trio albums: with J.J. Johnson (the great *We'll Be Together Again*); with bassist Niels-Henning Ørsted Pedersen (*Chops* and the out-of-print *Northsea Nights*); with guitarist Herb Ellis (*Two for the Road*); and with bassist Ray Brown and drummer Bobby Durham (*Portraits of Duke Ellington*).

Pass made two albums in the company of bassist Jim Hughart, drummer Colin Bailey and guitarist John Pisano, *Appassionato* and *Summer Nights.* Pisano has been a frequent collaborator, also appearing on *Whitestone, Duets,* both *Live at Yoshi's* sets and *Ira, George and Joe,* with Hughart and Shelly Manne on drums.

Pass's more varied dates include *Quadrant,* with Brown on bass, Milt Jackson on vibes and Mickey Roker on drums; *One for My Baby,* with Plas Johnson on saxophone, Gerald Wiggins on piano, Andy Simpkins on bass and Albert "Tootie" Heath on drums; and two Latin-jazz albums featuring percussionist Paulinho da Costa, pianist Don Grusin and others (*Tudo Bem!* and *Whitestone*). — J.S.

PASSPORT

★★ **Blue Tattoo (1981; Rhino, N.A.)**
★★★ **Talk Back (1989; Rhino, N.A.)**
★★★ **Balance of Happiness (1990; Rhino, N.A.)**
★★★ **Passport to Paradise (Atlantic, 1997)**

German saxophonist Klaus Doldinger (b. 1936) formed Passport in the early 1970s and became a pioneer in the burgeoning European fusion movement, performing at numerous festivals and releasing several albums in Germany before coming to the attention of U.S. record companies. While Passport's sound—sparse, angular playing over amplified rhythm sections—was novel at first, it lost its freshness over the years. Doldinger plugged on, working in a gray area somewhere between fusion jazz and pop rock. — J.S.

JACO PASTORIUS

★★★★ **Jaco Pastorius (1976; Epic, 1987)**
★★½ **Word of Mouth (1981; Warner Bros., 1988)**
★★★★ **Invitation (Warner Bros., 1983)**
★★★★ **The Birthday Concert (Warner Bros., 1995)**

Jaco Pastorius (né John Francis Pastorius III, 1951–1987) took the electric bass to the apogee of its creative and propulsive force in fusion. A big-band veteran when he emerged on the jazz scene, he became a cornerstone of the premier fusion band Weather Report after joining that group for one of its finest albums, *Heavy Weather,* in 1976. Largely in the Weather Report mode, *Jaco Pastorius* is a tour de force of exotic harmonics, hammered percussive effects, distortion, chordal work and driving rhythms, all in service to a sublime melodic sensibility informed by equal parts Charlie Parker and Jimi Hendrix. *Word of Mouth* was a troubled follow-up, but Pastorius rebounded in a return to his roots with *Invitation,* a big-band outing that features harmonica player Toots Thielemans, percussionist Don Alias, Randy Brecker and Jon Faddis on trumpets, Peter Erskine on drums and Bobby Mintzer on tenor and soprano saxophone.

Recorded near Pastorius's home in Florida in 1981, *The Birthday Concert* is a live career overview/celebration performed by a 21-piece band made up of his musician friends and colleagues from a variety of bands. Michael Brecker, the principal soloist throughout on tenor saxophone, turns in a fitting tribute to Jaco's precocious talent. — J.S.

BIG JOHN PATTON

★★★★ **Blue Planet Man (1993; Evidence, 1995)**

Hammond B-3 organist Big John Patton (b. 1935) came out of Kansas City playing blues-based R&B and jazz, accompanying Grant Green at one point, before recording for Blue Note with Lou Donaldson and later on his own in the 1960s. His style ranged from crowd-pleasing blues vamps to the kind of outside work that made him a natural collaborator with such experimental musicians as James Blood Ulmer and John Zorn.

Blue Planet Man, recorded for the Japanese King label, captures the diversity of Patton's approach on a set that is well grounded in blues nuance but jumps all over the place in its search for the unexplored nooks and crannies that can turn clichés into revelations. Zorn on alto saxophone heads a support cast that also includes Pete Chavez on tenor, Bill Saxton on tenor and soprano, Ed Cherry on guitar, Eddie Gladden on drums and Lawrence Killian on congas. — J.S.

CHARLEY PATTON

★★★★★ **Founder of the Delta Blues 1929–34 (1988; Yazoo, 1991)**
★★★★★ **King of the Delta Blues: The Music of Charlie Patton (Yazoo, 1991)**
★★★★★ **Masters of the Delta Blues: The Friends of Charlie Patton (Yazoo, 1991)**
★★★★★ **Charley Patton: The Complete Recorded Works (Peavine, 1992)**

So many facts are in dispute regarding the life and music of Charley Patton (1891–1934) that the best summary of the man's art may well be the succinct sentiment inscribed on his tombstone in Holly Ridge, Mississippi (which has the *-ey* ending for his name): THE VOICE OF THE DELTA, it reads. THE FOREMOST PERFORMER OF EARLY MISSISSIPPI BLUES WHOSE SONGS BECAME CORNERSTONES OF AMERICAN MUSIC. Even though others came before him, and others would follow him and gain acclaim far beyond the bounds of the Mississippi Delta, Patton's extraordinary and complex guitar style, the beauty and mystery of his often-abstruse lyrics and the haunted, chilling sound of his voice set him well apart from his predecessors and elevated his art to a standard by which succeeding generations of Delta musicians would be judged. So while it is historically inaccurate to call him the "founder" of the Delta blues, he at least rewrote the rules in his lifetime to such a point that his music is seen more as a starting point than as an extension of a style.

Just as his music held to no set pattern, so did his life as a black man in turn-of-the-century Mississippi have its quirks. For one, the Patton family did not sharecrop but farmed land rented from Will Dockery, who owned a huge Delta plantation near Cleveland, Mississippi; Charley's father, Bill, hired his own workers to supplement the family members and later owned businesses himself, including a drugstore. Charley had a ninth-grade education and was fairly well read. A restless sort, he traveled extensively, not only from plantation to plantation in the Delta, where he would perform at weekend dances, but also around the South and Southwest (he makes reference in "Down the Dirt Road Blues" to having visited Oklahoma's Indian Nation) and north as far as New York, further broadening his worldview and refining his personal style.

Yet it was to the Delta that Patton always returned and the Delta whose people and life inform his luminous canon—indeed, many of his friends, lovers and tormenters are singled out by name in various songs. Taken as a whole, though, these accounts, so explicit in lyric detail, paint a revealing portrait of the Delta in Patton's lifetime. The harrowing two-part "High Water Everywhere" recounts the terror attending the 1927 Mississippi River flood; on "34 Blues" he broadcasts the news of his being thrown off the Dockery plantation, names the man who chased him out, and recites the words he heard announcing his expulsion; "Tom Rushen Blues" describes the arrest of a friend in a song named after the Bolivar County deputy sheriff.

Patton's music is startling in its rhythmic complexity and structural innovation. His rhythmic devices have been traced to West African drumming; Patton further complicated his sound by disdaining any set rhythm pattern. As well, he often worked in 13½-bar verses instead of the standard 8- and 16-bar blues formulas, harkening back to a 19th Century folk-drumming style. His voice was a gruff instrument that took on added harshness after a 1929 incident in which his throat was slashed by a man enraged by Patton's flirting with his girlfriend. Still, he used it well as a percussive instrument, although that makes Patton's lyrics difficult to decipher.

In his later years Patton took up preaching and by all accounts was as effective in the pulpit as he was with a guitar in hand. Among the most moving of his recordings are his gospel numbers, which are nearly as numerous as his secular blues tunes. On most of these his lyrics are straightforward accounts of man humbled by his Lord's gift of mercy for sins confessed. Robert Johnson may have had a troubled relationship with his maker, but Patton comes across as a man who knew his Lord on intimate terms. "I Shall Not Be Moved" is the chilling entry among these songs, although the lesser-celebrated "Jesus Is a Dying Bed Maker" is nearly as powerful.

At his death of heart disease on April 28, 1934, Patton had been on a preaching binge, delivering a sermon every day of the week before his passing. According to a female friend who was with him at the end, Patton had fixed on a verse from Revelation 13: "Let your light shine that men may see your good work and glorify our Father which art in Heaven." According to this friend, Patton, then bedridden, said: "Did you hear that? My light been shining on each side. I let it shine for the young. I let it shine for the old. Count my Christian records and count my swinging records. Just count 'em! They even!"

The light does shine, and brilliantly so. The three-CD Peavine import *Charley Patton: The Complete Recorded Works* is the set to own, and offers a bonus in the estimable Jim O'Neil's superb liner notes, which make sense of the various tales surrounding Patton's movements, lineage and passions. The Yazoo discs offer lower-priced alternatives to the Peavine collection: The tracks on *Founder of the Delta Blues* represent many of Patton's now classic blues recordings, including "A Spoonful Blues," "High Water Everywhere" and "Pony Blues." *King of the Delta Blues,* on the other hand, focuses on Patton's gospel, preblues and country tunes. *Masters of the Delta Blues* is an anthology of recordings by Patton's contemporaries, friends and pupils (among them Son House, Tommy Johnson and Bertha Lee). Robert Palmer, author of *Deep Blues,* has referred to the three Yazoo titles together as representing "the finest introduction to pre–Robert Johnson Delta blues imaginable."
— D.M.

LES PAUL

★★ **The Fabulous Les Paul and Mary Ford (Columbia, 1965)**
★★★ **Chester and Lester (with Chet Atkins) (RCA, 1976)**
★★★★★ **Les Paul: The Legend & the Legacy (Capitol, 1991)**
★★★★ **Les Paul Trio: The Jazz Collector Edition (LaserLight, 1991)**
★★★★ **Les Paul and Mary Ford: The Best of the Capitol Masters (Capitol, 1992)**
★★★★ **16 Most Requested Songs (Columbia/Legacy, 1996)**

From their first release, 1948's "Lover," through their final Capitol hit, 1957's "Goodnight My Someone," guitarist Les Paul (b. Lester Polsfuss, 1916) and vocalist Mary Ford (1928–1977, b. Colleen Summers, she was rechristened by Paul when she joined his Trio in 1949, the same year she married the guitarist) made some of the liveliest, most inventive pop records of their time and were rewarded with public acclaim comparable to that of the most popular recording artists of the era. Moving to Columbia in 1958, they found their audience shrinking as rock & roll took over, although they still managed a Top 40 hit in 1961 with "Jura (I Swear I Love You)."

Ford sang in a pleasant if limited alto/soprano voice; when multitracked, she sounded like the Andrews Sisters. Behind her, often abetted by tape trickery, Paul worked out astonishing harmonic runs, some of them with music-box delicacy and poignancy, and unusual chord progressions. His smooth touch, flawless command and dexterous picking have elevated him to a status among guitarists nearly as legendary as his standing among electronics freaks.

Initially inspired by country-blues artists Deford Bailey and Sonny Terry, Paul developed a signature sound by osmosis: He listened to a wide variety of music and absorbed the most intriguing elements he encountered along the way: His single-string runs bring to mind those of Lonnie Johnson; his chordings and sustained phrasings evoke the style of Charlie Christian; an occasional thumb-picked bass line and fingerpicked lead suggest a Merle Travis influence. Working steadily on the road in the '30s and '40s provided him with ample opportunity to expand his own vocabulary with ideas inspired by other musicians who crossed his path without ever achieving fame on their own. In short, his style is so eclectic that it would be foolhardy to describe him as the child of any single instrumentalist or two—blues, country & western, jazz and pop voicings are all evident in his playing.

A host of contemporary guitarists pays homage to Paul; moreover, an entire industry—that of professional recording—honors the inveterate electronics tinkerer every time a new session begins. Paul's technological innovations of multitrack recording on disc, the solid-body guitar, eight-track tape recording and prototypical synthesizers and signal processors revolutionized the manner in which records are made to such a degree that to talk of studio technology at all is to discuss the pre-Paul era and the post-Paul era.

As for the music, the Capitol years are superbly documented on a four-disc boxed set, *Les Paul: The Legend & the Legacy,* which includes an entire CD of previously unreleased masters, 34 in all, as well as track-by-track liner commentary by Paul himself (buttressed by a first-rate biographical sketch courtesy of Stephen K. Peeples) and excerpts from the duo's radio shows and commercial spots. Three other CDs contain 75 tracks issued on Capitol between 1948 and 1958; of these, 5 showcase Paul in the pre–Mary Ford years, when he racked up 15 Top 30 singles on his own; 32 others, with Mary Ford, were Top 40 singles, including two chart toppers (1951's "How High the Moon" and 1953's "Vaya Con Dios"), 8 Top Fives and 17 total Top 10 entries. Fans on a tighter budget will find *The Best of the Capitol Masters* a good bang for the buck. It contains 20 tracks from the boxed set, and the liner booklet includes Paul's track-by-track commentary.

The Fabulous Les Paul and Mary Ford and *16 Most Requested Songs* are splendid surveys of the high points of the Columbia years, when the hits ended save for two more visits to the Top 40. Hits or no, Paul and Ford made wonderful records during these years. The former's choices as a soloist are often as unexpected as they are exhilarating, and Ford's voice has become a husky, mesmerizing wonder of romantic yearning. These two collections do justice to a productive time in the duo's career, when the quality of their work together often matched what they had done on Capitol, even if the sales figures indicated otherwise—a triumph of aesthetics over commerce.

When he formed his first Les Paul Trio in 1936, Paul hired Ernie Newton as his bass player and as rhythm guitarist and vocalist he brought in a fellow named Jim Atkins, whose brother Chet was on his way to making a name for himself as a picker. LaserLight's *Les Paul Trio: The Jazz Collector Edition* fills in some of the "lost" years in Paul's recording history pre–Mary Ford. Its 21 songs represent, according to the minimal liner notes, the trio "at the crest of their popularity" along with some radio performances dated circa 1947. The music is an unadorned delight—free of Paul's multitracking trickery—with the trio meshing beautifully on tunes ranging from the meditative (a beautiful take on "Embraceable You," with Paul alternating evocative single-note, Lonnie Johnson–style solos with flurries of notes suggesting love's roiling emotions) to the jubilant (a pop-cum-country take on "[Back Home Again in] Indiana," with Paul's flight of high-pitched notes voicing the joy of the journey back to sacred ground). All in all, the disc underscores Paul's mastery of technique and mood, lest anyone think his fanciful recordings in the '50s were more a showcase for the impish technocrat than for the player with heart.

Forty years after his brother joined up with Paul, Chet Atkins came around to join Les (the two had jammed together frequently over the years as their friendship grew) in laying down some licks for posterity on *Chester and Lester,* an engaging and invigorating supersession—no hype here—that feels improvised from first note to last, two old friends sitting around doing what they do best and about as well as any two people have ever done it. — D.M.

NICHOLAS PAYTON

★★★ **New Orleans Collective (1993; Evidence, 1995)**
★★★ **From This Moment (Verve, 1995)**
★★★★ **Gumbo Nouveau (Verve, 1996)**
★★★★★ **Doc Cheatham and Nicholas Payton (Verve, 1997)**

New Orleans–born Nicholas Payton (b. 1973) leads the new generation of jazz trumpeters, having already accomplished an incredible amount in his fledgling career. Payton's first professional gig came at the age of nine with the Young Tuxedo Brass Band, and as a teenager he studied under pianist Ellis Marsalis. At 19, he was tapped by legendary drummer Elvin Jones to be the musical director of Jones's ensemble. Jones knew he would be in good company; Payton's inspirations—primarily Miles Davis, Clifford Brown and John Coltrane—have pushed him to develop a pure and confident tone rarely heard in younger players.

Payton's Verve debut, *From This Moment,* doesn't quite live up to expectations. Though he is surrounded by a strong cast of supporting players, including guitarist Mark Whitfield and pianist Mulgrew Miller, the material rarely catches fire, and the subdued vibes work of Monte Croft is an ill-suited foil for Payton's gorgeous tone flights on the trumpet. There are glimpses of Payton's prowess: the spunky burst that lifts the solo on "It Could Happen to You" and the delicate phrasing on "Rhonda's Smile."

What a difference a year makes. *Gumbo Nouveau* crackles right out of the gate, with a white-hot version of "Whoopin' Blues." With a fresh approach to the New Orleans music he was raised on, *Gumbo Nouveau* proves that "When the Saints Go Marching In," "Way Down Yonder in New Orleans" and "L'il Liza Jane" are living, breathing examples of the Crescent City's contributions to improvisation in jazz. The closing track, "St. James Infirmary," shows Payton's gift for slow blues.

The album of duets with 92-year-old trumpeter/vocalist Doc Cheatham reaches stunning heights. Backed by a top-flight band of trad-jazz players, Payton and Cheatham trade dream solo after dream solo, invoking Louis Armstrong and King Oliver. Cheatham's sweet and charming vocals set the unhurried and luxurious pace as he and Payton stroll masterfully through the standards "Stardust" and "I Cover the Waterfront" and show a refined sense of playfulness on "Jeepers Creepers" and "Save It Pretty Mama."

New Orleans Collective, Payton's independently released debut, was recorded in 1992 as a showcase, featuring saxophonist Wessell Anderson, pianist Peter Martin, bassist Christopher Thomas and drummer Brian Blade. — S.J.

NIELS-HENNING ØRSTED PEDERSEN

★★★½ **The Trio (with Joe Pass and Oscar Peterson) (1973; Pablo, 1987)**
★★★★ **Jaywalkin' (SteepleChase, 1975)**
★★★ **Trio 1 (SteepleChase, 1977)**
★★★ **Montreux '77 (with Ray Brown and Oscar Peterson) (1977; Original Jazz Classics, 1989)**
★★★★ **Dancing on the Tables (SteepleChase, 1979)**

★★★ **Tivoli Gardens, Copenhagen, Denmark (with Stéphane Grappelli and Joe Pass) (1979; Original Jazz Classics, 1990)**
★★★★ **Double Bass (SteepleChase, 1988)**
★★★ **Hommage: Once Upon a Time (with Palle Mikkelborg) (EmArcy, 1993)**
★★★ **Pictures (with Keith Knudsen) (SteepleChase, 1994)**
★★★★★ **Ambiance (with the Danish Radio Big Band) (Dacapo, 1996)**
★★★ **Friends Forever (Milestone, 1997)**
★★★½ **Those Who Were (Verve, 1997)**

One of the greatest jazz musicians to come out of Europe, Danish bassist Niels-Henning Ørsted Pedersen, a.k.a. NHØP (b. 1946), is an astonishing virtuoso whose sensitivity for accompaniment has made him popular with everyone from Ella Fitzgerald and Oscar Peterson to Archie Shepp and Miles Davis.

Although he can be heard on myriad recordings as a sideman, NHØP's own recordings for SteepleChase showcase his extraordinarily dexterous and musical playing. *Double Bass* is an encounter with the great bassist Sam Jones, whose funky, blues-based playing is the perfect complement to the flamboyant Dane. Guitarist Philip Catherine, a frequent partner, is featured on *Jaywalkin'* and the out-of-print *Viking,* while American jazzmen John Scofield (guitar) and Dave Liebman (saxophone) do the honors on *Dancing on the Tables.*

An exceptional big-band collaboration between Pedersen and the Danish Radio Big Band, *Ambiance* balances superb bass playing with pithy writing and sharp orchestral passages. *Those Who Were* features Pedersen in settings with both European and American musicians, including the vibrant tenor saxophonist Johnny Griffin on two tracks. Pedersen's duet recordings with Joe Pass, Paul Bley, Martial Solal, Kenny Drew and Archie Shepp are also well worth looking for. — S.F.

ART PEPPER

★★★ **Surf Ride (1954; Savoy, 1991)**
★★★ **The Art Pepper Quartet (1956; Original Jazz Classics, 1994)**
★★★★★ **The Artistry of Pepper (1957; Pacific Jazz, 1992)**
★★★★★ **The Best of Art Pepper (N.A.; Pacific Jazz, 1993)**
★★★ **The Complete Aladdin, Vol. 1: Return of Art Pepper (N.A.; Blue Note, 1988)**
★★★★ **Modern Art . . . Aladdin Recordings, Vol. 2 (1957; Blue Note, 1988)**
★★★★ **The Art of Pepper, Vol. 3 (1957; Blue Note, 1988)**
★★★★★ **Art Pepper meets the Rhythm Section (1957; Original Jazz Classics, N.A.)**
★★★★★ **Modern Jazz Classics (1959; Original Jazz Classics, N.A.)**
★★★★ **The Way It Was! (1960; Original Jazz Classics, 1989)**
★★★★★ **Gettin' Together! (1960; Original Jazz Classics, N.A.)**
★★★★ **Smack Up (1960; Original Jazz Classics, N.A.)**
★★★★ **Intensity (1960; Original Jazz Classics, 1989)**
★★★ **Living Legend (1975; Original Jazz Classics, 1990)**
★★★ **I'll Remember April: Live at Foothill College (Storyville, 1975)**
★★★ **The Trip (1976; Original Jazz Classics, N.A.)**
★★★ **A Night in Tunisia (Storyville, 1977)**
★★ **No Limit (1977; Original Jazz Classics, 1990)**
★★★ **Thursday Night at the Village Vanguard (1977; Original Jazz Classics, 1992)**
★★★ **Friday Night at the Village Vanguard (1977; Original Jazz Classics, 1992)**
★★★ **Saturday Night at the Village Vanguard (1977; Original Jazz Classics, 1992)**
★★★ **More for Les: At the Village Vanguard, Vol. 4 (1977; Original Jazz Classics, 1992)**
★★★ **Live in Japan, Vol. 1 (Storyville, 1978)**
★★★ **Live in Japan, Vol. 2 (Storyville, 1978)**
★★★ **Laurie's Choice (1978; LaserLight, 1992)**
★★★ **Art Pepper Today (1978; Original Jazz Classics, 1990)**
★★★★ **Landscape (1979; Original Jazz Classics, 1991)**
★★★ **Straight Life (1979; Original Jazz Classics, 1990)**

★★★ **Winter Moon (1980; Original Jazz Classics, 1991)**
★★ **One September Afternoon (1980; Original Jazz Classics, 1991)**
★★★★ **Roadgame (1981; Original Jazz Classics, 1993)**
★★★ **Arthur's Blues (1981; Original Jazz Classics, 1991)**
★★★ **Art 'n' Zoot (1981; Pablo, 1995)**
★★★★★ **Goin' Home (1982; Original Jazz Classics, 1991)**
★★★★ **Tete-a-Tete (1983; Original Jazz Classics, 1995)**
★★★★ **The Complete Galaxy Recordings (Galaxy, 1989)**
★★★ **The Complete Village Vanguard (Contemporary, 1995)**
★★★ **San Francisco Samba (Contemporary, 1997)**

Art Pepper (1925–1982), the handsome and brilliant Los Angeles alto saxophonist who gained early acclaim as featured soloist with Stan Kenton's band, was perhaps as famous for his numerous heroin busts and decade in prison (described at length in his autobiography, *Straight Life*) as for his music. He will be remembered, however, as being among the most impassioned and personal alto saxophonists to emerge in the period dominated by Charlie Parker.

Some of the early Pepper recordings remain the best, and listeners should start with *Art Pepper meets the Rhythm Section* and *Gettin' Together!,* taped with Miles Davis's 1957 and 1960 accompanying trios, respectively; *The Art of Pepper, Vol. 3* a strong quartet with pianist Carl Perkins also well featured; and *Modern Jazz Classics,* arranger Marty Paich's 1959 settings of classic jazz tunes. Look for the currently unavailable two-volume *Night at the Surf Club* albums, taped live in 1952 with Hampton Hawes on piano. *The Artistry of Pepper* highlights Pepper's work with trumpeter Chet Baker.

Between 1960 and 1975, Pepper did time, lived at Synanon, scuffled and for the most part stayed out of the recording studio. After his return, he became prolific, generally with respected supporting players, but the results did not always come up to the level of his early work. The *Village Vanguard* albums, with George Cables and Elvin Jones, are typical of promising sessions that don't live up to their billing.

Among the last Pepper albums, the best are the currently unavailable *Among Friends,* a boppish throwback made in 1978; *Landscape, Roadgame* and the out-of-print *So in Love,* each of which contains fierce blowing and a good sense of Pepper's repertoire during his final period; *Art Pepper Today,* with its magnificent ballad "Patricia"; and the moving duets with pianist Cables on *Goin' Home,* Pepper's last recording session.

Pepper can also be heard on Savoy's *Black California* and *Cool California* anthologies and the Galaxy samplers *Five Birds and a Monk* and *Ballads by Four.*

Pepper's solid reputation continued to grow after his death with the posthumous release of *Tete-a-Tete.* The lavish Galaxy boxed set includes a wealth of previously unavailable material. — B.B./J.S.

DANILO PEREZ

★★★ **Danilo Perez (Novus/RCA, 1993)**
★★★½ **The Journey (Novus/RCA, 1994)**
★★★★★ **PanaMonk (Impulse!, 1996)**
★★★½ **Central Avenue (Impulse!, 1998)**

Pianist Danilo Perez (b. 1966) grew up in Panama, where his father is a Latin singer and bandleader. Strongly rooted in classical-music education, he gravitated toward jazz during college in the United States in the mid-1980s. He worked briefly with singer Jon Hendricks and saxophonist Paquito D'Rivera before trumpeter Dizzy Gillespie hired him for his United Nation Orchestra in 1989. Perez also has led his own band and worked with D'Rivera and trumpeters Claudio Roditi and Wynton Marsalis.

On his self-titled debut, a solid quintet session augmented by guest vocalist Ruben Blades, Perez explores his many musical influences. More autobiographical and radical in approach, *The Journey* uses original jazz material to blend the high-energy pianist's cultural and musical inheritances from Africa, Europe and the Americas. *Central Avenue* melds Perez's roots with the blues much as *PanaMonk* did so brilliantly with bebop. He also blends Middle Eastern melodies and instrumentation and Luciana Souza's ethereal vocals into his folk-influenced "jazz with rice and beans" music. — K.F.

BILL PERKINS

★★★ **Quietly There (1966; Original Jazz Classics, 1991)**
★★½ **I Wished on the Moon (Candid, 1992)**

West Coast multi-instrumentalist Bill Perkins (b. 1924) excelled on tenor and baritone saxophone as part of the Woody Herman and Stan Kenton orchestras during the 1950s, later as part of *The Tonight Show* band, the Lighthouse All Stars and as a sideman with Bud Shank. *Quietly There* is a quintet session co-led by pianist Victor Feldman featuring film soundtrack music. *I Wished on the Moon* is a larger-group album that pales in comparison with the work he did as a leader on a few dates and a sideman on many others that are now buried in history. — J.S.

PINETOP PERKINS

★★★★ **Boogie Woogie King (1976; Evidence, 1992)**
★★★ **After Hours (Blind Pig, 1988)**
★★★½ **Pinetop's Boogie Woogie (Antone's, 1992)**
★★★ **On Top (Deluge, 1992)**
★★★½ **Portrait of a Delta Bluesman (Omega, 1993)**
★★★ **Live Top (Deluge, 1995)**
★★★½ **Born in the Delta (Telarc, 1997)**

Born in Mississippi in 1913, pianist Willie "Pinetop" Perkins has a résumé that reads like a Who's Who in the blues. He played with Muddy Waters, Sonny Boy Williamson (Rice Miller), Robert Nighthawk and Earl Hooker, to name a few. With his extensive work as a sideman, he never enjoyed the fruits of a domestically released album until 1988: *After Hours* was recorded with the assistance of New York blues band Little Mike and the Tornadoes. Displaying Perkins's infectious boogie-woogie style, the album features Waters's "Got My Mojo Working," Jimmy Smith's famous instrumental "Chicken Shack," Jimmy Reed's "You Don't Have to Go" and Nighthawk's "Anna Lee," interspersed with Perkins's own "Sit in the Easy Chair" and "Thinks Like a Million."

Recorded in France, *Boogie Woogie King* documents the classic postwar-blues style. Accompanied by Waters's alumni guitarist Luther "Guitar Jr." Johnson, bassist Calvin "Fuzz" Jones and drummer Willie "Big Eyes" Smith, Pinetop injects his quintessential Chicago-by-way-of-the-Delta playing, and the rest is history. Included are versions of Robert Jr. Lockwood's "Take a Little Walk with Me" and Hudson Whittaker's "Sweet Black Angel." Especially scintillating are Perkins's glissandos on the opening number, "Pinetop Is Just Top." *Pinetop's Boogie Woogie* again features stellar personnel, including harmonica players James Cotton and Kim Wilson, guitarists Matt "Guitar" Murphy, Duke Robillard and Hubert Sumlin. Highlights include Robert Higginbotham's "High Heel Sneakers," Roosevelt Sykes's "Sunny Road Blues," Fleecy Moore's "Caledonia" and the Elmore James/Marshall Sehorn composition "Look on Yonder Wall."

On Top features the harmonica work of Jerry Portnoy and the National steel guitar of Paul Rishell. In fine form, Perkins covers Eddie "Cleanhead" Vinson's "Kidney Stew," Jimmy Yancey's "Yancey Special" and Waters's "Little Girl," as well as Big Maceo's version of "Worried Life Blues." *Portrait of a Delta Bluesman* is a survey of Perkins's career, featuring stories and narration by the artist and solo piano renditions of songs like Little Brother Montgomery's "Chains of Love," Howlin' Wolf's "Forty-Four" and Walter Davis's "Come Back Baby." *Live Top,* recorded in October 1994 during two performances in Maine, finds Perkins backed by a band called the Blue Flames. Both albums offer testimony to Perkins's mastery of the blues. — B.R.H.

BILL PERRY

★★★½ **Love Scars (Pointblank, 1996)**
★★★★ **Greycourt Lightning (Pointblank, 1997)**

Songwriter, guitarist and vocalist Bill Perry (b. 1959) is a promising new blues artist from upstate New York, whose straightforward debut consists of 11 original songs, performed with his band (bassist Eric Winter, drummer Papa John Mole and keyboardist Jeremy Baum). Though Perry has worked extensively as a sideman, he pointedly chose not to use guest performances in favor of showcasing his excellent group and putting the focus on his songs, several of which could possibly become future blues standards (particularly the title cut, the catchy "Settle Down, Fred" and the anthem "Fade to Blue"). Perry's impressive guitar playing alternates between a rich, rough-edged electric sound and superb acoustic-slide work. Perry became a regular performer at New York's Manny's Car Wash, where he went over so well that he and his group became the unofficial house band. By the time of *Greycourt Lightning,* he had matured into a budding blues star whose guitar playing is second to none. — J.Z.

OSCAR PETERSON

★★★½ **Oscar Peterson Plays the George Gershwin Songbook (1952; Verve, 1996)**

★★★½ **At Zardi's (1955; Pablo, 1995)**
★★★ **At the Stratford Shakespearean Festival (1956; Verve, 1993)**
★★★½ **Oscar Peterson Plays Count Basie (1956; Verve, 1993)**
★★★½ **Sonny Stitt Sits In with the Oscar Peterson Trio (1957; Verve, 1991)**
★★★½ **At the Concertgebouw (1957; Verve, 1994)**
★★★½ **Oscar Peterson Plays Porgy and Bess (1959; Verve, 1993)**
★★★½ **Oscar Peterson Plays the Cole Porter Songbook (1959; Verve, 1986)**
★★★ **A Jazz Portrait of Frank Sinatra (1959; Verve, 1985)**
★★★★ **Ben Webster Meets Oscar Peterson (1960; Verve, 1997)**
★★★ **The Trio (1961; Verve, 1986)**
★★★½ **The London House Sessions (1961; Verve, 1996)**
★★½ **West Side Story (1962; Verve, 1995)**
★★★ **We Get Requests (1964; Verve, 1986)**
★★★½ **Oscar Peterson Trio + 1 (with Clark Terry) (1964; Verve, N.A.)**
★★★ **Eloquence (1965; Verve, 1987)**
★★★ **Blues Etude (1966; Verve, N.A.)**
★★★½ **My Favorite Instrument (1968; Verve, 1990)**
★★★★ **Reunion Blues (1971; Verve, 1992)**
★★★½ **Tracks (1971; Verve, 1995)**
★★★½ **The Trio (with Joe Pass and Niels-Henning Ørsted Pedersen) (1973; Pablo, 1987)**
★★★ **The Good Life (1973; Original Jazz Classics, 1991)**
★★★ **The Giants (1975; Original Jazz Classics, 1995)**
★★★½ **Oscar Peterson and Harry "Sweets" Edison (1975; Original Jazz Classics, 1992)**
★★★½ **Ella and Oscar (with Ella Fitzgerald) (1975; Pablo, 1987)**
★★★½ **Oscar Peterson and Roy Eldridge (1975; Original Jazz Classics, 1992)**
★★★ **Oscar Peterson and Clark Terry (1975; Original Jazz Classics, 1994)**
★★½ **Porgy and Bess (with Joe Pass) (1976; Original Jazz Classics, 1994)**
★★★ **Tristeza on Piano (1976; Verve, N.A.)**
★★★ **Montreux '77 (with the Oscar Peterson Jam) (1977; Original Jazz Classics, N.A.)**
★★★ **Montreux '77 (with Ray Brown and Niels-Henning Ørsted Pedersen) (1977; Original Jazz Classics, 1989)**
★★★ **Jousts (1978; Original Jazz Classics, 1995)**
★★★ **The Paris Concert (with Joe Pass and Niels-Henning Ørsted Pedersen) (1978; Pablo, 1993)**
★★★ **The London Concert (1978; Pablo, 1993)**
★★★½ **Skol (with Stéphane Grappelli) (1979; Original Jazz Classics, 1991)**
★★½ **Digital at Montreux (with Niels-Henning Ørsted Pedersen) (Pablo, 1979)**
★★★½ **Nigerian Marketplace (Pablo, 1982)**
★★½ **Face to Face (with Freddie Hubbard) (1982; Original Jazz Classics, 1987)**
★★½ **If You Could See Me Now (Pablo, 1983)**
★★★½ **Two of the Few (1983; Original Jazz Classics, 1992)**
★★★ **A Tribute to My Friends (1984; Original Jazz Classics, 1996)**
★★½ **Oscar Peterson Live! (Pablo, 1986)**
★★★ **Time After Time (1986; Pablo, 1991)**
★★★ **Oscar Peterson and Dizzy Gillespie (Pablo, 1987)**
★★½ **The Personal Touch (Pablo, 1988)**
★★★½ **Oscar Peterson + Harry Edison + Eddie "Cleanhead" Vinson (Pablo, 1988)**
★★★★ **Compact Jazz: Oscar Peterson and Friends (Verve, 1988)**
★★★ **Compact Jazz: Oscar Peterson Plays Jazz Standards (Verve, 1988)**
★★★★ **Live at the Blue Note (Telarc, 1990)**
★★★½ **Saturday Night at the Blue Note (Telarc, 1991)**
★★★ **The Will to Swing/Oscar Petersen at His Very Best (Verve, 1991)**
★★★½ **The Essential Oscar Peterson: The Swinger (Verve, 1992)**
★★★ **Jazz 'Round Midnight (Verve, 1992)**
★★★ **Last Call at the Blue Note (Telarc, 1992)**
★★★ **Encore at the Blue Note (Telarc, 1993)**
★★★ **Three Originals (Verve, 1993)**
★★★ **History of an Artist (Pablo, 1993)**

★★★ **Oscar Peterson Plays My Fair Lady/The Music from Fiorello! (Verve, 1994)**
★★★ **Verve Jazz Masters 16 (Verve, 1994)**
★★★ **Verve Jazz Masters 37: Oscar Peterson Plays Broadway (Verve, 1994)**
★★★½ **The Complete Young Oscar Peterson (1945–1949) (RCA, 1994)**
★★★ **The Lamp Is Low (Four Star, 1995)**
★★★½ **The More I See You (Telarc, 1995)**
★★★ **The Song Is You: The Best of the Verve Songbooks (Verve, 1996)**
★★★ **Bursting Out with the All Star Band!/Swinging Brass (Verve, 1996)**
★★★ **The Jazz Soul of Oscar Peterson/Affinity (Verve, 1996)**
★★★ **Two Originals: Walking the Line/Another Day (Verve, 1996)**
★★★ **Oscar Peterson in Russia (Pablo, 1996)**
★★★★ **Oscar Peterson Meets Roy Hargrove and Ralph Moore (Telarc, 1996)**
★★★½ **A Tribute to Oscar Peterson: Live at Town Hall (Telarc, 1997)**
★★ **The Silver Collection (Verve, N.A.)**

An international jazz institution, Montreal-born pianist/composer Oscar Peterson (b. 1925) possesses the most overwhelming technique of the musicians from his era. His intention to play at faster speeds and more complex harmonic levels is both a blessing and a curse, however: His playing prowess drowns expression and becomes more of an impossible feat accomplished than a statement communicated. Peterson's virtuosity is in direct lineage to Art Tatum, who accomplished similarly astonishing keyboard pyrotechnics a generation before, but Tatum's approach, on the whole, came across as warmer.

Nevertheless, it would be a deeply ironic mistake to criticize Peterson for in essence being too good. His accomplishments give him a major role in jazz history. He was a superb accompanist when called upon in such a role (he excelled playing with vocalist Ella Fitzgerald) and a master of both up-tempo swing and ballad styles. Peterson built his reputation as one of the most prolix note-wielders on the notoriously solo-crammed jam sessions of the famous Jazz at the Philharmonic tours. Recorded in the '50s and early '60s, *Compact Jazz: Oscar Peterson and Friends* demonstrates Peterson's abilities in a variety of swing contexts—the friends include saxophonists Lester Young, Ben Webster, Stan Getz, Sonny Stitt and Flip Phillips, trumpeter Roy Eldridge, vibraphonists Lionel Hampton and Milt Jackson and vocalists Fitzgerald, Fred Astaire and Anita O'Day.

During the mid-'50s Peterson worked most frequently in a drummerless trio—his powerful and often percussive style left little room for a drummer. His right-hand man from the inception of his trio was bassist Ray Brown, an extraordinary player in his own right. Barney Kessel was the guitarist on *Oscar Peterson Plays the George Gershwin Songbook;* Herb Ellis played guitar on the *At the Concertgebouw, At the Stratford Shakespearean Festival* and *At Zardi's* sets. By the end of the '50s Peterson had arrived at his classic trio: Brown and drummer Ed Thigpen. This is the format in which he would record most frequently, although he would often augment it to a quartet or strip it down to duet exchanges and occasionally even revisit the drummerless trio.

Oscar Peterson Plays Count Basie features Brown, Ellis and drummer Buddy Rich, but the Brown/Thigpen lineup appears on *Oscar Peterson Plays My Fair Lady, Oscar Peterson Plays Porgy and Bess, Oscar Peterson Plays the Cole Porter Songbook, A Jazz Portrait of Frank Sinatra, The Silver Collection* (with mawkish Nelson Riddle strings), Verve's *The Trio, Eloquence, The Jazz Soul of Oscar Peterson/Affinity, The London House Sessions, West Side Story* and *We Get Requests. Bursting Out with the All Star Band!/Swinging Brass* is a big-band session. *My Favorite Instrument* and *Tracks* are solo outings. *Oscar Peterson Trio + 1* adds flügelhornist Clark Terry, a longtime collaborator with Peterson. Vibist Jackson appears on *Reunion Blues.*

Peterson returned to the drummerless trio in the early 1970s as he embarked on a prolific era at Pablo. The new format, featuring bassist Niels-Henning Ørsted Pedersen and guitarist Joe Pass, put out both Pablo's *The Trio* and *The Good Life* in 1973. Pass and Peterson (on clavichord) played a series of duets for a new reading of *Porgy and Bess,* and teamed up with Brown on bass for *The Giants.*

At Pablo, Peterson was placed in a wide range of musical settings, from the duets with Gillespie, Edison, Eldridge and Terry to the two-bassist concept (Brown and NHØP) on *Montreux '77* and the Jazz at the

Philharmonic–style jam, with Eddie "Lockjaw" Davis and Gillespie, from the same year. Peterson took on each of the trumpet kings—Terry, Eldridge, Gillespie, Edison and Jon Faddis—on *Jousts.* In '78 Peterson reunited with Pass and NHØP for *The Paris Concert.* The same year produced *The London Concert,* with drummer Louis Bellson and bassist John Heard.

Skol, with violinist Stéphane Grappelli and drummer Mickey Roker augmenting the Pass/NHØP trio, is a delightful session in which Peterson is doing as much listening as playing; the *Digital at Montreux* duet with NHØP is disappointingly dry. *The Personal Touch,* an uninspired quintet session additionally labored with a string section, is best left alone. *Nigerian Marketplace,* with drummer Terry Clarke joining NHØP, is a momentary return to form before the listless *If You Could See Me Now.* Milt Jackson's spirited vibes come to the rescue on the excellent duet album *Two of the Few. Oscar Peterson Live!* and *Time After Time* introduce a new quartet with Pass joined by bassist David Young and drummer Martin Drew. The summit meeting with the always delightful Edison and the soulful Eddie "Cleanhead" Vinson does not disappoint.

The indefatigable Peterson charged into the 1990s on the strength of a remarkable engagement at New York's Blue Note nightclub that yielded four releases. Reunited with Brown, Ellis and drummer Bobby Durham, Peterson adds emotional depth and softer edges to his playing. *The More I See You* is a warm sextet session with old friends Brown and Clark Terry joined by alto saxophonist Benny Carter, drummer Lewis Nash and guitarist Lorne Lofsky. *Oscar Peterson Meets Roy Hargrove and Ralph Moore* is an entirely successful cross-generational collaboration. Hargrove's great blues sense and emotional nuance allow him the free range of Peterson's palette, while NHØP, Nash and Ralph Moore on tenor saxophone more than hold up their end of the bargain.
— J.S.

RALPH PETERSON

★★★★ **The Reclamation Project (Evidence, 1995)**

★★★★ **The Fo'tet Plays Monk (Evidence, 1997)**

Drummer Ralph Peterson (b. 1962) was marketed as one of the young lions of late-1980s and 1990s jazz. Despite being placed in the context of a series of equally talented young players, Peterson failed to display a coherent vision on a series of disappointing, no-longer-available albums for Blue Note. On Evidence, however, Peterson produced an expressive vision with a "fo'tet" whose playing on *The Reclamation Project* is bigger than its names—Steve Wilson on soprano saxophone, Bryan Carrott on vibraphones and marimba and Belden Bulloch on bass. The same lineup covers nine Thelonious Monk compositions, including "Jackie-ing," "Played Twice," "Criss Cross" and "Brilliant Corners," on *The Fo'tet Plays Monk.* — J.S.

MICHEL PETRUCCIANI

★★★½ **Pianism (Blue Note, 1987)**

★★★★ **Power of Three (Blue Note, 1987)**

★★★½ **Michel Plays Petrucciani (Blue Note, 1988)**

★★★ **Music (Blue Note, 1989)**

★★★★ **Promenade with Duke (Blue Note, 1993)**

★★★½ **Live (Blue Note, 1994)**

★★★½ **The Best of Michel Petrucciani (Blue Note, 1994)**

★★★★ **Marvellous (Dreyfus, 1994)**

★★★★ **Conference de Presse (Dreyfus, 1995)**

★★★★ **Au Théâtre des Champs-Élysées (Dreyfus, 1997)**

★★★½ **Both Worlds (Dreyfus, 1998)**

French pianist Michel Petrucciani (1962–1999) became a major contemporary stylist despite the lifelong handicap of the growth-inhibiting bone disease osteogenensis imperfecta. Fascinated by music since his childhood spent in a household with a guitarist father and bassist brother, Petrucciani overcame his disability and showed great ability as a pianist. After playing in the family band, Petrucciani was introduced to the mainstream jazz world at age 15, playing with Clark Terry and Kenny Clarke.

He made his first recording at age 17, a duo with alto saxophonist Lee Konitz on a 1980 tour of France, and moved to the United States in 1982 to tour with Charles Lloyd. Petrucciani's early recordings are currently unavailable domestically, but the solo sessions *Oracle's Destiny* and *100 Hearts* and the trio recording *Live at the Village Vanguard* are worth searching out.

Petrucciani was a key figure in Blue Note's mid-1980s revival. *Pianism* features the same trio as on the Village Vanguard set, bassist Palle Danielsson and drummer Eliot Zigmund. *Power of Three* ups the ante considerably with the presence of soprano and tenor saxophonist Wayne Shorter and guitarist Jim Hall. Another powerful set, *Michel Plays Petrucciani* includes guitarist John Abercrombie and two rhythm sections featuring bassists Eddie Gomez and Gary Peacock and drummers Al Foster and Roy Haynes.

Interesting lineups including Joe Lovano on soprano sax, Gil Goldstein on accordion, a variety of rhythm sections and vocalist Tania Maria enliven *Music,* but its self-conscious bid for airplay distracts from Petrucciani's strengths. The solo-piano *Promenade with Duke* admirably shows off Petrucciani's stirring romanticism and melodic invention. *Live* is a fascinating two-keyboard band with keyboard wizard Adam Holzman. *The Best of Michel Petrucciani* is a useful collection from the Blue Note titles.

In the mid-'90s Petrucciani moved to the French label Dreyfus. The pianist opened up in his new surroundings with *Marvellous,* a trio with the great rhythm section of bassist Dave Holland and drummer Tony Williams augmented by a string quartet, and followed suit with the daringly unconventional piano/organ outing with Eddy Louiss, *Conference de Presse.*

From his earliest days as an unabashed disciple of pianist Bill Evans, Petrucciani has displayed remarkable gifts as a soloist. *Au Théâtre des Champs-Élysées* is his crowning achievement in this format, a collection of some of his favorite melodic themes extemporized with the romantic flair and vibrant swing of a keyboard master. The 40-minute-plus opener in this two-CD set, "Medley of My Favorite Songs," is a great piece of extended piano improvisations, accessible without reliance on cliché, a landmark performance by a critically underappreciated artist. The sextet recording *Both Worlds* teams Petrucciani's composing skills with the arrangements of Bob Brookmeyer into a strong brass odyssey unlike anything he did before on record. — J.S.

OSCAR PETTIFORD

★★★★ Deep Passion (Impulse!, 1994)
★★★½ Oscar Pettiford Sextet (Vogue Disques, 1996)

Bassist/cellist Oscar Pettiford (1922–1960) was an unsung hero of jazz who followed in the footsteps of Jimmy Blanton to establish the role of the bass as more than just a cog in the rhythm section. Pettiford was among the most sought-after players of his era, working with Duke Ellington, Thelonious Monk, Charlie Parker, Sonny Rollins, Miles Davis and Milt Jackson, as well as blues singer Wynonie Harris. He played throughout the Midwest as part of his family's band before coming to prominence in the 1940s playing with big bands led by Charlie Barnet, Duke Ellington and Woody Herman. He went on to form one of the first bebop groups, in partnership with Dizzy Gillespie, and to become an integral part of New York's 52nd Street scene during the bop era. He appears on Sonny Rollins's *Freedom Suite.*Pettiford was also an accomplished writer and arranger who pioneered the cello as a jazz instrument.

Despite his stature, Pettiford's own meager output as a leader is all but buried. Available on vinyl only, *The New Oscar Pettiford Sextet,* made for Charles Mingus's Debut label, features Pettiford on cello and Mingus on bass, with Julius Watkins's french horn blending beautiful tones against those strings, along with Phil Urso on tenor saxophone, Walter Bishop on piano and Percy Brice on drums.

Deep Passion is a big-band collection featuring tenor saxophonist Lucky Thompson, trumpeters Ernie Royal and Art Farmer, trombonist Jimmy Cleveland, pianist Tommy Flanagan and drummer Gus Johnson. *Oscar Pettiford Sextet* is the reissue of a 1954 session with drummer Max Roach, tenorist Al Cohn, trombonist Kai Winding, guitarist Tal Farlow and pianist Henry Renaud. Pettiford plays both bass and cello. If you're looking for more of Pettiford's cello work, it's worth seraching for the currently unavailable *My Little Cello.*
— J.S.

BARRE PHILLIPS

★★½ Aquarian Rain (ECM, 1992)

Classically trained bassist Barre Phillips (b. 1934) has played extensively in both classical and jazz settings and was part of Gunther Schuller's Third Stream attempt to bridge the gap between the two musics in the 1960s. Phillips continued to expand his boundaries in Europe, playing with a wide range of musicians including George Russell, Attila Zoller and Gong.

Phillips has made a series of probing albums over the years in a variety of contexts dating back to the late-'60s effort *Unaccompanied Barre.* Though most of the critically acclaimed recordings were for the ECM label, the only title remaining available under that imprint is the substandard *Aquarian Rain,* a bloodless group of electronically tweaked duets with percussionist Alain Joule.

Search out Phillips's work as a solo performer (*Journal Violone, Call Me When You Get There*), as part of the group Trio with saxophonist John Surman and drummer Stu Martin, in tandem with Dave Holland (*Music from Two Basses*), with Norwegian guitarist Terje Rypdal (*What Comes After*) and the breathtaking *Mountainscapes,* the Trio lineup augmented with guitarist John Abercrombie and synthesist Dieter Feichtener. — J.S.

ESTHER PHILLIPS

★★★ **Memory Lane: The Best Songs Little Esther Ever Recorded (1959; King, 1994)**
★★★ **And I Love Him (1965; Rhino, 1998)**
★★★ **What a Diff'rence a Day Makes (1975; Columbia, N.A.)**
★★★★½ **Confessin' the Blues (1975; Rhino, 1990)**
★★★ **Esther Phillips (1978; Just a Memory, 1995)**
★★★★½ **The Best Songs Ever (King, 1997)**
★★★★½ **The Best of Esther Phillips (1962–1970) (Rhino, 1997)**

Esther Phillips (1935–1984) used her unique voice to put her distinctive stamp on a wide range of material, from her early R&B days as a contemporary of Etta James, gigging with Johnny Otis's revue, to her nights as a denizen of Studio 54, performing as a disco queen. She will always be remembered most, however, for her earthy approach to blues, R&B and jazz.

Like James, Phillips was barely in her teens when she began scoring R&B hits backed by Johnny Otis's orchestra. These early sides—which document the evolution of rock & roll from R&B—are available on King's *Memory Lane: The Best Songs Little Esther Ever Recorded* and the more complete *The Best Songs Ever.* Phillips dropped out of the business for a while in 1954, returning eight years later—and really hitting her stride. The best introduction to Phillips's mature artistry is the double-CD Rhino set that anthologizes these years. It includes her 1962 comeback hit "Release Me," which led to a contract with Atlantic, for whom she cut some awesome sides. Her forte was putting her own spin on well-known songs by others: "And I Love Him" (the Beatles' "And I Love Her"), Van Morrison's "Crazy Love," Willie Nelson's "Hello Walls," Dylan's "Tonight, I'll Be Staying Here with You." No matter the genre, it all came out sounding 100 percent Phillips—soulful, with a jazzy feel. Still available is *And I Love Him,* her first album for Atlantic. *Confessin' the Blues* consists of seven tracks produced by Nesuhi Ertegun featuring Phillips backed by a jazz orchestra and six stripped-down sides (just piano, bass and drums) produced by King Curtis.

Plagued by heroin addiction, Phillips's recording career faltered in the early '70s; after drug treatment, she signed with Kudu, for whom she cut a series of bluesy jazz albums. The one still in print, *Esther Phillips,* documents her less than effective disco sound, as does *What a Diff'rence a Day Makes,* the 1975 album that gave her a disco hit with the title track. Unfortunately, Phillips lost her battle with substance abuse, and died of liver and kidney failure in 1984. — H.G.-W.

FLIP PHILLIPS

★★★½ **A Sound Investment (with Scott Hamilton) (Concord Jazz, 1987)**
★★★ **A Real Swinger (Concord Jazz, 1988)**
★★★ **The Claw: Live at the 1986 Floating Jazz Festival (Chiaroscuro, 1991)**
★★½ **Try a Little Tenderness (Chiaroscuro, 1992)**
★★★ **At the Helm—Live at the 1993 Floating Jazz Festival (Chiaroscuro, 1994)**
★★★ **Flip Wails: The Best of the Verve Years (Verve, 1994)**
★★★ **John and Joe Revisited (Chiaroscuro, 1996)**

Tenor saxophonist Flip Phillips (b. 1915) began his lengthy career in the swing era playing in his hometown of Brooklyn and went on to star in the Benny Goodman and Woody Herman orchestras as well as Norman Granz's Jazz at the Philharmonic all-star jam sessions, where his big-voiced, prolix solos drew the ire of some jazz critics who resented him for taking space from other players. His solos preserved on the Verve JATP series show him to be a robust and emotional player, however, and his musical tenacity served him well over a career that saw him still kicking at age 78 (on tenor) in front of a swinging quintet featuring bassist Milt Hinton and guitarist Bucky Pizzarelli on *At the Helm. A Real Swinger* is similar fare; *Try a Little*

Tenderness has him singing with strings. *A Sound Investment* features saxophonist Scott Hamilton and includes a cover of Hoagy Carmichael's "New Orleans." — J.S.

PIANO RED

★★★ Atlanta Bounce (1972; Arhoolie, 1992)
★★★ Blues, Blues, Blues (Black Lion, 1992)

Born William Lee Perryman in Hampton, Georgia, Piano Red (1911 or 1913–1985) was influenced by Fats Waller and Tampa Red. In 1936 he recorded some unreleased sides for Vocalion with Blind Willie McTell, then in the early '60s he became Dr. Feelgood by virtue of his Okeh hit "Doctor Feel-Good." *Atlanta Bounce* features Red singing and playing solo piano on all but five tracks that were recorded with a full band at Atlanta's Magnolia Ballroom on March 5, 1956. This live material, with its straight-ahead barrelhouse style, has a crackling excitement to it, while the other tracks on the album tend to sound a bit staid. Two of the live selections, "Rockin' with Red" and "Red's Boogie," were originally recorded for RCA Victor in 1950 and became a double-sided national hit for Piano Red the next year (he also had three other hits that year). Of the solo material, Red's boozy ruminations shine through on tracks like "Red's How Long Blues" and "Ten Cent Shot." *Atlanta Bounce* also contains seven previously unreleased tracks, including "Got You on My Mind" and "Boogie Time." *Blues, Blues, Blues* is a solo-piano recording of Red's performance at the 1974 Montreux Jazz Festival. — B.R.H.

ROD PIAZZA

★★★½ Harpburn (1986; Black Top, 1993)
★★★½ Blues in the Dark (Black Top, 1991)
★★★★ Alphabet Blues (Black Top, 1992)
★★★½ California Blues (Black Top, 1997)
★★★★ Tough and Tender (Tone Cool, 1997)
★★★★ Vintage Live: 1975 (Black Top, 1998)

Harmonica virtuoso Rod Piazza (b. 1947) played with the blues/rock outfit the Dirty Blues Band in the late 1960s before serving as an apprentice to harmonica master George "Harmonica" Smith for 15 years as a member of the group Bacon Fat. Piazza went on to form the Mighty Flyers, a backup band that included his wife, Honey Alexander, on keyboards. This band's live intensity is well documented on *Vintage Live: 1975.* As blues made a 1990s comeback, Piazza was well positioned to take advantage. *Harpburn* features former Canned Heat bassist Larry Taylor and guitarists Junior Watson, Hollywood Fats and the Flyers' own stringbender Rick Holmstrom. *Alphabet Blues* is an extremely well-played album; *California Blues* is nearly as good. *Tough and Tender* marks a return to top form for the band, with Piazza blowing his top on harmonica and Holmstrom matching him lick for lick. — J.S.

GREG PICCOLO

★★★½ Heavy Juice (Black Top, 1990)
★★★½ Acid Blue (Fantasy, 1995)
★★★½ Red Lights (Fantasy, 1997)

Vocalist/tenor saxophonist Greg Piccolo (b. 1951) was a founding member of the New England jump-blues band Roomful of Blues before leaving after more than 20 years to form a new group, Heavy Juice. The parting was amicable, as Roomful proved by pitching in on *Heavy Juice,* with Piccolo not straying too far from his previous role. By the time of *Acid Blue,* Piccolo had developed his own sound, mixing his big-band blues roots with the New Orleans influence of Earl King's "Always a First Time" and the Texas blues of Freddie King's "Someday After Awhile," both of which feature Piccolo on electric guitar. Ex-Roomful keyboardist Ron Levy also plays on *Acid Blue. Red Lights* offers more Piccolo on guitar, excellent support from Barry Seelen on Hammond B-3 organ and piano and the rollicking bookends "Old Maid Boogie" and "Moondog Boogie." — J.S.

BILLY PIERCE

★★★½ Epistrophy (1993; Evidence, 1995)

Tenor saxophonist Billy Pierce (b. 1948) grew up in Boston and learned his most important jazz lessons as a member of Art Blakey's Jazz Messengers from 1980 to 1982. After several disappointing records as a leader on the Sunnyside label, Pierce rose to occasion when the Japanese-based King Records gave him the chance to record *Epistrophy,* an album of material associated with his twin idols, Thelonious Monk and Sonny Rollins. Pierce is not afraid to invite comparison with Rollins by opening the set with a quirky version of "I'm an Old Cowhand," from the Rollins recording *Way Out West.* With Donald Brown on piano, Christian McBride on bass and Billy Drummond on drums, Pierce goes on to tackle such Monk fare as "Bye-Ya," "Ugly Beauty," "Epistrophy" and "Criss Cross." — J.S.

COURTNEY PINE

★★ **Journey to the Urge Within (Antilles, 1987)**
★★★ **Destiny's Song and the Image of Pursuance (Antilles, 1988)**
★★ **The Vision's Tale (Antilles, 1990)**
★★★ **Closer to Home (Antilles, 1990)**
★★★ **Within the Realms of Our Dreams (Antilles, 1991)**
★★★ **To the Eyes of Creation (Island, 1992)**
★★★ **Modern Day Jazz Stories (Antilles, 1996)**
★★★★ **Underground (Antilles, 1997)**

An English tenor saxophonist of Jamaican descent, Courtney Pine (b. 1964) spent his early years playing in reggae bands while woodshedding jazz. At age 22, he virtually revolutionized the English jazz scene single-handedly, with a similar (if not as thorough) effect as the Marsalis brothers had in the United States. Pine established the Abibi Jazz Arts organization, worked with virtually all the musicians passing through and toured with Art Blakey's Jazz Messengers.

Journey to the Urge Within is a sprawling, loosely postbop recording with the pretty but out-of-place "Children of the Ghetto" as a cornerstone. *Destiny's Song and the Image of Pursuance* flirts with reggae and makes a more cohesive statement, with a wonderful solo version of "'Round Midnight" at its heart. His next recordings follow in the postbop vein with various degrees of success. Two thirds of *The Vision's Tale* is classic jazz ("C Jam Blues," "Giant Steps") with a quartet including pianist Ellis Marsalis and drummer Jeff Watts, but it doesn't cook like it might. Similar in scope, *Within the Realms of Our Dreams* fares much better. "The Sepia Love Song" shows off Pine's way with a melody, while "A Raggamuffin and His Lance," Ornette Coleman's "Una Muy Bonita" and Wynton Marsalis's "Delfeayo's Dilemma" offer forums for extremely muscular blowing.

The soloing on *To the Eyes of Creation* is no less muscular, but the backing shows signs of maturation and less slavish devotion to the young-lion ethic. Perhaps his most lyrically melodic work, it also features synthesizers and overdubbing. Covers of the Skatalites' "Eastern Standard Time" and Bob Marley's "Redemption Song" set the stage for *Closer to Home,* Pine's reggae record. The personnel—percussionists Cleavie, Sly Dunbar and Drummie and baritone saxophonist Dean Fraser—are closer to reggae than jazz, but this does not prevent Pine from delivering some of his fiercest and most melodic playing.

Modern Day Jazz Stories brings together contemporaries like Cassandra Wilson, Geri Allen, Charnett Moffett and Mark Whitfield with old-guard hero Eddie Henderson and DJ Pogo. When it works, the scratching plays like hand percussion or occasionally sets up a deep hip-hop groove. When it doesn't, the DJ sounds forced into the more melodic postbop contexts. Yet through it all, Pine blows as fiercely as ever. *Underground* continues his collaboration with DJ Pogo, adding Wynton Marsalis's former rhythm section of Reginald Veal and Jeff Tain Watts, Cyrus Chestnut and cameos by trumpeter Nicholas Payton and guitarist Mark Whitfield. Both an homage and revamping of soul jazz, the recording has a looser format and everyone blows. Tunes like the title track and "Oneness of Mind" might have come off a Ramsey Lewis record if not for the scratching and samples. Pine's tenor and soprano work excels throughout. Chestnut plays some killer organ, but his piano on the album's straightest cut, "Silver Surfer," really stands out. — H.B.

MIKA POHJOLA

★★★★½ **Myths and Beliefs (GM, 1996)**
★★★★ **On the Move (GM, 1997)**

Pianist Mika Pohjola was born in 1972 in Finland, where he developed an interest in jazz by listening to his bassist father's playing and extensive jazz record collection. Art Tatum and Charlie Parker provided early inspiration, but classical music and Stevie Wonder were parallel influences. Pohjola went to study with Gary Burton at Berklee College of Music, then relocated in 1995 to New York.

Myths and Beliefs is an impressive debut from a pianist whose compositions are designed to offer him full expression on the keyboard. His simple, direct lyricism recalls Burton and Chick Corea on their collaboration *Crystal Silence.* Pohjola ruminates on ancient stories from the days of the Roman Empire with moods drawn from contemporary life. The quartet features great support from guitarist Mick Goodrick. Pohjola once again evokes dreamlike landscapes with his atmospheric compositions throughout *On the Move.* This time the quartet includes saxophonist Chris Cheek. — J.S.

DANIEL PONCE

★★★½ **Arawe (Antilles, 1987)**
★★★½ **Chango Te Llama (Mango, 1991)**

Cuban percussionist Daniel Ponce (b. 1953) is one of the greatest new-generation congeros, a supple and powerful player who's worked with Paquito D'Rivera, Dizzy Gillespie, Tito Puente and Eddie Palmieri. *Arawe* features an all-star cast including Yomo Toro on cuatro, Vernon Reid on guitar and Steve Turre on trombone. *Chango Te Llama* includes saxophonists Mario Rivera and Dave Sanchez. Also look for Ponce's fine (out-of-print) debut, *New York Now!*
— J.S.

JIMMY PONDER

★★★ **Mean Streets—No Bridges (Muse, 1987)**
★★★★ **Jump (Muse, 1988)**
★★★ **Come On Down (Muse, 1991)**
★★★ **To Reach a Dream (Muse, 1992)**
★★★ **Soul Eyes (Muse, 1995)**
★★★ **Something to Ponder (Muse, 1996)**

Guitarist Jimmy Ponder (b. 1946) is a groove-oriented soul-jazz player out of the Grant Green mold. The Pittsburgh native's big break came playing in Charles Earland's mid-'60s organ combo, and he went on to gigs with Lou Donaldson, Donald Byrd, Stanley Turrentine, Jimmy McGriff, Groove Holmes, Ron Carter and Roland Hanna. Ponder mixes pop titles with jazz standards, filtering them all through his burning R&B-friendly conception. *Jump* is the standout here, although it's worth looking for the out-of-print *Down Here on the Ground.*
— J.S.

JEAN-LUC PONTY

★★★½ **Electric Connection (1969; One Way, 1993)**
★★★ **More Than Meets the Ear (1969; One Way, 1994)**
★★★★ **Upon the Wings of Music (1975; Atlantic, N.A.)**
★★★ **Aurora (1975; Atlantic, 1990)**
★★★ **Imaginary Voyage (1976; Atlantic, 1987)**
★★★ **Cosmic Messenger (1978; Atlantic, 1987)**
★★★ **A Taste for Passion (1979; Atlantic, N.A.)**
★★★★ **Live at Donte's (1981; Blue Note, 1996)**
★★★ **Mystical Adventures (Atlantic, 1982)**
★★★ **Individual Choice (Atlantic, 1983)**
★★★½ **Open Mind (Atlantic, 1984)**
★★★ **Fables (Atlantic, 1985)**
★★½ **The Gift of Time (Sony, 1987)**
★★½ **Storytelling (Sony, 1989)**
★★★ **The Jean-Luc Ponty Experience (One Way, 1991)**
★★★ **No Absolute Time (Atlantic, 1993)**
★★★★★ **Le Voyage: The Jean-Luc Ponty Anthology (Rhino, 1996)**
★★★½ **Live at Chene Park (Atlantic, 1997)**

Virtuoso violinist Jean-Luc Ponty (b. 1942) excels in acoustic, electric and MIDI contexts and is one of the most accomplished soloists of his generation. A child prodigy from a family of classical musicians and teachers, his goal was to compose symphonies—until he heard New Orleans clarinetist Albert Nicholas's Paris-based jazz group and asked to sit in. Ponty's impressive technique came to the attention of the venerable French jazz violinist Stéphane Grappelli, who urged him to continue in the jazz idiom. Ponty's introduction to U.S. audiences came in 1967 when he was invited to play the Monterey Jazz Festival after winning the Miscellaneous Instrument and New Talent sections of *Down Beat*'s 1966 critic's poll. During that American stay, Ponty began playing with keyboardist George Duke; some of their work is available on *Electric Connection* and *More Than Meets the Ear.*

Ponty played with Frank Zappa on 1970's *Hot Rats* and several other Zappa projects and tours. His electric violin became one of the cornerstones of the fusion sound, and in the mid-'70s he debuted his own fusion outfit with the impressive *Upon the Wings of Music.* He went on to make a series of albums in a similar format, relying more on synthesizers in the '80s, beginning with *Individual Choice.* Though much of the sound's original excitement wore off through repetition, Ponty's technique continued to be impressive, yielding moments of brilliance throughout the catalog. *Open Mind,* with Chick Corea and George Benson, is a particularly good moment. *Le Voyage* offers an outstanding overview of Ponty's career that sticks to the high points of his fusion outings. On *Live at Chene Park* Ponty offers his own version of a career overview, leading a pumped-up quintet on five-string MIDI violin and six-string violectra.
— J.S.

POPA CHUBBY

★★★ **It's Chubby Time (Laughing Bear, 1993)**
★★★ **Gas Money (Laughing Bear, 1994)**

★★★½ **Booty and the Beast (Okeh/Sony, 1995)**
★★★★ **Hit the High Hard One (1-800-PRIME-CD, 1996)**
★★★★ **One Million Broken Guitars (Dixiefrog, 1997)**

Guitarist Ted "Popa Chubby" Horowitz (b. 1960) has been a fixture on the 1990s New York blues scene, helping make the Sunday-night jam at Manny's Car Wash essential on every blues fan's weekly calendar. A good songwriter, powerful vocalist and high-intensity string-bender, Horowitz began as part of New York's hard-core scene in such bands as Screaming Mad George and Disgusting, then as a sideman with Richard Hell and Pierce Turner before adopting the Popa Chubby persona and establishing himself as the '90s answer to Leslie West.

Popa Chubby's meteoric rise to blues prominence began when he won a nationwide talent contest and a spot in the 1992 Long Beach Blues Festival, released a pair of solid indie albums over the next two years, then followed by a major-label release on Okeh/Sony. *Booty and the Beast* is a hard-edged set produced by Tom Dowd, but Chubby is best heard on the incendiary live recording *Hit the High Hard One,* which features the gut-wrenching "Heart Attack and Vine," the minor hit "Sweet Goddess of Love and Beer" and the apocalyptic finale, "Wild Thing." — J.S.

GEORGE PORTER JR.

★★★½ **Runnin' Partner (Rounder, 1990)**
★★★½ **Things Ain't What They Used to Be (Transvideo, 1994)**
★★★½ **Funk This (Transvideo, 1997)**

As a founding member of New Orleans's legendary Meters, George Porter Jr. (b. 1947) was a cornerstone of late-'60s/early-'70s funk. *Runnin' Partner* finds Porter attempting to musically step outside that band's formidable shadow. The result is a well-conceived—albeit lightweight—album of originals, plus two Earl King songs thrown in for good measure. With healthy dollops of horn-inflected New Orleans funk, soul and R&B in the mix (occasionally supported by a sinewy groove), the arrangements and performances are actually superior to the songs themselves (except for King's "Don't You Make Me Act Ig'nunt" and "Rough Spots," upon which he guests). Other highlights include the funky instrumentals "More BTU's" and "D.T.P.," both of which illustrate Porter's musical looseness and spontaneity. *Things Ain't What They Used to Be* is a hot set recorded live in New Orleans. *Funk This* shows Porter's band settling into a comfortable studio groove. — B.R.H.

CHRIS POTTER

★★★ **Concentric Circles (Concord Jazz, 1994)**
★★★★ **Pure (Concord Jazz, 1995)**
★★★★ **Concord Duo Series, Vol. 10 (with Kenny Werner) (Concord Jazz, 1996)**
★★★ **Moving In (Concord Jazz, 1996)**
★★★★ **Unspoken (Concord Jazz, 1997)**
★★ **Vertigo (Concord Jazz, 1998)**

As a teenager, saxophonist Chris Potter (b. 1971) burst onto the jazz scene like a breath of fresh air. Born in Chicago and raised in South Carolina, he was discovered by trumpeter Red Rodney, who played with him at a local jazz festival. When Potter moved to New York at age 18, he began a four-year stint in Rodney's final band. He has also worked with drummer Paul Motian's Electric BeBop Band, the Mingus Big Band and pianists Marian McPartland and Renee Rosnes.

While the tenor saxophone is Potter's primary musical voice, he plays a variety of wind instruments and has developed a formidable soprano-sax sound. His strong debut, *Concentric Circles,* blends impressive originals and a pair of standards, with pianist Kenny Werner anchoring the band. *Pure* is a multifaceted quintet session, and Potter's duo recording with Werner sets a high standard for that format. His most challenging date, *Unspoken* consists entirely of originals and features John Scofield, Jack DeJohnette and Dave Holland. *Vertigo* is his deepest venture into free jazz but also his most disappointing project. While filled with original material, it is flawed by poor sound balance. *Moving In* teams Potter with pianist Brad Mehldau, bassist Larry Grenadier and drummer Billy Hart in explorations of original material that further develop his musical voice. — K.F.

BUD POWELL

★★★★★ **Jazz Giant (1950; Verve, 1988)**
★★★★½ **The Genius of Bud Powell (1951; Verve, 1988)**
★★★★ **Inner Fires: The Genius of Bud Powell (1953; Discovery, 1993)**

★★★½ Jazz at Massey Hall, Vol. 2 (1953; Original Jazz Classics, 1991)
★★★ Strictly Powell (1957; RCA, 1995)
★★★½ Swingin' with Bud (1958; RCA, 1995)
★★★½ The Scene Changes (1959; Blue Note, 1987)
★★★½ Bud in Paris (1960; Xanadu, 1994)
★★★ The Complete Essen Jazz Festival Concert (1960; Black Lion, N.A.)
★★★½ 'Round About Midnight at the Blue Note (1962; Dreyfus, 1994)
★★★ Bouncing with Bud (1962; Delmark, 1987)
★★★½ Salt Peanuts (1964; Black Lion, N.A.)
★★ Blues for Bouffemont (1964; Black Lion, 1989)
★★★ Bud Powell in Paris (1964; Warner Bros., 1995)
★★★ Strictly Confidential (1964; Black Lion, 1994)
★★★★ The Best of Bud Powell (Blue Note, 1989)
★★★★★ The Complete Blue Note and Roost Recordings (Blue Note, 1994)
★★★★ The Best of Bud Powell on Verve (Verve, 1994)
★★★★★ The Complete Bud Powell on Verve (Verve, 1994)
★★★★ Bud Plays Bird (Roulette, 1996)
★★★★ Jazz Profile (Blue Note, 1997)

As Leonard Feather put it long ago, "Bud Powell's status as the first and foremost of the bop pianists has seldom been disputed." Born into a musical family, Earl "Bud" Powell (1924–1966) was present for the early bop experiments at Minton's Playhouse and in 1943 made his first recordings as a sideman with Cootie Williams's band.

While with Williams, Powell was arrested and badly beaten by the police. He then began to display severe emotional problems that would follow him for the rest his life. From 1945 until his death, Powell was institutionalized numerous times, and his gradual deterioration is one of the great tragedies of jazz. Powell's erratic behavior was exacerbated by drug use, alcoholism and, later, tuberculosis. In spite of this, his playing was tremendously influential. The music he recorded in the late 1940s and early '50s displayed incredible technical virtuosity combined with advanced harmonic sophistication, blinding speed and an intense emotionality. While coming from the Art Tatum school of piano, Powell's art was often considered equal to that of Charlie Parker's.

The four-CD set *The Complete Blue Note and Roost Recordings* documents much of Powell's early work, including *Jazz Profile, The Scene Changes, Time Waits* (which is not great) and the out-of-print volumes of *The Amazing Bud Powell,* which capture Powell at his early peak, as well as the notable Roost recordings. *Jazz Giant* and *The Genius of Bud Powell* are both essential, sterling documents of Powell's playing from 1949 through 1951. Flourishing in the trio format, Powell illuminates *Jazz Giant* with his spectacular "Tempus Fugit" and standards like "Sweet Georgia Brown." *The Genius of Bud Powell* features Ray Brown and Buddy Rich on four cuts, three of which are different takes of "Tea for Two." The rest of this disc is solo piano showcasing the idiosyncratic comping of Powell's left hand in glorious battle with his lightning-quick right. These two releases, as well as *The Best of Bud Powell on Verve,* have been encompassed on the massive five-CD set *The Complete Bud Powell on Verve.*

Inner Fires is a spirited trio session with Powell's friend Charles Mingus on bass and Roy Haynes on drums. The three delve into compositions by George Shearing and Miles Davis as well as driving bop classics by Dizzy Gillespie ("Salt Peanuts" and "Woody 'n You"). *Jazz at Massey Hall, Vol. 2* unveils Powell with Mingus and the dynamic Max Roach on drums. There are also four cuts featuring bassist George Duvivier and drummer Art Taylor. Powell is in fine form and repeatedly blows right past his rhythm section.

Strictly Powell and *Swingin' with Bud* show Powell on the wane but still holding things together with impressive talent. *Strictly Powell* features his reliable accomplices George Duvivier and Art Taylor and is curiously relaxed, with occasional flashes of Powell's old virtuosity. The slightly more upbeat *Swingin' with Bud* uses the same rhythm section to better effect. *The Complete Essen Jazz Festival Concert* is well recorded and includes a guest appearance by Coleman Hawkins as well as the estimable rhythm section of Oscar Pettiford and Kenny Clarke.

'Round About Midnight at the Blue Note is a commendable live date from 1961 with Pierre Michelot and Kenny Clarke. *Bouncing with Bud* was recorded in Copenhagen and includes three tunes associated with Powell's old mentor, Thelonious Monk. Along with bassist Niels-

Henning Ørsted Pedersen and drummer William Schiopffe, Powell proudly hangs in there and does a thoroughly respectable job one more time. *Salt Peanuts* includes Johnny Griffin's tenor and may be considered Powell's last great performance available on disc. Poorly recorded, this French date is salvaged by his surprisingly energetic playing and remains a fitting testament to Powell's ability to rise to the occasion, even toward the end of his troubled career. — M.M.

PREACHER BOY AND THE NATURAL BLUES

★★★ **Preacher Boy and the Natural Blues (Blind Pig, 1995)**

★★★ **Gutters and Pews (Blind Pig, 1996)**

Songwriter, guitarist and vocalist Chris "Preacher Boy" Watkins (b. 1968) updates country blues with elements of ragtime, jug-band and country music, resulting in a buoyant, syncopated sound. The instrumentation on his albums includes mandolin, banjo, trumpet, saxophone, clarinet, trombone, tambourine, washboard, harmonica, kazoo, spoons and cowbell (thankfully not all at once) in addition to National steel, 6- and 12-string acoustic guitars, electric guitar, electric and upright basses and drums, divided among six fine musicians.

Watkins is somewhat like Keb' Mo' in his jazzing up of Delta blues styles but with a self-conscious retrosensibility more akin to Leon Redbone. The material on *Preacher Boy and the Natural Blues* is mostly very good, with the exception of "The Drive Goes On," a songwriterish number where Watkins's growly vocals bear a strong similarity to Tom Waits's and sound a bit forced. The best cuts, such as "Milk and Brown Sugar," "Epitaph" and the spooky "Like Me" highlight his wonderful work on National Steel. Watkins proved that his approach was no fluke on an equally eccentric follow-up, *Gutters and Pews,* which features original material such as "Down and Out in This Town" and "Back Then We Only Cared for Hell." — J.Z.

PRESERVATION HALL JAZZ BAND

★★★★ **New Orleans, Vol. 1 (Sony, 1977)**

★★★ **New Orleans, Vol. 2 (Sony, 1982)**

★★★½ **New Orleans, Vol. 3 (Sony, 1983)**

★★★½ **New Orleans, Vol. 4 (Sony, 1988)**

★★★★ **Best of Preservation Hall Jazz Band (Sony, 1989)**

★★★★ **In the Sweet Bye & Bye (Sony, 1996)**

The Preservation Hall Jazz Band practiced the traditional New Orleans style of collective improvisation, led by clarinetist Willie Humphrey Jr. (1900–1994) and trumpeter Percy Humphrey (1905–1995). These two players grew up along with jazz, Willie playing with the Young Tuxedo Brass band, King Oliver and Paul Barbarin, among others, Percy with the Eureka Brass band, George Lewis and others.

The historically important *New Orleans* series provides a detailed link to the earliest jazz performances and hints at the influences that came before jazz. *Vol. 1* opens with the traditional barnburner "Tiger Rag" and mixes spirituals with old folk tunes. Subsequent volumes don't always conjure the same excitement, and the singing becomes a little stilted at times, but the lengthy treatment of "Just a Closer Walk with Thee" on *Vol. 3* gives a good account of what funeral marches must have sounded like. *Vol. 4* is a strong collection of material highlighted by "Oh Didn't He Ramble" and "Bourbon Street Parade." *Best of Preservation Hall Jazz Band* does a good job of sampling highlights from the four discs.

The Humphreys are gone by the time of *In the Sweet Bye & Bye,* replaced by the virtuosic Dr. Michel White on clarinet and the new granddaddy of New Orleans jazz, Ellis Marsalis, on piano. This session covers similar musical ground in a more spirited fashion than the *New Orleans* recordings and proves that even approaching the next century, the oldest style of jazz still has plenty of vitality. — J.S.

RUTH PRICE

★★★ **Ruth Price (1961; Original Jazz Classics, 1991)**

Vocalist Ruth Price (b. 1938) carved out her reputation as a swing-influenced interpreter with Charlie Ventura, Red Garland, Harry James and Shelly Manne, among others. On *Ruth Price* she's backed by Manne and his group, including pianist Russ Freeman and tenor saxophonist Richie Kamuca, in a set at the Manne-Hole. — J.S.

JOHN PRIMER

★★★ **Stuff You Got to Watch (Earwig, 1992)**

★★★½ **The Real Deal (Code Blue, 1996)**

Blues guitarist/vocalist John Primer (b. 1946) is an accomplished Chicago-based session veteran with an impressive list of credentials including stints with Willie Dixon, Muddy Waters's final band and Magic Slim and the Teardrops. After establishing a local presence as a leader in Chicago on *Stuff You Got to Watch,* Primer shows his experience on *The Real Deal.* This engaging romp through a well-balanced collection of blues forms compensates for Primer's lack of virtuosity by referencing the right generic paradigms. Primer's debt to Muddy Waters is acknowledged on a knowing cover of "Blind Man Blues," and several originals demonstrate that he has learned his craft well. He's earned the right to mine this material, and he knows how to wrench every nuance out of the blues. — J.S.

MARCUS PRINTUP

★★★★ **Song for the Beautiful Woman (Blue Note, 1995)**
★★★ **Unveiled (Blue Note, 1996)**
★★ **Nocturnal Traces (Blue Note, 1998)**
★★★★ **Hubsongs (Blue Note, 1998)**

Trumpeter Marcus Printup (b. 1967) was pulled into the jazz fast lane in 1991 after pianist Marcus Roberts heard him at the University of North Florida. Soon he was touring and recording with Roberts, the Wynton Marsalis–led Lincoln Center Jazz Orchestra, drummer Carl Allen and singer Betty Carter. There's a natural soulfulness to his music, honed from his gospel-church upbringing in Georgia. His confident, evolving sound traces the warmth of Booker Ervin and Fats Navarro and the crispness of Lee Morgan, yet his conception is 100 percent Printup. The finest tunes on his debut recording, which has an unmistakable hard-bop lineage, are the originals.

Unveiled is more an ensemble session than a showcase for the leader. It features Printup with Roberts, drummer Jason Marsalis and Stephen Riley, an impressive new voice on the tenor sax. *Nocturnal Traces* fails to match the spirit and creativity of his prior works. Cofeaturing Tim Hagans and produced by Freddie Hubbard, *Hubsongs* is an outstanding feature for both Printup and Hagans that acknowledges the power and soul of Hubbard's playing in his prime without sounding derivative. — K.F.

PROFESSOR LONGHAIR

★★★★ **New Orleans Piano (Blues Originals, Vol. 2) (1953; Atlantic, 1989)**
★★★ **Rock 'n' Roll Gumbo (1974; Dancing Cat, 1985)**
★★★ **Live on the Queen Mary (Harvest, 1978)**
★★★ **Crawfish Fiesta (Alligator, 1980)**
★★★★★ **Mardi Gras in New Orleans (Nighthawk, 1981)**
★★★★ **The Last Mardi Gras (Atlantic, 1982)**
★★★★ **Houseparty New Orleans Style (Rounder, 1987)**
★★★★ **Mardi Gras in Baton Rouge (Rhino, 1991)**
★★★★★ **'Fess: The Professor Longhair Anthology (Rhino, 1993)**
★★★★ **Rum and Coke (Rhino, 1993)**
★★★★ **Big Chief (Rhino, 1993)**

As Jelly Roll Morton was to New Orleans music at the turn of the century, so was Henry Roeland Byrd, a.k.a. Professor Longhair (1918–1980), to the Crescent City's musical identity in the second half of the century. Post–World War II, New Orleans R&B and rock & roll are inconceivable minus the depth and Baroque grandeur of Longhair's signature keyboard voice. Born in Bogalusa, Louisiana, Longhair, who once told an interviewer that many of his relatives hailed from the West Indies, perfected the synthesis of mambo, rhumba and boogie-woogie rhythms that has suffused New Orleans music. With his indefatigable left hand, he maintained the rhythmic base of his work, having absorbed and broadened the styles of pioneers Jimmy Yancey and Pete Johnson, as well as those of a host of New Orleans barrelhouse giants (Tuts Washington, for instance) who came before him; while with his dexterous right hand he swooped, trilled and soared through the melody lines, bringing into play the Caribbean musics of his heritage and adding complexity in the form of the traditional country and blues quotations he worked into this blend.

Apart from his instrumental prowess, Longhair was a compelling singer, whose influence on succeeding generations is less obvious than that of his keyboard work, because in a city full of idiosyncratic vocalists, he may have been the most idiosyncratic of them all. Yelps, yodels and whistles were part of his trick bag, but that's not to dismiss the warmth or personality evident in his stylish approach. Having a sense of humor helped, too. His rocking interpretation of Hank Williams's "Jambalaya" finds him singing one verse in a deep, Fats Domino voice; likewise, on Muddy Waters's "Got My Mojo Working," he slurs some lyrics in a lascivious style that echoes

Elvis Presley's. The sound effects, the irresistible rhythmic assault and the unexpected vocal flourishes that produce great feeling make a case for Longhair as the greatest one-man band of all time.

Rhino's two-CD set, *'Fess: The Professor Longhair Anthology,* is the must-have, comprehensive overview of Longhair's career, beginning with his first and only R&B hit, "Bald Head" (released on the Dallas-based Star Talent label in 1949, it rose to #5 on the R&B chart), ranging through the key entries from the artist's catalog (including live cuts, among them the Longhair monuments "Hey Now Baby" and "Hey Little Girl," crash courses both in 'Fess's self-defined rhumba-boogie mode), and concluding with the previously unreleased "Boogie Woogie," the last recording Longhair made before his death in 1980. Nighthawk's *Mardi Gras in New Orleans* and Atlantic's *New Orleans Piano* collect Longhair's most important late-'40s and early-'50s recordings, including "She Ain't Got No Hair," "Mardi Gras in New Orleans," "Professor Longhair's Boogie" and "Tipitina." From 1964 to 1971 Longhair dropped out of music and worked as a manual laborer in New Orleans, until a talent scout for the New Orleans Jazz and Heritage Festival persuaded him to perform again, which he did until his death in 1980. *Crawfish Fiesta,* his final studio album, and *The Last Mardi Gras,* his final live album (recorded in 1978 at Tipitina's, named after the Longhair song), show no diminution in the master's touch nor in his feisty approach to the material. *Live on the Queen Mary* was the first live recording of Longhair's career, made at a 1975 party hosted by Paul McCartney. *Houseparty New Orleans Style* was Longhair's first postretirement recording, and it's notable for including more than the evergreens dotting most of the artist's releases. "Tipitina" is included, but so is "She Walks Right In" and "Cherry Pie," to cite a couple of interesting tracks. *Houseparty*'s companion volume, *Mardi Gras in Baton Rouge,* collects 18 tracks recorded in 1971 in Baton Rouge and in 1972 at Ardent Studios in Memphis; remarkably, neither disc is rendered superfluous by the essential Rhino title. *Baton Rouge* boasts endless delights for the Longhair faithful, not the least being a wonderful, rollin' and tumblin' Fats Domino medley made all the more impressive by comprising lesser-known titles from the Domino canon; on these tunes Longhair's approach shows precisely how much Domino learned from him in evolving an identifiable instrumental sound and a distinctive lyric phrasing. "Sick and Tired," a Top 30 single for Domino in 1958, is here as well (it's also on *'Fess*), with guitarist Snooks Eaglin constructing a blazing, staccato-rich solo run around and through Longhair's riotous disjointed boogie. *Rock 'n' Roll Gumbo,* originally issued in France in 1974 and released stateside in 1985 on George Winston's Dancing Cat label, teams the Professor with Louisiana blues guitarist Clarence "Gatemouth" Brown, who also adds some friendly fiddling to buttress Longhair on "Jambalaya." A fitting final tribute to Longhair's genius came with the 1993 release of *Big Chief* and *Rum and Coke,* live albums recorded over two nights in the early '70s at Tipitina's. In these sets Longhair pulls out all the stops in displaying the huge vocabulary at his command, whether it be the jubilant calypso of "Rum & Coca-Cola," the powerhouse R&B propelling the medley of "She Walks Right In"/"Shake, Rattle & Roll"/"Roberta" (both on *Rum and Coke*), the scalding mix of ragtime and jump blues on the instrumental "Mess Around" (from *Big Chief*) or the languorous, moody, slow blues of "Little Blues" (*Big Chief*). In a nice touch on *Rum and Coke,* Longhair pays tribute to James Booker with a buoyant take on the latter's "Junco Partner," yet another example of the great heart evident in Henry Roeland Byrd's art over the course of three decades. — D.M.

SNOOKY PRYOR

★★★½ Snooky Pryor (Paula, 1991)
★★★ Too Cool to Move (Antone's, 1991)
★★★ In This Mess Up to My Chest (Antone's, 1994)
★★★½ Snooky (Blind Pig, 1987)
★★★½ Mind Your Own Business (Antone's/Discovery, 1996)

Lambert, Mississippi–born Snooky Pryor (b. 1921) began playing harmonica professionally as a teen, going on to become a postwar Chicago-blues innovator. *Snooky Pryor* offers a sampling of his late '40s–late '50s output, including sides with such players as Floyd Jones, Moody Jones, Sunnyland Slim and Johnny Young, among others. Highlights are Pryor's signature song, the instrumental "Boogie" (the basis for Little Walter's "Juke"), the driving "Fine Boogie" and "Boogie Twist." Pryor plays acoustic harmonica on most cuts, but five tracks spotlight his electrified harp blowing. *Too Cool to Move* finds Pryor teamed with guitarist Duke Robillard, pianist Pinetop Perkins and drummer Willie "Big Eyes" Smith, to name a few of the players. High points include "Fire, Fire," "Bottle It Up and Go" and "Walkin' with Snooky."

On *In This Mess Up to My Chest* Pryor teams with guitarist Hubert Sumlin, Perkins and others. Pryor's trademark harmonica growl and vocals propel "When the Saints Go Marching In," as well as two live tracks ("Bluebird Blues" and "Judgment Day"), which were recorded at Antone's, the famed Austin, Texas, nightspot. These sides are well worth hearing for their beauty and passion. *Snooky* includes nine originals, including the driving "Broke and Hungry" and the ambling "Judgment Day." Also featured here is a plaintive version of Big Bill Broonzy's "Key to the Highway" and an effervescent reading of Sonny Boy Williamson's (Rice Miller) "Nine Below Zero." — B.R.H.

FLORA PURIM

★★★½ **Butterfly Dreams (1973; Original Jazz Classics, 1988)**
★★★½ **Stories to Tell (1974; Original Jazz Classics, 1991)**
★★★ **Encounter (1976; Original Jazz Classics, 1994)**
★★★ **Humble People (Concord Jazz, 1985)**

Brazilian vocalist Flora Purim (b. 1942) worked with percussionist (and later her husband) Airto Moreira and multi-instrumentalist Hermeto Pascoal in Brazil before coming to the United States in the late 1960s. She toured with Stan Getz, recorded with Duke Pearson and performed with the Gil Evans Orchestra. Purim came into her own as a charter member, along with Airto, of Chick Corea's Return to Forever, recording the magnificent *Light as a Feather* with that group. The two left Corea in 1973, the same year they collaborated on her debut album.

Butterfly Dreams, with Airto, keyboardist George Duke, tenor saxophonist Joe Henderson and bassist Stanley Clarke, showcases Purim's novel approach to vocals, using subtle electronic effects to highlight her eccentric sound. On *Stories to Tell* Airto and Duke are joined by a host of sidemen including guitarists Carlos Santana and Earl Klugh and bassists Ron Carter and Miroslav Vitous. *Encounter* is another all-star session with vocalist Urszula Dudziak, Airto, Carter, Duke, Henderson, Pascoal and McCoy Tyner. Purim and Airto have recorded infrequently since the 1970s. *Humble People,* with Latin percussionists Jerry Gonzales and Milton Cardono, is her best work from this period. — J.S.

IKE QUEBEC

★★★★ **Blue and Sentimental (1961; Blue Note, 1995)**

★★★½ **Heavy Soul (1961; Blue Note, N.A.)**

★★★ **It Might as Well Be Spring (1962; Blue Note, 1998)**

★★½ **Soul Samba (1962; Blue Note, 1998)**

Ike Quebec (1918–1963) was a soulful, big-voiced tenor saxophonist who played with force on uptempo material and had an effective, Coleman Hawkins–like affinity for ballads. He recorded prolifically in the '40s and '50s as a leader and sideman, but his extant catalog consists of material recorded in the years before his death from lung cancer in 1963. Quebec's playing on the title track of *Blue and Sentimental* shows him at his best. The Brazilian session *Soul Samba* is for dedicated fans only.
— J.S.

PAUL QUINICHETTE

★★★ **On the Sunny Side (1957; Original Jazz Classics, 1996)**

Tenor saxophonist Paul Quinichette (1916–1983) earned the nickname "Vice Pres" during his 1951–53 stint with the Count Basie band due to the resemblance of his sound to Lester Young's. After leaving the Basie orchestra, Quinichette led his own bands intermittently. *On the Sunny Side* is an enjoyable sextet session with alto saxophonists John Jenkins and Sonny Red, trombonist Curtis Fuller, pianist Mal Waldron, bassist Doug Watkins and drummer Ed Thigpen. Fans of Quinichette's sound should look for the cassette-only *Kid from Denver.* — J.S.

JAMES "YANK" RACHELL

★★★½ **Chicago Style (1987; Delmark, 1993)**

★★★ **Complete Recorded Works, Vol. 1 (Document, 1991)**

★★★ **Complete Recorded Works, Vol. 2 (Document, 1991)**

With very little competition—particularly in the amplified age—Yank Rachell (1910–1997) wrote the book on blues mandolin. Ry Cooder is one noted inheritor of his style, and many modern-day bluegrass mavens cite as influential Rachell's groundbreaking '30s recordings, as leader or as sideman with Sleepy John Estes or Sonny Boy (John Lee) Williamson, and as composer of such country-blues standards as "Diving Duck Blues" and "She Caught the Katy." Rachell performed up until his death at age 87.

Born near Brownsville, Tennessee, Rachell grew up in an era when blues bands shared the same acoustic-string lineup as early hillbilly bands. Rachell, also an accomplished guitarist, exhibited a distinctly advanced, rhythmically complex plectrum style. His earliest work is showcased on the Sleepy John Estes collection *I Ain't Gonna Be Worried No More* (Yazoo). The two-volume Document series gives an overview of his guitar and mandolin work with other sidemen (including Sonny Boy Williamson).

Of Rachell's more recent recordings on Delmark, only *Chicago Style* (recorded in 1979) is in print. Maintaining a rich, down-home feel with throaty country vocals on numbers like "Diving Duck" and "Going to St. Louis," the electric outing finds Rachell backed by a trio of veteran Chicago blues players (guitarist Pete Crawford, bassist Floyd Jones and drummer Odie Payne). A 1962 recording, *Mandolin Blues,* likewise boasts noteworthy accompaniment from Michael Bloomfield, Big Joe Williams, Sleepy John Estes and Hammie Nixon, and deserves reissue on CD. — A.K.

BOBBY RADCLIFF

★★½ **Dresses Too Short (Black Top, 1989)**

★★★ **Universal Blues (Black Top, 1991)**

★★★½ **There's a Cold Grave in Your Way (Black Top, 1994)**

★★★★ **Live at the Rynborn (Black Top, 1997)**

Guitarist/vocalist Bobby Radcliff Ewan (b. 1951) was just 17 when he traveled from the Maryland suburbs to Chicago in search of his hero, Magic Sam. After a brief immersion in Chicago's West Side blues scene, he shortened his stage name and returned to the low-profile Washington, D.C.–area blues-club circuit, then moved to New York, where he became a legendary but unrecorded club hero. In 1988 Ronnie Earl heard him and recommended him to Black Top Records. Combining the slashing style of Chicago blues and the rhythmic groove of funk, Radcliff usually plays in a trio where he handles both lead- and rhythm-guitar duties, melding the flashy solos reminiscent of Buddy Guy to the choppy syncopation of James Brown guitarist Jimmy Nolen into a distinctive funk-blues hybrid. Like Stevie Ray Vaughan, Radcliff is a much better guitarist than singer; he's so fast, in fact, he has to curb the temptation to play many more notes than are necessary, which he's learned to do over the course of his albums.

Dresses Too Short is his flashiest but least satisfying release, while *There's a Cold Grave in Your Way* is the most understated and the most rewarding. On the latter, occasional bursts of fast picking reinforce the beat rather than obscure it. Radcliff's modest voice, too, has become a rhythmic instrument, as he pushes the beat along with his shouts. The album includes tunes associated not only with John Lee Hooker, B.B. King, Magic Sam and Guy but also with Brown, Tyrone Davis and Kool and the Gang. By playing both the rhythm and the blues, Radcliff makes all these songs sound like parts of the same tradition. *Live at the Rynborn* is a high-intensity trio outing highlighted by the amazing covers "Improvisations on Honky Tonk," "Tramp" and "The Twist." — G.H.

THE RADIATORS

★★★★ **Law of the Fish (Epic, 1988)**
★★★★ **Zig-Zaggin' Through Ghostland (Epic, 1989)**
★★★★ **Total Evaporation (Epic, 1991)**
★★★★½ **Songs from the Ancient Furnace (Sony, 1997)**
★★★★★ **Live at the Great American Music Hall (High Sierra, 1997)**

Together for a decade before their major-label debut, the Radiators honed their craft in the smoke and sizzle of New Orleans bars. The years of silencing drunks and delighting dancers obviously paid off—this outfit cooks with real efficiency. Fond of Meters-like syncopations, they derive their core power from updating the swing and assurance of mid-'60s soul (Stax and Atlantic, rather than Motown). Guitarist/vocalist Dave Malone and keyboardist Ed Volker are the band's mainstays. A powerful singer, but never an excessive one, Volker shines on *Zig-Zaggin' Through Ghostland*'s "Red Dress" and "Meet Me Down in Birdland" and turns tender on the marvelous "I Want to Go Where the Green Arrow Goes," the best slow song on *Total Evaporation.* Produced by Jim Dickinson and featuring the Memphis Horns, *Total Evaporation* is the group's most varied album, but all the Radiators' records are tasty—timeless, bluesy rock & roll. *Songs from the Ancient Furnace* collects tracks from the Epic releases, but *Live at the Great American Music Hall,* a terrific San Francisco set in celebration of the Radiators' 20th anniversary, really shows what this band is all about. — P.E.

MA RAINEY

★★★★★ **Ma Rainey (1974; Milestone, 1992)**
★★★★ **The Immortal Ma Rainey (Milestone, 1975)**
★★★★ **Ma Rainey's Black Bottom (Yazoo, 1990)**

Billed on stage and records as "the Mother of the Blues," Ma Rainey (né Gertrude Pridgett, 1886–1939) is an artist for whom extravagant claims are justified. For example, at the turn of the century, when she was touring the South with a popular minstrel show, she heard a girl in a small town in Missouri perform a song bemoaning her faithless lover. Rainey was so moved by the song that she incorporated it into her act, much to her audience's delight. Blues at this time was still rural folk music, but Rainey, when asked what kind of song it was that she had added to her repertoire, replied, "It's the blues." In so doing, Rainey in effect liberated "blues"—the word and the music—from the fields and backwoods of rural black America and made it an accepted form of professional entertainment.

That's the least of her accomplishments. In terms of phrasing, attitude and showmanship, the Mother of the Blues had an impact on virtually every female blues singer—Bessie Smith, who may have been Rainey's protégée, and Billie Holiday being two of the most prominent examples. A flamboyant onstage presence, Rainey was given to adorning herself with headbands, feather boas, tiaras, dangling earrings, necklaces of gold and diamonds and dresses cut from expensive material; her teeth, as photos prove, were literally lined with gold. Her popularity so transcended that of other artists of her time that she became the pacesetter on the minstrel circuit, the acknowledged champion who was forever challenged but never vanquished.

Between 1923 and 1929 she cut over 90 sides for the Paramount label in Grafton, Wisconsin. Thirty-two of the best performances are on the *Ma Rainey* set, which contains the added bonus of authoritative liner notes by Dan Morgenstern. Rainey was always accompanied by outstanding musicians, illustrated here by tracks where she is joined by Louis Armstrong, Coleman Hawkins and Fletcher Henderson, among others; Armstrong's replies to Rainey's low-down vocalizing are a delight, especially on "See See Rider Blues." The sides upon which Rainey is accompanied only by guitarist Tampa Red and pianist Georgia Tom Dorsey are among the most moving blues performances ever recorded. There are moments when Rainey seems to be singing a cappella, so overpowering are her vocals. Dorsey has said, "She had that cry in her voice," and you can hear it on wrenching tunes like "Tough Luck Blues" and "Sweet, Rough Man."

The Immortal Ma Rainey and *Ma Rainey's Black Bottom* duplicate some of the material from the *Ma Rainey* set, but the bulk of the work on these two albums is unavailable elsewhere on domestic releases. On the import side, Document has collected Rainey's 1928 Paramount sessions on a single disc, simply titled *The Complete 1928 Sessions;* a more ambitious project is in the works at the Black Swan label, where all the Paramount sessions are being reissued chronologically in what will be a 10-volume set. — D.M.

BONNIE RAITT

★★★ **Bonnie Raitt (1971; Warner Bros., 1988)**
★★★★ **Give It Up (1972; Warner Bros., 1987)**
★★★★ **Takin My Time (1973; Warner Bros., 1988)**
★★★ **Streetlights (1974; Warner Bros., 1988)**
★★ **Home Plate (1975; Warner Bros., 1988)**
★★ **Sweet Forgiveness (1977; Warner Bros., 1987)**
★★★ **The Glow (1979; Warner Bros., 1988)**
★★★ **Green Light (1982; Warner Bros., 1990)**
★★★ **Nine Lives (1986; Warner Bros., 1990)**
★★★★ **Nick of Time (1989; DCC, 1996)**
★★★★ **The Bonnie Raitt Collection (Warner Bros., 1990)**
★★★★ **Luck of the Draw (1991; DCC, 1997)**
★★★½ **Longing in Their Hearts (Capitol, 1994)**
★★★★ **Road Tested (Capitol, 1995)**
★★★ **Fundamental (Capitol, 1998)**

When Bonnie Raitt (b. 1949) picked up four Grammys for her 1989 album *Nick of Time* she wasn't earning long-overdue credit. Rather the Grammys were testimony to the wisdom of hewing to a course that the artist knew to be right for her. Time and tide finally brought her to producer Don Was for *Nick of Time.* Which is not to suggest that Raitt's previous producers were hacks. Of the many with whom she has worked, only Paul Rothchild (whose credits include the Doors, Paul Butterfield Blues Band, Janis Joplin) misfired wildly, attempting to convert Raitt into a country-rock chanteuse on *Home Plate* and *Sweet Forgiveness.* Peter Asher, who produced *The Glow,* moved Raitt closer to the grit of her early albums even as he put a pop sheen on the proceedings. Looking back over Raitt's career leads one to the inescapable conclusion that the problem lay not in the producers but in the star. Simply put, it took a long time for Bonnie Raitt to grow up. As an artist she's always had the right idea—sliding in the blues she loves among a smattering of tough-rocking originals and smart outside material written by many of the best and brightest of her generation—but she hasn't always had undeniable presence. It's there sporadically on all of her Warners Bros. albums, and produces some exhilarating moments.

Give It Up is first-rate, with electrifying performances of Jackson Browne's "Under the Falling Sky" and Eric Kaz's tormented "Love Has No Pride," as well as her own forthright "Give It Up or Let Me Go." Thoughtful interpretations of songs by Kaz ("Cry Like a Rainstorm"), Browne ("I Thought I Was a Child") and Randy Newman ("Guilty") enliven *Takin My Time,* with Mississippi Fred McDowell's "Write Me a Few of Your Lines"/"Kokomo Blues" adding a raw-nerve edge to the proceedings.

On the otherwise muddled *Sweet Forgiveness* she delivers a delicate take on Paul Siebel's enigmatic "Louise" that approaches both Siebel's own definitive version and the subdued but stirring treatment given the song by Leo Kottke on his *Greenhouse*. But even her best work seemed too eclectic for its own good. Finally, she appeared too polished to be completely convincing as a blues singer, too gritty to be a pop singer, too restrained to be an out-and-out rocker.

By the time Raitt worked with Don Was, she was ready to make a statement. Was provided the rock-steady focus—crisp, stripped-down, bottom-heavy arrangements with Raitt's voice riding strong over everything, her slide guitar lines mixed hot and played tasty and soulful—and Raitt responded with one well-modulated performance after another. Where her singing had often been an example of studied casualness, she emerges with a voice easy, confident, free, robust and alive. The uptempo material—notably the hit single "Thing Called Love" (written by John Hiatt)—cooks righteously, and Raitt sounds utterly absorbed in its emotion. On meditative numbers such as the title song and Michael Ruff's "Cry on My Shoulder" she sings from knowledge learned the hard way.

So it is that she builds on these strengths on *Luck of the Draw,* which sounds of a piece with *Nick of Time.* Coproduced by Was and Raitt, the album serves up Raitt's forthright originals—"I ain't lookin' for the kind of man/Can't stand a little shaky ground/He'll give me fire and tenderness/And got the guts to stick around," she sings on "Come to Me"—and outside material that speaks most directly to her newfound assurance. Everything she touches reflects a gemlike luster. When she gets down with Delbert McClinton on "Good Man, Good Woman," their ebullience is infectious; by contrast, her yearning on "I Can't Make You Love Me" is profound and real, a serious turn inward to unburden the heart of sadness born of love gone wrong. A variety of moods, a variety of settings, Raitt's choices, regardless of the context, are impeccable.

Longing in Their Hearts is another good collection of songs, mostly Raitt originals, with guest appearances from Charlie Musselwhite on harmonica and Levon Helm on vocals. *Road Tested,* Raitt's first live album, showcases her gifts as a vocalist and guitarist in spades on what amounts to a greatest-hits collection. For *Fundamental,* Raitt switched producers, from Was to Mitchell Froom and Tchad Blake, an unfortunate creative decision. — D.M.

MICHAEL RAY

★★★★ **Michael Ray & the Cosmic Krewe (Evidence, 1994)**
★★★★ **Funk If I Know (Monkey Hill, 1998)**

Trumpeter Michael Ray (b. 1962) leads his New Orleans–based Cosmic Krewe on a panstylistic romp through free jazz, neoswing and second-line funk in a conception informed by two bands he performed with extensively, the Sun Ra Arkestra and Kool and the Gang. The band's lineup and conception is literally an outgrowth of the latter-day Sun Ra groups, which went for the kind of lush sonorities that grace these albums. On *Michael Ray & the Cosmic Krewe* Ray covers Sun Ra's "Discipline 27," "Carefree" and "Island in Space," along with Kool's "Champions" and four originals. His trumpet floats languidly through the arrangements, which are nudged along expertly by percussionist Steve Ferraris. *Funk If I Know* features guest appearances from organist John Medeski, drummer Delfeayo Marsalis and guitarist Trey Anastasio. — J.S.

OTIS REDDING

★★★★ **Pain in My Heart (1965; Rhino, 1991)**
★★★★ **The Great Otis Redding Sings Soul Ballads (1965; Rhino, 1991)**
★★★★★ **Otis Blue: Otis Redding Sings Soul (1965; Rhino, 1991)**
★★★★★ **The Soul Album (1966; Rhino, 1991)**
★★★★ **The Otis Redding Dictionary of Soul: Complete and Unbelievable (1966; Rhino, 1991)**
★★★★ **Live in Europe (1967; Rhino, 1991)**
★★★★ **King and Queen (with Carla Thomas) (1967; Rhino, 1991)**
★★★★½ **The Dock of the Bay (1968; Rhino, 1991)**
★★★★★ **The Immortal Otis Redding (1968; Rhino, 1991)**
★★★★★ **In Person at the Whisky-a-Go-Go (1968; Rhino, 1992)**
★★★★ **Love Man (1969; Rhino, 1992)**
★★★★ **The Best of Otis Redding (1972; Rhino, 1985)**
★★★★ **Recorded Live (1982; Rhino, 1992)**
★★★★★ **The Very Best of Otis Redding (Rhino, 1992)**
★★★★★ **Otis! The Definitive Otis Redding (Rhino, 1993)**
★★★★★ **Respect (Rhino, 1993)**
★★★★★ **The Very Best of Otis Redding, Vol. 2 (Rhino, 1995)**
★★★★★ **Dreams to Remember: The Otis Redding Anthology (Rhino, 1998)**

Otis Redding (1941–1967) was the premier Southern soul singer. Providing counterpoint to Motown, the Memphis-based sound Redding defined made the '60s R&B renaissance a glorious tension of complementary styles. While Motown was string-laden, melodic and tended toward pop, Stax-Volt/Atlantic, adhering more closely to gospel and blues roots, was horn-driven and primarily rhythmic, its fierceness the product of stellar solo vocalists and a lean rhythm section. Otis Redding remains its quintessence. Along with the Stax-Volt studio players—organist Booker T. Jones, guitarist Steve Cropper, bassist Donald "Duck" Dunn and drummer Al Jackson—he tested to the limits his quick musical intelligence. His horn parts alone were radically innovative—by employing trumpets as exclamation points, for example, he altered the syntax of the brass section in popular music, and his use of difficult, unexpected key signatures added density to the simple melodic lines his horn parts accompanied. Cowriting many of his hits with Cropper, Redding pared R&B down to its core—in Stax-Volt no note was redundant. All of Redding's technique, however, served emotion—and that emotion, celebratory or anguished, was conveyed by the urgency of his remarkable voice.

The title track to *Pain in My Heart* set the pattern for all his ballads to come—Redding triumphs at rendering agony. Signs of his virtuosity already appear in the almost teasing way he lingers over some lyrics and spits out others. *The Great Otis Redding Sings Soul Ballads* continues his rapid development as a style setter: "Mr. Pitiful" sums up his persona as a tortured romantic, and "That's How Strong My Love Is" demonstrates his skill at transforming gospel witnessing into erotic testifying. With *Otis Blue,* he achieves his first masterwork. "Respect" becomes not only a soul standard but a black-pride anthem; "I've Been Loving You Too Long (to Stop Now)" may be Redding's strongest ballad; the assertiveness of B.B. King's "Rock Me Baby" and Sam Cooke's "Shake" finds him as at home with blues and rockers as with ballads. His furious cover of the Stones' "(I Can't Get No) Satisfaction" is prescient—suggesting the spirit of such later R&B/rock fusioneers as Hendrix, Sly Stone and Prince. "Chain Gang" and the moody swing of "Cigarettes and Coffee" highlight *The Soul Album.* By the time of *The Otis Redding Dictionary of Soul,* he had arrived at another plateau. "Try a Little Tenderness," first recorded by Bing Crosby, is Stax-Volt at its most sophisticated; in an elegant, jazz-influenced setting, Redding, for all his customary fervor, delivers one of his most mature performances, smoky and at times almost languorous. "Fa-Fa-Fa-Fa-Fa (Sad Song)" is more typical Southern soul—hard, precise but swinging. *In Person at the Whisky-a-Go-Go* is dependably intense. From *King and Queen,* his duet with Carla Thomas, "Tramp" offers a rare display of Redding's sassy humor; their cover of Steve Cropper and Eddie Floyd's "Knock on Wood" is a driving sonic assault.

By 1967, the singer had reached a point of such assurance that he seemed riper for ever more ranging explorations of style, new shifts in tone. But even his record company didn't quite know what to do with the latest acoustic-guitar ballad, "(Sittin' on) the Dock of the Bay." The first soul singer to absorb the influence of Bob Dylan turns out a folk melody of indelible, simple force—his lyrics have all the immediacy of conversation, but he sings the line with an undertone of yearning that makes the record unmistakably soul music and the final triumph of his deep, short career. By the end of the year, the singer had died in a plane crash; given the potential suggested by *The Dock of the Bay,* as well as the consistent, challenging beauty of all the music he'd made up until that record's release, his loss remains immeasurable. The very thorough and excellently annotated anthologies—the four-CD *Otis!* and the two-CD distillation *Dreams to Remember*—are phenomenal. — P.E.

DEWEY REDMAN

★★★½ Musics (1979; Original Jazz Classics, 1995)
★★★★ Red and Black in Willisau (with Ed Blackwell) (Black Saint, 1980)
★★★★½ Living on the Edge (Black Saint, 1990)
★★★★ Choices (Enja, 1992)
★★★★½ African Venus (Evidence, 1994)
★★★★ School Work (Mons, 1995)
★★★★ In London (Palmetto, 1998)

Walter Dewey Redman (b. 1931) is one of the more underrated saxophone stylists to emerge from the free-jazz flurry of the mid-1960s. Raised in Fort Worth, Texas, he played in a high school band alongside Ornette Coleman, and both he and Coleman were mentored by a local tenor legend named Red Conner. He taught school in Texas during the 1950s and also served a stint in the Army before moving in 1961 to San Francisco, where he became affiliated with adventurous young musicians such as Pharoah Sanders and Donald Garrett. Reuniting with Coleman in 1967 in New York, Redman became a cornerstone of Coleman's group until 1974. During that time, he also recorded with Keith Jarrett's "American" quartet and Charlie Haden's Liberation Music Orchestra. In 1976 Redman formed Old and New Dreams with Don Cherry, Ed Blackwell and Charlie Haden, all alumni of Coleman's early groups and dedicated to keeping that tradition alive.

Versatile on several instruments including musette, clarinet and alto and soprano sax, Redman is best known for his innovations on the tenor saxophone. His big, bluesy, "Texas" tenor style incorporates both Middle Eastern influences and Coleman's harmolodic sensibilities. Redman began recording as a leader in 1966, but sadly, most of his early albums are out of print. *Look for the Black Star, Ear of the Behearer, Coincide* and *Tarik* are especially worth seeking out.

Musics showcases Redman in a semimainstream milieu. Along with drummer Eddie Moore, bassist Mark Helias and pianist Fred Simmons, Redman's healthy tone and sophisticated phrasing embolden a number of original compositions. A live collaboration with drummer Ed Blackwell, *Red and Black in Willisau* is a dynamic document of the pair's powerful harmonic flow. *Living on the Edge* is a noteworthy quartet date with pianist Geri Allen, bassist Cameron Brown and Eddie Moore. With this talented and immensely responsive band, Redman runs through the entire gamut of his instrumental abilities. Allen's cerebral piano work is the perfect counterpoint for Redman's earthy sax excursions. Playing free and forcefully one minute and down and dirty the next, Redman embraces his tenor and alto saxophones with the authority of an accomplished master.

Choices is particularly notable for the auspicious introduction of Dewey's son, Joshua Redman, who plays tenor while Dewey restricts himself almost exclusively to the alto and musette. *African Venus* again features Joshua on three cuts including a sensitive, swinging interpretation of Duke Ellington's "Satin Doll." Dewey's back-to-Africa motifs are absolutely exquisite, and his musette playing reaches yet another level of sophistication and nuance. Toward the end of the session Dewey reaches back and pulls out a rousing version of "Take the A Train" before finishing with Coleman's "Turnaround." — M.M.

DON REDMAN

★★★★ **Don Redman 1931–1933 (Classics, 1991)**
★★★ **Don Redman 1933–1936 (Classics, 1991)**
★★★ **Don Redman 1936–1939 (Classics, 1991)**

Alto saxophonist Don Redman (1900–1964) came to prominence during the 1920s as an arranger and soloist with the Fletcher Henderson Orchestra. Also a soprano saxophonist and vocalist, he went on to become the musical director of McKinney's Cotton Pickers before going out with his own big band in the 1930s. The anthology *Don Redman 1931–1933* covers all the highlights, including his signature number, "Chant of the Weed," the ahead-of-its-time "Shakin' the African" and a rocking arrangement of "I Got Rhythm."
— J.S.

JOSHUA REDMAN

★★★ **Joshua Redman (Warner Bros., 1993)**
★★★½ **Wish (Warner Bros., 1994)**
★★★★ **MoodSwing (Warner Bros., 1994)**
★★★ **Spirit of the Moment (Warner Bros., 1995)**
★★★★ **Freedom in the Groove (Warner Bros., 1996)**
★★★½ **Timeless Tales (for Changing Times) (Warner Bros., 1998)**

Tenor saxophonist Joshua Redman (b. 1969) did not walk a straight path in the career footsteps of his father, Dewey Redman, a former sideman to jazz adventurers Ornette Coleman and Keith Jarrett. Growing up in Berkeley, California, the younger Redman graduated first in his high school class and won a full scholarship to Harvard, where his primary playing experience was in the college jazz band.

After graduating in 1991, he put Yale Law School on hold to check out the New York jazz scene. He won the prestigious Thelonious Monk International Jazz Saxophone Competition that fall and inked a multiple-recording contract with Warner Bros. Industry hype helped jump-start his career, which he has sustained through talent, self-assurance and taking advantage of every playing opportunity to stretch his skills and increase his musical challenges. In addition to forming his own quartet, this invigorating player worked as a sideman with Joe Lovano (he's cofeatured on Lovano's 1993 Blue Note recording *Tenor Legacy*), Elvin Jones, Paul Motian, Jack DeJohnette, Red Rodney, Charlie Haden and his father.

Inspired primarily by Sonny Rollins and John Coltrane, Redman is a confident player who thoroughly enjoys the process of jazz—making intensely emotional music before a live audience. His material runs the gamut from the American songbook to James Brown, Eric Clapton and Stevie Wonder pop tunes as well as original compositions. His eponymous debut contains standards and original material performed with pianists Kevin Hays and Mike

LeDonne, bassists Christian McBride and Paul LaDuca and drummers Gregory Hutchinson, Clarence Penn and Kenny Washington. *Wish* teams him with a powerhouse band: guitarist Pat Metheny, bassist Haden and drummer Billy Higgins. The material is wide-ranging and challenging, with two tracks, "Wish" and Haden's "Blues for Pat," recorded live at New York's Village Vanguard. *MoodSwing* consists of entirely original material, songs designed purely to evoke a range of emotions in each listener. Because of his inspired approach, it is Redman's most intensely personal work to date, complemented by the fine playing of McBride, pianist Brad Mehldau and drummer Brian Blade.

Spirit of the Moment is an intense two-CD set recorded at the Village Vanguard with Redman's touring quartet during a one-week engagement in March 1995. Redman plays alto and soprano as well as tenor on *Freedom in the Groove,* his first quintet session. The addition of guitarist Peter Bernstein strengthened the cohesive sound of Redman's band, which has grown into a powerful unit. *Timeless Tales (for Changing Times)* finds Redman putting his own stamp on some favorite old and new standards from the likes of Gershwin, Kern, Berlin and Porter as well as Bob Dylan, Joni Mitchell, Prince, Stevie Wonder and Lennon/McCartney. — K.F.

DIZZY REECE

★★★½ **Blues in Trinity (1958; Blue Note, 1995)**
★★★★ **Asia Minor (1962; Original Jazz Classics, 1992)**

Jamaican trumpeter Dizzy Reece (b. 1931) worked out of Europe from the late 1940s with Don Byas and a number of European bands, playing bop-influenced jazz with solid taste and lyricism. *Blues in Trinity* is a London date with Donald Byrd on trumpet, Tubby Hayes on tenor saxophone and a rhythm section anchored by Art Taylor on drums. Reece moved to the United States at the end of the 1950s and recorded as a sideman as well as a leader. *Asia Minor* is a modal-influenced session with saxophonists Cecil Payne and Joe Farrell, pianist Hank Jones, bassist Ron Carter and drummer Charlie Persip. Reece was much admired by Dizzy Gillespie, who employed him in several touring bands, and Miles Davis, but most of his sessions are virtually impossible to find. Two worthwhile out-of-print '70s LPs are *Blowin' Away* and *Manhattan Project.* — J.S.

ERIC REED

★★★ **It's All Right to Swing (MoJazz, 1993)**
★★★★ **The Swing and I (MoJazz, 1995)**
★★★★ **Musicale (Impulse!, 1996)**
★★★½ **Pure Imagination (Impulse!, 1998)**

At age 18, Eric Reed (b. 1970) performed on a Midwestern tour with Wynton Marsalis; two years later he became Marsalis's regular pianist. He has also worked on occasion with Freddie Hubbard and Joe Henderson. Born in Philadelphia, Reed moved at age 11 with his family to Los Angeles, where he studied classical piano and played gospel music in his father's church. Stylistically, his sound comes out of Ahmad Jamal with a vibrant, inherent spirituality.

Reed's major-label debut, *It's All Right to Swing,* teams him with bassist Rodney Whitaker, drummer Gregory Hutchinson (then both members of the Roy Hargrove Quintet), alto saxophonist Wessell Anderson (a Marsalis band mate) and Marsalis himself on three tracks (listed for contractual reasons under his pseudonym, "E. Dankworth"). *The Swing and I* is a trio session with Hutchinson on drums and bass duties shared by Whitaker and Ben Wolfe. Gospel vocals supplement the trio on one of this session's several spirituals. *Musicale,* a strong mix of bluesy trio, quartet and quintet tracks, is another forceful showcase for Reed's Marsalis-influenced maturation as a conceptual songwriter and tastefully emotional player. On *Pure Imagination* Reed's trio puts a high-energy Tyner-esque imprint on Broadway's finest show tunes. — K.F.

JIMMY REED

★★★½ **Jimmy Reed at Carnegie Hall (Vee-Jay, 1962)**
★★★ **I'm Jimmy Reed (Vee-Jay, 1963)**
★★★★ **Jimmy Reed: The Legend, The Man (Vee-Jay, N.A.)**
★★★ **Now Appearing (Vee-Jay, N.A.)**
★★★ **Rockin' with Reed (Vee-Jay, N.A.)**
★★★ **Jimmy Reed at Soul City (Vee-Jay, N.A.)**
★★★★★ **The Best of Jimmy Reed (GNP Crescendo, 1974)**
★★★★ **Bright Lights, Big City (Chameleon, 1988)**
★★★ **Jimmy Reed Is Back (Collectables, 1993)**
★★★★★ **The Classic Recordings (Tomato, 1994)**

★★★★ **Lost in the Shuffle (32 Blues, 1997)**
★½ **Cry Before I Go (Drive Archive, 1998)**

Born in the Mississippi Delta on a plantation near Dunleith and raised by a sharecropper family that moved frequently to wherever work could be found in the fields, Jimmy Reed (1925–1976) was first inspired musically by Sonny Boy Williamson's (Rice Miller) King Biscuit Flour–sponsored radio broadcasts from KFFA in Helena, Arkansas. With his friend Eddie Taylor supplying indefatigable rhythm support, Reed began fashioning a distinctive approach to blues out of the Delta styles he heard on the Helena station and from the traditional country music he heard on the Grand Ole Opry's radio broadcasts.

Joining the black migration to the North in the late '40s, Reed settled in Chicago and worked a series of day jobs while trying unsuccessfully to establish himself in the Windy City's burgeoning blues scene. Reuniting with Taylor, he added harmonica to his sound—he had given it up when he began learning guitar years earlier—and the Reed style became whole: Taylor kept things grounded while Reed sculpted lazy, insinuating shuffle rhythms spiced with elemental blues progressions; tinny, crying harmonica lines; and a singing voice that was all nasal twang and drawl but engaging in its laid-back, friendly tone. In an era when blues giants walked the earth, Reed's medium-cool signature was like no one else's in the way the artist contained his fire even as that fire was consuming his audience. Troubles in love, troubles on the job, heartbreak, romance, reconciliation, making it through a day in one piece—if Reed's groove didn't hook his listeners, his lyric themes, rooted in commonplace experiences, more than did the job.

Following an unsuccessful audition for Chess, Reed landed at the newly formed Vee-Jay label, which he helped put on the map with his 1955 hit "You Don't Have to Go." For the next six years Reed was rarely off the charts and on occasion crossed over from R&B to the national pop chart. During that time, he built the monuments at which many young British rockers genuflected in the '60s: "Ain't That Lovin' You Baby," "Baby What You Want Me to Do," "Big Boss Man" (the rare song not written by Reed himself that became a hit) and, in 1961, the instant classic "Bright Lights, Big City." During the Vee-Jay years, Reed was teamed with some extraordinary musicians in the studio. Besides his ever-reliable partner, Eddie Taylor, he recorded for a time with Earl Phillips, a resourceful, dynamic drummer; guitarist Phil Upchurch, then a highly regarded newcomer; Curtis Mayfield on bass; versatile guitarists Lefty Bates and Lee Baker; and the veteran blues master Willie Dixon on bass (on "Big Boss Man," among other cuts). At first blush, Reed's sound may seem the epitome of simplicity. But in working so hard to keep it that way, these stalwart musicians did some of their finest work simply being ensemble players, with little in the way of individual moments of flash to mark their tenure with Reed.

Reed's catalog has been rounded out in fine fashion by the three-disc set *The Classic Recordings*. As per the title, Reed's best-known songs from the Vee-Jay years are here, along with B sides. In an unfortunate gaffe, however, the songs are not sequenced chronologically (1961's "Big Boss Man," for example, is the third song on disc one), nor is there any discographical information relating to session dates or personnel (although Pete Welding's notes make mention of the bands assembled for various tracks). Equally frustrating, the notes refer to numerous songs not included on any of the three discs. Ultimately, of course, the music carries the day on this essential set. *Bright Lights, Big City* and *The Best of Jimmy Reed* also do a superb job of charting the arc of Reed's Vee-Jay career, with less detailed liner notes but no less compelling music. Another solid overview of the best of the Vee-Jay years comes by way of *Lost in the Shuffle* on the new 32 Blues label headed by noted producer Joel Dorn (Roberta Flack, the Neville Brothers, Bette Midler, Rahsaan Roland Kirk, et al.), which has the added benefit of Bill Dahl's well-researched liner copy.

In May 1960 Reed made a triumphant concert appearance at New York City's Carnegie Hall, which Vee-Jay's *Jimmy Reed at Carnegie Hall* purports to document. The performances are uniformly first-rate, but there's nary a clap, whistle, cheer, cough, shout, or scream to be heard on what sounds for all the world like a series of studio performances.

On another supposed "live" album, *Jimmy Reed at Soul City,* the sound of audience chatter and tinkling glasses is easily audible, but at no point does Reed acknowledge the crowd, whose applause is identical from one track to another. But like the Carnegie Hall album, Reed's performances are commendable, if not revelatory, throughout. Reed's 1963 album, *I'm Jimmy Reed,* contains the original recording of "Honest I Do," a Top 10 R&B hit not included on *The Classic Recordings.* On this track, Reed was joined by Chicago jazz guitarist Remo Biondi, who added a new wrinkle to Reed's sound with a series of delicate, descending lines that serve as an instrumental counterpoint to Reed's vocal. This track alone raises the album to the level of being the most important of Reed's in-print releases apart from the greatest-hits collections.

Reed's final, unsuccessful years as a recording artist, when he was signed to ABC-Bluesway and Exodus, are represented in part by the fine Collectables album *Jimmy Reed Is Back,* containing 12 tracks from 1966 to 1971. Here Reed settles into his groove—doing as he advises on the second track, "Keep the Faith"—and gets solid support from Eddie Taylor, Lefty Bates and Phil Upchurch; his son Jimmy Reed Jr. is credited as the bass player on a few cuts, and on others Reed is joined by guitarist Louis Myers and drummer Fred Below, two of Chicago's finest. Among the highlights: the semiautobiographical blues "Just a Poor Country Boy," built on "Big Boss Man"; a raucous harmonica rave-up on "Tribute to a Friend," an homage to Sonny Boy Williamson; the deep, slow blues "I'm Leaving," which takes off behind Reed's soulful vocal. Drive Archive's entry, *Cry Before I Go,* a collection of recordings made for the Roker label in 1970, is an unfortunate experiment in updating Reed's sound with funk rhythm and wah-wah pedals galore. By the sheer force of his personality Reed pulls off some of this material, but on the whole this one's a must to avoid.

Reed died in August 1976 after suffering an epileptic seizure. His post–Vee-Jay years were marked by sporadic (and numerous canceled) performances, failed recordings and ill health resulting from alcoholism and epilepsy—a truly sad end for an artist whose music retained all its alluring immediacy, no matter the passing of time and trends. — D.M.

DIANNE REEVES

★★★	**Dianne Reeves (Alliance, 1987)**
★★	**Never Too Far (Alliance, 1990)**
★★★	**I Remember (Blue Note, 1991)**
★★★½	**Art and Survival (Capitol, 1994)**
★★★½	**Quiet After the Storm (Blue Note, 1995)**
★★★★	**The Grand Encounter (Blue Note, 1996)**
★★½	**The Palo Alto Sessions (Blue Note, 1996)**
★★★	**That Day . . . (Blue Note, 1997)**

Vocalist Dianne Reeves (b. 1956) occasionally brings jazz back into the orbit of contemporary popular music without breaching the etiquette or integrity of either genre. From her earliest three recordings on the defunct Palo Alto Records, condensed into *The Palo Alto Sessions,* she demonstrates a well-controlled, wide vocal range and an ability to scat. That she wrote some of the best material on these sessions, including the almost-hit "Better Days" (often called "The Grandma Song"), sometimes gets overlooked in these pyrotechnics. Billy Childs's piano and musical direction keep most of this music well grounded in jazz roots.

She reprises "Better Days" on her eponymous debut, and covers Duke Ellington as well. It almost seems she wants to show everything she can do, no matter how incongruous, all at once. Her voice is fabulous, scatting through "That's All" and skating over her full dynamic range. She also works with such talented folk as Childs, Herbie Hancock, Stanley Clarke and Tony Williams, and the album is produced by her cousin George Duke. Overall, however, it lacks focus and feels like an overpacked valise. Moving toward the pop side of Reeves's inclinations, *Never Too Far* is a bouncy but slight affair, with members of Take 6 and Earth, Wind and Fire lending a hand. She demonstrates what a full-voiced version of Rickie Lee Jones's "Company" can sound like and offers a surprisingly moving song, "How Long," inspired by an Elizabeth Catlett painting. While she employs some interesting pan-African touches and her voice is undeniable, many of the tunes don't reach that level of inspiration.

I Remember collects distinctive interpretations of hoary standards, recorded with a series of impressive bands. She reads "How High the Moon" in a style befitting the Abbey Lincoln pose she strikes on the cover. Her take on "Love for Sale" keeps the listener off balance with its tempo changes. She reads "Softly as in a Morning Sunrise" as well as any vocalist, accompanied by Charnett Moffett, Marvin "Smitty" Smith, Bobby Hutcherson, Greg Osby and others. The album also includes a stunning version of "Like a Lover," accompanied only by Kevin Eubanks's acoustic guitar, but a few questionable song choices ("I Remember Sky") mar the recording.

The Grand Encounter uses the idea of *I Remember* and kicks it up a few notches. With players like her mentor, Clark Terry, Harry "Sweets" Edison, Phil Woods and James Moody and a rhythm section of Kenny Barron, Rodney Whitaker and Herlin Riley, Reeves takes standards and bop evergreens and lives up to the title. Toots Thielemans keeps "Besame Mucho" from sliding into excess, and Bobby Watson blows smoke around "Cherokee." She also enjoys solid vocal companions: "Ha!" gets Lambert, Hendricks and Ross treatment, with Germaine Bazzle, Kimberley Longstreth, Terry and Moody, and she gives Joe Williams a run for his money on "Tenderly." — H.B.

JACK REILLY

★★★★ **Blue-Sean-Green (1968; Unichrom, 1995)**
★★★★ **The Brinksman (1981; Unichrom, 1995)**
★★★★ **Here's What I Like (1990; Unichrom, 1995)**

Pianist Jack Reilly (b. 1932) brings an intellectual force to his playing conception born of classical training, an interest in Eastern music and studies with Bill Evans and Lennie Tristano. *Blue-Sean-Green* is a trio date with bassist Jack Six and drummer Joe Cocuzzo that takes the listener through a hair-raising 57 minutes on one composition, "Halloween." The other two releases are solo-piano outings. *Here's What I Like* contains an original take on "I Got Rhythm"; *The Brinksman* includes tributes to Duke Ellington and Bill Evans. — J.S.

DJANGO REINHARDT

★★★★ **Djangology 49 (1949; RCA Bluebird, 1990)**
★★★½ **The Indispensable Django Reinhardt (1949–1950) (RCA Bluebird, 1983)**
★★★★ **Djangologie/USA, Vols. 1 and 2 (DRG, 1990)**
★★★★ **Djangologie/USA, Vols. 3 and 4 (DRG, 1990)**
★★★ **Rare Django (DRG, 1990)**
★★★ **Swing Guitar (Jass, 1991)**
★★★★ **Django Reinhardt and Stéphane Grappelli (GNP Crescendo, 1991)**
★★★★ **Django Reinhardt 1936–37 (Koch, 1991)**
★★★½ **Compact Jazz: In Brussels (Verve, 1992)**
★★★ **Django Reinhardt and Friends (Pearl, 1992)**
★★★★ **The Quintet of the Hot Club of France (Pearl, 1992)**
★★★ **Gypsy Jazz (Drive Archive, 1994)**
★★★ **Nuages (Living Era, 1994)**
★★★½ **Brussels and Paris (DRG, 1996)**
★★★ **The Best of Django Reinhardt (Blue Note, 1996)**
★★★ **Guitar Genius (Charly, N.A)**
★★★ **I Got Rhythm (Jazz Hour, N.A.)**
★★★ **In a Sentimental Mood (Four Star, N.A.)**
★★★★★ **Swing in Paris 1936–40 (Affinity, N.A.)**
★★★½ **Swing de Paris (1947) (Arco, N.A.)**
★★★½ **The London Deccas, Vol. 2, 1938–39 (JSP, N.A.)**

Guitarist Jean-Baptiste (Django) Reinhardt (1910–1953) developed a truly unique style that has been a touchstone for generations of guitarists. He had a breathtaking ability to string out melodic lines effortlessly and employ them inside glittering harmonic castles buttressed by daring octave leaps. A Belgian Gypsy, Reinhardt used the richly melodic folk materials available to him for raw material and played with a distinctive fingering technique due in part to a fire injury that left him with limited use of two fingers on his left hand. His bell-like tone on perfectly articulated single-note runs was a revelation to guitarists who had previously heard the instrument only in a rhythmic context.

Reinhardt was hard-pressed to find European players who could keep up with the sophistication of his rhythmic ideas, but his collaborations with violinist Stéphane Grappelli were an exchange of ideas between musical peers, even when the other members of the Quintette du Hot Club de France, their principal vehicle, plodded along desperately just to keep up. RCA's *Djangology* and the DRG *Djangologie/USA* discs give great accounts of Reinhardt's sublime moments with Grappelli, which are also well represented on the GNP and Koch sides.

The five-CD *Swing in Paris* is the mother lode, combining all of the indispensable pre–World War II recordings that demonstrate how far Reinhardt was ahead of all his European peers except Grappelli and how he could swing as mightily as the American giants who visited him—Coleman Hawkins, Rex Stewart, Benny Carter, Dicky Wells and Barney Bigard. — J.S.

EMILY REMLER

★★★ **Firefly (Concord Jazz, 1981)**
★★★ **Take Two (Concord Jazz, 1982)**
★★★ **Transitions (Concord Jazz, 1984)**
★★★ **Catwalk (Concord Jazz, 1985)**
★★★★ **East to Wes (Concord Jazz, 1988)**
★★★★ **This Is Me (Justice, 1990)**
★★★★ **Retrospective, Vol. 1: Standards (Concord Jazz, 1991)**
★★★ **Retrospective, Vol. 2: Compositions (Concord Jazz, 1991)**

Guitarist Emily Remler (1957–1990) was a Berklee College of Music graduate who went on to carve out a reputation in the jazz world during a brief but prolific recording career. Remler's stylistic debt to Wes Montgomery is apparent on her debut, *Firefly,* but on subsequent albums she expands stylistically, opening her music up to interesting collaborations, such as *Catwalk* and *Transitions,* both with trumpeter John D'Earth, bassist Eddie Gomez and percussionist Bob Moses. By the time of *East to Wes,* she had arrived at a crisper, more contemporary take on Montgomery bolstered by the forceful backing of drummer Marvin "Smitty" Smith, bassist Buster Williams and prescient pianist Hank Jones. On *This Is Me* Remler successfully integrates synth-guitar chromaticism into her approach. The *Retrospective* sets provide a useful overview of her career. — J.S.

REVOLUTIONARY ENSEMBLE

★★★★★ **Vietnam 1 & 2 (1972; ESP, 1993)**

This now-defunct trio, comprising Leroy Jenkins (b. 1932) on violin, Sirone (b. Norris Jones, 1940) on bass and trombone and Jerome Cooper (b. 1946) on drums and piano, was the most exciting new-music band of the '70s. Their basic violin, bass and drums instrumentation was perfectly balanced, allowing for maximum exploration without unnecessary assault. All three are demonic players, though each (especially the underrated Cooper) knew the value of restraint, and all three wrote intriguing material. Jenkins can also be heard on his own albums and with Anthony Braxton, Muhal Richard Abrams, Alice Coltrane and others; Sirone has recorded with Jenkins, Marion Brown, Dewey Redman, Roswell Rudd and Cecil Taylor; Cooper with Braxton and on the *Wildflowers* anthology.

Vietnam 1 & 2 is their incendiary but poorly recorded ESP debut, and the only record currently in print. *Manhattan Cycles,* like two other out-of-print discs, is a poorly recorded concert. The single composition (by trumpeter Leo Smith) sets the trio against prerecorded tape. *The People's Republic* is well produced and nicely programmed, though it lacks a bit of the fire heard on the concert albums.

The Revolutionary Ensemble disbanded in 1977, shortly after the concert performance documented on the Inner City release. The album captures much of the range, intensity and complementary spirit that made the Revolutionary Ensemble special. — B.B./J.S.

SONNY RHODES

★★★★ **Just Blues (1985; Evidence, 1995)**
★★★½ **Livin' Too Close to the Edge (Ichiban, 1992)**
★★★½ **Disciple of the Blues (Ichiban, 1992)**
★★★★ **The Blues Is My Best Friend (Kingsnake, 1994)**
★★★★ **Out of Control (Kingsnake, 1996)**

Texas-born Sonny Rhodes (b. Clarence Edward Smith, 1940) is an accomplished guitarist noted for his lap-steel playing, a terrific songwriter and exciting live presence with a tough, expressive vocal style. Despite solid credentials as a live performer and bandleader he has been overlooked by the recording industry over the years, releasing a couple of singles in Texas and San Francisco and several hard-to-find European albums.

Just Blues is a 1985 project his working band originally recorded for his own label, Rhodesway. Rhodes plays guitar and lap steel with a quartet augmented by a two-piece horn section in a spirited romp that takes the band through several originals, including the fine "House Without Love," the blues classics "I Can't Lose," "The Things I Used to Do," "Think," "It Hurts Me Too" and a tribute to mentor Percy Mayfield, "Strange Things Happening."

Rhodes resurfaced in the 1990s with a pair of solid albums on Ichiban before returning to top form on *The Blues Is My Best Friend,* with superb lap-steel playing and the topical "President Clinton." Rhodes turns up the heat on the aptly titled *Out of Control,* with a guest performance from guitarist Kenny Neal. — J.S.

BUDDY RICH

★★★½ **This One's for Basie (1956; Verve, N.A.)**

★★½ **Rich Versus Roach (1959; Verve, N.A.)**
★★★ **Big Swing Face (1967; Blue Note, 1996)**
★★★ **Ease On Down the Road (1974; Delta, 1996)**
★★★ **Live at Ronnie Scott's (DRG, 1980)**
★★★ **Time Being (RCA, 1987)**
★★ **Buddy Rich plays Selections from West Side Story and Others (LaserLight, 1996)**
★★★ **The Best of Buddy Rich: The Pacific Jazz Years (Blue Note, 1997)**
★★★ **Compact Jazz (Verve, N.A.)**

Buddy Rich (1917–1987) started as a vaudeville drummer before he was two years old and never lost the sense that he was the main attraction on the big stage. His astonishing feats of strength, stamina, speed and technique on the drums with the Artie Shaw and Tommy Dorsey big bands made Rich a featured sensation. But those same qualities led Rich as a leader to make overblown, bombastic recordings often plagued by bad judgment in material, driven by a cynical chase for pop hits. Even his best album, *This One's for Basie,* was obviously prompted by the fact that the Basie band had had a huge hit single the same year. *Rich Versus Roach* is a perfect example of Rich's failings; the two drummers sound like they come from different planets. For drum-solo buffs only. — J.S.

TOMMY RIDGLEY

★★★★ **The New Orleans King of the Stroll (Rounder, 1988)**
★★★ **She Turns Me On (Modern Blues, 1992)**
★★★★ **The Herald Recordings (Collectables, 1992)**
★★★★½ **Since the Blues Began (Black Top, 1995)**

One of the finest singers of vintage New Orleans rhythm & blues, Tommy Ridgley (b. 1925) possesses an impeccable sense of swing and phrasing that has gracefully aged over his career. His church-choir training gave Ridgley's voice the power to emerge from the fiercely competitive late-'40s scene at New Orleans's Dew Drop Inn, amid performers such as Ray Charles and Guitar Slim. After a tenure in Dave Bartholomew's band, Ridgley began recording on his own for a variety of labels including Imperial and Atlantic.

Both *The Herald Recordings* and *The New Orleans King of the Stroll* are excellent collections of Ridgley's early work. All the hallmarks of the cream of '50s and early-'60s R&B are present: funky shuffle drumming, a stacked horn section and piano figures doubling as bass lines. Ridgley's powers as front man and bandleader are formidable; he conducts his sidemen masterfully, while juxtaposing displays of vocal power on straight-ahead rave-ups with moving ballads. His Louisiana heritage helps make these recordings unique, with an unmistakable New Orleans joie de vivre pushing songs such as his well-known "Jam Up."

After decades of steady live work and on-and-off recording for small labels, Ridgley stepped back into the public spotlight in the '90s. *She Turns Me On* contains new versions of great Ridgley tunes such as "For You, My Love" and "Double-Eyed Whammy," with a crack band providing support; the thin production occasionally disappoints. Released just before his 70th birthday, *Since the Blues Began* finds Ridgley sounding richer than ever, tackling material like the hard-knuckled title track with youthful fire and a sage's wisdom. — S.J.

THE RIPPINGTONS

★★ **Tourist in Paradise (GRP, 1989)**
★★ **Kilimanjaro (GRP, 1990)**
★★ **Moonlighting (GRP, 1990)**
★★ **Welcome to the St. James Club (GRP, 1990)**
★★ **Curves Ahead (GRP, 1991)**
★★ **Weekend in Monaco (GRP, 1992)**
★★ **Live in L.A. (GRP, 1993)**
★★ **Black Diamond (Windham Hill, 1997)**
★★½ **The Best of the Rippingtons (GRP, 1997)**

The sound of success in the 1990s, the Rippingtons are on the leading edge of the smooth-jazz radio format designed as a lifestyle accessory. Guitarist Russ Freeman masterminds this concept, which buffs the edges off fusion to create a designer sound that presumably makes the demographically correct listener think of luxury cars and other expensive consumer items. Smooth-jazz fans will want *The Best of the Rippingtons,* which gathers a casting call of the genre's purveyors, including saxophonists Kenny G, Kirk Whalum and Eric Marienthal and vocalist Patti Austin. — J.S.

LEE RITENOUR

★★ **First Course (1976; Epic/Legacy, 1990)**
★★ **Captain Fingers (Epic, 1977)**

★★ **The Captain's Journey (1978; Discovery, 1994)**
★★ **Feel the Night (1979; Discovery, 1993)**
★★ **Banded Together (1979; Discovery, 1994)**
★★★ **Rio (1979; GRP, 1985)**
★★ **The Best of Lee Ritenour (Epic, 1980)**
★★ **Rit (1981; Discovery, 1994)**
★★ **Rit 2 (1982; Discovery, 1994)**
★★ **On the Line (GRP, 1985)**
★★ **Earthly Run (GRP, 1986)**
★★ **Portrait (GRP, 1987)**
★★★ **Festival (GRP, 1988)**
★★★ **Color Rit (GRP, 1989)**
★★★ **Stolen Moments (GRP, 1990)**
★★★ **Collection (GRP, 1991)**
★★★½ **Wes Bound (GRP, 1993)**
★★½ **Larry & Lee (with Larry Carlton) (GRP, 1995)**
★★½ **Alive in L.A. (GRP, 1997)**

An acolyte of Wes Montgomery and student of Joe Pass and Howard Roberts, Californian Lee Ritenour (b. 1952) has taken his intelligent guitar stylings and explored various fusions of pop, jazz and tropical rhythms. He's also been aggressive in his embrace of new recording technology and electronic instruments. But unlike so many technogeeks whose music winds up brilliantly recorded but emotionally sterile, Ritenour has by and large kept his eye square on the heart of the song and let the technology do its thing without intruding on the intended spirit of the work. All of his albums have their modest virtues, but the most durable ones feature Ritenour primarily on acoustic guitar and in a distinctly South American mode (*Rio, Festival,* and *Color Rit*). Notable among these is *Festival,* which features one of Brazil's most influential musicians, Caetano Veloso, whose "Vocee e Linda" (or "Linda," as it's titled here) is a moment of supreme beauty; Veloso's vocal is supported here with grace and sensitivity by Ritenour and a first-rate band. Breaking out of the mold a bit on *Color Rit,* Ritenour offers a commendable interpretation of the Isley Brothers' "I Can't Let Go."

It took a while to get around to recording a tribute to his inspiration, but his 1993 effort, *Wes Bound,* was worth the wait. An easy-swinging affair, this homage honors the style of a distinctive, influential guitarist by using his signature octave runs as establishing points for solos that mate Ritenour's economy of expression to Montgomery's robust sound. There are bursts of speed-picking that amaze in their dexterity ("Boss City"), but by and large the approach here places a premium on measured soloing rich in lyricism and rhythmic drive. One of the interesting experiments here is the loping Montgomery-style treatment of Bob Marley's "Waiting in Vain," as sung by Maxi Priest in a fit of barely contained erotic yearning.

A 1995 event, *Larry & Lee,* brought Ritenour and Larry Carlton into the studio together for an engaging set-to between distinctive stylists. With formidable musicians accompanying them (drummers Omar Hakim and Harvey Mason, bassist Melvin Davis, keyboardist Greg Phillinganes, synthesist and tenor saxophonist Larry Williams, among others), Ritenour and Carlton go to work on several original tunes that give them plenty of room for florid displays of complex soloing ("Crosstown Kids") as well as for lighter, lyrical, romantic dialogs on the order of the gently grooving "Low Steppin'." Elsewhere Joe Pass is honored with a vibrant duet on "Remembering J.P.," and Ritenour contributes "Reflections of a Guitar Player," a tasty bit of upbeat introspection with tart, angular single-string solos, to close the album on a thoughtful note.

Apart from these recommended titles, those seeking the essential Lee Ritenour are advised to opt for *Collection,* which offers 13 examples of the guitarist's varied excursions into fusion music dating back to 1981. This, along with any of the more recent recordings, is uniformly entertaining, intermittently challenging and guaranteed to deliver a pleasant surprise or two in its expert displays of a contemporary, mainstream, jazz-rooted guitar sensibility.

— D.M.

SAM RIVERS

★★★★★ **Streams: Live at Montreux (1973; Impulse!, 1989)**
★★★★★ **Dave Holland/Sam Rivers (1976; I.A.I., 1992)**
★★★★★ **Dave Holland/Sam Rivers, Vol. 2 (1977; I.A.I., 1992)**
★★★★ **Colours (Black Saint, 1983)**
★★★ **Lazuli (Timeless, 1990)**
★★★ **Concept (Rivbea, 1997)**

Versatile tenor/soprano saxophonist and flautist Sam Rivers (b. 1930) is an extraordinarily talented composer and arranger who has been in and out of the tradition, working with Serge Chaloff, Billie Holiday, the Miles Davis Quintet, with Cecil Taylor and Andrew Hill. In the 1970s his Studio Rivbea was a cornerstone of the New York loft-jazz scene. Rivers also worked as a blues and R&B session player, gigging with Jimmy Witherspoon and T-Bone Walker. The product of a gospel-singing family, Rivers moved to Boston in 1947 and studied at the Boston Conservatory but got his real musical education working seven nights a week in a variety of musical settings. He played on Tony Williams's 1965 Blue Note album *Spring,* recorded within a year of his debut as a leader on the same label, *Fuchsia Swing Song.*

None of Rivers's Blue Note material is available at this writing. The important *Fuchsia Swing Song,* with Williams and pianist Jaki Byard, demonstrates how Rivers was moving from a postbop conception into the free-jazz zone. *Contours,* a quintet session with trumpeter Freddie Hubbard and pianist Herbie Hancock, stays closer to the mainstream. On *Involution* Rivers has crossed over into free territory and would soon join Cecil Taylor's exploratory unit.

Rivers returned as a leader in the 1970s fully versed in the extremes of energy playing and outside-the-tradition conceptions. His energy and focus provided a nurturing ground for some great music at Studio Rivbea, and he turned out another series of mostly out-of-print albums for Impulse! and minor labels. The only Impulse! recording currently available is *Streams,* a live performance from the '73 Montreux Festival with Cecil McBee on bass and Norman Connors on drums. His magnificent duet albums with bassist Dave Holland continue the sublime exchange of ideas that graced one of the greatest albums of the 1970s, *Conference of the Birds. Colours* showcases Rivers's writing for large groups composed of saxophones, flutes, oboes and piccolo with no other accompaniment. These beautiful constructs reveal Rivers's vision of reed-and-wind–based coloratura in all its mass-winged glory. The more down-to-earth *Lazuli* quartet is less satisfying but geared toward a wider audience, an understandable move on Rivers's part, considering the lack of respect the industry has paid his catalog.

— J.S.

MAX ROACH

★★★½ **Max Roach Quintet Featuring Hank Mobley (1953; Original Jazz Classics, 1990)**
★★★★★ **Max Roach Plus Four (1957; Verve, 1990)**
★★★★★ **The Max Roach Four Plays Charlie Parker (1958; Verve, 1995)**
★★★★ **Deeds, Not Words (1958; Original Jazz Classics, 1988)**
★★★★★ **Percussion Bitter Sweet (1961; Impulse!, 1993)**
★★★ **Speak, Brother, Speak (1962; Original Jazz Classics, 1991)**
★★★★★ **We Insist! Freedom Now Suite (1963; Candid, N.A.)**
★★★★ **Freedom Now Suite: Live in Europe, 1964 (1964; Magnetic, 1993)**
★★★ **Featuring the Legendary Hasaan (1965; Atlantic and Atco Remasters, 1992)**
★★★★ **Birth and Rebirth (with Anthony Braxton) (Black Saint, 1978)**
★★★½ **One in Two—Two in One (with Anthony Braxton) (Hat Hut, 1979)**
★★★ **Pictures in a Frame (Soul Note, 1979)**
★★★★ **M'Boom (1980; Columbia/Legacy, 1994)**
★★★½ **Swish (1982; New Artists, 1993)**
★★★ **In the Light (Soul Note, 1983)**
★★★ **Collage (Soul Note, 1984)**
★★★★ **Historic Concerts (with Cecil Taylor) (Soul Note, 1984)**
★★★ **Survivors (Soul Note, 1984)**
★★★ **Scott Free (Soul Note, 1985)**
★★★½ **Easy Winners (Soul Note, 1985)**
★★★★ **Max and Dizzy: Paris 1989 (with Dizzy Gillespie) (A&M, 1989)**
★★★★½ **To the Max! (Bluemoon, 1991)**
★★★½ **Live at S.O.B.'s in New York (Mesa Bluemoon, 1992)**
★★★½ **The Long March, Part 1 (with Archie Shepp) (Hat Hut, 1993)**
★★★½ **The Long March, Part 2 (with Archie Shepp) (Hat Hut, 1993)**
★★★ **Mop Mop (Le Jazz, 1995)**
★★★★ **It's Time (Impulse!, 1996)**
★★★★ **With the New Orchestra of Boston and the So What Brass Quintet (Blue Note, 1996)**

Max Roach (b. 1924) stands alone among drummers in the latter half of the 20th Century. A pioneer involved in the birth of bebop, he went on to colead one of the 1950s' most important bands with trumpeter Clifford Brown and has since explored the possibilities of percussion ensembles with his groundbreaking M'Boom and with a contemporary marriage of classical and jazz in his double quartet. A thorough technician, Roach can play in the most crowd-pleasing manner on one session and the most theoretically challenging the next, yet it all flows from an overall conception that rhythms are a life force and a medium for change and enlightenment central to human understanding and communication.

Roach played with Charlie Parker in the early 1940s and studied drummer Kenny Clarke at Minton's where the early bop sessions were being held. At the age of 19 he took part in the first bebop recording session organized by Coleman Hawkins for Apollo Records. Later that year he played in bands led by Dizzy Gillespie and Benny Carter. Through the rest of the '40s, Roach played in a variety of groups with Parker, Hawkins and Miles Davis, among others. By 1954 he was leading the historic quintet with Clifford Brown, which was cut short by Brown's death in 1956. Roach went on to play with other talented young musicians including Sonny Rollins (with whom he'd already played in the quintet), Booker Little and George Coleman, a tenor saxophonist who worked with Miles Davis in the '60s.

Harmonic advances were central to Roach's conception, along with his muscular, logical timekeeping, and his small-band recordings were some of the first and finest examples of hard bop. *The Max Roach Quartet Featuring Hank Mobley,* his first recording date as a leader, also marks the debut of two musicians who would go on to stardom: tenor saxophonist Mobley and pianist Walter Davis Jr. The inspired Brown/Roach collaboration would never be duplicated, but Kenny Dorham, another Parker alumnus, was astonishingly good as a replacement. The Verve sides cover the period during Brown and then Dorham's stays in Roach's group. *Max Roach Plus Four* is a fiery session with Rollins and Dorham; *The Max Roach Four Plays Charlie Parker* session contrasts Dorham's trumpet against Mobley's or Coleman's tenor.

Deeds, Not Words is another fine hard-bop session with Little on trumpet, Coleman on tenor and Ray Draper on tuba, and *Speak, Brother, Speak* is a live recording with Clifford Jordan on tenor and Mal Waldron on piano. Waldron and Jordan, along with trumpeter Richard Williams, Julian Priester on trombone and Art Davis on bass, also appear on *It's Time,* a thematic song cycle that anticipates the experiments Roach would later undertake, in this case through the use of a chanting chorus across the album. Jordan, Priester and tenor saxophonist Stanley Turrentine appear on *Mop Mop. Percussion Bitter Sweet* takes Roach's experiments further, augmenting the Jordan, Waldron, Priester and Davis lineup with Little, Eric Dolphy and vocalist Abbey Lincoln on the riveting "Garvey's Ghost." The stage was then set for the historic political/musical statement *We Insist! Freedom Now Suite,* with Oscar Brown. Jr. joining Lincoln on vocals and Olatunji's percussion added to the mix.

In addition to his work with larger ensembles and African-inspired musical and political themes, Roach began making a series of challenging duet recordings. The two *Long March* recordings document a live duet performance with saxophonist Archie Shepp at a Swiss Jazz festival. *Birth and Rebirth* and *One in Two—Two in One* are more cerebral duets with Anthony Braxton, who plays alto, soprano and sopranino saxophones, contrabass clarinet, clarinet and flute. Roach's infamous meeting with pianist Cecil Taylor, *Historic Concerts,* is considered a turning point in Taylor's approach. *Swish* is another piano/drums duet, with Connie Crothers. *Max and Dizzy: Paris 1989* reunites the bop pioneers 45 years later in an inspired collaboration.

One of Roach's most interesting formats is the percussion ensemble featured on *M'Boom.* Roach presented this concept in live concerts during the '70s, and this recording utilizes tympani, vibraphones, marimbas, xylophone, Latin percussion, steel drums, gourds, chimes, parts of trap sets, bongos, timbales and a number of other small instruments for a lush, spiritual sound that overlaps African and avant-garde themes. *Live at S.O.B.'s in New York* is an excellent example of the ensemble's concert energy. Roach doesn't fully participate in the other M'Boom title, *Collage.*

Pictures in a Frame and *In the Light* feature Cecil Bridgewater on trumpet, Odean Pope on tenor saxophone, flute and oboe and Calvin Hill on bass. The same lineup, with Tyrone Brown on bass, appears on *Scott Free.* That lineup in turn, with percussionist Ray Mantilla added, is used in the first stage of Roach's next experiment, the double quartet, in collaboration with a string quartet on *Easy Winners.* On *Survivors* Roach takes on the string quartet by himself in what might be considered an extension of his duet experiments. *To the Max!* is an incredible recording that incorporates all the aspects of Roach's work over two sprawling, celebratory discs, highlighted by the "Ghost Dance" suite. The Bridgewater/Pope quartet, M'Boom, the Uptown String Quartet and a vocal choir all turn in superlative performances, and Roach even reprises his "Drums Unlimited" solo.

Roach's return to major-label status, *With the New Orchestra of Boston and the So What Brass Quintet,* is a major event in jazz history that might strike those who've followed Roach closely as something of an anticlimax. There's no questioning the quality of the music or performance, however, as Roach composes ambitiously for a lineup including Bridgewater, Steve Turre on trombone, Frank Gordon on trumpet, Robert Stewart on tuba and Marshall Sealy on French horn. — J.S.

MARCUS ROBERTS

★★★ **Truth Is Spoken Here (Novus/RCA, 1989)**
★★★½ **Deep in the Shed (Novus/RCA, 1990)**
★★★ **Alone with Three Giants (Novus/RCA, 1991)**
★★★★½ **As Serenity Approaches (Novus/RCA, 1992)**
★★★★½ **If I Could Be with You (Novus/RCA, 1993)**
★★★½ **Gershwin for Lovers (Columbia, 1994)**
★★★½ **Marcus Roberts Plays Ellington (Novus/RCA, 1995)**
★★★ **Time and Circumstance (Columbia, 1996)**
★★★★½ **Portraits in Blue (Sony Classical, 1996)**
★★★★½ **Blues for the New Millennium (Columbia, 1997)**

Pianist Marcus Roberts (b. 1963) first came to prominence in Wynton Marsalis's band, and like his onetime employer, Roberts sometimes worships the past at the expense of the present with a somber piety that robs jazz of its irreverent populism. Like his mentor, though, Roberts is such an astounding virtuoso and inspiring improviser that he eventually overwhelms all objections. There's room in jazz for those who apply the formal technical standards and refined precision of classical music to the tradition, and no one has pursued that approach more successfully since Duke Ellington's death than Marsalis and Roberts.

Blind since the age of 4, Marthaniel Roberts first learned piano in church, began nine years of classical lessons at age 12 and at age 13 fell under the spell of Art Tatum, James P. Johnson, Mary Lou Williams and other prebop pianists. Roberts was hired in 1985 as the pianist in Marsalis's band, where he displayed the chops and classicist mind-set to become the trumpeter's most important musical partner. Dubbed the "J Master" by his bandleader, Roberts recorded and toured with Marsalis for six years and made many return visits after leaving the band in 1991. In the meantime, he won the $10,000 first prize in the first annual Thelonious Monk International Jazz Competition in 1987.

Roberts's first three solo albums went to Number One on *Billboard*'s traditional-jazz charts. *Truth Is Spoken Here* finds the pianist playing his own compositions (as well as some by his biggest heroes, Ellington and Thelonious Monk) with such elders as Marsalis, drummer Elvin Jones and saxophonist Charlie Rouse, but the leader's playing impresses more than his writing does. *Deep in the Shed* is a big step forward: Working in quintet, sextet and septet settings with his former Marsalis band mates, Roberts shows a rare gift for building thick, elegant harmonies in the late-'50s tradition of Thelonious Monk and Miles Davis.

Roberts's most revealing albums may well be his three solo-piano explorations of older jazz traditions, because they showcase his best asset—his powerful, agile left hand. While most modern jazz pianists have allowed their left hands to be submissive servants of the right, Roberts worked hard at mastering the idioms of ragtime and stride and emerged with a left hand as capable and as assertive as his right. Roberts's hands operate so independently that they seem to be having a dialog. On *Alone with Three Giants,* he tackles six numbers each by Monk and Ellington plus three more by Jelly Roll Morton, though he sometimes seems intimidated by his models. He's much better on *As Serenity Approaches,* which includes 11 piano solos and 8 unaccompanied duets with Wynton and Ellis Marsalis and other members of the inner circle. Roberts is much more successful here at bringing to life the spirit of Morton and Fats Waller, both in their own compositions and in his tributes to them. Best is *If I Could Be with You,* which includes three compositions by stride master James P. Johnson, Scott Joplin's "Maple Leaf Rag," three traditional spirituals and tunes by Monk, Ellington, George Gershwin and Cole Porter. The pianist's unquestionable facility makes possible an irrepressible joyfulness.

Roberts served as musical director of the Lincoln Center Jazz Orchestra during its 1994 winter tour and used that experience as a springboard to his most ambitious album, *Portraits in Blue.* The centerpiece is a radical, half-hour reworking of Gershwin's "Rhapsody in Blue." Collaborating with a 50-member band drawn from the LCJO and the Orchestra of St. Luke's, Roberts brings the composition's subliminal jazz influences to the fore by muscling up the rhythm section and making it swing ever so forcefully. His own piano is part of that rhythm section, but it also steps forward for solos that tie Gershwin's 1924 ideas to many of the jazz movements that have since emerged. The album also includes a welcome revival of James P. Johnson's rarely heard orchestral piece "Yamekraw" and 13 minutes of Roberts's variations on Gershwin's "I Got Rhythm." He takes a more intimate, romantic approach on *Gershwin for Lovers,* which features 10 of the composer's pop songs reinterpreted for piano trio by Roberts, bassist Reginald Veal and drummer Herlin Riley Jr. Most of the songs are ballads, and the mood is sometimes too sedate, but Roberts plays beautifully, and Veal at times seizes the melody with impressive boldness.

Time and Circumstance is another piano-trio album, this time with 18-year-old bassist David Grossman and 19-year-old drummer Jason Marsalis. Roberts's liner notes explain how the 14 original pieces represent stages "in a life-long love affair," but they don't work as program music. The Monk-like rhythms are fascinating, but Roberts fails to come up with melodies as memorable as those of Monk or Gershwin. *Marcus Roberts Plays Ellington* simply collects 10 Ellington compositions recorded on four of Roberts's previous albums.

Blues for the New Millennium is at once retrospective and forward-looking, a large-band update of blues standards such as "Cross Road Blues" and "Jungle Blues" played with contemporary vitality. The interrelatedness of blues and jazz, and the role of that fusion in the future of American music, is nowhere better demonstrated. — J.S.

DUKE ROBILLARD

★★★½ **Swing (Rounder, 1987)**
★★★ **You Got Me (Rounder, 1988)**
★★★½ **Rockin' Blues (Rounder, 1988)**
★★★ **Turn It Around (Rounder, 1991)**
★★★★ **After Hours Swing Session (Rounder, 1992)**
★★★½ **Temptation (Pointblank, 1994)**
★★★½ **Duke's Blues (Pointblank, 1994)**
★★★½ **Dangerous Place (Pointblank, 1997)**
★★★½ **Duke Robillard Plays Blues (Bullseye Blues, 1997)**
★★★ **Duke Robillard Plays Jazz (Bullseye Blues, 1997)**
★★★½ **Stretchin' Out Live (Stony Plain, 1998)**

As a founding member and front man of the famed Roomful of Blues in 1967, Duke Robillard (b. 1948) spent 12 years honing his skills as a guitarist and singer. His subsequent career as a solo artist found him taking a more contemporary road, combining his interests in rock, pop, jazz and R&B and recording several albums that sound as authentic as they are soulful. The high points of two LP- and cassette-only releases, *Duke Robillard and the Pleasure Kings* and *Too Hot to Handle,* are collected on *Rockin' Blues,* a tough, smoldering set of songs that Robillard and his band the Pleasure Kings—bassist Thomas Enright and drummer Tom DeQuattro—seem to churn out effortlessly. Included here are the fine originals "Tore Up" and "Duke's Mood," as well as the Johnny Otis–penned title track and a version of Chuck Berry's "It's My Own Business."

Backed by tenor saxophone, keyboards, bass, drums and two guitars, *Swing* documents Robillard's love of jazz and includes a cool, sprightly interpretation of the Jay McShann/Charlie Parker composition "Jumpin' Blues," whose lyrics Robillard delivers with a laid-back intensity. Also present is a version of late saxophone giant Sonny Stitt's "Stitt's Bitts," which Robillard handles with a strong nod to bebop and a sly reference to the traditional reel "The Sailor's Hornpipe," which he briefly quotes in his solo, and originals like "Zot" and "Jim Jam," whose grooves and arrangements place them squarely into the thematic framework of the album. Featuring appearances by Jimmie Vaughan (whom Robillard succeeded for a short stint in the Fabulous Thunderbirds), Dr. John and pianist Ron Levy, Robillard and his Pleasure Kings spin through 10 tracks on *You Got Me,* including a blistering version of Snooky Pryor's "Judgment Day," Ike Turner's rollicking "You Can't Be the One for Me" and a smoky original called "You're the One I Adore."

Credited to the Duke Robillard Band featuring Susann Forrest, *Turn It Around* introduces Scott Appelrouth on bass and Doug Hinman on drums, as well as Louisville, Kentucky, native Forrest on vocals. Highlights include the ironically celebratory original

"Don't Look at My Girl Like That," on which a Rhode Island vocal quintet called the Pink Tuxedos adds punch to the song's chorus, and the first blues Robillard ever wrote, "I Think You Know," whose 10-minute length allows him to stretch out his soloing à la Stevie Ray Vaughan, to whom the song is dedicated. On *After Hours Swing Session* Robillard again looks to the past for cues, performing music that was either written or inspired by late-1930s jazz. Included here are songs associated with Nat King Cole, Tiny Grimes and the Benny Goodman Sextet: Especially riveting is Cole's "The Trouble with Me Is You," which Robillard and his band mates—including four Roomful of Blues vets—swing through with a studied abandon. Other highlights include Robillard's surprisingly fresh take on "Sweet Georgia Brown" and an original vibes- and baritone-saxophone–spiked blues called "Albi Ain't Here." *Duke Robillard Plays Blues* features guest shots from Dr. John and Jimmie Vaughan. — B.R.H.

FENTON ROBINSON

★★★★ **Somebody Loan Me a Dime (1974; Alligator, 1990)**
★★★★ **I Hear Some Blues Downstairs (1977; Alligator, 1991)**
★★★ **Nightflight (1984; Alligator, 1991)**
★★★½ **Special Road (1989; Evidence, 1993)**

The mellow passion and jazz-influenced phrasing of guitarist Fenton Robinson (b. 1935) have placed him at the forefront of modern Chicago blues since the early '60s. He cut his most famous composition, "Somebody Loan Me a Dime," in 1967, only to have it purloined two years later by Boz Scaggs, who with guitarist Duane Allman recorded a classic (and some say definitive) version of the song.

On *Somebody Loan Me a Dime,* Robinson's playing reflects a willingness to push the envelope. Backed by a deft stable of session players including rhythm guitarist Mighty Joe Young, Robinson's playing is an elastic high-wire act that doesn't sacrifice passion for the sake of technique (check the serrated final solo in "Country Girl"). An original called "Gotta Wake Up" features silken horn bursts and Robinson's sharp single-note runs, while "Texas Flood" becomes a vehicle for his amazingly fluid singing. *I Hear Some Blues Downstairs* features more fine playing, though Robinson's arrangements have become more progressive and jazzy. Robinson tears at the polished, ultrafunky backbeat of "Just a Little Bit" with fierce six-string salvos, then recedes for the slow blues of "West Side Baby," only to bounce back for the smooth, horn-spiked "I'm So Tired." A particular highlight of this album is Robinson's high-energy singing and playing on his interpretation of Howlin' Wolf's "Killing Floor."

Nightflight and *Special Road* were originally released on the Dutch label Black Magic. On the latter, recorded in Holland during a rare European tour, Robinson updates some of his obscure singles, including "7-11 Blues," "Nothing but a Fool" and the slow, insistent "Blue Monday," whose jarring central guitar riff is framed by the languid tenor-sax figures of Luther Taylor and Johan de Roos. Also included here is Robinson's smoky rendering of T-Bone Walker's "Love Is Just a Gamble" and his midtempo, menacing-yet-swinging interpretation of the Joe Lee Williams classic "Baby Please Don't Go." Robinson remains one of the great, underappreciated bluesmen. His recorded output has been sparse, but the quality of his albums is in no way proportional to their quantity. — B.R.H.

ROCKIN' DOPSIE

★★★ **Big Bad Zydeco (GNP, 1982)**
★★★ **Hold On (GNP, 1983)**
★★★½ **Good Rockin' (GNP, 1984)**
★★★ **Saturday Night Zydeco (Maison de Soul, 1988)**
★★★ **Louisiana Music (Atlantic, 1991)**

Offering good-time spirit in abundance, Rockin' Dopsie (né Alton Rubin, 1932–1993) parlays the raw essence of Big Easy zydeco. Cajun party fare—smoky vocals and zesty accordion—that combines the bounce of the polka and the grit of the blues, his albums are a consistent gas, but the Cajun-dialect takes on such New Orleans standards as "I'm Walkin' " and "I Hear You Knockin' " make *Good Rockin'* the standout. Recorded with a cast of zydeco all-stars rather than his usual Cajun Twisters, *Saturday Night* shows him at his most technically accomplished; *Louisiana Music* sounds almost slick. The unadorned charm of the earlier records provides fresher pleasure. — P.E.

JIMMIE RODGERS

★★★★½ **Train Whistle Blues (1958; Koch, 1998)**
★★★★★ **First Sessions, 1927–1928 (Rounder, 1991)**

★★★★★ **The Early Years, 1928–1929 (Rounder, 1991)**
★★★★★ **On the Way Up, 1929 (Rounder, 1991)**
★★★★★ **Riding High, 1929–1930 (Rounder, 1991)**
★★★★★ **America's Blue Yodeler, 1930–1931 (Rounder, 1991)**
★★★★★ **Down the Old Road, 1931–1932 (Rounder, 1991)**
★★★★★ **No Hard Times, 1932 (Rounder, 1991)**
★★★★★ **Last Sessions, 1933 (Rounder, 1991)**
★★★★★ **The Essential Jimmie Rodgers (RCA, 1997)**

In 1930 Mississippi-born "hillbilly" singer Jimmie Rodgers (1897–1933) engaged in a summit meeting of the highest order when he recorded "Blue Yodel No. 9" with Louis Armstrong on trumpet and Armstrong's wife, Lil, on piano. On this outing Rodgers made explicit an emotional link between jazz, blues and country. A year after the Armstrong sessions, Rodgers went against form again and recorded in Louisville with a black jug band. Rodgers evinced an uncanny ability to fit any type of song, be it an original composition, a cover version or something snatched from the public domain, to a singular and idiosyncratic approach that was truly multicultural in its disparate stylistic elements. Celebrated as he was for his evocative vocals (a bluesy tenor, he often employed what he termed a "blue" yodel—not bright, Swiss-style, but something darker and more haunting) and his stirring original songs, Rodgers's most valuable contribution to popular music was in expanding its boundaries.

This eclectic approach is hardly surprising, given Rodgers's background. He grew up surrounded by blues and country music. His mother died of tuberculosis when Rodgers was four; with his father away much of the time working on the railroad (Rodgers *fils* would follow in his footsteps later as a water carrier—he too was afflicted with TB and could not handle more physically demanding jobs, although his professional nickname was "the Singing Brakeman"), the youngster spent much of his childhood with relatives in Mississippi and Alabama. Traveling as much as he did, and listening to radio all the while, shaped his broad musical vocabulary.

Rodgers originally recorded for RCA Victor (*Train Whistle Blues* is a reissued RCA release); in 1997, the label issued *The Essential Jimmie Rodgers*, which gives a fine overview, covering the years 1927–1931. For the most part, though, his catalog had been in disarray for years until Rounder corrected the problem by reissuing all of the artist's studio recordings on eight CDs, each with thorough annotation by Rodgers's biographer, Nolan Porterfield. Listening to the discs in chronological order is one of the most exciting experiences available to a music lover: In terms of astonishing growth of artistic vision and breadth and depth of stylistic variation, Rodgers's catalog stands toe-to-toe with giants Louis Armstrong and Miles Davis.

First Sessions is largely Rodgers accompanying himself on guitar (the two original Bristol sides are here), then incorporating additional stringed instruments in the 1928 sessions as he begins stretching out his sound. *The Early Years* and *On the Way Up* show him expanding his repertoire and working with different combinations of instrumentalists. *The Early Years* includes tracks cut with an orchestra as well as three of the most famous recordings of Rodgers's career: "Waiting for a Train," "My Little Lady" and "Daddy and Home." *On the Way Up* includes two choice blues performances, "Jimmie's Texas Blues" and "Train Whistle Blues." On these, Rodgers is accompanied by a group of Texas musicians who went on to cut several important sides with him, including a notable soloist, steel guitarist Joe Kaipo. Also present is 17-year-old guitarist Billy Burkes, who became one of Rodgers's oft-imitated accompanists.

Riding High documents Rodgers at a time when he was one of the country's most popular recording artists. Its song selection includes tracks recorded in both Atlanta and Hollywood, where he delivered many of his most compelling performances. Lani McIntire's Hawaiians are on two numbers, as well as Bob Sawyer's Jazz Band, a contingent comprising piano, cornet, clarinet, banjo and tuba, on "My Blue-Eyed Jane." Commercially, *America's Blue Yodeler* represents a pinnacle for Rodgers, with its collection of tracks recorded in 1930 and 1931 encompassing many of his most popular sides, including the enduring "Blue Yodel No. 8" (or "Mule Skinner Blues") and the Armstrong side, "Blue Yodel No. 9," which finds Satchmo tentative at the outset but finally warming to his task and delivering a rousing, strutting solo. In keeping with the blues tradition, Rodgers allowed his bawdy streak to surface on occasion, as in "Let Me Be Your Side Track" and "The Mystery of Number Five."

Down the Old Road is both forward-thinking and static. Although the artist is treading water much of the time here, his sessions with the Louisville Jug Band produce ideas that Bob Wills and other Western swing pioneers would seize on some two decades later. *No Hard Times* and *Last Sessions* conclude this powerful legacy. Even with death approaching (he cut "Old Love Letters" while propped up on a cot, only two days before he died), Rodgers was still looking ahead to the next breakthrough. It is a testament to his brilliance that most of what he left behind remains in many ways as startling in its vitality and freshness as it was in its own time. — D.M.

CLAUDIO RODITI

★★ **Gemini Man (Milestone, 1988)**
★★★ **Slow Fire (Milestone, 1989)**
★★★ **Two of Swords (Candid, 1991)**
★★★★ **Milestones (Candid, 1992)**
★★★★★ **Free Wheelin' (Reservoir, 1995)**
★★★½ **Samba—Manhattan Style (Reservoir, 1995)**
★★★½ **Double Standards (Reservoir, 1997)**
★★★ **Mind Games (Summit, 1997)**

Trumpeter Claudio Roditi (b. 1946) moved to the United States from his native Brazil in 1970 to study at the Berklee College of Music in Boston. He quickly made his mark on the jazz scene as a first-rate soloist and ensemble player. While equally at home playing bebop or Latin jazz, he also has done much to blend jazz material with the rhythms of his homeland. Stylistically influenced by Miles Davis and Clifford Brown, he blends Latin fire with surgical articulation and deep feeling on both his preferred rotary-valve trumpet and flügelhorn. Roditi worked extensively with Cuban saxophonist Paquito D'Rivera and in Dizzy Gillespie's United Nation Orchestra and Jimmy Heath's big band.

Roditi's three earliest recordings reflect the Brazilian/bebop blend. The Brazilian lilt of his relaxed voice adds another texture to his music on several tracks of *Gemini Man* and *Slow Fire* but also lessens the overall impact of both discs. *Two of Swords,* split between a Brazilian quintet and a bop quartet, is much more interesting. *Milestones* is a live recording from New York's Birdland with D'Rivera and a stellar rhythm section—pianist Kenny Barron, bassist Ray Drummond and drummer Ben Riley. *Free Wheelin'* teams Roditi with saxophonists Andres Boiarsky and Nick Brignola in a superb tribute recording to late hard-bop trumpeter Lee Morgan. *Samba—Manhattan Style,* with Boiarsky and Greg Abate on saxes and Jay Ashby on trombone guesting on various tracks, fuses intense jazz soloing with exotic rhythms. *Double Standards* offers Roditi in two contexts, with two different bands performing Brazilian and jazz chestnuts. On the live recording *Mind Games* Roditi is special guest with a German octet at concerts in Munich and Berlin. — K.F.

RED RODNEY

★★★★ **Bird Lives! (1973; Muse, 1989)**
★★★ **No Turn on Red (Denon, 1989)**
★★★ **Then and Now (Chesky, 1992)**
★★★ **Fiery (Savoy, 1993)**

Trumpeter Robert Chudnick, a.k.a. Red Rodney (1927–1994), was a bop legend, one of Charlie Parker's musical accomplices and running partners during the heyday of 52nd Street. He came up playing in the swing-era big bands of the 1940s—Benny Goodman, Jimmy Dorsey, Stan Kenton, Woody Herman—and in 1949 took Kenny Dorham's place in Parker's group, where he established himself in less than a year as an accomplished bop player. In the '50s Rodney began a long-standing association with brass/reed player Ira Sullivan, recording several excellent albums, including the vinyl-only *Modern Music from Chicago* in 1955 and the out-of-print *Red Rodney 1957.*

Rodney retired to the Las Vegas session scene until the '70s, when he, along with alto saxophonist Charles McPherson, made the tremendous *Bird Lives!,* evoking Parker's spirit. He recorded several other fine albums for Muse, none of which remain in print, and a number of records for Scandinavian companies, the best of which, *Red Giant* on SteepleChase, is well worth searching out. — J.S.

ROY ROGERS

★★★★½ **Chops Not Chaps (1985; Blind Pig, 1992)**
★★★★ **Slidewinder (Blind Pig, 1987)**
★★★½ **Blues on the Range (Blind Pig, 1989)**
★★★★ **R&B (with Norton Buffalo) (Blind Pig, 1991)**
★★★½ **Travellin' Tracks (Blind Pig, 1992)**
★★★★½ **Slide of Hand (Liberty, 1993)**
★★★★ **Slide Zone (Liberty, 1994)**
★★★★★ **Rhythm & Groove (Pointblank, 1996)**

Roy Rogers (b. 1950) is a virtuoso slide guitarist and innovative songwriter whose bands deliver consistently high-powered performances. Rogers was also a mainstay in guitar legend John Lee Hooker's band for several years and produced the Grammy-winning/nominated albums that spurred Hooker's 1990s revival—*The Healer, Mr. Lucky* and *Chill Out.*

The San Francisco–based Rogers was recognized as the leading interpreter of Robert Johnson's Delta blues style as of his debut, *Chops Not Chaps,* which features astonishing versions of Johnson's "32-20 Blues," "Terraplane Blues," "Kind Hearted Woman" and "Judgment Day" as well as the chilling Skip James classic "Devil Got My Woman" and the Elmore James groove "Shake Your Moneymaker." The record also spotlights inventive keyboardist Phil Aaburg and harmonica whiz Norton Buffalo. The witty Rogers, whose parents named him after the cowboy star, closes the record with a snippet of "Happy Trails." *Slidewinder* showcases Rogers's dazzling slide-guitar technique, with guest shots from Hooker, whose band Rogers had been leading, and New Orleans great Allen Toussaint on keyboards. Keyboardist Mark Naftalin of the Butterfield Blues Band guests on the *Blues on the Range* sessions.

Rogers's modernization of country blues is most fully realized on *R&B,* an acoustic duet session with Buffalo (the title refers to their initials, not the music). The interaction between two players on unamplified instruments is breathtaking, and both musicians contribute excellent original material. The two reunited for *Travellin' Tracks,* which combines some dazzling live performance with studio sessions. *Slide of Hand* ups the ante to showcase Rogers on acoustic and electric guitars, National steel guitar and dulcimer in a variety of settings with help from Aaberg, Buffalo, Toussaint and NRBQ bassist Joey Spampinato. Rogers extends his mastery of the Johnson catalog with an acoustic reading of "Stones in My Passway" and showcases his own writing ability, particularly on the great "Don't Give It Up," "Rockin' at the Hey Hey" and "Change of the Season." *Slide Zone* adds more electric guitar on numbers recorded with Rogers's working band, the Delta Rhythm Kings, and includes two strikingly original acoustic pieces with Bela Fleck.

Rhythm & Groove is Rogers's masterpiece, an album that builds on his skills as a soloist, songwriter, vocalist and bandleader and moves boldly into a blues-rock direction without pandering or resorting to the usual clichés. "Vida's Place" is a vividly drawn evocation of a mythic roadhouse party scene, while "Call on Me" and "Feel My Care" offer unusually sensitive themes. "Shakin' Hands with the Devil" makes a compelling comment on the Oklahoma City terrorist bombers. Guitar playing remains the main event, though, and Rogers delivers with consummate bravado and taste. — J.S.

THE ROLLING STONES

★★★★★ **The Rolling Stones: England's Newest Hit Makers (1964; Abkco, 1986)**
★★★★★ **12 × 5 (1964; Abkco, 1986)**
★★★★★ **The Rolling Stones, Now! (1965; Abkco, 1986)**
★★★★½ **Out of Our Heads (1965; Abkco, 1986)**
★★★★★ **December's Children (and Everybody's) (1965; Abkco, 1986)**
★★★★★ **Big Hits/High Tide and Green Grass (1966; Abkco, 1986)**
★★★★★ **Aftermath (1966; Abkco, 1986)**
★★★ **Got Live If You Want It! (1966; Abkco, 1986)**
★★★½ **Between the Buttons (1967; Abkco, 1986)**
★★★ **Flowers (1967; Abkco, 1986)**
★★½ **Their Satanic Majesties Request (1967; Abkco, 1986)**
★★★★★ **Beggar's Banquet (1968; Abkco, 1986)**
★★★★★ **Through the Past, Darkly (Big Hits, Vol. 2) (1969; Abkco, 1986)**
★★★★★ **Let It Bleed (1969; Abkco, 1986)**
★★★★★ **Get Yer Ya-Ya's Out! (1970; Abkco, 1986)**
★★★★★ **Sticky Fingers (1971; Virgin, 1994)**
★★★★★ **Hot Rocks 1964–71 (1972; Abkco, 1986)**
★★★★★ **Exile on Main Street (1972; Virgin, 1994)**
★★★★★ **More Hot Rocks: Big Hits and Fazed Cookies (1973; Abkco, 1986)**
★★★½ **Goat's Head Soup (1973; Virgin, 1994)**
★★★½ **It's Only Rock 'n' Roll (1974; Virgin, 1994)**
★★★★ **Black and Blue (1976; Virgin, 1994)**
★★★★ **Some Girls (1978; Virgin, 1994)**
★★ **Emotional Rescue (1980; Virgin, 1994)**
★★★★ **Tattoo You (1981; Virgin, 1994)**
★★½ **Undercover (1983; Virgin, 1994)**

★★★ Dirty Work (1986; Virgin, 1994)
★★★★★ The Singles Collection (Abkco, 1989)
★★★½ Steel Wheels (1989; Virgin, 1994)
★★★★ Flashpoint (Rolling Stones, 1991)
★★★ Voodoo Lounge (Virgin, 1994)
★★★ Stripped (Virgin, 1995)
★★★ Rock & Roll Circus (Abkco, 1996)
★★★ Bridges to Babylon (Virgin, 1997)

The Rolling Stones' drummer extraordinaire, Charlie Watts (b. 1941) may have been exaggerating when he said the only thing his band has ever really tried to do is master the Chicago blues, but of all the '60s British rock & roll titans, the Stones indeed were the strongest and most successful champions of the form—and throughout their career, it's to black music that they've most often turned for inspiration. With Keith Richards's (b. 1943) guitar work a fond homage to Chuck Berry, and Mick Jagger's (b. 1943) vocals often a tribute to or a parody of blues and R&B belters, they've insisted largely on three-chord rock & roll. Swaggering in attitude, relentless in their emphasis on live performance, they've proved themselves inheritors of the essential R&B sensibility.

Mixing Rufus Thomas and Willie Dixon, Marvin Gaye and Sam Cooke, the Stones' first three albums are black-music primers of raw force; the blues appeal of *The Rolling Stones, Now!* makes it the strongest of the trio, but each was a revelation to white U.S. and U.K. teens. While a lesser album, *Out of Our Heads* features the breakthrough "(I Can't Get No) Satisfaction." Not only did the hit forecast Richards's mastery of the art of the riff, but in the lyrics the band found its central theme.

"Get off My Cloud" and "As Tears Go By" from *December's Children* show Jagger/Richards capable of writing equally effective rockers and ballads; and with *High Tide and Green Grass,* the group produced the best greatest-hits record of the mid-'60s. *High Tide*'s 12 cuts remain the triumph of a perfect rhythm section: Watts's backbeat—casual, unerring and swinging—is unrivaled; Bill Wyman's (b. 1936) bass lines fuse exactly with Watts's drumming; and Richards's guitar makes unabashed body music.

With *Aftermath,* Brian Jones (1942–1969) and Mick Jagger come into their own. The group's early reigning sex symbol, blues purist and de facto leader, Jones branches out—adding sitar to "Paint It Black," marimba to "Under My Thumb," dulcimer to "Lady Jane." A passionate elegance informs a number of the songs' arrangements; and while the sound remains intense, it isn't pop but a new way of rocking. On *Aftermath,* Jagger reveals his signature gift: Assuming a range of personae, he becomes the rock & roll actor nonpareil. The touching, inexpert mimicry of R&B stars that stamped his early singing gives way to an ironic virtuosity, the cockiness that would come to characterize all his postures.

Between the Buttons and its near-repeat, *Flowers,* continue the advance begun by *Aftermath.* "Let's Spend the Night Together" is one more bad-boy manifesto, and in "Ruby Tuesday," with its lovely flute passages, Jagger/Richards's melodic flair rivals Paul McCartney's. The Stones' one "experimental" album, a response to *Sgt. Pepper's,* is predictably shaky: On *Their Satanic Majesties Request,* the best work is done by outsiders—Nicky Hopkins's piano on "She's a Rainbow," John Paul Jones's orchestration of "2,000 Light Years from Home."

Returning to roots rocking, the Stones of *Beggar's Banquet* had become the Stones of legend. Outlaw anthems ("Street Fighting Man," "Sympathy for the Devil," "Stray Cat Blues") alternate with acoustic numbers of a country or country-blues turn ("Prodigal Son," "Factory Girl" and "Salt of the Earth"), and the album contains Jagger's best lyrics. Including "Honky Tonk Women," *Through the Past, Darkly* offers a review of the Stones' obsessions—sex and power—along with the tenderness of the outsider and an impulse toward romanticism. *Rock & Roll Circus,* the soundtrack of a live variety show hosted by the Stones, finds the band at a low point, overshadowed on their own gig by guest stars the Who.

The end of the decade brought *Let It Bleed,* a summing-up of the '60s Stones. (Brian Jones had died during recording, to be replaced by Mick Taylor [b. 1948].) Richards's guitar work on "Monkey Man" and "Midnight Rambler" flashes exuberant assurance; on "Love in Vain" and "Country Honk" he reasserts the band's blues and country sides; and on "You've Got the Silver" he tries out a kind of Dylan-esque vocalizing whose stark emotiveness contrasts with Jagger's increasing mannerism. On "Gimme Shelter," "You Can't Always Get What You Want" and "Live with Me," however, Jagger still sounds compelling.

With their best live set, *Get Yer Ya-Ya's Out!,* the Stones embarked upon an exceptional five-year period with Taylor. A graduate of John Mayall's Bluesbreakers, Taylor was an ace technician, his style somewhat recalling Eric Clapton's. Grafted onto the rhythm machine of the Stones, his playing produces iffy results—on *Sticky Fingers,* his work on "Moonlight Mile" helps lift the song into a majesty the group had never before achieved, but on the second half of "Can't You Hear Me Knocking" Taylor's runs make a great rocker descend into Santana lite. The record, however, stands as the classic "decadent" Stones album—Jagger's singing on "Sister Morphine" and "Wild Horses" finds few equals in its chronicling of exhaustion.

The Stones' final masterpiece, *Exile on Main Street,* remains the best double album in rock & roll history. Astonishing primarily for the guitar interplay—on "Tumbling Dice" Richards elevates riffing into grandeur, and Taylor's blues work is passionate throughout—the record is a triumph less of stellar moments than of relentless intensity. Sprung from a core of hyperdriven Chuck Berry–style rockers ("Rocks Off," "Rip This Joint"), *Exile* plunges into a soulful reexamination of the ethnic music that created the Stones. By now, however, they'd so completely absorbed the essence of the blues, Stax-Volt and country that songs like "Sweet Black Angel" and "Loving Cup" no longer pay tribute to their roots but extend beyond them.

Goat's Head Soup finds them drained of energy. Skill replaces fire; this is primarily Jagger's record, and his ballad work "(Angie," "Winter") is excellent, a little theatrical but not the parody singing he'd soon assume. Mick Taylor's swan song, *It's Only Rock 'n' Roll* is dogged by some of his most excessive playing ("Time Waits for No One"); and while its faster numbers offer dependable kicks, the album is the Stones marking time as "the world's greatest rock & roll band." With *Black and Blue*'s "Memory Motel" the band delivers its most anecdotal road epic; otherwise, the reggae tunes are good and crude, Jagger's singing achieves finesse, and the record debuts new guitarist Ron Wood (b. 1947). Formerly of the Faces (essentially a cheerier Stones sound-alike), Wood brought along none of Taylor's skill, but the Richards lookalike turned out to be more of a Stone than Taylor ever was, his devil-may-care rowdiness a cartoon version of their bad-boy pose.

By the time of *Some Girls,* Wood found his role—he'd fuse with Richards, the two guitarists becoming a rhythm juggernaut, their lead work a casual, conversational trade-off. With the album, too, the Stones came to terms with more contemporary black music; "Miss You" is disco, but they play it with more aggression than some of its "genuine" purveyors did, and the rest of the album's funk is tougher and more fluid than the kind they'd been working ever since *Goat's Head Soup*. With few exceptions, however, the late-model R&B they drew from lacks the subtlety of its '60s precursors—and the Stones rarely overcome the weakness of their sources.

Weakly echoing *Some Girls, Emotional Rescue* is the first Stones record that was merely bland, not even distinguished by the professionalism that came to stamp their later work. It was exactly the professionalism, however, that provoked the derision of their former fanatics—even though in other genres (blues, country, etc.), such honorable work is considered "carrying on the tradition." In the '80s the veteran Stones indeed proved cautious, but their alternate strategies—recycling the raucous sound of their glory days, or guardedly experimenting—sometimes deliver real pleasure. In their rawer style, *Tattoo You* is accomplished rock & roll; *Dirty Work* falters under the weight of its self-conscious primitivism. *Undercover,* with its strange, showy guitars and odd political consciousness, is a misguided attempt to keep current; *Steel Wheels* is all glossiness and craft, but of very high order. Remarkably, with 1994's *Voodoo Lounge,* a lean, sharp set, the band surprised even cynics by displaying a renewed energy. *Bridges to Babylon* employs late-1990s production techniques to update the band's sound.

While their classic individual records, of course, are essential to any understanding of rock & roll, the Stones' best-of collections aren't throwaways. *Hot Rocks* and *More Hot Rocks* are the best of the compilations, and *The Singles Collection* is magnificent. Relatively "unplugged," *Stripped* boasts a fine version of one of the band's concert staples, their reworking of Robert Johnson's "Love in Vain."
— P.E.

SONNY ROLLINS

★★★	**Sonny Rollins with the Modern Jazz Quartet (1953; Original Jazz Classics, 1988)**
★★★	**Moving Out (1954; Original Jazz Classics, 1987)**
★★★★	**Worktime (1955; Original Jazz Classics, 1982)**
★★★★½	**Tenor Madness (1956; Original Jazz Classics, 1987)**
★★★★★	**Saxophone Colossus (1956; Original Jazz Classics, 1987)**

★★★★ **Plus Four (1956; Original Jazz Classics, 1987)**
★★★½ **Sonny Boy (1956; Original Jazz Classics, 1989)**
★★★½ **Rollins Plays for Bird (1956; Original Jazz Classics, 1986)**
★★★★ **Sonny Rollins, Vol. 1 (1956; Blue Note, 1990)**
★★★★½ **Sonny Rollins, Vol. 2 (1957; Blue Note, 1989)**
★★★★ **Way Out West (1957; Original Jazz Classics, 1988)**
★★★★ **Tour de Force (1957; Original Jazz Classics, 1984)**
★★★★ **The Sound of Sonny (1957; Original Jazz Classics, 1987)**
★★★★½ **A Night at the Village Vanguard, Vol. 1 (1957; Blue Note, 1987)**
★★★★★ **A Night at the Village Vanguard, Vol. 2 (1957; Blue Note, 1987)**
★★★ **Sonny Rollins and the Contemporary Leaders (1958; Original Jazz Classics, 1988)**
★★★★★ **Newk's Time (1958; Blue Note, 1990)**
★★★★ **Freedom Suite (1958; Original Jazz Classics, 1989)**
★★★★ **The Quartets (1962; RCA Bluebird, 1986)**
★★★★ **The Bridge (1962; RCA Victor, 1996)**
★★★★ **What's New? (1963; RCA Bluebird, 1993)**
★★★ **Sonny Rollins on Impulse! (1965; Impulse!, 1988)**
★★★★ **Alfie (1965; Impulse!, 1986)**
★★★★ **East Broadway Rundown (1967; Impulse!, 1995)**
★★★★ **Sonny Rollins' Next Album (1972; Original Jazz Classics, 1987)**
★★ **Horn Culture (1973; Original Jazz Classics, 1987)**
★★★ **The Cutting Edge (1974; Original Jazz Classics, 1990)**
★★★ **Nucleus (1975; Original Jazz Classics, 1991)**
★★ **The Way I Feel (1977; Original Jazz Classics, 1991)**
★★★½ **Easy Living (1978; Original Jazz Classics, 1996)**
★★★ **Don't Stop the Carnival (1978; Milestone, 1989)**
★★★½ **Milestone Jazzstars in Concert (1978; Milestone, 1989)**
★★★ **Don't Ask (1979; Original Jazz Classics, 1996)**
★★★ **Love at First Sight (1980; Original Jazz Classics, 1992)**
★★★ **Sunny Days, Starry Nights (Milestone, 1984)**
★★★ **The Solo Album (1985; Original Jazz Classics, 1997)**
★★★★★ **The Essential Sonny Rollins on Riverside (Riverside, 1986)**
★★★★ **G-Man (Milestone, 1987)**
★★★½ **Dancing in the Dark (Milestone, 1988)**
★★★★½ **The Best of Sonny Rollins (Blue Note, 1989)**
★★★★½ **All the Things You Are (1963–1964) (RCA Bluebird, 1990)**
★★★ **Falling in Love with Jazz (Milestone, 1990)**
★★★ **Here's to the People (Milestone, 1991)**
★★★★½ **The Complete Prestige Recordings (Prestige, 1992)**
★★★ **Alternatives (RCA Bluebird, 1992)**
★★★ **Compact Jazz (Verve, 1992)**
★★½ **Old Flames (Milestone, 1993)**
★★★ **Plus Three (Milestone, 1996)**
★★★½ **Silver City (Milestone, 1996)**
★★★½ **Priceless Jazz (GRP, 1997)**
★★★★ **The Complete Sonny Rollins RCA Victor Recordings (RCA Victor, 1997)**
★★★★½ **The Complete Blue Note Recordings (Blue Note, 1997)**

Combining some of the melodic intricacy and flat-out attack of Charlie Parker and the bop pioneers with the assured swing and round, full tone of the tenor sax's original genius, Coleman Hawkins, Sonny Rollins (b. 1929) has been among that instrument's toughest players. While he achieved his peak during a brief period of dazzling inventiveness (1956–1957), he continued to make exciting jazz into the mid-'60s. His work since then has been uneven, although beginning in the late '80s he showed signs of a renewed vigor.

The staggering *Saxophone Colossus* remains his milestone. Playing with the superb backing of drummer Max Roach, pianist Tommy Flanagan and bassist Doug Watkins, Rollins not only flourishes the tonal power that's apparent also on such standouts as *Worktime* and *Tenor Madness,* but on the minor blues, "Blue Seven," debuts a style of improvisation that, rather than simply taking off from the piece's chord changes, works endlessly cunning variations on its central theme. The saxophonist's graceful playing on such albums as *Plus Four* and *Way*

Out West, influenced by the elegance of Lester Young, destroys hasty assessments of his style as exclusively that of the hard bopper who'd smoked through such assaultive music as *Worktime*—he proves himself capable of shimmering melody lines. The title track to *Freedom Suite* shows Rollins reaching for a freer, more abstract form of extended improvisation; the demanding set, again with Roach on drums, and with Oscar Pettiford on bass, stands as some of Rollins's most challenging work. Other examples of Rollins's mid-'50s strength can be found on *Sonny Rollins, Vol. 2:* The colossus is joined by Thelonious Monk and Horace Silver.

Rollins holed up from 1959 to 1961, practicing his horn on the Williamsburg Bridge above New York's East River, and returned in the company of guitarist Jim Hall, with a subtler, more fluid approach heard on *The Bridge* and *What's New?* Bluebird's *The Quartets,* which includes his 1962 breakthrough track, "The Bridge," compiles the best of this period. In the early '60s, as well, Rollins seized the chance to play with his early idol Hawkins and with such up-and-comers as pianist Herbie Hancock (hear the results on Bluebird's fine *All the Things You Are*).

After another spell of seclusion came Rollins's lighter work. He asserts himself on the live Montreux performance of *The Cutting Edge,* with, of all things, a duet with bagpipe on "Swing Low, Sweet Chariot," but many of his '70s recordings feature fusion fare that's well beneath his talents. By the middle of the next decade, though, he'd reemerged—*Sunny Days, Starry Nights* marks a return to grace; *The Solo Album* is remarkable in terms of sheer propulsion; *Falling in Love with Jazz* is a lovely set that includes fine accompanying work by Branford Marsalis and Jack DeJohnette. Of his most recent work, *Old Flames* is the darkest—and among the best. The late-'50s albums—including *Tour de Force, Way Out West* and *Newk's Time,* however, remain his standouts. — P.E.

ROOMFUL OF BLUES

★★★★ **Hot Little Mama (Varrick, 1985)**
★★½ **Dressed Up to Get Messed Up (Varrick, 1986)**
★★★½ **Glazed (with Earl King) (Black Top, 1987)**
★★★★ **Live at Lupo's Heartbreak Hotel (Varrick, 1987)**
★★★ **Dance All Night (Bullseye Blues, 1994)**
★★★ **Turn It On! Turn It Up! (Bullseye Blues, 1995)**
★★★ **Roomful of Blues (32 Blues, 1996)**
★★★½ **Two Classic Albums (32 Blues, 1997)**
★★★ **Under One Roof (Bullseye Blues, 1997)**

Roomful of Blues tackles jump blues, smooth West Coast blues, big-band jazz and New Orleans R&B with equal aplomb. Originally known for backing Big Joe Turner, B.B. King and Count Basie, the group launched the careers of Duke Robillard, Ronnie Earl and Ron Levy. Under the direction of Robillard and pianist Al Copley, the band formed in 1967 in Rhode Island, though its first solo album wasn't recorded until the late '70s. After two records (currently unavailable), Earl replaced Robillard, and following a stint with Eddie "Cleanhead" Vinson, the band signed with Varrick.

Hot Little Mama effectively showcases the group's swinging horn arrangements, Earl's tasteful, T-Bone Walker–influenced guitar playing and Greg Piccolo's heartfelt vocals. A disappointing follow-up, *Dressed Up to Get Messed Up,* suffers from overblown production, trite lyrics and the group's failed attempt to rock & roll. Though it is similarly overproduced, *Glazed* proves more enjoyable; a collaboration with Earl King, it offers midtempo soul and swing flavored by the New Orleans native's tender vocals. *Live at Lupo's Heartbreak Hotel,* Roomful's final and finest album for Varrick, captures a live performance at its favorite hometown haunt. Bursting with energy, the group turns in a cohesive performance, its liveliest horn riffs meeting raucous rhythms as Piccolo and Curtis Selgado sing their hearts out.

Almost a decade elapsed before the band's next album, during which time Earl exited. The group turns in a fair performance on 1994's *Dance All Night,* which witnesses the arrival of Sugar Ray Norcia, a vocalist better suited to the band's slower, more soulful material than its jump-blues rave-ups. For *Turn It On! Turn It Up!,* Norcia returned while Piccolo departed. Though *Turn It On!* lacks the instrumental strength of Roomful's previous efforts, it somewhat successfully covers new musical territory, taking another stab at rock & roll and exploring modern Texas blues. — J.K.

MICHELE ROSEWOMAN

★★★ **The Source (Soul Note, 1984)**
★★★★ **Quintessence (1987; Enja, 1993)**

★★★ **Contrast High (1988; Enja, 1990)**
★★★★½ **Occasion to Rise (Evidence, 1993)**
★★★½ **Harvest (Enja, 1993)**
★★★★ **Spirit (Blue Note, 1996)**

Pianist Michele Rosewoman (b. 1953) began playing at age six in her hometown of Oakland, California, and grew up incorporating into her style a wide range of influences, from jazz to soul to R&B to world music.

In the late '70s Rosewoman moved to New York to pursue her interest in Afro-Cuban music, and in 1983 she formed New Yor-Uba, a 14-piece Afro-Cuban band. The next year she was commissioned to write a piece for the Brooklyn Philharmonic Orchestra. *The Source,* recorded in Italy in 1983, is a solid debut on which Rosewoman showcases herself as an instrumentalist and composer in a quartet setting with Baikida Carroll on trumpet and flügelhorn, Roberto Miranda on bass and Pheeroan Ak Laff on drums.

Quintessence is a tour de force of Rosewoman's playing and arranging skills fronted by Steve Coleman on alto saxophone and Greg Osby on alto and tenor, and backed by the *simpatico* rhythm section of bassist Anthony Cox and drummer Terri Lyne Carrington. *Contrast High* pairs Osby with Gary Thomas on tenor and flute in a slightly less engaging matchup than *Quintessence. Occasion to Rise* is a powerful trio session with the excellent accompanists Rufus Reid on bass and Ralph Peterson on drums. In this setting Rosewoman's pianistic virtuosity is in full view. In addition to playing her own compositions she pays tribute to John Coltrane ("Lazy Bird"), Duke Ellington ("Prelude to a Kiss"), Charles Mingus ("Weird Nightmare"), Ron Carter ("First Trip") and Lee Morgan ("Nite Flite"). *Harvest* is a sextet date with saxophonists Thomas and Steve Wilson, bassist Kenny Davis, drummer Gene Jackson and percussionist Eddie Bobe. *Spirit* is another superb trio session, this time with Davis and Jackson, recorded at the 1994 Montreal Jazz Festival. Highlights include performances of Herbie Hancock's "Dolphin Dance," the title track, originally written by Maurice White for Earth, Wind and Fire, and Rosewoman's own "Independence Day," "Passion Dance Blues" and "For Monk." — J.S.

RENEE ROSNES

★★★ **Renee Rosnes (Blue Note, 1990)**
★★★½ **Without Words (Blue Note, 1993)**
★★★½ **Free Trade (with Free Trade) (Justin Time, 1994)**
★★★★ **One World (with Native Colours) (Concord Jazz, 1995)**
★★★★★ **Ancestors (Blue Note, 1996)**
★★★★½ **As We Are Now (Blue Note, 1997)**

Raised in western Canada, pianist Renee Rosnes (b. 1962) was classically trained in music from childhood through her college years at the University of Toronto. She was drawn to the jazz idiom by its sheer freedom of expression. In 1985, Rosnes moved from Vancouver to New York, where she found work in the bands of Joe Henderson and Wayne Shorter and later a slot in the Blue Note label's repertory unit, OTB. Through the mid-1990s she recorded regularly as a small-group leader while also working as first-call pianist in J.J. Johnson's sextet and the Carnegie Hall Jazz Band.

Rosnes's recordings are consistently excellent, showcasing a bright, lyrical style that draws from a wide range of influences but parrots no one. Her 1990 debut (now out of print) had a shifting lineup, including Branford Marsalis, Ralph Bowen and Wayne Shorter on saxes and a Herbie Hancock cameo. Also look for the out-of-print *For the Moment,* a 1990 quintet session with Henderson and Steve Wilson on saxophones, bassist Ira Coleman and drummer Billy Drummond, which also accentuates Rosnes's fine writing skills. *Without Words* is a trio session augmented by an understated string section arranged and conducted by Robert Freedman.

Free Trade was made during a 1994 trans-Canada tour with fellow Canadians Peter Leitch on guitar, Neil Swainson on bass, Ralph Bowen on sax and flute and Terry Clarke on drums. That same year, Rosnes formed the quartet Native Colours with saxophonist Ralph Moore and her regular touring trio mates, Drummond and bassist Larry Grenadier. Their first recording, *One World,* includes a mix of personalized standards and originals performed with upbeat buoyance and playfulness.

Ancestors is Rosnes's most personal and moving recording to date. Saxophonist Chris Potter, trumpeter Nicholas Payton, drummer Al Foster, bassist Peter Washington and percussionist Don Alias reinforce the strength of the material, predominantly written by Rosnes. Potter, Christian McBride and Jack DeJohnette joined Rosnes on *As We Are Now,* another exquisite outing that documents her creativity as a writer, player, bandleader and conceptualist.
— K.F.

BILLY ROSS

★★★ **The Sound: A Tribute to Stan Getz (Milestone, 1994)**

★★★½ **Woody (Contemporary, 1996)**

Tenor saxophonist Billy Ross (b. 1947) left Juilliard at 18 to hit the road with the Woody Herman big band and went on to play in several top Latin orchestras including Machito and his Afro-Cubans and Tito Rodriguez. He then moved to Australia before returning to the United States. He is a mainstay on the south Florida jazz scene, where he performs as part of the house band for the Univision television show *Sábado Gigante.*

The Sound is a tribute to Stan Getz, whose sensuous, breathy ballad tone Ross emulates. Ross underscores his common ground with Getz as part of different eras of Herman "Herds" with covers of Herman staples "Four Brothers" and "Early Autumn." *Woody* is a full-fledged Herman tribute peppered with material from Herman's legendary First Herd, including the classic "Woodchoppers' Ball." Ross frames the record with two of his own compositions, "Woody" and "For the First Herd." — J.S.

DR. ROSS

★★★★ **Call the Doctor (1966; Testament, 1994)**

★★★★ **Boogie Disease (Arhoolie, 1992)**

"I can get better, but I'll never get well . . . I got the Boogie Disease!" Such is the self-prognosis from the premier practitioner in the field of blues symptomology. Best known as a nonstop, one-man boogie machine, playing guitar, drums and harmonica simultaneously, Dr. Charles Isaiah Ross (1925–1993) actually began his blues studies solely as a harmonica prodigy. Heavily influenced by first-generation harmonica master Sonny Boy (John Lee) Williamson, he notched his first recordings as singer and harmonicist in Memphis's fertile early-'50s blues scene, accompanied by a variety of hot blues bands. From the same era (1952–1954), the excellent and complete Arhoolie album, *Boogie Disease,* collects almost all of Ross's early tracks, exhibiting his vocal and harmonica prowess on noteworthy tracks like the Delta standard "Shake 'Em on Down" and the slow and low-down "Down South Blues." *Call the Doctor* is a one-man-band outing for the good doctor, a solid display of his undiminished powers on harmonica ("Freight Train," "Mama Blues") and the increased depth of his blues reach ("Blues & Trouble"). In 1966 Ross was still suffering from his self-diagnosed disease, and the riff boogie "Cat's Squirrel" (covered by Cream on that band's debut album) is featured here as well. — A.K.

ROBERT ROSS

★★★★ **Rockin' the Rails (Blue Planet, 1991)**

★★★★½ **Darkness . . . to Light (Brambus, 1996)**

One of the finest guitarists on the New York blues scene, Robert Ross (b. 1949) was in the house band of the city's legendary Dan Lynch blues club. Ross learned the trade backing Lightnin' Hopkins, J.B. Hutto, John Lee Hooker and Brownie McGhee. "White Boy Lost in the Blues," from *Rockin' the Rails,* shows off the whole package—great voice, virtuoso guitar accompaniment and witty songwriting style. Ross flashes his dynamic slide-guitar playing all over *Darkness . . . to Light,* which also documents the emotional range of his songwriting, from edgy critique ("Record Biz") to comic relief ("Santa Claus Lost His Christmas List.") — J.S.

CHARLIE ROUSE

★★★★ **Takin' Care of Business (1960; Original Jazz Classics, 1991)**

★★★★ **Unsung Hero (1961; Columbia, 1990)**

★★★★ **Upper Manhattan Jazz Society (1981; Enja, 1992)**

★★★★ **Epistrophy (Landmark, 1989)**

★★★★ **Soul Mates (Uptown, 1992)**

Tenor saxophonist Charlie Rouse (1924–1988) came out of the Washington, D.C., post–World War II jazz scene, playing in big-band sections with Billy Eckstine, Dizzy Gillespie and Duke Ellington before moving to New York. In the 1950s Rouse was part of the hard-bop school of jazz, playing with Clifford Brown, Oscar Pettiford and Benny Green before coleading the unusual quintet Les Jazz Modes with French horn player Julius Watkins from 1956 until 1959. In '59 he began his famous association with Thelonious Monk, starting with the Town Hall concert and staying with him through the end of Monk's studio recording career, including his final dates for Riverside and all the Columbia recordings. Rouse's capacity for emotional expression, tempered by a dramatic tension and restraint within an arrangement, made him the perfect voice for Monk's demanding approach, elements that carried over to his own years as a leader.

Takin' Care of Business pairs Rouse with

trumpeter Blue Mitchell in front of the excellent rhythm section of pianist Walter Bishop, bassist Earl May and drummer Art Taylor. Mitchell pays tribute to Rouse's regular gig with his own Monk-ish composition "Blue Farouq," and the group plays two Randy Weston pieces, "204" and "Pretty Strange," along with the Rouse original "Upptankt." Later the same year Rouse recorded the first of three sessions collected on *Unsung Hero.* The sympathetic Taylor is back with bassist Reggie Workman for one of the two quartets on this set, which showcases Rouse in delicate settings, playing ballads that show his tremendous debt to Ben Webster. This beautifully understated album offers an interesting contrast to *Takin' Care of Business.*

Although Rouse worked with the Monk tribute band Sphere and recorded other out-of-print material, *Upper Manhattan Jazz Society* is his next available recording. This fine date features trumpeter Benny Bailey, pianist Albert Dailey, bassist Buster Williams and drummer Keith Copeland. Terminally ill, Rouse played his last public date at the 1988 Monk tribute concert, documented on *Epistrophy,* with a basic quintet consisting of trumpeter Don Cherry, pianist George Cables (Jessica Williams plays piano on one song), bassist Jeff Chambers and drummer Ralph Penland. Vibraphonist Buddy Montgomery expands the lineup to a sextet on two tracks.

Soul Mates is a magical 1988 session with Sahib Shihab's baritone saxophone joining Rouse on tenor and Claudio Roditi on trumpet and flügelhorn, Walter Davis Jr. on piano, Santi Debriano on bass and Victor Lewis on drums. By the time this recording was released, Rouse, Shihab and Davis had passed away. — J.S.

JIMMY ROWLES

★★★★★ Stan Getz Presents Jimmy Rowles: The Peacocks (1977; Columbia/Legacy, 1994)
★★★★★ Heavy Love (with Al Cohn) (Xanadu, 1978)
★★★★ Trio (Capri, 1989)
★★★★ Lilac Time (Kokopelli, 1994)

Jimmy Rowles (1918–1996) was a national treasure with an inimitably quirky approach to the piano, a razor-sharp wit and an encyclopedic knowledge of the American song. He could swing from a '20s pop ditty to a Wayne Shorter composition and feel perfectly at ease with both. Rowles was a West Coast fixture from the '40s on, until relocating in the early '70s to New York.

There he recorded *The Peacocks,* a revelatory session nominally led by Stan Getz, which showcases Rowles's talents in a variety of settings. His unavailable trio recordings for Choice and Xanadu are worth seeking out, as is the wonderful duet with bassist George Mraz, *Music's the Only Thing That's on My Mind,* on Progressive, and the magnificent Concord Jazz recordings Rowles made with bassist Ray Brown—*Tasty!* and *As Good as It Gets.* Rowles's out-of-print *Jimmy Rowles Plays Duke Ellington and Billy Strayhorn* is an intimate solo tribute to two of his greatest influences. His later work abounds with lovely examples of his harmonically astute, economically executed piano styling and charmingly craggy singing. — S.F.

ROYAL CROWN REVUE

★★★½ Mugzy's Move (Warner Bros., 1996)
★★★ Caught in the Act (Warner Bros., 1997)
★★★ The Contender (Warner Bros., 1998)

The Royal Crown Revue grew out of the rockabilly/roots-rock scene in Los Angeles in the early 1990s. Rockabilly style mutated into a neopachuco look as the band adopted zoot suits and tailored a soundtrack to accompany the clothes. The band's eccentric approach developed over a decade into a trend; ironically, as neoswing became a fad, Royal Crown Revue sounded less original. *Mugzy's Move* is a relaxed and unself-conscious record, the result of 10 years honing material played with love and confidence. "Trouble in Tinsel Town" is probably the best track in the neoswing movement; the album also includes singer Eddie Nichols in his most revelatory moment, covering Bobby Darin in "Beyond the Sea." Darin's finger-snapping clothes horse is the real stylistic reference of neoswing, just as the Las Vegas lounge scene is its ultimate direction. — J.S.

GONZALO RUBALCABA

★★ Giraldilla (Messidor/Rounder, 1990)
★★★ Mi Gran Pasión (Messidor/Rounder, 1991)
★★★★★ Discovery: Live at Montreux (Blue Note, 1991)
★★★ The Blessing (Blue Note, 1991)
★★★ Images: Live from Mt. Fuji (Blue Note, 1992)
★★★★½ Suite 4 y 20 (Blue Note, 1993)

★★★ **Rapsodia (Blue Note, 1993)**
★★★★ **Diz (Blue Note, 1994)**
★★★½ **Live in Havana (Messidor/Rounder, 1995)**
★★★ **Imagine: Gonzalo Rubalcaba in the U.S.A. (Blue Note, 1996)**
★★★ **Vol. 3—Messidor's Finest (Messidor/Rounder, 1997)**
★★★½ **Best of Gonzalo Rubalcaba (BMG/Milan Latino, 1997)**
★★★★ **The Montreal Tapes, Vol. 4 (with Charlie Haden and Paul Motian) (Verve, 1998)**
★★½ **Antiguo (Blue Note, 1998)**
★★★ **Flying Colors (Blue Note, 1998)**

Piano virtuoso Gonzalo Rubalcaba (b. 1963) is a member of one of Cuba's most vibrant musical families, bringing into the jazz realm a strong grounding in European classical music and the classically-influenced *danzones,* or Cuban ballroom-dance compositions. He took up piano at age 9, studying at the Amadeo Roldán Conservatory and Havana's Institute of Fine Arts, and by age 22 was touring Europe with his own fusion band, Grupo Proyecto (Projecto). Dizzy Gillespie first heard Rubalcaba at a jazz festival in Havana in 1985 and proclaimed him the best new pianist he had heard in ten years. A year later, bassist Charlie Haden heard Rubalcaba in Havana and arranged for appearances at the Montreal and Montreux jazz festivals that led to a lengthy recording contract with Blue Note. As a Cuban citizen, Rubalcaba was unable to tour in the United States until 1994, after he established legal residency in the Dominican Republic. While maintaining Cuban citizenship, he moved to Miami in 1997.

Rubalcaba possesses tremendous percussive technique, and musical ideas pour from him torrentially, but sometimes his restless explorations work against him. Three of his earliest releases (on Germany's Messidor label) show his immense stylistic range with unfortunate flaws in sound quality. *Live in Havana* is a vibrant blend of Latin and straight-ahead jazz; *Mi Gran Pasión* celebrates the *danzón* tradition with touches of jazz and classical piano; and *Giraldilla* is an electronic Latin fusion session with Projecto. *The Montreal Tapes, Vol. 4,* released under Haden's name, is a trio session with Rubalcaba and drummer Paul Motian that grandly documents Rubalcaba's first appearance in North America at the 1989 Montreal Jazz Festival. The intimacy of the music and depth of Rubalcaba's playing are forceful.

Discovery, the recording that made him a jazz world darling, is a trio session with Haden and Motian from Switzerland's Montreux Jazz Festival. It's one of his finest and most cohesive works. The live trio sessions that followed, *The Blessing* and *Images,* were recorded with Haden or John Patitucci and drummer Jack DeJohnette. *Suite 4 y 20,* recorded with his Cuban quartet (trumpeter Reynaldo Melian, drummer Julio Barreto and bassist Felipe Cabrera), reveals a very romantic and relaxed side of Rubalcaba's playing. *Rapsodia* is an electric and acoustic quartet session of original compositions and one cover; his fine Dizzy Gillespie tribute recording, *Diz,* includes bassist Ron Carter and drummer Barreto; and *Imagine* captures his first American performance with Haden and DeJohnette, in 1993, and a California concert a year later with his own quartet. It's loaded with energy and emotion but too often favors flash over substance.

Antiguo is a radical departure for Rubalcaba, a world-music suite that blends Afro-Cuban jazz with orchestral techniques, ritual chanting and other Latin flavors. While pointing to a new road he wants to travel, the route lacks the requisite passion. Rubalcaba and saxophonist Joe Lovano turn the duo format into an extended deep conversation on *Flying Colors.* — K.F.

HOWARD RUMSEY'S LIGHTHOUSE ALL-STARS

★★★ **Sunday Jazz à la Lighthouse (1953; Original Jazz Classics, N.A.)**
★★★ **In the Solo Spotlight (1954; Original Jazz Classics, 1990)**
★★★ **Howard Rumsey's Lighthouse All-Stars, Vol. 3 (1955; Original Jazz Classics, 1996)**
★★★ **Howard Rumsey's Lighthouse All-Stars, Vol. 6 (1955; Original Jazz Classics, 1989)**
★★★ **Lighthouse at Laguna (1955; Original Jazz Classics, 1990)**
★★★ **Jazz Invention (1955; Original Jazz Classics, 1989)**
★★★½ **Oboe/Flute (1956; Original Jazz Classics, 1991)**
★★★ **Music for Lighthousekeeping (1956; Original Jazz Classics, 1991)**
★★★½ **Mexican Passport (Contemporary, 1996)**

Bassist Howard Rumsey (b. 1917) was part of Stan Kenton's original 1941 band before going on to form his own group, the Lighthouse All-Stars. In 1949 Rumsey's band opened at the legendary Lighthouse jazz club of Hermosa Beach, California, and soon became a fixture there. The ensemble, featuring solid players such as tenor saxophonist Bob Cooper, trumpeter Conte Candoli, drummer Stan Levey, trombonist Frank Rosolino and pianist Sonny Clark, lays out a precise, understated appreciation of the "cool" aspects of bop that comes close to defining the West Coast sound, as this kind of playing became known. Rosolino shines on *Laguna.* Drummer Max Roach guests on *Oboe/Flute.* Listen for the Monk-ish overtones of Clark's blues phrasing on "Topsy," from *Music for Lighthousekeeping. Mexican Passport* is a good collection of early-1950s material featuring Chet Baker, Maynard Ferguson and Hampton Hawes. — J.S.

OTIS RUSH

★★★ **Mourning in the Morning (Atlantic, 1969)**
★★★★★ **Right Place, Wrong Time (1976; Hightone, 1985)**
★★★½ **Cold Day in Hell (Delmark, 1975)**
★ **Screamin' and Cryin' (1974; Evidence, 1992)**
★★★½ **Lost in the Blues (1977; Alligator, 1991)**
★★★½ **Live in Europe (1977; Evidence, 1993)**
★★★★ **Little Walter and Otis Rush: Live in Chicago (Quicksilver, 1982)**
★★★½ **Tops (Blind Pig, 1988)**
★★★★★ **1956–1958: His Cobra Recordings (Paula, 1991)**
★★★½ **Ain't Enough Comin' In (This Way Up/Mercury, 1994)**
★ **Blues Masters (with Little Walter) (Tomato, 1994)**
★★★★½ **So Many Roads: Live in Concert (Delmark, 1995)**
★★★ **Live & Awesome (Adelphi, 1996)**

Otis Rush (b. 1934) is one of the greatest, most influential electric blues guitarists ever. His extended, stinging, minor-key playing was a particular inspiration to rockers who wanted to live close to the edge: Rush continuously sounds as if he's about to hit the bum note that will send the whole thing crashing to the ground. His early Cobra sessions, cut when he was just 22 and collected on *1956–1958: His Cobra Recordings,* are the classic Otis Rush sides. These tracks, along with Buddy Guy's and Magic Sam's concurrent recordings for the same label, birthed West Side Chicago guitar, a ghetto-toughened, distinctly urban school of playing. This set includes "All Your Love," "I Can't Quit You Baby" and "Double Trouble," which years later supplied Stevie Ray Vaughan with his band name. Rush's heavily reverbed vocal histrionics and passionate soloing make these tracks among the most terrifying in all bluesdom.

Unfortunately, Rush's career has been marred by repeated setbacks, both professional and psychological. Following the demise of Cobra, Rush virtually disappeared from recording studios for a decade, tied up for several years by Duke Records, then bouncing from one bad deal to another. *Mourning in the Morning,* recorded for Cotillion with a fine backing band and a decent budget, should be a great album but somehow just misses the mark. In 1971 Rush signed a five-album deal with Capitol but never released a single album for the label. He cut one, the excellent *Right Place, Wrong Time,* which sat on the shelves for five years before seeing the light of day on Bullfrog, then disappearing again, only to be rescued by Hightone in 1985. A testament to Rush's vocal and guitar power when he is firing on all cylinders, it remains a blues classic. Occasionally obtrusive horn charts do little to dim his fire. Rush is also in fine form on the more relaxed, less consistent *Cold Day in Hell,* a raw, rough-edged album that succeeds most of the time. *Screamin' and Cryin'* is a horrifying document of an unstable man on a bad day. Fraught with errors and at times downright unlistenable, it is nonetheless a fascinating, tension-filled recording of a sensitive man publicly wrestling with his demons.

Over the years, Rush has been a wildly inconsistent live performer. When he's off, he may not be in the right key all night, but when he's on (far more often, thankfully), he remains a performer of absolutely devastating power. Hence, the abundance of live Otis Rush albums. *So Many Roads* is the best of a good bunch, an awesome document of Rush in peak form before an appreciative Japanese crowd, but you won't really go wrong with the more subdued *Live in Europe* (recorded in France in '77) or *Tops,* from the 1985 San Francisco Blues Festival. *Lost in the Blues* was cut in a Stockholm studio the same week *Live in Europe* was recorded but in 1991 was remixed with keyboards added, a dubious practice that yielded a great album. *Live & Awesome,* capturing some recent European shows, is frustratingly uneven—at times exhilarating and gut-wrenching, at others meandering and out of tune. In 1994 Rush released *Ain't Enough Comin' In,* his first new studio album in over 15 years. It's an impressive effort, though Rush's decision to pay tribute to his departed friend Albert King by slavishly copying him on several songs is a bit strange. Not surprisingly, he turns out to be the best of the hundreds of King imitators. — A.P.

PATRICE RUSHEN

★★ **Straight from the Heart (1982; Rhino, 1996)**
★★ **Anything but Ordinary (Sin-Drome, 1994)**
★★ **Haven't You Heard: The Best of Patrice Rushen (Rhino, 1996)**
★★½ **Signature (Antone's, 1997)**

Keyboardist Patrice Rushen (b. 1954) is a classically trained prodigy who recorded her first jazz album, the out-of-print *Preclusion,* featuring Joe Henderson, before she was 20. Though she exhibited immense talent as an instrumentalist, Rushen moved toward a more pop-oriented sound and began singing as well. Her Prestige catalog and many of the more dance-oriented recordings for Elektra are currently unavailable, but Rushen continued to be in demand for sessions and as a producer (of Sheena Easton). Easton and rapper Def Jef make appearances on *Anything but Ordinary.* The Rhino material documents her pop side. *Signature* is a bland smooth-jazz outing that sold well enough to garner a Grammy nomination. — J.S.

JIMMY RUSHING

★★★★ **Rushing Lullabies/Little Jimmy Rushing and the Big Brass (1959; Columbia/Legacy, 1997)**
★★★★ **The Essential Jimmy Rushing (Vanguard, 1978)**
★★★ **The Classic Count (Intermedia, 1982)**
★★★★ **The You and Me That Used to Be (RCA, 1988)**
★★★★ **Count Basie: Old Manuscripts, Broadcast Transcriptions (1944–45) (Music and Arts Programs of America, 1995)**

Born in Oklahoma City and raised in his hometown's melting pot of Texas blues, Western swing and traditional jazz, Jimmy Rushing (1903–1972) honed his unique style during the late '20s, when he spent hard, physically demanding years playing Southwestern theaters, dance halls and roadhouses with a traveling band called the Blue Devils, which included such extraordinary players as Count Basie, Lester Young, Hot Lips Page, Buster Smith and Eddie Durham, among others. By the time Rushing settled in with Bennie Moten's band in Kansas City in the early '30s, he had fashioned a distinctive disposition as a vocalist: forever ebullient, perennially optimistic, the brightest shade of blue this side of the sky. A big man nicknamed Mister Five by Five (a reference to his height and width), Rushing could deliver the saddest blues with a warm, soothing tone that implied better days ahead; he was ennobled, rather than diminished, by misfortune.

When Moten died in 1935, Basie formed his own group, with Rushing as its lead singer; the association, productive and prolific, lasted until 1950, when Basie broke up the band. Rushing made an effort to assemble his own band, but couldn't deal with the scope of the administrative duties and ended that experiment in 1952. Producer John Hammond, a longtime fan of Rushing's, produced for the Vanguard label in the mid-'50s a series of albums that teamed the singer with some of his mates from the Basie days. The late '50s and early '60s found Rushing in a variety of interesting settings while signed to Columbia and being produced by Irving Townsend and Teo Macero. *Rushing Lullabies* dates from this period. In 1971, working with producer Don Schlitten and a small band that included Zoot Sims and Al Cohn on tenor saxophones, Budd Johnson on soprano saxophone, David Frishberg on piano, Milt Hinton on bass, Ray Nance on cornet and violin and Mel Lewis on drums, Rushing cut 10 sides for RCA; these turned out to be his last recordings before his death in 1972. Through the decades, at every label stop, Rushing produced exemplary performances: What he has left behind is entertaining, exhilarating and instructive.

With Basie, Rushing established a style of singing that epitomized swing: He created a wonderful tension between band and vocalist by singing ahead of or behind the beat and generally toyed with the rhythm, stretching songs in new directions. He was at once a blues singer and a jazz singer, and his ability to work within both idioms had an incalculable influence on succeeding generations of jazz and popular-music vocalists.

The Classic Count collects 10 recordings

from the vintage Basie band of the 1940s, including some live performances; 4 tracks feature the young Rushing in readings of "Blue Skies," "I Never Knew," "Please Don't Talk About Me" and " 'Tain't Me." Unfortunately, there are no specific dates or personnel listings, and the skimpy liner notes are uninformative. A 1995 issue of Basie radio transcriptions, *Old Manuscripts* features the band in full flower with Lester Young on board (on tracks from 1944) and, on three cuts, Rushing handling lead vocals: On a driving, swinging version of "I'm Gonna Sit Right Down and Write Myself a Letter," he comes on ebullient and forceful, his swagger matching the instrumental braggadocio behind him; elsewhere he offers a heartfelt account of love's misfortunes in "Harvard Blues," couching his laundry list of woes in mock-serious terms as a series of academic missteps ("Reinhardt, Reinhardt, I'm a most indifferent guy"), and belts out a saucy "Basie Blues" over an arrangement that finds the Basie band cutting out like a freight train at full throttle.

The Essential Jimmy Rushing is a 14-track compilation of Vanguard highlights, and there isn't a bad cut among them. While his legend rests on his ability as a singer, Rushing developed into quite a good songwriter. Some of his better efforts are here, including several collaborations with Basie, a smoky, after-hours blues cowritten with boogie-woogie catalyst Sam Price (and featuring Price on piano) and that buoyant model of prevarication, "Sometimes I Do," penned by Rushing alone.

The deleted *Mister Five by Five* is, like the Vanguard album, selected highlights, these being from Columbia's Rushing vaults; and like all of Rushing's remaining in-print albums save the RCA release, it's devoid of or annoyingly vague about dates. The music is another matter entirely. Here Rushing is heard fronting big bands, quartets and, in one of the most remarkable moments of a remarkable career, a trio that includes Rushing on piano with support from bassist Walter Page and drummer Jo Jones. Three must-hear selections date from a 1960 reunion with Helen Humes, one of Rushing's female counterparts in the Basie band. Fronting a quartet of instrumentalists, these two extraordinary singers complement each other in grand style, Humes's sensuality being a soothing match for Rushing's earthy exuberance.

Finally, there is Rushing's last testament, *The You and Me That Used to Be.* The title song and several others—"My Last Affair," "When I Grow Too Old to Dream," "Fine and Mellow," "Linger Awhile"—have an endgame theme, but Rushing delivers them brightly. The last song sums up Rushing's point of view: "Thanks a Million" is sung with the gripping sincerity of a man taking stock. It's Rushing's most introspective moment on record and a touching coda to a monumental career. — D.M.

TERJE RYPDAL

★★★½ Odyssey (1975; ECM, 1994)
★★★½ Waves (1978; ECM, 1994)
★★★★ Descendre (1980; ECM, 1994)
★★★½ Eos (1984; ECM, 1994)
★★ Chaser (1985; ECM, 1994)
★★★ Blue (1987; ECM, 1994)
★★★ The Singles Collection (ECM, 1989)
★★★ Undisonus-Ineo (ECM, 1990)
★★★ Q.E.D. (ECM, 1991)
★★★★ Works (ECM, 1994)
★★★ If Mountains Could Sing (ECM, 1995)
★★★★ Skywards (ECM, 1997)

Norwegian guitarist Terje Rypdal (b. 1947) provides a fascinating glimpse into the evolution of the past quarter century of music. He studied at Oslo University, immersing himself in the possibilities of harmonically "free" jazz and learning the Lydian Chromatic Concept of Tonal Organization with George Russell, all the while paying close attention to the sonic innovations of Jimi Hendrix, Pink Floyd and Led Zeppelin. Rypdal emerged with a dense, introspective style characterized by notes that are stretched, bent and transmogrified into dramatic fragments. His use of bow technique and MIDI synthesizer applications gives his playing an alternatively romantic and abstract content as he wends his way through a career touching on fusion, Third Stream, power-trio and New Age styles while seldom surrendering to any of them.

After playing in saxophonist Jan Garbarek's group in the late 1960s, Rypdal formed an eccentric quartet, Odyssey, which recorded an eponymous album and *Waves.* The subsequent trio album *Descendre,* with Palle Mikkelborg on trumpet, flügelhorn and keyboards and Jon Christensen on drums, is a career high point. *Eos* is an atmospheric series of duets with cellist David Darling.

Rypdal spent the better part of the 1980s leading a power trio, the Chasers, which

recorded some of his most commercial and least satisfying work. He has since followed the ECM trend toward a more formal classical-oriented style—*Undisonus-Ineo* is a collection of orchestral works. *Skywards,* another classical-oriented outing, features excellent composition from Rypdal. Some of his best recorded moments are unavailable, but *To Be Continued* and *What Comes After* are worth seeking out.
— J.S.

SAFFIRE—THE UPPITY BLUES WOMEN

★ **Saffire—the Uppity Blues Women (Alligator, 1990)**
★ **Hot Flash (Alligator, 1991)**
★½ **Broadcasting (Alligator, 1992)**
★★ **Old, New, Borrowed and Blue (Alligator, 1994)**
★ **Cleaning House (Alligator, 1996)**

Saffire—the Uppity Blues Women, originally comprising bassist Earlene Lewis, guitarist Gaye Adegbalola and pianist Ann Rabson, are persnickety middle-aged women who look to the blues, gospel and their own crises for inspiration. Like their subsequent albums, the group's eponymous debut introduces their frank humor, which deals with being female in a patriarchal society, the aches and pains of middle age and the pursuit of younger men. Included here is their reading of Ida Cox's "Wild Women Don't Have the Blues," which speaks volumes about their credo without falling back on the obvious, sophomoric sexual clichés that litter their original songs. *Hot Flash* contains more of the same, but while the performances are adequate, the songs don't warrant repeat listenings.

Broadcasting sees the departure of Lewis and the addition of Andra Faye McIntosh on mandolin, fiddle and background vocals, yet the songs remain mostly subpar. Included here is a version of "OBG Why Me Blues," a humorous tale of a harrowing trip to the gynecologist, and a pared-down rendition of Louis Jordan's "Is You Is or Is You Ain't My Baby?" *Old, New, Borrowed and Blue* sees McIntosh take over bass duties as it maintains the group's "don't mess with me" stance, with "T'Ain't Nobody's Business," a song recorded by such figures as Bessie Smith and Billie Holiday, Sippie Wallace's "You Got to Know How" and a rendition of Ma Rainey's "Yonder Come the Blues." The choice of material on this album makes it the group's strongest, as their performances of bona fide classics seem to free their voices and playing. *Cleaning House* contains covers of Willie Dixon's "Love Me to Death" and Johnny Copeland's "Nobody but You" and mediocre originals like "I Want My Money Back" and "Rocket Ship." — B.R.H.

DOUG SAHM

★★★★ **Juke Box Music (1989; Antone's, 1997)**
★★★★ **Texas Tornado: The Best of Doug Sahm's Atlantic Sessions (Rhino, 1992)**
★★★ **The Last Real Texas Blues Band (Antone's, 1994)**
★★★ **Day Dreaming at Midnight (Elektra Nonesuch, 1997)**
★★★★ **"S.D.Q. '98" (Watermelon, 1998)**

WITH THE SIR DOUGLAS QUINTET

★★★★ **The Best of the Sir Douglas Quintet (Mercury, 1990)**

WITH THE TEXAS TORNADOS

★★★★ **Texas Tornados (Reprise, 1990)**
★★★½ **Zone of Our Own (Reprise, 1991)**
★★★½ **Hangin' On by a Thread (Reprise, 1992)**
★★★★ **The Best of the Texas Tornados (Reprise, 1994)**
★★★½ **4 Aces (Reprise, 1996)**

With a jukebox mind under his 10-gallon hat, Doug Sahm (b. 1941) has ranged from horn-heavy blues to country to psychedelia and even, at the start of his career, to a unique mix of garage funkiness and Merseybeat. The Sir Douglas Quintet's "She's About a Mover" started the trip, as the 1965 hit laid a moptop catchiness atop Augie Meyer's Vox organ syncopations and revealed a gift for eccentric fusions that would stamp the band's subsequent (out-of-print) efforts: *Honkey Blues*'s James Brown–ish horns are overlaid with San Francisco guitar noodling; *Together* is Latino swagger meeting the blues meeting C&W. *Mendocino* produced another hit in the flower-power title track; "At the Crossroads" is Doug doing Bob Dylan.

Through the years, Sahm has occasionally faltered; his guitar sounds better when he reins it in; and earnestness remains his singing's greatest virtue—but his musical imagination has paid off consistently in happy, novel ways. In the '90s Sahm served as a mainstay in the Texas Tornados, a rocking outfit that combined the swagger of R&B and the sass of Hispanic roots music. And with *The Last Real Texas Blues Band,* he led 14 crack players on a tour of tough blues numbers, ranging from Lowell Fulson's "Reconsider Baby" to Fats Domino's "My Girl Josephine." The 1992 Rhino anthology collects the best of Sahm's two Atlantic albums, including his brilliant version of Dylan's "Wallflower." *"S.D.Q. '98"* finds Sahm working with a combo formed in the spirit of the Sir Douglas Quintet, including his longtime collaborator Augie Meyers on keyboards and members of Austin, Texas, roots-rockers the Gourds. — P.E.

SAL SALVADOR

★★★ **The Way of the Wind (Jazzmania, 1994)**
★★★ **Lorinda's Kitchen (Jazzmania, 1996)**
★★★ **Second Time Around (Muse/Westside, 1996)**

Sal Salvador (b. 1925) is a swing-influenced guitarist from Connecticut who's made a handful of independent-label records, most of which are currently unavailable. His tasteful yet emotionally convincing style makes for consistently pleasant listening, and he has fronted exciting groups featuring such stalwart sidemen as Phil Woods and Sonny Stitt, yet he is among the ranks of many solid players who are overlooked by jazz history. Try to find the excellent *Juicy Lucy* and *Starfingers.* — J.S.

DAVID SANBORN

★★★ **Taking Off (1975; Warner Bros., 1988)**
★★★ **David Sanborn (1976; Warner Bros., 1989)**
★★★½ **Heart to Heart (1978; Warner Bros., N.A.)**
★★★ **Hideaway (1980; Warner Bros., N.A.)**
★★★ **Voyeur (1981; Warner Bros., N.A.)**
★★★½ **As We Speak (1982; Warner Bros., N.A.)**
★★★ **Backstreet (1983; Warner Bros., N.A.)**
★★★★ **Straight to the Heart (1984; Warner Bros., N.A.)**
★★★ **A Change of Heart (Warner Bros., 1987)**
★★★ **Close-Up (Reprise, 1988)**
★★★★ **Another Hand (Elektra, 1991)**
★★★ **Upfront (Elektra, 1992)**
★★★ **Hearsay (Warner Bros., 1994)**
★★★½ **The Best of David Sanborn (Warner Bros., 1994)**
★★★ **Pearls (Elektra, 1995)**
★★★ **Songs from the Night Before (Elektra, 1996)**

David Sanborn (b. 1945) possesses one of the most distinctive saxophone sounds in popular music and uses it to make records that are almost indistinguishable from one another. It isn't that he has nothing to say, for given the proper setting he shines as a soloist; nor is it that he lacks leadership ability, for his albums are packed with top sidemen and first-rate arrangements. It isn't even a question of quality, for Sanborn's jazz fusion avoids most of the usual clichés, never plays down to the listener and is enjoyable despite its maddening consistency.

So why the rut? Because Sanborn is essentially a groove player and tends to settle in the same groove from album to album, year to year. It rarely wears thin, in part because Sanborn has impeccable taste in rhythm sections, but mostly because he's one of the few saxophonists around who understands how to translate a soul singer's sense of time and line to jazz. As such, it hardly matters whether he's working a wah-wah pedal in "Butterfat" from *Taking Off,* squawking through the funk of "I Told U So" from *Backstreet* or soaring against the refrain of "You Are Everything" from *Close-Up;* his playing is equally solid, every time.

Granted, things do tend to improve when he makes changes or takes chances. *Heart to Heart,* for instance, augments the usual pop-fusion rhythm section with horns, at one point including the Gil Evans Orchestra (Sanborn is an Evans alumnus); *As We Speak* doesn't alter the backing tracks but switches Sanborn from alto to soprano for several tunes; and *Straight to the Heart* uses a live-in-the-studio strategy to add extra fire to the instrumental interplay.

Overall, only *Another Hand* stands out as a complete departure—and for good reason. Instead of his usual fusion sidemen, this album matches Sanborn with an odd mix of new-music types like guitarists Bill Frisell and Marc Ribot as well as mainstream jazz heavyweights like bassist Charlie Haden and drummer Jack DeJohnette. The result is some of the most inspired playing Sanborn has offered in 15 years and a much needed break in his musical routine.
— J.D.C.

DAVID SANCHEZ

★★★½ **The Departure (Columbia, 1994)**
★★★ **Sketches of Dreams (Columbia, 1995)**
★★★★ **Street Scenes (Columbia, 1996)**
★★★★ **Obsesión (Columbia, 1998)**

Saxophonist David Sanchez (b. 1968) belongs to a generation of younger jazz players from Latin America and the Caribbean who are extending the musical linkage between jazz and the rhythms of their birth countries. In his native Puerto Rico, he studied percussion and classical music before turning to the tenor saxophone. Moving to the United States after high school, he began working with Danilo Perez, Eddie Palmieri and Paquito D'Rivera before joining Dizzy Gillespie's United Nation Orchestra in 1991. Other collaborators have included trumpeter Tom Harrell and Slide Hampton's JazzMasters.

Sanchez has a muscular, confident tenor sound and plays soprano sax sparingly on his recordings. *The Departure,* his debut as a leader, is his most straight-ahead session, while *Sketches of Dreams* has a decidedly Latin tinge. Weighted toward original compositions, *Street Scenes* is a stellar celebration of his many swinging influences. Sanchez tastefully adds strings and more woodwinds to his band on *Obsesión,* a lush exploration of his musical roots through beloved Latin American standards plus one ringer—Ray Bryant's "Cuban Fantasy."
— K.F.

PHAROAH SANDERS

★★ **Tauhid (1966; Impulse!, 1993)**
★★★½ **Karma (1969; Impulse!, 1995)**
★★★ **Jewels of Thought (1969; Impulse!, 1998)**
★★★½ **Thembi (1971; Impulse!, 1998)**
★★★½ **Black Unity (1971; Impulse!, 1997)**
★★★ **Summun Bukmun Umyun (1972; Impulse!, 1998)**
★★★ **Pharoah Sanders (1977; India Navigation, 1996)**
★★★ **Rejoice (1981; Evidence, 1992)**
★★★ **The Heart Is a Melody (1982; Evidence, 1993)**
★★★ **Shukuru (1987; Evidence, 1992)**
★★★½ **Oh Lord, Let Me Do No Wrong (Dr. Jazz, 1987)**
★★★ **Prayer Before Dawn (1988; Evidence, 1993)**
★★★ **Welcome to Love (1991; Evidence, 1996)**
★★★ **Journey to the One (Evidence, 1994)**
★★★ **Crescent with Love (Evidence, 1994)**
★★★ **Message from Home (Verve, 1996)**
★★★½ **Priceless Jazz (GRP, 1997)**

While primarily a tenor saxophonist, Pharoah Sanders (b. 1940) blows alto and soprano with equal power—his tone rich and sometimes raw, his blues-based delivery sometimes almost assaultively dynamic. In the mid-'60s he played on John Coltrane's landmark *Ascension* and also worked with others among the cream of the avant-garde jazz crop—including Don Cherry and Alice Coltrane. His own aggregations of the late '60s and early '70s reflect his interest in non-Western idioms, free-form soloing and highly charged atmospheres; like Coltrane, Sanders embraces music as a vehicle for a highly personal mystic communication, even while the physicality of his style is abundantly apparent (check the strength of *Jewels of Thought,* especially the interplay with the bassists).

Unfortunately, such examples of Sanders at his toughest as *Love in Us All* (Impulse!, 1974), with its 20-minute powerhouse title cut, are out of print, but *Summun Bukmun Umyun,* a bold outing with Lonnie Liston Smith, has recently been reissued. *Karma, Thembi* and the unavailable *Love Will Find a Way* all found surprising commercial success. In the late '70s and early '80s, however, many critics attacked Sanders for going soft; *The Heart Is a Melody* counters that charge with its great long sax workout, "Ole." More recently, he's moved closer to traditional jazz, as evidenced by his ballad work on *Welcome to Love. Crescent with Love* is valuable, too: The horn playing recalls the sweeter Coltrane. — P.E.

ARTURO SANDOVAL

★★★ **To a Finland Station (with Dizzy Gillespie) (1983; Original Jazz Classics, 1992)**
★★★★ **Tumbaito (1985; Messidor, 1991)**
★★★ **Flight to Freedom (GRP, 1991)**
★★★★★ **I Remember Clifford (GRP, 1992)**
★★★ **Dream Come True (GRP, 1993)**
★★★★ **Danzón (Dance On) (GRP, 1994)**
★★★ **Arturo Sandoval and the Latin Train (GRP, 1995)**
★★★★ **Swingin' (GRP, 1996)**
★★★★ **The Best of Arturo Sandoval (BMG/Milan Latino, 1997)**
★★★½ **Hot House (N2K, 1998)**

Arturo Sandoval (b. 1949) began studying trumpet at age 12 and quickly became caught up in the improvisational excitement of jazz. He was heavily influenced by Dizzy Gillespie, who befriended and encouraged him during the trumpet master's occasional trips to Cuba. Sandoval performed with the Cuban Orchestra of Modern Music before becoming a founding member in 1974 of the Grammy-winning group Irakere, which blended jazz, classical and rock with traditional Cuban music. He formed his own band in 1981 and toured extensively through Latin America and Europe. During a 1990 European tour, Sandoval and his family walked into the American embassy in Rome and requested political asylum in the United States. He became a full-time member of Gillespie's United Nation Orchestra and intensified his own recording career.

With a strong tone and control, Miami-based Sandoval is an explosive player capable of solos that burn over diverse Afro-Cuban rhythms as well as jazz standards. His intense flurries and stratospheric high notes are sometimes offset by solos of sheer melodic beauty. *To a Finland Station* was recorded with Gillespie and a Finnish rhythm section on the spur of the moment when the master and protégé crossed paths in Helsinki. *Tumbaito,* a stunning work recorded in Spain with his Cuban sextet, captures the rich blend of influences Sandoval extended after his years with Irakere.

His first domestic recording, *Flight to Freedom,* features Chick Corea, Dave Weckl, Anthony Jackson and Ed Calle, as well as Sandoval's own band. For his carefully arranged Clifford Brown tribute, Sandoval steps away from the Latin context. His customary fire is harder to find on *Dream Come True,* a collaboration with pianist Michel Legrand and an orchestra that showcases his balladry.

He's back to his vibrant Cuban jazz roots on *Danzón,* a 1994 Latin Jazz Grammy winner with cameos by Gloria Estefan, Bill Cosby, Vikki Carr and Dave Valentin, and *Arturo Sandoval and the Latin Train,* with vocal support from Joe Williams, Celia Cruz and Oscar D'León. On the creative session *Swingin',* Sandoval spends less time in the trumpet stratosphere and far more conversing with a strong all-star peer group that includes Michael Brecker, Eddie Daniels, Mike Stern, John Patitucci and Joey Calderazzo. *Hot House* is Sandoval's excellent first effort at big-band Latin jazz, with his trumpet soaring over a lush rhythmic cushion. Tito Puente, Patti Austin and Michael Brecker are along for the ride.
— K.F.

JUMPIN' JOHNNY SANSONE

★★★★ **Crescent City Moon (Bullseye Blues, 1997)**

Jumpin' Johnny Sansone (b. 1956) ranks as one of contemporary blues' finest harmonica players, but he is much more than the latest slavish Little Walter disciple. After years of fronting blues bands in Colorado, Texas and the Carolinas and a stint as front man for guitarist Ronnie Earl's band the Broadcasters, Sansone now mixes the standard Windy City harp motifs with equal inspiration from sources such as veteran Chicago guitarist Lonnie Brooks's early Gulf Coast rhythm & blues sides, the Louisiana swamp pop of Bobby Charles and the zydeco accordion mastery of Clifton Chenier. Filtered through Sansone's keen songwriting—and brought to life with his robust voice and instrumental prowess—these touchstones come alive as a refreshing new entity.

Crescent City Moon is one of the strongest Louisiana records of the '90s; Sansone has absorbed the diverse musical roots of his adopted hometown, New Orleans, to powerful effect. "Give Me a Dollar" pays homage to the tap dancers on Bourbon Street with a raucous second-line groove and a supercharged slide solo from Sonny Landreth, and "Your Kind of Love" utilizes the Iguanas' horn section to color a sweet love song that wouldn't sound out of place on a vintage Shirley and Lee record. For an off-the-wall harp showcase, check out the quirky instrumental "Popeyes and a Hubig's,

Part 2." The title track is the record's tour de force, with Sansone's anguished vocal and funereal accordion figure breathing life into the tale of a downtrodden man whose friends have sold him down the river. — S.J.

MONGO SANTAMARIA

★★★★ **Yambu (1958; Original Jazz Classics, 1987)**
★★★★ **Afro Roots (1972; Prestige, 1989)**
★★★★★ **Our Man in Havana (1960; Fantasy, 1993)**
★★★★ **Mongo at the Village Gate (1963; Original Jazz Classics, 1990)**
★★½ **Mongo Introduces La Lupe (1963; Milestone, 1993)**
★★★★ **Sabroso (1963; Original Jazz Classics, 1993)**
★★★★ **Skins (Milestone, 1976)**
★★★★ **Summertime (1981; Original Jazz Classics, 1991)**
★★★ **Mongo y Su Charanga (Fantasy, 1987)**
★★★½ **Soy Yo (Concord Picante, 1987)**
★★★★ **Soca Me Nice (Concord Picante, 1988)**
★★★ **Olé Ola (Concord Picante, 1989)**
★★★★ **Live at Jazz Alley (Concord Picante, 1990)**
★★★★ **At the Black Hawk (Fantasy, 1994)**
★★★★ **Mongo's Greatest Hits (Fantasy, 1995)**

When Dizzy Gillespie and the Cuban conga player Chano Pozo collaborated on the song "Manteca," they suggested a new direction for jazz that another Cuban native, Mongo Santamaria (b. 1922), seized upon and broadened beyond imagination. Inspired by "Manteca" 's fusion of Cuban dance rhythms and harmonic ideas rooted in jazz composition (played with the improvisational feel of jazz solos), Santamaria delivered his own Afro-Cuban masterpiece in the form of 1960's "Afro Blue," in which a 6/8 tempo common to African folk music met a minor-key blues melody. Pressing the point, Santamaria made a greater impact on popular music three years later when his recording of Herbie Hancock's "Watermelon Man," itself an irresistible amalgam of blues, jazz and Afro-Cuban rhythms, became a Top 10 pop hit.

Born in Havana, Santamaria worked with bands in Mexico City before venturing to the United States in 1949. His first jobs were with the Perez Prado and Tito Puente orchestras; in 1958 he joined a group led by vibraphonist Cal Tjader that featured bassist Al McKibbon and pianist Vince Guaraldi. It was during his tenure with the Tjader group that he wrote "Afro Blue," which became a springboard for the formation of his own ensemble, a traditional Latin *charanga* band billed as Mongo Santamaria y Sus Ritmos Afro-Cubanos. This group made an impressive debut on the Fantasy label with *Yambu,* a collection of percussive songs reflecting the convergence of religious thought and music in the African tradition. Here the various conga players, led by Santamaria, employ the instrument's wide pitch range to its fullest effect, both rhythmically and melodically, in constructing lead voices and substructures that are in turn supported by other percussive instruments such as sticks, bongos, quinto, timbales and so forth. In addition to traditional Cuban rhumbas and other dances, the songs include religious dances dedicated to spiritual gods and philosophical treatises addressing the path trod by Cuba's common people. From a musical standpoint, the grand statement here is the song "Timbales y Bongo," which incorporates in its structure virtually every facet of the Afro-Cuban approach—call-and-response, shifting lead voices, solo mastery, themes and variations, etc.—and features Willie Bobo on timbales in an exciting tête-à-tête with Santamaria on sticks, as well as a spectacular display of virtuosity by Francisco Aguabella, who plays three conga drums simultaneously as the music reaches its fever pitch.

Afro-Cubanos evolved into the Mongo Santamaria Afro-Latin Group, populated by the likes of saxophonist and Sun Ra alum Pat Patrick and a promising keyboard player named Armando Corea, nicknamed Chick. This outfit's first album, *Go, Mongo!* (now packaged with the band's final Riverside album as *Skins*), featured some profound ethnic material (Santamaria's own composition "Carmela" being a standout) nearly as deep as that on *Yambu.*

The small but significant events that were *Yambu* and *Go, Mongo!* were followed by an even larger moment of consequence. In 1963 Santamaria recorded "Watermelon Man," bringing his own Afro-Latin rhythmic flourishes to the blues structure Hancock had designed. In addition to a signpost pointing toward the development of funk music in the '70s, "Watermelon Man" suggested a world-beat sensibility, a new wrinkle that broadened the fusion of pop and Latin influences pioneered in

America in the '40s by the Desi Arnaz, Xavier Cugat and Perez Prado orchestras.

Santamaria has gone on to become one of the most prolific writers and recording artists of his generation, producing a catalog of staggering variety and musical depth that is nothing less than the definitive textbook on Afro-Cuban styles. Start with *Afro Roots,* an essential primer for anyone wishing to understand Santamaria's history and the introduction of Afro-Cuban music to the American marketplace. This two-record set contains 21 sides recorded in 1958–59, marking Santamaria's first sessions as a bandleader. Always a magnet for top-flight musicians, Santamaria is joined on these tracks by the likes of the reliable Willie Bobo, Armando Peraza, Paul Horn, Pablo Mozo, Cal Tjader, Al McKibbon, Carlos Vidal, Vince Guaraldi and others. *Soca Me Nice* is an exciting exploration of *soca* (soul calypso) styles released at a time when the West Indian music was gaining some mainstream attention on these shores.

Throughout his career Santamaria has made the most of every recording opportunity available to him. His studio albums are uniformly strong, but he has used the live album as something of a bully pulpit to advance his multicultural musical agenda. Each title charts a specific course, similar to concept albums in their thematic unity. That they are invariably showcases for tasteful but breathtaking musical virtuosity is another matter entirely.

Mongo at the Village Gate, for example, recorded in 1963, opens with the Valerie Capers instrumental "El Toro." On this cut the flamenco melody is established by pianist Rodgers Grant via a brief quotation from "Watermelon Man," then the song blasts into orbit on the strength of a 3/4 Venezuelan rhythm pattern known as *joropo,* which the drums (by Frank Hernandez) and conga (Santamaria) pick up as the horn section (Marty Sheller, Pat Patrick, Bobby Capers) floats overhead. Ensemble and solo parts create a distinctly jazz feel, angular and searching in their upper register, punctuated by solo blasts of staccato notes working variations on the theme. Jimmy Heath's tribute to Santamaria, "Mongo's Groove," blends a lyrical Ellingtonian melody with a pulsating Latin groove for a nice change of pace; "Creole" follows, raising the temperature by summoning the energy of a marching band in drummer Frank Hernandez's rolling riff. The lightly accented samba groove of Rodgers Grant's "The Morning After" provides a peaceful palette for Marty Sheller's warm trumpet solo, announcing in its satisfied tone that the lovemaking didn't stop with the dawn of a bright new day. The set is rounded out by the driving "Nothing for Nothing," which gets its spirit from the 6/8 Yeza rhythm pattern common to the Cuban religious songs of Santamaria's youth; and, as a bonus track on the CD edition, "Para Ti," a 5:14-minute crash course in Afro-Cuban melodic and rhythmic sensibility.

A year before the Village Gate recording, Santamaria released two albums, *Mighty Mongo* and *Viva Mongo!,* recorded (except for a few cuts on the latter album) at the Black Hawk, then the leading jazz club in San Francisco. These have now been combined seamlessly into one CD, *At the Black Hawk,* a splendid demonstration of both the instrumental wizardry common to Santamaria's explorations and the tender lyricism that moves hearts as well as minds. While unexpected fusions are plentiful—from the opening cut, "Bluchanga," whose title indicates its intertwined blues and *charanga* styles, to the merry "Merengue Changa," another rhythmic summit of two contrasting forms complete with celebratory group singing—in many ways the most memorable passages occur on some of the standards. "Tenderly" finds the exemplary tenor saxophonist Jose "Chombo" Silva striking a moody Lester Young mode in developing this pop classic's graceful melody as the band lopes along, supporting him with a lively samba. Silva shines again on a mellow interpretation of "Body and Soul," as his controlled solo summons memories of Stan Getz's bighearted lyricism, favoring as it does a linear approach to the haunting original melody line rather than a showy flight that would undermine the delicate mood.

In contrast to the heat of the Village Gate set, the Black Hawk cuts show Mongo and his players in a more contemplative mode, their solos favoring emotional nuance over startling technique. On the 1990 *Live at Jazz Alley* (in Seattle), Santamaria and company explore the many song forms in his repertoire. "Manteca," "Para Ti" and "Afro Blue" are reprised here, but it's a measure of the song selections' strength that these warhorses don't dominate the proceedings. Santamaria's self-penned "Bonita" is a languorous funk *guajira* notable both for its sunny, lilting melodic theme and Ray Vega's soaring, delicate trumpet solo. Elsewhere the musicians negotiate the tricky rhythms of jazz mambos, Latin funk and a *danzón* in what amounts to a Baedeker to Latin music's most diverse points of interest.

The exception to the rule governing Santamaria's live albums is *Summertime,* titled so both because of its being recorded in July and for the George Gershwin tune that is the high point of an album containing only four cuts, the shortest being Alphonse Mouzon's "Virtue" at 7:24. But on this outing, recorded in Montreux, Switzerland, in 1980, Santamaria is teamed with two acknowledged giants in trumpeter Dizzy Gillespie and harmonica player Toots Thielemans. "Afro Blue" is Santamaria's showcase conga number, but at 13:41 everyone gets a chance to shine, especially Gillespie, who comes storming in shortly before the 5-minute mark with a trilling, shouting solo, then takes off into the horn's upper register and develops a crystalline countertheme over the band's roiling Latin rhythms. Thielemans seizes his moment (as does baritone saxophonist Allen Hoist) on the 11-minutes-plus consideration of George Gershwin's "Summertime." Bending notes; blowing hard, staccato phrases; turning the melody inside out on a lengthy quotation that is marked by alternating single- and multiple-note runs, Thielemans demonstrates both the sensitivity and the invigorating intellect that mark his sound signature. For sheer instrumental virtuosity, *Summertime* is hard to beat.

In general terms, the studio albums are less concerned with specific themes and variations developed through improvisation than with tightly constructed songs and incisive solo flights within an abbreviated framework. The least effective of these is his introduction of the fiery Latin vocalist La Lupe (*Mongo Introduces La Lupe*), not for lack of ideas but for La Lupe's vibrant but fairly one-note performance. On *Soy Yo,* Santamaria builds a bridge between contemporary black pop and Afro-Cuban with a steady percolating, conga-driven tempo supporting Sam Furnace's fluid, modulated alto sax in the lead role on the Anita Baker hit "Sweet Love," while a slow-grooving take (with bracing 6/8 interludes) on Sade's "Smooth Operator" is energized by Tony Hinson's dark, bluesy tenor-sax lead.

In a real sense, *Sabroso* and *Our Man in Havana* best define this intriguing artist. The former, recorded in the early '60s at the height of Santamaria's pop success, finds him not straying from his roots in pursuit of the commercial market's Holy Grail but instead plumbing ever deeper into the music that defined him before he began redefining it. With the usual stalwart supporting cast, Santamaria offers 13 examples of Cuban popular music as interpreted in the *charanga* instrumental and vocal style. *Pachangas, charangas, descargas,* mambos and *guaguancos* are represented in the song selection, each of which is played with specific instrumental lineups. This is Santamaria's Music Appreciation 101 course, and it's an effective lesson. Thanks to the detailed liner notes explaining the particulars, even newcomers to the Cuban song tradition will come away enlightened from their encounter with *Sabroso.*

Our Man in Havana finds Santamaria back in his native Cuba in 1960, accompanied only by the ever-reliable Willie Bobo and a team of Fantasy engineers. He had a mission: to honor the music of his homeland while at the same time subverting some ancient barriers. First he assembled a group of esteemed Cuban musicians among whose numbers sat Yeyito, Cuba's foremost bongo player; a top-flight flautist known simply as Julio; and most important of all, Nino Rivera, a master of the *tres* (a native six-string instrument that is something of a cross between a mandolin and a guitar) and a peerless, daring arranger. Unwritten rules passed down through generations prohibited certain instrumental pairings, such as flutes and bongos, in a specific type of group known as an *orquesta típica,* and the piano and the *tres* in the *conjunto* band. Santamaria disregarded both tenets and fashioned a groundbreaking orchestra that remains one of the most personable he has ever had on record. For these select personalities he composed or covered equally forward-thinking material; specifically, the original songs here largely combine the traditional with the mystical, all harkening back to traditional folk rhumbas and to religious songs common to Afro-Cuban cults. The result is an exhilarating blend of masterful ensemble and individual playing and deeply felt material that is by turns ruminative and jubilant, always speaking to the soul—an important recording whose fresh, vital aura, still undiminished, sets a formidable standard for contemporary musicians who would call themselves pioneers. — D.M.

SANTANA

★★★★ **Santana (1969; Columbia, 1994)**
★★★★ **Santana: Abraxas (1970; Columbia, 1998)**
★★★★ **Santana 3 (1971; Columbia, 1998)**
★★★★ **Caravanserai (Columbia, 1972)**

★★★★★ **Santana's Greatest Hits (Columbia, 1974)**
★★★½ **Borboletta (1974; Columbia, 1990)**
★★★★★ **Lotus (1974; Columbia, 1991)**
★★★★ **Amigos (Columbia, 1976)**
★★★ **Festival (1977; Columbia, 1990)**
★★★ **Moonflower (Columbia, 1977)**
★★ **Inner Secrets (Columbia, 1979)**
★★ **Marathon (Columbia, 1979)**
★★ **Zebop! (Columbia, 1981)**
★★ **Shangó (Columbia, 1983)**
★★ **Beyond Appearances (Columbia, 1985)**
★★½ **Freedom (Columbia, 1987)**
★★★★ **Viva Santana! (Columbia, 1988)**
★★★ **Spirits Dancing in the Flesh (Columbia, 1990)**
★★★★★ **Dance of the Rainbow Serpent (Columbia, 1995)**
★★★★ **Live at the Fillmore, 1968 (Columbia, 1997)**
★★★★ **Santana/Abraxas/Santana 3 (Columbia, 1998)**

CARLOS SANTANA SOLO

★½ **Carlos Santana and Buddy Miles Live (1972; Columbia, 1994)**
★★★ **Love, Devotion, Surrender (with John McLaughlin) (1973; Columbia, 1991)**
★★½ **The Swing of Delight (1980; Columbia, 1990)**
★★★ **Havana Moon (Columbia, 1988)**
★★★★ **Blues for Salvador (Columbia, 1988)**
★★★½ **Milagro (Polydor, 1992)**
★★★½ **Sacred Fire: Live in South America (Polydor, 1993)**
★★★ **Brothers (with the Santana Brothers) (Island, 1994)**

Formed in San Francisco in 1967, Santana fed that scene's appetite for lengthy open-air jams with an athletic mixture of blazing guitar and frenetic percussion. The band's novelty lay in employing the jam format for Latin music—leader/guitarist Carlos Santana (b. 1947), drummer Michael Shrieve and percussionist José "Chepito" Areas were the outfit's anchors; fusing Latin dance forms and bluesy rock, they achieved a synthesis that combined the familiar and the exotic. World-beat ahead of the time, Santana riveted Woodstock audiences with one of the most exciting stage acts of the festival—and Carlos's playing continues, throughout the band's career, to offer delight even when sometimes squandered on inferior material. *Live at the Fillmore, 1968* captures this era of the band well.

While the two-CD *Viva Santana!* serves as a sturdy career overview and the three-CD *Dance of the Rainbow Serpent* goes it one better, the band's first albums remain its strongest, and it's the 22-song live set, *Lotus,* that best captures Santana's considerable appeal. Throughout its history the band was marked by personnel changes, and this lineup is its strongest: With Leon Patillo, it had found a singer markedly more soulful than either original vocalist Greg Rolie or later mainstay Alex Ligertwood, and the entire eight-member unit achieves an instinctive symbiosis. Charging through early hits (Fleetwood Mac's "Black Magic Woman," Tito Puente's "Oye Como Va"), they're fiery and fluid; with Airto Moreira's "Xibaba (She-Ba-Ba)" and Richard Kermode's "Yours Is the Light," the group suggests its coming direction—jazz-rock fusion and flights into the mystic.

Because its rhythmic basis is so strong and the music itself a solid mix of genres, Santana's jazz fusion was generally successful (the band drew heavily on Miles Davis's *Bitches Brew*–period aggressiveness and rarely stooped to jazz lite). Carlos himself delves deeper into the form with *Love, Devotion, Surrender* featuring John McLaughlin, Billy Cobham and Jan Hammer of the Mahavishnu Orchestra, and *The Swing of Delight*—a kind of fusion supersession with Herbie Hancock, Wayne Shorter and Tony Williams—finds the guitarist exploring more complex chord structures and looser rhythms. With *Zebop!,* however, came a foray into a more mainstream pop style that, from the late '80s on, expanded to embrace more wholeheartedly the band's Latin roots (check *Spirits Dancing in the Flesh*).

On his own, Carlos Santana has flexed his guitar in a number of settings. An instantly recognizable musician—with a B.B. King–style clarity of tone, he achieves long, graceful lead lines that resemble a violinist's—Carlos sounds best when he's juxtaposed with heavy percussion. Becoming a devotee of Indian guru Sri Chinmoy in the early '70s (and taking the name Devadip: "light of the lamp of the Supreme"), he revealed a more introspective side when teamed with fellow Chinmoy disciples McLaughlin and Alice Coltrane. On the whole, his solo output has been spotty—from the excellent *Blues for Salvador* to the bland *Havana Moon,* the latter hosting such big-name (if unlikely) collaborators as Willie Nelson, the Fabulous Thunderbirds and Booker T. Jones. *Brothers,* joining Carlos with his guitar-playing brother Jorge and cousin Carlos Hernandez, is a representative set, stylish and intense. — P.E.

SAHEB SARBIB

★★★ Seasons (Soul Note, 1982)
★★★ It Couldn't Happen Without You (Soul Note, 1994)

Bassist Saheb Sarbib (b. 1944) has led a number of experimental groups out of his New York base, but his recorded output is sporadic and, even then, under-represented. *Seasons* finds Sarbib leading a quartet with drummer Paul Motian, alto saxophonist Mark Whitecage and reed player Mel Ellison in a challenging high-energy exchange. Sarbib's vinyl-only sessions with the Multinational Big Band (*Aisha* and *Live at the Public Theater*) are worth searching out. — J.S.

GRAY SARGENT

★★★★★ Concord Duo Series, Vol. 2 (with Dave McKenna) (Concord Jazz, 1993)
★★★★ Shades of Gray (Concord Jazz, 1993)

Guitarist Gray Sargent (b. 1953), a tasteful and inventive player who is extending the swing tradition on his instrument, labored in relative obscurity in and around Boston for more than a decade. That visibility problem eased in the early 1990s when he increased his traveling with the Illinois Jacquet Big Band and kindred spirit Dave McKenna and was summoned onto the weekend jazz-party circuit across the United States. In 1997 Sargent's credentials were strengthened further when singer Tony Bennett added him to his touring band.

While inspired by Kenny Burrell, Oscar Moore and any number of horn players, the self-taught Sargent has honed his own fascinating style. He accentuates single-note melodic lines with thick chords and adds playful and usually witty counterpoints that complement the solos of others. His own solos add fresh musical ideas or quotations that fit the moment.

Shades of Gray, his debut as a leader and composer, showcases the guitarist's artistry and features bassist Marshall Wood and drummer Ray Mosca, with pianist McKenna guesting on several tracks. The duo recording with McKenna reveals the deep and natural affinity the two have for each other's sounds and their instinctive way of supporting each other.

Sargent can also be heard on several other Concord recordings, including the *Concord All-Stars on Cape Cod,* The Newport Jazz Festival All-Stars' *Bern Concert '89,* McKenna's *No More Ouzo for Puzo* and trumpeter Lou Colombo's *I Remember Bobby,* plus several Ruby Braff sessions for Arbors Records. — K.F.

MARIA SCHNEIDER

★★★★ Evanescence (Enja, 1994)
★★★★ Coming About (Enja, 1996)

Composer and big-band leader Maria Schneider (b. 1960) moved into the top tier of jazz orchestra leaders with *Evanescence,* the debut recording by her superb big band, which has Monday nights reserved at Visiones in New York. Schneider worked as Gil Evans's assistant during the last three years of his life. Like Evans, she excels in building intricate layers of texture in her colorful works, allowing the band to build emotional intensity. Other influences include Bob Brookmeyer and Rayburn Wright, late teacher of arranging and composing at the Eastman School of Music in Rochester, New York, where Schneider received her master's degree in 1985. As a guest composer and conductor, Schneider has appeared with Finland's UMO New Music Orchestra, Sweden's Stockholm Jazz Orchestra and Norrbotten Big Band, the Danish Radio Big Band and the Cologne Radio Orchestra.

Dedicated to and inspired by Gil Evans, *Evanescence* is a very fine showcase of Schneider's formidable writing and arranging talents. Prime soloists include saxophonist Rick Margitza, pianist Kenny Werner and trumpeter Tim Hagans. Her second recording, *Coming About,* is strengthened by a stable band that has grown considerably with Schneider. In addition to her 30-minute "Scenes from Childhood" suite and other original compositions, it showcases a swinging, distinctly Schneiderish orchestral rearrangement of John Coltrane's classic "Giant Steps." — K.F.

GUNTHER SCHULLER

★★★★½ The Art of Scott Joplin (1977; GM, 1997)
★★★½ Symbiosis (GM, 1985)
★★★★★ Jumpin' in the Future (GM, 1988)
★★★½ The Art of the Rag (GM, 1989)

Without being—strictly speaking—a jazz musician, Gunther Schuller (b. 1925) had a profound influence on jazz through his invention of the term "Third Stream" to describe his bold fusion of European classical music and jazz. Schuller became known to jazz fans through his French-horn performance on several tracks of Miles Davis's *Birth of the Cool* sessions and on the Gil Evans/Miles Davis recording of *Porgy and Bess.* Perhaps his best-known contribution was his direction of Charles Mingus's sprawling *Epitaph,* performed at New York's Lincoln Center. With a formalist's mind and an explorer's heart, Schuller reveals his deep understanding of ragtime and the possibilities it offers within its strict limits in his work with the New England Ragtime Ensemble on *The Art of Scott Joplin* and *The Art of the Rag.* The title track of *Jumpin' in the Future,* originally written in 1947 but performed here by Orange Then Blue, a band led by Schuller's drummer son, George, is a challenging composition that resets the tone for many subsequent avant-garde jazz projects. — J.S.

DIANE SCHUUR

★★½ Deedles (1984; GRP, 1990)
★★★★ Diane Schuur & the Count Basie Orchestra (1987; GRP, 1990)
★★½ Pure Schuur (GRP, 1991)
★★★★ In Tribute (GRP, 1992)
★★★ Love Songs (GRP, 1993)
★★★ Heart to Heart (GRP, 1994)
★★★ Love Walked In (GRP, 1996)
★★★★ Blues for Schuur (GRP, 1997)

Diane Schuur, blind since her birth in 1953, grew up in Seattle with an abiding love of music and a strong voice influenced by virtually everything she heard. Originally a country singer, she was discovered by Stan Getz and quickly introduced to the jazz world, where the outstanding power, range and sheer personality of her singing won her immediate and abiding fans. She can belt like Helen Humes and sit perfectly inside the flow like Ella Fitzgerald. Her talents have been difficult to harness effectively, however, and in the wrong setting she has a tendency to overshoot the mark. Her breakthrough record was with the Count Basie Orchestra, where she was in total control riding the crest of the big band. Schuur probably would have thrived in the era of tinny or nonexistent PA systems when vocalists had to shout over the band.

In Tribute showcases her strength at getting to the heart of her influences, including Fitzgerald, Billie Holiday, Anita O'Day, Sarah Vaughan, Peggy Lee and Nancy Wilson. *Love Songs* is more of a pop outing. *Heart to Heart,* a collaboration with B.B. King, falls short of its intended mark. On *Love Walked In* Schuur handles a set of jazz standards expertly. *Blues for Schuur* is a mature work from a singer who has finally found the right tone for each setting within which she finds herself. — J.S.

JOHN SCOFIELD

★★★ Electric Outlet (Gramavision, 1984)
★★★★ Still Warm (Gramavision, 1986)
★★★ Blue Matter (Gramavision, 1987)
★★★½ Pick Hits Live (Gramavision, 1987)
★★★ Loud Jazz (Gramavision, 1988)
★★★½ Flat Out (Gramavision, 1989)
★★★★ Time on My Hands (Blue Note, 1990)
★★★ Slo Sco: Best of the Ballads (Gramavision, 1990)
★★★ Who's Who? (1990; One Way, 1997)
★★★ Rough House (Enja, 1991)
★★★ Meant to Be (Blue Note, 1991)
★★★★ Grace Under Pressure (Blue Note, 1992)
★★★½ Liquid Fire: The Best of John Scofield (Gramavision, 1994)
★★★½ Hand Jive (Blue Note, 1994)
★★★ Groove Elation! (Blue Note, 1995)
★★★★½ Quiet (Verve, 1996)
★★★½ A Go Go (Verve, 1998)

Guitarist John Scofield (b. 1951) has straddled postbop, funk and fusion styles over an eclectic career that his seen him play with Gerry Mulligan, Charles Mingus, Gary Burton, Lee Konitz, Billy Cobham, Dave Liebman and Miles Davis. He was already developing out of the soul-jazz tradition when Miles Davis tabbed him to play on *Decoy.* The Gramavision sides show him moving toward fusion after his time with Davis.

The exciting *Still Warm,* with Davis-band compatriots Darryl Jones on bass and Omar Hakim on drums, is the best from this period, although *Flat Out,* with organist Don Grolnick, comes close. *Electric Outlet* gets some good input from drummer Steve Jordan and alto saxophonist Dave Sanborn. Scofield faces off with guitarist Hiram Bullock on *Blue Matter* and keyboardist George Duke on *Loud Jazz. Pick Hits Live* is a Japanese recording of his working trio—Dennis Chambers on drums and Gary Grainger on bass.

On the Blue Note sides, Scofield moved back into the jazz mainstream with sensational results. *Time on My Hands* pairs him with tenor saxophonist Joe Lovano fronting the awesome rhythm section of bassist Charlie Haden and drummer Jack DeJohnette. The intriguing *Grace Under Pressure* is an album of ever-shifting textures explored by a group including second guitarist Bill Frisell, flügelhornist Randy Brecker, trombonist Jim Pugh, French-hornist John Clark and a rhythm section of Haden and Joey Baron.

Quiet is a masterpiece of acoustic textures recorded with bassist Steve Swallow, drummer Bill Stewart, saxophonist Wayne Shorter and Randy Brecker. Verve pushed him into a more commercial direction on *A Go Go,* teaming Scofield with the ecstasy soundtrack masters Medeski, Martin and Wood. — J.S.

E.C. SCOTT

★★★½ **Come Get Your Love (Blind Pig, 1995)**

E.C. Scott (b. ca. 1955) is a smooth and technically impressive blues and R&B vocalist from Oakland, California. Scott's gospel training is evident on her solid debut, *Come Get Your Love,* in the moving call-and-response exchange with her backup singers on the title track, one of the set's several good originals. Though her blues songs unfold in contemporary surroundings, like the local mall, they stick to the verities of love's ups and downs. Her sure-handed, Little Milton–influenced delivery marks Scott as a veteran performer despite her lack of recording experience. Several guitarists contribute to the proceedings, including label mate Chris Cain, who excels on two tracks, and her road guitarist Tim Landis, whose touch matches Scott's voice well when he lays off the effects. Too bad the production leans toward commercial studio tricks and electronic drums. — J.S.

JIMMY SCOTT

★★★½ **Regal Records: Live in New Orleans (1951; Specialty, 1991)**
★★½ **Very Truly Yours (1955; Denon, 1993)**
★★★★ **All Over Again (1960; Denon, 1994)**
★★★½ **Lost and Found (1969/1972; Rhino, 1993)**
★★★½ **All the Way (Sire, 1992)**
★★★½ **Dream (Sire, 1994)**
★★★★ **Heaven (Warner Bros., 1996)**
★★★½ **Holding Back the Years (Artists Only!, 1998)**

Trying to define or explain the ethereal passion of Jimmy Scott (b. 1925) is like grabbing at a blue wisp of smoke. Yes, his voice seems to suspend and even alter time and rhythm; pauses, dips and crescendos redirect classic standards (and, lately, pop and rock ballads); "All the Way," "Day by Day" and even "Slave to Love" are somehow never the same after one hears his version. And yes, his lugubrious vocals sound like a woman's: His upper-register voice is the result of a hormonal condition that locked that part of him in preadolescence. But if ever a balladeer carried the unlearned, rule-defying and emotionally laden mystery and promise of great jazz singing, it would be Scott.

Born in Cleveland, Scott began singing church music. The late '40s found him in Harlem, performing under the name "Little Jimmy Scott" and eventually joining the Lionel Hampton Orchestra. His recorded material from this time—including the minor hit "Everybody's Somebody's Fool"—reveals a strong, maturing vocalist, comfortable in the overlapping R&B and jazz idioms of the day. In 1951 Scott joined popular New Orleans bandleader Paul Gayten; the five tracks on a live album from that year show him in a tight, rhythmic groove, dramatically brandishing the operatic side of his voice; the deep subtleties and color of his phrasing were yet to come.

In the mid-'50s, Scott signed the Achilles' heel of his career: a long-standing, stifling contract with Savoy Records. It generated a series of lushly orchestrated (and therefore somewhat constricting to Scott's blossoming genius) sessions that relied on the reverb-heavy pop/jazz mannerisms of the day. Forgo *Very Truly Yours;* it's included in the 24-track *All Over Again,* which features stellar vocal workouts like "Imagination" and a heart-grabbing version of "Sometimes I Feel Like a Motherless Child."

By 1963 Ray Charles had founded his own label, Tangerine, and produced one album with Scott—to which he added sympathetic piano work—and immediately met fierce legal resistance from Savoy. The album's continued unavailability remains a tragedy.

Lost and Found anthologizes two Atlantic sessions produced in 1969 and '72 that had sadly languished in the vaults after Savoy again threatened legal action. For sheer power and poise, it can't be beat: cool readings of classic material ("Sometimes I Feel Like a Motherless Child," "The Folks Who Live on the Hill," the heart-stopping "Day by Day") confident backup (pianists Ray Bryant and Junior Mance, sax men Frank Wess and David Newman, guitarists Eric Gale, Billy Butler and David Spinozza), all sparsely arranged with an intermittent, tasteful string section. It's Scott at his peak, period.

By the late '70s—after one last, less-than-spectacular album for Savoy in '75—Scott had returned to his hometown, running the shipping department in a Sheraton and singing for old-age homes on the weekends. In 1991, when he sang "Someone to Watch Over Me," accompanied by Dr. John on piano, at R&B songwriter Doc Pomus's funeral, Sire Records president Seymour Stein ended his early retirement.

Scott's Sire output testifies to the timeless quality of his art even as a few cracks in his 70-year-old's timbre and a quirky vibrato have become apparent. *All the Way* is sombre and standard driven ("Angel Eyes" is a triumph) with Kenny Barron, Ron Carter and Grady Tate; *Dream* a warmer, more upbeat collection with fellow veterans Junior Mance and Milt Jackson; and most intriguing, *Heaven,* divining Scott's inherently deep, spiritual side with versions of traditional numbers ("Wayfarin' Stranger," etc.) with pianist Jacky Terrasson. Continuing the postmodern pattern of covering nonjazz material (and risking the pitfall of jazz-lite pablum), *Holding Back the Years* proves some silly love songs just lack proper interpretation: "Nothing Compares 2 U" and the title track are passable, but "Almost Blue" and "Slave to Love" are sublime. — A.K.

SHIRLEY SCOTT

★★★★ **Soul Shoutin' (1963; Prestige, 1994)**
★★★★½ **Queen of the Organ (1964; Impulse!, 1993)**
★★★½ **Blue Flames (1965; Original Jazz Classics, 1995)**
★★★½ **Roll 'Em (1966; Impulse!, 1995)**

Shirley Scott (b. 1934) grew up in the soul-jazz hotbed of Philadelphia and became one of the most popular post–Jimmy Smith organists, working in small groups, often with her husband, tenor saxophonist Stanley Turrentine. *Soul Shoutin',* a reissued twofer combining *The Soul Is Willing* and *Soul Shoutin',* shows the Scott/Turrentine connection in top form. *Queen of the Organ* is an incendiary live performance from 1964 by the Scott/Turrentine quartet. *Roll 'Em* is a mixed trio/big-band session of classic big-band material. — J.S.

TOM SCOTT

★ **Blow It Out (1977; Legacy, 1990)**
★ **The Best of Tom Scott (Columbia, 1980)**
★ **Desire (Elektra Musician, 1982)**
★ **Streamlines (GRP, 1987)**
★ **Flashpoint (GRP, 1989)**
★ **Them Changes (GRP, 1990)**
★★★ **Born Again (GRP, 1992)**
★ **Reed My Lips (GRP, 1993)**
★ **Night Creatures (GRP, 1994)**

Pop/jazz saxophonist Tom Scott (b. 1948) prefers playing lightweight fusion and covering popular rock material to following his initial interests as an interpreter of the work of Charlie Parker and Oliver Nelson. He achieved fame when his band, the L.A. Express, backed up Joni Mitchell on several albums and recorded "Jazzman" with Carole King. Since then, Scott's done a lot of work in Hollywood backing rock stars and working on soundtracks.

Born Again is the one standout in Scott's catalog, a return to his jazz roots for a mainstream sextet date bolstered by pianist Kenny Kirkland, trumpeter Randy Brecker and trombonist George Bohannon.

Scott may never live down his 1982 decision to work as Olivia Newton-John's musical director and flout the musicians' boycott of South Africa by playing 10 days at Sun City. — J.S.

GIL SCOTT-HERON

★★★ **Small Talk at 125th and Lenox (1972; Flying Dutchman, 1995)**
★★★ **Free Will (1972; Flying Dutchman, 1995)**
★★★ **Pieces of a Man (1973; Flying Dutchman, 1995)**
★★★ **The First Minute of a New Day (1974; TVT, 1998)**
★★★ **Winter in America (1974; TVT, 1998)**
★★★½ **From South Africa to South Carolina (1975; TVT, 1998)**
★★★★ **The Best of Gil Scott-Heron (1984; Arista, 1991)**
★★★½ **The Revolution Will Not Be Televised (RCA Bluebird, 1988)**
★★★ **Spirits (TVT, 1994)**

Pianist Gil Scott-Heron (b. 1949), along with the Last Poets, anticipated rap; his voice fashioned funky prophecy. Scott-Heron's '70s albums flourished serious intelligence notably lacking in the age of disco, and his political wordplay soared miles beyond contemporaneous "ooh-baby" sentiments. As a novelist (*The Vulture/The Nigger Factory*), poet and musician, Scott-Heron graced his laid-back soul with jazz embellishments borrowed from *Bitches Brew*–period Miles Davis. As shown by the title track and "Whitey on the Moon" from *The Revolution Will Not Be Televised,* the singer often leavened his class-struggle sermons with wit, and at his most direct ("Home Is Where the Hatred Is") he could summon all of the righteous fury—if little of the noise—of Public Enemy.

"Johannesburg," off *From South Africa to South Carolina,* gave him FM-radio airplay, but Scott-Heron has generally remained only a critical success. Playing with expert musicians (Bernard Purdie, Ron Carter, David Spinozza), he's made skillful records—but his vocals have lacked distinction, and an overreliance on the glossy flute work of Hubert Laws and Brian Jackson has sometimes blunted the rhythmic edge of his songs. "Re-Ron," a biting anti-Reagan diatribe off *The Best of Gil Scott-Heron* shows him working with a tougher sound, courtesy of Material's Bill Laswell—and his now out-of-print early-'80s work, as a whole, gained in force. After a decadelong studio absence, Scott-Heron reminded listeners of his significance with the trenchant, topical *Spirits.* Its hip-hop flavor updates his style, but the man's power of critique, and his urgent sense of commitment, remain intact. — P.E.

SON SEALS

★★★★½ **The Son Seals Blues Band (Alligator, 1973)**
★★★ **Midnight Son (Alligator, 1976)**
★★★½ **Live and Burning (Alligator, 1978)**
★★★★ **Chicago Fire (Alligator, 1980)**
★★★½ **Bad Axe (Alligator, 1984)**
★★★½ **Living in the Danger Zone (Alligator, 1991)**
★★★½ **Nothing but the Truth (Alligator, 1994)**
★★★★ **Live: Spontaneous Combustion (Alligator, 1996)**

Born in Osceola, Arkansas, in 1942, guitarist Frank "Son" Seals joined forces with Earl Hooker in 1963, fronting Hooker's Roadmasters for a spell before starting a 1966 stint with Albert King's band (playing drums). But it was not until 1971, when he moved permanently to Chicago, that Seals would begin to establish a reputation as one of the most fiery and distinctive blues guitarists of his generation.

Seals's self-titled first solo effort, released in 1973, is a monstrous recording featuring Johnny "Big Moose" Walker on organ. With Seals's fantastic playing and singing throughout, the album features some of his best songs: the slow-burning "Sitting at My Window," the funky, sinister "Your Love Is Like a Cancer" and the captivating, surging "How Could She Leave Me." Also in evidence is Seals's respect for the blues tradition, particularly illustrated by his passionate reading of Magic Sam's "All Your Love."

Midnight Son takes Seals in a different direction—with a horn section and a more sterile, less spontaneous feel. Originals like "On My Knees" and "Going Back Home" retain their smoldering immediacy, however. Seals is joined by James Cotton and B.B. King alumnus Alberto Gianquinto on keyboards and former Junior Wells/Hound Dog Taylor bassist Snapper Mitchum. *Live and Burning,* true to its title, finds Seals in his natural habitat—onstage. Recorded in the late '70s at Chicago's Wise Fools Pub, the album has an immediacy that can only be achieved in a cramped, smoky nightclub. With guests A.C. Reed on sax and Lacy Gibson on guitar, Seals and his band are loose yet tight, running through such numbers as the searing, staccato "Funky Bitch" and Reed's "She's Fine." Gianquinto joins the fray on one track, playing piano on a version of Little Walter's "Last Night."

Chicago Fire features a dose of sharp originals, including the slow blues "Leaving Home" and the urbane, funky "Gentleman from the Windy City." These are flanked by a version of the Steve Cropper/Wilson Pickett classic "I'm Not Tired," on which King Solomon's boogie-woogie piano cuts a prickly swath through a syncopated, four-part horn arrangement. *Bad Axe* and *Living in the Danger Zone* find Seals firing off ferocious riff after riff on a combination of originals and covers, and both benefit from a stripped-down instrumental approach; gone are the sweeping, multihorn arrangements. Although Seals's playing still has a hungry edge, these albums are the work of a polished player and bandleader. Peppered with funky vamps, the semislick *Bad Axe* features a tricky turnaround on "I Think You're Fooling Me" and the Meters-esque "Can't Stand to See Her Cry." The hilarious "Frigidaire Woman" and the nimble "Arkansas Woman" are among the standouts on *Danger Zone,* while a bent central riff and hovering flute create a foreboding intersection with Seals's cautionary lyrics on the title track.

Spontaneous Combustion was recorded live over a three-day period in June 1996 at Buddy Guy's Legends club in Chicago. Here Seals fronts a tight sextet, with whom he spins through tunes like the horn-spiked original "I Need My Baby Back" and a slow-burning version of Lowell Fulson's "Trouble Trouble." This release finds Seals sounding very much at home—onstage.

In an idiom packed with deft, impassioned players, Son Seals stands out. His original songs place him a notch above many of his talented Chicago contemporaries, while his fret work and singing always glow like a burning coal, whether on record or in person. — B.R.H.

BRIAN SETZER ORCHESTRA

★★★ **The Brian Setzer Orchestra (Hollywood, 1994)**
★★★ **Guitar Slinger (Interscope, 1996)**
★★★½ **The Dirty Boogie (Interscope, 1998)**

After leading retro-rockabilly band the Stray Cats to chart success in the 1980s, Brian Setzer (b. 1959) resurfaced as a big-band leader, kicking off the swing revival in the 1990s. It took nearly four years, but eventually his success illustrated that Setzer was ahead of the curve. His big-band debut's pastiche of '40s swing colored by his rockabilly, uptempo raunch and even his earlier new-wave irony made it palatable to young 1990s audiences. On the debut, the 16-piece Orchestra puts across such chestnuts as "There's a Rainbow 'Round My Shoulder" and "A Nightingale Sang in Berkeley Square" with knowing savoir faire. For *Guitar Slinger,* Setzer has even enticed Joe Strummer into embracing jump blues on "Sammy Davis City." *The Dirty Boogie* rocketed Setzer and company into the Top 10, yielding a hit with his repro version of Louis Prima's "Jump Jive an' Wail." — H.G.-W.

SHADOWFAX

★★★ **Watercourse Way (1976; Windham Hill, 1985)**
★★★ **Too Far to Whisper (1977; Windham Hill, 1986)**
★★★½ **Shadowfax (1982; Windham Hill, 1997)**
★★★ **Shadowdance (1983; Windham Hill, 1997)**
★★★ **The Dreams of Children (1984; Windham Hill, 1998)**
★★★½ **What Goes Around: The Best of Shadowfax (Windham Hill, 1991)**
★★★½ **Esperanto (EarthBeat!, 1992)**
★★★ **Magic Theater (EarthBeat!, 1994)**
★★★ **Shadowfax Live! (Sonic Images, 1995)**

Shadowfax is a California-based sextet that plays an eclectic amalgam of international styles in an early version of world music that evolved into easy-listening New Age sonorities. Originally a blues band, the group was built around lyricon player/saxophonist Chuck Greenberg, bassist Phil Maggini, guitarist G.E. Stinson and a shifting variety of percussionists. With a nod to Oregon and more than a little inspiration from Shakti, the group serves up a listenable pastiche highlighted by the interplay of Stinson and violinist Jamil Szmadzinski on the early Windham Hill material. Despite personnel changes, Greenberg managed to keep the group fresh and focused. The label switch brought new life, as Greenberg was rejoined by Maggini and percussionist Stu Nevitt for *Esperanto,* which features violinist Lakshminarayana Shankar and percussionist Emil Richards. — J.S.

SHAKEY JAKE

★★★½ **Good Times (1960; Original Blues Classics, 1994)**
★★★★ **Mouth Harp Blues (1960; Original Blues Classics, 1993)**

James Harris (1921–1990) was a vital force on the post–World War II Chicago blues scene, an original whose easy, expressive vocal style and inventive songwriting made him a popular club bandleader. He was also the uncle of guitarist Magic Sam. Born in Earle, Arkansas, Harris moved to Chicago at age seven but bounced back and forth between the two locales during the '30s before joining the Army. He picked up his nickname after the war for his reputation as a man who could throw hot dice. Hustling at craps was one of the keys to popularity on the social scene, and Harris became tight with blues kingpins Muddy Waters and Little Walter, sitting in on gigs with them before going out on his own. Harris's many songs were inspired, he claimed, by trips down to Chicago's Madison Street, where he would pick up hard-luck stories from the denizens of Skid Row. Apocryphal or not, the tale supports Harris's multifaceted understanding of blues storytelling, although he was as adept as many of his contemporaries in borrowing entire song structures from other performers.

His reedy, self-taught chordal harmonica style, fashioned out of his admiration for Sonny Boy (John Lee) Williamson, is featured on the trio session *Good Times* with organist Jack McDuff and guitarist Bill Jennings. Despite some good performances in this interesting context, the session's remastering leaves an unpleasant echoing distortion on several tracks. Ironically, harp is far less in evidence on *Mouth Harp Blues,* a smoldering quintet session including some lightning leads from Little Walter's guitarist Jimmy Lee Robinson. Harris's singing is right there, rhythmically intense yet delivered with squinty-eyed understatement. — J.S.

SHAKTI

★★★★½ The Best of Shakti (Moment, 1994)

This acoustic fusion project combined guitarist John McLaughlin in his post–Mahavishnu Orchestra phase with several Indian master musicians, notably Lakshminarayana Shankar on violin and Zakir Hussain and T.H. "Vikku" Vinayakram on tabla and other percussion instruments. McLaughlin developed a special guitar with a second set of strings crossing at an angle for drone and overtone effects. Shakti recorded three albums in the '70s, achieving wonderful results with this understated yet eloquently vibrant music. *The Best of Shakti* is derived from the out-of-print releases. — J.S.

KENDRA SHANK

★★★★ Afterglow (Mapleshade, 1994)
★★★★★ Wish (Jazz Focus, 1998)

The precociously talented Kendra Shank (b. 1958) is among the best of the rash of great young jazz vocalists to emerge in the 1990s. Her superb interpretive singing style is already well developed on *Afterglow,* which was coproduced by the great Shirley Horn and features pianist Larry Willis and alto saxophonist Gary Bartz. *Wish* is a multigeneric masterpiece, on which she brings new meaning to the folk standard "Black Is the Color of My True Love's Hair"; recasts James Taylor's "That Lonesome Road" as a jazz vehicle; chooses two masterful Abbey Lincoln covers, "Should've Been" and "Angel Face"; and includes a title track cowritten with vibraphonist Joe Locke. — J.S.

LAKSHMINARAYANA SHANKAR

★★★★ Who's to Know (ECM, 1980)
★★★★ Vision (ECM, 1983)
★★★ The Epidemics (ECM, 1985)
★★★½ Pancha Nadal Pallavi (ECM, 1989)

Indian violinist Lakshminarayana Shankar (b. 1950) had made a number of recordings of Indian classical music before coming to the attention of Western listeners through his extraordinary work in Shakti, which he co-led with John McLaughlin. After Shakti, Shankar worked briefly with Frank Zappa, who produced the out-of-print *Touch Me There.*

Who's to Know is close in spirit to the Shakti material, while *Vision* is a jazz outing with Jan Garbarek on a variety of saxophones and Palle Mikkelborg on trumpet and flügelhorn. *The Epidemics* is a quintet outing featuring another Zappa alumnus, guitarist Steve Vai. *Pancha Nadal Pallavi* is a session of Indian music. — J.S.

MEM SHANNON

★★★½ A Cab Driver's Blues (Hannibal/Rykodisc, 1995)
★★★½ Mem Shannon's 2nd Blues Album (Hannibal/Rykodisc, 1997)

Driving a taxi can be inherently blues-inducing, but Mem Shannon (b. 1959) has done what few cabbies ever get the opportunity to do—make an album to exorcise those blues. Hailing from New Orleans, the singer, songwriter and guitarist has obviously assimilated the city's rich musical history, as demonstrated by the horn-driven, funky sensibility of *A Cab Driver's Blues.* Like all good blues albums, *A Cab Driver's Blues* is decidedly autobiographical; one listen makes it clear that these stories couldn't be made up. Shannon's inspired singing and playing are augmented by snippets of actual conversations with his passengers; interspersed between songs, these add a palpable stamp of authenticity, originality and humor to standout tracks like the brooding, harmonica-drenched "Maxine" and the hilarious "My Baby's Been Watching TV." Shannon eventually found cab driving taking a backseat to his recording career and went into music full time to make *Mem Shannon's 2nd Blues Album.* — B.R.H.

SONNY SHARROCK

★★★ **Guitar (Enemy, 1987)**
★★★ **Seize the Rainbow (Enemy, 1987)**
★★★½ **Live in New York (Enemy, 1989)**
★★★★ **Highlife (Enemy, 1990)**
★★★★ **Ask the Ages (Axiom, 1991)**
★★★½ **Faith Moves (with Nicky Skopelitis) (CMP, 1991)**
★★★ **Space Ghost Coast to Coast (Cartoon Network, 1994)**

Sonny Sharrock (1940–1994) was one of the most challenging guitarists in contemporary music. As a sideman in some of Herbie Mann's most experimental bands as well as with Pharoah Sanders and as a member of Last Exit, Sharrock was the guitar's great free-jazz exponent. Ironically, he often said he saw his instrument as a saxophone with strings.

Most of his late-'60s and early-'70s recordings are long out of print. His "comeback" recordings, *Guitar* (a series of solo and overdubbed guitar pieces) and *Seize the Rainbow* (band recordings including Pheeroan AkLaff and Melvin Gibbs) grabbed a generation largely unfamiliar with his guitar pyrotechnics by the ears and tugged. *Guitar* offers a dazzling pinwheel of sound, with Sharrock playing glass-lightning guitar lines over his own guitar beds, while *Seize the Rainbow* unfolds in a less musically claustrophobic setting. The band gives him some breathing space, structurally, rhythmically and melodically, and Sharrock makes a fusion record that never loses track of either side of its delicate equation. An expanded version of this band plays tunes from both of these studio albums on *Live in New York.* Keyboard player Dave Snyder proves a wonderful foil for Sharrock, providing an anchor for his out-of-the-tradition sounds.

The early '90s found Sharrock releasing three albums almost simultaneously, under three different guises. *Ask the Ages* renewed his association with Pharoah Sanders. Along with Elvin Jones and Charnett Moffett, Sharrock created his most challenging record, interacting with Sanders to explore the edges of their harmonic possibilities. *Highlife,* made with his road band, sounds almost lighthearted, capturing Sharrock's melodic gifts and the group's high spirits. He does a beautiful variation on changes by art rocker Kate Bush and even gives the spiritual "All My Trials" an edge of fun. *Faith Moves,* his duet with Nicky Skopelitis, is perhaps the prettiest album Sharrock ever recorded.

Sharrock had just signed a deal with RCA and was at work composing when he died of a heart attack while exercising in his Ossining, New York, home. His last release was an EP of music for the Cartoon Network show *Space Ghost Coast to Coast.* — H.B.

ARTIE SHAW

★★★ **The Uncollected Artie Shaw and His Orchestra, 1938, Vol. 1 (Hindsight, 1979)**
★★★ **The Uncollected Artie Shaw and His Orchestra, 1938, Vol. 2 (Hindsight, 1979)**
★★★ **Original Big Band Recordings, 1938–1939 (Hindsight, 1987)**
★★★★ **Begin the Beguine (RCA Bluebird, 1987)**
★★★★ **The Complete Gramercy Five Sessions (RCA Bluebird, 1989)**
★★★★½ **Blues in the Night (RCA Bluebird, 1990)**
★★★ **Best of the Big Bands (Columbia, 1990)**
★★★ **The Last Recordings, Vol. 2: The Big Band (MusicMasters, 1990)**
★★★ **Artie Shaw and His New Music (Forlane, 1992)**
★★★½ **Frenesi: Featuring Begin the Beguine (RCA Bluebird, 1992)**
★★★★ **The Indispensible Artie Shaw, Vols. 5 and 6 (RCA Bluebird, 1992)**
★★★★ **The Last Recordings: Rare and Unreleased (MusicMasters, 1992)**
★★★ **More Last Recordings: The Final Sessions (MusicMasters, 1993)**
★★★ **The Essence of Artie Shaw (Legacy, 1994)**
★★★ **Free for All (Four Star, 1995)**
★★★½ **Greatest Hits (RCA Victor, 1996)**

Clarinetist Artie Shaw (b. 1910) led one of the most innovative and popular big bands of the '30s and '40s, but those two traits were constantly at odds with each other in his music. In 1936 he introduced the idea of using a string section in big-band swing, but when he began recording for Bluebird two years later he used standard instrumentation. The success of that band's '38 recording of "Begin the Beguine" made Shaw an international star and a popular rival of Benny Goodman.

Begin the Beguine documents the recordings of Shaw's acclaimed 1938–41 organization. Tenor saxophonists Tony Pastor and George

Auld, who were both aware of Lester Young's style, play beautifully, and sultry-voiced Helen Forrest does all the singing except for an exquisite Billie Holiday appearance on "Any Old Time." Shaw himself is the principal soloist, playing the clarinet with a soulful dedication that still sounds inspired. The precocious young drummer Buddy Rich brings his energetic style into the mix as well.

At the end of 1939, during the height of his popularity, Shaw made a celebrated and dramatic "retirement," disbanded his group and went to Mexico. He returned to recording in 1940 with a ponderous band that brought the strings and other orchestral arrangement ideas back into a grandiose mix. One of the compositions, "Frenesi," became a huge hit. At the same time, Shaw's small group, the Gramercy Five, was playing chamber jazz with remarkable lucidity and originality. Shaw himself was a consummate soloist who was complemented beautifully by trumpeter Billy Butterfield and the absolutely novel sound of Johnny Guarnieri's harpsichord.

The lineup on *Blues in the Night* includes such luminaries as trumpeters Roy Eldridge and Hot Lips Page, alto saxophonists Tom Mace and Les Clarke, trombonist Ray Conniff and drummer Dave Tough. The strings are still there, but the band isn't intimidated by them—the way Page cuts a Louie Armstrong–inspired trumpet solo through the strings on "Blues in the Night" has to be heard to be believed. This recording also collects material from Shaw's next band, which features wonderful playing from Eldridge and guitarist Barney Kessel in both large-group and quintet settings.

The Last Recordings once again places Shaw in a small-group setting that highlights the outstanding technique and expressiveness of his playing. Pianist Hank Jones and guitarist Tal Farlow also shine on the sextet dates; the big-band material is less interesting. The several greatest-hits packages are not the ideal way to hear this music, since Shaw's most popular material was not necessarily his best. — J.S.

WOODY SHAW

★★★½ **Blackstone Legacy (Contemporary, 1971)**

★★½ **Song of Songs (1973; Original Jazz Classics, N.A.)**

★★★ **Last of the Line (Cassandranite/Love Dance) (1974/1976; 32 Jazz, 1997)**

★★★★ **The Moontrane (1975; 32 Jazz, 1995)**

★★★★ **Little Red's Fantasy (Muse, 1977)**

★★★½ **The Woody Shaw Concert Ensemble at the Berliner Jazztage (Muse, 1977)**

★★★★½ **Rosewood (Columbia, 1978)**

★★★★★ **Stepping Stones: Live at the Village Vanguard (Columbia, 1978)**

★★★★★ **Woody III (Columbia, 1979)**

★★★ **Ichi-Ban (with Louis Hayes and Junior Cook) (Muse, 1979)**

★★★½ **For Sure! (Columbia, 1980)**

★★★★ **The Iron Men (Muse, 1981)**

★★★½ **United (Columbia, 1981)**

★★★★ **Lotus Flower (Enja, 1982)**

★★★½ **Master of the Art (with Bobby Hutcherson) (Elektra Musician, 1982)**

★★★½ **Night Music (with Bobby Hutcherson) (Elektra Musician, 1983)**

★★ **Time Is Right (Red, 1984)**

★★½ **Woody Shaw with the Tone Jansa Quartet (Timeless, 1985)**

★★★½ **Solid (Muse, 1986)**

★★★★ **The Freddie Hubbard and Woody Shaw Sessions (1987; Blue Note, 1995)**

★★★½ **Imagination (Muse, 1988)**

★★★ **In My Own Sweet Way (In + Out, 1989)**

★★ **Lausanne 1977 (as the Louis Hayes/Woody Shaw Quintet) (TCB, 1997)**

Woody Shaw (1944–1989) was the most creative mainstream-jazz trumpeter of the 1970s, the bridge from Freddie Hubbard to Wynton Marsalis. A former Jazz Messenger like Hubbard and Marsalis, Shaw was an exceptional hard-bop blower with a hard-edged tone and a marvelous fluency. He also worked with such avant-gardists as Eric Dolphy and Anthony Braxton, however, and this gave his harmonic concepts an unpredictability that set him apart from all the Lee Morgan revivalists of the era. Most important, Shaw rehearsed his combos and taught them his concept of jazz pieces that developed dramatically and told a story and weren't merely a series of solos.

All these accomplishments didn't gain him much in terms of money or lasting fame. It took him a long time to emerge as a bandleader, and soon after he did, his generation was shunted offstage by the "young lions" of the '80s. His name is hardly noted in jazz histories, but his 1975–1983 albums are still rewarding examples of the best postbop, analogous to the work of Dexter Gordon and McCoy Tyner during the same period.

Shaw was born in Laurinburg, North Carolina; his father was a member of the Diamond Jubilee Singers, a gospel group. Shaw grew up in Newark, New Jersey, and was playing in New York with Chick Corea in Willie Bobo's band at age 18. Eric Dolphy heard Shaw and invited the teenager to play on the *Iron Man* album. A year later, in 1964, Dolphy sent a plane ticket for Shaw to join him in Paris. A few days later Dolphy was dead, but Shaw went anyway and played with Bud Powell, Kenny Clarke and Johnny Griffin.

Shaw returned to the States for gigs with the three best hard-bop bands in the world: the Horace Silver Quintet, the Max Roach Quintet and Art Blakey and the Jazz Messengers. There were also collaborations with Joe Henderson in Los Angeles, with Bobby Hutcherson in San Francisco and with the Louis Hayes/Junior Cook Quintet in New York.

By now it was 1975, and for 12 years Shaw had been trying without success to jump-start his own career as a leader. In 1965 he financed his own sessions with Henderson, Ron Carter and Herbie Hancock, but they went unreleased until they appeared on 1974's *Cassandranite* (now available with *Love Dance* on *Last of the Line*).

In 1970 Shaw recorded an ambitious two-album set, *Blackstone Legacy,* which boasts two bassists (Carter and Clint Houston), two saxes (Gary Bartz and Bennie Maupin) and drummer Lenny White on extended arrangements of Shaw's compositions. It is an exciting set that balances the leader's hard-bop and open-ended tendencies, but it doesn't lead anywhere and was followed by *Song of Songs,* which features a less interesting cast.

In 1975 things began to turn around for Shaw. That year he released *The Moontrane,* which features a young, hungry band (including trombonist Steve Turre, pianist Onaje Allan Gumbs and drummer Victor Lewis) willing to work on Shaw's concept of evolving improvisation, where the movement from ensemble to solo and back again had a logic. The title track became Shaw's best-known composition, but it is typical of his striking melodic themes and harmonic builds.

Love Dance and *Little Red's Fantasy* follows the same approach, with the latter being more successful. In 1976 Shaw used the quintet he co-led with Hayes as the basis for an expanded septet (with Frank Foster and Slide Hampton) that he called the Woody Shaw Concert Ensemble. This group's one album, *At the Berliner Jazztage,* illustrates the leader's flair for working with dense horn harmonies.

In 1977 Shaw dipped back into avant-garde waters by recording *The Iron Men,* which went unreleased until 1981. This collaboration with Anthony Braxton, Muhal Richard Abrams and Arthur Blythe was inspired by Dolphy and finds Shaw stimulated by the strategic element of disorder in the arrangements.

When Dexter Gordon made his long-awaited return to North America in 1976 after 14 years of self-imposed exile in Europe, he picked the Woody Shaw/Louis Hayes Quintet to back him for his "Homecoming" tour. Shaw was a highlight of the shows, and the attendant press convinced Gordon's label, Columbia, to sign Shaw as a leader.

Shaw responded to the challenge by assembling and drilling a tight quintet (with Gumbs, Houston, Lewis and saxophonist Carter Jefferson) to handle his ambitious new music, which mixed bop and modal elements into arrangements built around dialogs within the band rather than the usual monologs. Shaw himself forsook the trumpet to play the mellow flügelhorn on slower tunes and the piercing cornet on faster numbers. He and Jefferson soon achieved a rare rapport that allowed them to shadow and counterpoint each other's lines even as they were being invented.

The first Columbia album (which added Joe Henderson to the quintet) was the impressive *Rosewood,* but it was soon eclipsed by the dazzling live album *Stepping Stones,* which illustrates how quickly the quintet was improving as a unit. In 1979 came the high point of Shaw's entire career, *Woody III,* which expands the quintet to a 12-piece ensemble for a three-part autobiographical suite and then uses various small combos for three more originals. Shaw's writing and arranging were never stronger than here, where he constructed massed, Mingus-like horn harmonies over hard-charging bop rhythms.

He never achieved that level again, though he continued to make good music. *For Sure* experiments with strings, voices and Latin flavors with mixed results, but it does welcome Bartz and Turre back into the Shaw camp. The

Stepping Stones lineup was gone by the time *United* appeared in 1981; Turre and Bartz provide excellent solos, but the session lacks the organic cohesiveness of the landmark late-'70s recordings.

Some of that unity was back on *Lotus Flower,* which features Shaw's working band of the time (Turre, bassist Stafford James, drummer Tony Reedus and pianist Mulgrew Miller) rethinking some of his best compositions.

The same quintet joined Bobby Hutcherson for two respectable releases, *Master of the Art* and *Night Music,* but Shaw was no longer writing much new music and seemed to be recycling his past. *Double Take,* a duo album with Hubbard, is devoted to standards (now available on the Blue Note *Freddie Hubbard and Woody Shaw Sessions* disc), as are *Solid* and *Imagination. Lausanne 1977* and *Time Is Right* are poorly recorded European concerts, but *In My Own Sweet Way* is a well-recorded, well-played 1987 Swiss session with Shaw and a pickup band playing mostly standards.

Shaw was legally blind and needed thick glasses to get around. In 1989, on his way to a memorial service for Roy Eldridge in New York, he fell off a subway platform and had his arm severed by an oncoming train. He died a few months later, never having enjoyed the recognition and remuneration his achievements deserved. — G.H.

GEORGE SHEARING

★★½ **George Shearing and the Montgomery Brothers (1961; Original Jazz Classics, 1989)**
★★★ **Jazz Moments (1962; Capitol, 1995)**
★★★ **Nat "King" Cole Sings/George Shearing Plays (1962; Capitol, 1991)**
★★★ **Blues Alley Jazz (Concord Jazz, 1980)**
★★★ **Two for the Road (Concord Jazz, 1980)**
★★½ **On a Clear Day (Concord Jazz, 1980)**
★★★ **Alone Together (Concord Jazz, 1981)**
★★★ **First Edition (Concord Jazz, 1982)**
★★★½ **An Evening with George Shearing and Mel Tormé (Concord Jazz, 1982)**
★★★ **Live at the Cafe Carlyle (Concord Jazz, 1984)**
★★★ **Grand Piano (Concord Jazz, 1985)**
★★½ **George Shearing and Barry Tuckwell Play the Music of Cole Porter (Concord Concerto, 1986)**
★★★ **More Grand Piano (Concord Jazz, 1987)**
★★ **Breakin' Out (Concord Jazz, 1987)**
★★★ **Dexterity (Concord Jazz, 1988)**
★★★ **The Spirit of 176 (Concord Jazz, 1989)**
★★★ **In Dixieland (Concord Jazz, 1989)**
★★★ **Piano (Concord Jazz, 1990)**
★★ **Mel and George "Do" World War II (with Mel Tormé) (Concord Jazz, 1991)**
★★★ **I Hear a Rhapsody: Live at the Blue Note (Telarc, 1992)**
★★★½ **Midnight on Cloud 69 (Savoy, 1993)**
★★ **My Ship (Verve, 1994)**
★★★ **That Shearing Sound (Telarc, 1994)**
★★★ **Walkin': Live at the Blue Note (Telarc, 1995)**
★★★ **The Best of George Shearing (Capitol, 1995)**
★★★ **The Best of George Shearing, Vol. 2 (Capitol, 1997)**
★★★ **Favorite Things (Telarc, 1997)**

Throughout most of his career, London-born pianist George Shearing (b. 1919) has demonstrated outstanding technique and worked as a fine accompanist to a wide range of vocalists from popular and cabaret music to jazz, including Cleo Laine, Nat King Cole, Billy Eckstine, Abbey Lincoln, Nancy Wilson and Ernestine Anderson. Some of his best work was backing up Mel Tormé and is rated in that entry.

Blind from birth, Shearing took stylistic cues from a variety of sources from Fats Waller to Herbie Nichols and developed a locked-hands approach to playing that became his trademark. He also composed the jazz standard "Lullaby of Birdland." While *Midnight on Cloud 69* compiles Shearing experimenting with bop on the same disc with such leading lights of the music as Charles Mingus, Red Norvo and Tal Farlow, he went on to make the popular but lighter-weight recording with the Montgomery Brothers and the even more pop-oriented fare of the Capitol recordings.

In the 1980s Shearing found the perfect home at Concord, where he made the recordings with Tormé as well as the solo *Grand Piano* sessions and collaborations with bassists Brian Torff

(*Blues Alley Jazz* and *On a Clear Day*) and Don Thompson (*Live at the Cafe Carlyle*), pianists Hank Jones (*The Spirit of 176*) and Marian McPartland (*Alone Together*), guitarist Jim Hall (*First Edition*) and vocalist Carmen McRae (*Two for the Road*).

Shearing remained a vital force well into his '70s, as the group recordings on Telarc document. *I Hear a Rhapsody* and *Walkin'* are live recordings from a 1992 engagement at the Blue Note in New York. The trio setting features bassist Neil Swainson and drummer Grady Tate. *That Shearing Sound* is a return to his classic quintet format with a front line of piano, vibes and guitar. Shearing plays solo on *Favorite Things.* — J.S.

KENNY WAYNE SHEPHERD

★★★ **Ledbetter Heights (Giant, 1995)**
★★★½ **Trouble Is . . . (Revolution/Warner Bros., 1997)**

Childhood guitar prodigy Kenny Wayne Shepherd (b. 1977) reveals his immense debt to Stevie Ray Vaughan on his solid debut recording, *Ledbetter Heights.* His high-energy, smooth-lined blues-rock playing has made the Shreveport native a popular figure on the Louisiana club circuit, including New Orleans, where he made his public debut as a 13-year-old sitting in with guitarist Bryan Lee. Shepherd expands on his strengths with *Trouble Is . . .* backed by Stevie Ray's own Double Trouble band and featuring a guest harmonica cameo from James Cotton. Shepherd shines on a high-energy cover of the Jimi Hendrix barnburner "I Don't Live Today." — J.S.

ARCHIE SHEPP

★★★★ **Four for Trane (1965; Impulse!, 1997)**
★★★★ **Fire Music (1965; Impulse!, 1995)**
★★★★ **On This Night (1966; Impulse!, 1993)**
★★★★½ **Mama Too Tight (Impulse!, 1967)**
★★★½ **The Magic of Ju-Ju (Impulse!, 1967)**
★★★★ **Live at the Donaueschingen Music Festival (MPS, 1967)**
★★★ **Attica Blues (Impulse!, 1972)**
★★★½ **There's a Trumpet in My Soul (Freedom, 1975)**
★★★ **A Sea of Faces (Black Saint, 1975)**
★★★ **Montreux One (Freedom, 1976)**
★★★ **Steam (1977; Enja, 1987)**
★★★½ **Green Dolphin Street (Denon, 1977)**
★★★½ **Trouble in Mind (SteepleChase, 1980)**
★★★★ **Looking at Bird (SteepleChase, 1980)**
★★★ **Down Home New York (Soul Note, 1984)**
★★★ **Little Red Moon (Soul Note, 1985)**
★★★ **California Meeting: Live "On Broadway" (Soul Note, 1987)**
★★★ **The Rising Sun Collection (Just a Memory, 1994)**

Playing alto and soprano but chiefly tenor sax, Archie Shepp (b. 1937) came to the fore in the '60s alongside John Coltrane, Don Cherry, Cecil Taylor and other representatives of a new, freer jazz that soared beyond the rhythmic and melodic tropes of the tradition. Influenced in the breadth of his tone by Sonny Rollins, Shepp played with abundant energy—his style was marked, however, by an occasional idiosyncratic, delicate romanticism (on *Live at the Donaueschingen Music Festival* he segues from free, intense blowing into a take on "The Shadow of Your Smile"). *Four for Trane,* Shepp's Impulse! debut, captures the characteristic deliberate rawness of his approach; *Fire Music* finds him exploring Duke Ellington; *On This Night,* a powerful quintet set, teams him felicitously with Bobby Hutcherson on vibes; *Mama Too Tight* incorporates R&B maneuvers; the drum-crazed *Magic of Ju-Ju* mines African music and reveals a wicked sense of humor—all of these albums flourish Shepp's dazzlingly eclectic approach. Adamantly political, he uses the orchestral idiom to examine the Attica prison riots in *Attica Blues;* with Semenya McCord on vocals, *There's a Trumpet in My Soul* continues to reflect Shepp's world-music interests—he tackles sambas and other Brazilian forms. More recently, he's turned his attention back to earlier jazz and bop; *Looking at Bird* is an excellent Charlie Parker set. — P.E.

JOHNNY SHINES

★★★½ **Masters of Modern Blues (1967; Testament, 1994)**
★★★½ **Johnny Shines with Big Walter Horton (1969; Testament, 1995)**
★★★ **Standing at the Crossroads (1971; Testament, 1995)**
★★★★ **Hey Ba-Ba-Re-Bop (1979; Rounder, 1992)**
★★★★½ **Johnny Shines and Robert Lockwood (Paula, 1991)**

★★★½ Back to the Country (Blind Pig, 1991)
★★★★ Johnny Shines (Hightone, 1991)
★★★★½ Traditional Delta Blues (Biograph, 1991)
★★★★ Mr. Cover Shaker (Biograph, 1992)

Too often considered a mere disciple of Robert Johnson, Johnny Shines (1915–1992) deserves greater recognition. Although Johnson influenced his playing, Shines didn't limit himself to Johnson's style of blues, continually reinventing himself by bringing contemporary sounds into his music and calling on the techniques of other country-blues musicians. After traveling with Johnson from 1935 to 1937, Shines moved north, cutting some of the first postwar Chicago-blues sides. He then released a number of quality singles on Chess and JOB, the latter now available on the shared title with Robert Lockwood compiled by Paula. Poor sales of the original recordings caused Shines to quit playing until his "rediscovery" in the mid-'60s.

Masters of Modern Blues, Shines's return to the studio, showcases his fine ensemble work in the classic Chicago style, with Big Walter Horton on harp, Otis Spann playing piano and Fred Below on drums. In addition to outtakes from these sessions, *Johnny Shines with Big Walter Horton* presents his 1969 recordings with Luther Allison, which feature bass-heavy arrangements and funky guitar work.

With the solo acoustic *Standing at the Crossroads,* recorded in '70, Shines returned to Robert Johnson's style; overall, it's his least moving work. That same year, however, he recorded the Hightone album that masterfully mixes stellar soul blues with solo acoustic numbers striking in their structural simplicity, vocal power and rhythmic drive.

Shines's new solo acoustic approach sparkled even brighter on the live record *Hey Ba-Ba-Re-Bop!* and a fantastic collection of country-blues standards, *Traditional Delta Blues,* both of which proved that Howlin' Wolf and Charley Patton had as much of an effect on Shines's music as Robert Johnson did.

On *Back to the Country* Shines sticks to vocals in the company of Snooky Pryor on harmonica and vocals and John Nicholas and Kent Du Shane on guitars. *Mr. Cover Shaker* features six worthwhile solo tracks from the sessions that yielded *Traditional Delta Blues* and seven songs recorded in '74 with Dave Bromberg's band, ranging from acoustic numbers to horn-driven blues and soulful ballads.

Though a stroke in 1980 slowed him, Shines continued to play until his death in 1992, leaving behind a satisfying legacy of adventurous music. — J.S.

MATTHEW SHIPP

★★½ Circular Temple (1990; Infinite Zero, 1994)
★★★ Zo (with William Parker) (1993; 2.13.61/Thirsty Ear, 1997)
★★★★ Critical Mass (1994; 2.13.61/Thirsty Ear, 1996)
★★★½ Symbol Systems (No More, 1995)
★★ 2-Z (with Roscoe Mitchell) (2.13.61/Thirsty Ear, 1996)
★★★★ Prism (Brinkman, 1996)

One of the most exciting musicians to emerge in the '90s, pianist Matthew Shipp (b. 1959) is a leading light among a group of like-minded New York–based improvisational players (including William Parker, David S. Ware and William Hooker) who play so-called "punk jazz." Rather than a fusion of the genres, Shipp's music is like punk in its ferocious intensity and purity of emotion. His style is so punishing that his hands are sometimes bloody at the end of a performance.

Sounding like a cross between Cecil Taylor, Bud Powell and "Blue" Gene Tyranny, Shipp leads his trio (Parker on bass and Whit Dickey on drums) through *Circular Temple*'s four-part composition, which ranges from foreboding massed chords and speedy glissandos ("Circular Temple #1") to fractured bop ("Circular Temple #2 [Monk's Nightmare]"). At times the music feels unfocused as Shipp tries to get too many ideas across at once.

A duo with bassist William Parker, *Zo* is filled with hyperactive nervous energy. Shipp occasionally allows a snippet of melody to surface in his improvisations, only to be dissected and splintered in the roiling maelstrom. In Parker and Shipp's hands, Gershwin's "Summertime" becomes less a paean to the season's languid ease than an evocation of the humid tension preceding a storm.

Critical Mass takes place in the storm's center: With the addition of violinist Mat Maneri, Shipp explodes his sound, placing the bass on the low end and violin on the high, with his piano and Dickey's drums mapping out and holding down a very broad center. Probably his most cohesive work to date, *Critical Mass* demonstrates a maturity to Shipp's playing not previously heard.

Though the solo pieces on *Symbol Systems* might seem a step back after *Critical Mass,* they actually permit Shipp to explore his more introspective side. There's a playfulness at work on songs such as "Clocks" and "Dance of the Blue Atoms"; "Bop Abyss" and "Algebraic Boogie" allow Shipp to pay homage to the styles of Thelonious Monk and Bud Powell.

Shipp collaborated with saxophonist Roscoe Mitchell on *2-Z,* his least distinctive recording. Out of deference or design, Shipp lays back on the majority of tracks, allowing Mitchell to call the shots. While Mitchell is an interesting player, Shipp sounds restrained and the album lacks the laserlike focus of *Critical Mass.*

Prism, a live recording of a 1993 trio date, is especially impressive, with Dickey taking charge of "Prism I," his liquid yet insistent drumming pushing Shipp and Parker into new territory. On "Prism II," Shipp's playing takes on a conversational tone, moving from damped, whispered bass notes into longer, graceful phrases that eventually turn into an attention-grabbing sheet of passionate chords. — S.M.

WAYNE SHORTER

★★★★ **JuJu (1964; Blue Note, 1996)**
★★★★ **Night Dreamer (1964; Blue Note, 1990)**
★★★★★ **Speak No Evil (1965; Blue Note, 1990)**
★★★½ **The Soothsayer (1965, Blue Note, 1990)**
★★★★ **The All Seeing Eye (1966; Blue Note, 1988)**
★★★★★ **Adam's Apple (1967; Blue Note, 1995)**
★★★★★ **Schizophrenia (1967; Blue Note, 1995)**
★★★½ **Super Nova (1969; Blue Note, 1988)**
★★★½ **Moto Grosso Feio (1970; One Way, 1993)**
★★★★★ **Native Dancer (1975; Columbia/Legacy, 1996)**
★★★½ **Etcetera (1980; Blue Note, 1995)**
★★ **Atlantis (1985; Columbia/Legacy, 1995)**
★★ **Phantom Navigator (Columbia/Legacy, 1987)**
★★★★ **The Best of Wayne Shorter (Blue Note, 1988)**
★★½ **High Life (Verve, 1995)**
★★★ **This Is Jazz 19 (Columbia/Legacy, 1996)**
★★½ **1 + 1 (with Herbie Hancock) (Verve, 1997)**
★★★★ **Jazz Profile (Blue Note, 1997)**
★★★ **Wayne Shorter (GNP Crescendo, N.A.)**

Wayne Shorter (b. 1933) must be acknowledged as one of the most important jazz musicians to emerge in the 1960s. A stunning saxophonist at ease on both tenor and soprano, Shorter in his career mastered hard bop, abstract jazz and jazz-rock fusion. In the 1960s Shorter was a vital member of Art Blakey's Jazz Messengers and several Miles Davis ensembles, including Davis's most influential quintet. Along with Joe Zawinul, Shorter cofounded the pioneer fusion band Weather Report.

Born in Newark, New Jersey, Shorter moved to Manhattan in the mid-1950s before serving a quick stint in the Army. By the late '50s, he had worked with Horace Silver and joined Maynard Ferguson's band, where he first played with Zawinul. With a tenor sound that drew influence from both John Coltrane and Sonny Rollins, Shorter was still developing his style when he became a member of Art Blakey's Jazz Messengers.

As Blakey's musical director from 1959 until 1963, Shorter was known for his forceful tenor playing and excellent compositional skills. His early recordings as a leader display his hard-bop playing, mirroring his work with Art Blakey. The GNP Crescendo reissue consists of some of his Vee-Jay recordings from this time. Though not as fulfilling as his Jazz Messengers work, it showcases his formidable abilities on the sax.

Shorter recorded aggressively as a leader (for Blue Note) while fulfilling his duties with Blakey and again with Miles Davis from 1964 until 1969. *JuJu* and *Night Dreamer* display Shorter as an evocative composer and a dynamic soloist with strong support from Coltrane sidemen McCoy Tyner and Elvin Jones. Subtly veering into progressive, postbop terrain, *Etcetera* (recorded in '65) reveals Shorter still under the influence of Coltrane but also evolving into a consummate ensemble player.

With *Speak No Evil* Shorter steps up and delivers his best, most uncompromising effort. Along with former Messengers mate Freddie Hubbard on trumpet and again showcasing Jones on drums, Shorter is joined by two of his partners from the Miles Davis Quintet, Herbie Hancock on piano and Ron Carter on bass. Featuring some of his finest compositions, Shorter and Hubbard explore advanced harmonic constructions while the inventive rhythm section plays some of the freer interactions permitted at that time.

The Soothsayer retains the services of Hubbard and Carter and features the uncanny drumming of Tony Williams. Shorter expanded his traditional quintet with the addition of James Spaulding on alto.

Shorter continues his flirtation with the avant-garde and once again expands his ensemble, this time to an octet, for *The All Seeing Eye.* With Grachan Moncur III on trombone and Joe Chambers attacking the drum kit, this is as energetic and challenging as any of Shorter's recordings and not to be missed. He pares things down to a quartet on *Adam's Apple.* Hancock's sensitive accompaniment and the telepathic interplay between bassist Reggie Workman and drummer Joe Chambers offset Shorter's tour de force of saxophone virtuosity.

In complete control of his instrument, Shorter struts and churns with a sextet of the usual suspects on *Schizophrenia.* By this time, there was no question as to the refined nature of Shorter's writing or his wisdom as a bandleader. Years with both Blakey and Davis had honed Shorter's skills to an unprecedented degree of musicianship and professionalism.

Both *Super Nova* and *Moto Grosso Feio* parallel Shorter's creative work with Miles Davis on seminal fusion albums like *In a Silent Way* and *Bitches Brew.* While Shorter unveils the soprano-sax stylings that would become synonymous with the Weather Report sound, bold new players like John McLaughlin, Chick Corea (on drums, vibes and marimba), Dave Holland and Jack DeJohnette also make important appearances. These complex recordings have held up well over the years and reveal a logical step in Shorter's musical development.

Shorter's emphasis on jazz-rock fusion makes *Native Dancer* that much more surprising. With its delicate embrace of Brazilian music and the American debut of singer Milton Nascimento, Shorter presents us with his final classic: His soprano playing was never better, and the vocal performances are particularly moving. *Native Dancer* is an album of understated beauty and gentle introspection, a true classic.

Shorter seemed to write less and less as he became consumed with Weather Report—nearly a full decade passed before he would record again as a leader. Unfortunately, *Atlantis* and *Phantom Navigator* both fall short of the quality expected. Immersed in the funk grooves of latter-day Weather Report and leaning more on the Synclavier, saccharine melodies and unnecessary vocals, *Atlantis* is a well-played, sophisticated bore. Although a bit more hard-driving, *Phantom* is equally underwhelming.

Still more fusion, *High Life* adds strings, reeds and horns, giving some depth, but the music is too slick to be deemed more than a passing fancy. — M.M.

HORACE SILVER

★★★★ **Spotlight on Drums (with Art Blakey and Sabu) (1953; Blue Note, 1989)**
★★★★★ **Horace Silver and the Jazz Messengers (1955; Blue Note, 1990)**
★★★★ **Six Pieces of Silver (1956; Blue Note, 1988)**
★★★★ **Blowin' the Blues Away (1960; Blue Note, 1987)**
★★★★ **Horace-Scope (1960; Blue Note, 1990)**
★★★★ **The Tokyo Blues (1962; Blue Note, 1996)**
★★★★ **Silver's Serenade (1963; Blue Note, 1998)**
★★★★ **Song for My Father (1965; Blue Note, 1990)**
★★★ **The Cape Verdean Blues (Blue Note, 1966)**
★★★ **The Jody Grind (1967; Blue Note, 1991)**
★★★★ **The Best of Horace Silver, Vol. 1 (Blue Note, 1988)**
★★★★ **The Best of Horace Silver, Vol. 2 (Blue Note, 1989)**
★★ **It's Got to Be Funky (Columbia, 1993)**
★★ **Pencil Packin' Papa (Columbia, 1994)**
★★★ **The Hardbop Grandpop (Impulse!, 1996)**
★★★ **Re-Entry (32 Jazz, 1996)**
★★★ **Further Explorations of the Horace Silver Quintet (Blue Note, 1997)**
★★★ **Jazz Profile (Blue Note, 1997)**
★★★ **Prescription for the Blues (Impulse!, 1997)**

Along with the work of Art Blakey and maybe one or two other musicians, the prime recordings of pianist Horace Silver (b. 1928) have come to epitomize the hard-bop movement that first blossomed in the late '50s. Born in

Connecticut, Silver was enlisted as a sideman in 1950 by the great saxophonist Stan Getz. While clearly influenced by the bop scene in general and pianist Bud Powell in particular, Silver also injected a healthy amount of blues and gospel references into his passionate playing. The net result of Silver's particular fusion is a widely imitated style that was described at the time as "soulful" or "funky" jazz.

After playing with Getz, Silver recorded some trio dates. Stretching out on his first session as a leader, *Spotlight on Drums* displays an energetic young Silver armed with a number of stylish compositions ("Opus de Funk") and invigorated by an extremely responsive rhythm section of Blakey (drums) and Sabu (congas).

Silver's next recording date would mark the beginning of a great jazz institution. While Blakey had used the name of the Jazz Messengers a few times in the late '40s, *Horace Silver and the Jazz Messengers* crystallized an archetypal instrumentation for many hard-bop ensembles and provided Blakey with a moniker for the ages. With the rhythm section of bass, drums and piano along with a simple front line of trumpet and saxophone, Silver and Blakey created a musical blueprint that both men would employ for decades. Featuring the strong solo/unison voices of trumpeter Kenny Dorham and tenor player Hank Mobley, Silver minted his funky compositions like "The Preacher" and "Doodlin'" and would go on to inspire countless gutbucket imitators.

After recording with Blakey, Silver left the Jazz Messengers but continued to maintain a series of small groups with very similar instrumentation. *Six Pieces of Silver* and *Blowin' the Blues Away* show the next two versions of the Horace Silver Quintet, both at the top of their fiery game. *Six Pieces* once again features the strong playing of tenor man Mobley, only this time it is Donald Byrd next to him on trumpet. *Blowin'* introduces the durable trumpet-and-tenor tandem of Blue Mitchell and Junior Cook. This great session also features Silver playing a couple of trio numbers with bassist Gene Taylor and drummer Louis Hayes. While he was never one of the greatest hard-bop soloists, Silver had clearly developed into an influential composer and bandleader.

While Horace Silver recorded for Blue Note for almost 30 years, a large number of his better albums on this label remain out of print. Still, available classics like *The Tokyo Blues* and *Song for My Father* are wholly representative of Silver as he went swinging into the '60s using his experience of touring Japan as a compositional context. *Tokyo* shows Silver enjoying one of his more stable quintets. Mitchell and Cook remain in place, each stepping forward with some hot soloing. "Song for My Father" is probably Silver's most famous composition (the piano introduction was even used by Steely Dan on "Rikki Don't Lose That Number") and continues to display him working with quality sidemen and great tunes.

While the rest of his '60s output is fairly consistent, the fixed structure of his ensemble's instrumentation on top of constant personnel changes results in a more generic sound—none stands out as exceptional or particularly different in terms of Silver's content or style.

In the 1970s Silver, tired of the instrumental format he had used so extensively, began to experiment with vocals as well as sessions featuring percussion and brass. His "United States of the Mind" series is long out of print and probably best forgotten. In the 1980s Silver released several interesting discs on his own Silveto label; these are now difficult to locate.

The 1990s found Silver eager for a major-label comeback and putting out discs with mixed results. *It's Got to Be Funky* and *Pencil Packin' Papa* are overproduced affairs that pale in comparison with his best work. There are flashes of the timeless Silver sound amid these updated grooves, but they ultimately fail to satisfy in spite of some all-star assistance by talented folks like Eddie Harris and Branford Marsalis.

The Hardbop Grandpop fares slightly better than the other recent releases and can be considered a move back to form. Remarkably, Silver seems to have regained some of the musical fire that he had been missing for decades. — M.M.

NINA SIMONE

★★★★	**At the Village Gate (1961; Blue Note, 1991)**
★★★	**Broadway—Blues—Ballads (1964; Verve, 1993)**
★★★★	**The Best of Nina Simone (1969; Verve, N.A.)**
★★★★	**The Best of Nina Simone (1970; RCA, 1989)**
★★★½	**Baltimore (1978; CTI, 1995)**
★★★½	**Let It Be Me (Verve, 1987)**
★★★★	**Don't Let Me Be Misunderstood (Mercury, 1988)**

★★★½ **Compact Jazz (Verve, 1989)**
★★★★ **In Concert/I Put a Spell on You (Verve, 1990)**
★★★★ **Pastel Blues/Let It All Out (Verve, 1990)**
★★★★ **Wild Is the Wind/High Priestess of Soul (Verve, 1990)**
★★★★ **The Blues (Novus, 1991)**
★★★½ **A Single Woman (Elektra, 1993)**
★★★★ **The Best of Nina Simone (Blue Note, 1993)**
★★★★ **The Essential Nina Simone (RCA, 1993)**
★★★½ **The Essential Nina Simone, Vol. 2 (RCA, 1994)**
★★★ **Live at Ronnie Scott's (DRG, 1994)**
★★★½ **The Rising Sun Collection (Just a Memory, 1994)**
★★★★ **The Tomato Collection (Tomato, 1994)**
★★★★ **Verve Jazz Masters 17 (Verve, 1994)**
★★★ **Porgy (LaserLight, 1995)**
★★★ **Live! (LaserLight, 1995)**
★★★★ **After Hours (Verve, 1995)**
★★★½ **Verve Jazz Masters 58: Nina Simone Sings Nina Simone (Verve, 1996)**
★★★½ **Anthology: The Colpix Years (Rhino, 1996)**
★★★ **Saga of the Good Life and Hard Times (RCA, 1997)**
★★★★ **The Ultimate Nina Simone (Verve, 1997)**

Dubbed the "High Priestess of Soul," Nina Simone (b. 1933) draws upon all manner of music—deep blues, jazz, traditional ballads, African songs, folk and pop. The angry political statement ("Mississippi Goddam," eulogizing civil rights martyr Medgar Evers, "Four Women," a black-power manifesto), the soulfully interpreted standard (the Gershwins' "I Loves You, Porgy," for which she won a gold record in 1959), the R&B wailer ("I Put a Spell on You") and the pop hit (the Bee Gees' "To Love Somebody") all are part of her repertoire. A skillful, understated pianist, she's also an inventive arranger; virtually all of her covers transform the originals into music more elegant, leaner, more haunting.

As a vocalist, Simone swings with a nearly austere finesse—her trademark is authority. Many of her individual albums are hard to find, but she's been served well by compilations—the Verve, RCA and Tomato discs are all outstanding. The Verve *Best of Nina Simone* concentrates on her mid-'60s material (she charted with "I Put a Spell on You" and "Don't Let Me Be Misunderstood"); the RCA *Best of Nina Simone* features cool takes on gems by George Gershwin, Bob Dylan, Leonard Cohen and Jimmy Webb. The concert set *Let It Be Me* is also exceptional, with Simone's gruff-graceful delivery taking on a more assertive edge.

The best intro to her work, though, is Novus's *The Blues:* With such ace musicians as drummer Bernard Purdie and guitarist Eric Gale, she essays Dylan's "I Shall Be Released" and Hoyt Axton's "The Pusher," sets Langston Hughes's "Backlash Blues" to music and, accompanied only by herself on piano, delivers one of her strongest performances with "Nobody's Fault but Mine." *After Hours,* a distillation of her seven late-'60s and '70s albums for Philips, is terrific—in both a trio setting ("Wild Is the Wind") or solo at the piano ("Don't Smoke in Bed"), she stuns.

While Simone sat out the early '80s, her reemergence finds her in fine form. *The Rising Sun Collection* is a spare reworking of her early, tough stuff; with *A Single Woman,* her first new set in more than a decade, she manages to wring from standards—and even Rod McKuen—stark, fresh passion. — P.E.

ZOOT SIMS

★★★★ **Zoot Sims Quartets (1951; Original Jazz Classics, 1992)**
★★★ **Morning Fun (1956; Black Lion, 1990)**
★★★ **That Old Feeling (1956; Chess, 1996)**
★★★ **The Rare Dawn Sessions (1956; Biograph, 1994)**
★★★ **Zoot! (1957; Original Jazz Classics, 1991)**
★★★ **Either Way (1961; Evidence, 1992)**
★★★★★ **Body and Soul (with Al Cohn) (1973; 32 Jazz, 1988)**
★★★ **Zoot Sims and the Gershwin Brothers (1975; Original Jazz Classics, N.A.)**
★★★★ **Zoot Sims Plays Soprano (1976; Original Jazz Classics, 1996)**
★★★ **Hawthorne Nights (1977; Original Jazz Classics, 1995)**
★★★★★ **If I'm Lucky (with Jimmy Rowles) (1977; Original Jazz Classics, 1992)**
★★★ **For Lady Day (1978; Pablo, 1991)**

★★★★★ **Warm Tenor (with Jimmy Rowles) (1978; Pablo, N.A.)**
★★★ **Just Friends (with Harry "Sweets" Edison) (1978; Original Jazz Classics, 1991)**
★★★★ **The Swinger (1980; Original Jazz Classics, 1995)**
★★★½ **Zoot Sims Plays Duke Ellington (1980; Original Jazz Classics, 1997)**
★★★ **Art 'n' Zoot (with Art Pepper) (1981; Pablo, 1995)**
★★★ **Blues for Two (with Joe Pass) (1982; Original Jazz Classics, 1991)**
★★★ **The Innocent Years (1982; Original Jazz Classics, 1995)**
★★★ **On the Korner (1983; Pablo, 1994)**
★★★★ **Suddenly It's Spring (1983; Original Jazz Classics, 1992)**
★★★ **Zoot Sims Plays Johnny Mandel: Quietly There (1984; Original Jazz Classics, 1993)**
★★★ **Somebody Loves Me (LaserLight, 1996)**
★★★ **The Best of Zoot Sims (Pablo, N.A.)**

A consummate mainstream saxophonist, Zoot Sims (1925–1985) embodied a marvelous combination of restraint and virility, the intensity of his up-tempo blowing matched only by the emotional depth of his ballads. One of the original Four Brothers in the Woody Herman big band of the '40s, Sims had an infatuation with Lester Young that is evident throughout his early sessions as a leader.

Sims evolved into one of the most dependable musicians of the '50s and '60s—any recording from this period is marked by his warm-toned yet tenacious blowing. Still, his playing reached a heightened maturity in the next two decades. The exceptional *Body and Soul,* a shared date with Sims's occasional tenor partner Al Cohn, has some particularly fine playing from Sims on both tenor and soprano. Signing with Pablo in the '70s, Sims found growing public exposure. *Warm Tenor* and *If I'm Lucky* are glorious recordings with superior support from pianist Jimmy Rowles and bassist George Mraz; all other sessions featuring Rowles are recommended listening. The Pablo recordings (reissued as Original Jazz Classics), which find Sims in a variety of settings, are consistently thoughtful and well produced. Seek out his late-career masterwork, the out-of-print *In a Sentimental Mood,* with bassist Red Mitchell, rich with Sims's expressive balladering. — S.F.

FRANK SINATRA

★★★★ **Swing and Dance with Frank Sinatra (1950; Columbia/Legacy, 1996)**
★★★★★ **Songs for Young Lovers/Swing Easy (1954/1955; Capitol, 1998)**
★★★★★ **In the Wee Small Hours (1955; Capitol, 1998)**
★★★★★ **Songs for Swingin' Lovers (1956; Capitol, 1998)**
★★★★★ **A Swingin' Affair! (1957; Capitol, 1998)**
★★★★★ **Where Are You (1957; Capitol, 1998)**
★★★★★ **Come Fly with Me (1958; Capitol, 1998)**
★★★★★ **Only the Lonely (1958; Capitol, 1998)**
★★★★★ **Come Dance with Me! (1959; Capitol, 1998)**
★★★★ **No One Cares (1959; Capitol, 1991)**
★★★★★ **Nice 'n' Easy (1960; Capitol, 1998)**
★★★★½ **Sinatra's Swingin' Session (1961; Capitol, 1998)**
★★★½ **Ring-a-Ding Ding! (1961; Reprise, 1998)**
★★★★ **Come Swing with Me! (1961; Capitol, 1998)**
★★★½ **Sinatra Swings (1961; Reprise, 1989)**
★★★½ **I Remember Tommy (1961; Reprise, 1998)**
★★½ **Sinatra and Strings (1962; Reprise, 1998)**
★★½ **Sinatra and Swingin' Brass (1962; Reprise, 1998)**
★★½ **Point of No Return (1962; Capitol, 1991)**
★★★★★ **Sinatra and Basie (1962; Reprise, 1990)**
★★★½ **Sinatra's Sinatra (1963; Reprise, 1991)**
★★ **Days of Wine and Roses, Moon River and Other Academy Award Winners (1964; Reprise, 1989)**
★★★★ **It Might as Well Be Swing (1964; Reprise, 1998)**
★★★★★ **September of My Years (1965; Reprise, 1998)**
★★★★★ **Sinatra—A Man and His Music (1965; Reprise, 1998)**
★★★★ **Strangers in the Night (1966; Reprise, 1998)**

★★★★ **Sinatra at the Sands (with Count Basie and His Orchestra) (1966; Reprise, 1998)**
★★★★ **Francis Albert Sinatra and Antonio Carlos Jobim (1967; Reprise, 1998)**
★★★★ **Francis A. Sinatra and Edward K. Ellington (1967; Reprise, 1998)**
★★★★ **Frank Sinatra's Greatest Hits, Vol. 1 (1968; Reprise, 1998)**
★★ **My Way (1969; Reprise, 1990)**
★★★ **Frank Sinatra's Greatest Hits, Vol. 2 (1972; Reprise, 1998)**
★★★½ **Ol' Blue Eyes Is Back (1973; Reprise, 1990)**
★★ **Sinatra—The Main Event Live (1974; Reprise, 1998)**
★★★★ **Trilogy: Past, Present and Future (1980; Reprise, 1998)**
★★★★ **L.A. Is My Lady (1984; Reprise, 1997)**
★★★★½ **Tommy Dorsey/Frank Sinatra: All-Time Greatest Hits, Vol. I (RCA, 1988)**
★★★★½ **Tommy Dorsey/Frank Sinatra: All-Time Greatest Hits, Vol. 2 (RCA, 1988)**
★★★★½ **Tommy Dorsey/Frank Sinatra: All-Time Greatest Hits, Vol. 3 (RCA, 1989)**
★★★★ **Capitol Collectors Series (Capitol, 1989)**
★★★★½ **Tommy Dorsey/Frank Sinatra: All-Time Greatest Hits, Vol. 4 (RCA, 1990)**
★★★★★ **The Capitol Years (Capitol, 1990)**
★★★★½ **The Reprise Collection (Reprise, 1990)**
★★★½ **Very Good Years (Reprise, 1991)**
★★★½ **Concepts (Capitol, 1992)**
★★★★★ **The Best of the Capitol Years (Capitol, 1992)**
★★★½ **Stardust (RCA, 1992)**
★★★★★ **Frank Sinatra: The Columbia Years, 1943–1952: The Complete Recordings (Columbia/Legacy, 1993)**
★★★★★ **The Best of the Columbia Years, 1943–1952 (Columbia/Legacy, 1993)**
★★½ **Frank Sinatra Duets (Capitol, 1993)**
★★★★ **Voice (Columbia/Legacy, 1994)**
★★★★ **The Essence of Frank Sinatra (Columbia/Legacy, 1994)**
★★ **Duets II (Capitol, 1994)**
★★★½ **I'll Be Seeing You (RCA, 1994)**
★★★★ **Song Is You (with Tommy Dorsey) (RCA, 1994)**
★★★½ **Frank Sinatra and Sextet Live in Paris (Reprise, 1994)**
★★★ **My Shining Hour (Drive Archive, 1994)**
★★★ **From the Top (Drive Archive, 1995)**
★★★½ **Sinatra 80th: Live in Concert (Capitol, 1995)**
★★★★ **Sinatra 80th: All the Best (Capitol, 1995)**
★★★½ **Frank Sinatra Sings Select Johnny Mercer (Capitol, 1995)**
★★★½ **Frank Sinatra Sings Select Rodgers and Hart (Capitol, 1995)**
★★★★ **16 Most Requested Songs (Columbia/Legacy, 1995)**
★★★★ **I've Got a Crush on You (Columbia/Legacy, 1995)**
★★★★★ **The Complete Reprise Studio Recordings (1995; Reprise, 1998)**
★★★★ **Everything Happens to Me (Reprise, 1996)**
★★★ **Frank Sinatra Sings the Select Sammy Cahn (Capitol, 1996)**
★★★★★ **The Complete Capitol Singles Collection (Capitol, 1996)**
★★★★ **Greatest Hits (with Tommy Dorsey) (RCA Victor, 1996)**
★★★½ **Sinatra Sings Rodgers and Hammerstein (Columbia/Legacy, 1996)**
★★★ **Live in Australia 1959 (with the Red Norvo Quintet) (Blue Note, 1997)**
★★★★★ **The Very Best of Frank Sinatra (Reprise, 1997)**
★★★★ **Portrait of Sinatra (Columbia/Legacy, 1997)**
★★★★ **Frank Sinatra Sings His Greatest Hits (Columbia/Legacy, 1997)**
★★★★ **Love Songs (with Tommy Dorsey) (RCA Victor, 1997)**

Earning him beyond question his legendary status, Frank Sinatra's (1915–1998) innovation and steady excellence were breathtaking. Himself a student of the sharpest jazz vocalists—divas Billie Holiday and Ella Fitzgerald in particular—he deployed his supple baritone with the cunning of a great jazz horn soloist: Consistently, his phrasing startles. And, gifted at melody and musical improvisation, he revealed almost a poet's sensitivity to language, discovering in the standards of American popular song (Cole Porter, Harold Arlen) fresh richness and in lesser lights (bard manqué Rod McKuen) unexpected depth. Finally, by means of his persona—charming and churlish, an underdog and a powerhouse—the perception of male vocalist was transformed. Here was a tough guy fearless at displaying astonishing vulnerability, a streetwise sentimentalist who stood the comforting model of singer (Nelson Eddy/Bing Crosby) on its ear and instead came across with something more grittily realistic yet infinitely more romantic. With Sinatra, singing loosened up, becoming a conversation in swing.

At first only the special attraction of Tommy Dorsey's orchestra, he so outdistanced his horn-playing mentors that he speeded the end of the big-band era that had brought him fame; after Sinatra (who'd learned much about phrasing from Dorsey's trombone), no instrumentalist would rival a singer as star in pop music. Sinatra's colloquialism, too, helped make American music the world's primary popular form: Before him, the style of mainstream singers had derived from bel canto, music hall and light opera; after Sinatra's attention to his (excellent) drummers and to jazz rhythm, popular music became more essentially grounded in African-American forms.

A good place to begin considering Sinatra's voluminous recording history is his collaboration with Dorsey's swing band: The four RCA Dorsey/Sinatra *All-Time Greatest Hits* compilations feature the voice that drove early-'40s' bobby-soxers crazy at New York's Paramount Theatre. Dorsey's swing band soars, and Sinatra's approach is that of a prodigy: He vocalizes with an almost eerie purity—it's the sound of a singer surprising himself with his skill. The often sappy material is cuddle-up music ("Head on My Pillow," "Shake Down the Stars," both on *Vol. 3*); the youth idol identifies fully with his devotees (who will not desert him but grow with him—later he would become one of pop's few stars to embrace aging, to wrest from a sense of mortality eloquent pathos).

In 1942 Sinatra left Dorsey, and *The Columbia Years* records his next decade (the 4-CD *Best of the Columbia Years* is more manageable than the 12-CD *Columbia Years, 1943–1952: The Complete Recordings*). With arranger/conductor Axel Stordahl crafting lush backdrops of strings and harps, this is Sinatra at his most romantic (and least jazzy), but already he's ahead of the game—the first singer to manipulate the microphone as other players work their horns, he whispers, strains and "talks," and the effective combat of Stordahl's orchestral classicism and Sinatra's saloon smarts yields stirring underlying tension.

The Capitol Years, The Best of the Capitol Years and *The Complete Capitol Singles Collection* find Sinatra coming into his own. Three arrangers—Nelson Riddle, Gordon Jenkins and Billy May—free him not only to swing but to get serious by treating lyrics with an unprecedented attention. On Riddle's *In the Wee Small Hours,* the blithe crooner has been replaced by the ruminative cosmopolitan; Sinatra comes across harder and bluer than ever before. Gordon Jenkins's *Where Are You* is Sinatra as pop Hamlet, anxious and intense. With Billy May's *Come Fly with Me, Come Dance with Me!* and *Come Swing with Me!,* Sinatra's effervescence and casual zest come to the fore; as cocky as his trademark snap-brimmed hat, the songs swing with risky exhilaration. *The Capitol Years* covers the hits, but also necessary are *Songs for Young Lovers, Songs for Swingin' Lovers, Only the Lonely, A Swingin' Affair* and *Nice 'n' Easy.*

Founding Reprise Records in 1961, Sinatra spent the decade working with a remarkable spectrum of arrangers (Riddle, May, Jenkins, Sy Oliver, Don Costa, Neal Hefti, Quincy Jones) and genre giants (jazz legends Duke Ellington and Count Basie, bossa nova artist Antonio Carlos Jobim and Latin-music maestro Eumir Deodato). Among the jazzier highlights are *Sinatra and Basie, It Might as Well Be Swing* and *Sinatra at the Sands* (all arranged by Quincy Jones) and the Jobim collaboration (the Ellington pairing doesn't match the Basie set, but it's fine nonetheless). From the standpoint of musical technique, Sinatra's later-'60s recordings lack the assurance of some of his previous work; if read, however, like a great psychological novel, this stretch of time is rich—by turns tentative, defensive and courageous, he fights the onslaught of rock, and on occasion cagily concedes to it; at times he gives in to self-parody, at others, he sings with a new, wounded wisdom. *The Reprise Collection* is hardly exhaustive in its study of the period, but it's a capable sampler: Its contents comprise a riveting autobiography. *The Very Best of Frank Sinatra* is a more complete overview of this period.

In 1980 Sinatra released his last epic, *Trilogy.* Don Costa's arrangement of "Theme from *New*

York, New York," gave the singer another signature tune to stand alongside "Nancy (with the Laughing Face)," "It Was a Very Good Year," "Strangers in the Night" and "My Way"; Gordon Jenkins provided embarrassing, inflated "Ol'-Blue-Eyes-Is-God" stuff; and Billy May resurrected the swinging '50s. A return to jazz (George Benson, Clark Terry and Lionel Hampton all guest-star), *L.A. Is My Lady* shows Sinatra working hard at swinging—and, in the main, marvelously succeeding.

While undisputedly proving the man's staying power, the *Duets* sets did Sinatra a disservice—pairing him with partners predictable (Liza Minnelli) and bizarre (Bono); they're mainly interesting in that they show how nearly every big-name guest sounds daunted; almost all oversing—a vice this titan never even considered. Offering a final grace note of proof, *Everything Happens to Me* is a nice one-CD intro. Comprising Sinatra's personal favorites of the 450 tunes he recorded for Reprise, it's a treat for Frank-ophiles and neophytes alike. Check how Sinatra often comes in just a bit behind the beat—it's a cool maneuver . . . and the essence of jazz. — P.E.

SUNNYLAND SLIM

★★★★ **Slim's Shout (1960; Original Blues Classics, 1993)**
★★★★ **Blues Anytime! (1964; Evidence, 1994)**
★★★½ **Be Careful How You Vote (1981; Earwig, 1990)**
★★★★ **Sunnyland Train (1983; Evidence, 1995)**
★★★★½ **Chicago Jump (1985; Evidence, 1995)**
★★★½ **House Rent Party (Delmark, 1992)**
★★★★ **Decoration Day (Evidence, 1994)**
★★★½ **Live at the D.C. Blues Society (Mapleshade, 1994)**

Born Albert Luandrew in Mississippi, writer, pianist and vocalist Sunnyland Slim (1907–1995) adopted his stage name in the late 1920s after witnessing the Sunnyland Train—which ran between Memphis and St. Louis—strike and kill two families within the span of a week. Repulsed, he wrote "Sunnyland Train," a song that would become his trademark. He went on to play the blues with virtually every important bluesman in the South, including Little Brother Montgomery, Memphis Slim, Big Walter Horton and Roosevelt Sykes. In the early '40s Slim relocated to Chicago, where he continued his affiliation with blues movers and shakers, namely Big Bill Broonzy, Sonny Boy (John Lee) Williamson, Hubert Sumlin and Muddy Waters. He recorded prolifically, and discographers assert that Slim played on more than 250 sides.

Slim's Shout finds Slim accompanied by a crack quartet that includes tenor saxophonist King Curtis and organist Robert Banks. Included here are such originals as "Sunnyland Special"—a rolling blues with limber solos by Curtis and Banks—and "Harlem Can't Be Heaven." Other standouts include a hiccupping, boogie-woogie reading of Big Joe Turner's "Shake It" and a swinging rendition of Leroy Carr's "Baby How Long." *Blues Anytime!* features a supergroup—Slim, Willie Dixon and Sumlin play in various combinations, and drummer Clifton James completes the ensemble. Recorded in East Berlin, highlights include Slim's "Every Time I Get to Drinking" and "It's You, Baby" and Sumlin's solo acoustic "When I Feel Better."

Compiled from two albums originally issued in the early '80s, *Be Careful How You Vote* includes appearances by a cast of musicians including guitarists Sumlin, Lurrie Bell and Magic Slim. Highlights include "Johnson Machine Gun," which he originally cut with Waters in 1946, and the title track, one of Slim's most poignant topical numbers. Consisting entirely of his solo piano and vocals, *Sunnyland Train* pays tribute to Slim's innovative piano style, which is stripped bare in this setting. Running through a combination of original and cover material, he touches on songs by Bessie Smith ("Backwater Blues"), Roosevelt Sykes ("Unlucky One"), Big Bill Broonzy ("I Feel So Good") and James Oden ("Goin' Down Slow"), among others. *Chicago Jump* spotlights Slim's band of the mid-'80s, an electric quartet of guitar, bass, drums and tenor saxophone. Slim's piano flourishes ice the cake, but he shares the grooves amicably with his combo, whose effortless swing is anchored by drummer Robert Covington. Particular highlights are an up-tempo rendition of Chuck Willis's "I Feel So Bad" and the title track, which is an update of "Bassology," a song Slim recorded in 1953.

House Rent Party collects sides Slim cut in 1949, including nine previously unissued tracks. He's backed by several prominent St. Louis players, including vocalist St. Louis Jimmy, guitarist and singer Jimmy Rogers and pianist, harmonica player and singer Willie Mabon.

Decoration Day is made up of tracks recorded in 1980 and '81 in a variety of locations. On almost every cut Slim is accompanied on blues harp by Carey Bell, whose serrated tone adds bite to his roiling piano figures. Highlights include the stinging original "Past Life" and a spare reading of Elmore James's "Dust My Broom." *Live at the D.C. Blues Society* documents a solo 1987 performance by an 80-year-old Slim, whose singing and piano style—particularly his clear falsetto and methodical left-hand work—are as spry as ever. — B.R.H.

CAROL SLOANE

★★★ Carol Sings (1979; Audiophile, 1985)
★★★★ The Real Thing (Contemporary, 1990)
★★★★★ Heart's Desire (Concord Jazz, 1992)
★★★★½ Sweet & Slow (Concord Jazz, 1993)
★★★★★ When I Look in Your Eyes (Concord Jazz, 1994)
★★★★ The Songs Carmen Sang (Concord Jazz, 1995)
★★★ The Songs Sinatra Sang (Concord Jazz, 1996)
★★★½ The Songs Ella & Louis Sang (with Clark Terry) (Concord Jazz, 1997)

Heavily influenced by the late Carmen McRae, vocalist Carol Sloane (b. 1937) is a no-frills performer who believes the basics are the key to the fine art of jazz singing. As a storyteller, she respects the intended melody, probes lyrics that have a deep meaning and avoids scatting as if it were the plague. Sloane began singing professionally at age 14 with a dance band in her native Providence, Rhode Island. Between 1958 and 1960 she toured with the Les and Larry Elgart Orchestra and temporarily subbed for Annie Ross in Lambert, Hendricks and Ross. The jazz world took notice of her first major festival appearance at Newport in 1961.

Carol Sings is highlighted by her interplay with alto saxophonist Norris Turney on his Johnny Hodges tribute, "Checkered Hat." Sloane's talent is secure, yet her delivery seems incomplete when compared with her consistently excellent 1990s body of work. *The Real Thing* teams her with Phil Woods (on alto sax and clarinet) and an all-star rhythm section. Tenor and flute player Frank Wess, a prime collaborator on *Carol Sings,* returns for the very strong *Sweet & Slow* and her Sinatra-tribute recording. Woods guests again on Sloane's poignant McRae tribute.

Each of these discs showcases the essence of Sloane's musicality: vocal clarity, spellbinding phrasing and, quite often, the sense that she has lived each and every lyric. While on a thematic roll with her back-to-back nods to McRae and Sinatra, Sloane had a much deeper link to McRae and her music, making that session the stronger of the pair. Old friend Clark Terry brings his trumpet and vocal talents to share in a fine update of the classic songbook material of Louis Armstrong and Ella Fitzgerald. — K.F.

BESSIE SMITH

★★★★★ Any Woman's Blues (Columbia, 1970)
★★★★★ The World's Greatest Blues Singer (Columbia, 1971)
★★★★★ Empty Bed Blues (Columbia, 1971)
★★★★★ The Empress (Columbia, 1971)
★★★★★ Nobody's Blues but Mine (Columbia, 1972)
★★★★★ Bessie Smith: The Collection (Columbia, 1989)
★★★★★ The Complete Recordings, Vol. 1 (Columbia/Legacy, 1991)
★★★★★ The Complete Recordings, Vol. 2 (Columbia/Legacy, 1991)
★★★★★ The Complete Recordings, Vol. 3 (Columbia/Legacy, 1992)
★★★★★ The Complete Recordings, Vol. 4 (Columbia/Legacy, 1993)
★★★★★ The Complete Recordings, Vol. 5: The Final Chapter (Columbia/Legacy, 1996)

Unlike numerous other pioneer artists, Bessie Smith (1894–1937) didn't have to wait for the CD revolution to bring some semblance of order to her catalog. In 1970, under the aegis of the late John Hammond, Columbia began releasing double-album sets of her work, and by 1972 almost every song the Empress of the Blues had left behind was back on the market. Come 1989 and the near-total demise of vinyl, yet another reissue program began with *Bessie Smith: The Collection*, a well-annotated overview of Smith's decade-long recording history; a more ambitious project was launched in 1991 with multi-CD boxed sets, five in all, under the rubric *The Complete Recordings,* which is exactly what it claims to be—166 Columbia and Okeh sides—and more.

Born in Chattanooga, Tennessee, Smith began performing on the street and by her late teens was a local star on the strength of her ratings in amateur shows. In 1912 her brother Clarence came through town as a member of the traveling

Moses Stokes minstrel show. Stokes's featured vocalist was Ma Rainey, whose widespread popularity had pretty well destroyed the notion that women couldn't, or shouldn't, sing the sort of hard blues common to male performers on the circuit. Smith joined up with Stokes, but Rainey's influence on the young singer appears to have been minimal. Musicians who were around at that time asserted that Smith already had developed a distinctive individual style that needed no further grooming; if anything, Rainey may have done the good deed of enlightening Smith to the ofttimes nefarious ways of showbiz types.

In 1923 Smith recorded her first sessions for Columbia (published reports exist of her having recorded for the Chicago-based Emerson label in 1921, but none of this work has ever surfaced), with producer Frank Walker, head of the label's race-records division. Her cover of Alberta Hunter's "Downhearted Blues" sold 780,000 copies in its first six months of release and catapulted Smith to headliner status; at the same time, her touring schedule expanded to include dates in Chicago, Detroit and Cleveland, a rarity considering that the black revues' rigorous tour schedules then were confined to the Southern states.

Smith's singing was fueled by rage and anger. Being both black and female—something of a double whammy in those prefeminist, Jim Crow days—she grew up conscious of artificial barriers constructed to prevent her from living a rich life of boundless opportunity. Her fierce passions were expressed tempestuously, thanks to her hair-trigger temper. Numerous tall tales abound of her attacks on others (being physically prepossessing, she seemed to fear no one, male or female), perhaps the most memorable coming on the occasion when she learned of her husband's infidelity and proceeded to trash both their hotel room and him. Deep blues is defined in her voice, in all its dark, brooding mood and chilling, nuanced moans and wails. The text of her songs, and the kinetic performances of them, suggest someone who is nursing deep wounds that may never heal completely.

Throughout the '20s Smith recorded with the best musicians of the era, but it was a fleeting session with Louis Armstrong that has justifiably entered into legend. In 1925, with pianist Fred Longshaw the only other player on the date, they recorded five songs—including a monumental summit of voice and instrument on "St. Louis Blues"—and challenged each other in the way geniuses need to be challenged in order to bring out their best. Theirs is one of the great conversations in blues history, preserved on *The Empress*, *The Collection* and on *Vol. 2* of *The Complete Recordings.*

Vol. 3 covers the years 1925–1928, when Smith was at the peak of her interpretive powers, her writing was at its sharpest and her recordings were instant classics ("I'd Rather Be Dead and Buried in My Grave," "Send Me to the 'Lectric Chair," "Muddy Water [A Mississippi Moan]" and "Backwater Blues" among the many standouts here). On *Vol. 4* the arc is still ascending in the years 1928–1931, when the material takes a revealing but disturbing personal turn in its bluest moments, offering a glimpse into the artist's tormented offstage life. "Me and My Gin," "Shipwreck Blues," "Empty Bed Blues" (parts one and two), "Nobody Knows You When You're Down and Out" and "I've Got What It Takes (But It Breaks My Heart to Give It Away)" tell a story as intimate and revealing as any artist has offered in this century.

The Depression upended Smith's career, although she continued to record into 1933, with her final sides being for Columbia subsidiary Okeh, a label that had rejected her 10 years earlier for being "too rough." These, along with her final Columbia sessions, are on *Vol. 5* and demonstrate an artist in transition. Still a magnet for top-drawer musicians, Smith was backed on the Okeh sides by the remarkable Buck Washington band, whose members included Washington on piano, Frank Newton on trumpet, Jack Teagarden on trombone, Chu Berry on tenor sax, Bobby Johnson on guitar, Billy Taylor on bass and, on the romping "Gimme a Pigfoot," a barely audible Benny Goodman on clarinet. At this stage of her career Smith isn't abandoning the blues, but she is moving away from the relentlessly downbeat, moaning approach that was her stock in trade in earlier years. Still direct and commanding, she adopts a lighter tone and a more jocular approach to her tales of romantic skullduggery, as if shrugging off her bad luck instead of railing against it. Behind her the band settles into a brisk pace that sets up some exciting solos, such as Newton's trilling trumpet turn and Washington's loping, lazy interjection on "Do Your Duty," a lighthearted, double-entendre scolding of a feckless lover. In fact, much of the Okeh material is of the wink-and-a-nudge variety, with Smith laughing and growling her way through risqué scenes such as those described in "Gimme a Pigfoot" and in the stark, steamy "Need a Little Sugar in My Bowl," one of her last Columbia recordings and a memorable one, with pianist Clarence Williams providing the sole, spare bit of instrumental accompaniment. For a little added oomph, *Vol. 5* also includes a disc containing a 70-minute interview with Smith's niece Ruby Smith, who recounts memories of her Aunt Bessie's life, some of them loving, some comical, some profane, some harrowing, all riveting.

Smith's legend endured, darkly, after she was fatally injured in a car wreck in Mississippi in 1937 and Hammond published an article in *Down Beat* in which he claimed, without any documentation to support his theory, that a white hospital's refusal to treat Smith led to her demise. So powerful was the cultural pull of this myth that Pulitzer Prize–winning playwright Edward Albee would reimagine it in his 1959 play *The Death of Bessie Smith.* The booklet accompanying *Vol. 5* settles this question by reprinting recollections from a 1971 interview with the doctor who found Smith's broken body on the side of the road and a letter from the doctor who treated Smith at Clarksdale's black hospital where, he writes, "we gave her every medical attention, but we were never able to rally her from the shock." Bessie Smith's death was a tragedy that didn't need John Hammond's outrageous fabrication to make it more heartbreaking. Focus, instead, on what remains—namely, her recordings. Resonant, stirring, troubling, electrifying, the art of Bessie Smith is a national treasure. — D.M.

BYTHER SMITH

★★★½ **Blues Knights (with Larry Davis) (1986; Evidence, 1994)**
★★★★ **Housefire (Bullseye Blues, 1991)**
★★★★ **I'm a Mad Man (Bullseye Blues, 1993)**
★★★★½ **Mississippi Kid (Delmark, 1996)**

Cousin to J.B. Lenoir, Byther "Smitty" Smith (b. 1932) is a straight-ahead, third-generation Chicago bluesman with a stinging, authoritative guitar style and a penchant for highly original and autobiographical songwriting. Having been tutored in a series of blues, R&B and gospel outfits, Smith first gained recognition in Europe in the early '80s.

Blues Knights catches him in full maturity while touring France in 1985 on a double bill with Larry Davis. With a stellar Chicago band, including guitarist Maurice John Vaughn and saxophonist A.C. Reed, Smith explores a range of textures and rhythms including reworkings of Sonny Boy Williamson's (Rice Miller) "Don't Start Me Talkin'" and Otis Rush's "Double Trouble" (recast as "Addressing the Nation with the Blues"). *Housefire,* another European production, showcases his full blues range, from slow numbers ("Live On and Sing the Blues") and funk excursions ("Martha Dear") to the soulful, begging-for-mercy vocals of "The Man Wants Me Dead." A bonus is an updated version of Detroit Junior's "Money Tree." *I'm a Mad Man* finds him in a Southern-soul setting, propelled by the Memphis Horns and a crack blues rhythm outfit led by organist Ron Levy. The title tune bristles with bad intent; Smith slides on "Get Outta My Way"; and "35 Long Years" is a slow-drag blues workout with suitably tasteful, understated guitar work.

Mississippi Kid is Smith's most focused, autobiographical title yet, retaining a larger horns-and-rhythm sound with a new Chicago-based backing group, the Night Riders. Retaining a requisite rough edge to his brand of the blues, this album finds him comfortable in his craft, building tight, moving portraits of his life. Stellar songs—the slow blues "White Robe," the roll-and-tumble rocker "Runnin' to New Orleans" and "Cora, You Made a Man out of Me," with its happy soul preaching—make this a standout. — A.K.

CARRIE SMITH

★★★½ **Confessin' the Blues (1977; Evidence, 1993)**
★★★½ **Every Now and Then (Silver Shadow, 1993)**

With her voluptuous alto, Carrie Smith (b. 1941) has spent her life singing gospel, blues, jazz and R&B. All these influences are evident—though jazz predominates—on the ebullient *Confessin' the Blues,* a compendium of tracks recorded in Toulouse and Miraval Studio, France; and Barcelona. *Every Now and Then* presents Smith's repertoire of jazz and R&B standards.
— H.G.-W.

CECILIA SMITH

★★★ **The Takeoff (Brownstone, 1993)**
★★★½ **CSQ, Vol. II (Brownstone, 1995)**
★★★ **High Standards (Brownstone, 1996)**
★★★½ **Leave No Stone Unturned (Brownstone, 1997)**

Ohio native Cecilia Smith (b. 1960) first made her mark as a vibes player on the Boston jazz scene before moving to New York in the early

1990s. She takes a hard-swing approach that shows the stylistic influence of vibist Bobby Hutcherson and guitarist Wes Montgomery. In addition to performing with her own band, she subs occasionally in the Spirit of Life Ensemble and works as a community music educator.

The Takeoff is a quartet session with pianist Frank Wilkins, drummer Ron Savage and bassist Lonnie Plaxico. The follow-up, *CSQ, Vol. II,* teams her with Wilkins, Savage, bassist Steve Kirby and saxophonist Billy Pierce. Javon Jackson joins Pierce in the reed section for Smith's wide-ranging *High Standards,* which also features guitar and vocals on two tracks. Trumpeter Cecil Bridgewater and saxophonists Gary Bartz and Greg Osby help fuel Smith's musical fire on *Leave No Stone Unturned,* a blend of standards and originals. — K.F.

JABBO SMITH

★★★★½ **1929–1938 (Challenge, 1997)**

Trumpeter/vocalist Cladys "Jabbo" Smith (1908–1991) was an important but sparsely recorded early jazz star who rivaled the young Louis Armstrong for his trumpet pyrotechnics. Born in Pembroke, Georgia, Smith also had in common with Armstrong an institutionalized childhood, growing up in Jenkins Orphanage in Charleston, South Carolina. He honed his skills as an entertainer early, made his reputation as the main soloist in the Erskine Tate band in the 1920s and recorded with Duke Ellington, banjo player Ikey Robinson and Fats Waller and the Louisiana Sugar Babes before leading his own groups.

Smith was not reluctant to take on Armstrong's Hot Fives, as the material on *1929–1938* demonstrates. His high-wire solos take impossible turns, while his relentless swing and creative scat and blues singing make you wish there was more of this unique talent preserved on record. In live performance he was a major force in jazz for years to come but remains relatively undocumented. — J.S.

JIMMY SMITH

★★★★ **The Sermon (1958; Blue Note, 1987)**
★★★ **Open House/Plain Talk (1960; Blue Note, 1992)**
★★★ **Midnight Special (1960; Blue Note, 1989)**
★★★ **Crazy! Baby (1960; Blue Note, 1989)**
★★★ **Back at the Chicken Shack (1960; Blue Note, 1985)**
★★★ **Bashin': The Unpredictable Jimmy Smith (1962; Verve, 1995)**
★★★ **I'm Movin' On (1963; Blue Note, 1995)**
★★★ **Prayer Meetin' (1963; Blue Note, 1988)**
★★★ **Any Number Can Win (1963; Blue Note, 1998)**
★★★★ **The Cat (1964; Verve, 1998)**
★★★★ **Organ Grinder Swing (1965; Verve, N.A.)**
★★★ **The Dynamic Duo (with Wes Montgomery) (1966; Verve, N.A.)**
★★★½ **Off the Top (Elektra Musician, 1982)**
★★ **Go for Whatcha Know (1986; Blue Note, 1996)**
★★★★ **Compact Jazz (Verve, 1987)**
★★★½ **Jimmy Smith Plays the Blues (Verve, 1988)**
★★★★ **The Best of Jimmy Smith (the Blue Note Years) (Blue Note, 1988)**
★★★½ **Prime Time (Milestone, 1989)**
★★★★ **Fourmost (Milestone, 1991)**
★★★ **The Cat Strikes Again (LaserLight, 1991)**
★★★½ **Sum Serious Blues (Milestone, 1993)**
★★★ **The Master (Blue Note, 1994)**
★★★ **Verve Jazz Masters 29 (Verve, 1994)**
★★★ **Jazz 'Round Midnight (Verve, 1994)**
★★★ **Damn! (Verve, 1995)**
★★★★ **Walk on the Wild Side: Best of the Verve Years (Verve, 1995)**
★★★ **Talkin' Verve: The Roots of Acid Jazz (Verve, 1996)**
★★★½ **Angel Eyes (Verve, 1996)**
★★★ **En Concert (RTE, 1996)**
★★★★ **All the Way Live (Milestone, 1996)**
★★★½ **Home Cookin' (Blue Note, 1996)**
★★★½ **The Master II (Blue Note, 1997)**
★★★½ **Jazz Profile (Blue Note, 1997)**
★★★½ **New Sound—New Star (Verve, 1997)**
★★★½ **Got My Mojo Workin'/Hoochie Coochie Man (Verve, 1997)**

The master of the Hammond B-3 organ sound in jazz, keyboardist Jimmy Smith (b. 1925) floored the New York jazz community during an engagement at the Cafe Bohemia in early 1956 and recorded his classic "The Preacher" for Blue Note around the same time. His soaring, hard-driving organ playing in a freewheeling trio format revolutionized that instrument's position in jazz. Behind him came a phalanx of organ combos, a style that became a staple of the black-nightclub circuit across the country. Smith was a pioneer of the soul-jazz scene, mightily influenced R&B arrangements, virtually invented the funk keyboard style and had a profound, if little understood, effect on 1960s and early-'70s rock bands, which used the B-3 extensively. From Memphis to London, Jimmy Smith was showing the way. It's not surprising that he resurfaced in the '90s as a prime target of samplers in the groove-oriented world of acid jazz.

Both of Smith's parents were pianists, and he was a child prodigy, playing in the Philadelphia area before he was a teenager. He studied bass and piano formally and gigged as a piano player before switching to organ. By the time Smith began leading his own trio in 1955, he had developed a revolutionary sound that bore little relation to the organ's history in the hands of Fats Waller and Count Basie, making a wild leap off the style of Wild Bill Davis. In addition to his dexterity with single-line improvisation and held notes, his raging swing and passion for the blues, Smith had a unique left-hand and foot-pedal technique that allowed him to be the bass player and chordal accompanist to his right-handed soloing—a one-man band.

From the late 1950s through early 1963 Smith was a featured member of the Blue Note cast, blowing up a storm with Art Blakey, Lee Morgan, Jackie McLean, Lou Donaldson and Curtis Fuller. Smith was his own bass player, so his combos included either Blakey or Donald Bailey on drums backing Smith and whatever brass player he was tackling at the moment. Blue Note's haphazard attitude toward these sessions leaves several great titles unavailable (although the timeless *Sermon* is in print), making *The Best of Jimmy Smith* essential.

Smith carried Verve through the rest of the '60s with some soulful work, including the epochal party record *Organ Grinder Swing*. By the '70s, he was a huge international star, recording in a variety of contexts, from all-ballad sessions to big-band material with Oliver Nelson arrangements. He went into semiretirement in the mid-'70s, opening a club in Los Angeles where he would sit in whenever the spirit struck him. By the '80s, he was back in full swing. *All the Way Live* is a terrific session matching Smith against the electrifying Eddie Harris on tenor, with Kenny Dixon refereeing on drums.

For the rest of the '80s, Smith knocked around from label to label, often making substandard recordings, particularly *Go for Whatcha Know,* a lousy comeback effort. *Off the Top* is the best release from this period, a live recording with Smith playing organ and synthesizer in an all-star lineup that includes guitarist George Benson, bassist Ron Carter, drummer Grady Tate and tenor saxophonist Stanley Turrentine. It wasn't until he made his way back to the music-friendly Milestone label that Smith found himself in the pocket again. *Prime Time* is a spirited return to form, and *Fourmost* is a hot live recording from the now-defunct New York nightclub Fat Tuesday's featuring Turrentine on tenor, Kenny Burrell on guitar and Tate on drums (plus one vocal). *Sum Serious Blues* is a full-band date featuring a six-piece horn section led by trombonist George Bohannon. More than 40 years after his ear-opening debut, Smith is still capable of playing the B-3 with unparalleled virtuosity. — J.S.

LEO SMITH

★★★★½ Divine Love (ECM, 1978)
★★★★ Mass on the World (Moers, 1978)
★★★★ Spirit Catcher (Nessa, 1979)
★★★★½ Go in Numbers (1980; Black Saint, 1993)
★★★★ Rastafari (Sackville, 1985)
★★★★½ Kulture Jazz (ECM, 1994)

Trumpeter Leo Smith (b. 1941) has a startlingly original conception that expands on experiments inspired by Miles Davis and Lester Bowie. Using a personally devised notation system he calls "ahkreanvention," Smith tries to combine elements of composed music and improvisation simultaneously. A devout Rastafarian who obviously feels an affinity for reggae rhythms, Smith is also well grounded in the blues, an influence he picked up from his father, Mississippi blues singer Alex "Little Bill" Wallace.

Go in Numbers is a hot live performance from the Kitchen in New York. *Kulture Jazz* utilizes all the elements in Smith's repertoire on an omnibus tour through blues and jazz history, with a country blues played on the kora and tributes to Billie Holiday and John Coltrane.

One of Smith's most impressive stylistic achievements is *Divine Love,* which features the remarkable "Tastalun," an ahkreanvention for three muted trumpets with Lester Bowie and Kenny Wheeler joining Smith. Other worthwhile imports include the live *Mass on*

the World; Spirit Catcher, a quintet recording (except for "The Burning of Stones," which features a second trumpet and strings); and an interesting drummerless session, *Rastafari.*
— J.S.

DR. LONNIE SMITH

★★★★ **Think (1968; Blue Note, 1988)**
★★★½ **Drives (1970; Blue Note, N.A.)**
★★★★ **Afro Blue (MusicMasters, 1993)**
★★★ **Foxy Lady: A Tribute to Hendrix (MusicMasters, 1994)**
★★★ **Purple Haze: A Tribute to Jimi Hendrix (MusicMasters, 1996)**
★★★★ **Afrodesia (LaserLight, 1996)**

Organist Dr. Lonnie Smith (b. ca. 1945) was an acknowledged master of the Hammond B-3 sound dating back to his work with the George Benson quartet; he has gone on to perform frequently with Lou Donaldson and to lead his own group. *Think* is an acid-jazz staple that features the hard-grooving guitar work of Melvin Sparks, trumpeter Lee Morgan and tenor saxophonist David Newman. Smith virtually disappeared as a leader during the 1980s before resurfacing with the brilliant *Afro Blue,* a hot trio session with guitarist John Abercrombie and drummer Marvin "Smitty" Smith. The two Hendrix tribute albums don't live up to their possibilities but *Afrodesia,* with guitarist George Benson and saxophonist Joe Lovano, is a white-hot groove. — J.S.

LONNIE LISTON SMITH

★★★½ **Cosmic Funk (1974; Flying Dutchman, 1995)**
★★★★ **Expansions (1975; Flying Dutchman, 1995)**
★★★½ **Visions of a New World (1975; Flying Dutchman, 1995)**
★★★★½ **Golden Dreams (1976; RCA Bluebird, 1992)**

Keyboardist Lonnie Liston Smith (b. 1940) grew up in Richmond, Virginia, under the influence of his gospel-singing father, who was a member of the Harmonizing Four for more than 40 years. He played with vocalist Betty Carter from 1963 to 1964, and from there he worked with Rahsaan Roland Kirk (*Here Comes the Whistleman*), Art Blakey, Joe Williams, Leon Thomas (*Spirits Known and Unknown*), Gato Barbieri (several classics including *Under Fire*) and Miles Davis (*On the Corner* and *Big Fun*) and was a key member of the Pharoah Sanders group from '69 to '71 before forming his own group, the Cosmic Echoes. His powerful, running style never lost the touch of gospel soul he grew up with, but his band's sound moved toward more overtly electrified, fusion excursions with increasingly mixed results. *Reflections of a Golden Dream* and *Astral Traveling,* long out of print, have been reissued (minus two tracks from *Astral Traveling*) as *Golden Dreams. Cosmic Funk* links Smith's vision with similar moves from George Clinton's progressive funk band of the same era. *Expansions* and *Visions of a New World* meld an Afrocentric world-music foundation with a utopian science-fiction theme that clearly inspires the band's performance.
— J.S.

WILLIE "THE LION" SMITH

★★★★ **1925–1937 (Classics, N.A.)**
★★★★ **1935–1937 (Classics, N.A.)**
★★★★ **1937–1938 (Classics, N.A.)**
★★★★ **1938–1940 (Classics, N.A.)**
★★★ **Pork and Beans (Black Lion, 1966)**

William Henry Joseph Bonaparte Bertholoff "Willie the Lion" Smith (1897–1973) was a jazz original who reigned as one of the baddest stride-piano players during the '20s and '30s heyday of Harlem's run as the jazz capital of the world. Duke Ellington cited Smith as a prime influence on his own playing, and his rhythmic inventions were not lost on the receptive ears of Thelonious Monk either. Smith's later work is still good but lacks some of the wild spirit of the 1920s and 1930s material on the Classics discs. There are a number of other Smith recordings that never made it to CD, and his out-of-print autobiography, *Music on My Mind: The Memoirs of an American Pianist,* is worth searching out. — J.S.

CHRIS SMITHER

★★★★ **It Ain't Easy (1984; Genes, 1989)**
★★★ **Another Way to Find You (Flying Fish, 1991)**
★★★½ **Happier Blue (Flying Fish, 1993)**
★★★½ **Up on the Lowdown (Hightone, 1995)**
★★★★ **Small Revelations (Hightone, 1997)**

Honing a synthesis of folk and blues for more than 25 years, Chris Smither (b. 1944) has quietly achieved a quasimythic status as an outstanding musician and composer. His first three albums—1970's *I'm a Stranger Too!,* 1972's *Don't It Drag On* (both out of print) and a 1973 unreleased LP, *Honeysuckle Dog,* featuring Lowell George and Maria Muldaur—

introduced Smither's dazzling facility on guitar and gruff, soulful voice. Smither's only '80s release, *It Ain't Easy,* originally on Adelphi in 1984, consists solely of his vocals and solo acoustic guitar performing three originals and several classic blues covers, including a doleful reading of Howlin' Wolf's "Sittin' on Top of the World" as well as "John Hurt Medley," a deft amalgamation of the legendary bluesman's canon, notably "Pay Day" and "Richland Woman Blues."

Another Way to Find You is likewise a solo acoustic effort, though not as accomplished as its predecessor. Recorded in late 1989 before an audience in a Boston studio, the album's material draws from Smither's earlier Poppy output, which feels ponderous in a live setting. There is little levity to counterbalance the weighty subject matter of originals like "Lonely Time" and "Don't It Drag On." The only notable exception is the virile, up-tempo "Love You Like a Man," a Smither song Bonnie Raitt made well known. His renditions of Elizabeth Cotten's "Shake Sugaree" and Blind Willie McTell's "Statesboro Blues" contribute to the album's rueful aura.

Happier Blue is both a terrific return to form and a departure. While it contains some of Smither's best writing to date, it also introduces a band (including saxophone and violin) to back his guitar and flesh out the arrangements. The combination yields Smither's most optimistic-sounding album, though the title track's lyrics seem to question the attitudinal shift ("I don't care what you say/Maybe I was happier blue"). Interspersed with songs by John Hiatt, J.J. Cale and Lowell George are several stellar Smither originals such as "Already Gone (Flatfoot Blues)" and "Mail Order Mystics," a song that John Mayall turned into a high-energy rave-up on his 1993 album *Wake Up Call.*

Up on the Lowdown, recorded in Austin, Texas, and produced by noted guitarist Stephen Bruton, also features a band, but it's instrumentally pared down in comparison with the flowery flourishes earmarking *Happier Blue.* This rootsy return serves Smither's style well, particularly on such sharp compositions as the title track, "Link of Chain" and "Bittersweet." His self-assured "I Am the Ride" exudes a confidence and a basic truth that can only be grasped through experience.

The Bruton-produced *Small Revelations* is a landmark Smither recording. It contains seven originals, including the tunefully pensive "Cave Man," the melancholy "Slow Surprise" and "Hook, Line and Sinker," a ragtime ditty featuring fine piano work by Riley Osbourne. Also included here are Smither's inspired versions of Elmore James's "Dust My Broom," Brownie McGhee's "Sportin' Life" and Jesse Winchester's "Thanks to You." — B.R.H.

MARTIAL SOLAL

★★★★ **Bluesine (Soul Note, 1989)**
★★★★ **Triangle (JMS, 1995)**

Born to French parents in Algeria in 1927, pianist Martial Solal was hailed as one of the greats by critics during the early '60s, but his low profile ensured virtual anonymity among U.S. record buyers. Gifted with amazing technical dexterity and harmonic knowledge, Solal is a highly cerebral player, which accounts for his occasional associations with Lee Konitz. Early Solal can be heard on Sidney Bechet's *When a Soprano Meets a Piano. Bluesine* is an excellent solo recital, while *Triangle* finds Solal alongside bassist Marc Johnson and drummer Peter Erskine. Solal's European work with his '60s trio and his big-band work are worth looking for as imports; and hear his score for Jean-Luc Godard's *Breathless.* — S.F.

JAMES SOLBERG

★★★★ **See That My Grave Is Kept Clean (Atomic Theory, 1995)**
★★★★ **One of These Days (Atomic Theory, 1996)**

Best known for his long association with Luther Allison, Milwaukee-area guitarist, vocalist and songwriter James Solberg (b. ca. 1950) is a formidable talent in his own right. His voice is all smoke and grit, but he sings feelingly and to good effect. He brings his touch to a wide variety of material on both albums, doing originals and new arrangements of old songs, and his guitar work truly shines on deep, spooky numbers like "Jimmy's Blues," "Bad Love," which he coauthored with Allison, "St. James Infirmary Blues" (from *Grave*) and "Litehouse Keeper" (from *One of These Days*). The arrangements are tight, and Mike Vlahakis's keyboard playing really shines. — J.Z.

SOUL REBELS

★★★★ **Let Your Mind Be Free (Mardi Gras, 1995)**
★★★★½ **No More Parades (Tuff City, 1998)**

The next step in New Orleans brass bands, the Soul Rebels have been opening eyes and ears at

Donna's, the hottest brass-band club in New Orleans. Snare drummer Lumar LeBlanc raps a steady stream, while Derrick J. Moss backs him up on bass drum. Damion Francois sings, then bleats the beats on tuba. Curtis Watson Jr. anchors the vocals and plays trumpet alongside Mervin Campbell, who doubles on flügelhorn. Steve and Ronell Johnson duel on trombones. William Terry is a triple threat on baritone, tenor and soprano saxophones, and Byron Bernard also plays tenor. *Let Your Mind Be Free* is a magical, high-spirited statement of purpose. The band throws down the gauntlet on *No More Parades,* a startling move that makes the Soul Rebels the Public Enemy of brass bands.
— J.S.

OTIS SPANN

★★★½ **The Blues Never Die! (1965; Prestige, 1990)**
★★★★ **Down to Earth: The Bluesway Recordings (1966/1967; MCA, 1995)**
★★★½ **Cryin' Time (Vanguard, 1969)**
★★★ **Bluesmasters (with Muddy Waters) (Tomato, 1995)**

In his abbreviated but important career, Jackson, Mississippi, native Otis Spann (1930–1970) played an integral part in defining the hard-edged, urban-blues sound as the pianist in Muddy Waters's powerhouse band in the '50s and '60s and in session work for virtually all of the stellar blues and rock & roll artists in Chess Records's employ. With Waters he was the epitome of versatility, staying discreetly and solidly in the background while Waters and Little Walter (and, later, James Cotton) wailed away on guitar and harmonica, and then stepping out to raise the intensity level a couple of notches with his tasty, right-hand glissandos and chromatic runs. With Waters he can be heard on all of the legendary Chess recordings and is captured in a live setting backing the blues master on a 1953 European date on Tomato's *Collaboration.*

Spann began his solo career while he was still working with Waters and others at Chess. Recording for the Candid label in 1960, he delivered a remarkable duet album, *Walking the Blues,* with Robert Jr. Lockwood. In 1963 the Storyville label brought him into a Copenhagen studio to beget *Otis Spann* out of sessions featuring a special guest appearance by Lonnie Johnson, and a year later British Decca released another long-player on which Spann was backed by Waters and Eric Clapton. Both the Candid and Storyville albums remain available as imports.

Stateside, Spann's most productive affiliation was with the Prestige label. 1965's *The Blues Never Die!* features Spann on piano throughout its 11 cuts and on vocals for 5 of those tracks. His impeccable keyboard work always overshadowed his singing, but here his personable voice is at its most engaging. Spann and his band mates—who include James Cotton on harmonica and vocals and a guitarist whose *nom de disque* of "Dirty Rivers" hardly disguises the identity of the fellow fashioning the slashing lead-guitar lines heard on several songs—blow red hot and blue through some Cotton originals and offer up rousing interpretations of Elmore James's "Dust My Broom" and Willie Dixon's "I'm Ready."

Muddy Waters's lively shuffle "Popcorn Man" opens Spann's first album for ABC-Bluesway, 1966's *The Blues Is Where It's At,* and signals the start of a festive session of slow, grinding blues and stomping rave-ups performed before an appreciative studio audience. Among the surprises here is a churning, dark-hued tale of love and jealousy, "Brand New House," written and originally recorded by Bobby Darin (!) and keyed here by guitarist Sammy Lawhorn's stinging exclamations and George Smith's foreboding, vibrato-rich wails on harmonica. Elsewhere, Waters himself contributes some razor-sharp slide licks to energize Spann's weary reading of a Waters original, "My Home Is in the Delta," and Spann the pianist takes center stage on a mellow instrumental closer, "Spann Blues," offering up some angular variations on a familiar blues theme and setting up the various instrumentalists for their solo turns.

The Blues Is Where It's At is now packaged with Spann's second Bluesway album, *The Bottom of the Blues,* on *Down to Earth: The Bluesway Recordings.* One of the consistent delights of this outing is the muscular, emotional harmonica support lent by George "Mojo" Buford blowing tender and wistful on aching laments such as Muddy Waters's "Look Like Twins," or hot and gritty when the mood gets lighthearted. Spann's wife, Lucille, makes a couple of outstanding turns here as well, engaging her husband in a sassy duet à la Carla Thomas and Otis Redding on "I'm a Fool" and lending some no-nonsense testifying in a supporting role on "Shimmy Baby." As if to make a point, Spann closes the album with

"Nobody Knows" and "Doctor Blues," which seem designed to stand as definitive stylistic statements of late-'60s Chicago blues. The former is a turgid slow blues, with Spann and Buford adding a sense of urgency in their instrumental sparring; the latter explodes off its launching pad on the strength of Spann's hammering attack, then settles into a driving groove over which Spann delivers an exhortatory vocal decrying his downcast state of affairs, as guitarist Sammy Lawhorn constructs terse, angular solos throughout.

Spann's last stop as a solo artist was with Vanguard, for which he cut the bristling collection of songs released in 1969 as *Cryin' Time.* In guitarists Barry Melton (of Country Joe and the Fish) and Luther Johnson, bassist Jos Davidson and drummer Lonnie Taylor, Spann had a band that could bring the fire on the boogie-oriented numbers and get down and dirty on slow grinders, with Spann himself turning in some exemplary performances on piano, particularly on the four-minute "Blues Is a Botheration," which affords him a variety of solo approaches as its mood shifts. Of note here is the title track, an instrumental featuring Spann working out on an organ, his left hand comping chords as the right constructs elegant, complex solo passages built on rapidly executed glissandos, legato phrases and trilling ostinatos. Lucille Spann turns up again, most movingly on the traditional "Blind Man," where her stirring gospel inflections suggest a personal involvement with the text's account of a man bereft of spiritual guidance. *Cryin' Time* was to have signaled the start of a full-bore effort at a solo career for Spann, who had planned to leave the Waters band. At the moment he was preparing to step out on his own, though, he was diagnosed with cancer. He died at age 40, less than a year after his initial Vanguard effort.
— D.M.

JOSEPH SPENCE

★★★★★ **The Complete Folkways Recordings 1958 (1959; Smithsonian Folkways, 1992)**
★★★★ **Happy All the Time (1964; Hannibal, 1985)**
★★★★ **Bahamian Guitarist: Good Morning Mr. Walker (1972; Arhoolie, 1990)**
★★★½ **Living on the Hallelujah Side (Rounder, 1980)**
★★★ **Glory (Rounder, 1990)**
★★★★ **The Spring of Sixty-Five (Rounder, 1992)**

"Discovered" in 1958 by blues archivist Samuel Charters on the island of Andros in the Bahamas, Joseph Spence (1910–1984) was working as a stonemason. The recordings Charters made that day reveal Spence's guitar mastery and unique style revolving around rhythm and melodic improvisation, influencing Ry Cooder, Taj Mahal and numerous other guitarists. Spence's earliest tracks are documented on *The Complete Folkways Recordings 1958.* Recorded at Andros's Fresh Creek Settlement on July 23, 1958, the album features for the most part religious tunes, including "There Will Be a Happy Meeting in Glory," "Face to Face That I Shall Know Him" and "The Lord Is My Shepherd," among others. Also included are such traditional folk songs as "Brownskin Gal," "Jump in the Line" and "Bimini Gal," all of which highlight Spence's formidable improvisational skills. Often Spence growled his lyrics and melodies (keeping his pipe in his mouth while playing), as illustrated by "Coming in on a Wing and a Prayer," the popular World War II song.

Bahamian Guitarist features 21 tracks recorded in 1971 that display Spence's incomparable skill as a player, as well as his tenuous handle on vocals. Highlights include "Sloop John B.," "Lay Down My Brother (I Bid You Goodnight)" and a song he calls "Will the Serpent Be Unbroken." It's actually the traditional country song called "Will the Circle Be Unbroken," and Spence admits halfway through the rendition that he doesn't know the words. The album's notes accurately credit Spence with "guitar and vocal sounds." *Happy All the Time,* produced by Paul Rothchild, features the spiritual "Out on the Rolling Sea," a classic anthem that Spence recorded for at least three other releases.

Living on the Hallelujah Side comprises live recordings made in Cambridge, Massachusetts, in 1972 and Nassau, Bahamas, in 1978. Though it's often difficult to unravel his vocal patois, Spence's playing speaks for itself. Included is the full spectrum of the guitarist's repertoire, including hymns, dance tunes and old pop songs, such as "Jesus on the Mainline," "When the Saints Go Marching In" and "Goodnight Irene." Also notable are the curiosity piece "Santa Claus Is Comin' to Town" and two songs—"I'll Be a Friend to Jesus" and the title track—that feature a female singer named

Blooming Rosalie Roberts. *Glory* and *The Spring of Sixty-Five,* though recorded 13 years apart, both feature the Pinder Family on vocals. *Glory* was recorded in 1978 and 1980 and includes such fare as "Old Time Religion," "Shake My Hand" and "Rock Daniel," all featuring accompaniment by Edith, Geneva and Raymond Pinder. *The Spring of Sixty-Five,* credited to Joseph Spence and the Pinder Family (who appear on every track), has a heavily spiritual feel. In general, Spence's earlier recordings are superior, but his latter-day efforts also hold treasures to be discovered. — B.R.H.

VICTORIA SPIVEY

★★★½ **Songs We Taught Your Mother (with Alberta Hunter and Lucille Hegamin) (1961; Original Blues Classics, N.A.)**
★★★★ **Idle Hours (with Lonnie Johnson) (1961; Original Blues Classics, 1987)**
★★ **Complete Recorded Works, Vol. 1 (1926–1927) (Document, 1995)**
★★ **Complete Recorded Works, Vol. 2 (1927–1929) (Document, 1995)**
★★ **Complete Recorded Works, Vol. 3 (1929–1936) (Document, 1995)**
★★ **Complete Recorded Works, Vol. 4 (1936–1937) (Document, 1995)**

Victoria Spivey (1906–1976), a.k.a. Jane Lucas, sang classic blues influenced by fellow Texan Blind Lemon Jefferson and in emulation of the legendary Bessie Smith. Spivey was a blues sex symbol of the '20s and went on to perform in a revue with her sisters Addie and Elton Spivey during the '30s, but her records, even with the remarkable guitarist Lonnie Johnson, were inconsistent. Spivey went on to form her own label in the early 1970s, recording local New York artists such as Sugar Blue as well as her own work, which compares favorably with the earlier recordings. Unfortunately the Spivey label is no longer active. — J.S.

SPYRO GYRA

★★ **Spyro Gyra (1978; Amherst, 1994)**
★★½ **Morning Dance (1979; Amherst, 1994)**
★★ **Catching the Sun (1980; Amherst, 1994)**
★★ **Carnaval (1980; Amherst, 1994)**
★★ **Freetime (1981; Amherst, 1994)**
★½ **Incognito (1982; Amherst, 1994)**
★½ **City Kids (1983; Amherst, 1994)**
★★ **Access All Areas (1984; Amherst, 1994)**
★★ **Alternating Currents (1985; Amherst, 1994)**
★½ **Breakout (1986; Amherst, 1994)**
★★ **Stories Without Words (1987; Amherst, 1994)**
★½ **Rites of Summer (1988; GRP, 1996)**
★½ **Point of View (1989; GRP, 1996)**
★★ **Fast Forward (GRP, 1990)**
★★ **Three Wishes (GRP, 1992)**
★★ **Dreams Beyond Control (GRP, 1993)**
★★ **Love and Other Obsessions (GRP, 1995)**
★★ **Heart of the Night (GRP, 1996)**
★★ **20/20 (GRP, 1997)**
★★ **Road Scholars (GRP, 1997)**
★★½ **The Best of Spyro Gyra: The First Ten Years (Amherst, 1997)**

Spyro Gyra has been remarkably consistent over the years, churning out album after album of pleasant but indistinguishable instrumental pop. Although the group's lineup shifts constantly—only saxophonist Jay Beckenstein, keyboardist Tom Schuman and mallet-percussionist Dave Samuels stick it out for all titles—the Spyro Gyra sound offers only the slightest variations: *Freetime* leans somewhat to funk, *Stories Without Words* has a Caribbean bent, *Fast Forward* is more openly influenced by Afro-Cuban rhythms and so on. Otherwise, almost any Spyro Gyra album will offer the same slick fusion grooves, polished ensemble playing and effortless, jazzlike solos.

So why bother? It depends on what you expect from the group. Although Spyro Gyra is a waste of time if what you want is the inspired serendipity of jazz, it does make excellent easy-listening fare. After all, the music is tuneful (particularly the pop-friendly *Morning Dance*), perky, unobtrusive and infinitely hipper than the Living Strings. — J.D.C.

SQUIRREL NUT ZIPPERS

★★★½ **The Inevitable Squirrel Nut Zippers (Mammoth, 1995)**
★★★½ **Hot (Mammoth, 1996)**
★★★½ **Perennial Favorites (Mammoth, 1998)**

Singers Jim Mathus and Katharine Whalen lead the Squirrel Nut Zippers, a cracked rearview vision of 1920s nostalgia filtered through the sensibility of the 1960s as seen from the 1990s. *The Inevitable Squirrel Nut Zippers* consciously evokes the hokum spirit of the brilliant Dan Hicks and His Hot Licks, who were only 30 years too early to cash in on the swing revival. What makes this a good thing is that the SNZ need to play well to pull it off. By the time of *Hot,* the band got its flavor-of-the-week brand from MTV via the video for "Hell," sure to be included on future "One-Hit Wonder" specials. The band proved that such notoriety didn't kill its sense of humor with songs like "Ghost of Stephen Foster" and "Pallin' with Al" on *Perennial Favorites.* — J.S.

JO STAFFORD

★★★ G.I. Jo (Corinthian, 1987)
★★★★ Jo + Jazz (Corinthian, 1987)
★★★★½ Greatest Hits (Corinthian, 1990)
★★★★★ Capitol Collectors Series (Capitol, 1991)
★★★★★ The Portrait Edition (Sony Music Special Products, 1994)

Born and raised in Long Beach, California, in 1917, Jo Stafford possessed a silky, feathery contralto voice and a somewhat emotionally ambiguous approach to a lyric that stand as the hallmarks of one of American popular music's most beguiling stylists. She began her remarkable career singing in a trio with her two older sisters. The Stafford Sisters soon became regulars on Los Angeles radio station KHJ and found their services in demand as background vocalists on recording sessions and in movies. In 1938 Stafford left the trio to join a male vocal septet, which became the Pied Pipers. Having caught the attention of Tommy Dorsey's arrangers, Paul Weston and Axel Stordahl, with their elegant, sophisticated vocal approach, the Pipers were invited to perform on Dorsey's New York–based radio show.

In 1939 Dorsey proffered an invitation to join his band, and the quartet, with Stafford as its lead vocalist, leaped at the opportunity. They were soon joined in the ranks by a new, unproven singer Dorsey held in high regard: Frank Sinatra. Backed by the Pied Pipers on his early recordings, Sinatra became an international sensation. At the same time, Stafford began to take solo spots in the Dorsey show. Her effect on listeners was immediate, and she soon became a major draw on the big-band circuit.

In 1942 songwriter Johnny Mercer founded his own label, Capitol Records, and hired Paul Weston as musical director. A Stafford fan, Mercer made the singer one of his first signings. She joined a stellar artist lineup that included, on the distaff side, Margaret Whiting and Peggy Lee. Beginning in 1944 and continuing through the 1950s, she proved herself more than worthy of a place in this pantheon. In the 1940s she cut 38 Top 20 singles, 10 of them double-sided hits, and twice won *Down Beat* magazine's Most Popular Artist poll. Testimony to her versatility is provided by a cursory glance at the material she plumbed during this era. Traditional popular songs by the great American composers were her meat and potatoes, but her recordings included country songs, Christmas carols, jazz numbers and a stirring reconsideration of some revered folk songs on the now out-of-print album from 1948, *Jo Stafford Sings American Folk Songs,* released in the wake of a Gallup poll that showed her to be the American public's favorite singer. Of her four Number One singles, "You Belong to Me" (1952, for Columbia) occupied the top spot for nine weeks, sold nearly 2 million copies and became, for all intents and purposes, her signature song as well as the definitive version of an oft-recorded standard.

Capitol Collectors Series documents this fruitful period. The material is first-rate, much of it bearing the composer credits of some of the towering figures in American popular music (Jerome Kern, Ira Gershwin, Cole Porter, Jimmy Van Heusen, Rodgers and Hammerstein, Jule Styne, Sammy Cahn and Johnny Mercer), and the performances are uniformly mesmerizing. Stafford's range may have been limited, but she had few peers when it came to inhabiting a song's emotional interior; point of view and character mark her readings.

Stafford left Capitol in 1951, following Weston to Columbia; a year later the two were married. She continued her string of hits through the late '50s, before rock & roll swamped the charts and effectively spelled the end of her generation's hold on American popular culture. Irked by what they considered bad taste in material on the part of Columbia A&R director Mitch Miller, Stafford and Weston created the alter egos of Darlene and Jonathan Edwards, whose playing and singing were purposefully off-key in service of trite material reflecting the new trends in the day's music. Though today they are little noted, the Edwardses released several albums in the late '50s into the early '60s and were moved to emerge yet again in the late '70s to lampoon the cultural folly they saw all around them. By 1960

Stafford and Weston were back at Capitol, although the hits had stopped; as the decade progressed, Stafford gradually receded from the scene, preferring to devote her time to raising her children, although she surfaced periodically on disc with albums for Colpix, RCA Victor, Dot and Sinatra's Reprise. In the '70s Weston and his son by Jo, Tim, founded Corinthian Records with a catalog consisting almost entirely of Stafford's Columbia recordings obtained as part of a settlement when she left the label.

The three-CD boxed set *The Portrait Edition* now stands as the definitive document of the Columbia years, with some of the early Capitol recordings represented, as well as four tracks by Jonathan and Darlene Edwards, among them a hilarious 1979 take on "Stayin' Alive." Her first recording with the Dorsey band is here, 1939's "Little Man with a Candy Cigar," along with gems on the order of a sprightly version of "The Trolley Song" with the Pied Pipers and a good sampling of her many duets with male vocalists, principal among them being those with Frankie Laine and Gordon MacRae, two singers whose muscular style well complements Stafford's wispy but authoritative counterpoint. Of special note here: a version of "Shenandoah," from the 1961 rerecording of the *Jo Stafford Sings American Folk Songs* album for Capitol, all Aaron Copland in its winsome, haunting strings redolent of a place fondly remembered even as it disappears, with Stafford's plaintive lament underscoring the landscape's enduring emotional pull.

The Corinthian albums survey Stafford's output from the '40s and early '50s, so there is some duplication between these titles and the recordings available in the boxed set and on the Capitol collection. Still, the offerings are choice, beginning with, of course, *Greatest Hits,* an essential album. "You Belong to Me" is included, as well as another Number One single from 1954, "Make Love to Me," based on a 1923 jazz instrumental called "Tin Roof Blues." For excellent examples of Stafford's versatility, check out "Jambalaya" and "St. Louis Blues." A gentle treatment of "Stardust" is a breathtaking journey through tenderness and longing, very nearly as compelling as Stafford's ethereal treatment of "I'll Be Seeing You." *Jo + Jazz* teams the singer with some first-rate players of her day, including tenor saxophonist Ben Webster, legendary alto saxophonist Johnny Hodges, trumpeter Ray Nance, former Billie Holiday pianist Jimmy Rowles, drummer Mel Lewis and others, with the superlative songwriter Johnny Mandel serving as arranger and conductor. The interpretations given "What Can I Say After I Say I'm Sorry" and "You'd Be So Nice to Come Home To" are remarkable musical moments, among many on this album. *G.I. Jo* is a collection of songs that were popular during World War II, including "You'll Never Know," "We Mustn't Say Goodbye," "I'll Remember April" and the enduring "I'll Be Seeing You." Whatever the song or the style, Stafford's is a voice that feels like home, one that burrows into your heart and takes up residence, enriching the soul more with every whispered phrase. — D.M.

JEREMY STEIG

★★★★ Something Else (1970; LaserLight, 1996)
★★★½ Outlaws (1976; Enja, 1993)
★★★½ Jigsaw (Triloka, 1992)

Jeremy Steig (b. 1942) is a virtuoso flautist who has expanded the instrument's range both technically and conceptually over a career that has been as influential as it has been underappreciated. In the mid-'60s, after working in a free-jazz context with Paul Bley and Gary Peacock, Steig formed the groundbreaking jazz-rock group Jeremy and the Satyrs, a prefusion touchstone. On *Something Else* Steig fronts an intriguing lineup of Jan Hammer on electric piano, percussionist Don Alias and bassists Eddie Gomez and Gene Perla. He and Gomez perform a series of stunning duets on *Outlaws.* Steig came out of retirement to make *Jigsaw,* a solid small-group session featuring Joe Chambers on drums and LeeAnn Ledgerwood on piano. *Wayfaring Stranger,* an out-of-print Blue Note album, is worth seeking out. — J.S.

LENI STERN

★★★½ Clairvoyant (Passport Jazz, 1985)
★★★ The Next Day (Passport Jazz, 1987)
★★★ Secrets (Enja, 1989)
★★½ Closer to the Light (Enja, 1990)
★★★ Ten Songs (Lipstick, 1992)
★★★ Like One (Lipstick, 1993)
★★½ Words (Lipstick, 1995)
★★★ Separate Cages (with Wayne Krantz) (Alchemy, 1996)
★★★★ Black Guitar (Leni Stern, 1997)

Guitarist Leni Stern is an inspired player whose best qualities have for the most part not been well represented on her recordings. She has twice been awarded the Best Female Jazz Guitarist honor by Gibson Guitars. A child prodigy on piano in her hometown of Munich, Stern (b. Magdalena Thora, 1952—she is married to guitarist Mike Stern) began playing guitar at age 11. She moved to the United States to study at the Berklee College of Music in 1977.

After moving to New York, she formed her own band in 1983 with drummer Paul Motian, guitarist Bill Frisell, bassist Harvie Swartz, pianist Larry Willis and tenor saxophonist Bob Berg. Hiram Bullock sympathetically produced the band's debut, *Clairvoyant.* Frisell did not return for *The Next Day,* which features an unlikely but refreshing fusion version of "Blue Monk" as a duet with Swartz. Otherwise, the originals show off Stern's range more than her chops, leaving ample room for the rest of the band to stretch out.

Secrets employs a three-guitar front line, with Stern's tone taking on a Larry Carlton–like quality contrasted against David Tronzo's incendiary slide work and some extraordinary saxophone playing from Berg. The other guitarist, Wayne Krantz, contributed the smoking title track, which is propelled by Don Alias's fiery percussion. *Closer to the Light* covers similar ground with less energy. David Sanborn plays alto saxophone on a couple of tracks, and Stern shows some expansion in her technique. Krantz's double stops on "All or Nothing" provide the album's highlight.

With many of the same musicians (Goines, Krantz, Chambers, Alias) and others adding their talents, like Badal Roy on Indian percussion, Gil Goldstein on keys and Billy Drewes on soprano sax, *Ten Songs* finds Stern exploring compositionally like she did on her debut but using her expanded chops. Texturally much more interesting than the previous two releases, the album spotlights Stern on Spanish guitar and slide. She leads generously, letting her band have as much of the spotlight as she takes. Both Bob Malach and Drewes cook on their sax parts, and Roy rules the tracks on which he plays.

Stern is the sole guitarist on *Like One,* which features Didier Lockwood on violin. *Words* is a more stripped-down band collaboration with keyboardist Joy Askew. *Separate Cages* reunites Stern and Krantz for an album of guitar duets.

After so many permutations in her musical direction and accompanists, Stern brought her musical vision into sharp focus on the excellent *Black Guitar,* a full-band lineup buoyed by some of Stern's most confident guitar playing and her surprisingly effective singing. — H.B.

MIKE STERN

★★★ **Upside Downside (Atlantic, 1986)**
★★★★ **Time in Place (Atlantic, 1987)**
★★★½ **Jigsaw (Atlantic, 1989)**
★★★★ **Odds or Evens (Atlantic, 1991)**
★★★★ **Standards (and Other Songs) (Atlantic, 1992)**
★★★★ **Is What It Is (Atlantic, 1993)**
★★★★ **Between the Lines (Atlantic, 1996)**
★★★★ **Give and Take (Atlantic, 1997)**

Guitarist Mike Stern (b. 1953) became well known through his featured role in the Miles Davis band of the 1980s. He went on to make a series of strong albums as a leader, and has been a mainstay at the downtown Manhattan jazz club the 55 Bar during the 1990s. *Time in Place* introduces the excellent lineup of Bob Berg on tenor and soprano saxophones, Jim Beard on keyboards, Jeff Andrews on bass and Peter Erskine on drums. Michael Brecker guests on tenor saxophone on *Time in Place* and on an electronic wind instrument on *Jigsaw.* Berg and Beard continue to form the core of Stern's band on *Odds or Evens,* along with percussionist Don Alias and either Anthony Jackson or Lincoln Goines on bass and Dennis Chambers or Ben Perowsky on drums. Stern moves in a more introspective direction on the Gil Goldstein–produced *Standards* (*and Other Songs*), with Randy Brecker guesting on trumpet.

Is What It Is features another great tenor contribution from Michael Brecker in support of a strong group of Stern originals. Beard returns on this album and is also heard on the richly textured *Between the Lines.* On *Give and Take,* a graceful session of standards and originals, Stern is unleashed in a trio format with bassist John Patitucci and drummer Jack DeJohnette. Guest performances are highlighted by a spectacular Brecker on tenor saxophone on the Stern-penned "Hook Up," "One Liners" and "Jones Street." — J.S.

SONNY STITT

★★★★ **Sonny Stitt/Bud Powell/J.J. Johnson (1949; Original Jazz Classics, 1992)**
★★★½ **Kaleidoscope (1950; Original Jazz Classics, 1991)**
★★★½ **Jazz at the Hi-Hat (1954; Roulette, N.A.)**
★★★★ **Sonny Stitt Sits In with the Oscar Peterson Trio (1957; Verve, 1991)**

★★★ Sonny Stitt (1958; Chess, 1990)
★★★ Stitt Meets Brother Jack (1962; Original Jazz Classics, 1992)
★★★★ Stitt Plays Bird (1963; Atlantic, N.A.)
★★★★★ Soul People (with Booker Ervin) (1964; Prestige, N.A.)
★★★★ Endgame Brilliance: Tune-Up!/Constellation (1972; 32 Jazz, 1997)
★★★ The Champ (1973; 32 Jazz, 1998)
★★ Soul Girl (1975; Paula, 1992)
★★★½ The Last Stitt Sessions, Vols. 1 and 2 (Muse, 1982)
★★★½ Soul Classics (Original Jazz Classics, 1988)
★★★ Autumn in New York (Black Lion, 1989)
★★★★ For Musicians Only (with Stan Getz and Dizzy Gillespie) (Verve, 1989)
★★★½ Prestige First Sessions, Vol. 2 (Prestige, 1992)
★★★ Compact Jazz (Verve, 1992)
★★★½ Verve Jazz Masters 50 (Verve, 1995)
★★ Night Letter (Prestige, 1996)
★★ Legends of Acid Jazz (Prestige, 1996)
★★★½ Jazz at the Hi-Hat, Vol. 2 (Roulette, 1996)

Alto, tenor and baritone saxophonist Sonny Stitt (né Edward Stitt, 1924–1982) began his career during the World War II years, a blind spot in jazz history due to a recording ban that confined the revolutionary development of bop to the clubs where it was being developed. Stitt's reputation as an alto player rivaled Charlie Parker's, sparking arguments about the authenticity of Stitt's sound.

Even though it's reasonable to believe Stitt's claim that he had arrived at a protobop style similar to Parker's before he'd ever heard Bird play, by the time Stitt was working in Dizzy Gillespie's band in 1945–46, Parker's shadow was so long that Stitt eventually ended the controversy by switching to tenor and didn't play alto again until after Bird's death in 1955.

Stitt worked profusely as both a sideman and a leader and was a particularly welcome participant in jam sessions such as the Jazz at the Philharmonic series. Only some 10 percent of this enormous legacy survives in print.

Stitt and Gene Ammons co-led a legendary two-tenor group during the early 1950s that has virtually disappeared from history aside from a couple of tracks on *Prestige First Sessions, Vol. 2.* Another Prestige record (now out of print), *Genesis,* has more. Stitt's abilities at the time are well represented, however, in the studio dates *Sonny Stitt/Bud Powell/J.J. Johnson, Kaleidoscope* and the two live quartet recordings *Jazz at the Hi-Hat.*

During the '50s Stitt played with the Jazz at the Philharmonic orchestra and with Gillespie in addition to his own groups. Most of this era's recordings are out of print, but the magnificent *Sonny Stitt Sits In with the Oscar Peterson Trio* documents a very successful meeting. *Verve Jazz Masters 50* is the better of the two Verve compilations.

In the '60s Stitt recorded organ-combo albums, often featuring Jack McDuff, notable for their consistent if interchangeable intensity. He may have set a record during this era for releasing albums with the word *soul* in the title, and his high-intensity style merited the description. Luckily the brilliant session with Booker Ervin, *Soul People,* is still available, as well as the compilation *Soul Classics.* Check out his Parker tribute, *Stitt Plays Bird,* from 1963, too.

Stitt experimented quite a bit in the '60s and early '70s, often with unsatisfying results, as when he started to play the electric Varitone sax, like on the compilations *Night Letter* and *Legends of Acid Jazz* (reissued at the height of that "sound," hence the misnomer title). *Soul Girl* pits Stitt against strings in an uncomfortable setting.

Stitt regained his greatest form during the last 10 years of his life in the more supportive setting of Muse Records (many of his Muse releases have been reissued on 32 Jazz). He lost nothing from his technique and played with as much (or more) emotion than he had as a younger man. *Tune Up!* and *Constellation,* quartet dates with Barry Harris on piano and Sam Jones on bass, represent Stitt's triumphant return; these two releases are now nicely combined on one CD, *Endgame Brilliance. The Champ* brings in Joe Newman's trumpet on a good quintet date. The out-of-print tributes to Gene Ammons and Duke Ellington, *My Buddy* and *Blues for Duke,* are worth searching out.

Stitt was only weeks from death when he recorded *The Last Stitt Sessions, Vols. 1* and *2,* but you'd never know it by listening to him play here. The posthumously released recordings offer a solemn tribute to a talent that burned brightly until the very end. — J.S.

DAVE STRYKER

★★★ **Passage (SteepleChase, 1991)**
★★★½ **Guitar on Top (Ken, 1992)**
★★★ **Strike Zone (SteepleChase, 1994)**
★★★ **Blue Degrees (SteepleChase, 1994)**
★★★½ **Full Moon (SteepleChase, 1994)**
★★★★ **Stardust (SteepleChase, 1995)**
★★★★ **Nomad (SteepleChase, 1995)**
★★★★ **The Greeting (SteepleChase, 1996)**
★★★★ **Big Room (SteepleChase, 1996)**
★★★★½ **Blue to the Bone (SteepleChase, 1997)**

Guitarist Dave Stryker (b. 1957) grew up in Omaha, Nebraska, where he began his career before moving to Los Angeles, then finally settling in New York in 1980. Stryker played in organist Jack McDuff's band, then with saxophonist Stanley Turrentine, where he soon received featured-role status (see the MusicMasters release *T Time*).

Stryker's debut recording, *First Strike,* was for a Japanese label in 1988. His acclaimed 1992 *Guitar on Top* album (released on a U.S. independent label) features pianist Mulgrew Miller, bassist Robert Hurst and drummer Victor Lewis. While the influences of Pat Martino and George Benson are evident, Stryker has a commanding sound of his own.

Stryker's SteepleChase albums are all drenched in a sweaty soul-jazz groove. *Passage, Strike Zone* and *Blue Degrees* are comparatively tame efforts. On *Full Moon,* Stryker's quartet covers Thelonious Monk ("I Mean You"), John Coltrane ("Wise One") and Ornette Coleman ("The Sphinx," "The Disguise") with aplomb. *Stardust* is a blazing set of standards recorded in a trio format with organist Joey DeFrancesco and drummer Adam Nussbaum. *Nomad* puts Stryker in front of the Bill Warfield big band. *The Greeting* is an excellent quintet date featuring six originals, Wayne Shorter's "Armageddon" and the McCoy Tyner–written title track. *Big Room* is a quartet session with saxophonist Rich Perry, bassist Ed Howard and drummer Billy Hart. *Blue to the Bone,* his finest album, expands the horn section to include tenor and baritone saxophones, trumpet and trombone. — J.S.

SUGAR BLUE

★★★ **Blue Blazes (Alligator, 1994)**
★★★½ **In Your Eyes (Alligator, 1995)**

Focusing on the harmonica's frequently ignored upper register, Sugar Blue (b. James Whiting, 1949) blows harp in a style all his own. Playing distorted notes quickly and forcefully, he makes his mouth organ sound like an electric guitar. Blue left his native New York for Paris in the mid-1970s, recording his first solo albums on the French label Blue Silver.

After moving to Chicago in 1982, Blue backed Willie Dixon for a decade before recording his domestic debut. On *Blue Blazes,* hollow production detracts from thoughtful arrangements and tight ensemble playing, but Blue's harp comes through loud and clear. The record features covers of classic Chicago-blues songs like "Back Door Man," but the few tunes Blue wrote himself ("Country Blues," "Out Till Dawn") are its real highlights. *In Your Eyes* takes many more chances than most contemporary blues records, grouping off key dirges ("In Your Eyes"), bluesy pop ("Bottom Line") and heavy-metal–influenced blues ("She"). Surprisingly, this musical gamble pays off, making *In Your Eyes* a rewarding disc. — J.K.

IRA SULLIVAN

★★★★ **Nicky's Tune (1958; Delmark, 1994)**

Washington, D.C., native Ira Sullivan (b. 1931) learned trumpet from his father and saxophones from his mother, giving him an unusual facility on both brass and wind instruments. During the 1950s he became a fixture on the Chicago jazz scene: In 1956 he joined Art Blakey's Jazz Messengers and stayed long enough to record with that band; later he recorded with J.R. Monterose. Sullivan made several albums with trumpeter Red Rodney in a fruitful group effort. *Nicky's Tune,* his only in-print outing as a leader, is a lively session featuring Jodie Christian on piano. — J.S.

MAXINE SULLIVAN

★★★½ **A Tribute to Andy Razaf (1956; DCC, 1991)**
★★★★ **Uptown (with Scott Hamilton) (Concord Jazz, 1985)**
★★★★ **Swingin' Sweet (Concord Jazz, 1988)**

Vocalist Maxine Sullivan (1911–1987) had a particularly fragile-sounding voice unsuited for the power of classic blues but well adapted to the nuances of swing and bop. She began her career with what was purported to be an exotic Claude Thornhill swing arrangement of the Scottish folk ballad "Loch Lomond."

Despite her creativity, Sullivan had a hard time shaking off the trappings of stardom. Still, she continued to record in very musical contexts until the 1950s, although most of this material has vanished. The Leonard Feather–produced *A Tribute to Andy Razaf* features Charlie Shavers on trumpet, Buster Bailey on clarinet, Jerome Richardson on alto and tenor saxophones and flute, Dick Hyman on piano, Milt Hinton on bass and Osie Johnson on drums. Sullivan resumed her career with a vengeance in the 1980s, recording a pair of excellent albums for Concord Jazz. Her worldly tone, backed by tenor saxophonist Scott Hamilton's quintet featuring John Bunch on piano, makes *Uptown* and *Swingin' Sweet* some of the best work of her life. — J.S.

HUBERT SUMLIN

★★★★ **Blues Anytime! (1964; Evidence, 1994)**
★★★½ **Hubert Sumlin's Blues Party (Black Top, 1987)**
★★★½ **Heart & Soul (Blind Pig, 1989)**
★★★½ **Healing Feeling (Black Top, 1990)**
★★★ **My Guitar and Me (Evidence, 1994)**
★★★★★ **Wake Up Call (Blues Planet, 1998)**

Hubert Sumlin (b. 1931) is one of the greatest guitarists to emerge from the Chicago blues scene, yet suffers from a lack of recognition because his best work has been as a sideman, particularly with Howlin' Wolf on that band's classic Chess recordings. One of 13 children in a farming family, Sumlin grew up desperately poor in the Great Depression and turned to music early, learning drums at age 10 and guitar at 11, leaving home to lead his own bands at 12. Sumlin played in the James Cotton band from 1951 to '53, and recorded with that group on the Sun label in 1954.

Sumlin first worked with Howlin' Wolf in 1954 and moved to Chicago the same year. Aside from a period during 1954–56, when he joined up with the Muddy Waters band, Sumlin remained with Wolf until his death, at which point he took over leadership of the band; he also worked as a sideman with the Eddie Taylor band and Magic Sam. Among his best solo albums is *Blues Anytime!,* recorded and originally released in East Germany.

Sumlin resurfaced in the 1980s to make a pair of albums for Black Top Records and *Heart and Soul,* which reunited him with Cotton, but Sumlin continued to be a diffident bandleader. That all changed, however, on the brilliant *Wake Up Call,* on which Sumlin is backed by members of New York's top session band, led by guitarist Jimmy Vivino. The group, which also backed pianist Johnny Johnson on his comeback albums, includes the former rhythm section from the Johnny Copeland band, bassist Mike Merritt and drummer James Wormworth. — J.S.

SUN RA

★★★★★ **Super-Sonic Jazz (1956; Evidence, 1992)**
★★★★ **Sound of Joy (1957; Delmark, 1994)**
★★★★★ **Jazz in Silhouette (1958; Evidence, 1992)**
★★★½ **The Futuristic Sounds of Sun Ra (1961; Savoy, 1993)**
★★★★ **Other Planes of There (1964; Evidence, 1992)**
★★★★★ **The Magic City (1965; Evidence, 1993)**
★★★★ **Monorails and Satellites (1966; Evidence, 1992)**
★★★½ **Holiday for Soul Dance (1969; Evidence, 1992)**
★★★★ **Atlantis (1969; Evidence, 1993)**
★★★½ **My Brother the Wind, Vol. 2 (1970; Evidence, 1992)**
★★★★ **Space Is the Place (1972; Evidence, 1993)**
★★★½ **Strange Celestial Road (Rounder, 1987)**
★★★½ **Reflections in Blue (Black Saint, 1987)**
★★★★ **Out There a Minute (Blast First, 1989)**
★★★★ **Mayan Temples (Black Saint, 1990)**
★★★½ **Hours After (Black Saint, 1990)**
★★★★½ **Sunrise in Different Dimensions (Hat Hut, 1991)**
★★★★ **Sun Song (Delmark, 1991)**
★★★½ **Sound Sun Pleasure! (Evidence, 1992)**
★★★★★ **Sun Ra Visits Planet Earth/Interstellar Low Ways (Evidence, 1992)**
★★★★★ **We Travel the Spaceways/Bad and Beautiful (Evidence, 1992)**
★★★★★ **Cosmic Tones for Mental Therapy/Art Forms of Dimensions Tomorrow (Evidence, 1992)**
★★★★ **Angels and Demons at Play/The Nubians of Plutonia (Evidence, 1993)**
★★★★ **Fate in a Pleasant Mood/When the Sun Comes Out (Evidence, 1993)**
★★★★ **Somewhere Else (Rounder, 1993)**

★★★½ At the Village Vanguard (Rounder, 1993)
★★★★★ The Singles (Evidence, 1996)

Herman Lee "Sonny" Blount (1914–1993) was a 20th Century renaissance man, a visionary and traditionalist who effortlessly bridged the chasm between the earliest forms of jazz and styles that lay unexplored by others at the time of his death. From New Orleans to swing to bop to free jazz to electronics to rap, Sun Ra, who began his career as Le Sony'r Ra, cruised along serenely, directing a mixed-media performance piece that combined light shows, elaborate costuming, exotic dancers, spoken-word features and one of the most accomplished large bands of the century, his Arkestra, which is still thriving years after his death. His influence runs as deep as his stylistic range, and he left his stamp on the music of several different cities. His sense of theater, his fascination with African roots and his thirst for unusual instrumentation were key influences on the important Association for the Advancement of Creative Musicians.

After he moved to New York at the beginning of the 1960s, Sun Ra's band helped define the new music scene on the Lower East Side in a residence at the legendary jazz club Slug's. In addition to its influence on the free-jazz movement and on John Coltrane, this band became a beacon to esoteric rockers, and many not-so-hidden Sun Ra references crop up in late-1960s rock. During the course of performances that sometimes ran six hours without interruption, like the 100-piece marathon band assembled for two mid-1980s concerts at the New York nightclub the World, Sun Ra deftly juggled swing arrangements by Fletcher Henderson, with whom he played, and Duke Ellington with searing blues stomps, free-jazz improvisations, gutbucket R&B, wild electronic excursions, introspective solo-piano passages, chanting Afro-beat rundowns, spoken-word sections where he'd grab members of the audience by the collar and declaim to them, gospel call-and-response exchanges, Saturnian rap sequences and New Orleans second-line funeral marches.

Sun Ra began putting together his musical vision sometime in his 30s while playing in a wide variety of contexts. He organized bands at Alabama A&M and performed in the Fess Whatley orchestra during the 1930s. He toured the South backing up such blues singers as Wynonie Harris and Lil Green before moving to Chicago in 1946, where he played in Henderson's band and finished out the '40s with Gene Wright's Dukes of Swing, after sitting in at the Club DeLisa. He worked for close to a decade at this glamorous club, arranging music to accompany extravagant floor shows and dance marathons. By the time he was ready to assemble his first Arkestra, Sun Ra had mastered the full range of swing, blues, bop and show music and was ready to put it all together in a visionary mix that would anticipate future styles in jazz, rock and R&B.

All of these experiences came into play when Sun Ra decided to form his own record company, Saturn (a.k.a. El Saturn), in 1954. That label is where the bulk of Ra's most important work appeared and is the subject of a magnificent reissue project organized by Jerry Gordon of Evidence Records. Evidence's most exhaustive work, *The Singles,* collects virtually every 45-rpm single supervised by Sun Ra and released on Saturn. These records, often pressed in lots of as few as 50 pieces, are part of the alternate reality that Sun Ra's recording history defines, a parallel-universe Top 40. The range of material included here is staggering: doo-wop, hard blues, New Orleans R&B, space music, teen ballads and holiday songs as well as the Arkestra's own music, including some of the familiar themes in previously unheard versions.

The Evidence CD reissues often combine two or three Saturn albums with related material. *Sound Sun Pleasure!* pairs the 1958 release of the same name with Sun Ra's earliest recording, a late-'40s session originally called *Deep Purple.* The material is mostly standards, with Ra backing Chicago vocalist Hatty Randolph on several tracks, including an atmospheric reading of Thelonious Monk's "'Round Midnight." Ra is already experimenting with otherworldly sounds on this set, playing a crude synthesizerlike device called a Solovox.

By the time Sun Ra started recording the Arkestra in 1956, after several years of nonstop performing and sleepless nights spent at endless rehearsals, the band had reached full stride. The vitality of this group is astonishing, and its innovative nature, so radical at the time, now sounds aggressively mainstream. That year saw the band record material included on Delmark's *Sun Song* as well as the Saturn/Evidence releases *Angels and Demons at Play, Sun Ra Visits Planet Earth* and the "official" debut of the Arkestra, *Super-Sonic Jazz.* Though "A Call for All Demons" and "Demons Lullaby" were recorded in 1956, the title track of *Angels and*

Demons at Play, which turns on a beautiful flute solo from Marshall Allen, was recorded in 1960. In between those two dates the band recorded the material for the Afrocentric release *The Nubians of Plutonia,* which is coupled with *Angels and Demons. Super-Sonic Jazz* demonstrates Sun Ra's early willingness to defy jazz conventions by using electric keyboards and bass, an attitude heretical to orthodox jazz tastes. Yet the band produced work of raw, exotic beauty, particularly "India" and "Super Blonde."

Ra was experimenting with modal improvisation in the mid-1950s, before Miles Davis and John Coltrane made breakthrough recordings using similar techniques. The band's first session, four tracks of which are also on *Sound of Joy,* appears on *Sun Ra Visits Planet Earth,* which opens with the incendiary "Reflections in Blue" and includes one of the band's most beautiful signature tunes, "Saturn." The Evidence reissue includes some more exotic 1958 material from the original Saturn release as well as the 1960 session *Interstellar Low Ways,* a space-music program piece that finished with one of Ra's famous themes, "Rocket Number Nine," later recorded by NRBQ and the Aquarium Rescue Unit.

Jazz in Silhouette showcases the Arkestra's tenor-saxophone giant, John Gilmore, and introduces another of the band's enduring themes, "Enlightenment." *We Travel the Spaceways/Bad and Beautiful* presents Sun Ra on "cosmic tone organ" and introduces another of his "hits," "We Travel the Spaceways." *Fate in a Pleasant Mood,* recorded in 1960 and '61, documents the Arkestra's final Chicago recordings in a mellower septet sound with some gorgeously phrased piano playing from Sun Ra and the terrific performance of bassist Ronnie Boykins. Marshall Allen's sprightly flute theme from "Kingdom of Thunder" was later appropriated by the Blues Project for "Flute Thing." *When Sun Comes Out,* a similar lineup's New York recordings from 1962 and '63, features the near-telepathic empathy on alto saxophone between Allen and Danny Davis and an eerie recording of "We Travel the Spaceways."

Cosmic Tones for Mental Therapy and *Art Forms of Dimensions Tomorrow* are collected together on one early-'60s package, notable for the influential "Infinity of the Universe." *Other Planes of There* is a free-jazz blowout that, for all its abstraction, has a trancelike beauty that flows from the spiritual cries of Gilmore and the Arkestra's other soloists, Davis, Allen, Pat Patrick, Walter Miller and Ronnie Cummings. *The Magic City,* recorded partly at the New York loft of African percussionist Olatunji, is a screaming "tribute" to Sun Ra's hometown of Birmingham that marks a creative high point for the possibilities of large-band free jazz and establishes Gilmore as one of the most important players of his generation.

Monorails and Satellites, a solo-piano recording, displays Sun Ra's unique style, which bridges the blues/postragtime architecture of Jelly Roll Morton with the angularity of Thelonious Monk and the ascent beyond traditional structure of Cecil Taylor. *Atlantis* refocuses the Arkestra's interest in creating music that evokes mythical and interplanetary themes while exploring the roots of African rhythms. Most of the album consists of clarinet over a bed of percussion instruments. *Holiday for Soul Dance,* also recorded during the late 1960s, returns to a format of standards arranged for small groups. He also continued his keyboard experiments—his synthesizer work on *My Brother the Wind, Vol. 2* was way ahead of its time, and few soundtracks of that decidedly eccentric era were as gone as *Space Is the Place,* which includes some rare footage of the Arkestra performing live and the magnificent vocals of June Tyson, who would go on to become an Arkestra mainstay.

Huge sections of the Saturn catalog, which numbers over 100 titles, remain to be explored. The releases as they exist now are among some of the most difficult-to-obtain jazz albums ever made. Other 1970s recordings are now out of print, but the Saturns beckon, with titles such as "Why Go to the Moon?," "Outer Space Employment Agency," the variations on "Discipline," "Media Dreams," "Saturn Research," "Constellation," "On Jupiter," "Seductive Fantasy," the breathtaking combination of "Springtime" and "Door to the Cosmos" and the epic "Sleeping Beauty."

The 1980s begin with the Arkestra's Henderson/Ellington side superbly represented on *Sunrise in Different Dimensions* and the space explorations continuing on *Strange Celestial Road,* a three-part suite. *Reflections in Blue* and *Hours After* show the Arkestra gravitating toward more traditional material. Other Saturns ("The Rose Hue Mansions of the Sun," "Dance of Innocent Passion") fill in the blanks. *Somewhere Else* is an excellent studio project using much of the same personnel as

Blue Delight. Mayan Temples, a well-rounded set, touches on all aspects of the Arkestra's greatness, including the leader's marvelous piano playing. Sun Ra, in failing health on *At the Village Vanguard,* can only sing and add limited synthesizer accompaniment to pianist Chris Anderson, but the Gilmore-fronted sextet plays in profound tribute to the maestro, whose time to leave the planet was obviously near. — J.S.

KLAUS SUONSAARI

★★★★ **Klaus Suonsaari, Niels Lan Doky and Niels-Henning Ørsted Pedersen Play the Music of Tom Harrell (Jazz Alliance, 1992)**

★★★★ **Inside Out (Soul Note, 1995)**

Finland native Klaus Suonsaari, born in 1959 to a family heavily into jazz, played piano for seven years before deciding at age 14 to become a drummer. At 16, he traveled to the United States to study percussion at the Eastman School of Music, then returned home to work with the sextet Blue Train, which was voted Finland's top jazz group in 1978. He later moved back to the United States to study composing and arranging at the Berklee College of Music, then headed to New York in 1985.

He has emerged as a strong conceptualist and empathetic timekeeper who can be an explosive soloist when the music warrants it. He teamed up with bassist Niels-Henning Ørsted Pedersen and pianist Niels Lan Doky on a very fine session exploring the extraordinary compositions of trumpeter Tom Harrell, with whom Suonsaari worked starting in the late 1980s. The sextet recording *Inside Out* contains equal parts Suonsaari originals (reflecting a strong Harrell compositional influence) and jazz standards. This tight band includes vibist Steve Nelson, reed player Scott Robinson, trumpeter Scott Wendholdt, pianist Renee Rosnes and bassist Ray Drummond. — K.F.

TIERNEY SUTTON

★★★★ **Introducing Tierney Sutton (Challenge, 1998))**

Jazz vocalist Tierney Sutton (b. 1963) found her niche as a vocalist on the Boston jazz scene in the early 1990s before moving to the West Coast, where she chairs the jazz vocals department at the University of Southern California. In 1998 she was one of 11 vocalists at the Thelonious Monk International Vocal Jazz Competition.

Her pure, sometimes sweet and always assured voice prioritizes respect for the song and the melody, as evidenced on *Introducing Tierney Sutton.* It includes a challenging blend of jazz standards and ageless choices from the American Songbook. Highlights include her update of the long-neglected "Old Country," first popularized by Nancy Wilson and saxophonist Cannonball Adderley, a funky rendition of Ellington's "Caravan" and an exquisite version of "It Never Entered My Mind." — K.F.

STEVE SWALLOW

★★½ **Home (1980; Wah Works/ECM, 1994)**

★★★½ **Carla (1987; Wah Works/ECM, 1994)**

★★★½ **Swallow (1992; Wah Works/ECM, 1994)**

★★★★ **Real Book (Wah Works/ECM, 1994)**

★★★★ **Deconstructed (Wah Works/ECM, 1997)**

One of the music world's great eclectics, bassist Steve Swallow (b. 1940) is better known as a sideman (particularly for Carla Bley) than as a soloist. An ephemeral, cogent bassist, he sets the poetry of Robert Creeley to music on *Home,* his first outing as a leader. The album, while pretty, lacks warmth. Sheila Jordan's vocals and Swallow's compositions tend toward archness reather than swing, despite anything David Liebman, Bob Moses or Steve Kuhn can do.

With the sterling help of Bley on organ and Larry Willis on piano, the follow-up, *Carla,* frequently rocks, especially when Hiram Bullock puts on an exhibition of funk guitar work. *Swallow* splits the difference between the two. Great playing by Gary Burton, John Scofield, Bullock and Bley's daughter Karen Mantler on harmonica and synthesizer more than make up for the lapses in soul and swing. "Ballroom" and "Thrills and Spills" find him at his best and most honest: strong compositions with sneaky time signatures but a funky bottom. Ever the stylistic chameleon, Swallow explores samba, salsa and soca. Yet many of the compositions suffer from lack of movement and dynamics.

With the help of an all-star cast, *Real Book* buys into the postbop neoclassicism of the 1990s, although Swallow can also be as prickly as a cactus, with titles like "Muddy in the Banks" and "Second Handy Motion." These compositions get far better than competent treatment from the likes of saxophonist Joe Lovano, pianist Mulgrew Miller, trumpeter Tom

Harrell and drummer Jack DeJohnette. *Deconstructed* is a solid collection of originals inspired by Tin Pan Alley tunes, with young neoboppers Chris Potter and Ryan Kisor on saxophone and trumpet. — H.B.

HARVIE SWARTZ

★★ **Full Moon Dancer (Bluemoon, 1989)**
★★★★ **In a Different Light (Bluemoon, 1990)**
★★★★½ **Arrival (Novus, 1994)**
★★★ **Spirits, Live at Vartan Jazz (Vartan Jazz, 1995)**
★★★½ **Love Notes from the Bass (Jazzheads, 1996)**

Harvie Swartz (b. 1948) entered music school as a piano player but changed his instrument to bass after hearing Scott LaFaro's expressive sound on Bill Evans's classic "Waltz for Debby." Swartz taught himself to play bass and was working in clubs in a matter of weeks. He drew attention in the early 1980s with his fusion group Urban Earth but remains best known for his enduring bass-and-voice duo association with artful jazz singer Sheila Jordan. In the 1990s Swartz has been highly regarded as a producer as well as a player.

Full Moon Dancer, an Urban Earth session augmented by vocals and electronic trappings, is pleasant but lacks the depth he has shown on other recordings. Swartz's two guitar-dominated works rank among his best recordings. *In a Different Light* features stunning combinations of duets, trios and quartets with drummers Winard Harper and Leon Parker (his recording debut) and five fine guitarists—John Scofield, Mike Stern, Mick Goodrick, Gene Bertoncini and Leni Stern—performing unhurried originals and standards. *Arrival* is an exceptional quartet session with guitarists Goodrick and John Abercrombie and drummer Marvin "Smitty" Smith. *Spirits, Live at Vartan Jazz,* a trio session recorded at a Denver club, features Jordan on two tracks. *Love Notes from the Bass* is a duo session with pianist Randy Klein, who wrote 9 of the 10 originals. The tunes and the duo format are a fine showcase for Swartz's rich, bold sound. — K.F.

ROOSEVELT SYKES

★★★★½ **The Return of Roosevelt Sykes (1960; Original Blues Classics, 1992)**
★★★★½ **The Honeydripper (1960; Original Blues Classics, 1993)**
★★★★½ **Blues by Roosevelt "The Honeydripper" Sykes (1961; Smithsonian Folkways, 1995)**
★★★★ **The Honeydripper's Duke's Mixture (1971; Verve, 1993)**
★★★½ **Complete Recorded Works, Vol. 1 (1929–1930) (Document, 1992)**
★★★★ **Complete Recorded Works, Vol. 2 (1930–1931) (Document, 1992)**
★★★½ **Complete Recorded Works, Vol. 3 (1931–1933) (Document, 1992)**
★★★★ **Complete Recorded Works, Vol. 4 (1934–1936) (Document, 1992)**
★★★★ **Complete Recorded Works, Vol. 5 (1937–1939) (Document, 1992)**
★★★★ **Complete Recorded Works, Vol. 6 (1939–1941) (Document, 1992)**
★★★½ **Complete Recorded Works, Vol. 7 (1941–1944) (Document, 1992)**
★★★½ **Complete Recorded Works, Vol. 8 (1945–1947) (Document, 1992)**
★★★★ **Complete Recorded Works, Vol. 9 (1947–1951) (Document, 1992)**
★★★★ **Complete Recorded Works, Vol. 10 (1951–1957) (Document, 1992)**
★★★½ **Gold Mine (Delmark, 1992)**
★★★½ **Hard Drivin' Blues (Delmark, 1995)**

Born either in 1906 in Elmar, Arkansas, or in St. Louis in 1913, Roosevelt Sykes began a long and prolific recording career in 1929, developing and expanding the role of the piano in modern blues music. He died in New Orleans in 1983. In the 1930s Sykes's piano could be heard behind virtually every St. Louis–based blues singer. He first earned his nickname, "the Honeydripper" (later a hit song for him), accompanying Edith North Johnson on "Honeydripper Blues."

The Return of Roosevelt Sykes represents the pianist at the peak of his form, displaying a deft handle on the keys that's sometimes reminiscent of players like Jimmy Yancey or Meade "Lux" Lewis. This work, recorded for the Bluesville label, contains a dozen tunes in Sykes's trademark "down home" rhythm & blues style. Of the many originals, notable are "Drivin' Wheel" (later covered by Junior Parker, the Butterfield Blues Band and others), "Stompin' the Boogie" and "Hangover." A remake of his 1936 hit "Night Time Is the Right Time" is also included here. Sykes's fine band on this date comprises Clarence Perry Jr. on tenor sax, Frank Ingalls and Floyd Ball on guitars and Armond "Jump" Jackson on drums.

On *The Honeydripper* Sykes fronts a different

cast of players, including the fantastic King Curtis on tenor sax. Interestingly, this session features an organist (Robert Banks) and a bassist (Leonard Gaskin) but no guitarists. Sykes penned eight of the nine tracks, including "Mislead Mother," a child's guileless perspective on his parents' marital turmoil that features a particularly piquant Curtis solo. Other highlights include the swinging, didactic "Jailbait" and the swirling, assertive blues "She Ain't for Nobody." *Blues by Roosevelt "the Honeydripper" Sykes* is a shift for Sykes, finding him in a solo setting, playing piano and singing. Produced by Memphis Slim, it features the instrumental "R.S. Stomp," on which Sykes demonstrates his remarkable ability with his left hand. Another standout is the up-tempo, twinkling "Ran the Blues Out of My Window." All in all, this album represents Sykes's solo-piano blues at its best.

As with all albums on the Austrian Document label, *Complete Recorded Works* is an exhaustive cataloging of Sykes's recordings, in chronological order. The 10 discs capture all of Sykes's output from 1929 to 1957 and are musts for completists and fans of quintessential piano blues. The sound quality of even the earliest recordings is very good, and Sykes can be heard in many different settings, from solo artist to bandleader.

The Honeydripper's Duke's Mixture finds Sykes playing piano and guitar. He's teamed again with Memphis Slim, who adds vocals and his own ivory work to this session. Cut in Paris in late 1970, the work contains Sykes's originals like "Ice Cream Freezer," "A Woman Is in Demand" and "Dirty Mother for You." Also featured are versions of the classics "Sweet Georgia Brown" and "Honeysuckle Rose." A particularly rueful version of Jimmy Oden's "Goin' Down Slow" is one of the album's most moving tracks.

Hard Drivin' Blues was recorded during 1962 and 1963 and features 17 Sykes compositions, including "Ho! Ho! Ho!," "We Gotta Move" and "Mistake in Life." On six tracks Sykes's solo piano and vocal are accompanied by Homesick James Williamson on bass and guitar. Of particular prominence are "Slidell Blues" and two boogie-woogie pieces, "North Gulfport Boogie" and "Run This Boogie," which represent Sykes's mastery of the "jive" style. *Gold Mine* is culled from a 1966 solo session in Europe and includes some newer Sykes compositions as well as classics like ".44 Blues," "Boot That Thing" and "Henry Ford Blues," all of which he had recorded nearly four decades earlier. — B.R.H.

GABOR SZABO

★★★½ **The Sorcerer (1967; Impulse!, 1990)**
★★★ **Bacchanal (1968; DCC, 1994)**
★★★ **Jazz Mysticism/Exotica (DCC, 1990)**

Hungarian guitarist Gabor Szabo (1936–1982) left his homeland for the United States after the 1956 invasion by the Soviet Union and studied at Berklee College of Music in Boston. He came to prominence as a member of the Chico Hamilton group in the early 1960s and later in the decade worked with Charles Lloyd and Gary McFarland before forming his own group. His loping, nimble approach incorporated elements of Hungarian folk music with Middle Eastern and Indian modalities for an engaging sound that made him an influential stylist for many younger players in the 1960s, particularly Larry Coryell. He made a series of well-received albums for Impulse!, the most popular of which, *The Sorcerer,* documents a live performance at Boston's Jazz Workshop. — J.S.

JAMAALADEEN TACUMA

★★★★ **Show Stopper (1983; Gramavision, 1990)**
★★★★ **Renaissance Man (1984; Gramavision, 1990)**
★★★ **Music World (1986; Gramavision, 1990)**
★★★ **Jukebox (Gramavision, 1988)**
★★★★ **House of Bass (Gramavision, 1993)**

Bassist Jamaaladeen Tacuma (b. 1956) arrived at one of the most effective fusions of new electric music on his dense, challenging debut, *Show Stopper*. The Philadelphia native combines the heady funk of Sly Stone, James Brown and Stevie Wonder with a unique understanding of Ornette Coleman's harmolodic contemporary-jazz conception. As part of Coleman's Prime Time band, Tacuma rivaled Coleman for center stage—he can be heard on the groundbreaking *Body Meta* and *Of Human Feelings*. He has also played with James "Blood" Ulmer (*Tales of Captain Black*), Walt Dickerson (*Serendipity*), Kip Hanrahan and the Golden Palominos. *Show Stopper* features one side with his own group, Jamaal (guitarist Rick Iannacone, drummer Cornell Rochester, percussionist Ron Howerton and alto saxophonist/metal clarinetist James R. Watkins), and one side with such luminaries as pianist Anthony Davis, alto saxophonist Julius Hemphill and Ulmer. Tacuma continued his sonic explorations on *Renaissance Man* with help from Coleman, David Murray, Vernon Reid and Bill Bruford, among others. *House of Bass* is a good collection of the Gramavision recordings. His later albums mine similar territory without reaching the heights of the first two recordings. — J.S.

TAKE 6

★★ **Take 6 (Reprise, 1988)**
★★★ **So Much 2 Say (Reprise, 1990)**
★★★½ **Join the Band (Reprise, 1994)**
★★★½ **Brothers (Reprise, 1996)**

Formed in 1987, Take 6, a male sextet living and recording in Nashville, has redefined the contemporary gospel group by blending aspects of hip-hop, classic American pop, jazz and soul stylings. Slick but less overtly commercial than, say, the Wynans, and given to deceptively complex harmonizing in the style of Lambert, Hendricks and Ross, Take 6 has as its sole purpose to illustrate how a deep and abiding faith in God is the answer to the problem of making it through a day.

As you listen, the passion of the voices cuts through, particularly when the men dig into the great old hymns such as "Mary" and "Get Away, Jordan" (from the group's self-titled debut album) and reinvigorate the songs with their stylish but affecting approach. *So Much 2 Say* updates the sound slightly and has better material. Notable among the new songs are "Something Within Me," "Sunday's on the Way" and "Where Do the Children Play?"

The appropriately titled *Join the Band* finds Take 6 doing precisely that, thanks to the support of some first-rate musicians who bring percolating rhythms, funky grooves beholden to Kool and the Gang, and some stirring, silky-smooth vocal interplay that suggests the influence of Boyz II Men. Significantly, this expanded sound palette buttresses a number of original songs whose lyrical content has grown considerably darker than the material on previous Take 6 albums. A thoughtful, probing effort is further enlivened by Ray Charles's ingratiating guest appearance on "My Friend," his rawboned ebullience playing off Take 6's smooth harmonizing, and Stevie Wonder checks in near the end for a gospel-cum-pop rave-up, "Why I Feel This Way," complete with a lilting harmonica solo from Wonder in between his urgent testifying. Working some swooping vocal variations on Brahms's familiar lullaby in the album closer, "Lullaby," lead singer McKnight employs his affecting tenor voice in a message that is both plaintive and peaceful, closing the album on an optimistic note and suggesting better days ahead. *Brothers* suggests both the soul-saving virtues of music (in a funky take on Maurice White's "Sing a Song") and the blessings bestowed on true believers in the gospel's message. Avoiding stridency, Take 6 makes its case in soulful tones buttressed by tight, driving but lush Quiet Storm–style arrangements. Theirs is a potent message and compelling, thoughtful music to boot. — D.M.

TAMPA RED

★★★★ **Bottleneck Guitar 1928–1937 (Yazoo, 1992)**
★★★ **Don't Tampa with the Blues (Original Blues Classics, 1992)**
★★★★ **The Guitar Wizard (Columbia/Legacy, 1994)**
★★★★½ **The Bluebird Recordings 1934–36 (BMG, 1997)**
★★★★ **The Bluebird Recordings 1936–38 (BMG, 1997)**
★★★ **Don't Jive Me (Bluesville, N.A.)**

With lyrics devoted to wine, women and the turn of a good double entendre, "hokum" blues was that last-gasp vestige of minstrelsy to sweep through popular, Prohibition-era American music. In its day, when blues bands, Western-swing ensembles and hillbilly units were all swinging "tight like that," there was no better purveyor of the hokum ethos than a light-skinned black bottleneck guitarist from Georgia. But to define Tampa Red (né Hudson Whittaker, 1904–1981) solely as the artist who brought forth such huge and influential "race" hits as "What Is It That Tastes Like Gravy?," "The Duck Yas-Yas-Yas" and the hokum anthem "It's Tight Like That" would be a disservice to the uncannily smooth, left-hand dexterity that established the measure by which all future bottleneck stylists would be gauged, from contemporaries like Blind Willie McTell and Robert Nighthawk to Earl Hooker and Ry Cooder. As well, he was an incredibly prolific songwriter—inventing in and out of the strict blues/ragtime molds and leaving a thick and prodigious songbook crammed with tunes that are still being played today.

In his day Tampa Red played with and/or influenced a multitude of legendary blues singers and stylists—from pianist Georgia Tom Dorsey and Ma Rainey in his native Georgia to Big Bill Broonzy, Robert Nighthawk, B.B. King and Freddie King during his latter years in Chicago. Long before John Lee Hooker or Lightnin' Hopkins made an art of label hopping, Tampa Red was recording under different names for a number of fledgling blues labels, pioneering the role of the blues virtuoso—a solo artist, a bandleader, a songwriter/producer *and* an in-demand studio guitarist.

Covering the blues-and-hokum high points from his early career, *Bottleneck Guitar 1928–1937* and *The Guitar Wizard* both offer a credible overview of Red's in-studio facets. The 14-track *Bottleneck Guitar* in particular covers tasteful solo slide performances ("You Got to Reap What You Sow"); hokum duets with his erstwhile partner Georgia Tom Dorsey ("If You Want Me to Love You"); Red's earliest extant recording, with tuba accompaniment ("Through Train Blues"); jug-band tunes ("Come On Mama, Do That Dance"); and accompaniment with various "classic" blues singers (Ma Rainey on "Black Eye Blues" and Madlyn Davis on "It's Red Hot"). *The Guitar Wizard* offers 17 songs and includes a stark demarcation between the ebullient spirit of Red's '20s recordings and the tempered topicality of heartfelt Depression-era tunes like "Turpentine Blues" and "Western Bound Blues."

By the mid-'30s, Tampa Red had relocated permanently to Chicago with its bustling recording industry, becoming a leading member of the Bluebird Records blues "mafia" and working exclusively with A&R man Lester Melrose. In fact, his home on South State Street became headquarters to the nascent scene, which grew to include the leading bluesmen in the city: harmonica legends Jazz Gillum and Sonny Boy (John Lee) Williamson, pianists Blind John Davis and boogie giant "Big Maceo" Merriweather and guitarists "Big Boy" Crudup, Big Joe Williams and a young Robert Lee McCoy (later "Nighthawk"). Together they defined the first cohesive Chicago blues sound, laying the groundwork for the electric-blues revolution of the mid-'50s.

Tampa Red's best midcareer recordings are in the midst of a complete reissue process by BMG. The well-packaged and -programmed double-disc collection *The Bluebird Recordings 1934–36* reveals various facets of his musical genius: his ability to turn street lingo into song ("Give It Up Buddy & Get Goin'"), his continuing penchant for pop-influenced melodies ("When I Take My Vacation in Harlem"), his strong and unfaltering blues sense ("Drinkin' My Blues Away") and his raucous, falsetto voicings that predate Buddy Holly's vocal tricks by 20 years. Speaking of predating, will someone check with Jimmy Buffett as to his indebtedness to Tampa Red's "Let's Get Drunk and Truck" for his song of almost verbatim title?

Red's sessions for Bluebird stretched well into the early '50s, and awaiting reissue are the long-lost original versions of such classics as "When Things Go Wrong with You" (popularized as "It Hurts Me Too" by Elmore James), "Crying Won't Help You" and "Anna Lou Blues" (both recorded by Robert Nighthawk, the latter as "Anna Lee"), "Black Angel Blues" ("Sweet Little Angel" in the hands of B.B. King) and "Love Her with a Feeling" (a Freddie King hit). Let's hope the wait is not too long.

Compromised by Tampa Red's failing health and the death of his wife, *Don't Tampa with the Blues* and *Don't Jive Me* caught only a shadow of the guitar master's former wizardry and mark his last recordings before he passed away.
— A.K.

HORACE TAPSCOTT

★★★★ **The Dark Tree, Vol. 1 (Hat Hut, 1989)**
★★★★ **The Dark Tree, Vol. 2 (Hat Hut, 1989)**

Born in Houston in 1934 and raised in California, Horace Tapscott began his career in the 1950s playing trombone in Lionel Hampton's band but switched to piano after being injured in an automobile accident. Tapscott became an important figure on the Los Angeles jazz scene, tutoring a number of young musicians, including Arthur Blythe, through his Pan Afrikan Peoples Arkestra.

Both volumes of *The Dark Tree* determinedly display Tapscott's musical strengths with a fine band featuring clarinetist John Carter, drummer Andrew Cyrille and bassist Cecil McBee. Most of Tapscott's recordings were released on his own Nimbus label and are currently unavailable although well worth seeking out. *Flight 17, The Call* and *Live at the I.U.C.C.* feature the Arkestra's high-energy performances of Tapscott's challenging compositions. *The Tapscott Sessions* collects a challenging series of solo compositions and improvisations.
— J.S.

HOWARD TATE

★★★★½ **Get It While You Can: The Legendary Sessions (Mercury, 1995)**

In the late 1960s Howard Tate (b. 1938) consummated the perfect marriage of blues and soul. Born in Georgia and raised in Philadelphia, Tate recorded an album's worth of material for Verve between 1966 and '68. Ace producer Jerry Ragovoy orchestrated the sessions, wisely matching Tate with masterful players like pianist Richard Tee and guitarist Cornell Dupree. Tate added a pinch of soul to classics like "Part Time Love" and "How Blue Can You Get" while maintaining their character as blues songs. Ragovoy penned most of the rest of Tate's material, crafting tastefully arranged, upbeat soul tunes that foresaw the work of Philadelphia producers Kenny Gamble and Leon Huff.

The two Tate gems that reached the R&B Top 20 had a strong effect not only on music fans but also on Tate's peers. "Ain't Nobody Home" was covered by B.B. King a few years after Tate cut the original. Hugh Masekela, Jimi Hendrix and the blues-rocking James Gang all cut versions of "Stop." While not a charter for Tate, "Get It While You Can" gave Janis Joplin a note-for-note blueprint for one of her best-loved recordings. Mysteriously, Tate disappeared from the public eye in the early 1970s, cementing his status as a lost soul legend. — J.K.

ART TATUM

★★★★★ **The Best of Art Tatum (Pablo, 1987)**
★★★★ **The V-Discs (Black Lion, 1989)**
★★★★★ **Solos (1940) (MCA, 1990)**
★★★ **Art Tatum at the Piano, Vol. 1 (GNP Crescendo, 1990)**
★★★ **Art Tatum at the Piano, Vol. 2 (GNP Crescendo, 1990)**
★★★★★ **The Tatum Group Masterpieces, Vol. 1 (Pablo, 1990)**
★★★★★ **The Tatum Group Masterpieces, Vol. 2 (Pablo, 1990)**
★★★★ **The Tatum Group Masterpieces, Vol. 3 (Pablo, 1990)**

★★★★ **The Tatum Group Masterpieces, Vol. 4 (Pablo, 1990)**
★★★★ **The Tatum Group Masterpieces, Vol. 5 (Pablo, 1990)**
★★★★ **The Tatum Group Masterpieces, Vol. 6 (Pablo, 1990)**
★★★★ **The Tatum Group Masterpieces, Vol. 7 (Pablo, 1990)**
★★★★★ **The Tatum Group Masterpieces, Vol. 8 (Pablo, 1990)**
★★★★★ **The Complete Pablo Solo Masterpieces (Pablo, 1990)**
★★★★★ **The Complete Pablo Group Masterpieces (Pablo, 1990)**
★★★★★ **Classic Early Solos (1934–1937) (Decca, 1991)**
★★★★★ **The Standard Sessions: 1935–1943 Transcriptions (1991; Music and Arts Programs of America, 1996)**
★★★ **Standards (Black Lion, 1991)**
★★★★ **20th Century Piano Genius (1992; Verve, 1996)**
★★★★★ **The Art Tatum Solo Masterpieces, Vol. 1 (Pablo, 1992)**
★★★★★ **The Art Tatum Solo Masterpieces, Vol. 2 (Pablo, 1992)**
★★★★★ **The Art Tatum Solo Masterpieces, Vol. 3 (Pablo, 1992)**
★★★★★ **The Art Tatum Solo Masterpieces, Vol. 4 (Pablo, 1992)**
★★★★★ **The Art Tatum Solo Masterpieces, Vol. 5 (Pablo, 1992)**
★★★★★ **The Art Tatum Solo Masterpieces, Vol. 6 (Pablo, 1992)**
★★★★★ **The Art Tatum Solo Masterpieces, Vol. 7 (Pablo, 1992)**
★★★★★ **The Art Tatum Solo Masterpieces, Vol. 8 (Pablo, 1992)**
★★★★★ **I Got Rhythm, Vol. 3 (1935–44) (Decca, 1993)**
★★★★ **California Melodies (Memphis Archives, 1994)**
★★★★½ **Fine Art & Dandy (Drive Archive, 1994)**
★★★★ **Tea for Two (Black Lion, 1994)**
★★★★★ **Piano Starts Here (Legacy, 1995)**
★★★★½ **The Complete Capitol Recordings (Blue Note, 1997)**

During his time, Art Tatum (1909–1956) was the greatest jazz pianist ever, and in some ways he has yet to be dethroned. He was the first jazz pianist whose sheer technique rivaled that of the Western classical virtuosi; in fact, Vladimir Horowitz was an unabashed fan of Tatum's playing. Count Basie referred to Tatum as the eighth wonder of the world. But Tatum's genius wasn't limited to the dexterity, speed and architectural intelligence of his playing. His pieces, no matter how fast, never sounded forced but had a natural pace to them, a sense of inevitability that allowed them to cascade from the keyboard like streams flying down a mountainside.

Tatum combined a background of classical training with a thorough understanding of the ragtime, stride, swing, blues and barrelhouse-boogie piano styles that informed jazz tradition. He was well versed in the masters who preceded him—Jelly Roll Morton, Earl Hines, James P. Johnson and particularly Fats Waller. Tatum also demonstrated a harmonic sophistication previously unglimpsed in jazz playing, a trait that made him a precursor of the bop movement and a profound influence on Bud Powell, among others.

Born in Toledo, Ohio, Tatum played classical violin as a child and studied piano at a conservatory. He arrived in New York in 1932 as the accompanist to vocalist Adelaide Hall; a year later he was astonishing the jazz world with his first solo pieces, beginning with an incredible reading of "Tiger Rag," available on the appropriately titled *Piano Starts Here.* Listening to these early solos, it's easy to believe that Tatum, who was legally blind, came upon his style in part from studying piano rolls, which often featured two players, and teaching himself to play both parts at once.

The Standard Sessions is a mother lode of solo Tatum, 61 pieces recorded in 1935, 1938, 1939 and 1943. The Black Lion *Standards* is a shorter collection of some of the same material. *California Melodies,* a series of radio transcripts from the private collection of David Rose, includes a Tatum performance with a Rose orchestral score. *Fine Art & Dandy* collects more radio transcriptions from 1939 and 1945. *The V-Discs,* recorded from 1944 to 1946 for distribution among the U.S. armed forces, are solo and trio recordings, including Tatum's 1944 performance at the Esquire Concert at New York's Metropolitan Opera House. *Tea for Two* collects rare recordings from a variety of sessions in the 1940s. *The Complete Capitol Recordings* contains trio sessions from 1949 and 1952, with Stewart and guitarist Everett Barksdale as well as more remarkable solo recordings.

During the last years of Tatum's life, producer Norman Granz undertook the project of recording him in a definitive series of solo and group sessions. *The Complete Pablo Solo Masterpieces,* a seven-CD boxed set of 119 solos recorded between 1953 and 1955, afforded Tatum the opportunity of codifying his genius and offering it up as a single, sustained pianistic vision. Some have complained that these versions of the songs aren't different enough from the originals recorded 20 years earlier, but there are actually subtle changes, and the fact that Tatum was more interested in fine-tuning his inventions than repudiating them only adds to their status as classics. This material (minus four tracks from a 1956 Hollywood Bowl concert) is also available on eight individual CDs.

The Complete Pablo Group Masterpieces is, in its own way, an even greater triumph in that Granz managed to place Tatum in more imaginative group settings than the pianist did on his own. These sessions, recorded between 1954 and 1956 and available as eight individual volumes or a six-CD box, place Tatum in the context of other legendary masters such as alto saxophonist Benny Carter and drummer Louis Bellson (*Vol. 1*); trumpeter Roy Eldridge (*Vol. 2*); vibraphonist Lionel Hampton and drummer Buddy Rich (*Vols. 3* and *4*); Hampton, Rich, trumpeter Harry "Sweets" Edison and guitarist Barney Kessel (*Vol. 5*); bassist Red Callender and drummer Jo Jones (*Vol. 6*); Callender, drummer Bill Douglass and clarinetist Buddy DeFranco (*Vol. 7*); and Callender, Douglass and tenor saxophonist Ben Webster (*Vol. 8*). — J.S.

ART TAYLOR

★★★★ **Taylor's Wailers (1957; Original Jazz Classics, 1992)**
★★★★ **Taylor's Tenors (1959; Original Jazz Classics, 1995)**

Drummer Arthur Taylor (1929–1995) grew up in Harlem, joined Coleman Hawkins's group in 1950 and later played with Bud Powell, Miles Davis, Thelonious Monk and John Coltrane, among others. By the mid-1950s he was leading his own group, Taylor's Wailers.

The CD bins don't reflect the hard-swinging Taylor's prolific recording career. All that are currently available are *Taylor's Wailers,* with Coltrane, Charlie Rouse and Taylor's old friend from Harlem Jackie McLean, and *Taylor's Tenors,* with Rouse and Frank Foster. The hard-to-find Enja release *Mr. A.I.* is a high-powered session from the early 1990s that is well worth searching for. — J.S.

BILLY TAYLOR

★★★½ **Separate Keyboards (with Erroll Garner) (1945; Savoy, N.A.)**
★★★½ **Cross Section (1954; Original Jazz Classics, 1989)**
★★★ **The Billy Taylor Trio with Candido (1954; Original Jazz Classics, 1991)**
★★★ **My Fair Lady Loves Jazz (1957; Impulse!, 1994)**
★★★½ **Billy Taylor with Four Flutes (1959; Original Jazz Classics, 1994)**
★★★½ **Uptown (1960; Original Jazz Classics, 1997)**
★★★½ **Solo (Taylor-Made, 1988)**
★★★ **We Meet Again (with Ramsey Lewis) (Columbia, 1989)**
★★★½ **It's a Matter of Pride (GRP, 1994)**
★★★½ **Homage (GRP, 1995)**
★★★½ **Billy Taylor Trio (Prestige, 1995)**
★★★½ **Where U Been (Concord Jazz, 1996)**
★★★½ **Music Keeps Us Young (Arkadia Jazz, 1997)**

Pianist Billy Taylor (b. 1921) came up in the '40s playing with Ben Webster, Dizzy Gillespie, Stuff Smith, Slam Stewart, Machito, Charlie Parker and Don Redman. In 1949 he formed his own quartet, which was converted into one of Artie Shaw's Gramercy Five lineups in 1950. During the early '50s Taylor was a fixture on the New York bop scene and a Birdland perennial. His tasteful, bop-derived style has continued to please listeners through his career. The urbane and well-spoken Taylor is also an effective teacher and promoter of jazz, having written several useful books and many perceptive critical articles on the subject as well as founding New York's Jazzmobile live-performance project. In the late '60s Taylor became the first black music director of a major television program, *The David Frost Show.*

The Original Jazz Classics discs are solid Latin-jazz outings. *Cross Section* features vocalist Machito; *Billy Taylor with Four Flutes* includes percussionist Chano Pozo, with Frank Wess, Herbie Mann and Jerome Richardson among the flutes. Much of Taylor's ensuing work is unavailable, including a number of recordings made for his own label, Taylor-Made. Fortunately his rare solo outing on that imprint, *Solo,* can be found in stores.

Taylor's recent work for GRP finds him in top form. *It's a Matter of Pride* uses bassist Christian McBride and drummer Marvin "Smitty" Smith in a trio augmented on several tracks by Ray Mantilla on congas and tenor saxophonist Stanley Turrentine. The recording includes sections of a suite Taylor wrote for Martin Luther King. *Homage* features two extended works—the title track, a tribute to many of Taylor's early influences, featuring his trio backed by the Turtle Island String Quartet; and an extended dance piece "Step into My Dream." — J.S.

CECIL TAYLOR

★★★½ **Jazz Advance (1956; Blue Note, 1991)**
★★★½ **Love for Sale (1959; Blue Note, 1998)**
★★★½ **Looking Ahead! (1959; Original Jazz Classics, 1990)**
★★★★ **Nefertiti—Beautiful One (1962; Freedom, 1997)**
★★★★★ **Unit Structures (1966; Blue Note, 1989)**
★★★★ **Cecil Taylor and the Jazz Composer's Orchestra (1968; ECM, 1990)**
★★★½ **Indent (1973; Freedom, 1988)**
★★★★★ **Silent Tongues (1975; Freedom, 1988)**
★★★½ **Dark to Themselves (1976; Enja, 1990)**
★★★½ **Air Above Mountains (1976; Enja, 1992)**
★★★★ **Embraced (with Mary Lou Williams) (1977; Pablo, N.A.)**
★★★½ **One Too Many Salty Swiftly & Not Goodbye (Hat Hut, 1978)**
★★★½ **The Cecil Taylor Unit (New World, 1978)**
★★★½ **3 Phasis (New World, 1979)**
★★★½ **It Is in the Luminous Brewing (Hat Hut, 1980)**
★★★★ **Garden, Part 1 (Hat Hut, 1981)**
★★★★ **Garden, Part 2 (Hat Hut, 1981)**
★★★★ **Historic Concerts (with Max Roach) (Soul Note, 1984)**
★★★★ **Winged Serpents (Soul Note, 1985)**
★★★★ **For Olim (Soul Note, 1986)**
★★★½ **Olu Iwa (Soul Note, 1994)**
★★★½ **The Great Paris Concert (Black Lion, 1996)**
★★★½ **Trance (Black Lion, 1997)**

Along with Ornette Coleman, pianist Cecil Taylor (b. 1929) is the master of modern, avant-garde jazz, a pioneer since midcentury and no less daring today. While his playing reflects Duke Ellington's elegance, Fats Waller's humor and Dave Brubeck's chordal density, his highly percussive style is unmistakable. Classically trained and influenced strongly by contemporary classical music, Taylor served an apprenticeship with Johnny Hodges before forming in the late '50s a stellar quartet with soprano saxophonist Steve Lacy, bassist Buell Neidlinger and drummer Dennis Charles. He then embarked on a lifelong experiment—crafting highly original, very demanding music.

His debut, *Jazz Advance,* is one of the more remarkable in jazz history—without forgoing entirely his blues base, he radically rethinks meter and tonal color, deconstructs standards and yet also nods back fondly to Ellington. *Looking Ahead!* consolidates Taylor's original gains: He unleashes his rhythm section, pays homage to Fats Waller and barrels toward a looser, freer sound. *Unit Structures,* as its title suggests, is a kind of gorgeous musical math, but math like Mondrian—striking, angular, extraordinarily fresh.

Taylor kept his ensembles fresh (working often with alto saxophonist Jimmy Lyons and drummer Sunny Murray); he cofounded in the mid-'60s the Jazz Composers' Guild and in the '70s taught at the University of Wisconsin. He puts flesh to his increasingly intricate theory on such landmarks as *Silent Tongues* and *The Cecil Taylor Unit; Gardens, Parts 1 and 2* and *For Olim* are solo-piano standouts—the playing is incendiary. *Winged Serpents* features a large band such free-jazz heavy hitters as trumpeter Enrico Rava, tenor saxophonists John Tchicai and Frank Wright, William Parker on bass and Gunter Hampel on baritone sax. — P.E.

EDDIE TAYLOR

★★★★½ **I Feel So Bad: The Blues of Eddie Taylor (1972; Hightone, 1991)**
★★★★ **Long Way from Home (1977; Blind Pig, 1995)**
★★★★ **My Heart Is Bleeding (1980; Evidence, 1994)**

Eddie Taylor (1923–1985) is best known for his guitar work on Jimmy Reed and John Lee Hooker recordings for Vee-Jay Records, but he was also a terrific singer and influential songwriter (the Rolling Stones covered the Robert Johnson version of his "Stop Breaking Down" on *Exile on Main Street*).

Taylor grew up in Mississippi, learning blues guitar from family friend Memphis Minnie as well as by listening to Charley Patton, Robert Johnson and Son House, among others, at house parties and juke joints. He moved to Memphis in 1943, soaking up the scene and squaring off against the likes of B.B. King and Robert Jr. Lockwood at open sessions.

After World War II Taylor began playing electric guitar and moved to Chicago in 1949 as part of the Southern migration that produced the blues explosion of the early 1950s. He played Maxwell Street and hung with fellow Mississippi émigrés like Muddy Waters and Reed, with whom he began recording in 1953—the two eventually developed a Midas touch. He went on to record with Hooker and others as a sideman, all the while making a series of remarkable records on his own.

I Feel So Bad is a stirring album dead center in the Chicago-blues tradition with Phillip Walker excelling on second guitar and George Smith's harmonica coming on like James Cotton's in the Muddy Waters band. The band rears back and slams the rhythm. Taylor's affinities with Hooker show on the hair-raising "Stroll Out West," and "Stop Breaking Down" gets a workout here too. The Reed signature tune "Going Upside Your Head" sounds right at home. The aptly titled *Long Way from Home* was recorded live with stripped-down accompaniment from guitarist Louis Myers, bassist Dave Myers and drummer Odie Payne Jr. Opening with a version of the show-stopping "Bad Boy," the record moves through some hot passes. All-star blues session *My Heart Is Bleeding* features special guests Carey Bell on harp, Hubert Sumlin on guitar and Sunnyland Slim on piano. In addition to the songs on the original release (Taylor's "Wreck on 83 Highway," "Blow Wind Blow" and "Lawndale Blues"), the CD reissue includes good moments such as Sumlin's "Gamblin' Woman" and Elmore James's "Dust My Broom." — J.S.

HOUND DOG TAYLOR

★★★★ **Hound Dog Taylor and the HouseRockers (1971; Alligator, 1989)**
★★★½ **Natural Boogie (1974; Alligator, 1989)**
★★★★½ **Beware of the Dog! (1976; Alligator, 1991)**
★★★½ **Genuine Houserocking Music (1982; Alligator, 1993)**

The music of Hound Dog Taylor (1915–1975) and the HouseRockers may have lacked subtlety, technique and variety, but the group made up for it with raw fervor. Born and raised in Mississippi, Taylor began playing guitar at age 20 and moved to Chicago five years later. By the late '50s, he had quit his day job to become a full-time musician. He and the HouseRockers had been gigging together for six years when Bruce Iglauer made them the first signing to Alligator Records in 1971.

Distilling and intensifying the sound of Elmore James, Taylor and his group attacked frenetic boogies, upbeat shuffles and a few slow blues. Taylor's nerve-rattling slide riffs and impassioned vocals lead the way, followed by the distorted bass lines of second guitarist Brewer Phillips and drummer Ted Harvey's jackhammer beats. This combination drives the band's impressive debut, *Hound Dog Taylor and the HouseRockers;* its less engaging second album, *Natural Boogie;* and *Genuine Houserocking Music,* a posthumously released assortment of outtakes. *Beware of the Dog,* the group's third album, brilliantly showcases the HouseRockers' live prowess as they began adding to their musical palette. — J.K.

KOKO TAYLOR

★★★★ **Koko Taylor (1969; Chess, 1988)**
★★★½ **South Side Lady (1973; Evidence, 1992)**
★★★★ **I Got What It Takes (1975; Alligator, 1991)**
★★★ **The Earthshaker (1978; Alligator, 1989)**
★★★½ **From the Heart of a Woman (1981; Alligator, 1989)**
★★★ **Queen of the Blues (Alligator, 1985)**
★★★ **Live from Chicago: An Audience with the Queen (Alligator, 1987)**
★★★ **Jump for Joy (Alligator, 1990)**
★★★★½ **What It Takes: The Chess Years (Chess, 1991)**
★★★ **Force of Nature (Alligator, 1993)**

More Howlin' Wolf than Bessie Smith, Koko Taylor (b. 1935) delivers Chicago blues with a gruff, powerful voice. After moving from Memphis to Chicago in the early 1950s, Taylor found work as a maid, spending her spare time sitting in at South Side clubs with Muddy Waters and Wolf. In 1964 Willie Dixon signed her to a management/production deal, and for the next eight years he wrote her songs, chose her musicians and arranged her material.

The swinging, upbeat tunes Taylor recorded for Dixon at Chess (and its subsidiary Checker) remain her best, filled with spooky guitar riffs and distinctive vocal phrasing. Her eponymous debut contains many of these tracks, but *What It Takes: The Chess Years* outdoes it, offering selections from Taylor's out-of-print second LP, *Basic Soul,* in addition to the finest tracks from her first record. Especially noteworthy are Taylor's signature tune, "Wang Dang Doodle," the last Checker blues release to reach the R&B Top 10, and the eerie gem "Insane Asylum," a duet with Dixon.

After leaving Chess in 1972, Taylor cut a few forgotten sessions in Europe before signing to Alligator Records in 1974. She then turned away from the sound of her Chess recordings, adopting a mix of rocking boogies and guitar-driven slow blues. Tight, blues-drenched arrangements and the crack playing of guitarists Mighty Joe Young and Sammy Lawhorn make a real winner of her first Alligator release, *I Got What It Takes,* but over her next three albums, Taylor's music grows increasingly formulaic. With *From the Heart of a Woman* she successfully tackles soul blues, turning in credible versions of "Something Strange Is Going On" and "I'd Rather Go Blind." She brings funk elements to *Jump for Joy* and adds rock to its successor, *Force of Nature.* None of these recordings measure up to her Chess output, but Taylor, who continues to perform regularly, retains her voice, which remains the same rough wonder it was in the 1960s. — J.K.

LITTLE JOHNNY TAYLOR

★★★½ Everybody Knows About My Good Thing (1972; Ronn, 1996)
★★★½ Ugly Man (Ichiban, 1989)
★★★★★ Greatest Hits (Fantasy, 1991)
★★★½ The Super Taylors: Little Johnny & Ted (Paula, 1991)

What a shame when two stellar artists share almost exactly the same name. With his diminutive moniker the only giveaway (on paper anyway) separating "LJT" from the better-known Stax soul/disco balladeer, this particular Johnny Taylor (b. John Young, 1943) established his name on disc with a less gritty, blues-focused style that hit paydirt with a number of tightly arranged R&B numbers in the mid-'60s.

Tennessee-born and Los Angeles–bred, Taylor as a teen spent time singing with gospel stars the Mighty Clouds of Joy, which helped to hone his plaintive delivery and improvisational skills. After changing course for deeper blues waters, Taylor furthered his training with the Johnny Otis Show. In 1963 he arrived at Galaxy Records with a number of self-penned tunes and an upper-register tenor not far off from his primary influence, Little Willie John.

Originally intended as the B side to "Somewhere Down the Line," "Part Time Love" hit immediately, making it one of R&B's most commercially successful singles; other hits included "You'll Need Another Favor" and "Zig Zag Lightning." He also recorded aptly chosen covers like Bobby Bland's "I Smell Trouble" and Little Willie John's "Big Blue Diamonds." All reflected a jaunty, horn-driven approach that never lost a concentrated blues punch, spiced with stinging guitar solos and balanced with urbane production values. A note of credit is certainly due to Galaxy's production/arranging team of Cliff Goldsmith and Ray Shanklin, who cowrote a few tunes and added the necessary studio magic to the majority of the tracks on the superlative *Greatest Hits* package.

Later years (1968 through the 1970s) found Taylor recording for the Louisiana-based Jewel/Ronn/Paula label family, finding success with Southern soul hits like "Everybody Knows About My Good Thing" and "Open House at My House." These recordings are available mostly on non-CD format, but *Everybody Knows About My Good Thing* and *The Super Taylors* offer a few slices of his Southern-fried soul hits, with added music by and duets with label mate Ted Taylor on the latter.

Taylor's most recent effort, *Ugly Man,* stands as a solid tribute to a blues singer whose soulful vocals and songwriting abilities remain undiminished in focus and strength. — A.K.

MELVIN TAYLOR

★★★★ Blues on the Run (1982; Evidence, 1994)
★★★★ Plays the Blues for You (1984; Evidence, 1993)
★★★★½ Melvin Taylor and the Slack Band (Evidence, 1995)
★★★★ Dirty Pool (Evidence, 1997)

Guitarist Melvin Taylor (b. 1959) is the embodiment of the 1950s and '60s Chicago single-note blues style and solid proof that the form is destined to thrive well into the next century. Like many of his blues contemporaries, Taylor was influenced by Jimi Hendrix and Buddy Guy, but he favors a clean, direct sound over distortion, making vibrato the old-fashioned way, with his fingers. He occasionally throws in some wah-wah effects, particularly in Hendrix-inspired settings, but his trademark is the well-articulated phrase played with biting force and velocity. Taylor was already turning heads as the 15-year-old leader of Chicago's Transistors before joining the Legendary Blues Band, but it wasn't until he traveled to Europe and blew away the French blues audience that he got a chance to record as a leader.

Blues on the Run is an impressive debut showcasing Taylor's roots on a quintet session covering Albert King ("Travelin' Man"), T-Bone Walker via Albert Collins ("Cold, Cold Feeling") and Kenny Burrell ("Chitlins Con Carne"). *Plays the Blues for You* is a rerelease of a French import with Taylor's trio augmented by keyboardist Lucky Peterson, highlighted by the Taylor originals "Talking to Anna Mae," "Born to Lose," "Groovin' in Paris" and the Wes Montgomery paean "Tribute to Wes."

Taylor really shines on *Melvin Taylor and the Slack Band,* a faithful reflection of the style he developed fronting a trio on Chicago's West Side. With bassist Willie Smith and drummer Steve Potts laying down a solid groove behind him, Taylor dazzles from start to finish, burning through such standards as "Texas Flood," "Tin Pan Alley," "All Your Love" and "T-Bone Shuffle," tossing in his own "Groovin' in New Orleans" and "Depression Blues" and climaxing with a taut, ringing version of the Hendrix classic "Voodoo Chile" before wrapping things up with a jazz-inspired instrumental cover of "Tequila." Having demonstrated his thorough assimilation of the Hendrix legacy, Taylor makes the logical jump into Stevie Ray Vaughan material on *Dirty Pool,* covering songs written by Vaughan and his main cowriter, Doyle Bramhall—"Too Sorry," "Telephone Song" and the title track—as well as blues standards by Willie Dixon ("I Ain't Superstitious"), Albert King ("Floodin' in California") and William Bell/Booker T. Jones Jr. ("Born Under a Bad Sign"). Taylor acknowledges his debt to Otis Rush on "Right Place, Wrong Time" and does a bang-up version of the Leiber and Stoller favorite "Kansas City." He closes the album with a soulful slow-blues reading of the classic "Merry Christmas Baby." — J.S.

PAUL TAYLOR

★★ **On the Horn (Countdown, 1995)**
★★ **Pleasure Seeker (Countdown, 1997)**

Denver-born saxophonist Paul Taylor (b. ca. 1966) utilized his smooth-jazz style as a sideman in the Keiko Matsui band. His bright, upbeat and deliberately lightweight approach owes much to David Sanborn's influence, although Taylor ventures as far into straight pop/R&B as you can go while still claiming to be a jazz player. *On the Horn* and *Pleasure Seeker* are for those on an easy-listening musical diet. — J.S.

JACK TEAGARDEN

★★★★ **Big Eight (1940; Original Jazz Classics, 1991)**
★★★ **Think Well of Me (1962; Verve, 1998)**
★★★★ **Jack Teagarden (1962; Best of Jazz, 1996)**
★★★★ **I Gotta Right to Sing the Blues (ASV/Living Era, 1992)**
★★★ **Teagarden Party (Parade/Koch International, 1995)**
★★★★★ **The Indispensable Jack Teagarden (RCA Bluebird, N.A.)**

Throughout his career, trombonist Jack Teagarden (1905–1964) was one of his instrument's best, a virtuoso whose faultless technique and rhythmic sophistication made him a key element of the crucial 1927 recordings led by Louis Armstrong. The effusive Teagarden later became a featured player in the Armstrong small groups of the post–World War II era and was also an effective vocalist on the traditional New Orleans jazz that he never deserted. *The Indispensable Jack Teagarden* is an essential album, a keen overview of Teagarden's career as a leader and a sideman in a range of contexts. Included here are his first recording as a leader, "She's a Great, Great Girl," terrific sides with the innovative tenor saxophonist Bud Freeman and Teagarden's definitive playing and singing on his calling card, "I Cover the Waterfront." — J.S.

SUSAN TEDESCHI

★★★ **Just Don't Burn (Tone-Cool/Rounder, 1998)**

Massachusetts native Susan Tedeschi (b. 1970) plays a mean blues guitar and has a soulful, urgent vocal style inspired by Bonnie Raitt, Janis Joplin and Etta James. Her debut, *Just Don't Burn,* appeared after Tedeschi made a name for herself as a live performer (she joined her first band at 13). It showcases Tedeschi's own songwriting and her authoritative take on well-chosen covers. Her own tunes (here, mostly ballads) aren't particularly memorable, and lack the conviction she gives others' material. She's at her best on uptempo numbers like "It Hurts So

Bad" and "Rock Me Right" (written by her producer/drummer Tom Hambridge). As Tedeschi finds her own voice, it will be interesting to see where she takes her emotive singing and muscular guitar work. — H.G.-W.

JACKY TERRASSON

★★★★ **Jacky Terrasson (Blue Note, 1995)**
★★★ **Reach (Blue Note, 1996)**
★★★½ **Rendezvous (with Cassandra Wilson) (Blue Note, 1997)**
★★★½ **Alive (Blue Note, 1998)**

Pianist Jacky Terrasson's daring approach to jazz piano draws heavily from the influence of Bud Powell and Thelonious Monk, coupled with the melodicism of Bill Evans. Born in Berlin in 1956 and raised in Paris, he studied classical piano from age 5 and became a jazz listener at 12. The jazz public caught on to him after he won the Thelonious Monk International Piano Competition in 1993, a success that led to a brief stint in Betty Carter's band and a recording contract with Blue Note.

The trio is his preferred format; his first two sessions include two strong collaborators—bassist Ugonna Okegwo and drummer Leon Parker, who works with a slimmed-down drum set. As a unit, they excel at dramatic changes in texture and dynamics. Terrasson's forte is reworking standards, often implying the melody as he digs deep for new harmonic possibilities and rhythmic vamps, dropping melodic hints along the way. His eponymous debut thunders with such marvelous invention.

Reach takes a subtler tack at times and favors originals over standards. His Caribbean-rhythm remake of "(I Love You) For Sentimental Reasons" offers a radical shift on a tune previously etched with Nat Cole's balladry. *Rendezvous,* a small-group session with singer Cassandra Wilson, reveals Terrasson's skills as a mood-setting, creative accompanist. *Alive,* from a 1997 appearance at the Iridium jazz club in New York, captures the deep sympatico of his trio with Okegwo and Parker. — K.F.

CLARK TERRY

★★★½ **Serenade to a Bus Seat (1957; Original Jazz Classics, 1992)**
★★★★ **Duke with a Difference (1957; Original Jazz Classics, 1992)**
★★★★ **In Orbit (1958; Original Jazz Classics, 1987)**
★★★½ **Top and Bottom Brass (1959; Original Jazz Classics, 1992)**
★★★★ **The Happy Horns of Clark Terry (1964; Impulse!, 1995)**
★★★ **Oscar Peterson and Clark Terry (1975; Original Jazz Classics, 1994)**
★★★ **Squeeze Me (1976; Chiaroscuro, 1989)**
★★★ **Memories of Duke (1980; Original Jazz Classics, 1990)**
★★½ **Yes, the Blues (1981; Original Jazz Classics, 1995)**
★★★½ **To Duke and Basie (Rhino, 1986)**
★★★ **Portraits (Chesky, 1989)**
★★★ **The Clark Terry Spacemen (Chiaroscuro, 1989)**
★★★ **Live at the Village Gate (Chesky, 1991)**
★★ **What a Wonderful World: For Louis and Duke (Red Baron, 1993)**
★★★ **Shades of Blues (Challenge, 1994)**
★★★★ **Mellow Moods (Prestige, 1994)**
★★★ **Talkin' Trash (with James Williams) (DIW/Columbia, 1995)**
★★★ **The Second Set (Recorded Live at the Village Gate) (Chesky, 1995)**
★½ **Big Band Basie (Reference, 1995)**

For more than 50 years Clark Terry (b. 1920), a veteran horn player and bandleader, has been a major influence on jazz trumpeters. Merging creative phrasing with relentless swing, Terry incorporates big-band and cool-bop styles in a personal approach to tunes and has been compared to Roy Eldridge and Dizzy Gillespie as a melodic innovator on the horn. Known for his upbeat, personal, dedicated and lyrical playing, the St. Louis native is a master of the blue-note scale, excelling at mid to up tempos and blues. Terry is steeped in tradition, having been a regular in both the Count Basie and Duke Ellington bands. He blazed new territory in the '50s and '60s through his harmonic explorations and innovative phrasings allied in tension with New Orleans and Dixieland rhythms, but he remains faithfully dedicated to the blues. Most of his numbers over the years have been originals, often composed on the spot and just as quickly left behind. The sound of Terry's horn is often described as happy and bright, and he clearly aims to make people feel good. In the tradition of Louis Armstrong and Gillespie, the trumpeter is also famous for his humorous scat singing; Terry's crowd-pleasing "Mr. Mumbles" routines, the parodic ravings of an incoherent hipster, have long been a staple of his concerts.

Terry's music is well represented on CD. The classic late-'50s Riverside albums (now Original Jazz Classics), produced by Orrin Keepnews, are noteworthy souvenirs from the postbop era. *Serenade to a Bus Seat* is a hard-swinging set of bebop and blues with Johnny Griffin, Wynton Kelly, Paul Chambers and Philly Joe Jones. *Duke with a Difference* is a collaboration with such notable Ellingtonians as alto saxophonist Johnny Hodges and tenor saxophonist Paul Gonsalves. *In Orbit* soars with an all-star quartet lineup of Thelonious Monk, Sam Jones, Philly Joe Jones and Terry on flügelhorn. *Top and Bottom Brass,* an unusual quintet date, features Terry's horn over Don Butterfield's tuba and Sam Jones's bass. Butterfield's virtuosic playing is deployed as a co–lead voice in the low register, while the rhythm section of drummer Art Taylor and pianist Jimmy Jones keeps the bottom-heavy combo swinging. Many of the heads feature octave doubling by Terry and Butterfield; "Top 'n' Bottom" became one of Terry's signature tunes. *Happy Horns* is a 1964 set with Ben Webster on tenor and Phil Woods on alto and clarinet. *Mellow Moods* collects a pair of early-1960s Moodsville sessions.

On *Yes, the Blues,* a mellow West Coast blues date, the leader lays out quite a bit in order to foreground the unusual reedy sonority of Eddie "Cleanhead" Vinson's alto sax, "Harmonica George" Smith's harp and Art Hillery's organ. *Memories of Duke,* a tribute to Ellington, features a quintet of Pablo regulars including Joe Pass and Ray Brown; Terry and Pass establish a nice accord, from fast ensemble playing to ballads.

A relaxed-sounding Terry flexes his chops on *Portraits,* a quartet recording featuring midtempo standards, scat singing and tributes to Eldridge and Gillespie. *The Clark Terry Spacemen* was the U.S. edition of the midsized (10-piece) band that toured the European festival circuit in 1988. With Al Grey on trombone and Phil Woods and Red Holloway in the saxophone section, the Spacemen's gently swinging arrangements have roots in Terry's late-'50s work with the Duke Ellington Orchestra. The tasteful charts leave plenty of room for virtuosic soloing and a happy feeling. The CD also includes a 19-minute interview.

The two Village Gate sets were recorded just before Terry's 70th birthday. The lively first release moves through jump, samba, blues, slow-ballad and waltz tunes. Saxophonist Jimmy Heath stands out on solos, Terry and drummer Kenny Washington strike a few sparks in a duet called "Brushes and Brass" and Terry does one of his trademark comedic scat routines on "Hey Mr. Mumbles." *The Second Set* contains more ambitious ensemble compositions, ballads, extended jams and audience participation, as well as a 10-minute interview. The Chesky CDs boast audiophile sound quality.

What a Wonderful World, a tribute to Armstrong and Ellington with trombonist Al Grey and bassist Ron Carter, has some occasionally lush arrangements but mostly lackluster playing. An odd mix has Terry's horn in the background much of the time, although his laid-back vocals are in decent form; producer Bob Thiele wrote several of the tunes. On *Big Band Basie* a desultory Terry sits in with DePaul University students reading big-band charts. *Shades of Blues,* a Dutch import recorded in Brooklyn, finds Terry's horn in good voice as he lays down a nice groove with old partners: pianist Charles Fox (a childhood friend from St. Louis), bassist Marcus McLaurine (Terry's regular bass player since 1981) and trombonist Al Grey. Highlights include a remarkable impromptu mumbling vocal on "Whispering the Blues" and an authoritative horn duet with Grey on "St. Louis Blues."
— T.M.

JIMMY THACKERY AND THE DRIVERS

★★★½ Sideways in Paradise (with John Morney) (1985; Blind Pig, 1993)
★★★ Empty Arms Motel (Blind Pig, 1992)
★★★★ Trouble Man (Blind Pig, 1994)
★★½ Wild Night Out! (Blind Pig, 1995)
★★★ Drive to Survive (Blind Pig, 1996)

Jimmy Thackery (b. 1953) is a gifted but ultimately frustrating guitar hero. He established his reputation in the '70s as the lead guitarist for acclaimed blues and boogie bar band the Nighthawks, flooring audiences with his mastery of a range of six-string styles from Albert King to Jimi Hendrix. When Thackery opted for a solo career in 1987, his own sound emerged triumphantly; he embellishes single-note picking with hints of echo and reverb, and his affinity for Hendrix crops up in deft wah-wah flourishes. Thackery is also a convincing singer with a surprising intuition for ballads, but his choice of material begs questioning.

Blues-rock guitar fans will find something to like on each of Thackery's releases; the problem is an unhealthy number of clunkers in the midst.

For every road anthem like "Empty Arms Motel" or "Drive to Survive," there's an abomination like "Cool Guitars," which just isn't tongue-in-cheek enough to redeem its stupid and sexist "I'm gonna sell the bitch's car" chorus.

For maximum sonic wallop, *Trouble Man* is Thackery's strongest effort. "Mercury Blues," "Bullfrog" and "She Needs Everything" pull off a high-wire mix of rockabilly and blues, and Thackery nails the sting of Albert Collins with a version of the Iceman's "Don't Lose Your Cool." Revealing the common threads of influence between Thackery and Stevie Ray Vaughan, "Hang Up and Drive" is a Texas-style shuffle. If Thackery can approach the level of Vaughan's songwriting in the future, he's a serious contender for the vacant blues-rock throne. — S.J.

TOOTS THIELEMANS

★★★½ **Man Bites Harmonica (1958; Original Jazz Classics, 1997)**
★★★★ **Live in the Netherlands (1980; Original Jazz Classics, 1992)**
★★★½ **The Brasil Project (Private Music, 1992)**
★★★½ **The Brasil Project, Vol. 2 (Private Music, 1993)**
★★★ **East Coast West Coast (Private Music, 1994)**

Jean "Toots" Thielemans (b. 1922) emigrated from Belgium in 1951 and settled in New York, where his virtuosic harmonica technique made him a sought-after session player. That's his harmonica solo on the *Sesame Street* theme. Thielemans began a long association with Quincy Jones in the late '60s. His playing appears on the soundtracks of *Midnight Cowboy* and *Sugarland Express* and on the Jones albums *Walking in Space, Gula Matari, Smackwater Jack* and *Mellow Madness.* He's also recorded with Oscar Peterson, J.J. Johnson, Zoot Sims, Bill Evans and Jaco Pastorius.

Thielemans has made a number of albums under his own name, but most of them are out of print. The two *Brasil Project* recordings place him in lush settings accompanied by a combination of Brazilian musicians and session stars Lee Ritenour on guitar, Mark Isham on trumpet and Dave Grusin on piano.

Live in the Netherlands is Thielemans at his best, performing in concert with bassist Niels-Henning Ørsted Pedersen and guitarist Joe Pass. *East Coast West Coast* is a collection of Thielemans's favorite compositions, including John Coltrane's "Naima" and "Giant Steps"; Thelonious Monk's "In Walked Bud"; Dizzy Gillespie's "Groovin' High" and "Con Alma"; and Paul Desmond's "Take Five." Recorded with two different lineups in New York and Los Angeles, the project features guitarists John Scofield and Robben Ford, pianists Lyle Mays, Bruce Barth, Herbie Hancock and Alan Broadbent, bassists Christian McBride and Charlie Haden, drummers Troy Davis and Peter Erskine, Mike Mainieri on vibes, Joshua Redman on tenor saxophone, Terence Blanchard on trumpet and Jerry Goodman on violin.
— J.S.

HENRY THOMAS

★★★★★ **Texas Worried Blues: Complete Recorded Works 1927–1929 (Yazoo, 1989)**

In only 23 extant recordings, songsmith Henry "Ragtime Texas" Thomas (1874–1930) provides the best glimpse of the full gamut of early–20th Century country music: square-dance songs, ragtime numbers and other danceworthy styles. In Thomas's day, the blues were just one shade in an itinerant musician's repertoire and all song styles were enjoyed by white and black country-music lovers alike. Thomas's mark—like that of many prewar bluesmen—was made decades later when such artists as Bob Dylan and Taj Mahal covered his songs ("Honey, Won't You Allow Me One More Chance?" and "Fishing Blues," respectively). But unlike most prewar musicians of any ilk, Thomas penned a song that would hit the Top 20 during the psychedelic '60s: Canned Heat changed his "Bull Doze Blues" to "Going Up the Country" and reached its high-water mark.

History aside, Thomas's output is also eminently enjoyable. One can easily imagine the jukebox role he filled at rural late-night country parties, playing a percussive, rhythmic guitar style and singing in a pronounced vibrato-laden voice a little less "shouty" than his contemporary Lead Belly. Accompanying himself with his trademark panpipes crafted from river reeds, Thomas was a one-man band.
— A.K.

IRMA THOMAS

★★★½ **Turn My World Around (1972; Shanachie, 1993)**
★★★½ **Safe with Me (1979; Paula, 1991)**
★★★★ **The New Rules (Rounder, 1986)**

★★★★ **The Way I Feel (Rounder, 1988)**
★★★ **Something Good: The Muscle Shoals Sessions (Chess, 1990)**
★★★★½ **Live! Simply the Best (Rounder, 1991)**
★★★ **True Believer (Rounder, 1992)**
★★★½ **Walk Around Heaven: New Orleans Gospel Soul (Rounder, 1994)**
★★★★ **Sweet Soul Queen of New Orleans (Razor & Tie, 1996)**
★★★★ **The Story of My Life (Rounder, 1997)**

Summing up 30 years in soul music, Irma Thomas's *Live! Simply the Best* is one of the great live R&B recordings. A scorching "Time Is on My Side" makes the better-known Rolling Stones version sound feeble; an Otis Redding/James Brown medley honors the masters; Crescent City classics like "Iko Iko" never were zestier; and Allen Toussaint's "It's Raining" is balladry of a heart-stopping order. Born in 1941, this powerhouse from Ponchatoula, Louisiana, debuted in 1958 with the swaggering "You Can Have My Husband (but Please Don't Mess with My Man)" and went Top 20 nationwide in 1964 with "Wish Someone Would Care." The consistent big time eluded Thomas, however, and she retreated to the congenial intimacies of New Orleans nightclubs. There, she reigns. *The Way I Feel, The New Rules, The Story of My Life* and *True Believer* are excellent recent Thomas releases. Deeply moving gospel soul, *Walk Around Heaven* exemplifies the Mahalia Jackson/Bessie Griffin tradition that she embodies. But *Simply the Best* is essential, nearly in a class with vintage Aretha Franklin. *Sweet Soul Queen of New Orleans* is the early career overview—and it's a stunner. — P.E.

LEON THOMAS

★★★ **Precious Energy: Live at Ethells (Mapleshade, 1993)**

Vocalist Leon Thomas (b. 1937) is woefully underrepresented on CD considering his career accomplishments and relatively high profile over the years. He spent much of the 1960s singing with the Count Basie band before making a tremendous impact with the Pharoah Sanders group in the late 1960s and early '70s, composing the lyrics to and singing "The Creator Has a Master Plan," which featured a unique yodeling technique Thomas derived from his studies of African vocalization. Thomas went on to international acclaim as the vocalist with Santana on the fusion masterpiece *Welcome* and its live counterpart, *Lotus.*

Precious Energy is an adequate representation of Thomas's talents but pales in comparison to some of his out-of-print works, particularly *The Leon Thomas Album* and *Spirits Known and Unknown.* — J.S.

DON THOMPSON

★★ **Winter Mist (Jazz Alliance, 1991)**

Canadian bassist Don Thompson (b. 1940) played extensively with John Handy, touring and recording with that group before settling down to session work in Canada. He has played bass on recordings by Lenny Breau, Jim Hall and Don Bickert. On his own Thompson also plays keyboards. *Winter Mist* is the only Thompson album available among several that were released. *A Beautiful Friendship* (Concord Jazz, 1984), with guitarist John Abercrombie, bassist Dave Holland and drummer Michael Smith, although only available on cassette, is worth searching out. — J.S.

LUCKY THOMPSON

★★★½ **Tricotism (1956; Impulse!, 1993)**
★★★ **Happy Days (1963/1965; Prestige, 1994)**
★★★★ **Lucky Strikes (1964; Original Jazz Classics, 1987)**

Tenor saxophonist Eli "Lucky" Thompson was born in 1924 in Detroit but made his mark in New York and Los Angeles with the same Billy Eckstine group that featured Charlie Parker and Dizzy Gillespie, then as a member of the Parker band that would also feature the young Miles Davis. (Thompson later appears on Davis's classic *Walkin'* album.) Thompson went on to play with the Boyd Raeburn and Stan Kenton big bands as well as fronting his own group before moving to Europe in 1957.

Tricotism reissues two sessions, one a trio date with Oscar Pettiford on bass and Skeeter Best on guitar, the other a series of quartets and quintets based around pianist Hank Jones and trombonist Jimmy Cleveland. *Happy Days* combines two Prestige sessions, one a tribute to Jerome Kern and the other a Barbra Streisand homage, which, naturally, covers "People." The excellent *Lucky Strikes* features Jones, bassist Richard Davis and drummer Connie Kay. Find the out-of-print *Accent on Tenor Sax* for Thompson at his best. — J.S.

GEORGE THOROGOOD AND THE DESTROYERS

★★★½ **George Thorogood and the Destroyers (1977; Rounder, 1992)**
★★★½ **Move It on Over (1978; Rounder, 1992)**
★★★ **I'm Wanted (Rounder, 1980)**
★★½ **More George Thorogood and the Destroyers (1980; Rounder, 1986)**
★★★½ **Bad to the Bone (Capitol, 1982)**
★★★ **Live (Capitol, 1986)**
★★★½ **The Baddest of George Thorogood with the Destroyers (Capitol, 1992)**
★★★ **Haircut (Capitol, 1993)**
★★★ **Let's Work Together: Live (Capitol, 1995)**
★★★ **Rockin' My Life Away (Capitol, 1997)**

Formed in Delaware in 1973, George Thorogood (b. 1952) and the Destroyers developed a rocking blues sound primarily centered around Thorogood's heavy guitar style and growling vocals. Based on recycled blues licks and a passion for rock & roll, the group's songs are heartfelt and immediately recognizable, though derivative. Their eponymous debut contains inspired versions of Earl Hooker's "You Got to Lose," Elmore James's "Madison Blues" and an eight-minute-plus rendition of John Lee Hooker's "One Bourbon, One Scotch, One Beer." This release serves as a model for each Thorogood album that follows, including the hugely successful *Move It on Over,* whose anthemic title track would become an FM radio staple. Also appearing on this album are inspired versions of Bo Diddley's "Who Do You Love," Brownie McGhee's "So Much Trouble" and Homesick James's "Baby Please Set a Date."

More George Thorogood and the Destroyers contains all covers, including Muddy Waters's "Bottom of the Sea," Elmore James's "Goodbye Baby" and Carl Perkins's "Restless." The album as a whole enjoys Thorogood's trademark guitar swagger and gritty vocals but loses the hunger of his earlier albums. *The Baddest of George Thorogood with the Destroyers* collects the high points of Thorogood's previously released material and is a reminder that Thorogood's skills as a player, though formidable, are actually a collection of Elmore James, John Lee Hooker, Chuck Berry, Bo Diddley and Rolling Stones riffs sewn together as if to form something new and original. — B.R.H.

BIG MAMA THORNTON

★★★★ **Ball n' Chain (Arhoolie, 1968)**
★★★½ **Sassy Mama (Vanguard, 1975)**
★★★ **Jail (Vanguard, 1975)**
★★★★ **Hound Dog: The Peacock Recordings (MCA, 1992)**

Blues belter Willie Mae "Big Mama" Thornton remains indelibly linked to rock & roll as the artist who recorded the original growling version of Leiber and Stoller's "Hound Dog" and her self-penned "Ball and Chain," the latter being the number with which Janis Joplin slayed a generation at Monterey in 1967. Cut from the Ma Rainey/Bessie Smith mold of physically imposing, big-voiced, free-spirited blues women, Thornton projects a tough but engaging presence on record, giving as good as she gets while also allowing a touching vulnerability to surface in her rough vocals from time to time.

Born in Montgomery, Alabama, Thornton (1926–1984) sang with her six brothers and sisters in their minister father's church, taught herself to play drums and harmonica and left home at age 14 to make a buck singing the blues. In the late '40s she settled in Houston, where Don Robey discovered her in 1951 and signed her to his Peacock label. A devoted road warrior, she maintained an ambitious touring schedule over the next few years, working steadily with bandleader Johnny Otis (who produced and played on several of her finest Peacock sides) and with other top names on the blues and R&B circuit, including Bobby "Blue" Bland and Johnny Ace (she shared a dressing room with Ace in Houston on Christmas Eve 1954, when he killed himself playing Russian roulette).

Hound Dog: The Peacock Recordings contains the essential documents on which Thornton's legend rests, starting with 1952's powerhouse version of "Hound Dog," produced by Otis, who also played drums on the session. Released in early 1953, the single topped the R&B chart that spring; although it was her only Number One record, she put together a number of compelling singles before leaving the label in 1957. Some of these make their first U.S. album appearance on this collection; taken as a whole, the 18 tracks here show Thornton, particularly in her work with Otis, evolving from the hard-driving, small-combo sound of "Hound Dog" to more sophisticated approaches involving Otis's big band with horns and the bandleader himself adding some tasty quotes on vibes on several numbers, particularly on the topical "Hard

Times." One of the rare gems here is a 1953 single, "Yes, Baby," released on Peacock's sister label, Duke, featuring Johnny Ace and Thornton in a smoldering duet. Their emotional displays are further heightened by Otis's relentless, driving arrangement sparked by a stinging guitar solo from Pete Lewis and a honking, protesting tenor-sax break courtesy James Von Streeter. A 1955 track, "You Don't Move Me No More," recorded with the Billy Harvey Orchestra (also a frequent road partner of Thornton's), finds Thornton sashaying confidently, and with a lighter touch than usual, through a tune notable for its rhumba feel and a scorching, distorted guitar solo by Roy Gaines that is all screaming three-note chords and serpentine single-string runs.

Post-Peacock, Thornton recorded for several labels. Many of these recordings are out of print domestically, but her tenures at Arhoolie and Vanguard in the '60s and '70s are documented in the releases noted in the discography. Arhoolie's *Ball n' Chain* is 16 tracks of vintage Thornton sessions dating from 1965 through 1968, recorded in London, San Francisco and Hollywood with some of the preeminent bluesmen on the planet. Five cuts find her fronting a band that includes Buddy Guy on guitar, Little Walter Horton on harmonica, Fred Below on drums, Eddie Boyd on piano and organ and Jimmy Lee Robinson on bass. They push Thornton—and she them—to some effusive performances. These, however, are no match for what transpires with the six tracks with Muddy Waters's band, whose members include Waters, James Cotton, Otis Spann, Samuel Lawhorn, Luther Johnson and Francis Clay. On these tracks Waters, Cotton and Spann rock the joint with their soloing, and Thornton sounds mightily possessed. Two tracks recorded in Hollywood feature a low-profile band that is more in-the-pocket rock & roll than the others, but Thornton rolls on undeterred. The transcendent moments here feature only Thornton and Mississippi Fred McDowell on two dark, deep Delta blues numbers that they wrote together, "School Boy" and the scary "My Heavy Load." Thornton's raw testifying—redolent of her roots in the church and not always apparent in her gruff blues numbers and novelty songs—has an immediacy and urgency lacking on the other fine songs in this collection, perhaps owing to McDowell's ragged-but-right percussive slide-guitar support. He's pushing the envelope on his solos, sometimes getting so carried away that he's doing little more than flailing the strings as he sets up Thornton's next sortie.

Sassy Mama, Thornton's first album for Vanguard (recorded in 1975), shows her less in the sassy mode of the title than in a thoughtful one on seven songs, all but two being her own compositions. The top-notch band here moves easily from down-and-dirty arrangements of blues (such as "Big Mama's New Love") to mellow, combo-style R&B, lending comforting ambiance to slow laments such as the 17-minutes-plus workout on "Mr. Cool," with Cornell Dupree's popping, robust solos and the steady-grooving organ fills provided by Paul Griffin challenging Thornton as drummer Jimmy Johnson and bassist Wilbur Bascomb keep the bottom nailed down.

Jail, Thornton's other in-print Vanguard title, was recorded live in 1975 at Monroe State Prison in Monroe, Washington, and at the Oregon State Reformatory in Eugene. Its 30 minutes plus of performances showcase impassioned performances of "Hound Dog," "Ball and Chain," Willie Dixon's "Little Red Rooster" and a scorching take of "Rock Me Baby." The show closes with a version of Edwin Hawkins's gospel standard "Oh Happy Day," again revealing a contemplative side of Thornton that rarely surfaced in her studio recordings. Had she taken a different route, she might have been one of the great gospel singers; instead, she became one of her generation's outstanding blues artists, albeit one whose spirited and ofttimes adventurous music never quite achieved the public acclaim it merited. Thornton died a sad case, penniless and obscure. Johnny Otis, who was there at the beginning, had since become an ordained minister, and presided over her funeral. — D.M.

HENRY THREADGILL

★★★★½ Spirit of Nuff . . . Nuff (Black Saint, 1991)
★★★★ Too Much Sugar for a Dime (Axiom, 1993)
★★★★ Song out of My Trees (Black Saint, 1994)
★★★★½ Carry the Day (Columbia, 1995)
★★★★★ Makin' a Move (Columbia, 1995)
★★★★½ Where's Your Cup? (Columbia, 1997)

With a spiritual zeal, saxophonist/flautist Henry Threadgill (1944–1995) pursued his obsession with sounds at the limit of human expression throughout a career that kept him firmly in the avant-garde as he explored world music and fusion. The Chicago native took formal training at the American Conservatory of Music but also played in school marching bands and gospel groups before spending the 1960s dividing his time between the Association for the Advancement of Creative Musicians and Chicago blues clubs. In the 1970s Threadgill formed the experimental band Air with bassist Fred Hopkins and drummer Steve McCall.

Several excellent Threadgill-led sessions from the 1980s are currently unavailable. *Just the Facts and Pass the Bucket,* a difficult-to-find recording, contains outstanding Threadgill compositions and is one of his best albums. *Rag, Bush and All* is also well worth searching out.

Threadgill's compositional interest in unusual lineups illuminates *Spirit of Nuff . . . Nuff,* performed by his Very Very Circus lineup of Curtis Fowlkes on trombone, Edwin Rodriguez and Marcus Rojas on tubas, Masujaa and Brandon Ross on guitars and Gene Lake on drums. In addition to his saxophone work, Threadgill plays a memorable flute solo on "First Church of This."

Too Much Sugar for a Dime, an extended series of heroin metaphors presented in Threadgill's deadpan style, is an even more adventurous combination of instrumentation, still tuba-powered but colored with Mark Taylor's French horn and, on three tracks, violins, vocals and percussion. The conception and performance of this material is continually impressive, but this composer, always looking for new visions, kept shifting his perspective.

Threadgill moved into an entirely different soundscape on *Song out of My Trees,* using Ted Daniel on trumpet and hunting horn, Tony Cedras on accordion, Diedre Murray and Michelle Kinney on cellos, Amina Claudine Myers on organ and harpsichord, Myra Melford on piano, Ross, Ed Cherry and James Emery on various guitars, Jerome Richardson on acoustic and electric bass and Gene Lake and Reggie Nicholson on drums.

Carry the Day is an exultant, big-screen world-music affair, with Threadgill playing alto, flute and bass flute in front of a Very Very Circus consisting of Taylor, Cedras, Rodriguez, Rojas, Ross, Masujaa and Lake as well as percussion, vocals and violin.

Makin' a Move combines several elements of the previous albums, from the pastoral *Song out of My Trees*–like opening track to the riotous brass exchanges that make up the bulk of the album and Threadgill in chamber-jazz settings with cellos and guitars. The dual tubas of Rodriguez and Rojas are particularly magnificent on this set. *Where's Your Cup?* continues Threadgill's panstylistic musical search, with Cedras and Ross excelling. — J.S.

STEVE TIBBETTS

★★★★ **Yr (1980; ECM, 1988)**
★★★ **Northern Song (ECM, 1982)**
★★★½ **Bye Bye Safe Journey (ECM, 1984)**
★★★½ **Exploded View (ECM, 1986)**
★★★½ **Big Map Idea (ECM, 1988)**
★★★ **The Fall of Us All (ECM, 1994)**

Guitarist Steve Tibbetts (b. 1954) is a self-taught virtuoso whose imaginative playing covers a wide stylistic range that seems more in the tradition of modal high-energy saxophonists like John Coltrane than it does any guitarist's. He also plays mandolin, sitar, keyboards and kalimba. Tibbetts came to public attention via *Yr,* an exceptional debut album recorded in his home studio in Minnesota.

Tibbetts is adept at building droning improvisations over a rich percussive background. Fellow Minnesotan Marc Anderson adds his own percussive ideas to the mix. The records are the most interesting sections pared down from marathon sessions. The beautiful *Bye Bye Safe Journey* is an unusual quintet with bassist Bob Hughes and two other percussionists alongside Anderson. *Exploded View* adds a chanting chorus. Cellist Michelle Kinney is included on *Big Map Idea.* — J.S.

BOBBY TIMMONS

★★★★ **This Here Is Bobby Timmons (1960; Original Jazz Classics, 1992)**
★★★★ **Soul Time (1960; Original Jazz Classics, 1994)**
★★★½ **Easy Does It (1961; Original Jazz Classics, N.A.)**
★★★½ **In Person (1961; Original Jazz Classics, N.A.)**
★★★½ **Sweet and Soulful Sounds (1962; Original Jazz Classics, 1997)**
★★★½ **Born to Be Blue (1963; Original Jazz Classics, N.A.)**
★★★★ **Workin' Out (1964/1965; Prestige, N.A.)**

Pianist Bobby Timmons (1935–1974) was one of the talented generation of jazz artists to emerge from Philadelphia in the 1950s, a key member of the late-'50s lineup of Art Blakey's

Jazz Messengers who later performed with Cannonball Adderley. A powerfully blues-savvy player, Timmons ranged from hard bop to soul jazz and funk, even touching on the '60s avant-garde. An important sideman, he also worked with Kenny Dorham, Lee Morgan, Hank Mobley and Kenny Burrell.

Timmons is best known for his compositions "Moanin'," written for Blakey, and "Dis Here" and "Dat Dere," written for the Adderley quintet. Timmons rode his funky tunes and down-home gospel groove to solo success beginning with the burning debut *This Here Is Bobby Timmons,* a trio session with bassist Sam Jones and drummer Jimmy Cobb (also the lineup on *Easy Does It*). Blakey joins Jones and trumpeter Blue Mitchell for *Soul Time.*

Workin' Out is a reissue of two early-'60s LPs, one with a group consisting of bassist Keter Betts, drummer William Hinnant and vibraphonist Johnny Lytle, the other with Wayne Shorter on tenor, Ron Carter on bass and Cobb on drums. The latter session includes a great version of Shorter's "Tom Thumb." *In Person* is a live trio date with Carter on bass and Albert Heath on drums. — J.S.

CAL TJADER

★★★½ **Mambo with Tjader (1954; Original Jazz Classics, 1987)**
★★★ **Latin Kick (1956; Original Jazz Classics, 1991)**
★★★½ **Tjader Plays Mambo (1956; Original Jazz Classics, 1996)**
★★★½ **Cal Tjader Quartet (1956; Original Jazz Classics, 1997)**
★★★ **Jazz at the Blackhawk (1957; Original Jazz Classics, 1990)**
★★★½ **Latin Concert (1958; Original Jazz Classics, 1991)**
★★★ **San Francisco Moods (1958; Original Jazz Classics, 1987)**
★★★½ **Monterey Concerts (1959; Prestige, 1989)**
★★★★ **A Night at the Blackhawk (1959; Original Jazz Classics, 1987)**
★★★ **Latino! (1960; Fantasy, 1994)**
★★★ **Stan Getz with Cal Tjader (1963; Original Jazz Classics, 1991)**
★★★★★ **Soul Sauce (1965; Verve, 1994)**
★★★ **El Sonido Nuevo (The New Soul Sound) (1966; Verve, 1993)**
★★★ **Plugs In (1969; DCC, 1995)**
★★★ **Primo (1970; Original Jazz Classics, 1993)**
★★★½ **Descarga (1972; Fantasy, 1995)**
★★★½ **Los Ritmos Calientes (1973; Fantasy, 1992)**
★★★★ **Tambu (1974; Original Jazz Classics, 1996)**
★★★★ **Amazonas (1976; Original Jazz Classics, 1995)**
★★★ **The Grace Cathedral Concert (1977; Fantasy, N.A.)**
★★★ **Here and There (1977; Fantasy, N.A.)**
★★★ **La Onda Va Bien (1980; Concord Picante, 1992)**
★★★ **Gózame! Pero Ya (1980; Concord Picante, 1990)**
★★★½ **The Shining Sea (1981; Concord Jazz, 1992)**
★★★ **A Fuego Viva (1982; Concord Picante, N.A.)**
★★★ **Good Vibes (Concord Picante, 1984)**
★★★ **Huracán (LaserLight, 1990)**
★★★½ **Heat Wave (with Carmen McRae) (Concord Jazz, 1992)**
★★★ **Black Orchid (Fantasy, 1993)**
★★★ **Cal Tjader's Greatest Hits (Fantasy, 1995)**

St. Louis–born vibraphonist/percussionist Cal Tjader (1925–1982) was a vaudeville tap dancer before becoming a drummer on the West Coast, where he joined Dave Brubeck's group as a percussionist in the late 1940s. In 1953 he became the vibraphonist in George Shearing's band, then began leading his own groups in 1954. Tjader had a simple but dramatically effective design for a small Latin-jazz group highlighted by the airy tone of his vibes and a relentless, driving groove. His first records were chamber-jazz outings with mambo themes; *Mambo with Tjader* made him popular with the dance-club set immediately, setting the stage for a career of careful and occasionally overpolite readings of West Coast salsa.

Tjader soon became a standard bearer for Latin jazz in the United States as his graceful runs and smoking percussion sections influenced other popularizers of the music such as Herbie Mann and eventually players from the next generation like vibraphonist Gary Burton and pianist Chick Corea. During his two runs at Fantasy, Tjader released more than 20 well-received LPs; the first run was between 1954 and '62 and featured sidemen like tenor saxophonist Stan Getz, *congeros* Armando Peraza and Mongo Santamaria, multipercussionists Willie Bobo and

Johnnie Rae and keyboardist Vince Guaraldi. *A Night at the Blackhawk* is a particularly good live set from this era driven by Bobo and Santamaria, who are also on *Latin Concert* and *Monterey Concerts.*

Tjader's mid-'60s work with producer Creed Taylor at Verve produced the popular "Soul Sauce (Guacha Guaro)," an adaptation of a Chano Pozo/Dizzy Gillespie composition. *El Sonido Nuevo* (*The New Soul Sound*) followed suit, but Tjader was not destined to follow a pop career track. Instead he returned to Fantasy and recorded in a variety of settings. Highlights of Tjader's second stint with Fantasy include the fine collaboration with guitarist Charlie Byrd, *Tambu, Heat Wave,* with vocalist Carmen McRae, the Airto Moreira–produced *Amazonas* and the live set *The Grace Cathedral Concert.* In his final recordings for Concord Picante, Tjader returned to his chamber-jazz approach. Though the playing is uniformly good, *The Shining Sea,* with tenor saxophonist Scott Hamilton and pianist Hank Jones, has the edge. — J.S.

CHARLES TOLLIVER

★★★★½ **The Ringer (1969; Black Lion, 1993)**
★★★★ **Grand Max (1972; Black Lion, 1991)**
★★★★★ **Impact (1975; Strata East, 1994)**

Charles Tolliver (b. 1942), a firebrand trumpeter out of Jacksonville, Florida, had his feet firmly planted in the bop tradition but reached out into freer expressions that eventually forced him out of the mainstream record business to cofound with pianist Stanley Cowell the Strata East label. As is often the case for the most creative and uncompromising jazz players, most of his output is currently unavailable.

As a sideman, Tolliver starred with Jackie McLean and Max Roach. One of his first albums as a leader, *Paper Man,* is well worth finding. *The Ringer* is a tour de force quartet with Cowell, bassist Steve Novosel and drummer Jimmy Hopps. *Grand Max,* a 1972 recording dedicated to Roach, features pianist John Hicks, bassist Reggie Workman and drummer Alvin Queen. This group also appears on the out-of-print *Live at the Loosdrecht Jazz Festival.* In the late 1960s and early 1970s Tolliver led an outstanding version of his Music Inc. band, with Cowell, bassist Cecil McBee and drummer Jimmy Hopps. This band was recorded live at a peak performance in the legendary New York jazz club Slug's. *Live at Slug's, Vol. 1* and *Vol. 2* are currently unavailable but are worth searching out.

The only Strata East Tolliver recording in print is the magnificent big-band outing *Impact,* with Cowell and McBee, featuring a five-trumpet front line led by Tolliver and Jon Faddis, four trombones led by Garnett Brown and a saxophone section including Harold Vick, James Spaulding and George Coleman. — J.S.

MEL TORMÉ

★★★ **It's a Blue World (1955; Bethlehem, 1994)**
★★★½ **Mel Tormé Sings Fred Astaire (1956; Bethlehem, 1992)**
★★★★ **Back in Town (1960; Verve, 1991)**
★★★½ **Swingin' on the Moon (1960; Verve, N.A.)**
★★★½ **Mel Tormé Swings Shubert Alley (1960; Verve, 1992)**
★★★½ **The Duke Ellington and Count Basie Songbooks (1961; Verve, 1990)**
★★★½ **Songs of New York (1963; Atlantic, 1983)**
★★★½ **That's All (1964; Columbia/Legacy, 1997)**
★★★½ **Right Now! (1968; Columbia/Legacy, 1997)**
★★★½ **An Evening with George Shearing and Mel Tormé (Concord Jazz, 1982)**
★★★½ **Top Drawer (Concord Jazz, 1983)**
★★★ **An Evening at Charlie's (Concord Jazz, 1984)**
★★★½ **Mel Tormé, Rob McConnell and the Boss Brass (Concord Jazz, 1986)**
★★★ **An Elegant Evening (Concord Jazz, 1986)**
★★★ **A Vintage Year (Concord Jazz, 1988)**
★★★★ **In Concert in Tokyo (Concord Jazz, 1989)**
★★★ **Night at the Concord Pavilion (Concord Jazz, 1990)**
★★★ **Live at the Fujitsu-Concord Jazz Festival in Japan '90 (Concord Jazz, 1991)**
★★ **Mel and George "Do" World War II (with George Shearing) (Concord Jazz, 1991)**
★★★½ **Reunion (with the Marty Paich Dek-tette) (Concord Jazz, 1992)**
★★★½ **Mel Tormé in Hollywood (Decca, 1992)**

★★★½ **Sing Sing Sing (Concord Jazz, 1992)**
★★★ **The Great American Songbook (Telarc, 1993)**
★★½ **Luck Be a Lady (LaserLight, 1993)**
★★½ **'Round Midnight (LaserLight, 1993)**
★★★ **16 Most Requested Songs (Columbia/Legacy, 1993)**
★★½ **The Best of Mel Tormé (Curb, 1993)**
★★½ **Easy to Remember (Hindsight, 1994)**
★★★ **A Tribute to Bing Crosby (Concord Jazz, 1994)**
★★½ **Velvet and Brass (with Rob McConnell and the Boss Brass) (Concord Jazz, 1995)**
★★★½ **Encore at Marty's (DCC, 1995)**
★★★ **An Evening with Mel Tormé (Concord Jazz, 1996)**
★★★★ **The Mel Tormé Collection (1944–1985) (Rhino, 1996)**
★★★ **Comin' Home Baby and Other Hits (Rhino, 1997)**
★★★½ **Compact Jazz (Verve, N.A.)**

Mel Tormé (b. 1925) is a distinctively mellow-toned vocalist whose smooth, melismatic delivery earned him the aptly descriptive nickname "the Velvet Fog." A gifted writer and arranger as well as a singer, his most famous composition is "The Christmas Song," cowritten with Nat King Cole. A more traditional stylist than his contemporaries Frank Sinatra and Tony Bennett, his roots are in plain view on the excellent *Mel Tormé Sings Fred Astaire;* nearly 40 years later he turns to them again on *A Tribute to Bing Crosby. Compact Jazz* collects trademark material recorded for Verve in the late 1950s and early 1960s. *Back in Town,* a 1959 recording with Mel Lewis on drums, Art Pepper on saxophones and Tormé's vocal group, the Mel-Tones, is a high point.

The Atlantic and Legacy titles show Tormé in excellent form during the mid-1960s. *Songs of New York* is a classic assemblage of songs romanticizing life in the Big Apple as it could only be viewed in the gilded age of the jet-setter. *That's All* is a defining moment in Tormé's career, reissued with previously unreleased material. *Right Now!* is a surprisingly effective set of covers of mid-1960s pop and rock hits.

Tormé's long and fruitful association with Concord Jazz began with a perfectly matched series of recordings with pianist George Shearing. *An Evening with George Shearing and Mel Tormé* features the duo accompanied by bassist Brian Torff; *Top Drawer* switches Torff for Don Thompson; and *An Evening at Charlie's* fills out the accompaniment to a trio with drummer Donny Osborne. *Sing Sing Sing* is a well-executed Benny Goodman tribute. *Mel and George "Do" World War II* is a mistaken exercise in sheer nostalgia.

Mel Tormé, Rob McConnell and the Boss Brass works but veers into self-parody and shows how difficult it is for Tormé to achieve the easygoing simplicity of his approach over and over again. *Reunion* is much more effective, as are the live sets *Night at the Concord Pavilion, Live at the Fujitsu-Concord Jazz Festival* and *In Concert in Tokyo. An Evening with Mel Tormé* shows him still going strong at age 70. — J.S.

ALLEN TOUSSAINT

★★★★★ **The Allen Toussaint Collection (Warner Bros., 1991)**
★★★★½ **Connected (NYNO, 1996)**

One of the masterminds of the modern New Orleans sound, Allen Toussaint (b. 1938) possesses talents as a singer, songwriter, keyboardist and producer that are as subtly powerful as the eddying currents in the Mississippi River at the backwards S it forms along the city's docks. His productions of classic material by Jessie Hill ("Ooh Poo Pah Doo"), Ernie K-Doe ("Mother-in-Law") and Chris Kenner ("I Like It Like That"), among others, are the stuff of legend. Oddly, the richly designed music he crafted on his own magnificent but overlooked recordings never produced hits for the elegant Toussaint.

The Allen Toussaint Collection reissues material from four albums' worth of his most interesting work, including *Southern Nights* and *From a Whisper to a Scream.* In the 1990s, Toussaint continued to produce for his own label, NYNO, including his own sprightly performed *Connected.* — J.S.

RALPH TOWNER

★★★★½ **Diary (1973; ECM, 1988)**
★★★★ **Solstice (1975; ECM, N.A.)**
★★★★ **Trios/Solos (1975; ECM, N.A.)**
★★★★ **Matchbook (1975; ECM, N.A.)**
★★★½ **Old Friends, New Friends (1979; ECM, 1991)**
★★★★ **Solo Concert (1979; ECM, 1987)**
★★★ **Blue Sun (ECM, 1983)**
★★★½ **Slide Show (ECM, 1986)**
★★★ **City of Eyes (ECM, 1989)**
★★★ **Works (ECM, 1991)**

★★★ **Open Letter (ECM, 1992)**
★★★ **Lost and Found (ECM, 1996)**
★★★ **Ana (ECM, 1997)**

Multi-instrumentalist Ralph Towner (b. 1940) is a master on 6- and 12-string and classical guitar and also plays synthesizer, French horn and cornet. His fertile musical imagination tends toward tonal subtlety and nuance and the use of space, especially on his solo work. Classically trained, Towner was a founding member of the remarkable chamber-jazz group Oregon, and his solo works explored an even more delicate sensibility than his work with Oregon.

His spectacular ECM debut, *Diary,* is a tour de force of Towner's solo guitar and piano playing and its novel experiments in time and tonality. The new sound given to his classic composition "Icarus" is a highlight. *Solo Concert,* recorded later in the decade, is nearly as good.

Towner found a sympathetic spirit at ECM in Norwegian multi-instrumental/sonic conceptualist Jan Garbarek. Garbarek is at his best on *Solstice,* which also features Eberhard Weber on bass and cello and Jon Christensen on drums. *Matchbook* is a wonderful exchange with vibraphonist Gary Burton, whose lucid approach to melody and harmonic invention brought out another side of Towner's sound. *Trios/Solos* is an essential recording.

Towner appeared to drift creatively in his solo work after the death of one of his partners in Oregon, master percussionist Collin Walcott, in a 1984 automobile accident. The troubling *Blue Sun* lacks the beauty of the other works; *Open Letter* is an unsuccessful sequel to *Diary,* with drummer Peter Erskine joining Towner; and *Works* is an oddly programmed and unsatisfying career overview.

Several of Towner's better ECM recordings are currently unavailable. *Batik* is a top-notch trio date with bassist Eddie Gomez and drummer Jack DeJohnette. *Sargasso Sea* is a splendid exchange with guitarist John Abercrombie, whose acerbic attack provides an illustrative foil to Towner's ringing 12-string chordal work. *Five Years Later,* another collaboration with Abercrombie, is another high point missing from the catalog. — J.S.

TREMÉ BRASS BAND

★★★★ **Gimme My Money Back (Arhoolie, 1995)**

The Tremé Brass Band is a New Orleans marching band directly connected to the funeral marching bands of second-line legend while featuring some of the genre's newest stars. Led by the shuffling snare beat cut by drummer Benny Jones of the Dirty Dozen and Chosen Few Brass Bands and Dirty Dozen compatriot Lionel Batiste Sr. on bass drum and vocals, Tremé sticks to mostly traditional material but slaps it around so nastily that it always sounds fresh. Kirk Joseph, another charter member of the Dozen and the son of New Orleans trombonist Waldren "Frog" Joseph, keeps things rolling with monster tuba blasts. The front line pits Fats Domino veterans Elliot "Stackman" Callier on tenor sax and Fred Kemp on soprano and alto against young lions Kermit Ruffins and James Andrews on trumpets and Corey Henry on trombone. Ruffins was coleader of Rebirth Brass Band; Henry of the Little Rascals Brass Band. Four live cuts with a slightly different lineup are included. — J.S.

THE TRENIERS

★★★★★ **They Rock! They Roll! They Swing! (Epic/Legacy, 1995)**

With unbridled energy and urgent vocalizings, twin brothers Claude (b. 1919) and Clifford Trenier (d. 1983) led their raucous big band through a series of devil-may-care and frequently off-color jump-blues and early rock & roll hits that distilled roadhouse blues spirit into such exclamatory anthems as "Go! Go! Go!," "It Rocks! It Rolls! It Swings!" and their signature curtain-riser, "Rockin' Is Our Business." In their day, besuited and appearing on the Dean Martin/Jerry Lewis–hosted *Colgate Comedy Hour,* the Trenier brand of rock & roll was then hailed as a showbiz novelty. The frenetic Treniers now seem ahead of their time, considering their ribald repertoire: Professor Longhair's "Bald Head," Richard Berry's "Get Out of the Car (Uh-Oh)," Roy Brown's "Good Rockin' Tonight" and 1952's "Poon-Tang!," the most extreme example of their lyrical license (with the built-in disclaimer, "A poon is a kiss/A tang is a hug"). A best-of package featuring songs recorded over a five-year span for Okeh (1951–55), *They Rock! They Roll! They Swing!* is a solid, hits-and-not portrait of the Treniers, featuring all the aforementioned songs as well as their highest charter, the baseball paean "Say Hey (The Willie Mays Song)." — A.K.

LENNIE TRISTANO

★★★★ **The Complete Lennie Tristano on Keynote (Mercury, 1994)**

★★★★ **Lennie Tristano/The New Tristano (Rhino, 1995)**
★★★★ **Intuition (Capitol, 1996)**

Lennie Tristano (1919–1978), pianist, teacher, leader and theoretician, was a reclusive, opinionated man who spent the last quarter century of his life teaching out of his Long Island home surrounded by an extremely devoted coterie of students. Since his death, Tristano's brilliance in the realm of sinuous, unclichéd improvisation in a less visceral bebop-derived style has gained wider appreciation, and much great music under his name has appeared.

The Complete Lennie Tristano on Keynote collects some of Tristano's earliest work, from 1946 to '47. *Intuition* includes an album's worth of material with tenor saxophonist Warne Marsh and tracks by Tristano's Konitz/Marsh quintet. Several out-of-print albums on Jazz Records are especially enlightening; these releases should be sought out. *Live at Birdland* (1949) contains quintet performances featuring Marsh, plus four 1945 piano solos that appear to be Tristano's first recordings. *Live in Toronto* (1952) is classic early Tristano played by a quintet featuring Lee Konitz and Marsh. *Wow* (1950) and *Continuity* (1964) also feature Konitz and Marsh.

Also currently unavailable, *Requiem* includes some of Tristano's greatest work. Part of the album is a 1955 recording that shows the pianist in early overdubbing experiments, plus live material from a New York club with star pupil Lee Konitz on alto. Completing *Requiem* is a stunning 1961 solo recital in which Tristano achieves the complex contrapuntal effects he was aiming at in 1955—this time without overdubs. — B.B.

DEREK TRUCKS BAND

★★★★½ **The Derek Trucks Band (Landslide, 1997)**
★★★★★ **Out of the Madness (House of Blues, 1998)**

Derek Trucks (b. 1979) grew up on the home schooling of his uncle Butch Trucks's band, the Allman Brothers, and has pursued a multifaceted guitar style that ranges from hard blues to free jazz, always in service of the almighty groove. Trucks is the goods, a naturally gifted player with a real thirst for musical expansiveness, and thus his playing is full of pleasant surprises, as he twists and turns his way cleverly around familiar blues and jazz tropes. He can evolve a stately evocation of Jeff Beck's fusion masterpiece "Blow by Blow" into a blistering slide solo inspired by the spirit of the Sky Dog himself, Duane Allman. Of all the under-20 guitar sensations on hand, he is both the furthest developed technically and the likeliest to improve even more. — J.S.

LUTHER TUCKER

★★★★ **Sad Hours (Antone's, 1994)**
★★★½ **Luther Tucker and the Ford Blues Band (Blue Rock'it, 1995)**

Guitarist Luther Tucker (1936–1993) moved from Memphis to Chicago with his family as a child and worked in Little Walter's band from 1952 to '58. Tucker was a sought-after guitarist on the Chicago scene in the late 1950s and '60s, doing stints with Muddy Waters, Sonny Boy Williamson (Rice Miller) and Sunnyland Slim, and later with Otis Rush and James Cotton. After moving in 1969 to the San Francisco area, he played on and off through the 1970s with John Lee Hooker and Charlie Musselwhite. *Sad Hours* is a solid groove of a session organized around the Austin blues regulars at Antone's, including drummer George Rains, saxophonist Mark Kazanoff and keyboardist Reese Wynans, and a whopping dose of class-A harmonica from the great Kim Wilson. *Luther Tucker and the Ford Blues Band* is an engaging set; the album also includes interview material with Tucker. — J.S.

MICKEY TUCKER

★★★½ **Blues in Five Dimensions (SteepleChase, 1990)**
★★★ **Hang in There (SteepleChase, 1994)**
★★★ **Gettin' There (SteepleChase, 1995)**

Keyboardist Mickey Tucker (b. 1941) worked in R&B and pop bands before building solid credentials as a sideman with Art Blakey, James Moody, the Thad Jones/Mel Lewis orchestra and Frank Foster. He recorded a series of albums under his own name for Xanadu and Muse, all of which are currently unavailable on CD (look for *The Crawl*), and went on to record for SteepleChase. *Blues in Five Dimensions* is the best of these, a solid quartet date with guitarist Ted Dunbar, bassist Rufus Reid and drummer David Jones. — J.S.

IKE TURNER

★★★★ **Ike Turner 1958–1959 (Paula, 1991)**

★★★★ **I Like Ike! The Best of Ike Turner (Rhino, 1994)**

However large the gap between Ike Turner's private morality and his public and professional conduct, the music he made, especially in the pre– and early–rock & roll eras, bespeaks a gifted, even visionary artist.

Born in Clarksdale, Mississippi, in 1931, Izear Luster Turner began playing piano as a child and almost immediately was worshipping at the altar of Sonny Boy Williamson's (Rice Miller) stalwart pianist, Pinetop Perkins, whom he heard regularly on the King Biscuit Flour radio show emanating from Helena, Arkansas. In his teens he took a job at Clarksdale's WROX station, mixing sound for the country and blues artists who often came through doing live shows. This led to his first professional job as a musician, accompanying bluesman Robert Nighthawk on piano during his Clarksdale-area gigs. By the late '40s, Turner had formed his own band, the Kings of Rhythm, comprising mostly Clarksdale musicians. B.B. King, newly signed to RPM Records himself, became the Turner band's benefactor when, in 1951, he recommended them to Sam Phillips, who was then cutting blues artists at his Memphis studio and leasing their masters to such labels as Chess and Modern. There, on March 3 (or 5, depending on the source), Turner and his band cut the song that in later years would be referred to by Phillips as "the first rock & roll record," meaning "Rocket 88," a rousing, up-tempo paean to the virtues of that model Oldsmobile. Featuring Turner's 13-year-old cousin Jackie Brenston on lead vocal, the song's lyrical sentiments were matched by the Turner band's ferocious rhythmic assault, buoyed by Ike's own unrelenting right-hand attack on the keyboards and Raymond Hill's exciting tenor-sax howls. Leased to Chess, the single topped the R&B chart on June 12 and remained on the chart until early September.

Turner's bands never made it back to such rarefied heights, but the years leading up to Ike's association with the former Annie Mae Bullock (Tina Turner) produced music of unflagging energy, wit and emotional depth from an array of sterling vocalists and first-rate musicianship, with Ike himself leading the way. *I Like Ike!* offers 18 examples of Turner's evolution from "Rocket 88" up to a trio session he cut in 1972. No mere musician and bandleader, he became a key behind-the-scenes player in the development of the '50s big-beat music that evolved into rock & roll. Introduced to Joe Bihari, owner of Modern/RPM Records, during a session at Phillips's studio, Turner became the label's chief talent scout, arranger, producer, writer and house pianist in addition to cutting sides with his own band. A number of label changes followed over the years, but at every stop Turner produced interesting music.

One of the first Modern efforts is here, the 1954 Turner-written and -produced single for Dennis Binder & His Orchestra, "I Miss You So," a steady-rolling track in the Roy Brown vein recorded in Clarksdale. Another Turner original, "Peg Leg Woman" (released in 1956 on the Vita label), is something of a "Rocket 88" rewrite fueled by Willie King's (Billy Gayles) Clyde McPhatter–style vocals. Of the many stellar vocalists who passed through Turner's stable, none matched gospel-bred belter Tommy Hodge for the sheer emotional charge of his gravel-voiced exhortations. The three tracks featuring Hodge show how smoothly Turner made the transition from the hard, blues-oriented approach of his early recordings to a more pulsating, R&B big-band groove in which instrumental soloing was kept to a minimum, the better to buttress the obvious force the featured singers brought to the table.

Still, Turner knew when to step out or to let others shine. Consider his 1959 composition "Matchbox": Behind Hodge's go-for-broke declaiming, Turner offers a counterpoint vocal via a stinging, slicing guitar solo that melds Freddie King with T-Bone Walker—a performance as remarkable for its heart as for its instrumental mastery. In an obvious play for the pop charts, Turner wrote and recorded the 1958 single "Boxtop," which, though failing commercially, is noteworthy for being Annie Mae Bullock's first appearance on record with her future husband; for Ike's own rare appearance as a low-down vocalist; and for another of his electrifying, compact solos. Included here in its first appearance on any reissue collection, "Boxtop" sounds like the sort of low-tech pop/doo-wop coming out of New York at the time. Check out Ike's fluid, spitfire picking—all Carl Perkins and Hank Garland in style—on the Kings of Rhythm's cover of Texas Playboy Leon McAuliffe's "Steel Guitar Rag," a track included on Ike and Tina's debut, *Dance with Ike & Tina Turner's Kings of Rhythm.* Finally, Ike steps out on his own on the 1970 track "Takin' Back My Name," with a snarling vocal, a riff lifted from the Stones' "Honky Tonk

Women" and lyrics that, one supposes, represent Ike's point of view in no-holds-barred fashion.
— D.M.

JOE TURNER

★★★★★ **The Boss of the Blues (1956; Atlantic, 1981)**
★★★★ **Big Joe Rides Again (1960; Atlantic, 1987)**
★★★★ **The Trumpet Kings Meet Joe Turner (1975; Original Jazz Classics, 1990)**
★★★ **Nobody in Mind (Original Jazz Classics, 1976)**
★★★★ **In the Evening (1976; Original Jazz Classics, 1995)**
★★★ **Things That I Used to Do (1977; Original Jazz Classics, 1995)**
★★★½ **Everyday I Have the Blues (1978; Original Jazz Classics, 1991)**
★★★ **The Midnight Special (Pablo, 1980)**
★★★★★ **Tell Me Pretty Baby (1980; Arhoolie, 1992)**
★★★★ **The Best of Joe Turner (1980; Pablo, 1987)**
★★★ **Have No Fear Joe Turner Is Here (Pablo, 1981)**
★★ **Boss Blues (Intermedia, 1982)**
★★ **The Very Best of Joe Turner (Intermedia, 1982)**
★★ **Roll Me Baby (Intermedia, 1982)**
★★ **Rock This Joint (Intermedia, 1982)**
★★★ **Life Ain't Easy (Original Jazz Classics, 1983)**
★★★★ **Blues Train (Muse, 1983)**
★★★★ **Kansas City Here I Come (Original Jazz Classics, 1984)**
★★★ **Patcha, Patcha, All Night Long: Joe Turner Meets Jimmy Witherspoon (1985; Pablo, 1996)**
★★★★★ **Big Joe Turner Memorial Album: Rhythm & Blues Years (Atlantic, 1986)**
★★★★★ **Big Joe Turner: Greatest Hits (Atlantic Jazz, 1987)**
★★★ **Flip, Flop & Fly (with Count Basie and His Orchestra) (Pablo, 1989)**
★★ **Joe Turner and T-Bone Walker: Bosses of the Blues, Vol. 1 (RCA Bluebird, 1989)**
★★★★★ **I've Been to Kansas City, Vol. 1 (MCA, 1990)**
★★★★ **Stormy Monday (Pablo, 1991)**
★★★ **Texas Style (Evidence, 1992)**
★★★½ **Shouting the Blues (Specialty, 1992)**
★★★★★ **Jumpin' with Joe: The Complete Aladdin and Imperial Recordings (EMI, 1993)**
★★★★★ **Every Day in the Week (Decca, 1993)**
★★½ **Shake, Rattle & Roll (Tomato, 1994)**
★★★★★ **Big, Bad & Blue: The Big Joe Turner Anthology (Rhino, 1994)**

"Boss of the Blues" Joe Turner (1911–1985) can lay legitimate claim to being a founding father of both rhythm & blues and rock & roll—this in addition to being regarded as one of the most powerful blues singers in history, a man of Promethean appetites and energy whose name was often preceded by the apt descriptive "Big" and whose Mack truck of a voice was unadorned by gimmickry. The straightforwardness of his approach was its own recommendation: Whether shouting it out or getting into what passed for a gentle, sensitive mode, Turner's voice remained a grand, stately instrument full of interesting colors. When he was in full flight, roaring over a big, swinging band with pulsating horns, he was like a force unleashed by nature, unstoppable and awe-inspiring in the primal force of his fury—"human thunder," as one critic described him. On slower, bluesier numbers, the tenderness in his phrasing could be heart-stopping in all its bountiful beauty.

Turner's career dates to the mid-'20s, when he landed a job tending bar in Kansas City, his hometown; as an extracurricular activity he took up shouting the blues with pianist Pete Johnson, and the two became a local sensation after settling in at the Sunset club. Turner, Johnson, Sam Price and Jay McShann became the key figures in a vital K.C. music scene that merged blues and jazz into boogie-woogie, which swept the country after Turner's and Johnson's 1938 appearance at New York's Carnegie Hall in the "From Spirituals to Swing" concert organized by John Hammond. "It's All Right Baby," the first Turner/Johnson recording, was made at the Carnegie Hall date; a few days later the musicians cut their first Vocalion sides, "Roll 'Em Pete" and "Goin' Away Blues." Turner remained in New York, holding forth regularly at Barney Josephson's Cafe Society boîte (along with fellow boogie pioneers Albert Ammons and Meade "Lux" Lewis) for the next four years. Shortly after his Carnegie Hall show, Turner cut his first sides for Vocalion, inaugurating a recording career that would span more than 40 years for a number of labels and produce a consistently high-quality body of work, invariably accompanied by the best musicians of his time.

The early groundbreaking sides are featured on several essential releases. *I've Been to Kansas City, Vol. 1* and *Every Day in the Week,* comprise, respectively, sessions cut in 1940–41 in New York and trio dates in Los Angeles (1941–42) and Chicago ('44); the latter CD also contains '60s sessions recorded in New York, including a new version of "Piney Brown Blues" featuring Panama Francis on drums. The three-CD *Big, Bad & Blue* presents a representative sampling of Turner's work through the years, as he essays material ranging from hard blues to boisterous R&B to swinging, jazz-flavored sides. Included here are the original "It's All Right Baby"; the 1939 Vocalion sides; recordings made in the late '40s to 1950 for National, Down Beat, Aladdin and Freedom; all of the critical Atlantic sides; and, from his latter years, single entries from his productive Pablo stint in the '70s, one cut released by LMI in 1974 and a cut from his final album as a leader, 1983's *Blues Train.* For one package, this is the must-have Joe Turner title.

Late '40s Joe Turner/Pete Johnson sessions for the Down Beat label are the focus of Arhoolie's 24-cut *Tell Me Pretty Baby.* Check out the blazing ensemble work—especially Johnson's hailstorm of right-hand staccato notes and Herman Mitchell's evocatively distorted guitar solos—on the 1948 instrumental "Rocket Boogie '88' (Pt. 1)," the model for Jackie Brenston and Ike Turner's "Rocket 88" that was recorded six years later at the Sun studio in Memphis and subsequently hailed by Sam Phillips as the first rock & roll record. Otherwise this collection shows the young Turner at his most powerful, using that big, smoldering baritone voice on material that allows him to show off his tender side ("Baby, Won't You Marry Me") as well as his swaggering one, while Johnson and his orchestra get a chance to flaunt their impressive chops on some potent instrumental interludes.

Still another brief era of Turner's '40s recording odyssey surfaces on Specialty's *Shouting the Blues,* featuring eight tracks cut in 1949 for the Houston-based Freedom label (other artists on this compilation include Big Maceo, the Don Johnson Orchestra, Smilin' Smokey Lynn and H-Bomb Ferguson). Backed by a small combo and horn section, Turner is heard here adding to the foundation that would become rock & roll in the next decade, particularly in the three sides featuring Goree Carter adding some rock-ribbed Lonnie Johnson–style guitar solos to the R&B groove. "Life Is a Card Game" and "Still in the Dark" stand with Turner's most persuasive performances in any style or era.

The Boss of the Blues (originally released in 1956) re-creates the fertile Kansas City period of Turner's career, reuniting him with the estimable Johnson and other first-rate players on the tunes that secured Turner's early acclaim, notable among the selections being "Cherry Red," "Roll 'Em Pete," "I Want a Little Girl," "Wee Baby Blues" and "Low Down Dog." These and other sides Turner cut in the late '40s constitute a harder-edged school of rhythm & blues than that being pioneered by Turner's brilliant contemporary Louis Jordan; thus it was only a short leap from Turner's style of R&B to early rock & roll, as indicated by the success of Turner's "Shake, Rattle and Roll" in a lyrically sanitized but hotly recorded cover version by Bill Haley and His Comets.

Signed to Atlantic in 1951, Turner proceeded to write his name large in rock & roll history with important genre-busting entries that blur the distinction between R&B and rock & roll and are formidable in their music, in their vocal performances, in their clever use of language and imagery. Of these the most prominent are "Flip, Flop and Fly," "Honey Hush," "Corrine, Corrina" and "Sweet Sixteen." This fruitful era is well documented on *Big, Bad & Blue, Big Joe Turner: Greatest Hits* and *Big Joe Turner Memorial Album: Rhythm & Blues Years.* A 1960 Atlantic release, *Big Joe Rides Again,* demonstrates the ease with which this masterful singer could adapt material to suit his personal style. Here he rolls through great popular ballads ("Until the Real Thing Comes Along," "I Get the Blues When It Rains," "Pennies from Heaven") and up-tempo blues ("Switchin' in the Kitchen") and drops in a soulful meditation in blues, "When I Was Young."

An unsettling gap in Turner's recording history is filled with the 1993 release of EMI's *Jumpin' with Joe: The Complete Aladdin and Imperial Recordings.* After his first flush of success and before moving to Atlantic, Turner saw some of his most commanding recordings released in 1947 on the Aladdin label, where for a brief, glorious moment in blues history he shared a studio with "Mr. Blues," Wynonie Harris, and beginning in 1950 on Imperial, a

West Coast label that was then mining New Orleans for talent. A frequent visitor to the Crescent City, Turner signed with Imperial in 1950 and headed to the J&M recording studio to lay down tracks with producer Dave Bartholomew and his powerhouse studio band (including, on Turner's first session, Imperial's newest star, pianist Fats Domino). One of the mysteries of Turner's career is why the Aladdin and Imperial years produced so little in the way of chart success, given the high quality of the music the artist recorded for both. However fallow those years may have been on the sales front, they find Turner delivering again and again. Consider the first four tracks on *Jumpin' with Joe,* wherein Turner and Harris battle it out in grand style, alternately sympathizing with each other in their troubles with faithless women or engaging in some feisty one-upsmanship over who is indeed the cock of the walk. Though far less popular with the general public than Turner, Harris could hold his own with the best, and do so in shouting style or in more reflective passages, as he demonstrates in his teamings with Turner. As for the Imperial sides, suffice it to say that Bartholomew did the artist justice in providing the most sympathetic framework for numbers that were both steamrolling house rockers and slow-grinding tales of woe.

Turner continued to record sporadically through the '60s, then found his career in high gear again come the '70s, thanks to producer Norman Granz, who teamed him with jazz giants Count Basie, Milt Jackson, Roy Eldridge and others on several recordings for the Pablo label (many of which have been rereleased on CD on Original Jazz Classics) that have a casual, jam-session feel. His authoritative singing undiminished by age, Turner, inspired by his stellar accompanists, came up with several terrific performances. Of note here are *Flip, Flop & Fly,* with the Count Basie Orchestra (recorded in 1972); *Nobody in Mind,* with Milt Jackson, Roy Eldridge and Pee Wee Crayton among the supporting cast; *In the Evening,* a moody set featuring Turner's swaggering, laconic take on George Gershwin's "Summertime"; a low-down deep-blues excavation of Leroy Carr's title track; a strutting, carefree and altogether hilarious reading of "I've Got the World on a String"; and a steady-grooving rethinking of "Pennies from Heaven," with Turner and alto saxophonist Bob Smith engaging in some witty vocal/instrumental repartee toward the end. Crayton's guitar work plays a stellar supporting role (as does tenor- and alto-sax man Sonny Stitt) on *Everyday I Have the Blues,* where the musicians work some new variations on tried-and-true material such as "Stormy Monday," "Shake Rattle and Roll" and the title track.

A remarkable summit meeting defines the whole of *The Trumpet Kings Meet Joe Turner,* a 1974 project that finds the sine qua non of blues shouters holding forth with a quartet of equally imposing trumpet masters in Dizzy Gillespie, Roy Eldridge, Harry "Sweets" Edison and Clark Terry. Each is given plenty of room to maneuver in four lengthy cuts—Terry's muted solo on "Mornin', Noon and Night," in which he sustains a triplet figure over the length of a chorus, is a tour de force of technique coupled to emotive power—and Turner is an affable host, commanding enough of the spotlight to make his mark, then stepping back to let the players establish their own points of view.

Among other titles here are the odd *Shake, Rattle & Roll* on Tomato, a disc about evenly divided between live and overproduced studio recordings, with the major plus of having an 18-page liner booklet written by blues authority Pete Welding but with the major negative of there being no information at all regarding session dates, personnel, producers or the locale and dates of the live cuts. Best guess, from the deeper, gravelly tone of Turner's voice, is that these sides are of late-'70s vintage.

Evidence's *Texas Style* comprises eight tracks cut in France in 1971, with Turner backed by a powerhouse trio of Milt Bruckner (piano), Slam Stewart (bass) and Jo Jones (drums). The musical reference point here is Kansas City in the '30s; the mood is festive in an after-hours way. Despite some well-worn material ("Cherry Red," "TV Mama," "Rock Me Baby"), Turner and company find ways to energize one another throughout this engaging, spirited get-together marked by authoritative singing and tight, inventive instrumental support—a good bang for the buck.

Only completists need bother with the Bluebird title, *Bosses of the Blues, Vol. 1,* with its eight sides of Turner and seven of electric-guitar pioneer T-Bone Walker recorded back to back in Los Angeles in 1969. Turner is backed by an unidentified orchestra conducted by Gene Page and a small combo, but the effort here is directed toward updating Turner's R&B sound for contemporary audiences, which succeeds in making the singer sound uncomfortable (on a woeful Philly-soul version of "Shake, Rattle and Roll" that prefigures the sort of pop disco Page would foist on an unsuspecting public a few years later) and, finally, bored (on a desultory "Corrine, Corrina").

In 1983 Turner got together with the equally legendary songwriter Doc Pomus to cowrite a new tune, "Blues Train," which became the centerpiece of Turner's final album. Coproduced by Pomus and Bob Porter, *Blues Train* rumbles and roars mightily, with Turner backed by Roomful of Blues and Dr. John on nine cuts that take him all the way back to Kansas City and bring him forward into the present.

Two years later, Turner proved conclusively that age and experience were virtues for a blues singer when he teamed with another master, Jimmy Witherspoon, for some low-down carousing on *Patcha, Patcha, All Night Long.* This is wonderful stuff, with Turner adapting to his diminished range with a series of lyric readings remarkable for their heart and personality; by contrast, Witherspoon comes on full of spit and vinegar, sounding like a tenor version of the younger Turner. Together these giants have a splendid time, whether turning up the heat on the title song or looking back poignantly at a lost love on the Turner-penned "Kansas City on My Mind," a song rife with metaphorical overtones for the Boss of the Blues. There's also time for a bit of lascivious fun on Leiber and Stoller's "The Chicken and the Hawk." *Patcha, Patcha, All Night Long* turned out to be the last great testament of a great singer. — D.M.

STANLEY TURRENTINE

★★★★ **Up at Minton's (1961; Blue Note, N.A.)**
★★★½ **Z.T.'s Blues (1961; Blue Note, 1988)**
★★★ **Ballads (1961; Blue Note, 1993)**
★★★ **Never Let Me Go (1963; Blue Note, 1992)**
★★★★ **Let It Go (1966; Impulse!, 1991)**
★★★ **Common Touch (1969; Blue Note, 1997)**
★★ **Salt Song (1971; Sony, 1997)**
★★ **Don't Mess with Mister T (1973; Columbia, 1988)**
★★★½ **Pieces of Dreams (1974; Original Jazz Classics, 1992)**
★★½ **Everybody Come On Out (1976; Original Jazz Classics, 1996)**
★★★½ **The Best of Stanley Turrentine (Blue Note, 1989)**
★★★ **The Best of Stanley Turrentine (Columbia/Legacy, 1990)**
★★★ **The Best of Mr. T (Fantasy, 1992)**
★★★★ **More Than a Mood (MusicMasters, 1992)**
★★★ **If I Could (MusicMasters, 1993)**
★★★½ **Time (MusicMasters, 1995)**
★★★ **Flipped (Drive Archive, 1995)**

The trademark of tenor saxophonist Stanley Turrentine (b. 1934) is a soulful, full-bodied tone that shakes the sweat off every note he hits. He learned the technique from his father, Thomas Turrentine Sr., who played saxophone for the Savoy Sultans in the late '30s. In the early '50s the younger Turrentine played in the Lowell Fulson band with Ray Charles on piano before taking jazz gigs with Tadd Dameron and rocking R&B with Earl Bostic. By the end of the decade, he'd made a name for himself with the Max Roach Quintet.

During the '60s he was in a working band with his wife, organist Shirley Scott, heard here on *Let It Go.* He recorded effectively with various small groups in a soul-jazz groove, using pianist Horace Parlan, bassist George Tucker and drummer Al Harewood on the out-of-print *Look Out,* then adding guitarist Grant Green for the terrific live set *Up at Minton's.* Green also took part in *Z.T.'s Blues,* with the stellar rhythm section of pianist Tommy Flanagan, bassist Paul Chambers and drummer Art Taylor.

Turrentine veered toward pop in the '70s, recording for CTI and Fantasy. The CTI dates are slick, heavily arranged affairs, the best of which, the out-of-print *Sugar,* features trumpeter Freddie Hubbard, guitarist George Benson and bassist Ron Carter. Carter also backs Turrentine on some of the Fantasy material. *Pieces of Dreams* was a hit for Fantasy, leading to eight more albums on the label, but only *Pieces of Dreams, Everybody Come On Out* and *The Best of Mr. T* remain available. Turrentine was unsuccessfully marketed as a contemporary R&B artist in the 1980s, a mostly disastrous encounter with synthesizers and click tracks that produced one standout session, the out-of-print Stevie Wonder tribute *Wonderland.*

At MusicMasters Turrentine has been presented as the venerable jazz great he is. *More Than a Mood* shows him back in top form surrounded by Freddie Hubbard on trumpet and flügelhorn, Cedar Walton on piano, Carter on bass and Billy Higgins on drums. — J.S.

McCOY TYNER

★★★½ **McCoy Tyner Plays Ellington (1964; Impulse!, 1990)**

★★★★ **Today and Tomorrow (1966; GRP, 1991)**
★★★★ **The Real McCoy (1967; Blue Note, 1987)**
★★★★★ **Sahara (1972; Original Jazz Classics, 1987)**
★★★★★ **Echoes of a Friend (1972; Original Jazz Classics, 1991)**
★★★★ **Song for My Lady (1973; Original Jazz Classics, 1987)**
★★★★ **Song of the New World (1973; Original Jazz Classics, 1991)**
★★★★★ **Enlightenment (1973; Milestone, 1990)**
★★★★★ **Trident (1975; Original Jazz Classics, 1992)**
★★★½ **Fly with the Wind (1976; Original Jazz Classics, 1992)**
★★★★★ **Supertrios (1977; Milestone, 1989)**
★★★ **McCoy Tyner 4 × 4 (1980; Milestone, 1993)**
★★★ **Double Trios (Denon, 1987)**
★★★½ **Inception/Night of Ballads and Blues (Impulse!, 1988)**
★★★★ **Uptown/Downtown (Milestone, 1989)**
★★★★ **Live at Sweet Basil (1989; Evidence, 1995)**
★★★★ **Revelations (Blue Note, 1989)**
★★★½ **Things Ain't What They Used to Be (Blue Note, 1990)**
★★★★ **One on One (with Stéphane Grappelli) (Milestone, 1990)**
★★★ **Bon Voyage (Timeless, 1990)**
★★★½ **Just Feelin' (Quicksilver, 1991)**
★★★ **Blue Bossa (LaserLight, 1991)**
★★★ **New York Reunion (Chesky, 1991)**
★★★ **Double Exposure (LaserLight, 1991)**
★★★★ **44th Street Suite (Red Baron, 1991)**
★★★½ **Remembering John (Enja, 1991)**
★★★½ **The Turning Point (Verve, 1992)**
★★★★ **Soliloquy (Blue Note, 1992)**
★★★ **Manhattan Moods (Blue Note, 1994)**
★★★ **Journey (Verve, 1994)**
★★★½ **Prelude and Sonata (Milestone, 1995)**
★★★★★ **Infinity (Impulse!, 1995)**
★★★★ **The Best of McCoy Tyner: The Blue Note Years (Blue Note, 1996)**
★★★½ **Autumn Moods (LaserLight, 1997)**
★ **What the World Needs Now: The Music of Burt Bacharach (Impulse!, 1997)**

Pianist McCoy Tyner (b. 1938) has a personally expressive and extremely influential approach to playing that emphasizes the instrument's percussive depth and harmonic density. His sheer power forces the piano into loquaciously ill-tempered dissonance while pursuing melodic lines of exquisite, hypnotic beauty. Through chromatic chord substitutions based on fourths and a single-line style that clusters notes like John Coltrane's saxophone scales did, Tyner achieves a uniquely orchestral sound on the piano. At the same time he never loses sight of the blues.

Tyner grew up in Philadelphia's jazz community, a close acquaintance of piano genius Bud Powell. He worked in the Art Farmer/Benny Golson Jazztet before joining fellow Philadelphian Coltrane in a musical partnership that reflected the dramatic changes of the 1960s and would have a profound impact on the future of jazz. This quartet, including bassist Jimmy Garrison and drummer Elvin Jones, recorded several of the greatest albums in jazz history and influenced generations of musicians to come.

Tyner began his career as a leader while still a member of the Coltrane quartet, recording both with and without the quartet for Impulse! His solo albums were clearly lighter fare than the quartet's epochal statements, and they enhanced Tyner's reputation as a piano leader who excelled in the trio format. *Inception,* part of a reissued twofer with *Night of Ballads and Blues,* shows that Tyner was more than prepared for the leader's role. The best of the Impulse! albums, *Today and Tomorrow,* features tenor saxophonist John Gilmore and trumpeter Thad Jones.

After leaving Coltrane, Tyner signed with Blue Note, just as that company was about to go into decline. Two years later he was shaken by Coltrane's death. Tyner's music went through a deeply personal and troubled period that, despite a lack of economic success, yielded profound musical benefits as Tyner took up the spiritual quest he once shared with Coltrane and explored the roots and crosscurrents of African and Asian musical influences. Tyner reconfigures the Coltrane quartet on *The Real McCoy,* reuniting with Jones along with Ron Carter on bass and Joe Henderson on tenor.

The swirling cross-cultural currents of the era and the emotional life, death and rebirth cycle Tyner experienced informed his next quartet, whose players reached a plane only the Coltrane quartet had previously inhabited. Night after night, often at New York's fabled Lower East

Side club Slug's, Tyner led Sonny Fortune on soprano and alto sax and flute; Calvin Hill on bass, percussion and reeds; and Alphonse Mouzon on drums, percussion, trumpet and reeds through possessed, vertiginous marathons of shamanistic discovery, exploring themes for hours on end as that magical last set sped toward dawn.

Somehow Tyner manages to condense this experience into a single album, the astonishing *Sahara.* Some of his greatest piano playing is here, marked by beautiful sections of African music where piano and percussion become an intricate interlace, and the powerful interaction between his keyboard-pounding trances and the inspired drumming of Mouzon, who has never sounded better. The same group appears on *Song for My Lady,* with flügelhornist Charles Tolliver, violinist Michael White and percussionist Mtume on two tracks. *Echoes of a Friend* is a solo-piano tribute to Coltrane. On *Song of the New World* Tyner switches to writing for large brass and string ensembles with Fortune and Mouzon still at the core of the proceedings.

On *Enlightenment,* a 1973 live recording from Montreux, Tyner returns to the blinding intensity of the quartet, with Mouzon joined by Azar Lawrence on soprano and tenor saxophones and Joony Booth on bass. Tyner strips the format down to a trio for the formidable *Trident,* with drummer Elvin Jones and bassist Ron Carter. He enjoyed widespread airplay with the string-driven title track of *Fly with the Wind.* The aptly named *Supertrios* is split between two sessions, one with Carter on bass and Tony Williams on drums, the other with Eddie Gomez on bass and Jack DeJohnette on drums. By contrast, *McCoy Tyner 4 × 4,* a series of all-star sessions, never seems to get off the ground.

Tyner's music is so demanding that he is not afforded the breathing space to be ordinary, leaving a brief period of consolidation during the 1980s, when he was without a major domestic recording contract, to appear like a slump. But Tyner is always a worthwhile listen, as the fine mid-'80s trio date with bassist Avery Sharpe and drummer Louis Hayes, *Just Feelin',* demonstrates. Even when he was unable to make major-statement studio albums, Tyner remained a transcendent live performer who flirted with greatness every time he sat down at the piano. The 1988 solo outing, *Revelations,* was recorded at New York's Merkin Hall, "live" but without an audience. A month later, before a packed house at the Blue Note, Tyner recorded *Uptown/Downtown,* introducing his big band, which went on to become a New York institution. Tyner's virtuosity was caught on a particularly good night in 1989 at New York's Sweet Basil and reissued by Evidence as *Live at Sweet Basil.*

Things Ain't What They Used to Be mixes solos and duets and features George Adams on tenor saxophone or John Scofield on guitar. *Blue Bossa* and *New York Reunion* are small-group sessions showcasing the more understated side of Tyner's approach, with an emphasis on Brazilian music. Tyner returns to his more muscular style on *44th Street Suite,* with Arthur Blythe on alto and David Murray on tenor saxophones blowing up a storm. *Soliloquy* is another beautiful solo-piano session recorded at Merkin Hall, and *The Turning Point* is an outing from the Tyner big band. *Prelude and Sonata* is a contemplative session with a group made up of the young lions of the 1990s: Joshua Redman on tenor saxophone, Antonio Hart on alto saxophone, Christian McBride on bass and Marvin "Smitty" Smith on drums.

Tyner found the perfect complement to his latter-day style in bassist Avery Sharpe, who had been in his various working bands for a decade when the brilliant *Infinity* was recorded. Aaron Scott, who had been playing drums with Tyner since *Live at Sweet Basil,* is another simpatico adjunct on a set capped by the magnificent tenor saxophonist Michael Brecker. *What the World Needs Now,* an album of Burt Bacharach compositions, is an ill-considered attempt at pop crossover. — J.S.

JAMES BLOOD ULMER

★★★★½ **Tales of Captain Black (1979; DIW, 1996)**
★★★★ **Are You Glad to Be in America (1981; DIW, 1995)**
★★★★½ **Odyssey (1983; Columbia, 1993)**
★★★★ **Live at the Caravan of Dreams (Caravan of Dreams, 1986)**
★★★½ **America Do You Remember the Love (Blue Note, 1987)**
★★★★ **Original Phalanx (DIW, 1987)**
★★★ **Blues All Night (In + Out, 1989)**
★★½ **Black and Blues (DIW, 1991)**
★★★ **Blues Preacher (DIW/Columbia, 1992)**
★★★ **Live at the Bayerscher Hof (In + Out, 1995)**

Like drummer Ronald Shannon Jackson and bassist Jamaaladeen Tacuma, guitarist James Blood Ulmer (b. 1942) is a disciple of Ornette Coleman and an exponent of the "harmolodic" funk Coleman introduced with his Prime Time band, although it must be pointed out that Ulmer was playing a similar style even before he met Coleman. *Tales of Captain Black* (which credits Ulmer as "James Blood"), in fact, features Coleman as well as Tacuma, and is thrilling to hear, though it is perhaps the guitarist's most demanding album. With *Are You Glad to Be in America,* Ulmer moves to a slightly more pop-oriented sound, working more off backbeat-grounded grooves on some tunes as well as singing on a few numbers. Unfortunately, the disparity between selections like the R&B-oriented title tune and the free-blowing "Revelation March" may be a bit much for some listeners.

Ulmer went on to consolidate his focus and to tone down the more experimental elements of his sound. His attempt to find a middle ground between rock accessibility and harmolodic freedom falters on two out-of-print albums but finds its footing on *Odyssey,* on which he abandons the multiband format for a bassless trio featuring violinist Charles Burnham. The sound is deeply blues-inflected yet freed from the usual level of cliché; unfortunately, the band did not find the audience it deserved. *Original Phalanx* returns to a dense, demanding sound coauthored by Ulmer's perfect match, drummer Rashied Ali and saxophonist George Adams. *Blues All Night, Black and Blues* and *Blues Preacher* find Ulmer searching unsuccessfully for a commercial hook to his approach.

Unfortunately, one of Ulmer's greatest albums, *Revealing,* with an outstanding performance from saxophonist George Adams and a rhythm section of Cecil McBee on bass and Doug Hammond on drums, is currently unavailable. Ulmer is a frequent collaborator with other musicians, including making a historic guest appearance on organist Larry Young's classic *Lawrence of Newark.* — J.D.C.

MICHAL URBANIAK

★★★★½ **Fusion (1974; Columbia/Legacy, 1998)**
★★★ **Take Good Care of My Heart (SteepleChase, 1985)**
★★★★ **Songbird (SteepleChase, 1990)**
★★★ **Manhattan Man (Milan, 1992)**
★★★½ **Some Other Blues (SteepleChase, 1994)**

Polish violinist Michal Urbaniak (b. 1943) was in the forefront of European jazz violinists by the beginning of the 1970s and released an impressive performance on the now out-of-print *New Violin Summit.* After moving to the United

States in the mid-1970s with his then wife, vocalist Urszula Dudziak, Urbaniak recorded a series of critically acclaimed fusion albums, *Fusion* being the only one currently available. It's a recording of passion, grace and dazzling beauty, a spiritually driven experiment from musicians who were dedicated to plumbing the possible interactions of their native Polish folk melodies with the jazz they grew up listening to on Radio Free Europe. The quintet, which utilizes Urbaniak's violin and soprano saxophone, Dudziak's wordless vocals, Adam Makowicz and Wojciech Karslak's keyboard embellishments and Czeslaw Bartkowski's drumming, plays with the singleminded purpose of explorers fired by the discoveries their music engendered.

Urbaniak has continued to record—mostly for SteepleChase, while expanding into synthesized sounds and the electric wind instrument the lyricon. Ironically, the best of the SteepleChase releases is the most traditional: *Songbird* proves that Urbaniak is at his best when the gimmicks take a backseat to the lyricism of his playing. On *Manhattan Man,* he is joined by keyboardist Herbie Hancock, harmonica virtuoso Toots Thielemans and drummer Lenny White. — J.S.

US3

★★½ **Hand on the Torch (Blue Note, 1993)**

★★★ **Broadway and 52nd (Blue Note, 1997)**

The most commercially successful band to fall under the loosely defined moniker of acid jazz, Us3 fits the genre by blending a number of musical styles including jazz, hip-hop, funk, rap and fusion. The brainchild of English producers Mel Simpson and Geoff Wilkinson, the group's *Hand on the Torch* raids (with permission and encouragement) Blue Note's prestigious back catalog, sampling such classic jazz cuts as Herbie Hancock's "Cantaloupe Island," Thelonious Monk's "Straight, No Chaser" and Art Blakey and the Jazz Messengers' "Crisis." On top of these archival samples, Wilkinson and Simpson have laid down fresh hip-hop beats and enlisted the talents of international rappers who deliver a fairly typical brand of laid-back yet sometimes annoyingly self-congratulatory raps. The extra punch supplied by modern instrumentalists, including saxophonist Ed Jones and trumpeter Gerard Presencer, helps to make this hybrid recording one of the smoothest—and possibly the slickest—acid-jazz records to date.

Broadway and 52nd follows pretty much the same format, but with less sampling (digging deeper into Blue Note's catalog for Wayne Shorter, Horace Silver and Lou Donaldson riffs), more instrumentalists and more aggressive rapping. Yet it somehow seems to be more an adaptation for the uninitiated jazz listener than a progressive sound. — G.E.

WARREN VACHÉ

★★★½ **With Scott's Band in New York City (with Scott Hamilton) (Concord Jazz, 1978)**
★★★★ **Iridescence (Concord Jazz, 1981)**
★★★ **Midtown Jazz (Concord Jazz, 1983)**
★★★ **Easy Going (Concord Jazz, 1987)**
★★★½ **Warm Evenings (with the Beaux-Arts String Quartet) (Concord Jazz, 1989)**
★★★ **First Time Out/Encore '93 (Audiophile, 1993)**
★★★★ **Horn of Plenty (Muse, 1994)**
★★★★ **Talk to Me Baby (Muse, 1996)**
★★★ **Live at the Vineyard (Challenge, 1996)**

Cornetist Warren Vaché Jr. (b. 1951) was tagged a traditional jazz musician upon his 1977 debut *First Time Out* (rereleased with *Encore '93*). And while he certainly has been a leader of a new generation of trad-jazz players and his early recordings find him mining that vein with excellent though occasionally boring results, it's a label that ultimately doesn't really do justice to his breadth. *Horn of Plenty*'s first two songs reveal much about the range covered by Vaché, moving from the hard-hitting bebop of "Eternal Triangle," a tune closely associated with Dizzy Gillespie, to the joyous Louis Armstrong barnburner "Struttin' with Some Barbecue." On both tunes, Vaché plays tag with tenor saxophonist Houston Person as pianist Richard Wyands pushes them along with a graceful swing. The album then moves through a varied repertoire, including Miles Davis's "All Blues" and "Bix Fix," a tribute to Bix Beiderbecke played as a duet with guitarist Joe Puma. This type of scope and depth make Vaché's Muse albums the best of his available work. On everything, he displays a smooth, graceful style and easy technical mastery over the trumpet, cornet and flügelhorn, but his later work is more confident and less easily pigeonholed. — A.P.

DAVE VALENTIN

★★ **The Hawk (GRP, 1979)**
★★ **Light Struck (GRP, 1986)**
★★★½ **Live at the Blue Note (GRP, 1988)**
★★★½ **Two Amigos (GRP, 1990)**
★★½ **Musical Portraits (GRP, 1992)**
★★½ **Red Sun (GRP, 1993)**
★★½ **Tropic Heat (GRP, 1994)**
★★★ **Primitive Passions (RMM/GRP, 1996)**

Flautist Dave Valentin, born in the Bronx in 1954, was a protégé of Herbie Mann's who quickly developed a pop-jazz approach that owes more to dance music than to Afro-Cuban roots. Though Valentin is a technically proficient player, his records suffer from heavy-handed production, and even during some of the more exciting moments he appears to be playing down to the listener. The *Live at the Blue Note* session suffers from none of these problems, and Mann brings out Valentin's best performance in *Two Amigos.* — J.S.

DAVE VAN RONK

★★½ **Black Mountain Blues (Smithsonian Folkways, 1960)**
★★★½ **Inside Dave Van Ronk (1962/1963; Fantasy, 1989)**
★★★½ **Hummin' to Myself (Gazell, 1990)**
★★★½ **The Folkways Years 1959–1961 (Smithsonian Folkways, 1991)**
★★★ **Going Back to Brooklyn (Gazell, 1991)**

★★★½ A Chrestomathy (Gazell, 1992)
★★★½ To All My Friends in Far-Flung Places (Gazell, 1994)
★★★½ A Chrestomathy, Vol. 2 (Gazell, 1995)
★★★ From . . . Another Time and Place (Alcazar, 1995)

Former merchant marine and pope of Greenwich Village's folk scene, Dave Van Ronk (b. 1936) is an American original—as unofficial tutor to a host of '60s singer/guitarists, he helped to introduce the blues to the white college audience that would soon embrace the music. Since the late '50s, he's made many records—almost all of them clean but not reverent readings of traditional blues and folk. *Inside Dave Van Ronk* combines the 1962 album of the same name with *Folksinger* (from '63) for a representative sampler of his finest work. "Cocaine Blues" is deadpan and chilling; "Talking Cancer Blues" brandishes a gallows humor; and "Poor Lazarus" is awesome—grit enters Van Ronk's voice, thrusting it past its usual carefulness, and he's seldom sounded more engaged or intense. His strength, embodied on *The Folkways Years 1959–1961*, remains lean versions of archival fare, which he saves from sounding nice by the zest of his attack.

A lot of Van Ronk's earlier work is out of print; of the more recent work, the ambitious double album *A Chrestomathy* is strong; *Hummin' to Myself* is a fine American songbook (Duke Ellington, Hoagy Carmichael, George and Ira Gershwin); *To All My Friends in Far-Flung Places* reunites the singer with many of his fellow roots-music revialists; *From . . . Another Time and Place* features new recordings of classic Van Ronk tunes. He has also made some children's records. — P.E.

THE VAUGHAN BROTHERS

★★★★ Family Style (Epic, 1990)

The album that blues-guitar fans, Texas branch, had been waiting years to hear was finally realized in 1990 but came clouded by the tragedy of Stevie Ray Vaughan's death shortly before its release. Apart from his family's considerable loss, modern blues was stripped of a giant. A triumph all around, *Family Style* provides bold displays of both the fire and the tenderness that marked the brothers' art, be it as influential instrumentalists or underrated vocalists.

Produced by Nile Rodgers, who keeps a hard sheen on the proceedings, *Family Style* shows off the Vaughans' guitars in tandem (a rousing twin-guitar workout on "D/FW") and apart but also showcases each man's affecting vocal style on several cuts. Of special note is Jimmie's laconic vocal over a steadily percolating rhythm track on "Good Texan." By the same token, Stevie Ray delivers a powerful blue-eyed soul plea for peace and understanding on "Tick Tock," his voice all smoky gray and a model of controlled urgency.

Guitar enthusiasts will hardly be disappointed, though. The brothers come on strong—Jimmie tough and economical, Stevie Ray robust and razor-edged—on a couple of blues-rock steamers, "Long Way from Home" and "Telephone Song." On "Brothers" they make the connection clear: The distinction between the two disappears as one angular solo melds into another, blood on blood, a fitting final gesture. — D.M.

JIMMIE VAUGHAN

★★★★ Family Style (with Stevie Ray Vaughan) (Epic, 1990)
★★★★ Strange Pleasure (Epic, 1994)
★★★★ A Tribute to Stevie Ray Vaughan (with Eric Clapton, B.B. King, Bonnie Raitt, Buddy Guy and Robert Cray) (Epic, 1996)

Family Style, the 1990 collaboration between Jimmie Vaughan (b. 1951) and his kid brother, Stevie Ray, was a revelation. Jimmie's terse, pithy mastery of the guitar was a known commodity from his 16 years with the Fabulous Thunderbirds, but it turns out that Vaughan also has a smooth, sometimes sultry singing voice, a deft songwriting hand and a cutting wit. Songs like "Good Texan" and "Hillbillies from Outer Space" crackled with the only thing Stevie Ray really lacked in his music—a sense of humor. *Family Style* was a success from beginning to end, and it should have launched a new phase in the careers of both brothers. Instead, Stevie Ray was killed before the album's release, and the grieving Jimmie disappeared for a few years. He reemerged with his true solo debut, *Strange Pleasure,* a joyous affirmation of life highlighted by a distinctly upbeat roadhouse party flavor, as well as a moving acoustic tribute to his late brother, "Six Strings Down" (cowritten with Art and Cyril Neville)—a stone-cold treat from beginning to end.

In May 1995 Vaughan convened a meeting of the blues royalty—B.B. King, Robert Cray, Buddy Guy, Eric Clapton and Bonnie Raitt—to pay tribute to his late brother. The results are captured on *A Tribute to Stevie Ray Vaughan,* with each artist performing SRV's songs and all of them coming together for the three final tunes, including a stunning take of "Six Strings Down." — A.P.

SARAH VAUGHAN

★★★★ **Sarah Vaughan with Clifford Brown (1955; EmArcy, 1990)**
★★★ **In the Land of Hi-Fi (Verve, 1956)**
★★★★ **Swingin' Easy with Sarah Vaughan and Her Trio (1957; EmArcy, 1992)**
★★★ **Sarah Vaughan's Golden Hits (Mercury, 1967)**
★★★ **Sassy Swings Again (1967; Mercury, 1983)**
★★½ **Send in the Clowns (1974; Columbia/Legacy, 1995)**
★★★ **Recorded Live (EmArcy, 1977)**
★★★ **How Long Has This Been Going On? (1978; Pablo, 1987)**
★★★ **Billie, Ella, Lena, Sarah! (Columbia, 1980)**
★★★★ **A Celebration of Duke (1980; Original Jazz Classics, 1990)**
★★★½ **Duke Ellington Songbook, Vol. 1 (1980; Pablo Today, 1987)**
★★★½ **Duke Ellington Songbook, Vol. 2 (1980; Pablo Today, 1987)**
★★★★ **Copacabana: Exclusivamente Brasil (1981; Pablo Today, 1988)**
★ **Songs of the Beatles (Rhino, 1981)**
★★★ **Sarah Vaughan and the Count Basie Orchestra: Send in the Clowns (1981; Pablo Today, 1989)**
★★★ **Gershwin Live! (Columbia, 1982)**
★★★ **Crazy and Mixed Up (1982; Pablo Today, 1987)**
★★★ **The Best of Sarah Vaughan (1983; Pablo, 1990)**
★★★★ **Sarah Vaughan & Billy Eckstine: The Irving Berlin Songbook (EmArcy, 1984)**
★★★★★ **The Complete Sarah Vaughan on Mercury, Vol. 1: Great Jazz Years, 1954–1956 (Verve, 1986)**
★★★★★ **The Complete Sarah Vaughan on Mercury, Vol. 2: Sings Great American Songs, 1956–1957 (Verve, 1986)**
★★★★★ **The Complete Sarah Vaughan on Mercury, Vol. 3: Great Show on Stage, 1957–1963 (Verve, 1986)**
★★★★★ **The Complete Sarah Vaughan on Mercury, Vol. 4: 1963–1967 (Verve, 1987)**
★★★ **Sassy Swings the Tivoli (EmArcy, 1987)**
★★★★ **Classic Jazz (Mercury, 1987)**
★★ **Brazilian Romance (CBS, 1987)**
★★★½ **Compact Jazz (Mercury, 1987)**
★★★★ **The Divine Sarah: The Columbia Years 1949–1953 (Columbia, 1988)**
★★★½ **The George Gershwin Songbook, Vol. 1 (EmArcy, 1990)**
★★★½ **The George Gershwin Songbook, Vol. 2 (EmArcy, 1990)**
★★★★ **Misty: Sarah Vaughan with Quincy Jones (Mercury, 1990)**
★★★½ **Golden Hits (Mercury, 1990)**
★★★ **The Roulette Years, Vols. 1 and 2 (Roulette, 1991)**
★★★ **A Time in My Life (Mainstream, 1991)**
★★½ **Sarah Slightly Classical (Roulette, 1991)**
★★★★ **Sarah Vaughan at Mister Kelly's (EmArcy, 1991)**
★★★ **The Singles Sessions (Blue Note, 1991)**
★★★★★ **Time & Again (Musicraft, 1992)**
★★★★★ **It's You or No One (Musicraft, 1992)**
★★★★ **Jazz 'Round Midnight (Verve, 1992)**
★★★ **Jazzfest Masters (Scotti Bros., 1992)**
★★★★ **The Essential Sarah Vaughan (Verve, 1992)**
★★★★ **Sarah Sings Soulfully (Roulette, 1992)**
★★★★ **16 Most Requested Songs (Columbia/Legacy, 1993)**
★★★½ **Jazz Masters 18 (Verve, 1994)**
★★★★ **The Benny Carter Sessions: The Explosive Side of Sarah Vaughan/The Lonely Hours (Roulette, 1994)**
★★★★ **The Essence of Sarah Vaughan (Columbia/Legacy, 1994)**
★★★½ **I Love Brazil (Pablo, 1994)**
★★★ **Jazz Collector Edition: Dizzy Gillespie, Sarah Vaughan, and Charlie Parker (LaserLight, 1994)**
★★★½ **Jazz Masters 42: The Jazz Sides (Verve, 1995)**
★★★★ **Sarah Vaughan Sings Broadway: Great Songs from Hit Shows (Mercury, 1995)**
★★★½ **Embraceable You (LaserLight, 1996)**
★★★★ **Compact Jazz Live! (Verve, N.A.)**

The late Sarah Vaughan (1924–1990) possessed a voice of such supreme majesty and dimension that to compare her with anyone else is a waste of time; she was a genre unto herself. While many singers could match the husky, sensuous timbre of her voice, Vaughan was in her own league when it came to controlling mood, melody line and phrasing. Demonstrating an impeccable command of dynamics, she developed a stylistic quirk—swooping from a warm alto to a cool soprano (she had a three-octave range—opera's loss, jazz's gain) and hitting the notes dead-on—that remains one of the most breathtaking displays of technique married to emotion in all of American music. A fearless improviser who improved with age, she embraced the harmonic innovations Charlie Parker and Dizzy Gillespie were pioneering in the '40s at the dawn of bebop and brought those concepts into the context of jazz vocalizing. And yet there was nothing cold or clinical about her singing: Above all else, Sarah Vaughan was about heart.

Vaughan began playing organ for and singing in her church choir in her childhood years. In 1942 the 18-year-old singer won an amateur contest at Harlem's Apollo Theatre, which brought her to the attention of Billy Eckstine, then a featured and widely popular vocalist with Earl Hines's band. On Eckstine's recommendation, Hines auditioned and then hired Vaughan, who stayed on for a year and then left to join Eckstine in his band, as did Parker and Gillespie (that group also included, at times, Fats Navarro, Miles Davis, Art Blakey and Dexter Gordon).

Her solo recording career (in '44 she had cut some sides as a member of Eckstine's band on the Deluxe and Continental labels) began in 1945 when she signed with the financially beleaguered Musicraft label, a two-year association that produced three Top 30 pop singles, one of which, 1948's "Nature Boy," peaked at #9. At Musicraft she was introduced to bandleader George Treadwell, whose orchestra backed her on her debut single, "Tenderly." Treadwell fell hard for the singer, began guiding her career and eventually became her husband.

When Musicraft went bankrupt in 1949, Vaughan jumped to Columbia and made an overt move into the pop field. Between her first Columbia hit, "Black Coffee," and her last, 1953's "Time," she had 14 Top 30 songs. It was with a move to Mercury in 1954 that she began to secure her legend. In two tenures there—1954 to 1959 and 1963 to 1967—she recorded practically every type of song that had been written (she even sang a selection from Handel's *Messiah* on the soundtrack for the film *Bob & Carol & Ted & Alice*) and set an imposing standard for any vocalist who would follow her and claim to be versatile. From Mercury she moved on to Roulette for a near-three-year stint before returning to Mercury for a final go-round; she closed the '60s without a recording contract.

Vaughan's career is now well represented on CD in all its phases, its last major gap being filled when Musicraft founder Albert Marx regained control of the label's master tapes and subsequently reissued the artist's earliest recorded work. Two albums of Vaughan's Musicraft sides are now in print, *Time & Again* and *It's You or No One,* and both reveal an important artist beginning to find her way. Backed sometimes by George Treadwell's orchestra, sometimes by a small combo, the young, feathery-voiced Vaughan demonstrates an uncanny knack for investing a lyric with precisely the proper emotion, some of them darker feelings she would come to know well in the course of a rocky personal life, although she had yet to experience those valleys to any great degree. Moreover, one is struck by her innate musicality at this early stage.

On the Musicraft sides Vaughan is most impressive in the small-combo format, where her voice rings cornetlike amid the ensemble work. One particularly sterling example of her prowess occurs on a low-down version of "Lover Man" (on *It's You or No One*). Backed by a quintet comprising Dizzy Gillespie on trumpet, Charlie Parker on alto sax, Al Haig on piano, Curley Russell on bass and Big Sid Catlett on drums, Vaughan weaves a scintillating spell with an airy, nonchalant vocal. Gillespie then bounces off Vaughan's reading to execute a complementary solo that is as haunting in its high, lonely notes as it is deft in its design. To hear the Musicraft recordings again is to hear an artist wise beyond her years in her sense of the singer's role in band and orchestral settings—and to hear some of the very best American popular music of that decade.

If Vaughan wanted to prove her point about singing pop, she did it emphatically at Columbia. The essential chronicles of these years include the 28-song, two-CD *Divine Sarah* set, which contains only two of her hits from the years in question; *16 Most Requested Songs,* a more thorough survey of hits only; and *The*

Essence of Sarah Vaughan, which blends a few hits with other noncharting orchestral outings. The latter two discs are heavy on tracks arranged and conducted by Percy Faith, who bathed the vocals in syrupy strings. Vaughan was better served by the fine musicians in the big bands she recorded with, particularly those under the direction of Joe Lippman in 1949 and especially by the incarnation of Treadwell's All Stars heard on eight tracks of *The Divine Sarah* and on four cuts on *16 Most Requested Songs.* The latter outfit included Miles Davis, Budd Johnson, Benny Green, Jimmy Jones, Billy Taylor and J.C. Heard, one of the most sensitive small ensembles Vaughan ever recorded with.

Moving to Mercury in 1954, Vaughan continued her pop-chart success into the late '50s with nine Top 40 singles between 1954 and 1959. Many of these were fine but unadventurous recordings, some in the pop-jazz vein of her best Columbia sides, others turning up the heat for the rock & roll era (notably her Top 10 single—and first million-seller—from 1959, "Broken Hearted Melody," a bouncy, minor-key tale of lost love given a marvelous reading by Vaughan, who used her upper register to suggest the lacerating pain and loneliness following an affair's end). But she also used these years to establish herself more as a peerless jazz and classic-pop interpreter. Several of her Mercury albums from the '50s have been returned to print on CD, and most are first-rate, particularly *In the Land of Hi-Fi* and the various *Songbook* surveys of specific songwriters (also Rodgers and Hart, on cassette only; Gershwin; and the potent teaming with Billy Eckstine on an Irving Berlin tribute on which the two singers bring new dimension to even the most well-worn songs). The most comprehensive overview of Vaughan's development in both of her stays at Mercury comes by way of the four-volume, multi-CD boxes titled *The Complete Sarah Vaughan on Mercury;* although some of her Mercury recordings are unrepresented in the collection ("Broken Hearted Melody," for one, and most of the cuts contained on *Sarah Vaughan's Golden Hits*), each volume also boasts a number of previously unissued tracks from various live and studio dates. *Vols. 1* and *2* of *The Complete* best demonstrate her growing confidence as a vocalist in a jazz context, while *Vol. 2* shows her bringing an assured intellect to classic American pop (included here are the tracks that became the Rodgers and Hart and Gershwin songbook albums, as well as three cuts with Eckstine from the Duke Ellington songbook sessions). *Vol. 3: Great Show on Stage,* is somewhat misleadingly titled, since all but a dozen of the tracks on its six discs were recorded in a New York studio; those actually recorded before an audience are taken from an August 1957 show at Chicago's Mr. Kelly's club—this material is now available separately in its complete form as the single CD titled *Sarah Vaughan at Mister Kelly's* (and can be found in part on her *Recorded Live* album). This quibble aside, Vaughan turns in some powerful performances backed by the Count Basie Orchestra (minus Count Basie) and on several cuts with Quincy Jones conducting and providing some subtle arrangements. Here Vaughan's first Mercury era ends.

In 1960 she signed with Roulette. While this period produced no Top 40 pop hits, she continued working with top-drawer arrangers and producers. Check out *The Singles Sessions,* primarily for its four excellent tracks arranged by Billy May ("The Green Leaves of Summer" being especially haunting). In 24 cuts *The Roulette Years, Vols. 1* and *2* provides the clearest snapshot of Vaughan's three-year stay at the label, which has the feel of a holding pattern, given that she went right back to Mercury when her Roulette contract expired. Not to suggest she ceased taking chances. *Sarah Slightly Classical* finds her working out her fabulous pipes on popular songs based on classical themes ("Be My Love," "Full Moon and Empty Arms"); unfortunately, the vocal readings are rather stolid, as if her reverence for the texts had shackled her improvisational instincts. Better representing her Roulette tenure is the spirited work heard on *The Benny Carter Sessions,* a compilation of songs released on albums titled *The Explosive Side of Sarah Vaughan* and *The Lonely Hours.* Here she is alternately loose and swinging, deliberate and tender, as the material demands, and the accompanying musicians give her ample room to reinvent each song in her own style. The appropriately titled *Sarah Sings Soulfully* is simply a marvel of simpatico instrumental support (especially by an uncredited organist, whose tasty fills on "A Taste of Honey" reinvigorate that oft-mishandled pop classic and who later steps in for some quiet vamping that adds a deeper shade of blue to a piercing version of "I Guess I'll Hang My Tears Out to Dry") in service to some of the most probing vocals Vaughan ever delivered in a studio setting. Here her performances are less about technique than about a heart laid bare, with all her mistakes and missteps offstage evident in each tear-stained phrase she sings.

Vol. 4 of *The Complete Sarah Vaughan on Mercury* wraps up the final four years of her Mercury history in six discs of material recorded in Copenhagen and New York, largely with Quincy Jones at the helm. Some of the Copenhagen sessions are also included on *Recorded Live.* Of note on *The Complete, Vol. 4,* are 12 1963 sides recorded in Copenhagen with the Sevend Saaby Choir (issued as the album *Vaughan with Voices,* now packaged as part of a twofer titled *Misty,* which comprises the aforementioned album and another titled *Vaughan and Violins,* both titles representing some of her most compelling collaborations with Jones). Her voice having matured into an earthy, husky timbre, Vaughan works expressive wonders on these heavily produced sides of delicately shaded, lyrically rich contemporary pop on the order of Mancini and Mercer's "Charade" and "The Days of Wine and Roses," along with poignant fare such as Hoagy Carmichael's "Blue Orchids" (done with a pronounced Rosemary Clooney vocal approach) and Kander and Ebb's winsome "My Coloring Book."

After leaving Mercury in 1967, Vaughan was without a label deal until signing in 1970 with Mainstream, which had been founded by Robert Shad, one of her Mercury cohorts. Some good music ensued, although the label's idea of framing her with period arrangements—orchestral disco soul heavy on thumping bass and cooing, silky background voices of no particular distinction—was ill-suited to Vaughan's style and temperament. On too many of these songs she's struggling to find a way through the muck around her. Still, a 1974 session produced a memorable version of Stephen Sondheim's oft recorded "Send in the Clowns" that was popular enough to become something of a theme song for Vaughan. A representative sampling of this period is found on Legacy's *Send in the Clowns* reissue of a 1974 Mainstream album. Six of the arrangements are by Gene Page, who was otherwise known for his success in the '70s soul-and-disco world; when writing, he seems to have forgotten to factor in an artist with a recognizable, individual style. Michel Legrand, who might have been expected to know something about sensitive arrangements, did the honors on "Wave," a beautiful Antonio Carlos Jobim song. Here Vaughan caresses it in loving fashion in the opening verses and is sailing along at an intoxicating, relaxed pace until she hits the bridge—then the dreamy mood is rent asunder by blaring horns and clanging percussion. An even greater disaster occurred in 1977, when Vaughan cut some Beatles songs in a jazz/funk setting; Atlantic purchased the masters of that session and released *Songs of the Beatles* on Rhino in 1981. Nothing works on this record, and only the most tenacious completists will find any reason to search it out.

From Mainstream the path took Vaughan to Norman Granz's Pablo label, where she was returned to and thrived in big-band and small-combo settings. Duke Ellington was a particular favorite of Vaughan's, and the obvious affection and scintillating intelligence she brought to his challenging material made her Ellington's foremost interpreter. Of the three strong latter-day examples listed, *A Celebration of Duke* comes strongly recommended, owing to the greater sympathy Vaughan exhibits with her small combo on this recording. But anyone who passes up the two-volume *Duke Ellington Songbook* will be cheated of hearing a stylist very near the top of her game on material in which she finds new wellsprings of meaning as she plumbs the lyrics for richer, more complex emotions. The Pablo years also featured her initial foray into Brazilian music on the delightful *I Love Brazil,* with its all-star Latin musician lineup (Antonio Carlos Jobim, Milton Nascimento, Dori Caymmi, et al.) adding subtle and supple instrumental ballast to the proceedings. On these recordings Vaughan sounds engrossed in the material and comfortable with the exotic arrangements, far more so than she did 10 years later on the stillborn *Brazilian Romance.*

Recent years have seen a spate of CD reissues of Vaughan's Mercury albums along with other collections of Mercury material that offer bang for the buck in a single disc. *Sarah Vaughan with Clifford Brown,* comprising sessions recorded in December of 1954, is one of the peak moments in the Vaughan catalog. In a loose, jam-session atmosphere, Vaughan delivers some of her most breathtaking jazz singing, becoming, in essence, another formidable instrumentalist in a lineup replete with same, including Brown, Herbie Mann on flute and tenor saxophonist Paul Quinichette along with Vaughan's steady trio at the time (subtle pianist Jimmy Jones, bassist Joe Benjamin and drummer Roy Haynes). Vaughan and her trio are showcased in splendid form as well on *Swingin' Easy,* which can be enjoyed for the sheer technical virtuosity on display or as a wee-small-hours respite from the daily grind. *Jazz Masters 18, Jazz Masters 42: The Jazz Sides* and *Compact Jazz Live!* are well-considered overviews of Vaughan the jazz singer, in contrast to *Golden Hits'* focus on the pop sides. In a sense, though, the virtuoso Vaughan is most vividly on display in the two-CD *Sarah Vaughan Sings Broadway: Great Songs from Hit Shows.* Working largely with Hal Mooney's orchestra in late 1956, Vaughan employed not only her stunning technical gifts but infused the proceedings with wit and palpable human feeling for the situations evoked in some of the theater's grandest songs. For some historical perspective, try Columbia's *Billie, Ella, Lena, Sarah!,* a collection of tracks by four of the greatest voices in jazz history. Vaughan's performances—"Nice Work If You Can Get It," "East of the Sun (West of the Moon)," "Ain't Misbehavin'," "Goodnight, My Love"—are from 1950, when she was backed by George Treadwell's Miles Davis–era All Stars, and offer the listener an opportunity to compare and contrast the singular approaches of these four beloved stylists.

Vaughan left Pablo in 1982 but continued working a demanding concert schedule for the rest of the decade. She passed away shortly after she was sent home from a concert tour after becoming too weak to perform. At the time of her death, she was in bed, watching a TV movie featuring her adopted daughter, Debra Lois. Life was richest for Sarah Vaughan when she was being a mother and being a singer. To the end, she did exactly what fulfilled her most. — D.M.

STEVIE RAY VAUGHAN

★★★	**Texas Flood (Epic, 1983)**
★★★½	**Couldn't Stand the Weather (Epic, 1984)**
★★★★	**Soul to Soul (Epic, 1985)**
★★★★	**Live Alive (Epic, 1986)**
★★★	**In Step (Epic, 1989)**
★★★★	**Family Style (with Jimmie Vaughan) (Epic, 1990)**
★★★★	**The Sky Is Crying (Epic, 1991)**
★★★★	**In the Beginning (Epic, 1992)**
★★★★★	**Greatest Hits (Epic, 1995)**

Among the generation of blues guitarists who came of age in the early '80s, only Robert Cray approaches the elusive combination of skill, influence and heart that Stevie Ray Vaughan (1954–1990) possessed to such an abundant degree (Vaughan's brother Jimmie sneaks in there as well on the strength of his powerful work with the Fabulous Thunderbirds). To be sure, though, Vaughan kicked the latest blues revival into high gear with his first two albums, *Texas Flood* and *Couldn't Stand the Weather,* which became unlikely best-sellers in the midst of a rock market being consumed by glossy, frigid technopop.

Texas Flood pays its debts to traditional Texas blues and R&B, sounding a tad muddy, the better to savor the slice-and-dice solos Vaughan delivers so fluidly. Stylistically, Vaughan was a true eclectic whose hard-driving, steely sound achieved individuality while incorporating quotes from Hubert Sumlin, Buddy Guy, T-Bone Walker, Lonnie Mack, Albert Collins, B.B. King, Elmore James and Jimi Hendrix. That's a broad palette, but it also illustrates how artfully Vaughan built on the best of what had come before to express the emotional extremes described in his lyrics and instrumentals.

Couldn't Stand the Weather finds Vaughan broadening out a bit beyond R&B to include a stirring rendition of Hendrix's "Voodoo Chile" and a Charlie Christian–Kenny Burrell flavor on the jazz-tinged "Stang's Swang." *Soul to Soul* represents Vaughan and his band Double Trouble's great leap forward. First the addition of keyboardist Reese Wynans expands the sound, adding textural possibilities that heighten the shifting moods of Vaughan's original material and, as best exemplified by his contribution to a version of Hank Ballard's "Look at Little Sister," to reveal previously hidden wells of feeling in the impeccably chosen cover versions. By this time Vaughan is showing more facility with melody in his songwriting, producing his first outstanding ballad in "Life Without Love." Vaughan had a tender side that he could express effectively with either a delicate vocal or wailing guitar solo. *Live Alive* sums up the first part of Vaughan's career with rousing sets recorded in Austin, Dallas and at the Montreux Jazz Festival. Of note is Jimmie Vaughan's special guest appearance on four tracks cut in Austin. *In Step,* Vaughan's last solo studio album, collects more well-turned originals, along with a tasty selection of Howlin' Wolf, Buddy Guy and Willie Dixon covers. Vaughan's own "Crossfire" is one of his peak solo turns in a pure, gut-wrenching style.

Vaughan's legacy has been ennobled by the releases issued since that horrible August 27, when he died in a helicopter crash. *In the Beginning* can be seen as something of a bookend to *Live Alive,* in that it was recorded April 1, 1980, shortly after Double Trouble had lost an extraordinary lead singer in Lou Ann Barton and a solid sax man in Johnny Reno, reducing its lineup to Vaughan, drummer Chris Layton and bassist Jackie Newhouse. Then pretty much an unknown commodity outside his Austin home base, Vaughan immediately quelled any concerns his followers might have had about the smaller band's limitations. The announcer (the show was broadcast live from a club by an Austin radio station) barely finishes the last word of his introduction before Vaughan comes blazing in with a firestorm of screaming notes and hell-bent-for-leather riffing on the Sonny Thompson/Freddie King instrumental rouser "In the Open," with his mates perfectly in sync and lacking nothing in the way of sound and fury—powerhouse stuff that served spellbinding notice of Vaughan's intentions to step out and stake his claim. A Vaughan original, "Slide Thing," follows, wherein the guitarist pays a huge debt to Elmore James, tosses in a taste of Freddie King–style macho picking, then establishes his own razor-edged voice. Alternating between James-ish howling slides and his own singular voice, you get the feeling Vaughan is doing nothing so much as constructing a dialog between himself (the new hotshot on the block) and James, slide-guitar master of yore. It's a tough, moving performance, both for the respect with which he announces his affection for James and for the sheer force of personality and soul evident in his own sound signature. A nine-song set neatly balanced between originals and covers, *In the Beginning* stands as a record of the first brilliant sparks from a gifted artist, whose growth, as *Live Alive* proves, shows how well the blues, far from being a static form, can embrace new ideas as long the artist's foundation is solid.

While there's certainly good reason to own all of Vaughan's individual albums, those fans on a limited budget, or newcomers to the Vaughan legend, are well advised to invest in the 1995 *Greatest Hits* set. For one, it includes a previously unreleased version of George Harrison's "Taxman," featuring a delicious, snarling, contemptuous vocal by Vaughan that is, pure and simple, one of his most glorious on record, and even more effective in being supported by his angry, swirling lead lines. All the obvious tracks recommend this can't-miss collection—among them "Texas Flood," "Couldn't Stand the Weather," "Little Wing"—as well as a fine accompanying booklet. Rather than the usual liner notes extolling Vaughan's great virtues and rehashing his biography, music writer and Vaughan confidant Dan Forte offers interview selections with the surviving members of Double Trouble (Wynans, Layton, bassist Tommy Shannon and Vaughan's friend and frequent songwriting collaborator Doyle Bramhall), who reconstruct Vaughan's and the band's growth by discussing the recording sessions and other details pertinent to each track's history. Their words, always interesting and ultimately poignant, underscore the heightened sense of loss they feel.

The lovingly assembled 1991 album *The Sky Is Crying* contains 10 studio performances recorded between 1984 and 1989, with only one track, "Empty Arms," having appeared in a different version on a previous Vaughan album (*Soul to Soul*). The tunes offer a good overview of Vaughan's stylistic range. Most pronounced is the nod to Albert King, but there are also touches of Kenny Burrell (whose "Chitlins Con Carne" is covered), Hubert Sumlin, Lonnie Mack (his classic "Wham") and, of course, Hendrix ("Little Wing"). The album closes on a somber note, "Life by the Drop," Vaughan's first recorded acoustic solo. It's a moment you don't want to end. — D.M.

JOE VENUTI

★★★ **Joe in Chicago 1978 (1979; Flying Fish, 1993)**
★★★★★ **Violin Jazz 1927 to 1934 (Yazoo, 1989)**
★★★ **Sliding By (Gazell, 1990)**
★★★★½ **Stringin' the Blues (Topaz Jazz, 1995)**
★★★ **The Fabulous Joe Venuti: 15 Jazz Classics (Omega, 1995)**
★★★½ **Pretty Trix (IAJRC, N.A.)**

Born in Italy and raised in Philadelphia, Giuseppe "Joe" Venuti (1894–1978) wrote the book on jazz violin and remained one of the greatest practitioners of stringed swing right up until his death. Venuti made a series of historic recordings with guitarist Eddie Lang between 1925 and 1933, when Lang died. The records, some duets and some with Venuti's Blue Four (with Jimmy Dorsey on clarinet, alto, trumpet and baritone sax; Frankie Trumbauer on C-melody sax and bassoon; and Benny Goodman on clarinet), are technically virtuosic presentations of relentlessly swinging music. *Violin Jazz 1927 to 1934* is the best collection of this material, followed closely by *Stringin' the Blues. Pretty Trix* comes from zany radio broadcasts, which feature Louis Prima, Red Norvo and trombonist/comedian Jerry Colonna.

Sliding By, Joe in Chicago 1978 and *The Fabulous Joe Venuti* are all from his return to the jazz circuit in the '70s. — J.S.

VIENNA CLARINET CONNECTION

★★★ **V.C.C. 001 (Pepperland, 1995)**

The Vienna Clarinet Connection, a quintet, takes jazz standards like "A Night in Tunisia," "Autumn Leaves" and "In a Sentimental Mood" and breaks up the melody into different lines for an eerie, Eric Dolphy–esque sound. There are some lighter moments as well, as in "The Drunken Girl from Ipanema." Principal soloist Helmut Hödl contributes the original "A Little Funky Song for Sheba." — J.S.

LEROY VINNEGAR

★★★★ **Leroy Walks! (1957; Original Jazz Classics, 1989)**
★★★ **Leroy Walks Again!! (1962; Original Jazz Classics, 1990)**
★★★ **Walkin' the Basses (Contemporary, 1993)**

Leroy Vinnegar (b. 1928) is known as "the Walker" for his unerringly precise and rhythmic timekeeping on the bass—"walking." A veteran of hundreds of West Coast jazz sessions, Vinnegar occasionally stepped into the spotlight; like the essence of Vinnegar's no-nonsense playing itself, these recordings are workmanlike projects that are unpretentious and enjoyable. *Leroy Walks Again!!* contains Vinnegar's lovely, elegiac "For Carl," dedicated to the legendary pianist Carl Perkins, who guests on *Leroy Walks!* West Coast favorite sons Teddy Edwards (on tenor sax) and Victor Feldman (on piano and vibes) acquit themselves well throughout. *Walkin' the Basses,* recorded three decades later, offers proof that Vinnegar's walking remains as solid as ever. — S.F.

EDDIE "CLEANHEAD" VINSON

★★★★ **Cleanhead's Back in Town (1957; Bethlehem, 1996)**
★★★★★ **Cherry Red (1967; One Way, N.A.)**
★★★★★ **Kidney Stew Is Fine (1969; Delmark, 1993)**
★★★★ **Jammin' the Blues (Black Lion, 1975)**
★★★ **Kidney Stew (1976; Southland, 1983)**
★★★½ **I Want a Little Girl (1981; Original Jazz Classics, 1995)**
★★★ **Blues in the Night: The Early Show (with Etta James) (Fantasy, 1986)**
★★★★ **Blues in the Night: The Late Show (with Etta James) (Fantasy, 1986)**
★★★½ **Oscar Peterson + Harry Edison + Eddie "Cleanhead" Vinson (Pablo, 1988)**
★★★★½ **Two Classic Albums (with Roomful of Blues) (32 Blues, 1997)**
★★★★ **Battle of the Blues, Vol. 3 (King, N.A.)**

Vocalist/saxophonist Eddie "Cleanhead" Vinson (1917–1988) was a living illustration of the interconnectedness of blues and jazz. The Houston native was already a talented alto saxophonist as a teenager and by the late 1930s was part of the outstanding Milton Larkin Orchestra's saxophone section alongside Arnett Cobb and Illinois Jacquet. Jacquet moved to Los Angeles in the early 1940s, joined Lionel Hampton's big band and immediately became a star via "Flying Home." When Jacquet went on to join Cab Calloway's band, he recommended Cobb to replace him in the Hampton band. Meanwhile, Vinson, who had been a big-band–style vocalist in the Larkin band, was touring with Big Bill Broonzy, who encouraged him as a blues singer. Vinson became a star attraction fronting the Cootie Williams Orchestra from 1942 to 1945, playing lead alto saxophone and singing. His showstopper was an intense version of the Joe Turner vehicle "Cherry Red." He also began to experiment with protobop instrumentals with this group along with its pianist, Bud Powell.

Vinson began recording as a leader in 1945 with a series of currently out-of-print jump-blues and jazz sides for Mercury, including the hits "Old Maid Boogie" and "Kidney Stew Blues." From 1949 to 1952 he made a series of classic blues sides for King, including remakes of several signature tunes. These cuts go in and out of print—currently the disc *Battle of the Blues, Vol. 3* collects some alongside recordings by Jimmy Witherspoon. Even as he was recording these blues sessions, Vinson was leading a jazz big band based in New York's Zanzibar club and later touring the country. He even worked in a band with John Coltrane, but their musical conception was too unique to interest any record companies in signing the group.

Two songs Vinson wrote during this period, "Tune Up" and "Four," eventually appeared on Miles Davis albums. In '54 Vinson rejoined the Williams band, then returned to Houston to put together a band with Cobb. Recorded with members of the Count Basie Orchestra,

Cleanhead's Back in Town bolsters his status as a terrific jazz performer. Another good jazz album, recorded in 1961 for Riverside with Cannonball Adderley, is currently unavailable.

By the end of the 1960s, the blues revival caught up with Vinson, who recorded for Bluesway with guitarist Michael Bloomfield on the great *Cherry Red.* Fortunately, the crucial 1969 release *Kidney Stew Is Fine* is still around; it's the only document of three of the most important Southwest blues figures in history playing together—Vinson, guitarist T-Bone Walker and pianist Jay McShann. Tenor saxophonist Hal "Cornbread" Singer, another jazz and blues veteran, is also on this set.

Vinson recorded a series of albums for Muse in the 1970s and '80s. The outstanding collaboration between Vinson and Roomful of Blues has been reissued by 32 Blues (in a twofer with Roomful's Joe Turner collaboration). *Jammin' the Blues* is a hot live session from the 1974 Montreux Jazz Festival costarring Singer. *You Can't Make Love Alone,* a currently unavailable disc recorded live at Montreux in 1971 with a crack R&B band and Larry Coryell on guitar, is also worth searching out.

I Want a Little Girl is a session of blues songs with a relaxed approach and jazz accompaniment. *Blues in the Night* is from a down-home live performance in which Vinson shares the spotlight with Etta James fronting a band led by saxophonist Red Holloway and featuring Jack McDuff on organ. — J.S.

MIROSLAV VITOUS

★★★ **Miroslav (1978; Freedom, 1988)**
★★★★ **Guardian Angels (1978; Evidence, N.A.)**
★★★★ **Journey's End (1982; ECM, 1991)**
★★★★ **Emergence (1985; ECM, 1994)**
★★★ **Atmos (with Jan Garbarek) (ECM, 1992)**

Miroslav Vitous (b. 1947) polished off an impressive childhood education in classical music by studying bass at the Prague Conservatory after starting out on violin. His love of jazz brought him to Boston's Berklee College of Music, then to New York, where he was a sought-after session player, working with Miles Davis, Herbie Mann, Chick Corea and others.

Vitous eventually became a founding member of Weather Report, but not before recording the landmark debut album *Infinite Search* (later reissued as *Mountain in the Clouds* but maddeningly unavailable now in any format).

All Vitous's available work is from the period after he left Weather Report. On *Guardian Angels* he teams up with guitarist John Scofield. *Miroslav* is a trio with percussionists Don Alias and Armen Halburian. John Surman's expressive reed work and perfect-touch backing from drummer Jon Christensen and pianist John Taylor ably flesh out the beautiful *Journey's End.* Vitous made a powerful solo-bass outing with *Emergence.*

Several other out-of-print sides for ECM, particularly *Miroslav Vitous Group,* are worth searching out. — J.S.

JERRY VIVINO

★★★½ **Something Borrowed Something Blue (DMP, 1995)**

Multi-instrumentalist Jerry Vivino (b. 1955) shows himself to be a crafty bandleader and arranger as well as a skilled improviser on a variety of woodwinds on this extremely well-recorded debut. Choosing a wide-ranging selection of jazz, blues and pop standards to share space alongside several original compositions, Vivino demonstrates a chameleonlike ability to coax a full palette of musical colors from his various instruments. Influences from Herschel Evans to Thelonious Monk and Rahsaan Roland Kirk to the jump-blues dance bands of the 1940s are in evidence throughout *Something Borrowed Something Blue.* Younger brother Jimmy Vivino sits in on guitar for three tracks.

Vivino deftly explores the longstanding symbiotic relationship between blues and jazz. The raucous joys of New Orleans R&B are revisited on Lee Allen's "Walking with Mr. Lee," which features a hot guitar solo from Jimmy. Vivino cuts a Memphis groove on alto sax with his soulful version of the Willie Mitchell/Al Green classic "Let's Stay Together" and takes the band through a tenor-sax–driven shuffle, the happy-go-lucky original "Done Deal." Vivino can be heard nightly as part of the Max Weinberg Seven on *Late Night with Conan O'Brien.* — J.S.

ABDUL WADUD

★★★★ **I've Known Rivers (Gramavision, 1982)**
★★★★ **Trio 2 (Gramavision, 1989)**
★★★★ **Oakland Duets (Music and Arts Programs of America, 1993)**

St. Louis–based cellist Abdul Wadud (b. Ron Devon, in 1947) was a key figure in the Midwest experimental-music scene of the 1970s, which eventually formed a huge part of the New York loft-jazz movement and the subsequent 1980s jazz renaissance. Wadud was part of the St. Louis new-music collective the Black Artists Group (BAG), a close relation to the Chicago-based Association for the Advancement of Creative Musicians (AACM).

Wadud's closest musical partner has been saxophonist Julius Hemphill. Wadud appeared on Hemphill's excellent *Dogon A.D.*, *Coon Bid'ness* and *Raw Materials and Residuals.* In New York during the 1980s Wadud recorded with pianist Anthony Davis and flautist James Newton (*I've Known Rivers* and *Trio 2*). He also appeared on Newton's awesome tribute to Charles Mingus, *Romance and Revolution,* and in alto saxophonist Arthur Blythe's band. *Oakland Duets* is another collaboration with Hemphill. — J.S.

COLLIN WALCOTT

★★★ **Grazing Dreams (ECM, 1977)**
★★★★ **Works (ECM, 1988)**

Multi-instrumentalist Collin Walcott (1945–1984) was a world-music pioneer who, in addition to receiving Western classical training, studied tabla with Alla Rakha and sitar with Ravi Shankar. His work with the Paul Winter Consort and Oregon and later collaborative efforts with Don Cherry in Codona stake him a major place in jazz history, but a handful of solo efforts add an important chapter to an all-too-brief saga. *Grazing Dreams* is a quintet session with Cherry, guitarist John Abercrombie, bassist Palle Danielsson and percussionist Dom Um Romao. *Works* is a career overview including material recorded with Oregon shortly before his death.

Unfortunately, the rest of Walcott's fine work for ECM is unavailable. *Cloud Dance* (1975), with Abercrombie, bassist Dave Holland and drummer Jack DeJohnette, is every bit as good if not better than *Grazing Dreams. Dawn Dance* (1981), a series of duets with guitarist Steve Eliovson, is also worth searching out. Walcott was tragically killed in a car accident while touring Europe in 1984. — J.S.

MAL WALDRON

★★★ **Mal-1 (1956; Original Jazz Classics, 1991)**
★★★★ **Mal/2 (1957; Original Jazz Classics, 1991)**
★★★½ **Mal/3: Sounds (1958; Original Jazz Classics, 1993)**
★★★½ **Mal/4 (1958; Original Jazz Classics, 1995)**
★★★ **Impressions (1959; Original Jazz Classics, 1992)**
★★★★ **Left Alone (with Jackie McLean) (1959; Bethlehem, 1996)**
★★★★ **The Quest (1961; Original Jazz Classics, 1992)**
★★★ **Free at Last (1969; ECM, 1989)**
★★★ **Black Glory (1972; Enja, 1995)**
★★★★ **Hard Talk (with Steve Lacy) (1974; Enja, 1996)**
★★★★ **Moods (with Steve Lacy) (1978; Enja, 1990)**

★★★★½ What It Is (1981; Enja, 1994)
★★★ In Retrospect (Four Star, 1982)
★★★★½ Sempre Amore (with Steve Lacy) (1987; Soul Note, 1993)
★★★★ Update (1987; Soul Note, 1994)
★★★★ The Git Go: Live at the Village Vanguard (1987; Soul Note, 1993)
★★★ Our Colline's a Treasure (1987; Soul Note, 1991)
★★★★ Live at Sweet Basil (1987; Evidence, 1992)
★★★½ Mal, Dance & Soul (1987; Enja, 1994)
★★★½ Dedication (Soul Note, 1988)
★★★★ The Seagulls of Kristiansund (Live at the Village Vanguard) (Soul Note, 1990)
★★★★ Left Alone '86 (Evidence, 1992)
★★★ Crowd Scene (1992; Soul Note, 1994)
★★★★ Quadrologue at Utopia (Tutu, 1994)
★★★ Where Are You? (Soul Note, 1994)
★★★ Blues for Lady Day (Black Lion, 1994)
★★★ Blood and Guts (ECM, 1995)
★★★ My Dear Family (Evidence, 1996)

Malcolm Earl Waldron (b. 1926) was one of the most strikingly original pianists to emerge as a leader in the 1960s, yet the meticulousness of his conceptual approach to music and the discipline of his technique kept him remarkably free of any of the excesses and creative dead ends that accompanied the search for new forms of expression characteristic of that decade's avant-garde jazz movement. That virtue was undoubtedly the product of what Waldron learned as an accompanist in the 1950s, notably as part of the Charles Mingus Jazz Workshop lineup that recorded *Mingus at the Bohemia* and *Pithecanthropus Erectus* and as Billie Holiday's pianist in the last years of her career.

The Original Jazz Classics material documents Waldron's years on Prestige. Of the best of these, *Mal/2* features John Coltrane on tenor saxophone, Jackie McLean and Sahib Shihab on alto and Bill Hardman on trumpet, while *The Quest* uses Eric Dolphy on alto saxophone and clarinet and Booker Ervin on tenor.

Left Alone is a superb collaboration with McLean. Waldron moved to Europe in the mid-1960s and didn't surface in the studio again until the end of the decade to make *Free at Last,* in which he explored the concept of harmonic freedom in a trio context.

Hard Talk and *Moods* document Waldron's felicitous collaboration with soprano saxophonist Steve Lacy, whose wit, originality and curiosity as a player match Waldron's conception perfectly. It doesn't hurt that both men are near-fanatic disciples of Thelonious Monk. *What It Is* is terrifyingly good stuff. Waldron and the brilliantly tortured tenor saxophonist Clifford Jordan pound on the gates of hell in this astonishing session with bassist Cecil McBee and drummer Dannie Richmond. Waldron continued on a roll with *Sempre Amore,* a triumphant series of duets with Lacy on a program of Duke Ellington–related material. *Left Alone '86* reprises the 1957 session, with McLean's alto joining Waldron in a heartfelt tribute to the tragic denouement of Lady Day's bittersweet life.

The Seagulls of Kristiansund and *The Git Go* were both recorded during an incendiary stand at the Village Vanguard with the outstanding lineup of Woody Shaw on trumpet and flügelhorn, Charlie Rouse on tenor saxophone and flute, Reggie Workman on bass and Ed Blackwell on drums. *Our Colline's a Treasure* is a more modest trio setting with bassist Leonard Jones and drummer Sangoma Everett. *Live at Sweet Basil* is credited to the Super Quartet, which features Lacy, bassist Reggie Workman and drummer Eddie Moore.

Mal, Dance & Soul is a probing trio session with bassist Ed Schuller and drummer John Betsch. Tenor saxophonist Jim Pepper makes it a quartet on one track; this lineup reappears on the fine *Quadrologue at Utopia.* — J.S.

JOE LOUIS WALKER

★★★ Cold Is the Night (Hightone, 1986)
★★★★ The Gift (Hightone, 1988)
★★★★★ Blue Soul (Hightone, 1989)
★★★★★ Live at Slim's, Vol. 1 (Hightone, 1991)
★★★★ Live at Slim's, Vol. 2 (Hightone, 1992)
★★★½ Blues Survivor (Verve, 1993)
★★★½ JLW (Verve, 1994)
★★★★ Blues of the Month Club (Verve, 1995)
★★★½ Great Guitars (Verve, 1997)
★★★★ Preacher and the President (Verve, 1998)

Guitarist Joe Louis Walker's 1986 debut, *Cold Is the Night,* was a startlingly complete entrée into the blues world. With his distinctive, percussive lead style, chugging rhythm playing, intelligent songwriting and gutsy, soulful singing, Walker

(b. 1949) sounded more like a veteran recording star than a green talent. Perhaps this was because his overnight emergence was 20 years in the making. As a teenager, the San Francisco native opened shows for the Jefferson Airplane as well as bluesmen Freddie King and Earl Hooker before leaving secular music behind to play gospel for a decade.

Since reemerging, Walker has made up for lost time, recording eight excellent albums in nine years—a rich body of work that marks him as one of blues' true artists and easily its finest contemporary practitioner. Each album features a tremendous range of material, from upbeat, gospel-inflected R&B to down-and-dirty acoustic Delta blues, from accordion-driven zydeco to burn-down-the-house slow-blues guitar extravaganzas, all of it performed with both precision and edgy intensity.

Walker hasn't cut a bad album, though Bruce Bromberg's and Dennis Walker's production of his debut is a little heavy-handed. He has since produced or coproduced every album himself with much better results. Either volume of *Live at Slim's* is a fine introduction to Walker's work, compiling versions of songs from his first three albums and displaying the full range of his talents. *Blue Soul* and *The Gift* are both impeccable collections of songs. Signing with Verve in 1993 seems to have given Walker more studio time, allowing him to pursue his ambitious agenda even further, embracing jazz, utilizing gospel quartets and charting ever-more-sophisticated arrangements. Occasionally, this ambition leads Walker to cram too much into the songs on *JLW* and *Blues Survivor,* but when he succeeds, the results are remarkably powerful. Everything clicks on *Blues of the Month Club,* coproduced by Booker T. and the MG's guitarist Steve Cropper: The title track is a witty pop blues; "Lost Heart" sounds like a long-lost Stax nugget; "Your Lyin' Eyes" is a bone-cutting acoustic blues; and several of these elements meld into a cohesive, totally original whole on "Second Street," a grinding midtempo rocker with jazz changes, powered by a fluid Delta-style slide line—heady stuff. On *Great Guitars,* he is joined by a host of his friends and heroes including Buddy Guy, Otis Rush, Bonnie Raitt and Clarence "Gatemouth" Brown. *Preacher and the President,* coproduced by Cropper in Muscle Shoals with the Muscle Shoals Rhythm Section backing up Walker, is a superb session highlighted by the title track, a timely satiric piece aimed at the hypocrisy of self-styled moralists. — A.P.

T-BONE WALKER

★★★★ T-Bone Blues (1960; Atlantic, 1989)
★★ Dirty Mistreater (1968; MCA, 1983)
★★★ Well Done (1970; Collectables, 1990)
★★ Joe Turner and T-Bone Walker: Bosses of the Blues—Vol. 1 (1972; RCA Bluebird, 1989)
★★★ I Want a Little Girl (Delmark, 1973)
★★★★ The Complete Recordings of T-Bone Walker, 1940–1954 (Mosaic, 1990)
★★★★★ The Complete Imperial Recordings, 1950–1954 (EMI, 1991)
★★★★★ The Complete Capitol/Black & White Recordings (Capitol, 1995)
★★★½ Stormy Monday (LaserLight, 1996)

Trace the arc of blues history from the country blues to big-band swing to postwar electrified urban blues to rhythm and blues to the dawn of soul music, and one name is everywhere: Aaron Thibeaux Walker, popularly known as T-Bone Walker. Through most of these eras, Walker was more than a mere participant—he was doing much of the reshaping of the landscape around him before moving on to discover new worlds.

Born into a musically inclined family in Linden, Texas, T-Bone Walker (1910–1975) took up guitar at age 13. Scrapper Blackwell, who accompanied blues pianist Leroy Carr, was an early influence on the young Walker, but two other blues giants would exert an even greater sway over his stylistic evolution. One was Lonnie Johnson, whom Walker was able to study during Johnson's frequent forays into the Dallas area; the other was the nonpareil country-blues guitarist/writer Blind Lemon Jefferson. From Johnson, Walker adopted a single-string soloing style that he developed into a voice that was direct, evocative, economical, inventive and tender or tough as the material demanded. Jefferson's uncommonly individual guitar stylings and lyrical folk poetry also left an indelible imprint on the budding artist, who absorbed the master's lessons while leading him around the Dallas streets where Jefferson played for tips. And it was Jefferson's raw, emotional approach that informed Walker's first recordings, "Trinity River Blues" backed with "Wichita Falls Blues," made in 1929 for Columbia, on which he was billed as Oak Cliff T-Bone, Oak Cliff being the section of Dallas where he lived. When that record didn't sell,

Columbia elected to dispense with a follow-up. By that time Walker had a full schedule playing with a group of school friends in the Lawson/Brooks big band, an affiliation that continued until 1934, when he headed west to Los Angeles's thriving R&B scene; his place in Lawson/Brooks was assumed by a promising young guitarist named Charlie Christian.

In 1939, while working with the Les Hite band, Walker was signed to the fledgling Varsity label and cut "T-Bone Blues," which brought him some attention, although he didn't play guitar on the session. Even so, he was then beginning his early experiments with the newest sonic innovation on the block, the electric guitar, and along with Christian and a handful of other players began breaking new ground. He signed with the nascent Capitol label in 1942 and made a statement with his early release "I Got a Break, Baby." Nearly a minute passes at the outset of that track with nothing but soloing from Walker, everything from frisky single-line runs; sustained bent notes; ostinato riffs morphing into screaming three-note chords; rich, legato phrases; speed-picked single notes cartwheeling one over the other. Then Walker the vocalist enters, casual but confident, swinging his phrases with Joe Turner–like assurance. The whole package was there, and from that foundation he would move on to write his name large on virtually every succeeding trend in black music up to his death in 1975.

In 1946 Walker jumped to another new label, Black & White, after the lifting of wartime restrictions on materials used for recording. The 50-plus songs he recorded in a variety of contexts over the next five years are now considered among the most important body of blues work ever committed to tape. In it are signposts to B.B. King's warm, single-string lyricism, Albert Collins's blazing, hard-picked attacks, Albert King's hearty but unusually tender voicings—the list goes on and on, encompassing about every important guitarist who came after him in the '50s, '60s and '70s. Moreover, he had the vocal chops to work persuasively in a number of styles. A mid-1949 session produced "Don't Give Me the Runaround," a languorous jazz/pop fusion in the style of the King Cole Trio, with Walker singing in a silky, seductive voice that could easily be mistaken for the smoky gray crooning of Cole himself; a swinging bit of Louis Jordan–style small-band novelty, "I Know Your Wig Is Gone"; and Walker's self-penned Mount Rushmore of a blues song, "Call It Stormy Monday But Tuesday's Just as Bad."

In 1950 Walker joined the Imperial label for what turned out to be a four-year stint that was an aesthetic extension of the marvelous Black & White years in its ongoing redefinition of modern blues. In addition to being a touchstone for musicians who came in his wake, Walker was a popular figure with the general public: a galvanic live performer, his club dates across the country invariably drew packed houses, and many of his '40s and '50s singles routinely peaked in the upper reaches of the R&B chart.

The Black & White and Imperial recordings are given a complete overview in Mosaic's pricey six-CD set, *The Complete Recordings of T-Bone Walker, 1940–1954.* Otherwise, *The Complete Capitol/Black & White Recordings* is, as its title suggests, the complete picture of Walker's early artistic breakthroughs, including "I Got a Break, Baby"; the first version of "Mean Old World" (which became a staple of his live shows and something of a signature song); two versions of "T-Bone Shuffle"; and the original and alternate versions of "Call It Stormy Monday But Tuesday's Just as Bad." This information is in abundance on *The Complete Imperial Recordings, 1950–1954,* along with all 52 songs Walker recorded for the label (minus 6 alternate versions excluded owing to space limitations), including several tracks cut in New Orleans with Dave Bartholomew and some of the same musicians who played on Bartholomew-produced Fats Domino recordings.

In 1955, with the rock & roll era dawning, Walker signed with Atlantic and over the next four years cut 15 sides with producers Jerry Wexler, Ahmet Ertegun and Nesuhi Ertegun. By the end of his Atlantic tenure, R&B, child of gospel and blues, was mutating into soul, child of gospel, blues, R&B and pop, and bringing with it a broad-based, young audience that regarded Walker's generation as yesterday's news, as these artists' declining sales figures indicated. Yet the Atlantic recordings, issued in 1960 as *T-Bone Blues,* were swept up in the folk and blues revival of that time and jump-started Walker's career, albeit on a smaller scale than he had experienced in the previous two decades. Working small clubs, colleges and festivals, he won a new following and gained recognition as an important jazz instrumentalist.

In 1968–69 Walker cut several sessions with jazz producer Bob Thiele, who surrounded him with the cream of Los Angeles's jazz-rock players (including Tom Scott on tenor sax). Ten of these are contained on MCA's *Dirty Mistreater,* seven on Bluebird's *Joe Turner and T-Bone Walker: Bosses of the Blues*. (Turner's eight tracks were recorded the day, before Walker's.) Both titles are mixed bags. Walker has some exemplary moments on the former—a terrific, weary vocal on "Stormy Monday" that is undercut by blaring horns; some terse, pungent solos spicing "Jealous Woman"—but the affair as a whole sounds cluttered, and the word *subtle* seems unfamiliar to the various players supporting the star. On *Bosses of the Blues,* Turner sounds bored with the proceedings, but Walker is at least engaged if not outright effusive. The feel throughout is loose and jam-session–like, with the various instrumentalists allowed ample solos, although by comparison Walker's guitar gets short shrift and sometimes is mixed too low. Of particular interest is a lively sparring match among the various instruments on Walker's relaxed interpretation of Memphis Slim's "Every Day I Have the Blues," a song long identified with B.B. King, one of Walker's most fervent admirers; King himself is the focus of an instrumental tribute, "For B.B. King," which allows Walker to repay the Blues Boy's effusive praise over the years with some tough, stinging soloing in the King style as filtered through Walker's sharp-edged sensibility. Other than the misstep of the slow blues "Vietnam," Walker's efforts here are pleasant but unremarkable on most counts. A live date recorded in 1968 (possibly in France, as Walker is heard to comment before one song, "I wish I could speak French so y'all could understand what I'm saying") and issued on LaserLight, *Stormy Monday* finds Walker at his gritty best vocally while delivering some scintillating guitar work, alternately sizzling or ruminative as the song demands.

Although 1973's *I Want a Little Girl* was Walker's final album before his death from pneumonia two years later, 1970's effort for the Home Cookin' label (now available on Collectables), *Well Done,* is the gem of the later years. The players, producer and recording dates are a mystery left unsolved by the perfunctory liner copy, but whoever decided to return Walker to a small-combo setting had the right idea. Walker energizes the place with his smoky, gritty vocals and gets off some startling solos along the way—check out "Good Boy," where he rips into the churning blues setting with a series of slashing, piercing, trebly lines, as a harmonica wails low and mean behind him. A droning organ establishes the moody ambiance for the dark-textured musings of "Please Come Back to Me," with Walker underscoring his own broken-hearted vocal with a series of extended, angular six-string discourses. Bobby Bland's hit "Farther on Up the Road" gets a confident, husky vocal reading from Walker as the band cooks steadily behind him without getting in the way of a tart, pointed guitar solo in the midst of the up-tempo workout. *I Want a Little Girl* concludes Walker's recording history on a swinging note that finds him putting some air into his sound as he opts for a terse soloing approach remarkable for its understated eloquence. Both albums boast an intimate, after-hours club feel and offer periodic displays of vocal and instrumental prowess. As final testaments of a great artist, these are worthy additions to the catalog. — D.M.

FATS WALLER

★★★ **A Legendary Performer (RCA, 1978)**
★★★★★ **Fine Arabian Stuff (Muse, 1979)**
★★★★★ **Fats Waller in London (1979; Disques Swing, 1984)**
★★★★ **20 Golden Pieces of Fats Waller (Bulldog, 1984)**
★★★★ **The Joint Is Jumpin' (RCA Bluebird, 1988)**
★★★★ **Classic Jazz from Rare Piano Rolls (Biograph, 1988)**
★★★★★ **Fats Waller and His Rhythm: The Last Years: 1940–1943 (RCA Bluebird, 1989)**
★★★★ **Low Down Papa (Biograph, 1990)**
★★★★★ **Turn On the Heat: The Fats Waller Piano Solos (RCA Bluebird, 1991)**
★★★½ **Fats and His Buddies (1927–1929) (RCA Bluebird, 1992)**
★★★★★ **Fats Waller and His Rhythm: The Middle Years Part 1 (1936–38) (RCA Bluebird, 1992)**
★★★★ **Ain't Misbehavin' (LaserLight, 1993)**
★★★★ **The Indispensable Fats Waller, Vols. 9 & 10 (1940–1943) (RCA Bluebird, 1993)**
★★★★★ **Fats Waller and His Rhythm: Breakin' the Ice: The Early Years, Part 1 (1934–35) (RCA Bluebird, 1995)**

★★★★★ **Fats Waller and His Rhythm: I'm Gonna Sit Right Down: The Early Years, Part 2 (1935–36) (RCA Bluebird, 1995)**

★★★★★ **Fats Waller and His Rhythm: A Good Man Is Hard to Find: The Middle Years, (1938–40) (RCA Bluebird, 1995)**

★★★★ **Last Testament: His Final Recordings (Drive Archive, 1996)**

What Memphis was to rock & roll, so was the Harlem of the 1920s to jazz piano. Foremost among the keyboard practitioners in that fertile upper-Manhattan scene was James P. Johnson, who linked the formalism of ragtime with the friskiness of stride. Johnson inspired a host of acolytes, none more important than his protégé Thomas "Fats" Waller. Waller (1904–1943) honored the ragtime tradition by building on it to point the way forward on the strength of his powerful left hand and nimble right hand that together made an orchestra of the 88 keys. As Johnson was an incalculable influence on the young Waller, so did Waller cast a giant shadow over the immortals who followed him, such as Count Basie, Art Tatum, Erroll Garner, Jaki Byard and Joe Turner. Apart from his influence, though, Waller left behind a wealth of recordings and some of the most beloved songs in all of American popular music.

Waller was an ambitious, driven youngster who by his teens was proficient on piano and pipe organ—at age 10 he began playing the latter at the Abyssinian Baptist Church, where his father was a preacher, and by age 15 he was playing organ accompaniment to silent films at Harlem's Lincoln Theater. When Waller's mother died, Johnson took the 16-year-old under his wing and tutored him on the piano (he also bought Waller his first pair of long trousers). Johnson also opened professional doors for Waller; when Johnson landed an out-of-town gig, he recommended the 18-year-old musician take his featured spot at Leroy's nightclub on 135th Street, which led to a recording deal with the QRS Music Roll company.

The next year, 1923, the Fats Waller saga really began: His first issued QRS piano rolls popularized swinging ragtime, or stride, piano; he made the first of numerous career-enhancing radio broadcasts; and he cowrote, with lyricist Clarence Williams, his first hit, "Squeeze Me." During the QSR years in the '20s, Waller was also introduced to a gifted lyricist, Andy Razaf; over the next decade-plus these two would cocompose not only some of Waller's most popular recordings but songs that have endured as American classics—"Ain't Misbehavin'," "Honeysuckle Rose," "Blue Turning Grey Over You," "Black and Blue" and others. In 1926 Waller made his big move to the Victor Talking Machine Company (soon to be RCA Victor), where he produced an important body of work—the heart of his legacy—with a sextet he dubbed Fats Waller and His Rhythm and became a star of international renown. For good measure, he composed two well-received musical comedies, 1927's *Keep Shufflin'* and 1929's *Connie's Hot Chocolates,* the latter providing Louis Armstrong a featured turn on Broadway singing "Ain't Misbehavin'."

The earliest period of Waller's career is now well documented on CD. *Classic Jazz from Rare Piano Rolls* contains Waller's earliest ragtime piano-roll recordings, beginning with his first, 1923's "Got to Cool My Doggies Now." *Low Down Papa* rounds out the QSR years in 13 tracks, including a piano duet between mentor and pupil, when Waller and James P. Johnson team (barely—Waller plays a few airy, right-hand trilling fills behind Johnson's hearty, swinging attack) on "Cryin' for My Used to Be," a 1927 recording.

From piano rolls, Waller went to records and to the small-combo settings that would serve him so productively throughout the remainder of his recording career. *Fats and His Buddies* charts the early years on Victor, when Waller recorded in a variety of contexts with some of the best jazz instrumentalists of the '20s and '30s. Aesthetically, the least successful of the sessions collected here are those by the Louisiana Sugar Babes, whose lineup included James P. Johnson on piano and Waller on organ. As tentative as this quartet sounds, though, with Johnson at times struggling to be heard over Waller's organ, an engaging ambiance is created on the poppish tunes they essay, including the engaging Razaf/Waller composition "Willow Tree" and two takes of the Rodgers and Hart standard "Thou Swell." Far more effective, on every level, is the quintet and nonet billed as Fats Waller and His Buddies on recordings made in 1929. The Louis Armstrong influence is heard loud and clear in Charlie Gaines's soaring trumpet solos, while on the irresistible pop confection "Lookin' Good but Feelin' Bad" Jack Teagarden makes his presence felt on vibraphone while the Four Wanderers deliver a smooth, spirited vocal.

The heart of the Fats Waller catalog is the exhaustive five-volume, multidisc sets (the two *Early Years* sets are two discs each; the two *Middle Years* sets are three discs each, as is the single-volume *Last Years* set) charting the recording history of Fats Waller and His Rhythm from 1934 through the final recordings made shortly before the artist's death from bronchial pneumonia. These attractive, thoroughly annotated boxes demonstrate, in precise chronology, Waller's strengths and weaknesses—and how he turned the weaknesses into strengths on memorable performances of several otherwise unremarkable numbers. To capitalize on Waller's outsized, ebullient personality and the public affection he engendered in bringing wit and an irrepressible sense of invention to his performances, RCA's music directors fed Waller much of his repertoire. To Waller's everlasting chagrin, he was often saddled with material that was so hokey it belonged in vaudeville, not on a record by one of the era's supreme artists. (Said his clarinet and tenor-sax player Gene "Honeybear" Sedric: "Fats was sometimes very unhappy about his music. You see, he was appreciated for his showmanship ability and for that amount of piano that he played on records, but very few of Waller's record fans knew how much more he could play than what he usually did on records.") Yet he dug into his songs, whether original or from other writers, and sold them, summoning all his consummate comic and interpretive skill to spin gold out of dross. The collection spans from 1934 to 1943 and shows some of the best music recorded by any American artist of that time, with many of the best songwriters of the first half century represented along with a good number of the best jazz players of the modern era, prebebop.

Other recommended titles include *Fine Arabian Stuff* and *Fats Waller in London,* which showcase Waller on the pipe organ, and *Last Testament: His Final Recordings. Fine Arabian Stuff* is taken from a single session recorded in 1939 and includes gospel, folk and turn-of-the-century popular songs; *Fats Waller in London* was recorded in two sessions, one in 1938, one in 1939, and is a splendid single-disc overview of one aspect of Waller's art. The tunes include two versions of "Ain't Misbehavin'," organ instrumentals of four gospel songs (including a moving "Go Down, Moses"), standards such as "That Old Feeling" and "I Can't Give You Anything but Love" and an ambitious impressionistic suite of songs written about six different London neighborhoods ("The London Suite").

Last Testament: His Final Recordings is Drive Archive's collection of 12 tracks cut on September 23, 1943, and issued on V-discs for military personnel stationed overseas during World War II. A delightful version of "Ain't Misbehavin'," with Waller's fingers in full, glorious stride form buttressing a playful, personable vocal, kicks off the session and sets the tone for an in-studio concert rife with Waller's infectious, earthy humor and a broad palette of emotional colors. The bill of fare includes a healthy serving of familiar tunes, but Waller throws in a few moving but lesser-known original gems, such as the winsome "There's a Gal in My Life." He closes out with a number composed especially for this occasion, "Bouncin'," which finds Waller doing as the title says, but on the organ rather than piano, overtly employing it as a jazz instrument well ahead of any other musician using it as such.

Finally, LaserLight's *Ain't Misbehavin'* serves as the closest thing to a single-disc greatest-hits set in the Waller catalog. Its 11 cuts include well-known material along the lines of the title song and "Honeysuckle Rose" (both featuring Waller solo on piano) as well as lesser-known but no less stirring moments such as Waller and trumpeter Hot Lips Page in a two-man game on "Blues for Two in B Flat," a solo-piano version of "Go Down, Moses" and an all-star rave-up—Waller, Jack Teagarden, tenor-sax giant Bud Freeman, guitarist Al Casey, bassist Cedric Wallace, drummer Zutty Singleton and Louis Armstrong on trumpet—on the Gershwins' "I Got Rhythm." In the end there is so much to admire about Waller's music that picking out highlights becomes an exercise in futility. The man's entire career is a highlight and stands as one of this century's grand moments in music.
— D.M.

GEORGE WALLINGTON

★★★★ **The George Wallington Trios (1953; Original Jazz Classics, 1990)**
★★★★ **At Cafe Bohemia (1955; Original Jazz Classics, 1993)**
★★★ **Jazz for the Carriage Trade (1956; Original Jazz Classics, 1985)**
★★★ **The New York Scene (1957; Original Jazz Classics, 1985)**
★★★ **Jazz at Hotchkiss (1957; Savoy, N.A.)**

George Wallington (b. 1924) was an early adherent of bebop piano. In 1943 and '44 he played for the first bop band on 52nd Street led by Dizzy Gillespie and Oscar Pettiford; later in the decade he wrote "Lemon Drop" for Woody Herman's classic big band, and his "Godchild" was recorded in Miles Davis's historic *Birth of the Cool* sessions.

The George Wallington Trios, featuring drummer Max Roach and at various times bassists Charles Mingus, Oscar Pettiford and Curley Russell, documents Wallington's complete absorption of Bud Powell's pianistic vocabulary. *At Cafe Bohemia* uses the cream of Detroit's jazz exports: Pepper Adams, Donald Byrd and Paul Chambers. *New York Scene, Jazz for the Carriage Trade* and *Jazz at Hotchkiss* all feature altoist Phil Woods and trumpeter Byrd.
— S.F.

JACK WALRATH

★★★ **In Montana (1980; Jazz Alliance, 1996)**
★★★ **In Europe (1982; SteepleChase, 1995)**
★★★ **Out of the Tradition (Muse, 1992)**
★★★ **Serious Hang (Muse, 1994)**

Trumpeter/flügelhornist Jack Walrath (b. 1946) has a tough, wide-open sound honed playing blues and R&B with Ray Charles and jazz rock with Cold Blood before joining one of Charles Mingus's later bands and eventually becoming the group's arranger when Mingus's health failed.

Walrath continued to pursue the Mingus tradition after Mingus's death, recording his first album, *Demons in Pursuit* (out of print), with Mingus drummer Dannie Richmond. Walrath followed his ties to Mingus on a second, also unavailable solo effort, *Revenge of the Fat People,* which includes "Duke Ellington's Sound of Love," Mingus's tribute to another master.

Walrath's wry sense of humor and fondness for the macabre overlay his musical adventurousness and fierce, energetic chops. *In Europe* features the incendiary "Duesin' in Düsseldorf." With his Masters of Suspense band, Walrath assails standards on *Out of the Tradition* and lays out on *Serious Hang.* Other out-of-print titles include *Killer Bunnies, A Plea for Sanity* and the trio set *Wholly Trinity.* — J.S.

CEDAR WALTON

★★★★ **Cedar! (1967; Original Jazz Classics, 1990)**
★★★★ **Soul Cycle (1969; Original Jazz Classics, 1995)**
★★★★ **The Maestro (1981; Muse, 1989)**
★★★★ **Cedar Walton Plays Cedar Walton (Original Jazz Classics, 1988)**
★★★½ **My Funny Valentine (1991; Evidence, 1995)**
★★★★ **St. Thomas (1992; Evidence, 1996)**
★★★★ **Among Friends (Evidence, 1992)**
★★★½ **As Long as There's Music (Muse, 1993)**
★★★★½ **Maybeck Recital Hall Series, Vol. 25 (Concord Jazz, 1993)**
★★★★ **Spectrum (Prestige, 1995)**

Keyboardist Cedar Walton (b. 1934) came up with Art Blakey's Jazz Messengers in the '60s before gigging with Freddie Hubbard, Kenny Dorham, Lee Morgan, Eddie Harris and others. Walton worked as a Prestige session pianist and later made a number of records under his own name for the label. A smooth and rhythmically exciting stylist, Walton fit the blues-based blowing-session concepts of most of the Prestige recordings, which are listed above under both Prestige and Original Jazz Classics reissue imprints. His careerlong relationship with drummer Billy Higgins begins on *Cedar!*

Walton tried his hand on electric keyboards during the '70s, recording for several labels with little success, and that material is now unavailable. From the mid-1970s he was involved in the far more satisfying acoustic project Eastern Rebellion, with Higgins, George Coleman (then Bob Berg) on tenor saxophone and Sam Jones on bass.

On *The Maestro* Walton is joined by Higgins and bassist David Williams as well as vocalist Abbey Lincoln. Look for the cassette-only *Piano Solos,* a beautiful acoustic set from 1981. Walton's strengths as a group player began to be surpassed by a genius for solo work that reached its apogee on the outstanding *Maybeck Recital Hall Series. Among Friends* is a mixed session consisting of trio music with Higgins and Williams, a guest appearance by Bobby Hutcherson on vibes for one track and a beautiful solo medley from Walton.

As Long as There's Music is a quintet session with Higgins and Williams joined by the front line of Terence Blanchard on trumpet and Jesse Davis on alto saxophone. *My Funny Valentine* and *St. Thomas* are live trio performances with Higgins and Ron Carter recorded at the New York nightclub Sweet Basil. — J.S.

MICHAEL WARD

★★★½ Laid Back (Ralph, 1998)

Not to be confused with the great percussionist of the same name who died in 1998, Michael Ward (b. ca. 1970) is a talented and versatile Louisiana violinist. He may be best known for his performance on Wynton Marsalis's *Blood on the Fields,* but he has done a lot of work in the blues field, playing with Louisiana guitarist Kenny Neal and others. Ward's debut, *Laid Back,* is a solid session of grooves for Ward to lay out on, which he does in engaging fashion. — J.S.

ROBERT WARD

★★★★ Fear No Evil (Black Top, 1991)
★★★★ Rhythm of the People (Black Top, 1993)
★★★★ Black Bottom (Black Top, 1995)

Guitarist/vocalist Robert Ward (b. 1938) started out playing in the 1950s on the Georgia juke-joint circuit. He developed a unique fingering technique, using his thumb instead of a pick, which allowed him to concentrate on rhythmically intense single-note solos in an echoing texture derived from his use of stereo Magnatone amplifiers.

By the early 1960s, Ward had moved to Ohio and become an in-demand session player, recording with Wilson Pickett and Eddie Floyd. Ward is the player behind the insistent guitar pattern of "I Found a Love," the 1962 hit for the Falcons, a vocal group featuring Pickett. Ward's own group, the Ohio Untouchables, was a local legend that eventually evolved into the Ohio Players. Ward worked as a session player at Motown before quitting the music business.

Ward resurfaced nearly 20 years later on the Black Top label with the eclectic 1990 recording *Fear No Evil,* a set that utilizes his gospel, soul and blues influences on a strong collection of originals accompanied by such stalwarts as George Porter Jr. on bass and George Rains on drums.

Rhythm of the People is a superbly crafted record that captures Ward's live sound more successfully than the comeback album. Rains and several bassists—Lee Zeno, Sarah Brown and Porter—really kick behind Ward's guitar playing, and the arrangements are augmented by a four-piece horn section. Ward slams through "A Good Man" and "The Real Deal" and recuts "I Found a Love."

Ward moved on to record the eccentric and diverse *Black Bottom,* an ongoing consolidation of his strengths with a view toward a new expression. Ward runs through a catalog of diverse moves, blending the R&B groove of "Lonely Man" and "Toehold," the slinky shuffle of "Soul Stroll," the heartfelt ballad delivery of "Silver and Gold," the hard blues of "Two Steps from the Blues," the swamp music of "Black Bottom" and the inspirational bent of "Help the Needy" and "Something Good Drivin' the Devil Nuts" into a coherent vision. — J.S.

DAVID S. WARE

★★★½ Flight of i (DIW/Columbia, 1992)
★★★ Third Ear Recitation (DIW/Columbia, 1993)
★★★½ Dao (Homestead, 1995)
★★½ Cryptology (Homestead, 1995)

A veteran player who has worked with Cecil Taylor, alto saxophonist David S. Ware (b. 1949) connects the free-form improvisation of New York's loft-jazz movement of the '70s with the new, more aggressive style of Matthew Shipp and William Parker. Strongly influenced by Sonny Stitt and Albert Ayler, Ware favors a gruff, grainy tone that swoops from harsh, quickly played scales to more legato, calmer passages.

Ware's most accessible album, *Flight of i* hews closest to traditional jazz harmonics while exemplifying his attempt to find what he calls the inner sound of his music. His versions of "There Will Never Be Another You" and Jerome Kern's "Yesterdays" show off his technical facility and his ability to wring unexpected variations from standards. In high relief is the epic, 17-minute free-jazz flight of "Infi-Rhythms #1," in which the band's circular riffing steadily splinters as the theme develops, eventually recombining with Shipp and Ware's syncopated, staccato arcs.

Third Ear Recitation extends *Flight*'s ideas, the more abstract songs bookended by two drastically different versions of "Autumn Leaves," demonstrating Ware's emotional range. *Dao* is a series of variations on a theme, with Ware and band moving from cathartic, almost punklike noise to moments of quiescent calm with an almost breathtaking ease. *Cryptology,* while possessing moments of great harsh beauty, is almost too personal and inner-directed. The epiclike title suite appears to start in midtheme and begins to cohere only after intense and repeated listening: In this case, the music is too repetitive and dense and the returns too small to justify the time spent decoding it. — S.M.

DINAH WASHINGTON

★★★★ **Dinah Jams (1954; EmArcy, 1990)**
★★★ **For Those in Love (1955; EmArcy, 1991)**
★★★★★ **In the Land of Hi-Fi (1956; EmArcy, N.A.)**
★★★ **The Bessie Smith Songbook (1958; EmArcy, 1986)**
★★★★ **The Fats Waller Songbook (1958; EmArcy, 1984)**
★★★ **What a Difference a Day Makes! (1959; Mercury, 1984)**
★★★★ **The Two of Us (with Brook Benton) (1960; Verve, 1995)**
★★★★ **Dinah Washington's Greatest Hits (Mercury, 1963)**
★★★ **Dinah '63 (1963; Roulette, 1990)**
★★★★ **The Jazz Sides (EmArcy, 1976)**
★★★★★ **A Slick Chick (On the Mellow Side) (EmArcy, 1983)**
★★★ **Dinah Washington Sings the Blues (Mercury, 1987)**
★★★★ **Compact Jazz: Dinah Sings the Blues (Verve, 1987)**
★★★★★ **The Complete Dinah Washington on Mercury, Vol. 1 1946–1949 (Mercury, 1987)**
★★★★★ **The Complete Dinah Washington on Mercury, Vol. 2 1950–1952 (Mercury, 1987)**
★★★★★ **The Complete Dinah Washington on Mercury, Vol. 3 1952–1954 (Mercury, 1988)**
★★★★★ **The Complete Dinah Washington on Mercury, Vol. 4 1954–1956 (Mercury, 1988)**
★★★★★ **The Complete Dinah Washington on Mercury, Vol. 5 1956–1958 (Mercury, 1989)**
★★★★★ **The Complete Dinah Washington on Mercury, Vol. 6 1958–1960 (Mercury, 1989)**
★★★★★ **The Complete Dinah Washington on Mercury, Vol. 7 1961 (Mercury, 1989)**
★★★ **Golden Classics (Collectables, 1990)**
★★★★ **Dinah! (EmArcy, 1991)**
★★★★★ **Unforgettable (Mercury, 1991)**
★★★ **In Love (Roulette, 1991)**
★★★½ **The Best of Dinah Washington: The Roulette Years (Roulette, 1992)**
★★★½ **Mellow Mama (Delmark, 1992)**
★★★★★ **The Essential Dinah Washington: The Great Songs (Verve, 1992)**
★★★★★ **First Issue: The Dinah Washington Story (The Original Recordings) (Verve, 1993)**
★★★★ **Jazz 'Round Midnight (Verve, 1993)**
★★★★ **Dinah Washington Sings Standards (Verve, 1994)**
★★★★ **Verve Jazz Masters 19 (Verve, 1994)**
★★★★ **Blue Gardenia: Songs of Love (EmArcy, 1995)**

It would be enough to assert that Dinah Washington (née Ruth Lee Jones, 1924–1963) was simply a great singer who could handle everything from gospel to jazz to pop, and leave it at that. If only the immediacy and emotional sweep of her vocals didn't demand more. What was going on with an artist who could come on so sassy and tough one minute, so demure and vulnerable the next? After you have marveled at Washington's extraordinary instincts—the three-octave alto voice, clear and bright, working behind the beat to heighten the tension; the way she bites off the final notes of a lyric, giving her reading a stylish twist that adds layers of emotional subtext; her precise phrasing, sometimes taut, sometimes airy, that is always in perfect sync with the intended mood—you are left with the big, imposing heart and appetite for life lived hard that informed her approach.

Born in Tuscaloosa, Alabama, Washington sang in and played piano for church choirs in her youth after her family migrated to Chicago. Inspired by the recordings of Bessie Smith and Ethel Waters, she developed a distinctive vocal style early on, enough so that she won first place in an amateur contest at Chicago's Regal Theater in 1938, when she was 15. Two years later she was touring with gospel legend Sallie Martin's seminal female gospel group, the Sallie Martin Colored Ladies Quartet. A year after joining Martin, she began singing for free in Chicago nightclubs, following her regular gig as a washroom attendant at Garrick's Stage Bar. Her big break came in 1942 when Louis Armstrong's manager, Joe Glaser, who gave her the stage name Dinah Washington, brought Lionel Hampton to one of her after-hours performances. Duly impressed, Hampton offered her a job with his band (sharing the vocal duties with Joe Williams) and launched her recording career on the Keynote label, chronicled on the two-CD set *First Issue: The Dinah Washington Story (The Original Recordings),* an intelligent summary of the key recordings from Washington's first 18 years on record, 1944–1962. Even as a teenager she turned heads with the assurance and intensity she brought to ballads and up-tempo blues songs, an early indicator of the versatility that was to mark her mature work.

As reported by various biographers, Washington's offstage exploits were legendary. She hadn't been long on the road with Sallie Martin when she decided she would serve God and Mammon both; whatever solace she took from the good book, she also indulged a growing addiction to feckless men, alcohol and life in the fast lane. At last count she was reported to have had nine husbands in her 39 years, though how many of them were legally betrothed to her remains in doubt. She had a reputation for tolerating hecklers during a show, then attacking them physically afterward. Club owners who attempted to shortchange Washington learned firsthand that she always got what she had earned, even if she had to threaten them with her pistol to get it. And few who came into contact with her escaped the sting of her profane tongue. However tortured the woman's inner life, though, when she opened her mouth to sing, out came one of the most compelling voices anyone had ever heard.

In 1945 Washington left Hampton's band and made her first recordings as a solo artist, cutting a dozen small-combo R&B sides for the Apollo label with session players—among them vibraphonist Milt Jackson and bassist Charles Mingus—organized by tenor saxophonist Lucky Thompson. Alternately swinging and moody, with outstanding soloing by the supporting musicians, these recordings, now issued on Delmark's *Mellow Mama,* are fairly narrow stylistically but offer a hint of things to come in Washington's approach to the material—delicate and wispy on the slow numbers (betraying a Billie Holiday influence), hearty and righteously forceful (redolent of the gospel singer) on the up-tempo songs. These recordings caught the attention of Mercury Records, and in 1946 Washington embarked on what became a fruitful 15-year association with that label and its EmArcy subsidiary that produced an incandescent legacy of jazz, blues, pop and R&B sides—in sum, a body of work comparable aesthetically to that of any vocalist of her generation and a benchmark by which succeeding stylists have been measured. Early on she was dubbed the Queen of the Blues, and so it was that in the late '40s and early '50s Washington was dominant on the R&B chart. In the early '50s Mercury began to reposition her for a broader audience by adding pop standards to her repertoire (fine by Washington, who once declared, "I can sing anything. Anything at all"). For several years white radio stations refused to play these recordings, but that didn't deter Washington. She simply delivered some of the classic pop albums of the decade, three of which, *Dinah Jams, In the Land of Hi-Fi* and the beautiful *For Those in Love,* remain in print in their original configurations. *Dinah Jams* is of particular interest, as it documents a classic session teaming the singer with a band including such jazz giants as Max Roach, Clifford Brown, Clark Terry and Junior Mance. Pop success came at last in 1959 with a Top 10 single, "What a Diff'rence a Day Makes," a languid ballad that had first been a hit in 1934 for the Dorsey Brothers Band—with Bing Crosby's brother Bob on lead vocal—as "What a Diff'rence a Day Made" (which was based on a popular Mexican song, "Cuando Vuelva a Tu Lado.")

In 1960 Washington was back in the pop Top 10 twice on the strength of inspired duets with Brook Benton, another great vocalist who came out of a gospel background and was then in the early stages of becoming a Top 40 fixture. This duo clicked on "Baby (You've Got What It Takes)" and "A Rockin' Good Way (to Mess Around and Fall in Love)," a couple of winning songs that found them engaging in friendly, flirtatious vocal banter and delivering the lightweight lyrics with sass, grit and good humor. Their winning chemistry carried over to an engaging album, *The Two of Us,* now back in print and featuring seven tracks not included on the original vinyl release.

The above-mentioned albums certainly belong in any Washington collection, but the big enchilada of her catalog is the exhaustive seven-volume CD collection *The Complete Dinah Washington on Mercury.* Here the course of an important career can be heard chronologically in all its peaks and valleys—with remarkably few valleys apparent—complete with a raft of previously unreleased tracks, newly discovered recordings and rare singles. In addition, each multidisc volume contains a booklet with insightful, thoughtful annotation of the pertinent recording history and blunt accounts of the personal dramas informing her work through the years.

Washington's last two years on record were spent with the Roulette label, where she stayed close to R&B ballads, blues and pop standards, working with small combos and orchestras. Addictions to prescribed weight-reduction pills and alcohol had taken a toll on Washington's voice—as is evident on some of the sides on Mercury's *Vol. 7*—and by this time she was straining to reach high notes, undermining some otherwise effective performances. But there are beautiful moments on the Roulette discs noted in the above discography—stirring, heartbreaking ballads and fresh perspectives on some timeless standards—that show her far from washed up. *The Best of Dinah Washington: The Roulette Years* is a good single-disc overview, but both *In Love,* with Don Costa's ornate arrangements, and *Dinah '63* are rife with touching, often poignant performances, especially on the standards.

Among other recommended individual titles from the Mercury/EmArcy catalog, two standouts are *A Slick Chick (On the Mellow Side)* and *The Jazz Sides,* each containing nearly 90 minutes of music. Both titles indicate the nature of the material therein; the latter is highly recommended, both for its superb 1955 Quincy Jones–arranged octet jam sessions and for its inclusion of two performances from the 1958 Newport Jazz Festival, these being Washington's only live recordings. *Unforgettable* can lay claim to featuring some of Washington's most penetrating ballad work, beginning with her Promethean interpretation of producer Clyde Otis's "This Bitter Earth," which kicks off the proceedings. Backed by an orchestra and a small combo whose sterling members include guitarists Barney Kessel and Rene Hall, bassist Red Callender and drummer Earl Palmer, Washington gets to work on 18 top-notch love songs—some made top-notch by the depth of feeling in her singing rather than by the quality of the writing—and fashions a document that explores the tumultuous emotions of a love affair in dramatic, insightful terms. These sessions from 1959, 1960 and 1961 find the artist in an easygoing, relaxed mood, her voice soaring gently over swelling strings or taking on a feathery, whispery tone on more subdued numbers, as the band provides her with the sort of sensitive support a vocalist lives for. Tried-and-true material such as "I Understand" and "When I Fall in Love" is reinvigorated by the singer's heartfelt readings, and had Nat King Cole not placed his stamp indelibly on "Unforgettable," Washington's sumptuous version included here might well be declared definitive (it did manage to make the Top 20 on both the pop and R&B charts in 1959). The CD also includes six bonus tracks, four of which had previously been issued only as singles.

An overdose of pills and alcohol ended Washington's life. Death came too soon, but her music has grown richer over the years. Listen to any of her solo recordings, from the Apollo days through the glory years with Mercury to the final sessions for Roulette, and you will be struck by how unique she was in her own time, and by how mesmerizing her voice remains in ours. — D.M.

GROVER WASHINGTON JR.

★★ **Inner City Blues (Motown, 1972)**
★★ **All the King's Horses (Motown, 1972)**
★★ **Soul Box, Vol. 1 (Motown, 1973)**
★★★½ **Mister Magic (Motown, 1975)**
★★ **Feels So Good (Motown, 1975)**
★★ **A Secret Place (Motown, 1976)**
★★ **Soul Box, Vol. 2 (Motown, 1976)**
★★ **Live at the Bijou (Motown, 1977)**
★★ **Reed Seed (Motown, 1978)**
★★ **Paradise (Elektra, 1979)**
★★ **Skylarkin' (Motown, 1979)**
★★½ **Winelight (Elektra, 1980)**
★★ **Baddest (Motown, 1980)**
★★ **Come Morning (Elektra, 1981)**
★★ **The Best Is Yet to Come (Elektra, 1982)**
★★ **Inside Moves (Elektra, 1984)**
★★½ **Anthology (Elektra, 1985)**
★★ **Strawberry Moon (Columbia, 1987)**
★★ **Then and Now (Columbia, 1988)**
★★ **Time Out of Mind (Columbia, 1989)**
★★ **Next Exit (Columbia, 1992)**
★★ **All My Tomorrows (Columbia, 1994)**

Saxophonist Grover Washington Jr. (b. 1943) came from a musical family, learning to play the saxophone at age 10 from his father. At 16 he left home to tour with the Four Clefs, then began playing blues and R&B with Philadelphia organ combos in the '60s, eventually becoming a session player first for Fantasy Records and then for Creed Taylor's CTI/Kudu organization. Taylor's '70s jazz productions were mostly faceless settings that had little to do with any individual player's personality, but Washington's professional music background made him a perfect cog in the machine. When Washington was asked by Taylor to substitute for Hank Crawford on a session, the result proved commercial enough to prompt the savvy Taylor to produce more records featuring Washington.

It didn't take long before Washington and Taylor hit paydirt with *Mister Magic,* a staple of both Quiet Storm and smooth-jazz radio formats. The easy-listening pop jazz produced by Washington relied on his languid tone stretched out over busy rhythm beds, a formula that varies little over a career that offers little in the way of fireworks but never fails to deliver the professional consistency that his undemanding fans crave.

Washington's consistency stretched over the decades and through various labels. In the '80s *Winelight,* with vocalist Bill Withers guesting on the hit "Just the Two of Us," became the apotheosis of mood jazz, winning two Grammys and selling over a million copies. In 1992 *Next Exit* became the seventh Washington album to hit the top spot on the jazz charts. — J.S.

TUTS WASHINGTON

★★★★ New Orleans Piano Professor (1984; Rounder, 1992)
★★★★ Tipitina's '78 (Tuff City, 1998)

New Orleans pianist Tuts Washington (1907–1984) was a mainstay on the live R&B scene in the Crescent City. *Tipitina's* is a good example of the kind of set one might have heard Washington play at one of the many local clubs in which he performed. Jelly Roll Morton–inspired blues, stride and boogie-woogie piano were Washington's fortes, and he dishes them out here from his deep, steaming pot of influences—everything from the barrelhouse of "Yancey Special" to the Neworleaniana of "Tee-Na-Nah," "Pool Hall Blues" and the Dixieland standard "Sweet Georgia Brown." — J.S.

WALTER "WOLFMAN" WASHINGTON

★★★ Wolf Tracks (Rounder, 1987)
★★★ Out of the Dark (Rounder, 1988)
★★★★½ Wolf at the Door (Rounder, 1991)
★★★½ Sada (Pointblank, 1991)
★★★★ Blue Moon Rising (4-Tune, 1994)
★★★★½ Funk Is in the House (Bullseye Blues, 1998)

Walter "Wolfman" Washington (b. 1944) makes first-rate New Orleans blues and R&B heading up the Roadmasters, a tough six-man crew of nightclub vets. Washington plays guitar with some of the sting and crispness of Albert King (his own skills honed working with Lee Dorsey and Irma Thomas)—and he sings with a swinging, casual power. Chiefly because of the Doc Pomus/Dr. John ballad "Hello Stranger" and the easiest, jazziest vocal performances Wolfman has mustered, *Wolf at the Door* is his strongest album—the brass arrangements, in particular, are stunning—but the man seems incapable of making music lacking in either kick or class.

Blue Moon Rising is a strong album featuring Washington's touring band on a mix of covers ("Fever" by Little Willie John and "Use Me" by Bill Withers) and originals. By the time of *Funk Is in the House,* the band had evolved to new heights of performance intensity. — P.E.

ROB WASSERMAN

★★ Solo (Rounder, 1983)
★★★★ Duets (MCA, 1988)
★★★ Trios (GRP, 1994)

Bassist Rob Wasserman (b. ca. 1950) is a tremendously versatile musician whose work skips easily through a number of genres. He's worked as a band member with such varied musicians as David Grisman, Stéphane Grappelli, Bob Weir and Lou Reed. Recorded live without overdubs, *Solo* showcases Wasserman's technique and melodic fluidity but lacks the variety of his best work.

Duets adds to the multifaceted artist's luster. He swings through "Over the Rainbow" with Grappelli, accompanies Aaron Neville on a beautiful reading of the Hoagy Carmichael classic "Stardust" and produces a rocking version of "One for My Baby and One for the Road" with Reed. The duo settings are generally spare, though he doesn't resist overdubbing this time.

Trios tried to be more pop and less of a Whitman's sampler, but that was the very quality that gave *Duets* its quirky charm. Some of the couplings are inspired, bringing together Chris Whitley with Les Claypool, Jerry Garcia with Edie Brickell and old friends Bruce Hornsby and Branford Marsalis. Except for the Willie Dixon/Al Duncan track, the spareness falls prey to the expanding number of players. Working with Wasserman, however, even the most plodding pop musician gets a dose of swing. — H.B.

ETHEL WATERS

★★★ Ethel Waters' Greatest Years (Columbia, 1972)

★★★★ **Ethel Waters on Stage and Screen 1925–40 (Columbia, 1989)**
★★★★½ **Cabin in the Sky (Rhino, 1996)**
★★★ **Miss Ethel Waters (Monmouth Evergreen, N.A.)**

Dignified and majestic, Ethel Waters (1896–1976) surmounted a troubled childhood on the streets of a Philadelphia red-light district to become the first black pop singer to gain widespread acceptance by black and white audiences alike. She then parlayed her success as a singer into a long-standing career as an actress acclaimed for her work in Broadway plays and in movies; in her later years she appeared regularly in evangelist Billy Graham's Crusades, moving the crowds with her powerful, teary-eyed gospel witnessing in song.

A petty thief, a gang leader at age 10, a wife at 13 and a divorcée at 14, the young Waters fit the profile of a dead-end kid. But after her marriage failed, she got religion, and for the remainder of her life, matters of faith dictated her style and course of action. Waters eschewed any artistic technique that might cast her as a blues singer, blues being a state of mind she had abandoned in her conversion. Her diction was precise, crisp, stately, unaccompanied by grunts, shouts, purrs or other suggestive ornamentation she associated with blues singers.

While her conservatism surely eased her passage into white society, it didn't diminish her ability to move listeners of all races. Between 1921 and 1938 she cut 26 Top 40 singles, the earliest sides recorded with Fletcher Henderson, the later ones featuring Benny Goodman. Her biggest hit came in 1933, when her original and still-definitive version of "Stormy Weather" remained Number One for three weeks. This followed by four years her first Number One, a mesmerizing rendition of "Am I Blue?" that topped the charts for two weeks. However accidental, she was a pioneer among black musical artists, and her success broadened the crossover opportunities for such artists as Louis Armstrong, Billie Holiday and Lena Horne.

Her most famous movie role came in 1943, when she joined an all-black cast in director Vincente Minnelli's first film, *Cabin in the Sky.* Teamed with Horne, Armstrong, Duke Ellington and others, Waters was featured in five numbers, including two powerhouse performances, "Taking a Chance on Love" and "Happiness Is Just a Thing Called Joe," all included on the Rhino soundtrack reissue. As a bonus, that CD also contains Waters's stirring version of the folk song "Dat Suits Me," which was deleted from the final cut, and a rare piano/vocal track of Waters singing the reprise to "Taking a Chance on Love."

In the '50s Waters became the first black actress to star in her own network TV series, *Beulah,* and she went on to appear in many of that decade's highly regarded dramatic shows. By then she had completed her most important work as a musical artist. In her later years she recorded some spiritual albums centered on the Southern gospel songs she favored in the Billy Graham Crusades, but these are all out of print.

Ethel Waters on Stage and Screen contains cuts spanning the years 1925 to 1940 and is the most essential of Waters's domestic recordings still available. Its songs include the original versions of "Stormy Weather," "Am I Blue?" and "Taking a Chance on Love." *Ethel Waters' Greatest Years* collects material from the '30s, but also includes her 1925 hit single "Sweet Georgia Brown." For a sampling of the live artist, *Miss Ethel Waters* contains concert performances from the '50s, including a terrific version of "St. Louis Blues." The import Classics label lists in its catalog an exhaustive overview of Waters's early career in six chronological volumes covering the years 1921 to 1934. Domestically, however, the definitive Waters collection, which would include a sampling of the gospel years as well as the critical secular material, remains an idea and nothing more. This great artist deserves better than her present semiobscure state. — D.M.

MUDDY WATERS

★★★★★ **The Best of Muddy Waters (1958; Chess, 1987)**
★★★★★ **Muddy Waters at Newport, 1960 (1960; Chess, 1986)**
★★★ **Muddy Waters Sings Big Bill Broonzy (1960; Chess, 1986)**
★★★★ **Muddy Waters Sings Big Bill Broonzy/Folk Singer (1960/1964; Chess, 1987)**
★★★★ **Folk Singer (1964; Chess, 1987)**
★★★★★ **Down on Stovall's Plantation (Testament, 1966)**
★★★ **The Real Folk Blues (1966; Chess, 1987)**
★ **Muddy, Brass and the Blues (1966; Chess, 1989)**
★★★ **More Real Folk Blues (1967; Chess, 1988)**
★★★ **Mud in Your Ear (1967; Muse, 1990)**
★★★ **Fathers and Sons (Chess, 1969)**

★★★★ **They Call Me Muddy Waters (1971; Chess, 1990)**
★★★★ **Live at Mr. Kelly's (1971; Chess, 1992)**
★★★ **The London Muddy Waters Sessions (1972; Chess, 1989)**
★★★ **Can't Get No Grindin' (1973; Chess, 1990)**
★★ **The Muddy Waters Woodstock Album (Chess, 1975)**
★★★★ **Hard Again (Blue Sky, 1977)**
★★★½ **I'm Ready (Blue Sky, 1978)**
★★★★ **Muddy "Mississippi" Waters Live (Blue Sky, 1979)**
★★★★ **King Bee (Blue Sky, 1981)**
★★★½ **Muddy & the Wolf (1982; Chess, 1986)**
★★ **Sweet Home Chicago (Quicksilver/Intermedia, 1982)**
★★★★ **Rare and Unissued (1982; Chess, 1991)**
★★★½ **Rolling Stone (Chess, 1984)**
★★★★★ **Trouble No More (Singles, 1955–1959) (Chess, 1989)**
★★★★★ **The Chess Box (Chess, 1989)**
★★★½ **Blues Sky (Epic/Legacy, 1992)**
★★★★★ **The Complete Plantation Recordings: The Historical 1941–42 Library of Congress Field Recordings (Chess, 1993)**
★★★½ **"Unk" in Funk (Chess, 1994)**
★★★★★ **One More Mile: Chess Collectables, Vol. 1 (Chess, 1994)**
★★★ **Chicago Blues Masters, Vol. 1: Muddy Waters and Memphis Slim (Capitol, 1995)**
★★★ **Muddy Waters Blues Band featuring Dizzy Gillespie (LaserLight, 1996)**
★★★ **Hoochie Coochie Man (LaserLight, 1996)**

Muddy Waters (1915–1983) stands in a select group of American musical artists whose work altered the landscape, reaching across the years to mark everything that has come in its wake. His 1950s recordings for the Chess label transformed his native Delta blues into a music with widespread popular appeal, both here and abroad, thereby laying a huge chunk of rock & roll's foundation. This he accomplished by giving the blues a new shape crafted by electric instruments and amplification; along the way he introduced a stop-time riff that has since become one of the most familiar sounds in blues and rock and penned eloquent, culturally revealing lyrics rooted in the folklore and traditions of African-Americans. Moreover, musicians who accompanied Waters always profited from his rigorous discipline, many of them going on to form their own bands and make important records. And while the blues is acknowledged as a limited musical form, Waters, sometimes solely through the sheer force of his own personality, demanded attention be paid to his work, even to noble but failed experiments such as 1966's *Muddy, Brass and the Blues.*

When he died, Waters left behind a substantial body of recordings, many of which remain in print. Most indispensable, naturally, are the Chess albums, which document the most fertile period of his artistry; but it would be a mistake to ignore his later work, because the man was still going strong in the late '70s, buoyed by an association with the Blue Sky label that paired him with Johnny Winter, whose energizing presence as producer reinvigorated Waters both personally and artistically. As for the Chess years, it's impossible to point to one or two compilations and pronounce either one definitive, although *The Chess Box* approaches such distinction. Simply put, Waters is so formidable a historical figure that a complete portrait is possible only by dipping into other titles in his extensive catalog.

Had Waters never made it out of the Delta, *Down on Stovall's Plantation* (a vinyl release on the Testament label) and its unabridged version on Chess, *The Complete Plantation Recordings,* would show only the raw beginnings of an artist much admired in his own region, albeit one whose style was imitative of other Delta giants who had preceded him or were his contemporaries; in fact, at the time of these recordings made by Alan Lomax for the Library of Congress, Waters's reputation for brewing the best moonshine whiskey in Mississippi's Coahoma County was on a par with his standing as a musician.

Born McKinley Morganfield in Rolling Fork, Mississippi, Waters grew up in Clarksdale on the Stovall Plantation, where he was raised by his grandmother, who bestowed upon him the nickname Muddy, to which his friends amended Waters. In 1932, when he was 17, he took up the guitar, taught by a friend. Waters's most direct influences were Charley Patton, Son House and Robert Johnson. House's sound is heard prominently in Waters's early bottleneck voicings, although on many of the Library of Congress recordings from 1941 to '42 he is working in the more complex, polyrhythmic style associated with Johnson. A neighbor owned a record player, as did Muddy's grandmother, and he was exposed to the music of Blind Lemon Jefferson, Lonnie Johnson, Tampa Red, Leroy Carr and other seminal blues artists, further broadening his musical vocabulary. In between "plowin' mules, choppin' cotton and drawin' water," as he described his duties at Stovall, he began to make a name locally by converting his one-room log cabin into a juke joint on weekends and providing music, drink and gambling for the attending revelers.

Folklorist Alan Lomax, heading up a field-recording team for the Library of Congress, came to Clarksdale in 1941 looking for Robert Johnson, unaware that he had been dead for nearly three years. Told that the man on Stovall's played a lot like Johnson, Lomax tracked down Waters at home and recorded him performing two songs; a year later he came back and recorded more sides, some with Waters playing solo acoustic; some with Waters and a primitive string band, the Son Sims Four; some with Waters and guitarist Charles Berry. Encompassing 18 sides in all, these recordings, cut in Waters's cabin, are raw, moving and suggestive of things to come. One of the 1941 tracks, "Country Blues No. 1," is descended musically and lyrically from House's "My Black Mama" and Johnson's "Walkin' Blues." Thus a pattern emerged: Over the course of his career Waters would make frequent figurative forays back to the Delta for material, building new songs out of folktales and fragments of choruses he had absorbed in his youth, adding new and sometimes bolder lyrics to material otherwise decades old. As for thematic focus, Waters's songs were in the Delta tradition of brooding ruminations on death and faithless love, aptly summarized in titles such as "You're Gonna Miss Me When I'm Dead and Gone," "You Got to Take Sick and Die Some of These Days" and "Why Don't You Live So God Can Use You?" Vocally he displays mastery of the nuances of Delta blues singing, but while the stark authority of his voice is commanding, he's not yet the overpowering presence he would become a few years later after relocating to Chicago.

In 1943 Waters packed his belongings in a suitcase and boarded an Illinois Central train, joining the mass exodus of black people out of Mississippi to greater opportunity in the North, Chicago in this case. In the mid-'40s he got his first electric guitar and began working with various combinations of musicians headed by an older Delta-born bluesman, Sunnyland Slim. With Slim and bassist Big Crawford he recorded some unsuccessful sides for the Columbia and Aristocrat labels, the latter a Chicago-based operation run by brothers Leonard and Phil Chess.

In 1948 Waters cut two Aristocrat sides in the Delta bottleneck style, "I Can't Be Satisfied" backed with "(I Feel Like) Going Home," which sold rapidly in Chicago and the South. By this time Waters was working clubs with a band that included Claude Smith on guitar, Jimmy Rogers doubling on guitar and harmonica, Baby Face Leroy on guitar and drums and Little Walter Jacobs doubling on guitar and harmonica. This configuration, which later included Elgin Evans on drums, began recording in 1950 and developed the hard-driving sound of modern urban blues on "Louisiana Blues," "She Moves Me," "Honey Bee," "Still a Fool" and "Long Distance Call," all heard (along with the early Aristocrat sides) on disc one of the three-CD *Chess Box.* "Louisiana Blues" was a significant track in that it was Waters's first recording to feature Little Walter's amplified harmonica and it was his first national R&B hit; also, it was the single that established the Chess label, which had been formed in early 1950 after the brothers Chess bought out their Aristocrat partner.

Leonard Chess was producing Waters in these days, and his lack of musical training worked to his and the artist's favor. Like Waters, Chess went on instinct and feel. He close-miked Waters's voice, so that it was bold and out front of the raging band; ditto for Little Walter's amplified harp, which was virtually a searing, soulful second voice. Between 1952 and 1954 bassist Willie Dixon penned three songs for Waters that became major R&B hits and, as subsequent years have shown, blues masterpieces—"Hoochie Coochie Man," "Just Make Love to Me" and "I'm Ready." That same year saw pianist Otis Spann and drummer Francis Clay (replacing Elgin Evans) join Waters and the band develop rhythmic innovations, such as stop-time patterns and a driving backbeat, that quickly found their way into other artists' songs. Disc one and the first half of disc two in *The Chess Box* document the groundbreaking period from 1947 through 1956 and demonstrate most dramatically Waters's growing confidence in his artistry. He was surrounded by great musicians, and in Dixon and Chess he had the support and advice of two studio-savvy mentors, one an artist himself, the other a technician, both of whom understood where this music was headed and knew how to get it there.

Come 1956 (and the second half of *The Chess Box*'s second disc), Waters's band was undergoing change. Late in the year Little Walter left to form his own band and was replaced by Junior Wells; in early '57 Rogers left and was replaced by one of the early masters of distortion, Pat Hare. This combination proved even more combustible than Waters's first band. Additionally, the late-'50s sides show, as critic Robert Palmer points out in his essay accompanying the boxed set, Waters's most overt use of gospel vocal techniques that had then become a common element of both Ray Charles's and Sam Cooke's work. Check out "Evil," "Diamonds at Your Feet," "Take the Bitter with the Sweet" and particularly "Good News" for examples of how Waters brought gospel-derived elements into the secular world of the blues.

In 1958 Waters and Spann toured England with great success, which led to a booking at the 1960 Newport Jazz Festival. Before that date, though, Waters appeared with Chicago blues pianist Memphis Slim at an Alan Lomax–organized concert at Carnegie Hall, released on a 1959 United Artists album titled *Folk Song Festival at Carnegie Hall.* Five of these performances survive on the Capitol Blues Collection entry titled *Chicago Blues Masters, Vol. 1,* along with 12 others probably recorded in New York in 1961. The performances themselves have their moments—a rather measured reading of "Hoochie Coochie Man" opens the set on an affecting note, and Slim's exhausting workout on "Boogie Woogie Memphis" astounds in its fleetness—and it's interesting to hear Waters joining Slim's band as guitarist on the latter's tracks, both live and in the studio. Not a towering entry in the Waters catalog, this, but one that is consistently interesting for the casual mastery both artists demonstrate. The live album from that date, *Muddy Waters at Newport, 1960,* was a substantial hit in England, where it had enormous impact on the then-emerging generation of young white blues musicians. It remains available and is one of the most important in the entire catalog, marked as it is by outstanding vocal performances from Waters and revelatory guitar support from Pat Hare. Waters's music from 1954 to this point, sealed by the Newport album, is what so inflamed the young musicians who formed the Rolling Stones, the Animals and the Yardbirds.

The early '60s brought new personnel into the band, including guitarists Buddy Guy, Sammy Lawhorn and Pee Wee Madison and drummers Willie "Big Eyes" Smith and S.P. Leary. This was a time of experiments, with Waters cutting an album on which horns were later overdubbed (a mistake), *Muddy, Brass and the Blues.* In 1969 a group of young American blues artists got together with Waters for their own salute to the master on the *Fathers and Sons* album. Two alternate takes from those sessions are featured on *The Chess Box*'s third disc, with Waters and Spann accompanied by Paul Butterfield, Michael Bloomfield, Donald "Duck" Dunn and Phil Upchurch, among others. Ever gracious, Waters took a backseat on the Muse recording from 1967, *Mud in Your Ear,* which he produced and contributed to as a sideman. Luther "Georgia Boy Snake" Johnson and Mojo Buford take the lead vocals and prove themselves gritty, effective shouters—Johnson's roaring take on Washboard Sam's "Diggin' My Potatoes" opens the disc on a blazing note—while Waters steps aside and allows Lawhorn to showcase his stinging, trebly lead-guitar style. Although it was recorded in a New York City studio, *Mud in Your Ear* has the feel of a late-night blowout in a rowdy South Side Chicago blues joint.

Other titles showcase the breadth and depth of Waters's blues over the years. *Folk Singer* is a return to the Delta blues, a stirring all-acoustic session with Waters and Buddy Guy on guitars, Willie Dixon on bass and Clifton James on drums. That title is now available on a recommended twofer CD with Waters's heartfelt homage to the towering figure who preceded him as the majordomo of Chicago blues, Big Bill Broonzy, *Muddy Waters Sings Big Bill Broonzy. The Best of Muddy Waters* is an excellent sampling of early tracks from 1948 ("I Can't Be Satisfied") through 1954, including the most crucial of the 1951–54 sides. *Rare and Unissued* is recommended as an adjunct to *The Chess Box,* as most of its tracks cannot be found elsewhere (the cassette version has no liner information, so *caveat emptor*); the other gem in this category is the *One More Mile* double CD of rare and obscure Waters recordings from 1948 through 1972. The real find here—if it's fair to single out any track or tracks as such on this estimable collection—comes in the form of 11 studio recordings made for broadcast in Switzerland in 1972. These feature Waters accompanied only by Louis Myers on acoustic guitar and George "Mojo" Buford on harmonica in what amounts to an unplugged set of Waters classics, performed Delta-style with only trace elements of Chicago informing the proceedings. Another fine live album (though there's nary a hint of an audience on it) from 1971, *Live at Mr. Kelly's,* features the Waters band with Pinetop Perkins on piano (Otis Spann died in 1970) and Willie "Big Eyes" Smith on drums, with James Cotton blowing some harsh, protesting harmonica solos on three cuts. Waters is at his fine, weary-voiced best on this outing, and the band is about note-perfect behind him with the Smith and Calvin Jones (bass) rhythm section especially coming up with a powerhouse performance. The 1972 album *The London Muddy Waters Sessions* united Waters with some of his British and Irish acolytes (Georgie Fame, Steve Winwood, Rick Grech, Rory Gallagher, Mitch Mitchell) for fair-to-middling results (some of these tracks, along with those cut in London by Howlin' Wolf, found their way onto the 1982 compilation *Muddy & the Wolf*).

Beware the hype on *Muddy Waters Blues Band featuring Dizzy Gillespie.* The first-rate band includes, in addition to Smith and Perkins, Jerry Portnoy on harmonica, Bob Margolin on guitar, Calvin Jones on bass and Guitar Junior on guitar, but Gillespie, despite a cover note indicating that he appears on the first six of the CD's dozen cuts, is inaudible until the fifth number, "So Long," and even on that one his shining moment is reduced to one brief solo burst at the end; he adds a warm, probing solo to the version of "Kansas City" that follows, then disappears altogether. The set as a whole is fairly incendiary Muddy Waters live, albeit lacking some of the deep emotions evident in the playing on *Live at Mr. Kelly's.*

Despite the presence of the Band's Levon Helm and Garth Hudson, plus Paul Butterfield, Waters's final Chess LP, *The Muddy Waters Woodstock Album,* released in 1975, is an uninspired effort, with the musicians trudging through their paces and Waters straining to get something out of half-baked material. *Sweet Home Chicago* contains some of the early-'50s tracks available elsewhere, as well as the rare "Goin' Home," a blues done gospel-style, with Waters backed by a female chorus.

Following the disappointment of the Woodstock album, Waters came roaring back two years later on the Blue Sky label, with the appropriately titled *Hard Again,* on which Johnny Winter provided the sensitive production touch otherwise lacking on some of the early-'70s recordings. Here Waters sounds like a young man again, singing with a fury that had been missing in recent years and cutting loose on some tough guitar solos. Old hands James Cotton and Bob Margolin, among others, are back on board; Jimmy Rogers shows up on the follow-up to *Hard Again, I'm Ready,* as does Walter Horton.

Muddy "Mississippi" Waters Live demonstrates what everyone who saw Waters in the late '70s learned: On any given night the man could cut down any other artist who stepped on a stage, a point he made explicit on this set with an explosive version of "Mannish Boy" performed as if it were freshly written. *King Bee* is a fitting final testament, with Waters mixing in some stirring originals ("Too Young to Know," "Sad Sad Day") with covers of Slim Harpo's "I'm a King Bee" and Arthur Crudup's "Mean Old Frisco Blues." *Blues Sky* is a recommended overview of the Blue Sky years, although its dozen stellar cuts will only drive fans back to the complete albums from which each was culled (probably the point of this set, anyway). The cover photo of *King Bee* shows Waters smiling beatifically and relaxing in an ornate chair. Atop the chair is a king's crown, which rests directly above Waters's head. It looks like a good fit. — D.M.

PATTY WATERS

★★★★ **Patty Waters Sings (ESP, 1965)**
★★½ **College Tour (1966; ESP, N.A.)**

With a crucifix on her forehead and a wide-ranging if somewhat disembodied voice, Patty Waters (b. ca. 1940) is an extremely offbeat artist. Recorded in 1965, her debut album, *Patty Waters Sings,* finds Waters backed by a jazz trio (piano, bass, drums) while she delivers a set of six standard if somewhat abstract torch songs. The real fun begins (and the album ends) with the seventh track, a rendition of "Black Is the Color of My True Love's Hair," an arresting, absolutely riveting 13-minute-plus epic. As Waters warbles the song's lyrics (consisting of nothing more than its title), trilling up and down the scale, holding some notes, cutting others short, repeating phrases as she deems fit, the band gamely attempts to follow. *College Tour,* a live album, focuses on Waters's more pedestrian side, and unfortunately, the CD lacks the original vinyl LP's Esperanto liner notes.
— S.M.

BOBBY WATSON

★★★ **Jewel (1983; Evidence, 1993)**
★★★★ **Advance (Enja, 1984)**
★★★½ **Gumbo (1984; Evidence, 1994)**
★★★★ **Appointment in Milano (Red, 1985)**
★★★ **Love Remains (Red, 1986)**
★★★½ **Round Trip (Red, 1987)**
★★½ **Solo Saxophone Album (Red, 1991)**
★★★★½ **Present Tense (Columbia, 1992)**
★★★½ **Tailor Made (Columbia, 1993)**
★★★★ **Midwest Shuffle (Columbia, 1994)**
★★★ **Urban Renewal (Kokopelli, 1995)**

Alto saxophonist Bobby Watson was musical director of Art Blakey's Jazz Messengers when Wynton Marsalis joined in 1980. Eight years older, Watson (b. 1953) had no trouble holding his own as a soloist with the trumpet prodigy, for he had a similarly rich tone and slashing attack. The tall, lanky Kansas native had a much different temperament, for he played with the greasy good humor of Cannonball Adderley and the lusty romanticism of Johnny Hodges, in contrast to Marsalis's cerebral severity. Severity is what the press and audiences wanted, however, and the undeniably brilliant Marsalis became a superstar while Watson enjoyed no more than modest success.

Watson deserved better, for he's one of the most engaging saxophonists of his generation. He is interested in everything—from John Coltrane–esque outside jazz to traditional swing, from hard bop to hip-hop—and he finds something interesting to say in each genre. This eclecticism may have undermined his marketability, but it has yielded a rich discography, though several Watson releases have fallen out of print or are available only as imports. Tying it all together is Watson's emotional openness, his willingness to slow down or risk a mistake in hopes of capturing a feeling.

Watson emerged as a composer on Blakey's albums, and two out-of-print albums on Roulette, recorded while he was still a Messenger, are in the same vein. After leaving Blakey, Watson formed a combo with two Betty Carter alumni—pianist Mulgrew Miller and bassist Curtis Lundy—and a rotating cast of drummers and guests. This group debuted on the out-of-print *Beatitudes* and came into its own on *Jewel,* a single-horn session credited to the Robert Watson Sextet, and especially on *Gumbo,* a triple-horn set (featuring Hamiet Bluiett and Melton Mustafa) credited to Bobby Watson and the Horizon Quintet.

This was hard bop in the swaggering, soulful style of Cannonball Adderley. If the band strutted like Ray Charles on the fast tunes, it was as romantic as Billy Strayhorn on the slow pieces. It showcased this aspect of its music on the out-of-print *Year of the Rabbit,* a gorgeous tribute to Johnny Hodges credited to Bobby Watson and the High Court of Swing. Fast or slow, the recordings relied heavily on the tuneful, splashy writing of Watson and Lundy, who also collaborated on the quartet session *Love Remains.*

Simultaneous to his work with Miller and Lundy, Watson recorded two dates with Italy's Open Form Trio, *Appointment in Milano* and *Round Trip.* The latter took its title from an Ornette Coleman composition, and both revealed Watson's ability to play aggressively within an avant-garde vein.

Watson landed a short-lived major-label American deal with Blue Note, which has since deleted Watson's recordings. *No Question About It* (1988) began a long and productive relationship with drummer Victor Lewis, who can be heard on all of Watson's subsequent albums. Lewis brought a combination of melodicism and fire to match Watson's own and pushed the leader to escape the bop straitjacket by exploring both more progressive modal settings as well as more populist R&B flavors. *No Question* leans in the progressive direction, with Frank Lacy and Roy Hargrove joining the leader for dense horn harmonies. *The Inventor* (1990) leans in the populist direction with a lighthearted calypso, seductive ballads and witty musical jokes. It all comes together on 1991's *Post-Modern Bop,* an album at once ambitious and accessible, hinting at what Charlie Parker might have sounded like if he'd been a fan of the Four Tops. Watson's final Blue Note outing, 1992's *New York Stories,* is an old-fashioned blowing session with Hargrove and Joshua Redman, but it includes the wild card of rockabilly guitarist Danny Gatton, who stimulates the jazzmen into some of their most down-to-earth playing. All the Blue Note recordings are worth seeking out.

Moving to Columbia, Watson stabilized his band around Lewis, Venezuelan pianist Ed Simon, Nigerian-American bassist Essiet Essiet and American trumpeter Terell Stafford. They made *Present Tense* as a quintet, extending the achievement of *Post-Modern Bop* into ever more adventuresome modal harmonies and ever more aggressive attacks. If the earlier recording was Watson's most accessible, the new one was his most rewarding. The same quintet made the sporadically brilliant live album, *Midwest Shuffle,* and the underrehearsed big-band album of striking Watson originals, *Tailor Made.*

Finally, in 1995, Watson made his long-resisted foray into pop-jazz fusion on *Urban Renewal.* Lewis was still on board, but the textures between the drums and saxophone are dominated by synthesizers, electric bass and electric guitar. The results are better than might be expected, because Watson and Lewis write such uncommon melodies and harmonies, but when they try to add vocals, the results are disastrous. Watson has also recorded as a member of the groups Superblue and the 29th Street Saxophone Quartet. — G.H.

JOHNNY "GUITAR" WATSON

★★★ **Ain't That a Bitch (1976; Collectables, 1994)**
★★★ **A Real Mother for Ya (1977; Collectables, 1994)**
★★★★ **Funk Beyond the Call of Duty (1977; Collectables, 1994)**
★★★½ **Giant (1978; Collectables, 1994)**
★★★ **Love Jones (1980; Collectables, 1994)**
★★★★★ **Three Hours Past Midnight (Flair/Virgin, 1986)**
★★★★ **Lone Ranger (Fantasy, 1995)**

In a blues, R&B and soul continuum rampant with macho bravado—from Robert Johnson and Muddy Waters to Marvin Gaye and L.L. Cool J—no bluesman assumed the alpha-male role as poetically, persistently and in as many styles as did the original "Gangster of Love": Johnny "Guitar" Watson (1934–1996). A Texas-born, L.A.-raised stringbender who stepped out of the T-Bone Walker/Clarence "Gatemouth" Brown school of strolling blues, Watson was among the first to push the technical possibilities of electric guitar; later he locked into a funk/R&B mantle during the disco '70s.

Watson's first recordings, for Federal in 1953, included the feedback-fueled "Space Guitar" (inspiring a young Frank Zappa) but are no longer available; nor are his later Federal singles: "Cuttin' In," "Highway 60" and the original "Gangster of Love" that so influenced fellow Texan Steve Miller. *Three Hours Past Midnight,* however, is an excellent overview of the young bluesman at his prime, all sparkling with his trademark, snappy guitar sound and propulsive horn arrangements. "Hot Little Mama," "Too Tired," "I'm Gonna Hit That Highway" and "Ain't Gonna Hush" (the answer song, featuring singer Cordella De Milo, to Big Joe Turner's "Honey Hush") are all period classics and have provided much fodder for such latter-day blues bands as Roomful of Blues and even Albert Collins.

In the '70s Watson discarded his blues/R&B mantle and plunged headfirst into the disco tide, never looking back; in this mode he produced a slew of albums that never really threatened the reign of Kool and the Gang or the Ohio Players (though his cheesecake album covers followed in the mode of the latter). *Lone Ranger* collects the best of the early '70s, highlighting a sardonic, street-hip songwriting talent on such numbers as "I Don't Want to Be a Lone Ranger" and "You Can Stay but the Noise Must Go." Watson's latter output has been reissued on the Collectables label, and though firmly rooted in the vamp-driven, boogie-booty feel of the time, the albums retain Watson's bristling guitar work and often put the *fun* back in *funky* with such polished workouts as "A Real Mother for Ya," "It's About the Dollar Bill" and a discoized "Gangster of Love." — A.K.

CHUCK WAYNE

★★★ **Tasty Pudding (1954; Savoy, 1995)**
★★★ **The Jazz Guitarist (1956; Savoy, 1995)**

Guitarist Chuck Wayne (1923–1997) was much in demand as a sideman on various 1940s bop dates, recording and/or playing with Lester Young, Slam Stewart, Barney Bigard, Woody Herman, George Shearing, Barbara Carroll and Gil Evans, as well as on his own. All of Wayne's own work is unavailable except for *Tasty Pudding* and *The Jazz Guitarist,* both of which feature Brew Moore and Zoot Sims on tenor saxophones. — J.S.

WEATHER REPORT

★★★ **Weather Report (1971; Columbia/Legacy, 1992)**
★★★★★ **I Sing the Body Electric (1972; Columbia/Legacy, 1990)**
★★★ **Sweetnighter (1973; Columbia/Legacy, 1996)**
★★★★★ **Mysterious Traveller (1974; Columbia/Legacy, N.A.)**
★★★★ **Tale Spinnin' (1975; Columbia/Legacy, 1994)**

★★★★ **Black Market (1976; Columbia/Legacy, 1991)**
★★★★★ **Heavy Weather (1977; Columbia/Legacy, 1992)**
★★★★★ **Live in Tokyo (1977; Columbia/Legacy, 1997)**
★★★ **Mr. Gone (1978; Columbia/Legacy, 1991)**
★★★ **8:30 (1979; Columbia/Legacy, 1994)**
★★★★ **Procession (1983; Columbia/Legacy, 1997)**
★★★½ **Domino Theory (1984; Columbia/Legacy, 1997)**
★★★ **Sportin' Life (1984; Columbia/Legacy, 1991)**
★★★ **This Is This (1985; Columbia/Legacy, 1991)**
★★★★ **Night Passage (Columbia/Legacy, 1991)**
★★★ **Collection (Griffin, 1994)**
★★★★ **This Is Jazz 10 (Columbia/Legacy, 1996)**

Keyboardist Joe Zawinul (b. 1932) and saxophonist Wayne Shorter (b. 1933) were well-known sidemen with Cannonball Adderley and Miles Davis, respectively, who had been prime movers in Davis's popular *In a Silent Way* and *Bitches Brew;* they formed Weather Report in 1971, with bassist Miroslav Vitous (b. 1947) as original coleader. The shifts in the band's music and personnel charted the pinnacles and pitfalls of jazz/rock fusion. Like its namesake, Weather Report was always changing, occasionally frustrating and quite often right on target.

The first album, *Weather Report,* with Alphonse Mouzon and Airto Moreira on drums and percussion, was an extension of the style first forged on *In a Silent Way*—lots of ensemble mood, few solos (except on Shorter's "Eurydice," the album's most substantial piece) and an overall feeling of incompleteness. "Orange Lady," a lovely Zawinul melody that never goes anywhere, typifies the problems of the album. *I Sing the Body Electric* features the first permanent touring version of the band, with drummer Eric Gravatt and percussionist Dom Um Romao. One half, recorded live in Tokyo, plus Zawinul's "Unknown Soldier" from the studio sessions, is the best recorded example of Weather Report's in-concert intensity. *Live in Tokyo* is more from the Tokyo concert. With *Sweetnighter* the band shows its intention to make funkier music more directed to the rock audience, and while Zawinul's long pieces "Boogie Woogie Waltz" and "125th Street Congress" have the beat, they dissipate into a blue haze of electric jamming.

From *Mysterious Traveller* on, Zawinul displays a much keener awareness of studio technique and a growing sense of how to integrate the various electronic keyboards; Vitous is replaced by the funkier electric bass of Alphonso Johnson, and a string of players fill the percussion chairs. This is the most successful album of this period, but excellent improvisations like "Cucumber Slumber" and "Blackthorn Rose" notwithstanding, all of these works lack energy, due to the contained percussion work and the overall technological veneer of the music. Most troublesome is the minimal presence of Shorter, one of the great contemporary musical minds, who tended to play less and took a less central role in the recorded ensembles as time passed (live performances were, fortunately, different).

Electric bassist Jaco Pastorius replaced Johnson in 1976 and quickly assumed coleader status with Shorter and Zawinul. Alejandro Acuna on drums and Manolo Badrena on percussion give the band a stable personnel who recorded *Heavy Weather,* its most commercial and one of its most challenging albums. "Birdland," the record's hit, shows the distance Zawinul has gone in his ability to use rock and studio techniques creatively, while "A Remark You Made" and "The Juggler" testify to his compositional range. Pastorius is simply the finest electric bassist around and a multifaceted composer as well; and Shorter, even pithier, contributes eloquent balladry on "A Remark You Made" and the infectious tune "Palladium."

After the overall success of *Heavy Weather,* which remains Weather Report's best-selling album, the end of the '70s saw another change in the percussion section. *Mr. Gone* was made with various drummers, including Peter Erskine, a young veteran of Stan Kenton's and Maynard Ferguson's bands. Erskine's big-band approach lent itself to the orchestral spreads of Zawinul's ensembles, and he joined the band permanently, the lone percussionist for a time, with hand drummer Robert Thomas Jr. added in 1980. By 1982 Pastorius, Erskine and Thomas had all departed, to be replaced on *Procession* by Victor Bailey, Omar Hakim and Jose Rossy.

Weather Report remained something different live, where the various twists of the tunes have been absorbed over time and the rhythms are looser. Still, Zawinul's music seems to restrict the role of the others. Complaints about Shorter's underuse grew tiresome, but Pastorius didn't seem to be getting his due either. Zawinul is ever more sure of his various keyboards and synthesizers, and *Night Passage* affords a particularly good example of his feeling for the sounds of the other players. Subsequent compositions often visit familiar territory, and (to judge by two nights of the concert tour summarized on *8:30* that I heard) so do the solos. Still, *8:30*'s format of three concert sides reprising earlier studio material, plus one new studio side, is a hard late-Weather survey to beat. Zawinul continued to command the proceedings with élan, fronting yet another lineup on *Procession,* with Victor Bailey on bass, Omar Hakim on drums and Joe Rossy on percussion. — B.B.

BOOGIE BILL WEBB

★★★★ **Drinkin' and Stinkin' (Flying Fish, 1989)**

Guitarist Boogie Bill Webb, born in 1924 in Mississippi and raised in New Orleans, learned to play guitar by listening to country-blues legend Tommy Johnson, who played at family fish fries. Webb's raw, personal approach to playing combines the roots of country blues with the funk and soul of subsequent electric styles in a stirring version of Southern juke-joint music. Though a few Webb singles have appeared on compilations, this is his only album, a wild excursion through blues history. Webb plays songs learned from Tommy Johnson ("Canned Heat"), Roosevelt Sykes ("44 Blues"), Lead Belly ("Red Cross Store Blues") and Lowell Fulson ("Black Nights"), as well as originals like the title track and the bizarre "You Can't Tell My Business After Dark," with King Curtis's "Soul Serenade" thrown in for good measure. He's backed ably by the Radiators' Reggie Scanlan on bass and musicologist Ben Sandmel on drums. — J.S.

CHICK WEBB

★★★★½ **Chick Webb and His Orchestra (1929–34) (Classics, N.A.)**
★★★★ **Chick Webb and His Orchestra (1935–38) (Classics, N.A.)**
★★★★ **Spinnin' the Webb (Decca, 1994)**
★★★ **Chick Webb (Best of Jazz, 1995)**
★★★½ **Standing Tall (Drive Archive, 1996)**

Drummer Chick Webb (1909–1939) came to New York from his native Baltimore in the mid-'20s and began leading his own group in 1926. *Chick Webb and His Orchestra (1929–34)* documents that band, which he led as king of Harlem's Savoy Ballroom, taking on all comers in nightly battles of the bands. His peers acknowledged Webb as the greatest percussionist of his era, and his band, with bassist John Kirby and players like Benny Carter on clarinet and alto saxophone and Jimmy Harrison on trombone, could swing with the best of them. The second Classics set shows that this later version of the band still pushed a mighty swing. Louis Jordan's vocals are featured on several tracks. *Spinnin' the Webb* collects material from 1929 to 1939.

By the time Webb went on to his greatest recognition behind his discovery of Ella Fitzgerald, the band was no longer always playing with as much energy, due to Webb's deteriorating physical condition. Fitzgerald kept the group going for two years after Webb died of tuberculosis. *Standing Tall,* live recordings from 1939, is a useful adjunct to a skimpy catalog that does not do justice to a jazz giant. — J.S.

EBERHARD WEBER

★★★★ **The Colours of Chloe (1974; ECM, 1991)**
★★★ **Silent Feet (with Colours) (1978; ECM, 1991)**
★★½ **Fluid Rustle (1979; ECM, 1991)**
★★★ **Later That Evening (1982; ECM, 1991)**
★★½ **Chorus (1984; ECM, 1991)**
★★★ **Orchestra (ECM, 1991)**
★★★ **Pendulum (ECM, 1993)**
★★★½ **Works (ECM, 1994)**

Bassist/cellist Eberhard Weber (b. 1940) was a child prodigy on cello in his native Germany. He began playing jazz in the 1960s with Wolfgang Dauner but emerged in the '70s with a compositional program influenced by European jazz, the American avant-garde and the minimalism of Steve Reich. Weber's music ranges from brilliantly innovative soundscapes brimming with new ideas to icy, dark-side-of-the-moon electronic classicism.

The Colours of Chloe is a truly original musical conception that dovetails magnificently with the exacting technical demands of Manfred Eicher's ECM Records, a watershed for European jazz. Weber became one of ECM's most visible figures, playing with vibist Gary Burton on *Ring* and *Passengers* and guitarist Ralph Towner on *Solstice* and organizing a series of his own groups. *Silent Feet* documents

Weber's band Colours, with ex–Soft Machine drummer John Marshall, Rainer Bruninghaus on keyboards and Charlie Mariano on soprano sax, nagaswaram and flute. *Fluid Rustle* finds Weber fronting another group with Burton, guitarist Bill Frisell and atmospheric vocalists Bonnie Herman and Norma Winstone. *Later That Evening* brings in Oregon's multi-instrumentalist Paul McCandless and pianist Lyle Mays. *Orchestra* contrasts solo bass with a large brass section. *Pendulum* is a solo set; *Works* a career overview. Amazingly, ECM has not reissued one of Weber's greatest recordings, *Yellow Fields. Little Movements,* another superior album, is also unavailable on CD, as are several others. — J.S.

BEN WEBSTER

★★★★★ **King of the Tenors (1954; Verve, 1993)**
★★★★★ **Soulville (1957; Verve, 1989)**
★★★★★ **Ben Webster and Associates (1959; Verve, 1988)**
★★★★ **Ben Webster Meets Oscar Peterson (1960; Verve, 1997)**
★★★★ **At the Renaissance (1960; Original Jazz Classics, 1992)**
★★★★ **Ben and Sweets (1962; Columbia, 1987)**
★★★★ **Soulmates (1963; Original Jazz Classics, 1991)**
★★★★★ **See You at the Fair (1965; Impulse!, 1993)**
★★★★ **Stormy Weather (1965; Black Lion, 1990)**
★★★★ **Gone with the Wind (1965; Black Lion, 1989)**
★★★★★ **The Jeep Is Jumping (1965; Black Lion, 1990)**
★★★★½ **There Is No Greater Love (1965; Black Lion, 1991)**
★★★★ **Ben Webster Meets Bill Coleman (1967; Black Lion, 1989)**
★★★★ **Masters of Jazz, Vol. 5 (Storyville, 1986)**
★★★★ **Ben Webster Plays Duke Ellington (Storyville, 1989)**
★★★★ **Ben Webster Plays Ballads (Storyville, 1989)**
★★★ **The Big Three (with Coleman Hawkins and Lester Young) (Signature, 1989)**
★★★★ **The Warm Moods (1989; Discovery, 1993)**
★★★★ **Compact Jazz (Verve, 1992)**
★★★★ **Jazz 'Round Midnight (Verve, 1993)**
★★★★★ **The Soul of Ben Webster (Verve, 1995)**
★★★★ **Verve Jazz Masters 43 (Verve, 1995)**
★★★★ **Music with Feeling (Verve, 1995)**
★★★ **Cotton Tail (RCA, 1997)**
★★★½ **Ben and Buck (Storyville, 1997)**

A dark horse in the stylistic battle that raged through the late '30s and '40s between the light-toned Lester Young and full-blooded Coleman Hawkins, tenor saxophonist Ben Webster (1909–1973) may have been the winner by a nose. Less flamboyant than either of those two stars, he was sentimental yet never embarrassingly so. His warm, at times breathy tone was more accessible than either Young's or Hawkins's. His use of growls and rasps could be superb, but it was his eloquent approach to ballads that most distinguished his playing. Webster was more concerned with touching his fans' hearts than dizzying their heads.

Born in Kansas City, Missouri, Webster began playing the violin before switching to the piano, an instrument he played until 1928, when he switched to alto sax. It wasn't until 1929 when he joined Billy Young's family band—where he first met and became lifelong friends with Billy's son Lester Young—that he moved to tenor. He began playing strictly tenor in late 1930 with Jap Allen's band. Webster rose fast through the bands of Blanche Calloway (Cab's sister) and Bennie Moten, where it first became apparent that he was a force to be reckoned with. He later replaced Lester Young in Fletcher Henderson's band. In the mid- to late '30s, Webster recorded in small groups with Teddy Wilson, Billie Holiday, Benny Goodman and others, and their works remain some of the finest jazz recordings ever made.

After subbing with Duke Ellington in 1935 and '36, returning to Henderson's band and briefly staying in Wilson's short-lived big band, Webster officially joined Ellington's band in 1940. His three years in that band produced much of his finest work, most of which is available on Bluebird's essential reissue *Duke Ellington: The Blanton-Webster Band.* Webster left Ellington in 1943, but after five years of playing in New York in small combos, he returned. The magic was gone, however, and a year later he left the group for good.

Signing with Verve in 1952, Webster made a string of classic recordings, the first of which,

King of the Tenors, is justifiably one of the most famous and beloved tenor records ever. Opening with a definitive reading of "Tenderly," this disc delivers classic after classic: "That's All," "Don't Get Around Much Anymore," "Jive at Six" and his Ellington-band showpiece, "Cotton Tail." *Soulville* continues this roll, adding ballads like "Lover Come Back to Me," a sinuous, sensual "Makin' Whoopee" and one of Webster's few self-penned stabs at near–rock & roll, "Late Date." Another spirited session, *Ben Webster and Associates,* highlighted by the Ellington standard "In a Mellow Tone," features trumpeter Roy Eldridge and tenor saxophonist Coleman Hawkins and reunites Webster with the man who first taught him scales on the sax, Budd Johnson. On *Ben Webster Meets Oscar Peterson* the two giants are supported by bassist Ray Brown and drummer Ed Thigpen.

The two-CD *Soul of Ben Webster* collects three albums: *The Soul of Ben Webster,* which he leads, Harry "Sweets" Edison's *Gee, Baby Ain't I Good to You* and Johnny Hodges's *Blues-a-Plenty,* on which Webster appears as a sideman. While the Hodges material may be the weak link here, all three albums showcase swing musicians in their prime. Significantly, Webster penned five of the seven tunes recorded in his session, although the most memorable number, thanks to a dreamy solo, is Billy Strayhorn's "Chelsea Bridge."

Before Webster left permanently for Europe in 1964, he made several near-classic American swan songs. *Ben and Sweets,* the pairing with trumpeter Edison, is sweet indeed; *Soulmates* is anything but, featuring the bizarre pairing of Webster with pianist Joe Zawinul (fortunately, Philly Joe Jones is there to hold things together). *See You at the Fair,* with Phil Woods, Pepper Adams, Hank Jones and other stellar support, again revisits several Ellington classics like "In a Mellow Tone" and "The Single Petal of a Rose."

Stormy Weather and *Gone with the Wind* were recorded in Copenhagen's Montmartre Jazzhus on a single very long night in January 1965 and find Webster's breathy delivery in high gear. Pianist Kenny Drew adds experience to both sessions as well as to *There Is No Greater Love,* which was recorded in Metronome Studios in Copenhagen and consists almost entirely of ballads. *The Jeep Is Jumping* strikes an ideal balance of blues, ballads and up-tempo numbers. Occasional fast songs like "Duke's in Bed" show that the big man could still growl if he wanted to. *Ben Webster Plays Ballads* and *Ben Webster Plays Duke Ellington* are mostly taken from Danish radio broadcasts from the late '60s and early '70s. *Plays Ballads* features a with-strings rendition of "Greensleeves" and "Stardust" with pianist Teddy Wilson. The *Masters of Jazz* collection is also mostly drawn from Danish radio broadcasts. Despite many titles in common with the other two Storyville collections, none of the performances is duplicated between volumes.

Those looking for a broad survey of Webster's work on Verve will be satisfied with any of the label's compilations. The *Jazz 'Round Midnight* collection is an amusing but effective attempt to package Webster's sexy solos into a disc for private "late-night" listening. — R.B.

KATIE WEBSTER

★★★½ **I Know That's Right (Arhoolie, 1987)**
★★★★ **The Swamp Boogie Queen (Alligator, 1988)**
★★★½ **Two-Fisted Mama! (Alligator, 1989)**
★★½ **No Foolin'! (Alligator, 1991)**
★★★½ **Katie Webster (Paula, 1991)**

Pianist Katie Webster (b. 1939) is something of a natural wonder, an all-American treasure whose songbook encompasses jump blues, boogie-woogie, R&B, low-down dirty blues, zydeco and gospel, all of it played with an elegant, classically trained touch. She is also a great singer, capable not only of gut-busting emotion but also the sort of subtle shading and phrasing that separates the wheat from the chaff in the world of vocalists.

By age 15, Webster had established herself as the best keyboardist in southern Louisiana, playing on hundreds of 45s, backing immortal swamp bluesmen like Lightnin' Slim, Lazy Lester and Slim Harpo, as well as zydeco kingpin Clifton Chenier, country crooner Warren Storm and Louisiana pop king Phil Phillips—that's her on the original version of "Sea of Love." Producer Jay D. Miller also cut a couple dozen tracks with Webster as the leader, all of which are collected on *Katie Webster.* You've probably never heard a teenager sound quite like Webster on "No Bread, No Meat." Lots of fun. From 1964 to 1967, Webster played organ with Otis Redding, who at the time of his death was attempting to free her from a contractual tie to Miller so he could record her.

Webster didn't record a solo album until 1987's *I Know That's Right,* featuring mostly original tunes and spotlighting her diversity, including three live solo-piano numbers. The production values of the Alligator releases are much higher, but none of them completely captures the full breadth of Webster's skills, though *The Swamp Boogie Queen* comes pretty damned close. With guest appearances by Bonnie Raitt, Robert Cray and Kim Wilson, the album leans more than it should on R&B chestnuts like Redding's "Fa-Fa-Fa-Fa-Fa (Sad Song)," but Webster performs them so well, it's hard to complain. The album also features a boogie-woogie instrumental, a few slow soul blues and an impromptu solo-piano tribute to her fellow bluespeople, "Lord, I Wonder." *Two-Fisted Mama!* and *No Foolin'!* find Katie alone with her touring bands, proving that she really doesn't need any celebrity help. Unfortunately, the material on *No Foolin'!* doesn't match Webster's talents, and for the only time in her recorded career, she sounds like she's consciously performing rather than just letting the music flow through her. — A.P.

MONSTER MIKE WELCH

★★★ **These Blues Are Mine (Tone-Cool, 1996)**
★★★ **Axe to Grind (Tone-Cool, 1997)**

Bluesboy Monster Mike Welch (b. 1979) plays on the verge of guitar greatness. He may have some growing up to do, but his ability, passion and attitude hint at his place in a league with blues veterans old enough to be his grandfather. The fact that he's shared stages with Junior Wells and Hubert Sumlin, released two albums and been likened to Stevie Ray Vaughan before graduating high school or getting his driver's license makes his talent even more noteworthy.

Welch (Dan Aykroyd dubbed him "Monster Mike" while he was playing at the Cambridge, Massachusetts, House of Blues) was eight when he received his first guitar and began emulating Magic Sam and Earl Hooker. By his 11th birthday, he was a fixture at Boston-area blues jams, making music with Ronnie Earl and Luther "Guitar Junior" Johnson. The influence of those legendary stringbenders is evident in his own ballsy, blazing 12-bar blues guitar and soulful baritone growl. *These Blues Are Mine* features Welch's explosive and expressive guitar work, proving that he is equally comfortable with rapid-fire spurts ("Lover and a Friend") and slow, powerful licks ("Cold Poison"). On *Axe to Grind,* he displays the same range, while his influences remain apparent, from the Beatles ("Palm of Her Hand") to danceable '50s instrumentals ("Elkmont Stomp"). His slow, driving blues number ("My Emptiness") sounds more personal, showcasing Welch's softer side with smoky vocals and delicate guitar work.

Although Welch's assured vocals and guitar-playing ability belie his youth, his lyrics—for the most part, youthful ruminations and tales of troubled teenage relationships—do not. And Welch has yet to transcend his formidable influences, but these albums still reveal a guitar honors student, poised to graduate to the big time. — A.A.

DICKY WELLS

★★★★ **Dicky's Blues (Topaz Jazz, 1995)**

Trombonist Dicky Wells (1907–1985) grew up in Louisville, Kentucky, before moving to New York in 1927, where he established himself as one of the great players with a growling, vocalizing vibrato sound and a musical sense of humor that became his trademark. He toured with Benny Carter, Fletcher Henderson and Teddy Hill before reaching his pinnacle as a member of the classic Count Basie band from 1938 to 1945. *Dicky's Blues* collects material from 1933 to 1941 with tenor-sax pioneer Coleman Hawkins, Basie and fellow Basie-ites Lester Young and Buck Clayton. He also recorded in a variety of contexts in Europe during the 1930s. Search out his great 1937 recording *In Paris,* now deleted from the Prestige catalog. — J.S.

JUNIOR WELLS

★★★★★ **Hoodoo Man Blues (Delmark, 1965)**
★★★★ **It's My Life, Baby! (Vanguard, 1966)**
★★★★ **On Tap (Delmark, 1966)**
★★★ **Blues Hit Big Town (Delmark, 1967)**
★★½ **Coming at You (Vanguard, 1968)**
★★★½ **Southside Blues Jam (Delmark, 1970)**
★★★ **Pleading the Blues (1979; Evidence, 1993)**
★★★★ **Harp Attack (with Carey Bell, James Cotton and Billy Branch) (Alligator, 1990)**
★★★★ **1957–1966 (Paula, 1991)**
★★★½ **1957–1963: Messin' with the Kid (Paula, 1991)**
★★ **Better Off with the Blues (Telarc, 1993)**
★★★ **Everybody's Gettin' Some (Telarc, 1995)**

★★★★ **Come On in This House (Telarc, 1996)**
★★★½ **Live at Buddy Guy's Legends (Telarc, 1997)**

Junior Wells (né Amos Blakemore, 1934–1998) is one of the five or six most important blues harmonica players of all time. At age 17 he was already a veteran accompanist when, in 1952, he replaced the immortal harmonica player Little Walter in Muddy Waters's band. He was still a tentative singer and front man, however, a fact illustrated on the disappointing *Blues Hit Big Town,* cut in 1953–54 and featuring a band that includes Waters and Elmore James. Wells's coming of age is apparent on *1957–1963: Messin' with the Kid,* a collection of his 1957–63 singles. He had really blossomed by 1965, when he cut his first proper album, *Hoodoo Man Blues.* Years of playing South Side blues clubs, often backed by guitarist Buddy Guy, honed Wells's chops as he developed an expansive, new, hardened style, adding heavy dollops of urban menace and James Brown–style protofunk to his traditional Chicago blues. *Hoodoo Man Blues* is not only Wells's finest moment but a modern blues masterpiece, which leaps out of the gate with "Snatch It Back and Hold It," a burst of funky R&B fun, and never looks back, with Wells and Guy constantly prodding each other to new heights.

It's My Life, Baby! is almost as strong, while *Coming at You* is weighed down by a superfluous horn section that only deadens the remarkable interplay between Guy and Wells. *Southside Blues Jam* is, as its name implies, a laid-back, deep-blues session. Featuring Waters's great pianist Otis Spann in his final recording, the album is worth owning if only for the set-closing "Trouble Don't Last Always," which begins with Guy yelling, "Roll the tape" and continues for seven minutes, as Guy and Wells improvise verses while Spann tinkles the ivories behind them. These albums also contain some of Guy's finest playing, finding an excellent middle ground, pushing the boundaries of the blues while still playing well-structured, thoughtful solos—not always the case in his later work.

On Tap is a laid-back, stone-cold treat, while *Pleading the Blues* is a decent, unessential slice of '70s Wells. After a long layoff, Wells returned to recording in 1993 with the distressingly lifeless *Better Off with the Blues,* then rebounded nicely with *Everybody's Gettin' Some.* The mostly acoustic *Come On in This House,* on which Wells is joined by young guitarists including Corey Harris, Sonny Landreth and John Mooney, is a remarkable achievement, a top-notch album cut years after Wells was written off as a creative force. *Harp Attack* was a 1990 harp players supersession, featuring Wells along with James Cotton, Billy Branch and Carey Bell. Everyone shines, highlighting the possibilities of the harmonica in the hands of the right person. Wells is still capable of delivering great live performances well into his '60s, as *Live at Buddy Guy's Legends* proves. — A.P.

KENNY WERNER

★★★ **Introducing the Trio (Sunnyside, 1990)**
★★★½ **Uncovered Heart (Sunnyside, 1990)**
★★★ **Press Enter (Sunnyside, 1992)**
★★★½ **Meditations (SteepleChase, 1993)**
★★★ **Copenhagen Calypso (SteepleChase, 1994)**
★★★★ **Gu-Ru (TCB Records, 1994)**
★★★½ **Paintings (Pioneer LDC, 1994)**
★★★★★ **Maybeck Recital Hall Series, Vol. 34 (Concord Jazz, 1994)**
★★★½ **Live at Visiones—Standards (Concord Jazz, 1995)**
★★★★ **Concord Duo Series, Vol. 10 (with Chris Potter) (Concord Jazz, 1996)**
★★★★½ **Unprotected Music (Double-Time, 1998)**
★★★★ **A Delicate Balance (RCA Victor, 1998)**

Kenny Werner (b. 1951) has emerged as one of the great improvising pianists of his generation, a musician of great skill and the understanding that he's not so much a player as a vehicle through which the music can flow. In that regard, this Brooklyn-born, classically trained musician is stylistically like Keith Jarrett and Bill Evans—a player of great depth and melodicism. Werner developed his jazz skills at the Berklee College of Music, then began musical associations with Charles Mingus, Archie Shepp, Lee Konitz, Gunther Schuller and the Village Vanguard Jazz Orchestra. In the 1990s he has worked frequently with trumpeter Tom Harrell and saxophonist Joe Lovano.

Introducing the Trio, *Press Enter* and the bold *Live at Visiones—Standards* were recorded with two longtime musical partners, bassist Ratzo Harris and drummer Tom Rainey. This team constantly unearths new musical discoveries in original and standard jazz material. The adventuresome *Uncovered Heart* puts Werner on the line with a first-rate band including Lovano, trumpeter Randy Brecker, bassist Eddie Gomez, drummer John Riley and percussionist Edison Cafe Adasilva.

Meditations and *Copenhagen Calypso* are early, artful solo piano sessions that reveal his depth and imagination. The former has classical underpinnings, while the latter favors the standard repertoire. *Gu-Ru* again teams Werner with Harris and Rainey and includes cameos by trumpeter Tim Hagans, saxophonist Billy Drewes and percussionist Jamie Haddad on one excellent Werner original "Shivaya." *Paintings,* recorded with a fine sextet plus special guests, presents Werner as composer, performer and conceptualist, offering original music inspired by works of some of the world's greatest painters—from Renoir to Picasso, Dali to Kandinsky.

Because of its sheer beauty, risk taking and flood of ideas, his contribution to Concord's Maybeck Recital Hall solo-piano series ranks as one of the best of that impressive lot. Werner's Maybeck duo recording with rising young saxophonist Chris Potter, a formidable tenor and soprano player, sets a new standard for recordings made without the comfort of a rhythm section.

Werner takes his inventiveness still deeper on *A Delicate Balance* with bassist Dave Holland and drummer Jack DeJohnette. *Unprotected Music* represents the art of surprise at its highest creative level. Werner, bassist Marc Johnson and drummer Joey Baron went into the studio and let the tape roll as they explored their collective chemistry on a couple of familiar tunes and open improvisations. The result is stunning.
— K.F.

FRANK WESS

★★★★ **North, South, East . . . Wess (1956; Savoy, 1993)**
★★★★ **Trombones and Flute (1956; Savoy, 1993)**
★★★★ **Opus in Swing (1956; Savoy, 1993)**
★★★★ **Jazz Is Busting Out All Over (1957; Savoy, 1993)**
★★★★ **Opus de Blues (1959; Savoy, 1993)**
★★★★ **Jazz for Playboys (1959; Savoy, 1993)**
★★★½ **Dear Mr. Basie (Concord Jazz, 1990)**
★★★★ **Entre Nous (Concord Jazz, 1991)**
★★★ **Tryin' to Make My Blues Turn Green (Concord Jazz, 1994)**

Frank Wess (b. 1922) is best known for his saxophone and flute playing alongside Frank Foster in the mid-1950s Count Basie band, one of Basie's most popular lineups and the creators of the 1956 hit "April in Paris." Wess was born in Kansas City but developed as a musician in Washington, D.C., where he played in the house band at the Howard Theater. After a military stint during World War II, he spent the late '40s touring with a variety of bands including those led by Billy Eckstine, Lucky Millinder and Bull Moose Jackson.

Wess became a huge star immediately after joining Basie in 1953 and established the flute as a mainstream jazz soloing instrument, although he also played tenor and alto sax in the group until his departure in 1964. His Savoy releases, made while he was in the Basie band, are related to his work there, often taking their titles from popular Wess arrangements in the Basie book and featuring fellow band members. The Concord releases show that Wess still had his chops into his 70s. *Entre Nous* documents the excellent, Basie-esque Frank Wess Orchestra in live performance. *Dear Mr. Basie* is a big-band session with trumpeter Harry "Sweets" Edison and a lineup of Basie-ites recorded live in Japan. — J.S.

STAN WEST

★★ **My Blues (Res-O-Nator, 1994)**
★★ **West Coast Slide (Res-O-Nator, 1996)**

California-based Stan West (b. 1946) isn't much of a vocalist, and his original material is weak—more message than feeling—but he's a wonderful slide guitarist. *My Blues* and *West Coast Slide* have a traditional blues feel, and Jeff "Dutch" Masters contributes some nice harp work. West's work is for the electric- and acoustic-slide aficionado only. — J.Z.

RANDY WESTON

★★½ **Get Happy (1955; Original Jazz Classics, 1995)**
★★★ **Jazz à la Bohemia (1956; Original Jazz Classics, 1990)**
★★★ **With These Hands . . . (1956; Original Jazz Classics, 1996)**
★★★½ **How High the Moon (1957; Biograph, 1997)**
★★★★★ **Tanjah (1973; Verve, 1995)**

★★★ **Carnival (1975; Freedom, 1987)**
★★★★ **Blues to Africa (1975; Freedom, 1988)**
★★★ **Berkshire Blues (1978; Black Lion, 1995)**
★★★★★ **The Healers (with David Murray) (Black Saint, 1987)**
★★★★ **Self-Portraits (Verve, 1990)**
★★★★½ **Uhuru Afrika/Highlife (Roulette, 1990)**
★★★★★ **The Spirits of Our Ancestors (Antilles, 1992)**
★★★★ **African Sunrise: Selections from The Spirits of Our Ancestors (Antilles, 1992)**
★★★★★ **Volcano Blues (with Melba Liston) (Antilles, 1993)**
★★★★ **Marrakech in the Cool of the Evening (Verve, 1994)**
★★★★½ **Monterey '66 (Verve, 1994)**
★★★ **The Splendid Master Gnawa Musicians of Morocco (Antilles, 1995)**
★★★★½ **Saga (Verve, 1995)**
★★★★ **Earth Birth (Verve, 1997)**

No matter who plays it, jazz is a fundamentally African-American music, and few have emphasized its African sources more than Randy Weston (b. 1926). His repeated visits and five-year African residency have resulted in a connection to source material that goes beyond sentimentality to an instinctual grasp of the land's polyrhythms, non-Western harmonies and trance chants. By marrying these elements to his grounding in Duke Ellington, Thelonious Monk, Art Tatum and Nat King Cole, Weston has balanced the African and American elements in jazz better than anyone other than Abdullah Ibrahim.

Weston was born in Brooklyn, the son of a West Indian Garvey-ite who championed Africa as the motherland. He grew up on his father's big-band records and his mother's A.M.E. church services, but it was Monk's live performances in the early '40s that converted Weston to modern-jazz piano. Weston's first recordings for Riverside and Dawn (now out of print) make clear how thoroughly he absorbed his mentor's style. Whether playing standards, his own compositions or Monk's, he plays the rests as carefully as the notes and makes the piano a percussive as well as melodic instrument.

Weston soon developed into a remarkable composer, able to come up with quirky, catchy themes that remain fascinating under countless harmonic shifts. His "Hi-Fly" is already a jazz standard, and several others are on their way to that status. Weston's big breakthrough as a composer came on the unavailable *Little Niles* album, a series of waltzes for his children, Niles and Pamela. The title tune, "Earth Birth," "Pam's Waltz" and "Babe's Blues" would stay in his repertoire for the rest of his career.

Weston hailed the African independence movement with *Uhuru Afrika,* which features the undulating African rhythms he had heard secondhand. He visited Africa on a State Department tour in 1961 and adapted Nigeria's high-life pop music into his landmark *Highlife,* which presents hybrid music that places American jazz harmonies on top of high-life themes and rhythms. *Uhuru Afrika* and *Highlife,* both featuring Melba Liston's big-band arrangements, were later reissued as a twofer.

Even as he was encountering African music on its own turf in the early '60s, Weston was assembling a terrific band at home: trumpeter Ray Copeland, drummer Lenny McBrowne and baritone saxophonist Cecil Payne. Detroit bassist Vishnu Bill Wood and Big Black, a hand percussionist who played in an authentic African fashion rather than the prevailing Latin style, filled out the sextet, who rehearsed and stayed together, developing the earthy rapport that marked Charles Mingus's groups of the same era. With tenor saxophonist Booker Ervin joining Payne, they recorded the live *Monterey '66,* which Weston himself has cited as one of his favorites.

In 1967 Weston moved to Tangier, Morocco, a North African city with a large community of Gnawans, black sub-Saharans with a lively, intact culture of their own. Weston ran a nightclub and an Afro-Caribbean festival there, and the Gnawan influence on his jazz shines on such superb albums as *Tanjah* and *Blues to Africa. Tanjah* finds Weston summarizing everything he learned in Morocco into a sumptuous, Ellington-esque song cycle with superb help from Liston. Weston lived in Morocco until 1972 and returns regularly.

When he returned to America, acoustic jazz had hit a commercial doldrums, and Weston's absence had only lowered his profile. *Carnival* was a spirited but loose jam at the 1974 Montreux Jazz Festival. Weston fell out of the spotlight during the late '70s and the '80s, but he made a triumphant return to prominence with the release in quick succession of three albums, all recorded over a three-day period on a big, booming Bosendorfer Imperial in Paris. Backed by bassist Jamil Nasser, percussionist Eric Asante and drummer Idris Muhammad, Weston pays tribute to his three major influences on the unavailable *Portraits of Duke Ellington* and *Portraits of Thelonious Monk,* and *Self-Portraits* (original compositions based on African sources). At 6 feet 7 inches, Weston is an imposing figure, and when he applies his outsized hands to the keyboard, the wide wingspan brings unacquainted notes into close proximity and the muscular force gives the pulse a percussive kick.

Weston then moved on to the most creative work of his career: *The Spirits of Our Ancestors* collects cultural meditations recorded with Gnawan singer/instrumentalist Yassir Chadly and American all-stars Dizzy Gillespie, Pharoah Sanders, Benny Powell, Billy Harper and Dewey Redman, as well as such longtime partners as Liston, Nasser, Muhammad and Big Black. Weston reprises many of his best compositions and adds the new "African Village Bedford Stuyvesant," an affectionate tribute to his childhood neighborhood, done once with solo piano and again with the whole band. Weston then examined the supports of the bridge between Africa and North America with an album devoted to the blues, *Volcano Blues.* With Liston's arranging help, he plays a Mississippi Delta blues, adds two Count Basie blues and fills in with his own takes on the form. Texas blues singer/guitarist Johnny Copeland appears on two numbers and gives the affair the juice of a juke joint.

The Splendid Master Gnawa Musicians of Morocco is a collaboration between Weston's piano and 11 Gnawan vocalists and percussionists; it's the most African and least American thing he's ever done and lacks the constant change of jazz. *Marrakech in the Cool of the Evening* is an elegant solo-piano album recorded in the Moroccan city. *Earth Birth* is a live recording from the 1995 Montreal Jazz Festival that gave Weston a chance to work with strings rather than the usual brass and reeds. He comes up with never intrusive, always sympathetic settings that bring out the romance lurking inside his best-known compositions. *Saga* plays on both the English meaning of the title, "a heroic, historical narrative," and the Wolof meaning, "African family," and features new pieces that sketch Weston's musical autobiography from his days as a young bebopper to his first encounters with Africa to his recent reemergence as an elderly grandmaster of jazz. It's an impressive album, partially because it tells such an imposing story—the tale of one of jazz's most underappreciated giants. — G.H.

KENNY WHEELER

★★★ **Gnu High (1976; ECM, N.A.)**
★★★ **1976 (Just a Memory, 1976)**
★★★ **Deer Wan (1978; ECM, 1991)**
★★★ **Double, Double You (1984; ECM, 1990)**
★★★ **Welcome (Soul Note, 1986)**
★★½ **Flutter By, Butterfly (Soul Note, 1988)**
★★★ **Music for Large and Small Ensembles (ECM, 1990)**
★★★½ **The Widow in the Window (ECM, 1990)**
★★★½ **Touche (with Paul Bley) (Justin Time, 1996)**
★★★ **Siren's Song (Justin Time, 1996)**
★★½ **Angel Song (ECM, 1997)**

Kenny Wheeler (b. 1930), a quietly gifted trumpeter, is a paragon of the inside/outside modern player. Purity of sound, warmth of palette and a steadfast aesthetic vision are the hallmarks of his style. Working in a post–Bill Evans harmonic idiom, he fuses chromaticism and lyrical solos, and the influence of late Miles Davis has clearly shaped his trumpet vocabulary. Well regarded by fellow musicians for his mature, elusive, introverted playing, the semireclusive Wheeler has developed a cult following. However, his intelligent, evocative and subtle music is dragged down a bit by subdued energy levels and a certain sameness of coloration and mood.

On *Gnu High,* Wheeler, Keith Jarrett, Dave Holland and Jack DeJohnette pursue sensitive ensemble improvisations in the atmospheric ECM house style. Though the group tends to meander, Jarrett is at his mid-'70s peak, playing beautifully, curbing his showier tendencies in favor of introspection. DeJohnette's polyrhythmic drumming functions as a melodic instrument, and Holland's bass is solid and sublime.

Deer Wan features lithe ensemble work from Jan Garbarek and John Abercrombie; *Double, Double You,* with Mike Brecker and John Taylor, drives harder. *Ensembles,* an ambitious two-CD set of Third Stream compositions combining quintet, vocalist and 19-piece wind orchestra, contains many interesting ideas, although some are overly drawn out. The hypnotic *Widow in the Window* has fine understated playing, especially from Wheeler and Abercrombie. *Touche* is a collaboration with pianist Paul Bley. — T.M.

ANDREW WHITE

★★★★ **Passion Flower (Andrew's Music, 1974)**
★★★★ **Collage (Andrew's Music, 1976)**
★★★ **Seven Giant Steps for Coltrane (Andrew's Music, 1977)**

Washington, D.C.–based Andrew White (b. 1942) is nothing if not unique. He has toured with Stevie Wonder and the Fifth Dimension on electric bass, recorded on that instrument plus English horn with Weather Report and has been a member of Julius Hemphill's Sax Sextet. As of fall 1997 White had transcribed 585 John Coltrane solos, arranged Coltrane's music for orchestra and recorded as a saxophone soloist (alto) with McCoy Tyner and on more than 40 albums (alto and tenor) for his own label, Andrew's Music. The first 30 of White's album covers are uniformly gold print on white background, with a version of his composition "Theme" nearly always included. Both *Passion Flower* and *Collage* are mid-'70s quartets, with Steve Novosel on bass and Blackbyrds Kevin Toney (piano) and Keith Killgo (drums) showing what they can do in a straight-ahead context. *Passion Flower* seems like a study of Coltrane's evolution, with White reflecting much of the spectrum in tenor solos on his own blues lines. *Collage* stresses some interesting arranging ideas and tune choices (Wayne Shorter's "Contemplation," Coltrane's "Just for the Love," Les Baxter's "Dock at Papaeta"). *Seven Giant Steps,* containing seven live, unaccompanied alto solos, supposedly based on Coltrane's "Giant Steps," is a bit indulgent even for White. — B.B.

BUKKA WHITE

★★★★ **Sky Songs (1963; Arhoolie, 1990)**
★★★★ **Legacy of the Blues: Bukka White (1963; GNP Crescendo, 1976)**
★★★★★ **The Complete Bukka White (Columbia/Legacy, 1994)**
★★★★★ **1963 Isn't 1962 (Genes Adelphi, 1994)**

Born in Houston, Mississippi, on the farm of his grandfather, the Rev. Punk Davidson, B.B. King's cousin Booker White (1909–1977), better known by his nickname, Bukka, received a guitar for his ninth birthday. A few years later he got serious about playing the blues after being introduced to and inspired by Charley Patton. Came the Depression and White hit the road, his wanderings taking him all over the South and as far north as Buffalo, New York. Big and strong, he was a skilled-enough athlete to make a living pitching two seasons for the Birmingham Black Cats, before moving on to Chicago in the late '30s and using his sledgehammer fists to support himself as a boxer. In the Windy City he established himself with the local blues crowd, befriending Big Bill Broonzy, and in 1937 was offered a chance to record by Lester Melrose of the Melrose Brothers publishing company, a concern that had been arranging recording sessions for locally based blues and jazz artists for nearly two decades. He was scheduled to go in for the date immediately upon his return from paying a social call on relatives in Mississippi.

Back in the Delta, he and a friend were ambushed one night by a fellow looking to settle an old score; White, who had come prepared for such an attack, promptly dispatched his would-be assailant with a gunshot to the leg. Arrested and sentenced to two years in the Parchman Prison Farm, he managed to get back to Chicago (either by jumping bail or through the auspices of Lester Melrose) to cut two original songs ahead of his imprisonment in Mississippi. Issued on the Vocalion label, White's single, "Pinebluff, Arkansas" backed with "Shake 'Em On Down," sold more than 16,000 copies—making it a bona fide hit among "race" records—with the shuffling, slightly bawdy "Shake 'Em On Down" becoming the favored side of the two; a year later Big Bill Broonzy offered an updated version of the song in his own "New Shake 'Em On Down," and several other blues artists covered the original version.

Upon his 1940 release from Parchman, White returned to Chicago to cut some new sides for Vocalion. Writing solidly for two days in early March, he came up with a dozen songs torn from the dark heart of his life experiences—songs about death, imprisonment, duplicitous women, the privations of poverty and the shiftless, aimless existence of the hobo he had once been. Singing in a deep, quavering voice and pounding hard chords on his guitar or razor-sharp slide lines (with Washboard Sam slapping out percussive support on washboard), White fashioned some of the most vivid imagery and soulful poetry the blues has ever known, work that stands easily alongside that of Robert

Johnson, Skip James, Son House and Charley Patton as monuments of the Delta style in its deepest form. Few Delta accounts of death's long reach are as harrowing as "Strange Place Blues," White's reflections on his mother's passing. In "When Can I Change My Clothes?" he protests the indignities of a prison regimen designed to destroy every shred of the inmates' dignity in the name of rehabilitation, a theme he plumbed to equally moving effect in "Parchman Farm Blues." "District Attorney Blues" finds him inveighing against a legal system that was especially unforgiving of black men's trespasses, a bold statement in 1940. "Fixing to Die Blues" is an interior monolog about the death experience imagined from the deceased's viewpoint, with White's propulsive riffing and stinging slide lines heightening the eerie narrative. This remarkable session, plus the two 1937 Vocalion sides, comprise *The Complete Bukka White,* as essential a Delta blues album as exists.

Although he continued playing live, 23 years would pass before White recorded again. By that time he was living in obscurity in Aberdeen, Mississippi, the Vocalion sessions a memory so distant they almost seemed like a dream. Guitar virtuoso John Fahey and his partner "Banana" Ed Denson, blues enthusiasts both, tracked him down and ushered him into a studio for the sessions released on *Legacy of the Blues,* another forceful, definitive personal statement straight from the Delta, and a live recording, *1963 Isn't 1962,* recorded at the Cabale in Berkeley, California. (A year later Fahey and Benson unearthed Skip James and got him back on record.) On *Legacy*'s collection of 11 songs, as blues scholar Samuel Charters observes in his liner notes, White sounds exactly as you would expect of a man who had been bottling up nearly two and a half decades of pain and abuse. *Legacy* finds White reprising a number of songs from his Vocalion catalog, but the textures in his singing and the ornamentation he has added to his slide style bespeak a richer, if sadder, personal history. To hear his lamentations in "Baby Please Don't Go," "Parchman Farm Blues" and "Poor Boy a Long Ways from Home" is to hear a man with hellhounds on his trail. This is a stirring, important document. While he continues to explore familiar themes on *1963 Isn't 1962,* White sounds like a man who has had a great burden lifted—as if, somewhere along the way, he has attained a survivor's spiritual state of grace. Echoes of Blind Lemon Jefferson and Lightnin' Hopkins abound in some of the story-songs here, and the personable manner of their telling recalls Lead Belly's genial style. Nevertheless, there are some harrowing moments, most notably on "Fixin' to Die," which is reprised here. He also makes a compelling personal statement out of another artist's song in adapting Charles Brown's "Driftin' Blues" to his own life experiences and recasting it as a disturbing Delta blues titled "Driftin' and Driftin'," its narrative pulled from White's own hard days riding the rails. Following these recordings, White returned to work steadily as a musician, playing before appreciative audiences during the blues revival of the '60s and reclaiming his rightful place of honor in the Delta blues pantheon.

The 60-minutes-plus of music contained in seven lengthy story-songs on *Sky Songs* are vintage examples of White's gift for improvisation (the title refers to White's observation that he didn't so much write songs as pull them from the sky), both verbal and instrumental. On two cuts, "Bald Eagle Train" and "Alabama Blues," White's rhythmic drive is buttressed by his buddy Big Willie Wayne's go-for-broke support on washboard (White always seemed to get the best out of his washboard players). While these minidocumentaries have a looser, more upbeat feel than his earlier material, the artist's view of human nature remains skeptical, of life tragic. Peace may never have been his, but Bukka White's striking imagery and powerful storytelling abound in instructive messages for those who would enter his forbidding world. — D.M.

JOSH WHITE

★★★ **Josh White Sings the Blues and Sings (Collectables, 1995)**
★★★★ **Josh White: Blues Singer 1932–1936 (Columbia/Legacy, 1996)**
★★★½ **Free & Equal Blues (Smithsonian Folkways, 1998)**

Country blues-folk artist Josh White (1915–1969) lived several different artistic lives: He started his career as a guitar-playing teen leading blind preachers through the Delta; then in the 1930s he began recording blues under the name Pinewood Tom and sacred songs with the moniker Joshua White, the Singing Christian. By the 1940s, his rather mellifluous vocals had brought the blues to a mainstream white audience; many of his compositions were topical, pointing out the inequities and horrors suffered by Black Americans. During the McCarthy era, White was pushed into naming names, losing the respect of the lefties who'd embraced him. He rebuilt his audience before his death, however.

White's early sides, including those by Pinewood Tom and the Singing Christian, are well documented on the Columbia/Legacy set. Backed by piano and/or acoustic guitar, the young White puts forth strong versions of a Delta repertoire, like "Milk Cow Blues" and spirituals, in his pleasant tenor. Informative, comprehensive notes accompany the set. The Collectables release presents a hodgepodge of White's later recordings (a mixture of blues, spiritual, folk and pop songs), including his versions of Lewis Allan's "Strange Fruit" and Jimmie Rodgers's "T.B. Blues." *Free & Equal Blues* is a well-annotated set documenting White's 1940s recordings captured by folklorist Moe Asch. Standouts include "Freedom Road" (with lyrics by Langston Hughes) and Cole Porter's "Miss Otis Regrets." — H.G.-W.

LENNY WHITE

★★★½ **Present Tense (Hip Bop, 1995)**
★★★½ **Renderers of Spirit (Hip Bop, 1997)**

New York drummer Lenny White (b. 1949) came on the scene in the late 1960s playing with the Jazz Samaritans, then with Jackie McLean before appearing on Miles Davis's historic 1969 *Bitches Brew* sessions. He went on to perform with Joe Henderson and Stan Getz, then joined Chick Corea's Return to Forever. His playing on that group's landmark *Hymn of the Seventh Galaxy* was a high point of the fusion style.

In the 1970s White made a series of solo albums that lack the focus of his work with Return to Forever and are now out of print, but at the same time he excelled as a producer, working on the fine Echoes of an Era project. White resurfaced in the '90s producing acid-jazz sessions, which led to the engagingly eclectic *Present Tense* and the quality postfusion outing *Renderers of Spirit* with bassist Stanley Clarke, keyboardist Geri Allen and saxophonist Michael Brecker. — J.S.

LILY WHITE

★★★★ **No Pork Long Line (Jazz Focus, 1997)**

Part of the flourishing Brooklyn jazz scene, Lily White (b. 1962) is a technically proficient and emotionally powerful saxophonist, adept at a multiplicity of styles. *No Pork Long Line* is a fine example of White's eclecticism, from the intricately arranged "If I Had Faith" (featuring guest Conrad Herwig on trombone), the atmospheric "Loss," the hip-hop friendly "Lumpy" and the playful "Circus Samba" to the nimble swing of "Annie Sprinkle Has My Hat" and the 5/4 romp of "Small Things, Tall Things." — J.S.

THE WILD TCHOUPITOULAS

★★★★★ **Wild Tchoupitoulas (1976; Antilles, N.A.)**

The Wild Tchoupitoulas are Mardi Gras "Indians"—that is, a "tribe" of Creoles who dress in elaborate, stylized Indian costumes to march and compete in Mardi Gras parades—fronted by the late George "Big Chief Jolly" Landry. Like many Mardi Gras Indians, the Wild Tchoupitoulas perform musical routines as part of their act—hence, Wild Tchoupitoulas. But because Landry happened to have a few nephews named Neville, the Wild Tchoupitoulas were able to recruit the Meters as their rhythm section, which lends their Indian numbers a solid grounding in New Orleans funk. As such, the album sounds as festive as a Mardi Gras album should; not only are the Tchoupitoulas' songs solidly soulful (particularly Landry's "Meet de Boys on the Battle Front"), but the album also includes a few songs from the Meters' repertoire, including "Hey Pocky A-Way" and the stirring "Brother John." *Wild Tchoupitoulas* is also the first recording to feature Meters Charles and Cyril Neville harmonizing with their brothers, Art and Aaron, a temporary combination that eventually (and without the Indians) became a full-time band: the Neville Brothers. — J.D.C.

JACK WILKINS

★★★★ **Merge (1977; Chiaroscuro, 1992)**
★★ **Alien Army (1991; MusicMasters, 1996)**
★★★ **Mexico (CTI, 1992)**
★★★ **Artwork (Koch, 1996)**

Jack Wilkins (b. 1944) is a warm-toned, limber guitarist comfortable with standards, bop, modality and everything in between. Besides being a showcase for the leader's inspired playing, *Merge* features the excellent support of drummer Jack DeJohnette, bassist Eddie Gomez and trumpeter Randy Brecker. *Mexico,* recorded 15 years later with altoist Phil Woods, pianist Albert Dailey and bassist Harvie Swartz, proves

Wilkins still had the goods, but *Alien Army* has too many fusion-lite overtones. — S.F.

REV. ROBERT WILKINS

★★★★★ **The Original Rolling Stone (Yazoo, 1989)**
★★★★ **. . . Remember Me (Genes, 1993)**
★★★½ **When I Lay My Burden Down (with Mississippi Fred McDowell and Furry Lewis) (Biograph, 1994)**

From Scottish bagpipe ballads to Morocco's Jajouka music and India's most time-honored ragas, music's ability to induce a meditative, trancelike state is universally shared and prized. In the blues world, a relatively small brotherhood of guitar pickers has likewise taken simple, repeated patterns and droning bass notes to the same spell-casting depth. In the '60s, Mississippi Fred McDowell excelled at this, but in the prewar era, no bluesman achieved the same hypnotic tranquility as did the "Reverend" Robert Wilkins (1896–1987).

With ethereal vocals, open tuning and intricate fingerpicking, Wilkins proved a seamless song sculptor, working out of the standard blues form. His "I'll Go with Her," "Rollin' Stone" (not the Muddy Waters classic), "Fallin' Down Blues" and "That's No Way to Get Along" each stand as separate tunes, breaking the blues' normal 12-bar mold and forgoing its A-A-B lyrical structure. His more upbeat numbers—"Alabama Blues," "Old Jim Canan's"—flirt with ragtime patterns but likewise exhibit unique construction. Offering all these, the Yazoo collection is the best document of Wilkins's accomplishments from 1928 to 1935.

A "rediscovery" in 1964 introduced to the folk circuit the bluesless Wilkins, performing a select number of Delta spiritual titles. Unlike many of his contemporaries, Wilkins had fortunately never laid his guitar down during his obscure years. Culled from never-before-heard tracks recorded in 1971, *. . . Remember Me* reveals the lion in winter, his clear and insistent picking patterns ringing like a bell on his electric guitar, while his slide work remained as strong and bristling as ever. His nine-minutes-plus take on Bukka White's "Streamline 'Frisco Limited" is the main attraction, and standards like "You Gotta Move" and "Just a Closer Walk with Thee" show off a warmer vocal approach that had foregone its stark and lonely edge. The Biograph title is from the same era, constituting an excellent comparison study on three distinct, gospel-centered Delta bluesmen (all perform revealing takes on the title track). — A.K.

BIG JOE WILLIAMS

★★★★ **Nine String Guitar Blues (1961; Collectables, 1995)**
★★★★ **Blues on Highway 49 (1961; Delmark, 1992)**
★★★★ **Walking Blues (1961; Fantasy, 1995)**
★★★ **Big Joe Williams at Folk City (1964; Original Blues Classics, 1995)**
★★★★ **Back to the Country (1965; Testament, 1994)**
★★★ **Classic Delta Blues (1964; Original Blues Classics, 1991)**
★★★★ **Stavin' Chain Blues (1966; Delmark, 1993**
★★★½ **Legacy of the Blues, Vol. 6 (1974; GNP, 1992)**
★★★★ **Shake Your Boogie (Arhoolie, 1990)**
★★★★★ **Nine String Guitar Wizard (Collectables, 1994)**
★★★★ **Have Mercy! (Tradition, 1996)**
★★★ **No More Whiskey (Evidence, 1998)**

Blues giant Joe Lee "Big Joe" Williams (1903–1982), a powerful and eccentric force as both a vocalist and guitarist, grew up in the Mississippi Delta and became a key practitioner of Delta blues. His work on the nine-string guitar is filled with the buzzing overtones and incidental rhythms central to the touchstone influences of the African diaspora in the Americas.

Williams had been going strong for more than 20 years when the late-1930s sides collected on *Nine String Guitar Wizard* were reissued. This is Williams at his best. *Stavin' Chain Blues,* 1958 duet recordings with his cousin J.D. Short on second guitar, is packed with the power of Williams's blues. *Nine String Guitar Blues, Walking Blues* and *Blues on Highway 49* are 1961 sessions of prime Williams performances. *Big Joe Williams at Folk City* is a 1962 solo performance at Gerde's Folk City, the Greenwich Village folk mecca. Williams sounds good but is unable to break the spell of the self-conscious crowd as he accompanies himself on kazoo. *Back to the Country* is just that, an authentic-sounding session with Jimmy Brown on guitar and violin and Willie Lee Harris on harmonica. *Legacy of the Blues, Vol. 6* is a stark solo set. *Shake Your Boogie* is a twofer reissue of *Tough Times* and *Thinking of What They Did.* On *Have*

Mercy! Williams is joined by Brownie McGhee, Sonny Terry and Lightnin' Hopkins. — J.S.

BUSTER WILLIAMS

★★★★ **Crystal Reflections (1976; 32 Jazz, 1998)**
★★★ **Something More (In + Out, 1989)**
★★★ **Tokudo (Denon, 1989)**

Bassist Buster Williams (b. 1942) established himself in the late '60s and '70s as one of the more distinctive sidemen on his instrument and has remained in demand ever since. For an early example of Williams's inventive powers, hear him on Herbie Hancock's *The Prisoner.*

Williams doesn't play shy on his own recordings; he gives himself lots of solo space. *Crystal Reflections* uses pianists Kenny Barron and Jimmy Rowles in separate trio tracks and includes a bass/vibes duet with Roy Ayers. *Tokudo* is a 1978 trio session with Barron and drummer Ben Riley, while *Something More* features saxophonist Wayne Shorter, drummer Al Foster and pianist Hancock but doesn't quite live up to expectations. Williams can also be heard to good advantage on Kenny Barron sessions. — S.F.

JAMES WILLIAMS

★★★½ **Alter Ego (1984; Sunnyside, 1993)**
★★★★ **Progress Report (Sunnyside, 1986)**
★★★★ **Magical Trio 1 (EmArcy, 1987)**
★★★ **Magical Trio 2 (EmArcy, 1988)**
★★★ **I Remember Clifford (DIW/Columbia, 1989)**
★★★½ **Meet the Magical Trio (EmArcy, 1990)**
★★★★½ **James Williams Meets the Saxophone Masters (DIW/Columbia, 1992)**
★★★½ **The Key Players (DIW/Columbia, 1994)**
★★★ **Talkin' Trash (with Clark Terry) (DIW/Columbia, 1995)**
★★★★ **Maybeck Recital Hall Series, Vol. 42 (Concord Jazz, 1996)**
★★★★★ **Truth, Justice and the Blues (Evidence, 1996)**

Heavily inspired by fellow Memphis player Phineas Newborn Jr., pianist James Williams (b. 1951) began making jazz imprints as a member of Art Blakey's Jazz Messengers from 1977 to '81. During a prior stint as a teacher at Boston's Berklee College of Music, he forged strong associations with other rising players, including saxophonist Billy Pierce and bassist John Lockwood, that have served him well through the present. After leaving Blakey's band, he worked with Dizzy Gillespie, Milt Jackson, Sonny Stitt, Bobby Hutcherson, Elvin Jones and Tom Harrell and began developing his own bands. He has also produced fine recordings for others, such as pianist Geoff Keezer.

Williams's earliest available sessions, *Alter Ego* and *Progress Report,* are stepping stones for a platoon of rising talents, including Pierce, guitarist Kevin Eubanks and drummer Tony Reedus. *Magical Trio 1,* with Blakey and bassist Ray Brown, is the strongest of the three *Magical Trio* sessions and marks the only time the two legendary Pittsburgh natives recorded together. *James Williams Meets the Saxophone Masters* features strong ensemble playing and head-to-head soloing from George Coleman, Joe Henderson and Pierce. *The Key Players* is a Williams-produced septet session with Williams, Keezer, Mulgrew Miller and fellow Memphis natives Donald Brown and Harold Mabern mixing it up on five pianos, supported by Reedus and bassist Christian McBride.

Williams's finest work has been in a straight-ahead jazz context in which his playing digs deeply into his roots. Two primary examples are the solo-piano showcase *Maybeck Recital Hall Series, Vol. 42* and *Truth, Justice and the Blues.* The latter features his innovative sextet, Intensive Care Unit. With vocalists Roger Holland and Miles Griffith, ICU blends jazz, blues and gospel—the core of American music—into a soulful kind of swing. It also celebrates something too often lacking in jazz in the 1990s—a cohesive group sound. — K.F.

JESSICA WILLIAMS

★★★★★ **Maybeck Recital Hall Series, Vol. 21 (Concord Jazz, 1992)**
★★★★ **Momentum (Jazz Focus, 1994)**
★★★★★ **Arrival (Jazz Focus, 1994)**
★★★★½ **Encounters (Jazz Focus, 1994)**
★★★★ **Inventions (Jazz Focus, 1995)**
★★★★★ **Intuition (Jazz Focus, 1995)**
★★★★½ **The Victoria Concert (Jazz Focus, 1996)**
★★★ **Joy (Jazz Focus, 1996)**

Keyboardist Jessica Williams (b. 1948) plays with a chameleonlike approach that engenders comparisons to Cecil Taylor, Keith Jarrett, McCoy Tyner, Chick Corea, Thelonious Monk, Herbie Hancock and Art Tatum. Not sounding like an acolyte, however, Williams animates her different moods with emotional conviction. She made a vibrant series of recordings in the 1970s and '80s—*Rivers of Memory, The Portal of Antrim, Portraits, Orgonomic Music* and *Update*—that pointed her out as a vibrant force on the contemporary jazz scene. Those records are no longer available, but she reemerged in the 1990s with a sound even more spectacular by virtue of its newfound restraint. Where Williams was once the dazzling purveyor of technique, with an energy that seemed to pour out of her, she now brings a new kind of subtlety and nuance to her performance. Instead of an ostinato played to breathtaking climaxes, Williams now has it boiled down to a simple phrase stated once and left to hang, as if in punctuation, before a rolling glissando of notes.

Momentum and *Inventions* are recorded with Williams's working trio of bassist Jeff Johnson and drummer Dick Berk. The melodic invention and structural freshness of her sound stamp her as a true original. *Momentum* consists of her own compositions and a collection of standards, including a beautiful "Autumn Leaves," Monk's "Shuffle Boil" and Jymie Merritt's "Nommo." *Invention* is a program of original compositions played by the trio, including tributes to John Coltrane ("Last Trane") and Toshiko Akiyoshi ("Toshiko"), capped off by a wondrous solo-piano version of "T 4 2." On *Encounters,* a special live trio date with bassist Leroy Vinnegar and drummer Mel Brown, Williams is in top form, starting with the extended Coltrane tribute "Introduction/Equinox," working through Randy Weston's "Berkshire Blues" and finishing with Monk's "We See."

Williams is at her most impressive on the solo-piano recordings *Intuition, Arrival, Maybeck Recital Hall Series* and *The Victoria Concert.* She summons up all her influences, from the afternoons of her childhood practicing endless classical scales to the rapturous nights spent drinking in the secrets of the masters. *Arrival* features two more brilliant takes on Monk's "Misterioso" and "Ruby, My Dear," Weston's "Blues for Strayhorn," a spiritual rendition of Pharoah Sanders's "The Creator Has a Master Plan" and a gorgeous piece of Ellingtonia, "Mood Indigo." *Intuition* is highlighted by Monk's "Green Chimneys" and "Monk's Dream," a delicate reading of the Miles Davis composition "Flamenco Sketches" and a wild celebration of the spirit of Rahsaan Roland Kirk, "Black and Crazy Blues." *The Victoria Concert* includes a gorgeous version of "I Want to Be Happy" via Sonny Rollins, "My One and Only Love" and "Mr. Syms" via Coltrane and Monk's "Straight, No Chaser." *Joy* is an ambitious concept album performed by Williams's sextet, but while it has some worthwhile moments, it falls short of her best work. — J.S.

JOE WILLIAMS

★★★ A Night at Count Basie's (1957; Vanguard, 1992)
★★★½ A Swingin' Night at Birdland (1962; Blue Note, 1991)
★★★★ Me & the Blues/The Song Is You (1963/1965; Collectables, 1997)
★★★★ At Newport '63/Jump for Joy (1963; Collectables, 1997)
★★★★ Joe Williams and the Thad Jones/Mel Lewis Orchestra (1966; Blue Note, 1994)
★★★★ Every Night: Live at Vine St. (Verve, 1987)
★★★ In Good Company (Verve, 1987)
★★★★ Joe Williams Live (Fantasy, 1991)
★★★★ Joe Williams with the Count Basie Orchestra Live at Orchestra Hall, Detroit (Telarc, 1992)
★★ Here's to Life (Telarc, 1993)
★★★ Feel the Spirit (Telarc, 1994)
★★★★ The Best of Joe Williams: The Roulette, Solid State & Blue Note Years (Blue Note, 1997)

Widely recognized as the last of the great big-band blues singers, Joe Williams (b. 1918) made his reputation playing with Coleman Hawkins, Lionel Hampton and Andy Kirk before joining the Count Basie Orchestra in 1954 to front one of the most popular versions of that group, in the vocal tradition of Jimmy Rushing. *The Best of Joe Williams* is an excellent overview of the most high-profile years of his career, including work with the Basie band, Thad Jones/Mel Lewis orchestra, Harry "Sweets" Edison, Jimmy Jones, Jimmy Mundy and Horace Ott. *Joe Williams and the Thad Jones/Mel Lewis Orchestra* is a perfect fit for Williams, making that album an important moment in his history. Williams is heard to best effect on *Joe Williams with the Count Basie Orchestra Live at Orchestra Hall, Detroit* and *Joe Williams Live,* with the Cannonball Adderley band, as well as *Every Night: Live at Vine St.,* in which Williams is backed by a simple quartet. *Me & the Blues/The Song Is You* and *At Newport '63/Jump for Joy* are important twofer repackagings of early 1960s material. — J.S.

LARRY WILLIAMS

★★★ **Here's Larry Williams (Specialty, 1959)**
★★ **Unreleased Larry Williams (Specialty, 1986)**
★★ **Hocus Pocus (Specialty, 1986)**
★★★★ **Bad Boy (Specialty, 1990)**

New Orleans–born Larry Williams (1935–1980) got his chance to record when Lloyd Price, for whom he had been playing piano (and, according to some accounts, serving as valet), bolted the Specialty label for ABC-Paramount. Seeing an open door, Williams walked through it in 1957 to the tune of two rocking Top 20 singles, "Short Fat Fannie" and "Bony Moronie." Subsequent singles failed to generate much chart action, and Williams's career soon hit the skids commercially. As an artist, however, he was still growing, and his later sides revealed a skilled lyricist developing, as well as a singer capable of more subtle textures than he had demonstrated on his up-tempo sides. In 1959 he was arrested for narcotics possession; subsequently, Specialty dropped him from its roster. After a brief stint at Chess, he moved over to Okeh as a producer. His name gained new currency in the mid-'60s thanks to the Beatles, who covered three of his songs ("Bad Boy," "Dizzy Miss Lizzy" and "Slow Down"). In the late '60s Williams teamed up with Johnny "Guitar" Watson on a version of "Mercy, Mercy, Mercy" to which the duo added their own lyrics. That minor hit was followed by a little-noticed, smoking album, *Two for the Price of One.* In January 1980 Williams was found dead in his apartment, apparently a suicide.

Bad Boy stands as the definitive Larry Williams album. Its 23 tracks include his most prominent singles and other inspired moments. His red-hot version of "Heeby-Jeebies" gives no quarter to Little Richard's own rollin' and tumblin' take; "Hocus Pocus" boasts an enthralling groove; "Iko Iko a.k.a. Jockomo" harkens back to the singer's New Orleans roots. *Here's Larry Williams* is his first album, complete with the artist's three famous singles and its original 1959 packaging. *Unreleased Larry Williams* is a fine complement to *Bad Boy,* containing alternate versions of "High School Dance," "Slow Down," "Bad Boy" and "Just Because," in addition to unreleased versions of songs still unavailable elsewhere. *Hocus Pocus,* with liner notes by Little Walter, is another treasure of unreleased material, notably "Hey Now Hey Now," a new interpretation of "Iko Iko"; a stirring ballad, "I Was a Fool"; a Latin-flavored version of "Bad Boy" called "Bad Boy Cha Cha"; and "Make a Little Love," minus background vocals originally supplied by Sonny Bono. — D.M.

LUCINDA WILLIAMS

★★★½ **Ramblin' (1979; Folkways, 1991)**
★★★½ **Happy Woman Blues (1980; Folkways, 1990)**
★★★★ **Sweet Old World (Chameleon, 1992)**
★★★★★ **Lucinda Williams (1988; Koch, 1998)**
★★★★★ **Car Wheels on a Gravel Road (Mercury, 1998)**

Louisiana-born rambler Lucinda Williams (b. 1953) is one of the best blues-based singer/songwriters to emerge in the 1980s. Her bruised vocals, richly textured songs and rootsy repertoire present a compelling picture of the underdog residents of Southern America.

Ramblin' shows Williams's first love, Delta blues and honky-tonk music; the album consists of covers of her favorites, ranging from Memphis Minnie's "Me and My Chauffeur" to Porter Wagoner's "Satisfied Mind." Her burgeoning songwriting powers began to emerge on *Happy Woman Blues,* which contains such worthy originals as "King of Hearts." Eight years later, she resurfaced with the brilliant *Lucinda Williams,* a showcase of her masterful songwriting. The album has since been reissued on CD, with some additional unreleased cuts and live tracks. Her next album, the lovely *Sweet Old World* was not quite as strong in the songwwriting department, but still a marvel. The long-awaited *Car Wheels on a Gravel Road* proved to be an astounding collection of Williams's songs, ranging from a revised version of the bluesy "I Lost It" (from *Happy Woman Blues*) to compelling character studies of small-town America and beautiful losers. Though not strictly a blues musician, Williams rather is a consummate artist who has absorbed the best of blues and country, creating her own unique, unforgettable sound. — H.G.-W.

MARY LOU WILLIAMS

★★★★★ **Zodiac Suite (1945; Smithsonian Folkways, 1995)**
★★★★★ **Town Hall '45: The Zodiac Suite (1945; Smithsonian Folkways, N.A.)**

★★★½ **Zoning (1974; Smithsonian Folkways, 1995)**
★★★★ **Live at the Cookery (1975; Chiaroscuro, 1992)**
★★★★ **Embraced (with Cecil Taylor) (1977; Pablo, N.A.)**
★★★★ **Solo Recital/Montreux Jazz Festival 1978 (1978; Original Jazz Classics, 1998)**
★★★★ **Mary Lou Williams and Meade Lux Lewis (Collectables, 1995)**
★★★½ **Key Moments (Topaz Jazz, 1995)**

Pianist, composer and arranger Mary Lou Williams (1910–1981) is one of the very few jazz artists whose accomplishments and interests span the entire history of the music leading up to the fusion era. She began her career in the 1920s touring the vaudeville circuit before marrying alto saxophonist John Williams and getting her start in jazz. In 1929 she joined Andy Kirk and his Clouds of Joy as an arranger, then as its pianist from 1931 to '42, during which time Kirk's band became one of the most prominent in jazz on the strength of Williams's compositions "Froggy Bottom," "Mary's Idea" and "Walkin' and Swingin'." Williams also wrote arrangements for Benny Goodman while in Kirk's group, then for Duke Ellington in the 1940s.

She went on to forge friendships with Thelonious Monk and Bud Powell in the late 1940s, associations that her advanced work as an arranger had foreshadowed musically. These friendships were not on immediate display due to her decision to move to Europe in the 1950s rather than continue in the antijazz political atmosphere in the United States. She returned to the States in 1954 with a missionary zeal to promote jazz and help the music achieve its rightful place in American history. She converted to Catholicism and became interested in writing lengthy spiritual compositions, at the same time developing an interest in the open-ended melodic and improvisational possibilities of free jazz.

Williams's masterpiece is her incredible 1945 *Zodiac Suite,* a composition in 12 parts, one for each sign of the Zodiac, played by a jazz group augmented by a full orchestra. Conceptually, the work was at least 20 years ahead of its time. On *Zoning* she leads a quartet through an experimental program that shows her interest in the possibilities of dissonance. She takes those ideas even further in her ear-opening showdown with Cecil Taylor, *Embraced. Live at the Cookery* offers an excellent example of the breadth of Williams's musical conception short of the experimental work, covering traditional jazz in a swinging, Earl Hines–inspired mode, as well as spirituals and blues. Far too little of her extensive recording history, including works for her own label, is available, and she is one of the most underrecognized master musicians in jazz history. — J.S.

ROBERT PETE WILLIAMS

★★★★ **Free Again (1960; Original Blues Classics, 1992)**
★★★★ **I'm Blue as a Man Can Be (Arhoolie, 1994)**
★★★½ **When a Man Takes the Blues (Arhoolie, 1994)**

If all blues music were somehow measured on a scale stretching from pure emotion to absolute structure, no blues artist would come closer to 100 percent passion—or farther from strict blues form—than Robert Pete Williams (1914–1980). With a total disregard for rhyme or consistent meter, Williams's stream-of-consciousness lyrics and slurred vocals act as counterpoint to familiar country-blues guitar riffs and patterns. His songs are as spontaneous and intensely personal as acoustic blues can get (many of his tunes were improvised on the spot), and at times he seems to be seriously displaced, invoking West African sonorities more than the music of his native central Louisiana.

A latter-day Lead Belly whose path luckily crossed that of blues researcher Harry Oster in 1959, Williams sang his way out of the Angola state penitentiary and by the early '60s became a favorite on the folk-festival/coffeehouse circuit. Though he recorded for a number of labels during that decade, the Williams titles currently available are drawn from his mostly solo recordings done while incarcerated or immediately after his release. The Arhoolie collections were compiled with devotion by guitarist and longtime fan Henry Kaiser; *I'm Blue as a Man Can Be* features the autobiographical "Pardon Denied Again" and the haunting "Louise" from 1970. *When a Man Takes the Blues* offers a number of spiritual songs as well as an 11-minute narration of Williams's earliest musical memories, his crime and conviction (the early-evening birds and crickets audible on his jailhouse recordings only enhance the Faulkner-esque mystery that his music conjures). In addition, his "Prisoner's Talking Blues" is a minimasterpiece, leading off the Arhoolie anthology *Angola Prisoners Blues. Free Again* features the achingly private "I've Grown So Ugly" and captures Williams (so to speak) postparole in 1960. — A.K.

TONY WILLIAMS

★★★ Spring (1965; Blue Note, 1987)
★★★★½ Emergency! (1969; Polydor, 1991)
★★★½ Turn It Over (1970; Polydor, N.A.)
★★★ The Joy of Flying (1979; Columbia/Legacy, 1997)
★★★½ Foreign Intrigue (Blue Note, 1986)
★★★★½ Lifetime: The Collection (Columbia, 1992)
★★★★ The Best of Tony Williams (Blue Note, 1996)
★★★½ Spectrum: The Anthology (Verve, N.A.)

Miles Davis may have gotten the credit for it, but jazz rock was actually Tony Williams's idea. It was Williams (1945–1997), while drumming for Davis, who introduced the trumpeter to guitarist John McLaughlin, and though Davis got into the studio with McLaughlin first (for the lovely, reflective *In a Silent Way*), it was Williams's band Lifetime that first afforded McLaughlin the opportunity to merge rock with jazz, on *Emergency!* Fusion starts there.

A child prodigy, Williams was well known in Boston jazz circles while still in his teens, and led his first sessions—for the fiercely avant-garde *Life Time* (now out of print)—at the ripe old age of 19. He didn't start experimenting with electric music, though, until the late '60s, when he formed Lifetime with McLaughlin and organist Larry Young (a.k.a. Khalid Yasin). Although the instrumentation recalls the organ trios led by the likes of Jimmy McGriff or Richard "Groove" Holmes, the music is something else again, gleefully indulging in volume and distortion, and coloring jazz's usual swing with the furious intensity of acid rock (although, to be honest, the playing is miles beyond the misdirected flailings of most psychedelic-era rock acts). Yet apart from "Spectrum," the songs don't "rock out" in any conventional sense of the term; indeed, it isn't until "Vuelta Abajo" from *Turn It Over* (which brings Cream bassist Jack Bruce aboard) that Williams and Lifetime latch on to the sort of riff-based structures necessary for rock-style repetition. (Williams also sings at points, though the less said about that, the better).

McLaughlin and Bruce left before Williams recorded the out-of-print *Ego* (though Bruce can be heard in an uncredited vocal on "Two Worlds"). Williams introduces an entirely new lineup with the also unavailable *Old Bum's Rush,* yet he doesn't fully attempt to cash in on the fusion craze he helped launch until *Believe It* and *Million Dollar Legs* (both out of print as well). Both are excellent albums, but the band broke up after it was unable to attract the arena-sized audience the music deserved. Taking one last stab at fusion, Williams cut *The Joy of Flying* with a variety of fusion stars, including Jan Hammer, George Benson, Tom Scott, Stanley Clarke and even a quartet featuring rockers Ronnie Montrose, Brian Auger and Mario Cipollina, but the album's most intriguing collaboration is with pianist Cecil Taylor on "Morgan's Motion"—and that wasn't fusoid in the slightest. Williams then began touring on more traditional jazz fare, fronting a combo including trumpeter Wallace Roney and pianist Mulgrew Miller; all records are very good, but *Foreign Intrigue* is a standout. — J.D.C.

HOMESICK JAMES WILLIAMSON

★★★★ Blues on the Southside (1964; Original Blues Classics, 1990)
★★★ Sweet Home Tennessee (Appaloosa, 1993)
★★★ Juanita (1993; Evidence, 1997)
★★★½ Goin' Back in the Times (Earwig, 1994)

Bottleneck guitarist Homesick James Williamson was born James Williamson or John Williamson or John William Henderson in 1904 or 1905 or 1910, most likely in Somerville, Tennessee. In 1937 he made his first recordings in Memphis, and he would go on to play with a litany of important blues figures, including Sleepy John Estes, Yank Rachell, Roosevelt Sykes and Big Joe Williams, among others. Williamson recorded frequently as a sideman and a leader, including a 1950s stint on bass and occasional guitar with the band of his second cousin Elmore James. In that outfit he played on several famous tracks including "The Sky Is Crying" and "Dust My Broom."

Blues on the Southside features 11 fine Williamson originals, including the undulating "She May Be Your Woman," on which his slide dances over the fret board like it's on fire, and the flowing "Homesick's Blues," on which his crying vocals stand at the fore. Also included here is a slow-burning rendition of the traditional "Stones in My Passway," spotlighting Williamson's rock-solid band—pianist Lafayette

Leake, bassist Eddie Taylor and drummer Clifton James—who provide a resonant underpinning for his compact slide-guitar figures. *Goin' Back in the Times* was recorded in Chicago in 1992 and features Williamson's solo slide guitar and vocals, except on three tracks—"They Call Me Hot Foot Homesick," "Crossroads Years Ago (Honeyboy Is a Friend of Mine)" and Lightnin' Hopkins's "Rocky Mountain"—on which Honeyboy Edwards lends his spirited guitar playing. The album also includes a ringing version of Memphis Minnie's "Kissing in the Dark" and a slow, tortured rendition of Yank Rachell's ".38 Pistol." *Sweet Home Tennessee* and *Juanita* were recorded in Nashville with local musicians in 1991 and 1993 respectively. — B.R.H.

SONNY BOY WILLIAMSON (RICE MILLER)

★★★★ **Down and Out Blues (1959; Chess, 1987)**
★★★★ **The Real Folk Blues (1966; Chess, 1987)**
★★★★ **More Real Folk Blues (1967; Chess, 1988)**
★★★★ **Bummer Road (1969; Chess, 1991)**
★★★ **In Paris: Sonny Boy Williamson & Memphis Slim (GNP Crescendo, 1973)**
★★★★ **One Way Out (MCA, 1976)**
★★★★★ **King Biscuit Time (Arhoolie, 1989)**
★★★★ **Keep It to Ourselves (Alligator, 1990)**
★★★★ **Trumpet Masters Vol. 5: From the Bottom (Collectables, 1991)**
★★★★ **Clownin' with the World: Sonny Boy Williamson and Willie Love (Acoustic Archives/Trumpet/Alligator, 1992)**
★★★★ **Goin' in Your Direction (Trumpet/Alligator, 1992)**
★★★★★ **The Essential Sonny Boy Williamson (Chess, 1993)**
★★★★ **In Europe (Evidence, 1995)**
★★★★ **His Best (Chess, 1997)**

A man fond of myth and mythmaking, Aleck "Rice" Miller (1910–1965), the younger of the two Delta blues musicians to take the name Sonny Boy Williamson, left a legacy that justifies his tall tales and eccentricities. Born in Glendora, Mississippi, Miller, who was also nicknamed "Footsie," "Goat" and "Little Boy Blue," began teaching himself to play harmonica at age 8. By age 14 he was performing around the Delta and hooking up with other traveling bluesmen, including Robert Johnson (one of Miller's tales is that he was present at Johnson's death), Johnson's stepson Robert Jr. Lockwood, Elmore James and Howlin' Wolf. After Miller adopted the name of the first Sonny Boy Williamson (John Lee Williamson, who had been recording for Bluebird), his career took a quantum leap forward. Suddenly he was in demand throughout the South, and in 1941 landed a steady, high-profile gig on the King Biscuit Time show emanating from KFFA in Helena, Arkansas. Blowing amplified harmonica with a small combo and playing high-octane blues over the airwaves, Miller pioneered a harder-edged style of blues that bloomed beautifully late in the decade when Muddy Waters, having migrated from the Delta to Chicago, plugged in his guitar and changed not only the blues but popular music as well. When Lillian McMurry launched her now revered Trumpet label, Miller was one of the first artists she approached about recording. Early sessions proved unproductive, but the artist finally found his groove in 1951 and laid down some of the strongest Delta blues sides extant.

A peerless instrumentalist whose most noted acolyte was Little Walter Jacobs, Miller exhibited superior command of the harp's tonal possibilities, employing it not only to accompany his vocals but in essence as a second singing voice. Without any help, though, Miller was a first-rate vocalist who could invest a gruff, half-spoken lyric with a moving immediacy born of the hard life and relentless pursuits of love and liquor that informed his self-penned songs. The Trumpet recordings on Arhoolie's *King Biscuit Time* encompass many of Miller's most important entries—"West Memphis Blues," "Mister Downchild," "Eyesight to the Blind," "Pontiac Blues"—and stand as one of the key documents in Delta-blues history. The CD also includes a live, four-song set from one of Miller's appearances on the King Biscuit show.

From the Bottom adds to the Trumpet-years legacy with 14 exemplary cuts from 1953 and 1954, including a previously unissued take of "From the Bottom" that finds young B.B. King blazing away on guitar. In addition to King's appearance, guitarist J.V. Turner engages Miller in some fiery instrumental interplay on four tracks recorded in 1954, showing himself well capable of playing in the big leagues with that era's better-known blues guitarists. Further

Trumpet recordings comprise *Clownin' with the World* and *Goin' in Your Direction.* The former features one side of Miller, another of his stellar, longtime accompanist, pianist Willie Love, who also is heard on four of Miller's cuts recorded in a Houston studio in 1953; the latter offers several tracks Miller cut for Trumpet between 1951 and 1954, including two with Arthur "Big Boy" Crudup on guitar, and another version of "From the Bottom," again with B.B. King on guitar.

In 1955 Miller, then living in Chicago, was signed to the Chess label's Checker subsidiary. His first single, "Don't Start Me Talkin'," recorded with Muddy Waters's band, climbed to #3 on the R&B chart, marking the onset of an eight-year chart run during which Miller became one of the label's most productive and popular artists, whose backing band invariably included many of the greatest names in the history of the genre. His fame took on an international dimension when he toured Europe in 1963 as part of the American Folk Blues Festival and dazzled the locals with the depth of his music. When the tour returned to America, he stayed behind, spending a year trying to establish residency in England; failing at that, he rejoined the tour when it played Europe again in 1964 and came back to the States decked out in two-tone suits and affecting a British accent.

In Europe collects five tracks recorded live at the American Blues Festival in Hamburg and Bremen, Germany. His accompaniment here tells a good part of the story: Hubert Sumlin and Matt Murphy on guitars; Sunnyland Slim and Otis Spann on pianos; Willie Dixon on bass; Bill Stepney and Clifton James on drums. Nine cuts are culled from Williamson's somewhat dicey set-to with the Yardbirds (comprising guitarist Chris Dreja, bassist Paul Samwell-Smith, drummer Jim McCarty and, on lead guitar, 18-year-old Eric Clapton) that was released in album form in 1966 as *Sonny Boy Williamson & The Yardbirds.* That album documented a sloppy, disjointed affair, owing in part to Miller switching to songs the group had not rehearsed with him. The tracks included on *In Europe* show something else: a band conversant in blues providing solid, propulsive backing for the blues master, who wails and moans his heart out and sounds like he was being given his money's worth by Clapton's intelligently conceived, sharply executed lead work, whether on an up-tempo blazer such as the classic "Mister Downchild" or a dark, churning lament on the order of "23 Hours Too Long."

In Paris: Sonny Boy Williamson and Memphis Slim is another document from those European years, this one being a live set cut in 1963 with Memphis Slim on piano. Before a respectful audience, Miller bares his soul, easing into a pain-wracked take on Elmore James's "The Skies Are Crying" (a variation on James's original title), with Slim providing sensitive accompaniment, before commanding the stage solo for powerful performances of "Your Funeral and My Trial" and "Explain Yourself to Me."

Between 1955 and 1964 Miller cut some 70 sides for Checker and Chess, and 45 are gathered on the aptly titled double-CD collection *The Essential Sonny Boy Williamson.* This is all prime Sonny Boy, something of a bible of the blues in its evocative songwriting, masterful musicianship and forceful vocal personality evident at every turn. Included among the classic tracks is the legendary "Little Village," complete with profane, contentious dialog between producer and label co-owner Leonard Chess and Miller—the same dialog that earns Miller's *Bummer Road* album, from which the song is culled, a parental-advisory sticker warning of explicit lyrics.

Elsewhere in the catalog, various Chess/MCA titles round out the artist's most fruitful years. *One Way Out* comprises Miller's early Chess sides, while *Bummer Road* maps sessions from the late '50s to 1960, and numbers both "Little Village" and Miller's skewed Christmas tale of legal imbroglio, "Santa Claus," powered by some ferocious guitar work by Robert Jr. Lockwood and Luther Tucker. In order, *Down and Out Blues, Real Folk Blues* and *More Real Folk Blues* pick up where *One Way Out* ends, taking Miller through the remainder of his Chess years; considered as a whole, these sides paint a bleak picture of Miller's interior life, thus constituting one of the saddest self-portraits a bluesman has ever painted as he moans his way through "Sad to Be Alone," "Your Funeral and My Trial," "Nine Below Zero" and "Somebody Help Me."

In some ways, *Keep It to Ourselves,* a 1963 studio recording made in Denmark and released stateside in 1990 by Alligator, is Miller's most engaging work. This session finds Miller, accompanied by guitarist Matt Murphy and Memphis Slim (with Bill Stepney on drums on one cut only), in a mellow mood, his voice warm and welcoming, his harp blowing languorous melody lines around his relaxed vocals, with Slim and Murphy staying obliquely in the background. In an intimate, front-porch setting unlike that on any other of his recordings, Miller rises to the challenge with some starkly rendered performances as haunting as they are personable. Without diminishing the Trumpet or Chess recordings, let it be said that *Keep It to Ourselves* has the feel of an artist making a big statement in an understated way. But then, that was Rice Miller's way—all those years spent in the Chess orbit of blazing meteorites like Muddy Waters, Howlin' Wolf and Little Walter, and he kept on doing his thing in the way only he could do it, stayed on the charts, made great music, influenced succeeding generations of blues musicians and left monuments paralleling those of his more celebrated label mates. A little under two years after these Denmark sessions, he was found dead in his apartment in Helena, where the legend had first taken root. What a glorious sound he left behind. — D.M.

SONNY BOY WILLIAMSON (JOHN LEE WILLIAMSON)

★★★★★ Blues in the Mississippi Night (1959; Rykodisc, 1990)

★★★★ The Original Sonny Boy Williamson: Southern Blues Classics (Collectables, 1995)

History has not been so kind to the original Sonny Boy Williamson (né John Lee Williamson, 1914–1948) as it has been to his like-named Delta acolyte who was born Rice Miller. Little Walter, James Cotton, Big Walter Horton and certainly Rice Miller were deeply indebted to Williamson, who transformed the harmonica from an accompanying instrument into a powerful solo voice and was a major draw on the Chicago-blues circuit from the time of his arrival there in 1937.

Born in Jackson, Tennessee, Williamson honed his chops touring the South with Sleepy John Estes before migrating to the Windy City, where he became one of the most frequently recorded and popular blues artists of his day. His unusual technique was to rapidly alternate between vocal and instrumental with such unerring timing that his colleague Big Bill Broonzy once described Williamson's style as being akin to singing and playing at the same time. Without question, Williamson is best remembered for his groundbreaking work as a harp player, and rightly so, since it became a hallmark of the Chicago blues sound; but he was also a personable, impassioned vocalist who took a conversational style and invested it with forceful feeling. While he was most effective on up-tempo material that he could rip and roar his way through, he was also capable of more subtle, deep-blues phrasing that brought different shades of emotion to a lyric passage. A prolific writer, his best-known song by far is "Good Morning Little Schoolgirl," a touchstone for countless American and British blues bands.

Unfortunately, Williamson's recordings are largely out of print domestically. Collectables has partially corrected this oversight on its 14-track collection *The Original Sonny Boy Williamson: Southern Blues Classics,* culled from recordings made between 1937 and 1944 when Williamson was being backed by Yank Rachell, Blind John Davis and Washboard Sam. Relative to Williamson's focus as a writer, the song selection surveys a wide range of topics, from standard mean-woman blues ("Check Up on My Baby") to economic deprivation ("Welfare Store") to blues mythology ("Joe Louis and John Henry"); once in a while Williamson plays the lovable fool, re-creating his fumbling attempt to pick up a woman—complete with all the bad lines that fail to win her favor—as the band stomps out a dance tune ("Jivin' the Blues"). The import Blues Classics and Document labels offer the most complete histories of this neglected but important artist, the former in three volumes, the latter in five.

Williamson also had a part in one of the most important blues recordings ever made, *Blues in the Mississippi Night.* In 1946 folklorist Alan Lomax traveled to Chicago to trace the roots of the blues in the tortured personal histories of Williamson, Broonzy and Memphis Slim, who spoke both in personal terms about their own lives and more generally—but vividly—about the daily humiliations, brutality and deprivations visited routinely on Mississippi's black population. The three artists requested that their names not be revealed out of fear of reprisals against their families and friends. The musical lessons imparted here are in the form of examples of each artist's work, as well as field chants and work songs common to the Delta people. Also included is an extensive booklet with a background essay by Lomax on the recording sessions, along with transcriptions of some of the dialog and thumbnail biographies of each artist. Anyone who wishes or pretends to understand the deepest origins of the blues must own this disc. — D.M.

CASSANDRA WILSON

★★½ Point of View (Verve, 1986)

★★ Blue Skies (Verve, 1988)

★★★ **Jumpworld (Verve, 1990)**
★★★ **She Who Weeps (Verve, 1991)**
★★★ **After the Beginning Again (1992; Verve, 1994)**
★★★★ **Live (Verve, 1992)**
★★★ **Dance to the Drums Again (DIW/Columbia, 1993)**
★★★★ **Blue Light 'Til Dawn (Blue Note, 1993)**
★★★★½ **New Moon Daughter (Blue Note, 1995)**
★★★★ **Songbook (Verve, 1996)**
★★★★ **Rendezvous (with Jacky Terrasson) (Blue Note, 1997)**

The voice of the M-Base Collective, Cassandra Wilson (b. 1955) displays an extremely wide range of influences and one of the most malleable jazz vocal styles this side of Betty Carter. *Point of View* only hints at this, with a stomping, soulful workout, "I Thought You Knew," and the Prime Time–inspired "Square Roots," sharing space with a tenderly read version of Miles Davis's "Blue in Green." M-Base buddies guitarist Jean-Paul Bourelly, saxophonist Steve Coleman and versatile bassist Lonnie Plaxico keep the proceedings interesting. With straight-ahead trios backing on standards, however, the follow-up, *Blue Skies,* never quite transcends the ordinary.

Wilson takes a huge step into harmolodic jazz funk on *Jumpworld.* Once again, her best material uses a guitarist (this time David Gilmore) as a foil. This album of originals (all but one Wilson's) takes a science-fiction approach on "Love Phases Dimensions." Tunes like "Phase Jump," "Warm Spot" and "Woman on the Edge" dance into free-jazz territory, while the ballads "Whirlwind Soldier" and "Lies" could pass for contemporary R&B. "Dancing in Dreamtime," a harmolodic ballad, is a harbinger of things to come. In this comfortably chaotic context, Wilson starts to find her voice. The process continues on *She Who Weeps,* with mixed results. Wilson starts to improvise more vocally, using her voice as an instrument, particularly on her startling reading of "Body and Soul." By comparison, *After the Beginning Again* sounds like backsliding. Accompanied by a guitarless quartet, Wilson scats nicely through "My Corner of the Sky" and squeezes the pathos out of "'Round Midnight" but doesn't really extend herself.

Live recording, from 1991, shows Wilson making the panstylistic connections between "Soul Melange," "'Round Midnight" and "Body and Soul." The disparate elements of the earlier records start to coalesce on *Dance to the Drums Again.* A collaboration between Wilson and Bourelly, with able support from pianist James Weidman and the understated base of Kevin Bruce Harris, this consistently focused album melds R&B, funk and rock influences with all the jazz components of her previous work. "Just Keep Thinking of Eubay" and "Rhythm of My Mind" afford her the opportunity to open up her voice, multitracking in several registers.

Even this couldn't prepare fans for her next direction, a stripped-down, almost totally acoustic album celebrating the roots and manifestations of the blues. *Blue Light 'Til Dawn* brings together music by Ann Peebles, Gene de Paul and Don Raye, Robert Johnson and Van Morrison in an organically melded package. Even her remake of "Redbone" improves on the version from *After the Beginning Again.* Backed predominantly by guitars, *Blue Light 'Til Dawn* displays nakedly what the Bourelly and Gilmore records only hinted at: Wilson's voice naturally responds to the instrument. Similar in concept and even broader in scope, *New Moon Daughter* rereads Son House, Neil Young, Hoagy Carmichael and U2. With Chris Whitley on resophonic guitar, she deconstructs "Strange Fruit" while bringing new nuances to Hank Williams's "I'm So Lonesome I Could Cry" and the Monkees' "Last Train to Clarksville." As remarkable as the covers are, *New Moon Daughter* also includes some of Wilson's best compositions, including the sambaesque "Little Warm Death" and the lilting "Solomon Sang."

Songbook and *Rendezvous* project Wilson's role as one of the most important vocal interpreters of standards into the next millennium. *Songbook* takes on "Let's Face the Music," "Sweet Lorraine" and "Baubles, Bangles and Beads." On *Rendezvous,* teaming with pianist Jacky Terrasson, bassists Lonnie Plaxico and Kenny Davis and percussionist Mino Cinelu, she takes familiar tunes and changes them utterly. "Tennessee Waltz" is reborn as a 6/8 shuffle blues. Her reading of "It Might as Well Be Spring" accentuates the melancholy, and her version of "If Ever I Would Leave You" squares it. She draws things out of these songs that even the composers wouldn't recognize. — H.B.

KIM WILSON

★★★★★ **Tiger Man (Antone's, 1993)**
★★★½ **That's Life (1995; Discovery, 1997)**

Vocalist/harmonica player Kim Wilson (b. 1951) moved as a child from Detroit to California, but he learned the secrets of the blues in Texas, backing the genre's masters as part of the house band at Antone's in his adopted hometown of Austin. Muddy Waters in particular took Wilson under his wing, teaching him lessons he put to good use when the Antone's band became the Fabulous Thunderbirds, with Wilson as co–front man with guitarist Jimmie Vaughan. The Thunderbirds went on to major-label success, but Wilson grew tired of the creative compromises required to sustain an MTV-oriented career and returned to the Antone's fold to realize his lifelong dream of recording an out-and-out blues record, *Tiger Man,* his solo debut.

Tiger Man's powerhouse lineup includes guitarists Duke Robillard, Junior Watson and Rusty Zinn, drummers George Rains and Fran Christina, bassists Preston Hubbard and Jack Barber and a horn section with a saxophone front line of jazz master Ronnie Cuber, Austin legend Mark Kazanoff and San Antonio great Rocky Morales. Wilson's harp playing has never sounded better, and he reaches a new level on vocals handling classic material by Johnny "Guitar" Watson, Roosevelt Sykes, Willie Dixon, Sonny Boy Williamson (Rice Miller) and Joe Hill Louis, as well as some originals. *That's Life* is a worthy follow-up that doesn't have quite the bristling focus of *Tiger Man,* possibly because Wilson was devoting some of his energy to reviving the Thunderbirds lineup along similar lines. There are several good originals here, particularly "Don't Bite the Hand That Feeds You" and "Humpin' to Please." — J.S.

SMOKEY WILSON

★★★ **88th Street Blues (1983; Blind Pig, 1995)**
★★★★ **Smoke 'n' Fire (Bullseye Blues, 1993)**
★★★½ **The Real Deal (Bullseye Blues, 1995)**
★★★ **Man from Mars (Bullseye Blues, 1997)**

It's a little hard to figure out why it took Robert Lee "Smokey" Wilson (b. 1936) so long to emerge on the national blues scene after running and performing the well-known Pioneer Club in Watts, Los Angeles for 20 years. He is a fantastic singer, with a gravelly, smoky voice, and a dynamic, in-the-pocket, high-energy guitarist with a distinct, rough-edged yet fluent style. He also performs with so much enthusiasm that it feels like he might jump out of the speakers at any minute. When he kicks off the delightful *Smoke 'n' Fire,* his first nationally distributed album, by shouting, "Here I go," there's no need to ask where he's headed.

The slightly uneven *Real Deal* features a few generic boogie numbers, but there's nothing boring or average about the way the Mississippi native tears into slow electric blues like "Rat Takin' Your Cheese" or belts out the joyously defiant "Not Pickin' Your Cotton," digging into the funky syncopated grooves with sly gusto to unleash toe-curling single-note bends.

Recorded in 1983, the solid *88th Street Blues* finds Wilson, backed by Rod Piazza and his band, running through a repertoire of traditional blues. He sings and plays with authority, but this is a decidedly less original album than any of the Bullseye sessions, which are dominated by Wilson's own impressive compositions and lent extra punch by organist/producer Ron Levy and a fantastic band. — A.P.

TEDDY WILSON

★★★★ **Teddy Wilson 1934–1935 (Classics, N.A.)**
★★★★ **Teddy Wilson 1935–1936 (Classics, N.A.)**
★★★★★ **Teddy Wilson 1936–1937 (Classics, N.A.)**
★★★★★ **Teddy Wilson 1937 (Classics, N.A.)**
★★★★ **Teddy Wilson 1937–1938 (Classics, N.A.)**
★★★★ **Teddy Wilson 1938 (Classics, N.A.)**
★★★½ **Teddy Wilson 1939 (Classics, N.A.)**
★★★½ **Isn't It Romantic (1946; Discovery, 1993)**
★★★ **Stomping at the Savoy (1967; Black Lion, 1991)**
★★★ **Air Mail Special (1967; Black Lion, 1989)**
★★½ **Meets Eiji Kitamura (1970; Storyville, N.A.)**
★★★★ **With Billie in Mind (1972; Chiaroscuro, 1995)**
★★★★ **Runnin' Wild (1973; Black Lion, 1993)**
★★★ **Blues for Thomas Waller (1974; Black Lion, 1990)**
★★★ **Teddy Wilson and His All-Stars (1976; Chiaroscuro, 1996)**
★★★ **Cole Porter Classics (1978; Black Lion, 1992)**
★★★ **Masters of Jazz, Vol. 11 (1980; Storyville, 1990)**

★★★ **Teddy Wilson Revisits the Goodman Years (1980; Storyville, 1990)**
★★★½ **Everytime We Say Goodbye (1990; Discovery, 1993)**
★★★★ **Alone (Storyville, 1995)**
★★★½ **How High the Moon? (Tradition, 1997)**
★★★ **Interaction (Drive Archive, 1997)**
★★★★ **Solo Piano: Keystone Transcriptions 1939–1940 (Storyville, 1997)**

Pianist Teddy Wilson (1912–1986) first made an impression on the jazz world with his hot solo work, which can be heard on the first of the Classics releases, but soon left his enduring mark as the consummate band pianist and accompanist on sessions featuring such greats as Roy Eldridge, Louis Armstrong, Benny Goodman, Ben Webster, Chu Berry, Benny Morton, Johnny Hodges, John Kirby, Cozy Cole, Ella Fitzgerald and Billie Holiday. Wilson was also a featured player in Goodman's historic swing band. His empathy with Holiday was extraordinary, and the structural approach to harmonics underlying his arrangements anticipates what would become the mainstream approach for piano accompanists. The Classics material covers everything up until Wilson's ill-fated touring band at the end of the 1930s. *Isn't It Romantic* collects solo and small-band recordings from 1944 to 1946 with trumpeter Buck Clayton and tenorist Don Byas.

Wilson was tragically overlooked by the U.S. recording industry from the 1950s on, a fact reflected in the hit-and-miss nature of his later catalog. Yet the elegant consistency of his approach, central to his genius in the 1930s, was still there 40 years later. While his later recordings vary in quality depending on his musical settings, the solo pieces glow with a kind of platonic logic. Wilson was a visionary in the sense that he was able to translate his imaginative thoughts through his playing with a seeming effortlessness. *With Billie in Mind,* the solo-piano tribute to Wilson's glory years with Lady Day, magically conjures her spirit. Wilson also shines on the solo-piano sets *Keystone Transcriptions* and *Alone,* and *Runnin' Wild,* recorded at the 1973 Montreux Jazz Festival.

— J.S.

JOHNNY WINTER

★★★★½ **The Progressive Blues Experiment (1968, One Way, 1990)**
★★★★★ **Johnny Winter (1969; Columbia, 1990)**
★★★★½ **Second Winter (1969; Columbia, 1990)**
★★★ **Johnny Winter Live! (1971; Columbia, 1989)**
★★★½ **Still Alive and Well (1973; Columbia, 1994)**
★★★ **Saints and Sinners (1974; Columbia, 1996)**
★★★ **Captured Live (1976; Columbia, 1990)**
★★★½ **Nothin' but the Blues (1977; Blue Sky, N.A.)**
★★★★ **Guitar Slinger (Alligator, 1984)**
★★★½ **Serious Business (Alligator, 1985)**
★★★½ **3rd Degree (Alligator, 1986)**
★★★★ **Let Me In (Pointblank/Charisma, 1991)**
★★★½ **Scorchin' Blues (Columbia, 1992)**
★★★½ **Hey, Where's Your Brother? (Pointblank/Charisma, 1993)**
★★★½ **Rock 'n' Roll Collection (Columbia, 1994)**
★★★½ **White Hot Blues (Columbia, 1997)**
★★★★ **Johnny Winter/Second Winter/Captured Live (Columbia, 1997)**

Johnny Winter (b. 1944) was the first of the contemporary guitarists to emerge from Texas in the 1960s, fusing blues content with the amplification dynamics of rock technology, and as such is one of the most subtly influential musicians of the last third of the 20th Century. Winter manages to combine the open-ended style of Lightnin' Hopkins and the Texas country-blues players, the rattling edge of Elmore James on slide, the string-bending power of Albert King and the melodic fluidity of T-Bone Walker into his own thoroughly unique style. Winter's solos move forward and sideways at the same time, and he sings in a growling howl inspired by Blind Lemon Jefferson. Winter, a partially blind albino, has let his musical interests lead him throughout a career notable for early experimentation and clear fascination with rock yet always at its best in a blues context.

Both of Winter's parents were musicians, and he grew up playing with his brother Edgar. The brothers began as a preteen ukulele duo playing local talent shows, but Johnny was leading his own band by the end of the 1950s. After playing in a variety of rock and blues bands and recording *The Progressive Blues Experiment,*

Winter burst onto the scene with his eponymous major-label debut, a stylistic tour de force that even he found impossible to duplicate. *Second Winter,* with its classic interpretation of Bob Dylan's "Highway 61 Revisited" and the astonishing "Fast Life Rider," was a razor's-edge split down the middle of blues and rock—music that simply defies categorization. *Johnny Winter* and *Second Winter* are also now available as a three-CD set with 1976's *Captured Live. Still Alive and Well* reaffirms Winter's commitment to blues before he ventured back toward rock for the next few albums.

Winter went on to produce Muddy Waters's *Hard Again,* a set in which Winter's exhilarating accompaniment galvanizes Waters to a performance on a par with his glory days. The experience had a profound effect on Winter, as shows on the terrific *Nothin' but the Blues.* Then, after a similar revival collaboration with a crepuscular Sonny Terry, he celebrated his full-scale return to the blues with *Guitar Slinger.* Winter has battled severe physical problems in the 1990s, but like the blues giants who inspired him, he seems determined to keep playing as if it were the only reason for living. His undiminished skills as a spontaneous creator of blues structures are evident on *Let Me In* and *Hey, Where's Your Brother?* — J.S.

JIMMY WITHERSPOON

★★★ **Feelin' the Spirit (1959; Legacy, 1994)**
★★★★★ **The 'Spoon Concerts (1960; Fantasy, 1989)**
★★★★ **Jimmy Witherspoon Sings the Blues (1961; Muse, 1980)**
★★★ **Baby, Baby, Baby (1963; Original Blues Classics, 1990)**
★★★★ **Evenin' Blues (1963; Original Blues Classics, 1993)**
★★★ **Blues Around the Clock (1963; Original Blues Classics, 1995)**
★★★★ **Some of My Best Friends Are the Blues (1964; Original Blues Classics, 1994)**
★★★½ **Blues for Easy Livers (1965; Original Blues Classics, 1996)**
★★★½ **Spoonful (with Robben Ford) (1975; Avenue Jazz, 1994)**
★★★★ **Live (with Robben Ford) (1976; Avenue Jazz, 1993)**
★★★ **American Blues (with Howard Scott) (1976; Avenue Jazz, 1995)**
★★★½ **Black & White Blues (with Eric Burdon) (1976; A-Street Blues, 1995)**
★★★½ **Spoon's Life (1980; Evidence, 1994)**
★★★½ **Rockin' L.A. (Fantasy, 1989)**
★★★½ **Spoon So Easy: The Chess Years (Chess, 1990)**
★★★★ **Blowin' in from Kansas City (Flair, 1993)**
★★★★ **Ain't Nobody's Business (Drive Archive, 1994)**
★★★★ **Spoon's Blues (Stony Plain, 1995)**
★★★★½ **Cold Blooded Boogie (Night Train, 1995)**
★★★½ **Live at the Mint (Private Music, 1996)**
★★★★ **'Spoon and Groove (with Groove Holmes) (Rykodisc, 1996)**
★★★½ **Jimmy Witherspoon with the Junior Mance Trio (Stony Plain, 1997)**

Vocalist Jimmy Witherspoon (1923–1997) was one of the few blues shouters whose voice and musical conception allowed him to captain some of the hottest blues/jazz bands in history. The big-voiced native of Gurdon, Arkansas, began his singing career in the service during World War II but became one of the top rhythm & blues singers after he joined the legendary Jay McShann group in 1944 and contributed to a series of McShann recordings, including "Ain't Nobody's Business," which went to Number One in 1949 and cemented his reputation. *Cold Blooded Boogie* and *Ain't Nobody's Business* document this period well. On the former we hear Witherspoon belting it out in front of the McShann group as well as some sides with veteran Count Basie tenor saxophonist Buddy Tate; the latter offers more McShann cuts along with tracks of Witherspoon burning it up in live performance.

He continued recording without great success in the '50s; the Chess sides from this era collected on *Spoon So Easy* are well worth a listen. In 1959 a spectacular performance at the Monterey Jazz Festival launched Witherspoon to new status in blues and jazz circles—he won *Down Beat*'s 1961 "New Star Male Vocalist" award. The essential, era-defining *'Spoon Concerts* documents the Monterey show, which features Witherspoon fronting an all-star band including trumpeter Roy Eldridge, tenor saxophonists Ben Webster and Coleman Hawkins, clarinetist Woody Herman and pianist Earl "Fatha" Hines and is a true crossroads of jazz and blues. On *Jimmy Witherspoon Sings the Blues* he's backed by the Savoy Sultans.

Witherspoon recorded prolifically from this point on, but only a fraction of his albums are currently available. On *'Spoon and Groove* he's fronting Richard "Groove" Holmes's organ trio. The Original Blues Classics discs are solid examples of his work in several top-notch jazz and blues lineups. *Evenin' Blues* features guitarist T-Bone Walker, and *Some of My Best Friends Are the Blues* finds Witherspoon fronting a big band conducted by Benny Golson. *Blues for Easy Livers* is a jazz session with trombonist Bill Watrous, reeds player Pepper Adams, pianist Roger Kellaway, bassist Richard Davis and drummer Mel Lewis. He went on to make a series of now out-of-print crossover albums in the late 1960s and early '70s, then recorded with War guitarist Howard Scott (*American Blues*) and blues rocker Eric Burdon (*Black & White Blues*) and began a long association with guitarist Robben Ford (*Spoonful*, *Live*). In 1980 he made the hard-edged *Spoon's Life* fronting a Chicago blues quintet. A year later he battled throat cancer successfully, and by the mid-1980s he was back in terrific form on the intense but unavailable *Midnight Lady Called the Blues. Rockin' L.A.* is a fine small-band live recording from 1988.

Witherspoon continued to be a vital force into the 1990s, as *Live at the Mint* amply demonstrates. *Spoon's Blues* is a terrific career retrospective covering traditionals, the originals "Spoon's Life Blues," "Sad Life" and "Past Forty Blues," McShann's "Lonely Boy Blues," Joe Turner's "Lowdown Dirty Shame" and Wynonie Harris's "Playful Baby." Witherspoon is backed by a worshipful band including the excellent guitarist Duke Robillard and saxophonist Scott Hamilton. The set also includes Witherspoon's spoken-word recollections of a life in the blues. — J.S.

CAROLYN WONDERLAND AND THE IMPERIAL MONKEYS

★★★½ **Play with Matches (Big Mo, 1995)**
★★★★ **Bursting with Flavor (Justice, 1997)**

Don't let Carolyn Wonderland's (b. 1972) purple hair fool you. She may look like an alterna-chick, but her albums prove she can sing the blues with the best of them. Wonderland's belting fronts one of Houston's favorite blues bands, the Imperial Monkeys.

Monkey membership has changed over years of club dates and two (out-of-print) independent recordings, but both *Play with Matches* and *Bursting with Flavor* feature drummer Leesa Harrington-Squyres, guitarist Eric Dane and bassist Chris King. This lineup's range is impressive: On *Matches,* the funky, bass-driven "Monkey Love" defies you to sit still, while the haunting final notes of "Fright of the Night" make you feel Wonderland's pain. *Bursting* moves from the syncopated groove of "Momma Don't Like My Friends" to the comic monolog on "Darlene" (courtesy of a 1981 Little Screamin' Kenny and the Sidewinders show).

Sometimes the lyrics become lost and unintelligible in Wonderland's rich, molasseslike voice, but hers isn't the most cerebral band, anyway. These tunes make you wish you were dancing and having another beer on a summer night in a Texas hole-in-the-wall. — A.A.

MITCH WOODS

★★½ **Steady Date with Mitch Woods & His Rocket 88's (Blind Pig, 1984)**
★★★ **Mr. Boogie's Back in Town (Blind Pig, 1988)**
★★★★ **Solid Gold Cadillac (Blind Pig, 1991)**
★★★½ **Shakin' the Shack (Blind Pig, 1993)**
★★★★ **Keeper of the Flame (Viceroy, 1996)**

One of the earliest contemporary roots bands to effectively mine the proto-R&B jump-blues of Louis Jordan and Ike Turner, pianist Mitch Woods (b. 1951) and His Rocket 88's grew out of a solid base in San Francisco during the 1980s to national prominence in the '90s as part of the popular revival of the swing-era dance the lindy hop. The band's effectiveness in the genre is well represented by its version of Jordan's "I Want You to Be My Baby" on *Mr. Boogie's Back in Town.* Woods teams up with Roomful of Blues on *Solid Gold Cadillac,* with a guest shot from Charlie Musselwhite on harmonica. *Shakin' the Shack* moves into New Orleans–influenced blues, a good fit with Woods's boogie-woogie keyboard style. *Keeper of the Flame* adds guitarists John Lee Hooker and Earl King and mouth-harp wizard James Cotton to the mix. — J.S.

PHIL WOODS

★★★ **Woodlore (1955; Original Jazz Classics, 1991)**
★★★★ **Pairing Off (1956; Original Jazz Classics, 1991)**

★★★ **The Young Bloods (with Donald Byrd) (1957; Original Jazz Classics, 1992)**
★★★½ **Bird Feathers (1957; Original Jazz Classics, 1992)**
★★★½ **Four Altos (with Gene Quill, Sahib Shihab and Hal Stein) (1957; Original Jazz Classics, 1992)**
★★★½ **Phil and Quill with Prestige (with the Gene Quill Quintet) (1957; Original Jazz Classics, N.A.)**
★★★ **Early Quintets (1959; Original Jazz Classics, 1995)**
★★★★½ **Rights of Swing (1960; Candid, 1988)**
★★★ **Pot Pie (with Jon Eardley) (1962; Original Jazz Classics, 1996)**
★★★★ **Sugan (1963; Original Jazz Classics, 1994)**
★★★ **A Live Recording, Vol. 1 (1979; Clean Cuts, 1991)**
★★★ **More Live (1981; Genes, 1995)**
★★★★ **Integrity (Red, 1984)**
★★★ **Gratitude (Denon, 1986)**
★★★½ **Bop Stew (Concord Jazz, 1988)**
★★★½ **Bouquet (Concord Jazz, 1988)**
★★★½ **Evolution (Concord Jazz, 1988)**
★★★½ **Flash (Concord Jazz, 1989)**
★★★ **Live from New York (1989; Quicksilver, 1995)**
★★★ **Here's to My Lady (Chesky, 1989)**
★★★ **All Bird's Children (Concord Jazz, 1991)**
★★★½ **Flowers for Hodges (Concord Jazz, 1991)**
★★★ **Full House (Milestone, 1991)**
★★★½ **Real Life (Chesky, 1991)**
★★★★ **At the Vanguard (Antilles, 1992)**
★★★★ **An Affair to Remember (Evidence, 1995)**
★★★½ **Mile High Jazz (Concord Jazz, 1996)**
★★★ **Into the Woods: The Best of Phil Woods (Concord Jazz, 1996)**

Phil Woods (b. 1931) grew up in Springfield, Massachusetts, playing an alto saxophone bequeathed to him by an uncle. He studied with Lennie Tristano and majored in clarinet at Juilliard but established himself as a hot Charlie Parker–inspired bop player in stints with Jimmy Raney, Dizzy Gillespie, Quincy Jones, Charlie Barnet and Benny Goodman in the '50s and '60s while also leading his own groups. Woods has worked in several formats, often doubling with alto saxophonist Gene Quill (see *Phil and Quill with Prestige* and *Pairing Off*) but most frequently showcasing his own aggressive bop style in a quartet (as on *Woodlore*), occasionally fleshing it out to quintets and sextets. He also stamped himself as an accomplished composer and arranger, drawing high praise for his five-part large composition *Rights of Swing,* with its obvious reference to Stravinsky's fascination with Parker and other bop players.

From 1968 to 1972 Woods lived in Paris, where he formed the European Rhythm Machine. After returning to the United States he established a new unit around drummer Bill Goodwin and bassist Steve Gilmore that continued for more than 20 years with only minor variations. His unique tone and attack on alto brought him past any accusations of being a Parker clone; he has turned out consistently fine music without pandering to trends. The live *Integrity* introduces a fine quintet with Tom Harrell on trumpet and flügelhorn and Hal Galper on piano. *Bop Stew* and *Bouquet* were recorded live in Japan. More recently, Woods has experimented with his Little Big Band, adding trombonist Hal Crook, baritone and alto saxophonist Nick Brignola and tenor saxophonist Nelson Hill to the lineup. *Real Life,* with its tribute to Woods's old partner, "Quill," is particularly good. *Here's to My Lady* is a quartet date with pianist Tommy Flanagan, bassist George Mraz and drummer Kenny Washington. Woods, an accomplished interpreter of ballads, covers offbeat standards on the quintet date *An Affair to Remember.* Woods has won multiple Grammys and many musicians' and critics' polls, but such honors have not ensured that the records remain in print, so check the cutout bins for more gems.
— J.S.

WORLD SAXOPHONE QUARTET

★★★★★ **W.S.Q. (Black Saint, 1981)**
★★★★½ **Revue (Black Saint, 1982)**
★★★★ **Live in Zurich (Black Saint, 1984)**
★★★★ **Live at the Brooklyn Academy of Music (Black Saint, 1986)**
★★★★½ **The World Saxophone Quartet Plays Duke Ellington (Elektra Nonesuch, 1986)**
★★★★★ **Dances and Ballads (Elektra Nonesuch, 1988)**
★★★½ **Rhythm and Blues (Elektra Musician, 1989)**
★★★½ **Metamorphosis (Elektra Nonesuch, 1991)**

★★½ **Breath of Life (Elektra Nonesuch, 1994)**
★★★½ **Moving Right Along (Black Saint, 1994)**
★★★½ **Four Now (Justin Time, 1996)**
★★★ **Takin' It 2 the Next Level (Justin Time, 1997)**

In 1977, when David Murray, Julius Hemphill, Oliver Lake and Hamiet Bluiett launched the World Saxophone Quartet, the idea of four horn players without a rhythm section didn't exist outside rehearsal rooms and the most obscure performance spaces. Despite that, the WSQ became the most important democratic jazz band of the '80s. The four saxophonists took some of their inspiration from the avant-garde; the honking, popping, squealing, whistling and rumbling sounds of the free-jazzers gave the sax not only a much broader spectrum of timbres but also an unprecedented percussive sound. The most important influences, though, came from the most traditional sources: the a cappella singing styles of Southern gospel quartets and Northern doo-wop groups—male-vocal outfits that demonstrated how four voices could create their own triad chords, lead lines, bass lines, counterpoint and rhythm without any outside help. These vocal influences became more and more obvious as time went by.

Bluiett's primary horn was the baritone sax (though he also played alto flute and alto clarinet), and he anchored the bottom. Murray was the main tenor voice (though he also played bass clarinet) and most ferocious soloist. Lake mostly played alto (in addition to soprano, tenor and flute) and had the best sense of humor, with a fondness for R&B flavors and wild tangents. Hemphill also played alto (as well as soprano and flute) and was the band's lyricist, the one most likely to come up with the emotionally arresting phrase.

The quartet's debut, the now unavailable *Point of No Return,* was recorded live at a German jazz festival and reveals four great blowers who haven't quite become a group yet. The band's first studio release, *Steppin' with the World Saxophone Quartet* (also out of print) shows the development of a true ensemble sound, thanks largely to the efforts of Hemphill, who wrote and arranged four of the six tracks. His efforts bear sweet fruit on *W.S.Q.,* one of the band's two best albums, which introduces their theme song, Bluiett's finger-snapping "Hattie Wall," and Hemphill's joyously melodic "Pillars Latino." The pieces are shorter, more sharply focused and more equally distributed among the members. Nearly as good is *Revue,* a studio project that includes four terrific Hemphill tunes, Murray's romantic ballad "Ming" and gospel and R&B tunes from Lake and Bluiett.

Hemphill's dominance reaches its peak on *Live in Zurich,* which begins and closes with a hypnotic processional take on "Hattie Wall" and includes six of his compositions. He also composed and arranged three of the six tunes on the subsequent *Live at the Brooklyn Academy of Music.* These two recordings are a testament to what a brilliant, underrated composer and player Hemphill was.

The WSQ's first American release is also its first album of nonoriginal material. *The World Saxophone Quartet Plays Duke Ellington* remains its best-selling album, thanks to the familiarity of the material, the crisp clarity of the recording and the imaginative, radical reworkings of the tunes. As far out as the WSQ take "Come Sunday," "Lush Life," "Prelude to a Kiss" and "Take the A Train"—filling these swing classics with nervous bop lines and modal tangents—they never lose the melodic thread or the essential romanticism. They apply the same populist romanticism to the 10 originals on *Dances and Ballads,* a career pinnacle. Among the highlights are Murray's tributes to Lester Young and R&B singer Little Anthony. The quartet returns to the successful standards formula on *Rhythm and Blues,* only this time the standards come from Otis Redding, Marvin Gaye, the O'Jays and Junior Wells.

Hemphill left the WSQ in 1990, and the band was never the same. His replacement, Arthur Blythe, was perhaps the only alto saxophonist with the chops, the tunes and the background to replace Hemphill, but by now the band members were too busy elsewhere to rebuild a sense of tight ensemble. *Metamorphosis* and *Four Now* (with John Purcell replacing Blythe) are promising collaborations between the new WSQ and three African drummers. *Breath of Life* departs from the central concept by adding singers and other players to the quartet. Eric Person replaces Blythe for *Moving Right Along,* which gets the WSQ back to its gospel roots with versions of "Amazing Grace" and John Coltrane's "Giant Steps." On *Takin' It 2 the Next Level* the band is backed by a conventional rhythm section. — G.H.

MARVA WRIGHT

★★★ **Heartbreakin' Woman (Tipitina's, 1991)**
★ **Marvalous (Mardi Gras, 1995)**

★★★½ I Still Haven't Found What I'm Looking For (Aim, 1995)
★★★★ Born with the Blues (Pointblank, 1996)

Marva Wright (b. 1948) didn't begin singing the blues until she was almost 40 years old. She sang gospel until she opened a show for Koko Taylor in 1987, launching a rapid ascent that has earned her the nickname "the Blues Queen of New Orleans." After honing her newfound creative outlet with grueling hours on Bourbon Street, Wright has graced numerous international stages and created a mixed catalog of recordings.

Her debut, *Heartbreakin' Woman,* is short on original material but long on soul. Personal and rousing readings of "The Sky Is Crying" and "Born Under a Bad Sign" are highlights, along with the funky Wright originals "Let's Make Love" and the title track. She packs the power of Etta James and the divine leanings of Mavis Staples in her stratospheric voice and seemingly unlimited lung power. But, as is the case with *I Still Haven't Found What I'm Looking For,* Wright has a tendency to lean on overworked material such as "Feel Like Breakin' Up Somebody's Home" and "Bring It on Home to Me." She is far better served by singing her own convictions, such as the naked confession "I'm Not Coming Back (The Battered Women's Song)."

Marvalous is a great concept—matching Wright with Al Green producer Willie Mitchell—but the stiff retro-'70s arrangements and more tired covers ("Down Home Blues") drain her vitality and originality. *Born with the Blues,* however, delivers on all of Wright's promise and more. Backed by a dream Louisiana band featuring guitarists Walter "Wolfman" Washington and Sonny Landreth and an ultrafunky rhythm section, Wright soars her way through a diverse set of 12-bar blues ("What's Wrong"), New Orleans R&B ("Three Times"), goose-bump–inducing gospel ("Pray") and one hook-filled original. — S.J.

JIMMY YANCEY

★★★★★ **Chicago Piano (1951; Atlantic, 1972)**
★★★★★ **Complete Recorded Works, Vol. 1 1939–1940 (Document, 1990)**
★★★★★ **Complete Recorded Works, Vol. 2 1940–1943 (Document, 1990)**
★★★★★ **Complete Recorded Works, Vol. 3 1943–1950 (Document, 1990)**

A true original, Jimmy Yancey (1898–1951) was an accomplished barrelhouse pianist throughout a career that began in the prehistory of jazz and blues playing at house parties in Chicago. As a child, he performed on the vaudeville circuit with his father, Mose Yancey, giving a command performance before King George V of England in 1913.

Yancey brought a quiet eloquence and nuance to the style that the rough-and-tumble barroom soundtrack genre often lacked. He recorded infrequently (and often with his wife, vocalist Estella "Mama" Yancey) during his lifetime. In addition to his music, he held down jobs such as playing baseball for the semipro Chicago All-Americans and working as a groundskeeper for the Chicago White Sox at Comiskey Park from 1925 to 1950.

Yancey's influence on pianists who copied the steady bass patterns that eventually became popular during the boogie-woogie craze of the 1930s eventually led to his discovery. The Document releases cover most of Yancey's recording career, which began in 1939. The Atlantic sides are reissues of an emotional session made just a few weeks before his death in 1951 with Mama Yancey singing on some tracks. — J.S.

YELLOWJACKETS

★★ **Yellowjackets (Warner Bros., 1981)**
★★ **Mirage à Trois (Warner Bros., 1983)**
★★ **Samurai Samba (Warner Bros., 1985)**
★★ **Shades (MCA, 1986)**
★★ **Four Corners (MCA, 1987)**
★★ **Politics (MCA, 1988)**
★★ **The Spin (MCA, 1989)**
★★ **Greenhouse (GRP, 1991)**
★★★ **Live Wires (GRP, 1992)**
★★★ **Like a River (GRP, 1992)**
★★★ **Run for Your Life (GRP, 1994)**
★★★ **Dreamland (Warner Bros., 1995)**
★★★ **Blue Hats (Warner Bros., 1997)**

One of the most successful of the postfusion "smooth jazz" groups, the Yellowjackets fashion a lightweight easy-listening sound—the perfect background music for the stereotypical understated cocktail party overlooking the beach. Glib and technically proficient but totally devoid of anything resembling soul, the band soldiered on through the 1980s selling LPs and inducing sleep. The arrival of multi-instrumentalist Bob Mintzer, who is adept on tenor and soprano saxophone as well as bass clarinet, for *Live Wires* gave the band a much-needed shot in the arm. — J.S.

THE YOCKAMO ALL-STARS

★★★★ **Dew Drop Out (Hannibal, 1998)**

Getting heavy airplay on New Orleans radio station WWOZ, the Yockamo All-Stars created one of the hands-down good-time New Orleans albums of the year. This wonderful tribute to the legendary days of '40s and '50s New Orleans

R&B is performed with verve and detailed technique by a coterie of local players who are central to the current identity and future of New Orleans music. — J.S.

LARRY YOUNG

★★★★ **Testifying (1960; Original Jazz Classics, 1991)**
★★★ **Young Blues (1960; Original Jazz Classics, 1994)**
★★★ **Groove Street (1962; Original Jazz Classics, 1994)**
★★★½ **The Art of Larry Young (1964; Blue Note, 1992)**
★★★★ **Unity (1965; Capitol, 1995)**

A wildly innovative keyboardist, Larry Young (1940–1978), or Khalid Yasin, as he renamed himself, expanded his roots in rhythm & blues combos to become one of the best young organists of the 1960s, playing with Grant Green, Lou Donaldson, Elvin Jones, Lee Morgan and Joe Henderson. By the end of the '60s Young was helping to create fusion, playing with John McLaughlin on *Devotion,* Miles Davis on *Bitches Brew* and the extraordinary Tony Williams Lifetime as well as sessions with Jimi Hendrix and Carlos Santana.

Testifying, Young Blues and *Groove Street* show Young blasting his way through soul-jazz trio and quartet sessions. *Unity* and *The Art of Larry Young* collect some of the burning sessions Young did for Blue Note; *Unity* is especially fine, with Elvin Jones matching Young's energy just as he did John Coltrane's, while tenor saxophonist Joe Henderson and trumpeter Woody Shaw (whose "Moontrane" is on this set) add their ideas to the conversation. — J.S.

LESTER YOUNG

★★★★½ **Master Takes with Count Basie (1949; Savoy, 1994)**
★★★★½ **Jazz Immortal Series: The Pres (1950; Savoy, 1993)**
★★★★ **The Lester Young Trio (1951; Verve, 1994)**
★★★★ **Pres and Sweets (with Harry "Sweets" Edison) (1955; Verve, 1991)**
★★★★½ **The Jazz Giants (1956; Verve, 1986)**
★★★★ **Pres and Teddy (1956; Verve, 1986)**
★★★★½ **Blue Lester (1956; Savoy, 1992)**
★★★★ **The Master's Touch (1956; Savoy, 1993)**
★★★★ **Lester Young in Washington, D.C., 1956, Vol. 1 (1980; Original Jazz Classics, 1993)**
★★★★ **Lester Young in Washington, D.C., 1956, Vol. 2 (1980; Original Jazz Classics, 1996)**
★★★★ **Lester Young in Washington, D.C., 1956, Vol. 3 (1981; Original Jazz Classics, 1996)**
★★★★ **Lester Young in Washington, D.C., 1956, Vol. 4 (1981; Original Jazz Classics, 1993)**
★★★★ **The Best of Lester Young (Pablo, 1987)**
★★★★ **Compact Jazz: Lester Young and the Piano Giants (Verve, 1988)**
★★★★ **Masters of Jazz: Lester Young (Storyville, 1988)**
★★★ **The Big Three (with Coleman Hawkins and Ben Webster) (Signature, 1989)**
★★★★ **Verve Jazz Masters 30 (Verve, 1994)**
★★★★ **The Complete Aladdin Sessions (Blue Note, 1995)**
★★★★★ **Lester Leaps In (ASV/Living Era, 1995)**
★★★★★ **This Is Jazz 26 (Columbia/Legacy, 1997)**
★★★★★ **The Kansas City Sessions (Commodore, 1997)**
★★★ **Pres (Collectables, 1997)**

Tenor saxophonist Lester Young (1909–1959) was one of the most inventive and singular soloists in jazz history. His light, feathery, almost altolike tone, his affinity for (and influence on) singers, his concentration on melody and his playing just behind the beat established a second, cooler school of thought and style in tenor playing, one that stood in direct opposition to the heated, more aggressive school of the other dominant tenor, Coleman Hawkins. Young was a major influence on bebop, both in terms of his unmistakable sound and his inimitable personality: His porkpie hat, sometimes unintelligible hipster lexicon and habit of holding his instrument at oblique angles inspired the beret-and-shades look that became such an integral part of the bopper mystique.

Born in Woodville, Mississippi, and raised in New Orleans, Young, who started out playing drums before moving to sax, was initially influenced by C-melody saxophonist Frankie Trumbauer. He began playing with his father Billy Young's band and later moved through the Blue Devils, the Bostonians, King Oliver's mid-

'30s band, a Count Basie–led combo, Fletcher Henderson's band (as a brief replacement for Hawkins) and, in 1936, the big band led by Basie. Young's finest recordings, those he made with the Basie band, are now scattered across Columbia's *Essential Count Basie* series, the Basie series on the French Classics label and numerous other compilations. A tantalizing, 17-cut slice of the Young riches in Columbia's vaults can be found on *This Is Jazz 26. Lester Leaps In* is also a good single-disc survey of this period.

In 1940 Young abruptly left Basie's band and began leading small groups, a role for which he proved unsuited: Most of his best recordings are as a sideman, not a leader. Before entering the Army in 1944, Young recorded three sessions for Savoy. Using Basie-band personnel on one session and a septet led by pianist Johnny Guarnieri and drummer Cozy Cole on the other, Young is routinely brilliant on tunes like "Jump, Lester, Jump." These fine sessions are now stretched and repeated across four albums. *The Master's Touch* is primarily alternate takes, while *The Pres, Master Takes* and *Blue Lester* duplicate many of the same tracks, and cuts from a fine 1949 session with drummer Roy Haynes are mixed into all four discs.

Whether Young's nightmarish experiences in the Army wrecked his psyche as well as his playing is among the deepest and most irreconcilable controversies in jazz history. There is even some debate over what those experiences were. Whatever occurred, Young returned from his year in the service a changed man—darker and less lively than before—but not broken and lazy. *The Complete Aladdin Sessions* offers proof that Young still had something to say and give after 1945. The 40 cuts in this collection were recorded between 1942 and 1948, and they show a man whose tone and attack have mellowed but who's still full of ideas and invention. Among the many highlights here are "Lester Blows Again," "Jumpin' at Mesner's," an odd sextet run-through of his old Basie blockbusters "One O'Clock Jump" and "Jumpin' at the Woodside" and a four-song session that Young recorded in 1942 with Nat King Cole on piano. Young's postwar solos are more angular than his more famous earlier work, showing the effects of his struggle to come to terms with bop, a form he helped inspire.

Masters of Jazz: Lester Young is an interesting hodgepodge of radio broadcasts of small-group dates recorded between 1951 and 1956. Also included is "Jumpin' with Symphony Sid," recorded in 1956, at Olivia Davis's Patio Lounge the night after the sets captured on the *Lester Young in Washington, D.C.* series. These four live Original Jazz Classics albums offer the most convincing proof that Young, despite a growing litany of emotional and physical problems, remained gifted and inspired to the end. Here he overcomes sluggish backing to again reach for heights, scaling most and making all the attempts shining voyages of discovery.

Of the Verve sessions, *The Jazz Giants* is the clear winner. Young's playing has a warm, full tone, and while his solos here are simpler and more direct than in the past, they exude a vigor and spirit that are patently Young. While they often contain soaring solos and sterling cuts, the rest of the Verve discs find Young's talents decaying, though still infinitely more interesting than that of his mob of imitators. *The Lester Young Trio* finds him with Buddy Rich but not entirely in sync. The first all-star pairing with former Basie-ite Harry "Sweets" Edison is scattered, and despite some great moments, Young sounds worse for wear and tear. *Compact Jazz* and *Verve Jazz Masters 30* collect many of the best cuts from the individual Verve albums.

— R.B.

MIGHTY JOE YOUNG

★★★★ **Bluesy Josephine (1976; Evidence, 1993)**

★★½ **Live at the Wise Fools (Quicksilver, 1990)**

★★★ **Mighty Man (Blind Pig, 1997)**

Steeped in the tradition of Chicago's postwar electric blues, guitarist Mighty Joe Young's (b. 1927) music often sounds more derivative than inspired. Though he throws modern flourishes into his adept playing, there's an almost intangible hunger that seems to be missing from his songwriting and axe work. After performing as sideman on projects by Albert King, Otis Rush and Billy Boy Arnold, Young released *Blues with a Touch of Soul,* his first solo effort, in 1971. While this cassette-only album is inconsistent, his best available release is *Bluesy Josephine,* which documents a 1976 recording session in Toulouse, France. Young's loose, B.B. King–influenced sound is in full evidence here, as he shows off five originals, including the earnest "Takes Money," to which pianist Willie Mabon contributes rolling boogie-woogie accompaniment. The album also includes Young's nine-minute interpretation of Eddie Boyd's "Five Long Years" and a soulful-yet-tame reading of the Robert Johnson classic "Sweet Home Chicago." Though he's a very capable Chicago guitarslinger cut from the cloth of classic blues, Young's playing doesn't have the tortured underpinnings that characterize much blues music, diluting its immediacy. — B.R.H.

FRANK ZAPPA

★★★★ Freak Out! (1966; Rykodisc, 1995)
★★★½ Absolutely Free (1967; Rykodisc, 1995)
★★★ Tis the Season to Be Jelly (1967; Rhino, 1994)
★★★ The Ark (1968; Rhino, 1994)
★★★★★ We're Only in It for the Money (1968; Rykodisc, 1995)
★★★½ Lumpy Gravy (1968; Rykodisc, 1995)
★★★½ Cruising with Ruben and the Jets (1968; Rykodisc, 1995)
★★★★★ Uncle Meat (1969; Rykodisc, 1995)
★★★★ Hot Rats (1969; Rykodisc, 1995)
★★★★ Burnt Weeny Sandwich (1969; Rykodisc, 1995)
★★★★ Weasels Ripped My Flesh (1970; Rykodisc, 1995)
★★★★ Chunga's Revenge (1970; Rykodisc, 1995)
★★★ Freaks and Motherfuckers (1970; Rhino, 1994)
★★★½ Fillmore East, June 1971 (1971; Rykodisc, 1995)
★★★½ Just Another Band from L.A. (1972; Rykodisc, 1995)
★★★★ Waka/Jawaka (1972; Rykodisc, 1995)
★★★★ The Grand Wazoo (1972; Rykodisc, 1995)
★★★½ Over-Nite Sensation (1973, Rykodisc, 1995)
★★★ Piquantique (1973; Rhino, 1994)
★★★½ Apostrophe (1974; Rykodisc, 1995)
★★★½ Roxy and Elsewhere (1974; Rykodisc, 1995)
★★★ Unmitigated Audacity (1974; Rhino, 1994)
★★★½ One Size Fits All (1975; Rykodisc, 1995)
★★★½ Bongo Fury (1975; Rykodisc, 1995)
★★★ Zoot Allures (1976; Rykodisc, 1995)
★★★★ Zappa in New York (1978; Rykodisc, 1995)
★★★ Studio Tan (1978; Rykodisc, 1995)
★★★ Saarbrucken 1978 (1978; Rhino, 1994)
★★★ Sleep Dirt (1979; Rykodisc, 1995)
★★★ Orchestral Favorites (1979; Rykodisc, 1995)
★★½ Sheik Yerbouti (1979; Rykodisc, 1995)
★★★ Any Way the Wind Blows (1979; Rhino, 1994)
★★★★ Tinseltown Rebellion (1981; Rykodisc, 1995)
★★★★ You Are What You Is (1981; Rykodisc, 1995)
★★★ Ship Arriving Too Late to Save a Drowning Witch (1982; Rykodisc, 1995)
★★★ The Man from Utopia (1983; Rykodisc, 1995)
★★★½ Baby Snakes (1983; Rykodisc, 1995)
★★★½ Thing-Fish (1984; Rykodisc, 1995)
★★★ Francesco Zappa (1984; Rykodisc, 1995)
★★★ Boulez Conducts Zappa: The Perfect Stranger (1984; Rykodisc, 1995)
★★★½ Frank Zappa Meets the Mothers of Prevention (1985; Rykodisc, 1995)
★★★½ Them or Us (1986; Rykodisc, 1995)
★★★★ Shut Up 'n Play Yer Guitar

(Complete Set) (1986; Rykodisc, 1995)
★★★★ **Jazz from Hell (1986; Rykodisc, 1995)**
★★★★★ **Joe's Garage, Acts I, II and III (1987; Rykodisc, 1995)**
★★★★ **Guitar (1988; Rykodisc, 1995)**
★★★★★ **You Can't Do That on Stage Anymore, Vol. 1 (1988; Rykodisc, 1995)**
★★★★★ **You Can't Do That on Stage Anymore, Vol. 2 (1988; Rykodisc, 1995)**
★★★★ **Broadway the Hardway (1988; Rykodisc, 1995)**
★★★★★ **You Can't Do That on Stage Anymore, Vol. 3 (1989; Rykodisc, 1995)**
★★★★★ **You Can't Do That on Stage Anymore, Vol. 4 (1991; Rykodisc, 1995)**
★★★ **Make a Jazz Noise Here (1991; Rykodisc, 1995)**
★★★ **Beat the Boots! (Rhino, 1991)**
★★★ **Playground Psychotics (1992; Rykodisc, 1995)**
★★★★ **You Can't Do That on Stage Anymore, Vol. 5 (1992; Rykodisc, 1995)**
★★★★ **You Can't Do That on Stage Anymore, Vol. 6 (1992; Rykodisc, 1995)**
★★★★ **Beat the Boots!, Vol. 2 (Rhino, 1992)**
★★★½ **The Yellow Shark (1993; Rykodisc, 1995)**
★★★★ **London Symphony Orchestra, Vols. 1 and 2 (1993; Rykodisc, 1995)**
★★★ **Ahead of Their Time (1993; Rykodisc, 1995)**
★★★½ **Civilization Phaze III (Rykodisc, 1995)**
★★★★½ **Strictly Commercial: The Best of Frank Zappa (Rykodisc, 1995)**
★★★★ **The Best Band You Never Heard in Your Life (Rykodisc, 1995)**
★★★ **Does Humor Belong in Music? (Rykodisc, 1995)**
★★★ **Lost Episodes (Rykodisc, 1996)**
★★★ **Läther (Rykodisc, 1996)**
★★★★ **Have I Offended Someone? (Rykodisc, 1997)**
★★★½ **Strictly Genteel: A Classical Introduction to Frank Zappa (Rykodisc, 1997)**

Relentlessly experimental, Frank Zappa (1940–1993) defied categorization. In a sly manner reminiscent of Andy Warhol's odd fusion of parody and homage, he worked at virtually all kinds of music—and whether he was guised as a jazz/rock fusionist, guitar virtuoso, satirical rocker, electronics wizard or orchestral innovator, his eccentric genius was undeniable. Cross Dion and the Belmonts with Harry Partch, and you get some idea of Zappa's musical sensibility; as a humorist—and humor was crucial to Zappa—he came on like a hybrid of Lenny Bruce and the Three Stooges (the influence of early risqué blues records, too, is significant). Elusive, indulgent, at times inscrutable, Zappa has a tone and intention that are often hard to determine—they seem calculated to provoke fury, awe and giggling. An early crusader against censorship, he was political—if sometimes perplexingly so—but his ultimate significance resides in his music. Brandishing as his motto a quote from his idol, the French avant-gardiste Edgard Varèse, "The present-day composer refuses to die!," Zappa was as much modern classical composer as pop legend—and the erasure of the lines between high and pop art that he premiered with his first band, the Mothers of Invention, remains one of the emancipatory gestures of the '60s. Zappa was also an accomplished blues guitarist and songwriter, with acknowledged debts to Johnny "Guitar" Watson and Jimi Hendrix, and a jazz composer and arranger who clearly enjoyed his references to Eric Dolphy and Oliver Nelson and employed jazz players from Jean-Luc Ponty to Michael Brecker in his bands.

With a riff aping the Stones' "Satisfaction," "Hungry Freaks, Daddy" provides the anthemic intro to *Freak Out!* Lyrically, the record's antilove songs and daft non sequiturs raise the rebel flag for the underdogs Zappa and the Mothers would henceforth champion; the music is both a triumph and mockery of blues, psychedelia, folk rock and doo-wop. Considerably more demanding, *Absolutely Free,* composed of fragmentary jazz allusions, vibraphone noodlings, chanting and operatic vocals, pushes the envelope even further; its determined messiness seems totally mad. On "Plastic People," a "Louie Louie" guitar motif disintegrates into free-form swinging, all in service of a poke at LBJ and American suburbia. And, with *We're Only in It for the Money,* with its orchestral segments and general ferocity, the Mothers achieve their masterpiece.

The prototype of the technically brilliant aggregations upon which Zappa would come to insist, the Mothers of 1967 was basically a crack rock outfit with woodwind capability. *We're Only in It for the Money* is in large part the musicians' work, but the vision is assuredly Zappa's. "Who Needs the Peace Corps?," "Flower Punk" and "Harry You're a Beast" are early exercises of his trademark themes: paranoia—both political and sexual; ridicule for the bourgeoisie; and a utopian insistence on completely free expression. In search of that goal, Zappa detoured from the Mothers by putting out *Lumpy Gravy,* his first solo work. Recorded with a 50-piece orchestra, this difficult and sometimes surprisingly lovely record of John Cage–ish modern music paved the way for the Mothers' second major set, *Uncle Meat.* A pastiche of 31 sound bites—either in the form of tape edits, nonsense phone conversations, "songs" or instrumental passages—*Meat* is an inspired monstrosity. There are lyrics, but they're secondary to the assault of glorious noise. A kind of musical version of William Burroughs's "cut-up" method of literary construction—the insertion of random passages within an otherwise narrative text—*Meat* reinvented pop music. The only problem was that this kind of zonked brilliance could never be "popular"—and *Meat* marks the coalescence of one of Zappa's characteristic stances, the cryptic prophet howling in the wilderness. A crossword-puzzle–style key to future Zappa music, this far-reaching set introduced one of Zappa's most memorable and oft-referenced instrumental themes, "Dog Breath," and included the first live Zappa guitar solo on the closing segment of "King Kong." At one point *Uncle Meat* was intended to be part of a 12-record Mothers documentary. Other pieces of this project appeared as *Burnt Weeny Sandwich* and *Weasels Ripped My Flesh.*

The quartet of *Weasels Ripped My Flesh, Chunga's Revenge, Hot Rats* and *Burnt Weeny Sandwich* is a high point of consistency but the last of the original Mothers of Invention. While members of the Mothers would resurface throughout his career, the band as such was kaput—and Zappa began working with a bewildering array of talents (Little Feat's Lowell George, violinist Don "Sugarcane" Harris, drummer Aynsley Dunbar, keyboardist George Duke). While there are vocals on all these albums, it is the music that matters. Propulsive neojazz alternates with gorgeous, classically derived pieces that nourish the grace or power of soundtracks for dreams. A collaboration with Captain Beefheart is *Hot Rats*'s nifty standout, "Willie the Pimp," and in "Peaches en Regalia" Zappa finds a music of majesty.

The next Mothers records, *Fillmore East, June 1971* and *Just Another Band from L.A.,* add ex-Turtles singers Howard Kaylan and Mark Volman, which only increases the yuks factor. *The Grand Wazoo, Waka/Jawaka* and *One Size Fits All* make for an impressive clutch of Mothers-less outings; *Over-Nite Sensation* and *Apostrophe* evoke a postmodernist hilarity that obscures the fact that Zappa was inventing a new genre.

Although Zappa's approach resists generalization, it became apparent by the mid-'70s that those albums that balanced humor with musical experimentation would be the ones to watch for. *Bongo Fury* is as strong a Beefheart performance as a Zappa one; *Zoot Allures* is comparatively bland, but *Sheik Yerbouti* is much less impressive than *Shut Up 'n Play Yer Guitar,* wherein Zappa simply turns loose his astonishing guitar playing. On *Joe's Garage* Zappa telegraphs his intentions to turn up the heat on political oppression of music in the next decade with this Swiftian theatrical piece about a future in which music is outlawed. The story is presented as a warning to young people about the evils of becoming a musician, but Zappa adds a surprise twist when Joe, languishing in the jail for musicians, plots his revenge in terms of the imaginary guitar solo "Outside Now." Zappa's guitar solos are culled from previous performances with the new tracks built up around them in a process Zappa called "xenocrony," or strange synchronization.

You Are What You Is, however, finds the naughty lad reclaiming the stand-up stage. But this time the musical parodies are varied enough to carry the day. Mock versions of reggae, ska, Journey-style power ballads and country music, and a hilarious takeoff on the Doors, produce the most inventive comedy he'd attempted in years.

The joke-predominant albums *Tinseltown Rebellion, Broadway the Hardway* and *Them or Us* are fairly tasty, especially the rock send-up *Them or Us,* but the real excitement is elsewhere. *London Symphony Orchestra, Vols. 1 and 2* finds Zappa in an all-orchestral setting, with impressive results; *Jazz from Hell,* with his executing virtually all the pieces on synclavier, displays his longtime mastery of music tech. Most ambitious, however, are his retrospectives—*Guitar,* a sequel to *Shut Up 'n Play Yer Guitar* that features 32 live solos recorded between 1979 and 1984; and the staggering *You Can't Do That on Stage Anymore* series. Twenty years in the making, the set presents previously unreleased live work from 1968 to 1988. *You Can't Do That on Stage Anymore* may well be the most ambitious live recording project ever attempted. Over the course of 12 CDs, Zappa offers a bird's-eye view of what his numerous bands sounded like at their best. By intercutting performances years apart without segues, Zappa intended the set to sound like one marathon performance that included all of his bands coming in and out of the mix on cue like individual musicians. In this respect, *You Can't Do That on Stage Anymore* is the ultimate expression of "conceptual continuity," Zappa's love for repeating the self-referential themes throughout the body of his work that give the entire output coherence. Absolute Frank-ophiles will enjoy *Beat the Boots!, Vol. 2.* Seven CDs of live work from 1968 to 1977 present the Mothers at their fiercest and sometimes most inspired. The set includes a massive scrapbook that loosely chronicles Zappa's career from high school to his scrape with the Parents Music Resource Center. Rhino has reissued the bootlegs as individual CDs.

The Yellow Shark is riveting—Zappa's most difficult compositions played by the 26-member Ensemble Modern. Together with *Boulez Conducts Zappa: The Perfect Stranger,* a "chamber music" piece, and *Francesco Zappa,* purportedly the canon of an 18th Century composer but in actuality Frank himself in a classical vein, *The Yellow Shark* is challenging, at times baffling, at times brilliant. With Rykodisc turning out a wondrous ton of Zappa releases since his death, there are a lot of "rarities" to choose from. Perhaps most engaging is *Strictly Commercial,* a brave attempt at a Zappa best-of. Seventy-six minutes of gems from 60 albums, it's impressive—and accessible. Three great Mothers collections, *Playground Psychotics, Ahead of Their Time* and, especially, *The Best Band You Never Heard in Your Life* (1988 big-band versions of vintage Frank) keep the anarchic spirit of that remarkable ensemble alive. Finally, the titles—and, of course, the contents—of two fine sets nicely hint at the range of the composer's accomplishment: *Make a Jazz Noise Here* broadcasts Zappa's insistence on the art of improvisation; *Does Humor Have a Place in Music?* begs rhetorically the question that's long dogged those who never quite "got" Zappa. Those who *did* don't need an explanation: It's all right there in the music.
— P.E.

JOE ZAWINUL

★★★	**Money in the Pocket/The Rise & Fall of the Third Stream (1966/1968; Rhino, 1994)**
★★★★	**Zawinul (Atlantic, 1971)**
★★★★	**Dialects (Columbia, 1986)**
★★★	**The Immigrants (Columbia, 1988)**
★★★	**Black Water (Columbia, 1989)**
★★★½	**Lost Tribes (Columbia, 1992)**
★★★★	**My People (Escapade, 1996)**
★★	**Stories of the Danube (Philips, 1996)**

Growing up in Vienna, Austria, keyboardist Joe Zawinul (b. 1932) was nurtured on European classical music, but his overriding love was for the jazz he heard on record and from occasional touring American musicians. In 1959 he moved to the United States and began a great jazz career.

After playing with Maynard Ferguson's big band and backing Dinah Washington, Zawinul joined the Cannonball Adderley group in 1961. As Adderley's pianist, Zawinul quickly became a major figure in the soul-jazz movement, composing several hits, including the durable "Mercy, Mercy, Mercy."

By the end of the '60s, Zawinul was branching out from the rootsy sound of the Adderley band into the sonic experiments that would create fusion. He recorded four albums pivotal in Miles Davis's evolution during 1969 and 1974: *In a Silent Way,* for which he composed the richly textured title track; the groundbreaking *Bitches Brew; Live-Evil;* and *Big Fun.*

In 1971 Zawinul went on to form Weather Report, where his fertile musical imagination incorporated a wide range of instrumentation and synthesized effects to create some of fusion's most inspired aural landscapes.

The Rhino twofer includes Zawinul's 1966 record *Money in the Pocket* and the 1968 release *The Rise & Fall of the Third Stream,* recorded with the Adderley rhythm section of bassist Sam Jones and drummer Louis Hayes. By the time of the 1971 session, *Zawinul,* the fusion experiment was much in evidence. Zawinul and Herbie Hancock team up on electric pianos with an impressive array of sidemen, including trumpeters Woody Shaw and Jimmy Owens, percussionists Joe Chambers, Billy Hart, David Lee and Jack DeJohnette, and two of Weather Report's cofounders, saxophonist Wayne Shorter and bassist Miroslav Vitous.

Dialects is an impressive display of Zawinul's conceptual genius with synthesizer textures; with the help of several violinists he constructs this elaborate soundscape from scratch. His post–Weather Report band, Zawinul Syndicate, employs a wide range of musicians and styles in a world music–based context. Zawinul reaches the apotheosis of this approach on *My People,* which includes guest vocals from Salif Keita. On *Stories of the Danube* he falls into the faux-symphonic trap that has captured so many of his classically trained peers in the jazz world.
— J.S.

DENNY ZEITLIN

★★★★ **Time Remembers One Time Once (with Charie Haden) (ECM, 1981)**
★★★ **Trio (Windham Hill, 1988)**
★★ **In the Moment (Windham Hill, 1989)**
★★★★★ **Maybeck Recital Hall Series, Vol. 27 (Concord Jazz, 1993)**
★★★★ **Concord Duo Series, Vol. 8 (with David Friesen) (Concord Jazz, 1995)**

Pianist Denny Zeitlin (b. 1938) has had the unusual distinction of maintaining dual high-profile careers for the past 30-odd years. He's been both a practicing jazz musician and a psychiatrist with a busy Bay Area office and teaching responsibilities in San Francisco.

Zeitlin grew up in a musical family in Chicago, where he picked up piano early. Though classically trained, he was intrigued by improvisation. He made his first four recordings for Columbia in the early 1960s after meeting producer John Hammond during a medical fellowship at Columbia University.

Through the years, he has recorded or performed with a broad stylistic range of musicians including Herbie Hancock, Wes Montgomery, Pat Metheny, Bobby Hutcherson, Joe Henderson and the Kronos Quartet. His available recordings fall into the solo, duo or trio format. Zeitlin clearly prefers the challenge and risk of duo performance.

One of those duo sessions, *Time Remembers One Time Once,* was recorded live at San Francisco's now defunct Keystone Korner with bass player Charlie Haden, who was a member of Zeitlin's earliest West Coast trio in the mid-1960s. It set a high standard for musical empathy in this format, as the pair turned intricate tunes inside out with their harmonic explorations.

In the Moment is a split session, the first half a trio format with bassist Joel DiBartolo and drummer Peter Donald, who also backed him on *Trio.* The second half consists of duets with bassist David Friesen. While it has some fine moments, it lacks cohesion.

His solo session, *Vol. 27* in Concord's Maybeck Recital Hall Series, is one of the most cerebral and wide-ranging presentations in this acclaimed collection of recordings at a small concert hall in Berkeley, California.

Zeitlin has developed a strong musical partnership with Friesen, with whom he has made duo concert appearances for more than 10 years. Friesen's muscular bass complements Zeitlin well. Their splendid Concord recording is the eighth in the Maybeck Duo Series. — K.F.

JOHN ZORN

★★★ **The Classic Guide to Strategy (1985; Tzadik, 1996)**
★★★½ **Voodoo: The Music of Sonny Clark (Black Saint, 1986)**
★★★½ **The Big Gundown (Icon Nonesuch, 1986)**
★★★½ **Spillane (Elektra Nonesuch, 1987)**
★★★½ **News for Lulu (hat Art, 1988)**
★★★½ **Spy vs. Spy: The Music of Ornette Coleman (Elektra, 1988)**
★★★ **More News for Lulu (hat Art, 1989)**
★★★★½ **Cobra (hat Art, 1990)**
★★★½ **Naked City (Elektra Nonesuch, 1990)**
★★★½ **Filmworks 1986–1990 (Elektra Nonesuch, 1992)**
★★★★ **John Zorn's Cobra Live at the Knitting Factory (Knitting Factory Works, 1992)**
★★★ **First Recordings 1973 (Tzadik, 1995)**
★★★ **Nani Nani (Tzadik, 1995)**
★★★ **The Book of Hearts (Tzadik, 1995)**
★★★ **Elegy (Tzadik, 1995)**
★★★ **Kristallnacht (Tzadik, 1995)**
★★★ **Redbird (Tzadik, 1995)**
★★★ **Bar Kokhba (Tzadik, 1996)**
★★★ **Film Works, Vol. 3 (Tzadik, 1997)**

★★★ **Film Works, Vol. 7: Cynical Hysterie Hour (Tzadik, 1997)**
★★★ **New Traditions in East Asian Bar Bands (Tzadik, 1997)**
★★★ **Film Works, Vol. 4: S&M (Tzadik, 1997)**
★★★ **Duras: Duchamp (Tzadik, 1997)**

An eminence of New York City's East Village arts scene, alto saxophonist John Zorn (b. 1953) mixes heavy influences (Ornette Coleman, modern classical music) with a puckish sensibility to come up with ultrachallenging records that sound like scores to dreamlike film noir. The quintessential postmodernist, he draws from a wealth of private obsessions (things Japanese; game-playing and strategizing; Warner Bros. cartoons composer Carl Stalling) and a bewildering range of musical styles, an art of collage. Craftily reassembling motifs and ideas from mainstream and "outsider" sources, he achieves a startling originality. Often disturbing, consistently ambitious, he's a spiritual partner of sorts with Frank Zappa, in his subversive undermining of any distinction between pop and high art; he also follows in the very American tradition of radical composers like Harry Partch. What makes Zorn credible is neither coyness, crassness nor ease (some of his pieces are furiously demanding). Instead, he's managed to infuse the sensibility of classic, hip jazz with his own fresher hipness and combine the best of both underworlds.

Zorn can get gritty, indeed—but with no sacrifice of skill. On *The Big Gundown* he collects a host of downtown talents—guitarists Arto Lindsay, Robert Quine, Vernon Reid and Fred Frith, as well as a clutch of other neojazz experts—and turns them loose on smart reworkings of Ennio Morricone's spaghetti-Western oeuvre. *Spillane,* notable especially for the blinding-fast time changes Zorn favors, combines film-noir atmospherics, funk and R&B. *News for Lulu* joins him with trombonist George Lewis and guitarist Bill Frisell for an expert bop set. *Naked City* mixes Coleman and Morricone remakes and brash reworkings of the *Batman* and James Bond themes alongside Zorn originals—again, it's dense, smart, exhilarating. His tribute records to Sonny Clark and Coleman feature some of his best playing; *Filmworks 1986–1990* may be the place for the Zorn novice to begin. The live *Cobra* may be his most representative set: Nearly 90 musicians engage in perplexing, astonishing play, sometimes beautiful, often abrasive. — P.E.

ANTHOLOGIES

AMERICAN FOLK BLUES FESTIVAL

★★★★ American Folk Blues Festival: '62–'65 (Evidence, 1995)

Like photographs from a family picnic, this five-disc boxed set frames a festive gathering of well-known blues faces—T-Bone Walker, John Lee Hooker, Muddy Waters and others—in informal and surprising combinations. Also like a photo album, it's probably best that the listener is familiar with the participants and their music to fully appreciate the proceedings captured here. This ample selection comes from a vast, well-recorded archive of both studio and stage recordings made during the first four years of the American Blues Folk Festival in Hamburg and Bremen, Germany. Typically, American electric and acoustic blues artists performed backed by a shared all-star pickup band—with varied results. When it works—as on some Muddy Waters tracks, for example—another audio glimpse of a legend is, thankfully, preserved. The awesome band lineup includes such stellar musicians as Willie Dixon on bass; Memphis Slim, Otis Spann or Eddie Boyd on piano; Matt "Guitar" Murphy, Buddy Guy or Hubert Sumlin on guitar; and Jump Jackson, Fred Below or Billie Stepney on drums.

Vol. 1 (1962) shows off the best Memphis Slim, T-Bone Walker, Sonny Terry, Brownie McGhee and John Lee Hooker performances. Vols. 2 and 3 (1963) feature Memphis Slim and Willie Dixon with Muddy Waters, Sonny Boy Williamson (Rice Miller), Otis Spann, Victoria Spivey, Big Joe Williams and Lonnie Johnson. Vol. 4 (1964) captures Williamson again, along with Howlin' Wolf, Hubert Sumlin, Sunnyland Slim, Lightnin' Hopkins, Sleepy John Estes and soul/blues singer Sugar Pie DeSanto. In 1965 the festival offered its most diverse selection, represented on Vol. 5: J.B. Lenoir, Mississippi Fred McDowell, John Lee Hooker, Buddy Guy, Big Mama Thornton, Roosevelt Sykes, Dr. Ross, Big Walter Horton and Eddie Boyd. — A.K.

AN ANTHOLOGY OF BIG BAND SWING

★★★★★ An Anthology of Big Band Swing: 1930–1955 (Decca, 1993)

Check out these bandleaders: Louis Armstrong, Benny Carter, Count Basie, Jimmy and Tommy Dorsey (together and separately), Roy Eldridge, Duke Ellington, Lionel Hampton, Erskine Hawkins, Fletcher Henderson, Woody Herman, Earl Hines, Stan Kenton, Jimmie Lunceford, Glenn Miller, Don Redman, Artie Shaw, Jack Teagarden, Chick Webb. Being an anthology derived from the Decca archives, this excellent double-disc set of big-band jazz recordings couldn't possibly miss in its coverage of the swing era's hit-making period, from its beginning in 1930 to its last reigning days in the mid-'50s. Producer Orrin Keepnews also gathers some great, toe-tappin' tunes that tell a tale of the times: These popular songs (from Ellington's "Rockin' in Rhythm" to Goodman's "One O'Clock Jump") were popular because they're *good.* The carefully arranged music (each track clocks in at around three minutes) allowed for some superb players to shine on their improvised solos. In addition to the aforementioned, the compilation features such stellar musicians as Red Allen (trumpet on "Saratoga Drag" and "Down South Camp Meeting"), Coleman Hawkins (tenor sax on "House of David Blues"), Sy Oliver (trumpet on "Avalon"), Charlie Parker (alto sax on "Swingmatism"), Ben Webster (tenor sax on "I've Got You Under My Skin") and trumpeter Buck Clayton and tenor-sax man Lester Young

(both on "Panassie Stomp" and "One O'Clock Jump"). Informative liner notes (including an amazing live photo of a young Hampton leading with his vibes) complete this five-star set.
— S.D.

ARHOOLIE BLUES COLLECTIONS

★★★ **Country Negro Jam Session (1959; Arhoolie, 1993)**
★★★ **Mississippi Delta Blues, Vol. 1 (1967; Arhoolie, 1994)**
★★★½ **Mississippi Delta Blues, Vol. 2 (1967; Arhoolie, 1994)**
★★★½ **I Have to Paint My Face: Mississippi Blues—1960 (1960; Arhoolie, 1995)**
★★★½ **Mississippi Delta Blues Jam in Memphis, Vol. 1 (1981; Arhoolie, 1993)**
★★★ **Mississippi Delta Blues Jam in Memphis, Vol. 2 (1981; Arhoolie, 1993)**
★★★½ **15 Down Home Country Blues Classics (Arhoolie, 1996)**
★★★★ **15 Down Home Urban Blues Classics (Arhoolie, 1996)**

Boasting a vast catalog of acoustic and electric blues (mostly the former), Chris Strachwitz's Bay Area–based Arhoolie label has been at it for almost 40 years, recording and reissuing a library of traditional American music. In the blues idiom, that includes some of the strongest recordings by such legends as Mississippi Fred McDowell, Lightnin' Hopkins, Mance Lipscomb and Clifton Chenier. With much to be proud of, Arhoolie shares its best on these collections. The more expansive (such as the *Blues Classics* volumes) and star-driven (*Mississippi Delta Blues Jam in Memphis*) prove the more enjoyable and illuminating of the lot; the other titles get to be a bit monochromatic.

More a solid look at the second-stringers than a greatest hits of the blues, *15 Down Home Urban Blues Classics* covers the most stylistic ground, featuring vintage blues and R&B reissues from the '40s and '50s (Sonny Boy Williamson's [Rice Miller] "Pontiac Blues," Big Joe Turner's "Wine-O-Baby Boogie"), plus selections from Arhoolie's own sessions from the next 15 years: boogie-woogie specialists (Piano Red, Big Joe Duskin, Katie Webster), hard-driving electric blues (Earl Hooker, Charlie Musselwhite and the incomparable Texas slinger Bee Houston). *15 Down Home Country Blues Classics* focuses on Arhoolie's forte—guitar-based rural bluesmen—with a veritable Who's Who of the tradition during the '60s: Mississippi Fred McDowell ("Frisco Line"), Lightnin' Hopkins ("Have You Ever Loved a Woman"), Mance Lipscomb ("'Bout a Spoonful"), Bukka White ("Columbus Mississippi Blues"), R.L. Burnside ("Poor Black Mattie") and even a folk incarnation of New Orleans string maestro Snooks Eaglin ("Country Boy Down in New Orleans").

Mississippi Delta Blues Jam in Memphis is a two-volume snapshot from the summer of 1969, at the first and last Memphis Blues Festival, which drew together a staggering collection of surviving acoustic-blues masters. Bukka White, Sleepy John Estes, Fred McDowell and Furry Lewis were all recorded on location by Arhoolie, preserving the rare moment and offering a generous sampling of the best of the blues old school. *Country Negro Jam Session* is a discful of evidence that the blues—through 1962 at least—was a shared rural tradition, one that most members of many communities were expected to know and perform. No blues masters or masterpieces here (well, Robert Pete Williams does make an appearance), just very down-homey renditions of such guitar, fiddle and harmonica standards as "Smokestack Lightning," "Jelly Roll" and even gospel tunes ("Sign of the Judgement").

The remaining titles chronicle two field trips that generated a load of vintage of-the-moment Mississippi blues. There's a sad sense of a world about to vanish on the tracks of *I Have to Paint My Face,* a Strachwitz production from 1960, with such findings as former jug-band star Sam Chatmon (performing the title track and "God Don't Like Ugly"), guitarists Big Joe Williams ("Texas Blues"), K.C. Douglas ("Mercury Blues"), R.C. Smith ("Lost Love Blues") and Wade Walton (with unnamed rooster adding ambiance on "Rooster Blues," naturally), and piano man Jasper Love ("The Slop"). Culled from recordings by producer George Mitchell, both volumes of *Mississippi Delta Blues* present many of the remnants of the Southern blues scene, circa 1967–'68. *Vol. 1* offers 23 tracks from a wide variety of minor blues stars—Do-Boy Diamond, Robert Diggs, Rosa Lee Hill—plus surprises like Robert Nighthawk (with Houston Stackhouse on guitar) and fife-and-drum leader Napoleon Strickland. More tightly focused on the juke-joint professionals, *Vol. 2* compares the work of three stalwarts—

R.L. Burnside, Joe Callicott, and Houston Stackhouse—the last serving a tribute to the late great Delta bluesman Tommy Johnson with small-band versions of "Cool Water Blues" and "Canned Heat." — A.K.

ATLANTIC JAZZ

★★★★½ **Atlantic Jazz: Soul (Atlantic, 1986)**
★★★★½ **Atlantic Jazz: The Avant-Garde (Atlantic, 1986)**
★★★½ **Atlantic Jazz: New Orleans (Atlantic, 1986)**
★★★ **Atlantic Jazz: Introspection (Atlantic, 1986)**
★★★★ **Atlantic Jazz: Fusion (Atlantic, 1986)**
★★★★ **Atlantic Jazz: Kansas City (Atlantic, 1986)**
★★★½ **Atlantic Jazz: Bebop (Atlantic, 1986)**
★★½ **Great Moments in Jazz (Atlantic, 1988)**
★★★★★ **Atlantic Jazz Legends, Vol. 1 (Rhino, 1993)**
★★★★ **Atlantic Jazz: Best of the '50s (Rhino, 1993)**
★★★★★ **Atlantic Jazz: Saxophones (Rhino, 1993)**
★★★★½ **Atlantic Jazz: Saxophones, Vol. 2 (Rhino, 1994)**
★★★★ **Atlantic Jazz: Keyboards (Rhino, 1994)**
★★★½ **Atlantic Jazz: Flutes (Rhino, 1994)**
★★★★ **Atlantic Jazz Vocals: Voices of Cool, Vol. 1 (Rhino, 1994)**
★★★★½ **Atlantic Jazz Vocals: Voices of Cool, Vol. 2 (Rhino, 1994)**
★★★★★ **Atlantic Jazz: Best of the '60s, Vol. 1 (Rhino, 1994)**
★★★★½ **Atlantic Jazz: Best of the '60s, Vol. 2 (Rhino, 1994)**
★★★½ **Atlantic Jazz: Best of the '70s (Rhino, 1994)**

Compilations were originally intended simply as aural catalogs, loss leaders to help introduce and sell individual titles to consumers. But the almost three decades' worth of material in the Atlantic jazz vaults have been offered and reoffered in so many instrumental, stylistic and chronological packagings as to constitute a primer on creative marketing and extreme catalog exploitation. It's to the credit of Nesuhi Ertegun—the large-eared visionary behind the label's many jazz explorations—that ranging from New Orleans traditional to the extremes of mid-'60s avant-garde, there's enough compelling material to make each collection stand out as a solid survey of its narrow focus. Thankfully, none attempts to be complete or all-knowing—just an enjoyable, ofttimes illuminating listen.

The 1986 stylistic releases cover their respective categories adequately but offer less material and information than subsequent repackagings by Rhino. Nonetheless, *Atlantic Jazz: Soul* is the most satisfying of these, with a clear mid- to late-'60s focus, including Eddie Harris's electric-sax workout "Listen Here," Ray Charles and Milt Jackson's languid "How Long Blues," Les McCann and Eddie Harris's well-known funk rave-up "Compared to What," Nat Adderley's "Jive Samba," Johnny Griffin's gutsy tenor with organ on "Twist City" and Yusef Lateef's tenor combined with Eric Gale's bristling guitar work on "Russell and Eliot." The trad-jazz revival of the early '60s—plus two Paul Barbarin tracks from 1955—is represented by the *New Orleans* title; Dixieland mainstays of the day like clarinetist George Lewis, trumpeter Joe "De De" Pierce, trombonist Wilbur de Paris, cornetist Ernest "Punch" Miller and the Eureka Brass Band put new life into second-line standards such as "Tiger Rag" and "Shreveport Stomp." On the opposite end of the jazz spectrum, the mid-'60s foundation of all that became free and contemporary (and its architects) is well covered on *Atlantic Jazz: The Avant-Garde:* Mingus's influential "Wednesday Night Prayer Meeting," Ornette Coleman's "Lonely Woman" and the Art Ensemble of Chicago's "Nonaah" are expected numbers, while the collection is spiced with uncommon surprises in Rahsaan Roland Kirk's "Black Mystery Has Been Revealed," John Coltrane's "Countdown" and his duet with Don Cherry, "Cherryco."

The six-track, virtuoso-driven *Fusion* checks out the early-'70s scene, after Miles Davis's jazz-rock excursions had made it all right to plug in, turn up and jam tirelessly. Feature tracks include pre–Weather Report Miroslav Vitous covering "Freedom Jazz Dance" with Joe Henderson, John McLaughlin and Herbie Hancock; Les McCann and Yusef Lateef combining with an all-star New York R&B session band on "Beaux J. Pooboo"; Klaus Doldinger's acclaimed German group Passport offering its tightly arranged, melodic vision on "Homunculus"; and electric violinist Jean-Luc

Ponty screaming through "Egocentric Molecules." Concurrent to the recordings on *Fusion, Introspection* offers gentle melodies and atmospheric crescendos, peeking in at the now slightly dated spiritual-jazz wave, when names like Hubert Laws ("Yoruba"), Charles Lloyd ("Forest Flower") and Keith Jarrett ("Standing Outside") pointed the way to the golden road of an unlimited New Age audience (two notable exceptions: Joe Zawinul's own composition "In a Silent Way" with Herbie Hancock on second electric piano and Keith Jarrett's too short "Standing Outside" with Charlie Haden and Paul Motian).

Atlantic also recorded many of the names that gave the territory-band tradition its swing, blues and drive, if 20 years after its heyday. On *Kansas City,* Big Joe Turner sings in a jazzy context, reprising his pre–rock & roll material like "Until the Real Thing Comes Along" and "Piney Brown Blues," Basie horn blowers Vic Dickenson and Buck Clayton riff through "The Lamp Is Low" and "Undecided," K.C. blues godfather Jay McShann ably handles "Jumpin' at the Woodside" and rerecords his first hit, "Confessin' the Blues," and connected more by stylistic proximity, Texas bluesman T-Bone Walker joins a West Coast outfit with Plas Johnson on sax and Barney Kessel on guitar for "Evenin'."

Pulling from a limited selection of appropriate material to satisfy its theme, *Atlantic Jazz: Bebop* is more important historically, a quick seven-track presentation of various one-off meetings: Dizzy Gillespie with members of the Modern Jazz Quartet ("Our Love Is Here to Stay") and with an all-star group featuring Thelonious Monk, Sonny Stitt and others, live in Europe in 1971 ("Allen's Alley"); Coltrane and Milt Jackson ("Bebop"); Monk and Art Blakey ("Evidence"); Sonny Stitt and John Lewis ("Ko-Ko"); plus Philly Joe Jones ("Salt Peanuts") and Max Roach ("Almost Like Me").

Great Moments in Jazz tries a little too hard to cram the entire Atlantic Jazz story into two discs and ends up the most pop-oriented of these collections, stuffing mellow, R&B-flavored artists like Gerald Albright and Freddie Hubbard in with cabaret vocalists Mel Tormé and Carmen McRae, along with the more significant contributions of Jimmy Giuffre, the MJQ, John Coltrane, Charles Mingus, Rahsaan Roland Kirk, Art Blakey and Thelonious Monk.

Rhino has recently taken over the reissue helm, with sporadic help from veteran producer Joel Dorn (whose work is scattered throughout the Atlantic catalog) and with an eye to satisfying the expanded expectations of a CD audience. All material was chosen with taste, a sense of history and an affection for a worthy anecdote now and again; each offers a well-programmed listening session, with no overlap of material between titles.

Atlantic Jazz Legends, Vol. 1 is a can't-miss, greatest-hits 12-tracker with notes explaining the who, the what and the why (these tunes were historically significant). The album yields such landmarks as Coltrane's "My Favorite Things," Les McCann and Eddie Harris's "Compared to What," Rahsaan Roland Kirk's "The Inflated Tear," Ornette Coleman's "Ramblin'," Mingus's "Wednesday Night Prayer Meeting" and Yusef Lateef's "Nubian Lady," as well as bluesy hits by Ray Charles ("Sweet Sixteen Bars"), David "Fathead" Newman ("Hard Times") and Mose Allison ("Your Mind Is on Vacation").

The saxophone volumes constitute the strongest of the instrumental packages—the first with the best-known and most enduring of Atlantic's '60s reed masterpieces (Coltrane's "Giant Steps," Coleman's "Lonely Woman," Eddie Harris's "Freedom Jazz Dance," Charles Lloyd's "Forest Flower" songs). *Vol. 2* is a more catholic study, unearthing such buried gems as postbop Leo Wright's "Blues Shout," Lee Konitz's "Topsy" and Sonny Stitt's "Parker's Mood," along with Kirk's "Old Rugged Cross," and John Coltrane's "Mr. P.C."

The first volume of vocalists is a generous 20-track focus on Atlantic's penchant in the '50s for mining the pop/cabaret vein, bringing over its own R&B hit makers like Ruth Brown, Big Joe Turner and LaVern Baker to join Mabel Mercer, Sarah Vaughan, Sylvia Syms and other tuxedoed and gowned balladeers. Even jazz impresario, pianist and singer George Wein appears, with an interesting reading of "I'm Through with Love." *Atlantic Jazz Vocals: Voices of Cool, Vol. 2* is a surprisingly rocking set, embracing a slew of well-known singers in more contemporary small-group contexts, including Betty Carter, Chris Connor, Mose Allison, Jimmy Scott, Mel Tormé, the Manhattan Transfer with Bobby McFerrin ("Another Night in Tunisia") and Aretha Franklin ("Crazy He Calls Me"). Bonuses include the Las Vegas glitz of Bobby Darin ("All Nite Long") and a subtly classical interpretation of "La Cantatrice" by Diahann Carroll and the Modern Jazz Quartet. The

Keyboards collection necessarily favors the soul/blues edge of the jazz field, with Ray Charles, Thelonious Monk, Junior Mance, Les McCann (with an orchestrally lush "Doin' That Thing") and old-time bluesman Jimmy Yancey. Highlights include Lennie Tristano's Third Stream workout "C Minor Complex" and tracks by the three kings of '70s jazz keyboards: Joe Zawinul, Keith Jarrett and Chick Corea (Zawinul's unaccompanied "My One and Only Love" is an emotive eye-opener). Herbie Mann, Rahsaan Roland Kirk, Charles Lloyd and "Fathead" Newman fire the *Flutes* album—culled mostly from the funk-and-fusion scene of the late '60s and early '70s. Newman's brilliantly arranged big-band number "The Thirteenth Floor" stands out, along with Kirk's trademark "nose-flute" performances.

Not surprisingly, the decade-focused anthologies present totally mixed bags, the '50s being a satisfying hodgepodge of traditional jazz (Shorty Rogers), cabaret (Chris Connor), blues (Big Joe Turner, LaVern Baker), R&B (Ray Charles) and modern (John Coltrane, Charles Mingus, Art Blakey). The '60s volumes define the Janus-like experimental/roots vision of Atlantic, from Mose Allison's street-hip songwriting and the blues-filled saxes of David Newman and Hank Crawford to the modern jazz trinity of Coltrane, Coleman and Mingus and the uniquely inspired black-music gumbo of Rahsaan Roland Kirk. Either volume from the '60s is a pleaser (*Vol. 2* earns the extra half star for including vocals and some hard-to-find numbers like Allison's "You Can Count on Me to Do My Part"). Weak only relative to the other decades, the '70s volume still swings its rock- and fusion-influenced way through 13 tracks featuring Eddie Harris, Charles Lloyd, Jean-Luc Ponty and Billy Cobham, plus more introspective material from Gary Burton and Keith Jarrett ("Moonchild"/"In Your Quiet Place"), the Modern Jazz Quartet ("Blues in A Minor") and a great vocalese singer deserving greater review—Oscar Brown Jr. ("A Ladiesman"). — A.K.

ATLANTIC RHYTHM & BLUES

★★★★★ **Atlantic Rhythm & Blues 1947–1974 (Atlantic, 1991)**

What to say beyond that this seven-CD boxed set offers a capsule history of the evolution of modern black music styles? Vol. 1 (1947–1952) focuses on urban blues, group harmony and New Orleans jump blues; over the course of the succeeding volumes, we hear Ray Charles evolving soul out of rhythm & blues, Chuck Willis merging rock & roll and R&B, Solomon Burke and Aretha Franklin bringing the church into their secular music, the rise of Southern soul in sessions cut in Memphis and at Muscle Shoals with Franklin, Otis Redding, Percy Sledge and others, early New Orleans pop in Barbara Lewis's first recordings and, in Vol. 7 (1967–1970), the last gasp of traditional soul via the great Tyrone Davis and Clarence Carter and the first stirrings of the soft black pop that dominated the mainstream in the early '70s. In addition to the obvious hits and classic tracks contained in this set, the first three volumes in particular include songs by artists who may not be in the pantheon but whose contributions were important: the Cardinals' "Wheel of Fortune," Harry Van Walls's "Tee-Nah-Nah," Joe Morris's "The Applejack," the Ivory Joe Hunter tracks on Vol. 3 and the Cookies as well. All in all, an extraordinary history of a once-great label whose artists, even the minor ones, had a spirit and style that remain invigorating and instructive to this day. — D.M.

BEFORE THE BLUES

★★★★ **Before the Blues, Vol. 1 (Yazoo, 1996)**

★★★★ **Before the Blues, Vol. 2 (Yazoo, 1996)**

★★★★½ **Before the Blues, Vol. 3 (Yazoo, 1996)**

Differentiating between preblues modal songs and true blues can take a trained ear—basically preblues material is simpler, one or two chords played harmonically in a few bars. These three volumes explore the predecessors to the blues—spirituals, folk ballads, breakdown dances and rags—that had been performed since before the Civil War in the rural countryside by both blacks and whites. Though the 12-bar form we know as the blues had already become pervasive by the time the first recordings were made, the older styles were still being performed—and were, fortunately, immortalized on disc. Taken from 1920s and '30s 78s and remastered to remove some of the surface noise, *Before the Blues,* along with its liner notes, preserves the music for both its educational and listening value. *Vol. 1* features such poignant sacred songs as "On Jordan's Stormy Banks We Stand," "Dying Mother and Her Child" and "Christian Soldier." *Vol. 2* captures the haunting character of early rural songs like Geeshie Wiley's "Last Kind Words Blues" and Blind Willie Johnson's "It's Nobody's Fault but Mine." *Vol. 3* documents the formative styles of artists who would later play the blues, including Memphis Minnie, Blind Boy Fuller, Furry Lewis and Mississippi John Hurt. — S.D.

THE BEST OF CHESS VOCAL GROUPS

★★★★ **The Best of Chess Vocal Groups (Chess, 1988)**

Though widely known for its pioneering role as a blues and rock & roll label, Chicago's Chess Records also had a long and illustrious history recording vocal groups in the 1950s and 1960s. Some of the very best came through Phil and Leonard Chess's door during that time and left behind some wonderful sides before moving on to greater success elsewhere; some inspired one-hit wonders came through as well before disappearing altogether.

Chess didn't specialize in any single area of group-harmony vocalizing; rather, the Chess brothers made their decisions based on what they thought would sell, without regard to stylistic consistency. *The Best of Chess Vocal Groups* shows an impressive range of group-harmony approaches that serve as portents of the split that would occur in black music in the '60s, with Motown cornering the market on pop soul while Stax purveyed a tougher, more blues-based brew. These considerations aside, the set also represents one of the last, best gasps of doo-wop, which faded into obscurity as the '50s ended.

Of special interest are a couple of moments that are significant in light of what came after. The Four Tops, for example, offer a tender rendition of "I Wish You Would" (recorded in 1956 and previously unissued) that couldn't be farther from the tough, spectacular records the group recorded a decade later for Motown. Similarly, the O'Jays close the album with a 1969 cut, "One Night Affair," an early Gamble and Huff production in which the production flourishes—especially the lush, zinging strings and close-miked drums—clearly presage the disco sound the duo would trade on in the following decade. At the opposite end of the spectrum were the Ravens, the dominant vocal group of the late '40s and early '50s, whose style influenced many of the groups included. Pretty much finished and lacking any of their original personnel in 1956, the group pulled it together for one spectacular moment, "(Give Me) A Simple Prayer," on which lead tenor Joe Van Loan hits a falsetto note that must be heard to be believed.

Elsewhere amid familiar items such as Lee Andrews and the Hearts' "Long Lonely Nights," the Marathons' "Peanut Butter" and the Dells' "There Is" are some vital but lesser-known recordings. The Students justify their immortal ranking among doo-wop fanatics with the driving "Every Day of the Week," while the Sensations' "(Put Another Nickel In) Music, Music, Music" and the Gems' "Dear One" showcase two outstanding female vocalists in Yvonne Baker and Vandine Harris, respectively. The Knight Brothers offer a soaring interpretation of "Temptation 'Bout to Get Me" that brooks comparison to Billy Stewart's original tour de force. — D.M.

THE BEST OF DOO WOP

★★★★ **The Best of Doo Wop Uptempo (Rhino, 1989)**

★★★★ **The Best of Doo Wop Ballads, Vols. 1 & 2 (Rhino, 1989)**

Two splendid surveys of the tender and the boisterous sides of doo-wop show off some of the best voices in the genre's history. *The Best of Doo Wop Uptempo,* including 18 cuts, begins and ends with the best of the Dell-Vikings ("Whispering Bells" and "Come Go with Me"), which bookend a rich variety of the various styles of doo-wop extant between 1954 (represented here by the Crows' jazz-inflected "Gee") and 1963 (Randy and the Rainbows' propulsive "Denise"). Those into reprogramming CDs are likely to become orgasmic over the options here. This combination is highly recommended: the Marcels' "Blue Moon," to Dion and the Belmonts' "I Wonder Why," to Randy and the Rainbows' "Denise," to the Silhouettes' "Get a Job," to the Dell-Vikings' "Whispering Bells," to the Mystics' "Hushabye," to the Elegants' "Little Star." Wonderful. And we haven't even touched Frankie Lymon yet!

Like *Uptempo, The Best of Doo Wop Ballads, Vols. 1* and *2* is mostly familiar ground as far as the tune stack is concerned: "In the Still of the Night," "Sincerely," "Daddy's Home" and so on. Still, these songs always seem fresh, owing to sometimes transcendent, often extraordinary, always deeply felt vocalizing. Thirty years after the release of the Jive Five's "My True Story," to cite one example, Eugene Pitt's lead vocal remains a mesmerizing display of nuance and phrasing in service of lyrics that would have made O. Henry proud. Lesser-heard gems such as "Lover's Island" by the Blue Jays and "Been So Long" by the Pastels are nice touches in a package that otherwise offers a murderers' row of doo-wop's heavy hitters. — D.M.

BLACK LEGENDS OF JAZZ

★★★ Black Legends of Jazz (Decca, 1994)

Looking back into the unique history of America, one can find atrocious events alongside incredibly wonderful occurrences, and sometimes these are inextricably related: Of course I'm referring to the forced emigration of enslaved Africans to North America and the development of jazz. Compiling a set of CDs under the honorific title of *Black Legends of Jazz* is one way of clarifying the importance of the music's innovators (excluding whites or others, you will still pretty much have a complete history); unfortunately, this set is hindered in its goal by being derived from basically one record company and ending with recordings made in 1959.

Decca began operation in the United States during the Great Depression, hence the preponderance of big bands. The inclusion of some artists is pretty much by default—their best or most representative sounds should be found from other labels' archives (the most pointed example is Charlie Parker, who recorded for Decca only when he was a part of Jay McShann's orchestra and had yet to reach his legendary status). The music included is terrific, however, and it's wrapped in a beautiful package, complete with well-written, lengthy liner notes. But unfortunately, the songs appear alphabetically—rather than grouped by genre or chronologically—which does not make musical sense. — S.D.

THE BLUES

★★★★ The Blues, Vol. 1 (1963; MCA, 1986)
★★★★ The Blues, Vol. 2 (1963; MCA, 1987)
★★★★ The Blues, Vol. 3 (1964; MCA, 1988)
★★★★★ The Blues, Vol. 4 (1965; MCA, 1988)
★★★★★ The Blues, Vol. 5 (1966; MCA, 1990)
★★★★ The Blues, Vol. 6: The Fifties Rarities (MCA, 1991)

These first-rate collections of urban and country blues, boogie and seminal R&B were originally released by Chess Records in the '60s as samplers of the label's extensive blues catalog. All of the big names are present and accounted for, as are lesser-knowns whose importance shouldn't be discounted. *Vol. 5* stands out, not only for the powerful Howlin' Wolf track "How Many More Years" but also for top-flight performances by Percy Mayfield ("Double Dealing"), Willie Mabon ("Seventh Son") and Memphis Minnie, one of the great female blues singers, who's represented by the naughty "Me and My Chauffeur." There's a good sampling of blues classics here—"Spoonful" by Howlin' Wolf, Muddy Waters's "Rollin' Stone," Little Walter's "My Babe" and others—mixed in with some nice surprises (the Chuck Berry selections are not the hits but some of the blues sides he cut for albums) to make each volume a winner. *Vol. 6: The '50s Rarities,* not a part of the original series, includes alternate takes of classics as well as some of the non–hit-maker obscurities. — D.M.

BLUES CLASSICS

★★★★★ Blues Classics (MCA, 1996)

Great artists, great music, great liner notes, great deal—three discs that, through the good fortune of over 40 years of classic recordings ending up under one corporate roof, are able to tell a most complete story on the evolution and effect of the blues in America.

MCA's current holdings include a rich and influential mother lode of stuff that includes catalogs of leading early blues labels, from the '20s (Vocalion, Brunswick) through the swinging days of big bands and early R&B (Decca), to the golden age of electric blues in the '50s and '60s (Chess, Duke and ABC-Bluesway). Translated to actual artists and performances, this means a glorious listening session that runs from Furry Lewis's "Billy Lyons and Stack O'Lee" and Leroy Carr's "How Long—How Long Blues" on disc one; to Big Joe Turner's "Piney Brown Blues," Louis Jordan's "Let the Good Times Roll" and Muddy Waters's "Long Distance Call" on disc two; to soulful tracks by Buddy Guy, Otis Rush and Bobby Bland on disc three, closing with B.B. King's 1969 opus "Paying the Cost to Be the Boss"/"The Thrill Is Gone."

As a greatest-hits, bowl-you-over introduction to the idiom, one would be hard-pressed to find better. Simple but classy packaging and informative but not overly academic notes mark this as one of the best of its kind. — A.K.

BLUES MASTERS

★★★★½ Vol. 1: Urban Blues (Rhino, 1992)
★★★★½ Vol. 2: Postwar Chicago (Rhino, 1992)

★★★★½ **Vol. 3: Texas Blues (Rhino, 1992)**
★★★★½ **Vol. 4: Harmonica Classics (Rhino, 1992)**
★★★★★ **Vol. 5: Jump Blues Classics (Rhino, 1992)**
★★★★★ **Vol. 6: Blues Originals (Rhino, 1993)**
★★★★ **Vol. 7: Blues Revival (Rhino, 1993)**
★★★★★ **Vol. 8: Mississippi Delta Blues (Rhino, 1993)**
★★★½ **Vol. 9: Postmodern Blues (Rhino, 1993)**
★★★½ **Vol. 10: Blues Roots (Rhino, 1993)**
★★★★★ **Vol. 11: Classic Blues Women (Rhino, 1993)**
★★★★½ **Vol. 12: Memphis Blues (Rhino, 1993)**
★★★★½ **Vol. 13: New York City Blues (Rhino, 1993)**
★★★★ **Vol. 14: More Jump Blues (Rhino, 1993)**
★★★★½ **Vol. 15: Slide Guitar Classics (Rhino, 1993)**
★★★★ **Vol. 16: More Harmonica Classics (Rhino, 1998)**
★★★ **Vol. 17: More Postmodern Blues (Rhino, 1998)**
★★★★ **Vol. 18: More Slide Guitar Classics (Rhino, 1998)**

You used to have to pay dues if you wanted to learn the blues, but thanks to the current reissue boom, you can get away with just going to the record store. Anyone interested in an overview of the music's development should proceed to Rhino's Blues Masters series. Why? This is the first major blues overview to avoid the single-label myopia that plagues most multiartist anthologies. That means *Urban Blues,* the first volume, can include Joe Turner's sassy "Chains of Love" (an Atlantic single) as well as Joe Williams's suave "Every Day" (currently part of the Verve catalog), while *Vol. 4: Harmonica Classics* features performances by Little Walter and His Night Cats (originally on Checker), Jimmy Reed (Vee-Jay) and the Fabulous Thunderbirds (Chrysalis). Also, the series is organized by subgenre, turning each album into a single-volume history lesson. So *Vol. 2: Postwar Chicago* shows how that scene developed from the Delta-derived approach of Muddy Waters, Johnny Shines and Sonny Boy Williamson (Rice Miller) to the electrifying big-city sound of Magic Sam, Buddy Guy and Junior Wells; while *Vol. 3: Texas Blues* traces the thread that runs from Blind Lemon Jefferson's "Matchbox Blues" through T-Bone Walker's "Call It Stormy Monday" to Stevie Ray Vaughan's "Flood Down in Texas." *Vol. 5: Jump Blues Classics* unearths such protorock gems as Wynonie Harris's "Good Rockin' Tonight," Tiny Bradshaw's "The Train Kept A-Rollin'" and Big Mama Thornton's "Hound Dog."

Three volumes will have an obvious appeal to rock fans—*Vol. 6: Blues Originals,* which assembles cover-ready classics like Elmore James's "Madison Blues" and Howlin' Wolf's "Back Door Man"; *Vol. 7: Blues Revival,* which traces the post–rock & roll blues, from Jimmy Reed to Paul Butterfield and Canned Heat; and *Vol. 9: Postmodern Blues,* which focuses on latter-day players like Albert Collins, Robert Cray and Stevie Ray Vaughan. Far more enriching, though, is *Vol. 8: Mississippi Delta Blues,* which pairs well-restored recordings from the '20s and '30s by Tommy Johnson, Charley Patton and Robert Johnson with later work by Muddy Waters, Robert Nighthawk and Elmore James. And anyone interested in the evolution of American popular music will be fascinated by *Vol. 10: Blues Roots,* which draws audible parallels like Robert Pete Williams and Furry Lewis.

Considering a woman made the first blues recording—"Crazy Blues" by Mamie Smith, which kicks off *Vol. 11*—having a single disc devoted to female singers is certainly worthy. This set displays the poignant stylings in blues vocals: from Ma Rainey's deep, soulful aches on "Countin' the Blues" to Bessie Smith's wise cries on "Nobody Knows You When You're Down and Out" and Billie Holiday's aching but smooth phrases on "Stormy Blues."

The regional history lessons continue with the Memphis and New York City volumes. The blues evolution into rock & roll can be heard on the Memphis disc: from early down-home groups like the Beale Street Sheiks—which included Frank Stokes, whose role in Memphis blues is comparable to that of Charley Patton's in the Delta—to the renown of B.B. King, to protorockers Rufus Thomas and Roscoe Gordon, who had R&B hits for the Memphis-based record companies Sun and Duke, respectively. The Big Apple's ballrooms called for the big bands to rock the blues: this disc shows how swing went from the boogie-woogie of Lionel Hampton to the dance beat of Alan Freed's Rock 'n Roll Band. Who continues the call for good times in *More Jump Blues*? Floyd Dixon on "Hey Bartender," Joe Liggins on

"Pink Champagne," Piano Red on "Jump Man Jump." Along with the harmonica, slide guitar's distinct sound is closely associated with that of the blues—and both benefited from amplification. *Vols. 15, 16* and *18* express the raw emotion in the wild, untamed tones of the blues turned way up. The first slide-guitar disc truly has the classics: From Elmore James's "Dust My Broom" to the Allman Brothers Band's cover of "Statesboro Blues." *Vol. 18* has the surprises: Eddie Jones, recorded on skid row in L.A., wails on one string (a wire streched over a pill-bottle bridge on a two-by-four amplified by a paint can) while rocker Chuck Berry slides on a pedal steel for "Blues for Hawaiians." *Vol. 17: More Postmodern Blues* stretches a little too far the "essential" character of the Blues Masters series. — J.D.C./S.D.

CHICAGO BLUES FROM THE '50S

★★★★ **Chicago Boss Guitars (Paula, 1991)**
★★★½ **Chicago Piano 1951–1958 from Cobra & JOB (Paula, 1991)**
★★★ **Chicago Blues Harmonicas (Paula, 1991)**

As the only domestic release to cull the best guitar blues from the short-lived (1956–58) Chicago independent Cobra Records, *Chicago Boss Guitars* is almost the only way to find the most enduring, influential and heart-stopping tracks by legendary stringbenders Otis Rush, Buddy Guy and Magic Sam (Capricorn's *Cobra Records Story* boxed set is the alternative). It won't win any awards for creative repackaging —one grainy photo of Magic Sam and session details are all that accompanies this disc—but with 20 tracks that include "I Can't Quit You Baby," "Double Trouble," "All Your Love" and "Easy Baby," one cannot find a better one-disc representation of Chicago's intense and urgent late-'50s West Side soul sound.

Another indie from the Windy City kicking it in the '50s was the JOB label. *Chicago Piano 1951–1958* presents the best ivory men of their generation, recorded by both JOB and Cobra and featuring legendary figures like Sunnyland Slim ("Highway 61," "'Fore Day Bounce"), Eddie Boyd (the classic "Five Long Years," "Hard Headed Woman"), Memphis Slim, Little Brother Montgomery and Lafayette Leake. There's much cross-pollination among the backup bands and material, but along with the odd piano-focused tracks on Chess Records anthologies, this CD is valuable proof of the rich legacy left behind by the pianists who were playing at the same time as, or behind, the better-known Muddys, Wolfs and Sonny Boys of the scene.

Chicago Blues Harmonicas volume also draws from the JOB and Cobra vaults, including a few known names (Snooky Pryor, Big Walter Horton) and lesser-knowns (John Lee Henley, Little Willie Foster). Louie Myers, leader of Little Walter's erstwhile backup group in the '50s, evokes his boss on "Bluesy." Sonny Boy Williamson's (Rice Miller) "Steady Rollin' Man" conjures Robert Johnson's spirit in a sparse, harmonica-and-bass fashion, while the best of the remaining tracks are those boasting excellent accompaniment—Big Walter's "Have a Good Time" features Otis Rush *and* Wayne Bennet on guitars, plus Willie Dixon on bass—on sensational compositions like Charles Clark's "Row Your Boat" (produced by Dixon). Next to Little Walter and Sonny Boy collections, this set rates as a solid intro to the '50s blues harp scene, Chicago style. — A.K.

COBRA RECORDS

★★★★★ **The Cobra Records Story (Capricorn, 1993)**

As tight as Chess Records' hold was on Chicago's black-music scene of the '50s and '60s, a number of independents managed to make their mark, profiting from the talents of those neglected and/or disappointed by the South Side blues giant. One of the most compelling was the short-lived Cobra, best known as the label that caught such second-generation stringbenders as Otis Rush, Magic Sam and Buddy Guy in their hard-hitting, creative prime and is now overviewed by Capricorn in a well-annotated and -packaged two-disc boxed set. Cobra had been the child of record-shop owner Eli Toscano, who would later gamble it away, but its music has endured and reached an incredibly international audience. With its signature West Side sound, Cobra provided the high-water mark by which a generation of British bluesmen (from John Mayall and Eric Clapton to Led Zeppelin and Peter Green's Fleetwood Mac) were first measured.

Chess's loss became Cobra's gain: Producer, composer and bassist Willie Dixon provided the creative spark and A&R direction for the party. Recruiting an all-star stable of blues session men from Chicago (Lafayette Leake, Odie Payne, Harold Burrage, Shakey Horton) and elsewhere (Ike Turner, Wayne Bennett) to record in the abandoned garage that was Cobra's studio, Dixon managed to write and/or capture some of the deepest and most urgent slices of blues of the era: Otis Rush's "I Can't Quit You Baby," Buddy Guy's "Sit and Cry (The Blues)," Magic Sam's "Easy Baby" and his rock & roller "21 Days in Jail," Shakey Horton's "Have a Good Time" and Betty Everett's "My Love." Cobra also released a variety of blues by its session men and other minor-league stars—Harold Burrage, Louis Myers and the Aces (Little Walter's backup band) and Ike Turner's Kings of Rhythm—and attempted to crack the doo-wop and rock & roll market with the Clouds' "Rock and Roll Boogie." Unbelievably, *The Cobra Records Story* marks the first time that these tracks have been made available domestically through a national major distributor. — A.K.

COLUMBIA JAZZ MASTERPIECES

★★½ **Jazz Sampler, Vol. 1 (Columbia/Legacy, 1987)**
★★½ **Jazz Sampler, Vol. 2 (Columbia/Legacy, 1987)**
★★★ **The 1930s—Big Bands (Columbia/Legacy, 1987)**
★★★ **The 1930s—The Singers (Columbia/Legacy, 1987)**
★★★★ **The 1930s—The Small Combos (Columbia/Legacy, 1987)**
★★★ **The 1940s—The Singers (Columbia/Legacy, 1987)**

Sony Music's vaults contain many of the most important recordings in jazz history, made for the Columbia, Vocalion, Okeh and Brunswick labels. The Columbia Jazz Masterpieces reissue program has done an admirable job releasing single-artist anthologies and essential albums (listed in this book under the artists' entries); unfortunately, the samplers and various-artist compilations are not very useful. Granted, the artists and song selections are all excellent, but the sets don't work as meaningful or cohesive groupings of material. Trumpeter Roy Eldridge, tenor saxophonist Chu Berry, trumpeter Cootie Williams and clarinetist/soprano saxophonist Sidney Bechet were always best known as players in others' orchestras; on *The 1930s—The Small Combos* they can be heard fronting their own groups, making this disc stand well on its own. The two samplers touch on music from the postswing eras in seemingly random order, without giving information about the tracks and which musicians appear on them: For example, Miles Davis's "Saeta" runs before Louis Armstrong's "Beale Street Blues," and you have to be knowledgeable enough to recognize John Coltrane's tenor-sax sound to know that's Trane playing on the Miles Davis Quintet's "Bye Bye Blackbird." The 1930s and '40s discs are limited in light of what's available in the label archives—what about bop in the '50s? Cool in the '60s? Fusion in the '70s? Columbia could have put together something to live up to the series name. These six discs just skim the surface rather than serve as an in-depth introduction for jazz neophytes or as a rarities set for jazz buffs. — S.D.

THE COMMODORE STORY

★★★★ **The Commodore Story (GRP, 1997)**

Historically significant as one of the first genre-focused companies originating as a true label of love, Commodore Records grew out of the legendary record store on New York's East 42nd Street that was as much a hangout for jazz's first generation of cognoscenti as it was a home for the musicians themselves. Commodore founder and jazz zealot Milt Gabler (whom Louis Armstrong later dubbed "Angel Gabler"), the son of a hardware retailer, took his jazz passion and created a label that released the odds and ends of jazz's commercial, "hot" heyday: studio outtakes, jam sessions, archival performances and other recordings deemed unissuable by the majors of the day.

An avidly annotated and enjoyably programmed two-disc set, *The Commodore Story* collects the best releases from the small label's 16-year history, beginning in 1938, including standout performances like the original take of Billie Holiday's premier protest song ("Strange Fruit"), Lester Young and the original Kansas City Six showing off their little big-band best ("Way Down Yonder in New Orleans"), Don Byas and Slam Stewart caught live ("Indiana"), even Jelly Roll Morton's intimate solo remembrances of New Orleans ("Mamie's Blues").

These were not all surplus tracks from other producers—Gabler was himself responsible for engineering some of the most memorable encounters of his day. In fact, the bulk of the gems on this collection owe much to his ability to play master chef, hand-picking and mixing the best soloists of the day and concocting incredibly tasteful moments. Almost half of the 40-track set is devoted to these one-of-a-kind meetings, including such rarities as Fats Waller with Eddie Condon ("[You're Some] Pretty Doll"), Benny Carter with Coleman Hawkins ("Smack"), Roy Eldridge with Chu Berry ("Body and Soul") and Art Tatum with Coleman Hawkins ("My Ideal").

The second disc further highlights Commodore's devotion to the solo stars of the Dixieland-to-swing transition and is arranged instrumentally: from trumpets (Hot Lips Page, Muggsy Spanier and Sidney De Paris) and trombones (Jack Teagarden, George Brunies and Miff Mole) to reeds (Pee Wee Russell, Bud Freeman and Chu Berry) and piano (Art Hodes, Albert Ammons, Willie "the Lion" Smith and Gabler's own favorite, Jess Stacy).

Sadly, Commodore never grew to any major commercial consequence—Gabler himself was later hired as an A&R man by Decca, where he became Louis Armstrong's longtime producer as well as making the influential R&B classics of Louis Jordan—but became another too-brief tribute to jazz's ongoing struggle of quality over quantity. — A.K.

DELTA BLUES

★★★★★ **The Roots of Robert Johnson (Yazoo, 1990)**

★★★★★ **Masters of the Delta Blues: The Friends of Charlie Patton (Yazoo, 1991)**

Robert Johnson did not create his incendiary style in a vacuum: Just as he influenced countless bluesmen, he was inspired by the Delta's Charley Patton and Son House. These two discs show how Patton and his contemporaries and/or students helped form the language of the blues that informed Johnson's style. Son House, the most direct connection between Patton and Johnson, appears on both discs with his "Preachin' the Blues." The song was recorded in a 1930 session organized by Patton (available from the sole existing 78). Johnson, who became a disciple of House shortly thereafter, soon incorporated the song into his repertoire (and recorded it in '36 as "Preachin' Blues"), making it his own. The liner notes for both discs give a thorough technical analysis of each song, clarifying the significance of such artists as barrelhouse pianist Louise Johnson (she reportedly had affairs with both Patton and House), Willie Brown (a student and early accompanist of Patton's who later also became lifelong friends with House), Lonnie Johnson (whose descending diminished chords Johnson copied) and Scrapper Blackwell (in whose guitar solos Johnson undoubtedly found inspiration). — S.D.

EVERY WOMAN'S BLUES

★★★½ **Every Woman's Blues: The Best of the New Generation (Shanachie, 1998)**

Women have been singing (and playing) the blues since its earliest recordings; in fact, Mamie Smith cut the very first blues record, "Crazy Blues," in 1920. In the '60s a handful of young white women (from Janis Joplin to Bonnie Raitt) began contributing to the genre. This anthology presents a mix of contemporary female blues voices, which carry on the legacy of their black and white sisters. These '90s women hail from all over the map, write original material and frequently play lead guitar. Sounds range from the blues-rock workout of Deanna Bogart's "Checks and Love Letters" to Alicia's solo-acoustic Delta blues–fueled "Love Me Like a Guitar." More standouts include excellent slide guitarist Rory Block's instrumental "Gone Woman Blues," the soulful Lady Bianca's "Ooh, His Love Is So Good" and Lucinda Williams's spine-tingling version of "Going Back Home" (backed by Taj Mahal on harmonica). All 14 tracks whet the appetite for more by each artist represented here. — H.G.-W.

EXCELLO RECORDS

★★★★★ **Excello Records, Vol. 1: Sound of the Swamp (Rhino, 1990)**

★★★★½ **Excello Records, Vol. 2: Southern Rhythm & Rock (Rhino, 1990)**

Take languid, slow-drag rhythm; spice with Afro-Cuban percussion, lonesome harmonica wails, New Orleans–style boogie piano; add blues lyrics sung in a slow, Southern drawl; simmer these elements in a sweltering, reverb-heavy stew, and what's yielded is Excello's instantly recognizable "swamp sound." As a measure of the wide and enduring influence of this unique musical recipe, try to imagine a world without Elvis Presley's "Baby, Let's Play House," the Rolling Stones' "Shake Your Hips" or "Sweet Black Angel" and the majority of music recorded by Creedence Clearwater Revival and the Fabulous Thunderbirds. Featuring a talent roster that included blues and R&B legends like Slim Harpo, Lightnin' Slim, Guitar Gable and Jerry McCain, the Nashville-based Excello so faithfully captured and distributed the music of West Louisiana/East Texas that it was claimed one could discern the crickets, frogs and mosquitoes behind the Crowley, Louisiana, studio in which most of these tracks were produced by the late Jay Miller.

Local fauna notwithstanding, these two discs make a perfect set, providing an excellent introduction to the twin facets of the fine, regional music that spun on Excello's distinctive bright-orange-and-blue label from the late '50s to mid-'60s. *Sound of the Swamp* covers Excello's blues side with all heavy hitters present—Slim Harpo ("Baby Scratch My Back," "Rainin' in My Heart"), Lightnin' Slim ("Rooster Blues," "Bad Luck Blues"), Guitar Gable ("This Should Go on Forever," "Congo Mombo"), Lazy Lester ("I Hear You Knockin'") and Lonesome Sundown ("My Home Is a Prison"). Also featured are juke-joint rockers like Joe Hudson and His Rockin' Dukes and dyed-in-the-wool rockabilly stars like Johnny Jano. *Southern Rhythm & Rock* tracks Excello's more "swamp-pop" experiments, including doo-woppers the Gladiolas ("Little Darlin'," which became a Top 10 hit for the Diamonds in 1957) and the Marigolds ("Rollin' Stone"); R&B shouters Rudy Green ("My Mumblin' Baby"), Lillian Offitt ("Miss You So") and Arthur Gunter ("Baby, Let's Play House"); Cajun crooners the Crescendos ("Oh, Julie"); and early rock & roll outfits Jerry McCain and His Upstarts ("My Next Door Neighbor") and the Blues Rockers ("Calling All Cows"). — A.K.

FATHER AND SONS

★★★★★ Father and Sons: Gospel Quartet Classics (Spirit Feel, 1990)

For anyone curious about gospel music's influence on R&B, doo-wop, soul and rock & roll singing styles, *Father and Sons* stands as an essential primer. The set features eight towering performances by the original Soul Stirrers, as headed by R.H. Harris, an innovator and stylist virtually without peer in American music. Also included are performances by the Five Blind Boys of Mississippi, with their redoubtable lead singer Archie Brownlee, a disciple of the Harris style, and the Sensational Nightingales, whose Julius Cheeks delivered his messages in a raucous baritone that influenced the macho school of soul epitomized by Wilson Pickett, Levi Stubbs and, certainly, James Brown. Cheeks, who joined the Soul Stirrers in one of their post-Harris incarnations, also had a hand in pushing Sam Cooke, one of Harris's luminous successors, to add a harder edge to his sweet vocalizing. If Harris is widely regarded as the most important male singer in gospel history, Brownlee and Cheeks are close behind. Harris is credited with creating the gospel-quartet tradition. In doing so he laid the groundwork for the earliest forms of rock & roll. To gospel he introduced the techniques of ad-libbing, chanting background repetition, singing in delayed time; his voice was light and clear and charged with emotion on every lyric, and he could swoop up into a falsetto that was a chilling exhortation to a higher power. Recorded between 1939 and 1948, the eight tracks amply demonstrate Harris's singular approach. The force of the Soul Stirrers' testimony is an overwhelming emotional experience that almost renders analysis moot. Music so perfect and so honestly felt begs to be left alone to work its magic on your heart.

Brownlee had a lustier voice than Harris, and his version of the Harris falsetto had the effect of a rather frightening series of shrieks, at once terrifying and beautiful expressions of the spirit moving. The 1952 track "Will Jesus Be Waiting," one of the Blind Boys' most explosive performances, is a potent example of Brownlee's intricate interaction with his fellow singers. The Sensational Nightingales were the vehicle for Julius Cheeks's forceful leads, which were often buttressed by spot-perfect baritone counterpoint courtesy of Paul Owens. *Father and Sons* features Cheeks and Owens on only one cut, "Vacant Room in Glory," and a later configuration of the Nightingales minus Owens on three other cuts. The latter group is heard on the album's most relentless report, the yearning "Somewhere to Lay My Head." When this CD is over, everything is over. Turn out the lights, lie there in silence and try to grasp what you've heard. — D.M.

FIRE AND FURY RECORDS

★★★★ The Fire/Fury Records Story (Capricorn, 1993)

By the early '60s, almost every major city could boast a black-owned R&B record label that recorded its own local artists, exporting that local sound to a national and often international audience. But New Yorker Bobby Robinson—yet another record-store owner turned label chief—proved the exception when his Fire and Fury labels started pumping out a respectable number of blues and R&B hits from his storefront location near Harlem's Apollo Theatre. Following an "if-it-sounds-like-nothing-else" release philosophy, Robinson almost exclusively depended on music imported from other locations for his hit output, be it New Orleans R&B (Lee Dorsey's "Ya Ya," Bobby Marchan's "There Is Something on Your Mind"), North Carolina blues (Wilbert Harrison's "Kansas City," Buster Brown's "Fanny Mae"), Atlanta vocal groups (Gladys Knight and the Pips' "Every Beat of My Heart") or Texas country blues or gutsy tenor sax (Lightnin' Hopkins's "Mojo Hand" and King Curtis's "Soul Twist," respectively). The fact that the label could claim no identifiable "sound" yet managed to leave its mark, taking even a straight-ahead blues artist like Elmore James onto the soul-filled charts of the mid-'60s (with "It Hurts Me Too") is a compliment to Robinson's promotional abilities and the label's influence.

The 51-track, double-disc box *Fire/Fury Records Story* is another well-researched, well-designed and loving tribute to one of R&B's most interesting independents, covering all the songs mentioned and many other gems from the vaults. Welcome rediscoveries include gritty blues rocker Tarheel Slim ("Number Nine Train"), Chicago guitar hero Mighty Joe Young ("Why Baby"), Little Richard's New Orleans crazed house band, the Upsetters ("Jaywalking") and Louisiana harmonica great Sam Myers ("You Don't Have to Go"), who later teamed up with Texas guitarist Anson Funderburgh. When Fire and Fury did turn attention to the New York R&B scene, a few local obscure denizens popped up—Noble "Thin Man" Watts caught the organ-and-tenor wave of 1960 with "Jookin"; the Latin-tinged R&B group sound was the Jay Cees specialty on "Just Say the Word"; a jive-talkin' Dr. Horse provided a lesson in early rap with "Jack, That Cat Was Clean"; and guitarist Jimmy Spruill's unique, distorted buzz-saw sound was the driving wheel on Harrison's "Kansas City" and his own instrumental, "Cut and Dried." — A.K.

GIANTS OF THE TENOR SAX

★★★★ Giants of the Blues Tenor Sax/Giants of the Funk Tenor Sax (1981; Prestige, 1990)

Disguised as a study of jazz's most typical lead instrument, this sleeper of a collection is actually more a celebration of the guts, grit and postbop swing that swept through small jazz bands from the late '50s through the early '70s. Underneath a pedestrian cover and title, a plentiful portion of lengthy riff-based jams and free-blowing sessions is hidden in this three-disc anthology, comparing and contrasting two popular schools within the postbop jazz world: the blues and funk. As the jazz world reembraced its blues roots in the early '60s, as the organ integrated itself into the jazz front line by reflecting the gospel and soul sonorities of the day, so the more R&B-driven horn blowers like Hal Singer and King Curtis found equal footing and respect with jazz legends like Coleman Hawkins, Gene Ammons and Sonny Stitt (all included herein).

Earning *Giants of the Blues Tenor Sax/Giants of the Funk Tenor Sax* its stars are standout blues sides like the understated Coleman Hawkins and Kenny Burrell matchup "Soul Blues," the distilled big-band charts of Buddy Tate's "No Kiddin'" and Jimmy Forrest's mood masterpiece "Bolo Blues." The funk side bristles with Stanley Turrentine's "Walkin'" (with the double-barreled guitars of Eric Gale and Lloyd Davis), the tenor matchup of Johnny Griffin and Edwin Williams on the uplifting, orchestrated gospel standard "Wade in the Water" and the tenor/organ duo of Rusty Bryant and Charles Earland on the satisfying, 11-minutes-plus of "Soul Liberation."

This package is one of the most enjoyable representations of the timeless music in the impressively large Fantasy catalog, including tracks from Prestige, Riverside, Milestone and Pablo Records. — A.K.

THE GOSPEL SOUND

★★★★★ The Gospel Sound (Columbia/Legacy, 1994)

Other than the blues, no other musical style so completely (and subtly) pervades the sound of America—rock, pop, commercial, alternative, whatever—as that of black gospel. It's a feel thing—evident not in structure, lyrics or actual songs but manifest in sanctified rhythms and ascendant arrangements, in close-knit harmonies and unbridled solo singing, even in deep moans and plaintive hums. Yet because of gospel's strict, self-imposed isolation from the brighter spotlight of the commercial arena, it probably remains the least-annotated and most-underappreciated chapter in the story of modern American music.

This two-disc set provides the most complete and illuminating road map to the gospel highway on retail shelves today, tracing all stops along the evolution of the music. A four-decade period is covered, from roadside, guitar-playing preachers or piano-pounding revivalists (Blind Willie Johnson, Arizona Dranes) to fire-and-brimstone preaching (Rev. J.M. Gates), from unschooled, dirt-floor church singers (Mitchell's Christian Singers) to smooth, jazz-influenced gospel quartets (the Golden Gate Jubilee Quartet), the solo stars of gospel's golden age in the '50s (Mahalia Jackson), Harlem choirs (Abyssinian Baptist Gospel Choir conducted by Alex Bradford) and the soulful pop hymnal of R&B-influenced vocal groups (the Staple Singers and the Dixie Hummingbirds).

The Gospel Sound does not pretend to be a greatest-hits package; Sam Cooke, Aretha Franklin and James Cleveland are not to be heard here. Instead, it offers the sound and story of gospel through 28 artfully chosen tracks, documenting the best gospel moments in Columbia Records' library. Credit is due to Tony Heilbut, the producer and researcher behind this project and a walking encyclopedia of gospel music. With back-of-the-hand familiarity and longtime devotion to the subject—and with the support of legendary Columbia producer John Hammond—he combed through the label's archives in the late '60s and fashioned this enduring collection. Twenty-odd years later, with no necessary changes or enhancement, the CD version of this package is a testament to its lasting importance and its uplifting and ear-opening effect. — A.K.

THE GOSPEL SOUND OF SPIRIT FEEL

★★★★★ **The Gospel Sound of Spirit Feel (Spirit Feel, 1991)**

Anyone feeling 'buked and scorned is advised to partake of a full-bore immersion in *The Gospel Sound of Spirit Feel,* a 27-cut, 90-minutes-plus journey to spiritual redemption through song. Twenty-two of the tracks are from gospel's golden era of 1946 through 1960 and afford listeners an overview of a time of tremendous stylistic innovation, when artists such as R.H. Harris, the Soul Stirrers' magnificent lead singer; Archie Brownlee (a Harris acolyte) of the Five Blind Boys of Mississippi; Sister Rosetta Tharpe and others altered gospel's course and, in the process, laid the foundation for doo-wop, R&B, soul and rock & roll. Even the pop sound of early girl groups such as the Chantels has its roots in the sassy harmonies of the Gospel All Stars backing Professor Charles Taylor on the 1956 track "New Born Soul."

While the thread of history is woven deeply into the fabric of this album—Clara Ward begat Aretha Franklin; Julius Cheeks begat Wilson Pickett; R.H. Harris begat Sam Cooke—the sheer power of the testifying herein overwhelms all other virtues. Certainly there is nothing in contemporary music to prepare one for the way Cheeks scorches "Sinner Man" with a fierceness and conviction that bespeak terrifying knowledge of the wages of sin. At the opposite end of the spectrum, Harris's gentle ebullience at the beginning of the Soul Stirrers' "Canaan" gives way to a frenetic ad-libbing style (which would later become standard procedure for gospel quartets) that culminates in an overpowering display of joyous anticipation in the repeated chanting of "I'm worthy," as six voices soar heavenward. Elsewhere, Mahalia Jackson and Marion Williams are given two cuts each that they turn into mesmerizing statements, the former being all classic, stately grandeur, the latter all sanctified, blues-tinged testimony to the power of faith.

The secular world creeps into the act in sly ways, too. With "99½" the album opens on a swinging note more common to R&B than to gospel at the time; it also pits Katie Bell's languid singing style against the younger Sister Rosetta Tharpe's highly rhythmic approach to a lyric (a harbinger of change in the gospel world when it was recorded in 1949); a 1953 track, "No Room at the Hotel," finds Sister Jesse Mae Renfro employing her most penetrating blues-gospel voice to inveigh against prejudice and management while adopting a pro-labor stance on the eve of the civil rights movement.

Such examples abound—someone influenced someone else; someone anticipated a trend, indeed a movement, well ahead of its time. Ultimately, though, this music isn't so much about history as it is about the often conflicting emotions we seek to control even as they control us. To anyone willing to embrace its bolstering spirit, *The Gospel Sound of Spirit Feel* reaches across the years to provide meaning, to provide solace, perhaps even to provide answers where once there were none. — D.M.

HOUSE OF BLUES

★★★½ **Essential Blues (House of Blues, 1995)**

★★★★ **Essential Blues, Vol. 2 (House of Blues, 1996)**

★★★★½ **Essential Women in Blues (House of Blues, 1997)**

★★★ **Livin' in the House of Blues: Smokey Blues (House of Blues, 1997)**

★★½ **Livin' in the House of Blues: Roadhouse Blues (House of Blues, 1997)**

As the House of Blues empire grows—nightclubs, radio show, Web sites—so does its presence in music retail (in CD stores and, of course, right next to the cash registers in its clubs, too). Its ability to leverage together some finely picked, cross-label blues collections shows off its marketing muscle and its ability to secure participation from various labels—but, most important to us, its good taste. On all titles, the producers picked well from a wide, mostly modern blues spectrum. As introductory vehicles to blues of the rough, roadhouse variety—a natural choice for a business promoting the live aspect of the music—the volumes kick and do not miss many of the big names.

Elmore James's "Dust My Broom," Howlin' Wolf's "Killing Floor" and Albert King's "I'll Play the Blues for You" are 3 of the 30 blues classics present on the not-perfect overview of postwar blues (Where's Muddy? Where's T-Bone?) on the double-disc *Essential Blues* package, complete with a well-written and graphically hip 60-page booklet, spoken commentary on each artist courtesy of Stanley Bennet Clay and an entertainingly programmed choice of tunes. *Vol. 2* dives deeper and wider—including Muddy Waters this time, as well as the more guitar-oriented (Buddy Guy, Magic Sam), soul-infused (Z.Z. Hill, James Brown, Robert Cray) and folky (Clifton Chenier) edges of the blues arena. Again, strong material was chosen, with finely annotated explanations in the booklet.

Including the requisitely large blues "mamas" —Big Mama Thornton, Big Maybelle, Big Time Sarah—*Essential Women in Blues* is the most ambitious of the House of Blues bunch, reaching further historically (prewar "classic" blues singers like Memphis Minnie, Ida Cox, Bessie Smith and Ma Rainey are featured) and stylistically (ditto with jazz vocalists Nina Simone, Hadda Brooks and Lil Green). Many inheritors of the tradition—Katie Webster, Marcia Ball, Rory Block—are included, too, tying together a neat two-disc study of the female perspective.

Both *Smokey Blues* and *Roadhouse Blues* begin to lose focus as the packaging process becomes redundant, with repeat names from previous House of Blues collections and a less exciting, more random approach to selections and style. — A.K.

JAZZ GUITAR CLASSICS

★★★½ **Guitar Player Presents Jazz Guitar Classics (Original Jazz Classics, 1990)**

Taken from sessions recorded between 1953 and 1974 for the Fantasy labels—Prestige, Pablo, Milestone, Contemporary and Riverside—this mostly monochromatic collection clearly favors the studied postbop, mellow stylings of the Tal Farlow/Kenny Burrell/Jim Hall school. The party does threaten to get a little out of hand with echoes of the "hot" scene from Eddie Duran ("Why Not?"), while the jump and R&B world is implied by tracks from Tiny Grimes ("Tiny Bean," with Coleman Hawkins) and Billy Butler (of the legendary "Honky Tonk" guitar solo, here heard playing the rare bass guitar on "The Thumb"). Wes Montgomery provides a slightly dispassionate "Bock to Bock" with the quartet he shared with his brothers Monk and Buddy. Fittingly, proper credit is given to the jazzman who first secured a bandstand seat for the amplified guitar: Barney Kessel offers a polite "Salute to Charlie Christian," while Joe Pass and Herb Ellis chase each other around one of Christian's signature pieces—the standout album closer, "Seven Come Eleven." — A.K.

JEWEL RECORDS

★★★ **Super Soul Blues, Vol. 1 (Jewel, 1991)**

★★★ **Super Soul Blues, Vol. 2 (Jewel, 1991)**

★★½ **Super Soul Blues, Vol. 3 (Jewel, 1991)**

★★★½ **Jewel Spotlights the Blues, Vol. 1 (Jewel, 1994)**

★★★½ **Jewel Spotlights the Blues, Vol. 2 (Jewel, 1994)**

A list including the likes of John Lee Hooker, Little Johnny Taylor, T-Bone Walker and Aaron Neville typifies the mixed bag of Southern-fried blues and soul artists that make up these collections. All are solid listening sessions, with an emphasis on the better-known tracks from the Jewel and Paula catalogs and a few unusual covers of better-known songs like "That's How Strong My Love Is" (Tommy Young), "Bad, Bad Whiskey" (Peppermint Harris) and "Never Been to Spain" (Tina Turner). Ultimately, bypassing *Super Soul Blues, Vols. 1–3* in favor of Capricorn Records' *Jewel/Paula Story* boxed set would offer the best two-disc representation of the label's best soul and blues tracks.

The two volumes of *Jewel Spotlights the Blues* head in a more straight-ahead blues direction, overlapping little with the *Super Soul Blues* series and adding spice to the stew with stellar tracks from the Cobra and JOB vaults (Otis Rush, Buddy Guy). There are the expected hits—Elmore James's "Dust My Broom," Buster Benton's "Spider in My Stew," the Carter Brothers's "Southern Country Boy," Little Joe Blue's "Standing on the Threshold" —plus a few surprises like latter-day Willie Dixon tracks (with a very young Kenny Wayne Shepherd on guitar), a talking blues from Lightnin' Hopkins ("Mr. Charlie") and a stinging slide instrumental from Earl Hooker ("Blue Guitar"). — A.K.

JEWEL AND PAULA RECORDS

★★★★ The Jewel/Paula Records Story (Capricorn, 1993)

Continuing its label-by-label survey of American blues and R&B independents, Capricorn's two-disc study of the north Louisiana–based Jewel/Paula record company is actually a tribute to a family-owned work-in-progress. Founded in 1963 by Stan Lewis, one more record-store owner turned impresario, Jewel/Paula bucked the trend of other major blues labels that had turned their attention to soul and R&B in the early '60s and remained committed to the blues. Not surprisingly, the first half of the collection serves a hearty sampling of music by blues legends like Lightnin' Hopkins, Memphis Slim, Roosevelt Sykes, Lowell Fulson, Charles Brown and John Lee Hooker. Nonetheless, soul—of a decidedly raw, Southern flavor—would become the mainstay of the Jewel/Paula catalog in the '70s, and would remain so through 1989, the date of the most recent song on this collection.

In addition to the above-mentioned luminaries, *The Jewel/Paula Records Story* also includes such one-hit blues wonders as the Carter Brothers, whose rough, roadhouse songs "Southern Country Boy" and "Booze in the Bottle" sound like New York's Holmes Brothers gone way country, and Little Joe Blue, whose smooth brand of the blues brings to mind Fenton Robinson and Larry Davis and whose "Standing on the Threshold" hit in 1969. Maintaining the same blues thread in feel and production, the second disc celebrates Jewel/Paula's Southern soul singers. Little Johnny Taylor leads the pack with his regional hits "Everybody Knows About My Good Thing" and "Open House at My House" (a later hit for Z.Z. Hill), along with singer/songwriter Bobby Patterson ("How Do You Spell Love," later covered by the Fabulous Thunderbirds, and "Right On Jody"). Other noteworthy regional jukebox stars included in this anthology are Buster Benton (whose 1979 hit "Spider in My Stew" was produced by Willie Dixon), Toussaint McCall ("Nothing Takes the Place of You" was an R&B chart topper in 1967), the down-home, suggestive funk of Bobby Rush ("Bowlegged Woman/Knock-Kneed Man") and the equally salty blues of Cicero Blake ("Dip My Dipper"). — A.K.

THE LEGENDARY BIG BAND SINGERS

★★★★½ The Legendary Big Band Singers: The Original Decca Recordings (Decca, 1994)

"Some folks say that swing won't stay/And it's dying out/But I can prove it's in the groove/And they don't know what they're talking about." This line June Richmond sings from "Wham! (Wham-Rebop-Boom-Bam)" could easily be the slogan for the swing revival of the late '90s. Although today's craze is more one-dimensionally focused on the big band's swinging dance appeal, it shouldn't be forgotten that in the big-band heyday of the '30s and '40s audiences not only dug the dancing, they clamored for the singers. This release gathers some of the biggest and most distinctive vocalists (and, in some cases, bandleaders) of the era: Cab Calloway, Louis Armstrong, Ella Fitzgerald, Dinah Washington, Jack Teagarden, Lionel Hampton. The songs range from the jaunty "Vol Vist Du Gaily Star"—where the onomatopoetic stylings of a singer billed as "Bon Bon" play well with the horns—to the sweet, clear pop of Fitzgerald's "When My Sugar Walks Down the Street." Don't be fooled by "I Wish I Knew"—knowing the effeminate voice belongs to Little Jimmy Scott somehow adds a dimension that shouldn't be missed (though it may have been missed often enough with the song's 1950 radio listeners). — S.D.

LEGENDS OF GUITAR

★★★★ Guitar Player Presents Legends of Guitar: Electric Blues, Vol. 1 (Rhino, 1990)

★★★★½ Guitar Player Presents Legends of Guitar: Electric Blues, Vol. 2 (Rhino, 1991)

Sponsored by *Guitar Player* magazine, this two-volume series spotlights the most inventive, individual and influential of the modern-day stringbenders. Beyond the headlining stars of the craft—B.B. King, T-Bone Walker, Muddy Waters—focus is shared with the lesser-knowns who added their distinctive guitar work to the blues of Bobby "Blue" Bland (Wayne Bennett), Howlin' Wolf (Hubert Sumlin) and Junior Wells (Buddy Guy). Adequate attention is given to all shades of the amplified-blues spectrum: slide masters (Elmore James, Hound Dog Taylor), country-based artists (John Lee Hooker, Frankie Lee Sims), second-generation Chicago stringbenders (Magic Sam, Otis Rush) and white-boy inheritors (Johnny Winter, Michael Bloomfield). It's not a perfect study; argument could be made for including Stevie Ray Vaughan and against the choice of Freddie King's later material or of Snooks Eaglin's more pop-style recordings. But both volumes capture the important milestones (*Vol. 1* covers a wider—and whiter—range, while *Vol. 2* is almost exclusively Texas and Chicago), and with 35 tracks between them, no blues-guitar student or fan should feel shortchanged. (The B.B. King track "You Done Lost Your Good Thing Now" on *Vol. 1,* with unaccompanied guitar on the intro and first verse, is itself reason for full satisfaction.) — A.K.

MASTERS OF JAZZ

★★★★★ **Masters of Jazz, Vol. 1: Traditional Jazz Classics (Rhino, 1996)**
★★★★½ **Masters of Jazz, Vol. 2: Bebop's Greatest Hits (Rhino, 1996)**
★★★★★ **Masters of Jazz, Vol. 3: Big Bands of the '30s & '40s (Rhino, 1996)**
★★★★ **Masters of Jazz, Vol. 4: Big Bands of the '50s & '60s (Rhino, 1996)**
★★½ **Masters of Jazz, Vol. 5: Female Vocal Classics (Rhino, 1996)**
★★★½ **Masters of Jazz, Vol. 6: Male Vocal Classics (Rhino, 1996)**
★★★ **Masters of Jazz, Vol. 7: Jazz Hit Singles (Rhino, 1996)**

While such comprehensive, cross-label reissues were unheard of only a few years ago, Rhino has managed to make them commonplace. All the volumes here can be accused of being subjective in their choice of material, but in the attempt to create a groundwork on which to build a fuller appreciation of a particular jazz style, they all succeed. For sheer enjoyment, *Vol. 1: Traditional Jazz Classics* and *Vol. 3: Big Bands of the '30s & '40s* are worth the investment—the others are ear-expanding and enjoyably so.

Appropriately, *Traditional Jazz Classics* kicks off with early Dixieland stars from both sides of the racial line—the Original Dixieland Five ("Tiger Rag") and King Oliver's Creole Jazz ("Sugar Foot Stomp")—and proceeds to celebrate the growth of the legacy through its first generation of composers (Jelly Roll Morton, Duke Ellington, Fats Waller), soloists (Louis Armstrong, Bix Beiderbecke, Benny Goodman, Sidney Bechet, Coleman Hawkins), arrangers (Fletcher Henderson) and singers (Bessie Smith, Louis Armstrong, Jack Teagarden). *Bebop's Greatest Hits* traces the notion of the virtuoso soloist through jazz's first revolution, from its first breaths in the fleet-fingered hands of Dizzy Gillespie ("Salt Peanuts") and Charlie Parker ("Ko-Ko," "Ornithology," "Yardbird Suite"), through the jam-happy tenors of Lester Young ("Jumpin' with Symphony Sid") and Dexter Gordon/Wardell Gray ("The Chase"), to the groundbreaking compositions of bop-era pianists Thelonious Monk ("'Round Midnight"), Bud Powell ("Bouncing with Bud") and George Shearing ("Lullaby of Birdland"). The 18-track story closes as bebop encountered and was integrated into other musical styles—big band (Claude Thornhill's "Anthropology"), cool (Miles Davis's "Move"), Afro-Cuban (Dizzy Gillespie's "Manteca") and the blues-rooted drive of hard bop (Clifford Brown/Max Roach's "Joy Spring").

Covering the sound to which America danced and swung, *Big Bands of the '30s & '40s* targets jazz's high-water mark as a commercial music, bypassing Glenn Miller and other pop-swing stars and concentrating on the originators like Don Redman, Fletcher Henderson, Chick Webb and Jimmie Lunceford. It also features the unexpected arrival of territory bands like Bennie Moten's and Andy Kirk's and follows with swing's best-known hits: Count Basie's "Jumpin' at the Woodside," Duke Ellington's "Cotton Tail" and Earl Hines's "The Father Jumps." The collection further catches the rise of star soloists—Charlie Parker with Jay McShann's orchestra on "Swingmatism"—as well as the song credited as the lead-in to the age of R&B, Lionel Hampton's "Flying Home" with the famed solo by tenor legend Illinois Jacquet. The definitions of both *big* and *band* are needfully expanded in *Big Bands of the '50s & '60s,* as jazz lost its function as dance music and economics forced a downgrade of the larger ensembles. This 15-track set concentrates on an era when larger jazz ensembles returned to pure musical invention and experimentation, with many forsaking the live stage for recording studios alone—beginning with the West Coast sound of Woody Herman ("More Moon") and the virtuoso/big-band counterpoint of Charlie Parker and His Orchestra ("I Can't Get Started"). Emphasis is next given to the most influential bandleaders of that era, including the master of instrumental color and texture, Duke Ellington ("The Mooche" in 1952), the rhythm maestro Buddy Rich (an awe-inspiring, gear-shifting "West Side Story Medley") and the man who almost single-handedly taught Broadway and Hollywood composers how to swing, Stan Kenton ("What's New?"). The remaining selections explore the progress of veteran bandleaders (Count Basie with Neal Hefti's "Cute" and Dizzy Gillespie with Gil Fuller/Chano Pozo's "Tin Tin Deo") and the new jazz guard (Cannonball Adderley's "African Waltz," Maynard Ferguson's "Maria" and Stanley Turrentine's "River's Invitation") and closes with the two pioneering arrangers of the mid-'60s: the avant-gardist Charles Mingus ("Better Get Hit in Yo' Soul") and the ubiquitous Oliver Nelson (Jimmy Smith/Wes Montgomery's "Down by the Riverside").

The remaining three collections deserve criticism for succumbing to a peculiarly narrow focus, overlooking important links from the overall jazz tradition. After dealing with the requisite legends Billie Holiday, Ella Fitzgerald and Sarah Vaughan, *Female Vocal Classics* drops off into cabaret land with Nancy Wilson, Chris Connor and Etta Jones—it would have been nice to hear more from the queens of classic blues (Bessie Smith), swing (Ivie Anderson), '60s socially conscious/experimental (Abbey Lincoln) and even avant-garde (Jeanne Lee). *Male Vocal Classics* gets going with the strident soul of Cab Calloway ("Some of These Days" rather than "You Gotta Hi De Ho") and Louis Armstrong, but where's Fats Waller's vocal dexterity? It then immediately bows to the novelty—Louis Prima, Dizzy Gillespie ("Ool-Ya-Koo")—missing out on various influential big-band stars (Al Hibbler, Jimmy Rushing) and again cuts off prematurely in the midst of the '60s blues/hard-bop era. Kudos, however, for including the gender-defying vocals of Chet Baker and Jimmy Scott and not forgetting the overlooked white-boy-lost-in-the-blues style of Jack Teagarden.

Leaning too singularly on the Atlantic and Blue Note modern approach to its subject, *Jazz Hit Singles* covers both the actual radio success stories (John Coltrane's soprano sax on the standard "My Favorite Things," Mongo Santamaria's take on Herbie Hancock's "Watermelon Man," Stan Getz's excursion on Antonio Carlos Jobim's samba "Desafinado") with other jazz tunes that bow to the three-minute, melody-and-mood approach to hit making: the Jazztet's "Killer Joe," James Moody's "I'm in the Mood for Love" and Donald Byrd's "Cristo Redentor." Again, if this anthology wants to follow its own rules, where's Cannonball Adderley's "Mercy, Mercy, Mercy" or Hugh Masekela's "Grazing in the Grass"? It seems it could have been more—expansive and inclusive—with little effort. — A.K.

THE MERCURY BLUES 'N' RHYTHM STORY

★★★★★ **The Mercury Blues 'n' Rhythm Story 1945–1955 (Mercury, 1996)**

As historical boxed sets go, this is one classy—and complete—package: 211 tracks on 8 discs recorded during R&B's first golden decade of 1945 through '55 by Chicago's then-young Mercury Record Company, all explained and celebrated in a thoroughly researched and well-written 87-page booklet.

Ten years covers a lot of R&B, and this collection offers many reasons why Mercury found itself a constant fixture on the R&B charts of the day. Leaving the rowdier, down-home blues of Chicago's South Side to Chess Records and other independent labels in the late '40s, Mercury opted for a more urbane approach—saxophone-led combos, boogie-woogie stylists and gentle R&B crooners. And in no way was it limited to the music of its hometown; within its first five years Mercury released hit singles by such diverse luminaries as T-Bone Walker, Eddie "Cleanhead" Vinson, Dinah Washington, Albert Ammons and even Big Bill Broonzy with a jazzy, sax-supported band.

These artists and many more grace the tracks in this anthology, divided into regional segments. Discs one and two peruse the "Midwest blues" with the names mentioned—Washington's ribald "Long John Blues" would make Clarence Thomas blush—and along with such piano masters as Sunnyland Slim and Memphis Slim. The next two discs cover the Southwest, highlighted by Kansas City bandleader Jay McShann, Texas bluesmen Lightnin' Hopkins and Smokey Hogg and early recordings by New Orleans piano legend Professor Longhair. The West Coast is the subject of discs five and six, including legendary rhythm-and-blues inventors Johnny Otis and Joe Liggins as well as a number of lesser-known jump bands and R&B shouters. Things really start jumping as the East Coast closes the Mercury story with two discs' worth of Eddie Vinson (including his classics "Cherry Red Blues," "Kidney Stew Blues" and his signature "Cleanhead Blues"), Helen Humes ("Jet Propelled Papa"), the manic Trenier Twins ("Hey Sister Lucy!"), more Dinah Washington and some early Screamin' Jay Hawkins.

If the smooth and mellow stylings of R&B crooners, the raw and wailing honk of sax players and the insistent energy of jump-blues bands feed your fire, then this is an unqualified must-have. — A.K.

NEW ORLEANS

★★★★½ **New Orleans Jazz and Heritage Festival 1976 (Rhino, 1989)**
★★★★★ **New Orleans Party Classics (Rhino, 1991)**

Like a big, bead-throwing parade coming down a Crescent City boulevard, these two titles capture the best music from the city's two best parties: Mardi Gras and the Jazz Fest.

New Orleans Party Classics captures the ain't-nothin'-but-a-party spirit of Mardi Gras, with a distinct R&B flavor. Professor Longhair's "Go to the Mardi Gras" and "Big Chief," the Hawketts' "Mardi Gras Mambo," Al Johnson's "Carnival Time," Dr. John's "Iko Iko" and various Mardi Gras Indian marching songs ("Meet de Boys on the Battlefront," "Hey Pocky Way," "Li'l Liza Jane") are among the must-have anthems included here.

Harkening back to the days when the outdoor, multistage festival was a little less crowded and a little more reliant on its hometown flavor, *New Orleans Jazz and Heritage Festival 1976* presents the stars that mattered most during the Jazz Fest's early years. Songsmith/piano man Allen Toussaint gets a star turn with five tracks, including "Shoorah, Shoorah" and the brilliant ballad "Freedom for the Stallion," along with Professor Longhair ("Tipitina," "Mardi Gras in New Orleans"), Irma Thomas ("Cry On" and "You Can Have My Husband but Please Don't Mess with My Man"), Lee Dorsey ("Workin' in a Coal Mine"), Ernie K-Doe ("Mother-in-Law"), Earl King ("Trick Bag") and even Texas guest Lightnin' Hopkins ("Baby Please Don't Go"). — A.K.

THE OKEH RHYTHM & BLUES STORY

★★★★ **The Okeh Rhythm & Blues Story 1949–1957 (Epic/Okeh/Legacy, 1993)**

Okeh's story is a weird but telling historical footnote in the evolution of the record industry. A veritable Lazarus of a label, it has been resurrected and reburied by its parent company, Columbia, at least four times since its inception, as a means to house the black-music department (first defined as "race" in the '20s, then "rhythm & blues" in the '40s and '50s, "soul" in the '60s and most recently as a weird amalgam of reissue projects and alternative R&B like Keb' 'Mo). This three-disc set peruses Okeh's third incarnation, from 1949 through '57, when Columbia Records decided—a bit belatedly—that it wanted in on the R&B party that was then catching fire.

Kicking off the proceedings with "Rock the Joint" by Chris Powell and the Five Blue Flames, this three-disc box is chock-full of shoutin', wailin', jumpin', jivin' and other R&B craziness that defined the times. It's a fun if pedestrian collection, with a lot of novelty tunes and a few influential tracks and recognizable artists among the set's 78 performances—Big Maybelle's "One Monkey Don't Stop No Show" and Big John and the Buzzards' "Your Cash Ain't Nothin' but Trash," for example. Other stars include New Orleans bandleader Paul Gayten and his vocalist, Annie Laurie, R&B harmony pioneers the Ravens and the D.C. doo-wop group the Marquees (featuring a young Marvin Gaye with guitar help from Bo Diddley).

There's also such proto–rock & roll ribaldry as Chuck Willis's early blues shouting on "I Rule My House" (which later softened into a more mellow and successful R&B mold for Atlantic Records), that legendary madman Screamin' Jay Hawkins with his classics "I Put a Spell on You" and "Little Demon" and finally two joyous slices of libido-on-the-loose by the Treniers and the Bill Davis Trio. The package includes enjoyable and well-researched liner notes by WFMU (New Jersey) deejay the Hound (James Marshall) and Peter Grendysa. — A.K.

THE ORIGINAL JAZZ MASTERS SERIES

★ **The Original Jazz Masters Series, Vol. 1 (da Music, 1994)**
★ **The Original Jazz Masters Series, Vol. 2 (da Music, 1994)**
★ **The Original Jazz Masters Series, Vol. 3 (da Music, 1994)**

★ **The Original Jazz Masters Series, Vol. 4 (da Music, 1994)**

There really should be a sign wherever fine boxed sets are sold, reading NO DUMPING ALLOWED. Plagued by absolute random ordering of material and paper-thin packaging without photos, booklets or even graphics, these four five-disc sets are clearly the result of a lazy decision maker making the lazy decision to pillage the entire Black Lion jazz catalog and thrust the sets as cheaply as possible onto the retail shelves. Important and legendary artists like Duke Ellington, Thelonious Monk and Coleman Hawkins are done a disservice by releases such as this, and jazz consumers yearning for well-thought-out reissues deserve better. — A.K.

THE R&B BOX

★★★★★ **The R&B Box: 30 Years of Rhythm & Blues (Rhino, 1994)**

Coined in 1949 by then-*Billboard* columnist Jerry Wexler to replace the "race music" moniker, "rhythm & blues" became the catchall term for popular black American music—an appropriate and enduring hyphenation for a long, rich, varied and voluminous tradition that grew from the blues, boogies and ballads of an earlier era. Ever the reissue zealots, Rhino took on the daunting task of distilling this legacy—at least a generous 30-year slice from 1943 to 1972—into 108 songs, to tell the story of how the music of a minority captivated and directed the course of popular American music in general, and how it was itself affected by its own success and its need to change and evolve.

Formalizing an informal sequence of cultural events and then neatly boxing the results is bound to leave some parts of the story untold. One could easily demand why James Brown's "Please, Please, Please" was included while his funk-founding anthem "I Feel Good" was bypassed. That *The R&B Box* works in its goal of being a complete and illuminating overview is due to the fact that 1) its producers were willing to make certain subjective choices from a mountain of timeless music; and 2) given Rhino's access to an enviable number of label catalogs, an inclusive and non-label-specific perspective was guaranteed. But the unavailability of material by certain artists caused the unfortunate exclusion of such luminaries as Sam Cooke, artists from Cincinnati's legendary King label (Wynonie Harris, the Five Keys, Roy Brown and others) and Stevie Wonder (though Motown is well represented otherwise).

The R&B Box unfolds its story through six discs, each constituting a chapter in the growth and proliferation of R&B. Jumpin' the Blues kicks off the party with Louis Jordan, R&B's first superstar, and catches the greatest and most gone jivers, honkers, shouters and wailers of the pre–rock & roll era: Joe Liggins, Roy Milton, Big Jay McNeely, Dinah Washington, Johnny Otis and doo-wop's first stop, the Ravens. The first disc, Teenagers Are Diggin' It, takes on the birth of rock & roll as white America began to take notice, from Jackie Brenston's "Rocket 88" through Big Joe Turner, Little Richard, Big Mama Thornton, Professor Longhair, LaVern Baker and a slew of vocal groups: the Five Keys, the Spaniels, the Clovers and the Moonglows. On Rockin' 'n' Rollin', Ray Charles's "I've Got a Woman" provides the intro to R&B's first golden age: Fats Domino, James Brown, the Five Satins, Big Maybelle, the Robins (later the Coasters), Clyde McPhatter, the Dells and Bo Diddley (considered a purely rock & roll artist, Chuck Berry is eschewed). Goin' Nationwide explores the second generation of R&B stars, from Little Richard (arguably better suited for the previous disc) to Jackie Wilson, Jerry Butler, the Flamingos, Dee Clark, Carla Thomas, Ernie K-Doe and the first hints of the gospel-infused sound that would become soul: Bobby Bland, Ben E. King and Etta James. Soul Brothers & Soul Sisters heralds the new arrival, with tracks by Solomon Burke, the Impressions, Esther Phillips, Don Covay and a host of Motown artists. Finally, The End of the Golden Age closes the R&B box with soul's high-water mark from Memphis and Muscle Shoals—Otis Redding, Sam and Dave, Eddie Floyd, Percy Sledge, James Carr and Aretha Franklin—and portends the smoothly orchestrated R&B of the '70s with the Spinners, Johnnie Taylor and Brook Benton. — A.K.

RCA VICTOR JAZZ

★★★★ **RCA Victor Jazz: The First Half-Century—The '20s–'60s (BMG, 1992)**

The most important music on this five-disc, decade-by-decade boxed-set study is from the earlier days of recorded jazz—from King Oliver, Louis Armstrong, Jelly Roll Morton and Sidney Bechet to Fats Waller and Duke Ellington.

Disc one digs into the '20s, celebrating the kings of Dixieland swing (Morton, Henry "Red" Allen and the Original Dixieland Jazz Band) and the Chicago and Kansas City inheritors (Benny Goodman, Bix Beiderbecke, Coleman Hawkins and Bennie Moten) plus the orchestrators of the new sound: Fletcher Henderson and Earl Hines. Featured as well is that early and most holy trinity of jazz piano: Morton ("Black Bottom Stomp"), stride king James P. Johnson ("Bleeding-Hearted Blues") and his star pupil, Fats Waller ("Handful of Keys"). The beginnings of swing are perused on the '30s disc, from Duke Ellington's "Daybreak Express" and Count Basie's "Moten Swing" to the first generation of star soloists: Artie Shaw's "Any Old Time" (featuring Billie Holiday), Lionel Hampton's "I'm in the Mood for Swing" (Benny Carter), Gene Krupa's "Swing Is Here" (Roy Eldridge), Benny Goodman's "Life Goes to a Party" (Harry James).

Disc three (covering the '40s) is the most diverse of this collection, kicking off with the three tracks for Ellington's classic 1940 ensemble with bassist Jimmy Blanton and sax legend Ben Webster ("Jack the Bear," "Concerto for Cootie," "Cotton Tail"), followed by a rundown of stellar instrumentalists: Django Reinhardt, Johnny Hodges, Coleman Hawkins and the geniuses who gave birth to bebop (Gillespie's Afro-Cuban hit "Manteca," Lennie Tristano's "Spontaneous Combustion" and Kenny Clarke's version of Thelonious Monk's "Epistrophy"). A variety of bop and hard-bop luminaries—Bud Powell, Art Blakey, Al Cohn and Zoot Sims—spice up the '50s disc, which also includes an intriguing mix of modern jazz composer/arrangers: John Lewis's "Two Degrees East, Three Degrees West," Charles Mingus's "Ysabel's Table Dance," Gil Evans's "Blues for Pablo" and George Russell/Bill Evans's "Concerto for Billy the Kid."

Except for one or two names (Gary Burton, Jackie McLean), the final disc proves the box's title, with all remaining artists belonging more to the first half of this century (Duke Ellington, Joe Williams, Lionel Hampton) than reflecting any important jazz developments since 1960. Still, within its 96 tracks, *The First Half-Century* is as accurate and important a listen as one can find from any one jazz label out there.
— A.K.

RISQUÉ RHYTHM

★★★ Risqué Rhythm: Nasty 50s R&B (Rhino, 1991)

Serving as a reminder that "rock & roll" itself was originally slang for "the wild thing," *Risqué Rhythm* returns to the early '50s and exhumes bump-and-grind treasures and truly blue blues. Actually, this raunchy stuff is pretty genial fare—broad double entendres, rather than smut. There's Dinah Washington singing about a trombonist and his "Big Long Slidin' Thing" and Moose Jackson bragging about his "Big Ten-Inch Record." Wynonie Harris, of "Good Rockin' Tonight" fame, contributes "Keep On Churnin' " and "Wasn't That Good"; the Toppers turn in the most brazen title, "(I Love to Play Your Piano) Let Me Bang Your Box." All nudging saxes, boom-boom drums and leering vocals, the playing is that of standard (i.e., very good) early R&B—and it's a kick to note that quite a few of these numbers were massive sellers in their day. The ultimate impression these songs give, however, is that of a loopy charm and blushing innocence—they're actually a form, no matter how marginal, of Americana, a nostalgic look back at a time when it was possible to be shocked. — P.E.

RIVERSIDE HISTORY OF CLASSIC JAZZ

★★★★★ Riverside History of Classic Jazz (1956; Original Jazz Classics, 1994)

Decades before the reissue rage of the CD era, there was a similar one when the long-playing record was new. In the '50s, record collectors treasured their pre–World War II 78s and wished for them to be reissued on LPs. Riverside was initially formed with that intent—though the founders, Orrin Keepnews and Bill Grauer Jr., and collectors were labeled by hipsters as moldy figs, old-fashioned, close-minded jazz purists who weren't hep to the sounds of bebop. (Riverside did eventually record such nontraditional artists as Bill Evans and Thelonious Monk.) Therefore, this reissue of reissued "classic jazz," typically small groups or solos emphasizing up-tempo rhythmic improvisations, sticks pretty much to recordings made in the '20s and those that are closely related to that period in American music, even if made later. The original '56 liner notes (pull out your magnifying glass) are reproduced in the CD booklet and describe the evolution of jazz and its coalescence in New Orleans—try to skim over the constant debunking that author Charles Edward Smith makes of others' debunkings, and just catch his enthusiasm for the music and the people who created it. The annotated discography (written by Keepnews for the later reissue) gives a clearer understanding of who's what and why—which is necessary because Riverside couldn't license recordings owned by the major labels, so the *Riverside History* includes some unfamiliar artists and songs recorded at a later time and place. The boxed set is divided into 10 volumes (one for each side of five long-players), now on three discs. Vols. 1 through 3 represent the development of jazz in the prerecorded era: from African drumming and early blues styles (chants, sermons, prison songs) to piano rolls of ragtime composers like Scott Joplin to what might be called "classic blues," performances by Ma Rainey, Bessie Smith and Blind Lemon Jefferson. The next six volumes culminate in New Orleans jazz and its direct descendants: boogie-woogie, Chicago and Harlem/New York styles. Then, for the final volume, it jumps over the big-band heyday (not enough improvisation, not enough technical prowess!) into the revivalist period of the early '50s when some of the older players came out of retirement/obscurity and younger players began focusing on traditional jazz. Perhaps narrow-minded, but this set is a unique historical overview. As Smith calls it, classic jazz "is the parent style, root and branch. For every jazzman, this is still the tree of hope." — S.D.

ROOTS 'N' BLUES: THE RETROSPECTIVE

★★★★★ Roots 'n' Blues: The Retrospective 1925–1950 (Columbia/Legacy, 1992)

Before the advent of artists & repertoire, before the advent of hit charts, and long before music was ever ruled by market considerations or demographic studies, absolute democracy ruled in the music marketplace: Practically anyone making music could cut a record. With no chart histories to steer by but with first-generation recording equipment in hand, a legion of recordists journeyed forth upon the social checkerboard of America and recorded whatever they could find. It was the '10s and '20s, record companies were in their infancy and the heyday of field recordings yielded a bumper crop of blues, minstrel music, hillbilly instrumentals, boogie-woogies, hokum anthems, sanctified sermons, holy-rolling choirs and shape-note singing.

Culled from a 25-year library of American folk music, the four-disc *Roots 'n' Blues* celebrates a kaleidoscope of musical wealth—focusing on the legacy of small labels that were absorbed and remain in Columbia's catalog (Okeh, Vocalion, ARC, etc.). The 107 tracks presented here were recorded between 1925 and '50 and together weave a multiethnic musical tapestry that was America. Like fading but telling snapshots of what was, the songs invite the listener into a world all but lost in the bland, homogenous '90s—the performances are sprinkled with regional details and idioms, reflecting topical subjects (Prohibition, the Depression, natural disasters, even the assassination of President McKinley) and more timeless themes (wine, women, salvation and the joys of cohabitation—as in Cliff Carlisle's "Onion Eating Mama").

Illuminating slices of life pop out—a bootlegger offers musical sips of moonshine to a customer ("Moonshiner and His Money"), a "classic" blues singer describes the physical attributes of her partner ("My Sportin' Man"), a country preacher delivers a protorap sermon ("Warming by the Devil's Fire"), a white country bluesman shows off his rag-guitar dexterity, philosophizing on man's need to be humble ("The Last Scene of the Titanic"). As well, a number of blues and country legends were discovered by the talent scouts of the day and are featured on tracks herein—Blind Willie McTell, Gene Autry, Albert Ammons, Bill Monroe, Charley Patton, even a rare "Burying Ground Blues" from 1946 by McKinley Morganfield (better known today as Muddy Waters).

In 1952 a small, left-leaning label out of New York called Folkways pioneered the first similar collection of the songs of the common man. The *Anthology of American Folk Music* celebrated the rich and varied folk music found on all the old, garage-sale 78s that no major labels saw the need to reissue at the time. (It was reissued on CD in 1997.) The Folkways label is no longer a commercial one (its recordings now belong to the Smithsonian Institute), but the lesson has been learned; this excellent boxed set is proof of just how far the majors have come in realizing the history that they're sitting on. — A.K.

SAVOY JAZZ

★★★★★ The Modern Jazz Piano Album (Savoy, 1995)
★★★½ Ladies Sing the Blues (Savoy, 1995)
★★★★ Giants of Traditional Jazz (Savoy, 1995)
★★★★ The Trombone Album (Savoy, 1995)

★★★ **Black California, Vol. 2: Anthology (Savoy, 1995)**

Among the first jazz catalogs to fall into the hands of archivists, the wealth of material in the Savoy Records library—from traditional and swing through bebop, R&B, modern jazz and early rock & roll—has been preserved and repackaged in entertaining, well-researched and well-annotated collections since the '70s. The Japanese giant Denon now owns Savoy and has wisely elected to keep these anthologies on the retail shelves.

The most compelling and historically important of the volumes above, *The Modern Jazz Piano Album,* covering 1946–1956, is an absolute must for any student of bebop composition and performance during and after its heyday. Just add Thelonious Monk's Blue Note sessions, and one has an entire generation of keyboardists who were translating the revolution according to Charlie Parker and Dizzy Gillespie: Bud Powell (with the short-lived Bebop Boys, who were Kenny Dorham, Sonny Stitt and Kenny Clarke), Lennie Tristano, Herbie Nichols (rare pre–Blue Note sessions), Dodo Marmarosa, George Wallington and the Kenny Clarke Quintet (with Horace Silver). The majority are caught here in the budding stage of their careers, with the real eye-opener being the inspired, chance-taking solos of the leader of the pack—Bud Powell in 1946—and the first breaths of Herbie Nichols's compositional genius, in '52.

For lovers of the brassy, bassy sound that is the slide-valve trombone, studies of the instrument are exceedingly uncommon. For rarity's sake—and given its arguably comprehensive view of the instrument as handled by its bebop and postbop masters—*The Trombone Album* merits recommendation. Covering a little over a decade's worth (1947–60) of Savoy trombonists, the disc calls itself "an aural scrapbook" that stretches from the smoothly stated J.J. Johnson in a small bebop band session (including the moody "Boneology" and aptly titled flag-waver "Riffette") and the energetic showman Frank Rosolino, with piano support from a young Barry Harris (a jazzed-up version of "Take Me Out to the Ballgame"), to the 1956 summit of Jimmy Cleveland, Benny Powell, Henry Coker and Bill Hughes providing a big-band, wall-of-'bones backup to Frank Wess's flute ("You'll Do" and the excellent romantic ballad "Wanting You") and Curtis Fuller in hard-bop glory and excellent accompaniment with Lee Morgan, Yusef Lateef and McCoy Tyner in 1960 ("Accident" and "Darryl's Minor").

Two well-known R&B divas of the '50s—Big Maybelle and Esther Phillips—show off their distinct sounds but not their Savoy hits on *Ladies Sing the Blues,* a collection that actually serves to spotlight three relative unknowns from an earlier R&B period (1944–1951). Tracks like "Sugar" and an energetic reworking of "Downhearted Blues" place Miss Rhapsody's 1944–1945 sessions directly in Bessie Smith's steps with an updated, swing edge, while the even more straight-ahead blues shouter Albinia Jones likewise keeps the tradition loud and alive with "Evil Gal Blues" and "Salty Papa." A real find here are the 1951 recordings "Me and Dirty Blues" and "Baby Please Come Home" by Linda Hopkins, an inspired, clear-throated singer with roof-raising power.

More of a general archival portrait than a collection of individual stars, *Black California, Vol. 2* brings to life the loose and bluesy California postwar jazz scene with various live and studio tracks by such West Coast luminaries as tenor legend Wardell Gray ("Blow Blow Blow"), drummer Kenny Clarke ("Strollin'," with Milt Jackson, Frank Morgan, Percy Heath and others), singer Helen Humes ("Rock Me to Sleep," "This Love of Mine"), Slim Gaillard singing "I'm Confessin'" and trumpeter and vocalist Russell Jacquet (brother of Illinois, on "Blues a la Russ" and "Wake Up Old Maid"). Proving the point that trad jazz can vary widely in scope and flavor, *Giants of Traditional Jazz* offers a hearty 24-track buffet of recorded delights from the late-'40s Dixieland revival, featuring clarinetists Sidney Bechet and Joe Marsala (the latter on the platter's four standout tracks with Eddie Condon, including the raucous "Clarinet Marmalade"), trumpeter Mutt Carey with veterans Albert Nicholas ("Cake Walking Babies") and Danny Barker ("The Entertainer") swinging sensationally and a Jack Teagarden showcase from 1952 ("Mighty Lak a Rose"). The collection ends with brass men and longtime band mates Ruby Braff and Vic Dickenson in an eight-song live set from Boston's famed Savoy nightclub in 1949.

— A.K.

SOUL SHOTS: A COLLECTION OF SIXTIES SOUL CLASSICS

★★★★★ **Soul Shots, Vol. 1, (Rhino, 1988)**
★★★★★ **Soul Shots, Vol. 2, (Rhino, 1988)**

★★★★★ **Soul Shots, Vol. 3, (Rhino, 1989)**
★★★★★ **Soul Shots, Vol. 4, (Rhino, 1989)**
James Brown, Aretha Franklin and the Stax-Volt gang may have ruled supreme, but a number of less-famous names made substantial contributions to the dictionary of '60s soul. That's the basis for this outstanding anthology series: There are plenty of big hits, but they are buttressed by other powerful performances that deserve to be called classic tracks. In essence, *Soul Shots* is an unabridged version of Epic's first-rate *Lost Soul* series of the early '80s, which showcases not only artists but disparate styles within the category of soul music. The scope is amazing in its inclusiveness—no base is left untouched, from blues to instrumentals to both the mellow and the boisterous sides of the male and female points of view. The blues set, *Vol. 4,* is especially strong, with Albert Collins, Z.Z. Hill and Roscoe Gordon joining the lineup and Little Richard being represented by one of the tracks cut when Jimi Hendrix was his guitarist. Also note on *Vol. 1* the presence of James Brown in top form on two cuts, "Night Train" and "I Got You." Add in the minor gems that make life worth living, and you get a classic collection. — D.M.

SOUNDS OF THE SOUTH

★★★★★ **Sounds of the South (1961; Atlantic, 1993)**
During its first 10 years, Atlantic Records covered a lot of musical bases, but no project matched the truly noncommercial effort to subsidize and release a series of field recordings in 1959 by the renowned ethnomusicologist Alan Lomax. It was the first time a leading label had attempted to put the most pristine and least acculturated music of the continent into the same record bins as Elvis Presley and Frankie Avalon.

Initiated as a reaction to the then-popular misconception that the Washington Square scene actually defined American folk music, 80 hours of reel-to-reel reality were collected, revealing a still-extant but slowly disappearing world of folk songs, church songs, spirituals, field hollers, work songs and roadhouse blues. The musical and geographical area covered is formidable—"from the Georgia Sea Islands to the Mississippi Delta," as the booklet promises. More than 100 performances offer a kaleidoscope of lone and collective voices and instruments—fiddle, mandolin, guitar, fife, hand drums, even comb in wax paper. Upon listening, an engaging study emerges of the cross-influences that typified the parallel musical development of white and black rural cultures.

Lomax's musical journey—his first with hi-fi stereo equipment—unfolds through this four-disc boxed set. The first disc, Sounds of the South/Blue Ridge Mountain Music, examines the separate and fused legacies of African and English song traditions, as they evolved from colonial roots through to white bluegrass and hillbilly, and black folk, blues and gospel traditions. Disc two, Roots of the Blues/The Blues Roll On, captures the constituent elements that, when they came together, generated the blues, America's most enduring musical form. From the rhythm and emotion of prison work songs, the verse structure and lyrical content of camp hollers, the boogie and bounce of ragtime guitar pieces and the voicelike wail of a solo harmonica, all is examined, followed by a study of the more conventional blues song, emphasizing the unique-entertainer, itinerant-jukebox and news-commentator roles of the blues performer in rural society. The more sacred side of the blues/gospel coin is covered by disc three, Negro Church Music/White Spirituals, a collection of both individual and group performances; solo singers, choirs, sermonizing preachers, congregations, lone guitarists, bluegrass ensembles and even the shape-note singing style, an eerie tradition unto itself, are featured. The fourth disc celebrates American Folk Songs for Children. Through tunes like "Frog Went a-Courtin'," "Hambone" and "Liza Jane," the real roots of double Dutch and other modern-day school-yard melodies and nursery rhymes are brought to light, ultimately revealing just how shared the American folk tradition had become by midcentury and how early in life the legacy is instilled and inherited.

Though the collection is more of the songs than the singers, of special interest are two future and influential folk legends who are first heard on these tracks. The lean, spiritual blues of Mississippi Fred McDowell debuts here with "Keep Your Lamps Trimmed and Burning" and other tunes, a few years before his better-known Arhoolie recordings would influence the Rolling Stones and Bonnie Raitt. As well, the totally pristine and timeless choral songs like "Blow Gabriel" as sung by Bessie Jones and the St. Simon's Island Singers would help shape the preblues, improvised vocal stylings of Bernice Reagon's Sweet Honey in the Rock. — A.K.

STAX/VOLT SINGLES

★★★★★ The Complete Stax/Volt Singles 1959–1968 (Atlantic, 1991)

A nine-volume collection gathering nearly 250 cuts of the toughest R&B ever made, *The Complete Stax/Volt Singles* is a wonder. Not only are the hits and experiments of the label's stars, from Otis Redding to Johnnie Taylor, fully represented, but the vast assemblage of knockout songs by lesser-knowns makes the compilation indispensable. There are enough so-so tracks to ground the Stax-Volt achievement in some kind of recognizable human reality (and to allow the gems to shine even more brightly), but the undiminished visceral immediacy of most of this music lends the label an almost eerie luminosity—it seems uncanny that so strong a sound was developed in so short a time, by so few a number of central players. Outmanned and outmonied, Stax never quite matched Motown in terms of sales, but compared with Motown's brilliant, irresistible pop soul, Stax's R&B cut straight to the bone—technically simpler, at its best it was music of a disturbing emotional depth; Motown pleased, Stax demanded. Quintessentially Southern, the Memphis-based label reflected the hard grandeur of America's most conflicted and most poetic region—and the fact that its ownership and a significant handful of its key musicians were white Southerners added to the creative tension.

White banker Jim Stewart and his sister, Estelle Axton, founded the label; some of its greatest writing and producing talent (Chips Moman, Spooner Oldham) were country boys; half of its peerless house band (guitarist Steve Cropper, bassist Donald "Duck" Dunn) wouldn't have looked out of place in Buck Owens's Buckaroos. But the '60s R&B Stax produced drew consistently from the gospel and blues roots of the genre; the songs were the colloquial poetry of African-American experience; and the stars were black. Otis Redding, Sam and Dave, Booker T. Jones, Isaac Hayes, Eddie Floyd and Rufus Thomas were Stax's legends; close behind came Rufus's daughter Carla (among the Stax set's treasures are cuts that reveal this singer's neglected greatness; the same holds true for Mabel Thomas), William Bell, Johnnie Taylor and Barbara Stephens. An instrumental powerhouse, Stax presented, in the Mar-Keys, a truly fearsome horn section (most imaginatively deployed by Redding) and boasted soul music's answer to rock & roll's Charlie Watts in the essentialist drumming of Al Jackson—even the acoustics of the studio itself (a refashioned theater) were magic, helping to deliver a mono sound stretched as tight as Jackson's snare-drum head.

The Stax set includes all the standards by Otis Redding (in moods ranging from "I Can't Turn You Loose" to "Try a Little Tenderness"), Booker T. and the MG's ("Green Onions," "Hip Hug-Her"), Sam and Dave ("Soul Man"); it ranges from stone blues (Albert King) to the high, weird humor of Rufus Thomas, from doo-wop to nascent funk. It's an epic collection.
— P.E.

SUN RECORDS

★★★★★ Blue Flames: A Sun Blues Collection (Rhino, 1990)

Today, more than 40 years after Sam Phillips opened the Memphis Recording Service at 706 Union Avenue, the very fact that a Sun Records actually existed once in this country's history remains remarkable. While it is forever linked with the birth of rock & roll, Phillips's creation was considerably more broad-based. Long before Elvis Presley stepped up to the microphone in 1954, Phillips was recording some of the most important blues artists in the South.

Blue Flames proves that Phillips's chops for spotting talent were developed well ahead of Presley's arrival. His Memphis Recording Service became a clearinghouse for the music made by some of Memphis's and Mississippi's most important blues artists, which Phillips then leased out to other labels prior to forming Sun in 1952 after one of his recordings leased to Chess, Jackie Brenston's "Rocket 88," topped the R&B charts. Brenston was a session player backed by Ike Turner and His Kings of Rhythm, and "Rocket 88" (which kicks off *Blue Flames*) was, according to Turner, a knocked-off item done solely for gas money. It is also a wild, incendiary romp that is often cited as the first rock & roll recording.

The cuts on *Blue Flames* chronicle Phillips's work from 1951 through 1954, primarily, and showcase a wide variety of blues styles and even one gospel number, "Forgive Me Lord," by the Southern Jubilee Singers. In B.B. King's "B.B. Blues" and James Cotton's "Cotton Crop Blues," you hear the roots of the urban blues and R&B styles these gifted artists helped pioneer; Rufus Thomas's "Bear Cat," an answer record to Big Mama Thornton's "Hound Dog," is a 1953 cut that fuses R&B and gutbucket-blues shouting;

"Terra Mae" features the legendary one-man band Doctor Ross in a stripped-down blues with accompaniment by Reuben Martin on washboard. Also notable is the inclusion of guitarist Pat Hare's "I'm Gonna Murder My Baby," a 1954 track. Hare, who was in essence a Sun session player (he can be heard to searing effect on the aforementioned "Cotton Crop Blues"), was an early, though probably unconscious, proponent of distortion; his blistering sound is instantly identifiable not only on Sun Records but in the work of any number of '60s guitar heroes. Hare went on to play in Junior Parker's band and to contribute some extraordinary lead-guitar work on Muddy Waters's *At Newport* album. But true to his word, in 1962 Hare did indeed murder his baby—his girlfriend, that is—and spent the last 16 years of his life in prison. — D.M.

SUPERBLUES

★★★★ **Superblues: All-Time Classic Blues Hits, Vol. 1 (Stax, 1990)**

★★★★ **Superblues: All-Time Classic Blues Hits, Vol. 2 (Stax, 1991)**

★★★★ **Superblues: All-Time Classic Blues Hits, Vol. 3 (Stax, 1995)**

Imagine a dusty jukebox in a roadside tavern in Mississippi, still stacked full of scratchy 45s, with names like B.B. King, Lightnin' Hopkins and Bobby Bland penciled in next to Z.Z. Hill, O.V. Wright and Irma Thomas. That same overlap of '60s and '70s soul, blues and R&B is to be found on these three volumes and offers a good argument as to why every good blues anthology need not limit itself to a strictly focused theme, artist, era or even to the blues. Stax's diverse, cross-label *Superblues* series emphasizes great artists and superb songs with adequate, if not overly academic, information. *Vol. 1* kicks off the series with 14 tracks, rounding up the usual suspects like B.B. King ("The Thrill Is Gone"), Bobby Bland ("I Pity the Fool"), Jimmy Reed ("Honest I Do") and Howlin' Wolf ("Killing Floor") with Southern soul stars like Little Johnny Taylor ("Part Time Love") and Ike and Tina Turner ("It's Gonna Work Out Fine") plus a Larry Williams and Johnny "Guitar" Watson duet ("Mercy, Mercy, Mercy"). The two follow-up titles follow suit even more generously (18 and 19 tracks respectively), with Guitar Slim, Sonny Boy Williamson (Rice Miller) and Albert King alongside O.V. Wright, Percy Mayfield and Gene Allison on *Vol. 2,* while *Vol. 3* boasts a satisfying mix of Elmore James, Billy Boy Arnold and Little Walter with Ted Taylor, Jimmy Liggins and Joe Liggins. — A.K.

SWINGTIME RECORDS

★★★★ **The Swingtime Records Story (Capricorn, 1994)**

When giants with names like Louis Jordan, Nat King Cole and Charles Brown ruled the "race" charts of the late '40s, a small R&B label out of Los Angeles was planning a novel strategy. Bucking the tradition of trying to create a full-service, everything-under-one-roof record company (later successfully employed by Berry Gordy), music entrepreneur Jack Lauderdale relied on the success of others—licensing or actually buying out the catalogs of smaller R&B labels. In this pioneering fashion, Swingtime Records managed a successful seven-year run (1946–1954) during R&B and gospel's golden age, introducing new stars like Ray Charles, Percy Mayfield, Lowell Fulson, Lloyd Glenn and Jimmy Witherspoon, and reviving the careers of veterans like Big Joe Turner, Charles Brown and Pete Johnson.

Capricorn's two-disc, 50-track boxed set packages the smooth, hip and urbane sound that Swingtime favored—more influenced than influential—making it a well-researched and illuminating study. The label proves its early mettle with Eddie Williams's original version of "Saturday Night Fish Fry," Pete Johnson's "Rocket Boogie 88, Part 2," Big Joe Turner's "Wine-O-Baby Boogie" and various chart-friendly tunes by Jimmy Witherspoon ("Times Gettin' Tougher" and "Ain't Nobody's Business, Part 1") and trendsetter and major B.B. King influence Lowell Fulson ("Every Day I Have the Blues," "Blue Shadows").

The Swingtime story—opening with jazz and swing influences but later beginning to point in a more rock & roll direction—can itself be seen through the tracks of its nascent star Ray Charles. At first a Charles Brown clone, singing sweet and mellow on tracks like "Someday" and "I'll Do Anything but Work," Charles arrived at a more individual, gospel-influenced stamp, which becomes apparent on the 1951 hit "Kissa Me Baby" (which first brought him to the attention of the fledgling Atlantic label). Add well-honed harmony-gospel groups like the Nightengale Jubalaires [*sic*] with "Rough and Rocky Road" and the Stars of Harmony offering "Where Shall I Be" to their roster, and it would seem that Swingtime had hit upon the perfect combination of influences and styles to cover every corner of the exploding R&B market. By 1950, it had even grown to include a house band led by its A&R and musical director, pianist Lloyd Glenn (whose bouncing instrumental "Chica Boo" topped the R&B charts that year).

But Swingtime's downfall proved the limits of its label-as-distributor formula, furthered by its decision not to emphasize a creative and exclusive relationship with its own artists. By the early '50s, Ray Charles and Big Joe Turner had moved on to Atlantic, Percy Mayfield to Specialty and, most devastating, Lowell Fulson and Lloyd Glenn had exited to Aladdin. The doo-wop unit Hollywood Flames provided Swingtime's swan song with the hit "I Know" in 1952, but as bluesman Playboy Thomas put it in one of the label's last releases, it was "The End of the Road Baby" (both songs are included here). — A.K.

CONTRIBUTORS

EDITOR

John Swenson (J.S.) has been a syndicated music columnist for United Press International since 1986, a ROLLING STONE contributor since 1975 and the author of numerous books on music.

REVIEWERS

Ann Abel (A.A.) is the assistant editor of Rolling Stone Press and a freelance writer living in Manhattan. Her work has appeared in *Time Out New York,* the *Albuquerque Journal* and *The ROLLING STONE Book of Women in Rock.*

Robert Baird (R.B.) is the music editor of *Stereophile* magazine. He has written for ROLLING STONE, *Pulse!, Request, Magnet* and *Down Beat.*

Bob Blumenthal (B.B.) is a regular contributor to the *Boston Globe,* the *Atlantic Monthly, Fi* magazine and other music publications.

Veteran music critic **Hank Bordowitz** (H.B.) has covered jazz, rock and non-Western music for more periodicals—and years—than he'd care to count. He is the author of *Bad Moon Rising: The Unauthorized History of Creedence Clearwater Revival.*

J.D. Considine (J.D.C.) began writing about jazz in 1977 for the *Baltimore Sun.* Since then he has written for a number of music publications including ROLLING STONE, *Musician* and *Guitar World.* He was also a regular on the VH1 show *Four on the Floor.*

Shawn Dahl (S.D.) is the former senior editor of Rolling Stone Press, the book division of ROLLING STONE, where she worked for the nine years following her college graduation in 1989. She coedited *ROLLING STONE: The Seventies* and *ROLLING STONE Raves: What Your Rock & Roll Favorites Favor.* She also codesigned the illustrated book *Pornstar* by Ian Gittler. She is currently the editor of *Time Out New York Guides.*

Greg Emmanuel (G.E.) is a freelance writer and an editor at *Time Out New York.*

Paul Evans (P.E.) has contributed to *The ROLLING STONE Album Guide* and *The ROLLING STONE Encyclopedia of Rock & Roll.* A teacher and writer living in Atlanta, he has written for the *Washington Post,* the *Los Angeles Times* and other publications.

Ken Franckling (K.F.) has been United Press International's jazz columnist since 1985. He is also a contributing writer/photographer for *JazzTimes, Down Beat, SwingJournal* and other publications. He is a winner of the ASCAP–Deems Taylor Award for excellence in music journalism and is also a freelance photographer specializing in music photography.

Steve Futterman (S.F.) has written about jazz for ROLLING STONE, the *Village Voice, High Fidelity, Musician* and the *Record* and has contributed to *The ROLLING STONE Encyclopedia of Rock & Roll.*

Holly George-Warren (H.G.-W.) is the coeditor of *The ROLLING STONE Album Guide, The ROLLING STONE Illustrated History of Rock & Roll, ROLLING STONE: The Seventies* and *The ROLLING STONE Encyclopedia of Rock & Roll,* for which she won the 1996 ASCAP–Deems Taylor Award. Her writing appears in

The Rolling Stone *Book of Women in Rock, The Encyclopedia of Country Music* and *Country on Compact Disc,* among other books. She also has written for a variety of publications, including Rolling Stone, the *New York Times* and the *Village Voice.*

Geoffrey Himes (G.H.) writes about music on a regular basis for the *Washington Post.* He has contributed to *The Blackwell Guide to Recorded Country Music* and *The Encyclopedia of Country Music.* He has also written about music for Rolling Stone, *Down Beat, Request,* National Public Radio, *Replay, New Country, Country Music, No Depression,* the *Baltimore City Paper, Fi, Crawdaddy, Musician, Sing Out!,* the *Baltimore Sun* and the Patuxent Newspapers. He lives in Baltimore with his wife, Elizabeth Cusick.

B.R. Hunter (B.R.H.) is a freelance music writer in New York City whose work has appeared in Rolling Stone, *Guitar* and *Rhythm Music.* He was a contributing editor at *Swing* magazine and is the author of *The Midnight Special 1972–1981: Late Night's Original Rock & Roll Show.* He also likes candlelight dinners, long walks on a moonlit beach, and detests scary movies, carnival rides and cigarettes.

Scott Jordan (S.J.) is associate editor and writes the "Bluesworthy" column for New Orleans' *OffBeat* magazine; his work has also appeared in *The B.B. King Companion,* the *Oxford American, The Musichound Guide to Blues, Blues Revue* and other publications.

Ashley Kahn (A.K.) has presented, spun discs by, written about, hauled equipment for and/or generally followed the spirit and advice of many of the jazz and blues artists herein. He is the coeditor of *Rolling Stone: The Seventies.*

Jordan Kessler (J.K.) is a former blues DJ at WKCR-FM in New York and a former contributor to *Blues Review* magazine. He is currently working for a civil rights group.

David McGee (D.M.), a New York–based writer whose work has appeared in Rolling Stone, *Spin, New Musical Express* and other publications, is the author of *Go, Cat, Go! The Life and Times of Carl Perkins, the King of Rockabilly.* He has also served as assistant curator for the Rock and Roll Hall of Fame and Museum.

Tom Miller (T.M.) is an anthropologist and ethnomusicologist who lives in Brooklyn. He worked as a disc jockey at radio station WKCR and is an award-winning composer, writer and curator. His current work is focused on the music of shamans and the history of phonography.

Steve Mirkin (S.M.) is a freelance writer based in Los Angeles. A contributor to *The Rolling Stone Encyclopedia of Rock & Roll* and *The Trouser Press Guide to '90s Rock,* his work has also appeared in Rolling Stone, *Entertainment Weekly,* the *New York Times, Spin,* the *Hollywood Reporter* and many other publications.

Mitch Myers (M.M.) is a psychologist and a freelance writer who lives in Chicago. He travels extensively and spends a lot of time on the phone.

Ted Panken (T.P.) has been broadcasting jazz and new music on WKCR in New York since 1985. He writes for *Down Beat* and *Jazziz* and has done numerous liner notes.

Alan Paul (A.P.) is a senior editor at *Guitar World* and the editor of *Guitar World Online* (*www.guitarworld.com*). He has also written for *The New Yorker, Entertainment Weekly* and *People.*

Manchild **Joe Van Plummer** (J.V.P.) was educated at the University of Wisconsin where he studied jazz history with bassist Richard Davis. He currently resides in Manhattan as a journeyman, trucker, freelance writer and musician.

Jennifer Zoggott (J.Z.) is a contributing writer for *Blues Review* and has written for *Blues Access, Blue Suede News* and *Folk Roots.* She was a contributor to *The Musichound Guide to the Blues* and is a cofounder of an e-mail discussion group devoted to the music of the Holy Modal Rounders, Michael Hurley and Jeffrey Frederick and the Clamtones. She lives in Brooklyn.

RECORD LABEL AND DISTRIBUTION INFORMATION

A&M
(see **Interscope Geffen A&M Records**)

Accurate
(division of Rounder)
288 Norfolk St.
Cambridge, MA 02139
(617) 628-0603

Ace Records
(see **Avanti**)

Acoustic Sounds
P.O. Box 2043
Salina, KS 67402-2043
(785) 825-8609

Adelphi Records
Genes CD Co.
P.O. Box 7688
Silver Spring, MD 20907
(301) 434-6958

ADP Records and Tapes
237 E. 26 St., Apt. 5H
New York, NY 10010
(212) 725-1853

Airwax Records
P.O. Box 288291
Chicago, IL 60628
(773) 779-2384

Alcazar/Alcazam! Records
(see **New Sound**)
P.O. Box 669
Waterbury, VT 05676
(802) 244-7845

Alchemy
61 Surrey Dr.
Cohasset, MA 02025
(800) 292-6932
www.alchemyrecords.com

Allegro Distribution
(handles many import labels, including **SteepleChase**)
14134 N.E. Airport Way
Portland, OR 97230
(800) 288-2007
www.allegro-music.com

Alley Way Records
P.O. Box 728
Anniston, AL 36202-0728

Alligator
P.O. Box 60234
Chicago, IL 60660
(773) 274-7538
www.alligator.com/store.html

Almo Sounds
360 North La Cienega Blvd.
Los Angeles, CA 90048
(310) 289-3080
www.almosounds.com

Altenburgh Records
P.O. Box 154
Mosinee, WI 54455
(715) 693-2230

Amblin Records
P.O. Box 15960
Lenexa, KS 66215
(913) 888-6774

Amherst
1762 Main St.
Buffalo, NY 14208
(716) 883-9520

Andrew's Music
4830 Dakota Ave. N.E.
Washington, DC 20017
(202) 526-3666

Angel/Capitol
304 Park Ave. S.
New York, NY 10010
(212) 253-3000
www.hollywoodandvine.com

Antone's
507 W. Avenue, Suite 200
Austin, TX 78701-2734
(512) 322-0617
www.antonesrec.com

Arabesque Recordings
(distributed by **Allegro**)

Arbors Jazz
1700 McMullen Booth Rd., Suite C3
Clearwater, FL 33759
(813) 726-7494
www.arborsjazz.com

Arhoolie
10341 San Pablo Ave.
El Cerrito, CA 94523
(510) 525-7471
www.arhoolie.com

Arista
6 W. 57th St.
New York, NY 10019
(212) 489-7400
www.aristarec.com

Arkadia
34 E. 23rd St., 3rd floor
New York, NY 10010
(212) 674-5550
www.arkadiarecords.com

Arrival
(distributed by **K-Tel**)

Ascending Productions
P.O. Box 688
Point Lookout, NY 11569
(516) 897-7532
www.erols.com/marlabb

Astor Place
740 Broadway, 7th fl.
New York, NY 10003
(212) 529-2600
www.smilecom.com

Atlantic
1290 Avenue of the Americas
New York, NY 10104
(212) 707-2000
www.atlantic-records.com

Atomic Beat
10390 Santa Monica Blvd., Suite 210
Los Angeles, CA 90025-5058
(617) 661-0401

Atomic Theory
106 W. 49th St.
Minneapolis, MN 55409
(612) 822-5988

Audiophile and **Jazzology**
1206 Decatur St.
New Orleans, LA 70116
(504) 525-1776

AudioQuest Music
P.O. Box 6040
San Clemente, CA 92674
(714) 498-1977

Aum Fidelity
P.O. Box 170147
Brooklyn, NY 11217

Avanti Records
(formerly **Ace Records**)
135 Fairmont Plaza
Pearl, MI 39208
(601) 939-6868

Avenue Jazz
(also distributed by **Rhino**)
11100 Santa Monica Blvd., Suite 2000
Los Angeles, CA 90025
(310) 312-0300

★

Bahoomba Music
847A Second Ave., Suite 294
New York, NY 10017
(718) 591-4382
www.bahoomba-blues.com

Baltimore Blues Society
P.O. Box 26250
Baltimore, MD 21210
(410) 329-5825

Barfly Records
906 Date St.
Las Vegas, NV 89108
(702) 646-4865

Barking Pumpkin
P.O. Box 5265
North Hollywood, CA 91616-5265
(818) 755-3700
www.zappa.com

Bear Family
P.O. Box 1154
D 27727 Hambergen
Germany
04-794-93000

Big Mo
2002 Gove Hill
Thetford Center, VT 05075
(802) 785-4225
www.bigmo.com

Biograph
P.O. Box 369
Canaan, NY 12029
(518) 781-3715

Bizarre/Planet
740 N. La Brea Ave., 2nd fl.
Los Angeles, CA 90038
(323) 935-4444

Black Lion
(see **d a Music**)

Black Saint
c/o Eurojazz Marketing
P.O. Box 160402
Sacramento, CA 95816
(516) 482-7325
www.blacksaint.com

Black Top
P.O. Box 56691
New Orleans, LA 70156
(504) 895-7239
www.blacktoprecords.com

Blind Pig
(division of **Whole Hog, Inc.**)
P.O. Box 2344
San Francisco, CA 94126
(415) 550-6484
www.blindpigrecords.com

Blue Moon
(distributed by **FTC**)

Blue Note
1290 Avenue of the Americas, 35th fl.
New York, NY 10104
(212) 492-5300

Blue Plate Music
33 Music Square W., Suite 102-B
Nashville, TN 37213
(615) 742-1250

Blue Wave Records
3221 Perryville Rd.
Baldwinsville, NY 13027
(315) 638-4286

Blue Thumb
(division of **MCA**)
www.mca.com/grp/blue

Bluemoon
(See **Mesa/Bluemoon**)

Blues Factory, Inc.
2911 Elmhurst Blvd.
Royal Oak, MI 48073
(248) 280-0363

BMG
(distributes **ECM, Flying Dutchman, Milan, RCA, RCA Bluebird, RCA Victor, Victor Jazz**)
1540 Broadway
New York, NY 10036
(212) 930-4000
www.bmg.com

Brownstone
P.O. Box 60163
Worcester, MA 01606
www.brownstonerecordings.com

Bullseye Blues
(division of **Rounder**)

Burnside Records
3158 E. Burnside
Portland, OR 97214
(503) 231-8943
www.burnsiderecords.com

★

Cadence Jazz Records
Cadence Bldng.
Redwood, NY 13679
(315) 287-2852

Capitol
1750 North Vine St.
Los Angeles, CA 90028
(323) 462-6252
or
304 Park Ave. S.
New York, NY 10010
(212) 253-3000
www.hollywoodandvine.com

Capricorn
83 Walton St.
Atlanta, GA 30303
(404) 320-8479
www.capri.corn.com

Catfish Records
7601 Shelton Rd.
Austin, TX 78725
(512) 385-5852

Cavity Search
P.O. Box 42246
Portland, OR 97242
(503) 243-3662
www.cavitysearch.com

Charly Distribution Ltd.
156-166 Ilderton Rd.
London SE15 1NT
England
0-171-639-8603

Chesky
335 W. 52nd St.
New York, NY 10019
(212) 586-7799
www.chesky.com

Chess
(distributed by **MCA**)

Chiaroscuro
830 Broadway
New York, NY 10003
(212) 473-0479
www.chiaroscurojazz.com

Cindy Lou's Musical Mail Order
1900 Elm Hill Pike
Nashville, TN 37210
(800) 224-6395

Classics
(division of **Allegro**)
2402 40th Ave.
Long Island City, NY 11101
(718) 937-8515
www.qualitime.com

Clean Cuts
(division of **Rounder**)

Collectables
P.O. Box 77
Narberth, PA 19072
(610) 649-7565
www.oldies.com

Columbia
550 Madison Ave.
New York, NY 10022-3211
(212) 833-8000
or
2100 Colorado Ave.
Santa Monica, CA 90404
(310) 449-2100
www.sony.com

Concord Jazz and Concord Picante
P.O. Box 845
Concord, CA 94522
(925) 682-6770
www.aent.com/concord

Contemporary
(division of **Fantasy**)

C.R.C. (Collector's Record Club)
GHB Jazz Foundation Bldg.
1206 Decatur St.
New Orleans, LA 70116
(504) 525-1776

CTI
(some releases available through **Sony**)
88 University Pl., 8th fl.
New York, NY 10003
(212) 645-9302

Curb
47 Music Square E.
Nashville, TN 37203
(615) 321-5080
www.curb.com

★

da Music
P.O. Box 3
Little Silver, NJ 07739
(908) 530-6887

DCC
(see **Dunhill Compact Classics**)

Delmark
4121 N. Rockwell
Chicago IL 60618
(773) 539-5001
www.delmark.com

Deluge
P.O. Box 1522
Scarborough, ME 04070
(207) 883-1712

Denon and **Savoy**
3343 Peachtree Rd. N.E., Suite 333
Atlanta, GA 30326
(404) 240-2940
www.denon.com

DGC
(see **Interscope Geffen A&M Records**)

Dionysus
P.O. Box 1975
Burbank, CA 91507
(818) 848-2698

Discovery
(see **Sire Records**)

DIW
(some releases distributed by **Columbia**)

DMP (Digital Music Products)
P.O. Box 15835
Park Sq. Station
Stamford, CT 06901
(203) 327-3800
www.dmprecords.com

Document
(also distributed by **Arhoolie**)
Eipeldauerstr. 23/43/5
A-1220 Vienna
Austria
1-257-1377 or 1-259-2743

Double-Time
P.O. Box 1244
New Albany, IN 47151
(812) 923-6122
www.doubletimejazz.com

Down Beat Magazine
102 N. Haven Rd.
Elmhurst, IL 60126
(630) 941-2030

Dreyfus
19 W. 44th St., Suite 1716
New York, NY 10036
(212) 944-1630

DRG Records
130 W. 57th St., Suite 6D
New York, NY 10019
(212) 582-3040
www.drgrecords.com

Drive Archive
10351 Santa Monica Blvd., Suite 404
Los Angeles, CA 90025
(323) 815-4900

Dunhill Compact Classics (DCC)
9301 Jordan Ave., Suite 105
Chatsworth, CA 91311
(818) 993-8822
www.dcccompact.com

★

Earthbeat!
P.O. Box 1460
Redway, CA 95560
(707) 923-3991

Earwig Music
1818 W. Pratt Blvd.
Chicago, IL 60626
(773) 262-0278
earwigmusi@aol.com

ECM
1540 Broadway, 40th floor
New York, NY 10036
(212) 930-4996
www.ecmrecords.com

Elektra
75 Rockefeller Plaza
New York, NY 10019
(212) 275-4000
www.elektra.com

EmArcy
(division of **Polygram**)

EMI-Capitol Music Group
1290 Avenue of the Americas
New York, NY 10104
(212) 253-3000
or
8730 Sunset Blvd., 5th fl.
Los Angeles, CA 90036
(310) 659-1700
www.emirec.com

Enja
(distributed by **Koch International**)

Entertainment Exclusives
403 Commonwealth Ave.
Boston, MA 02215
(617) 266-0038

Epic
550 Madison Ave.
New York, NY 10022
(212) 833-7442
www.sony.com

Eurojazz Marketing
P.O. Box 160402
Sacramento, CA 95816
(916) 455-4239

Evidence
1100 E. Hector St., Suite 392
Conshohocken, PA 19428
(610) 832-0844

*

Fantasy
2600 10th St.
Berkeley, CA 94710
(510) 549-2500
www.fantasyjazz.com

Fat Possum
P.O. Box 1923
Oxford, MS 38655
(800) 659-9794
www.fatpossum.com

Fedora Records
3840 N. Forestiere Ave.
Fresno, CA 93722
(209) 276-8317

Fish Tail
P.O. Box 2561
Iowa City, IA 52244
(319) 338-3614

Flying Dutchman
(distributed by **BMG**)

Flying Fish
(division of **Rounder**)

Fountainbleu
91-38 114th Street
Richmond Hill, NY 11418
(718) 847-3281
www.fountainbleu.com

Free Lance
(distributed by **Qualiton**)

FTC Distribution
8306 Wilshire Blvd., Suite 544
Beverly Hills, CA 90211
(310) 327-4232

*

Galaxy
(division of **Fantasy**)

Geffen
(see **Interscope Geffen A&M Records**)

GNP Crescendo
8480 Sunset Blvd., Suite A
West Hollywood, CA 90069
(323) 656-2614
www.gnpcrescendo.com

Good Time Jazz
(division of **Fantasy**)

Gramavision
(division of **Rykodisc**)

GRP
(see **Verve Music Group**)

Guitarchives
www.cyberstore.ca/guitarchives

★

Hannibal
(division of **Rykodisc**)

Hat Hut
(distributed by **Eurojazz Marketing**)
Box 521
Basel 4020
Switzerland
(916) 455-4239
www.hathut.com

Heartbeat
(distributed by **Rounder**)

Hightone
220 Fourth St., #101
Oakland, CA 94607
(510) 763-8500
www.hightone.com

Hindsight Records
c/o Michele Audio Corporation
P.O. Box 566
Massena, NY 13662
(315) 769-2448

Hip Bop
1600 Broadway, #910
New York, NY 10019
(212) 927-6756

Homestead
P.O. Box 738
Syosset, NY 11791-0738
(516) 677-6000
www.dutch-east.com

★

Ichiban
3991 Royal Dr.
Kennesaw, GA 30144
(770) 419-1414

I.M.G., Inc.
1900 Elm Hill Pike
Nashville, TN 37210

Impulse!
(see **Verve Music Group**)

In + Out
(division of **Rounder**)

India Navigation
177 Franklin St.
New York, NY 10013
(212) 219-3670

Infinite Zero
(distributed by **American/WEA**)

Interscope Geffen A&M Records
10900 Wilshire Blvd.
Los Angeles, CA 90024
(818) 777-1000

Intersound
P.O. Box 1724
Roswell, GA 30077
(770) 664-9262

Island/Mercury Group
825 8th Ave., 24th fl.
New York, NY 10019
(212) 333-8000

★

Jazzateria Recordings
112 W. 72nd St., Suite 2F
New York, NY 10023
(212) 724-0592
www.jazzateria.com

Jazz Corner Web Site
(information on many jazz artists)
www.jazzcorner.com

Jazzheads
1841 Broadway, Suite 1102
New York, NY 10023
(212) 977-9449
www.jazzheads.com

Jazz Letter Magazine
P.O. Box 240
Ojai, CA 93024
(805) 646-0835

Jazz Mania
270-272 W. 19th St.
New York, NY 10011
(212) 989-7200

Jazzology
(see **Audiophile**)

Jazz Tree
648 Broadway, Suite 703
New York, NY 10012
(212) 475-0415
(212) 475-0502

Jewel
(see **Paula**)

Justice Records
3215 W. Alabama
Houston, TX 77098
(713) 525-4400

Justin Time
5455 Paré, Suite 101
Montréal, Quebec H4P1P7
(514) 738-9533
www.justin-time.com

★

K-Tel
2605 Fernbrook Ln. N.
Minneapolis, MN 55447
(612) 559-6800
www.ktel.com

Keyesland Music
115 Johnson Town Rd.
Sloatsburg, NY 10974
(914) 753-6914

Kicking Mule
(division of **Fantasy**)

King Biscuit Flower Hour
www.king-biscuit.com

King Records
(distributed by **I.M.G., Inc.**)
Retail orders can be made through
Cindy Lou's Musical Mail Order

King Biscuit Flower Hour
18 E. 53rd St., 11th fl.
New York, NY 10022
(212) 758-4636

Knitting Factory Works
74 Leonard St.
New York, NY 10013
(212) 219-3006
www.knittingfactory.com

Koch International
2 Tri-Harbour Ct.
Port Washington, NY 11050
(516) 484-1000
(516) 484-4746
www.kochint.com

Kokopelli
P.O. Box 8200
Santa Fe, NM 87504
(505) 424-1250

★

LaserLight
1663 Sawtelle Blvd.
Los Angeles, CA 90025
(310) 453-9504
www.deltamusic.com

Legacy
(**Sony** label that reissues **Columbia, Epic** and other **Sony** label releases)
550 Madison Ave.
New York, NY 10022
(212) 833-8000
www.sonymusic.com

★

Maison de Soul
(distributed by **Flat Town Music**)
P.O. Drawer 10
Ville Platte, LA 70586
(318) 363-2177

Malaco
3023 West Northside Dr.
Jackson, MS 39213
(601) 982-4522
www.malaco.com

Mango
Island Records
825 8th Ave.
New York, NY 10019
(212) 333-8000

Mapleshade
2301 Crain Highway
Upper Marlboro, MD 20774
(301) 627-0525

Mardi Gras Records
3331 St. Charles Ave.
New Orleans, LA 70115
(504) 895-0441
www.mardigrasrecords.com

Matador
625 Broadway, 12th fl.
New York, NY 10012
(212) 995-5882
www.matador.recs.com

MCA Records
70 Universal City Plaza
Universal City, CA 91608
(818) 777-4000
www.mcarecords.com

Mercury
(see **Island/Mercury Group**)

Mesa/Bluemoon Recordings
(distributed by **Rhino**)
9229 Sunset Blvd.
Los Angeles, CA 90069
(310) 205-7445

Messidor
(Distributed by **Rounder**)

Milestone
(division of **Fantasy**)

Mosaic
35 Melrose Place
Stamford, CT 06902
(203) 327-7111
www.mosaicrecords.com

Motown
(see **Universal/Motown Records**)

Muse
(many **Muse** releases have been reissued on **32 Jazz**)

Music and Arts Program of America
P.O. Box 771
Berkeley, CA 94701
(510) 525-4583
www.musicandart.com

MusicMasters
9 Canterbury Rd.
Manalapan, NJ 07726
(609) 924-8878
musmasters@aol.com

*

New Sound
(formerly **Alcazar/Alcazam! Records**)
P.O. Box 669
Waterbury, VT 05676
(802) 244-7845

New Star
8955 Beverly Blvd.
Los Angeles, CA 90048
(310) 786-1600
www.newstarmedia.com

New World
701 Seventh Ave., 7th fl.
New York, NY 10036
(212) 302-0460

Nonesuch
75 Rockefeller Plaza, 8th fl.
New York, NY 10019
(212) 275-4910

North Country Distributors
(Red, Dreyfus, DIW)
Cadence Building
Redwood, NY 13679
(315) 287-2852
www.cadencebuilding.com

Novus
(distributed through **BMG**)

*

Okeh Records
550 Madison Ave.
New York, NY 10022-3211
(212) 833-8000

Omega
27 W. 72nd St.
New York, NY 10023
(212) 769-3060
www.omegarecords.com

1-800-PRIME-CD
111 E. 14th St., Suite 300
New York, NY 10003
(212) 366-5982
www.primecd.com

One Way
15 Industrial Park Rd.
Albany, NY 12206
(518) 489-3288
www.aent.com/oneway

Original Blues Classics
(division of **Fantasy**)

Original Jazz Classics
(division of **Fantasy**)

Orleans Records
828 Royal St., #536
New Orleans, LA 70116
(504) 837-5042

★

Pablo
(division of **Fantasy**)

Palmetto
71 Washington Place, #1A
New York, NY 10011
(212) 673-9394
www.palmettorecords.com

Paula, Jewel and **Ronn**
P.O. Box 1125
Shreveport, LA 71163-1125
(800) 446-2865

Pearl
(subsidiary of **Delmark**)

Postcards
Dept. SK
225 Lafayette St.
New York, NY 10012

Prestige
(division of **Fantasy**)

Private Music
8750 Wilshire Blvd.
Beverly Hills, CA 90211
(310) 358-4800

★

Qualiton Imports
24-02 40th Ave.
Long Island City, NY 11101
(718) 937-8515

Qwest
3800 Barham Blvd., Suite 503
Los Angeles, CA 90068
(323) 882-1300

★

Rabadash
P.O. Box 19384
New Orleans, LA 70179
(504) 486-2540
www.rabadash.com

Razor & Tie Records
214 Sullivan St., #4A
New York, NY 10012
(212) 473-9173

RCA Bluebird
(see **BMG Entertainment**)

Red House
P.O. Box 4044
St. Paul, MN 55104
(800) 695-4687
www.redhouserecords.com

Reprise
3300 Warner Blvd.
Burbank, CA 91505
(818) 846-9090
or
75 Rockefeller Plaza
New York, NY 10019
(212) 275-4500
www.repriserec.com

Res-O-Nator
346 W. Foothill Blvd.
Glendora, CA 91741
(626) 335-8777

Reservoir Music
276 Pearl St.
Kingston, NY 12401
(914) 338-1834

Rhino
10635 Santa Monica Blvd.
Los Angeles, CA 90025
(310) 474-4778
Rhino catalog: Rhino Direct
P.O. Box 6008
Tampa, FL 33660-0008
(800) 35-RHINO
www.rhino.com

Riverside
(division of **Fantasy**)

Ronn
(see **Paula**)

Roesch Records Inc.
25-13 Old Kings Hwy. N., Suite 272
Darien, CT 06820
(203) 838-5023

Rooster Blues
(also distributed by **Rounder**)
3516 Holmes St.
Kansas City, MO 64109
(816) 931-0383

Rounder
One Camp St.
Cambridge, MA 02140
(617) 354-0700
www.rounder.com

RSA Records
P.O. Box 790
Stoneridge, NY 12484
(914) 687-0912

Rykodisc
Shetland Park
27 Congress St.
Salem, MA 01970
(888) 2-EARFUL
www.rykodisc.com

*

Savoy
(see **Denon**)

Seaside
215 Corey Ln.
Middletown, RI 02842
(401) 849-1290

Shanachie Entertainment
13-17 Laight St.
New York, NY 10013
(212) 334-0284
www.shanachie.com

Shattered Music
9024 W. Sunset Blvd.
W. Hollywood, CA 90069
(310) 385-0193

Silvertone Records
137-139 W. 25th St.
New York, NY 10001
(212) 727-0016

Sire Records
(distributes **Sire, Discovery**)
936 Broadway
New York, NY 10010
(212) 275-4000

Smithsonian Folkways
955 L'Enfant Plaza, Suite 7300
Washington, DC 20560-0953
(202) 287-3251
www.si.edu/folkways

Songline Recording
2323 W. 2nd Ave., Apt. 1003
Vancouver, BC V6K1J4
Canada
(604) 737-1632
www.songlines.com

Sony
(distributes **Columbia, Epic, Legacy, Sony**)
550 Madison Ave.
New York, NY 10022-3211
(212) 833-8000
www.sonymusic.com

Soul Note
(distributed by **Euro Jazz Marketing**)
P.O. Box 160402
Sacramento, CA 95816
(916) 455-4239

Specialty
(division of **Fantasy**)

Stax
(division of **Fantasy**)

SteepleChase
(distributed by **Allegro**)

Stony Plain
P.O. Box 861
Edmonton, Alberta T5J2L8
Canada
(403) 468-6423

Sugar Hill Records
P.O. Box 55300
Durham, NC 27717-5300
(919) 489-4349
www.sugarhillrecords.com

Sunnyside Communications
348 W. 38th St., #12B
New York, NY 10018
(800) 654-0279
www.sunnysidezone.com

★
Telarc International
23307 Commerce Park Rd.
Cleveland, OH 44122
(216) 464-2313
www.telarc.com

Terra Nova Records
P.O. Box 455
Sumland, CA 91041
(818) 352-5593

Testament
(distributed by **Hightone**)

32 Records (32 Jazz, 32 Blues, etc.)
(distributes many titles formerly available on **Muse**)
250 West 57th St.
New York, NY 10107
(212) 265-0740
www.32.com

Tomato
(distributed by **Rhino**)

Tone-Cool Records
1 Camp St.
Cambridge, MA 02140
(617) 354-0700 x296
www.tonecool.com

Tradition
(division of **Rykodisc**)
www.traditionrecords.com

Trend
(division of **Discovery**)

Triple X
P.O. Box 862529
Los Angeles, CA 90086-2529
(323) 221-2204
xxx@triple-x.com

★
Unity
2916 Main St.
Santa Monica, CA 90405
(310) 581-2700

Universal/Motown Record Group
(distributes **Universal, Motown, Polydor**)
70 Universal City Plaza
Universal City, CA 91600
(818) 777-4000

Upstart
(division of **Rounder**)

★
Vanguard
2700 Pennsylvania Ave.
Santa Monica, CA 90404
(310) 829-9355

Varrick
(division of **Rounder**)

Verve Music Group
(distributes **Verve, GRP, Impulse!**)
555 W. 57th St.
New York, NY 10019
(212) 333-8000
(212) 603-7919

Virgin
304 Park Ave. S.
New York, NY 10010
(212) 253-3100
www.virginrecords.com

★
Warner Bros.
3300 Warner Blvd.
Burbank, CA 91505-4694
(818) 846-9090
www.wbr.com

Warner Jazz
75 Rockefeller Plaza
New York, NY 10019
(212) 275-4500
www.wbjazz.com

WEA
(distributes **Warner Bros., Elektra, Atlantic**)
111 N. Hollywood Way
Burbank, CA 91505
(818) 843-6311
or
75 Rockefeller Plaza
New York, NY 10019
(212) 275-4000
www.wea.com

Windham Hill
8750 Wilshire Blvd.
Beverly Hills, CA 90211
(310) 358-4800
www.windham.com

★

Yazoo
(division of **Shanachie**)